Dictionary of Jamaican English

Dictionary of Jamaican English

SECOND EDITION

Edited by

F. G. Cassidy *and* **R. B. Le Page**

UNIVERSITY OF THE
WEST INDIES PRESS
Barbados • Jamaica • Trinidad and Tobago

University of the West Indies Press
1A Aqueduct Flats Mona
Kingston 7 Jamaica

06 5 4 3 2

CATALOGUING IN PUBLICATION DATA

Dictionary of Jamaican English / edited by F. G. Cassidy and
R. B. Le Page. – 2nd ed.
p. cm.
Previously published: Cambridge: Cambridge University Press, 1980.
Includes bibliographical references.

ISBN: 976-640-127-6

1. English language – Dialects – Jamaica – Dictionaries.
I. Cassidy, Frederic Gomes, 1907–2000.
II. Le Page, R. B. (Robert Brook), 1920–.

PE3313.25C3 2002 427.9'7292 -dc-21

Cover design by Robert Harris.
Printed in the United States of America.

CONTENTS

PREFACE TO THE PAPERBACK EDITION

Prior to this edition of the *Dictionary of Jamaican English*, the Cambridge University Press has produced two editions (1967, 1980), the latter three times reprinted (1984, 1985, 1997), each coming very handsomely from that press, and bound, but at a production cost which made it necessary to charge a price beyond the reach of most Caribbean pockets.

With the death of Frederic Cassidy in June 2000, Robert Le Page, now the sole individual copyright owner, felt the full weight of popular pressure for a cheaper edition, and decided that this could best be achieved through collaboration between the Cambridge University Press and the University of the West Indies Press in Jamaica. This collaboration was readily agreed in a generous manner, Cambridge University Press making their typeface available to Jamaica for a very modest fee. No changes have been made to the text for this edition, which has been produced with the co-operation of the Department of Language and Linguistic Science of the University of York.

Heslington, York
February 2002

GENERAL INTRODUCTION

INCEPTION OF THE DICTIONARY AND SOURCES USED

The decision to compile a dictionary of Jamaican English of the most comprehensive and scholarly kind arose out of the agreement of the two editors in 1955 to pool their collections of material for this purpose. Up to that time the work had proceeded as follows:

F. G. Cassidy (FGC), who had himself been born and had spent his early years in Jamaica, returned to the island for the academic year 1951–2 as a Fulbright Research Fellow. During that year he read the relevant literature in the Institute of Jamaica, comprehensively up to 1850 and selectively thereafter, and extracted citations of Jamaicanisms.

In 1952, using a questionnaire based on that of the Linguistic Atlas of the U.S. and Canada, but adapted by him to Jamaican conditions, he visited every parish and recorded in the International Phonetic Alphabet the responses of some thirty informants (see *Jamaica Talk*, pp. 418–20, for a list of these). At the same time he made tape-recordings of the free speech of some forty more informants all over the island, telling of their activities as small cultivators, fishermen, hog-hunters, boat-builders, cane-planters, cattlemen, distillers, foresters, domestics, school-teachers, social workers, and recording tales, songs, biographies, and so on. These have been transcribed, classified with due regard to the language status and geographical distribution of the speakers, and added to the files. Citations from this field work are given as '1952 FGC' followed by the short name of a parish, e.g., 'StC'. The extensive collections which were the result of this year's work formed the basic file for the Dictionary.

In 1952 P. M. Sherlock, then Vice-Principal of the University College of the West Indies (UCWI), passed to R. B. Le Page (LeP) the original entries for a competition held by the *Daily Gleaner*, of Kingston, in December 1943, in which a prize was offered for the best list of 'dialect words and phrases'. The entries, of which there were several hundred, came from all parts of Jamaica, and ranged from a dozen or twenty words on a single sheet of paper to a hundred or more items on half-a-dozen sheets. A file was made from these, and the originals were passed on to the Dictionary by LeP. These word-lists presented special problems. They came mostly from people of limited education, and contained many spellings which were difficult to interpret, many definitions which were not easily understood. Most of the problems were cleared up by the inquiries made by those who, from 1953 on, worked on the Linguistic Survey of the West Indies, and by FGC on his return visits to the island in 1955, 1958–9, 1960, and 1961. Some puzzles, however, remained; but virtually all the items on all the lists have been entered in the Dictionary on the assumption that they constitute prima facie evidence for some linguistic feature or other which, if not explicable at present, may be explained in the future. The *Gleaner* competition citations are entered as '1943 *GL*' followed by the parish from which the entry came, when known. The original spellings and definitions of the competitors have been retained.

In 1953 the Linguistic Survey of the West Indies was started by LeP with the aid of a grant from the Carnegie Corporation of New York, and it was under the aegis, partly or wholly, of the Survey that Mrs Beryl Loftman Bailey (BLB) spent six months on field work in the island in 1956, and two years as a Research Fellow from 1960 to 1962; that Louise McLoskey (Mc) spent fifteen months from 1955 to 1956 doing field work in a number of parishes—especially Manchester, Portland and St Andrew—and in supervising field work done by students; that FGC paid his second (1955) and fourth (1960) visits to the island to check and collate his material and prepare the first drafts of the Dictionary; and that David DeCamp (DeC) spent the years 1958–60 as a Fulbright Fellow in Jamaica collecting materials for a dialect geography of the island and teaching at the UCWI. Citations in such cases are given by the date when the item was collected, the initials of the collector and the parish if known. They are normally in a phonemic transcription, followed by a translation where necessary. With the exception of Miss McLoskey's, each of these visits has resulted in independent publications (see the Bibliography); the Dictionary files were however placed at the disposal of all, and each, including Mc, contributed very valuable material to those files either from direct observation or from transcriptions of tape-recorded material already collected by LeP and others.

In 1954 LeP sent out a questionnaire, to various parts of the Caribbean, modelled physically on that of the Scottish Dialect Survey but redesigned for use by local interrogators working with local informants. Some twelve of these were completed in Jamaica by school-teachers or local welfare officers, working in each case with a middle-aged local informant of limited education. This source is cited as '1954 LeP' followed by the parish; the spellings used by the interrogators, who were instructed to spell words as they sounded, have been retained.

In 1955 FGC worked out the phonemic notation which is used throughout the Dictionary to represent the pronunciation of the folk dialect. This was first used in *Jamaica Talk*, and is given in Appendix I of that book. (See further under Format and Linguistic Introduction.)

Mr H. P. Jacobs, who had been collecting lexical items in Jamaica for many years, both from written sources and from his own observations, made available to the Survey both his advice and also that portion of his collections which had been transcribed into two manuscript books by Mr Astley Clerk. These books covered only about half the alphabet, for the period 1935 to 1948; they proved a helpful source, and are cited by the date of the observation followed by 'HPJ', followed by a parish when that was given. Where Mr Clerk had added his own notes, these are cited as 'A. Clerk in HPJ'.

In 1957 the Institute of Education of UCWI (now the University of the West Indies) enlisted the aid of school-teachers and teacher-trainees all over the island, in a study designed to establish the vocabularies available to Jamaican children of different ages. The spontaneous conversation of children in school playgrounds or in their homes was written down in any spelling that appeared suitable to conve-

the pronunciation. Miss Joyce Nation (JN) collated and analysed this material for the Institute, and then made it available to LeP, who extracted from it citations for the Dictionary. These are cited as '1957 JN', followed by the parish when known. The spelling of the original material has been retained.

Mrs Jean Brown, secretary to the English Department of UCWI for a number of years, gave a great deal of help in checking doubtful items and herself contributed a number of citations. These are identified as JB, preceded by the date. Smaller but valuable contributions were made by many students and staff at the University College and at the University College Hospital, as well as by individual members of the public who sent in their observations as the work on the Dictionary became known, or replied to letters of enquiry placed in the *Daily Gleaner*, or who were consulted on specific items. Citations from such sources are acknowledged by name, date and (where known) the parish. The staff of the University College Library were extremely long-suffering, being used as check-informants for a number of items during the editorial stages. The Botany Department placed their files at our disposal; reference is also made to articles printed in the *West Indian Medical Journal* (see the Bibliography, *WIMJ*).

EDITORIAL WORK

FGC was appointed chief editor of the Dictionary when collaboration was agreed upon in 1955. He had already by this time carried out one of the major tasks necessary—the collation of the material in the basic file with four dictionaries: The *Oxford English Dictionary* (*OED*), the *Oxford English Dictionary Supplement* (*OEDS*), the *Dictionary of American English* (*DAE*), and the *Dictionary of Americanisms* (*DA*). He had also, with the assistance of the staff of the Institute of Jamaica, made more positive identifications of many species of flora and fauna than the historical citations by themselves provided. (The Institute of Jamaica, its director, Mr C. Bernard Lewis, and several staff members—Miss P. B. Caws, Mr R. P. Bengry, Mr George Proctor, Miss Dulcie A. Powell and Mr Thomas Farr put the library, scientific collections, publications and other facilities most generously at his disposal throughout the period of compilation and editing of the Dictionary.)

Checking against the *English Dialect Dictionary* (*EDD*), the *Scottish National Dictionary* (*SND*), and the *Dictionary of the Older Scottish Tongue* (*DOST*) was necessarily less thoroughly systematic than that against the dictionaries listed earlier. For one thing, the *SND* and *DOST* were still appearing as the work on the *DJE* progressed; for another, lacking any consistent comparative phonology for JC and the various dialects of English, the search for cognates was bound to a certain extent to be one of trial and error, with intuitive awareness gradually sharpening as positive results were obtained. The latter qualification applies also to the extensive searches made of the African dictionaries available to us. Help in identifying Africanisms was given generously from time to time by Professor J. Berry and his colleagues at the School of Oriental and African Studies in London, but the greater part of this work was done by trial and error with dictionaries of widely differing calibre. To check whether one single item might be an Africanism sometimes involved the inspection of all lexical items under three or four different initial letters in five or more dictionaries. Quite apart from the fact that different African dictionaries use different orthographies and different conventions of alphabetizing, the Anglicized stress-patterns of some Jamaican Africanisms led to a supposed morphemic segmentation quite different from that under which the African original was finally located (see, for example, **JOHN CANOE** dʒoŋku-nu; **BUFFRO-BUFFRO** o-bò-fũro etc.). Again, the same qualification applies to the searches made of those dictionaries of American Spanish available to us. Both editors have spent a great deal of time—possibly a disproportionate amount of time—on the etymologies of Jamaicanisms. The scepticism of each in turn has served as a useful check on the enthusiasms of the other, so that we feel no far-fetched etymologies are advanced in these pages. We also feel quite certain, however, that many puzzles remain to be solved, and we have avoided dogmatism in doubtful cases, preferring simply to suggest a number of possibilities.

ACKNOWLEDGEMENTS

Acknowledgement should here be made once again to the Carnegie Corporation, since it was with Linguistic Survey funds that a great many reference works and expensive dictionaries were bought, without which the editorial work would have been impossible. The librarian of the UCWI, Mr William Gocking, made all his resources available to us, including—very often on permanent loan for long periods—the rare books of the West Indies collection; his staff could not have been more helpful or patient. Grateful acknowledgement must also be made to the Graduate School of the University of Wisconsin, which, from its research funds, gave FGC the equivalent of an entire year's support (one semester 1954–5, one semester 1963) for the preparation and editing, as well as funds for travel to Jamaica.

Once the format of the entries had been decided, FGC wrote up the entries from the files, which LeP was pre-editing. The slips were then typed on to stencils by the English department secretarial staff (Mrs Vera Read, Mrs Pauline Lyn, Miss Sonya Lyle) and eight complete sets of the seven volumes of mimeographed material were sent to interested persons for their comments. Finally, FGC made (1963) a complete revision of the MS, utilizing these often very helpful comments and the additional materials that had come into the files since the beginning of editing. The MS was sent to the Press in June 1963.

The Historical Phonology in its final form is predominantly the work of LeP. He has, however, built upon foundations laid in the first instance by FGC—who produced the original phonemicization of Jamaican Creole—and Mrs Beryl L. Bailey, and he has had the advantage of the phonological analyses made by David DeCamp, Louise McLoskey, and Alan S. C. Ross, whose help he would like to acknowledge.

METHOD AND FORMAT

The *Dictionary of Jamaican English* (*DJE*) is a historical, descriptive dictionary of the English language in all the forms it has taken in Jamaica since 1655, when it was introduced with the taking of the island by the English. The method followed is, in general, that of the *Oxford English Dictionary* (*New English Dictionary*), and those based on it for the United States: the *Dictionary of American English* (Craigie and Hulbert) and the *Dictionary of Americanisms* (Mathews), with dated citations, numbered senses, documentation of spelling-forms, etymologies (which *DAE* omits), usage labels, etc. This dictionary, however, faces a special problem not present for its predecessors: the fact that Jamaican English runs the gamut from standard educated usage no different in kind from other regional forms of English to dialectal folk usage, much of which has never been written down before.

The latter, customarily called 'the dialect' in Jamaica, is full of variations due both to geography and development. It is not 'dialect' in the sense in which that word applies to a local dialect in England, which latter would be largely of the same historical descent as Standard English. The better term for Jamaican dialect is 'creole', the term used by linguists today, which points to the origin of this folk speech as an amalgam of some features of English with others drawn from a large variety of African languages. (For a full account of the origins of Jamaican English see LePage, *Creole Language Studies I*, part 1; see also the Linguistic Introduction below.) It also contains loan features from other European languages spoken in the Caribbean. This creole speech, or dialect, is by no means homogeneous. It exists in rather archaic forms in some isolated settlements, and, being always under the influence of English as the language of prestige, adapts itself in varying degrees in the usage of communities, individuals, and social levels, to standard English usage.

What is here labelled as 'dialectal', therefore, refers to any linguistic feature characteristic of the Jamaican folk in both town and country: small cultivators, villagers, unskilled and many skilled workers, domestics, market people, and many others, for whom formal schooling has had little effect in daily life, and language is largely traditional, especially when they are speaking among themselves. The sounds, intonations, vocabulary, and syntax of these speakers differ markedly from those of educated speakers, who closely approximate or achieve standard English with Jamaican differences. It is possible to separate the vocabulary, as is done here, into dialectal and non-dialectal items, according to their being characteristic of the folk, on the one hand, or of educated speakers and writers on the other. Some dialect words are of very narrow range: they would be known only in a small community or only to individual speakers. Others are widespread among the folk but would not be generally known by the educated. Others again are well known to every Jamaican, though they might not be used normally by the educated. (And there are many words used by Jamaicans, educated or not, which would not be known to the outsider; but these are not 'dialectal'.)

It may be wondered why two such different types, the language of the educated and that of the folk, might not have been separated and treated in two dictionaries, one perhaps based on printed materials, the other on dialect sources, oral or written. The answer is that just because there is one continuous, gradual scale of usage between the extremes of these types, any sharp division made between them would have had to be arbitrary, tearing apart what is, in fact, a thoroughly interwoven fabric. It therefore seemed better to make a single dictionary, putting all together, but recognizing in a broad way the two foci of cultivated and folk usage by entering headwords in two ways, those words and phrases that follow traditional orthography (or for which no other was possible) being presented in capital letters, and those which are usually or altogether oral being put in lower-case letters and in a phonemic orthography, that is, one which represents the significant sound-units of the folk speech.

The kinds of words which have been considered 'Jamaican' in one sense or another for inclusion in the Dictionary are:

1. Words or senses now (or once) general in English but of which the earliest or latest record is in a book about Jamaica by one who had been there or otherwise had direct knowledge of the island. Examples: **ANATTA, BANJO.**
2. Words not otherwise especially associated with Jamaica, but recorded earlier or later, in a book about Jamaica, than they are known to be recorded elsewhere. Examples: **ALBINO, GRAPEFRUIT.**
3. Words, spellings, or senses used in Jamaica though not a part of the English language outside the Caribbean. (When these are known to be used elsewhere in the Caribbean, this fact is noted.) Examples: **BARRACOUTA, OBEAH.**
4. Dialect words which have been given written forms more or less in the manner of traditional orthography. Examples: **BIGE, JUNJO.**
5. Dialect words written down by their collectors in naive spellings, whose spoken form is unknown. Examples: **LASITA, BALEH.**
6. Dialect forms known only from oral sources. Examples: **nombari, talawa.**
7. Dialect forms which, though sometimes printed in dialect literature, have no established spelling and are known chiefly from oral sources. Examples: **singkuma, pere-pere.**

It may be noted that the first five types are entered in capitals, the latter two in lower-case letters.

FORMAT IN DETAIL

1. *Headword.* The capital-letter and lower-case entries just referred to are listed in a single alphabetical sequence throughout the dictionary. All known variant forms are entered (in capitals or lower-case letters as appropriate) and cross-referred to the main headword for treatment. Alternative forms of relatively equal frequency are given together as headwords, the one best supported by etymology, historical priority, or contemporary usage being given first (e.g. **ACKEE, AKEE**). Homonymous entries, when they are the same part of

speech, are followed by small superscript numbers to permit specific reference. When part of an entry-form is sometimes used, sometimes not used, that part is put in parentheses, e.g. **CROMANTY** (**ANT**), **bikaan**(**g**).

2. *Pronunciation.* Pronunciation is not shown when it agrees with Received Standard English; only variants are shown. Pronunciations of dialect forms are placed between diagonals, and are in the phonemic spelling used for all lower-case entries. They are only given, therefore, for capital-letter entries. If the latter, however, are illustrated by a single quotation in phonemic writing, the pronunciation is not repeated in the entry. No dialect pronunciation is given when the form corresponds regularly to the Standard English form (see the Linguistic Introduction), but variants are given when known. Accentuation is not shown (1) for monosyllables, unless to indicate a rising or falling diphthong; (2) when it is the same for all syllables of a word; (3) when primary and secondary stress vary freely. When shown, acute accent (´) placed over the vowel is used for primary, grave (`) for secondary, and no mark for weak stress. (Note: In etymologies from Twi and some other African languages these accents indicate variations of pitch. The practice of the source dictionary is followed.) Occasional sub-phonemic (phonetic) pronunciation variants are shown within square brackets.

3. *Part of speech.* In general the abbreviations used in *OED* are adopted, but not italicized and without following punctuation: sb adv pron conj prep int phr, etc. Exceptions are the *OED*'s *v* and *a*, for which vb and adj are used here to avoid confusion with *vide*, *ante*, etc. (See Abbreviations 2 below.) The part-of-speech categories of Standard English are not always applicable to the Jamaican folk grammar, where functions are often syncretized, or syntactic groups are susceptible of more than one analysis. In such cases, alternative labels are used, e.g. 'sb or vb'. Labels are applied in accordance with the function performed by the word in the illustrative quotation.

4. *Usage label. OED* labels are generally adopted, but not italicized and without following punctuation: obs rare dial, etc. A few, however, are given special senses: bot ornith, etc. indicate that the word is found chiefly or only in books—these are therefore not used for information or lore derived from dialect speakers. The label 'dial' refers here to Jamaican folk speech in any of its forms, as explained above. (See Abbreviations.) Labels are used only when necessary. Further details concerning usage are sometimes given in notes preceding the definitions.

5. *Spelling-variants.* Spelling-variants, when numerous, are given in chronological order preceded by the dates of appearance. A single date indicates one occurrence; inclusive dates (e.g. 1678–1803) show earliest and latest occurrences known; date followed by arrow (e.g. 1890→) shows earliest known occurrence of a word that is still in use; date preceded by arrow (e.g. →1760) shows use of the word up to that date (the latest known occurrence). Spelling variants are not listed when they are few, since they appear in the dated citations; nor are they shown when the *OED* treatment of the word is unaltered by Jamaican evidence.

6. *Etymology.* For English words no etymology is given except to correct or supplement existing ones. Simple etymologies (e.g. those going back to a current Spanish or French word) are carried back only one step. Complex etymologies,

especially those inadequately treated elsewhere, are carried back as far as possible. When single source-forms cannot be determined, as often is the case with African loan-words, related forms may be referred to. Etyma are given in lower-case italic type whether or not they are in some standard orthography. If necessary, Jamaican dialectal etyma in phonemic spelling are indicated as such.

7. *Dictionary reference.* When the present treatment antedates or post-dates that of one of the other historical dictionaries this fact is indicated by means of a date, an arrow, and reference to the other dictionary; thus '*ODS* 1829→' for **ARALIA** means that the earliest citation in the *Oxford Dictionary Supplement* is from 1829, but *DJE* has an earlier citation (in this case from 1756); similarly, '*OED* →1865' for **BEKNOWN** means that the latest citation in the *Oxford English Dictionary* is 1865, but *DJE* has later citations (1935, 1957). Inclusive dates from another dictionary are given when *DJE* has both pre- and post-dating citations. Entries that refer to no other historical dictionary are not treated in them and are therefore additions to existing lexicography. (Non-historical dictionaries and other sources are also referred to when appropriate.)

8. *Cross-reference.* Cross-references are made in capital or lower-case letters according to the entry form of the word referred to. They may be made at whatever point in the treatment is deemed appropriate. Reference is made primarily to words treated in *DJE*, secondarily to treatments elsewhere. When necessary for clarity, cross-references are preceded by 'Cf' or 'See', but any word given in capital letters, other than an actual entry-form, is a cross-reference to its treatment in its alphabetical position in *DJE* and should be looked up for additional information.

9. *Senses.* Senses are given in the presumed order of development and are preceded by digits; sub-senses are preceded by alphabetic letters. When citations illustrate more than one sense simultaneously (e.g. plant, fruit, derivative product), all senses are given together before the citations. When two or more etymologically related parts of speech are treated collectively, the treatment of each is preceded by a capital letter, as: A sb:, B adj:, C vb:, preceding the numbered senses. In such treatments the numbering of senses begins anew for each part of speech. Treatment is separate or collective according to convenience, depending on the number of senses, etymology, and other considerations.

10. *Definitions.* When the citation is a definition, or gives all the pertinent information, 'See quot' is used instead of a formal definition. When only a single citation has come to hand for any word, definition may be omitted. The citation then immediately follows the entry line.

11. *Variant names.* When there are or have been two or more names for the same thing, the chief treatment comes under the commonest name, and all others are referred to in alphabetical order following the definition: 'Also (called)'—e.g. **ANATTA**...once also called ACHIOTE, ROUCOU. This reference may come after the definition or at the end of the entry-line.

12. *Quotations.* Each sense is normally illustrated with one or more citations, giving, in order: (1) the date, (2) the author or informant (using short references—see Abbreviations and Bibliography), (3) the short title (only when date and author

do not sufficiently identify the source) or the parish or other place which an informant represents, (4) the words of the author in the exact spelling of the source; or, if that was oral, the phonemically spelled pronunciation between diagonals, followed, when necessary for clarity, by a paraphrase or 'translation' in standard English. (Such translations, when they were part of the source, are given as they appeared there. Those furnished by Linguistic Survey staff are italicized. Those added by the editors of *DJE* are italicized within square brackets.) If the treatment of a word in *OED* or other historical dictionaries is otherwise adequate, only earlier and later citations may be given.

13. *Acknowledgements and additional information for the second edition.*

(i) For this revised edition help has been generously given by a number of people. Professor James Sledd (University of Texas) read the text very closely for forgotten cross-references, typographical errors, and similar lapses, now repaired. Staff members of the University of the West Indies who were consulted or who volunteered items of information were Gertrude Buscher, Dennis Craig, Jean Small, and Rex Nettleford. Others who sent us additional material over the years, or who answered our 1976 appeal in the *Gleaner*, were: L. E. Duffey (St Ann), Mrs H. T. Landale (Kgn), C. Bernard Lewis (Kgn) and Miss L. G. Perkins (Munro College). All these are hereby thanked, with special gratitude for repeated valuable contributions from Jamaica's devoted scholar-citizen, Mr H. P. Jacobs.

(ii) The symbol **s** in the main dictionary indicates that further information is to be found in the revised Supplement. Where this symbol occurs before a cross-reference, it is to the Supplement entry.

(iii) Information about usage in other parts of the Caribbean has been generously supplied, as far as they were able to check in the time available, by Dr Walter Edwards (Guyana), Dr Donald Winford (Trinidad), Dr Richard Allsopp and staff of the Caribbean Lexicography Project (Barbados), Barbara Assadi and John Holm (Nicaragua) and Dr Colville Young (Belize). Items *known* to be used with closely similar form and meaning in these territories have been marked *G*, *T*, *BA*, *N*, *BL* respectively. When placed against a cross-reference the letters indicate that a particular form or spelling is known in that territory. We wish to express our thanks to all these contributors. The incidence of items in Sranan (marked *SC*) has been checked by FGC himself. Occasional evidence from other territories is shown by the name spelt in full e.g. Tobago.

(iv) We are indebted also to the editors of the *Scottish National Dictionary* for completing their work in time for us to reflect adequately the wealth of Scotticisms in use in Jamaica.

(v) After the revised text had gone to press Dr Hazel Carter, of the School of Oriental and African Studies, London, made a number of suggestions for Bantu etymologies for which we are grateful and which we have done our best to incorporate.

University of Wisconsin
November 1977

University of York

BIBLIOGRAPHY

1655 Calendar	*Calendar of State Papers*, Colonial Series V, s. a. 1655.
1655 Eye-Witnesse	S., I. (An Eye-Witnesse). *A Brief and Perfect Journal of the Late Proceedings and Successe of the English Army in the West-Indies.* London, 1655.
1657 Continuation	*A Book of the Continuation of Foreign Passages... Moreover, An Attempt on the Island of Jamaica.* London (Jenner) 1657.
1657 Ligon	Ligon, Richard. *A true and exact History of the Island of Barbados.* London (Moseley) 1657.
1657 True Des.	*A True Description of Jamaica, with the Fertility, Commodities, and Healthfulness of the Place...* London (F. M.) 1657.
1658 Doyley	[Doyley, Edward]. *A Narrative of the Great Success...* London (Hills and Field) 1658.
p 1660 State of Jamaica	*The State of Jamaica.* British Museum MS Egerton 2395 (Copy in Institute of Jamaica), p 1660.
1661 Hickeringill	Hickeringill, Capt. E. *Jamaica Viewed: with All the Ports.* London (Williams?) 1661.
1662 Stubbe	Stubbe, Henry. *The Indian Nectar... Chocolata.* London (J. C. for Crook) 1662.
1664 Intelligencer	*The Intelligencer. A letter from Jamaica, June 30,* London (Hodgkinson) 1664.
1671 Ogilby	Ogilby, John. *America: being the latest, and most accurate description of the New World...* London (1671).
1672 Blome	Blome, Richard. *A Description of the Island of Jamaica.* London (Milbourn) 1672.
1678 Blome	Blome, Richard. *A Description of the Island of Jamaica.* London (J. B. for Newman) 1678.
1679 Trapham	Trapham, Thomas. *A Discourse on the State of Health in the Island of Jamaica.* London (Boulter) 1679.
1683 Laws	*The Laws of Jamaica, Passed by the Assembly...* London (Hills for Harper) 1683.
1683 *Present State*	*The Present State of Jamaica.* London (Clark for Malthus) 1683.
1687 Blome	Blome, Richard. *The Present State of His Majesty's Isles and Territories in America.* London (Clark for Newman) 1687.
1687–9 Wright	Wright, Capt. Lawrence. *Log or 'Journall' of —, Commander of H.M.S. Assistance 1687–9.* Transcr. for Institute of Jamaica from Captain's Journal 68 P. R. O. Series.
1692 Earthquake	*A Full Account of the Late Dreadful Earthquake at Port Royal in Jamaica.* London (Jacob Tomson) 1692.
1693 Rev. Divine	A Reverend Divine. *The Truest and Largest Account of the Late Earthquake in Jamaica, June the 7th, 1692.* London (Buttler) 1693.
c 1695 Acts & Laws	*The Acts of Assembly & Laws of Jamaica.* No imprint (Institute of Jamaica) c 1695.
1696 Sloane	Sloane, Sir Hans. *Catalogus Plantarum Quae in Insula Jamaica Sponte Proveniunt...* London (Brown) 1696.

1696–7 Nevill	Nevill, Vice-Admiral. *Journal.* Phillipps MS 8606 in Institute of Jamaica.
1698 Ward	[Ward, Edward.] *A Trip to Jamaica: With a True Character of the People and Island.* London, 2nd ed., 1698.
a 1705 Ray (1713)	Ray, John. *Synopsis Methodica Avium et Piscium.* London (Innys) 1713.
1707 Sloane	Sloane, Sir Hans. *A Voyage To...JAMAICA, with the Natural History* (vol. I). London (B. M.) 1707.
1712 Walker	Walker, Rear-Admiral Sir Hoveden. *Journalls—A Continuation of...my Journalls.* MS in Institute of Jamaica, 1712.
1725 Sloane	Sloane, Sir Hans. *A Voyage To...JAMAICA, with the Natural History* (vol. II). London, 1725.
a 1726 Barham (1794)	Barham, Dr Henry, Sr. *Hortus Americanus.* Kingston (Aikman) 1794
1727 Merchant	An English Merchant. *Some Modern Observations Upon Jamaica.* London, 1727.
1730 Buggs	Southall, John. *A Treatise of Buggs.* London (J. Roberts) 1730.
1733 *Jrl. House of Assembly*	*Journal of the House of Assembly of Jamaica* various dates. (III 152 is the date here.)
1738 Articles of Pacification	Articles of Pacification with the Maroons of Trelawney Town, concluded March the first, 1738. Pp. xvi ff. in 1796 Assembly, q.v.
1739 Leslie	Leslie, Charles. *A New and Exact Account of Jamaica.* Edinburgh (Fleming) 1739.
1740 Importance	*The Importance of Jamaica to Great Britain Consider'd.* London (Dodd) [1740].
1740 Leslie	Leslie, Charles. *A New History of Jamaica.* London (Hodges) 2nd ed., 1740.
1750 Yellow Fever	*An Essay on the Bilious or Yellow Fever of Jamaica.* Kingston (Daniell) 1750.
1750 Hughes	Hughes, Griffith. *The Natural History of Barbados.* London, 1750.
p 1750 Kerr	Kerr, James. *Reasons why Lucea is more convenient...for the Spanish Trade.* Jamaica [p 1750].
1754 Landholders	*A List of Landholders in the Island of Jamaica.* Kingston (MS in Institute of Jamaica) 1754.
1756 Browne	Browne, Patrick. *The Civil and Natural History of Jamaica.* London (Osborn and Shipton) 1756.
1757 St Jago	*The St Jago Intelligencer.* St Iago, Ja. (Brett) 1757.
1757 White	White, Charles. *An Enquiry Concerning the Trade, Commerce, and Policy of Jamaica.* St Jago de la Vega (Brett) 1757.
1764–5 Gordon	Gordon, Lord Adam. *Travels in America and the West Indies 1764–5.*
	Mereness, Newton D. *Travels in the American Colonies.* New York (Macmillan) 1916.
1774 Long	[Long, Edward.] *The History of Jamaica, or General Survey of the Antient and Modern State of that Island.* 3 vols. London (Lowndes) 1774.
1775 Gazette	*The Jamaica Gazette.* Kingston (Weatherby) 1775.

1778 Present State	*The Present State of the West Indies containing an accurate description of what parts are possessed by the several powers in Europe.* London (R. Baldwin) 1778.
1781 Dancer	Dancer, Thomas. *A Brief History of the Late Expedition Against Fort San Juan...* Kingston (Douglass and Aikman) 1781.
1783 Dirom	Dirom, Alexander. *Thoughts on the State of the Militia of Jamaica.* [Kingston] (Douglass and Aikman) 1783.
1784 Dancer	Dancer, Thomas. *Bath Waters* I.
1787 Eclogues	*West-Indian Eclogues.* London (Lowndes, Philips) 1787.
1788 Act to Repeal	*An Act to Repeal Several Acts...respecting Slaves.* Santiago de la Vega (Douglass) 1788.
1788 Planter	A Jamaica Planter. *Observations upon the African Slave Trade.* London (Law; Faulder; Deighton) 1788.
1788 Beckford	Beckford, William, Jr. *Remarks upon the Situation of Negroes in Jamaica.* London (Egerton) 1788.
1788 Francklyn	[Francklyn, G.] *Observations...[on]...the Abolition of the Slave Trade.* Kingston (Strupar and Preston) 1788.
1788 Marsden	[Marsden, Peter.] *An Account of the Island of Jamaica.* Newcastle (Hodgson) 1788.
1788–9 M'Neill	M'Neill, Hector. *Observations on the Treatment of the Negroes in the Island of Jamaica.* London (Robinson) [1788 or 1789].
1789 Reports	*Two Reports...from...House of Assembly of Jamaica... on...the Slave Trade.* London (B. White and Son, *et al.*) 1789.
1790 Short Journey	*A Short Journey in the West Indies.* London (Murray, Forbes) 1790.
1790 Beckford	Beckford, William, Jr., *A Descriptive Account of the Island of Jamaica.* London (Egerton) 1790.
1790 Moreton	Moreton, J. B. *Manners and Customs in the West India Islands.* London (Richardson, Gardner and Walker) 1790.
1792 Edwards	[Edwards, Bryan.] *Poems, written chiefly in the West Indies.* Kingston (Aikman) 1792.
1792 Stewart	Stewart, James. *A Brief Account of the Present State of the Negroes in Jamaica.* Bath (Hazard) 1792.
1793 Edwards	Edwards, Bryan. *The History, Civil and Commercial, of the British Colonies in the West Indies,* vols. I, II. Dublin (Luke White) 1793.
1793 Mathews	Mathews, Samuel Augustus. *The Lying Hero...* St Eustatius (E. L. Low) 1793.
1794 Broughton	[Broughton, Arthur]. *Hortus Eastensis, or A Catalogue of Exotic Plants.* St Jago de la Vega (Aikman) 1794.
1794–7 Braco	*Journal and Account Book from Braco Estate, Trelawny, Jamaica.* MS covering in part the years 1794–7. Lent by Mr Fernleigh Gist (Seagram's, Jamaica).
1796 Assembly	Jamaica House of Assembly. *The Proceedings of the Governor and Assembly of Jamaica in Regard to the Maroon Negroes.* London (Stockdale) 1796.
1797 Higgins	Higgins, Bryan. *Observations...[on]...the Manufacture of Muscavado Sugar,* First Part.
1798 Evidence	*Evidence and Examinations taken before the Secret Committee of Safety.* St Jago de la Vega (Aikman) 1798.

c1800 Mansong — *The History and Adventures of Jack Mansong, the famous negro robber and terror of Jamaica.* Otley (William Walker) n.d.

1801 Dancer — Dancer, Thomas. *The Medical Assistant.* Kingston Aikman) 1801.

1801 Edwards — Edwards, Bryan. *The History, Civil and Commercial, of the British Colonies in the West Indies*, vol. III. London (John Stockdale) 1801.

1801 Higgins — Higgins, Bryan. *Observations...[on]...the Manufacture of Muscavado Sugar*, Third Part. St Jago de la Vega (Aikman) 1801.

1801–5 Nugent — Nugent, Lady Maria. *Journal* (1801–5). London (West India Committee) 1907, 1934.

1803 Dallas — Dallas, R[obert] C[harles.] *The History of the Maroons.* London (Strahan for Longman and Reese) 1803.

1807 Renny — Renny, Robert. *An History of Jamaica with Observations on the Climate* [etc.]. London (Cawthorn) 1807.

1808 Stewart — [Stewart, James of Trelawny.] *An Account of Jamaica and Its Inhabitants.* London (Longman *et al.*) 1808.

1811 Mathison — Mathison, Gilbert. *Notices Respecting Jamaica in 1808, 1809, 1810.* London (Stockdale) 1811.

1811 Titford — Titford, W. J., M.D. *Sketches Toward a Hortus Botanicus Americanus.* London (Stower) 1811.

1814 Lunan — Lunan, John. *Hortus Jamaicensis, or a Botanical Description...of Its Indigenous Plants hitherto known...*, 2 vols. Santiago de la Vega (Gazette) 1814.

1816 Subsistence — *An Act for the Subsistence, Clothing, and Better Regulation and Government of Slaves*, in John Lunan, *An Abstract of the Laws.* St Jago de la Vega (Gazette) 1819.

1817 Williamson — Williamson, John. *Medical and Miscellaneous Observations Relative to the West India Islands.* Edinburgh (Smellie) 1817.

a1818 Lewis (1834, 1845) — Lewis, M. G. *Journal of a West-India Proprietor.* London (Murray) 1834 (1845).

1819 Dancer — Dancer, Thomas. *The Medical Assistant.* Kingston (Aikman) 1819.

1819 Lunan — Lunan, John. *An Abstract of the Laws of Jamaica Relating to Slaves.* St Jago de la Vega (Gazette) 1819.

1820 Thomson — Thomson, James. *A Treatise on the Diseases of Negroes.* [Kingston] (Aikman) 1820.

182– Egan — Egan, Francis. *West Indian Pot Pourri.* Kingston (Francis Egan) 182–.

1821 Baillie — Baillie, John. *The Jamaica Distiller's Directory: A Treatise on Fermentation, Distillation, and Rectification.* St Jago de la Vega (Gazette) 2nd ed. 1821.

1823 Koromantyn — *Koromantyn Slaves: or West Indian Sketches.* London (Hatchard and Son) 1823.

1823 Roughley — Roughley, Thomas. *The Jamaica Planter's Guide.* London (Longman *et al.*) 1823.

1823 Stewart — Stewart, James. *A View of the Past & Present State of the Island of Jamaica.* Edinburgh (Oliver and Boyd) 1823.

1825 Shooting — *Account of a Shooting Excursion...in the Parish of Trelawny.* London (Harvey, Darton) 1825.

1825 Bickell	Bickell, The Rev. R. *The West Indies as they are*. London (Hatchard, Relfe) 1825.
1825 De la Beche	De la Beche, Sir H. T. *Notes on the present condition of the Negroes in Jamaica*. London (Cadell) 1825.
1826 Barclay	Barclay, Alexander. *A Practical View of the Present State of Slavery in the West Indies*. London (Smith, Elder) 1826.
1826 Williams	Williams, Cynric R. *A Tour through the Island of Jamaica...in the year 1823*. London (Hunt and Clarke) 1826.
1827 Hamel	*Hamel, the Obeah Man*. London (Hunt and Clarke) 1827.
1828 Barrett	Barrett, M. *A reply to the Speech of Dr Lushington*. London (Shackell and Baylis) 1828.
1828 Marly	*Marly; or The Life of a Planter in Jamaica*. Glasgow (Griffin) 2nd ed., 1828.
1828 Ordinances	*The Ordinances of the City and Parish of Kingston*. Kingston (Ja. Courant) 1828.
1828 Slave Law	*Slave Law of Jamaica: with Proceedings and Documents Relative thereto*. London (Ridgway) 1828.
1829– Almanack	*Jamaica Almanack for the year 1829–*. Kingston (Aikman) 1829–.
1830 Proprietor	A Jamaica Proprietor. *Negro Emancipation No Philanthropy*. London (Ridgway) 1830.
1831 Bleby	Bleby, Henry. *Death-Struggles of Slavery (1831)*. London (Hamilton, Adams) 1853.
1832 Letter from Legion	*A Letter from Legion to His Grace the Duke of Richmond*. London (Bagster) [1832].
1833 Baptist Missionaries	The Baptist Missionary Society. *Narrative of Recent Events connected with the Baptist Mission in this Island*. Kingston (Jordan and Osborn) 1833.
1833 Foulks	Foulks, Theodore. *Eighteen Months in Jamaica*. London (Whittaker, Treacher, Annott) 1833.
1833 Letter from Legion	*A Second Letter from Legion to His Grace the Duke of Richmond*. London (Bagster) 1833.
1833 Scott	[Scott, Michael.] *Tom Cringle's Log*. Edinburgh (Blackwood) 1833.
1833–4 Hosack (1876)	Hosack, W. *Jamaica: A Poem*. Kingston (De Cordova) 1876.
1835 Madden	Madden, R. R., M.D. *A Twelvemonths Residence in the West Indies*. 2 vols. London (Cochrane) 1835.
1835 Senior	Senior, Bernard M. *Jamaica, As It Was, As It Is*. London (Hurst) 1835.
1836 Widow	R., M., By a Widow. *A Young Englishman's First Residence in Jamaica*. Ashton (Orme) 1836.
1837 Belisario	Belisario, I. M. *Sketches of Character...of the Negro Population in the Island of Jamaica*. Kingston (Belisario) 1837.
1837 Macfadyen	Macfadyen, James. *The Flora of Jamaica Vol. I*. London (Longman *et al.*), Edinburgh (Black), Glasgow (Smith) 1837.
1837 Patterson	Patterson, Capt. John. *The Adventures of Captain John Patterson*. London (Boone) 1837.
1837 Slave's Diary	'Father Finlayson' of Penshurst Estate, St Ann. *Diary of a Slave (1827–38)*. MS in Institute of Jamaica.

1837 Sterne	Sterne, Henry. *A Statement of Facts, submitted to the Right Hon. Lord Glenely*. London (Chappell) 1837.
1837 Williams	Williams, James. *A Report of Evidence Taken at Brown's-Town and St Ann's Bay...Events since the 1st of August, 1834*. Falmouth (Castello) 1837.
1838 Kelly	Kelly, James. *Voyage to Jamaica and Seventeen Years' Residence in that Island*. Belfast (Wilson) 1838.
1839 M'Mahon	M'Mahon, Benjamin. *Jamaica Plantership*. London (Wilson) 1839.
1840 Barclay	Barclay, Alexander. *Remarks on Emigration to Jamaica*. London (Calkin and Budd) 1840.
1840–3 Chamberlaine	Chamberlaine, Dr Richard. 'Contributions to Ornithology', in *Companion to the Ja. Almanack* for 1840, 1842, 1843.
1843 Phillippo	Phillippo, James M. *Jamaica: Its Past and Present State*. London (John Snow) 1843.
1847 Gosse	Gosse, Philip H. (and Hill, R.). *The Birds of Jamaica*. London (Van Voorst) 1847.
1849 Coad	Coad, John. *A Memorandum of the Wonderful Providences of God*. London (Longman, etc.) 1849.
1849 Duncan	Duncan, Rev. Peter. *A Narrative of the Wesleyan Mission to Jamaica*. London (Partridge and Oakey) 1849.
1850 Macfadyen	Macfadyen, James. *The Flora of Jamaica Vol. II*. Jamaica (No t.p., never publ.) [1850, Date used by Fawcett and Rendle].
1851 Gosse	Gosse, Philip H. *A Naturalist's Sojourn in Jamaica*. London (Longman, Brown, Green and Longmans) 1851.
1854–5 *TJSA*	*Transactions of the Jamaica Society of Arts*. Kingston (DeCordova) 1854–5.
1858 Chambre	Chambre, Major. *Recollections of West-End Life*. Vol. II, chs. III–IX. London (Hurst and Blackett) 1858.
1859 Hill	Hill, Richard. *Lights and Shadows of Jamaica History...* Kingston (Ford and Gall) 1859.
1860 Trollope	Trollope, Anthony. *The West Indies and the Spanish Main*. London (Chapman, Hall) 2nd ed. 1860.
1862 Clutterbuck	[Hamley, William G.] *Captain Clutterbuck's Champagne*. Edinburgh and London (Wm. Blackwood and Sons) 1862.
1863 Waddell	Waddell, Hope Masterton. *Twenty-Nine Years in the West Indies and Central Africa*. London (Nelson) 1863.
1864 Grisebach	Grisebach, A. H. R. *Flora of the British West Indian Islands*. London (Lovell Reeve) 1864.
1867–8 *TJRSA*	*Trans. Ja. Royal Soc. of Arts & Agriculture New Series*, I, 4, 64. Kingston (De Cordova, McDougall) 1867–8.
1868 Hill	Hill, Richard. *On poisonous fishes*. Typescript, Institute of Jamaica.
1868 Russell	[Russell, Thomas.] *The Etymology of Jamaica Grammar*. Kingston (De Cordova, MacDougall) 1868.
1873 Gardner	Gardner, William J. *A History of Jamaica*. London (Stock) 1873.
1873 Rampini	Rampini, Charles I. G. *Letters from Jamaica*. Edinburgh Edinburgh (Edmonston and Douglas) 1873.
1875 Lawrence-Archer	Lawrence-Archer, J. H. *Monumental Inscriptions of the British West Indies*. London (Chatto and Windus) 1875.

1877 Murray *Feedin' 'Perrit*	Murray, Henry G. '*Feedin' 'Perrit': A lecture, Illustrative of Jamaica Mythology*. Kingston (De Cordova) 1877.
1877 *Kittle*	Murray, Henry G. *Manners and Customs of the Country a generation ago... Tom Kittle's Wake*. Kingston (E. Jordan) 1877.
1881 Harrison	Harrison, Thomas, Govt. surveyor. 'The Timber Supply of Jamaica', in *Handbook of Jamaica 1881, V*. Kingston (Govt. Printing Office) 1881.
1886 Hooper	Hooper, E. D. M. *Report upon the Forests of Jamaica*. London (Waterlow) 1886.
1887 Brassey	Brassey, Lady Annie. *In the Trades, the Tropics, and the Roaring Forties*. London (Longmans, Green) 1887.
1887 Ellis	Ellis, A. B. *The Tshi-Speaking Peoples of the Gold Coast*. London (Chapman and Hall) 1887.
1889 Sanguinetti	Sanguinetti, F. S. in *Victoria Quarterly*, May. Kingston (De Souza) 1889.
1890 Thomas	Thomas, Herbert T. *Untrodden Jamaica*. Kingston (Gardner) 1890.
1891 Fawcett	Fawcett, William. *Economic Plants...in Jamaica*. Kingston (Govt. Printing Estab.) 1891.
1891– *JIJ*	*Journal of the Institute of Jamaica*. Kingston (De Souza and Co.) 1891–1899.
1892 Cockrell	Cockrell, T. D. A. 'A provisional list of the fishes of Jamaica', in *Institute of Jamaica Bulletin, No. 1*.
1892 Day	Day, C. R. 'Native Musical Instruments', in Mockler-Ferryman, Capt. A. F., *Up the Niger*. London (Philip) 1892.
1893 Sullivan	[Sullivan, Caroline.] *The Jamaica Cookery Book*. Kingston (Gardner) 1893.
1894 Banbury	Banbury, Rev. [R.] T. *Jamaica Superstitions, or the Obeah Book*. Kingston (De Souza) 1894.
1894 Spinner	Spinner, Alice [Augusta Zelia Fraser.] *A Study in Colour*. London (T. Fisher Unwin) 2nd ed. 1894.
1896 Bates	Bates, William C. in *Journal of American Folklore* IX, XXXII, XXXIII. Boston (Houghton-Mifflin) 1896.
1896– Excelsior	*Excelsior race book*. Kingston (De Souza) 1896–.
1896 Heaven	Heaven, Violet. *Jamaica Proverbs & John Canoe Alphabet*. Kingston and Montego Bay (Aston Gardner) 1896.
1896 Trowbridge	Trowbridge, Ada W. in *Journal of American Folklore* IX, XXXV. Boston (Houghton-Mifflin) 1896.
1897 Heaven	Heaven, Violet. *The Negro Alphabet*. Kingston (Aston Gardner) 1897.
1897 *JJAS*	*Journal of the Jamaica Agricultural Society*. Kingston (Ja. Agric. Society) 1897.
1899 Hill	Hill, R. T. 'The Geology and Physical Geography of Jamaica', *Harvard Bulletin of the Museum of Comparative Zoology*, vol. XXXIV. Cambridge (Harvard University Press) 1899.
1899 Smith	Smith, Pamela Coleman. *Annancy Stories*. New York (Russell) 1899.
1900 Murray	Murray, W. C. *A Week's Rambling with Bra Quamin*. Savanna-la-mar (Cornwall Herald) 1900.
1902 Jordan-Evermann	Jordan, D. and Evermann, B. *American Food and Game Fishes*. New York (Doubleday, Page) 1902.

1903 Loscombe — Loscombe, A. R. 'English as spoken in the West Indies', in *The Gentleman's Magazine* vol. 294, 36–44. London 1903.

1905 Dodd — Dodd, E. A. ('E. Snod'). *Maroon Medicine.* Kingston (Jamaica Times) 1905.

1905 Smith — Smith, Pamela C. *Chim-Chim. Folk Stories from Jamaica.* London (The Green Sheaf) 1905.

1907 Jekyll — Jekyll, Walter. *Jamaican Song and Story.* London (Nutt) 1907.

1907 Reynolds — Reynolds, ? in *Jamaica Times,* 14 Dec. Kingston (Ja. Times) 1907.

1909 Harris — Harris, W. 'The Timbers of Jamaica', repr. from *West Indian Bulletin,* IX, 4, 297–328. [Kingston] (Advocate) 1909.

1909 Livingstone — Livingstone, Noel B. *Sketch Pedigrees of Some of the Early Settlers in Jamaica.* Kingston (Educational Supply Co.) 1909.

1909 Redcam — MacDermot, T. H. (pseud. Tom Redcam). *One Brown Girl And—A Jamaica Story.* Kingston (Ja. Times) 1909.

1910 Anderson-Cundall — Anderson, Izett and Cundall, Frank. *Jamaica Anancy Stories.* Kingston (Institute of Ja.) 1910.

1910 Fawcett — Fawcett, W. and Rendle, A. B. *Flora of Jamaica,* vol. I. London (Longmans) 1910.

1912 McK *Ballads* — McKay, Claude. *Constab. Ballads.* London (Watts) 1912.

1912 McK *Songs* — McKay, Claude. *Songs of Jamaica.* Kingston (Gardner) 1912.

1913 Fawcett — Fawcett, William. *The Banana Its Cultivation Distribution and Commercial Uses.* London (Duckworth) 1913.

1913 Harris — Harris, W. *Notes on Fruits and Vegetables in Jamaica.* Kingston (Govt. Printing Office) 1913.

1914 Fawcett — Fawcett, W. and Rendle, A. B. *Flora of Jamaica,* vol. III. London (Longmans) 1914.

p1914 Clerk — Clerk, Astley. *The Music and musical instruments of Jamaica.* Kingston (Astley Clerk) p1914.

1915 Cundall — Cundall, Frank. *Historic Jamaica.* London (Ballantyne, Hanson) 1915.

1915 De Lisser — De Lisser, H. G. *Susan Proudleigh.* London (Methuen) 1915.

1915 Wilson — Wilson, Sir James. *Lowland Scotch as Spoken in... Perthshire.* London (Oxford) 1915.

1916 Cruikshank — Cruikshank, J. Graham. *Black Talk.* Demerara (Argosy Co.) 1916.

1916 Dalziel — Dalziel, J. M. *A Hausa Botanical Vocabulary.* London (T. F. Unwin) 1916.

1917 Guppy — Guppy, H. B. *Plants, Seeds, and Currents in the West Indies and Azores.* London (Williams & Norgate) 1917.

1919 Cundall — Cundall, Frank. 'The Migration from Surinam to Jamaica', repr. from *Timehri* VI. Demerara (Argosy Co.) 1919.

1920 Fawcett — Fawcett, W. and Rendle, A. B. *Flora of Jamaica,* vol. IV. London (Longmans, Green) 1920.

1921 Franck — Franck, Harry A. *Roaming through the West Indies.* New York (Century) 1921.

1922 Beckwith — Beckwith, Martha Warren. 'Folk Games of Jamaica', in *Publications of the Folklore Foundation*, no. 1. Poughkeepsie (Vassar Coll.) 1922.

1922 Holbrooke — Holbrooke, Josef. *Jamaican Dances for the Young.* London (Goodwin and Tabb) 1922.

1923 Beckwith — Beckwith, Martha Warren. 'Christmas Mummings in Jamaica', in *Publications of the Folklore Foundation*, no. 2. New York (Vassar Coll.) 1923.

1923 Gowdey — Gowdey, C. C. 'The Principal Agricultural Pests of Jamaica', *Department of Agriculture: Entomological Bulletin*, no. 2. Kingston (Govt. Printing Office) 1923.

1923 Rattray — Rattray, Capt. Robert S. *Ashanti.* Oxford (Clarendon) 1923.

1924 Beckwith — Beckwith, Martha Warren. 'Jamaica Anansi Stories', *Memoirs of the Amer. Folklore Society*, vol. XVII. New York (Stechert) 1924.

1924 Beckwith *Hussay* — Beckwith, Martha Warren. 'The Hussay Festival in Jamaica', *Publications of the Folklore Foundation*, no. 4. Poughkeepsie (Vassar Coll.) 1924.

1924 Roberts — Roberts, Helen H. 'Some Drums And Drum Rhythms of Jamaica', *Natural History* 24: 241–51. New York (American Museum of Nat. Hist.) 1924.

1925 Beckwith — Beckwith, Martha Warren. 'Jamaica Proverbs', *Publications of the Folklore Foundation*, no. 6. Poughkeepsie (Vassar Coll.) 1925.

1926 Edmonds — Edmonds, Mrs F. S. *One Hundred Jamaica Recipes.* Kingston (Gleaner) 1926.

1926 Fawcett — Fawcett, W. and Rendle, A. B. *Flora of Jamaica*, vol. V. London (Quaritch) 1926.

1926 Roberts — Roberts, Helen H. 'Possible Survivals of African Song in Jamaica', *Musical Quarterly*, July 1926. New York (Schirmer) 1926.

1927 Anderson-Cundall — Anderson, Izett and Cundall, Frank. *Jamaica Negro Proverbs and Sayings.* London (Hazell, Watson and Viney) 1927.

1927 Beckwith — Beckwith, Martha Warren. 'Notes on Jamaican Ethnobotany', reprinted (with original pagination) in *Memoirs of the Amer. Folklore Soc.* XXI, 1928.

1927 Cundall — Cundall, Frank. *Chronological Outlines of Jamaica History*, 1492–1926. Kingston (Govt. Printing Office) 1927.

1927 Rattray — Rattray, Robert S. *Religion and Art in Ashanti.* London (Oxford University Press) 1927 (1954).

1927 Stafford — Stafford, Hurlburt. *The Orange Grove and Other Poems of the Jamaica Peasantry.* Montego Bay (Saint James Press) 1927.

1928 DeGoeje — DeGoeje, C. H., *The Arawak Language of Guiana.* Koninklijke Akademie van Wetenschappen te Amsterdam, 1928.

1928 Earle — Earle, F. S. *Sugar Cane and its Culture.* London (Chapman and Hall) 1928.

1929 Beckwith — Beckwith, Martha Warren. *Black Roadways.* Chapel Hill (University of North Carolina) 1929.

1929 Rattray — Rattray, Robert S. *Ashanti Law and Constitution.* Oxford (Clarendon) 1929.

1930 Jordan *Chk. List*	Jordan, D. S., Evermann, B. W. and Clark, H. W. *Check List of the Fishes...of North and Middle America.* A Reprint of Appendix X to the Report of the U.S. Commissioner of Fisheries for the fiscal year 1928. Originally issued February 1930.
c 1930 Clerk	Clerk, Astley. *Jamaican Folk Songs.* (Clippings from a lecture program.) Kingston (Institute of Ja.) c 1930.
1932 Williams	Williams, Joseph J. *Whence the 'Black Irish' of Jamaica?* New York (Dial) 1932.
1933 Beebe	Beebe, William and Tee-Van, John. *Field Book of the Shore Fishes of Bermuda.* New York and London (Putnam) 1933.
1933 Gaunt	Gaunt, Mary. *Harmony: a tale of the old slave days in Jamaica.* London (Ernst Benn) 1933.
1933 McK	McKay, Claude. *Banana Bottom.* New York and London (Harper) 1933.
1933 Williams	Williams, Joseph J. *Voodoos and Obeahs, Phases of West India Witchcraft.* London (George Allen & Unwin) 1933.
1934 Citrus	'The Cultivation of Citrus in Jamaica', *Dept. of Science & Agric. Bulletin 3 (New Series).* Kingston (Govt. Printing Office) 1934.
1934 Williams	Williams, Joseph J. *Psychic Phenomena of Jamaica.* New York (Dial) 1934.
1935–47 *HPJ*	Jacobs, H. P. *MS Collections of Materials on Language Usages in the West Indies,* copied with notes by Astley Clerk. 1935–47.
1936 Bond	Bond, James. *Birds of the West Indies.* Philadelphia (Academy of Natural Sciences) 1936.
1936 Fawcett	Fawcett, W., Rendle, A. B. and Moore, S. L. *Flora of Jamaica,* vol. VII. London (Quaritch) 1936.
1936 Hitchcock	Hitchcock, A. S. *Manual of the Grasses of the West Indies.* U.S. Dept. of Agric. Miscell. Pub. No. 243. Washington (U.S. Govt. Printing Office) 1936.
1936 Martinez	Martinez, Gene in *The Daily Gleaner.* Kingston (Gleaner) 1936.
1936 Olivier	Olivier, Lord [Sydney.] *Jamaica, the Blessed Island.* London (Faber) 1936.
1936 Rivero	Rivero, Luis Howell. *Collection of Fishes from Jamaica.* Repr. from *Handbook of Jamaica for 1936.* Kingston (Institute of Ja.) 1936.
1938 Williams	Williams, Joseph J., S.J. 'The Maroons of Jamaica', *Anthropological Series, Boston College Graduate School, III. 4 Dec. 1938.* Chestnut Hill, Mass. (Boston Coll.) 1938.
1940 Lynn-Grant	Lynn, W. G. and Grant, C. 'The Herpetology of Jamaica', *Bulletin of the Institute of Jamaica, Science Series,* no. 1. [Kingston] 1940.
1940 Perry	Perry, Louise M. *Marine Shells of the Southwest Coast of Florida.* Ithaca (Paleontological Research Institution) 1940.
1941 Kirkpatrick	Kirkpatrick, Oliver. *Country Cousin,* by John Canoe. A Selection of Dialect Tales Broadcast from ZQI. Kingston (Gleaner) 1941.

1941 Swabey	Swabey, Christopher. *The Principal Timbers of Jamaica.* Dept. of Science and Agric. Bulletin no. 29 (New Series) Jamaica. Kingston (Govt. Printer) 1941.
1941–54 *NHN*	Natural History Society of Jamaica. *Natural History Notes.* Kingston (Institute of Jamaica—Mimeographed) 1941–54.
1942 Bennett	Bennett, Louise. *Jamaica Dialect Verses.* Kingston (Herald) 1942.
1943 Bennett	Bennett, Louise. *Jamaican Humour in Dialect.* Kingston (Gleaner) 1943.
1943 *GL*	*Gleaner List.* MSS of Jamaican words and expressions collected in a contest, Dec. 1943. (On deposit at UWI.)
1943 Roth	Roth, Vincent. *Notes and Observations on Fish Life in British Guiana.* Georgetown (Daily Chronicle) 1943.
1944 Campbell	[Campbell, Granville.] *Jamaican Folk Songs.* Kingston (Montague's Music) [1944].
1945 Jacobs	Jacobs, H. P. in *Jamaica Historical Review,* vol. I. Kingston (Govt. Printer) 1945.
1946 Dunham	Dunham, Katherine. *Journey to Accompong.* New York (Holt) 1946.
1946–50 U. Newton	[Burke, Edmond N.] *Stories told by Uncle Newton.* Kingston (Jamaica Welfare) 1946–50.
1947 Bond	Bond, James. *Field Guide to Birds of the West Indies.* New York (Macmillan) 1947.
1948 Bennett	Bennett, Louise. *Mis Lulu Sez.* Kingston (Gleaner) 1948.
1948 Calypso	[*Calypso Tunes, with Words*] in Institute of Jamaica. Kingston (unpub. typescript) ?1948.
1949 Forbes	Forbes, Rosita. *Islands in the Sun.* London (Evans) 1949.
1949 Reid	Reid, V. S. *New Day.* New York (Knopf) 1949.
1949 Turner	Turner, Lorenzo D. *Africanisms in the Gullah Dialect.* Chicago (University of Chicago Press) 1949.
1950 Pioneer	Bennett, Louise, Clarke, Dorothy, Wilson, Una, and Others. *Anancy Stories and Dialect Verse.* Kingston (Pioneer) 1950.
1950 Jacobs	Jacobs, H. P. 'The Settlers of Morant', *W.I. Review,* XXIX (July 1950) 23–5.
1950 Smith	Smith, Victoria. *File List of Jamaican Fishes,* in Institute of Jamaica.
c 1950 Inst List	*List of the Plants of Jamaica.* Typescript, on deposit at Institute of Jamaica.
1950–1 Smith	Smith, Victoria. 'The Reef: Fish Fairyland of Jamaica', *NHN,* 1950–1. Kingston (Institute of Jamaica—Mimeographed) 1950–1.
1951 Proctor *Ferns*	Proctor, George R. 'The Ferns of the Hermitage Dam Area, Jamaica', *Occas. Papers of the Museum of the Institute of Ja.,* no. 5, 15 April 1951. Kingston (Gleaner) 1951.
1952 Kerr	Kerr, Madeline. *Personality and Conflict in Jamaica.* Liverpool (University Press) 1952.
1952 Topper	Topper, B. F. *How to Grow Pineapples.* Dept. of Agric. Ja. Extension Circular no. 49. Kingston (Printers Ltd) 1952.
1953 Bailey	Bailey, Beryl L. *Creole Languages of the Caribbean Area.* M.A. Thesis, unpub. (Columbia University) 1953.

1953 Moore — Moore, Joseph Graessle. *Religion of Jamaican Negroes.* Doctoral Diss., unpub. (Northwestern University) 1953.

1953 Murray — Murray, Tom. *Folk Songs of Jamaica.* London (Oxford) 1953.

1953–5 *WIMJ* — Asprey, G. F. and Thornton, Phyllis. 'Medicinal Plants of Jamaica', Parts I, II, III and IV, in *West Indian Medical Journal*, vol. 2, no. 4; vol. 3, no. 1; vol. 4, nos. 2 and 3. [Mona, Ja.] (UCWI) 1953–5.

1954 *FG* — Jamaica Agricultural Society. *The Farmer's Guide.* Glasgow (University Press) 1954.

1954 Howard — Howard, Richard. *The Vegetation on Bauxite and Related Soils in Jamaica.* Kingston (Institute of Ja. mimeographed publ.) 1954.

1954 Sherlock — Sherlock, Philip M. *Anansi, the Spider Man.* New York (Crowell) 1954.

1954 Stevenson — Stevenson, G. C. *Sugar Cane Varieties in Barbados, An Historical Review.* [Bridgetown] (Advocate) 1954.

c1954 Reckord — Reckord, Barry. *Della.* Typescript (on loan to LeP) c1954.

1955 Bennett — Bennett, Louise. Poems (cited by individual names) published in *The Star.* Kingston (Gleaner) 1955.

1955 Curtin — Curtin, Philip D. *Two Jamaicas.* Cambridge (Harvard University Press) 1955.

1955 Taylor — Taylor, Lady. *Introduction to the Birds of Jamaica.* London (Macmillan) 1955.

1956 Jeffrey-Smith — Jeffrey-Smith, May. *Bird-Watching in Jamaica.* Kingston (Pioneer) 1956.

1957 Bennett — Bennett, Louise. *Anancy Stories and Dialect Verse.* Kingston (Pioneer) 1957.

1957 *FFM* — Jamaica Agricultural Society. *The Farmer's Food Manual.* Glasgow (University Press) 1957.

1958 Yates-Thompson — Yates, C. S. and Thompson, R. W. 'Algunas notas provisionales sobre la toponimia española de Jamaica', *Proc. of Fifth Internat. Congress of Onomastic Sciences,* I, Salamanca.

1960 *CLS* — LePage, R. B. and DeCamp, David. *Creole Language Studies I.* London (Macmillan) 1960.

1960 *SAN Report* — Smith, M. G., Augier, Roy, and Nettleford, Rex. 'The Ras Tafari Movement in Kingston, Jamaica', *Institute of Social and Economic Research.* [Mona] (UCWI) 1960.

1961 BLB — Bailey, Beryl Loftman. *Grammar of Jamaican Creole,* typescript. unpub. Furnished by Author.

1961 *Ja. Talk* — Cassidy, F. G. *Jamaica Talk.* London (Macmillan) 1961.

1961 Katzin — Katzin, Margaret. 'It's All in the Life of a Country Higgler', in Kingston *Daily Gleaner*, 3, 10 and 17 September 1961.

1961 *CLS* — Le Page, R. B. ed. *Creole Language Studies II.* London (Macmillan) 1961.

1961 R. M. Murray — Murray, R. M. 'Quadrille Invitation', in Kingston *Daily Gleaner*, 6 August 1961, 20.

1962 BLB — Bailey, Beryl Loftman, *A Language Guide to Jamaica.* New York (Research Institute for the Study of Man) 1962.

1966 Navarro	Navarro, Tomás. *El Español en Puerto Rico.* Río Piedras (Editorial Universitaria) 1966.
1967–71 Guthrie	Guthrie, Malcolm. *Comparative Bantu.* Farnborough (Gregg Press) 4 vols. 1967–71
1974 Nazario	Nazario, Manuel Alvarez. *El Elemento Afronegroide en el Español de Puerto Rico.* San Juan (Instituto de Cultura Puertorriqueña) 1974.
1975 Tabouret-Keller	Tabouret-Keller, Andrée. 'Un champ sémantique: les noms d'identité raciale au Honduras Britannique' in *La Linguistique* 1975, part 1. Paris.
1977 Owens	Owens, Joseph. *Dread—The Rastafarians of Jamaica.* Kingston (Sangster) 1977.

DICTIONARIES AND GLOSSARIES CITED

Abraham, Hausa	Abraham, Major R. C. *Dictionary of the Hausa Language.* London (Austin) 1949.
Abraham, Tiv	Abraham, Capt. R. C. *A Dictionary of the Tiv Language.* Hertford (Austin) 1940.
ADD	Wentworth, Harold. *American Dialect Dictionary.* New York (Crowell) 1944.
Adams	Adams, Capt. John. *Remarks on the Country...from Cape Palmas to the River Congo.* 1823.
Alexandre	Alexandre, R. F. '*La Langue mõré*', tome 1. *Memoires de l'Institut français d'Afrique Noire.* (Ifan-Dakar) 1953.
Alvarado	Alvarado, Lisandro. *Obras Completas de Lisandro Alvarado.* 3 vols. Vol. 1, Glossario de Voces Indigenas de Venezuela. Caracas (La Nacion) 1953–5.
Bargery	Bargery, Rev. G. P. *A Hausa-English Dict'y. and English-Hausa Vocab.* London (Milford) 1934.
Barrère	Barrère, Albert and Leland, Charles G. *A Dictionary of Slang, Jargon and Cant.* 2 vols. London (Ballantyne Press) 1889, 1890.
Baumann	Baumann, H. and Westermann, D. *Les Peuples et les civilisations de l'Afrique.* Paris (Payot) 1948.
B and V	Berrey, L. V. and Van den Bark, M. *The American Thesaurus of Slang.* New York (Crowell) 1942, 1947.
Burrow-Emeneau	Burrow, T. and Emeneau, M. S. *A Dravidian Etymological Dictionary.* Oxford (Clarendon) 1961.
Carambula	Carambula, Ruben. *Negro y tambor.* Buenos Aires, Argentina (Ferfoglia, Baretto and Paskulin) 1952.
Christaller	Christaller, Rev. J. G. *Dictionary of the Asante and Fante Language, Called Tshi (Twi).* 2nd ed. Basel (Basel Evangelical Missionary Soc.) 1933.
Clarke	Clarke, Mary Lane. *A Limba-English Dictionary.* Freetown (Government Printer) 1929.
DA	Mathews, M. M. *Dictionary of Americanisms.* Chicago (University of Chicago Press) 1946.
DAE	Craigie, Sir William and Hulbert, James R. *A Dictionary of American English.* 4 vols. Chicago (University of Chicago Press) 1938.
Craven	Craven, Rev. Thomas and Chitambar, Bishop J. R. *The New Royal Dictionary: English into Hindustani and Hindustani into English.* Lucknow (Methodist Publishing House) 1932.
Doke	Doke, C. M., Malcolm, D. McKay and Sikakana, M. A. *English and Zulu Dictionary.* Johannesburg (Witwatersrand University Press) 1958.
EDD, EDG	Wright, Joseph. *English Dialect Dictionary* and *Grammar.* London (Oxford University Press) 1896–8, 1905.
Flacourt	Flacourt, Etienne de. *Dictionnaire de la Langue de Madagascar.* Paris (E. Leroux) 1905.
Focke	Focke, H. C. *Negerengelsch Woordenboek.* Leiden (Van den Heuvell) 1855.
Forbes	Forbes, Duncan. *A Dictionary: Hindustani and English... /and/ English and Hindustani.* London (Allen) 1848.

Friderici	Friderici, Georg. *Amerikanistisches Wörterbuch.* Hamburg (Cram, De Gruyter) 1947.
Greenberg	Greenberg, Joseph H. *Studies in African Linguistic Classification.* New Haven (Compass) 1955.
Grose	Grose, Francis. *A classical dictionary of the vulgar tongue.* London (S. Hooper) 1785.
Hause	Hause, H. E. 'Terms for Musical Instruments in the Sudanic Languages...', *Journal of the Amer. Oriental Soc.* Supplement no. 7 (January–March 1948).
Herskovits	Herskovits, Melville J. and Herskovits, Frances S. *Suriname Folk-Lore.* New York (Columbia University Press) 1936.
Homburger	Homburger, L. *The Negro-African Languages.* London (Routledge, Kegan Paul) 1949.
Malaret (1925)	Malaret, Augusto. *Diccionario de Americanismos.* (Con un Indice Cientifico de Fauna y Flora.) Mayaguez, Puerto Rico (Carrero) 1925.
Malaret (1937)	Malaret, Augusto. *Vocabulario de Puerto Rico.* San Juan (Imprenta Venezuela) 1937.
Mason	Mason, J. Alden. 'The Languages of South American Indians', in *Handbook of South Amer. Indians,* Smithsonian Institution, Bureau of Amer. Ethnology, Bulletin 143, vol. VI, part 3, pp. 157–317. Washington (U.S. Govt. Printing Office) 1950.
Melzian	Melzian, Hans. *A Concise Dictionary of the Bini Language of Southern Nigeria.* London (Kegan Paul) 1937.
Mendonça	Mendonça, Renato. *A Influência Africano no Português do Brasil.* 3rd ed. (1948). Porto (Livraria Figueirinhas) 1935.
Migeod	Migeod, F. W. H. *The Mende Language.* London (Kegan Paul, Trench, Trubner) 1908.
OED, OEDS	Murray, James A. H., *et al.,* Burchfield, R. W. *Oxford English Dictionary* and *Supplements.* Oxford (Clarendon) 1933, 1972, 1976.
Ortiz	Ortiz, Fernandez. *Los Instrumentes de la Musica Afrocubana.* 2 vols. Habana (Publicaciones de la Dirección de Cultura del Ministerio de Educación) 1952.
PADS	*Publications of the American Dialect Society.*
Partridge	Partridge, Eric. *A Dictionary of Slang and Unconventional English.* London (Routledge, Kegan Paul) 1949.
Pichardo y Tapia	Pichardo y Tapia, Esteban. *Pichardo novísimo: o Diccionario provincial...de voces y frases cubanas.* Habana (Selecta) 1953.
Radcliffe	Radcliffe, J. *Lectures on Negro Proverbs.* Kingston (de Cordova, McDougall) 1869.
Ramos	Ramos, Arthur. *O Negro Brasileiro. Biblioteca Pedagogica Brasileira Serie 5a—Brasiliana.* vol. 188. Sao Paulo (Companhia Editora Nacional) 1951.
Revollo	Revollo, Pedro Maria. *Costeñismos Colombianos.* Barranquilla [Talleres graficos de la Ed. Mejoras] 1942.
Robinson	Robinson, Charles Henry. *Dictionary of the Hausa Language.* Cambridge (University Press) 1925.
Rodman	Rodman, Hyman. 'Glossary of Slang Terms', in 'Family Relationships in a Lower-Class Negro Village in Trinidad', an unpublished Ph.D. thesis, Harvard University, pp. 167–78. Cambridge, Mass., 1957.
Rodriques	Rodriques, D. W. *Bananas...Economic History of Production and Trade...* Kingston (Government Printer) 1955.

Roig y Mesa	Roig y Mesa, Juan Tomás. *Diccionario Botanico de Nombres Vulgares Cubanos*. 2 vols. Ministerio de Agricultura Boletin No. 54. Habana (Seoane, Ferandez) 1953.
Rood	Rood, N. *Ngombe-Nederlands-Frans Woordenboek*, in Annalen van het Koninklijk Museum van Belgisch-Congo. Tervuren, Belgie (D. G. Michiels) 1958.
Santamaría	Santamaría, Francisco J. *Diccionario General de Americanismos*. 3 vols. Mexico City (Robredo) 1942.
Schneider	Schneider, Rev. G. D. *Cameroons Creole Dictionary, First Draft*. Bamenda, Southern Cameroons (mimeographed) 1960.
Simpson	Simpson, George Eaton. 'Jamaican Revivalist Cults', in *Social and Economic Studies*, v, xi, pp. 321–442. Mona, Jamaica (UCWI) 1956.
SND	Grant, William and Murison, David D. *Scottish National Dictionary*. Edinburgh (Scottish National Dictionary Association) 1941–76.
Tejera	Tejera, Emiliano. *Palabras Indijenas de la Isla de Santo Domingo*. Trujillo (Editora del Caribe) 1951.
W_2	Merriam-Webster. *Unabridged International Dictionary*. 2nd ed. (1934).
W_3	Merriam-Webster. *Unabridged International Dictionary*. 3rd ed. (1961).
Westermann	Westermann, Dietrich and Bryan, M. A. *The Languages of West Africa*. London (Oxford University Press) 1952.
Westermann, Ewe	Westermann, Dietrich. *Wörterbuch der Ewe-Sprache*. Berlin (Akademie-Verlag) 1954.
Wright	Wright, Richardson. *Revels in Jamaica*. New York (Dodd, Mead) 1937.
Yoruba Dicty.	*A Dictionary of the Yoruba Language*. London (Oxford University Press) 1953.
Zayas y Alfonso	Zayas y Alfonso, Alfredo. *Lexicografía Antillana*. 2 vols. Habana (Tipos-Molina) 1931.

ABBREVIATIONS

I. GENERAL

abbr abbreviation, abbreviated
absol absolute, absolutely
abstr abstract, abstractly
addr address
adj adjective
adv adverb
aph aphetic
app apparently
arch archaic
assim assimilation, assimilated
assoc association, associated
attrib attributive, attributively
auxil auxiliary
bot in botanical books
cent century
cf confer, compare
cit citation, cited
cogn cognate (with)
colloq colloquial, colloquially
compar comparative
concr concrete, concretely
conn connected, connection
const construction, constructed (with)
correl correlative
corresp corresponding (to)
cpd compound
def definite
demonstr demonstrative
deriv derivation, derivative
derog derogatory, derogatively
descr descriptive
devel developed
dial dialect, dialectal
diff different, differing
dimin diminutive
ellipt elliptical, elliptically
equiv equivalent
erron erroneous, erroneously
esp especially
estab established
etym etymology, etymological
euphem euphemism, euphemistically
evid evidently
ex example
exc except
excl exclamation, exclamatory
expl explanation
fig figurative, figuratively
folk-etym folk-etymology, -ical
freq frequent, frequently
gen generally
hist historical, historically
ibid *ibidem*, in the same place
ichth ichthyological, in books on fish
ident identified
indef indefinite, indefinitely
infin infinitive
infl influence, influenced
int interjection
interp interpreted, interpretation
interrog interrogative, -ly
intr intransitive
introd introducing, introduction
irreg irregular, irregularly
iter iterative
joc jocular, jocularly
lit literally
metaph metaphorical, metaphorically
metath metathesis
neg negative, negatively
obj object, objective
obs obsolete
occas occasional, occasionally
orig origin, originally
ornith ornithological, in books on birds
pass passive
perh perhaps
pers person, personal
phon phonetic
phr phrase
pl plural
poss possessive
ppl participial
pple participle
prec preceding
prep preposition
pres present
prob probable, probably
pron pronoun
pronom pronominal
pronunc pronunciation

prov	proverb, proverbial	superl	superlative
redup	reduplicative	techn	technical
refl	reflexive	trans	transitive
reg	regular, regularly	transf	transferred
rel	relative	transl	translated, translation
repr	represents	ult	ultimate, ultimately
resp	respective, respectively	uncom	uncommon
sb	substantive, noun	uncert	uncertain
sc	*scilicet*, namely, that is	unstr	unstressed
sg	singular	usu	usually
sp	spelling, spelt	var	variant, varying, various
spec	special	vb	verb
specif	specific, specifically	vbl	verbal
std	standard	vulg	vulgar, vulgarly
subj	subject		

2. CONTRIBUTORS, PARISHES, TOWNS, LANGUAGES, PUBLICATIONS, ETC.

Accom	Accompong, Maroon settlement in parish of St Elizabeth.
ADD	Harold Wentworth, *American Dialect Dictionary.*
Afr	African.
BA	Barbados.
BL	Belize.
BLB	Beryl Loftman Bailey. See bibliography.
CB	Common Bantu
CBL	C. Bernard Lewis, Director, Institute of Jamaica.
Clar	Parish of Clarendon.
CLS	*Creole Language Studies.*
DA	M. M. Mathews, *Dictionary of Americanisms.*
DAE	W. A. Craigie, *Dictionary of American English.*
DAP	Dulcie A. Powell, Botanist, Institute of Jamaica.
DeC	David DeCamp. See bibliography.
DOST	*Dictionary of the Older Scottish Tongue.*
Dut	Dutch.
EB	Eddie Baugh (Portland parish, 1957).
EDD	*English Dialect Dictionary.*
EDG	*English Dialect Grammar.*
Eld	Elderslie, Maroon settlement in parish of St Elizabeth.
Engl	English.
EP	Eunice Paul (St Andrew, 1956).
EWM	Elsie Woo-Ming (St Andrew, 1956).
FFM	*Farmers' Food Manual.*
FG	*Farmer's Guide.*
FGC	Frederic G. Cassidy.
Fr	French.
F & W	Funk & Wagnalls *Standard Dictionary.*
G	Guyana.
Ger	German.
GHC	Gabriel H. Coulthard, UCWI.
GHP	George H. Proctor, Botanist, Institute of Jamaica.
GL	*Gleaner* lists of dialect words gathered 1943, all parishes.
Gr	Greek.
Han	Parish of Hanover.

HPJ Herbert P. Jacobs, Collection of Notes on Jamaican language.
Irel Ireland.
Ja Jamaica.
JB Jean Brown (St Andrew, 1956).
JC Jamaican Creole, sometimes in citations Jean Creary (St Catherine 1958).
JH John Holm.
JHSB *Jamaican Historical Society Bulletin.*
JIJ *Journal of the Institute of Jamaica.*
JN Joyce Nation (St Andrew, 1957).
Kgn Kingston (Jamaica).
Ko Kongo
Lat Latin.
LeP Robert B. Le Page. See bibliography.
Man Parish of Manchester.
Mc Louise McLoskey (1956).
MED *Middle English Dictionary.*
MEL MacEdward Leach.
N Nicaragua.
NJL Mrs N. J. Lewis (St Catherine, 1961).
ODS *Oxford Dictionary, Supplement.*
OED *Oxford English Dictionary.*
PADS *Publication of the American Dialect Society.*
Pg Portuguese.
Port Parish of Portland.
RJO R. Jerome Owens (St Andrew, 1958).
RWT R. Wallace Thompson (St Andrew).
SC Surinam Creole.
SJR Shirley J. Reid (St Andrew).
SND *Scottish National Dictionary.*
Sp Spanish.
StAnd Parish of St Andrew.
StAnn Parish of St Ann.
StC Parish of St Catherine.
StdE Standard English.
StE Parish of St Elizabeth.
StJ Parish of St James.
StM Parish of St Mary.
StT Parish of St Thomas.
T Trinidad.
TJSA *Transactions of the Jamaica Society of Arts.*
Tre Parish of Trelawney.
TRSAA *Transactions of the Royal Society of Arts and Agriculture.*
UCWI University College of the West Indies, Mona, Jamaica.
UWI University of the West Indies.
W2 *Webster's International Dictionary*, 2nd edition.
W3 *Webster's International Dictionary*, 3rd edition.
West Parish of Westmoreland.

LINGUISTIC INTRODUCTION

The Historical Phonology of Jamaican English

Bibliography and abbreviations

Christaller, *Dicty*. Rev. J. G. Christaller, *Dictionary of the Asante and Fante Language Called Tshi (Twi)*. 2nd edn. Basel: Basel Evangelical Missionary Society, 1933.

Christaller, *Grammar*. Idem, *A Grammar of the Asante and Fante Language Called Tshi (Chwee, Twi)*. Basel: 1875.

CLS I, II — *Creole Language Studies* ed. R. B. Le Page. London: Macmillan, vol. I, 1960; vol. II, 1961.

Cooper — Christopher Cooper, *The English Teacher* (London, 1687), ed. Bertil Sundby. Lund: Gleerup, 1952.

Dobson — E. J. Dobson, *English Pronunciation 1500–1700*. 2 vols. Oxford: Clarendon Press, 1957; 2nd edn. 1968.

Douglas — *James Douglas On English Pronunciation* (MS *c.* 1740) ed. Börje Holmberg. Lund: Gleerup, 1956.

EDD — *The English Dialect Dictionary* ed. Joseph Wright. London: Oxford University Press (reprinted), 1961.

EDG — Joseph Wright, *The English Dialect Grammar*. London: Henry Frowde, 1905. (Also forms an appendix to vol. VI of *EDD*.)

EDGI — The Index to *EDG*.

Gimson — A. C. Gimson, *An Introduction to the Pronunciation of English*. Second (corrected) reprinting, London: Edward Arnold, 1965.

IPA — The International Phonetic Association and its Alphabet, as set out in *The Principles of the International Phonetic Association*. London: Department of Phonetics, University College, Gower Street, London, W.C.1.

Ladefoged — Peter Ladefoged, *A Phonetic Study of West African Languages*. Cambridge: Cambridge University Press, 1964.

Luick — Karl Luick, *Historische Grammatik der Englischen Sprache*. Oxford: Basil Blackwell (reprinted), 1964.

ME — Middle English.

ModE — Modern English.

OE — Old English.

OED — *The Oxford English Dictionary*. Oxford: Clarendon Press, 1933, 1961.

OF — Old French.

RP — 'Received Pronunciation', or the educated Southern British English dialect, as described by Gimson.

Westermann — Diedrich Westermann, *A Study of the Ewe Language* (1907) translated A. L. Bickford-Smith. Oxford: Oxford University Press, 1930.

Wyld — H. C. Wyld, *A Short History of English*. London: John Murray (3rd edn.) 1927.

I. INTRODUCTION TO SECOND EDITION

The discussion below of the historical phonology of Jamaican English, written for the first edition and here only modified in some minor respects, was intended to help the non-specialist as well as the specialist with those factors and processes which must be referred to in order to explain historically, as far as is possible, the pronunciations recorded in the dictionary.

LeP wishes to record his thanks to Anthony Warner, John Kelly and Paul Werth for their criticisms and help. It has not been possible to accept all their detailed suggestions, although a number have been incorporated in the text. It is likely that they would have been happier with a more wholesale revision towards an updated and more specialist approach. Something more needs to be said to justify the retention of the old version, beyond the very urgent need to keep the costs of reprinting as low as possible.

As we explain on p. xliii, educated southern British usage, or RP (Received Pronunciation), was taken as the external reference point. It would, it is true, have been preferable to speak of the Jamaican phonemes as *corresponding to*, rather than as *reflexes of*, those of RP. By using the latter term we indicated that the phonology still predicted accurately what interpretation Jamaican speakers would place on an RP pronunciation newly heard. As we noted, the reason for that was that RP and standard British usage had been since the nineteenth century the models—at least in principle, and to some considerable extent in practice also—for the Jamaican education system. Today that is no longer true. Educated Jamaican English provides its own model.

However, it remains true that by taking RP as the external reference point we were using one which was very fully documented by *OED* and various pronouncing dictionaries, and by Dobson and the authorities on which he relies.

We had noted that, assuming the Jamaican vernacular to have its origins in a creolized pidgin, the history of its phonology could not be reconstructed with any very great accuracy. To the processes of seventeenth-century pidginization, eighteenth-century creolization, and nineteenth- and twentieth-century gradual decreolization under the influence of education must today be added those induced by a growing sense of national and regional identity among Jamaicans. Since the first edition was prepared a great deal more work has been done both on the study of pidgins and creoles and on historical English phonology. Such studies as Chomsky and Halle's *Sound Pattern of English* (New York, 1968), Michael Samuels' *Linguistic Evolution with Special Reference to English* (Cambridge, 1972) and Roger Lass's *English Phonology and Phonological Theory* (Cambridge, 1976) have contributed (sometimes conflicting) views on the nature of the seventeenth-century English vowel system, and have re-interpreted the evidence of the orthoepists—for example, of Christopher Cooper. The *Survey of English Dialects* directed by Harold Orton has provided a great deal of evidence of modern dialectal pronunciations to add to that of the *English Dialect Dictionary* and the (incomplete for our first edition but now complete) *Scottish National Dictionary*. In spite of Roger Lass's (1976) dismissal of the tense/lax distinction as baseless in articulatory fact and useless in phonological theory, it nevertheless still seems to offer some insight into the possible re-interpretation of the seventeenth-century English system by West African speakers.

It would be gratifying if we could now establish a distinctive-feature representation of seventeenth-century pidgin English as a base line with as much certainty as some have of an abstraction known as Middle English. Unfortunately, it is still true that the comparable necessary work has not been done for West Africa.

We set out for comparison four vowel–phoneme systems. They have been reconstructed so as to give each set of phonemes as nearly as possible the same abstract status. The first is based on Christaller's 1881 description of Twi; the second, on A. C. Gimson's reconstruction, from the orthoepists and other sources, of Early Modern English (south-east Midlands educated usage); the third, on Gimson's description of modern RP, and the fourth, on FGC's description of Jamaican Creole. Some contrasts primarily of vowel-length in older varieties of English have been replaced in both JC and in RP (as Gimson notes) by contrasts primarily of vowel-quality, (although as noted in places below there is some fluctuation of length in relation to stress in JC). Early Modern English seems to represent a transitional stage in this change. Except where they reflect a primary phonemic contrast, therefore, the length-marks of Gimson's own symbolisations for Early Modern English and RP have been omitted. The corresponding systematic symbols used for JC in the remainder of the dictionary have been designed to make use of conventional type, and are set out in §2 below.

Wherever possible in the following pages the values of the Jamaican vowel-phonemes have been accounted for in terms of (*a*) the vowel-sounds of conservative seventeenth- or eighteenth-century English dialects or (*b*) their reinterpretation in terms of some West African system such as that of Twi or (*c*) pan-West African characteristics such as the incidence of nasality or (*d*) other general phonetic or phonological processes. Lacking any distinctive feature analysis which could help us to reconstruct the West African element it has not been possible to undertake a major recasting of this historical phonology in such a way as to make it more coherent for the specialist whilst retaining its value for the non-specialist. We have had to be content with minor revisions, and must ask the specialist to use it as a summary of the evidence rather than a systematic treatment. We wish to underline the point that resemblances between the phonology of JC and that of certain modern British or American dialects in some respects point to a comparable degree of conservatism along one or other continuum of sound-change rather than to a necessary direct connection.

Twi	Early Modern English	RP	JC
Monophthongs			
i u	i u	i u	i u
ɪ ʊ	ɪ ʊ	ɪ ʊ	ɪ ʊ
e o	o, ɤ		o
ɛ ɒ	ɛː, ɛ ə	ɛ ɜ ə ɔ	ɛ
æ (or a) ɑ	æ ɒː, ɒ	æ ʌ	aː, a
		ɑ ɒ	
Diphthongs			
'The vowels are as a rule short.' There are no glides or diphthongs. All except e and o can be nasalized	iu ui	ɪə ʊə	iɛ uo
	eu ou	eɪ	oʊ
	ɛi	ɛə əʊ ɔɪ	
	əi, əu ɔi	aɪ aʊ	aɪ

Phonetic transcriptions are given in the head of an entry only if it is necessary to draw particular attention to the pronunciation, and are then given in square brackets, thus: [ˈθrɪpəns].

2. THE PHONEMES OF JAMAICAN CREOLE

The phonemic symbols, used between diagonals thus: / ninggam-baiti /, have the following phonetic values in the broad dialect:*

Vowels and diphthongs

/ii/ long, high, tense, front unrounded; generally closer to cardinal 1 [i] than RP /iː/.
/i/ short, high, lax front unrounded; closer to cardinal 1 than RP /ɪ/.
/ie/ a falling diphthong [iɛ], [iɐ], with palatalization of preceding consonant.
/e/ short, mid-front, half-open, half-tense, generally more close and more tense than RP /e/.
/a/ short, open, central, unrounded, range [a], [ɐ], [ɑ].
/aa/ long, open, central, unrounded, range [aː], [ɐː], [ɑː].
/ai/ a falling diphthong, range [ɐi] to [ɐɛ].
/o/ short, centralized or mid-back, half-rounded, approximately [ɵ].
/ou/ a falling diphthong, range [ɐu] to [ɵu], [ɵʊ].
/u/ short, high back, rounded; closer to cardinal 8 [u] than RP [ʊ].
/uo/ a falling diphthong, range [uᵒ], [uᵓ], [uᵃ], [oᵓ].
/uu/ long, high back, rounded; closer to cardinal 8 than RP /uː/.

Consonants

/b/ [b] voiced bilabial stop.
/p/ [p] voiceless bilabial stop.
/d/ [d] voiced alveolar stop.
/t/ [t] voiceless alveolar stop.
/gy/ [ɟ] voiced palatal stop.
/ky/ [c] voiceless palatal stop.
/g/ [g] voiced velar stop.
/k/ [k] voiceless velar stop.
/m/ [m] bilabial nasal.
/n/ [n] alveolar nasal.
/ny/ [ɲ] palatal nasal.
/ng/ [ŋ] velar nasal—also used to denote nasalization in the preceding vowel; thus /dong/ *down* may represent [dɵŋ] or [dɵ̃].
/v/ [v] voiced labiodental fricative.
/f/ [f] voiceless labiodental fricative.
/z/ [z] voiced alveolar fricative.
/s/ [s] voiceless alveolar fricative.
/sh/ [ʃ] voiceless alveopalatal fricative.
/j/ [dʒ] voiced alveopalatal affricate.
/ch/ [tʃ] voiceless alveopalatal affricate.
/l/ [l] alveolar lateral.

* The RP sounds are denoted by the symbols used in Gimson. For some aspects of the description the terms used are those of K. Pike, *Phonemics* (Ann Arbor, 1947). Stated ranges of phonetic values are very approximate, based on the observations of Mc.

/w/ [w] bilabial semivowel.
/r/ [r] or [ɹ] alveolar trill, flap or semivowel.
/y/ [j] palatal semivowel.
h [h] is not a phoneme, but denotes oral friction accompanying the vowel as an allophonic variation in certain stressed positions.

3. RANGE OF DIALECTS COVERED

The Dictionary includes forms attested at any time between 1655 and the present day, from many different social levels. Furthermore, no speaker today at any level is consistently monosystemic in his usage—he may, according to his audience, speak in broad dialect or in a more educated form of Jamaican English. No description of the phonology can therefore represent accurately all the features represented in the dictionary; the description which follows is as generous as possible but is in general a description of the present-day Creole dialect rather than of Standard Jamaican; if the usage described is regarded as one end of a continuum, and RP (which is still to some extent the model language for Jamaican English) as the other, then the pronunciation of individuals may represent any point in the continuum. For example, the word *face* in the broad Creole English is pronounced with a falling /ie/ diphthong, /físes/; further up the educational ladder with a rising /ie/ diphthong /fiés/; further up still it may be a short, tense monophthong, /fes/, and the almost Anglicized speaker will of course say /féis/, although both elements of the diphthong here are liable to be closer and tenser than with the RP speaker.

4. HISTORICAL BACKGROUND

The historical background to the evolution of Jamaican English has been described in some detail in *CLS* 1, *Jamaican Creole*, and may be briefly summarized here. When the island was discovered on Columbus's third voyage it was inhabited by Arawak Indians. After 100 years of Spanish settlement these had been entirely wiped out, leaving only place and plant and animal names in use by the Spanish as linguistic evidence of their existence. Negroes were imported by the Spaniards from West Africa, and some of these escaped to the hills to form the first Maroon settlements. In 1655 Cromwell's expeditionary force took the island; nearly all the Spaniards were evicted or taken prisoner, and they in turn have left the same kind of, and almost as little, linguistic trace as the Indians. About 250 Maroons remained in the island.

Cromwell's force, under the command of General Venables, consisted of about seven to eight thousand officers and men, of whom about half had been drawn from various regiments in England and about half raised in Barbados and the Leeward Islands of St Kitts, Nevis and Montserrat. It is very likely that among the troops raised in the West Indies, West of England and Irish servants and, to a less extent, Scotch servants predominated. St Kitts, Nevis and Barbados had been settled since the 1620's and it is likely that by the 1650's the patterns of Creole speech in these islands were already formed, either independently, or on the common basis of a slave-trade pidgin English which in turn may have been influenced by an earlier Portuguese pidgin.* These colonies continued to supply settlers, and some slaves, for the new colony in Jamaica; in addition, indentured servants were sent from Ireland and the West of England, Bristol being the main port for Jamaica at the time. The main contact of the Negro slaves was with these indentured servants and poor whites, who acted as bookkeepers and overseers on the plantations, rather than with the planters themselves. The growth of the white population was slow compared with the Negro. By 1675 there were probably about nine thousand whites and nine to ten thousand slaves in the island; by the end of the century the white population was still not very much in excess of nine thousand, but the Negro population by this time was over forty thousand.

The slaves were brought from many parts of the West African coast, and a few even came from Madagascar; but in the first fifty years of the island's settlement the largest number from any one language-community were those from the Gold Coast (where the Royal Africa Company had factories) and its hinterland, speaking therefore one of the Akan-Ashanti languages; and the next largest number were from Dahomey, many of whom probably spoke Ewe. During the eighteenth century, as the rapacity inspired among the Africans themselves by the profits of the slave-trade led to civil wars and upheavals, and as the chief European nations in the trade—the Portuguese, Dutch, English and French—fought each other for factories and trading rights, captains were forced to go further and further afield for cargoes, while at the same time the demand for slaves in the West Indies and America grew immensely. Far larger numbers of slaves from the Bight of Benin, the Congo and Angola were eventually delivered to Jamaica by the time the trade was brought to an end in 1807–8; but by that time, as both the linguistic and historical evidence show, the Akan- and Ewe-speaking slaves were firmly established in a *Creole* society, speaking Creole English, despising newcomers from Africa and dominating the Maroon settlements which their runaways had joined, settlements which have since been centres of linguistic conservatism.

One might therefore say that the dominant features of the mould in which Jamaican Creole was formed were as follows:

1655–1700 Contact under conditions of duress between large numbers of West African slaves, lacking a common language although dominated by the Twi-Fante-Ga-Ewe-speaking groups, and comparatively small numbers of poorly educated bookkeepers and overseers from Britain, dominated by Western, Irish and Northern dialect speakers. The English speech of many of these in the early years had been conditioned by previous residence in the Leeward Islands or Barbados. The Jamaican contact took place in a West Indian environment which had its own common, distinctive, cultural flavour, so that the emergent pidgin was influenced by established Caribbean usages of Amerindian, Portuguese, Spanish, Dutch, French and English origin. In particular, its patterns may have been influenced by those already established over the previous century

* On this subject see R. W. Thompson, 'A Note on Some Possible Affinities Between the Creole Dialects of the Old World and the New', in *CLS* II, J. Voorhoeve, 'Historical and linguistic evidence in favour of the relexification theory etc.' in *Language in Society* 2, 1973, pp. 133–46 and R. B. Le Page, 'Processes of Pidginization and Creolization' in A. Valdman, *Pidgin and Creole Linguistics* (Bloomington, 1977), pp. 222–55.

for the pidgin Portuguese and subsequent pidgin English of the West African trade.

1700–1808 Contact between constantly growing numbers of new slaves—of whom an increasing proportion came from the Bight of Benin, the Congo and Angola—and the by-now established Creole-speaking slave-society; with an ever-diminishing amount of contact on the part of individual slaves with native English speakers of whom, as the century wore on, a higher proportion tended to be Scots.

During this period the Creole English became the accepted *lingua franca* of the island among the slaves, between Creole whites and slaves, in the growing community of free people of colour, and—in a less extreme form—among many of the Creole whites themselves. The use of metropolitan dialects of English was confined to expatriates, among whom the bookkeepers and artisans would soon get into the habit of using Creole.

At the end of the eighteenth century there was an influx of French-speaking refugees from Haiti. During the nineteenth century, education, particularly by missionaries, played an increasingly important part. There were fresh arrivals of indentured Africans in the middle of the century, many of them Yoruba-speaking, and importations also of Chinese, East Indian and Portuguese labour.

Through education, English was now the model language towards which the Creole moved; but on the other hand the dispersal of the former slaves away from the plantations into more remote communities of peasant-smallholders in the hills helped to conserve Creole speech and the arrival of new immigrants introduced fresh idiosyncratic features.

In the present century, the return of migrant labourers from Panama, other parts of Central America, and Cuba has introduced a number of Hispanisms into the island; increasing contact with the U.S., Canada and Britain, coupled with far greater educational opportunities and better communication in the island, has helped further to modify the local dialects.

5. HISTORICAL PHONOLOGY OF JAMAICAN ENGLISH: THE RESOURCES

In order to trace the historical development of the phonology of Jamaican English it would be desirable to have phonological descriptions of the chief English dialects and the chief African languages involved in the seventeenth and eighteenth centuries, and of the model language from the eighteenth century onwards. But whereas the English pronunciation of members of educated court and government circles in London has been described in detail from time to time from the sixteenth century to the present day,* no comparable work exists on other dialects, and hardly any detailed descriptions of West African languages were made before the nineteenth century. The *English Dialect Dictionary* and *English Dialect Grammar* of Joseph Wright were the first attempts at systematic synchronic and diachronic description of regional English dialectal usage, and

* For lists of such descriptions see Gimson, ch. 6, and Dobson, vol. 1.

although they contain a great wealth of material it is too patchy in consistency to enable us to reconstruct, say, the Bristol dialect or the Antrim dialect of the latter part of the seventeenth century with any kind of certainty. Since we have conserved for us in Jamaica and in current use today pronunciations and words which have passed out of use in England, *and since these are preserved within living systems so that their structural relationships are known*, Jamaica may itself turn out to be an important source of information about seventeenth to eighteenth-century regional English usage.

In general terms, it seems evident that the phonetic structure of seventeenth and early eighteenth-century English dialects was reinterpreted through the matrix of the phonology *either* of West African languages such as Twi or Ewe, *or* of a Portuguese-West African pidgin; that the resultant pidgin was rapidly Creolized, becoming the native language of Jamaican-born slaves; that subsequently Scots and, at a further remove until the nineteenth century, educated southern British English, have acted as model languages for the Creole, the educated version of which, as used by middle-class Jamaicans, has acted in turn as a model language for the uneducated version. We cannot reconstruct the process with any accuracy.

Considerable use has been made in the following pages of the descriptions of educated southern English usage provided by the seventeenth- and eighteenth-century orthoepists, particularly Gil (1619), Cooper (1687) and Douglas (*c.* 1740); of the descriptions of Twi by Christaller (1875) and of Ewe by Westermann (1907); and of the description of modern RP by Gimson. Gil, Cooper and Douglas were chosen because they were describing metropolitan English at periods significant for the settlement history of the West Indies. The descriptions of Twi and Ewe are the earliest of any great accuracy for these languages, but we have no means of knowing how close the nineteenth- and twentieth-century languages of West Africa are to those of the seventeenth century.

Since until recently RP had acted for some time as the model language for Jamaican English it is reasonable, in setting out the vowel and consonant phonemes of JC, to show them at the same time as reflexes of the appropriate RP phonemes, thus indicating what pronunciation a word newly borrowed from the model language would assume in Jamaica. Wherever possible an attempt has been made to relate Jamaican usage to phonological developments in England.

Dobson* has been used as the most convenient reference work on English pronunciation during the formative period of Jamaican Creole. Reference to his pages does not necessarily imply acceptance of his conclusions; but the opening sentences of his preface may well be quoted here with full endorsement:

> The central theme of this book...is that many elements went to make up the developing standard spoken language of the early Modern English period; that there were many variant pronunciations, many levels and styles of speech, co-existing at any time, and that the accepted norms of pronunciation of one generation were not merely apt to differ from, but were sometimes not even directly developed from, those of an earlier generation.

In each of the following sections the 'regular' equivalence between the

* See bibliographical index.

Jamaican Creole phonemic distribution and that of RP is stated first. An attempt is then made to list and, where possible, suggest an explanation for, forms which will be found among the citations in the Dictionary which do not fit the regular pattern.

6. ACCENT, INTONATION AND RELATED FEATURES

There is no space here for an extended discussion of what is meant by such terms as accent, prominence, quantity, stress and intonation in relation to English words and English utterances. A fairly detailed treatment will be found in Gimson, chapters 9 and 10.* The precise relationship between such factors as stress, pitch and quantity in determining the relative prominence of one syllable to another in English words is still under examination but it is beyond dispute that in RP words have well-marked patterns of relative syllable-prominence which are only overridden in connected speech by the demands of rhythm or rhetoric; in the word *undecided*, for example, the third syllable will always be the most prominent except where, in reply to the question 'So you are decided, then?', one would probably accent the first syllable: 'Nó, I am úndecided.' In those syllables which are not accented or given prominence in any way, vowel-quality is less determinate, and in such positions the *schwa*-vowel (or central [ə]) is often heard.

In a West African language such as Twi, on the other hand, 'every syllable of every word has its own relative tone or tones, equal with or different from the neighbouring syllables, being either high, or low, or middle. Besides this intonation, inherent in the original formation of words, there are also "grammatical" tones, by means of which different tenses are denoted' [Christaller, *Dicty*. p. xvi].

Since tone plays a *phonemic* role in Twi it cannot be involved in syllable-prominence in that, or in any other tone-language, in the same manner as in English. Nor, in view of the 'grammatical' tones, can the morphological and syntactic role of intonation be the same. As might be expected, the prominence-patterns of the syllables in English words and utterances are not easily recognized by West African ears, nor the tones of West African languages by English ears.

As a result, the relative prominence of syllables in JC tends to be very level. The *schwa*-vowel does not normally occur, nor is there the same loss of vowel quality in unaccented positions as in RP. Intonational distinctions similar to, though not identical with, those of RP do exist in JC, as between declarative and interrogative utterances. Isolated words, or words in declarative utterance-final position, normally have rising intonation in place of the falling intonation of RP, although not rising as high as that of interrogative utterance-final elements. But some part of the impression of rising intonation, as of the impression of word-final accent, which strikes the English ear may be due to *evenness* of accent or *evenness* of intonation where a *falling* cadence would be expected. The precise role of accent and intonation in the syntax of JC has yet to be studied by a trained Africanist.

* For comparison, see the American treatment by Hans Kurath, *A Phonology and Prosody of Modern English* (Heidelberg, 1964).

According to Christaller, all the vowels of Twi, normally short, may occur lengthened or doubled, the acoustic quality of the vowel being unaffected. In modern RP, on the other hand, the so-called 'long' vowels (as in *bead*, *bird*, *bard*, *board* and *booth*) are distinguished from the 'short' vowels (as in *middle*, *meddle*, *paddle*, *model*, *muddle*, *wooden*) by differences of quality which tend to carry with them differences of length. Some phoneticians—for example, Daniel Jones—have treated the qualitative differences as phonemically subordinate to those of length; more recent writers have tended to reverse this order of precedence. The considerable changes of vowel-quality which have taken place in English since the fifteenth century have greatly obscured the relationship between 'length' and vowel-quality, as may be seen from a study of the orthoepists; the fact that there is no consistent relationship between length in JC and length in RP reflects both the different roles of length in West African languages and English, and the changes which have taken place in English itself.

7. VOWELS AND DIPHTHONGS

/ii/ and /i/

JC /ii/ is the normal reflex of RP /iː/: /bliit/ *bleat* /bliid/ *bleed* etc.

JC /i/ is the normal reflex of RP /ɪ/ in both stressed and unstressed positions: /blingki/ *blinky*.

In emphatic, and sometimes in non-emphatic, contexts /ii/ can replace /i/: /iin/ *in* /hiich/ *itch* etc. Moreover, as noted below, there is some variation between JC /i/ and /e/. The Jamaican situation would appear to reflect two facts: first, educated English usage in the sixteenth to seventeenth centuries varied a good deal in respect to vowels derived from ME ī, ME ĭ and ME ē̜ (see Dobson II, §§ 10–12); secondly, [i] and [ɪ] appear to be allophones of the same phoneme in both Twi and Ewe. Thus JC /kril∼kriil/ *creel* /brim/ *bream* /siniki/ *sneaky* /hib∼heb/ *heave* /aslip∼asliip/ *asleep* certainly reflect the loss of 'quantity' as a basis of phonemic distinction, but as noted above (6) vowel-quality rather than quantity is in any case the primary basis of phonemic distinction in RP also, and Jamaican variations are paralleled by seventeenth-century variations in England.

Specific examples

In /kwiich oul∼kriich oul/ *screech owl* the development, as in RP, is from a form which began to replace the older *scritch-owl* only at the end of the sixteenth century, as an onomatopoeic modification of the latter; *scritch-owl* survived into the nineteenth century, and is preserved in a third JC alternant /krichúol/, but the dialectal evidence is insufficient to help with the provenance of the Jamaican forms.

JC /kiit/ *skate* derives from a pronunciation reflected by some of the sixteenth to seventeenth century β-forms recorded in *OED*: *skete* and *skeat*. The more normal development >RP /eɪ/ has equated the vowel in ON *skata* with that in ME *face*.

JC /fliim/ *phlegm* derives from a pronunciation [ɛː] attested by a number of sixteenth to seventeenth-century orthoepists (Dobson II, § 8) and by the older spelling *fleam*, whereas RP /flem/ is presumed to derive from a Middle English alternate pronunciation [flɛm] which did not become general until the eighteenth century.

JC /instral/ *entrails* /pilikin/ *pelican* /nitl ~ netl/ *nettle* /kirout/ *get out*! reflect the variation between [ɛ] and [ɪ] widely attested both by the orthoepists (Dobson II, §§ 75–80) and by *EDD* (see, e.g., *nether*, *nettle*, *never*).

JC /fipens/ *fivepence* is attested in England by Elisha Coles in his *Compleat English Schoolmaster*, a spelling-book published in 1674 (Dobson, I, pp. 346–50; II, § 12).

JC /kiba (~ keba)/ *cover* creolizes what was and still is a widespread English form [kɪvər], deriving from the OF strong form *cuevre* of *couvrir* (Dobson II, § 83; *EDGI cover*; *OED kiver*).

JC /hinka/ as a variant of /henka/ *hanker*, and /ginj/ *gange* may be due to the creolization of a vowel, raised beyond [æ] to [ɛ], from what was more usually [a] in the seventeenth century; the raised vowel [ɛ] may still be heard among rather old-fashioned or refined speakers of RP, and in popular London speech (Gimson 7.12 (3)).

JC /tida (~ teda)/ *t'other* creolizes dialectal English pronunciations whereby the more common fifteenth to sixteenth century ['ʊðɛr], giving modern ['ʌðə] in the south and ['ʊðə] in the north of England, became ['ɪðər] in large parts of Scotland.

In /(wip)ri/ *(whip)ray* and /fi/ *for*, JC /i/ is used as a reflex of the unstressed vowel, as it is in the final syllable of /pilikin/ *pelican*. It is possible, however, that in both /wipri/ and /pilikin/ there is some relic of African vowel-harmony.

JC /swiit/ *suet* may derive from earlier English pronunciations illustrated by the fifteenth to sixteenth-century spelling *swet*. (The variant developments from OF initial *su-* are illustrated in the modern English pronunciations of *sue*, *suite*, *suit*, *suet* and *sure* ([sjuː], [swiːt], [suːt], [suɪt], [ʃʊə].)

JC /dwiit/ *do it* seems to be a purely Creole development, probably by analogy with /dwiim/ *do (h)im* in the emphatic exclamation /awa dwiim?/ *what is troubling him*? As noted above, /ii/ can replace /i/ in emphatic contexts; with the stress in /du iim/ on the vowel of the second syllable, the first vowel has become a semi-vocalic element in a rising diphthong, perhaps under the influence of the common initial /dw-/ of the Akan dialects.

/ie/

JC /ie/ is the normal reflex of RP /eɪ/ in /iej/ *age* /fies/ *face* /pitieta/ *potato* /janikiek/ *Johnnycake* etc. The greatest number of words with this /eɪ/ diphthong in RP were pronounced with [aː] in ME, which in the fifteenth to seventeenth centuries was raised successively to [æː] and [ɛː] before being diphthongized to [ɛi]; or with [æɪ] or [ɛɪ] in ME, which had become [ɛː] by the end of the sixteenth century and so coalesced with the former set. The Jamaican pronunciation is a development from the further raising and diphthongization of this [ɛː] vowel; the diphthong was becoming general in England in the eighteenth century although it seems to have developed in Northern dialects as early as the first quarter of the seventeenth century. The modern RP [eːɪ] and [eɪ] date from the early nineteenth century.

EDGI, under *face*, records *feəs* from most parts of England, *fias* from Southern Scotland, Northumberland, Durham, Cumberland, Yorkshire, Lancashire, Oxfordshire, the Isle of Wight, Wiltshire and Dorset. It seems likely therefore that the quality of the Jamaican vowel is due to the influence of Northern and Scots dialectal usage.

The development of JC /ie/ before /r/ as in /mieri/ *Mary* /die(r)/ *dare* etc. is no different from that outlined above, since it was only after the Jamaican borrowing took place that [ɛː] before [r] developed into a different diphthong ([ɛə]) in polite English speech from [ɛː] before other consonants (Dobson II, § 204).

JC /ie/ in /die(r)/ *dear* (and emphatic *there*), /hie(r)/ emphatic *here*, /fie(r)s/ *fierce* is the regular reflex of RP /ɪə/; there is a greater tendency towards retention of the r-coloration in the JC diphthong than in RP, from which it has completely disappeared.

The fact that the vowels of *dare*, *dear* and *fierce* are pronounced with the same diphthong in JC reflects the situation in some dialects of English in the latter part of the seventeenth century; for the evidence, see Dobson II, §§ 201–4.

At the stage when words with ME ā (e.g. *fate*) were pronounced with [ɛː], they rimed with words which retained this vowel from Middle English (e.g. *great*). Many of these latter words which were pronounced by some with [ɛː] as late as the first quarter of the eighteenth century now have a shortened vowel: *threat*, *sweat*, *bread*, etc. Because of the overlap, there occurred a redistribution among the phonemes which have become in RP /eɪ/ and /e/ of words which in ME had [aː], [ɛː], and [ɛ], and the allocation of words has varied from one dialect to another. Dobson II, § 8, cites Gil as pronouncing *measure* with [ɛː]; *EDGI* records *hedge* with a long vowel from many parts of Scotland; JC has /mieja/~/meja/ *measure*, /iejag~ejag/ *hedgehog*, etc. Under this heading also probably belongs JC /kriedl/ *curdle* (and *cradle*), the development being [kʊrdl̩] > [krʊdl̩] > [krɛdl̩] > [krɛːdl̩] > JC [kriɛdl̩]. (*EDGI* records *krudz*, *krɒdz* from parts of Scotland, Ireland, northern and western England, and *kridz* from West Somerset.)

The pronunciation /fierin/ *fern* is probably due to the preservation of a form [feərn] (with a trilled [r]) < early seventeenth century [fɛːrn]—see Dobson II, § 8; *EDGI* records [feːrn] from Scotland, [fɪən] from North Derbyshire, [fɪərn] from the Isle of Man.

/tiek/, /miek/ occur alongside the regular /tek/, /mek/ for *take*, *make*, probably under the influence of the model language; the latter forms are dealt with below under JC /e/.

JC /tie/ *till* shows simply the loss of a final semi-vowel with consequent diphthongization of the preceding vowel. JC /petifiegin/ *pettifogging* occurs as an occasional emphatic variant of /petifagin/, and may be an individualism, as is also, probably, /safies/ *suffice*, recorded from a Portland Maroon.

/e/

JC /e/ is the normal reflex of RP /e/ in /get/ *get* /ded/ *dead* etc., and in /teg-reg/ *tag-rag* /tengki/ *thankyou* /skelyan/ *scallion* /plet/ *plait* etc. is a common reflex of RP /æ/. The dominant pattern here is that of the partial coalescence of a phoneme deriving from ME *ă* (as in *rag*) with one deriving from ME *ĕ* (as in *get*). But JC /a/ is a more common reflex of RP /æ/ than is /e/, while there is a good deal of variation between the two pronunciations as in /hangkra~hengkra/, /laba-laba~lebe-lebe/ etc. According to Dobson (II, § 59):

The evidence is slight, but is, I think, sufficient to show that in the sixteenth and seventeenth centuries there were two pronunciations of ME *ă* in use in StE: a more conservative [a], generally used by careful speakers until 1600 and probably still the more usual pronunciation among such speakers until 1650, which may have continued in occasional use until the end of the century; and a more advanced [æ], vulgar or popular in the sixteenth century, gradually winning wider acceptance in the first part of the seventeenth century, and generally accepted by careful speakers by about 1670.

If Christaller's ear can be trusted in respect to English,* [æ] ('a (thin) sound as *a* in *fat*') occurred in Twi in 1875. More recent descriptions of Twi do not list this vowel allophone, however; slightly higher is [ɛ], and slightly lower, [a]. In JC, [a]-vowels of English and of West African words have been preserved intact; [æ]-vowels have been raised to [ɛ] and assimilated, together with most English [ɛ]-vowels, to the phoneme /e/. In view of the paucity of our information about the phonemic structures of West African languages in the seventeenth century it is impossible to say whether the lack of [æ] in JC is due to its lack in West African, or to the fact that the dominant influence on JC was a more conservative English dialect than that spoken by Dobson's 'careful speakers' of 1670.

In /shet/ *shut* JC preserves a form recorded by the *EDGI* only in Shropshire, Oxfordshire, Hertfordshire and Norfolk; the *OED*, however, records that the Kentish form *shette* (used by Chaucer and Gower) was very common alongside *shit* (< OE *scyttan*), the prevailing form down to the end of the sixteenth century. Either *shet* or *shit* could give /shet/ in JC.

EDGI does not record [fɛs] for *fuss*. The etymology of *fuss* is uncertain; the first *OED* citation is 1701. The occasional form /fes/, which occurs in Jamaica alongside the regular /fos/, may have been influenced by a reflex of Scots *fash*, /fesh/, which has virtually the same meaning as *fuss* (and may indeed be the origin of that word).

In /ef/ *if* /hent/ *hint* /henda/ *hinder* etc. JC preserves a tendency shown in English dialects from the fourteenth century onwards, for ME [ɪ] to be lowered to [ɛ] (Dobson II, § 80). The evidence for the sixteenth to seventeenth centuries comes from South-Western, Northern, Eastern and vulgar London dialects. *EDGI* records *enðə(r)* from Oxfordshire, *endə(r)* from Dorset, *hendər* from Scotland. JC /get/ *girth* may be due to dialectal retention of the original ME [ɛr], the [r] being lost in Jamaica; but ME also had the forms [gɪrθ] and [gɪrt]; at all events, the JC borrowing antedates the general retraction of both vowels to [ə] before [r]. Dobson's evidence (II, § 213) is that the latter change was taking place in the later seventeenth century. /feril/ *fern* also preserves a vowel which antedates this change.

* 'The author has never had the advantage of living among or conversing with Englishmen more than a few weeks at a time, neither could he submit the manuscript or part of it to an Englishman before it went to the press...'—from the preface to the *Grammar*.

JC /lef/ *leave* /lep/ *leap* may be due to the use of the past-tense form for the present, but on the other hand *EDGI* records *lef* for *leave* from Somerset, and *EDD lep* for *leap* from Ireland, three Midland counties, Shropshire and Wiltshire.

/a/

JC /a/ in /pan/ *pan, upon,* /hat/ *hat, hot* etc., preserves two features of a number of seventeenth to eighteenth-century English dialects: first, the coalescence of ME *ŏ* with ME *ă* through lowering, unrounding and fronting to [a]—a pronunciation common as a fashionable vulgarism in Restoration comedy in, e.g., oaths, *Gad*! *Stap me*! etc.; second, the lack of that subsequent raising of [a] to [æ] which has taken place in RP and some other English dialects since the latter part of the eighteenth century. The fact that [æ] is rare in West African languages (see above, under /e/) has almost certainly reinforced the failure of JC to follow the model language in this raising. JC /a/ is thus the normal reflex of both RP /æ/ and of RP /ɒ/. There is, however, a tendency for initial /k/ and /g/ to be palatalized* where RP would have /æ/ or /ɛə/, but not where RP would have /ɒ/. Thus /ka ~ kya ~ kyaa ~ kyai ~ kyar ~ kyari ~ kye ~ kyeri/ *carry*, /kasha ~ kyasha/ *cashaw*, /kashu ~ kyashu ~ kushu/ *cashew* (*nut*), /kéchòp ~ kyáchòp/ *catch up*, /gyanda/ *gander*, /galawas ~ gyalawas ~ galiwas ~ galang-was/ *galliwasp* etc., but never */kyabla/ for /kabla/ *cobbler* etc. As in the case of /aa/, the palatalization may well be the result of the need to maintain a phonemic distinction where two vowels have become very close rather than identical in quality; it is noteworthy that it only came into English speech at the end of the seventeenth and during the eighteenth century when the values of the low back and low front vowels were tending to converge, and that it disappeared from polite English speech as [a] was raised to [æ]. It was still widespread in English dialects at the turn of the century (see *EDGI*). Palatal [ky] and [gy] are in complementary distribution with velar [k] and [g] in Christaller's description of Twi.

/kya/ *care* (~ /kie ~ kyie ~ kyer/) may, as the entry suggests, reflect a borrowing via Ewe or, alternatively, borrowing from a dialect in which the fronting and raising of the vowel before [r] had not gone further than [a]. *EDGI* records *kia*(*r*) from Yorkshire and Lancashire, *kjɒ*(*r*) from Oxfordshire, *kjɒə*(*r*) and *kjɒ*(*r*) from Lancashire, and palatal glides before front and central vowels from most parts of England.

/a/ occurs sometimes, either in variation with /aa/ or alone, for RP /ɑː/: /jagl/ ~ /jaagl/ *gargle*, /hash/ *harsh* etc. In compounds of *all*- and elsewhere before /l/ it replaces the normal /aa-/ even where this has not been reduced to /a/ by the reduction of stress (as in /aredi/ *already*): /azwiez/ *always*, /kal/ *call*, /tal/ *tall* etc. /a/ in the second syllable of /tambran/ *tamarind* is presumably due to some feeling of analogy with common iteratives such as /bram-bram/.

In /tara (~ teda ~ tida)/ *t'other*, /anada (~ aneda ~ anida)/ *another*, /talabred/ *thoroughbred*, JC /a/ is presumably due to borrowing from a dialect with [a] or [ɒ] in these words; Dobson (II, § 15) discusses those of his authorities who record a short low back vowel in *other*, and the *EDGI* records many modern dialectal variants.

* See below, *Consonants: palatal and velar stops.*

In /tambrik/ *turmeric* a variety of explanations can be offered for JC /a/; the word has such an obscure history that it is hardly worth guessing which explanation is correct. The spellings, *tarmaret*, *tormarith* and *tormerik* are all recorded (in *OED*); all indicate *possible* etymologies for /tambrik/, but it is simplest to derive this from a fifteenth-century /tar-/ pronunciation.

In /advaantij/ *advantage* /ninggam-baiti/ *lignum-vitae* /ruba ~ riba/ *river*, JC /a/ is one of the normal reflexes of the unstressed /ə/ of RP.* In /mashéted/ *emaciated* the stress has shifted, possibly through analogy with *machete*, so that /a/ is here the reflex of the unstressed vowel.

/aa/

JC /aa/ is the normal reflex of RP /ɑː/ in /paas/ *pass*, *past*, /glaas/ *glass*, /yaad/ *yard*, /haaf/ *half*, /faada/ *father* etc., and of RP /ɔː/ in /braad/ *broad*, /haakshaa/ *hawkshaw*, /yaak/ *York*, /paanz-beli/ *paunch-belly*, /laan/ *lawn*, /kaaz(n)/ *(be)cause(n)*, /aal/ *all* etc., etc. Where appropriate, however, a palatal initial consonant is retained in words of the first group as against a velar consonant in the second; thus /kyaad/ *card*, /kaad/ *cord*; /gyaadn/ *garden* /gaadn/ *Gordon*; /kyaan, kyaang/ *can't* /kaan/ *corn* or *scorn*, etc. Finally, in /klaat/ *cloth* /raatid/ *wrathèd* (or *wrothèd*), /maat-grass/ *moth-grass* /gaan/ *gone* etc., and in /daag ~ dag/ *dog*, JC /aa/ is the reflex of RP /ɒ/.

The historical phonology of the RP vowels concerned is complex and uncertain. What seems evident is that in the English usage transplanted to the West Indies—either originally, first to the Leeward Islands and Barbados, and thence to Jamaica, or subsequently in the form of polite upper-class usage as a model language for Jamaican Creole—the vowel-sounds of all the words listed above were sufficiently similar for them to be subsumed under one phoneme in JC, the value of which corresponded with, for example, Twi [ɑː]; and, secondly, that there was transplanted to or there developed in the West Indies the set of phonemic distinctions between palatal and velar initial consonants which must earlier have been a function of the distinction between front and back vowels.

The pattern for the first group of words is set by those which, according to Dobson, had [a] in Middle English, lengthened to [aː] because of the influence of the following consonant, and so pronounced in polite southern speech at the end of the seventeenth century. (In some dialects, however, particularly in the West and North, the lengthening before [r] was not to a low front-central, but a low back vowel, a pronunciation which survives in Mod E *Marlborough*—Dobson II, § 44.)

The pattern for the second group (other than *broad*) is provided by those words which, from one source or another, had a diphthong *au* in Middle English, which was monophthongized to low-back [ɒː]. According to Dobson (II, § 235) 'The evidence of the orthoepists shows that diphthongal pronunciations, at least in some words, survived in conservative speech until late in the seventeenth century'.

Thus on Dobson's reasoning, at the end of the seventeenth-century polite

* See below, *Vowels in final and relatively unstressed positions.*

English usage had a low front-central [aː] in the first group of words and a low back [ɒː] in most of the second group (though not in *lawn*). These two vowels are sufficiently close to have coalesced into the Jamaican [aː] whilst retaining their separate identity and developing separately in modern English. Such a hypothesis would also explain the retention in Jamaican of a feature which was appearing in some English dialects at the beginning of the seventeenth century—the palatalization of [k] and [g] before front vowels—and its use in JC to distinguish what would otherwise be awkward homophones such as *card* and *cord*.*

Other scholars, however (e.g. Luick), have assigned a different value, [ɑː], to the seventeenth-century pronunciation of the second group; such pronunciations certainly survive in a number of dialects (see *EDGI*, e.g., *call*, *talk*, *corn*) particularly in the north and west of England, and in the U.S.

In /braad/ *broad* /klaat/ *cloth* /raatid/ *wrathèd* /maat/ *moth* /daag∼dag/ *dog* the JC vowel again reflects a seventeenth-century English [ɒː], lengthened from ME ŏ or ă, and retained in many English dialects (Dobson II, § 53) (*EDGI*, e.g., *broad*, *cloth*). Apart from *broad*, the vowel has been generally shortened to [ɒ] in educated English speech, although some old-fashioned speakers still say [klɔːθ] etc. (cf. also U.S. [dɔːg] *dog*). The earliest evidence for [rɔːθ] *wrath* is Milton's spelling *wrauth* (1637).

There is a certain amount of variation between JC /aa/ and /a/: /naadi/ *noddy*, /nuoz-naat/ *nose-snot*, /daag/ *dog*, where the expected reflex would be /a/, as also in /straan/ *strand*, /maas nik/† *mastic*. JC /maav/ *mauve* (instead of the expected /muov/) is probably a 'spelling pronunciation' by analogy with such words as /saas/ *sauce*; the word was not borrowed into English from French until the mid-nineteenth century, and in England has always been pronounced to rime with *hove*.

JC /naavis/ *nervous* in contrast with the recorded /sovis/ *service* is the opposite of what might be expected. Thus the common late seventeenth- and eighteenth-century educated pronunciation was [sarvɪs], preserving here a vowel which in RP is now only retained in a few words such as *clerk*, *Berkeley* and *Derby*. *Nerve* was recorded by the seventeenth-century orthoepist Daines as already pronounced, according to Dobson's interpretation (II, § 213), [nərv]; the Jamaican pronunciation is thus more conservative in this case, and in the case of *service* more recent, than polite seventeenth to eighteenth century English usage.

/ai/

JC /ai/ is the normal reflex of RP /aɪ/ in /tail/ *tile* /grain/ *grind* /hais/ *ice*, and of RP /ɔɪ/ in /tail/ *toil* /grain/ *groyne* /hais/ *hoist* etc. In conjunction with the second group must be considered those words with labial glides after labial consonants: /bwai/ *boy* /pwail/ *spoil* etc.

Three main classes of words are involved: those in which ME [iː] as in *wif* > Mod E [aɪ] *wife* (Gimson 7.23 (4)), and two ME diphthongs, mainly in OF loan-words: [ɔɪ] (e.g. *choice*, *noise*) and [oɪ] or [ʊɪ] (e.g. *boil*, *point*) (Gimson 7.24 (4)). The second of these diphthongs coalesced in some dialects by the end

* See also under /a/ above, and below under *Consonants: palatal and velar stops.*
† There is probably an element of folk-etymology in this case: *Master Nick.*

of the seventeenth century with the [əɪ] which had developed from ME [iː] (Dobson II, § 262), and both together became [aɪ] in polite speech after 1700: [waɪf] *wife*, [dʒaɪn] *join*, [baɪl] *boil* etc. After about 1800, however, because of the *oi* spelling, the [dʒaɪn] pronunciation gave way in that group to RP [ɔɪ]. The first of the diphthongs, ME [ɔɪ], has retained this pronunciation in some dialects ever since in [nɔɪz] *noise* etc., to which group were added by analogy *boil* (ulcer), *groin, hoist, joist* which originally had ME [iː]; in other dialects, however, the pronunciation [əɪ] had been adopted for this group also by the end of the seventeenth century, though regarded as a vulgarism in polite speech in the eighteenth century. Jamaican pronunciation therefore derives from a dialect (or a period) in which all three diphthongs had coalesced as [aɪ], and one which was not or had not been affected by the spelling-pronunciation [ɔɪ] for the *join*-group.

There was, however, a tendency for the ME [uɪ] pronunciation to be retained after labial consonants when this diphthong had become [əɪ] in other environments; the Jamaican lip-glides after initial labials may be a relic of this later retention of the [ʊ] element in the diphthong (see below, *Consonants*, /w/).

The pronunciations [dʒaɪn] *join* [dʒaɪst] *joist* [naɪz] *noise* etc. are recorded in many counties by the *EDGI*, as is the [w] on-glide in *boy* etc.

In archaic speech, JC /ai/ is the reflex of RP /æ/ before [g] in /baig/ *bag* /flaig/ *flag* /haig/ *hag* /raigin/ *ragging* /laigz/ *lags*. Two further (rare) examples show assimilation to this group of a reflex of RP /ɒ/: /praig ~ prag/ *prog* /daig ~ dag/ *dog*. These pronunciations are today being replaced by the more normal /a/, but are retained in formulaic constructions, e.g., /uol haig/ *old hag*. Similar development of ME ă, but in different environments, is discussed by Dobson (II, § 63); otherwise the only documentation from England comes from the forms *baig* and *raig* recorded from South-mid Lancashire in *EDGI*.

/o/

JC /o/ is the normal reflex of RP /ʌ/ in /ogli/ *ugly* /kodl/ *cuddle* /bod/ *bud* etc. Possibly here JC pronunciation provides support for Luick as against Dobson (see Dobson II, § 93); Luick supposed that ME *ŭ*, in the process of unrounding and centralizing to RP [ʌ], passed through the stage of being an advanced and half-rounded *o* sound, and that it had this value in polite speech from the end of the sixteenth to the early eighteenth century. Dobson feels that Luick's '*o* sound' is a myth, and that the modern [ʌ] has been in use from the seventeenth century; if this had been so, however, it seems more likely that this phoneme would have been subsumed under /a/ in JC rather than /o/, since phonetically [ʌ] and JC /a/ are very close.

JC /o/ is the normal reflex of RP /ɜː/ in /kodl/ *curdle* /bod/ *bird* /wotlis/ *worthless* etc. The changes which took place in the ME vowels when they occurred before [r], as that [r] ceased to be trilled and became more and more—finally completely—vocalic, are too complex and uncertain to be dealt with in detail here as they are in Dobson II, part 3 (§§ 198–218). It would seem that words with ME *ĕr*, *ĭr* and *ŭr* (~ *ŏr*) plus consonant were by the end of the seventeenth century all being pronounced [ər] by educated speakers; the subsequent vocalization of the [r] has led to the lengthened [ɜː] in RP, but the [r] may have been lost independently in JC and the vowel borrowed may have been closer to [ɒ] than to [ə]. This may be the explanation of the fact that where, as with some speakers, r-coloration has been retained, the vowel remains /o/: /torkl/ *turtle* /form/ *fern* /torpmtaim/ *turpentine* etc.

In /boksha/ *Berkshire* JC has evidently borrowed from one of the many dialects of English (possibly from American English) in which, unlike RP, the ME [ar] pronunciation has not been preserved.

JC /sorop/ *syrup* may reflect a retraction of the front vowel before intervocalic [r] which has not taken place in RP (see Dobson II, § 213), but which is common in other dialects in England and America; the pronunciation may on the other hand derive from ME variants reflected in the spellings *surrop*, *surrope* (*OED* forms β 6, 7), whereas the spelling by the seventeenth century was standardized as *sirop*, *sirup* or *syrup*.

The pronunciation /todi/ for *steady* regularly heard in the phrase /tan todi/ *stand steady*, might help to date the phonology were it not that this phrase is probably a preserved military or seafaring phrase and so reflects a more conservative dialectal usage than normal. *OED* gives the spelling *study* from *The Mariner's Magazine c.* 1699; *studdie* is cited as a Scots form. *EDD* records *studdy* from Cornwall; *EDGI*, *studi*, south-west and south Northumberland, *stùdi*, Isle of Man.

JC /o/ occasionally replaces /uo/ as the reflex of RP /əʊ/:

/i-no/ *no*!	/nombari/ *nobody*
/joko-joko/ *joke*	

JC /ong/ is the regular reflex of RP /ɑʊn/:

/bongks/ *bounce*	/dong/ *down* etc.
/tong/ *town*	

In /habriko/ *albacore* /yosef/ *yourself* JC /o/ is the reflex of RP /ɔː/, the second example being due to lack of stress. In /loroks/ *rowlocks* and /kongk/ *conch* JC /o/ is the regular reflex of RP /ɒ/.

/uo/

JC /uo/ is the regular reflex of RP /əʊ/ as in /guot/ *goat* /uova/ *over* /huobaluk/ *overlook* /uondli (~onggli)/ *only* /kuot/ *coat* /puos/ *post* etc. The RP diphthong derives from a seventeenth-century monophthong (in polite English speech) [oː] or [ɔː].

JC /uo/ is the regular reflex of RP /oː/, conservative RP [ɔə], wherever that phoneme derives from a seventeenth century [uː], [oː] or [ɔː] before [r] (see Dobson II, §§ 145 ff. and § 165, Gimson 7.16): /kuot/ *court* /puotmantyuu/ *portmanteau* /puok/ *pork* /fuo/ *four* /duo-mout/ *doormouth* /muo/ *more* etc. The loss of [r] in ModE here has been accompanied by diphthongization of the preceding vowel and by lowering of the first element of the diphthong; in RP this diphthong has been monophthongized. The [r] was lost in polite English in the eighteenth century. It would appear that Jamaican English borrowed the seventeenth-century vowels, and that the [r] was lost in Jamaica independently, without the lowering of the vowels.

An alternative explanation is that the Jamaican pronunciation of both groups is borrowed from a conservative regional English dialect; *EDGI* records, e.g., *guet* (goat) from Northumberland, Cumberland, Yorkshire, Lancashire, Lincolnshire, Oxfordshire, Hertfordshire and Wiltshire; *kuəs* (course) from the same northern counties, Staffordshire, Warwickshire, Oxfordshire, Kent and Sussex.

JC /puoltris/ *poultice* /shuolda/ *shoulder* also seem to derive from a seventeenth-century English [uː] or [uːᵊ] pronunciation (Dobson II, § 174). JC /uovn/ *oven* is a common pronunciation in the island; it appears to be borrowed from a regional English dialect in which the short ME vowel was lengthened before [v]: *EDGI* records [oː] or [ɔː] from Wiltshire, Devon, Dorset, Isle of Wight, Somerset parts of Scotland, the Isle of Man.

JC /juosi/ *jersey* is not accounted for by any of the forms recorded in *EDD*.

In emphatic contexts JC /uo/ as in /wuoda ~ uoda (~oda)/ *other* /huogli (~ogli)/ *ugly* is the reflex of RP /ʌ/.

/ou/

JC /ou/ is the normal reflex of RP /aʊ/ as in /hous/ *house* etc. (with the exception noted under /o/ viz. that RP /aʊn/ = JC /ong/). The Jamaican pronunciation is close to that of some Northern English dialects (see *EDGI* e.g. *house, out*). ME [uː] began to be diphthongized in most English dialects (but not Scots) in the fifteenth century to [ʊu] and the first element was progressively lowered giving [əʊ] or [ʌ̈ʊ] in the sixteenth and seventeenth centuries. Jamaican [ɵʊ] is thus close to seventeenth-century Southern or later Northern English usage.

/u/

JC /u/ is the normal reflex of RP /ʊ/ in, e.g., /wud/ *wood* /fut/ *foot*.

In /juju (~juu)/ *dew* /chupid/ *stupid* JC /u/ is the reflex of RP /juː/ after a dental consonant (compare /nyuuz/ *news*). The sixteenth to seventeenth-century pronunciations antecedent to RP /juː/ are discussed at length by Dobson (II, 179–88, 143 ff. etc.) and Gimson (7.18 (4)) as well as by earlier writers such as Wyld and Luick. Both the short vowel and the assimilation of the palatal [j] to the preceding dental consonant to form an alveopalatal affricate can be paralleled from English dialects; the first stage of the reduction of initial [stj-] > [tj] (> [tʃ]) in *stupid* is dealt with below under *Reduction of Consonant Clusters*.

In /ruba (~riba)/ *river* /prusi/ *prissy* /fup (~fip)/ *fivepence* JC preserves an alternation between /u/ and /i/ well-attested by seventeenth-century orthoepists (Dobson II, §§ 81 ff.); the most common parallel in modern English dialects is a central or back vowel instead of a front vowel after [r] as in ['θrʊpəns ~ 'θrʌpəns ~ 'θrɛpəns ~ 'θrɪpəns] *threepence*.

/uu/

JC /uu/ is the normal reflex of RP /uː/ in e.g. /ontruut/ *untruth* /ruudnis/ *rudeness*.

There is a certain amount of alternation between JC /uu/ and /u/, particularly in final position (see next section).

Vowels in final and relatively unstressed positions

JC /i/, /e/, /a/, /o/ and /u/ can all occur in final position without diphthongization or loss of quality, whereas in RP this is true only of /ɪ/ (and this only in some varieties of RP—see Gimson 7.10 (3)). The use of these short open vowels in final position is a characteristic of Negro English, often indicated by the final spelling with *-h*; the feature is of course particularly common in African loan-words:

/wipri/ *whipray*	/bangkra/ *bankra* (a market basket)
/oli/ *early*	/mi no no/ *me no know, I do not know*
/pikni/ *pickney, child*	/we im a go/ *where is he going?*
/de/ *deh, there*	/combolo/ *cumbohloh, a companion*
/se/ *say*	/hou yu du/ *how do you do?*
/sense/ *senseh-fowl* (a fowl with no neck feathers)	/bagabu/ *bugaboo*
/sa/ *sah, sir*	/chuku/ *chookoo, a far-away place*
/mada/ *mother*	/patu/ *patoo, a nightjar*

In relatively unstressed positions JC /i/ and /e/ sometimes alternate:

/bin ~ ben/ *been* /if ~ ef/ *if* /jis ~ jes (~ jos)/ *just* etc.

The most common reflexes of RP unstressed /ə/ are JC /a/ and /i/:

/rieza/ *razor* /sekshan/ *section* /batam/ *bottom* /alaiv/ *alive* /bota/ *butter* /pilikin/ *pelican* /biesin/ *basin* /hevin (~ hebm)/ *heaven* /raskil/ *rascal* /bifuo/ *before* etc.

/giláant/ *gallánt* reflects the stress-pattern of the verb form, no longer much used in England.

The short vowels may also occur as *svarabhakti* vowels (see below, *Reduction of Consonant Clusters*), their use being apparently determined by vowel harmony:

/simit/ *smith*	/worom/ *worm*
/siniek/ *snake*	/sumaal/ *small*
/panchalam/ *Spanish elm*	/sunuorin/ *snoring* etc.

8. SEMIVOWELS AND CONTINUANTS; SYLLABIC CONSONANTS

In the most archaic specimens of Jamaican Creole (as exemplified by 'Bungo talk' and Anancy's ostensible 'tongue tie'), /y/ replaces both initial /l/ and initial /r/. (Both these sounds are rare initially in Twi.) Examples: /yikl/ *little* /yed/ *red* /yedi/ *ready* /yap/ *wrap* /yaga-yaga/ and /yeg-yeg/ *ragged.*

Syllabic /l̩/ and /n̩/ are common: /likl/ *little* /kaazn/ *(be)cause(n)* etc. Syllabic /m̩/ is not uncommon, sometimes replacing English /-n/ especially after labial consonants: /babm/ *bobbin* /torpmtaim/ *turpentine* /razm/ *rosin* /uopm/ *open* /stiibm/ *Stephen.*

The syllabic final [r] of seventeenth-century English (see Dobson II, § 324) has been generally replaced by JC /a/: /sobaz/ *Sobers* (the cricketer) /neba/ *never* etc.

9. CONSONANTS

Set out below are charts representing the consonants of English as described by Gil (1619) and Gimson (1965); of Twi as described by Christaller (*Grammar*, 1875), and of Ewe as described by Westermann (1907). (Some unfamiliar symbols and terms used by some of these authors have been replaced by the corresponding IPA symbols and terms.)

(i) *Gil's English consonants*, 1619

		Bilabial	Labiodental	Dental/alveolar		Palato-alveolar	Palatal	Velar/glottal	
Plosive	vd	b	—	—	d	—	—	g	—
	vl	p	—	—	t	—	—	k	—
Affricate	vd	—	—	—	—	dʒ	—	—	—
	vl	—	—	—	—	tʃ	—	—	—
Fricative	vd	—	v	ð	z	—	—	—	—
	vl	—	f	θ	s	ʃ	—	x	h
Rolled/flapped		—	—	—	r	—	—	—	—
Nasal		m	—	—	n	—	—	ŋ	—
Lateral		—	—	—	l	—	—	—	—
Continuant or semivowel		w	—	—	—	—	j	—	—

(ii) *Gimson's RP consonants*, 1965

		Bilabial	Labiodental	Dental	Alveolar	Post-alveolar	Palato-alveolar	Palatal	Velar	Glottal
Plosive	vd	b	—	—	d	—	—	—	g	—
	vl	p	—	—	t	—	—	—	k	—
Affricate	vd	—	—	—	—	(dr)	dʒ	—	—	—
	vl	—	—	—	—	(tr)	tʃ	—	—	—
Fricative	vd	—	v	ð	z	—	ʒ	—	—	—
	vl	(ʍ)	f	θ	s	—	ʃ	—	—	h
Nasal		m	—	—	n	—	—	—	ŋ	—
Lateral		—	—	—	l	—	—	—	—	—
Continuant or glide (semivowel)		w	—	—	—	r	—	j	—	—

(iii) *Christaller's Twi consonants*, 1875

		Labial	Dental	Palatal	Palato-labial	'Guttural'	'Gutturo-labial'	
Plosive	vd	b	d	gy	dw̆	g	gw	gŭ
	vl	p	t	ky	tw̆	k	kw	kŭ
Fricative	vd	—	—	—	—	—	—	—
	vl	f	s	hy	fw̆	h	hw	hŭ
Nasal		m	n	ny	ŋw̆	ŋ	ŋw	ŋŭ
Semivowel		w	r(l)	y	w̆	—	—	—

In some Fante dialects [t] > [ts] and [d] > [dz] before front vowels. The *Mfantsi Grammar* of Carr and Brown, 1868, says that t > [θ] before back vowels, and that hy = [ʃ]; [v], [z] and [ʒ] are known only in loan-words. (Paraphrase of Christaller's note.)

(iv) *Westermann's Ewe consonants*, 1907

		Bilabial	Labio-dental	Alveolar	Retroflex	Palatal	Labio-velar	Velar
Plosive	vd	b	—	d	ɖ	—	gb	g
	vl	p	—	t	—	—	kp	k
Affricate	vd	—	—	dʒ	—	—	—	—
	vl	—	—	ts	—	—	—	—
Fricative	vd	β	v	z	—	—	—	ɣ, h
	vl	ɸ	f	s	—	—	—	x
Nasal		m	—	n	—	ny	—	ŋ
Liquid		—	—	l, r	—	—	—	—
Semivowel		w	—	—	—	y(ỹ)	—	—

It is often not possible to be exactly specific about the provenance of this or that consonantal phoneme of JC. Most of the Jamaican usages which seem to be Africanisms can be paralleled in one or another of the British English dialects, as reference to *EDG* will show. It is true for example that [ð] and [θ] are rare in West African languages, although as will be seen from the above chart [θ] is described for Fante, a language closely related to Twi. In a great many contact-situations in various parts of the world English [ð] and [θ] are replaced, sometimes by varieties of [z] and [s], more frequently by varieties of [d] and [t]. But [t] also occurs for RP initial [θ] in a number of English dialects; initial [θr] > [dr] in a great many southern and western dialects, and > [tr] in many northern and eastern dialects (*EDG*, § 313); medial [ð] > [d] frequently (*EDG*, § 315); final [θ] > [t] regularly in the Shetlands and Orkney, and occasionally in other dialects, e.g., 'Lancashire mot, Gloucestershire māt, Oxfordshire mōt' for *moth* (*EDG*, § 316). Thus, whilst it is almost certain that the subsuming of English /d/ and /ð/ under Jamaican /d/, and of English /t/ and /θ/ under Jamaican /t/, are due to the lack of /ð/ and /θ/ in many West African languages, the possibility remains that in the speech of the Leeward Islands and of Barbadian settlers and white servants of the first half of the seventeenth century these processes had already begun without African influence.

Labial stops

JC /b/ = RP /b/ regularly in /biebi/ *baby* /bab/ *bob* etc.

~/v/ = RP /v/ in /beks/ *vex* /debl/ *devil* √shob/ *shove* etc.

/v/ is lacking in Twi and closely related West African languages.

/b/ for /v/ occurs sporadically in English dialects before /l/ or /n/, intervocalically, and finally in one or two words of French origin (*EDG*, § 279).

JC /p/ = RP /p/ regularly in /paasl/ *parsley* /tapi-/ *stop-it-* /pap/ *pop* etc.
= RP /k/ occasionally, mostly before /l/, in /plaba/ *clabber* (sour milk) ~*claver* (a quarrel), /plaa/ *claw* /hup/ *hook.* No similar change is recorded by *EDG* or by Dobson.

JC /p/ is followed by a palatal /y/ initially in a number of words of African origin—see /pyaa-pyaa/, /pyaka-pyaka/ etc.

Dental/alveolar stops

JC /d/ = RP /d/ regularly in /ded/ *dead* /duo-duo/ *dough-dough* etc.
= RP /ð/ commonly in /dat/ *that* /bada/ *bother* /briid/ *breathe.*
[ð] is rare in West African languages.
[d] occurs sporadically for [ð] initially, medially and finally in British English dialects—see *EDG*, §§ 311–17.
[d] ~ [ð] medially in a few words in seventeenth-century polite English usage—see Dobson II, § 383.
~ /g/ occasionally: /gyad/ *gag* /kende/ ~ /kengge/ (see kengge).
This change is not recorded in *EDG*.

JC /t/ = RP /t/ regularly in /tin/ *tin* /beta/ *better* /pat/ *pot.*
= RP /θ/ commonly in /tin/ *thin* /kati/ *Kathy* /simit/ *smith.*
[θ] is rare in West African languages.
[t] for [θ] is quite widespread, initially and finally, in British English dialects—see *EDG*, §§ 312–16.
= RP /k/ occasionally in /lit/ *lick.*
= RP /p/ occasionally in /polt/ *pulp.*

Palatal and velar stops

JC /gy/ is the reflex of seventeenth to eighteenth-century British /gy/ before low-front [a] and [aː] as contrasted with /g/ before low-back [ɔː] (see *Vowels*, /aa/, above). Thus JC /gyad/ *gag* /gad/ *God*, /gyaadn/ *garden* /gaadn/ *Gordon* etc. The palatalized /ky/ and /gy/ before front vowels were first noticed in England at the beginning of the seventeenth century, became the accepted polite usage in the eighteenth century, and survived in old-fashioned speech until the beginning of the present century (see Dobson II, § 379). It is assumed that they are retained in JC before /a/ and /aa/, whilst almost disappearing in other contexts, because of the coalescence in JC of the two English vowel phonemes; the existence of palatal /ky/ and /gy/ in Twi was undoubtedly of importance in their retention.

/gy/ occurs occasionally in other contexts: /gyanzi/ ~ /ganzi/ *Guernsey*, /gyou/ < Scots *gow* (see *SND*). In the case of *gargle* the form /jaagl/ occurs alongside the more normal /gyaagl/, the probable development being /gyaagl/ > /dyaagl/ > /jyaagl/ > /jaagl/.

JC /ky/ is the voiceless counterpart of /gy/, with the same status and explanation: /kyata/ *scatter* /kata/ *cotter*; /kyaan(g)/ *can't* /kaan/ *corn* etc. /kyou-kyou-kyou-kyou/ (q.v.) is probably echoic, but may be based on an Africanism.

JC /k/ = RP /k/ regularly in /kil/ *kill* /kodl/ *cuddle* /pika/ *pecker* /puok/ *pork* [but see /ky/ above].
= RP /t/ regularly before /l/ in medial position in /likl/ *little* /bikl/ *victuals* etc.; *EDG* (§ 283) records /brikl/ *brittle* Hampshire, /likl/ *little* Lancashire and Shropshire.
= RP /t/ occasionally intervocalically and finally: /priki-is/ *prettiest* /puyaak/ *Pouyat* (banana).
= RP /d/ finally in /punyaak/ *poniard.*
= RP final /p/ occasionally: /pak not/ *pop nut* (see **PARK NUT**) /huk wis/ *hoop withe.*

/-k/ is sometimes the velar equivalent of a glottal stop (as in Malay) after a final back vowel: /brak/~/bra/ *brother*, /kikombok/ *cucumber*, /muduk/~/mudu/ *a freak*, /patuk/~/patu/ *an owl*, /sak/~/sa/ *sister* etc. This feature is presumably an Africanism.

JC /g/ = RP /g/ regularly in /giet/ *gate* /guot/ *goat* /bagi/ *baggy* (*-pants*) /gig/ *gig* [but see /gy/ above].
= RP /d/ regularly before /l/ in medial position in /migl/ *middle* /krogl/ *cruddle* (dialect form of *curdle*) etc. No similar forms are recorded in *EDG*.
= RP /b/ occasionally before /l/ in medial position: /gagl/ *gobble* /gaglit/ *goblet*. (Not found in *EDG*.) Also occasionally intervocalically, as in /rogij/ *rubbish.*
= RP /k/ occasionally, as in /glami/ *clammy* (Not found in *EDG*.)

Nasals

JC /m/ = RP /m/ regularly as in /mout/ *mouth* /tamas/ *Thomas* /faam/ *form.*
= RP /n/ commonly, as in /metl/ *nettle* /pami/ *pan*(*i*) /ramsak/ *ransack.*
= RP syllabic /-n/ or /-in/ commonly after labial consonants and occasionally elsewhere, as in /babm/ *bobbin* /razm/ *rosin* (see above, *Syllabic semivowels*). *EDG*, § 269 states that /n/ has become vocalic /m/ after labials by assimilation in northern and south-western English dialects, and also often in those of the Midlands.
= RP /b/ occasionally, as in /komanansi/ *Cob Anancy* /min/ *been.*
= RP /h/ occasionally in /mamlit/ *hamlet.*

JC /n/ = RP /n/ regularly as in /nuoz/ *nose* /buoni/ *bony* /baan/ *born.*
= RP final /ŋ/ commonly as in /maanin/ *morning* /aianin/ *ironing* etc. Such pronunciations, confined however to the present participles as in *fishin'*, were vulgar and dialectal in the seventeenth century in England but became generally accepted in the eighteenth century; today they are old-fashioned or dialectal once more. (See Dobson II, § 377, Gimson 8.23 (4).)
= RP /l/ occasionally as in /ninggambaiti/ *lignum vitae* /wenshman/ *Welshman* /pinchaz/ *pilchers* (*pilchards*) /pinikin/~/pilikin/ *pelican.*
= RP /r/ (rarely) as in /nigretfl/ *regretful.*

JC /ny/ = RP syllable-initial /ny/ in /nyuuz/ *news*, /nyam/ *gobble up*. It is common in words of African origin (see esp. pp. 325–6), and occasionally replaces English initial /y/ when the form of the word suggests similarities to Africanisms, as in /nyong/ *young*. Conversely there is a tendency for African /ny/ to be reduced to /y/ as part of a general tendency to 'de-nasalize' and so de-Africanize initial pre-nasalized consonants; thus /nyanga/ > /yanga/, just as African /ntambu/ > JC /tambo/.

JC /ng/ = RP medial and final /ŋ/ in /ting/ *thing* etc.; this frequently in JC is reduced to nasalization of the preceding vowel, so that /dong/ *down* > [dǝ̃] etc.

= RP /ŋ/ before /k/ and /g/ regularly as in /hengka/ *hanker* /tingk/ *think* /finggl/ *finger* vb., etc.

Fricatives and affricates

JC /v/ = RP /v/ in /viniga/ *vinegar* /sovis/ *service* /maav/ *mauve*; but see /b/ above. As a hypercorrection JC /v/ occasionally occurs for RP /b/, as in 'savat' *Sabbath* (Russell) and 'truvel' *trouble* (Louise Bennett).

= RP initial /w/ in occasional archaic speech (see *Jamaica Talk*, p. 41) as in /vel/ *well* etc. (*EDG* does not record this feature, although it was immortalized by Dickens as a 'Vellerism' in *Pickwick Papers*.)

JC /f/ = RP /f/ in /fieva/ *favour* /kafi/ *coffee* /difran/ *different*.

= RP /p/ before /l/ occasionally, as in /zeflin/ *zeppelin*.

JC /z/ = RP /z/ in /zingk/ *zinc* /ruoziz/ *roses* etc.

= RP /l/ occasionally in /aazwiez/ *always*.

JC /s/ = RP /s/ in /saal/ *salt* /biesin/ *basin* /fies/ *face*.

= RP /ʃ/ occasionally before /r/ in /srints/ *shrimps* etc. (a characteristic of the Midland dialects in England—see *EDG*, § 338).

JC /sh/ = RP /ʃ/* in /shiema/ *shamer* /rashin/ *ration* /flesh/ *flesh*.

= RP /tʃ/ occasionally in /wish/ *which* etc.

JC /j/ = RP /dʒ/* in /jinal/ *ginal* /kojo/ *Cudjoe* /ginj/ *gange*.

= RP medial /ʒ/ in /pleja/ *pleasure* /akiejanali/ *occasionally* etc. /ʒ/ was not naturalized as an English sound until the seventeenth century; it is missing from Gil's list of consonants. It is also lacking in both Twi and Ewe.

= RP final /tʃ/ occasionally, as in /boj/~/boch/ *birch*.

(~jr) (~dy) = RP /dr/ in /jingk~jringk~dyingk/ *drink* /jaa~jraa/ *draw* /jai~jrai/ *dry*; /dy/ only among old-fashioned speakers. Many English speakers—including RP speakers—approach this pronunciation of /dr/—see Gimson 8.26 (2). The /dr/ combination occurs in Twi only in foreign loan-words.

= RP /g/ occasionally, as in /jaagle/ *gargle*.

JC /ch/ = RP /tʃ/* in /chienj/ *change* /hachit/ *hatchet*.

= RP /t/ occasionally as in /chiini/ *teeny*, /mancha/ < /manchinik/ < *Martinique* (*banana*).

(~/ty/) = RP /tj/ in /chupid/ *stupid* (for loss of *s* see below).

* The sounds in JC and RP are identical, but Gimson's symbols are different from those of this Dictionary.

(~/ty/) = RP /tr/, /θr/ in /chii~tyii/ *tree, three* /ching/ *string* /ch(r)uu/ *true, through*, etc.

= RP /sk/ occasionally, as in /toch/ *tusk(s)* (see **RING-BOAR**), after metathesis > /toks/ (see below, *Metathesis*).

= RP /ts/ occasionally, as in /kochi/ *curtsy.*

/l, r, w, y/ and [h].

JC /l/ = RP /l/ in /likl/ *little* /beli/ *belly* /kuul/ *cool.*

~JC /r/ = RP /r/ in /flitaz/ *fritters* /talabred/ *thoroughbred* /praimali/ *primary* /finggl/ *finger* vb. /brufil/ *Bluefields (cedar)*. The /l/~/r/ alternation is not a feature of English dialects, but is a very common feature of contact-varieties of English in many parts of the world. According to Christaller's description, [l] occurs in Twi only in loan-words, but in sóme Fante dialects it replaces Twi [r]. In Westermann's description of Ewe [l] and [r] are in complementary distribution.

= RP /n/ in /feril/ *fern* /malela/ *Manila (rope).*

JC /r/ = RP /r/ in /rak/ *rock(stone)* /grienj/ *grange* /maras/ *morass* and ĭs sometimes sounded as a trill or as r-coloration in final position also: /torkl/ *turtle*, /fuo~fuor/ *four* etc. In final position there is sometimes sandhi-alternation due to preservation before a vowel *vis-a-vis* loss before a consonant, as in many English dialects.

= RP intervocalic /d/ or /ð/ occasionally: /nombari/ *nobody* /tara/ *t'other* /impyurens/ *impudence.* Cf. *EDG*, § 299.

= RP /w/ rarely in /ripri/ (usually /wipri/) *whip-ray.*

= RP /w/ after /k/ in /kriel/ *quail.*

(~/l/) = RP /l/ in /shrip-shrap/ *slip-slop.* See above, /l/~/r/ alternation, under JC /l/.

JC /w/ = RP /w/ in /waata/ *water* /kwiel/ *quail* /bitwiin/ *between.*

= RP /r/ after /k/ in /kwisel/~/krichúol/ (*scritch-~*) *screech-owl.*

It is common as a glide (i) initially in emphatic contexts before /uo/ as in /wuopm/ *open* /wuol/ *whole*, and (ii) after /p/ and before /ai/, /uo/; after /b/ and before /ai/: /pwail/ *spoil* /bwail/ *boil* /ripwuot/ *report* etc. The evidence for such pronunciations in England in the seventeenth century is summarized by Dobson (II, §§ 431–2). Initial /w/ has disappeared in JC /uman/ *woman*, as in many English dialects; also in JC /ud/~/hud/ *wood.*

JC /y/ = RP /j/* as in /yaaz/ *yaws* /kyuua/ *skewer*. It is frequent as a palatal glide after /k/, /g/, qqv. Especially in old-fashioned speech JC preserves /y/ as an initial glide as in /yai/ *eye* /yeda/ *hither* /yeri/ *hear* /yuokwud/ < Eng. *oak* etc.

These /y/-glides, like the /w/-glides described above under /w/, were widespread in English dialects in the fifteenth to seventeenth centuries, and are discussed by Dobson (II, §§ 428–30); many examples are recorded by *EDG* from modern dialects—§ 248.

* The sound is identical, but Gimson's symbol differs from that used in the Dictionary.

JC [h] = RP /h/ initially and medially as in /haat/ *heart* /bihiev/ *behave*.

JC [h] does not, however, have phonemic status, as it does in RP where, e.g., *arbour* and *harbour* form a minimal pair. Initial [h] is frequently lost in unemphatic contexts and used as a hypercorrection in emphatic contexts: /aaba~haaba/ *arbour* and *harbour* /hanch/ *ants* /human~uman/ *woman* /habriko/ *albacore* /haaj/ *adze* /huda/ *would have* etc. Both the loss and the hypercorrect use are features of English dialects also.

= RP /w/ or /hw/ rarely in /hen/ *when*.

10. REDUCTION OF CONSONANT CLUSTERS, ASSIMILATION, METATHESIS ETC.

(1) Initial /sk/ /skr/ /sp/ /spr/ /st/ /str/ are frequently reduced by loss of /s/; this appears to have been the norm in older forms of JC and must be ascribed to the lack of those clusters in such languages as Twi: /kin/ *skin* /kraani/ *scrawny* /pwail/ *spoil* /prinj/ *springe* /tan/ *stand* /trangga/ *stronger*.

Under the influence of the model language the *s* is often restored (and frequently inserted also as a hypercorrection as in /skrosh/ *crush* /stanjariin/ *tangerine*), but it may nevertheless be long and syllabic, even to the point of producing a svarabhakti vowel. JC /s/ behaves in a similar way also before /m/ and /n/: /s̩kuul/ *school* (but /skrebi/, /skriil/, /skrosh/ etc.) /s̩maal/ *small*, /simit/ *smith* /sumuud/ *smooth* /s̩nuo/ *snore* /siniek/ *snake* etc.

(2) No trace remains in JC of initial *kn* or *gn*, although these were still commonly pronounced in seventeenth-century English, probably both as [hn]. No such cluster appears in Twi or Ewe, and it has of course disappeared also from RP since 1700.

(3) In medial and final position some consonants are assimilated to contiguous /s/ or /f/ and so lost: /yeside/ *yesterday* /fisla/ *fistula* /kris/ *crisp* /ris/ *wrist* (and thence by hypercorrection to /risk/ as in /ham-risk/ *hand-wrist*) /sef/ *self* /fif/ *fifth* /lif-op/ *lift-up*.

(4) Final clusters of *consonant + dental* are frequently reduced by loss of the dental: /uol/ *old* /san/ *sand* /kalek/ *collect* etc. In English dialects final /d/ is frequently lost after /l/ and /n/ (*EDG*, § 307), and final /t/ after /s, k, p, f/ (*EDG*, § 295).

(5) Assimilations:

/l/ > /r/: /aaredi/ *already* /aarait/ *alright*.

/l/ > /z/: /aazwiez/ *always*.

/d/ > /n/: /brénót/ *breadnut*.

/d/ > /l/: /mel/ *meddle* (although this may well have been borrowed as /mel/ from England—see *OED* Mell *v*[2]).

/m/ > /n/ through influence of adjacent alveolar consonant: /batn/ *bottom* /sinting/ *something*.

/n/ > /m/ through influence of adjacent labial consonant: /stiibm/ *Stephen* /uopm/ *open* /pimplo/ *pin-pillow*.

/t/ > /d/ in /sidong/ *sit down* etc.

Final nasals may be assimilated into a nasalization of the preceding vowel (see above under /ng/). Any final consonant(s) may be lost, sometimes with accompanying modification of the preceding vowel: /lii/ *little* /wa/ *what?* /bikaa/ *because* etc.

(6) *Metathesis.* Metathesis of /sk/ is common in /aks/ *ask* /hoks/ *husk* /baks/ *bask*; the first of these at least is common in English dialects, and the feature generally was common after back vowels in late West Saxon (see A. Campbell, *Old English Grammar*, 1959, § 440) and may well have survived unrecorded in English dialects at least to the eighteenth century—there is thus no need to think of it as a Jamaicanism.

Metathesis of /r/ and of /l/, also to be heard in English dialects (and common in children's talk), occurs commonly, e.g., in /kromuujin/ *curmudgeon* /kruchument/ *accoutrement* /prakapain/ and /pakrapain/ *porcupine* /slandaz/ *sandals* /flim/ *film* /pusl/ *pussley* /baazli/ *basil* /paasl/ *parsley* etc.

(7) *Metanalysis.* Examples: /nangka/ *anchor* /nej/ (*to set on*) *edge* /nel/ *ell.*

11. LOSS OF PRELIMINARY UNSTRESSED SYLLABLES (INCLUDING APHESIS)

The normal English tendency towards colloquial aphesis and loss of preliminary unstressed syllables ("'cos' for *because* etc.) has become a very common feature of JC: /gens/ *against* /kaazn/ *because* /pekta/ *inspector* /piini/ *subpoena* (see **PEENY** sb[2] dial.) etc. etc.

12. INTRUSIVES AND PARASITICS

Vowels:

Archaic JC tended to add /-i/ or /-a/ after a final consonant: /yeri/ *hear* /taaki/ *talk* /rata/ *rat* /uona/ *own.* In compounds these intrusives have a linking or perhaps svarabhakti function: /rakatuon/ *rockstone* /disaya/ *this here* /sochilaik/ *such like* etc. This feature probably reflects West African phonotactics. Other svarabhakti vowels are mentioned above under (1). They are found also in such occasional forms as /worom/ *worm* /feril/~/fierin/ *fern* /rosit/ *rust.*

Consonants:

Intrusive /-n/ is found in /fishnin/ *fishing* /huntnin/ *hunting* /waitnin/ *whiting* /aisnin/ *icing* /kanchaniil/ *cochineal* /blansam/ *blossom* /malanta/ *mulatto,* and finally in /wishn/ *which* /kaazn/ *because.* Intrusive /n/ is a sporadic feature in English (cf. *messenger, passenger* earlier *messager, passager*) and in the dialects—*see EDG*, § 267; Dobson II, § 438.

Intrusive initial /y/ and /h/ are dealt with above under /y/ and /h/; final /-k/ above under /k/.

Intrusive /b/ occurs in /tambran/ *tamarind*; /m/ in /nombari/ *nobody.*

Intrusive /d/ occurs in /uondli/ *only* /laiad/ *liar* (the latter being found also in English dialects; it is perhaps partly due to the unfavourable connotations of the suffix *-ard*, e.g., in *bastard, stinkard,* when applied to people).

Intrusive /t/ occurs in /diistant/ *decent* /wist/ *withe* (normally /wis/ in Jamaica).

Intrusive /l/ occurs in the nonce-form 'repatrilate' (Louise Bennett), a formation probably influenced by *dilate, relate* etc.

Intrusive /k/ is regularly heard in /bongks/ *bounce.* /r/ occurs after consonants in /puoltris/ *poultice* /shaatrij/ *shortage* /primenta/ *pimento* /maagrit/ *Margate* (*fish*)—the last case, however, being possibly influenced by a folk-etymology < *Margaret.*

Intrusive /w/ is heard occasionally after /s/ in /swagi/ *soggy* /swinj/ *singe* /swipl/ *supple* (usually /sipl/).

A[1] /a/ prep dial; < *a* (worn down proclitic, *OED a prep*[1]) or *at*. *G*

1. Of place: at, in, on.

1873 Rampini 63, 'Dem bush no grow a' logwood tree!' said Bob. 1877 Murray *Kittle* 10, When I dead put it a my coffin. 1956 Mc Man /ebri pikini get a bag a swiiti a di piknik/ *Every child got a bag of sweets at the picnic.* 1957 JN StAnn [Where are you off to?] A' tank fe wata mam. [What are you going to put it in?] A wan cheese pan.

2. Of time: at, in; cf. *OED a prep*[1], 8; sometimes derivable from *of*. *T*

1925 Beckwith 63 [Prov:] If I don't ketch you a moonshine, I wi' ketch you a' dark night. 1957 JN /mi get mi kop ful a tii a maanin taim/ *I get my cup full of tea in the morning.*

3. Of motion: to.

1873 Rampini 178 [Prov:] Mean man go a market two time. 1956 Mc Man /mi waak trii mail go a maakit/ *I walked three miles to the market*

A[2] /a/ prep dial; < *a* (worn down proclitic, *OED a prep*[2]) or *of*. Of. *BL G T*

1868 Russell 1, 'A give him fe de good "*a*" him children'. 1950 Pioneer 27, Takooma jump dung off a de tree; *ibid* 61, Bans a more man, *Lots more men.* 1956 Mc Man /ten kwaat a milk/ *Ten quarts of milk.*

A[3] /a/ pron dial; < *I*. (In written dialect spelt *I*, *A*, *Ah*.) I (alternative to the more common /mi/). *BL G T*

1877 Murray *Feedin' 'Perrit* 14, Ef de gal didn't 'peak, you neba would a notice it a sure [*You never would have noticed it, I'm sure*]. 1905 Dodd 5, Ah tek dis bush..an bwoil it down. 1922 Beckwith 12, 'Jump mek a see!' [*Let me see you jump!*] 1929 Beckwith 100, 'A don't mind the wet a wet, but de 'prain a 'prain me foot!', *I don't mind that I got wet*, etc. 1950 Pioneer 35–6, 'Me dear Bredda Wasp, a hooda gi yuh anyting ef yuh help me out..Ah wi gi yuh a bite'. 1956 Mc Man /a wanda if wi dina redi/ *I wonder if our dinner is ready.*

A[4] /a/ demonstr & rel pron dial; prob < *that*. *G*

A. demonstr: That.

1868 Russell 1 (Demonstr:) A man 'gainst de fence was ya yes-i-day.

B. rel: Who, which, that.

1957 JB /hím a wena mek naiz, mam?/ (*Do you mean*) *the one who was making the noise, Ma'am?*

A[5] /a/ vbl auxiliary dial; prob < *a-* as in *a-going*, *a-fishing* (cf *OED a prep*[1], 13b). Used before a verb to indicate durative aspect or progressive action in present or future; see quots. Cf also *DA*. *G*

1873 Rampini 90, A provision ground in full cultivation—'when it a-bloom', as the negroes call it—is a very picturesque sight indeed. 1950 Pioneer 35, All wen him have 'casion fe serious, him keep awn a laugh fe show him teet. 1956 LeP StAnd /him go a luk fi mi/ *He comes looking for me;* /mi hed a hat mi/ *My head is hurting me;* /mi a nyam mi dina/ *I am eating my dinner* (as opposed to /mi nyam mi dina/ *I* [*habitually*] *eat my dinner*), etc. 1957 JN StE, No—no—not a man a get this pretty one; *No, no; nobody shall have this pretty one.*

A[6] /a/ vb[2] dial; < *is*, and other forms of the verb *to be*. Am; is; are. *G*

1873 Rampini 181 [Prov:] When man a magistrate, crooked da follow him. 1956 Mc Man /him a i wosis man lib ina di distrik/ *He is the worst man living in the district;* /dem ya an dat we yu sel mi laas wiik a di siem?/ *Are these the same as those you sold me last week?* 1957 JN StE, You a me cousin so me coming to live wid you.

A[7] /a/ vb[3] dial; < *is*, and other forms of the verb *to be*; see also IS. Introducing (and often intensifying) statements or questions: It is, There is, There are; Is it?, Is there?, Are there? Also preceding interrog pronouns and adverbs similarly. *G N*

1877 Murray *Kittle* 25, Watchman say, 'a so?' Mudfish say 'yes..'. 1895 Banbury 21, A any way him run, oh, Me wi' pull he oh, [*Any way it is* (*that*) *it runs* (i.e. *wherever, no matter where it runs*)]. 1907 Jekyll 65, A fun me a make, *It's fun I am making*, i.e. I am only pretending. 1953 Reckord *Della* /a di siem we dem kaal wen Vai daata Laiza sik/ [*They called out in the same way when Vi's daughter Liza was sick*]. 1956 Mc Man /a hu ben sii-im wen im tiif di pitieta-dem?/ *Who is it* (*that*) *saw him when he stole the potatoes?*; /a mí duwi misef/ *It is I who did it myself.* 1957 JN /a wan litl griin buk mi riid it out av/ *It is a little green book* (*that*) *I read it out of;* /a bra guot duwit/ *It is Brother Goat* (*who*) *did it;* /a juok; a fuo in mi klaas/ *It is a joke; there are four in my class*; a what you writing so long? *What is it* (*that*) *you are writing so long?*

A[8] /a/ intrusive transition sound, dial; freq after *like*, *must*, etc., prob due to phonetic analogy with W. African languages (e.g. Twi). (In written dialect it may be attached to the preceding or following word.) *G*

1790 Moreton 156, You no twist like a-me! 1873 Rampini 180 [Prov:] Trouble neber set in like a rain. 1877 Murray *Feedin' 'Perrit* 15, Ef I did hab money I mus' a ben hab a dish [of turtle]. 1912 McKay 33, Me own a* true sweetheart. * There is a delicious caressing sound about this intrusive 'a'. 1942 Bennett 29, For me buy me ticket me owna self. 1950 Pioneer 35, Yuh mussa feel sweet wid yuh wing dem ee, Bredda Wasp? [*You must feel sweet with your wings, eh, Brother Wasp?*] 1957 JN /unu mos a en ron/ *You must have run.*

a see HA.

aachi sb; cf Ewe *atsíī*, a river fish. See quots; cf *aachibombo*.

1955 LeP StE (Eld), Archie, codfish cakes. 1959 DeC StJ /aachi/ saltfish fritters—dropped from the spoon into the pan (in contrast to /stamp/, which are molded in the hands).

aachibombo, aachibong sb dial; cf *aachi*; the source of the second element is not clear, but cf BUMBO and slang *bung*, anus. Codfish fritters; see quots.

1943 *GL* Tre, Achibong, achibung, saltfish fritters. 1952 FGC West /àchibómbo/ saltfish fried in flour paste; made by the Chinese; black-people eat this when they drink their rum. 1959 DeC Tre /aachi-bong/ saltfish fritters dropped from a spoon; West /aachi-bombo/ an obscene name for saltfish fritters, more politely called just /aachi/.

aaf see OFF.

aafta see AFTER.

aaftali see AFTERLY.

aaftawad(**z**) see AFTERWARD(S).

aai see AYE.

aaj vb dial; an unusual pronunc of *urge*; /oj/ would be expected. *G*

aal see ALL.

aamtik see ARM-STICK.

aan, aant see AUNT.

[**aapetebi usaka** phr dial; cf. Twi *apete*, vultures; *bi*, some, certain one(s); *nsa kã*, to obtain, receive, get; cf AHPETTI. A preserved African phrase; see quot.

1958 DeC Port (Moore Town) /aapetébi usáka/ a Maroon saying: 'the crows will eat you (when you are dead)'.]

aapetti see AHPETTI.

aarait see ALL RIGHT. *BL G*

aas-bed sb dial; etym uncert: the first element might represent *arse, ass, horse*, or some other word.

1958 DeC StAnd /ass-bed/ a rough bed, often made of boxes and boards.

aata see AFTER.

aazwez, aazwiez see AZWAYS.

aba see ABBA.

ABACK /abák/ adv dial; <*aback* (backward, behind), transf of sense from motion or position to time. Ago, in the past—normally used of an interval longer than minutes or hours. *T*

1952 FGC StE, About five weeks aback. 1956 Mc Man /a wiik abak/, but /faiv minit ago/. 1958 FGC StJ /trii diez abak/ *Three days ago.*

ABBA /aba/ proper name obs; <Fante *Ábà* or similar form. *BL*

1. Name for a female born on Thursday: a so-called 'African DAY-NAME'.

1774 Long II 427, Abba, Thursday. 1907 Jekyll 156 (Day) Thursday..(Girls) Abba. c1935 *Gleaner* [Prov:] Poor ketch Abba a low groun' him tun sarvant fe dorg. [*When poverty catches Abba on low ground, she becomes servant to a dog.*] 1955 LeP StT, Abba, girl born on Thursday.

2. A flat BANKRA basket; see quot.

1958 DeC Port /ába/ a flat /bangkra/, so called because /aba kyari hit a shap/ *Abba carries it to the shop.*

ABBAH see prec.

ABBAY, ABBEY /abé, ábe, ábi/ sb; 1811 abbay, 1815 1929 abba, 1851 ebby, 1947 abbey; <Twi *a-bé*, palm-tree. *SC obè-makka.*

1. The African oil-palm, *Elaeis guineensis*, which grows to a height of 20–30 ft; also the fruit of this tree, about 2 in. in diameter, resembling very small coconuts. (Sloane describes it under the name of Palm Oil-tree (1725 113, and 175 Tab 214). *Abbay* is however sometimes mistakenly applied to other oil-yielding palms, and Gosse's description is in fact of the MACAW or MACCA-FAT palm.)

1811 Titford xvi, Abbays (Elæis guineensis). The fruit of a species of palm, called oily palm, which produces palm oil..They have a fibrous, yellow, oily pulp over the stone, and when boiled are pleasant and wholesome. 1834 Lewis 108, The abba, or palm-tree. 1851 Gosse 239, Ebby Palms. 1925 Beckwith No 478 [Prov:] If you t'roat-hole no big enough, you no to swallow abba seed. 1954 LeP StE /ábi, ábe/. 1956 Mc StE, StT /abé/.

2. Transf to the fruit of the BROADLEAF tree. (The evidence is inadequate, as this tree is not native to the Kgn area.)

1943 *GL* Kgn, Abě, broadleaf seed.

ABBLY /abli/ adv and adj dial; ? <*ably*.

A. adv: More ably, ablier, better. (Jekyll glosses '*abbly no me*, except me', but cf NO, than.)

1907 Jekyll 11, Brother Annancy..say..'Not a man can do it abbly no me'.

B. adj: Able. Cf ABLY.

1959 DeC Port /yu wuon fain a maruun muor abli no mii fi gaid you/ *You won't find a Maroon more capable than I am at guiding you.*

abe sb dial; perh a var form of ABBA 2.

1959 DeC StJ /abé/ temporary trash bag made at the field of grass or trash.

abe see ABBAY.

ABEA QUATTY sb dial obs; the first element is unknown; cf. QUATTY.

1943 *GL* no addr, Abea quatty. A silver penny half-penny.

ABENG /abéng/ sb dial; <Twi *abɛŋ*, animal's horn, musical instrument, etc.

1. A cow's horn used as a musical instrument and for signalling, esp among the Maroons; see quot.

1890 Thomas 28, A glass of grog was served out all round, we gave three cheers, and Nelson produced the abeng, and with his eyes closed, and his body swaying to and fro, blew a tremendous triumphal blast which the north wind must have carried miles away among the woods and gorges below. 1913 Clerk 23, It is made of eight or nine inches of the small horn of a cow—sufficient of the tip is taken off to leave a hole the size of a pea. On the concave side of the horn and close to the smaller end, an oblong opening or mouth hole is made..about a quarter of an inch wide by about an inch long..The lips are placed to the oblong opening and the thumb covers the hole in the tip, the opening and closing of which gives a variation of about a tone..The Maroons have a regular code of signals for the Abeng which is never divulged to any but their own people. [Largely from Thomas.] 1956 Mc Man, 'The abeng (or akete) is still blown in Westmoreland as a summons when there is some communal job to be done'.—Minister living at Retirement.

2. By extension: A conch-shell or any other form of Maroon bugle. (See also SHELL and its cpds.)

abi see ABBAY.

abli see ABBLY.

ABLY /íebli/ adj dial; <*able*. Cf ABBLY. Able, capable.

1956 Mc StA /ef a íebli/ *If I can.*

ABONG erron for ABENG; see KIAKE.

ABOO see *abu*[1].

ABOUKANI sb obs; origin unknown, but cf *gyashaani*. A bull, in the 'language of the Accompong Maroons'; see quot.

1915 Cundall *Hist Ja* 336, The 'Colonel's' brother told us he knew more of their old language (Coromantyn) than any one else, but all we could get out of them was pig = bracho, bull = aboukani, cow = aboukress. From a philological point of view one views them with suspicion.

ABOUKRESS sb obs; cf ABOUKANI, and *-ess*. A cow.

ABOUT adj, adv, in technical use. s *bout* vb.

A. adj: Of a sugar mill: in operation, working.

1812 Underhill 329. 1832 Waddell 71. 1873 Rampini 70, In spring, when the mills are 'about', the number of accidents..in working them is..large. 1935 HPJ, 'Still the technical term'.

B. adv: In the phrase *to put about*: set in operation, start working. (Cf *OED put v*, 34 b.)

1790 Beckford II 49, The common practice at the beginning of crop, is to set-in all the able hands for one or two days previously to the putting about the mill, to cut as many canes as possible, that it may continue, when once set in motion. 1825 Bickell 71, For putting the mill about (viz. for making sugar) on a Sunday, there is a fine of £50. 1873 Rampini 74, He had paid £60 more to rig up the old mill, to 'put it about', as he phrased it.

ABRUCT adj dial rare; <*abrupt* (cf. *plaba* for parallel k/p alternation).

1943 *GL* StT, Crabit, abruct.

abu[1] /abu/ sb, chiefly attrib; 1754 1774 aboo; cf Twi *ɛ-bó*, grey potter's clay; *abo-abó*, stony <*abó*, stones, rocks.

1. A dark reddish-black or dun-coloured clayey earth occurring in shale-like formation in damp places; it has a sweetish taste and was once eaten by negroes—cf DIRT-EATING.

1754 Browne 64, The aboo earth, or clammy Marl. 1774 Long III 851–2, Aboo Earth (described). 1952 FGC StT /abu stuon/. 1956 Mc StJ, Tre /abu/.

2. Stony, slaty soil.

1943 *GL* StM.

abu[2] /abu/ sb dial; cf Twi *ɔ-bɔ́we*, a thick climbing plant; *bów*, odour, scent, smell. Among the Accompong Maroons: the jasmine, esp when used medicinally.

1956 Mc StE /abu—jesima trii/.

abuja, buja /abúja, búja/ sb dial; <Twi *obogyá*, glow-worm. A firefly (applied in the quots to both *Photurus* and *Pyrophorus* spp.). (The sense in quot 1958 may imply something inimical.) *SC bodjà.*

1956 Mc StE (Accom) /buja/ a firefly; word interchangeable with /piini/. 1958 DeC Port /abúja/ the small firefly with light from the tail. Informant quoted old 'Maroon proverb': /wen daaknis kech u, abúja chraik/ *When darkness comes upon you, the firefly strikes.*

aburu sb dial; cf Hausa *aburu*, =*iburo*, a cereal.. an important cereal mainly grown by Pagan tribes. (Bargery.)

1959 DeC Han, West /abúru/ a turned cornmeal mush, highly seasoned with country pepper. Used by the Guinea, Congo, and Nago peoples.

ACACEE sb obs, also attrib. =Acacia (cf *DAE* quot 1785). For a time, at least, *acacee* seems to have been the form favoured in the West Indies.

1756 Browne 251, Mimosa 1..The common *Acacia*, or Acacee-bush..Mimosa 6..The smooth Accacee.. Mimosa 7..The spreading long-winged Acacee, or Sensitive. 1835 Madden II 90, The common Acacia or Acacee bush, which..goes here by the name of Cashaw.

ACAJOU TREE sb obs; <Fr. *acajou*; cf. *OED acajou* (1725→) and CASHEW.

1696 Sloane 188, The Cashew or Acaju Tree.

ACAJOU WINE sb obs; cf ACAJOU TREE.

1707 Sloane xxix, *Acajou* Wine, made of the Fruit so called, is very strong, keeps not long, and causes vomiting; 'tis reckoned a good remedy in the Dropsie.

ACAJU see ACAJOU TREE.

ACCOM see *akam.*

ACCOMPONG sb; prob <Twi *Onyaŋkõmpoŋ*, a name for the Supreme Being, rendered into English as *Accompong* and understood to be a personal name (see 1793 Edwards II 70, 'The Koromantyn Negroes..believe that Accompong, the god of the heavens, is the creator of all things..', etc.). Though the names of tutelar deities were often taken as personal names (cf Christaller Appendix E 601), it is unlikely that this should have been; a similar personal name such as *Ɔkõàmpá* or possibly *Akyéampɔ̀ŋ* could have been understood by the whites as 'Accompong'.

[1. Personal name: One of the Maroon leaders, *Captain Accompong*, brother and second in command to Captain Cudjoe, who concluded the Articles of Pacification on behalf of the Maroons of Trelawny Town, 1 March 1738 (cf 1796 Proceedings etc., xvi, xxi). See quot 1803 below.]

2. Name of the Maroon village in St Elizabeth founded by this leader, and today one of the three chief Maroon settlements.

1774 Long II frontis map, Accompongs Town. 1803 Dallas 44–5, Cudjoe now augmented the body he had placed under the command of his brother Accompong, and established them on the northern borders of St Elizabeth..a place where there is still a town called Accompong after his name. [Current 1961.]

3. A Maroon from this village. Obs.

1803 Dallas I 120, But neither the Accompongs, nor any other of the Maroon bodies, could be induced to join in the rebellion.

4. By extension: A person of genuine Maroon origin.

1906 *Gleaner* 17 March [Letter from Colonial Secretary:] True Accompong by descent from Maroons.

ACHIBONG see *aachibombo.*

ACHIE see ACKEE.

ACHIOTE sb obs; 1662 achiote, achiotte, 1672 achiots; *OED* 1796→. =ANATTA.

1662 Stubbe 56, Achiotl (as it is called by Hernandez) or Achiote, as it is usually called (Mr Gage calls it Achiotte) ..It is a Tree, that grows every where in the West Indies, without cultivation; it is regarded as well for its use in Painting, as Physick. It is a tree of an indifferent bigness, leaved somewhat like to an Elm..the fruit grows out in a Cod containing thirty or forty grains, which..yield a juice of a pure Vermilion colour: out of these grains..is the Achiote so called made. 1672 Blome 14, Achiots or Anetto. 1683 Laws.

ACHIOTS, ACHIOTTE see prec.

ACHRAS sb bot; cf *WD 2.* Evidently used broadly of some *Sapota* tree or trees; see quot. (Not treated in the hist dictionaries.)

1826 Williams 290, An achras, which they call xylobocion..; the white achras (salicifolia).

ACKEE, AKEE /áki, hákii/ sb; 1793 aka, 1794→ akee, 1801 acqui, 1834 achie, 1835 acca, 1890→ ackee; <Kru *ā-kee*, and cf Twi *àŋkyẽ*, *áŋkyẽ*, a kind of wild cashew tree and its fruits; cf 1864 Grisebach 125, '*Blighia sapida*.. Akeesia africana, Tuss.'. *ODS ackee, akee* 1829→. *BL*

1. The tree *Blighia sapida*, introduced to Jamaica from W. Africa about 1778 (see quot 1794).

1794 Broughton 11, Nov. Gen. *The Akee [from] Africa [presented by] Dr. Tho. Clarke, 1778. * This plant was brought here in a Slave Ship from the Coast of Africa, and now grows very luxuriant, producing every Year large Quantities of Fruit; several Gentlemen are encouraging the Propagation of it. I do not know that it has hitherto been described. 1801 Nugent 28 Sept., The acqui, a tree that bears a large scarlet fruit, the inside of which, they say, when dressed is like a sweet-bread. 1811 Titford 59. 1835 Madden II 67, The acca-tree from Africa. 1913 Harris 23, Akee.

2. The fruit of this tree.

1793 Edwards I 203, Aka Another African Fruit, introduced by the Negroes. 1953 Murray 19 [Song:] Carry me ackee go a Linstead Market.

3. The edible flesh of this fruit; often eaten with SALTFISH.

1952 FGC StAnd /áki/ There is only one kind; the pod is the white part that you eat; the seed is at the end of the pod.

NOTE. In the E. Caribbean, where *Blighia sapida* is virtually unknown, *Melicocca bijuga* (the GUINEP of Jamaica) is called ackee.

ACKEEBUS vb dial joc; <ACKEE + *-bus*, schoolboys' pseudo-Latin.

1943 *GL* StC, Ackeebus, mix with ackee.

ACKEE WALK sb; <ACKEE + WALK sb. A plantation or grove of ackee trees. (Used here as a place-name.)

1936 Martinez in *Gleaner* 3 Oct. 35, see WAPPEN-BAPPEN.

ACKRA /ákra/ sb, also attrib; cf Yoruba, Igbo, Efik *akara*. A flat cake made from blackeye peas, fried in oil. *T*

1893 Sullivan 33, Ackra cakes. 1943 *GL* Clar, ackra. 1959 DeC West /akra/.

ACROBAT sb dial slang.

1958 DeC StM /akrobat/ a stupid fool.

ACTOR-BOY sb. One kind of JOHN CANOE dancer.

[1801 Nugent 25 Dec. Figures called Johnny Canoes. All dance, leap and play a thousand anticks. Then there are groups of dancing men and women..Then there was a party of actors..Then a little child was introduced, supposed to be a king, who stabbed all the rest.] 1837 Belisario plate 1, KOO, KOO OR ACTOR BOY. Such is the strange title, by which this Aspirant to Histrionic honors is designated..of late years, this class of *John-Canoe* has found but little inducement for the exercise of his talent. *Ibid* plate 3, 'Koo-Koo', or 'Actor-Boy'.

ada var pronunc of 'other'; cf *aneda*.

A DA MEK, A DAT MEK /a dá mek, a dát mek/ conj phr and int dial; <(it) *is that* (which) *makes*; cf. A[7]; cf. also A IT MEK, A SO MEK, etc. *G*

A. conj phr: That's why.

1877 Murray *Feedin' 'Perrit* 6, A dat mek all de week I da work, I can't hab no money. 1955 LeP StAnd /a da mek, yu si, di wait piipl../ *That's why, you see, the white people..*

B. int: That's why!—an intentionally mystifying answer made to an inquisitive person's question 'Wa mek?' (used by schoolchildren). Also simply as a taunt.

1955 LeP StE (Accom), [Story:] /Him go huom..tu hiz mada, se ma, evri die mi go a skuul, yen tída wan, an mi hav eniting, dem se 'a dá mek'. Wa mek dem de se so? Di ma se..you nuo wat ai wil du, ai goin giv yu a wip tumaro, an eni wan tel yu so agen, biit im/.

ado see EDDO.

A-DOOR, A DOORS see *aduo*.

ADOPI sb dial; < Fante *adɔ́pɛ̂*, a species of ape (Christaller). [In Brit. Guiana *adopi*—Cruikshank.]

1943 *GL* Man, Adopi, A little hairy creature said to live in the bush.

ADROO, ADRU see next.

ADRUE /adrú, adrúu, ajú, hàjú/ sb; 1725→ adrue, 1794 adru, 1817 adroo, 1929 hadrow, 1953 hadrue; cf Twi *adúru*, powder, medicine, drug, physic; Ewe *adrú*, moss used as a dressing for wounds.

1. A medicinal plant; esp in Jamaica *Cyperus articulatus*, a reed with a chive-like blossom which when crushed and mixed with rum is used as a dressing for fresh cuts and wounds. (Such preparations are also called ALL-HEAL or FRESH-CUT.) An infusion of the root was taken internally for diarrhoea and dysentery. *N*

1725 Sloane *Nat Hist* 361, P.121.1.2. At the end [of the entry in 1704 *Voyage* 121, *Juncus cyperoides creberrime geniculatus*..] *add*, An *Cyperus Americanus caulibus articulatis*..1.19. *At the end add*, Adrue of Mr *Barham* in his Manuscript Observations of *Jamaica* Plants. whose Roots strung, and worn by the Negroes take off the rammish Smell which some of them have. It hath the same Colour, Taste, Smell and Virtues of the Contra-yerva. 1794 Barham 163, Rushes..2. That which the negroes call *adru*. 1801 Dancer 363, *For strengthening the Stomach etc.* Adrue (*Cyperus articulat.*)..The Roots aromatic and stimulant. 1820 Thompson 147, Adrue.. In chronic diarrhoea..it is singularly efficacious. 1891 Fawcett 36, Adrue. 1952 FGC Han, Port /ajú/. 1953 *WIMJ* 244, *Cyperus articulatus* 1. Adrue (Hadrue). (Digests 1927 Beckwith.)

2. A preparation of this plant used as an ingredient in recipes (e.g. to drive away ghosts).

1929 Beckwith 94, Add 3d. hadrow, 3d. oil of life, 3d. oil of nohel..

3. Attrib.

1817 Williamson 1 301–2, Where vomiting was excessively troublesome..the Adroo tea, was found useful.

adruu see prec.

aduo /adúo/ adv dial; <*a-doors* (cf. *OED*, →1777), prob reinforced by such a form as Akuapem *àdṹo*, the yard of a native dwelling (*adiwo hɔ*, out of doors). Outside; out of doors.

1907 Jekyll 138, An' the Jar t'row him outside a door. When him get out a door old lady said:—[etc.] 1924 Beckwith 75, An' de wife detain de boy in de yard fo' de whole day until rain come de day an' wet up all Massa Jesus clo'es a-do'. Dis boy was Sammy de Comferee, an jus' t'ru Sammy de Comferee mek de clo'es a wet up a-do'. 1956 Mc StAnd /put it adúo—bot it iz óut adúo/ *Put it outside! But it is outside*; StT /lúk out die adúo, lúk out adúo/ *Look out there outside; look outside.* Also Clar, Man; not much used by young people.

[**ADVANTAGE** /adváantij/ vb tr dial; <*advantage* sb; also in Trinidad, etc. To take advantage of, cheat, ill-treat (someone). *BL G T*

1952 FGC StAnd /duon mek im adváantij yu/ *Don't let him take advantage of you.* 1957 LeP StAnd /no bada adváantij mi man/ *Don't try to cheat me, man!*]

ADVICE sb dial. A bit or piece of advice or counsel. *BL G T*

1924 Beckwith 156, De missis said to him, 'Out of you money an' t'ree advice, which one you rather?' He said, 'I rather de t'ree advice..' De t'ree advice—'Not to forsake de bridge which you cross; not to interfere in politics; you mustn't in haste in temper'.

afana /afána, aféna, afíni/ sb; cf Akyem *afaná*, sword, var *afena*, *afona*. The Maroon word for a cutlass, machete.

1935 HPJ Accom, Afenna—'Colonel Rowe's word for a machete'. 1943 *GL* Port, Affanna, cutlass. 1955 Mc Accom /afána/ 'Maroon language' word for a cutlass. 1957 LeP Accom /afíni/.

AFASIA, AFASYAH sb dial; <Ewe *afaɔ́éɛ* (or Akan *afaséw*) an inferior kind of yam (Christaller). A kind of wild yam.

1890 Milne-Home, quoted in 1896 Bates 128, *De Affassia.* A greedy father of a family will give no share of his yams to any of his household who do not know the correct name of the vegetable. It is discovered to be *Affassia.* 1943 *GL* Tre, Afasia, afasyah, a wild yam.

AFENNA, AFFANNA, afini see *afana*.

AFFASSIA see AFASIA.

AFO, AFOO see AFU.

AFRICAN /áfrikan, háfrikan/ sb and adj.

1. In Jamaica generally: Negro. Hence 'African talk' is broad dialect, or words thought to be of African origin. Freq derog. Cf BLACK AFRICAN. *G*

1947 U.Newton II 2, A heated iron comb is applied to the African kinks, producing nearly straight Indian Hair.

2. In St Thomas parish: A negro group living in the lowlands in the area of Morant Bay, its members, and their religious practices. (Moore 24; see quot).

1953 Moore 27–8, 'The *african* gods are from tribes and nations. Take *Manuka Vola*, he is a great ancestral zombie who now is so strong he become a strong earth-bound god of the whole *Congo* nation', etc.

AFRICAN ROSE sb obs. Unidentified plant.

1790 Beckford I 32, The bushy richness of the oleander and African rose.

aftawad(z) see AFTERWARD(S).

AFTER /áafta, áata, ta/ prep, conj, and int; 1868 ater (Russell 19); <*after*.

A. prep: 1. Of time: At intervals of, after an interval of (cf *OED after* prep II 7). *BL G*

1956 Mc Man /yu kyan get a bos aafta a houa/ i.e. *The bus runs every hour* (*so that you will not need to wait longer than that*).

2. Of manner: In imitation of, like (cf *OED after prep* IV 14). *G T*

1925 Beckwith 40, De young cock crow after de old one.

3. Denoting the aim or object of the verb: About, concerning (cf *OED after prep* I 5 b).

1957 JN Man, Let me look after your supper; I'll cut the bread. *Let me see about your supper.* *BA BL G T*

4. At, to (someone or something). *BL G T*

1805–16 Slave Court Records (cited by Rampini 138), 'He..said..I would get fum-fum [be whipped], as the busha was swearing after me very much'. 1907 Jekyll 49, An' that time Guinea-pig was laughing after Rabbit. 1951 FGC StAnd /dem a kaal aafta yu/ *They are shouting at you* or *calling for you;* /im truo rak stuon aafta di daag/ *He threw a stone at the dog.*

B. conj or conj-adv: 1. Since, inasmuch as. (Passing into next sense.) *BL G T*

1924 Beckwith 156, He said, 'De only way you will taste de odder piece, let I pluck out de odder eye'. De little boy said, 'What mus' I do after I hungry?' An' him pluck out de odder eye an' gi' him de balance of pone lef'. 1955 Bennett *Bad Foot*, But me blame yuh Bredda Nancy After yuh no got no right..Fe go start up any fight. 1956 Mc Man /yu no waan kyaa, man, aafta yu kyaan draiv i/ *You don't want the car, man, seeing that you can't drive it.*

2. Considering that. (*OED when* 9; cf AFTER WHEN, of which this may be an abbr.) *BL G T*

1873 Rampini 173, *Me* can't paint! After my grand-mother's husban' was a painter, *me* can't paint! [He means, 'Of course I can paint!']

C. emphatic word or int: 1. Introducing an expression of protest, showing annoyance or contempt, analogous to *Really! Good heavens!* (Perh < sense B 2.) *BL N*

1942 Bennett 33, Him sey..me shouldn' come soh far But atta me po' li Jackass Is nat noh mota kear. [*He says I shouldn't come so far, but really! my poor little donkey is not a motor car.*] *Ibid* 44, Noh tan up fronten me load mah, Gwan! Atta I doan care. 1960 DeC *CLS* I 172, 'atta ba'bia'buo de go kil yu. '*After* [*still*] *Babiabuo is going to kill you.*'

AFTERLY adv dial; <*after* adv + *-ly*.

1958 DeC StAnd /aaftali/ recently, in recent years.

AFTER-MEAL sb dial.

1958 DeC Port /aafta-miil/ food left from one meal to the next.

AFTERWARD(S) sb dial; <*afterward* adv. Food left over (which may be eaten afterward, or later). *BL*

1958 DeC StT /aaftawad, aaftawadz/ leftover food.

AFTER WHEN /aafta wen/ conj phr. Of temporal succession: when. *BL G*

1956 Mc StE /so aafta wen de went tu bed, de hie di naking/ *So after they had gone to bed, they heard the knocking;* /aafta wen di dopi ron gaan, di man go a yaad/ *After the duppy had run away, the man went into the yard.*

AFU, AFU YAM /áfu, háfu, áfo, háfo/ sb dial; 1814→ afou, 1873→ afoo, 1907 1927 hafoo, 1927→ affoo, 1934→ afu, 1943→ afo, haffoh, hafu, hafooh; cf Twi *afúw*, plantation, cultivated ground. A common variety of hard yellow yam. Sometimes the hard white yam, though this is usually distinguished as WHITE AFU. s *afu buosan*, RED AFU.

1814 Lunan II 309–10, Dioscorea..aculeata..This yam is called the Afou yam..; it is of a smaller size and its inside is of a yellow colour. 1873 Rampini 115, It is essentially the literature of a race, not of a nation..its subjects are almost exclusively drawn from the common daily incidents of a country life. 'It scarcely ever rises above Gungo peas and Afoo yams.' 1907 Jekyll 17, Me go buy me little salt fish an' me little hafoo yam. [Note:] hafoo (pronounced hahfoo, really afoo, an African word), a kind of yam. 1927 Stafford 26, She is cooking Hafoo-yam and sweet potato. 1934 Williams 35, The name of the common yellow yam in Jamaica is afu. 1943 *GL* StC, Haffoh; StE, Hafu; Tre, Afo, Yellow yam. StJ, Hafooh, Negro yam. 1955 LeP gen.

AFU LUCEA /áfu lúusi/ sb; see AFU. A white yam associated with the town of Lucea in Hanover; see LUCEA YAM.

1956 Mc Port /háfu luusi/. 1958 DeC gen /afu luusi/ an afu (yellow) yam which is whitish; resembles the LUCEA YAM; it 'have a greenish look' inside after peeling.

AFU PUMPUM sb dial; <AFU + PUMPUM.

1943 *GL* Kgn, A kind of yam.

AGAIN /agén/ adv. *BL G*

1. In negative expressions implying a change of state or action since an understood time: any more, any longer (cf *OED again, adv* 4). *BA T*

1956 Mc StE, see DINGHY. 1957 JN, I don't love him again, *I don't love him any longer*; I not sending to your shop again, *I will not buy from your shop any more.*

2. In negative expressions implying a reversal of something announced or expected: any longer, after all. *T*

1907 Jekyll 263, A man was reported to be dead. Next day came the intelligence: 'He don't dead again', he is not dead after all, he is not really dead. 1957 JN, No, a not gwine beat you again, *No, I don't intend to beat you after all*; He can't be coming again, if he's not here yet, *He can't be expected to come any longer, since he's not here yet.*

3. Also, in addition. (Cf *OED* A 5). *T*

1957 JN, We ave tree East Indian, tree ackees..Yes, an what again? Two hairy mango.., *We have three East Indian mangoes, three ackee trees..That's right, and what else? Two hairy mangoes..*; Me get me cup full a tea a maanin taim an papa gi me some a fe him again, *I get my cup full of tea in the morning, and Father gives me some of his in addition.*

4. Vaguely, as if seeking to recall something, or asking for its repetition (cf *OED again, adv* 7). *T*

1957 JN, What de pretty girl over Miss Dorothy name again? *Now what is the name of the pretty girl over at Miss Dorothy's?*

5. As a post-verbal intensifier.

1957 JN, Mama what you tink me hear again—'shop at the store with the mike at the door', *Mama, just what do you think I heard?* etc.

AGAINST see *gens*.

aganga sb dial; for *iguana* or perh *agama*.

1952 FGC StAnd /agánga/ lizard.

AGE-PAPER sb dial. A birth certificate. *G*

1950 Pioneer 47, Dem bun dem aunty wid de soup Back bite her wid de fish, Now dem dah nyam up her age paper Wid de main-course dish.

agidi /agídi/ sb dial; <Yoruba *Àgidí*, 'a prepared meal of Indian corn, as a staple food'; also as a loan-word in Ewe.

1. Among the 'Guinea people' of Hanover: A dish prepared from yellow yam, grated, mixed with flour and fried in oil.

1959 DeC Han /agídi/.

2. Among the 'Guinea', 'Congo', and 'Nago' people of Hanover and Westmoreland: A pudding made from the fine sediment of grated cornmeal, seasoned and boiled in a banana-leaf.

1959 DeC Han, West /agídi/.

AGNUS CASTUS sb obs; cf *OED*. A name once erroneously applied in Jamaica to the castor bean.

1774 Long III 712, Oil-nut-tree..Agnus-castus—*Ricinus Americanus*. 1794 Barham 120, Oil-nuts (Linn. *Ricinus communis*). These are so called from the great quantity of oil got out of them; and also vulgarly, but very erroneously, called *agnus castus*, they having no relation to that species; but everybody in Jamaica calls it *agnus castus*, or oil-leaves, which they put to their blisters instead of melilot, and use no other.

A-GO vbl auxil phr; <A[5]+*go*. Preceding another verb, this forms phrases expressing the future; cf similar use of GWINE. *G*

1957 JN StE, Mama this man a-go turn teacher too, *This man is going to become a teacher too;* They a go eat off all the ripe plum an guava off de tree, *They are going to eat up all the ripe plums*, etc.

AGRICULTURAL adj dial. Applied in recent years to certain varieties of plants: Introduced by the Department of Agriculture; see quot.

1952 FGC Port, agricultural calalu; StC, agricultural cassava. 1959 DeC gen, Agricultural banana—the Lacatan banana.

AGUE /íegyu, híego/ sb, also attrib. =*OED ague* 1, 'An acute or violent fever. *Obs.*'—but this survives in common use in Jamaica; also, *ague fever*. *BA G T*

AHA sb dial rare; orig unknown.

1943 *GL* no addr, Aha—a weed that grows on graves.

AHAM see AKAM.

AHM pron dial; <*him*. =HIM 2. See quot 1907 Jekyll 164.

AHOA see A-OAH.

AHPETTI sb dial obs; cf Twi *o-peyi*, a certain amulet (Christaller), *opete*, vulture, deity (Turner 96). See quots.

[1820 Letter from the Virgin Islands 148 (Tortola) And superstition is on the wane among the negroes; they seem to confess that whatever apettis (spells) their magicians could once effect, these have long since failed before superior Christian incantations.] 1826 Williams 145, Cato, holding up the amulet suspended from his neck (a bag containing among other things bones, teeth, and hair) cried aloud, 'While I wear this, Plato, no one can take me'. 'And I,' returned the other, 'have also an ahpetti, a charm, a better charm—I wear the white man's spell.'

AH WO see A-OAH.

ai see AYE, EYE.

aian see IRON.

ail see OIL.

ail-not see OIL-NUT.

airis mas see IRISH MOSS.

AISE sb dial; a common dial sp for EARS. *G*

1942 Bennett 25, All de strain me strain me aise. 1950 Pioneer gloss, Aise—ears.

A IT MEK conj and int phr; <(it) *is it* (which) *makes*. Cf A DA MEK, A SO MEK. *G*

A. conj: That's why, that's the reason.

1868 *TRSAA* I 66, A it meck you see Green-lizard always lib 'pon tree. 1877 Murray *Feedin' 'Perrit* 12, Becasin arter you drink you cross wusser mo an dog, sar. A it mek you ben da call me inday, sar, me no come sar, *That's why when you called me in there, sir, I did not come, sir.*

B. int phr:

1959 DeC StT, Di pikni den haig di bwai, sie tu im se, a hit mek, *The children teased the boy, said to him, 'A it mek!'*

aj sb dial; the regular folk pronunciation of *adze*. See also *haaj*. *N*

1952 FGC Man /aj/—right name is /adz/; also StAnn etc; StJ /haj/.

aju see ADRUE.

akam /akám, hákam/ sb dial, also attrib; 1814 1864 acom, 1854–5 accom, 1868 aham; <Twi *akám*, a wild and inferior yam.

1. A kind of wild yam which bears aerially on the vine; eaten when other food is scarce.

1814 Lunan II 310, *Dioscorea..bulbifera*..The negroes call this kind *Acom*, and they cultivate it on account of the fruit it bears on its stems; which is very irregularly shaped, of a brown colour, rough skin, about the size of Irish potatoes, which it much resembles in taste, either roasted or boiled. 1854–5 *TJSA* I 68, Accom Yam. Discoria [*sic*] bulbifera. 1864 Grisebach 781, Acom: *Dioscorea bulbifera*. 1868 Russell 6, *Aham*—A creeping plant..African. 1952 FGC Han, StAnn, StE, StM, Tre /ákàm/; StC, StM /hákàm/.

2. See quot.

1956 Mc Man /akám/, a growth on the ear resembling the yam; it is said to result from piercing the ear during the akam season.

akbil see HAWKBILL TURTLE.

AKEE see ACKEE.

akete /akéte/ sb; cf Twi *kète*, a flute or pipe made of a reed; Ewe *kete*, Gũ *okete*, flute.

1. Another name for the ABENG: the horn of a goat or cow used as a bugle, chiefly by the Maroons; but cf KETTAY.

1943 *GL* StE, Aketta, Maroon bugle. 1956 Mc StE, StT /akéte/. 1958 DeC Port, StM.

2. Since about 1930: The drums used in *buru* dancing; taken over about 1940 by Ras Tafari cultists in West Kingston.

1960 *SAN Report* 18, The old *burra* dance by which discharged prisoners were reintegrated with their slum communities was taken over into the Ras Tafari movement by Locksmen. The *burra* drums became known as *akete* drums and the old *burra* dance was replaced by the Niyabingi dance.

AKETTA see prec.

akra see ACKRA.

aksbil see HAWKBILL TURTLE. *BL N*

ALBECATO see ALLIGATOR PEAR.

ALBINO sb; cf *OED* 1777→. *G*

1774 Long II 49, The offspring of two Negroe-parents, if born with a white or light-coloured *reticulum*, is called an Albinoe.

ALBION sb. The name of a sugar-estate near Yallahs, used attrib in ALBION CANE and ALBION SUGAR; hence also BROWN ALBION and WHITE ALBION.

1802 Nugent 6 March, Breakfast at 6, and start for Albion. [Note:] 1939 Cundall *Nugent* 88, A well-known sugar estate, whence Albion sugar takes its name, as white vacuum-pan sugar was first made at this estate somewhere about 1870.

ALBION CANE sb. A variety of sugar-cane associated with ALBION estate.

1952 FGC StJ. 1958 DeC StT.

ALBION SUGAR sb; see ALBION.

1893 Sullivan 64, One-and-a-half-pounds of light brown or albion sugar. 1957 LeP StAnd, Albion sugar (current).

ALDER TREE sb; cf *OED alder sb*², and *DAE alder-bush.* See quot 1864; better known as BUTTON-TREE, BUTTON-WOOD.

1794 Barham Index. 1864 Grisebach 781, Alder tree, West Indian: *Conocarpus erectus.*

ALEWIFE sb, also attrib; cf *OED alewife*² 'An American fish (*Clupea serrata*) closely allied to the herring'; *DAE +alewife*, 'The branch herring'. In Jamaica, species of *Balistes* and *Aluterides*; usu called OLDWIFE. *BA*

1952 FGC StT /íelwàif/; Clar /íelwaif jàk/.

ALEWIFE JACK see prec.

ALIAS MAN sb dial slang; <*alias*+*man.* A confidence man; see *raabaaba.*

1961 Ja. Talk 217 /raabáaba/ means specifically 'an alias-man'..and more generally a coarse, rough-spoken person.

alibotn see ALLIBUTTON.

ALICADA see ALLIGATOR PEAR.

ALICE sb bot; perh < the name *Aloysia*, 'Sweet-scented Verbena'—cf *OED verbena* 2 b.

1935 HPJ, Alice—the light purple Verbena.

aligeta see ALLIGATOR.

alikasha /álikàsha, álikyácha, hálikàsha/ sb dial; < ARRACACHA.

1956 Mc StA /hálikàsha/; Port /álikyásha/—'a plant resembling carrot in colour and shape, also called RELISH'. 1957 LeP StE /álikàsha/.

A-LIMBER adj dial; cf *OED limber a*, 'gently waving, moving in a supple fashion'.

1912 McKay *Constab* 18, Fields of manchinic..Wid.. scalloped leaves o' blue, In de evenin' light a-limber.

ALL¹ /aal/ adv dial; obscurely elliptical for *all the way* (*to*), or the like, implying a great degree, an extreme. *BL G T*

1. An intensive (cf. *OED all* C 3) very commonly used to draw attention to something considered unusual or extreme: Even.

1924 Beckwith 48, An' dey let Anansi stay [in the oven] all roas' till he burst! 1950 Pioneer 35, All wen him have 'casion fe serious, him keep awn a laugh, *Even when he had occasion to be serious, he kept on laughing.* 1956 Mc Man /aal nou him nieli ketch/ *Even at this moment he is nearly there;* /som a dem get plenti plenti moni—dem kyan get op tu twenti-sevn poun—dem kyan get all op tu dat/ *Some of them get a great deal of money—they can get up to twenty-seven pounds—they can even get as much as that.* StA /bena—da kyan kil aal daag/ *Bena* [a trap]—*that will even kill dogs.* 1957 JN /yes, som drai an som drap, aal sii red liif drap, aal sii kaan stik drai op die tu/ *Yes, some dry and some drop, see even the red leaves drop, see even the ears of corn there are drying up too.*

2. In expressions of duration, number, extent, or degree: even up to, even as many as, even as far as, etc.

1924 Beckwith 95, Ol' Witch ask her, 'What de matter you' han?' Say, 'Not'ing, ma'am'. Even when it cut up all bleed, never say not'ing. [*Even when it was cut up to the point of bleeding, she said nothing.*] 1956 Mc Man /dem bie aal di end av Juun/ *They bear up to the end of June*; /dis iivning nou yu sii dem wan wan, bot a maanin taim yu sii aal siks wan taim/ *This afternoon now you will see an occasional one, but in the mornings you will see as many as six at a time.* StE /wi hav tu put in drien aal tuu fiit/ *We have to put in drains as deep as two feet.*

ALL² /aal/ conj dial.

1. No matter how much, however much; even though very much. *BA BL G T*

1950 Pioneer 41, Nancy sey..'Play louda man!' But all Bra Cockroach try, him did too hungry an weak, an not a soun' coulda come from him troat. 1957 LeP StAnd (Irish Town) /aal im waan im no mek op im main fi go/ *However much he wants to, he has not made up his mind to go.*

2. If even.

1957 JN /mi da lib fi go nuo di sii; aal a misa Jiemz an Juo se im go tu, den yu no si mi kyan go, dada?/ *I just live to go and know* [i.e. experience] *the sea. If even Mr James and Joe say they are going too, then don't you see that I can go, Daddy?*

ALL³ /aal/ adj dial. (Also locally in U.S.) Only, nothing but. *G*

1957 JN Man, Mi go pick all grapefruit since morning, *I've been picking nothing but grapefruit since morning.*

ALL AND ALL /aal an aal/ pron dial. Everything, absolutely all. *G*

1955 Bennett *Sweepstake*, An dis Is all an all me do. 1959 DeC StAnd /in go tel aal an aal in fren/ *He went and told every one of his friends.*

ALLEGATOR see ALLIGATOR PEAR.

ALL-HEAL /áal híil/ sb now chiefly dial; cf *OED all-heal* 2, 1597–1725. Any of several medicinal plants, e.g. ADRUE, but esp *Micromeria obovata*; also the curative dressings prepared from these plants.

a 1726 Barham (1794) 171, Self-heal, or Alheal. See PICKERING'S HERB. 1801 Dancer 367, Self-Heal or All-Heal (*Ruellia panicul*[*ata*]); *ibid* 373, Adrue—All-Heal. 1814 Lunan I 11, All-Heal—See Self-Heal. [But no further entry under Self-Heal.] 1864 Grisebach 781, All-heal: *Micromeria obovata.* 1955 *WIMJ* 81, Micromeria Viminea..Peppermint; Wild Mint; All-Heal.

ALLIBUTTON /álibòtn/ sb and epithet; origin unknown, but phonologically corresponding to *Halliburton.*

One who through foolishness, ineffectiveness, or lack of self-respect works without proper payment or wastes his labour futilely. Hence, also, a stupid or worthless person. Esp in proverbial rhyming phrases: see quots. (Also in St Vincent.)

1935 HPJ, 'Allibutton Wuk fe nuttin' (Man, StM, Tre). In northeastern St Ann 'mek allibutton' = to work and not be paid. 1943 *GL* Tre, Allibutton, A person who works for nothing; StM, Allybutton, silly person. 1956 Mc StE /a pórsn dozn máta imself—satisfai wi eniting—alibotn wok fi notn/ *A person (who) doesn't respect himself, satisfied with anything—Allibutton work-for-nothing.* 1957 F. E. F. Fraser *Gleaner* 25 March, During my younger days in lower St Andrew it was used chiefly by small boys deriding cabbies who went to funerals in the hope of their cabs being chartered (but which remained unchartered) in a context such as this: 'Alibutton, work for nuttin', Get 'im pocket Full o' button.' 1957 Ansell Hart 23 March (letter), In Montego Bay about sixty years ago there was a moron named Albert Reaburn. The saying was often applied to him by the boys around—Allibutton work fi nutt'n, or Allibutton good fi nutt'n.

ALLIGATOR /haligeta, aligeta/ sb; cf *OED*. The native crocodile of Jamaica, *Crocodilus acutus*. *BL G N T*

1661 Hickeringill 34, *Jamaica..Alligator* or *Indian-Crocodile*, an amphibious Creature. 1684 Laws *The Arms of Jamaica*, And for the crest an Alligator. 1873 Rampini 175 [Prov:] Alligator lay egg, but him no fowl. 1908 Caine 296, Alligators, or rather *Crocodilus acutus*, abound all along the south side of the island. [Current 1962.]

ALLIGATOR APPLE sb, also attrib; see quot 1774; cf *OED alligator* 3; some analogy to the earlier ALLIGATOR PEAR was prob felt also. *OED* 1886. The fruit of the tree *Annona palustris*; also the tree itself, usu called CORK-WOOD.

1756 Browne 256, *ANNONA* 4..The Alligator Apple Tree, or Cork-Wood..bears a fine sweet-scented fruit, of no disagreeable flavour; but it is said to be a strong narcotic and is not used on that account. 1774 Long III 832, Alligator Apple, or Cork-Wood..It grows in great abundance about the Southside lagoons..When they are ripe, and drop into the water, the alligators watch their falling, and at the proper season of the year, are said to subsist chiefly upon them. 1864 Grisebach 781, Alligator-apple: *Anona palustris*.

ALLIGATOR PEAR sb, also attrib; 1696 allegator, 1725 albecato, 1788 alicada, 1788→ alligator; prob by popular etymology < some such form as *albacatas* (see quot 1696), borrowed from Sp. *OED* (s.v. *avocado*) suggests that *alligator* here is a corruption of *avocado*, itself formed by popular etymology from Aztec [i.e. Nahuatl] *ahuacatl*; but as *allegator* and *avocado* were equally familiar to Sloane in 1696, it is more likely that both words go back through separate forms to the Nahuatl source. Entirely independent formation (cf ALLIGATOR APPLE, ALLIGATOR WOOD) is also a possibility. *OED* 1763→. The avocado pear, *Persea gratissima*; the name being applied to both the tree and the fruit. Also called BUTTER PEAR, LONG-NECK PEAR. *N*

1696 Sloane 185–6, Prunifera arbor, fructu maximo pyriformi viridi..Alvacatas *of Hawks*..Avocottes *of Hortop. Spanish Pear of Hughes*..Ahuacaquauhitl seu arbor querciformis butiraceo fructu. Hernandez..*The Avocado or Allegator Pear-tree.* 1725 Sloane 132–3, *Prunifera arbor..The albecato Pear-Tree,* Hisp. *Abacado; seu, Avocado.* 1788 Marsden 78, The Alicada, or, as the negroes call it, Alligator Pear. 1914 Fawcett 208–9, Alligator pear..*Persea americana*.

ALLIGATOR RUSH sb dial; so called because alligators hide among them. *Acrostichum aureum*; more commonly CRAB THATCH.

1943 *NHN* II 7.

ALLIGATOR WOOD sb; so called, according to Sloane, because its musk-scented bark resembles the characteristic scent of an alligator; cf *OED alligator*[2] 3. The tree *Guarea glabra*, also called MUSK WOOD, WILD ACKEE.

1696 Sloane 137, *Alleygator* or *Musk wood.* 1774 Long III 861, Hogshead Staves. Santa Maria, Gum Tree, Alligator Wood. 1886 Hooper 32. 1920 Fawcett 214–15, *Guarea..glabra..*Musk Wood, Alligator Wood, Wild Akee. 1952 FGC StT, /áligeta wúd/ 'It has a round seed; Indian conies feed on them'.

ALL OF THAT adv phr dial. Expressing emphatic agreement: Exactly! Just so! *G*

1955 FGC Man /aal a dat/.

ALL RIGHT /áa ráit/ exclamatory phr chiefly dial. A common greeting in passing, or in parting. *BA BL G T*

1942 Bennett 18 [As a train leaves] Kiss Tayma. Tell John howdy do! Hawl een yuh head! A' right! *Ibid* 29, Ah-right me gawn yaw Tayma. [Current 1962.]

ALL THE /aal di/ adv phr dial; cf ALL[2] 1. Preceding and introducing a common construction in which a word is repeated for emphasis: however much, no matter how much; see quots. *G T*

1837 James 8, Sometimes he will leave his wife in the gig, and go in to punish the people, and all the call his wife can call to him to leave off, no use. 1942 Bennett 25, But all de strain me strain me aise Me couldn' ketch a wud him sey. 1950 Pioneer 16, De pickney tun over one leaf [of the book] an Nancy se one picture a Puss..But all de tun de pickney tun, an all de look Anancy look, him never se himself.

ALL THE SAME adv phr dial. Used for 'just the same' (cf *OED same* C 3, 'a. Exactly in the same manner..b. None the less'). *BL G T*

1924 Beckwith 26, 'I'll knock you down with my right hand!' That hand stuck fast all the same. *Ibid* 151, Jack didn' know not'ing all de same, but jus' working his head.

ALL THE WHILE adv phr dial. Regularly, repeatedly, frequently; always. *BL T*

1957 JN Clar, I go to May Pen to buy things all the while.

ALLYBUTTON see ALLIBUTTON.

ALLY-COCO sb dial; origin unknown. Some kind of plant or fruit (cf alikasha)? (Perh only a nonsense refrain.)

1935 HPJ, Green guava, green guava, green guava so sweet, Ally-coco, ally-coco, ally-coco so sweet. (Chorus to the ring game 'Postman'.)

ALL YOU /áal yú/ pron phr dial derog; cf US Sth *you-all*, of which, however, this is not an exact equivalent. You and people of your kind.

1942 Bennett 11 [One woman insulting another:] Gwan, all yuh should'n walk a day, You clothes fava black-out. *Ibid* 13, Tantudy mah meck me sidung, Tap wriggle yuhself, cho, All yuh too high fe dis yah tram, [*Sit still, ma'am, let me sit down; stop moving yourself about!' People like you are too high-up to ride on this tramcar.*] *BA G*

ALREADY /arédi/ adv. Yet; in this sense dial.

1956 Mc Man /dem sel aredi?/ *Are these sold yet?* 1957 JN Bohemia /a wanda ef di bos ketch a lórimaz aredi/ *I wonder if the bus has reached Lorrimers yet. BL G T*

ALUMEE-SUPOTA, see SAPODILLA.

am /am/ 3d pers pron dial; <*him*; cf. HIM, AHM. Used objectively: him, her, it. *G T*

1956 Mc StA /a fi yu pikini, yu du az yu laik wid am/ *She's your child, do as you like with her;* /a hu dwiit? di wie di taim tan, mi kyaan uon am/ *Who did it? The way things are at the moment, I can't own to it.*

amasi /amási/ int dial; reduced form of *Lord-a-mercy* (*OED lord* 6 b). Exclamation of surprise, consternation, etc.; sometimes 'corrected' in written dialect to *Have mercy!*

1943 *GL*, amassy; ha massy = have mercy; Clar, A massy [corrected to Ha massy], A prayer.

AMATA ppl adj; poss < Sp *amada*, dear, beloved. A cant word of a Morant Bay cult, said to mean 'loved'.

1953 Moore glossary.

amba see AMBER.

AMBASANGFA sb dial; cf AMBER and *samfai*. = JACKFRUIT FOOT.

1943 *GL* Clar, Ambasangfa, a jackfruit foot.

AMBER /ámba/ sb dial; cf *OED amber* 4, 'A piece of amber used as an amulet to attract lovers. Obs.'. 1604, 1691. A talisman or the like used for divination in the practice of obeah and myalism; see quots.

c 1842 *Song* (in 1895 Banbury 21), Amba do know me, oh! 1895 Banbury 21–2, The 'amber' was a talisman by which they [the Myalmen] pretended to divine. Both the mial and obeahman use it. Anything through which they look at the obeah [i.e. the magical objects or charm]..is called an 'amber', the name is not confined strictly to the substance so called. 1907 Jekyll 171–2, 'Me amber hé! me amber ho!' [The singer is using an amber to help him find buried gold.] 1929 Beckwith 32–3, The 'amba' is, according to Mary Campbell, a fetich secured from the spirits of the dead by means of the myal dance. The dance takes place in the grave-yard. 'The spirits carry you dancing all through the bush, then you come back to the grave and the *amba* comes rolling to you over the ground.' Ewan had one of these fetiches in the shape of a transparent little ball with red lines about it and something blue inside, according to Mary's account. He soaked it in rum and kept it in a little pouch. 1959 DeC Kgn, One obeahman told me that to obtain his amba (which appeared to be a glass pendant from a lamp pull) he had exhumed the corpse of a hanged murderer and had removed it from the corpse's mouth.

AMBER JACK sb; *ODS, DA* 1897→. The fish *Seriola dumerili* and similar species, earlier called Amber-fish.

1873 Rampini 171, see quot s.v. HORSE-EYE CAVALLY.

AMBER-JACK CAESAR sb dial. A variety of the CAESAR fish that resembles the amber-jack.

1952 FGC StE, = BOTTLE-CAESAR.

AMBITION sb dial. Self-respect. *BL G T*

1952 FGC StM.

AMBITIONABLE sb dial; cf MANNERSABLE, etc. Ambitious.

1961 BLB Man /dem duon ambishanebl/ *They have no ambition.*

amblit see HAMLET.

AMBROSIA sb. A dessert made of local fruits: see quot.

1957 *FFM* 263, Genuine ambrosia is made with oranges, bananas, and grated coconut sweetened with powdered or granulated sugar.

AMELIA /amíilia, hemíila/ sb dial; evid from the proper name.

1. A kind of rough bed; also called FOUR-FOOTER.

1931 Martinez *Gleaner* 3 Oct. (HPJ). 1959 DeC Tre, A rough wooden bed.

2. See quot.

1959 DeC StT /amíilia/, a good bed, store bought, with decorated head and footboard.

AMEN-PREACHER sb dial rare; see quot. A nickname for the JOHN CROW, from its black plumage, and from the strong dislike for evangelistic missionaries felt by some at the time it was given.

1827 Williams 82, Abdallah told me they were called john-crows or carrion-crows till lately; but now, he said, they were called amen-preachers, because they finished everything, and eat it all up. 1940 HPJ, 'Still current'.

AMERICAN sb dial.

1. See FRENCH SET-GIRLS.

2. 1958 DeC StT, a coconut RUNDOWN.

AMERICAN BROOMWEED sb bot obs; cf. BROOMWEED. Macfadyen's name for *Abutilon americanum* (ident. 1926 Fawcett 101).

1837 Macfadyen 86, Sida Americana. *American Broomweed.*

AMERICAN JESSAMINE sb bot obs. A name, never much used, for *Ipomoea quamoclit*; also called BARBADOES SWEET-WILLIAM, INDIAN CREEPER, INDIAN PINK, RED BELL-FLOWER.

1756 Browne 155, Ipomea Quamoclit..The American Jessamine. This plant is cultivated in many of the gardens of Jamaica on account of its beautiful flowers and thick foliage. 1814 Lunan I 399, Browne calls it the *American jessamine*..It is also called *Indian pink.*

AMERICAN MARMALADE sb obs. The Mammee-Sapota, formerly called the 'marmalade tree', and its pulp 'natural marmalade'. (Cf. *OED marmalade* 2.)

1811 Titford 57, Mammee Sappota..the fruit is of an oval shape, with a thick brown rind, and a very luscious, sweet, yellow pulp, called American marmalade.

a-mi-du sb dial; < Ja dial A[7] + *me* + *do*, *It is I who do it* (or *have done it*). A kind of yam: see quot.

The local name (in upper Man, StE, Tre) for the native wild yam *Dioscorea trifida*. This is an 'obeah yam', planted in provision grounds to discourage thieves. If a thief steals from the ground, the owner cuts a branch of what has been stolen (or some other branch—practice varies) and beats the a-mi-du hard with it. When the vine withers, the thief will too; or he will suffer some bodily harm. The a-mi-du performs vengeance for the beating it has been given. (GHP.)

AMYRIS WOOD sb tech; < *Amyris*, the genus name. See quots.

1941 Swabey 29, Amyriswood..*Amyris balsamifera.* 1944 *NHN* II 94, It seems probable that at least three species [of *Amyris*] have been shipped abroad, formerly under the name of West Indian Sandalwood but now as Amyris Wood.

anabo /ànabó, hànabó/ sb dial; etym unknown, but cf FANCY-ANNA. A tree bearing a pretty, liquorice-flavoured bean.

1952 FGC StT, Port.

AN' ALL phr dial; < *and all*. A phrase which, placed after a noun or pronoun, means 'even including', and implies that the inclusion is unusual or surprising. (Cf ALL 1.) Cf also DOWN TO. *BL G T*

1907 Jekyll 147, Time get so hard Hog an' all a look work [*Everybody, even including Hog, is looking for work*]. *Ibid* 272, Busha Webb an' all a pick coco-finger. 1925 Beckwith 59 [Song:] De time so hard daag and all dey look work.

ANANCY, ANNANCY /anánsi, hanáansi, nánsi/ sb; [1859 Ananzi], 1868 Anansay, Annancey, 1873→ Nancy, Annancy, 1924 1929 Anansi, 1943 Nance, Anawnsy, 1950→ Anancy; <Twi *anànse,* spider, *Anànse,* the name of a deity. *BL N T*

1. The central character of numerous fables, West African in origin, and extremely popular in Jamaica and many other parts of the West Indies. Anancy, the spider, pits his cunning (usually with success) against superior strength; he also symbolizes greed and envy. *G*

[1859 Dasent Introd., In all the West Indian Islands, 'Ananzi' is the name of spiders in general, and of a very beautiful spider with yellow stripes in particular. The Negroes think that this spider is the 'Ananzi' of their stories, but that his superior cunning enables him to take any shape he pleases. In fact, he is the example which the African tribes, from which these stories came, have chosen to take as pointing out the superiority of wit over brute strength.] 1868 *TRSAA* I 65, Anansay..is the Jove, the Thor, the Bramah of negro mythology. His great strength is in his cunning, and in his metamorphic versatility; he out-Proteuses Proteus. His parentage is utterly unknown—nor indeed does it seem referred to in any of the Anansay stories. 1873 Rampini 116, The principal hero of this autochthonic literature is the large black Annancy spider. [1934 Williams 35, It is peculiar to the Ashanti to use a sobriquet of the Supreme Being or Creator *Ananse Kokroko,* the Great Spider.] 1950 Pioneer 25, De man suspeck 'Nancy but him nevah meck Anancy know, him study a brain fe work pon him. 1956 LeP, /náansi, hanáansi/.

2. A harmless spider, as distinct from SPIDERS, which term in the dialect is frequently reserved for the black poisonous variety: BLACK ANANCY.

1943 *GL* Port, Nance, spider. 1956 Mc StT. 1960 Institute of Jamaica exhibit, Anancy spider, *Heteropoda venatoria.*

3. Attrib, as in ANANCY ROPE, ANANCY STORY, ANANCY TOUGH-TOUGH, NANCY BAG, NANCY NEST, etc. *G*

ANANCY ROPE sb dial. Spider web.

1907 Jekyll 13, Spiders' webs of any kind are called Annancy ropes. 1943 *GL* Kgn, Anawnsy Rope, cobweb. 1950 Pioneer 17, Sometime wen de ole oman dem sleepy Anancy tie up dem face wid him rope. 1957 JN StAnn, The kitchen full of annancy rope.

ANANCY STORY, NANCY STORY sb; <ANANCY+*story.* (Found widely throughout the Caribbean.) *BA BL G N T*

An inclusive name for tales favoured among the peasantry (and Jamaicans in general as children), either a beast-fable (in which case it is usually of African origin, and specifically from Ashanti, with Anancy the spider as its prominent figure), or a 'fairy-tale' (in which case it is usually of European origin, at least proximately). Sometimes features of both types are combined. Cf 1924 Beckwith.

a 1818 Lewis (1845) 127–8, The negroes are also very fond of what they call Nancy stories, part of which is related, and part sung..Observe, that a moral is always an indispensable part of a Nancy-story. [Anancy does not appear in the examples given.] *Ibid* 133, It seems to be an indispensable requisite for a Nancy-story, that it should contain a witch or a duppy, or in short some marvellous personage or other. It is a kind of '*pièce à machines*'. 1877 Murray *Kittle* 17, Nobody would venture on a 'Nancy Story' till 'Red Head Thomas' came. 1907 Jekyll title-page, Annancy Stories, Digging Sings. 1950 Sherlock in Pioneer 14, Here, then, is a collection of Anancy stories and dialect verse.

ANANCY TOUGH-TOUGH sb dial. An unidentified wild plant—perhaps one recalling ANANCY ROPE; cf ANANCY WIS, *ti-tai.* Also *SC Anansi-tetéi.*

1952 FGC StT.

ANANCY WIS sb dial; <ANANCY+WIS.

1959 DeC StJ /anánsi wis/ a fine, black basket-withe.

anaris see HAND-WRIST.

ANATTA, ANATTO /anáta, anáto, náta, náto/ sb; 1670 1794 anotto, 1672 anetto, 1696 1801 arnotto, 1774 1794 anotta, 1854–5 arnatto, 1888→ annotto; cf Sp (Peru) *anate* < Island Carib *onoto,* but the derivation in English may be direct, or multiple, judging by the variations in early forms. (Cf Santamaría, Friederici.) *OED* a 1682→.

1. A low, shrubby tree, *Bixa orellana* (10–12 ft high), cultivated extensively in Jamaica as elsewhere in the tropics; once also called ACHIOTE, ROUCOU.

2. The dark orange-red berries (*c.* $\frac{1}{8}$ in. diam.) which fill the pod of this tree.

3. The dye obtained from the waxy red coating of these berries, used for colouring foodstuffs and in preparing a cordial.

1672 Blome 14, Achiots or Anetto. 1696 Sloane 150–1, Urucu *of Knivet..*Anato *of Leigh..*Anotto *of Ligon..* Arnotto. 1756 Browne 254, Bixa 1..The *Roucou,* or Arnotto Tree. This curious shrub is pretty frequent in the cooler vales of Jamaica..All the seeds of this plant are covered with wax, which..is what generally goes by the name of *Terra Orellana, Roucou,* and *Arnotto.* 1801 Dancer 371 (Index of Diseases and Country Remedies) Cough, Asthma, Consumption—Liquorice Vine—Calabash—Ochrow—Arnotto (etc.). 1854–5 *TJSA* I 60, Heart-leaved Arnatto. Bixa orellana. 1950 Pioneer 78, 'Im take ackee make soup 'im take natta calar i', *She takes ackee to make soup, she takes anatta to colour it.* 1956 Mc Man /anáto/; StAnd /natá, náta/; StT /anáto, náto/.

[Cf use of the word in StM place-names, which differs in form from use of the word otherwise: Long I opp 376, 1670 map, Anotto River; *Ibid* II frontis, 1774 map, Anotta Bay; Edwards III append, 1794 map, Anotta Bay; 1888 Liddell Map, Annotto Bay.]

ANAWNSY (ROPE) see ANANCY (ROPE).

ANBURY sb dial; ? <*hand*+*berry.* A fungal gall on a turnip or cabbage.

1952 *NHN,* Fungal gall..finger and toe, or anbury.

ANCH sb dial; an irregular form of ANTS showing change of /ts/ to /ch/.

1907 Jekyll 257 [Song:] Anch a bite me.

ANCHOVY PEAR sb, also attrib; 1696 1725 anchove, 1756 anchovie, 1774→ anchovy; cf *OED,* 1725→. The tree *Grias cauliflora*; also its fruit.

[1657 Ligon 38, 72, Anchove Pear.] 1696 Sloane 179, Palmis affinis malus Persica..*The Anchove Pear-tree.* 1774 Long III 810, Anchovy Pear, or West India Mango.. This beautiful tree is frequent in the mountains, as well as in low moist bottoms..The fruit is about the size of an alligator's egg, and much like it in shape, only a little more acute at one end, and of a brown, russet colour; when pickled it exactly resembles the *East India Mango..* 1864 Grisebach 781, Anchovy-pear tree. 1959 FGC StM /anchúovi/ used to have it for pickles years ago; haven't heard it for a long time.

ANCOOL, ANCUL see UNCLE.

anda /ánda, áanda/ prep dial; <*under*. =UNDER, of which the regular reflex in the dialect is /ónda/.

1943 *GL* Clar, Anda, under. 1956 Mc Man /dem haid aanda di bed/ *They hid under the bed;* /anda wan trii/ *Under a tree. BL*

AN' DEM phr dial arch; <*and them*. A phrase which, placed after a noun, forms the plural; see DEM. *G T*

1868 Russell 4 [Plurality is] indicated by the pronoun *dem*, joined to its corresponding noun by the conjunction *an*. Thus, De cow an dem: De horse an dem. 1962 Bailey 7, We say *Jan-dem* or *Jan-an-dem*..meaning.. John and company..This use is extended to animals also, so that a mother may ask her son 'yu go fiid di kou-an-dem yet?' meaning 'have you already fed the cow and the other animals?'

[**ANDIROBA** sb bot obs. An early native name (cf Amer Sp *anderoba*—Santamaría) never fully adopted in English; =ANTIDOTE CACOON.

[1696 Sloane 85, Ghandiroba vel Nhandi-roba Brasiliensibus.] 1794 Barham Index, Andiroba.]

andrin /ándrin, hándrin/ adj dial; perh <*under* + *-ing*; cf *anda*. Looking distressed, odd, queer; physically unattractive.

1943 *GL* Kgn, Andrin, queer; Clar, Handrin, anything that is funny, ugly, or irregular. 1954 LeP StAnd /láng an ándrin/ tall and unnaturally thin. 1956 Mc StT /ándrin/ distressed-looking, as if in trouble; Man /andrin/ not pretty.

aneda dial pronunc of ANOTHER, of which the regular reflex in the dialect is /anáda/. Cf BREDA. Also /anida/. *G*

1912 Jekyll 6, Vowels are sometimes changed out of mere caprice, as it seems. Thus we have *ef* for *if*..*anedder* for *anudder* (another), etc. 1943 *GL*, Aneda, another. 1959 DeC gen /aneda, anida/.

ANGEL-BIRD sb rare; ?from its manner of standing with golden wings spread. The JACANA.

(1935 HPJ.)

ANGELEEN see ANGELIN TREE.

ANGEL-FISH sb; *OED angel-fish*, 'A fish of the *Squalidae* or Shark family', but the 1784 citation refers to a chaetodon (the sense here); *DAE* 1709 citation (from N. Carolina) probably refers to one also. A name given to several representatives of the Chætodons, of which a number of beautifully marked varieties are found in the reefs from the Florida Keys to the West Indies. *G T*

1756 Browne 454, Chætodon 2..The striped Angel-fish. 3..The variegated Angel-fish. 1892 Cockrell, Angel fish..*Pomacanthus aureus*. 1953 Smith in *NHN*, Chaetodontidae: *Holocanthus tricolor* (known as angel fish or rock beauty)..*Pomacanthus paru*, the French angel-fish.

ANGELICA TREE sb bot; cf *OED angelica* 2, 1827 Angelica-tree, *Aralia*; *DAE angelica tree*, *Aralia spinosa*, 1785→. A short tree (8–15 ft high) flowering profusely at the tops of the branches and then bearing small, whitish, succulent berries; usu called GALAPEE.

1756 Browne 189, Aralia 1..The *Galapee*, or Angelica Tree. 1864 Grisebach 781, 306, Angelica tree: *Sciadophyllum Brownei*, 'their true congener'.

ANGELIN TREE sb bot; 1794 angelyn, 1864 1954 angeleen, 1909→ angelin; <Sp *angelín* or Pg *angelim*; cf *OED angelina*, 1663→. The tree *Andira inermis*, common in Jamaica along the river valleys; usu known as (BASTARD) CABBAGE-BARK.

[1696 Sloane 135, An Andira. Ibaiariba sive Angelin.] 1794 Barham Index, Angelyn-tree. 1864 Grisebach 781, Angeleen tree: *Andira inermis*. 1909 Harris 300, Bastard Cabbage Bark or Angelin. 1941 Swabey 16, Cabbage Bark—(Angelin, Wormwood). *Andira inermis*.

ANGEL-MAN sb dial obs. A practitioner of MYALISM; see quot.

1895 Banbury 20, The great mial procession about the year 1842 or '46..took its rise at Newman Hall estate in Saint James, and went through that parish, Westmoreland and Hanover, increasing as it went until it consisted of hundreds of deluded fanatics. They went by the name of 'Mial people'; they were also called *Angel men*. They declared that the world was to be at an end..etc.

ANGEL'S FOOD sb (cf *OED angel's food*, 1577 'strong ale'; *DA* 1881→ =angel cake). A dessert made by sprinkling grated coconut over sections of orange.

1893 Sullivan 44 (Recipe given).

ANGELYN see ANGELIN TREE.

ANGOLA PEAS sb bot; from their supposed place of origin: cf *DA* 1763→. GUNGU PEAS.

[1671 Ogilby 346–7, In the Caribby Islands:..Passion-flower, pease of Angola, Seven-Year Beans..] 1756 Browne 296, Cytisus 1..Pigeon or *Angola* Peas. This shrub is frequently cultivated by the negroes, because it is a perennial, and does not require so much care. It grows commonly to a height of four or five feet, and bears a great many pods. The seeds are much used among the poorer sort of people and reckoned a hearty wholesome pulse. 1774 Long III 787, Pigeon or Angola Pea. 1814 Lunan II 64, Pigeon or Angola Peas.

ANI sb ornith; the species name, <Amer Sp *aní* (Santamaría), from native onomatopœic name. The SAVANNA BLACKBIRD, *Crotophaga ani*.

[1725 Sloane II 298, *Ani Brasiliensibus Marcgrave*..*The Great Black-bird*..It haunts the woods on the edges of the savannas..] 1952 Carley in *Gleaner* March, Everyone knows the savanna blackbird, or 'ani' with its ugly ridged beak. 1956 Jeffrey-Smith 65–6, The Savanna Blackbird or Ani..All the while it uttered its cry of, 'Ah ni, ah ni'.

anida see *aneda*.

ANIMAL FRUIT sb dial; a children's word. A leaf gall.

1952 *NHN* StAnn, StJ.

ANISOU /ánisou/ sb; <Sp *anisado*, aniseed spirit (in Amer Sp the *d* is often lost, giving /anisáo/). A medicine for coughs, fevers, etc., made from aniseed and rum.

1915 DeLisser 46, I feel weak in me chest, an a little rum an anisou would help de feeling. 1952 FGC Man /ánisou/.

ANNANCY see ANANCY.

ANSWER BACK /aansa bak/ vb phr. To answer, reply to (without the pejorative force of Standard usage); but cf BACK-ANSWER. *BA G T*

1957 DeC StE /di bwai aansa bak an se, yes ma/.

ANTAGGANIS see next.

ANTAGONIST vb dial. To treat as an antagonist; to antagonize. *G*

1943 *GL* Port, Antagganis, to annoy.

antana sb dial; cf Twi *atẽnã*, a travelling net. See quot; also *tana, tena*.

1943 *GL* Clar, Antanna, a large string bag for carrying weight on the back. 1959 DeC Clar, StC /antána/.

ANT-BIRD, ANT-EATER see ANTS-BIRD.

ANTIDOTE (COCOON) sb; < *antidote* + *cocoon*, cf CACOON. The plant *Fevillea cordifolia*; also the bean which it bears, and medicinal preparations made from it; cf ANDIROBA, SABO.

1756 Browne 374, Fevillea 1..The Antidote *Cocoon*. This plant is frequent in the inland parts of Jamaica, and generally found climbing among the tallest trees in the woods. The seeds are very oily and frequently burnt by the negroes instead of candles..The kernels are extremely bitter, and frequently infused in spirits for the use of the negroes: a small quantity of this spirit opens the body and provokes an appetite, but a larger dose works both by stool and vomit. It is frequently taken to clear the tube, when there is any suspicion of poison. 1801 Dancer 363, Calabash Coccoon Antidote (*Fevillea scandens*). The Kernel, sliced and infused with Orange Peel, and a little Wild Cinnamon, in Rum, an excellent Bitter, and opening Medicine. 1864 Grisebach 781, Antidote-cocoon: *Feuillea cordifolia*. 1952 FGC StJ, StM, Tre, antidote /ántiduot-káakúun/. 1953 *WIMJ* 244, Fevillea Cordifolia..Antidote Cocoon; Segra Seed; Nhandiroba. The seeds are purgative and contain a bitter principle fevillin, tannin compounds and resins. *N* ~ *tree*

ANTIQUE LAMP sb obs. The shell of any of various land snails (*Cochleae*) from their distinctive shape. Also abbr as 'antique'.

1756 Browne 400–1, Cochlea 3..The Middle-sized Antique Lamp. Cochlea 4..The Antique Lamp with one tooth..Cochlea 6..The thin-edged Antique with an open navel..These are all land shells, and frequent in the woody inland parts of *Jamaica*.

ANTS /ants, ans, hans, anch, hanch/ sb dial; this is both the sg and plur form: 'ant' is not used in the dialect. Cf HANEN. *BL G N T*

ANTS-BIRD /áns bòd/ sb dial; *ants* (not *ant*) is the regular form.

1. The Arrow-headed Warbler, resident in Jamaica.

2. The Black-and-White Warbler, a winter migrant from N. America.

1936 Bond 320, Arrow-headed Warbler (*Dendroica pharetra*): Local names:—Ants Bird, Ant-eater; Guinea-hen Canary. *Ibid* 326, Black and White Warbler (*Mniotilta varia*) Local names:—Ants Bird; Ant-eater. 1940 HPJ, Anse-bird. A small black-and-white bird that eats ants. 1941→ *NHN*, Ant bird, *Mniotilta varia*. 1956 Jeffrey-Smith 84, Ants-bird.

ANTS-PICK, ANTS-PICKER sb dial; from its habit of picking ants off the trunks and branches of trees. The ANTS-BIRD.

1952 FGC StAnd, StM, Man, Han /ans pika/. 1959 Jeffrey-Smith letter, Antspick (West).

ANTS-WOOD sb. See quot 1914. *G*

1854–5 *TJSA* 1 63, Ant Wood. Prunus sphoerocarpus? 1914 Fawcett 259, Wild cassada, Ants' Wood (*Prunus myrtifolia*). 1952 FGC StT, 'Feed rabbit with leaves'; StE.

ANT-WOOD see prec.

ANYTHING pron dial. In phr: *to be anything*—to be any kind of relatives, to be related (to one another). *G T*

1957 JN Baillieston, Elain Grant—I don't know if she and Miss Gwen is anything.

ao, aoa see next.

A-OAH /aó, aóa/ int dial; cf Twi *àò*, what! why! hey! ay! fie! (Christaller). An exclamation of fear, surprise, acceptance or comprehension of a statement, etc.; equivalent to English *oh!*; now rather countrified.

1942 Bennett 22 [Exclamation of a country-woman who thinks she sees a ghost] Ah nahvas yaw..Gata dress-dung chile a-oah, [*I'm nervous, you hear?..Agatha, move over, child, oh!*] 1943 *GL*, Ahoa, Well!; StC, A wo; Man, Aow, Pooh! Ah! Surprise, sorrow. 1952 FGC StA /aóa/. 1957 JN StAnd, You na go tonight? Ah wo!, *You're not going tonight? Oh, I see!*

AOW see prec.

apali gront /apáli grónt/ sb; etym unknown. Some variety of the fish GRUNT.

1952 FGC StM.

APARTMENT sb; not equivalent to either Brit or US use. *G*

1958 DeC gen, Apartment, meaning a room of a house. In the country (and sometimes in town) the size of a house is described by the number of apartments.. kitchens and bathrooms are not counted, even when they are under the same roof.

apeke see APPECKEH.

APEMPAY sb dial; etym unknown. See quot and see SHOW-ME-TOWN, *jiji-waina*, s WINEY.

1959 L. G. Perkins letter, In my childhood I used to hear the St Ann peasantry say Apempay..This was the name applied to moth pupae which are often turned up in the earth, and it seemed to apply in particular to the large Hawk Moth pupae. The hinder parts of these pupae are capable of..making spasmodic jerks from side to side. It was believed that if one wanted to find any given direction, say to a certain town or village, you had only to hold Apempay upright by its head, and ask your question, when it would reply by pointing with its tail to show the right way. I think there was a special formula to be repeated when asking the question.

apempe see MAPEMPE.

APIMPE, pempe /apímpe, pémpe/ sb dial; cf Madagascar *ampembe, ampemby*, sorgho (Flacourt 150). See quot 1927; if the identification is correct, this is not the same as APEMPE.

[1707 Sloane 104, Milium Indicum arundinaceo..An Ampembe de Flacourt. p. 118?] 1927 Beckwith 11, Apimpe-grass. 1929 Beckwith 116–17, Another weed, which Wilfrid called 'Madam Fate', if tucked together with two kinds of grass called Bahama and Apimpe (*Eleusine indica*) into the belt of a man..will make him indolent. 1952 FGC StM /pémpe graas/.

APPECKEH /apéke/ sb; etym unknown. See quot and cf APEMPAY, *jiji-waina*.

1943 *GL* StM, Appeckeh, a pupating worm.

APPLE BANANA sb. A short, fat, sweet variety of banana. *BL G*

1913 Harris 2, There are several local varieties such as lady's finger, strawberry, apple banana, &c., that are smaller and much more delicately flavoured than the commercial banana, and are used as dessert fruits. 1952 FGC StAnd /iz di smaalis—it hav fi raip/.

APPLE MANGO sb. An apple-shaped variety of mango. *BL G*

1952 FGC StAnd, StJ.

AR pron; a dial sp for *her*; cf HAR.

1941 Kirkpatrick 9, see IN (ONE'S) SALT.

ARALIA /arielya, oriilya/ sb; 1756→ aralia, 1942 orellia; *ODS* 1829→.

1. The ANGELICA TREE or GALAPEE; in this sense only bot.

1756 Browne 189, Aralia..The *Galapee*. 1814 Lunan 1 313–14 (from Browne).

2. See quot 1953; this has been common for at least fifty years (FGC).

1942 Bennett 25, I was gwine to sen' pure orellia bush, As yuh wanted so-soh greens. 1952 FGC StT /ariélya/; StAnd /oríilya/. 1953 *WIMJ* 237, Aralia guilfoylei.. Aralia. The leaves are used in Jamaica to prepare tea for colds. It is common in gardens as a hedge-plant and is not indigenous.

ARCHANGEL sb bot obs. *OED, ODS, EDD* give Archangel as the name of various other plants. See quots.

1756 Browne 313, Eupatorium 2. Odoratum bisurtum.. The Archangel. This weakly shrubby plant is very frequent in the lower hills of *Jamaica*. 1814 Lunan 371 (from Browne), one variety of hemp-agrimony.

aredi see ALREADY. *BL G*

aribeka see ARRABECK.

arielya see ARALIA.

ARM-STICK sb dial; <*arm* sb+*stick* sb. A crutch.

1952 FGC Han /im háfi yùuz tùu áam stik/.

ARMY GIRL sb dial; also called BLUE GAL. A bright blue fish, *Hypoplectrus unicolor*.

1950 Smith Han, Port. 1952 FGC StJ, StM.

ARRABECK /àribéka, hàribéka/ sb dial; origin unknown, but cf Sp 'jararaca=*Arum dracunculus*; *Dracontium polyphyllum*'—Malaret. See quots.

1943 *GL* Man, Arrabeck, native wild potato used in making starch. 1952 FGC StM /hàribéka/—'red arrowroot, leaf an' stalk; de bearin' is mos' like ginger, reddish'.

ARRA-BUSY sb dial; first element unknown.

1943 *GL* Kgn, Arra-busy, busy-body.

ARRACACHA sb; *OED* →1832. The edible tuber of the plant *Aracacia esculenta*; in folk use, *alikasha*.

[1850 Macfadyen 189–90, Arracacia esculenta..The root.. is a large tuber, yellow or white.] 1893 Sullivan 36, Arracacha. This is a kind of yam, and has a peculiar flavour rather like parsnips; it is not common. It is cooked in the same way as yams are. 1913 Harris 23, Arracacha. *Arracacia xanthorhiza.* This vegetable..was introduced to Jamaica in 1822 and is grown on the slopes of the Blue Mountains. 1926 Fawcett 428–9.

ARRANSPRAT *see* HERRING SPRAT.

ARROW sb; *OED arrow* 7b, 1779→. *T*

1. *OED*: 'The flowering stem of the sugar-cane.' Sometimes specifically the stem alone. Esp in western Ja; also called FLAG.

1790 Beckford I 51 [The cane] from the centre of which shoots up an arrow, like a silver wand..from the summits of which, grows out a plume of white feathers. 1958 DeC StAnd, Arrow, distinguished from FLAG in that arrow is the stem that bears the flag.

2. Transf: The tassel that grows at the top of a stalk of corn (maize).

1952 FGC StJ. 1959 DeC Han, StE, StJ, West.

ARROW vb, also const with *out*; <*arrow OED* 7b. Of sugar-cane: to put forth an arrow, implying that the cane is ripe, therefore the top is not fit for replanting; hence ARROWED, ARROWING. *T*

1823 Roughley 85 [One must pay attention to] the age of the cane; the species it is of; ..if it has been arrowed, bored, or rat-eaten.. *Ibid* 254, The arrowed top is a pithy, almost hollow, sapless trunk, with little life, few eyes, and those mostly blind ones.. *Ibid* 256 [A plantation of canes] should not be a prey to arrowing. 1958 DeC Man /aro out/ what the cane does when it blossoms.

ARROW-HEADED WARBLER sb ornith.

1936 Bond 320, Arrow-headed Warbler (*Dendroica pharetra*): Local names- Ants Bird. 1956 Jeffrey-Smith 85.

ARROW-HEADED WORM sb. An intestinal worm found in young dogs. See quot.

1954 *FG* 711, The first worm to trouble the life of the young dog is called the 'Puppy Worm' or the 'Arrow-headed Worm'. It is up to six inches long, rather translucent, and lives in the small intestines.

ARTIFY vb dial; <*art*+*-ify*. To render artistic, to decorate.

1909 Redcam 29, All you pretty picture that you paste up on you house wall to *artify* de place and mek it look luxuriant.

ARUM sb bot. In Jamaica, once used specifically of *Dieffenbachia seguine* or DUMB-CANE; now obs in this sense.

1774 Long I 443, The stalk of the *arum* or *dumb-cane*, sliced and thrown into the boiling liquor [sugar], has sometimes been used.

AS adv dial; perh through confusion of use with *like*. Such as, like. *G T*

1924 Beckwith 9, Anansi says, 'O Mr Goolin! you couldn't tell me a word as dat!' 1959 DeC gen.

asam sb dial; cf ASHAM (to which the texture or colour may be likened).

1956 Mc StAnd /asam/ 'A type of cloth'.

ASCORDEN adv dial; <*as*+aphetic form of *according*. According.

1955 Bennett *Back to Africa*, Ascorden to dat, all dem blue eye wite American Mus go back a Englan'. 1959 DeC gen.

ase see HUSSAY.

ASHAM /àshám, háshàm, ashan/ sb dial; <Twi *o-siãm*, parched and ground corn. Indian corn or Guinea-corn parched, finely ground and mixed with sugar. Also called BLACK GEORGE, BROWN GEORGE, COCTION, KAK SHAM, SHAM-SHAM.

1943 *GL* Clar, Kgn, Port. 1952 FGC Port, StM. 1955 LeP Port, Áshan, parched corn ground up finely. 1956 Mc StE, StT. [1956 LeP British Honduras/kaan sham/.]

ASHES BUSH see ASHES-WOOD.

ASHES-WATER sb obs; cf *DAE, DA ash-water*, 1852 only. Water leached through or mixed with ashes and used as a remedy.

1877 Murray *Feedin' 'Perrit* 16, De word gi'e me a bu'nin' in me tomack dat was wus an any heartbun. I drink hashes water, an I eat roas' cawn, but it was no use.

ASHES-WOOD sb dial. A small tree (*Tetrazygia pallens*) which burns entirely to ashes but retains its shape.

1952 StAnn, Tre /háshish wùd/. 1961 DAP StC, Ashes wood (Sligoville), Ashes bush (Guy's Hill).

ASINEGO sb obs; 1672 assnegroes, 1683 asnegroes, 1739 asinego; *OED* →1685.

1672 Blome 22, Assnegroes and Mules (both wild and Tame) are very many. 1683 *Present State* 17, Some Mules and Asnegroes. 1739 Leslie 176, Asinego [still in use in Laws of Jamaica].

asinu see *asunu*.

ASNEGRO see ASINEGO.

A SO MEK int dial; see quot. Cf A DA MEK, A IT MEK. *G*

1960 CLS 167 /so wán díe, hím an wán nái litl skúulmiet.. kéch tu a kámbát. di bwái síe, a-so-mék!/ *So one day he and one small, little schoolmate..catch to a combat. The boy say, 'So make!'* [This idiom, literally, 'It is this which makes or causes it', is a common schoolyard taunt, roughly equivalent to 'I know a secret and I won't tell'.]

ASONO, ASOONAH, ASOONOO see *asunu*.

ASSAY see HUSSAY.

ASSISTANT sb dial. A coconut RUNDOWN (because, as a sauce, it assists the eater to get his food down).

1958 DeC Tre.

ASSNEGRO see ASINEGO.

ASSONO, ASSUNNA see *asunu*.

ASTHMA BUSH, ASTHMA-WEED sb. See quots.

1927 Beckwith 11, Asthma-weed. *Leptilon bonariense*.. For asthma boil with 'Love weed' and drink as tea (White). 1952 FGC StM /hazma bush/. 1953 *WIMJ* 242, Erigeron bonariensis..Asthma weed.

asunu /ásunù, asúnu, asínu, asúna, asúnuk, súnù, súnusùnu/ sb dial; 1868 Asono, 1924 Asoonah, 1929 Assono, 1943 Asoonoo, Assunna; <Twi *e-sóno*, an elephant.

1. The elephant, known esp as a character in Anancy stories; his identity is now often obscured.

1868 Russell 6, *Asono*—The Elephant. 'Purely African.' 1924 Beckwith 86, Asoonah is a big skin t'ing. When it come in you' yard it will sink de whole place. 1929 Beckwith 219–20, Tiger and Monkey, with Assono (a huge unknown), are the only actors in the story not local to the island. 1956 Mc Accom /asunu/ tones: ¯-_ or _¯-, an African word which occurs in Anancy stories; they [the Maroons] do not know the precise meaning, but it is something large and voracious. 1957 LeP StE /bra sunu sunu/—a character in Anancy stories. 1958 DeC Port /asunu/ a very large animal which used to live in Jamaica, Asia, India, Africa, and South America. It ate human flesh. It is now extinct.

2. An opprobrious epithet applied to somebody very big and/or very greedy.

1943 *GL* Clar, Kgn, Man, Port, StJ, Tre, Asoonoo, etc.; Assunna, A proverbial glutton. 1958 DeC Port /asunuk/ A big and stupid fool. 1959 DeC Tre /asúnu/, a /man hu iit plenti, grabalishas man/.

3. A very big corn dumpling.

1935 HPJ StE, and elsewhere.

ASWALE adv dial rare; by metathesis <*always*; cf AZWAYS.

1943 *GL* StE, Aswale, always.

ASWAYS see AZWAYS.

ATAO see ATTOO.

ater, ATTA see AFTER.

AT LENGTH AND AT LAST phr; cf *EDD long* 12 and *length* sb II, the parallel Scots phrases *at length and at long* and *at long and at last*, of which this appears to be a blend. A phr used in narration: Finally, ultimately. *G*

1956 JB StAnd, At length and at last. 1960 LeP StAnd.

ATTOO sb bot obs?; cf Igbo *atɵ*, a chewing stick. A plant (see quots) of disputed identity.

a 1726 Barham (1794) 5, *Attoo*—I never could find any other name for this plant, and that I had from a negro.. the root to the sight much resembles English liquorice, but of a bitterish taste..the negroes cleanse their teeth with this root..A certain gentleman recommended it to me as an excellent remedy in the dry belly-ache. 1811 Titford Expl to Plate IX 2, Twiggy Cassia (*Cassia viminea*) nat. of Jamaica..It is also called Atao, or Attoo. 1814 Lunan I 177, Chaw stick. Gouania..(He cites Barham's account).

ATTORNEY sb; cf *OED attorney sb*[1] 1, 2. In Jamaica, commonly: One who manages a property for an absentee owner. *G*

1774 Long I 389, It is notorious, that many of these estates are left without a due superintendency, by the practice of employing one attorney to take the management of several different and distant properties. 1788 Beckford 68, An Attorney is a man who has a delegated power to act for principals in England; but is essentially different in practice from an Attorney at law. 1828 Marly 23, For, with respect to attornies, he was uncharitable enough to say, that they eat up or destroyed estates, and that their study was not to make the interest of the proprietors their own, but to derange the affairs of the plantation, in order that they might be continued in the management, till the property under their charge belonged to themselves. 1835 Senior 103–4, Although some resident proprietors are excellent attornies, the opinion greatly prevails *out of the island*, that what is called a 'large attorney', that is, one holding several properties, is the most likely person to make a *sure return* and regular annual remittances. 1959 LeP Han, West, 'Attorney' still in use: 'Somebody who manages estates for other people'.

ATWEEN prep or adv dial; cf *OED* '*prep.* and *adv. arch.* and *dial.*' →1842. *G*

1943 *GL* West, Atween, between.

AUNT sb dial occas; <*aunt*. A stepmother. (The word is used usually in its English sense at all levels.) *BL G*

1955 LeP StT /aant/ stepmother. 1958 DeC StAnd.

AUNTIE ESSIE sb dial local; echoic: see next. The BANANA BIRD.

1956 Jeffrey-Smith 75, The varied song of Auntie Katie (or Auntie Essie, as she is also called) is heard to best advantage in February to March.

AUNTIE KATIE sb dial; echoic and personifying. The BANANA BIRD. *BL*

1936 Bond 357, Jamaican oriole (*Icterus leucopteryx*). *Local names:*..Auntie Katie (Jamaica). 1941 *NHN* I iii 7, the Orioles, or Auntie Katie..were fairly abundant in the region of Clydesdale. 1952 FGC StM /hánti kíeti/ 'imitation of the sound it makes'.

AUNTIE MAG /aanti mag/ sb dial. RED WATERGRASS (*Zebrina pendula*); also called CREEPING JENNIE, RED WANDERING JEW, ROLLING-CALF BED.

1952 FGC StE /anti mag/.

AURICULA sb bot obs; cf *OED*, for a different plant. See quot.

1811 Titford Expl to Plate VII 1, Auricula, or French Jasmin (*a[sclepias] gigantea*), is common in the Savannas of Jamaica, and grows seven feet high.

AVOCADO PEAR sb; 1657, 1672 avocatas, p1660 advocatas, 1683 aduecades; <Sp (cf *OED*), but somewhat anglicized in the 18th cent by analogy with *advocate*, lawyer, the meaning of the Sp word; the latter is <Nahuatl *ahuacatl* by popular etymology. *OED* 1697→. Currently known in Jamaica simply as PEAR; see also ALLIGATOR PEAR. The fruit of the tree *Persea gratissima*; also the tree itself. s. *BA G T*

1657 *Book of Continuation* 46, Avocatas, a wholesome pleasant fruit; in season in August. p 1660 *State of Jamaica* (MS Egerton 2395) fol 489, Advocatas. 1672 Blome 25, There are plenty of choice and excellent *Fruits* in this *Island*, as..Avocatas. 1683 *Present State* 21, Supotilla, Aduecades, Star-Apples.

a wa see WA. *G*

a warra see *wara BL*

AWAY FROM prep phr dial. Apart from, aside from, except.

1952 FGC StM, I always live here, away from sixteen months in America. 1958 DeC StT /fuud miin evating awie fram fruut/ '*Food*' *means everything except fruit.*

a we see WE. *G*

a wen see WHEN. *G*

A WO see A-OAH.

AYE /ái, áai/ int dial; prob <Twi *ai*, *aaì*, *aìi*, ah me! alas!, but cf Sp *ay*, Fr *aïe*, etc.; also *OED ay*, int. An exclamation of surprise, fear, etc. *T*

1858 Chambre II 165, The servants..contented themselves with exclaiming, 'Aye! Aye!' as they never fail to do whenever anything occurs to excite their astonishment. 1952 FGC StAnn /aay/ (Exclamation of a man in a car when it rounded a corner and suddenly met a bus coming toward it on a narrow road).

AYES, AZE sb dial; spellings for EARS. *BL G*

1941 Kirkpatrick 42, see quot s.v. EARS. 1943 *GL* StJ, Aze, ears.

AZESBAUMER sb dial; <*ears's* (poss sg) + uncertain second element.

1943 *GL* StC, Azesbaumer, ear drum.

AZWAYS adv dial; by assimilation of *l* to *z* <*always*. (An unusual pronunc; the usual dial one would be /áalwìez/.) Always.

1941 Kirkpatrick 5, 'So me azways wonder 'ow 'im get wey wid it'. *Ibid* 11, 'You mus' 'e know de class a man me mean, you asways see dem roun' town wid dem chis out'. 1952 FGC StAnn, Fishermen '/áazwez/ bring in pots into a safe place when northwest wind increase'. 1959 LeP StAnd /ázwiez/.

ba, baa /ba, baa/ sb dial; abbr of *baada* or BABA. Brother; used as a title or a term of address.

1946 Dunham passim, Ba' Weeyums. 1954 LeP StE /ba jash/ *Brother Joshua* (a reciter of folk-tales at Accompong). 1956 Mc Port /baa/.

baaba see BABA, BARBER.

baabi[1] /báabi/ sb dial; prob abbr <*Barbados*. A species of yam, also called BAJAN or RENTA YAM.

1943 *GL* Clar, Baubey yam, Barbados yam. 1956 Mc Man /baabi/.

baabi[2] sb dial; prob abbr <BARBECUE. A wooden platform fixed to a tree to enable a sawyer to stand on it and lop the tree. Also called *kyaaf*.

1956 Mc Accom /báabi/.

baabis see BONAVIST.

baabl dov see BARBLE DOVE.

baabl jak see BARBLE JACK.

baabri sb dial; ?<*Barbary*. Cf BABOON, BOURBON COCO. A species of COCO (*Colocasia*).

1956 Mc StT /báabri/.

baada /báada, báda/ sb dial; prob <*brother*; the lengthened vowel may be due to analogy with *baaba*.

1. A term of respectful address to a male relative, usu an elderly one.

1935 HPJ, Bada, 'Uncle'..really a term of respect to male relatives—brothers, uncles, or cousins..It is usually not applied to a father, but sometimes a man will be widely known by the term *bada*, so that even his children will speak of him as 'Bada Ben' (to quote an actual instance from Hanover). In this case the Kin-significance must be quite lost. There is no doubt but that this word is African..'Badi is uncle in Fulani, bada would be your uncle, badam is my uncle.'—Professor Westermann. 1943 *GL* Kgn, Bawda, elder male relative. 1956 Mc StE (Elderslie) /baada/ applied to any old man.

2. = Brother.

1943 *GL* Tre, Baudah, brother. 1956 Mc StE (Elderslie) /baada/ brother.

baag = bag.

baaj /baaj, baarj/ sb chiefly dial. By sound-changes normal in Jamaican dialect <*varges* or *vargis*, 16th-17th cent and later dialectal variants of *verjuice* (see *OED*), 'The acid juice of green or unripe grapes, crabapples, or other sour fruit, expressed and formed into a liquor; formerly much used in cooking, as a condiment, and for medicinal purposes. Also in comparisons as, *as sour* (*bitter*, *tart*, etc.) *as verjuice*.' In Jamaica the extremely acid grape-like berries of certain trees (see sense 1) were thought to be 'sour like baaj' (see sense 3) and the trees bearing them were thence called 'baaj' or SOUR BAAJ. *T*

1. Any of several trees popularly thought of as related because the fruits are similar in growing directly from the trunk and branches, in being pale- or greenish-yellow, and in being very acid or astringent: 1. *Phyllanthus distichus* (or *acidus*), formerly called OTAHEITE GOOSEBERRY, now commonly JIMBLING, or SOUR BAAJ (and by confusion occas BIMBLING); 2. *Averrhoa bilimbi*, early called BIMBLING but now JIMBLING and CHEREMILA; 3. *Averrhoa carambola*, also called CHEREMILA, JIMBLING, and SOUR BAAJ, but known too from its larger, finer fruit as CHINESE JIMBLING, COOLIE BAAJ, or TALL BAAJ. Note: Baaj, except in the phr 'sour as baaj' (see below) is confined to eastern Ja; CHEREMILA is largely confined to western Ja.

1935 HPJ, A sour fruit like 'chimbolin'..'Sour like baaj', literal and metaphorical. 1952 FGC StT /baaj/ same as jimbilin—used to take out stains [*Phyllanthus acidus*]; also another kind, colour of starapple [prob. *Syzigium jambolanum*]; also Port. 1956 Mc Port /soua baaj—siem az jombelin/.

2. JAMBOLAN. (This is due to confusion of the names, since this fruit differs in colour and taste from the others.)

3. In phr 'sour like baaj': extremely acid to the taste. Note: the phr is used throughout Ja; in the eastern area it may refer literally to the fruits. (It is historically earlier than sense 1: see etym note.) *T*

1935 HPJ, see sense 1. 1956 Mc StJ /di arinj soua laik baaj/.

BAAJAM sb dial; obscurely <*breadfruit*, cf BACHA.

1943 *GL* StAnd, Baajam, breadfruit.

baaji /báaji, báji/ sb dial; <Hindi *bhājī*, 'greens'. The East Indian name for CALALU, or spinach (more commonly used in Trinidad than in Jamaica). *G T*

1943 *GL* Port, Badgey. 1956 McStAnd /báaji/.

baakini /báakìni/ sb dial; <Bantu *bakini*, the dancers. (J. Berry.) **s.**

1. A RING GAME or PLAY usu constituting part of a NINE-NIGHT or other funeral observance. Cf sense 3. See SET-UP.

1943 *GL* Kgn, Bawkinny, Demoniacal manifestations at the death of one; Port, Barckiny, one who is not settled. 1956 Mc StE Accom, The expression is 'to play baakini', and the baakini is called 'play': /kom plie di baakini, mek di liedi si. Kom sho di plie/. The dancing is an essential part—baakini is only performed if the weather is dry enough to go out of doors and 'jump' it. The song is sung in parts; the words are:

Baakini oh! baakini.
baakil im pikini bakini kini oh!

1958 DeC several parishes /baakini/—The most common meaning is a specific ring game whose form of play varies from place to place but which is always played to the same song, a song whose refrain or bobbin runs /baakini tumbe baakini, baakini tumbe baakini/.

2. By extension, all ring play (just as ring play is more commonly called *Sally Water* from the ring tune of that name). (1958 DeC.)

3. By further extension, a funeral meeting, usu the one on the second night, characterized by ring play; also occasionally (e.g. StT), the entire series of funeral meetings, including those at which there is no ring play.

1929 Beckwith 83, In the Santa Cruz Mountains they build a bonfire, about which the men and boys play games while the women and girls stand by watching the sport. The occasion is called the 'Bakinny' or 'Back in i' [the grave]', as I believe. 1958 DeC several parishes.

baal, baalin see BAWL, BAWLING.

baal hed see BALD-HEAD.

baal-pliet sb dial; malapropism or folk-etymology for BALD-PATE. *G*

1952 FGC Han /bál-plíet/ (said repeatedly). 1959 FGC Kgn /báal-plíet/.

baam see BALM.

baami see BAMMY. *BL N*

baan /baan/ sb dial uncom; etym unknown, but cf BORN-NAME. See quot.

1935 HPJ, Barn, A form of address used instead of a person's name in the Milk River area because of a superstition that an alligator overhearing the real name would catch its owner.

baandi sb dial; cf Akoko (Yoruba) *bañjí*, a type of yam.

1. A type of COCO; cf BADU.

2. A large yam resembling COCO-HEAD.

1956 Mc Man /baandi/.

baan-die see BORN-DAY.

baan-niem see BORN-NAME.

baan-ya sb dial; <*born-here*. See quots.

1943 *GL* Clar, Bawnya, A native; Kgn, a person born in the district; StAnd, Bawn yah, born here.

baara, baaro see BARROW.

baarj see *baaj*.

baas see BOSS.

baasi, basi /báasi, bási/ sb dial; prob a familiarizing reduction of *basket*. (But cf EDD BASSIE, 'Scots—a large wooden bowl.. used for carrying meal from the girnal to the bakeboard'.) A basket.

1868 Russell 5, Base, Basket. 1943 *GL* Clar, Bausi, bausie, bas-se, basy—basket. 1955 FGC Man /bási/. 1956 Mc StE /báasi/.

baat see BATH.

baat-an-daa /báat an dáa/ sb dial; <Hindi, cf the more usual *daal-am-baat*. An East Indian dish of boiled rice and split peas porridge seasoned with garlic.

1943 *GL* StT, Baht-an-Dah, Coolie's mode of making corn cake. 1956 Mc Man /báat an daa/ a highly seasoned Coolie dish.

baazli /báazli/ sb dial. = Basil; cf WILD BASIL. *N*

1952 FGC, In general use. 1954 Kirkland 170 [Contents of a fever-bath, Portland:] Panjaba, dragon, basley tame, basley wild, etc.

BABA /baaba, baba/ sb dial; cf Yoruba *Baba*, father, master; Mandinka, etc., *Baaba*, my father.

1. Father, grandfather, or senior male member of a household; used as a title and term of respect.

1936 HPJ (Old Jamaican Folk Song): Baba gahn a-jail, oh! 1956 Mc StT /baaba/—'father'. 1960 DeC *CLS passim*, Baba Rowe.

2. Brother. (Cf *baada*.)

1946 Dunham 139, 'Baba' (brother), 'godbrother', and 'marsa' are terms of intimacy most used for a man of one's own age. 1956 Mc StAnd, StT /baaba/.

baba-lad /bábalàd/ vb dial; prob <BABA + *lad*, terms of intimacy and friendship. To flatter (someone) in an unctuous manner.

1943 *GL* StE, Babaladd—to soft soap somebody, to baby him. 1958 P. J. Patterson /bábalàd/—to rub somebody up the right way.

BABAT, BATBAT sb dial; prob by iteration <*bati*.

1943 *GL* Clar, Babat, bat-bat, the rump.

babis see BONAVIST.

babm see BOB, BOBBIN.

BABOON /báabúun/ sb dial; a derog term implying ugliness. The MACCA CRAB, or any similar crab of the family *Maiidæ*. *G*

1961 R. P. Bengry StAnd, So called by fishermen.

BABOON COCO sb dial; <*baboon* + COCO sb[1]. The TAYA.

1756 Browne 333, ARUM 10..*Colocasia Strongylorrhiza Zeylonica*..The Baboon or Hog *Cocco*. The root of this plant grows to a monstrous size, and is very coarse: it is.. planted chiefly for the hogs. 1814 Lunan I 212, *The baboon hog coco* or *taya*.

BABU sb dial now considered derog; <Hindi *bābū*; cf *OED baboo*. *BL G T*

1. A term for an East Indian, in general use in Jamaica among those of Negro descent.

1921 Franck 431, Hindu men, whom the overseers invariably address as 'Babu', do most of the cutting. 1943 *GL* Clar, Han, Kgn, Man, Port, StAnd, StJ. 1956 Mc Man /bábu/; StAnd /babú/.

2. Also attrib, as in *babu cloth*—East Indian cloth.

BABWA int dial; cf Twi *bóbṹóo!*

1868 Russell 21–2, Babwa! wonder. It must be observed that the interjection *babwa* is used only on estates and their vicinity, and is of African origin. Settlers in the mountainous parts would consider it disgraceful to be heard using such a word.

BABY /bíebi/ sb dial; <*baby*. s EYE-BABY.

1. The pupil of the eye (cf *OED baby sb* 3, 'The small image of oneself reflected in the pupil of another's eye' 1593–1682). *BA G*

1952 FGC Han, She has dark-eyes: the baby of the eye is good, but she's blind.

2. The bull's-eye of a target.

1949 U.Newton v 6–7, 'He has hit the baby? Whose baby? The baby of the Bull's Eye? Oh I see..the dead centre of it, eh?'

3. The 'eye' or softest part of a grain of Indian corn.

1956 Mc Man /bíebi/.

4. A newly developed ear of Indian corn; esp in phr 'to tie baby': to put out ears. (Perh because the ear hangs from the stalk as a baby hangs in a BACK-TIE on its mother's back.)

1935 HPJ, 'To tie bebe'—to put out the cob. 1952 FGC Tre /biebi/ new ear of corn. 1958 DeC StT /tai biebi/.

5. Also attrib in the common sense of 'an infant' (*OED baby sb* 1) in BABY FENNEL, BABY LIZARD, BABY PUZZLE, etc. *BA G*

BABY FENNEL sb dial; <*baby's*+*fennel*. A wild herb (prob *Foeniculum vulgare*) used to make TEA for babies.

1952 FGC Tre, Baby fennel, good for baby; thistle grows something like it.

BABY LIZARD sb. See quots; another name for the POLLY LIZARD. (Species of the genus *Sphærodactylus*.)

1835 Senior 80, The '*baby lizard*'..is extremely diminutive, as its name implies, and subsists merely on the smallest of the fly species. 1959 FGC StAnd, etc.

BABYLON /bábilàn/ sb slang or dial; <*Babylon*. (Sense 2 infl by Engl *bobby*?) s.

1. A biblical allusion often made by the RASTAFARI, hence, from their point of view, non-believers, white men; and from the point of view of their opponents, the Ras Tafari followers themselves. See quots.

1955 LeP Kgn (Trench Town), Babylon, white man. 1958 JB, A Ras Tafari follower, a contentious man, a trouble-maker.

2. A police constable, considered as their enemy by the RASTAFARI.

1943 *GL* Kgn, Port, Babylan, police. 1952 FGC Han /bábilàn/ district constable, policeman. 1956 Mc StAnd /bábilan/.

BABY PUZZLE sb dial; <*baby*+*posl* <Engl dial *pussley* (purslane), generalized in Jamaica and applied to a number of plants. Used for a woman in labour. See quots.

1929 Beckwith 198, Certain plants are called after their uses..'Baby-puzzle' is fed as tea to the new-born child. 1954 *WIMJ* 25, *Pilea microphylla*..Wild Thyme (Tim); Baby Puzzle; Lace Plant; Artillery Plant.

BABY'S BOOTEE sb. A flowering shrub *Sesbania grandiflora*.

1958 Brian Topper StAnd.

BACCALOW /bákalàu/ sb dial; <Sp *bacallao* or Pg *bacalhau*, codfish (probably brought back by farm labourers from Cuba or some other part of Latin America); cf *OED bacalao* 1555→1765. Salt-fish, or the dish SALTFISH-AND-ACKEE. s.

[1889 Sanguinetti 50, The well known compound dish of salt-fish and akee..was formerly known here as 'Bacallao', the Spanish equivalent of 'Codfish', its main ingredient.] 1943 *GL* Port, Baccalow. 1956 Mc Man, StAnd /bákalàu/ 'Spanish talk' for saltfish.

BACCEROE, BACCRA see BACKRA.

BACCRY sb dial; prob a familiarized form <BACKRA+-*y*.

1943 *GL* Clar, Baccry, white man.

BACHA sb dial; obscurely <*breadfruit*. The breadfruit; cf BAAJAM, BRAMBRA, BRESHE, etc.

1943 *GL* StAnd, Bacha, breadfruit.

BACHELOR BUTTON /báchila, báshila/ sb; cf *OED bachelor* 6 (applied to a variety of flowers), *DAE* 1836→ in this sense. In Jamaica & North America: chiefly the globe amaranth. *G*

1756 Browne 184, Gomphrena 1..Batchelor's-Button.. does however now grow wild about the town *Savannas*. 1814 Lunan I 40, Bachelors Button—*Gomphrena Globosa*. 1914 Fawcett 143. 1952 FGC StM /báchila bòtn/; Port /báchla/; Han, StC, Tre /bashila/; Han /báshala/.

bachila botn, bachla botn see prec.

BACK adv.

1. Used (as are other adverbs of direction) more freely in Jamaica than in England; often pleonastically (as, to return *back*), and often placed after another post-verbal adverb (as, come home *back*). *BA BL G*

1827 Hamel I 218 [Quadroon maiden:] I shall return back to my mother. 1907 Jekyll 54, An' they come home back. *Ibid* 70, An' Annancy went home back.

2. Again; as before; in return. *BL G*

1924 Beckwith 58, Every man go cut, soon dey cut de chip fasten back, *Every man went and chopped* [*at the tree*], *but as soon as they chopped, the chips fastened themselves back where they had been before*. *Ibid* 161, De goat was well frighten how to come out back. 1943 Bennett 2, Ah hooda tell tram wey fe goh An' 'fix-up' back de bus. [*I would tell the trams where to go, and repair the busses again*.] 1952 FGC Han, The man eat your lunch today an' you eat back his tomorrow. 1957 JB, 'Close back the door'—*Shut the door as it was shut when you came in*.

BACK-ANA-PITCH sb dial.

1943 *GL* StM, Back-ana-pitch, Burgundy pitch.

BACK-AND-BELLY (BILL) sb dial. A bill (machete, bush-knife) that cuts with both the back of the blade and the 'belly' or (curved) underside; hence, a hypocrite, a treacherous person. Cf BADGER-BILL, SPANISH-MACHETE.

1955 LeP Kgn, Back o' Belly, double-edged machete. 1956 Mc Man /bák an béli bíl/ a back-biter. 1957 DeC StT /bak-an-beli/ a cutlass [the same width throughout, with ogive point], sharpened on both sides.

BACK-AND-FRONT sb dial. =BACK-AND-BELLY.

1958 DeC Kgn /bak-an-front/.

BACK-ANSWER sb & vb dial; cf *OED back adv* 12c. *BA BL G T*

A. sb: A sharp retort.

1943 *GL* StJ, Back-ansa, back answer.

B. vb: To retort sharply, 'talk back to', answer back.

1950 Pioneer 34, Before you tank me fe carry yuh pon me head yuh dah..come back-answa me, [*Instead of thanking me for carrying you on my head, you are talking back to me!*]

BACK-BACK /bák-bàk/ vb dial; <*back* vb intr+*back* adv. Go backwards. *BA G T*

c1915 FGC StAnd. 1962 BLB 39.

BACKEARARY see BACCRY, BACKRA.

BACK FOOT sb dial; cf *OED back* a 1, →1870. Hind foot; the regular term in Jamaica though somewhat archaic elsewhere. *BL G*

1950 Pioneer 37, So him dress up himself, an as proud as any puss back foot, walks eena de gal yard. 1959 DeC Port /bra nansi waak an im bak fut laik a man/.

BACK-GULLY sb dial; <*back* sb+*gully* sb. The furrow along the spine. *G*

1907 Jekyll 257 [Song:] Anch [ants] a bite me a me back gully..'cratch me back.

BACK-JAMB sb obs (this is *OED* only quot, dated 1852). See quot.

1833 Scott II 335, A very handsome diningroom, situated in what I believe is called a back jamb, a sort of outrigger to the house, fitted all round with movable blinds, or *jealousies*, and open like a lantern to all the winds of heaven except the west, in which direction the main body of the house warded off the sickening beams of the setting sun.

BACK-LAND sb dial slang; cf *DAE back land(s)* 1681–1842. Transf from the literal sense: the buttocks.

1943 *GL* Clar.

BACK O' BELLY see BACK-AND-BELLY.

BACK-ON-THE-HAND sb dial. Some kind of children's game played with cashew nuts; cf *bakini*.

1948 U.Newton IV 35. (See CASHEW 2.)

BACKRA, BUCKRA /bákra, bókra/ sb chiefly dial, also attrib; 1740 bacceroe, 1774 bochara, 1868→ backra, 1954 baccra bakra; 1808 buckera, 1826→ buckra, 1940 1943 bockra; <Ibo, Efik *mbakára*, white man, he who surrounds or governs (cf. 1949 Turner 191). Also used in US (Gullah) and widely through Caribbean. *DAE* 1736→. In Jamaica the written form and educated pronunc make the first vowel *u* [ʌ], but in the folk pronunc it is almost always /a/, preserving the quality of the African source word. s BACKRA, BUCCRA. *BA T*

1. A white man or woman (the latter also *backra lady, backra mistress*, etc.); also, collectively, white people. *G N*

[1688 Behn *Oronooko* (1886) 67, Though as Oronooko afterwards said, he had little reason to credit the words of a Backearary; yet he knew not why, but he saw a kind of sincerity, and awful truth in the face of Trefry.] 1740 Importance 20, They [the negroes] say..England must be a large Place, and Scotland a small one; for Scots Bacceroes (which they call all white Men) all know one another, but *English Bacceroes no know one another*. 1808 Stewart 304, If me for have mistress, give me Buckera mistress, no give me Mulatto, them no use neega well. 1826 Williams 202, Buckra, I fear, is derived from Buccaneer. [A satiric derivation which some have taken seriously.] 1943 *GL* StC, Bockra, white man or woman; StC, Backra, white people; West, Backra, the white race. 1954 LeP Kgn, Port, StT, Bakra, white man; StAnn, Baccra; StE, Backra.

2. As a term of polite address, equiv to sir, master, boss; also a master or boss. *BL G*

1808 Stewart 262 [At Christmas] it suffices that Buckera gives them their three days; though the law appoints only two. 1837 Sterne 19, First day me tell buckra every thing. 1959 FGC gen in country, esp. from older people.

3. In reference to people of light enough colour to be associated with whites rather than negroes. *G*

1952 FGC Port /bákra/ an albino negro. 1954 LeP StT, Bakra, a mulatto.

4. One who, though not white, lives like a white man or moves in white society. Cf BLACK BACKRA, SAMBO BACKRA.

1868 Russell 15, Backra or buckra..is not used exclusively in referring to the white man, a brown or black gentleman is also called so in acknowledgment of his gentility, or genteel appearance; but this little 'privilege' (?) is only given him with his good morning or good evening, or when he is asked a favour, otherwise he is only 'gentleman' or 'smart fella'. Should he however, by his education and position, or money, move much in the upper class society, then he is said to turn 'pure-pure backra'. 1943 *GL* Port, Backra, a well-to-do-person. 1956 Mc Man /bakra/ Anyone (including black) with plenty of money—refers to social status, standard of living.

5. Attrib or adjectival: fit for the white man or master, hence, of good (or the best) quality, excellent. See as separate entries: BACKRA CALALU, BACKRA PINE, BACKRA YAM, etc.

1940 HPJ, Fine, outstanding, excellent, as 'a big bockra dog', where ownership by the white man is not necessarily implied.

6. Attrib or adjectival: introduced to the negro by the white man, hence by the former considered as characterizing or pertaining to the latter: *Backra book*, the Bible; *Backra swear*, an oath taken on the Bible; etc.

1808 Stewart 279, 226 (HPJ).

7. Used for the possessive, hence equiv to *my*. (The speaker's sense of possession evid makes him feel like a master.)

1940 HPJ, As a 'phrase' equivalent to 'my'..'Don't trubble bockra boots'—don't interfere with my boots.

8. A species of the genus *Phytolacca* [which is one type of CALALU], perh through confusion with BACKRA CALALU.

1952 FGC Port /bakra/ [plant like US pokeweed], berries make ink.

9. Prob the tree *Hernandia catalpifolia*; = WATER MAHOE.

1956 Mc Port /bakra/ a glossy-leaved tree, whose pale green fruit may be blown to produce a /swiit soun/ like a fife.

BACKRA-BETTERS sb dial; <BACKRA+ *betters* (cf *OED better sb* 7b). The sense seems to be, one who thinks himself the superior of a white man; see quot.

1958 DeC StT /bakra-betaz/ a name for an albino Negro.

BACKRA CABBAGE sb dial; <BACKRA 5 +*cabbage*. A small, fine variety of cabbage.

1940 HPJ, Bockra Cabbage: the Clarendon name for a small plant (cabbage?) called greengage in St Ann. (Marion.) 'It small an it eat fine.'

BACKRA CALALU sb dial; <BACKRA 5 +CALALU. The finest variety of calalu: *Amarantus viridis*; it is called 'white' (though the stalks are pale green) in contrast to 'red' calalu.

1952 FGC Port, StAnn, StC, StE, StJ, StT /bákra kàlalu/; StC, StT /bókra kalalu/. 1954 LeP Man, Bakra Kalalu, edible spinach.

BACKRA COUNTRY sb obs; <BACKRA 6 +*country*. *G*

1. Jamaica, to which the slaves were brought by the white man. [E.g. in a slave's speech, 'Since me come a bakra country'.]

2. England, the home country of the white man (in contrast to 'Negro-country'—Africa).

1940 HPJ, Backra country; England.

BACKRA-HALL sb dial arch; <BACKRA 6 +*hall*. The parlour of an overseer's house on an estate.

1828 Marly 51, Marly reached the buckra-house about the same time with the first book-keeper, when they found the carpenter waiting, to go and have a glass of grog along with them in the buckra-hall.

BACKRA-HOUSE sb dial arch; <BACKRA 6 +*house*. The overseer's house on an estate. *G*

1828 Marly 34, On Mr Marly's arrival at Water Melon Valley Buckra house (overseer's house,) Mr Samuels introduced him to his brother book-keeper. *Ibid* 45, The Buckra-house was pleasantly situated on an eminence, which commanded a beautiful prospect of hill and dale for miles around.

BACKRA PINE sb dial obs; <BACKRA 5 +PINE. A fine variety of pineapple.

1788 Marsden 86, A second sort is the Buckara, or White People's Pine.

BACKRA RUM sb dial; <BACKRA 5+*rum*.

BACKRA YAM sb dial; <BACKRA 5+*yam*. A fine or delicate variety of yam (in contrast to *Negro yam*).

1774 Long III 781, Negroe-Yam—Dioscorea, radice tuberosâ luteâ. White-Yam—Dioscorea, radice albâ aut purpureâ. Both these plants are cultivated here universally for food; but the former, which is of a yellowish colour, is coarse, frequently stringy, and not so much in esteem as the second, vulgarly called, by the Negroes, *bochara-yam*. 1958 DeC gen /bakra yam/ any high grade yam.

BACKSTOP see next.

BACK-STRAP vb dial; by intrusion of /r/ (a fairly common phenomenon) into /bakstap/, the dial pronunc of *backstop*; cf *DAE*. (This may be an individualism.) In cricket, to field deep behind the wicket. *G*

1957 JN Tre, Barbara, you back-strap meck me lick out the ball; *Barbara, you act as backstop so that I can hit out the ball.*

BACK-TIE sb obs; <*back* sb+*tie* sb. A piece of cloth tied on a negro mother's back in which she carried her baby.

1838 Kelly 34, There was a midwife on every estate, who reported the births, and brought the children to the overseer when a month old. She then received..certain clothing for the baby, always including a few yards of Osnaburg linen for the back-tie.

BACKWAY(S) adv; cf *EDD backway* adv, *backways* (Yorks). Backwards. *BL*

1946 U.Newton I 16, I fell off the chair backways. 1952 FGC StT, backways; StM, you stagger backway when you bite it.

BACK-WEIGHT sb dial.

1958 DeC StAnd (Dallas), A bag supported (while carrying it on the back) by a fold across the forehead.

BACRA see BACKRA.

bada compar adj dial; <*badder*. Badder, i.e. worse. *BL G T*

1957 JN, Fe you strongah-an dis; him no badda-an me; *Yours is stronger than this one; he's no worse than I am.*

bada see *baada*, BOTHER.

badarieshan see BOTHERATION.

BAD BELLY sb dial. Post-natal abdominal disease in a mother. *G*

1952 Kerr 30, No visitors should come [to the mother] except those who were present at the birth..Sometimes a yard stick or sticks of bitter cassava are put across the doorway. Anyone entering would have to step over them and this prevents the mother catching a bad belly.

BAD CANDLE, BAD LAMP sb dial. A candle or lamp used in 'sympathetic magic' practices: as it is burned, the life, health, luck, etc., of the person against whom it is directed is supposed to dwindle away.

[1934 Williams 107–8, *Lighting a candle on* [someone]: 'Fadder take pin and Fadder take candle, and him stick der pin in der candle, and him light der candle on you. Der candle him burn and him burn and him burn. And you waste and you waste and you waste. And when der flame touch dat pin—you die.'] 1954 Reckord 8, Da magic me sprinkle over him from distance touch him, candle, bad lamp, sicken him already.

BADDO(O) see BADOO.

BAD-FEELING /bàd-fíilin/ sb dial. A feeling of vague ill-health or malaise. *BL G N T*

c1915 FGC StAnd [Song:] Dip 'im, dip 'im Missa Bedward, Dip 'im fe cure bad-feelin'. 1946 U.Newton I 17, Guinea pepper for pain in the stomach; rum-and-camphor for bruises and cuts..and assafoetida..for bad feeling.

BADGER BILL, BAJU BILL /baja-bil bajobil, baju-bil/ sb dial; prob <*badge* (*EDD* v[2], 'To cut corn, peas, beans, &c. close to the ground by means of a badging-hook') +*-er*[1] +BILL; but cf also BADOO-BILL.

1. A machete of various shapes but characteristically sharpened on both sides—cf sense 2.

1958–9 DeC Kgn /baju-bil/ an old-fashioned usage for a very long (30 in.) cutlass [which broadens symmetrically toward an ogive point]; StAnd (Dallas) /baja bil/ a long machete, broad at the tip, sharp on both sides, used for billing grass or weeds—also called SAW BILL; StJ, a cutting tool used for husking coconuts around Montego Bay [with a short blade having a rounded hooked end].

2. Fig. A deceitful, dangerous person—cf BACK-AND-BELLY BILL, SPANISH MACHETE.

1943 *GL* Tre, Bajobil, a worthless person. 1955 LeP Kgn Bajabill, deceitful person.

BADGEY see *baaji*.

BADGO sb dial; perh <*badger*: cf BADGER BILL 2, or perh repr Sp *bajo*, low.

1943 *GL* Tre, Badgo, one of low rank.

BAD-HANDED adj obs.

1707 Sloane lii, see WELL-HANDED.

badis superl adj dial; <*baddest*. =Baddest, i.e. worst in conduct. (Often a euphemism for sexual misconduct.) *BL G*

1956 Mc Man /a him a di badis man ina di distrik/ *He's the worst-behaved man in the district.*

BAD LAMP see BAD CANDLE.

BAD-LUCKED, BAD-LUCKY /bàd-lókid, bàd-lóki/ adj dial. Subject to misfortune, frequently having bad luck. s. *BA BL G*

1943 Bennett 9, But me really bad-luckid mah, Me bad luckid; *ibid* 8, Some people is unfortunate, Me really bad lucky; *ibid* 38, Lacka how me badlucky, Mine you meck police arres' me.

BAD MANNERS sb phr dial. See quot. *G T*

a1818 Lewis (1845) 72, Whannica, in particular, assuring me very earnestly, that I never should have cause to accuse her of 'bad manners' again; for, in negro dialect, ingratitude is always called 'bad manners'. *Ibid* 154, He..was brought to me all rags, tears, and penitence, wondering 'how he could have had such bad manners as to make massa fret'.

BAD-MINDED adj dial. Ungenerous, thinking ill, evil-minded. *BL G*

1943 *GL* Port, Crumugin, a bad-minded person. 1951 FGC StAnd [Song:] I don' know, I don' know, why some people bad-minded so.

bado see next.

BADOO /bádu, bádo/ sb dial; 1929 baddoo, 1943 baddo, 1950 badoo; cf Dalziel, 'Hausa bădo, *Nymphaea lotus*, White Water-lily; the starchy rhizome and seeds are edible'. A variety of COCO with a large, light-red rhizome or 'head' that is eaten; it is considered less desirable than the regular cocos.

1929 Beckwith 17, The *baddoo* or *toaya* is a variety in which, as in Polynesia, the head is the part eaten. 1943 *GL* StC, Baddo head, headers tawna [tannier]; Tre, Bado, Baddoo, eddoes. 1950 Pioneer 71, A walk all dis day an a don't get eben a badoo fe carry home. 1956 Mc Man, StE /bádu/; StAnd /bádo/.

BADOO-BILL sb dial; <BADOO+BILL; or perh by folk etym from BADGER-BILL. A short blade or hoe, both edges of which are sharpened, and to which a handle may be attached; used for digging cocos, yams, etc.

1943 *GL* Kgn, Badoo-bill, kind of machette sharpened on both sides. 1956 Mc StC /bádu bíl/ a digging bill.

bad sidong sb dial; <*bad*+*sit-down*. =BAD-WAYS. *BL*

1943 *GL* no addr, Bad-si-dung, bad ways; Kgn, Badsi-dong, bad ways.

badu see BADOO.

BAD-WAYS sb dial. *BA BL G T*

1962 BLB 48 /badwiez/ mean disposition.

BAEJAY see *beje* sb[1].

baf adj dial; prob abbr of *bafan*. (But cf *EDD* BAFF adj.) Slow, backward.

1956 JB, Wa mek yu baf so? *Why are you so painfully slow?* Also /baf pikini/ a crippled or backward child. See *bafini*.

BAFAM see next.

bafan /bàfán, báfam/ sb dial; <Twi *bafáŋ* '1. *a child who did not learn to walk the first 2–7 years.. 2. rachitis, the rickets.. 3. sluggard, lazybones*', Christaller; often folk-etymologized to /baf-hand/.

1. =*bafini*. Also attrib.

1943 *GL* Kgn, Port, Baff-hand, a cripple; Port, Baffan, a baby slow to walk; West, Bafam, children who come to the age to walk and talk and cannot. 1958 DeC gen /bafan chail/.

2. See quot.

1943 *GL* Kgn, Baffan, freak.

3. A useless, clumsy person; applied as an epithet—e.g. to a clumsy maid-servant.

1956 Mc Man, StAnd /bafán/. 1957 DeC StT /bafan/ a stupid, clumsy woman, no good at housework.

BAFFAN, BAFF HAND see prec.

BAFFOON sb dial; cf PUFOON.

1943 *GL* Kgn, Tre, Baffoon, bad smell. 1959 DeC Kgn, breaking wind (?imitative of the sound).

bafini /bàfíni, báfini, bafáni/ sb and adj dial; Akyem *bafané*, meaning the same. (Cf also Fante *mfina*, Twi *anyinnaá*, a stunted person; see also FIN HAND.) A disfigured or crippled child; one who does not learn to walk properly.

1943 *GL* Kgn, Baffeney, a disfigured child; StAnn, Bafani, a defective. 1956 Mc StE /baféne, bafáani, báfini bíebi/ a child that doesn't learn to walk.

BAG sb dial; cf. *OED sb* 12, 'A baggy place, a fold'—in a horse's mouth, illust by only quot, 1572. *BA*

1958 DeC Tre, Bag, a soft kind of growth, growing downward from the roof of the mouth, which appears on mules, donkeys, and occasionally cattle; as it interferes with the animal's eating, it must be cut out by the farrier.

BAG-A-BACK sb dial; <*bag*+A[1]+*back*. A crocus bag borne on the back, and supported by its mouth being rolled and hooked over the crown of the head. Cf BACK-WEIGHT, WRAP.

1958 DeC Port, StT /bagabák/.

bagabu see BUGABOO.

bagampan sb dial; <*bag*+*and*+*pan*.

1. Rubbish, trash; cf *banggarang*[1].

[c 1915 FGC StAnd, 'Bag-an'-pan'—nickname of a junkman who plied between Halfway-Tree and Kingston.] 1958 DeC StT /bagampán/ rubbish, trash, junk.

2. A dustbin.

1958 DeC StT /bagampan/ A garbage can.

bagi /bági/ sb; prob dimin or familiar form of *bag*; cf *OED bag sb* 16.

1. A SIDE-BAG.

1958 DeC Port.

2. A baby's knickers.

1956 Mc Man, StAnd. 1957 JN, Mi want towell. Mi want bagie.

BAHAMA GRASS /bahíema, bíema/ sb; *DAE* 1890→. See quots. *G*

1808 Stewart 125, Plats of Bahama-grass (a plant which spreads rapidly, and forms a smooth and beautiful sward). 1864 Grisebach 781, Bahama-grass, *Cynodon dactylon*. 1952 FGC StAnd /bahíema/; StAnn /biéma/; StAnn, StC, StM /bíema/. 1953 *WIMJ* 246, Bahama or Bermuda grass; Dog's Tooth Grass. In some parts of the Island, at least, a tea made by boiling the roots is thought to be good for the kidneys.

bahiema see prec.

BAHLIMBO, BALIMBO int or sb dial; a word of uncertain origin, prob ult African—though the statement made in quot 1907 is suspect. A word of uncertain meaning, perh a name, used in the refrain of songs; see quots.

1907 Jekyll 212–13 [Song:] 'Me go to Morant Bay, Bahlimbo, Me see one Coolie gal, Bahlimbo..' 'Bahlimbo' is a nickname for a cheap sort of cloth, i.e. fabric of any kind. In Africa calicoes are called *limbo*. 1940 HPJ, Balimbo; Bahlimbo—A personal name found in Songs. Marion connected it with a children's game in which one of the characters was called the Limber Lawd. A tale about Limber-Limber-Lawd is a version of 'Drop, you drop'. (Astley Clerk: [Before 1 April 1940] a teacher told me that the word means Bro: Chatty, from *Ba*, *Bah*, meaning Brother, and limbo = talkative—both words he said were African.)

BAHOOT see *bahu*.

BAHT-AN-DAH see *baat-an-daa*.

bahu, bahul, bahut /báu, bàúl, bàhú, bahút/ sb dial; prob <*barrow*, perh also with infl <Fr *bahut* and/or Sp *baúl*, a large travelling chest. (The Fr word had the slang sense in the 19th cent of 'a dilapidated carriage'.) **s.**

1. A wooden box with long handles fore and aft for carrying small loads. Used esp for gravel in repairing roads.

1959 FGC Man /bahu hav tuu hanggl front, tuu behain/.

2. A hand-cart such as is commonly used by porters around the docks in Kingston and elsewhere for delivering small loads. Also called SKATE.

1943 *GL* StE, Bawu, a handcart. 1956 Mc Kgn /baú/ handcart.

3. A porter who pushes such a cart; hence also one who carries loads on his head, an errand-boy.

1943 *GL* Kgn, Bahul, cart boy; Port, Bahoot, an errand boy; StAnn, Bahule man, One who carry load on his head for a living; StE, Bawol, a handcart man. 1956 Mc StAnd /bahú, baú/ a handcart man.

BAHZOON sb dial. See quot.

1907 Jekyll 274, 'Dundooze'. .is a term of endearment. Others are. .bolow, bahzoon.

bai see BY.

baia see BYA.

baig see BIGE.

BAILING see BALING.

bain sb dial vulg; ? < *behind*. The buttocks.

c1919 FGC StAnd, Schoolboy expression: 'Yu bain!' (Your arse!)

baita fut see BITE-A-FOOT.

baiyeri yam sb dial; < Twi *bàyérɛ*. A variety of yam resembling YELLOW YAM.

1952 FGC StT /bàiyéri yám/.

BAJAN YAM sb dial; < *Bajan*, WI familiar form of *Barbadian*. See quots.

1943 *GL* StM, Bajan, Barbadoes yam. 1956 Mc Man /báabi/—'same as /bíejan/, /renta yam/.'

baji see *baaji*.

baju /bájù/ sb dial rare; origin unknown, but cf *baaji*. See quot. (Possibly a mishearing of BADOO?)

1956 Mc Man /bájù/ mashed up food; fufu.

BAKE BAMMY FOR (SOMEONE) vb phr dial; *bake* BAMMY *for*. = ROAST COCO or PLANTAIN FOR (SOMEONE).

1927 Anderson-Cundall 74 [Prov:] Mercy, Mana, John Crow a bake bammie fe him.

BAKE-THING /bíek-tìng/ sb dial; cp SALTING.

1. Bread (the general term in some parts of the island, e.g. StE). (Mc.)

1955 LeP StE (Eld), Bake tings, bread.

2. Anything prepared by a bakery—bread, cakes, rolls, pastry, etc. (Mc.)

bakini sb dial; ? < *baakini*, or perh conn with BACK-ON-THE-HAND. A game of jacks, played with cashew nuts. (This may be assoc with *baakini* as another funeral game, or be a separate word.)

1956 LeP StE (Eld) /bákini/ game of jacks played with cashews. 1957 JN StE, Backani over. A two you have. That a one game. 1958 DeC /baakini/ a game played with cashew nuts.

BAKINNY see *baakini*.

baklas see BOTTLE-ARSE. *BL*

bakl nek see BOTTLE NECK.

bakra see BACKRA.

baks /baks/ vb dial; by metathesis < *bask* (*OED* 1, →1530). To bathe.

1956 Mc Port /di wáata yuuz tu báks in/—(said of the lagoon at the mouth of a river below Moore Town) *The water is used to bathe in.*

BALAAM sb dial; < *Balaam* (cf *OED*), or *Balaam's ass*. A nickname for a donkey.

1943 *GL* Kgn, Balaam, donkey or ass; StAnn, Balam, a donkey.

BALACLAVA /balaklaba/ sb; cf *banikleva*. A town in St Elizabeth; see quot.

1958 DeC StE, The town of Balaclava /balaklaba/ is widely thought in that area to be derived from /baniklaba/, and some old people actually pronounce the name in that fashion. Everyone's story differs as to what the town has to do with sour milk.

balad, balyad /bálad, bályad/ sb dial; < *bollard* —cf *OED* 1844→. Also attrib. The thole-pin on a fishing canoe; also, transf, a rowlock.

1956 Mc StC (Old Harbour) /bályad/; Port Royal /bályad/ or /rálaks/.

BALAD PLATE, BALYAD PLATE sb dial; < *balad, balyad* + *plate*. The wooden block (bearing the *balad* or thole-pin) which is fastened to the gunwale of a fishing canoe.

1952 FGC StT /bályad pliet, báled pliet/.

BALAFOU sb obs; cf Bambara *bala*, Mandingo *bala:*, xylophone. An African musical instrument: a kind of harmonicon.

1823 *Koromantyn Slaves* 75, The Africans struck up a song of welcome, accompanying it with the tones of the balafou.

balaho[1] /bálaho/ sb dial; < Sp *balajú*; DA *balao, ballaho* 1867→. The beakfish *Hemirhamphus brasiliensis*. *N*

1854–5 *TJSA* I 144, Hæmirhamphus Braziliensis, Ballahoo. 1952 FGC StC /balaho/ small piper—grows no more than 14 inches.

balaho[2] /bálaho/ vb dial; < *ballyhoo*; cf next.

1952 FGC StC /balaho/ to flatter.

balahu /bàlahú/ adj or sb dial; cf *DAE ballyhoo* 3. s.

1. Boisterous; boisterous person.

1943 *GL* Kgn, Balla-hoo; Kgn, Ballahoo, vulgar.

2. A wasp.

1956 Mc StAnd /bàlahú/.

balaklaba see BALACLAVA.

BALAM see BALAAM.

balas-injin bluo vb phr dial; < *ballast*? + *engine* + *blow* (for *has blown*). An expression taken from the blowing of a whistle to rouse workers. (The identity of the engine has not been established. Perh a railway term?)

1958 FGC StT /bàlas-ínjin blúo/ time to get up!

balata see MULATTO TREE.

BALDHEAD sb cant. = CLEAN-FACED MAN.

BALD-HEAD (BUSH) sb dial; prob by hyper-correction < BALL-HEAD—see quot s.v.

BALD-PATE sb; cf *OED* quot 1883. See quots, and cf *baal-pliet*. *N*

1725 Sloane II 303, *Columba minor, capite albo*. .The Bald Pate. 1840 Chamberlaine 18, Bald Pate Pigeon (Columba leucocephala). 1955 Taylor 90, A medium-large blue Pigeon with a white head, usually seen high in trees and flying high in the air.

BALD-PLATE see *baal-pliet*.

BALEH /bálè/ sb dial; prob < Fr *balai*, broom.
1943 *GL* StT, Baleh, a broom.

balieri see BAYERE.

balikleva see *bani*.

BALING sb chiefly dial; abbr of *baling cloth*.

1. A kind of cloth: see quot.

1956 Mc Man, /bíelin/—a fabric used for bags, finer than crocus; it may be used to dry coffee on.

2. A container for produce being taken to market, made of this cloth.

1961 Katzin 3, Produce easily crushed..is packed in the basket; yams and cabbage in crocus bags and root vegetables in bailings. Carrots and escallions are laid in the bailings with the bunches alternating, so that the tops of one bunch are next to the roots of the next..Then the bailing is drawn together by the corners and tied very tightly to prevent movement and crushing in transit.

BALINSTEER sb dial obs.
1868 Russell 5, Note that..*b* is usually changed into *v*, and *v* to *b*; thus..Balinsteer, Volunteer.

BALLA-BALLA sb dial; prob imitative, or perh an iterative based on BAWL, or *balahu*. *G*
1943 *GL* StC, Balla-balla, a loud person.

BALLAD BUSH, BALLARD BUSH /bálad/ sb dial; etym unknown—possibly <*mallow*: see quot 1955. (*Ballard* is a common surname in Jamaica from the 18th cent however.) A shrubby plant of the Malvaceae family, *Urena lobata*.

1952 FGC Man, StE, Tre. 1955 *WIMJ* 145, *Urena lobata*..Ballard Bush; Bur or Indian Mallow. This plant is used to make tea for colds and is also employed by the poorer people for washing greasy dishes. 1957 JN StE, A ballad-bush—I see the bull-frog go in there.

BALL-HEAD /baal-hed/ sb dial; *ball + head* (unless the form BALD-HEAD for the same plant is the original one). A common weed which has spiky, ball-like flower heads strung on tall stems.

1955 *WIMJ* 81, *Leonotis nepetaefolia*..Pick Nut; Christmas Candlesticks; Ball Head; Bald Head or Bush; (Male) Bas' Cedar.

BALLOON sb dial.
1956 DeC StJ /balúun/ a very large round boiled dumpling—half pound of flour each.

BALLOONFISH sb dial. The swellfish; see quot.

1952 Smith in *NHN* 135, Lurking in the sea-grass [along the Palisadoes] could be spotted several small swellfish or bloaters (also known as puffers or balloonfish), *Sphoeroides testudineus* and *S. spengleri*.

BALL-PAN /bal pan/ sb dial; <*ball + pan*. See quot, and cf next.

1958 DeC StAnd /bal-pan/ a tiered pan carried by street vendors in Kingston..rectangular, about two feet long (though they vary in size a great deal), with three or four flat pans stacked..in some sort of frame.

BALL-PAN MAN sb dial. A vendor of meatballs and similar foods, which he carries about in a pan or box.

1912 McK *Ballads* 54, Waits de slimber ball-pan man.*
* A vendor of patties. (1955 FGC Kgn, StAnd, current.)

BALLS sb dial. *BA*
1958 DeC StC /baalz/ Cassava head rolled in balls and dried in the sun; later used to make porridge.

BALM /baam/ sb dial; prob < Engl *balm*, but cf also Twi *abam'*, name of a fetish, etc.

1. The 'healing influence' experienced at a BALM-YARD.

2. The 'treatment' applied to a patient at a BALM-YARD.

1929 Beckwith 132, For 'balm' he 'beats the patient with a wet calico and rams the abdomen with clenched fists' 1943 *GL* Clar, Balm, pocomania.

3. Abbr for BALM-YARD.

1950 Pioneer 53, Ef dem set a nine-day baby Ghose fe teck yuh life, Yuh can go a Mada Banna balm. 1951 FGC Man, People 'go to the balm'—e.g. that kept by Brother Matthews—for treatment.

BALM vb dial; < BALM sb or Engl *balm* vb; cf *OED*. To give treatment, physically or spiritually, at a BALM-YARD.
1943 *GL* Kgn, Balm, to heal. 1956 Mc Man /baam/.

BALM-MAN sb dial. A man who keeps a BALM-YARD.

1951 FGC Man, Brother Matthews, the balm-man near Old England; 1952 StE, Recipes 'from balm-man' including balm oils.

BALM OIL /bàam haíl/ sb dial. Any of the supposedly curative oils or other ingredients composing the medicines prescribed at a BALM-YARD.

1952 FGC StAnd, Balm oils: 'oil of rignam, ..oil of deadman, oil of cat-o'-nine, oil of peppermint', etc; StE, 'oil of calviry, oil of cade, oil of power, oil of salvation', etc.—to be bought at the DOCTOR-SHOP. [1952 Kerr 139, complete contents of a curative bath, including several balm oils.]

BALM-YARD sb dial.

The headquarters and ritual site of a BALM-MAN, or SHEPHERD, who administers herbal and other remedies (such as BALM OILS), and who leads at his YARD a form of worship with revivalist preaching and the singing of Sankey and Moody hymns accompanied by drumming and dancing which induce a trance-like state in the dancers; after which HEALING may take place, followed by a feast. (Cf JUMPING, POCOMANIA, TRUMPING, etc.) The Shepherd is also qualified to remove OBEAH by practice of 'White magic' (MYAL); sometimes he is himself an Obeah practitioner on the side.

1929 Beckwith 131–2, Obeah practitioners may act as doctors to cure the sick. Either they may visit the patient in his home, or they may keep what is called a balm-yard, where the patient is brought to be cured. 1952 Kerr 137, The balmyard is an extremely interesting phenomenon.. The mythology behind it is Christian but the magic is similar to any fertility cult.

BALSAM FIG sb bot. = BALSAM TREE 2.
1864 Grisebach 781, Balsam fig: *Clusia rosea*.

BALSAM HERB, BALSAM WEED sb bot; cf *OED balsam*. Any of several related aromatic herbs or weeds (*Dianthera americana*, *D. comata*, *D. reptans*); see quots. Now GARDEN BALSAM. *G*

1696 Sloane 59, Antirrhinum minus angustifolium, flore dilute purpureo *Balsam herb*. 1794 Barham 13, This herb is so called in Jamaica, and few or none know it by any other name, although it is a sort of *antirrhinum*. This in Jamaica smells, when rubbed in the hand, almost like melilot, or some pleasant balsam; and therefore they call it balsam-weed or herb, and make a balsam of it. 1814 Lunan 1 41, Balsam Herb 1. Dianthera americana.. Balsam Herb 2. Dianthera comata. 1864 Grisebach 781, Balsam-herb, *Dianthera repens* [*sic*], *ibid* 732, *D. reptans*.

BALSAM TREE sb; cf *OED balsam tree* 1695.

1. An early name for *Bursera simaruba*, now called BIRCH, etc. *G*

1696 Sloane 168, Terebinthus folio singulari non alato [etc.]..balsamum fundens..*The Balsam Tree*. 1725 Sloane 91. 1794 Barham 14–15, Balsam-tree..Bursera gummifera..This tree is so called because so much balsam comes from it, even from the bark, leaves, and fruit.. They grow in great plenty in Jamaica.

2. An early name for *Clusia flava*, or similar species. *G*

1756 Browne 236, The Balsam Tree. Clusia 1. This shrubby tree is frequent enough in Jamaica..grows mostly in the lower hills, and delights in dry ground. Wherever the trunk or larger branches of this tree are wounded, they throw out a thick resinous gum. 1814 Lunan I 41, Balsam Tree. *Clusia flava*. 1864 Grisebach 781, Balsam tree, *Clusia rosea*.

BALSAM WEED see BALSAM HERB.

BALTIMORE CRICKETER sb dial. The pilot fish, *Abudefduf saxatilis*, perh referring to its bands of bright colours. The reference to Baltimore is unexplained.

1952 FGC Port.

baltuu sb dial; cf such words as *bolo*, *tutus*, etc.

1958 DeC Port /baltuu/ a term of endearment.

baluun sb dial; origin unknown, perh < Engl *balloon*, but cf *baltuu*, BAHZOON.

1958 DeC Port /balúun/ a term of endearment.

baluun see BALLOON.

balyad see *balad*.

bam int dial; cf Twi *bàm* 'expressing the sound of *striking*, *clapping*, *lashing*, *falling*..(*bám bam bam, a good thrashing*)'—Christaller; Hausa *bam*, 'the sound of the slamming of a door'—Bargery. An imitative sound suggesting a sudden action (though not necessarily an audible one). Cf BAMMERLICHY. *BL G T*

1877 Murray *Feedin' 'Perrit* 4, As it drop so, I mek fe catch it—cho, bufo you could say 'Jack', bam, cold choke o, fish o, ebery bit gone in a sea; *ibid* 21, Him put him finger in a de nose; bam, de mus-muss bite him. 1956 Mc Man /yu shot yu mout, bam/ *You shut your mouth, just like that—bam!* StE /mi nak im bám bám/ *I hit him just like that—bam! bam!*

BAMBA sb dial; from redivision of /ab-amba/ as /a-bamba/.

1943 *GL* Kgn, Bamba, amber (e.g. ile o' Bamba).

bambai /bámbài, bá-m-bài, bómbài, búmbài/ adv and sb dial; <*by and by*; cf *EDD bamby*, Dev. and Cornw. Gen in Eng-based Créoles.

A. adv: Later; in a little while. *BL*

1877 Murray 10, Ef me wrong, well—monkey gie him dog name say—tay bam-by we all wi see. [*If I'm wrong, well—monkey gave his dog a name, and said, 'Wait a bit and we all will see'.*] *Ibid* 26, Mudfish say, 'Dis put me riber side make I smell riber water'. Him say, 'No, Mudfish! bambye you make me fool!' 1905 Smith 18, Bumby, long time after dis, Annancy tink him wi' try one more time. [Note:] By-and-by. 1943 *GL* Clar, Bumbie, later; Man, Bam-bam, bye-and-bye; StAnn, Bambye, Bumbye, later; Tre, Bamby, by-and-bye; West, Bamby, later on; also Han, Kgn, Man, StC, StE, StJ, StM.

B. sb: A portion of food put aside to be eaten later. Also called *iit-an-lef*, STAY-BACK, *wat-lef*, etc. *G*

1947 U.Newton III 30 (see *wat-lef*). 1956 Mc Man, StAnd /bá-m-bài/; StAnd /bómbài/. 1958 DeC StAnd /bámbài, bómbài, búmbài/.

bam-bam sb dial; a familiarized or childish form, prob also euphemistic: echoic (from beating on the buttocks), or perh <*bati* (cf *bem-bem*, prob <*belly*). Perh infl by *bum*. *G T*

1943 *GL* StM, Bam-bam, buttucks. 1959 DeC gen.

BAM-BAM see *bambai*.

BAMBOO ASHES sb. The very light ashes that remain after bamboo is burnt—symbolic of something negligible.

1873 Rampini 87, Thus, when he wishes to describe anything as very light and worthless, he says, 'It is like bamboo ashes'. c 1915 FGC StAnd, Current.

BAMBOO BED sb dial. A rickety bed that creaks like bamboos in the wind.

1958 DeC StT /bambu-bed/ Any rough wooden bed, usually made of boxes and boards; only occasionally is this made of bamboo.

BAMBOO COCO sb dial; prob <BOURBON COCO.

1952 FGC StJ /bámbu kùoko/ Bourbon coco; also StC.

BAMBOO HOUSE sb dial.

1955 LeP StAnn, Bamboo house, Building made from bamboo poles, with walls and roof of woven trash.

BAMBOO POT /bámbu pát/ sb dial. Cf *pata*. See quot.

1958 DeC Port /bámbu-pát/ a fowl-nest made of bamboo. Plant a stout log of bamboo upright so that the top is 3 or 4 feet above ground; split the topmost section..so as to produce about a dozen splints, all attached at the bottom, loose at the top, each splint being about 12 inches long; spread the splints outward and hold in position with a hoop of metal or withe; this produces a sort of raised basket, which is then lined with trash.

bambu see BAMBOO.

BAMBY(E) see *bambai*.

bami[1] see BAMMY.

bami[2] sb dial; <*bonny(-clabber)*; cf *bani*.

1958 DeC StT (Yallahs) /bami/ Sour milk. [Homophonous with *bammy(-cake)*, but the latter word not native to this district.]

BAMMERLICHY int dial; echoic, but in part analysable: *bam* + A^5 + LICK + *i* (= it). See quot.

1907 Jekyll 274 [Song:] Bammerlichy, bammerlichy, bam-by, I never see a woman dancing with a wooden leg. Note: At 'Bammerlichy' etc. the dancers imitate the stiff action of a wooden leg.

BAMMI(E) see next.

BAMMY /bámi/ sb, also attrib; 1893→ bammy, 1929 bammie; etym unknown, but cf Tupi *mbeiyú*, Guarani *mbeyu*, Mainland-Carib *meiú*, 'a kind of cake made of manioc' (Friederici); also Ewe *bampá*, ground maize cooked in water. A flat, round cake (about 1 in. thick) of cassava flour, baked in a heavy iron mould, or a pot or pan; cf BAMMY IRON, POT BAMMY. *BL N*

1893 Sullivan 38, Bammys are sold ready for cooking and are a sort of muffin. They are made out of cassava. 1905 *Maroon Medicine* 8, Provision for his journey—a gill bammy, a little pork..etc. 1913 Harris 28, Bammy Cakes [Recipe follows]. 1929 Beckwith 21, But for the choicest dish of all, the cherished 'bammie', the starch [of the cassava] must not be washed out at all. The grated cassava is put into a 'cutacoo'..In the morning the meal is taken out of the pocket, beaten, and sifted. The flour thus formed is mixed with salt and water and baked and turned like a flapjack on a hot griddle. 1955 LeP Port, Bami; StAnn, Bammy; StE, Baamy; StT, Bammi. 1956 Mc Man, StAnd, StE /bámi/.

BAMMY CHIPS sb dial. A folk name for what are commercially CASSAVA LACE CAKES.

1952 FGC West, 'Bammy chips, thin as paper—not made by Quashie'.

BAMMY IRON sb.

1958 DeC StC /bami aian/ A flat iron for baking BAMMY, like a *tawa*.

BAMMY PRESSER sb; <BAMMY+*presser*. A bag in which grated cassava is pressed to squeeze out the juice in making bammies.

1942 Bennett 28 [Insulting description:] Yuh nose favah bammy pressa, Yuh mout' look like it false.

BAMMY RING sb. An iron ring placed on the BAMMY IRON to contain the cassava in making bammies.

1959 DeC gen.

bamo /bámo/ int slang; <dial pron (in Cuba, Puerto Rico, etc.) of Sp *vamos*, let's go! (cf *DA vamoose*). Get out! Go away!

1943 *GL* Kgn, Bamo, Go away. 1956 Mc StAnd /bámo/ keep out, scram!

BAM SUKEY adv dial arch; <BAM+/suki/ etym unknown—perh partly echoic, or <some African word.

1. =BAM.

1877 Murray *Feedin' 'Perrit* 4, Dis [=*just as*] de head go get used to it [*sc* a hat], bam sukey, da dat time breeze da go blow it way in a sea.

2. See quot.

1943 *GL* StM, Bam-suki, Sound of a wooden foot.

ban /ban/ sb[1] dial; <*band*.

1. In CANE-BAND. *G*

2. A belt.

1957 JN StM, No tek you ban an lick me man, tek one whip, mek me go look one whip. *Don't take your belt to hit me, man, take a whip, let me go and look for a whip.*

ban /ban/ sb[2] dial; perh <*band*, group. See quot.

1958 DeC Tre, Ban: a unit of selling head-sugar; a 'standard' head weighs one and a half pounds; six such heads (or 9 pounds) make a /ban/. It is sometimes called a /ban/ even if all in one large head or (as for wet sugar) when in a tin, just so the weight is nine pounds; however, it is preferred to have it in six heads.

ban /ban/ vb dial; prob <*been*. Auxiliary of the past tense (apparently distinguished here from BEN).

1957 JN Tre, The Mail—it ban top a one tree an you ben give the man one orange, *The Mail Van—it stopped at a certain tree and you gave the man an orange*; It stop a office an me ban come out, *It stopped at the office and I got out.*

ban- see BANG-.

bana sb dial; analysed as a separate element out of *bana-wis*, a form of BONAVIST. A vine or WIS; usually in combined forms: *bana-bis, bana-string, bana-wis, hog-bana*, etc.

bana see *banna*.

banabiins, banabis see BONAVIST.

banaklaa sb dial; a variant form of *banikleva*.

1958 DeC StT /banakláa/ sour milk.

BANANA BARREL sb. A barrel-like container in which bananas were formerly shipped.

1907 Jekyll 20, Me wife, you know wha' we fe do. Make we get a banana barrel an' lay it on de bed, make him favour one man.

BANANA BESSY sb dial; cf BESSY 3. The BANANA QUIT.

1935 HPJ, Banana Bessy = Beeny quit.

BANANA BIRD /banána bòd/ sb; *ODS* 1713–1847. The Jamaican Oriole, *Icterus leucopteryx*; also called AUNTIE KATY, BANANA KATY, MA KATIE, WATCHY PICKET. (Sometimes also applied to the BANANA QUIT.) *BL N*

1725 Sloane II 311, *The Bonano Bird*. This is about five inches long..It frequents *Bonano* Trees, whence its Name. 1835 Senior 83–4, Another bird..called the 'banana bird', by reason of its principally subsisting on the ripe banana. 1873 Rampini 163, Black and golden banana birds..flitted out and into the mysterious recesses of the bush. 1936 Bond 357. 1955 Taylor 38.

BANANA BREEZE sb. A breeze strong enough (about 40 m.p.h.) to blow down banana trees.

1951 FGC StM.

BANANA CHIPS sb; cf *potato chips*. GREEN BANANAS cut into thin strips or slices and fried in hot fat. *BL*

1957 *FFM* 161.

BANANA CUDJOE /kójo/ sb dial; prob from its colours, *banana* implying yellow and CUDJOE blackness. The SPANISH HOGFISH, *Bodianus rufus*, in its dark colour phase, with yellow tail and belly, and dark back.

1952 FGC Port, StE, StT.

BANANA DRINK sb. See quot.

1707 Sloane LXIX, Bonano and Plantain Drinks are severally made by mashing of either of these ripe Fruits with water, till it comes to be pretty well mixed with the Fruits, then they let it stand in a Trough twelve hours, and draw it off.

BANANA FIG sb. A banana, usually whole, dried like a fig, whence the name. Also known as 'dried banana'.

[1725 Sloane 142, The fruit [of Plantains] cut long ways and dried in the Sun is thought to be as good as Figs so dried.] 1913 Harris 2, Banana 'figs' are prepared for export by several local factories and the demand for these dried bananas is steadily increasing. 1957 *FFM* 274–5, Banana-Figs..Select sound, just ripe, bananas. Line tray with waxed paper, peel bananas and lay in rows on paper. Cover with glass..and set in the sun..Repeat the process for about seven days, or until the bananas are quite dry.

BANANA FISH sb; from its colour. The SPANISH HOGFISH.

1950–1 Smith, Han (Lucea), *Bodianus rufus*, banana fish. 1952 FGC StJ, Banana fish 'have a black miggle [*middle*], yellow head and tail'.

BANANA FLIPS sb dial; cf *flips*.

BANANA KATIE sb dial; *katie* prob onomatopœic, cf AUNTIE KATIE, QUIT.

1. The Jamaican Oriole, *Icterus leucopteryx*; see BANANA BIRD.

1952 FGC StAnd, StAnn.

2. Transf, the fish *Bodianus rufus*, whose yellow and black colours are reminiscent of the colour of the bird.

1952 FGC StM.

BANANA MAT sb.

1955 LeP StAnn, Banana mat, mat made from dry trash or grass.

BANANA QUIT sb; *ODS* 1847. The Antillean Honey Creeper, *Coereba flaveola*; also called BEENY BIRD, BANANA YUOKI, etc.—see quot 1956.

1847 Gosse 84, Black and Yellow Creeper. *Banana Quit. Certhiola flaveola*, 1950 FGC Man, 'Banana quit—smaller than butter-bird'. 1955 Taylor 3, 8. 1956 Jeffrey-Smith 71, Black-and-Yellow Creeper..or Banana Quit..with many local names: Beany Bird in St Mary, Bessie Coban in St Thomas and Psyche and John Croppie in Trelawny.

BANANA SPIDER sb. A large spider, popularly called a 'tarantula', often found among bananas; see quot.

1949 *NHN* IV 35, Banana Spider, [also called] House Spider, Crab Spider, Brer Anancy, Daddy Long Legs.. *Heteropoda venatoria*.

BANANA TEA sb dial. An infusion or decoction made with the black fibres—the withered remains of the flower—from the ends of bananas. Said to be good for the nerves.

1952 FGC Port (Happy Grove).

BANANA WALK sb; <*banana* + WALK sb. A grove of banana trees. *BL*

1957 Bennett 86.

BANANA WATER sb dial. Water in which bananas have been boiled; cf BENEFIT.

1943 *GL* Kgn, Benefit, bannana water.

BANANA YOKEY /yúoki/ sb dial; <*banana* + ?*yoke* + *-y* familiarizing suffix. Perh ref to its colour. The BANANA QUIT. s.

1952 FGC Man.

BANA-STRING sb dial; <*bana* + Engl *string*. A vine used to tie things.

1943 *GL* Man, Ti-tie, banna string.

banavis, banawis see BONAVIST.

BANCHA, BANCHAN /bánchà, bánchàn/ sb dial; prob <*banana*, and by analogy with *mancha*. A banana.

1943 *GL* Clar, Banchan, banana. 1955 LeP StE (Accom) /bánchà, bánchàn/ banana; 'old-fashioned'.

BANCRA see BANKRA.

banda sb dial; cf Nafana *bendo*, Siti *bendere*, Dyoula *bennde*, a large drum (Hause 17–18).

1953 Moore gloss, Banda, baritone drum (African). [See AFRICAN 2.]

BANDI sb dial; evidently a nickname for a BADOO.

1943 *GL* Clar, Bandi, bado.

BANDOO see *banduu*.

BANDS /banz/ sb dial; <Engl *band* (*OED sb*[3]), perh reinforced by Fr *bande* (cf *DAE band* 5); cf also Mauritian Creole *banne* (<Fr *bande*) in the same sense. A great crowd; a great many; a great deal.

[1907 Jekyll 71, Annancy..tell them that he will have a bands of music playing in going home.] 1943 *GL* Kgn, Bans, large quantity, plenty. 1950 Pioneer 59, Dem put me fe tan up fronten Bans a big camera! *Ibid* 20, Bans a food controle an rationin' wasa gwan.

bandu see next.

banduu /bándù, bàndúu/ sb dial; <Fr *bandeau*. A kerchief or scarf as commonly worn by the women in Jamaica, around their heads, tied at the front. Also called HEAD-TIE, WRAP. *BL G*

[1827 Hamel I 305, Sebastian looked down, and beheld the Obeah man, attired as we have described him..with his crimson bandeau and his scarlet poncho.] 1943 *GL* Kgn, Bandoo, a head scarf. 1956 Mc Man /mek a bànduu/ to tie a scarf round the head; StAnd /bándu/ wrap.

BANG sb; cf *bangga*. A local name for *Clupea pseudohispanica*, a small fish of the herring family.

1892 Cockrell. 1935 HPJ, A small sea-fish, resembling a sardine, used as bait.

bang /bang/ vb dial; etym unknown, ?African. To swell up; cf BANG-BELLY, BELLY.

1935 HPJ, Yo' belly bang like kid swalla kissada water. 1956 Mc Man /bang/ to swell up in the belly.

BANGA sb dial; cf Twi *bɔ̃ŋ* [<Engl *band*], singing and dancing to a musical accompaniment. *G*

1943 *GL* Clar, Banga, to sing; Port, Banga, A type of Jamaican dance.

BANGA MACCA see *bangga maka*.

BANGANANCE see *banggarang*[2]. *G*

BANGARAM, BANGARANG see *banggarang*[1, 2].

bang-bang sb dial; Engl *bang* iterated. A stick used to beat clothes against a stone when washing them; shaped like a paddle. Also called a CLAPPER.

1956 Mc StAnd /báng-báng/.

BANG-BELLIED adj; BANG-BELLY + -ED[2] (*OED*). Having a large paunch.

1947 U.Newton III 20, I saw a long procession of ghosts of all types (long, short, fat, meagre, funny faced and good looking with one or two bang-bellied ones) marching up to the gate. 1959 DeC Kgn /likl uol bangbeli man/.

BANG-BELLY sb dial, also attrib; prob <past pple of *bang* vb (see above) + *belly*. 1. A swollen abdomen, as that of an ill-nourished child, a pregnant woman, etc.; a paunch; 2. a child showing malnutrition in this fashion. *G*

1935 HPJ, Bang belly, swollen stomach..Sometimes just paunch. 1956 Mc Man, StAnd /bángbéli/.

BANGERANG see *banggarang*[1, 2].

bangga /bángga/ sb[1] dial; cf Fante *ɛ-baŋ*, Twi *m̀màŋ*, a small species of herring, Mende and Freetown Creole *bóngà*, a small fish; cf also BANG. A small fresh-water fish like the English 'tiddler', about 2 in. long. (Possibly *Cyprinus* descr by Browne, 442.) *G*

1943 *GL* Kgn, Man, StAnn, StE, Trel, Banga, small fish. 1955 LeP StE (Accom). 1956 Mc Man, StE /bángga/.

bangga sb[2] dial. uncom. = *banggo nait*.

1960 DeC Port, see 1961 *CLS* 72.

bangga maka /bángga, bánggra máka/ sb dial; cf Philippine Sp *bonga* (<Tagalog *bunga*, *bonga*), the Areca Palm (*Areca catechu*, L.) and its fruit—Friederici. This may, on the other hand, be African—cf *bongka*, CULLABUNKA. The MACKA-FAT PALM.

1935 HPJ, Banga-macca, macca-fat. 1943 *GL* Port, Banga macka, edible palm. 1952 FGC Port /bángga màka, banggra/. 1956 Mc Port.

banggarang[1] /bánggaráng, bánggarám/ sb dial; prob imitative. Cf *banggarang*[2]. Rubbish; old, worthless stuff.

1935 HPJ, Bangaram, rubbish. 1943 *GL* Kgn, Man, Tre, Bangarang, rubbish; Port, Bungorung, old things. 1956 Mc Man /bánggaráng/ rubbish. 1958 DeC Man /banggarang/ a miscellaneous load of small articles on a truck, esp things that might rattle and roll about; StAnd /banggarang/ used chiefly of banana trash; StT /banggaros/ miscellaneous trash or rubbish.

banggarang[2] /bánggaráng, bánggaráns, bánggananś/ sb dial; prob imitative—cf *bang*, and *-ance*—but cf also Pg *banguelê*, riot, disorder—African term—(Mendonça). Cf *banggarang*[1]. A great noise or disturbance among people; quarrelling.

1943 *GL* Clar, Bangerang, pandemonium; Port, Bangarangs, riot; StT, Bangananance, trouble. 1955 FGC Man, Bangarang, noise. 1956 Mc Tre, Bangarang, a quarrel. 1958 DeC StT /banggarang/ a row, a riot; Kgn /banggarang/ riot, commotion, fight, but [with] a difference in syntax: /wat saat a banggarang dem a mek de?/—In rural Jamaica one would /kiip op/ a banggarang rather than /mek/ it.

banggaros see *banggarang*[1].

banggazuu sb dial; cf *banggarang*[1] and the familiarizing suffix *-u*; cf also *banggo baig*.

1958 DeC Port /banggazúu/ temporary trash-or-grass bag made in the field.

banggo, banggu baig sb dial; <Ko *mbangu*, basket (cf *bangga maka*, and BANKRA)+*baig*. See quots.

1956 Mc Man /bánggu bàig/ a long narrow bag made of 'thatch'. 1958 DeC StAnd /banggo/ a string bag supported by a strap across the forehead; StT /banggo/ a small cloth bag for matches, etc.

banggo nait sb dial; cf *banggo* and *banggarang*[2]. See quot, and cf SET-UP.

1958 DeC StT /banggo-nait/ a funeral meeting on the second through the eighth nights after a death, characterized by ring-games, stories, etc.

banggra maka see *bangga maka*.

BANG-GUT sb dial; <*bang* vb (see above) +Engl *gut*. =BANG-BELLY.

1943 *GL* Kgn, Bangut, Big Belly; Port, Bang-gutt, one with a large belly; StM, bang gut, big belly.

BANGIL see BANJA.

bangkin see BANKING.

BANG-KITTY int dial; origin uncertain, but cf Vai *ban* to be finished, *a ban* it is finished; Bambara *ban* to finish; Gullah *ban!* It is done! (Turner). Cf also BAM SUKEY.

1935 HPJ, Bang-Kitty, 'All right, O.K.'; an exclamation much used on pens and estates..by any person told to do anything who wishes to convey his comprehension of his instructions and his readiness to carry them out..Overseers and bookkeepers use it in ordinary conversation.. 'A Maroon word for "Yes".'

bangkra see BANKRA.

BANGLE sb; cf *OED*. *G*

1. A bracelet of any kind. *N T*

c1915 FGC StAnd (Bangle, the usual term). 1950 Pioneer 59, Tayma say she hooda len me All de bangle dem me need.

2. In the phr *Bangle and fandangle*: dress-up accoutrements.

1958 DeC StAnd /mi put an aal mi banggl an fandanggl dem an guo a toung/ *I get all dressed up fit to kill and go to town*. (Said by a man!)

bani, banikleva /báni, bániklèva, bàniklíeva, bàniklíeba, báliklèva, bami, bomi/ sb and adj dial; <*bonny-clabber*—cf *OED*. *G*

1. Sour, curdled; curdled milk.

1907 Jekyll 205, Thick sour milk allowed to stand and curdle is called 'barnyclebber'. 1943 *GL* StE, Bany, Curd-milk. 1954 LeP StAnn, Bannie, bommy, sour milk. 1956 Mc Man /báliklèva/ *curdled* (of milk); /di milk ton bani/ *The milk has become curdled (milk)* [The last word may be sb or adj]; StAnn /bomi/ sour milk. 1958 DeC Port /baniklieba, baniklieva/ sour milk; StT /bami/ sour milk.

2. The creamy froth on top of boiled cornmeal.

1956 Mc StAnd /banikleva/.

BANIAN DAY sb obs; 1826 banyan day; cf *OED Banian* 4 →1823.

A day on which (as on shipboard) no meat is served, hence a day of fasting or austerity (in allusion to the *Banian*, a Hindu sect). This is one of the many nautical expressions that were adopted in Jamaican use; its present folk form appears to be BEN JONSON'S DAY.

1826 Williams 252, I should have had a banyan day but for half a dozen eggs that Miss Louisa had the humanity to offer me, and a slice of Dutch cheese as hard as Pharoah's heart.

banikl /bánikl/ sb dial; <*barnacle*. A folk pronunc; the form that would be expected in the dialect is */báanakl/.

1952 FGC StAnn, StJ /bánikl/.

banikleva see *bani*.

BANJA, BANJO sb; 1739 bangil, 1790 bonjour, 1793–1868 banja, 1816 banjee, 1826 bonja, 1826 1835 bonjaw, 1835 bongau, bonjoo; etym prob African—cf *DA*; cf also *banza*, stringed musical instrument, African loan word into Brazilian Pg (Mendonça). *DA* earliest quot is from Jamaica: 1739 below. The most common form of the word in Jamaica was (and still is) /bánja/; the earliest form seems to have been /bánjíi/; a frequent one /bónjaa/ is closest to what became standard in the US and elsewhere. Also attrib.

The banjo, esp in its primitive form made with a gourd as the resonance chamber. See STRUM-STRUM, and Sloane's illustration of the instrument (1725). *BL G T*

1739 Leslie 326, They have other musical Instruments, as a Bangil, not much unlike our Lute in any Thing but the Musick. 1790 Beckford II 387, A bonjour, originally taken, perhaps, from a French word, as many have found their way by corruption among the negroes. 1816 Lewis 53, The sudden sounds of the drum and banjee, called our attention to a procession. 1823 *Koromantyn* 85, They found the slaves dancing to the sound of their rude African instruments, the banja..an imperfect kind of violoncello, played upon with the finger, like a guitar. 1826 Williams 21, Their gombays, bonjaws, and an ebo drum; *ibid* 101, A bonja. 1835 Madden I 184, Bongau; *ibid* II 7, Bonjoo; *ibid* II 153, Bonjaw. 1868 Russell 6, Banja. 1927 Anderson-Cundall 64 [Prov:] Banja gourd wan' go a sea..etc. 1956 Mc Man /plie bánja/.

BANJA vb dial; prob <BANJA sb.

1935 HPJ, Banja, To play the fool.—Georgie, who said it was not the same as 'banter'.

BANJEE, BANJO see BANJA.

BANJU SALE /bánju síel/ sb dial; <Ewe *gbandyo*, auction. See quots. **s.**

1943 *GL* StJ, Banju sale, A public sale. 1955 FGC Man /bánju síel/ a junk sale.

BANK sb; <*bank* (*OED sb*[1] and *sb*[3]). A game played with cashew nuts thrown into a hole in a bank of earth.

1949 U.Newton V 16, As played by children..'Bank' was an enjoyable thing. The banker dug a shallow hole in a bank of the road..[A player] would stand on the opposite side of the road, pitch (that is, throw) up his cashews one by one and collect two cashews for everyone of his which settled in the hole.

BANKING, BENKIN /bangkin, bengkin/ sb dial; <*bank* or *banking*; cf *DAE banking* vbl n[1] 2, a bulwark of earth; an embankment, 1853, 1872. A bank (of a river, alongside a road, etc.)

1943 *GL* StC, StM, Benkin, bank. 1953 Murray 49, Me jump off de deal bud Me jump pon de bankin, [*I jumped off the deal board, I jumped on the bank*]. 1958 Jean Creary StJ. *T*

BANK PARROT sb dial; <*bank* (*OED sb*[1] 5). A variety of PARROT FISH that is caught near undersea banks.

1952 FGC Port.

BANKRA /bángkra, bóngkra/ sb chiefly dial; 1868→ bankra, 1877 bunkra, 1895 bancra, 1934 bonkra; <Twi *bɔ̃ŋkărā*, Fante *baŋkraŋ*, 'a wicker-hammock or travelling basket' (Christaller).

A square-cornered basket made of palm 'thatch', with a lid and handle. Cf FOUR-CORNER BASKET, TWO-CORNER BASKET. This is normally larger than the CUTACOO, but in some localities they are identified, in others the size distinction is reversed (DeC).

1868 Russell 6, Bankra—A hand-basket. African. 1877 Murray *Feedin' 'Perrit* 4, I ben hab a de bunkra, but it tear up, an I trow it way. 1895 Banbury 7 [The obeah-man] never goes without a bancra, wallet or bag, in which he carries his 'things'. 1934 Williams 36, The Ashanti *bonkara*, a travelling basket, is the Jamaica bonkra, or as it is sometimes spelt bankra. 1946 Dunham 93, Square, covered 'bankra' baskets woven of thatch. 1955 LeP Man, Bankra, big market basket; StAnn, Bankra, basket for storing pickled meat, fish, etc.; StE, Bankra, palm-leaf bag. 1956 Mc Clar, Man, Port, StAnd, StAnn, StE /bangkra/.

BANKUP adj dial; evid folk-etym <*bankrupt*.

1943 *GL* StAnd, Bankup, bankrupt.

banna /bánná, bána/ sb dial; reduced <*banana*. A banana. (Used esp to or by children.)

1943 *GL* Man, Banna, banana; StM, Manchan, ban-na. 1956 Mc StAnd (Blue Mts) /bánná/ etc.; (Mt Charles) /bwai, a we yu get da banna/ *Boy, where did you get that banana?*

BANNABEES, BANNABIS, BANNER-BEANS see BONAVIST.

BANNIE see *bani*.

BANS see BANDS.

banta, bantan /bánta, bántán/ vb dial; <*banter* (cf *OED, EDD, DAE*, the sense of rivalry developing to emulation and imitation). See quots.

1943 *GL* Port, Bantan, to follow suit. 1955 FGC Man, Bantan, 'follow-fashion'. 1956 Mc Man /bánta/ to try to rival somebody by imitation, esp in dress; /im waak bántán/ he goes with the mob; he is indiscriminate in his choice of friends.

BANTER-SING /banta-sing/ sb dial; *banter* SING.

A group song, such as those sung by men digging yam-hills. ('Banter'—cf *banta*— refers to the group; it may also carry the ordinary sense of the verb, to tease, since these songs often allude satirically to local people and happenings.) See DIGGING MATCH, DIGGING SING.

1952 FGC StM /de sing aal saata banta-sing dat di men de kyan kyari aan/ *They sing all sorts of banter-songs that the men there can carry on.*

BANY see *bani*.

BANYAN DAY see **BANIAN DAY**.

banz see BANDS.

BAP, BAPS /bap, baps/ int and adv dial; echoic.

A. int: 1. Imitating the sound of a sharp or sudden stroke; cf KNOCK 2, quot 1924. *BL G T*

1868 Russell 19, Him knock me *bap* wid him fis. 1907 Jekyll 46–7 [Song:] Ballantony Bap! twee twee..Note: *Bap!* is the knock of the stick. 1960 *CLS* 151 /an im nák im sáid so, báp!/ *And she struck her side so, bap!*

2. Suggesting exactness or aptness. *BL G*

1935 HPJ, Baps! 'When a thing drops and hits where you want it.'

3. Accompanying a command: Instantly! This minute!

1943 *GL* Clar, Han, Kgn; StC, Baps, instantly.

B. adv: Describing a quick blow: thus, like this. *BL G T*

1956 Mc Man /yu lik im baps/ *You hit him 'baps'* (the exclamation is accompanied by a friendly slap)—said in a game of 'Tip you last'.

BAPTIST TICKET sb obs; <*Baptist*+ TICKET. A printed card given monthly to each member of Baptist congregations by which weekly attendance and offerings were recorded; they served as passes to church meetings.

1833 Foulks 111–12, On many of the revolted estates hundreds of 'Baptist tickets' were found.

BAPTIST WAR sb hist. The slave rebellion of 1832, for which the Baptists were blamed, since they had encouraged the slaves in demands for emancipation. See prec.

1833 Foulks 112, The rebellion was publicly distinguished by the negroes as 'The Baptist War'. 1863 Waddell 79 (year 1833), If we might be thus judged, we said, for the doings of people, who used our names to cover their own designs, then might the Baptist brethren be condemned for the late rebellion, as the insurgents employed their name to forward the scheme, and it was known as 'The Baptist War' among the negroes themselves. 1873 Gardner 277–8, On all sides it was asserted that the rebellion had been caused by the teaching of missionaries, and particularly by that of the Baptists and Wesleyans. The former, it was said, were the most guilty; indeed, the rebellion was frequently spoken of as the Baptist war.

bara /bára/ vb dial; an occas pronunc of BOTHER, usu pronunc /bada/ in the dial, here with flapped *r* for *d*; cf also *braa*.

1943 *GL* Clar, Barra, to worry. 1957 JN, Mi no know —no barrah mi.

bara sb dial; abbr of BARRACOUTA. *BL*

1959 FGC Kgn /bára ín de/ *There's a barracouta in there.*

BARACOOTER, barakuta, barakuuta see BARRACOUTA.

barampa /barampa, berampa/ sb dial; etym unknown.

1. Fallow land. (When ratoons are used, there is no replanting.)

1943 *GL*, Barampa, fallow land.

2. In ginger-growing districts: the old ginger root, planted the preceding year, on which ratoons form.

1935 HPJ Man, Berampa, Ginger ratoons, particularly near Christiana. (Mr Cresser.) 1956 Mc Man, StE /barámpa/.

3. (Evid from association with an old ginger root). See quot.

1956 Mc StE (Accom) /barámpa/ a sharp-tongued woman given to brawling; a woman who nags.

BA-RA-RAP int dial; echoic, but last syllable <*rap*: see quot. (Cf BRAGADAP.)

1907 Jekyll 160–1 [Song:] Ba-ra-rap ba-ra-rap ba-ra-rap me Benjiman. Note: Always *Benjiman* for Benjamin and the Bararaps culminate in a sharp final staccato *rap*. 1957 DeC StE /bàraráp, bàrararáp/ imitative of something falling or colliding.

bararieshan see BOTHERATION. *G*

BARBADOS BLACKBIRD sb obs? The KLING-KLING. Cf BLACKBIRD 2, SHINE-EYE 3. *BA*

1727 *Some Modern Observations* 18, One sort of *Blackbird* with a very large Bill, another with a small one called the Barbadoes Blackbird. 1756 Browne 476, The *Barbadoes* Blackbird. This bird is of a delicate form, and all shining black, except the iris which is whitish. The bill is..pretty thick at the base, of a conic form, tapering and arched moderately at the top. 1847 Gosse 217, TINKLING GRAKLE..*Barbados Blackbird. Quiscalus crassirostris.* 1873 Rampini 163, the Barbadoes blackbird, with its white glassy eye, occupied its leisure hours in picking the ticks from the backs of the cattle.

BARBADOS CABBAGE TREE sb obs. *Roystonea oleracea,* not native to Jamaica. (Ligon's 'Cabbage palm'.) *BA*

1756 Browne 342, Palma 2 *Caudice altissimo*..The *Barbadoes* Cabbage Tree. This is the most beautiful tree I have ever seen..it grows to a very considerable size.. The seeds..were first carried to Jamaica by the present Governor..Admiral Knowles.

BARBADOS CEDAR sb obs; prob a transl of Plukenet's *Cedrus Barbadensium* (Phyt. *t. 157, f. 1*). =JAMAICA CEDAR. *BA*

1756 Browne 158, Cedrela 1..*Barbadoes* Cedar..This tree was very common, and still continues to grow in many parts of the island.

BARBADOS CHERRY sb arch; *OED Barbadoes-cherry* 1858. The trees *Malpighia urens* or *M. glabra* and their cherry-like fruit. *BA*

1696 Sloane 172, *Cherry-tree or Barbados Cherries.* In Jamaica Insulæ hortis ubique colitur. 1756 Browne 230, Malpighia 3..The *Chereeze*, or *Barbadoes* Cherry Tree. This shrub has been but lately introduced to, or cultivated in *Jamaica.* 1814 Lunan I 48. 1913 Harris 4, Cherry, Barbados. *Malpighia glabra.*

BARBADOS COTTON sb bot obs. A variety of *Gossypium lapideum*; also called CHAIN COTTON, KIDNEY COTTON. *BA*

1811 Titford Expl of Plate VIII, *Gossypium*..the most common and the most productive in Jamaica is the Barbadoes Cotton. 1854–5 *TJSA* I 60, Barbadoes Cotton, Gossypium Barbadense.

BARBADOS GOOSEBERRY sb obs; *OED* 1876. A former name for *Pereskia aculeata* (WEST INDIAN GOOSEBERRY). *BA*

1756 Browne 237, Cactus 1..The Gooseberry, or *Barbadoes* Gooseberry Bush. 1814 Lunan I 414 [Cactus] pereskia..This is called sometimes *Barbadoes gooseberry.* The stem hath many prickles in tufts..the fruit about the size of a walnut, having..within a whitish mucilaginous pulp, containing small seeds like gooseberries.

BARBADOS GRAPEFRUIT sb obs.

1837 Macfadyen 131–2, Citrus Paradisi..There are also two varieties of this species. Var. α. *pyriformis*; Barbadoes Grape Fruit. Var. β. maliformis; Forbidden Fruit.

BARBADOS LIMPET sb obs. See quot. The first specimens systematically described were those found in Barbados, hence the name.

1725 Sloane 231–3, III *Patella minor rotunda*..Small white ribb'd *Barbados Limpet*.. VIII *Patella cinerea minor*..The Wart ribb'd *Barbados Limpet*.. IX *Patella cinerea cancellata*..Barbados *Thimble Limpet.*

BARBADOS PRIDE sb; *OED* 1885. *T*

1. The flowering shrub *Caesalpinia pulcherrima,* much used in hedges and medicinally. Also called DOODLE-DOO, FLOWER FENCE, RANGER, (WILD) SENNA, SPANISH CARNATION. See quots.

1756 Browne 225, Poinciana 1..*Barbadoes Pride.* This plant has been, I fancy, first carried to *Jamaica,* from some of the other colonies, of which it is a native: but it now grows wild in many places about Liguanea. 1801 Dancer 358, Barbadoes Pride—Tea of the Leaves and Flowers.—Syrup of the Flowers.—Powder of the Seeds. Dose, 1 dr. A cure for the Belly-Ache.. *Ibid* 362, *For promoting the Terms* in Women—Emmenagogues. 1864 Grisebach 781, Barbadoes-Pride: *Caesalpinia pulcherrimia* and *Adenanthera pavonina.* 1920 Fawcett 95. *BA G*

2. Applied occas to other plants; see prec quot.

BARBADOS SWEET WILLIAM sb bot; sp *Barbadoes.* See quots.

[1760 *OED*, 'Sweet William of Barbadoes'.] 1801 Dancer 357–8, *Such Plants as are Purgative*..Quamoclit, or Barbadoes Sweet William—The Root in Decoction. 1814 Lunan I 399, It is known by the name of *Barbadoes sweet-william*..(*Ipomoea quamoclit*). 1819 Dancer 381. 1864 Grisebach 788.

BARBADOS YAM sb. See quot. Also called BAJAN YAM, *baabi yam. BA*

1952 FGC StC, 'Barbados yam—white, has a heap of foot'—much like St Lucia and renta yams. 1959 DeC gen.

BARBARA ALLEN /báarbari álin/ sb.

1952 FGC Han, A bush with fine thistle-like flowers, purple below, white above, and a circular stem striped vertically with green.

BARBAROO sb or adj; ? <*Barbary.*

1935 HPJ, 'Him come from Barbaroo country'—said of a stranger.

BARBARY DOVE /barbri dov/ sb; cf *OED Barbary* 4c. See quots; more commonly called BARBLE DOVE.

1952 FGC Han /bárbri dòv/; StT, Barbary dove.

BARBARY PEPPER sb obs; cf *OED Barbary.*

1774 Long III 857 [A Synopsis *of Vegetable and other Productions of this Island*]..Spicery and Peppers.. Barbary.

BARBARY THORN sb bot obs; associated in some way with *Barbary*; cf *OED.* The shrub or tree *Pithecellobium unguis-cati*; see quot.

1814 Lunan II 2–3, Nephritic-Tree. Mimosa. Nat. or.—*Lomentaceae*..This is a small tree, from seven to ten feet in height..Browne..calls it the *black-bead shrub*; and it is also called *Barbary Thorn.* 1837 Macfadyen I 307, *Barbary-thorn.*

BARBECUE /báabikyùu, babikyuu/ sb; [1657 barbycu], 1756 barbakue, 1835 barbicue, barbecue; <Sp *barbacoa* <Taino; cf *OED* 5, 1855→. A rectangular platform, originally of sticks, now usually of stone or cement, on which coffee beans and other produce are spread in the sun to dry. *N T*

[1657 Ligon 89, the place where they unload [the canes], is a little platform of ground, which is contiguous to the Mill-house, which they call a Barbycu; about 30 foot long and 10 foot broad; done about with a double rayle, to keep the Canes from falling out.] 1756 Browne 163, Such as have large coffee-walks, should be provided with a convenient *barbakue*, or platform, to dry these seeds more commodiously upon. 1835 Senior 53, cf BARBECUE-FUL. 1959—Current throughout Jamaica. (Cf *baabi.*)

BARBECUEFUL sb. The quantity of coffee, etc., that covers a barbecue when spread out on it.

1835 Senior 53, At night, each barbicueful is safely pushed up into a centre compartment of the barbicue. 1958 DeC StT.

BARBEL DOVE see BARBLE DOVE.

BARBER sb dial; <*barber*. A labourer employed to cut down cane stalks or stumps left standing in the cane fields after a crop has been cut, as a measure against infestation by ants, etc.

1956 Mc StT /baaba/.

BARBERRY BULLET sb; <*barberry*+ BULLET. A tree having fruit and leaves much resembling the barberry, and tough wood.

1961 DAP Man, Barberry bullet, *Erythroxylon confusum*, Britton.

BARBLE DOVE /báabl dòv/ sb chiefly dial; 1935 barbel, 1949 barble, 1956 bauble; <*Barbary*, by dissimilation of *r*. Cf *OED Barbary* 4c, which, however, does not include *Barbary dove*; *OED barbel* 3 is prob misplaced, and belongs here.

1. A name in Jamaica transf from the caged BARBARY DOVE (*Streptopelia risoria*) to escaped similar doves and evid also to native wild doves of the genus *Zenaida*. (Cf the application in Haiti of *Barbarin* to the White-winged Dove, *Zenaida asiatica*).

[1756 Browne 469, Columba 9. *Minor subcinerea, pectore maculâ oblongâ nigrâ insignito.* The Barbary Dove..All these species, except the first and ninth, are natives of Jamaica..They are all wild, and feed on most sorts of wild grain.] 1935 HPJ, Barbel Dove: A small grey or greyish brown pigeon with white marks on the head and chest. Barbary dove? 1949 U.Newton v 26, Your willing uncle never shot barble doves, bald pates, white bellies, or chick-ma-chicks. 1952 FGC Han, StAnd /báabl dòv/—a whitish dove with a black mark round the throat; often tamed. 1956 Jeffrey-Smith 106, Bald Pates, Pea Doves and 'Baubledoves' are often to be seen in cages.

2. A nickname for a shilling—perh punning on 'bob'.

1943 *GL* StM, Barble dove, a shilling.

BARBLE JACK /báabljták/ sb dial; prob <*Barbary* (cf *OED* 4c, also *Barb*) +*jack* (*OED* 27b). See BARBLE DOVE. A large male donkey.

1952 FGC StAnd /báabljták/.

BARE /bíe, bíer/ adj dial; cf *OED bare* III. Mere; only; nothing more than; cf NAKED. *BL G*

1935 HPJ, 'A sie bare peeny walla', *I saw nothing but fireflies.* 1956 Mc Man /im gat bíe manggo ina im bag/ *He has only mangoes in his bag.* 1957 JN StAnn, 'Are there any bigger than you?' 'A bay small-picknу mam', *No, there are only small children, ma'am.*

BARGE see *baaj*.

BARGUADIER see BARQUADIER.

BARILLA sb; cf *OED* 1764→ for *Salsola soda*. The JAMAICA SAMPHIRE, *Batis maritima*.

1774 Long III 906, For the greatest quantity of merchantable barilla. 1914 Fawcett 35.

BARK vb dial; <*bark* sb. To polish (floors, etc.) with stems and leaves of plants.

1956 Mc StAnd, see JOHN-CROW BUSH.

BARKADERE see BARQUADIER.

BARK BATH sb obs; <*bark* (*OED sb*[1] 7) +*bath*. A medicinal bath in which the essential ingredient is quinquina bark.

1801 Dancer 91, The Intermittents of children are difficult to cure..they may be placed several times in the day, in a Bark Bath. *Ibid* 328, Bark Bath [recipe follows].

BARK JACKET sb obs; <*bark* (*OED sb*[1] 7) +*jacket*. Powdered quinquina bark sprinkled thickly upon a patient until it covers him like a jacket.

1781 Dancer 51, The method of sprinkling it plentifully over the surface of the body; if there be any moisture on the skin, a great part of it will adhere, and a sufficient degree of absorption take place, to render it beneficial. The efficacy of the bark jacket has been long known. 1814 Lunan I 489, Are not all these effects answered by bark jackets lately introduced into practice?

BARK-TREE sb; cf *OED* 'English name of the Cinchonas'.

1. The MAHOE, whose bark is stripped and used in making rope.

[1696 Sloane 95, lists 'Barks of trees of which they make Nets to lie on'.] 1756 Browne 284, The *Mohoe*, or Bark-Tree..The negroes, and country people, make all their ropes of it.

2. *Bucida buceras*, a source of tan-bark, etc.

1756 Browne 221, Buceras 1..The Black Olive, or Bark-Tree. It is reckoned an excellent timber-tree; and the bark is greatly esteemed among the tanners. 1774 Long III 749, Black-olive, or Bark-tree—*Buceras*..The bark, mixed with that of the mangrove tree, is much esteemed for tanning leather; and an excellent styptic water may be made from it. [1864 Grisebach 786, Olive-bark tree, *Bucida Buceras*.]

3. A general term for trees such as mango, fig, trumpet, etc., on whose bark edible mushrooms grow.

1952 FGC StJ.

BARKWOOD sb dial joc. A cigar, as if made from the bark-wood of a tree.

1952 FGC Han.

BARKY adj dial; cf *OED* 2, 'of the nature of bark', 1835 only. Of wood: that does not form splinters, but is flexible and may therefore be used to make rope.

1952 FGC StAnn, StM.

BARN see *baan*.

barn-ton sb dial; <*Barnton, Barrington* or some such name? Cf BULLINGTON CANE.

1958 DeC StAnd /barn-ton/ a kind of soft white cane.

BARNYCLEBBER see *bani*.

BARQUADIER sb arch; 1774 1823 1838 barquadier, 1790 barguadier, 1808 barquedia, 1940 barkadere; <Sp *embarcadero*, a wharf; the form is that of a French word, but no record of such has been found; this word, like some others, was probably gallicized by Englishmen. Cf *OED embarcadere*.

1. An export wharf. *BL*

1774 Long II 192, A place called the Cave, where the barquadier stands. This is built of timber, and projected to a considerable distance into the sea, for better conveniency of shipping goods. 1790 Beckford I 151, To the distant wharfs, or barguadiers. *Ibid* II 87, Barguadier. 1823 Roughley 6, The sugar and rum were suffered to remain too long on the estate or barquadier without shipping..requiring sometimes one-quarter to make up loss by ullage.

2. A place which has an export wharf; a shipping port.

1774 Long II 42 [Passage Fort] is a barquadier for Spanish Town, and most of the plantations in St Catharine, St Thomas in the Vale, and St John. The merchant ships which load from hence usually lye off the hospital of Greenwich, where they receive their cargo out of large boats, or lighters, there not being depth of water sufficient for vessels of burthen to come nearer the wharfs. 1808 Stewart 106, Many [estates] are necessarily placed at a great distance from the *barquedia*, or shipping place.

3. Attrib: *barquadier road*, a road from a property to the barquadier; *barquadier cattle*, cattle employed in drawing produce to the barquadier; *barquadier (waggon)*, a waggon used to transport produce to the barquadier, etc.

1863 Waddell 134 (year 1838), The 'barquadier road', led from Frankfort wharf [Ocho Rios] up the sides of the mountains. 1935 HPJ Tre, Barquadier road, waggon, cattle. 1940 Astley Clerk [in HPJ] 'Now "barkadere"'.

BARQUEDIA see prec.

BARRACODA see next.

BARRACOUTA /bàrakúuta, bàrakúta/ sb; see spellings in quots; cf *OED barracuda*. (The word is usually der from Sp; cf however quot 1756, and the Amer Sp word *baracutey*, of Cariban origin, meaning one who lives alone; also appl to a solitary bird. Santamaría.) = Barracuda. (The regular Ja pronunc and sp differ from Brit and US form.) Cf also *bara*.

1679 Trapham 65, see GRASH FISH. 1740 Importance 39, Herrings, Barracodas, Guar-fish. 1756 Browne 451, PERCA 2..The Paracuta, and Paracute. 1776 Long III 867, Paracuta. 1790 Beckford I 188, The savage baracooter. 1892 Cockrell index, Barracouta, barracuda. 1952 FGC Man, StAnn, StJ, StM /bàrakúuta/; West /bàrakúta/. *BL N T*

BARRACOUTA SLAVE, BARRACOUTA WAITING-BOY sb dial. Any of the small gaily-coloured fish (such as PORK-FISH) which swarm around the barracouta as if attending on him.

1952 FGC StJ, Barracouta slave; StA, StJ, StM, StT, West, Barracouta waitin'-boy.

BARRACUDA see BARRACOUTA.

BARRED GRUNT sb.

1952 Smith in *NHN* 141, The barred grunt, *Conodon nobilis*, is caught in Kingston Harbour and is found on the sandy shores of Texas, Jamaica, Martinique, Puerto Rico, and Brazil.

BARREL-BAG sb dial.

1907 Jekyll 90, Barrel-bag, a bag of the capacity of a flour-barrel.

BARROWBY BEAN sb; evid an erron form of BONAVIST.

1788 Marsden 74, The bean called Barrowby grows upon bushes to the height of seven or eight feet; it yields a yellow flower, after which comes a small pod that contains the beans.

(Note: The description fits GUNGO PEAS rather than Bonavist beans.)

BARROW-CROOK sb dial; evid <*barrow* (*OED*² *sb* a castrated boar—cf BOAR MACHETE) + *crook*.

1955 LeP Kgn, Barrow-crook, a machete with a hooked end.

BARSLEY see *baazli*; WILD BARSLEY.

BASCEDAR see BASS CEDAR.

BASE see *baasi*.

bashala botn, bashila botn see BACHELOR BUTTON.

basi see *baasi*.

basiida see BASS CEDAR.

BASKET HOOK sb dial; <*basket* + HOOK, a vine. Another name for BASKET WITHE or HOOK WIS.

1929 Beckwith 48, Round baskets are made of a withe called 'basket hook' treated like wattling. 1952 FGC StM, Basket hook, Very tall [i.e. long]; leaf is round; cut wis and split.

BASKET WITHE sb. Any of several plants used in making baskets: species of *Tournefortia*, *Chamissoa*, etc.—see quots.

1756 Browne 169–70, TOURNEFORTIA 3. Reclinata diffusa, & hirsuta, foliis ovatis..The Basket-Withe..it is generally used for dung-baskets about the country. 1864 Grisebach 781, Basket-withe: *Tournefortia volubilis*. 1914 Fawcett III i 128, *Chamissoa altissima*..Basket Withe. 1952 FGC StM /baaskit wis/ same as basket-hook—to make hamper; StAnn, Same as hook-wiss.

BASLEY see *baazli*.

BASS CEDAR /basíida/ sb; origin uncert: it was early confused (or identified) with BASTARD CEDAR, and the confusion persists today, but Fawcett's form implies a more likely source: *bass* (*OED sb*²) + *cedar*. *N*

1. Confused or identified with BASTARD CEDAR (*Guazuma ulmifolia*).

1826 Williams 40, In cases of drought, the cattle are fed with the leaves of the bread-nut tree and the ramoon, as well as with those of the bascedar.

2. The tree *Trema micrantha*.

1914 Fawcett 39, *Trema micrantha*..Bass Cedar, Jamaican Nettle Tree. 1952 FGC Han, StAnd, StM, StT, Tre /basíida/.

3. A name, prob erron, reported for BALLHEAD.

BAS-SE see *baasi*.

BASSECOTT sb; origin uncert, but cf *baasi*, *basi*, a basket, and *cut*, a section or partition. See quots.

1835 Senior 53, At night, each barbicueful [of coffee] is safely pushed up into a centre compartment of the barbicue, called a '*bassecott*', and covered with a tarpaulin. Next morning the contents of the bassecott are spread abroad on the barbicue. 1943 *GL* Kgn, Bassicut, a small barbeque within a larger one.

BASSICUT see prec.

BASTARD adj; cf *OED bastard a* 5b, 'applied to things resembling, but not identical with, the species that legitimately bear the name'. Common in Jamaica in the names of plants: see following entries. It is now tending to be displaced by WILD.

BASTARD ALOE sb obs. *Aloe vulgaris*.

1814 Lunan I 56, Bastard Aloe. Aletris..Hyacinthoides.

BASTARD BRAZILETTO sb. See quots.

1864 Grisebach 782, Bastard Braziletto: *Weinmannia pinnata* and *Sciadophyllum capitatum*. 1914 Fawcett 251–2, *Weinmannia pinnata*..Bastard Brazilletto, Wild Brazilletto.

BASTARD BREADNUT sb. *Pseudolmedia spuria*; also called MILK WOOD.

1914 Fawcett 45.

BASTARD BRYONY sb bot arch. *Cissus sicyoides*; now called PUDDING-WITHE.

1814 Lunan I 56. 1954 *WIMJ* 26.

BASTARD BULLY TREE sb. *Dipholis nigra*; also called RED or CHERRY BULLET.

1756 Browne 201, Achras? 6..The Bastard Bully-Tree. 1814 Lunan I 57, *Bumelia* species. 1864 Grisebach 782.

(BASTARD) CABBAGE-BARK = next.

BASTARD CABBAGE TREE sb. *Andira inermis*; also called ANGELIN or CABBAGE BARK TREE.

1740 Importance 54, The *Cabbage* Trees are of two sorts; the Mountain Cabbage Tree ; rows very high..the Bastard Tree is Timber. 1886 Hooper 29. 1952 FGC StM /báastad/ cabbage tree.

BASTARD CABBAGE-WOOD = prec.

BASTARD CEDAR sb; *OED* 1753. Cf also BASS CEDAR. The tree *Guazuma ulmifolia* and similar species.

1696 Sloane 135, *Bastard Cedar Tree.* Locis campestribus Insulæ Jamaicæ in sylvis apertioribus ubique abundat. a 1726 Barham (1794) 17 (cit Lunan I 60), Bastard cedar, as it [*Guazuma*] is here called; for what reason I know not, being in no respect like cedar..I take this tree to be of the mulberry kind, more than of the cedar: the flowers are like the line or lindal tree. 1814 Lunan I 59, Bastard Cedar. Bubroma..Guazuma..It is a native of Jamaica, and peculiar to the lowlands, forming a very agreeable shade for cattle, and frequently supplies them with food in dry weather. 1886 Hooper 29, Bastard cedar, *Guazuma tomentosa.* 1914 Fawcett 157, *Guazuma ulmifolia*..Bastard Cedar.

BASTARD CHERRY(-TREE) sb.

1. *Ehretia tinifolia.*

1696 Sloane 169, Ceraso affinis arbor baccifera racemosa..*Bastard Cherry-tree.* 1864 Grisebach 782. 1952 FGC StT.

2. *Coccoloba longifolia.*

1957 Howard 97, Common names: Wild Grape, Bastard Cherry.

BASTARD GERMANDER sb bot arch. *Stemodia maritima*; also called SEA-SIDE GERMANDER.

1814 Lunan I 61. 1864 Grisebach 784.

BASTARD GREENHEART sb bot. *Calyptranthes chytraculia.*

1756 Browne 239–40, Bastard Green-heart..This tree grows chiefly in the parish of St John, and is generally reckoned an excellent timber-wood. 1811 Titford 70. 1864 Grisebach 784. 1926 Fawcett 323, Bastard Green Heart.

BASTARD HEMP AGRIMONY sb bot arch. *Ageratum conyzoides.*

1814 Lunan I 62. 1864 Grisebach 784.

BASTARD HOOP WITHE sb. *Achyranthes altissima* and similar species.

1756 Browne 179, Celosia 2..Bastard Hoop-withe. 1811 Titford 49. 1814 Lunan I 4.

BASTARD IPECACUANHA sb bot. *Asclepias curassavica*; formerly called BLOOD FLOWER, now commonly called RED HEAD.

1756 Browne 183, Asclepias 2..Wild or Bastard Ipecacuanha. 1814 Lunan I 63, Bastard Ipecacuanha. Asclepias..Currassavica..It grows very common almost every where in Jamaica, and is called *red head* by the negroes. 1864 Grisebach 784. 1954 *WIMJ* 28 (see WILD IPECACUANHA).

BASTARD IRONWOOD sb. *Zanthoxylum fagara* or *Trichilia hirta.*

1756 Browne 216, Barbilus 1..Bastard Iron-wood..This tree is very rare in Jamaica. I have seen it only once in the woods back of *Bull-bay.* 1864 Grisebach 784, Ironwood, bastard: *Fagara lentiscifolia* and *Trichilia hirta.* 1941 Swabey 23, Ironwood, Bastard-(Saven tree). *Zanthoxylum fagara.*

BASTARD LEMON sb obs. The lime (*Citrus aurantifolia*): an early name.

1661 Hickeringill 10, Nature hath stor'd it..with Oranges, Lymes, (or bastard Lemmons,) Guavars.. Iamaica pepper. [1697 Dampier *New Voyage.*]

BASTARD LIGNUM-VITAE sb. *N*

1. *Polygala paniculata.* (This sense app obs.)

1756 Browne 287, Polygala 3..The Bastard *Lignum Vitæ* of the red hills..[so called] because it tastes not unlike the gum of that wood. 1814 Lunan I 447.

2. *Sarcomphalus laurinus.*

1756 Browne 179, Sarcomphalus 1..Bastard *Lignum Vitæ* Timber-wood..grows in many parts of the island.. and is looked upon as one of the best timber-woods. 1814 Lunan I 120. 1864 Grisebach 785. 1926 Fawcett 67. 1941 Swabey 24.

BASTARD LOCUST TREE sb bot. *Clethra tinifolia.*

[1673 Ligon 74, Bastard locust.] 1696 Sloane 165, Baccifera arbor calyculata foliis laurinis..*The bastard Locust Tree.* In pratis loci *Liguanee* dicti, &c. reperitur. 1814 Lunan I 65. 1864 Grisebach 785.

BASTARD MAHOGANY sb. *Matayba apetala*; also called COBY WOOD, COBY-NANCY, CROMANTY, RED WOOD, WANIKA.

1864 Grisebach 785, *Ratonia apetala.* 1914 Fawcett 56, *Matayba apetala.* 1952 FGC StE, StM, Tre.

BASTARD MAMMEE TREE sb. *Calophyllum jacquinii*; also called SANTA MARIA, WILD MAMMEE.

1696 Sloane 180, Mali persicæ Mameyæ dictæ..*Bastard Mammee Tree or Santa Maria.* In sylvis Jamaicæ Insulæ densis & opacis frequens est. a 1726 Barham (1794) 18. 1814 Lunan II 140, Bastard mammee or santa maria trees are very tall.

BASTARD MANCHIONEAL sb bot arch. *Cameraria latifolia.*

1756 Browne 182, Cameraria 1..The Bastard Mangeneel. This tree is frequent in Westmoreland and St James's; it..is said to be a good timber-wood, but is full of an acrid milky juice. 1814 Lunan I 66. 1864 Grisebach 785.

BASTARD MUSTARD sb bot. *Cleome* of various species.

1814 Lunan I 67. 1864 Grisebach 786.

BASTARD NICARAGO sb bot; <*bastard* +older form of *Nicaragua* (cf *OED*). *Cæsalpinia vesicaria.*

1756 Browne 227–8, Cæsalpinia 2..Bastard Nicarago. This prickly shrub is common about the *Ferry*, and the lower lands of *Liguanea.* 1814 Lunan I 110. 1864 Grisebach 786, Bastard Nicarago: *Cæsalpinia bijuga.* 1920 Fawcett 95, *C. vesicaria*..Indian Savin Tree, Bastard Nicarago, Jack Fish Wood.

BASTARD OKRO sb bot arch. *Malachra capitata*; also called WILD OKRO.

1756 Browne 281, Sida 10..Bastard *Ochro.* This plant grows chiefly in low rich bottoms, and is frequently met with in marshy places..The tender buds are full of mucilage.

BASTARD PLANTAIN sb bot. *Heliconia* of var species; also called WILD PLANTAIN. *BA G*

1814 Lunan I 69, Heliconia..Bihai..The seeds of the bastard plantain are greedily devoured by hogs. 1864 Grisebach 786.

BASTARD SAFFRON sb bot arch. *Carthamus tinctorius.*

1756 Browne 314, Carthamus 1..Bastard Saffron. This plant was introduced to *Jamaica* by the *Spanish* Jews, who still call it by the name of Saffron. It is cultivated in most of the gardens about *Kingston*; and the *florets* are frequently used in broths and ragoo's by most people there; especially the *Jews*. 1814 Lunan I 71–2, Carthamus. . Tinctorius.

BASTARD SARSAPARILLA sb obs. *Cissus sicyoides*; also called BASTARD BRYONY, CHINA ROOT, PUDDING WIS, WILD YAM.

1801 Dancer 363, China Root (*Smilax pseudochin.*)—Bastard Sarsaparilla, or Wild Yam. Decoction of the Root in place of true Sarsaparilla.

BASTARD SENNA sb bot obs. Some species of *Sesbania*.

1814 Lunan I 72, Coronilla. . 1.Valentina. . 2. Minima.

BASTARD SENSITIVE(-PLANT) sb bot. *Aeschynomene americana*.

1814 Lunan I 73 (Bastard Sensitive.) Æschynomene. . Only one species is a native of this island *americana*; three others have, however, been introduced. 1864 Grisebach 787.

basu /basú/ sb dial; perh to be connected with *baasi*. See quot; cf also *tana*.

1956 Mc Man, A bundle of ground provisions tied up in trash (e.g. a dry banana leaf) with a wis.

basu see *busu*.

BASY see *baasi*.

BAT /bat/ sb dial; < Engl *bat*; cf also EDD BAT sb[6], which gives evidence of the use of this sense in N. Ireland. (Common today in Ulster —RWT.) A very large moth (this is the common use in Jamaica); also, moths in general, or butterflies.

[1740 Importance 48, There are several sorts of *Butterflies*, as in *England*, and one great sort which has in the upper part of his Wings small Sinews like the *English* Batt.] 1851 Gosse 163, All Bats are called by the negroes Rat-bats, probably to distinguish them from Butterflies, to which they give the name of Bats. A little sable urchin came to me one day, and asked me in evident sincerity, 'Do you want to buy any Bats, Massa?' Then opening his hand he displayed two of our most common butterflies. 1952 FGC Han, Man, StAnd, StT, Tre, West.

bata see BATTER.

batamsaid see BOTTOM-SIDE.

BATBAT see BABAT.

BAT-BUSH sb dial. *Passiflora sexflora*; also called BAT WING, etc.

1952 FGC Tre, Bat-bush, same as goat-foot wis—from the shape of the leaf.

BATEAU /bato, batu/ sb dial; < Fr *bateau*; cf US usage for a light river boat (*OED*, *DAE*, *DA*). A rough raft-like structure; see quots.

1873 Rampini 169, Still yet another mode of fishing is with the 'bateau', an open kind of punt made of branches of trees loosely nailed together, in which the fisher squats, dropping his line over the bows of his uncouth skiff, and with the aid of a paddle no bigger than a cricket bat shifting his position from place to place. 1935 HPJ, Bateau: A kind of raft (constructed of some half-dozen logs tied together) used between Priestman's River and Port Antonio. 1943 *GL* Tre, Batu, a raft made of bamboo. *G N*

BAT-FISH sb dial; cf BAT, above, and SEA-BAT.

1. The pork fish or sea-butterfly—a Chaetodon.

1952 FGC StC, StM. Bat-fish.

2. See quot; the allusion is evid to the bright and variable colours.

1952 Smith in *NHN* 251, The vacas (locally called 'bat fish') *Hypoplectrus unicolor*, have so many variations in their theatrical colouring and markings that I have called them 'the court masquers'.

BATHE /bied/ vb dial; < *bathe* v. *OED*: '1 *trans*. (Now mostly reflexive or passive)'. . 1a quots →1796. In phr: *bathe (one's) skin*, wash (oneself). Cf WASH SKIN. *BA BL G T*

1956 Mc Man /go bied yu kin/ *Go and bathe your skin, wash yourself*.

Note: *bathe* is often used in Jamaica where *wash* would be the usual word elsewhere.

bati /báti/ sb dial; prob a hypocoristic abbr of *bottom* (*OED sb* 1b), but poss infl by *batie* (*SND* BATIE, BAWTIE, round and plump) or *butt* (*EDD* sb[2] 4, *DAE* n[3] 3). The buttocks; common among schoolboys and generally in the vulgar phrase /yù báti/ expressing anger, disdain, or general insult. *BL G T*

c1915 FGC StAnd (remembered). 1935 HPJ [Prov:] Wen breeze blow, fowl batty show. 1943 *GL* StJ, Batty, buttocks.

bati-man sb dial; < *bati*+*man*. A homosexual; a pederast. (1955.) *BL G T*

batlas see BOTTLE-ARSE. *N*

bato see BATEAU.

BATTER /báta/ vb dial.

1. trans. To flog.

1956 Mc StE (Accom), Batter, to flog someone.

2. trans. See quot.

1955 LeP StT, Batta, to cut awkwardly or hack with dull tool.

3. intr. To work very hard; to have a difficult time; see quots.

1912 McKay *Songs* 42, High people fabour t'ink it sweet Fe batter* in de boilin' heat. * Labour and sweat; toil and moil. 1958 DeC StT /batta haad/ to work hard and steadily in life; to keep one's nose to the grindstone.

4. intr. To knock loudly.

1959 DeC Kgn /mi guo an bata pan in duor/ *I went and knocked on his door*.

BATTER-BATTER /bátabáta/ vb dial; by iteration of *batter*. To beat severely.

1952 FGC Man (Christiana) [A country-woman, referring to the 1951 hurricane and the damage it did to her house and land:] 'Storm batter-batter me'.

BATTERY /bátri/ sb dial; prob < *battery*, *OED sb* 14.

1956 Mc Man (Banana Ground) /bátri/ the stone wall supporting the road at a culvert.

BATTLE sb; spelling for dial pronunc of *bottle*; it is still /batl/—also freq /bakl/. *BL G*

1833 Scott I 325, 'Hand us up a dozen bottles of spruce, do you hear?' 'Dozen battle of pruce!' groaned the old woman.

BATTY see *bati*.

batu see BATEAU.

BAT-WING sb dial; also called BAT-BUSH.

1927 Beckwith 18, see GOAT-FOOT (WIS). 1954 *WIMJ* 19, *Passiflora sexflora*. . Duppy Pumpkin; Bat Wing; Goat or Duck Foot; Passion Flower.

bau see *bahu*.

BAUBEY YAM see *baabi*[1].

BAUBLEDOVE see BARBLE DOVE.

BAUDAH see *baada*.

BAUDIES sb dial; evid related to *baada*, brother.

1943 *GL* Tre, Baudies, sister.

baul see *bahu.*

BAUSI(E) see *baasi.*

BAWDA see *baada.*

BAWL /báal/ vb; cf *OED bawl v* 2, 3; much more commonly used in Jamaica than in England or US, where it is now dial. *BA BL G T*

1. To shout.

1956 Mc StE (Accom) /im baal out dong de fo dem tu kom an help im/ *He shouted from down there* (in the ditch) *for them to come and help him;* /híe mista és báalin nóu/ *Listen to Mr S.* (a revivalist preacher) *shouting now.*

2. To wail, cry, weep.

1877 Murray *Feedin' 'Perrit* 7, Him say 'Wha you da bawl?' Me say 'You tink it no hot me?' 1941 Kirkpatrick 26, Dem Hitalian..can bawl back an' front as much as dem like, dem gettin' sandwich dis time. [*Those Italians..can cry out on both sides as much as they like, they're getting squeezed this time.*] 1947 U.Newton II 38, When we were tired to bawl [tired of crying] we watched the fire. 1956 Mc StAnd /elin a baal, ai waata, o, elin a baal, baal fi di dakta/ *Ellen's crying, eye-water, o! Ellen's crying, crying for the doctor.*

BAWLING vbl sb dial; <BAWL. Shouting, lamentation, or wailing. *BL G T*

1956 Mc StE (Accom) /a fyuu minit aafta, de woz a baalin uova naana yaad—naana iz ded/ *A few minutes later a shout (or wailing) went up in Nana's yard—'Nana is dead';* StAnd /sami daangki dedo, a mi yier di baalin/ *Sammy's donkey is dead, and I hear the lamentation.*

BAWNYA(H) see *baanya.*

BAWOL, BAWU see *bahu.*

BAY see BARE.

BAYAKUTA sb? dial; cf Yoruba *òkúta*, a rock, *abeokuta*, beneath the rock. (In Westmoreland is the settlement named Abbeacuta, evid after the village of Abeokuta in Southern Nigeria.)

1943 GL West, Bayacuta, rock.

[**bayawo** phr dial; cf Yoruba *gbe ni yawo.* (J. Berry.) A retained African phrase; see quot.

1959 DeC Han /bayawo/ 'Guinea' phrase used in Guinea Town meaning 'Are you married?']

BAYBERRY (TREE) sb bot; cf. *OED.* A species of PIMENTO; see quots.

1756 Browne 247, *Caryophyllus* 1..The Bayberry Tree.. the characters of this plant differ but very little from those of the following species..*Pimento,* or All-Spice. This sort is called the *Wild Cinnamon* or *Wild Clove tree,* by most people, both in *Antigua* and *Jamaica.* 1814 Lunan I 75, Bayberry, or Wild Clove..Myrtus acris. 1955 *WIMJ* 157, *Amomis caryophyllata* Kr. and Urb. (=Pimenta acris Kostel.) Common names: Bay Rum Tree; Bay Berry Tree; etc.

BAYERE YAM see *baiyere yam.*

BAY GRAPE sb bot. See quots.

1814 Lunan I 76, Bay or Sea-Side Grape. *Coccoloba Uvifera* etc. There are six species, natives of Jamaica. 1864 Grisebach 784, *Coccoloba.*

BAYHOO adj and sb dial; prob < Sp *viejo*, old, old man.

1943 *GL* Port, Biehu, an old man; StAnn, Bayhoo, old (Spanish); StM, Bayou, old man.

BAYJAM sb dial; perh a form of BAJAN, or else a blend of BAJAN+YAM.

1955 LeP StAnn, Bayjam, Barbados yam.

BAYOU see BAYHOO.

BAY RUM TREE sb. =BAYBERRY TREE.

1926 Fawcett 326–7, *Amomis..caryophyllata..*Wild Cinnamon, Wild Clove, Bay Rum Tree, Bay Berry Tree. 1955 *WIMJ* 157.

BAY-SIDED GRASS QUIT sb ornith obs. See quots.

1847 Gosse 253, Bay-sided Grass-quit..Of this very plain and unpretending species, but a single specimen has fallen into my hands..its fawn-coloured sides distinguish it from the females of the preceding two species. 1956 Jeffrey-Smith 95, Gosse described another grass quit of much the same general coloration..which he named the Bay-Sided Grass Quit (*Spermophila adoxa*)..Ornithologists today..would regard it, in the light of further knowledge of the genus *Tiaris,* as an age phase.

BEACH GRAPE sb. A less common name for the sea or seaside grape tree. *N*

1957 Howard 88, Beach grape, *Coccoloba uvifera.*

BEAD BUSH sb bot obs. An unidentified plant, placed in the genus *Trichilia.*

1814 Lunan II 319–20, The following new species of Trichilia is noticed in A. Robinson's manuscript; which he calls Bead Bush: Scandens, foliis simplicibus..etc.

BEAD TREE sb.

1. *Melia azederach*; *OED* quots 1668 (not clearly this) and 1852. Also formerly EVERGREEN BEAD TREE.

1811 Lunan I 79–80, Bead, Hoop, or Lilac, Tree. Melia.. Azedarach..The nuts are bored and strung for beads. 1920 Fawcett 215–16.

2. *Ormosia jamaicensis.* (The name was used earlier in Dominica and St Vincent for the related species *O. dasycarpa.*) See quots. Also called NICKEL, the more properly Jamaican name.

1909 Harris 310, Nickel, or Bead Tree (*Ormosia jamaicensis,* Urb.). This fine tree is known from Dominica, St Vincent, etc., but was not known to occur in Jamaica until the writer collected specimens of it on the slopes of Dolphin Head Mountain in 1906..Its seeds are hard, roundish, beautifully polished, and of a bright scarlet colour with a jet black spot at one end. They are used for making necklaces. 1941 Swabey 13.

BEAK sb dial. The 'comb of a chicken or peafowl'—evid from its having points.

1958 DeC StT.

BEAN BIRD sb dial. See quot; also called BUTTERFLY BIRD.

1956 Jeffrey-Smith 82, Redstart..*Setaphaga ruticilla..* Another local name is Bean Bird because it frequents the plant.

BEAN TREE sb obs [*OED, DAE,* applied to different plants]. In Jamaica, *Erythrina corallodendron*; now called RED BEAN TREE.

1696 Sloane 142–3, Coral arbor spinosa orientalis fructu obscure rubente..*The Bean-tree.* 1794 Barham 19, *Bean Tree..*In the island of Jamaica, they make fences of them, being very prickly.

BEANY BIRD, QUIT see BEENY BIRD, QUIT.

BEARD DRUMMER sb dial. A variety of DRUMMER having a 'beard' or barbel. (*OED* records this sense of *beard* but without quots or references.)

1952 FGC StC, Beard drummer.

BEARDED GRASS sb bot; cf *OED bearded* 2; *DAE bearded grass* 1805, *beard-grass* 1791→. Species of *Aristida.*

1756 Browne 135, *Aristida* 1..The bearded Grass..This plant is frequent in Jamaica..*Aristida* 2..The smaller bearded Grass. This plant is somewhat smaller than the foregoing.

BEARD-MAN sb cant. An adherent of the RASTAFARIAN cult; specif, one who wears a beard and plentiful hair, but trims them at times. Cf LOCKSMAN.

1960 *SAN Report* 23, The brethren fall into three categories: the Locksmen, whose hair is matted and plaited and never cut, neither their beards; the Beard-men, who wear their hair and beards but may trim them occasionally and do not plait the hair, but keep it clean.

BEARER sb dial. An officer of a Revival cult.

1953 Moore 89, see POST-HOLDER. 1959 DeC gen.

BEARING vbl sb dial; cf *OED vbl sb* 20, 1838 sole quot. That which a plant bears—a fruit, root, ear, etc.; the common country term in Jamaica.

1952 FGC StM, The bearing of aribeka is mos' like ginger; StT, Burn-nose has a white 'seed bearing'. 1959 DeC gen.

BEAR OFF /bìer áaf/ vb phr dial; cf. *OED bear v*[1] 42. Of a plant: to finish bearing, to complete its crop.

1956 Mc /aki trii bier aaf di ada die/ *The ackee tree finished bearing the other day.* 1959 DeC gen.

BEAST sb dial; cf Engl slang *beastly* (*OED adv* 2). An intensifying word: cf 'a *devil* of a..'.

1941 Kirkpatrick 30, So dem is in a beas' of a fix nung. [*So they are in a very difficult situation now.*] *G*

BEAST-DEAL sb dial; possibly a nonce-formation. A 'horse-trade' (cf *DAE*); a piece of bargaining or exchange: also metaphorical. ('Beast' is the common general term for an animal of the horse kind in the Jamaican countryside.)

1941 Kirkpatrick 31, Roosevelt an' Churchill mek a beas' deal dey dat almos' fe cripple 'Itler complete. Da bargain a fifty 'Merican warship fe base ovah de 'ole a de Wes' Indies.

BEAST-LICK sb dial; <*beast* (*OED* 3, in very common use in Jamaica) +LICK. A heavy, punishing blow (such as might be given to an animal); also metaphorical.

1941 Kirkpatrick 8, 'Itler been mekin' 'im bowler dem bowl off de wicket..but even dough dem get so much beas' lick, lak de St Paul Cathedral one..de batsman dem jus' rub de spat an' go right on battin'. [*Hitler has been making his bowlers bowl off the wicket..but even though they* [*the English*] *get such heavy blows, like the one* [*bomb*] *on St Paul's Cathedral, the batsmen just rub the spot and go right on batting.*]

BEAT vb dial trans and absol; cf *OED v*[1] 10c, 1770 and later (unspecified). To gain (the victory), win (a game); cf WIN. *BL G*

1907 Jekyll 42, I must beat the race. 1957 JN Tre, Count the run you meck, fe see which one a we de go beat, *Count the runs you make, to see which one of us is going to win.*

BEATER sb obs; *DA* 1784→. The smallest of the series of vats used in the manufacture of indigo.

1774 Long III 676, The second [vat] opens in the like manner into the third, or smallest. These latter are called batteries, or beaters.

BEATING VAT sb obs; *DAE* 1797 only. =BEATER.

1774 Long III 678, The clear water is then..drawn off, out of the beating-vat.

BEAT OUT BRUISED BLOOD phr obs. See quot. *G*

1833 Second Letter 22, After they have received thirty-nine or forty lashes with the whip, then to use the tamarind switches; the common expression is, 'beating out the bruised blood'.

BEAU sb dial arch or obs; cf *DAE beau* and *ODS*, *DA bo* (the latter however taken to be an abbr of *bozo* or *hobo*), 1893→. Cf next. A term of address to a man; prob the same as US *bo*; now virtually out of use in Jamaica. *BA*

1826 Williams 204, 'A buckra parson!' rejoined the sailor; 'you must not talk in that fashion, beau'. [1935 HPJ, Bo..A friendly vocative expression in Barbados.]

BEAU-STICK sb obs; the spelling *beautic* represents a dial pronunc /buo-tik/; BEAU (cf *OED beau* B and its cpds) +*stick* sb. A stick formerly carried by men who fancied themselves fashionable, partly for swagger and partly as a weapon (cf COCO-MACCA, STICK-LICKING, etc.).

1792 Stewart 19, In broils, or disputes [among the negroes], the beautic, or cudgel is wielded with dexterity. 1793 Mathews 14, His invectives against those Gentlemen, whom he terms Cowskin Heroes, I shall animadvert upon in its proper place; but I sincerely pray he may never come within reach of them, as it may put him to the disagreeable necessity of distinguishing them, in his second Edition, by the more remarkable appellation of the Bowstick Heroes.

BEAUTIC see prec.

BEAUTY adj dial; <*beauty* sb or abbr of *beautiful*. Beautiful.

1952 FGC StM /a byuuti wan/ *A beautiful one.*

bebe see BABY.

BE-BE, BE-BE-BE-BE adj dial; <*big*, showing degrees of comparison by iteration. *G*

1868 Russell 11, The adjective big and some others are therefore compared in two ways; thus, big, biger, bigis; and big, be-be, be-be-be-be. [=/bi-bi/ etc.]

bebrij see BEVERAGE. *G*

BECASIN see BECAUSEN.

BECAUSE conj dial (cf BECAUSEN). In full /bikáaz/; frequently reduced to /bikáa/, /káaz/ or /kaa/. *G T*

BECAUSEN /bikáazin, bikáazn, bikáang, bikáan/ conj dial; <*because* +-*n* suffix[1] (see below). Cf CAUSEN. *BL G*

1862 Clutterbuck 50, I admires you..becausin you is so genteel. 1868 Russell 20, Becausin (because). 1877 Murray *Feedin' 'Perrit* 9, becasin. 1943 *GL* StC, StJ, Becausen, because. 1956 Mc Man /unu fi draib gud bikaan di ruod rof/ *You are to drive carefully because the road is rough.*

BECAUSIN see prec.

BECOUNT sb in conj phr dial; prob </bi/ dial pron of *by*+'*count*, aphetic form of *account*; cf *bigens*. Account.

1907 Jekyll 15, Lumpy kill Miss Wenchy loss, on becount of young King Daniel.

BED sb dial; *OED* 1611 sole quot. =*bed*, *OED sb* 16 'The placenta or afterbirth. Obs.'

1929 Beckwith 57, The afterbirth or 'bed' must be carefully buried.

BED vb intr; possibly <*bed* (*SND* v[2]..Ork. 1929..to 'lodge' corn, to lay flat a growing crop. Gen in past pple *bedded*—i.e. 'lodged', laid flat—by rain and wind); however, possibly a simple extension of *bed* v, 'to lodge flat'—see *OED*; also LODGE. Of sugar-cane: to bend over to the ground when ready for cutting.

1956 Mc StT /di kyien bedin, di kyien bedid/ *The cane is*

bedding, the cane is bedded; /di kyien duon gaan tu bed/ *The cane has not become bedded down.* [There may be a play on words in the second example on *bed* sb, the earth in which the canes grow.]

BEDDING sb dial; cf *beje* 2. *G T*

1955 LeP Kgn, Bedding, old, ragged clothes.

bede[1] sb dial; cf Twi *ɔ-bɛdɛ́w*, Akan *ɔbɛdɛ*, a kind of basket roughly made of palm branches. Cf also *beje* 2.

1. A temporary bag made of grass or trash in the field.

1958 DeC Port, StE.

2. Palm-leaf thatch used for anything.

1958 DeC Port.

bede[2] /bede/ sb dial; perh familiarizing form of *bed*, but cf *beje*.

1958 DeC StE (Accom) /bede/ a rough wooden bed.

BEDGE see *beje* sb[1].

BED GLASS sb dial. A chamber-pot; also called *chimi*, *puo*.

1955 FGC Man.

BEDWARDISM, BEDWARDIST, BEDWARDITE sbs. <Alexander *Bedward*, name of a well known revivalist preacher (b 1859) and Shepherd of the 'Jamaica Baptist Free Church' established at August Town, StAnd, in 1894. In 1920 he announced himself as the incarnation of Christ and foretold his 'Ascension' for 31 Dec. of that year. The following year he was consigned to the Asylum. His Church still keeps his name alive at August Town.

1929 Beckwith 168 [The church] became the established home of Bedwardism. *Ibid*, This was a critical time for the Bedwardists. *Ibid* 167, The most remarkable of these prophetic groups in Jamaica, the cult called Bedwardite.

BEE-BEE sb dial; prob iteration of *bee*. An herbaceous plant (*Compositae*), also called CAMPHOR BUSH, CAMPHOR WEED, HALBERT WEED.

1928 Beckwith 11, Bee-bee..For a cold, boil and drink as tea. 1953 *WIMJ* 242, *Calea jamaicensis* L. Bee-Bee.

BEE BUR sb dial. The herb *Desmodium supinum*, also called BEE BUSH, MAN BACK, STRONG BACK, WILD PINDER.

1928 Beckwith 12, Bee-bur, *Meibomia supina* (L) *Britton*. 1954 *WIMJ* 18, *Desmodium supinum*..Bee Bur or Bush.

BEE BUSH see BEE BUR.

BEEF-APPLE sb.

1. The tree *Micropholis rugosa*, its fruit and wood.

1864 Grisebach 781, Beef-apple, *Sapota rugosa*. 1952 FGC StE /biif apl/ bear seed [i.e. *fruit*] like custard apple; worm breed in it; good timber.

2. = BEEFWOOD.

1952 FGC Tre, Beef-apple, same as beefwood.

BEEF BEAN sb dial.

1952 FGC Port /bíif bíin/ a large brown bean eaten with beef.

BEEF MANGO, BEEFY MANGO sb. A common variety of mango with a solid, 'beefy' flesh.

c 1915 FGC StAnd, Common: beef or beefy mango. 1952 FGC StAnd, StAnn, StJ, StT, Port, Beef mango.

BEEF THYME sb dial. A kitchen herb with a scent similar to that of thyme (though it is unrelated) and having a succulent leaf. Prob = FRENCH THYME, SPANISH THYME.

1952 FGC Port, see SPRICKLE-SPRICKLE.

BEEFWOOD sb; cf *OED* Beef-wood 2: 'Applied to various other trees, e.g...in Jamaica to evergreen shrubs or low trees of the genus *Ardisia* (N.O. *Myrsinaceae*).' *OED* 1756→. Various trees; see quots (not all of which furnish clear identifications, however).

1756 Browne 201, Achras 4..This tree is commonly called by the name of Beef-wood by most people in *Jamaica*, from the fleshy colour of the interior bark. [Prob *Micropholis*.] 1774 Long III 749, Locus or Lotus-Tree..Qu? Achras 4 of Browne..Beef-wood? 1811 Titford 57, There are also Beef-wood..[etc.], all hard, fine timber. 1826 Williams 290, As they ascended..they met with abundance of Santa Maria wood..; beef wood; etc. [1874 Grisebach 781, Beef-wood, red: *Ardisia coriacea*. Beef-wood, small-leaved white: *Schoepfia chrysophylloides*.] 1944 *NHN* II 81, *Pisonia obtusata*, Beefwood, Lob-lob Beefwood..The trees are not cut for any purpose by the people of the region but in other parts of Jamaica the species is used for firewood. 1952 FGC Tre, Beefwood—similar to white bullet, same as BEEF-APPLE; StAnn, StC, MAN BEEFWOOD = the HERRING-WOOD of StE and Tre; StAnn, StC, WOMAN BEEFWOOD (the soft variety) = *paplas*, Tre.

BEEFY MANGO see BEEF MANGO.

BEE HUMMINGBIRD sb ornith.

The smallest of the hummingbirds, no larger than a bumblebee which it resembles both in its darting hovering flight and the hum of its wings. (Difference of opinion exists as to its classification—see Jeffrey-Smith's discussion, 25–6.)

[1790 Beckford I 363, There is one species [of humming-bird] that is very little larger than an humble-bee; and this is by far the most beautiful of the kind. 1847 Gosse 127–34, Vervain Humming-Bird. *Mellisuga humilis*..It visits the spikes in succession, flitting from one to another, exactly in the manner of the honey-bee..The noise produced by the hovering..of Humilis is a hum, like that of a large bee.] 1936 Bond 215ff, Bee Humming-bird, *Calypte helenæ*. 1955 Taylor 5, The tiny Vervain or Bee Humming-bird (*Mellisuga minima*) which, with the exception of the very similar Bee Humming-bird (*Mellisuga helenæ*) of Cuba, is the smallest bird in the world.

BEENY /biini/ adj and sb dial; etym unknown, but cf Ewe *bii*, narrow, slender, small, lying close, and *ní*, it is, that is. (Cf also PEENY, CHEENY, and Engl *teeny-weeny*, which all suggest smallness phonosymbolically.)

A. adj: Tiny; cf BEENY BIRD, BEENY QUIT, of which this word is probably the first element.

1941 Kirkpatrick 53, Beeny—tiny, small. 1943 *GL* Clar, Beeny, small. 1956 Mc Man /wan biini wan/ a very small one.

B. sb: A 'little one', a child.

1943 *GL* StJ, Beeny, a child; Tre, Bīnī, child.

BEENY BIRD /bíini bòd/ sb dial gen; < BEENY + *bird*. A honey-creeper, *Coereba flaveola*; see quots.

1952 FGC Man /likl biini, biini kwit/; StAnd, StT /bíini bòrd/. 1955 Taylor 8, The Banana-quit or Beany Bird..is a tiny, gaily coloured bird. 1956 Jeffrey-Smith 71 (see quot under BANANA QUIT). 1956 Mc StE /bíini bòd/.

[The prevalent spelling is BEANY, which, however, is misleading—cf BEAN BIRD.]

BEENY QUIT sb dial; cf QUIT. = BEENY BIRD. s.

1952 FGC Man /biini kwit/. 1956 Mc Man /bíini kwìt/.

BEETWOOD sb bot. *Cyrilla racemiflora*; named from the beetroot colour of the timber —also called BLOOD WOOD.

1926 Fawcett 18. 1941 Swabey 14.

BEEZIE sb dial; <Ko *mbizi*, animal, flesh. A cant word of the 'AFRICAN' cult in StT; see quot.

1953 Moore 117, 'The *Kongo* word for flesh is *beezie*'.

bef adj dial; prob a form of *baf*, but cf also *EDD* BEFF sb (Scots) 'A stupid person', and BAFF a (North. & Dur.), 'Useless, worthless'.

1943 *GL* StE, Bef, useless.

BEFORE /bifúo, bufúo/ adj dial; cf *OED before a*, →1599. Used for the Standard *fore*; cf BEFORE-DAY, BEFORE-FOOT, etc. *BL G*

BEFORE prep dial; a development of *before*, *OED prep* II. Rather than; instead of. *BL G T*

1924 Beckwith 290 [Prov:] Darg say befo' him plant yam fe look like masquita' foot, him satisfy fe tun beggar. [*Dog says, rather than plant yams that will grow no bigger than mosquitoes' feet, he is satisfied to turn beggar.*] 1942 Bennett 39 [Prov:] Before me tumble dung me hole macka. [*Rather than fall down, I'll hold on to prickles* (or *a prickly plant*).] 1950 Pioneer 34, Before yuh tank me fe carry yuh pon me head yuh dah..come back-answa me. [*Instead of thanking me for carrying you on my head, you are talking back to me!*]

BEFORE-DAY sb dial. The earliest morning hours. *BA BL G*

1877 Murray *Tom Kittle* 27, Well, I go sleep till bufo day, nummo come yerry dem Eboe fellow—'Broke Whanica Penny comb Kill de debil moder'. [*Well, I went to sleep till early morning had hardly come, when I heard those Ibo fellows singing, 'Breaking Whanica's penny comb Killed the devil's mother'.*] 1958 DeC gen /bifúo-die/ the period from midnight or one o'clock to daylight. This is not an adverbial phrase any more. In most parishes a man would not 'come before day'; he would 'come in the before-day'.

BEFORE-FOOT sb dial; see BEFORE adj. Forefoot.

c1915 FGC StAnd, Current.

BEFORE-TIME sb, adj and adv dial; cf *OED beforetimes adv*, →1647, though this may be a new formation <*before*+*time*: see quots. *G*

A. sb: An era or period in the past. *BL*

1877 Murray *Kittle* 20, In a before time, quite ober da chookoo yonder, dere was a woman dere, did hab a little pickney. [*Long ago, in a distant country*, etc.] 1899 Smith 9, In a long before time in dis country dere lib Chim-chim bird.

B. adj: Belonging to earlier days. *BL*

1956 Mc Man /bifúotaim píipl/ *People of earlier times or olden days.*

C. adv: Formerly.

1826 Williams 5, He [Quashie] told me it was before time (according to his phraseology) a cotton tree, but now a fig tree. 1863 Waddell 121 (year 1836), Before time, minister, I was one of the biggest rogues ever was; but now I do try, and beg God to keep me from such bad ways. 1956 Mc Man /bifúotaim mi hie se../ *Formerly, I have heard it said..*

BEG vb dial. *BL G N T*

1. Used commonly in Jamaica where Standard Engl would use the unemphatic *ask*.

1877 Murray *Tom Kittle* 17, 'Beg you little water' &c were played. 1924 Beckwith 154, De snake said, 'Do, I beg you carry me go to me fader'. 1935 HPJ, Me a beg you fimme cloes, *May I have my clothes?* 1956 Mc StE (Accom) /a did beg Aastin dem tu klaim di trii/ *I asked Austin and the others to climb the tree.* 1957 JN StAnn, Beg Ess—she will give you; Tre, Im den beg one man fi carry him box an grip, *He then asked a man to carry his box and grip.*

2. In the phr *Beg you*, equiv to *Please* (=if you please), *please give me.*

1942 Bennett 29, Beg yuh move yuh foot deh mah. [*Please move your foot, ma'am.*] 1958 StAnd, etc. /beg yu a drap, sa/ *Please give me a lift, sir.*

BEG adj dial; for *begged* pa pple. Borrowed.

1925 Beckwith 19, Beg water can't bwoil cow 'kin, *Borrowed water can't boil a cow-skin.*

BEGAINST see *bigens*.

BEG-BEG adj dial; iterative form of BEG. Borrowed (with the implication that a little quantity is obtained from many people). *G*

1925 Beckwith 19, Beg-beg water, *borrowed water.*

BEGENS(E) see *bigens*.

BEGI sb dial; prob =*beje*.

1943 *GL* Port, Begi, matting made with coconut leaves.

BEG-YOU-LITTLE-WATER sb dial. A social game played at wakes and similar meetings.

1873 Rampini 85, The mourners indulge in such diversions as 'Hide and seek', 'Hot bran well buttered', 'Thread the needle', 'Beg you little water', and other boisterous games. 1929 Beckwith 78 (ref. to this passage).

BEHAVE vb dial. As a copula: to be in behaviour, to behave as. *G T*

1924 Beckwith 289, Marse Peter never go af'er no girl again. Marse Peter behave a good buckra massa af'er this. 1957 JN Mandeville, 'I will go to heaven if I behave a good girl'.

BEHIND-FOOT sb dial; cf BEFORE-FOOT. Hind foot.

c1915 FGC StAnd, Current.

BE IN MALICE see MALICE. *BL*

beje /béje/ sb[1] dial; etym uncert, but cf Twi *mpa-dùá*, bedstead, *mpatiá*, a short-legged bedstead; prob infl also by *bed*, familiarized (cf Scots *beddie*). A wooden bed; a rough or temporary bed; a 'shakedown'. (There is considerable local variation in application. DeC.)

1935 Astley Clerk (in HPJ), Bejjay, a simple bed, a shakedown. 1936 Martinez *Gleaner* 3 Oct. 35, A 'Bedge' (pronounced bayjay, the a being short). 1943 *GL* Man, Baejay, bejja. 1956 LeP StE (Eld) /beje/ a wooden bed nailed to the wall. 1956 Mc StAnd (Mt Charles) /béje bed/ made of mahogany but less grand than a four-poster; StE (Accom) /beje/ a temporary bed, a shakedown, anything—e.g. a piece of board lying on two chairs —fixed up as a bed to avoid lying on the floor.

beje /béje/ sb[2] dial; prob a variant form of *bede*[1].

1. See quot.

1958 DeC Man /beje/ a temporary bag or basket made of trash at the field.

2. See quot.

1958 DeC StT /beje/ old, ragged work-clothes.

BEJJA(Y) see *beje* sb[1].

BEKNOWN, BEKNOWNST ppl adj; cf *OED beknown*, <*beknow*, arch; →1865. Well-known; familiar.

1935 HPJ, Mr Rae is well beknown in the car business. 1941 Kirkpatrick 7, See ONE-ONE A 1. 1957 JB, 'Beknown and beloved' is a phrase often used in references to the members of a church congregation.

beks, beksbeks see BEX.

bela sb dial; prob <*belly*. *OED* has *belly sb* 5 d Obs., a glutton, quots 1526–1655. This Jamaican form however is prob an abbr of *belagot*.

1943 *GL* Man, Bela, a greedy person.

belagot /bélagot/ sb dial; <*belly*+*gut*. (The middle vowel /a/ is unexpected: the normal dial reflex would be /i/.)

1. Intestines, tripes; cf LICKY-LICKY 1950.

1935 HPJ, Bella-gut, cow-tripe.

2. Fig: something inward and intimate (as, family affairs)—cf BELLY-WORD. (In the citation there is a play on senses 1 and 2; it also shows how sense 3 was developed.)

1925 Beckwith 85, Me no hab big pot fe bwoil bella(?) gut! An expression employed to quiet a quarrel in the family.

3. A large cooking-pot (orig one large enough to cook cow-tripes after butchering). Also called *belapat*, BIG DADDY POT.

1943 *GL* Man, Billagut, a huge cooking pot. 1956 Mc Man /bélagot/ used only in a particular phrase [cf sense 2?]—otherwise /bélapát/; StAnd /bélagót/ = Big Daddy pot.

4. See quot.

1958 DeC StT /belagot/ a fat man, a glutton.

belapat /bélapát/ sb dial; =*belagot* 3.

1956 Mc Man /bélapát/ a huge cooking pot.

beli- see BELLY-.

belihat sb dial; <Engl *belly*+*hat*, hurt. *G*

1952 FGC, see CHICKEN-WEED. 1956 Mc Man /mi ha belihat/ *I have a bellyache.*

[Cf Stedman 1 120, Belly-hatty, or dry gripes. (Surinam.)]

beliwok see BELLY-WORK. *BL G*

BELLA sb dial; prob abbr of *belagot*—see 4.

1943 *GL* Man, Bella, greedy person.

BELLAGUT see *belagot*.

BELL-FLOWER sb; cf *OED bell-flower*, species of *Campanula*. *G*

1912 McKay *Songs* 103, Bell-flowers. . *Datura suaveolens*, whose great white trumpets flag as the sun gets hot.

BELL-PEPPER sb; cf *OED Bell* 12, *bell-pepper* 1707→. The largest of the *Capsicum* peppers; so called from their shape.

1696 Sloane 114, Capsicum latifolium. . fructu magno. . Americanum. . Bell Pepper. 1740 Importance 34, The Bell-Pepper is red when ripe; the Negroes will not use it, because it is not hot enough for them. 1794 Barham 30, The large hollow sort [of capsicum], called bell-pepper. 1814 Lunan 1 256, Bell Peppers.—Of which there are two kinds: the largest purple. . The other kind has a large heart-formed red fruit. 1952 FGC StM, See SCOTCH-BONNET PEPPER.

BELLY sb dial.

1. The condition of pregnancy; cf BELLY-WOMAN, SHOW BELLY. *BL G T*

1935 HPJ, Him ha' belly, *She's pregnant*; Him gi him belly, *He made her pregnant.*

2. The inner self—cf *belagot* 2, BELLY-WORD.

1925 Beckwith 114 [Prov:] Wha' woodpecker say in him belly hard fe answer. . What the woodpecker thinks is hard to guess.

3. A bulge in a dry-stone wall, or, the depression or partial break which forms in a dry-stone wall when the top retaining-stones fall away. *BA*

1956 Mc Man.

BELLY adj dial; <BELLY sb. *BL*

1943 *GL* Clar, Belly, pregnant.

BELLYACHE sb obs; abbr used absolutely following *the* for DRY BELLYACHE. See quots; and cf next. *T*

1679 Trapham 131–2, Cold. . cruciating the tender Fibres with obdurate contractions; wherein the sharp sting of the Bellyach lies. 1718 *Courant* 11 Feb. page 4, A White Man named John Swinstead. . very weak in his Hands and Legs, having once lost his limbs by the Belley-Ake.

BELLYACHE BUSH sb; cf *OED bellyache* and quot 1750. *Jatropha gossypifolia*, once used as a medicine for the DRY BELLYACHE. Now more commonly called WILD CASSAVA.

[1707 Sloane 129, Wild Cassada. . this is the most general remedy of the poorer sort in the dry Belly-ach.] 1814 Lunan 1 163, The leaves of the *gossypifolia, cotton-leaved jatropha, wild cassada*, or *belly-ache bush*, are quinquepartite. 1874 Grisebach 781, Belly-ache bush. 1920 Fawcett 312, Belly-ache bush.

BELLYACHE WEED sb obs. A plant (unidentified in 1926 Fawcett) of the family Cucurbitaceae, used formerly to treat the DRY BELLYACHE.

1696 Sloane 103, Colocynthis bryoniæ albæ folio, in quinque lacinias dentatas profunde secto, aspero, cathartico. Belly-ach weed. 1707 Sloane 228, Belly-ach-weed. . By what I saw, I question not but this is a Colocynthis. . This is counted an extraordinary Medicine against the Belly-ach. . It is accounted a very good Remedy against the Dropsie.

BELLY-BOTTOM CONCRETE sb dial slang.

1959 DeC StJ /beli-batam-kangkriit/ very large round boiled dumpling.

BELLYCARK see next.

BELLY-CORK sb dial; cf *EDD* BELLY-BUTTON, -NIPPLE.

1943 *GL* Man, Bellycark, navel.

BELLY-FEED sb dial; <*belly*+*feeding*. Feeding the belly; providing for food; or perh (more concretely) food, that which feeds the belly.

1924 Beckwith 54, De lady say de meaning 'Belly-feed no not'ing, but *mus'* somet'ing!' [*Feeding the belly* (or *food*) *is not something negligible, it is something important*]. . So Anansi set *him* fiddle, play, Bittle no somet'ing, what is somet'ing? [*If food is not important, what is?*]

BELLYFULL sb dial. A kind of cake.

1941 in HPJ, Grato: A white oblong cake, perhaps the same as bellyfull.

BELLY-GOD sb dial; cf *OED belly-god* 1, →1818; prob infl by *belagot*—see 4. A glutton.

1943 *GL* StT, Belly-god, A greedy person. 1956 Mc Man /im a beligad/.

BELLY-GUT see *belagot*.

BELLY-HOT, BELLY-HURT see *belihat*.

BELLY-LICK sb & vb dial; <*belly*+LICK. A style of dancing in which the partners rub their abdomens together. Also called MATTIE-BELLY. *BL G*

1952 FGC StAnn [Song:] Belly lik! 1960 LeP Kgn.

BELLY-WOMAN sb dial; <BELLY sb 1 +*woman.*

1. A pregnant woman. *BL*

1834 Lewis (1845) 124, *Their* title in Jamaica is rather coarse, but very expressive. I asked Cubina one day 'Who was that woman with a basket on her head?' 'Massa,' he answered, 'that one belly-woman going to sell provisions at the Bay..' It afterwards appeared that she was one of those females..in an interesting situation, and who, in consequence, were discharged from all severe labour; *ibid* 128. 1956 Mc Man /belihuman/.

2. Transf: a cutlass with a well-rounded blade.

1958 DeC StC /beliuman/ a cutlass (the Mother Thomas cutlass, so called because of its pregnant shape).

BELLY-WORD sb dial. A thing not spoken, kept within oneself; a secret.

1924 Beckwith 102 [A mother advising her daughter:] De firs' time you get a husban' you tell him all yo' belly-word? Save somet'ing!

BELLY-WORK /beli-wok/ sb dial; cf *EDD Belly-wark* sb 1, 'Gripes, colic'. Northern. See also WORK (ONE'S) BELLY. Diarrhoea.

1943 *GL* Clar, Belly work. *BL G T*

bem-bem /bem-bem/ sb dial; prob hypocoristic dimin of *belly*, iterated; cf Engl *tummy, tum-tum* <*stomach.* Used with children: stomach, belly.

1943 *GL* Kgn, Bem bem, stomach. 1955 LeP StE (Eld). 1956 Mc Man, StJ /yu bém-bem fúl/ *Your stomach's full.*

BEN vbl particle dial; <Engl *been* pa ppl, either as an independent development, or more prob from the Engl dial use of *been* (derived elliptically from *has been, have been*) in the sense of *was, were.* Though hardly recorded in any of the dictionaries consulted (*EDD* alone has an example, BE VII 2, from the Isle of Wight), this use of *been* is familiar in Engl and US dialect, e.g. *Where you been? I been eatin' me dinner. Now you been an' gorn an' done it—the boss been askin' for you.* Var forms in Ja are *ban, bin, en, hin,* MIN, *n,* WEN, qv as separate entries. *BA G* Tobago

1. Used without any other verb: was, were.

1954 LeP StE (Eld), She ben a good gal one time, *She was a good girl once.* 1957 JN Tre, The pickney jump up and glad to see me—them ben in a shop, *The children jumped up and were glad to see me—they were in a shop.*

2. As auxiliary to another verb to express past time: did (+infin), has or have (+past pple), was (+pres pple or its equivalent; see A[5], DA[3]), or simply the past tense of the other verb. (Cf *bena*[3].)

1868 Russell 16, The past tense is represented by the past participle of the verb to be *ben* (been); thus, Me ben tell you..*Ibid* 14, De fella dat ben tak de money sick. 1877 Murray *Feedin' 'Perrit* 15, Rankine kill a 'plendid turckle dis mornin'..ef I did hab money I mus' a ben hab a dish. [*If I had had money, I certainly should have had a dish.*] *Ibid* 16, Wha mek you ben ax me? [*Why did you ask me?*] 1943 *GL* Reported from 11 parishes. 1956 DeC /shi no hin kom ya/ *She hasn't been here.* 1957 JN Tre, The Mail—it ban tap a one tree an you ben give the man one orange, *The Mail stopped at a tree and you gave the man an orange.*

3. Combined with (and preceding) A[5], DA[3], FI[3], or DE[4] to show durative or progressive action in the past.

1837 Sterne 16, They come an call me; me been da sleep. [*I was sleeping.*] 1954 LeP StE (Eld), John an some more o'dem ben a it mango under de tree, *John and some others were eating mangoes under the tree.* 1956 Mc StE (Accom) /bot hou mi han ben a pien mi yeside, mi no ben kom/ *But because my hand was hurting me (so much) yesterday, I didn't come.* 1957 DeC gen /dem no wan him fi ben fi kom/ *They didn't want him to have come,* they were sorry that he had come.

bena /bena/ sb[1] dial; perh for *bender,* that which bends or is bent; cf *DOST bend* v 1 b, to cock or make ready for firing.

1956 Mc Port /bena/ a bird trap.

bena /bena/ sb[2] dial; prob <*bender.*

1956 Mc Man /uol béna/ an old, stooped person.

BENA see BEN 2. This form is frequently used by dialect writers for *ben a*; it is justified by the fact that *a* joins itself prosodically more often to *ben* than to the following verb. The same is true of the variants of *ben*: *bina, ena, wena,* etc. *G* Tobago

[**BENACA** imp dial; <Sp *ven acá,* Come here! An expression consciously foreign, affected by Jamaican labourers who have been in Panama, Cuba, etc. *BL*

1943 *GL* Kgn, Benaca, Come here!]

BENARE, BENARI see *bineri.*

BENCH DRUM sb dial; so called from its shape.

1837 Belisario Expl to Plate 3, The small square wooden frame, over which a goat's skin is tightly strained, is termed a 'Gumbay', 'Box', or 'Bench-drum', and by being briskly struck several times in quick succession with one hand, and once only with the other, produces a monotonous sound with but little vibration. [1913 Astley Clerk 20, repeating Belisario.]

BENDER sb dial arch or obs; 1790 bender, 1868 benta; <Twi *ɔ-bɛntá,* or some related dial form, infl by Engl *bend.* Also *SC benta.*

1790 Beckford I 216, The bender is an instrument upon which the Whydaw negroes, I believe, in particular excel. It is made of a bent stick, the ends of which are restrained in this direction by a slip of dried grass; the upper part of which is gently compressed between the lips, and to which the breath gives a soft and pleasing vibration; and the other end is graduated by a slender stick that beats upon the nerve, if I may so express it, and confines the natural acuteness of the sound, and thus together produce a trembling, a querulous, and a delightful harmony; *ibid* II 387, The bender..of which I have before spoken (with the omission however of a slender stick which the player..presses to the string a little below his mouth, to graduate the vibration). 1868 Russell 6, *Benta,* A rude musical instrument. 1929 Beckwith 211 (refers to earlier writers).

BENDS sb pl dial; cf *OED bend sb*[1] 2, and *band sb*[2] 9. The 'ribbon board' fastened outside the upper edge of a dugout canoe, below the gunwale.

1952 FGC Clar, StM.

BENEBA(H) pers name dial; <Twi *Àbẽnãã,* or related dial form. The DAY NAME given to a female child born on Tuesday; now almost extinct as such.

1877 Murray *Feedin' 'Perrit* 6, A little girl named 'Benebah'.

BENEFIT sb dial; cf *OED benefit sb* 3. In concrete and specific sense: the water in which any food (but esp banana) has been boiled.

1943 *GL* Kgn, Benefit, bannana water. 1956 Mc Port /benifit/ the water bananas have been boiled in, used as a healthful beverage, 1959 DeC gen.

BENG int dial; prob <Pg *bem* [bɛŋ], well, right, just, exactly.

1943 *GL* StM, Beng, fine. 1948 HPJ *Ja Hist Rev* 281, As the tree rights itself [in the story, the hero] shouts triumphantly 'Beng! Beng!' (*Beng* is an exclamatory word for 'good'.)

bengkin see BANKING.

BENGY sb dial; etym unknown, but cf BENKIN.

1943 *GL* Kgn, Bengy, a field.

BENI, BENIE pers name; cf BENEBA.

1873 Rampini 88 [List of day-names] Tuesday.. (Female) Benie, handsome. 1943 *GL* Kgn, Beni, name of a female born on Friday [evidently an error for Tuesday].

BENIERIE see *binieri*.

BEN JONSON DAY sb gen; perh <BANIAN DAY. (There may however be some connection with the story often related in slaving annals of one Ben Jonson, a negro slave-merchant on the West African coast in the 18th cent, who, having kidnapped and sold a young girl into slavery, was in turn kidnapped by her brothers, who then took him to the slave-ship and exchanged him for her.) The day before pay-day; a day of short provisions and austerity; a day when the prospect of life is unpleasant; a day of reckoning.

1943 *GL* Kgn, Ben gaunson day, Friday. 1954 LeP StAnd (From a number of informants). 1955 HPJ, Likely used by educated classes as well as dialect speakers. A beggar will be told, 'This is Ben Johnson day'—there is no money. Bank clerks used to call the 15th and last days of the month 'Johnson days' because they were days of reckoning.

BENKIN see BANKING.

BENTA see BENDER.

benta /bénta/ vb dial; <*venture*. To venture; to undertake something hazardous.

1943 *GL* Kgn, Man, Port, StAnn, StT. 1956 Mc Man /mi en waan go in a di waata bot mi kudn benta/ *I wanted to go into the water but I didn't dare; ibid* /mi kudn benta him/ *I didn't dare take him on* (in a fight).

bentasam adj dial; <*venturesome*; cf prec.

1. Ready to dare or to risk trouble.

1943 *GL* Kgn, Bentasam, troublesome; StAnd, Bentasom, venturesome.

2. Interfering, meddlesome.

1955 LeP StAnn, Bentasom in people's business, to meddle or interfere.

berampa see *barampa* 2.

BEREN, BERIN, beri-in see BURYING.

BERKSHIRE (HOG) /boksha/ sb dial. See quots.

1956 Mc Man, Berkshire hog, ugly, ill-featured. 1958 DeC common /boksha, boksha haag/ a 'pet' name (inoffensive) for a very black man.

BERMUDA GRASS see BAHAMA GRASS.

BERMUDA LOGWOOD sb; from its resemblance to logwood; the association with Bermuda is unexplained. The tree *Pithecellobium dulce*, and the closely related *P. unguis-cati*. Also called BREAD-AND-CHEESE.

1943 *NHN* I 11 20, These interesting trees are called by various names; common ones are 'Bread-and-Cheese', 'Black-Bead Shrub', 'Bermuda Logwood' and 'Cat's Claws'. The scientific name is Pithecolobium, and there are two kinds—..a tall tree..[and] a shrub..This latter form has become very popular as a hedge plant.

BERMUDAS CEDAR sb bot; cf *ODS Juniperus bermudiana* 1829→.

1756 Browne 362, Juniperus 1..The *Bermudas* Cedar.

BERMUDIAN GRUNT sb dial; cf *OED Bermudian*. A variety of the GRUNT fish.

1952 FGC West /bumúujan/ grunt.

berrin see BURYING.

BERSHEER see BUSHA.

BERTISS sb dial vulg; <*bati* or *buttocks*.

1943 *GL* StM, Bertiss, rump.

BESIDEN adv dial; <*beside* + *-n* suffix[1]. Besides.

1941 Kirkpatrick 38, Besiden me an' you know say muss muss cyan run 'pon grass bockle. [*Besides, you and I know that mice can run on broken glass.*]

besis /bésis/ adj dial; <Engl dial *bestest*. The very best; see quots. *BL G*

1943 *GL* StJ, Bestest. 1956 Mc Man, 'refers to conduct —means orderly, well-behaved'.

BESSE see BISSY.

BESSY sb dial; cf *EDD Bessy* sb[1]; poss also *Besom* sb[3]. Used epithetically (as in Great Britain and US) to imply affection or amused contempt: One who or that which exhibits certain aspects of common femininity.

1. A busybody who always puts in an appearance at public functions: cf BESSY KEEP-UP, BURYING BESSY, WEDDING BESSY, etc.

2. One who juts or bobs the bottom in stooping: cf BESSY DOWN, BESSY KICKUP, etc.

3. In other cpds, the names of birds, fish, etc.: BANANA BESSY, BESSY BIRD, BESSY COCKBURN, BESSY KREKRE, BUNGO-BESSY, etc.

BESSY BIRD sb dial; cf BESSY 3. The BANANA QUIT.

BESSY COBAN sb dial; cf BESSY 3; *Coban* may represent the name Coburn, or Cockburn.

1956 Jeffrey-Smith 71 (see quot under BANANA QUIT).

BESSY COCKBURN sb dial; cf BESSY 3, *Cockburn*, a surname, prob also puns on the common Jamaican use of *cock*, to stick up, since the fish has a 'high forehead'. A fish: see quot.

1892 Cockrell index, Bessy Cockburn = High forehead, *Vomer setipinnis*, *Selene argentea*.

BESSY CORCA sb dial; cf BESSY 3; *corca* prob represents CACA. A fish: see quots.

1892 Cockrell index, Bessy corca, *Monacanthus pardalis*. 1899 *Jnl Inst Ja* 614, *Monacanthus vetula*.

BESSY DOWN vb phr dial; from a ring game: see quot 1922. To bend or stoop. *BA BL G*

1922 Beckwith 53–4, Bessie Down. The players form a big ring with one in the center, and all sing. During the first four lines the one in the center claps time to the song. At 'Bessie down', she goes to each player in turn and places her hands on her shoulders. The player obeys the words of the song by crouching. At the next round they sing 'Bessie up' until all are standing again. 1943 *GL*, Bessy down, stoop down.

BESSY GOOBER sb dial; prob a var of BESSY COBAN—cf BESSY 3. The BANANA QUIT.

1935 HPJ, Bessy Goober: A bird. Beeny quit.

BESSY GROUPER sb dial; cf BESSY 2, 3 and GROUPER.

1956 Mc, A small mud fish.

BESSY KEEP-UP sb dial; cf BESSY 1.

1956 Mc Man /besi kip-op/ A child who is not allowed to mix with others.

BESSY KICK-UP sb dial; cf BESSY 2 and *OED Kick-up*. A bird which flirts or bobs its tail as it walks: see quots; also called BESSY SHAKE-UP, MARY SHAKEWELL, WHITEBELLY MAID, etc.

1847 Gosse 151, Water Thrush. *Bessy Kick-up—River pink..Seiurus Noveboracensis.* 1952 FGC Han, Bessy Kick-up—chirps as it moves, and kicks up; it says /bèsi kíkop/; also StM, StT.

BESSY KREKRE /bési krékre/ sb dial; < BESSY 3 + ? var of *kreng-kreng*.

1952 FGC Man, Apparently the name in Goory, Manchester, for COGWOOD, a very tough, crossgrained tree.

BESSY SHAKE-UP sb dial; cf BESSY 2. BESSY KICK-UP.

1952 FGC Man /bèsi shíekop/ 'shake itself when it walk —like dem boasy lady shake up dem hip'. 1956 Jeffrey-Smith 67, Most local names are derived from some characteristic call..or from a particular trait, as for example hopping dick, Bessie kick-up (though shake-up is even more expressive).

beta /béta/ sb dial; < Hindi *beṭā*, son. A little boy. (Known but not much used outside East Indian communities.) Cf *beti*. *BL G T*

1943 *GL* Clar, Beta..little boy (Indian).

beta see BETTER. Also s *beta no de*.

beti /béti/ sb dial; < Hindi *beṭi*, daughter. A little girl. (Chiefly among East Indians; the word is prob understood as the personal name Betty.) *G T*

1943 *GL* Clar, Beti, little girl; Kgn, Indians..Betty, A young girl.

BETTER /beta/ vb dial. To make someone ill 'get better'; to cure. Cf WELL vb. *G*

1956 Mc StE (Accom) /a simpl man gi him simpl ting an beta him/.

BEVERAGE /bébrij, brébij, bér-rij, bŕ-bij/ sb; cf *OED* 4b 'West Indian term for lemonade' 1834; *DAE* 1800, 1885. (The general Engl sense is current; the specifically US and WI sense is now chiefly dial in Ja.) See quots. *G*

[1657 Ligon 33, The eighth sort of drink is Beveridge, made of spring water, white sugar, and juyce of Orenges, and this is not onely pleasant but wholesome.] 1834 Scott (1859) 389, The bottle of Lemonade or Beverage as it is called in Jamaica. 1873 Rampini 165, A host of 'beverages' of which not the least acceptable was sweetened lime-juice and water, with just a soupcon of nutmeg and perhaps a teaspoonful of old rum to qualify the whole. 1893 Sullivan 114, New sugar..Mixed with water to which a squeeze of lime-juice has been added, they call it either 'cool drink' or 'beverage'. 1943 *GL* StJ, Bebridge, a drink made from sugar and water. 1956 Mc StE (Accom) /ber-rij, br-bij/ lime juice with new sugar and water. [1958 DeC Port /brebij/ aerated water.]

BEX /beks/ vb, ppl adj, and vbl sb dial; < *vex, vexed, vexing*. To anger, to be or become angry; angry; anger. (The senses are not always distinct.) See VEX. *BL G N*

1877 Murray *Kittle* 7, I don't know *how* to bex wid Tom. De boy sabe me life, else I would really bex wid him. *Ibid* 26, Ef him no been taste dis pork meat ya, it would a mek ebery body sick de bex him been da go bex [*If he had not had a helping of this pork meat here, it would have made everybody sick, the vexation with which he would have become vexed*]. 1896 Bates 122, When Ratta see dat, him bex..Anancy was mad bex. 1950 Pioneer 36, Wasp get bex an sey..him wi teck up de challenge. 1956 Mc /beks/ angry, annoyed. Also reduplicated: /beksbeks/.

BEYACCA /béyaka, bíaka, beyuka/ sb dial; etym unknown. (Derivation from Amer Sp *bejuco* /behúuko/ is phonetically unlikely—nor is the sense close.) Prob related to YACCA. The name of at least two species of *Sapium*: *cuneatum* and *jamaicense*, also called respectively BLIND-EYE and CANDLEWOOD.

[1909 Harris 300, BLIND-EYE or YUCCO (*Sapium cuneatum*, Griseb.). This tree appears to be found only in the western end of the island. It yields a valuable, lasting wood.] 1941 Swabey 14, BLIND-EYE—(Yucca, Beyacca, Gum tree, Milkwood, Cantu, Cantoo). *Sapium jamaicense.* 1952 FGC StAnn, Beyucca, = burn-eye, blind-eye, torchwood, cantu, candlewood; StE /bíaka/ used for fence-post; Tre /béyaka/ beyacca, 'the StE word for candlewood'.

beyaka, BEYUCCA see prec.

B. H. CANE sb; abbr for *Barbados Hybrid cane*. A variety of sugar-cane.

1952 FGC Port, StJ, B.H. cane.

biah see BYA.

biaka see BEYACCA.

BIB sb dial; cf *OED bib sb*[1] b, c. An apron. (Not a baby's bib, which is MOUTH-WATER.)

1956 Mc Clar, Kgn, Man; StAnd, Bib, shoemaker's apron.

bibi /bibi, biibi/ sb dial; etym uncert—cf *OED beebee* < Urdu *bībī*, lady..Now..applied to Englishwomen of lower rank, to a (native) mistress, etc.; cf also Fante *abɛbɛ*, pet, favourite, and Fr *bébé* (often pron in Engl /biibii/), baby, darling.

1. Mistress, sweetheart.

1943 *GL* StT, Bibi, mistress. 1956 Mc Man /im bibi/ his mistress.

2. An affectionate term of address to a friend, to a child, etc.; darling.

1956 Mc StAnd /kóm ya bíibi/ *Come here, dear.*

BIBLE POINTER sb dial. A preacher's assistant, at revivalist and similar meetings, who reads out the Bible text which the preacher then expounds.

1953 Moore 112, Bible-pointer, A woman who reads the psalms of a revival ceremony.

bibling sb dial; var of BIMBLING.

1959 DeC Han /bibling/ the tall barge fruit (i.e. *Averrhoa bilimbi*). [*Sic.* See *baaj*.]

BICHE, BICHY (TREE) see BISSY.

BICKLA sb dial; prob < **bittler*, Sc and N-Country form of **beetler* < *beetle* v, to beat, pound [cloth, in bleaching or washing]. Cf *EDD*.

1943 *GL* Port, Bickla, scrubbing board.

BICKLE, BITTLE /bíkl, bítl, víkl/ sb dial; < *victuals* (see Introd, Phonol). s GROUND~. Food of any kind, though sometimes a distinction is made between /bíkl/ = ground-provisions, and /sáalting/ = preserved meat and fish. Cf /grong-bikl/. /bikl/ is a more refined word than /nínyàm/ but less so than *food*. *BL G*

1868 *TRSAA* 1 65, One rich lady..got one big pen an' plenty ob bittle. 1877 Murray *Feedin' 'Perrit* 4, I carry my biscuit, I carry my candle, I eben carry boil bittle in dere. 1890 Thomas 69, Well, if you plant bittle (victuals —meaning ground provisions) here Monday, it bear Tuesday. 1943 *GL* general, Bickle, bittle. 1952 FGC StJ, StM /bikl/; West /bitl/. 1956 Mc Port /bikl, vikl/ used of anything eaten.

BICKLE-KIN sb dial; <BICKLE+*skin*. The skin of ground-provisions, etc.

1943 *GL* StAnd, Bickle kin, food skin.

BICYCLE-SKATE sb dial. See quot.

1958 LeP StAnd, Bicycle-skate, a name for the familiar home-made 'scooters' used by boys, made of rough wood and old car bearings.

bie see BEAR.

biebi see BABY.

bied see BATHE, BEARD.

BIEG see BIGE.

BIEHU see BAYHOO.

bielo krab /bíelo, bíero/ sb dial; origin unknown; but cf Sp *pelo*, hair. A crab that inhabits mangrove marshes and has hair on its feet.

1952 FGC Han /bielo krab/; StC /belo krab/ have hair on foot, live in mangro; back broad, round, have two color; StJ /biero, bíelo/ Spanish, have hair on toes, live in mangro, in marosh.

biema (grass) see BAHAMA GRASS.

biero see *bielo krab*.

BIEYA see BYA.

BIF adj dial; cf *ODS biff*, to hit, strike; the weight is perh suggested by the sound of a heavy blow.

1943 *GL* Tre, Bif, heavy.

BIG-AND-SO-SO adj and sb dial; *big*+*and* +SO-SO.

A. adj: Not very good despite the large size; large but of common quality.

1942 Bennett 4, She musa tink me fool. Cause me soh big an so-soh She no tink me wen go a school.

B. sb: Absolute use of the adjective: the name of a variety of mango that is large but has little flavour.

1949 U.Newton v 7, You know the mango they call Big-and-So-So?

BIG BED, BIG SIZE BED sb dial. A double bed. *G*

1955 LeP Man, Big bed, bed big enough for two; StAnn, Big size bed, bed big enough for two persons.

BIG-BELLY adj dial. Greedy. s. *BL G*

1925 Beckwith 81 [Prov:] Man coax you fe buy big belly horse, no help you fe cut grass.

BIG-BIG adj dial; iteration of *big*. Very large. Cf BE-BE. *BL*

1877 Murray *Kittle* 22, All gentlemen wid dem big big estate. c 1951 [Song:] Big-big Sambo Gal.

BIG-BUMP sb dial. A variety of sugar-cane having very large joints.

1959 DeC StJ /big-bomp/ a kind of cane.

BIG-COPPER sb dial.

1943 *GL* StC, Big copper, a name for a copper penny. ['Coppers' includes pence, half-pence and farthings.]

BIG DADDY POT sb dial. A very large cooking-pot.

1956 Mc StAnd /bélagot/ Big Daddy pot.

BIGE /baig/ sb dial; dial sp and pron of *bag*—one of a small group preserving an archaic form (cf HIGE, RIGE), the regular pronunciation being /bag/. A bag or anything similar; cf NATTA-BIGE. *G*

1907 Jekyll 228 [Song:] Wrap up in a crocus beig In a Sandy Hill. *Ibid* 30, Note: *Huyg* for Hag, as they say *buyg* for bag. . The sound will be best understood from the second example. Say *buy* and put a hard *g* after it. 1935 HPJ [Prov:] Empty bige cyan 'tan' up; only in proverbs and in folk tales. 1943 *GL* Kgn, Bige, bag (g hard); Kgn, Bieg, bag. 1956 Mc Man /baig/.

bigens /bigéns/ conj dial; prob <*by*+*gainst*. Cf also BECOUNT.

1. By the time (that). (*OED against*, B. *conj* or *conj advb b.* →1848.)

1943 *GL* Tre, Begense, by the time. 1956 JB StAnd /bigéns yu don de mi wi rédi/ *By the time you've finished I'll be ready.* 1958 LeP StAnd /bigens yu kom bak mi wi don/ *By the time you come back I'll have finished.*

2. In preparation for. (*OED against*, *prep* 18, →1875.)

1961 R. M. Murray, see SPLENDACIOUS.

BIG-EYE adj dial; cf 1949 Turner 233, interpreting Gullah 'big eye' (covetous) as a trans of Ibo *aɲa uku* 'covetous', lit 'eye big'. Greedy, covetous, selfish. *BL G*

1868 Russell 12, Big-eye people nubba is fe satisfy in dis wol. 1873 Rampini 87, 'Big-eye' is said of anyone who is greedy or covetous.

BIG-FAMILY sb dial. A tree with multiple trunks: see quots.

1943 *NHN* II 53, *Coccoloba krugii*—Big Family. This species branches from the roots giving rise to the local name. 1957 Howard 92, Big Family, Crabwood, *Coccoloba krugii*.

BIG FINGER /bìg-fíngga/ sb dial; by analogy with *big-toe* or contrast with LITTLE FINGER. The thumb. Cf BIG TUMPY. *G*

1943 *GL* Tre, Big finger, the thumb. 1950 Pioneer 46, Tom stop suck him big finga. 1952 FGC Man /big fingga/. 1956 Mc Man, StAnd /big finga/.

BIG-FOOT sb dial. A type of elephantiasis; cf also BIG-LEG. *G*

1820 Thomson 138, *The big foot* is very often observed to attack the offspring of such parents [*sc* those who had COCOBAY] after the age of puberty. I never heard of one who had got the elephantiasis before that period. 1956 Mc StE, see THOMAS MASU.

BIG FURUH (BIRD) sb dial; perh <*vireo*; but cf Sranan (Surinam) *foeloe* <*fowl*. A local name for *Vireo osburni*; cf LITTLE FURUH (BIRD).

1936 Bond 303, Blue Mountain Vireo (*Vireo osburni*). . 'Big Furuh Bird. .' *Range*:—Jamaica. 1949 *NHN* IV 27, Big Furuh. 1956 Jeffrey-Smith 50, Big Furuh Bird.

BIG GANG sb dial. The chief or main gang of cane-field workers. Cf GREAT GANG.

1788 Beckford 46, They [the tiers who tie the canes into bundles] are too weak for the labours of the big gang.

BIG GILL /bíg-jíl/ sb dial; by contrast with LITTLE GILL. Cf *OED gill sb*[3], 1, 'A measure for liquids, containing one-fourth of a standard pint. In many districts the gill is equivalent to a half-pint, the quarter-pint being called a *jack*'. *EDD*, GILL sb[7], one-quarter pint, but also very freq (esp N-Country) one-half pint, and occas a pint or quart. A measure of quantity = the standard *gill*, one-fourth of a pint.

1942 Bennett 9, An' yuh kean get gill a ackee Till yuh call fe big-gill ile. 1943 *GL* Kgn, Big gill, ¼ pint; Big Jill, gill. 1953 Murray 11, One big gill a coconut ile. . Big gill, One quarter pint.

BIGGY sb dial; <*big* + *-y*.

1959 DeC Tre /bigi/ noun meaning a man who is big and lazy.

BIG-HEAD adj dial; <*big-headed*. Big-headed—used in a somewhat depreciatory sense; cf LOGGERHEAD. *BL*

1957 JN StM, Every minute when me in a school one bighead boy a tump me because me dont lend him me pencil.

BIG-HEAD TOM-FOOL see BIG TOM-FOOL.

BIG-LEG sb; cf BIG-FOOT. Elephantiasis.

1820 Thomson 131, The elephantiasis or big leg.

BIG LUNATIC sb dial.

1955 LeP StAnn, Big lunatic, big, oafish man.

BIG MAN sb dial; cf *OED big* 3b. An adult man, grown man. *BL G*

1924 Beckwith 276, He says, 'From the day I'm born, never see a big man call me name, much more a little boy!'

BIG-MASSA sb dial; <*big* + MASSA; cf OLD-MASSA. God.

1910 Anderson-Cundall 23 [Prov:] Big Massa gib ebery man him own mout'-water fe swaller him own duckanoo. 1943 *GL* StC, Big massa, God. 1945 Jacobs 95, 'Gara-mighty-in-a-Tap' or 'Big Massa'.

BIGNADOW see next.

bignaduo sb dial; < /big-no-duo/ *big as a door* —cf NO, adv. See quots.

1910 Anderson-Cundall 8 [Prov:] Big no' door, no hab coco-head a barrel. Big no door = a bumptious person. 1943 *GL* Kgn, Bigmadow [*sic*], one who boast [*sic*]; Port, Bignadow, proud. 1958 DeC StAnd /bignadùo/ somebody who is putting on airs, going up in the world and displaying foolish and false pride.

BIG-PEOPLE sb chiefly dial. Adults. *BL G*

1952 FGC Port; (StAnd, remembered from c 1915). 1958 *Public Opinion* 27 Dec. 4, People were going in and coming out with presents. Big people and little children.

BIG PEPPER sb dial. The large, sweet Capsicum pepper (in contrast to the much smaller hot peppers such as bird-pepper or Scotch-bonnet).

1955 LeP StAnn, Big pepper, sweet pepper.

BIG SIZE BED see BIG BED.

BIG-SOMEBODY /bíg-sm-ádi/ sb dial. An adult or adults.

c 1915→ FGC StAnd and elsewhere, e.g. in the phrase /píkni and bíg-sm-ádi/ *Children and grown-ups*. 1952 FGC StM, Hard-ears = stubborn—a child or big-somebody.

BIG-THUMB, big-tom see BIG-TUM.

BIG TOM-FOOL sb dial. A bird; see quots.

1936 Bond 249, *Myiarchus validus*..Local names:—Big Tom Fool; Red Tom Fool; Big-head Tom Fool.. Range:—Jamaica. 1956 Jeffrey-Smith 48.

BIG-TREE sb attrib dial; <BIG-TREE BOY. Violent, bullying, gangsterish.

1941 Kirkpatrick 7, Dem is mekin' it dem job fe protec' we 'gains' any big tree idea 'Itler [Hitler] 'ave in 'im 'ead. 1959 DeC Kgn /big trii taak/ bullying talk.

BIG-TREE BOY, BIG-TREE MAN sb dial slang. One of the men who idle about (formerly haunting a large banyan tree in Victoria Park, Kingston) and take occasional jobs as porters, etc.

1912 McK *Ballads* 49, De Syrian grew astonished as he looked upon his load, Which de whoppin' big-tree boy had tumbled in de middle road. [Note:] Big-tree. A certain big tree in Kingston is the resort of idlers and vicious characters. 1958 *Public Opinion* [Title of serial:] Sam, the 'Big Tree' Man.

BIG TUM, BIG TUMPY sb dial; prob <*big* + *thumb* (/tom/), *stumpy*, cf LICKPOT, TUMPA.

1956 Mc StAnd /big tompi/ thumb. *BL G*

BIG-VOICE sb dial. The SEWI-SEWI, a small bird that is not often seen but has a conspicuous song.

1952 FGC StM.

BIG WINKY sb dial; <*big* + WINKY. [This is something of a misnomer, since this insect is distinctly different from the WINKY.] The PEENY or CANDLEFLY.

1907 Jekyll 89, The insect, which is the size of a cockchafer but rather longer, is commonly called Big Winky or Peeny.

BIG YARD sb dial or slang; <*big* + YARD. (Cf US slang *big house*.)

1943 *GL* StM, Big yard, prison.

bii-bii see BEE-BEE; CAMPHOR BUSH.

biini see BEENY.

bikaan(g) see BECAUSEN.

bikaa(z) see BECAUSE. *N*

bikaazin, bikaazn see BECAUSEN.

bikl, BIK'L see BICKLE.

BILAH SONG sb dial; Ko *mbila*, call or Kimbundu *mbila*, grave, sepulchre. A type of song sung at *kumuna* and other such ceremonies.

1953 Moore 173, It should be emphasized that *bilah* songs are in a dialect which is primarily English, but Jamaica country songs are in a language referred to, in this area [StT], as *african*. [Moore seems to have reversed the names. In his Appendix III he lists the names of 52 bilah songs.]

BILGE-WATER TREE sb obs. See quot.

1814 Lunan I 130, Cabbage Bark Tree. Geoffroya.. Inermis..There are two species, one of which is a native of Jamaica..This tree (which is called sometimes the *bilge-water tree*, from its disagreeable smell).

BILIMBI see BIMBLING (PLUM).

BILIOUS /bílyas/ sb dial; conversion of adj to sb (cf *DAE* 1870, as an abbr of *bilious fever*). Biliousness, indigestion. *BL G*

1952 FGC StE, Crack-saw tree is /gud fi bilyas/; StT, The monkey-fiddle plant is 'good for bilious'.

BILIOUS FEVER sb obs; cf *DAE* 1779→. Yellow fever.

1750 Williams i, The bilious, or yellow Fever, so called from the yellow appearance of the skin. *Ibid* iii, That no one hath yet endeavoured to explain to the Public the Nature and Causes of this fatal bilious, or yellow Fever of Jamaica, is somewhat Strange. 1808 Stewart 26, Bilious fever.

BILL /bil/ sb, chiefly dial; cf *OED bill sb*[1] 4. Specifically: the type of cutlass or MACHETE used for cutting cane, having a sharp hook at the end; also generically: any cutlass or machete. (Uses in early accounts of Jamaica—1661 Hickeringill 59, 1672 Blome 16—are in the English sense.) See also BILL-HOOK, CANE-BILL, HOOK-BILL, SPANISH BILL, etc. *BA G*

1739 Leslie 335 [The canes] are cut up with a Bill..(for they are too big to be mow'd with a Scythe, or cut with a Hook). 1952 FGC StM /bil/ short, cuts both sides, round handle, sharper than cutlass and broader. 1956 Mc Man, StC, StT, Bill, a machete; broad stumpy blade with a hook at one end and narrowing at the handle. Used esp to cut cane.

BILL vb, chiefly dial; <*bill* v^1 (*OED* last quot is 1833 below). Often const *down*. *G*

1. To clear (land, a path, etc.) by cutting down the bush or undergrowth.

1795 *Braco* 23 July, Great and Small Gangs cleaning and billing down the Guinea grass pasture. 1823 Roughley 307, If the land has any underwood upon it, it should be cut down..then billed down and hoed off from bushes and weeds. 1833 Scott II 372, A small footpath that had been billed in the bush. 1954 LeP StE, Bill, to clear the land by cutting bush. 1956 Mc StT, Bill, to clear land.

2. To cut low to the ground, esp cane or grass, with a bill (i.e. cutlass or machete).

1823 Roughley 284, All grass hoed off, six feet distance from the cane plants, and it should be billed down to 30 feet distance from it; so that rats will not have an asylum close to the plant canes. 1943 GL StT, Bill, to mow with a cutlass. 1956 Mc Man /im bil doun di graas/.

BILLAGUT see *belagot.*

BILL-BIRD sb obs; <*bill* (*OED* sb^2) +*bird.* An unidentified bird; evid one with a prominent beak. *N*=*toucan.*

1740 Importance 38, Among the curious are Flamingos, Corresoes, Cardinal Birds, Bill-Birds..Canary birds.

BILL-HOOK sb dial; *OED* →1857, 'A heavy thick knife or chopper'.

1958 DeC StAnd /bil huk/ a cutlass.

BILLY GREEN sb dial. The bird *Myiarchus stolidus.*

1956 Jeffrey-Smith 49, see RICKY-TEE.

bim, bimbim sb dial; abbr form of *bima*, also iterated. Occas vars of *bima.*

1956 Mc Man /bim/ also /bimbim/ a sore leg.

bima /bima/ sb dial; prob African, cf Ewe *abimo*, surface of a wound, Mende *gbalema*, a sore, an ulcer. Cf TIMBIM.

1. An old sore or ulcer on the foot or leg which does not heal easily.

1943 *GL* Kgn, Bimma, old sore (ulcer). 1955 FGC Man /bimà/ on foot; hard to heal.

2. A sore foot or leg.

1956 Mc Man /énibadi hav súo fút, kaal it bíma—'go bíed yu bíma'/ *If anybody has a sore leg, it's called 'bima' —'go and bathe your bima'.* StAnd /bima/ an enlarged foot.

3. A person with a leg lame from sores. (Uncert.)

1956 Mc Man.

bimbim see *bim.*

bimblim see next.

BIMBLING (PLUM) /bimbling, bimblim, blimblim, blimbing/ sb; <*bilimbi* (cf *OED*).

1. The trees *Averrhoa bilimbi* and *A. carambola*, and their fruit used for preserves and pickles. (Not always distinguished from JIMBLING.) Cf *baaj.*

1811 Titford 67, Bimbling plum, Averrhoa Bilimbi.. nat. East Indles. This has been introduced into Jamaica..[It has] a five-celled pome, of an acid taste, growing on the branches or trunk. 1837 Macfadyen I 184, Bilimbi or Bimbling..A tree seldom more than 15–20 feet in height..Fruit containing a strong acid..The tree.. was brought to Jamaica in the year 1793..It is now to be met with in several parts of the Island. 1935 HPJ, Blim-blim, A fruit growing in clusters from the tree-trunk; sour; of a yellowish green; about 4 inches long. Also called bimblings, blimbing, bilimbi, etc. 1956 LeP StAnd /bimblim/. 1957 JB StAnd, Grows on a shrub; looks like a small cucumber; found mostly in StAnn.

2. The tree *Phyllanthus acidus* and its fruit, which somewhat resembles the foregoing; more often called JIMBILIN, etc.

1893 Sullivan 82, Bimblings. A sort of berry, very acid indeed. These are generally made into preserve but they take an immense amount of sugar.

BIMMA see *bima.*

bin see BEN. *G*

bina see *bin* vbl particle. *G*

binaana see BANANA in cpds.

BINARI, BINARIE see *bineri.*

BIND-PEAR /báin-píe/ sb dial; prob <*bind* (though *vine* is phonologically possible) +*pear.* A type of climbing cactus or prickly-pear having red and white blossoms and greenish fruit.

1952 FGC StAnd.

bineri /binéri/ sb dial; <*Benaria*, said to be the name of a variety of banana formerly cultivated, now rare (Mr Sullivan). [?Benares.]

1943 *GL* Kgn, Binarie, benari, banana; StAnd, Benierie; Tre, Benare. 1955 LeP StE (Eld), Binari, banana. 1959 DeC Port, StE /binéri/ banana—a general word. Found by me only in Moore Town and Accompong, and there considered a relic.

bini see BEENY, BUSINESS.

BINIY, biniz see BUSINESS.

BIRCH (GUM, TREE, WOOD) /boch, boj/ sb; <*birch.*

The tree *Bursera simaruba*, its medicinal gum, and its wood. Formerly called BALSAM TREE, TURPENTINE TREE; now also INCENSE TREE, MASTIC, MULATTO TREE, RED BIRCH, WEST-INDIAN BIRCH.

1696 Sloane 167, Terebinthus major, betulae cortice.. *The Birch Tree.* Hæc arbor ubique frequens & obvia est in Jamaica & Canbeis [*sic*] insulis. 1725 Sloane 89–90, The Birch-Tree..has..a Trunc..cover'd with a brown, red, smooth, membranaceous outward Bark, falling off in round Pieces like to that of the English Birch, whence the Name. 1756 Browne 345, Terebinthus 1..The Birch or Turpentine Tree..This tree is very common in all the sugar-islands. 1886 Hooper 29, Birch, *Bursera gummifera.* 1920 Fawcett 205–7, B. Simaruba..Red Birch..The juice forms, on inspissating, a clear transparent gum-resin, 'budge gum', of a dark green colour. 1952 FGC Man /boch wud/ used for making matches; StAnd /boj trii/; StAnn /boj gom, boj wud/ lizards can't climb it; StC /boji gom/; StE /boch gom/ for boil on skin; StM /boj gom/ has a leaf like mahogany leaf, use for toothache; StT /boch, boch wud/ use as live fence; Tre /boj waata/.

BIRD-MOUTH adj dial; <*bird-mouthed.* Having been 'mouthed' or pecked by a bird.

1946 U.Newton I 26, Then I would pick the fruits, praying that some would burst or that some would be 'bird mouth' (that is picked by birds).

BIRD PEPPER /bod, bord pepa/ sb; cf *OED* 1786→, *DAE* 1785→. A variety of *Capsicum* peppers, small and conical, growing wild but easily domesticated, much used in cookery, and much favoured by birds; see also quot 1790.

1696 Sloane 112, An solanum capsicum dictum fruticosum siliquis exiguis surrectum..*Bird Pepper.* In *Madera* Jamaica & Caribeis Insulis, sylvis, frutetis, &

sepibus ubique sponte oritur. 1756 Browne 176, Capsicum 4..Bird Pepper. All these species of the *Capsicum* or *Indian* pepper (as it is called in *America*) are cultivated, or vegetate naturally in most parts of Jamaica.. The pods of this last sort dried, and pounded with a sufficient quantity of salt, is the *Cayan pepper* or *butter* of the *West-Indians*. 1790 Moreton 95, Turkies are the most difficult to raise..a small grain of bird-pepper, that grows in the country, given to each as soon as out of the shell, is serviceable. 1814 Lunan I 94. 1913 Harris 36, Bird pepper—*Capsicum baccatum*. 1952 FGC gen /bod pepa, bord pepa/. *BL G N T*

BIRD'S EYE PEPPER sb. *BA*

1954 *FG* 469, Bird or Bird's Eye Pepper, not cultivated, but growing half-wild.

BIRD TOMATOES sb. ?Small tomatoes, analogous to bird peppers.

1952 FGC StJ /bord tumatoz/.

BIRTH NAME sb. =DAY NAME, BORN-DAY NAME.

1929 Beckwith 59, According to the old custom recorded from the African Gold Coast, every child receives at birth a name depending on the day of the week on which it is born..it would seem as if the hesitation of some to have their 'birth name' known had no other motive than a dislike of nicknames.

BIRTH-NIGHT PARTY sb dial; <*birthnight* (*OED* 1, →1849; the term is virtually out of use in England, but is kept alive by folk observances in Jamaica). See quots. *BL G*

1952 FGC StAnd /bort nait/ party—a party given on the night of a baby's birth. 1959 DeC gen, Birth-night party: On the night of the birth of a child (or if the mother is too weak, a day or so later) friends come to the yard, are received by the father (who thereby acknowledges his paternity) and visit the mother in bed with the child. Gifts may be brought, and light refreshments are usually furnished.

BIRTH-PAPER sb dial. A certificate of birth; AGE-PAPER; cf also FREE-PAPER. *BL G*

1951 FGC StAnd, Heard from a servant.

BIRTH TREE sb. See quot. Cf NATAL TREE, NAVEL-STRING TREE.

1946 Dunham 113, But here in Accompong planting the navel cord is as important as it is in other parts of Jamaica. The navel cord and after-birth are planted under a tree, usually coconut or breadfruit, and that tree belongs to the infant for the rest of his life..and it and its produce descend to his children. Sometimes the tree is provided by the parents, sometimes by godparents or other relatives or friends..While a man may have much property and several single trees in various parts of the village, he always points to his birth tree with much pride. 1959 DeC StAnd, The 'birth tree' custom is still preserved here. [Cf 1826 Williams 17, where, though the word is not used, the story is told about a slave who claimed damages of his master for cutting off a branch of a calabash tree which, the slave said, had been planted by his godfather.]

bisi see BISSY.

BISSEY see BISSY.

BISSY (NUT, TREE) /bísi, bízi/ sb, now chiefly dial; 1696→ 1835 (1954) bichy, 1740 besse, 1774 biche, 1774→ bissy, 1927→ busy, 1943 bissey, bizzy; <Twi *bisé*, Ewe *bisí*, Aky *besẽ* the kola nut and the tree bearing it. The tree *Cola acuminata*, and its nut, valued for medicinal use. *N*

1696 Sloane 154, The Bichy Tree. In agris Dom. *Bourden* plantatam hanc arborem reperi. 1725 Sloane 60–1, The *Bichy-Tree*..The Seed brought in a *Guinea* ship from that country, was here planted by Mr Goffe in Colonel Bourden's Plantation beyond Guanaboa. It is called *Bichy* by the *Coromantin* Negro's, and is both eaten and used for Physick in Pains of the Belly. 1740 Importance 31, The *Besse*. 1774 Long III 855, Dissert Fruits.. Biche, or Bissy..not yet common. 1794 Broughton 34, Bichy Tree. 1891 Fawcett 33, *Cola acuminata*..Bissy, kola, cola. Seeds used like chocolate..said to be of great dietetic value. 1927 Beckwith 13, Busy-nut (Cole). See 'Cola-nut'. 1943 *GL* Clar, StC, Bizzy Seed, Bizzy Tree; Kgn, Bissy; Tre, Bissey, the Kola nut. 1952 FGC Port /bísi, bízi/ antidote, good for malaria, high blood pressure; StAnd /bísi/ can boil tea; StAnn /bísi/ 'kola nut' is the shipping name; StE, StJ, StM, StT.

BIT /bit/ sb now dial; cf *OED Bit sb*[2] 8b 1683–1883: 'Applied in the Southern States of N. America, in the West Indies, etc., to small silver coins forming fractions of the Spanish dollar, or (when these are obsolete) to their value in current money. Last century [i.e. 18th cent] the bit was generally the old Mexican real=⅛ of a dollar or about 6½*d.* sterling; later values assigned are a half pistareen or $\frac{1}{10}$ of a dollar, $\frac{1}{16}$ of a dollar, and (in some colonies) the value of 1½*d.* sterling.' s CURRENCY. *G*

1. The values given in Jamaican citations are sometimes in terms of sterling, sometimes in local currency; thus in 1780 the bit was worth 5¼*d.* sterling, but 7½*d.* in local currency. The coin itself seems to have disappeared from circulation during the first quarter of the 19th cent; the value referred to today is uniformly 4½*d.*, currency and sterling, and seems to have been so since the mid 19th cent.

1707 Sloane lxxxv, Ground-Doves are sold for a *Bitt*, or Real a Dozen. c 1715 William May MS. letter (in Foley *The Early English Monies* 129), For we can have nothing here under a Bit, i.e. 7½d, that being the smallest coin we have. a1726 Barham (1794) 136, Ryals 'which we call in Jamaica bits' (HPJ). 1774 Long I 582–3, The foreign coins at present used here in circulation..Ryal or bit 7½d current value.. *Ibid* 589, Table VII, Old Ryal or Bit piece. 1780 *Almanack* 84, A Table of Ryals or Bits In Currency and Sterling..Currency 7½d—Sterling 5¼d + 3/7ths. 1803 Dallas I lxviii, The lowest silver coin is called a *bitt*, equal to about 5d sterling. 1808 Stewart 59, Pesterines and bitts, at 1s. 3d. and 7½d (these are rare). 1835 Senior 124, The charge is seven-pence-halfpenny (called 'a bit'). 1873 Rampini 94, Bit, fourpence halfpenny. 1943 *GL* gen, Bit, 4½d. 1952 FGC Han, StM, Bit, 4½d.

2. In combinations, of which the most common are: /bít an fípans/ = 7½*d.*; /bít an fúopans/ = 8½*d.*; /bít an kwáti/ = 6*d.*; /fúobìt/ = 1*s.*6*d.*

1943 *GL* Kgn, Bit an' fupance=8½*d.* 1949 Reid gloss, Bit-&-fippence=7½*d.* 1957 DeC StAnd /bit and kwati/ =6*d.*

bita dampas sb dial; altered form of BITTER DAMSON.

1952 FGC StM /bìta dámpas/.

bitaz-tii see BITTERS-TEA.

BIT-BIT /bítbìt/ sb dial; by iteration of *bit*, symbolizing gradual accumulation. Bit upon bit; by small instalments (quasi-adverbial).

1950 FGC [Prov:] Bit-bit mek pound.

BITCH-WHEEL sb dial slang.

1958 DeC StT /bich-wiil/ a large round boiled dumpling.

BITCHWOOD sb now dial; by assoc with DOGWOOD, which it closely resembles. A variety of *Piscidia piscipula*, once thought to be a different species ('*Piscidia carthaginensis*', Linn). See quots.

1814 Lunan I 270, Dogwood Tree. Piscidia Carthaginensis. Browne calls this the *mountain dog-wood*, and observes that it is so like the foregoing, both in appearance and smell, as well as in the grain and texture of its wood, that it is difficult to distinguish the one from the other, until the fruit is observed, which, in this, is quite compressed and plain, without wings. It grows to nearly double the size of the other, and its wood..is rather darker, but equally good..It is found plentifully in Clarendon and Vere, where it is known by the name of *bitch-wood.* 1854–5 *TJSA* I 62, Bitchwood, *P. carth.* 1864 Grisebach 781, Bitch-wood: *Lonchocarpus latifolius.* [1920 Fawcett 81 calls this Dogwood; it is closely related but perh an erroneous identification (on Grisebach's part).] 1952 FGC StT /bichwud/ a specie [*sic*] of dog-wood—same as poison dogwood.

BITE vb dial; cf *OED bite v* 9a →1637. To hurt sharply; to sting with pain. *BL G*

1907 Jekyll 76, Till hungry [=hunger] bite them they no go 'way. 1924 Beckwith 100, When de yawzy bite me, me mudder kill a cow an' tek de blood an' wash me.

BITE-A-FOOT /baita fut/ sb dial; prob <*bite* vb+A[1] I+*foot.* See quots.

1956 BLB StJ /baita fut/ lights said to be seen at night during the period preceding Christmas. So called because they move along the ground, hence are thought to be biting the feet. Believed to be ghosts. [1958 Miss McKoy, UCWI student, says they are actually a type of glow-worm, but she does not know this name. They move in a circular motion on the ground. LeP.]

BITE-AND-BLOW vb phr dial; also used as adj or sb. To blow a cool breath on the place where one is biting, so that the bite is not felt; hence symbolic of successful deceit or soothing hypocrisy. See WHITE-BELLY RAT 2.

1900 Murray, Bra Quamin..was familiarly known as 'Bite and blow Tata'. 1952 FGC StT, Charlie Price rat is bite-an'-blow.

BITING-ANTS sb dial; <*biting*+ANTS. A species of small black ant that builds its nest in the earth and bites fiercely. *BA G*

1952 FGC Han /baitn ans/ black-ants; StAnd /baitn hants/; StT /baitn ans/ live in ground, come out when there's going to be a weather, heavy rain—have wings, take them off—some black, some reddish; also Tre.

BITING-WASP sb dial.

1952 FGC Han /baitn was/ have a comb like a bee.

bitl see BICKLE.

BITTER sb see SUSUMBA.

BITTER adj dial; <*bitter*, perh also infl by Twi *bὲtεε*, weak, infirm. In the phr *bitter for the disease* [*sc* yaws]: especially susceptible or disposed toward.

1820 Thomson 86, Old and sensible negro women will tell you, that the skin of such infants [those of yawy mothers] is forever after rendered *bitter* for the disease. *Ibid* 83, The natives say the *skin is bitter for the disease,* and they regard the patient as liable to constitutional symptoms at a future period of life.

[**BITTER ASH** sb dial; cf *OED bitter-*; Barham (quoted in Lunan I 96): 'its leaves [are] like the English ash'.

In St Christopher and some of the Windward Islands: the tree in Jamaica called BITTER WOOD; recently also used in Jamaica: *Picraena excelsa.* See quots.

1774 Long III 820–1, The quassi, quashee, or Surinam bitter-wood, was first noticed at Demerara..but, after its virtues came to be published, it was likewise discovered to be indigenous to the island of St Christopher, and some of the other Caribees..It grows in the mountains, and near the sides of rivulets. It is vulgarly called, by the Negroes, the *bitter ash,* and is used by them to promote abortion. But it is likewise proved, since the white inhabitants brought it into use, to be a great specific in dropsical cases..The following is the method of administering it in practice at the Windward Islands..It is uncertain as yet, whether or not we have the same tree in this island [Jamaica]. 1791 Lindsay, quoted in Lunan I 95, The *quassia polygama,* has long been known in Jamaica..With us it is called bitter wood, and in the windward islands bitter ash. 1920 Fawcett 201, *Picraena antillana*..Bitter Ash of the lesser Antilles, included by Swartz and other authors in the above species. 1954 *WIMJ* 31, *Picraena excelsa*..Jamaica Quassia; Bitter Wood; Bitter Ash.]

BITTER-BROOM sb dial; cf *OED bitter-* and BROOM-WEED.

A weed not certainly identified; the name is used in contrast to SWEET BROOM-WEED (*Scoparia dulcis*); it may be *Corchorus siliquosus,* usually BROOM-WEED (cf Grisebach 782, 1954 *WIMJ* 32).

1952 FGC StT, Bitter-broom, tansy; good for worms in cattle; keeps off fleas.

BITTER BUSH sb chiefly dial, also attrib; <*bitter-* (*OED*) +BUSH. *G*

Any of several shrubs of the N.O. *Compositae,* valued for medicine; in particular, varieties of *Eupatorium* and *Neurolaena lobata.* A bitter infusion or TEA made of the bark and leaves is used against colds, fevers, etc.

1854–5 *TJSA* II 41 [Send to England] Leaves of the Bitter Bush, and ditto [dried specimens of the plant] so as to ascertain if it be the *Eupatorium parviflorum*? 1893 Sullivan 113, Bitter Bush Tea. 1935 HPJ, Bitter-bush. A plant about three feet high, with bitter leaves and wood; good for fever, indigestion and liver. 1936 Fawcett 174–81, *Eupatorium odoratum, E. villosum, E. triste,* Bitter Bush. *Ibid* 269, *Neurolaena lobata,* Bitter Bush. 1952 FGC Man; Han /bíta bush/ similar to JACK-IN-THE-BUSH but smaller, finer, more velvety leaves and finer flowers; same as HONEY BUSH (Cedar Valley). 1953 *WIMJ* 242; 1955 *WIMJ* 75.

BITTER CASSADA or **CASSAVA** sb; cf SWEET CASSADA. *OED* s.v. *cassava* has one quot: a1818. The variety of *Manihot utilissima* which has a bitter, poisonous juice which must be expressed before the root may be used for food. *G T*

1740 Importance 35, Secondly, the bitter Cassada, the juice of which is Poison. 1950 Pioneer 80 [Song:] A bitter Cassada kill Joe Browne. 1952 FGC gen /bíta kasáva, kasáda/: use for starch.

BITTER CUP sb. *OED* 1876 only. A cup turned from *Picraena excelsa* or similar bitter wood, which discharges some of its bitter element into water poured into it, which liquid is then drunk as a stomachic. *G*

1880 Bentley & Trimen 57, The bitter-cups now frequently sold are manufactured from quassia wood. 1944 *NHN* II 94, Bitterwood or Jamaica Quassia..has been exported..for many years..In Jamaica 'bitter cups' are made of the wood.

BITTER DAMPAS sb dial; BITTER DAMSON.

1952 FGC StM /bìta dámpas/ bitter damsel.

BITTER DAMSEL sb; by folk-etym <BITTER DAMSON. The tree *Simaruba glauca,* its wood and fruit. Also called BITTER DAMPAS, BITTER DAN, BITTER DANDISON.

1941 Swabey 8, Some woods have a characteristic bitter taste: examples are Bitterwood (Quassia) and Bitter Damsel. 1951 *Gleaner* Oct?, Bitterwood is different from bitter damsel but the difference is difficult to discern until the wood is sawn up. Often a lot of bitter damsel comes into the shoe heel factories mixed with bitterwood. 1952 FGC Han, StAnn, StE, StT, Tre /bìta dámzl/.

BITTER DAMSON sb bot; cf *OED,* no quot. The tree *Simaruba glauca,* and its plum-like fruit. It is now generally called BITTER DAMSEL.

1778 Wright, see STAVEWOOD. 1814 Lunan I 521, This tree is known in Jamaica by the name of *mountain damson, bitter damson,* or *stavewood.* 1864 Grisebach 783. 1920 Fawcett 198–9.

BITTER DAN sb dial; by folk-etym < BITTER DAMSON.

1920 Fawcett 198–9, see STAVEWOOD. 1941 Swabey 14, Bitter Damson—(Bitter dan..). *Simaruba glauca.* 1952 FGC StE /bita dán/.

BITTER DANDISON sb dial; by folk-etym < BITTER DAMSON.

1952 FGC StT, Bitter dandison.

BITTER-GOURD sb dial; cf *OED* '*Citrullus colocynthus*' only quot 1755. A wild gourd, *Lagenaria vulgaris.* (UCWI Herbarium.)

1952 FGC StAnn /bìta gúod/ runs like pumpkin; StJ, has a long neck, use for sickness—pick leaf and spread with warm oil.

BITTER JESSE (or **JESSIE**) sb dial; <*bitter-* (cf *OED*) +a familiarizing personal name. A variety of yam: BITTER YAM, HIMBA. **s.**

1952 FGC StE /bìta jési/ bears underground, like yellow-yam.

BITTER ORANGE sb. The SEVILLE or SOUR ORANGE.

1837 Macfadyen 128, Bitter or Seville orange..The sweet and the bitter Oranges are considered, by De Candolle and some others, as distinct species. This cannot in my opinion be the case. 1920 Fawcett 188, *Citrus vulgaris*.. Bitter Orange.

BITTERS-TEA sb dial; <*bitters*+TEA. A stomachic drink made by boiling the leaves of any of the plants known as 'bitters'. *BL G*

1961 BLB 6 /yes, an yu dringk likl bitaz-tii tu/.

BITTERS UP vb phr; <*bitters* sb+*up*. To fill oneself with 'bitters'—here with rum; to become drunk. *G*

1877 Murray *Feedin' 'Perrit* 7, Well, sar, I gi'e him a mackarony. Him broke way wid it sir; him 'pen de whole mackarony in a rum, an bitters up himself, bad fashun.

BITTER-SWEET ORANGE sb. A variety of *Citrus vulgaris.*

1920 Fawcett 188, The Bitter-sweet or Seville-sweet Orange is a variety the flavour of the juice being sweet and pleasantly flavoured.

BITTER-TOBACCO sb dial. A local name for *Pluchea odorata* and *P. purpurascens.*

1952 FGC StM, Bitter-tobacco, a little tree, bears a red berry—good bitters; resembles crimp-edge tobacco; =COUNTRY IBO. 1955 *WIMJ* 76, *Pluchea odorata*.. Riverside Tobacco; Bitter Tobacco; *Pluchea purpurascens*..Bitter Tobacco; Wild Tobacco.

BITTER TREE sb obs. Prob for BITTERWOOD.

1740 Importance 50, The bitter Tree, the Wood of which is as bitter as Soot, is used for Bedsteds; Buggs nor Vermin will not come near it.

BITTER WATER sb dial; cf BITTER CASSADA.

1935 HPJ, Bitter water, The poisonous fluid expressed from Cassava. *G*

BITTER-WEED sb dial. See quots.

1914 Fawcett 124, *Chenopodium ambrosioides*..Mexican Tea, Hedge Mustard, Bitter Weed. 1952 FGC StE, Bitter-weed. 1954 *WIMJ* 24, Bitter Weed..fairly commonly employed in Jamaica as a vermifuge.

BITTER-WOOD sb; <*bitter-* (cf *OED*) +*wood.* Any of various trees and shrubs whose wood, bark, or berries are bitter, and therefore useful in medicine, as vermicides, etc. *N*

1. Species of *Xylopia*; also called LANCEWOOD. (Sometimes in this sense confused—as by Barham and Long—with *Picraena excelsa*; see sense 2.) Cf *OED bitter-wood*, 'The timber of a tropical American genus of trees *Xylopia*, or the trees themselves'—no quot.

1756 Browne 250–1, *Xylopicrum?* 1..The smaller Bitter-wood. 2. The larger *Xylopicron*, or Bitter-wood.. The wood, bark, and berries have an agreeable bitter taste, not unlike that of the orange-seed. 1814 Lunan I 97, Bitterwood. *Xylopia*..1. *Muricata*..Browne calls this the *smaller bitter wood*..2. *Glabra*..Browne calls this the *larger bitter wood.* 1914 Fawcett 199, *Xylopia*.. Bitter Wood.

2. *Picraena excelsa* (the most commonly intended tree), also called BITTER ASH, JAMAICA QUASSIA.

1791 Lindsay, in Lunan I 95, The *quasia polygama* has long been known in Jamaica..With us it is called bitter wood. 1837 Macfadyen 198, *Simaruba excelsa.* Lofty Bitter-wood. 1893 Sullivan 120, To destroy Blight on Plants. Four ounces of bitterwood. 1920 Fawcett 200–1, *Picraena excelsa*..Bitter Wood, Jamaica Quassia. 1941 Swabey 14. 1944 *NHN* II 94, Bitterwood..(Picraena excelsa) has been exported..for many years..it was used as a substitute for hops [by brewers]..Its principal use today, however, is in the manufacture of insecticides.

3. Obs. *Simaruba amara,* similar to BITTER DAMSON.

1837 Macfadyen 198, Officinal Bitter-wood..*Simaruba amara.*

4. Another member of the family Simarubaceae, more commonly known as MAJOE BITTERS.

1954 *WIMJ* 21, *Picramnia antidesma*..Majoe Bitters.. Bitter Wood.

5. Applied to *Neurolaena lobata,* properly BITTER BUSH. (This appears to be an error of Fawcett's perpetuated in *WIMJ.* Fawcett (1936, top page 271) quotes Barham for support, but Barham's description of a wood used for furniture cannot apply to *N. lobata,* which is a low woodless shrub.)

1936 Fawcett 269, N. lobata..Bitter Wood, Bitter Bush. 1955 *WIMJ* 75.

BITTER-YAM sb dial; cf BITTER JESSE. A type of WILD YAM; also called HIMBA.

1952 FGC StT /bita yam/; Tre /akam/ run like bitter yam but bear seed. 1955 LeP StAnn, Bitter yam, wild yam.

BITTLE see BICKLE.

BITTOE vb dial rare; etym unknown.

1943 *GL* StT, Bittoe, sit down.

bizi see BISSY.

bizniz see BUSINESS.

BIZZY see BISSY.

blaasam see BLOSSOM.

BLACK ANANCY sb dial.

The BLACK SPIDER; evid because *anancy* usually refers to harmless spiders, and *spider* to poisonous ones, and the *black anancy* is poisonous, some feel hesitation about the term; see quots.

1952 FGC Trel /blak anaansi/ not the same as black spider, though similar; Man /blak anánsi/ lives in thrash [*sic*]; there are three different sizes of anancy—the red-spot-belly kind is an anancy; when he gets big he turns spider.

BLACK-AND-WHITE CREEPER sb ornith obs; cf *DAE* 1811 applied to *Certhia maculata.* In Gosse's use: *Mniotilta varia,* now called ANTS-BIRD, Black-and-White Warbler, etc.

1847 Gosse 134.

BLACK-AND-WHITE DANCE sb dial cant. In the terminology of revivalist cults: a memorial dance sponsored by a family for one or more of its deceased members—so called because black and white insignia are worn. Cf next.

1953 Moore 148.

BLACK-AND-WHITE GIRL sb dial cant. An alternative name for MOTHER OF THE CUMINA; see quot.

1953 Moore 137–8, The female singer..is also referred to as the 'black and white girl' and is either a relative or appointed by the family holding the Cumina. The master of ceremonies of a Cumina dance wears a black and white cord placed around his neck, which is the badge of his office. A number of times during a ceremony the female singer will wear his black and white cord, especially at such times as when the master of ceremonies is not present or is possessed.

BLACK-AND-YELLOW CREEPER sb ornith. In Gosse's use: *Coereba flaveola*, now generally called the BANANA QUIT, etc.

1847 Gosse 84. (1956 Jeffrey-Smith 71, quoting Gosse.)

BLACK ANT(S) /blak ans, ~hans/ sb; <*black* +*ant* (in dial, *ants* is also sg.). Usually, a common variety of black ant (*Cremastogaster brevispinosa*) with an unpleasant smell, which builds its nest in trees. Also called STINKING ANTS. *BA BL G*

1740 Importance 48, There are large *black Ants*, which build on high Trees, and others on the Ground; they destroy other Vermin. 1835 Senior 79, The common '*black ant*' is a terrible plague, finding its way into everything eatable. 1952 FGC Han, Man, StAnd, StT /blak (h)ans/. 1954 *FG* 607, Tree-nesting Ants. This species, commonly known as the 'black ant', is usually found in colonies or nests, and occurs most commonly on mango, avocado and citrus trees..They [have]..a disagreeable odour emitted on coming in contact with the person.

BLACK-ART MAN sb dial.

1950 Pat Wilmot StAnd, Black-art man, Obeahman.

BLACK ASHES (WOOD) sb. See quot.

1961 DAP StE, Black ashes = Ashes-wood, *Tetrazygia pallens*.

BLACK-BACK sb dial. A water-bird, prob the Black-necked Stilt (*Himantopus himantopus*). (Cf Gaylor 72.)

1952 FGC StC /blák bák/ same as cock-soldier—has a high cry: /ku/ very rapidly as often as ten times; a walker, has yellow feet, white belly, black back.

BLACK-BACK(ED) SPRAT sb. A variety of sprat, perh *Harengula macrophthalmus*.

1820 Thomson 41, The black-backed sprats, which are in general injurious, if laid one night in salt pickle, may be eaten with safety. 1952 FGC StJ, StM /blak bak sprat/ use for bait.

BLACK BACKRA sb dial; <*black*+BACKRA; cf SAMBO BACKRA.

1958 DeC StT /blak bakra/ a term of respect for a black man.

BLACK BANANA sb dial. Some variety of banana?

1927 Beckwith 12, Black-banana. For diarrhoea, cut a stalk of black banana, beat it, wring the juice into a table-spoon and add salt.

BLACK BANANA-BIRD sb dial; <*black* +BANANA BIRD. =BLACKBIRD 3.

1936 Bond 360, Jamaican Blackbird..*Local names*: Black Banana Bird, etc..*Range*:—Jamaica. 1956 Jeffrey-Smith 76, Another member of the oriole family is known as the Black Banana Bird.

BLACK-BEAD SHRUB sb bot. *Pithecellobium unguis-cati*, whose glossy black seeds are strung in necklaces. Also called BREAD-AND-CHEESE.

1756 Browne 252,4. Mimosa *Fruticosa..seminibus compressis, atronitentibus*..The Black-bead shrub, or large-leafed *Mimosa*. 1920 Fawcett 146. 1943 *NHN* I 11 20.

BLACK BEE sb. A small dark wild honey-bee, evid indigenous.

1959 O. P. Cousins Kgn, The black bee..is small and dark in colour with no characteristic marking. Honey and comb are dark in colour. Found mostly in hollow trees and is sometimes caught and reared by interested bee keepers. However, due to its poor honey-making characteristics (quantity and colour) it is not very popular and is only found with a few unimproved bee keepers. Present-day apiaries tend to be a cross between the common black bee and imported types.

BLACK BERRY sb dial. See quot. *BL*

1943 *NHN* II 82, *Sapindus saponaria*—Black Berry..The district name [on Portland Ridge] is derived from the black seeds; in many other areas it is known as 'Soap Berry' as the pericarp may be used as soap.

BLACKBERRY (BRAMBLE) sb. See quots.

1814 Lunan I 98, Blackberry Bramble. *Rubus Jamaicensis* ..It differs..from the common bramble of Europe in having..the flowers and berries smaller. 1913 Harris 3–4, There are two blackberries native of Jamaica, and apparently they are confined to Jamaica. 1914 Fawcett 260–1, *Rubus..jamaicensis*..Blackberry, Bramble.

BLACK BETTY (PEAS) sb. A variety of beans (prob *Vigna unguiculata*); see quots.

1814 Lunan I 434, *Calavances*, or *red bean*, and *black-betty*..the bean of the former is red, that of the latter black. They are both wholesome food, of which the negroes in general are very fond. 1873 Rampini 91, Black Betty. 1929 Beckwith 19. 1952 FGC Port, StAnd /blák béti/ size of cow peas but black.

BLACK-BILLED PARROT sb ornith. See quots.

1936 Bond 166, *Amazona agilis*..*Local name*:—Black-billed Parrot..*Range*:—Jamaica. 1956 Jeffrey-Smith 55, Our parrots owe their local names to the colour of their bills. The black-billed parrot..has bright red feathers.

BLACK-BILLED STREAMER-TAIL sb ornith. The humming-bird *Aithurus scitulus*: 'This form should perhaps be regarded as a subspecies of *A. polytmus*' (Bond). Cf STREAMER-TAIL.

1936 Bond 213, Black-Billed Streamer-Tail. 1956 Jeffrey-Smith 24, From 1903 I knew of the existence of a black-billed streamer-tail in Portland and the adjoining parish of St Thomas.

BLACK-BILLED WHISTLING DUCK sb ornith. See quot.

1956 Jeffrey-Smith 137, The Black-billed Whistling Duck, or West Indian Tree Duck (*Dendrocygna arborea*), was once very common..Its legs and feet are black, as is its bill.

BLACK-BILL PARROT sb dial. A variety of PARROT FISH.

1952 FGC StM.

BLACK-BILL SPRAT sb dial. A variety of sprat (unidentified).

1952 FGC Port /blak bil sprat/ about three ounces, has double scales and is tough.

BLACKBIRD sb; cf *OED*: 'In North America the name is given to other birds' [than *Merula turdus*]. Any of at least three species of birds, but currently most often that of sense 1. *BL T*

1. *Crotophaga ani*, one of the commonest

Jamaican birds; it has a large, parrot-like beak and feeds on the parasites of cattle. Also called ANI, BLACK PARROT, BLACK WITCH, LONG-TAILED CROW, OLD SLUT, SAVANNA BLACKBIRD, TICK-BIRD.

1725 Sloane 298, *The Great Black-bird*..The Bill was three-quarters of an Inch long and black, the under mandible being straight, the upper of a singular Make.. for it was arch'd. 1847 Gosse 282, Savanna Blackbird; *ibid* 287, In July I found a Blackbird's nest. 1952 FGC Han, Man, Port, StAnd, StAnn, StM, StT /blak bord/. 1955 Taylor 11, *Crotophaga ani*..In Jamaica it is widely known as the Blackbird and sometimes as the Tick-bird.

2. Applied sometimes (today incorrectly) to *Quiscalus niger*, the KLING-KLING. Also called BARBADOS BLACKBIRD. *BA*

1725 Sloane 299, *The Small black-bird*..The Bill is black, one Inch long, pointed with no rising as the other of the same Name hath, and like a Magpyes. 1943 *GL* Tre, Cling-cling, the Blackbird.

3. Applied sometimes to *Nesopsar nigerrimus*, the Jamaican Blackbird. Also called BLACK BANANA BIRD, CORPORAL BIRD, DUPPY BIRD, TRELAWNY BLACKBIRD, WILD PINE SERGEANT.

1756 Browne 469, Turdus 1. Niger, rostro palpebris pedibusque luteis, alis macula oblonga alba insignitis. The Blackbird. This bird is a native of *Jamaica*, and not uncommon in the cooler woods, where it chiefly lives. It differs but little, either in size or make, from the *European* Blackbird. [1936 Bond 360, The Jamaican Blackbird.]

BLACK BLAST sb obs; cf *OED blast sb* 6b 'A disease of the sugar cane', 1756, and YELLOW BLAST.

1790 Beckford I 53, The black blast attaches itself to the stem, and the leaves of the canes; it is likewise an accumulation of insects; and..they will..in a great measure suppress their vegetation.

BLACK BUG sb dial. A large black wasp or hornet? Cf BLACK BEE.

1952 FGC Man, Black bug, a wasp, or insect similar to a big wasp.

BLACK BULLET, BLACK BULLY-TREE sb. A variety of BULLETWOOD.

1864 Grisebach 782, Bully-tree, black: *Dipholis nigra*. 1941 Swabey 15, *Dipholis salicifolia*..Black Bullet. [*Dipholis nigra*..Red or Cherry Bullet.] 1952 FGC StAnn, Tre, Black bullet; StT, Black bully-tree, one of the three kinds of bulletwood, the other two being white bullet and neeseberry bullet.

BLACK BULLFINCH sb ornith. The BLACK SPARROW.

1956 Jeffrey-Smith 102.

BLACK CANDLEWOOD sb.

1. *Amyris balsamifera*, when the wood is of a darker variety; cf RED and WHITE CANDLEWOOD.

1864 Grisebach 782, Candlewood, white and black: *Amyris balsamifera*. 1920 Fawcett 192.

2. =BLACK SWEETWOOD, *Ocotea floribunda*.

1914 Fawcett 212.

BLACK CANE sb dial. A dark-stemmed variety of sugar-cane. *G*

1952 FGC StE, StJ, StM, StT.

BLACK-CAP vb dial; <*black cap* sb; cf *OED* 1, '*Black cap*: spec. that worn by English judges..when passing sentence of death upon a prisoner'. To pass sentence of death upon.

1951 FGC Kgn, 'Him gwine black-cap him!'

BLACK-CHEEKED YELLOW-THROAT sb ornith obs. In Gosse's use: the bird *Maryland Yellow-throat*.

1847 Gosse 148.

BLACK CHERRY sb obs. The tree identified by Fawcett & Rendle as *Eugenia disticha*, by Proctor as *E. axillaris*.

1696 Sloane 173, Black Cherries. 1725 Sloane 107, *Black-Cherries*. The Branches of this Tree are cover'd with a brown Bark, with white Spots on it here and there; the Leaves set one against another, exactly like those of the *Myrtus Latifolia*, the Fruit stands on a small..Footstalk, is like Black Cherries, whence the name, having a very thin black Skin..[etc.]. 1814 Lunan I 98, Black Cherry. Myrtus Cerasina.

BLACK COCO sb. A variety of *Colocasia esculenta*, dark and hard; prob the same as COMMANDER COCO.

1823 Roughley 404, Cocoas or eddoes..there are several kinds of them; the bourbon..and the country white and black cocoas, which are small, more prolific, more nourishing, drier, and more agreeable to the negroes, but which take a longer time to become ripe.

BLACK CRAB /blák kráb/ sb; cf *OED crab sb* 1..'*Black crab*, a land-crab of the Antilles, *Gecarcinus ruricola*, so called from the marking of its carapace'. Quots 1779, 1885, both from Jamaica.

1756 Browne 423, Cancer 16..The Black or Mountain-Crab..These creatures are very numerous in some parts of Jamaica..They live chiefly on dry land and at a considerable distance from the sea; which, however, they visit once a year, to wash off their spawn, and afterwards return to the woods and higher lands..When the black crab is fat and in a perfect state, it surpasses every thing of the sort, in flavour and delicacy. 1835 Madden I 199, Black crabs and wild guinea-fowl. 1952 FGC StAnd, StAnn, StJ, StM, StT, West /blák kráb/. 1957 *FFM* 222, The black crab (in season) is considered a delicacy.

BLACK DOCTOR-FISH sb dial. A variety of the DOCTOR FISH: prob *Teuthis hepatus* (in contrast with BLUE DOCTOR-FISH). It is actually dark brown.

1952 FGC StAnn, StC, StE, StM /blák dákta físh/.

BLACK DOG sb[1] dial obs; cf *OED* †1, 'A cant name, in Queen Anne's reign, for a bad shilling or other base silver coin. *Obs.*' Quots 1706 →1724. A coin (prob of silver) current in the WI during the 18th cent. It was of the lowest value. Cf CHANGE BLACK DOG FOR MONKEY.

[1793 Mathews 59, Upon opening the stocking..[they] found half dollars, quarter dollars, pistreens, bits, half bits and black dogs to the amount of thirty odd pounds. (St Kitts)]. 1873 Rampini 175 [Prov:] Black dog (a small coin) buy trouble; hundred poun' no clear him.

BLACK DOG sb[2] dial. Any of at least two plants: BLACK SAGE and a type of fern. See quots.

1952 FGC StAnd, Black dog, black sage. 1952 FGC StC, Black dog [so called because] the bone of the ferm [*sic*] is black. 1956 BLB Man /blak dag form/.

BLACK DOR sb obs; <*black* + *dor* (cf *OED*). A type of beetle. *BL*

1756 Browne 430, Curculio 4..The *Jamaica* Clock or Black Dor. This species is very common about the houses in *Jamaica*, and keeps generally in ground-rooms and pantry's.

BLACK DRUMMER sb dial. A variety of the DRUMMER fish.

1952 FGC StE /blák dróma/.

BLACK DUKE (COCO) sb dial. The COMMANDER COCO; see also DUKE COCO.

BLACK-EYE MULLET sb dial. A variety of the river mullet. Cf s RED-EYE MULLET.

1952 FGC Port.

BLACK-FACE(D) GRASS-QUIT sb ornith; cf GRASS-QUIT. The bird *Tiaris bicolor.*

1936 Bond 382, *Local names:*—..Black Sparrow.. Black-faced Grass Quit. 1956 Jeffrey-Smith 95, The Black-face Grass Quit..is less handsome than the yellow-face but more readily recognized.

BLACK-FIN SHARK sb. Among Jamaican fishermen: the largest of the deep-sea sharks in local waters.

1952 FGC StC (Old Harbour) /blák fin sháak/.

BLACK-FOOT JUMPING-DICK sb dial. One of the two kinds of Jamaican thrushes, both locally called JUMPING-DICK; this is *Turdus jamaicensis.*

1944 *NHN* II 130, Black-foot jumping-Dick = glass-eye thrush.

BLACK GAULIN sb obs. The bird now called BLUE GAULIN.

a 1705 Ray (1713) 189, see GAULIN. 1725 Sloane Tab 263, Ardea cœruleo-nigra. The black gaulding or blew gaulding.

BLACK GEORGE sb dial rare; cf BROWN GEORGE.

1955 LeP StE (Eld), Black George is the Brown George (parched corn ground up finely) mixed with wet sugar.

BLACK GIANT see BLACK JOINT(ER).

BLACK GINGER sb obs; cf *OED ginger* 1: '*Black ginger*: The unscraped root, from the E. Indies'. Quot 1707. See quot.

1707 Sloane lxviii, At twelve months end, when the Stalks and Leaves are withered, 'tis Hough'd up, clear'd of its Fibrils, Stalks and Strings, by a Knife, or the Hand, then wash'd in fair water, put in a Basket about a hundred Pound at a time, and boil'd in a Kettle for a quarter of an hour, then expos'd to the Sun and dried. Though Rain comes, it hurts it not; this is the Black Ginger. Fresh Roots must be boil'd in fresh water.

BLACKGUARD adj dial; cf *OED*, →1857; now replaced in England by *blackguardly.*

1943 *GL* Port, Blaggard, outrageous.

BLACK-HEART FIDDLEWOOD sb arch; cf FIDDLE-WOOD. A timber tree: *Citharexylum quadrangulare* (Grisebach).

1756 Browne 265, Citharexylon 2..Black-heart Fiddlewood. This tree grows chiefly in the low lands, and *Savannas*..one of the hardest and best timber-trees in the island..The berries are sometimes eat by the negroes. 1774 Long III 862, Black-heart Fiddle Wood. 1811 Titford 79. 1814 Lunan I 291–2, Black-Heart (Fiddlewood). Branches quadrangular.

BLACK HOG LOBSTER sb dial. A variety of LOBSTER; also called *pagro.*

1952 FGC StT, Black-hog lobster, a stumpy black one; = /págró/.

[**BLACK IRONWOOD** sb bot; cf *OED ironwood*..'Black Ironwood, *Condalia ferrea* of N. America', no quot.

1926 Fawcett 65, Krugiodendron ferreum Urb..*Condalia ferrea* Griseb..Black Iron Wood.]

BLACK JACK /blák ják/ sb dial; cf *DAE* 6, quot 1883; fish not identified. A black or dark-coloured variety of the jack fish. *BA*

1952 FGC StC, StE, StM.

BLACK JANGA sb dial. A dark variety of the river prawn called *jangga.*

1958 DeC common /blak jangga/ a black, stubby variety of /jangga/ found in small streams and springs; also called /tompa kwa-u/.

BLACK JINNY sb dial rare; <*Jinny*, a feminine name to corresp to *George.* A variant, perh jocular, of BROWN GEORGE; cf also BLACK GEORGE.

1954 LeP StAnn, Black Jinny, parched corn ground up finely.

BLACK JOINT(ER) /blák jáint, blák jáinta/ sb dial; *black* + JOINTER. One kind of PEPPER ELDER: *Piper nigrinodum*; see quot 1914.

1914 Fawcett 22, Black Jointer..*Shrub* 10 ft. high. *Branches*..jointed, black. 1927 Beckwith 12, Black-giant (joint). *Piper nigrinodum*..For fever, boil the twigs both for bath and tea. 1952 FGC Han /blák jáinta/; StE, Tre /blak jaint/. Cf s WHITE JOINTER.

BLACK JUCK sb dial; <*black* + DUKE, in var pronunc /juuk/. A variety of coco said to be the same as BOURBON COCO; see DUKE and quot 1935.

BLACK JUMPER sb. A spider of the family Salticidae; see quot.

1756 Browne 418, Aranea 2..The black Jumper. This spider is frequent in the country parts of Jamaica, especially in the parish of St Mary's. It is a very remarkable jumper.

BLACK LANCEWOOD sb bot; cf LANCEWOOD. See quots.

1814 Lunan I 438, Uvaria Nigra. Black Lancewood.. The negroes make lances of the wood, whence its name. 1914 Fawcett 202, *Oxandra lanceolata* Baill..*Uvaria lanceolata* Sw..Black lancewood..A straight-growing *tree*, to 30 ft. high..The wood is tough, strong and elastic. 1941 Swabey 23.

BLACK-LEGGED GAULIN sb; <*black-legged* + GAULIN. One type of WHITE GAULIN: *Egretta thula.*

1847 Gosse 334, Black-legged gaulin..Egretta *candidissima.* 1949 *NHN* IV 180, Black-legged gaulin, *Egretta thula*, with its black bill, black legs and yellow feet.

BLACK MANGO sb. A variety of mango which remains green when ripe, not acquiring the bright colours of many other mangoes. Also called GREEN SKIN, KIDNEY, MILK HEAD, PAPER-SKIN MANGO. *BL*

c 1915 FGC StAnd, common; 1952, many parishes. 1954 *FG* 475 [Varieties of mangoes:] Black. Of delicate flavour, small, colour green when ripe. Skin very thin.

BLACK MASTIC sb bot obs; cf *OED mastic* 3, 'A valuable timber tree of the West Indies and Florida, *Sideroxylon Mastichodendron*', 1657(Ligon)→. See quots.

a 1726 Barham (1794) 103, There are in Jamaica three sorts of trees called mastick; *viz.* black, white, and yellow. 1814 Lunan I 57–8, Bastard Bully Tree. Bumelia nigra.. This is the common bastard bully tree, a native of Jamaica, and but an indifferent timber; it is the black mastic of Barham.

BLACK MINT sb dial. A medicinal herb. (Prob *Mentha viridis.*)

1927 Beckwith 12, Black-mint. *Mentha*—. Boil for tea.

BLACK-NAYGA sb dial; <*black* + NIEGA. *G* A negro; the 'black' is not altogether redundant, as it refers to the darker, more purely

African negroes. The term is used by negroes about negroes and is not necessarily insulting.

1907 Jekyll 227 (see s.v. NAYGA). 1912 McK *Ballads* 49, How you sell wha' no wut gill self to black naygur for a bob. 1924 Beckwith 66 [Prov:] If you follow wha' black neger say, you lose you' way. 1954 LeP StAnn, Black negro, negro.

BLACK-NAYGA HAM sb dial joc; < BLACK-NAYGA (possessive) + *ham*. Codfish, a very common food among the negroes from slavery days forward.

1954 LeP Man, Black nayga ham, saltfish.

BLACK OLDWIFE sb dial. A variety of the OLDWIFE fish. See quot.

1854–5 *TJSA* I 145, Black Old Wife..*Balistes ringens*.

BLACK OLIVE sb bot; cf *OED olive sb*[1] 1b, only quot 1756 Browne. The tree *Bucida buceras*, the fruit of which resembles an olive. Also called BARK TREE (2), OLIVE BARK-TREE, and (most commonly today) WILD OLIVE.

1756 Browne 221, Buceras 1..This tree is called the *Black-Olive* in *Jamaica*; but in *Antigua*, where it is equally common, goes by the name of *French Oak*. 1774 Long III 749. 1801 Dancer 368. 1926 Fawcett 306–7, Olive Bark Tree, Black Olive. In salt marshes on the sea-coast.. *Tree*, 30–60 ft. high. 1941 Swabey 27.

BLACK PAN sb dial; cf BURN-PAN.

1954 LeP StAnn, Black pan, cooking pot hung from a stick.

BLACK PARROT sb[1] dial; cf *OED parrot-fish*. A dark variety of the PARROT fish.

1952 FGC StAnn, StC /blák páarat/.

BLACK PARROT sb[2] dial; cf *OED parrot sb* 1. The blackbird *Crotophaga ani*, in allusion to the shape of its beak.

1956 Jeffrey-Smith 65, Everyone in Jamaica knows the blackbird, or the black parrot, to give it another of its local names.

BLACK-PEPPER-BRAIN sb dial. A derog name: see quot. Cf PICKY-PICKY HEAD.

1960 SJR StAnd, When a boy has very short hair which grows close to the scalp in little balls of fluff (very negroid) it or he is called 'black-pepper-brain'.

BLACK PIG sb dial. A small black edible sea-fish with a thick lip, caught in pots; also called SEA GOD-A-ME.

1952 FGC Port, West, Black pig.

BLACK PINEAPPLE or **PINE** sb. A variety of pineapple formerly common in Jamaica.

1756 Browne 192–3, Bromelia 2..The Black Pine-Apple. Bromelia 3. The Queen Pine-Apple. These last two species are more common than the first [*sc* Sugar-loaf Pine-Apple]; their fruit is generally larger and roundish, but grows seldom yellow, even in the surface. 1952 Topper 6, At Clonmel (St Mary) it [the Red Spanish variety] is known as the 'Black' Pine. 1959 Alma Norman StC, Black pine is similar to Ripley but remains black in colour even when ripe. It grows only in some areas and is found for sale mainly in Kingston.

BLACK ROCK SWEETWOOD see ROCK SWEETWOOD.

BLACK SAGE sb dial; cf *OED sage sb*[1] 3. In Ja: Any of at least two herbaceous plants whose leaves are used to make medicinal 'teas'. See quots 1953–5. *BA G*

1927 Beckwith 12, Black-sage. *Varronia globosa* Jacq. For tightness in the chest, boil and take as tea. 1952 FGC Han, StAnd, StAnn, StE, StM, Tre /blàk siej/ (*Lantana crocea* or similar species). 1953 *WIMJ* 238, Boraginaceae..*Cordia globosa*..Black Sage; John Charles; Gout Tea. 1954 *WIMJ* 25, Verbenaceae..*Lantana crocea*.. Wild Sage; Black Sage. 1955 *WIMJ* 71, Boraginaceae.. *Cordia cylindristachya*..Sage; Black Sage. In some parts of Jamaica this species appears to replace *C. globosa* as black sage and is used in the treatment of colds and indigestion.

BLACK SHOT sb obs; cf *OED shot sb*[1], '†21 a collect. sing. Soldiers armed with muskets or other fire-arms..*Obs*..†b. A soldier armed with a firearm. *Obs. rare*.' Quots 1572–1706.

1. (Collect sg.) Such a band composed of trusted negroes.

1793 Edwards (1801) III 310, These garrisons were composed of white and black shot and baggage negroes, who were all duly trained. 1803 Dallas I 38, To this force [regular soldiers and militia] was attached a number of confidential negroes, called Black-shot, Mulattoes, and Indians..[from] the Mosquito shore..The Black-shot and Mosquito Indians proved of great service.

2. (Sg.) A trusted negro permitted to bear firearms.

1736 House of Assembly (see WHITE SHOT). 1825 *Shooting Excursion* 6, A party of eleven whites..accompanied by about twelve black shots.

BLACK SHRIKE sb ornith. In Gosse's use: The Jamaican becard or JUDY.

1847 Gosse 187. 1956 Jeffrey-Smith 69.

BLACK SILK sb dial; cf *OED silk sb* 5a. A dark-coloured variety of SILK-SNAPPER fish (Lutianidae).

1929 Beckwith 33, Pot fish are..snappers; mullet..silk of the red 'sun-silk' and the black varieties. 1952 FGC StM /blak silk/ = black snapper in Kingston.

BLACK SNAKE sb; *OED* uses Gosse's designation.

1. In Gosse's use: The snake now designated as *Alsophis ater*.

1851 Gosse 228, The most common Ophidian reptile in Jamaica is the Black Snake..*Natrix atra*, mihi.

2. In present Ja use: A snake peculiar to the island: see quot.

1940 Lynn-Grant 125, *Dromicus funereus* (Cope) 'Black snake'..Glossy slate black above; underneath almost as dark except throat and neck..Apparently confined to damper, forested parts of the island.

BLACK SNAPPER sb; cf *OED snapper sb*[1] 6; *DAE*, *Lutjanus caxis*, 1799→. In Ja: any of several similar fishes; see quots. *BL*

1854 *TJSA* I 142, *Centopristes rufus*—black snapper. 1873 Rampini 171, The grouper, the black snapper, the old wife, the mud-fish. 1892 Cockrell list, Black snapper, *Lutjanus stearnsii* and *L. jocu*. 1952 FGC Port, StAnn, StC, StE, StJ, StM /blak snapa/.

BLACK SPARROW sb; cf *OED sparrow* 2, 1771→. In Ja: a variety of the Greater Antillean Bullfinch, *Loxigilla violacea ruficollis*; also called BLACK BULLFINCH, COCK SPARROW, COFFEE BIRD, COTTON-TREE SPARROW.

1725 Sloane 311, *Passer niger, punctis croceis notatus*..The Black-Sparrow. 1952 FGC Han, StAnn, StT /blak spara/ black bird, red under chin—go about in flocks, destroy corn. 1956 Jeffrey-Smith 102.

BLACK SPIDER /blàk spáida, blàk páida/ sb; cf *DAE*, 1832→. The poisonous spider *Latrodectus mactans* (known in US as the *black widow*); also called GROUND-ANANCY, RED-ARSED SPIDER, RED-TAILED SPIDER. *G*

a 1726 Barham (1794) 6–7, I knew a gentlewoman in Jamaica that was bit or stung with a black spider (which is venomous here) upon one of the fingers, which immediately inflamed and pained her up to the elbow and shoulder. 1811 Titford Expl. to Plate VI 4, The roots and seeds..cure the bites of serpents and stings of scorpions or black spiders. 1949 *NHN* IV 15. 1952 FGC Man, StT, Tre, West /blàk spáida/ big; long legs, sharp sting; lives in earth with web.

BLACK STAINY see STAINY (BANANA).

BLACK-STICK CASSAVA sb dial. A variety of CASSAVA having a black 'stick' or stem. *G*

1952 FGC StT.

BLACK-STICK MAIDENHAIR sb dial; cf *OED maidenhair*, and STICK; cf also WHITE STICK.

1955 *WIMJ* 79, *Adiantum tenerum* Sw. Maidenhair Fern; Black-stick Maidenhair. This species of maidenhair fern..is used to make tea for colds.

BLACK SWEETWOOD sb bot; cf *OED sweetwood*, 'A name for various trees and shrubs, chiefly lauraceous, of the West Indies and tropical America..Black Sweetwood, *Strychnodaphne (ocotea) floribunda*'. No quot.

1914 Fawcett 212, *Ocotea floribunda*..Black Sweetwood, Black Candle-wood..A *tree* 30–60 ft. high.

BLACK SWIFT sb ornith; cf *OED swift sb.* See quots.

1847 Gosse 63, Black Swift. *Cypselus niger.* 1955 Taylor 82, The Black Swift (*Cypseloides niger*) and the Collared Swift..are residents in Jamaica..Often seen together hawking in small flocks high among the mountains. 1956 Jeffrey-Smith 21, Black Swifts (*Nephoecetes niger*)..are found in the mountains. [This authority follows Bond (1936, 199) in naming the genus.]

BLACK-TAIL GRUNT sb dial. A variety of the GRUNT fish.

1854–5 *TJSA* I 142, *Hæmulon caudimacula*—black tail Grunt.

BLACK-THROAT GRASS-BIRD sb ornith. The BLACK-FACED GRASS-QUIT (*Tiaris bicolor*).

1917 Panton in *Ja. Times* 3 Nov., The black-throat grass-bird.

BLACK UP /blák óp/ vb[1] and ppl adj dial [these two are indistinguishable in many constructions]; <*black* (or *block*, which is also /blak/ in the dial). To become very drunk; very drunk. *BL G*

1943 *GL* StAnd, Black up, Drunk. 1954 LeP Kgn (Trench Town), Dat night fi-her husban black-up, black-up, couldn't black-up no more. 1956 Mc Kgn /a núo bái fiti kókokóla, gét blak óp/ *I know a boy who 'ate' coca-cola, and got very drunk.*

BLACK UP /blák óp/ vb[2] dial. Of the sky: to become overcast, heralding rain. Also *set up for rain. BL G*

1954 Reckord 17, Sky black up fi rain.

BLACK VELVET sb dial. The tree *Colubrina ferruginosa*, evid ref to the appearance of the wood (or perh the seeds).

1926 Fawcett 68, Greenheart, Snake Wood, Black Velvet, Wild or Mountain Ebony..*Seeds*..roundish, black, shining..used for making necklaces and other ornaments. 1941 Swabey 30, Black Velvet..occasionally used in inlay work.

BLACK VERVINE sb dial; <*black* + VERVINE.

1927 Beckwith 12, Black-verryvine (vervain). *Valerianodes cayennensis*..As a purge for an animal.

BLACK WASH sb dial joc.

1. SUGAR-AND-WATER, prob alluding to its dark colour (or perh as being a common drink among negroes).

1943 *GL* Clar, Black wash, Sugar & water. 1955 FGC Man.

2. Coffee, from its colour.

1943 *GL* Kgn.

BLACK WASP /blak was/ sb dial; *DAE* 1789 without identification. A small black wasp that builds a mud nest, chiefly in houses.

1952 FGC Port, StAnd.

BLACK WATER int dial; perh <*back water* (*OED back v.* 15b). An exclamatory formula used to terminate a group song; also BOG WALK.

c 1953 Wilson in *Gleaner*, Black water!..The bomma's cry to end a jamma sing.

BLACK-WATER sb dial; cf *OED water sb* 17, 'Used to denote various watery fluids found in the human or animal body, either normally or in disease'. See quots.

1952 FGC StAnd /blák-wáata/ horse gather black-water in frog-part of foot [i.e. under the hoof] after blacksmith has pricked him; also StT.

BLACK WATTLE /blák wátl, blák wákl/ sb. Any of various trees: see quots. *G*

1936 Fawcett VII 133–4, *Viburnum villosum*..a shrub or small tree..Black Wattle. *Ibid* 134–5, *V. alpinum*..a large shrub or small tree..Black Wattle. 1943 *NHN* II 82, Black Wattle. A tree..with fluted trunk and black, rough bark. The wood is white and slightly under medium hardness. 1952 FGC StAnn, Black wattle, 'the Portland name for Wild mahogany, Wanika, Coby wood, Cob Anancy'.

BLACK WHITE sb dial, often used epithetically.

1956 Mc StAnd /blak wáit/ a black person with plenty of money; a rich negro.

BLACK WILLOW sb bot. *BA*

1914 Fawcett 231, *Capparis cynophallophora*..Black Willow, Zebra Wood.

BLACK WITCH sb. The JAMAICAN BLACK-BIRD.

[1884 Coues (1903) 604, *Crotophaga ani*..Black Witch.] 1936 Bond 177, *Crotophaga ani*..[Jamaican names:] Black Witch; Long-tailed Crow; Tick Bird; Savanna Blackbird.

BLACK WITHE /blak wis/ sb; cf *OED withe sb* 3b, 'The creeping plant *Heliotropium fruticosum* of Jamaica, the stems of which are used for making baskets', quot 1847. Any of several kinds of 'wis' or vine: see quots.

1847 Gosse 373, The gradual predominance of marsh plants, *sagittaria*, ginger-fern, bulrush, and black-withe. 1927 Beckwith 13, Black-wis (vine). *Passiflora pallida* L. 1952 FGC StM, Tre /blak wis/ used to make baskets; also to make scent.

BLACKY sb dial. An unidentified fish, said to be a nuisance to fishermen's lines.

1952 FGC StJ.

BLACKY-BLACKY /bláki-bláki/ sb and adj dial; <*black* + *-y* (cf *OED*), the whole iterated. The soot on a pot that has been on the fire; sooty from the fire.

1956 Mc Man /yu skriep af di blaki-blaki/ *You scrape off the soot;* /di gyali blaki-blaki/ *The galley is sooty.*

BLADE sb dial.

1959 DeC StJ /blied/ the blossom on corn [i.e. maize]: /i bluo blied/ *The blossom is flowering out.*

blak op see BLACK UP.

blak wis see BLACK WITHE.

blam int dial; ult echoic, perh African; cf *bam.* See quots. *G*

1943 *GL* no addr, Blam, an exclamation showing that something fits where it is thrown; StC Blam, to make a sharp sound. 1959 Louise Bennett (to LeP), Blam, used just in the same way as *bam.*

blangsam, blansam see BLOSSOM.

blasam see BLOSSOM.

BLAZER sb dial. See quot.

1958 DeC Port /blíeza/ small sticks used as firewood.

BLAZES JANE sb dial. (Vegetables are frequently given people's names—cf MISS KELLY peas, etc.)

1952 FGC StT, Blazes Jane, peas—very fine.

BLEAK sb dial. A period of BLEAKY weather.

1958 FGC StT, A bleak comes on—cloudy, foggy. *G*

BLEAKY /bliiki/ adj common; cf *OED* →1797. Of the weather: with dull or overcast sky. *BL G*

1952 LeP Kgn, Bring your car in for ducoing on a bleaky morning, not bright. 1956 Mc Man /blíiki máanin—i gwoeng fie tidé/ *It's dull this morning—it's going to be fair today*; StE /wen di maanin bliiki, di die gud/ *When the morning is overcast, the day is good.*

BLEBE vb; a dial sp for *believe.*

1877 Murray *Kittle* 10, see ME 1.

BLEED vb trans; <*bleed* vb intr, cf *OED* 3, 'Of plants: To emit sap when wounded'; prob also infl by sense 9, 'To draw or let blood from, *esp.* surgically'. *BL G*

1823 Roughley 233, But in no instance, when they are ordered to be trashed, should any of their joints be bled (a common phrase with planters, when green trash is forced from the joints, and their fibrous veins exposed to the sun, and made to drip their vital juices).

BLEEDING-HEART sb; cf *OED bleeding ppl a* 5, 'Bleeding-heart, the popular name for several plants' (but not those so called in Jamaica). See quots. *BL*

1. 1874 Grisebach 781, Bleeding-heart: *Colocasia esculenta.* [Cf EDDO.]

2. 1914 Fawcett 131, *Amarantus paniculatus*.. (Bleeding Hearts), found in gardens, is allied to *A. tristis.* [Cf CALALU.]

3. 1952 FGC West, Bleeding-heart, = MOSES-IN-THE-BULRUSHES.

blimbing, blimblim see BIMBLING (PLUM).

BLIND /blain/ adj dial; cf *OED* 11 a, 'Closed at one end'. Of a cow's nipple: Not open, not giving milk.

1952 FGC StAnd /blain/.

BLIND /blain/ sb; cf *OED.*

1. A jalousie. *BL T*

1956 Mc StAnd [Song:] /se mi waanda we musu get in de—musu waak truu blain/ *Say I wonder how (where) mouse got in there—mouse walked through the blind.*

2. An awning. *G T*

1958 FGC StAnd /blaind/ an awning.

3. (Plur) The blinkers on a horse.

1943 *GL* Port, Blines, blinkers.

BLIND adv dial; <*blind* adj. As an intensifier: entirely, utterly (as if one were blind). See quot. *G*

1956 Mc Man /yu rang, sa—blain rang/ *You're wrong, Sir—utterly wrong.*

BLIND-EYE /bláin-ái/ sb dial; <*blind* vb + *eye.* The tree *Amyris balsamifera,* whose inflammable resin is liable to irritate the eyes of axemen trying to chop it down.

1952 FGC StAnn, Tre, Blind-eye = BEYACA, BURN-EYE, CANDLEWOOD, CANTU, TORCHWOOD.

BLIND OATH sb dial. A lie.

1958 DeC StT /tiek blain uot/ to tell a lie.

BLINKER sb. The firefly now commonly called BLINKY.

1851 Gosse 113, Of the two kinds of luminous beetles which we possess..the *Lampyris,* which we call the *Blinker*..is usually found on the trunks of trees.

BLINKY /blíngki/ sb; <*blink* vb + *-y.* The small, soft-bodied species of firefly (*Photuris jamaicensis*) with feeble intermittent light under its 'tail' (in contrast to the large click-beetle with luminous 'eye' on its head, the PEENY-WALLY). (Some Jamaicans confuse the two.) Also called STRANGER, WINKER, WINKY, etc. *N*

1917 Hammett in *Ja Times* 29 Sept., It would also be interesting to know if the 14 species of Blinkies (Lampyridae) are common in any part of Jamaica. 1924 Beckwith 11, Blinkie* an' Anansi was gwine in a wood.. * (Fire-flies are common in Jamaica). 1929 Beckwith 110, Falconer related an amusing story which he heard from a member of the West Indian regiment in 'Serlion' [Sierra Leone] West Africa, of the obeah sold in that part of the world..'Little blinkie [fireflies] head and wing and shell-shell, that's what the Obeah Men sell to the country people. 1943 *GL* Port, StE, Blinky. 1952 FGC Han, Port, StAnd, StT, Tre /blingki/; Han, If you go to bed at night and see blinky inside the housetop, stranger coming; StAnd, Blinky has light underneath, and cuts it off. 1956 Mc Clar, Port /blingki/.

BLOODBERRY sb dial.

1. A low shrub with scarlet berries that resemble drops of blood. See quot 1914.

1914 Fawcett 156, *Rivina humilis*...Bloodberry. *Plant 2–3 ft high.* 1952 FGC StAnn, Blood-berry and GUMA are both called PICKNEY-MUMMA.

2. An unidentified tree.

1952 FGC StM, Blood-berry—tall tree, nuff [i.e. many] branches.

BLOOD-CLOTH sb dial.

1956 Mc /blod-klaat/ sanitary towel.

BLOOD-FLOWER sb obs; cf *OED blood sb* 19. *Asclepias curassavica,* valued as a styptic, emetic, and vermifuge, now most commonly called RED HEAD.

a 1726 Barham (1794) 22, Blood-flower. It is so called from its stopping bleeding when all other remedies have failed; and is so well known in Jamaica that it needeth no particular description. 1811 Titford Expl. to Plate VII 1. 1814 Lunan 1 63–4, Bastard Ipecacuanha..Barham calls this plant blood-flower..It..is called *red head* by the negroes. 1953 *WIMJ* 237.

BLOOD WIS /blod wis/ sb dial; <*blood* + WIS, presumably so called because of the tonic properties of the root.

The JAMAICA SARSAPARILLA, *Smilax officinalis,* a climbing vine whose roots may furnish a drink said to 'sweeten the blood'; it was also used formerly against venereal disease.

1952 FGC Han /blod wis/ sarsaparilla.

BLOOD-WOOD sb bot; cf *OED*: a Jamaican tree is named (*Gordonia haematoxylon*) but without quot or ref.

1. The tree *Laplacea haematoxylon* and its

blood-red wood—whence the name; also called IRON WOOD.

1835 Senior 25, No mahogany, with a French polish, can assume a finer face than the bullet-tree and blood-wood floors exhibit after this operation [*sc* polishing]. 1837 Macfadyen I 116–17, Blood-wood. 1920 Fawcett 188–9, *Laplacea haematoxylon*..Bloodwood..The wood is of a deep red colour, very hard.

2. The tree *Cyrilla racemiflora* and its wood; see quots. Also called BEETWOOD.

1920 Fawcett 18, C. racemiflora..Blood Wood, Beet Wood. 1941 Swabey 14, Bloodwood (Beetwood). 1946 *NHN* III 61, The bark of the tree is red, the sapwood is cream, whilst the heartwood is a beautiful red; hence the local name—'Blood-wood'.

BLOOD WORM sb. The larva of the midge *Chironomus*, from its colour.

1946 *NHN* III 54, If the larval case was touched or irritated, the larvae crawled out. They were striking in colour, bright red, resembling small worms—they are commonly known as 'Blood Worms'.

BLOODY-GUM sb obs. A spiral univalve or sea-snail, the opening of whose shell has two processes like teeth, with reddish coloration at their base. Cf WHITE GUM.

1756 Browne 399, Nerita 7..The Bloody-Gum.

BLOSSOM /blásàm, bláasàm, blánsàm, blangsam/ sb chiefly dial; cf *OED* 1 b, 'Also said of grain, grass, etc.' 1769, 1868. (The lengthening and nasalization of the first vowel are not what would be expected. They occur for ordinary senses of the word as well as those below.)

1. The sugar-cane ARROW or FLAG.

1952 FGC StE, The cane shoots out a /blánsàm/ in December.

2. The 'tassel' that shoots from the top of a stalk of maize.

1952 FGC StE /blánsàm/; StT /blásàm/.

3. The 'beard' that issues from an ear of maize.

1952 FGC StT.

BLOW[1] /bluo/ vb dial.

1. intr. Cf *EDD blow* sb[2] & v[3]; *OED* v^2 1: 'To burst into flower; to blossom, bloom.' Archaic or poetic in England, US, etc., but common in Ja. *G*

1924 Beckwith 189 [Riddle:] Me fader got a rose-tree in him yard; eb'ry night he blow, an by time de fe clean, eb'ry one gone.—Stars. 1954 LeP StAnd /di rúoz blúo/ *The rose is blooming;* /di bód blúo out/ *The bud has burst into blossom.*

2. trans. To produce by blooming.

1788 Marsden 24, Ocro..blows a yellow flower. 1956 Mc StE /di kien bluo an aro/ *The cane produces as a flower an 'arrow'.*

BLOW[2] /bluo/ vb intr dial; used absolutely for *blow* (*a*, *the*, *its*, etc.) *horn*; cf also *OED* v^1 15 a. Of a car or truck: to sound its horn. *G*

1952 FGC StAnd (Said angrily by a pedestrian startled by a car coming quietly up behind him:) /wái yu no blúo?/. 1957 JN StAnn, One truck and one car—Mi never see it and mi only hear it when it blow and mi frighten.

BLOW-BLOW sb; iterative baby-talk. *G*

1955 BLB StJ /bluo-bluo/ a toy whistle. Also called FEE-FEE.

BLOWER sb dial slang; <*blow* vb, Engl and US slang, to spend (money) freely. *G*

1943 *GL* StAnd, Blower, a spender.

BLOW-FIRE sb arch. The OLD HIGE or OLD SUCK, a witch believed to go about at night enveloped in flames and suck the blood, especially of infants.

1895 Banbury 32, Knives and forks, and sometimes the bible, are placed at the head of the infant to scare away the 'blow-fire'.

BLOWING vbl sb; cf *OED* v^1 10, 26. Accidental overflowing within a rum still. See quot.

1823 Roughley 212, Stills should never be quite filled; six or eight inches should be left empty at the top, to prevent accidents by blowing, or sending the liquor or low wine down the worms, instead of low wine from the liquor still, and rum from the low wine still. *G*

BLOW-NOSE sb dial. Nasal mucus. See JOHN-CROW BLOW-NOSE.

BLUE adj and adv dial; cf US usage in *blue blazes*, *blue norther*, etc.; cf also BLUE FIRE. As an intensifier, esp in connection with hunger (cf BLUE MAAGA, BLUE SQUALL): hungry. *G*

1935 HPJ, Blue, adverbial intensive, 'used in slavery times'. 1943 *GL* Man, Blue, to be hungry.

BLUE-BADAS sb dial; perh <BLUE-BAIZE.

1956 Jeffrey-Smith 70, The exquisite general coloration of the male, violet blue, accounts for 'Blue Baize' and 'Blue Badas'.

BLUE-BAIZE /bluu biez, bluu bej/ sb dial; <*blue-baize*, a kind of cloth formerly much used for work-clothes. Cf *DAE baize* quot 1732: a runaway slave wearing *blue baize*. The ORANGE QUIT, a bird of a conspicuous blue colour.

1936 Bond 312, Orange quit (*Euneornis campestris*). *Local names:*—..Long-mouthed Quit; Blue Baize; 'Swee'; Feather-tongue; Sour-sop Bird. 1955 Taylor 45. 1956 Jeffrey-Smith 69–70.

BLUE-BELLY sb obs; evid by contrast with WHITE-BELLY, an early established name. A kind of dove or wild pigeon: prob the MOUNTAIN WITCH is meant, which is known widely as the BLUE DOVE.

1740 Importance 38, White-belly, blew-belly, and red Doves.

BLUE-BILL PARROT sb dial. One variety of the PARROT fish.

1952 FGC StM.

BLUEBIRD /bluu bod, bluu bord/ sb, also attrib; fig use, ameliorative, alluding to the bluish colour of the leaves. Some understand the word as BLUE-BUD.

1. A variety of sweet-potato.

1952 FGC Port, StJ /bluu bord/ the leaf is blue; StAnn, StC, StT /bluu bod/ the root has a white skin, top of plant is blue.

2. A variety of cassava, also called LOUISA.

1952 FGC StAnd /bluu bod/ has bluish leaves at top, is a yellow-heart cassada; StAnn /bluu bod/ = Louisa, has a yellow skin; StT /bluu bod/ a sweet cassada.

BLUE BOOT /blúu búut/ sb dial; <*blue* + *boots*. A synonym for 'Sunday-best clothes'.

1935 HPJ, Me no yable fe go wi ju, becausin me no hab de money fe buy blue-boot, an wid outn blue-boot me cyan go up four-an-twenty 'teps. 1952 FGC StM, Wear me blue boot go up eleven steps (i.e. to court).

BLUE-BUD = BLUEBIRD.

1954 *FG* 439, Other lesser-known varieties [of sweet-potato] are Blue Bud and Mother Edwards.

BLUE CANE sb dial. A variety of sugar-cane with a blue-striped stem. RIBBON CANE.

1952 FGC StAnn.

BLUE CHICKWEED sb. *Salvia alata.*

1942 *NHN* I 6 11 (see quot under HOUSE-SIDE WEED).

BLUE COCO sb dial. A bluish variety of coco; =*lef-man.*

1952 FGC Han. 1958 DeC common /bluu koko/ also /lefman/ names for a bluish coco.

BLUE DOCTOR-FISH sb. A variety of DOCTOR FISH—prob *Teuthis coeruleus.*

1854–5 *TJSA* I 143, Acanthurus caeruleus, Blue Doctor Fish. 1952 FGC StE, StM /blùu dákta físh/.

BLUE DOVE sb.

1. A bird identified by Bond as *Geotrygon versicolor.*

1936 Bond 156, Crested Quail-Dove (*Geotrygon versicolor*) *Local names:*—Blue Dove; Blue Partridge, Mountain Witch.

2. *Columba caribaea*; see quots.

1952 FGC StAnn, Blue Dove; StM, Blue dove—like baldpate, but not bald; StT, Blue dove—in high woodland, looks just the same as pea-dove but is bigger; StT, Blue dove—feeds chiefly on the ground, called BLUE PIGEON in St Elizabeth but not here.

BLUE-DRAWERS /bluu draaz/ sb dial joc; cf *OED drawers sb pl*, 'A garment for the lower part of the body and legs'.

A pudding of boiled corn- or cassava-meal, so called because it is tied up in a piece of banana leaf (which is bluish) for boiling. Also called *dokunu.*

1943 *GL* Kgn, Blue drauz, banana pudding (ducuno); StM, Blue-drawers, sweet cassava or corn cakes boilt wrapped in green banana leaves. 1952 FGC StAnn /bluu draaz/ take corn cake mixture, tie in banana leaf with banana bark, boil till boilt; StJ /bluu draaz/ same as duckanoo, tie-a-leaf: banana leaf is blue. 1956 McPort, StAnd.

BLUE-FACED BOOBY sb ornith. The bird *Sula dactylatra.*

1936 Bond 12. 1956 Jeffrey-Smith 133.

BLUEFIELDS CEDAR sb. A tree found plentifully near Bluefields, Westmoreland, and resembling Jamaica Cedar. Its identity is uncertain; see quot.

1952 FGC StAnn /brúfil síida/ in StAnn, St Elizabeth, Trelawny; StJ /blúufiil síida/ called so in St Elizabeth: called gold-spoon, May-day mahogany in StAnn.

BLUE FIRE sb dial; cf BLUE, *blue devil*, etc. Serious trouble. *G*

1907 Jekyll 142, So, sister, I ha da go home, will be blue fire when I catch Puss. . Dog say:—'Ah, me man, will be blue fire!'

BLUE FLY sb dial. =GINGY-FLY.

1952 FGC Man, Blue fly, /gínggi flài/.

BLUE-FOOT sb[1], also attrib; cf *OED blue a* for the many pejorative connotations of that word; cf also PARTRIDGE.

1. A prostitute.

1935 HPJ, Blue-foot, a prostitute. 1943 *GL* StT, Blue-foot, base, common girl.

2. An outsider, stranger to a certain district.

1952 Miss P. Caws StT, Blue-foot man, an outsider who has come in (through marriage, business, etc.) to live—said by people in StT; current ten years ago.

3. A negro.

1954 LeP Port (Moore Town), Bloo fut, negro.

4. A term of abuse (perh related to sense 2 or 3).

1929 Beckwith 83 [Song:] Lick him with a stick, Get up, you brute, blue-foot brute!

BLUE-FOOT sb[2] dial. An unidentified bird mentioned in the widely-sung song 'Chi-Chi-Bud-O'.

1951 Murray 24, Some a Blue-foot.

BLUE-GAL sb dial; perh by allusion to the BLUES AND REDS. A small blue fish; also called ARMY GIRL.

1950 Smith, Han, Port. 1952 FGC StJ, StM /bluu gyal/.

BLUE GAULIN sb; <*blue* + GAULIN. The common name for the herons *Flordia caerulea* and *Ardea herodias. BA*

a1705 Ray, see GAULIN. 1725 Sloane Tab 263, Ardea cœruleo-nigra. The black gaulding or blew gaulding. 1847 Gosse 337, Blue Gaulin. . The slender contour of this bird, its arching purple neck, its filamentous crown-plumes, and the long pointed scapulars arching down over its back, combine with its graceful motions and delicate hue to give this bird an aspect of peculiar elegance. 1955 Taylor 64, In Jamaica birds of this group are almost always referred to as Gaulins. Those most likely to be seen are the Great Blue Heron. .etc. 1956 Jeffrey-Smith 121, The Little Blue Heron. .—our Blue Gaulin.

BLUE-GAY sb dial; prob var of BLUE-BAIZE, perh under folk-etym infl, since *baize* is no longer current. The ORANGE QUIT.

1956 Jeffrey-Smith 70, As the bird has a reddish throat it is known as 'Blue Gay', in St Elizabeth.

BLUE HOLE sb topogr.

1. A small body or pool of salt or fresh water having a remarkably blue colour (usually due to the purity of the water which has been filtered through limestone formations). Freq a generic term in place-names.

[1774 Long II 192, The road leading into Westmoreland from St Elizabeth crosses the boundary at a place called the Wells, and proceeds. .till it reaches Bluefields. Near this part stands, on an elevated spot, the dwelling-house of Mr Wh—e, called Bluehole.] 1890 Thomas 72, In the first mile we came upon one of the loveliest 'blue holes' I have ever seen. .Great parapets of laminated limestone. .walled it in on both sides. Ferns and shrubs overhung its damp mossy edges, and mirrored their fairy forms in water of the deepest, loveliest blue, a blue that made you long to tear off your clothes and jump headlong and lave your limbs in it. 1929 Beckwith 102, There is a 'blue hole' near Lucea in Jamaica where the Spaniards are supposed to have sunk 'a table of gold'. [1959—place-names: *Blue Hole* (Han, Port, StAnn, StC, StJ, West), *Blue Hole Valley* (West).]

2. A deep place in a river, also called STONE HOLE.

1907 Jekyll 7, One day Annancy an' Bro'er Tiger go a river fe wash 'kin. Anancy said. . :—'Bro'er Tiger, as you are such a big man, if you go in a de blue hole with your fat you a go drownded'. 1961 *Gleaner* 29 June 1/6, Mr Ralph Dennis. .drowned in a 'blue hole' called Middle Dam, Sunday afternoon. .the deepest part of the water.

BLUE-JEAN PARROT sb. A variety of PARROT fish presumably the colour of blue-jean cloth; perh the same as the BLUE PARROT. Cf BLUE-BAIZE.

1952 FGC StM.

BLUE-LIGHT sb dial; by some diabolical association?—cf *OED blue devil.* A coarse, vulgar, or indecent expression.

1943 *GL* StM, Blue-light, bad word; StT, Blue-light base, vile expression.

BLUE MAAGA adj dial; <BLUE+*maaga*. In a state of great distress or starvation.

1826 Williams 205, see *maaga*. 1958 DeC StT /bluu maaga/ starving—worse than /maaga/.

BLUE MAHOE sb; <*blue*+MAHOE; cf *OED mahoe*, quot 1866. The common mahoe tree (*Hibiscus elatus*) and its wood. The wood has a bluish cast.

1814 Lunan II 319, The variety with red flowers is called the Blue Mahoe, it is an excellent timber tree..It has been observed that the wood of the blue kind..appears purplish when cut with iron. 1864 Grisebach 785, Mahoe, blue: *Paritium elatum*. 1926 Fawcett 141, *Hibiscus elatus*..Blue or Mountain Mahoe, Cuba Bark. 1941 Swabey 24. 1952 FGC Man; StAnn, Blue mahoe = turtleshell mahoe; Tre, Blue mahoe = turtle-fat mahoe.

BLUE MOUNTAIN DUCK sb. A petrel (*Pterodroma hasitata*) now extinct in Jamaica, though it once nested in the Blue Mountains, whence the name.

1847 Gosse 437, In the Blue Mountains, high up towards their summits, is a curious *burrowing* bird, which they call the Blue-Mountain Duck. It is described as having webbed feet, and a hooked parrot-bill. This description would indicate a species of *Alca*. It inhabits holes in the cliffs, and is said to burrow to the extent of ten feet. 1936 Bond 6, Black-Capped Petrel (*Pterodroma hasitata*) *Local names*:—Blue Mountain Duck. 1941 *NHN* I 2 9, Blue Mountain Duck (*Pterodroma jamaicensis*, Bancroft.)

BLUE MOUNTAIN VIREO sb ornith. A vireo early observed in the Blue Mountains of Jamaica, though found elsewhere in the island.

1936 Bond 303, Blue Mountain Vireo (*Vireo osburni*). *Local name*:—'Big Furuh Bird..' *Range*:—Jamaica. 1956 Jeffrey-Smith 50.

BLUE MOUNTAIN YACCA sb bot. A type of YACCA (*Podocarpus urbanii*) that grows in the higher parts of the Blue Mountains, Jamaica.

1941 Swabey 32.

BLUE PARROT (FISH) sb. A blue variety of PARROT fish; cf BLUE-JEAN and BLUE-PETER PARROT. *BA*

1756 Browne 447, Mormyra 3..The blue Parrot-fish. 1950 Smith, Blue parrot, *Scarus coeruleus* (Negril).

BLUE PARTRIDGE sb ornith.

1. A ground pigeon now extinct; see quots.

1847 Gosse 324, The woodsmen speak of a Blue Partridge, and a Red-necked Dove; the former is figured by Robinson, and is no doubt a ground pigeon. 1941 *NHN* I 2 9, Blue Partridge (*Zenaida plumbea*, Gosse) a ground pigeon figured by Robinson, probably made extinct by the mongoose.

2. A local name for the Crested Quail-Dove.

1936 Bond 156, *Geotrygon versicolor*..*Local names*:—Blue Dove, Blue Partridge, Mountain Witch..*Range*:—Jamaica.

BLUE PEA FLOWER sb bot; cf *OED pea-flower*..b. 'Name for several West Indian leguminous plants having such flowers, as.. species of *Centrosema* and *Clitoria*.' 1825→.

1814 Lunan I 101–2, Blue Pea Flower. Clitoria..1. Brasiliana..2. Virginiana..3. Galactia.

BLUE-PETER PARROT sb dial.

A variety of blue PARROT fish, perh in its colouring resembling the Blue Peter (a blue flag with a white square in the centre) (note also, however, US use of Blue Peter for a coot: *DA blue* a 3); cf BLUE PARROT.

1952 FGC StJ.

BLUE PIGEON sb. *Columba caribaea*, more commonly called RING-TAIL (pigeon). *BA*

1840 Chamberlaine 20, Blue pigeon, *Columba Caribbœa* (2)—Lin. 1936 Bond 147, Ring-Tailed Pigeon (*Columba caribaea*) *Local names*:—Ring-tail; Blue Pigeon..*Range*:—Jamaica. 1952 FGC Man /blùu píjin/; StT, Blue dove—called blue pigeon in St Elizabeth, not here.

BLUE-QUIT sb; <*blue*+QUIT. Two distinct birds: LONG-MOUTHED and SHORT-MOUTHED BLUE-QUIT, which see; see also quots below.

1847 Gosse 238, *Euphonia Jamaica*..A short stumpy bird, and rather inelegant from the shortness of its tail, the Blue Quit reminds me of the Nut-hatches. 1936 Bond 368, *Pyrrhuphonia jamaica*..*Local names*:—Blue Quit; Cho-cho Quit; Short-mouthed Quit. 1955 Taylor 37, *Pyrrhuphonia jamaica*..This very small bird is known locally as..the Short-mouthed Blue-quit. *Ibid* 45, The Long-mouthed Blue-quit (*Euneornis campestris*) has a variety of local names, Blue Baize, Orange Quit [etc.].

BLUE ROAN sb dial; <*blue*+*roan*. A variety of PARROT fish, evid assoc through its colour with that of a blue-roan horse (or other animal: cf *OED roan a* and *sb*[1] Aa, B1b quot 1789).

1951 FGC StE, Blue-roan, a very bright-coloured reddish-blue fish, caught near Pedro bluff. 1952 FGC StE /bluu ruon/; StT /bluu ruun/ a parrot, heliotrope colour.

BLUES AND REDS sb obs.

The rival factions of SET GIRLS: the troupes of negro or coloured girls who vied with each other in Christmas and New Year fancy-dress parades in the late 18th and early 19th centuries. See quots.

1790 Beckford I 389, At Christmas the negroes upon neighbouring estates are divided, like other communities, into different parties: some call themselves the blue girls, and some the red: and their clothes are generally characteristic of their attachment. 1808 Stewart 263–4, On new year's day it was customary for the negro girls of the town ..to exhibit themselves in all the pride of gaudy splendor, under the denomination of *blues* and *reds*. a1818 Lewis (1845) 25, It seems that, many years ago, an Admiral of the Red was superseded on the Jamaica station by an Admiral of the Blue; and both of them gave balls at Kingston to the '*Brown Girls*'; for the fair sex elsewhere are called the 'Brown Girls' in Jamaica. In consequence of these balls, all Kingston was divided into parties: from thence the division spread into the other districts; and ever since, the whole island, at Christmas, is separated into the rival factions of the Blues and the Reds (the Red representing also the English, the Blue the Scotch), who contend for setting forth their processions with the greatest taste and magnificence.

BLUE-SPROUT sb dial. A variety of NEGRO YAM having blue sprouts.

1954 LeP StE.

BLUE-STRIPED CAVALLA sb.

1952 Smith in *NHN* 225, *Caranx ruber*, the blue-striped cavalla, is the handsomest of these [fish].

BLUE-STRIPED GRUNT sb.

1952 Smith in *NHN* 223, *Haemulon seiurus*, the blue-striped grunt, is a robust, elongate, compressed fish.. Yellowish with ten, blue, horizontal stripes on the head and body.

BLUE-SWEE sb dial; <*blue*+SWEE. The BLUE BAIZE bird or ORANGE QUIT. *G*

1952 FGC StT /bluu-swii/ eats oranges; very smart—hard to catch: called OBEAHMAN CUNNY.

BLUE-TAIL sb; cf *DAE blue-tail*, applied (1890) to a skink. The Blue-tailed Lizard *Celestus duquesneyi*.

1940 Lynn-Grant 105–6, *Celestus duquesneyi* Grant, 'Blue-tail'..The only blue-tailed *Celestus* known.. Known only from Portland Point.

BLUE-TOP sb dial. A variety of cassava of which the upper leaves are bluish.

1952 FGC StE.

BLUE TUMPA sb dial; <*blue*+TUMPA. A variety of PARROT fish that is blue and stumpy; cf BLUE PARROT.

1952 FGC StE /bluu tompa/ blue all the way through. 1958 DeC StT /bluu tompa/ a large parrot-fish.

BLUE-VINE (YAM) sb dial. A variety of NEGRO YAM of which the vine is blue.

1952 FGC StJ/blúu váin yam/; StM, Blue-vine, same as /moshéla/—huge, may weigh 100 lb. 1954 LeP StE (Eld), Blue vine and blue sprout: two varieties of Negro Yam.

BLUE-WEED sb dial. The weed *Blechum brownei*, with small blue flowers.

1952 FGC StJ, Blue-weed, same as dead-man-bones.

BLUFF adj, sb and vb dial; cf *OED bluff a* 2, *v*[1] 3.

A. adj: Big, clumsily large.

1912 McKay *Ballads* 13, Do it *so*, you mountain man; Car' behin' de bluff lef' foot, Seems i' frighten fe de boot!

B. sb: A rebuff, an insult.

1912 McKay *Ballads* 34, Ef we are smokin' cigarette, He [the 'bummer'] wants a part of it too; An' ebery bluff you gi'e to him, He's answer got to fit you.

C. vb: To insult.

1943 *GL* Han, Bluff, to insult.

BLUFF MANGO sb dial; <BLUFF adj+ *mango*.

1933 HPJ, The Bluff Mango is so called from its size.

BLUJONGO sb dial; prob based on *bludgeon*, but perh also infl by JUNKA (STICK).

1943 *GL* StE, Blujongo, A club.

BLUNDER /blonda/ sb dial; cf *OED blunder sb* 1, →1774. A quarrel or disturbance.

1958 DeC Man /duon guo der an mek a blonda/.

bluu bod, bluu bord see BLUEBIRD.

bluuda trii sb dial rare; etym unknown. The HOG APPLE (*Morinda citrifolia*).

1952 FGC StAnn /bluuda/ tree, monkey-berry.

BO see BEAU.

-bo suffix dial; perh represents BEAU, but cf Twi *-fó*, person, possessor. Suffix: a person of the kind, or possessing the quality, expressed in the element to which it is attached. Cf GREY-BO, *ha-buo, kiebo*, etc.

BOAR, BOW (MACHETE) /buo, buor, buoz, buorz/ sb dial; etym uncert: *bow* (*OED sb*[1]), *boar*, and some other words (*bore, beau*) are equally possible phonetically; on the side of sense, *bow* seems the most likely, but some evidence favours *boar*. There are at least two specific shapes involved—see quot 1958—but they may not always be kept distinct; nevertheless shape is prob the basis of the names. If *boar* is a genuine part of the meaning, it may refer to the somewhat tusk-like shape. Cf *sou, suod*.

1954 LeP Port, StT, Bou, curved machete; StAnn, Boars, Boze, curved machete. 1956 Mc StT /buo/ a curved machete; StAnd /buoz/ machete with a blunt hooked end—useful for climbing hillside, point dug into ground, but /it hav aal yuus/. (In StT called /uk paint/.) [Blade tapering to a semicircularly recurved end.] 1958 DeC Port /buor mashiet/ a cutlass..[with blade broadening to a large, gradually recurved point]; also /buo mashiet/; StT /buo/ a cutlass..[with straight blade broadening toward a symmetrically arched point].

BOARD[1] sb attrib or adj. *Board* is commonly used in Jamaica where *wooden* would be used elsewhere, esp attrib. Cf also BOARD SHOES, BOARD SLIPPERS, etc. *BA BL G T*

1905 Smith 25, An' at las' dey come to a little stream, an' over it a board bridge. 1958 DeC StT /buod handl/, /buon handl/: respectively the FLARE and SOU machetes, even though the handles are not always wooden and bone. Apparently in earlier times the flare handle was always wooden, the sou handle always of bone.

BOARD[2] /buod/ vb dial; <*board* vb. To grasp, take hold of.

1877 Murray *Feedin' 'Perrit* 8, Dis time, sar, I boad a piece o' tick, I go back in a de room; as I go in so I hit him, wop, wop. *Ibid*, Him boad de two side o' de coonoo, begin da rock..Him rock, I bawl!

BOARD-HANDLE sb dial. The FLARE machete; cf BOARD[1], quot 1958.

BOARDING HOOK sb. A gaff used to get a large fish into a boat.

1952 FGC StJ /yùuz búodn-ùk/ to get kingfish into /kúnu/.

BOARD SHOES sb dial; BOARD[1]+SHOES. *G*

1956 Mc Man /buod shuuz/ home-made sandal with a wooden sole.

BOARD SLIPPERS sb dial; BOARD+*slippers*. =BOARD SHOES. *G*

1952 FGC StAnd /búod slípaz/—Chinaman always wear them; StM.

BOAR-FISH sb dial; cf *OED boar-fish* for other species. The hogfish.

1892 Cockrell list, Boar-fish, hog-fish, pig-fish, *Lachnolæmus suillus*.

BOAR-GUM (TREE), BOAR-TREE, BOARWOOD sb; 1696, 1725 boar-tree, 1900→ boarwood tree, 1935→ boar-gum (tree). Two distinct trees (not always clearly distinguished by writers): *Rhus metopium* and *Symphonia globulifera*. See quots. Cf also HOG DOCTOR-TREE, HOG-GUM (TREE).

1696 Sloane 167, Terebinthus maxima..*Hog Doctor-Tree* or *Boar-tree*. 1725 Sloane 90–1, *Hog Doctor-Tree*, or, *Boar-Tree*..It is affirm'd very confidently in this Island by people who pretend to have seen it, that wild Hogs when wounded, by natural Instinct, come to this tree, where, by rubbing its Balsam on their Wounds, they are cured, from whence this Tree hath its common name. 1900 Murray 12, Among these stalwart forest kings you will catch a glimpse of a boarwood tree. 1926 Fawcett 9, Sloane gives the name Doctor Tree [*sic*] or Boar Tree to this tree [*Rhus metopium*], and Browne calls it Hog Gum Tree, but Macfadyen..shows that these names belong to *Symphonia globulifera* Linn. f. (*Moronobea coccinea*). 1935 HPJ, Boar-gum Tree, the same as coonoo-coonoo. 1941 Swabey 14, Boarwood—(Jamaica Sumach, Hog Doctor, Poison Wood, Burnwood) *Rhus metopium*. *Ibid* 22, Hog Gum—(Boarwood). *Symphonia globifera*. 1952 FGC StT /buo gom/ tree, good for cuts.

BOARS see BOAR.

BOAR TREE, BOARWOOD see BOAR-GUM.

BOASIFY /búosifài/ adj and adv dial; 1869 bosify, 1907 boastify, 1943 boasify; <*boast*+ -IFY. The sp *boastify* represents an unnatural pronunc that would be used only by a speaker being affected, or one conscious of the formation of the word. For etym cf also BOASY,

BOASY NAKED. *G*

A. adj: Puffed up with pride; showing off.

1877 Murray *Kittle* 5, Dat Mass William Hinds, you see da, him is a regular wa dem call *bosify Bony*. [Bony = Bonaparte]. 1907 Jekyll 246, When a Jamaica boy has money in his pocket he gets 'boastify'. 1943 *GL* Kgn Boasify, conceited.

B. adv: Proudly, swaggeringly.

1957, Bennett 29, Anancy dress up himself..an step boasify eena de gal yard.

BOAST WOOD sb; prob a mistaken 'normalization' of BOAR-WOOD via the form *boar's-wood. (Since the dialect reduces *-st* > *-s*, the writer 'restored' a *t*.)

1944 *NHN* II 142, The Boast Wood with its dark green foliage.

BOASY /búosi, buosti/ adj dial; < *boast* + *-y* (*OED* suffix[1])—cf also *boastive* (*EDD* Stf). Coincidental infl of African words is also possible: cf Yoruba bọ́si [ˈbɔːsi], to be all right, to be successful.

1. = BOASIFY: proud, vaunting, conceited; see also BOASY NAKED. *G*

1952 FGC Man, Bessy Shake-up [is a] small yellow-looking bird—shakes itself as it walks—'like dem /búosi/ lady shake up dem hip'. 1954 Reckord *Della* 4, Me run down de road an see Shepherd boasy wheel him staff like regimental sergeant-major.

2. Showily dressed; well dressed; attractive. (Prob a development from 1, perh influence also from BEAU.)

1935 HPJ, Bosy, spruce, fine, showy. 1943 *GL* StJ, Bosey, show-off or dressed well. 1956 Mc Man /shúo di liedi hou you búosi/ *Show the lady how prettily you are dressed*. /wát a búosi frák/.

3. Phr: *Boasy 'pon not'n*, to be boastful or conceited without warrant. *BL*

1954 LeP StAnn, Bosty pon nutten, to boast. [The definition takes *boasy* as a verb here, but it is prob an adjective.]

BOASY sb dial; < BOASY adj.

1. A boastful person. *G*

2. A much dressed-up man. See quots.

1954 LeP Man, Boasi, Word to describe man—elegantly dressed up; StAnn, Boasy, a boastful person; StT, a boastful person. 1956 Mc StAnd /búosi/ a boastful person; one who shows off.

BOASY NAKED adj phr dial; < BOASY + *naked*. See quot; the sense is not clear—perh the ref is to shameless showing-off. (Cf *barefaced*.)

1956 Mc Man /búosi níekid/ used of a person who boasts a lot.

BOATSWAIN /búosn/ sb; cf *OED*—this is one of the several nautical terms that were brought ashore in transf senses in Jamaica.

1. One of the 'officers' on a sugar estate, formerly in charge of a slave gang or overseeing the work of the sugar mill. Also, in present use, any similar headman in charge of labourers.

1774 Long II 319 note, Boatswain of the mill. The Negroe who attends the mill-gang, or feeders. 1823 Roughley 338, An ostensible slave officer, called the boatswain of the mill, should always be put in commission, whenever the mill is at work. 1839 McMahon 44, He then called the boatswain of the yard, to punish all hands in the boiling-house. 1943 *GL* West, Boson, a Headman. *G*

2. A prison officer having direct charge of prisoners.

1798 Evidence 2, They were sent with the boatswains of the gaol, to cut wood. 1837 James 7, All the drivers and the boatswains in the yard, is people that sentence to the workhouse for life. 1889 Sanguinetti 51, In our prisons till lately we had 'Boatswains' instead of 'Warders' and divided them into 'Watches'. 1943 *GL* Tre, Bous'n, a prison officer. 1959 Alma Norman StC, Bosun, a guard in charge of prisoners.

BOB vb dial; < BOB sb. To sing the bob or refrain of a song.

1956 Mc StAnd /dem bab di chuun—uol im juo/ *They sing the refrain of the tune 'Hold him Joe'*.

BOB, BOBBIN /bab, babm/ sb dial; cf *OED bob sb*[1] II, 'The refrain or burden of a song', quots 1606–1788; *bobbin* evid represents **bobbing* vbl sb.

1907 Jekyll 158, One man starts or 'raises' the tune and the others come in with the 'bobbin', the short refrain of one or two words which does duty for chorus. 1907 Myers in Jekyll 284, There is one feature of the above-quoted 'Angola' song which is also shared by the modern songs of this collection, namely, the presence of 'bobbins' or short refrains. c 1953 Wilson 'Digging Songs' *Gleaner*, Bobbin: The short refrain sung by diggers at the end of a series of lines sung by the Bomma. 1956 Mc StAnd /báb iz—tùu dé/ *The refrain is 'To-day'*; /ˈmongki jaa buon so swiit'—dat iz di babm av it/ *Monkey jaw-bone so sweet—that is the refrain of it.*

BOBA-MAH see BUBA-MAT.

BOBBY BROWN sb dial. A variety of sweet potato. (Cf the Twi practice of naming yams after the men who first grew them—Christaller, s.v. *ɔ-dé*.)

1952 FGC StT /babi broun/ a round, red type of sweet potato.

BOBBY HANSON sb dial. A variety of cassava. Cf BOBBY BROWN.

1952 FGC StE /babi hansn/ cassada.

BOB COOK sb dial. One of the species of *Dipholis* (presumably not *D. salicifolia*, which is GALIMETA WOOD). Cf BOBBY BROWN.

1952 FGC StE, Bob Cook, San Domingo Bullet—similar to Galimeta.

BOBO /bóbò búobò/ adj[1] and sb[1] dial; < Sp *bobo*, dunce, fool (*bobón*, a great idiot or simpleton). Perh also infl by Twi *bɔ́ɔbɔɔ*, quiet, phlegmatic, dull, sluggish. *G*

1. See quots. (*BL* /bubu/)

1943 *GL* StAnd, Bobo, a fool ('Spanish'); Kgn, StM, Bobo, foolish. 1954 LeP StE, Bobo, an ugly, fat, oafish fellow. 1956 Mc StAnd /búobo/ a bad man, dishonest.

2. A fish: see quot. [1902 Jordan 257 lists *bobo* as the name of a mountain mullet in Cuba.]

1952 FGC StC /bóbo/ a flat fish, most like puppy-mouth; puppy-fish; catfish.

BOBO /búobò/ adj[2] and sb[2] dial; prob iterative < Fr *beau*, beautiful, perh also infl by Ewe *bɔbɔ*, smooth, sweet, effeminate.

1. Pretty.

1943 *GL* StC, Bowbo, pretty; StJ, Bobo, pretty. 1955 FGC Man /buobuo/ pretty.

2. See quot.

1943 *GL* StAnd, Bowbo, child's dress.

BOB-TENNER /báb-téna/ sb dial; < Engl slang *bob* + TENNER. One shilling and sixpence.

1943 *GL* Clar, Bob-tenna, 1/6d. 1952 FGC Han /bábténa/ 1/6d, fourbit. s CURRENCY.

boch see BIRCH.

BOCHARA-YAM see BACKRA YAM.

BOCKRA see BACKRA.

BOCO see POCO.

BODILY /bádili/ adj dial. Of persons: tall and thin.

1958 DeC StT /badili/ pertaining to a tall thin person.

BODOO sb dial; ?abbr of RUBADOO. A drum.

1943 *GL* StE, Bodoo, drum.

BODY-COME-DOWN /bádi kóm-doun/ sb dial. Prolapse of the rectum.

1959 Mrs Robinson, UCWI Preventive Med.

bof sb dial; prob represents Engl *buff*, perh in allusion to the colour.

1958 DeC Port /bof/ same as /fufu/: food pounded soft in a mortar.

bof tiit see BUFF TEETH.

bogobi, bonggobi /bógobi, bónggobi/ sb dial; cf Mende *bóngà*, a small fish, also perh Twi *koóbi*, Ewe *kǒbì*, species of river fish. A small, round, fresh-water fish (cf *bangga*); also called *gadami*, SAND FISH.

1826 Barclay 331, A large lagoon near where I resided, part of which is covered with reeds, abounds with a small kind of fish, from 3 to 4 inches long, called by the negroes bugabees or bungabees. 1952 FGC Port /bonggobi/ = /gadami/; StC /bónggobi/ = Sand fish; StT /bogobi/.

BOGRO, BOGRO-BOGRO /bógro, bógru, búgra/adj dial arch; etym unknown, though said to be an Africanism (Russell).

1. See quots.

1868 Russell 10, Bogro-bogro—Coarse. Wa me fe do wid dis bogro-bogro ting. 1873 Rampini 127, Him curse him moder for a 'bogro-bogro' (coarse)..'nana' (old woman). 1935 HPJ, Bogro-bogro, 'applied to stout people'. 1959 LeP, from Miss McKoy (UCWI student) /bugra-bugra/ 'rugged'.

2. In combin: bogro salt, bogro corn.

1868 Russell 6, Bogro-sal, Coarse mine-salt. 1935 HPJ, Bugru corn, A large species of (imported) Indian corn. 1952 FGC StJ, Tre /bogro/-salt being replaced by 'coarse salt'. 1955 LeP StAnd /bogru kaan/ said by a higgler in Papine market to be a white kind of maize used for making cornmeal.

[In Antigua /bákrà/ = coarse, fat, rough.]

BOG-RUSH sb; *OED* has no quots; *DAE* 1817–8, *Schoenus setaceus*. A rush of the genus *Schoenus*, growing characteristically in bogs.

1814 Lunan I 103, Bog Rush. *Schoenus* [ten species are listed].

BOGUE /buog/ sb also attrib; prob < *bog*, esp in the Scottish form [bo:g] (cf Craigie *bog* 1 b and *SND* spellings *bog, boag, boge, bogg, bowg*), a marshy place. In this connection one may note that in quots 1672 and 1756 the word is joined with Scottish surnames. The derivation < Sp *boca*, mouth, referring to a river gorge, is condemned by Yates & Thompson (1958, p 5) in connection with *Bog Walk*; note, however, quot 1683 below. A generic element in a number of Jamaican place-names: boggy or swampy land from which water runs out. *BL N*

1672 Blome Map (printed 1671), Duncan's bogg (St James), Dry bagg [*sic*] (StAnns). 1683 *Laws* Map, Boga Creek (St Catherine). 1756 Browne 26, Mendsy's Bogue, in St Anne's; *ibid* 66, Mendzey's-Bog, in this parish.

Current: Bogue (Clar, StC, StE); Bogue Islands (StJ—in mouth of Montego river); Bogue Hill (Man & StE).

BOG WALK int dial; perh < *back water* (cf BLACK WATER), folk-etymologized to the form of the place-name *Bog Walk* (St Catherine). An exclamatory formula used to terminate a group song.

1948 U.Newton IV 17, 33, Bog-Walk! (A shout used to end songs between a leader and a group—e.g. 'Chichi-bud'.)

BOG-WALK PINE sb obs; < *Bog Walk* + PINE. A variety of pineapple, associated in some way with Bog Walk (St Catherine)—perh once grown esp there.

1774 Long III 792, The bog-walk pine, of a compressed form, and deep green coat.

BOILING HOUSE sb; *OED* 1712. The building in which the cane juice is evaporated in manufacturing sugar. *G*

1839 McMahon 44, see quot s.v. BOATSWAIN 1.

boj (waata) see BIRCH.

boja sb dial; prob < *budge* (*OED* sb^5 'Obs. slang' meaning a 'sneak thief') + *-er*[1] (*OED*).

1958 DeC StM /boja/ an undependable no-account person.

boji gom see BIRCH.

bojo /bójò/ sb dial, also attrib; perh a variant of *beje* sb[2].

1. A cloth or straw bag with a loop by which it can be slung over the shoulder; used for carrying victuals to the field. Cf HENG-'PON-ME, LEAN-'PON-ME, etc.

1956 Mc StE (Accom) /bójò/. 1959 DeC StJ /bojo, bojo-bag/ a side-bag (any size) of canvas or crocus bag.

2. See quot, and cf *beje* sb[2].

1959 DeC Han /bojo/ a temporary trash bag made at the field.

boki see BUCKY.

bokra see BACKRA.

boksha (haag) see BERKSHIRE (HOG).

boksn see BUXEN.

BOLANGENA sb obs; < Amer Sp *berengena*, with the common substitution of *l* for *r*. The egg-plant. Cf also BROWN-JOLLY, VALANGHANNA.

1756 Browne 173, Solanum 1..The Brown-Jolly, or *Bolangena*..This plant..was first imported into Jamaica by the *Jews*..It generally bears a number of large berries.

BOLLO sb dial; etym unknown—perh conn with BOLOW, in the sense of fellow-workers. Relief work in hard times; emergency employment.

1943 *GL* (No addr), Bollo, a system of relief works; Port, Relief work.

BOLOW /bólo/ sb dial, often appellative; prob an abbr of COMBOLO.

1. A fellow, comrade, friend.

2. A sweetheart, lover.

1907 Jekyll 245 [Song:] Colon bolow *gone a Colon.. * Bolow, comrade; *ibid* 274, A term of endearment.. bolow. 1943 *GL* Kgn, Bollo, sweetheart, lover, friend; Tre, Bollow, my friend.

bombai see *bambai*.

BOMBAST MAHOE sb bot; cf *OED bombast* 1 b attrib. →1653, and MAHOE. The tree *Ochroma pyramidale*; the 'bombast' is referred to again in another of its names: DOWN TREE; the flower resembles that of the MAHOE.

1756 Browne 286, Hibiscus 10..The Bombast *Mohoe*, with very large leaves. 1814 Lunan I 271, *Ochroma lagopus*..This tree is also called bombast mahoe.. 1926 Fawcett 153, Bombast Mahoe. 1941 Swabey 19.

BOMBAY MANGO sb. A fine variety of mango, named for its place of origin.

1913 Harris 12, see quot s.v. EAST INDIAN MANGO. 1954 *FG* 475, Bombay mango, A comparatively late importation from India.

bombo see BUMBO.

bomi see *bani.*

BOMMA sb dial; prob <Engl and Scots *bum* (cf *SND bum* v[1] 2, 'To make a droning sound, used of musical instruments, esp the bagpipes, also of a person singing or reading in a droning or indistinct manner'; also *OED v*[2], 'To hum loudly, to boom') + *-er*[1] (*OED*). Cf JAMMA.

c 1953 Wilson 'Digging Songs' in *Gleaner*, Bomma, the leader in the group singing of work songs.

BOMMY see *bani.*

bomp-a-chuot sb dial; <*bump* + A[1] 1 + *throat.* The Adam's apple.

1956 Mc Man, see quot s.v. *wail paip.*

BON sb dial; prob <*band* (*OED sb*[3] 4, attrib, e.g. as in *band drum*); cf *banda.* (Engl *band* was borrowed into Kimbundu as *bǎŋ̀*, a European soldier's drum.)

1923 Beckwith 41 [Song:] Bon gone a' Rose Hall.—Rose Hall is a famous old estate..'Bon' is the big drum. [Cf also photograph of 'Bon drum' from Lacovia opposite title-page of Beckwith's collected *Jamaica Folklore.*]

BONA /bona/ sb dial; etym uncert—perh <Twi *mpǎnã, mpě̃na*, lover, sweetheart. See quots.

1952 Murray 18 [Song:] Cantinny me bona Prim, Prim—Note: Me bona, A term of endearment. 1958 DeC gen /bona/ 'darling', 'putus'.

bonabis see BONAVIST.

BONACE BARK TREE sb bot; etym uncert: the sole source is Browne, from whom later writers repeat the name. If it was pronounced in three syllables it may represent Amer Sp *bonasí*, a native Central American name of *Hamelia erecta* or other species (Santamaría, Mesa). By folk-etym it produced BURN-NOSE BARK. The trees *Daphnopsis occidentalis* and *D. tinifolia.*

1756 Browne 372, Arbor 19, The Bonace Bark Tree.. This tree is common near *Monteca bay*..The bark makes very good ropes..The seeds have a sharp biting taste. 1814 Lunan I 106–7, Bonace Bark. 1864 Grisebach 782, Bonace-bark.

BONAVIST /bánavìs, bánabìs, bónabìs, bánawìs, bánabìinz, báabís, bábis/ sb; 1655 bonuist [1657] 1696 1864→ bonavist, 1740 bonnavest, 1788? bannavis, 1912 bannabees, 1913 bonovist, 1929 bannabis, banner bean; <*Bona Vista. OED* derives this from Italian *buona vista*, but a *DAE* citation records the tradition, known in Jamaica, that the name refers to the place of origin, the island of Bona Vista (Boa Vista, Cape Verde Is.), from which the beans were imported into the New World. *DAE* 1682→. An edible bean (Leguminosae), *Dolichos lablab.* See also BROKE-POT PEAS. *BA*

1655 Eye-Witnesse Account 19, Bonanoes, Bonuist, Plantans, Pine-Apples. [1657 Ligon 24, At the time we came first there (*sc.*, Barbados), we found both *Potatoes, Maies* and *Bonavists*, planted between the boughes.] 1696 Sloane 67, Phaseolus maximus perennis..*White bonavist. Ibid* 68, *Red bonavist.* 1864 Grisebach 782, Bonavist, *Dolichos Lablab.* 1912 McKay *Songs* 15, Watch de blue bannabees..Some call it 'broke-pot' peas. 1929 Beckwith 19, 'Bannabis' (Banner bean)..'Time nebber too long fe Bannabis bear bean', says an old-time proverb inculcating the rewards of patience. 1943 *GL* Port, Banabis. 1952 FGC StT, Port /bánavis/; StAnn /bónabìs/; StJ /báabís/; etc. 1956 Mc Man, StAnd /bánabìin, bánabìs, bá-bis/.

bon-bon sb dial; iterative <*burn* (or *burnt*). *T*

1. Any burnt food.

1956 Mc Man /gi mi di bón-bon/ *Give me the burnt part.*

2. Specif.—See quot. *BL G*

1956 Mc Man, Bun-bun—burnt rice at the bottom of the pan—some people like it. 1962 BLB 50.

bonchakii, bonchi see BUNCH-O'-KEYS, BUNCHY.

BONE /buon, buun/ sb chiefly dial; <*bone. G*

1. The hard centre rib or stalk of a plant leaf, esp that of large compound leaves, used for making mats, etc.

1952 FGC Man, Fern bones—used to make mats for drying ginger; StAnn, Napier grass has a 'bone like cane', StC, 'Black-dog' fern so called because the bone is black; StM, Bone of leaf make basket. 1956 Mc StAnd /di buon av di banana liif yuuz fi mek mat/.

2. The stems of ganja after the leaf has been taken for making cigarettes; they are usually steeped in white rum, or boiled and the water added to rum, to give it a more intoxicating effect.

1958 DeC gen /him juk it op wid buunz and pepa/ *He gave it a stronger 'kick' with 'bones' and pepper.*

3. See quot.

1958 DeC gen /buonz/ the ribs of a bamboo basket.

BONE-BASKET sb dial. See quot.

1958 DeC Tre /buon baskit/ any basket which has *bones*, i.e. hook-withe or swipple-jack ribs, and bamboo wattling. Thus a /groun baskit/ and a /hanggl baskit/ are two kinds of /buon baskit/ but a /bangkra/ is not.

BONE-DANGER sb dial.

1952 FGC StM, Bone-danger—a kind of shellfish having sharp spines, so that it is dangerous to step on.

BONE-HANDLE sb dial. A local name for the sow machete; cf BOARD[1], quot 1958.

BONE-IN-A-VALLEY sb joc dial or slang.

1958 DeC StM /buon-in-a-vali/ a thin person.

BONEYARD MAN sb dial or slang; cf *DAE boneyard*, cemetery, 1872→. *G*

1958 DeC StM, Boneyard man, a very thin person.

bong sb dial rare; perh <Twi *ɔ-bóŋ* hole, hollow, cave, den of animals.

1954 LeP StE, Bung—a dirty, untidy house.

BONGAU see BANJA.

bonggi see BUNGAY.

bonggo see BUNGO.

bonggobi see *bogobi*, and supplement.

BONGGY see BUNGAY.

bongka /bóngka/ sb dial; cf Twi *ɔ-bɔ̃́ŋ*, rind, bark + articulative *-k-*, + A[8].

The CABBAGE PALM tree, its branch, or the sheath or 'bough' (lower part of the leaf or branch, which in growth is closely wrapped around the trunk and less-developed sheaths); also applied to other palm trees and their branches. The sequence of senses is uncertain, whether the sheath or the tree is primarily so named, but the sheath has had many uses: formerly for roofing, and as a cradle for a child, and still as a mat on which to dry produce, and by children as a sledge for sliding down grassy slopes. See also *bubakin, buunakin,* CULLABUNKA, KANDA.

1940 HPJ, Bunka, the fallen limb of a coconut tree. 1943 *GL* Port, Boonkah, bough of a coconut tree; StAnd, Bunkah, tree limb; StM, Bunka, bough; No addr, Bunkah, the dry bough of a palm. 1952 FGC StM /bóngka/ Cabbage palm: use to beautify a yard; StT /bongka/ Mountain cabbage: heart of trunk can use as cabbage, leaves as thatch, children play like 'sledge' in sheath. 1959 LeP StAnd /bóngka, búunakin, búbakin iz aal di siem ting—kyábij paam bou. Wi yuuz dem tu skiet an/.

bongkas sb dial; perh a form of prec. See quot.

1956 Mc Man, A piece cut from the second head 'built' by yellow-yam. Yellow-yam bears a first head, which is cut off; a second head forms, and a piece cut from this is called /bóngkas/.

bongkra see BANKRA.

bongks see BOUNCE.

BONGO see BUNGO.

BONITO JACK /baníita jak/ sb dial. The bonito fish. *BA*

1952 FGC StM, StT.

BONJA, BONJAW, BONJOO, BONJOUR see BANJA.

BONKRA see BANKRA.

BONNET PEPPER sb obs; cf *OED* which has no quot. A former name for the SCOTCH-BONNET pepper.

1740 Importance 34, Bonnet-Pepper, Hen-Pepper and Bird-Pepper, all used in Soops or Pickles. 1814 Lunan I 356, Bonnet Peppers.—These have a large turbinated fruit, not furrowed like the bell peppers, but very shining.

BONNY see *bani.*

bon-pan see BURN-PAN.

BONSORO see *bousarou.*

bontong see BURN-TONGUE.

bonvist see BONAVIST.

BOOBA see BUBA.

BOOBO see BUBU.

BOOBO-YAGGA see *buguyaga.*

BOOBY BIRD sb. Any of the birds (not true boobies) that lay BOOBY EGGS. *BL N*

1956 Jeffrey-Smith 135, The Bridled Tern (*Sterna anaethetus*) and the Sooty Tern (*Sterna fuscata*) as well as the Noddy (*Anous stolidus*) are known as 'booby birds'. Their eggs are gathered by the thousands from the cays off the mainland. .and brought to Kingston for sale on the streets.

BOOBY EGG(S) sb; cf *OED booby* 2. The eggs of BOOBY BIRDS, sold as food by street vendors in Kingston (and elsewhere in Jamaica). *BL*

1873 Rampini 25–6, He who sold booby eggs had nothing to do with the vendors of eggs of ordinary poultry. 1929 Beckwith 52, 'Han-y he-egg!' cry the egg vendors, or 'Booby he-egg! booby he-egg! bwoil an' raw, booby he-egg!' These pretty brown spotted booby eggs, about half the size of a hen's egg, are a favourite breakfast dish. 1956 Jeffrey-Smith 133, and cf BOOBY BIRD quot 1956.

BOOCHOUNOU sb dial; cf *bununus, bululups,* and other phonosymbolic creations suggesting kissing or nuzzling.

1943 *GL* Port, Boochounou, baby.

BOOD see BOOTH.

BOOF /buf/ adv dial; echoic. A word suggesting the short, dull sound made by something lumpish striking the ground, or the like. Cf BOOPS, WOOF, etc. *BL*

1905 Smith 21, Ticky-Picky Boom-Boom Boof! [The noise made by the yams as they chase Tiger down the road.] c 1915 FGC StAnd, remembered in telling of Anancy stories, e.g. when Anancy's children fall from the ceiling to the ground, they go /buf/.

BOOFOO see BUFFO.

BOOGOOYAGA, BOOGOO YAGGA, BOOGU-YAGGA see *buguyaga.*

BOOK AND KEY sb; cf *OED book sb* 4a, the Bible. *G*

The name of a kind of 'trial by ordeal' still practised in the West Indies: A key is inserted in the Bible at an appropriate text—e.g. the commandment which the person being tried is alleged to have broken; should the accused be guilty, when he swears his oath while touching or holding the key the Bible will either fly open or fall to the ground. Details of the procedure vary. An early description is in 1835 Madden II 100, The Book Ordeal; a recent one (for Trinidad) is in V. S. Naipaul, *The Suffrage of Elvira.*

BOOKIE sb dial; familiar formation <BOOK-KEEPER. *G*

1956 Mc StT /bukii/ book-keeper on an estate.

BOOK-KEEPER sb. An assistant subordinate to the overseer on a sugar estate; in the 18th cent, usually a white indentured servant. See quots. *BA G*

1788 Beckford 89, Book-keepers are in subordinate command to the Overseers, they attend the still-houses in crop, and out of crop, the the [*sic*] field. There are many so little deserving the name they bear, that so far from being able to calculate accounts they cannot many of them even read. 1828 Marly 51, This refreshment [grog] they had some need of, more especially the book-keepers, who had remained in the field under the sun for such a length of time. 1889 Sanguinetti 52, But we have 'Barracks' on estates for lodging book-keepers in. 1956 Mc StT, The book-keeper is under the overseer and over the head-man.

BOOLOOLOOPS see *bululups.*

BOON adj dial; <*boon,* good, goodly (*OED* →1686). Good, goodly.

1794 (Ms 1711) Barham 7 [A sick negro in Jamaica when given arrowroot juice:] He said he found his heart boon. (HPJ.) 1957 JB /him i wan buun pikni/ *He was a good child.*

BOONA, BOONAKIN, BOONASKIN see *buna, bunakin.*

BOONKAH see *bongka.*

BOONOONOOS, BOONOONOONOOS see *bununus.*

BOOT sb[1]; prob metaph <*boot.*

1952 FGC StE, Boot, nit, or young peanut when just formed on the plant.

BOOT sb[2] dial; cf *OED boot sb*[1] (esp 2, *obs*), and the phr *to boot.* Money gained in a bargain, or earnest-money to bind a bargain. (The sense here is not clear.)

1943 *GL* StAnd, Boot, money on a bargain.

BOOTH /buud, buut/ sb dial; <*booth*—cf *OED* sb 1: 'A temporary dwelling covered with boughs of trees or other slight materials. *arch.* in gen. sense'. A temporary shelter, usually of bamboo poles and palm thatch, as erected for dances, wedding festivities, or on the beach or by the roadside.

1912 McKay *Songs* 130, I'll go to no more dancing booth. 1943 *GL* Port, Bood, a hut. 1952 FGC StAnd, Coconut leaves make shed or /buut/ or summer house; StJ, Coconut leaves thatch hut, make /buud/ and arch when someone going to married. 1954 LeP Man, Board, a thatched hut. 1955 LeP Port, Bood, building made from bamboo pole, etc.

BOOTIFOOT /búutifùt/ sb dial; <*boot* + *-y* or *-ie* + foot. (The presence of *bootee* in this compound is doubtful; diminutive *-y* or *-ie* (*OED -y* suffix[6]) is very commonly used in Ja dial; or this may be *OED -y* suffix[1], 'having the qualities of'.) A variety of chicken with heavily feathered legs and feet, so that it seems to be wearing boots.

1940 HPJ, Bootifoot, a fowl with feathers on lower legs. 1952 FGC West /búutifùt/.

BOOTOO see *butu*.

BOOT-SHOE sb dial; <*boot* sb + *shoe* vb. A semicircular plate of metal placed under the heel of a boot or shoe to prevent wear.

1956 Mc StAnd /buut shuu/.

BORE /buor/ vb dial; <*bore*, vb. *BL G*

1. trans. To push (oneself) through a crowd or other obstruction (cf *OED bore* v^1 1 d, 'to penetrate, make one's way through (a crowd)', only quot 1732. Cf also BUMP-AN'-BORE. *BA*

1943 *GL*, see POT-HOOK 2. 1950 Pioneer 52, Se dem yah Dah push an 'queeze an bore. 1956 JB /a wé im a búor imself go?/ *Where's he pushing himself to?*

2. Passive use of Engl active *bore*: to be penetrated.

1952 FGC StJ, Sea-bladder very soft—as you touch it it bore.

BORE-NOSE sb dial arch, also attrib; for *bored-nose* or *bore-nosed*. An epithet: see quot.

1940 HPJ, Bore-nose—applied to coolies because they wear nose-jewels. (But, 'you see hole bore a mi nose?' refers to the stupidity of the African.)

BORER sb dial; <*borer*.

1. Cf BORE 1.

1960 HPJ in *Gleaner* 9 May, The old 17th century sense still universally known in Jamaica: the *borer* penetrates a crowd and can pick a pocket in the confusion.

2. A kind of sea urchin. Cf *OED* v^1 1 b.

1952 FGC Port, West, Borer, a white sea-egg with short, thick prongs.

BORING vbl sb dial; <BORE. Pushing one's way through a crowd. *G*

1957 Bennett 76, Ee-hee, now fe de borin'. Gimme All de ticket George.

borki adj dial; prob for *bulky*. Stout.

1952 FGC Tre, When soil is poor /di banaana duon gruo borki/.

BORN /baan/ ppl adj dial; cf *OED born pple* and *a* B 1 a. Related or connected by birth; cf *baan-ya*, BORN-DAY, BORN-NAME, etc. *BL G T*

1955 LeP StE (Accom) /Nuo mi chail, mi no rieli yu baan mada/ *No, my child, I'm not really your true mother (who bore you).*

BORN-DAY /báan-dìe/ sb dial. The day-of-the-week on which one was born, as reflected in one's DAY NAME.

1868 Russell ix, Chapter II..Proper Nouns:—'Born days' with their general signification. 1907 Jekyll 156, Poor me little Cubba boy, barn day no Cubba? (Note:) 'is not my born-day (birthday) Cubba'. 1940 HPJ, Barn-day (Jekyll) seems anomalous, but Georgie knew it. 'Me barn-day no' Cubba', i.e. 'I was not born on a Thursday'. 1956 Mc Man /kojo/ is a born-day name.

BORN-DAY CLOTHES sb dial. See quot.

1962 BLB 48 /baan-die kluoz/ very short clothes.

BORN-DAY NAME, BORN-NAME /báan-nìem/ sb dial. = DAY NAME.

1935 HPJ, Barn-name, the name given to a child according to the day on which it was born, in the Twi manner.

BORN NEAR THE PLANTAIN ROOT phr. Truly and thoroughly of the country.

1873 Rampini 15, The two planters, evidently 'born near the plantain root', who thought Jamaica was going to the devil.

BOROUTEN prep dial; this sp represents a pronunc [bəˈrautn̩] for WITHOUTEN (see Introd, Phonology; cf also BECAUSEN, etc.).

1943 *GL* StAnd, Borouten, without.

borstin stail see BURSTING STYLE.

bos see BUS, BUST.

BOSEAU sb dial; perh <BEAU + SO.

1943 *GL* Clar, Man, Boseau, a pet name.

BOSEY see BOASY.

bos-mi see BUSS-ME.

BOSON see BOATSWAIN.

BOSSU see *busu* sb[1].

bosta sb dial; etym uncert: this could equally well represent *buster* (now chiefly US—cf *DAE* 1 b, 'An animal or thing of unusual size or quality') or *Busta*, the affectionate nickname of Sir Alexander Bustamante, popularly considered a 'buster', a champion of the common man, and a tough article. Cf BUSTA BACKBONE.

1. A locally-made sandal, the sole of which (and sometimes the upper part) is made from old automobile tyres. Also called *masha*, POWER SHOES, etc.

1956 Mc StAnd /bosta/ a rough sandal of car tyre.

2. A very tough kind of sweet, also called BUSTA BACKBONE, STAGGERBACK.

1943 *GL* Man, Busta, A tough brown sweet made of head sugar and grated coconut. 1952 FGC StM /bosta/ staggerback; black and tight.

bostin stail see BURSTING STYLE.

BOSUN see BOATSWAIN. Also s BOSUN YAM.

BOSY see BOASY.

bota- see BUTTER-.

BOTHER /bada/ vb colloq; <*bother* (*OED v* colloq 3). *G*

1. In negative constructions (*Don't bother* /no bada/), sometimes with reflexive pron: I forbid you (to do something); it's no use (your doing something)—so don't waste your effort. *BA*

1942 Bennett 44, Noh bada show off 'bout a fe Yuh money, data lie! [*Don't show off about its being your money; that's a lie!*] 1956 Mc StE /nó báda kom in yier yu no/ *It's no use coming in here, you know!*

2. As above, with an added note of warning: Be careful not to; see that you don't. *BL*

1956 Mc StAnd /no bada maak yu pikni/ *Mind you don't mark your child.* (Said to a pregnant woman.)

3. As a polite refusal (/no bada/). [Questionable.] *BL*

1956 Mc Port (Moore Town), Would you sing us one of the old-time songs?—/no bada/ *I'm sorry, but I won't.*

4. Refl: To trouble oneself; to waste one's time; const *with. BL*

1956 Mc Man /dem káal i shúga an wáata aa bébrij—dem duon báda wid lemaniéd/ *They call it 'sugar-and-water' or 'beverage'—they don't use the word lemonade.*

BOTHERATION /bàdaríeshan, bàraríeshan/ sb common; cf *OED*, 'Formerly also bodderation'; quots →1867. A vexation or annoyance (somewhat stronger than the sense in Std Engl); also concretely: a thing or a person that is a source of much annoyance. *BA G T*

1943 *GL* (many parishes). 1946 U.Newton I 15, The man was a botheration. 1956 Mc Man /báraríeshan/. 1957 JN, Me don't like no botheration when mi a do nothing..Mi can't stand no worries you know.

botri see BUTTERFLY.

BOTTLE-ARSE /bátlás, bátl-ás, báklàs/ (cf *OED bottle-arsed* in a different sense). A small blood-sucking fly whose abdomen becomes red and swollen—whence the name. *BL N*

1725 Sloane II 226, *Culex niger minor. A Bottle-Arse. Moustiques de Rochefort* which bite without Noise..This Fly is very small, no larger than a Pin's Head, the Body is very black, the Wing's grey, the other Parts scarce perceivable. 1740 Importance 48, *Bottle-Arses* is a small Fly with a large Breech; they are chiefly in the Country; they will suck the Blood where they fasten till they are full. 1952 FGC Han, Man, Tre /bátlás/ etc.

BOTTLE-CAESAR sb dial. A variety of the CAESAR fish shaped somewhat like a bottle.

1952 FGC StE /bátl síiza/ same as amber-jack caesar—longer, rounder, thicker [than ordinary caesar].

BOTTLE-COD ROOT sb bot; presumably so named from the shape of the root being like that of the *cod* or belly of a bottle. A shrubby tree or plant identified both as *Capparis cynophallophora* and *C. flexuosa*. The root was formerly used medicinally.

1814 Lunan I 107–8, Bottle-cod Root. Capparis..1. Cynophallophora..The root is large, yellow, fleshy, and tastes strongly like horse-raddish. 1854–5 *TJSA* I 60, Bottle Cod Root. 1914 Fawcett 234, *Capparis flexuosa* L .. Bottle-cod Root..*Shrub* or *tree* 8–25 ft. high.

BOTTLE-FISH sb; cf *OED*, listed without quots.

A fish which may puff itself up until it resembles a bottle; specifically *Canthigaster rostratus* (the 'smooth bottle-fish'); formerly also applied to *Diodon liturosus* and other SOURSOP FISH. The first is also called locally *jeje*, PUFF-FISH, PUFF-GUT, TOAD-FISH, TOADY.

1756 Browne 456, Ostracion 2..The prickly Bottle-fish.. Ostracion 3...The Bottle-fish. 1820 Thomson 41, The fish found in the West-Indies to be most deleterious are the barracuta..King-fish..smooth bottle-fish (ostracion glabellum). 1952 FGC Port, StAnn, StC, StJ, StM, West /batlfish, baklfish/; 'is poison', 'tease the belly and it swells', 'flat bottom, smooth—head round and sharp'.

BOTTLE-FLY sb obs (cf *EDD, DAE*, which list the word in a different meaning). See quot; the ref is prob to the PEENY.

1838 Kelly 16, Of these [fireflies] there are several varieties; the bottle-fly is the largest..There is another, a smaller kind..alternately shewing and withholding their light, which is feeble in comparison with that of the bottle-fly.

BOTTLE-MOUTH PARROT sb dial; cf BOTTLE-NOSE PARROT. A variety of PARROT-FISH having a bottle-like mouth.

1952 FGC StM, Bottle-mouth parrot—blue but not entirely.

BOTTLENECK sb chiefly dial.

1. Another name for the ALLIGATOR or AVOCADO PEAR, from the shape of the fruit.

1952 FGC Port /baklnek/ alligator pear.

2. The false fruit of the prickly CHO-CHO.

1956 Mc Man /bakl nek/ false bearing of /maka chuocho/.

BOTTLE-NOSE PARROT sb dial; cf BOTTLE-MOUTH PARROT. A variety of PARROT-FISH having a bottle-like nose.

1952 FGC StJ, Bottle-nose parrot. 1952 Smith in *NHN* 203, *Scarus acutus*, which is called 'the bottle-nose parrot-fish' in Long Bay, St James.

BOTTOM-SIDE /bátamsàid/ adv or prep dial; <*bottomside*, in nautical usage, which in turn may be infl by coolie pidgin. [*Bottomside* is more frequent in the E. Caribbean than in Ja.] Cf TOPSIDE. *G*

1943 *GL* StC, Battam side, below.

BOTTOMSIDIN adv or prep dial; <*bottomside* (cf BOTTOM-SIDE) + -*n* suffix[1].

1943 *GL* StC, Bottomsidin, below.

bou sb dial uncom; perh <*bow sb*[1] (*OED*). A path or track made by wild hogs and followed by the hog-hunter.

1952 FGC Tre /yu tek a bou aafta di hag..yu fala likl bou op an doun in di mountin/.

BOUGHTED vb form dial; <*bought* + -*ed*[1] (*OED*). An overcorrection (or other unorthodox form); the normal dial past-tense form is *buy* or *did buy*. *G*

1868 Russell 15–16 [In the dialect the verb is never inflected for number, person, or tense] 'except in few cases when usually the irregular verb, past tense, is inflected to express the past tense; thus, I boughted a horse for ten pounds 'talin money'.

BOUL sb dial; perh var of *bahu*, but see BOLOW.

1943 *GL* Kgn, Boul, a labourer.

boulin /bóulin/ sb dial; perh <*bowline* (*OED* records the spellings *bolin, bowlin, boulin* from 17th cent). The tarpon.

1952 FGC StC /boulin/ = /sabilo/ = tarpon.

BOUNCE /bongs, bongks/ vb gen colloq; <*bounce* vb (cf *OED*: 1. To beat, thump, trounce, knock. Trans and intr; obs since 18th cent). *BL G*

1. Trans. To hit or knock (someone or something) with a sudden blow. *BA*

1940 HPJ, Bounce, to 'barge' into, 1935 Trinidad, Tobago. Jamaican: very common, not purely working class. 1942 Bennett 33, Mota kear..crawl up backa-we.. An' bunks we to glory. 1956 Mc StE (Accom) /yu bongks im/ *You hit him*; StAnd (Dallas) /mi a sing, him a bongks mi/ *I was singing—he bumped (shoved) me.* 1959 LeP StAnd /yu bongks mi/—(a common accusation in a minor car collision), *You ran into me!*

2. In various phrases: A. active: *bounce up against*, to run into (somebody or something),

bounce off, to knock off, dislodge; B. passive: *bounce down*, to be knocked down.

1955 LeP StAnd /him bongks op gens mi/ *He banged into me.* 1956 Mc StE (Accom) /di man bongks aaf di latch an ron in/ *The man knocked off the latch and ran in.* 1957 JN, We play ring and we play all kine of something and if you don mind sharp you bounce down.

BOUNCE-AND-SPAN sb dial; cf *bonce, bounce, boss and span* (1955 *PADS* 23 12). *G*

A marble game: one player throws his taw out, the other throws his as close as he can to it; if he gets within a span of the first, he wins. (Though in its origin *bounce* was a name for a taw, in the Ja game it evid refers to the throwing of the taw.)

1952 FGC Han /bóngs an spáan/.

BOURBON /borban/ sb attrib.

An element in the names of various plants, usu superior varieties, brought to Ja from the island of Réunion in the Indian Ocean at the end of the 18th cent, the island being at that time (since 1642) named *Bourbon* in honour of the French royal family. See next entries.

BOURBON CANE sb; <BOURBON+*cane*. A superior variety of sugar-cane. *BA*

1811 Mathison 60, The Bourbon cane has been established in Jamaica within the last fifteen years. 1814 Lunan II 205, The Bourbon or Otaheite cane, which was brought here in the year 1796..This cane is of a much larger size than any other. 1823 Roughley 287–8, The Bourbon cane is a..more productive plant than other species.

BOURBON COCO sb. A variety of coco—see BOURBON; informants do not agree on its identity—see quots.

1823 Roughley 404, Cocoas or eddoes are the most lasting and durable ground provisions..There are several kinds of them; the bourbon, which is large but rather soft..etc. 1929 Beckwith 17, Great variety of names attached to the coco in different localities..In Mandeville were enumerated..the 'White Stalk'.. 'Sinket', and 'Burban'. 1940 HPJ, Burban: same as 'black juck'—a kind of coco. 1952 FGC StAnn /bórban kòko/ black, softer; StC /borban/ = white commander; StJ /borban/ white, medium hard, = bamboo coco.

BOURBON COTTON sb obs. See quot. (Also in Barbados, etc.)

1814 Lunan I 241 [quot from Bryan Edwards, *Hist.W.I.*], A kind of cotton, called the *Bourbon*, was introduced into this island in 1795, being sent from the East Indies by Mr Atkinson, of Bengal, to his brother.

bousarou /bóusaróu/ sb dial; etym unknown.

1. Some kind of masking or fancy-dress entertainment.

1940 HPJ, Bonsoro, a dance or game in connection with the John Canoe. [Misread for 'bousoro'?] 1943 *GL* StM, Bow-so-row, country dance; West, Bowsorowd, dressed in different loud colours. 1955 FGC Man /bòusaróu/ dress up, masking—like John Canoe.

2. See quot; the word *row*, an uproar, may enter into this extension of meaning.

1956 Mc Man /bóusaróu/ an uproar, a noisy meeting, etc. (The term was used of revivalist meetings, with reference to the drumming, singing, and jumping involved.)

BOUS'N see BOATSWAIN.

bout see ABOUT. Also s *bout* vb.

bout-bout prep dial; iteration of *bout*. Around and about; repeatedly, back and forth, about.

1868 Russell 19, A see a man da walk bout-bout de place. [Current.] *G*

'BOUTEN prep dial; aphetic form of *about* + *-n* suffix[1]. About.

1912 McK *Songs* 42, 'Nuff rock'tone in de sea, yet none But those 'pon lan' know 'bouten sun.

bov vb dial; etym uncert: perh <*above*. (Cf Trinidad *boof* vb, reprove; sb, scolding, reprimand.) To affect (someone) with a sense of oppression (implying that he feels troubled, even threatened, and does not know how to respond).

1956 Mc Man /di wie di ting bov mi, a kudn se a wod/ *I was so astonished by it that I was speechless.* (Usually refers to someone else's behaviour—BLB.) 1959 DeC, *Bov*—I've encountered it many times and am reasonably certain that it is English *above*..Note that this sentence [see quot 1956] could be altered to /di wie di ting tan bov me../ with no change in meaning. [1960 BLB letter, There is absolutely no implication, not even metaphorically, of taking a literal position over someone.]

BOW (MACHETE) see BOAR (MACHETE).

BOWBO see BOBO.

BOW-FOOT adj dial; for *bow-footed*, cf FOOT. Bow-legged. Cf K-FOOT. *G*

1952 FGC Han /buofut/.

BOW GRUNT sb dial; the meaning of 'bow' is uncertain—cf *gyalanbuo*, if pronunc is /buo/ but it may be /bou/. A variety of the GRUNT FISH, perh having distinctive markings or shape.

1892 Cockrell list, Bow grunt, *Hæmulon fremebundum.*

BOWIE sb dial; <*bow* (*OED sb*[1]) + *-ie*. A kite (evid in allusion to the common type of Jamaican kite, which is hexagonal and has the top section bowed forward). *BL*

1943 *GL* Kgn, Bowie, kite.

BOWL-HAT /búol át/ sb dial; perh <*bowler hat*, but there appears to be an element of fresh formation <*bowl*+*hat*. Any hat with a round crown: a bowler, pith-helmet, etc. *G*

c1950 FGC StAnd, Bowl hat. 1960 LeP Kgn /búol at/ also /élmàt/ a pith helmet, esp as worn by the govt messenger rank.

BOWSOROW see *bousarou*.

BOWSTICK see BEAU-STICK.

BOX vb chiefly dial; cf *OED box v*[2], obs since 18 cent exc in phr 'to box one's ears'. To strike or hit; a common word. *BA BL G T*

1924 Beckwith 24, So Anansi open his right han' an box de 'tump. His right han' fasten. He said to de 'tump, 'If you no let me go I box you wid de lef' han'!' 1957 JN StJ, So bra anancy box him im han fasen..im tek im belly box him im belly fasen.

BOX-ABOUT sb dial or slang; <*box* (*OED v*[1] 13, '*To box about*: to sail up and down, often changing the direction'); prob also partly in sense of *OED box v*[2]. See quots. *G*

1958 DeC StT /baksabout/ of a man: a loafer or idler—of a woman: a trollop; StAnd /baksabout/ a promiscuous woman, one who is unable to maintain a stable sexual partnership, or one who is unable to find steady employment—often said of a woman who has several children by different fathers: /dat gyol notn bot a baks-about/ (Irish Town)—/mi no waan fi bi no baks-about/—one of Mattie's lines in 'Quashie Lady' (1958 pantomime).

BOX-AND-BOARDS sb dial.

1958 DeC Port /baks-an-buodz/ a rough bed, sometimes literally made of boxes and boards. 1958 FGC StT.

BOX AROUND vb phr; cf BOX-ABOUT. To go from place to place without steady employment. *G*

1952 FGC StJ /wi jos baks aroun an trai tu get likl work tu kiip guoin/.

BOX DRUM sb. A name for one type of GOMBAY, which is square, or is actually improvised out of a box.

1837 Belisario Expl. to Plate 3 (see quot s.v. BENCH DRUM).

BOX-FISH sb.

1953 Smith in *NHN* 13, *Lactophrys bicaudalis*, the box-fish, is a most interesting creature..close relative [of] the cow-fish..The body is three-angled..Hard body and tail.

BOXWOOD sb; *OED* lists *Jamaica boxwood* without quot or ref, and identifies as *Tecoma pentaphylla*, but this name has not been found in Ja botanical works, and *boxwood* is used of a different tree. The tree *Vitex umbrosa*. (Identity of trees referred to in quot 1952 is unknown.)

1909 Harris 300, Boxwood, or Fiddlewood (*Vitex umbrosa*, Sw.). This is a moderate-sized tree, found in the mountains. Used for framing houses, and for general purposes where a lasting timber is required. 1941 Swabey 14, Boxwood—(Fiddlewood). *Vitex umbrosa*..No data are available concerning this tree. 1952 FGC StAnn, StT /bakswud trii/ for timber.

BOY sb dial. A sucker of the coco plant (*Colocasia*).

1925 Beckwith 52 [Riddle:] Gal in a wall, boy in a coco hole..The sucker, called 'boy', from the tuber of the coco plant which goes into the hole for planting.

BOYA see BOYO.

BOY-BOY sb dial; iterative <*boy*. A number of miscellaneous boys.

1952 FGC StAnd [A man explaining the true cause of gravel being thrown (according to popular belief) by duppies:] /dem bwaay-bwaay haid—trii ar fuor—truo grabl, mek piipl se hous haantid/.

BOYO /bóyo, búoyo, bóya/ sb dial; <Amer Sp *bollo* (in E. Cuba *boyo*—Pichardo), a roll of dough (corn, cassava, plantain, etc.) seasoned and baked, boiled, or fried (contents and methods of cooking varying locally). Chiefly in Portland parish: the *dokunu*. *BL*

1940 HPJ, Boya, Bua: Duckanoo, apparently in Portland, where *boya* and *blue drawers* were commonest names. 1943 *GL* Port, Boyo, boiled pudding; Port, Buoyough, another name for cornmeal duckanoo; StT, Boyo, a cake of cornmeal and sugar. 1952 FGC Port /boya/ = /dokunu/. 1958 DeC Port /boyo, buoyo/ = dokunu, boiled pudding.

BOYSIE sb dial; prob <*boy* + *-sy* (cf *OED*), and perh with infl also from *-ie*. *BA BL*

1954 LeP StT, Boysie, son.

BOZE see BOAR MACHETE.

BRA /bra/ sb dial; 1907 Bro'er, 1924 Brar, 1943→ Bra; reduced <*brother*. *BL G N T*

1. = Brother. As a term of address, BRA is yielding place to BREDDA; cf also *ba*, *baa*, BAADA, BABA, BRARA. It is equivalent to 'Mr' (which is also frequently used—cf Jekyll passim), and may be applied to any man, or in Anancy stories to any male animal.

1877 Murray *Kittle* 24, see *sa*, *sar*. 1907 Jekyll 9, Bro'er Tiger. 1924 Beckwith 57, Brar Dog. 1943 *GL* Port, Tre, Brer, brother. 1950 Pioneer 16, Bra Puss. 1954 LeP StE (Eld), Bra, Brother. Bra may be applied to any man.

2. In other senses of 'brother'.

1943 *GL* Clar, Bra, friend.

BRA adj dial; <*braw*, brave. Brave.

1941 Kirkpatrick 19, 'Im a trimble nung an' 'im doan bra lak 'im use fe was.

braa /braa/ vb dial; reduced <*bother* (usually pronunc in the dial /báda/) with common interchange of *r* for *d* and syncope of first vowel; cf *bara*.

1940 HPJ, Braugh, 'Mallan saw woman braugh me'—line in Maroon Coromanti folk-song (1931). 1943 *GL* StAnd, No braa me—don't bother me.

braad-paint see BROAD-POINT.

braata /bráata/ sb chiefly dial; <Sp (Mexico, Colombia) *barata*, adj, cheap, sb, a bargain sale (Santamaría). (*DA* etym s.v. *brotus* 'Cf British dial *brot(t)*, scraps, fragments, a small quantity' is phonetically inadmissible, nor is the sense close enough.) The folk pronunc preserves the Sp vowels better than does the 'educated' pronunc repr by the spelling 'broughta'.(See *Amer. Speech* 42.194–6.) *BL G*

1. A little amount of the same, as of some foodstuff that one is buying, added on for good measure. Cf MECK-UP, NYAPA.

1912 McK *Songs* 38, No two bit o' brater Wid shop-keeper Marter. [Jekyll's note erroneously takes 'brater' to mean 'brother'. In the poem the speaker is rejoicing that he is out of debt to shopkeeper Martha and no longer forced to petty bargaining.] c1915 FGC StAnd (remembered as current, and then spelt 'broughta' or 'brawta'). 1943 *GL* Clar, Brawta, Brata, an addition, make up. 1952 FGC Han /bráatá/ mek op.

2. See quot.

1958 DeC StAnd /braata/—This used to mean the extra gift at a shop (a practice no longer followed); recently it has come to mean the free thirteenth pound of ground provisions.

braba-braba sb dial; app a 'stretched form' of *bra-bra* 2.

1952 FGC StM /braba-braba/ mistaken speech.

BRABILA sb bot obs; perh <Amer Sp *albarillo*, *Ximenia americana* (Santamaría). A shrub and its fruit, of uncertain identity. See quot 1814.

1756 Browne 370, Brabila 10. *Fruticosa & spinosa*..The prickly *Brabila*, with smooth oval leaves..I found this shrub near the beech at Port Antonio, where it grows to the height of eight or nine feet, or better. The fruit has all the flavour, and much of the appearance, of the European plumb; but the shell of the seed is smooth, and the pulp and skin of the fruit of a pale red colour. The leaves and footstalks are all of a pale green. 1774 Long III 826 (Account from Browne); *ibid* 855 (among 'Dissert Fruits') Brabila. 1814 Lunan II 156, Ximenia americana..This is thought to be Browne's *brabila*.

BRABO /bráabo/ adj and sb dial; prob <Sp *bravo*. See quots.

1943 *GL* StAnn, Brabo, an out-law, full of noise. 1956 Mc Man /bráabo/ quick to anger, 'easy-vex'.

BRABO vb dial; ?from prec, or perh a var of *pra-pra*.

1943 *GL* Port, Brabo, lay hold on.

BRA-BRA sb obs; some kind of symbolic word—cf DAB-A-DAB from this same source, and modern BRAGADAP. See quot.

1774 Long II 427, The Negroes seem very fond of reduplications..as..*dab-a-dab* (an olio, made with maize, herrings, and pepper); *bra-bra* (another of their dishes)..[etc.].

bra-bra /brábrá/ sb dial; echoic—cf Twi *bĭrebĭre*, brawl, noisy quarrel, loquacity; cf also *braba-braba.*

1. 1943 *GL* West, Brabra, brawling or loud talking.

2. 1956 Mc Man /brábrá/ 'bad language', i.e. not grammatical English.

BRAC sb dial; prob <BRA+*k*. =BRA, brother.

BRACHO sb dial obs; prob <Twi *p'rakó*, hog, swine, porker, <Pg *porco*. A pig; see quot s.v. ABOUKANI.

BRACKEN sb. In Jamaica applied properly to *Pteridium caudatum*, improperly also to the net-ferns (*Gleichenia* spp). *G*

1954 *FG* 579, There are six different species of Net-fern occurring in Jamaica..They are often mistakenly called 'Bracken'.

BRACKET FLOUNDER sb obs; *bracket* prob refers to shape or structure. A type of flounder.

1774 Long III 867, Sea-Fish..I shall enumerate such as are the most in esteem; *viz.* Black snapper..Flounder, Soal..Dolphin, Bracket flounder [etc.].

BRACKISH adj dial. Of a beverage; tasteless (because not having enough sugar). Not used of plain water. *G*

1960 Leandro cartoon in *Gleaner* 3 July, 'Sugar price up'. 'Well, we will have to start drinking our tea brackish for a change'. 1960 P. Wilmot StAnd, Brackish —used of all beverages, but especially of bush teas when they haven't enough sugar and milk in them and so have an insipid taste and appearance.

BRAFIN sb dial; obscurely <*breadfruit*; cf also FINEY. The breadfruit; cf BAAJAM, *brambra*, and other nicknames.

1943 *GL* StAnn, Brafin, breadfruit.

brag sb dial; etym uncert: perh <Amer Sp *braga*, a rope cinch or strap, perh abbr of BRAGADAP 6.

1952 FGC StT /bragz/ rope straps used to hold oars to gunwale of fishing canoe.

BRAGADAP /bràgadáp, bràgadáps/ sb[1] dial; No formal etymology for this word has been worked out; it appears to be phonosymbolic, expressing basically the ideas of *roughness* (stone wall, soil, perhaps rope), assoc with *toughness*, and, when applied to foods, with *quick preparation* and *simple or coarse materials* (fritters, dumplings, etc.). The echoic element imitates sounds of foods being 'slapped together' (cf BRA-BRA, DAB-A-DAB, etc.) and (see sb[2] below) the sudden stopping of something in motion (cf BAP(S), BARARAP, BRAP, BRIGGADIM, etc.).

1. A codfish (or other fish) fritter; =STAMP-AND-GO.

1940 HPJ, Braggadap, A name given to a kind of fish fritter made, without picking the fish, by wrapping dough round it. 1943 *GL* StC, Bragadap, fritters. 1952 FGC StAnd /bragadap/ saltfish fritters.

2. Thick flour paste (such as fritters would be dipped in); flour-and-saltfish sauce.

1957 DeC StAnd (Irish Town) /bragadap/ a thick flour paste used to thicken stew or gravy; Clar, a white sauce of flour and saltfish.

3. Unsweetened foods made chiefly of flour: a dumpling, a scone, or the like; see quots.

1954 LeP StE (Eld), Bragadap, a fried dumpling. 1958 DeC Tre, Bragadap, a round, flat, boiled dumpling; StJ /bragadap/ here meaning a baking-powder biscuit [US usage, =scone]; Port, here means johnny-cake; West, A water cracker or similar wafer.

4. Sweetened foods made chiefly of flour or the like: a common cake, large or small; a bread-pudding; a corn pudding.

1943 *GL* Kgn, Brag-a-daps, A kind of cake. 1958 DeC StJ /bragadap/ a common large cake baked with cake flour, sugar, baking powder, etc., and often frosted; Man, here meaning a hard, sweet cake, like a bulla only thicker, sells for a penny in the shops; StAnd, StT, a pudding consisting mainly of stale bread and sugar, baked; StJ, a dish of whole-kernel corn boiled with sugar and milk; Han etc., Coconut candy.

5. Another name for RENTA YAM; the sense connection is uncertain: it may be with flour, it may be with stone (see quot 1956), or with the general idea of toughness. Cf BRAGADAP WALL, BRUGUDU.

1952 FGC Tre /bragadap/ so we call renta fos time, *We formerly called renta yam so.* 1956 Mc Man /brágadáp/ another name for Barbados yam (also called..renta). This yam grows best over stone.

6. Anything big, esp a fat woman; the association is prob with dumplings.

1958 DeC StAnn.

BRAGADAP sb[2] dial; echoic: cf sb[1]. *T*

1. A sudden stop; a motion that comes to a sudden stop; a sudden motion. *G*

1959 DeC Han, Man, StE, StJ, West /bragadap/ a sudden stop; you /mek a bragadap/ if you suddenly rein in a mule, stop in your tracks when running, or slam on the brakes of a car.

2. See quot, and cf BARARAP.

1959 DeC Han, West /bragadap/ lively dance music.

3. Something that makes a creaking or clacking noise when in motion: see quot. *G*

1959 DeC Han /bragadap/ a creaky, noisy wooden bed; Port, StAnd, StC, StT, a fisherman's rope oarlock; StC, Man, a metal oarlock pin.

4. A funeral wake celebration. Cf SET-UP.

1960 DeC West, in 1961 *CLS* 72.

BRAGADAP int dial; phonosymbolic or echoic, suggesting suddenness—and prob also infl by the wide currency of BRAGADAP sb.

1. A call to a mule or donkey to make it stop. (Assoc with sb[2] 1.)

1958 DeC Man, StE, StJ, West.

2. An exclamation of excited pleasure made while dancing. (Assoc with sb[2] 2.) *G*

1958 DeC Clar.

BRAGADAP WALL sb dial; cf BRAGADAP sb. A rough stone wall (very common in Jamaica).

1940 HPJ, Bragadap-wall, A stone wall made without mortar.

bragampan adj and sb dial; cf BRAGADAP, of which this may be a variant form, carrying the sense of toughness or solidity.

A. adj: See quot.

1943 *GL* Port, Braganpan, immovable.

B. sb: See quot.

1958 DeC Port /bragampán/ fried green bananas.

brag-brag sb dial; a denasalised form of *brang-brang*, which see; poss also infl by *brog*, *brag* (See *EDD Brog*, Yks *brag* 3, A branch of a tree, a broken bough, a short stick; *brogwood*, brushwood.)

1958 DeC StE /brag-brag/ small sticks used for firewood.

BRAGGA sb dial; prob < Sp or Pg *braga*, swaddling band, rope cinch around an animal's belly, etc. See quots. *G*

1943 *GL* Kgn, Bragga, shirt folded around the waist; StT, Bragga, a peasant woman's dress folded and tied up at her waist to make the dress shorter.

BRAGGADAP see BRAGADAP.

BRAGGING-TOM /bragin-tam, braigim-taam/ sb dial; a personalizing nickname bearing phallic symbolism. BARBADOS YAM or some other white variety that has a relatively long tuber.

1954 LeP Man, Braggin Tom, white yam; Port, Braigimtaam, Barbados yam (used mostly for the slimmer kind). 1956 Mc Man, Braggin Tam, snake yam.

BRAGING sb dial; ? < *bragging*.

1943 *GL* StT, Braging, ring game.

bragin-tam, braigim-taam see BRAGGING-TOM.

BRAIN sb dial; < *brain*. A clever ruse. *G*

1950 Pioneer 18, Anancy..study a brain fe work pon Ticks. 1952 FGC Han, To work a brain, a tricky device.

BRAINIST sb dial; < *brain* + *-ist*.

1954 LeP Kgn, Brainist; StAnn, Braines', a crafty, cunning person.

brak see BRAC.

BRAKE-AXE see BREAK-AX.

BRAM sb dial; perh < *branle* (cf *OED sb* 2, 'A kind of dance, and the kind of music suitable to it'). *BL G*

1940 HPJ, Bram, A bruckkins of a somewhat higher class; an outdoor festival, a 'hop'. 1943 *GL* Clar, Bram, dance. 1954 LeP Kgn /bram/ a small party.

BRAM adv dial; echoic. A sound suggesting a sudden motion or one which stops suddenly. Cf BRAP. *G T*

1868 Russell 19, De trap fly *bram*, an' cut off de puss foot. 1940 HPJ, Bram: the tramp of a person with heavy boots. 1942 Bennett 32, Sametime de bus tap bram. [*Immediately the bus stopped 'bram'!*]

BRAMBLE sb dial; < *bramble* (*EDD* sb 4, 'Withered branches, twigs, &c., which are gathered for firewood'—Nth Ireland). See quots; cf also BRAM-BRAM. *G*

1954 LeP StAnn, Bramble, wood used as kindling for a fire. 1956 Mc Man, StAnd /brambl/; StE (Accom), The smallest branches of tree, put together in bundle, like fagot. 1958 DeC Port /brambl/ = BRAM-BRAM, GRENG-GRENG, etc., i.e. small sticks for firewood.

brambra sb dial; prob (with iteration of the first part of the word) < *bread-fruit* (cf BAAJAM, BACHA, and other nicknames); but cf Twi *brámmbraŋŋ*, big of growth. The breadfruit.

1952 FGC Port /brámbra/ the biggest breadfruit—easy to roast.

BRAM-BRAM, BRANG-BRANG, BREM-BREM /bram-bram, brang-brang, brem-brem/ sb dial; iterative formed on the base of BRAMBLE, and prob with analogical infl from other iteratives of the same or similar meaning, as GRANG-GRANG, JENG-JENG, etc. (Cf also Fante *brambram*, Twi *fràmfram*, blazing, flaming.) Kindling wood, small bits of stick or wood for burning.

1943 *GL* Kgn, Brang-brang, brambles; StE, Brem-brem, small-wood. 1954 LeP Man, Brambram, wood used as kindling for a fire; StE (Eld), Brem-brem. 1958 DeC StE (Accom) /bram-bram/ firewood, esp. bits and pieces of wood.

BRAN sb dial; < *brawn* (*EDD* sb², 'A boar, pig', perh specif in the Yks form *bran*). A boar, usually a castrated one.

1943 *GL* Clar, Bran, a castrated boar; Kgn, Bran, boar. 1955 FGC Man /bran/ a boar, not castrated. 1956 Mc Man /bran/ a male pig when small, called /buor/ when grown.

BRANCHED CALALU sb bot. *Solanum nigrum* or *S. nodiflorum*; in folk usage usually called GUMA.

1756 Browne 174, The branched Caleloe..is very common in the low lands of *Jamaica*..[Though] equally common in *Europe*, and of a virose heavy smell and very narcotic quality in these cold climates [it] is void of both in *Jamaica*, where it is daily used for food and found by long experience to be both a pleasant and wholesome green. 1864 Grisebach 782, Calalu, branched: *Solanum nodiflorum*.

BRANG-BRANG see BRAM-BRAM.

BRAP, BRAPS adv dial; echoic, perh an elided form of BARARAP; cf BRAM. A sound suggesting suddenness, or sudden cessation of motion. (Cf BRAGADAP int and sb².) *BL G*

1942 Bennett 6, Ef dem gi me wan aeroplane Fe fly ovah Germany, Yuh hooda se' 'ow war stap brap, An' po' Englan' go free.

BRARA sb dial arch; < *brother*, with common substitution of *r* for *d* by assimilation. Cf also BRA. *G*

1868 Russell 5, Bra-ra—Breda, Brother.

BRASELITEA see BRAZILETTO.

BRASHAE, BRASHEH see BRESHE.

BRASILETTA, BRASILETTO see BRAZILETTO.

BRASS sb dial or slang; < *brass*, money (*OED* 3a† →1775); cf also *brass farthing*. A penny.

1943 *GL* StAnd, Brass, 1 penny. 1952 FGC Han, A brass, one penny.

BRASS CANNON sb dial. A variety of sweet-potato with a brassy colour and longish shape.

1952 FGC StT /bras kyanan/ sweet potato, tallish, red skin.

BRASS-HEAD sb attrib; or for *brass-headed*, ppl adj. A negro having the reddish cast of hair that comes from a diet low in proteins.

1950 Pioneer 79, Brass Head Jimmy tief corn pork.

BRAUGH see *braa*.

BRAWTA see *braata*.

BRAYSHAE see BRESHE.

BRAZELETTO, BRAZELITTA see next.

BRAZILETTO /bràziléta, bràzilíta/ sb, also attrib; < Sp *brasilete*, prob 'hispanised' by the English alteration of *-e* to *-o* (cf *palisado*, *bastinado*, etc.); in Colombia there is a form *brasileto* applied to the brazil tree and its wood, but this appears to be more recent. (Santamaría.) Cf *OED* 1656, 'Brazeletto or Jamaica wood'.

'One or more species of dye-wood, inferior to Brazil-wood, imported from Jamaica and adjacent islands'—*OED*. The tree *Peltophorum brasiliense* and its wood. *N*

1657 Continuation 45, Brasil, and Brasiletto, excellent for dying, sold in these parts. 1696 Sloane 213, Brasiletto. In pratis & collibus Insulæ Jamaicæ abundat. 1756 Browne 227, Cæsalpinia 1..Brasiletto..This tree grows in every part of *Jamaica* where the soil is dry and rocky: it is an excellent timber-wood..The wood is elastic, tough, and durable; and bears a fine polish: it is of a beautiful orange-colour, full of resin, and yields a fine full tincture by infusion; but is seldom cut for the dyers use in *Jamaica*. 1797 *Braco* 27 Jan, Great Gang Cleaning & Cutting Grass on Braselitea pastures. *Ibid* 30 Jan, At Brazelitta. 1920 Fawcett 90, Braziletto.

BRAZILIAN COTTON sb obs. *Gossypium lapideum.*

[1725 Sloane 68, That of Brasil has many seeds conglomerated.] 1793 Edwards II 271, The most profitable sorts for general cultivation seem to be, the..Small-seed, and the Brasilian. 1837 Macfadyen I 72, Gossypium Brasiliense. *Chain-Cotton*..It is probable that this variety was brought from Brazil, as it was known in the time of Sloane, as well as that of Edwards, by the name of Brazilian cotton.

BRAZIL MACKA sb dial; <*brazil* + MACKA. *Mimosa bimucronata.*

1920 Fawcett 134, Shrub or tree to 25 ft. high, with (or occasionally without) prickles..Brazil Macca..Used for making hedges. 1952 FGC Tre /brázil màka, bráazíl/ for live fence; different from /kasha maka/—grow tall tree.

BREAD sb gen; <*bread* (*OED sb*[1] †3 →1643).

1. A loaf of bread of any size. [Also Grenada, 1934.] *BA BL G T*

1940 HPJ, Bread: Loaf (in advertisements even). 1956 Mc Man /sel mi a bred/ *A loaf of bread, please.* 1959 LeP StAnd /mi jos goin fi bai a bred/.

2. Fig. A livelihood. *BL G*

1940 HPJ, Bread: Livelihood, e.g. the things a man hab to do fe a bread.

BREAD-AND-CHEESE sb. The shrub and tree *Pithecellobium unguis-cati* and *P. dulce*, from the appearance of the black bean sandwiched in a white, fleshy aril. Formerly called NEPHRITIC TREE, BARBARY THORN, DOCTOR LONG; now also BERMUDA LOGWOOD, BLACK-BEAD SHRUB, CAT'S CLAW. *BA G*

1943 *NHN* I 11 20 (see quot s.v. BERMUDA LOGWOOD).

BREADFRUIT sb; for sense 2 cf *OED* 1697→.

1. Evid = BREAD-KIND.

1788 Marsden 19, They..raise more ground-fruit, bread-fruit, and vegetables.

[2. The tree *Artocarpus incisa* and its fruit; in Jamaica this word has entered into many compounds, which see as separate entries. *BA G T*

1794 Broughton 30, Artocarpus incisus. Bread Fruit Tree. Otaheite.—347 plants of the breadfruit arrived 5 Feb. 1793 [on] HMS Providence [and] were distributed through the Island.]

BREADFRUIT PARROT-FISH sb dial. A variety of PARROT fish thought to be shaped like the breadfruit (or its blossom?).

1952 Smith in *NHN* 202, *Scarus croicensis*, known around St Mary as the 'bread-fruit parrot-fish', is elongate and evenly tapering in body form.

BREADFRUIT REMEDY sb dial; <*breadfruit* + REMEDY. Coconut RUN-DOWN; a tasty sauce which improves the bland or somewhat insipid breadfruit.

1958 DeC StM /bredfruut remidi/ coconut run-down.

BREADFRUIT ROSE sb rare; of doubtful authenticity. The common garden flower, the oleander.

1951 Kingston *Gleaner*, Sept.

BREADFRUIT SWORD sb. The blossom of the breadfruit tree, esp as used to make a crystallized confection.

1957 *FFM* 251, Crystallised Breadfruit 'Sword' or Blossom..Pick breadfruit swords when just ripe (before they become brown and hard). Soak for 15 minutes, etc.

BREAD-GUT sb dial. See quot.

1925 Beckwith 100 [Prov:] Quattie bread-gut fill monkey belly...'bread-gut' as the soft part of the bread is called.

BREAD-KIND sb; *ODS* 1697→. (A word very common in Jamaica up to the end of the 19th cent, and still well known.) The type of vegetable or fruit of a starchy kind which may serve as a substitute for bread (see quot 1952). Cf FISH-KIND, MEAT-KIND. *BA N*

[1690 Dampier 214.] 1733 *Jrl House of Assembly* III 152, Now all bread-kind is rooted up. 1756 Browne 332 [Coco root] is more valuable, and supply many of the poorer Sort of people with what they call *Bread-kind*, in those parts of the world. 1873 Rampini 91. 1933 McKay 316, Breadkind, general name for the staple vegetables and fruits. 1952 FGC StE, Breadkind—corn-meal, flour, punkin, sweet potato, yam, green-banana, yampi, badu, dasheen, breadfruit, coco, rice, bammy.

BREADNUT /brénót, brénàt/ sb, also attrib; *OED* 1756→.

1. The tree *Brosimum alicastrum*, its wood, and its edible seed. It has been valued from the early days of the colony for its fruit and timber, and because the leaves make excellent food for cattle during dry seasons. *BA G N T*

1683 Laws Map (SE of Montego Bay:) Breadnut Hills. 1740 Importance 53, The Berry or Bread-Nut, when ripe, is sweet and luscious; and when green, if Hurricanes happen to blow down their Plantane Walks, supply their Place as Food. a 1726 Barham (1794) Index 23, Bread-Nut Tree..Why this is so called I cannot tell, unless it be upon the account of the wild hogs feeding upon its fruit. 1868 Russell 5 [Peasant pronunciation:] Bra-nat, Breadnut. 1952 FGC Port, StE, StJ /brénót/; also (more deliberate pronunciation) /brédnót/.

2. The breadfruit (*Artocarpus incisa*); perh initially through some confusion. See quots 1913.

1913 Harris 26, Three kinds are known here, the 'white-heart', the 'yellow-heart' and the seeding sort, the latter being known also as breadnut. 1952 FGC StT, Port, Breadnut, also a name for breadfruit.

BREADNUT ZEBRA-WOOD see RAINBOW WOOD.

BREAK see BROKE.

BREAKAWAY see BROKE-'WAY.

BREAK-AX /brok-aks/ sb; *OED* only quot 1756. One of a number of plant-names of the same pattern, perh modelled on or translating Sp *quiebra-hacha* (cf also *quiebra-arado*, *quiebra-muelas*, *-ollas*, *-piedras*, *-plato*, etc.—Malaret); this pattern is also known in Africa (cf *Hausa kariye gatari*, break-ax, the name of some hard-wood trees—Dalziel 58), but if there is a connection with the Caribbean names, the direction of the influence is unknown.

1. The tree *Sloanea jamaicensis* and its very tough wood.

1756 Browne 250, Sloanea? 1..The large oval-leafed *Sloanea*, or Brake-axe Tree..is said to be pretty common in the mountains of St Ann's, and esteemed as one of the best and largest timber-trees in the wood: though so very hard, that it is found a difficult matter even to cut it down; and from thence it takes its common appellation. 1926 Fawcett 90, *Sloanea jamaicensis*..Break-axe tree, Iron Wood, Lignum durum. 1952 FGC StAnn, 'Break-ax wood' in StC and StAnn, 'Comb-wood' in Man and Tre, 'Pop-nut' in St E, 'Puss-head' in StT; StE /brok-aks/ = greenheart—very hard center.

2. See quot.

1943 *NHN* II 82, *Krugiodendron ferrei*—Broke Ax. The wood is very hard. [1926 Fawcett 65, *Krugiodendron ferreum*..Black Iron Wood.]

BREAKFAST /brekfas, brekfaas, briekfas/ sb chiefly dial and rural. The second meal of the day, taken usually from 11 to 12 o'clock. (Cf SECOND BREAKFAST.) *BA G T*

1946 U.Newton I 10, Come back here before breakfast time (the Chapelton way of saying 'lunch-time'). 1952 FGC StE /brekfas/ 11.00—pumpkin, sweet-potato, fish, etc; StJ /brékfás/ 12 o'clock; StM, Breakfast—better-off people's name for the early meal—for poorer people, the 12 o'clock meal; Tre, 11–12 o'clock; West, black people in adjoining district have /briekfas/ from 10–12. 1954 LeP StE (Eld), Breakfus, = second meal (about 12). 1956 Mc Man /brekfaas/ about 1 or 2 PM; StAnd, StE /brekfaas/.

BREAKFAST-BASKET sb dial; < BREAKFAST + *basket*. A basket in which the midday meal is carried. *G*

1959 DeC StJ /briekfas-baskit/ small, square-bottom bankra.

BREAK FRIEND WITH vb phr dial; cf BROKE, break. To terminate friendship, to fall out with. *BL G*

1907 Jekyll 45, An' from that day Snake broke friend with Annancy.

BREAKFUS see BREAKFAST.

BREAKING /brókin/ vbl sb; < BROKE 3. The gathering of a crop, or that which is gathered.

1929 Beckwith 17, One year after planting, the first 'breaking' is ready, but the [coco] head may be moled [*sic*] up for nine months more for a second breaking.

BREAKING-DOWN sb dial. A cause of decay. *G*

1952 FGC StJ, No jobs—that is just the breaking-down of the Island.

BREAKNECK /brók-nek/ sb dial; < BROKE, break + *neck*. *G*

1. A bird-trap which catches the bird by the neck.

1929 Beckwith 36, The *chokie* or 'breakneck' employs a string.

2. See quot.

1952 FGC Han /broknek/ a marble game for any number of players. Draw a long line, place marbles on it; everybody pitches his taw trying to get it as close to the line as possible without going over (breaking your neck). Winner takes all; then set again.

BREAK-STOMACH see BRUCKTUMMUCK.

BREAK TOP vb phr; cf BROKE 5. To burst out at the top.

1958 DeC Man /brieks tap/ verb for what the corn does when it blossoms.

BREAK-UP sb, also attrib; < *break-up* (*OED sb*, 'break-up party' 1843). The breaking-up or termination (of a school term). *BA BL G*

1957 JN Tre, Teacher tell we say dat Christmas we going have break-up concert.

BREAST /bres/ sb dial; < *breast*. The udder of a cow (or other milch animal). *BA BL*

1952 FGC StAnd, StM, StT, West—[regular usage throughout Jamaica].

brebij see BEVERAGE. *G*

brebre see BREY BREY.

BRECHA see BRESHE.

BRECHIE, BRUTCHIE NEGRO sb obs; ? Ibo—cf quot 1823. See quots.

1820 Thompson 4, Those negroes, who have in their own country undergone the operation of having the greater portion of the skin on the brow and forehead removed; they are called here *Brechie negroes*. [1823 Adams 133–4, A class of Heebos, called Breeché..Breeché, in the Heebo language, signifies gentleman, or the eldest son of one.. Before attaining the age of manhood, his forehead is scarified, and the skin brought down from the hair to the eye-brows, so as to form a line of indurated skin from one temple to the other. This peculiar mark is distinctive of his rank, the ordinary mark of the Heebo being formed by numerous perpendicular incisions on each temple.] 1828 Hamel I 104, They did not presume to such familiarity with the Brutchie, by which they understand a king or prince.

breda /bréda/ sb dial; 1837 breder, 1868 breda, 1943→ bredder, bredda; an early established but irregular pronunc of *brother* (the dial pronunc that one would expect is /broda/ but this occurs far less often). *BL G T*

1837 James *Slave's Diary* passim, Breder, brother. 1868 Russell 5, Bra-ra—Breda, Brother. 1943 *GL* Clar, Bredda, bredder—brother.

BREDDA, BREDDER, BREDER see prec.

BREED vb dial; cf *OED* 1b, 1513 only. To cause to conceive, to make pregnant. *BL G N T*

1940 HPJ, Breed: to get with child. 1949 Reid 53, Bro' Heze only stopped breeding Ma Lucy because he could find no more names for the pickneys.

BREEDING-VEIN sb dial. Varicose veins (accompanying pregnancy).

1952 FGC StAnd /bríidn víen—woman jinarali hav it/.

BREER see *brrr*.

BREEZE sb dial; cf *OED sb*² 3, 'A gentle or light wind'.

1. A strong wind; a wind accompanying a storm. *BL G N T*

1940 HPJ, Breeze: This word frequently means quite a strong wind. 1951 FGC StT, Breeze, the hurricane of 17 Aug.

2. The breath, literally or metaphorically, as believed to carry a good or evil influence from spirits. *BL G*

1952 FGC StAnd, Three-foot-horse. If 'im buck you up a' night 'im blow bad breeze 'pon you. 1953 Moore 158 [In Cumina celebrations:] When good spirit come, he carry a good breeze; but when sick spirit comes, evil spirit bring a high breeze. You can tell by looking at the person. 1955 Bennett *Cricket History*, And so de duppy blow good breeze.

3. Slang: Air, hence freedom—in phr—see quot. Cf BREEZE vb, and the common simile 'as free as air, the breeze'. *G T*

1940 HPJ, 'Give me a breeze' = give me air, clear off.

4. Slang: Small change. (Cf metaphorical uses of *air*.)

1952 FGC StM, Breeze = small change: 'One pound an' breeze'. 1957 DeC, Breeze, always small change, less than a shilling.

BREEZE vb dial or slang; cf BREEZE sb 3. In phrases: *Breeze me a bit*, give me air, clear off; *Breeze me ase* (i.e. my ears), said to a talker (=give my ears freedom). *G*

1940 HPJ.

BREEZE-MILL sb now dial; by analogy with *windmill.*

1. A windmill (such as those formerly used on sugar estates to pump water, etc.).

1788 Marsden 27, Water in a reservoir or tank, supplied, as often as occasion requires, by a breeze mill of such a construction that it is set a-going by one man: It has sails like ours in England and the water is thrown up by pipes into the tank, as well as various parts of the boiling-house. 1826 Barclay 53, A perfect thicket was reared up, to the serious injury, not only of the mansion-house, but also of the breeze-mill, when the wind was northerly. 1952 FGC StE, 'Breeze-mill' more common than 'windmill'.

2. A child's toy having vanes that spin in the wind.

1952 FGC Man, Use breeze-mill to frighten birds away; StE, West, a child's toy.

BREEZE-PUMP sb. A pump operated by power from a BREEZE-MILL.

1796 Braco 10 May, Mr Cooper mended the Breeze pump this Day. *Ibid* 11 May, The Breeze pump got out of order and cannot get any Water.

BREGALEGBASH quasi-vb dial; echoic, imitating the sound of falling and impact—cf the similar words BRIGGADIM, BRAGADAP, etc.

1943 *GL* StE, Bregalegbash, to fall to the ground.

brej sb dial; cf BRAC: this form seems an example of the play with words and sounds that is often indulged in; or it may be an abbr of **breja* < *breda* (BREDDA).

1958 DeC StT /brej/ affectionate word for brother.

brekfaas, brekfas see BREAKFAST.

BREM-BREM see BRAM-BRAM.

BRENGEH sb dial rare; etym unknown.

1943 *GL* Man, Brengeh, pretty.

BRER ANANCY SPIDER sb; cf BRA, ANANCY.

1949 *NHN* IV 35, Brer Anancy spider, *Heteropoda venatoria.*

BRESHA, BRESHAY see next.

BRESHE /breshe/ sb dial; for spelling-forms see quots; etym uncert—prob < *breadfruit*, with word-play (cf the many other nicknames for breadfruit: BACHA, BRAMBRA, BUKU, etc.).

1. Breadfruit.

1943 *GL* Clar, Breshay, Bresha, Brayshae; StAnd, Bressha; StC, Brecha; StJ, Brashae; West, Breshay. 1952 FGC StJ /breshe/. 1954 LeP StAnn, Bresha; StE, Brasheh; StT, Breshe. 1955 Mc StAnd /breshe/ generally breadfruit—however, according to one person /úonly wen it rúos/. 1955 HPJ, Bresha..breshay.. bresheh (probably the best form)..One informant said it was applied only in times of plenty (heavy breadfruit crop). [Cf BREY BREY.]

2. See quot. (A rare, evid transf, use.)

1943 *GL* StAnd, Bressha, turned corn meal.

BRESHEH, BRESSHA see prec.

BREY BREY /brebre/ sb dial; cf Twi *bèbĕree*, much, many; plentiful.

1943 *GL* West, Brey brey plenty.

BRIAL /bráial/ sb dial; < *briar*, by common substitution of *l* for *r*.

1868 Russell 5, Brial, Brier. 1929 Beckwith 52 (see next).

BRIAL WIS sb dial; BRIAL + WIS. A common wild species of *Smilax.*

1927 Beckwith 13, Brial-wis (vine). *Smilax*—. 1929 Beckwith 52, Both China and 'brial wis' are to be beaten up with the sarsaparilla [to make a drink]. 1955 *WIMJ* 82, Bryal Wys (Withe). Like China root and sarsaparilla this Smilax sp. is used in tonics.

BRICE vb or ppl adj; etym unknown, but connection with *brace* (*OED* v^1) or *braced* (*OED ppl* a^1) is not impossible.

1943 *GL* StM, Brice, constipate.

BRICK-MOULD sb ?obs. [*OED* lists *brick-mould* but without def or quot; presumably it meant a mould in which bricks were shaped.] This is < *mould*, friable earth. See quots.

1774 Long III 686, Plants...removed...from a husky, impoverished piece of ground into a clayey, loamy, or brick-mould soil..may bear large, succulent berries. 1793 Edwards II 210, Next to that, is the soil which in Jamaica is called *brick-mold*; not as resembling a brick in colour, but as containing such a due mixture of clay and sand, as is supposed to render it well adapted for the use of the kiln. It is a deep, warm and mellow, hazel earth, easily worked.

BRIDE sb dial; < *bride* (*OED* 2, quots c 1440–1598). A bridegroom.

1924 Beckwith 142, When dinnertime, Jack, de bride, come out an' say, 'Frien's, we soon have dinner'. 1946 Dunham 109, A host of relatives and friends on both sides, and the two brides. For some time I could not figure out where the groom was or why another bride. Then I finally extracted from Mai that the husband is also 'bride'.

BRIDE-MAN sb dial; cf *OED* 2 '*Obs.* or *dial.*' →1830. See quots.

1956 Mc Port (Moore Town) /bráidman/ the 'best-man' at a wedding (responsible for leading in the chief bridesmaid and the bride). 1962 BLB 22.

BRIDLE-MOUTH PARROT sb dial. A variety of the PARROT fish having markings about the mouth that resemble a bridle.

1952 FGC StM, Bridle-mouth parrot—has red markings.

BRIEF sb dial slang; etym unknown, but cf *EDD brief* adj 4, 'Clever, apt, keen'.

1956 Mc StAnd, Brief, Person who plays the fool or clowns, joker.

briekfas see BREAKFAST.

bries /bríes/ vb dial; etym uncert: ? < *brace.*

1955 LeP StAnd, To make the most of, take advantage of: /a sii yu briesin di sonshain/ (with reference to a towel hung on the line to dry).

BRIGGADAM-BIFF, -BRIF, BRIGGADIM see BRIGIDIM (-BAM).

BRIGGIN see BRIGIN.

BRIGHT adj dial. In phr: *eyes too bright, eyes bright so*, bold, looking boldly. *BL G*

1956 Mc StAnd /hou yu ai bráit so—yu ái tuu bráit/ *Why are you looking so boldly—you're bold-eyed*; StT /hou yu hai brait so/ (when staring at someone with big eyes, significantly).

BRIGIDIM (-BAM), (-BIFF) adv dial (and sb); echoic, imitating the sound of something tumbling (and, with added element, falling hard), prob with concurrent infl of such words as Twi *bìrim* (*bìrim-bìrim*), a sudden fit, start; suddenly, at once; *ɔhwee ase b.*, he fell down plump! bounce! *bìrìd twem*, all at once, suddenly. (Christaller.) *BL G T*

1889 Sanguinetti 52, A late Chief Justice was quite 'nonplussed' when a witness before him described a man as falling down 'briggadam brif'; and the expression is still sometimes used. It may be that the noise of a falling body is meant to be expressed, but we hazard the conjecture that it had its origin in the noisy gambols of the 'Rigadoon'. 1940 HPJ, Briggadam-biff—When anyone falls down; Bruggudum biff; 'I hit him biff! and he fall down briggadim!' 1943 *GL* StE, Brigidimbam, sb., A clean jump over. 1956 Mc StE (Accom) /faal doun brigidim/ to fall full-length, fall flat.

BRIGIN /ˈbraigin/ adj dial; prob for *bragging* (cf /baig/ for *bag*, /haig/ for *hag*, etc.); however the form *briggin* may indicate some conn with US dial *biggity*, which has var forms *briggity*, *brigaty*, etc., and the sense conceited, proud, haughty. (Cf also *OED* s.v. *bigot*, the first citation, *bigin*, *bigot*.)

Haughty, proud; ostentatious; self-importantly calling attention to oneself. Also *fig*.

1940 HPJ, Briggin: When a person in a higher position gives himself airs (Marion). Brigin ribber (i.e. spated) nebber drown somebody—[Cp 'Barking dogs don't bite'.] Two-bits nebber brigin like one fippeny (Miss Reynolds) —[Cp Banbury 40, 'Two-bits nebber braggin as one fipenny'.]

brikl-brikl adj dial; iteration of *brickle* (*OED*). *G*

1958 DeC StE /brikl-brikl/ brittle, crumbly; counter-flour is used along with kwa-kwa in making dumplings because /bier kwakwa de a likl brikl-brikl/ [*Bare kwakwa —kwakwa by itself—is a little crumbly.*]

brim sb dial; the regular pronunc of *bream* (the fish) though */briim/ would be expected. Also in south-east US.

1952 FGC StC, StE, StT, West, etc. /brim/.

BRIM GRUNT sb dial; <*brim*, bream + *grunt*. The variety of grunt also called *brim*—e.g. *Diplodus argenteus*, family *Sparidæ*.

1952 FGC Port, StJ, StM /brim gront/.

BRING COME vb phr dial; prob infl by the Twi (and other African languages') manner of combining verbs (here, redundantly). Bring (it) here. *G T*

1907 Jekyll 4, Bring come. Bring it here. 1950 Pioneer [41, Sista Fowl bring nuff drinks an tings fe eat come gi Anancy]; *ibid* 64, You carry any more bring come? [*Have you brought any more here?*] 1957 JN Clar, Tek up di baby bring come.

BRING DOWN vb phr dial; cf COME DOWN 2. To cause to flow or flood. *G*

1873 Rampini 57, But during the 'seasons' the rains in the mountains 'bring the gullies down' as it is called, and the dry water-courses become raging torrents, overflowing their banks.

bringgl see BRINGLE.

BRINGING IN THE AUGUST MORNING phr sb. *G*

1953 Moore 119, Celebration on the eve of Emancipation Day.

BRINGLE /bríngl/ adj, sb, and vb dial; <*brindle* (*OED v dial*, 'To be irritated, to show resentment, to bridle up').

A. vb: To become angry.

1943 *GL* Tre, Bringle, to become cross.

B. adj: For *brindled*: Angry, fierce.

1941 Kirkpatrick gloss, Bringle, fierce. *Ibid.* 17, Dem sailor 'board it mus' 'e bringle bwoy. W'en dem go fe fight nutten stop dem.

C. sb: Evid from the vb, but in a favourable sense—lively emotions or sensations.

1943 *GL* StAnd, Bringle, good feeling.

BRING OUT vb phr obs; cf *OED bring v* 21b →1607. Produce, bring to birth. *G*

1823 Roughley 149, When the cow happens to calve..or brings (as they say in that country) her calf out.

BRING UP vb phr dial; cf *OED bring v* 27e. In absolute sense: to arrest and hale into court.

1942 Bennett 34, Yuh meck dem bring up Dora sey She ovah work har mule. 1950 Pioneer 93, Now because o' you dem gone bring me up. *BA BL G*

BRINJAH sb dial rare; etym uncert, but cf BANJA vb.

1943 *GL* Man, Brinjah, a comical person.

B'RO see *brrr*.

BROAD-BASKET sb dial. A large basket of woven bamboo without a handle and with sides turned somewhat inward, used for carrying ground provisions and the like.

1959 DeC StAnd /braad-baskit/.

BROAD BEAN sb; *OED* 1783→. A variety of *Phaseolus lunatus*, named for its shape. *BL G*

1756 Browne 293, Phaseolus 12. Maximus perennis.. The Broad Bean. This plant is cultivated more for the sake of its shade, and speedy growth in arbours, than for its seeds; tho' these are known to be both wholesome and palatable, and frequently used at the best tables in the island. 1837 Macfadyen 282, Broad-Bean. 1920 Fawcett 64.

BROAD CUTLASS see DeC in 1961 *CLS* 70.

BROADLEAF (TREE) sb; cf *OED*, quots 1756→. The tree *Terminalia latifolia*, and its wood. *G*

1696 Sloane 184, Arbor maxima..folio longissimo latissimoque. *The broad-leaf Tree.* 1941 Swabey 15, Broadleaf—*Terminalia latifolia*..A tall tree..The trunk is usually very straight and devoid of branches below 50ft. The wood..is often used for shingles and barrel staves, but by far its chief use is as boards. The bark is also in great demand for use in tanneries. 1952 FGC StAnd, StAnn, StE, StJ, StM, Tre /bráadliif/.

BROADLEAF BUSH sb dial. An unidentified shrub. *G*

1952 FGC StT, Broadleaf bush—has a leaf similar to mackerel bush.

BROAD-LEAF CALALU sb dial; <*broad-leaved* + CALALU. Identity uncertain, but prob the cultivated 'spinach', *Amarantus viridis*. *G*

1952 FGC StAnd, Broad-leaf calalu.

BROADLEAF CONCH sb dial; cf BROADLEAF and CONCH. A variety of large conch whose shell opens out with a broad, leaf-like appendage.

1952 FGC StC /bráadliif kongk/ pink inside.

BROAD-LEAFED BROOMWEED sb bot; cf BROOMWEED 1. Browne's name for *Sida jamaicensis*, preserved by some botanists, but not generally. (It may represent a genuine folk-term—cf other uses of 'broadleaf'.)

1756 Browne 280, Sida 5..The broad-leafed Broom-weed..It grows very much like the second species of Melochia. 1814 Lunan I 494–5, ref to Browne. 1926 Fawcett 111–12, *Sida jamaicensis*..Broad-leafed Broom Weed.

BROAD-LEAVED CHERRY (TREE) sb bot. The tree *Cordia macrophylla*. *G*

1696 Sloane 184, Prunus racemosa, foliis oblongis hirsutis maximis, fructu rubro..The broad-leav'd Cherry-tree. 1814 Lunan I 197–8, Cordia..2. Macrophylla..This tree, is called the *broad-leaved cherry*..The leaves are a foot and a half long, very large and rough; the berries are the same size as those of the clammy [cherry]. 1864 Grisebach 782, Cherry, broad-leaved: *Cordia macrophylla*.

BROAD-LEAVED SCREW TREE sb bot obs. An early name for the SCREW TREE.

1811 Titford 82, Broad-leaved screw-tree, *Helicteres Jamaicensis*..The capsule is twisted in a spiral form.

BROAD-OUT vb dial. To spread widely. *G*

1941 Kirkpatrick 10, Yessiday de fiel' broadout so much dat sometime de batsman coulden see de fiel'er dem. 1943 *GL* Clar, Prawlout [=*sprawl out*]—to broad out, ugly sitting down.

BROAD-POINT sb dial. A type of cutlass or MACHETE.

1958 DeC StAnd /braad paint/ a machete (the short, 20 in., flare).

bro-bro sb dial; iterative <*brow*. The eyebrow.

1956 Mc Man /ái bró-bro/ eyebrow; StAnd /bró-bró/ (not all speakers).

bro-bro see BRU-BRU.

BROGOBILLI sb dial; BROGO- is unknown, BILLI prob <*Billy* (cf *OED Billy*[1,2]). Cf also *bogobi*.

1943 *GL* StAnn, Brogobilli, a kind of worm.

brok sb dial; ?abbr of BRUCKINS. Entertainment (stories, etc.).

1955 Mc StAnd (Mt Charles) /éniwan no anánsi brok kyan kóm/ *Anyone who knows Anancy-stories (etc.) can come.*

brok see BROKE, BRUCK-, BRUK-.

brok-aks see BREAK-AX.

BROKE /brok/ vb dial; also sp *bruk*, *bruck*; <*broke*, past tense and participle of *break*, for which it is used in all senses.

1. In ordinary trans senses of break. *BL G N*

1877 Murray *Kittle* 17, Ef I catch John Joe I wi broke him neck. 1907 Jekyll 199 [Song:] Me go da Galloway road, Gal an' boy them a broke rock stone, Broke them one by one..[etc.] 1952 FGC Port, etc., Broke rock-stone —game.

2. In ordinary uses of the participle: *broke*, *broken*; also as passive. *BL G N*

1921 Franck 424 [Prov:] Better fe water trow 'way dan gourd fe bruck. 1957 JN Port, Me not doing any home work cause me slate bruk. (I.e. *broke* or, more likely, *is broken*.) 1959 LeP StAnd /mi brok/ *I'm broke, have no money*.

3. To gather or harvest (a crop, esp one which actually requires detaching the fruit); also with *in*. (Cf *OED break v* 33; *DAE* v 4 1837→.)

1790 Beckford I 313–14, The grain is ripe and requires to be gathered, or, as it is called in Jamaica, to be broken in ..When the negroes break in the Indian, or the great corn. 1797 Braco 16 Jan, Great Gang..went to Gordon Bank to break Corn. 1912 McKay *Songs* 102, Her pa an' ma about de fiel' Are brukin' sugar-pine. 1952 FGC Man, Kling-kling..eat off peas or corn that's ready to /brok in/; StC /brek/ reap (corn).

4. Elliptically for 'break into a run' or the like.

1896 Bates 122, As him tas' it so, an' tas' how it sweet, him bruck (broke, seized the fowl and fled)..Dem tell him, him bruck a'ter Puss. [*They told him, he set off instantly after Puss.*] *G*

5. In phrasal combination with adverbs: /brok/ +*away*, *down*, *in*, *out*, *up*, etc. (See as separate entries.) *BL G*

6. In phrasal combination, or compounded, with noun objects: /brok/+*kitchen*, *neck*, *pot*, *stomach*, *top*, etc. (See separate entries.) *BL G*

BROKE A FIGHT /brok a fait/ vb phr dial; <BROKE, break+A[5]+*fight* vb (i.e. break out fighting). To start fighting suddenly, to break into or begin fighting. *G*

1942 Bennett 15, Ef any man gi gains Miss Knib, meck Up yuh mine fe we bruck a fight; *ibid* 18, Ah feelin' good dis mahnin' or Ah hooda bruck a fight.

BROKE AWAY vb phr; <BROKE, break+*away*. *G*

1956 Mc StC /im brok awe di siel/ *He takes down the sail.*

BROKE AX see BREAK-AX.

BROKE FOOT /brók-fùt/ sb dial joc; <BROKE vb+FOOT. The first pregnancy of an unwed girl. Cf TUMBLE DOWN.

1960 BLB.

BROKE-KITCHEN sb dial; also attrib; <BROKE, break+*kitchen*. A dog, because it breaks into the kitchen.

1943 *GL* Clar, Bruk-kitchen, dog. 1955 FGC Man /brok-kichin daag/.

BROKEN LANGUAGE /bruokng langwij/ sb dial. Sub-standard speech, the Jamaican folk dialect; also called BAD TALK, *patwa* (patois), etc. *BA BL G T*

1956 Mc StE (Accom) /kokoté—dat óul-taim bruoken langwij/ *'Kokote'—that is old-fashioned folk speech*; StAnd /iz not dat shi waan, iz di bruokng langwij shi waan/ *That is not what she wants,—she wants every-day speech.*

BROKE OUT vb phr dial; cf BROKE 3. To gather a crop; to *break in*.

1924 Beckwith 23, Tink you say a me a t'ief you corn.. if dem broke out you corn, how you say a me? (If *they* picked your corn, how can you say it was I?)

BROKE-OUT sb dial; <BROKE vb+*out*. A quarrel; a falling-out. *G*

1954 LeP StE (Eld), Dem ha a single bruk out.

BROKE-OVER /brók-úova/ adj dial; <BROKE past pple+*over*. Beyond limits, gone to excess, unruly; see quot.

1959 StE (Potsdam), Mother to child: 'Yu too bruk-over'..means 'forward'—would be used by an adult to a child who takes something without asking. Not used much between adults here.

BROKE-POT PEAS sb dial; <BROKE, break +*pot*; cf Sp *quiebra-ollas* (*Acnistus aggregatus* —Malaret) and BREAK-AX. The BONAVIST BEAN, so nicknamed because it takes so long to cook that it 'breaks the pot'.

1912 McKay *Songs* 15, Watch de blue bannabees..Some call it 'broke-pot' peas, It caan' bruk we bu'n-pan. 1959 FGC, still widely known.

BROKE-STONE sb dial; <BROKE 6, broken +*stone*.

1929 Beckwith 11, Whitestone (the common linestone or 'bruk stone' used in mending roads).

BROKE-UP /brok-op/ vb phr dial; <BROKE 5, break+*up*. *G*

1956 Mc StAnd /brok op/ to wriggle the body in a dance. [Cf BRUCKINS.]

BROKE-'WAY /brókwé/ sb dial; <BROKE+ *'way*, away, for *breakaway*.

1. A landslip or landslide.

1943 *GL* StM, Bruck way, landslide. 1952 FGC Tre /brokwe/ rundown, landslip; StT /brókwè/.

2. The bare place from which the landslip fell.

a 1938 Anon, marginal note written alongside passage (1826 Williams 279–80, The side of the hill was broken away, and hurled to the bottom of the ravine, possibly by an earthquake), The breakaway terminates in a rocky cliff..Called now Newington Breakaway. 1952 FGC StAnd /brokwe/ the place a landslip slipped from.

brokinz see BRUCKINS.

brok-nek see BREAKNECK.

BROO see *brrr*.

BROOBROO see BRU-BRU.

BROOK-CAKE for *brute-cake*; see GRATER BRUTE.

BROOM-WEED sb chiefly dial; <*broom* (*OED* 3) +*weed*, evid a new combination, though perh infl by *broom* as the name of a plant (*OED* 1). *N*

1. Various species of *Sida* (*S. glomerata*, *S. urens*, *S. procumbens*, etc.) which are used to make brooms; they also have medicinal and other uses.

1740 Importance 35, The Broom-Weed bears a small yellow Blossom, the Stalks of which boil'd in Water cure the Itch..but the Blossom kills Poultry. 1756 Browne 280, The broad-leafed Broom-weed. 1794 Barham 24, Broom-weed. This plant is so called by the negroes in Jamaica..because they make a broom with it..but it hath no resemblance to the English broom, being of the mallow kind. 1926 Fawcett v 107–8, *Sida*..Broom Weed. 1952 FGC Han, StAnn, StC, StM, StT /brúum-wíid/; Tre /brúung wíid/; StE /bróunwiid, brúumwíid/.

2. The similar *Melochia pyramidata*.

1756 Browne 276, Melochia 2..The smaller *Melochia* or Broom-weed.

3. *Corchorus siliquosus*.

1756 Browne 147–8, Coreta 1..Broom-weed..it is generally used in beesoms by the negroes. 1926 Fawcett 85, *Corchorus*..*siliquosus*..Broom Weed.

4. *Scoparia dulcis*. See SWEET BROOMWEED.

BROOM-WEED MALLOWS sb bot obs; cf BROOMWEED. In Browne's use: *Malvastrum coromandelianum*.

1756 Browne 282, Malva 4..The Broom-weed Mallows. [1926 Fawcett 104.]

BROUGHTA see *braata*.

broun wiid see BROOM-WEED.

BROUSE sb or vb? dial rare; evid by some irreg devel <*bruise*: cf *OED brouse* as a 15th–16th century spelling of *bruise*.

1943 *GL* StAnd, Brouse, bruise.

brouts sb dial.

1959 DeC StAnd /brouts/—a general derogatory epithet, used always with some color term but apparently used of all colors and classes: /go we, yu wait brouts yu/.

BROWN ALBION (SUGAR) sb. A type of locally made light-brown sugar, also called simply ALBION SUGAR. (Cf COOLIE-FOOT SUGAR.)

1943 *GL* StM, Brown Albion Sugar, Coolie foot.

BROWN-BEARDED COTTON sb obs. A variety of cotton formerly cultivated in Jamaica: see quot.

1793 Edwards II 270, Brown Bearded [Cotton].—This is generally cultivated with the species last mentioned [*sc* Common Jamaica], but the staple is somewhat finer, and the pods, though fewer in number, produce a greater quantity of wool. 1814 Lunan I 240 (ref to Edwards).

BROWN DUSK /broun dos/ sb dial arch; cf *OED brown a* 1, dusky, dark..'Now only poetic'. See quots.

1956 Mc StAnd /broun dos/ evening twilight, time between 6–7 PM approximately. 1958 DeC StT /broun dos/ an old-fashioned word for FIRST DUSK.

BROWNED-NOSE sb.

1892 Cockrell list, Browned nose, deepwater cod, *Brotula barbata*.

BROWN GEORGE sb dial; cf *OED* in diff senses, 1688→.

1. A confection consisting basically of dry corn parched and ground or pounded fine and mixed with sugar and salt; some recook it. This kind is also called ASHAM or HASHAM. Cf BLACK GEORGE.

1929 Beckwith 20, Brown George is parched dry corn beaten fine in a mortar and eaten with sugar and salt. 1943 *GL* Man, Brown-george, parched corn grounded and recooked in boiling water with sugar and salt. 1954 LeP Man, Brown Gawrge; StE (Eld), Brown George, parched corn ground up finely.

2. A confection made of sugar and coconut.

1952 FGC Tre, Brown George—take corn, parch it, beat it, sieve it, turn it with coconut milk, squeeze out milk and put on fire till it gets hard. 1956 Mc StE (Accom) /broun jaaj /sugar and coconut.

BROWN GIRL sb gen.

A mulatto or coloured girl; the word in the plural was used formerly in allusion to the beauty of these girls, and to their supposed amorousness and accessibility. *G*

1827 Hamel I 239, I caught them philandering together this morning. These brown girls are the devil incarnate: they fly at a pretty fellow as a parcel of sharks rush at a piece of salt beef. a 1818 Lewis (1845) 25, Both of them gave balls at Kingston to the 'Brown Girls'; for the fair sex elsewhere are called the 'Brown Girls' in Jamaica.

BROWN-JOLLY (BERRY) sb obs; by folk-etym <*brinjal*, egg-plant (cf *OED*). The egg plant; the name was never much used.

1756 Browne 173, Solanum 1..The Brown-Jolly or *Bolangena*..This plant..was first imported into Jamaica by the *Jews*..It generally bears a number of large berries. 1774 Long III 772, Brownjolly; *ibid* 854, Pot-herbs and Greens..Branched calalue. Brownjolly berry. Calalues. 1813 Titford 53 (see under EGG FRUIT).

BROWN MAN sb. s. *G*

1. A coloured man, between black and white. (The term may be used neutrally, but among negroes it often carries resentment or scorn—see quot 1927.)

1826 Williams 92 (see PARATEE). 1877 Murray *Kittle* 6, An old brown man named John Marshall. 1896 Bates 125, Mr Murray, the 'brown man' mentioned in the previous article. 1927 Anderson-Cundall 30 [Prov:] Brown man wife nyam [eats] cockroach a corner, sabe money fe buy silk dress. 1960 LeP StAnd, A brown man is someone who does not have very negroid features, a fairly light skin and straightish hair—a mulatto but fairly light skinned.

2. Hence, one who is better off in general than a black man: see quot.

c 1953 LeP West, I was asking my garden-boy why he came to Kingston for work, and he said, 'There aren't many brown men to give you work in Westmoreland'. I asked him what he meant by a brown man, and he said, 'Rich man'. I said, was I rich?—he said, yes; was I a brown man?—'Oh no, Doc—you're a foreigner'.

BROWN-MAN'S FANCY sb. A common wild-flower often planted in gardens (*Vinca rosea*); see quots.

1927 Beckwith 13, Brown-man's fancy (pink periwinkle). *Apocynaceae*. For a cold, boil and drink as tea. 1954 *WIMJ* 32, *Vinca rosea* L. . . Periwinkle; Ram-goat Rose; Brown Man's Fancy; Old Maid.

BROWN OWL sb. The owl *Pseudoscops grammicus*. *G*

1840 Hill in *Almanack* (ref 1847 Gosse 22), After sunset the Brown Owl, seated on the dead limb of a tree in some savanna, makes little circuits of about thirty feet diameter, and returns to perch again. 1936 Bond 189, Jamaican Owl. . *Local name:*—Brown Owl. 1957 Jeffrey-Smith 11, Our brown owl is peculiar to Jamaica and is also known as the Horned Owl.

BROWN PARROT FISH sb obs? A brown variety of the PARROT fish.

1756 Browne 447, Mormyra 2. . The little brown Parrot-fish.

BROWN PETRIL sb obs.

A former (perhaps mistaken) name for the Black-capped Petrel (*Pterodroma hasitata*). (Cf 1936 Bond 6, 'Formerly nested in the Blue Mountains of Jamaica. . *Local names:*—Blue Mountain Duck'.)

1774 Long II 128, Bull-finches, and brown petrils: the latter are said to be very numerous on the higher parts of the Blue Mountains, where they breed in holes made in the earth.

BROWN RAT sb. The rat. *G*

1851 Gosse 445–6, The Brown Rat. . though it is at this time by far the most numerous of these vermin. . is of comparatively recent importation. The negroes are said to distinguish it by the name of the *George* Rat. [q.v.]

BROWN-SKIN adj chiefly dial; for *brown-skinned*. Mulatto, or similar colour. *BA BL G T*

c 1951 StAnd [Song:] Brown-skin gal, stay home an' mind baby. 1954 LeP StT, Brown skin, someone whose skin is light brown.

BROWN SNAKE sb; cf *DAE*, *DA*, 1832→ for different snakes. *Dromicus callilaemus*. (Identity uncert in quot 1790.)

1790 Beckford I 368–9, I was once very severely bitten by a little brown snake. . I should not have mentioned this trifling incident, did not a vulgar error prevail that makes this reptile of every species entirely harmless. 1823 Stewart 85, The yellow, the black, and the brown snake, the last being the smallest of the three. 1940 Lynn-Grant 123, 'Brown snake' [quoting Gosse's descr (1851, 384–5) of the 'Spotted-Chinned Snake':] Colour reddish-brown above, softening to white below. An oblong mark of deep brown passes along the summit of the head.

BROWN WIDOW sb; by analogy to *black widow*. The spider *Latrodectus geometrica*, of a brown colour.

[1949 *NHN* IV 15, The black spider, *Latrodectus mactans*. . [and] *L. geometrica*, the brown species.] 1954 *NHN* VI 77, The brown widow spider.

brrr int dial; cf the same in Norway, Poland, etc. (The expl offered in quot 1940 is most unlikely.) Noise produced by vibrating the lips sharply while expelling breath, used as a signal to make a horse, mule, or donkey stop.

1940 HPJ, B'ro, A curious sound to stop donkeys. The Spanish *burro*, a jackass. . cp *buru*, a donkey, Portuguese loan-word in Mpongwe. 1943 *GL* StAnd, Breer, to stop an ass; Tre, Broo, stop. 1952 FGC StJ /brrr/! [Used by a local man driving a horse-drawn vehicle.]

BRU-BRU adj dial; cf Twi *búru*, slovenliness, sluttishness, etc., prob here iterated.

1. Disorderly, untidy—applied to a variety of things.

1940 HPJ, Bru-bru:—'Like you don't do anything good' (Marion). 1943 *GL* Clar, Bru-bru, untidy; Tre, Broo-broo, shaggy.

2. Applied specif to people: Lower-class, of no account.

1941 Kirkpatrick gloss, Bru-bru, unimportant, insignificant. 1943 *GL* no addr, Bro-bro, under class affairs. [This may be an absolute (substantive) use.]

3. Forming sb compounds: *bru-bru dance*, *bru-bru race*, etc. See quots.

1940 HPJ, Brubru dance—A dance made up of all sorts of people among the lower classes (Astley Clerk). 1940 HPJ, A *bru-bru* race was a 'scratch' race-meeting in the country, with all sorts of queer entries (Mr Rutty); it means a 'scratch' race meeting in Kingston or any other part of the island, when any sort of entries are allowed. I have known more than one 'brubru' race on the Kingston Course up to six years ago (Astley Clerk). 1959 LeP Clar, Bru-bru races—still held in the country parts, esp. to try out unknown horses; anyone can enter and you can ride as you wish—'no rules about jostling or anything like that'.

BRUCK see BROKE. *G*

BRUCK-DOWN MALE sb dial; cf BROKE 4.

1954 LeP StAnn, Bruck-down male, man who limps.

BRUCKINS /brókinz/ sb dial; for pronunc cf BROKE; for sense see *break* (*OED v* 24), and cf esp *DA* '*breakdown*, a noisy, rollicking dance of rustic origin', *Ethiopian breakdown*, *Negro breakdown*, etc.

1. A lively, vigorous dance or similar entertainment.

1940 Astley Clerk in HPJ, The only people who use the 'brukkins' are the peasantry. . they are danced [in] the open air. . The Jamaica brukkins, or Shay Shay, is quite a different dance to the Spanish Mento or any other similar Spanish dance. I would connect the Jamaica Dialect words, 'Bruck' and 'Brukkins' with the particular (or syncopated) rhythm in which this class of Jamaica Folk Dance is broken up, and played—a syncopation outstandingly Jamaican. 1943 *GL* StC, Bruckins, a dance. c 1948 *Calypso Tunes*, When Big Mattie dance inna London Town, Whether brukins, mento or Samba, Parisian gəl haffi sit dung tight An' grudge de gal from New London. 1954 LeP Man, Dem have one big [brʌk]ings = big party.

2. News (i.e. that which one learns when another 'breaks the news'. Cf *OED break v* 24).

1943 *GL* StAnn, Bruckings, news.

BRUCKSY adj dial; <BROKE, broken + *-sy* (*OED*). Broken up.

1943 Bennett 2, Me ha' six pickney an'. . Dis dutty, brucksy baskit yah Is dem ongle support. 1957 Bennett 74, Bear wickedness how t'eatre brucksy Chair wan' bruck me back.

BRUCKTUMMUCK sb dial; <BROKE 5, break + *stomach*. A hill so steep that it seems to break the stomach of one who tries to climb it.

1943 *GL* StM, Brucktummuck, steep hill.

brufil siida see BLUEFIELDS CEDAR.

BRUGGUDUM BIFF see BRIGIDIM-BAM.

BRUGO sb dial rare; perh clipped form of BRUGUDU.

1943 *GL* StE, Brugo, refused articles.

BRUGUDU /brugudu, brogadu/ sb dial. A type of soil having a mixture of clay and gravel; it is considered poor for most crops.

1899 Hill 61, 'Bruggadoo', as the black clays at the railway cut [near Richmond, StJ] are called. *Ibid*, Creeping blue, black, and red clays known in Jamaica as Bruggadoo. 1940 HPJ, Brŭgudŭ, Broogoodoo, A soil of clay and pebbles mixed, good for Bananas (Sam Burke); All over the island, 'poor soil' (W. G. Stuart). 1955 LeP StE (Eld) /brugadu/ stony soil.

BRUISE vb dial.

1954 LeP StT, Brooz, to cut awkwardly or hack with a dull tool.

BRUKINS, BRUKKINS see BRUCKINS.

BRUK STONE see BROKE-STONE.

BRUSH sb dial. <*brush* (OED *sb*[2] 3b). The 'silks' that hang from an ear of maize.

1953 FGC StAnn /brosh/ the corn-silk.

BRUSH-BRUSH sb dial; iterative <*brush* (*OED sb*[1]). Small bits of wood or sticks, usually for kindling.

1943 *GL* StE, Brush-brush, chip, bramble. 1955 FGC Man /brosh-brosh/ small sticks. 1956 Mc StE /brosh-brosh/ twigs, fine wood used for firewood that flares up quickly but doesn't burn for long.

BRUSH-TAIL DOCTOR-FISH sb dial. A variety of the DOCTOR-FISH having a brush-like tail.

1952 FGC StM.

BRUTCHIE NEGRO see BRECHIE.

bruung wiid see BROOM-WEED.

BRYAL WYS see BRIAL WIS.

BUA see BOYO.

BUAW sb dial obs; perh merely an inexact pronunc of 'bullock', but see quot.

1774 Long II 427, There are some other words, that are remarkable for the different senses in which they are used, viz..Buaw, (Original Import) Devil, (Common Import) Bullock (Negroe phrase), (Dialect) Mundingo.

BUBA /buba/ sb dial; prob Guiana Arawak *buba*, the palm *Irearta exhorrhiza* (1928 De Goeje 265). *SC bóeba.*

1. The dry leaf or bough of a palm (coconut, cabbage, etc.).

1943 *GL* Tre, Buba, part of coconut plant; StT, Booba, coconut boughs when dry. 1954 LeP StE (Eld), Booba, thatch for roofing. [In Jamaica, thatch is made of palm leaves.]

2. In compounds: BUBA-MAT, BUBA-SKIN, BUBA-TREE. (See as separate entries.)

3. Fig. See OLD BUBA.

BUBAKA sb dial rare; perh conn with BUBA. Some sort of weed or 'bush' that is a trouble in cultivated ground.

1943 *GL* West, Bubaka, bad bush in cultivation.

BUBA-MAT /buba-mat/ sb dial; <BUBA+*mat*. A sheath of the cabbage-palm (from the lower part of the branch), used for a mat.

1943 *GL* no addr, Boba-mah, the broad part of the leaf of a Jamaica palm (the cabbage palm). 1952 FGC StJ /búba-mat/ sheath of the cabbage palm, used [by children] to slide down hill.

BUBA-SKIN /búbakìn/ sb dial; <BUBA+*skin*. The dry (fallen) bough of a palm tree, esp the sheath at the lower part of a cabbage-palm leaf. Cf *bongka*, *buunakin*, CULLABUNKA, KANDA.

1943 *GL* Man, Bubbakin, cabbage palm leaves; StC, Bubboa-kin, the dry bough of a palm tree. 1955 FGC Man /buba-kin/. 1959 LeP StAnd /bóngkà, búunakin, búbakìn iz aal di siem ting—kyabij paam bou. wi yuuz dem tu skiet an/.

BUBA-TREE /búba tríi/ sb dial; <BUBA+*tree*. The CABBAGE PALM TREE.

1943 *GL* StC, Bubba tree, Cabbage Palm Tree; West, Bubboa tree, cabbage palm tree.

BUBBAKIN, BUBBA TREE see BUBA-SKIN.

BUBBIE see BUBBY.

BUBBOA-KIN, BUBBOA TREE see BUBA-SKIN.

BUBBY /bobi, bubi/ sb dial; <*bubby* (*OED bubby*[1] '*obs*. or *dial*.' →1725); US dial (Wentworth). A woman's breast. (Already considered vulgar in the 18th cent—see quot 1790.) *BA BL G N T*

1790 Moreton 116 [Examples of Creole talk:] 'Pray, miss Louisa, will you permit me to help you to a bit of the turkey; it is very fine!' 'Tank you, sir, *wid* all my *haut*.' 'Pray, miss what part do you like best?' 'Sir, Ise don't love turkey rump—Ise love turkey bubby.' 1943 *GL* Clar, Kgn, StAnd, StAnn, StJ, StT, etc., Bubby, Bubbie, breast. 1956 Mc Man, Port /bobi/.

BUBBY-BITER /bóbi-bàita/ sb dial. See quot; =TITTY-BITER.

1960 NJL StC, A thing just like a tadpole, but not getting any bigger, swimming in rivers; girls apply them to their breasts 'to develop them'.

BUBLIC see PUPA-LICK.

BUBLOON sb dial arch; for *dubloon*.

1943 *GL* Clar, Bubloon, £3. 4. 0.

BUBU /bubu/ sb dial; cf Fon *bũbũ*, insect; prob with coincidental English infl—cf BUGABOO 1. See also BOBO sb[1]. *SC boebóe.*

1. See quot.

1943 *GL* Kgn, Boobo, worm.

2. See quot.

1943 *GL* StC, Bubu, a frightened person.

3. Nasal mucus; cf BUGABOO. *BL*

1943 *GL* Kgn, Bu-bu, matter in the nose. 1955 FGC Man /bubu/ come out of nose.

bubububububububu int dial; <Mende *bubu*, to fly (Turner 68).

1955 Emmanuel Rowe (StE—Accom), [In telling the story of how Bobiabu flew from one cotton tree to another, suggests the sound of his flight:] /bubububu-bububu/. 1960 CLS 175.

bubus sb dial; cf *dudus*.

1958 DeC Port /bubus/ affectionate name for a child.

BUCCANEER sb; cf *OED*: the first quot is that given here. *G*

1661 Hickeringill 33–4 [The Spaniards] are not able with all their skill and strength to root out a few Buckaneers, or Hunting French-men, that follow their Game, in despight of them, though they cannot number three hundred at a general Rendezvouse.

BUCK /bok/ vb chiefly dial; cf *OED v*[6] 'dial. and U.S.—a corruption of butt' →1860.

1. trans. To strike with the horns—regularly said of cows and goats; also of human beings who butt with the head. *BL N*

1900 Murray 8, An when you come pon buckin pint an rum drinkin pint, you is a nyamps side o' she. When she buck me de berry house shake. 1950 Pioneer 26, Anancy sey, 'do Sista Nanny-goat, buck me offa dis tree noh'.

2. trans. To strike (any part of the body) against something. *BL N*

1940 HPJ, 'A buck me foot', I have struck my foot (against something). 1956 Mc StE (Accom) /mi bók mi fút/ I stubbed my toe (on a stone).

3. intr. Said of a part of the body: To strike something. Also const *on*. *BL*

1907 Jekyll 87, Him travel till him go an' buck on a house. The way the night was so dark he never see the house, he just buck on it. 1940 HPJ, Me foot buck: My foot has struck something.

4. In the phr to buck (one's) *right*, *left*, *good*, etc. *foot*, to have a sign of good or bad fortune to come. *BL*

1943 Bennett 20, Come Rufus shake me han Me buck good foot at las' me dear Me goin' to Englan'. 1952 FGC Han, If you buck you lef' foot—bad luck; StAnd, Buck im lef' foot, buck im right foot.

5. To come upon, to meet (unexpectedly). Usually in the phr BUCK UP. *BL N*

1943 *GL* Port, Buck, meet.

6. intr. To protrude, stick out or up (said of the forehead, toes, etc.).

1950 Pioneer 46, Same way Tom forrid buck, [*Just so Tom's forehead protrudes*].

7. intr. To search; const *for*.

1958 DeC Port /dem stil a bok fi Anansi fi arés im baksaid put a jiel/ *They are still searching for Anancy*. . etc.

BUCKARA PINE see BUCKRA PINE.

BUCK-BUCK sb dial; iterative <BUCK. The TRUNK-FISH (or COWFISH), which has horns, and which rocks on its hard base like a cow seeming to 'buck' one.

1950 Smith in *NHN* 135, Lurking in the sea-grass [along the Palisadoes] could be spotted. . one species of cowfish ('buckbuck'), *Acanthostracion quadricornis*. 1952 FGC StE /bokbok/ 'the Clarendon name for the trunkfish'; /bokbok/ same as scuttle, cunnybuck, trunkfish.

BUCKERA see BACKRA.

BUCKET PAN sb dial. Redundantly: a metal bucket (i.e. a pan which is a bucket).

1955 Bennett *Pleasuration*, Wid bucket pan eena him han.

BUCK FLY sb dial; <BUCK vb+*fly*. A small fly which meets you by getting into your eye.

1952 FGC Port, Buck fly—catch you in your eye when you're driving or riding; a lot flying together in Lent.

BUCKI MASSA see BUCKY MASSA.

BUCKLE /bokl/ vb dial; cf *OED v* 3d quot a 1605 only. To grab, take hold of firmly; more often BUCKLE-HOLD. *BL G*

1868 Russell 17, *Bokle*, To catch by surprise; thus, A bokle de chap sa.

BUCKLE-FOOT sb dial; <*buckled*+FOOT. s.

1952 FGC StAnd /bokl fut/ knock-knee. *G*

BUCKLE-HOLD /bokl-huol/ vb dial; <BUCKLE+*hold*. (Cf *OED button-hold*.) To BUCKLE, to grasp and hold firmly. *G*

1942 Bennett 32, Leggo me han' yaw sah Me noh mel yuh, soh me keahn tell Wey yuh buckle-hole me fah. 1950 Pioneer gloss, Buckle-hold, =to hold tightly. 1955 Bennett *Cricket History*, Missus de bwoys was gran! Fe buckle hole *two* century Pon *one* six wicket stan!

BUCK-MOUTH sb dial; <BUCK 6+*mouth*. *G*

1940 HPJ, Buck-mouth, a mouth with projecting upper teeth. Also adjectivally.

BUCKRA see BACKRA.

BUCK-TOE sb dial.

1. A toe which protrudes or sticks up. *G*

2. A small crayfish (that is shaped like a buck-toe or which 'bucks' a wader's toe?).

1912 McKay *Songs* 82, Watchin' de bucktoe under de shadow. . in de stream.

3. Attrib: *buck-toe shoes*.

c 1915 FGC StAnd, Buck-toe shoes—men's shoes in style at this time with a toe or cap raised into a point.

BUCK UP /bókóp/ vb phr dial; <BUCK+*up*.

1. To meet, encounter, come upon; also const *against*, *on*. *BL*

1924 Beckwith 34, I go in Dead country an' buck up Brar Dead; *ibid* 95, See s.v. BUGABOO 1. 1940 HPJ, To buck up on a person is to meet him unexpectedly. 1952 FGC StAnd, If him buck you up a night, *If he happens upon you at night*; Tre, I never buck up dat, *I have never encountered that*. 1956 Mc Man /mi jos bok i op/ *I just came upon it* [a turtle on the beach]; StE (Accom) /mi bok im op iina ruod/ *I met him on the road* [a sudden and unwelcome encounter].

2. In the phr *buck up on*: to bump into. *BL*

1957 JN Man, Mi was running and Beverly Boucher buck up on mi mam. It a hurt me.

BUCK-UP /bókop/ sb dial; <BUCK UP, vb phr. A social gathering or meeting; see quots.

1956 Mc StE (Accom) /wi havin bokop tunait/ *We are having a 'do' tonight* (so please give us our money to buy cigarettes, etc); /bokop/—a gathering of people, not for any one special purpose—/eni miit—plenti piipl miit tugeda/.

BUCKY sb dial arch; perh <*buck* (cf *DAE* sb 3 or 4) +-*y* or abbr of. A man.

1958 DeC StAnd, StT /boki/ man; word now archaic and seldom heard any more except in the common proverb /ebri seki tu dem boki/.

BUCKY MASSA sb dial; prob a familiarized form of BUCKRA+MASSA—see quot 1924; but cf also MACKY MASSA. A term of address, respectful, affectionate, or pleading.

[1924 Beckwith 288, Massa Peter was a funny sort of a buckra massa.] 1940 HPJ, Bucky: An adjective found only in vocations, as 'Mi Bucky Missis'. Dear, good. from Buckra. (Astley Clerk: in everyday use.) 1943 *GL* Tre, Bucky Massa, one of high rank; West, Bucky massa, a pleading word. (Also Tre, Bucky, kind.) 1947 U.Newton III 20, 'Do sir! I won't do it again. Do bucki massa!!'

BUDGE (GUM, TREE, WOOD) see BIRCH.

BUDJOE sb dial rare; etym unknown.

1943 *GL* StM, Budjoe, soup.

budu sb dial; etym unknown. Cf BUTTER-DOUGH.

1959 DeC Han /budu/ a cake made of sugar, flour, butter, and spice, turned over in pot when half done. The name /bragadap/ is used for the same thing.

budum /bùdúm/ sb or adv dial; <Twi *bŭrŭm*, noise of something heavy falling to the ground. A loud sound; loudly. *BL G* (*see over*)

c 1915 FGC StAnd, Mi faal doun go 'budum'! 1958 BLB StJ, see *fi*[3] 2.

BUFA-BAW sb dial; etym obscure—perh conn with BUBA, palm leaf; the second element may represent *bag* or *basket*; cf *baasi, bahu.*

1954 LeP Kgn, Bufa-baw, palm-leaf bag. I think baw is short for basket.

BUFF /bof/ sb dial; abbr of obs BUFF-JACKET.

1958 DeC Port /bof/ same as /fufu/ food pounded soft in a mortar.

BUFFALO sb and attrib dial; <*buffalo*, perh infl by BUFFO. Fig: a large and stupid person; big; stupid.

1943 *GL* StAnn, Buffulo, big. 1958 DeC StT /bófalo/ a name for a stupid fool.

BUFF (HOUSE) sb obs; evid <*above* (cf *bov*) +*house*. (Also StKitts, Antigua, etc.)

[1834 Wentworth I 161, The 'great house' is a term commonly applied by the Negroes [in the Virgin Islands] to the proprietor's dwelling, in contradistinction to their own. As it usually stands on an elevation, it has also acquired among them the name of 'the Buff', a corruption of the word, *above*.] 1873 Rampini 162, The little fishing hamlet of Bluefields. . at the Buff* or Great House of which Gosse resided while studying the natural history of the island. . * Buff, contraction for 'above'. The Great House or Mansion house of an estate is generally situated on a little hill; hence the name. 1940 HPJ, Buff: The 'great House', or European residence on a property. Obsolete, and only traced in place-names, e.g. Buff Bay. Buffe Bay River, Sloane, 'History', I. viii. 1707.

BUFFITY /búfiti, búfti/ a dial; <BUFFO+-*ety*: cf COCKATY, etc. See quots. *BL*

1954 LeP Man, Buffity, Somebody who is very fat and clumsy. 1958 DeC Port /bufti/ derogatory epithet meaning foolish and fat and stupid.

BUFF-JACKET sb obs; a variant of *buff-coat* (*OED* †3, quot 1688, 'Buff-Coat [is] a soft Bread eaten hot with Butter'). Cf BUFF.

1725 Sloane 142, Plantains. . are likewise boil'd in the Skins, peel'd and beat to a Paste, form'd like a Dumplin, and call'd Buff-Jacket.

BUFF-MOUTH sb dial; cf BUFF TEETH.

1940 HPJ, Buck-mouth [q.v.]. . Marion said this was 'bove mout' (almost buff-mouth).

BUFFN-BAFFN sb dial rare; etym unknown (but note that Engl *buff* and *baff* both mean a stroke or blow: perhaps the cake is beaten or thumped during preparation).

1943 *GL* Kgn, Bŭffn-baffn, A kind of flour cake.

BUFFO, BUFFU /bufu, bufo/ adj dial; cf Ewe *bofaa*, broad and thick, Twi *bɔ̀fõõ*, swollen. Big, heavy, and unwieldy; cf also BUFFITY, BUFFRO-BUFFRO, BUFU-BUFU, BUFUTO. *BL*

1940 HPJ, Bŭffŭ, a variant [of Buffootoo]. 1943 *GL* StE, Buffo, big; StM, Boofoo, unwieldy; Tre, Buffoo, big. 1954 LeP Man, Buffo; StE, Buffu, somebody who is very fat and clumsy.

BUFFRO-BUFFRO adj dial arch; iterative <Twi *o-bò-fŭro*, a lazy, good-for-nothing fellow.

1. Clumsy, stout. (The sense better suits that of BUFU-BUFU, BUFUTU, etc., than that of the Twi word; perh these more current words had some influence here.)

1868 Russell 10, Clumsy, stout. What a buffro-buffro man! African. 1873 Rampini 127, A. . 'Buffro-buffro' (clumsy). . old woman. 1940 HPJ (Astley Clerk:) Buffro-buffro—Gladys says she has heard it used by her and other children, and thinks it means bigness, i.e. *overbig, clumsy*.

2. A nickname or 'secret word' for a breadfruit.

1940 HPJ, Buffro-buffro: One informant said it meant *breadfruit* in secret or *gipsy language*, by which was meant a secret jargon or slang used by children. (Astley Clerk:) Old Cookie says she has heard it used in the sense of 'breadfruit'.

BUFF TEETH sb dial; perh <*buff* (*OED* v^2), to puff out; but cf BUFF (HOUSE). Protruding teeth. *G*

1952 FGC Han /bóf tíit/; StM, Buff teeth—teeth sticking out.

BUFFU see BUFFO.

BUFO see BEFORE.

bufu see BUFFO.

BUFU-BUFU adj and sb dial; iterative—cf BUFFO, BUFFU, and BUFFRO-BUFFRO. Equivalent to or increasing the effect of BUFFO: Very big, clumsy, stupid, worthless.

1943 *GL* Kgn, Bŭffoo-bŭffoo, big and clumsy; StE, Buffo-buffo, very big; StJ, Bufu bufu, short, squat; West, Buffu-buffu, big, but of no value. 1958 DeC gen /bufu-bufu/ a name for a stupid fool.

BUFUTU /bufútu/ adj or sb dial; <BUFFU, in some way extended (-*tu* is unknown). =BUFFO: big, clumsy, and of little value despite the size. Cf Ko *bufutu*, stupidity. *BL*

1940 HPJ (and Astley Clerk), Buffootoo, bulky, strapping, hulking. 1943 *GL* Kgn, Bŭfootu, big and unshapely; West, Bufuto, big, but of no value. 1954 LeP StT, Bufutu, Someone who is very fat and clumsy. 1955 Bennett *Pleasuration*, Dem dah. . got big pleasuration Becausen Clem buffooto daughter Pass examination!

BUGABEE see *bogobi*.

BUGABOO /bàgabú/ sb dial; 1774 bug-a-bugs, 1868→ bagabo, 1943→ bagaboo; <*bugaboo* in its various senses (cf *OED, EDD, bug, bugaboo, buggey-bo*, etc.), with prob reinforcement from African words, e.g. Fon *bũbũ* (*bobõ*), insect, Bambara *buba*, termite, Ewe *baba*, termite. Cf BUBU. S BOGA.

1. A general word for various insects, worms, and the like; specifically, a. A termite; b. A caterpillar; c. A louse; d. A bed-bug; e. A spider. See quots.

1774 Long II 427, The negroes seem very fond of reduplications, to express a greater or less quantity of any thing; as. . *bug-a-bugs* (wood-ants). 1868 Russell 6, Bagabo—A caterpillar. African. 1924 Beckwith 95, Eh! me mamma sen' me fe water I buck up agains' all kind of bugaboo, meet all kin' of insect! 1943 *GL* Man, Bagaboo, caterpillar, bed bug, or chink; Tre, Bugaboo, insect, Bagaboo, spider; West, Bagabo, any disdainful little thing. 1952 FGC Han, Man, Tre, West /bagabu/ caterpillar; Man, also Grandy Mary, forty-leg. 1955 FGC Man /bàgabú/ worm, lice, etc.—*not* caterpillar.

2. Cf *EDD*, 'A hobgoblin or ghost'.

1774 Long II 416, They [the negroes] firmly believe in the apparition of spectres. Those of deceased friends are called *duppies*; others, of more hostile and tremendous aspect, like our raw-head-and-bloody-bones, are called *bugaboos*. 1943 StC, Bagaboo, something frightful or ridiculous; Kgn, Bagaboo, Jamaican Sandman. [This may not belong here.]

3. Nasal mucus, esp when dry; cf *EDD bug* sb[3], *boggle* sb. *BA*

c 1915 FGC StAnd /bagabu/ a nursery word for nasal mucus. 1943 *GL* Port, Bag-a-bu, dried cold in nostril. 1956 Mc StAnd /bágabú/ nose-snot (no other meaning known).

BUGGO-YAGGA see *buguyaga.*

BUGO sb dial rare; prob some alteration of *bag.*

1943 *GL* Tre, Bugo, a field bag.

BUGO-BUGO adj dial; cf *buguyaga.*

1943 *GL* West, Bugo-bugo, rough and crusty.

BUGOYANGA see *buguyaga.*

bugu-bugu fly sb dial; prob related to BUGABOO, BUBU 1. A maggot-fly; see quot.

1952 FGC Han /mini-mini flai/ is not like /bugu-bugu flai/.

buguyaga adj and sb dial; a word of mixed elements, evid compounded in Jamaica—cf BUBU, BUGABOO, BUGO-BUGO for the notion of something ugly, repulsive, unclean, and Ewe *yaka, yakayaka,* disorderly, confused, untidy, slovenly; cf also Hausa *buguzunzumi,* a big fat untidy person.

1. Worthless, slovenly, clumsy, etc.

1942 Bennett 27, Yuh an' yuh buggo-yagga fren'. 1943 *GL* Kgn, Boogooyaga, good-for-nothing; Port, Buguyaga, big and clumsy; Port, Buggo-yagga, a loose-looking person or thing. 1950 Pioneer gloss, Boogooyagga, unkempt, untidy person.

2. Used substantively and fig: see quot.

1943 *GL* StT, Boobo-yagga, old clothes bundle; used as an abuse to those who delight in wearing old clothes.

3. Used substantively of diseases: see quots.

1943 *GL* Man, Bugoyanga, a native name for gonohorhea [*sic*]; StAnn, Buggo-yagga, sore.

4. Perh by confusion with BUGABOO 1—see quot.

1943 *GL* StAnn, Buguyegeh, chrysallis.

5. A dance of some kind—perhaps a low-class or indecent one? Cf *buru.*

1943 *GL* Kgn, Boogu-yagga, dance.

BUGUYEGEH see prec.

BUILD, BUILD UP vb dial; <*build.*

1. To produce by growing.

1956 Mc Man, A piece cut from the second head built by yellow-yam.

2. In the phr *to build (up) a squall,* to prepare a storm. (Said of the weather or sky, when heavy rain-clouds roll up.) *BA G*

1952 FGC StC /it bil a skwaal/; StM /bildin op a skwaal/.

buja see *abuja.*

buku sb dial; prob <*breadfruit* with familiarizing word-play: cf BRESHE.

1956 JB /buku/ word for breadfruit used by young children—'Ripe buku no good fe pikney'.

BULB sb tech. The underground tuberous rhizome of the banana tree.

1913 Fawcett 3, The banana plant has no seed but is propagated by young plants which bud from the underground tuberous stem, or 'bulb', as it is called, of an older plant. This bud at first gets all its food material from the parent bulb, but very soon forms leaves and roots of its own.

bulflinsh sb dial; var (perh folk-etym) of *bullfinch.*

1952 FGC StT /bulflinsh/.

BULKIN sb dial; <*bulkin* (*OED obs,* quots 1583–1616); cf also *EDD bullkin.* A partially grown bull calf. (Evidence only from Manchester.)

1954 LeP Man, Bullkin, bull. 1956 Mc Man /bulkin/ a bull not fully matured—the various stages are /kaaf/ when born, /bulkin/; /bul/ when fully grown; /stiir/ when castrated.

BULLA sb dial; prob <Amer Sp *bollo,* bread, roll. (Santamaría.) s. *SC bóloe.*

1. A round, flat cake, sometimes with a hole in the middle—see quot 1947. Considered tough and reliable.

1940 HPJ, Bulla: A local cake, much enjoyed by our peasantry—made of flour, sugar, etc. . Also called cartman's hymn-book. 1947 U.Newton III 10, A bulla was a cake made by humble people from the cheapest grade of flour called 'cake flour' with a worthwhile addition of locally made 'wet' sugar (molasses) and a pinch of 'drinking soda'. Of a circumference of five inches, a thickness of three-quarter inch, a colour near to dark brown and a taste bordering on that of the famed 'nectar and ambrosia', it was something that had an instant and constant appeal to small boys, big girls, poor women and hungry men. 1952 FGC StM /búla/ butterdough; West /bula/ a cake of flour and brown sugar—also old bread with sugar added, made into a cake. 1954 LeP Man, Bullah; StAnn, Buller; StE, StT, Bulla.

2. See quot; the sense connection is not clear (this may be a different word).

1943 *GL* no addr, Bullah, the eyeless piece of the sugarcane.

3. An insult. (This may be a verb.)

1943 *GL* StE, Bulla, insult.

4. A blow.

1955 Bennett *Miss W.I. Wed,* De police-man gi her one big Bulla an run her weh.

BULLAH see prec.

BULL-APPLE TREE sb bot obs. The BEEF-APPLE (*Micropholis rugosa*); the name would seem to mean a fruit eaten by cattle (cf ALLIGATOR APPLE, etc.).

1756 Browne 166, Butneria 1. . The Bull-Apple-tree. . in St James's. . The fruit is very like a pomegranate both in size and form. 1864 Grisebach 782, Bull-apple tree: *Sapota rugosa.*

BULL BLUE GINGER sb dial. A variety of ginger.

1952 FGC Man (Christiana), Bull blue ginger is one kind.

BULL-BUCKER sb dial. A man who thinks he is strong enough to butt a bull; a belligerent person; a bully. =DUPPY-CONQUEROR.

1943 *GL* StAnn, Bull bucker [no explanation given]. 1959 Mr J. E. Bowen, The word 'bull-bucker' as used in Westmoreland means someone who is assuming power over others. . 'Bull-bucker' is often used in combination with 'duppy conqueror', thus:—'You are bull-bucker and duppy-conqueror, but you can't frighten me'. 1959 O. P. Cousins Kgn, Bull-bucker refers to a notorious Bad man in an area.

BULL-COW sb dial. A bull. (Cf MAN-COW.)

1942 Bennett 41, Yuh musa hear sey Tahta lahs Him black an w'ite bull cow? 1956 Mc StAnd /búkou, bulkóu/ a bull. *BA BL G; SC bòeroe-kau.*

BULLDOG (BOOT), (SLIPPER) sb chiefly dial. Rope-soled slippers—perh in allusion to their toughness or tenacity; now no longer sold.

1907 Jekyll 171, You have got long boots, while I must put up with 'bulldogs', rope-soled slippers. 1912 McK *Ballads* 52, Print frock an' old bulldog boots Tatters all t'rough wear and tear, She is waitin'..Our mess-woman, mudder Mell. 1959 O. P. Cousins Kgn, Bull Dog Boots.. a Canvass top shoes with rope like fibre soles. Used to be sold in shops during the 30's and late 40's. 1959 Mrs E. B. Hoyes Kgn, Bull-dog slippers or boots were really made of rope or a fibre very much like rope and my mother tells me they were sold at one shilling and six pence per pair in her day.

BULLER see BULLA.

BULLET (TREE) sb; by false division of BULLY-TREE, with folk-etym infl of *bullet* (cf Fr *boulet de canon*). A later form (now the prevailing one) of BULLY (TREE). *BL*

BULLET-TREE GUM sb; cf *OED bully sb*[4]: *bullet-tree* 1796→. A gum extracted from the BULLET TREE. *BL*

1740 Importance 44, The *Bullet Tree* Gum is a Horse Purge.

BULLET (TREE) WOOD sb; <BULLET+ *wood*. Another name for the BULLET (TREE) or its wood; see BULLY (TREE). *BL*

BULLFROG sb gen. A toad: see quots. *BL G*

1940 Lynn-Grant 15, There are no representatives of the genus *Bufo* indigenous in Jamaica. The genus is represented in the island, however, by the introduced 'Marine Toad' which in Jamaica, is commonly known as the 'bullfrog'. 1943 *NHN* II 70, *Bufo marinus*..[was] introduced into Jamaica from Barbados 1844 by a Mr Anthony Davis—a planter..It is the only species of toad in Jamaica and though it is commonly called 'Bull Frog', it should not be confused with the true frogs.

BULLFROG PLANTAIN sb dial. An alternate name for FROG BANANA, FROG PLANTAIN.

1956 Mc StE /bufrag plaanten/ a variety of plantain.

BULL GANG sb colloq; perh service slang: the soldiers put to doing useless tasks.

1956 Mc StT /búl gyang/ the gang of workers on a sugar-estate which does all the odd jobs.

BULL-HEAD PINE sb dial. A variety of pineapple which is shaped like a bull's head—relatively large and heavy; cf BULL PINE.

1952 FGC StAnd /búled pain/.

BULL-HEAD THATCH PALM sb dial. App the same as BULL THATCH.

1952 FGC West, Bull-head thatch palm, with extra-big leaves.

BULL-HEAD (WENCHMAN) sb dial. A fish thought of as of the 'wenchman' type (cf WELSHMAN) but with a large head.

1952 FGC StJ /búled wenshman/; West /bulhed/ longer than /gadami/ same shape, scale finer, round head, can eat.

BULL-HOOF /búlúf, búlóf/ sb dial; <*bull*+ *hoof*, though the second pronunciation implies that there has been some confusion with *hough*. The leaf is shaped like the print of a bull's hoof.

1. *Passiflora rubra.*

1756 Browne 328, Passiflora 12..The Bull-hoof, or *Dutchman's* Laudanum. 1801 Dancer 365. 1926 Fawcett 239–40, *Passiflora..rubra*..Bull Hoof.

2. *Bauhinia divaricata.*

1920 Fawcett 116–17, *Bauhinia..divaricata*..Mountain Ebony, Bull-Hoof. 1952 FGC StAnn /bulof, bulúf/ 'called butterfly tree in Portland'; StE /bulof, bulhof/ same as Moco John.

3. Some species of *Peperomia*—perh *alata.*

1944 *NHN* II 142, The large-leaved Peperomia known as 'Bull Hoof'.

BULLINGTON CANE sb dial; ?a surname—cf *barn-ton*. A variety of sugar-cane.

1952 FGC StT, Bullington cane.

BULLOCK'S HEART APPLE sb bot rare; evid a transl of Fr *cœur de bœuf* (cf 1914 Fawcett 198). A name for the CUSTARD APPLE.

1866 *Treas Bot, Bullock's Heart*, a name given to the fruit of *Anona reticulata*. [From *OED*.] 1954 *FG* 477, The Custard Apple—sometimes called 'sugar apple' and 'bullock's heart apple'..The fruit is heart-shaped, with a thin skin that attains a pinkish tinge when ripe.

BULL PINE sb dial; <*bull*+PINE. A variety of pineapple; prob = BULL-HEAD PINE.

1952 FGC StE /bul pain/.

BULL'S FACE sb obs?; cf *DAE, DA bull-face*, quot 1800. See quot.

1707 Sloane lxiii, Tobacco..is of several sorts..: that with the broad leaves is call'd Bulls Face.

BULL-STONE MANGO sb dial; <*bull*+ *stone* (*OED sb* 11). A variety of mango thought to resemble a bull's testicles.

1952 FGC Port /búltúon/ mango.

BULL THATCH sb; <*bull*+THATCH. (1864 Grisebach 514 mentions '*Sabal taurina*, Lodd.' as occurring 'in gardens as introduced from Jamaica or Trinidad'. This species designation suggests that 'bull thatch' was already the common term before 1864.)

1. The tree *Sabal jamaicensis*; also its leaves and wood.

1942 *NHN* I 4 9–12, *Sabal jamaicensis*, Broad Thatch, Bull Thatch, Jamaica Palmetto. 1943 *NHN* II 89, The Bull Thatch found on Portland Ridge is *Thrinax parviflora* and not *Sabal jamaicensis*. The latter is a species also known as Bull Thatch which occurs in the central parishes.

2. *Thrinax parviflora*; cf BULL-HEAD THATCH PALM.

1943 *NHN* II 53, *Thrinax parviflora*—Bull Thatch. The leaves are used for thatching but they are very inferior to Silver Thatch leaves. The Bull Thatch tree is usually stouter than the Silver Thatch but not as tall. The trunk of this palm is hard and durable.

BULLY sb dial.

1952 Smith in *NHN* 187, It is with the squirrel-fish, *Holocentrus ascensionis*, with which we head our list..its scaly cloak, which shimmers with the iridescence of rich scarlet-gold brocade makes me consider it the handsomest of the reef-fishes. Its good looks, however, do not seem much appreciated by the fisherfolk of St Mary and St James for they have given it the appellation of 'bully'.

BULLYRIGE vb dial; a phonetically irregular form of *bullyrag*: cf *baig, haig*, etc. *G*

1943 *GL* Kgn, Bullyryge, torment. 1959 Mrs E. B. Hoyes Kgn, Every village has at least one person who bullies (bully-rige) his or her way into public notice. This he or she gets away with until one day his or her match comes into view.

BULLY (TREE) sb also attrib; prob <*bully*, bullace (cf *EDD*); *OED* refers also to Fr *boulet de canon*, applied to this or similar trees, as a possible source of infl. Cf BULLET (TREE). **s.**

Various similar trees; in Jamaica the usual form today is BULLET (TREE, WOOD, etc.), and it is applied chiefly to *Dipholis nigra* and *D.*

salicifolia. For various alternate names see quot 1941. *N*; *SC bortri* (Focke).

[1657 Ligon 14, Loftie trees, as the *Palmeto, Royall.. Bully, Redwood*..etc.] 1696 Sloane 206, Anona maxima.. The Bully Tree In sylvis montosis ubique nascitur.. non vero specie à præcedente [*sc* Naseberry] differens. 1725 Sloane 172, The Bully-Tree. This, which is of the same kind with the *Nisperas*, only a larger Tree and smaller Fruit. a 1726 Barham (1794) 25, Bully-tree. This is so called by the Jamaicans, for its fruit when ripe is as black as a bully or damson, but in shape of a Lucca olive. 1774 Long II 205, The window shutters are of bullet-tree-wood (so called, because an inch-board of it is bullet-proof). [This is prob folk-etym.] 1864 Grisebach 782, Bully-tree: *Sapota Sideroxylon* and *Myrsine læta.* 1890 Thomas 43, Tall trees surrounded us on every side; mountain guava, bullet-tree, cogwood. 1941 Swabey 15, Bully Tree. See also Bulletwood, Mountain Bullet, Black Bullet, Cherry Bullet, Red Bullet, White Bullet, White Bully, Sapodilla Bullet..There is much confusion in local nomenclature. 1952 FGC StT /búlitwud/.

bulu sb dial; prob abbr of next.

1959 DeC Han /bulu/ pet name for a child or sweetheart.

bululups /búlúlúps/ sb dial; one of many phonosymbolic words of endearment—cf *bununus*, etc. *BL*

1950 Pioneer 51, De ongle ting ah want me lickle Booloo-loops, is yuh! 1958 DeC Tre /bululups/ affectionate term to a child or (more frequently) to a sweetheart.

BUM /bum/ vb slang; cf US *bum* vb (*DA* 2), to beg, but the Jamaican pronunciation is different: It would be close to the presumed etymological one of Ger *bummeln*, but may perh imply some North of England connections. *BA BL G*

1912 McKay *Ballads* 35, Bumming: cadging, begging for gifts. The *u* has the value of *oo* in book.

bumbai, BUMBIE see *bambai.*

BUMBLE FOOT see PUMBLE FOOT.

BUMBO /bómbo, bumbo/ sb dial vulg; prob of multiple derivation: cf Partridge, '*Bumbo*, occ. *bombo*. The female pudend: mid-C 18–19, West Indian; orig a negroes' word. Grose 1st. ed.' Cf also 1889 Barrère *D. of Slang*, etc. African origin is also claimed in the earliest quot (1774), and cf Zulu *-bumbu*, pubic region. However, there has prob been concurrent infl of Engl *bum* and perh also Amer Sp *bombo*, both meaning the buttocks, rump. *BL*

1. See quots.

1774 Long II 427, There are some other words, that are remarkable for the different senses in which they are used; viz..Bumbo, (Original Import,) Alligator, (Common Import,) *Pudendum muliebre*, (Dialect) Mundingo. 1943 *GL* Kgn, Bumbo; StAnn, Bunbo; no addr, Bumbo, The private part of a female. 1952 FGC Han /bombo/.

2. The buttocks.

1940 HPJ, Bumbo: Possibly also 'posterior'. (Astley Clerk:) Really same as Chaucer's *arse.* Timne (Sierra Leone) *a-bombo*, i.e. labia. 1943 *GL* Kgn, StAnn. 1959 DeC West /bombo/ is the common word here; /raas/ is known but seldom used; /bombo/ on the other hand, is hardly known around Kingston.

BUMBO CLOTH sb dial; cf prec. *BL*

1956 Mc /bombo klaat/ sanitary towel.

BUMBY(E) see *bambai.*

BUMP sb dial; <*bump*, cf also BUMPY BANANA.

1. A small bit of anything. *BA*

1942 Bennett 10, 14—cf FARTHING BUMP. 1943 *GL* Clar, Bump, a small bit.

2. One of the nodal rings that separates two 'joints' of sugar-cane. *BL*

1956 Mc StT, On each /bomp/ is an /ai/ and this is what shoots.

3. The crest of a hill; the part of a road at the top of a hill. *G*

1956 BLB Man, The bump: this is where the village square is often located../sel di pimento op di bomp/ i.e. at one of the shops in the square.

BUMP-AND-BORE sb and vb dial; <*bump* + *and* + BORE. Pushing and jostling in a crowd in an effort to get ahead of others; to push and jostle. *G*

1955 Bennett *Back to Africa,* Wat a debil of a bump-an-bore, Rig-jug [*sic*] an palampam! 1958 DeC Kgn /yu ha fi wiet, man; yu ha fi bomp an buor/ (i.e. to get into the Labour Office).

BUMP-A'-THROAT sb dial; <*bump-at-throat*; cf RUM-BUMP.

1956 Mc Man /bompa chuot, bompa truot/ Adam's apple.

BUMP-BUMP /bomp-bomp, bombomp/ sb and vb intr or adj; iterative <*bump.* A skin rash or disease in which the skin itches and is covered with bumps; to be affected with this skin condition.

1952 FGC StAnd /ringworm/—ketch it in dirty water—you skin all /bómbómp/. 1958 DeC StAnd /bomp-bomp/—the itch, SCRATCH-SCRATCH.

BUMPER /bompa/ sb dial or slang; <*bumper*, i.e. one who has a bump—abbr of RUM-BUMPER. A habitual rum-drinker; a drunkard.

1943 *GL* StAnd, Bumper, drinker of rum; Port, Bumpa, drunkard.

BUMP-JAW sb dial ?obs; cf the Spanish name given in quot, which means 'big-head(ed)'; a small fish (*Monosira stahlii*) is called *cabezón* in Cuba and Puerto Rico (Santamaría).

1854–5 *TJSA* I 144, *Gobius smaragdus*—Cabazona of Cuba: the Bump Jaw.

BUMPY (BANANA) sb dial; cf BUMP. A name or nickname for a small variety of banana.

1952 FGC StE /bompi banana/.

bumuujan see BERMUDIAN.

bun sb dial; prob abbr of *bununus.*

1958 DeC Port /bun/ an affectionate word for child or sweetheart.

buna, bunakin /búnakin, búunakin/ sb dial; prob cogn or var of BUBA-SKIN. See also *bongka.* The bough of a palm-tree, and its sheath. **s.**

1943 *GL* StM, Boona, sheath of palm-tree; StM, Boonakin, bough of palm tree. 1955 FGC Man /búnakin/. 1959 LeP StAnd /búunakin/. (See BUBA-SKIN quot 1959.)

BUNA-SKIN see *buna, bunakin.*

BUNBO see BUMBO.

BUN-BUN see *bon-bon.*

BUNCH sb tech. = COUNT BUNCH; in the banana industry, a bunch of bananas having 9 HANDS or more; in use for 40–50 years. **s.**

1951 Murray 3 [Banana Loaders' Song:] Six han', seven han', eight han', Bunch! 1952 FGC StM, 9 hands or more = 1 'count bunch'; 8 hands = ¾ bunch; 7 hands = ½ bunch; 6 hands = ¼ bunch; bunches of less than 6 hands are not bought for export.

BUNCH-O'-KEY /bònchakíi/ sb dial; <*bunch of keys*. Varieties of sweet-potato and of cassava that are supposed to resemble a bunch of keys, from the way the tubers spread out.

1952 FGC StE /bònchakíi/ cassada; StJ /bònshakíi/ sweet potato—white, like bunch of keys. 1956 Mc Man /bonchákii/ type of sweet potato.

BUNCHY /bónchi/ sb[1] dial; prob familiarized form of BUNCH-O'-KEY, but cf also Twi *ɔ-bàŋkyẽ*, the cassava. (The Twi word may be a loan as the plant is American.) A type of sweet-potato.

1952 FGC StC /bonchi/ the inside have a purple looks; StJ /bonchi/ big, yellow outside with red stripe.

BUNCHY sb[2] dial; evid <*bunch*+*-y*. A nickname for the buttocks.

1943 *GL* Clar, Bunchy, rump.

BUNDLE /bondl, bonggl/ sb dial; <*bundle*. A bunch of vegetables (thyme, SKELLION, pumpkin, etc.) prepared and tied together and so sold in the markets for making soups; *leginz*. *G T*

1958 DeC StAnd /bondl, bonggl/ for /leginz/; also StT.

BUNDOOSE vb dial; etym unknown.

1943 *GL* StE, Bundoose, to hang idle around.

BUNG sb dial; cf Twi *ɔ-bóŋ*, hole, hollow, cave, den of animals; no conn with Engl *bung* seems possible.

1954 LeP StE (Eld), Bung, dirty, untidy house.

BUNGA see BUNGO.

BUNGABEE see *bogobi*.

BUNGAY, BUNGY /bonggi/ sb arch; 1788 1835 bungay, 1877→ bungy, 1943 bungey, bonggy; prob African (cf Amer Sp *bongo*, a large dugout canoe and the tree (usually of the *Bombaceae*) from which it was made. Friederici, 'possibly African'. Cf Hausa *bungu-bungu*, a canoe made from dum or deleb palm-wood.) The form *bongo* has been borrowed into US (cf *DA*), but the Jamaican form is distinctive in ending, *-y* perh representing a familiarizing suffix.

1. Originally a large dugout canoe used for carrying freight; later applied to a built boat.

1788 Marsden 32, The stores are carried down the river.. in a large boat called a *bungay*, made out of the cotton-tree, and capable of carrying five or six hogsheads. 1835 Senior 22, [Black River] is navigable for immense boats, called 'bungays', for many miles up. 1877 Murray *Feedin' 'Perrit* 21, Me good sar, de shoes dis faber a ole bungy. 1939 Grant in *Gleaner* 13 June, Bungies..large flat bottomed boats. 1943 *GL* no addr, Bonggy, a large river boat. 1952 FGC Han /bonggi/ a big lighter; West /bonggi/ used till fifteen years ago,—now a 'lighter'.

2. See quot.

1943 *GL* Tre, Bungey, small boat.

BUNGEY see prec.

bungguz man see next.

bungguzu /búngguzu/ sb dial, also attrib; perh <Twi *bòné*, bad, evil, wicked (cf *ɛ-bòné*, evil, wickedness; *ɔ-bonsám*, wizard, sorcerer) + GUZU.

1. =OBEAH.

1940 HPJ, Bungozu: said to mean sorcery. 1943 *GL* Tre, Bungguzo, obeiah; Tre, Bunggusu, science; West, Bunguzu, obeah.

2. Attrib. Cf *buzuman*.

1959 DeC Han, West /bungguz man/ obeah man.

BUNGO /bónggo/ sb dial; cf Hausa *bungu*, 'A nincompoop, country bumpkin..Often also applied to one of unprepossessing appearance', Bargery. Possibly both this and the Jamaican word have a common origin with one or more of the tribal names for the Bantu, Semi-Bantu, or Pigmy peoples between the Niger Delta and the Congo, the negroes of this area being held in contempt by the more north-westerly nations. (Cf CONGO, CONGO-MAN as opprobrious epithets.) Among the Semi-Bantu of the Cross River area are the Baboungo; among the Pigmies of the Congo are the Bongo, and Bongo is also frequent as a tribal name in the region of the Nile–Congo–Niger watershed. (See Baumann & Westermann, *Les Peuples et les Civilizations de l'Afrique*, 1948, pp. 289–95.) s

1. In Jamaica an insulting term meaning very black; ugly; stupid; a country bumpkin; 'African'; etc.

1912 McKay *Ballads* 13, Right tu'n, you damn' bungo brut'! [Note:] Bungo: black African. 1942 Bennett 6, Me always get out cross w'en uncle Cuss me bungo fool. 1943 *GL* throughout Jamaica, Bungo, bongo—'a real African', 'black and ugly', 'illiterate, coarse, crude', 'a fool', etc. 1952 Murray 58–9 [Song:] 'One bungo man come fe court me'—'Bungo' meaning an African. 1955 LeP StE, Bongo, very black and worthless. 1956 Mc StAnd /im fieba bonggo/ *He favours a Bungo*, i.e. he is very ugly; StAnn, StT /bonggo/ very black person; Man /yu bonggo yu/ *You idiot!*

2. Attrib, as in *bungo bee*, *bungo man*, *bungo talk*, etc. See as separate entries.

3. Iterated and attrib, as in *bungo-bungo bus*.

1957 JN, One day I get on the Bungo-Bungo bus driving to Kingston; but the Chi-Chi bus drive sweeter. [Bungo-bungo bus: an old-fashioned and consequently broken-down bus used in the country; the CHI-CHI bus is more modern.]

BUNGO BEE sb dial; evid <*bumble-bee* infl by BUNGO, but poss a new comb BUNGO+*bee*. A large black bumble-bee: the carpenter bee *Xylophaga mordax*.

1952 FGC Port /bonggo bii/.

BUNGO-BESSY sb dial; <BUNGO+BESSY. A woman whose busybody qualities are considered retrograde, lower-class, or highly undesirable.

1940 HPJ, To call a man a 'Bungo' man is abusive.. 'bungo-bessi' may therefore be abusive.

BUNGO-BUNGO see BUNGO 3.

BUNGO MAN sb dial; <BUNGO+*man*.

1. See quot.

1952 Kerr 144, The [kumuna] dancers are supposed to be true 'Bongo men' or Africans. They sing songs during the dance which they say are in Bongo language.

2. A term of address used among Rastafarians.

1961 *Gleaner* 8 June 1/9, 'Bongo Man', the witness explained, was the name Rases used for calling one another.

BUNGO OKRO sb dial; <BUNGO+OKRO. A short, thick, coarse type of okro.

1952 FGC Port /bonggo okra/ tree pure white, bears in March; StAnn; StT /bonggo okro/ same as coolie okro.

BUNGORUNG see *banggarang*[1].

BUNGO STORY, BUNGO TALE sb dial; cf BUNGO 2. A type of story formerly popular among peasants in which the stupidity of Bungo people (sometimes Congo, etc.) was illustrated. Cf NAYGA-TRICK.

1940 HPJ, A bungo tale is an African tale.

BUNGO TALK sb dial; < BUNGO + *talk* sb. See quot; cf also BUNGO MAN, quot 1952.

1940 HPJ, 'Bungo stories' deal with ignorant, stupid, bush people. 'Bungo talk' is the language of such people. 1956 Mc StAnd /bónggo taak/ the entirely uncultivated speech of the illiterate.

BUNGOZU see *bungguzu*.

BUNG-SHELL sb obs?; origin obscure: perh a kind of SHELL (or copper used in sugar-making) that had bung-holes. (However, this may poss represent *bomb-shell*.)

1877 Murray *Feedin' 'Perrit* 21, You eber see Fingal? Deres a fellah hab a nosehole, eh, sar. A regela bung-shell of a nose.

BUNGUZUNG sb dial vulg; cf Engl *bung*: the similarity to *bungguzu*, since no sense connection seems possible, is prob coincidental. Cf BUMBO.

1943 *GL* Kgn, Būngūzung, the anus.

BUNGY see BUNGAY.

BUNKA, BUNKAH see *bongka*.

BUNKA-FOOT sb dial; etym unknown, but cf Engl slang *bonk*, imitative of a wooden hammering noise, and cf *bongkas*. *G*

1940 HPJ, Bunka-foot, club foot, wooden foot.

BUNKRA see BANKRA.

BUNNATO sb dial rare; < Sp *boniato*, sweet-potato.

1943 *GL* Tre, Bunnato, sweet potato.

BUNPAN see BURN-PAN.

BUN-'TOMACH sb dial rare; < *burn* vb + *stomach*. See quot. (The sense is not clear, unless potatoes are considered indigestible.)

1943 *GL* Clar, Bun-'tomach, potatoes.

BUNTUNG /bontong/ sb dial; < *burn* + *tongue*. A variety of mango which 'burns' or tastes sharp on the tongue. *BA*

1949 Reid gloss, Buntung, a species of mango.

BUNTUNG JACK sb dial ?obs; evid < *burn(t)* + *tongue* + *jack*. *BA*

A variety of the jack fish. The sense is not clear; if the name means *burn-tongue* (cf BUNTUNG mango) it may refer to the taste; if it means *burnt-tongue* (cf BURN-FIN JACK) it may refer to the black colour of the tongue. The former is more probable.

1851 Gosse 290, The Jacks..are members of the great Mackarel family: they are distinguished as Buntung Jack, Round-headed, or Ground Jack, and Cavally Jack.

bununus, bunununus /búnúnús, búnùnúnùs/ adj and sb dial or slang; a phonosymbolic creation—cf *bululups*—but it may have been infl by Sp *bueno*, *bueno-bueno*, or the like. *BL*

A. sb: A term of endearment.

1943 *GL* Kgn, Bunoo-nunos, sweetheart; boonoonoonoos, darling, etc. 1950 Pioneer gloss, Boonoonoos, a term of endearment. 1955 LeP StE /bununus/ pretty one.

B. adj: Very pretty, beautiful, wonderful, glorious: a term expressing a burst of favourable enthusiasm.

1943 *GL* Kgn, StJ, Boonoonoonoos, very pretty, pretty. 1949 U.Newton v 24, Oh it was a day of joy and glory. Horatio would describe it as a 'boonoonoonoose' day. 1955 Bennett *Touris*, Yes me had a boonoonoos time. *Idem*, *A Well-Deserving Ting*, We mus answer de call To de gran' and great exciting Boonoonoonoos Red Cross Ball!

buo see BOAR, BOW (MACHETE).

buobo see BOBO.

buon see BONE.

buor, buorz see BOAR, BOW (MACHETE).

buosan /búosàn/ sb dial; ?for BOATSWAIN, folk-etym of Twi *abosí*, a species of yam (BAYERE). **s** *buosan*, *afu* ~.

1. Another (less common) name for PUMPUM yam.

1935 HPJ, Boäsun, A kind of yam, the same as pum-pum. 1956 Mc Man /buosan/ same as pum-pum, denkě.

2. See quot.

1956 Mc Man /buosan/ a piece cut off a yam, 'which goes on swelling'. 1961 BLB (West) /buosn/—the part of a yellow yam which grows after the foot has been cut.

buosn see BOATSWAIN and prec.

buoyo, BUOYOUGH see BOYO.

buoz see BOAR, BOW (MACHETE).

bup /bup/ vb dial; echoic: cf Engl. and US *bop*, etc. To strike, hit. *G*

1943 *GL* West, Bup, to strike or hit. 1959 LeP StAnd /i bup im an di nuoz/ *He hit him on the nose.*

BUR-BARK sb ?obs; < *bur* + *bark*. An early name for one kind of BUR-BUSH: *Triumfetta Bartramia*.

1756 Browne 233, Triumfetta 2. The Bur-Bark..Pericarpium. *Capsula..ab apice ad medietatem setis validis uncinatis armata*..The bark is tough and strong, and serves for ropes.

BUR-BUR /bór-bór/ sb dial; iterative < *bur*. *G*

1. Burs in general; a collection of burs.

1942 Bennett 47, Nuff bur-bur an' dutty all ovah him clothes, [*His clothes all covered with burs and dirt*].

2. Various bur-bearing plants—see BUR-BARK, BUR-BUSH, BUR-MALLOW, BUR-ROOT, BUR-WEED, WILD BUR.

1952 FGC Port /bor-bor/ (has spikes of small pink-purple flowers); StE, 'same as /balad/'; StT, a name for /bor-bush/ but there is another /bor-bor/ with lots of small reddish-brown burs along stems, = /wail bor/.

BUR-BUSH /bor-bush/ sb dial; < *bur* + BUSH.

1. Varieties and species of *Triumfetta*.

1926 Fawcett 81, *Triumfetta*..Bur-weed, Bur-bush. 1954 *WIMJ* 32.

2. *Priva lappulacea.*

1952 FGC StM /bor-bush/ green seed—can hold to clothes. 1955 *WIMJ* 160, *Priva lappulacea*..Clammy Bur, Bur Bush, Fasten-'pon-Coat.

BUR GRASS sb; cf *OED* 1834 only, for a species of *Carex*? Various species of *Cenchrus* having sharp burs.

1725 Sloane 361, Mr Barham in a Manuscript of the Plants of Jamaica saith that this which is call'd Burrgrass, green, or dry, is hearty Food for Horses. 1813 Lunan I 126, Bur-grass. Cenchrus. 1954 *FG* 226, Burr Grass (*Cenchrus echinatus*). *Ibid* 586, The Burr-grass is an annoying weed because the fruiting heads are covered with sharp spines.

BURKE (SWEET-POTATO) sb dial; evid from the surname. A local variety of sweet-potato, prob introduced or grown by someone named Burke. *G*

1952 FGC StAnd /bork/ sweet-potato, red outside, white inside.

BUR-MALLOW sb bot. *Urena lobata*; cf BUR-BUR 2.

1955 *WIMJ* 160, *Urena lobata*..Ballard Bush; Indian or Bur Mallow.

BURN vb dial; <*burn v*[1], *OED*. *G*

1. To rub off the skin by sudden abrasion, causing a sensation similar to that produced by a burn.

c1915 FGC StAnd (remembered). 1957 JN Man, Fall down when I was coming to school..a was running. I tun back and bun me knee. It not too bad now.

2. Of shoes: To cause the feet to burn (cf *OED v*[1] 3a).

1907 Jekyll 166, Boots..are the outward and visible sign of being well-to-do. They hurt him, 'burn him' as he says, but no matter.

BURN-ANTS sb dial. Small red ants whose sting is very sharp or 'hot'.

1952 FGC Port /born-ans/.

BURN BAD CANDLE see BAD CANDLE.

BURN-BURN see *bon-bon*.

BURN-EYE /born-ai, bon-ai/ sb dial. One of the local names for *Amyris balsamifera*, whose resin irritates the eyes when it is chopped down.

1952 FGC StAnn (see BLIND-EYE); Tre, =torch-wood, but 'burn-eye' is the most common term—used for fence-posts, railway sleepers, but must burn the bark first.

BURN-FIN JACK sb dial; <*burnt*+*fin*. A variety of the jack fish with a fin that looks black, as if it had been burnt.

1952 FGC StE /bórnfín ják/.

BURN-FIN (SNAPPER) sb dial; <*burnt*+ *fin*. A variety of the snapper fish with black at the base of the pectoral fins as if it had been burnt. (Prob the same as the WI 'Black-finned Snapper', *Lutianus buccanella*).

1952 FGC Port, West /bórnfin/ round, red—underneath fin has a little black; StC, StJ, StM, StT /bónfin/ or /bónfin snápa/.

BURNING MOUNTAIN sb dial.

1956 Mc StE (Accom) /bornin mountn/ a plant with large red leaves.

BURNING-STICK sb obs? A torch.

1839 McMahon 31, I had to go to the field, and call the list by the light of a burning-stick.

BURNING-TO vb phr obs. Of cane-syrup which is being evaporated: being burnt to the inside of the copper when it gets too hot. *G*

1797 Higgins 109, Some new expedient is necessary, to prevent the burning-to which is manifested.. by the hissing heat of the copper.

BURN-MARK, BURN-MARKED sb and adj; <**burnt-mark*, a mark that is burnt, a brand, +-*ed* (*OED* suffix -*ed*[2]). A brand; branded.

c1695 *Acts & Laws* 97, Ear markt, or burn-markt Cattle shall belong to the right Owners, if claimed at any time.

BURN-NOSE (BARK) /bónuoz, bórnuoz, bórn nùoz/ sb chiefly dial; <*burn*+*nose*, evid altering BONACE by folk etym. The trees *Daphnopsis occidentalis* and *D. tinifolia*, whose bark is said to burn the nose of one who smells it. (But cf quot 1941.)

1814 Lunan I 106–7, Bonace..there is a larger species of this known by the name of burn-nose bark, so called from its supposed effects on those who smell it closely. 1854–5 *TJSA* I 8, *Daphne tinifolia*. Burn-nose Bark. 1926 Fawcett 288. 1941 Swabey 16, Burnnose—Botanical identity not yet established. 1952 FGC StE /born nuoz/ —/bon yu fies tu/; StM /bónuoz/—use bark for mat, rope, whip; StT /bornùoz/ has a white 'seed bearing'—birds eat it—has thick bark, can make rope; Tre /bórnuoz/—baldpates feed on berries.

BURN-PAN, BUNPAN /bon pan/ sb dial; <*burnt*+*pan*. A cooking pot of thin metal blackened from being on the fire. *G*

1927 Stafford 26, In a burnt-pan she is cooking Hafoo-yam and sweet potato. 1929 Beckwith 47, The pail-shaped tin which constitutes the ordinary cooking-vessel is called a 'bu'n pan' from the black look it gets. 1954 LeP Kgn, StE, Bunpan.

BURN-PAN HAT sb dial arch; <BURN-PAN +*hat*. A top-hat, from its shape and blackness resembling the cooking pot; cf US *stovepipe hat*.

1907 Jekyll 26, Snake go an' borrow..long coat an' burn-pan hat an' the whole set out of clothing. 1924 Beckwith 65, Brer Rabbit put on his bonpon hat an' coatie an' spectacle. 1940 HPJ, Bunpan Hat: silk hat—'topper'. Obsolescent.

BURN-SIDE (COFFEE) sb dial. See quot.

1929 Beckwith 22, The first fruit [of coffee] which ripens in August is called 'Burn Side', because only one side shows red, and is harvested for home consumption.

BURN THE COLOUR, BURNING COLOUR vb phr tech. To burn sugar (caramelize it) for use in colouring rum.

1952 FGC Tre, Then we burn the colour..use sugar in burning colour.

BURN-TO-HELL PEPPER sb dial. The hottest *Capsicum* peppers—e.g. CURL-FINGER.

1952 FGC Port /born-tu-hel pepa/—red, like finger.

BURN-TONGUE cf BUNTUNG.

BURNT-PAN see BURN-PAN.

BURN WANGLA vb phr dial; <*burn*+ WANGLA. To put OBEAH (upon someone) by burning wangla seeds. See quot 1895.

1895 Banbury 10, Sometimes application is made for the purpose of punishing thieves. A curious custom is connected with this, which prevailed in the western parts of the island formerly, and we believe to some extent still. It is called 'Burning wanglo'. The seed of this plant is procured, and with pepper and salt is burned on the road where the thief is known to travel over night. This has the effect, the people believe, of 'catching' the thief. That is, it throws out the King's evil ('cocoaba') upon him. Such a dread was entertained of the potent effects of this grain when used in this way, that very often the thief restored overnight what he had stolen. 1955 Bennett *Oonoo Lie!*, Me naw bun wangla fe oonoo.

BURN-WEED sb obs; <*burn* sb+*weed* sb. *Datura stramonium*, alluding to its use in an ointment against burns, etc.

1756 Browne 167, Datura 1..The Thorn-apple or Burn-weed..All the parts of this plant are remarkably narcotic..they are commonly made into ointments, and applied in scalds and other painful sores.

BURN-WOOD sb dial; <*burn* sb or v+*wood*.

1. In Lunan's use: A species of *Comocladia* (prob *C. pinnatifolia*).

1814 Lunan 475, Maiden-Plum Tree. Comocladia.. integrifolia..This is sometimes called *burnwood* or *papaw-wood*, and grows very commonly in Jamaica.

2. JAMAICA SUMACH (*Rhus metopium*). The juice blackens indelibly anything it touches.

1864 Grisebach 782, Burnwood of Negroes: *Rhus Metopium.* 1926 Fawcett 9, *Rhus metopium*..Jamaica Sumach, Burn Wood. 1941 Swabey 14, Boarwood—(Jamaica sumach, Hog Doctor, Poison Wood, Burn Wood). *Rhus metopium.*

BURR-FISH sb dial.

1953 Smith in *NHN* 12, *Chilomycterus antennatus*, the burr-fish, resembles the porcupine fish except for the noticeable fact that the spines are short, stiff, immovable, and triangular.

BURR-GRASS sb bot; cf *OED* 1834, *DAE* 1829→. A type of grass (cf quots 1864, 1954) which has burs, and is a good fodder. (Applied to more than one species.)

1725 Sloane 361, Mr Barham in a Manuscript of the Plants of Jamaica saith that this which is call'd Burrgrass, green, or dry, is hearty Food for Horses. 1774 Long III 765, The Dutch, burr, cross, speckled, and manna grasses are among the best for fodder in the lower situations. 1864 Grisebach 782, Burr-grass: *Panicum glutinosum. Ibid* 552, Hab[itat] Jamaica..in mountain-woods. 1952 FGC StAnn; StE /bor grass/—same as Dutch grass. 1954 *FG* 226, Burr Grass (*Cenchrus echinatus*).

BUR ROOT sb dial. Another name for a type of BROOM-WEED—a low bush with purple flowers and 5-part seed pod (family *Malvaceæ*).

1951 FGC Man; 1952 FGC StT.

BURSTING STYLE /borstin stail, bostin stail/ sb dial. Very vigorous manner.

BURTLIN'S PLAGUE sb dial; evid < *Burtlin*, surname + *plague*, sb.

1952 FGC Port /bórtlinz plíeg/ dry it and make mats with the leaves, pads for horses, etc.

buru /búru/ sb dial, also attrib; 1940→ buru, burru, 1943 burroo, bhuroo, boor-ru, burao, 1960 burra; cf Twi *búru*, filthiness, sluttishness; Yoruba *buru*, wicked. Cf *bru-bru*. *BL*

1. A type of dancing, sometimes vulgar, or an occasion upon which there is such dancing. Spec, funeral-celebration dancing.

1940 HPJ, Buru—A kind of dance which Marion remembers being held in Kingston.—somewhat indecent. Mr Thompson says 'Indecent, with posturing of the hip'. 1943 *GL* Clar, Bhuroo, a common-place dance; Kgn, Burroo, a rustic dance; StJ, Burru, a dance or picnic; StM, Boor-ru, a kind of celebration for 9 days after a person dies. 1954 LeP StE, Burru—general term for a dance or wild party—when the dance gets hot and wild. 1956 Mc Man /búru dans/ rough, not properly run dance.

2. A place where wild or indecent dancing is done.

1955 FGC Man /búru/ Low-down dancing place.

3. A type of music—esp drumming—such as is used for buru dancing; also a drum, and a group of musicians who play buru dance music.

1943 *GL* Kgn, Burru, drum; StT, Buru, an orchestra composed chiefly of drums at different pitches; No addr, Burru, yuletide negro music.

4. A cult similar to KUMUNA, in which wild dancing to drums is a prominent feature.

1943 *GL* StE, Burao, religious fanaticism; West, Buru, crude religion. 1958 DeC StT, etc /buru/ some sort of semi-religious order..most or all adherents are ex-convicts. They beat kumina drums and use the kumina songs and dances but apparently without any real belief in it.

BUR-WEED /bor wiid/ sb dial. Various species of *Triumfetta*, which bear many burs.

1837 Macfadyen 109, *Triumfetta*. Bur-weed. *Ibid* 110, From the tenacity with which the capsules hook themselves on the clothes of travellers, the French Colonists give the plant the name of '*Les Cousins*'. [Also listed 109–11, Common Bur-weed, Mallow-leaved Bur-weed, Rhomb-leaved Bur-weed.] 1926 Fawcett 81 (cf BUR-BUSH). 1952 FGC StAnn, StT /bór-wíid/.

BURYING /berin, beri-in/ vbl sb dial; cf *OED burying vbl sb* 1 b →1787, '*Obs.* or *dial.*' A funeral—the common dial term. *BA BL G N*

1877 Murray *Kittle* 9, Old Tom communicated the fact to Sam, that he had left him sole heir, and that he was to give him 'a good berrin'. 1943 *GL* Kgn, Beren, berrin, funeral. 1956 Mc Man /beri-in/.

BURYING-BESSY sb dial; < BURYING + BESSY. A woman who comes to every burying or funeral proceedings. Cf WEDDING BESSY. *BL*

1877 Murray *Kittle* 16, It was known that she never missed a wake. Hence her enemies used to call her 'Berrin Bessy'. She hated the name.

BURYING-YARD sb dial; < BURYING + YARD. See quot. *BL*

1958 DeC StT /beri-in yaad/ 1. A funeral celebration on the afternoon of the first or second day; rum is drunk and songs sung, etc., while the coffin is being made and the grave dug. 2. The dead man's yard from the time of death until he is buried; after that the yard is called the /ded yaad/ (Penlyne Castle). 3. Funeral wake on the first through the eighth nights (Middleton).

BUS /bos/ sb arch or obs; < *bus*, vehicle for public transportation.

A horse-drawn buggy for public hire. (This vehicle began to be displaced by the taxicab in the 1920's. When electric trams began also to be displaced by motor omnibuses in the 1930's, the latter introduced 'bus' in a different sense—the usual one outside Jamaica—which is now virtually the only one, esp as the horse-drawn vehicle has itself almost disappeared.)

1873 Rampini 16, So hailing a ''bus', as the Kingston cabs are called, we started to seek the hotel. 1907 Jekyll 76, Bus..the buggies which ply for hire in Kingston are so called.

bus /bus/ int and sb gen; echoic. A sound imitating the effect of something falling with a dull thud; hence something disappointing, an occurrence that fails to come up to expectation. *G*

1915→ FGC StAnd (Remembered in such a sentence as, 'The whole affair was a /bus/!').

BUSH /bush/ sb chiefly dial; < *bush* (*OED sb*[1]; sense 9 is very common in Jamaica: 'Woodland ..applied to the uncleared or untilled districts in the British Colonies which are still in a state of nature..'—see sense 1 below). *G*

1. Wild or uncleared woodland and thickets; hence, a place of refuge for runaways; also contrasted with settled places. *BL T*

1825 Bickell 24, Poor blacky..sure of other punishment, ran away; nor could his master get him back..he was in the bush,* as it is termed;.. * Viz. in the woods. 1895 Banbury 43 [Prov:] Trubble da a bush, Anancy bring i da house. 1905 Smith 13, Now dese two, Annancy an' Chim-Chim, get to know each oder in de bush. [Current today; cf TAKE BUSH.]

2. The wild plants or brushwood (singly or collectively) that grow in uncleared lands or in

land taken out of cultivation. 'Bush' is commoner in folk usage than 'weed' or 'plant'.

1907 Jekyll 158, To clear the ground..the brushwood, or bush, as it is called, is chopped down with the cutlass. 1940 HPJ, Bush: The vegetation on 'ruinate' land. (Not applied to virgin forest.) *BL T*

3. A branch or bunch of leaves taken from a plant or tree: usually '*a piece of* bush'. (Cf WATER-BUSH.) *BL T*

1940 HPJ, Bush: a part or portion of a plant—'bring-cum piece a dat Mango bush'.

4. Any plant used in folk remedies, in teas, and in other domestic ways. Also the tea itself. Cf BUSH DOCTOR, BUSH TEA, COLD-BUSH, TEA-BUSH, etc.; and the names of particular plants, as ASTHMA-BUSH, RINGWORM-BUSH. (A specific use of *OED sb* 1.) *BL T*

1952 FGC StAnd /dríngk búsh agens fíiva/.

5. Specifically: the concoction of an OBEAH-MAN, in which medicinal or poisonous herbs are an important ingredient.

1834 Madden II 93, It appeared in evidence that he went to a negro hut, and asked for some fire to light his pipe; that he was seen to put some *bush* (herb) into the pipe.. He was accused of being an obeah man. 1895 Banbury 7, The person must not stop on the way, look behind, or look to any one, nor allow rain to wet him on the way, as this would either tend to destroy the efficacy of the 'bush', as it is sometimes called..They affirmed that obeah was found in the pocket of the unfortunate man [who had broken his neck in a fall from a horse]..and that..in returning with his 'bush', rain caught him, and hence his misfortune. 1927 Anderson-Cundall 25, You can' fight bushman, tek' 'way him bush. [Cf BUSH-DOCTOR, BUSH-MAN—current names for an OBEAHMAN.]

BUSHA /búsha/ sb orig dial, now gen colloq; 1790 obisha, 1826 bersheer, 1826→ busha, 1835 busher; <*overseer*. (Several impossible 'sources' have been proposed. Apart from *overseer* the only word which may possibly have affected the derivation is *caboceer* (*OED*), which had a form *cabosheer*, head-man, chief.) Cf *OED* 1832→. *SC basjà.*

1. An overseer on any kind of estate; in general charge. Also as a term of address.

1790 Moreton 149, 'Hecta *nebba* will make puncheon for you, Obisha'. *Ibid* 153, 'No use me ill, Obisha!' 1826 Williams 202, Overseer, first corrupted to Oberseer, is now Bersheer or Busha. 1828 Marly 63, The overseer.. The Busha, as the people called him. 1835 Madden I 92, He..takes an hour's exercise in the cool of the morning on horseback if he is a great man, and a busha, but on foot if he is..poor. *Ibid* 124, Bushers. 1907 Jekyll 188, Overseers of the estate..Bushas as he calls them—a word said to be derived from Pasha—are often satirised. 1956 Mc StT (cf BOOK-KEEPER).

2. As a term expressing respect; formerly applied to white men, now to any man of some local position. See quots.

1958 DeC Man /busha/ polite name (also used in addressing the person) for a brown man of some social and economic standing, esp. a property owner; StT, cf PENNER 2.

BUSHA HOUSE sb chiefly dial; for BUSHA'S *house*. The overseer's dwelling on a sugar estate (or other similar property).

1863 Waddell 30, In the beginning of February [1830] we took up our abode at Cornwall, in the old 'busha house', which had been repaired for our use.

BUSH-BAG sb dial; <BUSH 2 or 3+*bag*. Also called *antana, intete, kana, gwanggu-bag, nambu, nangku, pata, tana.*

1959 DeC StAnd /bush-bag/ a temporary bag made of grass or trash at the field.

BUSH-BATH sb chiefly dial; <BUSH 4+*bath*. A bath of hot water in which local herbs have been steeped. Also called FEVER-BATH. It is applied to the body with a cloth, and followed by a rub-down with rum. **s.** *G T*

1927 Beckwith 7–8, An extremely common remedy today 'for cold, fever or numbness' is the so-called 'bush-bath' of which Sloane writes. [1707 Introd liv]..Sarah Crawford names as wild plants suitable for the bath 'Leaf-of-Life', 'Horse-bath', 'Fiddle-wood', 'Black-giant', 'Rose-mary', 'Orange', 'Black-sage', 'Wild-barsley', 'Strong-back', 'Fever-grass'. 1957 Bennett 92, Tercentenary Bush Bath an Walla walla committee.

BUSH CLOTHES sb dial; <BUSH 1+*clothes*.

1958 DeC Port, StM /bush kluoz/ old ragged clothes.

BUSH-DOCTOR sb dial; <BUSH 4 or 5 +*doctor*. One who practises herb remedies; esp one who practises obeah under the guise of medicine—a euphemism for OBEAHMAN.

1873 Rampini 131–2, Under the style and title of a 'bush doctor', he wanders from place to place, exacting 'coshery' from his dupes on all hands. 1907 Jekyll 241, In every district there is an Obeah-man, or Bush-doctor, as he is often called, from his supposed knowledge of herb simples. *BL G N*

BUSHER see BUSHA.

BUSH FENCE sb dial; <BUSH 2 + *fence*. (*DA* has *bush fence* quot 1790 in diff sense.) A fence made by planting a thick hedge of (usually prickly) bushes. (Many plants are favoured for this purpose in Jamaica, e.g. Barbados pride, Cat's-claw, Jerusalem candlestick, etc.)

1950 Pioneer 18, Anancy chop off him goat head an push it eena de tick bush fence between him an Ticks yard.

BUSH-FIGHT vb obs; cf US *bush fighter, bush fighting* (*DA*). To fight in the BUSH by stealth, not by the rules of organized warfare. *G*

1827 Hamel II 279, 'Oh!' replied Fillbeer, affecting to be satirical, 'ever while you live send red-coats to bush-fight in the woods of the tropics; and cocked hats for the officers'.

BUSH LIZARD sb; <BUSH 1 or 2+*lizard*.

1940 Lynn-Grant 89, *Anolis lineatopus lineatopus* Gray, 'Bush lizard'.

BUSH-MAN sb dial; <BUSH 5+*man*. An OBEAHMAN or BUSH DOCTOR.

1873 Rampini 139, He knows Fisher. He is a Mungola man. He is a bush man—an obeah man. 1895 Banbury 9, The chief resort to the '*Bushman*' is to injure, either to kill outright, or to afflict with a sore leg, *kings evil*, or some other direful distemper, for life. 1943 *GL* Man, Bush man, obeah man.

BUSH TEA sb; <BUSH 4+TEA. See quots.

1953 *WIMJ* 2 233, The use of local plants for medicinal remedies is a very prevalent practice in Jamaica. Among the poorer families, the morning meal frequently consists of nothing more than a cup of bush-tea prepared by steeping the leaves in hot water. 1957 *FFM* 353, Medicinal Plants and Bush 'Teas'..The use of 'bush teas' is widespread amongst this class of Jamaican. These are prepared from the leaves, seeds and roots of an enormous variety of plants, of which over two hundred have been listed. *BA BL G N*

BUSINESS /bizniz, biniz, bini/ vb dial; <*business* sb, evid by abbr of 'have business'. To be concerned (with something)—usually in negative. (This may show indifference or caution.)

1910 Anderson-Cundall 5 [Prov:] When cow mek fight horse no business dey. 1940 HPJ, 'A doan business wid dat', I have nothing to do with that..I do not concern myself with that. 1942 Bennett 35, Me kip fur fram dem far—'cockroach Noh biniz a fowl yard'. 1943 *GL* no addr, Biniy, business. 1950 Pioneer 44, Mos' a de gal dem up deh never Business wid concert. *BA G*

BUSQWINE sb dial rare; etym unknown. s.
1943 *GL* Kgn, Busqwine, a silly person.

BUSS-BELT /bos-belt/ sb dial; *burst-belt*. A paunchy man. *G*
1961 R. M. Murray in *Gleaner* 6 Aug, 20, Yes, eberybody will sartain go, Longilala Sam an buss-belt Joe.

BUSS-ME /bos mi/ sb dial joc; <*buss*, kiss +*me*. A variety of sugar-cane.
1959 DeC StJ /bos-mi/ name of a kind of cane.

BUSSOU vb dial; <*buss* vb, to kiss (which is itself current) + -U. See also *busu* sb[1].
1943 *GL* StE, Bussou, to kiss.

BUSSU vb dial rare; perh conn with BESSY vb, or BUTU.
1943 *GL* no addr, Bussu, to stoop.

BUSTA see *bosta*.

BUSTA BACKBONE sb dial; <*bosta*, abbr of *Bustamante's*+*backbone*. =*bosta* 2.
1952 FGC StJ /bósta-bákbùon/ iron cunny.

busu /búsu/ sb[1] dial; cf 'BÚZIO: concha de mariso usada como valor monetário entre os negros do Brasil' (Mendonça). A small edible fresh-water snail (*Neritina virginea*) often used in soup. (A word found almost exclusively in Portland parish.)
1929 Beckwith 194, The Rio Grande (famous for a fresh-water mussel called *bossu*, out of which is composed a favorite soup). 1940 HPJ, Buzu..in Rio Grande, the smallest shellfish, used for bait; Busso, a river shellfish, a whelk (Port); Bussoo, has a small shell, crawls in rivers, comes up in sun-hot to the stones, is caught and put in soup. 1943 *GL* Clar, Bassoo, a river snail; Port, Bussou. 1952 FGC Port /búsu/ 'smaller than wilks'; StT /búsu/ 'in the Rio Grande'. 1954 LeP Kgn, Bussoo, shellfish (general term). 1958 DeC Port /busu/ a small creature in a shell about the size of a marble, shaped like a lower-case letter *e*..Found in upper Rio Grande. The Maroons scald them to get them out of the shell to eat.

busu sb[2] dial, also attrib; cf Twi *-busu-* in such cpds as *abusu-dé*, a wicked, mischievous thing, *o-busufó*, a wicked mischievous man. See quot.
1956 Mc StE (Accom) /búsu fúul, púl yu músu/, /ignoran, fraitful porsan/ quarrelsome, objectionable person. [Twi *mmusú*, mischief.]

BUSUBUSU sb dial; iterative perh <*busu* sb[2].
1954 LeP StT, Busu-busu, someone very fat and clumsy. 1956 Mc StT /busubusu/ fat, clumsy.

BUSY(-NUT) see BISSY.

BUTA sb dial cant; cf Ko *mbuta*, adult. In AFRICAN cult use of St Thomas parish: A man.
1953 Moore gloss, Buta, man.

BUT, BUT-BUT sb dial; abbr <*butterfly* and sometimes iterated. A butterfly.
1924 Beckwith 2, Brer Tiger see Brer But pass an' ask Brer But to loose him. *Ibid* 44, But-but an' Hanansi dem gwine up to town. 1929 Beckwith 220, Of insects, Duck ant, 'But-but' (butterfly), Tumble-bug.

BUTLERESS sb gen; *OED* quots only c 1615, 1860; in Jamaica the word was common until the 1930's. A female domestic who serves at table.
1915 FGC StAnd (in regular use). 1952 FGC StM /bótlarès/.

BUTOU see *butu*.

BUTRIE see BUTTERY.

BUT STOP see STOP.

BUTTA sb dial rare; cf W. Ko *buta*, bow.
1940 HPJ StE (Accom), Butta (or būta), A bow & arrow used for shooting birds; the arrow being made from cane-arrow.—Col. Rowe.

BUTTER-BIRD sb; *OED* 'U.S.', and only quot 1883. The American Bobolink (*Dolichonyx oryzivorus*); also called OCTOBER BIRD, OCTOBER PINK, PINK.
1790 Moreton 42, Quails, Guinea-hens, butter-birds, plovers. 1840 Chamberlaine 25, The Butter-Bird (*Emberiza oryzivora*). 1847 Gosse 229, Butter-Bird. Ortolan..In ordinary seasons this well-known bird arrives in vast numbers from the United States, in the month of October. 1952 FGC Man /bota bord/. 1956 Jeffrey-Smith 77, They used to be in great demand for the table. They were regarded as a *bonne-bouche*, hence one of the local names, butter bird.

BUTTER-BUN sb dial; <*butter-bun*. A nick-name for a small fish (perhaps Cockrell's BUTTER-FISH).
1952 FGC StAnn /bóta bón/ small, green colour, has a pretty spot on the side like a button.

BUTTER-DOUGH sb chiefly dial. A kind of sweet cake.
1907 Jekyll 253–4 [Song:] Sake a the young gal butter-dore, James Brown a shake him shoulder. (A butterdore, more properly butter-dough, is a kind of cake.) 1943 *GL* Clar, Butter doe; StAnd, Buttahdoe; StT, Butter-doe, a very sweet Cake. 1952 FGC StM /botaduo/ round, cakish, made with sugar—same as bulla.

BUTTER-FISH sb gen; cf *OED*: 'The Spotted Gunnel, so called from its slimy skin' 1674→. A common fish of various colours and spotted; fishermen say the name comes from its colour, though this is not always like that of butter. Cf, however, the Latin species name, *fulvus*.
1892 Cockrell list, Butter-fish, *Enneacentrus punctatus*. 1952 FGC StAnn, StC, StE, StJ, StM, West /bota fish/. 1952 Smith in *NHN* 250, *Cephalopholis fulvus ruber*..is locally known as butterfish..St Mary..St James.. *Cephalopholis fulvus punctatus*, also known in Jamaica as 'butterfish'..is scarcely distinguishable from the above except for colouration. *BA G*

BUTTERFLY BIRD sb. See quot; also called BEAN BIRD.
1956 Jeffrey-Smith 82, *Setaphaga ruticilla*..Locally it is known as Butterfly Bird, a name given not only because of its lovely colouring, but also because of its method of flight.

BUTTERFLY TREE sb. The *Bauhinia* genus of trees, from the resemblance of their bi-lobed leaves to the half-spread wings of a butterfly. (The flowers also attract butterflies strongly.)
1951 FGC Man; 1952 FGC StAnn, Said to be the Portland name for what in StAnn is called BULL-HOOF.

BUTTER-HIND sb dial; <abbr of *butterfish* +*hind*. A butter-fish; it resembles the *hainz*.
1952 FGC StAnn /bota-hainz/ = butterfish; yalla colour.

BUTTER-JACK sb dial. A variety of the jack fish of a yellow colour, whence the name.
1952 FGC StE, Butter-jack, yellow-jack.

BUTTER-PEAR sb dial. An alternative name for the 'pear' (AVOCADO), alluding to its buttery flesh. Cf the former name MIDSHIPMAN'S BUTTER. *G*
1952 FGC StJ /bota pier/ the flesh is red [i.e. yellow-orange coloured].

BUTTER-ROOM sb dial; evid a 'rationalized' form of BUTTERY.

1956 Mc StE (Accom) /rón in di kichin, in di bóta ruum nou, bring wan a duoz bangkra de fo mi/.

BUTTERY /botri/ sb dial arch; <*buttery*. (Cf US usage: arch, =pantry.) A storeroom or storage bin (off the kitchen, under the house, etc.) where foodstuffs (esp ground provisions) are kept. *BA*

1943 *GL* StM, Buttery, pantry; Tre, Buttrey, store house; Tre, Butrie, a room where foodstuffs are kept. 1952 FGC Tre /botri/ storeroom—white people call it 'pantry'; West /botri/ under the house, where ground provisions are kept—old fashioned except among humbler people—others say 'pantry'. 1956 Mc Man, StE /bótri/.

BUTTO see *butu*.

BUTTON vb obs?; cf *OED* 5 →1772–84. Of a plant: to begin to form tubers.

1823 Roughley 406, Cocoas will require two moldings and three cleanings, before they begin to button or bear at the roots.

BUTTON BUSH sb. See quot; 'button' perh refers to the fruit or seed, though both are very small. (*Borreria laevis*.) Cf BUTTON-WEED.

1944 *NHN* II 142, The Button Bush, *Boreria laevis*.

BUTTON MANGROVE sb; <*button*+*mangrove*. The BUTTON TREE, which grows among mangroves and somewhat resembles them.

1926 Fawcett 309–10, *Conocarpus*..*erecta*..Button Tree, Button Mangrove, Button Wood. 1941 Swabey 16.

BUTTON TREE sb; cf *OED* 1725→. *Conocarpus erecta*; see quot 1926.

1696 Sloane 135, *Button tree*. In arenosis maritimis prope *Passage fort*..copiose crescit. 1725 Sloane 18, Button Tree..The tops of the Twigs are branch'd, sustaining at first some small roundish Heads..These augment to so many round red Balls, something resembling the Cones of Alder, or like Buttons, whence the Name. 1864 Grisebach 782, Button-tree: *Conocarpus erectus*. 1926 Fawcett 309–10, C. erecta..Button Tree, Button Mangrove, Button Wood.

BUTTON-WEED sb dial; cf *OED*; *DAE* 1817–8→. Species of *Spermacoce*, esp *S. tenuior*, and prob also the closely allied genus *Borreria* (cf BUTTON-BUSH). Also called IRON GRASS, MAN-HEART, MONGOOSE GRASS. *N*

1811 Titford 39–40, Slender Button Weed, *Spermacoce Tenuior*, called also Iron Grass..Rough-haired, thorny, and shaggy Button Weed, are natives of Jamaica. 1927 Beckwith 13, *Borreria lævis*..and *verticillata*. 1952 FGC Man; Tre, Button-weed, = man-heart, mongoose grass. 1954 *WIMJ* 20, *Borreria lævis*..*B. verticillata*..Button Weed or Bush.

BUTTON WOOD (TREE) sb; *OED* 'The genus *Conocarpus*'. (Cf *DA* 1674→ for spp of *Platanus*.) *Conocarpus erecta*; also called BUTTON TREE. *BL N*

1756 Browne 159, Conocarpus 2..The Button-tree, or Button-wood. 1877 Murray *Kittle* 11, A nightingale overhead, seated on a dry twig of a button wood tree, caroled forth his matin song. 1886 Hooper 31, *Conocarpus erectus*, Buttonwood. 1952 FGC Tre /bótnwùd/ Bright red berries, smooth like cherry—bird feed on them—grow in sea, sea washes roots.

BUTTREY see BUTTERY.

BUTT SNAPPER sb; cf *OED butt*, flatfish +*snapper*. A variety of snapper fish; see quots.

1892 Cockrell list, Butt snapper, *Lutjanus buccanella*, = schoolmaster.

BUTTU see next.

butu /bútu/ vb dial arch; cf Twi *butuw* (Akan *butu*), Ewe *bútu*, to overturn, turn upside down. To stoop down; to squat on the heels. Also const *down*.

1943 *GL* Man, Butto, stoop down; Port, Buttu, stoop; Port, Butou, to squat; StAnd, Butto, to sit on one's feet; Tre, Bootoo, stoop down. 1955 FGC Man /butu/ stoop, squat on heels—old-time. 1956 Mc Clar, Man, StAnd /butu doun, butu dong/.

BUTUDU adj dial rare; perh a form of BUTTER-DOUGH.

1943 *GL* Kgn, Butudu, fat.

buunakin see *buna, bunakin*.

buunz see BONE.

BUXEN sb dial; perh <Twi *abosí*, a species of yam.

1943 *GL* Man, Buxen, a small edible local wild yam.

BUY LOAD vb phr dial. Of a higgler: to buy from growers produce which will make up the load she takes to market.

1961 Katzin 3, On Wednesday, Miss A left her yard at dawn to buy 'load'.

buzan sb dial; <*bosom*.

1956 Mc Man /búzan/ the space between the breasts. (A breast is /bobi, titi, bres/.)

buzu sb and int dial; cf Twi *busu*—as in *abusudé*, a wicked thing, wicked deed, ill luck, disaster, *o-busufó*, a wicked man; Ewe *busú*, evil, ill-luck, etc. Cf *guzu*. Luck (usually bad); obeah; see quots.

c 1915 FGC StAnd /buzu/—an exclamation used in boys' games to bring an opponent bad luck. 1940 HPJ, Boozoo, a somewhat indeterminate word, implying 'luck' (Astley Clerk: good luck) or duppy. (Astley Clerk: never heard this last). 1943 *GL* Tre, Boozoo, Obeah.

buzu-hed sb dial; <*buzu*+*head*.

1958 DeC StT /buzuhed/ a name for a stupid fool.

buzuman sb dial; <*buzu*+*man*, the latter being an exact transl of Twi *-fó*—cf *buzu*. = GUZU-MAN.

1956 Mc StAnd /búzumán/ Obeahman.

BUZZOO-YAKKO sb dial; etym unknown, but cf *buguyaga, buzu*. See quots.

1940 HPJ (Cruickshank 10, quoting Jekyll), A sidebag or napsack, according to Jekyll who says it is a local word (i.e. not widely distributed). 1943 *GL* Man, Buzzoo yahko, a side bag, slung with strap round neck.

bwaai, bwai sb dial; <*boy*. This pronunc is still very common among dialect speakers; it preserves in the diphthong an 18th cent Engl pronunc (cf the rhymes of Pope and others), and labialization of *b*. **s.** *BL* Tobago.

BWILE sb or vb. A dial sp representing the folk pronunc /bwail/ for 'boil'. Cf BWOIL. *BL*

1942 Bennett gloss, Bwile: boil.

BWIVILOUS sb? or vb? dial; etym unknown.

1943 *GL* StC, Bwivilous, boil.

BWOIL sb or vb. A dial sp representing the folk pronunc /bwail/ for 'boil'. Cf BWILE. *BL*

1905 Dodd 5, A bwoil it down an mek some tea.

BY conj dial rare; <*by*, cf *OED* 2 1 d, 'quasi-*conj*..*Obs*. exc. *Sc*.' *G*

1. 'By the time that, when, after.' (*OED*.)

1907 Jekyll 81, By Pig on the tree fulling up his basket here come Wolf. *Ibid* 83, He climb up the chimbley, an', by he fe get to the top, the pot of boiling water was long time ready waiting for him.

2. By the fact that, because.

1907 Jekyll 129, An' Cock by him catch the tief takes the corn. [*Cock, because he caught the thief, got the corn.*]

BYA /báia/ vb dial; <Engl *-bye*, as in *rock-a-bye*, etc.; cf *OED bye-bye*[1]. To lull a child to sleep.

1912 McK *Songs* 117, She knelt by the babe An' byaed* her on de cot.. * A verb formed from hushaby. 1943 *GL* Clar, Bieya, hush; StE, biah baby, to hush lullaby. 1956 Mc Man /Yu bai-a di biebi tu bed/.

BYA-BABY sb dial; <BYA+*baby*.

1943 *GL* StE, Biah Baby, a lullabye.

BYE-CHILD sb; <*by*+*child*. See quot.

1873 Rampini 81–2, Concubinage is a universal institution, and bears with it no disgrace. The offspring of such connexions—'bye-children', 'out-children', or 'love-children', as they are called,—generally follow the mother.

CA see *kya*.

CA, CAA see CARRY.

CAANDIERT see SCORN-THE-EARTH.

CABA-CABA sb dial; =*kap-kap*, q.v. See quot; this may be the same as the *kap-kap*, which, however, is black. (Cf *kaba-kaba*.) *G*

1943 *GL*, Caba-caba, the largest kind of Jamaica red ants.

CABAN sb dial; ?<*caban*, ME and EMnE sp of *cabin*; cf Sp *cabaña*, a hut. A platform of green sticks on which pork is jerked; cf PATTA.

1890 Thomas 87, This is called about the Blue Mountain Valley a 'patta', while among the Maroons, and in the Cuna-Cuna district it is known as a 'caban'.

CABBAGE sb; cf *OED sb*[1] 3, 1638→.

1. The inner sheaf of young leaves of the CABBAGE TREE: the part that is eaten. [Not specif Jamaican.] *G N*

1725 Sloane 116, The outwardmost Leaves Footstalks inclosing those within it, and they others, at last they all surround the Gemma or Germen, which is the leaves not yet sprouted, and this is what is call'd the Cabbage, which being kept from the Light and Air is very tender and delicate.

2. The upper portion of a sugar-cane, between the cane itself and the leaves; it is planted, esp in the fall planting, as it is the surest to 'strike', or take root. Also called the SEED.

1956 Mc StT (Serge Island sugar estate) /kyabij/.

CABBAGE freq abbr of CABBAGE BARK or TREE.

CABBAGE BARK sb; *OED* 1777 only. *BL*

1. The medicinal bark of the CABBAGE BARK (TREE).

1814 Lunan I 244, The ill success of the cabbage-bark in a few cases.

2. In folk use, the Cabbage Palm, in allusion to the broad sheath below the bough—cf CABBAGE SKIN.

1952 FGC StAnd, Cabbage-bark bears berries like macka-fat.

CABBAGE-BARK (TREE) sb; cf *OED* 1777 sole quot.

Andira inermis, the tree, and its bark (CABBAGE-BARK or erron CABBAGE-TREE BARK) used as an anthelmintic medicine; now commonly called WORMWOOD (TREE); also ANGELIN, BASTARD CABBAGE-WOOD, and formerly BILGEWATER TREE. *BL*

1814 Lunan I 130–1, Cabbage Bark Tree..it is chiefly remarkable on account of the quality of its bark, which has been found to be an excellent vermifuge. 1920 Fawcett 84–5, *Andira inermis*..Cabbage Bark Tree, Bastard Cabbage. 1952 FGC Port, Cabbage-bark—when moon is full, peel bark and give to children for worms; also StAnn, StE, StT.

CABBAGE-LEAF TOBACCO sb. A variety of tobacco with a broad leaf.

1952 FGC StE.

CABBAGE PINE sb obs?; <*cabbage*+PINE. A variety of pineapple.

1740 Importance 30, The *Pine Apple* or *Ananias* [*sic*], is a very rich and delicious Fruit..There are three Sorts of them; the Cabbage, the Orange, and the Sugar-Loaf.

CABBAGE SKIN sb dial. Another name for the CABBAGE-TREE, alluding to the broad lower sheath of the bough which has several uses. Cf *buba-mat*.

1952 FGC Port, 'Cabbage-skin—can eat heart, use shank to cover and dry seeds'; StM, 'Cabbage-skin—straight, very tall; bough very broad when it hoks [husks] from the tree'.

CABBAGE TREE sb, also attrib; *OED cabbage-tree* 1725→. The *Areca* or some other palm with edible terminal bud. *N* ~ *palm*.

[1655 Eye-Witnesse 18, Of Limon, Orange, Coco, Cabage, Palmeeto..there are great plenty [in Santo Domingo].] 1661 Hickeringill 13, All sorts of fruit-bearing Trees, as Orange-trees, a sort of Cabbage trees, rag'd with berries, &c. 1679 Trapham 44, The many salt springs near Cabbage Tree bottome, and the neighbouring places. 1952 FGC StJ, 'Cabbage—like coconut, but has bark—buba-mat'.

CABBAGE-TREE BARK sb. The bark of the CABBAGE-BARK TREE (not of the CABBAGE TREE), used medicinally.

1782 Stewart, in Lunan I 248–9, Anthelmintic..all other medicines [than cowitch] given with the same intention, except cabbage-tree bark. 1814 Lunan I 244, I laid aside the cabbage-tree bark.

CABBAGE-WOOD sb. Another name for the CABBAGE-BARK (TREE).

1952 FGC Port, Cabbage bark, cabbage wood.

CABELIAU, CABILLIAU see *kyabiyo*.

CABOOSE sb dial; cf *DA* 1, 'Obs', →1874.

1943 *GL* Kgn, koobooce—a small house; StE, Coboose, small house. 1943 *GL* Kgn, Caboose, bag. [Error for *cutacoo*?]

CA! CA! int and vb dial. A call to encourage draft animals.

1833 Scott II 370, The *ca ca 'ing*, like so many rooks, of the children driving the mules and oxen in the mills.

CACA sb (also attrib), vb and int dial; origin uncertain, prob multiple—cf Sp and Fr *caca*, excrement, Mende *ka*, waste matter (Turner 102), Twi *kắŋkãŋ*, stinking.

A. sb: A widely known word for excrement, filth, or anything dirty. The noun, by itself, is used as an interjection. Also attrib in CACA-BELLY, CACA PILOT, etc. *BL G N T*

1790 Moreton 131, The yellow snake says to her poor black wench who she is learning to be a stitcher..'Dat will nebba do foa me, garl! Wind him so! Work him so! Hold him so! Jig him so! Kackkaw foa you!' 1943 *GL*, Kakka Int. What a mess!; Tre, Ka ka, excreta; West, Cacca, dung. 1952 FGC StM [The fish] caca-pilot goes after caca.

B. vb: See quot.

1943 *GL* StAnd, Cacca, The act of passing ones stool.

CACAA see COCOA.

CACABAY see COCOBAY.

CACA-BELLY, COCK-A-BENNY sb dial; CACA+*belly*. A fish similar to the GRUNT, with a dark under-belly, whence its name. (Cf the Kakabelli of British Guiana: *Poecilia vivipera* —Roth 229.) *G*

1910 Anderson-Cundall 18 [Prov:] Cock-a-benny tun yellow-tail. [Someone plain or ugly has dressed himself up in fine clothes—usually derisive. Cf YELLOW-TAIL.] 1952 FGC, Caca-belly feeds between river and shallow sea.

CACANABU see *kakanabu*.

CACAO-NUT-WALK sb obs. =COCOA-WALK sb[1].

1707 Sloane lxxi, At Guanaboa, in the time of the Spaniards, were great Chocolate or Cacao-Nut-Walks.

CACA PILOT sb dial; cf CACA. A type of pilot fish that is said to go after dung.

1950–1 Smith, *Abudefduf saxatilis: pilot fish*, StM, *coco pilot*, Pt Antonio, *sheepshead*, Lucea. 1952 FGC, StC, StM, West.

CACCA see CACA.

CACHIMBA sb dial rare; < Amer Sp *cachimbo*, a smoking-pipe; < Kimbundu *quixima, kixima* (Friederici).

1943 *GL* Clar, Coch-imba, clay pipe. 1956 Mc Man /kachímba/ pipe, 'in Cuban language'; StE (Accom) /kachímba/ is the Spanish word, /kachimbu/ the Kromanti word.

CACK see COCK.

CACKY-QUAW sb dial; partly onomatopoeic, but cf also *cock*, to turn or stick up, and quot. A bird not clearly identified; perhaps the clapper-rail *Rallus longirostris*. See quot.

1847 Gosse 376, I have not heard it utter any sound; but Robinson, in describing two that were brought to him alive in October 1760, says, 'their cry was very low, and resembled that of a Coot, when at a great distance.. Several..were killed accidentally, by the negroes at work; as they are so foolish as to hide their heads, and, cocking up their rumps, think they are safe, when they are easily taken..The negroes in Clarendon call it *Cacky-quaw*, by reason of its cry, which consists of three articulations; the negroes in Westmoreland call it *Johnny Ho*, and *Kitty Go*, for the same reason'.

CACOA see COCOA.

CACOON /káakúun, kákúun/ sb; 1696 1794 1920 cocoon, 1814 1864 1920 cacoon; etym unknown: *OED*: '?A native African name'; but Sloane cites *Hortus Malabaricus* part 8, p. 59, 'Perim-kaku-valli', the second part of which may be the etymon: Telugu *perim.. valli*, great climbing-plant; *kaku*, (?)vomit: cf Tamil, Kannada *kakku*, Gondi *kakkānā*, to vomit (Burrow-Emeneau), and cf ANTIDOTE COCOON. *OED cocoon* 1756→ 'Obs. form of Cacoon'; *cacoon* 1854→. In Jamaica *cocoon* is still the 'educated' form; *cacoon* seems to have been and is regularly the folk form.

1. A climbing shrub, *Entada gigas*, used for its strong withe; the Maroons drape the vine and leaves around themselves for camouflage; also its bean (about 2 in. wide by ½ in. thick) used to make purses, etc., and as food. Also called MAFOOTOO WITHE.

1696 Sloane 68, *Cocoons*. Reperitur loco *the Thickets* dicto ultra montem Diabolo..& aliis sylvis mediterraneis Insulæ Jamaicæ. 1814 Lunan I 137–9, Cacoons.. Mimosa Scandens..It climbs up the tallest trees, and spreads itself in every direction by means of its *cirrhi* or claspers, so as to form a complete arbour, and to cover the space of an English acre from one root. This circumstance has a bad effect on the trees or bushes so shaded.—the leaves drop off, the tree gradually rots, and the limbs fall down by the weight of this parasite..The pod is perhaps the largest and longest of any other in the world, being sometimes eight or nine feet in length, five inches broad, jointed, and containing ten or fifteen seeds. These seeds are brown, shining, flattened, very hard, and called *cacoons*. 1864 Grisebach 782, Cacoons, *Entada scandens*. 1920 Fawcett 124–5. 1952 FGC Port /kákúun/; also StE.

2. *Crudia spicata* and its bean, which closely resembles that of *Entada gigas*.

1920 Fawcett IV 212–22, *Crudia spicata*..Cacoon.

CACOON ANTIDOTE sb obs. A medicine made from the ANTIDOTE CACOON.

1820 Thomson 163, Coccoon Antidote. Slice a few of the kernels, add the powdered bark of the wild cinnamon; a pint of rum. It operates likewise as a purge.

CACOON POTATO sb dial; ? < *coccoon*, grub +*potato*.

1940 HPJ, Cawcoon potato: a potato eaten by worms.

CACTUS FENCE sb slang. An asylum; this probably refers to Bellevue Hospital, Kgn, which has such a fence.

1943 *GL* Man, Cactus fence, asylum.

CAESAR sb, also attrib; etym uncertain; *W2* lists it thus without explanation, but *seizer* is equally possible phonologically and semantically. The fish *Bathystoma rimator* (*W2*). Cf AMBER-JACK CAESAR, BOTTLE-CAESAR.

1929 Beckwith 33, Pot fish are..snappers; mullet..; silk..; goat and Caesar. 1952 FGC StM /siiza/ same as BAIT-BARKER—take the bark off—eat bait in pot; also StE.

CAESAR-BUSH sb dial; etym unknown (perhaps this should be 'seizer'). See quot.

1952 FGC StJ, Bachelor button, with large dried heads—/siiza bush/.

CAESAR GRUNT sb dial. =CAESAR.

1952 FGC StC, StE. 1952 Smith in *NHN* 221, *Bathystoma rimator*, the Caesar grunt, is elongate and compressed.

CAESAR OBEAH sb dial. A common wild plant: see quot.

1955 *WIMJ* 159, *Hyptis capitata*..(Wild) Batchelor's Button; Caesar Obeah; Wild Hops; Iron Wort.

CAESARWOOD sb bot. One of the types of ROSEWOOD. (The name is unexplained.)

1920 Fawcett 176, *Zanthoxylum rhodoxylon*..Rosewood, Caesar-wood. 1941 Swabey 29.

CAFFILUS see SCROFULOUS.

CAJACIA sb bot obs; etym unknown. *Euphorbia hyssopifolia* (Fawcett), formerly used as a medicine against poison, the DRY BELLYACHE, etc.

1679 Trapham 138–9, So far the Doctor to his excellency, referring to the Plant it self under the name of Cajacia, called by the Spaniard Erudos Cobres; Which in English is a Snakeweed. 1756 Browne 235, Euphorbia 4..The small erect Spurge..is the *Cajacia* of *Trapham*..who extolls it as an excellent ingredient in baths, for people afflicted with the dry belly-ach. 1814 Lunan II 196–7, *Euphorbia hirta*. The creeping hairy spurge..may be given with success in most diseases arising from a lentor or spissitude of the juices—*Cajacia*, alias *caacica*.

CAKE-HEAD sb chiefly dial; cf COCO-HEAD, HEAD SUGAR, etc. See quot.

1907 Jekyll 76, A knife and fork being handed to a bridesmaid she takes off the cake-head, which is a small top tier or addition to the cake proper.

CALABAN /kàlabán, kàlbán/ sb dial; 1707 clavanne, 1707 1725 clavanie, 1847 calamban, 1868 calibean, 1873→ calaban; <Engl dial (Somerset) *callyvan*, 'A pyramidal wicker trap..used to catch birds' (*EDD*). (This word must have been early spread in the Caribbean, prob by negroes: cf Cuban *caravana*, a bird trap—Malaret.) A box-like trap made of sticks, used to catch ground-walking birds. **s.**

1707 Sloane lxxxv, Ground-Doves..are taken with Clavannes, and wild Cassada Seeds for Bait. 1725 Sloane 305, Clavanies or Traps made of Reeds. 1868 Russell 6, Calibean, A basket snare for birds..African. 1873 Rampini 164, 'Calabans', baited with peas or pulse. 1905 Smith 14, Annancy try to ketch Chim-Chim by springes, an Calaban,* an' lime.. * Bird trap. 1929 Beckwith 35, The most complex of these trapping methods is the calaban, made like a rustic flowerpot. 1943 *GL* Port, Colaban, Cone-shaped bird trap being set on the ground; also Tre. 1949 U.Newton v 26. 1952 FGC Han, Man /kàlabán/.

CALABASHA sb dial; evid <Sp *calabaza* (the Std form *calabash* comes through Fr).

1943 *GL*, Coobla—small calabasha.

CALABASH BROOM sb dial.

1952 FGC StC, Calabash broom, old-fashioned name for ironweed, dog-tongue.

CALABASH ESTATE sb obs. In the phrase *To carry sugar to Calabash Estate*: to steal sugar from the mill, a calabash-full at a time, supposedly to take it to a place so named.

1828 Marly 36, I trust, however, that your attention will be such, that you will put it out of the power of any of them, to carry sugar from the curing house to Calibash estate..; *ibid* 43, Calibash estate comprehends the whole island of Jamaica.

CALABASH NUTMEG sb. See quots.

1854–5 *TJSA* I 59, Calabash Nutmeg. Monodora myristica. 1864 Grisebach 782, Calabash-nutmeg: *Monodora Myristica.*

CALABASH PUMPKIN sb dial. A variety of pumpkin with a shell-like skin similar to that of the calabash.

1952 FGC StAnd, StC.

CALABOOSE vb dial; cf *DA* →1857. To catch or imprison.

1943 GL StM, Calabuse, to take hold of.

CALALOE, CALALOO see next.

CALALU /kálalu, kálilu, kólalu/ sb; 1696 1707 culilu, 1748 caliloo, 1756 calaloe caleloe, 1756 1835 calaloo, 1774 colalue, 1774 1814 calalue, 1811 colilu, 1814 calalu, 1835 1948 callalu, 1913 calulu, 1946 callalloo; <Amer Sp *calalú*, Pg *carurú*, a rich soup or stew in which one or more kinds of calalu leaves are the chief ingredients <Tupí *caárurú*, a fat or thick leaf (Mendonça). (Such an African word as Gẽ *kalalu*, broth, soup, is probably a loan from this.) **s.** Also **s** CATALUE.

1. The name given to several plants having edible leaves, eaten as greens, in soups, medicinally, etc.; the kinds are BRANCHED, GREEN, MOUNTAIN, PRICKLY, SMALL-LEAVED, SPANISH, SURINAM CALALU. *BL G N T*

2. A thick soup (the usual Sp Amer meaning); in Jamaica this is usu *calalu soup*. *BA BL G T*

3. In recent use (esp among the folk) the word is further generalized to include any leaves eaten as greens. INDIAN KALE was early considered a calalu; see COCO-CALALU.

1696 Sloane 49, Caruru Brasiliensibus..*Culilu, or Caterpillars.* In locis campestribus post pluvias ubique copiosè luxuriat. 1707 Sloane 143, Culilu..when the leaves are stript off, and boiled as a Sallet, [it] is one of the pleasantest I ever tasted..likewise 'tis shred and boiled in Pottages of all sorts..It is eat as Spinage. 1864 Grisebach 782, Calalu: *Phytolacca.* 1946 Dunham 94, She is still there, fingering a bunch of 'callalloo' greens and haggling over the price. 1952 FGC StAnn /kólalu/; StM /kálilu/ a soup: also means Indian kale, spinach, etc.; StM /posli kalalu/ *Purslane greens.* 1956 Mc Port (Referring to the leaves of taya) /dis iz di kalalu av it—yu yuuz it laik kiel tu mek pepa pat/.

CALALUE see prec.

CALAMANTE sb dial; a variant form of CROMANTY, of which cf sense 4. See quot s.v. COBY-NANCY; the identification may be incorrect, however.

CALAMBAN see CALABAN.

CALAPAVER, -OR, -RE see CALIPEVA.

CALAPEE see CALLIPEE.

CALAPIVER see CALIPEVA.

CALASH, CALASHTE int obs; origin unknown.

1868 Russell 22, Interjections: calash or calashte! Indifference.

CALAVANCE sb; cf *OED* so spelled 1829→.

[1634 Herbert *Trav* 182, Carauances or Indian Pease.] 1696 Sloane 72, Calavances. 1697 Nevill 24 June, Calavanseys. 1756 Browne 292, Calavances, or Red Pease. 1794 Barham 28, Calavances..a small white pea resembling the kidney.

CALEDONIA sb dial; from the opening words of a song popular about 1944–5.

1954 LeP Kgn, Caledonia; StT, Kalidounia, someone very fat and clumsy.

CALELOE see CALALU.

CALEMBE, CALIMBE /kalémbe/ sb dial; calimbe, kalembey, kelembi; cf Gũ *kãlĩmɔ*, a slave (hence, perh, a slave dance), and Amer Sp *calémbe*, rags, tatters. (Cognate with the Gũ word is Fɔ̃ *kanumɔ*, a slave, which is prob the source of Amer Sp *candombe*, a boisterous negro dance—see Westermann, Malaret, etc.)

A dance of African origin, and the music and song that went with it (see quots). It is now less practised than formerly, and is falling into disrepute.

1924 Beckwith 177, The dance [Cumbolo] (also called 'calimbe') is performed at wakes, two men holding a couple of sticks parallel while a third dances upon them to the strains of the song. 1929 Beckwith 83, At a wake.. They 'dance Calimbe' in an antic caper upon a pair of sticks held horizontally by two other players. 1940 Astley Clerk in HPJ, 'Kelembi' being the name of one of the oldest song-dances sung in Jamaica by the African (not European) slaves—as an Orchestral piece my Orchestra played it at Myrtle Bank, and other places during the Tourist seasons of 1912–18..[It is] *a classic.* 1943 *GL* West, Kalembey, Pocomanian jump. 1955 FGC Man /jòmp kalémbe/—an old-time dance; not necessarily pocomania.

CALEMSHA sb dial obs; an off-form of, or an error for CALEMBE.

1940 HPJ (Song) Monkey, monkey, play de fiddle Mek de bahboon dance calemsha. [A. Clerk knew the song with 'Kelembi' instead of 'calemsha'.]

CALEPEAVER see CALIPEVA.

CALIBASH see CALABASH.

CALIBEAN see CALABAN.

CALICO WEED sb. A plant similar to WILD MINT (*Commelina*); evid so named for the mottled colour of the leaves.

1952 FGC Han.

CALILOO see CALALU.

CALIMBE see CALEMBE.

CALIPASH see CALLIPASH.

CALIPEE see CALLIPEE.

CALIPEVA, CALIPAVER /kàlifíeva, kyàlifíeva, kyàlifya/ sb; 1756 calapaver, 1774 calipever, 1790 calapavre, 1808 calapavor, 1826 calapiver, 1833 calipiver, 1858 calipiva, 1893 calepeaver; <Pg *carapeba*, *carapeva* <Tupí *acarapeba*, *corapeba*, the fish *Diapterus rhombeus*. (Friederici.) *OED calipeva* 1833→. (There is no clearly established spelling, though 'calipever' is perh more common than others. The *OED* 'calipeva' is retained here as one which recognizes the claims of etymology, pronunciation, and orthography. The educated pronunciation varies between [ˌkjælɪˈpivə] and [ˌkjælɪˈpevə]; the folk pronunciation (see above) has *f* for *p*, etc.)

In Jamaica, the fish *Mugil liza*, a large sea and river mullet (by fishermen usually called 'Califavor mullet'), esteemed as a delicacy. *N*

1756 Browne 451, Mugil 2..The Calapaver..This fish is so like the foregoing [Mullet], both in habit and appearance, that it is generally thought to be the same species in a more perfect state: it is commonly about two feet or better in length, and is looked upon as a very delicate fish. 1774 Long II 48, Calipever. 1790 Beckford I 234, Calapavre. 1808 Stewart 87, Calapavor. 1826 Barclay 328, Calapivers. 1858 Chambre II 73, Calipiva. 1952 FGC Port, StAnn, StC, StE, StJ, West (Fishermen: /kàlifíeva, kyàlifíeva molit/).

CALIPEVER, -PIVA, -PIVER see prec.

CALL /kaal/ vb dial; cf *OED call v* II.

1. To name. *T*

1952 FGC StAnd (A bystander speaking to a man who is giving the names of vegetables grown locally): 'You no call cabbage yet?'

2. In the phrase *call* (possessive noun or pronoun) *name*: to mention, speak. *BL*

1956 Mc StE (Accom) /a dis kaal yu niem/ *I just mentioned your name.*

CALLALLOO, CALLALU see CALALU.

CALLAPEE see CALLIPEE.

CALLAWAMPUS adj dial: a blend of, or an analogical formation to US *callithumpian*, *catawampus*, etc. See *DA*. Big, stout, fine, grand.

1943 *GL* StA, Callawampus, something grand. 1956 Mc Man /kalawampus hed, kalawampus fut man/ (Of a person, a pig, etc.) /kalawampos/ big, fine, stout.

CALL-DOG sb dial joc. A fish too small for human consumption (so one calls the dog to eat it).

1943 *GL* Tre, Call-dog, small fish.

CALLEPEE see CALLIPEE.

CALLIPACH see next.

CALLIPASH sb arch; 1698 callipach, 1802 callipash; prob <Sp *carapacho*, carapace, shell. Cf *OED calipash* b, 1749→. That part of the meat of a turtle which is next to the shell. *N*

1698 Ward 14, Sea-Turtle..The Belly is call'd Callipee, the Back Callipach. 1802 Nugent 121, Pepper-pot, and callipash and callipee, at Mr Mowat's.

CALLIPE see next.

CALLIPEE sb arch; 1679 calapee, callapee, 1698 1802 1838 callipee, 1707 callepee, 1740 callipe; prob from some Amer Ind word, cf Cent Amer Sp *calapé*, fricassee ('guisado') made with turtle's meat cooked in the shell (Malaret), prob from the same source. Cf *OED calipee*.

That part of the meat of a turtle which is next to the plastron.

[1657 Ligon (1673) 36, Then lifting up his [a turtle's] belly, which we call his *Calipee*, we lay open all his bowels.] 1679 Trapham 61, When the Callapee (for such is called the belly part) is baked, it vies with Venison. 1698 Ward 14, see CALLIPASH. 1707 Sloane lxxxviii, The Callepee, or under part of the Breast or Belly, bak'd, is reckon'd the best piece. 1740 Importance 39, Turrapine, or Land-Turtles, Callipe, or Sea-Turtles; this last is a great Dish baked with forc'd-meat Balls, and some say it tastes of all sorts of Flesh. 1838 Kelly 15, I found that I could relish turtle callipee.

CALULU see CALALU.

CAMAROUN(G) see COME-AROUND.

CAMFOR YAM see *kyamfya yam*.

CAMIEJER sb dial; prob <*scavenger*.

1943 *GL* Clar, Camiejer, acts like a crow.

CAMPEACHY LOGWOOD sb.

1954 *WIMJ* 30, *Haematoxylum campechianum*..Logwood; Campeachy Logwood; Campeachy Wood.

CAMPHOR BUSH or **WEED** sb dial. A common wild plant thought to have the smell of camphor.

1955 *WIMJ* 157, *Calea jamaicensis*..Camphor Bush or Weed; Halbert Weed.

CAMPHOR TREE /kyámfyà/ sb; cf *OED*, applied to other trees. See quots. *G*

1794 Broughton 12, *Laurus Camphora* Camphire Tree [from] Japan [brought by] Dr Tho. Clarke, 1775. 1811 Lunan I 144, The *camphire tree* is very near akin to the *cinnamon tree*..This tree is mentioned in the Hortus Eastensis as having been introduced into this island by Dr Clarke, in the year 1775, and has since been successfully cultivated in several parts of the island. 1955 *WIMJ* 158, *Cinnamomum camphora*..Camphor Tree.

CAMPHOR YAM see *kyamfya yam*.

CAN vb dial. Used for StdE *do* or *will*, esp in negative statements. *BA*

1907 Jekyll 44, An' he call again 'Puppa, Puppa!' an' he couldn' hear [*didn't hear anything*]. 1952 FGC Port /mi waif kyaan kom?/ *Why doesn't* (*or won't*) *my wife come?* 1956 Mc StE (Accom)/tiiman shuuz kyaang fit im/*Teeman's shoes won't* (or *don't*) *fit him;* /aal itaim a did trai tu get di prap-kaan to prap, it kudn prap/ *Though I kept trying to get the pop-corn to pop, it wouldn't pop.*

CANADA FLEABANE sb bot.

1936 Fawcett 197, *Erigeron canadensis*..Canada Fleabane. 1954 *WIMJ* 29, *E. canadensis*..Canada Fleabane; Dead Weed.

CANADIAN DUST sb dial joc.

1958 FGC StT, Canadian dust—shop flour.

CANANA see *kanana.*

CANCRO see CYANCRO.

CANDLE-FLY sb; cf *OED* in diff sense. A firefly; see quots. *G*

1740 Importance 48–9, There are two sorts, which are not only innocent but beautiful by Night, casting Beams of Light like Sparks of Fire thro' the Air; they are called *Candle-Flies.* 1907 Jekyl 89, Candlefly, A large firefly. 1952 FGC Man, StAnd, StT, Candle-fly, old-time name for peeny-wally.

CANDLEWOOD /kyandlwud, kyanglhud/ sb; cf *OED* 2, and JAMAICA CANDLEWOOD.

In Jamaica: at least four trees whose resinous wood has been used for candles and torches: 1. Some species of *Zanthoxylum* (quot 1811); 2. *Sciadophyllum capitatum* (quot 1864); 3. *Peltostigma pteleoides* (quot 1920); 4. *Amyris plumieri* (quot 1920). Cf also BLACK, RED, WHITE and YELLOW CANDLEWOOD.

1811 Titford 128, Citron wood. A tree of the West Indies, called also Candle Wood; the leaves are like Bay leaves, with a black berry similar to Pimenta; the wood has a fine grain and takes a good polish. 1827 Hamel II 83, The woman was as black as pitch, as Roland could distinguish by the light of a piece of candlewood which she kindled. 1864 Grisebach 782, Candle-wood: *Sciadophyllum capitatum.* 1920 Fawcett 181, *Peltostigma pteleoides*..Candle Wood; *ibid* 192–3, *Amyris plumieri*.. Candle-wood. 1944 *NHN* II 94, Their common names in Jamaica are Candlewood or Torchwood (*Amyris* spp), so called because even the green wood will burn strongly and consequently torches made from the wood are used by peasants and woodmen.

CANDY-BOWL sb dial. A box (about 24× 16× 8 in.) with wood bottom and frame and glass sides and top, in which sellers of candies and cakes carry and display their wares. In its early form it was presumably bowl-like.

1942 Bennett 10, Candy lady, candy mam..Buy candy.. de pickney..y'ey dem a tare out like him want Hickmatize me candy-bole.

CANE-BAND sb. A band (made of withe or other material) used to tie cut sugar-canes into bundles. *G*

1790 Beckford II 64, A gang of negroes..collect them into bundles, and tie them with cane-bands together. 1956 Mc StT, etc.—/kien bàn/.

CANE CUTLASS see DeC in 1961 *CLS* 75. A cutlass used to cut sugarcane.

CANE-HOLE sb. The furrows in which PLANT-CANES are planted. *G*

1788 Marsden 29, The deep furrows made with the negroes' hoes; these furrows or cane-holes are remarkably strait and exact. 1837 Sterne 262, It appears that digging cane-holes is a very arduous undertaking. 1839 McMahon 160.

CANE KNIFE sb dial. A cutlass; specifically, a hooked, square-ended bill.

1958 DeC StT.

CANE-LIQUOR sb; *OED cane sb*[1] 10, 1875 only quot. The expressed juice of the sugar-cane.

1774 Long 445, The cane liquor..should be brought into the coppers as free from dirt and trash as possible. 1811 Mathison 53, The lime is administered to the cane-liquor in a cold state.

CANELLA sb bot; cf *OED* 2, 1756→. Cf RED CANELLA. The tree *Canella winterana* (=*C. alba*), and its bark, used medicinally.

[1725 Sloane II 88, This is not the true Cortex Winteranus tho' sold for it, but it is describ'd by Clusius, under the Name of *Canella alba.*] 1756 Browne 275, *Canella,* or Winter's Bark..This tree is very common in all the lower woods, and rocky hills of Jamaica, where it grows without any care..The bark of this tree is the *Canella alba* of the shops: it is a pungent warm aromatic. 1811 Lunan I 194, Cinnamon, wild. Canella. 1955 *WIMJ* 157, Canella winterana Gaertn. (=C. alba Sw.)..Wild Cinnamon; White Cinnamon; Whitewood Bark; Canella; False Winter's Bark.

CANE-PIECE sb; <*cane*+*piece* (*OED sb* 2b, *DAE* n 2). Cf DOG CORN-PIECE. *G*

1. A field in which sugar-cane is grown. *BA*

1774 Long III 901, All these different species [of rats] agree, in committing most dreadful havock on neglected foul cane-spieces [*sic*]. 1790 Beckford I 155, The cane-pieces upon mountain estates are generally at a considerable distance from the pastures. 1801 Nugent 39, We took a cross road, through a sugar plantation, or rather cane-piece, as it is called. 1839 McMahon 117, I was ordered to line cane-pieces for the second gang.

2. Attrib in CANE-PIECE RAT, CANE-PIECE SENSITIVE PLANT, etc.

CANE-PIECE CAT sb joc obs; euphemistic. The CANE RAT, when made an article of food. Cf CANE-RABBIT.

1834 Lewis (1845) 109, To fill up my list of Jamaica delicacies, I must not forget to mention, that I did my best to procure a Cane-piece Cat roasted in the African fashion. The Creole negroes, however, greatly disapproved of my venturing upon this dish, which they positively denied having tasted themselves..However, I tasted it, as did also several other people, and we were unanimous in opinion that it might have been mistaken for a very good game soup, and that, when properly dressed, a Cane-piece Cat must be excellent food.

CANE-PIECE RAT sb; cf CANE-PIECE. = CANE RAT.

1851 Gosse 444, The cane-piece rat. 1873 Rampini 48, Him pop into de supper-room, like a half-starved cane-piece rat.

CANE-PIECE SENSITIVE PLANT sb bot. *Cassia glandulosa*; the roots were once used in decoction as an antidote for vegetable and fish poisons, or boiled for a common drink.

1801 Dancer 366, Cane-piece sensitive plant, *Cassia chamæcrista.* 1814 Lunan I 151, Cane-Piece Sensitive Plant..This is frequently met in cane-piece intervals. It..has a few branches, with numerous small pinnated leaves, which collapse immediately on being touched. 1864 Grisebach 782.

CANE-RABBIT sb obs. The CANE-RAT, in allusion to its being eaten. Cf CANE-PIECE CAT.

1790 Moreton 22, *Old Hector and Sambo*—for the pains in their stomachs, to eat plenty of homony and fungee; plantation eels and cane rabbits will not hurt them.

CANE-RAT sb; *ODS* in a different sense. *G*

1707 Sloane lxxxvi, The Cane-Rats are numerous, of a gray colour, cheap, large, and very good Victuals. 1774 Long 900, The larger [field-rat] is of a light-ash or greyish colour, on the back, and other parts, except the belly, which is intirely white. This subsists almost wholly upon the sugar-cane, and therefore generally termed the cane-rat..they are not an article of food with the white inhabitants, though highly esteemed among the plantation Negroes.

CANE-TOP sb; *DAE, DA* 1826→. The upper leaves of the sugar-cane, from which the ARROW grows; they are used for PLANT-CANES, as feed for cattle, etc. *BA G*

1739 Leslie 332, The Flags or Cane-Tops of them exceed nine Foot Stalk and all..These Cane-Tops make very good Food for Horses and black Cattle. a1818 Lewis (1845) 108 (Journal entry 1816), The fresh plants are cane-tops. [1958 current.]

CANGA /kangga/ vb dial; cf *OED Congo dance.* To dance—a word of AFRICAN cult use.

1953 Moore gloss.

CANGATONY see *kanggatuoni.*

CANIP(E) see GUINEP.

CANKER-BERRY sb bot; *OED* 1756 only. *Solanum bahamense.*

1756 Browne 174, Solanum 5..The Canker Berry.. both the stem and branches are every where full of sharp thorns. The berries are bitterish, and thought to be very serviceable in sore throats. 1811 Titford 46, Canker-berry..is considered a specific for a cankerous mouth. 1814 Lunan I 152. 1864 Grisebach 782.

CANKSNOT see *kangksnot.*

CANNA see *kana.*

CANNANAPO, CANNANNA-POO see *kananapo.*

CANOE see *kunu.*

CANTA see *kantu.*

CAN'T DONE /kyáan dón/ adv phr dial; abbr of *it can't be done*, there's no end to it. Cf CAN. Extremely, 'no end'. [It follows the adjective or verb which it modifies.]

1952 FGC StAnd, Spirit-weed smell very strong—can't done!; StM, It nice can't done. 1954 LeP StE, Me lub fe shake foot caan' done. 1955 Bennett *Denbigh Show*, Dem enjoy demself kean done. 1956 Mc /hing ogli kyaang don/ *He is exceedingly ugly.*

CANTOO, CANTU see *kantu.*

CAP-BERRY sb bot. *Nectandra patens*; also called SWEETWOOD.

1914 Fawcett 216.

CAP-BERRY SWEETWOOD sb bot. *Nectandra coriacea*; also called PEPPER-LEAF SWEETWOOD, SWEETWOOD, SMALL-LEAVED SWEETWOOD.

1914 Fawcett 217. 1941 Swabey 31.

CAPE MULLET /kíep mólit/ sb dial. A sea mullet, the same as JUMPING MULLET.

1952 FGC StAnn, StC.

CAPILLARY-PANICLED BROOMWEED sb bot obs; cf BROOMWEED. In Macfadyen's use: *Sida paniculata* (ident. 1926 Fawcett 114–15).

1837 Macfadyen 83, Sida capillaris. *Capillary panicled Broom-weed.*

CAPITAL K sb dial; from the shape: K. A K-FOOT; knock-knees. *G*

1943 *GL* StM, Capital-K, knock-kneed. 1952 FGC Han /kyápital kíe/ knock-knee.

CAPOOSE[1] sb obs; 1790 capouse, 1801 capoose; perh < Pg or Sp *capuz*, a cowl; cf also Venezuelan Sp *capúza*, arrow-head (Alvarado I). Each of the pivots on which the rollers in sugar-mills formerly turned; they were shaped like cones rounded at the top and flanged below. Cf CUT CAPOOSE.

1790 Moreton 47, These rollers [are] coged all round, and supported on the mill bed..on small pieces of metal about the size and shape of whipping-tops, called capouses. 1794 Edwards (1801) II diagram facing page 223, C. pivot to each roller, called the capoose.

CAPOOSE[2] see CUT CAPOOSE.

CAPOUSE see CAPOOSE[1].

CAP-OYSTER sb obs. A type of shellfish, so called from its shape.

1756 Browne 413, Stola 5..The small white cap-Oyster. Stola 6..The small yellow cap-Oyster.

CAP (SHEET) sb. A flat piece of wood covering a dugout canoe above the gunwales at bow and stern and affording a hand grip for lifting it.

1952 FGC StJ /kyap av di kunu/; StM /kyap-shiit/.

CAPTAIN sb dial. The SHEPHERD of a revival group.

1953 Moore 56 (StT).

CAPUCHINE sb bot obs; *OED capuchin* 3.

1756 Browne 322, Impatiens 1..The Capuchine, or Balsamine.

CARAMANTEE see CROMANTY.

CARANAMPO, CARANAPU(M) see *karanapo.*

CARATO see CORATOE.

CARD sb dial. A piece used in the game of dominoes. *BL G*

1958 DeC StAnd, etc. /kyaad/ a domino. Although the game is called dominoes, each piece is called a *card* rather than a *bone* as in the U.S. /hou moch kyaad yu ha nou?/

CARD GUM sb dial. A plant of the genus *Clusia.*

1961 DAP Man, Card gum, *Clusia* spp.

CARE see *kva.*

CARE HOW conj phr dial; abbr of some such phr as 'I don't care how'. No matter how. *BL G*

1912 McKay *Songs* 53, A man can't eben ketch a mac, Care how him 'train him neck.

CARENCRO see CYANCRO.

CARETA see *kyarikta.*

CARIBBEE BARK TREE sb bot.

1936 Fawcett 11–12, *Exostema caribæum*..Caribbee Bark Tree, Jamaica Jesuit's Bark..The bark of these species was formerly used as a febrifuge.

CAROACHIES, CAROACHY, CAROCHI see CAROCHIES.

CAROCHIES, CAROCHY /karúochiz, koróchi/ sb chiefly dial (usually plur); < Amer Sp *corotos*, playthings, tools of trade, chattels, trumpery, trash, stuff (Puerto Rico, Venezuela, Colombia). Things of little value; rubbish.

1877 Murray *Tom Kittle* 10, 'What de use of dem, "corrosis" bout de place ya?'..The 'corrosis' referred to Old Tom's conchological and other marine collections. Sea fans in any quantity were nailed on the walls. 1940 HPJ, Carochi, Rubbish. 1943 *GL* Kgn, Corochi, rubbish; Tre, Carrochis, Rubbish. 1955 HPJ, *Caroachy, carouchie, caroachies.* Like Banagarang, but I think more common. 1956 Mc Man /go áan go ték op yu uol korúochi dem/ *Take away your old rubbish.*

CAROLINE PEAS /károlàin, kyárolàin, kàlláin/ sb dial; cf *OED Carolina, Caroline*, but the reason for this application is unknown. A small variety of BLACK-EYE PEAS.

1952 FGC StAnd, StAnn, StE. 1954 *FG* 422, The Caroline is also similar [as black-eye peas are, to cow peas] in all respects, but has a slightly pink border around the eye.

CAROUCHIE see CAROCHIES.

CARPI, CARPIE see CORPIE.

CARRA-CARRA see *karakara.*

CARRION CROW see CYANCRO.

CARROCHIS see CAROCHIES.

CARROO-CARROO see *karakara*.

CARROT MANGO sb.

1837 Macfadyen 222, The Carrot Mango, a large fruit with the pulp hard, and in taste, somewhat resembling the root which gives it its designation.

CARRY /ka, kya, kyaa, kyai, kyar, kyari, kye, kyeri/ vb dial; sp in dialect *kea, caa*, etc.

1. In the archaic English and dialectal American sense (cf *OED* 5, *DAE* 2): to conduct or take (a person, animal, etc.) along with one.

1697 Nevill 6 May, To gett me 9 Pylots to carry us through the Virgin Islands. 1950 Pioneer 24, Anancy.. carry har go gi de king. 1956 Mc Man /mek mi kya daangki go lang noung/ *Let me take the donkey away with me now. BL G N T*

2. Characteristically followed by another verb of motion. [Examples usually illustrate sense 1 also.] *G T*

1837 Sterne 19, An massa——come back and shove me, and carry me go. 1950 Pioneer 35, Bredda Anancy was a pos'man, an him usual kea letta goh, kea letta come, up an dung every day. 1952 FGC StM /lèt mi kyár di báskit kom shúo yu/. 1956 JN Tre, Aunt Dolly, you going carry me go a concert tomorrow night mam?

3. In the imperative phrase *carry come*: Bring it (here). This is one of several similar phrases (cf BRING COME, CARRY COME) prob reflecting West African verb syntax. *T*

1943 *GL* StC, Ca come, bring it. 1956 Mc StC /kyai kom/. 1956 JN, Carry come mek mi fix it up. 1959 FGC StAnd, etc.

4. Fig (cf *OED* I): To bear, to have upon oneself.

1956 Mc StJ /shi kyari gud iej/ *She carries a good age—is quite old. G*

5. Refl (cf *OED* 33): To keep or comport (oneself). *G*

1956 Mc Clar /dem duong kyeri demself taidi/ *They don't keep themselves tidy.*

CARRY-ALL sb dial; cf *DA carryall*, 'Orig. a light one-horse vehicle'.

1958 DeC StT /kyari-al/ a four-wheeled handcart.

CARRY COME vb phr dial. See CARRY 3.

CARRY-GO-BRING-COME sb dial; see CARRY 2. Tale-bearing; a tale-bearer.

1943 *GL* StC, Carry-go-bring-come, tale-bearing. 1956 BLB Man /cho! him a riel kyari-go-bring-kom/ *Oh! he's a real tattler.*

CARRY-ME-SEED sb dial. A small wild plant which has its flowers (and seeds) usually hanging in pairs beneath the leaves; see quot. Also called CHAMBA BITTER, GRIPE-WEED, *mirazmi bush*, PICKNEY-'PON-BACK, QUININE WEED, RICE BITTERS, SEED-UNDER-LEAF, WILD TAMARIND, etc.

1954 *WIMJ* 31, 1955 *WIMJ* 159, *Phyllanthus niruri*.. Carry-me-seed; Chamber Bitter.

CARTMAN DUMPLING sb dial; <*cartman's* + *dumpling*; cf next.

1958 DeC Port /kyaat-man-dompling/ a very large round boiled dumpling.

CARTMAN'S BIBLE sb dial joc.

1. A BAMMY.

1940 HPJ, Cartman's Bible (i.e. bammie).

2. A substantial biscuit or cake made with coconut: the cartman 'swears by it'.

1952 FGC StE.

CARTMAN'S CHEESE sb dial joc. Salt-fish.

1940 HPJ, Cartman's cheese (i.e. saltfish).

CARTMAN'S HYMN-BOOK sb dial joc. A BULLA cake.

1940 HPJ, Cartman's hymn-book (i.e. buller).

CART-WHEEL sb dial; cf DRAY-WHEEL. *BL*

1958 DeC StT, etc. /kyaat wiil/ a large dumpling.

CASARA sb dial; <CASSADA; a spelling which recognizes flapped *r* for *d*. *BL*

1868 Russell 5, Bra-ra, Bredda..Casara, Cassava.

CASAVA sb; *OED* (s.v. *cassava*) *casava* 8–9 (i.e. 1800's to 1900's). An early spelling of *cassava*.

1657 Continuation 50, There being not much Casava in the Country.

CASHAW /kásha, kyásha/ sb; presumably <*acacia*, but cf Akan *kasɛ́*, thorn.

1. The shrub or small tree *Prosopis juliflora* (and similar species); it is extremely prickly and is used chiefly for fence posts.

1774 Long 838, Smooth Acacia, or Cashaw..It is esteemed a good timber wood, and used for building small craft, and wharf piles, on account of its being offensive to the worm, tough, and lasting. 1811 Titford 106, Acacia or Cashaw, Mimosa Tortuosa..A troublesome, prickly shrub, in the low lands of Jamaica, and almost impossible to eradicate. It continues green in the driest weather. 1839 Hill 29, The Prosopis Juliflora of De Candolle (the common Cashaw of the southern plains of this island) is a familiar instance of extreme durability and rapid maturity of growth in a tree that is not deciduous. 1920 Fawcett 128. 1952 FGC StAnd, StAnn /kyásha/ use for live fence; StE, Cashaw, called 'compound tree'; StM /kásha/ has heart like logwood; burn for charcoal; StT /kásha/ very prickly, same as puss-claw; Tre /kásha máka/ grow thick; macka turn back—cow can't go through it.

2. In folk use, generalized to refer to other prickly shrubs.

1943 *GL* Clar, Casha, prickles.

CASHAW GRUNT sb dial; from the mottled brown markings on its back, resembling CASHAW wood. A variety of GRUNT; it has yellow stripes between grey scales, and does not grow as large as other grunts.

1952 FGC StC, StE /kásha grónt/.

CASHEW /káshu, kýashu, kúshu/ sb, also attrib; for forms see quots; <Fr *acajou* <Pg *acaju* <Tupí *acajú*; *OED* 1703→.

1. The tree *Anacardium occidentale*, its fruit (see CASHEW APPLE), and its nut. *BA BL G N T*

p 1660 Ms Egerton 2395 fol 489, Supotillia, advocates, Cashues, prickell peares. 1662 Stubbe 137, Nor do the fruits of Jamaica Cushu equal the feeding of the tree of Life. 1671 Ogilby 339, Cashuds, Custud-Apples..Pine-Apple. 1679 Trapham 59, Citrons, Pomegranates, Cushewes, Grapes. 1696 Sloane 188, The Cashew or Acaju Tree. 1774 Long III 725, Cashew, or Cashou Tree. 1790 Moreton 22, *Samuel*—for his sores, to bathe them in the decoction of limes and cushue leaves. 1894 Spinner 82, Cachews. 1941 Swabey 17, Cashew. 1943 *GL* Clar, Cooshu, cashew.

2. Any of several children's games in which cashew nuts in their shells are used much as marbles would be. *BL*

c 1915 FGC StAnd, 'Let's play kushu'. 1948 U.Newton IV 35, At Bartons and at Four Paths, the popular cashew games were 'knock-and-go-along', 'standing', 'Chink-up' and 'back-on-the-hand'. At Chapelton we bigger ones did not play those childish games. We played 'bank'.

CASHEW APPLE sb; <CASHEW + *apple*. The 'fruit' of the CASHEW tree (actually a fleshy stem) below which the nut (the true fruit) grows.

1740 Importance 32–3, The Cashew Apple and Nuts grow upon trees about the size of Dwarf Apple-Trees in England..The Nut appears before the Apple, which is red or yellowish; it is a very juicy Fruit, and eats very tough; they roast them to put them into Punch; and when stew'd or bak'd they eat like Marmalade..Some put the Apple into Rum, which they esteem the better for it. 1952 FGC Port /kushu apl/ has bottle-neck.

CASHEW BIRD sb; *OED* 1852 only, for a different bird; cf also *OED curassow*. Another name for the ORANGE BIRD (*Spindalis nigricephala*).

1847 Gosse 231, Cashew bird = orange bird. 1936 Bond 370, Jamaican Spindalis..Cashew Bird.

CASHEW GUM sb. The gum that exudes from the CASHEW tree.

1740 Importance 44, The *Cashew-Gum*, for the Stone and Gravel is reported to be a certain Cure.

CASHOU, CASHU, CASHUD, CASHUE see CASHEW.

CASOM see THROW SARCASM.

CASSADA /kasáda, kisáda/ sb; 1661 cassauder cassawder, 1740→ cassada; *OED* a 1642→, but some forms found in Jamaica (see quots) are lacking. *BL G N*

1. Cassava. The form 'cassada' was once prevalent generally, and still is so in the folk speech. *BA*

1661 Hickeringill 16, Plantanes, Cassauder, Sugar Canes, &c. 1740 Importance 34–5, Cassada, of which there is three sorts, first the sweet they eat the Root roasted; secondly, the bitter Cassada, the juice of which is Poison..the third sort is the wild Cassada. 1820 Sheldon 388, The Caribs had another sort of manioc among them which has not any poisonous or offensive quality. In Jamaica it is called cassada. 1943 *GL* StE, Kisada, cassava. 1952 FGC StAnd, StAnn, CtC, StJ /kasáda/; StE /kisáda/.

2. WILD CASSADA, so called by abbr.

CASSADA BALLS sb dial. = BALLS.

1959 DeC Han /kasada baalz/ moist cassava from which the juice has been pressed, formed into balls to be dried and later used.

CASSADA BREAD sb dial. *BL G N*

1707 Sloane xxix, see quot under PERINO. 1954 LeP StE, Kissada Bread—cake made from cassava flour..very thin and often dried in the sun to make it hard and crisp.

CASSADA HALYARD sb dial; the second element is uncert, but such metaphorical nick-names for foodstuffs are common.

1959 DeC West /kasada haliad/ a lump of bitter cassava boiled in water and eaten as food.

CASSADA HEAD, CASSAVA HEAD sb dial; cf *OED head sb* 9, 10. Flour made from cassava root that has been grated, squeezed, and dried.

1954 LeP Port, Kasaada ed; StE, Kissada head; StT, Kassaada head. 1958 DeC StAnd, Cassava head, = kwa-kwa flour, COUS-COUS.

CASSADA JOHNNY-CAKE sb dial.

1954 LeP StAnn, Cassada johnny cake, dumpling made from cassava flour.

CASSADA LUMP sb dial. See LUMP.

1958 DeC StE /kasada-lomp/—cassada head. [A lump of cassava put into soup.]

CASSADA MARBLE sb dial; the name alludes to the marble-like seed. The WILD CASSADA.

1927 Beckwith 14, Cassada-marble (Wild cassada)..A speedy cure for constipation is to cut it up, boil, and drink as tea. 1954 *WIMJ* 30, *Jatropha gossypifolia*.. Wild Cassada; Bellyache Bush; Cassada Marble.

CASSADA PONE sb dial. *BL G T*

1954 LeP Man, Kisada pone, cake of cassava flour.

CASSADA RIDER sb dial; <CASSADA + RIDER. GOAT-HOOF WIS.

1952 FGC StAnd, Cassada rider—goat-hoof wis.

CASSADA TRASH sb dial. = CASSAVA HEAD.

1958 DeC Port.

CASSADA WOOD sb bot; evid from resemblance to the wood of WILD CASSADA.

1926 Fawcett 38–9, see MUTTON WOOD.

CASSADA YAM sb obs? A variety of the NEGRO YAM with a smooth skin.

1814 Lunan II 308, see NEGRO YAM.

[**CASSAREEP** sb now uncom; 1855 casserip, 1873→ cassareep; cf *OED* 1832→. 'The inspissated juice of the cassava, which..forms the basis of the West Indian pepper-pot' (*OED*). See quot 1959. *BA G*

1855 *Trans Ja Soc Arts* II 41, I have never been able to get Casserip. 1873 Rampini 64, For here [in Chapelton], was I not introduced to 'pepper-pot' and mountain mullet? Not the Demerara pepper-pot with its evil-smelling and still more evil-tasting Cassareep sauce.. but a rich succulent potage.. *Ibid* 91, Cassava..from whose poisonous root is extracted the well-known cassareep, the foundation of almost all our sauces. 1913 Harris 28, Cassareep is the juice of bitter cassava root. 1959 DeC StJ /kasariip/ a dish made by taking the poisonous cassava water which is wrung or pressed out, boiling it down until it is thick and black. Although once common in Montego Bay, now people are generally afraid to eat it for fear of the poison. Apparently, however, no-one ever suffered any ill effects.]

CASSAUDER see CASSADA.

CASSAVA BAG sb dial.

1958 DeC Tre /kasava-bag/ a thatch or crocus bag used for pressing cassava.

CASSAVA LACE CAKE sb. A very thin wafer made of cassava meal; toasted, buttered, folded in two, and served for tea.

c 1915 FGC StAnd, Common. [Still so 1959.]

CASSAWDER see CASSADA.

CASSIA-STICK TREE sb bot; from the resemblance of the bean to a stick. *OED* 1756 only. The *Cassia fistula*.

1756 Browne 223–4, Cassia 1..The Cassia-stick Tree. 1774 Long 730. 1864 Grisebach 782. 1920 Fawcett 102.

[**CASSIE FLOWER** sb; evid <*acacia*; cf ACACEE.

1920 Fawcett 139, *Acacia Farnesiana*..Cassie Flower.. The distilled flowers yield a delicious perfume.]

CAST sb dial; <*cast* (*OED sb* 5b), prob with analogy to *cast-net*, a common word in Jamaica.

1943 *GL* Kgn, Cast, lasso to catch a horse. *BL*

CAST /kyaas/ vb dial; cf *OED cast v* †56. Of an eye: to look obliquely; cf CAST-EYE. *BA G*

1943 *GL* Clar, Keas, to look indirectly.

CASTE sb; cf *OED* 1 b: only quot 1760; cf also current US use, perh abbr of *half-caste*—e.g. Nebraska. A person of mixed blood.

1774 Long II 28, Free Blacks and Casts, make up the greatest part.

CASTEE sb obs; <CASTE sb, +-*ee*, on the analogy of *mustee*. A quadroon, or person of one-eighth negro and seven-eighths white blood. See quot. Cf Sp *castiço* (Santamaría).

1740 Importance 16, There are also Mulattoes and Mustees; the first are from a Negroe and white Man; the other is from the second Generation; and the third are called Castees; several of these are free.

CAST-EYE sb; cf *OED cast sb* 33, 'Cast of the eye, a slight squint', and *cast v* 7. An eye that looks obliquely or does not focus properly; a cock-eye. *BL G*

1952 FGC Han, StAnd, StAnn, StM.

CAST-NET DRUMMER sb dial. A type of DRUMMER that is often caught with a cast-net.

1952 FGC StE /kyaasnet droma/.

CASTOR-OIL NUT sb obs. *BL*

1801 Dancer 359, Castor-Oil Nut (Ricinus am[ericanus]).

CAT sb[1] and vb; *OED sb* 8 →1846, *v* 3 →1865. A switch made from branches of the tamarind tree. See quot. *G*

1933 McKay 316, The tamarind switch or its equivalent, used for flogging prisoners in Jamaica: cat is the abbreviation of cat-o'-nine-tails and is employed as noun and verb.

CAT sb[2] chiefly dial; for *cats*. Rubber-soled canvas shoes; more often called PUSS BOOTS.

1943 *GL* StAnd, Cat, cheap canvas shoes.

CATATIC see *kata-tik*.

CATAWIA see *katawaia*.

CATCH /kech/ vb dial; this pronunciation is also common in Engl dial and colloq speech generally.

1. In the language of OBEAH: to capture a SHADOW, either to enthrall it or to liberate one enthralled: cf also SHADOW-CATCHING; also, to find a lost living person, treating him as if dead —see quot 1895.

1826 Barclay 191, When him set obeah for summary (somebody), him catch dem shadow and dem go dead. 1895 Banbury 30, Delay is incurred in looking out an obeah or mial man to '*catch*' the child, believing that it could not be found without such aid, being hidden by the duppies.

2. To take, to have (usually something involving action). *BL G*

1957 JN StE, Me a go ketch a daance, hey de radio a play, *I'm going to have a dance, since the radio is playing.*

3. To break into action, as, quarrelling, fighting. (Cf *OED v* 44, to catch fire.) *BL G*

1907 Jekyll 270, 'Me no min dé a concert the night When Martha an' Pompey catch a fight'..People are always said to 'catch fight' when they come to blows. 1950 Pioneer 34, Dog run dung pon Puss an de two a dem ketch a fight, *Dog ran down upon Puss, and the two of them began fighting.* 1955 LeP StE (Accom) /di bwai went tu skuul di neks die. wen im go dem kech di kwaril agen/.

4. Causative, of fire: to cause to catch (*OED v* 14b), to kindle and cause to spread or increase. Cf CATCH UP vb phr 3. *BA BL G T*

1956 Mc StE (Accom) /wen diiz (kien trash) drai, wi tek i an kyech faia ona de/ *When these (cane trash) are dry, we use them to kindle a fire under there.*

5. To get (something unpleasant); cf *OED v* 30. *BA BL G*

1942 Bennett 47, Him sey him was gwine to paradise, An' lickle mose him ketch jail.

6. Passively: to be caught. *BL G T*

1952 FGC West, Shrimps hardly ketch round this end, *Very few shrimps are caught in this part of the island.*

7. Absolutely: to arrive at a place (specified or understood).

1877 Murray *Tom Kittle* 22, Cho! him put on de pur [spurs] when him most catch, maam. 1942 Bennett 42, Him mighta Dead before me ketch, *He might die* (or *be dead*) *before I arrive.* 1950 Pioneer 52, Tengad we ketch home safe [*Thank God we got home safely*]. 1957 JN Tre, A wander ef the bus ketch a Lorrimers aready.

8. To arrive at or attain a point in time, a stage of development, a condition, or the like.

1952 FGC Tre, When syrup doesn' catch to sugar yet—don' turn sugar—is molasses. 1956 EP [A woman, on hearing that a baby was two months old:] /shi kech dat aredi?/ *She's as old as that already?* 1956 Mc Man /i kyechin shieki/ *It is becoming shaky. Ibid* /im kech im fried; mi kech mi fried/ *He became frightened* (*and began to act cautiously*); *I became frightened*, etc.

CATCH-ME-TIME sb dial; for *catch my time*. See quot.

1924 Roberts 246, The flutist played various tunes known to the people as *sha-shas*..catch-me-times, mentos, reels, lanciers, two-steps, and others. Many of these dance tunes are presumably taken from Scottish airs or from old English dance music.

CATCH-UP /kéchop/ sb dial.

1. A light 'between-times' meal; a snack.

1943 *GL* StJ, Ketch up, a light meal. 1958 DeC StT, etc.

2. Flour, grated coco, or the like, added to a mixture (a cookery recipe) to bind it together.

1958 DeC StC.

CATCH UP /kéchòp, kyáchòp/ vb phr dial; cf *OED catch v* 53. *BA*

A. trans: 1. To gather and capture. *G*

c 1915 FGC StAnd [Song:] Waterman Trinity very good man, Ketch up him hen an' put dem in pen. [Cf 1922 Beckwith 13.]

2. To tie up hurriedly or loosely. *G*

1942 Bennett 20, Me ketch up me head an' goh look 'bout har.

3. To kindle (a fire); cf CATCH 4. *G*

1952 FGC StM /kyách op di fáia/.

4. To support, sustain; cf CATCH-UP sb.

1942 Bennett 48, Is 'ow me da go ketch up me bady Ef me keahn get milk fe buy!

B. intr: 1. To germinate; cf *DA catch* v 1. *G*

1956 JN Clar, I can get orange seeds to plant, and it grow. When you water it, it ketch up quick.

CATCH UP WITH vb phr dial; cf *DA catch* v 5. To find out about or to understand the purpose or action of (someone); cf US *catch on.*

1956 JN StAnd, A catch up wid yu—yu tekin down me notes. I talk to dis teacher an you write down what I say—tink a don' know, no? *BL G*

CAT-CLAW see CAT'S-CLAW.

CATERPILLARS sb obs. A former name for *Amarantus viridis* (or other species), from the appearance of the flowering heads. Cf CALALU, quot 1. [Also in British Guiana—see 1927 Anderson-Cundall 26.]

1696 Sloane 49, Culilu, or Caterpillars. 1707 Sloane 143, Caterpillars or Culilu.

CAT-NAIL sb arch or obs; cf CAT'S-CLAW 3.

1814 Lunan II 245, see SUSUMBA.

CAT-O'-NINE adj dial; <*cat-o'-nine-tails*, whip. Severe, punishing. *BA G T*

1952 FGC Han [Song:] Disya yier no tan laka laas yier gaan—a kyatanain yier. [*This year is not like last year—it's a cat-o'-nine year.*]

CATRAO sb obs; etym unknown. An unidentified fruit.

1657 Continuation 46, Catrao, a very sweet luscious fruit, green of colour, and much like a Mulberry in shape and bignesse.

CAT'S-CLAW sb bot obs; transl <*unguis cati*, the species name, or Sp *uña de gato* for the same or similar plants; *ODS* 1898→.

1. *Pithecellobium unguis-cati*; now more often called BREAD-AND-CHEESE. (Probably also in early use applied to FINGRIGO and other plants with recurved prickles.)

1801 Dancer 359, Nephritic Wood, Cats-Claw (*Mimosa, unguis cati*). 1814 Lunan I 375, If the salve is intended to dry up a sore, the juice of the cats-claw may be added. 1837 MacFadyen 306–7 (see quot s.v. NEPHRITIC TREE). 1943 *NHN* I II 20 (cf. BERMUDA LOGWOOD).

2. *Galactia parvifolia*, from the claw-like upturned keel of the flower. Obs.

1756 Browne 294, Dolichos 6..Cats-Claws. This little plant is frequent about *Old-harbour*. 1814 Lunan I 166, Cat-Claws. Dolichos..Filiformis. (Cites Browne.)

3. ? = CAT-NAIL.

1952 FGC StAnn, Cat's claw or Cat-claw, similar to susumba but has more prickles; the fruit is like a tiny garden-egg.

CATTA see COTTA.

CATTER FOOT see *kyata fut*.

CATTLE-MAN sb; cf *OED* 1878→ (*DAE, DA* 1864→ in a different sense). A man employed to tend cattle.

1790 Beckford II 65, The cattle-men and the mule-boys, the trash-carriers, the feeders, and the watchmen who attend the pens, should all be allowed warm clothing in crop-time.

CATTLE-MILL sb obs; *DA* only 1848. 'A mill operated by animal power.'

1718 *Courant* 5 Aug 3/2, To be Sold, a Sett of Coppers and a Sett of Mill-work for a Cattle-Mill.

CATTLE-PEN sb; cf *OED* 1837→.

1790 Beckford I 198 [Those] who are obliged to watch the cattle-pens upon the summits of the hills at night.

CATWOOD sb dial. A small tree with whitish wood (unidentified).

1952 FGC StAnn.

CAUCHIE see *kaachi*.

CAUDRY phr dial rare; etym unknown: the first element may be <*care*.

1943 *GL* Man, Caudry, I don't care.

CAUKIE sb dial; prob var of *gaaki*.

1954 LeP StE, Caukie, somebody who is credulous.

CAUSEN conj dial; /káazn, káan/ aphetic form of BECAUSEN, often further reduced. Because.

1912 McK *Songs* 14, We caan' lie down..Causen we job must finish soon an' good. 1943 *GL* StAnd, Causen, because. 1950 Pioneer 64, Cow ah fan him tail, causen de gingy fly dem ah bodder him. 1956 Mc StAnd /yu shuda en mek mi nuo ma, kaan mi da en waan sintin fi memba yu/ *You should have let me know, Ma'am, because I would have wanted something to remember you by*; Man /wi gí-im niem pátu káan him so hógli/ *We call him 'Patu' because he's so ugly. BA BL*

CAVALLA, CAVALLEE see CAVALLY, HORSE-EYE CAVALLY.

CAVALLY sb; 1820 cavallee, 1873 carvallhy, 1892 covally; cf *OED cavally*, quots 1634→ but not these spellings. *BA N*

CAVALLY JACK /kubáali, kúbàali, kóvàali, kóváli, kóvoli, kubáalo, kobálo/ sb dial; CAVALLY + JACK. *Caranx hippos*, a fish well known around the coasts of Jamaica. *BA*

1952 FGC Port, StAnn, StC, StE, StJ, StM, StT, West.

CAVANA CANE see *kyabana*.

CAVEACH /kobíich/ sb now dial; the most reduced form of Sp *escabeche*, pickled fish; also called ESCOVEITCHED and SCAVEECHED FISH. *OED* 1822 only. *N*

1962 BLB Man /kobíich físh/.

CAVE-HEAD sb dial; cf CAVY.

1954 LeP StAnn, Cave-head, a crafty, cunning person.

CAVE-HEADED adj dial; cf CAVE-HEAD, CAVY.

1952 FGC StM, Cave-headed, wise in spending; cute. 1954 LeP StE, Cave-headed, steady, reliable.

CAVE SWALLOW sb obs. *Petrochelidon fulva*, now called the Cliff Swallow.

1847 Gosse 64, Cave swallow, *Hirundo pœciloma*.

CAVY adj dial; <*cagey*, cf *DA*; also Lat *cave*, beware (English school slang).

1952 FGC Han /kíevi/cagey; won't spend at all.

CAWCOON see CACOON.

CAWOBENA sb obs; < Sp *caobana*, < Carib, archaic name of the *caoba*, Cent Amer, Puerto R. (Malaret). The mahogany or similar trees (*Swietenia* spp). Cf COBY-NANCY.

1657 Continuation 45, Cawobena, a tree of six fathome about, a fine red, excellent good for beds, tables, or building.

CAWVAW sb obs; ? < *kava*; cf *OED*, 1817→.

1707 Sloane lxii, Molossus [molasses] Drink is called *Cawvaw*.

CAY /kái, kíi/ sb; 1683 coi, 1693 1707 1782 key, c1695 1847 kay, 1697 kee, 1707 cayo, 1774 caye. The oldest pronunc, repr Sp *cayo*, was [kai] or [kɔi]; later came [kei] and [ki:]. The spelling favoured on maps is still *cay*. *OED cay* 1707→. An offshore islet, low and sandy, sometimes also rocky, and usually with some vegetation. *BL N*

1683 *Laws of Jamaica* (Map), Sand Coi, Brasilett Coi, Gun Coi, etc. 1693 *Truest & Largest Account*, A multitude of whose Corps floated a great many days after..till at last some were sunk, others dispers'd by the Sea-breeze, some to one place, some to another, upon the Keys to the Leeward of the place. c1695 *Acts & Laws* 96, The Kays lying off Port-Royal. 1697 Nevill's *Journal* 24 May, Two sloops to look for them, one to lye of Poynt Pedro Kees, and the other to lye off Porta Merant Kees. 1707 Sloane lxxxvi, I went from Port-Royal in a Boat to *House Key* and *Gun Key*, or *Cayo*, so called from the Tryal of Guns from the Fort; they shooting thence at a Cask set up here. They were defended by Coral and Astroites Rocks to the South, and were very small Islands, with some few Bushes on them. 1774 Long II 69, Six small cayes, or little sandy islands. 1952 FGC West /kii/.

CAYA see *kaya*.

CAYAN-BUTTER sb obs; 1725 cayen, 1756 cayan, 1794 kyan; cf *OED Cayenne*, and Ja *kayan*. See quots.

1725 Sloane II 378, Salt ground with it [*sc Capsicum* or BIRD PEPPER] makes the universal Indian Sauce, call'd by some Cayenbutter. Mr *Barham* MS. 1756 Browne 177, The pods of this last sort [BIRD PEPPER] dried, and pounded with a sufficient quantity of salt, is the *Cayan pepper* or *butter* of the *West-Indians*. 1794 Barham 30, Commonly called kyan butter.

CAYAN-PEPPER /kayáan, káyan/ sb now dial; cf *OED Cayenne* etym note. The pronunc /káyan/ is illust in *OED* →1796; also, 'The somewhat archaic pronunc. (kəi:an·) survives from the older form'—and is represented in Ja by /kayáan/. A type of Capsicum, as a fruit and as a condiment. *BA*

[1756 Browne 177, see CAYAN-BUTTER]. 1952 FGC StC /káyan pèpa/; StAnn, StJ /kayáan pèpa/ devil pepper, the hottest of all.

CAYE see CAY.

CAYEN-BUTTER see CAYAN-BUTTER.

CAYENNE- see CAYAN-.

CAYO see CAY. *BL*

CEDAR sb dial. An albino negro.

1958 DeC Tre /siida/. Informant says the source is in an old riddle: /chiip cheri bier siida/ [*cheap cherry bears cedar*—the Jamaican cedar having a fruit that resembles a plum but is inedible] the answer to which is an albino Negro.

CEDAR (TREE) sb; cf *OED* this sense 1725→. *Cedrela odorata*, also called JAMAICA CEDAR, WEST-INDIAN CEDAR. *BA BL G*

1655 Eye-Witnesse 18, Of..Cabage, Palmeeto, Ceadar, Mastick..are great plenty [in Santo Domingo]. 1657 Continuation 45, Cedar, the best in all the Indies, usefull for all purposes, as Oake in England. 1696 Sloane 183, Pruno forte affinis arbor maxima, materie rubrâ laxâ odoratâ..*The Cedar tree*. In Jamaicæ Insulæ mediterraneis & montosis sylvis ubique crescit. [Current 1963.]

CEIBA sb bot; < Sp *ceiba*; *OED* 1812→. *BL*

1790 Moreton 40, The ceiba, or silk-cotton tree, out of which canoes are made. 1807 Renny 85, The ceiba or wild cotton-tree..The ceiba, when hollowed out, has been known to furnish a boat.

CEITFUL /siitful/ adj (and sb) dial; aphetic form of *deceitful*. Speaking wrong of, deceiving or distrusting (someone). *BL G*

1900 Murray 15, You is a ceitful, good fe nuttin man. 1925 Beckwith 41 [Prov:] Ceitful fire roast plantain, 'cong-a-so' 'crape it. 1950 Pioneer 20, If yuh ketch anybody dah 'ceitful pon yuh, yuh got right fe teck wey everyting dem got. *Ibid* 21, Lawd a Massi, me noh mean fe ceitful, but is how Peel-head a goh a barba an she no got a 'kench' a hair pon her head. 1954 LeP StAnn, Ceitful, somebody who is always gossiping (adj.); StT, Ciitful, hypocrite, a deceitful person.

CEITFUL vb trans dial; cf CEITFUL adj. To speak ill of; to gossip about. *BL*

1954 LeP StAnn, Wi a ceitful Mary—*We are talking about Mary*.

CELANDINE see *salandain*.

CENTIPEDE, CENTIPEE see *santapii*. *BA G*

CEP conj dial; reduced form of *except*. *G*

1868 Russell 19, Cep (except).

CERASEE /sòrosí, sórosi/ sb; 1740 sourasea, 1794→ cerasee, 1893 sorasee, 1943 serouci surrosy cerosee cirosee; etym unknown—poss < Fr *céracé*, waxy, but in the light of the folk pronunc and quot 1794, an African source seems more likely. (Cf Twi *nsuró*, a climbing vine). *Momordica charantia* and *M. balsamina*; valued in Jamaica as a 'tea-bush' to clear the blood, etc.; also noted for its bitterness: cf OLD-CERASEE. *BL*

1740 Importance 35, The Sourasea, or Ladies-slipper, grows on a small wire, and has a small pale Blossom which bears a yellow Pod, which opens upon its being incloased in one's Hand, and has a Seed like a Melon Seed incloased. 1794 Barham 38, Cerasee and Cucumis is the name that negroes and some others give to a plant growing in great plenty in Jamaica. 1864 Grisebach 782, Cerasee. 1893 Sullivan 114, Cerasee or sorasee. This they boil [*sc* the leaves] as tea. 1943 Bennett 7 [Names of local songs:] Den we have 'Jig Bang' and 'Chichi Bud' An 'Bitta Cirosee'. 1952 FGC Han, StAnn, StE, StM, StT, etc.

CEREMONE vb dial; back-formation from *ceremony*, *ceremonial*, or the like.

1943 *GL* no addr, Serremone, to grieve over.

CEROSEE see CERASEE.

cha, CHA see CHO.

chaa see CHAW.

chaaklit see CHOCOLATE.

CHACCA-CHACCA, CHACKA-CHACKA see CHAKA-CHAKA.

CHACK see CHOCK.

CHACKALADA see CHAKLATA.

CHACKAMPECKLE sb dial rare; poss < CHAKA(-CHAKA) + *and* + *speckled*.

1943 *GL*, Chackampeckle, confusion.

CHACKRA adj dial; cf CHAKA-CHAKA.

1943 *GL* Kgn, Chackra, untidy.

CHACLATTA, CHACLETTA see CHAKLATA.

CHAIN sb; cf *OED chain sb* 9b →1850; *DAE* →1909. A linear measure equal to 66ft, the most common measure used in Jamaica for distances of less than a mile. (Regularly used on Parochial Road signs.)

1921 Franck 418, Information as to distance is given in 'chains' if at all, the customary answer being a non-committal 'not too far, sah'.

CHAIN COTTON sb obs. A variety of cotton in which the seeds come in a bunch as if chained together. See quot 1926.

1793 Edwards II 271, *Kidney Cotton*, so called from the seeds being conglomerated or adhering firmly to each other in the pod..likewise called *Chain* Cotton. 1811 Titford Expl to Plate VIII, Chain cotton, *gossypium*. There are six species. 1854–5 *TJSA* I 60, Chain Cotton, Gossypium Brasiliense. 1926 Fawcett 147, *Gossypium lapideum*..Chain Cotton.

chaini wis see CHINA WITHE.

chak see CHOCK.

CHAKA-CHAKA sb, adj, and adv dial; iterated form of Gẽ *tyáka*, Ewe *tsáka*, to mix, to be mixed. A. sb: Disorder; B. adj: Disorderly, irregular; C. adv: in a disorderly or irregular manner.

1868 Russell 10, *Chaka-chaka*—Disorderly..De boy clothes so chaka-chaka. *Ibid* 20, Adverbs of quality.—..chaka-chaka. 1873 Rampini 127, Him curse him moder for a..'chaka-chaka' (disorderly)..'nana' (old woman). 1943 *GL* no addr, Chacka-chacka, in an irregular manner; StJ, scattered about; Kgn, Chacca-chacca, not done in a proper way; Port, Chaka-chaka, untidyness. 1954 LeP StT, Chakka chakka doti hows, *A dirty, untidy house*. 1958 DeC Port /chaka-chaka/ wet, sloppy, and muddy.

CHAKALADA see next.

CHAKLATA /chàkláta, chòkláta, chàklíta/ sb now dial; 1868 chaklata, 1873 chocolata, 1935 chocolatter, 1943 chaclata, chaclatta, chackalada, chaklitta, choclata, chocklata, chucklatta, 1954 chacletta. <Sp *chocolate*.

Among the country folk of Jamaica, the first solid food taken in the day: usually what was left over or put aside from the day before—bammy, yam, bread, etc. Some combine it with TEA, others take it later; the word therefore applies not only to the food, but to the meal at which it is eaten.

[1679 Trapham 51–2, It must be for health and continuance of strength to eat at least four times in twenty-four hours, *viz.* Chocalata at six in the morn, at Ten dine more sparingly than the English, at four afternoon repeat Chocalata, between seven and eight a plentiful supper.] 1868 Russell 6, Chaklata—A light meal before work or school—Purely African. 1873 Rampini 77, A group of negroes, who were taking their *chocolata* (breakfast) under a tree, after their morning labours in the field. 1943 *GL* Clar, Chackalada, cold overnight, Chac-la-ta, food with tea; Tre, Chaklitta, Breakfast, Chocklata, Toasted overnight food; StC, Chuck-latta, lunch; Clar, Chaclatta, a light dinner. 1947 U.Newton III 24, Then we had our early morning breakfast ('choclata' to be correct), each of us boys getting a whole tin of 'whatever you want'. 1952 FGC StJ /chàkláta/ at 8 a.m.—a little boiled food with tea—same as 'tea'; also StE, StM, Tre, West; StAnn /chòkláta/; StM /chàklíta/. 1954 LeP StE, Chacletta, first meal of the day (7 a.m.).

chaklita, CHAKLITTA see CHAKLATA.

CHALK-KA-LINDOO adj dial rare; etym uncert: *chalk* evid indicates whiteness—*lindoo* perh <Sp *lindo*, pretty.

1943 *GL* Port, Chalk-ka-lindoo, Whiter than snow.

CHALLA /chala/ int dial; <Hindi *chalo*, int, away, begone, come away. *G*

1943 *GL* Clar, Port, StJ, Challa, go quickly; Kgn, Challa, go away—Coolie word. 1955 FGC Man /chala/ 'move off!' (not violent), 'I'm going'.

CHAMBA /chamba/ vb and ppl adj dial; <*Chamba*, a people of N-E Nigeria and Cameroon, who had a very striking method of tattooing or cutting the skin of the face: cf 1793 Edwards II 125, 'Some of the Negroes of the Gold Coast..(the *Chamba* Negroes for instance) appear to me to use the same, or nearly the same, marks as the savages of New Zealand; *viz.* deep incisions on each cheek drawn circularly from the ear to the mouth'. *G*

A. vb: To cut roughly, to disfigure.

1943 *GL* Kgn, Chamba, to cut with a dull tool; StC, Chamba, cut up, disfigure. 1954 LeP Man, Chamba, to cut awkwardly or hack with a dull tool.

B. ppl: Cut up; furrowed.

1942 Bennett 47, De whole a him face chamba up [Gloss:] Cut or disfigured. 1956 Mc Man /sens yu faal doun, yu fies chamba hop/ *Since you fell down, your face is all cut and bruised.*

CHAMBA BEEZER /chámba bíiza/ sb dial; <CHAMBA+*beezer*, an untraced word (perh rel to *baize*?—cf BLUE-BAIZE). The Black-and-White Warbler, its striped appearance making it seem scratched or cut.

1952 FGC Han /chámba bíiza/. 1958 W. Adolphe Roberts, letter, I knew *chamba beezer* in southern Manchester in my boyhood as the name of the black-and-white creeper.

CHAMBA BITTER /chamba/ sb dial; <CHAMBA+*bitter*, sb. =RICE BITTERS.

1952 FGC StT /chámba bíta/. 1955 *WIMJ* 159, *Phyllanthus niruri*..Carry-me-seed; Chamber Bitter.

CHAMBA-CHAMBA /chamba-chamba, chama-chama/ vb dial; iterative <CHAMBA vb. See quots. *G*

1943 *GL* StC, Chamma-chamma, to mince up. 1954 LeP StAnn, Chamba-chamba, to cut awkwardly or hack with a dull tool.

CHAMBER see CHAMBA.

CHAMPONG adj dial; cf CHAMPONG-NANNY. Meaning uncert.

1940 HPJ, Coromanty verse: Champong kotakoo carry mi amba hay! [*Champong cutacoo, carry my amber, hay!*—cf AMBER, CUTACOO.]

CHAMPONG-NANNY sb dial; prob <Twi *Akyéampɔŋ*, a personal name (cf ACCOMPONG) +NANA, grandmother. A rather vague figure, semi-legendary; by folk-etym the first element is now taken to be the word *champion*, hence also a bully, or the match for a bully (properly, a female).

1943 *GL* Kgn, Champung-nanny, the oldest ancestor of the negroes; a bully. Tamponanny, champion. 1955 FGC Man /champong nani/ man or woman likes to fight. Means 'champion'. 1959 Mrs E. B. Hoyes Kgn [A woman challenging a bully:] 'Me a champung nanny!'

CHANGEABLE ROSE sb bot obs; trans of species name *mutabilis*+*rose*. The hibiscus flower frequently described by early travellers as changing colour in the course of the day.

1792 Edwards 12 [Note:] Commonly called the China rose; but improperly: It is the *hibiscus mutabilis*, or changeable rose, of Linnæus. 1814 Lunan I 175, Changeable Rose..large handsome flowers. The single are composed of five petals, which spread open, and are at first white, turn to light flesh colour after they bear the action of the sun for some hours, and contract and close for the night, to be ready for the like changes the ensuing day.

CHANGE BLACK DOG FOR MONKEY vb phr prov. Perh with play on words—see BLACK DOG. To get no good out of an exchange; to be as badly off as before. *BL*

1925 Beckwith 24, see CHANGIE FE CHANGIE. 1959 FGC StE (Black River), To change black dog for monkey.

changga bed sb dial; perh =JAGGAY, but cf JANGA-MANGA. A crude, makeshift bed covered with old, torn bed-mats; a derogatory term.

1956 Mc StE (Accom), The remark /gó we go lài dóng an yu chángga/ is a /bad kos/—a serious insult. See also TEAR-UP (TEAR-UP) quot 1956.

CHANGIE FE CHANGIE phr dial; <*change* +-Y². Proverbial phrase: one thing for another very much the same; an exchange in which one gains little or nothing. *BL*

1910 Anderson-Cundall 35 [Prov:] You gi' monkey fe black darg, a change fe change. 1925 Beckwith 24, Changey fe changey, black daag fe monkey..implying that a change is often for the worse. 'Monkey' is often used as the symbol for the colored man and 'black dog' for the full black. 1940 HPJ, Changie fe changie, black dawg fe monkey.

chapaalin /chapáalin/ sb dial; by metathesis (via */trapáalin/) <*tarpaulin*.

1956 Mc Man /chapáalin, chrapáalin/ tarpaulin.

chaplen sb dial; <*Chaplin* (for Charlie Chaplin). *G*

1956 Mc Man /chaplen/ a moustache.

chapmachik, chapnachik sb dial; a variant or parallel form of CHICK-MAN-CHICK, TAP-NA-CHICK, etc. *BL*

1952 FGC StAnn /chapna-chik/—Hopping Dick. 1956 Jeffrey-Smith 153, Birds to be seen at Runaway Bay and Vicinity..Hopping Dick, 'Chop-ma-chick' *Turdus aurantius.*

CHAPUNKO sb and adj dial; etym unknown: some influence from *punk* (cf *DA* 5b) is possible.

1943 *GL* Port, StM, Chapunko, one who won't try to look refined; worthless.

CHARKO sb; perh erron for GUACO?

1940 HPJ, A white-flowered climbing plant.

CHARLES PRICE RAT sb; 1774→ Charles-Price (rat), 1828 Sir Charles Price, 1834 1858 Sir Charles Price's Rat, 1851 Price's Rat, 1952 Charlie Price Rat, 1952 Charl Price; see quots.

A rat (the CANE-PIECE RAT) mistakenly believed to have been introduced to Jamaica by Sir Charles Price (1708–72), a planter and Speaker of the Assembly, in order to combat cane rats. See quots 1774, 1933. *BL*

1774 Long 899, The largest is commonly called the Charles-price rat, and obtained its name from having been first observed here about the time when the late Sir Charles Price, Baronet, returned hither from Europe ..They are no other than the water-rat of Europe.. amphibious, and found in holes on the banks of rivers, and the sides of ponds. 1828 Marly 53, The negroes.. are very partial to rats, and have denominated them Sir Charles Price, thereby commemorating an event, that..I do not at present recollect to have seen..observed in any of the authors who have written respecting this island..This Sir Charles Price..to get rid of the mice and small rats which then pestered the colonists..sent to the Mosquito shore, and had a number of the large ones imported. 1836 Lewis (1845) 89, Sir Charles Price's rats, as they are called. 1933 Cundall in *Gleaner* 9 Mar, A particular species of rat—the largest in the island—known as the 'cane-piece rat' or the 'Charles Price rat' on the assumption that it was introduced into Jamaica by him; but Richard Hill, who investigated the matter for Gosse and obtained the family tradition on the subject from George Price, of Worthy Park, a great grandson of Sir Charles Price, came to the conclusion that the animal, which Price introduced from South America and in the eyes of the negroes had strong rat characteristics was no rat. Several were let loose at the Decoy, and at Worthy Park, but they did not survive. They may possibly have been a species of opossum. 1935 HPJ, Charles Price, a large rat with reddish streaks on the back, eaten by blacks at least till 1920. 1952 FGC StAnd /cháal práis/; StT, Charlie Price rat.

CHARLEY DUMPLING sb dial. =SPINNER.

1958 DeC StAnd /chaali dompling/.

CHARLEY SWEET-POTATO sb dial.

1952 FGC StE /cháali/ sweet potato—named for a man.

CHARLIE PRICE, CHARL PRICE see CHARLES PRICE RAT. *BL*

CHAT sb+v dial; cf *OED chat sb*[1] †1 'Chatter; idle or frivolous talk, prating, prattle, small talk' →1768. Still current in Jamaica. Idle talk; chatter; gossip. (Verb and noun are sometimes indistinguishable.) *BA BL G T*

1927 Stafford 41, You too lub chat, *You're too fond of idle talk* (or *of talking idly*). 1942 Bennett 34, Yuh kean gwahn chat, but doan fegat yuh gwine reap wat yuh sew.

CHAT-CHAT vb dial; iterative <CHAT. To gossip continually. *G*

1958 DeC Port (Moore Town) /mis lashi/ a man who /chat-chat/ all the time; a male gossip.

CHATTERING-CROW sb obs. The GABBLING-CROW.

1725 Sloane 298, *Cornix nigra garrula..A Chatering Crow,* or, *a Cacao Walke.*

CHATTY-CHATTY sb dial; iterative <*chatty.*

1954 LeP StT, Chatti-chatti, somebody who is always gossiping. *G*

CHAW sb dial; cf *OED chaw sb*[2] 'An act of chewing; also, that which is chewed..' →1833. Something to eat; food; a meal; cf MORNING-CHAW. *BA*

1940 HPJ (Song) For him chaw will be right Mango-time. 1943 *GL* StC, Chaw, something to eat. 1958 DeC Port /chaa/ a between-meals snack.

CHAWSTICK sb now dial; <*chaw* sb or vb +*stick* sb. CHEWSTICK, *Gouania lupuloides*: see quots.

1756 Browne 172–3, The Chaw-stick..is generally kept to rub and clean the teeth..[it] is frequently used to ferment, and give a flavour to..cool drinks. 1774 Long II 271, The chaw-stick..A species of rhamnus. It is of a bitter taste..It is cut into small junks, of three or four inches in length; one extremity of which, being first soaked a little while in warm water, is soon formed into a soft brush by chawing; from whence it derives its popular name. 1811 Titford 67, Chawstick is a species of Banisteria. 1954 *WIMJ* 30, *Gouania lupuloides..*Chew or Chaw Stick.

CHEATING sb dial; <*cheat*; cf *OED sb*[1], 8 (no quots). A card game—evid *cheat. G*

1949 U.Newton V 29, Card games: All Foes. Cheating, Strip Me.

CHECK sb; cf *OED sb*[2], *ODS* 3, *DAE* (in somewhat different senses). Small spaces left undug between cane holes.

1823 Roughley 269, The negroes, when they are digging the piece, observing where to leave the checks, or small undug spaces.

CHECK-CHECK sb dial; iterative of *check* sb or adj; cf CHECKY-CHECKY. A local name for the bird *Vireo modestus,* alluding to the chequered effect of the plumage.

1949 *NHN* IV 27, Check-check or Little Furuh.

CHECK HOLE sb; <CHECK+*hole.* A cane-hole, one of a series with undug spaces between; see quot.

1823 Roughley 268, It would be adviseable, then, where the land is rather steep, to bind it here and there, by digging check, or chequered holes.

CHECKS sb dial; prob a form of CHENKS. A small piece. (Like *scraps,* etc., this is the singular form.)

1943 *GL* Clar, Checks, scraps.

CHECKY-CHECKY /cheki-cheki/ adj dial; iteration of *checky.* Checked, chequered. *G*

1952 FGC Man, The diver is a checky-checky bird.

CHEENI, CHEENIE see next.

CHEENY, CHEENY-WEENY /chiini/ adj. and sb dial; prob <*teeny* (*OED a*[2]), palatalized and affricated. *BL T*

1943 *GL* Clar, Cheeny, a small bit; StJ, Cheeni, small, tiny; also StE; Clar, Cheenie-weenie, a very tiny bit. 1954 LeP StE, Cheenie, very small, tiny, adj.

CHEESE-BERRY sb. *Rubus ellipticus,* a bush and its fruit growing wild in the Blue Mts; named from its yellow berries. (Introduced into Jamaica in 1894.)

1952 FGC StAnd; also 1958.

CHEESE MANGO sb dial. A variety of mango that has the smell and taste of cheese.

1952 FGC StM.

CHEESE-PAN sb dial; < *cheese* + PAN. A tin in which cheese was imported, used as a vessel holding from 2 to 3 quarts.

1956 JN StAnn [What are you going to put the water in?], A wan cheese pan.

CHEESE PINE sb dial; < *cheese* + PINE. A variety of pineapple, also called (American) SUGAR PINE.

1952 FGC Port, StT, Tre.

CHEESY TOES sb dial. A wild plant whose pods are thought to resemble toes.

1954 *WIMJ* 31, *Stylosanthes hamata*..Donkey Weed; Lady's Fingers; Cheesy Toes; Pencil Flower.

chekre sb and adj dial; etym unknown, but cf CHAKA-CHAKA.

A. sb: A worn and broken basket.

1955 FGC Man /chekre/ a basket, much worn and broken up.

B. adj: Shabby; in poor condition.

1943 *GL* StJ, Checkrey, shabby or il-looking.

CHEMIST BILL /kémis bíl/ sb dial; for *chemist's* + BILL. Cf quot 1873 below, and DOCTOR-SHOP KNIFE.

1. A cutlass sharpened on both sides.

2. A deceitful person, one who will turn against or betray one.

[1873 Rampini 87, A deceitful, double-faced man is said to resemble 'an apothecary's knife', which cuts both ways.] 1958 DeC /kemis bil/ 1. A cutlass sharp on both sides. Informant claims that /kemis/ is the name of the firm that makes it, but I have never seen one. 2. Metaphorically, a traitor, a turncoat. [Cf SPANISH MACHETE.]

CHENK(S) sb dial; perh < *chunk* + the *-s* added by over-correction to many nouns. A piece or part of something, usually small. Cf. next.

1942 Bennett 4, Me stop an ax har wats de time..De pickney tun-roun' tell me say Is lickle chenks to eight. 1943 *GL* Kgn, Chenks, a very small piece of anything. 1950 Pioneer 41, Anancy nyam off everyting an nevah gi Cockroach a 'chenks'. 1954 LeP StE, Chenk, something little, of no importance.

cheps sb dial; prob < CHECKS, with substitution of *p* for *k* as in several other words; possibly also influenced by *chips*.

1956 Mc Man /jos a likl chiini cheps mam/ *Just a little tiny bit, ma'am.*

CHEQUERED GRAPE TREE sb bot; from the markings on the fruit—see quot. The tree *Coccoloba venosa*; cf CHIGERY GRAPE TREE.

1754 Browne 210, Coccolobis 3..uvis minoribus punctatis..The chequered Grape-Tree. 1914 Fawcett 120, *C. venosa*..Chequered Grape Tree.

cheramiina see CHEREMILA.

CHEREEZE sb bot obs; perh < *cherry* under the infl of Fr *cerise*, or an attempt to render the folk form of *cherries* (the grammatical singular).

1756 Browne 230, Malpighia 3..The *Chereeze*, or *Barbadoes* Cherry Tree. This shrub has been but lately introduced to..*Jamaica*..The fruit is of the same size and make with our common *English* cherries.

CHEREMILA /chèrimíil, chèremíila, chèrimíilya, chèrimílyan, chèrimíinya, chèremíina/ sb; for variant spp see quots; < Pg *cheramela*, the genus *Averrhoa* (< Malay *chĕrmai*) partly altered by folk-etym (*cherry-*, *-million*). (There is no connection with CHERIMOYA.)

1. Esp in western parishes: The tree *Phyllanthus distichus* (or *P. acidus*) and its fruit; also called JIMBLING, *baaj*, etc.

1913 Harris 10 (See quot s.v. JIMBLING). 1940 HPJ, Cheri-malia, A country name for the jimbolin. 1952 FGC StM, West /chèrimíilya/; StJ /chèrimíinya/. 1959 DeC Han /cherimiil, cherimiila, cherimiilia/; West /cheramiina/ the small round barge fruit. 1959 O. P. Cousins Kgn, Cherry-Melia or Jimbelin..The shape is very much like a cherry but..more segmented and flattened at the stem..The name cherry-million is sometimes used which seems to suggest the profuse number of fruits clustering on the stem.

2. See quot.

1959 M. Jeffrey-Smith letter, *Cherrymelia* is a name I have heard applied to the naseberry, though this is far from general.

CHERI-MALIA, cherimiil(a), cherimiilya, cherimilyan, cherimiinya see prec.

CHERIMOYA /chérimáia, jérimáia/ sb; < Amer Sp *chirimoya, chirimoyo*, < Quichua *chirimuyu*; the first part has been assimilated to *cherry* by folk-etym. The fruit *Annona cherimolia.*

1794 Broughton 19, Annona Cherimoya [Introduced] 1786. 1893 Sullivan 78, Cherrymoyer. 1952 FGC StAnn, StT /chérimáia/; 1955 StAnd /jérimáia/.

CHERRY BULLET sb dial. The RED BULLET (TREE), from the colour of the wood.

1941 Swabey 15, Cherry Bullet [also called] Bulletwood etc.—see BULLY (TREE). 1952 FGC StAnn, StC, StE, Tre.

CHERRY-CHEEK MANGO sb dial. A variety of mango; descriptive.

1952 FGC Port, Cherry-cheek mango—can eat green.

CHERRY-MELIA, CHERRY-MILLION see CHEREMILA.

CHERRY-PEPPER sb dial; *OED* 1832 only. A variety of capsicum; from its shape and colour.

1774 Long III 857 [Kinds of peppers] Cherry pepper. 1952 FGC StM, Cherry-pepper, 'round like gennep'.

CHERRY RIPE adj phr; < *ripe as a cherry*. The stage of ripening at which coffee berries are harvested.

1835 Senior 52, As soon as the berries are what is called '*cherry ripe*', or a little before crop commences, the negroes gather them in baskets. 1956 Mc StE (Accom) /yu kyan sel it cheri raip/.

CHEWSTICK sb; modernized form of CHAWSTICK. *N*

1835 Madden II 49, A species of rhamnus, which has got the name of chewstick, from the use to which it is converted by the Creoles and coloured people. 1933 McKay gloss, Chewstick, the stem of an acid climbing plant with which the peasants clean their teeth; also used to flavor ginger beer. 1935 HPJ, Chewstick, a 'wiss'..much used for cleaning teeth. 1956 Mc Man /chuu stik/.

CHEW-WATER /chuwáata/ sb dial. *G*

1. Water left over from cooking food, usually fed to the pig.

1956 Mc Man /chuwáata/.

2. A derisive name for thin soup.

1943 *GL* Kgn, Chuwater, inferior soup.

CHICANEY /chikíeni/ sb and adj dial; prob < *chicane* + *-y*, familiarizing suffix, or perh reduced < *chicanery*.

A. sb: Trickery; a trick.

1935 HPJ, Chicaney: (*Ch* is hard)..When you play a person a nasty trick. 1943 *GL* Port, Chickeeny, unfair tricks.

B. adj: Tricky.

1912 McKay *Ballads* gloss, Chicaney, tricky.

CHICHI /chichi/ sb dial; prob from some African form indicating small size, such as Ewe *tyítyi*, to be close or tight like meshes, or *títi*, small, tiny. Cf *tichi*.

1. The dry-wood termite *Cryptotermes brevis*.

1943 *GL* West, Chi Chi, a kind of termites; also Man, Port, Tre, West. 1952 FGC Han /chichi/—white thing resembling caterpillar; tough, horny beak; destroys furniture and softer-natured wood. Also StAnd, West.

2. The fæcal pellets or 'dust' of this termite; also called chichi dust.

1952 FGC StAnd; also Man.

chichibu see *kitibu*.

CHI-CHI BUD /chichi bod, -bord/ sb dial; <*chi-chi* (imitative of sounds made by birds) +*bird*. (Possibly infl by *chick*.) A singing bird or singing birds.

1953 Murray 24 [Song:] A Chi-Chi Bud—oh! Some a dem a halla, some a bawl.

CHI-CHI BUS /chichi bos/ sb dial; *chi-chi* (imitative of the hiss of air) +*bus*. A modern passenger bus with hissing pneumatic doors.

1950 Pioneer 53, Me wi haffe stop car-drivin An go sponge pon chi-chi bus! 1956 JN, see BUNGO 3.

CHICHI-CROW sb dial rare; cf etym of CHICHI, and TICHICROW.

1943 *GL* no addr, Chichi-crow, a small or undersized person; StAnd, Chi-chi-cro, an undersized person, a pygmy.

CHICHI-MUS sb dial; cf etym of CHICHI, and MUS-MUS. A nickname for the little finger—apparently meaning 'little mouse'.

1943 *GL* StAnd, Chi-chi-mus, the little finger.

CHICK-CHICK sb dial; reduplication of *chick*. A small chicken or baby chick. *BA G*

1956 JN Man, Me see the chicken dem inna the garden—chick-chick dem won't come—the mother is calling them also.

CHICKEN BITTERS sb dial. =CHICKEN WEED.

CHICKEN NET sb dial; 'net' here prob for 'nut'—cf *nit*.

1954 *WIMJ* 30, *Miconia laevigata*..Chicken Net; Johnny Berry; Indian Currant Bush.

CHICKEN-WEED sb dial. *Salvia serotina*, the seeds of which are eagerly eaten by chickens, and sometimes choke chicks. *G*

1952 FGC Han, StAnn, Chicken-weed; Tre /chikin wiid bita—fi beli-hat—foul iit di siid/. 1954 *WIMJ* 31, *Salvia serotina*..Chicken Weed or Bitters; Wild sage.

CHICKLING sb dial; cf Amer Engl *chitling*. Chitterlings.

1873 Rampini 25, Vendors of tripe and 'chickling'.

CHICK-MAN-CHICK /chík-màn-chík, chík-ma-chík, chík-mi-chík/ sb dial; prob <TRICKING-CHICK. Cf CHIP-MAN-CHIP, TWOPENNY-CHICK. The bird *Turdus aurantius*; also called HOPPING DICK, MOUNTAIN DICK, etc. *BL*

1943 *GL* Kgn, Chickmanchick, Hopping Dick. 1949 U.Newton v 26, Your willing uncle never shot barble doves, bald pates, white bellies or chick-ma-chiks. 1952 FGC StAnd, StT /chik-man-chik/. 1955 Taylor 96, Chick-me-chick.

CHIEF sb cant; ironic use of *chief*. A dupe: used as a term of address by a SAMFAI MAN to his prospective victim.

1940 HPJ, Chief, a dupe. 1952 FGC Han, 'Chief in town; jinnal mus' dive', *The gull has come to town; the cheat must disguise his intentions.* 1954 LeP Kgn, Chief, someone who is credulous.

chieni wis see CHINA WITHE.

chiganit see CHIGGER-NUT.

CHIGA, CHIGER, CHIGGER *see* JIGGER. *BA*

CHIGGERFOOT see JIGGERFOOT. *BA*

CHIGGER-NUT /chìganít/ sb dial; <CHIGGER +*nut*; cf also *nit*, below. A small wild plant with nut-like fruit; it is used against chiggers. See quots.

1952 FGC Han, StAnn, StT, Tre /chìganít/ used to kill jiggers; same as horse-bath; like cooper-hook. 1955 *WIMJ* 160, *Tournefortia hirsutissima*..Chigger Nut.

CHIGGER-TOE sb dial; <CHIGGER+*toe*. *BA G*

1942 HPJ, Chigger-toe—a man with a toe eaten by jiggoes.

CHIGISE see JIGGER.

CHILD /chail/ sb dial; cf *OED sb* → 1610. *BA G*

1. A young woman.

1950 Pioneer 94 [A mother speaking to a grown daughter:] Noe pay her any mine me-chile. 1956 Mc, A young woman (used in areas where pikini is used for 'child').

2. A girl friend or lover.

1943 *GL* Kgn, Chyle, girl friend; StC, Chile, lover.

CHILLAM see next.

CHILLUM /chilom, chilong/ sb dial; <Hindi *chilam*, the part of a hookah which contains the burning tobacco. A pipe for smoking GANJA; also generally of any pipe for smoking. *G T*

1943 *GL* Kgn, Chillam; StC, Chillum; StM, Chelung; Tre, Chillum, Chilum, East Indian smoking pipe. 1952 Kingston *Gleaner*, about 16 April, Chillum pipe. 1952 FGC Man, Smoke ganja in a /chilong/—a six-inch straight tube—has no shank. 1958 DeC Kgn /chilóng/ a pipe for smoking ganja..made of clay..shaped like a child's straight toy horn..held vertically while smoking. A marble is placed in the bowl before the pipe is filled; this covers the hole in the bottom of the bowl and allows the smoke to get through but stops the ganja fibers from falling down into the smoker's mouth.

chilom, chilong, CHILUM see prec.

CHIMBLIT sb, also attrib dial; cf Engl dial forms of *chimney*: *chimbley*, etc. + *-et*, diminutive. The glass chimney of a kerosene or similar lamp.

1943 *GL* StC, Chimblit, lampshade. 1955 FGC Man /lamp chimblit/.

chimbolin see JIMBLING.

CHIM-CHIM sb[1] dial; etym unknown. The name of a bird, character in some ANANCY STORIES.

1905 Smith 9, Chim-chim Bird him buil' him nest on de top of de grass..An' in de evenin' when de north breeze blow, de nest go up and down and rock Breda Chim-chim Bird to sleep.

CHIM-CHIM sb[2] dial; reduplication of *chim-* <CHIMNEY.

1. In children's use: A chamber-pot.

c1915 FGC StAnd, Chim-chim, nursery form of *chamber-pot.* 1943 *GL* Kgn, Chim-chim, chamber-pot.

2. See quot.

1958 W. Adolphe Roberts letter, Chim-chim is excrement, not the pot. The latter is chimmy.

CHIMMEY, CHIMMY sb dial; dim and familiar formation <*chamber*+-*y* (*OED* -*y*[6]). (Cf *chimpey*, euphemism used in Birmingham, England: Mc.) In children's use: A chamber-pot. *BL G*

1952 Kerr 38, At nights as soon as the children are old enough they are wakened and put on the chimmey. 1955 FGC Man /chimi/ bed glass. 1956 JN StT, A teck out me mother chimmey and wash it out in the morning time.

CHIMPUNG, CHING-PUNG sb dial; ?a supposed imitation of Chinese speech. *G*

1943 *GL* Tre, Chimpung, a Chinaman; Ching-pung.

CHINA, CHINESE, CHINEY BANANA /chaini/ sb. A small, fancy variety of banana tree and fruit (*Musa cavendishii*) introduced from China in 1846.

1907 Jekyll 195–6 [Song:] Carry banana, a Chiney banana..The China banana is a stout low kind which withstands wind: the fruit is, however, coarse. 1913 Harris 2, The Chinese or dwarf banana..The individual fruits are shorter and thicker than those of the common banana. 1952 FGC Port, StAnd, StAnn, StJ, StM, StT /cháini banána/.

CHINA CANE sb dial. An unidentified plant.

1929 Beckwith 129, see PAIN-COCO.

CHINA-DRINK sb. A COOL-DRINK made with China root.

1707 Sloane lxxi, To make *China*-Drink. Take four or five handfuls of the Root..It is of a red Colour, and a very pleasant Drink.

CHINA, CHINEY GUAVA sb. A kind of guava also called PURPLE or STRAWBERRY GUAVA.

1913 Harris 9, *Psidium Cattleianum..China guava*..The pulp is fleshy, soft and juicy, purplish-red next the skin but white in the centre, sweet and acid, with a strawberry-like flavour. 1952 FGC Port /chaini gwaava/—has leaf like coco-plum.

CHINAMAN sb.

1. A Chinese; in Jamaica the term is now considered derogatory by many. *G*

1959 *Gleaner* 26 July etc.

2. dial. A farthing, because it is a small coin.

1943 *GL* StAnd, Chinaman, farthing. 1955 *GL* Man.

CHINA PLAGUE sb dial joc; cf CHINESE ITCH. CRATCH-CRATCH or some similar skin affliction; a recent name.

1958 DeC StC /chaina plieg/.

CHINA, CHINEY SHOP sb dial. A shop run by a Chinese. (In Jamaica the retail grocery trade is very largely in the hands of the Chinese.) *G N T*

1942 Bennett 26, We strole eena de Chiney shap Lack up! Lack up! we cry Ah laaf fe se' Chiney-man run. 1958 LeP StAnd, 'Kerosene? Try any China shop—any grocery'.

CHINA WITHE /chíeni wis, chaini wis/ sb now dial; cf *OED China root.* A name for any of several large-leaved climbing vines, including China root, COCO-WIS, FIVE-FINGER, SEVEN-FINGER, WICKER-WIS. (The term has become generalized.)

1794 Barham 210, The most noted for use in tying things together, are the prickly-pear withe, the China withe, the pudding withe, &c. 1864 Grisebach 782, China-wythe: *Smilax Balbisiana.* 1952 FGC StAnn, StE, Tre /chíeni wis/ big wild coco-wis; StM /chaini wis/ five-finger, seven finger, wicker wis.

CHIN-CHILLY adj dial; cf *OED chinchy*, niggardly, stingy →1653, and US dial, +*li*. Cf also CHI-CHI. See quot (which, however, gives a mistaken analysis; the word should be analyzed as *chinchy li*).

1868 Russell 11, Chin-chilly, small. Gie me chinchilly bit. African.

CHINCH MANGO sb dial; <*chinch*+*mango*. A variety of mango that smells like bedbugs.

1952 FGC Port.

CHINESE BANANA see CHINA BANANA.

CHINESE HAT sb. A common garden shrub, *Holmskioldia sanguinea* so called from the shape of the flower bract; also called JAPANESE HAT, JAPANESE UMBRELLA.

1951 May Jeffrey-Smith in Kingston *Gleaner* 7 Sept.

CHINESE ITCH sb dial; cf CHINA PLAGUE.

1959 DeC West /chainiiz ich/ ringworm infection of the skin.

CHINESE JIMBLING, CHINEY JAMBOLAN sb chiefly dial. *Averrhoa carambola* (as distinct from *A. bilimbi*, which is plain JIMBLING).

1958 DeC StAnd /chainiiz jimbilin/ the tall [i.e. long] variety of /baaj/ or *jimbilin*, the same which in eastern StT is called *coolie-barge*. 1959 Mrs E. B. Hoyes Kgn, There is also another specie referred to as the 'Chiny Jambalan' (Chinese) also called 'sour-barge'. This is a much bigger fruit, oval in shape with peg-shaped indentations running from top to bottom around the fruit, green in colour turning to yellow as it ripens.

CHINESE LEMON sb. The shrub *Triphasia trifoliata.*

1837 Macfadyen 124, Three-leaved Triphasia..This is a very common shrub in our gardens. It generally receives the name of the Chinese lemon. The fruit is red and juicy, the size of a small gooseberry..It is a native of China. 1920 Fawcett 183.

CHINESE, CHINEY NET sb dial. A fishing net, used in shallow water, that is drawn together in a circle to trap the fish within.

1952 Smith in *NHN* 186, This nurse shark, I understand, is not a very popular bait and is only used when one is caught by accident in a 'chinese net'. 1952 FGC StJ /chaini net—mek a sorkl wid it/. 1960 FGC Kgn.

CHINESE ROSE sb obs; 1756 Chinaise. A former name for China Rose (cf *OED* China 2b (*b*): *Hibiscus Rosa-sinensis*).

1756 Browne 286, Hibiscus 7..The Chinaise Rose.. cultivated..for flowers.

CHINESE, CHINEY YAM sb. See quots.

1952 FGC StC /cháini yám/ same as chiney sweet-potato, grows a bunch of small ones, 'want bear like pinda' [*Bears very much like peanuts*]; StM /cháini yám/ much like Irish potato. 1954 *FG* 446, The Chinese Yam. This is a variety of the white yam.

CHINEY sb dial; *OED* 'Obs. form of *China*'. This is the regular folk form in Jamaica for a Chinese (*OED* 1b, Obs; →1634); often used attrib (as in the foll comb), in which case it usually implies small size and sometimes a less robust variety. *BL G T*

1912 McKay *Ballads* 53, Not a gill me caan' get when Chiny dah dun fe him cash.

CHINEY APPLE sb dial. A fruit similar to the European apple in shape and external appearance but much smaller and of a greenish-yellow colour when ripe: *Zizyphus mauritiana*. Also called COOLIE PLUM.

1958 FGC StAnd /chaini apl/.

CHINEY BANANA see CHINA BANANA.

CHINEY CABBAGE sb dial. A form of cabbage that has a loaf-shaped rather than a round head. *G*

1952 FGC StE /cháini kvábij/.

CHINEY COW-PEAS sb dial. A variety of *Vigna unguiculata* (cf 1920 Fawcett 67, China Pea).

1952 FGC StC /chaini kou piiz/ have a white eye, long stalk—can eat young—vine grows like yam plant.

CHINEY-EXTRA sb slang; dial pronunc of *China* (=*China root*; cf CHINA WITHE) + dial pronunc of *extract*, sb. By a play on words (China-extract being an extract of China-root): the offspring of a Chinese and a negro. (The more common term is CHINEY-RIAL.)

1940 HPJ.

CHINEY GUAVA see CHINA GUAVA.

CHINEY JAMBOLAN see CHINESE JIMBLING.

CHINEY OKRO sb dial. A variety of okro, with a short, whitish, ribbed pod.

1952 FGC StE, StM /cháini ókro/.

CHINEY PORTLAND sb dial; < CHINEY + PORTLAND (YAM). A variety of yampi with pink flesh.

1952 FGC StC /chaini puotlan/.

CHINEY-RIAL sb dial; CHINEY + RIAL. The offspring of a Chinese and (usually) a negro, or (sometimes) a white or East Indian.

1955 G. Coulthard StAnd /cháini ráial/ a person of mixed Chinese and negro ancestry. 1956 Mc Man /cháini ráyal/ a person who is half Chinese, half white. 1958 DeC StC /chaina raial/ the child of a Chinese man and a black or East Indian woman.

CHINEY SWEET-POTATO sb dial. = CHINEY YAM.

1952 FGC StC.

CHINEY YAM see CHINESE YAM.

CHING-PUNG see CHIMPUNG. *G*

CHINK sb dial; *OED*: 'Obs. form of *chinch* sb.[1]' →1756. A bedbug. *BA*

1756 Browne 434, Cimex 1..The Chink or Bug. 1935 HPJ, Yu fas as chink An jus as tink [*You're as impertinent as a bed-bug, and just as ill-smelling*]. 1943 *GL* Clar, Kgn, StE, Chink, bedbug. 1952 FGC Man, StT, Tre, West /chingk/; StT /chingk bog/.

CHINK-STICK sb dial slang; < CHINK + *stick*.

1958 DeC StT /chingk-stik/ a rough bed of boards..so called because usually infested with bugs.

CHINK-UP sb dial; cf *OED chink* v[4] + *up*. A game (similar to a marble game) played with cashew nuts.

1947 U.Newton II 12, Clovis told me that he meant to play cashews—the setting going thus: the boy who is asked to set the other places as many cashews as he can afford, usually two, in the hands of the other boy, who now begins playing a game called 'chink-up'. In this game the player throws out the cashews on the ground, flicks cashew No. 1 to hit No. 2 and No. 3 to hit No. 4. If he succeeds, then the other boy has to set him again and the game continues until he fails, when the other boy becomes the player.

CHINK-WEED sb dial. A plant whose leaves are used to drive away bedbugs.

1952 FGC StT, Chink-weed.

CHINK WOOD sb dial. A local name for COCKROACH WOOD, from its odour.

1952 FGC Tre.

CHIP, CHIP-CHIP BIRD sb dial; onomatopœic. American warblers, when they migrate to Jamaica in winter; see quot 1955.

1952 FGC StT, Chip, a bird with a black cheek. 1955 Taylor 16, Their presence is often first realised when one hears a persistent 'chip, chip, chip' coming from bushes or undergrowth. This is the only note likely to be heard from these birds in Jamaica since their true song is chiefly restricted to the breeding season in North America. It is also the origin of their local name of Chip-chip Birds.

CHIP-CHIP sb dial; iterative < *chip* sb. Chips of wood used for starting a fire. *G*

1958 DeC Port.

CHIP-MAN-CHIP /chíp-màn-chíp/ sb dial. The bird CHICK-MAN-CHICK. *BL*

1952 FGC StT /chíp-màn-chíp/ same as hopping-dick—has long red legs, long beak.

CHIPPIN' CHICK sb dial. The GOLDEN WARBLER.

1956 Jeffrey-Smith 86, At Port Morant these engaging warblers are known as 'Chippin' Chicks'.

CHO /cho, cha, chu, chot/ interj; 1827 1830 1862 cha, 1835 1943 chu, 1862 chaw, 1868 chow, 1877 → cho, 1907 tche, 1943 chut; perh < Ewe *tsóò*, interj of astonishment, anger, impatience, disappointment, or Twi *twéaa*, interj of uttermost contempt. (Engl *tcha* can, hardly be the source—*OED* quots only 1844, 1887—but may have reinforced it.) (Also Cent Am Island Carib and Dominican Créole—D. Taylor.)

An exclamation expressing scorn, impatience, annoyance, disagreement, expostulation, etc.; usually independent; also preceding a statement or question. *BA BL G N*

1827 Hamel I 333, 'Cha!' said the Negro.. 'I say *cha*, master attorney, when you say I want to be free..' 1835 Madden II 150, Who care for Willyforce neger? Hi chu! who have the imperance to call him free neger? 1877 Murray *Kittle* 25, Dem say, 'Cho man, who da go boder with you?'; *Feedin' 'Perrit* 8, Cho! as I put de mug to my head—woy, I blige to pit it out. 1907 Jekyll 98, Hog say:—'Tche! you can't play'. 1924 Beckwith 111, And she said, 'Oh, cho! nonsense!' 1943 *GL* Port, Chu sa, no sir; West, Chut, not so. 1950 Pioneer 17, De ole ooman sey 'cho Anancy dat shouldn't worry yuh'. 1956 Mc Man /cha man/ Exclamation of depreciation.

CHOBY /chúobi/ sb dial; perh < Engl *chub* + *-y* (*OED -y*[6]). A small fish, same as TICKY-TICKY.

1952 FGC StT /chúobi/.

CHOCHO /chúochúo, chocho/ sb, also attrib; 1756→ chocho, 1790 1935 chota, 1835 chuchu; < Brazilian native name *chuchu*, but cf also Cuban (Oriente) *chote* < Amer Sp *chayote*, with which the form CHOTA is prob conn. The climbing vine *Sechium edule* and its fruit, eaten throughout Jamaica as a vegetable. *BL N*

1756 Browne 355, The *Chocho* Vine..is now cultivated in many places in Jamaica. 1794 Broughton 32, Sicyos *angulata* Chocho Vine. 1814 Lunan I 182, Cho-cho. 1835 Madden II 67, Callalu, ochro, chuchu. 1873 Rampini 91, A handsome cho-cho vine, whose pear-like fruit is one of the most useful vegetables of the tropics. 1933 McK 316, Chocho, a vegetable apparently kin to the melon family, much valued by the peasants. 1952 FGC Port, StAnn, StC, StE, StJ, StM, StT /chúochùo/.

CHOCHO ARBOUR /aba, hava/ sb dial; <*arbour*, the /v/ being substituted for /b/ by confusion or over-correction, and the stressed vowel shortened. An arbour made with cho-cho vines.

[1814 Lunan I 182–3, Cho-cho. . The vine bears fruit all the year long, and makes very good arbours, as they run and spread much.] 1956 Mc Man /chó-cho háva/ a wooden frame over which cho-cho vine is trailed; StAnd /chúo-cho ába/.

CHOCHO BIRD sb dial. = CHOCHO QUIT.

1948 *NHN* III 177, The Euphonia (*Pyrrhuphonia jamaica*), although apparently common, was a new addition to my bird-list. . I heard a very persistent sweet warbling, which the gardner told me was a 'Cho-cho bird' (the local name), and then I saw a small blue-grey bird flying out of the same place. 1955 Taylor 37–8, This very small bird is known locally as the Cho-cho Bird. . It is especially fond of mistletoe berries and the young shoots of the cho-cho.

CHOCHO QUIT sb dial; CHOCHO + QUIT.

1. The SHORT-MOUTH(ED) (BLUE) QUIT. See quot 1956.

1952 FGC StAnn /chúochuo kwít/ like Soursop Bird [i.e. the long-mouthed Blue-quit]. 1956 Jeffrey-Smith 93, Blue quits owe a local name of Cho-cho Quits to their destructive habit of eating the tender shoots and very young fruit of the cho-cho vine.

2. The LONG-MOUTH(ED) (BLUE) (QUIT).

1952 FGC StAnn /bluu bej/ have a round beak; boys call them cho-cho quit.

CHOCHO WOOD sb dial; CHOCHO + *wood*. ? *Symphonia globulifera*.

1952 FGC Tre, Chocho wood, very soft; same as HOG-DOCTOR.

CHOCK /chak/ adv dial; cf *OED chock adv*. Separately, or in such common phrases as *chock here*, *chock there*, etc.: exactly, fully, entirely, all the way. *BA G*

1912 McK *Songs* 15 [Beans] Run ober mango trees, 'Pread chock* to kitchen doo'—* Right up. 1943 *GL* Port, Chaka, far [i.e. all the way to]; Kgn, Chakya, right here; StJ, Chack deh, quite there; Chack yaunder, quite yonder; Chack, far away. 1960 *CLS* 164 /uol líediríeza másh chák tu di bák/ *The old lady's razor was smashed all the way to the back*.

CHOCK /chak/ vb dial; origin uncert, but perh a development from CHOCK adv (or sb), suggesting something made fast or firmly done. To take the lead in singing songs, hymns, etc.; to sing the verse (as a BOMMA does) while others come in on the refrain (or BOBBIN). *BA G*

1956 Mc Man /sómbadi chák it óut/; /chak di him/ *To call out the hymn*.

CHOCK AND BELAY adj or adv phr dial; <*chock* or *chocked and belayed*, tightly fastened, well stowed—a nautical phrase.

A. adv: Altogether rightly, perfectly; B. adj: Full, fully provided.

1943 *GL* Chack and billay, perfectly. 1955 FGC Man, The market is /chák an bilíe/ with things.

CHOCK STICK sb dial; cf *OED chock sb* 3 + *stick*. A piece of wood used to prop up a fisherman's *kunu* (boat) when it is on land; a chock. *G*

1956 Mc StC /chak tik/.

CHOCLATA, CHOCOLATA see CHAKLATA.

CHOCOLATE (TREE) /cháaklit/ sb dial, also attrib; *OED* 3, quots 1755, 1794, 'Erroneously applied to the cacao-tree, its fruit or seed. *Obs.*' Still current in Jamaica, however, where it serves to make distinction from *cocoa* (cacao), *coconut*, *coco(-root)*, etc.

The tree *Theobroma cacao*, its fruit pods, and the seeds (formerly called *cacao-nuts*, *cocoa-nuts*, CHOCOLATE-NUTS) from which chocolate and cocoa are made.

1814 Lunan I 183–4, Chocolate Tree. Theobroma. . There is only one species, the cacao. . The *cacao* or chocolate tree grows in a handsome form to the height of twelve or sixteen feet. 1952 FGC Port /cháakalit/; StAnd /cháaklit/ the outside of the pod has some peg-peg [protuberances]; StJ /chaaklit/ when it is parched and prepared to drink; StC /cháaklit tríi/. 1956 JN StC, Him plant pear tree an' mango an' chocolate an' banana tree.

CHOCOLATE NORTH (CHOCOLATE GALE) sb obs. A NORTH wind strong and cool enough to harm the CHOCOLATE trees. (CHOCOLATE GALE may not have been specifically Jamaican.)

1699 Dampier II ii i 39, The next day having a brisk N.W. Wind, which was a kind of a Chocolatta North; *ibid* III vi 62, The wind continues at N.W. blowing only a brisk gale, which the Jamaica seamen call a Chocolate North. [1867 Smyth *Sailor's Word-book, Chocolate gale*, a brisk N.W. wind of the West Indies and Spanish main.]

CHOCOLATE-NUT (TREE) sb obs; *OED* only quot 1751. The cacao-tree; cf also CHOCOLATE.

1790 Beckford I 236, A grove of coco or chocolate-nut trees. 1807 Renny 152, *Cocoa*, or the *chocolate-nut*, is a native of. . South America, from whence it was conveyed to Santo Domingo and Jamaica.

CHOCOLATE WALK sb obs. = COCOA WALK sb[1].

1707 Sloane lxxi, see CACAO-NUT-WALK.

CHOCOLATTA see CHOCOLATE.

CHOICE vb dial; <*choice* sb. To choose.

1912 McK *Songs* 35, But you choice* your way.—* Choose, have chosen. 1943 Bennett 11, Ah gwine ch'ice De one in de bes' position.

CHOKE KNOT sb dial. A slip-knot. *G*

1952 FGC Tre, Use /chuok-nat/ to catch wild hog.

CHOKE-ME /chuok-mi/ sb dial joc; cf COLD-CHOKE. FUFU; a nickname alluding to its thick, cloying consistency.

1958 DeC StT.

CHOKESTAY sb; <*choke* (*OED sb*[2]) + *stay* sb. A choke-band on a horse or mule.

1823 Roughley 160, With platted noseband, headstall, and chokestay.

CHOKEY see next.

CHOKIE /chúoki/ sb dial; <*choke* + *-ie* (cf *OED -y*[6]). A snare which catches a bird by means of a loop that chokes it.

1925 Beckwith 42 [Prov:] Don't draw chokie mek bird see you. 1929 Beckwith 36, The *springe* and *chokie* are placed upon a branch. . The *chokie* or 'breakneck' employs a string for the same purpose. 1935 HPJ, Chokey (Chokie), A kind of bird-trap. 1956 Mc Clar /chúoki/ bird snare made of wis /kech an im nek/; also Man, StAnd.

choklata see CHAKLATA.

choko-choko sb dial; echoic. The sound made by something moving back and forth, specifically, a file sharpening a cutlass; cf CHOOKOO-CHOOKOO. *G*

1956 Mc Port /choko-choko/ (repeated a number of times).

choko-choko adj dial; cf prec. The basic meaning seems to be movement of a back-and-forth kind (cf CHOOKOO-CHOOKOO 2), hence scattering or disintegration.

1959 DeC Han, West /choko-choko/ an adjective of vague meaning: a yam hill is likely to go /choko-choko/ if the earth is too loose.

chom /chom, chron/ vb dial; on the basis of regular sound changes this could be derived from *thrum* (*OED* v^3 5, to beat (a person), quots 1604–1823) or from *churn*, the sense in each case being close but not exact; as *churn* exists independently, however, probability favours *thrum*. But an echoic origin is not impossible—cf TUMTUM; and the US word *chum*, refuse of fish, may be related (see *DA*).

To beat or pound (usually) some vegetable product, or (sometimes) other material, so as to separate an unwanted part. Also const *out*.

1943 *GL* StJ, Chum, to thresh in a mortar. 1952 FGC StE /chom it/ (i.e. take the seeds out of cucumber, or the trash from coffee); Tre /get bush an chron it/ for mulch [evid means 'beat or strip the leaves off the branches']. 1955 FGC Man, Chum, country people say: pulping coffee beans, and so on. 1956 Mc Man /chóm out píis av klúoz/ to wash clothes roughly, half-wash. (In Jamaica clothes are often beaten with a flat piece of wood in washing.)

chomp vb dial; < *tromp*, cf US dial, var of *tramp*.

1956 Mc StAnd /dem chomp aroun at baamyaad/ *They tromp around at the balm-yard.* [Cf TRUMP AND LABOUR.]

CHONEY sb dial; prob <*Johnnie*, cf US euphemism for a chamber pot or toilet bowl.

1943 *GL* StE, Choney, beg-glass [i.e. BED GLASS].

CHOOKA-CHOOKA /chúka-chúka/ vb and ppl adj dial; variant of CHAKA-CHAKA. (Cf Fr Créole *tchotcho*, half-wash. D. Taylor.) To do (something) carelessly; specif, to half-wash clothes. *G*

1943 *GL* Kgn, Chooko-chooka, to half-wash. 1955 FGC Man /chuka-chuka/ same as /chaka-chaka/ not well done. 1956 Mc Man /yu jos chuka-chuka hit/ *You only half-washed it.*

CHOOKOO /chúku/ sb dial arch; prob <CHOCK, which usually suggests a long distance away, +-U. A far-away place; hence a vague 'country', therefore spelt with an initial capital letter; cf CHUCO HANNAH.

1877 Murray *Kittle* 20, In a before time, quite ober da chookoo* yonder, dere was a woman.. * 'Chookoo' is the African synonym for a 'far countree'. *Ibid* 24, Once upon a time in a Chookoo dere was hard time dere. 1935 HPJ, Terra incognita: back o' beyond. A stranger who makes trouble can be told: 'Yu cum fram Chukoo to mek trubble.' 1943 *GL* West, Chuku, far distance.

CHOOKOO-CHOOKOO sb (or vb) dial; echoic, perh also infl by CHOCK adv and/or CHOOKOO.

1. The sound made by something moving or being shaken back and forth; cf *choko-choko*. *G*

1940 HPJ, Chookoo-chookoo, used in describing a moving noise.

2. See quot; this may represent a verb.

1943 *GL* Tre, Chookoo-chookoo, go and come.

CHOO-LE see CHUREY.

CHOOPID see CHUPID.

CHOP /chap/ vb dial.

1. intr. Of a cock: To beat its wings before crowing.

1956 DeC StE (Accom) /kák de cháp fi díe-lait/.

2. trans. To inflict a wound on (someone) with a machete. *BA G T*

1790 Moreton 84, He gave strict orders to the watchmen ..to chop and murder them. 1954 LeP StE, Chap, to cut with a machete. 1958 LeP StAnd, 'Man chops three women in August Town'.

3. trans. To hit with a chopping blow. *G T*

1894 Spinner 84, Not long before Brown, the barman, had actually 'chopped' the coachman, greatly to the damage of the latter's thick skull, and..'chops' and blows more or less serious were neither infrequent nor harmless among the coloured domestics.

4. transf. In revival and POCOMANIA ceremonies: To *chop down*—when a SHEPHERD causes a possessed person to fall to the ground.

1953 Moore 102, A crowned warrior could not be chopped down by a shepherd. A man chopped down has no power himself, but is using the power of another man in possession. The shepherd achieved the chopping down by throwing lighted matches into the outer dancing area. After the third match, the warrior fell.

CHOP-MA-CHICK see *chapmachik*.

CHOPPED DEVIL sb dial; cf *OED devil*. CUT BRUTE or PICK-ME-ROUND.

1929 Beckwith 45, Cocoanut cakes called, if cut, 'chopped devil', if grated, 'grata brule' [*sic*; error for *brute*].

CHOPPING DOWN vbl sb phr cant; see CHOP 4.

CHOP TEN vb phr dial; a parallel formation to CUT TEN.

1957 Bennett 11, Him dress off himself, goh eena de buggy, chap him ten, an start play de figgle. 1958 DeC StT /chap ten/ the same as /kot ten/ i.e. to cross one's legs.

CHORURO WATER sb dial; prob an old local place-name, *Chorreras*, waterfalls, the source of *Ocho Rios*. A local name for a sauce made of coconut oil and other ingredients half boiled down; better known as DIP-AND-COME-BACK.

1943 *GL* StM, Cho-ru-ro watäh, half-boiled cocoanut oil.

chot see CHO.

CHOTA sb dial; cf CHOCHO. The CHOCHO; so called in western Jamaica as far east as Man.

†1790 Beckford II 190, Those plants that creep upon espaliers, and form themselves into bowers and shady walks, such as the chota, the grenadilla, etc. 1940 HPJ, Chota, a Montego Bay and Falmouth word for *Chocho*. 1959 DeC StJ /chuota/ a chocho; apparently the common form in Adelphi and frequently encountered throughout the western parishes.

CHO-TICK see CHUO-STICK.

chot-pot int dial; a 'stretched form' of *chot*.

c 1915 FGC StAnd /chót-pòt/. 1943 *GL* StM, 'Chut-put, You are talking nonsense'.

CHOWY /chóui/ adj dial; < *chow* vb (*OED*, 'A variant form of *Chew* in all senses, formerly in general use, but now dialectal') +*y* (*OED* $-y^1$ 3). Resilient to pressure of the teeth, 'chewy'; hence, of a root, no longer fit to eat—in condition for planting, because it will soon sprout.

1943 *GL* Port, Chowie, springy. 1955 FGC Man /chóui/ of a root: sticky, gluey, not good to eat; getting ready to spring.

CHRISTIAN vb obs; *OED* →1684.

p 1781 Dr Moseley in 1934 Williams 120, Quashee, before he set out on the expedition, got himself christianed, and changed his name to James Reeder.

CHRISTIANABLE adj dial; (the formation is unorthodox: its elements so combined should mean 'fit to be christened'—cf CHRISTIAN, MANNERSABLE). Christian-like. *G*

1907 Jekyll 144, By Dog get in de house Quashy was in already sitting down look quite meek an' christianable.

CHRISTMAS BEAN sb dial.

1952 FGC StM, Christmas beans, like sugar-beans, flat, but much bigger.

CHRISTMAS BIRD sb dial. (1) The black-and-white warbler (*Mniotilta varia*), (2) The redstart (*Setaphaga ruticilla*); so called because these birds are thought to migrate to Jamaica about Christmas time. *BL*

[1935 Bond 326, Migrants..They are variously known to the natives as 'northern birds', 'cold birds', 'dingy birds', 'Christmas birds'.] 1952 FGC Port, Christmas bird, black-and-white striped. 1956 Jeffrey-Smith 83, I saw a female redstart, or Christmas Bird (to give it one more of its other names) behaving like an ants bird.

CHRISTMAS BUR sb dial; perh an error for CHRISTMAS BUSH 2. ?*Eupatorium odoratum*, best known as JACK-IN-THE-BUSH.

1952 FGC StC, Christmas bur.

CHRISTMAS BUSH sb. Various plants whose blooming is associated with Christmas time: 1. Poinsettia. 2. JACK-IN-THE-BUSH. 3. Similar kinds of *Eupatorium*. *G*

1952 FGC StAnd, Christmas bush, poinsettia: StM, StT, Sometimes said for /jákini búsh/; StAnd, A wild flower resembling the wild aster.

CHRISTMAS CANDLESTICKS sb. The common weed which about Christmas time sends up tall stalks strung with ball-like flower-heads; cf BALD-HEAD, BALL-HEAD.

1955 *WIMJ* 159.

CHRISTMAS FISH sb dial. A small fish, blue all over (unidentified); caught around Christmas time.

1952 FGC StAnn.

CHRISTMAS GAMBOL sb bot obs.

A convolvulaceous plant, *Ipomœa sidifolia*, which flowers conspicuously about Christmas time, and 'gambols' over the tops of other plants; Long also applies the name to Browne's Convolvulus 5—what may have been the SEA-SIDE POTATO, *Ipomœa pes-capræ*, see quot 1774.

1756 Browne 153–4, Convolvulus 7..Christmas-Gambol. This plant is common about *Spanishtown*, and spreads very thick upon all the bushes that grow near it; it blooms about *Christmas*, and bears a great abundance of white flowers. 1774 Long III 833, Christmas Gambol.—Convolvulus Polianthos..The first species grows generally near the sea, and is very common in many parts of the island..The second is common about Spanish Town, spreads very thick about all the bushes near it; blooms about Christmas and bears a great number of white fragrant flowers. 1864 Grisebach 782, Christmas-gambol: *Ipomœa sidifolia.*

CHRISTMAS GRASS sb. = PIANO GRASS.

1915 W. Harris in *Daily Chronicle* 20 Sept, It is..known as 'Christmas grass' because at that season of the year the plumes of flowers and seeds waving in the breeze are a noticeable feature in the pastures of Trelawny.

CHRISTMAS MANGO sb dial.

1952 FGC StAnd, Christmas mango, come in at Christmas time.

CHRISTMAS OKRO sb dial.

1952 FGC Port, Christmas okro, short and thick.

CHRISTMAS PEA sb.

1. The GUNGU PEA.

2. The JERUSALEM PEA. See quots.

1814 Lunan II 64, Pigeon or Angola Pea..they..continue in bearing for several months of the year, about Christmas; and therefore sometimes called in Jamaica the *Christmas pea.* 1952 FGC StJ, 'Christmas peas, the St Catherine name for Jerusalem peas'.

CHRISTMAS POP sb dial.

1. A vine; perh CHRISTMAS GAMBOL?

1952 Astley Clerk, Christmas pop, a vine with bell-shaped flower, very much in evidence about Christmastide.

2. The blossom of LEAF-OF-LIFE, which children squeeze in their fingers to make them pop.

1952 FGC StAnn.

CHRISTMAS PRIDE sb; *OED* only 1756. See quot 1864.

1756 Browne 267, Ruellia 1..Christmas Pride. This plant is very common about *Spanish Town*..where it generally blows in the months of *December* and *January*: and makes a very beautiful appearance among the bushes, in that bleak season of the year. 1814 Lunan I 189–90. 1864 Grisebach 782, Christmas-pride: *Ruellia paniculata*

CHRISTMAS ROSE sb. JACK-IN-THE-BUSH.

1936 Fawcett 175, *Eupatorium odoratum*..Archangel, Christmas Rose. 1954 *WIMJ* 29.

chron see *chom.*

CHU, chu see CHO.

CHUB GRUNT sb dial. A variety of GRUNT similar to the chub.

1952 FGC StJ.

CHUB SQUIRREL sb dial. A variety of the squirrel fish similar to the chub.

1952 FGC StE /chób skwéril/ smaller than squirrel, and round, short, thick.

CHU(-CHU) vb dial; converted from an int.

1943 *GL* Clar, Chu, to drive hogs; StAnn, Chu-chu, drive pig.

CHUCK vb dial; < *chuck* (cf *OED* v^2).

1943 *GL* Kgn, Chuck, push.

CHUCK-LATTA see CHAKLATA.

CHUCK-UP (MAN) adj and sb dial; cf *OED chock* adv, 'as close and tight as can be'; also *chock-full.* This could equally well have developed, in Jamaica, from a past pple *chocked* (or *chucked*) + *up*.

1943 *GL* StM, Chuck-up, short and stout. 1954 LeP StAnn, Chuck-up, Chuckup man, someone who is very fat and clumsy.

CHUCO HANNAH sb dial; < CHOOKOO + ?Twi *ahànnú*, two hundred, *ahánnúm*, five hundred. A long distance away; a place far away.

1943 *GL* Clar, Chuco Hannah, Distance.

CHUCS vb dial; prob < *chuck*, but cf *shuks* vb[1].

1943 *GL* Tre, Chucs, to hand a person something and take it back quickly.

CHUKOO see CHOOKOO.

CHUKU vb dial; var of CHOOKA-CHOOKA.

1943 *GL* StJ, Chuku, to wash carelessly.

CHUM see *chom*.

CHUNDARI(E) sb dial; cf Hindi *chunari*, a kind of dyed cloth.

1943 *GL* StC, Chundarie, dress; Tre, Chundari, A dress.

CHUNKY PIPE see JUNKA-PIPE.

CHUNTA sb dial; < Hindi *chimtā*, *synnthā*, tongs.

1943 *GL* Clar, Chunta, fire tongs.

chuoki see CHOKIE.

chuok-mi see CHOKE-ME.

CHUO-STICK sb dial; ? < *chow*, food (or perh *chow—OED*: 'A variant form of CHEW.. formerly in general use, but now dialectal') + *stick* sb. Cf CHAWSTICK, CHEWSTICK.

1943 *GL* Port, Chuo-stick, Sharpened stick used as a fork; Port, Cho-tick, Wooden cooking fork.

CHUPID /chupid, chupit/ adj dial; < *stupid*. A common folk pronunciation showing normal reduction of /st-/ > /t-/ and affrication of /ty/ before /u/; sometimes also devoicing a final /d/.

1868 Russell 11, *Chupit*, Stupid. 1877 Murray *Feedin' 'Perrit* 4, An wha hot me, da de chupid 'tory him hab fe da tell you. 1935 HPJ, Chupid, stupid. 1943 *GL* StJ, Choopid, stupid. *BL G T*

[**CHUPON** sb tech; < Sp *chupon*, sucker.

1954 *FG* 352, Cocoa plants, sown from seed, at first produce 'chupons'—straight stems with leaves growing in all directions from the stem.]

CHUPS sb and vb dial; prob onomatopœic, but cf Sp *chupar*, to suck.

1. The sound made by sucking the teeth (see quot), or an instance of the making of this sound; to suck the teeth. The *chups* expresses disdain, impatience, or a sense of having been wronged, when one is not in a position to *say* so (e.g. when a servant is made to do something against his will). *BA G T*

1950 HPJ, Jamaican (i) vb to suck teeth, (ii) sb sucking of the teeth; (Astley Clerk:) The sound produced by the tongue lightly resting near the lower front teeth and the breath being quietly drawn or sucked in..'Noh chups pan mi', do not suck your teeth on me. Cf SUCK TEETH.

2. To kiss.

1960 LeP Kgn /im chups mi/ *He kissed me.*

CHUREY, CHULEY sb dial; < Hindi *chhurī*, knife. (On the substitution of *l* for *r* see Introduction, Phonology.)

1943 *GL* Kgn, Choo-le, Knife, Coolie word; StT, Churey, A knife.

CHUT see CHO.

CHUT-PUT see *chot-pot*.

chuuta adj dial; evid < *tutor*, for *tutored*.

1958 DeC St /chuuta/ (of a person) more mature, more sensible.

CIATACU see CUTACOO.

CIGAR BUSH sb. *Eupatorium dalea* (locally in Blue Mts, Liguanea, etc.); the flower has a long white tube, which may account for the name.

1936 Fawcett 176.

CIGARETTE BEETLE sb.

1923 Gowdey 61–2, The Cigarette Beetle, *Lasioderma serricorne*, Fab. After tobacco leaves have been cured and baled or the finished product—cigarettes, cigar and pipe tobacco—packed away in boxes it is subject to the attack of this insect both in the larval and adult stages.

CIGAR FLOWER sb. A wildflower, so called near Newcastle, having a long, tube-like, deep scarlet bloom: *Cuphea platycentra*.

1951 FGC Man [Painting by Mrs Brenda Sutton, Bromelia estate, of a flower obtained near Newcastle, StAnd].

CIMBAL see SYMBOL.

CINDER sb dial.

1956 Mc Man /sinda/—Fire-stone used to support pot.

CIRCASSIAN BEAD TREE, BEAN, PEA-TREE, or **SEED** sb bot. The tree *Adenanthera pavonina* (introduced to Jamaica in 1802) and its bean—or pea-like fruit; also called JOHN-CROW BEAD, LADY COOTE BEAN, RED-BEAD TREE, etc.

1814 Lunan II 315, This is known by the name of *Grand Anther* or *False Flower Fence*: In Jamaica, where it has been pretty generally cultivated, and has thriven well, it has been called *Circassian pea-tree*, from the beauty of the pea, of which necklaces are made. 1873 Rampini 155, There, too, trailed the Circassian bean (*Adenanthera Pavonina*), whose seeds are said to be so constantly uniform in weight. 1909 Harris 311, Red-Bead Tree (*Adenanthera pavonina*, Linn)..The scarlet seeds, known as Circassian seeds, are used for making necklaces, etc. 1920 Fawcett 128, Circassian Seed. 1941 Swabey 13, Circassian Bead Tree.

CIRCLER sb dial. A small round boiled dumpling.

1958 DeC StT.

CISTERN sb dial; cf *OED* 2a, 'A laver', →1756–7. A wash-hand basin.

1942 Bennett 20, Me two pung goblet an' cistan me chile Mash up, mash up. [*My two-pound water-pitcher and basin..have been smashed.*] 1954 LeP Kgn, Cistern, a washing place.

CITRON WOOD sb bot obs; cf *OED citron* 7, only quot 1712. See CANDLEWOOD 1, quot 1811.

CITRUS WALK see WALK.

CLABBER-CLABBER sb dial; iterative < *clabber* sb. Sour milk. Cf *bani kleva*.

1958 DeC StT /klaba-klaba/.

CLABUB sb and adj dial; < *clabber*, sb (cf *OED*). See quots. (Cf *bani-kleva*.)

1943 *GL* Kgn, Clabubs, coconut half boiled down. 1955 FGC Man, Same as RUN-DOWN—Clabub is the word used in StT and Port. 1943 *GL* StC, Clab-up, peas soup. 1955 FGC Man, Thick, heavy, overboiled.

CLAD see *klad*.

CLADDY CREAM, CLODDY CREAM /kládi kriim/ sb dial; cf CLAD, CLOD, and *clotted cream*. Sour milk.

1958 DeC Port.

CLAM vb dial; cf *OED clam v*[1], of which this is prob an extension; cf also CLAMMISH, from which this may be a back-formation. To pucker the mouth with astringency. *G*

1935 HPJ, Clam: to make the mouth dry: 'stainy fruits clam the mouth'. Clammy cherry..a white berry which 'clams'.

CLAMMISH adj dial; cf *OED clammish,* sticky, viscous →a 1678. Said of fruits or the like: astringent to the tongue, tending to pucker the mouth; cf CLAM vb. *G*

1951 FGC Kgn, Macca-fat have a clammish taste.

CLAMMY adj and vb dial; < *clammy,* adj; cf CLAM, CLAMMISH. *BA G*

A. adj: Sticky.

1958 DeC Port /fonji/—coconut milk boiled with cassava flour to a /klami/ porridge.

B. vb: To make sticky; const *up.*

1952 FGC StAnd, Clammy-cherry clammy-up you hand.

CLAMMY BROOM-WEED sb bot obs; cf BROOM-WEED. In Macfadyen's use: *Sida glutinosa* (ident 1926 Fawcett 113).

1837 Macfadyen 83, Sida nervosa. *Clammy Broom-weed.*

CLAMMY-BUR sb dial. A wild plant whose leaves stick closely against the skin or to clothing.

1927 Beckwith 25, Clammy-bur..'Rattle-weed'. For a cold, boil and drink as tea. 1954 *WIMJ* 31, *Priva lappulaceae*..Clammy Bur; Rattleweed; Styptic Bur; Velvet Bur.

CLAMMY-CHERRY sb; *DAE* only 1889. The tree and fruit of *Cordia collococca. BA G*

1696 Sloane 169, Ceraso affinis arbor baccifera racemosa ..Clammy Cherries. 1774 Long III 790, Clammy-cherry..This beautiful tree grows to a considerable size in the lowlands. The berries come out in clusters of a fine red colour, about as big as a middling cherry, having a soft, sweetish, clammy pulp, inveloping a number of small seeds. 1814 Lunan I 197, Clammy Cherry. Cordia collococca. 1864 Grisebach 782. 1952 FGC StAnd, Clammy-cherry clammy-up you hand; also StM, StT.

CLAMMY MILK sb dial; cf CLAM, CLAMMY. Thick sour milk; both astringency and stickiness may be alluded to.

1958 DeC StC /klami milk/.

CLAMP /klamp, klamps/ sb dial; < *clam* by folk-etym under the infl of *clamp* vb. A large bivalve mollusk, also called 'mussel'.

1956 Mc Port Royal /klamp, klamps/ the same form given by two or three people. The name is derived from the fact that it is supposed to open and clamp on you.

CLAMPAS sb dial rare; perh for *clamper.*

1943 *GL* StM, Clampas, eater.

CLAPPER /klápa/ sb and vb dial; cf *OED clapper* I.

A. sb: 1. A piece of wood used to beat clothes on a flat stone in the river when washing them. Cf *pata* sb[2]. *G*

1956 Mc Clar /klapa—sonting yu tek biit kluoz/.

2. A stick used in cultist ceremonies to make a rhythmic percussion against a post.

1953 Moore 172 [Used at CUMINA ceremony:] A clapper or catatic, which is a flat stick beat against the center post of the dancing booth.

3. A squib or fire-cracker, esp a large one. (Etym here perh due to Chinese pronunc of *cracker* as *clacker,* then with *p* for *k* as in some other words. RWT.)

1943 *GL* StT, Clappers, scribs [i.e. squibs]. 1958 DeC /klapa/ any firecracker (common).

B. vb: To strike a hard blow. (Perh < *clobber.*)

1941 Kirkpatrick 12 [In cricket:] 'Im jus' keep 'im 'ead cool an' clappers 'im wid a coupla good shat.

CLAPPY sb dial; < *clap* + *-y.* Board slippers which make a clapping sound as the wearer walks. Cf CROPPIE. *G*

1955 FGC Man /klapi/.

CLARIFIER sb obs; cf *OED* 2, 'a large metallic pan or cauldron used in the clarification of sugar', 1822→. *G*

1797 Higgins 42, Grand boilers have been abandoned, and..clarifiers have been introduced; *ibid* 45, As small clarifiers set to separate fires bring waste..of fuel, and large ones spoil the sugar, every effort for the restoration and improvement of grand boilers..ought to be encouraged.

CLARY see (WILD) CLARY.

CLASS LEGISLATION sb obs. Legislation designed by Jamaican planters to hamper the small-settler class and force them to work on estates for wages. Examples of such legislation were the Police Acts of 1835 and 1838, and the Vagrancy Acts of 1834 and 1839. *BA*

1955 Curtin 130, Other 'class legislation', as it was called in Jamaica, was discovered and dis-allowed by the home government.

CLATE vb dial; cf *clat* (*EDD* v[3]), to clout. slap, cuff.

1943 *GL* StE, Clate, knock, beat.

CLAVANIE, CLAVANNE see CALABAN.

CLAW /klaa/ sb dial. A MACHETE having a semi-circularly recurved end which forms a hook or 'claw'.

1959 DeC West /klaa/ a cutlass of shape [as described].

CLAW-FISH /klaafish/ sb dial; by folk-etym < *crayfish* or *crawfish. G*

1956 Mc StAnd (Dallas) /klaafish hav wan han lang, wan shaat yu no/ *The crayfish has one hand* [i.e. claw] *long, one short you know.*

CLAXUN sb dial rare; perh < *Clarkson.* (Cf BUXEN.) Evid a variety of the DASHEEN coco.

1943 *GL* Tre, Claxun, dasheen.

CLAY-CLAY sb dial; iterative from *clay.* A lot of clayey material.

CLAYING vbl sb; *OED* 1822. The process of using clay to remove molasses from sugar, thus making it whiter.

1793 Edwards II 238, The French planters probably think otherwise, upwards of four hundred of the plantations of St Domingo having the necessary apparatus for claying, and actually carrying on the system.

CLEAN adj and vb dial.

A. adj: Bald, hairless. *BA G*

1956 Mc StE (Accom) /a klíin héd kyáan dák/ *A bald head can't be trimmed.*

B. vb: Of day or morning: To become light. Cf DAY CLEAN. *G*

1873 Rampini 92, From early morning, 'when day just clean', as the negro idiom has it, the roads..are thronged. 1907 Jekyll 60, He knew that the Cock going to crow when day clean, an' 'creech owl going to know when day is cleaning an' go away. 1956 Mc Man /díe jes a klíin/ *Day is just breaking*; Port /az di díe klíin/ *As the day breaks.*

CLEAN-FACED MAN sb cant. An adherent of the RASTAFARIAN cult who nevertheless does not wear the characteristic beard or long hair. Cf BALDHEAD. *G*

1960 *SAN Report* 23, Thirdly there is the Baldhead or 'clean-faced' man who is not obviously distinguishable from the ordinary Jamaican except by some article such as the yellow, green and red pompom or scarf. Clean-faced men are mostly employed.

CLEAR vb, adj and adv dial.

A. vb: To solve (a riddle).

1952 FGC Han, They give riggles; the genius is the one who clears it.

B. adj: Light in complexion. *BL G N T*

1954 LeP Kgn, Clear skin, skin light brown. 1956 Mc Man, One person may be /kliera/ than another.

C. adv: All the way; entirely. (Cf *OED* A 19a, B 5). Cf CHOCK. *G T*

1956 Mc StE (Accom) /antil im riich kliia in Kingstan/ *Until he got right into Kingston*; Man /fling i klía we/ *Fling it right away.*

CLEAR-COLOUR PEAS sb dial. A variety of bean contrasted with MIX-PEAS, which have mixed colours; both usually applied to *Phaseolus vulgaris.*

1952 FGC StC /klíe kòlr píiz/.

CLIED see *klaid.*

CLIMBING MELON sb. The 'wild melon' *Cionosicys pomiformis.*

1926 Fawcett 264.

CLIMBING SORREL sb bot obs; cf *OED sorrel sb*[1] 4 only quot 1864. *Begonia glabra.*

1756 Browne 203, Rumex 1..The large climbing Sorrel. This plant is very common in the woods of *Jamaica.* 1814 Lunan I 199, Climbing Sorrel. Begonia acutifolia.

CLING-CLING, CLINKLING see KLING-KLING.

CLOD see *klad.*

CLOSET-MAN sb dial; < *closet*, latrine + *man.*

1943 *GL* Clar, Closet-man, sanitary inspector. *G*

CLOSE-UP SHOE sb dial.

1956 Mc StE (Accom) /klúoz-op shuu/ a front-lacing (lady's) shoe.

CLOT OF BLOOD sb dial rare.

1929 Beckwith 39, Seven stars 'come out in May and scatter in June'. It is these stars that cause the heat, and they are called 'clot of blood'.

CLOUD SWIFT sb ornith. See quot.

1955 Taylor 82, The Collared Swift (*Streptoprocne zonaris*), which is also known as the Cloud Swift. 1956 Jeffrey-Smith 21, The name cloud swift is due to the fact that this bird soars above the high mist-covered mountains. It is seen in large numbers in the Blue Mountains, in Portland and St Thomas. Occasionally it descends to sea-level.

CLOVEN-BERRY sb; cf *OED cloven ppl a*, quots 1725, 1756. The shrub and fruit of *Casearia hirsuta.*

1696 Sloane 173, Frutex baccifer..*Cloven Berries.* In collibus sylvosis *red hills.* 1794 Barham 63, Cloven-Berries. I have seen of these frequently..From the flowers flow out black berries, about the bigness of small sloes, cleaving into two for the most part; whence the name. 1814 Lunan I 201–3. 1926 Fawcett 216.

CLUCKING-HEN sb; 1679→ clucking, 1727 clocking; cf *OED clucking ppl a*, b, quots 1847, 1860. The bird *Aramus scolopaceus*, similar to the rail and crane. Quots 1740 and 1840 prob refer to other birds, and there is evidence that the name is not strictly applied today. s.

1679 Trapham 67, Wild Fowl, such as Ducks..Pigeons.. Parreketoes, clucking Hens, Guinny Hens. 1727 Merchant 18, In the Woods and Savanahs are likewise Clocking Hens, Carrion Crows..etc. 1740 Importance 38, The Clucking Hen, speckled with black and white like the common Guinea Hen; they are large as Capons, with a red Bill and Feet, and eat Fish. 1840 Chamberlaine 78, The Jamaica Heron—Clucking Hen—by some called Qua bird. 1952 FGC Han, Man, StAnn, StM /klòkin hén/. 1956 Jeffrey-Smith 113, The Clucking Hen was given its local name because of its note as it roamed the mountain solitudes in Gosse's day, but today it is oftener seen in the lowlands.

CLUCKING LIZARD sb dial; perh < *croaking* with substitution of *l* for *r* (see Phonology), or perh a new formation. The CROAKING LIZARD.

1952 FGC Man, StAnd, StT /klókin lízad/.

CLUCKING-LIZARD BEAN sb. A variety of BONAVIST bean.

1952 FGC StC /klókin lìzad bíin/—tall pod, red seed, type of /bána bíin/ or /bánabís/.

CLUSTER-FRUIT sb obs. The grapefruit, which grows in clusters on the tree.

a 1818 Lewis (1845) 77, One between an orange and a lemon, called 'the grape or cluster-fruit', appears to me quite delicious.

CLY adj dial; < *cloyed.* See *klaid. BL*

1935 HPJ, Cly, from a boy at Jamaica College, = clied (cloyed).

COAH see COUSIN.

COAL BOY sb obs. A man employed to carry coal into a steamship. *G*

1873 Rampini 15, One after another in a long line, men and women, black as the coals they carried, chanting a wild recitative, and walking with that peculiar swing which is characteristic of the black race all over the world, they trooped up the gangway to empty their baskets in the hold. These 'coal boys', and still more so the 'coal girls', are a peculiar class.

COAL BUSH sb dial. The place in the BUSH where charcoal is burned.

1956 JN StT (Yallahs), Me mother sell coal. And she look after the baby. Dem go at coal bush and carry coal and do sewing.

COAL GIRL sb obs. A woman employed to carry coal into a steamship. See COAL BOY.

COAL MANGO sb dial. A variety of mango with a dark skin.

1952 FGC StJ /kuol manggo/.

COAL-POT sb. A black, cast-iron, charcoal stove, having a round foot (about 8 in. diameter and 6 in. high) and a shallow pot-like top with a metal grill; it is used widely in Jamaica for cooking, heating irons, etc. *BA G*

1940 HPJ, Coal-pot Jamaica (also Trinidad, Tobago, Virgin Is.).

COAL-SKILL sb dial; *coal* + overcorrected form of *kill* (= kiln); cf *DAE coal-kiln* →1847. A kiln for burning charcoal.

1952 FGC Man /kuol-skil/.

COARCHER, COATIER see COURTIER.

COBA-COBA see *koba-koba.*

COB-ANANSI see COBY.

COBBA-COBBA see *kaba-kaba.*

COBBLER /kábla/ sb attrib dial; cf *OED* 2 →1811. A workman who is not good at his job.

1956 Mc Man, An inferior workman: a /kabla kyapinta, kabla shuu mieka/. 1962 BLB 58.

COBBLER, COBBLER-FISH, COBBLER-JACK /kabla/ sb dial; etym uncert: this may be a folk-etym <Pg *cavallo* (or Sp *caballo*)—see CAVALLY, or it may be assoc with the *cobbler-fish* of *OED*: 'A West-Indian fish, *Blepharis crinitus*, having long rays likened to a cobbler's strings'. (No ref or quot.)

1. A fish having long extensions to the fin; see quot.

1892 Cockrell index, Cobbler-fish, *Trachynotus falcatus*.

2. A fish similar to the CAVALLY.

1929 Beckwith 33, A seine is used at Alligator Pond to catch cobbler; 'cavally' (Gosse thinks from the Spanish *cavalho* [*sic*]) and 'hard bone' jack. 1952 FGC StC, StM, StT /kabla jak/.

COBBUG see *kabob*.

COBELL /kobél/ sb dial; <*cabal*, *EDD* 2, 3.

1. A loud noise and confusion.

2. A quarrel, a fight.

1943 *GL* Kgn, Cubel, Scandal or noise; Cobell, quarrell or loud noise; also Port, StAnn, StJ. 1956 HPJ, Cobell, confusion, quarrel, or loud noise. Please note, confusion means 'fray', 'uproar'. *To raise a cobéll* is to cause a quarrel actually leading to a fight.

[**COBIA** see *kyabiyo*.]

COBICH, COBITCH see CUBBITCH.

COB-NUT sb bot; cf *OED* 1866→. The tree *Omphalea triandra*.

1801 Dancer 357, Cob-nut (*Omplalea* [*sic*] *diand*). 1814 Lunan I 203–4, *Omphalea nucifera*, Cobnut..In Jamaica it is known in some parishes by the name of *pig* or *hog* nut. 1920 Fawcett 320.

COBOCA sb dial rare; etym unknown, but cf Sp *boca*, mouth.

1943 *GL* StE, Coboca, a good speaker.

COBY, COBY-WOOD, COBY-NANCY /kuobi, kuobinansi, kobanansi, komanansi/ sb dial; prob <Sp *caoba*, mahogany; the older *caobana* (cf CAWOBENA) is prob the source of *coby-nancy* and its variants, produced by folk-etym in Jamaica. In Spanish America *caoba* is applied to the genus *Swietenia* basically, but also to species of *Eucalyptus* (Roig y Mesa) and *Podocarpus* (Santamaría). *Coby* may owe its form in part to Ewe *kɔbi*, ochre-coloured earth.

1. Prob at first applied to *Swietenia mahogani*, but evidence is lacking; the place-name *Lacovia* (St Elizabeth) is thought to preserve it (<Sp *la caoba*).

2. Applied generally to BASTARD MAHOGANY, *Matayba apetala*, which has a red wood similar to that of mahogany. *N*

1926 Fawcett 55–6, *Matayba apetala*..Wanika, Cromanty, Bastard Mahogany, Coby, Red Wood. 1941 Swabey 18, Comanancy, Cobywood. 1952 FGC Tre, Coby-wood; StAnn, In St Ann and St Catherine this is the same as cobanansi, and it is also called wanika, wild mahogany, black wattle. Also StE.

3. ?A mistaken identification: see quot.

1943 *NHN* II 68–9, Sideroxylon foetidissimum(?)-· Calamante, Cobynancy..In other parts of Clarendon [than Portland Ridge] it is probably one of the several species of Sideroxylon included under the name of 'mastic'.

COCAATY, COCATY see COCKATY.

COCASHA sb dial rare; etym unknown.

1935 HPJ (from Col. Rowe, Accompong), Cō-casha, A medicinal wild-pine, Cromanty.

COCCO see COCO.

COCCUS WOOD, COCUS WOOD sb dial; 1920 cocus, 1941→ coccus; origin unknown. The trade name for the timber of West Indian or Jamaican Ebony. See quots.

1920 Fawcett 26, Brya ebenus. West Indian Ebony, Cocus Wood. 1941 Swabey 20, Coccus wood, West Indian Ebony. 1943 *NHN* II 45, *Brya ebenus*—Ebony (rarely, Coccus). 1944 *NHN* II 61, The West-Indian Ebony..Its trade name is Coccus wood to distinguish it from the true ebony. *Ibid* 94.

COCHANEIL, COCHENEAL see COCHINEAL.

COCHIMBA see CACHIMBA.

COCHINEAL sb, also attrib; 1672 cochaneil, 1756 cocheneal, 1893 cochineal; cf *OED*.

1. (Additional spelling.) Cf also *kanchaniil*. *BA*

1672 Blome 14, Cochaneil is produced by a plant that grows in this Isle.

2. Attrib: see quots.

1756 Browne 237, Cactus 4..The Cocheneal *Indian*-Fig. 1893 Sullivan 121, Toona or Cochineal Plant. The natives esteem this most highly.

COCK sb also attrib dial; cf *OED* *sb*[1] III. A male lizard. *BA*

1952 FGC Man, The cock one sticks out his gill.

COCK vb dial; cf *OED* *cock* *v*[1] 3. *BL T*

1. intr. To extend from at an angle; to stick *up* (*off*, *out*, etc.), with respect to something lying in another direction. *BA G*

1943 *GL* Port, Cock up, to turn up, turned up. 1956 Mc, Him yase cack aff fram him hed. [*His ears cock off from his head.*]

2. trans. To turn (something) at an angle decidedly away from its normal position, or from the thing or place to which it is adjacent or attached; with *up* (*off*, *out*, etc.).

1950 Pioneer 48, Yuh no haffe cock it up so high Me se de eight poun boot. 1956 JN, You thief you! Any time I hold you by you foot and cock you up you will find out!

COCK-A-BENNY see CACA-BELLY.

COCKADEWIE sb dial; cf Twi *akókɔ-duɔ̀dúà*, the yellow wagtail. An unidentified bird.

1943 *GL* Port, Cockadewie, A species of bird.

COCKATTY see next.

COCKATY /kákati, kákiti/ adj and sb dial; for spellings see quots; prob <Twi *kakaté*, unmanageable, unruly; perh infl also by Engl *cockety* (cf *EDD*) lively, vivacious, pert; disposed to domineer. *G*

1. adj: Boastful, proud, selfish.

1943 *GL* Clar, Kack-a-te, Cocaty, proud; Kgn, Cockaty, cockatty, independent, Kackatie, proud; Port, Cocaaty, Neglect former duties to show independence; StAnn, Cacaty, Proud; StJ, Kakaty, Proud, selfish; StT, Cackaty, Proud; also Kakiti.

2. sb: A boastful, selfish person; a fussy, pernickety person.

1943 *GL* Port, Kackatie, A boastful person; Cakatty, A selfish person. 1954 LeP StE, Cockaty, a fussy, pernickety person.

COCK-COPPER sb tech obs. A copper vat for evaporating sugar-cane juice with a cock to let the juice flow out.

a 1818 Lewis (1845) 43, The juice..passes through a wooden gutter into the boiling-house, where it is received into the siphon, or 'cock-copper', where fire is applied to it.

COCKCRAW sb; prob folk-etym form of CRAW-CRAW.

COCK-CROW sb; cf *OED* →1880. Used in somewhat specialized senses: see quot 1826. *G*

1826 Barclay 317, They designate the hours of the night by the crowing of the cocks—'before cock crow', signifies before two o'clock; then follows 'second cock-crow'—then 'cock crow fast'—and, lastly, 'day cut', or dawn. 1827 Hamel II 195, Where was Mr Fairfax? Hamel had sent him notice before cock-crow. 1925 Beckwith 116 [Prov:] When cock crow fas' fas', day soon light.

COCK HERRING-WOOD see HERRING-WOOD.

COCKLE-FISH see CUCKOLD-FISH. *N*

COCKLE'S INCREASE, COCK-NA-CRIS, COCKOLD'S INCREASE see CUCKOLD'S INCREASE.

COCKPIT sb, also attrib.

1. A valley, often 500 ft or more deep, with very steep sides usually heavily wooded and difficult of access—the characteristic terrain in several parts of Jamaica, but esp in south-western Trelawny and south-eastern St James; freq in phr 'the cockpit country'. Cf *OED* 4, 1803→.

1683 *Laws* Map, Cockpit Savana [near Old Harbour]. 1740 Leslie Map, Pedro's Cockpits [in 'St Marie's' just west of Moneague]. 1803 Dallas I ii 39, The grand object of a Maroon chief in war was to take a station in some glen, or, as it is called in the West Indies, Cockpit, enclosed by rocks and mountains nearly perpendicular, and to which the only practicable entrance is by a very narrow defile. 1899 Hill 25, 'The cockpit country', as it is locally called..the cockpits are limited to a rough district embracing the corners of Trelawney and St James..The cockpits are primarily deep funnel-shaped sinkholes, from which the drainage percolates downward into the cavities and fissures of the underlying rocks..The pits vary in depth from shallow circular basin-like depressions surrounded by low mammillary hills..to deep-sided sinks often 500 feet in depth. 1927 Beckwith 4, Near Maggotty at the entrance to the Cockpit country. 1952 FGC gen; Tre /kakspit mountin/.

2. In a sugar-mill house: the area in which the mill is placed, circular and below the main level. (Cf *OED* 3, the nautical usage prob transf here.)

1823 Roughley 189, The cock-pit should always be kept clean, and the cogs free from impediments of trash and dirt.

COCKROACH APPLE sb bot obs; cf *OED*. *Solanum aculeatissimum*; today called COCKROACH POISON, COCKROACH BERRY, etc.

1756 Browne 173–4, Solanum 2..Love Apple, and Cockroch Apple. This plant is a native of Jamaica..The smell of the apples is said to kill the Cockroches.

COCKROACH BERRY, BUSH, MACKA, POISON, or **WEED** sb chiefly dial. In various parts of Jamaica (see quots): *Solanum aculeatissimum*, both plant and fruit; formerly called COCKROACH APPLE.

c 1915 FGC StAnn (Moneague), Cockroach poison—the ripe fruit is broken and put into cupboards to combat cockroaches. 1944 *NHN* II 58, The genus *Solanum*.. includes..the Cockroach Poison, a thorny shrub with large bright orange coloured berries..which are very poisonous. 1952 FGC StM, Cockroach berry; Port, Cockroach bush; StAnn, Cockroach macka, Cockroach weed—and some call it Cockroach poison or Duppy tomato. 1954 *WIMJ* III 31, *Solanum aculeatissimum*, Cockroach Poison.

COCKROACH GRASS sb dial; cf MOTH GRASS. A local name for *Vetiveria zizenioides*: see quot.

1954 *FG* 226, The name Khus-Khus is the Indian name for this aromatic grass which is also sometimes known as 'Cockroach' grass and 'Khas-Khas'.

COCKROACH LOBSTER sb dial. A variety of sea crayfish with body flattened so that it resembles a cockroach; also called LOBSTER'S MUMMA, SEA-ROACH.

1952 FGC StJ, Cockroach lobster, same as sea-roach.

COCKROACH MACKA, COCKROACH POISON see COCKROACH BERRY.

COCKROACH TREE sb bot obs.

1756 Browne 219, Melastoma 1. *Subarborescens*..The Cock-roch Tree. 1819 Dancer 374, Cockroach Tree, Melastoma. 1826 Williams 290, Some species of the cock-roach tree (melastoma).

COCKROACH WEED see COCKROACH BERRY.

COCKROACH WOOD sb dial; note variant names. ?*Prunus myrtifolia*; if this identification is correct, this is also called ANTS-WOOD, CHINK WOOD, etc.

1952 FGC Tre, Cockroach wood, same as chink wood, cassada; it is used to make axe sticks, and has a rank smell [whence its name].

COCKS vb dial or cant; <*cog* (*OED* v^3: 'it would seem that "cogging" generally designated some sleight of hand, made use of to control the falling of a die'). Of dice: to fall (evid by means of some trick) to the advantage of one player. *BL*

1936 Martinez in *Gleaner* 3 Oct 35, A delightful place this west end [of Kingston], you will get a 'juk' [stab] with a 'pinta' [knife] if the dice should 'cocks' and you argue over it.

COCKSCOMB sb dial; altered, perh by folk-etym <COCKSTONE.

1956 JN Port, Cockscomb, Large-grained red peas with darker red stripes.

COCK'S HEAD sb bot; *OED* 1884→. See quot 1864.

1794 Barham 125, *Onobrychis* or *cock's head*. This has a woody brown-coloured stem..the tops are long spikes of flowers, papilionaceous, of pale purple colour. 1814 Lunan I 306, *Hedysarum tortuosum*. (Quotes Barham.) 1864 Grisebach 783, Cock's head: *Desmodium tortuosum*.

COCK-SOLDIER sb dial. The stilt; cf CRACK-POT SOLDIER.

1952 FGC StC /kàk súolja/ same [as] black-back.

COCK SPARROW sb dial. The BLACK SPARROW. *BA G*

1952 FGC StM /kak spara/ black bird, red under throat, short beak; eat corn, ackee.

COCKSPUR sb also attrib; from the shape of prickles.

1. FINGRIGO: *Pisonia aculeata*.

a 1726 Barham (1794) 114, Its prickles are short and crooked, as the cockspur-tree is. 1756 Browne 358, The Cock's-Spur or Fingrigo. 1774 Long 755, Fringrigo [*sic*], or Cockspur..The seeds are glutinous and burry, sticking so fast sometimes to the ground-doves, and pea-doves (which feed upon them), as to prevent their making use of their wings. 1914 Fawcett 151. 1952 FGC StAnd, Cockspur—same as single-go, puss-claw.

2. SUSUMBA.

1952 FGC StM, Cockspur resembles wild coffee, with white flowers; it bears round berries.

COCK'S-SPUR see prec.

COCKSTONE (PEAS) sb; *OED* 2, only quot 1756, '*Obs.*' A large variety of kidney-bean, red or of mixed colours: *Phaseolus vulgaris*; named from its resemblance to the testicle of a cock.

1756 Browne 291, Phaseolus 5..The Kidney-Bean, or Cock-stone. 1814 Lunan I 433, This useful vegetable, of which there are numerous varieties, known by the name of *cockstones*, grows very plentifully in Jamaica..Seeds several, ovate or oblong, kidney-shaped, smooth, and shining; they vary exceedingly in shape and size, but particularly in colour, being white, black, blue, red, and variously spotted. 1952 FGC Port, Cockstone, peas, black and white; StAnn, white, with black stripes; StC, big red ones; StM, red, named from their shape; StT, bigger than ordinary red peas.

COCK-TEETH adj dial; < COCK vb + TEETH for *tooth(ed)*. Having teeth that stick out angularly. See next. *G*

COCK-TEETH PARROT sb dial; < COCK-TEETH + PARROT. A variety of PARROT fish with teeth that stick out of its mouth and are twisted. *G*

1952 FGC StC.

COCO /kuoko/ sb[1]; 1740–90 cocoa, 1756 cocco, 1788→ coco, 1864 cocoe; etym uncert—poss: (1) A Polynesian name imported with the plant (cf Hawaiian *kokole*, fifth generation of a *taro* plant; Rarotongan *taro-koa-koa*, a variety of *Colocasia*; (2) A new formation made by W.I. negroes—cf *coco (nut)*; (3) A W.I. dial form of *Colocasia* (cf the similarly formed JACK SPENCE, *simi-kantrak*, SINGLE-BIBLE, TRIMONA, etc.). The Twi *kóòkó*, *koókó* are thought to be loan-words from Jamaica, whence one variety of the plant was introduced into Africa (Christaller). Cf also Fanti *koko*.

1. The plant *Colocasia*, esp *C. esculenta*, and its edible tuber, the 'coco root'. (The rhizome and the leaves are also eaten: cf COCO-CALALU, COCO-HEAD, COCO-LEAF.) Also extended to include similar plants of *Xanthosoma* spp which have no tubers but of which the rhizome is eaten—specifically BADU, DASHEEN, EDDO, TANYA or TAYA.

1740 Importance 39, They make use of Yams..the Cocoa Root, Potatoes. 1756 Browne 332, Arum 4..The purple *Cocco*..Arum 5..the white *Cocco*. 1814 Lunan I 212, The following are the kinds principally cultivated in Jamaica: *purple coco..white coco..Surinam coco..San Blas coco..St Kitt's coco..baboon hog coco* or *taya*. 1823 Roughley 404, Cocoas or eddoes are the most lasting and durable ground provisions..There are several kinds of them. 1864 Grisebach 783, Cocoe: *Colocasia esculenta*. 1929 Beckwith 17, Next to yam in importance of the tubrous vegetables is the coco..The great variety of names attached to the coco in different localities suggests that both nomenclature and variety have a local range.

2. In present folk use, a general term for many plants having leaves like those of *Colocasia*, e.g. FIVE-FINGER, SEVEN-FINGER, etc.; cf COCOWIS.

COCO sb[2]; perh < COCO sb[1]; poss also ref to *coco(nut)* = head. But cf also Amer Sp *bicoque*, in Bolivia, a bump on the head, a blow given on the head with the knuckles. (Santamaría.) A lump which develops rapidly on the head, neck, etc., following a blow. *T*

1877 Murray *Feedin' 'Perrit* 7, I hit de back a me head.. a coco raise up in a me head back, big as a mango. 1946 U.Newton I 16, I fell off the chair backways and collected one of those things known to small boys as 'Cocoes'; *ibid* 26, And that breadfruit gave me a 'coco' (don't you know the sudden swelling called a 'coco') on my head.

COCOA an early spelling for COCO.

COCOABA, COCOABAY see COCOBAY.

COCOA OAK sb. A tree resembling the oak, and used to shade young COCOA (i.e. cacao) trees.

1954 FG 352, Cocoa..Get plants that are grown from specially selected trees. Be sure to provide good shade.. Quickstick and Cocoa oak.

COCOA PIECE sb chiefly dial; < COCO (or perh COCOA) + *piece*. A field where cocos (or possibly cocoa trees, though this would normally be a COCOA-WALK) are grown.

1837 Sterne 17, Me no been there, me go da cocoa piece.

COCOA-PLUM see COCO-PLUM. *BL*

COCOA-POD /koko-pad/ sb dial. The pod in which cacao (or cocoa) beans are contained. *G*

1956 Mc.

COCOA TEA sb dial; cf *OED cocoa* 4 1855 only; and cf TEA. (Cf Fr Créole *dite kako*, du thé cacao. D. Taylor.) Cocoa used as a drink.

1952 FGC Man, Cocoa tea, cocoa to drink; StM, Bissy.. make tea much like cocoa tea. *BA G T*

COCOA-TREE sb; cf *OED cocoa* 4 'the cacao-tree', only quot 1707. The cacao tree, *Theobroma cacao*. *G*

1790 Beckford I 236, There, a grove of coco or chocolate-nut trees protrude their bulbous and purple pods from the rinds of the stems and branches. a1818 Lewis (1834) 258, Near the cocoa-tree.

COCOA-WALK sb[1]; 1661 cacoa-walk, 1671→ cocoa walk, 1679 cacaa walk, 1774 cacao walk; < *cacao* or *cocoa* + WALK. A plantation of cacao (or cocoa) trees, usually placed in rows, with other trees between to shade them.

1661 Hickeringill 19, The Cacoa-Walks, which are not few in this Island, some of them containing ten or twelve Acres of Ground..The Trees are about the bignesse of our largest Plum-trees in England, orderly set, like our Orchards, at the distance of 6 or 7. foot from each other.. and naturally skreen'd and shaded from the piercing rayes of the Sun. 1671 Ogilby Map opposite p 336, 'Cocoa walks' in Clarendon. 1679 Trapham 35, A Cacaa Walk..wherein the Cacaa and Plantain Trees are orderly and successively ranged the one to shelter the other. 1774 Long I 601, The ill success the English have at this time in their cacao walks. 1929 Beckwith 17, The coco..is often planted..in a cocoa or coffee walk.

COCOA-WALK sb[2] obs; imitative of the birds' chattering, and with folk-etymological reference to COCOA-WALK sb[1]. The JABBERING CROW.

1725 Sloane 298, *A Chatering Crow*, or, *a Cacao Walke* ..It frequents the Mountains, where it loves to be always making a chattering Noise, different from that of any of the European Crowes.

COCOBAY sb dial; 1788–9 cocaby, 1801 1820 coco-bay, 1807 cacabay, 1814 coco bay, 1830→ cocobey, 1834 cocoa-bay, 1895 cocoaba, 1929 cocobay, 1943 cocobeh; < Twi *kokobé*, leprosy. Cf *OED cocoabay*. **s.** Also **s** COCOA-BAG.

1. A kind of leprosy or elephantiasis once prevalent among negroes in Jamaica. *G*

1788–9 McNeill 35, Some of these disorders are not only dreadful, but often incurable. These are the *Yaws*..the *Bone-ache*, and the *Cocaby*. 1801 Dancer 230, *Hilary* makes the Elephantiasis different from the Leprosy—*Heberden* describes both them, and the Coco-Bay, as being all one Disease. 1814 Lunan I 59, The decoction of the inner bark is..celebrated for its efficacy in curing the coco bay or elephantiasis, or joint evil. 1873 Rampini 26, One wretched creature, suffering from that particular form of the disease [leprosy] which goes by the African name of 'coco-bay', asked us for an alms.

2. Transf to YAWS and similar diseases. *G*

1895 Banbury 10, Burning wanglo [to punish a thief].. throws out the *king's evil* ('cocoaba') upon him. 1943 *GL* Tre, Cocobeh, yaws. 1956 HPJ, Cocobey, a rough skin like that of a lizard.

3. A whitish exudation from the frog or toad, believed to cause the disease.

1943 *GL* Kgn, Cocobey, a white liquid emitted from the skin of the frog; No address, Cocobey, a white milk from the frog; Clar, Cocobay, Matter from frog.

COCOBAY-MAN sb dial. One affected with COCOBAY; a leper. *G*

1910 Anderson-Cundall, see TAKE SHAME. 1925 Beckwith 60, You tek shame, you shake cocobay-man hand [*A fear of offending will make you shake a leper's hand*].

COCOBEH, COCOBEY see COCOBAY.

COCO-BREAD sb dial; the sense of *coco* is uncert. See quot.

1959 DeC Tre /koko-bred/ a baked 'dumpling' made by pounding dumpling dough out flat, folding over once, then baking. A more descriptive name for the same thing is /pakit-buk/. (No idea what it has to do with /koko/.)

COCO-CALALU sb; <COCO + CALALU.

1. INDIAN KALE, with a small, edible leaf; an early name.

1740 Importance 34, Callaloe of three Sorts, Top-a-Top, or the Cocoa-Callaloe [*Colocasia*]; another Sort grows like Brocoli and eats like Spinage [*Amarantus*]; and the Mountain-Callaloe [*Phytolacca*].

2. The common, uncultivated varieties of Colocasia, sometimes fed to animals.

1952 FGC StM, Coco calilu, riverside calilu.

COCOCHAWYER sb and adj dial; prob a form of COCO-TAYA. A mean or insignificant person.

1943 *GL* StAnn, Cocochawyer, mean, low, not countable.

COCO CRAB sb dial; the sense of *coco* is uncert.

1952 FGC Port, Coco crab, same as jackass crab; West /koko krab/ bigger than sea-crab, reddish, with rough back and toes.

COCOE see COCO.

COCO-EYE sb dial; <COCO sb² + *eye*.

1935 HPJ, Coco-eye, a swollen eye; an eye that has been bunged up.

COCO-FINGER sb obs; <COCO sb¹ + FINGER. A coco, from the tubers' shape, and perh also from their spreading out from the rootstock somewhat like fingers.

1834 Lewis (1845) 55, Their most valuable and regular supply of food arises from the coco-finger, or coccos, a species of the yam, which lasts all the year round. *Ibid* 69. 1907 Jekyll 272 [Song:] Come go da mountain go pick coco finger. [Jekyll notes that this is an old usage, no longer current.]

COCO-HEAD sb chiefly dial. *BL*

1. The rootstock or rhizome of the COCO plant, as distinct from the tuber, which is a COCO.

[1814 Lunan I 212, All the kinds are easily cultivated by cuttings from the main stem or root, commonly called the head, after the plant ceases to produce its esculent roots.] 1823 Roughley 405, Some good, ripe, dry coco heads, with good vegetating eyes, let them be cut into plants. 1873 Rampini 180 [Prov:] When cocoa-head meet rich soil, de root bore de ground. 1952 FGC StAnd, Port, etc.

2. Fig. A stupid person.

1943 *GL* StAnd, Coco-head, a dunce. 1955 FGC Man.

COCO-LEAF sb. *BL*

1. The leaf of the COCO plant; used as food for animals, to tie things in, etc.

1940 HPJ [Riddle:] My fader hab a tank in him yawd, wen i rain plenty i noh ketch eny wata, but wen i drizzle it hol plenty wata. [Answer:] Coco-leaf. [A heavy rain bends the leaf down and spills the water.]

2. Transf and slang: A pound-note (from its green colour).

1943 *GL* Clar, Coco leaf, a pound note. 1955 FGC StM.

COCO-MACCA /kókomáka, kókumáka, kúkumáka, kùkumakyák/ sb dial; <Amer Sp (P. Rico, Cuba, etc.) *coco macaco*, or the Fr equivalent *coco-macaque*, the tree *Bactris plumeriana*, and the stick made from its trunk or stem, noted for its hardness; assimilated to MACCA.

A heavy stick or bludgeon (originally one made from the cocomacaco tree). *G*

[1830 *Negro Emancipation No Philanthropy* 18, The soldiers use the coco macac (a species of heavy jointed cane) in a most arbitrary and sometimes cruel manner.] 1941 Kirkpatrick 22, She wi' step een an' t'row cooku makyac 'pon dem. 1943 *GL* Clar, Cocu macca, a rough stick; Clar, Cucko-macca, club to fight with; Kgn, Cuckoo-maca, a stick; StAnd, Cucu macca, walking-stick. 1944 Campbell *Sweetie Charlie*, Sweetie Charlie a go bus' Mattie head wid 'im coco-macca. 1952 FGC StAnn /kúku máka/ cane.

COCO MEAL sb; <COCO + *meal*. Meal made from the coco root, esp to make bread and biscuit.

1855 *TJSA* II 41, Coco Meal and Second Meal—Quaqua Starch.

COCONUT sb; dial pronunc /kuoknat, kuoknit/. *G*

COCONUT BRUSH sb. A brush for scrubbing and polishing floors, made by sawing off horizontally the top of a dry coconut husk, just above the nut. (Used throughout Ja. FGC.) Cf JOHNNY-COOPA-LANTAN.

COCONUT CAKE sb. = CUT CAKE. *G*

COCONUT CREAM sb. A thicker form of COCONUT MILK 2. *G*

1893 Sullivan 65–6, Cocoanut Cream. Grate a cocoanut. Pour a quart of boiling water on it and skim when cold. Some people merely put the grated cocoanut in a coarse cloth and wring out the juice. It is a great addition to tarts, entrées, or savories.

COCONUT DROP sb. A confection made by boiling small bits of coconut meat in spiced brown sugar fondant and dropping this so as to form lumps or rough cakes; also called CUT BRUTE, etc. *G*

1952 FGC StE, StJ, West, etc.

COCONUT JELLY sb. The unripe jelly-like flesh of the coconut; it is scooped out and eaten. Cf JELLY COCONUT. *BA BL G T*

1958 FGC StAnd, Known to me for the past forty-five years; it has certainly been in use from long before.

COCONUT MILK sb; not entered in historical dictionaries. (Cf *OED milk sb* 3, 1757.)

1. Obs. The slightly cloudy liquid inside a green coconut—what would today be called COCONUT WATER in Jamaica. *BA BL G T*

1826 Barclay 314, It contains also about a pint of delicious juice, called '*cocoa-nut milk*'.

2. The white, thickish liquid obtained by grating the flesh of a ripe coconut, pouring water over, and squeezing. It is used as a sauce for stewed fruits, etc. Also called COCONUT CREAM. *BL G T*

1725 Sloane 41, The [grey Nicker] Beans beaten and us'd with Coco-Nut Milk are good for Ruptures. 1893 Sullivan 65, 'Ricey Cocoa'. Half-a-pint of rice. Cocoanut milk. Nutmeg, spice, sugar, rosewater. Boil a pint of rice very soft, and add to it while hot some cocoanut cream, nutmeg, etc..(1959 FGC, current.)

COCONUT SAUCE sb dial. A coconut RUNDOWN. *G*

1958 DeC StT /kuokonot saas/.

COCONUT WATER sb; *ODS* 1834→. The natural liquid inside an unripe coconut; it is slightly cloudy with a mildly salt-sweet taste. Cf WATER COCONUT. *BA G T*

1817 Williamson i 96, As a refreshing and nutritious drink, cocoa-nut water may be mentioned. (1958, current throughout Jamaica.)

COCO-PLUM sb; 1683 coquer plum, 1727 coco-plumb, 1756 cocco plumb, 1814, 1933 cocoa plum, 1912 cocoaplum, 1914 coco-plum, 1941 cocoplum; <Sp *icaco, hicaco* <Taino *hikako*, Island Carib *hikáku* (D. Taylor); *OED* 1676–99→. *BL N*

1. The tree or shrub *Chrysobalanus icaco*, and its fruit, which is eaten raw or preserved, the seed or nut being considered a delicacy.

1683 Laws map, Coquer Plum B[ay] (shown east of Alligator Pond). 1727 *Observations* 13. 1756 Browne 250. 1814 Lunan I 211. 1933 McK 316, Cocoaplums: an indigo blue berry, favourite among children.

2. Mistakenly applied to the OTAHEITE APPLE.

1958 Mc StJ (Cambridge).

COCO-PLUMB see prec.

COCO ROOT see COCO sb[1].

COCO ROSE sb dial; COCO sb[1]+ROSE. Some species of *Colocasia* that has a sweet-scented flower.

1952 FGC Port, Coco rose, wild arum.

COCO-TAYA sb; <COCO sb[1]+TAYA, here misprinted or erron 'poyer'. The taya (which is a kind of coco).

1834 Lewis (1845) 77, For the vegetables I cannot say so much; yams, plantains, cocoa-poyers, yam-poys, bananas, &c.

COCO-WIS sb dial; <COCO sb[1]+WIS. Any of several vines or climbing plants having large leaves similar to those of *Colocasia*.

1952 FGC Port, Coco-wis, same as wis-maami; StE, China-wis is a big, wild coco-wis; StM, Some call house-wis coco-wis; StT, Coco-wis is five-finger and other leaf —the roots use to tie thatch.

COCO-WOOD sb dial; the sense of *coco* is uncert. See quots. (Quot 1898 may refer to COCCUS WOOD.)

1864 Grisebach 783, Coco-wood: *Inga vera*. 1898 Hill 213, Bitter woods, lancewood bars, satinwood, ebony, coco-wood, lignum-vitæ..are more or less prominent [among woods exported from Jamaica]. 1952 FGC StM /kúkuwùd/ used for firewood, children eat berries.

COCTION /kakshan, kaksham/ sb dial; origin uncertain: perh <*coction* (cf *OED*), which was applied on sugar estates to the process of boiling the cane juice down to make sugar—but cf also *concoction*, of which this may be an abbr. The form 'Kak Sham' is prob infl by ASHAM.

A confection of parched guinea corn heated with sugar, made into balls or cubes, and usually coloured pink (very much like US 'popcorn balls').

1952 FGC StC /kakshan/ To make, parch the guinea corn, put in a pot with sugar, at the end ball it; StM /kákshán/ Guinea corn sweetened and coloured. 1959 O. P. Cousins Kgn, Kak Sham..is made from 'popped' Guinea Corn cemented together by a syrupy mixture of sugar and other flavour. The cake which is usually cuboidal or prismatic may be coloured red or left in its natural brown colour. Quite common with sweets pedlars in Kingston.

COCUS see COCCUS WOOD.

COCYA sb dial rare; <Amer Sp *cocuyo*, firefly. (Ult <Taino. D. Taylor.)

1943 *GL* Clar, Cocya, firefly.

COD vb dial; abbr of COW-COD. To whip or beat.

1955 Bennett *Me Dream*, Sometimes she fetch me aise a box Sometime she cod me back.

COD-PEPPER sb; cf *OED* *sb*[1] 1727. Capsicum of any variety, as distinct from JAMAICA PEPPER, PEPPER-ELDER, etc.

1671 Ogilby 338, Cod-pepper [grows] very plentifully. 1672 Brome 13, Codd-pepper which is so commonly used in all the West Indies, grows plentifully here. 1725 Sloane 147, Cod-pepper, capsicum.

COFFEE /kaafi/ sb dial. =BREAKFAST; used chiefly in the country; cf CHAKLATA, TEA. *G*

COFFEE BIRD sb; cf *OED* 'a kind of bullfinch..found in Jamaica which builds its nest in coffee trees'. The Greater Antillean Bullfinch (*Loxigilla violacea*).

1936 Bond 386, Coffee Bird. 1949 Forbes 55, An orange bird, a 'blue quit' and a 'coffee-bird' are among the 200 known species. 1956 Jeffrey-Smith 102, Then the Black Sparrow, or Black Bullfinch, or Coffee Bird (to give it a few of its names), is seen in numbers on these [fustic] trees.

COFFEE LIZARD sb. See quot; the name prob refers to the brownish coloration.

1940 Lynn-Grant 92–5, *Anolis opalinus* Gosse..Known only from Jamaica..a very common little species known throughout Jamaica as the 'coffee lizard'.

COFFEE MOUNTAIN sb obs; cf MOUNTAIN. An estate in the mountains on which coffee is grown.

1798 Evidence 20, Have you..sold a coffee mountain, and negroes, called Ginger-Hall..? 1801 Nugent 29, Intend to drive to Mr Lewis's Coffee Mountain. 1825 Bickell 197, I was walking out with a Mr Jackson..who had a coffee mountain near; *ibid* 248, Sometimes, coffee mountains are bought well established, in full bearing. 1828 Marly 58, To embark in wild speculations, of bringing in new sugar ground or forming coffee mountains, whenever a transitory rise in price of these commodities took place. 1839 McMahon 227, Took charge of Mr Gibb's Coffee Mountain.

COFFEE PIECE sb; cf *OED piece sb* 2b, *DAE* 2. A plot of land on which coffee is grown. *G*

1873 see MOUNTAIN. 1890 Thomas 53, A piece of land at the entrance of the woods that was formerly a coffee piece. 1946 U.Newton 16, Such work as 'picking up the yard' or 'running down the coffee piece for some brush-wood'.

COFFEE STEM BORER sb.

1943 *NHN* II 70, Coffee Stem Borer, *Apate terebrans*.

COFFEE TEA sb dial; cf TEA. Coffee used as a drink. *BA G N*

1952 FGC Port, Coffee tea, coffee to drink.

COFFEE WALK sb; <*coffee*+WALK. *G*

1839 McMahon 222, Ridge Pen and Coffee-walk, two properties which adjoined each other.

COG sb dial rare; prob <*cog*, a coin, cf *OED sb*[4] 3 →1729.

1943 *GL* Tre, Cog, one shilling.

COGWOOD sb; *OED* 1725 →1814. *Zizyphus chloroxylon*, a valued hardwood native to Jamaica; see quot 1756.

1725 Sloane 85. 1756 Browne 187, The Greenheart or Cogwood Tree. . The wood is very tough and hard, and observed to answer better than any other sort for the coggs used in the rolls of a sugar-mill. 1886 Hooper 32, Cogwood, Ceanothus chloroxylon. 1926 Fawcett 64.

COLABAN see CALABAN.

COLALUE see CALALU.

COLD-BUSH sb dial. Any plant which is considered a good medicine for colds: Aloes, Leaf-of-life, Water-grass, etc. (A list of plants actually so used is in *WIMJ* 36–7.) *G*

1940 HPJ, Cold-bush. 1955 *WIMJ* 155, This species continues in use as a cold bush.

COLD-CHOKE sb dial; <*cold*+*choke* (cf *OED sb*[1] 1b: prison bread). A jocular name for cold food, which is hard to swallow.

1877 Murray *Feedin' 'Perrit* 4, I eben carry boil bittle in dere, cold choke, when I da go fishinin'. 1959 DeC West /kuold chuok/ left-over food eaten at a later meal.

COLD LIQUOR sb. The freshly squeezed juice of sugar-cane (before it is boiled to make sugar). *G*

1890 Thomas 73, He hospitably invited us to his sugar-mill. He cut a few canes, and there being no draught beasts on the spot, five or six of the men harnessed themselves to the mill and ground enough 'cold liquor' for the whole party. 1950 Pioneer 64, While dem all ah chaw [sugar-cane], him show de fus cow one big bottle him did hab, full up wid cole-liquor, an ax him ef him want taste it.

COLD TEMPERING sb. A method of tempering sugar (starting crystallization) formerly practised; see quot.

1811 Mathison 53, A different method has been lately practiced. . which is principally experienced in the improved quality of the sugar. . This process is distinguished by the term '*Cold tempering*', according to which the lime is administered to the cane-liquor in a cold state in a vessel, contrived for that purpose, called the receiver; to which no fire is applied during any part of this early process. . At the expiration of fifteen or twenty minutes the clean saccharine liquor is fit to be drawn off by cocks suitably placed in the receiver.

COLD WIS sb dial; *cold* (*OED sb*[6] 4) +WIS. A withe or vine used as a medicine against colds; cf CHIGGER-NUT quot 1955, and COLD BUSH.

1955 *WIMJ* 71, *Tournefortia hirsutissima* L. Chigger nut; Cold Withe; Horse. . Bath.

COLIC MINT sb dial; see CULLEN MINT quot 1954.

COLIC WEED sb dial. A common wild plant used medicinally against indigestion or 'colic'.

1954 *WIMJ* 28, *Achyranthes indica*. . Devil's Horsewhip; Devil's Riding Whip; Devil's Backbone; Colic Weed; Hug-me-close.

COLLAR vb; <*collar* (*OED v* 4, 5). With following prepositions: to take firm hold. *G*

1950 Pioneer 20, Anancy calla awn pon Jackass an teck wey all a de grass outa him cart.

COLLARED SWIFT sb ornith.

1955 Taylor 82. (Cf CLOUD SWIFT.) 1956 Jeffrey-Smith 21, The broad white band around the neck has given it the name of the Collared Swift (*Streptoprocne zonaris*).

COLLINS sb dial; prob from a trade name. A kind of MACHETE.

1958 DeC StT /kalinz/ a cutlass.

COLO-COLO see *kolo-kolo*.

COLON BIRD /kolon bod/ sb; origin unknown. A mythical bird with a habit of hopping on one leg.

1956 Mc StE (Accom) [Prov:] Ef yu go to di kolon bod an yu see 'im jump 'pan wan fut, an yu jump an wan fut, remember ef yu slip, yu wil shit. [I.e. What is good for the gander is not necessarily good for the goose; or as a warning, Do not mock mysterious things: you may come to grief.]

COLON BUSH sb dial; associated in some way with *Colon*, Panama. Said to be a former name of JOHN CHARLES.

1952 FGC StAnn /kálan bush/.

COLONIAL (CHURCH) UNION sb obs exc hist. An association of planters and others, formed in 1832 and active into 1833, aimed at opposing dissenting sects and their missionaries whom they considered responsible for the slave insurrections of 1831–2. (See Gardner 279 ff.)

1835 Madden I 281, The colonial unions which had been established since the termination of the rebellion [1832], now openly set the power of the executive at defiance. The attorney-general had declared these societies to be illegal. *Ibid* 284, Colonel Hilton, the president of the St Anne's Colonial Union, had convened a meeting, at which very strong resolutions were passed. . censuring the Governor. 1863 Waddell 76 (Year 1833), The 'Colonial Church Union' was. . formed. . for the purpose of expelling all 'Sectarian' missionaries from the island. *Ibid* 79, The patronage of the 'Kirk', offered by the Colonial Union, and its pretended favour for a time to our mission, we did not court, nor warrant, nor even avail ourselves of.

COLON MINT see CULLEN MINT.

COLT'S FOOT sb bot; cf *OED* 2, 'in W. Indies, *Piper peltatum* (*Pothomorpha*)'.

1864 Grisebach 783, Coltsfoot: *Pothomorpha*. 1914 Fawcett 26, *Piper umbellatum*. . Colt's-foot. 1954 *WIMJ* 31, *P. umbellatum*. . Cow or Colt's Foot.

COLU sb dial; an early form of *cola*—cf *OED*.

1814 Lunan I 87, The negroes in Jamaica call it *bichy* or *colu*, where the seeds are used by themselves, or mixed with capsicum, for complaints in the belly.

COMANANCY see COBY.

COMB-CLAWED CRAB sb obs.

1756 Browne 421, Cancer 3. . The comb-clawed Crab. This species is both rare and curious; it is very large, and the claws are grooved on one side and indented on the other, so as to resemble a comb and comb-case in some measure.

COMBOLO /kómbolò/ sb dial; 1907 combolow, 1924 cumbalo cumbolo, 1943 cumbohloh, 1943 1950 combolo; etym uncert: the word seems to be primarily the name of an African song-dance, in which the phrase 'we all a Combolo' meant *we are all dancing the Combolo* (i.e. treating *combolo* as a verb); this phrase, however, came to mean *we are all companions* (cf Cuban *cúmbila*, comrade, friend—Malaret; S and Cent Am Sp *cumpa*, Mex *compa*, familiar abbr of *compadre*, fellow, companion; also Sp *compañero*, comrade, mate. There may be other African words involved—cf Kimbundu *camba*, comrade—Mendonça). BOLO (BOLOW) may be an abbr of this, or perh an independent element to which *com-* has been prefixed.

1. A traditional African song-dance; this word appears to be a metathetic variant with CALEMBE, though which is primary is uncertain. See quots.

1924 Beckwith 177, 'But Bruddie, dat ol' Cumbolo dat was singing las' night!'—'Den you mus' come let we dance de Cumbolo, Susan, we all a Cumbolo!' (sing and dance). [Note:] The dance (also called 'calimbe') is performed at wakes. *Ibid* 288, Sarah Findley was an old-time negress who lived in a little hut far out in the bush. She danced to the song with a queer jumping motion like boys playing leap-frog and with all the agility of a young girl. The dance as a wake game is performed upon two parallel bars held by four men. One informant called it dancing 'Calimbe'.

2. A comrade, companion, friend.

1907 Jekyll 177 (Song) We all a combolow, John Thomas; [Note, 178:] 'Combolow' is comrade oh! 1943 *GL* Kgn, Combolo, friend or companion; StJ, Combolo, company.

3. A sexual partner.

1957 DeC Port, StC /kómbolò/ Sexual partners or companions.

4. An old machete. (To the Jamaican countryman, his machete is a constant companion.)

1943 *GL* StM, Cumbohloh, old machete.

COMBOLOW see prec.

COMB-WOOD sb dial. *Sloanea jamaicensis*, from the close-packed spikes, like the teeth of a comb, with which the seed capsule is covered. Also called BREAK-AXE, IRON WOOD, LIGNUM DURUM, POP-NUT, PUSS HEAD.

1952 FGC StAnn, Comb-wood, same as break-axe, etc. (Said to be so called also in Man and Tre.)

COME[1] /kom, kong, kum/ vb dial; <*come*. *BA G*

1. As a command, without the idiomatic adverbs (e.g. *here*, *along*, *in*) of Std English.

1952 FGC StAnd, Come! (in answer to a knock on the door); Come, no? (Said to a lagging child.)

2. Before another verb with the effect of preparing for it, thus of giving it prominence or greater force. *T*

1950 Pioneer 34, Before yuh tank me fe carry yuh pon me head yuh dah shake-up shake-up yuhself, an a come back-answa me.

3. Following another verb of motion, with quasi-adverbial effect; also with adverbs following. *T*

193– HPJ, 'Massoo i' carry me cum', *Lift it up and bring it here to me.* 1956 Mc Man, We walk it down [from Bull Savanna to Alligator Pond] but we drive an' bus come up; StE /mi kyaang waak kom out/ *I can't walk out.*

4. Repeated before another verb, with conjunctive force. *BL*

1877 Murray *Kittle* 18, Dis naga man come come collar me de same like a say me da him sexis [*This black man comes and collars me just as if I were the same sex as he*]. 1952 FGC StAnd [Mother, to her child:] Come-come tek yu food.

COME[2] /kom/ vb dial; <*become*, or perh <*come* as abbr of *come to be*. To be, become, come to be. *BL G N*

1868 *TRSAA* I 66, Missis wi' sen' fe you breakfus; him mus' a da put i' up tay i' come 'nough, 'nough. *She must have put it away until it becomes plenty.* 1873 Rampini 182 [Prov:] Yellow snake an' fowl no compartner [prob for 'come partner']. 1943 *GL* Kgn, Lard how yu com so, What's wrong with you. 1952 FGC StT (Tape record of Fan Me Soldier Man) /wen di biebi kom baan-uo, di faada gaan a kantinjen/ *When the baby comes to be born, oh, the father is gone in a Contingent.* 1956 Mc StAnd /wen i kom kuol/ *When it cools.*

COME-AN'-GO-'LONG sb dial. =RAM-GOAT-DASHALONG.

1940 HPJ, Come-an-goh-lang, 'dash along' (a weed).

COME-AROUND /komaroun, kamaroun, kamarong/ sb dial; by folk-etym <Amer Sp *camarón* (cf Santamaría: the basic meaning seems to be a beggar or parasite).

1. A day-labourer or casual worker, not at regular work. *N*

2. Hence, a loafer, a petty thief or cheat.

1912 McK *Songs* 74, Day-labourers, men and women, in Kingston streets and wharves, famous for the heavy weights they carry, are called come-arounds. 1943 *GL* Kgn, Comaroun, scuffler; Tre, Camaroun, A person who loafs at shop place; Clar, Camaroung, a trickster.

COME-BETWEEN sb dial.

1. A derogatory term for an albino negro (who 'comes between' black and white). Also called QUAW (3).

1958 DeC StT /kom-bitwiin/.

2. A between-meals snack.

1958 DeC StT.

COME DOWN vb phr dial; cf *OED come* 56.

1. Said of the soft palate when it becomes inflamed and enlarged. *G*

1820 Thomson 75, They [negroes] are, however, liable to inflammation of the *uvula and amygdaloid glands* in the severest forms. The palate enlarges (comes down, as they call it), and the throat is much inflamed.

2. Said of a river or other watercourse: to flood. *G*

1907 Jekyll 101, At last the river come down carry him gone. 1951 Murray 47 [Song:] De ribber ben come dung, An' me couldn' get ovah.

COME-HERE-FE-HELP-WE, COME-TO-HELP-US, sb dial; see quot 1929. ST VINCENT YAM.

1929 Beckwith 16, 'Come-here-fe-help-we' Wilfrid called the St Vincent because it keeps so long in the earth, and propagates itself by seed, so that one planting will sometimes perpetuate itself for fifteen years and serve the people in hard times. 1942 Bennett 44, Me have—rento, mosela wite An' come-to-help us yam. 1954 LeP Man, Port, StE, Come-to-help-us, St Vincent yam.

COME-SEE sb dial. A variety of mango; the name implies that the fruit is famous and means 'eat it and see for yourself'.

1943 *GL* Port, Kumci, A mango peculiar to St Mary; StM, Come-see, a mango.

COME SEE ME /kòm-sí-mi/ vb phr and sb dial.

A. vb phr: Used to invite or entice someone or something—in the quotation, an incantation: Come to me, within my control. *G*

1924 Beckwith 52 [Anansi, singing a song intended to draw Goat into his yard so that he may eat him:] Meat a da me yard, Meat, come see me. (Repeated.)

B. sb: A ratoon or sucker of a plant, which comes up and draws attention to itself. Cf COME-SEE.

1943 *GL* Tre, Come-see-me, ratoon plants.

COMES-UP sb dial; cf *OED come v*, 69 f. Impudence; self-obtrusion.

1912 McK *Ballads* 34, You'll soon see'm pokin' up him nose Wid him bareface an' comes-up.

COME TOGETHER sb dial. To coagulate, to set. *BA G*

1956 Mc StAnd, For corn pone, grater the corn with sugar, leave until it come together.

COME-TO-HELP-US see COME-HERE-FE-HELP-WE.

COMFEREE sb dial arch; etym uncert—perh < Fr *confrère* (cf 1898 Robert Hill 287 on use of this word by Haitian peasants as a term of polite greeting). Both form and meaning of this word show confusion; it survives in a song in which the words may be originally African now garbled, and this may itself be affected by folk-etym.

1924 Beckwith 75–6, Sammy the Comferee..It was a woman had one son, an' it was a boy dat very unruly by him mudder an' fader..Dis boy was Sammy de Comferee. [Sammy goes to Massa Jesus' yard, is detained all day by his wife, so that Massa Jesus' clothes are wet by rain. Massa Jesus makes Sammy climb a red-hot pole—he sings the song while climbing it—which melts him entirely to fat. If Sammy had not been so pretty, none of this would have happened.] 1924 Beckwith 76 [Song:] Ah, me Sam-my de Con-fa-ri-a-e-ro, Gi-ra no, ah, in din ro. 1926 Roberts 349 [Song:] A mi Sammy di Con-fa-ri-a ir rōw Gi-ra no a in din rōw.

COMFORTER adj dial, compar degree; < *comfort*(able) + *-er*. More comfortable.

1956 BLB, From a song about a little hut in the hills: /i likl, bot i komfata/.

COMICAL /kámikl/ adj and sb dial; cf *OED comical* 5. Not serious, frivolous, fussy; as a sb, one who makes a fuss or foolishly finds fault.

1943 *GL* Clar, Cammicle, scorner. 1954 LeP StE, Camickle, a fussy, pernickety person. 1956 McMan /kámikl/ fussy over food. *BL*

COMING ppl adj; cf *OED* 1, where *coming* usually precedes the noun. In expressions of time, this follows the name of the day or month. (Its counterpart is GONE.) *BA BL G T*

1956 Mc Man, StC /satide komin/ next Saturday.

COMMANDER (COCO) /komáanda, kománda/ sb dial. A widely used name for a hard variety of coco, the name suggesting its superior quality. Also called DUKE, LEF'-MAN.

1927 Anderson-Cundall 31 [Prov:] Commanda coco an' white yam no bear togedda. 1943 *GL* Port, Commander cocoa, juk cocoa; StM, Coomannda coco, lefman coco. 1952 FGC Port, StAnd, StAnn, StC, StJ, StM, StT.

COMMON BROOMWEED sb bot obs; < *common* adj + BROOMWEED. Macfadyen's name for *Sida jamaicensis* (ident 1926 Fawcett 111).

1837 Macfadyen 77, Sida Jamaïcensis. *Common Broom-weed.*

COMMON-GRASS sb dial; < *common* sb + *grass*. A kind of grass which grows on commons or meadows.

1952 FGC StM.

COMMON LETTER sb dial; < *common* adj + *letter* sb. A small or lower-case letter of the alphabet. *G*

1959 Miss M. Bramford, StAnd; also others.

COMMON MANGO sb; < *common* adj + *mango*. A variety of mango not considered choice; also called HAIRY, STRINGY or YELLOW MANGO. *BL*

1952 FGC Port, StAnd, StE, StM /káman mánggo/. 1954 *FG* 475 (see quot s.v. HAIRY MANGO).

COMMON PIN sb gen; < *common* adj + *pin*. An ordinary metal pin. *BL G T*

1962 BLB 58.

COMPANY vb dial; cf *OED* →1814; *EDD* Sc. →1897. To give companionship to. *G*

1956 Mc Man /iz a litl popi di misis gyíev mi tu kompani mi/ *It's a little puppy the mistress gave me to keep me company.*

COMPARTNER see COME[2]. s.

COMPELLANCE WEED sb dial; < *compel* + *-ance*. A cant term, prob originating in BALM use (cf OIL OF COMPELLANCE): GANJA, under the infl of which one feels compelled to act.

1943 *GL* no address, Compellance weed, ganja.

COMPELLING POWDER sb dial. A cant term (cf OIL OF COMPELLANCE): a powder supposed to be able to compel someone to love another. *BL G*

1940 HPJ, *Compellin-powder*, Tempting-powder or 'stay-home'. An obeah charm to secure somebody's love.

COMPOUND TREE sb. A local name for CASHAW; being extremely prickly it can be used for fences to form compounds.

1952 FGC StE.

CONCENTINA sb dial. A concertina.

1907 Jekyll 132, Annancy get a concentina*..An' when Annancy go down Annancy was playing..An' when the mumma hear, the music was so sweet she commence to dance. * *Concentina*, always with this *n*.

CONCH see *kongk*.

CONCHS-NUT see *kangksnot*.

CONCONSA see *kongkongsa*.

CONCONTAY, CONCONTEY see *kongkonte, kongkote*.

CONCRETE sb dial slang. A jocular name for various hard or solid starch foods with peas or beans mixed in (evidently representing the cement and the gravel), specifically RICE-AND-PEAS, MUSA; see quots.

1943 *GL* StAnd, StAnn, Concrete, cooked rice and peas. 1958 DeC Port, TURNED CORNMEAL with peas (i.e. MUSA), allowed to cook until it is very hard.

CONCUBINE sb dial; cf *OED*: as applied to a woman, quots →1815, and to a man →1540.

1954 LeP StAnn, Concubine, lover or sweetheart (man or woman). *G*

CONCUBINE LIFE sb dial.

1956 Mc StAnd /kángkyubàin láif/ living together unmarried; also Port.

CONEY see INDIAN CONEY.

CONFARIA see COMFEREE.

CONFEREE sb dial rare; obscurely <*confer* or *conference*?

1940 HPJ, Conferee, conversation; Miss Reynolds suggests this was the origin of 'Sammy the Conferee'.

CONFUSION sb dial; perh <*confusion OED* 6, prob infl in meaning by *contention*. A quarrel, often leading to a fight. *BL G*

1873 Rampini 95, 'Confusions', in negro parlance, do occasionally take place..But, as a rule, quarrels seldom occur. 1907 Jekyll 61, So Annancy begin to raise a confusion over it..An' 'creech-owl began to cry. *Ibid* 135–6, One day Mr Annancy an' Monkey, made a bargain to kill Tiger, an' they didn' know how to make the confusion for Tiger was Monkey godfather..An' that time Puss was passing when the confusion occurred. 1912 McK *Songs* 14 [Note:] And we cannot complain, for this would 'bring confusion', *i.e.* cause a row.

CONFUSION vb dial; <*confusion* sb. To confuse. *BA G*

1941 Kirkpatrick 39, Dem a scatter scatter demself lak w'en pan 'ead [policeman] run dung dem gambler bwoy.. an' dem all run diffran way fe confusion de pan 'ead.

CONG see COUSIN.

CONGASO see *kongkongsa*.

CONGEA /konja/ sb; from the genus name. A vine which trails luxuriantly over trees: *Congea tomentosa*.

1940 HPJ, Conja, a vine with a pink, four-petalled flower. 1959 FGC StAnd [kɔndʒə].

CONGO /kangga, kanggo, konggo, konggu/ sb now chiefly dial; 1757 Conkaw, 1774→ Congo.

1. The African country of origin of many Jamaican negroes; also attrib. *G*

1757 St Jago *Intelligencer* 14 May (Advertisements for runaway slaves), Of the Conkaw Country..speaks very little English..Three men..of the Congo Country. 1790 Moreton 153 [Song:] If me want for go in a Congo, Me can't go there! Since dem tief me from my tatta, Me can't go there!

2. A negro from the Congo region. *G*

1774 Long II 352, The Congo's, Arada's, Quaqua's, and Angola's, particularly the latter, who are likewise the most stupid. 1828 Kelly 21, The Mongolas, the Mandingoes, the Eboes, the Congoes, &c., formed into exclusive groups, and each strove to be loudest in the music and songs.

3. Among the folk today, used to suggest blackness (cf CONGO FLY, etc.), stupidity, backwardness, and other mostly unfavourable qualities. (The Congo were later comers than Gold Coast and Guinea negroes, whose Jamaican-born descendants looked down on them.) Also attrib. Cf Bantu *nkongo*, slave. *G*

1929 Beckwith 4, Even today the term 'Congo' refers to one who is the butt of his fellows. *Ibid* 215, An occasional noodle story told of a 'congo nager', like that of the slave who, sent to bring home a clock from the repair shop, kicked it to pieces because it persisted in striking. 1943 *GL* Kgn, Bungo, Congo man; Tre, Congo, a foolish negro. 1954 LeP StAnn, Congo, very black negro.

4. A fish; cf *kanggatuoni*.

1943 *GL* StAnd, Kongu, fish.

CONGO ANTS sb dial; cf CONGO PEGGY.

1952 FGC Man /Kongo hants/ I hear of it, don't know it.

CONGO BREADFRUIT sb dial; cf CONGO 3. A variety of breadfruit having a rough skin, and not as fine eating as others; it is contrasted for quality with FINEY.

1952 FGC StAnn /kanggo bredfruut/.

CONGO CHIGGER sb dial. The chigger (cf *DA*), evidently thought of as having come from the Congo. *G*

1952 FGC Tre /kangga chiga/.

CONGO FLY sb dial; cf CONGO 3.

1952 FGC Tre /konggo flai/ a black fly.

CONGO-JOE sb dial; CONGO+*Joe*, personifying name (cf ROGUING JOE); cf, however, JO-PAN, which also implies that this element refers to a container.

1943 *GL* Kgn, Congo-jo, Bag made of pa[l]m leaves of the thatch tree, to carry ground provisions from ground to peasants' homes.

CONGO MAHOE /konggo/ sb; <CONGO 1 +MAHOE. See quots.

1814 Lunan I 469–70, It grows but rarely in the island of Jamaica, in coppices near the coast. Its common name is Congo mahoe, the negroes affirming that it came originally from Africa. *Sw*[*artz*]. Sloane says it grew on the Red Hills very plentifully. 1837 Macfadyen I 70, This plant has probably received from the Negroes the name of *Congo-Mahoe*, from its resembling some plant, bearing the name of Mahoe, in their native country. 1926 Fawcett 139, *Hibiscus clypeatus*..Congo Mahoe. 1952 FGC Man, Tre /kónggo mahúo/.

CONGO PEAS sb; the etym or learned form of the name GUNGO (PEAS). *OED* 1866 only. *G*

1837 Macfadyen I 296, Cajanus bicolor. *Pigeon or Congo Pea*. 1864 Grisebach 786. [Occas in present use. FGC.]

CONGO PEGGY sb dial; cf Okwawu *kàŋkaŋ*, a kind of big ant (if this is the source of the first element, it has undergone folk-etym change) + *Peggy*, personifying name.

1868 Russell 6, Congo peggy, A large species of ants. 1952 FGC Tre, Congo Peggy, red ants.

CONGO PLAIT /kongo plet/ sb dial. A style of hair-plaiting using only two portions of hair (rather than the usual three) and rolling one over the other continuously round the head, bringing in fresh portions continually. *G*

1956 Mc StE (Accom).

CONGOSAH, CONGOSAW, CONGOSO see *kongkongsa*.

CONGO-TONY see *kanggatuoni*.

CONGO-WORM sb dial; prob <CONGO+ *worm*, but cf *kanggatuoni* 2.

1943 *GL* StM, Cungo-wurrum, Worm that supposedly eats the body after burial.

CONGRY /kanggri, konggri, kanggriil, kanggwi/ sb dial; <*conger eel*; cf *DA congeree*, 1884. Various fish of the family Muraenidae: *Gymnothorax funebris*, and others. *BL*

1756 Browne 444, Muræna 3, The Congre. [This may be merely a spelling-variant of *conger*.] 1877 Murray *Feedin' 'Perrit* 6, Him worser an any congree in a sea.

1952 FGC Port, StC, StJ /kanggri, kanggriil/ green; StM, Green /kanggri/; West /konggri/ bigger type than murrey—dark, not speckled. 1956 Mc StC /kanggwi/; Kgn /griin kanggri an mori kanggri/.

CONJA see CONGEẠ.

CONKANTE see *kongkonte.*

CONNA sb dial; prob < Hindi *kūnḍā*, the refuse of rice.

1943 *GL* Jones Pen, Conna, fine rice thrash, used for feeding pigs.

CONNECTION sb dial rare; perh malapropism for CONFUSION or CONTENTION.

1955 Mc Clar /kom tu kanékshan/ to quarrel, fall out.

CONNU see JOHN CANOE A 1. quot 1774.

CONOO see *kunu.*

CONOO-MONOO see *kunu-munu.*

CONQUINTAY see *kongkonte.*

CONSEQUENTIAL sb dial; perh by omission of *being* before *consequential* adj (or by abbr of *consequentiality*). Self-importance.

1896 Bates 38 [Prov:] Consequential mek crab hab no head. c 1915 FGC StAnd, Him have too-much consequential. 1927 Anderson-Cundall 34.

CONSHEBA see *kanshiiba.*

CONSIDER (ONE'S) HEAD vb phr dial. To consider in one's head; to think deeply. Cf STUDY. *BL G*

1950 Pioneer 66, Brer Tiger nebber get de chance fe ketch Brer Nancy an him consider him head long time fe fine a way fe ketch him.

CONSTAB sb dial; abbr of *constable* or *constabulary. G*

1907 Jekyll 206 [Song:] 'Wheel him, Constab, wheel him'..A girl is the delinquent and the 'Constab' (constable, pronounce *con* as in *con*stant) is inside the ring with her, lightly beating her with a twig or pocket-handkerchief. 1912 McK [Title:] Constab Ballads. 1943 *GL* StJ, Constab, policeman.

CONSTAB MACCA sb dial; < CONSTAB + MACCA. Burs—evid used generally here; cf POLICE MACCA.

1942 Bennett 46, (Of a Ras-Tafari man who has escaped from a meeting that was raided by the police by crawling on his face) Mass John come back fram pinnicle Yuh want see him beard Muma Yuh kean tell ef i meck outa hair or Outa constab macka.

CONSTAB TICKS sb dial; cf CONSTAB. Cattle ticks—so called in StM because they are striped—an allusion to the policeman's trousers. *NHN.*

CONSUMPTION BUSH sb dial. Any kind of plant that is used as medicine against consumption; see quot.

1952 FGC Tre, Consumption bush: jockey-saddle, dog-tongue; also StM, StT—other plants.

CONSUMPTION CURE sb dial = CONSUMPTION BUSH.

CONSUMPTION WEED sb dial. Any of the plants so called that are used against consumption: *Emilia sagittata, Peperomia pellucida,* and others.

1927 Beckwith 18, Grease-bush. *Emilia sagittata..* 'Consumption weed'. For a cough boil as tea. 1952 FGC Han, Port, Consumption weed, same as rat-ears. 1954 *WIMJ* 29. 1955 *WIMJ* 160 (see MARIGOLD).

CONTO see *kantu.*

CONTOO see next.

CONTOON sb; prob < Twi *o-kũntṹ*, Ewe *kuntú*, woollen cloth, flannel, etc., prob infl also by *cantoon* (*OED*: 'A strong kind of fustian..' 1688, and later in dictionaries). Both words refer primarily to fabrics; it is possible that *cantoon*, imported to Jamaica, was identified by the slaves with the cloth called *o-kũntũ* in Africa. (The spelling *cuntung* shows velarization of the final nasal—a common feature of the folk pronunciation.)

1. A kind of heavy cloth (evid used for work clothes).

1940 HPJ, Cuntung—a kind of thick serge..Belisario mentions *contoon*, a cloak..[see quot below].

2. A heavy woollen cloak made of this cloth, used by labourers.

1827 Hamel I 17, 'And what are these?' he added, taking up some garments that lay on the floor, a contoo, and an instrument of music, a bonjaw. *Ibid* 18, He..attired himself in the contoo of his invisible host. 1837 Belisario 4 (unnumbered, under 'Creole Negroes'), A field-Negro with his Kilmarnock cap..a blue checked shirt, Oznaburgh trowsers, and contoon, or cloak made of dark blue woollen-cloth called Pennistone, complete the ordinary costume of the Praedial labourer.

CONTRAJERVA see next.

CONTRAYERVA sb bot; cf *OED*: 'Sp; = "counter herb", *i.e.* one used as an antidote'. In Jamaica: Species of *Aristolochia* (see quots) which have been valued esp as antidotes. *N*

[1672 Blome 14, Here are likewise Contrayerna [*sic*], Cyperas, Aloes..with many other Druggs.] 1707 Sloane lv, One of the greatest remedies of the Planters living here to prevent Diseases, or the ill effect of what they call ill Fumes or Vapours, is an infusion of the Seeds of that kind of *Aristolochia* called *Contra Yerva.* 1756 Browne 329, Aristolochia 1..The *Contra-Yerva* of the south side of *Jamaica.* This plant is a climber..The root has a strong smell, and is deservedly looked upon as a warm attenuant, and an active diaphoretic and stomachic: it is administered in infusions, and greatly used among the slaves in *Jamaica*..Aristolochia 3..The *Contra-Yerva* of the north side. The roots of this plant are used on the north side of the island, where it is most common, in the same manner as those of the first species are on the south side. 1794 Barham 44–5, Contrayerva..This is so called in Jamaica from its great efficacy against poisons, but it is in no respect like the Spanish contrayerva. (Index) *Aristolochia odorata.* 1887 D. Morris in Kew Bulletin 12 7, In Jamaica, this term is invariably applied to a species of *Aristolochia*, while roots of *Dorstenia* are there called Spanish Contrayerva. 1914 Fawcett 106, Contrajerva of the north side (Browne)..*Aristolochia trilobata*..Contrajerva of the south side (Browne)..*A. odoratissima.*

CONVERSATE vb dial; back-formation from *conversation.* To talk. *G*

1958 EP StAnd /yu kyaan kanvisiet laik dat, man/ *You can't* [*shouldn't, mustn't*] *talk like that, man.* (The person spoken to was muttering insults.)

CONY sb; < *cony*, cf *OED.* The INDIAN CONY.

1952 FGC StT /kúoni/ grazy.

CONY-BUCK, CUNNY-BUCK /konibok, konibo/ sb dial; prob < Engl *cony* (cf *cony-fish*) + *buck* (cf BUCK-BUCK); cf also CUNNY. The pronunc /koni-/ was the regular one in 17th–18th-cent England. The TRUNK-FISH.

1952 FGC Port /konibok, konibo/ trunk-fish; also StC, StT. 1956 Mc Kgn, StC /kónibok/ trunk-fish.

COO see KU.

COOB /kub/ sb dial; <*coob*, a hen-coop (cf *EDD*). Transf meanings: see quots. *BL G*

1943 *GL* Port, Coob, a cage; StAnd, Coub, jail. 1956 Mc StAnd /kub/ a large wire pen for animals, a coop (for goats and fowls).

COOBALEY sb dial; origin unknown.

1943 *GL* Port, Coobaley, a game.

COOBITAY see *kubaiti*.

COOBLA, COOBLATA sb dial; cf Ewe *ákobidɛ̀*, a small calabash with a handle. A small or young calabash, or a portion of the shell, used as a drinking vessel, to make a pot-spoon, etc.

1943 *GL* Tre, Coobla, small calabash for drinking; Cooblata, small marrow calabash, Pot spoon.

COOEY see *kuy*.

COOK-HOUSE sb dial; cf *OED*.

1953 Moore 133, Cook-house, where an obeahman mixes his medicines and potions.

COOK RAM see next.

COOK-ROOM sb; cf *OED* b, 1707→1818. A separate room or building used as a kitchen.

1707 Sloane xlvii, The Kitchens, or Cook-Rooms here, are always at a small distance from their Houses. . There are no Chimneys or Fire-places in their Houses, but in the Cook-Room. . This word is used to signifie their Kitchen, and is a Sea word, as many others of that Country. 1774 Long II 319, *Cook-room*. Kitchen. 1802 Nugent 98, The kitchen, or cook-room, as it is called in this country. 1808 Stewart 14, Cook-room, as it is here called. 1943 *GL* Clar, Cook ram, kitchen.

COOKU MAKYAC see COCO-MACCA.

COOK-UP sb; cf *OED v* 2, 3. A dish of meat, rice, and vegetables cooked up together. *G*

1956 Mc StT (see *daal* 2). 1957 *FFM* 152, Cook-up. (Recipe given.)

COOL (COLOUR) adj (and sb) dial; cf US 'jive-talk' of the 1940's and after in which *cool* is a term of approval. See quots. *G*

1956 Mc Man, A *sambo* has /kuul kolo/. 1958 DeC StT, Cool, A complimentary racial term, meaning dark but clean-cut. 1960 SJR StAnd, cool skin = olive skin—very dark black but with a fine, smooth, slightly purplish skin.

COOL COPPERS vb phr obs; <*cool*+ *copper* (*OED sb* 3). By a figure of speech derived from sugar-making: to relieve (oneself) from the heat, or to reduce the heat of activity; see quots.

1802 Nugent 96, When I expressed my regret at parting with Mr Simon Taylor, he said, 'I am very sorry, too, Ma'am, but good Almighty God, I must go home and cool coppers'. I thought really he was going home, to have all the large brass pans emptied to cool, that I had seen the sugar boiling in. .; but I found he meant that he must go home, and be abstemious, after so much feasting. 1835 Senior 115, Cool one's coppers, to have a drink.

COOL-DRINK /kúul-dringk/ sb. A drink, fermented or unfermented, especially intended to allay thirst in warm climates, and to cool the drinker. (In present use the sense is shifting, the drink itself being cooled before serving.)

1707 Sloane lxii, Perino, before described is the wholesomest of all cool Drinks. 1756 Browne 285, Red Sorrel. . the decoction of them, sweetened and fermented, is what people commonly call Sorrel Cool-drink, in America: it is a small diluting liquor, that is much used in all our sugar-colonies, and reckoned very refreshing in those sultry climates. 1774 Long II 314, What is still preferable [to rum], is the *cool drink*, prepared here by many of the free Negroe and Mulatta women, who vend it cheap to the soldiers. . This drink, when cool and depurated, is racy and pleasant, extremely wholesome, and, if taken in too large quantities, intoxicates in some degree, but without causing any ill effect. 1790 Moreton 105, Cool drink or mauby. 1893 Sullivan 114, New Sugar. . Mixed with water to which a squeeze of lime-juice has been added, they call it either 'cool drink' or 'beverage'. 1958 FGC StE, Would you like a cool-drink? /kúul-dríngk/ not /kúul dríngk/. *BL G*

COOLER sb. A device used in many Jamaican houses to keep them cool; it may be a box-like construction with jalousies built around a window, or a slatted wooden awning hinged so that it may be set at various angles to the house.

1952 FGC StAnd, StM, etc. *G*

COOLIE sb, also attrib; cf *OED*. An East Indian; formerly a neutral word, now used derogatively by many non-East Indians, and objected to by East Indians. (East Indians began coming to Jamaica as indentured labourers in 1834–8, and on a larger scale after 1845.) *BA BL G T*

1862 Underhill 271, The estates' negroes exhibit no hostility or jealousy towards the Coolies, and do not seem to fear that their employment will either depreciate wages, or drive them from the estates. 1907 Jekyll 265 [Song:] Me da Coolie sleep on piazza with me wrapper round me shoulder. 1924 Beckwith 209, A path where a poor coolie-man and his family had to cross. 1940 HPJ, Coolie, East Indian. 1943 *GL* Kgn, Ah-ta, flour. Coolie word. 1955 LeP StT, Coolie-man kyaan win! (Bustamante, at an election meeting in which his candidate was opposed by an East Indian.) 1956 JN StM, Live with mi grannie in Belfield Works. Grannie is a coolie.

COOLIE BAAJ sb dial; COOLIE + *baaj*. The fruit of *Averrhoa carambola*: see CHINESE JIMBLING quot 1958.

COOLIE CALALU sb dial. A type of CALALU grown especially by East Indians, who are skilful vegetable gardeners. *G*

1952 FGC StC /kuuli kalalu/ has a blue stalk, big and fat.

COOLIE DUPPY sb dial. The ghost of an East Indian, believed to be one of the most troublesome haunters.

1940 HPJ, Coolie duppy (or ghost), the strongest and most malignant spirit used by Obeahmen. 1955 Bennett *Pleasuration*, Big noise eena Cudelia yard, Bra Charles and Sista Clem Dah jump and kick an gwan like Coolie-duppy deh pon dem!

COOLIE-FOOT SUGAR sb dial. Muscovado sugar; the nickname comes from the fact that what was spilled and stepped upon by East Indians bagging it at sugar factories was swept up and sold very cheap.

1926 Edmonds 30, Sprinkle with currants, cinnamon and mixed spice, and coolie foot sugar (muscovado sugar). 1943 *GL* StM, Coolie foot, brown Albion sugar. 1952 FGC StE, StJ, StM, Coolie-foot sugar, muscovado.

COOLIE OKRO sb dial; < COOLIE + OKRO. A coarse variety of okro (?eaten by coolies).

1952 FGC StT, Coolie okro = Bungo okro.

COOLIE PEPPER sb. A type of *Capsicum*; see quot.

1952 FGC StJ /kuuli pepa/ big, hot, red when ripe Coolies grow it.

COOLIE PLUM sb dial. A fruit shaped like a very small apple; recently introduced to Liguanea plain: *Zizyphus mauritiana*. Also called CHINEY APPLE.

1952 FGC StAnd, Coolie plum is round, same size as red-coat plum ,same seed, but a green looks, and the tree have prickle. 1957 *FFM* 102, Fruits, such as mangoes, 'coolie plums', guavas, etc., are eaten in large amounts when in season.

COOLIE-RIAL sb dial; COOLIE+RIAL. A person of mixed East-Indian and negro stock.

1935 HPJ, *Coolie ryal*: Child of Coolie and Creole. 1955 FGC StAnd /kùuli-ráial/.

COOLIE WEED sb dial. The fern *Anemia underwoodiana*.

c 1950 GHP Port.

COOLMASSA see SCHOOLMASTER.

COOLOO COOLOO see *kulu-kulu*.

COOMANNDA COCO see COMMANDER.

COON sb dial; perh <*cone*?

1. A felt hat.

1943 *GL* StAnd, Coon, felt hat.

2. A manner of wearing a hat, shaping it so that it is low in front, high at the back; also attrib. *G*

1955 FGC Man, Coon-shape.

COONFOODOO sb dial rare; ?familiarizing alteration of *confidant*. (Cf COMBOLO.)

1943 *GL* StE, Coonfoodoo, companion.

COONO-MOONO see *kunu munu*.

COONOO see *kunu*.

COONOO-COONOO /kúnu-kúnu/ sb dial; prob from the fact that the trees are found at *Cuna-cuna Pass* (Blue Mts)—the pass itself prob being named after the mountainous 'Akuna Kuna Country', inland from Old Calabar (cf 1863 Waddell, map facing p. 242). A timber tree, prob *Symphonia globulifera*.

1890 Thomas *Victoria Qrly* May 68–9, Coonoo-coonoo, A large tree, also called boar-gum and gracie-wood. 1890 Thomas *Untrodden Jamaica* 23, But the most striking in appearance was the 'gracie-wood', or 'coonoo-coonoo',—it bears both names. It is of immense girth, its trunk profusely garnished with knots and excrescences of varying size, and its branches twisted in every direction. 1935 HPJ—see quot s.v. BOAR-GUM.

COONOOH see *kunu*².

COONOOMOONOO see *kunu-munu*.

COONTOONG adj dial rare; <Twi *kȭntũŋŋ*, large, bulky, huge; dark; clumsy.

1943 *GL* StE, Coontoong, horrible looking.

COOPER('S) HOOP or **HOOK** sb; formerly used by *coopers* to make *hoops* for casks. BASKET WITHE. *G*

1952 FGC Tre, Cooper-hook, a wiss. 1955 *WIMJ* 158, *Chamissoa altissima*..Cooper's Hoop; Basket Withe.

COOPER WITHE sb. See quot.

1914 Fawcett 156, *Trichostigma octandrum*..Hoop Withe, Cooper Withe..The common names indicate its uses.

COOSHU see CASHEW.

COOT vb dial; by back-formation <*cooter*; cf *OED coot v*¹, '? *Obs.*', 'Of tortoises: to copulate', 1667–1750; and *DA cooter*, a turtle; also Turner, *kuto*, 'a salt-water turtle (a totem of some of the noble clans of Gambia)'. The likelihood is that African slaves brought the noun *kuto* to the Caribbean, that it was later applied to land turtles in the southern US; and that the verb, developed from the noun, was applied at first to sea tortoises (as it still is) and thence transf to snakes, etc. *N*

Of sea-turtles and other reptiles: to copulate.

1851 Gosse 319, This knotting [of yellow snakes in coupling] is called by the negroes 'cooting', perhaps from the Spanish *Coito*. 1952 FGC StM, Sea-turtle coot; cooting is when two turtles go together.

COOTER sb dial; <Bambara *kuto*; see COOT. A floating decoy made of cottonwood with a head to simulate a sea-turtle; used in connection with a TURTLE NET.

1952 FGC StM /kuuta/—decoy; when the male turtle comes to coot, fishermen catch him.

COOTIKOP, COOTO sb dial; echoic.

1. The sound made by a donkey walking briskly.

1940 HPJ, Cootikop, cuticap, sound for the patter of a donkey's feet. 1943 *GL* StE, Cooto, sharp walking of an ass.

2. Transf: A rough wooden bed (evid from its legs' clacking on the floor).

1959 DeC Tre /kutikap/—a rough wooden bed.

COOTO see prec.

COOTOO BAG sb; abbr of CUTACOO+*bag*.

1889 Sanguinetti 50, When out-shooting [*sic*] in the country districts your guide will perhaps speak of his 'Cootoo' bag.

CO-OUH see COUSIN.

COOY, COOYE, COOYH see *kuy*.

COP-COP see *kap kap*.

COPPER COLOUR sb dial. A colour term of different local applications—see quots. *BL G*

1954 LeP StAnn, Copper colour, mulatto. 1958 DeC StT /kapa kola/ a euphemistic name for an albino negro.

COPPER LEAF sb. A descriptive name for a common garden plant; see quot.

1955 *WIMJ* 157, *Acalypha wilkesiana*..Copper Leaf; Red Hedge; Croton; Headache Bush.

COPPER WEED sb dial. A mossy growth on the copper keels of ships.

1940 HPJ, Tre (Falmouth).

COPPERWOOD sb obs. Light wood and brush formerly used as fuel to heat the coppers in sugar-making.

1790 Beckford I 254, The trees..have been recently felled for copperwood..the copperwood for the use of the curing-house and still-house. 1823 Roughley 100, Cutting copper-wood.

COPPUSE see CUT CAPOOSE.

COQUER PLUM see COCO-PLUM. *BL*

CORAL-BEAN TREE sb; from the colour of the fruit. *Erythrina corallodendron*. Also called *maatel*, NEVER DEAD, RED BEAN TREE, SPANISH MACHETE, SWORD ROSE or TREE.

1756 Browne, see RED BEAN TREE. 1774 Long III 696, The Spaniards take a branch of *coral bean tree*, and set it S.S.W. (in Jamaica it should be N.N.E.) at a small distance from the plants, and inter-mixed between the rows. These slips will grow up with the cacao, and defend it from blowing, violent weather; *ibid* 915, Coral Bean-tree. 1814 Lunan I 233, CORAL or RED BEAN TREE. *Erythrina Corallodendron*. 1864 Grisebach 783, Coral-bean tree.

CORAL BELLS sb. CORAL VINE. (The flowers are not shaped like bells, but they may be thought to hang so.)

1952 FGC StAnd, Coral bells.

CORALLENA sb; prob alteration of CORALILLA by analogy with *-ina*[2] (*OED*). CORAL VINE.

1952 FGC StAnd, Corallena /koralíina/.

CORALILLA sb; < Sp *coralillo*. CORAL VINE. *BA*

1914 Fawcett 122, *Antigonon leptopus*..Coralilla. 1959 FGC StAnd, common.

CORAL PEPPER /kóril pépa/ sb now dial. A type of *Capsicum*—see quot 1814.

1774 Long III 857, Spicery and Peppers..Cherry, Ram's-horn, Coral, &c. 1811 Titford xiii, Coral pepper. 1814 Lunan I 357, Coral peppers—These are called so from their long, slender, singularly twisted, shape and shining red colour, resembling corals. 1952 FGC StT /koril pepa/ long, red.

CORAL TREE see CORAL-BEAN TREE.

CORAL VINE sb. A vine with conspicuous coral-coloured flowers that climbs over shrubs and trees: *Antigonon leptopus*. Also called CORAL BELLS, CORALLENA, CORALILLA.

1952 FGC StAnd, Coral vine.

CORAM sb dial rare; etym unknown—perh a nonsense-form to make the rhyme. Dung.

1924 Beckwith 205 [Riddle:] Limb fell lamb; down fell lamb in the cow coram.—Limb falls, knocks lamb into the cow-dung.

CORATO see next.

CORATOE /kàráto, kàrató, kárito, kyárat/ sb; 1696 curaca, 1740 corito, 1756 curaça, 1756 1774 coratoe, 1794 corato, 1794 1893 currato, 1851 1940 keratto, 1935 carato; < Amer Sp *caraguatá* < Guaraní *carawatá*, species of Bromelia, wild-pine. The commonest name in Jamaica for *Agave americana*. See also *OED Maypole*. *N*

[1679 Trapham 147, A..plant not unlike the species of Caragauta or Manguey or Metle a large strong and thick leaved and succulent Plant, whose leaves if broke afford a thick roapy juicy bitumen not unlikely to appearance of the white or black Amber.] 1696 Sloane 117–18, Maguey Mexicanis..*Curaca*. In collibus saxosis sterilioribus & aridioribus Insulæ Jamaicæ frequenter nascitur. 1740 Importance 36, The *Corito* bears a thick leaf about five Foot long; they use it..to scower..pewter. 1756 Browne 199, Agave 1..Coratoe, or Curaça. There are but few plants more common than this in Jamaica. 1774 Long III 710, Great American Aloes, or Coratoe—Agavè. 1794 Barham 49, Currato; *ibid* 94, Corato. 1851 Gosse 31, The great Keratto, or American aloe. 1893 Sullivan 123, Currato for whitening dressers. 1952 FGC Port /karato/ flog it out, get t'read, can twis' rope; StAnn /kàrató, kárito/ similar to manila, or sisal—use for live fence, plait for whips; StE /kárito/ is the correct name, but we (Bull Savanna) call it maypole.

CORATOE-JUICE sb. The soapy juice of the CORATOE, used as a substitute for soap, as a bleach, for medicine, etc.

1820 Thomson 73, Frequent warm washings, with soap or coratoe juice. [Cf CORATOE quot 1893.]

CORKERS sb slang obs; cf *OED caulker* 3, 'A dram, a "drop" of liquor'. 1808→. Rum punch—alluding to its filling up the cracks? (The form is plural, but the sense seems to be singular, unless the word refers to individual drinks of punch.)

1808 Stewart 198, He can drink strong rum punch (denominated *corkers* here) and smoke segars, or chew tobacco, with the oldest and most confirmed sinners of his acquaintance.

CORKSCREW (PLANT) sb. *Helicteres jamaicensis*, so called from the spirally-twisted fruit.

1952 FGC StC (Little Goat Island), Corkscrew plant. 1954 *WIMJ* 30, Helicteres jamaicensis..Corkscrew; Screw Tree.

CORKWOOD sb; cf *OED*, only quot 1756.

1. *Annona palustris*; see quots.

1756 Browne 256, *Annona* 4..The Alligator Apple Tree, or Cork-wood..is most commonly found in soft marshy places, and bears a fine sweet-scented fruit, of no disagreeable flavour; but it is said to be a strong narcotic.. The wood of this tree is so very soft, even after it is dried, that it is frequently used by the country people, instead of corks, to stop up their jugs and calabashes; from whence it has now universally obtained the name of *Cork-wood* in *Jamaica*. 1774 Long III 832, The wood of this tree is so extremely light, that..it makes excellent floats for fishing nets. 1914 Fawcett 197, *Annona palustris*..Alligator Apple, Cork Wood.

2. *Ochroma lagopus*; see quots.

1814 Lunan I 271, *Ochrona lagopus*..The wood is very lax and spungy, being fit for nothing but to make corks, and is used as such by fishermen, and therefore called by some the cork-tree: others stop bottles with it. 1864 Grisebach 783, Corkwood: *Anona palustris* and *Ochroma Lagopus*. 1941 Swabey 19, Corkwood, Down Tree, Bombast Mahoe, Balsa Wood.

CORN /kaan/ sb. An ear of maize; common in markets and generally. *BA BL G T*

1907 Jekyll 126, An' when the corns beguns to ripe Crab begin to lose the corn. 1926 Edmonds 20, Choose young, tender corns, and plunge into boiling water.

CORN-CORN sb dial; iterative < *corn* sb—evid suggesting the many small bits.

1959 DeC Han /kaan-kaan/ corn hominy.

CORNER sb dial. A variation; see quot. (Perhaps an individualism.)

1907 Jekyll 173, On asking if that [*sc* a one-line song] was all, Levi, the contributor, said:—'It no have no more corner', it hasn't any more corners, or 'turnings' as they generally say, what we call variations.

CORN FUNJU sb dial; < *corn* + FUNGEE, with the final vowel altered evid by assimilation to the first. A FUNGEE (a dish usually made of banana) made of maize.

1943 *GL* StAnn, Corn funju, Beaten corn boiled.

CORN-GRASS sb dial. A type of grass (*Setaria barbata*) with a leaf shaped like that of maize—relatively broad and with prominent length-wise veins—though very much smaller (about 6 in. long).

1952 FGC StAnn /káan gráas/.

CORN-HEAD sb dial. An ear of maize.

1952 FGC StE.

CORN-MEAT sb chiefly dial; for *corned meat*.

1954 LeP Kgn, Man, StE, Corn meat, salt meat. *BA BL G*

CORN-MOUTH sb dial. The top of an ear of maize. *G*

1952 FGC StJ, The beard comes from the corn-mouth.

CORN-PEPPER sb dial; evid < *corning* + *pepper*. Hot capsicum peppers used in corning meat. *BA G*

1954 LeP Kgn, Corn-pepper, hot peppers.

CORN PONE see PONE 3. *BA G*

CORN-STICK sb dial. *SC karoe-tiki*.

1. The cob of an ear of maize; corncob. *G*

1910 Anderson-Cundall 4 [Prov: see next]. 1924 Beckwith 115 [Prov:] When bottle hol' rum, corn'tick get drunk. 'When the bottle holds rum, the cornstick (which serves as a cork) gets drunk.' 1952 FGC Port, Corn-stick use to scrub clothes; also StJ.

2. Transf: The tree *Hernandia jamaicensis*; also called PUMPKIN WOOD.

1963 GHP Institute of Ja, C. B. Lewis has..recorded the name..'Cornstick'.

CORN-TURN sb dial uncom; <*corn*+*turned*. TURNED CORNMEAL.

1959 DeC West /kaarn-tarn/ turned cornmeal.

COROCHI see CAROCHIES.

CORO-CORU see *karakara*.

COROMAI sb obs; prob Amerindian: cf the fish *kuramai* of the Courentyne R., Guiana (1943 Roth 73).

1756 Browne 451, The Calapaver, or Coromai.

COROMANTEE, COROMANTIN see CROMANTY. *G*

CORPIE /kaapi/ sb dial joc; familiarized <*corporal*. A policeman. *G*

1941 Kirkpatrick 20, Lak w'en corpie ketch dem bwoy a nick dice a Race Course. 1942 Bennett 43, Ah beg yuh pardon Carpi, lawd! Noh kea me a jail sah! 1943 *GL* StC, Carpie—corporal. 1948 U.Newton IV 35, Constable Cambridge who told us..'stop your gambling (strong word, Corpi!) and your indecent actions'. 1956 Mc Clar, Man, Port, StAnd /káapi/.

CORPORAL BIRD sb; <*corporal* sb+*bird*.

1936 Bond 360, Jamaican Blackbird (*Nesopsar nigerrimus*). Local names: Black Banana Bird; Corporal Bird; Wild Pine Sergeant.

CORRO-CORRO see *karakara*.

CORROJUNGO sb dial; prob symbolic, perh under infl of CAROCHIES; cf also *junk*. **s.**

1943 *GL* Kgn, Corrojungo, rubbish.

CORROMANTEE see CROMANTY.

CORROSIS see CAROCHIES.

COSCOS see *koskos*.

COSSIE sb dial; prob <*cosset*, 'a lamb, colt, &c, brought up by hand' (*EDD*).

1943 *GL* StT, Cossie, a he goat.

COST vb dial; cf *OED v* 2. To put (one) to the expense or trouble (of doing something). *G*

1877 Murray *Kittle* 6, Him is a man ef you go a him yard him neber mek ef you come out, cepin him gie you a drink, ef e even coss him fe go truss it..[*even if he is forced to go and get it on credit*].

COSTA RICA sb. A variety of sweet-potato.

1929 Beckwith 18, 'Costa Rica' is a white potato.

COT sb ?obs; cf *DA* 1800, 1835, *cot*=sofa. A planters' term for a settee, said to be derived from nautical usage.

1774 Long II 319, *Cot*. A settee.

COTCH /kach/ sb, vb, ppl adj; <*scotch*, cf *OED sb*[2] 'a block placed under a wheel..to prevent moving or slipping', *v*[2] 'to block or wedge (a wheel, log, gate, etc.) so as to keep from moving or slipping'. There is evidence recently of merging of sense with CATCH. *G*

A. sb: Anything which supports, esp temporarily (usually literal but may be metaphorical); a temporary resting place.

1943 Bennett 14, Dis ole 'oman can get a kotch, Se' seat yah ole lady. 1959 LeP West, I'm coming up to Kingston —you can give me a cotch to-night?

B. vb: To support (something, oneself, etc.) in any way; specif, (1) to lean (on things) for support when walking, (2) to lodge temporarily, (3) to plant in a shallow hole.

1942 Bennett 13, Matty come katch yah soh [on the edge of a tram seat]. 1950 Pioneer 50, So me cotchin' wid Mass U, Miss Q, Sta P., an Cousin B., Dem ongle got one lickle room But two big mango tree. 1954 LeP StE (Eld), Kotch, to plant, not very deeply. 1955 Bennett *Bad Foot*, But Bra Nancy get a bad kick For him still a walk an cotch.

C. ppl adj: Scotched, blocked, immovable, stuck in place. (In this sense sometimes identified with 'catch'.)

1912 McK *Ballads* 46 [Title of a poem:] Cotch Donkey; Ko how de jackass lay do'on in the road; An' him ondly car' little bit o' load. Kue, jackass, git up! Tan up 'pon you foot!..him always cotch. 1958 FGC StAnd, Freq in such a phrase as 'The window /kach/—I can't move it'. [*The window is stuck.*] 1959 LeP StAnd [One student speaking of another:] He was cotchin' deadly. [*He was standing in one spot instead of dancing.*]

COTCH-UP sb dial; <COTCH+*up*; cf CATCH-UP, which has the same meaning but differs in sound and source. A light, quick meal that stays hunger or supports one temporarily.

1952 FGC West /káchop/.

COTOBO sb dial rare; ?<*Catawba* (cf US use for melons, grapes, etc.).

1943 *GL* StT, Cotobo, The Seville Orange, so called at Glengoffe.

COTTA[1] /kata/ sb dial; cf Ko *nkata*, headpad, Twi *katá*, to cover, overspread, protect, etc., *ŋkata-hɔ̃*, cover, covering. **s.**

1. A circular pad (about 6 in. diameter), traditionally made of plantain-leaf but also of twisted cloth, placed on the head to protect it and to steady a load borne on it. It was formerly used also in token of divorce—see quot 1774.

1774 Long II 413, The Negroes use their heads, instead of their shoulders, or backs, for carrying all sorts of burthens; with a dried plantain leaf they plait a circular pad, which they call a *cotta*; upon this, the load rests, and preserves their wool from being rubbed off..The cotta serves likewise for another purpose; on the voluntary divorce of man and wife, it is cut in two, and each party takes half. 1929 Beckwith 47, A gourd..poised upon the head by means of a ring-shaped pad of banana trash or handkerchief called a 'cotta'. [*Ibid* 63, reference to tearing a handkerchief in two as a token of divorce.] 1933 McK 316, Cotta, a rough chaplet made of dried bark, leaves, or straw used by the peasants in bearing loads upon their heads. 1943 *GL* West, Catta—pad to put on head to carry load with ease. *BL G* Krio, Cameroon (JH)

2. Transf: The crest or top-knot of a bird; the knot of a woman's hair.

1952 FGC Man, There's a /kata/-like, brush-top on a jumping-dick, *The jumping-dick bird has a crested head.* 1954 LeP Man, Cota, head pad; word also used when a woman puts up her hair in a 'bun'. 1956 Mc Man /nón a i chíkin dem nó ha káta/ *None of the chickens has a top-knot.*

COTTA[2] sb dial; 1790 cotter, 1826 cotta; ultimately echoic—cf *kata-tik*. [Cf the *cutter* drum of Trinidad, Tobago, Grenada. (A. C. Pearse.)] A percussion instrument, a drum or something like it, see quots. *G*

1790 Beckford I 390 [Of negroes:] The very children, so soon as they are able to walk, at the first sound of the cotter..put their little elbows in motion—their feet shortly follow. *Ibid* II 387, A cotter, upon which they beat with sticks. 1826 Williams 26, An incessant hammering was kept up on the gombay, and the cotta (a Windsor chair taken from the piazza to serve as a secondary drum).

COTTAHEAD sb dial; < COTTA + *head.* Prob the Jamaican Yellow-Crowned Elaenia (*Elaenia cotta*—Bond); the adult has a yellow head-patch or small crest; see quot.

1952 FGC StT, Loggerhead has a big head but is smaller than pechary; same as Tom Fool and Cottahead—has a cotta on his head.

COTT-A-WIRE see *katawaia.*

COTTAWOOD sb obs (exc as a place-name); see quots: *Cottawood* is a Jamaican place-name not found elsewhere. The first element may well be < Twi *katá*, to cover, conceal, protect, etc.

1733 *Jrl Assembly* 132, Disobeying their orders, in refusing to march into Cotter-Wood, in search of the rebels. 1803 Dallas I 29–31, Previous to the year 1730 a party of them [Maroons] separated from the others, and distinguished themselves by the name of the Cottawoods; having, it is supposed, originally come from a place so called, near the present Maroon Charlestown, in the parish of St George's..At subesquent periods smaller bodies of the Cattawood [*sic*] party attached themselves to this chief [Cudjoe]..The name of Cottawood was preserved among the descendants of that tribe and the original body of negroes under Cudjoe were distinguished by the appellation of Kencuffees, in which line the succession of their chiefs continued. [1847 Gosse 321, Often when riding through the Cotta-wood, a dense and tangled coppice near Content, I have been startled by the loud whirring of one of these birds.]

COTTER see COTTA[2].

COTTON CASSADA sb dial. A type of cassava root of cottony consistency.

1952 FGC StAnd.

COTTON-FLY sb obs (*OED cotton sb*[1] 10).

1756 Browne 435, Bruchus 1..The Cotton-Fly. This little insect is chiefly of a scarlet colour..The caterpillars of these flies are frequently pernicious to cotton-bushes.

[**COTTON TREE** sb; *OED* 1670→. In Jamaica, the *Ceiba pentandra*, a very large tree, used principally for dugout canoes; it is also the subject of superstitious awe among peasants, having been taken to correspond to the sacred Akata tree of Ashanti religion. (See 1927 Rattray I.) See GOD-TREE 2. Also attrib.

1696 Sloane 159–60, Gossipium arboreum maximum spinosum..The Cotton Tree. 1756 Browne 277, The Silk Cotton-Tree..The trunks of the full-grown trees serve for *Conoas.* 1837 Macfadyen 92, West India Cotton-tree..Perhaps no tree in the world has a more lofty and imposing appearance, whether overtopping its humbler companions in some woody district, or rising in solitary grandeur in some open plain. [See GOD-TREE 2.] 1877 Murray *Kittle* 6, His favourite cotton tree canoe. 1960 Rowe in *CLS* 178, see PITCH 2.] *BL N*

COTTON-TREE SPARROW sb. *Loxigilla violacea*; see quot 1955.

1873 Rampini 42, A large ceiba or cotton tree..The little cotton-tree sparrows make their nests in its branches. 1955 Taylor 40, The Jamaican Bullfinch is more strictly described as the Greater Antillean Bullfinch..It has a variety of local names, the commonest being Black Sparrow and Cotton-tree Sparrow. 1956 Jeffrey-Smith 102, I think that cotton tree sparrow is a misnomer, for always I have noted that the bird flies low.

COTTON-TREE WORM sb. The MACACA worm, formerly eaten as a delicacy.

1707 Sloane xxv, Great esteem was set on a sort of *Cossi*, or Timber-Worms, call'd Cotton-Tree-Worms, by the Negroes and Indians.

COTTON-WEED sb. The wild plant *Gnaphalium americanum*, which has white cottony hairs above the seeds by which they are blown about.

1936 Fawcett 206..Cotton-weed.

COUAGE see COW-ITCH.

COUCHEY see *kochi.*

COUDIN, COUN see COUSIN.

COUHAGE see COW-ITCH.

COUNT vb dial; cf *OED count v* 4, 'to esteem, value, hold of account (*obs.*)'. *BL*

1924 Beckwith 103, She got a brudder name of Collin. She didn't count de brudder. De brudder tell her, said, 'Sister, dat man you gwine to marry to, it is a snake'..So she never count her brudder till her brudder save her life.

COUNTER FLOUR sb dial; < *counter* (*OED sb*[3] 4) + *flour.* A cheap grade of flour sold in bulk over the counters of shops; cf CAKE FLOUR.

1957 DeC StAnd (Irish Town) /kounta floua/.

COUNT LASHER sb dial slang; < *count* (*OED sb*[2]) + LASHER.

1958 DeC, A local Don Juan.

COUNTRY COCO sb obs; cf *OED country* 13, →1703. A native COCO (in contradistinction to imported ones).

1823 Roughley 404, There are several kinds of them; the bourbon..and the country white and black cocoas. *Ibid* 405, Two patches of bourbon, and two of country cocoas.

COUNTRY DISEASES sb obs; cf *OED country* 13.

1. A disease characteristic of or endemic to a country.

1661 Hickeringill 80 [In Jamaica] there is no Countrey Disease (as at Virginia and Surinam) endemically raging throughout the Isle; nor any new and unheard of distempers that want a name.

2. Specifically, the dropsy.

1679 Trapham 93, The..epidemick, called the Dropsie or Country Disease, to which many Servants and neglected persons especially are obnoxious. 1774 Long II 569–70, The *dropsy* was formerly so common in Jamaica, that it went by the name of the *country disease*..It is now grown uncommon.

COUNTRY IBO sb dial; < *country* (*OED* 13) + *Ibo*, African tribal name. Evidently a local name for *Pluchea odorata* or *P. purpurascens*; cf BITTER TOBACCO. *BL N*

1952 FGC StM /kóntri híbo/ Bitter-tobacco, a little tree, bears a red berry—good bitters; resembles crimp-edge tobacco.

COUNTRY LANGUAGE sb obs; cf *OED country* 13 →1703. The language of one's country of origin; one's native language.

1733 *Cal State Papers*, Col 75 ii, A short time after one of the rebels called to the party and told us in his country language that if we would not kill him he would come in. We promised him very fair by one of our negroes.

COUNTRY MARK sb obs; cf *DA* 2 1754→. Tattoo marks or scars on the skin of a slave characteristic of the country or people in Africa from which he or she came.

[1707 Sloane liv, There are few Negros on whom one may not see a great many Cicatrices or Scars..these Scarifications are common to them in their own Countries, and the Cicatrices thought to add beauty to them.] 1757 St Jago Intelligencer 14 May, A New Negro Boy, named *Oroonoko*, without any Mark, except that of his Country Marks, of which, he has several in the Face. 1825 Bickett 39, Brown, a Nago, 4 ft. 11 in. no brand mark, has country marks on his temples. 1873 Rampini

33–4, 'Barrackie fe handie'..said one fellow with filed teeth and face tattoed with his 'country marks'.

COUNTRY NAME sb obs. The name given to someone in his native country; a slave's African name in contrast to his European one.

1793 Edwards II 104, *Adam* (a Congo) a boy as I guess about fourteen, his country name *Sarri*, came from a vast distance inland, was waylaid and stole, in the path about three miles from his own village, by one of his countrymen. *Ibid* 105, Oliver, from *Assiantee*—his country name Sang—a young man.

COUNTRY PEPPER sb; <*country* (*OED* 13, 14) +*pepper*. Capsicum pepper, thought of as characterizing Jamaica or the Caribbean colonies (*OED* sense 13); in present use it seems rather to be understood as referring to rural districts (*OED* sense 14).

1873 Rampini 53, A dinner..highly seasoned with 'Scotch bonnets', or some other of the many varieties of the 'country peppers' (Capsicum). 1952 FGC StAnd, StJ (Current in markets).

COUNTRY QUA sb dial; <*country* (*OED* 14) +QUAW. A bumpkin.

1955 FGC Man /kontri kwa/ raw country boy.

COUNTRY SCAR sb obs. A COUNTRY MARK.

1828 Marly 52, An ill-made African negro..much marked on the face with country scars.

COUPLE BENCH sb. A bench or pew in church in which married couples are placed.

1907 Jekyll 77, see 'TURN T'ANKS.

COURTEN vb dial; <*court* vb+-*n* suffix². To court. *BL G*

1907 Jekyll 14, The King Daniel was courtening to Miss Wenchy, an' the day when they was to get marry.. (etc.). 1957 Bennett 10, Wen she grow big, nuff-nuff man come fe cou'ten her.

COURTIER /kúotya, kúorcha/ sb now arch dial; cf *OED* †2 'one who courts; a wooer', →1766. One who is courting, a lover (male or female), an 'intended'.

1907 Reynolds 18, I am freely consent to be you coatier and we can fix up tings fe de weddin to tek place. 1907 Jekyll 73, Rabbit says he is looking for a courtier. 1913 E. R. Nichols MS Poem (HPJ), Coarcher. 1924 Beckwith 93, And the courtyer's mother waked him up and gave him eight eggs..*Ibid* 103, One day she saw a coal-black man, pretty man. 'he said, 'O mudder, dis is my courtier!'

COURTINGSHIP sb dial; blend of *courting* and *courtship*. Courtship, the act of courting. *G*

1924 Beckwith 108, One day in de yard he saw a man, big stout man. He put co'tin'ship to her. De woman said yes.

COUSCOUS¹ /kuskus/ sb dial; cf *OED couscous*.

1. Gruel of various kinds, e.g. MUSA, QUA-QUA, TURNED CORNMEAL, etc. *BA G*

1868 Russell 7, Cuscus—Gruel of any kind whatsoever. African. 1943 *GL* Tre, Cus-cus, grated bananas cooked in oil; boiled casava bamy; gen, cassava flour. 1952 FGC StE /kuskus/: put parched corn, beaten and sieved, in a pot with hot water; turn till it comes hard, put in pan, smooth it; slice like pone, eat with pear, salt-fish, or mackerel. 1958 DeC Han, Kgn /kuskus/ or /kuskus head/ cassava head, qua-qua flour; StJ, Grated banana boiled in water; Tre, A junk of bitter cassava boiled in soup, =/raip/.

2. Transf to other substances resembling flour or gruel; see quots. *G*

1935 HPJ, Cuss-cuss. Khus-khus, Fine charcoal; the last (or fourth) stage of dirt obtained by grinding from the sugar-cane roots—a sugar-refinery term. 1959 DeC Port /kuskus/—the dry, loose crumbs which are brushed off a bammy after baking.

3. Further transf—through assoc of dust or dirt? See quot.

1959 DeC Kgn /kuskus/—old and ragged work clothes.

COUS-COUS² see KHUS-KHUS.

COUSCOUS HEAD see COUSCOUS¹1 quot 1958.

COUSIN /kózn, kóz, kódn, kóng, kó, kó-u, kó-a/ sb dial; preserved in the senses listed in *EDD* 1, 4. (Most of these forms, and both meanings, can be paralleled in the Sth US.) A relative outside the immediate line of descent: an uncle, aunt, nephew, niece, cousin; freq as a familiar title or term of address. *BL G*

1946 Dunham 138, 'Cousin, ha' you dis ev'nin'?' 'Me well, Mars' Teddy.' No special relationship is signified by these terms, except that of close friendship. 1954 LeP Man, Cuddin, Cung; StE, Couz, Coun. 1956 Mc Man /ko, kong/; /ko ján/ *Cousin John*..

COUTEAU sb obs; cf *OED* →1782. A cutlass or machete.

1803 Dallas I 54, On the left side he [Cudjoe] wore a mushet, or couteau, three inches broad, in a leather sheath.

COUZ see COUSIN. *BL*

COVER, COVERING vb and vbl sb dial. A ceremony for the dead; see quots.

1774 Long II 421–2 [A month after the wife's death] a fowl is dressed at his [the widower's] house, with some messes of good broth, and he proceeds, accompanied by his friends, to the grave. Then begins a song, purporting, that the deceased is now in the enjoyment of compleat felicity..They then lay a considerable heap of earth over the grave, which is called *covering it*, and the meeting concludes with eating their collation, drinking, dancing, and vociferation. 1929 Beckwith 84, In Long's day a feast with song and dance went with the 'covering'. [See further TOMB DANCE, TOMBING.]

COVITCH see CUBBITCH. *BL*

COW sb dial slang.

1940 HPJ, Cow. A word used by the lowest classes to indicate a man who spends his money on a woman and is then left in the bush; because he is a 'milch-cow'.

COWAGE see COW-ITCH. *BL*

COW APPLE sb.

1. See quot. (The identification does not, however, agree with the description.)

1940 HPJ, A large (poisonous?) fruit, growing in five folds or segments green and brown, the small, 20 in. long. Identified at Hope as *Barringtonia speciosa*.

2. Another name for ALLIGATOR APPLE.

1943 *NHN* II 7, Cow-apple (*Anona palustris*)..This plant is poisonous to cattle and is avoided by those animals which graze on the higher flats.

COWBIRD sb. *Coccyzus minor*; see quot. *N*

1956 Jeffrey-Smith 90, The black-eared cuckoo or mangrove cuckoo..sometimes called cowbird, but not known to be parasitic in its habits.

COWBOY (PINE) /kóubwái páin/ sb dial; *cowboy* (derogatory—see first quot) +PINE. A short, stout variety of pineapple.

1952 Topper 9, In certain areas small, degenerate, 'scratch-mouth' Red Spanish plants are called 'Cow Boy'. 1952 FGC Port, StAnd, StAnn, StJ, StM, StT. 1954 *FG* 392.

COW-CATCH sb dial.

1943 *GL* Kgn, Cow-catch, nettle.

COW-COD sb dial; prob <*cow* (also applied to bulls) +*cod* (cf *OED sb*¹ 4), with transfer of sense from scrotum to pizzle, from which whips were made. *BL*

1952 FGC StT, Cow-cod, a whip.

COW-FISH sb; cf *OED* 3, 1885 only. The fish *Acanthostracion quadricornis*, whose horned head is cow-like; also called TRUNK-FISH. *G*

1950 *NHN* IV 136, The cowfish has very little freedom of movement indeed; it is encased in a hard shell formed by the fusion and solidification of the scales. 1952 FGC StC /kou fish/.

COWFOOT (LEAF) sb dial. A common plant with large rounded-cordate leaves (thought to resemble a cow's hoof), juicy, with an aromatic odour, much favoured in local medicinal preparations. (*Piper umbellatum*; now reclassified as *Pothomorphe umbellata* and *P. peltata*.) *N*

1893 Sullivan 113, Cowfoot leaf. The leaves are boiled and used as a drink when one has a troublesome cough. 1952 FGC Han, Port, StAnn, StE, StT, Cowfoot (leaf). 1954 *WIMJ* 31, *Piper umbellatum*..Cow or Colt's Foot.

COWFOOT MANGO sb dial. A mango considered to resemble a cow's foot.

1952 FGC StAnn.

COW GALL (BITTER) sb dial; *cow*+*gall*+*bitter* (*OED sb* 2). A plant used as a stomachic, evidently considered to be like the gall of cattle.

1952 FGC StAnn, Tre, Cow-gall (bush), a bitter bush, similar to jack-in-the-bush. 1955 *WIMJ* 159, *Neurolaena lobata*..Cow Gall Bitter; Halbert Weed; Bitter Bush or Wood; Goldenrod.

COW-GUT sb dial or slang; from some fancied resemblance.

1943 *GL* StM, Cowgut, tin lamp.

COW-GUT WIS sb dial. A vine so called from its toughness.

1952 FGC StAnd /kou-got wis/.

COWHAGE see COW-ITCH.

COW-HEAD sb dial. The name of one traditional member of a JOHN CANOE troupe, who wears a head-dress bearing the horns of a cow or bull.

1940 HPJ, Cowhead, An oxheaded John Canoe masquerader (suppressed by the police in Spanish Town, Xmas, 1933) [Astley Clerk: and in Kingston long before that.] 1952 FGC Han, Bull, usually called Cow-head: a man with cow-horns over a mask, tie with rope around waist. (Anyone who tries to discover his identity may be struck.)

COW-HOOF, COW-HOUGH sb dial. Local variants of COWFOOT (LEAF).

1952 FGC StM /kouhof, kouhuf/.

COW-ITCH sb dial; cf *OED cow-itch, cowage*.

1. Specifically (and not limited to Jamaican use) the climbing vine *Mucuna pruriens* and its beans covered with fine stinging hairs; in Jamaica (and esp in attrib use) the sense is generalized to include anything that irritates the skin upon contact: COW-ITCH BUSH, CHERRY, WEED; SEA COW-ITCH; etc. *BA BL G N T*

2. Fig. As the type or symbol of something extremely irritating.

1877 Murray *Kittle* 18 (Said to a notorious scold:) Me no know what kin o' cowitch dem rub pon you tongue so!

COWITCH BUSH, WEED sb dial. A wild plant with oblong-lanceolate leaves having stinging hairs beneath and on the stems: CREEPING COWITCH. *G*

1952 FGC StC, Tre, Cowitch bush; StM, Cowitch weed.

COWITCH CHERRY sb; <COW-ITCH+*cherry*. Cf *OED* quots 1725→1878. One species of the BARBADOS CHERRY, *Malpighia urens*.

1696 Sloane 172, *Couhage Cherry*. Circa urbem *St Jago de la Vega*..ad ripas fluvii *Cobre* appellati in frutetis crescit. 1725 Sloane II 106, Cowhage Cherry. 1920 Fawcett 227, *Malpighia urens*..leaves with stinging hairs..beneath..Cowhage or Cowitch Cherry.

COWITCH WEED see COWITCH BUSH.

COW LAW-BOOK sb dial. The omasum of the cow, known in England as the 'leaves' or 'manyplies'—words descriptive of its appearance.

1925 Beckwith 29 [Prov:] Cow read dem law book in a dem belly. 'Cows read the law in their bellies.' Tripe is called 'the cow's law-book' because it folds up like a book. *Ibid* 14 [Prov:] Not fe de want a tongue mek cow can't talk; he read all law in him book. 1927 Anderson-Cundall 24.

COW-MAN DUMPLING sb dial; prob <*cowman*, cowherd+*dumpling*. Cf CARTMAN DUMPLING.

1958 DeC Port /kou-man-dompling/ a very large round boiled dumpling.

COW-NECK sb dial.
See quot 1943

1900 Murray 8, Dis backra pickney from Tong is gwine to gie you a wet [drink of rum], but you mus satisfy wid cow neck. 1943 *GL* StM, Cow-neck—New white proof rum. 1955 FGC Man.

CO-WORKER sb dial cant. A title given to initiates in a St Thomas revivalist cult, equivalent to BEARER or POST-HOLDER.

1953 Moore 89.

COW-PLAATO sb dial; <*cow*, for *cowhide*+a fancifully altered form of *plait*, in Jamaica normally pronounced /plat/.

1943 *GL* StM, Cow-plaato, whip of cowhide.

COWSKIN sb obs. A dish once eaten by slaves.

1826 Williams 14–15, 'Cowskin'..cow or ox hide (the hair of which is first singed off) boiled to a jelly, with yams, cocos, ochro, and other vegetables; a famous mess, of which the little negroes made a most hearty meal.

COWSKIN HERO sb obs. A nickname for a sugar-estate manager, alluding to his power over the slaves by way of the *cowskin* whip. (Perh a nonce term.)

1790 Moreton 55, When they become cowskin heroes, or managers, [they] are totally ignorant of instructing their overseers or negroes..(if they know nothing about distilling). [1793 Mathews 14, His invectives against those Gentlemen, whom he terms Cowskin Heroes, I shall animadvert upon in its proper place.]

COW-TAIL sb dial. An unidentified wild plant used in making a cough medicine. (Possibly the COW-TONGUE fern.)

1893 Sullivan 109, To make Calabash syrup..some liquorice bush, one or two cowfoot leaves, one or two cowtail leaves, and some garden balsam.

COW-TONGUE sb dial.

1. A fern with large single leaves whose shape and roughness are considered like those of a cow's tongue. See quot 1955.

1952 FGC Kgn, Cow-tongue; also Port, StAnn, StC,

StE, Tre. 1955 *WIMJ* 160, *Polypodium phyllitidis*. . Cow Tongue.

2. A dumpling rolled like a SPINNER, then flattened and grooved to the shape of a cow's tongue.

1958 DeC StAnd /kou tong/.

COW-TONGUE TOBACCO sb dial. A variety of tobacco named for the shape of the leaf: see quots.

1952 FGC StAnn, Cow-tongue tobacco, with long leaf—old-time people say; StM, Cow-tongue leaf, long but narrower than Spanish leaf.

COZ see COUSIN. *BL*

CRAAB /kraab/ vb and ppl adj dial; prob <*crab* (*OED* v^2), but cf *kraap*. (Cf Nth Ireland *scrab*, to scratch. RWT.)

1943 *GL* Port, Craab, to rake with claws; clawed.

CRAAL see CRAWL.

CRAB-BASKET sb dial. A type of hand-basket with two sections side by side, each round-bottomed and covered, and with a handle going over the middle; it is adapted to gathering crabs. *G*

1956 Mc Clar /krabáaskit/ also called /hanbaaskit/.

CRABBIT adj dial; cf *OED crabbed*: the older form, which continued in England till the 18th century, and later in Scotland, is preserved in Jamaica; cf also *SND*. Cruel; rough; grasping; greedy.

1941 Kirkpatrick gloss, Crabbit, ferocious. 1943 *GL* Clar, Crabbit, cruel; StAnd, Crabit, cruel; StAnn, Crabit, craven; StE, Crabit, rough, cruel; StM, Crabbit, greedy.

CRABBY /krabi/ sb dial; a familiarized form of CRAB-YAWS.

1943 *GL* Tre, Crabi, Yaws at the bottom of the foot. 1956 Mc Clar /krabi—yaaz we kom onaniit yu fut batam/ *Crabby—yaws which come underneath your foot-sole.*

CRAB-CATCHER sb; cf *OED* 1699→ for other spp. A common name for certain American, and esp West Indian water birds such as the Green Heron; applied in Jamaica also to the night herons and others: see quots.

1756 Browne 478, Ardea 5. . The Crab-catcher. . Ardea 6. . The small red-winged Crab-catcher. . Ardea 7. . The larger Crab-catcher. 1936 Bond 26, Black-Crowned Night Heron (*Nycticorax nycticorax*). . Crab Catcher; *ibid* 28, Yellow-Crowned Night Heron (*Nyctanassa violacea*). . Crab Catcher. 1955 Taylor 68 (cf GREEN GAULIN).

CRAB-EYE (PEAS), CRAB'S-EYE (PEAS) sb dial.

1. A common variety of bean thought to resemble a crab's eye.

1952 FGC Port, Crab-eye peas, brown and white; StAnd /krab-ai piiz/ dark brown with irregular white longitudinal stripes; StC /krabz-ai/ mix-peas; StJ, Crab's-eye, brown with black stripe.

2. JOHN-CROW BEADS.

1920 Fawcett 43, Wild Liquorice. . Crab's Eyes. 1954 *WIMJ* 28, *Abrus precatorius*. . Red Bead Vine; Crab's Eyes; Lick Weed. . etc.

CRAB-EYE JACK sb dial. A variety of the jack fish whose eyes are thought to resemble those of a crab.

1952 FGC StM, Crab-eye jack.

CRABIT see CRABBIT.

CRABLIGHT sb dial. A tree whose wood was used for torches in hunting crabs at night. (Prob one kind of CANDLEWOOD.)

1847 Gosse 409, Tall and dense wood, consisting chiefly of manchioneel, crablight, sweetwood, and tropic-birch.

CRABN see CRAVEN. *BL*

CRAB RUM /kraab rom/ sb dial. A name for a common grade of rum, probably alluding to its sharp or irritating effect.

1952 FGC Han /kraab rom/ Estate rum, bought directly from the sugar estate.

CRAB'S-EYE PEAS see CRAB-EYE PEAS.

CRAB-SPIDER sb; *OED* only 1861.

1. A spider very common in Jamaican gardens; see quot 1756.

1756 Browne 419, Aranea 5. . The Crab-spider. This species is very like a crab in the general form of the trunk, but the head and breast are small and distinct. It is very common in St Mary's. *Ibid* Tab. 44, 5. 1960 Institute of Ja exhibit, Crab spider, *Gasteracantha cancriformis*; also members of the *Thomisidae.*

2. Another name for the BANANA SPIDER, *Heteropoda venosa*, referring to its crab-like appearance.

1949 *NHN* IV 35.

CRAB-THATCH /kráb tách/ sb dial. The ferns *Acrostichum aureum* and *A. danaefolium*, growing in swampy lands, which form a thick cover for the crabs that live there. Also called ALLIGATOR RUSH, GOLDEN FERN (2).

1952 FGC StJ /kraab tach/; Tre /krab tach/.

CRAB WEED sb dial.

1943 *NHN* II 7, Crab weed (*Gomphrena decumbens*).

CRAB WITHE /krab wis/ sb dial.

1914 Fawcett 140, *Alternanthera ficoidea*. . Crab Withe, Rupture Wort.

CRABWOOD sb dial. Various trees thought to resemble crabs in one way or another; see quots. *G*

1920 Fawcett 329–30, *Gymnanthes lucida*. . Crab Wood. . The wood is heavy, hard, close-grained. . It is rich dark brown streaked with yellow. 1943 *NHN* II 25, Crab-wood, the mustard shrub (*Capparis ferruginea*). . Wood said to smell like dead crab. 1957 Howard 92, *Coccoloba krugii*. . Common names, Big Family, Crabwood.

CRAB-YAWED adj; <CRAB-YAW + *-ed*[2] (*OED*). Affected with crab-yaws.

1790 Moreton 158, Mimba, crabyarv'd [*sic*], and Grace with canker'd nose.

CRAB-YAWS /krab-yaa/ sb dial; <*crab* (*OED* sb^1) +*yaws*. A form of Frambœsia which affects the palms of the hands and esp the soles of the feet in two distinct ways: see SPUR YAWS, RUNNING YAWS. *SC kraboe-jássi.*

1739 Leslie 329, 'Tis long before they can be cured [of the Yaws], two Years is the soonest; and that which they call the Crab-Yaws is never removed. 1801 Dancer 223, The soles of the feet are affected with what is called the Crab-Yaws. 1820 Thomson 95, There are two distinct diseases included under this name. The one is a painful affection, resulting from the fungus of the yaw finding difficulty in penetrating the hardened cuticle on the soles of the feet or hands; the other is a disease of the cuticle itself, and in no way connected with any previous disease.

1952 FGC Han /krábyáaz, skrábyáaz/ cut-up-cut-up under foot-bottom; Man /kráb yáa/ footsole or hand-middle, skin gets thick, then bursts; StAnd /kráb yáaz/ on foot-bottom, makes your toes pop-pop. 1959 DeC Han /krobi aas/ a disease of the feet; beginning with violent itching, the feet develop huge blisters which finally break into open sores. [Note: the word *scrub* is perh understood here by folk-etym.]

CRA-CA see CRA-CRA.

CRACASA see *krakasa*.

CRACK-CRACK sb dial; iterative <*crack*, fissure. Ringworm: a name descriptive of the effect it has on the feet.

1958 DeC Port /krak-krak/ athlete's foot.

CRACKER (CANE) sb dial.

1958 DeC StC /kraka/ a popular name for a variety (B 4362) of sugar-cane, because it cracks easily.

CRACK-POT SOLDIER sb dial. The Black-necked stilt, *Himantopus himantopus*, evidently for its military posture; 'crack-pot' is unexplained. Also called COCK-SOLDIER, BLACK-BACK, etc.

1955 Taylor 72, In Jamaica it is also known as the Soldier or the Crack-pot Soldier.

CRA-CRA /krakra/ adj and adv dial; <Twi *krà kra*, restless, excited; cf also CRAW-CRAW. Nervous; therefore erratic, clumsy, careless, etc.

1868 Russell 10, Cra-ca [*sic*], adj.—Careless, nervous, clumsy. Dis boy well cra-cra; *ibid* 18, De man walk so cra-cra. 1873 Rampini 127, An' him curse him moder for a 'cra-cra' (careless)..'nana' (old woman). 1894 Banbury 43, Cra, cra:—Harum, scarum:—Mad-headed, too hasty and quick at anything. 1935 HPJ (Abuse:) Yu faba cra-cra. [This could belong with CRAW-CRAW.] 1943 *GL* Clar, Cra-cra, erratic.

CRAFILOUS see SCROFULOUS.

CRAFT /kraaf/ vb dial; <*craft* sb.

1959 LeP (from Jean Creary) Kgn, StAnd /kraaf/ to trick, deceive, esp. in matters of love; to put somebody's nose out of joint. Most common in Kingston.

CRAHSS see CROSS.

CRAKING DRUMMER sb dial; <*craking* (cf *OED* crake v^1, 'to utter a harsh, grating cry', said of birds) +DRUMMER. A variety of the DRUMMER fish; cf CROAKING DRUMMER.

CRAMOOCHIN see next.

CRAMOUCHIN /kramúuchin, kromúuchin, krumúuchin, kramúujin, kromúujin, krumúujin, kramújin, kromújing, kramónjin, kromónjin, kumuujin/ adj and sb dial; prob by metathesis <*curmudgeon*.

With many shades of meaning: primarily, *deceitful*, whence *underhand*, *sly*; secondarily, *grasping*, *envious*, *conceited*; also as a less specific term of condemnation including such senses as *lazy*, *worthless*, *disagreeable*. The adj easily becomes a sb meaning *deceit*, *envy*, *worthlessness*, etc.

1929 Beckwith 50, The chorus of a 'hard time' song runs: Annotto can't sell, the price is unfair, Pimento a blossom and drop..Hard time a carry the day..For they won't put cramouchin' [grudging] away. 1935 HPJ, Cramoochin: (i) Grasping; studiously grabbing and keeping whatever comes one's way; (ii) Nursing concealed enmity..(iii) Disagreeable. 1943 *GL* Kgn, Crumuchin, sly; Kgn, Krūmoochin, deceitful; Port, Crumuging, conceited; Port, Crumugin, a bad minded person; StC, Crumuchin, subtle; StC, Krumoogen, deceptions; StT, Crumugine, hypocritical; StT, Krumungin, cynical, covert—evil person; Tre, Krumouchin, to envy the enjoyment of another; Tre, Cremuchin, underhand, deceitful. 1952 FGC StM /kromunjin/. 1956 Mc Man /kromúchin/ underhand; StE (Accom) /kramújin man wi tiif yu no/ *A cramouchin man will steal, you know*; /kumuujin/ two-faced, deceitful.

CRAMPIFY adj dial; <*cramp*+*ify* (*OED*), for *-ified*.

1943 *GL* Kgn, Crampify, adj, unfriendly.

CRAN sb dial; etym unknown.

1943 *GL* StM, Cran, banana.

CRAN-CRAN, CRANKCRAN see *kran-kran*.

CRANKY, CRENKY /krangki, krengki/ adj dial; cf *OED cranky* a^1, 1, 'Sickly, in weak health, infirm in body'. Very lean or thin (sometimes abnormally so). *BL G*

1943 *GL* Tre, Krenky, lean or thin. 1955 FGC Man /krangki/ thin. 1955 LeP StE (Eld) /krangki/ thin and feeble. 1958 DeC StAnn /krengki/ very thin or maaga; StT /krangki/ adj, pertaining to a tall, thin person.

CRAPS sb dial; <*scrap*, by reduction of initial /sk/ and overcorrect suffixing of /s/. *G*

1940 HPJ, Craps, scrap.

CRATCH /krach/ vb dial; prob a preservation of *cratch*, which lasted in English literary use into the 16th century, when *scratch* (evidently a modification of it) began to replace it (cf *OED cratch v*). *BL G*

1. To scratch. (Early evidence for the form.)

1833 Scott II 377, Great luxury to creole gentleman and lady, dat chiger; sweet pain, creole miss say—nice for cratch him, him say.

2. To irritate (the skin, mucous membrane, etc.).

1952 FGC Tre, Dumb-cane /krach/ bad.

3. To itch.

1956 Mc Man /mi yái a krách mi/ *My eye is itching.*

CRATCH-CRATCH sb dial; iterated form of CRATCH, prob also infl by CRAW-CRAW. See quots; cf CRATCH-KIN.

1954 LeP Kgn, Man, Cratch-cratch, dry, itching rash on the skin. 1956 Mc Man.

CRATCH-KIN sb dial; presumably from an adjectival form of CRATCH, +*kin*, skin. A dry, itchy skin-rash; cf CRATCH-CRATCH.

1956 Mc Port.

CRAVEN /kríebm, kríevn, kríebin, kríevin/ adj and sb dial; <*craving ppl a* (*OED* 2, →1818).

A. adj: Craving, greedy, avaricious. *BL G*

1924 Beckwith 143, An' dat was de end of de craving man, Uncle Green, an' Jack take all his riches. 1940 HPJ, Crābn, Greedy, craving [Astley Clerk:] avaricious. 1943 *GL* StAnn, Craven, crabit; StT, Craven, covitch. 1950 Pioneer 17, Anancy..walk home wid Puss an sey 'tap Bra Puss is how you dah play so nice wid Rat an noh eat him yet? Yuh no know sey Rat is nice meat?' Hear Puss wid him craven self, 'true Bra Nancy?' 1952 FGC Man, Ganja adds to appetite, makes you craven, calls for something sweet.

B. sb: Greed, being greedy. *BL G*

1940 HPJ [Prov:] Crabn choke puppy, *Greed choked* (or *chokes*) *the puppy.*

CRAVEN DICK sb dial; cf CRAVEN. *G*

1943 *GL* StT, Craven Dick, Greedy person.

CRAW-CRAW /kraa-kraa, kra-kra/ sb dial; sb dial arch; 1790 cockcraw, 1801→ craw-craw, 1820 kra-kra; cf *OED*: 'app. a Dutch Negro name, from Du. *kraauw* scratch, *kraauw-en* to scratch, to claw..A malignant species of pustulous itch, prevalent on the African coast, especially about Sierra Leone'; 1863→. Cf also Twi *kɔ́ré*, a cutaneous eruption, a kind of itch in the skin; and CRA-CRA. See quots. *G*

1790 Moreton 163, The diseases peculiar to black women, *i.e.* yaws, ringworm, cockcraws, clap, pox, &c. 1801 Dancer 234, Negroes are liable also to a particular species of Itch, called Craw-Craws. 1811 Titford Expl. to Plate IX 2, A strong decoction, is applied to ring-worms, or crawcraws, and for crabyaws the negroes' feet are soaked in it many days. 1820 Thomson 73, Kra-kra is a corrupted Eboe word. It appears in large superficial crustaceous blotches, chiefly about the buttocks. 1943 *GL* StJ, Craw-craw, Itch.

CRAWFISH, CRAYFISH (CANE) sb dial; <*crawfish*, crayfish + *cane*. A variety of sugar-cane with stripes, thought to resemble the crayfish.

1952 FGC Port /kráafish/ cane—has stripes; StM /kráafish/ or /kríefish/ cane; StT, Crawfish cane—has a seam on it. 1959 DeC Port /kriefish/ a kind of cane.. white with blue vertical stripes; StAnd /kraafish/ a soft cane with brown stripes like a crawfish.

CRAWL /kraal/ sb now dial; 1660 crawle, c1695→ crawl, 1774 craal; <Colonial Dut *kraal*, cf *OED sb*². *BL*

1. *OED*: 'An enclosure, pen, or building for keeping hogs (in the West Indies). *Obs.*' Quots 1660, 1707, both from Jamaica, where the word is still in use; cf PIG CRAWL.

1660 Hickeringill (1661) 13, They build two or three little Houses, or more; by them called a Crawle, and in these, they first inclose these tame Hogs, with which they begin their stock, and there feed them; that after (being let out) they will come to the haunt, at the sound of a Horn. c1695 *Acts & Laws* 111, None shall hunt any Gang of Dogs within 4 Mile of any Crawl. 1707 Sloane xvii, Swine fed at *Crawles* are in very great plenty. These Crawles, or Houses and Sties built for feeding and breeding Hogs, are kept by some Whites, *Indians* or Blacks. 1774 Long I 345, The word Craal being commonly used in the West-Indies to signify a place where provisions are planted, and hogs bred. 1956 Mc StE /a did hav a smaal kraal jos die wi tuu pig/ *I had a small crawl just there with two pigs*; also Clar.

2. A similar, staked enclosure in the sea, in which marine creatures are penned; cf TURTLE CRAWL. *N*

1934 Kingston *Gleaner* 15 March, The fish are transferred alive to a crawl.

CRAWLE see prec.

CRAWLEY-BOB sb joc obs; perh an individualism. Some kind of insect or crawling creature.

1862 Clutterbuck 288, The frolics of moths, bats, crickets, fiddlers, cockroaches, and a host of winged insects..Whenever a crawley-bob succeeded in charging her, she sharply chid her attendant.

CRAWL-UP vb phr dial; <CRAWL + *up*. To make like a CRAWL, to surround with a protective enclosure.

1956 Mc Man (Alligator Pond) /da wai a kraal-op di plíes, put di maka de/ *That's why I crawl(ed)-up the place and put the prickly bushes there* [to protect a young coconut tree].

CRAWNY /kráani/ adj dial; <*scrawny*; cf *OED*, 'US..lean, scraggy'. *BL G*

1. See quots.

1943 *GL* Clar, Crawny, small; Port, Crawny, meagre.

2. See quots.

1943 *GL* Clar, Crawny, nasty-looking; StJ, Crawny, unclean looking.

CRAYFISH (CANE) see CRAWFISH (CANE).

CREASE sb dial. A crack. *G*

1956 Mc StAnd (Dallas) [Song:] /musu waak tru kriis, musu waak tru blain/ *Mouse came in through the crack. Mouse came in through the jalousie.*

CREATE EXCITEMENT (ON) vb phr dial; perh malapropism for *incitement*. *G*

1958 DeC, to pick a fight, arouse someone's ire: /duon kriíet eni eksáitment an mi nou/.

CREBAY see *krebe*.

CREBBA sb dial; etym uncert—perh conn with *scrape*, which has the dial forms /kríep/ and /kráap/ (emphatic), perh with *crab*, which has the dial forms /krab, kraab/.

1943 *GL* StT, Crebba, scrapping [*sic*, prob for *scraping*].

CREEL /kril, kriil/ sb dial; cf *OED*, latest quot in this sense, 1860. See quots.

1956 Mc West /kril/ the baskets used on donkeys to carry load. 1959 DeC Han, StJ, West /kril, kriil/ a donkey-hamper; this is the common word through most of Hanover and Westmoreland, parts of St James. [Elsewhere HAMPER.]

CREEP vb trans dial. To pull fish or lobster pots up from the bottom of the sea with a CREEPER.

1956 Mc StC /kriipa—dem tek it kriip di pat/.

CREEPER sb dial; <*creep* + *-er*. A device for raising fish-pots from the bottom of the sea, consisting of a four-pronged metal hook on the end of a cord or rope.

1952 FGC StJ /kriipa—mek it wid fuor sprang/.

CREEPING COWITCH sb dial; <*creeping* + COWITCH. A creeping or twining plant the branches of which (like cowitch beans) are armed with stinging hairs. *G*

1756 Browne 336, Tragia 1..The creeping Cowhage.. The plant is very common in Jamaica, and well known on account of its sharp itching hairs. 1920 Fawcett 306, *Tragia volubulis*, Creeping or Twining Cowitch.

CREEPING JENNY sb. A common wild plant that runs along the ground; also found in gardens; see quot.

1954 *WIMJ* 32, *Zebrina pendula*..Red Water Grass; Creeping Jenny; Wandering Jew; Rolling-Calf Bed; Ginger.

CREEPING OX-EYE sb bot. A common wild plant with yellow, daisy-like flowers; see quot 1936.

1756 Browne 321, Buphthalmum 4. Hirsutum; foliis trilobis..The larger creeping Ox-eye. Both these last species are natives of *Jamaica*. 1811 Lunan II 25, Ox-eye, Creeping. Silphium..Trilobatum..creeping along the ground..and smelling aromatically..It grows on the banks of rivers and in low marshy lands. 1936 Fawcett 227, *Wedelia trilobata*, Creeping Ox-eye. 1954 *WIMJ* 32, *Wedelia trilobata*..Wild or Running Marigold; Marygold; Creeping Ox-eye; Water Weed.

CREEPING SENSITIVE-PLANT sb bot obs. Prob *Mimosa viva*.

1801 Dancer 366, The creeping sensitive plant; the prickly sensitive plant (Mimosa).

CREMUCHIN see CRAMOUCHIN.

CREN-CREN, CRENG-CRENG see *kreng-kreng.*

CRENKY see **CRANKY.**

CREOLE sb also attrib; cf *OED, DAE, DA.* s.

1. Anyone born, or anything grown or produced, in the West Indies or nearby territories, as distinct from one born or something grown elsewhere: see quots. The term was frequently misunderstood outside the West Indies, where it was taken to be a racial term implying full or partial Negro ancestry; this misunderstanding contributed to its disuse in Ja. *BA BL G T*

1740 Importance 14, The chief Distinctions among the Inhabitants are, of Whites and Blacks, Slaves or Free. The Whites are the *Creols* or Natives with English, Scots, Irish, French, who are either Planters, Merchants, or Factors: The first generally reside there, the other often return forwards and backwards to England. *Ibid* 18, The *Creol* Negroes greatly value themselves as much superior on that account, as an ancient *Britain* would himself to a *Norman*, and are afraid of the wild Negroes. 1774 Long II 261–2, The native white men, or Creoles, of Jamaica, are in general tall and well-shaped..This, indeed, has also been remarked of the Creole Blacks. 1798 Evidence 25, Some of the latter description of negroes.. when acquainted with the English creole language, may communicate ideas..prejudicial to the interest of the colony. 1835 Senior 67, Many people are impressed with the idea, that a *creole* must have been born of black or coloured parents. Such a notion is ridiculous. The meaning of creol is precisely this: *an individual born in the West Indies, of white parents!* 1838 Kelly 32, The term 'Creole' has no reference to colour, as is commonly supposed by Europeans, but merely means 'native'. We speak of a Creole horse, or of any vegetable or esculent not common to the country, as the Irish potato, which, when cultivated on the mountains, are called Creole potatoes.

2. In folk use: A coloured or white person of Jamaican parentage, not Chinese, East Indian, Maroon (considered more purely African), etc. For discussion of comparable (not identical) ethnic use in Belize see 1975 Tabouret-Keller. *G T*

1940 HPJ, Nowadays, it is usually employed..to designate 'coloured people', particularly to distinguish them from the Chinese. 'So-and-so' (naming a Chinese girl born of Chinese parents in Jamaica) 'is not a creole'. 'Such-a-one' (naming a Jamaica born girl whose father was Chinese and whose mother was coloured) 'is half a creole'. Marion, asked if a certain hunter was a Maroon, replied, 'He is a creole', and when questioned said Maroons were not Creoles but more like Africans.. Bertha: 'A creole is a Jamaican: a Creole can be white'.

3. See quot.

1940 HPJ, *Creole,* a lowland people, term applied to coastlanders by Upper Clarendon people.

CREOLE BREADFRUIT sb. A Jamaican variety of breadfruit, as distinct from the St Kitts ('SINKIT') breadfruit.

1935 HPJ StAnd (Stony Hill), Creole-breadfruit.

CREOLE CRAB sb obs. *G*

1756 Browne 422, Cancer 10..The Creole-Crab. This crab is very like the *Sherigo*..; Cancer 13..The larger hairy Creole-Crab with prickly claws.

CREOLE-WOMAN sb dial.

1943 *GL* Han, Creole-ooman, mixed blood of West-Indians and Spanish Americans.

CREOLIAN sb now dial; 1675 croyolien; 1730→ creolian; cf *OED* 1702→.

1. One born in the West Indies of European parents; a Creole.

1675 Lord Vaughan *Letter* in MS Edgerton 2395, The island is exceeding healthfull, the Children which are Borne in it thrive exceedingly, so that the Croyoliens and natives will in a few yeares make a great People. 1730 Southall 11, At first he refused, believing me (as I found by his discourse) to be a *Creolian*, whom the Negroes in general hate; but upon my convincing him I was an *Englishman*..the good Chear prevail'd. 1808 Stewart 303, The fair Creolian [ed. 1823 Stewart 330 (the corresponding passage), The fair creole].

2. See quot. (The form shows metathesis; the development of meaning parallels that of CREOLE.)

1943 *GL* Clar, Kerōlin, negro.

CREOLISM sb; 1873 creoleism; cf *OED* in different sense; *DAE, DA,* 1895. An expression characteristic of Creole speakers. *G*

1873 Rampini 13, Here 'in the hills', to use a Creoleism, is the favourite abode of the better class of Jamaica society.

CREOLIZE vb; cf *OED* only 1818. Cf UNCREOLIZED. To lounge elegantly in the manner of the inhabitants of warm climates.

1802 Nugent 155, After breakfast, the usual routine; writing, reading, and creolizing.

CREPE SOLE sb dial joc. A *tuoto,* or round flour cake.

1943 *GL* StAnd, Joe Louis or crepe sole, toto.

CRESSHY sb dial; cf *EDD cresh* (Yks), cress + *-y* familiarizing suffix.

1943 *GL* StJ, Cresshy, water cress.

CRIB sb dial. A slatted box sometimes used like a HAMPER: a pair are slung one on each side of a donkey or mule.

1958 DeC gen.

CRICKET LIZARD sb. *Sphaerodactylus parkeri,* named from some association with the cricket—see quots.

1940 Lynn-Grant 76, Habits.—Found under trash in company with *S. argus henriquesi, Celestus c. crusculus* and striped cricket. The similarity of marking of the cricket and lizard gives the latter its name of 'cricket-lizard'. 1952 FGC Man /krikit lizad/ creeks-creeks-creeks like cricket.

CRI-CRI see CRY-CRY.

CRIER sb dial; cf *OED,* and CRY.

1. A piece of leather put into a locally made boot or shoe by request, to make it squeak; also QUEE-QUEE.

1873 Rampini 173, He contracted with a shoemaker in the town to make another pair. But alas! when they were sent home he found that the faithless tradesman had omitted to put 'criers' into them, although he had paid him..for this luxury. 1940 HPJ (also Astley Clerk), the pride of the uneducated Negro's heart, and the louder it cries 'de mo' i sweet mi'—in church it used to often stop the parson.

2. Attrib: *criers boot,* boots with criers.

1922 Beckwith 39 [Song:] You see me Beaver hat, You see me criers boot.

CRIMP-HOUSE sb obs; cf *OED crimp* 2. A house in which seamen were harboured by crimps.

1828 Ordinances..Kingston, 11, 91–2, An ordinance relative to houses commonly called crimp-houses, and persons commonly called crimps.

CRINGY adj dial; perh <*cringe* + *-y,* but cf QUINGY. *G*

1943 *GL* Tre, Cringy, small.

CRINK-UP vb dial; <*crink,* crinkle (cf *OED* →1888) + *up.*

1958 DeC /kringk op/ vb. for what a bammy does around the edges as it bakes; you turn the bammy /wen yu sii de ej kringk op/.

CRIPS sb dial; metathesized <*crisp*.

1. The 'crackling' of pork; cf *OED crisp sb* 5: '*obs.* exc *dial.*' *G*

1950 Pioneer 21, Sista Peel-head Fowl..teck weh all de tings wat him [*sc* Anancy] teck fram de oder people dem an de lickle 'crips' weh him had fe himself.

2. Among fishermen: the squid.

1952 FGC StE /kríps/ between lobster and sea-cat; have big eyes; like jelly but firm; have edge, not tentacle.

CRIS see *kris*.

CROAKER sb; cf *OED* 1, 'An animal that croaks'. A CROAKING-LIZARD.

1952 FGC StT, West /kruoka/; also StAnd.

CROAKING DRUMMER sb dial; for second form cf *OED crake v*, =croak. A variety of the DRUMMER fish.

1952 FGC StE /krúokin dróma/—very noisy; same as /kríekin dróma/ Mongalar drummer.

CROAKING-LIZARD /krókin, krókng, krúokin lizad/ sb; cf *OED* s.v. *lizard* 1885 only. A common lizard, *Aristelliger præsignis*, which makes a distinctive croaking sound at night.

1835 Senior 80, The 'croaking lizard'..looks hideous, is grey mottled, and has a large head. He generally takes up his abode under the shingles, and issues a most disagreeable and piercing croak. 1851 Gosse 75, A singular croaking sound above his head causes him to look up; and then he sees clinging to the rafters, or crawling sluggishly along with the back downward..Lizards, of form, colour, and action very diverse from those he has seen before. It is the Gecko or Croaking Lizard..Its appearance is repulsive, I allow, but its reputation for venom is libellous and groundless. 1940 Lynn-Grant 67. 1952 FGC Port, StT /krókin lízad/; Port /krókng lizad/; Man /krúokin lízad/.

CROCODILE sb dial. A kind of MACHETE.

1958 DeC StT /krakadail/ a cutlass [with parallel sides and a lobed end at a slight angle]..So called from the picture of an alligator which is stamped on the blade as a trade mark.

CROCUS /krókos, krúokas/ sb; 1790→ crocus, 1808 crookas, 1823 croocas, 1863 crooks(?), 1905 cruckcuss; prob from its use to bag saffron ('crocus'): cf Avis, *Amer. Speech* 1955. *BL G*

1. A coarse material, formerly of linen, now of hemp, jute, or the like, widely used for making CROCUS BAGS (its chief present use), formerly, like Osnaburg, used for the clothing of slaves. (Not Jamaican in origin—cf *DA* 1689→.) *BA*

1767 *Jrnls Assembly* (quoted in 1814 Lunan II 237), The most expeditious way of obtaining the juice is by straining it through an hair-cloth, crocus, or coarse blanket. 1790 Beckford I xlix, For every three pieces of crocus, or osnabrug, loose—0 0 7½. 1863 Waddell 193 (year 1842), Their Obea articles, wrapped in old crooks, and some ill-looking compound in bottles, were produced to the amazement of the court. [*Crooks* is prob a misprint.] 1952 FGC StM /krókos bag/ is made of /krúokas/.

2. Said to be a type of great-coat—see quot. (The cloth described, however, seems to be Penistone rather than Osnaburg, so this quot is open to question.)

1808 Stewart 232, Both men and women [slaves] are also provided with great coats (or crookas, as they call them) of blue woolen stuff. (Ed. 1823, 269, sp *croocas*.)

CROCUS BAG /krókos bág/ sb; <CROCUS+*bag*. (This is the only Ja form—in US *crocus sack* and *croker sack* are also used.) A bag made of CROCUS, widely used as a receptacle for agricultural produce, etc. Formerly a synonym of *Osnaburg bag*. *BA BL G*

1873 Rampini 98, I had a crocus (Osnaburg) bag with breadkind on my back and my machette in my hand. 1905 Dodd 30, The 'cruckcuss bag', or bag of sack-cloth. 1942 Bennett 42, Pass de crocus bag femme. 1952 FGC StM, see CROCUS.

CROCUS BUSH sb dial; perh <*crocus*, CROCUS+BUSH. CHIGGER NUT. (The hairiness of the plant may be the basis of comparison with CROCUS.)

1953 *WIMJ*, see HOG HOOK. 1954 *WIMJ* 31, Tournefortia hirsutissima..Chigger Nut; Crocus Bush; ?Hog Hook.

CRODUCK sb dial; ?<*crow-duck*.

1943 *GL* StAnn, Croduck, a smart person.

CROMANTY /kròmánti/ sb, also attrib; 1757 Corromantee, 1757→ Coromantee, 1774 Coromantin, 1790 Caramantee, 1794 Koromantyn, 1909→ Cromanty; from the name of a town and settlement area of the Gold Coast, variously spelt Coromanti, Kormantyn, Koromanti, Cormantine, etc. Cf also CARAMANTE.

1. The place of origin of many of the slaves brought to Jamaica in the late 17th and early 18th centuries. (See 1960 *CLS*.) *G*

[1651 Cal. State Papers 1574–1660 355, Approving report of the Council of Trade concerning the trade to Guinea..the Council state their opinion that 20 leagues on each side of the two chief factories, or residences by the sea coast, the fort of Cormantin, and the river Cerberro, near Sierra Leone, may be granted to the present Adventurers, with exclusion of trade to all others for 14 years.] 1757 St Jago Intelligencer 14 May [Advertisement for a runaway slave:] Man of the Corromantee Country..speaks no English.

2. A negro brought from and identified with this area; in Jamaica, those who escaped and joined the MAROONS came to dominate them and gained a reputation for fierceness. *G*

1757 St Jago Intelligencer 14 May [Advertisement for runaway slaves:] 1 Ebo, 1 Angola, 1 Mundingo, 1 Coromantee. 1774 Long II 472–3, Coromantins. The Negroes who pass under this general description are brought from the Gold coast; but we remain uncertain, whether they are natives of that tract of Guiney, or receive their several names of Akims, Fantins, Ashantees, Quamboos, &c. from the towns so called, at whose markets they are bought..However, whether they are brought from some distance inland, or are the refuse and outcast of the several provinces whose names they bear; it is certain they are marked with the same characters, which authors have given to the natives of this part, who are said to be the most turbulent and desperate of any on the coast of Guiney; and that, were it not for their civil divisions, they would become dangerous neighbours to all the surrounding states. 1794 (1801) Edwards III 324, In the year 1760..The Koromantyn slaves, in the parish of St Mary, rose into rebellion, and the Maroons were called upon, according to treaty, to co-operate in their suppression. *Ibid* 326, A party of them, indeed, had afterwards the merit..of killing the leader of the rebels. He was a young negro of the Koromantyn nation, named Tackey. 1803 Dallas I 30, A considerable body of slaves had quitted the upper settlements in Clarendon, and were carrying on a war against the White inhabitants, under a negro called Cudjoe..these people were Coromantees, and their leader a brave and enterprising man. 1907 Reynolds 18, But you, a cromantee like you, wha you hab? You doan eben own a cow horn, let alone anyting else for de supportance of a wife.

3. The 'secret language' of the Maroons; also attrib.

1803 Dallas I 33, The Coromantee language, however, superseded the others, and became in time the general one in use [among the Maroons]. 1929 Beckwith 198, Certain plants are called after their uses—'Heal-it-and-draw', 'See-me-contract', and 'Search-me-heart'—names referred to as 'Kromanti talk'. 1935 HPJ, Philip Williams, of Maroon descent (knew Accompong well) said Cromanty was spoken by old-time people, and used in funerals in songs.

4. A local name for the tree *Matayba apetala*, which grows in the hills and is reputed for its tough wood. *N*

1890 Thomas 68, Bullet-tree, Coromantee..Santa Maria, and numerous other trees..towered skyward on every side [in the Johncrow Mts]. 1909 Harris 303, Cromanty ..A fairly common tree in woods of the interior hills..It is a most useful hardwood, suitable for all purposes, and especially for exposed situations. 1926 Fawcett 55–6, *Matayba apetala*..Wanika, Cromanty, Bastard Mahogany, Coby, Red Wood. s *pampandam*.

5. Attrib and comb (see also separate entries below).

1929 Beckwith 193, There were three classes of Kromanti songs, the 'jaw-bone', of a comparatively mild variety; the 'new war songs', of stronger power; and the 'old war songs', most powerful of all. 1935 HPJ (Mrs C. Stephenson), She knew an old African..when she was a little girl in Vere (ca 1895)..He used to come to sweep the yard, and one day he had stopped working to talk to her. A young bookkeeper, a Mr Maine, came up, and asked him, without looking at her, why he was not getting on with his work. She interposed: '*I* started talking to him, and he has only wasted a few minutes'. Mr Maine took no notice of her, but abused the African, who drew himself up and answered him. Maine said, 'I wish slavery were here again so that I could lay this whip about your shoulders'. The African replied: 'For that I will lay the Coromantee Curse upon you and the hand with which you wish to lay the whip about my shoulders, shall destroy you'. Mr Maine killed himself some years later. Mrs S. could never learn the Curse, tho' the African lived to be very old..He died about 1920.

CROMANTY (ANT) sb; <CROMANTY+*ant*. A large stinging ant, prob the same as the *kapkap*.

1851 Gosse 141, You may sit for hours..without disturbing a city of those formidable warriors, the great-jawed Corromantee Ants (*Odontomachus*). 1943 *GL* Kgn, Cromanty, A specie of black ants. 1952 FGC Han /krománti/ big size black ant—size of red-ants; lives in ground; has claw; sends liquid poison in you.

CROMANTY FLUTE sb; <CROMANTY+*flute*. A musical instrument in use among the CROMANTY negroes of Jamaica.

1790 Beckford I 217, The Caramantee-flutes are made from the porous branches of the trumpet-tree, are about a yard in length, and of nearly the thickness of the upper part of a bassoon: they have generally three holes at the bottom; are held, in point of direction, like the hautboy; and while the right hand stops the holes, in the left is shaken, by one of the party, a hollow ball that is filled with pebbles. 1802 Nugent 101, The Coromantee flute is a long black reed, has a plaintive and melancholy sound, and is played with the nose.

CROMANTY TALK see CROMANTY 3.

CRONGOE (YAM) /krongo, kronjo/ sb now dial; prob <*Crongoe*, tribal name+YAM. A type of wild yam.

1824 Barclay 438, The Crongoe yam, which roasted would bear comparison with the best Irish potatoes, grows wild in the fields that have been thrown out of cultivation. 1943 *GL* Port, Krunga, yam; Crungo, a yam; StT, Krunjo, African Yam. 1954 LeP Port, Kronjo, wild yam.

CROOCAS see CROCUS.

CROOK, A kind of MACHETE. See DeC in 1961 *CLS* 75.

CROOKED sb dial. Crookedness. *G*

1873 Rampini 181 [Prov:] When man a magistrate, crooked da follow him. [*When a man is a magistrate, dishonesty follows him.*]

CROOK-HAND sb dial. *G*

1958 DeC StT /kruk-han/ a twisted hand; in this district (Old Pen) opposed to /fin-han/ which means a withered but not twisted hand.

CROOKIE sb dial; origin unknown—conceivably an alteration of Twi *Kɔnnɔre*, the name of Anancy's wife (*ɛ-Kɔ́nnɔre*, a species of spider). In the NANCY STORIES, the wife of Anancy.

1873 Rampini 116, The other personages who figure in the tales are Annancy's wife Crookie, and Tacooma his reputed son. 1905 Smith 43, An' Annancy bawl out to him wife Crookie..An' Crookie bawl out.

CROOK-POINT see CROOK.

CROOKS see CROCUS.

CROP sb; cf *DAE* 2, *DA* 1623–78 'Obs.' Current in Ja. The period during which sugar-cane is being harvested and sugar made; also in phr: *during crop, in crop, out of crop*, etc. Cf TAKE OFF CROP. *BA BL G*

1788 Beckford 45, They seldom continue in the field, out of crop, after sun-set. 1788–9 McNeill 5, During *Crop*, every Negro is allowed to eat as much of the *cane*, and drink as much of the *hot liquor* from the coppers, as he chuses. 1839 McMahon 34, The slaves were never allowed more than four or five hours' rest every night, even out of crop. *Ibid* 43, The cattle you have killed this crop. *Ibid* 45, This scene, however, during crop, was several times repeated. 1952 FGC StT, Out of crop is a great time of hardship.

CROP-BASKET sb dial; <*crop* sb+*basket*.

1959 DeC Port /krap basket/ made of hook-withe, oval, open, has handle.

CROP-OVER sb; *ODS* only 1894. *BA BL G*

1. The end of the sugar-cane harvest, and the celebrations or amusements connected with it.

1826 Barclay 10, The day on which the last of the canes are cut down upon a sugar plantation, flags are displayed in the field, and all is merriment. A quart of sugar and a quart of rum are allowed to each negro on the occasion, to hold what is called crop-over, or harvest-home. 1828 Marly 46, A day..when the making of sugar for that year was finished, or as it is termed, crop over. As customary in the country at crop over, a number of the neighbouring overseers..were invited.

2. Fig. The completion of NINE-NIGHT, the last of the funeral celebration.

1953 Moore 118.

CROPPIE sb dial; prob <CLAPPY, with common change of *l* to *r* and 'standardized' spelling of /a/ as *o*.

1943 *GL* Port, Croppie, board slippers.

CROP-TIME sb. =CROP. *BA G*

1782 Considerations 44–5, 49, The season of the year wherein it is natural to expect an Enemy is the season of all others most inconvenient and distressing to draw off the attention of the Planter and the white people from their estates. The crops must be sacrificed..The season I allude to (commonly called crop-time). 1788 Marsden 18, They..are allowed two days in a week out of crop-time to till it. 1839 McMahon 188, In crop time, they were used as bags.

CROSS /kraas/ sb, adj, and adv dial; 1907 crahss, 1935 crass.

A. sb: A misfortune or adversity; often in plural. Cf *OED sb* 10b. Also in phr 'The cross is on (someone)'. *BA BL G*

1940 HPJ, Cross—Used in the curious expression 'The cross is on us', towards Easter, when the Devil and the powers of evil are particularly active, disturbing people and leading to many minor physical disasters. 1942 Bennett 45, Me no like Tung at all..De wan no mo week me spen' deh Me meet crosses! eh! eh! [*I don't like the city at all; in the single week I spent there I had such misfortunes!*] 1955 FGC Man /kraasiz/ bad luck.

B. adj: Fierce tempered. (Cf *OED a* 5, the sense of which is, however, weaker than this.)

1907 Jekyll 136, An' Tiger get cross begun to lick. 1924 Beckwith 102, The cow is so cross he has to turn stick an' stone to live amongst the cow. 1940 HPJ, Crass, Cross; fierce (of dogs). 1952 FGC StT /kraas kou/—one that bucks; StJ /barakuuta somtaim veri kraas/. *BA BL G N*; *SC krássi*

C. adv: Cf *OED adv* 3, 'In an adverse or unfavourable way; contrary to one's desire or liking'.

1954 LeP StJ, My brother writes the dry has gone cross on him, *The drought has seriously affected him.*

CROSS-AND-PILE prep and adv dial; <*cross and pile*, cf *OED sb* 21b, 'The two sides of anything; one thing and its opposite'. Alternately from side to side; zigzag (with respect to). *BA*

1946 U.Newton I 11, I rested for a few moments before walking 'cross-and-pile' the hill to reach my destination. 1947 U.Newton III 11, We walked zigzag or as we used to say 'cross and pile' down the hill. 1952 FGC Tre, Cross-and-pile.

CROSSBAR sb dial; also attrib. A fish of the mackerel family distinguished by stripes in the form of a crossbar; see quots.

1952 FGC StE /kráasbár/ same as queenfish—different shape from kingfish and softer flesh—mouth pointed like alligator; StM, Crossbar kingfish has stripes—/gá-ú/ is plain; StT, Crossbar mackerel—out in the deep.

CROSS-CUT vb dial. To interrupt another person's speaking.

1873 Rampini 101, W. (indignantly)—Don't cross-cut (interrupt) me, sa!

CROSS GRASS sb ?obs. A grass of uncertain identity—perh what Browne (136–7) called 'cruciated' grass (*Chloris cruciata*).

a 1726 Barham (1794) 69, There are about fifteen sorts of the cypress and galangal kinds, which are counted specifics against pestilential diseases..The cross grass hath the same virtues. 1774 Long III 765, The Dutch, burr, cross, speckled, and manna grasses are among the best for fodder.

CROSS-PASS sb dial; <*cross* adj, +PASS, path. A cross-path; a place where paths cross; a crossroads. *SC krássi-passi.*

1907 Jekyll 115–16, So they meet at a cross-pass..*Cross-pass*, cross-path. [1924 Beckwith 250, When he (Dead) ketch to a cross-path.]

CROSS-STICK /kráas tìk/ sb dial.

1956 Mc StAnd /kráas tìk/ rung of a ladder.

CROTCHITY see CRUTCHETY.

CROWN BREAD sb. A fancy loaf of bread in the shape of a crown. *G*

1912 McK *Songs* 130, I only took two set o' dance An at de bidding* tried me chance; I buy de big crown-bread fe you—* An auction of loaves of fine bread, profusely decorated by the baker's art, is a feature of rustic dances. [Current, 1958, FGC.]

CROWNED SHEPHERD sb dial. The title of highest rank (except for 'Father') in a single Revival band (StT).

1953 Moore 83.

CROWNING TABLE sb dial. See quot.

1953 Moore 109, Crowning table, the Sixth Revival service, essentially a service of ordination.

CROWN SHELL sb dial. A type of conch having the shape of a crown.

1952 FGC StM, Crown shell.

CROYOLIEN see CREOLIAN.

CRUCKCUSS see CROCUS. *BA*

CRUFF /krof/ sb dial; <*scruff*, 'A mean, worthless fellow; a wastrel', *EDD* sb[2] 8. See quots. *BA*

1943 *GL* Clar, Cruff, sluggard; StM, Cruff, uncouth person, one rough in manner; also Kgn, Man. 1954 LeP StE, Cruff, coarse, illiterate man. 1955 FGC Man /krof/ a worthless person—has no intention of uplifting [himself]. 1958 DeC gen /krof/ a stupid fool.

CRUFF /krof/ adj dial; <CRUFF sb, cf *EDD* sb[2], '1, Scurf..; 2, A thin crust or covering of any kind; a film; a rind'. Prob also infl by *rough*, through similarity of form and meaning. Cf CRUFFY, CRUFTY.

1. Of the skin: scabby, scurfy. *BL*

c 1915 FGC StAnd /Yu skin krof fi truu/ *Your skin is very rough.* 1956 McMan, The scabby state the skin gets into from not washing: /dem fut krof/ *Their feet are scabby.*

2. Of the skin or other surfaces: naturally rough. *BL*

1952 FGC Man, The green lizard is the /uol krof wan/.

3. Of a person's manners: coarse, uncouth.

1961 BLB 22 /mi bena kos dem hou dem krof/ *I was berating them for being so rough and crude.*

CRUFFIE-ROUCHEN, CUFFIE-ROUSIN sb dial; var forms of *kofi-routn*: prob with folk-etym infl of CRUFFY and of *rouse*.

1954 LeP StE (Eld); StAnn.

CRUFFY adj dial; <*scruffy* (*EDD* 1, 3) or CRUFF + -*y*. Scurfy; rough. *G*

1868 Russell 11, Cruffy, rough. 1943 *GL* Tre, Cruffy, rough.

CRUFTY adj dial; <CRUFF sb + -*ty*.

1943 *GL* Port, Crufty, coarse looking.

CRUMUCHIN, CRUMUGIN(E), CRUMUGING see CRAMOUCHIN.

CRUMUNA see *kumuna.*

CRUNGE vb dial; <*scrunge*, *EDD*, 'To crush, squeeze, crowd; to press'—chiefly North-country.

1943 *GL* Port, Krunge, crush or squeeze.

CRUNGO see CRONGOE YAM.

CRUST /kros/ sb dial; <*crust.* *G*

1956 JB gen /kros/ A long strip of dough rolled over, baked, and cut into sections (like Swiss roll made of crust, but with no filling).

CRUSTY adj dial.

1. See quot; the association is probably with the scabs or scurf of a CRUFF or CRUFFY person —a frequent one, in which the state of the skin is taken as symptomatic of every kind of backwardness.

1958 DeC Port /krosti/ a vague derogatory epithet meaning foolish, backward, illiterate, etc.—e.g. a /krof/ is defined as a /krosti/ man.

2. Of the complexion: see quot, and cf COOL (COLOUR).

1960 SJR StAnd, 'Crusty' describes a very black, unpleasant complexion; contrasts with cool-skin.

CRUTCHETY adj dial; prob <*crotchety* but infl in meaning by *crutch*.

1943 *GL* StAnd, Crotchity, Broken down, feeble; StM, Crutchety, unsteady.

CRUTCH-STICK sb dial. A saddle-like wooden frame which supports the hampers on a donkey or mule.

c 1940 HPJ, According to Ina, the crutch or crotch stick is simply the stick or board which supports the two hampers.

CRUTCHUMENT see *kruchument*.

CRY vb dial; cf *OED v* 12, →1781, '*Obs.*' Of shoes: to squeak; cf CRIER. *BL G*

1929 Beckwith 204, Instead of the shoes crying 'Ne' pass! ne' pass!' they will cry 'Love! love!' 1946 U.Newton I 37, The sun was pleased with our shining appearance, if not with our 'crying' shoes. And how those shoes squeaked!

CRY ppl adj dial; for *crying* <CRY vb. Squeaking. *G*

1910 Anderson-Cundall 41 [Prov:] Cry shoe no good fe listener.

CRY-CRY adj and sb dial; iter <*cry* vb. *BL G*

A. adj: 1. Fretful; constantly crying. *T*

1860 Radcliffe 5 [Prov:] Cry cry pickney nebar hab right. 1940 HPJ, Cry-cry, querulous, peevish (of child).

2. Transf. Of boots with CRIERS: squeaky.

1940 HPJ (Astley Clerk), Him wear cri-cri boot.

B. sb: Weeping; constant flow of tears. *BA T*

1935 HPJ [Folk Song:] Oh! de cry-cry tun me a fool-fool gal, Wata run a mi eye. [*Oh, my weeping turns me into a foolish girl*, etc.]

CRY UPON vb phr dial; cf *OED cry v* 2, 17 →1606. To supplicate (implying a sense of injury in the subject); to complain to, make a complaint or claim against. *G*

1924 Beckwith 69, And after it grew her goat ate it off. She cried upon the goat and told it that she wanted the peas. *Ibid*, The river took it away from her. She cried upon the river, and the river said it didn't have anything to give her but a fish.

CU see KU.

CUB, CUBBY sb; <*cub* (+-*y*). A young donkey. s CUBBY.

1951 FGC StAnd (Current for past 40 years). 1956 Mc StE, Cub, cubby, young donkey.

CUBA see CUBBA.

CUBA BARK sb. The tree *Hibiscus elatus*, and its bark; see quots.

1864 Grisebach 783, Cuba-bark: *Paritium elatum*. 1926 Fawcett 141–2, Blue or Mountain Mahoe, Cuba Bark.. The lace-like inner bark was at one time known as Cuba bark from its being used as the material for tying round bundles of Havana cigars.

CUBAN BANANA sb dial. A variety of very small banana.

1952 FGC Port, Cuban banana, fig banana.

CUBAN CANE sb dial. A type of sugar-cane thought to have been brought from Cuba.

1952 FGC Port.

CUBAN CONGO see GUNGU (PEAS) quot 1913.

CUBAN PETCHARY sb. A petchary said to be found in Jamaica; it can hardly be *Tyrannus cubensis*, however, which is not known far beyond Cuba; and the description fits the usual Jamaican bird, *Tyrannus dominicensis*.

1952 FGC Han, Cuban pechary, shorter—like the loggerhead—has a yellow center stripe in the head.

CUBAN PLANTAIN sb dial. A type of plantain thought to have been brought from Cuba.

1952 FGC StT, Cuban plantain, has stouter seeds but short and clumsy.

CUBBA /kúba/ sb; 1774 1793 Cuba, 1851 1873 Cooba, 1943→ Cubba, 1943 Koobah, 1954 Couba; cf Twi *A`kúwá*, woman's third day-name.

1. The DAY-NAME of a female born on Wednesday. *G*

1774 Long II 427, Cuba, Wednesday. 1793 Edwards II 33, In sprightly Cuba's eyes look gay. 1851 Gosse 233, Wednesday..Coóba. 1873 Rampini 88, Wednesday.. Cooba, stout. 1927 Anderson-Cundall 95 [Prov:] Poor Ketch Cubba a low groun', him turn sarvent fe darg.

2. A servant (but the sense of 'casual' is uncert); see quot.

1943 *GL* Kgn, Koobah, casual domestic.

3. Transf. See quot; cf also MISS CUBBA.

1943 *GL* StAnd, Cubba, a womanish man.

4. See quot; sometimes a slut.

1943 *GL* Clar, Cubba, companionship.

CUBBA-CUBBA see *koba-koba*.

CUBBAGE see CUBBITCH.

CUBBENA /kúbina/ sb; 1774 Cubbenah, 1851 Cubena, 1873 Cubbena, 1943 Cubina; cf Twi *Kwàbénã*.

1. The DAY-NAME for a male born on Tuesday.

1774 Long II 427, Cubbenah..Tuesday. 1851 Gosse 233, Tuesday, Cúbena (Coo-bena). 1873 Rampini 88, Tuesday, Cubbena, inventive. 1954 LeP Man, Coubenna, boy born Thursday. [Evid a confusion.] *G*

2. (By confusion with CUBBA.) Name of a female.

1940 HPJ, Sometimes the name is feminine: 'Let down rope, Cubben', Cubben''. 1943 *GL* StT, Cubina, a country woman of the peasant class.

CUBBENAH see prec.

CUBBICH, CUBBIDGE see next.

CUBBITCH /kóbich, kobij/ adj and sb dial; 1862 cubbich, 1907→ cubbitch, 1935 cubbidge, cubbage, 1943 cobich, cobitch, covitch, 1954 cubbisch; <*covetous*, cf *OED* 2, 'greedy, grasping, avaricious'. *BL G*

A. adj: See quots.

1862 Clutterbuck 233, Dis brown lady too bad, cubbich as a 'tar-apple tree. 1907 Jekyll 51, Cubbitch..'is used only in the sense of close-fisted'..A cubbitch man 'will not part with what he has'. 1940 HPJ, Cubbidge: greedy, stingy, mean. Cubbitch, cubbage are other forms of spelling:—'Cubbitch as 'tarapple' tree, which never lets its ripe fruit fall. 1943 *GL* Clar, Cobich, to be mean; StT, Covitch, craven. 1954 LeP Man, StAnn, StE, Cubbitch, cubbisch, someone who is mean.

B. sb: Greed, avarice.

1958 FGC, Common in such statements as /im wi ded fi kobich/ *Greed will be the death of him*.

CUBBITCH-HOLE sb dial. The hollow below the skull at the back of the neck, which, if pronounced, is taken as a sign that one is CUBBITCH. *BL*

1935 HPJ, Cubbitch hole, hollow in the back of the neck (supposed to be a sign of greed). 1943 *GL* StAnd, Cobitch hole, back of neck; Tre, Cubbitch hole, Intercomplexal fossa. 1946 U.Newton I 28, The 'cubbitch hole'—the ditch at the back of the head. 1956 Mc Man /kobich hùol/.

CUBBITCHNESS sb dial rare; < CUBBITCH + *-ness*. The state or quality of being CUBBITCH; see also CUBBITCH-HOLE.

1946 U.Newton I 30, Then he pushes that pair of scissors, one end of which is broken, down into my tender hole of cubbitchness.

CUBBY see CUB.

[**CUBBYU, CUBBY YEW** see *kyabiyo*.]

CUBEL see COBELL.

CUBENA, CUBINA see CUBBENA.

CUBUB see *kabob*.

CUBU-CUBU /kúbukúbu/ sb dial; poss by iteration < Twi *kobi*, a kind of rum or brandy.

1943 *GL*, Cubu-cubu, Stolen factory rum.

CUCHE sb dial; evid a familiarized form of *cashew* or *kushu*, both of which are accented on the first syllable in dial pron.

1943 *GL* Clar, Cuche, cashew.

CUCHIE see *kochi*.

CUCKOLD-FISH sb; < *cuckold* + *fish*, so called from the horns it bears on its 'forehead'. This 18th-century witticism has been forgotten, however, and folk-etymology has converted *cuckold* > *cockle*. (*OED* only 1757.) The fish *Acanthostracion quadricorne*. Also called TRUNK-FISH. *N*

1756 Browne 457, Ostracion 5..The Trunck-fish.. Ostracion 6..The Cuckold-fish..The two last species are so like each other that they can be distinguished only by the horns that shoot from above the eyes of the latter. 1892 Cockrell, Cockle-fish, *Ostracion quadricorne*.

CUCKOLD'S INCREASE sb obs; 1756 1837 cuckold's increase, 1873 cockle's increase, 1893 cockle creas, 1913 cockold's increase cock-na-cris; *cuckold* alludes to the 'horns' formed by the pods. As with CUCKOLD-FISH, the joke has been forgotten and *cuckold* has become *cockle*; in folk speech the name is still further reduced. *OED* only quot 1756. The bean *Vigna unguiculata*.

1756 Browne 292, Phaseolus 9..Cuckold's-Increase. 1837 Macfadyen I 288, Usually two, but never more, of the flowers perfect the fruit. This bean, from the pods standing out together like a pair of horns, commonly receives the name of 'Cuckold's Increase'. 1873 Rampini 91, Pease and pulse of all kinds—..the 'Cockle's increase' (not unlike Antibilious Pills in appearance). 1893 Sullivan 25, The mutton is excellent done..with cockle creas peas. 1913 Harris 33, In addition to the black-eye the forms known in Jamaica are Cockold's Increase or 'Cock-na-cris'; Quick Increase; Lady Pea, Cow Pea, &c.

CUCKO-MACCA, CUCKOO-MACA see COCO-MACCA.

CUCKOO /kuku/ sb dial; cf Ewe (Yehwe dialect) *kukú*, corn dumpling. (Engl *cook* has been adopted into several African languages: Twi, Ewe *kúkù*, Hausa *kuku*, etc., and may play a part here.)

1943 *GL* StM, Cuckoo, meal cock [*sic* = 'cooked'] with ockro.

CUCU MACCA see COCO-MACCA.

CUDDIN see COUSIN.

CUDJOE[1] /kojo/ sb dial arch, cf Fante *Kodwo*, Twi *Kwàdwó*.

1. The DAY-NAME for a male born on Monday.

1774 Long II 427, Male..Cudjoe..Monday. 1851 Gosse 233, Monday—Cúdjo (Coo-jo). 1873 Rampini 88, Monday—Cudjo, strong-headed. 1954 LeP Man, Cudjoe, boy born on Wednesday. [Evid a confusion.] 1956 Mc Man /koio/ born-day name, nickname. 1957 LeP StE (Eld) /kojo/ A Maroon name only. *G*

2. Hist. A chief of the MAROONS, brother of ACCOMPONG; see quot. *G*

1738 *Articles of Pacification with the Maroons of Trelawney Town*, Whereas Captain Cudjoe, Captain Accompong, Captain Johnny, Captain Cuffee, Captain Quaco, and several other negroes..have been in a state of war and hostility, for several years past, against our sovereign lord the King. [From 1801 Edwards III 313.]

3. Transf. A slave-driver.

1827 Hamel I 164 [The slaves retired] to handle the hoe or the bill for the less dignified [than Combah], though not less arbitrary cudjoes in the plains below—the drivers; whose whips..cracked till the very mountains repeated the sound.

4. In compounds: cf BANANA CUDJOE and prob *kojoruba*.

CUDJOE[2] /kojo/ sb and vb dial; prob < *cudgel*, infl in form by CUDJOE[1]. *BL*

A. sb: A heavy stick or cudgel.

1940 HPJ, Cudjoe: cudjel [*sic*] (country word). Quarko Sam ca 1816. 1956 Mc StE (Accom) /kójo/ walking stick. In phrase /a trúo mi kójo pán yu/ *I throw my cudgel on you* [*I will beat you with my stick*.]

B. vb: To beat with a stick.

1956 Mc StE (Accom) /mi a kojo yu/ *I will hit you*.

CUENTA /kwenta/ sb dial; prob < Sp *cuenta*, but cf Fante *akóntàá*, account, calculation, reckoning, < Pg *conta*.

1943 *GL* StT, Cuento, business; Clar, kwenta; Man, quenteh; StM, quenta.

CUENTO see prec.

CUFFEE /kófi/ sb dial; 1774→ Cuffee, 1873→ Cuffie; < Twi *Kòfí*.

1. The DAY-NAME for a male born on Friday; arch or obs. *G*

1774 Long II 427, Male..Cuffee..Friday. 1851 Gosse 233, Friday—Cúffee (Coo-fee). 1873 Rampini 88, Friday—Cuffie, hot-tempered. 1954 LeP Man, Cuffee, boy born on Friday.

2. Hist. One of the captains of the Maroons —cf CUDJOE[1] 2. *G*

3. As a derogatory term: a backward or stupid person, unable to speak clearly; one easily fooled. *BL*

1943 *GL* Port, Cuffie, uncivilized. 1952 FGC Han /yu tingk aim a kofi/ *You think I'm a gull, a fool*. 1955 FGC Man /kófi/ an easily fooled person; loggerhead person; don't have much speech.

4. Transf. A shrimp.

1943 *GL* Port, Cuffie, shrimp.

CUFFEE WOOD sb dial; ? < CUFFEE 3 + *wood*. See quot.

1926 Fawcett 217, *Zuelania Guidonia*..Cuffey Wood, Silver Wood, Glass Wood..The timber is used for building.

CUFFEY, CUFFIE see CUFFEE.

CUFFIROUTEN, CUFROUTIN see *kofiroutn*.

CUHI, CUIE see *kuy*.

CUJORUBA see *kojo-ruba*.

CUKRO adj dial; prob a form of CRA-CRA.

1943 *GL* Port, Cukro, big, old, tough.

CULILU see CALALU.

CULLABUNKA sb dial; first element unknown, second element <*bongka*, cabbage palm. See quot; prob the cabbage palm.

1907 Jekyll 118–19, An' that time Annancy went an' climb a cullabunka tree..*cullabunka*, a kind of Palm.

CULLEN MINT /kólon/ sb dial; origin uncert: perh for Dr Wm Cullen, whose *Materia medica* appeared in 1789, and whom Bryan Edwards II 227 and Lunan II 24 mention. A common herb, *Lippia geminata*, considered to have medicinal properties. (Prob also other similar plants: quot 1952 seems to refer to some species of *Lantana*; in quot 1954 the plant is unidentified.)

1952 FGC StAnn, StT /kólon mint/ sage with a pale flower. 1954 Kirkland 170 (Port—Contents of a fever-bath) Colon mint, ram goat regular, sweet broom, etc. 1954 *WIMJ* 30, *Lippia geminata*..Colic Mint; Guinea Mint; Cullen Mint.

CULLOLO sb dial; prob a familiarized, assimilated form of COMBOLOW.

1943 *GL* Man, Cullolo, friend.

CULLU CULLU see *kulu-kulu*.

CULTIVATION sb chiefly dial. A cultivated field, a GROUND. *G*

1943 *GL* Tre, Grong, cultivation.

CULTIVATOR sb dial. A small farmer. *G*

1929 Beckwith 20 (see TALKING). 1954 LeP StT, Koltivieta, man who makes living by growing and selling market crops. 1956 Mc Man, StAnd /koltivieta/.

CUMAMA /kumama/ vb phr cant; poss <Engl *come* (in dial often pronounced /kum/) +*mama*. A word of the AFRICAN cult (StT): cf Ko -*kumama*, come, arrive.

1953 Moore gloss, Cumama, calling dead mother.

CUMARTE /kumarti/ vb phr cant; the first element is poss < Engl *come* but cf prec. A word of the AFRICAN cult (StT).

1953 Moore gloss, Cumarte, calling spirits.

CUMBALO see COMBOLO.

CUMBAY see KUMBAY.

CUMBOHLOH, CUMBOLO see COMBOLO.

CUM-CUM-TEK see *kongkonte*.

CUMINA, CUMMINA, CUM-MO-NA see *kumuna*.

CUNCHUNTIA, CUNCUNGTA, CUNCUNTEH, CUNCUNTEY see *kongkonte*.

CUNEP see GUINEP.

CUNG see COUSIN.

CUNGCUNGSEH see *kongkongsa*.

CUNK see *kongk*.

CUNNIE see CUNNY.

CUNNIE-MO'N-FATHER sb; <CUNNY+ *more than father*. In Anancy stories, one of Anancy's sons; the name describes his character—he is (and figuratively represents) the son who is cleverer or trickier than his father, and the stories relate contests between the two.

1924 Beckwith 27–8, Anansi has seven children. He ask them how they would like to name. Six of them like different name, but one boy say he would like to name 'Cunnie-mo'-than-father'. So for every tack [trick] Anansi put up, Cunnie-mo'n-father break it down.

CUNNO see *kunu*.

CUNNU-MUNU see *kunu-munu*.

CUNNY /kóni/ sb and adj dial; 1873→ cunny, 1924→ cunnie; <*cunning*. *N*; *SC kóni*.

A. sb: Cunning, craftiness; a trick, tricks.

1873 Rampini 176 [Prov:] Cunny (cunning) better dan 'trong (strength). 1935 HPJ, How many cunnie have you? Tricks—Annancy stories. 1950 Pioneer 40, Bredda Nancy, wid him usual cunny.

B. adj: Cunning, clever, shrewd; tricky.

1873 Rampini 179, see RATTA. 1924 Beckwith 9, Him says to himself, 'Ha! if I didn't cunnie, I wouldn't get dis big barrow t'day'. 1943 *GL* StAnd, Cunny, smart. 1956 Mc Man /kóni/ knowing, shrewd; /bra nansi iz a kóni man/ *Brother Anancy is a cunning man*.

CUNNY-BUCK see CONY-BUCK.

CUNOOMOONOO see *kunu-munu*.

CUNTAPEACHY see *kontapiichi*.

CUNTUNG see CONTOON.

CUNUMUNU see *kunu-munu*.

CUPID'S PAINTBRUSH sb; a var of CUPID'S SHAVING-BRUSH.

1944 *NHN* II 84, The Cupid's Paintbrush with its tiny pink flowers.

CUPID'S SHAVING-BRUSH sb bot. A weed with a flower resembling a shaving-brush; see quot.

1936 Fawcett 273, *Emilia sonchifolia*..Cupid's Shaving Brush.

CUPPY /kopi/ sb dial, also attrib; <*cup*+ dimin or familiarizing -*y*; coincidental infl of Ewe *ákobidě*, a small calabash with a handle, is also possible. See quot.

1956 Mc Man, A /kópi/ is a small packy (a calabash cut down and used as a drinking or eating vessel), probably decorated for table use; also StAnd /kopi shel/ calabash used as a drinking vessel.

CUQUELA /kukwela/ vb phr cant; for the first element cf CUMAMA, CUMARTE—second element unknown. A word of the AFRICAN cult (StT).

1953 Moore gloss, Cuquela, calling day.

CURACA, CURAÇA see CORATOE.

CURCULIO sb; *OED* 1756→. *OED*: 'A Linnæan genus of Beetles', etc.

1756 Browne 429, Curculio 1..The streaked shining Curculio. This beautiful insect is generally about an inch in length. 1774 Long II 125, see PAPILIO (FLY).

CURE-FOR-ALL sb dial. A local name for the wild plant *Pluchea odorata*, descriptive of its supposed medicinal qualities.

1954 *WIMJ* 31, Riverside Tobacco; Wild Tobacco; Sweet-scented Fleabane; Cure-for-all.

CURER sb obs. A device formerly used for draining the molasses from sugar while it was curing; see quot. *G*

1790 Beckford II 79, It was formerly the universal custom to introduce curers, or thatch-sticks, about seven in number, into the hogsheads, previously to the potting of the sugar, in order to form drains for the discharge of the molasses..These sticks are, I believe, now almost entirely exploded; the sugar certainly cures full as well, if not better, without them.

CURL-FINGER PEPPER sb dial. A type of FINGER-PEPPER with curled or twisted pods. *G*

1952 FGC Port, Curl-finger pepper—like finger, red, burn to hell.

CURRANS TREE see CURRANT TREE.

CURRANT-CACTUS sb bot. Jamaican 'mistletoe' (*Rhipsalis cassutha*), whose berries resemble currants.

1756 Browne 238, The slender parasitical Currant-*Cactus* or *Indian* Fig. This plant is pretty frequent in *St Mary's*, and grows chiefly on the largest trees in the wood, hanging commonly to the length of three or four feet from its fastening, or root. 1814 Lunan I 412–13, Cactus pendulus. (Ref to Browne.) 1926 Fawcett 284–5, *Rhipsalis cassutha*..Mistletoe, Currant Cactus.

CURRANT TREE sb bot. Certain bushes or trees whose fruit resemble currants.

1. *Jacquinia armillaris.*

1696 Sloane 167, Arbor, baccifera, laurifolia, fructu corallino..*Currans Tree.* In Jamaicæ septentrionalibus ad littus marinum..collegi. 1814 Lunan I 390, Jacquinia armillaris..Sloane, from the resemblance of the berries to currants, called this plant currant-tree. 1864 Grisebach 783, Currant tree: *Jacquinia armillaris.*

2. *Beureria succulenta* and its various forms.

1794 Barham 49, Currant-tree. This is so called because its fruit is of the shape and bigness of a currant..Index: *Ehretia bourreria.* 1814 Lunan I 255–6, Currant Tree. 1864 Grisebach 783, Currant tree..*Beureria succulenta* and *havanensis.*

CURRATO see CORATOE.

CURROO-CURROO see *karakara.*

CURRY /kóri/ sb dial; <*curry* sb. A coconut RUN-DOWN without curry powder. (Originally the dish had curry, however—see quot 1893.)

[1893 Sullivan 95, Cocoanut curry..Take the jelly of a very young cocoanut; boil it in its own water with a little cinnamon &c, adding curry powder to taste.] 1958 DeC StT /kóri/—name for a coconut run-down.

CURRY-COMB PAN sb dial.

1956 Mc Man /kori kuom pan/ a sardine tin with holes pierced in it, used to curry a donkey.

CURRY GOAT sb dial; <*curried goat.* A popular Jamaican dish favoured for celebrations and large gatherings. It appears to have been introduced by East Indians.

[1943 *GL* Port, Melvin—broth of curried goat.] 1952 FGC StJ, Curry goat—Coolie bring it in; StM /kori guot/; also general.

CURTSEY, CURTSY see *kochi.*

CURUTRIMENT see *kruchument.*

CUSCUS see KHUS-KHUS.

CUSH sb dial or slang; prob conn with COUS-COUS, and US *cush* (cf *DAE*).

1943 *GL* Kgn, Cush, money; also elsewhere.

CUSHEW(E) see CASHEW.

CUSHION STAR sb. A large, thick-bodied starfish (*Oreaster reticulatus*) that appears padded like a cushion.

1960 Inst of Ja exhibit.

CUSHU(E) see CASHEW.

CUSS /kos/ vb and sb dial; <Engl dial *cuss*, curse. *BL G T*

A. vb: Followed by the word that is the 'curse' or insult (quasi cognate object): To use strong or insulting language about (someone).

[1907 Jekyll 151, *Cuss*, abuse. It does not imply swearing. To swear is to *cuss bad word.*] 1912 McK *Songs* 66, You.. put you' back agains' de wall An' cuss our teacher fool. 1925 Beckwith 88 [Prov:] No cuss alligator long mout' till you cross riber. [Cf *ibid* 65.] 1942 Bennett 6, W'en uncle Cuss me bungo fool. *BA*

B. sb: An insult; a piece of abuse.

1956 Mc StE (Accom), A /bad kos/ a serious insult; /'go we go lai dong an yu changga' iz a bad kos/ *'Go away and lie down on your rag-bed' is a violent insult.*

CUSS-CUSS see COUS-COUS, *koskos.*

CUSSEYE sb; presumably <CUSS+*eye.* A small fish; see quot.

1942 *NHN* I 8 5, Cyprinodon jamaicensis—Cusseye.. The eyes are black surrounded with gold. [The illustration shows them as relatively large and prominent.]

CUSSING /kosin/ vbl sb dial; <CUSS, perh with infl also from *koskos.* A quarrel; an 'insulting-match'. *BL G*

1956 Mc /dem a ha wan big kosin/ *They are having a big quarrel.*

CUSTARD /kostad/ sb dial. Applied in popular use to such custard-like substances as sour milk (cf CLABUB, CLAD, etc.), coconut sauce (cf RUN-DOWN, etc.), and the like.

1943 *GL* StC, Dip and fall back, Custard and oil. 1958 DeC Port /kostad/ sour milk.

CUSTARD APPLE sb; also attrib; *OED* 1657→, *ODS* attrib 1819. The tree *Annona reticulata*; its custard-like fruit. *BA BL G N T*

[1657 Ligon (1673) 11, Every one a dish of fruit..the first was Millions, Plantines the second, the third Bonanos..the sixth the Custard Apple.] p. 1660 *State of Jamaica* MS Egerton 2395 489, Soursops, Custard Apples..besides plantings Pines &c. 1696 Sloane 205, Anona maxima..*The Custard Apple-Tree.* (Current.)

CUSTOM vb or ppl adj dial; <*accustomed.* To be accustomed, make it a custom. *BL G T*

1955 Bennett *Street Bwoy*, Ah doan custam fe talk bad wud It dis fly outa me mout [*I'm not accustomed to use bad language—it just flew out of my mouth*].

CUSTOS sb; abbr of *Custos Rotulorum*—cf *OED custos* 2.

1. In Jamaica, the principal magistrate of a parish; he is also the Governor's adviser on matters of his parish. See quot 1934.

1738 Articles of Pacification xviii, They shall apply first to the custos, or any other magistrate. 1793 Edwards I 209, The vestries are composed of the custos and two other magistrates. a 1818 Lewis (1845) 111, On opening the Assize-court for the county of Cornwall on March 4, Mr Stewart, the Custos of Trelawny, and Presiding Judge, said, in his charge to the jury, he wished to direct their attention in a peculiar manner to the infringement of slave-laws in the island. 1827 Hamel II 135, The custos of the parish was the magistrate who had signed the warrant. 1828 *Ordinances* 3, The freeholders..may assemble..at such public place..as shall be appointed for the purpose by the *custos rotulorum* of the said parish. [Margin:] Custos, &c. to appoint time and place of first election. 1934 Cundall in *Gleaner* 27 Feb p. 6, In the early days [1668, first mention of Custos Rotulorum found in Jamaican sources]..Custodes had little more than civil power. Later on, however, they appear as Custodes Rotulorum and Chief Judges of the Common Pleas, appointed with special reference to Magisterial affairs, and they seemed to have been the channel through which the Government sent its instructions to the Magistracy of the various parishes..As a matter of practical politics a Custos has always been supposed to be the head of the parish and chairman of the magistrates, in other respects primus inter pares. His office has popularly been supposed to be equivalent to that of a lord-lieutenant of a county at home..[Quot from a letter of W. Baggett Gray, 1920:] It thus appears that the Custos in Jamaica performs at least one of the functions of the Lord Lieutenant in England, viz: the recommendation of magistrates. This may have given rise to the (irresponsible) opinion I have heard expressed that a Custos in Jamaica might be regarded as taking the place of a Lord Lieutenant in a county in England. But strictly, I believe the position of the Lord Lieutenant is military and not civil.

2. Transf. See quot.

1954 LeP Man, Kostas, a man who, though small, commands respect.

CUT /kot/ vb dial; cf *OED cut v* 3, 30, 35. *G*

1. To pain sharply (prob transf from the sense of whipping, *OED* 3). (Also in Dominican English. D. Taylor.) *BL*

1956 Mc StAnd /mi bóuil kóting mi/ *My bowels are hurting badly.*

2. To execute a dance-step, a gymnastic caper, or any similarly active or formalized movement (*OED* 30, →1844). See also CUT CAPOOSE, CUT GRECIAN, CUT TEN. S CUT YANGA.

1895 Banbury 16, He took to his heels..the snake 'cutting papa-licks' (somersaults) after him all the way. 1940 HPJ [Prov:] De tune yu deh play noh de one me deh cut [*The tune you are playing is not the one I am dancing to*].

3. To express, to pronounce; to speak in a high-flown or mystifying manner; see further the phrases CUT ENGLISH, CUT LANGUAGE, CUT UNKNOWN TONGUE.

1868 Russell 17, Here one can always judge of the pecuniary affairs of the 'boasters', by the style and manner of their language. When they 'cut' the purse is not over light, and fields (especially coffee) look promising. When they give out a long drawling jargon, things are not in an overpleasing condition. 1942 Bennett 1, Yuh want hear har cut Spanish, [*You should hear her speak Spanish!*] 1950 Pioneer 61 [Two Jamaicans are visiting Paris:] Den bans a more man gather roun Start cut language pon we. 1952 Kerr 129, I tried a Latin tag from the Æneid on Mother Evangeline as an experiment. She replied 'cutting nine'. I asked what this meant. She said she realised I was talking spirit language and her spirit told her to answer with these words. 1955 FGC Man [Why do they call it 'Mozela' yam?], I don't know—they just cut it that way.

4. To reveal.

1927 Anderson-Cundall 50 [Prov:] Nyam fambly bittle, but no cut fambly 'tory, [*Eat with the family but don't give out family affairs—don't make public what should be private.*]

CUTACOO /kótakú, kótokúu/ sb dial; 1826→ cutacoo, 1943 cutocoo cuttoque ciatacu kotoku kutoku; <Twi *kotokú*, bag, sack, pouch, etc. Cf also Bantu e.g. Ko *nkutu*, bag.

1. A field-bag or basket made of woven palm-thatch (sometimes of canvas, hemp, etc.), usually with a cover, hung at one's side from a strap over the shoulder. It is used by hunters and cultivators. Some associate it with the obeah-man as the container for his 'things'. Cf BANKRA. Also called CONGO-JOE, DARK LANTERN, *hamasak*, *hangkra*, *heng-pan-mi*, *liin-pan-mi*, *nambu*, NAMSACK, ROGUING TOM, SHORT-BAG, SIDE-BAG, SIDE-POCKET.

a 1818 Lewis (1845) 127 (year 1816), A negro song.—'Me take my cutacoo (*i.e.* a basket made of matting), and follow him to Lucea'. 1826 Williams 278, A cutacoo (a small basket) which contained his [a Blue Mountain Peak guide's] pipe, some tobacco, a flint, steel, and touchwood, not forgetting a bunch of plantains. *Ibid* 344, The young man..grappled with Cuffie..and at last succeeded in wresting the cutacoo from his grasp. The contents were..an old snuff-box, several phials..some dried herbs, teeth, beads, hair, and other trash; in short, the whole farrago of an Obeah man. 1952 FGC StM /kotaku/ word formerly much used for a bag, waterproof, of hemp, strapped over shoulder, taken to field; also West.

2. A thatch bag or basket in which grated cassava-root is pressed to expel the juice and produce the meal for making BAMMY.

1940 HPJ, in St Elizabeth a cassava strainer. 1943 *GL* Clar, Cutacoo, a bag used for pressing cassava; Man, Cuttoque, basket for pressing cassava. 1952 FGC Man /kotaku/.

3. Applied more generally to baskets of various kinds: see quots.

1925 Beckwith 29 [Prov:] Crab walk too far him wi' go a cutacoo..A 'cutacoo' is a flat fish-basket woven out of shredded palm-leaves. 1943 *GL* Port, Cutacoo, Sort of bag used by people when fishing; StM, Kotoku, suspended safe of split bamboo. 1952 FGC Tre /kotoku/ *big*—ship things to Kingston in them.

4. Transf. The HEDGEHOG fish, from its appearance when puffed up.

1952 FGC Port /kotaku/ hedgehog or soursop fish, when it swells up; also West.

5. Fig. The belly.

1956 Mc StE (Accom) /kotoku/ belly.

CUT-AWAY /kótwé/ sb and vb dial; <*cut*+*away*. *G*

A. vb: To become detached from a point of support; to collapse; to slide or fall.

1943 *GL* Clar, Cut-wa, fail, collapse. 1952 FGC Tre /him kot we ge inta di huol dat we/ *He slides and falls into the hole (loses his footing).*

B. sb: A landslide; also the earth itself, and the place from which it became detached.

1952 FGC StM /kót wé/.

CUT-BRUTE sb arch; <*cut* past pple+*brute* <Fr *brut(e)*, unrefined. A coconut CUT-CAKE.

c 1910 FGC StAnd, still current.

CUT-CAKE sb, chiefly dial.

1. A confection made with bits of chopped (occas also grated) coconut in a brown-sugar fondant. Cf GRATER-CAKE.

1947 U.Newton III 16, Juniors..like to eat parched corn, cut cake, tiealeaf, grated cake, coconut biscuits. 1952 FGC StM, Cut-cakes—make with wet sugar; when nearly cooked, drop in a little grain sugar. 1956 Mc StAnd /kót kiek/ identified with /kúoknàt kíek/; Port /kót kíek/ same as /gríeta kíek/.

2. A cake made with flour and intended to be sliced.

1956 Mc Man, Cut cake—a cake for slicing, made in a /laata/. 1958 DeC Port /kot kieks/ meaning not the coconut and sugar confection, but rather a cake baked with flour in a large pan, then cut in diamond shapes.

CUT CAPERS see next.

CUT CAPOOSE /kót kapúus/ vb phr dial; 1934→ capoose, 1943 coppuse; <CUT 2+an element of uncertain origin, though its form and meaning are quite clear. The phrase is often derived from *cut capers* (and some dialect writers render it so) but this is inadmissible, the accentuation being quite different and the sense too general. CAPOOSE (q.v.) is identical in form but there is no certain connection of meaning. *Capoose* in this sense may tentatively be analysed as </ka-/ (*OED ker-*, said to be US, though *DA* questions this, and evidence

in *EDD* s.v. *carfuffle*, etc. favours its being ultimately Gaelic) +*pouse*, push, thrust, etc. (*EDD*: Sc, Ir, North- and West-country), *capoose* thus being imitative of the motion of a rider on a horse.

1. To rise and fall in the saddle when riding a horse; by extension, a movement similar to this. (Often alluding—as in the story of Anancy's proving that Tiger was his father's old riding-horse—to the rider's superiority to the horse and the shame of the latter's subjection.)

[1925 Beckwith Prov 718, Puppy nyam ratta done, him cut capers 'pon John-crow. 'When the pup has eaten a rat, he chases the crows'; applied to one who has food given him and goes away without thanks.] 1934 HPJ, Capoose, capers. Motion of a rider up and down in the stirrups [Astley Clerk *et al*]. . [Prov:] Wen puppy nyam ratta bone him cut capoose pon John Crow. . [Extravagant description of a cat's ears:] Him yase cack off fram him head like ratta de cut capoose dung Mt Diablo, *His ears stick out from his head like a rat riding a horse down Mount Diablo.* 1943 *GL* Clar, Capoose, up and down saddle action when riding; Port, Cut capoose, to ride a horse at a brisk trot; West, Coppuse, a style of horse-riding. 1947 U.Newton III 6, Cut capoose—hold on to something before you, then rise from and fall gracefully and rhythmically to your seat. 1950 Sherlock in Pioneer 13, Ineffective people should not brag because 'You never see mus-mus cut capoose pon cow back'.

2. See quot.

1958 W. Adolphe Roberts *Letter*, 'Cut capoose' is also to leap in the air and then cross the feet like a ballet dancer.

CUT CARD sb and vb dial; < *cut cards*. *BA G*

A. sb (plur): Cards used in divination. *BL*

1935 HPJ.

B. vb: To throw the dice. [Cf also CARD, =a domino.]

1943 *GL*.

CUT CEDAR BOARD vb phr dial joc. Fig. To snore (i.e. to make a sound like someone sawing cedar boards).

1952 FGC StM /im a kót síida bùod/ *He's snoring.*

CUTCHIE, CUTCHY see *kochi*.

CUT DOWN vb phr intr dial. To fall in price.

1956 Mc StAnd /kélyan kót dong, yaa/ *Skellion has gone down in price, you know.* G

CUT ENGLISH vb phr dial; cf CUT 3. To use the language in a (supposedly) high-flown way, polysyllabically, with malapropisms, overcorrections, and other unorthodoxies, to impress those with less education than oneself.

1868 Russell 16–17, In trying to 'cut English', the most elegant form of the verb is the past tense of the verb to be, and the past participle used together, or with another verb, thus, A was ben told you of it. *Ibid* 13, In attempting to improve the Personal Pronouns ('cutting English'), some rather awkward faults are made.

CUT EYE vb phr chiefly dial; < CUT 2+*eye*. To catch (someone or something) with the eyes, then quickly close them and turn or toss the head aside. The purpose of the action may be to avoid temptation (quot 1950), but it is usually directed against another person (as when it is an 'evil eye' that is cut—cf CUT-EYE BEAN), and it is usually insulting (cf CUT-EYE). Insult and temptation may combine into provocation (quot 1957). *BA BL G T*

1950 Pioneer 23, Anancy. . se' plenty more cane but him cut him y'eye an pass dem. 1956 Mc /wé yu kót yu ái áata mi fó/ *What did you cut your eye after* (i.e. *at*) *me for?* 1957 JN, To cut one's eye is to toss one's head away from a man's glance in a contemptuous but sexually provoking fashion: Little girl, to a little boy, 'You come a me yard' (cutting her eyes) 'Come if you name man'.

CUT-EYE sb dial; < CUT EYE. The action of 'cutting' one's eyes at someone as an insult or mark of scorn. *BL G T*

1947 U.Newton III 14, That evening at private class, the Lopez group exchanged many cut-eyes and suck-teeths with the Stephensons.

CUT-EYE BEAN sb dial; < CUT EYE+*bean*. A large bean (*Canavalia ensiformis*) planted at the borders of provision grounds to protect them from the evil eye; it is also put to other superstitious uses. Also called OVERLOOK BEAN, etc.

[1851 Gosse 153–4, see HORSE-EYE BEAN.] 1929 Beckwith 28, To keep a neighbor from casting a 'grudgeful eye' at a fine field crop, plant the horse-eye bean. . also called 'cut-eye bean', at the top and bottom of the field. *Ibid* 76, In Mandeville it is the cut-eye bean that is used to plant down the ghost. 1940 HPJ, Cut-eye: The horse-eye bean, so called because its presence in a 'ground' will protect the latter from the evil eye ('cutting' bean).

CUT GRECIAN vb phr dial; < CUT vb 2+ *Grecian*, prob < *Grecian bend* (*OED*). Said of a woman: to walk in a self-consciously 'stylish' way. Also GRECIAN.

1943 *GL* StE, Cut Greshan, walk proudly. 1955 FGC Man /kót gríishan/ walk stylish, step cute, full of themself.

CUTICAP see COOTIKOP.

CUT JACK vb phr; < *cut*+JACK. To cut up and divide a JACK (large johnnycake); hence, generally, to eat.

1958 DeC Port.

CUT LANGUAGE vb phr dial; cf CUT 3, ~ENGLISH. To use language, to speak—especially in a high-flown or mysterious way, impressive to the hearer. *G*

1940 HPJ, A did hear dem [Maroons] cut language. [cf CROMANTY 3]. 1956 Mc St (Accom), To /spíik difran langgwij/ to 'speak with tongues', speak in an unknown language. Obeahmen use meaningless words and language to impress their clients. Adepts in pocomania and revivalists also /kot langgwij/; /di obyaman kom, kot a litl langwij/.

CUTLASS /kotlas, kotlis/ sb. An agricultural implement developed from and similar to the military cutlass; =MACHETE. The words are virtually interchangeable throughout Jamaica, and there are more than sixty other local names.

1788 Marsden 35, The road was rendered so intricate that the negroes were under the necessity of cleaning them with sharp cutlasses. 1826 Williams 66, He showed me a machet, or cutlass, made by one of his own blacksmiths, of a very excellent temper. 1896 Trowbridge 287, An' De't'. . mos' catch Nancy, an' mos' hit him wi' him cutlas. 1952 FGC gen /kotlas, kotlis/. *BA G T*

CUTLASS-BEAN sb dial. The SPANISH MACHETE tree, *Erythrina velutina*; also called SWORD TREE, etc.

1936 HPJ Clar, Cutlass-bean, A tall tree with a bright crimson flower, long and narrow, looking just like a machete.

CUTLASS (FISH) sb; cf *ODS* 1884. The highly esteemed food-fish *Trichiurus lepturus*, named for its shape. *G T*

1854–5 *TJSA* I 143, Cutlass Fish, Trichiurus lepturus. 1892 Cockrell, Cutlass-fish. 1893 Sullivan 8, Cutlas. This is a long ribbony fish. 1952 FGC Port: StE /kótlás/

flat, shine, good for frying; StM, StT, Tiger shark follow cutlass in rainy weather.

CUTOCOO see CUTACOO.

CUT OFF vb phr intr dial; cf *OED* 55 d. To die suddenly. *G*

1956 Mc Man /shi dúon sík, shi jos kot áaf/ *She wasn't ill, she just died suddenly.*

CUT ONE-SIDED vb phr.

1954 LeP Kgn, Cut one sided, to cut awkwardly or hack with dull tool.

CUT PUSS sb dial slang; <*cut*, castrated (*OED ppl a* 7) + PUSS.

1958 DeC StT /kot pus/ a fat and effeminate man.

CUTRUMENT see *kruchument*.

CUT-STONE sb dial; etym uncert. A small black ant with a narrow thorax and pointed abdomen, having a strong smell.

1952 FGC Tre /kótúon, kòtstúon/.

CUTTA adj dial; etym uncert: perh <*cut* past ppl + A[8], with poss infl of *cutty* adj, short, and prob analogy with JUNKA, short. Short.

1905 Smith 37, An' put on de ole cutta frock.

CUTTA-CUTTA sb dial; echoic—cf TOOK-TOOK.

1940 HPJ, A calabash with a hole bored in it, used as a water-vessel.

CUT TEN vb phr dial; <CUT 2 + *ten*, in the sense of the Roman numeral X.

1. To make the sign of the cross (as a religious symbol to ward off evil, etc.).

1907 Jekyll 175–6, One of the most dreaded Duppies is 'Rolling (*i.e.* roaring) Calf'..'If Rolling Calf catch you, give you one lick, you dead'. Your only chance is to run, and you must keep on 'cutting ten' (making the sign of the cross), and the pursuing monster has to go round that place ten times.

2. To cross the legs, esp at the knees while sitting. Cf CHOP TEN.

1942 Bennett 12, Soh ah start fe feel quite supportant, An' ah cut me ten an all dat. 1956 Mc StAnd [Song:] /di baaba a kot im ten a/ *The barber is crossing his legs.*

CUTTER /kóta/ sb dial.

1. Any fish that cuts or breaks fish-pots; a CUTTING-FISH.

1952 FGC Port, Cutter, the nurse—cuts pots; StF /kótaz/ all fish that cut pots: nurse, barracouta, large snapper, shark; StAnn, Cutter = /kótnfish/ snapper—has saw on back; West /kóta/.

2. A tin-opener. *G*

1956 Mc StE (Accom) /kota/.

CUTTING pple cant; <*cutting*. A word of revivalist cults, metaph transf from agricultural senses, but also having superstitious associations (e.g. with CUT-EYE); it enters into various phrases: see quots.

1953 Moore 82, Cutting and clearing, 'cutting off evil and clearing it away'; *ibid* 108, A cutting and clearing table, [a service (cf TABLE)] to 'set up a power to get away from trouble'; *ibid* 85–6, Cutting shepherd, [an officer who] 'determines whether there is any evil influence coming into a meeting and is charged with the duty of cutting it out before it can do any damage'. He uses candles or other lights to 'control the spirits' in a meeting.

CUTTING BEAN sb dial. = CUT-EYE BEAN; see quot 1935.

CUTTING-FISH /kótnfìsh/ sb dial. Any fish that cuts or breaks fish-pots; a CUTTER.

1952 FGC Port, Cutt'n fish; StAnn /kótnfìsh/ cutter; also StM.

CUTTING-GRASS sb dial. A kind of grass with sharp saw-toothed edges (*Cyperus ligularis*). *BL N*

1952 FGC Han, Cut'n grass; Port /kótn graas/ cuts you—good for clearing eyes; StC.

CUTTING UP THE BLACKBIRDS vb phr slang obs; cf *OED cut v* 3. Whipping the slaves.

1787 *WI Eclogues* 26, What they [slave-drivers] in a facetious tone have been heard to term, cutting up the black-birds.

CUTTOQUE see CUTACOO.

CUTTOVAM sb dial rare; etym unknown.

1943 *GL* StAnd, Cuttovam, Cassava cakes, bammy.

CUTTY-CUTTY adj dial; iterative <*cutty* <*cut* sb + *-y*[1] (*OED*). Much cut—said of cut glass. (Cf CUT-UP-CUT-UP.) *G*

1942 Bennett 20, Yessiday she mash t'ree big-gill glass An' wan cutty-cutty ice pitcha.

CUT UNKNOWN TONGUE vb phr dial; cf CUT 3. To mutter, speak, or shout nonsensical syllables which purport to be in a mysterious language; this is practised by obeah-men, pocomanians, revivalists, etc., supposedly when under possession by spirits. *G*

1942 Bennett 30, An' every mawnin..Ah keas [*cast*] me y'eye an' stap me breath An cut some unknown tongue. Wen me deh pon haste me cut it shart An' sey 'skarash ni-toe' But wen me ha' mo' time me sey 'Ski bam bam chinka po'.

CUT-UP-CUT-UP adj or sb dial; iterative <*cut up*. *G*

1952 FGC Han /skrab yaaz/ cut-up-cut-up under foot-bottom.

CUT-WA see CUT-AWAY.

CUWAUDA ?adj dial rare; etym unknown.

1943 *GL* Tre, Cuwauda, hard.

CUWEDIE /kuwidi/ vb phr cant. A word of the AFRICAN cult (StT). s.

1953 Moore gloss, Cuwedie, calling dead.

CUYA(H) see KU.

CYANCRO /kayang-kro, kyángkrò/ sb dial; 1940 cyancro, 1943 kiang-cro, cancro; phonetically reduced by loss of the first *r* <*carrion-crow*. The JOHN-CROW. *G N*

1924 Beckwith [21, Carencro's* House with a Key.. * Crow's name in French stories]. *Ibid* 80, An Harry said, 'Do, me good kyan-crow, tek we up on you wing, carry we away'. 1940 HPJ, Cyancro, another form for Jancro, crow. 1943 *GL* StAnd, Cancro, crow; Kiang-cro, the crow (bird).

DA[1] /da/ demonstr pron and adj dial; <*that*. That; that one. Cf DAT, DARA, DARI. *BA BL G T*

1843 Phillippo 48, Da buckra da come again. [*That white man is coming again.*] 1877 Murray *Feedin' 'Perrit* 15, But a'ter you eat all, da de piece o' red herrin ears you lef..[*But after you ate everything, that (there) piece of red herring's ear you left.*] 1942 Bennett gloss, Dah, dat: that.

DA[2] /da, do, du/ prep dial; also sp *dah*; prob <DE[3] + A[1]. = A[1]: at, in, on, to. *BL G*

1837 Sterne 19, Massa —— come da night too, so tell we, we no must speak anything at all. 1873 Rampini 177 [Prov:] Hand da bowl, knife da troat. [(*His*) *hand is in* (*my*) *bowl*, (*his*) *knife is at* (*my*) *throat*—said of a treacherous person.] 1877 Murray *Kittle* 10–11, Me ben bad man, worser more an all man wha ben lib da worl. *Ibid* 26, Watchman dance so, till de sweat drop off da him face. 1895 Banbury 21 [Mial song, 1842–46:] Token show da night, oh! [This is an allusion to a comet then visible, and to the expected end of the world.] 1942 Bennett 22, Nex' time me come a-tung, Dah Penny shelta me wi' stay. 1958 DeC Western parishes /du huom/ = *at home*; *du* used only with *home*. /him dide du huom/ *He is at home*.

DA[3] /da/ vbl auxiliary dial; prob < DE[4] + A[5], but cf Twi *da*, lie, be situated, live, remain, rest, etc. = A[5]: A less common auxiliary of durative or progressive action, present, past, or future. (DA[3] + a verb is equivalent to *to be* + a present participle.)

1826 Williams 297 [Song:] Hi! de Buckra, hi! You sabby wha for he da cross de sea..? [*Do you know why he keeps on crossing the sea?*] 1837 Sterne 17, Q. How many Christmases since this happen? A. This Christmas da come make four. 1873 Rampini 181 [Prov:] When man a magistrate, crooked da follow him. 1877 Murray *Kittle* 10, I da go trabel, [*I'm going to travel*]. 1941 HPJ [Prov:] Man da walk, dead da watch him. 1950 Pioneer 17, As me dah pass Puss yard, me hear Puss muma dah tell him sey..etc. [*As I was passing..I heard Puss's mother telling him*..etc.]

DA[4] vb dial, arch or obs; prob < DE[3] + A[6], but cf Twi *da* (DA[3]). = A[6]: Forms of vb *to be*. *BL*

1834 Lewis 254 [Song:] If da me eat Mammy Luna's pease, Drowny me water, drowny, drowny! [*If it is* (or *was*) *I who ate*..etc.] 1873 Rampini 176 [Prov:] Ebry day da fishing day, but ebry day no fe catch fish. 1877 Murray *Kittle* 10, Buckra da buckra, naga da naga. [*Whites are whites, blacks are blacks.*] 1895 Banbury 21 [Song:] Dandy obeah da ya, oh! [*Dandy obeah is here, oh!*]

DA[5] /da/ vb dial; prob < DE[3] + A[7], but cf Twi *da* (DA[3]). = A[7]: A word introducing statements and giving emphasis: It is, There is, etc. *BL G*

1837 Sterne 19, Massa ——..tell we, we no must speak anything at all..da dat make me no been speak every thing to buckra. 1877 Murray *Feedin' 'Perrit* 11, Da so me da go sabe me money. [*It is like that that I'm going to save my money.*] *Ibid* 15, Da de piece o' red herrin' ears you lef, da hit me da eat. [*That* (*there*) *piece of red-herring ear you left, it's that that I'm eating.*] 1942 Bennett 35 [Prov:] All fish nyam man, Dah shark wan get de blame. [*All fish eat men, it is shark alone that gets the blame.*]

DA[6] int dial.

1941 HPJ, Da—Used as a taunting phrase to provoke a fight—accompanied by insolent stare. (Astley Clerk: Is this Jamaica dialect? [He connects this with A DA MEK.])

daadi /daadi/ sb dial; < *daddy*; cf *maami*; perh with coincidental infl from African words such as Fante *dadaa*, *dadaw*, old. A respectful name or term of address for a father, an older man than oneself, an elderly man. Cf BABA. *BL G T*

1941 Astley Clerk in HPJ, Daddy. 1943 *GL* Clar, Dawdie, father; StAnd, Dardy, dady.

daaflii /dáaflíi/ sb dial; a reduced form of *dog-flea*.

1943 *GL* Clar, Dawfli, fleas; Man, Daflee, flea.

daal sb dial; < Hindi *dalnā*, *dāl*, split peas; also as an abbr of *daal-am-baat*. *BA G T*

1. In the specific sense: see quot.

1943 *GL* no addr, Daul, Indian name for split peas.

2. Generalized as referring to East Indian dishes: see quot.

1956 Mc StT /daal/ a Coolie cook-up: 1. Flour sauce; 2. A Coolie dish [see above]; 3. Green mango chutney.

daal-am-baat sb dial; < Hindi *dāl*, split peas + *and* + Hindi *bhāt*, rice. A favourite East Indian dish of rice and split peas; cf also *baat-an-daa*. *G*

1943 *GL* Kgn, Dal an Bahat, East Indian—rice and peas; Port, Dall and baut, An Indian sauce; StC, Dal-am-bath, Peas and rice cooked East Indian style; StM, Daul an baut. 1955 FGC Man /dàalambáat/. 1956 Mc StT /dáalambáat/.

daangki see DONKEY.

DAB-A-DAB sb dial; prob < some African word, not found—cf quot 1942; but cf also various echoic words imitating the sound of food preparation, e.g. TUM-TUM, and perh BRAGADAP; cf DABAH-DA.

1774 Long II 427, Dab-a-dab (an olio, made with maize, herrings, and pepper). 1941 HPJ, Dabbadah, Dabadab [ref to Long] Obs. (Astley Clerk:) I am not so sure that it is obsolete, for I am certain that I have heard it used inside half a dozen years ago. [1941 HPJ, Dabadab, In Dahomi, a corn-flour dumpling boiled hard. Duncan I 239, II 38. It is so called from its shape.]

DABAH-DA, DABBAH-DA sb dial; cf DAB-A-DAB.

1943 *GL* StC, Dabbah-da; StE, Dabah-da, cocoanut custard.

DABBLE vb dial. *G*

1. To get (something or someone) wet and dirty by dipping in or splashing with muddy water; const *up*. (Cf *OED* 1.)

1956 Mc StT /duon dabl yosef op ina dat mod/.

2. Fig. To meddle or interfere. (Cf *OED* 3b →1794.) *BA*

1954 LeP StE, Dabble, to meddle or interfere. 1956 Mc StE.

DACAS sb dial obs; prob repr *Dorcas* (see *ODS*, *DAE*) with transf of sense from the Dorcas Society to a garment given out by it, perh by abbr of some such phr as *dorcas dress*. Note: The expected dial pron would be /daakas/; this has evid become /dakas/, as implied by the rhyme in quot 2 and the back-formed *docker* of quot 3.

A skirt, petticoat, or some similar woman's garment; see quots.

1790 Short Journey I 153 [Of a slave being whipped:] Her eyes they swore held too much water For *Shif* and *Dacas* too were wet, And look! her eyes were streaming yet. *Ibid* 154, While loud she bray'd like any jack-ass, Simkin himself untied her dacas. a1818 Lewis (1845) 130, She returned to her aunt..related that an old woman in a red docker (i.e. petticoat) had made her a great lady, and then departed in triumph.

DACK see DOCK.

DADA see DAY-DAY.

DA-DA-DE /dádadè/ demonstr pron dial rare; < *that* + DE[1]; cf DARADEH. That (one) there.

DA DAT MEK phr dial; < DA[5] + DAT + MEK. = A DA MEK. *BL G*

1837 Sterne 19, see DA[5].

da-de demonstr pron or adj dial; < DA[1] + DE[1], = Engl dial *that-there*. (The object may come between: /da wan de/.) That (one). *G*

1877 Murray *Feedin' 'Perrit* 15, Da de piece o' red herrin' ears. [*That-there piece*..etc.] 1943 *GL* Tre, Dahdeh, that.

DAFLEE see *daaflii*.

DAGO sb dial; prob the same as US *dago*, < Sp *Diego*, James, though the sense connection here is not clear. See quot; a native? (Cf attrib uses as separate entries below.)

1943 *GL* StJ, Dago, one quite accustomed to a place.

DAGO adj dial; prob attrib use of US *dago*, < Sp *Diego*, James, used as a term of contempt. See quot; the sense is vague, though clearly unfavourable. *BL*

1943 *GL* Kgn, Dago, bad (Spanish).

DAGO CRAB sb dial; < DAGO adj or perh sb + *crab*. A kind of crab that is only partly good to eat.

1952 FGC StM /diego krab/—eat only claws: the back will drunk you.

DAGO GROUPER /díegó grúpa/ sb dial; < DAGO adj or perh sb + *grouper*. A variety of the grouper fish caught in deep water.

1952 FGC StE /diegó/ the largest kind of /grúpa/; you have to go over the shoal in deep for them.

DAH see DA.

daig sb dial rare; an irreg pronunc of what would normally be /dag/ or /daag/, on the analogy of *baig*, *haig*, etc.

1943 *GL* StJ, Daig, dog.

dain adj dial; prob < *dying*, but perh also infl by *damn* (for *damned*), similarly used in StdE. An intensive word, heavily stressed; cf GOD.

1958 BLB Man /yu si mi dain traial/ *You see my terrible trial*. (See also last quot s.v. FE-SOSO.)

DAL-AM-BATH, DAL AN BAHAT, DALL AND BAUT see *daal-am-baat*.

DAMPA sb dial; etym unknown.

1943 *GL* Kgn, StE, Dampa, vitality.

DAMSEL (BERRY) sb dial; < *damson*; cf BITTER DAMSEL. The fruit of *Chrysophyllum oliviforme*, also called DAMSON-PLUM.

1942 HPJ, Damsel, A fruit 'like 'tarapple but smaller' and stains the mouth. 1952 FGC StAnd /damzl-beri/ one inch, pointed, colour of /starápl/ and tastes like it. 1956 Mc Port /damzl/ small fruit which stains.

DAMSON PLUM sb bot; from the resemblance of the fruit to a damson plum. The fruit and tree of *Chrysophyllum oliviforme*; this name has been changed by folk-etym to DAMSEL (BERRY). Also called WILD STAR-APPLE. *G*

1756 Browne 171, Chrysophyllum 2..The Damson Plumb..is found wild in many parts of Jamaica, but seldom grows to any considerable size. 1813 Lunan I 259, Damson-Plum. Chrysophyllum..monopyrenum.. This tree never attains the size of the star-apple. 1864 Grisebach 783.

DAMSON TREE sb bot; from the resemblance of the fruit to a damson plum. The tree *Syzigium jambolanum*; more often called JAMBOLAN.

1926 Fawcett 352, The Jambolan or Damson tree.. berry in cultivated plants often as large as a pigeon's egg, purple-black, edible, somewhat astringent.

DANCE THE (TREAD)MILL vb phr obs. To tread a treadmill—in allusion to the leaping motion of the treader.

1837 James 4, To dance the mill. [Several times.] 1838 Kelly 53, To work in chains and dance the treadmill.

DANCING BOOTH sb dial.

1. In the general sense: see BOOTH, and quot 1912 McK *Songs* 130.

2. Specifically: see quot.

1953 Moore 61, Dancing booth—temporary building in which Revival, Revival Zion, Pocomania, and Cumina ceremonies are conducted.

DANDAH sb dial; cf *gang-gang*.

1943 *GL* StAnd, Dandah, old woman.

DAN-DAN sb and adj; prob < *dandy* by iteration of first syllable, but cf Yoruba *dãdã*, good, beautiful. *BL T*

A. sb: 1. A baby's dress. *BA G*

1943 *GL* Kgn, Dan-dan, baby's dress; Port, Dan-dan, frock. 1956 Mc Port /dandan/ infant's dress.

2. See quot.

1943 *GL* StM, Dandan, shirt without a collar.

3. A man (evid one who dresses up). *G*

1943 *GL* Clar, Dandan, man.

B. adj: Pretty, prettily dressed. *G*

1943 *GL* StAnn, Dandan, pretty. 1955 FGC Man /dandan/ dress pretty; dandy.

DANDELION /dàndiláian/ sb chiefly dial; < *dandelion*, from its diuretic qualities; like the European dandelion, it is also called PISSABED in Jamaica. *G*

1. The shrubs *Cassia ligustrina* and *C. occidentalis* (and perh other spp). See quots.

1927 Beckwith 15, Dandelion. *Cassia occidentalis* L.. For pain, fever or a cold, boil the leaves and drink as tea. The shelled seeds may be parched and beaten as a substitute for coffee. 1952 FGC Han, Port, StAnn, StC, StE, StM, StT, Tre /dàndiláian/. The man kind is coarser, the woman kind has a finer leaf, smaller seed. 1953 *WIMJ* 239, *C. occidentalis* L. Wild Senna; Dandelion; Stinking Weed or Wood; John Crow Pea; Wild Coffee..The drink prepared from them has a reputation for usefulness in kidney and bladder troubles and malaria.

2. Also applied to *Chaptalia nutans*.

1959 UCWI Herbarium.

DANDY /daandi/ sb and adj dial; < *dandy*.

1. In senses closely corresp to English and US uses: a very much dressed-up person; finely dressed, pretty. (The pronunc differs, however.) *BA G*

2. In phrases: DANDY BOY, DANDY DUDE, etc.

DANDY-BOY sb dial; cf DANDY 2. *BA G*

1943 *GL* StAnd, Dandy-bwoy, sweet, fine, well-dressed.

DANDY DUDE sb dial; cf DANDY 2 and DUDE.

1. A dandy, a dude, a man dressed up finely.

1943 *GL* Kgn, Dandy dude, a dressed person. 1954 LeP StT, Dandy dude, man 'dressed to kill'. *BA G*

2. In the phrase *To walk dandy-dude*: see quot.

1956 Mc StT, Tre /waak daandi-duud/ to kick out the legs in walking, as the result of a deformity.

DANDYMITE sb dial; by folk-etym < *dynamite*.

1941 HPJ, Dandymite—dynamite. Also the name of a 'Blue' [song]. 1943 *GL* StM, Dandymite, dynamite.

DANDY-SHANDY sb; < *dandy*, fine (cf US use) + *shandy*, a drink (cf *OED shandy-gaff*). Some kind of non-alcoholic aerated drink.

1947 U.Newton II 9 [We] drank rivers of aerated waters like dandy-shandy and cream-soda.

DANIEL'S GREAT GUN sb dial; perh < *Daniell* inventor of electric battery cell, etc.

(cf *ODS*). The plant more commonly called DUPPY GUN.

1942 *NHN* I 6 11, In the dry areas are associated..Duppy Gun or Daniel's Great Gun (Ruellia tuberosa), Noyeau Vine..etc.

DARA, DARI /dára, dári/ demonstr pron arch; <*that* (see Introd, Phonology) +A[8] or -I. Forms of *that* formerly very common, now much less so /dat/ being the gen dial form. Also in plural: those. Often combined with DE.

1839 McMahon 211, Alla could be dead since dary [since that time]. 1868 Russell 14–15, Demonstrative adjectives. Sing. Dis, da or dat, or da*ri* (*i* as in lick)..Observe that 'dari' is nearly obsolete, da and dat being more used. 1942 Bennett 15, Me due out a daradeh street corner me chile, Half-pass seven. 1956 Mc StAnd (Mt Charles) /mi sikin a hyie dari bwai a brad kyas nou/ *I'm sick of hearing that fellow broadcasting now*; /dari chaini hin ing kom a jimieka fi kom luk riichnis/ *Those Chinese have come to Jamaica to make money*; /mama, a dara yaa taak/ *Mama, you've said it!*

DARADEH see prec.

DARDY see *daadi*.

DARG see DOG.

DARI see DARA.

DARK adj dial; cf *OED* 9 '*Obs.* exc *dial.*' →1875.

1. In ref to the eyes: weak-sighted; partially or totally blind. *BA G*

1952 FGC Han, Put obeah on a woman, she start to have dark eyes—the baby of the eye is good, but she's blind. 1956 Mc Man /mi gyetin uol—kyaan sii gud—ai daak/ *I'm getting old—can't see well—eyes are failing*; StE (Accom) /aris trobl wid daak ai/ *Horace's sight is not good.*

2. Fig. Stupid, unintelligent. (Cf *OED* 10 →1837.) *G*

1948 Bennett 24, Is de ignorantiss, darkiss Set a fool me ever meet. 1956 Mc StAnd, StT /daak/ stupid, unintelligent. 1962 BLB 52.

DARK (UP) vb phr dial; *OED dark v 'arch.* or *dial.'* To turn dark. *G*

1957 JN StJ, see GUINEA PEPPER.

DARK GRUNT sb. A variety of the GRUNT fish, evid of dark colour.

1756 Browne 449, The Red Mouth, or dark Grunt. 1774 Long III 867, Sea-Fish..I shall enumerate only such as are the most in esteem; *viz.* Black-snapper..Silver shad, Dark grunt..etc.

DARK-LANTERN sb dial joc; <*dark-lantern*, 'a lantern with a slide or arrangement by which the light can be concealed', *OED*. A SIDE-BAG evid from its shape.

1958 DeC StT /daak lantan/ a sidebag or namsack.

DARK NIGHT sb dial. A nickname for the darker, purpler yampi, by contrast with the MOONSHINE yampi, which is light purple or white.

1941 HPJ, Darknight, The darker (or more purple) Yampie.

DARK-SAMBO sb, also attrib; <*dark*+*sambo*. A man or woman having about one-fourth white, three-fourths negro ancestry, hence relatively dark, though not black.

1951 *Gleaner* Sept? (Report of escaped prisoner), Dark-sambo. 1958 DeC gen, Dark-sambo, a relatively favourable racial term for a person about three-fourths black, with smooth skin and 'good' hair.

DARRO, DARRU see next.

DARU /dáru/ sb dial; <Hindi *dārū*, strong liquor; an East Indian word well known and to some extent used by non-East Indians. Rum. *BA G*

1943 *GL* Clar, Kgn, Port, StAnd, StAnn, StJ, StM, StT; Daru, darro, darru, rum.

DARY see DARA.

DAS /das/ conj dial; <*that*. (Less common than /dat/.) That, so that.

1877 Murray *Feedin' 'Perrit* 12, Him say sar, das when me see you drink you rum, me mus'n't come close you. 1941 Kirkpatrick 25, Dem doan seem fe know das cockroach doan biniz een a fowl fight. 1952 FGC Tre /fiks it bak das in duon nuo/ *Fix it the way it was so that he doesn't know.*

das for *that's*. *G*

DASH vb chiefly dial; cf *OED* 2 →1833.

1. trans. In common use in Jamaica where *throw*, *fling*, and other words would be preferred elsewhere. Also const, *away*, *down*, *out*, *up*, etc. *BA G N*

1941 HPJ, Dash—Throw; hurl: Dash away this water; dash the stone at him. 1956 Mc StE (Accom) /im dásh op som dós in mi fies/ *He threw some dirt into my face*; /az di dangki dásh im dóun so bám/ *As the donkey knocks (the boy) down with a thud.*

2. intr. To move vigorously; rattle about. *G*

1956 Mc Port /dash op/ to rattle about. 1958 DeC gen /dash/ to move vigorously during sexual intercourse.

DASH sb; abbr of *dash-board* (cf *OED* 3).

1956 Mc StAnd /dash/ A projection over a door to keep water out.

DASHALONG sb dial; see RAMGOAT DASH-ALONG.

1. A shrub much used in folk medicine: *Turnera ulmifolia.*

1940 HPJ, see COME-AN'-GO-'LONG. 1951 FGC Man /dáshalang/. 1954 *WIMJ* 32, Dash Along.

2. *Cassia occidentalis.*

1959 UCWI Herbarium.

[**DASHEEN** sb chiefly dial; cf *ODS* 1913. A variety of coco of which the 'head' (rhizome) is eaten: it has no tubers. Cf BADU. *G N T*

1952 FGC Han, StAnn, StE, StJ, StM, StT /dàshíin/. 1954 *FG* 447, The Dasheen is a comparatively recent importation from the East, where it is very largely grown..The leaves are distinguished from other varieties by having less pointed and more rounded leaves, with a purple tinge along the veins and in the centre.]

DASHER sb dial or slang; cf *OED* 1. A 'dashing' person, hence, a dandy, a lover; a term of approval. *G*

1941 HPJ, Dasha: (i) Lover, 'masher'—While me dasha like me..Moore Town Maroon Song 1898–192–. (ii) A finely dressed person. (iii) 'Dasha', a word meaning a lover, but the M[oore] T[own] Maroons call the Governor their 'dasha'. Osborne, 1 Sept 1930.

DASO see DE-SO.

DAUBING /dáabin/ sb dial; <*daubing*. *G*

1943 *GL* Han, StJ, Daubin', a thrashing or flogging.

DAUF adj dial rare; prob <*daft*, timid—cf *EDD* 5.

1943 *GL* West, Dauf, bashful.

DAUL AN BAUT see *daal-am-baat*.

DAVID'S ROOT sb bot obs; etym unknown. A plant valued for medicinal use: *Chiococca alba.*

1756 Browne 164, Chiococca 1.. Snow-berry, or David's-root.. The root of the plant has much the same bitter acrid taste with the *seneka* snake-root, and has been a long time used as a strong resolutive and attenuant in those colonies: I have known it administered with great success in obstinate rheumatisms, and old venereal taints; nor is it intirely useless even in the *Spina Ventosa* (commonly called Boneake). 1801 Dancer 363. 1811 Lunan II 175. 1936 Fawcett 68–70, *Chiococca..alba..*Snowberry, David's Root.

DAWBI-DAWBI adj dial; evid iterative <*daub* +*-y*, but cf also DABBLE.

1943 *GL* StM, Dawbi-dawbi, dirtying.

DAWDIE see *daadi*.

DAWFLI see *daaflii*.

DAY see DE.

DA-YA, DE-YA /da-ya, de-ya, di-ya/ adv or quasi-vb dial; <DA[4], DE[1,3]+YA. *G*

1. There; to be there.

1912 McK *Ballads* 70, You dih-ya 'douten use. [*You are there without use, to no effect.*] 1952 FGC StE /it dáiya/ *It's there.*

2. Here; to be here. *BL*

1864 Russell 15, Alla two de pick'ni dem da ya. [*Both of the children are here.*] 1943 *GL* Tre, Diah, here; StAnn, Imdya, he is here; West, Dayah, it is here. 1943 Bennett 33, Dung to ice deh yah. [*Even ice is here.*]

DA...YA demonstr pron phr dial; cf *da-de*, that. This. *G*

1960 BLB 9 /da wan ya uol/ *This one is old.*

DAYAH see DA-YA.

DAY-CHANGE sb dial. The time of day when it changes from morning to evening: see quot.

1958 DeC StAnd /die chienj/ 1–2 p.m. *G*

DAY CLEAN sb and vb phr dial; <*day*+ *clean* vb or adj, evid the abbr of a phrase: *when day is clean*, or *when day cleans*; or a loan-transl from African. Cf Fr Créole *ju netye*, jour nettoyé (D. Taylor). Daybreak. *G T* Gullah, Krio, Tobago.

1907 Jekyll 80, He wake an' start away the same hour. He travel till day clean. *Ibid* 83, Day is clean when you can see to walk. 1924 Beckwith 189 [Riddle:] Me fader got a rose-tree in him yard; eb'ry night he blow, an by time de fe clean, eb'ry one gone.—Stars. 1956 Mc StAnd /die kliin/ time of day just about sunrise; Man /díe jes a klíin/ applies to time about daybreak when you can just recognise people. 1959 DeC Kgn /die kliin/ day break (both as a noun and as a verb).

DAY CUT sb and vb phr dial; cf DAY CLEAN. Daybreak.

1826 Barclay 317, 'Day cut', or dawn. [Cf COCK-CROW.] 1952 FGC Han, Day-cut, sunrise; StM /die da kot/ dawn is coming.

DAYDA see DAY-DAY.

DAY-DAWN sb dial; <*day*+*dawn* sb. Dawn.

1956 Mc StAnd /wen kóming an die-dáan/ *When it's coming on to dawn. G*

DAY-DAY /díe-díe, díe-dè/ excl or int; cf *OED*: '*day, day!* a childish expression for "good day", "good-bye"'. →1784. (Cf Lesser Antillean *dédé*, good-bye <Fr Créole *adié, adé* <Fr *adieu* with reduplication. Douglas Taylor.) Good day! Good-bye!

1896 Trowbridge 287, *Deh-deh, deh-deh.* What a negro woman says when dropping a courtesy to a superior. 1943 *GL* Clar, Dayda, Goodbye; Port, Dada, Good Bye; StAnd, Day deh, goodbye; StJ, Daydeh, good-bye or good-day; StM, Dayde, Goodbye, adieu; West, Dey dey, Goodbye. 1955 FGC Man /díe díe/ goodbye.

DAYDE, DAYDEH see DAY-DAY.

DAY DRUMMER sb dial. A variety of the DRUMMER fish that is caught in the daytime.

1952 FGC StC /díe dròma/.

DAY GROUPER sb dial. A variety of the GROUPER fish that is caught in the daytime.

1952 FGC StM; StJ /díe grùpa/.

dayi /dáyi/ sb dial; etym unknown. A variety of CASSADA: see quot.

1952 FGC StAnd /dáyi/ a long-time cassada [i.e. not recently introduced], bitter, can eat when young.

DAY-MORNING sb dial; <*day* sb attrib +*morning*. *G*

1943 *GL* Port, Day-morning, daybreak.

DAY-NAME sb; <*day*+*name* sb. The name formerly given (following African custom) to negro children according to their sex and the day of the week on which they were born. The system is or was used where Ashanti slaves were taken in the Caribbean, with local variations. The more common term today among the Jamaican folk is BORN-DAY NAME. Cf also BIRTH NAME. The names themselves survive only in pejorative senses. *G T*

[1774 Long II 427, Many of the plantation Blacks call their children by the African name for the day of the week on which they are born; and these names are of two genders, male and female; as for instance:

Male	Female	Day
Cudjoe,	Juba,	Monday.
Cubbenah,	Beneba,	Tuesday.
Quâco,	Cuba,	Wednesday.
Quao,	Abba,	Thursday.
Cuffee,	Phibba,	Friday.
Quamin,	Mimba,	Saturday.
Quashee,	Quasheba,	Sunday.]

1946 Dunham 114, In the old days a Maroon baby was given a 'day name' as well as a Christian name. This is done only rarely now. 1953 Moore 67. [Cf DeCamp in 1967 *Language* 43.139–49.]

DAY-PEEP sb dial; <*day*+*peep* sb. *G*

1958 DeC StAnd /die-piip; piip av die/ dawn.

DE[1] /de/ adv dial; sp in dialect writing *de, deh, dey*, etc.; early writers often do not represent this, though it was undoubtedly used—they spell out *there* or *dere*; <*there*. *BL G T*

1. There.

1907 Jekyll 239 [Song:] Obeah down dé. 1912 Jekyll in McK *Songs* 8, *Deh..*may be either an adverb (there) or an auxiliary verb. 1952 FGC StM /a líe di foul a líe de?/ *Is the hen laying there?*

2. Passing into DE[3], so that the word is interpretable as adverb (*there*) or verb (*to be*).

1956 Mc StE /mi néva de in di choch/ *I am never at church.*

DE[2] /de/ prep dial; <*there*; perh also coincidentally <Ewe *ḍa, ḍe*, to, towards ('following a verb of direction', Turner 192). To. (=A[1] 3, which is, however, far more freq.) *G*

c1919 FGC StAnd [Song:] /go de lang pan fi waata/ *Go to Long Pond for water.*

DE[3] /de/ vb dial; in dialect writing also sp *deh, day, da* (but it is not the same as DA); <*there*, DE[1], which takes the place of the omitted verb *to be*—poss also with coincidental infl from some African word or words such as Twi *dè*, be —cf Christaller *dè*, v 4 (though this word has other and commoner meanings) or Ewe (Agu dial) *ḍe*, to be. *BL G N*

1. With words or phrases of place or location (*where, anywhere,* etc.): For parts of the verb *to be. T*

1877 Murray *Feedin' 'Perrit* 7, Bufo I know whi side I day, him let go him fist pon me mout lip. [*Before I know where I am*..etc.] 1907 Jekyll 178 [Song:] Whé mumma dé? *Ibid* 246 [Song:] Matilda dé 'pon dyin' bed. 1952 FGC StAnd, Snake waitin'-boy—/eniwe im de, sniek duon lef far/ *Wherever he is, a snake is not far off*; StAnd [Policeman speaking to people awaiting trial at court:] /éniwe yu dè wi káal yu/ *Wherever you are, we'll call you.* 1954 LeP StE, Fe me boat deh pon water ebery day.

2. Without reference to place or location: For parts of the verb *to be.*

1873 Rampini 177 [Prov:] John Crow say him de dandy man when him hab so-so fedder. [*The John Crow says he is a dandy though he has plain feathers.*] 1942 HPJ (quoting Simmons 14), Tax man deh pan me. [*The tax-collector has descended upon me,* or *is upon me.*] *Ibid,* Kingston pickney noh willin to de wi you.

DE[4] /de/ vb dial; also sp in dialect writing *day, deh, dey*; < DE[3]. *G*

1. As an auxiliary verb of durative or progressive action, = A[5], DA[3]. (DE + a verb = *to be* + present pple.) About as common as DA, but less so than A. *BL*

1873 Rampini 177 [Prov:] Man eber so hearty, dead day watch him. [*Though a man be ever so healthy, death is watching him.*] 1907 Jekyll 225 [Song:] who dé go married you? [*Who is going to marry you?*] 1925 Beckwith 81 (cf DEAD sb 2). 1955 LeP StE (Accom) [Recording of Story of Bobiabo:] /wa mek dem se so?/ [*Why do they say that?*]../wa mek dem de se so?/ [*Why do they keep on saying so?*] 1956 Mc StE (Accom): /mi de kom/ *I am coming.*

2. Transf. Expressing intention, determination, certainty. (Evid a parallel devel to that of Engl *will,* which may express simple futurity or determination to act, etc.; cf also *going to* with the same force.)

1943 *GL* StAnd, Deggo, sure to. [Presumably in such a phrase as /him dé go dwíit/ which might mean simply 'he's going to do it' or 'he's sure to do it!']

DEAD /ded/ vb intr dial; < *dead* adj. By ellipse of the verb *be,* so that the adjective carries the force of the verb: to be dead, to die.

1826 Williams 177, When they [negroes] were old and 'ready to *dead*'. 1837 James 7, When she faint she drop off the mill, and look as if she dead; all her fellow apprentice set up crying, and ask if she going to dead left them. 1907 Jekyll 224 (see quot s.v. GINGER PIECE). 1955 Bennett *Relief Fund,* Wen horse dead, cow fat. 1956 JN StJ, If hell get any more fire the people will faint and dead as they reach. *BA BL G T*

DEAD /ded/ sb dial; < *dead* adj; cf *OED dead* B; poss infl by such nominal uses of the adjective as Fr *un mort,* Sp *un muerto. G*

1. A dead body, a corpse. *BA BL T*

1942 HPJ, Dead, a dead person, corpse. 1943 *GL* Clar, Kip wake—A whole night singing when one has a dead. 1954 LeP Kgn, A dead; StT, Ded, a dead body.

2. The spirit of the dead; a duppy or ghost.

1873 Rampini 177 (cf DE[4]). 1895 Banbury 19 (cf DEATH). 1925 Beckwith 81 [Prov:] Man dey walk, dead dey watch him. Man nyam well, but duppy deh a yeye-corner dey watch him. *BA BL*

3. Death (the verbal idea is prob latent). *BL*

1873 Rampini 176 [Prov:] Dead better dan punish. [*Death is better than punishment,* or *To die, to be dead is better than to be punished.*] 1925 Beckwith 35, Daag say him mama dead don't hurt him like a overnight rain. 1956 Mc Man /it waz an aafu ded/ It was an awful death.

4. Personified in proverbs, stories, etc.: *Brother Death, Mr Dead.*

[1907 Jekyll 31, Brother Deat' no 'peak. So Annancy begin fe talk to himself: 'Bro'er Deat' say me fe go make up fire..'] 1924 Beckwith 34, Wife, I go in Dead country an' buck up Brar Dead. 1925 Beckwith 64 [Prov:] If Mr Go-'way no come, Mr Dead wi' come..a threat implying that if a man does not leave he may get killed.

DEAD adv dial; cf *OED dead* C 2, utterly, entirely, absolutely, quite. (Cf *ODS dead-sure.*) Certainly, for sure, at once. *BA BL G*

1956 Mc StAnd /áask fi sís, an dem núo déd iz mí/ *Ask for Sis, and they'll know for sure it's me.*

DEAD-AND-WAKE sb dial; < DEAD vb + *and* + *wake* vb. The sensitive-plant (*Mimosa pudica*) which closes its leaves together immediately it is touched and opens them again in a few minutes.

1927 Beckwith 15, Dead-and-wake (Sensitive-plant)... For a cold, boil with 'Devil's-back-bone' and drink as tea. 1941 HPJ, Ded-&-Wake, A local country name given to the sensitive plant. 1943 *GL* Man, Dead-an-wake, the sensitive plant. 1952 FGC Han, StE, Tre /dèd-an-wíek (maka)/. 1954 *WIMJ* 30, *Mimosa pudica*..Shame Weed; Sensitive Plant; Shama; Shame-a-Lady; Shut Weed; Dead and Awake.

DEADED past pple dial rare—perh an individualism; < DEAD vb, evid an overcorrection.

1956 Mc StE (Accom) /dem kil mi dédid/ *They will kill me dead. G*

DEAD FLESH sb dial. Proud flesh; excessive granulation tissue on a wound. *BA G*

1952 FGC Han, StAnd, StM /ded flesh/ proud flesh, when a sore not clean; Man /ded flesh/—right name is rotten flesh; also Tre.

DEAD LIMB sb dial. *G*

1958 DeC StAnd (Irish Town, Red Light) /ded lim/ any limb or branch [of a tree] which won't bear and must be pruned is called dead even though it is usually green and alive.

DEAD MAN BONES sb dial; cf use of the term (*DAE*) for *Linaria vulgaris.* A low wild plant (*Blechum brownei*) having medicinal uses; also called BLUE WEED, JOHN BULL, LOOK UP.

1952 FGC StM /ded man buon/—for cold, and if you are going in decline.

DEAD-NETTLE sb bot obs; cf *OED.* In Browne's use: *Pilea grandiflora.*

1756 Browne 337, Urtica 6..The larger Dead Nettle, with smooth leaves.

DEAD STORY sb dial; < *dead* adj + *story.* A happening, or a report of a happening, which one has not seen oneself, and which is therefore open to doubt. See LIVE STORY.

DEAD WASH sb tech; < *dead OED a* 12 + *wash* sb. In the manufacture of rum: The residue in the vats after fermentation has ceased. It is run into the still, boiled, vaporized, and condensed to produce rum.

1952 FGC Tre.

DEAD-WATER, DEATH-WATER /ded-waata/ sb dial; < DEAD sb 1, a corpse + *water.* The water with which a corpse has been washed—see quots. (Beliefs concerning it are African in origin.) *BL G*

1941 HPJ, Dead-wahta: the water thrown out of a house of mourning. It must not be walked in, as you will get ulcers and soon die; unless you spit in it. E.R.N. 1908. [Astley Clerk:] Could this superstition have had its origin at the time some 100 odd years ago when small-pox played havoc in Jamaica and the belief spread that to bathe in the water which had washed the corpse would give the bather the small-pox and its then consequent death, And yet, I had an aunt then a child who, because of her love for her father, did this very thing and escaped scot-free. 1953 Moore 38, Death-water, dead-water, The water used to wash a corpse ceremonially before burial. (It must not be poured down the drain, but out in the yard, and it's bad luck to step over it.)

DEAD-WEED sb dial; < DEAD + *weed. Erigeron canadensis.* See quots. Cf also DEATH-WEED.

1927 Beckwith 15, Dead-weed..Boil as tea for a baby or with 'Death-weed' as below. 1954 *WIMJ* 29, *E. canadensis L...*Canada Fleabane; Dead Weed.

DEAD-YARD sb dial; < DEAD sb 1. *BL*

1958 DeC East Ja /ded-yaad/ the dead man's yard *after* he has been buried. Before that it is called the BURYING YARD.

DEAF-EARS /déf-íez/ adj and sb dial; < *deaf* + *ears* (which is sing or pl). Deaf; a deaf person. *G*

1941 HPJ, Def-aise, deaf, a deaf person.

DEAF-EARS CRAB sb dial; < DEAF-EARS + *crab*.

1. A crab with a small body and one very big claw which it holds up like a deaf man cupping his hand to his ear.

1941 HPJ, Deaf-ear Crab, a kind of crab. 1952 FGC StM /def-iez krab/ small body, one big claw.

2. Transf. A deaf person.

1941 Astley Clerk in HPJ, One whose ears are as deaf as the crab.

DEAH-DEAH sb dial; phonosymbolic and prob African.

1943 *GL* Clar, Deah-deah, weakling.

DEALING STICK sb dial; < *dealing* pple; cf *deal* vb + *stick* sb. A stick to which magical properties have supposedly been given to 'deal with' inimical spirits.

1934 *Gleaner* 30 Jan (in 1934 Williams), Lucea—Ebenezer Clarke is convicted of imposing on Newton Brown, a shoemaker at Mount Pleasant, who reports having been informed by Clarke that 'Duppy is on me and my shop'. He is to receive a 'dealing stick' that is to be kept in his shop 'to keep away the duppy'.

DEATH sb; a 'corrected' form of DEAD sb 2. The spirit of a dead person.

1895 Banbury 19, The communication with spirits, or 'deaths'. The mialman harms by depriving persons of their 'shadows' or setting the 'deaths' upon them.

DEATH-WEED sb dial; < *death* + *weed*.

A wild plant used in obeah and myal practice (prob a species of *Solanum*, or perh of *Phytolacca*) to cause seeming death (from which the patient could be 'brought back to life'), to 'drive duppy', etc. Cf BRANCHED CALALU, MYAL WEED. (This is evid a different plant from DEAD-WEED.)

1927 Beckwith 16, Death-weed..White would 'mash it up properly with the other "Dead-weed" and with "Love-weed", add (laundry) blue, assafoetida, vinegar, a little fine salt, and cork it up tightly in a bottle or the cork will fly out. Rub it on the wound or over the body if you think there is a duppy (spirit) about. Anything contrary you feel, it will take that all away'. I was unfortunately unable to secure a specimen of this valuable weed. 1946 Dunham 159, He had been far in these hours before dawn, and had brought me back obi weed, snake root, and death weed. I must sleep with the snake root under my pillow always, and put the obi weed and death weed in separate bottles of rum.

DEBTMENT sb dial; < *debt* + *-ment*. Indebtedness.

1927 Anderson-Cundall 60 [Prov:] A pound a fretment no pay a gill a debtment.

DED see DEAD.

DE DA, DEDAY see *di-de*.

DEDE see *didi*.

DEEBU /díibu/ sb dial; said to be 'African'. In AFRICAN cult use: blood, maternal blood-relations.

1953 Moore 27, My deebu are my mother and her sisters and brothers, her mother and all her children. *Ibid* gloss, deebu = blood.

DEE-DEE, DEE-DI, DEEDY see *didi*.

DEEP adj dial; < *deep*, profound. An intensifying word: very great, extreme, utter. See quots. Cf also DEEP ENGLISH, READ. *BA BL G N*

1952 FGC Man, Deep curve in a road, a very sharp or acute-angled turn. 1956 Mc StE (Accom) /a diip strienja—iz di fos hi bigin tu vizit dis huom/ *A complete stranger—this is the first time he has been here.*

DEEP ENGLISH sb dial; cf DEEP, showing high degree; here high quality rather is shown. = HIGH ENGLISH (the more common term): the language of the educated, or an attempt to achieve it. *G*

1907 Jekyll 160, Here is the story in plain English, 'deep English' as the Negro calls it, not understanding it well. [Jekyll has himself misunderstood the metaphor.] *Ibid* 232, So, if they were trying to talk 'deep English', for 'Adela da jump' they would substitute 'Adela is jump' and think it quite right.

DEEP-WATER EEL sb. *G*

1892 Cockrell list, Deep water eel, *Conger conger* (the true conger eel).

DEEP-WATER SHAD sb dial. Another name for the ordinary shad fish.

1952 FGC StC /díip-wàata shád/.

DEEP-WATER SILK sb. A variety of SILK fish caught in deep water.

a1818 Lewis (1834) 104, Of the Sea Fish which I have hitherto met with, the Deep-water Silk appears to me the best. 1952 FGC StJ /díip wàata sílk/.

DEEP-WATER SNAPPER sb. A variety of the SNAPPER fish caught in deep water. *BA G*

1756 Browne 448–9, Coracinus 6..The black Snaper, or Deep-water Snaper. This fish grows to a pretty considerable size, and is deemed one of the best fishes in America ..Coracinus 9..The deep water red Snaper.

DEEP-WATER WENSHMAN sb dial; < *deep-water* + *wenshman*. The *kanggatuoni*.

1952 FGC StJ, StM /díipwàata wénshmàn/ resemble SATIN fish; same as ROUND-HEAD CONGO-TONY.

DEEP-WATER WHITENING see WHITING.

DEESTANT see *diistant*.

DEF adj dial; < *death*. An intensifying word, heavily stressed; cf similar use of GOD.

1907 Jekyll 171, 'I never do him one def ting', a single thing. 'Def' is emphatic, but is not a 'swear-word'.

DEGAY see *dege* sb.

dege, dege-dege /dége, dégi/ adj dial; cf Ewe *ḍeká*, single, alone, solitary, and Twi *atɛkɛ́*, short.

1. Only, sole, single.

1943 *GL* Man, Deggeh, only, single, solitary; StJ, deggeh-deggeh, single, also Han. 1950 Pioneer 18, De one deggeh goat me have you teck grudgeful kill him [*The one single goat I have, you become envious and kill it!*].

2. By transf of meaning from small number to small size: little, small. (Some quots also illustrate sense 1.)

1956 Mc Man /wán dege wan wi hab/ *We only have this one little thing;* /iz di wán dége peni mi hav/ *It's the one single* (or *mere*) *penny I have.* 1957 EB Port /dege/ One only, single, solitary, short.

dege /dége, dégi/ sb dial; prob the same as *dege* adj.

1. As a name. (This may be a different word.)

1907 Jekyll 163 [Song:] De-gay, Bell a ring a yard oh!.. The bell is ringing up at the house, says one of the slaves to Degay the head-man, and we want our breakfast. *Ibid* 198–9 [Song:] Deggy house a burn down do, de Gay. [The meaning is not clear, and seems to include some of the nonsense sounds usual in refrains.] 1922 Holbrooke t.p., Deggy Dance [listed among 'Digging Sings'].

2. A (good) friend—from the sense of exclusivity in the basic meaning 'only, sole'? (*dege* adj 1).

1943 GL StM, Good deggeh, good friend.

3. A short man (< *dege* adj 2). Cf also *dogi.*

1943 *GL* Kgn, Deggy, a very short man.

DEGGEH, DEGGY see prec.

DEH see DE.

DEH-DEH see DAY-DAY, *di-de.*

DEH SO see *de-so.*

DEH YAH see DA-YA.

DE LAURENCE sb dial, also attrib; < *De Laurence,* a Chicago publisher of books on occult subjects, banned from Jamaica. Witchcraft; loosely, obeah.

1960 DeC StAnd, etc. /dilárans/.

DEM /dem, deng/ 3rd pers pron plur dial; < *them.* Corresponding to all case-forms of StdE: they, their, them. *BA BL G N T*

1868 Russell 12–18, The personal pronouns are..Plur. 3rd person *Dem,* all cases Mas. Fem. Neuter. 1907 Jekyll 32, Me see enough yam, me fe peel dem put dem a fire. *Ibid* 77, I can't count dem to you, for dem dé all over me body. [*I can't count them..for they are*..etc.] 1960 BLB 7 /deng gi mi siks mont taim/ *They gave me six months' time.*

DEM demonstr adj plur dial; < *them.* Those; of that particular kind. *BA BL G N T*

1953 Bailey 27, *dem pikni*—children in whom the speaker has some special interest.

-DEM /dem/ plural-forming particle; < DEM, prob the pers pron rather than the demonstr, though both may have taken part in the development: cf 1868 Russell 13, 'The third Personal Pronouns are used in a sentence immediately after the noun with which it agrees, as a second subject to emphasize the noun..thus, De man him mus be mad'. This use of *dem* perh led to its reduction to an unstressed postposed morpheme of plurality. But its close juncture to the prec noun better implies reduction < AN' DEM; cf US dial *and them.* *BL G N T*

1. A suffix indicating the plural.

1868 Russell 8, Plurality is..indicated..By the pronoun *dem,* immediately following the noun and joined to it by the Copulative Conjunction, *an,* in most cases; thus—De horse an dem hard fe ketch..Sometimes *an* is omitted; as, De boy dem cleber; De crab dem bery sweet. [Use of *an* is now uncom. 1959 FGC.] 1907 Jekyll 114 [Normalized:] So the Cow them hear what the master said. [*So the Cows heard*..etc.] 1912 Jekyll in McK *Songs* 8, The reader will soon master the mysteries..of *dem* tacked close to its noun, to show it is plural. 1952 FGC StAnd /di wás-dem/ *The wasps.*

2. A suffix indicating association in a group.

1953 Bailey 21, *Jan-dem* or *Jan-an-dem*—John and his bunch.

DEM-DA see DEM-DE.

DEM-DE /démdè/ demonstr adj and pron dial; < *them* + *there.* Cf next. Those. *BL G*

1868 Russell 14, The plural of da, dat or dari, is dem, with the adverb da (thère), (*a* in *da* as in lay) making *dem da* = those..Dem ya hat wite, but dem-da black. 1943 *GL* Tre, West, Demdey, those.

DEM-YA /démyà/ demonstr adj and pron dial; < *them* demonstr pron + *here.* Cf prec. These.

1868 Russell 14, The plural of dis is 3rd person pronoun dem, with the addition of the adverb ya (here), making *dem ya* = these. [Cf DEM-DE.] 1942 Bennett 22, But dem yah a-noh femme foot [*But these are not my feet*]. 1943 *GL* Tre, West, Demyah, these. 1952 FGC StAnd /dem-ya a hag plom/ *These are hog-plums.* *BL G*

DENKE sb dial rare; cf CB *-*dèngè,* pumpkin.

1942 HPJ, Denkẽ, The real name of *pum-pum,* a large round yellow yam, the same as böasun.

depa /dépa, dípa/ sb dial arch; cf Twi *ɔdepá ne,* yam (of the first type listed by Christaller s.v. *ɔ-dé*).

1943 *GL* Clar, Depa, negro yam. 1954 LeP Man, Dippa, negro yam. 1956 Mc Man /dípa/.

de-pan /dépan/ vb phr dial; < DE[3] + *upon* (cf *OED upon* 4c, 10d, etc.). To be engaged in an action or activity of some kind; to be in a state of continuing or repeated action. *G N*

1942 HPJ, 'Me cyant stap, depan hace'. *I can't stop, I'm in a hurry.* 1953 Murray 41–2 [Song:] Judy deh pon dyin'. 1958 DeC /im depan pient di waal/ *He goes on painting the wall;* /im depan rien/ *It goes on raining;* /im depan 'duon do it'/ *He keeps saying 'Don't do it'.*

DESHA see DIS-YA.

DE-SO /désò/ adv dial; < DE[1] + SO. A more emphatic expression than either of its components separately: there! Cf *ya-so.* *G*

1877 Murray *Feedin' 'Perrit* 4, I see William Hinds tek da same nut ile daso rub him head. [*That very same nut-oil there.*] 1955 Bennett *Back to Africa,* For a right deh so you deh! [*For you are right there!*] 1961 BLB 23 /dát shap dé-so mi a gó/ *It's to that shop over there I'm going.*

DESSERT sb dial.

1958 DeC Port /dizót/ a snack between meals.

DESTANT see *diistant.*

DESTROYER sb dial; from Biblical influence?

1954 LeP StAnn, A distraya, a deceitful man.

DESTRUCTFULLEST adj dial; < *destruct-* (analysed out of *destructive, destruction,* etc.) + *-ful* + *-est.* Most destructive.

1952 FGC StAnn, Parrakeets are the most destructfullest birds.

DEUCE /juus/ sb dial; < *deuce*[2] (*OED, a*).

1. The devil to pay, a deuce of a row, a great conflict. *G*

1955 LeP StE (Accom) [Story:] /dis maanin it wil bi juus wid mii an bobiabuo/ *This morning there will be a great fight between me and Bobiabo.*

2. In phr *to deuce*: Extremely.

1962 BLB 27 /it wie tu-juus/ *It weighs a great deal* [*It's heavy as the devil*].

DEVIL- attrib, in compounds usually = *devil's*; pronunc /debl, devl/. *G*

DEVIL-DAMNATION PEPPER sb dial joc. Very hot capsicum peppers.

1952 FGC StT /débl dàmníeshan pépa/—very hot!

DEVIL-ENGINE sb dial.

1942 HPJ, Devil engine: Steam-roller (children's word).

DEVIL-HEAD adj or sb attrib dial; < *devil* + *head* (which may be a survival of *-head*, -hood, but is more likely to be a use of the independent noun.) Wicked, diabolical.

1954 LeP StAnn, Bad children are devil-head.

DEVIL-HELL PEPPER sb dial. = DEVIL-DAMNATION PEPPER.

1952 FGC.

DEVIL-MAN sb dial; < *devil* + *man*.

1954 LeP Kgn, Black like a devil-man, very black negro. (Devil-man is the blackest person in Mr John Canoe Dance.)

DEVIL PEPPER sb dial. Red capsicum pepper; also called DEVIL-DAMNATION, DEVIL-HELL, RED-DEVIL PEPPER.

1952 FGC StC /devl pepa/ the hottest; StJ /débl pepa/ = /kayáan pepa/.

DEVIL RAIN sb dial. Rain that falls when the sun is shining. See quots. *BL G*

1952 FGC Port, Devil rain; sunshine and rain together: 'the devil and his wife fighting for a piece of hambone', heard at school. Also StC, StT.

DEVIL'S BACKBONE sb dial. = DEVIL('s) HORSE-WHIP. The sharp burs are all along the whip-like flowering stalk.

1927 Beckwith 16, Devil's-back-bone. . For a cold, boil as tea. 1954 *WIMJ* 28, see DEVIL('S) HORSE-WHIP.

DEVIL'S-BEAN sb bot; ? Jamaican.

1864 Grisebach 783, Devil's-bean: *Capparis cynophallophora. Ibid* 18, Hab[itat]. Jamaica. . Dominica. . St Lucia. . Trinidad.

DEVIL('S) HORSE-WHIP sb dial. Either of two closely related weeds with tall, flexible stems having sharp burs along them; see quots 1954, 1959. s OLD WOMAN'S RAZOR.

c 1915 FGC StAnd. 1927 Beckwith 16. 1952 FGC Han, StAnn, StM /débl háas wip/; StT, devil's horse-whip. 1954 *WIMJ* 28, *Achyranthes indica*. . Devil's Horsewhip; Devil's Riding Whip; Devil's Backbone; Colic Weed; Hug-me-close. 1959 UCWI Herbarium, *Achyranthes indica, A. aspera*.

DEVIL'S RIDING WHIP sb dial. = DEVIL'S HORSE-WHIP.

1954 *WIMJ* 28, see prec.

DEVIL'S TRUMPET sb.

1954 *WIMJ* 29, *Datura stramonium*. . Thorn Apple; Devil's Trumpet; Trimona; Jamestown (Jimson Weed).

DEVIL'S WOOD sb obs; *ODS* 1832→ for other trees. *Thevetia neriifolia*. See quot.

1811 Titford 128, Cerbera, Class 5, Ord. 1. The wood of this tree is so excessively foetid that it cannot be burnt. It is called Devil's Wood.

DEW vb dial; < *dew v* (*OED* 1 →1726). Cf JUJU. *G*

1942 HPJ, Fe dew: to rain slightly.

DEW-DEW see JUJU.

de-wid /dé-wìd/ vb phr; < DE[3] 2 (in pregnant sense) + *with*. To be living with (someone) in concubinage. *G*

1943 *GL* Clar, De wid, along with, concubinage. 1956 EB Port (Pt Antonio) /de wid/. 1956 Mc StT /yu no dé wid yu swiitaat man/ *You are not living with your sweetheart*.

DEY see DE.

DE-YA see DA-YA.

DEYDEY see DAY-DAY, *di-de*.

di /di/ adj dial; the regular dial pronunc of *the*.

1. Used for definite article as in Std Engl, but not alwavs where it is required there. *BL G T*

2. Used with demonstrative force (= English *that*) preceding a personal name, indicating increase of formality and some displeasure. *G*

1958 DeC StE (Accom) [In a story of a witch who has been thwarted repeatedly by Andrew:] /an so shi wash di Andro/ [*And so she washed that fellow Andrew*]. (Also in conversation, occas, DeC.)

DIAH see DA-YA.

DIAL /dáial/ sb dial arch; prob < *dial*, sundial, face of a clock—cf *OED sb*[1]. In the phrase (evidently found only or chiefly in story-telling): *as shine as dial*, very bright. Cf SHINE adj.

1958 DeC Man [Story:] /hiz suod waz az shain az daial/—I have no idea what /daial/ is here, nor could the man who used it in a story explain it—he said it's just a saying meaning it was very shiny.

DIANA'S PAINT-BRUSH sb. = CUPID'S SHAVING-BRUSH.

1952 FGC Man.

DIBI-DERI, DIVI-DERI sb obs. A plant valuable for tanning (see quot 1837); now reclassified as *Caesalpinia tinctoria*.

1837 Macfadyen I 327, Coulteria tinctoria. *Dibi-Deri*. . This valuable shrub has been lately introduced into the Island by Henry Bright, Esq., and promises to be a great acquisition. The pods abound in the tannin principle. 1854–5 *TJSA* I 62, Dibi deri. Coulteria tinctoria. 1864 Grisebach 783, Divi-deri.

DICKY-BIRD BERRY sb chiefly dial. The tree also called SALTWOOD (*Neea nigricans*); evid because the berries are eaten by small birds.

1949 *NHN* IV 28. 1961 DAP StE (Quickstep), Dicky-bird berry—Salt-wood.

DID see DO.

DIDA sb; perh a blend of TITA and DADA.

1956 Mc Man /dída/ father.

DIDDE, DIDDEH, DIDDEY see *di-de*.

DIDDY see *didi*.

di-de /dí-de, dé-de/ adv or vb phr dial; in dial writing sp *didde, diddey, diddeh, didey, de da, deday, deh-deh*, etc.; prob iter of DE, or DE[3] + DE[1]. There; is, are there; was, were there. *BL G*

1877 Murray *Kittle* 22, Him come out ya—him de da, sir. [*He has come out here—he is there, sir.*] 1910 Anderson-Cundall 28, Wha' you see carrin, crow da dey. Where you see carrion you will find the John Crow. 1942 HPJ, 'Gentleman diddeh'—There's a man at the door 1943 *GL* StAnd, Deh-deh, to be at a place, there; Tre, Didey, there; West, Deday, it is there. 1950 Pioneer 63, When him reach him fine say cow no did-deh, dem all gone way. [*When he arrived he found that the cows were not there, they had all gone away.*] 1956 Mc no addr /if eni ada piiz dide/ *If there had been any other peas.*

DIDEY see prec.

didi /dídi, diidi/ sb and vb dial; iterative, prob euphemistic—no etym source found. (Cf however Ewe *ḍiḍi*, to let down, to lower.) Cf *duodo*. *BL G*

A. sb: Excrement, dung.

1942 HPJ, Diddy; deedy: excrement; evacuation; particularly used by children's Nanas or Nurses. 1943 *GL* Tre, Dee dee, excreta. 1957 JN (Lowe River), Marlene, yu step pon di dankey dee-di.

B. vb: To defecate.

1924 Beckwith 145 [Story:] Again the foolish brother said, 'I want to dédé!' So he did, and the robbers caught some. 1943 *GL* Clar, Deedy, defacates; Port, Dede, to ease the body.

didl see *dil*.

die-die see DAY-DAY.

DIFFERENT-DIFFERENT adj dial; iterative <*different*. Very miscellaneous; scattered. See quots. *G*

1950 Pioneer 56, Bans a different-different knife and fork An spoon an tarra-tarra! 1952 FGC StAnn, Cucumber—/difran-difran/ part they plant it. [*They plant cucumbers in many different kinds of places all about.*]

DIGESTER sb; cf *OED* 4. A large cast-iron pot with a cover, used for cooking soup. Cf JESTA.

1952 FGC Kgn. [From Mr D'Aguilar, hardware dealer.]

DIG FOOT vb phr. To run away fast. *BL*

1931 BLB Man, Man, yu beta dig fut!

DIGGER, DIGGER-STICK sb dial. A short blade on a wooden handle—used for making holes, digging potatoes, etc.

1956 Mc Man /diga stik/; StAnd (Mavis Bank) /díga—fi jam pii an dig patieto/; StAnd (Dallas) /diga/ also /jama/. 1957 EB Port /diga stik/ instrument used to dig up yam, etc.

DIGGING-BILL sb dial; <*digging* ppl+*bill*, agricultural knife. A sharp knife, used as a tool for digging; =DIGGER, JAMMA.

1956 Mc Man /digin bil/. 1957 EB Port /digin bil/ metal spike for digging.

DIGGING-MATCH sb dial.

1942 HPJ, Digging-match: A communal planting. A number of people (usually country people) agree to clear and plant their 'grounds' in turn, working together. [Astley Clerk:] Drink (and sometimes food) is provided by the owner of the 'ground' being cleared and planted out for all taking part. 1952 FGC StM, In a /digin mach/ a group of neighbours meet at one man's ground. He furnishes rum, and breakfast around 2 o'clock. They sing banter-sings—the more rum the more singing. They may dig 200 yam hills in a day. 1957 EB Port, In Port Antonio area.

DIGGING-SING sb dial; <*digging* ppl+*sing* sb. The type of group singing which regularly accompanies communal digging. (Cf DIGGING-MATCH.)

1907 Jekyll 158, To the other class of songs [than Ring-tunes] belong the 'digging-sings' used, together with rum, as the accompaniment to field labour..Nothing more joyous can be imagined than a good 'digging-sing' from twenty throats. 1922 Holbrooke t.p., Digging Sings.

DIGGING-SONG sb; the normalized form of prec. *G*

1942 Astley Clerk in HPJ, Diggin'-songs: The certain class of local Folk song sung on the occasion of a diggin'-match, the singing of which (led by a 'professional' diggin match singer) lightens the labours of the diggers.

digi-digi-out adj dial; <*dig*, past pple+-I, together iterated to show repeated action, +*out*. Much dug, pecked, or bitten out. *G*

1956 Mc Man /digi-digi-out/—said of cabbage leaves eaten by worms, fowls, etc.

digl-dagl vb dial; iterative showing repeated or continued action: the source is uncertain, but cf Engl *diggle, daggle* (*OED*). To lurk suspiciously (as a thief, etc.).

1956 Mc Man /di mán dígl-dagl roun di plíes/.

DIG SECOND vb phr; cf DIG FOOT. To put a car into second gear in order to get up a hill.

1931 BLB Man.

DIH-YA see DA-YA.

diistant adj & vb dial; <*decent*, with intrusive /t/. *BL*

A. adj: Decent.

1900 Murray 4, Deestant pusson. 1941 Kirkpatrick 5, Deestant people. 1957 EB Port, Adj /diistant/ decent. Common in Portland.

B. vb: To make (oneself) decent or tidy; const *up*.

1957 Bennett 49, Dem..start destant up demself an wipe De grease offa dem mout.

DIKKITAP sb dial; prob <DE[1]+*ki*, clear (cf *kirout*, clear out) +*top*.

1942 *GL* Port, Dikkitap, a high place—(away on top).

dil, dil-dil sb dial; <*dilly*[2] (*OED*); also iterated. A duck; usually a young one.

c1915 FGC StAnd /dil-dil/ duckling. 1943 *GL* StE, Dil-dil, duckling. 1952 FGC StAnd, StM, West /dil/; StAnn /didl/.

DILDO (PEAR) (TREE) sb; <*dildo*[2] (*OED* →1756). Two species of cactus so named for their phallic shape: *Cereus peruvianus* and *C. gracilis*. s TORCH CACTUS. *BA*

1696 Sloane 197, Cereus crassissimus, fructu intus & extus rubro..The larger Dildo tree..Cereus altissimus gracilior, fructu extus luteo, intus niveo..Dildo Tree the lesser or Torchwood. 1740 Importance 37, The Torch-Thistle is called there the Dildoe Tree; it grows wild in large Bushes. 1756 Browne 238, Cactus 8..Dildo Pear Tree (larger)..Cactus 9..Dildo Pear Tree (smaller). 1794 Barham 51, Some merry person gave it the name of dildo; but in other places it is called flambeau, torch-wood, or prickle-candle, it being in the shape of four candles joined together. 1926 Fawcett 279, *C. peruvianus*..Dildo. Dry parts of Jamaica on southern side. 1952 FGC StAnn, StE, StM, StT /dildo/—grows round sea-side; is bad macka—gives you blood-poisoning; also name for a small variety.

DILLY-DALLY adj dial; *OED a*, 1888→. Procrastinating. *BA G*

1868 Russell 17, Thomas is a dilly-dally fella.

dima, dimo sb dial uncom; etym unknown, but cf *bima*, RUCKODIMMO, *timbim*. A persistent sore; a lame foot.

1943 *GL* StM, Dimmo, lame foot. 1956 Mc Clar /dima—uol suo we neva wel/ *An old sore that never heals.*

din-din sb dial rare; etym unknown, but cf GINGY-FLY etym and Gullah *dindi*, a small child (1949 Turner 192).

1958 DeC (Accom) /din-din/ undersized, puny person.

dindi-okro sb dial; cf Ewe *diŋaa*, sticky, viscous, slimy+OKRO, one of the chief properties of which noticed by the folk is sliminess. One of the local names of the common climbing cacti, of triangular or polygonal cross-section: *Cereus triangularis, C. grandiflorus.*

1952 FGC Tre /díndi ókro/wall-okro; grows on wall; same as sipple-okro, god-okro.

DING-DING sb dial rare; etym unknown.

1943 *GL* StM, Ding-ding, tripe. *BA*

DINGHY /dinggi/ sb dial; evid <*dinghy*, a boat. A two-wheeled buggy or cart formerly widely used. See quots. *BA*

1942 HPJ, Dinghy: a light trap, now called a 'fly'; like a 'bus' but with no cover. . The same as parry-cart. 1943 *GL* Port, Dingy, two-wheeled buggy; Tre, Dingy, a Buggy. 1952 FGC West /dinggi/ = /pári-kyàat/: two-wheel cart for carrying people. 1956 Mc StE /dinggi/ a buggy, with a cover. The Chinese use them in Kingston, I was told, and there was one in St James. The thing is obviously rare now: /yu duon sii dhem agien/. This was differentiated (Accompong) from /flai/, which is a buggy without a cover.

DINGIMINNEY see next.

dingki(-mini) /díngki-míni, dingki, dingkii/ sb dial; etym uncert: cf Twi *adéŋkũm*, a women's play; Ko *ndingi*, lamentation, funeral song.

1. A type of RING-PLAY or dancing usually practised in connection with funeral ceremonies; also the ceremonies themselves. See quots. Cf SET-UP.

1936 Clarke in *Gleaner* 7 Aug, Young people congregate at nights in the villages all over the island to sing the catchy tunes, jump 'dinkie-minie' and indulge in practices which condemn them to degradation. 1942 HPJ, Dinkie-minie, to jump—dance the pucku? 1943 *GL* Clar, Dinky-minny, a ring play; Kgn, a fanatic religious rite; StM, Dingiminney, country dance—ninth night. 1951 Murray 6 [Song:] 'Ada'. . First heard in the hills of StMary at a 'Dinky'. 'Dinkies' are the ninth night celebrations after a funeral, when at midnight the mourners abandon themselves to gaiety and the occasion becomes a festive affair. 1958 DeC eastern Port and adjoining part of StT /dingki-mini/—1. A peculiar jumping dance to drums, somewhat similar to poco jumping but involving more vertical height in the jumps; at certain climactic points the dancer bends one leg at the knee and makes a long series of high leaps all on the other foot (as in hop-scotch, only there is no forward motion. 2. A funeral meeting on the second to eighth nights after death (usually only one of these nights, though occasionally there will be two), a meeting at which this dance is performed. 3. Such a funeral meeting even if the dance is not done, with ring games substituted.

2. Attrib as in *dingki sang*, etc.

1952 FGC StM, After somebody has died /dingkii—giem an daans—sing dingki sang/.

DINKIE-MINIE see prec.

DINKY /dingki/ sb dial; perh <US *dinkey*. Machine or device for threshing rice. s DENKY.

1943 *GL* StT, Dinky, apparatus made of wood used for thrashing rice. 1952 FGC Han /díngki/ local machine for thrashing rice. 1956 Mc StE, West /dingki/ a device used for threshing rice: a board, which is stepped on at one end.

DINKY(-MINNY) see *dingki(-mini)*.

DINNER /dina/ sb dial. *G*

1. The meal at the end of the day: at any time between 3 and 6 o'clock. *BA T*

1952 FGC StE /dina/ around 3 o'clock; StM, 5 or 6 o'clock—poorer people: the big meal at night; StJ, 4–5 o'clock, when people /kom fram grong/: the biggest meal; Tre, 3 o'clock or later; West, 5–6 o'clock. 1954 LeP StE (Eld), Dinner, third meal of the day (5 p.m.).

2. See quot.

1958 DeC StC /dina/ a funeral celebration held about forty days after death; includes a feast, singing, games etc., lasting nearly all night; most common among East Indians but observed by many Negroes also.

DIP vb dial; <*dip* vb.

1. Abbr for *to dip into others' affairs. BA BL G*

1954 LeP Man, To dip, to meddle or interfere. 1956 Mc Man, Dip, dip ina, to interfere. 1957 EB Port.

2. To strike lightly. See *fi*³, quot 1958.

dipa see *depa.*

DIP-AND-COME-BACK, DIP-AND-FALL-BACK, DIP-AND-SHAKE-OFF sb dial joc; descriptive of the action of one dipping food into a sauce which runs back along one's hand, or falls back into the bowl, or of which one shakes off the surplus. <Scots '*dup in un shaak aaf*, dip (your bread) in (the dish) and shake off (the dripping)', 1915 Wilson 201.

1. A sauce made basically with coconut milk, fish, and seasoning. (The details of the recipe vary locally.) Also called ASSISTANT, BREADFRUIT REMEDY, CHORURO WATER, (COCONUT) RUNDOWN, COCONUT SAUCE, CURRY, DIP-DIP, *dipidens*, DIVIDEN-AN-FLABUB, *dolo, dozi*, DUCK-AND-SHAKE-BACK, ELBOW-GREASE, *flabob, freke, frigasi*, GRAVY, JOHNNY RUN-DOWN, *kobijong, kuochi waata, lef-aan*, LONG ROAD, *malongkontong*, MULGRAVE, PAKASSA, *plaba, plomi, rege*, REMEDY, ROUND-THE-ROAD, STEW-DOWN, SWIMMER-DOWN, *tap-i-a-paas.*

1943 *GL* Man, Dip an fall back, a white sauce made of seasoning, butter, water, flour, fish; StM, Dip and shake off, half-boiled coconut oil; Tre, Dípanfalback, a sauce made of flour and cocoanut milk. 1952 FGC StAnn, Port, Dip-and-come-back, coconut milk and fish (shad, herring), salted, peppered, boiled down to sauce; StM, Dip-and-fall-back. 1956 Mc Man, Port, StAnd /dip an faa bak/; StAnd /dip an shiek bak/. 1958 DeC StAnd /dip-an-fal-bak, dip-an-shiek-bak/; StT /dip-an-kom-bak/—coconut run-down.

2. Also locally: FLOUR SAUCE.

1956 Mc StAnd /dip-an-faal-bak/ sometimes said instead of /floua-saas/ (in which case /rondoung/ is said for sense 1).

dip-and-shake-back spoon sb dial. (see prec.) A large spoon, usable in a large cooking pot; evid used in making DIP-AND-SHAKE-BACK.

1956 Mc StAnd /díp-an-shiek-bák spúun/ A very big spoon, used to stir /belagot/.

DIP-DIP sb dial; iterative <*dip* vb, suggesting repeated action. A coconut RUNDOWN; evid also other sauces. *BA*

1942 Bennett 13, Now we can start fe nyam. Me gat de dip-dip yah Tayma, Pass de yabah wid de yam. 1943 *GL* Port, Dipp-dipp, cocoanut sauce; StAnd, Dip-dip, pickle. 1958 DeC Port, Dip-dip, a coconut run-down.

dipidens /dípidens/ sb dial; etym uncert: the base is clearly *dip* vb, and the ending prob *-ence* (*OED*: suffix forming abstract nouns). Cf DIVIDEN(-AN-FLABUB).

1. A coconut rundown, or similar sauce.

1943 *GL* Kgn, Dipodence, coconut half boiled down to oil; StM, Dipidense, gravy. 1955 FGC Man /dípidens/. 1959 DeC StJ /dipidents/ a coconut run-down.

2. A peppery sauce. *BA*

1943 *GL* Tre, Dipidense, pickle pepper.

DIPIDENSE, DIPODENSE see prec.

DIPPA see *depa*.

DIPPISH adj dial; <DIP+-*ish*. Meddlesome, interfering.

1954 LeP StAnn, Dippish, to meddle or interfere.

DIRECT adj dial. Certain, specific. See quot.

1959 DeC Port /ai nuo a dirék spat an a ruod/ *I know of one particular place on the road* (where a duppy always appears). *BL G*

DIRT sb dial; 'corrected' from DUTTY sb. The ground, the earth. *BL G*

1956 Mc StE /lúk an dórt/ *Look on the ground* (for oranges shaken from a tree).

DIRT-EATING sb obs or hist; <*dirt*+*eating* vbl sb. *OED* 1817–34.

1. The action of eating 'dirt', that is certain kinds of clayey earth (cf ABU EARTH), to which many negroes were formerly addicted.

2. The disease in which this eating of dirt becomes habitual: geophagy—also called EARTH-EATING, MAL-DE-STOMACH, STOMACH-EVIL.

1791 Lindsay (quoted in 1814 Lunan I 95), That species of pica called dirt-eating, so fatal to a number of negroes. 1796 Braco 22 Oct, Pompy Died was very much Bloated, proceeding from excessive dirt eating and debility. 1801 Dancer 170–1, Malacia Africanorum *vel* Pica Nigritum—the Disease of Dirt-Eating among Negroes..Angola Negroes, who are more particularly addicted to Dirt-Eating than any others. 1817 Williamson I 110 etc., The stomach evil, or dirt-eating. 1820 Thomson 44, Dirt-Eating. This is one of the most serious complaints connected with a deranged state of the stomach and digestive organs. The countenance and complexion become so changed, that the disease is obvious at first sight. *Ibid* 47, With adult negroes the most frequent cause of their being addicted to dirt-eating is the temporary relief given to the melancholy, attendant on the idea of their being under the influence of witchcraft.

DIRTY see DUTTY.

DIRTY BUNDLE /dóti bónggl/ sb dial; <*doti* +*bundle*. *BL*

1943 *GL* StJ, Dutty bungle, an untidy person.

DIRTY-FACE PARROT sb dial. One type of the PARROT fish.

1952 FGC StJ /dóti fles párat/.

DIRTY MOTHER see DUTTY MUMA.

DIRTY SHIRT sb dial joc. A BULLA cake; cf KHAKI PATCH.

1956 Mc StAnd /dóti shót/ another name for a bulla.

dis /dis, des/ adv dial; <*just*: cf Engl and US dial *jist, jest*. Just. *G*

1877 Murray *Kittle* 26, Mudfish say, 'Dis put me riber side make I smell riber water'. 1942 HPJ, Dis: Just (adv). 1956 Mc StAnd /mi des hafi ha di main/ *I'll just have to imagine it* or *dream of it*; StE /a dis kom/ *I've just arrived.*

DIS demonstr pron or adj dial; regularly reduced <*this*. This (one). *BA BL G*

DISAH see DIS-YA. *BL*

DISAYA, DIS-YA /dísaya, dís-yà, dísh-yà, dísa, désa/ demonstr adj or pron dial; <DIS (+A[8])+YA. This, this one. Equivalent in meaning to DIS but more archaic. *BL G*

1933 McK 316, Disayah, this here, this one. 1942 HPJ, Desha, A middle Jamaican form of *dis-ya*. 1942 Bennett 22, Nex' time me come a-tung, Dah Penny shelta me wi' stay Noh dis-yah berrin-grung. 1943 *GL* Tre, Disah, this. 1952 FGC StAnd /dish ya wan ya/ *this (-here) one here.* 1956 Mc StAnd /a dísaya mán mi en sí laas wíik/ *This is the man I met last week;* /dísaya píkini wósa han a húman/ *This child is worse than a woman.* Note: The pronunciation appears to be either /disaya wan/ or /disya/.

DISAYAH see prec.

DIS SIDE see SIDE.

DISTANT sb dial; prob <*distance*, the final /s/ being treated as plural inflection, and therefore omitted. Distance. *G*

1907 Jekyll 78, When they get to a distant. *Ibid* 155, mile an' distant, to the distance of a mile. 1952 FGC Han [Story:] /wíil man máil an dístan/.

DISTEMPER OF THE COUNTRY sb obs. A disease characteristic of a particular country; cf COUNTRY DISEASE.

1740 Importance 15 [They] get dry Belly-achs or Fevers; and then their Imprudence is termed the Distemper of the Country.

divel op /divél óp/ vb phr dial; by back-formation <*develop*, analysed as *devel up*. Cf *gel op*. To develop, grow; to grow back. *BL G*

1941 Kirkpatrick 50, Bulletin say it develinup into a large scale hattack. 1952 FGC StC /wín iz divélin op/ *The wind is rising, a strong wind is developing*; also StA 1959. 1960 *CLS* 154 /in sie, bíer óp, mi gúd tríi, bíer óp!..di tríi divélop/ *Bear up, my good tree, bear up!..The tree grew back.*

DIVE UP vb phr dial. To dive down and bring (something) up. *BA BL G*

1956 Mc Man /duoz pilikan daiv op di fish/ *Those pelicans dive for fish.*

DIVIDEN(-AN-FLABUB) sb dial; evid a var of *dipidens*: there may be some connection with *dividend*. Cf REMEDY.

1. A coconut RUNDOWN.

1943 *GL* Kgn, Dividen-an-flabub, cocoa Nut sauce.

2. See quot.

1958 DeC Port /devidént/ Whole bananas boiled in a rundown.

DIVI-DERI see DIBI-DERI.

DIVI-DIVI /díbidìbi/ sb; <Amer Sp *dividíve* (*dividivi, dibidibi*), applied to several spp of *Cæsalpinia*, ult Cariban (Cumanagoto); *OED* 1843→. The tree *Cæsalpinia coriaria* and its beans, valued in tanning.

1837 Macfadyen I 330, *Cæsalpinia coriaria. Divi-divi*, or *Libi-dibi*..This, like the *Coulteria tinctoria*, is a very valuable plant, and promises..to be of great advantage to the Island. 1854–5 *TJSA* I 62, Divi-divi. 1920 Fawcett 96, *C. coriaria*..Divi-divi, Libi-dibi..The pods are rich in tannin and are used by tanners for the same purposes as sumach.

DIVING DAPPER, DIVING HOPPER sb dial; evid reformed from *didapper*. The Least Grebe, *Colymbus dominicus*.

1952 FGC StM /daivin dapa/ like a /dil/; black, dives in ponds. *Ibid* StAnn /daivin hapa/—water bird, in ponds, dive suddenly. 1956 Jeffrey-Smith 135, They disappear at the slightest provocation, thus earning the local name of Diving Dapper.

di-ya see DA-YA.

DO /du/ vb[1] dial; <*do*, perform, make; sometimes combined with following pron—cf *dwiit*.

1. Trans. To move. *BA BL G*

1956 Mc Man [A woman, protesting that she had not

raised her arm, as a man claimed she had:] /a néva dú mi hàn sò at áa/ *I never put my arm up like that at all!*

2. To do harm to, cause trouble to, hurt.

1837 Sterne 19 [Him] say suppose we no speak, nothing will do we, we all will get clear. 1907 Jekyll 110, Make me nyam ahm, nothing goin' to do me voice. [*Let me eat them—it won't harm my voice.*] 1943 *GL* StJ, A wa dweem, what is wrong with him. 1956 Mc StAnd /mi wudn waan notn du dem at aal/ *I shouldn't like anything to happen to them*; /mi no min te yu se notn du mi/ *I didn't tell you that there was anything the matter with me.* 1958 DeC gen /wa du yu?/ *What's the matter with you?* /notn gwain du yu/ *Nothing is going to hurt you. BA BL G*

3. As the auxil of an imperative (cf *OED* 30 a, b), usually immediately preceding it, but sometimes with parenthetical elements between: I beg you! Please! (Or, Please do not!) (Rather more frequent and more emphatic in Jamaica than in Britain.) *BA BL G*

1863 Waddell 31, Missis, me beg you a lilly o'meal to make pap for my pickaninny, him sick. Do, my good Missis. 1924 Beckwith 154, De mare said, 'Do, you kyan' slip off dis rope off me head?' 1946 U.Newton I 36, 'Do Teacher! A won't dweet again' [*Please don't beat me!*]

4. In the phrase *do over*: to kill. Obs.

1790 Moreton 84, When the skeleton of a slave, who had been 'done over' [killed and buried secretly] in this manner..was found.

DO /du/ vb² dial; <*do*, auxil; evid from loss of *be* from *do be* and such phrases, and transf of its function to *do*. Cf *EDD*. *G*

1. = To be, in its simple forms. (Usually in the negative, and not emphatic.)

1942 HPJ, Don': Isn't; aren't..It don' good again, i.e. it is of no use now. 1956 Mc Man /shuu di daangki mek im duon liem/ *Shoe the donkey so that he won't be lame*; Man, But goatfish is a sweet fish /ríeli i dú mam/ *It is indeed ma'am.* 1957 JN Clar, Me did in the school, *I was in the school*; Clar, Why you don't eat it? Because it don't nice; StAnn, Don't it right mam? *Isn't that right ma'am?*

2. = To be, as an auxil. *G*

1956 Mc StE /a blóuz is dír fo yú da duon wash/ *There is a blouse of yours there that isn't washed* (or *has not been washed*). 1957 JN, I was to take cutlass but Sarah say you did gone, long time, I didn't bother. [*But Sarah said you were* (or *had*) *gone, long ago.*]

3. In the phr appended to a question, *don't it?*: Isn't that true? *G*

1958 DeC gen /duont it?/ an echo question which is invariable in form like French *n'est-ce pas?* /yu ben tu toun, duont it?/—/gad iz lov, duont it?/.

DOA-DOA see DOUGH-DOUGH.

DOAH, DOUGH conj dial. Spellings used in dialect writing for /duo/ the dial pronunc of *though*. *BL G*

1941 Kirkpatrick gloss, Dough, though. 1942 Bennett gloss, Doah: though.

DOCEY see DOLCE.

DOCK /dak/ vb and sb dial; <*dock* (*OED* v¹, sb² 7 *obs*).

A. vb: trans. To cut the hair, give a haircut; intr. To have the hair cut; (of the hair) to be cut.

1956 Mc Man /a wáan tu dák mi héd/ *I want to have my hair cut*; StE (Accom) /a klíin héd kyáan dák/ *A bald head can't be trimmed.*

B. sb: A haircut. *BL*

1943 *GL* Kgn, Dack, haircut. 1956 Mc Man /roun dak/ a man's haircut cut low round sides with brush in front.

DOCKER see DACAS.

DOCO sb dial uncom; cf. Ko *dyooko*, manioc.

1943 *GL* StC, Dōco, potato.

DOCTOR sb joc; cf *OED* 6b.

1. The sea-breeze which rises in mid-morning and blows landward with healthful effect.

1740 *Hist Ja* II 21, The people here give it [the sea-breeze] the name of Doctor, and truly it deserves the Title. 1777 *Jamaica* 11, Sweet doctor! waft me to some purling rill. [Note:] The sea breeze; so called from its salubrious effects. 1808 Stewart 20, He who resides near the ocean..is comforted and refreshed by the daily sea-breeze..the poor half-parched seaman hails it by the *healing* appellation of the *doctor*. 1959 FGC StAnd etc, still current, though perhaps less so than formerly.

2. An obeah-man: cf BUSH-DOCTOR.

DOCTOR BIRD /dakta bod, dakta bord/ sb chiefly dial; from the bird's dark plumage and from its habit of 'lancing' flowers with its long beak (either by entering the corolla or by piercing its base from the outside); among the folk there are also associations with obeah (cf DOCTOR 2), the bird being believed to have magic properties (cf quot 1952 below). *BA*

1. The tody (*Todus viridis*) or robin (erroneously taken by early writers to be a humming-bird). Obs.

1826 Williams 36, Here are several sorts of humming-birds, and the doctor-bird, or robin, having a green body with a red throat.

2. The humming-bird (of any type); in earlier use, esp of the MANGO HUMMING-BIRD.

1847 Gosse 89, The appellation by which the Mango Humming-bird is familiarly known to the negroes in the colony, is that of 'Doctor bird', which, however, is sometimes applied also to Polytmus [the Long-tailed humming-bird]. It is thus explained by Mr Hill:—'In the old time, when costume was more observed than now,—the black livery among the gayer and more brilliant Trochilidæ represented the Doctor. It might with equal propriety have been the parson; but parsons were less known than doctors, in the old times of the colony'. 1942 HPJ, The Aruacs regarded the Humming-bird as the incarnation of their dead warriors, and the name *God-bird* also applied to it, and the supernatural awe attaching to it suggests that the Indian belief has been taken up by the blacks in a modified form, and that 'doctor-bird' is 'medicine-man's bird'. 1952 FGC Port, Han /dakta bod a koni bod —haad bod fi ded/ *Doctor-bird is a clever bird—a bird hard to kill.* [These are the words of a widespread song; it sometimes alludes to the magic powers of the Maroons, associated with obeah.] Also StAnd, StAnn, StM, StT. 1956 Jeffrey-Smith 24–5, The Mango Humming Bird..is the largest, or 'Blackest Humming Bird' mentioned by Sloane, and probably owes its local name of doctor bird to this dark colouring. But the peasants will give you another reason. They say these birds 'medicine the plants'. They have observed them puncturing the blossoms.

DOCTOR BUCHANAN BUSH or **WEED** sb dial. A wild plant, unidentified.

1952 FGC Man /dakta búkanan wiid/; West /dakta bókanan bush/.

DOCTOR DICK sb dial; perh named after someone who introduced or developed this variety, or because it comes quickly to cure hunger.

1958 DeC Port /dakta dik/ the 'old-time' Lucea yam, which bears in only six months.

DOCTORESS, DOCTRESS sb obs; cf *OED doctress* 2. A woman put in charge of the sick slaves in a HOTHOUSE.

a 1818 Lewis (1845) 110, When I visited him the next morning, he bade the doctoress tell me that massa had sent him no soup the night before. 1823 Roughley 91, I shall first advert to the hothouse or hospital doctor or doctress, (as they are termed in Jamaica,) midwives, &c., a most fearful fraternity. 1839 McMahon 37, I had on three blisters at once, and an old woman, the hot-house doctress, was sent to dress them.

DOCTOR FISH sb; from the pair of sharp spines (likened to the doctor's lance) at the base of the tail.

1. An unidentified fish, or perh a misapplication of the name. (*OED* takes it to be the present-day fish of the family *Acanthuridae*, but the description is clearly of some other.)

a 1818 Lewis (1845) 52, One of the sailors took up a fish of a very singular shape and most brilliant colours..He had a large round transparent globule, intersected with red veins, under the belly, which some imagined to proceed from a rupture..But I could not discover any vestige of a wound; and the globule was quite solid to the touch; neither did the fish appear to be sensible when it was pressed upon..Its name is the 'Doctor Fish'.

2. Fish of the genus *Teuthis* (or *Acanthurus*), esp *T. hepatus* (also called BLACK DOCTOR-FISH). *T. coeruleus* is the BLUE DOCTOR-FISH. *N*

1756 Browne 454, Teuthis 1..The Doctor..ad caudam lanceolâ mobili armatum. 1854–5 *TJSA* I 143, Acanthurus chirurgus—Doctor Fish. 1892 Cockrell list, Doctor fish, *Teuthis hepatus, T. coeruleus.* 1952 Smith in *NHN* 10–11, Family *Teuthidae.* This is the family of the doctor-fishes.

DOCTOR JOHN sb dial. A medicinal plant. See quots.

1927 Beckwith 16, Doctor John. Croton Wilsoni Grisebach..'The strongest of all the weeds,—it works with "Yellow-senda"'. 1954 *WIMJ* 29, *Croton wilsonii Gr.*. Pepper Rod; Doctor John; ?John Charles or Charlie.

DOCTOR LONG sb; prob for a physician by this name who successfully used the plant in medicine: see NEPHRITIC TREE, BREAD-AND-CHEESE. *Pithecellobium unguis-cati*; see quots.

1811 Titford Expl to plate IX 6, Nephritick Tree, or Cat's Claw (*Mimosa Unguiscati*)..a long scarlet pod, with black seeds, kidney-shaped and half surrounded with a white poppy down substance, which the negroes resemble to the fat surrounding the kidney..Browne calls it the Black Bead shrub..It is also called Doctor Long. 1942 *NHN* I 6 11, Bread-and-Cheese or Doctor Long (*Pithecolobium unguis-cati*) which is used for hedges.

DOCTOR MAN sb obs. A male hospital attendant; cf DOCTORESS.

1863 Waddell 113 (year 1836), Two were carpenters, one a blacksmith, one a head-constable, and one a 'doctor man', or hospital attendant.

DOCTOR McKATTY = MCKATTY BUSH.

DOCTOR PLAY sb obs?

A sort of dramatic performance, in origin an English mummers' play, formerly practised during Christmas holidays in which a Doctor, a stock character, brought back to life a supposedly dead warrior, king, lady, or the like. He was regularly represented as deaf, blind, or himself in need of medical attention. (See 1923 Beckwith 12–17; cf also E. K. Chambers, *English Folk Play* 8, 50 ff.)

1929 Beckwith 197, At evening in the big empty hall [Harmony Hall, below Accompong] the black overseer impersonating the 'play-acting' dialogue of an old 'doctor play'.

DOCTOR'S GUM sb. Prob an error for HOG-DOCTOR (TREE) 2.

1864 Grisebach 784, Gum, doctor's: Rhus Metopium.

DOCTOR SHOP sb now dial; for *doctor's shop.* A dispensary, chemist's shop, or druggist's. *BA BL G*

1775 *Gazette* 25 March, A store house, hot house and Doctor's shop. [1812 Williamson I 284, Though the most effectual remedy consists in change of air, people will not have recourse to it, in place of getting to town.. where..old women's nostrums [are] administered, and the doctor's shop absurdly resorted to.] 1893 Sullivan 123, At most 'doctor shops' (chemists). 1947 U.Newton III 25, And the crowds going down to the 'Doctor Shop' to see the Christmas Tree with 'Doctor' Fraser, the Dispenser. 1952 FGC Han /bai hiiling hail at dakta shap/ *Buy healing-oil from doctor-shop*; StC, oil from doctor-shop to cure pain in ears.

DOCTOR-SHOP KNIFE sb dial; <DOCTOR SHOP + *knife.* =CHEMIST BILL.

1959 LeP remembered.

DOCTOR TREE sb; evid an abbr of HOG-DOCTOR TREE.

1926 Fawcett 9.

DOCTOR WOMAN sb dial obs? =DOCTORESS.

1837 James 18, There was no doctor woman, nor any woman whatever to attend to the sick people.

DOCTRESS see DOCTORESS.

DODGE /daj/ vb dial; <*dodge* vb (cf *OED* 1).

1. intr. To hide or secrete oneself, esp so as to watch somebody else while being unseen oneself. *BA BL G*

1924 Beckwith 3, Anansi go to a grass-root an' dodge. *Ibid* 58, Tiger went in de day and dodge in de ground. 1943 *GL* Kgn, Dadge, hide.

2. trans. To hide from (someone) so as to observe his actions. *BL G T*

1924 Beckwith 19, And the two go back from Nanci yard and just dodge him now and hear his wife call. *Ibid* 61, So one day when Fowl go out, he go half way an' put down de plant an' dodge him.

3. trans. To hide (an object). *G*

1952 FGC StAnn /evriting im fain, i daj i/ *Everything he finds, he hides.* 1960 BLB 7 /koni de daj ing fies/ *Cunny is hiding his face.*

DODGING-QUAIL sb dial; cf DODGE. Prob the GRASS-DODGER. (The head is striped somewhat like that of a quail.)

1952 FGC StAnd /dájin kwíel—likl wan—daj aal in-a graas/. 'Quail' are larger and can whistle.

DODO see DOUGH-DOUGH.

DO-FE-DO see *du-fi-du.*

DOG-BITTER sb dial; for *dog's bitter* (cf *OED bitter sb*[1] 2). A wild plant (*Pluchea purpurascens*) considered a good 'bitter', or stomachic medicine.

1952 FGC StT /dáag-bíta/—same as wild-tobacco.

DOG-BLINE-ME sb dial slang; evid a euphemism for *Gorblimey* (cf *ODS*, which shows that the word has been applied to various garments). Cf also G-B. *BA*

1943 *GL* StM, Dog bline me, ankle boots with buckles.

DOG BLOOD[1] sb dial; for *dog's blood.* A TEA-BUSH (*Rivina humilis*) that bears small, very bright red berries that look like drops of blood. Also called JUBA BUSH—and see quots.

1952 FGC StAnn, Dog-blood, Fall-down bush, timi-timi—for bruises and drink as tea; StM, has a red stem, small white flowers. 1955 *WIMJ* 160, *Rivina humilis*.. Dog Blood; Bloodberry.

DOG BLOOD[2], **DOG LIVER** sb dial; for *dog's*+*blood* or *liver*. A variety of sweet-potato named for the colour of its flesh.

1952 FGC StAnn /dág blód/ sweet-potato, very red, bears well; StC /dáag líva/ sweet-potato, red inside.

DOG-CALL sb obs?; cf DOG-DRIVER. Sense uncert: A call such as might be used for dogs, either a particular device (such as a horn or whistle), or a particular way of blowing with a horn, whistle, or the like. See quot. (A nick-name for a bosun's whistle?)

1833 Scott I 197, As we drove up to the door, the overseer began to bawl, 'Boys, boys!' and kept blowing a dog-call. All servants in the country in the West Indies, be they as old as Methuselah, are called boys.

DOG CORN-PIECE sb dial; for *dog's corn-piece.* Usually in phr 'To be in-a dog corn-piece', a dangerous place, an uncomfortable situation, since the owner (dog) is a watchman and one is liable to be taken for a thief. See quots.

1910 Anderson-Cundall 9, You get in a darg corn-piece. 'Darg corn-piece' is said to be a corruption of 'quandary'. [This is most unlikely.] 1925 Beckwith 125, You get in a darg corn-piece..'into a dog's corn-field'; i.e. into serious difficulty. 1943 *GL* Clar, Darg Carn-Piece, quandary. 1955 FGC Man, In-a dog corn-piece, in trouble.

DOG DEAD phr dial; for *the dog died* or *is dead.* See quot. There may be an allusion to the well-known story 'The dog died' in which this statement leads to the revelation of a whole series of troubles. *BA*

1943 *GL* StM, Darg ded, hard luck.

DOG-DRIVER /dáag-dráiba, dág-dráiva/ sb dial; *dog*+*driver* or DRIVER.

1. The manager (or sometimes another officer) on a sugar-estate. The term implies that he treats the labourers under him like dogs. (Cf *OED dog sb* 3a.)

1793 Mathews. 1956 Mc StT (Serge Is) /dáag dráiva/ manager of the estate.

2. A policeman. This is a strongly derisive term, sneering at the policeman because he must drive away stray dogs.

1912 McK *Ballads* gloss, Dog-driver: nickname for a policeman. 1943 *GL* Port, StC, etc, Dawg driber, dog driver, police. 1952 FGC Han /dág dráiva/ district constable. A 'dog' is a man who gets into trouble, especially with women. 1956 Mc Man /dáag draiva/—The term is one of abuse in Burnt Ground—produced with giggling and the comment that you'd probably be jugged for using it!

doge see *dogi*.

DOG-FLEA WEED sb dial.

1953 *WIMJ* 243, *Parthenium hysterophorus* L. Wild Wormwood; Dog-flea Weed; Whitehead; Mugwort; Bastard Feverfew..Country people use it to prepare a decoction for colds and to make a bath for fleas on dogs.

DOG-GRASS sb dial. A plant (the sugar-cane top?) eaten by dogs as a remedy: see quot. Cf also DOG'S-TAIL GRASS.

1774 Long II 552, Even the dogs in this island..are not less fond of sugar. I have known a well-fed animal of this species, who was commonly dieted from a plentiful table, and never tasted carrion by way of *bon bouche* without suffering severely for it; on these occasions he used a quantity of what is here called *dog-grass*, sufficient either to make him disgorge, or compose, his stomach, probably, by the fixed air contained in that plant.

dogi, dogi-dogi /dógi, dóge/ adj and, by absol use, sb dial; cf Bambara *dogo*, small, short (Turner 77), and Gã *atɛkɛ́*, short, Twi *atɛkɛ́*, a short-legged fowl. Cf *dege* adj 2.

A. adj: 1. Short, small.

1943 *GL* StJ, Duggi, short, little; StJ, Duggie-duggie, short and clumsy. 1956 Mc Clar /dogi/ little and low; Port /doge, dogi/ short, small.

2. In cpds: *dogi man*, *dogi fut* and esp *dogi hen*, *dogi foul*. See as separate entries.

B. sb: 1. A short, stocky person.

1954 LeP Man /dogi/ short, thickly built person. 1955 FGC Man /dógi/ dogi man, short.

2. A short-legged variety of chicken.

1943 *GL* Kgn, Duggy, a small hen; Tre, Duggi, a small kind of fowl. 1956 Mc StAnd /dógi/ a small hen.

dogi foul sb dial; <*dogi* A 2+*fowl*. =*dogi hen*.

1952 FGC StAnd /dógi foul/ have short foot, low to ground. 1956 Mc Clar, StT /dogi foul/.

dogi fut sb or adj dial (for *dogi-footed*); <*dogi* A 2+FOOT.

1942 HPJ, Ducky-foot: short legged. [Cf *dogi hen*.]

dogi hen sb dial; <*dogi* A 2+*hen*. The forms with *ducky* show folk-etym by assoc of the chicken with ducks, which are comparatively short-legged, low to the ground, and clumsy in walking.

1912 McK *Ballads* 30, Ducky hen, Note: a small short-legged variety of hen. 1942 HPJ, Ducky-hen.

dogi man sb dial; cf *dogi* A 2.

1956 Mc StE, StT /dógi man/ a short person.

DOG LIVER see DOG BLOOD[2].

DOG MUMA sb chiefly dial; for *dog's*+MUMA. A children's game in which a big girl, chosen as 'Muma', has a set dialogue with the others, at the end of which they insult her (see quot) and run away; she catches one and beats her thoroughly. Another Muma is chosen and the game continues.

1960 May Jeffrey-Smith, *Letter* [End of the dialogue:] M. Who taught you dat manners? Ch. Dog Mumma. M. Who is Dog Mumma? Ch. YOU!

DO-GOOD (MAN) /dúgúd, dúgúdz, dúugúd man/ sb dial; <*do*+*good* sb+*man*. An OBEAH-MAN, alluding to his supposed powers of healing. Cf MYAL MAN.

1942 Bennett 20, Me had fe get two do-good man Ef yuh wen hear de ghose bawl wen dem ketch him Yuh hooda swear is rat eena de pan. 1943 *GL* StC, Dugud, obeah man; Tre, Dugudman, Obeiahman. 1954 LeP StE, StT, Man who professes to kill or heal by magic, Do-good-man, Du gud man. 1956 Mc StAnd (Bellevue) /dúgudzman/; StT /dúgud man/. 1958 DeC StAnd (Red Light) /duu-gud; duu-gud man/ Obeah man.

DOG SENNA sb; cf *OED dog sb* 18d.

1953 *WIMJ* 239, *Cassia obovata* Collad. Jamaica Senna; Port Royal, Dog..(etc.) Senna..This senna is still said to be used here as a substitute for the official sennas.

DOG'S TAIL sb dial.

1953 *WIMJ* 238, *Heliotropium parviflorum* L. Wild Clary; Dog's Tail; Sage.

DOG'S-TAIL GRASS sb bot; cf *DA* 1857→ for *Eleusine indica*. The grass *Leptochloa virgata* (Griseb.).

1814 Lunan I 266, Dog's-Tail Grass. Cynosurus..This name is derived from two Greek words signifying dog's-tail, which the grass resembles.

DOG'S-TONGUE, DOG-TONGUE[1] sb; from the shape of the leaf.

1. The wild plant *Pseudelephantopus spicatus.*

1936 Fawcett 165, *P. spicatus*..Dog's Tongue. 1952 FGC Han, StC /dag-tong/iron-weed. 1955 *WIMJ* 160, Iron Weed; Packy weed; Dog's Tongue.

2. The wild plant *Sansevieria.*

1952 FGC West /daag-tong/.

DOG'S-TOOTH GRASS sb bot; a transl of the Genus name: *Cynodon.* (Not specifically Jamaican.)

1953 *WIMJ* 246, *Cynodon dactylon Pers.* Bahama or Bermuda Grass; Dog's Tooth Grass. In some parts of the Island, at least, a tea made by boiling the roots is thought to be good for the kidneys.

DOG-TAIL PEPPER sb dial. A variety of capsicum pepper, thought to resemble a dog's tail.

1954 *FG* 469, Pepper..Dog Tail. Long (about 3 in.), not very stout, terminating in a blunt-pointed end, very pungent, very red when ripe.

DOG-TEETH SNAPPER, DOG-TOOTH SNAPPER /dáag-tíit/ sb dial; from its having teeth like those of dogs. A variety of the snapper fish, variously identified with others, the same or similar: see quots. s BAD-BOTTOM~.

1854–5 *TJSA* I 142, Messoprion cynodon—dog-tooth snapper. 1892 Cockrell, School-master snapper, black snapper, butt snapper, dogteeth snapper—*Lutjanus jocu.* 1952 FGC Port, StM /dáag-tíit snapa/ = old-shoe; StJ = /manggro-said snapa/; StC = /sha-shwa, hevi-led, silk, satn snapa/.

DOG-TONGUE[1] see CONSUMPTION BUSH, DOG'S-TONGUE.

DOG-TONGUE[2] sb dial; from its shape.

1958 DeC StT /dag-tong/ a creased spinner dumpling; = COW-TONGUE.

DOGWOOD (TREE) sb also attrib; < *dog-wood,* prob from the resemblance of this tree when in bloom to European dogwoods (perh also in part from the use of a decoction of the bark to rid dogs of mange).

In Jamaica: trees of two related genera: 1. *Piscidia piscipula* and 2. *Lonchocarpus latifolius.* See also BITCHWOOD, POISON DOGWOOD.

1. 1696 Sloane 143–4, Coral arbor polyphylla..A kind of Wood with which the Indians take their Fish..Dogg-wood Tree. In Insulæ Jamaicæ sylvis campestribus ubique crescit. 1740 Importance 51, Dog-wood is red, black, blue, and other Colours; it is a beautiful heavy Wood. The Bark of this Tree cures Dogs of the Mange. 1754 Browne 296–7, Dog-wood. 1837 Macfadyen 258, Piscidia Erythrina. Common Dogwood. 1920 Fawcett 84, *P. piscipula*..Dogwood..The whole tree, but especially the bark of the roots, contains *piscidin,* which is sedative and hypnotic..The pounded bark is thrown into streams to intoxicate fish. 1952 FGC StAnd, StAnn, StE, StM, StT /dáagwúd/—for fence posts; to poison fishes.

2. 1920 Fawcett 81, *L. latifolius*..Dogwood.

DOH see *duo.*

dok, dokun sb dial; abbr of *dokunu.*

1958 DeC Port (Moore Town) /dok/ Short for /dokun/ variant of /dokunu/ (in this community roasted rather than boiled).

dokantiil /dòkantíil/ sb dial; < *duck + and + teal*: the names of two birds combined as one—cf *duckinmallard DAE* 1806, 1923, 'An old name' reported from NY, NC, Fla. By folk-etym the word may now sometimes be thought of as *duckin' + teal.* The general name for wild birds of the type of ducks and teal: prob, from its commonness, the Blue-winged Teal, as well as similar ducks.

[1790 Beckford I 321, The sportsman now pursues the duck and teal, the snipes, the pigeons. 1873 Rampini 164, Duck and teal came to us from the neighbouring ponds.] 1952 FGC Han, Man /dòkantíil/ looks like duck; StAnn, One kind of bird, not two; also StC, StJ, StT.

dokun see *dok.*

dokunu /dókunu, dúkunu, dúkuno/ sb chiefly dial; 1740 1934 duckano, 1868 duckonoo, 1893→ duckoonoo, 1907 duckanoo, 1929 duckunoo, 1943 duccunu, 1954 dukunoo; < Twi *ɔ-dɔ̀kono,* boiled maize bread.

A kind of pudding made of some 'starch' food (plantain, green banana, cassava flour, esp corn meal) sweetened, spiced, traditionally wrapped in plantain or banana leaf, and boiled (in some localities baked or roasted): a favourite peasant dish. Also called BLUE DRAWERS, BOYO, TIE-A-LEAF; cf also MUSA. *BL,* Haiti (JH).

1740 Importance 29, The Fruit [of the Plantain]..when boil'd in its Leaves..is called *Duckano* (*i.e.* Pudding or Dumpling). 1868 Russell 6, Duckonoo—Corn boiled in balls, and then toasted. African. 1893 Sullivan 87, Cornmeal Duckoonoo..A cupful of cornmeal boiled thick with some butter..sugar..flour and a little spice. Let it cool. Then roll up in bits of plantain leaf and bake. 1929 Baillie 5, Duckunoo of green banana. 1943 *GL* Port, Duckoonoo, roasted pudding; Tre, Duccunu, a mixture of cornmeal, sugar and bananas boiled. 1952 FGC Port, StAnn, StC, StJ, StM, West /dokunu/; StJ, StM /dukunu/; StJ, Made with coco or coco head. 1956 Mc Port /dukunu/ Grated sweet-potato or corn, cornmeal, and coconut milk, cooked in a leaf in a pot; StAnd, Ground potato, yam, banana as well as flour may be used /biek intu a pat, a dochi/ harder than pone; StE, Dumpling made from /kisáada/ flour.

DOKUNU MANGO sb dial; < *dokunu + mango.* A variety of mango that resembles the dokunu? Or, as HPJ suggests, an allusion to the DOKUNU TREE.

1907 Jekyll 110, Then Blacksmit' say:—'Min' mustn' eat no duckanoo nor guava by the way, else you voice turn rough again'. Tiger gone making his way..As he get halfway he see guava an' duckanoo, an' being him so thirsty he say:—'Make me nyam ahm, nothing going to do me voice'. *Ibid* 113 [Note:] Duckanoo, a kind of mango. 1942 HPJ, Duckanoo Tree—A fabulous tree on which duckanoos are supposed to grow. Jekyll says that there is a duckanoo Mango; but this seems to be a mistake.

DOKUNU TREE sb; < *dokunu + tree.* An imaginary tree that bears dokunus; it figures in certain ANANCY STORIES.

1924 Beckwith 31, Den was a hard time. Anansi had a Duckano tree had some Duckano on it..Tacoomah..pick off all, lef' one. 1934 Williams 36, The fabulous duckano or dumpling-tree which is so frequently met with in Jamaica Anansi stories is derived directly from the Ashanti word dokono, boiled maize-bread.

DOLCE /duosi, dosi/ sb; 1893→ dolce, 1894 dosey, 1943 docey; < Pg *doce,* sweetmeat. The *l* is not and prob has never been pronounced in Jamaican use; in spelling it prob is due to infl of Sp *dulce,* cognate with the Pg word.

1. A preserve made from fruits (usually guava, but sometimes mango or others) boiled down

with sugar and strained: when cold it solidifies to a jelly-like consistency. Cf GUAVA CHEESE.

1893 Sullivan 67. Dolce. (Recipe given.) 1894 Spinner 82, The delicious guava 'dosey'. 1927 Stafford 6, Grenadilla and orange and guava For dolces and rose-marmalade. 1942 HPJ, Dolce: (pr dō-sie). 1943 *GL* Tre, Docey, a soft sweet made from the pulp of the guava fruit. 1952 FGC StJ, StM, StT /dúosi/. 1957 *FFM* 276, Jew-plum Dolce..(Recipe given).

2. Transf to various other sweet concoctions: see quots. Cf also *dozi*.

1943 *GL* Tre, Dulsi, a cake made of plenty ginger and sugar. 1952 FGC Tre /dósi/ grater cake.

DOLLY BASKET sb dial; for *dolly's basket*. Plants of *Aristolochia* species, so called from the shape of the seed pod, which opens and hangs like a diminutive basket.

1959 UCWI Herbarium.

DOLLY POT sb dial. A mess cooked by children in play. *G*

1957 *FFM* 100, Children..make 'dolly pots' with any material within their reach.

dolo sb dial; etym unknown.

1958 DeC StT /dolo/ a coconut run-down.

DOMINO BIRD sb; <*domino*, a half mask (cf *OED* 1 b). See quot.

1956 Jeffrey-Smith 87, The Maryland Yellow-Throat (*Geothlypis trichas*) is very inconspicuous compared with the last-named..The male, however, has a most distinctive broad, black mask separated by a tiny light-coloured band, hardly noticeable in the field. This bird is very appropriately named the Domino Bird.

domp sb dial; abbr of *dumpling*.

1958 DeC StC /domp/ short for dumpling.

dompumuot see DONE-PROMOTE.

DONE /don/ adv dial; <*done*, reduced from some such phr as *and am* (or other part of the verb *be*) *done*. Cf GONE. Placed after a verb (and its object or objects, if any), usually concluding the clause, and indicating the completion of the action expressed by the verb: completely, altogether. *BA BL G N*

1839 McMahon 58, We pray to God to take poor nega, before Buckra kill him done. 1877 Murray *Feedin' 'Perrit* 9, When him drink done, him fling de bottle in a sea. 1905 Dodd 48, Yes, sah, me feed him dun dis long time. 1942 Bennett 42, Teng Gad we sell off dun. [*Thank God we've sold everything off*.] 1956 Mc StE (Accom) /chó man, íit dón!/ *Cho, man! Finish eating!*

DONE /don/ vb dial; <*be done* (or the older *have done*). Cf *OED do* 17. An imperative expression referring to an action that another is engaged in: Stop (doing that)! *BA BL G*

1957 EB Port /don/ imperative, Stop!

DONE-PROMOTE /dómpumùot/ sb dial joc slang; perh from some such ambivalent statement, by someone looking at the sandals, as 'I see you done-promote (have been promoted)!' Sandals made from worn-out automobile tyres. Also called POWER shoes, etc.

1943 *GL* Clar, Dunpromote, powa (sandals). 1956 Mc Clar /dóm pu muot kot a taya—samplata kot a leda/ *Done-promotes are cut from tyres—samplatters are cut from leather*.

dong /dong/ adv dial; <*down*. A common pronunc of *down* in written dialect often sp *dung*. (See Introd, Phonology.) *T*

1942 Bennett gloss, *Dung*: down; *Dunga*: down at.

dong-an-tek sb dial; for *down and take*. A children's game similar to PEE-GEE.

1958 JC StC.

donggl /donggl, donggil/ sb dial; <*dunghill*.

1. A dunghill; *The Dungle* is a local name for a section of West Kingston where there was a rubbish heap—cleared away in 1940.

2. See quot. *BL*

1958 DeC StT /donggl/ rubbish, trash.

3. Attrib use of prec.

1956 Mc [Prov:] /meni a buon yu sii a donggil hiip kom aafa gud man tiebl/.

donjin sb dial; prob var of *donggl*, dunghill, but evid also assim to *dungeon*.

1956 Mc Man /donjin/ rubbish or manure heap. Also place where sweepings from street or market are put.

DONKEY /dángki, dáangki/ sb dial; <*donkey*.

1. Attrib in various senses closely related to the standard one, sometimes with the suggestion of something less than the best; also as a euphemism for jackass. See separate entries below.

2. A breadfruit; cf also JACKASS.

1956 Mc StAnd (Dallas) /dáangki/ breadfruit. 1957 EB Port, same.

DONKEY BLIND sb dial or slang; <*donkey* + BLIND sb 3; a derisive term. See quot.

1956 Mc StAnd /dáangki bláin/ a district police officer, so called because of his badge.

DONKEY BREADNUT sb dial; <DONKEY 1 + BREADNUT. A weed fed to rabbits; 'breadnut' alludes to the use of the leaves of this tree as feed for cattle: 'donkey' implies that it is not real breadnut.

1952 FGC Tre /dángki brénàt/ collard—feed rabbit.

DONKEY-EYE sb dial; from the appearance of the seed. = HORSE-EYE BEAN, the seed of *Mucuna sloanei* and prob also *M. urens*.

1952 FGC StAnn /dángki hái/ grows on vine, four in pod.

DONKEY MILK see DONKEY('S) MILK.

DONKEY PRICE sb dial; for *donkey's price*. A price that only a stupid person would pay: see quot. *G*

1958 DeC gen /dangki prais/ an exorbitant price /a no mi a touris; no bada gi mi no dangki prais/—a good phrase for use in the market.

DONKEY-RIDE sb. A pick-a-back ride: carrying a child on one's shoulders and back. *G*

1952 FGC StM, Donkey-ride, pickaback.

DONKEY-ROPE sb dial. Tobacco leaves wound together to form a 'rope' ($\frac{1}{2}$–1 in. diam), which is coiled for carrying; at market the amount sold is cut off as a single piece. (Often a euphemism for JACKASS ROPE.)

1927 Stafford 14, The men with 'donkey-rope' their pipes re-light. 1952 FGC StAnd, StT /dángki rúop/ tobacco.

DONKEY('S) MILK sb dial; evid so named for its white, milky juice. A bush or small tree *Stylosanthes hamata*, which has a milky juice; = DONKEY WEED 2.

1952 FGC StAnn /dangki milk/ always chop out of pasture; will take off warts.

DONKEY WEED sb dial.

1. An unidentified plant.

1952 FGC StAnn. 1955 FGC Man /dángki wíid/ runs on the ground, looks like thyme, good for tea.

2. = DONKEY('S) MILK.

1954 *WIMJ* 18, *Stylosanthes hamata Taub.* Donkey Weed; Pencil Flower; Lady's Fingers; Cheesy Toes.

DON PATINHO'S MONEY sb obs; < Pg *patinho* a simpleton, a stupid fellow. See quot.

1740 Importance 69, Great Quantities of Spanish Coin have been returned from this Island, the Planters not reserving a Bit for their own Use, except Pistorines, nick-nam'd by them Don Patinho's Money.

DON'T-CARE /dóng-kya/ sb and adj dial; < *don't care. BA G*

A. sb: Carelessness; indifference; irresponsibility; irresponsible lavishness.

1910 Anderson-Cundall 16, Don't kyar keep big house. [*Incautious spending keeps a large house.*] 1913 McK *Ballads* 84, Don't-care: nonchalance; indifference; *ibid* 37, When I think of our oppressors Wid mixed hatred an' don'-care. 1942 HPJ, Don' ca'—don't care (i) Indifference; lack of interest.

B. adj: Indifferent, careless. *T*

1912 McK *Ballads* 84, Don't-care: Inattentive; *ibid* 13, But seems unno don'-ca', Won't mek up you' min' fe larn. 1942 HPJ, Don' ca'—don't care..(ii) adjectivally; indifferent, careless.

DON'T IS phr dial; < DO vb² 2 + *not* + *is*. (An *it* has evid been lost before *is*.) Isn't it?

1952 FGC StM /duont iz somting laik dat/ *Isn't it something like that?*

DOOBA prep or adv dial; prob for DE¹ + *over*.

1943 *GL* Tre, Dooba, over.

DOODLE-DOO sb obs; cf *ODS doodle-doo*, 'Playful shortening of Cock-a-doodle-doo', but the application in the name of this plant is not clear, unless the spur-like prickles are alluded to. Cf COCKSPUR. (Also in Virgin and Windward Is.) BARBADOS PRIDE. (*Caesalpinia pulcherrima.*)

a 1726 Barham (1794) 10, The Barbados flower fence, 'commonly called in Jamaica *doodledoes*'. (HPJ; also 1814 Lunan I 51.) 1873 Rampini 155, The roads were bordered with a flower-fence of Barbadoes pride (*Poinciana pulcherrima*), or in negro idiom, 'doodle-doo'.

DOOL /duul/ vb dial; var of DUDE.

1943 *GL* StC, Dool, to dress up.

DOOMA see *duma*.

DOOR-MOUTH /dúo-móut/ sb dial; for *door's-mouth*. A loan-translation, or re-use in English of an African metaphor: cf Yoruba *iloro enu*, threshold (lit, porch mouth); Hausa *baki*, a mouth, an opening, an entrance, etc. (Cf J. H. Greenberg *Ess. in Linguistics* 70.) A doorway, or the place just outside the doorway of a small house or hut. See quot 1942. Cf also ADUO. *BL G*; *SC doro-móto*

1864 Russell 5, Doe-mout, Threshold. 1873 Rampini 121, Then Annancy took his spurs and stuck them into Tiger's side, till he drove him right up to de lady's door-mouth. 1907 Jekyll 77, Door-mouth includes not only the opening, but also the whole space just outside the door. 1942 Astley Clerk in HPJ, Doa-mout: The Jamaica peasantry sit more on the *last tread* of the outside step *leading up*, than on the door mouth itself. I think our qualification for this use should be remembered. 1952 FGC Han, The boys running away from the Three-foot Horse 'ran to the house door-mouth, got into the house'.

DOORPEEP sb obs; < *door-peep*. A fanciful creation offered as the source of DUPPY (quite without basis).

1895 Banbury 27, The word *duppy* appears to be a corruption of *doorpeep* (something peering through the keyhole). Duppies are ghosts.

DOOSE sb dial rare; etym uncert: perh conn with *dude*—cf DUUDA.

1943 *GL* Clar, Doose, a walking stick.

dopi see DUPPY.

dorty see DUTTY.

dos see DUST.

DOSEY, dosi see DOLCE.

dosi, dosing dial pronuncs for *dusky*, *dusking*.

1958 DeC StC /i dosi out nou—i dosing op/ *It's getting dark (outside).*

DOTED adj dial rare; cf *OED* 1 →1728. *BL*

1943 *GL* StAnn, Doted, foolish.

doti see DUTTY.

DOUBLE BILL sb dial; < *double* + BILL sb.

1954 LeP StE (Elderslie), Double bill, double edged machete.

DOUBLOON sb now dial and arch; cf *OED*. A guinea. Cf also DUB. s CURRENCY

[1942 HPJ, Dubbleloon: A doubloon, or Spanish coin once used in Jamaica. 'Quattie buy trubble, an dubbleloon cyant clear it', a saying Marion [a servant] had from her grandmother—but Marion did not know what a Doubloon was.] 1943 *GL* Clar, StT, Dub-blune, One guinea.

DOUGH see DOAH.

DOUGH-BOY /dúo-bwài/ sb dial; cf *OED* →1887 '*Naut.* and *Colonial*', *DA* →1843. *G*

1959 DeC StJ /duo-bwai/ general name for any kind of dumpling.

DOUGH-DOUGH /dúoduo, dúodo, dódo/ sb dial; iterative < *dough*.

1. Dough, esp in its soft, unbaked state.

1943 *GL* StJ, Dodo, dough. 1956 Mc Man, StAnd /dúodo/ dough before baking.

2. Insufficiently baked, hence doughy, bread-stuff or cake.

1957 EB Port /duodo/ Noun. Pastry or cakes improperly baked. No other meanings known in Port Antonio area.

3. Bread.

1956 LeP Kgn, Man, dou-dou, doa-doa, bread.

4. A kind of sweet cake. Cf TOTO.

1942 HPJ, Dodo: A kind of cake made from flour, sugar, and a good deal of soda. Some people say that *dodo* used to be made into the shape of some four-legged animals, others that it was 'ginger-cake' and always contained ginger. But the application of the term *dodo* seems to vary from place to place..Ina [a servant] said that the word was definitely *dough* (which she described) and that it had no connection with *toto*. 1959 DeC Han, West /duo-duo/ a sweet cake baked of flour, sugar, soda, coconut milk.

5. A round bread-roll made from left-over dough.

1956 Mc Clar /duo-do/ Noun. Little round rolls made from pieces of dough left over from bread-baking. 1958 DeC Port /dodo/ a roll made of yeast dough scraped from the trough after making bread.

6. A dumpling: see quots.

1958 DeC StT /dodo/ a spherical boiled dumpling, one inch in diameter; Tre, a spinner dumpling; StJ, a boiled dumpling like a spinner but much longer (12–18 in.), coiled up before boiling.

DO UP /du op/ vb phr dial.

1956 Mc Man /im du op imself/ he dirties his pants (by evacuation).

DOUTEN /dóutn/ prep dial; aphetic form of */widóutn/ < *without* + *-n* suffix[1].

1912 McK *Ballads* 70, Yet you dih-ya 'douten use. [*Yet you are there without any use.*]

DOVE /dov/ sb dial; < *dove* sb. An officer in a revivalist cult who coos like a dove during ceremonies.

1942 HPJ, A revivalist performer (girl?) making a cooing noise. 1953 Moore 112–13, Dove, queen dove—One of the officers of a Revival ceremony. c 1954 Reckord *Della* typescript 21, Then a beautifully-wailed note..signals the entrance of the white-dove.

DOVE-WOOD sb; cf *OED* no quot. The tree *Alchornea latifolia* and its wood.

1864 Grisebach 783, Dove-wood: *Alchornea latifolia*. 1920 Fawcett 296, Dove Wood. 1941 *NHN* I 3 9, Other species that occur at this altitude are..Dove wood. 1954 *WIMJ* 157, Loblob; Dove Wood; Jimmy Wood.

DOWN adj. In spate; cf COME DOWN 2. *G*

1860 Trollope 29, One hears that this river or that river is 'down', whereby it is signified that the waters are swollen.

DOWN /doun, dong/ prep dial; for *down at*. (Also in London vulgar speech. LeP.) At, down at. *G*

1957 JN Clar, Mrs Rickman, down Trout Hall, mam; StE, Tree a we de here wid we father but one down Mountainside live wid Missa Rogers. [*Three of us are here with our father but one at Mountainside lives with Mr R.*].

DOWN-COTTON sb dial; < *down* sb + *cotton*. A small wild shrub somewhat resembling the cotton bush and producing a kind of down. (*Hibiscus*, perh *H. clypeatus* or *H. pilosus*.)

1952 FGC Tre /dong katn/ has pale yellow flower. [= Han informant's WILD MAHOE.]

DOWN TO conj phr dial; cf current Engl colloq. Even including. (The sense is as if one had gone through a list *down to* the last, and even unexpected, items.) Cf AN' ALL. *BA BL G*

1943 Bennett 33, Plenty tings fe eat..—dung to ice deh yah. [*Plenty of things to eat..—even ice is here.*]

DOWN TREE sb; cf *OED*, listed without quot. The tree *Ochroma pyramidale*, named for the downy fibres it produces. See quot 1926.

1740 Importance 54, The Down Tree is like it. 1774 Long III 737, The down-tree is another species [of *Bombax*]..They are found at Oake's plantation in Clarendon, on the banks of the river Pindar, and some other parts. 1873 Rampini 61, The air was filled as with a mist with the floating flakes of the 'down' tree. [Chapelton.] 1926 Fawcett 152–4, Ochroma pyramidale..Cork-wood, Down Tree, Bombast Mahoe, Balsa-wood (of continental America). Common in the lower mountains..*Capsule* 3 dm. 1. and more; when mature, the outer husk falls off, and the down expands, and looks somewhat like a hare's foot, whence Swartz's specific name [lagopus]. It contains a large quantity of silky cotton-like fibres of a pale reddish colour. *Wood*..very porous and absorbent of water, the lightest of all woods, lighter even than true cork. 1941 Swabey 19, Down Tree.

dozi sb dial; prob a var of DOLCE.

1952 FGC StM /dózi/ dip-an'-fall-back, round-the-road.

DRAB MULLET sb arch or obs?

1854–5 *TJSA* I 143, Mugil capitulinus—drab mullet: long ears.

DRAGON sb dial; from its red colour, by association with the bush DRAGON (BLOOD). A variety of sweet-potato with a red skin and stem.

1952 FGC StC /dragan/ an old-time potato: outside red, slip red.

DRAGON(-BLOOD) sb; cf *OED dragon's blood* 1704→ of other plants. The plant *Calodracon sieberi*; see quot 1952.

1864 Grisebach 783, Dragon's blood: *Calodracon Sieberi*. 1952 FGC StT, Dragon-blood, A plant with reddish leaves (similar to those of wild-pine) at the top of a stalk several feet high—visible at a distance, therefore used to mark property lines; Tre /dyagan/ it plant a line, *Dragon, it's planted at lines*. 1954 Kirkland 170 [Contents of a bush bath:] Wisdom weed, panjaba, dragon, etc. [Identity uncertain.]

DRAGON CUTLASS sb dial; the sense of DRAGON is unknown, but there may have been a dragon imprinted on the blade; cf CROCODILE.

1958 DeC Kgn /dragan-kotlas/ a cutlass..[narrow parallel blade with point tapered from blade to back].

DRAGON WITHE sb; the sense of *dragon* is not clear: cf DRAGON(-BLOOD). A climbing plant *Heteropteris laurifolia*.

1920 Fawcett 233, H. laurifolia..Dragon Withe, White Withe. 1942 *NHN* I 6 11, Thickets of Dragon Withe (*Heteropteris laurifolia*)..are to be found further from the lagoon.

DRAPE sb or vb dial or slang.

1943 *GL* Kgn, Drape, arrest.

DRAW vb dial.

1. trans. In expressions where Std Engl would not use 'draw': To pull, pull up, etc. (Cf *OED* 39.) *BA BL G*

1877 Murray *Feedin' 'Perrit* 9, Him say, 'Now, mek we go draw de fish pot'. As we draw it it hab plenty fish. 1927 Anderson-Cundall 45 [Prov:] You want fe know if mauger dog hab teet', draw him tail. [*If you want to know whether a thin dog has teeth, pull its tail*].

2. intr. Of a liquid: To ferment. (Cf *OED* 41.)
1952 FGC StM, It will draw, ferment. *BA BL G*

3. trans. Of the sugar-cane: To produce (its flower or ARROW). (Cf *OED* 46.)

1958 DeC StE /i draa aro/—what the cane does when it blooms.

4. intr. Of a swelling: To diminish. Of a person: To lose flesh. Also const *down*. *BA*

1952 FGC Han, The swelling is drawing; Man, The swelling /draa/; StAnd /it draa dong/; Tre, swelling draw down. 1956 BLB Man /im no fat agen—im draa/.

5. trans. In the phr *draw snore*: To snore. Cf DRAW BUNGY.

1960 *CLS* 162 /dát a hóu in sóun slíip só, yu nuo, an in de dráa snúo/ [*That is how sound asleep he is, you know, and he is snoring*].

6. trans. To conjure away by magic means. Cf *OED* 26.

1961 Katzin 3, Cloves of garlic, small limes [etc.]..are put..in the pockets of the bib as a charm against thieves or people who can 'draw' money.

DRAW BUNGY vb phr dial; < *draw* + *bungy*, a bung? From the sound of drawing the bung from a cask: To yawn or snore?

1952 FGC Han /draa bonggi/ to yawn. 1956 Mc Man /draa bóngi/ to snore.

DRAW (ONE'S) HAND vb phr. To make a gesture (perh a particular one) with the hand. See quot. *G*

1877 Murray *Feedin' 'Perrit* 14, As she left the house, Georgey called at her through the window—'Mek hase come, yah. Tenpance wut o' de bes''. (Drawing his hand.) [A prearranged signal.] She brought the liquor, and while Georgey was helping his friends, she made frequent signs to him, taking the money out of her mouth..'Wha's matta?' said Georgey. 'Nuttin' sar, no mo as me ben see you draw you han', me know say da de long nine me fe buy sar, an a de change me hab da me mout fe gi'e you'.

DRAWING HALL sb; cf *drawing-room.*

1954 LeP StAnn, Living place in the house: drawing hall. (Hall is usually used as a dining room esp in a small house.)

DRAW-RAIL sb; cf *DA draw-bar.* One of the wooden rails forming part of a fence or wall which may be drawn aside to make an opening through it.

1947 U.Newton II 9, Let's slip through the short-cut, under the logwood trees, over the draw-rails, through the rectory grounds.

DRAY-MAN BIBLE sb dial; for *dray-man's bible.* A large round cake made of flour and water—very filling. The sense of the nickname is that the dray-man 'swears by it'.

1943 *GL* Clar, Dray-man bible, big round cake, =please-me; Han, Drayman bible; StAnn, Dray-man-bible.

DRAY-WHEEL sb dial; cf CART-WHEEL.

1956 Mc Man /drie wiil/ a big dumpling. 1958 DeC StAnd /drie wiilz/ large dumplings.

DREADLOCKS sb cant. Hair uncut and plaited, as worn by the most fully committed adherents of the Ras Tafari cult. **s.**

1960 *SAN Report* 12–13, From the earliest days, many Ras Tafari brethren had worn beards..At Pinnacle, a further development occurred, probably after photographs of Somali, Masai, Galla and other tribes in or near the Ethiopian border had become current. This was the plaiting of long hair by men known as the 'men of dreadlocks' or simply 'locksmen'. These men of dreadlocks were the Ethiopian Warriors and the self-declared Niyamen.

DREAM vb dial. Of a spirit: to visit a living person through a dream and inform him of something. (Usually intr, but see quot 1953.) *G*

1929 Beckwith 88, The spirits of the dead..come to him in dream, a mode of appearance called 'dream to me', or in a waking vision, spoken of as 'show himself to me'. 1942 HPJ, Dream: Appear in a dream to. 1952 FGC Han, She [a dead woman's spirit] dreamed to another woman to tell the boy he was saved only by being her own son. 1953 Moore 158, Probably, when you sick, say a month or two, and can't get better, and when you may have a dead, he come and dream you; say such-and-such a place trouble you. Then you must look after it.

DRENCHING-HORN sb; cf *OED* →1737, *DAE* →1858. An animal's horn used as a tube through which to get medicine down an animal's throat.

1952 FGC StAnn, Drenching-horn, to give cow medicine against worms.

DREPUSS see DRESS-PUSS.

DRESS DOWN, DRESS UP vb phr dial; cf *OED* dress *v* 4. Transf from military use (an order to a line of drilling men to move sidewise until each has space enough): move over (e.g. along a bench). *BA BL*

1942 Bennett 31, I can jus' dress dung lickle more. *Ibid* 22, 28. 1943 *GL* StC, Dress up, move up.

DRESS-PUSS /drés-pùs/ sb (and perh vb) dial; for *dressed-puss.* A person much dressed up, or overdressed.

1943 *GL* StAnd, Drepuss, overdress. 1954 LeP Man, To walk, as some good looking women do, in a provocative fashion: Dress puss. 1956 Mc Man, Someone overdressed: /him fieba drés-pus/. 1957 EB Port /dres-pus/.

DRESS UP see DRESS DOWN.

dresta sb dial; for *dresser* (*OED sb*[1]). A recorded pronunc showing intrusion of /t/; the usual dial pronunc is /dresa/.

1956 Mc Port /dresta/.

DRESTED ppl dial; for *dressed.* An overcorrected participle; in dial it is usually /dres/ as in the quot.

1943 *GL* StAnd, Drested, dress.

DRINK YALLAHS WATER vb phr dial. An expression from St Thomas parish, alluding to the Yallahs River at its western boundary: to come into the parish (as a stranger—not altogether welcome).

1952 P. B. Caws, 'Current ten years ago'.

DRIP sb obs; cf *OED sb* 1880→. Usually plural: stands on which SUGAR-POTS were set to drain during the process of refinement. *G*

1739 Leslie 339, The hot Liquor would run out, but the Pots are stopt with a Twig till they are set upon the Dripps.

DRIVE vb trans dial. To drive off or chase away. Cf RUN. *G*

1907 Jekyll 64, Me a drive fly. [*I am driving away flies.*] 1927 Stafford 32, Row enough to—'Dribe de Debbil!' 1929 Beckwith 117, All the herbs used to 'drive duppy' are so used because of the relation believed to exist between them and the activities of human life. 1950 Pioneer 65, Cow..busy ah drive de gingy-fly dem wid him tail.

DRIVE GOOD! int or vb phr chiefly dial; on the analogy of WALK GOOD! A call at parting with someone driving a car: Safe journey! *BL G*

1958 FGC StAnd.

DRIVER sb; cf *OED* 2c 1823→.

1. Obs. One who caught wild horses for sale, a HORSE-CATCHER.

1739 Leslie 177, Nor shall [anyone] drive or ride in any Savannah as a common Horse-catcher, without first giving security for their Honesty..No common Driver or Horse-catcher shall sell or barter any Horse, Mare or other Cattle, without bringing two sufficient Evidences to vouch for him.

2. The man, himself usually a slave, in charge of a gang of slaves. (Now hist.) *G*

1790 Beckford II 47, The driver follows with his knotted stick, and his whip flung carelessly across his shoulder.. the negroes follow, and he shows them upon what part of the piece to begin. a 1818 Lewis (1845) 93, However, this was sufficient to induce his head driver, who had been brought up in his own house from infancy, to form a plot among his slaves to assassinate him..No one suspected the driver. 1942 HPJ, Driber: Driver—the head slave in charge of a gang—up to 1838.

3. Since emancipation and today, the man who gives orders to a team of workers. (*Gleaner*—Mc.) Also of the head woman of a group of women (formerly DRIVERESS). *BA G*

1943 *GL* West, Driber, head woman.

DRIVERESS sb obs; <DRIVER+*-ess.* See quots.

1823 Roughley 105, Negro children, after they pass five or six years, if..healthy, should be taken from the nurse in the negro houses, and put under the tuition of the driveress, who has the conducting of the weeding gang. 1935 Senior 60, And a driveress to the small one [*sc* gang].

DROGO BOWL sb dial; <DROGUER (cf DROGUER 2) + BOWL as in CANDY BOWL. A box with glass panels—a sort of portable showcase—in which small articles and dress goods are hawked about. **s.**

1894 Spinner 46–7, Old Aunt Maria, the Droguer woman, who lived over the way..Angie loved the Droguer woman..The child often thought that when she grew up she would like to be one herself, and have a 'Drogo bowl', and sell tapes and laces, collars and pieces of print, as Aunt Maria did. 1942 Astley Clerk in HPJ, The drogo bowl is still to be seen on the roads in and out of Kingston.

DROGUE /druog/ vb; cf *OED drog* →1805, 'a backform from *Drogher*..' but the spelling implies that *o* is short, whereas in Jamaica the vowel is diphthongal. *G*

1. To transport goods in droguers.

1835 Steele 74, Drogging sugar and produce for ships. (HPJ.) 1952 FGC StM /druogin/.

2. Hence to transport anything heavy.

1942 HPJ, Drogue: carry—'You want fe see dem a drogue them home', from Madam Satan (Blue).

DROGUER /drúoga/ sb; cf *OED drogher*, 1782→.

1. A coasting vessel carrying freight. (Gen WI). *G*

1774 Long II 598, Vessels..(not including coasters, or droguers). 1791 *Laws* 31 Geo III cap 3 cl 13, Indians must not be entrusted with the command of droggers. 1816 MacDonald 99, That he had besides Two vessels (droggers). 1873 Rampini 30, Paying freight per droghers. 1942 HPJ, Droguer (the *o* is long): A coasting vessel of small draught. 1952 FGC StT, West /druoga/.

2. transf. One who carries about a stock of articles for sale. Also attrib.

1894 Spinner 46–7 (see DROGO BOWL).

DROP /drap/ vb and sb[1] dial; <*drop*. *G*

A. vb: To leave (off) (a communication or the like). (Cf Engl colloq 'drop me a line'.) *BL T*

1956 Mc StE /a wanda ef yu wud bi so kain as to mek a drap a mesaj a da hous de/ *I wonder if you'd be so kind as to let me leave a message at that house.*

B. sb: 1. Something that drops.

1943 *GL* Kgn, Kalban, bird drop. [It is a trap which drops over the bird.]

2. A free ride in a vehicle, at the end of which one is 'dropped off'. (Common.) *BL T*

1956 Mc StAnd /yu kyan gi mi a drap doun, mam/.

DROP /drap/ sb[2] dial; abbr of COCONUT DROP. A coconut sweetmeat made of coconut cut into very small bits and cooked in sugar till thickened, then dropped on to a pan to harden. Cf CUT CAKE. *BA T*

1943 *GL* Clar, Drops, coconut cake. 1954 LeP StE, Drops, cake made with coconut. 1956 Mc StE /draps/ or /kúoknàt dráps/.

DROP, DROP-DROP sb[3] dial.

1958 DeC Port /draps/ or /drap-drap/gratered banana boiled in a rundown.

DROP-DOWN sb dial. Prolapse of the oviduct in hens; also attrib, or absol, a hen with prolapsus.

1942 HPJ, Drop-down: a hen that has a dropping or droop at the back, due to inability to lay. Such a hen is said to 'put on gown'.

DROP OFF vb dial. To cause to drop off. *BA*

1934 Williams 126, see PEACE-CUP.

DROP-PAN sb; see quot. A gambling game of the lottery type in which tickets are bought, put into a pan, and the pan 'dropped' as a means of drawing the winning tickets. Cf *tai shiin.*

1943 *GL* Kgn, Woppy, Tyshin, drop pan terms; StT, Dropan, Chinese game. 1952 FGC Han /drápan/ a gambling game: a book of tickets /tái shiin/ with numbers from 1 to 36, each representing something..Buy a ticket; later there's a drawing to see which ticket wins.

DROPPER sb dial; <*dropper.*

1. A tin into which NEW SUGAR is poured to form a SUGAR HEAD.

1952 FGC Tre /drápaz-tin—drap di shuga in dem/.

2. A small finger-shaped dumpling that is dropped into the liquid in which it is boiled.

1958 DeC Port /drápaz/ spinner dumplings.

DROP-SHORT sb dial or slang. One who limps: description of the action of his leg.

1954 LeP Kgn, Drop-short, a man who limps.

DROP-TRASH (CANE) sb dial. A variety of sugar-cane which naturally drops its dry leaves, and therefore does not need to be 'trashed' by hand. Cf TRASH-MYSELF.

1952 FGC StT /drap-trash/ cane.

DROP YELLOWTAIL sb dial; one which has 'dropped' a roe. One kind of YELLOWTAIL fish: see quot.

1929 Beckwith 33, Pot fish are..yellowtails of the 'maiden' (small) and 'drop' (large) [varieties].

DROWN sb dial; <*drown* vb. A flood.

1959 DeC Clar /wen di droun kom/ *When there's a flood.* Reg in Upper Clarendon.

DROWND, DROWNDED vb dial; <Engl dial *drownd(ed)*. Used for all parts of the verb: drown. *BL G*

1877 Murray *Feedin' 'Perrit* 9, De drownded him da want drownded me didn't hot me like dat word. [*The drown he wanted to drown me* (i.e. the fact that he wanted to drown me) *did not hurt me like that word.*] 1957 JN no addr, Gen if you drop in there you go so far far down, you must drowned; Tre, An i deep! deep! deep! an in drounded me. [*And it was deep, deep, deep, and it drowned me.*]

DRUDGE (IN ONE'S BOOTS) vb (phr) dial. To wear boots or shoes habitually or to work in (the alternative being to wear them only to dress up).

1942 HPJ, Mi noh a drudge in a mi boots (i.e. I am not over-using my boots). [Astley Clerk: not working in them.] 1955 LeP StAnd, Q. Do you wear shoes? A. Well, I don't drudge (i.e. I don't wear shoes habitually).

DRUDGING ppl adj dial. In cpds: drudging boots, drudging clothes, = *working* ppl adj.

1956 Mc Clar /danggarii is drojin kluoz/ [*Dungarees are working clothes*], Man /drojin kluoz/ also /drojn buut/; Port /drojin kluoz/ clothes worn at home, working clothes.

DRUMMER /droma, jroma, joma/ sb[1]; cf *OED* 4a 1725→. A fish which makes a sound resembling drumming against the underside of boats and elsewhere. *BL G N*

1679 Trapham 65, The choice Mullet brings up the next division crowded with various Snappers,..Pilchers, Sprat, Drummers. 1725 Sloane 290, Guatucupa Brasiliensibus..The Drummer-Fish. 1899 *JIJ* II 613, Drummer, = Conodon. 1952 FGC Port, StAnn, StE, West /dróma, jróma, jóma/.

DRUMMER /droma, jroma/ sb[2] dial; cf *OED* 4b 1847 only. The cockroach *Blaberus discoidalis*, which 'drums' with its head against woodwork in houses.

1952 FGC Tre /jroma/ big gray roach, come from foreign.

DRUM PAN sb dial.

1929 Beckwith 47, The gasolene drum lately introduced is locally distinguished from the kerosene as the 'jo pan' or 'drum pan'.

DRUMWOOD sb dial. A kind of tree which, having soft inner wood, is easily hollowed to make drums; see quot 1961.

1952 FGC StAnn, Drumwood, parrotwood; StT, Drumwood /jínarali hálo/; Tre, Drumwood, glasswood. 1961 DAP Man, Drum wood—*Alchornea latifolia* Sw., also *Turpinia occidentalis* (Sw.) G. Don.

DRUNK, DRUNKEN vb dial; <*drunk, drunken*, adj, prob with some confusing infl of *drown* (exc sense 4).

1. To drown, or half-drown, by keeping in water too long.

1826 Barclay 325, He returns, and his prisoners [crabs] being by this time 'drunkened' (half drowned), they tumble out along with the plug of grass and are caught.

2. Of food: badly cooked, having had insufficient heat, etc.

1942 HPJ, Drunk, to drown (not drunken)..applied to meat which does not get enough heat to roast it..Also applied to peas. Food thus treated hardens and is useless.

3. Of clothing: badly washed. Also with *up*.

1956 Mc Man /yu dróngk op di klúoz/.

4. To render drunk or as if drunk. *BL G*

1952 FGC StM, Dago crab—can eat only claws: the back will drunk you. 1955 FGC Man, Cow-neck is bad rum that drunks you very quick.

DRY adj dial; <*dry* adj. *G*

1. Entirely bare of hair; quite bald. Cf DRY-HEAD, DRY-SKULL.

1956 Mc StE (Accom) [Story:] A. /a goin down a baaba shap goin get a trim/. B. /yo hed drai laik mi baksaid nou/. A. *I'm going down to the barber's for a trim.* B. *Your head's as bald as my backside now.*

2. Cf DRY-EYE.

DRY vb dial or slang; <*dry* vb. To deprive a person of everything he possesses. Perh limited to children's use in games. *BA G*

1947 U.Newton II 13, Meanwhile leave me to think of Clovis and the next game of cashews, for, mark this down, I am determined to 'dry him' which was our way of saying that I meant to skin, fleece, break or reduce him.

DRY sb; prob abbr of *dry time.* A period of dry weather; a drought. *BL*

1952 FGC StAnd /shi drai aaf in a di drai/ *She* [a cow] *dried off during the time of dry weather.* 1954 LeP StAnd, I heard from Bernard—he says over there [i.e. on the North Coast] the dry's gone cross on him. 1956 Mc Man, Drought: /eni taim yu hav drai/ you take these leaves to feed donkeys, etc.

DRY BELLYACHE sb obs; *DAE* quots 1723, 1757 prob refer to the same disease as this; *DA* has quots 1694, 1899, 1947 with only one definition, though these quots refer to different conditions. A painful and often fatal constipation of the bowels, very common in the early days of the colony. Also called DRY COLIC; KNOT-GUT may have been the same.

1679 Trapham 130–1, If any thing hath dismal aspect in the Indies, it is this Disease of the Dry Belliach..Even there where the Sun showers his most plentiful heat..cold taken between the hot Tropicks if seated in the region of the Belly, &c..Cramps the Muscles of the Abdomen and tender Fibres of the Guts with the contractings of the torturing Bellyach. 1698 Ward 15, That Fatal and Intolerable Distemper, The Dry Belly-Ach; which in a Fortnight, or Three Weeks, takes away the use of their limbs, that they are forc'd to be led about [by] Negro's. 1740 Importance 42, The dry Belly-ach..does not prevail now so much as it did formerly..which is attributed to their not drinking their Punch so strong or sweet as before, nor made with Brandy; Rum, by Experience, being found a more wholesome Liquor. 1784 Dancer *Bath Waters* 1. The Dry *Belly-ache* seems to have been the complaint in which the good effect of the Bath waters were first most eminently experienced.

DRY BUBA sb dial; <*dry* + BUBA. One who resembles a dry palm branch: see quot.

1959 DeC Han /drai buba/ used for a tall thin person, a /langgulaala/.

DRY COLIC sb obs. = DRY BELLYACHE.

1790 Beckford II 302, The dry cholic, a disease which is now, in a manner, expelled from the country by the fortunate introduction, and more general use, of honest porter and Madeira wine.

DRY DROPSY sb obs; <*dry* (*OED* 11b) + *dropsy*. The name formerly given to a feverish condition; see quot.

1707 Sloane clii, I had heard very much of a dry Dropsie, a Distemper that was said to be very Mortal to many of this Island, both Whites and Blacks, and was pretended to be a very strange Disease (as it would have been, had it answer'd to its Name) and proper to this Climate..I found this to be the beginning of a Consumption, and perfect Febris Hectica, having no Symptoms, but such as are common to our English, and all other Hectics.

DRY-EYE adj dial; for *dry-eyed*. Barefaced.

1943 *GL* Han, Dry-yeye, bareface. [1956 Mc StAnd (Mt Charles) /gýal yu ai drái laik páach-káan/ *Girl, your eyes are as dry as parched corn*—said to a bold, shameless girl.] 1960 LeP StAnd /draiyaid/ brazen. *BA G*

DRY GIN sb dial slang. GANJA, which has an intoxicating effect when it is smoked.

1936 Martinez in *Gleaner* 3 Oct p. 35, Here is the hotbed of ganja smoking, for the men and women take their 'dry-gin', 'maconi weed' and 'herb' as they wish.

DRY-HEAD sb dial; <DRY adj 1 + *head*.

1. A head with scanty hair (more than a DRY-SKULL, less than a BALD-HEAD). *BL G*

1942 HPJ, Dryhead: (i) a head with scanty hair. 1956 Mc StAnd /drai-ed/ with very short hair.

2. A person with a dry-head (sense 1). *BL G*

1942 HPJ, Dryhead: (ii) dryhead man, woman..'Yo' cuss me dryhead'. [*You insult me by calling me 'dry-head!'*]

3. In ANANCY STORIES: Dryhead, or Bredda Dryhead, a character never clearly delineated, but dangerous, having magical powers (he is hard to get rid of), and prob to be visualized as skull-like.

1924 Beckwith 27, 'Dry-head is a man always hide himself in the bush to eat up what Anansi or Tacoomah have', Parkes says. He figures as a kind of old man of the sea in the Anansi stories. 1942 HPJ, Dry head—dry kull—dry skull—a mythological character (Death?). 1950 Pioneer 86, [Anancy] heard something drop like a cocoanut off a tree..It was no fruit Anancy saw, but Bredda Dry Head on the ground.

DRY-HEAD adj dial; for *dry-headed*; see DRY adj 1. Bald or becoming bald; used of women and as a term of insult. *G*

1933 *Outlook* 30 Dec, You only lef' fe..go a prison, an' das would be de bes' place fe a ginger-toe, dry-head gal like you! 1958 DeC Port /drai-hed/ bald or balding (used only of a woman, or occasionally in stories of a guinea-hen who is referred to as Sister Guinea-Hen).

DRY JUMP vb dial; <*dry* (*OED a* 13) +JUMP. See quot.

1953 Moore 60, Dry jump, a derisive expression describing the activities of pocomania groups, who are jumping without really having 'the spirit'—so the other cultists feel.

DRY-SKULL sb dial.

1. An entirely bald person—more so than a DRY-HEAD or BALD-HEAD. *G*

1956 Mc StAnd /drai skol/.

2. A synonym of DRY-HEAD sb 3, which see, and see quot 1942.

DRY-WEATHER ESTATE sb. An estate in the area of lesser rainfall.

1839 McMahon 244, Some [properties] are called planting estates, which are generally in the interior of the country; and others are called dry-weather estates, which range along the whole of the south side of the island.

DRY YAWS sb dial.

1. The variety of CRAB-YAWS generally called RUNNING YAWS.

1959 A. D. Simons, UCWI Preventive Med.

2. In the phrase to SCRUB DRY YAWS.

du see DA[2].

DUB sb dial arch or obs; abbr of DOUBLOON.

1877 Murray *Kittle* 28, Bony mek de Dubs fly..Bony mek de Guineas fly.

DUBBLELOON, DUBBLUNE see DOUBLOON.

DUCCUNU see *dokunu.*

DUCHESS GRASS sb dial; by alteration, perh folk-etym, of DUTCH GRASS.

1952 FGC Han /dochis graas/.

DUCK-AND-SHAKE-BACK sb dial; a variant of DIP-AND-SHAKE-BACK, etc.

1958 DeC StT /dok-an-shiek-bak/ a coconut run-down.

DUCKANO, DUCKANOO see *dokunu.*

DUCK ANT sb; cf *OED* 1851→. The 'Damp Wood' termite (*Nasutitermes pilifrons*); it is white and has somewhat of the squat shape and the gait of a duck. *N*

[1707 Sloane xvii, These Poultry are all fed on Indian or Guinea Corn, and Ants Nests brought from the Woods, which these Fowls pick up and destroy mightily.] 1835 Senior 77, Another terrible plague is the '*duck ant*', or wood ant..it is flat, has feet, and emits a very offensive smell. 1942 Astley Clerk in HPJ, Unlike the Wood Ant..the Duck Ant works *outside* so that as a rule you can see him and destroy him. 1952 FGC gen /dok ans/; Han, Brownish body and black beak, feed on wood, smell strong, will build a whole nest overnight, look like ducks; Tre, build big black nest on tree, head part hard, batty soft, white. 1954 *FG* 659, Duck Ants..The species which commonly destroy lumber in the country parts are those which have nests in the soil, or which build conspicuous dark-coloured nests on trees..As all termites shun light, and die when exposed to dry air.. they never walk in the open, but remain within the tunnels or mud-covered pathways which they construct.

DUCK-APPLE sb dial. The tree *Morinda citrifolia*, more often called HOG-APPLE.

1952 FGC Port (Castle Comfort) /dók ápl/.

DUCK-DUCK sb dial rare; perh a var of TICKY-TICKY? (Astley Clerk).

1942 HPJ Port, Duck-duck: small fish eaten by mudfish.

DUCK-FOOT (WIS) sb dial. A small vine with a leaf shaped like a duck's foot: *Passiflora sexflora.*

1927 Beckwith 11, *Passiflora sexflora* Juss. 'Duck-foot.' 1952 FGC StM /dok fut wis/ goat-hoof. 1955 *WIMJ* 31, *P. sexflora*..Duppy Pumpkin; Passion Flower; Bat Wing; Goat or Duck Foot.

DUCKONOO, DUCKOONOO, DUCKUNOO see *dokunu.*

DUCK-PICKNEY sb dial. A duckling. *G*

1910 Anderson-Cundall 21 [Prov:] Hen 'gree fe hatch duck egg, but him no 'gree fe teck duck-pickney fe swim.

DUCKY-FOOT see *dogi-fut.*

DUCKY HEN see *dogi hen.*

DUDE /duud/ sb dial; cf *DA dude.*

1. See quot. This is prob an abbr of *dude's clothes*, or the like.

1954 LeP StT, Dood, very smart clothes.

2. A lover, 'young man', 'boy friend'. In this sense perh infl by *dudus. G*

1951 Murray 41–2 [A girl is roasting a coco in expectation of a visit from her young man:] Posen me roas' i' an' de Dude no come?

dudu sb dial; cf *dudus. G*

1957 DeC StE (Accom) /dudu/ penis.

dudus sb dial; prob phonosymbolic, but cf Twi *adɔ́de*, a pet, darling, and Fr *doux-doux*, fem *doux-douce*. One of a number of similar pet-words produced by pursing the lips as if to nuzzle or kiss—cf BUNUNUS, DUNDUS, TUTUS, etc.: a darling. *G T*

1958 DeC Port /dudus/ affectionate name for a child. (The informant, a young mother, insists there is no connection between /dudus/ and /dundus/—was horrified when /dundus/ was suggested; this means only an albino and would never be used of a normal child.)

DUFF /dof, duf/ sb dial; cf *OED sb*[1]. See quots. (This is one of the nautical words that came ashore in Jamaica.)

1943 *GL* Clar, Duff, dumpling. 1958 DeC StAnd /dof/ large dumpling; StJ /duf/ *sic*, though undoubtedly related to /dof/: a large round dumpling.

DUFFIDIA see next.

dufidaia /dùfidáia/ adj and sb dial; etym unknown—perh African.

1. A dwarfish, stunted person.

1943 *GL* Clar, Duphidia, like a Dwarf; Duffidia, stunned [*sic*].

2. See quot: the sense is not clear, but perhaps supports 'stunned' in the prec quot.

1955 FGC Man /dùfidáia/ careless-going person.

du-fi-du /dú-fi-dú/ sb dial; <*do-for-do*. One action for another; tit for tat. Chiefly in proverbial use and in unfavourable sense; but used also in suggesting that a reward is due ('one good turn deserves another'). *G*

1873 Rampini 176, Do fe do (tit for tat) no harm. Do fe do mek Guinea nigger come a' Jamaica. [The latter sentence may be an allusion to negroes selling fellow-negroes into slavery, but see next quot.] 1924 Beckwith 42, Do-fe-do is no harm, but do-fe-do mek bockra bring Guinea-coast neger come a Jamaica..'"Do as you would be done by" does no harm, but "do as you would be done by" did not prevent white men from bringing the Guinea-coast negro to Jamaica'.

DUG /dog/ vb dial; <*dug*, past ppl of *dig*; the less common form (the usual one being *dig*) of the verb *dig*, in all uses. (It is due to confusion or overcorrection.)

1952 FGC StM /dog di ort/ *Dig the earth*; StM, Starch-bean bulbs is dugged out.

DUGGI, DUGGIE, DUGGY see *dogi*.

DUGO-LOW adj or sb dial rare; etym unknown.

1943 *GL* Kgn, Dugo-low, plenty.

DUKE COCO /dyuuk, juuk, juk kuoko/ sb dial also attrib; for spellings see quots; <*duke*+*coco*. (With the shortening of the vowel from *uu* to *u*, there seems now to be some confusion with *juk*.) A coco (*Colocasia cordata*) given a title of honour because of its hardness (cf COMMANDER, LEF'-MAN cocos). Poss named in adulation of the Duke of Wellington.

1855 *TJSA* II 41 [Letter from England printed:] I should be thankful for good samples of the following also, for our Museum:..Jew Coco Biscuits. [Editor's addition:] (?Duke). 1935 HPJ, Burban Coco—'same Black Juck'. 1943 *GL* Port, Juk cocoa, commander cocoa. 1952 FGC Port /jùkúoko/ commander—very hard; StC /dyuuk kuoko/ in Portland = lef'-man, black commander; StT /dyuuk/ white and black: black duke = commander—very hard; StT /juuk/ = commander. 1956 Mc StAnd /juuk hav pingki kolo; minti hwait rait truu/ *Duke has a pinky colour; Minty is white right through.*

DUKKUM dial; echoic. See quot, and cf ITTY-ITTY-HAP.

1942 HPJ, Dŭkkŭm, an onomatopoeic sound imitating the tramp of the three-legged horse (a duppy).

dukuno, DUKUNOO, dukunu see *dokunu*.

duma /dúma/ vb dial; cf Hausa *'duma*, to thrash. To thrash, flog, beat.

1943 *GL* Clar, Dooma, flog; Kgn, Dumma, Ebo word = to flog. 1955 FGC Man /dúma/ to flog. 1956 Mc Man /a guoin dúma yu iina yu bak/ *I am going to thump you on the back*; StE (Accom) /ték yu fis dúma him/ *Take your fist and beat him.*

DUMBARTON, DUMBY /dòmbáatn, dómbi/ sb slang; cf *dounby* in Urquhart tr Rabelais *Gargantua* XIII. In children's euphemistic use: the buttocks.

c 1910 FGC StAnd.

DUMB CANE /dòm, dòng kíen/ sb; cf *OED* 1696→1830. A plant (*Dieffenbachia seguine*) somewhat cane-like, the acrid juice of which renders the tongue and mouth temporarily dumb. See also LUCKY LILY. *G N*

1696 Sloane 63, *The poisoned Cane of* Ligon. p. 69. *The dumb Cane.* 1707 Sloane I 168, If one cut this Cane with a Knife, and put the tip of the Tongue to it, it makes a very painful Sensation, and occasions such a very great irritation of the salivary Ducts, that they presently swell, so that the person cannot speak..and from this its quality, and being jointed, this *Arum* is called Dumb-Cane. 1927 Beckwith 16, Dumb-cane. The juice of the root is said to be used to poison an enemy. Rubbed upon the hat band it will produce insanity, according to intelligent informants in Port Antonio. 1942 HPJ, Dumb-cane..used in Obeah. 1952 FGC Port, StM, StT, Tre /dómklen, dòngkíen/—like LUCKY LILY; antidote—put it on poisonous cuts; /krach bad/—poison to kill rats. 1956 Mc StE (Accom) /dom kien/; /dom kyeal/.

DUMB KALE sb dial; a phonetic var of prec, perh infl by INDIAN KALE. = prec; see quot 1956.

DUMB-RETURNER, DUMB-TURNER sb arch or obs; cf *OED dumb a* 6. A device in a sugar-mill which turned the canes which had passed through the first sets of rollers and fed them back between the latter sets, thus relieving many slaves of a dangerous task.

1793 Edwards II 223 [The canes] having passed through the first and second rollers, they are turned round the middle one by a circular piece of framework, or screen, called in Jamaica the *Dumb-returner*, and forced back through the second and third. 1873 Rampini 70, If a feeding-board was set up before the rollers, and a 'dumb-turner' or semi-cylindrical piece of wood placed at the back of the central cylinder to assist the entrance of the canes between the two last rollers, the danger..would be minimized.

DUMB-THING sb dial; sg or plur. A domesticated animal. **s.**

1942 HPJ, Dum-ting..[Song:] Take away my land and dumting, sell out me berrin spot.

DUMBY see DUMBARTON.

DUMMA see *duma*.

DUMPLING /domplin, domplen/ sb dial. *BA*

1942 HPJ, Dumpling: Besides the English meaning this word now also signifies *Johnny Cake* in Jamaica. 1956 Mc Man, StAnd, Dumpling, Johnny-cake. May be fried or boiled. Made from /kisada/ flour.

DUMTING see DUMB-THING.

DUN dial sp of DONE.

DUNCY adj dial; a familiarized or affectionate term perh <*dunce* +*-y* or *dundus*[2] +*-y*.

1943 *GL* StAnn, Duncy, sweet, nice.

DUNDAR see next.

DUNDER /dónda/ sb; < Sp *redondar*, to overflow —cf *OED* 1793→. *N*

1. The scum from the coppers in which sugar-cane liquor was formerly evaporated. Some of it was used to start the fermentation for rum.

1788 Marsden 27, The skimmings of the cane juice and the refuse of the two first coppers, called *dunder*, are carried by lead gutters to the still-house.

2. The lees from the rum-still, used to start fermentation in making rum.

1774 Long II 564, A proportion of volatile oil is likewise produced in the process of distillation, by the action of the fire upon that saccharine matter in the distilling liquor, which has continued unchanged by fermentation, and adheres to the still, in form of what is generally called dunder. 1793 Edwards II 241, Lees, or, as it is called in Jamaica, *dunder*..The use of dunder in the making of rum, answers the purpose of yeast in the fermentation of flour. It is the lees or feculencies of former distillations; and some few planters preserve it for use, from one crop to another; but this is a bad practice. Some fermented liquor therefore, composed of sweets and water alone, ought to be distilled in the first instance, that fresh dunder may be obtained. 1803 Nugent 86, The smell of the dunder, as it is called, made me so sick. 1827 Hamel II 190, I tell you you are the scum of the earth—worse than the trash of the sugar cane, and the dunder of the still. 1929 Beckwith 24, This scum is called the 'dundar' [*sic*]. 1959 FGC, Current.

DUNDER CISTERN sb. A cistern in which DUNDER is stored.

1790 Beckford II 32, A large butt..is likewise a necessary appendage of this part of the building, as are a dunder-cistern and a tank for the reception of the worms. 1793 Edwards II 240, For working these stills and worms, it is necessary to provide, first, a dunder-cistern, of at least three thousand gallons

DUNDO sb obs; cf Ewe *ạdọndó*, small drum, Ngombe *ndundu*, drum; Yoruba *dùndún*, a kind of drum; Hausa *dundufa*, a long, narrow drum. (The word was evid not wholly naturalized.) (Hause lists some twenty words similar to these from W Afr, pp 41–4.) A small type of drum used by slaves.

1823 *Koromantyn* 85, They found the slaves dancing to the sound of their rude African instruments, the banja, the dundo, and goombay. The dundo is a complete tabor.

DUNDOOZE, DUNDOZE see *dundus*².

dundu sb dial; var form of *dundus*¹ 1.

1942 HPJ StAnd, Dŭndoo: Albino. (Two informants.) 1956 Mc Port /dúndu/ an albino.

DUNDU sb dial and perh slang; prob to be conn with *dundus* 2—cf *combolo* applied to a machete.

1943 *GL* Clar, Dundu, razor.

dundun sb dial; a hypocoristic form of *dundus*², from iteration of first syllable.

1959 DeC StJ /dundun/ pet name for child or sweetheart.

dundus¹ /dúndus/ sb dial; cf Ko *ndundu*, albino, white man, European.

1. An albino negro.

[1774 Long II 49, A nation of these Albinoes are said to inhabit somewhere in the central part of Africa, who are weak and of low stature, and do not mix with the Blacks. They are called Dondos, or Mokisses, by the natives.. They are likewise said to be educated in the science of priestcraft, or witchcraft, and to fill the chief offices at Loango in all religious affairs and superstitious ceremonies.] 1943 *GL* Kgn, Dundus, a very red man. [In folk use 'red' includes orange and yellow.] 1955 FGC Man /dundus/ a person with whitish colour, of black parents; quaw. 1956 Mc Man, StE /dundus/ negro albino. Note: 'dundus' seems to be a word of wider application than /kwa-o/. [I.e. it has this sense and also sense 2.]

2. A freak; someone who is not up to the mark of normality.

1943 *GL* Kgn, Dundus, a freak of nature; StAnd, Dun-dus, undersized. 1956 Mc Man, StE /dundus/ peculiar, inferior, subnormal person. 1957 EB Port /dundus/a freak. Not 'undersized'. 1958 DeC Port, cf *dudus*.

dundus² /dundus/ sb dial; evid a var of *dudus*. A darling, a much-loved one.

1907 Jekyll 274, 'Dundooze' (or dundoze, for it is rather hard to catch the vowel) is a term of endearment [between lovers]. 1950 Pioneer 78 [Song sung by a young man to a girl who is smothering him with attentions:] Gal you want fe come kill me fe Dundus. 1952 FGC StAnn /dundus/ term of affection used by an older person to a young girl or boy.

DUNG, DUNGA see *dong*.

DUNG BASKET sb obs; *dung* (*OED sb* 5) + *basket*. A basket formerly used by a slave to carry manure to the cane-fields. *BA*

1823 Roughley 90, He should have the handicraft watchmen bring in an ample supply of..ropes for mules.. trash and dung baskets, lining pegs, rat springs, &c. [1925 Beckwith 91, cf DUTTY sb 2.]

DUNGOYAH vb phr;? < *don't care*; see *kya*.

1943 *GL* StM, Dungoyah, don't care.

dunju sb dial; a variant of *dundus*¹ 1.

1958 DeC Port /dunju/ an albino Negro.

DUNPROMOTE see DONE-PROMOTE.

dunzdap sb dial; a variant of *dundus*¹ 1, much altered (by word-play?).

1959 DeC Tre /dunzdap/ an albino negro.

duo /duo/ adv dial; a form of *aduo*.

1943 *GL* Kgn, Doh, outside.

duodo /dúoduo, dúodo/ vb¹ dial; < Fr *dodo*, baby-talk for *dormir*, to sleep. *BL G*

1942 HPJ, Dodo: Sleep of children. 'Him dodo.' 1943 *GL* Port, Dowdo, sleep. 1955 FGC Man, 'Come /dúodo/'—said to baby. 1956 Mc StT, Mothers tell baby /duodo/—it mean 'to sleep'.

duodo, duodu, duudu vb² and sb dial; a word used chiefly to and by children: origin uncert, but cf DO UP, the first element of which may underlie this; also *didi*. (Cf *duudu*, defecate, in Brit Engl baby-talk. RWT.) *BL G*

A. vb: To defecate.

B. sb: Excrement, dung.

1956 Mc Man /him duodo wen im do op himself/. 1957 EB Port /duudu/ to defaecate. 1957 JN Lowe R. [Children playing with a dung-beetle:] Yu drawin di do-du an a carry im a go put in de do-du.

duodo, duo-duo see DOUGH-DOUGH.

duodu see *duodo* vb².

duosi see DOLCE.

DUPHIDIA see *dufidaia*.

DUPPY /dópi/ sb; 1774→ duppy, 1827 duppie, 1868 duppe: cf Bube *dupe*, ghost. Cf *OED* 1774→. *BA*

1. The spirit of the dead, believed to be capable of returning to aid or (more often) harm living beings, directly or indirectly; they are also believed subject to the power of OBEAH and its practitioners who can 'set' or 'put' a duppy upon a victim and 'take off' their influence. (The duppy was once clearly distinguished from the BUGABOO—see quot 1774—and the SHADOW, but these distinctions are now obscured or lost.) *BL N*

1774 Long II 416, They [*sc* negroes] firmly believe in the apparition of spectres. Those of deceased friends are *duppies*; others, of more hostile and tremendous aspect.. are called *bugaboos*. 1826 Williams 87, Abdallah asked his friend whether *Duppy* did not live there underneath; but Pompeius, with an air of disdain, replied, 'that he did not believe Duppy; that Duppy was all lies'. 1827 Hamel II 221, He is no spirit, Michal, but a man like me.. Who ever told of a duppie whose step was audible? 1868 Russell 6, Duppe—A Spirit. African. 1929 Beckwith 92, The headman at Burnt Ground wore turkey red as a guard at night, but Parkes thinks duppies like red, are sometimes seen in it themselves, and follow it when they see it, but 'take themselves away' for blue. 1956 Mc StE (Accom), Obiaman summons 'duppy' from the grave in the following way. He goes along to the selected grave at night and calls the duppy by name. If there is no answer, he takes some rum he has brought, throws it on the grave, and calls the duppy again. If the duppy does not respond to this kindness, he tries bullying: he takes some unpleasant, blinding things such as pepper and turpentine, which he has also brought with him, and mixes them in a bottle, and makes a hole in the grave and threatens to pour in the mixture and burn up the duppy if he does not come. The duppy then comes. Some duppies are the ghosts of people who refuse to lie down—the duppy comes around of his own accord.

2. Personified as Brother Duppy in Anancy stories.

1924 Beckwith 21, Once Brer Duppy make his house in de air..So Bredder Nansi come to find out Duppy house..An' Bredder Duppy take some boiling water an' t'row on him an' he was dead. 1942 HPJ, A proper name: Bro. Duppy, a super-natural being, probably man-eating.

3. In the game of noughts-and-crosses (in Jamaica tii-taa-tuo): a drawn game.

1952 FGC Han /dopi/ when a game of tii-taa-tuo comes out even—i.e. when nobody wins.

4. Attrib and comb: see as separate entries.

[1851 Gosse 186–7, Duppy's melon*..Duppy is a spiritual personage of whom negroes are terribly afraid; it might be rendered 'hobgoblin'. The habit of naming things that are considered uncouth, or in some way unpleasing, as *Duppy's* this or that, is analogous to the practice which prevails in our own country, of appropriating things to the Devil; as 'Devil's Squeaker' (the Swift), 'Devil's Coach-horse' (the Rove-beetle), &c.]

DUPPY BIRD sb dial; <DUPPY+*bird*. Any bird associated in popular superstition with DUPPIES—esp the GI'-ME-ME-BIT, GROUND DOVE and WILD-PINE SERGEANT: see quots.

1942 HPJ, Duppy bird, the ground dove, which is said to frequent burial grounds, and of which it is believed that if it flies into the Church, someone will die. 1947 U.Newton II 34, Of course we were careful not to shoot 'Duppy Birds'. I nearly shot one one day..If I had shot that bird, I would have died..He said that all Ground Doves were 'Duppy Birds'. 1956 Jeffrey-Smith 76, Wild Pine Sergeant..Its silent, almost furtive method of feeding among these [wild pines] has given it the name of 'duppy bird', in Hanover.

DUPPY CALALU sb dial; <DUPPY+CALALU. The common wild calalu with red stems and prickles—the latter perh responsible for the association with duppies: *Amarantus spinosus*.

1952 FGC StT /dópi kálalù/ has prickles, red stems.

DUPPY CAP, DUPPY CUP sb dial; for *duppy's cap*.

1954 LeP Man, Duppy cap, mushroom. 1956 McMan /dopi kop/ an inedible fungus, which grows on a stem, with top like an umbrella.

DUPPY-CATCHER sb dial. An OBEAH-MAN; this name shows how the concept of the SHADOW, formerly distinct, has become absorbed into that of the DUPPY. Cf SHADOW-CATCHER.

1929 Beckwith 96, 'They rescued Walker and took him away to Good Hope. And they got a smart man called duppy-catcher and he put him [i.e. the duppy] in a bottle, and when we saw the bottle we saw a sort of fly in the bottle. And Walker got better'. 1958 DeC Man /dopi-kecha/ obeah man.

DUPPY CHERRY sb dial; <DUPPY+*cherry*. The CLAMMY CHERRY.

1942 Astley Clerk in HPJ, Duppy cherry—a cream coloured fruit or berry, clammy in taste, hence also called clammy cherry, that grows in bunches—flowers, very pretty and white, in clusters. 1943 *GL* Kgn, Duppy cherry, wild cherry.

DUPPY-CONQUEROR sb dial or slang. A belligerent or bullying person; a derisive epithet often coupled with BULL-BUCKER.

1943 *GL* no addr, Duppy conqueror, champion. 1955 FGC Man, Duppy-conqueror, a fighter. 1959 Mrs E. B. Hoyes Kgn, 'Bull-bucker' is not complete without 'duppy-conqueror'. The by-gone Jamaican feared two things above everything else, a 'bucking' (butting) bull and a 'duppy' (ghost)..[One challenging a bully says:] 'Come sah you a bull-bucker, duppy-conqueror', etc.

DUPPY CUCUMBER sb dial.

1952 FGC StM /dópi kukúmba/ = /dopi pongkin/. [DUPPY PUMPKIN.]

DUPPY CUP see DUPPY CAP.

DUPPY DARNING-NEEDLE sb dial. A plant of uncert identity; see quot.

1952 FGC StAnn, Duppy darning-needle—a 'garden flowers' much like cockspur [i.e. cockscomb] but shape like duppy darning-needle; StC, same as picknut. [This is prob erron.]

DUPPY FEE-FEE sb dial; <DUPPY+FEE-FEE. The plant MONKEY FIDDLE, which makes a squeaking sound when two bits are rubbed across each other.

1942 HPJ, Duppy fee-fee, the Monkey-fiddle..*Pedilanthus tithymaloides.*

DUPPY FIDDLE(-STICK) sb dial. The plant MONKEY FIDDLE.

1952 FGC StC, Duppy fiddlestick; StM, Duppy fiddle.

DUPPY FLY-TRAP sb chiefly dial; for *duppy's fly-trap*. The plant *Aristolochia grandiflora*; see quot.

1942 *NHN* I 8 9, Perhaps one of our most curious plants is that locally known as 'Duppy Fly-trap'. It is a vine with large heart-shaped leaves and it produces a flower that is weird, both in shape and colouring. It is a wild relative of the much smaller, and better known, Dutchman's Pipe..It gives off, at times, a most disagreeable odour, as of putrefying flesh. This attracts flies which enter the bulbous cavern in the centre.

DUPPY GUN sb; for *duppy's gun*. The plant *Ruellia tuberosa*, whose tiny cigar-shaped seed-pods, when dampened, burst with a sudden explosion, whence the name. Also called DANIEL'S GREAT GUN, MENOW WEED, SNAP-DRAGON, SPIRIT LEAF or WEED, *tempe*, TRICK-WEED.

c1915 FGC StAnd, Duppy-gun. 1942 HPJ, Duppy-Gun, a charming little wayside purple flower, beloved by children who put the seeds into their mouths, the moisture causing the seed to 'pop'. 1942 *NHN* I 6 11. 1952 FGC StM, Duppy-gun.

DUPPY MELON sb dial. Prob the same as WILD MELON (*Cionosicys pomiformis*).

1851 Gosse 186–7, A luxuriant gourd called the Duppy's melon, has entwined in the limbs of the cedar, and sends down a hundred vines which dip their tangled mazes into the water. 1942 HPJ, Duppy-melon, a gourd.

DUPPY NEEDLE sb dial.

1961 DAP Man, Duppy-needle—prickles; also another name for Larn-manners.

DUPPY PEAS sb dial. Species of wild peas (*Crotolaria verrucosa* or *C. retusa*) which look like edible peas but are not. The dry pods rattle loudly when the bush is moved or shaken.

1952 FGC StAnd, Duppy peas—have white or purple flowers.

DUPPY PINDAR sb dial; <DUPPY+PINDAR. A plant whose beans closely resemble peanuts: see quot.

1942 *NHN* I 6 11, Among the smaller shrubs and recumbent herbs are..Duppy Pindar (*Canavalia obtusifolia*)..etc.

DUPPY POISON sb dial.

1954 *WIMJ* 30, *Morinda Royoc* L...[Common names:] Red Gal; Strong Back; Yaw Weed; Duppy Poison; Yellow Ginger.

DUPPY POP-GUN sb dial. = DUPPY GUN.

1958 FGC StAnd.

DUPPY PUMPKIN /dopi pongkin/ sb dial.

1. Any of various plants of the family Cucurbitaceae: see quots. The fruit is usually pumpkin-like, though inedible.

1927 Beckwith 16, Duppy pumpki . *Cayaponia*—. 'For a stiff neck, wind it about the nec' , and if anyone asks you what it is there for, break off one of the pods and throw it at him and he will have crick neck too', probably, though this was not stated, relieving the first sufferer. 1929 Beckwith 89, The gourd-like fruit of a vine called 'duppy pumpkin'. 1946 *NHN* III 60, The 'Wild Ackee'..was in fruit as well as the 'Duppy Pumpkin'—*Fevillea cordifolia*—which had climbed over the 'Monkey Tamarind'. 1952 FGC StAnn /dopi pongkin/—called it so as a child —not edible, nobody has any use for it, it just stays; StM,

Has a vine like cerasee, fruit like small /mós mèlan/. 1959 UCWI Herbarium, Duppy pumpkin, *Cayaponia racemosa*, etc.

2. Also applied to a plant of the family Passifloraceae: see quot.

1954 *WIMJ* 31, *Passiflora sexflora* Juss...[Common names:] Duppy Pumpkin; Passion Flower; Bat Wing; Goat or Duck Foot.

DUPPY RIDING-HORSE sb dial. The stick-insect, or the praying mantis (*Orthoptera*).

1952 FGC Tre /dopi raidin haas/ stick insect.

DUPPY SOURSOP sb dial. The Mountain or Wild Soursop, *Annona montana*. It closely resembles the soursop, but the fruits are inedible.

1952 FGC StE /dopi souwasap/ for fence posts, makes best furniture, gun-stocks, sleepers, birds won't eat it; Tre, Duppy soursop—near Maggotty, StE.

DUPPY TOMATO sb dial. The plant also called COCKROACH POISON or WEED, POISON TOMATO, etc.: *Solanum aculeatissimum*.

1952 FGC StAnn /dópi tumátis/ has more prickles than 'cat-claw'—similar fruit, deadly poison; some call it 'cockroach weed'.

DUPPY UMBRELLA sb dial. *BA*

1942 HPJ, Duppy umbrella—a mushroom. 1955 RWT, Duppy umbrella = junjo (mushroom). (Jamaica and elsewhere in BWI.) 1957 EB Port /dopi ombrela/ mushroom.

DURING CROP see CROP. *BA*

DURING THE WHILE conj phr dial. While.

1953 Moore 38 (recorded in Morant Bay, StT, 1950).

DUSKY BOOBY sb ornith obs; <*dusky* + BOOBY. In Gosse's use: The sooty tern, *Sula fusca*, one of those which lay BOOBY EGGS.

1847 Gosse 417, Dusky booby.

DUSKY EARED-OWL sb ornith. In Gosse's use: The Jamaican BROWN OWL (*Pseudoscops grammicus*) alluding to its dark colour and feather-tufts.

1847 Gosse 19–20, Dusky Eared-Owl..General plumage above dusky brown..Egrets of about ten feathers, forming conical *horns* about 1 inch high, giving the countenance a great resemblance to that of a cat. 1956 Jeffrey-Smith 11, Dusky-eared Owl [*sic*].

DUST /dos/ sb dial; <*dust*. Small change. (A lightly disparaging word.) *G*

1956 Mc Port, Money /briiz/ also /dos/.

DUSTY ROTI sb dial; for etym see s. *G T*

1958 DeC StC /dosti roti/ a very thin roti (about ⅛th inch) as opposed to the usual ½ inch.

DUTCH ACCOUNT sb joc obs; cf *OED Dutch reckoning*. An account that is confused (or falsified?), perhaps deliberately, in favour of its maker.

1828 Marly 23, Old Marly, therefore, would not venture the fruits of his industry into such hands, supposing, that when he returned, he would find a Dutch account of his crops.

DUTCH GRASS sb; cf *OED* 1640 only.

1. *Cynosurus indicus*, a common grass in Jamaica. (The reason for the name is not known.)

1696 Sloane 33, Dutch Grass. In pratis Insularum Jamaicæ & Barbados ad semitas copiosè provenit. 1756 Browne 137, Gramen 4..Dutch Grass. This plant is very common in all the swampy bottoms round the Island, and grows sometimes very luxuriantly in the mountains. 1854–5 *TJSA* 1 68, Dutch Grass. Cynosurus Indicus.

2. *Panicum molle*: reclassified as *Panicum purpurascens*.

1864 Grisebach 783, Dutch grass: *Panicum molle*. 1959 UCWI Herbarium, Dutch grass, *Panicum purpurascens*.

3. *Stenotaphrum secundatum*.

1959 UCWI Herbarium: Dutch grass.

4. Other applications of uncertain authenticity.

1927 Beckwith 16, Dutch-grass (*Eleusine indica* Gaertn.). Wilfrid uses it as a tea for fever and boils it for a bath with 'Madam Fate' and tall Bahama grass. These three together he uses as a charm. 1952 FGC StE /doch graas/ bur grass.

DUTCHMAN'S LAUDANUM sb bot arch; *OED* 1756 only. An older name for BULL-HOOF (*Passiflora rubra*) alluding to its former use as a substitute for laudanum.

1756 Browne 328–9, Passiflora 12..The Bull-hoof, or *Dutchman's* Laudanum..Both the syrup and decoction of the plant is now much used in the leeward parts of the island..and is said to answer, effectually, all the purposes for which the syrup of poppies and liquid laudanum are generally administered. 1926 Fawcett 240. 1955 *WIMJ* 159.

DUTCH POT, DUTCHY (POT) sb dial; cf *dutch oven*. An iron pot with handles and three or four feet, which may be covered and have fire heaped over as well as under; used for baking, sometimes frying. s DUTCHY MAID.

1943 *GL* Clar, Dutchie, a small pot. 1955 FGC Man /dòch úovn/ have three foot, cover; /dóch pàt/—no cover. 1956 Mc Man /doch pat/ the preferred term; /áian pát, dóchii/ occasionally; StAnd /dochi/. 1958 DeC Port /dochi/ a heavy iron pot with cover; short for *Dutch pot*.

DUTCH RUNNER sb arch; cf *OED Dutch* 2, 3 and *runner* 12c. A type or variety of the bean *Phaseolus vulgaris*.

1837 Macfadyen 283, *Phaseolus compressus*..Of this species there are two varieties; α. *humilis*, or the *poor man's pea*: β. *major*, the *common Dutch runner*. They are both much esteemed, and are very generally cultivated. 1920 Fawcett 64.

DUTCHY (POT) see DUTCH POT.

DUTTY /dóti/ also overcorrected as /dórty/ sb dial; <Twi *dɔ̀tέ*, soil, earth, clay, mud; infl by Engl *dirt, dirty*. *BL G*

1. Earth, soil; the ground. (There is no necessary sense of uncleanness.)

1943 *GL* many parishes, Dutty, earth. 1950 Pioneer 63, Brer Nancy leggo piece ah de cane mek it drap boof! pan dutty side ah one ah de cow dem. [*Brother Anancy let go a piece of the cane and made it drop boof! on the ground beside one of the cows.*] 1954 LeP /óuta dóti/ *Outside on the..clean ground in the yard.* 1955 Bennett *Gawn a Match*, Rain a come but dutty tough.

2. Excrement, dung. (Cf *OED dirt* 1 →1830.)

1910 Anderson-Cundall 20 [Prov:] Fowl dream say him hab gout a him foot, same time when him wake a nuttin but dutty. 1925 Beckwith 91 [Prov:] Ole basket no good fe not'ing but to carry dutty in. [Cf DUNG BASKET.] 1943 *GL* several parishes, Dutty, excrement. 1952 FGC Tre, Tumble-bug roll /dangki dorti/—live in it.

DUTTY adj dial; in dialect writing, a sp for *dirty*—infl by DUTTY sb and by phonological change—see Introd.

1. In ordinary senses: Dirty. *BL G T*

1950 Pioneer 96, Dis 'oman scrub de floor, She lick an' pran de dutty room.

2. Of a person: Having the skin broken out with the sores of yaws.

1960 CLS 158 /hím dóti, yu núo, an ha súor an brúok óut, ál di yáaz káb dem dé pan im/ *He is dirty, you know, and has sores and is broken out, all the yaws scabs are on him.*

DUTTY MUMA /dóti múma/ sb dial; < DUTTY adj + MUMA. A children's game, prob the same as DOG MUMA.

1957 JN (Mt Pleasant), Girl: I like to play ring games, dutty mumma, and I like to sing and dance; (Troy), Girl: Wi run up and down [at school, in the recess] and play Dutty Muma and them beat we and wi roll in a dut [dirt]; (Yallahs) Play dirty mather.

DUTTY POT /dóti pát/ sb dial; < DUTTY adj + *pot*. A children's mud-pie game: see quot.

1957 JN StAnn [Schoolgirl:] We play duty pat. [Teacher's note:] Playing in earth. Making pudding, soup, cakes, etc. out of earth with water.

DUUDA sb dial; prob conn with *dude*—perh for **duder*, in the sense of playing the dude. Cf DOOSE.

1943 *GL* Tre, Duuda, walking stick.

duudu see *duodo*.

duuna pan sb dial; perh < Cent Amer Island-Carib (and St Vincent) *dúna*, water (< Karina *túna*) + *pan* (Douglas Taylor). A large metal receptacle for water: see quots.

1956 Mc Man /dúuna pán/ a tar drum used as a water pan; StAnd, a kerosene tin for carrying water; StE (Accom), A big, wide bath-pan with two handles; StE (Eld), A cylindrical metal container for water.

DWARF CEDAR sb bot; *DAE* 1850 for a small-sized Northern cedar. *BA*

1914 Fawcett 72, *Pilea grandifolia*..Dwarf Cedar.

DWARF ELDER sb bot obs; see quot. DWARF CEDAR (*Pilea grandifolia*).

a 1711 Barham (1794) 55, Dwarf elder..Linn. *Urtica grandifolia*. [This plant is so called because it something resembles the European dwarf-elder, being a short plant, with a round jointed stalk and a reddish fruit; but its leaves are much like the large English nettle. Quoted in 1813 Lunan I 276.] 1864 Grisebach 783, Dwarf Elder: *Pilea grandis*.

DWARF KIDNEY BEAN sb. A variety of *Phaseolus vulgaris*, resembling, but smaller than, the kidney bean.

1837 Macfadyen 283, Phaseolus nana. *Dwarf Kidney-bean*..is a native of the East Indies, but is now extensively cultivated in this Island. 1920 Fawcett 64.

DWARF MANGO sb. *G*

1837 Macfadyen 222, 10. The dwarf Mango; growing in the upper mountains, size of a small plum, of no account as a fruit.

DWEET, DWIT see *dwiit*.

dwiim = duu + im see DO vb[1] 2.

dwiit /dwíit/ vb phr dial; in dial sp dweet, dwit; < *do it*. A dial pronunc in which stress has shifted to the vowel of *it*, which has become lengthened, the vowel of *do* has been syncopated: /dúu it/ > /dúwit/ > /dwíit/. Cf *dwiim*.

c 1915 FGC StAnd, remembered as common. 1946 U.Newton I 36, 'Do Teacher! A won't dweet again!' 1952 FGC StAnn [Of the preparation of coffee berries:] /hán mashíin kyan dwíit/ *A hand-machine can do it*; StM [Of the use of DANDELION seed as a coffee substitute:] /paach an draa as kaafi—hou wii dwiit/ *Parch and draw as coffee—how we do it*. *N*

dyuuk kuoko see DUKE COCO.

E[1] /i/ pron dial; < *it*. A spelling for *it* in dialect writing; the usual ones, however, are *i, i'* and *he*. *BL*

1877 Murray *Kittle* 6, Him gie you a drink, ef e even coss him fe go truss it [*If it even costs him to get it on trust*].

E[2] /e/ particle dial; cf A[8], *-i*, *-u*. A sound (far less common than /a/ or /i/) added to words ending in consonants; this is prob a relic of the adaptation of English words to W Afr sound-patterns. *BL*

1956 Mc Man, see /wishe paat/ WHICH PART.

EAR-DOVE sb obs; cf *OED* 1725 only. Prob the *Zenaida aurita*: the name is descriptive—see quot; it is equivalent to the species-word though whether the Latin translates the English, or the contrary, is uncertain.

1705 Ray *Synopsis* 184, Turtur auritus. Ear Dove. 1725 Sloane 304, An Ear Dove..it had two Spots of each side of the Neck of a dark Colour, whence the name of *Ear-Dove*.

EARS /iez, hiez/ sb dial; by dialect writers also sp AISE, AZE, etc.; for *ear*. *G*

1. The regular dial singular form (as well as the plural) for *ear*. *BA T*

1952 FGC StJ [Of the cap-sheet of a *kunu*:] /wi liiv it wit a híez so yu kyan huol it tu lif it/ *We leave it with an ear* (sidewise extension) *so you can hold it to lift it*.

2. Hence in cpds: EARS-CORNER, the tender place around the ear; EARS-HOLE, the hole of the ear; EARS-RING, an earring. *BL*

1900 Murray 8, You don't hab no nose agen. It change place wid you eas corner. 1925 Beckwith 17 [Prov:] Bad wud an' ear-hole never agree. 1941 Kirkpatrick 42, Unnu keep unnu ayes 'ole to de grung an' listen out fe 'im. 1946 U.Newton I 30, Yes, the trimmer comes to the 'ears corner'. I jump and he sticks me with the scissors. 1952 FGC StAnd, StAnn /íezring/. 1956 Mc Man, StAnd /íez-húol/.

EARSES /íeziz, yíerziz/ sb dial; false plur of *ears* treated as sg. *G*

1943 *GL* StE, Yerzes, ears.

EARTH-BOUND GODS sb dial. In the cant of the AFRICAN kumuna cult (StT), supposed deities. See quot.

1953 Moore 205–25, The earthbound gods of African cumina: Macoo (= Shadrak), Appei (= Meshak), Beeco (= Abendigo) [*sic*]..etc. [Moore lists over 70 such names, a conglomeration of Biblical, Classical, African or pseudo-African, etc., with lore about them.]

EARTH-EATER sb obs. A DIRT-EATER: one afflicted with geophagy.

1808 Stewart 273, The negroes are subject to a strange craving of the stomach for earth: earth-eaters are common upon almost every plantation..An elderly negro..considered a *mud-cake* as preferable to any other provisions. 1823 Stewart 307.

[**EAR-WIGGING** vbl sb legal slang obs; prob punning on the insect *earwig* and the lawyers' *ears* and *wigs*. See quot.

1835 Senior 116, The parties [to a legal action] now meet for the first time in battle array; all their forces mustered, and every manœuvre practised to gain information as to the probable result: this is called 'ear-wigging'.]

EAS see EARS.

EASE (ONE) UP vb phr dial. To be easy on (someone); to harm or punish less than one might. *BA BL G*

1950 Pioneer 19, Hear Anancy: 'Bredda Ticks, ah sorry fe yuh soh ah gwine ease yuh up'.

EASTER BUG sb. An insect that appears in large numbers around the Easter season.

1952 FGC Man, Easter bug—'similar to May bug, but not the same'.

EAST INDIAN sb; opposed to WEST INDIAN.

In compounds: (1) Of plants, etc., referring to origin in the general area of India, Indo-China, Polynesia, etc.—cf EAST INDIAN MANGO, etc. (2) Of people, referring to those brought to Jamaica from India chiefly from 1845 to 1847 and from 1883 to 1885 as indentured labourers, and who now compose about two percent of Jamaican population. *BA G T*(2)

EAST INDIAN MANGO sb. A variety of mango considered among the choicest.

1913 Harris 12, Serious efforts are now being made to distribute in large numbers grafted plants of the choicer East Indian mangoes, especially the superb type known as '*Bombay*'. 1952 FGC StAnd, StAnn, StM, StT /hiistíndyan/.

EAST INDIAN OKRO sb. A cucurbitaceous fruit that is eaten in much the same manner as okro, and resembles it somewhat in colour and shape. See quot.

1926 Fawcett 261, *Luffa acutangula*..East Indian Ochra..the fruit.. while still young, and not more than 4 inches long, is an excellent vegetable. It is peeled, boiled, and served dressed with butter, pepper and salt, or is used as an ingredient in curries.

EASY-TO-BROKE sb dial; cf BROKE.

1955 *WIMJ* 148, *Boerhavia scandens* L. Rat Ears; *Easy-to-Bruck*. This plant is used to make tea for colds and is also considered to be an excellent treatment for marasmus ('mirasmy') in children.

EASY-VEX adj dial; <*easy* adv+*vexed*.

1956 Mc Man, /iizi-véks/ quick-tempered.

EAT /íit, híit/ vb dial. In passive sense: To be eaten. *G*

1952 FGC StT etc. /di béri-dem kyàang híit/ *The berries can be eaten* (*are edible*).

EATABLE GOOTOO see GUTU.

EAT-AN'-LEF' see *iit-an-lef*.

EATING-MATCH sb dial joc; on the analogy of *boxing-match*, etc. A feast. (Latterly, an actual contest in eating.)

1868 Russell 2, Eating-match, a feast. 1873 Rampini 85, And then ensues a feast or 'eating match'. [At a wake.] 1960 FGC current.

EBBY-PALM sb obs: The ABBAY palm is evidently intended, but Gosse has misidentified it.

1851 Gosse 464, Palm-trees, chiefly..the Fan-thatch.. and the bristling Ebby-palm (*Acrocomia sclerocarpa*).

ebelait see EBOE-LIGHT.

EBOE, IBO sb; African.

1. The country of origin of the Eboe or Ibo people, in present SE Nigeria.

1790 Moreton 153 [Song:] If me want for go in a Ebo, Me can't go there!

2. An African people of SE Nigeria; one derived from this stock. They were looked down upon by the Cromanty negroes. *BL G*

1757 *St Jago Intelligencer* 14 May [Runaway slaves:] 1 Ebo, 1 Angola, 1 Mundingo. 1774 Long II 403–4, the Ebo men are lazy, and averse to every laborious employment; the women performing almost all the work in their own country..the Ebo women labour well. *Ibid* 424, the Ebos, the Papaws, &c. 1793 Edwards II 52, The slaves purchased on this part of the coast, have the general denomination of Eboes; probably from Arebo, the name of a village..on the river Benin. 1877 Murray *Kittle* 27, Yerry dem Eboe fellow—'Broke Whanica Penny comb.. Kill de debil moder'.

3. A person of light or yellowish colour: cf RED EBOE.

[1793 Edwards II 73, We are now come to the Bight of Benin, comprehending an extent of coast..of which the interior countries are unknown, even by name, to the people of Europe. All the Negroes imported from these vast and unexplored regions..are called in the West Indies Eboes..In complexion they are much yellower than the Gold Coast and Whidah Negroes; but it is a sickly hue, and their eyes appear as if suffused with bile, even when they are in perfect health.] 1942 HPJ, Marion said people in the country gave the name of Eboes to people who were neither black nor sambo: Eboes were red—the father and mother of an Eboe were both red. (Yellow seemed to be the colour really meant..) 1943 *GL* Kgn, Hebo, a red person; No addr, Ebo, a person of less colour than a mulatto.

EBOE DRUM sb arch. A type of large drum favoured by the EBOES.

a 1818 Lewis (1845) 39, their music consisted of nothing but Gambys (Eboe drums), Shaky-shekies, and Kitty-katties. 1826 Williams 21–2, they again assembled on the lawn before the house with their gombays, bonjaws, and an ebo drum, made of a hollow tree, with a piece of sheepskin stretched over it.

EBOE-LIGHT /èbeláit/ sb; occas sp *ebolite*; EBOE+light, sb. The tree *Erythroxylon areolatum*, at one time used for torches (cf its other name TORCH-WOOD), later for walking-sticks; a stick made of this wood.

1864 Grisebach 783, Eboe-light or Eboe-torchwood: *Erythroxylum brevipes*. 1912 McK *Ballads* 49, All dem boys wid eboe-light dem, dem is waitin' deh fe me..But me eboe-light wi' sure talk, of dat you can have no doubt. Note: Sticks made of eboe-light or torchwood. 1952 FGC StE /èbeláit/ used for walking stick; StJ, sp *ebolite*.

EBOE-TAYA sb dial obs; <EBOE+TAYA. Some kind of COCO, evid assoc with the EBOE people. (Perh confused with EDDO?)

1790 Beckford II 143, the Eboetoyer is raised with most success in brick-mould land, upon the banks of rivers..It has heads and fingers like the coco; is apt to scratch the mouth if not properly boiled; but is otherwise an agreeable root, and in taste resembles an artichoke bottom.

EBOE TORCHWOOD, EBOLITE see EBOE-LIGHT.

EBONY /ebini, hebini/ sb; cf *OED* 1 b, and ref to quot 1725, though there is none.

1. The tree *Brya ebenus* or its wood, which somewhat resembles true ebony. *BA*

1696 Sloane 140, Ebony. In sylvis campestribus Ins. Jam. a 1726 Barham (1794) 56, Ebony..Its heart, or inner part, is as black as jet. 1868 Russell 5, Hebiny, Ebony. 1952 FGC StAnd, StE, etc. /ébini/.

2. A switch made of prickly branches of ebony, formerly used to punish slaves.

1788 Marsden 41, He used to give them the further discipline of *ebonies*, which is something like our birch with short prickles.

ECHINI STONES sb obs. The shells of dead sea-eggs.

1774 Long II 49, The astroites, or star-stones and brontiæ, hedge-hog and echini stones are found in great abundance on the coast.

eda /éda/ pron dial; <*other*. The less common dial pronunc of *other*, the usual one being /áda/; cf *aneda*, *breda*, etc. *G T*

1956 Mc Man /dísaya rúod sháata dan di éda/ *This road is shorter than the other;* /di éda píkni ráng/ *The other child was wrong.*

[**EDDO** /édo/ sb; 1721 edy, 1756 edye; 1727→ eddo, 1788 eddow, 1864 eddoe; cf Fante *edwó*(*w*), yam, *ndwo*(*w*), root. *OED* 1685→;

not limited to Jamaica. The edible root or tuber of *Xanthosoma* spp and sometimes of *Colocasia esculenta*: a former name, never very common, for the TAYA. **s.** *BA G N T*

1721 *Courant* 28 June, there is also a Plantain-Walk[,] Piece of Ginger, and Edys, and a Garden. a 1726 Barham (1794) 56, Eddo. There are three or four sorts of them: Piso calls them *taiaoba*, and from thence came the word *tayas*; but they are the largest sort, and are apt to cause a heat in the throat. 1756 Browne 332, The old roots are generally called *Scratch Coccos*, from a little pungency with which they are always impregnated; and the young ones that shoot round the top, *Edyes*. 1788 Francklyn 22, Corn, yams, cocos, or eddowes. 1864 Grisebach 783, Eddoe; *Colocasia esculenta*. 1952 FGC Han /édo/ = /hag-taaya/—grows on dry ground; StM /ádo/ vaguely recalled.]

EDDY WASP sb.

1943 *NHN* II 47, The parasitic wasp (*Eretmocerus serius*): locally christened the 'Eddy Wasp', in honour of Mr W. H. Edwards, our Government Entomologist, which was introduced from Cuba in 1930 to control the Citrus Black Fly.

EDGE-TEETH see *nej-tiit*. *G*

EDGE-UP adj dial or slang; prob for *edging-up*. Companionable, friendly, eager to be acquainted. *G*

1943 *GL* StJ, Rakish, hedge-up, companionish.

EDOH-EDOH int dial; cf Twi *adwó èè*, a call for attention. 'A call used by hill people' (StE, Accompong); see quot.

1951 Murray 36 [Song:] Edoh-edoh..House an' lan' a buy fambly oh!

e-e /e-e/ int dial; two short midfront vowels preceded by glottal stops and in close juncture, with falling pitch: spelt *eh-eh*, and pronounced [ʔεʔε]; infl from English *eh* is phonologically unlikely; cf Twi *èì*, *éèì*, interj expressing surprise, astonishment: indeed! *G T* Antigua.

An interjection showing surprise, often amused surprise, sometimes worry; sometimes used tauntingly.

c 1915 FGC StAnd [ʔεʔε], exclamation of surprise. 1942 Bennett 45, De wan no mo week me spen' deh Me meet crosses! eh! eh! [*The one mere week I spent there* (in the city) *I had many troubles. Oh dear!*] 1943 GL StE, Eheh, an exclamation of jest; West, Eheh, look here. 1957 Bennett 7, Wich part him ever hear smady dance John-Cunoo widout dress-up, eh-eh!

EE /iing/ int dial; a prolonged, nasalized high-front vowel, said with rising pitch: sp *ee*; it corresponds in use to English *eh?* and prob comes from it. The pitch also corresponds to the English; the nasalization may be due to African influence. Cf *iim*, *iin-hiin*. *G T*

Eh? (Asking for repetition of a statement, or for agreement.)

1942 Bennett 47, Ah bex soh tell ah Keahn talk. Wat a trial ee Miss Vie? 1943 *GL* StC, Ee? what? 1950 Pioneer 35, Yuh mussa feel sweet wid yuh wing dem ee, Bredda Wasp. [*You must feel delightful with your wings, eh, Brother Wasp?*]

EE-HEE, EE-HI, EENHI see *iin-hiin*.

EEN, EENA see *iin*, *iina*.

EENA HIM SAAL see IN (ONE'S) SALT.

EENO see *i-no*.

EERIE adj dial; prob < *airy* (cf *OED* 6c,d), lively, gay, etc.; perh also having the sense of 'putting on airs'. Fashionable, stylish, gay, like a beau in dress and appearance. **s.**

a 1818 Lewis (1834) 201, 'Massa, please, me want one little coat..for wear when me go down to the Bay'.—'And why should you wear a little coat when you go to the Bay?'—'Massa, please, make me look eerie (buckish) when me go abroad'. So I assured him that he looked quite *eerie* enough already; and that..there could not be the slightest occasion for his being a bit *eerier* than he was. *Ibid* 118 [Song:] Hey-ho-day! neger now quite eerie (*i.e.* hearty).

EF /ef/ conj dial; < *if*; cf US dial pronunc.

A common (but not the prevailing) pronunc of *if*. *G*

1868 Russell 20, Ef (if). 1956 Mc StE (Accom) /ef im kom bak/ *IF he comes back*. The *ef* is emphatic, expressing strong doubt.

efn /éfn/ conj dial; < *if* + *-n*, suffix[1]. If. *G*

1957 JB StAnd /efn mi kom dong a nait, it wi tuu haad fi kom op bak/.

ef yu bad phr dial. If you dare. *BL G*

1957 JN Albert Town, 'Barbara come let we go over de so go play, the boys too provoking. Lawd hear wha him say, "Dweet ef you bad!"'. *Barbara, let us go and play over there, the boys are too provoking. Lord, did you hear what he said? 'Do it if you dare!'*

EGG FRUIT sb obs; cf *ODS* 1887, *DA* 1817. The GARDEN EGG (egg-plant).

1811 Titford 53, Egg Fruit or Mad Apple, *Solanum Melongena*..It is called in India Branjaw, in Jamaica, Garden Egg and Valanghanna, Brown Jolly or Bolangena.

EGG LILY sb chiefly dial. A type of lily that produces a fruit about the size and shape of a hen's egg: *Hymenocallis arenicola*.

1952 FGC StAnn, Egg lily.

EGG PUNCH sb obs? A beverage similar to egg-nog. *BL*

1839 Mc Mahon 185, Two or three of them coming in company together, the resident overseer calls for egg-punch, and directs the young females upon the estate at once to be assembled together, for the purpose of a dance.

EGG-TRASH sb dial; < *egg* + TRASH. Egg-shells.

1927 Beckwith 11, For a woman in labour, make it into a tea with 'egg-trash' (shells) and drink luke-warm.

EGSVANTAGE see *egvaantij*.

eguma sb dial; prob < *egg* + GUMA. A small weed (*Phyllanthus niruri*) which has tiny ball-like flowers in rows under the leaf stems.

1952 FGC StC, /eguma/, the Clarendon name for the little balls on the under side of leaf of the wild tamarind weed that's like rice bitters; used by midwives.

egvaantij sb and vb dial; for sp see quots; < *advantage*. An occasional pronunciation; cf ADVANTAGE.

1877 Murray *Feedin' 'Perrit* 8, 'Wha' you mean fe tek a egsvantage o' me, becausin' you see I da sleep'. Sis I, 'No egsvantage at all, sar, git up'. 1942 Bennett 19, She no know de eggvantige dem teck wid de chile Wen she go teck dat deh fo-fool exam. 1943 *GL* Kgn, etc., Egvantige, advantage.

EH see EE.

EH-EH see *e-e*.

EHNEE see *iin-hiin*.

EIDON sb dial cant. In the language of the St Thomas AFRICAN cult: see quot.

1953 Moore 160, Eidon = baby duppies who died before christening, are even more dangerous for they can never be identified and have no human knowledge.

EIL-NUT see OIL-NUT.

EKKA prep dial rare; etym unknown.

1943 *GL* StM, Ekka, out of.

ELBOW-GREASE sb dial; cf *OED*. A coconut RUNDOWN; the name alludes to the continued stirring necessary in cooking it. *G*

1958 DeC StT.

ELDER TREE sb obs. PEPPER-ELDER.

1756 Browne 122, Piper 2..The Elder-tree.

ELEPHANT FOOT CANE sb dial.

1952 FGC StJ /élifant fút kíen/ a stout type of cane that resembles an elephant's foot [i.e. leg].

ELEPHANT('S) EAR sb.

Any of several plants: 1. *Pithecellobium cyclocarpum*, from the shape of the seed-pod (1959 UCWI Herbarium); 2. *Argyria bracteata*, from the shape of the leaf (1958 LeP StAnd); 3. The leaves or the plants of various species of *Arum* or *Colocasia*; 4. The fern *Elaphoglossum crinitum*, from the shape and hairiness of its leaves. (c 1915 FGC StAnd.) *BA*

ELEPHANT'S FOOT sb; cf *ODS* 1817–18. Species of plants including *Elephantopus mollis*, the genus-name and common-name referring to the shape of the lower leaves of *E. scaber*.

1811 Titford 90, Rough-leaved Elephant's Foot. Elephantopus scaber..native of Jamaica..It is common on the north side. 1936 Fawcett 164, *E. mollis*..Elephant's Foot. 1955 WIMJ 158.

ELEVEN-PLAIT /lebm plat/ sb dial. Having eleven plaited strips of palm sewn side by side: see quot.

1877 Murray *Kittle* 19, His broad-brimmed *chapeau* was made of palmetto straw in the style that is known in the trade as *''leven plait'*.

ELEVEN STEPS sb dial. A phrase symbolizing the court-house, hence arrest and trial. Cf FOUR-AND-TWENTY(-STEPS).

1952 FGC StM, Take him up eleven steps, take him to court; Me wear me blue-boot go up eleven steps. 1955 FGC Man /levm tep/ court house.

ELLINAYARD sb dial; etym unknown; analyzable in several ways; the last element is evid YARD. See quot.

1943 *GL* no addr, Ellinayard, A group of three stars appearing always in November.

elmat see HELMET.

EMBARRASSED adj dial; *embarrass(ed)* perh blended with *barrow(s)*? Pregnant; in application to a man, perh means castrated.

1960 Dr W. Harper UCWI, To call a woman an embarrassed sow or a man an embarrassed hog is one of the direst insults among the Jamaican populace.

EMBO int dial rare; cf Ewe *mbó*, good! just so!; Carambula: *embó*, witchcraft.

1943 *GL* StE, Embo, an address to birds meaning 'pitch there', alight.

EMMA BEAN sb dial; etym unknown, but perh named after a woman who grew them successfully. A type of large bean (unidentified).

1952 FGC StT /ema biin/.

en 3rd pers pron; evid a var form of *him*, but 'distinguished almost consistently by this speaker from /im/' (JN), /en/ evid being pretty regularly a fem form. She (and occas other pers prons).

1957 JN StAnn, Q. Where is Miss V? I would like to see her. A. 'En dung a yäd. Q. No, Sonia, I am just coming down from there and she is not there. A. 'En no dung deh 'm. Q. Where is Uncle Charles? A. Im a sleep.

en auxil vbl particle; <*ben*, been. An auxiliary particle equiv in meaning and use to BEN, WEN, though less common than either; it is used to form past-time verbal expressions. **s** *heng*.

1943 *GL* Clar, Inda, were or was; Tre, Endey, was. [These would be used in such a sentence as, 'Me no know you en da go', *I did not know you were going.*] 1952 FGC Han /ef yu en truo mi we/ *If you had thrown me away*. 1957 JN StJ [Boys playing marbles:] My set aright, mi e go (/mi en go/) fi mi taa an mek wi play now. [*I went for my taw—let's play now.*]

-EN see *-n*.

ena see prec.

ENGET vb or adj dial; etym unknown, but cf *EDD angish* 2, poverty-stricken (Irel).

1943 *GL* StC, Enget, to be hungry.

ENGLISH BATATA sb obs; cf *DA* 1750→. The 'Irish' potato (*Solanum tuberosum*).

a 1726 Barham (1794) 153, Potatoes, *or* Batatas. Convolvulus..they exceed, in my opinion, the Irish or English *batata*.

ENGLISH CALALU sb dial; perh so called in contrast to SPANISH CALALU. The cultivated 'spinach' calalu: *Amarantus viridis*.

1952 FGC StAnn, /íngglish kálalu/—broad green leaves, thick stalk.

ENGLISH FLOUR sb arch or obs. Wheat flour, formerly imported from England; local flour would be cassava flour.

1893 Sullivan 85, etc., English flour, wheat flour.

ENGLISH PLANTAIN (LEAF) sb; 'English' is used to distinguish this from the plantain fruit and tree (*Musa paradisiaca*). The common weed, *Plantago major* (*tropica* Grisebach). See quots.

1814 Lunan II 70, Plantain, English. Plantago..For an hæmorrhage of blood, take..English plantain leaf. 1927 Beckwith 17, English plantain..For sore eyes, boil, strain, and wash the eyes with the tea. 1952 FGC StC, StT /ingglish plantn liif/ good for eyes. 1954 *WIMJ* 19, *Plantago majqr* L. English Plantain. The leaves of this species are rich in potassium salts and contain citric acid.

en-hen see *iin-hiin*.

ENKIE sb dial; etym unknown.

1954 LeP StE (Elderslie), Enkie, short, thickly-built person.

ENTOH vb dial rare; etym unknown.

1943 *GL* StC, Entoh, to turn round.

ERECT BROOMWEED sb bot obs; cf BROOMWEED. In Macfadyen's use: *Sida salviæfolia* (ident 1926 Fawcett 117).

1837 Macfadyen 80, Sida erecta. *Erect Broomweed.*

ERYSIPELAS PLANT sb.

1955 *WIMJ* 71, *Heliotropium indicum* L. Clary; Wild Clary; Turnsoles; Scorpion Weed; Erysipelas Plant. This species is occasionally used in Jamaica in the same way as *H. parviflorum*. Lunan claimed that a decoction is diuretic..etc.

ESAU sb dial; <*Esau*, the Biblical character. Rum; perh with some allusion to Esau's loss of his birthright?

1958 DeC Port (Moore Town) /iisaa/, rum, especially white rum.

[**ESCOBYOUN** sb mil; prob <Sp *escobillión*, a swab, sponge, tube-cleaner. Evid soldiers' slang: soup; implying that the soup is made from swabbings or scourings?

1943 *GL* Kgn, Escobyoun, Soup served to soldiers (J.T.V.).]

ESCOVEITCHED FISH sb; <Sp *escabeche*, pickled fish +*-ed*. This is a 'corrected' form; the word is usually found in the reduced forms SCAVEECHED FISH or CAVEACH.

1889 see quot s.v. SCAVEECHED FISH. 1957 *FFM* 158, Escoveitched Fish [recipe given].

ESPEUT /espyuut/ sb chiefly dial; <the surname of W. B. *Espeut*, who introduced the mongoose to Jamaica. The mongoose.

1943 *GL* StT, Espeut, nickname for mongoose. 1952 FGC StAnd /héspyuut/.

ESSENCE /èsént, ésen, ésn/ sb; <*essence* (*OED* 10, 'a fragrant essence; a perfume, scent. Somewhat *arch*.') →1855. The folk-pronunc regularly loses final /s/ as if it were a plural inflection. Perfume, scent. (The regular term in shops.) *G*

1952 FGC StE /tèk di flóuwaz mèk èsént/ *Take the flowers to make perfume.*

ESTATE sb; *DAE* 1742→. 'A landed property' (*OED*). In Ja specif: one where sugar-cane is grown. *BA G T*

1671–2 *Jrnls Assembly* 5, An act in Sir Thomas Modyford's time, entitled 'An act for quieting men's estates against dormant titles'. 1835 Senior 38, These properties are denominated *estates*, where the sugar, rum, and molasses are produced. The *plantation* is a more general term, and comprehends those on which are cultivated coffee, pimento, ginger, cotton, arrow-root, and other minor products. 1847 *Memorial of House of Assembly* 24 Dec, Estate—a sugar property.

ETAHOTI APPLE see OTAHEITE APPLE.

ETHIOPIA APPLE sb dial; by folk-etym <*iitiuoti* or similar var of OTAHEITE APPLE.

1960 LeP StAnd, Ethiopia apple, the Otaheite apple.

[**ETTOW** sb bot; evid a Tahitian word, introduced with the plant in 1793. *Cordia sebestena.*

1794 Broughton 6, Cordia[,] Ettow Otaheite H.M.S. Providence 1793. 1814 Lunan I 1, The *ettow*, a variety of the *cordia sebestena*..is said to be a good dyewood. 1864 Grisebach 783.]

etu sb dial; cf Twi *tòw*, to cast away, *tow poŋ*, give a banquet or entertainment, *ɛtów*, tribute, toll, tax; to collect taxes. (Christaller.) Evid a preserved Africanism: see quot. Cf SET-UP.

1959 DeC Han /etu/ a funeral celebration involving great expense and usually a feast. (Berry found that this is also used of a wedding feast; he associates it with a Twi(?) word for fees or expenses connected with feasting.)

EVELING /iivlin/ sb dial occas; by lambdacism <*evening*. s.

1868 Russell 18, In the evening, kobite, or good eveling. 1952 FGC Tre /shi kom bak in di iivlin/. 1956 Mc StE (Accom) /dis iivlin/.

EVENING /iivnin/ sb dial; cf US old fashioned rural use; cf EVELING. The part of the day from about 3 (or even earlier) to 5 P.M. *BA G N*

1952 FGC 'This evening'=after 1; West, 'Good evening' [said to someone arriving at 3.30]; StM /iivnin/ 3 till 5; StT, Evening—four o'clock going on. 1956 Mc Man, Port, Evening /iivnin/=afternoon: used very commonly in morning as greeting both in Moore Town and Banana Ground; StAnd, When is it evening? From one o'clock.

EVERGREEN BEAD TREE sb bot obs. The HOOP TREE, *Melia azederach.* Cf also BEAD TREE, WEST INDIAN LILAC.

1811 Titford 64, Evergreen bead tree, or Indian Lilac, *Melia Sempervirens*..nat. Jamaica.

EVERY BIT quasi-pron phr dial. Used of people: all; every one. *G*

1956 Mc StE (Accom) /yu síi hou shr'li-dem, ebri bít a dem gáan, líiv yu hie/ *You see how Shirley and the others, every one of them, have gone, and have left you here.*

EXTRA adj, adv, sb and vb dial; <*extra* adj.

A. adj: 1. Extravagant (in self-assertion, boasting).

1954 LeP Kgn, Be extra, to boast.

2. Extravagant (in being annoying, making objections).

1958 BLB Man /im tuu ekstra/ *She's too fussy.*

B. adv: Extravagantly: also in the phr *go on extra*.

1924 Beckwith 132, The godmother was so annoyed she cut out her tongue and left her there weeping extra. 1958 DeC gen, In the phrase 'Go(ing) on extra'—to behave extravagantly; /no bada guoing an ekstra with mii/.

C. sb: An extravagant person (in making a fuss, etc.).

1954 LeP StAnn, Extra, fussy, pernickety person.

D. vb: To boast.

1958 DeC, Extra, to boast.

e-ye /e-yé/ int dial arch; prob <Northeast Engl dial forms of aye: Nhb *eyeh*, Linc *eye*, w York *eea*, *eeah* (*EDD*); cf New England (etc.) *ayuh*, and Twi *yée*, *yê*, a reply to a call, showing that it has been heard. An occas pronunc of *aye*, corresponding to *i-ne*, no.

1943 *GL* Clar, Port, Eyey, yes; Clar Eyéh, yes; Kgn, Ayah, yes.

EYE see *hai*, *yai*.

EYE-BRIGHT sb; cf *OED*, appl to *Euphrasia officinalis*. *Euphorbia thymifolia*; so called from its use as an eye medicine.

1725 Sloane 371, The Juice drop'd into the Eyes takes off Spots after the Small-Pox, it is in great use in Jamaica for that, and call'd Eye-Bright. Mr Barham in his MS. a 1726 Barham 180–2. 1864 Grisebach 783, Eyebright: *Euphorbia maculata.*

EYE-BRUBRU, -BRUSH sb dial; prob folk-etym. Eyebrow(s).

1943 *GL* StAnd, Yeye brubru, eyebrow. 1956 Mc Man /yai-brosh, hai-/ eyebrow.

EYED PALLETTE-TIP see PALLETTE-TIP LIZARD.

EYE SASH-WINDOW sb dial joc. The eyes' sash-windows: eyeglasses.

1943 *GL* StE, Yey sash window, spectacles.

EYESIGHT sb slang.

1943 *GL* StAnd, Yeyesight, 'hush money'.

EYE-SKIN /yái-kín/ sb dial. Eyelid or eyelids.

1943 Bennett 3, Well lawd, wen har y'eye kin come dung She fava dead smaddy. 1943 *GL* Clar, Yi kin, eyelids.

EYE-WATER sb dial; cf *OED* →1845, but this may be a loan-translation—cf MOUTH-WATER. Tears. *BL G N*

1950 Pioneer 24, De door open an ongle her daughta y'eye wata was een de room. 1955 Bennett *Bad Foot*, Koo how y'eye wata dah flow. [*See how the tears are flowing!*]

FAADA see FATHER.

faam, FAAM see FORM, *form*.

faas see FAST.

faawod see *farad*.

FACCIE see *fasi*.

FACETINESS sb dial; <FACETY+*-ness*. Impudence, rudeness.

1942 Bennett 18, Ah hooden stan' har facetiness Far we wasen company.

FACETY /fíesti/ adj dial;? <*face* sb+*t* (*OED* 'parasitic *t*')+*-y*: apparently parallel to FACEY, but cf Surinam Creole *fiésti*, dirty, nasty (Focke), and Engl *fist* sb², a stink (*OED*). Impudent, bold, rude, overbearing.

1943 *GL* StC, Fasty, proud, bigoted; StT, Facety, impertinent. 1956 Mc Man /fíesi/ or /fíesti/—alternatives; StE (Accom) /fíesti/ cheeky, bold; Tre /fíesti/ impudent (used of a child who back-answers). 1957 JN Rural Hill, Yuh too untrute! What, de woman is a fasty woman! Hou yuh mean to send and tell me dat, woman?

FACEY /fíesi/ adj dial; <*face*, cf *OED* 7, 'impudence, effrontery, "cheek"', +*-y*. Impertinent, rude, 'forward'. Cf FACETY. *BL G*

1929 Beckwith 88, Although good spirits also come back to earth 'to make holiday', as some say, only a bad spirit is 'facey' enough to show himself to you. 1933 McK gloss, Facey: brisk, forward. 1943 *GL* Port, Facy—rude; Port, Facey—fierce [this seems to imply a belief that the words are related]; StAnn, Facey—premature [cf 'forward']. 1957 JN StAnn, What a facey gal. Lick him back. Him too facey.

FACT-AND-(A-)HALF /fak-an-aaf/ sb dial. A lie.

1942 HPJ, Fac-an-alf—A lie.

FACUMA see *fiekuma*.

FACY see FACEY.

FADGE vb dial; cf *OED* →1789. To manage as well as one can; to contrive to get on. *BA BL*

1942 HPJ, Fadge: make things work together in spite of disharmony and inconveniences. (Said of a man who was starting a cultivation and working for wages at the same time.) 1943 *GL* Kgn, Faj, to manage, I must faj fe meself. 1955 FGC Man, Fadge for yourself.

faia-bon see FIRE-BURN.

faia-kiti see FIRE-KITTY.

faivaz sb dial; a pronunc of *fibres*.

1952 FGC StM /haloz—yu trip it—tred iz faivaz, mek hanbag, bedruum shuuz/ *Aloes: you strip it, the thread is fibres*, etc.

FAJ see FADGE.

FALALINE, FALLALINE see FOLLOW-LINE.

FALL-DOWN-BUSH sb dial. A wild plant whose lower leaves are shrubby (*Rivina humilis*): the species-name and 'fall-down' evid allude to the same effect.

1952 FGC StM, Fall-down-bush, dog-blood, timi-timi; for bruises; drink as tea.

FALLING /fáalin/ vbl sb dial. A cascade, a waterfall.

1907 Jekyll 145, One day brother Annancy always set him fish-pot in a river ober a fallin' fe catch jonga.

FALLING-MATCH sb; <*falling* vbl sb (cf *ODS* 7) +*match*, contest. 'When somebody wants to get a lot of trees felled, he summons the men to a "falling match"—i.e. he asks them to come and help! He generally supplies food and drink.' Mc. Cf DIGGING-MATCH.

1956 Mc StE /men aks plenti men in di fiil tu faal plenti triiz—faalin-mach/.

FALL RAIN sb; cf *DAE* 13 quot 1852 only.

1823 Stewart 40, the autumnal or *fall rains*, as they are called by the planters, fall in October and November.

FALL ROUND vb phr dial; cf *OED fall v* X. To take up a position with respect to something. *G*

1958 DeC /dem faal roun di trii fi bigin kot it; dem faal roun di fiil fi bigin huo it/.

FALSE HOG-GUM sb; <*false*+HOG-GUM.

1864 Grisebach 784, False Hog-gum: *Rhus metopium*.

FALSE TUNA sb dial; <*false*+TUNA. A variety of TUNA cactus not considered the 'true' one.

1952 FGC StAnd (Pt Henderson) /faals tuuna/.

FALSE WINTER'S BARK sb bot. See CANELLA, and quot 1955.

FAMBILY, FAMBLE see FAMILY. *G*

FAME sb dial rare; cf *OED* 1 →1855. A report, rumour. (Evid preserved in story-telling style; not heard in conversation.)

1956 Mc StE (Accom) [Story:] /di fiem spred a hou hanaansi hiiting piipl/ *The report (rumour) spread of how Anancy was eating people.*

FAMILY /famili, fambili, faambli/ sb dial; <*family*. A relative; freq plur and mutual: relatives, relations, kin. *BA BL G*

1942 Bennett 12, Is Emeriah dah yuh muma bwoy? Den tap-tap, we dah fambily! [*Is Emeriah your mother, boy? Then hold on, we are relatives!*] 1943 *GL* West, Famble, relative. 1952 FGC StAnd, Flying ants are 'family to duck-ants'; West, Me and him is family. 1956 Mc StE (Accom) /him mi fambili, wi a fambili yu no/ *He's a relative of mine, we are relatives, you know.* 1957 EB Port /faambli/—cousin or any blood relation.

FAMOUS sb dial cant. An AFRICAN 'god'.

1953 Moore 146, The god who keeps the gate, Famous (or Kish), is invoked and fed so that there will be a spirit guard at the gate to control the spirit world.

FAN vb dial. *G*

1. To wave, swing back and forth like a fan. *T*

1907 Jekyll 106, Anancy say: 'Bro'er Cow. .fan you' tail with strength.' 1950 Pioneer 64, Cow ah fan him tail.

2. To have sexual intercourse with.

1951 Murray 51 [Song:] Fan Me Solja Man. .Gal yuh character gawn.

FAN BROOM, FAN THATCH /fan bruum, fan tach/ sb dial; <*fan* sb +THATCH. A small round-leaved thatch palm: from the leaves are made *thatch*—the material used in weaving hats and making brooms, ropes, etc.

1851 see quot s.v. EBBY-PALM. 1952 FGC StAnd /fan-tach/; StC /fan-bruum/—a small-leafed thatch without trunk: heart-leaves used for jippi-jappa hats.

FANCY-ANNA sb dial; by folk-etym <*Poinciana*. A name applied to a number of trees or other plants, mostly having conspicuous flowers: *Poinciana regia, Adenanthera pavonina*, etc.

1952 FGC StT /fànsi-ána/—Poinciana; StM, the red-bead tree; StAnn, Fancy Anna vine.

FANCY-BASKET sb. A basket prettily designed and made, with more decorative weave, colours, etc., than the common ones. *BA*

1958 DeC Kgn, StJ (Montego Bay) /fantsi-baskit/.. What is called fancy basket in Kingston and Montego Bay is in several districts of St James called a /liediz baskit/ or a /tuuris baskit/.

fandanggl, fandanggo see next.

FANDANGLE vb dial; <*fandangle* sb. To decorate with FANDANGOES; const *up*. *G*

1956 Mc Man /im fandánggl op imsèlf/ *He dressed himself up elaborately.*

FANDANGLE, FANDANGO /fandangas, fanggandanggas/ sb dial; cf *OED fandango*, esp 3. *G*

1. Elaborate or fussy decoration superimposed on a person, a piece of clothing, a building, etc. *BA*

1943 *GL* Port, Fangandangas, carving; StAnd, Fandangas, a fussy way of dressing. 1955 FGC Man /fandanggas/ dress-up: a person, a Christmas tree, etc. 1956 Mc Man /fandánggas, fandánggl/ elaborate bodice to a dress. 1957 EB Port /fandanggas/ decoration.

2. Foolishness.

1943 *GL* Port, Fandangas, foolishness. 1957 EB Port /fandanggas/ foolishness.

fanggandanggas see prec.

FANNY-BUSH sb dial; prob <*Fanny*, personal name +BUSH: prob assoc with a woman herbalist by this name. An unidentified 'tea-bush'.

1952 FGC StAnn /fáni-bùsh/ similar to piaba; has velvety leaves, looks like flax; wash plate with it.

FANNY COCKBURN, FANNY CORCA /fàni kákbòrn, fàni káaka/ sb dial; evid <personal names. The TURBOT.

1952 FGC StC.

FAN THATCH see FAN BROOM.

farad /fárad, fárid, fórod/ adj dial; <*forward*—cf nautical pronunc. 'Forward', impertinent, rude. *BL G*

1943 *GL* Clar, Farrid, forrad; Kgn StC, Farrad; StE, Furrud, impertinent.

FARINE sb dial rare; ? <*foreign*.

1943 *GL* StJ, Farine, unbleached calico.

FARRAD, FARRID see *farad*.

FARTHING BUMP /fáadn bómp/ sb dial. A small bit of cheap sugar-candy.

1942 Bennett 10, One no mo' farden bump she buy! *Ibid* 14, Me haffe gi' har wan farden bump Fe my-sen up har t'roat. [*I had to give her a farthing-bump to moisten up her throat.*]

FAS', FASS see FAST.

fasi /fasi/ sb and adj dial; <*farcy*, disease of horses; also 'communicated to men' *OED* 2 →1865.

1. A general term for sores on the skin, eruptions, and even abrasions.

1943 *GL* No addr, Fassy, eczema. 1954 LeP StE, Faccie, dry itching rash on the skin. 1959 Mrs Robinson, UCWI Preventive Med /fási/ used generally for sores, abrasions, cuts on the legs, etc. 1962 BLB 26 /go-we go wash yu fasi/ *Go bathe your sores* [an insulting expression].

2. Dirty.

1956 Mc StAnd /fási wáata/ dirty water.

FASSY see prec.

FAST /faas/ adj and vb dial; usually spelt *fast*, but also *fas*, *fass*, and once *fauce* in dialect writing; <*fast*, quick. *BL G N*

A. adj: Interfering; meddlesome; presuming or impudent; quick to intrude in others' affairs. *BA T*

1873 Rampini 100, He told me..that I was too d--n fast, and I was too mannish. 1910 Anderson-Cundall 28, John Crow say him a dandy man, but him put on bald head fe mek fas' s'mody fine fault wid him. 1924 Beckwith 54, Monkey didn't want Bredder Spider to marry his daughter as he thought Bredder Spider was too fast and beneath him. 1933 McK 316, Fass, impudent, officious. 1943 *GL* StC, Fauce, inquisitive. 1956 Mc Man /im tuu fass/ *He butts in*; StAnd /a no fi yu bizniz—yo tuu faas/ *It's none of your business—you interfere too much!*

B. vb intr: To meddle, interfere. *N*

1900 Murray 11, Look, yah boy, I tell you not fe fass wid my biness. 1954 LeP Kgn, StAnn, StT, Faas, fast, to meddle or interfere. 1956 Mc Port /yu gwain faas in di piipl-dem sese?/ *Are you going to interfere in those people's quarrel?*

FAST-BREEDING FRUIT sb dial; by folk-etym <FORBIDDEN FRUIT. The FORBIDDEN FRUIT.

1952 FGC StE /fáas-bríidn fruut/ bigger than grapefruit.

FASTEN vb dial. To become fastened, to get stuck, to be stuck. *BL G*

1924 Beckwith 24, Anansi open his right han' an' box de 'tump. His right han' fasten. 1950 Pioneer 18, Now me goat Bredda Ticks him fas'en eena de bush yah. 1957 JN StJ, Im buck him, im head fasten[,] im tek im belly box him im belly fasen.

FASTEN-MAN-COAT, FASTEN-'PON-COAT sb dial; cf FASTEN. *Priva lappulacea*, a plant whose burs stick to the clothing. See quots.

1952 FGC StC /fáasn-màng-kúot/—old-fashioned name for this is rocky-bur; use for mirazmi when a child's hair turns red. 1955 *WIMJ* 155, *Priva lappulacea* L. Clammy Bur; Bur Bush; Fasten-'pon-Coat..This species continues in use as a cold bush.

FAST-FAST MOUTH sb dial; <FAST, iterated; cf next.

1912 McK *Songs* 37, For people possess fas' fas' mout': For those who are too quick with their mouths.

FAST-MOUTH /fáas-móut/ adj dial; <FAST +*mouth*. Impertinent in speech; rude-mouthed. *BL G*

1877 Murray *Kittle* 13, Look, ya, you is a fast mout gal. Unoo woman is a bery fast mout people.

FASTNESS sb dial; <FAST+*-ness*. Impudence; interference; meddling. *BA BL G T*

1877 Murray *Feedin' 'Perrit* 17, She sprang up..pulled his hair, scratched his face with her hands, and then told him to 'take that for his fastness'.

FASTY see FACETY.

FAT sb dial; cf *OED sb*[2] 2 →1577.

The inner substance of something, esp if it is somewhat juicy or mucilaginous, though not necessarily oleaginous. It is used of vegetable juices (see FAT-BUSH), honey or the like.

1910 Anderson-Cundall 46, See *was-was*. 1952 FGC Tre, see RED WASP, THIRSTY.

FAT quasi-vb or vb dial; <*fat* adj. To give off oil.

1929 Beckwith 15, The cocoa is prepared by..pounding the white kernels in a mortar until they 'begin to fat', that is, to exude oil.

FAT-BUSH sb dial; <FAT sb+BUSH 4.

1. A plant which produces a thick juice (evid one of the *Malvaceæ*).

1952 FGC StC, Fat-bush, a large-leaved bur bush with leaves something like cotton-bush leaf.

2. Prob erron for 'fit-bush'; see quot.

1927 Beckwith 27, see SPIRIT WEED.

FATHER sb dial cant; cf *OED* 1 b, 6 b.

1. Fig, in phr *a father of a*: a big one. *BA G*

1941 Kirkpatrick 12, Dem gwine get such a fader of a lickin' dem we never fit go een a de ring again.

2. A rank and title among revivalist sects.

1953 Moore 83, This high office may be reached only by a crowned shepherd, who, after serving for a considerable period of time, becomes so respected by his own and other bands that he is advanced to the calling of Father.

FATHER-IN-LAW /faadan-laa, faada-laa/ sb dial. A stepfather. (Cf MOTHER-IN-LAW.) *BA*

1954 LeP Man, Faada-lah, stepfather; Port, Faadanlaw, stepfather. 1956 Mc Man, Port, StAnn, StE /faadan-laa/. 1957 JN StT, Yes mam, me father-in-law mam. [Said by a girl of 7: her step-father or 'common-law father'.]

FATIGUE /fitíig/ vb dial; cf *EDD* Fattigued [*sic*] 2. annoyed (Norfolk). To provoke, to annoy; also in phr *fatigue (one's) dice*. *BA G*

1943 *GL* Port, Fetigue, to provoke or fret. 1955 FGC Man, Fatigue, to tease. 1956 Mc Port /dùon fitíig mi/. 1961 BLB 16 /no fitíig mi dáis, ma, yú gó bóut yu bízniz/ *Don't annoy me, mam: go your way.*

FATTEN-BARROW sb dial; <*fatten*+*barrow* (*OED sb*[2]). Certain wild plants used to fatten pigs and other livestock; esp *Synedrella nodiflora.*

1942 HPJ, Fatten-barrow: a small plant with a pink, many-petalled flower. 1952 FGC StAnn, StC, StJ /fátn-bára/—a plant with a tiny yellow flower (something like Spanish Needle) in the corner of the leaf-stem: leaves rough like calalu. 1957 LeP StAnd (Irish T.) /fátn bàro/—A green stuff with large lanceolate leaves, growing wild in the woods, used as food for pigs and rabbits. Also called Jack o' the woods. 1957 EB Port /fatn baro/—Shrub with yellow flowers, fed to rabbits, guinea pigs, goats, cows, etc.

FATTEN-GROUND sb dial.

1958 DeC StT /fatn-groun/ Sour milk, so-called because it is of no use except to throw out and so fatten the ground.

FATTOON sb dial; <*fat*+*-oon*, or perh a blend of *fat* and *balloon*, or the like. A very fat person.

1952 FGC Han /fàtúun, fàtúun mán/.

FAT-WEED sb dial. Prob erron for FIT-WEED.

1927 Beckwith 17.

FAUCE see FAST.

FAUM see FORM.

FAVOUR /fíeba, fíeva/ vb chiefly dial; cf *OED* 8, resemble, -1867, 'Now *colloq.*' *BA BL G*

1. To resemble. (This is *OED* 8: see above; also in US dial use; not specif Jamaican, but widespread.) *N*

1862 Clutterbuck 42, Here he come, faba king. 1877 Murray *Feedin' 'Perrit* 9, Man you mout pretty! It dis faber a tun tomattis. [*Man your mouth's pretty! It just looks like a tomato turning in colour.*] 1956 Mc Man /im fieba im faada/ *He resembles his father;* /dem fieba twín/ *They are as alike as twins.*

2. To seem; to appear. Also with conjunctions *like*, *se*, etc.: it appears as if.

1873 Rampini 118, It favour like you have a suspich 'pon me, ma'am. (It looks as if you were suspicious of me.) 1912 McK *Ballads* gloss, Fabour say—it seems as if, as though, that; favour know—seem to know. 1956 Mc Man /i fieba so/ *It looks like it*; /it fieva yu huol ar out/ *It looks as if you've caught her out* (i.e. she doesn't know the answer); /i fieva me bok op som liezi smari dis maanin/ *It looks as if I met some lazy person this morning.*

FAWN see FORM.

FAYCOMER see *fiekuma*.

FE see *fi*, FOR.

fe /fe/ int dial; <Twi *f̃ẽ̀*, a challenge to fight. An exclamation by which one accepts a challenge to fight: see quot 1955.

1943 *GL* Clar, Fay, a word used in threatening. 1955 FGC Man, A: 'Say /fe/ and I knock you!' B (accepting the challenge): 'Fe!' (They begin to fight.)

FEATHER sb. The FLAG or flowering tassel of the sugar-cane.

a 1818 Lewis (1845) 108. (See quot s.v. FLAG.) 1942 Astley Clerk in HPJ, The feathers in a good breeze is [*sic*] a sight worth seeing.

FEATHER /feda/ vb dial.

1. trans. In tree-pruning: see quot.

1958 DeC StAnd, To feather: to remove (usually just with the fingers) all the small shoots and unwanted buds from the 'mother' and 'mother branches'.

2. intr. Const *up*: see quot, and cf *OED* 3.

1952 FGC StT /feda op/—of a tree: to get its leaves again after it has been bare.

FEATHER-FOOT sb dial, also attrib; for *feather-footed*. A variety of chicken, rather small, that has thickly feathered feet. Also called BOOTIFOOT.

1952 FGC StT /fédafùt/—a fowl with feathers on its feet.

FEATHER STAR sb. A star-fish (*Nemaster* spp) having fine, feathery 'points' or 'legs'.

1960 Inst of Ja exhibit.

FEATHER-TONGUE sb. The ORANGE QUIT, *Euneornis campestris.*

1847 Gosse 236, Feather-tongue or Sour-sop bird—(Rob MSS)..The tongue of this species, pencilled and barbed at the tip, might give it a place among the Honey-suckers. 194– *NHN*, Feather-tongue, long-mouth quit. 1956 Jeffrey-Smith 70 (full list of common names).

FEED vb dial. In passive sense: To be fed. *BL G*

1951 Murray 21 [Song:] How de pickney fe feed? *How are the children to be fed?*

FEED-FEED sb dial; iterative <*feed*. Food in small quantities.

1951 FGC StAnd, The trumpet tree has no fruit, 'only little feed-feed for birds'.

FEEDING vbl sb; <*feeding vbl sb* (*OED* 2, 'Now *rare*'.) That which one feeds upon: food, a portion or piece of food. Cf also FEEDING-TREE.

1907 Jekyll 124, Every feedin' Blackbird go fe pick, Annancy say that one a fe him.

FEEDING-TREE sb dial; <FEEDING+*tree*. A tree from which birds get food; esp their favourite food tree.

1907 Jekyll 123, Blackbird have a feedin' tree in a sea. An' every day Blackbird go an' feed. 1921 *Gleaner* 6 Apr, The pair [of humming-birds]..came regularly every evening to a tree in our garden..They only deserted us after their feeding tree had been destroyed by a hurricane. 1942 HPJ, Feedn-tree: A tree from which birds derive their food; particularly the tree they prefer. 1953 *NHN* v 206, 'Pimento as Feeding Tree for Birds'.

FEE-FEE /fíifì/ sb[1] chiefly dial; echoic.

1. A toy whistle or squealer: they are of different types but make shrill high-pitched sounds. Also called BLOW-BLOW. *G*

c 1915 FGC StAnd /fiifi/ a whistle. 1943 *GL* Port, Feefi; Tre, Fefi, a toy whistle. 1947 U.Newton III 24, Fee-fee—a noise-maker blown by a deflating balloon attached to a squealer.

2. A wild pea-flower and its vine (*Centrosema plumierii*): see quot 1837.

1837 Macfadyen 253, Clitoria Plumieri. *Large* Pea-Flower..They are commonly called the *fee-fee*, from the noise made by the negro children in blowing through the flower. 1920 Fawcett 45, Fee-fee. 1933 McK 316, Fee-fee—flower of a wild vine children use as whistles. 1952 FGC StT /fiifi/ a running vine with pale purple pea-flower which can be whistled in.

3. The imitation of a wheezing, whistling sound such as that of heavy, impeded breathing.

1956 Mc Man /yu chés go fii-fii/ when you have asthma; StE (Accom) [Story: a child is breathing heavily or snoring in sleep] /im go fii, fii/. [Vowels prolonged and slightly nasalized.]

4. Also attrib and comb: see as separate entries.

FEE-FEE sb[2] dial; origin uncert: prob an error for FUFU, or perh representing FEED-FEED.

1907 Jekyll 132, Tacoma carry a brass mortar to made it a present to the old lady to beat her fee-fee. *Ibid* 134, *fee-fee*, food.

FEE-FEE BUSH sb dial; <FEE-FEE sb[1] +*bush*. A wild bush having pea-flowers like those of the FEE-FEE vine.

1952 FGC Han /fiifi bush/; blossom yellow, white; it whistles.

FEE-FEE DOVE sb dial; <FEE-FEE sb[1] +*dove*. The GRASS QUIT.

1942 HPJ, Feefee dove, an alleged bird (from its note?). 1959 M. Jeffrey-Smith letter [Maid from StJ:] 'The fee-fee dove is the grass quit. They call it so because it sound like a fee-fee'.

FEE-FEE LAMP sb dial; <FEE-FEE sb[1] +*lamp*. A small oil-lamp shaped somewhat like a whistle.

1942 HPJ, Feefee lamp, used in houses.

FEEL vb chiefly dial; const with infinitive. To feel inclined or disposed (to do or to have something). *BA BL G T*

1942 Bennett 38, De fus time ah did feel fe laaf But now me tempa flame. 1942 HPJ, 'I noh feel to eat', I have no inclination to eat—Universal. 1956 Mc StAnd /mi duon fiil tu du notin/ *I don't feel like doing anything*; StE /im didn fiil tu go tu bed yet/.

felam sb dial; <*film*, *OED* 4, 'A morbid growth upon the eye'), but cf *felon*, a small abscess or boil (*OED*). *BL*

1956 Mc Man /félam/ A big white growth in a donkey's eye. 1957 EB Port /felam/ A growth in the eye, but not only of donkeys.

FELIX sb dial; < *Felix*, said to be onomatopœic (see quot) but also a pers name. (Perh alludes to Felix, the indestructible cat of a popular song of the 1920's.)

1959 DeC StJ /fiiliks/—a very large dumpling; West, a large, round boiled dumpling kneaded in order to make it tough; so called because it is supposed to make the sound /fiiliks/ when you bite into it.

FELWORT sb bot obs; cf *OED*, where the plant is identified differently. A former name for the DUPPY-GUN (*Ruellia tuberosa*), referring to its gentian-like flower.

a 1726 Barham (1794) 179, Spirit-leaf. This plant is well known in Jamaica by this name..It is also called *felwort*. *Ruellia clandestina* L.

FENAY see next.

fene /féne/ vb dial; cf Twi *fẹ̀*, to vomit, *nẽ̀*, to cack, *m-fénãŋ*, bile thrown up from the stomach; Fante *fenã*, to be troubled; Limba *feño*, to faint, *feñoi*, to faint, gasp; Bambara *fono*, to vomit; Ewe (Gẽ dial) *afɛ̃nu*, (West dial) *fénu*, filth, *fenyí*, trance.

1. To feel direct physical illness and show its effects: to vomit, to faint.

1943 *GL* Clar, Man, Fennay, fennea, to vomit, swoon. 1955 FGC Man, I frighten so till I nearly fene. [Some citations under sense 2 preserve some effect of this sense.]

2. In a vaguer sense: to feel intense pain, discomfort, trouble.

1941 Kirkpatrick gloss, Fenay—have a hard time. 1943 *GL* StC, Fenneh, to suffer. 1956 Mc Man /ef di gúot bók yu, yu féne/ *If the goat butts you, it will hurt*; /ef a lík yu, yu féne/ *If I hit you, you will feel it*; /mi tíit a mek mi fene/ *My teeth are giving me trouble, are paining me.*

3. Transf and neg: To treat with disdain. [There seems to be an echo of sense 1.]

1957 StE (Eld), 'She ask me a question, a wouldn't even fene on her'—*I didn't take any notice of her.*

fengke-fengke see FENKY-FENKY.

FENKAY see FENKY-FENKY, FLENKEE.

FENKY-FENKY /fengki-fengki/ adj (and sb) chiefly dial; etym uncert: the iterative form suggests an African source, but none has been found; perh <*finicky*. Also FRENKA-FRENKA.

1. Physically not robust; slight, puny.

1943 *GL* StM, Fenkay, slight, not vigorous. 1956 Mc Man, Of a person: thin, slim, skinny—/yu luk fengke-fengke/. 1958 DeC Port /fengke-fengke/ adj, sickly and weak, no good as a worker.

2. Cowardly, effeminate, prone to tears; foolish, fussy, making difficulties.

1943 *GL* Kgn, Fenky-fenky, coward; StAnd, Cry-cry; Try Again, Foolish; Tre, Effeminate. 1950 Pioneer 31, Bra Patto consida lickle den him sey, 'Ah hooda really like fe goh, but me hear sey de gal dem dunga 'Oman Tung fraid a feader (feather) an me got so much feader dem mighten like me'. Hear Anancy, 'Cho Bra Pattoo yuh too fenky-fenky'.

FENNAY, FENNEA, FENNEH see *fene*.

fere(-fere) adj and sb dial; perh a var of *pere-pere*, but cf Twi *ɛ-fére*, pot-sherd, piece, fragment of a pot.

A. adj: See quot.

1956 Mc Man, Ragged, dishevelled, showing loose ends; e.g. of a hat with the straw fraying and pulling out, of hair: /yu híe luk fere-fere/ *Your hair is untidy.*

B. sb: Remnants, left-overs, things of small value.

1956 Mc Man [Prov:] /di tik we nak a jege wi nak a fere/ *The stick which will hit a rag will hit a jag*, i.e. Don't gloat over another's misfortunes: you may be the next victim. 1957 EB Port /fere-fere/ adj and noun. Remnants, small or undeveloped.

feril sb dial; by substitution of *l* for *n* <*fern*; cf *fierin.*

1954 *FG* 579, In some districts these ferns [*sc* bracken and net-fern] are called 'Ferril'. 1956 Mc Port /féril, féri/—Two types of fern: one has thorns, the other trails over rock.

FERM, ferm see *form.*

FERN-LEAF sb. The silky oak tree; so called because of its fern-like leaves.

1941 Swabey 27, Oak, Silky—(Fern-leaf). *Grevillea robusta.*

FERN MOSS sb bot; cf *OED* 1698→.

1696 Sloane 12, *Fern moss.* In sylvis umbrosis ad radices arborum frequenter invenitur.

FERN-TREE sb bot; cf *OED* 1827 only. The tree-fern.

1756 Browne 95, *Asplenium*..the small Fern-tree..It is very difficult to distinguish it from the Fern-tree, with which it has been generally confounded; *ibid* 104, *Polypodium* 41. Arboreum maximum..The Fern-tree. 1793 Edwards II 232, This gentleman..recommends the use of..ashes of wood calcinated, such as pimento-tree, dumb-cane, fern-tree, cashew or logwood.

FERN-WOOD sb bot obs. An unidentified tree.

1740 Importance 54, Fiddle-wood and Fern-Wood. *Popinax,* which has a very faint offensive smell.

FERRIL see *feril.*

FE-SOSO adv phr dial; <*for*+so-so. Just as (it) is, plainly, simply, with no underlying motive.

1943 *GL* StAnd, Fesoso, for so. 1958 BLB Man /Yu miin yu rieli dis dwiit fi súoso?/ *You mean you just did it out of the kindness of your heart?* [In a conversation:] Q. /Mek im kil di guot, duo? /*But why did he kill the goat?* A. /Nat a dain ting misis; im dis kil im fi súoso/ *For no earthly reason, mam; he just killed it for fun.*

FESS, FESS-FESS adj and sb dial; <*fuss* sb. Fussy; fussiness.

1943 *GL* Kgn, Fess, fussy. 1958 BLB Man /fes-fes/—used mostly of the fretfulness which is characteristic of teething children. It is of course carried over to similar irritable behaviour of children; adults would rather be either FUSSIFY or FUSS-FUSS.

FET sb dial cant; ?for *fate*, or abbr of *fetish.* A gamblers' term: Good luck; bad luck.

1942 HPJ, Fet: Good luck, evil luck..If a gambler who wishes to change his luck says—'Ah put fet on you', he refers to..good luck.

FEVER BUSH sb dial; <*fever*+BUSH 4. Any plant supposed to furnish good medicine against fever. Cf COLD BUSH. *BL*

1905 Dodd 13, But of all de medicine and fever bush I know, none cure you so quick as dis. 1959 current (FGC).

FEVER GRASS sb. A kind of grass (*Cymbopogon citratus*) considered a good remedy in fevers. Also called LEMON GRASS. *BL G N*

1893 Sullivan 112, Fever grass is a fragrant smelling lemony grass; it is excellent in fever just boiled and sweetened. 1927 Beckwith 17, Fever-grass. [Mistakenly identified with Dutch-grass.] 1952 FGC StAnn, StC, Tre /fíiva-grass/. 1953 *WIMJ* 246, Fever Grass; Lemon Grass. This is one of the important oil grasses..Lunan says it was introduced into Jamaica about 1800 and that it was used in his day to make a cooling drink for fevers.

FEVER-TREE sb obs; cf *OED* 1876, *DAE, DA* 1868, for different trees. An early name for the castor-oil tree (*Ricinus communis*).

1740 Importance 46, The Fever-Tree, as they call it, is the Agnus Castus, or chaste Tree, but it is rarely apply'd to such uses in Jamaica; the leaves are used to dress Blisters, and a Lamp Oil is made of the Nuts.

FEVER WEED sb. A plant more widely known as WILD PINDER: *Desmodium supinum.*

1955 *WIMJ* 150, Fever Weed..is said to be an excellent hæmostatic..Wright recorded its use among poor people as a diaphoretic in cases of colds and slight fever.

FEW-SEEDED COTTON sb obs. A variety of the cotton plant: the fruit has relatively few seeds.

1854–5 *TJSA* I 60, Few-seeded Cotton, Gossypium oligospermum.

fi[1] /fi, fo/ prep dial; <*for.* *BL G*

1. In various senses now uncom or somewhat arch in StdE: *swear for*=swear against, because of; *frighten for*=be afraid of.

1924 Beckwith 23, Callalu a swear fe ol' 'ooman; ol' 'ooman a swear fe callalu.. 'Callalu (Jamaica greens) curses the old woman, the old woman curses the callalu'; implying a threat that although helpless to prevent it, 'If you trouble me, I will trouble you'. 1950 Pioneer 64, Brer Nancy tek de Cow..an tell him, 'Ah dis put dis ya rope pon you fe hender de pickney dem from frighten fe you..'

2. In various prep phrases: FOR (THE) BETTER, all the more; FOR PURPOSE, on purpose; FOR TRUE, truly, indeed.

fi[2] /fi/ occas /fo/ possessive particle dial; in dial writing usu sp *fe, for*; <*for*, preceding a pronoun, or occas a person's name or identifying phr, and closely joined to it, with equal stress on both elements (unless contrastive stress is involved). Belonging to (thus /fí-mí/ belonging to me, my, mine; /fí-ján/ belonging to John, John's, etc.). *BL*

1826 Williams 194, Hi! da for me bible book. 1873 Rampini 180 [Prov:] To-day fe me, to-morrow fe you. *Today is mine, tomorrow will be yours.* 1929 Beckwith 91, Care must be taken in throwing out water at night to warn the family spirits who may be near. 'Mind yourselves, me family', or 'good people', they cry, or, 'Anybody fe we move!' 1942 Bennett 12, She is a sista to femme sista Lize. *Ibid* 42, Pass me fe Leah tumpa knife. [*Pass me Leah's short knife.*] 1954 LeP StE, Fe him load bigga than fe you. 1956 Mc Man /da wan de fi di shapmaasa buot de/ *That is the shop-keeper's boat*; *ibid* /fi yu kunu gaan a sii?/ *Has your boat gone out?* 1959 Miss Bramford StAnd [In paternity cases in court:] This woman has a baby for you? *A baby of yours?*

fi[3] /fi/ occas /fo/ particle introd infin; in dial writing sp *fe, fo', for*; < the *for* of *for to* (*OED for* II). *BL G*

1. To (as introducing an infinitive verb).

1788 Marsden 49, See NYAM A vb. 1790 Moreton 153, If me want for go in a Ebo, Me can't go there! 1873 Rampini 178 [Prov:] No ebry ting you yerry good fe talk. 1907 Jekyll 145, See if you one can manage fe take out de fish-pot. 1956 Mc StE /dem te yu fi plaan pain/ *They tell you to plant pine.* 1957 JN StT, A like fe play with me sister mam.

2. In modal expressions (obligation, compulsion, etc.—cf StdE *You are to sit here*), where Ja dial omits the verb *to be*, and some of the modal force is shifted to *fi* making it quasi-auxiliary: Must, should, ought to, have to.

1943 *GL* Man, I fe tan dey, It has to stay there. 1958 BLB StJ /yu fi mikies kom/ *Hurry back;* /so mi dip 'budum', yu fi ongli dip so 'tip'/ *When I strike loudly, you must only make a little tap.* 1961 BLB 51 /im no fi kwik fi nak biga-an-imself/ *He should not be quick to strike someone bigger than himself.*

FIAH-BUN see FIRE-BURN.

fiba, FIBBA see PHEBA. *G*

fi beta see FOR (THE) BETTER. *G*

fibini sb dial; <*forbidden* (*fruit*). The FORBIDDEN FRUIT.

1943 *GL* Clar, Fibinnie, grapefruit. 1952 FGC Port, /fibini/ long-neck shaddock.

FIDDLER BEETLE, FIDDLER BUG sb. Any beetle of the genera *Prepodes* and *Pachnæus*, so called perh because of their shape (see quot 1954) but more likely because of the buzzing noise they make when cutting around small branches of trees. Cf also POLICEMAN, MY LADY.

1952 FGC Tre /fidla bòg/ cuts around branches and lives in wood. 1954 *NHN* VI 166, There are some ten known species of Fiddler Beetles in Jamaica—so called because the shape of the body resembles that of an old-time fiddle.

FIDDLE-WOOD sb bot; cf *OED* 1703→. A tree of the genus *Citharexylum* (which word this name virtually translates) species *quadrangulare* and *surrectum* Gr., and its wood, once much used in making fiddles and other musical instruments. The name is also applied to other trees—see quot 1941. *BA*

1696 Sloane 170, Fiddle Wood. In sylvis campestribus circa urbem *St. Jago de la Vega* ubique reperitur..ex cujus ligno citharæ & panduræ fiunt. 1756 Browne 265 Black-heart Fiddle-wood..White Fiddle-wood..the Green-heart Fiddle-wood..The long-spiked Fiddle-wood. 1814 Lunan I 292, Fiddle-wood..is very durable.. From its durable quality the French gave it the name of *fidelle* wood, which we have corrupted to *fiddle*. [This explanation is false.] 1927 Beckwith 17, Fiddle-wood. One of the ingredients of a bath for cold or pain. 1941 Swabey 14, Boxwood—(Fiddlewood). *Vitex umbrosa* Sir. *Ibid* 20, Fiddlewood—(often confused with *Petitia domingensis*). *Citharexylum quadrangulare* Jaq..Fiddlewood—*Petitia domingensis* Jacq. 1952 FGC StAnn, StM, StT, Tre.

fi di beta see FOR (THE) BETTER. *G*

fiekuma sb dial; the first element is prob Tahitian *fe'i*, mountain plantain; the second has not been found, but cf *singkuma*. A variety of the MAIDEN PLANTAIN.

1934 *Ja Times* 19 May, With regard to varieties grown locally, there are the 'horse' plantain, the giant, and three kinds of maiden, perhaps more, these being 'sepre', 'phacoma' and 'tiger'. 1942 HPJ, Faycomer, A kind of plantain larger than the maiden plantain, smaller than the horse plantain. 1943 *GL* Tre, Facuma—plantain. 1952 FGC StJ /fiekùma plantin/—big bunch, plenty hand; StM, /fiekùma/ maiden plantain.

FIELD-TRIBULUS sb bot obs. The wild plant *Kallstroemia maxima* (formerly classed in genus *Tribulus*); now called POLICE MACCA.

1756 Browne 220, Tribulus? 2..The field Tribulus.. This creeping plant is something like the foregoing, both in size and disposition: it grows in all the pastures. 1774 Long III 720, The field-tribulus..is something like the Turkey-blossom, so common in the lowlands, and which is another species of the tribulus.

fierin /fíerin/ sb dial; the preservation of a palatalized form of *fern* (cf *OED* '7..*fyrne*'). Cf also *feril*, *form*, *fyaan*.

1956 Mc Man /fierin/ bracken. 1952 FGC Man /fíerin búonz/ fern bones [cf BONE].

FIFER /fáifa/ sb dial; <*fifer*. The TRUMPETER fish, from the shape of its mouth.

1952 FGC Port /fáifa/—/trómpita/.

FIG BANANA sb dial. A very small variety of banana. (Not the same as BANANA FIG.) *G*

1952 FGC Port, Fig banana—Cuban banana; StM, Fig banana, very small.

FIGGLE /fígl, fígel/ sb dial; <*fiddle*; cf Introd, Phonology.

1950 Pioneer gloss, Figgle—fiddle. 1952 FGC StC, StT /figl/. 1956 Mc Man /im plíe im uon fígel/ *He blows his own trumpet.*

FIG-INDIGO sb obs. A form in which indigo was once prepared, being dried in lumps somewhat resembling figs.

1725 Sloane II 383, If the Mud be put on Cloath strech'd out and dry'd in the Sun [instead of being put in boxes and cut in squares], 'tis call'd Fig-Indigo. When it ferments it grows very hard. Mr Barham in MS.

fiiba see PHEBA.

fiiko sb dial arch; < Sp *ficha*, a silver piece of 5 centavos (P Rico, Hond). A small coin—see quots. s CURRENCY.

1941 Kirkpatrick gloss, Feeco—cent, penny. 1943 *GL* Clar, Feko, 3*d*. 1952 FGC StM, /fíiko/—hardly used; ? = 3*d*.

FILTERING STONE sb obs exc hist; cf *OED filtering vbl sb*, 1812. A large flower-pot-shaped container cut out of porous stone, formerly widely used to purify and cool water.

1790 Moreton 23, In wet weather..all the filth and dirt which is dispersed over the country is washed away, and circulates in every current, for which reason filtering stones are used, which not only purify, but cool the water amazingly. *BA*

fi-mi-lieta sb dial joc; <*for-me-later*. Left-over food.

1958 DeC StC /fi-mi-lieta/ sb, leftover food.

FIND (ONESELF) vb phr refl. To go hurriedly, get to or away from a place (with a suggestion of danger or threat). *G T*

1907 Jekyll 75, An' Gaulin fly out of the door mouth an' find himself right up in the air. *Ibid*, The boy come down off the tree an' find himself back to his yard.

FIND-FAULT adj dial; < *to find fault*, vb phr. Fault-finding, hard to please. *BL G*

1950 Pioneer 37, Once upon a time dere was a very fine-fault an pick an choose gal livin' in dis country.

FINE adj chiefly dial; cf *OED* 7d, 'Very small in bulk or thickness; extremely thin or slender'. →1821. *BL G*

1952 FGC StJ, see TICKY-TICKY sb[1]; StT, see SUGAR-ANT. 1954 *FG* 710, The Pimply Gut Worm..is about one-third of an inch long and very fine.

FINE-LEAF sb dial. SWEET BROOMWEED (*Scoparia dulcis*), which has a small compound leaf.

1927 Beckwith 28, 'Sweet-broom', 'Fine-leaf', 'Sweet-weed'. For stoppage of urine, take boiled as tea.

FINE-PLAY NIGHT sb dial. Any of the nights, from the second through the eighth, of funeral wake observances: in contrast to the first night (burial) and the ninth night (full-scale celebrations with games, dancing, etc.). Cf SET-UP.

1958 DeC Port /fain-plie nait/ funeral wake on second through eighth nights.

FINE SHAMER sb dial. = SHAMER, and referring to the smallest variety (cf 1920 Fawcett 134), contrasted with SHAMER MACCA.

1952 FGC StAnn /shíema máka an fáin shíema/.

FINEY /fáini/ sb dial; <*fine* adj + *-y*. A type of breadfruit.

1952 FGC StAnn, Finey, a floury white kind of breadfruit.

FINGAHLITE see FINGER-LIGHT.

FINGER sb; cf *OED* 8 1702→, in more general sense.

1. A single banana or plantain, from its shape, and as being one of many joined together in a HAND; also called SEED.

1907 Jekyll 196, Banana bunches are reckoned by the number of hands they contain, the separate bananas being called fingers. 1913 Fawcett 44 see s BUNCH.

2. A single tuber of the COCO, which is more or less finger-shaped: cf COCO-FINGER.

3. Attrib. Cf FINGER MANGO, FINGER PEPPER, etc.

FINGER vb see FINGLE.

FINGER-AND-TOE sb dial.

1952 *NHN*, Finger-and-toe, the fungal galls on turnips and cabbages.

FINGER-HEAD sb dial. The tip of the finger.

1952 FGC Tre /fingga-hed/ fingertip.

FINGER-LIGHT sb dial; cf *light-fingered*. A thief.

1943 *GL* StAnd, Fingahlite, thief.

FINGER MANGO sb.

1837 Macfadyen 222, 9. The finger Mango; a long fruit resembling in shape the human finger, of no value.

FINGER PEPPER sb. A variety of *Capsicum* pepper shaped like the finger.

1756 Browne 176, Capsicum 3. Fructu conico oblongo majori. Finger Pepper. 1774 Long III 857, Peppers.. Barbary, Finger, Cherry. 1959 Current in markets (FGC).

FINGER-SMITH sb dial slang; <*finger* + *smith*, workman (a generalized sense, omitting the limitation of working with metals). A thief.

1956 Mc Clar /finga smit/—/skofla/ [scuffler].

FINGER-SPLIT sb dial.

1959 DeC West, /fingga-split/ a SPINNER dumpling; small, finger-shaped, boiled.

FINGLE /fínggl/ vb dial; by lambdacism <*finger* vb. To finger, feel, touch, handle; it may have both favourable senses (fondle, caress) and unfavourable ones (handle harmfully). Also const *up*. *BA BL G*

1907 Jekyll 34, You can't fingle (finger) temper lime as you have a mind; it cut up you hand. 1912 McK *Ballads* 30, Where's you tender han', mumma, Dat would fingle up me jaw When de fever burned so deep..? 1942 Bennett 44, Teck yuh han' outa me bankra! Noh fingle up me pear! 1943 *GL* Clar, Fintle, To touch up friendly, feel up; Tre, Fingle, Usually objectionable—touching with the fingers. 1944 Campbell *Iron Bar*, When ah drink w'ite rum an ah tumble down, me na want dutty gal come fingle me. 1952 FGC StAnd, Duppy fingle a man food—make him sick.

FINGRIGO sb; etym uncert, perh <*fingery* + *go*, in allusion to its hooked prickles and its climbing and spreading habit; *OED* 1707→.

1. *Pisonia aculeata*; also called COCKSPUR, PUSS-CLAW, SINGLE-GO.

1696 Sloane 137, Rhamnus an potius Lycium Fingrigo Jamaicensibus dictum forte Katu-Karu-Walli. Hort[us] Mal[abaricus]..*Fingrigo*. Locis campestribus sylvosis Insulæ Jamaicæ ubique crescit. [*Katu-karu-walli*, sharp-thorn climbing-plant. Burrow-Emeneau.] a 1726 Barham (1794) 60, *Fingrigo*. I believe some negro gave the name, for it is very full of hooked prickles, like cock-spurs; and some call the plant so, which is well known in Jamaica. 1774 Long III 755, Fringrigo [*sic*]; *ibid* 916, Fingrigo. 1864 Grisebach 783. 1914 Fawcett 151. 1943 *GL* Tre, Finigo, shrub with large hooked thorns.

2. Other conspicuously prickly plants: see quots.

1756 Browne 252, Mimosa 5. Fruticosa, spinis aduncis undique armata; cortice cinereo..Fingrigo, or the thorny Mimosa. This prickly shrub is frequent in most of the sugar colonies, especially in *Antigua*..It grows in a tufted form, and seldom rises above five or six feet from the ground. 1814 Lunan I 296–7, Fingrigo or Cockspur: Pisonia..aculeata..There is another small prickly plant called *fingrigo*, the *mimosa cinerea*, described under the name *sensitive plants*. *Ibid* II 167–8, *Mimosa*..2. *cineraria*. (Quotes Browne.)

FIN-HAND /fin-han/ sb dial; ?<*fin* sb + *hand*.

1958 DeC StT /kruk-han/ a twisted hand; in this district (Old Pen) opposed to /fin-han/ which means a withered but not twisted hand. *BA*

fini-fini sb dial, also attrib; etym uncert, but cf Ewe *finya-finya*, soft, weak, for sense 1.

1. Thin, bony, sickly-looking (person or animal).

1956 Mc Man /fini-fini/.

2. Obeah; an obeahman; cf PHINNEY MAN.

1943 *GL* West, Finny finny, obeah. 1959 DeC Han /fini-fini/ obeahman.

FINIGO see FINGRIGO.

FINISH vb intr dial; <*finish* vb trans. Of a quantity or supply of objects: to be exhausted; also followed by an infinitive. *BL G T*

1912 McK *Songs* 31, Banana finish sell. [Note:] The selling of the bananas is over. 1959 Current in markets and shops: 'Orange finish!' *Oranges are sold out* (FGC). 1961 Katzin 17, Miss A sent her to the bakery..where she had heard bread was selling for a penny under the usual price, but Mamie soon returned, saying: 'The bread is finished'.

FINNY FINNY see *fini-fini*.

FINTLE see FINGLE.

FIP sb dial; abbr of FIPPENCE or FIPNEY. A threepenny bit; threepence. Since the fivepenny piece was and the threepenny piece is the smallest silver piece, the word is used fig: a very small amount of money. s CURRENCY.

1943 *GL* Man, Tre, etc., Fip—3*d*. 1952 FGC StM /fip/ —/trópèns/.

fipans, fipens see FIPPENCE.

FIPNEY, FIPNI see next.

fipni, fipini sb dial; abbr of *fivepenny piece*. A threepenny bit; threepence. See FIP, FIPPENCE. s CURRENCY.

[1808 Stewart 59, Tenpenny and five penny pieces; the latter is the smallest coin in use, there being no copper coin in circulation.] 1943 *GL* Tre, Fipni, threepence. 1952 FGC Han /fípini/—3*d*. 1956 Mc StJ /fipini/.

fi popas, fi porpas see FOR PURPOSE. *G*

FIPPANCE see next.

FIPPENCE /fípens, fípans, fúpans/ <*fivepence*; cf *OED*→1823 sb dial. s CURRENCY.

1. A fivepenny bit. (See *fipni* quot 1808.) *BA N*

1826 Williams 196, Me bet you fippance me mek you go. 1873 Rampini 177 [Prov:] If you see a fippence, you know how dollar is made. (See *ibid* 94, quoted s.v. GILL sb².)

2. A threepenny bit; threepence.

1927 Anderson-Cundall 19 [Prov:] Bit old, it tun fippence. 1952 FGC StM /mák-an-fúpans/ one shilling and threepence. 1956 Mc Man /fípans/ threepence. 1957 EB Port, same.

FIRE /faia/ vb dial; <*fire* vb. *G*

1. To crack a whip loudly, making a sound like a gun being fired.

1828 Marly 50, The driver fired his whip as a signal for work to stop. *Ibid*, The whip was sometimes fired behind them [*sc* slaves] to keep them in line, but seldom did any require to be touched with it. 1924 Beckwith 22, Tacoomah..get one whip an' go to clear place. He fire de whip an' say, 'Ah no me, sah!'

2. To shoot (something other than a gun).

1924 Beckwith 75, He had not'ing to do but fire bow an' arrow all day..An' one day he tek up him bow an' arrow an fire de arrow an' de arrow drop in a Massa Jesus yard. *BA BL T*

FIRE-BURN /fàia-bón/ sb dial; also attrib. *BL*

1. See quot. *G*

1942 Astley Clerk in HPJ, Fiah-bun: In Jamaica it refers to a place destroyed (ruins left) by fire—and, or to the place where a fire has been. Kingston after the Earthquake fire of 1907 was one big 'fiah bun' place.

2. A fire.

1958 BLB Man /fàia bón/ also refers to the actual fire.

FIRE-CATCHER sb dial. Ragged clothes (fit only for kindling fire).

1958 DeC StT /faia-kecha/ old ragged work clothes.

FIRE-CHIP sb dial; <*fire* sb+*chip* sb. *G*

1954 LeP Kgn, Fire-chip, wood for kindling a fire.

FIRE DOWN TOWN int phr dial; abbr of <*there is a fire down-town*. A demand for rapid and generous service; see quot.

1958 DeC Port, StAnd /fáia dóun tóun!/—shouted by men in bar while bartender pouring out rum; usually accompanied by pounding on bar and shouts of /bráata/.

FIRE-FIRE adj dial; iterative <*fire* sb.

1956 Mc Man /fáia-fáia/ quick-tempered.

FIREFLY sb dial; perh because it bears fast (flies like fire). (No connection with the insect seems indicated.)

1956 Mc StE (Accom) /fáia-flài/ a kind of negro-yam; quick-bearing.

FIRE-HORSE sb dial; <*fire* sb+*horse*. A kind of jelly-fish that irritates the skin sharply upon contact: it 'burns like fire'.

1944 *NHN* II 155, A small Cyanea, locally known as 'Fire Horse' can raise huge weals on the arms and legs.

FIRE-KITTY /fáia-kíti/ sb dial; <*fire*+/kiti/ in *kitibu*; the basic sense seems to be that of brightness, burning: hence *fire-kitty* is a redundant compound. Cf also Twi *kìtikiti*, violent commotion, tumult.

1. An over-energetic person.

1956 Mc StJ /fáiakíti/ a busy-busy person, i.e. over-energetic.

2. A fiery, turbulent, or brazen person.

1943 *GL* Man Fire-kitty, an outlaw person. 1955 FGC Man /faia-kiti/ an outlaw or outrageous person. 1955 LeP StE (Eld) /faia kiti/ a mischief-maker.

FIRE-LANTHORN sb; <*fire*+*lanthorn*, lantern. The redstart (*Setophaga ruticilla*); also called BEAN BIRD, BUTTERFLY BIRD, CHRISTMAS BIRD.

1956 Jeffrey-Smith 82–3, He is black, but under the wing and on his side are vivid red feathers and in flight these flash into view, hence the name of redstart. Spanish-speaking people call it candelita, 'little torch-bearer', for the same reason..Yet another name, Fire-Lanthorn, recalls its distinctive colouring.

FIRE-SHELL sb obs; <*fire*+SHELL. A shell (conch or horn) blown as a warning of fire.

a1818 Lewis (1834) 70, I find that my negroes were.. kept up all night by a fire at a neighbouring estate. On these occasions a fire-shell is blown, and all the negroes of the adjoining plantations hasten to give their assistance.

FIRESIDE sb dial. In Jamaican peasant kitchens, the edge of a raised platform of earth faced with logs, on top of which the fire is built; also the whole platform. *BA G*

1954 LeP StT, Fireside, a cooking place. 1956 Mc Clar, Man /faia-said/ the side of the built-up part on which fire is built in 'kitchen'.

FIRESIDE SHAD sb dial; <FIRESIDE+*shad*. A type of the shad fish with a somewhat burnt appearance.

1952 FGC StE /fáiasáid shad/—/mákabák shád/.

FIRESTICK sb chiefly dial; cf *OED*: some uses diff or more specif in Jamaica. *G*

1. A stick fit for burning, or usable as kindling.

1873 Rampini 178 [Prov:] Old fire-stick no hard fe catch. 1954 LeP StT, Fia tik, wood for kindling a fire. 1958 DeC StT /faia stik/ small sticks for starting fires, equiv to greng-greng etc.

2. A burning stick, a stick on fire.

1826 Williams 109, Dem poke you wid fire stick [in hell]. 1862 Clutterbuck 118, [He] stole off the stall a cigar, which he lighted on turning the next corner, begging a 'fire-tick' for that purpose. 1956 Mc no addr /tek faia bot no tek mi faia tik/ *Take fire, but don't take my fire-stick.*

3. A stick used as a poker for the fire.

1956 Mc StAnd /faia tik—lang stik fi shob di faia/.

FIRE-STOKER /faia-tuoka/ sb dial. A tree whose wood is good fuel; see quot.

1961 DAP Man, Fire-stoker, *Cestrum* spp?

FIRE-STONE sb dial. *BL*

1956 Mc Clar, Man /faia stuon/ the stone the pot is rested on in cooking.

FIRE-TOP-FIRE-BOTTOM sb dial. =TOP-AND-BOTTOM.

[**FIRST** /fos, fors/ sb; cf *DAE, DA*, 1862→. First time or occasion (on which something happens).

1924 Beckwith 48, Anansi say, 'Brar, I t'ink I know you!' De Monkey said, 'No, sah, a de firs' me an' you buck up!' 1942 Bennett 17, Is de fus Tom look soh clean. 1956 Mc StE (Accom) /iz a fors dat a man eva kil a neks wan/ *It's the first time that a man has killed another.*]

FIRST BELLY-PAIN sb dial joc. A woman's first child.

1954 LeP StAnn, Fus belly pain first born child.

FIRST-CUP sb dial.

1956 BLB Man, First-cup—First cup of coffee or tea or chocolate, to clear chest of gas, and get one ready for breakfast. 1958 DeC StAnd /fos-kop/ the early-morning meal.

FIRST DUSK sb dial.

1958 DeC StT /fos dos/ the time of day when it is starting to get dark—a slangy word used only by young people: BROWN DUSK is the word used by older people.

FIRST FEEL sb dial slang.

1958 DeC StT /fos fiil/—first chance, first opportunity; /let a hab di fos fiil/ means 'Let me go first'.

FIRST GANG sb obs. The GREAT GANG.

1793 Edwards II 128–9, The Negroes are divided into three sets or classes, usually called *gangs*; the first consisting of the most healthy..etc. 1796 *Braco* 27 June, First Gang Digging Cane Holes on No 10. Second Gang Cutting plants.

FIRST-NIGHT sb dial. The first night of NINE-DAY observances: the wake or SET-UP. *G*

1958 DeC StT, see WATCH-DEAD.

FIRST TIME sb dial. Earliest opportunity.

1924 Beckwith 102, De firs' time you get a husban' you tell him all yo' belly-word? Save somet'ing! [*At the first opportunity after you get a husband you tell him all your secrets?*] *BL G*

FIRST-TIME adv dial; abbr of such a phrase as *in the first times*. Formerly; in the past.

1912 McK *Songs* 75 [A woman telling off a big countryman turned policeman:] 'Cos you wear Mis'r Koshaw clo'es You t'ink say you's de only man, Yet fus' time ko how you be'n 'tan'. 1941 Kirkpatrick 19, Fuss time you ting 'im woulda go see any a dem odder people; eeno—'im use fe order dem fe come..Is diffran nung. 1952 FGC StM, Not like first-time [=long ago]. 1955 FGC Man, They used to have a lot of custard-apples and cherimoyas firs' time. *G N T*; *SC fósi-tem.*

fi-saatn /fi-sáatn/ dial pronunc of *for certain*. *G*

FISH sb dial. Any sauce, relish, or other food (not necessarily containing fish) that accompanies the staple starch food: from the fact that fish is a traditional component of sauces used by the Jamaican peasantry.

1956 Mc StAnd /hókro is a ting wi yuuz az fish—a vejetebl laik/ *Okro is a thing we use as fish—a sort of vegetable*; Fish includes cabbage, okro, susumba, as well as fish or meat; /fish iz relish: saalfish, jangga, kyebij, susumba/ *'Fish' is relish: saltfish, crayfish, cabbage, susumba.*

FISHEN /fishin, fishn/ vb dial, usually in pres pple; though sense is identical, this can hardly represent OE *fiscnian*; it probably is an infinitive form from the pres pple of the regular vb *fish*: /fishin/ < /fishing/. Cf *-n* suffix[2]. To fish.

1877 Murray *Feedin' 'Perrit* 4, When I da go fishinin'. 1907 Jekyll 74, The river side where Gaulin is fishening. 1912 McK *Songs* 82, We used to fishen in old Carew Pen. 1952 FGC Port /fishinin/ pres pple, used several times by two different fishermen; StE, Use soldier as bait in /fishnin/. *BL G T*

FISHERMAN BASKET sb dial.

1958 DeC StT /fishaman baskit/..the common long oval basket with a handle.

FISHERMAN BIRD sb dial. *N*

1952 FGC StC, Fisherman bird, kingfisher.

FISH-EYE sb obs. The thrush *Turdus jamaicensis*, with strikingly shiny eyes: also called GLASS-EYE, SHINE-EYE, WHITE-EYED THRUSH, etc.

1842 Chamberlaine 26, Fish-eye, glass-eye, *Merula leucophthalma.* 1847 Gosse 142, Fish eye, *Merula Jamaicensis.* 1956 Jeffrey-Smith 35.

FISH-HEAD sb dial slang; <*fish-head*, the head of a fish, eaten by poorer people and considered a delicacy by some. A tip; a bribe; 'graft'. *BL*

1956 Mc Man /fishéd/ a tip (money). 1957 EB Port /yu no gwain get fished/ *You know you will benefit.* 1959 LeP StAnd, There was a great 'Fish-head' rumpus in the KSAC in (I think) 1955 or 1956, when a JLP member accused a PNP man of accepting fish-heads (i.e. bribes).

fishin see FISHEN.

fish-in-a-migl sb dial; for *fish-in-the-middle*. See quot.

1958 DeC StT /fish-in-a-migl/ a fried dumpling made by flattening the dough, covering with a layer of saltfish, folding over, rolling into a ball, then frying.

FISHING-BAG sb dial.

1958 DeC StT /fishim-bag/ also /shaat-bag/—a small (6–12 in. sq.) bag with handles, often used by hunters and fishermen.

FISH-KIND sb dial; formed on the analogy of BREAD-KIND, MEAT-KIND, etc. Any kind of fish used as food.

1952 FGC StE, Eat it with fish-kind; StJ, 'Salting' is any fish-kind—herring, mackerel, saltfish; West /fishkain/ salting.

FISH KNIFE sb dial. A cutlass with long blade of even width and point tapered from edge to back; used by fishermen. *G*

1958 DeC StT /fish naif/ cutlass; either or both sides may be sharpened according to the fisherman's preference.

FISH-LOUSE sb; *OED* enters without quot or ref.

1756 Browne 418, Pediculus 3..The Fish-Louse, or Sea Cock-Roach.

fishn see FISHEN.

FISH-TAIL FERN. A cultivated fern with fronds dividing at the tips like a fish's tail (*Nephrolepis davallioides furcatus*).

1952 FGC StAnd, Fish-tail fern—current.

FISH-TEA sb dial; <*fish*+TEA. A soup or broth the chief ingredient of which is fish; the water in which fish was boiled, drunk as a beverage. *BL*

1952 FGC StE /fish tii/ fish soup. 1959 DeC West /fish tii/ a broth made by boiling down scallion and thyme with fish.

fisla sb dial; <*fistula.*

1956 FGC Port, Stone-bruise bush is good against /fisla/ on finger.

fi so-so see FESOSO.

FIT adj or quasi-vb dial; cf *OED* 5. *G*

1. (To be) nearly ripe; abbr of such a phrase as *fit to cut*, *fit to gather*.

1924 Beckwith 24, Anansi don't wait upon his food till it is ripe, but dig out an eat it. Tacoomah wait until it fit to eat it. *Ibid* 35, When it begun to bear he go an' look at it, an'..he say it will soon fit. 1950 Pioneer 71, It hab fe last tell de peas an corn fit, an dem don't ready as yet. 1956 Mc Man /wen dem fit, dem yelo; dem gríin bot dem wél fít/.

2. (To be) fitting—used characteristically in negative phrases of warning or prohibition: *you better fit*, it would be more fitting for you; *you don't fit*, *you wouldn't fit*, *you couldn't fit*—You'd better not, you wouldn't dare.

1933 *Outlook* 30 Dec, 'You is a wutless tief, an' a betch you a box you'. 'You wouldn' fit!' declared Mary-Ann scornfully. 'Wouldn' fit?' screamed Selina, rushing at her sister with upraised hand. 1942 HPJ, Fit..Used also expletively, like 'forsooth', 'yu betta fit do so & so' —'yu couldn' fit do it'. West Somerset, *better fit*, it would be better. 1956 BLB Man /yu duon fit liiv dis hous tide/ *You dare not leave this house today.*

FIT vb dial; cf *OED* †4, 'To be well adapted or suitable for; to answer or satisfy the requirements of'. →1749. *BL G*

1956 Mc Man /misiz wud laik dis plies, dis plies fit yu/ *This place would suit you.*

FIT int colloq or slang; <*fit* adj. An exclamation of approval: Good! *G*

1956 Mc StAnd /fit, man!/—Bravo! Good! 1959 FGC StAnd, current.

FIT BUSH sb dial; <*fit*, seizure+BUSH 4. FIT-WEED. *N fits bush.*

1954 *WIMJ* 24, *Eryngium foetidum* L. Fit Weed or Bush; Spirit Weed. A decoction of the plant is used for colds and fits in children. The plant is also rubbed on the body for fainting fits and convulsions. Since it is said to have magical properties in connection with protection from duppies (ghosts) this may explain its use in convulsions, fainting and hysteria for which it has long been employed in Jamaica.

fi truu see FOR TRUE.

FITSWEED see FIT-WEED. *N*

FITTAGO sb; etym unknown.

1943 *GL* no addr, Fittăgo, the smallest of plantains.

FITTISH adj dial; <FIT adj 1+*-ish.* Coming, or pretending to be, close to maturity.

1942 HPJ, Fittish, adj. [Applied] when little girls play woman and are womanish.

FITT-WEED see next.

FIT-WEED sb now chiefly dial; <*fit*, seizure +*weed. OED* 1756 only. First in Barbados, 1750. A small wild plant (*Eryngium foetidum*), very strongly aromatic, used to revive people from fainting and other fits.

[1750 Hughes 229–30, The Fit-Weed. This is a small Plant, seldom rising above six Inches high..A Decoction from this Plant is looked upon to be very efficacious to cure Fits.] 1756 Browne 185, Eryngium 1..The stinking *Eryngo*, or Fitt-weed..All the parts of this plant are reckoned very powerful antihisterics. 1774 Long III 846, Fit-Weed. 1811 Titford 50, This plant grows in Jamaica, and is a common remedy against hysteric affections, whence the Negroes call it Fittweed. 1942 HPJ, Fits-weed—nice smelling, for headaches. 1952 FGC StJ; StT, fit-weed, spirit-weed; Tre, spirit-weed, myal-weed. 1957 EB Port /fits wiid/.

FIVE int. In boys' games, a cry which entitles one to five seconds' immunity from being caught. *G*

1952 FGC Han, To get a rest [while playing *hide and whoop*, etc.], cry 'five!'.

FIVE-FINGER sb, also attrib; <*five*+*finger* (*OED* 8). (*OED* has *five-finger* for other plants, not for this.) The climbing vine *Syngonium auritum*, so called because the leaves develop 3, 5, or 7, but usually 5, subdivisions or 'fingers'; also called SEVEN-FINGER. *G*

[1814 Lunan I 298, Arum..auritum..This plant is very common in Jamaica, running upon trees, and is very remarkable, as being the only species of *arum*, in this island, furnished with compound leaves..The leaf has three lobes in the young plant, but, as it acquires age and strength, throws forth ears from the outward leaves, until it has frequently seven divisions, the hinder ones appearing like spurs to the others.] 1854–5 *TJSA* I 68, Five finger arum[,] Arum auritum. 1952 FGC StAnn, StM, StT /fáiv-fíngga/—five little branch on leaf: one kind of COCO-WIS. [Evidence of extension of the term to other climbing plants:] StM, =China-wis, wickerwis, etc.; Tre, larger than /makyati bush/, =MILE-WALK.

FIVE O'CLOCK BUSH sb dial. A tree of uncertain identity (perh young GUANGO or WOMAN'S TONGUE) which is said to close its compound leaves together at about 5 P.M. *G*

1952 FGC StT.

FIX vb dial; cf *OED* 6. To put (a person) under the influence of obeah so that he must do something. *G*

1942 HPJ, Fix..A man charged with stealing cigarettes and Rum said that 'a man fix him to steal every second of the day'. [Astley Clerk:] 'I wi fix yu' is a common threat, meaning 'I will obeah you so that you must do it'. 1962 BLB 54 /fiks/ put under obeah spell.

flaa-flaa (occas /flaan-flaan/) sb dial; etym unknown: ?<*flour.*

1. A codfish fritter.

1943 *GL* Clar, Flaw, Flitters; Kgn, Flaw-flaw, Chinese fritters; Port, Fla-fla, Fry friters; Port, Flawn-flawn, fritters; made of flour. 1954 LeP Kgn, StE, Codfish cakes—flaw-flaw; Man, flaa-flaa. 1955 FGC Man /flaa-flaa/ flour-and-codfish fritters.

2. Flour.

1943 *GL* Port, Flaw-flaw, flour.

flaa-flaa, flaai-flaai adj dial; etym uncertain: cf *EDD flaws*, intermittent showers, hence perh *flaa-flaa*=wet; but there may be some African word combined—e.g. Ewe *flofloflo, floyafloya*, porous, loose, spongy; the second form prob repr *flaa*+*-y* iterated.

1956 Mc Man /di párij fláa-fláa/ *The porridge is watery;* /nó go úoba dá-de flá-i-fla-i plíes/ *Don't go through that wet (muddy) part.*

FLABADASH sb dial; phonosymbolic in part, but prob chiefly <*flabber*+*dash*, suggesting a quickly-made and flaccid substance. Some kind of sauce—perh hastily made of flour and water, or the like.

1943 *GL* StT, Flabadash, sauce. [1943 *GL* Clar, Flabba, saucge (*sic*) without meat and fish.]

flaba-flaba /flába-flába/ adj dial; cf *EDD flabber*, to hang loosely, w Yks.

1. Worthless, good-for-nothing.

1956 Mc No addr /go we, yu likl flaba-flaba sinting yu/ *Get away, you little good-for-nothing.*

2. Fat, thick-set. *G*

1955 LeP StE (Eld) /flaba-flaba/ fat, thick-set.

FLABBY adj dial. See quot. *G*

1943 *GL* Port, Flabby, swarthy.

flabob, flombo, flombob sb dial; prob ult <Engl *clabber*: cf the other Jamaican variants CLABUB, *plaba*, etc. The forms beginning with *flom-* may also be infl by Sc *flummery*, 'A kind of food made by coagulation of wheat flour or oatmeal' (J.)—*OED.* A coconut RUNDOWN, or some slight variation of it: see quots.

1952 FGC StJ /flómbób/ to make, add a drop of flour to ROUND-THE-ROAD. 1955 LeP StE (Eld) /flabob/ coconut which has not been boiled down to the oil. Like molasses to sugar. 1958 DeC Tre /flombo/ common local name for a coconut rundown.

fla-fla see *flaa-flaa.*

flag see FLAG, FLOG.

FLAG /flag/ *sb*; cf *OED flag sb*[1] 2. See also *flaig.*

1. The flowering spike that shoots from the top of the mature sugar-cane, and somewhat resembles a flag flying from a pole; also called ARROW, BLOSSOM, FEATHER, TASSEL. (For map showing distribution see DeC in 1961 *CLS* 69.)

1739 Leslie 332, Some Canes will not rise above three Foot high, and others six, and the Flags or Cane-Tops of them exceed nine Foot Stalk and all. a1818 Lewis (1845) 108, The fresh plants are cane-tops; but those canes which bear *flags* or feathers at their extremities will not answer the purpose. 1952 FGC StAnd, StAnn, StT /flag/ of cane—/kíen-flág/. *N*

2. The similar blossom of maize.

1952 FGC StAnd, StC /flag/ the corn tassel.

FLAG /flag/ vb dial; by conversion of FLAG sb. Of cane, corn, etc.: to produce a FLAG.

1952 FGC StAnn /dat kaan suun flag/ *That corn will soon tassel out.*

flaig sb dial; a var pronunc of FLAG: cf *baig*, bag, *haig*, hag, etc. s *flaig* vb.

1956 Mc no addr /flaig/ tassel on sugar-cane.

FLAIRTAIL see FLARE-TAIL.

FLAMBOYANT sb occas; <Fr *flamboyant*, the same tree. The tree *Poinciana regia*, with its very bright red or orange flowers; usually called Poinciana, and by the folk FANCY-ANNA.

1920 Fawcett 98. *BA BL G T*

FLAME TREE sb uncom; evid a trans of Fr *flamboyant*, the same tree. The tree *Poinciana regia*; also FLAMBOYANT. *G*

1920 Fawcett 98.

FLAMING CANDLE sb dial.

1959 Lawton Kgn, Flaming candle—a lamp improvised from a condensed milk tin.

FLARE /flea, flie, flier/ sb dial. A MACHETE: see quot.

1958 DeC Port /flea/ a machete whose blade broadens slightly at the tip, but less so than OPEN-GUARD. Poss identical with open-guard, but 4 informants in Portland say not. [Later revised by DeC: 1961 *CLS* 70, 73.]

FLARE-TAIL sb dial; cf FLARE+*tail*. A MACHETE more or less flared at the end of the blade.

1954 LeP Kgn, flairtail, a curved machete. 1958 DeC StT /flier-tiel/ a cutlass. 1962 BLB 54 /fliertiel/ cutlass with flaring end.

FLASH vb dial; by phonetic substitution or simplification <*splash*, *slash*, *thrash* resp.

1. To splash. *G*

c1915 FGC StAnd, Don' flash di waata pan mi! 1952 FGC StAnd, Put leaves on top of water in a pail: /henda di waata fram flash out/.

2. To slash. *G*

1924 Beckwith 148, He flashed off three of the giant's heads.

3. To thrash.

1942 HPJ, 'Hin flash him like dawg flash mongoose'.

FLAT-BUR sb dial. An unidentified plant; =WOMAN STRONG-BACK.

1952 FGC StC /flat-bor/.

FLAT-FLAT adv dial; iterative <*flat*. Extremely flat, as flat as possible. *BL G*

1942 Bennett 47, Him dah lidung now Flat-flat pon him belly.

FLAT GRASS sb. Carpet grass (*Axonopus compressus*).

1954 *FG* 217, Flat grass assumes dominance in the higher rainfall belts.

FLATHEAD DRUMMER sb dial. A variety of the drummer fish with a flat head.

1952 FGC StC /flátèd dróma/.

FLATTY-CUT sb dial; <*flat*+-*y*, familiarizing suffix +*cut* (cf *cutworm*).

1952 FGC West /flátikòt/ a tiny, flat, red tick.

FLAW(-FLAW) see *flaa-flaa*.

FLAWN-FLAWN sb dial; a nasalized variant of *flaa-flaa* sb.

flea see FLARE.

FLEA-BANE sb bot; cf *OED*, of various other plants. Species of *Vernonia*—see quots.

1811 Lunan I 298–300, Flea-banes. Conyza. (Four spp listed.) 1864 Grisebach 783, Fleabanes: *Vernonia arborescens*. 1936 Fawcett 157, *V. anthelmintica*..Flea Bane. 1954 *WIMJ* 32, *Vernonia divaricata*..Old Man Bitter Bush; Fleabane.

FLECTA see next.

flekta sb dial; aphetized <*reflector*. A lamp: see quots.

1943 *GL* Kgn, Flecta, old lamp. 1955 FGC Man /flekta/ new or old lamp.

FLENKAE-FLENKAE adj dial; var of FENKY-FENKY.

1943 *GL* No addr, Flenkae-flenkae, meager.

FLENKEE /flengki/ sb dial; etym unknown. A revivalist cult.

1943 *GL* No addr, Fenkay, a superstitious cult. 1953 Moore 58–9, Flenkee, a revivalist cult. 'Convince Flenkee', name of such a group in Morant Bay area. 1958 DeC No addr /flengki/—some sort of religious order or cult.

FLESH-KIND sb dial; on the analogy of BREAD-KIND, FISH-KIND, etc.

1958 DeC /fleshkain/—a category of edibles which includes meat, fish (dried and fresh), eggs, cheese, ackee, and calalu (the last two because always eaten with fish or meat). Common throughout western Han and West.

flie, flier see FLARE.

FLIGHTY /flaiti/ adj dial. See quots. *BA BL G*

1943 *GL* StJ, Flighty, fiery or brazen. 1955 FGC Man /flaiti/ outlaw; fiery, brazen. 1957 EB Port /flaiti/ excitable.

fliik sb dial; prob by lambdacism <*freak*.

1958 DeC Port /fliik/ an albino [negro].

fliim sb dial; =*phlegm*, *OED* form α; →1709.

1952 FGC Man, Ganja takes off /fliim/ from chest.

FLING-ME-FAR sb dial joc. A RUNDOWN, perhaps alluding to the Anancy story of the jar or hole in the ground which flung far away anyone who put his hand into it.

1959 DeC Han /fling-mi-far/ a coconut run-down; also occurs commonly as /fling-mi-for/.

flips vb or quasi-vb dial; by phonosymbolism, perh with *flip* as base, but poss also (by the kind of alteration found in *flash*<*splash*, *slash*) with infl from *slip*. Cf also FLUPS. To slip suddenly away from one.

1955 Bennett *Long mout Doris*, She linga, an de good good man Jus 'flips' outa her han!

flips sb dial; etym unknown, but cf prec. A dish made with banana or plantain cooked in various ways: see quots.

1958–9 DeC Han /flips/ ripe plantain sliced and fried in coconut oil; StT /flips, banana flips/ whole green banana or plantain boiled in a rundown; West /flips/ a ripe banana rolled in pie dough and baked.

flitaz see next.

FLITTER /flitaz, flutaz/ sb dial; <*fritter*—cf Engl and US dial; /flitaz/ may be sing or plur.

1. Flat, fried codfish cakes. *BL*

1943 *GL* Tre, Flutas, 'fritters'. 1954 LeP Man, StAnn, Flitters, codfish cakes. 1956 Mc No addr /flitaz/ fritters (flat fried cakes made of flour, perhaps with egg, with fish, etc., added).

2. Attrib. *BL*

1948 Bennett 51, Sta Kate flittas-foot gal. [*Sister Kate's flat-footed girl*].

FLOAT vb dial. To cause a foodstuff to 'rise' when cooked, making it lighter. *BA G*

1952 FGC StM, Baking powder helps to float things.

FLOATING BOAT sb dial slang. See quot.

1958 DeC Tre /fluoting buot/ local term for cooked breadfruit.

FLOATING BULLET sb dial slang. A cooked breadfruit (which is large and spherical).

1943 *GL* StAnn, StM, Floatin' bullet, breadfruit. 1956 Mc StAnd /fluoten bulet/ usual word is breadfruit. 1962 BLB 54 /fluotn bulit/ breadfruit which rises to top of cooking.

FLOATING BUOY sb dial joc. See quot.

1956 BLB StT /fluoting bui/ a dumpling made of flour and baking soda which rises to the top during cooking.

flobo sb dial; cf *flabob*, prob of same origin. Cf also *flips* sb.

1959 DeC StJ /flobo/ whole green banana boiled in a rundown.

FLOCK vb dial; cf *OED v* 4a only quot 1609. 'To crowd upon, throng (a person).' *OED. G*

1943 Bennett 21, But dose bwoys ovah dere Wi' flock we like how dese gals flock De soljas ovah here.

FLOG /flag/ vb intr dial; <*flog*, vb trans. To be beaten. *BL G*

1958 DeC StT /al di tach flag rait aaf/ *All the thatch was blown off the house* (*in the hurricane*).

FLOG-ALL sb dial. A superior variety of sweet-potato which is thought to flog or beat all others.

1952 FGC StAnn /flág-ál/ whitish; StC /flágàal/ reddish, white inside, bears more than the rest; StJ /flágáal/ dry, yellow outside, white inside; StM /flág-háal/ red, bears more, 5 months as against 6 months [for other types]. 1954 *FG* 439, The most popular variety, both for eating and for good returns, is the Flog-all.

floksi see FLUXY.

flombo, flombob see *flabob*.

FLOOLOOLOOPS see *flululups*.

FLOOR BED sb. *G*

1954 LeP StAnn, Floor bed, bed or mattress on the floor.

FLOORING vbl sb; cf *OED* 2. In some country parts, the common word rather than 'floor'. *BL*

1956 Mc Man, Flooring, floor (which word is not normally used): /swíip di flúorin/.

FLORENCE /flaarents/ sb dial; the familiarizing name *Florence*, perh with a pun on *floor*. A temporary bed on the floor. Cf FLOOR BED.

1959 DeC Han /flaarents/ a rough mattress laid on the floor; in most parts of Jamaica this is called a *shakedown*.

FLOUR-BARREL sb dial. A variety of sweet-potato that is round, large, and white inside.

1952 FGC StAnd /flouwa baril/ very mealy, red; StC /floua baril/ white and roun'; StM, white, can be 10–15 pounds.

FLOUR BAT sb dial; <*flour* + BAT. A type of large moth that is covered with a powdery substance.

1958 DeC Port /floua-bat/ a bat-moths [*sic*] of about 3 in. wingspread, covered by a great deal of powder.

FLOUR-SAUCE sb dial.

1956 Mc StAnd /flóua sáas/ a dish made with flour, fish or meat, etc., and boiled.

FLOUR YAM sb. A fine floury white yam.

1790 Beckford II 140, The negro-yam is rather bitter, and by no means so substantial as the other species, which is distinguished by the appellation of flower-yam, to denote its superiority. 1952 FGC Port, StC, StM /floua yam/ big, white, fine grain, one straight yam. 1954 *FG* 444 (see s.v. WHITE YAM).

FLOWER-FENCE (OF BARBADOS) sb; *DAE* 1762→. The shrub *Cæsalpinia pulcherrima*, used for fences or hedges; now more often called BARBADOS PRIDE. *BA*

1696 Sloane 149, Flour fence of Barbados..In Insulæ Jamaicæ..ubique spontanea reperitur. 1873 Rampini 155, The roads were bordered with a flower-fence of Barbados pride (*Poinsiana pulcherrima*). 1920 Fawcett 95 (see s.v. BARBADOS PRIDE).

FLOWER-PRIDE sb bot rare; <FLOWER (-FENCE) + (BARBADOS) PRIDE.

1864 Grisebach 783, Flower-pride: *Cæsalpinia pulcherrima.*

FLOWERS sb dial as sing. *BL N T*

1. A flower.

1907 Jekyll 14, Miss Lumpy..show him a flowers in the pond. 1952 FGC StAnn, It have a white flowers. [Regularly elsewhere among dial speakers.]

2. Also in comb: *flowers-garden, flowers pot*, etc.

1905 Smith 20, Hi! me Annancy mus' hab one flowers garden like a buckra.

FLOWER YAM see FLOUR YAM.

flululups, flups adv, sb, vb, and int dial; essentially echoic.

A. adv: Imitating the sound of a liquid being drunk quickly and to the dregs; *flups* would appear to represent a shorter drink than *flululups*.

1955 LeP StE (Eld) /di man dringk it aaf flululups/—not a drop was left. 1955 FGC Man /a dringk it aaf flups/—at one quick swallow.

B. sb: 1. See quots.

1956 Mc Man /flúlulups, flululúps/ noise made in drinking. 1958 FGC StT /flululups/ sound made when 'slupping' soup.

2. Rubbish, the remnants or left-over bits of anything—e.g. meat, paper, etc.; fig, nonsense.

1943 *GL* StM, Floolooloops, useless meat. 1957 EB Port /flululups/ remnants of meat. 1958 DeC Port /flululúps/ (1) banana trash, (2) waste paper. 1959 DeC Kgn, Nonsense, foolishness; /yu taakin pyuur flululups, man/.

3. The sound of slippers dragging when someone walks. *G*

1956 Mc West.

C. vb: See quot.

1958 DeC StT /flululups/ to suck up liquids in a noisy manner.

D. int: An exclamation of appreciation (perh to be conn with sense B 2).

1957 DeC StE (Accom) /flululups/—exclamation on hearing a joke, expressing appreciation.

flups see prec.

FLUTAS, flutaz see FLITTER.

FLUTE sb dial. *BL*

1. A fife. *BA G*

1907 Jekyll 216, The music consists of three 'flutes' (fifes), two tambourines..etc.

2. Another name for the FIFER or TRUMPETER fish.

1952 FGC StE /fluut/ trumpeter: long, narrow, with red stripes, mouth pointed and opens at the end.

FLUXY /floksi/ adj dial; <*flux*, diarrhoea + -*y*. Of a green fruit or other similar substance: liable to cause the flux; hence (lit or fig) immature, premature. *BL*

[1943 *GL* No addr, Flux, a disease caused by eating green fruits. (Cf *OED* 1—1854.)] 1943 *GL* StC, Fluxy, immature. 1955 FGC Man, Fluxy—of a fruit or other things not fit. 1957 EB Port /floksi manggo/ below standard.

FLY vb causative; cf *OED* 9d 1676, 'fly the cork', 1876. To cause to fly out. *BA G*

1912 McK *Songs* 58, Just like how yeas' get strong an' sometimes fly de cark [cork].

FLYING-ANTS sb. The winged phase of the dry-wood termite, which flies about, then sheds its wings to begin a new phase. *BL G T*

1952 FGC Port, StAnd, Flying ants: black, slightly red; live in a high nest on the ground; 'family to duck-ants'.

FLYING HORSE sb colloq or slang. In schoolboy parlance: a bent pin or similar sharp device placed on a chair as a practical joke.

1950 U.Newton VI 19, I rose from my chair with remarkable agility when a 'Flying Horse' touched me.

FLYING PEN, FLY PEN sb; cf *OED fly v*[1] 4c. A field upon which cattle are penned temporarily so that they may manure it with their droppings; used on sugar estates, etc.

1790 Beckford II 202, It will be very difficult..to ascertain which method of manuring answers best—that of flying pens, or dropping dung into the holes. 1839 McMahon 249, Twenty acres of the most suitable land should then be penned over, by what are called flying-pens, taking in about an acre to each pen. A sufficient quantity of cattle to manure this should at once be turned on. 1952 FGC StJ, The 'fly-pen' is used upon Hampton estate, St James.

FLYING SAUCER sb slang. Nickname for policeman mounted on a motorcycle: the corps was established when 'flying saucers' were in the news (about 1950).

1951 FGC Kgn, StAnd.

FLYING SUCKER sb dial. A young banana plant that has begun to grow and to leaf out well.

1957 DeC StAnd (Irish Tn) /flái-in sóka/ a banana sucker 3–4 feet tall; these are considered the best.

FLY PEN see FLYING PEN.

FLY-PENNING vbl sb; <FLY PEN treated as a vb, or *fly* abstracted and prefixed to *penning*, vbl sb.

1942 HPJ, Fly-penning: Keeping cattle penned on fields that are to be fallowed. 1952 FGC StJ, The system of 'fly-penning': before replanting canes, pen cattle in the field one week to manure it, then remove them to another.

FLY-UP sb dial; <*fly* (*OED v*[1] 4) + *up*. A type of trap, used to catch birds and animals, in which a stick or small shrub is bent over, baited, and held with a trigger: when the quarry trips this, the stick flies up—whence the name. [Man informant may have confused this with a CALABAN.]

1956 Mc Man /flai-op/ a sort of tower built of sticks—used to catch dogs, cats, mongoose; Port /flai-op/ to catch /pus ar daag/; StAnd (Dallas) /flai-op/ identified with /bena/, a kind of trap that is set on the ground, for catching dogs as well as birds (?).

FO' see *fi*.

FOACE see FORCE.

FOFO see FUFU.

FOGIE sb dial; ? < FUNGEE; cf FUGGI.

1943 *GL* Port, Fogie, broth.

fok-aroun sb dial vulg; <*fuck* vb + *around*, with allusion to the stirring.

1. One of the names for a coconut RUNDOWN.

1958 DeC StT /fok-aroun/ coconut rundown.

2. See quot.

1958 DeC StT /fok-aroun/—gratered green banana boiled in a run-down.

FOLLOWER sb tech. A banana sucker not transplanted but left at the root of the parent plant to produce the succeeding crop.

1912 Levy in *Jrl JAS* (quot 1913 Fawcett 40), One size of Follower may be left throughout the field.

FOLLOW-FASHION adj and sb; cf *OED follow v.* 8. *G*

A. adj. Imitative; tending to copy what is done by others.

c 1915 FGC StAnd, Child, you too follow-fashion. 1924 Beckwith 49 [Prov:] Follow fashion Juba neber bwoil good soup.

B. sb. Imitation (with the implication that it may not be wise).

1873 Rampini 176 [Prov:] Follow fashion break monkey neck. 1921 Franck 424 [Prov:] Follow fashion mek monkey cut him tail.

FOLLOW-LINE /fála-láin/ sb dial; <*follow* vb + *line* sb.

1. A stranger who comes from another district along a hill track (Jekyll only) or along a railway track (the usual explanation). See quots. The connotation is unfavourable.

1907 Jekyll 269, Strangers are called 'follow-line' because, as they come down from their homes in the higher hills, they walk in strings..This walking in Indian file is necessitated by the narrowness of the track. 1943 *GL* Clar, Fallaline, a newcomer; StJ, Falaline, one who is always walking about; StT, Follow-line, Man who leaves one parish for another, travelling by foot on railway track. 1956 BLB StJ /a fi-mi kos dat; yu waak bai die, yu pich bai nait—yu falaláin, yu kom fraang yaanda/ *That's my favourite curse-word. You walk by day, you take shelter at night; you are a 'follow-line'; you have come from distant parts.*

2. See quot. (Perh erron.)

1954 LeP Port, Fala lain, negro.

fongk see FUNK.

fonji see FUNGEE.

FONK see FUNK.

FOOD sb dial; <*food*, perh infl in sense by close assoc with FUFU. In specific sense: 'starch' foods, esp the farinaceous tubers. *BA*

1954 LeP StAnn, Food—bread, yam. 1956 Mc StAnd, Q. What is food? A. /iz yam, kuoko, pitieta, domplen mam/ *It's yam, coco, potato, dumpling, Ma'am.*

FOOD-KIND sb dial; formed on analogy of BREAD-KIND, FISH-KIND, etc.; cf FOOD. Foods of the 'starch' kind: yam, coco, potato, bread-fruit, cornmeal, etc.

1942 Bennett 38, Me teck har een, buy some food kine, An' load wan baskit well.

FOO FA /fúu fá/ interrog phr; <*for*+*who*+*for*: cf *fi* possessive particle+*who*=whose, which has been telescoped with *who..for*. Whose?

[1942 HPJ, F'oo: fe who: Whose—A f'oo; or a fe-oo dis?] 1943 *GL* StM, Foo fa? whose? 1959 Mrs Lyn StAnd /fuu fa uon?/ *For-who-for own is this*, i.e. *Whose is this?*

FOO-FOO sb see FUFU.

FOO-FOO, FOOL-FOOL /fuu-fuu, fu-fuul, fuul-fuul/ adj dial, also absol; iteration of *fool* with vocalization of *l*. Cf also FOOL. *BL*

1. Credulous, simple, easy to take advantage of; hence also oafish, illiterate, generally stupid.

1868 Russell 11, Dis man fool-fool fe toro (true). 1950 Pioneer 55, Wich one a we more foo-fooler? 1954 LeP Man, StT, Somebody who is credulous—Foo foo, fool fool; StAnn, A fool-fool man, coarse, illiterate man; StT, Fool fool, big oafish man. 1956 Mc StAnd /yu folo dem fufuul uol taim piipl? yu ki yosel/ *You listen to those foolish old-fashioned people? You'll kill yourself.*

2. As a vague term of condemnation: stupid, silly, annoying—applied also to things: stupidly contrived.

1956 LeP StAnd /dem fuul-fuul aianin-buod de/ *Those foolish contraptions of ironing-boards.* (Said by a workman when one collapsed on him.)

FOOL sb dial; cf FOOL-FOOL. Abstr: Simplicity, stupidity. *G*

1950 Pioneer 36, De whol a de nex week Wasp wid him fool fly up an dung, carry de bag a letta.

FOOL-FOOL see FOO-FOO.

FOOLTIE sb dial; <*fool*+intrusive transitional /t/+*-ie*.

1943 *GL* StAnd, Fooltie, a fool.

FOOL UP vb phr dial. To play tricks on, make an utter fool of. *BL G T*

1957 JN No addr, You mus' tell mi when mi come you know mam. No bother fool mi up.

FOOLY sb dial; <*fool*+*-y*. The LOGGERHEAD PETCHARY, which is too trusting.

1952 FGC Man /làgahéd fúuli/.

FOOT sb dial; cf cpds: TUMPA-FOOT, WOODEN-FOOT, etc. The leg. ('Leg' is sometimes used for the thigh, in which case 'foot' is from the knee down.) [This is an inheritance from W Africa—cf 1929 Rattray I 53, 'Curious as it may seem there is not any word to distinguish "leg" from "foot" in these [Ashanti] languages, and the same applies to "hand" and "arm"'.] *BL G N T*

1907 Jekyll 46, Puss them have them junka 'tick secretly in a them trousies foot. [*The cats had their clubs hidden in their trouser-legs.*] 1943 *GL* Clar, Shenk, part of foot. 1956 Mc Man /dem hav anada bord agen, a lang-fut wan—dem kaal duoz gaalen—dem fut lang/ *There's another bird, a long-legged one, called gaulin—their legs are long.*

FOOT vb dial; cf *OED v* 7. To follow close on the heels of (someone), tread in (someone's) footsteps.

1956 Mc StE (Accom) [Children walking along the road:] /fut im!/.

FOOT-AND-FOOT adv dial. Step for step; together. *G*

1962 BLB 24 /fut-an-fut/ side by side, together. 1956 BLB StJ /mi an Aida waak fut an fut go out de/.

FOOT-BOTTOM sb dial; <*foot*+*bottom*. The sole of the foot. *BL G*

1877 Murray *Feedin' 'Perrit* 9, I wi' kiss you foot bottom. c1915 FGC StAnd [Song:] /Mi wi daans di shie-she, Mi wi daans di kach-riil, Mi wi daans til di huol a mi futbatam piil/. 1956 Mc Clar, see quot s.v. CRABBY.

FOOT-MAT sb. *G*

1954 LeP Kgn, Foot mat—mat made from dry trash or grass.

FOOT-PAD sb dial.

1956 Mc StE (Accom) /dát a banáana tróngk—ték it mek fút-pad/ *That is banana trunk—it is used to make door mats.*

FOOT POST-HOLE sb dial joc; for FOOT'S *post-hole*. Long boots that come far up the leg—alluding to their looking like deep holes.

1943 *GL* StC, Foot pose ole, long boots. 1956 Mc Port /fut puos uol/—long boot—same as /waata buut/.

FOR ALL TIME adv phr dial. For good, once and for all. *G*

1956 Mc Man /Yu kom for aal taim? No, mi gwoing bak doun/ *Have you come for good? No, I'm going home again.*

FORBIDDEN FRUIT sb; *DAE* 1751→. A citrus fruit (*Citrus paradisi*) in size between the SHADDOCK and GRAPEFRUIT; cf quot 1893. Also called FAST-BREEDING FRUIT, *fibini*. *N*

1756 Browne 309, Citrus 9..The Forbidden Fruit, or smaller Shaddock Tree. 1774 Long III 799. 1801 Nugent 36, Forbidden and grape fruit, in clusters. 1893 Sullivan 74, This is somewhat larger than a grapefruit. It is called 'forbidden fruit' because of three brownish marks on the outside peel, supposed to be Eve's finger marks as she plucked the fruit. 1920 Fawcett 190, *C. paradisi*..Grape Fruit, Forbidden Fruit, Pomelo.

FORCE /fuos/ vb dial; cf *OED v* 8 →1863. 'Now *rare*'. *G*

1. To press, use force; also *fig*, to insist.

1942 Bennett 10, Me couldn' get peas widout pepper, All de foace me foace. [*No matter how much I insisted.*]

2. In phr *Force up* (someone or something) *upon*: To obtrude. *BL*

1956 BLB gen /mi no nuo a we dem a fuos op demsef pang mi fa/ *I don't know why they insist on trying to associate with me.*

FORCE ACE adv phr dial; by folk-etym <*post-haste*.

1907 Jekyll 63, An' he..take his tumpa bill coming to Cow force ace fe chop off Cow's neck. *Ibid* 65, *force ace*, post haste.

FORCED CROP sb obs. A crop (of sugar-cane) for which the land and the labour force are used to absolute capacity, or beyond the sound limits, in order to produce the largest possible yield.

1839 McMahon 141–2, During the time of making these forced crops, the labourers were driven with the cart-whip from morning till night.

FORCE-FIT adj dial; for *forced-fit*—cf *OED forced ppl a* 5+FIT. See quot; cf FORCE-RIPE.

1956 BLB Man /fuos-fit/—Premature (used of a fruit). Precocious (of a child; of a dog that had a litter while still a puppy).

FORCE-RIPE adj dial; for *forced-ripe*—cf *OED forced ppl a* 5+*ripe*. Prematurely ripened; precocious; said with unfavourable connotation of young people acting like adults.

c1915 FGC StAnd, You is a force-ripe pickny! 1943 *GL* Clar, Fuba, 'force ripe'. 1959 current. *BA BL G T*

FORE-DAY(-MORNING) adv phr or sb dial; <*fore* (aphetic form of *before*) + DAY (+ MORNING). The time of day just before day-break; dawn. *BA BL G T*

1943 *GL* Port, Fo-day-mānin, Before day break. 1952 FGC StT /wen it komz aan tu fuor-die/ *When it comes close to dawn.* 1970 HPJ, Heard Kgn: Befo'-day morning.

FORE-EYED (MAN) see FOUR-EYE(D) MAN.

FOREIGN sb or adv dial; abbr of *a foreign land.* (Cf Royal Naval parlance: *going foreign*, going to a foreign station. LeP.) A foreign land, abroad; usually preceded by prep: A[1], *from*, *in*, *to*, etc. *EDD* Scot., Irel.

1942 HPJ, 'Him gahn foreign, missus', 'Him was in foreign but him cum back now'. 1952 FGC Man /jiga flii—a ting kom fram farin kom hier/; Tre, Drummer, big, gray roach, come from foreign. 1956 Mc Man /go a faran/ *Go abroad*; StE /dem sen tu farin/ *They are sent abroad.*

FOREIGNER sb dial. A travelled person. *G*

1943 *GL* Clar, Foreigner, one travel to foreign lands.

FOREIGN FLOUR sb dial. Imported wheat flour (in contrast, e.g., to locally made cassava flour).

1958 DeC Tre, wheat flour of any grade.

FOREIGN-UP vb phr. To make (something) appear to be foreign.

1950 Pioneer 61, Den me sey me want fe learn it to, Me haffe buckle dung, Screw up me mout an roll me y'eye An foreign up me tongue.

FOREIGN MARKET sb dial; cf FOREIGN. See quot.

1961 BLB Tre, Any of the big parish markets to which people of Trelawny take their produce, e.g. Falmouth, Montego Bay, etc. On Friday evenings they load their donkeys and set out for /farin maakit/. The term does not seem to be in use outside of this parish.

FORE-TIME adj dial; aphetic form of BEFORE-TIME. *G*

1956 Mc Port /fúotaim, fótaim/—old-fashioned, of olden days

FORGOT /figát/ vb dial; < past tense or pple of *forget*. To forget. *BL G*

1942 Bennett 34, Yuh kean gwahn chat, but doan fegat Yuh gwine reap wat yuh sew [*sic*]. 1950 Pioneer 17, An dem won't fegat it. *Ibid* 60, Lawd me never wi fegat de night.

FORKED PEPPER sb. A kind of *Capsicum* pepper with two points.

1814 Lunan I 357, Forked, or double pointed peppers.

FORK-FERN sb obs?; evid for *forked fern*. In Lunan's use: Ferns of the genus *Acrostichum*.

1814 Lunan I 301, Fork fern. Acrostichum..Eighteen species have been discovered in Jamaica.

FORK-TAILED HUMMING-BIRD sb. See quot.

1849 Hill 'Letter' in *Gleaner* 2 Mar, 1921 11, Polytmus is the long-tailed humming bird; your specimen, being what is usually spoken of as, fork-tailed, the long outer feathers being not yet developed.

FORKY-FORKY adj dial; iterative <*fork* + *-y*. See quot.

1942 HPJ, Forky-forky rack-tone is in an Anancy story, apparently 'jagged', but said by narrators to mean 'woodlands', though only in Anancy stories.

form /form, ferm/ sb dial; the prevailing dial pronunc of *fern*. (Cf also *feril, fierin, fyaan.*)

1952 FGC Han, StC, StM, Tre /form/; Tre /ferm/; StE /faam/.

FORM /faam/ vb dial; cf *OED* 4, *EDD* 5. To pretend to be, to pretend to be in (a certain condition); to feign. *Form fool*: act like a fool.

1912 McK *Ballads* 70, Yet you..Only formin' like de juice; An' dem caan' see..Dat you 'pon malingering. 1924 Beckwith 28, Cunnie-mo'n-father was lying down underneath the table fawning sleep; *ibid* 37, So he fawn sick, very very sick; *ibid* 45, Anancy got vex an' box him Tumblebug fawn dead. 1925 Beckwith 74 [Prov:] If you want fe know you' frien' from you' enemy, form drunk lay down. 1942 Bennett 14, Pickney wey yuh dah linga fah? Move aff an' don't form fool. 1943 *GL* Port, Faam, pretend; StC, Faum, pretend. 1947 U.Newton II 36, One day I tried to use the new 'High English' at Burrell Run. Sam started the crew laughing by asking: 'A (is) what Newsy a form?' So I had to use one language at school and another at Burrell Run. 1950 Pioneer 66, Ah don't mean ah really gwine dead, ah only gwine form dead. 1957 Patient at UCWI clinic /di kuk di tel mi mi faamin, bot it nat so/ *The cook told me I was shamming sick, but it's not so. BL*

FOR-ME-LATER see *fi-mi-lieta.*

FOR PURPOSE /fi popas, ~ porpas, ~ paapos/ adv phr. On purpose; intentionally.

1950 Pioneer 23, It look lika sey de people do fe purpose an lef cane j'int dem eena Anancy way. 1957 EB Port /fi popas/ on purpose. 1962 BLB 34 /fi-paapos/ on purpose.

FORRAD see *farad.*

FOR (THE) BETTER /fi beta, fi di beta/ adv phr. All the more. *G*

1907 Jekyll 130, Tiger bawl for Fire a stop, but Fire coming for the better. 1943 Bennett 3, Rouge an' lipstick meck de wrinkle Dem tan up fe betta. 1950 Pioneer 65, Anancy..bawl out, 'Wha mek you a fan you tail ah fe me yard?..' Den Cow say, 'De gingy-fly dem ah bodder me me frien..' An him go on ah fan him tail fe de better. 1957 DeC StE /shi hiel out fi di beta/ *She called out all the louder;* /it rien fi di beta/ *It rained all the harder.*

FOR TRUE /fi-trúu, fi-chúu/ adv phr dial; <*for true*, cf *OED for* 19b. In truth, truly, indeed. *BA BL G N T* Gullah Krio, etc.

1790 Moreton 125, A man, for true. 1862 Clutterbuck 143, He too honest for true! 1943 *GL* Tre, Fichu, Is it true[?]. 1950 Pioneer 64, Fe you chewstick sweet fe truu, me frien.

FORTY-SHILLING WORD sb slang. Any indecent word for the saying of which one may be fined forty shillings.

1961 C. Lindo StAnd.

fos see FIRST, FUSS.

FO TO PANG see *fruutapang.*

FOU-FOU see FUFU.

FOUR-AND-TWENTY(-STEPS) sb dial. See quots. Cf also ELEVEN STEPS.

1942 HPJ, Four-and-twenty steps—used to describe any specially imposing building. 1943 *GL* Man, Four-and-20, court-house.

FOUR-BIT sb dial; <*four* + BIT. One shilling and sixpence (four times $4\frac{1}{2}$*d.*); also called BOB-TENNER.

1943 *GL* Tre, Foubit, One shilling and sixpence; (also several other parishes). 1950 Pioneer 81, Him give me one cockeye fourbit Me take it me buy one silk dress. 1952 FGC Han, StM /fuobit/.

FOUR-CORNER BASKET sb dial. A rectangular thatch basket.

1958 DeC StT /fuo-kaana baskit/ a bankra.

FOUR EYE see FOUR-EYE(D) MAN.

FOUR-EYE, FOUR-EYE(D) MAN /fuo-yai man/ sb dial; < FOUR-EYED + *man*. (Not '*fore*'-

eyed.) An obeah-man or myal man, who supposedly has second sight.

1929 Beckwith 144, A Myal Man is called a fore-eyed man because he alone has the power to see where the shadow is nailed or the obeah is buried. 1942 HPJ, Fo-yeye—a short word for obeahman. 1943 *GL* Port, Fo'-yeye-man, obeahman; StAnd, Fou yeye man, obeah man. 1954 LeP Kgn, Four-eye; Port, Fou-yai man; StE, Four-eye-man—man who professes to kill or heal by magic.

FOUR-EYED adj and sb dial. Having 'second sight', being supposedly able to see spirits; absol as a noun, one believed to be able to see spirits. See next.

1895 Banbury 19, 'Mial people'..are said to be '*fo-yeyed*' (four-eyed,) that is, they can see spirits and converse with them. *Ibid* 24, The *foyeyed,* or those that can see spirits.

FOUR-EYE PUSS sb dial slang; cf *OED four-eyes* 1874.

1943 *GL* No addr, Four yeye puss, a person wearing glasses.

FOUR-FOOT AMELIA sb dial slang. A flimsy or roughly made bed; see quot.

1936 Martinez *Gleaner* 3 Oct 35, The furnished ones [*sc* huts] only carry a shelf and a 'Bedge'..or a 'Four foot Amelia', on which the occupant is supposed to sleep.

FOUR-FOOTER see prec.

FOUR-O'CLOCK FLOWER sb; *OED* 1756→. *BA*

The common garden flower (of various colours) *Mirabilis jalapa,* said by Barham to have got its name from opening and closing every four hours; other writers generally say that the name comes from the flowers opening daily at about 4 P.M.

1696 Sloane 91–2, *The Four a Clock Flour.* In agris Insulæ Jamaicæ & ad sylvarum..abundat. 1707 Sloane 211, The four a Clock Flower..It..usually opens its Flower about four a Clock, whence the name. a 1726 Barham (1794) 62, Four o'clock Flower. This plant is so called in Jamaica from its opening and shutting every four hours, night and day, as they have observed there. 1835 Madden II 50. 1914 Fawcett 147, *Mirabilis jalapa*.. Four o'clock, Marvel of Peru.

FOUR O'CLOCK TREE sb dial.

1. Trees of the genus *Bauhinia,* said to fold their leaves together at about 4 P.M.

1952 FGC Port, Four o'clock tree.

2. = FIVE O'CLOCK BUSH (Guango or similar trees).

1952 FGC StAnn, StM, Four o'clock tree.

FOURY sb dial; <*four* + -*y*, familiarizing suffix. In children's play (as in marbles) a piece worth four of another kind.

1952 FGC Han /fúori/ a red horse-eye, which is worth four gray nickers.

FOWL-BONE sb dial; for *fowl's-bone.* The wild shrub *Miconia lævigata,* so called because the stems are thought to resemble chicken bones.

1952 FGC StAnn /fóul-búon/ grows to a small tree, white when stripped; also StAnd, Tre. 1955 *WIMJ* 145, *Miconia laevigata* DC. Chicken Net; Fowl Bone; Sage; White Wattle; Long-leaf-Jointer.

FOWL-FOOT GRASS sb. = FOWL-TOE GRASS. *G*

1954 *FG* 228, Iron-Grass (Goose Grass, Fowl-Foot Grass) (*Eleusine indica*). This grass, a native of India, is common on open ground and waste places throughout the West Indies.

FOWL-ROOST sb dial. A fish also called *panggra*: see quot.

1952 FGC StE /fóul-rúus/—have mess in belly; gray and black kinds.

FOWLSHIT PINE sb dial. A variety of pineapple of an unpleasant greenish, caca-d'oie colour.

1952 FGC Port /fóulshit páin/.

FOWL-TOE GRASS sb dial. A type of common grass with a blossom shaped like a chicken's foot, with three 'toes' spread in one direction, and one in the other. Same as FOWL-FOOT GRASS.

1952 FGC StC /fóul-tùo gráas/—from the shape of the blossom; used against worms in babies.

FOX LEAF sb dial; origin of name unexplained.

1955 *WIMJ* 160, *Pluchea odorata* (L) Cass...Riverside Tobacco; Bitter tobacco; Fox Leaf.

FOX-TAIL sb dial.

1943 *GL* Man, Fox-tail, native wild flax.

FOX-TAIL GRASS sb; *OED* 1597–1813. A kind of grass with fluffy reddish spikes that resemble a fox's tail. See quot 1864. *N*

1803 Dallas I 83, Small cottages covered with thatch, or a long grass called the Foxtail. *Ibid* 84, The rest of it was over-run with a species of fern and Foxtail grass. 1811 Titford 37, Fox-tail grass, *Alopecurus Indicus.* 1826 Williams 290, The great fox-tailed grass. 1864 Grisebach 783, Foxtail-grass, *Anatherum bicorne* and *macrurum.* 1877 Murray *Feedin' 'Perrit* 4, It red de same like o fox tail grass. 1952 FGC Han /faks-tiel grass/ fluff from top used to stuff pillows.

FRAH-FRAH sb or vb dial; cf Twi *fráfrà,* to mingle oneself or associate with.

1943 *GL* Kgn, Frah-frah, gossip.

FRAID sb dial uncom; <*afraid*; also US—cf Went.

1. A ghost; also personified.

1948 U.Newton IV 7, A night will come when you shall meet Mr Fraid and you are going to regret it. *Ibid* 8, At last I can tell Pupa that I see two Fraids. *Ibid* 9, He shouted: 'Run Big Fraid: Little Fraid After You'.

2. Fear. In phr *to catch one's fraid*: to become cautious through fear. *BL*

1956 Mc Man /im kéch im fried/ she thought twice, she acted cautiously.

FRAID /fried/ adj dial; <*afraid.* Afraid, frightened. *BA BL G T N* (vb, = *to become* ~).

1956 Mc Man /im fried an im hed gruo; im taat get fried/ *She became frightened and her head grew; she began to get frightened.*

FRAIDY-FRAIDY adj dial; iterative <FRAID + -*y*. Timid, fearful, afraid.

1956 Mc No addr /cho, unu tuu friedi-friedi/ *Ha! you are too scared!*

FRAM, fram see FROM.

FREAK see *fliik.*

FRECKLE-NATURE sb dial.

1958 DeC StT /frekl niecha/ name for an albino Negro.

FREE-MASON sb obs. A kind of wasp that builds a nest of mud.

1756 Browne 439, Apis 5. *Subfusca innocua alvearis lutosis.* The Free-Mason. These insects live in small societies, and make their cells of mud.

FREENESS sb dial; <*free* + *-ness*. Something given free, without cost. (Cf Trinidad, a free feast.) *BA BL G T*

1957 Bennett 21, Once upon a Chrismus time, a kine rich gentleman was givin' wey beef an butta an bread to poor people..Well, Bredda Nancy hear bout dis ting an goh fe get some a de freeniss. *Ibid* 90, Freeniss..Is wa meck Jamaica people Dem like free sinting soh?

FREE-PAPER sb dial; *DAE* 1838→.

1. A document of manumission or emancipation from slavery. *G*

1831 Bleby 3, I was several times informed that the slaves ..were generally under the impression, that Mr Burchell was gone to Europe to obtain their freedom, and would at Christmas, when he was expected to return, bring out their 'free paper' with him. 1833 Baptist Missionaries 26, On Sunday, December 24, Steven James, a slave on Chatham estate, Trelawny, went to Mr Knibb, at Falmouth, and informed him that the people were saying, 'Free-paper was come out, and they would not work after Christmas'.

2. In phr *free-paper burn* (a slave's pass or TICKET has been burnt): one's holiday is over —one must get back to work again. *BL*

1889 Sanguinetti 52, And the other common phrase 'your free paper is burnt' as signifying that 'your leave is up', is referable to the curtailment of liberty when a slave's pass was destroyed. c 1915 FGC StAnd, 'Free-paper burn'—holidays are over: a phrase used by school-children and others. (1960 Current..FGC.)

FRE-FRA sb dial; prob phonosymbolic: cf *fere-fere*, FRAH-FRAH, *freke* vb., *frekete*, FLULULUPS.

1943 *GL* Clar, Frefra, things of little value.

freke sb dial; perh <*frigasi*, run-down. A dish in which coconut milk half boiled down to oil is the base, and other ingredients may be added. (Evid only in Port and StT.)

1943 *GL* Port, Freckey, freckay, half-boiled oil; StT, Freckey, Coconut milk, tomatoes and pepper cook together. 1958 DeC StT /freke/ coconut rundown.

freke vb dial; cf *freke-freke*.

1957 DeC StE (Accom) /freke/ to smash something to nothing.

freke-freke adj dial; iterative—cf *freke* vb, *frekete*.

1956 Mc Man /freke-freke/ shaky, unstable; used, for ex, of a house that looks about to tumble down.

frekete adj dial; cf *fre-fra*, *freke-freke*.

1943 *GL* StM, Freketeh, no value.

freketem int dial; cf *freke-freke*, *frekete*.

1956 Mc StE (Accom) /freketem/ 'When you throw down anything'—apparently an exclamation expressing rejection, 'That's no use!'

fren see FRIEND vb.

FRENCH ANGEL-FISH see ANGEL-FISH.

FRENCH CHURCH sb dial obs. The Roman Catholic Church: see quot.

1934 Williams 107, The first priest to become well known through the Jamaican 'bush' was a Frenchman, and the Catholic Church came to be known in consequence as the French Church.

FRENCH COTTON sb.

1. A variety of the true cotton, cultivated in the French islands: *Gossypium hirsutum*.

1756 Browne 282–3, Gossipium 1..French cotton. This shrub is planted in a few gardens in Jamaica, but is not much cultivated: for the Cotton is not thought to be so good; and the seeds are so small, that it is a difficult matter to separate them from the wool. 1793 Edwards II 271, *French* or *Small-seed*, with a whitish beard. This is the cotton in general cultivation in Hispaniola. Its staple is finer, and its produce equal to either of the three species last mentioned. 1864 Grisebach 783, Cotton, French: *Gossypium hirsutum* and *Calotropis procera*.

2. A plant which produces tufted seeds similar to those of cotton: *Calotropis procera*. Also called FRENCH JASMINE, MILKWEED.

1864 Grisebach 783, see quot above.

FRENCH GUAVA TREE sb. *Cassia alata*. Also called RINGWORM BUSH.

1820 Thomson 74, Then wash [ringworm] with the juice of the French guava-tree or ring-worm bush (*cassia alata*).

FRENCH JASMINE sb bot. The shrub *Calotropis procera*; also called FRENCH COTTON, MILKWEED.

1756 Browne 183, The Auriculas or French Jasmin. This shrub is now common in all the Savannas about Kingston and Old Harbour. 1811 Titford Expl to Plate VII 1, French Jasmin, *Auricula gigantea*. 1864 Grisebach 784, French jasmine: *Calotropis procera*.

FRENCH KILN sb ?obs. A type of kiln formerly much used (and still somewhat) for burning lime: see quot. (In dial /skil/.)

1774 Long III 849–50, Most of the planters, who use the Jamaica lime, burn it in circular, conical piles, ranging the strata of stone and wood alternately from the bottom to the top, which they bring to a point..The conical or French Kiln before mentioned.

FRENCH LIME sb. A cultivated, fine variety of the lime: *Citrus aurantifolia*.

1814 Lunan I 452, The *French lime* tree, as it is called, is to be found in many parts of Jamaica; it is of a larger growth than the other [*sc* sweet lime], and shoots more into the regular form of a tree. 1954 *FG* 317, *French Lime*. The principal lime grown. Propagated from seed. A small fragrant rinded fruit. Supplies the commercial lime oil.

FRENCH OAK sb; cf *OED* 1829 only.

1. The common timber tree *Catalpa longissima*; see quot 1941.

1740 Importance 50, The *French Oak* was first planted here, as was one Cypress-Tree by Sir N. Laws, both thrive very well. 1756 Browne 264, French Oak..This beautiful tree is now cultivated in many parts of Jamaica.. Its numerous flowers, and slender siliques, add a peculiar grace to its growth. 1814 Lunan I 309, Bignonia longissima. It is known in Jamaica by the name of French oak; the French call it *chene noir*. 1941 Swabey 33, Yokewood —(French Oak, Mast Wood, Jamaica Oak). *Catalpa longissima*.

[2. In Antigua: the tree *Bucida buceras*.]

FRENCH PHYSIC-NUT sb; cf quot 1814. *Jatropha multifida*, also called SPANISH PHYSIC-NUT, and, as the name indicates, used as a purge; this variety is considered better than the common physic-nut.

a 1726 Barham (1794) 141, There are three or four sorts of these trees; but one..differs very much from the rest.. they are called French physic-nuts, and their purging quality is more strong than any of the other sorts. 1756 Browne 348, Iatropha 3..French Physic Nut. This plant is pretty much raised in Jamaica, and forms no small ornament in many of their flower-gardens..The seeds are purgative, but so very violent in their operations that they are now but rarely administered. 1814 Lunan II 63, This plant is now very common, and, having been first introduced into the French islands from the continent, is known by the name of *French physic-nut*. 1920 Fawcett 313, Spanish, or French Physic Nut..cultivated and apparently indigenous in Jamaica and West Indies generally.

FRENCH PLANTAIN sb dial. A variety of plantain (*Musa paradisiaca*) that has shorter and yellower fruit than ordinary.

1952 FGC Port, French plantain, short, very yellow inside; StT, yellowish when green, seeds shorter.

FRENCH SET-GIRLS sb obs. Troupes of young women (cf SET sb) who celebrated Christmas in the French Creole fashion—see quot. Also s FRENCH SET DANCERS.

1837 Belisario Expl to Plate 7, French Set-Girls. This set is as much distinguished for the neatness of style in their dress, as their general deportment; differing in these respects greatly from all others..The French Sets.. are invariably observers of taste and decorum..During the eventful year 1794..many respectable families took flight [from St Domingo]..On becoming fixed residents [of Jamaica], they formed themselves into three Bands or Sets at Christmas, denominated 'Royalists', 'Mabiales', and 'Americans'. The former was composed wholly of Creoles of St Domingo..the 2d, of Africans from Congo, and the latter of a portion of both..They have their Queen, and allow male companions to join in their dances, during which, two drums, or 'Tamboos' are played, and an instrument shaken, called a 'Shaka': the voices of those who are not dancing, chime in, and together form a lively and inspiriting sound..The tasteful style in which the French Girls tie their kerchiefs on their heads, has ever been the envy of the Creole negroes of Jamaica, who make ineffectual efforts to imitate it. There are frequently twelve in a set, exclusive of males.. Thirty or forty pounds formerly were collected during the Christmas and New-Year's holidays, and that sum was expended in a grand repast..In the present day.. this description of pastime has greatly declined—the change no doubt having been effected by the degree of civilization to which the negroes have attained—the majority considering it disgraceful to join in such vulgar doings!!

FRENCH SORREL sb; cf *OED* 1829→ for spp of *Rumex* and *Oxalis*. An early and once common name for the plant *Hibiscus sabdariffa*, used to make the 'sorrel' drink of Christmas holidays. (This formerly common name is now usually abbr to 'sorrel'.)

1696 Sloane 99, *French Sorrel*. In hortis Jamaicæ Insulæ sata ubique provenit hæc alceæ species. a 1726 Barham (1794) 275–6, French sorrel, *Hibiscus sabdariffa*. 1811 Titford xiv, French Sorrell. 1954 *WIMJ* 30, *H. sabdariffa* L...Red, French or Indian Sorrel; African Mallow.

FRENCH THYME sb. The aromatic plant *Coleus aromaticus*, having an odour similar to that of ordinary thyme.

1952 FGC Port, StC, StM, StT /frénsh táim/. 1955 *WIMJ* 80, *Coleus aromaticus* Benth. French or Spanish Thyme. Country Borage. This species, a native of Java, is cultivated to some extent in the West Indies where it is used for seasoning. In Jamaica it is sometimes used in decoctions employed as cold remedies.

FRENCH WEED sb. A species of WATER-GRASS: *Commelina longicaulis*; used in making 'tea' against colds.

1864 Grisebach 783, Frenchweed: *Commelyna cayennensis*. 1954 *WIMJ* 29, *C. longicaulis*..Water Grass; French Weed.

FRENCH-WOMAN sb dial. A fortune-teller or obeahwoman.

1929 Beckwith 37, Betting was high, and even white men have acknowledged their indebtedness to the mysterious powers of the 'French woman' who occupied..a house backing upon the Kingston race course; *ibid* 106, There are Obeah Women too, who have the same power and are similarly employed. Parkes says the 'French women' have the most wisdom of all and are the most to be feared. 1942 HPJ, Frenchwoman: Obeahwoman, sorceress, fortune-teller.

FRENKA-FRENKA adj dial; var of FENKY-FENKY.

1943 *GL* Port, Frenka-frenka, delicate.

FRESH adj and absol as sb dial.

A. sb: Fresh meat (in contrast to salt, or SALTING). *BA*

1907 Jekyll 140 [Fowl Hawk speaks to John Crow:] Look you, sir, if you see the picny, nice fresh fe we mouth..You will get a good bag of fresh.

B. adj: 1. Without salt; hence insipid, without much flavour. *BL G T*

1958 G. Coulthard StAnd, 'Fresh', said of food—insipid. 1960 LeP StAnd, Fresh—tasteless because not seasoned in cooking, i.e. not enough salt.

2. Bare, mere.

1942 Bennett 3, Monday me sell ongle two pence.. Tuesday an Wednesday one tro-pence, Yessiday—Fresh quatty!

FRESH-CUT sb dial. A herb used especially as medicine for fresh cuts. More than one plant seems to go by the name: *Dianthera pectoralis* has been identified.

1927 Beckwith 17, Fresh-cut..For a cut bind on the bruised leaves as a plaster to check the bleeding.. Forbes and Wilfrid boil it as tea for a cold. 1952 FGC Port, Junjo-mitta is like fresh-cut, but more viny; StM, Fresh-cut, mos' like milkweed—beat it up, mix with /kyámfyà/ [camphor]; StAnn, StT. 1953 *WIMJ* 234, *Dianthera pectoralis* Murr. Fresh Cut; Garden Balsam [Trinidad]..The leaves are bruised, alone or with rum, and applied as a plaster.

FRESH-WATER SNAPPER sb obs. A fish: see quot. *G*

1725 Sloane II 289, Mugili affinis fluviatilis pisciculus.. The Fresh-Water Snapper..It is to be found with the Mullets in all fresh Water Lakes and Rivers of the Island.

FRET ON vb phr dial. To fret for, grieve for.

1956 Mc Man /di bíebi nó frét an yú?/ *The baby doesn't fret for you? (miss you?)*.

FRETRATION sb dial; <*fret* + /r/ by assimilation + *-ation*. A state of worry or fret; cf FRIGHTRATION.

1950 Pioneer 60, Me never se' car run so fas' Or so much street so broad, Me life eena fretration Wen me cross a Boulevard.

FRETTENATION /frètn-íeshan/ sb dial; <*fretting* + *-ation*. Fretting, worry, anxiety.

1907 Jekyll 145, Then Brother Rabbit commence to cry now, an' the frettenation in a Rabbit he say he kill somebody an' he know they going to hang him, an' next day Rabbit dead. *Ibid* 146, Frettenation, probably fright, but may have something to do with fretting. 1956 Mc StE (Accom) /meni píipl kyaan bie fretn-ieshan/ *Many people can't bear worry*. Also Man.

FRIEND /fren/ vb dial; cf *OED* 2 →1604. *G T*

1. To make friends with, be a friend of; also in phr *friend up with*.

1934 HPJ in *Gleaner* 13 Mar p. 12, Kick darg him fren' you, feed him him bite you. 1942 Astley Clerk, in HPJ, The word *fren* is one well known to me, in fact, an everyday word among the people—'Ef yu cyan beat a man, fren him', i.e. make him your friend. 1950 Pioneer 63, Him wuk him head fe fine out how fe mek de cow frien him, den him can get some ah dem meat. *Ibid* 64, Den dem all frien up wid Brer Nancy, an him invite de fus one..ah him yard.

2. To take (another) as a sexual companion without marriage; cf FRIENDING. *BL*

1952 Kerr, 60 While dancing he spoke to her asking if she would be a friend of his. She said if he wanted to friend her he would have to go to her mother and ask her.

FRIENDING vbl sb dial; <FRIEND vb. Concubinage. Cf CONCUBINE LIFE. *BA G T*

1953 Moore 25, Friending—the most informal and variable of the three types of conjugal relations (the other two being formal church-performed marriage and common-law marriage).

frigasi sb dial; <*fricassee. BA*

1958 DeC StT /frigasi/ a coconut run-down.

FRIGHTEN sb dial; <*frighten* vb, or perh <*fright* sb + -*n* suffix[1]. Fright, feeling of being frightened. *BA G*

1907 Jekyll 87, The frighten in him, him say 'No'. [*He felt so frightened that he said 'No'.*]

FRIGHTRATION sb dial; <*fright* + /r/ by assimilation + -*ation*. A state of fright or worried excitement.

1950 Pioneer 45, De 'ole Districk got frightration On dis ceremonial day.

FRINGE /frinj/ sb dial; <*springe*.

1956 Mc StAnd /frinj/ a bird snare consisting of a loop of string hung over a branch to fall by the fruit where the bird is likely to peck. Also Port.

FRINGRIGO see FINGRIGO.

FRISCO sb chiefly dial; prob < Sp *refresco*, cold beverage. A COOL-DRINK made with milk, egg, ice and flavouring, shaken together.

1950 U.Newton VI 31, Candies, fudge, frisco, ginger beer, syrup and sherbet. *BL N fresco*

FRITTER see FLITTER.

FROCK-BACK sb dial; for *frock's back*; cf NECK-BACK. The back of a woman's dress. *BL G*

1956 Mc StE /yu frák bák duon stíe so gud/ *The back of your frock is not right.*

FROCKY adj dial; <*frock*, N Engl form of *frough*, liable to break, brittle (cf *OED*, *EDD*) + -*y*; *OED* lists *froughy*, which survives in US dial. Friable, easily broken, worthless—said of wood.

1942 HPJ.

FRO-FRO[1] /fro-fro/ sb dial; perh < Sp *fósforo*, a friction match; but cf also Twi *fràfrafra*, brightly (burning), *fràmfram*, blazing, flaming. Fire; matches.

1943 *GL* Kgn, Port, Tre, Fro-fro, fru-fru, matches; Man, Fu-furo, matches. 1955 FGC Man, Fire in general: 'give me a light of fro-fro'.

FRO-FRO[2] sb dial; etym uncert: cf Sp (Cuba) *frío-frío*, a leguminous tree, perh *Cassia biflora* (Roig y Mesa).

1943 *GL* No addr, Fro-fro, a large tree of the Guango family.

FROG sb; cf *frog*, railway switch-plate. A device used in twisting rope: a truncated cone of wood having three lengthwise equidistant channels through which the three strands being twisted run.

1952 FGC StE.

FROG BANANA or **PLANTAIN** sb dial. A short, squat, thick-skinned variety of banana or plantain: it has some of the tartness of plantain, but if thoroughly ripe can be eaten uncooked like banana. *G*

1952 FGC Port, StAnd, StJ, Frog banana; StM, Frog plantain, same as Whitehouse.

FROM /fram, fran/ prep and quasi-conj chiefly dial; cf *OED prep* 3, C *quasi-conj*→1602. *BA G*

A. prep: 1. 'Indicating a starting-point in time, or the beginning of a period' (*OED*); ever since (a specific time). (In this sense Jamaican usage favours *from* over *since*.) *BL N*

1950 Pioneer 71, Dem belly empty fram marnin. 1956 Mc StAnd /ai duon get eni fram maanin—iz uonli laas nait ai hav/ *I haven't received any [bread] all day—I've only got last night's*; StAnd /mi dá ya fram laas wiik/ *I've been here since last week.*

2. In phr *from time*, ever since a distant but unspecified time in the past. *BL N*

1873 Rampini 73, His cooper's shop, with its heaps of old barrels carefully collected 'from time' to hold his then ungrown sugar. 1907 Cundall in Nugent (1934) 10, It had been the custom 'from time' (as the saying is in Jamaica) for the Governor..to be entertained. 1956 Mc StE /mi no lov i fram táim/ *I never liked it from the beginning.*

3. In phr *from long time*, long ago. *BL*

1956 Mc StE /hi set di fishpat fram lang taim mam/ *He set the fish-pot a long time ago, ma'am.*

B. quasi-conj: From the time when; usually from a time early in one's life and ever since. Esp in set phrases: *from me born*, *from me a little boy*, *from me was a child*, *from me was at me knee*, *from my eyes were at my knees*, etc.: see quots.

1910 Anderson-Cundall 35, Same time Annancy 'tan' from him barn. 1942 Bennett 34, From me bawn me nevah se' noh-Bady chat lacka yuh. 1942 P. B. Caws StAnd [Rude man on a dray, to the dignified and silent driver of two large white oxen:] From you start to eat beef you think you eat off one o' dem yet? 1947 U.Newton III 27, I've been handling cats from my eyes were at my knees [*since I was knee-high*]. 1951 Letter in *Gleaner* 7 Sept [Han sugar-estate worker:] I have been paying taxes from I was a young man. 1952 FGC StAnd /fràn míi a likl bwáai/ *Ever since I was a small boy.* 1956 Mc StAnd /frám mi waz át mi níi/. 1958 LeP StAnd, They're the kind we've been using from ever since.

FRONTEN /frontn/ prep dial; <*front*, for *in front of*, + -*n* suffix[1]: cf BECAUSEN, WITHOUTEN, etc. Before, in front of. *G*

1943 *GL* StAnd, Fronten, in front of. 1950 Pioneer 59, Dem put me fe tan up fronten Bans a big camera! 1962 BLB 34, Fronten, facing, across from.

FROOT-A-PANG see *fruutapang*.

FROZY /fruozi/ adj dial; cf *OED*, *EDD frowzy*. Mouldy; stale- or ill-smelling. *BL G N*

1943 *GL* Clar, StE, Frozy, bad-smelling, mouldy. 1955 FGC Man /it smel fruozi/ moldy. 1956 Mc Clar, Man /fruozi/. 1957 EB Port, Frozy, stale, sour-smelling—esp of clothes and people.

FRUFF sb dial; prob conn with *frough*, *frow*, brittle, of which *EDD* lists forms in -*f* from Cumberland and Northamptonshire; no noun is recorded, however.

1943 *GL* StM, Fruff, pieces of meat

FRU-FRU see FRO-FRO.

FRUIT-A-PANG see *fruutapang*.

FRUTINEAH sb dial; by rhotacism <*flutina*, a kind of accordion (*OED* 1859; cf also 1907 Jekyll 217).

1943 *GL* Tre, Frutineah, accordion.

fruutapang /frúutapáng, frútapàng, fútapàng/ sb dial; < Sp *fruta*, fruit + *pan*, bread, or some Amer Sp dial form **frutapan*. Breadfruit.

1943 *GL* Clar, Han, Kgn, Port, StJ, Fruit a pang, Fo to pang, etc., breadfruit. 1954 LeP Man, StAnn, Froot-a-pang, Fruit-a-pang—breadfruit.

FUBA, FUBBA /fúba/ adj dial; cf Ko *mfuba*, unfit or ill-formed fruit or nut. Of fruit: unfit, forced ripe, hence withered.

1943 *GL* Clar, Fuba, fubba—unfit, force ripe, withered.

FUFOO see next.

FUFU /fúfù/ sb dial; <Twi (*e-fúfu*, a white thing) *fufúú*, 'The common food..consisting of yam..plantains..cassada..cut into pieces and boiled..pounded [to] a tough, doughy mass. This, in the shape of a round lump, is put into the soup..and eaten with it.' Christaller. *ODS foo-foo* 1851→. Cf also FOOD. *BL G*

1. Starch food boiled and pounded; it may be eaten so, or further prepared and cooked. It is less made than formerly, but the word is still known throughout the Island. *N*

1739 Leslie 35, And boil it with beat Maiz or Indian Corn (which they call *Fu Fu*). 1826 Barclay 437, A negro ..would greatly prefer his own good substantial dish of foo-foo, composed of eddoes, ochras, and mashed plantains, made savoury with rich crabs, and pungent with Cayenne pepper. 1868 Russell 6, Foo-foo—Diff. vegetable food, beaten into one mass and eaten with 'pepper pot', hot soup..African. 1943 *GL* reported from most parishes: Fufu, fufoo, fofo, foo-foo. 1955 Bennett *Food Alphabet*, F is fe fufu, when yuh lose you teeth.

2. In a looser sense: mashed or grated FOOD.

1956 Mc Man /fúfu/ food mashed up (for old and toothless folk). 1959 DeC StAnd /fufu/ gratered banana boiled in a run-down.

FU-FURO see FRO-FRO.

fufuul see FOO-FOO adj.

FUGGI sb dial; prob <FUNGEE with loss of /n/; cf FOGIE.

1943 *GL* Kgn, Fuggi, early breakfast.

FULL /ful/ adj and vb now dial; <*full* adj. s.

A. adj: Said of fruit: fully grown, though not yet beginning to ripen. (Cf *OED* 1e; cf also FIT, TURN.)

1790 Beckford II 144, I have known the plantain shoot forth, and the fruit become full, according to the term adopted by the negroes, and which expresses the first state in which it is fit for use, in less than eleven.. months. *Ibid* 146. 1959 FGC current. *BA BL G T*

B. vb: To fill. (Cf *OED* v^2 1 →1627–47.)

1797 *Braco* 1 Aug, 12 Carrying Dung & fulling Carts. 1877 Murray *Kittle* 21, George Filby..used to come dere..and used to da full me daughter Molly head wid all kind of stories. 1950 Pioneer 63, So him mek haste go back ah yard, so full him long bag wid cane. *BL G N T*

FULL BAIT sb. See quot.

1851 Gosse 211, The negro fisherman takes a wire hook (No. 1. or 2.) as large as a goose-quill, which he throws overboard, baited with a sprat, but in a peculiar fashion. One side of the sprat is split nearly off, remaining attached only by the tail; this is allowed to hang free; and a slice from the back and one from the belly are allowed to hang in the same way. The hook is then passed in at the mouth, out at the gills, and again through the middle, and the head is tied to the top of the hook: another slice is then put upon the hook, and made to hang down. This is designated a 'full bait'.

FULL-EYE(S) sb chiefly dial; cf *OED full a* 12d, *full-eyed*, 'having full eyes' 1688. Bulging or protruding eyes. Cf PULP. *BA G*

1952 FGC StAnd /ful hai/ eyes that pulp out; StM, Full eyes, sticking out; Tre.

FULLING-UP FENCE sb dial; cf FULL vb. A kind of fence in which logs are filled (between posts) directly on top of each other, rather than with spaces between, forming a solid barrier.

1952 FGC StE /fúlinòp fens/ seen near Frenchman's Bay.

FULL-MOUTH (BEAN) sb dial; <FULL vb +*mouth*. A type of large bean that fills the mouth.

1868 Russell 5, Full mout, A large kind of beans. 1952 FGC StC /ful mout/ beans in bluish pod; StE /ful-mout/ plant it on moon-full and it grows well.

FULL-POT sb dial; <FULL vb+*pot*. A large variety of sweet-potato, thought to fill the pot.

1952 FGC StE /ful-pat/—yellow, round.

FUM, (FUM-FUM) /fom, fom-fom/ vb dial; prob onomatopœic, but poss also infl by an African word. (The iterated form is usually a noun, FUM-FUM.) *OED* 1790 only.

1. To beat or flog. *BL*

1790 Moreton 154–5, Then missess fum me wid long switch. 1826 Williams 190, Me tell 'em massa Wilforce fum fum mo no nine and tirty. 1873 Rampini 138, When I went home busha did fum me. [From Slave Court Records, Port, 1805–16.] 1943 *GL* Clar, Kgn, Fum, to flog. 1957 DeC StE (Accom) /fom/ (not /fom-fom/)—to flog or beat.

2. To pound in a mortar.

1895 Banbury 28, His wife in the kitchen 'fumming tum tum' (pounding yams to swallow with soup).

FUM-FUM /fom-fom, fum-fum/ sb dial; <FUM(-FUM) vb. *OED* 1885 only.

1. A flogging, a beating. *BL*

1774 Long II 427, The Negroes seem very fond of reduplications..as..*tie-tie, lilly-lilly, fum-fum*. 1862 Clutterbuck 289, 'Hi-yi-yi-yi!' howled Bunchy; 'me goin' for get fum-fum: me will dead. Oh, my king!' 1873 Rampini 138, He..gave me a bush to chew, and said if I went home without it I would get fum-fum, as the busha was swearing after me very much. [From Slave Court Records, Port, 1805–16.] 1943 *GL* Kgn, Tre, Fum-fum, beating, flogging. 1956 Mc StE /yu gét fóm-fom/ *You get a flogging*.

2. Food pounded in a mortar—cf TUM-TUM. (The form may be affected by analogy to FUFU.)

1958 DeC StT /fum-fum/ a name for fufu, i.e. food pounded in a mortar.

3. A mortar.

1959 DeC StJ /fumfum/ a mortar.

FUNDA /funda/ sb dial; prob < Sp *fonda*, inn, restaurant. See quots.

1943 *GL* Man, Funda, a kitchen or fireside. 1955 FGC Man, Funda, fireside. 1956 Mc Man /fundá/ place where one eats; an eating place, café.

FUNDAY see next.

FUNDE (DRUM) sb dial; etym unknown. A small, double-membraned drum, not strung tight, used to give the syncopation in drumming for *buru* dancing.

1943 *GL* no addr, Funday, the predominant music in Burru. 1960 *SAN Report* 18, Burra has three distinctive drums known as the bass, funde, and repeater.

FUN-FUN adj dial; iterative <*fun*. Done in fun or in play, for amusement or as a game. (Chiefly a children's word.) *G*

1946 U.Newton I 20, What we liked was the 'Picking' and the 'hug-up' for we had to hug up to dance. That was fun to us and fun-fun love making. *Ibid* II 14, Whenever we children..needed some pork, fish or salt beef for our fun-fun cooking.

FUNGA, FUNGE see next.

FUNGEE /fonji, funji, funju/ sb dial; < Kimbundu (Angola) *funzi*, cassava mush (1949 Turner 89.) 1. Corn or cassava meal boiled down till it is hard—now more often called cornmeal pone, MUSA. Other ingredients may be added—see quots. *BA*

1790 Moreton 22, For the pains in their stomachs, to eat plenty of homony and fungee. *Ibid* 150 [Lament of a slave whose wife has left him:] My fungee, alas! is unboil'd. 1868 Russell 7, Funge—Corn parched and beaten. African. 1929 Beckwith 20, 'Funga' is a mixture of corn meal and flour boiled in a pot with okra. 1943 *GL* Clar, Fungie, turned cassava meal. 1956 LeP StE, Corn funju, beaten corn boiled. 1957 DeC StE /funji/ banana or corn boiled in coconut milk with meat-kind. Banana funji or corn funji.

2. In later, transferred senses:

1958 DeC Port /fonji/—coconut milk boiled with cassava flour to a /klami/ porridge; StT /fonji/ gratered green banana boiled in a run-down; Port /funju/ (same as preceding).

funji, funju see prec.

FUNK /fongk/ sb dial; cf *OED funk sb*², 'A strong smell or stink; also, tobacco smoke'.

1. Poor tobacco (which smells bad when smoked).

1943 *GL* StM, Fonk, very poor tobacco; Tre, Funk, low grade tobacco. 1954 *FG* 371, The very over-ripe and usually much broken leaves [of tobacco], which have for so long been touching the ground, are of not much value and should be cut off. These leaves are called 'fonque' leaves. [This spelling, in the context, implies that the writer thought the word was Cuban (Spanish).]

2. See quot.

1943 *GL* no addr, Funk, a tinder box.

3. A kind of crude torch: see quot; also called SORE TOE.

1958 DeC West /fongk/ a bottle-torch made by filling a soda bottle with kerosene and inserting a piece of rag or wad of paper for a wick.

FUNK-BUSH sb dial; <*funk*+BUSH. An unidentified wild plant used in bush medicine; the name probably refers to the odour.

1952 FGC StE, Funk-bush, some call it wild wangla; will heal /di wound/.

FUNKIFY adj dial; for *funkified*—cf -FY; cf also *SND funky*, a bad temper, dudgeon, huff, tantrum.

1943 *GL* StM, Funkify, precocious, rude.

FUNNEL sb dial. Specific uses.

1952 FGC StJ /fonil/ in a fish-pot, the conical aperture through which the fish enter; Tre, in a /laim skil/ (*lime kiln*) the tube or opening at the center of the cone where the fire is applied and which serves as a chimney.

FUNNEL STICK or **SWITCH** sb dial. The shrub or small tree *Pisonia discolor*; it has long flexible stems—the reason for 'funnel' in the name is not clear.

1943 *NHN* II 82, Funnel Switch, A curious small tree.. The twisted trunk a mass of vermiculate ridges, dull wine coloured bark with silver-grey patches. *Ibid* 1947 III 98, *Pisonia discolor* (which is known as 'Funnel Stick' on Portland Ridge) with its straggling branches.

FUNNY-A-'KIN adj dial; <*funny*, peculiar, +A¹+*skin*. See quot; this may be a euphemism for YAWSY-SKIN.

1943 *GL* Port, Funniakin, not good looking.

FUNO /funu/ pron dial; <*fi*+*unu*. Cf FOO FA.

1943 *GL* West, Funo, yours.

FUP /fup/ sb dial; abbr of *fupans*, FIPPENCE.

1955 FGC Man, Fup, 3*d*. s CURRENCY.

fupans see FIPPENCE.

FUPS adj dial; prob abbr of *fupans*—cf FUP. Transf from FUP (FIPPENCE) as the smallest piece of money? Very small, tiny.

1943 *GL* StC, Fups, tiny.

fups adv and vb dial; onomatopœic—cf *flups*.

A. adv: Quickly, suddenly, in a single rapid action.

1956 Mc Man /di daag it aaf iz fuud fups/ *The dog gobbled up his food;* /mi drág i wé fram im fúps/ *I pulled it away from him suddenly.*

B. vb: In phr *fups off*: To eat very quickly, gobble up.

1956 Mc Man /di daag fups-aff him dina/—used also of a /kriebn/ child.

FURRUD see *farad*.

FURUH BIRD /fúru/ sb dial; prob < *Vireo*; other bird names have been similarly altered—cf JACK SPENCE. The *Vireo modestus*—cf LITTLE FURUH BIRD. *BL*

FUS-FUS /fos-fos/ adj dial; iteration of *first*. The very first. *BL G*

1942 Bennett 40, De fus-fus day she go a school Dem put har eena slate!

FUSSIFY /fósifài/ adj dial; for *fussified*: cf FUNKIFY, TRICKIFY. See quot.

1954 LeP StT, Fussifai, fussy, pernickety.

FUSS TIME see FIRST-TIME.

fuu-fuu, fuul-fuul see FOO-FOO.

-FY /-fài/ suffix dial; <*-fied*<*-fy*+*-ed*, on analogy of such words as *dandified*, *fancified*, etc. Added redundantly to adjectives (themselves sometimes unorthodox) ending in -y: cf FUNKIFY, FUSSIFY, HEATIFY, TRICKIFY, etc. *G*

fyaan sb dial; the preservation of an old form of *fern* (cf *OED*, '6 Sc. *farne*'). Cf also *feril*, *ferm*, *fierin*, *form*.

1912 McK *Songs* 23, To gellop ober fyahn an' ditch.

FYAHN see prec.

ga /gaa, ga/ vb or vb phr dial; <*go*+A (which may be of more than one source: see below).

1. Go to (a combination of *go* with A¹), occas used, though *go a* is more usual.

1957 JN No addr, Mi gat one sister a go ga England [*I have a sister who is going to go to England*].

2. In phr *go-'long*, see *galang*. *G*

gaa sb dial; <*grand*, *granny*, *grandy*, *gang-gang* or similar form.

1958 DeC Port /gaa/ affectionate word for grandmother.

gaaki see GAWKY.

gaalin see GAULIN.

GAB vb dial; cf *OED* v^1 4, quasi-*arch.* To brag, boast. *BL G*

1943 *GL* Kgn, Gyab, boast.

GABBLING CROW sb obs?; *OED* 1756 only. The JAMAICAN CROW (*Corvus jamaicensis*), or JABBERING CROW.

1727 *Observations* 18, Barbadoes Blackbird, Gabling Crows, Loggerheads. 1756 Browne 473, The gabbling Crow. This Bird is a native of Jamaica..They are extremely cautious and watchful, very noisy, and seem to imitate the sounds of most syllables in every language in their gabblings. 1847 Gosse 209, Jabbering Crow. Gabbling Crow.

GABLING CROW see prec.

GADAME, gadami, GADAMIE see GOD-A-ME.

GAD BUSH see GOD-BUSH.

gadi see GODDIE.

GA-GE sb obs; etym unknown.

1868 Russell 6, Ga-ge—Rum. African.

gagl vb, dial pronunc of *gobble.*

gaglit see GOGLET.

GAHD O' ME see GOD-A-ME.

GAIT sb dial; <*gait*, manner of walking. Liveliness of movement. *G*

1960 G. Castor Han [From local informant speaking of a horse:] /im hab tu moch giet/ *He's too lively.*

galang /gálàng, gáláng/ vb phr; <*go along.* The first /a/ may represent the *a* of *along*, or may be due to vowel-harmony with the second /a/ or perh both. To go along; freq used imperatively: Get along! *G*

1942 Bennett 34, see MOUT-A-MASSY. 1943 *GL* StE, Gallang, go on; Clar, Han, Kgn, StAnd, StAnn, StM, StT, Tre, West, Galang, go along, go on, move ahead, go away, etc. 1950 Pioneer 34, Dem galang, galang soh till dem ketch eena Dog yard.

GALAPEE TREE, GALIPEE TREE sb; *OED* 1756 only.

1. See quot 1926.

1756 Browne 189, Aralia 1..The *Galapee*, or Angelica Tree. 1814 Lunan I 313, Galapee or Angelica Tree. *Aralia* 1 arborea..2 capitata..3 sciodaphyllum [*sic*]. 1926 Fawcett 419–20, *Gilibertia..arborea..*Galipee, Angelica tree.

2. See quot.

1864 Grisebach 783, Galapee tree: *Sciadophyllum Brownei.*

galawas, galangwas see GALLIWASP.

GAL-GAL /gyal-gyal/ sb dial; iterative <*gal*, girl. A daughter: an affectionate appellation. *G*

1954 LeP StT, Gal-gal, daughter.

GALIMETA (WOOD) /gyalimenta, gelimenta/ sb, the latter form dial; etym unknown—prob a native Amerindian word. The folk form has intrusive /n/ prob on analogy of *pimento* /primenta/ etc. The 1814 form is pseudo-Hispanic. *OED* only 1756. See quot 1864.

1756 Browne 201, Achras? 8..The White Bully-Tree, or Galimeta-wood..It is..most frequently found in the lower lands, especially about Liguanea and Mangeneel. 1774 Long III 749, They had resource to the galimeta bark, and administered it with good success [instead of Jesuit's Bark]. 1814 Lunan II 320, Spanish Elm and Gallimento. 1864 Grisebach 784, Galimeta-wood: *Dipholis salicifolia.* 1952 FGC StT /gèliménta, gyàliméntà/ black and white bullet; StAnn /gyalimenta bulit/.

GALIPEE TREE see GALAPEE TREE.

galiwas see GALLIWASP.

GALL /gaal/ sb dial; abbr of *watergall* or *weathergall*, cf *OED water-gall* 2, 'a secondary or imperfectly formed rainbow; also applied to various other phenomena in the clouds that are believed to portend rain. Now *dial.*'

1952 FGC StJ /gaal/ like rainbow—the short part, never entire; sign of weather.

GALLANG see *galang.*

GALLANT /gilánt, giláant/ vb dial; <*gallant* vb, cf *OED* 3 b, 'To gad about idly, "gallivant" *Sc.*' →1880. To go about idly, frivolously; to flirt.

1943 *GL* StAnd, Gielant, to roam about aimlessly; Kgn, StT, Gillant, Gillaunt, to skylark, flirt. 1957 EB Port, To fritter away time in frivolities /yu gilaant tuu moch yu tu/.

GALLANTING ppl adj dial; <*gallanting*, *OED* →1869. See quots and cf GALLANT.

1943 *GL* Clar, Gilaunten, gelanhngtin [*sic*], frivolous, to play or laugh in an unbecoming way. 1955 FGC Man /gyaláantin/ gone fooling around, instead of doing duties.

GALLAWOSS see GALLIWASP.

GALLEY /gyali/ sb dial; cf *OED* 4, 'The cooking-room or kitchen on a ship'. *G*

1. A cooking place, kitchen.

1943 *GL* Clar, Galley, fireplace, or to prepare food. 1954 LeP Man, Galley, cooking place. 1956 Mc Man /di gyalii blaki-blaki/ *The galley is sooty.*

2. A cooking pot. (Mc 'Any pot that can be put on the fire.')

1943 *GL* Clar, StM, Galley, pot. 1954 LeP Man, Galli, cooking pot.

GALLEY-WASP see GALLIWASP.

GALLIMENTO see GALIMETA WOOD.

GALLINIPPER sb obs; origin uncert: the first element may be vaguely augmentative, the latter may show folk-etym: that which nips. *DAE* 1709→. 'A large mosquito' (*OED*) or some other stinging insect.

1683 *Present State* 20, The most Offensive thing in this Island..Gallinippors, from their Biting.

GALLIPOT sb; *OED* has *gallipot* in other senses.

1. A gum used as a substitute for *gum elemi.* Obs. *N*

a 1726 Barham (1794) 57, Take care it be not factitious, which is made of turpentine and oil of spike, and is called *gallipot.*

2. See quot. (Cf *EDD galley* sb^1...A leech.)

1942 HPJ, Gallipots: or Sea-cockroaches. Edible sea-worms.

GALLIVACHE see next.

GALLIWASP /galawas, gyalawas, galiwas, galang-was/ sb; 1683 gallivache, 1725→ galli-wasp, 1801 gally asp, 1808 gallow-wasp, 1835 galley wasp, 1940 gally-wasp gully asp yellow-wasp; dial sp 1907 gallawoss; etym unknown, but the word may be ult Amerindian—cf the Amer Sp words *garrobo*, lizard similar to the iguana, *guaripéte*, small lizard (Santamaría, Alvarado); it has repeatedly undergone folk-etym alterations. *OED* 1725→. Cf also *EDD gally* vb, to scare, frighten.

The common name of two (or more) species of lizards, *Celestus crusculus molesworthi* and *C. occiduus hewardii* (cf Lynn-Grant 104, 106) native to Jamaica. Their bite was formerly considered fatal, but they are quite harmless. *N*

1683 *Present State* 20, And in some parts of the North there's little ugly Creatures, called by the English Gallivaches, whose bite is Mortal to Dogs, Goats, &c. 1725 Sloane II 334, Galliwasp. 1801 Dancer 313, The Gally Asp, a large species of Lizard. 1808 Stewart 83, The gallow-wasp is an ugly..animal. 1834 Lewis (1845) 59, A Galli-wasp, which was killed in the neighbouring morass, has just been brought to me. This is the alligator in miniature, and is even more dreaded by the negroes. 1907 Jekyll 221, The Gallawoss—a Lizard with a gold eye and an undeserved reputation for biting. 1940 Lynn-Grant 104–6, 'Gally-wasp'..'Galliwasp'; 'gully-asp'; 'yellow wasp', etc. 1952 FGC Port /gálawas, gàlangwás/; StAnd /Gyálawas/ snake waiting-boy; StT /galiwas/ shine, live in stone wall, will sting or bite, old people say must get to water before he does [or you die]; West.

GALLOP see *gel op*.

GALLOW-WASP, GALLY ASP, GALLY-WASP see GALLI-WASP.

GAL-PICKNEY HUSBAND sb dial. See quot—jocular or nickname? *G*

1954 LeP Kgn, Gal-pickney husband, son-in-law.

GAMBOGE THISTLE sb bot. The thistly wildflower *Argemone mexicana*.

1801 Dancer 357, Yellow, or Gamboge Thistle. 1811 Titford Expl to Plate IX 1, Gamboge thistle..contains a lacteous juice, which turns in the air to a consistence of yellow colour, not distinguishable from gamboge. 1914 Fawcett 222, *Argemone mexicana*..Prickly Poppy, Gamboge Thistle, Mexican Thistle. 1954 *WIMJ* 17, Mexican Poppy..Gamboge or Yellow Thistle. Steggerda reported that this plant is used for colds, especially in children.

GAMBY see GOMBAY.

GAME-STOCK sb dial; <*game* (*OED* 2c: An object of ridicule) +*stock* by analogy with *laughing-stock*. An object of derision; a laughing-stock.

1943 *GL* Kgn, Pappy show, game stock. 1956 Mc Man /gíem-stàk/ person who does things to make others laugh. 1957 EB Port /gíem-stàk/.

GANAH sb dial rare. =CERASEE.

1943 *GL* Clar, Ganah, cerosee.

gana-gana sb dial; etym unknown, but cf GRANG-GRANG 2.

1959 DeC Han, West /gana-gana/ old ragged work clothes.

GANDELOW adj dial obs; etym unknown. A word forming part of a traditional song, and evidently meaning 'superlative'.

1907 Jekyll 26 [Song:] My eldes' sister, will you open the door oh? Fair an' gandelow steel. My door is bar with a scotran bar.

GANDER /gyanda/ vb dial; cf *OED*, '*v. dial* to wander aimlessly'. →1886. To walk or run.

1943 *GL* Kgn, Ganda, to run; StC, Gyanda, run. 1955 FGC Man /gyanda/ run or walk.

GANGA see *gang-gang*, GANJA.

gangalii sb dial; etym uncert, but evid based on *gang*. A bully.

1943 *GL* No addr, Gangalee, a conqueror; Kgn, StM, Gangali, gongali, a bully; Kgn, Gang-ga-lu, bad person. 1955 FGC Man /gàngalíi/.

GANG-DRIVER sb; <*gang*+DRIVER. One who is in charge (under a HEADMAN) of a gang of sugar-cane workers. *BA*

1956 Mc StT, The hierarchy is..manager..overseer.. bookkeeper; /hédman/ who is in charge of all the gangs; /gyang draiva/ who is in charge of a gang.

GANGFRARA sb dial cant; etym unknown. Said to be 'Maroon' (as distinct from 'African') in a St Thomas revival cult. See quot.

1953 Moore gloss, Gangfrara /ganggfrara/. An initiate and dancer among the Maroons.

gang-gang sb chiefly dial; <Fr *gan-gan*, granny, by hypocoristic iteration of *grand* (*-mère*).

1. A grandmother.

1943 *GL* Kgn, Ganggang, grandmother. 1951 FGC Man, An old /gáng-gàng/. 1956 Mc Man /gang-gáng/ grandmother.

2. By transf or extension: An aunt.

1943 *GL* StM, Ganga, aunt.

GANG-GANG adv dial; iterative of *gang* sb (*OED* 10). In a gang or group.

1927 Anderson-Cundall 93, see ONE-ONE adv[2].

[**GANJA** /gánjà/ sb; <Hindi *gānjā, gānjhā*, the hemp plant. *OED* 1800→. The spelling 'ganga' is erron. s MACONI WEED; s WEED.

The plant *Cannabis sativa*, whose leaves are smoked and chewed as a narcotic; it also has medicinal properties. It was introduced to Ja in the 19th cent by East Indians, and the word has entered into local combinations.] *BL G T*

GANJA STICK sb. *G*

1953 Moore 141, Ganja stick—a device for smoking ganja.

ganzi /gánzi, gyánzi/ sb dial; <*guernsey* (*OED* 2a). A garment—usually a sweater—made of closely knitted woollen or similar material.

1943 *GL* No addr, Gansie, an overall. 1956 Mc Man /gé(r)nzi/ woollen cardigan. 1957 EB Port /gyánzi/ —woollen cardigan or any knitted 'T shirt'. 1959 FGC Man, StE /ganzi, gyanzi/ a sweater.

GARABATA sb dial; <Amer Sp *garabato*, auxiliary hooked tool used by a machete-man in field-work (Santamaría 5); prob not wholly naturalized—but cf WAMPARA. A hooked stick with which plants are held ready to be cut with a machete.

1943 *GL* Tre, Garabata, a piece of stick with a crutch used in weeding grass with a cutlas.

GARAGARA adj dial rare; etym unknown.

1943 *GL* StAnd, Garagara, tall out of shape.

GARAMIGHTY-IN-A-TAP sb dial; <*God-Almighty-into-top* (i.e. in heaven). God.

1945 Jacobs 95, see BIG MASSA.

GARDA see GUARDER.

GARDEN BALSAM sb bot. See quots. Also called BALSAM HERB or WEED.

1756 Browne 118, DIANTHERA 3. Garden Balsom..ten or twelve inches in height. 1864 Grisebach 784, Garden-balsam: *Dianthera pectoralis*. 1954 *WIMJ* 29, *Dianthera pectoralis*..Fresh-cut; Garden Balsam.

GARDEN BITTERS sb.

1927 Beckwith 18, Garden-bitters. *Artemisia* ——. For stomach-ache boil and drink as tea..Boil it with

'Chicken-weed' and add salt for constipation. 1954 *WIMJ* 28, *Artemisia* sp. . Garden Bitters.

GARDEN EGG sb gen. The egg-plant, *Solanum melongena.*

1811 Titford xiii, Garden Egg. (Solanum Melongena.) Cut in slices, parboiled and fried, resembles fried eggs. 1913 Harris 31, Garden Egg. . It is grown to a considerable extent in Jamaica, especially by coolie market-gardeners near Kingston. 1952 FGC several parishes /gyàadn-ég/.

GARDEN-GATE MANGO sb dial. A tough variety of mango.

1952 FGC StM /gyáadn gíet manggo/.

GARLIC PEAR TREE sb bot; *OED* 1725→. A tree or shrub (*Cratæva tapia, C. gynandra*) which smells of garlic and bears a somewhat pear-shaped fruit, whence the name. *N*

1696 Sloane 206, Anona trifolia. . fructu. . allii odore: *The Garlick Pear-tree.* a 1726 Barham (1794) 64, Garlic-Pear. . very common in Jamaica. 1854–5 *TJSA* 1 60, Gynandrous Garlic Pear Tree *Cratæva gynandra.* Round fruited Garlic Pear Tree *Cratæva tapia.* 1914 Fawcett 235, Garlic Pear tree.

GARMAN DICK /gáaman dík/ sb dial; <*gorman,* old form of *gourmand* (cf *OED*) + Dick.

1954 LeP StE, Garman Dick, a greedy person.

GARSHAN BULL, GARSHANNI see *gyaashani.*

GASH sb and vb dial; prob <*gash,* cut, slash, but there may be the same kind of alteration as in FLASH = splash, slash.

A. vb: To flash (a light, lightning, or anything shining).

1907 Jekyll 86, Every gash Candlefly gash [*Every time Candlefly flashed his light*]. 1924 Beckwith 180, So de duppy gash his teet' at him an' he run. [This is *not* 'gnash'.] 1955 FGC Man, Gash—flash (of lightning, etc.).

B. sb: A flash (of light, lightning, etc.).

1907 Jekyll 86 (see above). 1943 *GL* StT, Gâsh—flash, as in lightning. [This may be intended as a verb.]

GASHY sb dial; cf Twi *ɔde-kwasea,* a type of yam.

1943 *GL* Kgn, Gashy, a wild yam.

GASO see GUZU.

GATEAU see *gato.*

GATETY see next.

GATEY sb dial; <*gate* + *-y,* familiarizing suffix: cf WATCHY, watchman.

1943 *GL* StAnd, Gatety, gateman.

gato /gáto, gráto/ sb dial; prob < Fr *gateau,* cake.

1. A name applied to various kinds of cake, bread, or biscuit. *G*

1942 HPJ, Gateau, Cake, at Red Lights, near Newcastle. . Gratteau, gratta, a kind of bread. 1943 *GL* Clar, Gotta, a hard biscuit made from the leavings of bread dough; Kgn, Gratto, a flat bread; StJ, Gatto, large biscuit. 1955 FGC Man, Gratto, flat bread. 1957 EB Port /grato/ flat, round bread.

2. See quot.

1959 DeC Port /gato/ a dumpling which is rolled out flat, folded over, then folded again to produce four layers, then boiled or (usually) baked.

GATTO see prec.

ga-u sb dial; etym unknown.

1952 FGC StM /gá-ú/ kingfish—the plain one; the 'crossbar' has stripes.

GAULDING see next.

GAULIN /gaalin/ sb; a1705 1756 gaulding, 1834 gawling, 1847→ gaulin, 1943 gauling, 1950 gawlin; prob <*gawlin,* a W Scots word: '1703 M. Martin *Western Islands* 71: The Gawlin, is a fowl less than a Duck; it is reckon'd a true Prognosticator of fair weather for when it sings fair. . good weather always follows' (*SND*); and cf quot 1907 below. However there may well be coincidental influence from Sp *gallina* (Pg *gallinha*), hen (or a dial form thereof); applied in various derived and combined forms in Spanish America to many birds, esp to water birds; *gallinazo* is applied to one of the birds called *gaulin* in Jamaica: *Ardea herodias* (Santamaría). Cf *OED gaulin, 'Jamaica',* a 1705→. *BA BL G N*

Certain herons, egrets, and similar birds: see separate entries under BLACK, BLUE, GREEN, GREY CRESTED, LITTLE, NIGHT, RED, RED-NECKED, WHITE GAULIN.

a 1705 Ray (1713) 189, *Ardea alba major nostras.* The largest White Gaulding. . *Ardea cœruleo-nigra.* The Black or Blew Gaulding. 1834 *WI Sketch Book* i 221, A few gawlings, sparrowhawks, and wild pigeons, were the only birds that particularly claimed our attention. [Tortola.] 1847 Gosse 334, The Gaulins, or Egrets, are usually shy. 1907 Jekyll 75, Gaulin, the Egret. In stormy weather the egrets leave the sea-side and fly up into the country to fish in the streams. 1943 *GL* Port, Gauling, gaulin. 1952 FGC Han, Man, StAnn, StC, StM, StT /gáalín/. 1956 Jeffrey-Smith 120, The term 'gaulin', like that of quit, is applied in Jamaica to birds of quite different genera.

GAULING see prec.

GAWKY /gaaki/ sb dial; *OED* →1876, *EDD* →1892, Engl and Sc dial. A fool, an easy dupe.

1943 *GL* Port, Ghaki, idiot; StAnd, Gawky, fool. 1955 FGC Man /gaaki/ idiot. 1956 Mc Man /yo uol gaaki yu/ *You old fool, you!*

GAWLIN, GAWLING see GAULIN.

GAWN see GONE.

G.B. sb dial slang; initial letters of GOD-BLIND-ME (cf *ODS*). Cf also DOG-BLINE-ME. (*Gorblimey*) = GOD-BLIND-ME.

1952 FGC StM /jíi-bíi/ gym shoes. 1956 Mc StAnd, StT /jii-bii/ boots lacing in front with buckles at side.

GELANHNGTIN see GALLANTING.

gelimenta see GALIMETA-WOOD.

GELL vb dial; ? <*gull;* cf *gyou.*

1942 HPJ, Gell: to stuff (with lies).

gel op /gél óp, gyél óp/ vb phr dial; by back-formation < /gélop/ *gallop,* analysed as *gal up.* Cf *divel op. G*

1. To gallop; to go fast.

1952 FGC StAnn /ing gyélin òp/ *he is galloping.* 1956 Mc StE /di háas waz gyélin óp an dóun in a i káman láik eni wáil ánimal/ *The horse was galloping up and down in the common like a wild creature;* Man /di háas gel óp/ *The horse gallops.*

2. Transf. To boil rapidly.

1956 Mc Man /di pat a gel óp/ *The pot is boiling.*

GELL-GELL sb dial; etym unknown—cf *dill-dill,* duckling.

1943 *GL* StC, Gell-gell, ducklings.

GEM sb; used absol for *gem of thought*—cf *OED* 2b. In school slang: One of the gnomic or proverbial sayings taught to schoolchildren.

1946 U.Newton I 37, Our multiplication tables, our gems, our scripture passages and our recitations. [1947 *ibid* III 12, Or in the words of one of our school gems of thought: 'The heights by great men, reached and kept, etc.'] *BA*

GENAL see *jinal.*

GENAP, genep see GUINEP.

GENG-GENG sb dial; evid iterative < /geng/ pronunc of *gang.*

1943 *GL* Kgn, Geng-geng, ill-clad, noisy children.

GENIAL see *jinal.*

GENIP see GUINEP.

gens prep dial; cf *OED against* 4, near, adjoining, 'Still *dial.*' This, however, must be the abbr of 'from against'. From near; from.

1956 JB StAnd /wi kom gens Penfiil/ *We come from near Penfield. Ibid* /kom gens/ *To come from* (a place). *BL*

GENTLEMAN'S-COMPLAINT sb dial euphem. Gonorrhoea.

1927 Beckwith 19, see HOGWEED 2. 1943 *GL* StC, Genkleman-complain, Gonnerrhea.

GEORGE /jaaj (fut)/ sb also attrib dial; perh the personal name. Cf THOMAS MASU, TIM-BIM. A leg, or part of it, that is sore or badly swollen, and does not get better. Also called a JACKFRUIT FOOT.

1943 *GL* StT, George, a sore toe. 1955 FGC Man, Not only the toe—a foot too. 'You have a George to keep', hard to be better. 1956 Mc StAnd /jaaj fut/ thickened, swollen leg, elephantiasis.

GEORGE RAT sb dial; see quot. Perh assoc with BROWN GEORGE. =BROWN RAT.

1846 Hill in 1851 Gosse 445–6, The Brown Rat has a good deal of fulvous intermingled with grey in its coat, and though it is at this time by far the most numerous of these vermin, it is of comparatively recent importation. The negroes are said to distinguish it by the name of the *George* Rat. This name is a curious coincidence with the historic scandal that, under the name of the *Hanoverian* Rat, assigns a similar introduction to the ship that brought the Brunswick family to the British shores.

gere sb dial; etym unknown. See quots. Cf SET-UP.

1943 *GL* StT, Gerre, a dance, carried on the night following person's death, chiefly in the country parts. 1959 DeC Han, Port, StJ /gere/ a funeral meeting normally on the first night (though a few coastal districts use this for the meeting on the second night). Characterized by ring-games, Anancy stories, etc. A few Sankeys may be sung at the beginning of the night, but generally the program is secular.

GERMAN /jáaman/ sb dial. (A settlement of German peasants and artisans was made in 1835 in the area around Seaford Town, Westmoreland, where their descendants still dwell.)

1. A poor white. (The second citation may not be so specific, but may merely indicate a distinction of origin.)

1942 HPJ, Jarman, Girman: A poor white (applied to Scots near Moore Town?). 1959 DeC West /jaaman/—what the Negroes of Seaford Town call one of the Germans there; the German himself would say /jarman/.

2. A type of fish: see quot. Perh for *germon*—See GEROOM.

1952 FGC StM, German, yellowish, poor; with stripes around; size of rolling-pin [fish]—eight inches.

GERMAN TRUMPET /jáaman trómpit/ sb dial. Shrubs of the genus Datura (prob *D. stramonium* and *D. suaveolens*), from the shape of the flowers.

1952 FGC StC, StM, StT /jáaman trómpit/ big white flower—used to scrub floors.

GEROOM sb obs; prob for *germon*—OED 1860 →. The fish *Germo alalunga* or similar species.

1713 Ray 159 [Fishes of Jamaica:] *Harengus major*.. a Geroom. 1725 Sloane 282, A Geroom. This was twelve Inches long, and two broad..They are taken at Old Harbour, and brought to Market where I had it, the Snout is longer and sharper than that of a Herring, and the Fins and Tail are larger.

GERRE see *gere.*

GET vb[1] intr dial; abbr of some such phr as *get there*; but cf *OED* 25, a trans vb corresp to this, →1712. *BA BL*

1. To arrive (at a place). Cf REACH.

1907 Jekyll 86, Them travel till at last them get; *ibid* 102, They travel the whole night until daylight an' never could get.

2. To succeed (in doing something).

1956 Mc Man /im wan tu se somting bot im jos kyaan get at aal/ *He wants to say something but he just can't succeed at all.*

GET vb[2] intr dial; <*get*—cf *OED* 26, the active vb corresp to this, which is passive. To be begotten. *BA*

1956 Mc StE (Accom) /mi get hie, mi baan hie, mi lib hie/ *I was conceived here, born here, I've lived here.*

get /get, gyet/ sb dial; <*girt* sb, girth. A girt or girth.

1956 Mc Man /ef yo dráa táit gét an im níebl yo kíl im/ *If you draw a tight girth on his navel you'll kill him.*

GHAKI see GAWKY.

[**GHANDIROBA** sb obs; a var form of ANDIROBA, NHANDIROBA.

1696 Sloane, see NHANDIROBA, also SABO. a1726 Barham (1794) 113, *Nhandiroba*, or *ghandiroba*. The first time I met with this plant was in St Thomas in the Vale.. A French gentleman some years past..told me, that the Spaniards call them *avilla* and that they were worth their weight in gold to expel poison (1814 Lunan I 22–3).]

GHOST CRAB sb. A whitish nocturnal crab: see quot.

1946 *NHN* III 31, Abundant along the seashore were small flattened Ghost crabs (*Ocypoda albicans*) that burrow in the sand and come out at night to feed on any refuse washed up by the waves.

GI see GIVE.

GIANT /jaiant, jaian/ sb, usu attrib. In the names of various plants: *Giant plantain; Giant purple cane; Giant sweet-potato.*

1952 FGC many parishes.

GIBRIDGE sb dial; <*gibberish. BA BL G*

1943 *GL* Kgn, Gimridge, foolishness; StM, Gibridge, foolishness.

gidibo sb dial; cf *agidi*, cornmeal or grated yam dishes + *-bo* (? as in GREY-BO, *kiebo*, etc.) person. A type of large breadfruit; this is one of the many nicknames for breadfruits, meaning something like 'starch-food fellow'. (Personification of staple foodstuffs is common among the peasantry.)

1956 Mc StE (Accom) /gídibo/ A very large type of breadfruit, about the size of a jackfruit. It has prickles.

GIE see GIVE.

GIELANT see GALLANT.

GIE-ME-ME-BIT see GI'-ME-ME-BIT.

giem-stak see GAME-STOCK.

GIG /gig/ sb; cf *OED* 1 'a whipping-top' *Obs.* → a1793.

1. A boy's spinning-top. *N*

c 1915 FGC StAnd, Gig, a spinning-top, usually of wood, spun with a string held in the fingers. 1943 *GL* No addr, Gig, a top.

2. A game played with gigs.

1952 Kerr 49, If bats are needed for playing, for instance in cricket or tops in a game called 'gig' then the bigger children make them.

3. A dumpling of size and shape like a top.

1958 DeC Port /gig/ a small (less than 1 in.) spherical boiled dumpling.

GIGGER see JIGGER.

GIGGIWIRE sb dial; etym unknown, but cf *Kitibu* and its variants, and *jijiwaina.*

1943 *GL* StM, Giggiwire, fire fly.

giichi adj dial; etym uncert—perh <*geach*, thief (OED 'sb slang ?Obs.' 1821→). A stingy or mean person. *BL*

1952 FGC StM /giichi/ mean, 'him han' tight'.

GIL see GILL.

gilaant, gilant see GALLANT.

GILAUNTEN see GALLANTING.

GILL /gil/ sb^{1}; cf *OED sb*^{1} 2. The extensible, bright-coloured dewlap or 'fan' under a lizard's throat.

c 1915 FGC StAnd (The regular word). 1952 FGC StAnd, The cock one sticks out his /gil/.

GILL /jil/ sb^{2}; cf *OED sb*^{3}, and 2 below.

1. A measure of quantity, $=\frac{1}{4}$ pint; cf BIG-GILL, GILL-GILL, LITTLE-GILL. *BL G*

2. A quantity of money (three-farthings) equivalent to one-half QUATTY, i.e. one-eighth of sixpence. The name is presumably transf from sense 1, *quatty* corresp to *big-gill* and *gill* (money) to *little-gill* (quantity). Now arch.

1873 Rampini 94, The negro nomenclature of coins is as follows:—Bill [*sic*: error for Gill], three farthings; Fippence, threepence; Bit, fourpence halfpenny; Joe, sixpence; Mac (macaroni), a shilling. 1879 De Montagnac 70, I buy a gill clay pipe. 1894 Spinner 83, I sell it for a gill an' a quattie a-piece. 1943 *GL* most parishes, Gill, jill, three-farthings. 1952 FGC Han /jil/—$\frac{3}{4}d.$ 1956 Mc Man /jil/ three-farthings, half a /kwáti/. These old coin names no longer used however. s CURRENCY.

GILLANT, GILLAUNT see GALLANT.

GILL-GILL /jil-jil/ adv dial; iterative <GILL sb^{2} 1. By small quantities. *G*

1924 Beckwith 44, Him buy everyt'ing in de whole town gill-gill.

GILPIN sb dial; abbr of JOHN GILPIN.

1956 Mc Man /gilpin/ A type of mashet with hooked point. 1958 DeC StM /gilpin/ A cutlass.

GI'-ME-BREEZE sb dial joc. Old work-clothes, which, being torn, 'give me breeze'.

1958 DeC StT /gi-mi-briiz/—old ragged work-clothes. Also /beje, faia-kecha/. *G*

GI'-ME-ME-BIT /gímimibít/ sb dial; echoic with folk-etym. The bird *Chordeiles minor*, also called Night-hawk, MOSQUITO-HAWK, PIRAMIDIG. This is one kind of DUPPY BIRD.

[1847 Gosse 33, About an hour before the sun sets, we hear a loud, abrupt, and rapid repetition of four or five syllables in the air above our heads, resembling the sounds, *piramidig*, or *gi' me a bit*, or perhaps still more, *wittawittawit*.] 1900 Murray 8, Married an Gie-me-me-bit a one ting—tek me up you tek up trouble, put me dong, you put dong trouble. 1943 *GL* Port, Gimmie-mebit, a bird. 1952 FGC Man /gimimibít/ bird size of /pichiiri/, long wings, flies in evening and cries gi'-me-me-bit; StAnd, StT. 1956 Jeffrey-Smith 12, Gie-me-me-bit.

GI'-ME-TROUSERS phr dial; supposedly onomatopœic. Imitation of the sound a cock makes when it crows.

1958 DeC Port /di kak se gi-mi-trouzaz/ day is dawning.

gi-mi-briiz see GI'-ME-BREEZE.

gimimibit, GIMMIEMEBIT see GI'-ME-ME-BIT.

GIMNINEETIE, GINNINEETIE sb dial.

1943 *GL* No addr, Gimnineetie, ginnineetie—a play [i.e. game] in which the girls clap each others' hands.

GIMRIDGE see GIBRIDGE.

GINAL see *jinal.*

GINEP see GUINEP.

GINGER /jínja/ sb dial; <*OED ginger sb.* CREEPING JENNY (*Zebrina pendula*)—from the similarity of the leaves.

1951 FGC Man.

GINGER GRASS sb. See quots. *G*

1814 Lunan II 35, *Panicum..glutinosum..*Native of Jamaica in the southern parts, in the woods of the highest mountains. It is called *ginger grass*, on account of the width of the leaves. The great clamminess of the spikelets, whence its trivial name, is peculiar to this species. 1864 Grisebach 784, Ginger-grass: *Panicum glutinosum.*

GINGER-LILY sb. Either of two species of plants having lily-like flowers and roots like those of ginger: see quots. *BA G*

c 1915 FGC StAnd, Ginger lilies growing near Newcastle. 1948 *NHN* III 131, Where once were numerous species of ferns hardy plants of the yellow Ginger Lily—*Hedychium Gardnerianum*—were to be seen. This Ginger Lily was introduced at the Cinchona Gardens and has spread very rapidly. 1952 *NHN* V 115, Several plants are confined to higher elevations on the Newcastle road partly through dependence on moisture..It is likely that..*Hedychium coronarium* (Ginger-lily), and *Macrocnemum jamaicense* fall into this category.

GINGER PIECE sb; <*ginger+piece.* A field of ginger. [Here, evid a place-name.]

1907 Jekyll 224 [Song:] So so ride you ride a Ginger Piece, All the gal them a dead fe you..'all the girls are dying for you'.

GINGER-TOE adj dial; for *ginger-toed*: cf TOE. Having splayed toes like the 'toes' of ginger roots; or, more vaguely, as an insulting epithet. *BL*

1933 *Outlook* 30 Dec, You only lef' fe..go a prison, an' das would be de bes' place fe a ginger-toe, dry-head gal like you!

ginggi adj dial. Small; poss <GINGY-FLY.

1943 *GL* Clar, Gingie, small. 1956 LeP StE (Eld) /ginggi/ small.

GINGGY sb dial; <DINGHY, perh infl by *ginggi* adj.

1943 *GL* Clar, Ginggy, a two-wheeler horse-drawn carriage.

GINGIE see *ginggi.*

GINGLE see *jinggl.*

GINGY-FLY /gínggi flài, gíng-gìng flái, jinji flai/ sb dial; <Bantu *ginggi*, fly. Any of various small flies, esp those which fly about the face, open cuts, etc., and annoy one. *BL*

1905 Smith 56, Annancy go out an' get him frien' Gingy-Fly: (dat is a blue-bottle). 1942 HPJ, Gingy-fly: A small fly. (The *g* is hard in both cases)..Supposed to spread yaws. 1943 *GL* StC, Gingy fly, sand fly. 1950 Pioneer 64, Cow ah fan him tail, causen de gingy fly dem ah bodder him. 1952 FGC Man /gínggi flài/—blue, nasty little fella, has eggs in it, lays them on face of sore, name is from the sound they make; Tre /gíng-gìng flái/ rounder than horse-fly; StAnd /jinji fly/ same as maggot-fly; West /ginggi flai/—a small, bothersome person is like a gingy-fly. 1955 FGC Man /ginggi/ don't bite, but come to cuts; smaller than sour-fly.

gini- see GUINEA-.

ginj vb and sb chiefly dial; <*gange* vb: cf *OED.* (Used elsewhere in WI also.)

A. vb: 1. To protect the part of a fishing-line above the hook by twisting wire around it, or by fastening the hook to one end of a length of wire (the ginj) and the line to the other end.

c 1917 FGC StAnd /ginj/ verb or noun—a piece of copper wire about 2 feet long, joining line and hook: to ginj the hook or line—to use such a ginj. 1942 HPJ, Ginge, Ghinje (1) To secure a hook to a fishing line by twisting wire round them both.

2. To strangle (evid by twisting a ginj or piece of wire about the throat).

1942 HPJ, Ginge..: To strangle.

3. To stuff with lies. (To choke or strangle with lies?)

1942 HPJ, Ginge..: To stuff with lies.

B. sb: A piece of wire on a fishing-line to prevent the fish from severing it.

c 1917 FGC StAnd (see above, A. 1).

ginjing vbl sb; <*ginj* vb; cf *OED ganging vbl sb*[3]. =*ginj* sb.

GINNAL see *jinal.*

GINNINEETIE see GIMNINEETIE.

GIRMAN see GERMAN.

GIROUT see *kirout.*

GIRRIE vb dial; <*get out* or *clear out*—cf *kirout* int. To drive a dog out.

1942 HPJ, Girrie: Chivy (a dog). From *get out!* <to geróu! girrie. Hence a verb, like English *shoo.*

GISADA see GIZADA.

GIVE /gi, gib, giv/ vb; often reduced in dial (as also in Engl, Scots, US, etc., dial) to /gi/ and in dial writing sp *gi, gi'* or *gie. BL G*

1. In ordinary senses of *give.*

2. Through loss or suppression of the direct obj, a quasi-intr vb: to give something to.

1950 Pioneer 72, Him tek up one and him gie de littlest pickney [i.e. *he gave it to the smallest child*].

GIVE COCO FOR YAM vb phr dial. To give as good as you get.

1862 Clutterbuck 182, Nelson..tell him he quite ready whenever Boney liked to come, and he gib him coco for yam.

gizaada see next.

GIZADA /gizáada/ sb; < Sp *guisar*, to prepare food, *guisada* past ppl fem, prepared, hence a preparation. (*Guisado*, stew, fricassee; also Pg.)

1. An open tart filled with grated, sweetened, and spiced coconut. Also called sweet-cake. *N*

1893 Sullivan 52, Gisadas. These are open tartlets. [Recipe given—chief ingredient coconut.] 1943 *GL* Clar, Gizardar, A tart made of pastry and grated cocoanut; Man, Gizarda, a native cocoanut cake; StM, Gizzada, sweet crimped edge cakes centered with shredded coconut. 1952 FGC StE, StJ, StM /gizáada/.

2. See quots.

1954 LeP StE, Gizaada, baked dumpling with sweetened grated coconut on top. 1957 EB Port /gizaada/ [same definition].

gizada /gizáda/ sb dial; < CASSADA. WILD CASSADA.

1952 FGC Tre /gizáda, kisáda/ cockroach-wood.

GIZARDA, GIZARDAR, GIZZADA see GIZADA.

GLABROUS-LEAVED BROOMWEED sb bot obs; cf BROOMWEED. In Macfadyen's use: *Sida pyramidata* (ident 1926 Fawcett 115).

1837 Macfadyen 82, Sida dumosa. *Glabrous-leaved Broom-Weed.*

glami /glami/ adj dial; prob <*clammy* (*EDD* 6, 'Moist, clammy, damp and cold; slimy'). Sticky and elastic. *G*

1952 FGC StJ Tie-teet' sugar, boiled till it gets /glami/ sort o' stretch [i.e. stretchy]; Tre, Fufu: [beat] yam, coco, or green banana, make it come togeda—/glami/.

GLASS-EYE sb; *OED* 1847 only.

1. The Jamaican thrush (*Turdus jamaicensis*); see quot 1847.

1842 Chamberlaine 26, Glass-eye, *Merula leucophthalma.* 1847 Gosse 142, Glass-eye. Shine-eye. Fish-eye..The common names of this bird are bestowed in allusion to the tint of the iris of the eye: this, as Mr Hill observes, 'is not absolutely white, but so transparently suffused with a hue of olive, that the eye has the look of very common glass'. 1944 *NHN* II 128–30. 1952 FGC StT, Grass-eye. [Cf GRASS-BOTTLE.] 1956 Jeffrey-Smith 34–5.

2. The SOLITAIRE.

1936 Bond 292, see WHISTLER.

GLASS-EYE BERRY sb. A berry favoured by the GLASS-EYE (THRUSH), whence the name.

1847 Gosse 142, Glass-eye berry..a Scrophularious shrub.

GLASS-EYE MULLET sb dial. A variety of mullet having prominently glassy eyes.

1952 FGC Port, Glass-eye mullet, a river fish.

GLASS-EYE SHARK sb dial. A variety of shark having prominently glassy eyes.

1952 FGC Port, Glass-eye shark, ordinary, flat head.

GLASS-EYE TAPNACHIK sb dial. The GLASS-EYE thrush (the TAPNACHIK being another, quite similar thrush).

1952 FGC StAnn /gláas-ài tápnachik/.

GLASS-WOOD sb. A tree (*Zuelania guidonia*) whose wood is brittle; when it is chopped, the chips fly like glass.

1926 Fawcett 217 (see CUFFEE WOOD). 1952 FGC Tre, Glass-wood—drumwood; seen in upper Clarendon.

GLEAN vb dial; <*glean*, 'to..pick up ears of corn..left by the reapers' *OED.* To reap (corn). *G*

1952 FGC StT.

GLIMPSE sb dial. An albino negro: perh in allusion to his weak, squinting eyesight.

1959 DeC StK /glimps/ an albino Negro.

GO /go, gu/ vb dial; dial sp: *goh, gu*; <*go*, with coincidental infl of Twi *kɔ̀*, to go (Christaller, sense 7: 'In connection with other verbs, *kɔ* frequently supplies the place of an Eng. *adv.* or *prep.*: *a*) the place of the *adv.-away*, denoting removal..*b*) together with a noun of place it supplies the place of a *prep.*, denoting a direction *towards* a place.') Cf 1 and 2. *G*

1. Following and completing another verb of action: and go, to go, going. Sometimes it is virtually redundant. *BL*

1837 Sterne 19, see CARRY 2. 1956 Mc Man /dem kómpini mi go chák a Túol Gíet/ *They accompanied me all the way to Toll Gate;* /mi hafi swim swim go/ *I had to swim and swim (when my boat capsized)*; StE /wen di bwai líiv go húom/ *When the boy left for home, or left to go home;* [Man pointing to the funnel of a fish-pot:] /dat a we di fish waak go in/ *That's where the fish go in.*

2. After another verb and preceding a noun of place: to, for.

1959 FGC /yu a tek di bos go Kingstan?/ *Are you taking the bus to (or for) Kingston?*

3. Vaguely auxiliary: similar to colloq 'go and'; cf also COME[2].

1907 Jekyll 16, An' what you go go buy, Miss Princess? *Ibid* 255 [Song:] You cut off the fowl head an' boil it with feather, So the baby go born with feather. [*So the baby was born*, etc.] 1950 Pioneer 93, Policeman a come fe go mek a row, All because o' you.

4. With covert allusion to OBEAH: *go to someone*, seek an obeah-man; *go away for (someone)*, get an obeah-man to put obeah on (someone).

1873 Rampini 139, the whole estate said they would go to somebody to kill busha. They all agreed to look out for a man for that purpose. (From Slave-court Records, 1805–16.) 1942 Bennett 20, So dem gu weh fe har an' de po' chile Goh step ovah dem obeah jeng-jeng.

GO quasi-adv; cf GO vb. Away; often correl with *come*, the two meaning movement away and back, to and fro or from, back and forth, one way and the other. *G*

1950 Pioneer 35, Durin dis same time Bredda Anancy was a pos'-man, an him usual kea letta goh, kea ketta come, up an dung every day. 1956 LeP StE (Accom) /wen im si doun in a di katn trii so, di katn trii liin go, im liin kom wid im/ *When he sat in the cotton tree, then, the cotton tree leaned one way, it leaned the other way with him.*

GOADIE, GOADY see GOURDY.

GO ALONG see *galang*.

GOAT-FISH sb; cf *OED goat* 4b, 1885. In Jamaica: *Upeneus maculatus.*

1851 Gosse 208, see KING MULLET. 1951 Smith in *NHN* v 187, The two goat-fish *Upeneus maculatus*, which I saw vomited from the stomach of a large grouper.

GOAT-FOOT, GOAT-KNEE, GOAT-SHANK CANE sb dial. A variety of sugar-cane which has prominent nodes or knobs at the joints, whence the name.

1942 HPJ, Goat-shenk, said by a black boy to be the name of a kind of sugar-cane. 1952 FGC Port /gúot níi/ has knobs; StJ /gúot-shángk kíen/ the St Catherine name —same as /tuod ai/ of Westmoreland; StT /gúot fút/ not an estate cane, jointy.

GOAT-FOOT (WIS) sb chiefly dial. Two species of *Passiflora*, small wild vines whose leaves seem cloven like a goat's foot; see quots 1954, 1955. *G*

1927 Beckwith 18, Bat-wing, *Passiflora sexflora* Juss. 'Duck-foot', 'Goat-foot'. For cold and fever boil with 'Velvet-leaf' and drink as tea. 1952 FGC StT, Goat-foot wis—duck-foot wis. 1954 *WIMJ* 31, *P. sexflora*..Duppy Pumpkin; Passion Flower; Bat Wing; Goat or Duck Foot. 1955 *WIMJ* 159, *P. rubra*..Goat Hoof; Goat Foot; Bull Hoof; Dutchman's Laudanum.

GOAT-FRIEND sb obs? See quot.

1814 Lunan I 326, Goat Friend. Aegiphila..*Tetrandria monogynia*..This generic name is derived from the Greek words for the English name, goats being fond of it.. [3 spp listed].

GOAT HOOF see GOAT-FOOT (WIS).

GOAT-HORN OKRO sb dial. A variety of okro which twists somewhat like a goat's horn.

1942 HPJ, Goat-horn: A kind of Ochro. 1952 FGC StAnn /guot haan okro/ have fine prickle.

GOAT-HOUGH TREE /guot-hof/ sb dial; <*goat's hoof* (though the pronunc implies confusion with *hough*, hock). The *Bauhinia* tree, from the shape of the leaf.

1952 FGC StM /guot-hof trii/ = bull-hoof.

GOAT-KNEE CANE see GOAT-FOOT CANE.

GOAT-MOUTH sb dial. *T*

1. A mouth like a goat's, believed to indicate the possession of prophetic powers and the power to inflict bad luck, disease, etc. *BA BL*

1943 Bennett 19, Wat me say boun fe happen yaw, For me have bad goat mout. 1957 JB /guot mout/ Prophecy of evil, making evil sure to happen: /wiet til guot mout kech yu/. [Dialog:] A: 'Ef yo do that, you will get sores.' B: 'Don't bother put goat-mouth on me.' 1957 EB Port /guot mout/ bad luck: To set goat-mout on someone.

2. By personification: *Mr Goat-mouth*, one who predicts or threatens evil.

1873 Rampini 87, A person addicted to making biting speeches [is] 'Mr Goat-mouth'.

GOAT-PEPPER sb obs; *OED* 1836 only. A type of *Capsicum* pepper that has a goat-like odour.

a 1726 Barham (1794) 30 [Capsicum, types 15 to 20:] These are called goat-peppers, for they smell rank like a ram-goat. 1740 Importance 34, Goat-Pepper is yellow when ripe. 1756 Browne 176, Capsicum 2. *Fructu cordiformi minori luteo.* Goat pepper. The smell of the fruit of this species is very differently received in the world; some find it extremely agreeable and reviving, while others think it as rank and disagreeable. It is much used in all the sugar colonies. 1814 Lunan I 356, Goat Peppers..are all of a beautiful shining yellow colour.

GOAT-ROOT sb dial. SPIRIT WEED; the name alludes to its very strong odour.

1952 FGC StC.

GOAT-SHANK CANE see GOAT-FOOT CANE.

GOAT-TURD sb dial. An unidentified plant.

1912 McK *Songs* 15, Though some call it goat-tud. [Note:] Goat-droppings—the name of a poisonous plant, somewhat resembling bannabees [BONAVIST peas].

GOAT-WEED sb; cf *OED* 1756→.

1. Two plants of the family *Scrophularineæ: Capraria biflora* and *Stemodia durantifolia*—the name apparently due to the shape of the leaf.

1756 Browne 268, The shrubby Capraria, or Goat-weed. This plant is very common in Jamaica; it grows about most houses in the lower Savannas: The leaves are narrow at the bottom, and stand on very short footstalks. 1864 Grisebach 784, Goat-weed: *Capraria biflora* and *Stemodia durantifolia.*

2. The plant *Lantana trifoliata*, which has a strong, pungent odour.

1927 Beckwith 18, Goat-weed. *Lantana trifolia* L. For a cold boil and drink as tea. 1954 *WIMJ* 30, *L. trifoliata* ..Wild Sage; Goat Weed.

GOD sb attrib dial. An intensive word, heavily stressed. (Parallel to 'damned'; cf also JESUS, LAW.) *BL G*

1952 FGC StAnd, Not one God piece of food! *Ibid* /evri gaad die mi kom bak, yu banaana gaan/ *Every blessed day when I come back, your bananas are gone.*

GODAHAW sb dial; prob onomatopœic. A donkey.

1943 *GL* StE, Godahaw, an ass.

GOD-A-ME /gádamì/ int and sb dial; <GOD + /a/ (of uncertain origin, perh representing *of*, perh analogous to *a* in *God-a-mercy*) + *me*. (*OED God-damn(-me)* cannot be the source, as neither accentuation nor sense corresponds.)

A. int: An exclamation expressing great distress, fear, expostulation, etc.

1912 McK *Ballads* 46, Lard! me Gahd o' me! Him got one lee' cratch.

B. sb: A small Jamaican river-fish—see quots. (The stories told to explain the name are *ex post facto* concoctions; the actual naming must have involved some situation in which the exclamation could be appropriately applied, perhaps to indicate the fear of the fish when being fished for.)

a1818 Lewis (1836) 104, Mud-fish, snappers, god-dammies, groupers, and grunts! 1942 HPJ, God-damy: A black mudfish with a high smell. . All the creatures had been given their names but the godda-mi forgot his, and went to God to ask him what it was. He knocked at the door and God called out, asking, who was there. The fish answered, 'God, a-mi'. God asked what his trouble was, and the fish said he had forgotten his name. God said: 'To prevent you from forgetting in the future, your name shall be, "God-a-mi"'. 1943 *GL* StAnd, Gadamie; StAnn, Gadame; Tre, Godame. 1947 *NHN* III 93, The Mud-fish is non-migratory. . One remarkable feature about this fish is its ability to live out of water for much longer periods than any other river fish, except the God-a-me. *Ibid* 95, The God-a-mi is perhaps the least known of all river fishes in Jamaica, perhaps because as far as is known they are only to be found in any quantity in the Cabaritta River in Westmoreland and the Black River in St Elizabeth. . They are small chocolate-brown fish and do not attain a length greater than about five inches. 1952 FGC Han /gádami/ fish caught in pots of very fine mesh—buy by the calabash, string and sell in season, dry them, salt, and fry crisp; Port /gádami/ = /bóngobi/; StAnn /gàdamí/ has a red beard [barbel]; StE /gádami/ live in rivers in St Mary, under rocks, say 'God-a-me' when the rock is raised; West /gádami/ plenty together in river after rain—Sav-la-Mar; black, head round, 6–8 in.

GOD-BIRD /gad-bod/ sb dial.

1. The humming-bird. The name indicates folk belief in its supernatural properties; it has the reputation of being very clever and a hard bird to kill. Cf DOCTOR BIRD. *G*

1868 Russell 5, God-bud, humming bird. 1943 *GL* StE, Gad-bud, humming bird. 1956 Jeffrey-Smith 26, At Quickstep [StE] I heard the name 'God bird' given to this bird. Now in StAnn, the youngest member of the family, the spoiled darling is called God bird. Mere smallness of size does not explain the connection.

2. The youngest, petted member of a family.

1956 Jeffrey-Smith 26, see prec quot.

GOD-BLESS BOY, GOD-BLESS GIRL sb dial. See quot.

1954 LeP Kgn, God-bless boy, God-bless girl, one born on a Sunday.

GOD-BLIND-ME /gaad-blain-mi/ sb dial joc; cf *ODS Gor-blimey*. Showy shoes; from the exclamation of one beholding them. Also called G.B.

1956 Mc StAnd, StT /gaad-blain-mi/ boots lacing in front with buckles at side. 1957 EB Port.

GODBROTHER sb dial; *OED* only 1571. *BL*

1946 Dunham 139, Godbrother, a term of intimate address for a man of one's own age [in Accompong].

GOD-BUD see GOD-BIRD.

GOD-BUSH sb chiefly dial. Parasitic bushes of the family Loranthaceæ; the name indicates a recognition among the folk of their 'supernatural' quality because they grow without ever touching the ground. Cf GOD-OKRO.

1850 Macfadyen 198, Loranthus occidentalis. *West-India Mistletoe*. . It grows commonly on trees, particularly the *Pear* (Laurus Persea), and it receives the name of the *God-bush* from the Negroes. 1851 Gosse 131, But what interests me most in this place is a flourishing Misseltoe, or God-bush, as the negroes call it. It is growing on a Soursop (*Anona muricata*), a tree which it principally affects, over-spreading every branch, and effectually, though gradually, killing its supporter. 1864 Grisebach 784, Gadbush [*sic*]: *Arceuthobium gracile*. 1914 Fawcett 88, The members of this family [*Loranthaceæ*] are generally known by the popular names, Godbush and Mistletoe. 1943 *GL* Clar, Kgn, Gad bush, God bush, mistletoe. 1952 FGC StC, StM /gádbúsh/ good tea-bush, never grows on ground. 1954 *FG* 580, Of some twenty-one different kinds of God-bush parasites occurring in Jamaica. . etc.

GOD-COTTON sb dial; cf GOD-BUSH, GOD-OKRO. A kind of fibrous or webby material—see quot; the name implies some consciousness of supernatural power, perh in its production, or because of its use in medicine. Also called PAIN-A-EARS.

1952 FGC StC /gád-kátn/ spun by a worm, usually on the back of a cassada leaf. Good for pain in the ears.

GODDA-MI, GOD-DAMMY see GOD-A-ME.

GODDIE /gádi/ sb dial; /*god* (*mother*) + *-ie*. Godmother; an intimate or affectionate term. *N*

1924 Beckwith 132, When the ninth night came, godmother came in and stole away the baby and put a cat in the bed. . When the nine nights went round again, the goddie went to the bed, took the baby (etc.). 1943 *GL* Port, Gaddie, godmother. 1947 JN StAnd, We stopped at Shirley's Godmother. . Goddie said it's because I did not leave the room when Hermine had mumps.

GOD-FIRE sb dial. A blister on the toe; so called because it burns (the significance of 'God' here is uncertain however—cf GOD, intensive word).

1959 Mrs Robinson, UCWI Preventive Med.

GOD-FOOD sb dial; prob 'food sent by God', a godsend; cf COME-HERE-FE-HELP-WE. Breadfruit.

1940 HPJ, Breadfruit—better known as 'God-food' by the masses.

GOD-HORSE sb dial; cf Hausa *dokin Allah*, Allah's horse, the mantis. *BA G*

1. The stick insect; also the praying mantis. Formerly, SPANISH HORSE.

1952 FGC Man, Port, StT /gád háas, gád-áas/ stick insect. 1956 Mc StT /gad (h)áas/—/it badi taal, leg taal/. A mantis. 1958 DeC StAnd /gad-aas/ a walking-stick insect.

2. Fig. See quot.

1958 DeC StT /gad aas/ a tall thin person, langulala.

GOD-OKRO /gad-okro/ sb dial. *Cereus triangularis*; 'God' refers to its seemingly supernatural growth on trees with no roots touching the ground; for 'okro' see quot 1913.

1913 Harris 33, The flower of the God-ochro is one of those known as 'night-flowering Cactus'. . The crimson fruit, known as 'Strawberry pear' contains a pleasant, sweet pulp enclosing numerous black seeds. The scaly buds of the plant are used as an ingredient in soups, and as a culinary vegetable it is equal if not superior to the ochro. 1926 Fawcett 280, *Cereus triangularis,* Prickly Withe, God Ochra. 1944 *NHN* II 44, Another creeper with triangularly shaped stems, from which aerial roots arise, is known as the..God Ochra. 1952 FGC StT /gád-ókrò/ triangular cactus.

GOD'S-BIRD sb. The NIGHTINGALE.

1942 Astley Clerk in HPJ, Gods-bird—this name is also applied to the Jamaica Mock-bird because of his extraordinarily magnificent voice and wonderful repertoire.

GOD-SICK sb dial; for GOD-SICKNESS. See quot. (The meaning is prob less specific than this quot suggests.)

1954 LeP StE (Eld) God sick, bad cough accompanied by a fever.

GOD-SICKNESS sb dial. See quot.

1942 HPJ, God-sickness: An illness sent by God, not caused by sorcery..Any sickness regarded as a 'visitation'.

GOD-TREE sb; *OED* 1866→ for other plants.

1. Some type of Indian Fig, from its 'supernatural' manner of growth by dropping roots which become new trunks, or by its being considered sacred. Cf GOD-BUSH.

1756 Browne 110, Ficus 5..The wild Fig tree or Indian God-tree..This monstrous tree is..a poor despicable creeper in its tender state: it seldom fails when it meets with a proper support..for it throws out many new appendixes..the roots frequently emit new shoots..and thus one plant is sometimes observed to raise a whole grove.

2. =COTTON TREE (*Ceiba*).

1837 Macfadyen 93, God-tree (Cotton-tree)..Even the untutored children of Africa are so struck with the majesty of its appearance, that they designate it the *God-tree,* and account it sacrilege to injure it with the axe; so that, not unfrequently, not even the fear of punishment will induce them to cut it down. Even in a state of decay, it is an object of their superstitious fears: they regard it as consecrated to evil spirits, whose favour they seek to conciliate by offerings placed at its base.

GO-FAR /gó-fór/ sb dial. The TURBOT fish, because it can serve several people (as food).

1952 FGC StE /gó-fór, tórbit/ could share to a lot of people.

GOGGLE-EYE sb dial; cf *OED goggle-eyed,* →1844; *goggle-eyed Jack* →1884–5. Attrib in the names of various fish having large, prominent eyes: *Goggle-eye jack* (*Trachurus crumenophthalmus*), *goggle-eye snapper, goggle-eye sprat. BA*

1854–5 *TJSA* I 143, *Caranx plumieri*..goggle-eye Jack of the market. *Ibid* 142, *Priacanthus boops*—goggle-eye snapper. 1929 Beckwith 33, Goggle-eye jack. 1952 FGC Port, StAnn, StC, StM /gágl-ái (jak)/. 1952 Smith in *NHN* 186, Herring or 'goggle-eye sprat', *Harengula pensacolæ caribaea.*

GOGGLE OFF vb phr dial; <*gobble+off.* To gobble up. *G*

1956 Mc Man /im gágl áaf im fúud/.

GOGLET /gaglit/ sb dial; *OED goglet*[2] 1688 only. A dial pronunc of *goblet,* illustrating the freq substitution of back stop-consonants for front. (See Introd, phonology). *BA G*

1862 Clutterbuck 84, Glasses, goglets and ice. 1942 Bennett 20, An' now she come mash up me gaglet. 1943 *GL* StC, Guglit, goblet. 1956 Mc Man /di gaglit at di tank said/ *The jug by the tank* (for taking up water).

GOH see GO.

GOIN', GOING see GWINE.

GOIN' PAAH /goin paa, goin puu/ vb phr dial <*going past.* The latter part of a street-vendor's cry advertising the wares she is carrying by, the first being the name of the thing for sale.

1942 Bennett 2, Ripe banana goin' paah! *Ibid* 3, Buy you ripe—..goin' paw; *Ibid* 38, Ripe plantain goin' pooh! Green Gungoo goin' poo!

GOLD-CUP sb dial.

1927 Beckwith 22, 'Water-weed', 'Gold-cup'. b. *Wedelia trilobata* (L) Hitchc.; *gracilis* L. For a cold, boil and drink as tea with sugar.

GOLDEN APPLE sb; transl <Fr—cf POMME D'OR. *BA*

1. The vine *Passiflora laurifolia* and its fruit.

1926 Fawcett 235–6, *P. laurifolia*..Golden Apple, Water Lemon..Fruit..the size of a large hen's egg. 1952 FGC StAnd, StAnn, StM, StT, Golden apple (or golden cup). 1954 *FG* 482, The Golden Apple. This is a well-known member of the Passiflora family.

2. The fruit of *Spondias dulcis,* the OTAHEITE PLUM. (This is prob an error.) *G*

1864 Grisebach 784, Golden apple, *Spondias dulcis.*

GOLDEN FERN, GOLD FERN sb.

1. A small-leaved fern growing in the hills, having gold-coloured spores: *Pityrogramma sulphurea.*

1873 Rampini 76 [Near the Bullhead, Clar:] Then stray specimens of the golden fern appeared. 1951 Proctor *Ferns* 8, *Pityrogramma sulphurea*..Gold Fern.

2. The large-leaved lowland and swamp-land fern *Acrostichum aureum.* Also called CRAB THATCH.

1943 *NHN* II 7, Golden fern.

GOLDEN ROD sb.

1. *Neurolæna lobata.* 1864 Grisebach 787. 1955 *WIMJ* 159.

2. *Bidens reptans.* 1954 *WIMJ* 28.

GOLDEN SPOON sb. The tree *Byrsonima coriacea* and its wood (if Grisebach's application of the common-name is not mistaken). See GOLDSPOON.

1864 Grisebach 784, Golden-spoon, *Byrsonima cinerea.* [Cf 1920 Fawcett 222, *B. coriacea.*]

GOLDEN SWALLOW sb ornith. The swallow *Lamprochelidon euchrysea*; see quot 1936.

1847 Gosse 68. Golden swallow. *Hirundo euchrysea.* 1936 Bond 262, Golden swallow..Local names:—Swallow; Rain Bird..Upperparts, sides of head and chin bright metallic green, bronze-green, or, to a slight extent, bluish green, with a golden gloss on the mantle and scapulars. 1956 Jeffrey-Smith 19.

GOLDEN WARBLER sb ornith. *Dendroica petechia*; also called CHIPPIN' CHICK.

1936 Bond 315, Golden Warbler. 1956 Jeffrey-Smith 85, The Golden Warbler..is found by the seaside, and well merits its local name of Seaside Canary, Mangrove Warbler, and Mangrove Canary.

GOLD FERN see GOLDEN FERN.

GOLDFINCH /gúolfínsh, gúolfrínsh, gùolfrínj, gùulfrínj/ sb; cf *OED.* In Jamaica: *Spindalis nigricephala*; see quot 1936.

1936 Bond 370, Jamaican Spindalis..Local names:—Goldfinch; Orange Bird; Cashew Bird; Spanish Quail; Mark-head; Silver-head..Head and neck black..back, scapulars, rump and upper tail-coverts yellowish olive-green, more yellowish posteriorly and at juncture of black of hind neck. 1952 FGC Man /gùulfrínj, gùolfrínj/ —Mark-head, Yam-cutter; StAnd /gúolfrínsh;/ StM, StT /gúolfínsh/.

GOLD-FRINGE /guolfrinj/ sb dial; by folk-etym < GOLDFINCH.

GOLD-LACE GRUNT /gúol-líes gront/ sb dial. A GRUNT fish with markings that resemble gold lace.

1854–5 *TJSA* I 142, *Hæmulon quadrilineatum*—gold lace grunt. 1950 Smith, Goolia's grunt.

GOLD-LACE PARROT sb dial. A variety of the PARROT fish with markings resembling gold lace.

1952 FGC StJ.

GOLDSPOON sb. The tree *Antirrhœa jamaicensis*, and its wood, used for furniture, which when polished resembles a gold spoon.

1936 Fawcett 60, *A. jamaicensis*..Gold Spoon, Wild Mahogany. 1941 Swabey 21, Goldspoon—(Susan Wood, Pigeon wood, May Day Mahogany)..Wood is of a light red colour: fairly closely grained. Good substitute for mahogany: Planes well and takes a good polish. 1952 FGC StAnn, StE; Tre /gúol spúun/ called Bluefields Cedar in StE, May Day Mahogany in StAnn.

GOLD-TAIL PARROT sb dial. A type of PARROT fish with gold-coloured tail.

1952 FGC Port, StM, Gold-tail parrot.

GOLDYLOCKS sb bot; cf *OED goldilocks*, for different plants.

1. Ferns of the genus *Trichomanes*.

1756 Browne 86, The small creeping Trichomanes or Goldylocks. 1814 Lunan I 329, Goldy Locks. Trichomanes..There are seventeen species natives of Jamaica.. 1. Membranaceum..The plant looks somewhat like a moss. It was found..in Sixteen-Mile-Walk, growing on trunks of trees.

2. *Gnaphalium americanum*: see quot.

1936 Fawcett 206, *G. americanum*..Cassidony, Cudweed, Goldylocks, Cotton-weed.

GO-'LONG see *galang*.

GO-LONG-GO sb dial; cf *galang* + GO, vb. A character in Anancy stories (see quot); since he can be picked up easily but (like the Old Man of the Sea) is difficult to dispose of, the name probably means that he *goes along* with the one who picks him up.

1924 Beckwith 38, He saw Mr Go-long-go come up. [Note:] 'Go-long-go' corresponds with 'Dry-head' in other versions.

GOMBA, GOMBAH see next.

GOMBAY, GOOMBAH /gombe, gumbe, gumba/. Spellings: 1774 goombah, 1793–1946 goombay, 1943 goombey; 1790 gomba, 1827 1835 gombah, 1863 gomby, 1929 gombay; 1790 1837 gumbay, 1793 1828 gumba, 1833 gumbi, 1836 1863 gumby, 1913 gumbie, 1924 gumbé, 1943 gum baa; 1836 gamby. Prob < Kongo *ŋgoma*, *ŋkumbi*, drum.

1. A drum; various types have borne the name (cf quots 1774, 1929), but all seem to be played with fingers rather than with sticks. *BL G N*

1774 Long II 423–4, The goombah, another of their musical instruments, is a hollow block of wood, covered with sheepskin stripped of its hair. The musician holds a little stick, of about six inches in length, sharpened at one end like the blade of a knife, in each hand. With one hand he rakes it over a notched piece of wood, fixed across the instrument, the whole length, and crosses with the other alternately, using both with a brisk motion; whilst a second performer beats with all his might on the sheep-skin, or tabor. 1790 Beckford II 387, A gomba, which they strike with their hands; a drum; a box filled with pebbles. a1818 Lewis (1834) 80 (year 1816), Their music consisted of nothing but Gambys (Eboe drums), Shaky-shekies, and Kitty-katties; *ibid* 193, So instantly the drums and gumbies left off beating; the children left off singing. 1913 Clerk 19, There was the Gumbie, a barrel-shaped drum, some six feet in length, made out of pieces of hollow trees—and the Goombah, a hollow block of wood; and the Goombay, a rustic drum formed of the trunk of a hollow tree. They were, of course, all covered with skins, goat or sheep. [The definite association of special names with special drums is prob not valid.] 1924 Roberts 247–9 (Photograph and description: a small, square, stool-like drum with a goat-skin head held taut by pressure of an inner frame wedged up from below; played with the hands). 1929 Beckwith 149, Two of these gombay drums I saw in St Elizabeth were owned by Myal Men, and the third was in the possession of the Maroons..All were of the same pattern and quite different from Valentine's gombay at Port Antonio or from the gombay in Belisario's drawing.. nor was Miss Roberts..able to trace the pattern to an African original. Yet all gombays alike are played with the fingers with the peculiar rhythm of the myal songs, and seem to be related to the practice of obeah. 1953 Moore 172, Three drums, one playing drum and two bandas, played together are referred to as *gomba* [by the AFRICAN cult].

2. Attrib: *gombay-man*, one playing a gombay; a GOMBAYER. *G*

1833 Scott I 350, In the same way all the other crafts and trades had their Gumbi-men, Horn-blowers, John Canoes, and Nondescript.

3. Transf, from the association of the drum with other African characteristics: see quot.

1943 *GL* Man, Goombey, a very black person.

GOMBAYER sb obs; < GOMBAY + *-er*. One who plays a gombay.

1826 Williams 22, One of the gombayers in old regimentals.

GONE /gaan/ vb dial; < *gone*; or perh reduced < *going*. Going; am (or other form of the verb *to be*) going. (Used as full or auxil vb; *gone* is also used for pple as in Std Engl.) *BA BL G*

1877 Murray *Kittle* 26, 'Bra Watchman, me gone, yerry!' Watchman jump after him, but bufo you coulda say 'Jack', Mudfish gone. 1896 Trowbridge 287, *Me gone.* I am going. 1907 Jekyll 110, Tiger gone making his way fe go eat the gal fe meat. 1912 McK *Ballads* 47, Now because o' you Dem gone bring me up. 1943 Bennett 31, Him sey him gawn, hear me, 'goodbye'. [*He says he is going; I say, 'goodbye'.*] 1955 Bennett *Pleasuration*, Me kean stop Jane, me gone next door.

GONE /gaan/ adv dial; as if reduced from some such phrase as 'and is gone', but prob also representing the tendency (as in Twi and other W African languages) to use verbs adverbially. Cf also BRING, COME, DONE. Following a verb expressing movement (e.g. *fly*, *run*, *walk*, etc.): away. *BL G*

1952 FGC StAnd, Snake Waitin'-Boy—have leg, but just wiggle-wiggle and run gone.

GONE adj chiefly dial; < *gone*. Following noun of time: past, last (*OED a* 3b). *BA BL G*

1956 Mc Man /sátide gáan/ *last Saturday*; /laas wiik gaan/ *last week*; StE (Accom) /disémba gáan/ *last December*.

GO-NO-MORE sb dial. A place to which one cannot go again. (Perh an individualism or nonce creation.)

1952 FGC StJ /gó-no-mo/.

GOOD-BELLY adj and sb dial; cf Engl *good-hearted*. Good-natured, kindly; benevolence.

1877 Murray *Kittle* 25, Bambye *good-belly pigeon come dere come drink water..*Good natured. 1927 Anderson-Cundall 63 [Prov:] Good belly mek nanny-goat da out a do' [*Good nature causes the goat to be left outdoors*]. 1942 HPJ, Good-belly: benevolent, benevolence.

GOOD-LUCKED /gúd lókid/ adj dial; cf BAD-LUCKED. Fortunate. *BL G*

1943 Bennett 8, De 'oman soh good luckid dat She meet wid accident. [Not ironic: she got money out of it.]

GOODLY adj dial. Used ironically or sarcastically: see quot. *G*

1942 HPJ, My goodly cousin take away ebery thing an doan bring dem back.

GOOD NIGHT int dial; in contrast to Brit usage, 'said only at parting', *OED*. See EVENING. A common greeting at meeting someone in the evening. *BA BL G T*

1959 FGC StAnd, Goodnight, sir. (Said by watchman arriving at his post for the night.)

GOOLIA'S GRUNT see GOLD-LACE GRUNT.

GOOLY BEAN see GULLY BEAN.

GOOMA see GUMA.

GOOMBAH, GOOMBAY, GOOMBEY see GOMBAY.

GOOMER see GUMA.

GOONGO, GOONGOO see GUNGO (PEAS).

GOONSO, GOOSOOM, GOOSUNG, GOOZOO see GUZU.

GOOTOO see *gutu*.

GOPHER CEDAR sb dial; prob in allusion to the wood of which Noah's ark was to be made: *Gopher* (*OED sb*[2]) +*cedar*. Some variety of cedar?

1952 FGC StM /gúofa síida/.

GORMANDIZER sb dial.

1. A worm or its chrysalis: see quot.

1952 FGC Han /gármandáiza/—chrysalis; destroys crops; sometimes makes a web.

2. A 'sucker' or shoot on a plant. (Cf Fr *gourmand* in this sense.)

1934 *Citrus* 5, Pruning: Save for regular suppression of 'Gormandizers', no pruning should be done for one year. 1952 FGC StE, Gormandizer, a sucker on a tomato plant, i.e. a new stem in the angle of a leaf. 1958 DeC StAnd /gaamandaiza/ any water sucker (including a man-limb) which saps the strength of the tree.

GORU /goru, goro/ sb dial; <Hindi *gorū*, cow.

1943 *GL* Kgn, StT, Goro, goru, a cow. Coolie word.

GOSSAMER SPIDER sb dial; *OED* 1802 only. See quot: evid a general term.

1952 FGC StAnd /gásma spáida/ biting one, big, no web; another kind always travel with egg, black, many legs, make web.

GOTTA see *gato*.

GOTTO sb dial joc; prob <*got to*, indicating that one can afford nothing better—cf WA-FI-DU hat.

1943 *GL* StT, Gotto, a rope-soled shoe.

GOUDY, GOURDIE see next.

GOURDY /guodi/ sb dial; <*gourd*+-*y*. A large calabash usually used for carrying water: it is whole except for a small hole through which the water is poured. *N*

1942 HPJ, Gourdie: A common term for 'gourd'—'Kip yu secret inna yu gourdie'. 1954 LeP Port, Goady; StE, Goadie; StT, Goudi, all 'calabash'. 1956 Mc StAnd, StE /guodi/ calabash with hole, used for carrying water.

GOURDY PEPPER sb dial; <GOURDY+*pepper*. A type of *Capsicum* pepper; named for its shape?

1952 FGC Port /gúodi-pépa/ fairly hot.

GOUT TEA sb dial. The plant *Cordia globosa*, used in making a medicinal tea. See quot 1953.

1864 Grisebach 784, Gout-tea. 1953 *WIMJ* 238, *Cordia globosa* H.B.K. Black Sage; John Charles; Gout Tea. This species is used in Jamaica to prepare a tea as a general beverage and for colds and 'tightness in the chest'.

GOUZOO MAN see GUZU-MAN.

GOVERNESS sb dial cant. A female officer in POCOMANIA and revivalist cults; see quots.

1929 Beckwith 176, The Pukkumerian leaders are called 'governors' or 'shepherds'. Each shepherd has attached to himself a good-looking young woman (not his wife) who acts as his confederate under the name of 'governess' or sometimes 'shepherdess'. The two have a secret code of speech which the spirits are supposed to speak. 1952 Kerr 127, The Pocomania Shepherd has to have mothers and the chief female figure who is called a governess. 1953 Moore 88, Governess, a special female officer in the Revival cult group (St Thomas).

GOVERNOR sb.

1. A chief slave, in charge of other slaves, on a sugar estate. Obs. *G*

a 1818 Lewis (1845) 156, He set about forming a conspiracy against Sully, the present chief governor, and boasted, on various estates in the neighbourhood, that he would take care to get Sully broke, and himself substituted in his place. *Ibid* 164, I must begin by displacing the trustee, the physician, the four white book-keepers, and the four black governors.

2. The male officer in a Pocomania cult. See GOVERNESS, quot 1929.

GOVERNOR APPLE sb obs; for *Governor's apple*.

1942 HPJ, Governor Apple: Mangosteen. Once there was only a single tree, the fruit of which was reserved for the highest official.

GOVERNOR BREAM sb. A variety of the bream fish—presumably a superior one.

1892 Cockrell list, Governor bream, *Anisotremus virginicus*.

GOVERNOR CANE sb dial. A variety of sugar-cane; the name probably implies superior quality—cf COMMANDER COCO, DUKE COCO, etc.

1912 McK *Songs* 87 [Note:] Governor cane; a yellow-striped sugar-cane.

GOWRIE see RINGED GOWRIE.

goyaak /gòyáak/ sb dial; prob <*Pouyat*—cf POUYAT BANANA. A banana.

1943 *GL* StJ, Goyak, Go yawk, banana; Tre, Guark, banana; also Goyark, and Kgn, StAnd, StE, West. 1954 LeP StE (Eld), Goyawk—banana. 1955 FGC Man /gòyáak/.

GOYAK, GOYARK, GOYAWK see prec.

graaf, graf vb dial; perh <*grasp*, or transf from US *graft*, to obtain by dishonest or parasitic means. (Cf DA 2.) To desire, seek greedily. Const *after*, *up*.

1957 DeC StAnd /im graf afta piiz/ to long for, desire. 1958 DeC StE /graaf op/ to pick up (something) eagerly and greedily.

graafnas adj dial; <*graaf*+-*nous* (linking *n* or /n/ <-*ing*, +-*ous*). Selfish, covetous.

1958 DeC StE /graafnas/ adj. for a selfish and covetous person: /hin waan fi graaf ebriting/.

graam op vb phr dial; prob var of *gaam op* (=Engl and US dial *gaum*).

graandi see GRANDY.

graas see GRASS.

graas bakl or **batl** see GLASS BOTTLE.

graba sb dial; perh =*grabber*, but this may be folk-etym, and the source may be Sp—cf GRABAT, GARABATA.

1958 DeC Man /graba/ a cutlass [with a hooked or turned back end]..so called because it is sharp on the inside of the hook and can grab the material to be cut.

GRABALICIOUS, grabalishas, GRABARICIOUS, grabarishas see *gravilishas*.

GRABAT sb dial; prob <Sp *garabato* (cf GARABATA), with folk-etym alteration.

1942 HPJ, Grabat: A kind of boathook used by fishermen for getting a large fish quickly into the boat.

GRABBER see *graba*.

GRABBLE /grabl/ vb[1] dial; cf *OED grabble* 1, grope, perh with folk-etym infl of *gravel*. *BL*

1. To scratch or dig in, or as if in, gravel.

1942 HPJ, Grabble: To scratch (like a hen). [Astley Clerk:] The meaning..is well known to me and is still.. much used by our lowest classes.

2. Const *out*: to dig out of the earth.

1942 HPJ, Grabble: To gravel out (dig out) cocos.

GRABBLE vb[2] dial; cf *OED grabble* 5, seize, →1857. *BA G*

1942 HPJ, Grabble: To catch on to somebody (to grapple) as rarely in English.

GRACIE-WOOD see GRACY-WOOD.

GRACY, GRAZY sb dial; perh conn with *graze*, vb; cf GRACY-WOOD. The Indian Cony (*Capromys brownei*).

1943 *GL* Kgn, Gracey—wild rabbit. 1952 FGC StT /griezi/—same as /kúoni/. 1957 EB Port /gráasi/ Injin coney.

GRACY-, GRAZY-WOOD sb dial. See quot 1890.

1890 Thomas 23, The most striking in appearance was the 'gracie wood', or 'coonoo-coonoo,'—it bears both names. It is of immense girth, its trunk profusely garnished with knots and excrescences of varying size, and its branches twisted in every direction. Its roots are generally hollowed out by Indian coneys, who prefer them as a dwelling to those of any tree. 1944 *NHN* II 142, The huge Gracy Wood with a light coloured bark..The coney was reported as common in the rocky slopes. 1952 FGC StT /griezi-wúd/ big, usually hollow, Indian conies live in hollows—but good hardwood.

GRADGO sb dial; etym unknown.

1943 *GL* Tre, Gradgo, hopish [hoppish?] walking.

GRA-GRA sb dial rare; a counterpart to GRI-GRI: see quot. With vaguely threatening or prophetic suggestion: a consequence, something which comes after (and is worse). (GRI-GRI is the first part, the forerunner or cause.)

1925 Beckwith 42, Dis a only de gri-gri, de gra-gra deh behin'. 1927 Anderson-Cundall 64.

gra-gra wud sb dial; cf *grang-grang*. Kindling wood.

1958 DeC StAnd /gra-gra wud/ small sticks for lighting the fire.

GRAIN SUGAR sb chiefly dial. Granulated sugar.

1952 FGC StM, Make 'cut cakes' with 'wet sugar'.. drop in a little grain sugar.

GRAMBAY /grambe/ sb dial; etym unknown. Some kind of locally made light shoe or slipper.

1943 *GL* StJ, Grambay, kind of shoe; Tre, Grambea, grambeh, a sandal made of old tyres; footwear. 1955 FGC Man /grambe/ a shoes.

grambe, GRAMBEA, GRAMBEH see prec.

GRAMPA TAATA sb dial; <*grampa*, grandfather+TAATA, father. One who (through incest) is both the father and grandfather of a child; also as a term of address.

1960 SJR StAnd /grámpa táata/.

GRANADILA EBONY see GRANADILLA (EBONY).

GRANADILLA see *grandidila*.

GRANADILLA (EBONY) (TREE) sb arch; <Sp *granadillo* (Cuba, etc.), *Brya ebenus* (Roig y Mesa, Santamaría); *OED* 1864 only. The tree now generally called EBONY or JAMAICA EBONY.

1657 Continuation 45, Severall sorts of wood..1. Grandillio, of a reddish black colour, and heavy as Ebony, used much in these parts for bedsteads. p 1660 State of Jamaica 611, Lignum vitee, Speckle wood, Granadila Ebony and others wch are frequently exported. 1672 Blome 11 Lignum-Vitæ, Ebony, Granadilla, and many other. 1864 Grisebach 784, Granadilla Tree: *Brya Ebenus*.

GRANADILLO TEMPLE sb. Meaning unknown.

1924 Beckwith 202 [Riddle:] High as the world; red as blood but not blood; blue as indigo, but not indigo; High as granadillo temple.—Rainbow.

GRANADITTA sb. A type of passion flower and its fruit; see quot 1926.

1926 Fawcett 236, *Passiflora ligularis*..is a native of tropical America and is cultivated in Jamaica under the name 'Granaditta'. It differs from *P. maliformis* in the leaves being broader and deeply cordate..[etc.]; the fruit is about the size of an orange and contains an agreeable pulp. 1933 Harris, *Bull. Dept. Agric. Ja.* n.s. ii 166.

GRAND COPPER sb obs; cf *OED grand* 7 +*copper* 3. The first and largest copper (whence the name) in the series formerly used in evaporating cane liquor to make sugar.

1790 Moreton 48, The largest..is called the grand copper, and [it is] the first that is filled with liquor; as soon as it is full, and tempered with a small quantity of Bristol lime and lye-water, the black boiler cries out, 'Fia! gran-coppa!' i.e. Fire! Grand copper! at which vociferation a blazing fire is instantly put to the grand copper. 1793 Edwards II 233, The evaporating boiler, commonly called the *grand copper*.

GRANDE, GRANDEE, GRANDI(E) see GRANDY.

GRANDE-GRANDE see GRANDY-GRANDY.

grandidila sb dial; <*granadilla*, the first element prob by folk-etym. A granadilla (*Passiflora quadrangularis*).

1952 FGC AtAnd, StAnn, StJ /gràndidíla/. 1957 EB Port /grandidila/.

GRANDIDITA sb dial; perh <GRANADITTA (cf *grandidila* <GRANADILLA), but the fruit is unidentified.

1942 HPJ, Grandidita, A kind of fruit.

GRANDILLIO see GRANADILLA (EBONY).

GRANDMA-HAIR sb dial; cf GRANNY-BEARD. A type of MACHETE with a broad, flaring, turned-back end.

1959 DeC StJ, West /grama hier/.

GRANDMARKET sb also attrib; prob <Fr *grandmarché*. An especially large market held at stated times or special occasions.

1905 Smith 15, Now de nex' gran' market day, Chim-chim come to town. 1947 U.Newton III 25, Grand-market—market on Dec. 24 (Chapelton, 1924).

GRANDY /graandi, grandi/ sb dial; <*grand* (reduced out of *grandmother* or *grandam*) + *-y*.

1. A grandmother; also used as a title and term of address.

1873 Rampini 182 [Prov:] You no see mammy, you seek grandy (grandmother). 1942 HPJ, Grandy Di—The name of a Maroon nurse in the Harrison family of St Thomas (1865). *Ibid*. 'In Kingston, if you call people grandy, them cuss you and say dem noh old; in the country if you don't call them grandy, they complain.' 1943 *GL* Clar, Grandĕ, grandmother. 1954 LeP StAnn, Grandie, grandmother (sometimes used).

2. As a term of address: A woman older than oneself, e.g. (as in quot) to a mother.

1873 Rampini 125, Den him turn to him moder Fowl an' say, 'Grandie, if any come to you, ask you fe give him de flute..[etc.]'. An' him moder say, 'Yes, sa! me hear'. Den Hawk say, 'An', Grandie, you mus' hab my breakfas' ready'.

3. A midwife; on estates in slavery times her duties included the rearing of infants. (Cf US dial *Granny-woman*, midwife.)

a 1818 Lewis (1834) 124, There ought to have been a third child, born at seven months, whom the graundee had reared with great difficulty. 1820 Thomson 115, The midwife on every estate should have a house built for her..To these apartments the pregnant woman is to be removed shortly before the expected time of her delivery and placed under the sole direction of the *grandee*, as they call her. 1943 *GL* StC, Grandi—midwife, maternity nurse. 1955 FGC Man /graandi/ not /grandi/—midwife. 1958 DeC StAnd /grandi/—a midwife; in this district /naana/ means only old grandmother never midwife.

GRANDY adj and adv dial; <*grand* + familiarizing *-y*. In vaguely favourable sense: Great, fine; very. (Examples in quot 1828 do not always ring true, and are too frequent.) Less used today than formerly.

1828 Marly 135, It hab be a grandy big estate, much grandy better dan Paradise to leeward; *ibid*, a grandy big serpent..it would make him Ebe much grandy savey.. Gor Amighty hab be grandy much angry..[used *passim* as an indiscriminate augmentative in reports of supposed negro speech]. 1942 HPJ, Clever, nice. (Used also in other Islands.)

GRANDY-GRANDY adj dial obs; iterative < GRANDY.

1774 Long II 427, The Negroes seem very fond of reduplications..as..*grande-grande* (augmentative size, or grandeur).

GRANDY MARY sb dial. A small myriapod worm, with jointed carapace and many small legs, which curls up when touched.

1952 FGC Man /grándi míeri/ or /graandi/—black body, lots of white legs; inch to inch and a half long; rolls up in ring. Also StAnd, etc.

GRANDY SUN sb dial; < GRANDY adj + *sun*. See quot, and note two senses.

1958 DeC Port /grandi son/ both the sun when it looks very large just before setting, and also the time of day when this happens.

GRANGE sb and vb dial; <*grainse*, a fish spear or harpoon (*OED grain sb*[2] 5 b).

A. sb: A pronged fish-spear. *N*

[a 1818 Lewis (1834) 43 (year 1815), The five-pronged grainse, which arms his hands.] 1942 HPJ, Grange: A two-pronged fork for killing fish first noticed..in Falmouth Harbour, Hence to grange.1952 FGC StJ /grenj, grienj/.

B. vb: To fish with such a spear. (See quot 1942 above.)

grang-gran sb; iterative <*gran*, grandmother (*EDD*). Cf *gang-gang*.

1957 DeC StAnd /grang-gran/ affectionate term for Grandmother.

GRANG-GRANG, GRAN-GRAN /grang-grang, grang-gran, gran-gran/ sb dial; cf Twi *krann*, wild, entangled.

1. Bits of sticks, dried shrubs, brambles, etc., used as kindling. This is one of several terms of similar structure and meaning: BRAM-BRAM, BRANG-BRANG, *kran-kran*, *kreng-kreng*, JAG-JAG, etc. s GRANGI-GRANGI.

1943 *GL* Clar, Grang-Grang, Fine Wood; Kgn, Gran-gran, bramble; StM, Grang-grang, small pieces of shrub dried for fuel; Tre, Grangrang, Bramble. 1953 Murray 15 [Song:] Me tek piece-a grang-grang, Me trow 'pon de water.

2. Rubbish.

1955 FGC Man /grang-grang/ old rubbish.

GRANKE sb dial obs; etym unknown.

1868 Russell 6, Granke—The cock-roach. African.

GRANNY sb dial; <*granny*, grandmother.

[1. Pet name for a grandmother.] *BL G T*

2. Pet name for a grandfather.

1943 *GL* Man, Grannie, grandson, grandfather or grandmother.

3. A grandchild.

1943 *GL* Man, see quot above. 1946 Dunham 19, Granny, grandchild. 1952 FGC StE /grani/ grandchild. 1956 Mc Man /graní an likl gráni/ *Grandmother and grandchild*; StE (Accom) [Old woman speaking:] /mi grani kyie mi/ *My grandchildren look after me*.

GRANNY-BEARD, -HAIR sb dial; for *granny's beard, hair*; cf GRANDMA-HAIR. A type of machete with flaring, curved-back blade.

1959 DeC Han /grani bierd/; 1961 *CLS* 70.

GRANNY'S TINDER-BOX sb obs. See quot.

1890 Thomas 72, A novelty among the nocturnal noises [in the John-Crow Mountains] was 'granny's tinder-box'..It is the name applied to the noise made by a large cricket, I presume, which exactly resembles the striking of flint and steel together with a regular cadence.

GRAN'-PICKNY sb dial; <*grand-* + PICKNY. A grandchild. *G*

1950 Pioneer 16, Anancy wasa pass one ole oman yard, an him see her gran pickney outa de doorway. 1956 Mc Man /síks a mi granpikni [or /gran-pikini/] dem lib wid mi/ *Six of my grandchildren live with me*.

GRAPEFRUIT sb; *ODS* 1851→. The fruit *Citrus decumana*, which grows in clusters like grapes. [Lunan's explanation of the name is erron.] *BA G T*

1814 Lunan II 171, There is a variety known by the name *grape-fruit*, on account of its resemblance in flavour to the grape; this fruit is not near so large as the shaddock. a 1818 Lewis (1845) 77 (year 1816) (see CLUSTER-FRUIT). 1913 Harris 8.

grapo sb dial; etym unknown, but cf *graba*. A kind of MACHETE with a hook at the tip.

1958 DeC StM /grapo/ a cutlass.

GRAPPLE vb dial. *BA G*

1958 DeC StT /grapl/ to pick up and carry something heavy. Cf PAWN, *stagalang, tagalang*.

GRASH FISH sb obs; prob <*grash*, to gnash (*OED* quots 1563–1607)—cf such other fish names as DRUMMER, GRUNT, etc. A type of fish which (judging by the name) made a gnashing sound when caught.

1679 Trapham 65, The choice Mullet brings up the next division crowded with various Snappers..Barracoota, Gar fish, Grash fish, Mud fish [etc.].

GRASS sb dial.

1. In compounds frequently used of plants not at all grass-like, though growing in patches covering the ground: see WATER-GRASS, HOG-GRASS, etc. *G*

2. Added in an explanatory way or redundantly to complete names of plants that are not grasses: =plant.

1912 McK *Ballads* 30, Look de 'panish-needle grass Growin' by de gully pass. [Cf SPANISH NETTLE.] 1952 FGC Port, Old-man's-beard grass.

GRASS-BELLY sb dial.

1942 HPJ, Grass-belly: The swollen stomach of a horse that has eaten too much grass.

GRASS-BIRD sb; *OED* in this sense 1847→.

1. The bird more generally known as GRASS QUIT. (Identity in quot 1740 is uncertain.)

1740 Importance 38, Grass-Birds, Parrots, Parokets [etc.]. 1847 Gosse 251–2, The Grass-bird very frequently selects a shrub, on which the wasps have built, fixing the entrance close to their cells..The Grass-birds remind me much of the European Sparrow. 1907 Jekyll 191 [Song:] On the carpet you must be happy as the grass-bird on the tree. 1927 Anderson-Cundall 125, A stem a grass-seed, an' only grass bud (bird) can climb i'. 1952 FGC StAnd, StM, Grass-bird, grass-quit.

2. Another name for the SWEE-SWEE.

1942 HPJ (Theo McKay).

3. See SAVANNA GRASS-BIRD.

GRASS BOTTLE /graas bakl, graas batl/ sb dial; <*glass bottle*. A piece or pieces of broken bottle(s). *G*

1941 Kirkpatrick 38, Me an' you know say muss muss cyan run 'pon grass bockle. 1942 HPJ, Grass-bottle: glass bottle in a broken state, often used for shaving. 1943 *GL* StM, Grass backle, broken glass.

GRASS BREAM /graas brim/ sb dial; <*grass* +*brim*, bream. A variety of the bream fish, evid one which lives in the sea-grass—cf GRASS GROUPER, GRASS GRUNT, GRASSY-GROUND PARROT.

1952 FGC StE /graas brim/ brown fish.

GRASS-COPPER sb dial rare (perh an individualism); <*grasshopper*. A grasshopper.

1952 FGC Tre /gràskápa/ yellow, brown; some pink, some green.

GRASS CRAB sb obs? A small purplish crab with a raised, many-pronged shell; presumably named for living in the grass.

1756 Browne 422, The Grass-Crab. This curious little shell-fish is but rarely met with in Jamaica, though a native of that island.

GRASS-CUTTER sb obs. A member of a GRASS-GANG. *G*

1839 McMahon 141–2, The labourers were driven with the cart-whip from morning till night..even grass-cutters, from seventy years old and upwards, were exposed to the same barbarous atrocities.

GRASS-DODGER sb dial; see DODGE. *Ammodramus savannarum*; also called GRASSHOPPER SPARROW, GRASS PINK, TICHICRO.

1936 Bond 394, *Ammodramus savannarum..Local names:*—Savanna bird; Grass-dodger; Grass Pink; 'Tichicro'. 1952 FGC StM /graas daja/ like grass-bird, with stripes. 1956 Mc Man /graas daja/ a bird, catch in ground snare (calaban).

GRASS-EYE see GLASS-EYE.

GRASS-GANG sb obs. One of the gangs of slaves on sugar estates, usually the younger or weaker ones, employed in gathering grass and other fodder for cattle. *G*

1774 Long I 450, The young boys and girls, or what are commonly called the grass-gang, may, with the slightest instruction, cut and lay the junks [of cane] in the furrow.

GRASS GROUPER sb dial. A GROUPER or similar fish that lives in the sea-grass.

1854–5 *TJSA* I 142, Serranus outalibi—yellow velvet fish: grass grooper.

GRASS GRUNT sb dial. A variety of the GRUNT fish that lives in the sea-grass.

1952 FGC StT, Grass grunt.

GRASS HAMLET see HAMLET.

GRASS-KNIFE sb dial. A grass-hook or long-handled sickle. *G*

1958 DeC StT /graas naif/ a tool consisting of a curved blade, sharpened on the concave side, 12–18 in. long, fastened to a stick as a handle. Used for billing grass and—with a very long handle—for cutting coconuts.

GRASS-LICE sb. Very tiny ticks that lurk in grass, whence they get upon cattle.

1912 McK *Ballads* 31, Ef you 'low de sun fe grow, Grass-lice wi' sure mek you know.

GRASS PARROT sb dial. A variety of the PARROT fish which lives in sea-grass; prob =GRASSY-GROUND PARROT.

1952 FGC StM /gráas párat/.

GRASS PENN (or **PEN**) sb obs; cf *OED* 1790 only. A property or small estate on which grass is grown for cattle-feed and small stock is raised—see quots.

1774 Long II 124, A number of little grass-penns, with good houses on them, are dispersed about the neighborhood [of Half-way Tree], chiefly the property of merchants in Kingston, who occasionally retire to them from the hurry of business; *ibid* 152, A small grass-penn, stocked with sheep and goats. 1790 Moreton 58, A grass-penn, or farm, is a better property, and is attended with less trouble and expence than a sugar plantation. Not many years ago, grass-penns were considered as despicable objects for enterprizing adventurers to hunt after..but latterly there has been..improvements.

GRASS-PIECE sb. A field in which grass is grown. *BA BL*

1756 Browne 174, The branched Caleloe..grows frequently in the grass pieces. 1837 Sterne 2, A thief had gone over his fence into his grass piece. (1959 Current, FGC.)

GRASS PINK sb; see quot 1956; *OED* 1894 only. The TICHICRO.

1847 Gosse 242, Grass Pink or Savanna bird. 1952 FGC StAnd /graas pingk/ little bigger than grass-bird, and back same colour, but pink underneath. 1956 Jeffrey-Smith 99, *Ammodramus savannarum*. Such a plain little bird to have so long a name! but that of Savanna grass bird does indicate its habitat and another, Grass Pink, its habit of lying low among the grass, occasionally uttering a monotonous 'pink-pink'.

GRASS QUIT sb; <*grass*+QUIT. A finch of the genus *Tiaris* of which there are two species in Jamaica: see BLACK-FACE and YELLOW-FACE GRASS QUIT. (Also BAY-SIDED GRASS QUIT.)

1847 Gosse 249, Grass-Quit; *ibid* 252, 253. 1955 Taylor 6–7, The Grass-quits belong to the Finch family and have the typical stout conical beaks of seed-eating birds.. These little birds are very common all over Jamaica both in gardens and in open country and even in the middle of towns. 1956 Mc Man /graas kwit/.

GRASSY-GROUND PARROT sb. A variety of the PARROT fish, prob the same as GRASS PARROT.

1892 Cockrell list, Grassy ground parrot. *Sparisema radians*.

GRATER /grieta/ vb; <*grater* sb. To grate, to scrape into fine bits with a grater. *BA BL G N*

1952 FGC StE, Grater green bananas, make porridge, make 'spoon drops' with gratered green bananas; StT, Grater the nut of coconut to get milk. [So for past 40+ years.] 1956 Mc StAnd /yo gríeta kasáada fós/. 1958 DeC gen /grieta/ verb: to grate. The country (and many a Kingston middle-class) Jamaican.

GRATER sb dial. A musical instrument: a stick with many notches used for percussion.

1953 Moore gloss, Grater—used by AFRICAN cult. *BL*

GRATER BRUTE sb; <*grater* (for *gratered*) +*brute* (<Fr *brut*, crude, unrefined). Cakes made of grated coconut cooked in a fondant of unrefined 'wet' or 'new' sugar. Now more often GRATER CAKE.

c 1915 FGC StAnd, *Grater brute*—common. 1929 Beckwith 45, Coconut cakes called..if grated, 'grata brule' [*sic*]. 1942 HPJ, *Grater-bruit (brew)*..Grater brŭ: brook-cake; Grater cake. 1943 *GL* StAnd, Grater brute—coconut puff. 1952 FGC StJ /gríeta brùut/; other informants doubtful.

GRATER CAKE sb; for *gratered cake*—cf GRATER vb. =GRATER BRUTE but is displacing it, and white sugar is now often used instead of brown.

1952 FGC StE, Grater cake, made with white sugar. 1954 LeP Port, StAnn, StE, Grater cake—cake made with coconut. 1956 Mc Man /grieta kiek/ cake made of coconut and sugar only. 1958 DeC Port /grieta kieks/ a confection of grated coconut, sugar, etc.

grato, GRATTA, GRATTEAU, GRATTO see *gato*.

GRAUNDEE see GRANDY sb.

GRAVE-DIGGER sb; *OED* 1851→. A kind of wasp that nests beneath the earth, a digger-wasp.

1756 Browne 438, Apis 2. Rufescens innocua, sub terram nidulans. The Grave-Digger. 1851 Gosse 145–6, The Grave Digger. On the earthen floor of the building.. a good many large wasp-like Flies may be observed in the hottest part of the day, briskly flying to and fro. It is a species of Sphex. 1952 FGC Tre, Grave digger—builds nest; big one is black, small one blue; kill /páida, anánsi/.

GRAVEL vb dial; <*gravel* sb. =GRABBLE vb¹.

1907 Jekyll 158, The loose soil is then piled up into small mounds in which the yam-heads will be placed. The object of the mound is to enable the proprietor to see easily at any time how the tuber is getting on, by just 'gravelling' it a bit with his hand. *G*

GRAVEL-GRAVEL sb dial; iterative <*gravel*. Gravelly land.

1952 FGC StC, Gravel-gravel—the kind of ground where spirit-weed grows.

gravichas see *gravilishas*.

gravila sb; etym unknown. Some kind of bush, unidentified.

1952 FGC StT /grávila/.

GRAVILICIOUS see next.

gravilishas /gràvilíshas, gràbalíshas, gràbaríshas, gravíchas/ adj dial; evid <GRABBLE +*-ish*, +*-ous*, but (esp in the sense of 'greedy') this may be analogical to *delicious*, or the like. Covetous, selfish, CRAVEN; greedy. *BL*

1943 *GL* Clar, Gravalicious, greedy; Port, Graba'-licious, craven, greedy. 1952 FGC StM /gràvilíshas/ craven, greedy. 1954 LeP Kgn, Grabalicious; StE, Gravilicious (adj)—a greedy person. 1958 DeC Man /gravíchas/ selfish, covetous. 1959 FGC Man, Grabaricious.

GRAVY sb dial. *G*

1959 DeC Han /grievi/ coconut run-down.

GRAY- see GREY-.

GRAZY see GRACY.

GREASE-BUSH sb dial; <*grease* sb+BUSH 4 (this is prob an independent formation having nothing to do with the US name). See quots.

1927 Beckwith 18, Grease-bush. *Emilia sagittata*.. 'Consumption-weed'. For a cough boil as tea. So called because it will take grease off the plates like soap. 1953 *WIMJ* 242. 1961 DAP Man, Grease-bush, *Parthenium hysterophorus* L., Removes grease from hands.

GREASY-BUSH sb dial; <*greasy*+BUSH. An unidentified wild plant; cf GREASE BUSH.

1952 FGC Han /gríisi-bùsh/ same as Hanover bur-bush—has small 5-part seeds or burs.

GREAT BEAN sb obs. The Broad or Sugar Bean, *Phaseolus lunatus*. (Cf 1920 Fawcett 64.)

1696 Sloane 66, Phaseolus maximus perennis, semine compresso lato, nigris maculis notato..*The great Bean*. 1707 Sloane 175.

GREAT BLUE SWALLOW sb obs. In Gosse's use: A variety of the Purple Martin (*Progne subis dominicensis*).

1847 Gosse 69, Great Blue Swallow. *Progne Dominicensis* ..As closely allied to the Purple Martin..I long mistook the present bird for that well-known species.

GREAT CALTROP sb obs; <*great*+*caltrop*. POLICE MACKA.

1774 Long III 720, The great caltrops, or the field-tribulus..a creeping plant, growing in all the pasture-lands of Jamaica.

GREAT COPPER sb obs; cf *OED great* 6. The GRAND COPPER in a sugar factory.

1790 Beckford II 76.

GREAT CORN sb obs; cf *OED great* I. 'Thick, coarse..composed of large particles.' →1614.

1790 Beckford I 314, The Indian, or the great corn.

GREAT-COTTON sb obs. If Long's identification is correct: *Adansonia digitata*. The similarity to 'cotton' may refer to the tree as compared with the Ceiba, the common 'Cotton Tree' of Jamaica.

1774 Long II 41 [In Spanish Town] are two trees called baobab, or the great-cotton, described by Adanson, in his account of Guiney, from whence the seeds were brought and planted here.

GREAT-FLOWERED CREEPING CEREUS sb bot obs. In Titford's use (translating *Cereus grandiflorus*): the Night-blooming Cereus.

1811 Titford 70, Great-flowered Creeping Cereus..is a native of Jamaica. The flower opens in the night and continues only six hours.

GREAT GANG sb obs. Formerly on sugar and other estates, the gang composed of the strongest slaves to whom was assigned the heaviest work. *G*

1795 *Braco* 1 June, Great gang or cutters, 48. Small gang or Tyers, 15. 1823 Roughley 307, To plant..this piece of land in guinea-grass, I would set in the great gang. 1825 De la Beche 6, The great gang, as the first class of negroes is denominated. 1839 McMahon 33, I left my own gang to go and speak to Lally, who was superintending the great gang.

GREATMENT adj dial joc; <*great*+*-ment* meaninglessly added following another word ending in *-ment*.

1960 Pat Wilmot StAnd, see HEATMENT.

GREAT PEPPER sb obs. A large variety of *Capsicum* pepper; see quot.

1811 Titford 46, Great Pepper, A large species, of the size of a peach, green or red, and frequently used for pickling.

GREAT WATER HORSETAIL see WATER HORSETAIL.

GRECIAN vb dial; abbr. To CUT GRECIAN.

1952 FGC StT [Song:] What's the use o' you Grecian?—Gal, you character gone!

GREEDY sb dial; <*greedy* adj or *greediness* sb. Greed. *BL G*

1873 Rampini 177 [Prov:] Greedy (greed) choke puppy. 1925 Bec with 55, same. (1960 Current. FGC.)

GREEN BALSAM sb obs; descr. The medicinal juice of the tree *Calophyllum jaquinii*.

1837 Macfadyen 136–7, see SANTA MARIA.

GREEN BUSH sb; <*green*+BUSH 3.

A children's game (much played in primary school) in which a player forfeits all valuables on his person if he does not have a piece of green bush upon him when another player calls the phrase.

1958 JC StC, Green bushit. (1961 Current. FGC.)

GREEN CALALU sb; cf species name. A commonly cultivated variety of CALALU, finer than the wild, red-stemmed kinds.

1814 Lunan 1 142, Calalu..*Amaranthus viridis*. Green. 1864 Grisebach 782, Green Calalu. 1914 Fawcett 131, *Amarantus viridis*..Common Garden Calalu, Green Calalu, Spinach. 1954 *WIMJ* 28.

GREEN CORN sb. See quot. *BA BL T*

1913 Harris 30, Maize..The young cobs or ears, while still tender and succulent..are known as 'sweet corn', or 'sugar corn' and are roasted and eaten. The matured cobs, before the seeds get dry and hard, are also gathered and sold in the markets as 'green corn' and in this state they are boiled and eaten.

GREEN EBONY sb.

1. Another name for JAMAICA EBONY (*Brya ebenus*), alluding to the colour of the wood.

1864 Grisebach 783, Green or West Indian Ebony: *Brya Ebenus*.

2. The shrub *Securinega acidoton*.

1920 Fawcett 266–7, *S. acidoton*..Green Ebony..'the whole plant has a good deal of the appearance of a young Ebony' (Browne).

GREENGAGE sb dial; <*greengage* (without much appropriateness) emphasizing 'green'. In StAnn: said to be what is called BACKRA CABBAGE in Clarendon.

1940 HPJ.

GREENGAGE CHOCHO sb dial. A local variety of the CHOCHO.

1952 FGC StAnn.

GREEN GAULIN sb; <*green*+GAULIN. The Little Green Heron.

1936 Bond 25, *Butorides virescens*..Gaulin; Little Gaulin; Least Pond Gaulin; Green Gaulin; etc. 1955 Taylor 68, The Little Green Heron..is also known as the Green Gaulin or Crab-catcher..It is an abundant bird and is present on nearly every pond, swamp or river in Jamaica.

GREEN GUANA sb dial. A bright green lizard (which can change its colour to dark brown) with a saw-toothed process down its back and tail (*Anolis garmani*). Also called GREEN LIZARD.

1851 Gosse 142, see VENUS LIZARD. 1952 FCC StE, StT/griin gwáana/.

GREENHEART (TREE) sb; so called from colour of wood. s ~ FIDDLEWOOD. *BL G*

1. The tree *Zizyphus chloroxylon* and its wood, also called COGWOOD.

1756 Browne 187, The Greenheart..This tree is common in many parts of the mountains, and rises by a strong branched trunk to a very considerable height; the inward bark is of a light blood colour, and incloses a strong greenish timber within the sap. 1807 Renny 85, Many of them..of an enormous size..; pigeon-wood, greenheart, braziletto. 1926 Fawcett 64, *Z. Chloroxylon*.. Cogwood, Greenheart.

2. The tree *Colubrina ferruginosa* and its wood; see quot 1926. (It is of the same family as 1.)

1864 Grisebach 784, Greenheart: *Colubrina ferruginosa*. 1926 Fawcett 68, *C. ferruginosa*..Greenheart, Snake Wood, Black Velvet, Wild or Mountain Ebony.

3. The tree *Sloanea jamaicensis* and its wood; see quot 1941.

1886 Hooper 30, Greenheart, *Sloanea jamaicensis*. 1941 Swabey 21, Greenheart—(Breakaxe, Ironwood, Lignum durum)..The heartwood is very dark in colour, readily distinguished from the sap wood.

GREEN HUMMING-BIRD sb obs.

1. An old and erroneous name for the bird *Todus viridis*, which is still often mistaken for a humming-bird. The GREEN TODY.

1725 Sloane 306–7, Rubecula viridis elegantissima.. Green Sparrow, or, Green-humming Bird. [Description and picture given.] [1756 Browne 476, Todus I. *Viridis, pectore rubro, rostro recto*. This little bird is hardly larger than the green Humming-bird. (Browne refers to the passage from Sloane, but does not seem to recognize that he identified the two names—Browne speaks of the green humming-bird as if it were separate, perh thinking of the Vervain humming-bird.)]

GREEN HUNTER CHUB sb ichth obs. A fish; see quot.

1854–5 *TJSA* 1 142, Serranus coronatus—green hunter chub.

GREEN JACK sb. A variety of the Jack fish; see quots.

1854–5 *TJSA* 1 143, Caranx Bartolomæi—green Jack. 1892 Cockrell list, *Caranx bartholomæi*, green jack. 1952 FGC StAnn, StE, StJ, StT /griin jak/.

GREEN-LEAF YAM sb dial. A variety of yam having especially green leaves. *G*

1952 FGC StJ.

GREEN LIZARD sb; cf *DAE, DA* 1709→ applied to *Anolis caroliniensis.*

1. The larger green lizard, also called GREEN GUANA (or merely GUANA), which can change its colour to dark brown (*Anolis garmani*). *BA*

[1835 Senior 80, The *large green* species..is sometimes designated the '*chamelion lizard*'.] 1868 *TRSAA* I 65, Annancey and Green-Lizard..Annancey say to Green-lizard..[etc.]. 1940 Lynn-Grant 83, Green Lizard, 'Guana. *Anolis garmani.*

2. The smaller green lizard; it too can turn brown. See quot. *BA T*

1835 Senior 80, The small green lizard..sometimes designated the 'chamelion lizard'. 1940 Lynn-Grant 85, *Anolis grahami grahami*..'Small green lizard'.

3. Transf. A deceitful person or traitor, because he changes colour.

1954 LeP Kgn, Green-lizad, deceitful person. 1958 DeC gen /griin lizad/ a traitor, a turncoat.

GREEN MANGO sb arch or obs; cf BLACK MANGO, YELLOW MANGO.

1837 Macfadyen 222, 4. Green kidney-shaped Mango, a fruit of a luscious sweetness.

GREEN PARROT (FISH) sb. A green-coloured variety of the PARROT fish.

1756 Browne 447, Mormyra 4..The green Parrot-fish of Catesb[y]..All these fishes are frequent in the seas about Jamaica, and pretty constant in their colours, which induced me to look upon them as different species. 1952 Smith in *NHN* 201, *Sparisoma viride*, or Green parrot-fish, is likewise an attractive creature..Colour of specimen observed: The ground colour was greenish-blue.. [etc.]. 1952 FGC StE /griin párat/.

GREEN PEA-SHELL sb obs.

1756 Browne 399, Nerita 17. Minima viridis, quandoque variegata. The small green nerite, commonly called the green Pea-shell.

GREEN SEA-EGG sb. The common sea-urchin *Toxopneuste variegatus*, green, with short spines.

1960 Institute of Ja exhibit. Green sea-egg. (Seen by FGC.)

GREEN-SEED COTTON sb obs exc hist; *DAE* 1775 *green-seeded cotton.* A type of cotton, *Gossypium hirsutum*(?); see quot.

1793 Edwards II 268–9, the cotton-wool..consists of two distinct kinds, known to the planters by the names of Green-seed Cotton, and Shrub Cotton..Green-seed cotton is of two species; of one of which the wool is so firmly attached to the seed, that no method has hitherto been found of separating them, except by the hand.. The other sort has larger seeds, of a duller green than the former. 1814 Lunan I 239–40.

GREEN-SKIN MANGO sb. Another name for the BLACK MANGO; its skin remains mostly green even when ripe. *G*

1952 FGC StE, StJ /griin-skin manggo/.

GREEN SPARROW sb obs. An old name for the bird *Todus viridis.*

1725 Sloane II 306–7, see GREEN HUMMING-BIRD. [1743–51 Edwards t 221, quoted in 1756 Browne 476.]

GREEN-STALK (COCO) sb dial. A variety of coco that has a bright green stalk.

1929 Beckwith 17, The 'Sally' and 'Minty' and the 'Green 'talk', named for its vivid green stalk. 1952 FGC StM /griin-staak/ coco is white, soft.

GREEN TODY sb ornith; transl of Lat name. *OED tody* 1773→. The bird *Todus viridis*; more often called ROBIN (REDBREAST).

1847 Gosse 72, Green Tody. 1956 Jeffrey-Smith 28–30

GREEN WITHE /gríin wís/ sb; *OED* 1725→. The leafless climbing orchid (*Vanilla claviculata*), valued for medicinal properties; see quots.

1696 Sloane 198, Cereo affinis scandens..caule..glabro succulento saturate viridi. *Green With.* 1707 Sloane cxix, She went into the Country after she had lost the use of her Limbs. She recovered them in some measure, by degrees, with the help of the *Green With*, and some Salves, and came to her perfect health. 1854–5 *TJSA* I 67, Green Wythe. 1910 Fawcett 17, Greenwithe. 1952 FGC Tre /gríin-wís/ a 6-sided running cactus; bake it, 'queeze out water, mix with rum and rub on for pain.

greng-greng sb dial; var of *kreng-kreng.* A device above a fireplace for curing meat; more commonly *kreng-kreng.*

1956 LeP StE (Eld) /greng-greng/ brick-work over fire for curing meat.

GREY-BELLY RAT sb dial; cf BITE-AND-BLOW. Fig: One who does things surreptitiously.

1943 *GL* StT, Grey Belly rat, doing things in the quiet.

GREY-BO, GREY-BOO sb dial; <*grey*+ -*bo.* An albino negro—see QUAW 3. s.

1958 DeC 27 /grie-buu/ a name for an albino Negro.

GREY BOZA sb dial; <*grey* +perh <Sp *bozal*, a negro recently come from Africa, one who speaks Spanish badly, a stupid or torpid person (Santamaría). Cf also, however, the US *bozo.*

1958 DeC StT /grie bóuza/ an albino Negro (derogatory).

GREY CRESTED GAULIN sb ornith obs. An egret or heron not clearly identified: prob the Great Blue Heron (*Ardea herodias*).

1756 Browne 478, Ardea 1..The grey crested Gaulding. This bird is one of the largest of the tribe in Jamaica: the greatest part of the head is black; but the crown, and a little space about the eyes, is white; and the rest of the body of an even grey colour.

GREY GRUNT sb. A fish of the genus *Hæmulon*, perh *H. macrostomum* or *H. plumieri.*

1725 Sloane 290, *The Gray-Grunt.* This was seven inches long..It was all colour'd over with yellow and white Lines, running from Head to Tail. 1952 FGC StC, StE /gríe grónt/.

GREY JANE, GREY JOE sb dial; <*grey* +personal name; cf GREY-BO, GREY BOZA.

1958 DeC Tre /grie juo/ derogatory term for albino Negro. 1959 DeC Han /grie jien/ an albino Negro.

GREY JUMPER sb. A spider; see quot. Cf BLACK JUMPER.

1756 Browne 419, Aranea 3..The grey Jumper. This is an elegant, active, little spider; but seldom spins a web, depending chiefly on its agility in catching its prey. It is very frequent about the houses in Kingston.

GREY LIZARD sb obs. A lizard, prob *Anolis lineatopus*—cf 1940 Lynn-Grant 91, '*A. lineatopus coxi*..Male not brown, but definitely a gray lizard'.

1725 Sloane 333, Lacertus cinereus minor..*The least light Brown*, or, *Grey Lizard.*

GREY MAHOE sb. A variety of the BLUE MAHOE.

1864 Grisebach 785, Grey Mahoe: *Paritium elatum*, var. *macrocarpum.*

GREY MOUNTAIN-SANDERS sb. A tree of uncertain identity: see quot.

1881 Harrison in *Handbook* 142, Grey Mountain Sanders. (Bucida ——?). This is a very good timber, saws readily makes a fine board, darker in color than the yellow sanders and not so satin-like in appearance but takes a fine polish.

GREY NICKER (or **NIKAL**) sb; <*grey*+NICKER. The plant *Cæsalpinia bonducella* and its ash-coloured fruit, a hard seed with which boys play games. It is also used medicinally. The folk pronunc is always /níkal/.

1952 FGC Han /níkal/ one yellow is worth ten grey ones. 1953 *WIMJ* 239, Although grey nicker is considered superior, the seeds of both species are dried and ground and used like coffee to prepare a drink which is thought useful for kidney trouble, diabetes and high blood pressure.

GREY-PEOPLE sb dial; cf GREY-BO, GREY JANE, GREY JOE, GREY PUSS.

1958 DeC Port /grie piipl/ polite name for albino Negroes.

GREY PETCHARY sb; <*grey*+PETCHARY. The bird *Tyrannus dominicensis*; see quots.

1847 Gosse 170, It is along the sea-side savannas and pastures, and among the adjacent hills and valleys, that the migratory flocks of the Grey Petchary swarm at the beginning of September. 1956 Jeffrey-Smith 40, Generally the term petchary is limited to the migrant grey petchary (*Tyrannus dominicensis*) which arrives in the spring and leaves us at the end of September. . The black ear coverts, the greyer shading on the breast, the dark grey head all mark the grey petchary.

GREY PLOVER sb; *OED* identifies as *Squatarola helvetica*. See quots.

1725 Sloane 318, *Pluvialis viridis*. . The Grey-Plover. So call'd in Jamaica by the Inhabitants. 1955 Taylor 69, Other kinds pass through as migrants, notably the Black-bellied or Grey Plover (*Squatarola squatarola*).

GREY PUSS sb dial; <*grey*+PUSS.

1958 DeC Tre /grie pus/ derogatory term for an albino Negro.

GREY SNAKE sb; cf *OED*. The snake *Alsophis ater*.

1863 Wood *Nat. Hist.* III 134 (*OED*), The Grey Snake of Jamaica (*Dromicus ater*).

GREY SNAPPER sb. A variety (or more than one) of the SNAPPER fish; see quot 1835. *G*

1835 Madden II 84, The gray snapper (*Coracinus fuscus*) is occasionally poisonous. 1952 FGC Port /gríe snápa/ mutton snapper—grow big; StAnn, Grey snapper is slow poison if you eat it—cook it, try it with a gold ring; StC /gríe snapa/ bigger than black snapper; StJ; StM, same as /manggro snapa/.

GREY-WHITE NIGGER sb dial; an insulting term.

1954 LeP StAnn, Grey-white nigger—mulatto.

gried-aian sb dial; irreg pronunc of *gridiron*; perh infl by *grate*?

1958 DeC StAnd /gried-aian/ the flat iron sheet used for making bammy (presumably from *gridiron*, but the vowel here is certainly /ie/).

GRI-GRI sb dial rare; etym uncert: perh vaguely conn with *gree-gree*, fetish (*OED*), but more likely phonosymbolic, especially as coupled with GRA-GRA. The first and lesser of two unpleasant things, of which GRA-GRA is the second. (GRI-GRI may be the cause or merely the forerunner of GRA-GRA.)

1925 Beckwith 42, see GRA-GRA.

GRINDER sb dial; by folk-etym < /grain/, folk pronunc of *groyne*. A groyne (such as those built to keep rivers in their channels, to cause deposition of sand along the seashore, etc.).

1942 HPJ.

GRINDING-CATTLE sb obs. The cattle used in turning the mill in early manufacture of sugar.

1679 Trapham 26, Commodious Stables for the grinding Cattle, lodging for the Over-seer.

GRING-GRING sb dial; var of *kreng-kreng*, *grang-grang*, etc.

1942 HPJ, Gring-gring, bramble?

GRIP BASKET sb dial. *G*

1959 DeC West /grip baskit/ a flat straw basket carried at the side like a grip; sometimes this has rigid reinforcement so that it looks like a grip, sometimes it is merely the flat BANKRA.

GRIPE-WEED sb dial; <*gripe* (*OED sb*[1] 2) +*weed*. The small wild plant *Phyllanthus niruri*, also called CARRY-ME-SEED, used in a 'bush tea'.

1943 *NHN* II 6, Gripe weed, *Phyllanthus niruri*. 1952 FGC Man, Gripe-weed, has little balls under the leaf.

GRIT sb dial or tech; cf *OED grit sb*[2].

1959 DeC West /grit/ the coarse part of the washed and wrung cassava which remains in the sieve, as opposed to the flour which passes through the sieve.

GRITTY-GRITTY adj dial; iterative <*gritty*. Rough or covered with bumps. *G*

1957 DeC StAnd, You can tell a lemon from a lime because the lemon skin is more /griti-griti/.

GROANING vbl sb dial cant. In Revival and similar cults: The heavy sucking in and expulsion of breath during dancing—cf also LABOUR. *G*

1953 Moore 70.

gro-gro parat sb dial; prob <GRUGROO+*parrot*. A variety of the parrot fish that is not thought well of.

1952 FGC StC /gro-gro parat/ is darkish.

GRO'L /gruol/? vb dial; <*growl*. An irregular dial pronunc; the normal form is /groul/.

1912 McK *Ballads* gloss, Gro'l: growl.

gron dov, groun dov see GROUND DOVE.

grong and cpds see GROUND and cpds.

grong-gad sb dial; <GROUND+*god*.

1. A stone; stones.

1943 *GL* Kgn, Grung-gad, stones; Port, Grungad, stone; StAnd, Grung gawd, rock stones; StE, Groundgod, a stone. 1955 FGC Man /grong-gad/ any stone.

2. See quot.

1943 *GL* Kgn, Grung gad, a scare-crow.

grong-tel-him-wod phr dial; for *ground-told-him-words*. A phrase used by one explaining some action or change of mind: he has heard a voice from the ground (i.e. from the spirit of an ancestor or dead relative).

1943 *GL* StM, Grung-tell-him-wud—timely advised.

GROS MICHEL BANANA /gruos, gros, gras, +míchel, máikal/ sb; <Fr *gros Michel*, big Michael. A favourite variety of banana, large and of fine flavour. Also called JAMAICAN, MARTINIQUE, POUYAT and WHITEHOUSE BANANA.

1913 Fawcett 16, see MARTINIQUE BANANA. 1952 FGC Port, StAnn, StM, StT, Tre, etc. 1954 *FG* 288, The *Gros Michel* variety of bananas is highly susceptible to Leaf Spot disease. 1957 *FFM* 337, The Gros Michel variety of banana. . was introduced from Martinique by the French botanist Jean François Pouyat around 1835 and first planted at his StAndrew coffee plantation Belle Air. . until as late as the nineties the Gros Michel banana was commonly called *Martnick* by the country people of Jamaica. *BA T*

GROSS sb dial, perh an individualism; <*gross*, a mass. A large number of fish swimming together; a school. cf *OED* sb[1] B+5.

1952 FGC StAnn /grupa ron in a gruos/ *Groupers go in schools.*

GROUND /grong, groun/ sb chiefly dial; *OED* 10b *Obs.*→1733, but cf *EDD*—common in Engl. dial, esp SW, W, N & Scotl. A field or piece of cultivated land; used with or without an article; sometimes for the earlier NEGRO-~, PROVISION-~, etc. *BA G N*

1873 Rampini 90, The only labour which is cheerfully performed by the negro in Jamaica is that which he bestows on his own 'provision ground'. Of these 'grounds' each negro has at least one. 1942 Astley Clerk in HPJ, Groun, Grung..the country people's provision grounds. 1943 *GL* Tre, Grong, cultivation. 1950 Pioneer 33, Bredda Puss wasa tie up him food fe leff him grung goh home. 1954 LeP Kgn, Ground—small holding cultivated by owner. 1956 Mc Man /mi a go a grong nou/ *I am going to (my) field now*; StE /foul liiv fi grong/ *Fowl set off for his field.*

GROUND /groun/ vb dial; <*ground* past pple of *grind*, by overcorrection or occasional variation: /grain/ is the regular vb. *G*

1952 FGC StT [Preparing chocolate:] Pick pods, take out seeds, dry and parch and ground them.

GROUND ALTAR sb dial cant. An 'altar' marked or placed on the ground in POCOMANIA ceremonies.

1953 Moore 95–6, Ground altar: An area at least 36 feet across, level. In centre, a triangular stone, the 'power key'. A chicken is sacrificed and its blood poured upon, around, and under the stone; a black cloth is placed over, and a white cloth on top of that. The altar is 3 concentric circles scratched into the earth; the inmost represents God the Father, the second God the Son, the third God the Holy Ghost. In the circles are placed candles, flowers, fruits (by Revival cults, also a Bible).

GROUND ANANCY sb dial; <*ground*+ ANANCY. The type of spider which lives on or in the ground; the ref appears to be to *Latrodectus*, the BROWN WIDOW and Black Widow.

1952 FGC Port /gróng anánsi/ dangerous: brown bad, black worse.

GROUND BASKET sb dial; <GROUND+ *basket*. A large round basket that is taken to one's GROUND to bring out GROUND PROVISIONS. Cf BONE-BASKET. *BA G*

1952 FGC StE /groun-baskit/ frame is of rose-apple or hoop-wis, other parts of /bambu/; Tre /grong-baskit/ made of hook.

GROUND-CALALU sb dial. Cultivated CALALU, grown in one's GROUND, as opposed to the common wild kinds.

1952 FGC StE /gròng kalalú/.

GROUND-CLOTHES sb dial; <GROUND+ *clothes*. Old, ragged clothes such as are only fit to be worn while working in one's GROUND.

1958 DeC StT /groung-kluoz/ ragged old clothes.

GROUND-COCO sb.

1. Some variety of *Colocasia esculenta*: INDIAN KALE. (Here *ground-* prob contrasts with *tree-*, i.e. cacao.) Obs.

1740 Importance 30, There is also the Ground-cocoa, which grows like Potatoes, with a broad Leaf, in the shape of a Heart; this is called Callaloe, and is a pleasant Sauce to salt Meat.

2. *Eulophia alta.*

1910 Fawcett 113, *E. alta*..Ground Coco, Wild Coco. In wet clayey soil in shady places..Leaves very long, lanceolate [etc.].

GROUND DOVE sb; cf *OED* 1792→. The smallest of the Jamaican doves, which feeds and is usually seen on the ground: *Columbigallina passerina.* In folk belief it is a DUPPY BIRD. *BA BL G N T*

1679 Trapham 67, Pigeons of various sorts, Turtle Doves, ground Doves, Parrats, Parreketoes. 1725 Sloane 305, Turtur minimus guttatus..*A Ground Dove.* They feed on the Ground as Partridges. 1840 Chamberlaine 19. 1952 FGC Han, StAnn, StT /groun dov/; StAnd /gron dov/.

GROUND-FRUIT sb obs. Evid =GROUND PROVISIONS. (Cf BREADFRUIT 2.)

1788 Marsden 19, they..raise more ground-fruit, bread-fruit, and vegetables.

GROUND-GOD see *grong-gad.*

GROUND-HUT sb dial. A shelter at a provision ground.

1943 *GL* Kgn, Padda, a peasants ground-hut.

GROUND ITCH /groun ich, grong~, gron~/ sb; *OED* 1823 only, *DAE, DA* 1857. An affliction formerly very prevalent in which the soles of the feet (or in animals the hooves) become sore and itch very much. It is now understood to be the effect of the hookworm organism entering the foot. *BA G N*

1823 Roughley 130, Mules..with soft pervious hoofs, which often split, and contain deep-seated crab-yaws and ground-itch. *Ibid* 191, see GROUND-ITCHED. 1952 FGC Han /groun ich/ on foot-bottom; Port, Use Maroon weed against ground itch; StAnd /gróngich/; Tre /gronich/. 1959 Mrs Robinson UCWI Prev Med, Ground-itch, the beginning of hookworm, the sore spot at which the organism entered the foot.

GROUND-ITCHED adj; <GROUND-ITCH+ *-ed*[2] (*OED*). Affected by ground-itch.

1823 Roughley 191, Little trash should be permitted to lie about the mill-yard..to make swampy, spungy foot-passages, impeding the carriers, and giving them tender and ground-itched feet.

GROUND IVY sb obs. An unidentified plant.

1740 Importance 44, The Indian Arrow Root, Ground-Ivy and China Root are some of them [*sc*, plants used in 'teas'].

GROUND JACK sb. A variety of the Jack fish which stays close to the sea bottom. See quot.

1851 Gosse 290–1, These bold and voracious fishes are members of the great Mackarel family: they are distinguished as Buntung Jack, Round-headed, or Ground Jack, and Cavally Jack.

GROUND LIZARD /gróng lízad/ sb; *OED* 1792→. The lizard *Ameiva dorsalis*, that lives in the ground and remains on the ground (not climbing trees). *BA G T*

1756 Browne 462, Lacerta 2..The large spotted Ground Lizard..Lacerta 4..The small Ground Lizard. 1940 Lynn-Grant 109–11, Ground lizard..It emerges from its burrow after the sun has warmed the ground around 8 or 9 A.M.; retires during the heat of the day and reappears for a few hours in mid-afternoon..A friendly, interesting animal that well repays watching. 1952 FGC Man, StAnd, StE /grong lizad/.

GROUND ORCHID sb. The kind of orchid that grows on the ground: not arboreal. *BA T*

1873 Rampini 78, We found the summit of the hill to be an almost level plateau, covered with grass, and ground orchids, and wild starch.

GROUND-PROVISIONS sb chiefly dial; also in Grenada, St Lucia, Tobago, *BA BL G N T*; *OED* 1827 only. The crops of starch-foods (yam, coco, sweet potato, cassava, etc.) that are raised in a GROUND.

1808 Stewart 100, A very excellent law..exists here relative to ground provisions (as they are called), or roots, by which all estates and other settlements are required to have ten acres of such provisions for every hundred negroes..These roots, or ground provisions, are so productive (particularly the yam), that the constant labour of one negro would almost be competent to feed fifty. 1943 *GL* Port, Grung-bikkle—Ground provisions.

GROUND-RAT sb dial. Presumably a rat which stays on or in the ground, but this may represent GROUND. *G*

1924 Beckwith 181 [Story:] Ground-lizard and Ground-rat were two friends.

GROUND-SHAKE, GROUND-SHAKING sb dial. An earthquake.

1838 Kelly 43, The Negroes call the earthquake 'ground-shake'. 1907 Jekyll 111, He commence to tell her mother that him hear a great rolling like groun' shaking while ago outside. *Ibid* 113, groun' shaking, earthquake.

GROUND SWITCH sb obs; the sense of 'ground' is not clear, but cf GROUND. See quot.

1725 Sloane 383, This is call'd Lance-wood, and of the Succors of it are made, what are call'd in Jamaica Ground Switches for whipping the Negroes..Mr Barham in MS.

GROUND TAMARIND sb dial. The small plant *Desmanthus virgatus*, which has leaves similar to those of the tamarind, and grows close or down to the ground.

1920 Fawcett 131–2, *D. virgatus*..Ground Tamarind.. *Shrub* erect, 2–4(–6) ft. high, or branches diffuse or prostrate..*Pinnæ* 2–5(–7) pairs.

GROUND-TELL-HIM-WORDS see GRUNG-TELL-HIM-WUD.

GROUND-THUNDER sb dial.

1. Thunder that seems to roll heavily or low along the ground.

1907 Jekyll 110, He [Tiger] nyam until he unrestful an' come his voice after was like groun' t'under.

2. Fig. See quot.

1943 *GL* Kgn, Grund tunda, some-one who grows very slowly.

GROUND-VICTUALS /grong-bikl/ sb dial. Food from the provision ground.

1943 *GL* Port, Grung-bikkle, ground provisions.

GROUND-WORKER sb dial; GROUND + *worker*. A cultivator.

1954 LeP Port /grong-worka/ man who makes a living by growing and selling market crops.

GROUPER /grúpa/ sb; 1679 1756 grooper, 1873→ grouper; <Pg *garoupa*, fish of this kind, prob of Cariban origin (cf Carib *garupu*, clay dish or saucepan); cf also Sp (Mex, S Cal) *garopa* for a similar fish; *OED* 1697→. Certain food fish of the genus *Epinephelus*, related to the Hamlets and Rock-fish. *BA BL G N T*

1679 Trapham 59, Rock fish, Stone bass, Cavallies, Groopers, Jacks, Grunts [etc.]. 1756 Browne 448, Corocinus 2..The Grooper. 1873 Rampini 171, Much more quaint lore about..the grouper, the black snapper.. and the parrot-fish, did we glean from our negro boatmen. 1952 Smith in *NHN* 187, A large grouper, *Epinephelus striatus*.

GROUT sb dial; cf *OED grout sb*[1] 4, sediment, dregs, lees, grounds.

1. The coarse waste material left after cassava has been sieved and the flour separated.

1958 DeC Han /grout/.

2. See quot; the connection in meaning with the basic sense is probably through contrast between the usable part of the plant (root) and the waste part.

1959 DeC West /grout/ the green, above-ground portion of any food-bearing plant.

groutn sb dial; in some way conn with *grout*, thin fluid mortar (*OED sb*[2]) or the corresponding verb (*OED v*[1]) to fill up with thin mortar, either as <*grouting*, pple, or as <*grout* + *-n* suffix[1]. Coarse river sand (gravel) used to mix with cement.

1956 Mc StAnd /gróutn/.

GROWING STAKE, ~ STICK, GROW-STAKE, ~-STICK sb chiefly dial.

Any of several fast-growing trees which are planted as fence-stakes, take root quickly, and form live posts. Trees favoured for this use are birch, maiden plum, maranga, plum, Spanish machete, and others. Also called GROW-POST, perh GROW-QUICK, and QUICK-STICK. Local preference leads to use of the term specifically for one or another plant: see quots.

1926 Fawcett 416–18, *Oreopanax..capitatum*..Woman Wood, Threefingered Jack, Growing Stick. 1949 Forbes 67, Glyricidia, 'Grow Quick' to the natives. [Doubtful—perh represents 'Grow-stick' or 'Quick-stick'.] 1952 FGC Port, Grow stake [*Gliricidia sepium*], called Moses-weed in Kingston; StAnd, Growing stake [*G. sepium*], St Vincent; StAnn, Growin' stake /gro-in stik/ plum used for this; StM, Growin' stake used for fence, quick-stick too; StT, Grow stake, for example, maiden-plum, birch, never-dead [*Erythrina velutina*]; Tre, Growing stake, use never-die /pánya-màshiet/. 1955 *WIMJ* 158, *Gliricidia sepium*..Quick stick; Grow Stick, Growing Stake; Maranga.

GROW-POST sb dial. = GROW-STAKE.

1926 Fawcett 16–17, Hog Plum..The branches grow readily when planted in the ground, and are much used in this way for fence-posts..Spanish Plum..The branches are used like the former species as 'grow posts'.

GROW UP vb phr dial; *grow* used causatively. To rear (a child, etc.). *G*

1907 Jekyll 79, The father died, so the mother grow them up herself.

GRUBBER BROAD-HEAD sb. A fish: see quot.

1892 Cockrell list, Grubber broad-head, *Stolephorus productus*.

GRUDGE /groj/ vb dial; cf *OED* 3 →a 1661. To envy, be jealous of (someone). (The thing about which one is envious is not expressed as direct object.) *BA BL G T*

1924 Beckwith 152, De girl was so pretty, one of de men dat in de vessel grudge Jack an' fling Jack overboard. c 1948 *Calypso Tunes*, see BRUCKINS. 1956 Mc Port /yu hav sonting, hi groj yu fo it/.

GRUDGEFUL /grójful/ adj and sb dial; cf *OED*: the sense-development of this adj parallels that of GRUDGE. *BA BL*

A. adj: Envious. *G*

1929 Beckwith 28, see CUT-EYE BEAN. 1951 Murray 22 [Song:] But a grudgeful dem grudgeful kill Sammy. [*But it is because they were envious that Sammy was killed.*] 1956 Mc Port, Jealous, envious. /im grojful/.

B. sb: Envy, jealousy.

1950 Pioneer 18, De one deggeh goat me have you teck grudgeful kill him. [*The only goat I have, you become envious and kill it!*] *Ibid* 35, Same time grudgeful start grow eena Anancy an him study a way how fe mash up Wasp life.

C. sb: Abbr for MARY GRUDGEFUL.

GRUGROO adj dial; etym unknown—perh African. Valueless, worthless.

1943 *GL* StE, Grugroo, invaluable [*sic*].

GRUGUDO sb dial; etym uncert: perh one of the nicknames produced by 'word-play' from GROUND-DOVE, though the first part may also be echoic. The GROUND-DOVE.

1943 *GL* StE, Grugudo—ground-dove.

GRUNG see GROUND.

GRUNG TUNDA see GROUND-THUNDER.

GRUNT sb; *OED* 1713→. Certain food fish esp of the genus *Hæmulon* which make a grunting noise when caught. See also BLACK-TAIL~, GREY~, RED-MOUTH~, YELLOW~. *BA BL G N*

1679 Trapham 65, Groopers, Jacks, Grunts, Porgoes. 1952 FGC Port, StE, StM, StT, West, etc. /gront/.

GU see GO.

GUACO (BUSH) /gwáako, gwáaku, kwáako, kwáaku/ sb; < Sp (Cuba, etc.) *guaco*, plants of genus *Mikania*, of Arawakan origin (Roig y Mesa, Pichardo). By folk-etym this has also become QUACO BUSH. Cf *OED* 1822–34→ for the substance extracted from the plant. Any of several wild plants of the genus *Mikania*, thought to have medicinal properties: see quots.

1854–5 *TJSA* I 64, Guaco. Mikania Guaco. Mexican Guaco. Guaco scandens. 1927 Beckwith 25, Quaco-bush. *Mikania*—. 'Gwaco.' For diarrhoea, grind the leaf, add salt. 1943 *GL* Tre, Guaka, a wild green bush, which has a strong smell, and is often used to clean the floor. 1952 FGC Han, StT /gwáako/; Han, StAnd, StC, StM /gwáaku/; Port, StT, Tre /kwáako/; StE /kwáaku/. 1953 *WIMJ* 242, *Mikania* spp. Guaco or Gwaco Bush..is used as a cold remedy and a decoction of the leaves is also used to bathe the skin for itch.

GUAKA see prec.

GUANGO /gwánggo, gwánggu/ sb; < Amer Sp *guango*, the trees *Samanea saman* and *Albizzia lebbek*, prob < Quichua *huáncupa*, rope, cord (Santamaría). *ODS* has only quot 1871 in altogether diff sense. The large shade-tree *Samanea saman*, and its pods, which are eaten by cattle. *N*

1886 Hooper 31, Guango, Pithecolobium (Inga) saman. 1920 Fawcett 152, *Enterolobium..saman*..Guango. 1941 Swabey 21, Guango—(Saman, Rain Tree). *Samanea saman*..The heartwood is of a distinctive red colour when freshly cut but assumes a dark chocolate brown tone when seasoned..It is ornamental and makes an extremely attractive furniture wood. 1942 Bennett 41, De Bull dah li-dung undah Neat' wan gwangu tree. 1952 FGC StC, StM, StT /gwánggu/; Port, StAnd, StT /gwángoo/.

GUARD /gyaad/ sb dial. *G*

1. A 'magic' object placed in or by a planted field as a protection against thieves: it threatens the thief with reprisal by evil spirits. Formerly called a PUNTEE.

1928 Beckwith 10, There is no doubt that the belief in 'guards' against theft has been encouraged by the whites as a means of protecting crops.

2. Any object or combination of objects worn by or kept near a person to ward off evil spirits. See quots. *BL*

1929 Beckwith 71, Before the coffin is carried out of the yard a bereaved wife or husband should put on a 'guard' of a large square of black cloth with a white cross marked upon it with chalk, and should wear this for four or five months. *Ibid* 88, A person born with a caul has this power to see duppies without their harming him, although some say the faculty can be removed by wrapping up a piece of the caul in black ribbon and keeping it as a 'guard'. *Ibid* 112, A modern guard consists in four padlocks, one for each corner of the house. 1952 FGC StAnd, Get a /gyaad/ to wear round neck. 1953 Moore 54, Guard, Anything which protects from evil spirits—e.g. crucifixes, rings, charm-medals.

GUARDER /gyaada/ sb dial; <*guard* (cf GUARD-FISH) + *-er*. = GUARD-FISH.

1942 HPJ, Garda: Garfish..St Thomas.

GUARD-FISH /gyáad-físh/ sb dial; by folk-etym <*gar-fish*. Any of the fish with long, beak-like jaws (such as LONG-JAW, PIPER, etc.), with which (as the understanding is) they 'guard' themselves. *N*

1892 Cockrell list, Guard-fish, *Tylosurus gladius*. 1952 FGC Port, StC, StT, West /gyáad-físh/.

GUARK see *goyaak*.

GUATEMALA INDIGO sb obs.

1774 Long III 675, There are three species of it, the common, the *guatimala*, and the wild..the wild indigo is preferable to either.

GUBGUB PEAS sb dial; cf *DA goober* 1834→; 'peas' is sing/plur. The peanut. (*Gub-gub* has never had much currency in Jamaica, however; far more current is PINDAR and *peanut* the common term.)

[1774 Long III 788, Pindals, or ground-nuts..They are nourishing, and often given as food to Negroes on voyages from Guiney, where they pass under the name of *gubagubs*.] 1924 Beckwith 4, A man plant a big field of gub-gub peas. [Note:] Tall bush peas, one of the commonest and most prized of Jamaica crop [*sic*]. [Either the name has been transferred to GUNGU PEAS, or Beckwith has confused them.]

GUDO-GUDO sb dial; etym unknown, but prob African. Cf CULLABUNKA, *bongka*.

1943 *GL* Clar, Gudo-gudo, the leafstalk of a kind of palm.

GUGLIT see GOGLET.

GUG-NUT sb dial; by word-play from *coconut*?

1942 HPJ, Gug-nut: said to be another name for the nut of the *abbi* Palm. [I.e. ABBAY.]

GUI see GWINE.

GUINEA BIRD sb obs; cf *OED* 1836. A negro imported from Africa (in contrast to a CREOLE). Transf from the name of an actual bird, the guinea-hen, this usage was disdainful. *BA G*

1774 Long II 410, The Creole Blacks..hold the Africans in the utmost contempt, stiling them, 'salt-water Negroes', and 'Guiney birds'.

GUINEA-CHICK sb chiefly dial; also attrib.

1. A guinea-hen or -fowl; this is a common term in Jamaica, though 'guinea-hen' is more frequent in compounds.

1952 FGC StAnd, StAnn, StE, StT /gíni chík/ lay plenty egg in bush; more watchful than /daag/.

2. Attrib, in allusion to the black-and-white chequered or speckled plumage of the guinea-chick: see quots.

1952 FGC StAnn, One kind of conger-eel has guinea-chick colour; guinea-chick lobster favour guinea-chick.

GUINEA-CHICK LOBSTER, GUINEA-HEN LOBSTER sb dial; <GUINEA-CHICK or -HEN + LOBSTER. A variety of sea crayfish that is much speckled, like the guinea-hen (or guinea-chick).

1952 FGC StAnn /gínichik lápsta/ has spots—favour guinea-chick; Port, StC, StJ, StM, West /gíni(h)èn lápsta/ small, speckle, cries like a guinea-hen when you catch it.

GUINEA-CORN GRUNT sb dial; <*guinea-corn* + GRUNT. A variety of the GRUNT fish which has a mottled colour-pattern resembling guinea-corn.

1952 FGC StE.

GUINEA-CORN YAWS sb dial obs. One of the types of YAWS in which the skin became mottled, therefore resembling guinea-corn.

1820 Thomson 83, There are several varieties in the appearance of the eruption for which the negroes have distinct names, as the *watery yaws, ring-worm yaws, Guinea corn yaws.* The causes of these different shapes are obscure.

GUINEA-GRASS sb. A grass (*Panicum maximum*) introduced from Africa or 'Guinea': see quot 1834. *BA G N*

1756 Browne 366, Holcus 2..Guinea Grass. This plant.. is frequently cultivated in Jamaica, to supply their stabled and working cattle with food. 1834 *Sketch Book* ii 9, A very different result attended the accidental introduction of *Guinea-grass* into Jamaica in 1744. The seed of it came as food for some birds sent from Africa as a present to the chief justice, but the birds dying it was thrown away. The eagerness of the cattle to eat the grass which sprang from it suggested the idea of cultivating it, which has been continued with great advantage to the planters. 1864 Grisebach 784. 1955 *WIMJ* 80, Guinea grass is used to make tea for fevers.

GUINEA-HEN PARROT sb dial. A variety of the PARROT fish speckled like a guinea-hen.

1952 FGC StE /gínihèn párat/ speckle.

GUINEA-HEN QUOK sb dial; <*guinea-hen* + QUOK. The night heron when in its speckled plumage: see quot.

1847 Gosse 346, A specimen was shot in April, in the spotted plumage, which is supposed to indicate youth.. In this state it is sometimes called the Guinea-hen Quok, from the white spots on the grey ground.

GUINEA-HEN ROOT sb dial. The root of the GUINEA-HEN WEED.

1942 HPJ, *Guinea-hen root* or *weed*—a plant with a bad smell when the leaves are broken.

GUINEA-HEN WEED sb; *OED* 1829 only. The strong-smelling wild plant *Petiveria alliacea*, used in medicinal preparations, but disliked generally for its taste: see quots.

1696 Sloane 64, Verbenæ aut scorodoniæ..allij odore. *Guiney hen weed.* In sylvis umbrosis oritur. 1740 Importance 45, The *Guinea Hen Weed* is a little Bush the Cattle feed on, the Root of which scraped they put into their hollow Teeth when they ake. 1814 Lunan I 354–5, Guinea-hen-weed. *Petiveria..alliacea..*grows plentifully in Jamaica..It is much coveted by Guinea hens, whence the name is derived. 1864 Grisebach 784, Guinea-hen's weed. 1893 Sullivan 26, Mutton with Guinea Hen Weed. Avoid this altogether..the detestable taste of the weed. 1952 FGC StAnn, Guinea-hen weed, has a harsh smell, burns nostrils—used for headache; StM, good for fever; Tre, = HEADACHE WEED: rub up and inhale for a fit; also StAnd, StC, StT, etc. 1954 *FG* 584, The Guinea-hen Weed is from all standpoints one of the worst weeds in Jamaica. Its tough, wiry stems are a pest in gardens, its sharp-pronged seeds stick to clothing and animals, and when eaten by cows the leaves impart a foul odour and taste to milk.

GUINEA-MAN sb; cf *OED* 3 1830→. A man born in Africa.

a 1818 Lewis (1845) 155, On hearing of this fresh instance of devilism, I asked her mother 'how she came to have so bad a daughter, when all her sons were so mild and good?' 'Oh, massa,' answered she, 'the girl's father was a Guinea-man.'

GUINEA MINT sb dial. The plant *Lippia geminata*, known to have been used medicinally in Africa ('Guinea').

1954 *WIMJ* 25, Colic Mint; Guinea Mint; ?Cat Mint; Cullen Mint. The fresh leaves..are commonly made into a tea..for indigestion and flatulence..In Africa Lippia spp. are employed for a variety of complaints.

GUINEA PEPPER sb; *OED* →1832. *Capsicum* pepper (an old name still current in Jamaica). *G*

1957 JN StJ, It name Guinea Pepper—a it first dark up when de rain goin start [*It is the first thing to turn dark when rain is about to fall*].

GUINEA-SHIP /giniship/ sb dial; <*Guinea* + *ship*, a ship bringing slaves from 'Guinea' or Africa. A large number or crowd of people.

1924 Beckwith 188 [Riddle:] Me fader hab a Guinea ship o' nager; eb'ryone o' dem a t'ree foot. 1956 Mc Man /im hab wan huol giniship a pikni/ *she* (or *he*) *has a very large number of children;* /a huol giniship a piipl iina di trok/ *a whole crowd of people in the truck*; [referring to successful result of the year's school-exams:] /a huol giniship pas dis ya/.

GUINEA TAMARIND sb chiefly dial. See quot; 'Guinea' perh means no more than 'foreign', and 'tamarind' refers to the similarity of the leaves (and perhaps pods) to those of the Tamarind.

1943 *NHN* II 45, *Albizzia berteriana*—Guinea Tamarind. This and a very similar species also called 'Guinea Tamarind' grow in scattered patches..It is said that the two species can only be differentiated when in fruit—this species being the one with shorter pods.

GUINEA WEED sb dial. = GUINEA-HEN WEED.

1927 Beckwith 18.

GUINEA YAM sb. A variety of yam like WHITE YAM but coarser grained. *BA*

1814 Lunan II 310 [Dioscorea] oppositifolia..This is called Guinea Yam, from the plants having been first brought from Africa; it bears a yam much resembling the negro yam in taste and consistence. 1942 HPJ, *Guinea yam*, a kind of yam resembling white yam, but coarser. 1943 *GL* Port, Crunjoe, guinea yam. 1952 FGC Port /gini yam/ like white yam, bigger grain; StAnn /gini yam/ kind of white yam but harder nature, grow very big in good soil; StC /gini yam/ = /sii yam/ —big, white inside. 1958 DeC gen, The Guinea yam is white and large, very clean skin, no hair on it, it 'have no foot'.

GUINEA YARD sb obs. A building or enclosure to which new slaves were brought after debarkation: a nickname.

1826 Barclay 224, A court of equity established in a Guinea-yard in the West Indies, to hear and decide on the titles to the slaves brought in, would certainly have been a novelty in judicature.

GUINEP (TREE) /ginep, genep, kinep/ sb, also attrib; 1756→ genip, 1788 genap, 1790 canip(e), 1811 cunep, 1893→ guinep, 1913→ ginep; <Amer Sp *quenepo*, Melicocca spp, and *quenepa*, its fruit, <Arawakan; *OED* has wrong etym and consequently wrong pronunciation: the initial sound is /g/, never /j/; the /k-/ form, now less common, better represents the source word: the /g-/ forms may possibly show some analogy to GUINEA. (The

standard spelling 'genip' misrepresents both etymology and pronunciation: of the other prevalent spellings, *ginep* is ambiguous (*g* before *i* may be either /g/ or /j/); *guinep* has therefore been given preference.) *BA G N* /kinep/.

The tree *Melicocca bijuga* and its fruit: see quots.

1756 Browne 210–11, Melicoccus 1..The Genip Tree. This tree was brought to Jamaica from Surinam, and is cultivated with great care by one Guaf, a Jew. 1788 Marsden 78, The Genap bears a fruit about the size of a magnum bonum plumb..nothing in the world can be more delicious than the pulpy juice of this fruit. 1790 Moreton 41, Canipes. 1801 Dancer 305, Strangulation.. Accidents of this nature..happen..oftener to children, from swallowing Genip Stones, than any other cause. 1811 Titford xv, Cunep, or Honey Berry. 1893 Sullivan 79, Guineps. These stain terribly. 1913 Harris 7, Ginep..The flowers are succeeded by clusters of green or greenish-yellow fruits, each about the size of a pigeon's egg, with a tough skin and usually one large seed which is surrounded by pulp with a pleasant grape-like flavour. The seeds are roasted and eaten like chestnuts. 1942 HPJ, *Kinep* still in Trelawny. 1952 FGC StE, StM /genep/; StAnd, StAnn, StJ /ginep/.

GUINEY see GUINEA.

GULGE sb dial; cf *EDD gulch*, a glutton; fat, ill-shaped person.

1943 *GL* StAnd, Gulge, large marble.

GULGULA sb dial; etym unknown.

1943 *GL* Tre, Gulgula, a mixture of sugar and flour cooked in oil.

GULLY[1] /goli/ sb and adj. **s.**

A. sb: [1. In the usual sense: *OED*, 'a channel or ravine worn in the earth by the action of water'.] *BA T*

2. A small stream. *G T*

1912 McK *Songs* 102, De gully* ripples 'cross de glade. **Brook.* The word is more generally used in the sense of precipice.

3. A precipice. (See prec quot.) *T*

4. (See suppl.)

B. adj: Of the nature of gully land: washed out, having deep washed-out places in them.

1823 Roughley 269, Steep places..Those spots are generally poor and gully, and disfigure a cane piece.

GULLY[2] see RED GULLY.

GULLY ASP see GALLIWASP.

GULLY BEAN sb dial joc. SUSUMBA, which grows wild in poor lands.

1942 HPJ, Sesumber—Black people call it 'Gully bean'. 1943 *GL* Clar, Gooly bean—sushumber. 1952 FGC Port, StAnd, StC, StM, StT /gólibíin/ poorer people say; = /susumba/.

GUM /gom/ sb dial. In various local uses for sticky or binding substances: see quots. *G*

1956 Mc Clar /gom/ used as a device for catching birds—the gum is taken from a tree, melted and then spread on a branch; /pred an tik—di gom uol im/ [= bird-lime]. 1958 DeC Tre, We add counter-flour to cassada head for gum [i.e. to stick it together], otherwise it /kyaan mesh/, will be too /shali/, so that it /mash/. *Ibid*, Gum, the asphalt on a road.

GUMA /gúma/ sb dial; 1814→ gooma, 1814 goomer, 1927→ gumma, 1927 gumba, 1954 guma; cf Bambara *gumbi*, a herb causing in horses an infectious diarrhoea (Turner 194); also Surinam Creole *Agoéma*, a solanaceous plant used as greens (Focke).

The plant *Solanum nigrum*, which grows wild and is eaten as CALALU, and also used medicinally; in strong doses it is cathartic and somewhat narcotic.

1814 Lunan I 142, Calalu, branched (*Solanum nigrum*). This plant is commonly called *gooma* or *goomer* calalu, and grows very luxuriantly in new grounds. 1927 Beckwith 18, Gumma..The berry is used for poisoning cockroaches. 1943 HPJ [Prov:] Ole lady sware fe gumma an gumma swear fe ole lady [i.e. she eats it and it 'physics' her]. 1952 FGC gen /gúma/ young leaves edible, berries not eaten; will draw boils; also for stomachache, colds. 1954 *WIMJ* 23, Branched Calalu; Guma; Black Nightshade. This plant has long been in use in Jamaica as a green vegetable and pot herb..It is said to be good for the blood and as an aperient.

GUMBA, GUMBAA, GUMBAY, GUMBE see GOMBAY, GUMA.

GUMBER sb dial rare; cf *DA gumbo*, okra, etc. Mucilaginous or slimy juice.

1943 *GL* Tre, Okra, a 'pod-like' green vegetable containing gumber.

GUMBESH sb dial rare; cf Ko *ngombe*, goat.

1943 *GL* Port, Gumbesh, goat.

GUMBI, GUMBY see GOMBAY.

GUMMA see GUMA.

GUM TREE sb; *OED* this sense 1756 only. In Jamaica: *Sapium jamaicense.*

1756 Browne 338, Sapium 1..The Gum Tree..This tree..yields a great quantity of resin..which generally serves for the boiling-house lamps..and is much used for bird-lime. 1814 Lunan I 361. 1864 Grisebach 784, Gum tree: *Sapium laurifolium.* 1920 Fawcett 325, Gum Tree, Milk Wood.

GUM WOOD sb. In Jamaica: *Tetrochidium rubrivenium.*

1920 Fawcett 318, Gum Wood. 1952 FGC StAnn, Gumwood, a soft-nature wood, leaves much like soursop, gum used to catch birds.

GUN-CAP BUSH sb dial. An unidentified bush.

1952 FGC StM, Gun-cap bush—it favour gun-cap when it blow the flowers.

GUNDY sb. A common abbr for SOLOMON GUNDY.

1942 HPJ.

GUNFIRE sb; cf *OED* 1823, 1833 quots.

1. The firing of a gun as a signal of time at certain hours. Formerly used, for example: a morning gun at 5 A.M.; a 6 P.M. gun warning ships to anchor off Port Royal; an 8 P.M. gun: lie outside the harbour. A noon gun was fired at Up Park Camp until 'late 1921 or early 1922' (Col. David Smith 1961).

1801 Nugent 51, 30 Oct. Up at gunfire. *Ibid* 53, 6 Nov. Drive to the Penn at gunfire [see Cundall's note]. 1958 DeC StAnd /gon-faia/ name of a time of day; not dawn, as in most places, but noon, because they used to fire a gun every noon at Up Park Camp.

2. Fig. A sound indicating that something is happening.

[1948 Bennett 82, We fix up fe action, but not A gun noh fire yet.] 1960 BLB Man /mi neva hier gonfaya bout im/ *I have never heard a sound about him.*

GUN-FOOT sb dial joc; for *gun-feet.* Long trousers, especially narrow tubular ones.

1942 HPJ, Gunfoot:..(Trousers) with very narrow legs. Marion..said it was because of their small size. 1948 U.Newton IV 35, We *soared into long pants!!!* The boys called them 'gun foot'..that was sheer envy.

gunggo, gunggu see GUNGO (PEAS).

gunggu man, gungguz man sb dial; variants of GUZU-MAN.

1959 DeC Han /gunggu-man/; Han, West /gungguz man/ obeahman.

gunggus sb dial.

1952 FGC Han /gunggus/—'work gunggus on you'—witchcraft device; for example, aromatic oil to give headache or to break up pocomania meeting.

GUNGO (PEAS) /gúnggu, gúnggo/ sb; 1867→ gungo, 1893 goongoo, 1912 gungu, 1927 goongo; cf Ko *ngungu*, pea(s). *BL*

1. The pea *Cajanus cajan*, which grows on a shrub 4–10 ft high; the pea is roundish; it is favoured for soup and frequently cooked with rice. Also called ANGOLA, CHRISTMAS, NO-EYE, PIGEON, CONGO PEAS, SEVEN-YEAR PEAS. *G*

1867 *TJRSA* I 64, [Negro literature] scarcely ever rises above Gungo peas and Afoo yams. 1913 Harris 34, The Gungo Pea, Pigeon Pea, or Congo Pea is doubtfully a native of India. . In Jamaica this plant is commonly cultivated at all elevations up to 4000 feet. . There are several varieties known as No-eye Pea, Morgan Congo, Cuban Congo, etc. 1920 Fawcett 71–2, Gungo Pea. 1927 Stafford 26, Soup of goongo peas and salt-fish. 1952 FGC StAnd, StAnn, StC, StE, StJ, StT /gúnggu (píiz)/; Port /gúnggo/. 1956 Mc Man /gunggu/; Man, StAnd /gunggo/.

2. In the phr *To have gungo a line with* (someone), to be the neighbour of; in neg, to have no dealings with. See quot and note.

1912 McK *Songs* 38, [Me have] No weight lef' behin' me No gungu a line fe De man who was usual to worry me life. [Note:] Friends plant their gungu (Congo peas) together, and, in picking the crop, are not particular about the line between their properties. When they cease to be friends, they have *no* gungu a line. The phrase is equivalent to 'to have no truck with'.

3. Attrib in *gungo leaf*, *gungo walk*, etc. Cf WALK.

1893 Sullivan 121, For a Sore Throat. Boil a handful of goongoo leaves. 1951 Murray 50 [Song:] Matty run a mile an' a half eena gungo walk.

gungu flai sb dial; var of *ginggi flai*.

1956 BLB StJ /gungu flai/ small flies.

GUNGU PEAS see GUNGO PEAS.

gunzu see GUZU.

guodi see GOURDY.

guolfinsh, guolfrinsh, guolfrinj *see* GOLDFINCH.

GURANDEAN sb dial; etym unknown.

1943 *GL* StAnn, Gurandean, a smart person.

GUSOUN MAN see GUZU-MAN.

GUSSUE, GUSU see GUZU.

GUTTER sb dial; cf *OED* 5, →1712; 6.

1. The spine, backbone—evid transf from the depression down the back of the spine, which is (by a similar metaphor) called the BACK-GULLY.

1956 Mc Man /gota/, also /pain/.

2. The space between yam hills.

1958 DeC Man.

3. Any other groove or channel: see THREE-GUTTER BED, THREE-GUTTER MACHETE. *G*

GUTU /gútu/ sb dial; etym uncert: cf Mende *gutu*, short.

1. A small, dark fish: Gosse's 'Sand Gootoo' —see quot 1851—which he names *Tetraodon ammocryptus*.

1851 Gosse 287, Between Bluefields and the Creek, our attention is attracted by some little Fishes, the largest not exceeding four inches in length, which shoot hither and thither in the shallows close to the water's edge. . if alarmed [they]. . seek to hide among the sea-grass, or attempt to bury themselves in the sand. The Negroes call them Sand-Gootoo, to distinguish them from a kind of *Scarus*, which they designate as Eatable Gootoo. 1943 *GL* StT, Gotto, a fish. [This could be sense 2 equally well.]

2. A variety of PARROT, usually GUTU PARROT.

1851 Gosse 287 (see above 1, 'eatable gootoo'). 1943 *GL* West, Gutu, parrot fish. 1953 FGC StC /gútu párat/ tan, darkish; StE /gútu párat/ smaller species of parrot, brownish, not bought by truck [for sale in town]; StJ /gùtú párat/ darkish, lets out pus from gut.

guula sb dial; etym unknown.

1956 Mc StAnd (Dallas) /gúula/ a crayfish, 'lobster'.

guulfrinj see GOLDFINCH.

guznik-man see GUZU-MAN.

GUZU, GUZUM /guzu, gusu, guzum, guzung, gunzu/ sb dial; 1868 gaso, 1900 guzzoo, 1922→ goozoo, 1943 goonso, goosoom, goosung, gussue, gusu, guzu, guzum; cf Twi *kã ntam gu. . so*, to conjure, and Kimbundu *nguzu*, strength, power, force. Cf *buzu*, *bunguzu*.

1. Some kind of deity or ancestral spirit in Ashanti religion?

1922 Beckwith 83 [Alphabet:] G is for Goozoo, all nigger papa.

2. An act of obeah, or witchcraft. *BL*

1868 Russell 7, Gaso—A single piece of obeah. African. 1929 Beckwith 105, In Jamaica, 'goozoo' is equivalent to obeah; you may say 'working goozoo' as well as 'working obeah'. 1943 *GL* Kgn, Goosoom, guzum, obeah or magic; Man, Gussue, Obah witchcraft; Port, Goosung, Witchcraft; StAnd, Goonso; StC, Gusu, Gunzu; Tre, Guzu.

3. An obeahman; more often GUZU-MAN.

1900 Murray 8 [To an obeah-man:] Hullo, old Guzzoo! 1957 DeC StAnd /guzúng/ obeah man.

GUZU-GUZU sb dial; iterative < GUZU.

1958 DeC Port /guzu-guzu/ obeah man.

GUZUM see GUZU.

GUZU-MAN /guzu-man, guzun-man, gunzu-man, guznik-man/ sb dial; < GUZU + *man*. An OBEAHMAN.

1954 LeP Kgn, Gusoun man; Man, Gouzoo man; StE, Guzzuman—man who professes to kill or heal by magic. 1956 Mc Clar, Man, StT /gúzuman/ Obia man. 1959 DeC StJ /guznik-man/ obeahman: informant remembers the word being used in his childhood; West /gunzu-man/.

guzung see GUZU.

guzun-man, GUZZUMAN see GUZU-MAN.

gwaako, gwaaku, GWACO see GUACO.

gwai, gwain, GWEN see GWINE.

GWAN /gwan, gwaan/ vb phr and sb dial. *BL*

1. Dial spelling for *go on*. *G*

1950 Pioneer 18, Cho Anancy[,] no gwan so.

2. A going-on, activity. (As a sb this is prob a nonce use.)

1942 Bennett 5, Him see de enjin comin dung Fire dah jump an prance, Him hear de train dah puff an blow An gwan wid bans a gwans [*And go-on with lots of activity*].

gwanggu-bag sb dial; etym not clear; perh conn with the GUANGO tree.

1958 DeC StT /gwanggu-bag/ a temporary bag made of trash or grass at the field.

GWAP /gwap/ vb dial; echoic. To swallow food or drink hastily; to gulp. Cf *wap*[2].

1943 *GL* Kgn, Gwap, to swallow food hastily; Man, Gwat, to drink; StE, Guapo, to swallow. 1954 LeP Man, Gwap i dung, to drink. 1955 FGC Man /gwap/ to swallow food hastily.

GWAPO, GWAT see prec.

GWINE /gwain, gwai/ pres pple dial; <*going*. This is an archaic pronunc, preserved also in US, etc. Going; as a main vb participle, it alternates with GONE; as an auxil vb it alternates with A-GO (A[5]+*go*) to show 'progressive' present tense or future tense. *BA BL G*

1942 Bennett gloss, Gwine: going. 1957 JN no addr, I gwen to buss da puss deh brain; StAnn [Boy spraying spider web with water from tap:] Spray Nancy next. Nancy you gui dead; a gui spray you next. (See NANCY NEST.)

GWOYOU vb dial rare; etym unknown.

1943 *GL* Port, Gwoyou, to bluff or fool.

gyaashani /gyáashàni, gyáasháni/ sb; a name, cf ABOUKANI. A bull in a well-known folk tale: see quots.

1890 Milne-Home (in 1896 Bates 128) [Story:] *Garshan Bull.* How a boy kills a bull, and marries the King's daughter. 1942 HPJ, Gárshanni: Name of the bull in some versions of 'the little boy who avenged his mother'. 'Garshanni, Garshanni, come here, The green tree shall stan' An' the dry tree shall fall.' 1958 FGC StT /gyáasháni/ in Anancy story.

gyad vb dial; prob var of *gag*. (Cf the corresp *t*/*k* alternation e.g. /lit/ for *lick*.)

1956 Mc Man /gyad/ To force something down the throat.

gyalan-buo parat sb dial; etym uncert: the first element is prob *gallant* (but may be *gallon* <*galloon*, cf US *ten-gallon hat*, etc.), the second element may equally well be *beau* (more probable if first element is *gallant*) or *bow* (more probable if first element is *gallon*, *galloon*). The markings of the fish are responsible for the name, but folk-etym may enter; possible originals may therefore be *gallant-beau*, *gallant's bow*, or *gallon-bow*.

1952 FGC StE /gyálan búo páràt/ brownish scales, yellow stripe, yellow bow across the head, from mouth to lower jaw.

gyalawas see GALLIWASP.

gyali see GALLEY.

gyalimenta (**bulit**) see GALIMETA WOOD.

gyana-gyana adj dial; cf Ewe *ganyaa*, bulging, *gãnagãna*, stiffly bowed, curved, bent.

1956 Mc StE (Accom) /gyana-gyana/ flabby, loose, bloated.

gyanda see GANDER.

gyanzi see *ganzi*.

gyou sb or vb dial; <*gow*, a fool, a stupid creature (*SND* [gʌu, gjʌu]). Perh conn with *gull*, a simpleton.

1. Falsehood.

1943 *GL* Kgn, Geow, noun, falsehood.

2. Pretentiousness; to act pretentiously.

1955 FGC Man /gyóu/ making yourself big. (Noun or verb.)

GYPSY /jipsi/ sb dial.

1943 *GL* Clar, Jipsy, secret language.

h- /h-/ dial. Sound frequently prefixed to initial stressed vowels—see Introd, Phonology.

HA vb dial; cf *OED have v* (*γ* form); also freq reduced to /a/. One of the several forms of *have*, a preservation of earlier English and Scots usage. *BL G T*

1942 Bennett 16, Me ha' wan numba nine crepe sole. 1956 Mc Man /dem ha lat av it/; /a wan dege wan mi de ha/ *I've got just one*; StE /mi ha fiiba a mi hed/ *I have a fever in the head.*

haaj vb dial; a folk pronunc of *adze*. See also *aj*.

1960 DeC *CLS* I 170 /an di bwái sí dóun an táát a háajin di kátn tríi fɪes/ *And the boy sit down and start adzing the cotton tree's face.*

haakshaa see HAWKSHAW.

haal-baat, haas-baat see HORSE-BATH.

HAB vb dial; a sp of *have*. *G*

HABALOO sb; <*hullabaloo*, with poss infl also of *hubbub*—i.e. perh a blend word.

1943 *GL* Port, Habaloo, confusion.

HABBIE(**-HABBIE**) /hábi/ vb phr dial; <HAB, have+I, it. (To) have it.

1942 HPJ [Prov:] Habbie-habbie noh waant it, but noh habbie da ded fe it. *To have it aplenty is not to want it, but not to have it is to long for it.* Noh ketchie noh habbie. *Not to catch it is not to have it.*

HABBLE vb dial; <Sp *hablar*, to speak.

1943 *GL* StM, Habble, to talk or speak.

habi see HABBIE.

habriko /hábriko/ sb dial; <*albacore*. The albacore.

1952 FGC StC /hábriko/.

ha-buo sb dial; <*ha-* etym unknown +*-bo*.

1959 DeC StJ /há-buo/ an albino Negro.

HACHEBAT sb dial rare; perh <ACROBAT.

1943 *GL* Kgn, Hachebat, old wretch.

HACKLE vb dial; cf *OED sb*[1].

1. trans. To treat roughly; to trouble, harass.

1942 HPJ, Hackle: To harass; upset (a person); to over-urge a horse. 1953 Moore 158, When you get a sick better..African spirit come, we kill a goat, we get the blood, we mix it with rum, and we wipe it from you head straight down to your feet and during the while we have you in the ring. Meantime, the drums knock you and hackle you, and probably by daylight, you come back a strong man.

2. intr. To work hard.

1943 *GL* Clar, Hackle, to do hard working.

HADROW, HADRUE see ADRUE.

HAFFE /háfi/ vb phr dial; a common dial sp for HA+FE. *G*

1942 Bennett gloss, Haffe: have to.

HAFFOH, HAFOO, HAFOOH, HAFU see AFU. *G*

HAG, haig see HIGE.

HAGA-LAGA adj dial; cf *logo-logo* adv.

1943 *GL* StT, Haga-Laga, plenty.

HAGARIAN sb dial; <*hog*+*-arian*, cf RUMARIAN. Rough, hoggish; cf HOGANEERING.

HAGGANEERING see HOGANEERING.

hagvongga /hàgvóngga/ sb dial; <*hog*+ *-vongga*, beetle, as also in *nyuuzvongga*: a form of *-monger*. (This may be an individualism as both words are from the same informant.) The dung-beetle; the association with the hog may be through its 'rooting' in the ground.

1952 FGC Port /hàgvóngga/—TUMBLE-TURD.

hai /hai/ sb dial; a common pronunc of *eye*. (For initial /h/ see Introd, Phonology.) (*OED* 14–17th cent.) *G*

1952 FGC StAnd /di was-dem sting hai—eni taim yu luk pan dem nong/ *Wasps sting your eyes—any time you look at them, now*.

HAIG see HIGE.

hail-not see OIL-NUT.

HAIL OUT /híel òut/ vb phr dial. *G*

1957 DeC no addr /hiel out/ to call out; /shi hiel out fi William/.

hain, hainz sb dial; the reg dial pronunc of *hind*, the fish (*OED sb*[1] 2). *N*

1952 FGC StJ /ainz/; StE, West /hain/; StAnn, StC, StT /hainz/.

HAIRY CERASEE sb bot.

1814 Lunan I 174, *Momordica charantia*..this is called the *hairy cerasee*. 1850 Macfadyen 140, Hairy Cerasee.. the fruit of this species..supplies one of the ingredients of the celebrated *pepper-pot* of the West Indies.

HAIRY MANGO sb. A variety of mango with hairy flesh; also called COMMON MANGO. *BA BL*

1952 FGC StAnd, StAnn, StE, etc. /híeri mánggo/. 1954 *FG* 475, Mangoes..Common or Hairy. Very plentiful. Ripens a bright yellow.

HAIRY-SKIN MANGO sb. A variety of mango with hairy flesh and a thick skin.

1947 U.Newton III 9, Choice number elevens, black mangoes and hairy-skins. 1952 FGC StJ, Hairy-skin (mango), so in StC, called /paas manggo/ in Man, has a round point and is stringy.

haj see *aj*.

haju see ADRUE.

haka-haka vb dial; iterative based on *hack*, or perh an alteration of *saka-saka* under infl of *hack*.

1956 Mc Man /háka-háka/ to cut with something blunt.

haks-bil torkl see HAWKBILL TURTLE.

HALBERT WEED sb; <*halbert*+*weed*; *OED* 1756 only. The common wild plant *Neurolæna lobata*; applied also to *Calea jamaicensis*, a close relative.

1756 Browne 315, Santolina 2..foliis serratis, hastatis.. This plant..is an excellent bitter, and much used in America, where a spirituous infusion of the tops is generally kept at most plantations. 1801 Dancer 364, Halbert weed (*Calea jamaicensis*). 1814 Lunan I 363, *Calea lobata*..From the shape of the leaves, Browne called this plant *halbert-weed*. 1864 Grisebach 784, Halbert-weed: *Neurolæna lobata*. 1936 Fawcett 269, *N. lobata*..Halbert Weed, Bitter Wood, Bitter Bush, American Golden Rod, Cow Gall. 1955 *WIMJ* 159, *Neurolaena lobata*..Halbert Weed; *ibid* 157, *Calea jamaicensis*..Halbert Weed.

HALF-A-FOOT adj and sb dial. Wooden-legged; a wooden-legged person. *G*

1927 Anderson-Cundall 82 [Prov:] Half-a-foot man go a market from Friday. 1942 HPJ, Half-a-foot, adj., wooden-legged. Also a noun: Half-a-foot dance deh him fambly yard.

HALF-DAY sb dial. *BA G*

1958 DeC StAnd /haaf-die, aaf-die/ noon, midday; so called because half the working day still remains. See also QUARTER-DAY, THREE-QUARTER DAY.

HALF-INCH sb and adj dial.

A. adj: Inadequately equipped.

1962 BLB 56 /haaf-inch/ ill equipped for task.

B. sb: An inferior workman.

1956 Mc Man /haaf inch/ a workman not good at his job.

HALIFAX MUTTON sb joc. SALTFISH, as being imported from Halifax.

1873 Rampini 54, A dish of 'Halifax mutton', as the planters jokingly call salt fish. 1943 *GL* StAnd, Hallifax mutton; StM, Halifax mutton, codfish.

halikasha see *alikasha*.

HALL sb.

1. Obs. See quots.

1860 Trollope 20, the inns in Kingston rejoice in the grand name of halls. Not that you ask which is the best hall..but such is the title given to the individual house. One is the Date-tree Hall, another Blundle's Hall. 1873 Rampini 17, We were landed at the door of a large and desolate-looking building, which the driver informed us was the 'Hall' (for by this grand name are inns known in Jamaica) to which we were bound.

2. The living-room in a small house (common in the country parts). *BL G N*

1924 Beckwith 10, An' Tiger was layin' down in de hall middle, an' all de chil'ren an' de wife, dem all upon house-top. 1954 LeP StAnn, Hall, living place in the house. 1956 Mc StAnd /haal/ living room. 1957 EB Port /haal/ living room.

HALLA, HALLAH dial sp of *holla* /hála/. *BL*

HALLING vbl sb and pple obs; <*hall*, hoe, an overcorrection or a new form devel <*haw*, *haugh*, 17 and 18th-cent forms of *hoe* (cf *OED*). (This may not be specifically Jamaican.) Hoeing.

1808 Stewart 112, A heavy and stiff clay may be ploughed; this is necessary to be done some months previous to halling, in order that the land may have time to pulverize. This mode of tillage on such soils, is performed with considerable less labour than by merely halling the ground, which is a most severe and harassing task to the negroes.

hamasak sb dial; <*haversack*, prob infl by the synonymous *namsack*.

1958 DeC Port /hamasak/ namsack or side bag, i.e. a small satchel in which victuals are taken to the field.

hamasi /hamási/ sb dial; <*have-mercy*. A wire container for storing food, hung over the fire-place. Also called *hangkra*.

1956 Mc Man /wi kaal i hamasi/ (Tones: low-high-mid).

hamblit see next.

HAMLET /amblit, hamblit, mamlit/ sb dial; origin unknown, but cf Santamaría *amilote*.. Pescado blanco de los antiguos lagos de Méjico. A variety of BUTTERFISH caught around the coasts of Jamaica.

1951 Smith, Hamlet. *Holocentrum ascensionis*, Lucea; *Myripristes jacobus*, StM; *Pristipomoides macrophthalmus*, Holland Bay, StT. 1952 FGC /graas amblit; hamblit; mamlit/ butterfish; West, 'Rock butterfish /laik grupa, bot ketch hit regyula/'.

ham-baskit see HAND-BASKET.

HAMLET-BIRD sb dial. The BLUE GAULIN; see quot.

1956 Jeffrey-Smith 125, Fishermen in Runaway Bay have a special name for white gaulins and for blue gaulins. They call the former 'Yaller-Tail', and the latter 'Hamlin' and 'Hamlet-Bud Dem' because they say that when the birds fly in flocks the fish that bear these local names are then 'running'.

HAMLIN see prec.

HAMPER sb chiefly dial. One of a pair of large baskets made to be hung at the sides of a donkey or mule; a pannier. They are chiefly used for taking produce to market. Also called CREEL.

1873 Rampini 181 [Prov:] When jackass carry salt, him lick de hamper. 1943 *GL* no addr, Hampah, contrivances for use on a donkey. 1956 Mc Man StAnd /hámpa/.

HAMPER BASKET sb dial. A large market basket made of materials similar to those of a HAMPER, divided somewhat at the middle suggesting the pair of hampers, and with a handle going over at this mid-point.

1954 LeP StAnn, Hamper basket. 1958 DeC common /hampa baskit/.

HANCH sb dial; cf ANCH, ANTS and HANEN. A dial spelling of *ants*.

1894 Banbury 41 [Prov:] You tek time you fine hanch gut, *If you are patient and careful, you can find an ant's guts.*

HANCRA see *hangkra*.

HAND /an, han/ sb chiefly dial; <*hand*.

1. The arm (cf FOOT = leg): any part or all of the arm, including the hand. (This usage is now less common than it once was.) A one-armed man = 'one-hand'; cf also HAND-ELBOW, HAND-HANGER. *BA G N*

2. The claw of a crab, lobster, etc.

1956 Mc StAnd /klaafish hav wan an lang, wan shaat, yu no/ *The crayfish has one claw long, one short, you know.*

3. Side. (A preservation, cf *OED sb* 4, now uncommon in Std Engl.) *BL G*

1924 Beckwith 43, Anansi tol' Goat to walk on the hand where the hole is an' he walk on the opposite side. 1957 JN Kgn, I use to go to a nex school..across Mountain View over on that han.

[4. One of the connected groups of bananas which cluster along the stem, forming a bunch. Gen, but not specifically Jamaican. *BA BL G*

1907 Jekyll 196 (see FINGER 1).]

HAND-BACK sb dial. *BL*

1956 Mc Man /hán-bak/ back of the hand.

HAND-BASKET sb. A small round basket of light withe or the like, used chiefly for carrying food. *G*

1868 *TJRSA* I 66, Green-lizard teck one han' basket o' boil rice. 1958–9 DeC StAnd, West, etc. /ham-, han-, hand-, handl-baskit/ a small round basket, usually made of withe, covered, no handle, primarily used 'to carry dessert to white people'.

HAND-BELLY sb dial uncom. The hollow of the hand.

1956 BLB StE (Accom) /han-beli/ the palm of the hand.

HAND-ELBOW sb dial; <HAND 1 + *elbow*. The elbow. (One of a number of redundant forms: cf HEAD-SKULL.)

1956 Mc Man /hán elbó/ the elbow.

HAND GO HAND COME vb phr arch. Help in return for help, esp a monetary advantage rendered in return for one received: quid pro quo, 'Ka me, ka thee'.

1839 McMahon 174, By this piece of policy he makes fully five hundred a year out of the pen-keeper. Such transactions are termed in Jamaica, 'hand go, hand come'; meaning, if you assist me, I will assist you.

HAND-HANGER sb dial.

1956 Mc StAnd /an hanga/ arm sling.

HANDLE-BASKET sb dial. A basket with a handle. (Sometimes also called HAND BASKET, though not all these have handles. Cf also BONE BASKET.) *G*

1958 DeC StAnd (Irish Tn).

HAND-MIDDLE /han-midl, han-migl/ sb dial. The hollow or palm of the hand.

1952 FGC Han, StAnd, Han'-middle scratch you, will get money; Man, Crab-yaw come on foot-sole or hand-middle; StAnd, Fistula /kom in a di han-midl/. 1956 Mc Man, StAnd /han-migl/ palm of the hand—'palm' was used for the whole hand (Burnt Ground). 1957 JN StAnn; EB Port.

HANDRIN see *andrin*.

HANDS-PEG sb dial; <*hands* + *peg*, pole. A pole manipulated (as a lever) with the hands.

1958 DeC StT /hanz-peg/ a pole used as a lever to move any heavy weight.

HAND-STOCKING sb dial joc. A glove.

1954 LeP StE. 1955 FGC Man.

HAND UP vb dial or tech. To tie up in bunches or 'hands'.

1952 FGC StAnn, Tobacco, han it up for sale.

HAND-WRIST /han-ris, han-risk/ sb dial; *OED* →1809.

1956 Mc Man /han-riis/; StAnd /han-risk/ wrist. 1962 BLB 56 /hanris/ wrist.

HANEGAL sb; a dial sp for /híenjal/ angel.

1943 *GL* StAnd, Hanegal, angel.

HANEN sb dial arch or obs; perh basically <*ant* (now /hants/), but prob coincidentally infl by Twi *hãnii*, a black ant.

1868 Russell 5, Hanen, The Ant.

HANG- see HENG-.

HANG DOG phr dial; <*hang* + *dog*, but the sense of the combination is not clear. Cf, perh, the US expression 'till the last dog is hung'—till all the provisions at a party are exhausted and it must stop.

1943 *GL* StM, Hang darg, plentiful.

hanggra see next.

hangkra /hangkra, hanggra/ sb dial; <Twi *hãŋkáre*, circle, anything circular, hoop, rim of a wheel, and prob also infl by Akyem *haŋkăra*, hearth, fireplace. The first syllable is prob reinforced by infl of Engl *hang*.

1. A hoop, rack, hook, or the like, of metal or basket frame hung above the fireplace to cure and preserve meat or fish. Also called *hamasi*, *kana*, KEKRIKE, *kreng-kreng*, *pata*.

1943 *GL* Man, Hankra, an interlaced iron hoop, etc.; Man, Hancra, hanging basket for meat; West, Hangra; no addr, Hankra. 1955 FGC Man /hangkra/ hang up hook, smoke meat. 1959 DeC West /hangkra/ same as /kreng-kreng/ a rack on which to dry meat or fish.

2. See quot.

1959 DeC /hangkra/—a side-bag of canvas, crocus, or thatch.

HANGMAN sb dial.

1. As a term of insult: see quot. *BA*

1862 Clutterbuck 55, Now, *hangman* is the very lowest term of negro reproach.

2. See quot.

1959 P.B. Caws StAnd, Hangman—the animal that is trained to lead other cattle (cows, prob also sheep, goats) to the butcher to be killed.

HANG-'PON-ME, HAN-PON-ME see *heng-pan-mi.*

HANGRA, HANKRA see *hangkra.*

HAN-YA-HUO sb dial rare; etym uncert, but cf Twi *o-nyǎ*, slave, and *w̆óo*, terrified, afraid.

1943 *GL* StAnd, Han-ya-huo, a very foolish person.

hapin-dik, hapn-dik see HOPPING-DICK.

HARD adj dial. Old. *G*

1961 BLB 8 /mi get haad nou/ I have become quite old now.

HARD-AISE, ~-AZE see HARD-EARS.

HARD-BACK sb dial; *OED* 1750 Hughes *Barbados.* Any kind of beetle with chitinous wing-covers.

1923 Gowdey 16, The White Grub or Hard Back, *Ligyrus tumulosus*..The life history of this beetle has not been worked out..The White Grub or Hard Back, *Lachnosterna jamaicensis*..The larvae of this beetle are similar to those of the preceding species. (1960 Current.)

HARD-BONE JACK sb dial. A variety of the Jack fish.

1929 Beckwith 33, On the towing line are caught 'ocean' and 'hard bone' jack. 1952 FGC StC /háad bùon ják/; StE, Hard-bone jack is the young of the /gágl-ò ják/; StT.

HARD-BOUND adj and vb dial; <*hard-bound a, OED* only 1735.

1951 FGC StAnd [Prov:] Is not one day hard-boun' old daag—*It takes more than one day to constipate an old dog,* A warning or threat that an injury will not be forgotten. 1952 FGC Han /háad bóun/ constipated /káastiv/.

HARD-EARS /háad-íez/ adj and sb dial. *BA G*

A. adj: Obstinate; stubborn; disobedient. *N*

1868 Russell 12, Hard-aze—Disobedient, wilful. Hard-aze people nubba prasper. 1877 Murray *Kittle* 25, Bra me ben tell you say you mustn't come ya; da you hard ears you take so come ya. 1896 Heaven [Prov:] Hard-aize pick[n]ey walk two time. [1907 Jekyll 111, Black-smit' get vex, tell him he going to lick him down with the iron, for his ears hard. (He has disobeyed instructions.)] 1952 FGC Han, StM, Tre /haad-ie(r)z/. 1956 Mc Ste /wat a ard irz gal/.

B. sb: Obstinacy, disobedience.

1956 Mc Man /yu tínk yu gwain kóm hía spáil di ada píkniz wid yu háad-iaz/ *Do you think you can come here and spoil the other children with your disobedient ways?*

HARD-EYE(S) adj dial. Disobedient. (This may be an error for *hard-ears.*)

1873 Rampini 87, Hard-eyes [is said] of people who are wilful or disobedient. 1896 Heaven [Prov:] Hard eye pick[n]ey neber go good.

HARD FOOD sb dial. See quot. *BA G*

1956 Mc Port /háad fúud/ =Starch foods, yam, potato, coco. Here /fuud/ (also /bikl/) is used for anything edible, including meat and fish.

HARD-HEAD DRUMMER sb dial. A variety of the DRUMMER fish that has a hard head.

1952 FGC StC /háad-éd dróma/.

HARD MANGO sb.

1. The same as TURPENTINE MANGO.

1837 Macfadyen 222, The hard or turpentine Mango, resembling the last [*sc* Parrot Mango], but of a yellow colour, with the pulp hard, and only fit for stock.

2. The COMMON or YELLOW MANGO.

1952 FGC StM /háad mánggo/ common-mango.

HARD MORRIS sb dial or slang. A tough, rough fighter.

1941 Kirkpatrick 41, Jus' fe mek de 'ole pitcha perfec' dem 'ard morris people a Jugo-Slavia run out dem coward government. *Ibid* 45, Dem mekin' ghos' fool dem ef dem t'ing say we gwine fight wid any less 'ard morris tactics counta we lose dem buildin'. 1960 BLB Man /háad máris/ one that can hold his own against all odds.

HARDNESS sb dial; cf *OED* 1b, →1790. Hardship. *G*

1956 Mc /yu miit a lat a haadnis mam/.

HARD-PAY MAN sb dial. A man who does not pay his debts, from whom it is hard to collect money owed (or who finds it hard to pay what he owes?). *BL*

1952 FGC Han, StM /háad-píe màn/. 1958 DeC Port /haad-pie man/, one who won't pay his debts; generally used for Quashie.

HARD SHOES sb dial. Shoes entirely of leather (rather than canvas, rope, rubber). *G*

1942 Bennett 16, Ah wear number eight in hard shoes But sence war me kean buy dem again. Me ha' wan numba nine crepe sole but it tear.

HARD-SOCKS sb dial. Canvas shoes with a thin crepe rubber sole.

1942 Bennett 20, Kean even buy wan hard-socks fe har foot Much more fe buy two-pung tilet [toilet] set. 1953 *GL* Port, Puss or hard socks, crept [sic] sole.

HARD THOMAS sb dial; prob an allusion to the Apostle 'doubting Thomas', as one hard to convince.

1958 DeC StT /haad tamas/ a stubborn man.

HARD-UP vb dial; cf *OED hard* 1, →c 1440. This is not a preservation but a new form converted <*hard* adj, +*up.* To become hard; of milk: to curdle and solidify.

1956 Mc Man /di mílk háad-óp/ The milk thickens (when bad).

HARD YAM sb chiefly dial. A kind of white yam that lasts well. *G*

1952 FGC Han, StC, StJ, StT /háad yám/.

haribeka see ARRABECK.

hariki see next.

HARK-YE /hàrikí/ vb dial arch; cf *OED hark v* 2c, →1838.

1. The imperative phr *hark-ye* preserved.

1943 *GL* Man, StAnn, Harrick, hariki, listen.

2. The phr used simply as a verb—cf *harkee.*

1955 FGC Man /hàrikí/ to listen to someone; listening. 'Old-fashion!'

HARRICK see prec.

HARRIGAN adj dial uncom; etym unknown —poss conn with *harridan* or *hooligan*?

1943 *GL* West, Harrigan, ragged.

HARRY-HARRY sb dial; etym unknown.

1943 *GL* StM, Harry-harry, rum.

HARSH BARK or **BATH** see HORSE BATH.

hash /hash/ adj dial; <*harsh*. A common dial pronunc of *harsh*, which would be expected to be /haash/. *G*

1952 FGC Tre /it hash an yu tong/ *It's harsh on your tongue.* 1956 Mc Man /kingstan bai hav riili hash tempa tu kil di gorl/ *That Kingston boy must have had a really savage temper to kill the girl.*

HASHAM see ASHAM.

hashish sb dial arch; <*ashes*, usually pronounced /háshiz/ in dial today, but early also /háshish/, the last sound perh altered by assimilation to the medial /sh/. *BL*

1868 Russell 5 [List of Nouns:] Hashish, Ashes. 1868 *TJRSA* 1 66, A' night him 'blige fe go a fireside, creep all in a hashish, all 'bout. 1942 HPJ, Mrs Harris remembered 'hashish' quite distinctly. Heard also at Cherry Garden.

HASOONOO see ASUNU.

HASTY adj dial; cf *OED* 4, →1878. Lively, quick-tempered. *BL G*

1954 LeP Kgn, Hasi; StAnn, Hasty.

HASTY sb dial; <*hasty* adj, or perh abbr of *hastiness*. Haste, hurrying, hastiness.

1907 Jekyll 107 [Song:] Lard! Lard! hasty kill me dead oh! *Ibid* 108 [Note:] Hasty, haste.

hat[1] vb, sb, adj and adv dial; <*hurt*, prob falling together with *hot* in sense (through assoc of heat with pain) and ultimately in form, both becoming /hat/. The expected dial form of *hurt* would be */hot/ or */hort/; if either of these once existed it must have been lost through this kind of syncretism. In dial sp usu *hot*. *SC hátti*, Gullah *hot*.

A. vb: To hurt (trans or intr). *BL*

1877 Murray *Feedin' 'Perrit* 7, Him say, 'Wha you da bawl?' Me say, 'You tink it no hot me?' 1942 Bennett gloss, *Hat*: hot or hurt. 1956 Mc Man /mi hed a hat mi/; /main yu hat yusef/ *Be careful you don't hurt yourself.*

B. sb: Pain, hurt.

Cf *belihat*. [Though 'pain' is the usual word, /hat/ appears in such expressions as /mi kyaan bier di hat/ *I can't stand the pain.*]

C. adj: Hurtful, painful. *BL*

1927 Anderson-Cundall 71 [Prov:] De higher de horse de hotter de drop.

D. adv: Painfully. *BL*

1960 BLB Man [A patient recommending a dentist to another for his easy extractions:] /mi no tel yu se im no teki out hat?/ [*Didn't I tell you he doesn't take it out painfully?*]

hat[2] dial pronunc of Std Engl *hat*, *hot*; see HOT.

HATCH vb dial. Of seeds: to germinate.

1952 FGC StAnn (2 informants).

[**HATO** sb obs; <Sp *hato*, cattle ranch. A cattle ranch; the word was used early in place-names, but never fully naturalized.

1774 Long 1 237, The savannahs were by the Spaniards formed into what they called hatos..Hato signifies a flock. 1873 Gardner 15 [Early place-names:] Hato of Morant, Hato of Liguany.]

HAULIE /háali/ sb dial; <*haul* + *-ie*, familiarizing suffix. A device with a slip-knot, used to catch fruit-eating birds: a string or withe is looped and the loop hung in front of a hole in a fruit; when the bird comes to eat, the string is 'hauled' and the bird caught by the neck. Also called CHOKIE.

1952 FGC Man, Use /haali/ to ketch blue-baize.

hava see CHO-CHO ARBOUR.

HAVE A MALICE see MALICE.

HAWK BILL or **HAWK'S-BILL TURTLE** sb. Not a Jamaicanism as such, but the dial pronunc /aksbil, haksbil/ (rather than */haaks-/, which one might expect) imply some effect of folk-etym, as if the word were being understood as *ox-* or *axe*-bill, the latter esp possible because of the common use of *bill*, a large agricultural knife. *BL G*

1952 FGC Port, StC, StE, StJ, StT, West /aksbil/; StAnn /haksbil/; StM /akbil/.

HAWKSHAW sb dial or slang; prob <US *hawkshaw*, a detective, spy, with pun on *hawk* —see next.

1958 DeC StT /haakshaa/ a greedy, miserly person; = /redai/.

HAWK UP vb phr dial; <*hawk* (*OED* v^1).

1943 *GL* StJ, Hawk up, to take things greedily. 1962 BLB 56 /haakop/ v. take greedily.

HAY int dial. One of the syllables with which the lines of songs are commonly ended, meaningless, but furnishing a vowel sound which the singer may prolong. Cf also OH, YE.

1931 Astley Clerk (in 1942 HPJ), Mallan saw hay hay.. Me amba hay..etc.

H.B. CANE sb dial; reversal of B.H. CANE? Said to be a variety of sugar-cane.

1952 FGC StM /híech bíi/.

HE pron[1] dial; prob renders a pronunc of HIM (= she) such as /in, ing, hin, hing/ in which the nasality of the vowel has been ignored. She.

1907 Jekyll 52, An' when the old lady receive the message from Annancy, he send to the ground to tell the old-witch boy.

HE /i/ pron[2] dial; a sp which implies that the sound /i/ has been intended for *he*, whereas /i/ is normally <*it* when used as obj. It. *G*

1895 Banbury 21 [Song:] Dandy obeah da ya, oh! Me wi' pull he, oh!

HEAD sb chiefly dial.

1. The rhizome of coco, the piece of yam that is planted, etc.—cf COCO HEAD, YAM HEAD.

2. The inner solid part of cabbage, nutmeg, etc.: see quots. *G*

1956 Mc Man /hed/ heart of a cabbage, lettuce; StAnd, the inner part of nutmeg that is used (skin, mace, shell, and finally the head).

3. The flour of cassada (evid as being the important part, that is used)—cf CASSADA HEAD.

4. A solid cylinder of hard crude sugar—cf HEAD SUGAR, SUGAR-HEAD.

5. In phr: *To have one's head turned*—see quot. *G*

1953 Moore 34 [In Pocomania and Revival cults:] Living dancers and drummers who have been possessed are described as people who have had their 'heads turned', at which time they join the ranks of the zombie world. It is clear that what is considered to happen in possession is a phenomenal change of the personal spirit; it is described as being like an electrical shock, and once accomplished, is indelible.

6. Head of hair, the hair on the head. (*OED* 4, →1832.) *G*

1961 BLB 25 /luk hou yu bon yu hed tie i nyam-aaf/ *See how you have burnt your hair so that it has now all fallen off.*

HEADACHE BUSH or **WEED** sb; *OED headache-weed* ref 1884.

1. *Hedyosmum nutans* (and similar spp), used as a remedy for headache; see quot 1814. *G*

1814 Lunan I 367, Head-Ache-Weed. Hedyosmum.. Two species were discovered by Swartz in Jamaica. 1. Nutans..The leaves of this plant have an aromatic odour, and, when bruised and smelled, are good for relieving pains in the head, whence the English name has been derived. 1864 Grisebach 784, Headache-weed. 1914 Fawcett 28, *Hedyosmum*..Headache Bush..*H. nutans*..*H. arborescens*.

2. *Piper* spp, i.e. PEPPER ELDER, etc.

1944 *NHN* II 142, *Hedyosmum* sp. and *Piper* sp.—Headache bush.

3. *Petiveria alliacea*, see quot.

1952 FGC Tre, Headache weed, = GUINEA-HEN WEED—rub up and inhale for fit.

4. *Acalypha wilkesiana*, see quot.

1955 *WIMJ* 78, Headache bush; Croton. Both in Jamaica and in other West Indian islands the leaf of this ornamental is used as a headache poultice. Sometimes the leaves are moistened with bay rum but they may be used alone.

HEAD-BACK sb dial. The back of the head.

1877 Murray *Feedin' 'Perrit* 7, I hit de back a me hed.. a coco raise up in a me head back, big as a mango. (1960 current.) *BL*

HEAD BOILER sb; < *head* sb attrib, + *boiler*. (The hyphen in the quot is misleading, making *head* appear to be dir obj of *boil*.) A workman in charge of the evaporation of the sugar-cane juice in a sugar factory boiling-house. *BA G*

1839 McMahon 38, He sent me to the boiling-house, as the mill was then about, and after a few days he told me that the two head-boilers were most rebellious rascals.

HEAD-HAIR sb dial; cf HEAD-SKULL. The hair on the head. *G*

1900 Murray 7, Look ya unoo betta tek aff dis ting aff a me head hair.

HEAD-HEAD sb dial; iterative < *head*. The refuse left after CASSADA HEAD or flour has been sieved out.

1958 DeC Tre /hed-hed/ cassava trash.

HEADMAN sb. The man in general charge of the labourers on an estate. *G*

1823 Stewart 261, When the young negro is *promoted* to an office of superintendence and responsibility..he is prone to exercise but little moderation in his new *office*.. He himself has been domineered over by a driver, or head-man; it is now his turn to domineer over others. 1894 Banbury 7, He had got it [*sc* obeah] to 'kill' someone whose situation he wanted as headman on a neighbouring pen. 1907 Jekyll 188, The gangs on private estates are under a head-man, who is responsible to the Busha. 1956 Mc StT, The hierarchy is:..*manager;* /busha/—*overseer;* /bukii/—*bookkeeper;* /hédman/ who is in charge of all the gangs and answers both to /bukii/ and /busha/.

HEADMAN JOHN-CROW sb dial; also JOHN-CROW HEADMAN. A white JOHN-CROW, acknowledged as a leader by the black ones.

1956 Jeffrey-Smith 2, Any crow showing partial albinism ..is called the 'parson'..Another local name for the 'parson' is 'Headman John Crow'. 1956 Mc StAnn /hédman jángkro/ white crow.

HEADS-AND-TAILS sb. A game played by children: The first player holds two pins side by side in his fingers, covering the ends, and asks, 'Heads or tails?' The second player guesses—if right, he gets the pins; if wrong he gives a pin. 'Heads': both pin-heads together; 'tails': one head and one point together. *G*

1948 U.Newton IV 28–9. (Chapelton, 1920's.)

HEAD-SKULL sb dial. The skull. ('Head' is redundant; cf HAND-ELBOW, ROCK-STONE, etc.)

1877 Murray *Feedin' 'Perrit* 4, Make comb go crape me head kull go gie me sore head. 1925 Beckwith 76 [Prov:] Jackass dead, you tek him hed-'kull so hol' honey. 1946 U.Newton I 28, see *kongk*.

HEAD SUGAR sb. Sugar made into 'heads' (see HEAD 4); these are usually cylindrical, of diameter greater than height.

1952 FGC StE; StM /héd shúga/—no /sórop/ at all—boiled dry, then they ball it.

HEAD-TIE sb dial; prob a simple cpd—something with which the head is tied, but cf *head-tire*, a biblical word, which may have had some infl on this. *G*

1956 Mc StAnd /éd-tái/ a head scarf.

HEAL-AND-DRAW, HEAL-I'-AND-DRAW sb dial. *Chaptalia nutans*, indicating its medicinal properties.

1927 Beckwith 19, Heal-i'-and-draw..To draw out a boil, grind the leaf, add oil or grease, and clap upon the boil. 1952 FGC StE, Heal-an-draw = white-back. 1954 *WIMJ* 29, *Chaptalia nutans*..Kema Weed; Whiteback; Heal-I-and-Draw; Lion's Tail; Dandelion.

HEALING TABLE sb dial cant. In Revivalist cults: a service whose purpose is to cure.

1953 Moore 108.

HEAR vb dial. *G T*

1. Followed by sb or pron: a phr introducing a direct quotation—equiv to 'says he', 'said I', or the like. See NO[3] 3, quot 1950.

1942 Bennett 39, Hear her to me—'Ah call out mah'. [*Says she to me*—etc.] 1943 Bennett 31, Him sey him gawn, hear me, 'goodbye'. [*He says he is going; I say, 'Goodbye!'*]

2. In the phr *hear me*, appended to an emphatic statement to lend further emphasis, e.g. 'I not goin' deal wid him, hear me!'—equiv to '*I can tell you!*' (Current. FGC.)

HEAR-SO sb dial; abbr of some such phr as *I hear it is so*. Rumour, gossip. *BL G*

1957 Bennett 48, Hear-so, hear-say, sey-sey, su-su, All dem rumour weh dah fly Spring from grudgefulness an malice Ten to one chance dem is lie!

HEARTFUL adj dial; < *heart* (*OED* 11) + *-ful*. Courageous.

1942 HPJ. 1957 EB Port /haatful/—courageous.

HEARTY adj chiefly dial; cf *OED* 7, 'In sound health, having good appetite and spirits; vigorous, hale', →1858. Used more freq in the Jamaican countryside than in current Std Engl. *BL G*

1956 Mc StE (Accom) /a dúon háati—ha fiiba a mi héd/ *I'm not very well—have a fever in my head*; A: /hou yu du?/ B: /haati, mam/; A: /hou di biebi?/ B: /shi haati mam/.

HEATIFY adj dial; for **heatified*; cf -IFY. Heated up, hot.

1956 Mc Man /a fiil ˈhiitifai/ *I feel heated, hot.*

HEATMENT sb dial joc; prob in origin a clumsy illiteracy, now quoted as a joke: <*heat* + *-ment*. Heat. *G*

1960 Pat Wilmot StAnd /di híitment iz gríetment/ *it's very hot.* Common.

HEAVY adj dial.

1. See quot.

1942 HPJ, Hebby: Heavy. Curious as a word with a partial taboo—it must not be used of children, you must use some word like 'weighty'—it is the corpse that is 'heavy'.

2. In phr *heavy to deliver*: close to giving birth.

1956 Mc StE (Accom) /hevi tu deliva/. *BA*

HEAVY-CHEST sb dial. Illness affecting the breathing; oppression in the chest. *G*

1955 *WIMJ* 80, *Hyptis capitata*..It is regarded as valuable medicine for 'heavy chest' and asthmatical breathing in babies.

HEAVY-LEAD SNAPPER sb dial. A variety of the snapper fish; the sense of 'heavy-lead' is uncertain—perh it feels as heavy as lead.

1952 FGC StC /hévi-lèd snápa/, same as DOG-TEETH SNAPPER.

HECATEE see HICATEE.

HEDGEHOG FISH /íejág, éjág, íechág/ sb now dial. A common name for the porcupine or SOURSOP FISH: *Diodon liturosus* and similar species. *BA N*

1851 Gosse 244, Specimens of the Hedgehog-fish, or Sea-Porcupine (*Diodon*), are frequently carried home by mariners and it is not uncommon to meet with one hung up as a curiosity in houses in England; where it is sure to attract attention from its globose figure, bristling on every side with stiff sharp spines. 1952 FGC StAnn, StJ, West /íejág/; Port /íechág/; StJ /éjág/.

HEDGE-UP see EDGE-UP.

hedn sb dial; prob for *heading, vbl, sb.* = CASSAVA HEAD.

1858 DeC Port /hedn/ cassava flour or quaqua flour.

HE-JACK sb dial; <*he*+*jack*(*ass*). A jackass or male donkey. (*He* is redundant.)

1943 *GL* Man, Hejack. 1962 BLB 57 /hiijak/ male donkey.

HELMET /élmàt/ sb dial; the pronunc implies folk-etym infl of *hat*, as if the sense were **helm-hat*. A pith-helmet. See BOWL-HAT, quot 1960.

HELP vb dial. Of food: to go along with some other kind of food, to piece it out. (Often there is a sense of complementation: the tasty to flavour the insipid, the bland to soften the sharp, etc.) *G*

1958 DeC gen, Ackee is to *help* saltfish, rundown to *help* fish [*sic*: 'food'—i.e. yam, or other starch vegetable—was prob intended], etc.

HELP (DOWN, ON, UP) /help, hep/ vb phr dial. To handle a load (of provisions chiefly), getting it *up* or *on* the head for carriage, or *down* off the head to sell it, etc. (Direct or indirect object may come between *help* and the adv.) *BA G*

1907 Jekyll 48, So they put Dry-bone into the bag, an' Rabbit ask Guinea-pig to help him up. An' Guinea-pig help him up. 1924 Beckwith 125, Anansi went on before an' stood beside the timber trying to help it on again. *Ibid* 89, An' she sen' Lydia fe water, give him a big jug.. Lydia was crying dat de jug is too hebby an' him kyan't get no one to help him up. 1947 U.Newton II 26, We [wood gatherers] were getting ready to 'help up' and leave when we felt drops of rain. 1955 Bennett *Gawn a match* [Higgler speaks:] An be de time me help dung Everybody deh pon spot. 1956 Mc Man /a jos hep op mi baaskit/ *I had just got my basket on to my head.* 1958 DeC StAnd /help, hep op/ to lift up a load and place on one's own or another's head.

HELP-UP sb dial; <HELP UP vb phr. Help given by another person to get a load on the head. *G*

1960 FGC StAnd /beg yu gi mi help-op/.

HEN sb dial; etym unknown: prob to some extent echoic, through abruptness or shortness. A small bit; in negative const: not the least bit.

1868 *TJRSA* I 65, Annancey si' down, nyam it off clean —no gi' po' Green-Lizard *hen*..Annancey si' down nyam i' off clean again, an' no gi' po' Green-lizard a *hen*.

hen conj dial; var of /wen/ *when.*

1957 DeC StAnd, StE /hen i sii dat/ *when he saw that.*

HENDER vb dial; perh preservation of Engl *hender*, an occas 15–16th-cent var of *hinder*, or an independent local development.

1943 *GL* StC, Hender, prevent. 1950 Pioneer 64, Ah dis put dis ya rope pon you fe hender de pickney dem from frighten fe you. 1952 FGC StAnd, Water-bush /henda/ de water from flash out.

HENG vb dial; a common var of *hang*: a preservation of the Engl var which continued into the 16th cent, or perh a local development. Hang; also in several cpds and phrs: see separate entries. *BA BL G*

1877 Murray *Feedin' 'Perrit* 8, I say, 'Tom dem wi heng you'. 1942 Bennett gloss, *Heng*: hang. 1950 Pioneer 46, Same way Tom forrid buck, same way May bottom lip heng dung.

heng-pan-mi sb dial; <*hang-upon-me.*

1. A SIDE-BAG or NAMSACK.

1929 Beckwith 48, The 'hang-'pon-me', also of thatch, is a square pocket hung from the neck. 1946 Dunham 93, Flat 'han-pon-mes' which are thrown over the right shoulder to carry food. 1952 FGC Tre /heng-pan-mi/ basket.

2. See quot; cf also next.

1958 DeC StT /heng-pan-mi/ ready made trousers.

heng-pan-niel sb dial; <*hang-upon-nail.*

1. Clothes that are hung on a nail, hence out-of-shape, untidy.

[1910 Anderson-Cundall 8 [Prov:] No hang you clothes all 'pon one nail.] 1942 Bennett 27, Goh wey yu favah heng 'pon nail. [This could poss be sense 2.] 1943 *GL* no addr, Heng-pan-nail, out of shape.

2. Ready-made clothes (which hang from a nail in the shop).

1943 *GL* Kgn, Heng-pon-nail, ready-made clothes. 1958 DeC StM /hang-pan-niel/ in some districts means old ragged clothes; in others, means ready-made clothes.

HENKA /héngka/ vb dial; <*hanker*, but perh also infl by analogy with HENG, hang. To hang about after another person hoping to get something from him, esp at meal-time, hoping for food. (This is the current form, formerly HINKA.)

1943 *GL* Clar, Henka, wait upon; Man, Henkah, to loaf, to beg, to depend on; StAnd, Henker, to loaf; Henkah, watching food not yours. 1954 LeP StE, Henka, hanging around another to get some of the food he has.

HENKAH, HENKER see prec.

HENKING pple dial; evid < **henk*, abbr of HENKA.

1943 *GL* Port, Henking, to sponge.

HEN-PEPPER sb ?obs; evid < *hen*+*pepper* —cf BIRD PEPPER. A variety of *Capsicum* pepper.

1740 Importance 34, see BONNET-PEPPER. 1774 Long III 857, Spicery and Peppers. Ginger..Jamaica Black Pepper, Indian Pepper..Bird, Olive, Hen, Barbary.. etc.].

hent vb dial; ?< *hint*; for the sound-change involved, cf HENDER.

1958 DeC /hent/ to plan or think out.

HEP sb dial; etym unknown.

1943 *GL* Man, Hep, a bet or challenge.

HERCULES see YELLOW HERCULES.

HERRING-JEW sb chiefly dial. A contemptuous term for an immigrant Jewish or Syrian trader. It is supposed that these people (who are now rich) once peddled salt-fish around.

1960 LeP StAnd.

HERRING ROLL sb obs. An account formerly kept on sugar estates: the list of slaves, with the number of herrings given to each.

1828 Marly 104, That same evening, [he] entered her name in the estate's books, Malvina, at the same time, giving out the statutory quantity of clothing for the young stranger, and inserting her name in the herring roll, at two herrings a-week.

HERRING SPRAT /hérin, héring, érin/ sb dial. Species of *Harengula*, caught in nets close to shore and used as bait.

1952 FGC StE, StM, West /herin, hering sprat/ small, flat, shine, has scales and gold stripe, smaller than herrin', live in with Jacksprat. 1953 Moore 280, Arran-sprat—Morant Bay 1950.

HERRING-WOOD sb dial. The tree *Pisonia fragrans*.

1952 FGC StAnn /herin-wud/ the name in Tre and StE for the MAN BEEFWOOD of StAnd and StC; StE /herring-wud/—a coarse thing, but not hard; StE, Cock herring-wood is harder than ordinary herring-wood; StT, Herring-wood—no insect bores it, if dry will last three generations, but won't stand water—a common stick.

HIB /hib/ vb dial; < *heave*. Use of /b/ for /v/ common, but change of /ii/ to /i/ not. s *heb*.

1. To throw, toss; freq in phr /hib-i-ya/ *toss it here*, and the like. *BL*

1943 *GL* Clar, Hibby, throw or fling; Kgn, Hib, ibbia, to throw; Port, Hib; StAnd, Ibbia; Tre, hib. 1955 FGC Man /hib/ to throw rather than hand something.

2. See quot. *BL*

1954 LeP StAnn, Hib, to lift something heavy.

HIB-AN'-DROP, hib-an-kech vb phr, usually used as a sb; < HIB+*and*+*drop*.

1. To lift and then drop (the body): to limp; hence, as a sb, one who limps.

1954 LeP Man, Hib-an-drop—a man who limps. 1956 Mc Man /hib-an-drap, hib-an-kech/ a person who limps.

2. Fig. One who takes you up and drops you, one not reliable as a friend.

1956 Mc Man /hib-an-drap/ a person sometimes friendly, sometimes not.

HIBBERT BEAN sb bot; cf HIBBERT PEA. A variety of the bean *Phaseolus lunatus*.

1837 Macfadyen 281–2, Prolific or Hibbert Bean..This bean is well deserving of cultivation, and is little inferior to the Lima bean, to which indeed it bears a considerable resemblance. It bears throughout the year..I have met with it growing wild in fences in Liguanea. 1864 Grisebach 781. 1913 Harris 25. 1920 Fawcett 64.

HIBBERT PEA sb bot; see quot 1837. A variety of the bean *Phaseolus vulgaris*? See quot 1920.

1837 Macfadyen 280–1, *Phaseolus gonospermus*. Hibbert Pea..The seeds..have not only the appearance but also a great deal of the sweet taste of the common Pea..The name of *Hibbert Pea* is commonly given, from its having been, accord[ing] to report, introduced into this Island, from Madeira, by one of the Hibbert Family [?Geo. Hibbert, British botanist]. 1920 Fawcett 64, *P. vulgaris*..(Hibbert Pea)?

HIBBUP see HIB-UP.

HIBBY, hib-i-ya see HIB.

HIB-UP vb phr; < HIB+*up*—parallel to LIF'-UP. To walk provocatively; lifting the body, strutting.

1954 LeP StAnn, Hibbup, to walk, as some good-looking women do, in a provocative fashion.

HICATEE sb arch or obs; < Sp *hicotea*, a land-tortoise < Island-Arawak (Friederici). *OED* →1756. Perh not spec. The fresh-water turtle *Chrysemys palustris*. *BL N*

1698 Ward 14, They have Iguanas, Hickeries [*sic*], and Crabs..the second a Land-Tortoise. 1756 Browne 466, Testudo 5..The *Hicatee*, or Land Turtle. 1774 Long III 868, Hecatee or land turtle..Some of these have been known to live thirty years. 1851 Gosse 421, Some of the old writers mention, among the animals of Jamaica, a Tortoise, to which they assign the name of Hicatee..we may consider it to have been a true terrestrial species, one of the *Testudinidæ*; but whether actually indigenous or imported, is doubtful. 1873 Rampini 164, If we could feast on hicatee (land-turtle) and black crab.

HICKERIE see prec.

HICKRY sb dial; etym unknown.

1943 *GL* StAnd, Hickry, nonsense.

HIDE vb obs slang. See quot.

1790 Moreton 84, He gave strict orders to the watchmen to hide every slave which they might find breaking the corn or canes; *i.e.* to chop and murder them, and bury them secretly.

hiego see AGUE.

hiez, iez sb; dial pronunc of *ears*, ear.

1942, 1943, etc., see AISE, AZE. 1956 Mc Man /dá man de ha wán híez/ *That man has one ear.* (Also /iez/.)

higa-higa adj or sb; etym unknown.

1956 Mc StJ /higa-higa/ (an) erratic, nervous (person).

HIGE /haig/ sb dial; < *hag*, one of a group of words (cf *bige*, bag, *bullyrige*, bullyrag, etc.), in which the regular dial reflex would be /hag/ but the irregular /haig/ appears instead.

1. Usually in the form OLD-HIGE, and its compounds. *G*

2. =OLD-HIGE 3. *G*

1958 FGC StT /haig, ùoláig/ = /kyitibu/—big one, shine eyes.

3. The name of a magic tree with dangerous properties (in the Anancy story 'William Tell').

1907 Jekyll 29, An' in the yard there was a tree, an' the tree no man can fall it. Any animal at all go under that tree it kill them, an' the name of the tree is Huyg. An William Tell wanted the tree to cut down. An him offer a cow to any man that kill the Huyg.

HIGE /haig/ vb dial; <HIGE sb; cf also *hag v.* (*OED* 3, →1854 'now dial.'); cf also Engl *heg*, Sc *haig* (*SND* s.v. *Hagg*). To trouble, annoy, bedevil.

1943 *GL* Kgn, Hige, to fatigue; Port, Hige, to annoy. 1958 DeC gen /haig/ to nag, rail at someone as Old Hige would do: /shi haig im, haig im so-tel im kil ar/.

HIGGLER sb; cf *OED higgler* 2, 'an itinerant dealer..a huckster', now little used in England, but in common use in Jamaica. A seller of any kind of small produce or goods; formerly an itinerant peddler, now also one who brings produce into a market to sell. *G*

a 1818 Lewis (1845) 180, When a white man dies, who happens to possess twenty negroes, he will divide them among his brown family, leaving, perhaps, five to each of his four children. These..have..to maintain their owner by some means or other..the most frequent being the travelling about as higglers, and exchanging the trumpery contents of their packs and boxes with plantation negroes for stolen rum and sugar. 1873 Rampini 25, Higglers of all descriptions were vigorously plying their trade. Coolies with baskets of vegetables on their heads; girls with cedar-boxes full of sugar cakes of every kind; boys with bundles of walking-sticks; vendors of tripe and 'chickling'; men with trays of king-fish. [Description continues 2 pp.] 1943 *GL* Port, Higgler, one who peddles. 1952 FGC Han /hígla/ sells anything—food, cloth, even scrap iron. 1956 Mc Man, Port, StT, (i) Peddler, (ii) Person who sells things in market. 1961 Katzin 3, The link between the isolated, small farmers and the market is the country higgler, usually a woman of the neighbourhood or a nearby area, who walks and buys produce to take to the market. Some country higglers spread their goods in the markets and sell directly to house buyers, and others sell to town higglers, town residents who rent stalls in the markets where they buy at wholesale and sell at retail.

HIGGLER BASKET sb dial. The kind of basket used by higglers for produce.

1958 DeC StT /higla baskit/ a large, open, round basket.

HIGGLERING pple dial; <**higgler* vb +-*ing*. Carrying on the activity of a HIGGLER.

1942 Bennett 39, Doah ah doan like higglarin..ah sell aff everything. *G*

HIGH adj chiefly dial.

1. High in the social scale. (Cf *OED* 5.)

1942 Bennett 13, Tantudy mah meck me sidung, Tap wriggle yuhself, cho, All yuh too high fe dis yah tram. [*People like you are too high in the world to ride in this tram.*]

2. Proud, haughty, arrogant. (Cf *OED* 14.)

1954, LeP Kgn, StAnn, Proud, high: dem gwan high.

3. In high style. Slang.

1954 LeP StAnn, Gal you high! =*you are wearing a very pretty dress.*

HIGH adv dial; <prec. To a high degree; very much.

1952 FGC StAnd /di was-dem sting hai/ *The wasps sting sharply.*

HIGH COLOUR sb. A type of complexion, or one having that complexion. *BA BL G T*

1960 LeP StAnd, High colour: describing someone of very light skin, though brown.

HIGH ENGLISH sb dial. The English of education; cultivated language, in contrast to 'bad language', the folk speech. *G*

1947 U.Newton II 36, One day I tried to use the new 'High English' at Burrell Run. Sam started the crew laughing by asking 'A..what Newsy a form?' [*What is Newsy pretending to be?*] So I had to use one language at school and another at Burrell Run.

HIGH-FOREHEAD sb dial. The fish *Vomer setipinnis* or *Selene argentea* (Cockrell), from the shape of the head.

1892 Cockrell index, Bessy Cockburn, =High forehead.

HIGH-STEAM adj dial slang; prob repr 'high steam' but 'high esteem' is possible. Very good, superior.

1942 Bennett 23, An ah 'ope to keep awn strikin' Tell some ighsteem jab ah get.

hii int dial. A call to stop a mule or donkey. Cf BRRR.

1943 *GL* Tre, Hee, stop. 1958 DeC StAnd /hii/ a call to stop mules or donkeys.

hiich see ITCH.

hiit-an-lef see EAT-AN'-LEF'.

HILL'S NIGHTINGALE sb ornith. The 'Nightingale' or Mocking Bird *Mimus gundlachi hilli*, named for Richard Hill, ornithologist friend of Gosse.

1955 Taylor 10, It should be added that in the dry limestone country of the Hellshire Hills and Portland Ridge there is another Mocking-bird which is larger and darker than the ordinary species. This is Hill's Mocking-bird (*Mimus gundlachii*). It is never seen except in its limestone haunts.

HIM /m, n, ng, im, in, ing, hm, hn, hng, him, hin, hing, am, aam/ pron dial equiv to all 3rd person forms, sg or pl, and all genders, of the StdE pronoun. *BL*

1. For feminine forms = she, her (possessive or obj).

a 1818 Lewis (1845) 130, Me see one old woman without him head. 1837 Belisario Expl. to Plate 8, Him [*sc* my wife] gone, so lef me. c 1931 Astley Clerk Songs, Miss Matty..come back to him mammy gown. 1956 Mc StE /yu háfi lúk pan ing an gríiv/ *You have to look at her and grieve*; Man /hin hózban ben blàk-óp/ *Her husband got drunk.*

2. For neuter forms = it (subj or obj), its.

1907 Jekyll 164 [Song:] The one shirt I have ratta cut ahm..[Note:] The broad 'ahm' (for him, it), is more used now by the Coolies than the Negroes. 1952 FGC StAnn /gàgl ái—hng ái bíg/ *The goggle-eye (fish)—its eyes are big.*

3. For masculine forms = he, his, him.

1877 Murray *Kittle* 13, Him Say, Mass Sammy..etc. 1943 *GL* Man, In dine dey, he is in there. 1952 FGC StAnn /shúb àaf in kúnu/ *Shove off his boat.* 1954 LeP Kgn, Him can' bad no more, *He can't be worse than he is.*

4. For plural forms = they, their, them.

1790 Moreton 156, You no work him like a-mè! *You don't make them* [the hips] *move as I do* [in dancing]!

-him /him, im/ demonstrative suffix dial; <HIM. That; used like a demonstr adj in conn with names, emphasizing them.

1961 BLB 17 /Mis Anji-him pudong kasaava waata a im yaad/ *Miss Angie put cassava water out in her yard. Ibid* 22 /in fak, Dorval-him en biga an aal/ *In fact, Dorval was the biggest one of all.*

HIMBA /himba, imba, yimba/ sb dial; <Ibo *mba*, a yam root. (Used also in Haiti.) A kind of edible wild yam that grows in shady places in the high woods.

1924 Beckwith 38, An' he see a wil' thing called *himba* an' he dig it to cook with the meat. 1942 HPJ, Himba, Imba, Himber. 1943 *GL* Kgn, Imba, Yimba, edible tuber much prized, grows wild in hilly woodland; Man, Himba, wild yam. 1952 FGC StE, Tre /hímba/. 1955 FGC Man /himba/ bitter yam, bitter Jessie.

HIMBER see prec.

HIN see BEN.

hin int dial uncom; etym unknown: perh a reduced, nasalized form of 'here'. An exclamation to call attention: Here! *G*

1958 DeC /hin, tek it/ *Here! take it.* So far only found in context of giving.

hinigran sb dial; etym unknown.

1958 DeC StT /hinigrán/ an albino Negro (insulting).

hinikwiti see INIQUITY.

hinjan yam see INDIAN YAM.

HINKA(-HINKA) vb dial; <*hanker*; cf also HENKA.

1864 Russell 17, Hinka, Hanging after for the purpose of getting something; thus: Don't hinka-hinka after de backra massa so.

HIPSAW vb dial obs; cf *DAE, DA, hipsesaw*, lower-class dance, quots 1830, 1832; <*hip*+Twi *sàw*, to dance, to shake, perh with coincidental infl of Engl *saw* vb, to move to and fro (*OED* v^1 2). A hip-shaking dance—see quot.

1790 Moreton 156–7 [Song used by slave girl while dancing:] Hipsaw! my deaa! you no do like a-me! You no jig like a-me! you no twist like a-me! Hipsaw! my deaa! You no shake like a-me! You no wind like a-me! Go, yondaa!

hip-shaat(id), hip-shad(id), hip-shatid, HIP-SHATTED, HIP-SHOD see next.

HIP-SHODDED /hip-shadid, hip-shatid, hip-shaatid, hip-shad, hip-shaat/ adj and sb dial; <*hip-shot*, having the hip out of joint+redundant *-ed* (*OED*), often altered by folk-etym as if <*short*(*ed*). Lame; as sb, a lame person. *BA G*

1954 LeP, A man who limps: Kgn, hip-shod; StAnn, Hip-shodded, Hip-shatted; StE, Hip-shodded. 1956 Mc Man StAnd /híp-shátid/; Man /híp-shaat/; StT /hip-shádid/. 1957 EB Port /hip-shaatid, -shatid/ lame.

HIT /hit/ pron dial; <*it* or its earlier form *hit*, preserved also in Engl dial elsewhere. (Not specif Jamaican, but regular in the folk speech here in stressed positions: cf I^1, its counterpart in unstressed positions.) It. *G*

1877 Murray *Feedin' 'Perrit* 15, Da hit me da eat. [*It's that that I'm eating.*] 1960 Current in such a phrase as /a hit mek mi se so/ *That's what makes me say so.* (FGC.)

hitioto apl see OTAHEITE APPLE.

HITLER BOOT sb dial; remembered but no longer used; <*Hitler*, German war-leader +*boot*. A loose shoe or sandal locally made during the second world war ('Hitler war') from cast-off automobile tyres. Also called JUMP-AND-JIVE.

1952 FGC Han /hítla búut/ motor tyre shoes, invented during war time.

HITTOE sb obs; African tribal name, prob the same as Ito, 'a small section near Arochuku' (i.e. near Calabar) speaking a dialect of Ibibio infl by Igbo. (Westermann-Bryan.) A man or woman of the Hittoe people.

1825 Bickell 42, James Grant, a Hittoe, 5 ft. 6 in. has country marks on his breast.

hn, hng see HIM.

hoch, hot see HUTCH, HUT.

HOCKALENAH sb obs; African? *Sesamum orientale*; an old name, prob never fully naturalized; the common folk name later came to be WANGLA.

1696 Sloane 60, Sesamum veterum..*Hockalenah.* A Nigritis in agris frequenter seritur. [*Is frequently sown in the fields by the Negroes.*]

hodiop adj or sb; etym unknown, but cf *EDD huddimuk, huddy-box,* in which *huddy-* means surreptitious. Crooked; crookedness.

1943 *GL* StT, Hudiup, crookedness. 1955 FGC Man /hódiòp/ crooked; 'You is hodiop', not straightforward.

HOGANEER, HOGANEERING adj or ppl adj dial; <*hog*+*-an*, a linking syllable of little or no meaning, +*-eer* (*OED*, 'in many of the words so formed there is a more or less contemptuous implication') (+*-ing*). Hoggish, greedy; rough. Cf HAGARIAN.

1943 *GL* Kgn, Hagganeering, piggish. 1955 Bennett *Pedestrian Crosses*, Hear dah hoganeer man dah blow!

HOG-APPLE sb dial. The tree *Morinda citrifolia* and its fruit, which is eaten by hogs. Also called *bluuda*, DUCK APPLE, HOG BERRY, INDIAN MULBERRY, JUMBY CHO-CHO, MONKEY BERRY, PIG'S APPLE. *N*

1952 FGC Port, StM /hág-ápl/ leaf is good for headache: put it on and get the ease.

HOG-BANNER sb dial; <*hog*+BANNER. A wild withe with a large leaf, used as food for hogs. (Cf HOG-MEAT.)

1952 FGC StE.

HOG-BERRY (TREE) sb, also attrib.

1. The tree *Byrsonima coriacea* and its fruit. (The reason for the name is unknown; presumably hogs eat the fruit.)

1855 *TJSA* II 41, I should be very thankful to receive from Jamaica samples..of Hog-berry Bark. [This may be a confusion with HOG-DOCTOR tree, the bark of which was considered highly medicinal.] 1920 Fawcett 221–2, *B. coriacea*..Locus-berry tree, Lotus-berry tree..Locust tree, Hog-berry tree. 1941 Swabey 24. 1952 FGC Han, StAnn, StM /hág béri/ same as /lókás/ can eat berries; berries size of susumba, black or brown, grow in bunch; use to tan leather.

2. One of the names of *Morinda citrifolia*, more often HOG APPLE.

1952 FGC StE, StM /hag-beri/.

HOG COCO sb dial. A type of *Colocasia* or *Xanthosoma* that is fed to hogs. Also BABOON COCO.

1756 Browne 333, Arum 10..Hog Cocco..it is of an easy growth, and planted chiefly for the hogs, which it is said to fatten very well. 1814 Lunan I 212, The *baboon hog coco* or *taya*..every part of the plant [is] very coarse, and is therefore principally planted for the purpose of feeding hogs.

HOG DOCTOR (TREE) sb dial.

1. Another name for BOAR-GUM (TREE). The medicinal properties of its gum are said to have been discovered when wounded wild hogs were seen to rub themselves in it. *Symphonia globulifera.*

2. *Rhus metopium*; according to Fawcett (1926, 9), the assignment of the name to this tree was an error of Sloane's followed by Browne but corrected by Macfadyen. But see quots.

1941 Swabey 14, Boarwood—(Jamaica sumach, Hog Doctor, Poison Wood, Burn Wood). *Rhus metopium.* 1952 FGC Tre /hag dakta/=Chocho wood, very soft.

3. *Moronobea coccinea.*

1837 Macfadyen 225, Rhus metopium. *Jamaica Sumach*..This shrubby tree has long been confounded with the *Moronobea coccinea*, the true Hog-gum tree. [Cf HOG-GUM (TREE) quot 1886.]

HOG-GRASS sb dial. Bracken, which is the shelter of wild hogs in the hills. See GRASS.

1952 FGC Port, StT, Hoggrass, /brákin/ thick-grown mass of low ferns.

HOG-GUM (TREE) sb; *OED* 1756→. = BOAR-GUM, HOG-DOCTOR.

a 1726 Barham (1794) 74, Hog-gum (Linn. *Rhus metopium*). 1727 *Observations* 8, With many sorts of Gums, but not minded, except the *Gum Guiaci* and *Hog Gum*. 1774 Long III 723, *Hog-gum Tree.*—Metopium. 1886 Hooper 32, Hog Cum [*sic*]. Moronobea coccinea. 1926 Fawcett 9, see BOAR-GUM; *ibid* 198, *Symphonia globulifera*, Hog Gum Tree.

HOG HEAD sb dial. See quot; the name perh indicates resemblance to a hog's head in the shape of some part of the plant.

1955 *WIMJ* 82, Smilax sp. (?balbisiana Kth) *Hog Head*. Like other *Smilax* spp. this is said to be used in tonics. The root is described as shorter and fatter than that of china root, though our specimen appears to be the same species.

HOG HOOK sb dial; < *hog* + HOOK. An uncertainly identified plant: see quot.

1953 *WIMJ* 238, *Tournefortia hirsutissima* L. Chigger Nut; Crocus Bush; ?Hog Hook. Used both internally and externally in the treatment of colds, coughs and fevers.

HOG-HUNTER sb obs. In specific sense: Any of the men who hunted wild hogs and sold their meat for use on ships. (Cf the word *Buccaneer* in its early sense.) These were at first white men in various islands; in Jamaica the term became applied to the negroes later called MAROONS, some of whom still hunt wild hogs.

1803 Dallas I 26, Fugitive negroes, now designated by the appellation of Maroons, or hog-hunters. 1827 Hamel I 175, see PIGEON-SHOOTER. 1890 Thomas 88, see NANNY-THATCH.

HOG MANGO sb dial. *G*

1952 FGC StAnn, Hog mango—like Kidney Mango, but full of worms.

HOG-MARKET SOMEBODY sb dial ?obs; cf SOMEBODY; cf HOGANEERING.

1873 Rampini 87, An ill-mannered man is a 'hog-market somebody'.

HOGMEAT, HOGSMEAT sb now dial, also attrib; < *hog's* + *meat*, food (*OED* 1). A term long applied to various plants, chiefly trailing or climbing plants, that have been gathered to feed hogs: specifically *Boerhavia decumbens* and (POISONED HOGMEAT) *Aristolochia grandiflora*.

1756 Browne 329, Aristolochia 2..poisoned Hog-meat. [Cf HOGWEED.] 1811 Titford 31, Hogmeat—hogweed (Boerhaavia). a 1818 Lewis (1845) 57, I desired that an action of oblivion might be passed in her favour, and away she went, quite happy, to pick hogs' meat. *Ibid* 86, The beautiful flowers of 'hogsmeat', and other creeping plants. 1873 Rampini 180 [Prov:] When bull ole, you take hog-meat tee-tie (the trailing stem of a wild convolvulus) fe tie him. 1942 HPJ, Hogmeat: A shrub with big white flowers like the wandering Jew. 1943 *GL* StT, Hog-meat, A creeping withes, used as hog-fodder. 1952 FGC Han, Hogmeat—hog-string; StAnd, StAnn; StM, Milk wis, most like hogmeat; StT, wild vine, purple flower.

HOG-MINT sb dial. A wild bush (unidentified; perh *Zebrina* species?).

1952 FGC StAnd, Hog-mint, not the same as hogmeat—has a red stem and many small flowers.

HOG-NOSE (MULLET), HOG-SNOUT MULLET sb. A variety of mullet valued as a food fish.

1756 Browne 451, Mugil 3..The Mountain or Hog-snout Mullet. 1876 Hosack 96, And shoals of hog-nose mullets there in dark seclusion dwell. 1952 FGC Port, Hog-nose (mullet)—only in the river.

HOG-NOSE SKATE sb dial; cf *kiet, kiit*. A variety of skate with a nose like a hog.

1952 FGC Port /hag-nuoz skiit/.

HOG NUT sb dial ?obs. See quot; = PIG-NUT[1].

1814 Lunan I 203–4, Cob Nut. *Omphalea nucifera*..in Jamaica it is known in some parishes by the name of *pig* or *hog* nut.

HOG PLUM (TREE) sb, also attrib; *OED* 1697→. The tree *Spondias monbin* and its plum-like fruit, neglected because it is coarse and prone to be wormy; hogs eat it. *BA N T*

1696 Sloane 182, Prunus Brasiliensis fructu racemoso.. *Hog Plumb-tree*. 1788 Marsden 78–9, The Hog Plumb is a native of the island, grows in the fences as the sloes with us, is not unpleasant to the taste. 1820 Thomson 96, The favourite negro cure [for crab-yaws] is boiling them. They place their feet in a large kettle, adding some particular bush or bark, generally that of the *mammee* or *hog-plumb*; here they soak them for several days. 1913 Harris 18, see SPANISH PLUM. 1926 Fawcett 15–16, *Spondias Monbin*..Hog Plum..The branches grow readily when planted in the ground, and are much used in this way for fence posts..the fruit..is not [*sic*] liable to be attacked by the fruit fly.

HOG-POP sb obs. See quot; for possible identification see NIGHTSHADE 2.

a 1726 Barham (1794) 116, They [Virginia potatoes] are full of a moist whitish pulp, in which lie many small roundish seeds, like those of the nightshades, or what we call the hog or red-pop in Jamaica.

HOG-SLIP sb dial; < *hog* + *slip*, from the resemblance to the sweet-potato vine. OED only 1750, Barbados; still current in Jamaica. The HOGMEAT vine.

1835 Senior 28, Hogslip = wild vine, convolvulus. 1952 FGC Han, Hog-slip, same as hog-meat.

HOG-SNOUT MULLET see HOG-NOSE MULLET.

HOG-STRING sb dial. = HOGMEAT.

1952 FGC Han, Hog-string—hogmeat.

HOG-TEETH PARROT sb dial. A mauve-coloured variety of the PARROT fish with teeth like a hog's tusks.

1952 FGC StC /hágtiit páaràt/—it's /maav/.

HOG-THOMAS sb dial slang. A cruel, rough person. Cf HOGANEERING. *BA*

1943 *GL* StAnn, StT, Hog-Thomas, rough and cruel. 1960 BLB Man /him a raa hag-tamas/ often heard in Manchester.

HOGWEED sb; *OED* 1707→.

1. Common wild plants of the genus *Boerhavia*, fed to hogs, which like them very much.

1696 Sloane 91, *Hoggweed*. Locis glareosis in Insula Jamaica ubique abundat hæc herba, porcino generi gratissima. 1756 Browne 123, Boerhaavia 1. Diffusa..2. Sarmentosa..Hogweed..The weed is frequently gathered for the hogs, and thought to be very fattening and wholesome food for them. 1914 Fawcett 147–8, Boerhavia.. Erect, diffuse, or climbing herbs, woody at the base.. Hog Weed.

2. The Solanaceous shrub *Physalis angulata*, or some similar one.

1927 Beckwith 19, Hog-weed (?)*Physalis angulata*. For 'gentleman's complaint', grind it, mix with water and drink. 1954 *WIMJ* 22, *Physalis angulata* L. Poisonous Cape Gooseberry; Hog Weed; Winter Cherry.

hoks sb & vb dial; by metathesis <*husk*.

A. sb: The outer, unused or inedible covering of coffee, coconut, beans, etc. *BL G N T*

1952 FGC Port, StAnn, StJ, StM, StT /hoks/; StM /hos/.

B. vb: 1. To take the edible or usable part of an agricultural product out of the waste part. Also const *out*. *BL G*

1943 *GL* StAnd, Hux, shell out. 1956 Mc StAnd /mi hoks i fran di pad/ *I husk it (gungo peas) from the pods*; [Of the 'seed' of 'chocolate':] /jos hoks i out an put i fo drai/.

2. To remove the waste part of a vegetable product from the rest. *G*

1952 FGC StM, Palm bough when it /hoks/ from the tree.

3. Fig. To chop or break open or seriously injure, as one would a vegetable product in husking it.

1877 Murray *Kittle* 8, Ef any man say das I beholdin to him, I will hux him mout in a minit. *Ibid* 18, You hear dat? Ef I hux dis gal mout, anybody can blame me sir? 1943 *GL* Port, Hux, to chop. [This may be literal.]

HOLD /huol, uol/ vb dial. *BA*

1. To get or catch hold of; prevent from getting away. *BL G*

1905 Dodd 5, De pain hol' her dat way. *Ibid* 51, Ah wish..ah could a hol de man dat tief me fowl. 1924 Beckwith 42, Anansi..put his han' down in the hole an' something hol' the han'. He said, 'A who hol' me?'

2. In the phr *hold one's road*, to go directly or quickly to a place. (*OED* 7d →1795.) *G*

1868 *TJRSA* I 66, By de time him say dat him hol' him road, sa; him run like a 'tief, an lef Green-lizard 'pon tree wid all de meat. 1950 Pioneer 64, An the two ah dem hol' dem road fe Brer Nancy yard.

HOLD-UP sb dial. A pole-trap.

1956 Mc Clar, A type of trap for catching dogs. There are two kinds /flai op/ and /huol op/ or /puol/.

HOL', HOLE vb dial; sp for *hold*. *G*

HOLE sb dial. A grave. *BL G*

1833 Scott I 205 [Funeral song:] I say, broder, you can't go yet. When de morning star rise, den we put you in a hole. c 1930 Astley Clerk MS Songs No. 9, Put marble stone to me head to me feet Give me a hole wide and deep. 1943 *GL* Han, 'Ole, grave.

HOLE-HOLE sb dial; iterative <*hole*. Many holes; hole after hole. *G*

1952 FGC StC /likl-likl huol-huol/ many small holes.

HOLING GANG sb obs. A gang (of slaves) on a sugar estate digging cane-holes together.

1790 Beckford I 315, I had the picture of a holeing gang that was very naturally..described.

HOLLAND BLIND sb dial; <*Holland*, cloth +*blind*, a window-shade. A roller shade.

1952 FGC StM, Curtain, also called Holland blind.

HOLLY-ROSE sb bot; *OED* →1700. The plant *Turnera ulmifolia*, better known as RAM-GOAT DASH-ALONG.

a 1726 Barham (1794) 75, Holly-rose or sage-rose. Vulgarly so called; in Latin *cistus*. Sir H. Sloane mentions a sort in Jamaica..Linn. Turnera ulmifolia. 1864 Grisebach 784, Holly-rose: *Turnera ulmifolia*. 1954 *WIMJ* 32, Dash Along; Sage or Holly Rose.

holo sb dial; cf BOLOW 2. See quots.

1943 *GL* StC, Holo, wife; 1959 DeC West /holo/ a pet name for a sweetheart.

HOLY GHOST PLANT sb. An unidentified plant.

1873 Rampini 145, There was the Holy Ghost plant, with its pure white petals, shrouding the snowy dove within. (Seen in Mandeville.)

HOMAN sb; dial sp for *woman*, though less common than OMAN, OOMAN. *G*

1907 Jekyll 162 [Song:] Bad homan oh! nyam an' cry.

homoch adv phr dial; for *how much*.

HONEY BANANA sb. A variety of banana.

1957 JN StE (Elderslie) /oni/ name for banana.

HONEY BERRY sb obs; transl of genus name. An old name for the GUINEP, *Melicocca bijuga*.

1811 Titford xv, Cunep, or Honey Berry (*Melicocca*).

HONEY BUSH sb dial. An unidentified plant of the *Compositæ* family, similar to JACK-IN-THE-BUSH.

1952 FGC StT, Honey-bush—spikes with small purple flowers among tiny leaves; lower leaves much cut.

HONEYCOMB ROCK sb; <*honeycomb* sb +*rock*; cf *OED honeycomb stone* 1753 only. 'Honeycombed' (quots 1899) may be formed with *OED -ed*[1] or *-ed*[2]. A type of alabaster with very sharp surface: see quot 1725.

1725 Sloane 337, Marmor cinereum superficie cavitatibus donata. Honey Comb Rock. The greatest part of all the Rocks I have seen in this Island, are of this Stone, many Hills are mostly made of it. It is whitish and soft like Alabaster, the Grain of it is very fine, so that it seems to be made of Clay, and has no appearing Pores in it..The natural Surface..has many Holes in it, like those of a Honey-Comb, whence its Name. 1886 Hooper map, The John Crow Mountains, a great plateau of honeycomb rock. 1890 Thomas 19, Surely boots can be procured with soles of strength enough to withstand the ravages even of honeycomb rock. 1899 Hill 25, In many places the surface is marked by jagged honeycombed rocks, between which grows a dense tropical foliage. *Ibid* 79, This formation is of cavernous or 'honeycombed' texture and weathers into irregularly crystalline limestone.

HONEY DRAM sb; *DA* 1834 only. A kind of drink: see quot.

1907 Jekyll 70, Honey dram: The ingredients are honey, water, chewstick, ginger and rum. When mixed, the dram is put in the sun to ripen.

HONEY MINT sb. An unidentified plant.

1952 FGC Tre, Honey mint, =scarlet mint.

HONEYSUCKLE sb.

1. The GOLDEN APPLE 1. Obs.

1756 Browne 327, Passiflora 3. Foliis ovatis..[etc.] This plant..is a climber, and spreads, like the Granadilla, so as to be frequently employed in arbours. [Ident 1926 Fawcett 237.] 1814 Lunan II 40.

2. *Bidens reptans*; see quot.

1953 *WIMJ* 241, *Bidens reptans*..Marigold; Golden Rod; Honeysuckle; McKitty or McCathy Weed. The shoots are used in decoction as a cold remedy.

honggl see *onggl*.

HOOD see WOOD; also for *would*.

HOODANCE see WOOD ANT.

HOODIAS see *huodyas*.

HOOK /huk/ sb[1] dial; <*hoop*, a ring; but cf the very widespread Sp *bejuco*, pronunc /behúuko/ flexible plant or vine. See Introd, phonology, lix.

1. A barrel-hoop. *BL*

1956 Mc Man /di báril ha húk róun i/ *The barrel has hoops round it.*

2. Any of several flexible shrubs or vines that were used to make barrel hoops for sugar estates; they are used today to make the frames of large baskets, donkeys' hampers, etc. Cf COOPER HOOK, HOOK WIS, WILD HOOK, etc.

3. An iron ring, part of the apparatus for making BAMMY.

1958 DeC StE /huk/ the iron ring, often called a hoop, used with the iron in making bammy.

HOOK sb[2] dial; abbr of names of machetes beginning with this word; see below.

HOOK-AN'-BANG sb dial. =next.

1958 DeC StT /huk-an-bang/ a cutlass.

HOOK-AN'-DRAW /huk-an-draa, huk-an-jaa/ sb dial; <*hook* vb + *and* + *draw* vb. A kind of MACHETE with a hook on the end of the blade with which the user hooks and draws toward him the thing to be cut. *G*

1958 DeC Man /huk-an-draa/ a hooked machete with the inside of the hook sharp; Port /hukanjaa/ a cutlass.

HOOK-BACK sb dial; etym uncert: *hook* may be noun or verb, *back* may be noun or adv, the senses being respectively a machete that has a hook on its back, or one that hooks back. A kind of hooked MACHETE.

1958 DeC StAnn /huk-bak/ a cutlass.

HOOK BILL, ~ CUTLASS, ~ MACHETE, sb dial. =HOOK-AN'-DRAW. *BA G*

1961 *CLS* 75, see map showing distribution of thirty variant terms.

HOOKIE see *huki, huku.*

HOOK-MOUTH sb dial. A MACHETE with strongly recurved rounded end.

1958 DeC Kgn /huk-mout/ a cutlass [as described].

HOOK-POINT sb dial. =HOOK-AN'-DRAW.

1952 FGC Man West /huk-paint mashiet/ hooky, turn-point. 1956 Mc StE; StT /uk-paint/ machete—also called BOAR.

HOOK-STICK sb dial; for *hooked-stick. G*

1958 FGC StAnd, Hook-stick, A stick held in the left hand to support the weight and to protect the foot, by one cutting close to the ground with a machete. It has a hook which can be used to pull at bushes which one is cutting. (Also called GARABATA.)

HOOK VINE see next.

HOOK WIS (or **WITHE**) sb dial. =HOOP-WITHE.

1952 FGC StAnn /huk wis/ = BASKET WIS; StM /huk vain/ cut and shaped in making baskets.

HOOKWORM BUSH sb dial. An unidentified plant.

1952 FGC StAnn, Hookworm bush, fine seeds, peculiar druggy smell, inconspicuous flower.

HOOP-CUTLASS sb dial; <HOOK-CUTLASS. (This development of /p/ < /k/ is the reverse of that found in *hoop* > HOOK.)

1958 DeC StAnd /hup kotlas/ a hooked cutlass.

HOOP TREE sb bot; see quot. The tree *Melia azederach* and its varieties.

1774 see LILAC. 1811 see BEAD TREE 1. 1837 Macfadyen 167–8, *Melia sempervirens.* Hoop-tree..This shrubby tree, although now very common, is probably, as it is not noticed by either Sloane or Browne, an introduced plant..The branches being long and supple, it has been proposed to employ them in making hoops. 1920 Fawcett 215–16, *M. Azederach*..Hoop Tree, West Indian Lilac, Bead Tree.

HOOP WITHE (or **WIS**) sb; *OED* 1847, 1884.

1. The plant *Trichostigma octandrum,* whose branches were used to make barrel hoops.

1756 Browne 149, Rivina 2. Sarmentosa..The Hoop Withe..The stalk is very tough and flexible, and often made into hoops, when there is a scarcity of those imported from Europe or North-America. 1811 Titford 41, Climbing Rivina, or Hoop Withe. 1914 Fawcett 156, *T. octandrum*..Hoop Withe, Cooper Withe.

2. The plant *Colubrina asiatica,* a naturalized plant, also used for hoops.

1864 Grisebach 784, Hoop-withe: *Rivina* and *Colubrina asiatica.* 1926 Fawcett 69–70, *C. asiatica*..Hoop Withe.. Bushy shrub..with long trailing branches.

HOOP WOOD sb; *OED* 1756. The tree *Zygia latifolia,* from whose wood hoops were made.

1756 Browne 279, Zygia 1..Horse-wood, or Hoop-wood..This shrub is very common in St Mary's: it grows chiefly in low moist lands..The wood is pretty tough, and sometimes cut for hoops. 1920 Fawcett 150, *Z. latifolia*..Horse Wood, Hoop Wood.

HOOTIAH sb dial uncom; etym unknown. (Perh <*hutia,* the Indian cony?)

1943 *GL,* Hootiah, one who lives in bushes.

HOPPING DICK sb; *OED* 1874 ref. A well-known Jamaican thrush, *Turdus aurantius,* with a characteristic hopping gait. Cf TRICKING-CHICK, CHICK-MAN-CHICK.

1847 Gosse 136, Not unfrequently we are startled by a shrill scream in some lonely place, and out rushes the Hopping Dick, jumping with rapidity across the road, almost close to our horse's feet. He greatly reminds me of the English Blackbird, in his sable plumage, and bright yellow beak, but especially when hopping along the branches of some pimento tree, or upon the sward beneath. 1952 FGC Han /hápn-dík/; StAnn /hápin-dík/.

HOPPISH adj dial; <*hop* + *-ish.* Limping.

1954 LeP StT, Man who limps: hoppish.

HORIZONTAL ANGEL-FISH sb ichth rare. The blue angel-fish, whose elongated fins form horizontal lines above and below it, tapering to thin tips behind.

1892 Cockrell list, Horizontal angel-fish, *Holocanthus ciliaris.*

HORN-BLOWER sb. Prob =HORN-MAN.

1833 Scott I 350, see GOMBAY 2.

HORNED LOBSTER sb obs. The Jamaican sea crayfish: LOBSTER.

1756 Browne 424, The Horned Lobster, or Great Cray-fish.

HORN-HEAD sb dial. The horned trunk-fish *Ostracion quadricorne.*

1952 FGC StE /haan-hed/ trunkfish with horns.

HORN-MAN sb dial; prob a loan-translation of Twi *abɛ́ŋfó*: cf ABENG. Among the Maroons, a man who blew the horn, giving signals.

1803 Dallas I 89, The Maroons had a particular call upon the horn for each individual, by which he was summoned from a distance, as easily as he would have been spoken to by name, had he been near. *Ibid* 70–1, One of Quao's men, a hornman..the hornman was acquainted with the treaty..Captain Adair made a halt, and ordered his guide to blow his horn. The Maroons knowing by the information given by the sounds that they proceeded from the missing hornman, returned an answer with one of their horns. 1929 Beckwith 193, In Accompong the 'horn man' calls out the name of the dead through a conch, and everyone listens to the signal.

HORN SHARK sb dial. The hammer-head shark, so called from the branched shape of its head, as if it had horns. *G*

1952 FGC Port, West /háanshâak/ shovel-head, hammer-head.

HORNY-CONY, HORNY-MONEY sb chiefly dial; <*horny* (from the protruding dorsal spine) +*cony* (common in names of fish, cf CONY-BUCK), or the form *money*, evid a folk-etym alteration, and perh an individualism. The file-fish *Monacanthus tomentosus*, or similar species; quot 1952 prob refers to the HORN-HEAD.

1854–5 *TJSA* I 145, *Monacanthus tomentosus*—Horny Cony. 1952 FGC West /háani-mòni tróngkfish/ the kind with horns.

HORNY OWL sb dial. The Jamaican Brown Owl (*Pseudoscops grammicus*). Also DUSKY EARED-OWL.

1952 FGC StE /hàaniyóul/. [1956 Jeffrey-Smith 11, Our brown owl is peculiar to Jamaica and is also known as the Horned Owl, but the so-called 'horns' are really tufts of feathers erect on the head, above the circular facial discs.]

HORSE BARK see next.

HORSE-BATH /haas-baat/ sb dial. A common weed used (among other things) to scrub horses. Also called CHIGGER-NUT.

1927 Beckwith 19, Horse-bath. (Near Accom, StE.) 1952 FGC Tre /háas-báat/ = /háal-báat, chíganít/. 1955 *WIMJ* 71, *Tournefortia hirsutissima* L. Chigger Nut; Cold Withe; Horse (Harsh) Bark (Bath?).

HORSE BEAN sb; cf *OEDS* 1684→, *DA*, for other plants. In Jamaica: *Canavalia ensiformis*, because of its large size and perhaps from its use as cattle feed.

1696 Sloane 68, Phaseolus maximus, siliqua ensiformi.. *Horse Beans.* In hortis Insulæ Jamaicæ frequenter seritur; circa urbem St Jago. 1837 Macfadyen 291–2, see OVERLOOK BEAN. 1920 Fawcett 61–2, *C. ensiformis*.. Horse Bean, Overlook Bean, Sword Bean, Jack Bean.. Experiments seem to show that the food value of this bean for cattle is great, as indicated by Church's analysis [in India].

HORSE-BURST sb; cf Sp *revienta-caballos* (Malaret). =HORSE-POISON, where see quot 1851.

c 1950 Inst List, Horse-burst, *Isotoma longiflora*.

HORSE CASSIA sb; see quot 1725; *OED* quotes 'Webster 1864'. The tree *Cassia grandis*.

1696 Sloane 146, *Horse Cassia*. In sylvis campestribus Jamaicæ Insulæ..frequens est pulcherrima hæc arbor. 1725 Sloane 44, Horse-Cassia, from its being given to purge Horses by Farriers. 1774 Long III 731, The pulp of the *horse-cassia* is likewise a purgative, but so violent and griping in its operation that it is never administered except to horses. 1920 Fawcett 101, *C. grandis*..Horse Cassia..The pulp is used like that of *C. fistula*, but is coarser and more powerful.

HORSE-CATCHER sb obs; *OED* 1740. One who caught wild horses for sale, =DRIVER 1.

1739 Leslie 178, If any Driver or Horse-catcher shall fraudulently or designedly put any false Mark, or deface any old Mark, he shall for such Offence be guilty of Felony. No common Horse-catcher shall ride or drive in any Savannah, without giving 100*l*. Bond.

HORSE-EYE BEAN sb; *OED* 1700–50. *BL*

1. The vine and the large round seeds of *Mucuna urens* and *M. sloanei*. (1920 Fawcett 52–3 makes a distinction, giving the first as OX-EYE and the second as HORSE-EYE, but it is not general. *OED* definitions are erron.)

1696 Sloane 69, Phaseolus Brasilianus frutescens lobis villosis pungentibus maximus..*Horse-eye Bean.* 1740 Importance 45, The *Horse-ey'd Bean* has a rough Pod upon which the Cow-Itch grows; the Bean is round and black like a large Eye. 1814 Lunan I 382–3, Horse or OX-EYE BEAN. *Dolichos urens*..with a black hilus almost round them, looking like a horse's eye. 1864 Grisebach 781, Horse-eye Bean: *Mucuna urens.* 1952 FGC Port /háas ái/ play marbles; StM /háas hái/.

2. Applied to the hard round seeds of the NICKER Tree.

1952 FGC Han /háas ái/ play with: use marble as /taa/; one red [i.e. yellow] horse-eye is worth two ordinary ones.

3. Confused with the HORSE BEAN.

1851 Gosse 153, It is the Horse-eye bean (*Dolichos ensiformis*) bearing large, sword-like legumes, with white oval beans.

HORSE-EYE CAVALLY sb dial; cf CAVALLY. A variety of the CAVALLY fish thought to have eyes like a horse's. *BA*

1854–5 *TJSA* I 143, Caranx fallax—quaretereba of Margrave, horse-eye cavalla. 1873 Rampini 171, Quaint lore about..the amberjack and the horse-eye Carvallhy.. did we glean from our negro boatmen.

HORSE-EYE JACK sb dial. A variety of the Jack fish with eyes thought to resemble a horse's; perh the same fish as prec—see CAVALLY JACK.

1952 FGC StJ, StM /háas-ái ják/ have a round forehead.

HORSE-EYE MULLET sb. A variety of the Mullet fish with eyes thought to resemble a horse's.

1854–5 *TJSA* I 143, Mugil equinoculus—horse eye mullet.

HORSE-EYE WENSHMAN sb dial. A variety of the WENSHMAN fish with eyes thought to resemble a horse's.

1952 FGC StJ /háas-ái wénshmàn/ same as WHITE WENSHMAN.

HORSE-FOOT COCO sb dial. A variety of coco (also called MARANGA COCO), which resembles a horse's foot.

1952 FGC StC, StM /háas-fút kúoko/ same as maranga, grows on a long neck, a yard from the head.

HORSE-HEAD sb dial. One of the traditional figures in the JOHN CANOE masquerade, who wears a horse's head mask or the actual skull of a horse. It may be historically related to the 'hobby-horse' figure of English mumming.

1943 *GL* StM, Horsehead, related to John Cunnu—chief dress, skeleton head of a horse. 1951 P. Hickson *Gleaner* 25 Oct, 'John Canoe' popularly called 'Juncoonu'.. 'Juncoonu' commonly called 'horse-head'..was demoralising and the dances were vulgar..only a little before World War II the police did all it could to suppress it..many people were taken to court for dancing horse-head, it was so vulgar.

HORSE-KIND sb; <*horse*+*kind* on the analogy of *mankind* and perh also from the frequency of this type of comp in Jamaican use: BREAD-KIND, FISH-KIND, FOOD-KIND, MEAT-KIND. Animals of the equine sort: horses, mules, donkeys.

1936 Olivier 36, 'Hay-Grass', and..guinea grass..offer good feeding for horsekind and cattle. 1956 Ja Dept Agric (Veterinary & Livestock) [Title of pamphlet:] *Common Diseases of Horsekind.*

HORSE PLANTAIN sb now chiefly dial. A large variety of the plantain (*Musa paradisiaca*). *G*

1725 Sloane 143, The greatest Sort which is rank, is called Horse-Plantain. The larger Pleasant-Plantain. The least Sort called Maiden-Plantain, is reckon'd the most pleasant of any. 1950 Pioneer 70, Him meet him old frien, Brer Rat..wid a big bunch a horse plantain pon him head. 1952 FGC Port, StAnd, StAnn, StE, StJ, StM, StT /háas pláantin, háas pláantn/ has few seeds but very stout.

HORSE POISON sb; *ODS* 1851 only. Any of several plants poisonous to horses, but esp *Isotoma longiflora*; see quots. Also called HORSE-BURST.

1851 Gosse 80, Among them peeps forth a lovely white blossom, resembling a star at the extremity of a long and slender tube. This, notwithstanding its treacherous beauty, is one of the most venomous of plants (*Isotoma longiflora*), commonly called Horse-poison, from its fatal effects on those animals, if they chance to eat it; causing their bodies to swell until they actually burst. 1854–5 *TJSA* I 65, Horse Poison—Hippobroma, Isotoma longiflora, Lobelia longiflora. 1955 *WIMJ* 73, *Isotoma longiflora*..Madam Fate; Star Flower; Horse Poison.

HORSE PURSLANE sb bot; *OED* 1828 ref. The plant *Trianthema portulacastrum*; 'horse' refers to its being rather thick and coarse.

1696 Sloane 89, Portulacæ affinis folio subrotundo succulento..*Horse-Purslane.* Post pluvias..circa urbem St Jago. 1864 Grisebach 784, Horse-purslane: *Trianthema monogynum.* 1914 Fawcett 168, *T. Portulacastrum*.. Horse Purslane.

HORSE-RADISH TREE sb bot; *OED* 1859→. The tree *Moringa oleifera*—see quot 1811. *G*

1811 Titford Expl to Plate VII 6, Horse-radish tree, or Moringa..The roots when scraped are used as horse-radish to which they are very similar. 1837 Macfadyen 324, Moringa..Horse-radish Tree. 1914 Fawcett 248. 1955 *WIMJ* 146, *Moringa oleifera* Lam. Horse-radish Tree; Ben Nut Tree; Moringa (*Maranga*). The tree is not native to Jamaica but is grown to some extent as an ornamental.

HORSE-TONGUE sb dial.

1959 DeC Han /haas-tong/ a dumpling, finger-shaped, but flattened, creased, and boiled. (Also called COW-TONGUE, DOG-TONGUE, etc.)

HORSE-WOOD sb; *OED* 1756 only. The tree *Zygia latifolia.*

1756 Browne 279, see HOOP-WOOD. 1864 Grisebach 784. 1920 Fawcett 150. 1952 FGC StAnn /haas wud/ similar to dogwood—clearer-coloured bark; StM, Horse-wood, very hard, has half-moon shaped green bean—use for live fence.

hos see *hoks.*

HO SENNY HO phr dial; <Chinese—prob Hakka dialect. A widely known phrase used in greeting Chinese shopkeepers; the conventional answer is MOW SENNY. **s.**

c1916 FGC Kgn /hou seni mau/. 1943 *GL* Kgn, Ho senny ho—how business. Mow senny—business bad. 1960 F. Milner StAnd /huo seni huo/ greeting.

HOT[1] adj dial; <*hot* adj. **s.**

[1. In Std Engl senses—not specif Ja.]

2. Of a drum: invested by spirits of the dead—see quot.

1953 Moore 126, Hot—Said of drums at Cumina ceremony when the fast rim beat indicates the presence of zombies in the drum.

HOT[2] a sp for dial *hat,* hurt. *BL*

hot see HUT.

HOT-AND-NICE sb slang. A meat patty.

1948 U.Newton IV 15, Had sardines, drum-and-fife crackers and a 'hot and nice' for lunch.

HOT BELLY sb dial; <*hat,* hurt+*belly.* Pain in the belly; cf BELLY-HOT, the more common term. *G*

1955 *WIMJ* 80, *Hyptis capitata*..Boiled to make tea, this species..is used in the treatment of colds, 'hot belly' and perhaps constipation.

HOT BOY sb dial slang. A young man of young 'blood' about town. Cf LION.

1960 LeP StAnd.

HOT BRAN WELL BUTTERED sb. A game, formerly a favourite in the country.

1873 see BEG-YOU-LITTLE-WATER. 1877 Murray *Kittle* 17, 'Hide and seek', 'Hot bean [*sic*] well buttered', 'Thread the needle', 'Beg you little water', &c., were played in their turns amidst much boisterous merriment. 1929 Beckwith 78, Hot bran well buttered.

HOT-HOUSE sb obs; etym uncert: HOT, hot or hurt, or the two blended, +*house*; *OED* 6, 1828 only.

1. A hospital for slaves, usually on a sugar estate. Obs.

1707 Sloane ciii, One Prince, a lusty Negro, had been ill of the Yaws..and flux'd for it in one of the Chirurgeons Hot-Houses at Town, where being kept extremely hot, and abridg'd of Victuals, he..broke open the Door and ran home. 1788–9 McNeill 8, He [*sc* a sick slave] is put into a house particularly appropriated to the purpose (a lazaretto or *hot-house,* as it is generally called) he is attended by a practitioner of medicine. 1801 Nugent 40, There is an excellent hospital on this estate, which is called a hot-house, where the blackies appear particularly comfortable, and well taken care of.

2. Attrib in *Hot-house doctor, keeper, woman.* See quots.

1790 Beckford II 17, The Hot-house..has a narrow piazza in front, at the end of which is a small apartment for the nurse or hot-house woman. 1827 Hamel I 244, The hothouse keeper indulged him with a plentiful dose of grog. 1835 Madden I 154, The hot-house doctor is generally a negro disqualified by age or infirmity for labour in the field. He has charge of the medicines.

HOT-OVER sb dial; <*hot* vb+*over.*

1958 DeC Man /hat-uova/—left-over food, heated again for a later meal.

HOUND /houn/ sb dial.

1942 HPJ, Houn (hound): an intensive word, esp in the phr *hound of a* preceding the noun to be intensified. He gave him hound of a licking.

HOUNDISH /hounish/ adj dial; *OED* →1849 in other senses.

1942 HPJ, Hounish:—greedy.

HOUSE sb.

1942 HPJ, House: The top of a cocoanut tree trunk, where the fronds branch off.

HOUSE-A-BLAZES adj dial. An intensive phr: altogether, utterly.

1943 *GL* StT, House-a-blazes, out and out.

HOUSE-A-HAN' sb dial joc; <*house*+A[1] I +*hand.* An umbrella.

1943 *GL* StAnd, StC, StE, House-a-han, umbrella. 1959—well known (FGC).

HOUSE ANT sb; cf *house fly.*

1943 *NHN* II 70, House Ant, *Monomorum* sp.

HOUSE JOHN CANOE sb; <*house*+JOHN CANOE. One of the types of John Canoes traditionally a part of Christmas masquerades. See quot.

1837 Belisario Expl to Plate 3, House John-Canoe. The house* is usually constructed of pasteboard and coloured papers—it is also frequently highly ornamented with beads, tinsel, spangles, pieces of looking-glass, &c. &c... *The specimen as given in the print, although *a plain one,* has been selected to shew an evident attempt (however humble) at West Indian architecture—the scalloped pillars..to the balconies so universally attached to dwellings.

HOUSEKEEPER sb arch.

1. Euphemism for the coloured mistress of a white planter, esp during the 18th and early 19th centuries. *G*

a1818 Lewis (1845) 87, These brown housekeepers generally attach themselves so sincerely to the interests of their protectors..that they commonly retain their situation..This kind of connexion is considered by a brown girl in the same light as marriage..and I am told that, except on these terms, it is extremely difficult to obtain the favours of a woman of colour. 1823 Stewart 326, She beheld with envy the gay, showy, and dissipated life which many of the companions of her youth led; who, being the *housekeepers* of men of fortune, were enabled to dress finely, and dash about in style in their carriages, attended by servants in livery; while she, poor woman, was obliged to toil from morning to night. 1839 McMahon 186, see WIFE.

2. As a satiric figure in the John Canoe masquerade.

1837 Belisario Expl to Plate 2, There is another Set, denominated 'House-keepers', who never *dance* in their progress through the streets.

HOUSE-LIZARD sb. Lizards of the kinds that frequent dwellings—in contrast to ground lizards, tree lizards, etc. They would include var brown and green species of *Anolis*. *G N T*

1952 FGC Man, StT, House-lizard.

HOUSE-SIDE WEED sb.

1942 *NHN* I 6 11, In the dry areas are associated Wild Indigo..Blue Chickweed or House-side weed (*Salvia alata*), Duppy Gun..[etc.].

HOUSE SPIDER sb. A type of spider common in dwellings. Also called ANANCY.

1949 *NHN* IV 35, House spider, *Heteropoda venatoria*.

HOUSE WASP sb. The common wasps, which build nests (both of mud and of wood-pulp) on verandas, under the eaves of houses, etc.

1952 FGC Han.

HOUSE WEED sb. A general term for small ground-creeping plants used commonly in garden beds around dwellings: species of *Commelina*, Creeping Jenny, etc.

1952 FGC StM.

HOUSE WIS sb dial; <*house*+*withe*. Any kind of vine or 'wis' used to tie the thatch on to the roof or walls of a house.

1952 FGC StM /hous wis/ wis used in thatching house—some call it coco-wis.

[**HOWDY** int dial; cf *OED*: in Britain this became dial or provincial in the 17th cent but was preserved in America. In the 19th cent it was often assoc with negroes—cf *OED* quot 1894. *DAE* 1863→. A greeting. *G N*

1833 Foulks 47, The labourers..meet..and the noisy *how d'ye* good humoredly goes round.]

HOW IS IT? phr dial. A greeting. *BA G*

1956 Mc Man /ou iz it?/ *How are things? How are you?*

HOW-MUCH /hómoch, húmoch/ conj phr dial. *BL G*

1. As much as; in neg context: however much, no matter how.

1943 *GL* Port, Whomuch, how much. 1952 FGC StC /hómoch yu kyaan híit/ *as much as you can eat*. 1956 Mc /hu moch/ an alternative form to /hou/ only in this collocation.

2. How many. (Cf MUCH.)

HOW-YOU-DO /hou-yu-du/ phr chiefly dial; <*how do you do?* A friendly greeting. *BA G*

1774 Long II 427, In their conversation, they confound all the moods, tenses, cases, and conjugations, without mercy: for example..*me glad for see you* (*pro*, I am glad to see you); *how you do* (for, how d'ye do?). 1958 FGC StAnd [Returned Jamaican meeting a friend at Palisadoes airport:] How you do, man?

hud see WOOD; also for *would*.

HUDIUP see *hodiop*.

HUFF vb dial; <*hough* sb, evid understood as meaning 'hoof'—cf BULL HOOF, GOAT-HOUGH TREE. To scratch with the hoof. *BA*

1907 Jekyll 79, Wolf said:—'I will huff an' I will cuff an' blow you house down'. *Ibid* 83 [Note:] Huff, scratch with the hoof.

HUG-ME-CLOSE sb dial.

1. A common weed having burs that cling to clothing: *Achyranthes indica*. *BA*

1954 *WIMJ* 28, see COLIC WEED.

2. Moss, that clings close to trees and rocks.

1952 FGC StAnn, Hug-me-close, moss; also Man.

HUG-ME-TIGHT sb dial. The fern *Polypodium exiguum*? (A rare fern from the upper Blue Mountains—the identification is doubtful.) *BA*

1927 Beckwith 19, Hug-me-tight. *Polypodium exiguum* Hew. For 'female weakness', boil this fern as a bath. 1953 *WIMJ* 246, According to Beckwith..; 1954 *WIMJ* 31, *Polypodium exiguum*..? Hug-me-tight.

HUGOO, HUGUY sb; <Chinese?

1943 *GL* StC, Hugoo, Chinese dance; StC, Huguy, Chinese dancing hall.

huk-an-bang see HOOK-AN'-BANG.

huk-an-draa, huk-an-jaa see HOOK-AN'-DRAW.

huki, huku sb dial; familiarized forms of *hook*, abbr of *hook-machete*. See *-u*.

1952 FGC Man /huki/ machete. 1954 LeP StE, Hookie—machete with hooked end. 1956 Mc StE /huki/ also called /huk-paint, ton-bil/. 1958 DeC StAnd (Irish Tn) /huku/ a cutlass.

HULLO sb dial uncom.

1943 *GL* Man, Hullo, an indifferent person.

huluuz sb dial; prob phonosymbolic—cf *bululups*, *dundun*, and similar terms of endearment.

1958 DeC Port /hulúuz/ affectionate term used to a child.

[**HUMBLE PLANT** sb obs; cf *OED* 1664→ for *Mimosa pudica*. Confused by Long, whose descr suits *M. pudica*, not BLACK-BEAD SHRUB.

1774 Long III 780, It has also some affinity to the black-bead shrub, or large-leafed mimosa, of Jamaica; a shrubby sensitive, and called, by some, the *humble plant*, which has a declining prickly stalk, with pods growing in clusters, with prickly coverings.]

HUNG vb obs; a new vb formed by conversion <past pple of *hang*. To set up on a supporting framework.

1797 *Braco* 16 Mar, Masons hunging a Copper at the Wharf to boil Salt for the Mules. *Ibid* 22 Mar, 3 Masons and Labourers hunging a Copper at the Wharf. *Ibid* 23, 24 Mar, etc.

HUNGER vb dial arch or biblical?; in StdE no longer literal. To be hungry.

1956 Mc StE (Accom) /hi hongga/ he feels hungry.

HUNGRY sb dial; <*hungry* adj; or perh for *hungriness*. Hunger. *BL G*; *SC hángri.*

1839 McMahon 57, Poor nega da dead we [*with*] hungry. 1950 Pioneer 41, Lawd Bra Nancy, me dah dead fe hungry se ef yuh can get lickle sinting fe me eat noh. 1956 Mc Man /moma, a daien fi honggri/; Hungry ketch dem. 1958 DeC StE /honggri/ a noun meaning hunger: /mi kyaan sliip fi honggri/; StAnd /honggri a gi mi hel/.

HUNGRY TIME sb dial. A season or period during which food is scarce. *G*

1868 *TJRSA* I 65, One big big hungry time, when nobody can't get nutten fe nyam, Annancey say to Green-lizard..[etc.]. 1907 Jekyll 123, One day, height a hungry time, Blackbird have a feedin' tree in a sea. (1959 current. FGC.)

HUNTEN vb dial uncom; <*hunt* vb + *-n* suffix[2]. Cf FISHEN. To hunt. *BL*

1952 FGC StJ, Go huntnin' wild hog.

HUNTER sb; *OED* ref, no quots. The bird *Hyetornis pluvialis.*

1847 Gosse 277, Hunter. Old Man.—Rainbird..The appellation of Rainbird is indiscriminately applied to both this and the preceding [*sc Saurothera vetula*], as is, in a less degree, that of Old Man. I use a term by which I have heard it distinguished, in St Elizabeth's, perhaps derived from the perseverance with which it 'hunts' (i.e. searches) for its prey. 1956 Jeffrey-Smith 63 (ref to Gosse).

HUNTERMAN sb dial. 1. A hunter. s. *BL N*

1907 Jekyll 137, A old lady have two son, one name Dory Dunn an' one name Tumpa Toe..an' Dory Dunn is a hunterman.

HUNTING SHEPHERD sb dial cant. An officer in Revivalist cults: see quot.

1953 Moore 85, A hunting shepherd..has the duty, principally, to hunt out every part of the yard..before the service begins. He also meets the good spirits formally; and the bad spirits who might harm the service.

HUNU see UNU.

huodyas adj dial; prob <*odious*, but there may be concurrent infl <Twi *ahũ-de*, a fearful thing; terrible things. Cf HOOTIAH.

1943 *GL* Port, Hoodias, terrible. 1956 EB Port /húodyas/ terrible.

huonyan see *uonyan*.

huoti hapl, huoti hiiti hapl see OTAHEITE APPLE.

huovn sb dial; an occas var of *uovn*.

HURRO-HURRO sb dial uncom; etym unknown.

1943 *GL* StAnn, Hurro hurro, cow tripe.

HURRY-COME-UP sb chiefly dial; cf *OED come v* 69 f, '*Come up*, To rise in rank or position. *Obs.*' quots →1561.

A. sb: 1. One who rises rapidly in the world. (The term often implies discredit.) Cf NEW-NAYGA, SINCE-WHEN. *G*

1933 McK 68, Tack was in peasant parlance, a hurry-come-up. That was the native word for *nouveau riche*, only more inclusive, as it meant not merely a have-nothing who had risen to be a have-something, but also one of bad reputation. 1943 *GL* Han; StM, Hurry-come-up, newly rich. 1949 Reid gloss, A hurry-come-up man, a parvenu.

2. Grown up rapidly.

1943 *GL* StAnd, Hurry-come-up, grown up quick.

B. adj: Done hastily, therefore poorly.

1957 EB Port /hori-kom-op/ not properly done; hurried.

C. vb: See quot.

1957 EB Port, To do something over-hastily, poorly.

HURT see *hat*.

huse see HUSSAY.

HUSK see *hoks*.

HUSSAY /ásè, húsè, wuse/ sb chiefly dial; <*Husain*, name of the younger grandson of Mohammed, shouted during celebration of the Muharram in commemoration of his murder with his brother Hasan. An annual festival among East Indians, traditionally including a dramatic representation of Husain's fate.

1924 Beckwith *The Hussay Festival in Jamaica* (see bibliography). 1943 *GL* most parishes, Assay, festival; Hossay; Hussay, East Indian festival. 1952 FGC StM, Coolie make /wuse/: sing and have stick-licking dance; also do horse dance.

HUT, HUTCH /hot/ sb dial. A temporary and flimsy structure with roof and sometimes walls, for cooking, shade, protection from rain, etc. Cf *pata*, THATCH HOUSE, *tatu*. *BA G*

1956 Mc Clar /hot/ a shelter consisting of roof only. StAnd /hoch/ by road for sheltering cement; Man /hoch/ a small house of wattle and daub walls; Port, A /hoch/ has walls, whereas a *pata* hasn't.

huutiya sb dial; *huut* abbr of *bahut* + *-ier*. A man who pushes a bahut.

1956 LeP /húutiya/ a rough handcart man.

HUX see *hoks*.

HUYG see HIGE.

I[1] /i/ pron dial; <*it*. A dial pronunc-form of *it* used in unstr positions (the stressed counterpart generally being /hit/). It is freq misunderstood for HE and so written. *BL G*

1873 Rampini 178 [Prov:] No catchie, no habie. [*If you don't catch it, you won't have it.*] 1942 Bennett 42, Yuh Well want i soh noh pose. [*You want it very much, so don't pretend.*] 1944 Campbell *Sweetie Charlie*, Hab im trouble a' yard, Mattie car' i down de street. 1957 JN StJ, The road right wey the red rock deh, i go roun so right back a dat hill.

I[2] /i/ article dial; <*the*. A pronunc-form: a further reduction beyond the usual /di/ for *the*.

1957 JN StJ, A wey i marble tun? [*Where did the marble go?*] See wey i bush de chop. [*See where the bush there is chopped.*] 1960 BLB 6 /ing gi wan a i pikni i faya/ *He gave one of the children the fire.* *BL G*

i see HE, IT. *BL*

-i /-i/ additive sound dial arch; historically prob due to the infl of W African languages (e.g. Twi) in which words may end only in vowels or sonorants: hence to other consonants /-a/ /-i/ /-u/ were added in Jamaican creole, more or less on principles of vowel harmony. This feature of creolism may be seen better preserved in Sranan (Surinam); it is an archaism in Jamaican creole.

Meaningless sound-element; its use today, however (except as established in songs, proverbs, etc.), indicates old-fashioned dial speech. Cf CHANGIE FE CHANGIE, TALKY-TALKY, YERRY, etc. *BL G*

1826 Williams 108–9, Brar!—You tink say when you die, you dead for true?..You tink say—Deady come, trouble come no mo? [Note:] 'Deady' = death. 1952 FGC Tre, Vervine—fe purge blood an' such-i-like.

IBBIA see HIB.

IBER vb dial rare; etym unknown, but cf Twi *bẽrà*, come, let us go!

1943 *GL* StC, Iber, to travel.

IBO, IGBO see EBOE.

ICENING sb dial; <*ice* vb + -*n* suffix² + -*ing*. Icing (on a cake). *G*

1952 FGC West /ais-n-ing/.

iebli see ABBLY.

iechag, iejag see HEDGEHOG FISH.

iegyu see AGUE.

iez see AZE, EARS, *hiez*.

IF /if, ef/ introd interrog word dial; the abbr of some such phrase as *I wonder* (*if*, etc.), or *Did you ask me* (*if*, etc.). *G N*

1. Introducing a question.

1960 FGC StAnd /if yu iz a good kecha/ *Are you a good catcher?*

2. Introducing the repetition of a question which (having not been fully understood) is repeated to make sure that that *was* the question: if, whether. *T*

1956 Mc Man, 'Did you like ——?' '/if ai did laik ——?/' *Did you ask me whether I liked* ——?; StAnd, 'Do you know where X is?' '/ef a duu nuo..?/' *Did you ask me if I know where X is?*

IF LIFE SAVE, IF LIFE SPARE phr dial; ellipt <*if my life is saved* or *spared*. A proviso added to a promise or prediction that one will do something at a future time: if my life is spared, God willing. *BL G T*

1956 Mc Man /mi kom orli mam, ef laif siev/ *I shall come early, Ma'am, if I'm spared.* 1958 DeC /if laif spier/ a standard formula used when arranging an appointment.. = D.V. 1959 FGC StAnd, I will come to see you tomorrow, if life spare. 1959 DeC StAnd (Irish Town) /if laif siev/.

-IFY adj-forming suffix dial; for -*ified* (as in *fancified, dandified*) but used to form words for which Std Engl has no corresp form in -*ified*. = -*ish*; connoting disapproval ranging from amused superiority to harsh scorn. See FUNKIFY, HEATIFY, JOKIFY, etc. *G*

IGNORANCE sb dial; evid parallel to IGNORANT. Obstinate or overbearing anger.

1942 HPJ, see next. *BL T*

IGNORANT /ígnaran, hígnaran, ígnoran/ adj dial; evid a malapropism for *indignant*, though the regular sense is sometimes mingled in.

1. Angry; quick to anger. *BA BL G T*

1942 HPJ, A person beside himself with rage, or obstinately blind in his overbearing conduct, is 'ignorant', and his frame of mind is 'ignorance'. 1952 FGC StAnd, StAnn /ígnaran/ indignant. 1956 Mc StE, Mind the mule get /ígnoran—im wi kík yu/ *Be careful that the mule doesn't get annoyed—he will kick you.* /yu wáan mek mi ígnoran?/ *Do you want to make me lose my temper?*

2. Arrogant, overbearing; ill-mannered.

1942 HPJ, see quot in 1 above. 1956 Mc Clar /hígnaran/ rude, ill-mannered. *BA BL G T*

IGHSTEEM see HIGH-STEAM.

I-HI, IHING see *iin-hiin*.

iim int dial; cf *iing, iin-hiin*, etc., in which a nasalized high-front vowel corresp to StdE vowels farther back. A sound made to fill a gap in speech when one is thinking of the next thing to say or trying to recall something; equiv to *uh* or *um*.

1952 FGC Port /iim/.

iing see EE.

iin prep dial; spelt in dial writing *een*; <*in*. A common dial pronunc of *in* (though the usual pronunc at all levels is /in/): in. *BL G*

1950 Pioneer 16, One big picture a rat lie dung een deh ..Anancy gi out..me mus een deh to.

iina, ina /íina, ína/ prep dial; sp in dial writing *in a, eena*; prob <*in, iin* + A⁸, though also infl by *into*—cf INTO. A common variant of *iin*: in, to, into. *BL*

1790 Moreton 153 [Song:] If me want for go in a Congo, Me can't go there!..Since massa go in a England, Me can't go there! 1833 Scott I 205 [Funeral song:] When de morning star rise, den we put you in a hole. 1943 *GL* most parishes, Eena, into. 1950 Pioneer 16, One big picture a Puss..eena de book. 1952 FGC StAnd, One kind of snail /liv ina bush/. 1956 Mc Man /shi tán wi mí íina díe/ *She stays with me during the day.*

iin-hiin /íin-híin, én-hén/ int dial; two nasalized, long high-front vowels (occasionally short mid-front) in close juncture, the first prec by glottal stop, the second by /h/ said with rising pitch: sp variously (see quots) and pronounced [ʔĩ:hĩ:], occasionally [ʔẽhẽ]; corresponding to US colloq *uh-huh*, but prob < Twi *ɛhẽẽ, interj* implying affirmation, approbation, assent... *yes!* Cf *in-in*. *T*

1. Yes.

1943 *GL* Clar, Ehnee; Port, Eẽ-hi; StAnn, Eenhi, Ihing; Tre, Eenhi; West, I-hi; all = yes. 1950 Pioneer 48, Ee-Hee Missis, is me same one Sidung yah all de time. 1952 FGC StAnn, Angel fish /én-hén/ like angel is butterfly. 1956 Mc StE /iin-hin/ yes.

2. In phr /iin-híin nòu/: see quot.

1960 BLB Man /iin-hiin nou/ taunting phrase said by one child to another in warning that he must be prepared for punishment for evil doing—usually accompanied by flipping of fingers.

iit-an-lef /íit-àn-léf/ sb dial; <*eat-and-leave*, or *eaten-and-left*: cf *lef*. Food left over from one meal, and saved to be eaten later. (Usually from night till the next morning.) *G*

1956 Mc Man /íit-an-lif/; StAnd /iit-an-lef/. 1958 DeC StT /hiit-an-lef/ left-over food. 1958 FGC StT /iit-an-lef/ chaklata.

ìitiuoti see OTAHEITE APPLE.

iivlin see EVELING.

ika vb dial; reduced <*nicker*, to neigh.

1952 FGC StJ /di kuolt ika—di mier ika/.

ILE /ail/ sb dial; the commonest pronunc of *oil*. (Found in Engl dial elsewhere, but the regular form in Jamaica.) Oil. (Also in cpds—see separate entries.) *BL*

1942 Bennett 19, Dem ax de po' pickney all 'bout British Isles W'en is ongle t'ree ile she know good[:] Kerosene ile fe de lamp, Castarile wen we sick An' cokenat ile wey we trow 'pon we food.

ILE A — see OIL OF —.

IMBA see HIMBA.

IMPERANCE see next.

IMPURENCE sb dial arch; <*impudence*, an example of substitution of /r/ for /d/.

1825 Shooting 10, Impurence. 1835 Madden II 153, Him say 'imperance to massa'.

IMPROVE vb dial. To gain weight—prob a euphemism.

1953 LeP StAnd, Miss' Cruickshank improve too much. [Putting on too much weight before having her baby.]

IMPROVER sb dial. Meaning uncertain—a switch?

1950 Pioneer 81, Dem tek bamboo make improver.

IN /in/ vb[1] dial; prob <*been*: equivalent therefore to BEN, EN, MIN, WEN. Was, were.

1943 *GL* Clar, Inda, were or was [followed by a verb]. 1956 Mc Clar /a in jos wan cheks mi tek/ *It was just one small piece I took;* /a in wan rieni nait mi kom dong/ *It was one rainy night I came down.*

in, ing vb[2] dial; a pronunc of *is*, produced by loss of *s* /z/ and nasalization of *i*.

1956 Mc StE (Accom) /so mi ing gaan nou/ *I am going now.* 1958 DeC Man, In (phonetically just nasalized /i/) verb meaning 'is': /if somting in kompólsari, yu kyaan duu beta, yu has tu guo/.

ina see *iina*.

IN ARROW phr; cf *OED arrow* 7b, 'The flowering stem of the sugar-cane', 1779→. Of the cane plant, individually or collectively: in flower, having 'shot' its arrow or arrows. *G T*

1790 Beckford I 50, A field of canes, when standing in the month of November, when it is in arrow (or full blossom) is one of the most beautiful productions. 1960 Still current (FGC).

INCENSE TREE sb; cf *OED*, for other trees.

1. A less common name for the BIRCH tree *Bursera simaruba*, alluding to its resinous gum.

1920 Fawcett 205–6, *B. Simaruba*..Red Birch, West Indian Birch, Turpentine Tree, Incense Tree, Mastic Tree..All parts abound with a glutinous balsamic juice of a turpentine odour. 1941 Swabey 13. 1955 *WIMJ* 157.

2. See quot. (Doubtful for Jamaica.)

1864 Grisebach 784, Incense tree: *Moschoxylon Swartzii*.

INCH MEASURE sb dial; cf *OED* 1851 only.

1956 Mc StE (Accom) /inch meja/ a tape-measure. Now, I think, old-fashioned or regional. 1960 BLB Man, Inch measure—not at all archaic or old-fashioned..I ask for tape-measure only in the store; in the house it is inch-measure. *BA G*

IN CROP see CROP.

INDIAN sb attrib, or adj.

1. In compounds: American Indian. See INDIAN ARROW-ROOT, INDIAN CONY, INDIAN PEPPER, etc.

2. In compounds: an occas abbr for EAST INDIAN. See INDIAN HAIR, INDIAN RIAL, etc.

INDIAN ARROW-ROOT sb; <INDIAN 1 +*arrow-root*: cf *OED* Arrow-root.

1696 Sloane 122, Canna Indica radice alba alexipharmaca..*Indian arrow root*. In hortis Jamaicæ & Caribearum Insularum. 1756 Browne 112–13, Maranta 1.. Indian Arrow-root. This plant is cultivated in many gardens in Jamaica, where it is..thought to resist the force of poisons very powerfully. 1801 Dancer 366, Indian arrow-root. 1952 FGC StM /ìnji nára/—whitish-green leaf.

INDIAN BELL-PEPPER sb obs; cf INDIAN PEPPER, BELL-PEPPER.

1707 Sloane lxxi, I saw them likewise here Preserve, or Pickle Green Indian-Bell-Pepper. Before it turns red, this Capsicum is cut and cleansed from its Seeds..[etc.].

INDIAN CAILE see INDIAN KALE.

INDIAN CONY sb; <INDIAN 1+*cony* (*OED* 4). *OED* 1796 only. The rodent *Capromys fournieri*, native to Jamaica, once very common and an article of food; now surviving in a few localities. Cf GRACY. *N*

1683 *Present State* 19, see RACCOON. 1756 Browne 484, Mus 2..the large brown *Indian* Coney..Mus 3..The small *Indian* Coney..the third, which is a native of *Jamaica*, and smaller than either of these two, differs but little..except the tail, which is short and stumped. 1952 FGC Man /injin kuoniz/ are destructive, eat cocos, live in stone holes—dogs seek them out like mongoose.

INDIAN CREEPER sb obs; <INDIAN 1 +*creeper*. See quots.

1814 Lunan I 399, Indian Creeper. Ipomœa..quamoclit..It is known by the name of *Barbadoes sweet-william*. Browne calls it the *American jessamine*..It is also called *Indian pink*, or *red bell-flower of America*. 1819 Dancer index, Indian creeper, =Barbadoes Sweet William. Ipomoea Quamoclit.

INDIAN CURRANT BUSH (or **TREE**) sb; <INDIAN 1+*currant-bush*; *ODS*, *DA*, for the coral berry only.

1. The plant *Miconia laevigata* and similar species, with fruits somewhat resembling currants.

1756 Browne 219, Melastoma 3..The smaller shrubby Melastoma, or Indian Currant-Tree. 1814 Lunan I 403–5, Indian currant-bush. Melastoma..14 Lævigata.. Browne calls this particularly the Indian currant-tree. 1864 Grisebach 783, Indian Currant bush: *Miconia*, *Clidermia*, etc. 1953 *WIMJ* 251, Miconia lævigata.. Chicken net; Indian Currant Bush; Johnny Berry.

2. The plant *Clidemia hirta* (of the same family, *Melastomaceae*), and similar species.

1864 Grisebach 783 (see quot above). 1953 *WIMJ* 251, *Clidemia hirta*..Indian Currant Bush, Soap Bush.

INDIAN GOD-TREE see GOD-TREE.

INDIAN HAIR sb; <INDIAN 2+*hair*. Long, straight, coarse hair (in contrast to curly or kinky hair).

1947 U.Newton II 2, see VISIT (ONE'S) INDIAN COUSIN. 1960 NJL StC /ínjan/ hair.

INDIAN KALE /ìnjin kíel/ sb; <INDIAN 1, in recent years sometimes taken to be INDIAN 2 +*kale*; *DAE*, *DA* 1810→.

1. Plants of the closely related genera *Xanthosoma* and *Colocasia*, the leaves of which are cultivated and eaten as greens and in soups: they are one type of CALALU.

1696 Sloane 62, *Indian Caile*, or *Tajas the lesser*. In agris ubique diligenter excultum provenit. 1793 Edwards I 195, To my own taste, however, several of the native growths, especially the chocho, ochra, Lima-bean, and Indian-kale, are more agreeable than any of the esculent vegetables of Europe. 1893 Sullivan 32, Indian Kale. 1913 Harris 32, Kale, Indian. *Xanthosoma atrovirens*.. The young leaves are boiled, chopped fine and dressed with butter, pepper and salt, and make an excellent.. spinach. 1943 *GL* Port, Injin Kale, a vegetable. 1952 FGC Port, StAnd, StAnn, StC, StJ, StM, StT /ìnjin kíel/—waan favor coco, like coco leaf, make good soup.

2. Attrib.

1957 *FFM* 215, Indian Kale soup.

INDIAN MALLOW sb bot; <INDIAN 1 +*mallow*. The plant usually called BALLARD BUSH: *Urena lobata*.

1864 Grisebach 785, Indian Mallow: *Urena*. 1955 *WIMJ* 160, Ballard Bush; Indian or Bur Mallow.

INDIA(N) MULBERRY sb bot; <INDIAN 2 +*mulberry*. Species of *Morinda*. (The name appears to apply better to *M. royoc*, which has

a fruit close to the size of a mulberry, than to *M. citrifolia* (HOG APPLE), whose fruit is larger than a hen's egg.) See quots.

1814 Lunan I 416–17, Indian Mulberry. Morinda.. Royoc..Browne notices four kinds of..morinda..Long calls it yaw-weed, but gives no reason why it is so called. 1864 Grisebach 784, India-Mulberry: *Morinda citrifolia*.

INDIAN PEPPER sb obs; <INDIAN 1 +*pepper*; *OED* quots 1578, 1596. 'Old name for capsicum' (*OED*).

1774 Long III 857, Spicery and Peppers..Jamaica Black Pepper, Indian Pepper, Bell..&c.

INDIAN PINK sb; <INDIAN 1+*pink* sb.

1. =BARBADOS SWEET-WILLIAM.

1814 Lunan I 399, see INDIAN CREEPER. 1864 Grisebach 784, Indian-pink: *Ipomoea Quamoclit.*

2. See quot.

1953 *WIMJ* 249, *Spigelia anthelmia* L. Pink Root; Worm Grass; Indian Pink; Pink Weed.

INDIAN RIAL sb dial; <INDIAN 2+RIAL. The offspring of an East Indian and a negro. Cf CHINEY-RIAL.

1958 DeC StC /indi-in raial/.

INDIAN SAVIN TREE sb bot; <INDIAN 1 +*savin*+*tree*. *Cæsalpinia vesicaria*: an old name kept up in botanical works.

1696 Sloane 149, Sena spuria arborea spinosa..sabinæ odore. *Indian Savin Tree*. Circa locum *Passage fort*. 1814 Lunan I 111, *Cæsalpinia bijuga*..Sloane calls this Indian savin tree. 1837 Macfadyen I 329, *Cæsalpinia bijuga*. Indian savin Tree..All parts of this tree give out, when bruised, a strong balsamic scent. 1920 Fawcett 95, *C. vesicaria*..Indian Savin Tree.

INDIAN SHOT (FLOWER) sb; <INDIAN 1 +*shot* sb: cf *OED* 1760→. The wild and the cultivated varieties of *Canna indica*. See quots.

a 1726 Barham (1794) 76, Indian shot..This is so called from its seed being round, black, and so hard, that, blown through a trunk or pith, it will kill small birds. 1740 Importance 35, The Indian Shot-Flower is about the Size of the Sweet-William, has a pod which bears round black Seeds, which are used by the Negroes to shoot with. 1864 Grisebach 784, Indian-shot: *Canna*. c 1915 FGC StAnd, current.

INDIAN SORREL sb bot; <INDIAN 1 +*sorrel*. *Hibiscus sabdariffa*; usually merely called SORREL.

1814 Lunan I 418, Indian Sorrel. Hibiscus..subdariffa [*sic*]..The flower-cups and capsules..are the only parts used..a decoction of them sweetened, is what is commonly called *sorrel cool-drink*. 1864 Grisebach 787, Indian or Red Sorrel: *Hibiscus Sabdarifa*. 1954 *WIMJ* 30, *H. sabdariffa* L., Red, French, or Indian Sorrel; African Mallow.

INDIAN SPIKENARD sb bot obs; <INDIAN 1 +*spikenard*; see PICK-NUT. One or more of the plants of the *Labiatæ*.

1696 Sloane 64, *Indian Spicknard*. In pratis circa urbem St Jago..[etc.].

INDIAN VINE sb; <INDIAN 1+*vine*. A wild grape vine.

1811 Titford 47, Grape Vine, *Vitis vinifera*..There are fifty-two varieties..Indian Vine or Water Withe, thrives in the Red Hills of Jamaica.

INDIAN YAM /ínjin, hínjan/ sb chiefly dial; <INDIAN 1 (nowadays thought of as 2 in contrast to NEGRO YAM) +*yam*. A small, fine white yam: the YAMPI.

1814 Lunan II 308–9, Dioscorea..triloba..This is known by the name of Indian Yam in Jamaica..This is the smallest and most delicate of all the yams. 1823 Roughley 407, The Indian yam though floury, and delicate, is not much planted, is capricious and hard to be reared, and therefore not much in use. 1864 Grisebach 789, Indian yams: *Dioscorea trifida*. 1913 Harris 42–3, *Indian yam* or Yampee is *Dioscorea trifida*. 1943 *GL* Port, Injin yam, yampie. 1952 FGC StC /injin yam/ yampy; StM /hindian/ or /hinjan yam/; StT /inji-yam/ yampy. 1958 DeC Port /hindi-in yam/ Same as the /yampi/.

INDIGO BERRY sb bot; *OED* 1866 only. A shrub bearing berries that stain blue—whence the name. (*Randia aculeata*.)

1756 Browne 143, Randia 1..This small shrub..is frequent in the low lands..The pulp of these berries.. stains paper or linen of a fine fixt blue colour. I have tried it on many occasions. 1814 Lunan I 426, Indigo Berry. Gardenia..aculeata. 1864 Grisebach 784, Indigo-berry: *Randia aculeata*. 1936 Fawcett 53–4, R. aculeata..Indigo Berry, Ink Berry, Box Briar, Prickle Bush.

INDIGO HOOK sb obs; <*indigo*+*hook* (*OED* C 1). A curved knife used in reaping indigo. (Indigo has not been grown as a crop in Jamaica since the first half of the 18th cent.)

a 1726 Barham (1794) 77, The weed will be fit to cut in six weeks time, which is done with a crooked knife, in the shape of a sickle, but not jagged, and are called indigo-hooks.

ing see *in, ing*.

INGA TREE sb bot; *OED* 1756→. The tree *Inga vera*, with a distinctive ridged pod.

1756 Browne 253, Mimosa 10..The Inga Tree, or large-leafed Sensitive. This shrubby tree is pretty frequent in St Mary's. 1814 Lunan I 428, Inga-Tree..each pod contains a great many quadrangular soft peas, lying close together in a white sweet pulp, which is eaten by negroes. 1864 Grisebach 784.

INGH-INGH see next.

in-in /ín-ín/ int dial; two nasalized short high-front vowels in close juncture, each preceded by a glottal stop, said with falling pitch: [ʔĩʔĩ]; corresponding to US colloq *unh-unh*, but prob <Twi *ɛ̃hẽ́ẽ, no!* Cf *iin-hiin*. No.

1943 *GL* Tre, Ingh-Ingh, No. 1952 FGC /in-in/. (The first syllable may sometimes be longer than the second.)

INIQUITY /hínikwìti/ sb dial.

1. Specifically applied: OBEAH.

1958 DeC Port /hínikwiti/ obeah.

2. As a nickname: Various foods (see quots); here weakened to mean little more than a suggestion of triviality or a minor 'botheration' that one only pretends to condemn.

1958 DeC StAnd /hínikwiti/ a small dumpling, a spinner; Tre (Lowe R.) /ínikwìti/ a small fried johnny cake; Tre (Warsop), common local name for a coconut rundown.

injin yam, inji yam see INDIAN YAM.

INK-BERRY sb; *OED* lists (b) without ref or quot. =INDIGO BERRY.

1864 Grisebach 784, Ink-berry: *Randia aculeata*. 1936 Fawcett 53.

IN MI SAAL see IN (ONE'S) SALT.

INNO, INO see next.

i-no /inó/ int dial; prob formed on the analogy of *e-ye*, yes. An occas pronunc of 'no', corresponding to *e-ye*, yes. Cf UNNO[1].

1941 Kirkpatrick 19, Fuss time you ting 'im woulda go see any a dem odder people; eeno—'im use fe order dem fe come..Is diffran nung. 1943 *GL* Man, Port, StJ, Eeno, no; Clar, Enoh, Ino, no; StJ, Tre, Inno, no. 1956 Mc StAnd /ino/ no.

IN (ONE'S) ACKEE adj phr dial; a parallel const to IN (ONE'S) SALT; see SALT-FISH 2. Feeling well-fed and energetic.

1941 Kirkpatrick 9, Bwoy Hinglan' wuz in a ar ackee, runs wuz comin' fa'ser nung.

IN (ONE'S) SALT /in (a) mi saal, iina dem ~/ adj phr dial. Lit: Well provided with SALT, having had plenty to eat; hence (usually today), feeling happy, cheerful, full of energy. Cf Engl slang 'full of beans'.

1912 McK *Songs* 131, So de young man was in dem sall, *So the young men had a fine time of it.* 1933 McK 317, In mi saal: having a good time. 1942 Bennett 14, Wat a way we deh go fast doah! De train eena him saal. 1943 *GL* StM, Inna-him-saal, Strong, well fed.

IN-STINE-DOW sb dial; ? < *instant* + *dough*.

1943 *GL* StT, In-stine-dow, Banana grate and Boil in cocoanut milk.

INSTRAL /instral/ sb dial; < *entrails*. The inwards of an animal (or fruit); tripes. *BA BL*

1943 *GL* Han, Instral, intestines. 1952 FGC StE /instralz/ is /straip/ from the /mou/ of the animal; StJ, Instrals of fish /traip, pig-got/; StJ, For pain use the instral of the bitter-gourd.

INSULTIVE adj dial; < *insult* vb + *-ive*. Insulting. *G*

1959 FGC Man.

INTERFERENCE adj and quasi-vb dial; < *interference* sb.

A. adj: Interfering.

1942 Bennett 19, Dah 'oman Miss Matty intaferance yuh se' Like dip har mout' eena people affair.

B. quasi-vb: Be interfering; interfere, meddle.

1900 Murray 11, Yes sah, roses and bull dag is de two wussis ting fe a man fe interferance wid.

INTERVAL sb; cf *OED* 3. An access road through a cane-field or similar cultivation. See quots.

1790 Beckford I 170, I think it of great consequence in Jamaica, to have dry and ample intervals. *Ibid* 171, It is scandalous to think how much in general these intervals are neglected, and how much they are cut up in the time of planting by the wains that constantly traverse them. 1823 Roughley 221, Intervals in cane pieces. 1956 Mc StT /intavál/ Road or avenue between cane or banana pieces along which vehicles can drive. (The space between rows of cane is the 'furrow'.)

intete /intéte/ sb dial; < CB *-*tètè*, Ko *ntete*, hamper. See quot.

1958 DeC Port (Millbank, Moore Town), (1) A temporary bag of grass or trash made in the field. (2) A special sort of basket that used to be used to carry jerked meat down to sell at Port Antonio market: Bend a stick of rose-apple, bringing the two ends together and tying with string, so as to form a tear-drop shape; plait thatch to form a basket with this as the rim; make another basket identical with this one (each looking something like a fisherman's landing-net); tie the blunt ends of the two teardrop frames together, with the two thatch bags pointing out in opposite directions; this hinges the two halves together so that the *intete* remains closed if the points of the two teardrops are held together but can easily be opened by separating them.

IN THE HILLS phr. See quot; this is prob not distinctively Jamaican.

1873 Rampini 13, Behind and above rose the magnificent range of the Blue Mountains..here 'in the hills', to use a Creolism, is the favourite abode of the better class of Jamaica society.

IN THE LONG WAY adj phr slang. Of a drink: Plentiful rather than strong. *G*

1833 Scott I 185, see LONG DRINK.

INTO prep dial; prob overcorrection of *iina*, though the meaning of INTO is more limited. Within, inside (of), in. (There is no motion implied, but a state of rest; the dial equiv of Std *into* is IN or *iina*.) *BL G*

1907 Jekyll 78, As Monkey passing, Tiger was into a stone-hole an' jump out on the fellah an' catch him. 1924 Beckwith 20, Anansi live into a tree with wife and children. *Ibid* 59, After Crab gwine home, he rej'ice into him, he singin', 'T'ank God..' 1956 Mc StE /wat klaas hi iz riiding intu?/ *What class is he in?* /dem liv tugeda intu a luonli katej/ *They live together in a lonely cottage*; /evri híe intu iz héd wáit/ *Every hair in his head had turned white.* 1957 JN Kgn, Gracie stayed into the room with me.

ipiapa, ipiyapa see YIPPI YAPPA.

IRISH sb dial; abbr of *Irish potato*. An Irish potato. (The regular form used in markets and kitchens, by cultivators and higglers.)

IRISH BRIDGE or **DRAIN** sb; 'Irish' here probably represents something done the easy way or less thoroughly than it might be, as seen by the English. See quot.

1957 LeP StAnd, etc., Irish bridge or drain, A concave section of a road, esp of a mountain road, paved so as to allow a stream to cross it without washing away the otherwise dirt surface.

IRISH MOSS sb; cf *OED* 1845 only. The edible seaweeds *Chondrus crispus*, and *Gracilaria* species, found around the coast of Jamaica and sold in markets.

1952 FGC Port, StM, StT /aírish más, aíris más/ at seaside, gleaned by old woman; easy to digest, good for heart, etc. 1955 *WIMJ* 158.

[**IRISH POTATO** sb; *OEDS* 1664→. This usage was chiefly colonial during the 17–18th cents, now gen American; in 18th-cent England the term for the same tuber was 'English potato'; 'Irish potato' thus became a mark of the Colonial; see quot. (Cf also *pitieta*.) *BA N*

1793 Mathews 133 [Some West Indians visiting in England try to pass for Englishmen; they ask for 'Irish potatoes':] What you saw said the landlord, are not Irish, they are English potatoes: pray gentlemen are you not Creoles?]

IRON CUNNY sb dial; evid < *iron* + CUNNY. A kind of very tough, hard sugar candy; = BUSTA BACKBONE.

1952 FGC StJ /áian kóni/.

IRON DIGGER sb dial.

1958 DeC StT /aian-diga/ a planting spud about 2 inches wide, fitted with a wooden handle.

IRON FEED sb dial; < *iron* + *feed*. A very 'solid' dish—see quot.

1943 *GL* StM, Iron feed, Corn meal cooked with rice.

IRON GRASS sb.

1. *Spermacoce tenuior* and similar species. *G*

1756 Browne 141, Spermacoce 5. Scandens..The Iron-grass, or climbing Spermacoce. 1811 Titford 39–40, Iron-grass—button-weed. 1814 Lunan I 127–8, Spermacoce..iron grass. 1952 FGC Tre, Iron grass—packy-bush.

2. *Eleusine indica*.

1952 FGC StAnn, Iron grass, grows like beach grass—running grass. 1954 *FG* 228, Iron-Grass (Goose Grass, Fowl-Foot Grass) (*Eleusine indica*). This grass..is common on open ground and waste places throughout the West Indies.

IRON SHRUB sb; *OED* lists without quot or ref. The shrub *Sauvagesia brownei*.

[1756 Browne 179, Iron 1. The slender reclining Iron.. This beautiful little plant rises, generally, in an oblique direction..The plant is very rare.] 1814 Lunan I 430, Iron-Shrub. Sauvagesia..There is only one species, a native of Jamaica. 1864 Grisebach 784. 1954 *WIMJ* 31, *Sauvagesia brownei*..Strong Back; Iron Shrub.

IRON WEED sb chiefly dial. Weeds supposed to give strength when used to make a tonic. See quot 1955. *G*

1952 FGC Han, StC /aian wiid/ dog tongue; Tre, Iron weed—packy weed. 1955 *WIMJ* 158, *Elephantopus mollis*..Elephant's Foot; Iron Weed. *Ibid* 160, *Pseudelephantopus spicatus*..Iron Weed; Packy Weed; Dog's Tongue.

[**IRONWOOD** sb; cf *OED* Ligon *Barbados* 1657→. Applied in Jamaica to at least three trees: *Turpinia occidentalis*, *Sloanea jamaicensis*, *Laplacea haematoxylon* (cf 1926 Fawcett 38, 90, 189 resp) which have very hard wood.] *N*

IRONWORT sb bot. The wild plant *Hyptis capitata*.

1794 Barham 81, Ironwort (Linn. *Clinopodium vulgare*). 1955 *WIMJ* 159, see CAESAR OBEAH.

is /is/ sb dial; <*miss*. A dial pronunc of 'Miss' used in greetings.

1943 *GL* StC, Iss Jane, Good morning Miss Jane.

IS /iz, hiz/ vb dial; for *it is*. =A[7]: Introducing statements and questions, and often making them more emphatic; similarly introducing interrog pronouns and advs. *G T*

1873 Rampini 109 [From a letter:] But his I take this liberty to inform you..[etc.]. 1950 Pioneer 17, Is Anancy meck it. *Ibid* 18, Is accident. *Ibid* 19, Ef me gi yuh de cow, is wat me gwine teck meck me livin? 1952 FGC Man, Is Coolie bring it in, *Coolies introduced it* (*sc* ganja). 1957 JN, You no love me, is Roy you going to make live with you.

ISLE OF — see OIL OF —.

ISS see *is*.

IT see HIT, I.

ITALIAN JASMINE sb.

1952 FGC StAnn, Italian jasmine—deadly nightshade.

ITCH /hiich/ sb dial; <*itch*. In common application (and pronunc): Various skin diseases; see quot 1959. *G*

1952 FGC Han, Land-pussley good for /krach-krach/ or /hiich/ on baby skin; StM, When children have /hiich/ bathe them with snake-cap. 1959 O. D. Simons, UCWI Preventive Med /hiich/ used about various skin conditions, as impetigo, eczema, dermatitis.

ITCH-ITCH sb dial; iterative <ITCH.

1958 DeC Port /ich-ich/ a dry rash.

ITCHY-BAMBA sb dial; <*itchy* + ?Sp *bamba*, a negro (Sto. Domingo—Santamaría 3). See quots. *BL*

1943 *GL* Tre, Itchy-bamba, skin disease. 1954 LeP StT, Itchi-bamba—dry, itching rash.

itiuoti apl see OTAHEITE APPLE.

IT IS impers const phr; by partial adaptation by a dial speaker toward StdE: as a plural const, this is dial. See IS. There are. *G*

1952 FGC Man, It is two sort of dem, green, and black.

'ITTE adj dial; <*little*. Anancy's way (representing BUNGO TALK) of saying 'little'. (In other stories he says *yikl*.)

1924 Beckwith 8, Anansi say, 'If dem tak dem *big* banana trash tie me, I wi' be glad, but if dey could a tak dat 'itte bit o' banana t'read tie me, I should be *so* sorry!'

ITTIOTTO see OTAHEITE APPLE.

ITTY-ITTY-HAP imitative phr; the first part is echoic, the last syllable prob =*hop*. The sound made by the THREE-FOOT-HORSE (a bugaboo or ghost) running on its three feet.

1907 Jekyll 35, He got on his horse an' start off itty-itty-hap, itty-itty-hap, until he get home.

JAACK TREE see JACKFRUIT.

jaagl vb dial; <*gargle* by palatalization of /g/ to /gy/ and affrication to /j/. To gargle.

1927 Anderson-Cundall 61 [Prov:] Frog nebber jagle him troat till him tas'e fresh water. Jagle = gargle. *The croaking of frogs is usually more pronounced after rain.* 1959 FGC StAnd /jaagl/ gargle.

jaaj, jaaj fut see GEORGE.

jaak puok see JERK PORK.

jaaman see GERMAN.

jaan tuwit see JOHN CHEWIT.

JABBERING CROW /jablin, jabin/ sb; 1740 javaline, 1847→ jabbering; OED lists, no ref or quot. The Jamaican crow (*Corvus jamaicensis*), which flies in flocks and makes noises likened to human speech. Also called CHATTERING CROW, COCOA-WALK, GABBLING CROW, WELSHMAN.

1740 Importance 38, Carrion-Crows..Javaline Crows, which are eatable; Bonana Birds. 1847 Gosse 209, In the wildest part of the mountain regions of Jamaica..where a narrow track..leads through the dark and damp forest to some lonely negro ground, the traveller is startled by the still wilder tones of the Jabbering Crow. So uncouth and yet so articulate..are these sounds..[etc.]. 1890 Thomas 69, Later in the day I got a 'jabbering crow', a bird almost exactly resembling the English raven. 1952 FGC Han, StAnn, StM /jáblin krúo/; Man /jabln kruo/.

JABBLING CROW see prec.

JABBY sb[1] dial rare; etym unknown, but see next.

1943 *GL* Man, Jabby, Male donkey.

JABBY sb[2] dial; etym unknown.

1943 *GL* Man, Jabby, Any thing slack, dirty or untidy; Man, Jabby, filt [i.e. filth].

jabin kruo see JABBERING CROW.

JABORAND sb obs; cf *OED jaborandi*, 1875→.

1801 Dancer 366, Jaborand or Colts foot (*Piper reticulat.*).

JACA TREE see JACKFRUIT.

JACK sb[1] dial. *BL*

1. See quot.

1959 DeC Port /jak/ a large johnnycake fried in a large pan.

2. A crook used in Revival ceremonies.

1953 Moore 93, [The] swivel (or 'jack' as one shepherd called it).

JACK sb[2]; *OED* 1897→, *DAE* 1883→. A common food fish; freq in comb. *BA BL*. Cf *SC djakki*.

1697 Trapham 59, The choice Mullet brings up the next division crowded with various Snappers..Groopers, Jacks, Grunts, Porgoes. 1851 Gosse 290, Buntung jack, Round-headed jack, Ground jack, Cavally jack. 1959 FGC (current throughout the Island).

JACK sb[3]; see next.

JACKA vb dial; abbr of *Jack-o'-both-sides* (OED *Jack sb*[1] 36). See quots.

1943 *GL* StE, Jacka, to play on both sides in games; No addr, Jakka, playing for both sides in cricket. [1956 BLB Man, Jacka—known to me as Jack or Jack-on-both-sides. This was the role given the odd man or least talented player.]

JACKASS sb dial joc; see quot 1868. A breadfruit; also attrib.

1868 Russell 5, To pad or saddle a jackass (culinary business) is to roast it, but to ride it and gallop it is to eat it with no bad apetite [*sic*]. 1952 FGC StAnd, Jackass—breadfruit. 1956 Mc Man, In /jakaas maakit/ breadfruit market.

JACKASS BLIND sb dial or derisive slang; i.e. a blind or blinder for a jackass. Transf. A district constable, so called from the supposed appearance of his badge—cf PAN-HEAD.

1956 Mc StAnd.

JACKASS BREADNUT sb dial; cf BREADNUT. The plant *Clibadium surinamense*, which has small fruits that jackasses and other animals relish.

1927 Beckwith 19, Jackass-breadnut..For a cold drink it as a tea. 'Goats and rabbits love it.' 1954 *WIMJ* 29, Clibadium surinamense..Jackass Breadnut.

JACKASS BUR sb dial. An unidentified plant with burs.

1952 FGC Han.

JACKASS CORN sb dial. A hard, crisp biscuit. See quots 1947, 1954.

1943 *GL* StC, Jackass corn, a hard cake got from coconut; Tre, Jack-ass-corn, hard-baked biscuit. 1947 U.Newton II 31, Miss White's Jackass Biscuit..a famous hard biscuit called Jackass Corn. Like the Jackass it was faithful, long-serving and tough. 1954 LeP StE, Jackass Corn is very thin and hard and crisp and when being eaten sounds like the eating of corn by a donkey.

JACKASS CRAB sb dial.

1952 FGC Port, Jackass crab, same as coco crab.

JACKASS-EARS TREE sb dial; from the shape of the leaves. Prob *Cordia macrophylla.*

1952 FGC StE, Jackass-ears tree, same as lobby-lobby.

JACKASS MILK (BUSH) sb dial. An unidentified plant.

1952 FGC StM, Jackass milk bush.

JACKASS ROPE sb dial. Locally grown tobacco, twisted into the form of a long 'rope' (½–1 in. in diameter) which is coiled or tied in a ball for market. Also euphemistically, DONKEY ROPE.

[1803 Dallas I 110, The leaves were dried and prepared for use by the [Maroon] men, who twisted them into a kind of rope..which they rolled up in balls, and carried out in the same manner to the different estates for sale.] 1943 *GL* Kgn, Port, StAnn, StM, Jackass-rope, twisted tobacco. 1952 FGC StAnd, StAnn, StM /jákáas rúop/ twis' tobacco.

JACK BUSH sb. = THREE-FINGERED JACK 2.

1961 DAP.

JACK FISH WOOD sb. An error for TACK FISH WOOD (i.e. STOCKFISH WOOD).

1920 Fawcett 95, *Cæsalpinia..vesicaria..*Jack Fish Wood.

JACK-FRUIT /jákfrúut/ sb; (1794 jaca tree), 1808→ jack-fruit, 1814 jaack tree, 1864 jack tree, 1941 jakfruit; cf *OED jack sb*[4]. (The form 'jack-fruit' 1830 only quot.) The tree (early called *jaca* or *jaack* tree), its wood, and esp its large bulbous fruit, whose pulp and seeds are eaten: *Artocarpus integrifolia.*

1794 Broughton 30, Indian Jaca Tree [from] East Indies [brought to Jamaica by] Lord Rodney, 1782. 1808 Stewart 93, Exotic fruits established of late years in the island are the mango..the bread-fruit, the jack-fruit. 1814 Lunan I 388, Jaack-Tree. Artocarpus..integrifolia.. This beautiful and excellent fruit tree was brought to Jamaica in his Majesty's ship Providence, in the year 1793, at the same time that the breadfruit was introduced. *Ibid* 112, *Jaack tree.* 1913 Harris 10, Jack-fruit..bears very large fruits on the trunk and old branches. The fruits are frequently 40 to 50 lbs. in weight..The yellow, pulpy mass which surrounds the large seeds is eaten by the natives who appear to relish it, but it has such a strong, disagreeable odour that Europeans seldom use it. 1941 Swabey 23, Jak-fruit..Wood hard..bright yellow, beautifully marked, takes a fine polish.

JACKFRUIT FOOT sb dial; < JACK-FRUIT + FOOT. A leg swollen and rough (from elephantiasis or similar disease) so that it resembles a jackfruit.

1942 Bennett 29, Me hear sey Him ha' wan big jackfruit foot. 1943 *GL* Port, Jack-fruit foot, Swollen foot; StM, Barbados leg. 1956 Mc Clar, StAnd /jak fruut fut/ swollen thickened leg.

JACK-FRY sb dial. Very small fish, taken to be young jack.

1956 Mc StAnd (Port Royal) /jak-frai/.

JACK-IN-A-BOX sb; *OED* 1752–9→. A plant of uncertain identity. The name was applied to *Hernandia sonora* (other Jamaican citations 1774–1814), but the description here suggests possible confusion with JACK-IN-THE-BUSH.

1740 Importance 35, Jack-in-a-Box is a white Flower.

JACK-IN-THE-BUSH /jákini (búsh), jákana búsh, jákna búsh/ sb now chiefly dial; cf *OED*, listed without quot or ref, for another plant. Also called ARCHANGEL, BITTER BUSH, CHRISTMAS BUR(?), BUSH, or ROSE. One of the best known of Jamaican 'tea-bushes', widely used as a remedy: *Eupatorium odoratum.*

a 1726 Barham (1794) 165, A large white sage, with white flowers, and commonly called in Jamaica *jack in the bush. Ibid* 96, Washing the sores..then laying over them a leaf of the jack in the bush, until their sores were healed. 1811 Titford Expl to Plate IX 5, Lantana inermis—another species, commonly called Jack in the Bush. 1893 Sullivan 114, 119, 120, Jack-in-the-bush [in bush tea and bath]. 1936 Fawcett 174–5. 1952 FGC Han, StAnd, StE, Tre /jákinibúsh, jákini/; Port, StAnn, StM /jáknabúsh/; Han, StC /jákana búsh/; StM, StT, sometimes called Christmas bush.

JACK MANDOŔA /ják mandúora/ rarely /jakmanchuo/ phr dial; var of *Jack a Nory* in Engl nursery rhyme. See *Stud in Linguistics.. McDavid*, Univ Alabama 1972, 25-8. *T*

1. The first part of a formula traditionally used to end an ANANCY STORY: it may be concluded 'me no choose none' (there are several variations—see quots), and the sense seems to be 'this is not directed at anyone in particular'—but with the implication that if the shoe fits, one may put it on.

1868 *TJRSA* I 66, Jacmandorah, Don't want none! 1877 Murray *Kittle* 26, This story was duly applauded, and wound up with the usual 'Jack Mandora'. 1907 Jekyll 9–10, *Jack Mantora me no choose any*..All Annancy stories end with these or similar words..Among the African tribes stories we know are often told with an object. The Negro is quick to seize a parable, and the point of a cunningly constructed story directed at an individual obnoxious to the reciter would not miss. So when the stories were merely told for diversion, it may have been thought good manners to say: 'This story of mine is not aimed at any one'. 1924 Beckwith 10, Jack man dora, choose none! 1952 FGC StM /jakmanchuo—mi no chuuz non/.

2. Used also to end a bout of riddling: see quot.

1942 HPJ, Jackmandory, Jackmandoreh: A word or expression said by the questioner at the last riddle to show that he will answer no more riddles. It means, 'I am done, and so are you'.

JACK MARIGGLE sb dial. = JOHN MARIGGLE.

1943 *GL* Kgn, Jac me riggle, bony fish.

JACKO /jáko/ adj or sb dial; cf *OED Jocko*, also *Jacko*, a chimpanzee. A credulous person. *BL*

1943 *GL* StAnd, Jacko, foolish. 1954 LeP StE, Jacko—somebody who is credulous. 1956 Mc StAnd /jako—dem duon ruul demsefs prapali/. To a person who is stupid, fails to catch a point, one says /go ahed, jako/.

JACK-ON-BOTH-SIDES see JACKA.

JACK-PANIA, JACK-PANNIER see next.

JACK-SPANIARD /jàk-pánya/ sb now dial; cf *OED* as the name for a WI wasp: *Jack sb*[1] 37, 1843→.

1. A gad-fly. (Now obs.) *BA*

1833 Scott I 360, They begin the interview..their horses fretting and jumping all the time—and if the Jack Spaniards or gadflies be rife, they have..to spur at each other..like a knight Templar and a Saracen.

2. A type of fowl or chicken with few feathers; those which it has are reddish, whence the name.

1942 HPJ, Jack Pannier: a senseh fowl..A naked chicken with nothing but three long wing feathers that turn to the head at a later stage. Feathers gradually grow in patches. They are great fighters and keep off the mongoose. 1943 *GL* Man, Jackpania, chick with very little feathers; Port, Jackpannier. 1952 FGC StAnd /jàk pánya/ no feathers except on wings and a little on head; StAnn, Jack Spaniard.

JACK SPENCE sb dial; by folk-etym from its scientific name. The bird *Jacana spinosa.*

1952 Carley in *Sunday Gleaner* Mar [Jacana:] I saw a crowd of these one April on a pond near Black River; the local people call them 'Jack Spence'—a neat corruption! s POND COOT.

JACK SPRAT sb dial. The young or 'sprat' of the JACK fish.

1952 FGC Port /jak sprat/ bigger than black-bill and yellow-bill; StAnn, young jack; StE, has no scale.

JACK TREE see JACK-FRUIT.

JACMANDORAH see JACK MANDORA.

JACOB BANANA sb dial.

1952 FGC Port /jíekob/ short, fat: resemble fig banana, but seed is bigger; must be very ripe to eat.

jaga-jaga adj dial; prob a variant of *jag-jag*, but cf also Ewe *dyaga-dyaga*, stretched out, spread, sprawled.

1943 *GL* Tre, Jagger-jagger, unequal or untidy.

JAGGAY ~, JAGGIN ~, or JAGU MAT /jáge, jágin, jágu/ sb dial; etym uncert, prob multiple: cf *jag-jag*, *jege-jege*, and other such words meaning ragged—cf also Ewe *dzagoo*, twisted, and Jamaican *-u*. A mat made from trash, bark, or the like, used to sleep on.

1942 HPJ, Jaggay mat, jaggin mat: A mat made from banana 'rush' and used to sleep on, being put on beds in the country; [also] an old torn mat. 1956 Mc StAnd /jagu mat/ a mat made from bark of fig tree, used for sleeping on.

jag-jag adj or sb dial; cf *EDD jag(g*, a rag or shred of raiment; gen in plur—rags, tatters; splinters; a branch of broom or gorse; a large bundle of briars. This may be simply an iterative from the English word, but it is also one of a group of similar words in which African infl seems probable—cf *jeg-jeg*, *jeng-jeng*, and their variants. Cf also *kreng-kreng*, *jaga-jaga*, *yagga-yagga*, *yeg-yeg*.

1. Branches or trash used for firewood when dried, for mulch when green.

1956 Mc Man /jag-jag/. Also StE (Elderslie).

2. Torn, ragged, shabby; as a noun: torn clothing, rags.

1956 Mc Man /jag-jag/—/ef éniting tíer op an lúk bád/.

JAGLE see *jaagl*.

jagu mat see JAGGAY MAT.

jagwa taak sb dial; prob blend <*jargon* and *patois*, both current in folk speech, the latter being a synonym of this; +*talk* sb.

1956 Mc Man /jagwa taak/ the local speech /jaagan, patwa/.

JAH /ja/ sb dial cant; prob <*Jah*, Jehovah (cf *OED*). A deity in the cults of 'Maroons' (here meaning St Thomas and other nearby hill folk). Also in Rastafarian use.

1953 Moore gloss, Jah—a god, among 'Maroons'.

JAKKA see JACKA.

jak puok see JERK PORK.

JALOUSIE, JALOUSY see JEALOUSY. *BA*

JAM vb[1] dial; perh altered <*jab*, but cf next. To force in something pointed; to prick, pierce.

1907 Jekyll 260, A man will often stroke his picker (pickaxe) and say: 'He no a come out if he t'ought him face would a jam so a dirty', he would not have come out if he had thought his face was going to be thrust so hard into the ground. 1941 Kirkpatrick 24, You know ef you jam eben de smalles' a 'ole een a balloon..all de air wi' leak out. 1943 *GL* Kgn, Port, StT, Jam—prick. 1956 Mc Man /jam/ to prick—a bigger prick than is expressed by /juk/; StAnd /maka jam yu, maka juk yu/ express the same thing. *G*

JAM vb[2] dial; prob back-formation <JAMMA understood as 'jammer'.

1954 LeP StE, Jam, to plant out plants.

JAM-A-CORNER /jám-a-káana/ sb dial; see variant forms in quots; <*jam*, force tightly +A[1]+*corner*. Also attrib.

1. A rough bed, usually one so weak that it has to be supported by being fastened into the corner of the room. Also somewhat better, but simple, beds.

1942 HPJ, A rough bed—can be shoved anywhere. 1954 LeP StE, Jam-a-corna, a rough wooden bed having only two legs, and one side is nailed to the wall. 1956 Mc StAnd /jam tu di kaana/. 1958 DeC Port /jam-a-kaana, jam-it-tu-kaana/; StT /jam-tu-di-kaana/.

2. Other roughly made structures: see quot.

1956 Mc StAnd /jam op kaana/ an unfinished structure (back porch, that looked rather like a /tatu/—but wasn't!); /jam-a-kaana hot/ a rough hut, made of grass and sticks, built on a cultivation—used as shelter from rain, for cooking or sleeping in.

JAMAICA, JAMAICAN the first element in many cpds (listed separately). Note: 'Jamaica' is the older and more frequent form, 'Jamaican' almost wholly of the 20th cent.

JAMAICA BARK, JAMAICA JESUIT'S BARK sb bot; for *Jesuit's-bark* cf *OED*. (*OED* lists *Ja. Bark* without quot.) The tree *Exostema caribæum*, the bark of which was once used as a substitute for Jesuit's Bark.

1801 Dancer 363, Jamaica bark (*Cinchona*; viz. *C. Caribbœa—C. Brachycarpa—C. Triflora*). These are indigenous species of the Jesuits or Peruvian Bark, and are successfully employed, like that. 1864 Grisebach 784, Jamaica-bark: *Exostemma*. 1936 Fawcett 11–12, *Exostema caribæum*..Caribbee Bark Tree, Jamaica Jesuit's Bark.

JAMAICA BEAN sb obs. The SUGAR BEAN.

1756 Browne 292, Phaseolus 10..The Jamaica Bean, or Sugar-Bean.

JAMAICA BILBERRY sb bot; *OED* lists without quot. *Vaccinium meridionale*; see quots.

1811 Titford 60, Jamaica bilberry, or Whortle Berry.. Nat. of Jamaica in the Blue Mountains..They make a good rob or jelly. 1864 Grisebach 781.

JAMAICA BLACK PEPPER sb. The plant now generally called JOINT WOOD.

1774 Long III 857, Jamaica Black Pepper. 1955 *WIMJ* 159, Piper Amalgo L...Joint Wood; Jamaica Black Pepper.

JAMAICA BOXWOOD see BOXWOOD.

(JAMAICA) BUTTERCUP sb. The wildflower *Tribulus cistoides*, with prominent yellow flowers. Cf TURKEY BLOSSOM.

[c1915 FGC StAnd, Buttercup.] 1954 *WIMJ* 27, Jamaica or Kingston Buttercup; Police Macca; Turkey Blossom; Kill Buckra. s RACECOURSE MACCA.

JAMAICA BUTTON SHELL sb obs; *ODS* 1895.

1725 Sloane 229, Trochus, sive Cochlea terrestris, minor, alba, rotunda, testa-tenui..Jamaica Button Shell..as large as a Nut-meg.

JAMAICA CANDLEWOOD sb. *OED* (s.v. *candlewood*) identifies this as *Gomphia guianensis*, which is today *Ouratea jamaicensis* (Fawcett). We have no other record of this name; *OED* gives no supporting quot; the only quot given from Jamaican source is for WHITE CANDLEWOOD. The existence of this name is therefore in question.

JAMAICA CEDAR see JAMAICA(N) CEDAR.

JAMAICA CHERRY sb. A large wild fig whose red fruit somewhat resembles a cherry.

1864 Grisebach 782 Cherry, Jamaica: *Ficus pedunculata*.

JAMAICA CLOCK sb; cf *OED clock sb³*. A beetle—see quot.

1756 Browne 430, Curculio 4..The *Jamaica* Clock or Black Dor..common about houses.

JAMAICA COTTON sb obs. See GREEN-SEED COTTON.

JAMAICA DEAL sb dial. A tree of unidentified species, tall and straight, and used for making deal boards.

1952 FGC StC.

JAMAICA DOGWOOD sb. *Piscidia piscipula*; cf DOGWOOD.

1955 *WIMJ* 161, Jamaica Dogwood.

JAMAICA EBONY sb; *OED* only 1756. See EBONY.

1756 Browne 299. 1814 Lunan I 277–8.

JAMAICA GARLIC sb obs. An erroneous name: see quot.

1814 Lunan I 317, Besides the common garlic, the *gracile*, or African garlic, has also been introduced from Africa; and has been erroneously termed *Jamaica garlic*, from the circumstance of Hinton East, esq. having sent the seeds from this island to England in the year 1787.

JAMAICA GRAPE(-VINE) sb bot. The WATER-WITHE.

1756 Browne 178, VITIS. I..the Jamaica Grapevine, commonly called Water-withe. 1835 Madden II 49, Jamaica grape-vine. 1864 Grisebach 784, Grape, Jamaica: *Vitis caribœa*.

JAMAICA HEATHER sb. The small wild shrub *Polygala paniculata*, which resembles heather.

1951 Mrs Brenda Sutton (Mandeville), Jamaica heather has a strongly aromatic root. Nobody seems to mention this.

JAMAICA HOT SAUCE sb. See quot.

1952 FGC Port, Jamaica hot sauce: boil chochos till tender; dice; add vinegar, mustard, curry, sugar, pepper, salt, pimento; bottle it. It looks like mustard sauce.

JAMAICA JESUIT'S BARK see JAMAICA BARK.

JAMAICA LEPROSY sb rare.

1929 Beckwith 129, Banbury says if one burns wangla with pepper and salt in a road which a thief passes, it will give the thief Jamaica leprosy, called 'cocobay'.

JAMAICA LONG-GRAIN RICE see LONG-GRAIN RICE.

JAMAICA MAHOGANY sb. The tree *Swietenia mahagoni*, and esp its wood, used for furniture.

1837 Macfadyen I 176, It was from this Island that the supply for Europe was in former times principally obtained, and the Old Jamaica Mahogany is still considered superior to any that can now be procured from any other country. 1941 Swabey 25.

JAMAICA MANDARIN ORANGE sb bot; cf *OED* 1866, *Jamaica Orange*.

1864 Grisebach 786, Orange, Jamaica Mandarin: *Glycosmis citrifolia*.

JAMAICAN /jamíekan/ sb dial. Among the folk: a term used contrastively with Chinese, East Indian, Creole, etc. for a Jamaican negro. It is used euphemistically to avoid the unfavourable connotations of negro, NAYGA, etc.

1959 DeC StC.

JAMAICAN BANANA sb. A variety of banana (the MARTINIQUE BANANA) which was so successfully cultivated in Jamaica for export that it became known as Jamaican. *G*

1913 Fawcett 16.

JAMAICAN BECARD sb ornith.

1936 Bond 259, Jamaican Becard (*Platypsaris niger*). Local names:—Judy (male); Mountain Dick (female). 1956 Jeffrey-Smith 69.

JAMAICAN BLACKBIRD sb ornith. See BLACKBIRD 3.

1936 Bond 360. 1956 Jeffrey-Smith 76.

JAMAICA(N) CEDAR sb. See quots.

1920 Fawcett 218, Jamaican, West Indian, Spanish, or Honduras Cedar. 1955 *WIMJ* 145, *Cedrela odorata*.. Jamaican..Cedar. *Ibid* 161, Jamaica Cedar.

JAMAICA(N) NETTLE-TREE sb bot. *Trema micrantha*—see quots.

1814 Lunan I 395, Jamaica Nettle-Tree. Celtis.. micrantha..is frequent in Clarendon and about the Ferry, and is known by the name of *bastard fustic.* 1864 Grisebach 786, Nettle tree, Jamaica: *Sponia micrantha.* 1914 Fawcett 39, Jamaican Nettle Tree.

JAMAICA NIGHTINGALE sb. The NIGHTINGALE.

a 1818 Lewis (1845) 90, Two Jamaica nightingales have established themselves on the orange-tree which grows against my window, and their song is most beautiful. This bird is also called 'the mocking bird', from its facility of imitating. 1960 Current (FGC).

JAMAICAN THRUSH see GLASS-EYE I.

JAMAICAN WOOD PEWEE sb ornith.

1956 Jeffrey-Smith 148, The Jamaican Wood Pewee or Stupid Jimmy, *Blacicus caribæus pallidus* (Bond) were fairly common in the region [around Clydesdale].

JAMAICAN YELLOW-CROWNED ELAENIA sb ornith.

1936 Bond 255, Jamaican Yellow-Crowned Elaenia (*Elænia cotta*)..Range: Jamaica. 1956 Jeffrey-Smith 50.

JAMAICAN YELLOW-CROWNED FLYCATCHER sb ornith.

1947 Bond 149, Jamaican Yellow-crowned Flycatcher (*Myiopagis cotta*)..A rare, but widespread, Jamaican flycatcher, most numerous in the Blue Mountains.. *Range*: Jamaica. 1956 Jeffrey-Smith 150.

JAMAICA OAK sb bot. =YOKEWOOD.

1941 Swabey 33.

JAMAICA ORTOLAN sb obs. The RICE BIRD or PINK: *Dolichonyx orizyvorus.*

1873 Rampini 164, The Jamaica ortolan (*Motacilla*) from the pastures.

JAMAICA PEAS sb obs. *Phaseolus lunatus*, the Lima bean; also called SUGAR BEAN.

1696 Sloane 67, Phaseolus major perennis, floribus spicatis..*Jamaica Pease.* 1707 Sloane 176.

JAMAICA PEPPER sb obs exc hist; *OED* 1660 only. Allspice, today called PIMENTO in Jamaica. *N*

1660 Hickeringill (1661) 12, see *OED.* 1662 Stubbe 14, The most delicate spice called Jamaica-pepper. *Ibid* 47–8, This spice hath a most delicate smell, and such, as resembles an Orange stuck with Cloves. 1672 Blome 45. 1782 'Account of the Island of Jamaica', *European Magazine* 257. 1955 *WIMJ* 161.

JAMAICA QUASSIA sb bot. See quots.

1920 see BITTER-WOOD 2. 1941 Swabey 14, Bitterwood—(Quassia, Jamaica Quassia). *Picraena excelsa.* 1954 *WIMJ* 31.

JAMAICA RED PEAS sb. *Vigna unguiculata*, now simply called RED PEAS.

1696 Sloane 71–2, Phaseolus erectus major, siliqua tereti, semine rubro..*Jamaica Red Pease.* In agris Insulæ Jamaicæ ubique seritur & provenit. 1707 Sloane 183.

JAMAICA ROBIN sb. =ROBIN, the Green Tody.

1951 FGC StAnd.

JAMAICA ROSE sb bot. The wild shrub *Blakea trinervia.*

1850 Mafadyen 95–6, Blakea trinervia..is commonly designated the 'Jamaica Rose'. 1851 Gosse 68, The edges of the woods are occupied by..Melastomaceous shrubs..Among them stands conspicuous for beauty *Blakea trinervia*, whose expanded crimson flower has received the name of the Jamaica Rose. 1864 Grisebach 787, Rose, Jamaica or wild. 1926 Fawcett 400.

JAMAICA SALMON sb arch. The CALIPEVA.

1833 Scott (1862) 239, Cold calipiver—our Jamaica Salmon. [1893 Sullivan 8, Calepeaver. This fish is sometimes called the Salmon of Jamaica.]

JAMAICA SALOP sb bot obs. A species of *Sassafras.*

1756 Browne 325, Satyrium 10..The Jamaica Salop.

JAMAICA(N) SAMPHIRE sb bot. See quots.

[1756 Browne 356, Batis 1. Maritima..The Samphire of Jamaica.] 1864 Grisebach 787, Samphire, Jamaica: *Batis maritima.* 1914 Fawcett 35, B. maritima..Barilla, Jamaican Samphire.

JAMAICA(N) SARSAPARILLA sb bot.

1953 *WIMJ* 249, Smilax..ornata..Jamaican Sarsaparilla. 1954 *Ibid* 33, Jamaica Sarsaparilla.

JAMAICA SATINWOOD sb bot. =YELLOW SANDERS.

JAMAICA SCREW-TREE sb bot. =SCREW TREE.

1837 Macfadyen 89, Helicteres Jamaicensis. Jamaica Screw-tree.

JAMAICA SENNA sb bot.

1953 *WIMJ* 239, *Cassia obovata* Collad. Jamaica Senna; Port Royal, Dog, Senegal, Tripoli, or Italian Senna.. Stated to have been introduced into Jamaica in the seventeenth century by a slave, this senna is still said to be used here as a substitute for the official sennas.

JAMAICA SHAMROCK sb. *Oxalis corymbosa*, so called from the shape of the leaf.

JAMAICA SORREL sb. =SORREL: *Hibiscus sabdariffa.*

1750 Williams 48, Jamaica Sorrel or the Jelly of it dissolved in Barley Water [for yellow fever].

JAMAICA SUMACH sb bot. *Rhus metopium*; see also HOG-DOCTOR TREE, BOAR TREE, HOG GUM, etc.

1837 Macfadyen 225, Rhus Metopium. Jamaica Sumach..This shrubby tree has long been confounded with the *Moronobea coccinea*, the true Hog-gum tree. 1864 Grisebach 788. 1926 Fawcett 9, Jamaica Sumach, Burn Wood. 1941 Swabey 14.

JAMAICA TEA GOATWEED sb bot obs. *Capraria biflora*; now called GOATWEED, WEST-INDIA TEA.

1811 Titford 79, Jamaica tea goatweed, or Sweet Weed, *Capraria Biflora.*

JAMAICA TURKEY sb joc or derisive. The JOHN-CROW.

1925 Beckwith 76, Jamaica turkey does fly high..'The Jamaica turkey (a popular name for the carrion crow) flies high'; employed as a jeer at one of poor family who rises in the world and puts on airs. 1956 BLB, Folk-etymology has it that a 'Bajan' (Barbadian), when he came to Jamaica and saw a john-crow for the first time, remarked, 'Jamaica turkey does fly high'.

JAMAICA WALNUT sb bot. The tree *Picrodendron baccatum* and its fruit.

1696 Sloane 214, Jamaica Wallnuts. Loco Guanaboa dicto in sylvis crescunt, unde fructus mihi dati adferebantur. 1756 Browne 346, The Jamaica Walnut. Juglans foliis oblongis..etc. 1864 Grisebach 788. 1920 Fawcett 273.

JAMAICA WHITE sb slang.

1960 LeP StAnd, Jamaica white: Local term for a person who looks white but is known by everybody in Jamaica to be slightly coloured. 1960 SJR StAnd, see RED NAYGA.

JAMAICA WILD CLARY sb bot obs. See quot.

1811 Titford Plate IV 4; descr ii, Jamaica wild clary (sativa sclarea).

JAMAICA WILLOW see WILLOW.

jam-a-kaana see JAM-A-CORNER.

JAMAL SONG see JAMMA 1.

jamba sb dial; evid <*Jambosa*, the genus name. The Otaheite apple tree (*Jambosa malaccensis*) or similar species.

[1913 Harris 2, Captain Bligh..in 1793 brought three varieties of this fruit..the two from Timor were called 'Jambo iremavah' and 'Jambo maree'.] 1952 FGC StT /jamba/ a softwood tree with large glossy leaf.

JAMBLING see JAMBOLAN.

JAMBO BITTER sb dial; cf *jamba*, quot 1913. An unidentified plant.

1942 HPJ, A St Thomas 'bush'.

JAMBOLAN sb; 1850 1864 jambolana, 1893 jamblang, 1913 jimbolan, 1913→ jambolan, 1959 jambalan jumboline; <the species name; cf *OED*, applied to a diff tree.

The tree *Syzigium jambolanum* and its fruit, 'naturalized in Jamaica' (Grisebach); there is confusion, because of the similarity of the names, with BIMBLING and JIMBLING, entirely different fruits, though all are called *baaj*.

1850 Macfadyen 105, Syzigium jambolanum. The Jambolana Tree. 1893 Sullivan 81–2, Jamblangs. These are large long narrow very dark blue black fruit, not very common but very much liked when they can be had. They are nice in their raw state and excellent as a preserve. 1913 Harris 10, In the West Indies it is known as Jambolan, Jimbolan..The fruit, which is sometimes nearly as large as a pigeon's egg and of a purple colour, is eaten but it is rather astringent. 1926 Fawcett 352, Syzigium Jambolanum..The Jambolan or Damson tree. 1959 V. M. Hadden StJ, Jumboline, A very small, oval, purple fruit..Unlike the other two [Cherry-melia, Jimbilin] this fruit is very sweet when ripe.

JAMBOLANA see JAMBOLAN.

JAMBO PARROT sb dial; sense of 'jambo' unknown. A variety of PARROT fish.

1952 FGC StC /jambo paarat/.

JAM-FORK sb dial; JAM vb[1] + *fork*. A four-pronged fork used to catch crayfish.

1956 Mc Port /jám-fáak/.

jam-it-tu-kaana see JAM-A-CORNER.

JAM-JAM sb dial obs. Some kind of musical instrument, evid of the percussion type. (The genuineness of the name is in doubt; it may rest on a misunderstanding of JAMMA.)

a1818 Lewis (1834) 345, I am sadly afraid..that the rewards after death which Christianity offers will be outweighed by the pleasures of eating fat hog, drinking raw rum, and dancing for centuries to the jam-jam and kitty-katty.

JAMMA /jama/ sb dial; prob from a number of similar or related African words referring to social gatherings, singing, etc.: Bambara *jama*, an assembly, company, Mandingo *dʒama* 'many' (Turner 98); cf also Twi *gyàm*, to condole with, express sorrow, grief or sympathy at the death of someone's relation; *e-dwóm*, song, hymn, etc.; Ngombe *jambo*, refrain; *gyama-dúdu*, a large kind of drum. The US *jam* (and recent *jam-session*) may be of similar source: cf *DA*. Also attrib: see BLACK WATER int.

1. A folk song, in Jamaica sung primarily to accompany communal field-digging (e.g. when planting yams), secondarily to accompany dancing and games at wakes, etc. The singers are led by a BOMMA, and the song comments on local happenings.

1926 Roberts 356, This version much resembles the prevalent Jamaican topical songs, comic or Jamal songs, as the people call them. 1933 McK 316, Jamma, field and digging song. 1943 *GL* Kgn, Jamma, a kind of dance at picnics, etc. c1953 Wilson, A jamma is not a poetical production by any means..the charm lies in the tune, the voice of the bomma, and the rhythmic swing of the workers. 1956 Mc Man /jama—yu hier a stuori an put it in a sang/—sung at set-up, on road work, etc.

2. A digging implement, esp one adapted to digging yams. Cf DIGGING-BILL. (Derived from sense 1 or perh a different word altogether —cf JAM vb[2].)

1943 *GL* Kgn, Jamma, a digging implement; pickaxe or mattock. 1952 FGC Han /jama/ tool for digging yams. 'Take out yam without jamma', expr meaning something unusual. 1956 Mc StE /jama/ iron spike, tool for digging.

3. Transf. See quot. Cf also JAM-POST.

1956 Mc Port /jama/—a fence post, gate post (made of tree trunk or branch).

jam-op-kaana see JAM-A-CORNER.

JAM-POST sb dial joc; <*jam*, force tightly + *post*.

1959 DeC Port /jam-puos/ a rough bed whose legs are fastened to the floor.

jam-to-di-kaana see JAM-A-CORNER.

jan (and compounds) see JOHN in compounds.

JANATAN, JANITON sb dial; ? <*Jonathan*, perh an allusion to 1 Samuel xx, 35. See quots.

1943 *GL* Tre, Janatan, small field. 1954 LeP StAnn, Janiton—a smallholding that the owner cultivates by himself or with his family.

janatan bush sb dial; <*Jonathan*, perh conn with JANATAN, + BUSH. An unidentified plant, used medicinally.

1952 FGC StAnd /janatan bush/ very green leaf, purple blossom, good for TB, consumption.

janchuu, jan chuuit see JOHN CHEWIT.

JANCRO see CYANCRO, JOHN-CROW.

JANE DENIS sb dial. A variety of sweet-potato, prob named after the woman who introduced or grew it successfully.

1952 FGC StAnd /jien denis/ [is] red, very nice and dry.

JANGA see *jangga*.

JANGA-MANGA sb dial slang; prob a 'stretched' form of JANGA, transf to human beings. A person of the lowest type. *G*

1943 *GL* Port, Janga manga, lowest type.

JANGAW see next.

jangga /jangga/ sb dial; 1893→ sp 'jonga' and pronounced accordingly by those meeting the term in print, but never in folk speech. Cf Doulla-Bakweri (in Cameroons pidgin) *ñjaŋga*, crayfish (G. D. Schneider). Cf BLACK JANGA. A river prawn (*Macrobrachium jamaicensis*) used locally as an article of food.

1893 Sullivan 4, Jonga Soup. Is prepared similarly to cray fish or bisque soup. *Ibid* 8, Jongas are a kind of small cray-fish which are often found in our mountain rivers. 1929 Beckwith 51, Fresh-water shrimps, called *jonga*, from the mountain streams. 1943 *GL*, reported from Clar, Kgn, Port, StAnd, StT, etc.; sp 'janga' 6 times, 'jangaw, jonga' once each. 1952 FGC Port, StAnn, StC, StT /jangga/.

jang-ho /jángho/ sb dial. The GUARD-FISH: see quot.

1952 FGC StC /jánghu, jángho/ guard-fish with top jaw long; piper has long lower jaw.

jang-jang see JAN-JAN.

jangko fies sb dial; <Ewe *dzoŋ'kɔ*, sorcerer +*face*. A mask worn in the JOHN CANOE celebration.

1956 Mc StAnd (Describing the Jancunu:) /dem put an jangko fies/ *They put on masks.*

jangko riid sb dial; etym uncert, but this is prob for John-crow weed, i.e. JOHN-CROW BUSH.

1956 Mc StJ /jángko riid/—a plant with a strong smell; used for fever; also for washing clothes: rubbed into the fabric, the juice will remove stains easily.

jangkra(-) see JOHN-CROW.

jangkunu, jankunu see JOHN CANOE.

JANGRA adj dial; prob Afr: cf CHAKA-CHAKA. See quots.

1943 *GL* Han, Jangra, untidy or careless-looking; StJ, ugly; Tre, rough. 1955 FGC Man /janggra/ ragged.

jani see JOHNNY.

janibijani int phr dial; cf Ewe *dzáni*, to be beautiful (Twi *gye aní*).

1959 DeC Port (Moore Town) /janibijani/ common greeting of one Maroon to another.

JANITON see JANATAN.

JAN-JAN, jang-jang sb dial; nasalized variants of *jag-jag*. Small bits of wood or rubbish; specif, kindling.

1943 *GL* Man, Jan-jan, small pieces of wood. 1958 DeC Man /jang-jang/ miscellaneous trash or rubbish; Tre /jang-jang/ small sticks used for firewood.

JAN-TANUP /ján tán-op/ sb dial; for *John stand-up*, prob an allusion to the 'staff of life'.

1943 *GL* StM, Jantanup, bread.

jan tu hit, jantu wit see JOHN CHEWIT.

JAPANESE HAT sb; cf also CHINESE HAT. A common garden shrub (*Holmskioldia sanguinea*) so called from the shape of the flower bract.

c1920 FGC StAnd, current. 1952 Carley in *Gleaner*, Humming birds..exhibit no shyness. They will..come in the house after the blossoms of 'Japanese hat'.

JAPANESE UMBRELLA sb. =JAPANESE HAT.

1959 DAP StAnd.

JAR PIPE sb dial. Common sewer pipe, made, like jars, of earthenware.

1952 FGC StAnd.

JAVALINE CROW see JABBERING CROW.

[JAVA PLUM sb bot. The tree *Eugenia jambolana*, and its fruit. (*OED* no quots.)

1913 Harris 10, In the West Indies it is known as *Jambolan, Jimbolan, Java Plum, Jack Plum,* &c.]

JAWBONE sb arch or obs. *BL N*

1. A musical instrument of rattling type (cf GRATER), consisting of a horse's jawbone: see quot 1837.

[1790 Beckford II 387, Their musical instruments.. consist of the jaw-bone of an animal, from which is produced a harsh and disagreeable sound.] 1837 Belisario Expl. to Plate 3, The instrument from which the [Jaw-Bone] 'John Canoe'..derives his title..is simply the lower jaw of a horse, on the teeth of which, a piece of wood is passed quickly up and down, occassioning [*sic*] a rattling noise.—To loosen the teeth, the Jaw is hung in the smoke for several days. 1929 Beckwith 210, The gourd rattle, and the jawbone vibrator.

2. Attrib: see quots.

1837 Belisario Expl to Plate 3, The 'Jaw-Bone John Canoe'..[is a] non-descript compound, in half-military, half-mountebank attire..His regimental coat and sash, are invariably retained, whatever changes may take place in the other parts of his costume—and as a rule without exception, he (in common with the whole of the John-Canoe fraternity) always wears a mask, with a profusion of dark hair. 1929 see CROMANTY 5. 1942 HPJ, Jawbone song: A kind of Maroon Song at Moore Town—From a custom of wearing jawbones of animals at Xmas time? [Cf 1961 *Ja Talk*. 262.]

JAW-FALL(ING) sb obs; erron definition in *OED*, 2. An infantile disease once prevalent: a type of lock-jaw.

1774 Long III 713, The retension of this excrement [the meconium in new-born infants] has been fatal to multitudes, by bringing on mortal convulsions, generally known here by the name of jaw-falling. 1789 *Two Reports..House of Assembly*..28, The tetanus of locked-jaw; a disorder which the negroes call the jaw-fall. *Ibid* 29, Immediately before death, a general relaxation comes on, and the lower jaw falls on the breast. 1801 Dancer 269, Though the terms Jaw-Fall and Lockea-Jaw are used synonimously, the Jaw-Fall proper signifies that state of the Disease, where the mouth either remains open..or else where the Chin falls down on the Sternum. 1820 Thompson 119, The disease has no right to be called *jaw-fall*, for that symptom rarely supervenes; and when it does, it is only during the last stages, and in consequence of paralysis.

JEALOUSY /jelasi, jalasi/ sb; Anglicized form of *jalousie*—cf *OED* →1834; this pronunc is still current in Jamaica. Also attrib. A jalousie: a slatted blind, formerly wooden, now also of glass or metal, fixed into a window frame, and able to be opened or closed. *BL G T* (archaic).

1774 Long II 22, Sashes [are] more generally in use, to which are added jealousy-shutters, or Venetian blinds, which admit the air freely, and exclude the sun-shine. 1835 Senior 15, The houses have..Venetian blinds, or, as they are there termed, jalousies (pronounced 'jelassee') by which they are both lighted and ventilated. (1960 Current, FGC.)

jega /jéga, jíega/ sb dial; <*jagger*, a fishing boat that tends another. *OED* β-form *jagar* is closest to this. A sail used aft on a *kunu* behind the skipper.

1952 FGC StM.

jege[1], jege-jege[1], jeg-jeg sb and adj dial; prob var of *jag-jag*.

1. Small bits of kindling wood. Cf *jigi-jigi*.

1956 Mc StE /jeg-jeg/ a big heap o' bramble pile up in one place. 1958 DeC StT /jege-jege/ small sticks used for firewood; trash or rubbish.

2. Rags, tatters, torn clothing and the like; also adjectivally, ragged, torn.

1942 HPJ [Song:] Me sleep pan jeggay mat, oh! [Cf JAGGAY MAT.] 1954 LeP StE, Jeggeh—old ragged clothes. 1955 FGC Man /jeg-jegz/ rags. 1956 LeP StE /jege-jege/ jagged. 1956 Mc StE /a jége-jege yu gat áan/.

jege[2], jege-jege[2] sb dial; onomatopoeic.

1. A rattling noise.

1956 Mc Man /di drie gwaan jege-jege/ *The dray made the sound 'jege-jege'.*

2. Something that makes a rattling noise.

1954 LeP StE /jege/ the cashew nut without a kernel, which rattles when shaken. 1956 Mc Man /tek di biebi jege-jege gi mi/ *Give me the baby's rattle.*

3. A form of gambling—see quot.

1956 Mc Clar /jege/ an old plate, blue and white is broken into pieces, which are shaken up. What the betting is made on I did not discover.

jege-man sb dial; prob < JIGGEY + *man.*

1958 DeC StT /jege-man/ an obeah man.

JEGGE sb (or vb?) dial; cf JIGGEY, JIGIFU.

1943 *GL* StT, Jegge—fool.

JEGGEH see *jege*[1].

JEGGI sb dial uncom; etym unknown.

1943 HPJ, Jeggi, A pretty white sea-shell; A white cowri; said to be Yoruba (? Lagos dialect).

jeg-jeg see *jege*[1].

jeje sb dial; etym unknown. The bottlefish; see quot 1950.

1950 Smith West (Negril), Jejea, *Canthigaster rostratus.* 1952 FGC Port, West /jéjè/.

JEJEA see prec.

JELASSEE see JEALOUSY.

JELLIDOE sb dial; < JELLY + a euphonizing syllable. The name for a JELLY COCONUT, shouted by vendors (the voice going falsetto on the end of the last syllable).

1930 FGC StAnd /jèli-dúo/ (and other var forms). 1954 LeP Kgn, Jellidoe, coconut sold in the street for water and jelly.

JELLY (COCONUT) sb; the abbr form is dial. An unripe coconut sold in the streets ready for the water to be drunk and the jelly eaten.

[1834 WI Sketch Book ii 15 (Basseterre), The coco-nut, in this unripe state, contains only a thin coating of the nut. . merely a transparent mucilage, whence it has acquired the name of the 'jelly coco-nut'.] 1954 LeP Man, Jeli, Jelly Kokenat; StAnn, Jelly. *BL G*

JELLY-MOSS sb. A gelatinous 'moss'; prob actually a fungus of the family *Collemaceae.*

1756 Browne 80, Collema viscosa, foliacea, inequalis. The foliaceous Jelly-moss. I have observed this mossy substance once in Mangeneel. 1952 FGC StAnn, Jelly moss. . doesn't have leaves but grows like the fat of something green—/veri swagi-laik/.

jempe adj dial uncom; etym unknown, but cf Twi *gyé*, frenzy, madness.

1956 Mc StE (Accom) /jémpe/ irresponsible, unstable, 'half-mad'.

jempe lamp sb dial; evid < *jempe* + *lamp.*

1956 Mc StE (Accom) /jempe lamp/—the small tin oil-lamp without shade, also called /tinin lamp/.

JENGA-GENGA sb dial; prob var of *jenge-jenge.* Miscellaneous objects, 'stuff'.

1943 *GL* Clar, Jengã gengã, 'Extras'.

JENGEH, jengge-jengge see next.

jen-jen, jeng-jeng, jengge-jengge sb or adj dial; nasalized variants of *jeg-jeg*, etc., but perh also with coincidental infl of such a word as Ngombe *jengé*, disorder. Cf also *jag-jag.*

1. Lopped branches of trees and bushes, used for firewood when dry, for mulch when green.

1956 Mc Man /jeng-jeng/.

2. Torn clothing, rags; also adjectivally, torn, ragged.

1943 *GL* Clar, StAnd, jen-jen, old ragged clothes; Kgn, Port, jeng-jeng. 1954 LeP Man, Jengeh—old ragged clothes; Port, StE, Jeng-Jeng. 1956 Mc Man /jengge/ also /jen-jen, jen-jeng/. 1958 DeC Tre /jengge-jengge/ old, ragged work clothes.

3. Ironically.

1942 HPJ, Jengeh: flashy finery.

4. Specif. The small rubbishy objects which an OBEAHMAN uses—his THINGS.

1942 Bennett 20, De po' chile Goh step ovah dem obeah jeng-jeng.

JENKOVING sb obs exc hist; etym unknown, but cf Gã *kofeŋ*, a horn which one blows; a blown horn. A musical instrument: see quots.

1739 Leslie 326, They have other musical instruments, as. . a *Jenkoving*, which is a way of clapping their Hands on the Mouth of two Jars. 1914 Clerk 22, Jenkoving. . two jars with medium-sized mouths over which the performers brought down their hands.

JEREMIAH sb dial; by folk-etym < *cherimoya.* The cherimoya fruit.

1942 HPJ, Jeremiah: Cherimoya. 1952 FGC Man /jèrimáia/.

JEREMY sb dial; prob from the name of the individual who introduced or produced it. A large, long-bearing variety of coco.

1929 Beckwith 17, In Mandeville were enumerated. . the 'Lef' Hand' [erron for *lef-man*] as the hardest, the 'Jeremy' as the biggest. 1952 FGC StC /jerimi/.

JERK vb; cf *OED jerk v*[2]. To preserve pork or beef after the manner of the Quichua Indians by drying it in the sun, originally without salt.

1707 Sloane xvi, Swine. . running wild in the Country, are shot or pierced through with lances, cut open, the Bones taken out, and the Flesh is gash'd on the inside into the Skin, fill'd with Salt and expos'd to the Sun, which is call'd Jirking. 1774 Long II 319 [Among sea-faring terms current ashore in Jamaica:] To jerk. To salt meat and smoak dry it. 1803 Dallas I 91, I know not whence the word *jirked* is derived, but it signifies cutting or scoring internally the flesh of the wild hog, which is then smoked. 1890 Thomas 87, The men set to work at once to prepare for 'jerking' the pigs. (See also *pata* sb[1] 1, *caban.*)

JERKED HOG sb obs; cf JERK, *jork puok.* See quots.

1790 Beckford I 330, The negroes smoak and dry this animal, from whence the pieces thus smoaked, obtain the appellation of *jirked hog*; and it is, when thus cured, a very savoury and a pleasing relish. 1802 Nugent 95, The first course was entirely of fish, excepting jerked hog. . which is the way of dressing it by the Maroons.

JERKIN sb dial arch; < *jerkin* (*OED* →1868). See quots.

1943 *GL* Kgn, Jerkin, a little child's dress. 1955 FGC Man, Child's dress—old-fashioned.

JERK PAN sb dial. A pan used in jerking meat.

1956 Mc StAnd, see next.

JERK PORK /jork puok/ sb dial; for *jerked pork*—cf JERKED HOG.

1. Smoked pork.

1952 FGC StM /jork puok/.

2. A stew of pork and vegetables.

1952 FGC StJ /jork puok/ boil in pot, brown in /huovn/ with garlic, skellion, country pepper /honyan/; cut in pieces. 1956 Mc StAnd, Kill a hog, put it in a deep pot with butter and spice, and steam it. Then put it in a jerk pan. Irish potatoes, etc. may be added. /jak, jaak, jork, jorkin puok/—the commonest being /jork/.

JERRY vb dial; < *jeer* + *-y.*

1943 *GL* Clar, Jerry, to mock or imitate; StM, Jerry, jeer. 1962 BLB 58 /jeri/ mock, jeer.

JERUSALEM CANDLESTICK sb; from the shape like a branched candlestick. The tree *Cassia alata*.

1952 FGC StAnn, StM, StT, Tre; Jerusalem candlestick—'round stem, green, like fingers scattered all over the tree'. 1956 Mc StAnd.

JERUSALEM PEAS sb; the name may be due to the blood-red flowers—an allusion to the Crucifixion? A variety of the bean *Phaseolus mungo*.

1910 Barclay *JJAS* (in 1913 Fawcett 33), Jerusalem peas can be planted immediately the [banana] plants appear.. The vines will soon cover the ground, and they do not run so much as the velvet bean or the Bengal bean.. The Jerusalem peas last longer than cowpeas. 1913 Harris 34. 1952 FGC Port, StAnn, StC, StJ, StM; very small red or brown peas.

JERUSALEM THORN sb; an allusion to Christ's crown: see quot 1873.

1. The prickly shrub *Parkinsonia aculeata*.

1756 Browne 222, The Jerusalem Thorn. This shrub was first introduced to Jamaica from the main, but it now grows wild..it has been originally cultivated for the use of inclosures. 1790 Beckford I 32, The singular appearance of the Jerusalem thorn. 1873 Rampini 155, The Jerusalem thorn..is popularly supposed to be the plant with which our Saviour was crowned. 1920 Fawcett 98. 1947 U.Newton II 6, There was a robber around.. In the clump of bush, in the Jerusalem thorns.

2. *Acacia catechu*: see quot.

1837 Macfadyen 314–15, *Acacia Catechu*. This tree appears to have been introduced into the Island many years since. In some districts it has been planted to form fences and has received incorrectly the name of the Jerusalem Thorn.

JESEN /jesn/ adv dial; <*jes* (dial pronunc of *just*) +-*n* suffix[1].

1933 McK 316, Jesen—just.

JESMY see next.

JESSAMY /jesimi/ sb dial; *OED* →1733. The jasmine tree. *G*

1912 McK *Ballads*, Jesmy: jasmine. 1924 Beckwith 74, A pretty tree name of Jessamy. (1960 Current, FGC.)

JESSIE sb dial; see BITTER JESSE.

1942 HPJ, Jessie—'A bitter yellow-yam introduced by the Spaniards', Col. Rowe. A Maroon 'thought this was the *nigger-yam*'.

JESTA (POT) sb dial; aphetic form of DIGESTER.

1. A heavy, originally iron, cooking pot with a long handle, and often a cover. (Not the same as DUTCH POT.)

1950 Pioneer 36, Anancy get one iron jesta dutch pot an bore out two hole. 1952 FGC StAnd, StM, Tre, West. 1955 FGC Man /jesta/—pot with long, straight handle; iron or enamel.

2. Less commonly: A pot with a spout; a kettle.

1943 *GL* Clar, Jester, a tea pot. 1956 Mc Man, StAnd /jesta, jesta pat/.

JESTER see prec.

JESUS /jiizas/ sb attrib dial. An intensive word, heavily stressed. Cf GOD. *BL G*

1961 FGC StAnd /nàt wàn jíizas shílin im no gi mi/ *Not one cursed shilling did he give me!*

[**JETICI** sb dial; prob Amer Ind: cf Ewe *dzete, dzeteé, dzetı*, Gɛ̃ *edyete*, sweet-potato (batata) perh from this word. A drink made from the sweet-potato by American Indians.

a 1726 Barham (1794) 116, From the fresh roots of this plant the natives [Virginia Indians] make a drink which ferments, and is called *mobby*, or *jetici*, which they fuddle and get drunk with, as they do with potatoe mobby in Jamaica.]

jetosi sb dial; etym unknown.

1952 FGC StT /jétosí/ the water mahoe tree.

JEW sb dial slang.

1956 G. Coulthard StAnd, Jew, used of any well-to-do person, presumably white; no racial or religious significance.

JEW COCO see DUKE COCO.

JEW FISH sb; *OED* 1697→. A fish (*Promicrops itaira*) early considered a delicacy. By fishermen now called JUNE FISH. *BL G N*

1679 Trapham 65, The Jew fish crowds to be one of the first three of our most worthy Fish..affording a most firm well relished flesh throughout his whole bulk, but a most eminently delicious head..etc.

JEW-HARP DRUMMER sb; from its having markings resembling a jew's-harp. A variety of DRUMMER fish.

1892 Cockrell list, Jew harp drummer, *Larimus breviceps*.

JEW-JEW RAIN see JU-JU (RAIN, WATER).

JEW PLUM sb; origin unknown, but prob in some way descriptive; freq replaced by the dial term JUNE PLUM. An egg-sized plum, greenish-yellow, with coarse flesh and spiny, hard seed; eaten raw and often cooked.

1913 Harris 18, *Spondias dulcis*..The Jew Plum..was introduced to Jamaica in 1782 and again in 1792. 1952 FGC Port, StAnd, StAnn; StM /júu plóm/ with a green skin—turns yellow; stew them.

JEYES /jiez/ sb; abbr of *Jeyes' fluid*. A common household disinfectant, also used in home remedies. s JEYESEY-AISE. *BA G*

c 1915 FGC StAnd, 'Jeyes' mixed with 'sivl-orange' and used to clean floors. 1947 U.Newton III 36, In vain the tooth was stuffed with healing oil, jeyes, creosote. 1952 FGC StM /jíez/ used in medicine against fever; Han, used against ghosts—see SEAL vb.

jien-jien an tataz sb phr; <*Jane-Jane and 'tatoes*; cf *EDD* for many aphetic forms of 'potato'. See quot.

1959 DeC Port /jien-jien an tataz/ johnnycakes and fritters; /jien-jien/ is apparently..used..only in this phrase.

JIG vb dial or slang. Of a woman: to walk in a provocative fashion. *BA G*

1954 LeP StE (Elderslie).

JIGGA NANNY sb dial; ?<*jigger*, one who jigs +*Nanny* (cf NANNY THATCH). The dancer at the centre of a singing ring-game (e.g. *Ball Gone Roun'*). Cf s MAWGA-NANNY.

1922 Beckwith 92 [Song:] Pass de ball an' de ball gwine roun', Jigger Nannie tell me say de ball gwine roun'. 1951 Murray 17, Jigga Nanny—Principal dancer. 1957 JN Man, Chiga nani.

JIGGEH see JIGGEY.

JIGGER /jíga, chíga/ sb; 1756 chiger, 1788 gigger, 1792 chigise (perh representing an overcorrected folk form), a 1818 chiga, 1835→ jigger, 1942 jiggoe; for etym see s. 'Chigger' is less frequent than 'jigger'. Also attrib. The chigoe, formerly a common cause of deformity among negroes. *BA BL G N T*

1756 Browne 418, The chigoe or Chiger. This insect is very frequent and troublesome. 1788 Marsden 30, The chegoe, or gigger..gets imperceptibly under the skin.. where..it lays eggs. 1792 Stewart 9, An insect called *a chigise*, is excessively troublesome. a 1818 Lewis (1845) 109, The most general of negro infirmities..is chiefly occasioned by the *chiga*. 1835 Madden I 88, Pray take care how you walk without your slippers; these jiggers, you know, produce frightful consequences. 1952 FGC StT, Tre, West /chiga, chiga flii/; Man, StAnd, StT, West /jiga/.

JIGGER-FOOT sb and attrib dial. *BA*

1. A foot infested or deformed by JIGGERS. *G T*

2. As a place-name symbolizing a poor, backward place. (Ref is to the 1865 uprising.)

1907 Jekyll 187–8 [Song:] War down a Monkland, war down a Morant Bay, war down a Chiggerfoot.

3. In the nickname JIGGER-FOOT (MARKET): a market considered to be frequented by the poorest people, symbolized by their having 'jigger-foot'.

1942 HPJ, Jiggerfoot market—popular name of a market in Kingston; there are others so called in St Thomas and St Catherine also. 1961 Katzin 10 [A country higgler speaking:] I don't know that girl..for a tief. That's the second time that woman from Chiggerfoot do that to me. When you lose your character for a shilling, that bad!

JIGGER NANNIE see JIGGA NANNY.

JIGGER-NIT sb dial; <JIGGER+*nit*. The egg or newly hatched young of the JIGGER, imbedded in the flesh; it must be removed to prevent bad sores. *G*

1942 Astley Clerk in HPJ, Jigger-nit is the egg or hatched young still in the toe.

JIGGEY sb dial cant; etym uncert—perh <*jig* vb (cf *OED* 2b), alluding to the 'pulling' of obeah. Cf also *jege*[1]. A talisman consisting of a bunch of herbs or their seeds, used by MYAL or OBEAH men.

1923 Beckwith 52, An amber bead used to be employed as a fetich object in myal practices. In Lacovia a glass marble takes its place today. 'Jiggey' is another fetich, in the form of the seeds of an herb a bunch of which the myal dancer brings out of the bush after the dance..To 'pull' the disease is to extract..the evil spirit which an Obeah-man has sent to torment the patient; this task it is the part of the Amber or the Jiggeh to perform. 1928 Beckwith 10, The obeah-man uses as a charm the seeds of a certain plant (unidentified) called 'jiggey' which are supposed to be given him by 'Death' at a dance when 'Death is pleased with him'. 1929 Beckwith 155, Some [songs]..like..the lively 'Oh, me ambah!..Pull i' me ambah, jiggey!' employ the very phraseology of the Myal Man's art.

JIGGING sb dial; <*jigging* vbl sb (*OED*).

1956 Mc Man /jígin/—A dance; dancing à la West Indian.

JIGGOE see JIGGER. *BA*

JIGIFU vb dial; prob <JIGGEY+*fu*, fool (cf FOO-FOO[2]).

1943 *GL* Port, Jigifu, to fool one.

jigi-jigi sb dial; a variant of *jeg-geg*, *jege-jege*[1].

1959 DeC West /jigi-jigi/ small sticks used for firewood.

jigi-jigi vb dial; <*jig*, iterated on analogy of *jege-jege*[2], suggesting repeated movement back and forth.

1956 Mc [Riddle:] 'Giggi-giggi all about de corners'. [Answer:] A broom.

jiji-waina sb dial; *ji-ji* (? < jig-jig, suggesting its motion) +*winder*. A larva which is used in a children's game: it is held in the hand, a verse is repeated, and it is then supposed to twist until it points in the direction of a place, etc.

1943 *GL* StC, Jiji-wina, a little dark brown animal; in hand, twis in any direction. 1955 FGC Man /jiji-waina, -wina/ when wood rotten..[it's] like a worm but with a slight shell—twists itself. s WINEY.

jiko sb dial uncom; evid African (but not listed by Christaller). Said to be a DAY NAME.

1956 BLB StJ /jíko/ a day name.

jil, JILL see GILL[2].

JIMBELI, jimbelin see JIMBLING.

JIMBELI, jimbelin, jimbili, jimbilin, jimblin see next.

JIMBLING /jímbilin, jímbelin, jímblin, jímilin, jímbili, chímbolin/ sb; <BIMBLING under infl of JAMBOLAN. (Both the forms of the names, and their applications, show confusion. See *baaj*.)

1. The tree *Phyllanthus distichus* (or *P. acidus*), and its extremely acid fruit, pale greenish-yellow, which come out in clustérs from the trunk and branches of the tree.

1894 Spinner 82, Justina..could manufacture the delicious guava 'dosey', and preserved 'Jimmielins' and cachews. 1913 Harris 10, Jimbling. *Phyllanthus distichus*..It is also known as *Otaheite gooseberry*, and *Cheremila*, and was brought to Jamaica from the island of Timor in 1793. The fruit..is about the size of a gooseberry, pale green in colour and ribbed. It is very acid and astringent. 1935 HPJ, see *baaj*. 1952 FGC Port, StAnd, StAnn, StM, StT /jimbilin/; StM, Sour as hell —boil, throw away the first water, make like jelly with sugar. 1956 Mc StAnd /jimbelin/; Port /jombelin, jumbelin/ small sour fruit, good stewed for jam. 1959 E. M. Falconer StC, Jimbeli or Jembeli as I know it is a very acid sort of cherry colour lime green to yellow.

2. See quot. (The description suits the JAMBOLAN, which, however, Sullivan describes somewhat differently.)

1893 Sullivan 81–2, Jimblings—A small blueish black fruit very stainy to the taste but fresh and juicy. They make an excellent preserve.

JIMBOLAN see JAMBOLAN.

JIMBOLIN, jimilin, JIMMIELIN see JIMBLING.

JIM CROW'S NOSE see JOHN-CROW (BLOW-) NOSE.

JIMMY-SWING sb dial slang; similar to Engl and US slang or dial expr, but not found in dictionaries.

1943 *GL* StAnd, Jimmy Swing, common people; StM, Jimmy Swing, ill-fed lad.

JIMMY WOOD sb dial. =DOVEWOOD.

1954 *WIMJ* 157, see LOB-LOB. 1955 *WIMJ* 78.

JIMPIREE sb dial; for *jamboree*, though perh borrowed directly from East Indians in Ja.

1943 *GL* Port, Jimpiree, spree.

jinal sb and adj dial; <*general sb*. For pronunc cf *ADD*: US sp *gin'ral*, *giner'l*, 1941 e. Texas *Negro* [ˈdʒĩnl̩]. A clever person; hence esp a crafty, tricky person: a 'crook'. (There are overtones of connection with obeah.) *BL*

[1925 Beckwith 40, Gin'al..general.] 1941 Kirkpatrick gloss, Jinal, crafty person. 1943 *GL* Kgn, StC, Jinnal, a smart person; Man, StC, Ginal, a sly cunning person, smart; Port, Ginnal, a crook; StAnd, StC, Genal; Kgn, Genial, one who plays smart. 1952 FGC Han, 'Chief [=dupe] in town; /jinal/ mus' dive!'; StJ, 'Him is a /jinal/ man!'

jing-bang sb dial; cf *EDD*, but Ja senses are depreciatory.

1. A crowd of people, noisy, dirty, etc.—riff-raff, rabble.

1943 *GL* Kgn, Jing-bang, a ragged noisy crowd. 1956 Mc Man /jing-bang/ a group of low-class, idle, chattering people.

2. A low-class, noisy, dirty person; spec a degraded woman.

1943 *GL* Clar, Jing-bang, a degrading girl. 1955 FGC Man /jing-bang/ a noisy person.

3. See quot. (In this sense prob infl by *jeng-jeng*.)

1957 G. Coulthard StAnd, Jing-bang, old bits and pieces of rubbish, clothes, etc.—'carochies'.

JING-JING sb dial; onomatopoeic.

1943 *GL* StE, Jing-jing, bangle.

jinggl vb dial; cf *OED jinkle, jiggle*. To shake, disturb. *G*

1942 Bennett 20 [Speaking of a clumsy servant who breaks things, and alluding to the superstition that if you kill spiders or trouble birds'-nests your hands will tremble:] De gal musa dah gingle bud nes' Meck she start mash up me funicha.

jingki (mini) sb dial; var of *dingki-mini*.

1943 *GL* StAnn, Jinkiminnie, party. 1958 DeC Port /jingki(-mini)/.

jinji see *din-din*.

jinji flai see GINGY-FLY.

JINNAL see *jinal*.

JINNA RUMBLE sb dial or slang.

1943 *GL*, Jinna Rumble, two pieces of sticks for walking.

JIP HAT sb dial or slang; abbr of JIPPI-JAPPA.

1948 Bennett 19, She..Grab Amy ole dutty jip hat An jam awn pon her head. 1956 Mc Port /jip hat/.

JIPPI-JAPPA /jípi-jápa/ sb; <*Jipijapa*, Ecuador: a form preserving the Spanish sp of the initial consonants, though the pronunc is changed. Cf by contrast YIPPI YAPPA. Also attrib. A kind of cream-coloured straw (properly from *Carludovica palmata*) used to make hats; also the hat itself. *BL*

c1915 FGC StAnd (remembered). 1933 McK 317, Jippi-jappa, local name for hats similar to Panama hats. 1943 *GL* StA, StE, Tre, Jippy-Jappa. 1952 FGC StAnd, StM /jípi-jàpa/ straw. 1956 Mc Port /jipi-japa hat/.

JIPSY see GYPSY.

JIRK see JERK.

JOBBING GANG sb obs; cf *OED job sb*² 2. Also attrib. A gang of slaves—see quots. *G*

1790 Beckford I 139, After a public misfortune [e.g. a hurricane]..the jobbing gangs were engaged with avidity. 1825 Bickell 50–1, Jobbing gangs; that is, gangs of Negroes belonging to men who have just land enough to raise provisions for their slaves and themselves..These gangs (generally from twenty to forty stout male and female Negroes) are hired out by proprietors and managers to do the heaviest parts of labour on sugar estates, and to repair roads, &c. 1825 De la Beche 34, Jobbing gang negroes, those belonging to the free brown and black people..Jobbing gangs are (I believe) by no means so numerous as they formerly were. 1839 McMahon 49–50, Mr Adam Steel, the proprietor of an extensive jobbing gang, induced me..to take charge of his gang as overseer. His gang was employed in jobbing on estates in that and the neighbouring parishes.

JOB CART sb dial. *G*

1958 DeC StC /jab kyaat/ a four-wheeled handcart.

jobo sb dial cant; etym unknown. In the jargon of St Thomas cults: blood.

1953 Moore gloss, Jobo—blood, a Maroon word.

JOCATO (CALALU) /jòkotó, jòkató, jòkatú, jòkatá, jòkotú, jòkutú, jùkutó, jùkutú/ sb dial; 1774 juckata, 1801 jucato jacatoo, 1913 jockato, 1914 jocato, 1927 1943 jocoto, 1943 jukoto, juckoto, 1943→ jokoto; cf Twi *ɔ-dókoto*, growing wild, and perh also Ewe *dzukuwi*, *dyukuwi*, a plant of Solanum type, used in soups.

The plants *Phytolacca rivinoides* and *P. icosandra*, used as a soup-green and in folk remedies. Also called MOUNTAIN CALALU.

1774 Long III 771–2, Mountain Calalue, Pokeweed, Surinam or Juckata Calalue—*Phytolacca assurgens ramosa*. 1801 Dancer 229–30, Cutaneous complaints..The *Phytolacca*, or Pork-Weed, has been used in America. A species of it here, the *Jacatoo Caleloe*, is also used. *Ibid* 368. 1913 Harris 27, Calalu, Jockato..The plant is very acrid, but the young leaves and shoots are carefully boiled and make an excellent spinach. 1943 *GL* StAnn, StE, StC, Tre. 1952 FGC most parishes. 1954 LeP StE, Calalu is the cultivated variety [of edible spinach]. Jokoto grows wild in virgin soil.

JOCKEY('S) SADDLE sb; descriptive. The JAMAICA ROSE: *Blakea trinervia*.

1941 *NHN* I 3 9, Jockey's saddle..is commonly found twining irregularly over trunks and branches. 1952 FGC Tre /jáki sádl/ [use as medicine] for cold; 'also in Manchester'.

JOCK-IN-THE-BUSH see JACK-IN-THE-BUSH.

JOE sb obs; cf *OED Joe sb*² 2, 'A fourpenny piece'. Sixpence. (Not to be confused with *Joe sb*¹, a general WI word—cf *OED*.)

1873 Rampini 94. (See GILL² 2.) s CURRENCY.

JOE BIRD sb dial. A pelican—cf OLD JOE.

1952 FGC StC /juo bod/.

JOE CLARK sb dial; said to be named after a local man. The bonito fish.

1952 FGC StE /júo kláak/.

JOE LOUIS sb dial slang; named after the American boxer. A kind of large, solid cake made with a pound of flour, a pound of sugar, etc. Also called UNCLE JOE.

1943 *GL* see CREPE SOLE. 1952 FGC StE.

JOHN BAILLIE sb; from the name of the author of *The Jamaica Distiller's Directory* (2nd ed 1821). *BA*

1. A stick of pulled sugar-candy flavoured with peppermint, made and sold locally.

1929 Beckwith 45, Pulled pink and white peppermint sticks called 'John Barley' [*sic*]. 1952 FGC StE (Black R.), John Baillie—long twisted sticks of peppermint.

2. Sugar that has become very sticky or tough.

1952 FGC StJ /jan bieli/ sugar boiled till it 'tie-teeth'; StM, sugar that becomes stiffy-like; Tre, a tough sugar —syrup dry out too much.

JOHN BARLEY error for prec.

JOHN BARNET sb dial; prob named after a man who introduced or grew it successfully. A variety of sweet-potato with white flesh.

1952 FGC StAnd, StC /ján báanit/.

JOHN-BELLY-FULL sb dial.

1943 *GL*, John-Belly-full, an iron axe for breaking stones.

JOHN BULL (TREE) sb; origin unknown.

1. See quots.

1926 Fawcett 145, Thespesia..populnea..Sea-side Mahoe, John Bull Tree. 1952 FGC StM /jan bul/.

2. =DEAD MAN BONES?

1952 FGC Man. (Identification uncert.)

JOHN BUSH sb dial; <*John*+BUSH.

1953 *WIMJ* 234, *Blechum brownei* Juss. Wild Hops; John Bush.

JOHN CANOE /jángkunu, jàngkunú/ sb; 1774 John Connú, 1801 1863 Johnny Canoe, 1816→ John-Canoe, 1825 1926 Joncanoe, 1826 1827 Jonkanoo; attempts to represent the dial pronunc: 1943 jancunoo, jankoono, jan-kunnah, 1949 Jan Cunnoo, 1951 Juncoonu. By folk-etym from some such form as Ewe *dzonɔ*, sorcerer +*kúnu*, something deadly, a cause of death; or Ewe *dzoŋ'kɔ*, sorcerer's name for himself +-*nu*, man: thus, a 'witch-doctor'. See *jangko fies*. (For earlier attempts at the etymology see quots and *DA Johnkannaus*, only quot 1861.) Also attrib. *BL*

A. sb: 1. The leader and chief dancer of a troop of negro dancers. He wears an elaborate horned mask or head-dress, which, by the end of the 18th and early 19th cents, had developed into or been replaced by the representation of an estate house, houseboat, or the like (never a canoe). The celebration takes place during the Christmas holidays, the John Canoe leading the other masqueraders in procession singing and dancing, with drums and noisy 'music', and asking for contributions from bystanders and householders. In the more elaborate celebrations there were different kinds of John Canoes (cf JAWBONE, COW-HEAD, HORSE-HEAD, etc.).

1774 Long II 424–5, In the towns, during Christmas holidays, they have several tall robust fellows dressed up in grotesque habits, and a pair of ox-horns on their head, sprouting from the top of a horrid sort of vizor, or mask, which about the mouth is rendered very terrific with large boar-tusks. The masquerader, carrying a wooden sword in his hand, is followed with a numerous crowd of drunken women, who refresh him frequently with a sup of aniseed-water, whilst he dances at every door bellowing out John Connú! with great vehemence..This dance is probably an honourable memorial of John Conny, a celebrated cabocero at Tres Puntas, in Axim, on the Guiney coast; who flourished about the year 1720. He bore great authority among the Negroes of that district..In 1769, several new masks appeared; the Ebos, the Papaws, &c. having their respective Connús, male and female. 1801 Nugent 65, After Church, amuse myself very much with the strange processions, and figures called Johnny Canoes. All dance, leap and play a thousand anticks. a 1818 Lewis (1845) 246, The sudden sounds of the drum and banjee, called our attention to procession of the *John-Canoe*, which was proceeding to celebrate the opening of the new year at the town of Black River. The John-Canoe is a Merry-Andrew dressed in a striped doublet, and bearing upon his head a kind of pasteboard houseboat, filled with puppets, some sailors, others soldiers, others again slaves at work on a plantation, &c...[He watches the SET GIRLS also parading.] ..John Canoe made no part of the procession [of girls]; but he and his rival, John Crayfish (a personage of whom I heard, but could not obtain a sight), seemed to act upon quite an independent interest, and to go about from house to house, tumbling and playing antics to pick up money for themselves. *Ibid* 36, A young mulatto carpenter..now begged me to notice the smaller of the two John-Canoe machines..And indeed it was as fine as paint, pasteboard, gilt paper, and looking-glass could make it! Unluckily, the breeze being very strong blew off a fine glittering umbrella, surmounted with a plume of John-crow feathers, which crowned the top. *Ibid* 37, The John-Canoes are fitted out at the expense of the rich negroes, who afterwards share the money collected from the spectators during their performance, allotting one share to the representator himself. 1826 Barclay 11–12, [The SET GIRLS] have always one or two Joncanoe-men, smart youths, fantastically dressed, and masked so as not to be known. Thus equipped..they proceed to the neighbouring plantation villages..Some refreshment is given to them, and the Joncanoe-men, after a display of their buffoonery, commonly put the white people under requisition for a little money, to pay the fiddler. 1827 Hamel II 102, Who the devil are you?..what do you come here for, dressed up like Jonkanoo Tom Fool? 1828 Marly 293–4, A principal attraction was John Canoe and his wife, each accoutred in a manner truly fantastical.. but John very prudently carried a small imitation of a canoe, into which he and his wife, with their attendants expected the donations of onlookers to be deposited..John and his wife danced without intermission, often wheeling violently round, for a great number of times, and all the while singing, or, in more correct language, roaring an unintelligible jargon..Their performance was truly hideous. 1837 Belisario Expl to Plate 5, The term *John-Canoe* has had many derivations applied to it, amongst others, that it has arisen from the circumstance of the negroes having formerly carried a house in a boat or canoe; but it is perhaps more consistent to regard it, as a corruption of *Gens inconnus*, signifying, 'unknown folks', from their always wearing masks. 1949 U.Newton V 30–1, 'It's nearly five o'clock [A.M.] and the "Jan Cunnoo" are coming. News of the "Jan Cunnoo" bounced me vertical [out of bed] quicker than you'd think.. 'Jan Cunnoo dem merry eh, Massa? Dem dress nice'. It was true..In the true Christmas spirit they had dressed themselves to look hideous and amusing so as to entertain us..scores of them, of the Satanic host I mean. Some with horns, some with tusks, some with heads of donkeys and horses but with the feet of men.

2. Transf. The house or houseboat carried by the John Canoe dancer.

1826 Williams 25–6, First came eight or ten young girls marching before a man dressed up in a mask with a grey beard and long flowing hair, who carried the model of a house on his head. This house is called the Jonkanoo, and the bearer of it is generally chosen for his superior activity in dancing. 1863 Waddell 17–18 (Event from year 1829), Christmas came on, when the slaves had three holidays..Companies of young men paraded the estates, carrying a fanciful and gaily painted structure, called a 'Johnny Canoe',* and followed by a crowd singing and beating the gomby..*A corruption, doubtless, of some African word.

3. The festival or celebration centering about John Canoe. Originally this was African, but elements of the English morris-dances and especially of the French carnival 'sets' (cf BLUES AND REDS) were absorbed into it, and certain stock characters from all these sources became established (see quot 1952). Also in phr 'to make John Canoe'. *N*

1825 Bickell 214, At Christmas, when I first arrived there [Kingston], one could hardly sleep at night, or drive through the streets in the day time, for the crowds of Slaves that were parading and thronging all parts, in a heathenish and noisy manner, making John Canoe, as they term it, according to the customs of Africa; but latterly this practice has been falling off very much, and most of those who had become Christians were ashamed to join in it. 1952 Kerr 143–4 [A list and description of the characters in a 'masquerade' or 'John Canoe' dance group].

4. A buffoon, a foolish person (transf from sense 1).

1956 Mc StAnn /jangkunu/ a clown, a buffoon.

5. Foolishness.

1943 *GL* Clar, Jankoono, silly things.

6. Attrib, passing into adjective. Cf *kunu* adj.

1943 *GL* Kgn, etc., Jancunoo, ugly.

B. vb: To have a John Canoe celebration.

1858 Chambre II 151–2, Reds and the Blues..—sometimes also going by the name of 'Johnny Canoeing'. On the north side of the island it is a splendid affair, but on the south side it is just the reverse. In the latter instance, the negroes dress themselves in bulls' hides, with the horns on, into which they are sewn, and go bellowing about the streets, butting all the people they meet. This is the remnant, most probably, of some superstitious African ceremony.

JOHN CHARLES (or **CHARLIE**) sb dial. *BL*

1. The wild plant *Hyptis verticillata*, used medicinally.

1952 FGC Han, StAnn, StC, StM, etc. /jan chaalz/—bush good for cold, fever—has square, purplish stem, minty leaf; Han /jan chaali/; StE /jan chaa/. 1955 *WIMJ* 80–1, *Hyptis verticillata*..This is the plant usually meant by 'John Charles'. It is a favourite cold bush used alone or with others.

2. The wild plant *Cordia globosa*, used as a 'tea bush' for colds.

1954 *WIMJ* 29, *Cordia globosa*..Black Sage, John Charles or Charlie, Gout Tea.

3. The wild plant *Croton wilsonii* (uncert).

1927 Beckwith 19, John Charles (doubtfully identified with Doctor John). 1954 *WIMJ* 29, *Croton wilsonii*.. Pepper Rod; Doctor John; ?John Charles or Charlie.

JOHN CHEWIT, JOHN CHEWI sb; see forms in quots below; imitative of the bird's call. The black-whiskered vireo, *Vireo calidris* (or *V. olivaceus*).

1839 see SWEET JOHN TUWHIT. 1847 Gosse 194, John-to-whit..the accent..is most energetically on the last syllable. 1933 McK 317, Johntuhit, little singing bird. 1936 Bond 304, Local names:—John-to-whit; John-chew-it; John Chewi. 1942 HPJ, John-twit, John-chuwit. 1952 FGC Han, Man, StAnd, StAnn, StM/ján chúuit/; StC, StM /ján chúui/; StAnn /jan tu hit/; StT /jántu wit, jáan tuwít/. 1956 Jeffrey-Smith 52, John Chewy.

JOHN-CHUWIT, JOHN-TUWHIT see prec.

JOHN CRAYFISH sb obs. A rival of JOHN CANOE, q.v. A. 1: quot a1818.

JOHN CROPPIE sb dial; *croppie* may refer to the bird's 'cropping' the fruits. The bird *Cœreba flaveola*; see BANANA QUIT, quot 1956.

1956 Jeffrey-Smith 71, John Croppie.

JOHN-CROW /jángkro, jángkra/ sb; a folk-etym formation from its former name (still extant) CARRION CROW, which was reduced in popular pronunciation to CYANCRO /kyangkro/ whence by affrication of /ky-/ to /ty-/ and voicing to /j/—both common phenomena in the folk speech—the form /jangkro/. Concurrent influence of such an African word as Ewe *doŋgró*, a large kind of fowl with sparse plumage, is not impossible. The supposed association with the Rev John Crow (quot 1943) is apocryphal. Gardner (*Hist Ja* 91) mentions this clergyman and his unpopular sermon, but makes no connection with the bird. The sermon took place in November 1689 (Coad 99), but the first record of the bird's being called 'John-Crow' is from 1826. (It may be noted that the US *Jim Crow* was first recorded in 1828—cf *DA*.) Also attrib.

1. The red-headed turkey-buzzard *Cathartes aura*. *BL N*

1826 Williams 82, The dead carcass of a mule, on which a score of john-crows were holding an inquest. 1836 in *Parlmt Papers* 1837 IV No 510 Let I, The complainant and constable..found the carcase so offensive, decomposition having taken place, the vermin and John-crows having also devoured a part. 1873 Rampini 121–2, The Carrion Crow or Turkey Buzzard..Their sense of smell is exquisite. 1943 Jeffrey-Smith in *NHN* (Radio broadcast 18 Aug), The Rev. John Crow, a clergyman from Ireland, exhorted his congregation not to complain of their ill-treatment..In contempt they named the bird, whose black plumage and red neck recalled the hated preacher—'John Crow'.

2. Fig. As a favourite figure in proverbs, tales, etc., the bird often symbolizes the unfavourable traits attributed to the negro by other negroes.

1873 Rampini 177 [Prov:] John Crow neber make house till rain come. John Crow tink him own pickny white. John Crow say him de dandy man when him hab so-so fedder [*plain feathers*]. *BL*

3. In its character as a scavenger, esp in the phr *John-crow roasting plantain for* (*someone*), a prediction of the person's imminent death or downfall. (The john-crow is reputed to know when someone is dying, and to perch on the roof in anticipation; the roasting of a plantain implies the expected meal.) See ROAST COCO. *BL*

1925 Beckwith 116 [Prov:] When John Crow see mauger cow, him roas' plantain fe him. 1960 Pat Wilmot StAnd.

4. In a nonsense-rhyme, with allusion to the bird's supposed vanity (see sense 2).

1959 FGC StE, 'What's the news?' 'John-crow wearing Peafowl shoes.'

JOHN-CROW BEAD(S) sb chiefly dial. *BL*

1. The seeds of the vine *Abrus precatorius*, scarlet peas with a prominent black spot about the hilum; freq strung for necklaces, and, as the species name suggests, used for rosaries. Also called CRAB-EYE, JOHN-CROW EYE.

1873 Rampini 155, The liquorice vine (*Abrus precatorius*), whose scarlet and black spotted seeds ('John Crow or Jumby beads') are well known in this country as necklaces. 1954 *WIMJ* 17, Red Bead Vine; John Crow Beads; Crab's Eyes; Wild Liquorice; Liquorice Vine; Lick Weed.

2. Applied to other red seeds, from trees, as the CIRCASSIAN SEED, RED-BEAD TREE.

1952 FGC StAnn, StM, Johncrow bead—Red-Bead tree, Fancy-Anna.

JOHN-CROW BEAN sb dial. =JOHN-CROW BEAD. *BL*

1952 FGC StE /jangkro biin/.

JOHN-CROW (BLOW-)NOSE sb dial; <JOHN-CROW (for *John-crow's*) +BLOW-NOSE (or *nose*).

1. A fungus-like parasitic plant (*Scybalium jamaicense*) that resembles the red head of the John-crow with its prominent nostrils. Also JOHN-CROW NOSE-HOLE.

[*ODS*: 1866 Treas. Bot., Jim Crow's Nose, a West Indian name for *Phyllocoryne*.] 1942 HPJ, John Crow blow-nose. 1943 *GL* Kgn, Jan cro blow nose, species of mushroom. 1952 FGC StAnn, John-crow blow-nose, jonjo. 1956 Mc StAnd /jangkra bluo-nuoz/ a red fungus. 1958 JB StAnd /jankro bluo nuoz/—fungus growth; unpleasant smell; 2 in. tall, pinkish red (like raw steak); branched growth (like veins in liver).

2. The red flowers of *Spathodia campanulata*, from which a lot of moisture can be squirted.

c1909 D. Levy StE (Black River), As a child we always used to hear the black-people call it 'John-crow blow-nose'.

JOHN-CROW BUSH sb chiefly dial; origin unknown. *Bocconia frutescens*; also called PARROT WEED, *salandain*, WILD CARROT.

1914 Fawcett 223, John Crow Bush. 1952 FGC Man, StT, John-crow bush—/salandain/. 1956 Mc StAnd /jáangkra bush/—dem tek it /baak/ de house [the plant is used to polish floors, etc.].

JOHN-CROW EYE sb dial. =JOHN-CROW BEAD 1. *BL*

1952 FGC StAnn, John-crow eye—bean, grow on vine.

JOHN-CROW HEADMAN sb dial. An albino JOHN-CROW, to which the black john-crows defer. Also called HEADMAN JOHN-CROW, KING CROW, (JOHN-CROW) PARSON. *BL*

1956 Mc StM, John-crow Parson, John-crow Headman—White Crow.

JOHN-CROW JACKET sb dial slang; an allusion to the John-crow's black plumage.

1952 FGC StM, John-crow jacket, the Black Maria or police waggon.

JOHN-CROW LAMP sb dial; ?because it is black with a red 'head' (the flame); or perhaps merely depreciatory—cf JOHN-CROW 2. See quot; cf also *jempe lamp*.

1959 DeC West /jangkro-lamp/ a small lamp made of tin with no chimney.

JOHN-CROW NOSE sb dial. The bladder of a cow.

1956 Mc StJ (Cambridge) /jangkro nuoz/.

JOHN-CROW NOSE(-HOLE) sb dial; <JOHN-CROW (for *John-crow's*) +*nose*(*-hole*).

1. =JOHN-CROW BLOW-NOSE.

1864 Grisebach 785, John-Crow's-nose: *Phyllocoryne jamaicensis*. 1942 HPJ, John-Crow nose or nose-ole, a fungus with a putrid smell which even the John-crows take for carrion. 1952 FGC StT, John-crow nose-hole. 1956 Mc Man, StAnd /jángkra nuoz, nuoz-uol/.

2. Other similar fungi, not red.

1956 Mc Man /ján kro núoz huol/—A fungus, black, yellow or grey, which grows out of the ground on a stem. It is inedible.

3. See quot; the allusion is prob to sense 2 of JOHN-CROW (BLOW-)NOSE.

1956 BLB StJ /jangkro nuoz/—/waata maa/—a cow's bladder. [See WATER MAW.]

JOHN-CROW PACKER sb dial. A withe or vine (unidentified).

1952 FGC StAnd /jángkro páka/ use to tie up bundles of wood.

JOHN-CROW PARSON see JOHN-CROW HEADMAN.

JOHN-CROW PEAS sb dial. The wild shrub *Cassia occidentalis*. *BL*

1927 Beckwith 15, Dandelion..'John Crow Pea', 'Wild Senna'..The shelled seeds may be parched and beaten as a substitute for coffee. 1953 *WIMJ* 239, John Crow Pea.

JOHN-CROW'S NOSE see JOHN-CROW NOSE (-HOLE).

JOHN-CROW VULTURE sb ornith. =The JOHN-CROW.

1847 Gosse 1.

JOHN GILPIN sb dial; origin unknown—perh a trade name. Cf also *SND gilpin*, a big, stout person. Cf GILPIN. A cutlass with curved back and flaring blade.

1958 DeC StAnd /jan gilpin/.

JOHN MARIGGLE /marígl, mirígl, marídl/ sb dial; <*John*, a personalizing element + /mirígl/ 'mariggle', from the phrase with which popular riddles begin—see RIDDLE. The bony-fish, *Elops saurus*, considered a very tricky fish.

1892 Cockrell, list, John Mariggle. 1902 Jordan-Evermann 87, John Mariggle. 1950 Smith, John Mariddle (Bogue Is.). 1952 FGC StC, StE, StJ, StM /jàn marígl/—tricky, very strong, fight hard, jump and try to shake out hook.

JOHNNY BERRY sb dial. =CHICKEN NET.

JOHNNY BLINKY sb dial; <*Johnny*+ BLINKY.

1959 DeC Port /jani blingki/ the small firefly with light from the tail.

JOHNNY-CAKE sb now chiefly dial; an Americanism (cf *DA*) of uncertain origin, but prob Indian; earliest record of Johnny-cake is 1739, of Journey-cake 1754, but evidence about their relationship is indeterminate. In Ja the senses are different from that in US: baked maize bread.

1. A sort of scone of flour or other starch ingredient, baked (or 'roasted' on a griddle). (Gen urban and somewhat out of fashion.) *BL N*

1893 Sullivan 90, JOHNNY CAKE. Flour..soda..lard.. butter..mix into a dough..roll about ½ an inch thick, cut in rounds with a small tumbler..bake on the gridiron. 1907 Jekyll 54, He asked his grandmother to get six Johnny-cake roast, an' he put it in his namsack, an' he travel in the wood. 1926 Edmonds 19, Johnnycake. To 2 boiled and crushed cocos put 1 egg, a little butter and flour sufficient to make a dough, roll out and cut in rounds, toast on gridiron. 1943 *GL* Port, Rootie—East Indian journey cake.

2. A dumpling, fried or boiled. (But see quot 1959.) (Mostly rural and very widely used.)

1952 FGC StE /jánikíek/ mix with flour, roll it out, fry in frying pan with coconut oil; soda makes it swell: soft inside /krips/ outside; StJ, West /jánikíek/—like dumplin—mix cornmeal or plantain porridge with water, salt; roll it in many little pieces; boil. 1958 DeC, Three people insisted that /joni-kiek/ or /jorni-kiek/ was a 'better pronunciation' than the allegedly rustic /jani-kiek/ 'because you often take these along on a journey'. 1959 DeC /janikiek/. In the eastern and central parishes this is distinct from *dumpling* in that johnnycake is always fried, whereas dumpling is a general term, usually meaning boiled but also including the fried. In the western parishes, however, all distinction is lost, and both a johnnycake and a dumpling can be either fried, boiled, baked, or roasted.

3. In a proverbial expression indicating disappointed hopes or expectations.

1958 D. Levy StE (Black R.), To go out a johnnycake and come back a dumpling.

JOHNNY CANOE see JOHN CANOE A. 1. quot 1801.

JOHNNY-COOPA-LANTAN sb phr; <*Johnny Cooper's lantern*, in part onomatopœic: cf KNOCK JOHNNY COOPER. The rhythmical sound made 'by good old-time house-cleaners' cleaning the floors on their knees with a coconut brush. 'Lantern' refers to its being done in the early morning by lantern light.

1943 HPJ, Johnny-coopa-lantan.

JOHNNY HO sb dial obs; imitative of the bird's cry. See CACKY-QUAW.

JOHNNY RUN-DOWN sb dial; *Johnny* is personifying. =RUN-DOWN.

1943 *GL* StAnd, Johnny run down, a kind of sauce. 1955 FGC Man.

JOHN'S GRASS sb; prob named after a local person who introduced or grew it successfully.

1954 *FG* 240, Para or John's Grass. [*Panicum purpurascens.*]

JOHN STAGGER-BACK sb dial; alluding to its toughness, which makes one stagger back when trying to bite a piece off. Cf STAGGER-BACK. See quot.

1943 *GL* StM, John-stagger-back, codfish fritters.

JOHN-TO-HEAL sb dial; descriptive of its curative properties. Prob *Asclepias curassavica*, today called RED-HEAD, etc.

a 1818 Lewis (1834) 63, As I had desired him to bring me any native flowers of Jamaica, this evening he brought me a very pretty one; the negroes, he said, called it 'John-to-Heal', but in white language it was *hoccoco-pickang*; it proved to be the wild Ipecacuanha.

JOHN-TO-WHIT, JOHN-TUHIT, JOHN TWIT see JOHN CHEWIT.

JOINTER, JOINTER BUSH sb dial; <*joint* +-*er* (+BUSH), the stems having prominent nodes which resemble joints. *Piper nigrinodum* and *P. jamaicense*. (The distinction indicated in *WIMJ* is not held to by the folk.)

1952 FGC StAnd, StE, StT, Tre /jainta/—has jointed stem. 1954 *WIMJ* 19, Jointer Bush; Black Joint (Giant); Black Jointer. ['Giant' is due to a mishearing by Beckwith of the dial pronunc: /jaint/ joint.] 1955 *WIMJ* 151, Jointer..Used in the same way as other [*Piper*] species.

JOINT-EVIL sb obs; *OED* →1683. A form of leprosy, more often called COCOBAY.

1801 Dancer 232, Leprosy and Coco-Bay, or Joint Evil. *Red Disease of Guiana.

JOINT WOOD sb dial; descriptive of the nodes on the stems. The shrub *Piper amalgo*, used medicinally.

1886 Hooper 30, Joint wood or pepper-elder. 1893 Sullivan 120, Leaves of ackee, sour-sop, joint-wood, pimento. 1914 Fawcett 20. 1954 *WIMJ* 19, *Piper amalgo* L. Joint Wood; Pepper Elder. The young stem and leaves of this species provide a decoction for flatulence.

JOINTY BENNA sb dial; <*jointy*, alluding to the prominent nodes (cf JOINTER, JOINT WOOD) +*benna*, perh for *bender*.*/*

1914 Fawcett 24, *Piper otophyllum*..Jointy Benna.

JOKIFY adj dial; for **jokified*—cf -IFY. Prone to jokes or jollity.

1943 *GL* StAnn, Jokify, jocular. 1950 Pioneer 31, Once upon a time Patto (night owl) was a very jokify an happy man. 1954 LeP StAnn, A buffoon, jokefy. 1942 Bennett 28, Noh frowns pon me yaw pickney..Yuh muma know lang time sey Ah so me jokify.

joko-joko vb dial; iterative—cf *juk-juk*. To poke or jab repeatedly. *G*

1959 DeC Han, West, In frying /dof/, /yu joko-joko im op, mek di fat sok in a hit/.

jombelin see JIMBLING.

jombi, JOOMBIE see JUMBY.

JONAH ROD sb dial; for *Aaron's rod*? An unidentified small reed.

1952 FGC West.

JONGA see *jangga*.

jongkuto /jóngkutò/ vb and sb dial; cf Tw *adwoŋku-tɔ̃*, limping. *SC djanka.*

A. vb: See quots.

1955 FGC Man /jongkuto/. 1943 *GL* StAnn, Jocoto, StM, Junkoto, to stoop down.

B. sb: See quot.

1943 *GL* Junkoto, a stooping position.

jonjo see JUNJO.

jon-jon sb dial; etym unknown. One of the plants of genus *Heterotrichum*—perh *H. umbellatum.*

1952 FGC StT /jon-jon/.

JONKRA WEED sb dial; ? < JOHN-CROW.

1946 Dunham 156–7, Jonkra weed = 'obi weed'—used in obeah practices; said to be poisonous.

JOOK see *juk.*

JOOKY-JOOKY see *juki-juki.*

JOOTAH see *juuta.*

jork, jorkin puok see JERK (PORK).

JOSEPH'S COAT sb. Applied to a small wild species of *Euphorbia.*

1951 FGC Man, Joseph's coat—wild poinsettia, red and dark-green.

JOSIE, JOSSIE see *juosi.*

jos lef fi see *lef* 4.

JOURNEY-CAKE see JOHNNY-CAKE.

JOUSI see *juosi.*

JUBA sb dial; cf Twi *A'dwówa.*

1. The DAY-NAME for a female born on Monday. *G*

1773 *Ja House of Assembly Rec* 6 465, Juba [HPJ]. 1873 Rampini 88, Monday..Juba, clever.

2. Symbolic of various traits of character, apparently including caution, imitativeness, etc.

1925 Beckwith 49 [Prov:] Follow fashion Juba nebber bwoil good soup. 1943 HPJ [Prov:] Jew-jew rain faal Jooba turn back [*When dew falls, Juba turns back*].

3. Transf. A fish similar to the hind. *G*

1952 FGC StE /júba/ fish like rock-hind or butter-hind, but smaller than /mamlit/.

JUBA('S) BUSH sb dial; <JUBA+BUSH. A wild plant used medicinally: *Iresine paniculata.* (Perh also similar bushes.)

1864 Grisebach 785, Juba's bush. 1914 Fawcett 145. 1927 Beckwith 20, Juba-bush. *Rivina humilis*..Number one medicine—what it can't cure are hard. 1954 *WIMJ* 30.

JUBAWAREN sb dial; <JUBA+?*wearing.*

1943 *GL* Tre, Jubawaren, hard. [?As tough as Juba.]

JUCK see *juk.*

JUCK-CUM-PENG sb dial; app in large part onomatopoeic, though by folk-etym *juk* may be present in the first element, and perh underlying the whole, Twi *a-dwoŋku-bɛ̃ŋ*, pains in the hip, coxalgia (which causes hobbling). An imitation of the sound made by a wooden-legged person walking.

1943 *GL* West, Juck-cum-peng, walking of a wooden-foot man.

JUDY sb dial; <*Judy*, woman's name. The male of *Platypsaris niger*; see MOUNTAIN DICK.

1847 Gosse 187, Black Shrike..this species..is not uncommon in the mountain districts of Jamaica, where, from the remarkable diversity in the appearance of the male and female they are distinguished by separate local names. The black male is known by the feminine appellation of Judy, while the chestnut-headed female receives the masculine soubriquet of Mountain Dick. 1936 Bond 259. 1956 Jeffrey-Smith 69.

JUG sb dial. A stalk of bamboo ten feet or so long, with the internal joints pierced to make it a single receptacle for water. It is carried over one shoulder.

1952 FGC StT /jog/.

JUGAR sb dial uncom; etym unknown.

1954 LeP Kgn (Trench Town), Big market basket, Jugar.

JUICE see DEUCE.

JUJU, JUU (RAIN, WATER) /juu, juju/ sb dial; <*dew* (+*rain*, *water*). *BL*

1. Dew; very light rain. *G*

1927 Anderson-Cundall 88, Ju-ju water wet me a marnin' time. 1943 HPJ, Jew-water, Dew. 1943 *GL* Kgn, StAnn, Ju-ju, dew. 1955 FGC Man /ju-ju waata/ water forming on leaves. 1962 BLB 58 /juu-waata/ dew; *ibid* /juu-juu-rien/ rain as light as dew; /i dis a juu-juu/ *it's only a mist.*

2. Stagnant water.

1943 *GL* Port.

juk /juk/ vb and sb dial; 1877→ jook, 1936→ juk, 1943→ juck; cf Fulani *jukka*, spur, poke; knock down, as fruit; Cameroons pidgin *čuk*, injection; *čuk-am*, pierce, prick, etc. (G. D. Schneider.) **s.**

A. vb: 1. To prick, pierce, poke, jab, stab—usually done suddenly. (By far the most frequent sense.) *BA BL G N T*

1877 Murray *Kittle* 23, Wen me see him so wid de begnet [*bayonet*]..me ting say de man da go jook me wid it. 1941 Kirkpatrick 53, Juk, stick. 1943 *GL* Clar, Juck, to pick from; West, Juck, to stick. 1952 FGC Port, StAnn, West /juk/—stingin'-grouper, if it juk you it poisòn you. 1955 Bennett *Vengeance*, An him teck him long fork juck me.

2. Vulgar. To have sexual intercourse with (a woman). *BL G T*

1943 HPJ, The non-literal use of this word Imogen regarded as profoundly shocking. 1958 DeC Clar.

3. With *up*: To add stimulus or power of stimulation to.

1958 DeC Clar [Referring to mixing ganja in rum:] /him juk it op wid buunz an pepa/. See BONE 2.

B. sb: 1. A jab, stab, prick. See COCKS. *BL G T*

2. Specif. A hypodermic injection. (Also medical and veterinarian slang.) *BL G*

1943 *GL* StM, Jook, injection.

juka stik sb dial; <*juk* vb+*-er*+*stick* sb. A dibble. *G*

1956 Mc Man /júka stík/ a sharpened stick used for digging.

JUK COCOA see DUKE COCO.

juki-juki adj dial; *juk* + *-y*/*-ie*(*OED*), iterated. *G*

1. Perforated, punctured.

1943 *GL* Port, Jooky-Jooky, Perforated with holes. 1956 LeP StE (Eld) /juki-juki/ pockmarked.

2. Pricking continuously or persistently.

1955 FGC Man.

juk kuoko see DUKE COCO.

juk-maka sb dial slang; <*juk* vb+*maka*, prickle(s).

1943 *GL* Tre, Juke-macca, A cunning fellow. Sharp enough to prick a thorn.

JULIAN MANGO sb dial uncom. =ST JULIEN.

1952 FGC StAnn /júulyan mánggo/.

JULIE (MANGO) see ST JULIEN. *BA G*

JULY-AUGUST sb dial. A type of *dokunu*. (Eaten in late summer?)

1958 DeC Port /julai-aagos/ made of corn-meal, potatoes, currants, rose water, sugar, and seasoning.

JULY FIFER sb dial. An insect that makes a shrill noise in July—prob the cicada.

1952 FGC StT /júulái fáifa/.

juma vb dial uncom; ?cf Twi *àdwũmã*, work, sb.

1958 DeC StE (Accom) /juma/ to shake (someone).

JUMBAY see JUMBY.

jumbelin see JIMBLING.

JUMBIE see JUMBY.

JUMBOLINE see JAMBOLAN.

JUMBY /jombi/ occas /jumbi/ sb dial; cf *ODS*. Cf CB e.g. Banoo *njambe*, God. Mainly E. Caribbean; DUPPY usu in Ja. See quots. *BA G T*

1873 see JOHN-CROW BEAD(S). 1943 *GL* Port, Joombie, West, Jumbay, a ghost. 1956 LeP StE (Eld), Duppy is more commonly used for the harmless ghost, Jumbie for the ghost that is set on one to do him harm.

JUMBY CHO-CHO sb dial. *Morinda citrifolia*, whose fruits look like stunted cho-chos.

1952 FGC Port /jombi chocho/ duck-apple.

JUMBY MAN sb dial; <JUMBY+*man*. *BA G*

1. A man having magical powers.

1905 Smith 13, Annancy..sometime him mek' himself big, an' sometime little, an' him was half man an' half spider—a sort of jumbe* man. *Evil spirit.

2. Specif. An OBEAH-MAN.

1956 Mc Man /jombi man/.

JUMBY TOWN sb dial. The place where the jumbies live.

1942 Bennett 22 [A woman who thinks she has seen a duppy here in Coronation Market (Kingston):] Coronation market fe true Dis yah dah Jumby Tung.

JUMMA sb dial rare; etym unknown.

1943 HPJ, Jumma, a dish made of peas.

JUMP vb dial. To dance with the jigging, up-and-down motion characteristic of African dancing, and, lately, of Revivalist and POCO-MANIA meetings. *G*

1907 Jekyll 208, 211, see JUMP SHAMADOR. 1942 Bennett 32, Se po' Miss Hayes outside dah gwa'n Like she dah jump poco. 1953 Moore 113, Revivalists..jump until noon. 1954 Reckord [Said by one of two young men watching the preparations for a balm-yard or pocomania session:] Old nayga goin' jump tonight. 1956 Mc StE (Accom) [Of the poco-man:] /in jomp a nait an sliip a die taim/. 1958 DeC StT /jómp riváival/—to participate in a poco-like ceremony, either at a church or at a funeral.

JUMP-AND-JIVE sb dial slang; <US slang *jive*, jazz. Slippers or shoes made from old automobile tyres. They began to be made locally about 1940. Also called HITLER-BOOT, POWER, etc.

1952 FGC Tre /jómpanjáiv/ auto-tyre shoes.

JUMPER sb dial. In spec Ja uses: see quots.

1. 1756 Browne 419, see BLACK, GREY JUMPER. 2. 1956 Mc StAnd /jompa/ a small river fish, 2 or 3 in. long. 3. 1943 HPJ, Jumpers, Puckumen, revivalists.

JUMPING vbl sb dial; <JUMP. See also JUMP-UP.

1956 Mc Man /jompin/ a dance, a wild party.

JUMPING CHARY sb dial; source of 'chary' unknown. The *jangga.*

1952 FGC StT /jompin chieri/ Janga; long joint.

JUMPING-DICK sb chiefly dial. =HOPPING-DICK.

1873 Rampini 67, The full rich notes of a mocking-bird, or a jumping dick from a neighbouring tree. 1936 Bond 286. 1952 FGC Man, StAnd /jompin dik/—/sii-im iina di trash/ like him jump on one foot; nearly big like nightingale; darkish.

JUMP(ING) MULLET sb dial. A sea mullet which leaps from the water at a sudden noise; the same as CAPE MULLET. *G*

1952 FGC StC /jómp(in) mólit/.

JUMP SHAMADOR vb phr dial arch; <JUMP I +unknown element, but cf Fr *chambard,* tumult, a shindy. A phrase used in ring dances, partly as a refrain, urging the dancers on.

1907 Jekyll 208, Wheel an' take your pardner, jump shamador!..'Shamador' is possibly a corruption of 'camerado'. *Ibid* 211, Jump Shamador, me darling. 1922 Holbrooke t.p., Jump Shamador (listed among 'Ring Tunes').

JUMP-UP sb dial.

1. A JUMPING; dancing, originally in connection with funeral or other such meetings, now also simply social. Cf SET-UP. *BA G N*

1954 LeP StE, General term for dance or party—Jump-up. 'Buru' and 'jump-up' are used when the dance gets hot and wild. 1956 Mc Man /jomp-op tunait/ *There's a dance tonight.* 1959 DeC StT /jomp-op/ a funeral meeting on the second night, with ring-play, dominoes, etc.

2. The larva of the mosquito—from its wriggling movements.

1952 FGC Port /kikfut/ jump-up.

JUMPY sb dial. Larva of the mosquito; =JUMP-UP 2, KICK-FOOT.

1936 Letter in *Gleaner* 12 Oct, Jumpies.

JUNA /juuna/ sb dial; from a personal name? Perh two diff words are involved here. A type of fish: see quots.

1927 Beckwith 91, A man and a woman had but one daughter..The girl was engaged to a fish, to another young man too..When she go to the river, she had to sing a song that the fish might come out—Dear old Juna, dear old Juna. 1952 FGC StE /júuna/ the smaller species of whipray—a skeat [*skate*].

JUNCK see JUNK.

JUNE FISH sb dial; by folk-etym <JEW FISH; cf JUNE PLUM. =JEW FISH. *BL G N*

1873 Rampini 176 [Prov:] Ebry haul of de net no catch June fish. 1893 Sullivan 11, June fish. A cottony fish. 1952 FGC gen, Port /juun-fish/ 300 to 500 pounds; StAnn, have yalla complexion; StT, eats like a cow-foot.

JUNE PLUM sb chiefly dial; by folk-etym <JEW PLUM. Cf JUNE FISH. The plum *Spondias dulcis.*

1942 HPJ, Jew-plum..Sometimes called *June plum*—but it is ripe even in December. 1952 FGC Kgn, StAnd, StJ, StM /júun plóm/.

JUNE POLE, JUNE PRIDE sb dial. The MOUNTAIN PRIDE—*Spathelia* species.

1952 FGC StAnn, June pole or June pride, similar to maiden plum—deep pink flowers, visible far off.

JUNE ROSE sb. The bush with showy white, pink, or purple flowers, *Lagerstroemia indica.*

c 1915 FGC StAnd; current 1960.

JUNGA sb dial rare.

1943 *GL* Port, Junga, a fishing lance.

JUNGO, JUNGU, JUNJA see next.

JUNJO /jónjo, júnjo, júnju/ sb dial; etym uncert: the word appears in various forms in several parts of the Caribbean, always as a dial word and in association with negroes, implying African origin; no clear proof of this has been made, however, and a contrary theory derives the word <Fr *champignon.* For discussion see Thompson, *Ja Hist Soc Bull* IX 117–18; Sandmann, *Nueva Rev de Filol Hisp* IX 383–5; Thompson, *Amer Speech* 33 170–5 (1958); Cassidy, *Ibid* 36 101–4 (1961). *G*

1. Any kind of fungus or fungus-like plant, edible or inedible, growing on the ground or on wood.

1895 Banbury 41, You po' fe meat, you nyam jungo. [*If you're badly off for meat, you'll eat mushrooms.*] 1925 Beckwith 39 [Prov:] De man who fall de cotton-tree a no him who pick de junjo. 1929 Beckwith 14, An edible fungus called 'junjo' which grows abundantly on the trunks of cotton and fig trees and in damp places. 1943 *GL* West, Junjo, mushroom. 1952 FGC StAnd /jonjo/ we call it—white people call it /múshrúum/; StJ /báak-trii jónjo kyan iit/ *mushrooms that grow on the bark of trees are edible.* Also most other parishes. 1959 DeC Port /junju/ edible fungus.

2. Mould, mildew. *BL*

1925 Beckwith 23 [Prov:] Bull ole, junjo grow 'pon him back. 1943 *GL* Kgn, Port, Jonjo, junjo, mildew.

3. See quot.

1961 R. P. Bengry, Junja—*Ascidia nigra,* a black Ascidian often seen in numbers on old piles, etc., in the sea.

JUNJO FLY sb dial. A small fly (cf SOUR-FLY) of bluish colour. *BL G*

1952 FGC Port /jonjo flai/ come when anything is sour; StT /junju flai/ come to white plantain plant.

junju see JUNJO.

junju-mita sb dial; ? <JUNJO; second element unknown. A wild plant or BUSH (unidentified), used medicinally.

1952 FGC Port /jùnju-míta/—like FRESH-CUT, but more viny and with blue berries.

jun-jun sb dial. A wild plant, similar to *Miconia* species, having a heart-shaped leaf with frilly edges.

1952 FGC StT /jun-jun/.

JUNK /jongk/ sb and vb now chiefly dial; <*junk* (*OED*) *sb*² 2, 'A piece or lump of anything; a *chunk*'. (In Std Engl today, 'chunk' would be used, but 'junk' is still current in New England.) *G*

A. sb: 1. A piece of a plant (e.g. sugar-cane, sweet-potato) cut off and planted to make a new crop. (First *OED* quot ref to sugar-cane: 1764.)

1756 Browne 130, Poorer lands require four or five juncks [of cane], but two or three are generally sufficient in a rich mellow soil. *Ibid* 154, The [sweet-potato] plant.. is cultivated by laying a few short juncks of the stem, or larger branches in shallow..trenches.

2. A large piece or lump, esp of meat. (Transitional to *OED* sense 3.) *BA N*

1827 Hamel II 281, The camp kettles seethed with junks of beef and pork. 1943 *GL* StM, Junk, a large bit. 1950 Pioneer 47, Koo de junk a ham an turkey Dat deh one lef pon her plate.

B. vb: To cut into junks or chunks. (*OED* quots chiefly from Ja.) *BA*

1823 Roughley 307, If the land has any underwood upon it, it should be cut down, junked, and sent home by mules to the works, for copper-wood. 1956 Mc Man /yu jongk yam/ when the yam is cut and left out of soil; Port /yu has to jongk taaya aafta yu dig it/ *cut taya into pieces.*

JUNKA /jungka/ adj dial; evid < JUNK + A[8].

1. Short, cut off short, broken off; hence chunky, sturdy. *G*

1943 *GL* Tre, Junka, broken, or piece. 1950 Pioneer 35, Anancy wid him junka brain [*Small but sturdy*].

2. Esp in cpds—see JUNKA PIPE, JUNKA STICK.

JUNKA(-PIPE), JUNKY-PIPE sb dial; < JUNKA + *pipe*. A tobacco pipe with very short stem.

1826 Williams 40, He [an escaped slave] and his companions sit. . and smoke their jonkas, or pipes about two inches long, until the evening closes in. 1873 Rampini 91, Lying under a tree with a 'junky' (cutty) pipe in his mouth. 1905 Smith 37, An' tek' her chunky pipe.

JUNKA-STICK /jòngkatík/ sb dial; < JUNKA + *stick* sb. A stout truncheon. *G*

1907 Jekyll 221, Junka stick, a short stick. *Ibid* 112, Him catch up one big junka 'tick an' lick down de wife. 1950 Pioneer 37, She grab a junka-a-'tik [*sic*] and she an her family beat Anancy.

JUNKOTO see *jongkuto*.

JUNKY adj dial; < JUNK sb + *-y*/*-ie* (*OED*). Short, having been junked or cut off. See JUNKA. *G*

1873 Rampini 129, Him [an ole-witch] tie on him junky (short) blue frock roun' him waist.

JUNK YAM sb dial; < JUNK sb 1 + *yam*.

1. See quot.

1943 HPJ, *Junk' yam*: a yam cut at the top and left to ripen in the ground.

2. See quot.

1956 Mc StAnd /jongk yam/: A sort of white yam, stout, produced from a piece cut off a yam and put back to grow. Renta, guinea, and flour yam are suitable for junking.

juosi /juosi/ sb dial; < *jersey*. Cf *ganzi*.

1. A woman's blouse.

1943 *GL* Port, Josie, a blouse. 1954 LeP StE, StT, Josie, Jousi—a woman's blouse.

2. A sweater. *G*

1958 FGC Man, StE.

3. A baby's dress.

1943 *GL* Kgn, Jossie.

JURRO-DOH sb dial; cf CHORURO (WATER) + ? the *-doe* of JELLIDOE.

1943 *GL* StC, Jurro-doh, half-cooked cocoanut oil.

JUST LEF' FE see *lef* 4.

JUTA see *juuta*.

juu see DEW, JUJU.

juuk kuoko see DUKE COCO.

juuna see JUNA.

JUU RAIN see JUJU (RAIN).

juus see DEUCE.

juuta /juuta/ occas /juta/ sb dial; < Hind *jūta*, shoe, slipper. A general term for shoes or boots.

1943 *GL* Kgn, Juta, shoes—Coolie word; also Clar, Port, StAnd, StAnn, StM, StT. 1950 Pioneer 49, Suede boot, kid boot. . Patent, plastic. . Big jootah, lickle jootah.

-k /k/ suffix dial; a simple phonetic element (voiceless closure after back vowels). This sound is occasionally added, seemingly for phonetic reasons, without changing the meaning of the base; see *brak*, *kikombok*, *muduk*, *patuk*, *sak*.

ka see CARRY.

ka, kaa see BECAUSE(N), CAUSEN. *BL G*

kaachi /kaachi/ sb dial; < Amer Sp *cacho*, a conch shell (or animal's horn)—1937 Malaret, + *-y*/*-ie* (*OED*). A shell or whistle blown as a warning, to tell the time, etc.; originally on estates, now also at factories.

1943 *GL* Kgn, Cauchie, train whistle; Man, Cauchie, A loud warning blown with a shell when danger is afoot. 1955 FGC Man /káachi/—factory whistle, tell time. 1956 Mc Man /kaachi/—factory whistle signalling knock-off time (12 noon and 4 PM) 'Sound like a train whistle'. 1956 LeP StE (Eld), A conch-shell blown on estate.

kaal see CALL.

kaan see CAUSEN, CORN. *BL G*

kaanigrong see SCORN-THE-GROUND.

kaaz(n) see BECAUSE(N). *BL G*

kaba-kaba /kábakába, kóbakóba/ adj and sb dial; cf Yoruba *kábakàba*, adv, confusedly, not smoothly. *G*

A. adj: Poorly done, worthless.

B. sb: Someone or something that is worthless. Cf *meke-meke*.

1943 *GL* StM, Cobba-cobba, Common quantity; also Port. 1956 Mc Man /kába-kába—pîipl hu no dúu tingz intu a díisen wîe/ *People who don't do things decently*; StJ /kabakaba/ worthless. 1956 LeP StE (Eld) /kabakaba/ No-good work; work that is carelessly done.

KABANGKA vb dial rare; origin unknown.

1943 *GL* Clar, Kabangka, to leave one fretting on his lover.

KABEH sb dial; etym unknown.

1943 *GL* StC, Kabeh, a stupid person.

kabob /kabob, kabog/ sb dial; < *cobweb*, the first form reduced phonetically, the second further altered by folk-etym. Cobwebs, and the dust and soot that gather on them from a kitchen fire.

1943 *GL* Clar, Cobbug, After smoke reaches the thatch of the kitchen it forms a thicky substance which mixes with the spider's web; Tre, Cubub, a deposit from smoke generally formed at the top of kitchens. 1955 FGC Man /kábob/ cobweb, black stuff that gathers on it. 1956 Mc Clar /kabób/ in 'right language', cobweb; also Man; StE.

kach see COTCH.

kacha /kácha/ sb dial; prob a variant form of *katiia*, *katya*, but perh also infl by the sense of COTCH vb, as if this were something on which to cotch, or rest temporarily. The explanation offered in quot 1958 is questionable, as it should produce /kecha/ not /kacha/. *G*

1958 DeC StAnn /kácha/ A wooden bed that folds up; hence it is likely to 'catch you up'. 1959 DeC Kgn /kacha/ a rough bed whose legs are permanently planted in earth or nailed to floor.

kachriil see KATREEL.

kachuchu /kachúchu/ sb dial uncom; perh <Amer Sp *cachucho*, a kind of metal pot, a small vessel (Chile—Santamaría); a small boat (Cuba).

1956 Mc Man /kachúchu/ paper bag.

KACK-A-TE, KACKATIE see COCKATY.

KACKKAW see CACA.

kafiroutn, kafirouzn see *kofiroutn*.

KAGGA sb dial; etym unknown, but cf US dial *cag*, keg. A ring around a KYNANDO drum.

1952 Kerr 145.

KAIA see *kaya*.

kaia-kaia sb dial; prob var of *kyaa-kyaa*.

1959 DeC StJ /kaia-kaia/ old and ragged work clothes.

kail droma sb dial; etym of first element uncert (but cf *EDD scale* sb[4], of which one form is *skile*). A variety of the DRUMMER fish.

1952 FGC StT /kail/ drummer, or /skail/—has spines, many colours.

kaiwaama sb dial; <Amer Sp *caguama* or *caivana* (Tejera) <Galíbi *kahuane* (Pichardo), the tortoise *Chelonia caouanna* (Schweigger).

1952 FGC StM /káiwáama/ a large turtle—hawkbill.

KAKA see CACA.

kakanabu /kàkanabú/ sb, also attrib, dial; <*cock-and-a-bull(-story)*, but there may be coincidental infl from CACA. Cf *OED Cock-and-bull, cock-and-a-bull.* Foolishness, nonsense.

1943 *GL* Kgn, Kakanaboo, foolishness; Kgn, Cock na Bul, false story; Kgn, Cock & a bull story, contrary talk; StAnn, Cacanabu, irrelevant; Tre, Ra-ka-na-bul—African, foolishness. 1955 FGC Man /kàkanabú/ talking nonsense.

KAKANCOMO vb dial; origin uncert, but the word *cock* (or perh CACA) may be one element. Cf *kakanabu.*

1943 *GL* StE, Kakancomo, to boast.

KAKATY, kakati, kakiti see COCKATY.

KAKKA see CACA.

KAK SHAM see COCTION. *G*

kalaban see CALABAN.

KALAMAZOO /kàlamazúu/ sb dial; a manufacturer's name <*Kalamazoo*, Mich.

1. A motor-driven milk trolley.

2. A passenger-carrying diesel car.

1943 *GL* Man, kalamazoo, milk trolley; Port, Passenger-carrying unit.

kalban see CALABAN.

KALEMBEY see CALEMBE.

kalops sb dial; prob <*scallops*. Trouble, difficulties.

1956 Mc Man /shi gat kalops/ *She got into trouble.*

kam sb dial; an exclamatory sound imitating a sudden, short noise. (Cf also Twi *kãm*; used with a negative, it has the force of 'hardly'. Christaller.)

1. The sound of a gun that fails to fire. *G*

1956 Mc StE (Accom) /di gon mek kam/ *The gun made a little sound (but did not go off).*

2. Suggesting something of little or no substance; =KEM.

1956 BLB Man, Common in the statement /fran di taim him a go a skuul, in duon nuo kam/ *Though he has been attending school for a long time, he has learnt nothing at all.*

kamarong, kamaroun see COME-AROUND.

kamu kyat sb dial; perh for *kana*, a device for drying meat in a kitchen +*cat*. Cf *pata-kyat.*

1954 LeP Port, Kamu kat, thief. 1956 Mc Port /kamu kyat/ a thief.

kana /kána/ sb dial; etym unknown—prob African.

1. A vessel or wire device by which meats are hung over a kitchen fire to preserve them (by smoking); more often *hangkra* or *hanggra.*

1943 *GL* West, Canna, Vessel for preserving meats over fire. 1959 DeC West /kana/ here meaning same as /kreng-kreng/—a rack for drying meat or fish.

2. See quot.

1959 DeC Man /kana/—a temporary field bag made of grass or trash.

kanana sb or adj dial; abbr or by-form of next. A word indicating that there has been nothing said, or no answer given when one was expected; see quots. Used both declaratively and interrogatively.

1935 HPJ, Canana: Constantly used by the grandmother of A. E. T. Henry in two senses: (*a*) Haven't you heard me? (*b*) There was no reply. 1943 *GL* StAnn, Canana, silent.

kananapo /kànanapú, kànanapó, kàanapé/ sb, adj, or adv dial; var of *karanapo.*

1. A marked silence; a failure to answer a question asked; as an adj, silent; as an adv, silently.

1943 *GL* Clar, Cannanapo, no answer; Kgn, Kananapo, no answer. 1955 FGC Man /kànanapú/ saying nothing. 1956 EB Port /im dis sidong de kaanape/ *He just sat there silently.*

2. See quots.

1935 HPJ, Cannanna-poo, a look of disdain. 1958 DeC StAnd /kananapu/ a word of contempt in an argument, about equivalent to sucking the teeth.

kanchaniil /kànchaníil/ sb dial; <*cochineal* with intrusive /n/. The cochineal cactus.

1952 FGC StE, Some say /kànchaníil/—swipple-pole is the usual name; StT, same as /tuuna/; also StAnn.

kanchini adj dial; perh conn with CHEENY.

1954 LeP Port /kanchini/ very small, tiny. (Old-fashioned.)

KANDA /kánda, kónda/ sb dial; cf Mende *kanda*, skin (J. Berry), and Cameroons pidgin *kanda*, skin, hide, bark (G. D. Schneider). A palm bough, especially the large lower sheath which holds it to the tree. See BUBA and its compounds.

1943 *GL* Port, Kanda, a palm bow; Konda, thatch palm. 1955 FGC Man /kánda/ cabbage skin, buba mat.

KANGAROO GRASS sb; see quot. An erroneous name for CHRISTMAS or PIANO GRASS.

1915 Harris in *Daily Chronicle* 20 Sept, It was called 'Kangaroo grass' through an error in identification many years ago. But the true 'Kangaroo grass' of Australia and Tasmania..is a different species.

KANGA-TONY see *kanggatuoni.*

kangga, kanggo see CONGO.

kanggatuoni sb dial; etym uncert: the first element is prob CONGO 3 (but cf Kongo *ŋkaŋka*, a fish—Turner); the second element is perh conn with the Ewe base *tɔn-* (Fã *tɔnĩ*, a water spirit, Gũ, Fɔ̃, Gɛ̃ *tɔ̣nɔ*, a stream, etc.). For sense 2 cf Ewe *tɔnyĩ*, an earthworm which by night stings sleepers. Cf Ko *nkamba, ntondi*, eel.

1. Applied by fishermen to various similar fish (DEEP-WATER WENSHMAN, POOKY SQUIRREL), alluding to their blackness. Cf WELSHMAN.

1940 HPJ, Congatong [prob miscopied by A. Clerk], A pinkish fish. 1943 *GL* West, Canga-toney, small fish. 1952 FGC Han /kànggatúoni/ same as Tommy, Wenshman; Port, same as Pooky, Wenshman; StC, same as Squirrel, Welshman; StE /kànggatúoni/ is the Portland name for /skwéril/; StM, same as Deep-water Wenshman; also StAnn.

2. A worm, often used for fish bait.

1943 *GL* StAnn, Kanga-tony, a kind of earthworm.

kangkarish adj dial; prob <*canker*+-*ish*[1] (*OED*); cf such other words as *cankerous, cankery*: *EDD, SND.* Of foods: spoiled.

1958 DeC StAnd /get kangkarish/—to spoil.

kangksnot sb dial; <*conchs*+*nut.* A fruit (*Passiflora maliformis*) whose edible pulp is enclosed in a nut-like shell (evidently thought of as resembling that of a conch). Also called SWEET-CUP.

1943 *GL* Port, Canksnot, the sweet-cup. 1952 FGC Port /kangksnot/ grows on a vine, has a hard shell; same as sweetcup.

kani /káni/ sb and vb dial; familiarized abbr of *consumption* (cf US slang *con*): *con*+-*y*. A bad cough with fever; to have a bad cough or cold.

1943 *GL* StC, Kanny, to have a cold. 1954 LeP StE, Cannie; StT, Kanni: bad cough accompanied by fever.

KANNY-DOH sb dial; <*kani*, cough+an unknown element evidently meaning 'person'.

1943 *GL* StC, Kanny-doh, a person who has a cold.

kanshiiba sb dial rare; etym unknown.

1952 FGC StT /kànshíiba/ a kind of wis [withe].

KANSHUCO sb dial rare; etym unknown.

1943 *GL* StE, Kanshuco, same kind.

kantu /kantu, kyantu/ sb dial; 1868 canta, 1929 conto, 1941 cantoo, cantu; <Twi *ɔ-kãntõ*, candlewood. Any of several trees whose resinous wood burns easily and is used for torches. (*Amyris* species; *Peltostigma pteleoides.*) See also CANDLEWOOD, TORCHWOOD.

1868 Russell 6, Canta—The torch wood. African. 1929 Beckwith 128, 'I got a wood that I call conto—short name is lightwood—such as old people make torches of'. 1941 Swabey 14, Cantoo, cantu. 1952 FGC Man /kyántú/ same as candlewood, torchwood; StAnn /kántú/ is the Trelawny word for candlewood, torchwood.

KANUBA /kanuba/ sb dial cant; origin unknown. In AFRICAN cult use: spirit.

1953 Moore 27, 'Spirit is called *kanuba*. Kanuba comes from the father, his father and father's father'.

kape /kapé/ sb dial; echoic. A name for the PEENIE(-WALLIE), a light-giving click-beetle, from the noise it makes. (Cf next.)

1952 FGC Man /kápé/.

kapkap sb dial; onomatopoeic. The ant *Odontomachus hæmatodes*, which makes an audible sound with its mandibles, whence its name. *G*

1943 *GL* no addr, Cop-cop n. A large kind of ant. Also Kgn, Man, Port, West. 1943 *NHN* II 70, 'Kap-kap'. 1952 FGC Man /kápkàp/ big, long black one that lives under dirt, has a very bad sting; you can hear the mouth knock together. Also StT, Tre.

karakara /karakara, karokaro, korokoro, krokro, kurukuru, krukro/ adj and sb dial; for forms see quots; etym uncert: the form appears African—cf Hausa *k'arak'ara*, rough plastering. Rough, rocky, bony, etc.; something rough or rocky. *G*

1943 *GL* Clar, Tre, Cara-cara, stony; Tre, Kara kara, stony; Kgn, Curroo-curroo, rough; StAnd, Kruk kro, rough; Tre, Carroo-carroo, rough; StJ, West, Carra-carra, rough stones; StC, corro-corro, bone; Man, Coro-coru, bony meat; Kgn, Karra-karra, a thicket. 1948 Bennett 68, Kooroo-kooroo face. 1958 LeP Han /kurukuru/ rocks and stones in a field.

karanapo /kàranampó, kàranapú, kàranapúm/ sb dial; cf Twi *krãnã, krãnãã, krãnanana*, silent, absolutely still, perfectly quiet. =*kananapo.*

1896 Bates 122, Him ax dis one..Him say him no know. Him hax tarra one, caranampo (silence). Him ax noder one, caranampo, till Ratta come up. 1935 HPJ, Caranampo: silence. 1943 *GL* Kgn, Caranapu, Caranapum, silence; StC, Kar-ā-nā-pō, no answer.

karato, karito see CORATOE.

karokaro, KARRA-KARRA see *karakara.*

karuochiz see CAROCHIES.

karuozin sb dial; <a var of CAROCHIE+-*ing.*

1958 DeC Port /karúozin/ old worthless furniture, pieces of metal, and similar junk.

KASAADA, kasada see CASSADA.

kasha, kasha maka see CASHAW.

kashu see CASHEW.

kaskas see *koskos.*

KASSAADA see CASSADA.

KASSAR sb. An unidentified fish; perh a mistake for *hassar* (*Hoplosternum littorale*). (Roth 229.)

1953 Moore 280.

kata see COTTA and cpds.

kata-kata vb and past ppl dial; <*scatter*, reduced to *kata* and iterated. *G*

1955 LeP StE (Eld) /kata-kata/ to scatter; scattered, dotted about.

kata-tik /kátatík/ sb dial; <*kata*, ultimately echoic (cf COTTA[2]) +*tik* <*stick.* See quots.

1953 Moore 137, The stick, or catatic, is played by striking it against the center pole of the dancing booth; *ibid* gloss, Cata 'tick, Percussion stick (=clapper) used in cumina (African).

katawaia /kátawáia/ sb dial; prob introd to Jamaica by East Indians—cf *OED cot sb*[4], 'ad. Hindī *khāṭ* bedstead, couch..(:— Prākrit *khaṭṭā*, Skr., *khaṭwā*)'. Cf also the synonymous *katya.* The form *Cott-a-wire* implies folk-etymology—but see quot 1958. Cf also *katiia.*

1943 *GL* Clar, Cott-a-wire, a rough wooden bed; Catawia, bed. 1958 DeC Port, StT, etc. /katawaia/

a narrow bed or cot. 'My informants have not interpreted this as cot-of-wire, but say it may be of wood, canvas, or metal.'

katch see COTCH.

KATECHA sb dial rare; in some way conn with CACHIMBA?

1943 *GL* StC, Katecha, pipe.

KATIE see AUNTIE ~, BANANA ~, MA ~.

katiia, katya sb dial; prob another form of *katawaia*, and of the same source. Cf also *kacha*. *G*

1943 *GL* no addr, Catya, a bed. 1959 DeC Han, West /katiia/ a folding cot or bed made of wood and canvas; both the bed and the name are associated with East Indians—'An Indian word, not an English word'.

KATREEL /katriil, kachriil/ sb dial; <*quadrille* with the latter syllable assimilated to *reel*. (Prob sometimes understood as *Scotch reel*, which may be homonymous: /kachriil/.) A quadrille. *G*

c 1915 FGC StAnd [Song:] Me wi' dance de shay-shay, Me wi' dance de /kachriil/. 1961 R. M. Murray, Is nuttin I lub as de square katreel, I out fe dance till me two foot peel.

kaya /káya/ sb dial; etym unknown. *Polanisia viscosa*, and evid also some similar species of *Cleome* (both genera are Capparidaceæ).

1942 *NHN* I 6 11, Caya (a *Cleome*). 1952 FGC Man /kaya/ a weed similar to strong-back, with a small, 3-part leaf. 1958 E. Robertson UCWI Herb, StAnd, The weed *Polanisia viscosa*, whose seeds are eaten by ground doves. Called *kaia* by a boy in Gordon Town.

kayaan, kayan sb dial; cf CAYAN-PEPPER. A condiment; =CAYAN-BUTTER, of which this word is prob an abbreviation.

1943 *GL* Port, Ka-yawn, mixture of pepper, salt, pimento.

KA-YAWN see prec.

KEA see CARRY.

KEAN see CAN'T.

KEASHI sb dial; etym unknown.

1943 *GL* StE, Keashi, kieshi, underpants.

KEAT see *kiet*.

KEBBA neg particle dial rare; etym unknown.

1943 *GL* Port, Kebba, no.

kech see CATCH.

KEEAY vb or int dial; perh <*clear*; cf *kirout*.

1943 *GL* StE, Keeay, leave.

KEEL-HAULING /kíi-háalin/ sb dial; cf *OED*. A flogging. *G*

1943 *GL* StJ, Key-haulin, a flogging.

KEEP /kiip, kip/ vb. (Locally current in US: *DA* →1908.) To carry out an activity or ceremony at the due time or in the due manner; esp in phr: *Keep spell*, *Keep wake*, *Keep wedding*. Cf *OED keep v*23 & *spell sb*³ 2c 1828. *BA BL G T*

1801 Dancer 33, The watchfulness of nurses, soldiers on their posts, persons keeping spell on plantations, &c. 1825 De la Beche 7, The negroes are..divided into two spells, which relieve each other every twelve hours..the drivers..do not keep spell. 1943 *GL* Clar, Kip wake, A whole night singing when one has a dead. 1956 Mc Man /dem kiip miitin/ *They hold meetings*. 1957 JN Man, They are going to keep the wedding at the church.

KEEP-BUSY sb dial joc. A skin affliction that makes one want to scratch oneself.

1958 DeC StT /kiip-bizi/ a skin affliction equivalent to SCRATCH-SCRATCH.

KEEPING-BACK ppl phr dial. An obstacle; a cause of refusal.

1951 FGC Man [A man explaining why he was not accepted for agricultural labour:] The thing that was my keeping-back was my teeth.

KEEP(ING) COMPANY sb dial. A SET-UP or wake. *BL*

1958 FGC StT, Keeping company—the first night in the series of nine nights spent in funeral ceremonies.

KEEPING THE PASSOVER vb phr slang obs. See quot.

1862 Clutterbuck 187, Keeping the passover was, however, only a phrase at that time in vogue in Jamaica..It meant spreading out one's kit or stock of clothes for the purpose of airing them..Its etymology was this: of yore the phrase had been, *Holding a Rag Fair*, or a *Monmouth Street*, the displays being much like those of the children of Israel. One day, however, it flashed across the brain of an officer, who was a profound orientalist, that there was some historical connection between the passover and old clothes.

KEEP MALICE see MALICE. *BL*

KEE-ROOT see *kirout*.

keke /keke/ sb¹ dial vulg. The female sexual organs.

1943 *GL* Tre, Keykey, Female organ. 1958 DeC gen /keke/ noun, 'obscene and coarse', female genitalia.

keke /keke/ sb² dial; echoic, but cf also Twi *kekáw*, bark, cry, scream, howl, etc. A croaking-lizard.

1943 *GL* StE, Keke, Croaking lizard.

keke vb dial; echoic—cf *keta-keta* vb and sb¹. To laugh, giggle, titter, cackle. *G*

1955 LeP StE (Elderslie) /duon keke-keke/ and run here when I am talking. (Giggle, cackle.) 1956 Mc Man /yu keke keke keke/; StE /keke/ laugh, giggle cackle.

KEKRIKE sb dial; cf *kreng-kreng*.

1916 Jekyll (as quoted in Cruikshank 10), A hoop over the fire to smoke meat.

KELEMBI see CALEMBE.

KELLION see next.

kelyan sb dial; <SKELLION. Scallion, escallion.

1943 *GL* StE, Kellion, skellion. 1956 Mc StAnd /kélyan kót dong, yaa/. See CUT DOWN.

KEM int dial; var of *kam*. A short, sharp sound suggesting a very little bit. *G*

1943 Bennett 29, One time him wasa gwan soh bad, Me glad ah was female, For as a po' man meck mistake Sey 'kem' him gawn a jail.

KEMA WEED sb dial; etym unknown, but cf Mende *kema*, a magician (Turner 108). The weed *Chaptalia nutans*.

1927 Beckwith 19, see HEAL-AND-DRAW. 1955 *WIMJ* 75, *Chaptalia nutans*..Kema Weed. This plant (usually called 'whiteback') is still used to make tea. Application of the juice to wounds is an old remedy.

kemis bil see CHEMIST BILL.

KEMPS /kemps/ sb dial; prob <*skimp* (cf *EDD* 5). A small portion or quantity. Cf KENCH.

1943 *GL* Port, Kems, small amount; StAnn, Kemps, small bit. 1950 Pioneer 56, see *warra-warra*. 1955 LeP StE (Eld) /jos wan likl kemps mi tek/ *I took just a little bit*.

KEMPSY adj dial; <*kempt* (cf *OED* →1867) + transitional *s* + *-y*. Smart, neat, dressed up.

1956 Mc Man /yu a kémpsi/ *How smart you look!*

KENCH sb dial; <*kinch EDD* sb[4], 'A small portion or quantity'. See quots. *G*

1950 Pioneer 21, She noh got a 'kench' a hair pon her head. *Ibid* 56—cf KEMPS. 1954 LeP StE (Eld), Something little, of no importance—kench.

KENCUFFEE sb obs; cf the name CUFFEE. A name of the body of MAROONS who were the original followers of Cudjoe; one of Cudjoe's captains, named Cuffee, may be alluded to here. See COTTAWOOD.

KENDEH sb dial; var of *kengge* 2. See quot.

1943 *GL* Man, A hard wooden ball hewn out by schoolboys to suppliment [*sic*] the more expensive cricket ball.

kengge /kéngge/ sb dial; etym unknown—prob African. (The central idea seems to be that of roughness or coarseness.)

1. A sore on the foot. (Cf YAWSY-KENGE.)

1943 *GL* Kgn, Kengae, Sore on foot (g hard). 1955 LeP StE (Eld) /kengge/—same as /timbim/ a perpetual sore.

2. A ball roughly hewn out of wood. (Cf KENDEH.)

1956 Mc Man /kengge/ a ball made of wood.

3. See quot.

1956 Mc StE (Accom) /kéngge/ low, undisciplined people, the lowest social class, the dregs of a community.

KENNE-KENNE sb dial obs; see quot. Ashes. (How much currency this word had is uncertain.)

1774 Long II 427, There are some other words, that are remarkable for the different senses in which they are used; viz..Kénne-kenne, Original import: Small-sand, Common import: Κόνις, Græc. *Cinis*, Lat. Mundingo.

KENNY see PUT AND KENNY.

KEPS sb dial; a sound suggestive of brevity; cf KEMPS. *G*

1957 Bennett 14, An before me could say keps dem married.

KERATTO see CORATOE.

KEROLIN see CREOLIAN.

KEROUT see *kirout*.

keta-keta vb and sb[1] dial; echoic—cf *keke* vb.

1956 Mc Man /im kéta-kéta áal taim/ *She is everlastingly giggling;* /aafta dem finish dem keta-keta don/ *When they have got over their giggling.*

keta-keta sb[2] dial; cf Twi *kétewa*, small, *kẹ́tẹkẹtẹ*, very small, tiny; cf also TICKY-TICKY.

1956 Mc StE (Accom), StJ /keta-keta/ small fish, another name for *bangga*.

KETCH see CATCH.

KETTAY sb dial; a parallel form of AKETTA (though KETTAY represents the final vowel better, and is closer in sense to its source).

1943 *GL* No addr, Kettay sb. A flute blown to call friends together.

KETTO sb dial; etym unknown. See quot.

1943 *NHN* II 68, *Hypelate trifoliata*—Ketto, Bastard Lignum Vitæ. The wood is extremely hard, heavy and tough, light yellow to pale brown in colour.

KEY sb dial cant; <*key* (*OED sb*[1] 3). In Revivalist use: the physical means (e.g. a stone, a shepherd's crook, a cloth, a specially dedicated churchyard, etc.) through which spiritual powers are supposed to be controlled.

1953 Moore 52, Key—control-point through which spiritual powers can come.

KEY-KEY see *keke* sb[1].

K-FOOT sb dial; *K*+*foot*. (But cf also *OED kay, key*, esp quot 1895.) A leg (or both legs) bent inward at the knee so that one 'knocks' the other and forms with it the shape of the letter K; cf CAPITAL K. *G*

1952 FGC StM /kíefùt/ favour letter K, knock-knee.

KHAKI PATCH sb dial joc. A BULLA cake; cf DIRTY SHIRT.

1956 Mc Man /káaki pách/ another name for a bulla.

KHAKI STICK sb dial.

1943 *NHN* II 25, Khaki stick—*Capparis flexuosa*..Name probably derived from the colour of the young branches.

KHAS-KHAS see COCKROACH GRASS.

KHUS-KHUS /kuskus/ sb; cf *OED cuscus*[2], 'The long fibrous aromatic root of an Indian grass, *Andropogon muricatus*..', *khus-khus*. A perfume made from the roots of the grass *Vetiveria zizenioides* (which are also used to make fans, to scent linens, etc.). *BA*

1935 HPJ, Cuss-cuss, 'Khus-Khus', an essence made of the roots of the wayside grass of similar name by the now Benjamin Mfg Co..Kingston.

KHUS-KHUS see COUSCOUS.

KHYA-KHYA see *kyaa-kyaa*.

KI, KIE int dial arch; perh related to KU. An exclamation of surprise, amusement, satisfaction, etc. (Also Gullah: 1949 Turner 196.)

a 1818 Lewis (1845) 95, 'Dere massa coat! and dere him chair him sit in!..And oh! ki! dere massa pye-glass!' *Ibid* 105, Upon which Nato had the impudence to burst into a fit of laughter—'Oh, ki, massa, doctor no need be fright; we no want to hurt him'. 1868 Russell 20–1, Interjections..*Kie!* Admiration, satisfaction.

KIAH-KIAH see *kyaa-kyaa*.

KIAKE sb dial rare; 'Maroon talk', therefore presumably African, but no source has been found. Cf *kaachi*. The ABENG.

1929 Beckwith 193–4, The horn was called *abong* [*sic*]—'just like saying ah-h!' and also *kiake*, but a third and secret name he would not divulge.

KIANG-CRO see CYANCRO.

kiba /kíba, kéba/ vb and sb dial; dial sp kiba, kibba, kiber, keiba; <*kiver*, Engl, Ir, Scot, US dial form of *cover* (*EDD*).

1. To cover. *BL*

1943 *GL* StAnd, Kibbarin, covering; StAnn, Kiber, cover; StE, StJ, Kibba, cover; Tre, Kiba, to cover. 1950 Pioneer 31, A jacket an a was'coat..wi keiba yuh up soh dat de gal dem kean se' yuh feader.

2. To lie upon like an incubus.

1900 Murray 7, You little beas' I kill you tiday! A mek duppy kibber you.

kiba-bak sb dial; evid <*cover*+*back*—something to cover one's back. A THATCH HOUSE or HUTCH.

1956 Mc Clar /kiba bak/ A house with wattled walls and thatch roof—also /tach ous̩/.

KICK sb dial or slang; cf US slang *white mule*, gin, whisky. See quot. *G*

1958 DeC Port, StAnd /kik/ a drink of white rum (known as 'mule'). Used alone or in the phrase 'Kick of rum': 'Let's stop at the bar for a kick'.

KICK-AND-BUCK sb dial, also attrib; <*kick* +*and*+BUCK.

1. A water-tank or cistern of rammed clay, in which the clay is 'kicked' and 'bucked', or pounded, inside the cistern until it becomes impermeable to water. See quot 1929.

[1821 Baillie passim, where ramming of clay in cisterns, or around sunk vats, is spoken of frequently.] 1905 Dodd 1, From one corner stretched a small barbecue, which against one corner fed a small, 'kick-um-buck' tank. 1929 Beckwith 11, Two kinds of tank are in use, the square and the 'kick and buck'..—a name derived from the method of finishing..The 'kick and buck' is generally smaller than the square tank and is cheaper of construction. After the hole is dug, a plaster made of equal quantities of red earth and lime mixed dry and stirred until sticky is applied to the dampened sides of the tank, and two men with heavy mallets, one to hold and one to pound, beat it in hard and level and smooth it with a trowel. About the top of the tank they build an edge of squared stones and mortar about three feet above the ground..A mason also is needed to finish the bottom.

2. Fig. Used to symbolize a cheap or inadequate type of masonry.

1943 *GL* No addr, Kick and buck, Sparing or scant mason work.

KICK-FOOT sb dial. The larva of the mosquito—from its jerky, wriggling movement.

1952 FGC Port /kikfut/ jump-up.

KICK JACK vb phr dial.

1958 DeC StT /kik jak/ sb. to cut and eat /jak/ a large johnnycake, hence to eat in general. See also JACK, CUT JACK.

KICK-SHINE sb dial; <*kick* (<*kick up OED v*[1] 9a) +*shine* (*OED sb*[2] 2), a disturbance, row, fuss.

1943 *GL* StM, Kick-shine, Noisy quarrel.

KICK-UP vb and sb dial; cf JUMP-UP.

A. sb: A dance, dancing. *G*

1956 Mc Man /yu ná go kík op/ *Aren't you going dancing* or *to the dance?*

B. vb: To dance.

1956 Mc Port /kik op/ To dance; a dance.

KICK-UP see BESSY KICK-UP, LAND KICK-UP.

KIDNEY BASKET sb dial; from its shape.

1959 DeC Port /kidni baskit/ of hook withe, oval, open, with handle.

KIDNEY MANGO sb dial. A variety of mango of kidney shape. *BA*

1952 FGC Port, StAnd, StAnn, StE, StJ, StM, StT. 1959 DeC Han /kidni manggo/ the mango which is called *black mango* in Kingston.

KIE see KI.

kiebo sb dial; <*kie-* etym unknown +*-bo*.

1959 DeC Port /kiebo/ an offensive word for a person of medium brown skin.

KIESHI see KEASHI.

kiet, kiit /kíit, kíet/ sb[1] dial; <*skeat*, *OED* β-form of *skate* (16th–18th cent), and *skate* itself, by regular dial reduction of *sk-* > *k-*; the full forms are also known. The skate fish (genus *Raia*).

1944 HPJ, Keat—A large flat fish (of devil fish class) found near Lucea. Skate? 1952 FGC Port /skíit/; StAnn, StC /kíet/; StJ /kíit/; StM, West /kíit, skíit/.

kiet sb[2] dial; perh for *pate*: a number of other dial words alternate *p* and *k*—cf *plaba*, PLAW, etc.

1959 LeP [Ja students at Oxford:] /todi im kiet/ [*study his pate?*] rack his brains.

kiit see *kiet* sb[1].

kikombok sb dial; <*cucumber*+*-k*.

1956 Mc Man /kíkómbok/ a form for 'cucumber'.

KILL-BUCKRA sb dial; <*kill* vb+BUCKRA. The JAMAICA BUTTERCUP (*Tribulus cistoides*), which flourished at the season of fevers when many white men died, and was therefore thought to cause their death. **s.**

1940 HPJ, Kill-buckra, a wild flower..(Tribulus cistoides). 1944 HPJ, Kil-bockra, a wayside weed, the Jamaica buttercup. 1954 *WIMJ* 31, Jamaica or Kingston Buttercup; Police Macca; Kill Buckra; Turkey blossom.

KILL HOG vb phr dial arch. To have a feast (of hog, etc.) as a means of announcing formally to the community that one's daughter has reached the marriageable age; a former custom among the Maroons.

1803 Dallas I 115, Although this feast was intended by the family as a signal to the young men for making an offer, the girl herself usually preferred a state of celibacy for some years after it was publicly known *that she had killed hog*.

KILL-KILL vb dial; iterative <*kill*. To do a great deal of killing, or repeated acts of killing.

1826 Barclay 304, The report which I have heard from.. many African negroes..'Guinea good—but country fight country, and kill kill too much—wish to go back? no'. *G*

KILL OBEAH vb phr dial. To perform the actions necessary to nullify the effects of OBEAH. (Cf PULL.) *G*

1895 Banbury 13, To put the object causing the disease, which has been 'pulled', into a basin, and to throw lime juice and ashes over it..is called 'killing' the obeah.

KIMBO vb and sb dial; aphetic form of *akimbo*.

A. vb: To place the arms akimbo. *BL*

1943 *GL* Port, Kimbo, to place both knuckles on your waist.

B. sb: Evid=hip, but perh the phr 'pon me kimbo' means 'akimbo' by itself (since 'hand' can mean the entire arm). *G*

1943 Bennett 22, Ah put me han' pon me kimbo Ah meck a sudden movement.

KIN (SKIN) sb or vb dial. *G*

A. sb: Skin, in various collocations where it would not be used in Std Engl: see quots; often virtually=body. *BL*

1835 Madden I 156, She had *pain in her kin!* (pain in the skin means every sort of external ill that negro flesh is heir to). 1956 Mc Man /go bíed yu kín/ *Go and wash* (more than the face); /mi gwain lík yu skín/ *I'm going to give you a beating* (cf tan your hide).

B. sb or vb: Abbr for KINCAT or KINOBA, or for KIN TEET.

1943 *GL* Kgn, Kin, turn; Clar, Kin, grin.

KINCAT sb and vb dial; <*skin the cat*, cf *DA skin* v 10.

1943 *GL* StC, Kincat, somersault; Tre, Kincat, to turn over; Kgn, Kincat, to overturn.

kinep see GUINEP.

KING int dial. An exclamation expressing surprise, annoyance, etc. Freq preceded by another word, as *oh*, *my*, and the like. The allusion is probably to God, but cf quots.

1862 Clutterbuck 289, 'Me will dead. Oh, my king!' 1873 Rampini 47 [Of Santiago de la Vega (Spanish Town):] In its streets the struggle between cavaliers and roundheads was enacted as fiercely as at home, and a local antiquary, the Honourable Richard Hill, states in one of his works that the common negro ejaculations of 'My father' and 'O King!' used to express surprise or astonishment, date back from these times. 1907 Jekyll 42, Him..say:—'My goodness King! a whé me a go do? 1912 McK *Ballads* 70, S'ep mi King!—So help me God. 1943 HPJ Kgn [A woman in Duke St:] Jesu King! 1944 HPJ, King: An interjection expressing surprise and dissatisfaction, particularly common in compounds such as 'My King!' (or O King! O my King! my gracious King! my goodness King!) [Astley Clerk: The only one I recognize is the first, 'My King!']..Cf perhaps Ri! King! an Irish exclamation of surprize [*sic*] and similar terms in Scots Gaelic: A Righ! O King.

KING CROW sb dial. An albino JOHN-CROW; also called JOHN-CROW HEADMAN.

1943 Jeffrey-Smith in *NHN* II 9. 1956 Jeffrey-Smith 2, It is quite common to see cases of partial albinism; but sometimes..the plumage is entirely white. He is then known as 'King Crow' and bird-watchers will tell you that he has the pick of anything in the nature of carrion.

KING-FREE adj dial obs. Said of the children up to six years of age at the time of emancipation (1 Aug 1834) who, by that 'royal' enactment received complete manumission from slavery, whereas all other slaves from six years of age upward remained bound for a time under the apprenticeship system. (Cf Bell & Morrell, *Select Doc. on Brit. Colonial Policy*, 1928, 389: Abolition of Slavery Act 1833.)

1944 HPJ, King-free: born not more than seven [*sic*] years before Aug. 1, 1834.

KING FRUIT =KING ORANGE.

KING MULLET sb. See quot. *BA G*

1851 Gosse 208, There was a pair of King-mullets (*Upeneus maculatus*, Cuv.), called also Queen-mullet, and, from its depending beards..Goat-fish. This is a beautiful fish.

KING ORANGE sb. A variety of the mandarin orange: *Citrus nobilis*. (Normally known as King Fruit. LeP.) *T*

1913 Harris 15, Orange, Mandarin..There are several recognized varieties or types of this exquisite fruit. *King*.—This has a large fruit which is rough and of a dark-orange colour. It appears to be the only variety shipped from Jamaica. 1920 Fawcett 189, King Orange. 1954 *FG* 316, Orange Group..Other varieties include the..Tangerine, Tangelo, King.

KING PINE sb obs; *OED king sb* 13c (a), only 1668. A large variety of the pineapple. (*OED* and other dictionaries that follow erroneously define it as 'the pine-apple'. Cf PINE.) First used in Barbados. *G*

[1657 Ligon 83, There are two sorts of Pines, the King and Queen Pine: The Queen is far more delicate..The King Pine..is commonly the larger Pine. I have seen some of them 14 inches long, and sixe inches in the diametre.] 1774 Long III 792, The smooth-leaved, or king pine.

KING RASTA sb dial; <*king* + RASTA. A name for the Emperor Haile Selassie of Abyssinia given by the RASTAFARIAN cult in Jamaica, who call him 'Son of King Solomon by the Queen of Sheba'.

1933 *Gleaner* 16 Dec, as reported in 1960 *SAN Report*.

KINGSTON BUTTERCUP sb. The wild plant *Tribulus cistoides*, very common around Kingston, not found inland or on the north side.

1954 *WIMJ* 31, see KILL-BUCKRA.

KINGSTON LIZARD sb dial. The ground lizard (*Ameiva dorsalis*), found chiefly in the south side lowlands and therefore associated with Kingston.

1952 FGC StT, Kingston lizard—ground lizard.

KINNUP see KIN-UP.

KINOBA, kin uova vb or vb phr dial; <*skin* vb + *over*; cf KINCAT. To turn (something, oneself) over; do a somersault.

1943 *GL* Han, Kinoba, turn over. 1959 DeC Tre /kin it uova/—to move something, as a log, by turning it end-over-end.

KIN OLD see next.

kin-oul /kinóul/ sb dial; <*skin* + *owl*. A witch or HIGE, believed to shed her skin by night, take the form of an owl, and fly out to suck people's blood. Cf OLD SUCK.

1943 *GL* StC, Kin owl; West, Kin old, old witch. 1955 FGC Man /kinóul/ witch—get out of their skin, go and suck people's blood.

KIN TEET /kin tiit/ vb phr dial; <*skin* vb + *teeth*. *BA*

1. trans: To draw the lips back, revealing the teeth; to grin, to laugh, usually with pleasure, sometimes with chagrin, etc. *G*

1925 Beckwith 88 [Prov:] No everybody wha' 'kin dem teet' wid you a you frien'. 1950 Pioneer 94, Go 'kin you teet' an show you smile. 1955 Bennett *Pleasuration*, Dem dah treat de gal like queen, all She dah do is kin her teet! 1956 Mc /yu kín yu tíit/ To laugh showing the teeth; to laugh enthusiastically.

2. intr: With *teeth* as the subject: to be uncovered by the lips.

1958 DeC Clar /a tiit kin/ the teeth have 'skinned'—i.e. *he is dead*, the face has taken on the death grimace which exposes the teeth.

KIN-TEET sb dial; from prec. A showing of the teeth; a grin; a smile. *BA G*

1925 Beckwith 88 [Prov:] No every 'kin teet' a 'kin teet'..*Not every laugh is an honest laugh.*

KIN-TEET adj dial; from vb. With protruding teeth. *G*

1956 BLB Man /di kin-tiit gyal/.

kin tiit see prec.

KIN-UP vb dial; <*skin* vb + *up*. To turn up (one's lip) in disgust or disdain. *G*

1956 BLB Man /im kin op im tap lip laik im smel sinting bad/ *He turned up his upper lip as if he had smelt something bad.*

KIN-UP past ppl adj dial; <*skinned* + *up*. Turned up; cf KIN TEET. *G*

1943 *GL* StM, Kinnup, turned up. 1955 Bennett *Breeze Pass*, Wid dem nose an mout-lip kin-up like pet dog a view pig-sty.

kip see KEEP.

kirout /kiróut, kìiróut/ int dial; perh <*clear out!* but prob <*git out!* An exclamation of abrupt dismissal; =Get out! (And like this phrase, it may also be used less strongly to express disbelief.)

1943 *GL* Clar, Kee-root, Get away; Kgn, Kirout, Clear out; Kgn, Kirout, Girout, Go away; Kgn, Kir-owt, Get out; Port, Kerout, Get off. 1955 FGC Man /kìróut/ to drive someone away in an abrupt manner.

KIROWT see prec.

kisada, KISSADA see CASSADA, *gizada*.

KISSIDY sb dial; imitative of the bird's call. A local name for the JUDY (*Platypsaris niger*).

1956 Jeffrey-Smith 69, Other local names recall its song, viz: 'Kissidy' as it is termed in Manchester, and 'London City', at Windsor in Trelawny.

KITCHEN-BITCH sb dial.

1. See quot.

1959 DeC West /kichin-bich/ a small lamp made of tin with no chimney.

2. See quot.

1959 DeC Port (Moore Town) /kichin bich/ a man who hangs about the kitchen all the time.

KITCHEN-CRUMB sb dial. =KITCHEN-BITCH 2.

1959 DeC Port (Moore Town) /kichin krom/.

KITCHEN-DRESSER sb dial. A shelf or cupboard in a kitchen where food is kept. *G*

c1915 FGC StAnd [Prov:] When kitchen-dresser fall down, maaga dog laugh. (1960 Current, FGC.)

KITCHEN-KEY sb dial.

1. A man who lingers about a kitchen.

1943 *GL* Clar, Kitchenky, a man who loves the kitchen. 1955 FGC Man /kíchin kii/ a man hang about the kitchen.

2. See quot.

1956 Mc Port /kichin kii/ A mark left by soot on the face or clothes in the kitchen.

kitibog see next.

kitibu /kitibú/ occas /chichibú, kichibú, kikibu, kyitibu, kitibog, tichibú/ sb dial; perh <Twi *kétee*, *kétekete*, adj and adv, bright, brightly, in full lustre; for second element cf Fanti *bũbũ*, insect, prob with coincident infl of English *bug*.

1. The click-beetle or firefly *Pyrophorus plagiophthalmus* with two luminous spots on its thorax often mistaken for eyes. Cf *tichibu*.

1943 *GL* Port, Kitty-boo, Kittaboo, firefly; Port, Kittibo, Peonie Waalie; StT, Kittyboo, firefly. 1952 FGC StT /kìtibú/ firefly with two shining eyes—same as 'moony'. 1958 DeC StAnd (Irish Town) /kitibu/ firefly.

2. A meddlesome person. Cf FIRE-KITTY.

1955 LeP StE (Eld) /kitibog/ not a firefly, but a mischief-maker: somebody always involved in quarrels.

kitibu afu sb dial; <*kitibu*+AFU. A kind of yam with prominent eyes (like the firefly); see quot.

1958 DeC Port, StT /kitibu afu/ a variety of afu 'with plenty eyes'.

kitibum sb dial; evid symbolic of the sounds and actions. (Hardly to be conn with *kitibu*.) An entertainment at which there is dancing, singing and other lively amusement. *G*

1956 Mc Man /kítibum/ a gathering given over to /jompin, singin, aal saat av fuulishnis/; /yu náa go a kítibum tunáit?/ *Aren't you going to the kitibum tonight?*

KITTABOO see *kitibu*.

KITTER vb dial; prob <*skitter* (cf *EDD*).

1943 *GL* StAnd, Kitter, to run away.

KITTIBO see *kitibu*.

KITTY sb, esp dial; cf *OED kitty*². Preferred in Jamaican use over *kitten*: a cat, often but not necessarily a young one. *G*

1956 JN Kgn, I saw the kitty's mother; come here kitty white-foot; Man (Mandeville), Why the kitty open its mouth to cry and no sound come out?

KITTY-BOO see *kitibu*.

KITTY-GO sb dial rare; imitative of the bird's cry. The CACKY-QUAW.

KITTY-KATTY sb dial obs?; prob echoic—cf *katatik*. A simple percussion instrument of wood, beaten with two sticks.

a1818 Lewis (1834) 345, see JAM-JAM. p1914 Clerk 22, The Kitty-Katty, or any flat piece of board on which they beat with two sticks.

KITTY-UP sb dial; cf Twi *kɛtɛ́*, a mat, the usual bed of the natives. [Reid's statement that this is 'sailor slang' is questionable.]

1949 Reid gloss, Kitty-up, old-fashioned sailor slang for a bed.

klad sb and vb dial; of uncert source: on phonological grounds (see Introd) equally well derivable from *clod* or *clad* (*EDD*: *clad* sb, a clod of earth), and on semantic grounds best derived from *clot* sb and vb.

1. sb: Sour milk.

1958 DeC Port /klad/.

2. vb: To congeal on; to make sticky.

1958 DeC StC, Cane is fit to cut when the juice /klad yu han/.

klaid ppl adj chiefly dial; earlier pronunc of *cloyed*. Cloyed; satiated with excess of food. (The normal dial form would not retain *-ed*—cf CLY.) *BL N*

1935 HPJ, Clied—cloyd, satisfied, surfeited. Cly also.. The word is remarkable as an apparent survival of a verb with a distinct past participle. 1956 Mc Man /mi nyám píe tel mi klaid/ *I ate pears until I was sick.*

klaid vb dial; <*klaid* past pple—see prec. To cloy, to surfeit.

1956 BLB Man /it gwaing klaid yu/ *It will cloy you.*

klieri, klierit see (WILD) CLARY.

KLING-KLING /kling-kling/ sb; 1847 clin-kling, 1943→ cling-cling, 1956 kling-kling, imitative of the bird's cry. The bird often called in books the TINKLING GRACKLE, *Quiscalus niger*. Other imitative names are TIN-TIN, TING-TING, TING-LING; also called BARBADOS BLACKBIRD.

[1774 Long III 893, Their note is somewhat like the creaking of an inn-keeper's sign in a high wind, or the handle of a grindstone; at other times it more resembles the gentle squeak which may be formed by means of a comb and paper. They vary frequently both the key and the tone, making altogether a very whimsical kind of concert.] 1847 Gosse 219, It is to the first of these notes that the bird before us owes his local names of Tinkling, Tintin, Clinkling, and, among the Spaniards of St Domingo, Chinchiling. 1943 *GL* Tre, Cling-cling, The Blackbird. 1952 FGC Han, Man, Port, StAnd, StM, StT /kling-kling/. 1952 Carley *Sunday Gleaner* (March), Cling-cling..grackle. 1956 Taylor 11, Kling-Kling, A bird of medium size with shining black plumage, pointed beak, a pale yellow eye and long boat-shaped tail.

KNAUM see NYAM.

KNIFE-AND-SCISSORS MAN sb dial. An OBEAHMAN, so called from the symbolic use he makes of knives and scissors to indicate his supposed power to cut off evil, etc. Cf CUTTING.

1952 Kerr 140, I do not like the knives and scissors men. They do bad things. They are the only ones who put things on people.

KNIFE-HANDLE SHELL sb obs. A kind of bivalve shellfish, so named for its shape.

1756 Browne 412, Solena 1..The Knife-handle shell.. It is naturally of an oblong form, and almost the same breadth the whole length.

KNIT sb ornith obs; a variant of (or error for) *knot* (*OED sb*², the red-breasted sandpiper).

1847 Gosse 354, Knit, *Tringa Canutus.*

KNOCK vb dial; various specif senses of *knock.*

1. Of the spirits of the dead: to strike (someone) so as to cause sudden illness or disease.

1895 Banbury 28, The 'deaths' are believed capable of returning for any relative or friend, or anyone who injured them in life. This they effect by 'putting hand' upon them, or 'knocking' them. Persons taking in suddenly with convulsive fits are thought to be knocked by duppies, especially children and young infants.

2. To flap the wings—cf CHOP 1.

1924 Beckwith 105, So de cock commence to eat de corn ..knock him wing bap bap bap bap! After he knock him wing, he crow.

3. To beat (a drum). *G N*

1956 Mc StE (Accom) /dem nak di drom/.

4. In phr *to knock water,* to drink rum. *G*

1959 DeC gen /nak wata/—to drink rum /a duon nuo if in gwaing gi mi a shiling to guo an nak mi wata out a ruod dis iivning/.

KNOCK-AND-BLOW sb; see quot. A nickname for round cream biscuits.

1960 J. Lewis StAnn, 'Knock-and-blow' originated on sailing vessels, where weevils were always present and ate the ship's biscuit. One would have to *knock* out the weevils and *blow* out their dust.

KNOCK-AND-GO-ALONG sb dial. The marble game of 'chase' or 'boss and span', played with cashew nuts. (Cf *PADS* 23.)

1948 U.Newton IV 35, At Bartons and at Four Paths, the popular cashew games were 'knock-and-go-along', 'standing', 'Chink-up' and 'back-on-the-hand'. At Chapelton we bigger ones did not play those childish games. We played 'bank'.

KNOCK AND RUN sb dial. A form of cricket (= *Tip-and-run, OED tip vb*¹ 1 b).

1957 JN StJ, Play knock and run.

KNOCK-AN'-STAN'-UP sb dial. = LICK-AN'-'TAN'-UP.

1924 Beckwith 201 [Riddle:] Knock an' stan' up.—Mat.

KNOCK JOHNNY COOPER vb phr dial. In waxing a floor with a COCONUT BRUSH: To imitate the rhythmic sound made by a cooper fastening hoops on rum casks. Cf JOHNNY-COOPA-LANTAN.

1956 BLB Man, A favourite pastime among children used to be to see who could /nák jànikúpa/ loudest, sweetest, and longest. The competition would of course be judged by the expert—the house cleaner, whom we were supposed to be helping in her task.

KNOT-GUT sb dial; < *knot* vb + *gut.*

1933 McK 317, Knot-gut—fatal constipation.

KNOW ABOUT /núo bóut/ vb phr; by suspension of the object of *about,* which is a secret. To have heard a piece of news; to know about some fact or event that not everyone has heard of.

1957 EB Port, 'Oh, you know 'bout'—You're in the know.

KNOW WHAT O'CLOCK vb phr dial. To know what is going on. *BA*

1960 *CLS* 150 /bot di yóng mán núo wát aklák/ *But the young man know what o'clock* [*is aware of the situation*].

KNOW-YOU sb dial; by folk-etym < Fr *noyau,* the name of the plant in Guadeloupe, so called because the leaves give off the smell of the essence of noyau. (A. Questel, *La Flore de la Guadeloupe,* 1943.) A wild plant (*Ipomoea dissecta*) used as a purge (which fact probably explains the folk name).

1952 FGC StAnn /núoyu/—leaf all in points, something like /sorasi/; Tre /núoyo/—a kind of small wis like bat-bush, red flower, ripe pods burst like ackee—also /yúoyo/. 1953 *WIMJ* 243, *Ipomoea dissecta*..Know You..said to be used as a cathartic.

KO see KU.

ko int dial; prob < Twi *kɔ,* go!, or similar form; cf COOY.

1943 *GL* StAnd, Kough, To go on. Said to horses, mules & donkeys.

ko, ko-a see COUSIN. *G*

koba-koba adj dial; etym unknown. See quots.

1943 *GL* Kgn, Cubba-cubba, worthless; StM, Coba-coba, worthless. 1955 FGC Man /kóba-kóba/. *G*

kobalo see CAVALLY JACK.

kobanansi see COBY.

kobi sb dial; < Twi *kóbὲ,* a species of yam. A variety of yam grown in the cockpit country of St James.

1956 Mc StJ /kobi/.

kobich see CUBBITCH.

kobiich see CAVEACH.

kobij see CUBBITCH.

kobijong sb dial; prob a form of *kyabiyo,* alluding to salt fish in the run-down. See quot.

1958 DeC Port /kobijong/ coconut run-down.

KOBITE see *kubaiti.*

kochi /kóchi/ sb and vb dial; < *curtsy,* cf *OED sb* 3, *v* 1. Curtsy.

c1915 FGC StAnd [Formula of politeness:] /kóchi fi líedi, bóu fi jéngklmàn/ *Curtsy for ladies, bow for gentlemen.* 1943 *GL* Clar, Cutchie, to bow; StJ, Couchey, kertsy; Tre, Cuchie, a bending of the knees to show thanks. 1956 Mc Clar /mek kochi/ to drop a curtsey; Port /im drap kochi/. 1957 Bennett 29, cutchy.

kodl sb dial; < *curdle. BL*

1959 DeC StJ /kodl/ sour milk; informant associates the word with *cuddle.*

kodn see COUSIN.

kofi-roba sb dial; < CUFFEE (cf *kofi-routn*) + prob the same second component as in *kojoruba.*

1958 DeC Man /kofi-roba/ ringworm infection of the skin.

kofi-routn /kòfiróutn, káfiròutn/ occas /káfiròuzn/ sb and adj dial; 1935 kuffyrouten, 1943 cuffirouten, cufroutin; prob < CUFFEE + *routing* (cf *OED rout v*⁸, 'to poke about, rummage; ..to tear up, scoop out', etc.).

A. sb: A skin disease—eczema or something similar; cf *kojoruba,* which is identified with this by some, and is of parallel formation.

1940 HPJ, Marian insisted that Kuffy-routen and King's Evil were quite distinct. 1943 *GL* Clar, Cuffirouten, eczema; Tre, Cufroutin, exzema. 1955 FGC Man /kòfiróutn/.

B. adj: Scruffy; by extension, low-class, low-quality—used as an insult. [The pronunc /káfiròutn/ appears to be increasing here, with folk-etym associations with *coffee*.]

1959 Mrs Landale StAnd, 'Formerly heard in the country'. 1959 Mrs Robinson, UCWI Preventive Med; also /káfiròuzn/.

kojo-ruba /kòjorúba/ sb dial arch; etym uncert —prob <CUDJO[1] (as a number of skin diseases are associated with African, as distinct from Creole, negroes) +an altered form of *rub*? Eczema or some similar disease.

1943 *GL* Man, Cujoruba, a disease; StE, Kojorubba, eczema. 1955 FGC Man /kòjorúba/.

KOJORUBBA see prec.

kolo-kolo adj dial; ? cf *korokoro* sb[1].

1959 DeC StJ /kolo-kolo/ adj (of a man) shiftless, unreliable, no-account.

komananansi see COBY.

komaroun see COME-AROUND.

konakunda vb phr dial cant; prob altered <*can come*. A cant word of the AFRICAN cult (StT).

1953 Moore gloss /konakunda/ can come.

KONDA see KANDA.

kong see COUSIN. *G*

konggo, konggu see CONGO.

kongk /kongk/ sb and vb dial; 1935 cunk, 1943→ kunk. The regular folk pronunc (instead of /kangk/ as would be expected) of *conch* (sea-shell; the edible shellfish; snail shell) and *conk* (to strike on the head; a blow on the head—cf Engl and US slang, Berrey and Van den Bark 702 20, etc.). *BL*

1935 HPJ, Cunk—a snail, snail-shell, conch. 1943 *GL* StC, Kunk, to tap in the head; West, Kunk, a limited blow in the head; Kgn, etc. 1946 U.Newton I 28, We boys called that area the head skull. And it was great fun to us to kunk (you know, biff with the finger) one another on the head skulls. *Ibid* 30, He kunks me in the head with the back of the comb.

kongkongsa, kongkonse /kòngkòngsá, kòngkònsé/ sb, adj, and vb dial; spellings: congaso, congoso, congosaw, congosah, conconsa, cungcungseh; <Twi *ŋkoŋkonsá*, falsehood, deceit, hypocrisy. (Folk-etym analyses: 'Congo-so', 'come-come-say', etc.) *SC gongosà*.

A. sb: 1. Deceit, flattery. *G*

a 1818 Lewis (1845) 64, One species of flattery (or of *Congo-saw*, as we call it here) amused me much this morning. 1835 Madden II 149, He is generally a shrewd, plausible fellow—has a good deal of Congo saw, or, in other negro parlance, sweet mouth. 1943 *GL* Kgn, Congo-saw, flattery; StAnd, Congosah, deceit. 1955 FGC Man /kòngkònsé/ flattery.

2. A deceitful person; one who shows unfair partiality. *G*

1910 Anderson-Cundall 37 [Prov: see next]. 1925 Beckwith 41 [Prov:] Ceitful fire roast plantain, 'cong-a-so' 'crape it. [Beckwith takes this to mean 'cunning', but it probably means that the deceitful man and the congaso are two of a kind and in league.]

3. Trouble or falling out between people, presumably due to deceit or hypocrisy. (This may, however, be erron for *kaskas*.) *G*

1873 Rampini 119, 'I don't want to hab any conconsa (argument) wid you, Breda', replied Tiger.

B. adj: Deceitful. *T*

1943 *GL* Kgn, Deceitful—'You too congosah'; Tre, Congoso, deceitful; also StAnn.

C. vb: To be deceitful, to connive; to flatter, to curry favour.

1943 *GL* StM, Cungcungseh; to connive, curry favour.

kongkonte, kongkote /kòngkònté, kòngkoté/ sb dial; 1873 conquintay, 1935 cuncunteh; dial sp cuncuntey, cuncungta, concontey, conkante, cunchuntia, kung-kung-teh, cum-cum-tek; <Twi *kokònté*, plur *ŋkoŋkònté*, cassada or plantains cut in pieces and dried; Gã *koŋkoŋte*, manioc flour. (This tends to be analysed by folk-etym as *come-come-take*.) *BL*

1. Flour made from cassava, plantain, or green banana; it is eaten as porridge, in the form of dumplings, etc. *G N*; *SC gongoté*.

1873 Rampini 73, An old, old woman..was drying thin slices of plantain on the sun-baked stones preparatory to pounding them into flour (called *conquintay*) for porridge. 1935 HPJ StM, Cuncunteh—banana cut in strips, sun-dried, and gratered. 1943 *GL* Kgn, Concontey, cassava flour; Port, Cunchuntia, dried banana; StC, Conkante, dumplings; StT, Cun-cun-tey, banana dried in sun; StT, Kung-kung-teh. 1952 FGC Port /kòngkoté/ green-banana flour: dry green bananas, pound and sift, use as baby-food, etc.; StM /kòngkònté/ slice green bananas, dry, pound, sift, make porridge or dumplings.

2. Fig. As the type of toughness or hardness.

1943 *GL* Clar, Cuncungta, denoting hardness.

konibok, konibo see CONY-BUCK.

konja see CONGEA.

kontapiichi, kontong, piiji int chiefly dial; origin uncert, but prob <*counter*, against +PEE-GEE; the parts may be used together or separately.

A formula or 'call' used in play by children to claim something seen. It may be countered by the other child's crossing the fingers or saying 'bar'. As with such games, methods of play and 'rules' vary considerably, as do the terms and their use.

1940 HPJ, Cuntapeachy [Astley Clerk: *kuntapeachie*], A word used by children—if the one has anything desired by the other, the latter can claim it by pronouncing the word if the former's fingers were not crossed. [Others know the word as *kuntung*, or as *peijy*.] 1943 *GL* Port, Cuntung, a game lapping two fingers.

kontong see prec.

KOOBAH see CUBBA.

KOO-KOO sb ?obs; cf Hausa *k'uk'u*, the sound made by the intestines in a scrotal hernia, the sound made by a horse that is a 'roarer'; *kuka*, rumblings in the abdomen. One type of JOHN-CANOE, or member of a John-Canoe band: see quot.

1837 Belisario Expl to Plate 5, Through the kindness of a friend, we are enabled to furnish the following derivation of the term *Koo-Koo*. It appears that many years back, this John-Canoe performed in pantomimic actions *only*, consisting of supplications for food—as being demanded by his empty stomach. At each request, an attendant chorus repeated 'Koo-Koo'; this was intended in imitation of the rumbling sound of the bowels, when in a hungry state.

KOOMOONA see *kumuna*.

KOO (YAH) see KU.

KORAH sb dial; prob var of CHUREY.

1943 *GL* StJ, Korah, Piece of knife.

kori see CURRY.

korochi see CAROCHIES.

korojonggl sb dial; cf such words as CAROCHIES, *korokoro*, +*jungle*. See quots.

1959 DeC StAnd, (1) General trash, rubbish, and junk if piled around the yard so thick that the place is 'like a jungle'. (2) Thick bush growing up around a yard making the place like a jungle.

korokoro sb[1] dial; ? iteration of the first part of /korochiz/: cf CAROCHIES.

1956 Mc Man /korokoro/ an abbreviated form of carochies.

korokoro sb[2] see *karakara*.

KOROMANTYN see CROMANTY.

kos, kosin see CUSS, CUSSING.

koskos, kaskas sb dial; < Twi *kasákàsa*, to dispute, contend in words, but identified often with Engl dial *cuss* < *curse*, from which it has derived the prevailing pronunciation. A dispute or quarrel; a 'row'. *BL*; *SC kosi-kósi*.

1873 Rampini 176 [Prov:] Cuss-cuss (calling names) no bore hole in my skin. 1943 Bennett 15, Dat marga gal Wingy Want put me eena kus-kus An big lian story. 1943 *GL* Tre, Coscos, quarrel; Kaskas, trouble; also Clar, Kgn, StAnn, StC, StM, StT, West. 1950 Pioneer 33, Anancy never like fe se' two people live neutral, so him start fe carry lie and story between dem, and start big kaskas. 1956 Mc Man /yu riez a kóskós ef yu tróbl áants an dem stáat tu ríez/ *You raise a koskos if you disturb ants and they start to come out at you.*

kot see CUT.

kotaku see CUTACOO.

KOTCH see COTCH.

kotla sb dial; ? < *cutlet*.

1958 DeC StAnd /kotla/—same as /rof/—a special kind of saltfish fritter..commonly sold by vendors in Kingston who..carry it about in a /bal-pan/.

kotlas, kotlis see CUTLASS.

kotoku(u) see CUTACOO.

kotwe see CUT-AWAY.

ko-u, KOUNG see COUSIN.

kovaali, kovali, kovoli see CAVALLY JACK.

koz, kozn see COUSIN.

kraani see CRAWNY.

kraap vb dial; prob < *scrape*, but cf CRAAB.

kraas see CROSS.

krach-kin sb dial; < *scratch-skin*. =next. *G*

1954 LeP Port, Dry, itching rash on skin—krach-kin.

krach-krach sb dial; iterative of *krach* < SCRATCH. A skin affection that 'scratches' the skin; the itch. *G*

1952 FGC Han /krach-krach/ a skin disease: bumps on skin from bad blood; Han, Lang-pussley good for /krach-krach/ on baby's skin; also StAnd, StM. 1954 LeP StT.

krach kuoko see SCRATCH COCO.

krakasa /krákasa/ sb dial. The palm *Thrinax rex*; see quots.

1943 *NHN* I 11 12, The last of the Jamaica fan palms is a very striking and interesting tree..The only place where this palm grows is on the steep escarpments and limestone rocks of the John Crow Mountains—it is known locally as Cracasa and the leaves are used for thatching. 1952 FGC Port /krákasa/ like round-thatch. (1963 Proctor Institute of Ja—Britton & Harris: *Thrinax rex*.)

krakra see CRA-CRA.

KRA-KRA see CRAW-CRAW.

krak-saa sb dial; perh folk-etym *crack-saw*—cf BREAK-AX. A tree said to furnish a good medicine for indigestion.

1952 FGC StE /krak-saa—trii, gud fi bilyas/.

kramonjin, kramujin, kramuuchin, kramuujin see CRAMOUCHIN.

krangki-mini sb dial; < CRANKY + *Minnie*, woman's name? (Cf *Bessie*, etc., used similarly); cf also *dingki(-mini)*.

1958 DeC Port /krangki-mini/ a tall thin man.

kran-kran /kran-kran, krang-kran/ sb dial; a var form with GRANG-GRANG, KRENG-KRENG, etc.

1. Dried yam vines or other small branches or twigs, used for firewood or mulch.

1943 *GL* Clar, Crankcran, dryed yam vines.

2. A basket used to hang meat over a fireplace.

1956 Mc Clar, Man.

KRAPE-KRAPE sb dial; iterative of /kriep/ reduced form of *scrape*. *G*

1943 *GL* StAnd, Krape-krape, scrapings.

krebe /krébe/ sb dial; etym unknown.

1. A legacy.

1943 *GL* Port, Cre-bay, legacy. 1955 FGC Man /krébe/ legacy.

2. Old worn-out or useless stuff.

1958 DeC Port /uol krebe/ old and ragged work clothes. 1960 LeP StAnd /krebe/ old things.

3. Something odd or queer; strange goings-on.

1960 LeP StAnd, 'I can't stand all that praying and /krebe/ at Mass'.

kregl sb dial; < *cruddle* sb. Cf *krogl*.

1958 DeC Port /kregl/ Sour milk or milk thickened by boiling.

kre-kre sb dial; echoic; cf *keke* sb[2].

1958 DeC StE (Accom) /krekre/ a croaking lizard.

krengke adj dial.

1959 DeC Tre /krengke/ A variant of /krengki, krangki/ meaning thin, *maaga*.

KRENG-KREH see next.

kreng-kreng /kreng-kreng, kreng-kre, kren-kren/ sb[1] dial; cf Twi *kyerɛ́ŋkyɛ́*, basket.

1. Brambles (presumably as fit for use as kindling-wood)—cf KRAN-KRAN, GRANG-GRANG.

1943 *GL* StM, Kreng-kreng, bramble.

2. An old basket (this assimilates to senses 1 and 3, being both a collection of sticks, and a container).

1943 *GL* StAnd, Kren-kren, old basket.

3. Specifically, a basket or similar container hung above the fire from the roof of a kitchen where it will receive the smoke, used to preserve and store meat or fish; also called a *hangkra*.

1927 Anderson-Cundall 49, Yeye can' tek meat out cren-cren. [*Your eye(s) can't take the meat out of a kreng-kreng.*] 1943 *GL* Clar, Kgn, Creng-Creng, A basket hanging from the roof of a kitchen for storing meat or fish; StM, Kreng-kreh, Suspended safe, also *kotoku.* 1958 DeC StC /kreng-kreng/ a rack hung in the kitchen to smoke fish or meat.

kreng-kreng sb² dial; perh conn with *kreng-kreng* sb¹ 1. Rocky or stony land; sharp stones in the land.

1954 LeP StE (Eld), Rocky, stony land, creng-creng. 1956 Mc StE (Accom) /kreng-kreng/ sharp stone /wi buor yu fut/.

kreng-kreng CALALU sb dial; perh related in source to OKRO; but cf *kreng-kreng* sb¹.

1952 FGC StAnd /kreng-kreng kalalu/—when dat boil, stay like okro.

KREN-KREN see *kreng-kreng.*

krepe /krépe/ sb dial; <Fr *crapaud,* or a dial form—cf Canadian Fr *crapais.*

1956 LeP StAnn /krepe/ frog.

krichuol sb dial; a common pronunc of *screech-owl.* Cf QUICHOLE. *BL*

1907 Jekyll 62, 'Creech-owl sounds like creechole. 1952 FGC Han, Man, StAnd, StAnn /krichúol/ occas /kríchuol/.

kriedl sb dial; prob <*cruddle.*

1958 DeC Port /kriedl/ sour milk.

kriel vb dial; var of QUAIL vb.

kriep see SCRAPE.

kriich oul see SCREECH OWL.

kriil, kril see CREEL.

kris /kris, krisp/ adj dial; <*crisp.*

1. Stiff, not pliable. (Cf *OED a* 6a.)

1952 FGC StAnd, Wild-yam not good to tie bundles of wood /it tuu kris/.

2. Of a manner of walking: conscious of one's value, beauty, etc.; proud. Hence generally, proud. s CRISS-MISS.

1954 LeP Man, Walk lakka cris Miss; Port, Kris, proud; StAnn, Crisp, to walk, as a good-looking woman does in a provocative fashion.

krobi-aas see CRAB-YAWS.

krofi-routn sb dial; <*kofi-routn* with CRUFFY blended into the first element.

1958 DeC StAnd /krofi-routn/—also /skrofi-routn/ a rash.

krogl ppl adj dial; <*cruddled,* cf *EDD cruddle.* Cf also above, *kregl.*

1956 Mc Man /krogl/ curdled.

krokin, krokng lizad see CROAKING LIZARD.

kromanti see CROMANTY.

kromonjin, kromujing, kromuuchin, kromuujin see CRAMOUCHIN.

kruchument sb dial; <*accoutrement,* with aphesis and metathesis. See quots.

1943 *GL* Port, Crutchument, Cutrument, old things, superfluous articles; StM, Curutriment, tools. 1955 FGC Man /krúchument/ things fit to throw away. 1958 DeC Port /kuchiment/ general trash or rubbish.

KRUK KRO, krukro see *karakara.*

krukru busu sb dial; etym of *krukru* uncert, cf CRA-CRA, nervous +*busu,* a shellfish.

1956 LeP StAnd /krúkru búsu/ somebody who retires into their shell.

KRUMOOCHIN, KRUMOOGEN, KRUMOUCHIN, KRUMUNGIN, krumuuchin, krumuujin see CRAMOUCHIN.

krumuna see *kumuna.*

KRUNGA see CRONGOE YAM.

KRUNGE see CRUNGE.

KRUNJO see CRONGOE YAM.

kruokas see CROCUS.

KU /ku, ko, (ki)/ int or vb (imperative only) dial; [a1818 ki], 1912 1943 ko, 1927 qui, c1930→ coo, 1933→ ku, 1943→ koo, 1943 kuo, 1943→ cu. Prob a reduced form of *look,* or /luku/ (<*look*+-*u,* an early and still existing form of *look*); this form therefore appears to coincide with Engl dial *K* or *Ka,* recorded in the midland shires, which *EDD* describes as 'An abbreviation of "look" in *comb.* with var *adv.* to form exclamatory phr.'. Examples include *K'out*! look out! *Kyander*! look yonder! *Ka here*! look here! To the last corresp Ja /ku ya/.

Look (at)! See!, esp with advs or preps of place; also as a warning. [The first quot may belong with KI.] *G*

[a1818 Lewis (1945) 134, A negro was brought to England, and the first point shown him being the chalky cliffs of Dover, 'O ki!' he said; 'me know now what makes the buckras all so white!'] 1912 McK *Songs* 75, Ko 'pon you' jam samplatta nose, [*Look at your damned nose, flat as a sandal.*] 1927 Stafford 27, But whenever Dumpah hears it, 'Qui yah!' shouts he in amazement. c1930 Clerk 10, Coo pan de invite wi jes been get. 1933 McK 317, Ku, look. 1943 *GL* StJ, Lookoo ya, look here; StM, Luku ya, look here; Clar, Kuyah, look here; StE, Cuya, look here; Tre, Cuyah, be careful; Han, Kuo-ya, look here, Luko-day, look there; Port, Kudae, look there; Clar, StAnn, StC, Koo, look; Clar, Cu, look. 1950 Pioneer 16, Koo Bra Rat! [*Look at Brother Rat!*]; Massi me massa! Koo yah lawd! [*Mercy my Master! See here, Lord!*] 1956 Mc Man /kú hou di kyát a wáshin im fíes wid im fut/ *See how the cat is washing his face with his paw.*

kubaali, kubaalo see CAVALLY JACK.

kubaiti /kubáiti/ dial arch; <*goodbye-to-ye.* Goodnight; good-bye.

1868 Russell 18, In the evening, kobite, or good eveling. Kobite means properly good night, and is only used as a parting compliment. 1943 *GL* Kgn, Coobitay, good-bye. 1955 FGC Man /kubáiti/ goodbye—'old-time'.

kubu-kubu see CUBU-CUBU.

kuchiment, kuchument see *kruchument.* *G*

KUDAE see KU.

KUE see *kuy.*

KUFFY-ROUTEN see *kofi-routn.*

kuku /kukú/ vb dial; cf *sangkuku.*

1956 Mc Man /kukú doun/ to stoop down.

ku ku ku ku int dial; prob reduced <*come,* which is often pronounced in dial /kum/—cf similar reductions in calls to animals: US *co-boss, cu-day,* etc.; perh in part imitative of the birds' clucking.

1958 DeC StAnd /ku ku ku ku/ call to chickens.

kulu-kulu /kulukulu/ adj and sb dial; origin unknown, but prob African (cf e.g. Yoruba *kólù,* to collect together).

1. Plentiful.

1943 *GL* Kgn, Kulu-kulu, plenty; StM, Cooloo cooloo, plentiful; West, Cullu cullu, plenty. 1955 FGC Man /yam iz kulukulu/ plenty.

2. Pure rum. (This may be a different word; cf also CUBU-CUBU.)

1943 *GL* StM, Kulu kulu, pure rum.

KUMBAY sb dial; variant form of GOMBAY.

1943 *GL* Port, Kumbay—A aferican drum; Port, Kumbay —a Maroon drum; West, Cumbay—funny music.

KUMCI see COME-SEE.

kumina, kumona see next.

kumuna /kúmuna, kúmona, kúmina, krúmuna/ sb dial; 1943 koomoona, cum-mo-na, cum-mina, crumuna, 1953 cumina; etym not clear: two or more words of related meaning are prob combined—cf Twi *kɔ̀m*, to dance wildly in a state of frenzy or ecstasy ascribed by the natives to the agency of a fetish, *ŋkóm-moa*, spirit of possession (Christaller); Kimbundu *kumona*, to see; possession (Turner). **s.**

A religious dance ceremony held on the occasion of a birth, betrothal, NINE-NIGHT, memorial, etc., at which the dancers are believed to become possessed by ancestral spirits; they perform difficult feats, fall unconscious, etc.

1943 *GL*, Cummina, n., a cult performance at night; Port, Koomoona, a native dance, Cum-mo-na, African dance; StT, Krumuna, native dance. 1953 Moore 39, Cumina, A ceremonial memorial dance for the dead—the first of which may be held within the first year, often on the first anniversary of the death of the individual. *Ibid* 117, Public Cumina dances begin usually at sundown Friday and last till sundown Saturday.

kumuujin see CRAMOUCHIN.

KUNCHIN sb dial; cf *OED kinchin sb* 1 b, a child, a kid.

KUNG-KUNG-TEH see *kongkonte*.

KUNK see *kongk*.

KUNTAPEACHIE, KUNTUN(G) see *konta-piichi*, PEE-GEE.

kunu /kúnu/ sb dial; <Bambara *kunu* (cf Gullah *'kunu*, Turner 118), a boat, the sense perh reinforced by Engl *canoe* (but note diff accentuation). A fishing boat, a canoe; regularly pronounced /kúnu/ in folk use. *N*

1756 Browne 277, A *Canoa*, *Conoa*, or *Conoo*, is but a junk of some large [silk-cotton] tree, hollowed as much as the dimensions of its axis will bear..They are sometimes very large..people frequently venture twenty or thirty leagues from the shore in 'em. 1877 Murray *Feedin' 'Perrit* 8, Him tek up de paddle..we shub off coonoo. 1943 *GL* Clar, Cunno—a dugout boat. 1952 FGC StAnd, StC, StM, StT, West, etc. /kúnu/.

kunu adj dial; cf Ewe *kúnu*, something enormous or dangerous; also JOHN CANOE, and UGLY.

1943 *GL* Man, Coonooh, ugly.

kunu-kunu see COONOO-COONOO.

kunu-munu /kúnu mùnu/ sb and adj dial; for spellings see quots; origin uncert, but cf *kunu* adj, ugly, of which *munu* may be an echoic extension. A stupid person; (one) easily taken advantage of. *BL G*

1935 HPJ, Cŭnŭmŭnŭ [coonoo moonoo, Astley Clerk], Fool-fool, easy-natural. 1943 *GL* Man, Cunoo moonoo, a novis, a slight person; Port, Coono-moono, someone who works for nothing; StAnd, Cunnu-munu; StAnn, Cunumunu, credulous. 1949 Reid gloss, Conoo-monoo, colloquialism for a gullible person.

kuo see KU.

kuobi sb dial; perh ref to its colour—cf Ewe *kɔbĩ*, ochre-coloured earth.

1. A kind of sweet-potato; cf WHITE KUOBI, YELLOW KUOBI.

1956 Mc Clar /kúobi/ a type of sweet potato.

2. In the phrase *a pinch of kuobi*: see quot. (This may not be the same word.)

1956 Mc Clar /pinch a kuobi/ 'a miserable little bit'.

kuobi, kuobinansi see COBY.

kuochi waata sb dial; poss conn with SANG-KOCHIE or MACOOCHE, but the contents are quite different.

1959 DeC West /som kuochi wata/ coconut run-down.

kuoknat, kuoknit see COCONUT.

KUO-YA see KU.

kurukuru see *karakara*.

kushu see CASHEW.

kuskus see COUSCOUS, KHUS-KHUS.

KUS-KUS see *koskos*.

kutikap see COOTIKOP.

kutoku see CUTACOO.

kuy /kúy/ int dial; spellings: 1912 kue, 1943 cooy, cooye, cooyh, cooey, cuie, cuhi, kuy; <Twi *kɔ̀ɛ̀*, go! An exclamation to make a donkey move forward.

1912 McK *Ballads* 46, Kue, jackass, git up! Tan 'pon you foot! Dis ya load no load, you's a lazy brut. 1943 *GL* Clar, Cuie, To drive donkey; Cooyh, cuhi, This word is used when driving donkeys which means to go on; StAnn, Coo-ey, get on; StE, Cooye, driving an ass; StT, Cooy, go on; Port, Kuy, go away.

KUYAH see KU.

kwaab sb dial; ?<QUAW blended with *squab*.

1958 DeC StAnd /kwaab/ an albino negro.

kwaako, kwaaku see GUACO.

kwaamin see QUAMIN.

kwabla sb dial; perh a blend of *squab* + *gobbler*.

1956 Mc Port /kwabla/ a young turkey. (The grown male is /piikak/!)

kwabz sb dial plur or quasi-adj; <*squab*, the unfledged young of birds or hairless young animals. (*OED*, *EDD*.)

1. Companions, equals.

1943 *GL* Clar, Kgn, Port, StAnn, StT, Quabs—companions, equal; Kgn, Port, Squabs. 1955 FGC Man [With disdain:] I and he is not /kwabz/.

2. Specif. Sexual partners.

1957 EB Port.

KWACKWA, kwakwa see QUAQUA.

KWENTA see CUENTA.

kwii-kwii see QUEE-QUEE.

kwisel sb dial derog; <*kriich oul* < *screech-owl*; cf *krichuol*, QUICHOLE.

1958 DeC Tre /kwisél/ albino negro.

kwou sb dial; prob for QUAW, or *craw-(fish)*. =TUMPA QUAW, BLACK JANGA.

1958 DeC gen /kwou/ a black and stubby variety of /jangga/ also called /blak jangga/.

kya /kya/ vb dial, usually const in negative; <*care.* Note: the Ewe language adopted Engl *care* in the forms *kià, kiè*, e.g. in the expression 'I don't care' (Westermann); /kya/ may therefore have been brought to Jamaica rather than developed here, or it may have been brought by some negroes and independently developed here by others. (The palatal *-y* was present in the English word when it was borrowed, and is preserved in dialect elsewhere—cf *ADD care* 1 b.) Adaptations toward StdE pronunc, and spelling-pronunciations, are now frequent: /kyíe, kyér/ etc.; cf CARE HOW.

Care; in neg, also: don't care, no matter. *BL*

1924 Beckwith 200 [Riddle:] No ca how time hard, one coco full pot. 1943 *GL* Man, Mi no kya, I don't care. 1956 Mc /no kyá hou im hóri op/ *No matter how much he hurries.*

kya, kyaa see CARRY.

kyaaf sb dial; prob abbr <*scaffold. BL*

1956 Mc StE (Accom) /kyaaf/—a platform used by sawyers in felling big trees; it is tied to the tree at the required height. Also called /baabi/.

kyaa-kyaa sb dial; etym unknown. Cf *kaia-kaia.*

1943 *GL* Tre, Khya-Khya, old clothes. 1954 LeP StAnn, Old kiah-kiah, clothes (general term). 1956 Mc StAnn /kyaa-kyaa/ old clothes.

kyaan, kyaang see CAN'T. *G N*

kyabiyo sb dial; a form of the word (*OED*) *cabilliau, cabeliau*, codfish; or a readoption of the related Fr *cabillaud*, Du *kabeljauw*. The name is used in Bermuda in other forms: *Cubby Yew, Cobia* and *Cubbyu*, for the fish *Rachycentron canadus*—cf 1933 Beebe 113, 171. A fish of uncertain identity.

1952 FGC StC (Old Harbour) /kyàbiyó/ a fish with flat head, dark colour, one stripe; same type as sucking-fish, but fuller.

kyai see CARRY.

kyamfya yam sb dial; < Twi *ŋkámfé*, a type of yellow yam. The form of the second syllable is prob infl by Engl *camphor* in its older form 'camphire', which is the common Ja folk usage: /kyámfya/. AFU YAM.

1943 *GL* Clar, Camphor yam, afou; Camfor, yellow yam. 1956 Mc Man /wúman kyángfyá/ name applied to yellow yams when they are getting scarce.

KYAN-BUTTER see CAYAN-BUTTER.

KYAN-CROW see CYANCRO.

kyandlhud see CANDLEWOOD.

kyangkro see CYANCRO.

kyantu see *kantu.*

kyar see CARRY, *kya. G*

kyarat /kyárat/ sb dial; a folk-etym form of CORATOE.

1959 LeP StAnd (Irish Tn) /kyárat/ coratoe.

kyari see CARRY.

kyarikta, kyarita sb dial; pronunc of *character.*

1868 Russell 20, Me peak fe de good a him charicta. 1943 *GL* Port, Careta, character. *G*

kyasha see CASHAW.

kyashu see CASHEW.

kyat vb dial; <*scat* int and vb (cf *OED*). To speak to (a child, etc.) sharply to make it go somewhere.

1956 Mc StAnd /kyat di chail bak hya/ *Scold the child and send it back home.*

kyata fut vb phr dial; <*scatter+foot* (i.e. to scatter one's feet).

1943 *GL* Kgn, Catter foot, to run. 1956 Mc StE (Accom) /sí im kyáta fut/ *See him run away!*

kye, kyeri see CARRY.

KYNANDO sb dial; cf Yoruba *kanaŋgo*, smallest hour-glass shaped drum. (Hause 42.) See quot.

1952 Kerr 145, The name of the Bass drum is Kynando, that of the other, Plain Case. Kynando has a ring around it called a Kagga and is made of breadfruit wood. Plain Case is made of trumpet wood.

kyou-kyou-kyou-kyou int phr. See quot.

1958 DeC Port /kyou-kyou-kyou-kyou/ etc.—a sound imitative of any kind of destruction; heard in an account of a man chopping another, of a ship breaking up on the rocks, of a hurricane blowing down a house, and of a two-car collision.

kyuua stik see SKEWER-STICK.

kyuu(-kyuu) see Q, QQ.

laad-mi-don sb dial; from the exclamation evoked from one who must go to the institution: 'Lord, I'm done for!'

1. An almshouse.

1943 *GL* Port, StAnn, Laud me done, poor house, almshouse.

2. A tuberculosis sanatorium.

1943 *GL* Man.

laama /láama/ sb dial joc; from /laa, ma!/ Lord, ma'am!, the exclamation from a beholder when the clothing is seen; cf SHALL-I, *wa-fi-du.* Clothing for a special occasion; often, but not necessarily, new clothes.

1943 *GL* Clar, Lawma, a new dress. 1955 FGC Man, A dress, not necessarily new, not so grand. 1956 Mc Man /láama/ any new article of clothing long waited for. 1957 DeC StE (Accom) /laama/ special clothes, for particular function, e.g. Christmas dance.

laas see LOSS.

laata sb dial; < Sp *lata*, tin plate. A sheet of tin or shallow pan for baking.

1943 *GL* StAnd, Lawta, tin sheet. 1955 FGC Man /láata/ tin baking sheet. 1956 Mc Clar, Man /laata/ flat tin tray for baking.

laba vb dial; cf *EDD*: *lab*, to blab; *lab*, a chatterbox. The present form is prob also in part echoic. Cf also *labrish.*

1954 Reckord *Della* typescript 18, Yu skin black but yu mouth must be white from labber wid de white man.

labaduori sb dial; <*Labrador* (source of saltfish—cf HALIFAX MUTTON) +*-y*, diminutive or familiarizing suffix.

1958 DeC StT /labaduori/ a saltfish fritter.

laba-laba adj[1] and sb[1] dial; iterative of *laba* <*lab*, to blab, let out secrets (cf also *lab* sb, a chatterbox) *EDD*; perh with additional echoism. Talkative; a talkative person, a chatterbox. *G*

1955 FGC Man /laba-laba/—person chat a lot. 1960 LeP Han, Cho! yu tu labba-labba.

laba-laba sb[2] dial; cf *lebe-lebe.*

1958 DeC StE (Accom) /laba-laba/—an excessive, wasteful amount of anything.

laba-laba sb[3] see LOBLOLLY TREE.

laba-laba, lobo-lobo adj[2] dial; cf *EDD lob* sb[1], a lump, and *lubber*, a lout; a heavy, awkward person. *BL*

1956 Mc Man /laba-laba, lobo-lobo/ fat and thick set.

LABBER see *laba.*

LABBRISH, LABERISH, LABRIS see *labrish.*

labilabi see LOBLOLLY TREE.

lablab see LOBLOLLY SWEETWOOD.

LABOUR(ING) see TRUMP(ING).

labrish adj, vb, and sb dial; evid <*lab* vb, to blab, let out secrets (*EDD, OED*) + *-er* + *-ish.* (Since the Std parts of speech are not clearly separable in the dialect, another analysis of the word is possible.)

A. adj: Talkative, gossipy; hence unreliable, untrustworthy.

c1948 *Calypso Tunes,* Woman wa mek you labrish so [?] Shut up you mouth an' gwan. 1958 DeC StT /labrish/ adj—pertaining to an unreliable, no-account person.

B. vb: To chatter, gossip, bear tales.

1943 *GL* Kgn, Man, Port, StAnd, StAnn, StC, Labbrish, Labris, To chat plenty a story; to give plenty news; to talk much. 1954 LeP StE, Laberish, to chat or gossip; StT, Labrish.

C. sb: Idle talk, gossip; stories; news.

1942 Bennett 2, Me 'ave a lot a labrish fe tell yuh. *Ibid* 4, Gimme, Dela, all De labrish from yuh yard. 1943 *GL* Kgn, Man, StC, Labrish, Careless talk, gossip, story, news; StAnn, Labbrish, story. 1954 Reckord *Della* typescript 19, Me hear what you hear, labrish. So me believe nutten.

LABRISHER sb dial.

1943 *GL* Kgn, Labrisher, chatterbox.

LACATAN sb dial joc; transf: the Lacatan banana is relatively short.

1958 DeC StT /lakatan/ a short, stout person—opposite of /langgulala/.

LACE-BARK sb; see quot 1756; *OED* 1756→. The tree *Lagetta lagetto* and its bark.

1756 Browne 371, Frutex 16..The Lagetto, or Lace-Bark Tree..The bark is of a fine texture, very tough, and divides into a number of *laminæ,* which spread into thin webs not unlike lace. 1864 Grisebach 785. 1926 Fawcett 287, Lagetta..Trees with a network of inner bark (bast fibres)..Lace-bark. 1941 Swabey 23, Lace Bark (Lagetto, Whitebark)..This is a very small tree or shrub, and is not a timber tree. It is prized for its bark.

LACEBUG sb. The lacewing fly.

1954 *FG* 599, 644, 645, 647, Lacebug; Index 824/2 Lacewing bug.

LACE CAKE see CASSAVA LACE CAKE.

LACE PLANT sb dial.

1. A fern (of any kind).

1952 FGC StAnd, Lace plant—common fern.

2. *Pilea microphylla.*

1954 *WIMJ* 25, Wild Thyme (Tim); Baby Puzzle; Lace Plant; Artillery Plant.

LACKEY(-DOG) sb dial; <*lackey OED* 2, a hanger-on, a camp-follower + *dog.* A lurking, cowardly dog.

1943 *GL* Kgn, Laky, a laped tail [= *lap-tailed*] greedy dog. 1955 FGC Man /laki-daag/ lurking, cowardly. 1956 Mc Man /láki daag/ A dog that wanders from place to place and gets scraps to eat. One may say of a person /jos laik a laki daag/.

LADY('S) BASKET sb. A basket of decorated thatch straw (or similar materials) used by women for travelling.

1929 Beckwith 49, Very pretty 'lady' baskets are made for a girl's trips to the city. 1958 DeC, see FANCY-BASKET.

LADY COOTE BEAN sb; <*Lady Coote,* wife of Sir Eyre Coote, Lieut.-Governor of Jamaica 1806–8.

1. = CIRCASSIAN BEAD TREE.

1864 Grisebach 785, Lady-Coot [*sic*]: *Adenanthera pavonina.*

2. Prob erron for LADY NUGENT'S ROSE.

1889 Sanguinetti 52, We are indebted to our Governors and their wives..for a few appellations, as..the 'Lady Coote', a snowy white wild flower which flourishes luxuriantly around Stony Hill.

LADY FAN sb. The tree *Carludovica palmata,* used to make hats, fans, etc.

1943 *NHN* I 11 12, A plant which is being increasingly used is the Jippi Jappa or Lady Fan—although this is generally considered to be a palm it really comes from a different family, closely allied.

LADY FANCY (CANE) sb; this could represent *lady's fancy* (sb or adj) or the personification *Lady Fancy.* A variety of ribbon cane.

1952 FGC Port, Lady Fancy, whitish canes with dark stripes.

LADY MUSGRAVE sb obs; for the wife of Sir Anthony Musgrave, Governor of Jamaica, 1877–83.

1889 Sanguinetti 52, Not long ago, a wide, coarse straw hat turned up on one side and artistically decorated with ribbons went by the name of 'Lady Musgrave'.

LADY NUGENT'S ROSE sb; for the wife of Lieut.-Gen. George Nugent, Lieut.-Governor of Jamaica 1801–6. The wild plant *Clerodendron fragrans.*

1889 Sanguinetti 52 (see LADY COOTE BEAN). 1960 UCWI Botany Dept, Lady Nugent's Rose.

LADY('S) FINGER(S) sb.

1. Various plants, specif *Stylosanthes hamata.*

1954 *WIMJ* 31, Donkey Weed; Lady's Fingers; Cheesy Toes; Pencil Flower.

2. Various fruits or vegetables of long and slender form: *Lady('s)-finger banana, okro, pepper.*

1913 Harris 2, Lady's finger banana (see APPLE BANANA). 1952 FGC StAnd, StAnn, StM, StT /liedi-fingga okro/ tall, smooth, round, slightly bent; StC, StT, Lady's-finger okro; StM, Lady's-finger pepper, long, hot.

LADY'S SLIPPER sb; *OED* etc. in other senses. In Jamaica: *Clitoria ternatea,* from the shape of the keel of the flower. *BA G*

1951 FGC Man, Lady's slipper, a wild pea growing on the ground and up over bushes; usually blue, sometimes white, sometimes purplish.

laga-laga vb dial; cf *lag*, drag (*OED* v^2 3). = *logo-logo* vb.

1958 DeC StC.

laga-laga sb dial; cf *logo-logo* adv.

1943 *GL* StT /laga-laga/ plenty.

LAGETO see next.

LAGETTO sb; *OED* 1756→. The LACE-BARK tree.

1696 Sloane 137, Laurifolia arbor..cortice interiore in telas plurimas linearum æmulas extensili..Lagetto. 1725 Sloane II 22, Lageto. 1926 Fawcett 287.

laigz sb dial; etym uncert: this may represent Engl *lag* (cf *baig* = bag, *haig* = hag, etc.), a term used in games (marbles, etc.) and perhaps here of gambling.

1. A chance, an opportunity to gain something.

1943 *GL* no addr, Lyges, chances or favours. 1955 FGC Man, I get a /laigz/; I /tekin a laigz/ off a sweepstake ticket.

2. A trick, a wily device; trickery.

1941 Kirkpatrick 5, Mass B a work a ligues, you know! *Ibid* 40, Bredder Tacooma nebber use so much ligues fe ketch bredder Sinake as wat de capen a de British fleet use 'pon de Hitalian dem.

3. Influence through friends; 'pull'.

1960 F. Milner StAnd, 'How did you get through so fast?' 'I have laigz!'

laka /laka/ normalized /làika/ conj dial; <*like* + A[8]. For dial sp see quot 1943. *BL*

1. A common equiv of StdE *like*, differing only in form. *G*

1790 Moreton 156, 1873 Rampini 180, see A[8]. 1877 Murray *Feedin' 'Perrit* 4, see FOX-TAIL GRASS. 1943 *GL* gen, lacka, lacky, laka, lakka. 1956 Mc Man /him en tuu waiz fi go du sinting laka dat/ *He is too wise to do a thing like that.*

2. In phr *laka se* (see *se*, conj): As if.

1956 Mc Man /him ron laka se dem set daag ata him/ *He ran as if they had set dogs after him.*

laki daag see LACKEY(-DOG).

lala sb dial; evid a phon var of *nana*, grandmother.

1958 DeC StT /lala/ grandmother.

LAMP vb dial or slang; prob from the obeah phr BURN BAD LAMP. To trick (someone), to deceive, befool. **s** *lamp* vb, sb.

1960 EB Port, *Lamper* is well known to me (and to others of my acquaintance). I remember a time a few years ago when it was very popular (verb *lamp*) among schoolboys in Kingston. 1960 LeP StAnd, lamp—to trick, to pull a fast one on someone; He's lamping you—he's fooling you.

LAMP BAT, LAMP FLY sb dial; <*lamp* + BAT. A moth which flies into lamps, often putting them out.

1952 FGC Han /lamp-bat/ hovers around light. StAnd /lamp-flai—hout di lamp at nait/; smaller than bat.

LAMPER sb dial or slang; <LAMP vb + *-er*. One who tricks another, esp one who makes a practice or profession of it.

1954 LeP Kgn, A crafty, cunning person, lamper. 1960 LeP StAnd, Lamper, a man who fools you up, tricks you (financially and otherwise).

LAMP FLY see LAMP BAT.

LAMP-LIGHT sb dial. The time of day when lamps are lighted. *BA*

1958 DeC StAnd, StT /lamp-lait/—a time of day, 5–6 P.M.

LAMP-OUTER sb dial; <*lamp* + *out* vb + *-er*.

1958 DeC StAnd /lamp-outa/ a small firefly (so called because he 'outs' his lamp).

LANCE see WALK AND LANCE.

[**LANCEWOOD** sb also attrib; *OED* 1697→. Trees of the genus *Oxandra*; cf also BLACK LANCEWOOD.

1707 Sloane lvii, For Negligence, they are usually whipt by the Overseers with Lance-wood Switches. 1740 Importance 50, Lance-Wood, of which the wild Indians make their Lances, is a hard Wood, and has a particular dark Colour. 1873 Rampini 75, Whilst bamboos and lance-wood and foliage of all descriptions shaded our path. 1914 Fawcett 201–2, *Oxandra*..Lancewood.]

LAND BREEZE sb; *OED* 1667→. A wind which blows from land out to sea. *BA BL N*

p1660 *State of Ja* MS Egerton 2395 fol 489b, From Eight at night till nine in the morning it frequently blowes westerly w[ch] they call Land breezes; wth this wind the vessels git out of the Harbours. 1687 Blome 5, These Easterly Winds commonly blow till about six or seven in the Afternoon, and then they change to the West; which the Islanders call Land-Briezes, because they blow off the Shoar. 1890 Thomas 44 [In the mountains:] The cold land breeze among the forest trees.. The keen land breeze drove me back to the hut. (1960 current. FGC.)

LAND KICK-UP sb dial; <*land* + *kick-up*, to flirt or bob the tail in walking. The Jamaican local name for the Oven-bird.

1847 Gosse 151–2, When walking or standing, the tail is continually flirted up in the manner of the Wagtails, whence the local name of *Kick-up*..*Land Kick-up. Seiurus aurocapillus.* 1956 Jeffrey-Smith 89.

LAND-MAN sb dial. One who collects the rent of a WAPPEN-BAPPEN.

1935 Martinez in *Gleaner* 3 Oct 35, the 'lan man' as he is better known, always comes armed on rent collecting days, which..is fixed for Sunday morning.

langge adj dial cant; cf LANGO; also Ewe *leŋgee*, tall, thin. In the usage of the St Thomas AFRICAN cults: tall, straight, long.

1953 Moore gloss.

langgulala /lánggulála, lánggulàala, lànggilála/ sb dial, also attrib or adj; origin uncert, but cf Hausa *langalanga*, a tall person of slight build; anything long and slender. Cf also LANGO, *lengge-lengge*.

1. A very tall, thin person. Often used as an epithet.

1943 *GL* StAnn, Longgulawla, a tall person,—(mostly by men) a curse; StE, Langolala, very tall; StT, extra tall person. 1954 LeP Man, Longu laala; StAnn, Longalaala; StE, Longulāla—very tall man. 1948 U.Newton IV 5, But is what sweet the langulala boy? 1956 Mc StE (Accom) /lánggulàala/ A very tall thin child or woman—the word is not here used of a man: the corresponding term applied to a man is /lengge-lengge/. 1961 DeB in *Gleaner* 6 Aug 20, Langoo-lawla; R. M. Murray *ibid*, Longilala.

2. Drawn out, straggling.

1943 *GL* Tre, Langy la la, straggling.

LANGO adj dial; cf *long* + *-o*.

1943 *GL* StE, Lango adj—tall.

LANGOLALA, LANGOO-LAWLA, LANGYLALA see *langgulala*.

LANTERN-JAW SNAPPER sb dial; descriptive. See quots.

1950 Smith, *Priacanthus arenatus* is called *lantern jaw* (Pedro Bay.) 1952 FGC StJ, StM, Lantern-jaw snapper—much like pot snapper; jawbone thinner; slightly pink with two spots about the tail.

LAP vb dial; *OED* v^2 3 →1876; arch in most senses, but current in Jamaica. *BL*

1. To wrap, enwrap.

1952 FGC StM, Sea-cat—cousin to octopus; claw you and lap you. 1957 *PFM* 219, Lapped Herring..Dip herring into egg mixture and fry in hot fat.

2. To fold; specif, of a dog's tail, to fold under; also fig: to show signs of shame, to restrain presumption. *G*

1956 Mc Man /im a shiema-daag—lap im tiel/ *He's a shamer-dog—he turns his tail under between his legs.* 1956 BLB Man [Said to a cheeky child or servant:] /yu beta lap yu tiel an bihiev yusef/; *ibid* /misis mi en so shiem, mi dis lap mi tiel kom we/ *I was so ashamed I quickly slunk away.*

LAPPER /lapa/ sb dial; <LAP+-*er*. A fritter with salt-fish folded in, or a ball of salt-fish covered with flour.

1958 DeC Clar /lapa/ a fritter covered with saltfish and then 'lapped' over; Kgn, see ROUGH.

LAP-TAIL adj dial; for *lap-tailed*: see LAP. With its tail between its legs. *BL*

1943 *GL* Kgn, see LACKEY(-DOG).

LAPWING sb; *OED* in diff sense. Applied in Jamaica to the WHITE-WING DOVE. *G*

1847 Gosse 304, Whitewing Dove (Lapwing). 1952 FGC Han, StT /lapwing/=white-wing; feed in trees; go about in company. 1956 Jeffrey-Smith 107, Another local name is Lapwing.

LARRY sb dial; cf *EDD Larry* sb^2, liquid mortar, grout.

1943 *GL* StM, Larry, thick soup.

LAS see LOSS.

LASH vb dial slang; cf *EDD* 15: *lash*, to work at anything with great vigour. To fornicate; to move violently during sexual intercourse. *BL G*

1958 DeC general.

LASHER sb dial slang. See quot. *G*

1958 DeC general /lasha/—a man renowned for his sexual adventures. Hence COUNT LASHER as a nickname../lash larúu/ is a nickname with similar meaning, but I have no clue to the second element.

LASITA sb dial; etym unknown.

1943 *GL* Kgn, Lasita, dog.

LAST-LAST adj dial; iterative of *last* adj. The very last. *BL G*

1912 McK *Ballads* 50, see RAISE.

LAST LICK sb. A children's game in which each tries to touch, tap, or in some way strike the other last before parting. *BA BL G*

1947 U.Newton II 15, Stones were among my best friends ..For giving 'last licks' to speedy school mates, I found them ideal..until, one day, when I was giving 'last lick' to a little girl the stone collided with her mouth.

LAS'Y /laasi/ sb dial; <*last* adj or sb +-*y*. The last or youngest child in a family.

1912 McK *Songs* 89, To buy drops fe las'y* son..*Lasty (lahsty), pet name for the Benjamin of a family.

LATE sb dial; cf *EDD* 'in the late', Scots. A late hour of the day. *BL G*

1924 Beckwith 100, Travel de whole day till late tek dem.

LATED adj dial; aphetic <*belated. OED* 'poet'; →1898. Made late, delayed, behind time. s. *BA BL G*

1907 Jekyll 81, Wolf come an' call:—'Little Pig, you ready?' Pig say:—'You lated; I go and come back already'.

LAUGHY-LAUGHY adj dial; iterative of *laughy. G*

1947 U.Newton III 8, He was what we call a very 'laughy-laughy boy'. You know he liked to laugh at jokes and to poke fun at people.

LAW sb attrib dial; from the sense of *law* as a source of power or punishment. An intensive word, heavily stressed. See GOD.

1962 BLB 24 /if a kech yu, a giv yu a laa fom-fom tide *If I catch you today I'll give you a sound thrashing.*

LAWMA see *laama*.

LAWTA see *laata*.

LAWYER FOOT sb dial joc; evid from the metaphor of the feet, like a lawyer, being one's means of evading the law. To apply lawyer foot: to run away.

1956 BLB StJ /aplai laaya fut/ make one's escape.

LAY-HIM-STRAIGHT adj phr dial. That lays (something) straight—specif, a preparation for straightening hair.

1950 Pioneer 21, She get one big horsemane comb, one bristle-comb brush an a jar of lay-him-straight hair dressin.

LAZY adj dial. Said of wood that won't hold fire or continue to burn once ignited.

1952 FGC Man.

LEAD DRUM /liid drom/ sb dial. A drum that leads the rhythm—more highly pitched than the *banda*; a PLAYING DRUM.

1953 Moore 127.

LEAF-OF-LIFE sb. *Bryophyllum pinnatum*, any leaf of which, dropped on the ground, sprouts a new plant at each indentation in its edge. (This probably explains the origin of the name, but its medicinal uses are also associated.) *G*

1927 Beckwith 20, Leaf-of-life..For a cold or fever, boil 5 yam leaves with one 'Leaf-of-Life', and drink as tea. 1952 FGC Port, StAnn, StM, StT /liif-av-laif/; StE /liif-a-laif/; Tre /liif-ang-laif/. 1953 *WIMJ* 243, Leaf of Life. The leaves of this succulent are much used for colds.

LEAF-SPOT DISEASE sb. A disease of bananas in which spots appear on the leaves as the first obvious symptom. *BA*

[1903 Earle in *Jrl N.Y. Bot. Gard.* iv, 1914 Fawcett 94, The 'banana spot disease', spread so rapidly that very prompt measures had to be taken, and the plants were destroyed by fire.] 1954 *FG* 288, Spraying banana fields with a copper fungicide for the control of Leaf Spot disease has been a regular..routine in banana cultivation in Jamaica ever since the disease became virulent in 1936..[The fungus is] *Mycosphacrella musicola.*

LEAN-'PON-ME see *liin-pan-mi*.

LEANY adj dial; *OED* →1602.

1958 DeC StT /liini/ adj.—very thin, maaga.

LEAST POND GAULIN sb ornith. The GREEN GAULIN.

LEATHER-COAT (JACK) /láda-kúot/ sb; cf *OED leather-jacket* 1770→. A fish of the jack type with a tough skin: *Oligoplites saurus.*

1756 Browne 452, Saurus 1..The Leather-coat..This species is distinguished from the rest of the tribe by its striated skin. 1952 FGC StE /láda kúot/—shine, have tough skin; StJ, silvery-looking, take off skin; StM /lada-kuot jak/.

LEATHER-COAT PLUM sb arch or obs; see quots. A variety of the SPANISH PLUM.

1756 Browne 229, There is a variation of this plumb, called the *Leather-coat*, from the appearance of its skin; but this proceeds from the dry soil in which it is produced. 1837 Macfadyen 227–8, Spondias purpurea. *Leather-coat* or Red Spanish-Plum..It is not liable to be infected by insects, from the thickness of the rind serving as a protection against their attacks.

LEAVE-OVER sb dial; for *left-overs*.

1958 DeC StT /liiv-uoba/ left over food.

LEBBAY-LEBBAY, LEBBEY-LEBB see *lebe-lebe*.

LEBBY sb dial; etym unknown.

1943 *GL* StE, Lebby, full, heavy breast.

lebe-lebe adv and sb; etym unknown—prob echoic or symbolic; cf *laba-laba*.

A. adv: Wastefully.

1943 *GL* Kgn, Lebbey-lebbey, in a wasteful way.

B. sb: Noisy, excessive chatter.

1943 *GL* West, Lebbay-lebbay, bad talking. 1955 FGC Man /lebe-lebe/ making a lot of noise.

leda /léda/ sb dial; pronunc of *ladder*; the normal dial reflex would be /lada/. (But cf /lada/occas for *leather*, as in LEATHER-COAT.) *BL*

LEEWARD sb; also attrib. Cf WINDWARD. *BA*

1. The westward part of the Island.

1774 Long II 319, The many nautical, or seafaring terms of expression, in use here among the planters from time out of mind, were probably introduced by the first English settlers; who, for some years, alternately followed privateering, and planting. I shall enumerate a few of them, with their explanation: *Cook-room.* Kitchen. *Leeward.* Every place situated to the Westward. *Windward.* The contrary. 1828 Marly 135, It hab be a grandy big estate, much grandy better dan Paradise to leeward.

2. Attrib. In a westward position or direction.

1731–2 *Jrl Assembly* 55, That four flying parties be constantly kept out, one at each of the aforesaid settlements, to scour the woods adjacent; the windward parties to consist of fifteen whites and thirty-five blacks, and five of the said whites to be officers; and the leeward parties of eight white men and seventeen blacks.

lef /lef/ vb dial; <*left*, past tense or pple of *leave*; one of a small number of verbs in which, in the dialect, the past rather than the present form of StdE became the base. *BL G N*

1. trans: Leave. *T*

1873 Rampini 124, Den Hawk spring 'pon Ground Dove, an' tear up him feathers..an' lef (leave) him fe dead 'pon de dirt. 1950 Pioneer 86, Left me alone, Bredda Anancy. 1956 Mc StAnd /mi sari yu afi lef wi kompani nou/.

2. intr: Leave. *T*

1956 Mc St And /mi aamuos redi fi lef nou/.

3. repr Engl passive: Be left, remain, remain over. *T*

1950 Pioneer 72, De one dat lef him gie him wife.

4. In impers phr developed from sense 3, (*jos, uonli*) *lef fi*: (only, merely) to remain (to do something, or for something to happen), to be just short of; to be all but, nearly (reaching a point, condition, or point of action).

1933 Perkins in *Outlook* 30 Dec, You only lef fe..go a prison. [*It only remains for you to go to prison, Nothing is left for you but to go to prison.*] 1941 Kirkpatrick 2, 'Im heat heat [*kept on eating*] tell 'im belly jus' lef' fe bus. 1943 Bennett 8, One fire spark fly t'ru de door, Pass ovah Joseph cap, Jus leff soh fe bun my puff-sleeve. *Ibid* 19, An me heart dis leff fe bruck up. 1958 DeC /i lef fi go rien/ *It's just about to start raining;* /mi jos lef fi go torn aan di mashiin/ *I'm just about to turn on the machine, it only remains for me to turn on the machine.*

lef-aan sb dial; <*left-on*, leave on (the fire), in contrast to *tap-i-a-paas*.

1958 DeC StT /freke; lef-aan/ names for a coconut run-down.

LEF' HAND COCO see next.

lef-man (koko) sb dial; *lef* 3+*man*: the one who remains. A variety of coco valued for its hardness which makes it keep well, though it takes long to cook. The name suggests these enduring qualities. Also called COMMANDER, DUKE COCO. (Sometimes, BLUE COCO.)

1877 Murray *Feedin' 'Perrit* 15, Him gi'e me dis piece o' lefman cocoa. 1910 Anderson-Cundall 3, Lef'man cocoa 'tick 'pon you belly rib. 1929 Beckwith 17, In Mandeville were enumerated the 'Lef' Hand' [error for *lef-man*] as the hardest..etc. 1952 FGC gen /léf-mán koko/; StC, very hard, can stay in ground 3 years; old-time name for Commander, Duke.

lega /léga/ sb dial; like *leda*, an unexpected pronunc of *ladder*. (LeP.)

lege-lege[1]**, legi-legi** vb dial; iterative of a base of uncert origin—cf such Engl words as *lag*, *lug*, and also Ja *logo-logo*.

1. To go slowly.

1943 *GL* Tre, Leggy leggy—linger.

2. To move something heavy slowly and with difficulty.

1958 DeC StAnd /legi-legi/ to drag, heave, or alternately pick up and put down a heavy object. Tre /lingga-lingga wid/ to heave a heavy and awkward load along; equiv to /lege-lege/.

lege-lege[2] sb dial; cf *lege-lege*[1] to which this is prob allied through association of mass and quantity; cf also Ngombe *légɛlɛgɛ*, to be full, be filled, fill itself; Ewe *logoo*, fat, paunchy.

1. Plenty, abundance.

1943 *GL* Kgn, Leggeh-leggeh, plenty.

2. See quot.

1956 LeP StE (Eld), lege-lege, fat, loose skin.

3. Of mixed quality. (Perh a diff word.)

1958 DeC StE (Accom) /lege-lege/ some good, some bad—e.g. of produce, or of a group of men.

LEGGINS see next.

leginz sb dial; < Fr *légumes*. A bunch of soup-vegetables (skellion, pumpkin, thyme, sometimes a slice of carrot, cabbage, etc.) tied up and sold in markets. (Prob introduced by French émigrés from Haiti—cf 1835 Madden I 104.)

c 1915 FGC StAnd /léginz/ for soup. 1954 LeP StAnd, Leggins, vegetables. 1956 Mc StE /leginz/—soup vegetables..tied together in a bundle.

lego /légo (bíis)/ adj dial; <*let-go*.

1. Let-go, loose, disorderly, out of control. *G*

1943 *GL* Kgn, Leggo, unkept. 1952 FGC StE, a /légo/ head of cabbage = open, 'it don't tie' therefore it does not form a head.

2. attrib, in phr *lego-beast*: an animal or person without an owner or protector, that runs wild; anyone of loose morals.

1943 *GL* Port, Leggo beast, one that is under no control; StAnd, Leggo beese, wild, runabout. 1956 Mc Man /légo bíis/ a tramp, a person without friends or protectors; implies also badly behaved. 1958 Dr Figuerroa StAnd, also applied to a loose woman.

LEMBEY sb dial; etym unknown, but cf *timbim.*

1943 *GL* StC, Lembey, an old sore.

LEMON GRASS sb, also attrib; from the odour. The lemon-scented grass *Cymbopogon citratus.* Also called FEVER GRASS. *BA G N*

1801 Dancer 90, [For a recurrent fever] the patient may go to bed an hour before the period of its return, and get into a perspiration by drinking some warm sangree —brandy toddy—ginger tea—lemon grass tea. 1814 Lunan I 442, Lemon Grass..This plant, which was introduced about fifteen years ago, has been pretty generally cultivated, and has thriven well, in most parts of Jamaica..The root is strong, woody, and tastes something like lemon peel, but more bitter. 1953 *WIMJ* 246, Fever Grass; Lemon Grass. This is one of the important oil grasses, producing lemon grass oil which is used medicinally and in perfumery. 1954 *FG* 226, Fever Grass or Lemon Grass..It grows in tufts and has a very sweet odour.

LENGA-LENGA, lengge-lengge, lenggi-lenggi adj and sb dial; cf Ewe *leŋgee*, tall, thin; Hausa *langa-langa*, a tall person of slight build. Cf *langgulala.* As adj: Tall, slender; as sb: A tall, slender person.

1943 *GL* StT, Lenga-lenga, slender. 1956 Mc StE (Accom) /léengge-léengge/ tall and thin (person)—the vowel exaggeratedly long to emphasize the length of the person. 1958 DeC StT (2) /lenggi-lenggi/ a tall thin person.

LENKIE /lengki/ adj dial; <*lanky*, perh with concurrent infl of Ewe *leŋgee*, tall, thin. *G*

1954 LeP StE, Lenkie, meagre, thin.

LENNON adj or sb attrib; etym uncert: perh <*lemman*, lover, beloved; but cf *EDD lenno*, a child, Scots. See quot.

1924 Beckwith 72 [Song: the mother's spirit, in guise of a snake, sings to her boy:] Come take me up, Come take me up, Simon Tootoos, lennon boy.

LENOOCO adj dial rare; etym unknown.

1943 *GL* StE, Lenooco, very short.

LEOPARD SKIN sb obs. A skin condition in negroes in which the pigment is lost in spots or patches. See quot.

1820 Thompson 4, This peculiar secretion is liable to disease, particularly on the hands and feet, giving rise to a singular mottled appearance, which is called leopard skin.

lep vb dial; <*leap*, cf *EDD* vb and sb[2], *lep*, Irel and Engl midlands. To walk briskly.

1943 *GL* Kgn, Lep, to walk. 1955 FGC Man /lep/ walk briskly.

LESSER BROOMWEED sb bot obs; cf BROOMWEED. In Macfadyen's use: *Sida spinosa* (ident 1926 Fawcett 111).

1837 Macfadyen 79, Sida minor. *Lesser Broom-weed.*

LET-GO (BEAST) see *lego.*

LEWIS DALEY sb dial. A variety of sweet-potato.

1929 Beckwith 17 [In Mandeville:] the 'Lewis Daley' is long and big.

li /li/ occas /lii/ adj dial; a reduced form of *little*, and prob in the second example of Engl dial *leetle*, but there may be concurrent Afr infl, cf Gullah *li*, young, small, recently born (Turner 198). Little. *BL*

1912 McK *Songs* 33, Stealin' one lee kiss! 1943 *GL* no addr, Li, little. 1956 Mc StAnd /da li gal ya/ *That little girl*; StE /li yaazi-kin fela/ *Little yaws-skinned boy.*

LIAD see next.

LIARD /láiad/ sb dial, also attrib; <*liard*, cf *EDD*, Somerset, Devon, Cornw. A liar.

1862 Clutterbuck 53, You is a cussed liard. 1943 *GL* StAnd, StC, Liard, Liad, liar. 1955 Bennett *Oonoo Lie!* All de lie gwine do de liard dem Is rotten off dem tongue! 1957 JN StM, What a liard boy! *BL G N T*

liba, liba-spat see LIVER, LIVER SPOT.

LIBIDIBI sb bot; *OED* (s.v. *divi-divi*) 1853→. = DIVIDIVI.

1837 Macfadyen 330. 1920 Fawcett 96. 1941 Swabey 19. 1954 *WIMJ* 28.

LIBWELL adj or sb dial; <*live-well.* Reckless; (one who is) too free in spending.

1925 Beckwith 78 [Prov:] Lib'-well can't lef' berry-well alone. 1927 Anderson-Cundall 84 [Prov:] Libwell man go tell gubner [Governor] howdy. 1943 *GL* StJ, Libwell, reckless.

LICCA TREE sb bot; *OED* 1756→. *Zanthoxylum spinosum.*

1756 Browne 207, Sapindus 2..The Licca Tree. I found this shrub in the Borough in St James's: it is remarkable for the prickliness of its trunk, which seldom exceeds seven or eight feet in height. 1864 Grisebach 785. 1920 Fawcett 178, see SUARRA WOOD.

LICK /lik/ occas /lit/ sb and vb; cf *EDD lick* 13. This word is far more commonly used in Jamaica than in Britain or US in these senses—more than *hit*, *strike*, or other synonyms. *BL G*

A. sb: 1. A stroke, a blow. *BA*

1907 Jekyll 175–6, If Rolling Calf catch you, give you one lick, you dead. 1957 JN, Bull-frog dem dead yet?.. Must get a lick off a him.

2. Absol in plur: see quot. Obs. *T*

1833 *Second letter from Legion* 27, This ebony bush.. contains a very small but sharp species of prickle; it is tied up in bundles like a birch rod. In some cases, after the punishment is inflicted with the whip, the licks, as they call them, are also inflicted with this ebony bush.

B. vb: 1. To hit, strike, beat. *BA T*

1907 Jekyll 136, An' Tiger get cross begun to lick, an' de first man him lick was his godson. 1956 Mc Man /bat yuuz tu lik baal/ *A bat is used to strike a ball*; StE /im gwoin lik di daag/ *He is going to hit the dog.* 1957 JN Bohemia, What a facey gal! Lick him back..Bus him mouth. Lick him again.

2. With postposed adverbs: *lick up*, stir up, fling up; *lick down*, beat or fling to the ground; *lick 'way*, strike off. *BA T*

1837 James 6, He raise up his stick three times to lick me down. I said, you can't lick me down, Sir, the law does not allow that. 1907 Jekyll 111, Blacksmit' get vex, tell him he going to lick him down with the iron. 1950 Pioneer 98, De big backra car dem A lick up de dus' in a we face. 1958 Rowe StE (Accom) /shi lik doun wan a di laim a doti/ [*She flung one of the limes to the ground.*] 1960 *CLS* 145 /lit/. 1961 BLB [To a man chopping branches off a tree:] /lik we di wan pan yu han/.

3. To run fast. *BA*

1956 Mc StE /im lík húom/ He dashed home.

4. In the name of the game *lick and run*: one child taps another and runs away; cf LAST LICK.

1957 JN Clar, I love to lick and run.

LICK AN' PRAN vb phr dial; abbr phr *to give a lick and a promise.* To tidy up.

1950 Pioneer 96, Dis 'oman scrub de floor, She lick an' pran de dutty room.

LICK-AN'-'TAN'-UP see *lik-an-tan-op.*

LICKERISH adj dial; *OED* 2 →1879. Of persons: 'Fond of delicious fare'; greedy.

1943 *GL* Kgn, Lickrish, like dainty things—sweet mouthed; StJ, Lickrish, greedy. *BA G T*

LICK-FOOT sb dial; <LICK vb+*foot,* i.e. where one beats one's feet (*foot* is also plur).

1954 LeP StAnn, Dance or wild party—lickfoot.

LICKING-MATCH sb dial. A free-for-all fight with sticks; a brawl.

1907 Jekyll 46, They made a bargain between themselves that, when the Ratta deep in dancing, Doba must out the lamp, then the licking-match commence.

LICKING-STUMP sb.

1907 Jekyll 155, Lickin' stump—a bee-tree-stump, with honey trickling out that one can lick.

LICKLE see *likl.*

LICKPOT sb dial; *OED,* 'Lickpot *obs.* 1. A name for the first finger' →c1475. The forefinger. *BA*

1943 *GL* StT, Lickpot, the first finger. 1956 Mc Man StAnd /lik-pat/ the forefinger, the others being /long-man/ (middle finger) /ring-man, likl-man, big-tom/ (thumb).

LICKRISH see LICKERISH.

LICK STICK vb phr; <LICK vb+*stick* sb; see STICK-LICKING. =PLAY STICK.

LICK-WEED sb dial; perh abbr of LICORICE, which enters into other names. *Abrus precatorius.*

1927 Beckwith 20, Lick-weed (Licorice)..Administered to babies or to adults for constipation, mashed in a mortar and boiled like tea. 1954 *WIMJ* 28 (cf JOHN-CROW BEAD).

LICKY-LICKY adj dial; iterative of *licky,* which may be <*lick* vb, but prob also assoc with LICKERISH. *BL*

1. Enjoying food and variety in food; being choosy about food.

1925 Beckwith 13, Licky-licky fly follow coffin go a hole..Greed causes a fly to follow a coffin into the grave. 1950 Pioneer 56, Doah me no got long bella-gut An me no licky-licky, Me can put weh a hearty meal. 1952 FGC StM, Licky-licky—pick a bit here and pick a bit there of different things.

2. Sponging; cf HENKA, HINKA(-HINKA).

1956 Mc Port /liki-liki/ man—person who calls in hope of getting something to eat. Also /lik-lik/.

LICKY-LICKY sb dial; =LICK vb+*i* (he) iterated. See quot and transl; Beckwith's spelling obscures the construction.

1924 Beckwith 180, An' he see a horse an' lick de horse.. Horse said de licky-licky no hurt him, but de 'brute' him call him. [*Horse said it wasn't that he licked him that hurt him, but that he called him 'brute'.*]

LICORICE see LIQUORICE.

lidi sb dial; prob a name, *Liddy,* for *Lydia.* A variety of sweet-potato, white both inside and out.

1952 FGC StC /lidi/.

lidong see LIDUNG.

LIDUNG /lidong, lidoung/ vb dial; <*lay,* lie +*down,* in dial sp reg 'dung', representing the pronunc /dong/. Lie down. *BA BL*

1942 Bennett 47, Him dah lidung now Flat-flat pon him belly. 1943 *GL* StAnd, Lidung, to lay down; StJ, Lidung, lie down.

LIE-AND-STORY /lai-an-tuori/ sb dial; <*lies and stories.* Gossip, slander. *BA BL*

1943 *GL* StJ, lian tory, carrying of news; no addr, Lie an story, gossip. 1950 Pioneer 33, see *koskos.*

LIE DOWN see LIDUNG.

LIE DOWN SET vb phr dial. Lie in wait.

1912 McK *Songs* 49, An' grass-lice lie do'n set.*.. *Waiting for us.

LIFFUP see LIF'-UP.

LIFT-COAT PEPPER sb dial; descr—see quot. A variety of *Capsicum* pepper.

1952 FGC Port /lif-kuot pepa/ very hot, lifts coat like a woman.

LIF'-UP /líf-op/ vb dial; ellipt from some such phr as *lift up one's feet, lift up the anchor,* etc.

1. To move, go away from a place. *G*

1943 Bennett 23, She sey, Jamaica man Wen dem ready fe liff-up Walk wey an leff you one. 1955 Bennett *Gawn a match,* Dem done nyam off me big-big lunch An lif up gawn dem ways!

2. To 'shut up shop' and go away.

1942 Bennett 11, Me day liff up now yah Dinah, Lacka ow dem lock up store An' everybady dah go home, Me naw go sell much more.

3. To move rapidly away on one's feet, or by some other means.

1941 Kirkpatrick 18, But no, dem lif' up an' try fe run. [Said of naval vessels.] 1943 *GL* Clar, Lif'-up, go faster.

4. Of a bus or other vehicle: To drive or go fast.

1942 Bennett 43, De bus a liff-up now bwoy! Wat a way de breeze feel sweet! 1943 *GL* Port, Liffup, drive fast.

LIGHT adj dial; <*light* adj, referring to weight, or perh *OED* 22, dizzy, giddy. Weak. *BA BL*

1956 Mc StAnd /ef dem duon iit fuud, dem tu lait—dem kyaang wok trang/ *If they don't have something solid to eat* (to begin the day) *they're too weak—they can't work well.*

LIGHT vb intr dial; *OED* v^2 1b →1596. To dawn; (of morning light) to break. Also const *out.*

1924 Beckwith 93, The boy went after the Old Witch man and overtake him and mash one of the egg, and day light. 1951 Murray 2, Day da light an' me wan' go home. 1952 FGC StT /die a lait out/ *Dawn is breaking.*

LIGHT A CANDLE ON see BAD CANDLE.

LIGHT-'PON-'TICK see MOONLIGHT-'PON-'TICK.

LIGHTWOOD sb; *OED* of other trees.

1929 Beckwith 128, see *kantu.*

LIGHT-WORK PEOPLE sb obs. The THIRD GANG on a sugar estate in slavery times, who did the lightest work.

1838 Kelly 19, The coffee is then picked—broken berries and triage carefully taken out by light-work people and invalids.

LIGNUM DURUM sb bot; <Lat *lignum durum,* hard wood.

1. *Sloanea jamaicensis,* =BREAK-AX 1.

1926 Fawcett 90, Lignum durum. 1941 Swabey 21, Greenheart—(Breakax, Ironwood, Lignum durum)..This is a tall, slender tree..Its terrific weight, density and strength are well known.

2. *Ocotea staminea*, =SPICEWOOD.

1914 Fawcett 213, Lignum dorum [*sic*]. 1941 Swabey 24. 1952 FGC StAnn /língkum dóro/ make shingles.

LIGNUM RORUM sb bot; see quot 1837. The tree *Zanthoxylum spinosum* ('a very variable species'—1920 Fawcett 179).

1696 Sloane 137, Lauro affinis, Terebinthi folio alato, ligno odorato candido, flore albo..Lignum rorum. 1837 Macfadyen 191, Swartz informs us that this tree is known in Jamaica by the name of *Lignum rorum*, being a corruption of *Ligno Rhodio*, which it resembles in giving out, when rubbed or heated, a strong odour. 1920 Fawcett 178, see SUARRA WOOD.

LIGNUM-VIT, LIGNUMVITA, LIGNUM-VITEE see next.

LIGNUM-VITÆ /nínggam-baiti, ningkam-baiti/ sb; p1660 lignum vitee, 1661 lignum vit, 1790 lignumvita; *OED* 1655→. The tree *Guiacum officinale*, and its very hard wood, used for furniture, etc., and medicinally: see quots. *BA*

p1660 State of Jamaica 611, Lignum vitee, Speckle wood, Granadila Ebony and others wch are frequently exported. 1661 Hickeringill 17, Gum Guiac. Lignum vit-Trees, Cassia, &c. 1790 Moreton 22, Mars—for the weakness in his joints, to drink plentifully of the decoction of lignumvita. 1920 Fawcett 163–4, Lignum vitæ..The wood is very fine, close, and even in grain; it is durable and tough, splitting with very great difficulty..Guiacum resin is obtained from the wood. 1927 Beckwith 23, Nigum-bitey (Lignum vitæ)..'To cure any bruise' of man or beast grate the gum, mix it with rum, and bind it on the injured place. 1943 *GL* StAnd, Ningambity—Lignumvitæ.

LIGUES see *laigz*.

liin-pan-mi sb dial; repr *lean-upon-me*. =*heng-pan-mi*.

1956 Mc StE (Accom) /liin-pan-mi, lin-pan-mi/ a basket, made of straw, which is hung over the shoulders by a string. It has a cover which slips right over the basket.. the handle passes through the cover. 1958 DeC StC /liin-pan-mii/ = /namsak/.

lik-an-tan-op sb dial; <*lick and stand up*. Large mats made of banana-leaf ribs, or river rushes, etc.; so called because they are coarse and stiff enough to stand leaning if firmly placed so.

1943 *GL* Clar, Lick-and-tan-hop, a long hard mat made of the stems of banana leaves. 1955 FGC Man /lik-an-tan-op/ coarse river-rush mat; hang on veranda; will stand leaning.

LIKE-A see *laka*.

LIKE WHAT adv phr; prob ellipt from *like I don't know what*, or the like. An intensifying or emphatic phrase, said when words fail: extremely, inexpressibly. *G*

1958 JB StAnd, He's fresh like what! *He's fresh as anything, extremely fresh.*

liki adj dial; a reduced form of *little*; cf *li, lili*, and next.

1952 FGC Tre, Guma has a /blak liki siid/.

likl /likl/ emphatic /liikl/ adj dial; reduced forms of *little, leetle*; cf *li*. Dial sp *lickle*. Little. *BL T*

1942 Bennett 10, Lady wid de pretty lickle bwoy Buy candy. 1952 FGC Tre /baklas flai—liikl blak wan/. 1957 JN, lickle bit.

likl-likl adv dial; iterative of *likl*. Little by little, bit by bit, in small quantities.

1952 FGC StAnd /yu mos duu it likl-likl/; StAnn, Cabbage, carrot, radish, beet, lettuce—/aal likl-likl gruo dem hier/ *Everybody here grows them in small quantities.*

likrish see LIQUORICE.

LILAC sb; *OED* in diff sense. The tree *Melia azederach*, now called WEST INDIAN LILAC.

1774 Long III 753, Lilac, or Hoop-Tree—*Syringa baccifera*. 1790 Beckford I 32, The tufted plumes of the lilac. 1801 Dancer 363, Lilac—Hoop Tree (Melias).—Bark of this tree, Dr Roxburgh says, is used in the East-Indies for the Peruvian Bark. 1814 Lunan I 79–80, Bead, Hoop, or Lilac, Tree..This is a native of Syria..and thrives well in Jamaica.

lili adj dial; iteration of *li*, a reduced form of *little*; dial sp: *lillie, lilly, lily*. s LILLY-LILLY. *G*

1803 Dallas I 113, 'Tap, Massa Governor,' said he, 'top lilly bit'. 1943 *GL* StAnn, StC, StJ, StM, Tre, Lily, lillie—little. 1954 LeP Kgn, Very small, tiny—lille bit. 1956 Mc StAnd /gal, get lili sinting rob op yosef/ *Girl, get a little of something to rub yourself with.*

lili-chiini adj dial; <*lili*+CHEENY. Tiny-little.

1943 *GL* StE, Lilichini, very small.

LILLE, LILLIE, LILLY, LILY see *lili*.

LILY TROTTER sb dial; from its habit of walking on water-lily leaves. The bird *Jacana spinosa*. s POND COOT.

1952 Carley in *Gleaner* March?, The lily trotter..has long splayed toe[s] to enable it to walk easily upon pond vegetation and water lily pads.

LIMA BEAN sb; *OED* 1858→, *ODS* 1831→, *DA* 1822→. A variety of *Phaseolus lunatus*.

1756 Browne 292, Phaseolus 6..The Lima Bean. This climbing plant was introduced to Jamaica some years ago, and is since much cultivated. 1774 Long III 786, Lima bean..This is esteemed the most delicious bean in the world. 1793 Edwards I 195, see INDIAN KALE. 1814 Lunan 434, Lima Bean—This is perennial. *BA T*

LIMBA see next.

LIMBER /limba/ adj and vb dial; cf *OED*, 'supple, flexible, lithe and nimble'. *BL G*

A. adj: Slender; easily bending.

1912 McK *Ballads* 18. 1943 *GL* Tre, Limber, slender. 1955 FGC Man /limba/ slimmy-like.

B. vb: To bend.

1943 *GL* StE, Limba, to bend. 1951 Murray 10, Sake a de pain a back me kean limba [I can't bend].

LIMB-LIMB adj dial; iterative of *limb*. Full of stalks, stalky.

1952 FGC StE /bakra kalalu/ low, limb-limb, but tall, grow straight up.

LIMBO adj dial.

c1940 HPJ, Limbo, talkative.

LIME-BLOSSOM, LIMEY sb dial. An unidentified bird; see quot.

1952 FGC Han /láimi, làim bláasam/ belly resembles a ripe lime; wings black; comes out after rain.

LIME MANGO sb dial. A variety of mango which smells like the lime fruit.

1952 FGC StM.

LINGER-LINGER WITH vb phr; iterative of *linger*. *G*

1958 DeC Tre, see *lege-lege*[1].

LION sb dial slang.

1960 LeP StAnd, Lion—a 'blood' about town, a 'hot boy'.

LION-ANT sb ?obs; cf *OED*, which, however, puts together citations for the *ant-lion* (genus *Myrmeleon*) and this (which is genus *Formica*); the first quot in this sense: 1774. An ant (*Formica leo*); see quot.

1756 Browne 439, Formica 1..The Lion-Ant. These insects are frequent in Jamaica..The male is of a beautiful greenish blue about the head and breast, but of a brown colour, like the others, behind.

LION-FISH sb; descr. A name for certain Scorpænas.

1892 Cockrell list, Lion-fish—*scorpæna plumierii* and *scorpæna grandicornis.*

LION'S TAIL sb. The plant *Chaptalia nutans*, more commonly called KEMA WEED, WHITE-BACK, HEAL-I'-AND-DRAW.

1954 *WIMJ* 29.

LION-TONGUE sb dial; descr. A local name for the *Sansevieria*, from the shape of the leaf.

1952 FGC West, Lion-tongue.

LIQUOR sb dial; *OED* 3 →1718. A liquid; a non-alcoholic liquid. *BA*

1788–9 M'Neill 5, During Crop, every Negro is allowed to eat as much of the cane and drink as much of the hot liquor from the coppers as he chuses. 1956 Mc StAnd /klen líka/ cane juice.

LIQUORICE (BEAD, VINE) /líkrish/ sb. The vine *Abrus precatorius* and its black-spotted red seeds (JOHN-CROW BEADS). *G*

1802 Nugent 87, In the hedges we saw clusters of the red (Liquorice) beads, sold in the jewellers' shops in England. They grow on a sort of vine, and are in pods, like peas. 1837 Macfadyen I 274, Wild Liquorice-vine.. The roots of this plant are sold, in the streets of Calcutta, as a substitute for those of the common Liquorice of Europe. The leaves also have a similar taste. 1864 Grisebach 785. 1952 FGC StM, Tre /líkrish/ red seeds with black eyes, = John-crow bead.

LIQUORICE-WEED sb bot. The plant *Scoparia dulcis*. Also called SWEET BROOMWEED.

1756 Browne 145, Scoparia 1..The Liquorish-weed, or sweet Broom-weed. This plant..grows by a very branched stalk and rises generally to the height of eighteen or twenty inches. 1814 Lunan I 455, Liquorice-weed. 1864 Grisebach 785, Liquorice-weed, *Scoparia dulcis.*

LISP-TONGUE see next.

lis-tong adj and sb dial; < *lisp* + *tongue*. Having a lisp or speech impediment.

1956 Mc Clar /lis-tong piipl stama/. 1962 BLB 62 /listong/ a lisp.

liti adj dial; a reduced form of *little*.

LITTLE adj; in dial pronunc reduced to various forms—see *likl, yikl, liki, lili, liti, li*. In dial literature sp LICKLE, LEE, LI', etc. *BL G*

LITTLE BIT adj dial; < *little bit* sb phr. Small, tiny. *G*

1954 LeP Kgn, Very small, tiny—lille bit. 1957 JN Arlington, Me have one broder a school and one de a yard. One name Faren and one name James. James lickle bit. (Gesture—hand knee high.) StT [Boy, age 7:] Dennis the Menace can swim? Him foot little bit so, littler than mine.

LITTLE CHRISTMAS sb dial obs. An old nickname among slaves for the Easter holiday.

1707 Sloane lii, They have Saturdays in the Afternoon, and Sundays, with Christmas Holidays, Easter call'd little or Piganinny, Christmas, and some other great Feasts allow'd them for the Culture of their own Plantations.

LITTLE DOG sb dial.

1958 DeC Man /likl daag/ a spinner dumpling.

LITTLE FURUH (BIRD) sb dial; cf BIG FURUH (BIRD). A local name for *Vireo modestus.*

1936 Bond 303, Jamaican Vireo..Local names:—Sewi-sewi; 'Furuh Bird'; 'Little Furuh Bird'. 1949 *NHN* IV 27, *Vireo modestus*—Check-check or Little Furuh. 1956 Jeffrey-Smith 50.

LITTLE GAULIN = GREEN GAULIN.

LITTLE GILL /likl jil/ sb dial. A measure of quantity: one half of the standard gill or BIG GILL.

1959 FGC StAnd.

LITTLE GRANNY sb dial. A grandchild.

1956 Mc Man, see GRANNY 3.

LITTLE JOHNNY sb dial. A small, finger-shaped, round or flattened dumpling.

1959 DeC StJ /likl jani/.

LITTLE MORE adv phr dial; abbr of some such phr as *in a little more time*. In a short while. *BA G*

1961 BLB 7 /yu hafi go a di paipsaid likl muo/ *You have to go to the pipe shortly.*

LITTLE MOST /likl muos/ adv phr dial; evid a 'superlative' or emphatic form of 'a little more', implying a condition or stage just short of some other. Almost, nearly.

[1839 McMahon 210, My good busha—him will die—a lilly mo him die dis morning.] 1877 Murray *Feedin' 'Perrit* 4, Little mose dem would a hab fe smoke him de same like o when dem smoke horse [for the glanders]. 1950 Pioneer 37, De gal did like de way Anancy dress up an lickle mos' she say 'yes'. 1955 Bennett *Europe an' Jamaica*, Lovely Lucerne was gay Little mos' it woulda lovely like De sea dung a Mo Bay. [*It was almost as lovely as the sea down at Montego Bay.*]

LITTLE PIG-FISH sb dial; see quot. Species of small fish, including *Abudefduf saxatilis* and *Microspathodon chrysurus.*

1951 Smith in *NHN* 204, The pilot fish..and the yellow-tailed demoiselle..[are] known around St Mary as 'little pig-fish' because 'him greedy, all time teef de bait'.

LITTLE TOM FOOL sb; see quot 1847.

1. The Sad Flycatcher of Jamaica; see quot 1936.

1847 Gosse 168–9, Foolish Petchary. Little Tom-fool.. It manifests, perhaps, less fear of man than even its congeners, often pursuing its employment of catching insects though a person stand beneath the twig which it has chosen as a station. If it does remove it usually perches again a few yards off, and sits looking at the stranger. 1936 Bond 249, *Myiarchus barbirostris*..Little Tom Fool.

2. The flycatcher *Contopus* or *Blacicus caribæus.*

1955 Taylor 41, The Antillean Pewee (*Contopus caribæus*)..Little Tom Fool. 1956 Jeffrey-Smith 49, see RICKY-TEE.

LITTLE WHILE adv phr dial; by ellipsis of related adjectives or prepositions of StdE.

1. A little while ago. *BA*

1950 Pioneer 17, Bredda Rat, me got bad news fe you; lickle wile as me dah pass Puss yard, me hear Puss muma dah tell him sey..him fe ketch Rat an eat him. 1961 BLB Kgn /we yu se likl wail?/ *What did you say just now?*

2. For a little while.

1954 Reckord *Della* typescript 12, Little while him open himself out to me, call me pretty colour word..etc.

LITTLE WOMAN sb dial; see quot. A local name for the plant *Salvia serotina.*

1955 *WIMJ* 81, Salvia serotina L. Chicken Weed; Little Woman..In former times it has been considered abortifacient and has also been used for a variety of female disorders.

LIVE GOOD vb phr dial. To be on good terms.

1956 Mc Man /wi a liv gud/. *BA BL G*

LIVELY UP vb phr dial. To make lively.

1948 Bennett 3, Yuh haffe lively up yuhself.

LIVER, LIVER-SPOT /liba, liba-spat/ sb dial; descr of the colour and markings of skin; cf *OED liver sb*[1] 7. A mulatto. *BL*

1943 *GL* StC /liba, liba spat/—mulatto. 1955 FGC Man, Liver-spot.

LIVER-SPOT MANGO sb dial. A variety of mango that has brown markings on the skin resembling 'liver spots' (*Chloasma*).

1952 FGC StAnd /líva spàt mánggo/.

LIVE STORY sb dial; <*live* adj + *story*. A happening, or a report of a happening, which one has actually witnessed.

1929 Beckwith 96, This is a live story; I saw it with my eyes—can't doubt it; only doubt a story I hear, that is a dead story.

LIZA /laiza/ sb dial; perh a personal name, but note that there is an American species of mullet named *liza.* (*DAE* 1883→.) A salt herring.

1943 *GL* StAnn, StT, Liza, herring. 1955 FGC Man /laiza/ salt herring, tall and straight; used to be cheap.

LIZARD CANE sb dial. An unidentified plant.

1956 Mc StJ /lizaad kien/ a plant—good for washing clothes.

LIZARD CUCKOO sb ornith. The bird *Saurothera vetula*, a cuckoo characterized by its habit of eating lizards.

1936 Bond 176, Jamaican Lizard Cuckoo..*Local names:*—May Bird, Old Woman Bird, Rain Bird. 1949 Forbes 54–5, The lizard-cuckoo and the rain bird or old man bird seem to like the colossal Guango tree. 1956 Jeffrey-Smith 63–4.

LIZARD LOOKING-GLASS sb dial; for *lizard's*, etc. A mushroom.

1952 R. W. Thompson [From a young woman, Clar:] Lizard looking-glass—jonjo, mushroom.

LIZARD TAIL sb. The garden plant *Arthrostema fragile*, from the way its jointed stems break off.

1960 DAP Inst. of Ja.

LIZARD-TONGUE sb dial. The fern *Polypodium piloselloides*, from its shape.

1959 DAP Inst. of Ja.

LOBBY-LOBBY sb dial; perh <*lob*, hang down + *-y*, iterated; referring to the leaves. (Another name is JACKASS EARS TREE.) The tree *Cordia macrophylla*. See LOBLOLLY TREE.

1952 FGC StE /lábilábi/; Tre /lábalába/. 1963 Proctor Inst. of Ja, Known in St Mary as 'Jackass Ears', in St Elizabeth as 'Lobby-lobby'.

LOB-LOB /lablab/ sb dial; prob a form of *loblolly*—see LOBLOLLY TREE. The tree *Alchornea latifolia.*

1954 *WIMJ* 157, Loblob; Dove Wood; Jimmy Wood. 1955 *WIMJ* 78, The leaves of the lob-lob are utilised by some as a tooth-ache cure.

LOB-LOB BEEFWOOD, LOB-LOLLY ~

1944 *NHN* II 81, *Pisonia obtusata*, Beefwood, Lob-lob Beefwood. See BEEFWOOD.

LOBLOLLY sb dial; cf *OED* 1, 'thick gruel or spoon-meat..a rustic or nautical dish or simple medicinal remedy'. Taken as a type of something soft, without firmness, weak or characterless. Cf use in compounds.

1826 Williams 110, Here a voice cried out, 'Sneezer, you lie—you puckerie yourself—you good for nutten, wibble wabble loblolly,—.' The fair sex were offended at his defamation.

LOBLOLLY SWEETWOOD sb.

1. The tree *Ocotea leucoxylon.*

1864 Grisebach 788, Loblolly Sweet-wood; *Oreodaphne Leucoxylon.* 1914 Fawcett 211, *Ocotea..leucoxylon..* White-wood, Loblolly Sweet-wood. 1941 Swabey 31, Sweetwood, Loblolly (Whitewood). [Also listed: Capberry Longleaf, Timber, and Yellow Sweetwood.] 1952 FGC StAnn /lablab swiit-wud/.

2. The tree *Sciadophyllum Jacquini* (1926 Fawcett 419: *Gilibertia arborea*), usually called GALIPEE or ANGELICA TREE.

1864 Grisebach 785.

LOBLOLLY TREE or **WOOD** sb. (*Loblolly tree* earlier in Barbados.)

Trees of the genus *Cupania*, or, specifically, *C. glabra*, noted for the softness of their wood.

[1725 Sloane 130, Prunus racemosa..Arbor Indica baccifera verbasci foliis lanuginosa, Loblolly Barbadensibus dicta.] 1756 Browne 178, Cupania 1..Loblolly-wood. This shrubby tree is pretty common..the leaves are pretty large and the wood soft and useless, from whence its name. 1837 Macfadyen 161–2, Cupania. Loblolly-wood..1. Cupania glabra. Glabrous Loblolly-wood.. 2. Cupania apetala. Apetalous Loblolly-wood. 1864 Grisebach 785, Loblolly tree. 1926 Fawcett 54–5, *C. glabra*..Loblolly tree.

LOBLOLLY WHITEWOOD sb; *OED* identifies as *Nectandra sanguinea* (TIMBER SWEETWOOD); but Fawcett takes it (with question) to be *Ocotea leucoxylon* (LOBLOLLY SWEETWOOD). A tree of uncertain identity.

1756 Browne 214, Laurus 2. Foliis venosis ovatis.. Loblolly Whitewood, or white Sweetwood..its berries are as large as cherries, plump and black.

LOBLOLLY WOOD see LOBLOLLY TREE.

lobo-lobo see *laba-laba* adj[2].

LOBSTER /labta, labtaz/ sb; cf *OED* 16. The Jamaican crayfish, *Palinurus argus*. *BA*

1725 Sloane 271, Sea Lobster..They are found with the other Crustacea and are not counted so good Meat as the commoner Sort of Lobster. 1756 Browne 424, Astacus 1..The Horned Lobster, or Great Cray-fish. This species is very frequent in the harbours of Jamaica..It has no claws, but in the room of these is supplied with a pair of large aculeated tapering horns. 1826 Williams 40, He eats *soldiers* and crawfish, which he calls lobsters. 1899 *JIJ* II 613, The common Jamaica lobster, *Palinurus argus*, occurred. (1960 Current, FGC.)

LOBSTER'S MUMMA sb dial. = COCKROACH LOBSTER.

1952 FGC StC /lábstaz múma/.

LOCKSMAN. A fully committed member of the Ras Tafari cult, who wears his hair long and plaited.

1960 *SAN Report* 12–13, see DREADLOCKS.

LOCUS-BERRY or **LOTUS-BERRY TREE** sb; the hesitation between the forms *locus* and *lotus* goes back at least to Plukenet's *Alma-*

gestum (1696), p 225 (so 1725 Sloane 86): *locus* is evid an early colloq reduction of *locust*, and Browne recognizes both; Macfadyen recognizes instead *lotus*, and gives his reason, which, however, he admits to be only presumptive; phonetically the words represent a common alternation between *k* and *t*, and either might have so originated from the other; in Jamaica, printed sources favour priority of *locust* and *locus*, and *locus* is the only current pronunciation. *OED* 1756 only.

The tree *Byrsonima coriacea*.

1727 *Observations* 13, Along the sandy Beaches, wild Grapes and wild Cherries, Locust Berries, Cocoa..etc. 1756 Browne 230–1, Malpighia 6..The Locus-berry Tree..Malpighia 7..The larger Locus-berry Tree. *Ibid* 214–15, The Volkameria..It seems to have a near resemblance to the Locust-berry tree, which we have placed among the *Malpigiæ*. 1837 Macfadyen 147, Lotus-berry Tree..This is a common but a very beautiful tree, graceful in its port, and..conspicuous for its profuse golden-coloured flowers. The fruit is very palatable, and deserving of a place at the dessert. It has received, I presume, the name of *Lotus berry*, from its resembling in taste, that of Ziziphus Lotus. 1920 Fawcett 221–2, *B. coriacea*..Locus-berry tree..Lotus-berry tree..Locust tree, Hog-berry tree. 1952 FGC Port, StAnd, StAnn, StM, StT /luokas/. *N* /luokas/ (JH).

LOCUST-ALE sb obs; *OED* only 1693: cf *locus sb*².

1707 Sloane lxii, Locust-Ale is Cane-Juice clarified, mix'd with Rum.

LOCUST BERRY see LOCUS-BERRY.

LODGING-HOUSE sb obs.

1860 Trollope 19, Inns in Jamaica are called lodging-houses, or else taverns.

LOFT sb dial. A storage-space set high within a kitchen. *BL*

1943 *GL* Man, Pattah, a loft in the kitchen.

LOFTY BITTER-WOOD see BITTER-WOOD 2.

LOFTY-GRASS sb bot obs.

1814 Lunan I 464, *Fuirena..paniculata*..This is called *lofty-grass* on account of its height.

LOFTY QUASSIA sb bot obs. Jamaica Quassia (*Picræna excelsa*).

1811 Titford 65, Lofty Quassia, Q. Excelsa, is also a native of Jamaica.

LOGGERHEAD FOOLIE sb dial. = LOGGERHEAD PETCHARY.

1952 FGC Man /lágahed fúuli/ have big head, black cap —foolish bird.

LOGGERHEAD FRY sb dial. Small fish with big heads: specif, *Hepsetia stipes*.

1854–5 *TJSA* I 143, Atherina stipes—Loggerhead fry. 1952 Smith in *NHN* 138, Attractive little silversides or atherinids, *Hepsetia stipes*..known..in Jamaica [as] 'loggerhead fry'..[with] a broad head, large eyes, a fairly large protractile mouth..etc.

LOGGERHEAD MOSQUITO sb. A type of mosquito, large and slow, whence the name.

1756 Browne 427, Culex 4. Major torpida fusca. The Loggerhead Muskeeto. This insect is much larger than either of the others.

LOGGERHEAD (PETCHARY) /lágahèd pichíeri/ sb; named from its having a large head and being foolishly bold; cf *OED* 1657→, Barbados.

The name applied in the British West Indian islands to various similar birds: in Jamaica specifically to *Tolmarchus caudifasciatus jamaicensis* (evid this in quot 1725), *Myiarchus tyrannulus* (quot 1847).

1725 Sloane 300, Sitta, seu picus cinereus major capite nigro. A Loggerhead. They are common in the Savannas among the Bushes, and let Men come so near them that they knock them down with Sticks, whence they have the Name of Loggerheads. 1847 Gosse 186, Red Petchary. Loggerhead. Great Crested Flycatcher. 1936 Bond 245; 247, Loggerhead. 1952 FGC Han, StAnd, StM, StT /lágahèd pichíeri/ have big head, not afear of nobody; have centre-stripe yellow in head—like a log on head.

LOGGERHEAD TORTOISE sb obs; *OED* 1772–84→. The loggerhead turtle. *BL*

1707 Sloane lxxxviii, There is a sort of Loggerhead Turtle or Tortoise at Jamaica, very little differing from the common sort, only in every part less, and having the Brest of a yellowish white colour.

logi-logi, log-log, logo-logo adj and sb dial; cf Engl *log*, *loggy*, *lug*, etc. Heavy; therefore slow, sluggish, stupid; as sb: a person having these characteristics. *BL*

1952 FGC StAnn [Of the loggerhead bird:] Has a big /logi-logi/ head. 1956 Mc StE /log-log/ slow, lazy, slothful (person or animal). 1958 DeC StC /logo-logo/ a stupid fool.

logo-logo vb dial; cf *lug* (*OED* 3), drag or move with difficulty. To move (or try to move) something heavy.

1943 *GL* Kgn, Luggo-luggo, moving a heavy weight; Tre, Lugo-lugo, to carry. 1955 FGC Man /logo-logo/ moving what you can scarcely manage—makes you stumble. 1958 DeC StC /logo-logo/ to lug something terribly heavy; Kgn, Here apparently means to attempt unsuccessfully to lift a very head load: /mi logo-logo wid i bo mi kyaan masu dat basket/ *I logo-logoed with it but I can't lift that basket.*

logo-logo adv dial; cf *logo-logo* vb. (Presumably conn through the common idea of weight.) See quot and cf *kulu-kulu* 1.

1943 *GL* StC, Luggo-luggo, in great amounts.

LOGWOOD CHIPPER sb; cf *OED logwood* 2c.

1. Men who fell logwood trees and chip off the bark so that the dyewood is prepared for sale.

1790 Beckford II 114, The logwood-chippers, whose axes are heard to resound from the depths of the wood.. Some are felling the heavy timber, and some with their bills are lopping the branches; while others, sitting upon the roots or stumps, are chipping off the bark.

2. Transf: The ANTS-BIRD: see quot.

1956 Jeffrey-Smith 84, In the western parts of the Island it is known as Logwood Chipper, because it frequents those trees and makes a chipping sound as it busily seeks its food.

LOGWOOD CUTTER sb. = LOGWOOD CHIPPER.

1725 Sloane vii, Another Danger to them is the being stung prodigiously by Mosquitos, by which many of the Loggwood Cutters have died [in the 'Bay of Campeche'].

LOGWOOD WALK sb. A WALK of logwood trees.

1948 U.Newton IV 6.

log-log, logz sb dial; prob <*lug*, to pull, drag or *lug* sb, something heavy; both the forms that appear are collective in effect, the first indicating this by iteration. Rubbish; things to be thrown away.

1956 Mc StE /log-log/ Rubbish, waste, refuse. 1958 DeC Man /logz/ miscellaneous trash or rubbish.

LOMAS adj dial; etym unknown—the latter syllable may represent *-ous*. (Perh by metathesis of /lúonsam/ lonesome—BLB.) A word of uncertain meaning; it usually modifies, *land*, *world*, or the like, and appears to suggest a yearning emotion. See quots.

1929 Beckwith 182, Thompson called the land of the dead 'Lomas land'..One of his songs runs: You no remember de year Robert Bryan was kill? Poor t'ing, poor t'ing. Dead and gone to Lomas land! 1943 *GL* Kgn, Lomas, troublesome (e.g. Dis lomas wo'l'); Port, Lomas, extensive; StM, Lomas, land of the living.

lomp, lomp-lomp see LUMP.

lompi-lompi see LUMPY-LUMPY.

LONDON CITY sb dial; imitation of the bird's call. A local name for the JUDY; cf KISSIDY.

LONELY (IN THE WEATHER) adj dial joc; alluding to the person's being far away from other people with his head 'in the clouds'. A tall, thin person.

1958 DeC StT /luonli, luonli-ina-weda/.

LONEY see *luoni*.

LONG adj dial.

1. Of persons: Tall. *G*

1873 Rampini 181 [Prov:] When man no done grow, him neber should cuss long man. 1954 LeP Kgn, StAnn, A very tall man—long man. 1957 JN StM, Me fraid because me see one long man a walk pan the road and me think a duppy.

2. Of persons: Apt to go to great lengths, to extremes.

1957 JN, 'He's a long man, you know'—*he will carry an argument to extremes.*

3. Of things: Stretched out.

1907 Jekyll 258, The cabbage was not done enough, so that it was ropy or 'long', as they aptly describe it.

LONG vb[1] dial; see LONG OUT.

LONG vb[2] dial; <*long v*[2] *arch.* (*OED*). To belong (in terms of origin); to come from.

1956 Mc StE /wie shi lang?/ *Where is she from?*

LONGALAALA see *langgulala*.

LONGAS sb dial; <*long* + *arse* or perh *-ous*.

1954 LeP StT, A very tall man—longas.

LONG-BAG /láng-bág/ sb dial. A large bag or sack: see quots.

1907 Jekyll 149, When they ready to start the father give them a long bag full with money. 1925 Beckwith 94 [Prov:] One t'ief no like fe see anoder carry long bag. 1958 DeC Port /lang-bag/ crocus bag rolled at the mouth so as to hook over crown of head.

LONG BELLY, LONG GUT sb dial. A greedy person. *BL G*

[1950 Pioneer 56, Doah me no got long bella-gut..Me can put weh a hearty meal.] 1956 Mc Man /lang beli, lang got/ a greedy person.

LONG-BUBBY SUSAN sb dial; <*long* + BUBBY + *Susan*. A duppy—see quot.

1929 Beckwith 99, Long-bubby Susan is characterized by breasts which touch the ground and which she throws over her shoulders when attacked.

LONG CERASEE sb obs. Evid *Momordica charantia*. (Fawcett lists a variant *M. abbreviata*, which perh furnishes the contrast.)

1811 Titford xiii, Long cerasee. 1850 Macfadyen 138.

LONG COLLIN sb dial; cf COLLINS.

1958 DeC StT /laang kalin/ old-fashioned name for a cutlass of 'sword' shape [long, slender, same width throughout, ogive point].

LONG-DAY BIRD sb dial; see quots. The GLASS-EYE, *Turdus jamaicensis*.

1936 Bond 284, White-eyed Thrush..Glass-eye; Gray-eye; Long Day Bird. 1944 *NHN* II 130, The glass-eye thrush [is called] Long-day bird because it is heard singing during the long days only. 1952 FGC StT, Long-day bird = shine-eye; whistles 'long day coom!'

LONG-DAY HOPPING-DICK sb dial. = LONG-DAY BIRD.

1956 Jeffrey-Smith 156.

LONG DRINK sb; cf *OED long a* 1 g. A drink having a lot of liquid, therefore taken more for dilution and cooling than for its alcoholic strength: COOL-DRINK, small-beer, etc., rather than strong or concentrated spirit. *BA G*

[1833 Scott I 185, An agent for a number of proprietors.. rather posed me, by asking me during dinner, if I would take anything in the *long way* with him which he explained by saying he would be glad to take a glass of small beer with me.] 1859 Trollope (1860) 47, A long drink is taken from a tumbler, a short one from a wine-glass. 1873 Rampini 55, A breakfast cupful of black coffee, sweetened with brown sugar, and another 'long drink' of rum and water will complete the evening's entertainment.

LONG DUMPLING sb dial.

1958 DeC StT /lang-dompling/ a dumpling, finger-shaped but flattened, creased, and boiled.

LONGEST adj dial; superl of LONG adj 1.

1958 DeC StT /laangis/ adj for tall thin person.

LONG-FINGER PEPPER sb dial. A variety of *Capsicum* pepper shaped like a long finger.

1952 FGC StC /lang fingga pepa/.

LONG FLARE sb dial; cf FLARE. A machete with slender blade of the same width through two-thirds of its length, but a broadened end and somewhat canted point.

1958 DeC Port /láng flíer/.

LONG-FOOT CRAB sb dial. A crab with a very long claw (*Lupella forceps*). Prob = LONG-SHANKED CRAB.

1961 R. P. Bengry StAnd, So called by fishermen.

longga sb dial cant. In the AFRICAN cult 'language' of St Thomas: water. s.

1953 Moore gloss, Langa, water.

LONG GAR sb dial. An unidentified fish; perh = LONG-JAW (GARFISH).

1952 FGC StE /láng gyár/.

LONG GAULIN sb dial; etym uncert: evid transf from the name of the bird GAULIN. A tall or long person or thing: see quots.

1956 BLB Man /lang gaalin/ term applied to a very tall person. 1958 DeC Port /lang gaalin/ a kind of fresh-water fish used for making soup in Portland. Same as /riva gaalin/.

LONG-GRAIN RICE sb dial joc; fig, the banana having the shape of a grain of rice, and the boiled banana being used as a starch food. Banana, or, specif, a boiled green-banana. *BA*

1943 *GL* StM, Long grain rice, green banana boiled; No addr, Jamaica long-grain rice, banana. 1956 Mc Man, Long-grain rice, general term for banana.

LONGGULAWLA, LONGILALA see *langgulala*.

LONG-JAW (GARFISH) sb. The needle-fish, genus *Tylosurus*.

1851 Gosse 288–9, That species of *Belone*, called indiscriminately Piper or Long-jaw. 1892 Cockrell list, Long-jaw—*Tylosurus notatus, T. euryops.* 1952 FGC Port, StAnn, StM /láng jáa/ same as /gyaad fish/—both jaws long; StJ /lang-jaa gyaa fish/.

LONG-JOINT sb dial. The name of a plant used medicinally (see quot); prob = JOINTER.

1954 Kirkland 170 [Contents of a fever-bath:] Colon mint, ramgoat regular, sweet broom, quackno, long-joint.

LONG-LEAF BITTER-BUSH sb dial. Perh *Neurolaena lobata*—cf BITTER BUSH.

1952 FGC Han, Long-leaf bitter-bush. If your back is scratched up, bathe, and rub your back with it.

LONG-LEAF JOINTER sb dial; cf JOINTER.

1955 *WIMJ* 145, *Miconia lævigata*..Chicken Net; Fowl Bone..Long-leaf-Jointer..Our informants..have all been consistent in describing it as used in bush baths for colds and fever.

LONG-LEAF (or **-LEAVED**) **SWEET-WOOD** sb. The tree *Nectandra antillana*.

1864 Grisebach 788, Long-leaved Sweet-wood: *Nectandra leucantha.* 1914 Fawcett 215, Shingle-wood, White-wood, Long-leaved Sweet-wood. 1941 Swabey 31, Longleaf Sweetwood.

LONG-MACHETE sb dial.

1958 DeC StE /lang-mashiet/ a cutlass with broad blade gradually curving to a point; sharpened on only one side.

LONG MANGO sb dial. A variety of mango longer than most varieties. *G*

1952 FGC Port, StM, Long mango—long, flat; has dots on it when ripe.

LONG-MOUTH(ED) (BLUE) (QUIT) sb. The ORANGE QUIT (*Euneornis campestris*).

1936 Bond 312, Orange Quit; Long-mouthed Quit; Blue Baize..etc. 1955 Taylor 37, see SHORT-MOUTH(ED) (BLUE) QUIT. 1956 Jeffrey-Smith 70, The somewhat thick but fairly long and sharp bill gives it a local name of Long-mouthed Quit, abbreviated to 'Long Mout'' at Quickstep.

LONG-NECK PEAR sb dial. A variety of the AVOCADO pear in which the upper part is somewhat attenuated; = BOTTLENECK 1.

1952 FGC StJ /langnek pier/.

LONG NINE sb dial; cf *DAE Long nine*, a cheap cigar. A cheap grade of rum.

1877 Murray *Feedin' 'Perrit* 12, Beneba, go buy.. fippance wut o' de long nine.

LONG OKRO sb. A variety of okro with long pods.

1696 Sloane 98, Alcea maxima, malvæ rosæ folio, fructu pentagono, recurvis, esculento, graciliore & longiore.. Long Okra. In hortis ubique plantatur & provenit. 1952 FGC StE /lang okro/.

LONG OUT vb chiefly dial; cf Engl *loll out*. To protrude, stick out; also causative.

1924 Beckwith 104, Snake..going into one hole an' long out his head. 1946 U.Newton I 26, How I 'long out my mouth' when Mami was not looking! *Ibid* 34, Some latecomers begin to laugh at me. One 'longs out' her tongue at me. 1955 Bennett *Miss West Indies Wed*, Me see one head wid de two Y'eye Dah bulge an tongue long out Like mawga dog dat set fe lick bread. 1955, 1957 UCWI Medical staff [Order to patients being examined:] Long-out your tongue. *G*; *SC lánga*.

LONG PEAS sb. A bean similar to cow peas, but with a larger seed and a longer pod. Evid a species of *Dolichos*.

1952 FGC StJ /lang-piiz/.

LONG PEPPER sb.

1. *Piper aduncum* (ident 1914 Fawcett 24)—according to Sloane, Leigh's term.

1696 Sloane 44, Piper longum folio nervoso pallide viridi, humilius..An Long Pepper of Leigh.

2. A variety of *Capsicum* pepper that has long fruit.

1952 FGC StE /lang pepa/.

LONG-RAIL MAT sb dial; 'rail' refers to the strips of trash or bark used in making the mat. = *jagu mat*.

1956 Mc StAnd /lang-riel mat/.

LONG ROAD sb dial; alluding to the time it takes to prepare. A coconut run-down.

1959 DeC StJ /laang ruod/.

LONG-SALT /lang-saal/ sb dial; < *long* + SALT. Salt herring or other pickled fish.

1943 *GL* Kgn, Long saul, herring; StM, StT, Long sall, herring, pickle fish. 1955 FGC Man /long-saal/ same as ONE-EYE CUFFY.

LONG-SHANKED CRAB sb obs.

1756 Browne 421, Cancer 4..The larger long-shanked Crab with delicate prickly arms, and slender toothed claws..Cancer 7..The large long-shanked Crab with a variegated shell.

LONG-TAIL sb. Ellipt for the LONG-TAILED DOCTOR BIRD.

1847 Gosse 99, The Long-tail is a permanent resident in Jamaica. 1951 Murray 25, Some a Long-tail. 1956 Jeffrey-Smith 22, Sometimes one sees an adult long-tail without one of its streamers. It has no doubt lost it in combat, for the males are very pugnacious.

LONG-TAILED CROW sb. The bird *Crotophaga ani*—not a crow but allied to the cuckoos, 'crow' no doubt alluding to its black plumage.

1936 Bond 177, Ani..*Local names:*—..Black Witch; Long-tailed Crow; Tick Bird; Savanna Blackbird (Jamaica).

LONG-TAIL(ED) DOCTOR BIRD sb; descr. = LONG-TAIL(ED) HUMMING-BIRD.

1936 Bond 212–13, *Local names:*—Doctor Bird; Long-tail Doctor Bird. 1956 Jeffrey-Smith 22, Long-tail Doctor Bird; *ibid* 144, Long-Tailed..etc.

LONG-TAIL(ED) HUMMING-BIRD sb; descr; *OED* 1868 only. The male of *Aithurus polytmus* or *A. scitulus*; also by extension the female.

1725 Sloane 309, Mellivora avis maxima, mas..The long Tail'd Humming Bird. 1847 Gosse 97, Long-Tailed Humming-Bird. This is the gem of Jamaican Ornithology. Its slender form, velvet crest, emerald bosom, and lengthened tail plumes, render it one of the most elegant even of this most brilliant family. 1951 Jeffrey-Smith in *Gleaner* 7 Sept.

LONG-TAILED PEA-DOVE sb. The Mourning Dove.

1955 Taylor 91, see PALOMA. 1956 Jeffrey-Smith 112, The Mourning Dove (*Zenaida macroura*)..is distinguished by its long, pointed tail, to which it owes the local name of Long-Tailed Pea Dove.

LONG-TEETH DRUMMER sb dial. A variety of the Drummer fish having long teeth.

1952 FGC StC /lang-tiit droma/.

LONG-THATCH (PALM) sb. The kind of thatch-palm with a long leaf (in contrast to those with a round leaf—cf ROUND THATCH).

1890 Thomas 71, The trees that surrounded us were principally thatch, of the 'long', and 'silver' or 'pimento', varieties; and we saw the tracks of recent thatch-cutters. 1952 FGC Port, StE, StM, StT /láng-tách/.

LONG-TIME adv and adj dial. *BA G T*

A. adv: Long ago.

1942 Bennett 21, Me did tink me always hear sey Missis Queen bannish slavery lang time. 1956 Mc StE /wat a ard irz gal! lang lang taim a tel ar go a shap!/ *What a disobedient girl! I told her ages ago to go to the shop!*

B. adj: From long ago. (Cf *OED* 18.)

1952 FGC StAnd, Is a long-time cassada, *This variety of cassava was introduced long ago*, or *has existed for a long time.*

LONGULALA, LONGULAALA see *langgulala.*

LONG WHIP sb obs. A whip with a long lash, used in driving cattle.

1833 *Second Letter from Legion* 26, The back..is bared, and the infliction is made generally with the long whip or cat-o'-nine-tails.

LONI see *luoni.*

LOOK vb dial; cf *OED* 6a, d, etc.: now mostly arch or dial in Engl. *G*

1. To look for, seek, try to find. *BL N*

1907 Jekyll 79, Me son, a time fe you go an' look you own living. 1954 LeP StAnn, To hunt for food—look grub. 1956 Mc StAnd /him ing kom a jimieka luk riichnis/ *He came to Jamaica to look for riches.*

2. To find and gather (to bring back). *BL*

1924 Beckwith 3, An' de two sister go an' look a bundle a wood. 1947 U.Newton II 25, Arthur and I joined a group of boys to 'look wood'. 1956 Mc Man /iz a pilikin, mam—dem luk fish/ *It's a pelican, ma'am—they're looking for* (or *catching*) *fish.*

3. To visit; also const *for*. *BA BL*

1956 Mc Man /im nó kom lúk fo im máda/ *He hasn't been to see his mother*; StAnd /dis láng taim mi neba ben sii yu—ming gáan lúk de áda wán/ *I haven't seen you for so long—I am going to see the other one(s).*

4. With various following prepositions differing from StdE usage.

1957 LeP StAnd, O.K., Sir, I'll look on it. *I'll look about it*, or *see about it*. 1957 JN Clar, I didn't look on the clock (i.e. *look at*).

LOOK-LOOK vb dial; iterative of *look* vb. To keep on looking for some time. *G*

1942 Bennett 45, Me tan-up tan-up 'bout de place, Look-look pon everything.

LOOKO' see *luku.*

LOOKOO YA see KU.

LOOKS sb sg dial; by overcorrection or confusion. Look. (A plural form used with singular meaning.) *BL G*

1952 FGC StAnd, Coolie plum..it have a green looks; StC, Sweet potato..the inside have a purple looks.

LOOK-UP sb dial. A low wild plant (*Blechum brownei*) the ends of whose stalks turn upward from the ground (whence the name).

1952 FGC Man /luk-op/ also 'dead-man's-bones'.

LORD see *laad.*

loroks sb dial; <Scots *loorach*, rag, tattered cloth. See *SND*. Anything old and rubbishy.

1943 *GL* Clar, Lurucks, old clothes. 1955 FGC Man /lóroks/ jeng-jeng, anything old. 1960 LeP StAnd /lóroks/ old junk—'very common'.

LOST /laas/ vb dial; sp lahs, las, lass; <*lost*, one of a small number of verbs which in the dial takes the past-tense form of StdE as its base; conceivably also by conversion of *loss* sb. To lose. *BA BL G N T*

1941 Kirkpatrick 8, 'Im lass 'im temper so much dat 'im tek up de ball an fire it after de spectator dem. 1942 Bennett 41, see BULL-COW. 1951 Murray 8, Las kean fine—*Lost and cannot be found.*

LOTS sb sing dial; by overcorrection or confusion with *lots of*. A lot, a great deal.

1907 Jekyll 60, Annancy tell 'creech-owl that he will get a lots of drink. 1950 Pioneer 50, Brer Nancy used to hab a lats a trouble. 1952 FGC StAnn, A lots of work.

LOTUS-BERRY see LOCUS-BERRY.

LOUISA (CASSAVA) sb dial; prob for someone who introduced or successfully grew it. A variety of cassava root.

1952 FGC StAnn /luuíiza/ yellow, with a yellow skin.

louji sb dial; cf *louch* vb and sb, to slouch, a sloucher (*EDD*) + *-y/-ie.*

1959 DeC Han /louji/ adj for a man who is big, hulking, stooped.

LOVE-APPLE sb obs. Applied early in Jamaica: *Solanum aculeatissimum.*

1756 Browne 173–4, Solanum 2..Love Apple, and Cock-roch Apple. This plant is a native of Jamaica, and makes a beautiful appearance when adorned with its large yellow berries.

LOVE BUSH or **WEED** sb. Plants of the genus *Cuscuta*, which grow parasitically on bushes and appear as bunches of conspicuous orange-red threads. Folklore has it that one will succeed in love if a piece one puts on another plant grows: hence the name. *BA G*

1814 Lunan I 266, Cuscuta Americana..The negroes of Liguanea mountains call it *love-bush*. I saw it winding about a young tree where a negro woman had thrown it, on purpose to propagate it. 1927 Beckwith 21, Love-weed..For asthma, boil with 'Asthma-weed' as tea..to induce love in one who hates you, rub the body especially the back of the neck with the plant, 'then clap your hands and hold them up palm outward when you see the person coming'..Repeat the words 'By Saint Peter, James and Paul' meanwhile. 1954 *FG* 582, The common Love-bushes of Jamaica comprise about four species of *Cuscuta*..Because they are parasites..and have a very serious effect on their hosts, they should be discouraged.

LOVE-DANCE sb arch or obs. See quot.

1826 Williams 22, They divided themselves into parties to dance, some before the gombays, in a ring, to perform a bolèro or a sort of love-dance, as it is called, where the gentlemen occasionally wiped the perspiration off the shining faces of their black beauties, who, in turn, performed the same service to the minstrel.

LOVE-WEED see LOVE-BUSH.

LOW-DOWN adv dial. *G*

1868 Russell 18, Adverbs: place—low-dong (below) fur (far) ya (here)..etc.

LOW-RUN adj chiefly dial. Underhanded, scoundrelly.

1956 BLB Man, Low-run—used of a person who supports you before your face, and then knifes you as soon as your back is turned. 1961 E. N. Burke Kgn, He's really a low-run man.

LOWS sb plur; ellipt for *low-wines*. Low-wines, i.e. the result of the first stage of distillation in rum-making.

1821 Baillie 13, You must lose none of your dunder from the liquor still, and only throw away the residuum of that dunder, and the lowes of your rum still.

LOW STOMACH sb dial. A feeling of weakness in the digestive system; queasiness and loss of appetite.

1927 Beckwith 26, See-me-contract..For worms or 'low stomach' drink as tea.

LUCEA AFU sb dial; <LUCEA (YAM) +AFU. =AFU LUCEA.

1957 LeP StE /lúusi àfu/.

LUCEA YAM /luusi, lusia/ sb; <*Lucea*, town in parish of Hanover +*yam*. A variety of yam: see quot 1954.

1952 FGC gen /luusi yam/. 1954 *FG* 445, The Lucea yam, a soft, white, well-flavoured yam, is grown in the hills of Hanover and in the hills bordering Western Westmoreland. It is the yam most liked by purchasers in our markets, and it seldom retains its texture when planted anywhere else but in Hanover and the borders of Westmoreland. 1956 Mc StE /lusia/ Negro yam.

LUCK adj dial; <*luck* sb or *lucky* adj. Lucky, fortunate.

1953 Moore 153, If the mother gets twins, they are very luck and very strong. The zombies love them.

LUCKY-BORN sb dial.

1954 LeP Kgn, Name for a boy born on Thursday—Lucky-born.

LUCKY-BOX, LUCKY-PACKET sb; cf *OED lucky-bag*. A box of sweets with a small favour or 'prize' inside. (What the favour proves to be is subject to chance.)

c 1910–20 FGC Kgn-StAnd, Lucky-packet. 1942 Bennett 9, Yuh face look like a sey Yuh draw it outa lucky-box.

LUCKY LILY sb. The white-spotted variety of DUMB-CANE (*Dieffenbachia seguine*), a common garden plant. Folklore has it that if money is placed at the root, more will come to you: hence the name.

1952 FGC StT, Tre.

LUCKY LIZARD sb dial. A POLLY lizard.

1952 FGC Port, Lucky lizard—like a toy, harmless, small, yellowish-suedish.

LUCKY-PACKET see LUCKY-BOX.

LUGGAGE sb dial; cf *OED* 2a →1693.

1959 DeC StJ /logij/ miscellaneous trash, rubbish, junk.

LUGGO-LUGGO, LUGO-LUGO see *logo-logo*.

LUKO-DAY see KU. *G*

luku vb dial; <*look*+*-u*. (*Luku* was probably a part of the lingua franca of the slave trade.) Cf also *luculucu* <Engl *look*, used in Cuba by negroes (Pichardo 434). Cf KU. Look! Look at, see! *BL G*; *SC lōekoe*.

1910 Anderson-Cundall 40 [Prov:] Ratta say if man chop after him, dat no kill him, but if him say, 'looko' rat' dat is wos. 1956 Mc /yuutin, luku ya/ *Ewton (?), look here!*

LUKU YA see KU. *BL G*

lulu sb dial; cf *DA looloo*, something exceptionally fine. (This word may be an independent creation, however: cf such others as *bululups*—of a phonosymbolic kind.)

1943 *GL* Clar, Lu-lu—feminine lover. 1955 FGC Man /lulu/—a boy-friend or girl-friend. Old-time word.

LUMP, LUMP-LUMP sb dial. Cassava head: moist cassava from which the juice has been wrung or pressed.

1958 DeC StE /lomp; kasada-lomp/; StJ /lomp-lomp/.

LUMPY-LUMPY adj or sb dial; iterative of *lumpy*.

1. A spinner dumpling.

1958 DeC StT.

2. See quot.

1959 DeC Han /lompi-lompi/ adj or noun: a dumpling (any shape) made with too much water; it goes to pieces in the water and must be removed.

LUMVOTUVO phr dial rare. s.

1943 *GL* Port (John's Hall), Lumvotuvo, your belly is big.

LUNCH CAKE sb dial.

1958 DeC StT /lonch kiek/ a bammy cake.

LUNDY sb dial; cf Zulu *londa*, a sore or wound.

1943 *GL* Kgn, Lundy, ulcer; StC, Lundy, ulsore.

LUNG-PLUNG sb dial; etym uncert, perh repr *lump-lump*. Flour sauce.

1943 *GL* StC, Lung-plung, sauce. 1955 FGC Man /long-plong/ flour sauce—old-time word.

luokal-miidiuokal sb dial; for *local mediocre*, altered to make a rhyme.

1958 DeC StM /luokal-miidiokal/ an undependable no-account person.

luoni adj and vb dial; <*lone*, alone +*-y*, hypocoristic.

A. adj: Of a baby: Standing or just learning to stand alone.

1943 *GL* Port, Loni, when a baby just learns to stand. 1960 LeP StAnd, The baby's /luoni/ trying to walk by itself.

B. vb: Of a baby: To stand or to demonstrate that it can stand alone.

1956 BLB Man, This action includes the outstretched arms with which the child balances. When he no longer needs arms to balance he has ceased to /lúoni/. 1960 LeP Kgn / jais, luoni fo mi/ *Joyce, stand by yourself for me.*

luonli see LONELY.

LURRUCKS see *loroks*.

lusia, luusi yam see LUCEA YAM.

luudi giem sb dial; evid <*ludo*.

1958 DeC StAnd /luudi giem/ a game played with pebbles or cashew nuts as counters, moved on board according to throws of dice.

LYGES see *laigz*.

MA /ma/ sb dial; etym prob dual: cf Twi *mmá*, woman, coinciding with a reduced form of *ma'am* or of *mama*. The vowel is sometimes nasalized, but without affecting the sense. (The StdE vowel of *Ma* is longer and lower than the Ja /a/.) s.

Mother; Madam; also as a title of respectful or affectionate address. *BA BL G N*

1793 Edwards II 82, In addressing such of their fellow-servants as are any ways advanced in years, they prefix to their names the appellation of Parent, as *Ta* Quaco, and *Ma* Quasheba; *Ta* and *Ma*, signifying Father and Mother, by which designation they mean to convey not only the idea of filial reverence, but also that of esteem and fondness. 1950 Pioneer 52, Wa kine a nize dat mah? [*What kind of noise is that, ma'am?*] 1951 FGC Man [Servant answering mistress:] [mã] (said with rising pitch), *ma'am?* 1955 LeP recording Rowe, story of 'Ba-biabuo' /im se, mã [rising pitch], a nuo yu a mi ma [falling pitch]—shi se, nuo mi chail, mi no rieli yu baan mada/.

maaga /máaga/ adj dial; 1826→1924 maugre, 1910→ mauger, 1943 maga marga mauga, 1950 mawga; prob <Pg, Sp *magro*, thin, but cf also *maager*, lean, thin, scraggy (*EDD*: Shetlands and Orkney); also perh infl by Dut

mager, lean. Most of the written forms, though intended to represent dial pronunc, 'correct' it to correspond to StdE sounds, making the vowel [ɔ]. Also s MAWGA-NANNY.

Thin, lean; by implication often, underfed, half-starved. *G N T*; *SC mángri.*

1826 Williams 205, Him mus' run fas, till he sweat blue maugre to h—ll. 1837 James 11, I was quite maugre and hungry that time, quite different to what I stand now. 1873 Rampini 179, Sharp spur make maugre horse cut caper. 1907 Jekyll 262, You take junka 'tick fe go lick maugre dog. 1952 FGC Man, Mosquito is long /máaga/ little trashy thing with long legs. 1956 Mc gen /máaga/ the regular word for 'thin' (which is scarcely used).

maaga-man sb dial; <*maaga*+*man.* A spinner dumpling, long and thin.

1958 DeC Port, Tre.

maaginiet vb dial; ?<*homogenate.* To bind a loose mixture of ingredients together.

1958 DeC StT /wi ad di wait floua to di kwakwa tu maaginiet it tu geda/.

maa-i /máa-i/ sb dial; cf Hindi *mā,e, mā,ī,* a mother. An East Indian woman; also used as a term of address. *G*

1943 *GL* Port, StC, Mawi, naui, nahhe, woman (East Indian); Port, Moel, old woman. 1955 FGC Man /maa-i/ East Indian woman.

maak graas sb dial; <*maat*, by substitution of *k* for *t.* =MOTH GRASS.

1956 Mc Port /maak graas/ grass with long sharp blades, roots of which are called /kus-kus/.

maama, mama /máama, mámá/ sb dial; etym prob dual; cf Twi *mmá, mmaa,* woman, coinciding with Engl *mamá,* or US *máma.* A term of address to any woman. *BL G N*

1954 LeP Man, Mahma, mother; StAnn, Mamma, stepmother (usually the same term is used for both mother and stepmother). 1956 Mc Clar /máama/ a title used for any old woman; StAnd /mama/ a term of address used in speaking (familiarly) to any woman; StE, A term of address used to a strange woman /maanin mama/ (to me).

MAAME see next.

maami /máami/ sb dial; prob a more intimate form of *maama*, as indicated by *-i.* Cf also SEA-MAHMY, SHRIMP MAAMI. A mother, esp one's own; also a term of address. *BA BL T*

1907 Jekyll 253 [Song:] James Brown, you mahmy call you. 1943 *GL* Clar, Mawmie, mother; Tre, Māmi, mother. 1946 U.Newton I 12, 'Good evenin' Mami..' Mami looked cool and dangerous. 1954 LeP Port, StAnn, Mother—Maame, Marmie.

maama-man, mama-man sb dial; <*maama* +*man.*

1. A man who does women's work; an unmanly man. *T*

1943 *GL* Kgn, StC, Mamaman, man who does kitchen jobs—worthless man; StAnd, Mawma man, too exact at home; StM, Mamaman, a man who acts woman-like. 1955 FGC Man /mama-man/. 1958 DeC Port /maama man/.

2. A man who makes a living by growing and selling market crops.

1954 LeP StE, Maama-man.

maas, maasa sb dial; reduced forms of *master.* Cf next. Formerly: master; now: Mr, but rather more informal and even intimate; toward older people, respectful. *BA G N*

1946 Dunham 139, Marsa—term of intimate address for a man of one's own age. 1950 Pioneer 50, So me cotchin' wid Mass U, Miss Q, Sta P., and Cousin B. 1956 Mc /maas/—shortened form of /maasa/: used affectionately, or intimately, with name of person when addressing or speaking of them, e.g. Maas Taam=Master Tom. /maasa/ is reserved for an employer or person for whom one holds high respect either because of social standing or age.

maasa-niega, maas-niega sb dial arch; <*maas, maasa*+*niega.* A fellow-negro; a friend. Also exclamatory. *SC massra-níngre.* s.

1826 Barclay 239, 'Massa-nigger! wharra dem Buckra no savi?..' *[Fellow-servant! What is it the white people do not know?]* 1877 Murray *Kittle* 10, 'And when I bury tree day, mek me mass nega dem kill da white fowl in a coob..' *Ibid* 13, On the third day after Tom's burying, his 'mass-negers' proceeded to carry out the old man's wishes. 1896 Bates 125, Massnega is a fellow-servant, male or female. 1943 *GL* StJ, Massaneaga—a friend. 1955 FGC Man /maasa-niega ooo!/—exclamation of surprise over some happening.

maas graas see MOTH GRASS.

maas nik sb dial uncom; <MASTIC, with loss of *t* and intrusion of *n* at syllable juncture, and evid with folk-etym personification: 'Mas' Nick.' The Mastic tree.

1952 FGC StE /máas ník/ tree.

maas-wud sb; this pronunc might represent MASTWOOD, which however is not especially light, or *moss wood* (otherwise unattested).

1958 DeC StT /maas-wud/—a light wood used for fish-pot buoys.

maata-stik see MORTAR-STICK.

maatel sb dial; <Fr *immortelle*, immortal; the tree is also called NEVER-DEAD. In Jamaica, *Erythrina corallodendrum* or *E. velutina*, the CORAL-BEAN TREE, frequently used for live fences because it will grow when a stick is merely stuck in the ground.

1952 FGC StM /máatèl/ Spanish machete, blows a red flower.

maat graas see MOTH GRASS.

MAC sb dial; familiar abbr of MACARONI. A shilling. s CURRENCY.

1873 Rampini 94, see GILL sb². 1943 *GL* Kgn, StM, etc., Mac—1s. 1950 Pioneer 93, Ef dem summons me, mek me pay few mac. 1952 FGC Han, StM /mak/ shilling, one bob.

MACACA /makáka, makáko, makóka, makóko, mákakú, makwáka, makwákwa, makángka, makónggo/ sb dial; 1756 macacca, 1873 macoco, 1943 maccacoo mak-kah-kah makwaka maquaka macca; etym uncert: the word is prob Afr, cf Ko *koka* (pl *makoka*), beetle. Connection with the name of the monkey is not impossible: Sp *macaca* (ultimately from Angola—Friederici). In the Guianas, *macaco, ~ca* is a worm (larva of a fly) that gets under the skin of men or animals. (Santamaría.)

In early use, a large wood-boring beetle and esp its grub that was considered a delicacy; now any grub or grub-like worm.

1756 Browne 277, But when it [*sc* the cotton-tree] falls, it becomes a nest for Macaccas and other insects. *Ibid* 429, Lucanus 1..The Macacca Beetle. This is the largest insect of the fly kind I have observed in Jamaica; it is about two inches and a half in length..This insect breeds in the decayed trunks of trees, particularly those of the plumb and silk-cotton trees; where their large caterpillars, commonly called Macaccas..are studiously sought for by some people, who think them a very great delicacy. 1873 Rampini 42, In the buttresses of its [*sc* the cotton-tree's] trunk reside a colony of macoco beetles, a delicacy as dear to the negro as the snail or frog to a Frenchman. 1943 *NHN* II 70, Fifteen May Bugs [*Ligyrus tumulosus*] the larvæ of which would have been the destructive white grubs of macca [*sic*] worms. 1943 *GL* no addr, Mackanka, a ringed, fat, creeper that lives in rotten wood; StAnn, Maquaka, a kind of worm; StC, Mak-kah-kah, an earth worm; Tre, Maccacoo, larva of a large moth; Maquaka, an earth worm that eats ground provisions. 1952 FGC Man, Port, StT, Tre, West. 1955 FGC Man /màkakú, makúku/ 2-inch white worm from rotten wood; ugly, fatty-like; not eaten any more. 1959 G. Underwood UCWI /macáca/ a generic term for grubs and beetle-larvæ.

MACACCA see prec.

MACADAM sb dial slang; <*macadam*, a type of road, and the material of which it is made. A codfish fritter; the name alludes to its flatness and toughness. *BA*

1952 FGC StAnn /mákadám/.

MACAGINAL sb dial; blend of *McDonald* and *jinal*, clever, tricky. An almanac published annually whose prognostications and general lore are much attended to by the populace of Jamaica.

1943 *GL* StC, Macaginal, McDonald's Almanac.

MACALICKI SU sb; prob imitative of the bird's call—but these imitations are usually pretended to be actual sayings, and this may be analysed as MACCA+LICK+I+SU. An unidentified bird.

1943 *GL* StAnn, Macalicki su, a bird.

MAC-AND-FIP, -FIPNI, or **-FIPPENCE** /mak-an-fip, -fipni, -fipans/ sb dial; <MAC+*and*+FIP, etc. One shilling and threepence.

1943 *GL* Kgn, StM, Mak an fi pans—1*s*. 3*d*.; Tre, Macafipney—1*s*. 3*d*. 1958 DeC StAnd /mak an fip, mak an fipni, mak an fipens/—1*s*. 3*d*. s CURRENCY.

MACANFLAKE sb or vb dial; cf MALIFLAKING.

1943 *GL* StE, Macanflake, damage.

MACARONI sb arch; the name probably alludes to the frequent use of the coin as a tip given by a gentleman or macaroni; *OED* 5, 1834→. s CURRENCY.

1. A coin valued at a quarter of a dollar or the like amount; one shilling. Since 1969=10c Ja.

1808 Stewart 59, The silver coins are dollars (6*s*. 8*d*.), half dollars, and quarter dollars, or maccaronies as they are here popularly called. 1834 Lewis (1845) 121, I also gave..every child a maccarony (fifteen pence) as a parting present. 1835 Madden II 150, Buckra of course rewards with a smile, or, what is still better, with a maccaroni, the fidelity of blackie. 1877 Murray *Feedin' 'Perrit* 7, Him 'pen de whole mackarony in a rum. 1943 *GL* Tre, Macaroni—1*s*.

2. The small fish called 'chub'.

1952 FGC StE /mákaróni/ go in groups; short (2 inches), thick in body, brown scales; some people (Kgn) call them /chob/.

MACARY BITTER /makari/ sb; cf Hausa *makari*, an antidote, +*bitter* sb. [There is prob no connection with *Macorí*, *macurije*, native names in Cuba of *Matayba* spp.] The shrub *Picramnia antidesma*, one of the first medicinal herbs noticed by writers as having been used by negro herb-healers. Cf MAJOE (BITTER), the usual name today. Quot a1726 is prob erron.

a 1726 Barham (1794) 96, It is also called Macary bitter, from its growing in great plenty in the bay of Macary, and being a very bitter plant. 1774 Long I 348, Macari Bahia..perhaps it may derive..from the Indian word Macarij (which signifies bitter), and allude to the tree commonly called the Majoe, or Macary-bitter, which grows in great abundance along this part of the coast. 1837 Macfadyen 224, Majoe or Macary Bitter..The leaves are bitter with a sweetish taste, resembling that of the liquorice..The bark, however, is the part which has been principally employed in medicine..in constitutional affections, connected with syphilis and yaws..as a tonic ..and in intermittent fever. 1920 Fawcett 202, P. antidesma..Majoe Bitter, Macary Bitter. 1954 *WIMJ* 31.

[**MACAW** sb; =*macaw*[1] (*OED* 1668→). The large parrots (genus *Ara*) so called generally today, now extinct in Jamaica. *BL N*

p 1660 *State of Jamaica* (MS Egerton 2395) 489, Of wild fowl infinite store as of..Snipes, Plouers, parrots, turtles, parachytoes wth Machawes, and very many other. 1683 *Present State* 18, Great variety of Pidgeons, Turtles, Parrots, Maces [*sic*], and other Birds, whose flesh is good, and Feathers finely coloured. 1823 Stewart 79, the maccaw is become very scarce.]

MACAW BUSH sb bot; <*macaw*—but in what sense is uncertain; perh macaw birds fed on them (turkeys did—cf the name TURKEY-BERRY); more likely this is an early example of *macaw* as a sp for present MACCA: these bushes were also called CAT-NAIL and are well known for their numerous, recurved prickles. *OED* 1866.

The SUSUMBA bush.

1814 Lunan II 245, Solanum..mamosum..Stem prickly, herbaceous..prickly branched; prickles bending downwards; leaves alternate, on long prickly pedicels..midrib prickly below..*macaw bush*. 1864 Grisebach 785, Mackaw bush: *Solanum mammosum*.

[**MACAW (PALM** or **TREE)** sb bot; cf *OED macaw*[2]: 'Prob. repr. one or more Carib words; cf Arawak (Guiana) *macaya*, *macoya*, the macaw-palm'. Cf also Brazilian *macauba*, palms of genus *Acrocomia* and their fruit. Cf Friederici s.v. *macáuba* and *mucujá*. Earliest use of the name in English is from Barbados. (The *macaw* bird may take its name from this tree.)

The palm tree *Acrocomia sclerocarpa*, noted for its being heavily armed with sharp black prickles.

1657 Ligon 72, The Macow is one of the strangest trees the Iland affords. 1696 Sloane 177–8, Palma tota spinosa major, fructu pruniformi..The great Macaw-tree. In pratis Insulæ Jamaicæ frequenter crescit. a 1726 Barham (1794) 93, Macaw-Tree. So called from a large bird that feeds upon the fruit of this tree, which is of the palm kind..It hath a black, flat round nut..covered over when ripe with a yellow pulp..which the macaw greedily swallows. 1756 Browne 343, The Mackaw Tree. This tree is very common in most of the sugar-colonies..The Great Mackaw Tree. The fruit of this kind differs but little from that of the small Mackaw tree: the husks of both are full of oil..The negroes say that this is the tree which yields the true palm oil. 1811 Titford 111, Maccaw Palm, Cocos butyracea..An oil or butter prepared from it is in constant use among the Indians in their food..The great Maccaw Tree, *C. Aculeata*.. [Jamaica]. 1864 Grisebach 785 Mackaw Tree: *Acrocomia sclerocarpa*.]

MACCA /máka/ sb chiefly dial; <*macaw*, the palm *Acrocomia sclerocarpa*, in reference to its formidable prickles, a striking characteristic which distinguishes it from other palms. A prickle, or prickles of any sort, on plants, animals, etc. (Cf numerous compounds.)

1910 Anderson-Cundall 31 [Prov:] De man dat hab on boot must go befo' so' mash macca. 1943 *GL* StJ, Macca, prickle; StM, Macka, a prickle; general. 1946 U.Newton I 17, There was soft grease—applied warm—for prickles ('macca' to us children) in the fingers or toes. 1954 Reckord *Della* typescript 23, Is not de window, is yu confusion. Yu in a one big, dark, maka-covered land. 1956 Mc Man /di karato hav di maka in di said bot di saisal hav uonly di wan maka in di tap/; StAnd /maka juk yu/ or /maka jam yu/. *BL*; *SC makkà*.

MACCA-BACK DOCTOR sb dial. A variety of DOCTOR FISH, perhaps BLUE DOCTOR FISH, having a spiny dorsal fin.

1952 FGC StAnn /mákabàk dákta/ blue.

MACCA-BACK (SHAD) sb dial. Small fish (one of the kinds called 'shad') that have sharp spines on the dorsal fin.

1892 Cockrell list, Macca back = silver fish, *Gerres rhombeus*. 1943 *GL* Port, Mackaback; StAnd, Maccabak, small sea fishes. 1952 FGC Port, StC, StE, StJ, StM, StT, West /mákabàk shád/.

MACCA-BACK SPIDER-RIAL sb dial. See SPIDER-RIAL. ('Macca-back'—spiny backed—adds to the monstrosity of the imaginary creature.)

MACCA BREADFRUIT sb dial. A variety of breadfruit (*Artocarpus altilis*) with a rough, spiky skin. Also called MONKEY BREADFRUIT.

1952 FGC Port, StT /maka bredfruut/.

MACCA BUSH sb dial.

1. Formerly perh applied specif to one bush: The MACAW BUSH.

2. In present use: any BUSH having prickles on it.

MACCA CALALU sb dial. *Amarantus spinosus* or PRICKLY CALALU.

1954 *FG* 587, Macca Kalalu. . Unlike the closely related garden Kalalu, this unpleasant weed has sharp spines located in pairs at the base of each leaf. These can be a danger not only to the cultivator, but also to such stock as may dare to browse on it.

MACCA CHOCHO sb dial. A very prickly variety of chocho.

1956 Mc Man /máka chócho/.

MACCA, MACCACOO see MACACA.

MACCA CRAB sb dial; <MACCA + *crab*. A crab having sharp points on its shell (*Stenioconops furcata*). Also called BABOON.

1961 Seen in Institute of Ja exhibit (FGC).

MACCA-FAT (PALM) /máka-fát/ sb; <*macaw* (palm) +*fat* sb, alluding to the oil from the tree and fruit. (*OED* 1858→.)

Specifically, the MACAW tree *Acrocomia sclerocarpa*, but this has not been clearly distinguished from the Guinea palm (*Elæis guineensis*) or the Gru-gru palm (*Acrocomia fusiformis*), and since all have similar oil-bearing fruits the name *macca-fat* has been applied to the latter two also.

[1756 Browne 343, The Mackaw Tree. . The rind of the fruit which is pretty thick, yields a fattish substance, not unlike, or inferior to, the real palm-oil.] 1801 Dancer 362, Mackaw Fat or Oil of the Guiney Palm (*Elais Guiniensis*). 1873 Rampini 71, Clumps of wild ginger, Macca-fat palms—surely the most graceful of all that graceful tribe. 1942 *NHN* I 6 13, The Jamaica Macca Fat or Gru-gru Palm is now referable as one species, *Acrocomia fusiformis*. 1943 *GL* StM, Macka-fat, Fruit of the Gru-Gru Palm. 1950 Pioneer 24, Anancy goh to Ma Kayke an ax her wat fruit Dora did like bes' of all, an Ma Kayke tell him sey Dora did love macka-fat. 1956 Mc StAnd, StT /mákafát/—little nut with trash like a coconut and nut inside; a palm with spikes up trunk and on fronds.

MACCA FERN sb dial. A kind of tree fern with many spines. s PRICKLY FERN.

1951 Proctor 8, *Hemitelia horrida*, macca fern. 1952 FGC Port /maka/—tree fern; makes charcoal. 1959 D. Powell Inst of Ja, *Cyathea horrida*, macca fern.

MACCA FISH sb dial. The porcupine or SOURSOP fish—another name alluding to its sharp spines.

1952 FGC StC /maka fish/.

MACCA GRASS sb dial. Some species of *Equisetum*.

1956 Mc StAnd, Umbrella plant—/maka graas/.

MACCA ROBIN see MOCO ROBIN.

MACCARONI, MACCARONY see MACARONI.

MACCA YAM sb dial. A variety of yam that has prickles on the vine.

1952 FGC StJ /máka yám/. 1956 BLB Man /máka yám/ a variety grown in StJ.

MACHET(TE), MACHETTO see next.

MACHETE /mashét, mashíet/ sb; 1803 mushet, 1808 machetto, 1826 1827 machet, 1873 machette, 1929 machete, 1943 mashet; cf *OED matchet* 1598→1887, with first-syllable stress, but in Ja, as spellings indicate, stress has in the past been, as now, on second syllable; ult <Sp *machete*; quot 1808 spells with pseudo-Sp *-o*; other spellings have pseudo-Fr form, dropping the third syllable of the Sp word. The Sp spelling is now Std.

= CUTLASS, the words being interchangeable throughout Ja: a large agricultural knife 2½–3 ft long. There are ten distinctive types differing as to shape, method of sharpening, etc., which adapt some to special uses. See the individual names (more than 60): DeC in 1961 *CLS* 70–1, 73–5. *BA BL G T*

1803 Dallas I 54, On the left side he [Cudjoe] wore a mushet, or couteau, three inches broad, in a leather sheath. 1808 Stewart 292, Their [*sc* the Maroons'] arms were a light fusee and powder-horn, a machetto, or short sabre. . etc. 1826 Williams 66, A machet, or cutlass, made by one of his own blacksmiths. 1873 Rampini 98, I had a crocus (Osnaburg) bag with breadkind on my back and my machette in my hand. 1952 FGC all parishes /mashét, mashíet/.

MACHIATED see *mashieted*.

MACKA(-FAT) see MACCA-FAT (PALM).

MACKARONY see MACARONI.

MACKAW TREE see MACAW (PALM or TREE).

MACKENZIE BOY sb dial; said to be <*mechanic boy*, but this is questionable.

1956 Mc StE (Accom) /makenzi bwai/ a mechanic.

MACKENZIE (PARROT) sb dial; etym unknown. A kind of wrasse, identified by local fishermen as a variety of PARROT FISH: *Halichoeres radiatus*, or similar species.

1952 Smith in *NHN* 190, *Halichoeres radiatus* the pudding wife. . In general shape it much resembles the coral wrasse. . For some mysterious reason it is known in St James as 'McKenzie' or more affectionately as 'Mr Mac.' 1952 FGC Port /makenzi parat/ = red-belly parrot; StM /makenzi parat, veri sripl, lang an krengki/; West /màkénzi skwáb/ = red parrot.

MACKEREL BUSH sb dial; from the shape of the leaf? An unidentified shrub.

1952 FGC Port, Mikonia?

MACKEREL MANGO sb dial. A variety of mango that tastes like mackerel.

1952 FGC StM /mákril mánggo/.

MACKEREL PLANTAIN sb dial. A variety of plantain with flattened fruits resembling the mackerel.

1952 FGC Port /makril plaantn/.

MACK EYE sb dial; etym unknown.

1943 *GL* StT, Mack eye, offspring of two dense blacks.

MACKEY (MASSA) see next.

MACKY, MUCKY /maki, moki/ adj dial arch; cf Twi *makyẽ*, int, good morning! By back-inference from MACKY MASSA: good, fine. (Also, more emphatically: merciful.)

1790 Moreton 158, Twist, wind and wriggle with the mackey beaux. 1943 *GL* Clar, Mucky—merciful. 1955 FGC Man /máki/—howdy-do; old-time, when /mek kochi/ [*In olden times, when one curtseyed, one would say* /máki/].

MACKY, MUCKY MASSA sb or int dial arch; <MACKY+*massa*, master, sir. A greeting: How do you do, Master—hence also (quot 1877) a phrase showing submission and respect.

1790 Moreton 157 [Slave girl doing a dance and singing:] You work him, mackey massa! You sweet me, mackey massa! A little more, my mackey massa! 1877 Murray *Feedin' 'Perrit* 9, Say me mucky massa..Hollar mek all de fish in a sea hear you call me sweet mucky massa. 1943 *GL* StAnd, Mukky massah, mercy master. 1960 UCWI Hospital patient (old woman) /yés máki máasa/.

MACKY, MUCKY MASSA adj dial; <prec. Pretending, for fun, to be a superior person—playing master to someone else.

1943 *GL* StAnn, Mucky-massa, superior in jest.

MACOCO see MACACA.

MACONGO TURTLE sb; etym uncert: cf 1949 Turner 127, *makɔŋgɔ* (Kongo)—persons having some physical deformity.

1873 Rampini 167, There was a Macongo turtle caught at Negril in 1843, which weighed a ton.

MACOO sb dial cant. In the language of AFRICAN cults: The god who causes a possessed zombie to climb up poles and trees backwards.

1953 Moore 140.

MACOOCHE sb dial; perh in some way related to SANGKOCHIE, <Sp *sancocho*; cf the Colombian *Machucho*, a dish of rice and meat or fish stewed together, <*sancocho macho* (Revollo).

1943 *GL* Man, Port, Macooche—soup. 1955 FGC Man /makúuchi/—soup: 'Indian word'.

MACOW see MACAW (PALM).

MAD vb trans dial; cf *OED v* 1 →1863.

1. To drive mad (with anger, envy, astonishment, etc.); to infuriate, to astonish.

1941 Kirkpatrick 13, De R.A.F. mad dem [*sc* the Germans] wid all de explosive dem a drap ebbery night 'pon dem war material factory. 1960 LeP StAnd /mi goin mad dem wid mi dres/.

2. Const *off*: To make (someone) mad with jealousy. (Ironic through exaggeration.)

1954 LeP StAnn [Said of a man very elegantly got up:] Coo yah, him want mad we off.

MADA CANTINNY sb dial.

1951 Murray 18, Mada Cantinny. Character in an Anancy story, whose name was only known to the animals she fostered. Anancy, disguised as a girl, learned her name from Bra Crab, one of her 'children', and Mada Cantinny sang this song to each animal in turn, asking if it were responsible for divulging her secret.

mada-faia, mada-pepa see MOTHER-FIRE.

MADA FATE sb dial; this would be the normal dial reflex of *Mother* Fate, but the plant meant is *Madam* Fate, q.v. This may be an erroneous form or a second name.

1943 *GL* Kgn, Madafate, a trailing plant used as medicine.

MADAGASS sb arch; <*Madagascar*. (Cf 1960 LeP in *CLS* 1 69.) A negro of Madagascar origin, or of similar type. See quot.

1873 Gardner 97, The term Madagass is still applied to certain light-complexioned negroes, especially to those whose hair is less woolly than common. These are found in families where there is a very slight mingling of European blood; and the name therefore only indicates that there was a period when people light in complexion and possessing rather straight hair were known in the colony by that term.

MADAM sb. Term applied to an immigrant Chinese woman, wife of Chinese shopkeeper, etc. Cf *mushe* 1.

MADAM FATE sb dial. A wild plant (*Isotoma longiflora*) having poisonous properties and supposed also to have magic ones. See quots.

1927 Beckwith 21, Madame Fate..If you don't feel like working, cut it up with tall Bahama grass and Apimpe and put into a bottle, then fill it up with rum and rub it on the face and hands. To make a man stop working, tuck the three plants into his belt and he can't work. Or lay them at the top and bottom of his piece of ground and he can't work. 1952 FGC Port /mádam fiet/ a night-shade bush—long tubed white flowers—poisonous certain times of year. 1955 *WIMJ* 73, Madam Fate; Star Flower; Horse Poison. In Jamaica this plant appears to have a reputation not unconnected with magic. 'When looking for it do not call its name or you will not find it' and again 'It will keep away harm—anything that threatens you'.

MADAM SIT-DOWN sb dial. Cf PUMPUM YAM. See quot.

1952 FGC StC /mádam sídòng/ a white Portland yam with a big round bottom.

MAD-ANTS sb. A type of ant that runs about very quickly and erratically, as if mad: *Prenolepis longirostris*.

1952 FGC Man /mad-ants/—/mad az di dikans/; Port, Raffle ant used to call mad-ants; StAnd /mad ans/ run like mad but don't bite; StT, Tre..

mad-dem sb dial joc; <MAD+*them*. Some very fancy kind of pudding which astonishes others (or makes them mad with envy?).

1943 *GL* StM, Mad dem, pudding with soft top.

MAESTIFINO see MUSTIFINA.

MAFEENA see next.

mafiina sb dial; <Pg *mofina*, miserable, wretched, unfortunate, paltry; perh reinforced by Fante *mfina*, a stunted person. A poor, ineffectual person for whom nothing turns out well and who is resigned to paltriness.

1942 Bennett 36, Me a po Muffeena noh missis Fe me luck is dis like mud Me noh bizniz wid a t'ing noh. 1943 *GL* StC, Mafeena, muffeena, poor person, refined, effeminate, ineffectual. 1955 FGC Man /maffina/ very poor, much reduced; keep out of trouble: Me is poor /maffina/—don' business wid trouble.

MAFOOTOO WITHE sb; cf Fante *ε-mã*, very, plentifully, *futuw*, rank, abundant, thickly grown. The CACOON vine, *Entada gigas*.

[1756 Browne 362, Cocoon..This plant is frequent in most of the woods on the north side of Jamaica, and climbs with great ease to the top of the tallest trees where it frequently spreads over many of the neighbouring branches.] 1814 Lunan I 137, Cacoons, or Mafootoo wythe..Mimosa Scandens. 1864 Grisebach 785, Mafootoo-withe. [1907 Dolf Wyllarde, *Mafoota*. (Title of a novel taken from name of an estate.)] 1920 Fawcett 125.

MAGA see *maaga*.

MAGGICH /mágich, mágij/ sb dial; cf *EDD*: *maghoges*, maggots (Wexford, Irel); derived from *maggot* by change of *-ts* (of plur form) > *-ch*, and voicing of *-ch* > *-j*. Maggot or maggots. *BL*

1943 *GL* Kgn, Maggich; Port, StAnn, Maggitch; StC, Magige. 1962 BLB 62 /magij/ maggots.

MAGGIE /mági/ sb dial or slang; etym unknown. Handcuffs.

1943 *GL* Kgn, StJ, Maggie, handcuffs, manacles. 1955 FGC Man /mági/ handcuffs.

MAGGITCH, MAGGOT see MAGGICH.

MAGIC vb dial; < *magic* adj or sb. To perform magic upon, to bewitch.

1952 FGC StM, Samfai man—a man that magic you.

magich, MAGIGE, magij see MAGGICH.

MAGNET sb dial; cf the idea of 'personal magnetism'. The psychic power or influence that one person may exert upon another. It may be exerted through the eye—see OVERLOOK.

1952 FGC StM, When a baby has been 'over-looked' it is because 'the magnet of people too strong for it'. Man, Him have a strong magnet.

mah see MA.

MAHHE see *maa-i*.

MAHMA see *maama*.

MAHMY see *maami*.

MAHO see next.

MAHOE sb; cf *OED* 1666→.

1. Any of several species of *Paritium*; also of similar trees—see compounds. (In this sense not a Jamaicanism, but note spellings.) *N*

1683 *Laws of Ja* map, Mohoe Garden. (*OED* this sp 1866.)

2. The bark or wood of this tree. Also attrib. (*OED* 1897.)

a 1726 Barham (1794) 95, The bark of those trees is often called *maho*. 1837 Sterne 17, They..tied him with a piece of maho bark, broad, but not twisted.

MAHOE ROPE sb; < MAHOE 2 + *rope*. Rope made from the bark of the mahoe tree.

[1756 Browne 284 (see BARK TREE 1).] 1827 Hamel I 320, He took from under his frock two or three fathoms of mahoe rope, which he told Roland he always carried to hang those who violated their sacred oaths. (1960 Current, FGC.)

MAHOE ROSE sb. A shrub with flowers resembling those of the MAHOE tree: *Malvaviscus sagræanus*.

1926 Fawcett 133, see MORASS BARK.

MAHOGANY sb[1]; cf Friederici: ult < Island-Arawak of Puerto Rico *maga*, later developed in some obscure way into *magahoni*, whence Linnæus's *mahagoni*. *OED* 1671→. The tree *Swietenia mahagoni* and its wood. *BA*

p 1660 State of Jamaica 661, Many sorts as Ceadr., Mahogeny, Lignum Vitee..and others wch are frequently exported. 1671 Ogilby America 338, Here [in Jamaica] are..the most curious and rich sorts of Woods, as Cedar, Mohogeney, Lignum-vitæ, Ebony [etc.]. (*OED*). 1756 Browne 17, While the Mahogany tree grew in the more convenient parts of this Island, it furnished another very valuable branch of its exports. *Ibid* 158, Mahagony. 1837 Macfadyen 176, It was from this Island that the supply for Europe was in former times principally obtained, and the Old Jamaica Mahogany is still considered superior to any that can now be procured from any other country. 1927 Beckwith 21, Mahogany..For cold or fever, the leaves are used as an ingredient in a bath and also drunk as tea. 1952 FGC StE /miágini/ StM /mahágani, mahágini/.

MAHOGANY sb[2] dial; evid for the name of the tree or wood, but the reason is unknown.

1943 *GL* Tre, Mahageny—shad. 1952 *FGC* Tre /mihágini/ shad, ale-wives.

MAID sb dial. A local name for the sting-ray *Urolophus jamaicensis*.

1961 R. P. Bengry, Commonly called 'maid' by fishermen: the sting-ray.

MAIDEN PLANTAIN sb; cf *maid plantain* of Trinidad, etc.; 'maiden' implies small size. A variety of plantain with relatively small individual fruits but large bunches. *N*

1725 Sloane, see HORSE PLANTAIN. 1934 *Ja Times* 19 May, and 1942 HPJ, see *fiekuma*. 1952 FGC Port, StAnd, StAnn, StE, StJ, StM, StT /míedn pláantn/.

MAIDEN PLUM (TREE) sb; *OED* 1725→.

1. Trees of the genus *Comocladia*; despite quot 1740, the tree does bear a plum, and the name is prob due to the delicacy of the flowering stalk.

1696 Sloane 184, Prunus racemosa, caudice non ramoso, alato fraxini folio non crenato, fructu rubro subdulci. The Maiden Plumb-tree. 1740 Importance 31, There is a Tree which they call the Maiden Plumb Tree, which has a beautiful Leaf, but never bears Fruit. 1814 Lunan I 475–6, *Comocladia integrifolia*..This plant is so similar in habit to the *spathelia simplex* (see mountain pride) that it is difficult to distinguish them from each other when not in flower, for which reason they have both been confounded by the name of maiden-plum. 1926 Fawcett 11, *Comocladia*..Maiden Plum. (Ten species listed.)

2. Erron: The MOUNTAIN PRIDE (fide Lunan—see quot 1814 above).

MAIDEN PULLET sb now dial. A young hen that has not yet produced eggs.

1790 Moreton 115 [For a feast] four capons, two maiden pullets (as they call them), twenty-four pigeons..lost their lives! 1942 FGC West /medn pulit/ fowl 1–1½ years that don't lay. [Also /miedn/.]

MAIDEN SUCKER sb. A banana sucker or young tree that has not yet borne fruit: see quot.

1913 Fawcett 25, The best for general purposes in planting are 'maiden suckers', that is, suckers about eight months old which have taken on adult foliage, and passed beyond the stage when the leaves are narrow in proportion to their length—'sword suckers'.

MAIDEN YELLOWTAIL sb dial; a young fish which has not yet produced eggs. A variety, or stage in growth, of the YELLOWTAIL fish: see quot.

1929 Beckwith 33, see DROP YELLOWTAIL.

MAIN SHEET sb slang arch or obs; *OED* 2 1882→. A mixture of rum and water.

1873 Rampini 164, To wash down all the delicacies we had penn punch..main sheet, sangaree, man dram, and a host of 'beverages'. 1889 Sanguinetti 51, A pleasant mixture of rum and water kept ready mixed in a bottle and exposed to the cooling influences of the breeze..is called 'Main Sheet'.

MAIN-WOOD sb. The sides of a sea-going *kunu*.

1956 Mc StC (Old Harbour) /mien uud/.

MAJA, MAJER see *meja*.

majo see next.

MAJOE (BITTER) /májo, máju/ sb; said to be a personal name (see quot a 1725): cf also Mende *majo*, the leading woman of the Sande, a female society into which nearly all the girls are initiated—still used as a personal name among Gullah negroes in US (Turner 127).

The shrub *Picramnia antidesma*; formerly called MACARY BITTER.

a 1726 Barham (1794) 96, This admirable plant hath its name from Majoe, an old negro woman so called, who, with a simple decoction, did wonderful cures in the most stubborn diseases, as the yaws, and in venereal cases. 1774 Long I 348, Some very notable cures, in cases of inveterate ulcers, the yaws, and venereal distempers, were some years ago performed by an old Negress, named Majoe, in commemoration of whom it took its name. 1801 Dancer 363, Stomachichs, Tonics..Majoe Bitter. 1952 Kerr 26, One recipe is as follows, cirque [*sic*] viva.. castor oil, rice bitters, and mojo bitters. 1952 FGC StAnn /máju/ use for /yaa/; StM /majo/ hextra bitter, used against /yaa/; Tre /manjo, majo/ bitter bush, red seeds.

maju see prec.

mak see MAC.

maka see MACCA.

makaka, makako, makaku see MACACA.

maka-maka adj dial; cf *meke-meke*.

1958 DeC Port /maka-maka/ wet, sloppy, muddy.

mak-an-fip, -fipni, -fipans see MAC-AND-FIP.

makangka see MACACA.

makaroni see MACARONI.

makati bush see MCKATTY BUSH.

MA KATIE sb dial; imitative of the bird's cry and personifying. The BANANA BIRD. *BL*

1955 Taylor 38, The Jamaican Oriole (*Icterus leucopteryx*) is known locally as the Banana-bird..the Ma Katie or the Auntie Katie.

MAKE /mek/ vb and adv dial; <*make* vb. Note: The normal dial reflex of this word would be */míek/ but it is always /mek/ (cf /tek/ for TAKE). This corresp exactly with, and prob preserves, the Engl dial pronunc [mɛk], common in the NW and W of England (*EDD*). (So also [mɛk, tɛk] in Sierra Leone Krio, Cameroons Pidgin.) *SC méki*.

A. vb: 1. In normal StdE senses, not specif Ja: produce, do, cause, force, etc.

2. Allow, permit, let. *BL G N*

1862 Clutterbuck 306, De dogs come tear we—make we run*..*Let us run. 1877 Murray *Kittle* 8, Mash her up and turn her adrift. Dont mek no man handle my canoe. 1947 U.Newton II 5, Look after the coffee; don't make rain wet it. 1956 Mc gen /mek a sii/ *Let me see;* /mek wi go nou/ *Let us go now.*

B. adv: As an introductory interrog word (ellipt < WA MEK): Why? *BL G*

1957 Bennett 81, Lick Rena pon har mout' an ask Her 'meck she chat soh much?' 1961 BLB 12 /mek im no iit im dina?/ *Why doesn't he eat his dinner?*

MAKE A BABY vb phr dial. To be pregnant—usually in pres pple form. *BA G T* Grenada; *SC méki pikíen.*

1952 FGC StAnd /shi mékin a bíebi/.

MAKE A FOOT vb phr obs; by the usual dial use of *foot* for *leg*, <*make a leg*. To make an obeisance.

1827 Hamel II 182, The Negro bowed, and made a foot—as the dialect has it.

MAKE FOUR EYES vb phr dial. Of two people: to look each at the other, to have sight of one another (implying intimate conversation). See SIX EYES. *BA G*

1949 Reid 374, Another example of an easily understood dialect usage is that of saying that two people 'make four eyes' instead of saying that they look at each other. 1955 FGC Man, Is long time since you an me mek four eyes. [i.e. since we have had a meeting or seen one another.] 1956 BLB Man /fi-mi ai ang fi-him no mek fuor/ [*We don't see eye to eye*].

MAKE HASTE see *mikies*.

MAKE (ONE) KNOW vb phr dial; ellipt <*make one know* (*what's what, who's the boss,* or the like). To scold, punish, etc. *BL G*

1912 McK *Ballads* 31, Ef you 'low de sun fe grow, Grass-lice wi' sure mek you know*..*Give you beans. *Ibid* 49, We boys beneat' de big-tree really mean fe mek you know. (1956 Current, BLB.)

MAKE PAPPA STAY AT HOME sb dial. The alleged name of one of the plants used to concoct a 'fever bath'.

1954 Kirkland 170 (Port).

maketi sb dial; ?cf MCKATTY BUSH.

1956 Mc Port /makéti/ a type of coco with white flesh.

MAKE-UP /mék-òp/ vb phr and sb dial.

A. vb: 1. A command by a buyer to a seller demanding full quantity, or something extra. (See the noun.) *BA G*

1952 FGC StAnd /mék-òp/ *Add some!*

2. trans or intr. Of the face: to distort or be distorted with a set expression of anger or some similar emotion. *G*

1877 Murray *Kittle* 27, I wake Peter. My good sir, Peter mek up one face! nuff fe cruddle any milk! 1942 Bennett 45, De man meck up him face dis lacka Wen it set fe rain. 1955 Bennett *Bad Prayers,* She stare pon me, her face meck up Like she was eena pain.

3. To have one's mind made up; to intend (*OED* 96k); to plan, to plot. *G*

1956 Mc Man /wi mék op fi gó éniwie/ *We are decided to go anyway.* 1956 BLB Man /mèk-óp/ agree, plan together, plot.

4. To prepare (a corpse) for burial.

1953 Moore 38, Then a man come and they make him [*sc* the corpse] up. Make him up means that they take something, a piece of calico about eight feet long and they pass it to the head and to the feet..[etc.].

B. sb: A little extra amount given by the seller to the purchaser to make it a bargain; *braata*. *BA G*

1952 FGC Han, StM /mék-òp/ a little more of something being bought. 1956 Mc, The market woman withholds a yam or two when she makes her sale, then awaits the inevitable /we di mek-op?/ The addition of this item satisfies the customer.

MAKE UP TIME vb phr dial. *BA G*

1958 DeC StT /mek op taim/ to pass the time; /an dem mek op taim se wel dem gwain tu kil bra taiga childran/ *and they passed the time by saying that they would kill brother Tiger's children.*

maki see MACKY.

MAK-KAH-KAH, MAKWAKA see MACACA.

MAKLA-MAKLA adj dial obs?; etym unknown.

1868 Russell 10, Bad taste from too many mixtures. Dis is a makla-makla drink. African.

makoka, makoko, makonggo, makwaka, makwakwa see MACACA.

MALAHACK vb dial; cf *EDD*, '*malahack*, to cut or carve in a slovenly, awkward way..Of a horse or donkey: to become disabled or worn out by hard work'. To treat an animal roughly or cruelly; to chop it. (Cf US *mollyhawk*, *ADD*.)

1943 *GL* Kgn, Malahak, cruelly choping an animal. 1955 FGC Man /malahak/ manhandle, treat roughly or cruelly.

malanta, malantan see MULATTO. s MALANTANG.

malanti (bush) sb dial. An unidentified bush.

1952 FGC Han /malánti/ a weak bending and running shrub, along the road by the sea; tiny white flowers in flat bunches; bees favour it.

malasis see MORASS (WEED).

malata, malato see MULATTO.

malava, malawa sb dial; cf Kongo *malavu*, Kikongo *malavu*, Tshiluba *maluvu*, palm wine or other spirits. (Turner 128.) Rum.

1943 *GL* Port, Malawa, rum. 1953 Moore StT /malava/—rum.

MAL DE STOMACH sb obs; <Fr *mal d'estomac*. Geophagy; DIRT-EATING.

[1817 Williamson i 110, What is known by the name of *mal d'estomac* among the French; among the British, the stomach evil, or dirt-eating.] 1823 Stewart 307, The most peculiar disease to which the negroes are subject is *mal de* stomach, being a strong and irresistible craving of the stomach for earth.

MALE BALSAM-APPLE sb bot obs.

1814 Lunan I 173, *Momordica balsamina*..This is called *smooth-leaved cerasee*, or *male balsam apple*.

(MALE) BAS' CEDAR sb dial; <*male*+BASS CEDAR; but the plant is so different from BASS CEDAR that the reason for the name is hard to imagine. Perh erron.

1955 *WIMJ* 159, *Leonotis nepetæfolia*..Pick Nut; Christmas Candlesticks; Ball Head; Bald Head or Bush; (Male) Bas Cedar.

malela, manila sb dial; <*Manila*, fibre used for rope, etc. The fibre of sisal, used similarly.

1952 FGC StAnn /manila/ called /kàrató/ in Portland, sisal in St Catherine; StM /maléla/ has a tall shooting, white flowers—plait it to make rope.

MALEMBA, MALEMBE int dial uncom; cf Ko *malembe*, greeting.

1943 *GL* Man, Malembe, Good morning (African); Port, Malemba, morning; malemba paungam, good morning.

MALICE sb dial. In various phrases of similar meaning: *to be in malice, have a malice with, keep malice*, etc.: to be in a quarrel with, not on speaking terms, refusing to make up with, looking for opportunities to harm. *BA BL*

1955 Bennett *Foot Works*, Ef yuh heel dem dah kip malice, An dem teck oat' [oath] no fe jine, Dem we haffe curb dem tempa Wen dem come eena dis line. 1956 Mc Man /fran dat wi hiina malis—wi no piik tu wan aneda/, /ef yu hav a malis wi a paasan yu mos waan im/ (before you attempt to kill him).

MALIFLAKING vbl sb; cf MACANFLAKE, MALAHACK; *mollyhawk* (*EDD, DA*). A beating or drubbing.

1900 Murray 8, Hullo, old Guzzoo! How is you mout'. You want anader maliflakin. *Ibid* 9, He was gleefully explaining the 'maliflakin'.

MALLA-MALLA vb dial unc; by iteration of *malla*, prob <*mall*, to beat (*OED Maul v.*,.. To beat,..to hammer). But cf MALAHACK.

1943 *GL* Tre, Malla-malla, beat or pound.

MALLET WOOD sb dial; used for furniture, perhaps turned for mallets? If equation with Wild Guinep is correct, this is the tree *Exothea paniculata*, and its wood. *G*

1952 FGC StAnn, Mallet wood, wild guinep.

MALLOW-LEAVED BROOMWEED sb bot obs; cf BROOMWEED. In Macfadyen's use: *Sida althæifolia* (ident 1926 Fawcett 117).

1837 Macfadyen 81, *Mallow-leaved Broom-weed.*

MALO adj or adv dial; <Sp *malo*. Bad; badly. *BL*

1941 Kirkpatrick 19, T'ings gwine so malo wid im. 1943 *GL* Kgn, Malo, Spanish, bad; StAnd, it mawlo, it bad.

malongkontong sb dial; etym unknown, but cf *konkonte* and LUNG-PLUNG. A coconut rundown.

1958 DeC Port /malongkontóng/.

mama see *maama*.

MAMA MAN see *maama-man*.

MAMI see *maami*.

mamlit see HAMLET.

MAMMA see *maama*.

MAMMA SHRIMP sb obs; cf SHRIMP MAAMI. A crab somewhat longer than it is wide, and appearing somewhat shrimp-like.

1756 Browne 422, Cancer 11..The Mamma-Shrimp.. It was found by some of the fishermen in the harbour of Kingston; and is represented here of the natural size. (Tab 42 f 2.)

MAMMA-YAW sb dial; cf Fr *maman-pian*: both the Fr and Engl words prob being loan-translations from Afr langs. The large central pustule of yaws about which the smaller ones cluster.

1801 Dancer 222–3, There is generally one pustule larger than the rest, called the *Master* or Mamma Yaw. *Ibid* 226, *Mamma-Yaw*—This sometimes remains after all the others are healed. 1820 Thomson 84 (see MASTER YAW). 1959 O. D. Simons UCWI Prev Med /maami yaa/—still in use.

MAMMEE APPLE /maami/ sb; *OED* 1683→. The fruit of the tree *Mammea americana*. (Guttiferæ.) *BA N*

1657 Continuation 46, Fruits..4. Mamesappole, tastes like Marmalet. 1826 Williams 290. 1913 Harris 12.

MAMMEE BARK sb. The bark of *Mammea americana*.

1820 Thompson 96, They place their feet in a large kettle..here they soak them for several days..They wash with a strong bath of mammea-bark immediately afterwards.

MAMMEE GUM sb dial.

1740 Importance 44, Mammee-Gum the Negro Doctors use for the Chigoes.

MAMMEE SAPOTA /sapúota, supúota/ sb; cf *OED* 1693→. The tree *Calocarpum mammosum*, one of the Sapotaceæ.

p 1660 State of Jamaica 489, Coconutts, Mannills [*sic*, misread for *mammees*], Manill supotas, supotillia.. [etc.]. 1672 Blome 25, There are great plenty of.. Fruits..as Guavars, Mamees, Alumee[*sic*]-Supotas, Suppotillias, Avocatas..[etc.]. 1696 Sloane 181, The Mammee-Sapota. 1740 Importance 52, The Mamme Suppotta bears a large Fruit in a Shell, which is very delicious, but scarce. 1959 E. M. Falconer in *Letter*; Mamie Supporter or Suppota. A fruit nearly like papa or pawpaw.

MAMMEE TREE sb; *OED* 1725→. The tree *Mammea americana*. *G*

1696 Sloane 180, The Mammee Tree. In omnibus sylvis montosis Insulæ Jamaicæ abundat. a 1726 Barham (1794) 99, Mammee-tree. 1864 Grisebach 785.

MAMMICK vb dial; <*mammock*, to break or cut into pieces, to crumble, tear, mangle (*EDD*). To manhandle (an animal, etc.). **s.**

1943 *GL* StM, Mammick, rough handled and hurt. 1955 FGC Man /mámik/ same as /malahak/.

MAMMY sb dial cant. In the language of Revival cults: A leading woman; = SHEPHERDESS.

1929 Beckwith 160, The women who thus become active Revivalists are called mammies, the men, soldiers. They are led by a 'captain' and a principal mammy..who in turn may be directed by a head captain and mammy for a large district.

MAMMY PLANT sb dial; origin uncert. Possibly the Mammee tree?

1929 Beckwith 87, If you plant the seed of a 'mammy plant' or of a pumpkin vine, a relative will die, says one of Cundall's informants.

ma mod sb dial; perh <MA+*mud*: cf *EDD mud-fat*, very fat indeed.

1956 Mc Man /ma mód/ very big, fat (woman).

mampala /mampáala, mampáalo, mámpala/ sb dial, also attrib; <Amer Sp (Colombia, Cuba, etc.) *mampolón*, a common cock, not a fighting-cock.

1. A man deficient or aberrant in his masculinity: impotent, effeminate, homosexual, etc. As a term of insult to a man this is among the most violent.

1943 *GL* Port, StE, Tre, Mampala, mampawla, mamparla—effeminate, low minded. 1952 C. B. Lewis Kgn /mampáalo/ the worst possible insult; means generally, the lowest possible thing, specifically, abnormal sexuality of any kind. 1960 LeP Kgn, Means homosexual but is commonly used as a curse: Get away, mámpala—get away, you mámpala-man you!

2. See quot.

1955 FGC Man /mampáala/ a man that meddles in women's business, abuses women. Used as an insult.

3. See quot.

1943 *GL* Kgn, Mampala, male crab.

MAMPARLA, MAMPAWLA see prec.

MAN sb; cf *OED* 4e. *BA BL G N T*

1. A fellow, friend: used by and of members of either sex in situations of informal or familiar conversation, as a term of address or of attention-getting. Frequent at all social levels. (This usage is prob an influence from the north and west of England, Scotland, Wales, Ireland, where it is more frequent and characteristic than elsewhere in Britain, though no more so than in Jamaica and other parts of the WI)

1877 Murray *Kittle* 7, To this Old John used to rejoin, after regarding Tom with a comical mixture of affection, and displeasure, 'Cho, go 'bout you business, man; you is a chupid boy'. 1950 Pioneer 31, Hear Anancy, 'cho, dat ish shmall mattas man, me wi kea yuh go'. 1954 LeP StAnn, Man, you strong!

2. A fellow, a person: the informal generic; sometimes used to avoid direct reference to oneself or another person. Chiefly dial.

1924 Beckwith 11 [A story in which animals are personified:] when I see a cow lie down, I go up an' run me han' inside of de cow an' hol' de man tripe, so I never out of meat. *Ibid* 41, So when Cow go long, pass him, Cow say, 'Chuh! man fool! man kyan't work groun' 'pon rock-stone!' [Cow is calling Anansi a fool without actually naming him.] 1956 Mc /yu si a man in jepit a dem laif, an you a laaf / *You see me in jeopardy of my life, and you laugh!* 1957 JN [A schoolgirl speaking to other children:] No-no, not a man a get this pretty one. *No no, nobody is going to have this pretty one.* (It's mine!)

MAN- sb attrib dial. Male, or having masculine characteristics (e.g. rough or hairy skin, larger size, harder flesh); sometimes redundant. See as first element in separate entries. Cf also WOMAN-, quot 1868. *BL G*

MAN AFU sb dial; <*man* attrib + AFU. An afu yam that grows a straight root. See quot.

1958 DeC gen /man afu/ an afu yam whose food 'grow straight' but 'it grow watery and not good'. A distinct variety?

MANANA /manyána/ sb; <Sp *mañana*, tomorrow. Widely known and to some extent used as a conscious Hispanism: tomorrow. *BL*

1943 *GL* Clar, Port, StAnd, Manana, tomorrow.

MANATEE GRASS sb; cf *OED*. The marine herb *Thalassia testudinum*.

1696 Sloane 5, Juncus marinus..Manati grasse. Copiose fluctuantem circa promontorium *Point Pedro* dictum observari & collegi. 1814 Lunan II 250, Turtle or Manatee Grass. Zostera..marina..This plant is the same as the European one, and grows frequently in the shallow sandy bays of Jamaica, and is the common food of the manatee, the turtle, and trune [i.e. trunc] fish. 1864 Grisebach 785.

MANATEE STONES sb obs. See quots.

1707 Sloane lxxxv, The Manati Stones are brought from thence [*sc* Porto Plata], and taken from behind the Ears of that Animal, each Ear having one. [1725 Sloane 329–30, The Manati..They have Stones in their Heads, good for the Diseases of the Liver burnt and powder'd, taken in a Morning with white Wine, it takes away the Pain in the Kidnies, breaks the Stone, and brings away with Urine the Sand.]

MANATEE STRAP sb obs. A strap or whip-thong of manatee hide.

1707 Sloane lvii, Beating with Manati Straps is thought too cruel, and therefore prohibited by the Customs of the Country. [1756 Browne 459–60, The Manatee..the skin, which is very thick, being cut into regular pieces, makes fine riding switches.]

MAN-BACK sb dial; for *man's back*. Species of *Desmodium*—see quot.

1954 *WIMJ* 18, Wild Pinder; Strong Back; Man Back; Bee Bur or Bush. *D. supinum* and probably other Desmodium species are used quite commonly to make tea for pains in the back. The whole plant is boiled either alone, or with other plants.

MAN BEEFWOOD see BEEFWOOD, quot 1952.

MANCHA, MANCHAN, MANCHI, MANCHINIC(K) sb dial; <*Martinique* (banana). Nicknames for the Martinique banana—now also generalized: any banana.

1912 McK *Songs* 30, Green Mancha mek fe naygur man; *ibid* 117, She look 'pon de Manchinic* tree, Not a piece of mancha fe eat..*Martinique, the best variety of Banana. Hence mancha for banana. 1943 *GL* Tre, Mancha, mansha; Clar, Manchinick; StT, Manchi. 1954 LeP StAnn, Mancha—Banana. 1956 Mc StE (Accom) /manchan/ general term for banana—now old-fashioned.

MAN-COW sb dial. A bull. *BA G*

1868 Russell 9, Gender..By prefixing the word Man and Oman.—This is done to animal as well as vegetable names; thus—Man-cow, Oman-cow, Man-prementa, Oman-prementa. 1956 Mc StAnd /mán kòu/ a bull.

MAN DANDELION sb dial. The shrubs *Cassia occidentalis* and *C. ligustrina*, higher, and with larger, coarser leaves than WOMAN DANDELION.

1952 FGC StM.

MANDINGO. A negro of Mandingo (=Madinka, Malinke, etc.) -speaking origin, from the area of present Senegal and (French) Guinea.

1828 Kelly 21, see CONGO 2.

MANDRAM sb arch; etym unknown; *OED* quots 1756→1845. See quot 1756.

1756 Browne 177, There is a mixture made and used in some of our colonies, called Mandram..which seldom fails to provoke an appetite in the most languid stomachs. The ingredients are sliced cucumbers, eschalots or onions cut very small, a little lime-juice, and Madeira wine, with a few pods of bird or other pepper well mashed and mixed in the liquor. 1873 Rampini 164, see MAIN SHEET.

MAN DUMPLING sb dial. A very large round dumpling. (It is uncertain whether the sense is 'size of a man' or 'fit for a man', both suggested by bigness.)

1958 DeC StT /man dompling/.

MANGERINE /mànjaríin/ sb; <*mandarin* (orange), or the Fr form *mandarine*, and by analogy to TANGERINE. *BL*

1943 *GL* Tre, Mangerine, A fruit of the tangerine family.

mangkishim sb dial unc; etym unknown: the word has the appearance of an Africanism but nothing like it has been found.

1958 DeC Port (Moore Town) /mangkishim/ noun: death, apparently in abstract sense; /hin no fried fi mangkishim/—*He doesn't fear death.* In speaking of a particular person's death, one would use the word /det/.

MANGO BIRD = MANGO HUMMING-BIRD.

MANGO BUG sb dial. The cricket—so called because it 'comes in' the same time as the mango.

1952 FGC Tre /manggo bog/ black, has two big eyes that pulp out.

MANGO COLOUR sb dial.

1958 DeC StT /manggo kola/ name for an albino Negro.

MANGO HUMMING-BIRD sb; the origin of 'mango' here is unknown: it can hardly refer to the fruit so called—see Gosse's suggestion, quot 1847; *OED* 1782 only.

The largest of the Jamaican humming-birds: *Anthracothorax mango.*

1847 Gosse 88, Mango Humming-Bird *Lampornis mango*..For what reason Linnæus applied the trivial name of Mango to this Humming-bird I have no knowledge; that it could have no connexion with the mango tree is evident, since that tree was not introduced into the western world till long after his time. It was perhaps a native name. 1936 Bond 208, Jamaican Mango Hummingbird. 1956 Jeffrey-Smith 24, The Mango Humming Bird..is not so called 'because it frequents a kind of fruit tree called the Mango'..as stated by A. G. Adams.

MANGOLA DRUMMER see MONGOLA DRUMMER.

MANGO PAPAW sb. A variety of papaw: see quot.

1814 Lunan II 37, The long mango papaw makes a pickle little inferior to the East Indian mango. The rounder fruit, when ripe, is boiled and eaten with any kind of flesh meat.

MANGROVE see MANGROW.

MANGROVE CANARY see SEASIDE CANARY.

MANGROVE CRAB sb. *OED* 1756. See quots.

1756 Browne 422, Cancer 15..The Mangrove Crab. This species is very common in all the low and marshy lands bordering upon the sea. It is often used by the negroes, but said to be sometimes poisonous. 1960 Institute of Ja exhibit, Mangrove crab, *Goniopsis cruentata.*

MANGROVE GRAPE (TREE) sb bot. The Sea-side Grape, *Coccoloba uvifera. N* MANGROW ~.

1696 Sloane 184, The Mangrove Grape-tree. 1756 Browne 209, The Mangrove or Sea-side Grape. 1814 Lunan I 77. 1864 Grisebach 784.

MANGROVE HEN /mánggro hén/ sb; so called from its living among mangroves; *OED* 1847→. The Clapper Rail *Rallus longirostris.*

1843 Chamberlaine 83, Rallus Virginianus? The country people call it the mangrove hen. 1847 Gosse 364, 367. 1952 FGC StC /manggro hen/ darker than /naadi/ (=noddy). 1956 Jeffrey-Smith 116, The mangrove hen is brownish above with a deep cinnamon neck and breast.

MANGROVE WARBLER see SEASIDE CANARY.

MANGROW /mánggro/ sb dial; the Jamaican folk form preserves the early *mangrowe* (*OED* 1613), the predecessor of *mangrove*, both being folk-etymologies based on Pg *mangue* or Sp *mangle. BL N; SC mángro.*

1952 FGC Tre, Han, and generally /mánggro/—mangrove.

MANGY /míenji/ adj dial; cf *OED* 3 'beggarly, mean' →1694. *BL*

1943 *GL* StC, Mangey, mean.

MAN-HEART sb dial. A wild herb, also called BUTTON-WEED, believed to furnish a good heart medicine.

1952 FGC StAnn, Tre /màn-háat, mànáat/—good for the heart.

manifak vb dial; cf *OED manufact sb*, →1691, of which this may be a corresp vb; more prob it is a back-formation <*manufacture vb.* To prepare a product for use or sale.

1952 FGC Clar, To /mánifàk/ all these herbs; Man, Ginger..is hard to /mánifák/.

manila see *malela.*

MANISH see MANNISH.

MANJABULA sb dial; etym unknown.

1943 *GL* StC, Manjabula, coconut shell.

MAN JACK sb; etym unknown—cf *OED manjak* (a West-Indian word for certain sticky or tarry substances) which may have some connection. *OED* 1864. *BA*

1. The tree *Cordia macrophylla.*

1854–5 *TJSA* I 8, Cordia macrophylla, Broad leave Cherry, or Man-Jack. 1864 Grisebach 785, Manjack.

2. Some kind of Ficus.

1944 *NHN* II 143, A Ficus known locally as Man Jack.

3. See quot.

1952 FGC StAnn /mán-ják/ the Portland name for watermahoe.

manjo see MAJOE.

MAN-LIMB sb chiefly dial. A term in pruning trees: see quot. Cf GORMANDIZER.

1957 DeC StAnd /man lim/ a water sucker shoot which grows from a limb or branch. This may shoot up several feet in one season..until it tops the rest of the tree, then branches out. A man-limb must be cut as soon as possible.

MANNARSABLE, MANNASABLE see MANNERSABLE.

MANNAS see MANNERS.

MANNASLY see MANNERSLY.

MANNERS adj dial; by abbr of *mannerly* or by conversion of *manners* sb. Mannerly, well-mannered. Cf MANNERSLY, MANNERSABLE. *BL*

1877 Murray *Feedin' 'Perrit* 11, Dem country people is a mannas set o' people; dem bring up dem pickney berry mannas.

MANNERSABLE adj dial; <*manners*+*-able*. Mannerly; polite.

1900 Murray 4, Teks my egsvice and larn to be mannarsable! 1942 Bennett 4, She mannasable, wen we meet She allways bow an' smile. 1960 LeP StAnd, Mannersable, having good manners.

MANNERSLY adj dial; <*mannerly* with intrusive *s* or by blending with *manners*. Mannerly. Cf MANNERS, MANNERSABLE.

1943 *GL* Kgn, Mannasly, polite.

MANNISH adj dial; <*man*+*-ish*. Forward, impertinent; said of either sex. *BL G N T*

1868 Russell 18, Ga lang yanda sa, you too manish. (Go away from me sir, you are too froward [*sic*].) 1873 Rampini 100, He further added—You are too d--n fast, you are too mannish. 1925 Beckwith 44 [Prov:] Lilly darg always mannish a him massa door-mout'.

MAN-O'-WAR BLADDER or **BLUBBER** sb dial; abbr of *Portuguese man-o'-war*+*bladder* or *blubber*, jellyfish. The Portuguese man-o'-war. *BA*

1952 FGC StC /mánowar blóba/—have a bad sting; StT /mánawar bláda/—type of jelly-fish, float on surface.

MAN-O'-WAR HAT sb dial obs? A hat (shaped like an admiral's?) of woven thatch-palm.

1877 Murray *Feedin' 'Perrit* 4, I ben had a plendid man-o'-war plat hat. I mek it merely wid a long crown.

MAN-O'-WAR YAGER sb dial; <*man-o'-war*, fighting ship+*yager*, hunter (see *OED jager*, *yager*, and cf *galley-worm*). This must be an old name for a ship of chase, assimilated, in its application to the worm, to a galley, with many oars.

A myriapod or galley-worm. More commonly called GRANDY MARY.

1958 FGC StT /mánawà íega/ 1000-leg worm.

MAN PIMENTO sb dial. The male pimento tree.

1868 Russell 9, see MAN COW.

MANSHA see MANCHA.

MAN-SUCKER sb dial. See quot.

1957 DeC StAnd /mán-sóka/ a very large banana sucker, at least four feet tall.

MAN-TO-MAN sb dial; evid from the phrase *man to man* (*OED* 4 h) implying directness, firmness, or the like.

1. The wild plant *Peperomia pellucida*, more commonly called RAT EARS.

1952 FGC StC, StM, StT, Man-to-man—same as rat-ears; make bush tea, good for cold.

2. A large, round, boiled dumpling.

1958 DeC Man /man-tu-man/.

MANTRY-MAKER sb arch; <*mantua-maker*. Cf *OED* →1886.

1943 *GL* StJ, Mantry-maker, dressmaker.

MANUMISSION sb. Concr: A written document declaring the manumission of a slave; a FREE-PAPER. *G*

1777 *Jamaica, a Poem* 30, Manumission..An Instrument in writing used by masters in giving freedom to their slaves.

man-wi-di-jakit sb dial joc. A DOKUNU, alluding to its 'jacket' of banana-leaf.

1959 DeC Han /man-wi-di-jakit/ a dokunu (boiled).

MAN YAM sb obs. A variety of the NEGRO YAM having a rough, hairy skin.

1814 Lunan II 308, see NEGRO YAM.

MAPEMPE /apémpe, mapémpe, pémpem/ sb dial; origin unknown: Afr in appearance, but no source word has been found. Various species of Spurge, used medicinally.

1927 Beckwith 21, Mapempe..'Milkweed', 'Milk-tea', 'Pempe'..For pain in the back, boil as tea. Horses on the estate are bathed with it to prevent irritation. 1952 FGC Man /pempem/; StAnn /apémpe/; Tre /mapémpe/. 1953 *WIMJ* 245, Euphorbia hirta..E. hypericifolia.. E. hyssopifolia..E. lasiocarpa..E. prostrata..—Spurge; Milkweed or Tea; Mapempe; Pempe. It is possible that all these..species are used in a similar manner to make tea for colds and indigestion..The juice is also said to remove warts.

MAQUAKA see MACACA.

marang see next.

MARANGA /marángga, maráng/ sb chiefly dial, also attrib; <Sp *marango*, from same source as *Moringa*, the genus name.

1. The tree *Moringa oleifera*, the HORSERADISH TREE.

[1814 Lunan I 385–6, Guilandina..The *moringa*, or horseraddish tree, has been very erroneously referred to this genus..Being of quick growth, this pretty little tree is frequently planted in Jamaica for fences and along garden walks, and is generally known by the name of *moringa*.] 1893 Sullivan 121, Marenga Root as a cure for Rheumatism. Marenga root steeped in rum..Marenga Oil. Oil is expressed from the marenga plant. 1952 FGC StM /marángga/ quick-stick; boil bush, good for fever. 1955 *WIMJ* 146, Horseradish Tree; Ben Nut Tree; Moringa (Maranga).

2. The tree *Gliricidia sepium*, to which the name has been transf from sense 1 because of the similarity of the use for live fences.

1952 FGC StE /marángga/ fine-leaved, like /lickrish/; StM /marang/. 1955 *WIMJ* 150, Quick Stick; Grow Stick; Growing Stake; Maranga. Under the name of Maranga, this species was pointed out to the authors as an ingredient of baths for fever and pain..The same common name has been given on other occasions..It seems likely that not only the name but the uses had been transferred from Moringa.

marangga see MARANGA, and MELANGA.

maranta sb dial; prob <Twi *omurấtònì*, mulatto (itself <Pg *mulato*, Engl *mulatto*). A mulatto.

1943 *GL* Kgn, Maromta, mulatto. 1955 FGC Man /maránta/, /myùláta/.

marasis, marast see MORASS (WEED).

MARBLE-HEAD MULLET sb. A mullet or similar fish presumably having a 'marble' or calculus of some sort in its head.

1952 FGC Port, marble-head mullet.

MARENGA (OIL, ROOT) see MARANGA.

MARE'S TAIL sb. *Russelia equisetiformis*, a common garden plant with drooping hair-like stems.

MARE-TAIL SQUIRREL sb dial. A variety of the squirrel fish: see quot.

1952 StE /mare-tail skweril/.

MARGA see *maaga*.

MARGARET GRUNT sb dial; <*Margate* (by folk-etym—cf *OED Margate-fish*) + GRUNT. Where—whether in England, Jamaica, or elsewhere—this change was made is unknown, but it corresponds to the very common Jamaican folk custom of giving personal names to birds, fish, plants, etc. s BASTARD MARGARET.

A variety of the GRUNT fish.

1892 Cockrell list, Margaret grunt—*Hæmulon gibbosum*. 1952 FGC StC, StE, West /máagrit grónt/.

MARIAH sb dial. A cat.

1943 *GL* Kgn, Mariah, puss.

marigl see MARINGLE.

MARIGOLD /míeri gúul/ sb; cf *OED*; the dial pronunc in Jamaica preserves that of 17th-cent England. *BA*

Two distinct types of wild plants: *Bidens reptans*, and various species of *Wedelia*. Botanical works do not identify these until relatively recently, but the name must have been adopted into folk use by the 18th cent at latest.

1756 Browne 322, Calendula..Marygold. 1814 Lunan I 498. 1864 Grisebach 785, Marygold: *Wedelia carnosa*. 1927 Beckwith 22, Marigold a *Bidens reptans*..For difficulty in menstruation, boil with 'Cerasee' and drink.. b *Wedelia trilobata*..For a cold, boil and drink as tea with sugar. 1952 FGC Han, Port, StAnd, StC, StM /míeri gúul/ two kinds—follow cow to know the good kind; make good tea for baby, for biliousness, clean bowels and tongue. 1954 *WIMJ* 22, *Bidens reptans*.. Marigold; *ibid* 170, *Wedelia trilobata*..Wild or Running Marigold; Marygold; Creeping Ox-eye; Water Weed. 1955 *WIMJ* 160, *Wedelia gracilis*..Marigold; Consumption Weed.

MARINGLE vb dial; <*mariggle*, as in JOHN MARIGGLE; cf also RIDDLE. To deceive, to trick.

1941 Kirkpatrick 17, Dem wi' soon fin' out dat 'Itler was maringling dem.

MARK vb dial; cf *OED* 11c, etc.

To cause a mark to appear on the body, according to the beliefs that (1) if one touches one's own body, when describing an injury that has occurred to another, one will be 'marked' in the place touched; (2) if a pregnant woman touches her body while expressing a desire for some particular thing to eat, the baby's body will be marked at the corresponding spot with an image of the food desired. *BA BL G*

1956 Mc StAnd /main yu maak yuself/ *Be careful that you don't mark yourself!* /no bada maak yu pikni/ *Don't mark your child!* [I would rather give you what you desire than see you do so.]

MARK-HEAD sb chiefly dial; prob for *marked-head*. The Jamaican Spindalis: see quots.

1936 Bond 370, *Spindalis nigricephala*..Local names:—Goldfinch; Orange Bird; Cashew Bird; Spanish Quail; Mark-head; Silver-head..Head and neck black, relieved by a broad superciliary stripe, malar stripe and..patch on chin. 1952 FGC Man /máak héd/ has about four marks in the head—same as Goldfinch, Yam-Cutter; StT /mark-hed/.

MARKING FERN sb. Ferns of the genus *Pityrogramma* and others that leave the mark of their silvery or golden spores on the skin when pressed against it.

1952 FGC StC, StAnn, Tre, Marking fern /stamp an yu haam/—same as /blak dag form/.

MARK WORK vb phr dial. Said of an agricultural labourer: to chop round about a piece of land that is to be cleared, by way of laying claim to that area, which he will return to clear later.

1952 FGC Han, StAnd.

MARL HOLE sb. A hole dug into limestone rock to take out marl. *BA*

1835 Senior 105, In a deep cavity, of a somewhat crumbling rock, near the road-side, which they term a 'marl hole', are seen, probably, from ten to twenty men. 1952 FGC Tre /maal huol/ a hole in the bank along a road from which marl has been dug for road construction. 1956 Mc Man /maal huol/ limestone quarry.

MARLIE HILL CASSADA sb; <*Marlie Hill*, St Catherine. A local variety of cassava.

1952 FGC StE /maali hil/ cassada.

MARMIE see *maami*.

MAROMTA see *maranta*.

MARON see next.

MAROON sb; <Fr *marron*, wild <Sp *cimarron*, wild, untamed. (Cf *OED maroon sb*² and *a*², 1666→.) The term did not have widespread use in Jamaica until about the middle of the 18th century.

1. A hunter of wild cattle in the Caribbean islands, who did not live in a fixed settlement but roamed about at large. Obs.

1661 Hickeringill 67, French Buckaneers, or Hunting Marownaes [in the Hispaniola]..who live by killing the wild Beeves for their Hides; and might grow rich by the Trade did not their lavish Riotings in expence (at the neighbour-Tortudoes) exceed the hardship of their Incomes. Their comfort is that they can never be broke whilest they have a Dog and a Gun; both which, are more industriously tended then themselves.

2. A runaway negro belonging to any of the groups who, in Surinam and the West Indian Islands, took refuge and formed communities in the hills. In Jamaica the nucleus of the Maroon body consisted of slaves (negroes and mulattoes) released by the fleeing Spaniards in 1655 when the English took the Island along with three settlements of runaways. These were later reinforced by other runaway slaves. In 1738 they concluded a treaty of peace with the English. (See LeP, 1960 *CLS* I, 8–9 and Chap VII.) *N*

1744 Long II 341, Whilst the officers were at dinner, attended by very few of their men, the Marons rushed suddenly from the adjacent woods, and assaulted them.. The Marons were repulsed..but the militia did not think fit to pursue them far. 1796 Edwards ii–iii, The main body, under the command of a negro named Juan de

Bolas..at length solicited for peace..A large party, however (who had now acquired the name of Maroons), remained in their retreats among the mountains. 1803 Dallas I 33, The term Maroon had been hitherto confined to the body of original Spanish fugitives, and it was not till about the year 1730, when Cudjoe had become formidable..that he and his people were included in the appellation. 1935 HPJ [From Kingston servants:] Maroons are not Creoles; they are a different race—more like Africans. 1953 Moore 29–30, He got *shref-shref*, which come from the father's family alone, which is spirit..My *shref-shref* is very strong because it comes from the Maroons.

MAROON BLISTER sb dial; <*Maroon*+*blister*, a vesicatory medicine (*OED* 3).

1. Some strongly aromatic plant, used against headache.

1952 FGC StE, Tre /marúun blísta/ like yam-vine: rub leaves and inhale, has a /hash/ [=harsh] scent; rub up leaf—smells: apply to forehead for headache.

2. A medicament made with a leaf of TUNA.

1952 FGC StT /marúun blísta/—heat leaf of /túuna/ wrap in cloth, apply to head, etc.

MAROON FLUTE sb. =CROMANTY FLUTE.

1952 FGC StM.

MAROON LANCE sb; <MAROON+*lance*. *Exostema brachycarpum*, a small tree, said to have been used by the Maroons to make lances.

1936 Fawcett 11, Maroon lance.

MAROON LILY sb; from the colour. The plant *Hippeastrum puniceum*.

1927 Beckwith 22, Maroon-lily..For sores and lameness, scrape the bulb clean..and apply as a plaster. 1953 *WIMJ* 235, Red Lily; Maroon Lily.

MAROON WEED sb; <MAROON+*weed*. Species of *Echites*: see quots.

1927 Beckwith 22, Maroon-weed. *Echites echites.* For a sore leg, bruise the plant and make a poultice. 1952 FGC Port, Maroon's weed—rub with rum against fever; also for ground itch. 1953 *WIMJ* 237, *Echites umbellata*.. Maroon Weed; Savannah Flower.

MAROON WITHE /marúun wís/ sb dial; <MAROON+*withe*. The wild plant *Tournefortia hirsutissima*.

1952 FGC Tre /marúun wís/—/aas baat/ [horse bath]—can boil bath, tea.

MAROSH see MORASS.

MAROWNAES see s MAROONER.

MARRIED, MARRY TO vb dial; by confusion of the Engl passive const (there being no formally distinct passive in the dial): *to be married to* is reduced to *to married* or *to marry to*, both used actively. *To married* is thus the basic vb form. *BA*

1. To marry; to be married. *BL G N T*

1873 Rampini 106 [Letter of courtship:] I will be truly wish that I could maried to you know [now]. 1877 Murray *Feedin' 'Perrit* 9, Nobody no da go married to him. 1907 Jekyll 72, Parson Dog won't married me. 1950 Pioneer 22, De king..sey him hooda like fe get her fe married to; *ibid* 28, Him quick mek weddin feas' an married 'im daughter to Anancy. 1952 FGC StJ /dem mek buudz an aach/ with coconut leaves when someone going to married. 1956 Mc Man /bra nansi want tu mari tu di king daata/; StE /hi want tu get wan a duoz daataz tu mari tu/. 1957 JN Tre, see MEMBA.

2. To couple something in short supply (and much in demand) with something not much wanted, so that one must purchase the latter in order to have the former.

1942 Bennett 44, Pumpkin? yuh wi Haffe buy cho-cho wid i, Dem married, same like 'ow cassada Married to yampi..Ef dem no sell off by a mahnin Me wi married dem to pear. 1952 Kerr 58–9, Soap and rice are popular gifts, as the shopkeepers in the country tend to 'marry them'. (Only sell them with goods in plentiful supply.)

MARRIED sb dial; for *marriage*, by change of final /j/>/d/, or perh by ellipsis <*being married*. Marriage. *G*

1900 Murray 8, see GI'-ME-ME-BIT.

MARSA see *maas*.

MARSHAL (SWEET-POTATO) sb dial; <*Marshal*, an honorific title (cf Duke, Commander, etc.). A local variety of sweet-potato.

1952 FGC StT /maashal/—also /red maashal/.

MARSHMALLOW sb arch or obs. The *Sidas*, of which there are at least a dozen in Jamaica; now mostly called BROOMWEED.

1814 Lunan I 492, Sida..marshmallows of Jamaica.

MART GRASS see MOTH GRASS.

MARTIAL-LAW sb dial. A time of upset and unruliness. (Allusion is to the uprising of 1865.)

1943 *GL* Clar, Martialaw, Great uproar, noise; Man, Mashalah, Former slave riot. 1955 FGC Man /mashaláa/—Old time.

MARTINETISM sb; *OED* 1835→. Use of the whip.

1825 De la Beche 19, It is much to be regretted, that considerable *martinetism* exists on some properties, with regard to the time when the negroes ought to assemble.

MARTINICO ROSE see MARTINIQUE ROSE.

MARTINIQUE BANANA sb. A favourite type of banana in Jamaica—also called GROS MICHEL and formerly POUYAT; see also the nickname MANCHA.

1913 Fawcett 16, An improvement on the ordinary fruit occurred in Martinique and eighty years ago M. Jean François Pouyat..was..sufficiently alive to its importance to introduce it into Jamaica. This variety, called at first the Pouyat banana, or the Martinique banana, has become the only one that is cultivated in Jamaica, Costa Rica, and elsewhere for export, and is known now as the Jamaican or Gros Michel banana. 1957 *FFM* 337.

MARTINIQUE ROSE sb. *Hibiscus rosa-sinensis*; see quot 1814.

1814 Lunan I 176, The seeds were first brought by the French to Martinico, and hence it is sometimes called the *Martinico rose.* 1873 Rampini 145, Our daily nosegay was formed of..gigantic lilies of exquisite hue and delicate odour, of clove-scented carnations, and Martinique roses.

MARUSS see MORASS.

MARY BUSH sb dial; prob named for a woman named Mary who used it successfully in healing. Also called PUDDING-WITHE. The common wild vine *Cissus sicyoides*, much used in folk medicine; see quots.

1927 Beckwith 22, Mary-bush..See Wild Yam. 1954 *WIMJ* 26, Pudding Wys (Withe); Snake Withe (Wys) or Bush; Wild Yam; Mary Bush; Yaws Bush; Bastard Bryony; Scratch Wys. The leaves, chopped and mixed with fat or 'quailed' and rubbed with castor oil, provide a plaster for boils and bruises.

MARY-COAT-BLUE sb dial. The supposed cry of a PEA-DOVE, hence a name for the bird.

1952 FGC Han.

MARY DOUGAL sb dial. A variety of sweet-potato.

1952 FGC StJ /míeri dúugl/ have a black slip, white potato.

MARY GOULD see MARIGOLD.

MARY GOULD MANGO sb dial; descr? A variety of mango in some way assoc with the MARIGOLD.

1952 FGC StAnd /míeri gúul mánggo/.

MARY GRUDGEFUL sb chiefly dial; <*Mary*, the woman's name, here probably broadly personifying +GRUDGEFUL. Any of several insects or worms which destroy plants or produce (as if in spite): the cut-worm, the millipede, and most commonly the green stink bug.

1923 Gowdey 73, The Green Stink Bug, *Nezara marginata*..This species is known locally as the 'Mary Grudgeful'. It is a large green bug which emits a disagreeable odour..This bug sucks the young foliage and the juice from the fruit. 1952 FGC StT, Mary Grudgeful —a millipede; West, Mary Grudgeful—a cutworm. 1954 *FG* 595, 596, Mary Grudgeful [the Green Stinkbug].

MARYLAND sb dial. A local variety of sweet-potato.

1952 FGC StT /míerilán/—white.

MARY'S BALSAM sb obs; transl the name of the tree it comes from +*balsam*. The medicinal juice of the SANTA MARIA.

1837 Macfadyen 136–7, see SANTA MARIA.

MARY SHAKEWELL sb dial; <*Mary*, personifying +*shakewell*, a pseudo-surname descriptive of the movement of the bird. The BESSY KICK-UP.

1952 FGC StT.

MARY'S TEARS sb; perh by alteration of MARE'S-TAIL. *Russelia equisetiformis*, commonly planted in gardens; the flower is a long, drooping, slender, bright-red tube, whence the name.

1952 FGC StAnd.

MARY-SUCKY-BABY sb dial; a personifying name suggesting some connection with a nursing mother. The vine *Melothria guadalupensis*, also called WILD CERASEE.

1927 Beckwith 22, Mary-sucky-baby..For a stiff neck, wind it about the neck. (Mandeville.)

MARY-SYRUP MANGO sb dial; <*Mary*, personifying name +*syrup*. A variety of mango—presumably juicy and sweet.

1952 FGC StAnd /míeri-sórop/ mango.

MARY-WITHE sb dial. =MARY BUSH.

1952 FGC StE /míeri wìs/—soldier wis.

MARZELLA YAM see *mozela yam*.

MASACOCO sb dial; <*maasa*+COCO. An eddo (which is considerably larger than the ordinary coco).

1943 *GL* Tre, Masacoco, eddos.

MASALA /masála, mazála, maasaala/ sb dial; <Hindi *masálah*, spices, condiments. A highly seasoned East Indian stew or curry. *G T*

1943 *GL* Han, Mazala, stew; Port, Massalah, Indian curry; StAnn, Mazala, stew; Tre, Masala, măsawla, a dish, curry. 1955 FGC Man /mazála/ East Indian dish.

MASAWLA see prec.

MASH vb chiefly dial; <*smash* by normal dial reduction of *sm*->*m*-, but coinciding in some uses with StdE *mash*. *BL*

1. To strike with a 'smashing' blow, bruise, smash, crush; hence to destroy, spoil. (Senses shade into one another.) *BA G T*

1862 Clutterbuck 121, 'She will make you a good wife.. You must have patience, you know'. 'So me hab, massa..' Me mash him head tree or four time, but he no better. 1925 Beckwith 66 [Prov:] If you don' mash ant, you don' find him gut. 1942 Bennett 20, Yessiday she mash t'ree big-gill glass An' wan cutty-cutty ice pitcha. 1943 *GL* StAnn, Mash—broke up; StC, Mash—to break up or to step upon. 1951 FGC StAnd [Pedestrian to motorist:] /yu gwain mash mi?/ 1953 Reckord *Della* typescript 2, Shepherd..mash dem in him mout like ripe banana. 1956 Mc Man /im bádi get másh aal úova/.

2. To seduce or rape. (Prob not from *mash* *OED* v^2.)

1958 DeC gen.

3. Phr: *He* or *she couldn't mash ants*: he or she has no spirit or vigour, is weak or cowardly; also good-naturedly: he or she would never think of harming another. *BA*

c 1920 FGC StAnd [Expressing disdain of a meek man:] He couldn't mash ants! 1956 Mc StAnd /mi ha wan pikini mievis ya—laka in kyaan mash aants—an a hel baka it/ *I have a child Mavis, who looks as if she couldn't squash ants (butter wouldn't melt in her mouth), and she's a devil behind it.* 1956 BLB Man, He couldn't mash ants—would not dream of hurting anyone by word or deed.

MASH sb dial. The small-change left after spending from a larger piece of money or banknote; =MASH-MASH 3.

1943 *GL* StM, Mash, the difference in exchange of goods.

MASHA MASHA vb phr dial; =MASH vb + A^3 + MASH vb + A^5. See quot and transl; Beckwith's spelling misrepresents the construction.

1924 Beckwith 180, Him run under de bridge mash a Rolling Calf. Said, 'Masha masha no hurt me, but de frighten you frighten me!' [*The smashing* (into Rolling Calf) *which I experienced did not hurt me, but the frightening you gave me!*]

MASHER /másha/ sb dial joc; <MASH vb+-*er*. Locally made shoes or sandals formerly with rope soles, later of automobile-tyre rubber.

1943 *GL* StM, Masha, sandal made from rubber tyre. 1959 E. M. Falconer Spanish Town, Bulldog Boots are also vulgarly called masha. They used to be made in canvas uppers, brown, and a sort of corded soles..in the 1930's.

mashet, mashiet see MACHETE.

masheted /mashéted, mashíetid/ adj dial; origin uncert: prob an aphetic form of *emaciated*, poss blended with MASH and/or MACHETE. In bad condition, of ill appearance; specif, one showing the effects of the yaws.

1943 *GL* Port, Mashyated—wrecked, dilapidated. 1957 Bennett 74, Yuh se how t'eatre ole machiated Chair bruck dung wid me? 1960 *CLS* 156 /nou ándro waz a uol wich bwái, a púor líkl..ándro úol and mashéted.. di líkl yáazikin bréda/ *Now Andrew was an old-witch boy, a poor little..Andrew old and masheted..the little yawsy-skinned brother.* 1962 BLB 63 /mashietid/ in bad condition.

MASH-FLAT vb phr dial c. slang; <MASH vb +*flat*, prob alluding to the driver's pressing the accelerator pedal flat to the floor. To drive a motor vehicle very fast.

1942 Bennett 12, All of a sudden wan neda man Halla out loud, Mash flat! 'Mash flat,' me sey, 'dat a riggle, An' me kean fine nat a clue.' 1943 *GL* StC, Mash-flat, drive fast.

MASH-MASH sb dial arch or obs; iterative of MASH vb converted to sb.

1. Anything that has been reduced to small pieces.

1943 *GL* StAnd, Mash mash, pieces. 1952 FGC StAnd /nótn léf bot likl másh-màsh/.

2. Fish broken or disintegrated into small bits.

1790 Moreton 146, Vegetables of one kind or other relished with 'mash mash', or rotten herrings. 1868 Russell 5, Mash-mash—Fish broken in small bits.

3. Small coins, 'small change'; also attrib.

1943 *GL* Kgn, Mash-mash, Small change. 1956 Mc Man /mash-mash moni/.

MASH-MOUTH /mash-mout/ sb or adj dial; <MASH, smashed+*mouth*, representing StdE *mouthed*. Having a mouth that has been, or appears, crushed. (Often used as an insulting epithet.) *BA BL G*

1877 Murray *Feedin' 'Perrit* 9, Da you mash mout wife you lef home. 1956 Mc /mash-mout/—term applied to person who has lost the front teeth, and whose mouth therefore has the appearance of being squashed.

MASH-MOUTH DRUMMER sb dial. A variety of the drummer-fish—see prec.

1952 FGC StT /másh-mòut dróma/.

MASH-UP vb dial; also for past pple; <MASH vb+*up*.

1. Beat, break, smash, crush; the sense passing into spoil, destroy. (Both active and passive senses.) *BL G N T*

1837 James passim, She was mashed up..her shins were mashed up. 1905 Smith 21, So him take him cutlass an mash up all de ground wid it! 1924 Beckwith 10, I's a man dat's so fat, if I drop on de bare eart' I's goin' to mash up. 1956 Mc Man /hag a mash-op mi groun/ *Hogs are tearing up my garden*; StAnd /dat wedin mashop/ *The wedding fell through*. 1958 Rowe (in 1960 *CLS* I 161) /dís wótlis bwái de ya de másh óp mi arîenjment/ [*This worthless boy here is spoiling my plan*].

2. Fig. To get, or to get someone, into difficulties; to suffer, or to cause, much trouble.

1924 Beckwith 23, Why Brar Hanansi, a you been mashin' me up?*..*Colloquial for 'getting me into trouble'. 1942 Bennett 20, Lawd me life mash up, mash up, mash up, Me noh know 'ow me gwine meck it out! 1956 BLB [Of a person who has fallen far below his former condition:] /im mash-op fi truu/ *He has gone to the dogs*.

3. In reference to health: Feeling ill. *BL T*

1956 BLB /láad, a máshop—fresh kuol a mashop mi laif/ *I'm feeling rotten indeed—a fresh cold is making me ill.* 1956 Mc St And/mi kyaan mash op no muo/ *I couldn't feel worse.*

MASHYATED see *masheted*.

MASHY-MASHY adj dial; <MASH+-*y*, iterated. Squashy, pulpy. *G*

1900 Murray 13, It mek a man feel dis de same as a ober ripe mango, ober sweet and mashy-mashy.

MASKIT sb dial; reduction of *mosquito*; usually /máskíta/ but cf Fr *moustique*.

1943 *GL* StC, Maskit, mosquitoes.

MASS see *maas*.

MASSALAH see MASALA.

MASSAMBIE sb dial; cf *Masambei*, medicinal plant in Santo Domingo (Tejera)—species of *Cleone*. Some kind of plant like aloes; cf MAZAMBREY.

1943 *GL* StE, Massambie, Mozambique aloes.

MASSANEAGA, MASSA-NIGGER see *maasa-niega*.

MASSA-TENKY sb dial arch; <*master*, +*thank'ee*. Cf TENKY-MASSA.

1943 *GL* Tre, Massa tenke, gift.

MASSHU see *masu*.

MASSI-FI-TENGAD sb dial joc arch; <*mercy-for-thank-God*.

1943 *GL* StE, Massi-fi-tengad, a slip (underwear).

MASSLE see *masu*.

MASSNEGA, MASS-NEGER see *maasa-niega*.

MASSOO, MASSOU, MASSU see *masu*.

MASS TOM sb dial; <*maas*+*Tom*.

1943 *GL* StAnn, Mass Tom, the shark.

MASTER, MASTER AND HIS COCK sb dial; from the roles assigned to players. (Cf 1922 Beckwith 13, *Master and Boy*.) Games played by adults at a SET-UP.

1952 Kerr 134, Jack pot (a gambling game). Master. Master and his Cock. These three all involve a playful flogging as a penalty.

MASTER YAW sb dial; *OED* 1744 (misprinted '1774').

1801 Dancer 223, see MAMMA-YAW.

MASTIC (TREE) sb bot; cf *OED* 3 1657→.

1. The BIRCH tree, *Bursera simaruba*, whose gum was used as a substitute for Gum Mastic. Cf *maas nik*.

1655 *Eye-Witnesse* 18, Of Limon, Orange..Ceadar, Mastick, and Lignum vitæ trees, there are great plenty. 1837 Macfadyen I 229–30, Bursera gummifera..It receives from the English colonists the name of *Birch*, from the bark having a resemblance to that of the tree which bears that name in Europe. The French call it *Gummier*, from the resin it affords; and the Spaniards *Almicigo*, or Mastic-tree. 1920 Fawcett 206. 1941 Swabey 13.

2. =MAST-WOOD. (This mistaken identification is prob due to analysis of *mastic* as *mast-stick*— -*st* of the first syllable being normally reduced >-*s*, and *st*- of the second syllable >*t*- in the dial.)

1943 *NHN* II 24, *Tabebuia leucoxylon*—Mast Wood, Yoke, Mastic. 1952 FGC StAnn, Mast-wood is same as mastic.

MASTIFF-BAT sb; cf *OED* 1851→. In Gosse's use: The bat *Nyctinomus brasiliensis*, from its mastiff-like muzzle.

1851 Gosse 159, The Chestnut Mastiff-Bat. *Ibid* 162, the family assured me that after these Mastiff-bats had emerged a few hours, they invariably returned into the hole again.

mastop, mastuu vb or vb phr dial; prob <*masu it up*. To lift.

1958 DeC Man /mastóp, mastúu/—variants of *masu*, to lift /pliiz mastop dat luod nou—mi kyaan mastuu i/.

MAST-WOOD sb; from its use to make masts for sailing craft? (*OED* for diff tree.) *Catalpa longissima*; the name was not noticed in books until recently.

[1814 Lunan I 309, This is an elegant upright tree, forty feet high, and upwards..It..is generally looked upon as an excellent timber tree..It is known in Jamaica by the name of *French Oak*.] 1909 Harris 316, Yokewood, Mast-wood, French Oak, Spanish Oak. 1941 Swabey 33, Yokewood—(French Oak, Mast Wood, Jamaica Oak).. Grows in the dry coastal plains..particularly common along the coast.

masu /másu/ vb dial; 1833 massu, 1924 massoo, 1943→ masu, 1943 massou, masshu, 1959 massle; <Twi *mā́sú*, raise, lift. To lift, pick up.

1833 Scott I 343, 'Here, Pilfer, Pilfer', to his black valet, 'give me my stick, and massu* the chair, and run home..' *Massu—lift. 1924 Beckwith 96, At de las' cross-road she massoo one [egg], an' see a big Ol' Witch man tear her up kill her. 1943 *GL* Man, Massou, lift up; StAnn, Masu, lift up; StT, Masshu, lift. 1954 LeP Man, Port, StE, To lift something heavy—masu.

MATILDA BUSH sb dial; prob after a woman named Matilda who used it successfully. An unidentified plant.

1952 FGC Han, Matilda bush—for sore foot.

matrash /matrásh/ sb dial; by folk-etym <MATRASS, infl by TRASH: see quot 1958. Mat or mattress material, or a mattress.

1952 FGC StE /mátrásh/—the leaves of cattails, used in making mats. 1958 DeC Man /matrásh/—mattress (so called because filled with trash).

MATRASS /matrás/ sb; <Scots *mattrass* (see *SND*). The common Ja form for *mattress*. *BA BL G*

MATRIMONY sb; cf *OED* 6, 1892. A dessert made of a mixture of starapple and orange.

c 1920 FGC StAnd. 1957 *FFM* 145, Matrimony..Wash star apples and remove pulp. Peel oranges and remove in sections. Mix, and add cream and sugar. Chill and serve.

MATTA-MATTA sb dial; iterative of *matter*. A lot of matter, or miscellaneous non-distinctive matter.

1868 Russell 4, Some nouns of one or two syllables are in using repeated; as mud-mud, matta-matta.

MATTER vb dial; <*matter* vb (*OED* 3 →1892). *BA*

1. To care about, pay heed to, take seriously.

1956 Mc StE /de tretn mi, an a neva mata dem/ *They threaten me, but I pay no attention to them.*

2. Refl: To show respect for (oneself), have self-respect.

1955 FGC Man /dem duon mata demself/. 1956 Mc StE /álibotn—a pórsn dozn máta imself—satisfai wi eniting/.

MATTIE-BELLY sb dial; cf *EDD matie* or *mattie*, a herring taken before its belly is full of roe, but just nicely formed. =BELLY-LICK.

1958 DeC Port /mati beli/ Mattie-belly, a kind of dance with a great deal of abdominal contact—/yu rob di gyal beli haad/.

matukla sb dial; etym unknown—prob Afr.

1958 DeC StAnd /matukla/ obeah man.

MAUGA, MAUGER, MAUGRE see *maaga*.

MAUI see *maa-i*.

MAUVE, MAUVISH /maav/ adj; dial pronunc implies the Engl pronunc [mɔ:v] behind, rather than [mo:v].

MAW-CHEN /mau-chen/ adj phr; <Chinese. Used in Chinese shops: without money.

1943 *GL* Clar, Maw-chen (or mow-chen), out of cash.

MAWGA see *maaga*.

MAWI see *maa-i*.

MAWLO see MALO.

MAWMA MAN see *maama-man*.

MAWMIE see *maami*.

MAXI, MAXY sb dial slang; <MAC + *-sy* familiarizing suffix; perh also infl by the personal name *Maxie*. A MAC, a shilling.

1943 *GL* StAnd, Moxy; StAnn, Maxy; Tre, Maxi—one shilling.

MAY BIRD sb; cf *OED*, *DAE*, *DA* for diff birds.

1. The Yellow-Billed Cuckoo.

1839 Hill in 1840 *Almanac* 33, A third species of the Old Man Bird..spoken of by the Bird shooters under the name of the May bird, has been brought to me. It is a yellow-billed Cuckoo..The visit of the May bird, as it migrates..is one of the precursors of the Spring rains in this Island. 1847 Gosse 279, Yellow-Billed Cuckoo. May-bird. *Coccyzus Americanus*.

2. The Jamaican Lizard Cuckoo—from its similarity to the preceding, though this does not migrate.

1936 Bond 176, *Saurothera vetula*..Local names:—May Bird; Old Woman Bird; Rain Bird. 1956 Jeffrey-Smith 63, The name May-bird is given to both the Jamaican lizard cuckoo..and the yellow-billed cuckoo..which is only a summer visitor arriving just before the May rains.

MAY-BUG sb; cf *OED* for diff senses. Beetles of various kinds which are in evidence about the month of May; esp the round-backed brown beetle called the June-bug in the US (genus *Phyllophaga*).

1952 FGC Man, StAnd, StT /míe-bóg/ come near May; some blue, some brown; different from Easter bug.

MAY-DAY (HUMMING) BIRD sb obs. The MANGO HUMMING-BIRD.

1849 Hill—Letter in *Gleaner* 2 Mar 1921, I now write forwarding a drawing of the bird I have asked for, which for distinction's sake I will call the May Day Humming Bird..The spangled crest and green-bordered tail are very marked distinctions of the May-day bird.

MAY DAY MAHOGANY sb; from the May Day Mountains, where the tree is native. The tree *Antirrhœa jamaicensis*, whose wood resembles mahogany. Cf GOLDSPOON.

1941 Swabey 21, May Day Mahogany..Good substitute for mahogany: Planes well and takes a good polish. 1952 FGC Tre, May-day mahogany—same as gold-spoon.

MAY-FLOWER sb bot arch or obs; from its resemblance, when in flower, to the English *may* tree. *OED* 1864. Trees of the genus *Dalbergia*: *D. brownei* and *D. ecastaphyllum*. *BL*

1837 Macfadyen 300, Sea-side May-flower. *Ibid* 300–1, Meadow May-flower..The white fragrant flowers of this lowly tree, come out in great profusion after the rains in spring, and have been compared to those of the Hawthorn, which blossom about the same period of the year. 1864 Grisebach 785, May-flower.

MAZALA see MASALA.

MAZAMBREY sb dial. =MASSAMBIE.

1927 Beckwith 22, Mazambrey..See 'Sinkle Bible'.

McCATHY WEED see next.

McKATTY BUSH, WEED, or **WITHE** /makáti, makíti/ sb dial; prob conn with Dr McKatty, of Doctor's Cave, Montego Bay.

1. A wild vine used medicinally.

1952 FGC Tre /makáti bush/=Dr McKatty; good for colds; has round, thick leaf, has tendrils, climbs. 1955 FGC Man /makáti wis/.

2. A wild shrub used medicinally: *Bidens reptans*.

1953 *WIMJ* 241, McKitty or McCathy Weed. The shoots are used in decoction as a cold remedy.

McKENZIE see MACKENZIE (PARROT).

ME /mi, mii/ pron dial; etym prob multiple: Engl *me* (in its full and reduced forms [mi:], [mɪ]) coinciding with Twi *me*, Fante *ɛme*, I, me, my, which assimilate to *mi* before verbs with close sounds. (Christaller.) *G*

1. The first personal pronoun singular, without distinction of case: I, me, my. (Usually unstressed.) *BL N T*

1877 Murray *Kittle* 10, Him no da blebe me. [*He won't believe me.*] You see dat shark tail nail ober me [my] bed head. 1943 *GL* StJ, Migarn, I am going.

2. Emphatic in the phr *me boy* (cf POOR ME BOY!) expressing self-pity. *BA*

1924 Beckwith 50, Anansi come down an' said, 'Lawd! dat's a lot me bwoy meet up t'-day!'

3. Introducing a number of common conversational phrases or exclamations which do not literally apply to the person addressed: *me son, me boy, me gal*, etc. (*Me* unstressed.) *BL T*

1941 Kirkpatrick 2, T'ings a 'appen fas' dese days me son. 1942 Bennett 9, Yuh kean get onion widout yuh buy Tomatis now me chile! 1943 *GL* StAnd, Me-mara-me-ded, What is this! [An exclamation of surprise or disbelief: *My mother I'm dead!*]

MEAGRE BROWN adj phr or sb dial. A racial or colour term, not necessarily unfavourable: see quot.

1958 DeC StT (White Horses) /miiga broun/ adj. for a very light brown man, not derogatory; (Bethel Gap) /miiga-broun/ derogatory, brown and rough (perhaps pocked) skin.

MEANING-TIME adv dial; overcorrection for *meantime*. Cf. DURING THE WHILE.

1952 FGC StT /miining taim/ meantime (said twice).

MEAT-KIND sb chiefly dial; formed on the analogy of BREAD-KIND. Any meat used for food, as distinct from fish, vegetables, etc.

1952 FGC Port, StAnn, StE, StJ, West /míit-káin/—beef, pork, mutton, etc.

MEAT-WATER sb dial. The water in which meat was boiled, used as soup.

1943 *GL* StM, Meat water, soup.

MECHANIC sb dial; cf *OED* B 1, prob infl by *antics*, and perh also by *machination*. A contrivance, a device, a trick—usually involving some physical action.

1907 Jekyll 207, The most laughable antics, 'mechanic' as they call it, are indulged in [in playing a ring game]. 1924 Beckwith 122, So lot of men went to the house an' try all sort of mechanic; the chil' wouldn't talk.

MECK see MAKE. *G*

MECKAM-PECKAM adj dial uncom; etym unknown: the verb *peck* may have some infl, and cf *mek-mek*.

1943 *GL* no addr, Meckam-peckam, Unusually fault-finding.

MEDICINE vb dial; *OED* *v* 1 →1889. To treat medicinally.

1956 Jeffrey-Smith 24–5, see DOCTOR BIRD.

meja /méja, míeja/ sb or vb dial; a common pronunc of *measure*. *BL*

1943 *GL* Clar, Maja, Majer, measure. 1952 FGC StAnd /méja/.

mek see MAKE.

MEK-MEK sb[1] and adj dial; iterative of *mek*, make, used in pregnant sense of making trouble; cf arch Engl *make-bate*.

A. sb: A quarrel; quarrelling.

1943 *GL* Kgn, Mek-mek, a quarrel or confusion. 1956 Mc StE (Elderslie), Always in some mek-mek or other.

B. adj: Quarrelsome.

1958 DeC StE (Accom) /mek-mek/ of a person: quarrelsome.

MEK-MEK sb[2] and vb dial; iterative of *mek*, make, implying repeated actions, contradictory, annoying, and the like.

A. sb: A fussy, pernickety person.

1954 LeP StE, Mek-mek.

B. vb: To hesitate, to be indecisive; to make a half-hearted attempt.

1943 *GL* Clar, Meck-meck, to hesitate, lingering. 1960 Pat Wilmot StAnd /him mek-mek at it/.

mek-mek, meke-meke sb[3] and adj[2] dial; cf *mucky*. s *peke-peke*.

A. adj: With too much liquid; messy; sloppy; muddy.

1943 *GL* Kgn, Meckay-meckay, sloppy, watery; StM, Meckay-meckay, nasty. 1958 DeC Port /mek-mek/ adj. for muddy (road or field). 1960 Pat Wilmot StAnd /meke-meke/ same as /poto-poto/ but used mainly about food.

B. sb: A liquid mess.

1957 J. Walker /mi gaan kuk meke-meke/ *I'm going to hash something up.*

meki-man sb dial; perh <MEK + *i*, it—i.e. the man who produces some desired effect: cf DO-GOOD MAN, SERVICE MAN. An OBEAH-MAN.

1958 DeC Port /meki-man/ obeah man; StT /miki man/.

mek-so /mek-so/ sb dial; <MAKE + SO. The way things are or have been made.

1927 Anderson-Cundall 75 [Prov:] Sabby-so mek mek-so 'tan so. *On the understanding of a thing depends how it is accomplished.* [Or better, *Understanding why things are as they are makes one leave them so.* FGC.]

MEL see MELL.

MELANGA /marángga/ sb dial; <Amer Sp (Bolivia) *malanga*, a variety of coco. (Alvarado.) A fine variety of coco (*Colocasia esculenta*). s.

1952 FGC StM /marángga/ same as horse-foot coco, grows far from the head—one yard. 1954 *FG* 447, The Melanga is a large, soft, white variety, excellent for the table and deserving of more extensive cultivation. It is exceedingly popular in Cuba.

MELASSES see MOLASSES-CISTERN.

MELL vb trans dial; <*mell* (*OED* v^2 8 *intr.*). To meddle with; to trouble, annoy, interfere with. *SC méri.*

1912 McK *Ballads* gloss, Mell: meddle. 1942 Bennett 32, Leggo me han' yaw sah Me noh mel yuh, soh me keahn tell Wey yuh buckle-hole me fah. 1958 JC StC, Don't mel me—*don't annoy me.*

MELON THISTLE sb bot; *OED* 1731–3 only.

1811 Titford 70, Melon thistle, *Cactus Melocactus.* 1814 Lunan I 502. 1850 Macfadyen 172. 1926 Fawcett 283, *Melocactus communis* Turk's Head, Turk's Cap, Pope's Head, Melon Thistle.

MELVIN sb dial uncom; etym unknown.

1943 *GL* Port, Melvin, broth of curried goat.

MEMBA vb dial; by aphesis <*remember. BL G*

1. To remember. *N*

1950 Pioneer 17, De ole oman dem mus memba fe talk bout him. 1956 Mc Man /jíen no mémba we mi en tél im sé/ *Jane doesn't remember what I told her.* ('Memba'—the regular word.) 1957 JN Tre, You memba when uncle did married?

2. To remind.

1950 Pioneer 17, Every night me wi come memba you something bout meself fe talk.

membaraiz vb dial; prob blend of MEMBA vb with *memorize.* This may be an individualism.

1956 Mc StAnd /membaraiz/ to remember.

MEMORIAL (TABLE) sb dial; cf *OED a* and *sb* 2. See quots.

1953 Moore 108, Memorial table—a Revival service, usually 2½ years after the burial, and once a year after this if desired. 1958 DeC StT /memúorial/ a funeral celebration held two or three months after death.

mempau sb dial; <Hakka Chinese (RWT). Bread.

1943 *GL* Clar, Kgn, StAnd, StT, Mempou, mempaw, bread. 1955 FGC Man /mempau/ bread—Cuban word?

men auxil vb dial; <BEN. =MIN.

1957 JN Clar (Mocho), A no soh ih men tie, *It was not so it was tied, that's not how it was tied.* 1958 DeC StAnd /men de/ is more common than /ben de/ around Irish Town.

MENOU WEED see next.

MENOW WEED sb obs; cf *OED*: etym uncert; perh Afr—cf Umbundu *mena*, to sprout, Kongo *mena*, to grow. The weed *Ruellia tuberosa*, now usually called DUPPY GUN.

1756 Browne 268, see SNAP-DRAGON; It is remarkable for its oblong fleshy roots; which are frequently used in fevers, among the negroes. 1814 Lunan II 191, Menou weed [quotes from Browne].

MENTO /ménto/ sb; etym unknown; African? A dance—originally a digging-song; sung and danced at wakes and at other entertainments; a two-step, and much like the shay-shay.

[1929 Beckwith 214, see SHAY-SHAY.] 1943 *GL* Man, Port, Tre, Mento, A kind of dance. 1952 FGC Han /mento/ is working song /minto/ is danced at wake; StM /mento/ you dance and wind-up yourself. 1963 R. Nettleford UWI, The Mento is a Jamaican ballad form with a strong rhythmic figure; it is thought to have been brought by Jamaicans returning from work in Cuba. Tunes like 'Dip and Fall Back' and 'Jamaica Farewell' have this character. 1963 T. Murray UWI, I had been told that the Mento was a kind of 'coda' to a song, a part that had a stronger rhythmical content suitable for dance movement..Usually it is a section that can be repeated ad lib. It is common for the percussion to be more prominent at this part.

MENYA-MENYA adj dial; the form appears African, but no source word has been found. (Perh iterative <Fr *menu*, slim, spare.)

1868 Russell 10, Menya-menya—Slender. Wat a menya-menya pickni? African. *Ibid* 18, minya-minya.

MERENGUE /mirénggi/ vb dial; <Amer Sp *merengue*, a dance introduced in Puerto Rico in 1842 as a substitute for the Spanish *contradanza* (Malaret). To dance the *merengue*; to dance in lively fashion. *G*

1950 Pioneer 41, Se yah de music sweet yu se'! All de fowl dem start fe yanga an merrenge roun' de room. [1963 T. Murray UWI, Merrengue has a shuffle step, the knees working from side to side. The tempo is slower than that of the yanga and 'easier' in character.]

MERINO /maríina, moríino/ sb; cf *OED* 2, 'A soft woollen material..originally manufactured of merino wool'. Knitted underwear, especially for children; now usually of cotton.

c 1915 FGC StAnd, I've torn my merino. 1924 Beckwith 69, The man gave her a moreen. She went a little further and saw a cow-boy. She gave him the moreen. After he had worn it out, she cried upon him for it. 1951 FGC StAnd, Have her wear a merino. 1952 FGC StAnd /maríina/ underwear; if made of calico, 'undershirt'. *G T*

MERRENGE, MERRENGUE see MERENGUE.

MERRY vb dial; <*merry* adj; cf SPREE vb. To make merry.

1924 Beckwith 60, She..never went in where everybody in de house merrying himself, went to de kitchen.

MERRY-WANG sb obs; etym unknown—if this is not the folk-etym of some foreign word, it may be a direct coinage: *merry* + **wang*—onomatopœic, like *twang*? (Cf MERRYWING, mosquito, and note that the Hawaiian *ukulele* means 'flea'.)

A musical instrument imitating the guitar, made by negroes—see quot; the prototype of the banjo—cf BANJA, STRUM-STRUM.

1774 Long II 423, Their *merry-wang* is a favourite instrument, a rustic guitar, of four strings. It is made with a calibash; a slice of which being taken off, a dried bladder, or skin, is spread across the largest section; and this is fastened to a handle, which they take great pains in ornamenting with a sort of rude carved work, and ribbands. [1929 Beckwith 211.]

[**MERRYWING** sb obs; <Fr *maringouin* (or Sp *maringuin*), a mosquito. *OED* 1671→1750. (The term was used earlier and later in the eastern Caribbean.) A mosquito.

1657 Ligon 62, And next to them [*sc* Musketos] Meriwings, and they are of so small a size, and so thin and aereall, as you can hardly discern them, but by the noise of their wings..: Where they sting, there will rise a little knob, as big as a pease, and last so a whole day. 1671 Ogilby 340, In some parts of the Countrey there are also a sort of stinging Flies, call'd *Muschilli* and *Merrywings*, but the English quarters are little infested by them. 1672 Blome 29, Here are also Muskettoes and Merry-wings, a sort of stinging Flies. 1683 *Present State* 20, The most Offensive thing in this Island are divers sorts of Flies called Mery-wings, from their Noise. 1725 Sloane 225, Culex e fusco cinereus major. Marigoui ou Marigouin. Abbeville..The Merrywing, or Common Mosquito. 1839 Hill in 1840 *Almanac* 38, The Lady and Gentleman Merrywings (Maringouin) as the Windward Islanders call the Gnat.]

MERY-WING see prec.

mese-mese see MESSY-MESSY.

MESH vb[1] dial; cf *OED* 3b.

1958 DeC Tre /mesh/—to hold together, to cohere; /gom/—anything binding or cohesive; e.g. we add counter-flour to cassada head for *gum*, otherwise it /kyaan mesh/.

MESH vb[2] dial; =MESS.

mes-mes see MESS-MESS.

MESS /mes, mesh/ vb dial; <*mess*, ordure (*EDD* v² 4). To defecate. *BA BL G T*

1952 FGC StAnd /main di biebi mes imself/. 1958 DeC gen /hin trai an in trai bot in kyaan mesh/.

MESS-AROUND /més aròun/ sb dial; <*mess* vb + *around.* A kind of cake—evid one that has to be stirred a lot.

1943 *GL* StAnd, Mess aroun, cake; StAnn, A cake made of flour.

MESSENGER sb. A flat ring of paper passed around a kite-string and driven up it by the wind.

1912 McK *Songs* 80, Messengers—Round slips of paper, which go twirling up the kite string.

MESS-MESS, MESSY-MESSY adj dial; iteratives <*mess* sb and *messy* adj; cf MEK-MEK adj².

1958 DeC StE (Accom) /mes-mes/ wet and sloppy—e.g. of a road or ground; StAnd /mese-mese/ sloppy, wet, muddy.

MET sb dial; etym uncert: the past tense of *meet* does not exist in dial otherwise; perh <*meeting*. A public gathering: a church assembly, a fair, a dance, etc.

1907 Jekyll 47, The father say: 'Get 'way, Sir, you little fellah you! It is the worst fe carry any little boy out fe met*'..*Met, dance, spree, picnic are convertible terms. 1943 *GL* Kgn, Meth, a fair. 1954 LeP StE, Dem a hab a big met. 1956 Mc StE /im wén tu i mét—dem háks im, wá yu há fi go sé/—*He went to the meeting—they asked him, What speeches are you going to make?* 1958 DeC Port /met/ a church or revival meeting.

METH see prec.

metl-rash sb dial, also attrib; <*nettle-rash*; cf also /nitl/ another variant. 'Nettle rash'—here, a skin condition resembling this, but not caused by nettle.

1952 FGC Man /metl rash/ bumps on skin, from the blood.

MET-POT sb dial; <MET+*pot*. A large cooking-pot or cauldron. Cf *belagot* 3.

1949 Reid gloss, Met-pot—large pot used in cooking for gatherings.

METTLE /metl/ sb dial; <*nettle*. See quot.

1943 *NHN* I II 7, Cow-itch, Nettle, Stinging Nettle, also corrupted into Nittle, Mettle, etc., *Tragia volubilis* (Euphorbiaceæ) is a slender herbaceous creeper found throughout the lowlands and the limestone plateau.

MEXICAN THISTLE sb bot; *ODS* 1906. *Argemone mexicana.*

1837 Macfadyen 20–1, Mexican or Gamboge Thistle.. This plant, as its specific name indicates, was supposed at one time to be peculiar to Mexico. It has however been found in all warmer parts of the globe..It is common in all the West India Islands. 1914 Fawcett 222, Prickly Poppy, Gamboge Thistle, Mexican Thistle. 1954 *WIMJ* 28.

MIAL see MYAL.

MICE sb sing dial; <*mice* plur; cf *teeth, lice,* and other mutation plurals in which the plural form of StdE became the only dial form. A mouse. *G N*

1943 *GL* StT, Musmus, a mice.

MICHAEL sb dial; a personifying name. A kind of cake; cf BULLA.

1952 FGC West /máikal/ a better kind of bulla; made at local Co-op bakery.

MICHELIN (TYRE) /míchilín/ sb dial joc; <*Michelin* brand of automobile tyres which advertises with a pneumatic man.

1. A BULLA.

1956 Mc Man, Another name for a bulla cake: /míchilin táia/.

2. A dumpling.

1958 DeC Port /michilin/ a large round boiled dumpling.

3. A very fat person.

1956 BLB Man /im a riel michilin/.

MID-DAY sb dial.

1958 DeC StT /mid-die/ the midday meal.

MIDDLE adj dial; ellipt for *middle of the. BA* The middle, or centre of the (time or place named). (The normal word-order of modification in both StdE and Ja dial is here reversed. The thing whose centre is in question should normally precede the word *middle*—cf *hand-middle*, etc. But see next entry. *G*

1907 Jekyll 4, You middle hand. The middle of your hand. 1925 Beckwith 82 [Prov:] Man in a middle room no need buy ile. 1956 Mc Man /di daag lidong iina di migl ruod/—*The dog is lying in the middle of the road.*

MIDDLE-DAY sb dial; cf MIDDLE. Midday.

1950 Pioneer 70, One day now him walk about all day till middle day, him no fine nuttin so him lay down so sleep under one big shade tree, tell de sun cool. 1957 JN Man, When I was four in the middle day my teeth started to change. 1960 Pat Wilmot StAnd /in di braad migl-die/. *BL N*

mieri see MARY.

mieri guul see MARIGOLD.

miimi sb dial; a var form prob of mixed origin —cf MA, *maami, mama, mima, muma*, etc. An affectionate name or term of address for a mother, grandmother, etc.: see quots.

1943 *GL* StAnd, Mee-me—name by which old women are called. 1954 LeP StT Miimi—grandmother. 1956 Mc StT, Affectionate term for mother or grandmother. 1960 Pat Wilmot StAnd, The sort of name you call your grandmother or great-grandmother.

mikies /mikíes, mekíes/ vb phr dial; <*make haste*, pronounced as a unit. *BL G N*

miki-man see *meki-man*.

MILADY sb dial. A type of coco: see RED MILADY, WHITE MILADY. See also MY LADY.

1952 FGC StE /malíedi/ coco.

MILE MONEY sb obs. The money paid for the return of a runaway slave, proportioned to the number of miles his captor had had to bring him. See quots.

1718 *Courant* 5 Aug 3, Whoever will take him up and bring him to the Overseer of the said Estate..shall have 10*s*. besides Mile-Money. [1739 Leslie 229, Whoever shall take up a Run-away-slave, shall bring him to his proper Owner, if known, and receive for their Pains 1*s*. *per* Mile for the first five, and 8*d*. *per* Mile for all over, the whole not exceeding 40*s*.] 1788 *Act to Repeal* 21, Mile-money, at the rate of one shilling per mile for the first five miles, and sixpence per mile afterwards. 1803 Dallas I 97, After the treaty with Cudjoe..a law was passed..allowing, besides the usual reward, mile-money for every run-away produced alive. 1828 *Laws* 88, Mile-money [still in force].

MILE-WALK sb dial. Some kind of large-leaved vine—prob FIVE-FINGER—which 'walks a mile' (grows a long distance from its root).

1952 FGC Tre, Mile-walk—same as Five-finger, but leaf is more like coco-leaf.

MILK(-HEAD) MANGO sb dial. A variety of mango that exudes a milky juice from the stem when picked green.

1952 FGC Port, Milk-mango—milk comes out when green. 1959 DeC Han /milk-hed/—the mango which is called *black mango* in Kingston.

MILK PAN sb; <*milk*+PAN. A large tinned metal container for carrying gallons of milk.

1957 JN Fairfield, I see plenty cars and trucks with people and food and milk pan. 1960 S. J. Reid StAnd, Milk pan—the kind of big milk-container women used to carry on their heads when selling milk—hold 10 gallons or so.

MILK-TEA sb dial. A number of herbs (genus *Euphorbia*) which have a milky juice and are used in medicinal or fortifying teas.

1927 Beckwith 22, Milk-Tea..See Mapempe. 1953 *WIMJ* 245, see MAPEMPE.

MILK TREE sb. The plants *Euphorbia brasiliensis* and *E. thymifolia*. *N*

1955 *WIMJ* 162, Milk Tree.

MILK WATTLE sb. An unidentified tree presumably having a milky sap and resembling the WATTLE-WOOD.

1943 *NHN* II 82, Milk Wattle—A small tree..with light brown flaky bark..The sap is said to be irritating but I did not find it so, nor did any of my men.

MILKWEED sb; *OED* 1706→ for diff plants. In Jamaica: almost any shrub which exudes a milky juice; but esp the euphorbiaceous plants —cf MILK-TEA, MILK TREE.

1927 Beckwith 22, Milkweed—'Strong-back' a *Parsonsia Parsonsia*..b..'Mapempe'. 1954 *WIMJ* 29, *Cuphea parsonsia*; 30, four species of *Euphorbia*; 1955 *ibid* 158, two more species of *Euphorbia*.

MILK WITHE /milk wis/ sb.

1952 FGC StM, see HOGMEAT. 1954 *WIMJ* 30, *Funastrum clausum*..Milk Wys (Withe).

MILKWOOD sb; *OED* 1725→ for 1.

1. *Pseudolmedia spuria*; also called BASTARD BREADNUT.

1696 Sloane 136, Laurifolia arbor venenata..Milk-wood. a 1725 Barham (1794) 103, Milk-wood, *Brosimum spurium*. 1756 Browne 369–70, Milk-Wood..This tree is pretty frequent in St Mary's..It is reckoned among the timber trees. 1774 Long III 863, Milk Wood. 1854–5 *TJSA* I 8, Milk Wood. 1864 Grisebach 785, Milkwood. 1914 Fawcett 45, Milkwood.

2. *Sapium jamaicense*; also called GUM TREE.

1920 Fawcett 325, Gum Tree, Milk Wood. 1941 Swabey 14, see BEYACCA. 1952 FGC StE /milk wud/ same as blind-eye, burn-eye, beyaca—hardest wood in Jamaica.

3. *Cecropia peltata*; also called TRUMPET TREE.

1944 *NHN* II 142, The Trumpet Tree..(Known locally [near Corn Puss Gap] as Milk Wood), with its large peculiar leaves.

4. *Rauwolfia nitida*.

1961 W. E. Fulford Man, Ident by DAP, Institute Ja.

MILLET REED sb obs.

1756 Browne 138–9, Arundo 4..The larger Millet Reed..This plant is very common in the woods, and rises by its slender and branched stalks to the height of six or seven feet.

MILL-GANG sb obs. That gang of slaves who tended the sugar-mill while it was in operation, feeding in the canes, etc. *G*

1774 Long II 319 note, Boatswain of the mill. The Negroe who attends the mill-gang, or feeders.

mima sb dial; cf *miimi*, *mama*. A term of address: Mother.

1952 FGC Han /mima/ mama, muma. 1956 Mc Man /mima/.

MIMBA sb obs; Afr. The DAY NAME for a girl born on Saturday.

1774 Long II 329, Mademoiselle, instead of modish French, must learn to prattle gibberish with her cousins Mimba and Chloe.

MIN /min/ auxil vb dial; a var of *bin*, BEN (with simple substitution of a bilabial nasal for a bilabial stop). The auxiliary of past tense constructions, corresponding (according to context) to StdE *had*, *was*, *did*.

1868 *TRSAA* I 66, You frighten me; suppose you min kill me. [*Suppose you had killed me.*] 1907 Jekyll 112, Me no min tell you fe bring home me daughter [?] [*Didn't I tell you..?*]. *Ibid* 270, Me no min de a concert. [*I was not there..*] 1942 Bennett 42, Ef Sue noh min nyam har fry fish.. [*If Sue had not eaten her fried fish.*]

mina auxil vb phr dial; <MIN+A[5]; cf BENA. Indicating past progressive tense of the verb *be*, or of some other verb which follows it (*mina*).

1954 LeP StT /jan an dem ada wan min a iit manggo anda trii/ *John and the others were eating..* 1958 Dec StAnd /bot yu nuo, fos taim mi an him mina gud fren/ *Formerly I and he were good friends.*

MIND /main/ vb dial; <*mind*, take care. To be careful lest, to see that one does not—usually in imperative expressions, warnings or threats.

1877 Murray *Kittle* 18, 'As for you,' rejoined Maria, 'you better mine dat you blink eye that you hab dere'. [*Be careful that you don't blink your eye.*] 1942 Bennett 38, Mine you meck police arres' me. [*Be careful or you'll make the police arrest me.*] 1956 Mc Man /main yu faal doun/ warning to a child. 1956 BLB StE /main yu tek op a kuol doun de/ *Mind you don't catch cold.* *BA BL G T*

MINE see prec.

mingki sb dial; a phonetic var of *blingki* (cf BLINKY)—cf MIN var of *bin*, BEN. A small firefly. But cf Ko *minikamalenge*, firefly.

1958 DeC StT /mingki/.

MINGLING PAIN sb dial; prob <*mingling*, but perh infl by /migl/ middle. A kind of pain felt during pregnancy.

1952 Kerr 28, The mother must not drink too much water..she must not eat eggs because they cause 'minglin' pains.

MINGO sb; prob < Sp *Mingo*, a person alluded to in popular phrases as being elaborately dressed. The 'scrawled filefish' (1933 Beebe & Tee-Van 241)—*Alutera scripta*, an olivaceous fish with light-blue and black spots, and light-blue streaks. See also QUASHIE 2.

1756 Browne 456, Balistes 3. Subcinerea maculata minor.. The Mingo. 1892 Cockrell list, Mingo—*alutera scripta*.

mini-blista sb dial; prob represents *Minnie*, a personifying feminine name, +*blister* repr the colour of an albino's skin, appearing as if blistered.

1959 DeC West /mini-blista/ a female albino Negro.

MINI-MINI adj and sb dial; etym prob multiple—cf Twi *mini-minã*, small stinging flies (cf sense B 2 esp); Hausa *minīnī*, plur *minīminī*, emphasizes smallness; perh also derivs of Lat *minimus*, smallest, in Engl and other langs. *BL*

A. adj: Very small.

1943 *GL* Tre, Minny minny, small. 1952 FGC Han /mini-mini/ very small.

B. sb: 1. Small, shining specks of water vapour.

1943 *GL* StM, Mini-mini, water vapour.

2. Small flies.

1943 *GL*, Mini mini, small flies. 1952 FGC Han /minimini flai/ is the smallest. 1955 FGC Man /mini-mini/ sour-flies.

3. The kind of small, bright 'spots' that one seems to see when struck on the head, or as an effect of smoking ganja.

1952 Kerr 130, Now in one centre where ganga was frequently taken we were told that when it was smoked people saw little figures that they called mini-mini. 1952 FGC Man /mini-mini/ something that shines or glitters when you get a blow on the head—or what one who smokes ganja sees. 1955 FGC Man, If they knock you you see /mini-mini/.

MINNY-MINNY see prec.

minti kuoko see MINTY COCO.

minto see MENTO.

MINTY COCO sb dial; etym uncert—no conn can be made with *mint*—it does not have a minty flavour; the personifying name *Minty* (for *Aminta* or the like) is possible, but positive evidence is lacking. A white soft variety of coco (*Colocasia esculenta*) that takes only six or seven months to mature.

1929 Beckwith 17, see SALLY COCO. 1942 Bennett 10, But me nevah know sey Lucea yam Did wed minty cocoa. [For the sense of 'wed' here cf MARRIED 2.] 1950 Pioneer 20, Yuh noh got noh minty cocoa can gi me fe plant noh sar? 1952 FGC Port, StAnd, StAnn, StC, StJ, StM, StT /minti kuoko/. 1956 Mc Man, Port, StAnd /minti/—white, soft, smooth /kuoko/.

MINYA-MINYA see MENYA-MENYA.

MIRASMAS, MIRASMI, mirazma see next.

mirazmi sb dial, also attrib; ult <Lat *marasmus*, emaciation, wasting from malnutrition, the medical term in Engl; the form in *-i* may be due to the suffix *-y*, or perh to Fr *marasme*. Emaciation, wasting from malnutrition—a common condition in infants. *T*

1943 Bennett 17, Se' de marga man wat hol'in' han' Wid de nice fat lady, She musa feel like she dah hol' A mirasmi baby! 1952 FGC StT, Trumpet leaf good for baby /mirazma/. StC, Fasten-man-coat—use for /mirazmi/ when child's hair turns red. 1957 *FFM* 26, There is no particular form of starvation—it's generalized starvation and we give it a polite name of *mirasmas* as we don't want to tell the woman her child is starving to death. [This spelling reflects the dial form of the word; elsewhere in this volume it is spelt *marasmus*.]

mirazmi bush sb dial; <*mirazmi* + BUSH. One of the names of the common weed *Phyllanthus niruri*, used against marasmus of infants, and for various diseases. Also called CARRY-ME-SEED. S BABY-GRIPE BUSH.

1952 FGC StAnd /mirazmi bush/—baby-gripe bush, when baby have cold, get thin, cure with this.

mirigl see MARINGLE.

MISS sb. In dial use, by itself or prec a name: a term of address of politeness and respect which does not imply recognition of superiority, greater age, that the woman is unmarried, or other such difference. *BL G T*

1942 Bennett 3, Ah glad fe se yuh Miss Dela, Step right inside me dear. 1959 JB, Miss B, used by one on familiar terms to address Jean Brown. 1959 LeP StAnd, Miss D—an impersonal form of address such as might be used by a higgler to a Jamaican in the market.

MISS CUBBA sb dial; <*Miss* + CUBBA.

1955 FGC Man /mís kúba/ a man who meddles in woman's affairs.

MISSES see next.

MISSIS /mísis, misís/ sb dial; <*mistress*. A title or term of address applied to an upper-class woman of any age, or to a woman as a polite form. This is more formal than MISS; it is about equivalent to *lady*. *BA G N*

1790 Moreton 154, Then missess fum me wid long switch. 1844 *Hongkong Register* 5 Mar, An English Lady, who went to make purchases in Jamaica, accompanied by her black maid, was repeatedly addressed by the negro shopman as 'massa', whereupon her sable follower exclaimed..'Why for you call my missus "massa"? Stupid fellah!—him's a she'. 1912 McK *Songs* 64, In peaceful solitude Rests de body of our Missis Queen,* Victoria de Good..*Always so called in Jamaica. 1924 Beckwith 5, Tiger was walking to a yard an' see two young misses, an' he was courting one of the young misses..Anansi.. said, 'Oh yes! I see Mr Tiger, but I tell you, missus, Tiger is me fader ol' ridin'-horse'. 1950 Pioneer 48, Eee-Hee Missis, is me same one Sidung yah all de time.

MISS JANE sb dial; symbolic of femininity. (Cf *OED Miss Nancy*.)

1958 DeC Port /mis jien/ a man who can cook.

MISS JANEY BUSH sb dial; prob used by a woman known as Miss Janey.

1952 FGC StT /mis jieni bush/ an unidentified plant.

MISS LASHEY sb dial; symbolic of femininity. (Cf *OED Miss Nancy*.)

1958 DeC Port, see CHAT-CHAT.

MISS RITTY sb dial; prob named after a woman who used it for successful cures. An unidentified 'tea bush'.

1952 FGC Han /mis riti/—a small tree, makes red tea; does not grow here, but they sell it in Kingston; leaf kind of velvet.

MISSUS see MISSIS.

MR MAC sb dial; abbr of *Mr Mackenzie*. A kind of wrasse—see MACKENZIE (PARROT).

MISTLETOE sb.

1. Species of the family *Loranthaceæ* (as elsewhere; not specif Jamaican).

2. The Currant Cactus, *Rhipsalis cassutha* (not properly a mistletoe, but widely so called).

1850 Macfadyen 182. 1926 Fawcett 285, Mistletoe.

MISTRESS /místris/ sb chiefly dial. Used as a formal title (preceding a name), or a term of address, more formal than MISSIS, and to a married woman. *BA BL G T*

MIX, MIXED, or **MIXTURE PEAS** sb dial. Mottled or parti-coloured beans, such as CRAB-EYE PEAS.

1952 FGC StAnn /mikst piiz/; StC /miks piiz/; StM /mikscha piiz/.

MIX-UP-MIX-UP vb or adj dial; iterative <*mix-up* or *mixed-up*. Mingle; mingled. (The iterated form suggests a greater degree.) *G*

1942 Bennett 12, Das de ting wid our fambily We noh mix-up mix-up wid stranger No sar, we gwan jus' like rayalty. [*We are not mixed-up* or *We do not mix-up indiscriminately*.]

MOCHO sb; cf the Mocho Mts. A place symbolic of remoteness—a rough, uncivilized place.

1943 Bennett 10, Suppose me..goh introduce Yuh to a stranga As me..son wat lately Come from 'Merica! Dem hooda laaf afta me, bwoy..Dem hooda sey me lie, yuh wasa Spen time a Mocho.

MOCO /móko/ sb now dial.

1. An African tribal name of doubtful identity; according to Bryan Edwards, the Moco slaves were shipped from Bonny as 'Eboes'; yet he uses the name as a separate one, and it was certainly so used in Jamaica. (In Sierra Leone the word *Móko* is used for all people coming from the region of the Calabar and Cameroon

rivers. J. Berry.) Cf the Ja place-names Mocho (Clar), Mocho Mts. *G*

1774 Long II 379, The Mocas not only worship, but eat, snakes; now adore, and presently devour, their deity. 1793 Edwards II 75, Many tribes among them, especially the Moco tribe, have been, without doubt, accustomed to the shocking practice of feeding on human flesh. 1825 Bicknell 35 [In the Trelawny Workhouse:] Tom, a Moco, 5 ft. 3 ins... *Ibid* 40, Neptune, a Moco.

2. Now used as symbolic of ugliness or backwardness (cf quot 1793 above); cf compounds, and *moko-*; it also suggests the remoter places, as in phr *back Moko way*, back-of-beyond.

MOCO JOHN sb dial; <MOCO+*John*, a personifying name. The wild tree *Bauhinia divaricata*, found plentifully in upland and mountain regions.

1943 *NHN* II 45, *Bauhinia divaricata*—Mokka John, Goat Hoof. 1952 FGC StE, Tre /moko jan, moko jaan/.

MOCO ROBIN sb dial; <MOCO+*robin* (*OED*). (*Moco* has derogatory connotations: cf the species name.) The Lizard Fish; see quot.

1892 Cockrell list, Mucco Robin, *synodus foetens*.

MOEL see *maa-i*.

mogl sb dial; perh <*muggle*, a muddle, confusion, disorder (*EDD*), or directly <*muddle*.

1958 DeC /mogl/ a stupid fool.

MOJO see MAJOE.

moka-moka, moko-moko adj dial; by iteration prob of an altered form of *muck* or *mucky*, but cf *mek-mek*, *meke-meke*. Muddy, wet and sloppy. *G*

1958 DeC Port /moka-moka/ adj for muddy road or field; StJ /moko-moko/ adj: wet, sloppy, muddy (of a road).

MOKKA see MOCO.

moko-jii sb dial; etym uncert: MOCO is prob the first element, but the second is unknown otherwise. Cf MOCO JOHN. See quots.

1943 *GL* Kgn, Mucko-gee—a country-man. 1955 FGC Man /mòko jii/—not clever.

mokomdash adj dial; etym unknown: the first element may be related to MOCO.

1943 *GL* West, Muckumdash, ugly. 1955 FGC Man /mókom dásh/ ugly.

MOLASSES-CISTERN sb; *DAE* 1833.

1807 Renny 136, The curing-house is a large, airy building, provided with a capacious melasses-cistern.

MOLASSES GRASS sb; from its sticky juice, which smells like molasses. The pasture grass *Melenis minutiflora*, also called WYNNE GRASS.

1954 *FG* 240, Molasses or Wynne Grass..The chief value of this grass lies in its ability to grow on areas of low fertility.

MOLOPLUNTO sb dial uncom; etym unknown.

1943 *GL* Port, Moloplunto, Banana dumpling in coconut milk.

MONEY-CUFFEE sb dial; <*money*+CUFFEE. Somebody who is well off and spends freely. (*Cuffee* being parallel to *fool* in similar English and American slang usages.)

1895 Banbury 43, Money Cuffie:—A fellow who can afford it, and rather makes a boast of his means.

MONEY FLY sb dial. A wood-boring beetle, bluish in colour. Popular lore has it that when the beetle flies out of his hole in the wood, one will get money. *BL G*

1952 FGCSt T.

MONEY-MUS' /moni-mos/ sb dial; prob <*Monymusk*, a well-known Jamaican sugar estate, but prob punning also on *must* (i.e money must come). Cf MUST POWDER. The LUCKY-LILY—a plant which brings you money if you plant some at its root.

1952 FGC Port /moni mos/.

MONGALAR DRUMMER see MONGOLA DRUMMER.

MONGOLA sb; an African tribal name (related to Angola). An African of Mongola origin. (Like other such tribal names, it has survived only in unfavourable senses, implying ignorance, stupidity, backwardness.)

1825 Bickell 38 [In St George's Workhouse], Diana, alias Susanna Grant, a Mungola. *Ibid* 41, Robert, a Mungola. 1826 Barclay 113, The most ignorant African negro, a Mongola even, would laugh.

MONGOLA DRUMMER /monggola, monggala, monggela, monggolo, manggola, monghela, mongala, mangela, man-grela/ sb; <MONGOLA+DRUMMER. A croaker (though popularly classed as a DRUMMER)—the fish *Micropogon fournierii*.

1834 Madden I 268, Ditto [*sc* Snapper], or Mangola Drummer, caught about Hunt's Bay. 1854–5 *TJSA* I 142, Mungola drummer. 1892 Cockrell list, Mongalar drummer—*Micropogon fournierii*. 1929 Beckwith 33, Jack; snit; drummer and 'mungala' drummer. 1952 FGC StC /mònggéla/; StE /monggolo/; StM /mán-géla, màngréla/; StT /mong-hela/.

MONGOOSE sb dial; a word referring to colour? (The mongoose is light brown and has reddish eyes.) See quot.

1958 DeC StT /mangguus/ a name for an albino Negro.

MONGOOSE GRASS sb dial. =BUTTON WEED.

1952 FGC Tre.

MONGOOSE WEED sb dial; the stem is said to be 'the colour of mongoose when ripe'. The wild plant *Borreria lævis*.

1952 FGC StC, StE, StM, StT /mangguus wiid/.

MONGST /mongs, mongks/ prep dial; aphetic form of *amongst*. Between. *BA BL G*

1956 Mc Man /di haas tan op mongs di tuu kou/ *The horse is standing between the two cows.*

MONK BAT sb. 'The *Molossus nasutus* of Jamaica' (*OED*).

1851 Gosse 294, I examined forty-three..and if I was surprised before at the extent of their gregarious habits, I was still more astonished to find that of this number, every one was of the male sex..The habit so strongly reminded me of a herd of monks, shutting themselves up in a convent, that I thought the species might well be designated as the Monk Bat.

MONK (BEETLE) sb obs. A beetle with a cover of the thorax which looks like a cowl over the head, whence the name.

1756 Browne 430–1, Bupestris 1. Fusca minima rugosa.. The Monk..The *scuta*, or cover of the thorax, is very large in proportion to the rest of the body, and serves as a cover for the head of the insect.

MONKEY-BERRY sb dial. The tree *Morinda citrifolia* and its fruit.

1952 FGC Man, StM /mongki beri/

MONKEY BREADFRUIT sb dial. A kind of breadfruit (not common) with a prickly exterior; also called MACCA or PRICKLY BREADFRUIT.

1952 FGC StT. 1956 Mc StE (Accom), A rather rare type of breadfruit /mongki brefruut/.

MONKEY-FACE sb dial; cf *OED* →1765. A grimace. *T*

1943 Bennett 3, For wen she laugh it like she Dah meck up monkey face. 1946 U.Newton I 31, The boys make monkey faces at me and I return the compliment with interest.

MONKEY-FIDDLE sb dial; see quot 1956. The plants *Pedilanthus tithymaloides* and *P. angustifolius*, growing wild and cultivated in gardens. *BL*

c1915 FGC StAnd, Monkey-fiddle. 1952 FGC StC, StT /mongki figl/. 1956 Mc StJ /mongki figl/—with smooth round stem, two pieces of which, when rubbed against each other, produce a pleasant sound as of a fiddle.

MONKEY IRON sb dial.

1952 FGC West /mongki aian/ boil coconut with sugar till it burns; hard to chew!

MONKEY-JESUS sb dial slang.

1943 *GL* Kgn, Monkey-Jesus, ugly person.

MONTEGONIAN sb; <*Montego*+*n*+*ian*, cf *Kingstonian*, *Oxonian*, *Devonian*, etc. An inhabitant of Montego Bay.

1924 Beckwith 206, Once as I was crossing the Montego Bay bridge, I met a Montegonian fellow.

MONTSERRAT PINE(APPLE) sb obs. A variety of pineapple brought in from Montserrat.

1774 Long III 792, The smaller green or yellow pyramidal or Montserrat.

MOOCHU vb dial; <*mooch*, pilfer, sponge, etc. (*OED*, *EDD*) +-*u*.

1943 *GL* no addr, Moochu, to beg.

MOODOO see *mudu*.

MOOMOO see MUMU.

MOON sb and vb dial; from the association of the lunar month with the period of human menstruation. (Cf also Amer Sp (Venezuela) *mono*, menstrual period—Alvarado.) *BA BL*

1958 DeC gen, 1. noun—menstruation. 2. vb.—to menstruate, /him no muun fi trii mont nou/ *She has not menstruated for three months now.*

MOON-FULL sb dial; <*moon* sb attrib +*full* sb. The full of the moon; the time of full moon.

1952 FGC StE, Full-mouth beans: 'plant it on moon-full and it grows well.'

MOON-GLOW sb urban slang.

1958 DeC StT /muun-gluo/ racial term: light brown skin, generally favourable connotations.

MOONIE sb chiefly dial; <*moon*+-*ie*. The firefly PEENY-WALLY. *N*

1917 Hammett in *Ja Times* 29 Sept, I have been given a clic-beetle ¾ or 1 in. long, caught in Mandeville, identical in form and action to our moonie, only it had no sign of any phosphorous. 1943 *GL* West, Moonie, firefly. 1952 FGC Han, StT, West /muuni/ same as KITIBU—has two shining eyes—the bigger firefly.

MOONIE-KITTY sb dial; <MOONIE+first part of *kitibu*. The firefly PEENY.

1959 DeC West /muuni-kiti/—the large firefly with light coming from the head; children toss these back and forth between them, calling out /muuni-kiti aal yu mie, yu hous a bon, yu pikni a bon/.

MOONLIGHT-'PON-'TICK sb dial joc arch; <*moonlight-upon-a-stick*—a piece of grotesque folk humour—cf HOUSE-A-HAND, FOOT-POST-HOLE, etc.

1943 *GL* Kgn, Moonlight pon 'tick, Gas lamp. 1956 BLB Man, Also /lait pan tik/, /muunshain pan tik/.

MOONSHINE sb dial; *OED*, 'now *rare* or poetic'. Moonlight. Often used to suggest a pinkish colour. *N*

1948 U.Newton IV 7, Though but 13 years of age, Joshie Barnes knew much about corn-shelling parties, moonshine revels.. including the playing of moonshine-baby and night-time errand running.

MOONSHINE BABY sb dial; <MOONSHINE +*baby*.

A game, played at full moon, in which children bring bits of broken crockery to a barbecue, choose a girl as 'moonshine baby' who lies still on the barbecue while the others outline her with the bits of crockery, which reflect the moonlight; the amusement comes from the players' remarks while outlining the 'baby' and later filling in the outline with more mosaic bits. (E. N. Burke.) See prec.

MOONSHINE DARLIN' sb dial; <MOONSHINE+*darling*. See quot.

1951 Murray 17, Note:..'Moonshine Darlins' are dances held out-of-doors when the moon is full. Anyone can join in the fun, whether invited or not, and refreshments are brought by those participating.

MOONSHINE DRUMMER sb dial; cf MOONSHINE SNAPPER. A variety of the DRUMMER or similar fish.

1952 FGC StM, Moonshine drummer—round head.

MOONSHINE GRUNT sb dial; cf MOONSHINE SNAPPER. A variety of the GRUNT fish.

1854–5 *TJSA* I 142, Hæmulon chromis—Moonshine grunt.

MOONSHINE-'PON-'TICK see MOONLIGHT-'PON-'TICK.

MOONSHINE SNAPPER sb dial. A variety of SNAPPER of pinkish colour and with large glassy eyes (whence the name); see quots.

1950 Smith *Priacanthus arenatus* is called..*moonshine* (Lucea); *P. cruentatus* is..*moonshine* (Montego Bay).

1952 FGC StC, StJ, StM, StT /muunshain snapa/ pink with white, glassy eye; West /muunshain/ big bright eyes, reddish colour; flatter than snapper. s SHINY-MOON~.

MOONSHINE YAM sb dial; from the colour. Red St Vincent yam ('red' meaning, as in many other instances, yellow or light orange).

1952 FGC StC /muunshain yam/.

MOONSHINE YAMPI sb dial.

1956 Mc StT /muunshain yaampi/ a type of yampi, red coloured. (Cf MOONSHINE YAM.)

MOONTAIL PARROT sb dial. A variety of the PARROT fish.

1952 FGC StAnn.

MOOSA see MUSSA.

MOOSHEMAN sb dial; <*mushe*+*man*. See *mushe* I (ref to samfi game).

1943 *GL* Kgn, Moosheman, trickster.

MOOS-MOOS see *mus-mus* sb[1].

MORASS /márás, maráas, máras, marós, morás, márósh, marást/ sb chiefly dial, also attrib; *OED*, 'The word is now confined to literary use, exc. in some parts of the West Indies, where it survives with the pronunciation mǫ·ras.' This does not quite describe actual Ja pronunc, q.v. above.

1. A moist or swampy piece of land covered with vegetation: see quot 1952. Also attrib. *BL G*

1683 *Present State* 7, Belly-aches, caused..sometimes by ill chosen Seats when they Plant in low Valleys..or by Mountains or Morossos, and have too much rain. 1727 *Observations* 12, But your Lagunes, Morasses, and Swamps might be drained. 1873 Rampini 181 [Prov:] When morass catch fire, land-turtle look for mangrove tree. 1952 FGC Han /marós/ St And /márás/ have water, constant running gutter; StAnn /maráas/ rushy, salt or not, but none here—Black River way; StAnn, Wild duck go around pools, /morás/; StE, wild starapple grow in maras place; StJ, bielo crab live in manggro, in marosh; StT /máras/—large trees on it, rushes and reeds; Tre /márás/ where rushes, crab-thatch, mangrove grow. 1954 LeP StE, Land that is swampy—Maruss. 1956 Mc StAnd /maraas/ swampy land.

2. As an abbr of MORASS-WEED. *BL*

3. See quot. (This is of doubtful validity: the name of the material may have been taken as the name of the product.)

1946 Dunham 4, Marosh—a mat of river reeds on which a mattress is laid.

MORASS BARK sb; <MORASS, here perh referring to the kind of land on which the shrub is often found growing +*bark*, referring to the use of the bark locally as a source of fibre. *Malvaviscus sagræanus*; see quot.

1926 Fawcett 133–4, *M. Sagræanus*..Sugar Bark, Morass Bark, Mahoe Rose..The bark of the young shrubs makes a fine, white, and very strong hemp.

MORASS (WEED) sb; <MORASS 1 +*weed*.

1. *Ceratophyllum demersum.*

1756 Browne 345, Ceratophyllum 1..the Morass, or Morass-weed. This plant is very common in all the brackish waters in Jamaica; and generally used to cover whatever fish or water-plants they carry a long way to market; for it retains a deal of moisture, which keeps them fresh and cool for a considerable time. 1864 Grisebach 785, Morass-weed. 1914 Fawcett 187, C. demersum..Morass Weed.

2. Extended to include other kinds of water plants—e.g. seaweeds anchored to stones on the sea-bottom; also perh to mosses, though evidence is not clear.

1943 *GL* Port, Marass, moss. 1956 Mc Kgn /maráas/ bright green seaweed, anchored; also sea-grass; StAnd /marasis, malasis/ (so said by children).

more see MURREY.

MOREEN see MERINO.

MOREST /múoris/ adj dial; <*more* compar +*-est* suffix of superl. Most.

1833 Scott I 50, De coloured peoples, never fear, Ah, him lob him de morest nor any oder. 1868 Russell 9–10, Good, goodis; Bad, badis;..More,..moris; Wosa, wosis. A hab de moris mango.

MORGAN CONGO see GUNGU (PEAS) quot 1913.

mori see MURREY.

MORINGA see MARANGA.

MORNING-BREAKFAST sb dial. The earliest meal of the day, in peasant custom. *G*

1958 DeC Port /maanin brekfas/ morning meal, opposed to just /brekfas/ the noon meal; StT /maanin brekfas/ equiv to TEA—distinct from Breakfast, the noon meal.

MORNING-CHAW sb dial.

1935 HPJ, Maanin-chaw, a light meal in the early morning (=chocolatter).

MOROSSO see MORASS.

[**MORTAR** sb dial. A mortar made by hollowing out a log or piece of tree-trunk. It stands vertically, as the tree-trunk would. Still in use in the country parts. *BA G T*

1956 Mc Man /maata/—a hollowed-out lump of wood; things (e.g. coffee, kisaada) are pounded in it with a /maata tik/.]

MORTAR STICK sb. A heavy pole of wood used to pound up produce or foodstuffs in a traditional wooden mortar. It makes a handy weapon, and is often treated as such. *G*

1873 Rampini 129–30, Hi! de ole witch get angry!..him fling him mortar stick over him shoulder, an' go 'long fe find out who tell de Prince dis ting..So him..take him mortar stick, an' beat Toad till him lie down like dead. 1924 Beckwith 45, An' tek a morter-stick an' lick upon head an' kill de pic'ny. 1952 FGC StAnn /maata stik/ a stick used by fishermen to kill fish.

MOSELLA see *mozela yam.*

MOSES WEED sb dial: prob a confused allusion to Aaron's rod—cf Bible, Numbers 17. The tree *Glyricidia sepium*, which grows very easily and quickly bursts into flower.

mosi vb dial; <*must* + *-i*. (Despite the translations, /i/ here is not <*is* though it coincidentally takes the position that forms of the verb *be* would have in StdE.) Must. *G*

1943 *GL* Man, No mussi—it must be. 1957 JN Clar, June look here. No pull up mi hair. You mussi no ha fe yu. [*You must not have any of your own!*] StJ, Musi pichary. [*It must be a petchary.*] *Ibid.* From this long time we no get any rain, a tonight i musi going fall.

moskafiim see MUSTIFINA.

MOSQUITO-BOOT sb obs.

1774 Long III 884. In those places where they are very numerous..the usual guard for the legs is the muskeeto-boot, or a kind of half-trouzer, made of linen, tied above the knee, and reaching to the shoes.

MOSQUITO BUSH sb dial; *OED* 1750 only.

1954 *WIMJ* 247, *Ocimum micranthum*..Wild Barsley; Mosquito Bush; Wild Basil. Used as a general beverage. For fever and pain the decoction is taken as a drink and also as a bath.

MOSQUITO HAWK sb obs. A large moth, popularly thought to hunt mosquitoes.

1756 Browne 438, Phalæna 1..The Muskeeto Hawk.. it is never abroad but in the earlier hours of the night, when the Muskeetos are most troublesome, which gave rise to its common appellation; most people imagining that it feeds on these insects. 1788 Marsden 57, They have a rooted enemy in an insect about the size of a bat, called the musquitoe-hawk.

MOSQUITO WOOD sb; < the *Mosquito* shore, where it was found + *wood.* The tree *Mosquitoxylum jamaicense* and its wood.

1909 Harris 309, Mosquito wood..This tree was unknown to science until described by Professors Krug and Urban in 1899..The tree is found in woods in the parishes of St Elizabeth, St James, Hanover, and Westmoreland. *Ibid* 318, Musquito-wood. 1926 Fawcett 9. 1941 Swabey 26, Mosquito Wood..The tree is common in the wetter sections of St Elizabeth and Westmoreland. 1952 FGC StE /màskítawud/.

MOTGREATEN phr; typographical error for 'me t'reaten', *I threaten* (Louise Bennett).

1955 Bennett *Me Dah Drive*, Me bruck up all de corner dem, An ben up all de curve, Motgreaten all de lamp pos' dem, Me shimmy an me swerve.

MOTHER sb dial.

1. A female officer in a Revival religious group. *G*

1953 Moore 56; *ibid* 87, Mother = crowned shepherdess —the highest female office; the highest is also a Wheeling Mother; and there are still other offices: rambling mother, warrior mother, hunting mother, cutting mother, spying mother, water mother.

2. A similar officer in *kumuna* cults.

1953 Moore 137–8, The qualifications for a Mother of Cumina are predicated upon a knowledge of folk songs and a great deal of strength to withstand the strong zombies who come close and sometimes enter to possess her..she is the chief assistant to the master of ceremonies; her singing is, therefore, only one part of her duties.

3. The rhizome or central rootstock of a coco plant, from which the tubers grow.

1958 DeC StC /mada/ The large tuber of a coco [*sc* the rhizome] as opposed to the buttons—the small, edible, replantable knobs.

MOTHER (BRANCH, LIMB) sb dial. One of the main branches or limbs of a tree: see quots.

1958 DeC StAnd /mada/ or /mada lim/ one of the main limbs branching out from the lowest main crotch of the tree. Normally there are two of these. (A tree-pruning term.) /mada branch/ a sound and useful branch coming from one of the mother limbs. The purpose of pruning is to leave a proper number of well distributed mother branches on two sound mothers.

MOTHER CANTINNY see MADA CANTINNY.

MOTHER EDWARDS sb dial. A variety of sweet-potato with yellow flesh.

1952 FGC StAnn, StC, StE /mada edwardz, mada hedwad, mada edwod/—yellow, round; inside favour punkin; ready in 3 months. 1954 *FG* 439, Other lesser known varieties are Blue Bud and Mother Edwards.

MOTHER FATE see MADA FATE.

MOTHER-FIRE, MOTHER-PEPPER adj dial; evid by personification of *fire* and *pepper* (two hot things).

1956 Mc Man /máda-fáia, máda-pépa/ quick-tempered.

MOTHER-GOAT sb dial.

1954 LeP StAnn, She goat, mother-goat.

MOTHER-IN-LAW sb dial; cf *OED* 2 = Stepmother, 'Now regarded as incorrect'. Quots 1516–1848.

1. A stepmother. *BA*

1954 LeP Kgn, Man, Port, Stepmother—Madan-lah, madanlaw, maadanlaw. 1956 Mc Man /mi madaanlaa, mi madarinlaa/ father's wife who is not her mother.

2. Fig. A confection of sugar and grated coconut.

1958 DeC StT /madanlaa/.

MOTHER LOBSTER sb obs; cf SHRIMP MAAMI. A variety of sea crayfish (cf LOBSTER); from the description this appears to be what is now called the QUEEN LOBSTER.

1756 Browne 424, Astacus 6..The Mother Lobster. This species is very rare, and seldom seen in Jamaica, though a native of those seas. It has no claws; but, instead of these, it is supplied with two broad, articulated and compressed defenders, that stretch forward from the fore-part of the head, one under each eye.

MOTHER LOOK-UP sb dial. A small wild plant (*Blechum brownei*) which seems to turn its stems and leaves up as if looking; 'mother' probably alludes to its medicinal uses. Cf LOOK-UP.

MOTHER OF (THE) CUMINA see MOTHER 2.

MOTHER-PEPPER see MOTHER-FIRE.

MOTHER THOMAS sb dial.

1. A variety of sweet-potato.

1952 FGC StM /mada tamas/—red.

2. A kind of MACHETE: see quots.

1952 FGC StE /màda támas/ one kind of open-guard machete. 1958 DeC Kgn /mada tamas/ here meaning a cutlass of any shape after it is worn down so far as to be useless.

MOTH GRASS /maat graas/ occas /maak, maas/ sb chiefly dial. Also erron sp Mart grass. KHUS-KHUS grass, whose aromatic roots are used to keep moths out of clothing.

1952 FGC Port, StM, StT /máat gráas/—put root in tin-case—keep /maat/ from cutting clothes; StT, People say /maat grass/ but /maas graas/ is correct. 1954 *FG* 225–6, Khus-Khus or Mart [*sic*] Grass (*Vetiveria Zizenioides*) ..The roots are often sold in Jamaica for packing in clothing to keep it from moths.

MOTOMPY sb dial rare; cf Twi *mmɔ̀tɔ*, fresh + *mpɛ̀*, matter found sometimes, esp after a night's sleep, in the corner of the eye.

1943 *GL* Man, Motompy, refuse of the eye.

MOULD (UP) vb dial; cf *OED* v^1 2 →1837. To heap mould or earth around the roots of a plant such as maize, yam, etc.; to hill up.

1912 McK *Songs* 14, see SO B 3. 1924 Beckwith 71, When de corn grew up, he went back to mol' it. As he started, the v'ice says, 'Who mol' corn deh?' 1956 Mc Man, To form yam-hill /yu muol op di uol/ (the yam hole). *BA G T*

MOUNT vb dial. To sit astride of (and play) the PLAYING DRUM of the *kumona* cult.

1953 Moore 136, Drummers begin on the *banda*..The man mentioned above played the *banda* at Cumina dances for six years before he was permitted to 'mount' the playing drum.

MOUNTAIN sb now dial; cf COFFEE MOUNTAIN. A small plantation in the mountains, esp for crops that grow better at an altitude.

1764 Gordon 378, I attended him also to his Farm (Penn) and to his Mountain, which is cool and pleasant. 1853 Bremer II 417, The highest aim of the negro is to be able to purchase his own little plot of ground, a 'mountain', as it is called, where he can erect for himself a birch-bark hut..and grow sugar-cane, or maize and edible roots. 1873 Rampini 92, The negro often rents a piece of land as a ginger 'mountain', a tobacco 'field', or a coffee 'piece', according to locality. 1957 JN StAnn, 'Where is Uncle Charles now?' 'A' mouten.' 'Doing what?' 'Gone dig food.' 'What does he do with the food?' 'Cook a mouten.'

MOUNTAIN BASTARD BULLY-TREE sb obs. Perh = MOUNTAIN BULLET.

1756 Browne 201, Achras? 7..The Mountain Bastard Bully-Tree.

MOUNTAIN BAY sb bot; *OED* 1895 of diff tree. In Jamaica: 1. *Quiina jamaicensis* (cf 1926 Fawcett 205), also called VELVET SEEDS; 2. *Calyptranthes discolor* (*ibid* 324).

MOUNTAIN BROOM TREE sb bot. The shrub *Baccharis scoparia.*

1756 Browne 316, Chrysocoma?..The Mountain Broom Tree. This is a native of Jamaica; and there found only in the coldest parts of the mountains..It resembles our European Broom, and is the only tree, of the same appearance, I have observed in that country. 1814 Lunan I 520. 1864, Grisebach 782. 1936 Fawcett 199, Mountain Broom Tree, Bitter Broom.

MOUNTAIN BRYONY sb bot. The climbing vine *Cayaponia racemosa.*

1756 Browne 355, Bryonia 1..The Mountain Bryony.. it runs a great way, and bears small roundish berries. 1814 Lunan I 118 (quotes Browne). 1926 Fawcett 269, Wild Cerasee, Mountain Bryony..All parts of the plant are intensely bitter.

MOUNTAIN BULFINCH sb obs? The Jamaican Spindalis (*Spindalis nigricephala*).

1847 Gosse 231, Cashew-Bird. Mountain Bulfinch (Rob.) —Orange-bird.

MOUNTAIN BULLET or **BULLY-TREE** sb. The tree *Dipholis montana.*

1864 Grisebach 782, Mountain Bully-tree; *Dipholis montana.* 1941 Swabey 15, Mountain Bullet or Bully Tree.

MOUNTAIN CABBAGE (TREE or **PALM)** sb; *OED* →1796. The palm *Euterpe oleracea*, with a terminal bud that is eaten like cabbage.

1740 Importance 54, see BASTARD CABBAGE TREE. 1864 Grisebach 782, Cabbage-palm, Mountain: *Euterpe oleracea.* 1913 Harris 26–7, Cabbage, Mountain..The mountain cabbage palm is a native of Jamaica and the West Indies generally..The portion used for cooking or for pickling is the heart of young leaves or cabbage as it is called. 1952 FGC StE, StJ, StT /mountn kyabij/ = wild cabbage—heart of trunk can use as cabbage; StM /mountn paam/. *N*

MOUNTAIN CALALU sb; see CALALU. *Phytolacca* species; also called JOCATO.

1740 Importance 34, Callaloe of three Sorts, Top-a-top, or the Cocoa-Callaloe; another Sort grows like Brocoli, and eats like Spinage; and the Mountain-Callaloe. 1754 Browne 232, Phytolacca 2..Mountain *Calaloe*, or Poke weed. This plant is a native of *Jamaica*, and commonly found in all the cooler hills and mountains of the island.. The leaves and more tender shoots are frequently used for greens, by the negroes. 1814 Lunan II 78–9, Poke-weed or Mountain Calalue. Phytolacca. 1. Decandra.. This plant is also known by the name of *Surinam* or *jukato calalue*, red-weed, and fox-glove. It is very common in Jamaica..This plant is the same as the red-weed or poke of Virginia and New England. 1914 Fawcett 159, *Phytolacca rivinoides, P. icosandra*, Mountain Calalu, Jocato, Poke Weed.

MOUNTAIN CINNAMON sb bot.

1926 Fawcett 209, *Cinnamodendron corticosum*..Mountain Cinnamon, Red Canella.

MOUNTAIN COCK sb; *OED* for diff birds. The HOPPING DICK.

1740 Importance 38, The Mountain-Cock or Tricking-Chick, which digs up their Corn. 1756 Browne 469, The Mountain-Cock. 1952 FGC StT, Mountain cock—sings well. Its cry: 'Tilly, Tilly, plant corn, plant corn; t'ree-t'ree, four-four, peas an' corn'. Same as hopping-dick.

MOUNTAIN COWITCH sb bot. = SMOOTH-LEAVED COWITCH.

1920 Fawcett 303, *Acidoton urens*..Mountain Cowitch. 1944 *NHN* II 57, The Mountain or Smooth Leaved Cowitch, a widespread shrub, is more difficult to avoid as the stinging hairs are confined to the margins of the leaves and are not readily noticed.

MOUNTAIN CRAB sb; alluding to the habitat. The BLACK CRAB.

1756 Browne 423. 1793 Edwards I 95 [quotes from Browne]. 1835 Madden II 266, I cannot conclude this account without a few words concerning the mountain-crab, which is the most celebrated of Jamaica delicacies.. [Refs to Edwards, Du Tertre, Browne]..However distant they may be from the sea, they go down to it once a year to deposit their spawn.

MOUNTAIN CRAYFISH sb. See quot.

1952 FGC Han /mountn/ crayfish—larger than 'ol' 'oman' and has claws.

MOUNTAIN DAMSON sb; *OED* 1814→. The tree *Simaruba glauca.*

1778 Wright, see STAVEWOOD. 1811 Titford 65, Mountain Damson, or Stavewood tree, Simarouba Quassia; nat. Ja. 1814 Lunan I 521, This tree is known in Jamaica by the name of *mountain damson, bitter damson*, or *stavewood.* 1920 Fawcett 198–9, Bitter Damson, Bitter Dan, Mountain Damson, Stave Wood..*S. amara*..occurs in some of the West Indian Islands, but is wrongly stated by Linnæus fil. to be a native of Jamaica. 1941 Swabey 14.

MOUNTAIN DICK sb.

1. The female of the Jamaican Becard, the male being called JUDY.

1847 Gosse 187, see JUDY. 1936 Bond 259, *Platypsaris niger*..Mountain Dick (female). 1956 Jeffrey-Smith 67.

2. Prob by confusion with MOUNTAIN COCK, applied to that bird (*Turdus auranteus*).

1952 FGC StAnd, Mountain Dick = chick-man-chick; StM, = chick-man-chick—always hopping; says /kúling/.

MOUNTAIN DOGWOOD sb bot obs. = BITCHWOOD. 'Mountain Dogwood', and the distinction it implied, have been abandoned by botanists.

1756 Browne 297, The Mountain Dog-wood. This tree is so like the foregoing, both in appearance and smell.. that a man can hardly distinguish the one from the other, until he observes the fruit. 1837 Macfadyen 259, *Piscidia Carthaginensis.* Mountain Dogwood.

MOUNTAIN DOVE sb. Prob = MOUNTAIN PIGEON.

1952 FGC StM, Mountain dove—more of them in StAnn.

MOUNTAIN EBONY sb.

1. The tree *Bauhinia divaricata*, also called BULL-HOOF, MOCO JOHN.

1696 Sloane 150, Mountain Ebony. In montibus sylvosis Insulæ Jamaicæ ubique abundat. 1756 Browne 286–7, Bauhinia 1..Mountain Ebony. 1837 Macfadyen 351, Bauhinia porrecta. Mountain Ebony. 1920 Fawcett 117.

2. The tree *Colubrina ferruginosa.*

1926 Fawcett 68, Greenheart, Snake Wood, Black Velvet, Wild or Mountain Ebony. 1941 Swabey 30, Mountain Ebony..occasionally used in inlay work.

MOUNTAIN GRAPE (TREE) sb. Various species of *Coccoloba*; some of these are *C. plumieri, C. laurifolia, C. krugii* (see 1914 Fawcett 122).

1756 Browne 210, Coccolobis 4..The Mountain Grape-Tree. This tree is frequent about the Cross in Clarendon: it grows to a considerable size, and is looked upon as a fine timber-wood. 1864 Grisebach 785, Mountain-grape, black: *Guettarda longiflora.* Mountain-grape, common: *Coccoloba tenuifolia.* Mountain-grape, large-leaved: *Coccoloba Plumieri.* 1914 Fawcett 113, 122. 1961 DAP, Mountain or Wild Grape: *Coccoloba swartzii.*

MOUNTAIN GRASS sb. *Tricholæna insularis*, Gr. See quots.

1756 Browne 365, Andropogon? 4..Mountain-Grass. In this plant the foot-stalks of the flowers are covered with a long white down. 1854–5 *TJSA* I 68, Mountain grass. *Andropogon insulare.*

MOUNTAIN-GREEN sb bot. In Grisebach's use: MOUNTAIN PRIDE.

1864 Grisebach 786, Mountain-green: *Spathelia simplex.*

MOUNTAIN GUAVA sb; *OED* 1756 only. *N*

1. *Psidium montanum* (but note quots under 2).

1756 Browne 239, Psidium 2..The Mountain Guava. This is one of the largest trees in the woods of Jamaica.. It makes very beautiful walking-sticks. 1864 Grisebach 784. 1886 Hooper 28. 1941 Swabey 26, Mountain Guava—*Psidium montanum Sw. Myrtaceæ.* A very tall tree up to 100 ft with a girth of about 7 ft..It is..used in making gun-stocks.

2. Transf to other trees having smooth-barked trunks; these include *Calyptranthes zuzygium* and species of *Coccoloba*—see quots.

1740 Importance 53, There is also a Mountain *Guaver* Tree, which bears a Fruit, tho' not eat by Man or Beast, but is esteem'd an Everlasting in Buildings. 1943 *NHN* II 53, *Coccoloba* spp.—Mountain Guava and Mountain Grape. There are at least five species of this genus growing in the area and all except *C. Krugii* are known as either Mountain Guava or Mountain Grape. *Ibid* 89, The identification of the Mountain Guava as *Psidium montanum* is definitely an error. The species on Portland ridge to which they refer is *Calyptranthes zuzygium.*

MOUNTAIN MAHOE sb. =BLUE MAHOE. *N*

1756 Browne 284, Hibiscus 1..The Mountain Mohoe. This tree grows commonly to a considerable size: it is frequent in the inland woods about Bath..The wood is of a dark olive colour. 1837 Macfadyen 68, Hibiscus elatus. Mountain Mahoe..This is a lofty tree with a straight stem, and affords a valuable timber, much prized, especially by cabinet-makers, having, when worked up and polished, the appearance of dark green variegated marble. 1926 Fawcett 141, Blue or Mountain Mahoe, Cuba Bark.

MOUNTAIN MULLET sb, also attrib. A small fish caught in mountain streams and considered a delicacy. *N*

1756 Browne 451, Mugil 3..The Mountain or Hog-snout Mullet. 1802 Nugent 79, There was a new fish, the Mountain Mullet, very small, but excellent. 1835 Madden I 199, A dinner of turtle and calipever, mountain mullets, ring-tailed pigeons, black crabs, and wild guinea-fowl. 1876 Hosack 98, A mountain-mullet feast he spread.

MOUNTAIN NASEBERRY-BULLY TREE sb bot. See quot. (This may be Browne's MOUNTAIN BASTARD BULLY-TREE.)

1864 Grisebach 786, Mountain Naseberry-bully Tree: *Sapota Sideroxylon.*

MOUNTAIN OLIVE sb. *Buchenavia capitata*; also called MOUNTAIN WILD OLIVE, WILD OLIVE.

1801 Dancer 363, Yellow Saunders or Mountain Olive.. The Bark, in Decoction cures Venereal Complaints. Negroes call it Negressa. 1952 FGC StAnn, Mountain olive (in Portland).

MOUNTAIN OWL sb. The Brown Owl?

1756 Browne 473, Strix 1. Rufescens miscella..[etc.]. The Mountain Owl.

MOUNTAIN PARTRIDGE sb. The Jamaican BLUE DOVE (1), BLUE PARTRIDGE (2), or MOUNTAIN WITCH: *Geotrygon versicolor. N*

1725 Sloane 304, The Mountain Partridge. This Sort of Pigeon, is ten Inches long..[etc.]. They are found in the woody Mountains near the Angels, where they feed on Berries. They are accounted very good Food. 1840 Chamberlaine 22, Mountain partridge—Columba montana—Lin. 1847 Gosse 320, Partridge dove. Mountain partridge. *Geotrygon montana*..I am convinced that our Partridge dove is the *montana* of Linnæus.

MOUNTAIN PIGEON. The RING-TAILED PIGEON; an old name.

1725 Sloane 302–3, The Ring-Tail'd Pigeon. This was fifteen Inches from the Bill to the end of the Tail..They are call'd Mountain Pigeons, tho' sometimes they are found amongst the Savanna Woods, as in the Month of January.

MOUNTAIN PLUM sb bot. The small tree *Ximenia americana.*

1837 Macfadyen 121, Ximenia montana. Mountain-Plum..Not uncommon; Port-Royal Mountains..Drupe size of the Plum of Europe, yellow, smooth, shining, one-seeded. 1864 Grisebach 786.

MOUNTAIN PRICKLY-YELLOW sb. The tree *Zanthoxylum martinicense*; also called MOUNTAIN SATIN-WOOD.

1961 DAP, Institute of Ja.

MOUNTAIN PRIDE sb. *Spathelia simplex*, a small tree which, when in bloom, spots the mountainsides with patches of rose-lavender colour.

1814 Lunan I 524–5, Mountain Pride. Spathelia. This tree rises by a single slender stem like the palms..The pyramid of flowers, which issued from its summit..had a most magnificent appearance. 1839 Hill in 1840 *Almanac* 34, The Spathelia Simplex, or Mountain Pride, uprears, from the mountain forests, its plume of purple flowers. 1920 Fawcett 193.

MOUNTAIN SATIN-WOOD sb. The tree *Zanthoxylum martinicense*; also called MOUNTAIN PRICKLY-YELLOW.

1961 W. E. Fulford Man, and DAP, Institute of Ja.

MOUNTAIN SOURSOP sb. The tree *Annona montana* and its fruit.

1837 Macfadyen 7–8, Mountain or Wild Sour-Sop.. This, at first sight would appear to be nearly allied to *A. muricata.* On examination they will be found to be distinct species. The fruit is dry and not edible. 1914 Fawcett 195.

MOUNTAIN SPARROW sb obs; *OED* 1738 for diff bird. Prob the BLACK SPARROW.

1756 Browne 467, Fringilla 1. Minor pulla, fronte & uropigio rufescentibus. The Mountain Sparrow. This is a native of Jamaica, but keeps chiefly in the woods.

MOUNTAIN SUPPLE-JACK sb. The climbing shrub *Serjania equestris.*

1837 Macfadyen 156, Serjania equestris. Mountain Supple-jack..Stem shrubby, climbing to a considerable height on neighbouring shrubs and trees. 1926 Fawcett 43.

MOUNTAIN SWEET-CUP sb. The vine *Passiflora edulis* and its fruit.

1913 Harris 21, Sweet Cup, Mountain..A strong woody climber, native of Brazil, but naturalized in the higher regions of the Blue Mountains where it produces fruit in abundance. 1926 Fawcett 234, Mountain Sweet Cup.

MOUNTAIN SWEETWOOD sb. *Misanteca triandra*, commonly simply SWEETWOOD. (Ident 1914 Fawcett 205.)

1864 Grisebach 788, Mountain Sweet-wood.

MOUNTAIN TAMARIND sb obs. =WILD TAMARIND 1.

1756 Browne 252, The mountain or wild Tamarind Tree. This is a native of Jamaica..it grows to a very considerable size, and is looked upon as an excellent timber-wood.

MOUNTAIN WILD OLIVE sb bot. =MOUNTAIN or WILD OLIVE.

1814 Lunan II 311, Mr Anthony Robinson..calls it *Yellow-Saunders* or *Mountain Wild Olive.* 1926 Fawcett 308, *Buchenavia capitata*..Yellow Sanders, Mountain Wild Olive.

MOUNTAIN WITCH sb; *OED* only 1847. The Crested Quail-Dove, *Geotrygon versicolor.*

1823 Stewart 78, Solitary birds..the white-belly or white-breast, the mountain-witch, the partridge pigeon. 1840 Chamberlaine 19, Mountain Witch. 1847 Gosse 317–18, At a distance its first note is inaudible; and the second, reiterated at measured intervals, sounds like the groaning of a dying man. These moans, heard in the most recluse and solemn glens, while the bird is rarely seen, have probably given it the name of Mountain Witch. 1952 FGC Man /móuntn wích/ as you brok a stick it stop and fly up and look about; Man, Mountain Witch of Manchester is Blue Dove of Portland; StM /mountn wich/ big bird like partridges that runs in mountains. 1955 Taylor 93–4, The Mountain Witch. .occurs only in Jamaica. .The first sight of it is usually on a forest path, and when disturbed it does not take readily to the wing, but waddles rapidly away stopping at intervals and looking back at its pursuer with a curious bobbing gesture.

MOURNING TABLE sb dial cant. See quot.

1953 Moore 38, In a Revival group, at a memorial service for the dead, a '*mourning table* is set and a minister of the Revival cult, known as a *shepherd,* comes to conduct the service'.

MOUSE-COLOUR PARROT sb dial. A variety of PARROT FISH.

1952 FGC StM.

MOUSSA see MUSSA.

MOUTAGRAM sb dial joc; <*mouth*+suffix on the analogy of *telegram.*

1943 *GL* Kgn, Moutagram, a source of false news; chatterbox.

MOUT-A-MASSY sb dial joc; <*mouth*+*have* +*mercy*; cf *amasi.*

1. One who talks too much.

1942 Bennett 34, Mouta Massi Liza yuh no hear Yuh muma dah call yuh? Meck yuh mout' so galang galang. 1943 *GL* Kgn, Mouta massy, a chatterbox; Port, Mouta-massey, noisy; StAnd, Mouta massy, Talk too much. 1954 LeP Kgn, StE, Somebody who is always gossiping —Mout-a-massy.

2. A hypocrite.

1954 LeP Kgn, Hypocrite, mout-a-massy.

MOUTAPHONE sb dial joc; <*mouth*+suffix on the analogy of *telephone, gramophone.* =MOUTAGRAM.

1943 *GL* StAnd, Moutaphone, chat chat line.

MOUTEN see MOUNTAIN.

MOUTH /mout/ sb dial. *G*

1. The edge of a cutting-tool (i.e. the part that bites).

1956 Mc Man /aks-mout/ head of axe; Port /di mout we fi chap di graas/ *The side of a cutlass for cutting the grass.* 1957 DeC StE (Accom) /uol liediz suod-mout ton rait uoba/ *the old lady's sword-edge turned right over.*

2. Fig. Excessive talk: chatter, gossip; hence further, malicious talk, rude, impertinent language. See the numerous compounds, esp MOUT-A-MASSY, MOUTH OFF, MOUTI-MOUTI. *BL*

MOUT'-HAB-NUTTIN-FE-DO sb dial. The chatterer who gives misinformation.

1910 Anderson-Cundall 35, Mout' hab nuttin fe do, him say Annancy grow, same time Annancy 'tan' from him barn. [*The chatterbox says Annancy has grown, but Annancy hasn't changed since he was born.*] 1943 *GL,* Mout' hab nuttin fe do, the idle talker.

MOUTH-LIP sb dial; <*mouth*+*lip.* The lip. (This is one of a number of such pleonastic formations—cf HEAD-SKULL, ROCK-STONE, etc.).

1877 Murray *Feedin' 'Perrit* 7, Him let go him fist pon me mout lip. 1956 Mc Man /móut-lìp/.

MOUTH-MUSIC sb dial. A mouth-organ or harmonica.

1958 DeC Port /mout-myuuzik/ harmonica.

MOUTH-OFF vb trans dial; <*mouth* sb, converted to vb (rather than from existing verbs, which are of diff sense) +*off.*

1952 FGC Han /anaangsi mout-aaf bra taiga wel/ *Anancy speaks insultingly to Bra' Tiger.* 1956 Mc StAnd /im jos don mout-aaf di dakta—im aask ar ef shi no don wid im yet, far im waang go huom/ *He has just spoken rudely* (or *been saucy*) *to the Doctor—he asked her if she was not done examining him. .*etc.

MOUTH-STACHE see *mout-stash.*

MOUTH-TAX sb dial; <*mouth,* implying strong language, insult, etc. +*tax.* See quot.

1934 *Gleaner* 17 March, Hinds explained to the Court that by 'mouth taxes', he meant fines imposed by the Court on persons for using indecent and obscene language.

MOUTH-WATER sb dial; prob a loan-translation from one or more Afr langs, e.g. Ibo *ɔno-mmiri,* mouth-water, *aŋa-mmiri,* eye-water; Mandingo *ŋgaya,* eye-water, a tear. (Turner, 90, 234.)

1. Saliva. *BL G*

1910 Anderson-Cundall 23, see BIG-MASSA. 1956 Mc Man /móut-wàata/ saliva.

2. A baby's bib.

1956 Mc Man.

MOUTH-WATER-CLOTH sb dial joc; <MOUTH-WATER 1 +*cloth.*

1943 *GL* StM, Mouth-water-cloth, Necktie.

MOUTI-MOUTI adj or sb dial; iterative <*mouthy.* A chatterbox, gossip. *BL G*

1942 Bennett 3, Yuh know mouti-mouti Dinah? Har mout' galang-galang soh tel. 1943 *GL,* Mouti-mouti, tale bearer. 1954 LeP StT, Somebody who is always gossiping—mowti-mowti.

mout-na-fi-yu sb dial; lit 'mouth not yours' —but it may mean either 'someone else's mouth', or 'something not intended to be said to you'.

1956 Mc Man /móut-na-fi-yú/ a tale-bearer.

mout-stash sb dial; by folk-etym <*moustache.* A moustache. *G*

[1952 FGC StJ /móustáach/ moustache.] 1956 Mc Man, StAnd /móut-stásh/ moustache. 1957 JN StT, Look at my mouth-stache.

MOW-CHEN see MAW-CHEN.

MOWEL see *maa-i.*

MOW SENNY phr dial; <Chinese. 'Business bad.' The conventional reply to the greeting HO SENNY HO.

MOWTI-MOWTI see MOUTI-MOUTI.

MOXY see MAXI.

mozela yam /mozéla, mazala/ sb dial; etym unknown. A type of very large but somewhat coarse yam, with white or yellowish flesh.

1929 Beckwith 15, The Marzella is the largest yam in size, but somewhat coarse and poor eating. 1952 FGC Han, StC, StE, StJ, StM, StT /mozéla yam/ giant, weighs 100 pounds; blue vine; white, yellowish inside. 1954 *FG* 445, The mosella is a prolific bearer. .This yam is a soft white, well-flavoured, good eating yam, but the texture varies in different districts. 1956 Mc Man /mozéla/. 1958 DeC StE /mazala/.

MUCCO ROBIN see MOCO ROBIN.

MUCH adj dial.

1. Many—esp after *how, so.* *BA BL G T*

1956 Mc Man /ai riili duon nuo hou moch mailz/; StE /hou moch yu kyach sins maanin/. 1957 JN StAnd, So-much children don't come to dat school like dis one.

2. In phr *how much* = what number. *T*

1956 Mc StE /ho móch chapter/ which (what number?) chapter?

MUCH MORE adv phr; evid by ellipse of the negative, or by dependence on the preceding one. Following a negative expression (or similar one): much less. *BA BL G*

1912 McK *Songs* 59, Dere is no star fe light de way, much more de white roun' moon. 1924 Beckwith 276, He says, 'From the day I'm born, never see a big man call me name, much more a little boy!' 1946 U.Newton I 9, We were so glad and frightened to be in the car that we could hardly *breathe*, much more *touch*.

MUCHU adj or sb dial; < Sp *mucho.* *BL G*

1943 *GL* Kgn, Muchu, Spanish, plenty.

MUCKASHANDY sb dial; prob partly fanciful, but *muck* and *shindy* have slang meanings that may be present here. See quot—some kind of lively entertainment. ('Masquerade' is also used about JOHN CANOE.)

1943 *GL* StJ, Muckashandy, masquerade.

MUCKO-GEE see *moko-jii.*

MUCKUMDASH see *mokomdash.*

MUCKY adj dial. See quots.

1943 *GL* Kgn, Mucky, bad smell. 1956 Mc Man /moki/ sour, stale-smelling; also /fruozi/.

MUD sb tech; < *mud,* dregs—cf *OED sb*[1] 2b →1856. The last impurities remaining from the milling of sugar-canes.

1952 FGC West, After the cane juice has been filtered for the last time, the residue, called 'mud', is dried and returned to the fields as manure.

MUD adj dial; < *muddy* adj or < *mud* sb. Muddy.

1956 Mc StE /mi fut tuu mod/ my feet are too muddy.

MUDFISH sb; cf *OED,* earliest quot for an Amer mudfish 1699. Any of several fish which stay in the mud, close to the bottom of the sea or rivers: the name is widely applied and identification of references in literature often impossible. See quot 1952. *BL G N*

1679 Trapham 65, The choice Mullet brings up the next division crowded with various Snappers..Gar fish, Grash fish, Mud fish, Cat fish..[etc.]. 1725 Sloane 285–6, Truttæ congener, piscis lævis fluvatilis..The Mudd Fish. This was about seven inches long..it has.. almost a square Tail, all the Skin except the white Belly, is covered over with small Scales; partly white or yellowish and partly black. 1756 Browne 450, Pelmatia 2..the mud-fish. 1854–5 *TJSA* I 144, Phylipnus dormitator—the mud fish. 1873 Rampini 171, Much more quaint lore about..the old wife, the mud-fish and the parrot-fish, did we glean from our negro boatmen. 1877 Murray *Kittle* 25, Mudfish shake himself, den begin fe sing. 1952 FGC West /mòdfish/—name here for gadami; Port, like bungoby, gadami, but bigger; StE, call /niega-man/ —children fish for them with pin and thread; StM, StT, found only in river; also StA, StC, StJ.

MUD-HOOK sb dial; see quot. The 'deep-water eel'.

1952 FGC StM /móduk/ push dem tail through mesh of fish-pot and hook it to the bottom [of the sea].

MUD JACK sb dial. Some variety of the Jack or similar fish.

1952 FGC StC, StM /mod jak/.

MUD-MUD sb dial. A lot of mud.

1868 Russell 4, Some nouns of one or two syllables are in using repeated; as mud-mud, matta-matta. (1960 Current, FGC.)

MUD SNAPPER sb. Some variety of snapper or similar fish that lives close to the muddy bottom.

1952 FGC StT /mod snapa/ yellow stripes against pale pink.

mudu, muduk sb dial; cf Hausa *muduk'uk'i,* a person of unprepossessing appearance; cf also *-u,* and *-k.* An albino negro.

1943 *GL* StT, Moodoo, A freak. A kind of voodoo 'white'. 1958 DeC StAnd /muduk/ albino negro.

MUFFEENA see *mafiina.*

MUGICLE /mógikl/ sb dial; < *mug* + *-icle* on the analogy of *cannicle, pannicle.*

1957 DeC StE /mogikl/ any kind of mug or drinking vessel.

MUGWORT sb bot; *OED* 1866 only. The plant *Parthemium hysterophorus.*

1794 Barham 106, Mug-wort. There is a herb in Jamaica called mugwort, that grows in all or most of the poor grounds. 1814 Lunan II 299 (cites Barham). 1864 Grisebach 786. 1936 Fawcett 215, P. Hysterophorus.. Wild Wormwood, Bastard Feverfew, Mugwort. 1953 *WIMJ* 243, Dog flea Weed; Whitehead; Mugwort; Country people use it..to make a bath for fleas on dogs.

MUKA /múka, móka/ vb dial; etym unknown, poss < **mucker,* to reduce to muck?

1943 *GL* Kgn, Muka, crush with the gums. 1955 FGC Man /múka/ some say; = MUMBLE.

MUKKY MASSAH see MACKY, MUCKY MASSA.

muku sb dial; ? < MOCO.

1956 Mc Man /taak muku/ talk nonsense.

MULATTO /maláta, malánta, malántan, maláto/ sb. s MALANTANG. *BA G*

1. Strictly, a person having one black and one white parent; less strictly, one of equal degrees of black and white parentage, as the offspring of mulatto parents in the stricter sense. (In this sense, not a Jamaicanism; cf *OED.*) Citations illustrate folk pronunciations.

1943 *GL* StC, StE, Malata, mulatto, mulattoo. 1958 DeC Port /malántan/ a mulatto.

2. Loosely, any person with light-brown or yellowish skin. Among negroes, not a favourable term.

1956 Mc Man /maláto/ a light-coloured person, described as 'red'.

MULATTO-COLOUR sb.

1827 Hamel I 242, The cocked-hat too..had the look of an old campaigner, being tanned by sun and rain into a good wholesome mahogany Mulatto-colour.

MULATTO TREE sb; from the colour of the bark, which is smooth and varies from yellowish to coppery. *N*

1941 Swabey 13, Birch, West Indian (—Mastic, Red Birch, Turpentine tree, Incense tree, Mulatto tree)..Tree.. with characteristic smooth papery chestnut-coloured bark. Wood soft, light and white in colour, not durable. 1951 FGC StAnd /maláta/ tree—birch.

MULATTO TURTLE sb. A turtle similar to the Hawksbill.

1873 Rampini 167, Of the various species of turtle which are known in Jamaica—the green turtle, the hawk's-bill, the mulatto or yellow turtle, the trunk and the Macongo, the green is the only kind sold as food. 1952 FGC StC /málata torkl/ have big head; like /aks bil/.

MULATTO WOOD sb. An unidentified tree. (The description as 'timber tree' makes it unlikely to have been MULATTO TREE.)

1774 Long II 128, A yellow timber-tree, called here Mulatto-wood..very common.

MULE(-BACK) JACK sb dial. A variety of the Jack fish having a back thought to resemble that of a mule.

1952 FGC StC /myuul jak/; StE /myuul-bak jak/.

MULE-RIAL /myúul-ráial/ sb dial; <*mule*+ RIAL. A hinny—offspring of a horse and a she-donkey; it is smaller than a mule, which makes 'rial' applicable.

1952 FGC StAnd, StT /myúul ráial/. 1956 Mc /myuul rayal/ the offspring of a she-donkey and male horse.

MULGRAVE sb dial; evid for the Earl of Mulgrave, Governor of Jamaica 1832–4, who was intimately associated with emancipation.

1959 DeC StJ /molgriev/ coconut run-down.

MULLUBUH sb dial uncom; etym unknown: the last syllable poss related to *bu*, bug.

1943 *GL* Port, Mullubuh, nastiness.

MUM /mum/ sb rural; cf MA. A form of address to a female, esp to a small girl; also a term of endearment. *BL*

1957 JC StJ, Tre /mum/ form of address to females, especially small girls; not heard in Kingston since 1945, though common in the country. 1960 NJL StC, Mum, used so much that it has become a pet-name for a little girl; not heard in Kingston.

muma sb dial; a variant of *mama*, *maami*, etc.; cf MA. (Cf the corresp *pupa*.) Mother. *BL G T*

1942 Bennett 34, Yuh no hear Yuh muma dah call yuh? 1950 Pioneer 71, Me gat tree pickney an dem mumma up a yard. 1954 LeP StE, Mumma—mother. 1956 Mc Clar /muma/.

muma-breda sb dial; <*muma*+*breda*.

1954 LeP Kgn, Uncle, mumma bredda.

mumbi krab sb dial; etym unknown.

1952 FGC StT /mumbi/ a crab used for bait; soft back, hair on feet and back; live in holes in swamp.

MUMBLE vb dial; *OED* →1847. To crush food with the gums. *G*

1955 FGC Man /mombl/ moka.

MUMBLE-HEAD COW sb dial; prob <*pommel* (cf *OED*)—cf PUMBLE-FOOT. A cow without horns.

1960 J. Lewis StAnn, Mumblehead cow is a pollhead cow. 1960 G. Coulthard StAnd, Mumblehead cow—cow without horns.

MUMMA see *muma*.

MUMMA-BREDDA see *muma-breda*.

MUMMOU, MUMMU see next.

MUMU /mumu/ sb dial; cf Ewe, Twi, *mumu*, deaf-and-dumbness; Mende *múmú*, Efik *imum*, Mandinka *muumunee*, a dumb person. *G*

1943 *GL* StAnn, StJ, Mumu, mute, clown; West, Mummu, slow of speech; Port, Mummou, backward, no initiative; Moomoo. 1956 Mc Man /múmu/ dumb (not common); StE, silent, stupid person, e.g. at school.

MUNDELLA WEZA phr dial uncom; <Ko *mundele*, white man + *u-iza*, he comes. A preserved Africanism: see quot.

1943 *GL* Port, Mundella weza—white man is coming.

MUNGALA or **MUNGOLA DRUMMER** see MONGOLA DRUMMER.

MUNJAY sb dial; poss <Fr *manger*, food, grub.

1943 *GL*, Munjay, large dumpling.

MUNNU sb dial or slang?; etym unknown, but cf *muuna*.

1943 *GL*, Munnu, romance.

MUNTUNG sb dial; etym unknown.

1943 *GL* Kgn, Muntung, plenty.

muoli flai sb dial; cf PEENY-MOLLY. A kind of firefly.

1956 Mc Man /muoli flai/—? Jack-o'-lantern—same like flash-light.

MURREY; MURREY CONGRY /móre, móri/ occas /maré/ sb dial; cf OED *moray*, also *murrey*, said to be accented on final syllable. The moray eel.

1952 FGC Port, StJ /móre, mórí/ black spotted eel; StAnn /maré/ pale and sort of green, smaller than conger-eel—one kind has a guinea-chick colour; West /móré/ black and white, brown and white—will bite, very cross—have to hurry up and kill it. 1956 Mc StAnd /mori kanggri/ is speckled eel, /griin kanggri/ is green eel.

MURRO-MUTTO sb dial; etym unknown.

1943 *GL* StAnd, Murro-mutto, poor cooking.

MURROPY sb dial uncom; etym unknown.

1943 *GL*, Murropy, small fishes.

MUSA, MUSE see MUSSA.

MUSHAE, MUSHAY see next.

mushe /mùshé/ sb dial arch; <Fr *monsieur* (pronounced /mosyóe/).

1. A Chinese.

1943 *GL* Kgn, Mushay, name given to an Oriental; Man, Mushe, Chinaman; StAnn, Mushay, a China man —a master mind of the samfi game; StC, Mushae.

2. A Syrian.

1943 *GL* Kgn, Mushay, Syrian peddler. 1955 FGC Man /mùshé/ an Oriental or a Syrian.

MUSIC-MAN sb dial; *OED* only quot 1866; this is doubtless an independent local formation, and may represent loan-translation from an Afr lang. A musical performer, musician. *BL*

1950 Pioneer 40, Once upon a time Cockroach was a very good music-man an everybody wat have a dance always want Bredda Cockroach fe play fe dem. 1952 FGC Han /myuuzik man/ play for dances; StT /Nou, iz pik op iz myuuzik man, wich iz trii kakruoch, dat i tuk intu a guodi/. (See 1961 *Ja Talk* App II.)

MUSKEETO- see MOSQUITO-.

MUSK FLY sb obs; *OED* 1665 only. See quot.

1725 Sloane 208 XVI. Scarabæus Capricornus dictus major, viridis suave olens..The Musk Fly..The Head, Thorax above and below, and Sheaths for the Wings.. are all of a shining green Colour..I met with it in a Wood..It smelt very strong and not unpleasantly.

MUSK MALLOW sb obs; *OED* only 1785 for this. The MUSK OKRO.

1794 Barham 107, Musk-mallow..its leaf is like the okra; its fruit is as big as the round okra, and hexangular. The seed of this plant smells as fine as any musk.

MUSK-MELON /mós mélan, mósmílan/ sb dial; transf for reason unknown. Any of certain composite bushes—see quots. *BA*

1927 Beckwith 23, Musk-melon, see 'Sheep-bur'. *Ibid* 27, Sheep-bur. *Acanthospermum humile*..'Musk-melon'. 'White-cleary.' For headache and fever, drink as tea. 1953 *WIMJ* 242, *Eupatorium macrophyllum*..Hemp Agrimony; Musk Melon?

MUSK OKRO sb bot; *OED* 1756 only. The shrub *Hibiscus abelmoschus* and its musky seeds.

1756 Browne 285, Hibiscus 4..Musk Okro. The seeds of this plant, when grown to full maturity, have a strong and perfect smell of musk. 1801 Dancer 357, Musk ochra; *ibid* index, Musk ochrow. 1837 Macfadyen 67, Musk Okra..The seeds..are said to be emetic..They are sometimes employed to adulterate genuine musk. 1926 Fawcett 142, Musk Ochra, Musk Seed, Wild Ochra. Naturalized and cultivated.

MUSK WOOD sb bot; *OED* quots sense 1, 1725→; sense 2, 1866.

1. The tree *Guarea glabra*, of musky smell.

1696 Sloane 137, Lauro affinis arbor..lignum moschum olente. *Alleygator or Musk-wood.* a 1726 Barham (1794) 107, Musk-wood. 1854–5 *TJSA* I 61, Muskwood or Alligator Wood. *Guarea trichilioides.* 1920 Fawcett 215, Musk Wood, Alligator Wood, Wild Akee..All parts of this tree, especially the bark, have a strong smell of musk. 1941 Swabey 27.

2. The tree *Trichilia moschata.*

1837 Macfadyen 170–1, 3. Trichilia moschata. Common shrubby Muskwood..B.T. moschata, var. Octandra. Octandrous shrubby Muskwood. 1864 Grisebach 786, Muskwood: *Moschoxylum Swartzii.* 1920 Fawcett 211.

mus-mus /mus-mus/ sb[1] dial; iterative of an older English (Scots, etc.) pronunc of *mouse*: *EDD moose, moos, mūs. SC moisi-móisi.*

1. A mouse.

1868 Russell 5, Moos-moos, Mouse. 1877 Murray *Feedin' 'Perrit* 21, One o' dese you mus-muss go pon de nose, walk all ober it, lick off de grease. 1905 Smith 49, An' dere was a *Moos-moos lib, an' Moos-moos name was Moos-moos Atoo. *Mouse. 1943 *GL* most parishes, Mus-mus (also Muss-muss), mouse, mice [this may be sg number]. 1952 FGC Man /mus-mus/. 1958 DeC StAnd, StJ /mus-mus/.

2. A rat, or young rat.

1943 *GL* Kgn, StAnd, Tre, Mus-mus.

mus-mus sb[2] dial; iterative of the base syllable of MUSSA.

1958 DeC Port /mus-mus/ same as musa, either corn or cassava.

MUSMUSS, MUSS-MUSS see prec.

MUSQUITOE- see MOSQUITO-.

MUSSA /músa/ occas /múse/ sb dial; etym uncert, but prob Afr (cf e.g. Ngombe *mosɔ́sɔ̀mbɔ́*, banana) and ult <Arabic *mawzah*, banana, from which the genus name *Musa* and the old word *muse* (*OED sb*[4]) both come. (Since the manioc was taken from America to Africa, the use of banana as a foodstuff came earlier in Africa.) **s.**

1. A dish made basically of turned meal or flour, with or without other ingredients. Cassava appears to be the most widely used, banana and corn meal also. (These words may be prefixed to designate the various kinds.)

1868 Russell 6, Muse—Cassava in form of a thick paste. African. 1943 *GL* Port (2), Mussa, moussa, green banana grated and boiled with coconut milk; StM, Mussa, quick pudding made with cassava flour, pepper and seasoning; Clar, StC, Mussa, Mussah, 'turned' corn-meal. 1952 FGC StT /banána músé/ grate green bananas, mix with flour into dumplings, boil in rich coconut milk, highly seasoned—'a *beautiful* dish'; StJ, Tre, Cassada /músa/. 1955 FGC Man /músa/. 1956 Mc StE, Mussa: A thick paste made by boiling cassava meal with shredded salt-fish and fat. It should be turned or stirred during cooking.

2. As symbolic of something soft: see quot.

1900 Murray 9, 'You raskill' replied Quamin, 'I gwine mek moosa a you tiday boy.' [He threatens him with a stick.]

MUSSAH see prec.

MUSSI see *mosi.*

MUSTAFENIA see MUSTIFINA.

MUSTARD SHRUB sb bot; *OED* 1756 only. The shrub *Capparis ferruginea.*

1756 Browne 246, Breynia 3..The Mustard-shrub.. This plant is common in all the Savannas, and low lands about Kingston..All the parts of the plant have a strong pungent smell and taste, like most of the mustard tribe.. *Ibid* 247, Crateva 3..The Mustard-shrub. 1814 Lunan I 109. 1914 Fawcett 233, Mustard shrub..The plant has a pungent smell and taste, whence the common name.

MUST CAN vb phr dial; <*must*+*can*, be able: *can* in this sense is still used in Engl and US dial after *shall, may*, etc., but is unrecorded after *must*, where it is common in Ja. Must be able to. *BL G*

1943 Bennett 18 [Woman calling to conductor on a train that is full and beginning to move:] Noh leff me sar, meck me come een, Ah mus can fine a space. 1952 FGC StM /him mós kyan dùu it/.

MUSTEEFINO see next.

MUSTIFINA, MUSTIFINO /mostifíina, moskafíim/ sb arch; 1825 mustiphino, 1828 mustiphini, 1833 maestifino, 1834 musteefino, 1924 mustafenia; <*mustee, mestee*, the offspring of a white and a quadroon (*OED*) + Sp *fino, fina*, fine, refined. (Cf *OED mustafina*, a 1818→.)

The offspring of a mustee with a white, i.e. one having one-sixteenth negro and fifteen-sixteenths white parentage.

a 1818 Lewis (1834) 106, From the mulatto and white comes the *quadroon*; from the quadroon and white the *mustee*; the child of a mustee by a white man is called a *musteefino*; while the children of a musteefino are free by law, and rank as white persons to all intents and purposes. 1825 Bickell 111, Mustiphino. 1828 Marly 94, A Mustiphini or Quadroon. 1833 Foulks 26, The pallid and sickly looking Maestifino. 1924 Beckwith 288, Massa Peter was a funny sort of a buckra massa. He was 'mustafenia' (white by law). Massa Peter an' me, we go to school together. 1958 DeC Man /mostifíina/ a racial term 'meaning one-fourth black'; complimentary; now old-fashioned but still used. Port /moskafíim/ a 'vex-word' of very bad connotation, used of a light brown man.

MUSTIPHINI, MUSTIPHINO see prec.

MUST POWDER sb dial; <*must*, implying compulsion +*powder*; cf OIL OF COMPELLANCE. A 'magical' powder (cf BALM OIL) which can supposedly ensure good luck. *BA*

1942 Bennett 290 [Of a sweepstake ticket:] She.. sprinkle it wid mus-powdah An' ile a-boun' fe win.

musu sb[1] dial rare; cf Twi *mmusú*, mischief. Appar only preserved in a fixed phrase: see quot.

1956 Mc StE (Accom) /búsu fúul, púl yu músu/ *stop your nonsense.*

musu sb² dial; <*mus*, base of *mus-mus*+*-u*. Mouse.

1956 Mc StAnd, see CREASE.

MUTTON sb obs; cf *ADD, mutton corn* 1821→. Tender young ears of maize roasted.

1774 Long III 762, Great Corn, or Indian Maize..The ears..are often gathered before they are thoroughly ripe; and, being roasted, form a dish known here by the name of *mutton*.

MUTTON OWL sb dial; cf MUTTON SNAPPER; *owl* may refer to large or prominent eyes. An unidentified fish.

1952 FGC Port, Mutton-owl—the book name for Round Robin. [This seems confused; perh it means 'the book name is Round Robin'—if so, the fish is *Decapterus punctatus*.]

MUTTON SNAPPER sb; cf *OED* 1867 ref, no quot. One or more species of the genus *Mesoprion*—fishes of the snapper kind. *BA*

1867 *TRSAA* I 25, Mutton snapper, ?*Mesoprion campecheanus*. 1892 Cockrell list, Mutton snapper—pot snapper. 1952 FGC Port, StAnn, StC, StE, StJ, StM, StT, West /motn snapa/—grow big; the best; like reef snapper but not so red; same as gray snapper. 1958 DeC StT /motn snapa/.

MUTTON WOOD sb bot.

1926 Fawcett 38–9, *Turpinia occidentalis*..Iron Wood, Cassada Wood, Wild Cassada, Mutton Wood..Tree 20–30 ft. high.

muu vb dial; a reduced form of *move*.

1956 Mc Man /múu da sínting fran dé/ *Move that thing from there*.

muun see MOON.

muuna sb dial vulg; <MOON+*-er*? The female sexual organs.

1958 DeC gen /muuna/.

MYAL /mail/ sb dial; cf Hausa *maye*, 1. Sorcerer, wizard; 2. Intoxication; 3. Return. (All of these senses are present in the Jamaican use of the word.) Attrib in MYAL DANCE, MAN, WOMAN, etc.

1. A form of witchcraft not clearly distinguished from OBEAH: though some myalists sought to represent themselves as the undoers of the evil done by Obeah (see quot 1863, etc.), this distinction is neither early nor consistent, and may be no more than a defence made against the whites' opposition to Obeah. The practices of obeahman and myalman were much the same, though the early MYAL DANCE (1) offered itself as a rite of resurrection, hence as curative. See quots. See also MYALISM, SHADOW CATCHER, SHADOW CATCHING, POCOMANIA.

1863 Waddell 137 (Year 1838), The *Myal* system..must not be confounded with *Obea*, to which indeed it was wholly opposed. It affected to cure the sicknesses..which the Obea produced. The Myal practitioners counted themselves angels of light, and called those of the opposite craft angels of darkness. 1868 Russell 6, Myal—Excitement bordering on madness. African.

2. In recent use in AFRICAN and similar cults: formal possession by the spirit of a dead ancestor, and the dance done under possession. See quots.

1952 Kerr 141, It is interesting that myal now means dancing with a spirit in a trance. It may be a new development of the word or it may be that the old writers never got the real meaning of the word. 1953 Moore gloss, Myal /mail/ formal possession by a known god or ancestral zombie, usually at a ceremonial (AFRICAN). *Ibid* 162, Myal possession has three phases: 1, receiving the god—falling to the ground or being rooted to the spot; 2, the individual gives his body to the god or ancestral zombie. Individual has no consciousness of what is happening—he dances, leaps, spins, etc.; 3, the controlled dance of the god or spirit possessing the individual, who is now spoken of as a zombie. He regains partial consciousness. *Ibid* 143, The possession dance of a dancing zombie is called *myal*. *Ibid* 143, But not all possessions can be spoken of as *myal*.

MYAL DANCE sb dial; <MYAL+*dance*.

1. A dance by which members were initiated into a Myal society by being apparently rendered dead and then being revived by an obeahman.

1774 Long II 416, Not long since, some of these execrable wretches in Jamaica [*sc* Obeahmen] introduced what they called the *myal dance*, and established a kind of society, into which they invited all they could. The lure hung out was, that every Negroe, initiated into the myal society, would be invulnerable by the white men; and, although they might in appearance be slain, the obeah-man could, at his pleasure, restore the body to life. The method by which this trick was carried on, was by a cold infusion of the herb branched calalue*; which, after the agitation of dancing, threw the party into a profound sleep. In this state he continued, to all appearance lifeless..till on being rubbed with another infusion (as yet unknown to the Whites), the effects of the colalue gradually went off, the body resumed its motions, and the party, on whom the experiment had been tried, awoke as from a trance, entirely ignorant of any thing that had passed since he left off dancing. *This herb is a species of solanum.. The myal gentry make the infusion with rum. In regard to the other infusion, which puts an end to its operation, we can only conjecture. a 1818 Lewis (1834) 354–5, The Obeah ceremonies always commence with what is called, by the negroes, 'the Myal dance'. [A full account follows.]

2. A dance performed under the effect of 'spirit possession' in the AFRICAN cult and similar ones. (See MYAL 2.)

MYALISM sb; <MYAL+*-ism*. The profession or practice of MYAL.

1843 Philippo 248, Myalism, as well as Fetishism, were constituent parts of Obeism. 1863 Waddell 188–9, In July 1842 the delusion broke out again in one of its principal seats, Flower Hill; and a company of its agents invaded Blue Hole to cleanse that estate from its sins and miseries. They were sent by God, they said, to purge and purify the world..It was the strangest combination of Christianity and heathenism ever seen..We..were attracted to the village by the noise of the Myal proceedings..*Ibid* 191, The following notice of their proceedings appeared in the county paper, on the 21st September [1842]:—'Myalism has lately extended its ramifications over a section of country, including sixteen estates, from Iron Shore to Moor Park. This extraordinary superstition has evinced itself in fearful paroxysms, bordering on insanity, accompanied with acts of violence on those who attempt to restrain it. Lately a set of these people took possession of a meeting-house on Palmyra estate, and commenced their orgies by singing, or yelling, and dancing in the most frantic excitement. The overseer and bookkeeper, attempting to restrain them, were assaulted with stones and other missiles, with a degree of ferocity perfectly demoniacal.' *Ibid* 193, They were yelling, wheeling round, and striking against one another in a frightful manner..One young man was beating himself, and spinning about, till he fell down in convulsions..One of them had been at our school. Next morning he wept, and said he did not know what was the matter with him. Soon after he rolled on the ground, and then ran up and down like a mad dog. I took hold of them, and they trembled all over, with eyes fixed and staring.

MYALIST sb; <MYAL+*-ist*. A practitioner or adherent of the MYAL cult.

1863 Waddell 193, One of the speakers described a rare scene he had witnessed among the Myalists the previous evening.

MYALL see MYAL.

MYAL MAN sb dial; <MYAL+*man*. A male practitioner of MYAL.

1774 Long II 417, Not long ago, one of these myal men, being desirous of seducing a friend of his to be of their party, gave him a wonderful account of the powerful effects produced by the myal infusion, and particularly that it rendered the body impenetrable to bullets. 1835 Madden II 97, There are two descriptions of obeah; one that is practiced by means of incantations; and the other by the administering of medicated potions—in former times, it is said of poisons, and these practitioners were called myal men. 1862 Clutterbuck 156, There was another class of impostors calling themselves Myallmen, who asserted that they had the power of reanimating dead bodies. 1863 Waddell 137–8, It was part of the art and power of a Myal man also to *catch the shadow* of a deceased person and retain it for purposes of necromancy..This kind of work was long kept a secret..The delusion went to the length of supposing that the shadow could be lost even before death..I knew a girl about sixteen years of age, who was greatly afflicted with the idea that she had lost her shadow. Someone had stolen it, she said. 1895 Banbury 19, Mialman. (Cf *OED*.)

MYAL-SONG sb dial; <MYAL+*song*. A song of the kind sung by MYALISTS.

1927 Beckwith 4, William Forbes..an old Myal-song leader near Maggotty at the entrance to the Cock-pit country.

MYAL WEED sb dial; <MYAL+*weed*. The common weed *Eryngium fœtidum*, which has a powerful aromatic odour and is used to revive people in a faint or a fit. (This may be the weed unknown to Long—cf MYAL DANCE, quot 1774—with which the dancer, supposedly dead, was resuscitated.) Cf BRANCHED CALALU, DEATH-WEED.

1952 FGC Tre, Myal-weed—spirit-weed, fit-weed.

MYAL WOMAN sb dial. A female practitioner of MYAL.

1863 Waddell 137 (Year 1838), He and his wife had gone to a Myal woman, of great repute on Iron Shore estate, for a cure. That woman's mode of practice being *secundum artem nigram*, or of a genuine African kind, was one we discouraged, as both unlawful and deceptive. Her system was to extract from the diseased body the vitiating substances, which some unknown enemy had, by magic arts, imbedded there. By sucking, or sneezing, or retching, she caused the pins, glass, or nails to be extracted from the sufferer's flesh.

MY LADY sb dial. The yellow and blue-green striped variety of *Prepodes vittatus* (the FIDDLER BEETLE), the gay stripes representing those of a lady's dress. Cf MILADY.

1954 *NHN* VI 166.

n /n/ pron dial; <*him*. A form of *him* (which may stand for any form of the StdE 3rd pers pron). Cf *EDD* EN, *pron*.

1952 FGC StT /kech di baal an kot-n/ *Catch the ball and cut it*. 1912 McK *Ballads* 55, De officer won' t'ink Dat a bobby's wutten price: worth his price.

n /n/ vb auxil dial; var form of BEN.

-n /n, ng/ suffix[1] dial; an intrusive sound with no certain origin, though well supported by examples such as BECAUSEN, CAUSEN, DOUTEN, FRONTEN, *jesn*, *wishn*, etc. *BL G*

-n /n/ suffix[2] dial; perh <*-ing*, or merely an intrusive syllabic nasal. Cf FISHEN, HUNTEN, ICENING, s *frainin pan*. *BL G T*

na vbl particle dial; <*n*, vb auxil+A[5]; cf *bena*[3].

1873 Rampini 165, Truly we rose from every meal with grateful hearts and could with unction repeat the negro grace, 'Tank you, me fader, fe all me na swallow' [*for all I have been swallowing*, or *have swallowed*].

NA /na, no/ conj dial; <Scots *na*, *nor*, than. (*OED na* →1535, superseded by *nor* →1883.)

1. With the comparative degree: than.

1826 Williams 190, More no nine and tirty. 1895 Banbury 39 [Prov:] Jamaica long mona rope.

2. With the positive degree: as. *BL*

1925 Beckwith 30 [Prov:] Cubbitch no 'tar-apple. 'Stingy as a star-apple.' 1941 Kirkpatrick 8, Fe we eyesight sharp no razor.

na see NO[1], NO[3].

naa adv dial; prob <*no*, not+A[5], but note Engl dial forms of *no: naa, naah, naw*, etc. (*EDD*). Not, followed by a progressive tense of a verb.

1942 Bennett 10, Ef yuh naw buy wey yuh stop fah! [*If you're not going to buy anything, what do you stop for?*] 1950 Pioneer 18, Bredda Ticks, i naw go soh. Bad tings a go happen between me an yuh. *BL G*

naadi sb dial; pronunc of *noddy*, the sea-bird (*Anous stolidus*); the expected reflex of the Std Engl word would be */nadi/.

1952 FGC StC /naadi/—noddy. 1956 Mc StC /naadi/ —a sea-bird: dives for fish.

NA'AM vb dial; etym unknown; poss <*alarm* aphetized and with *n* for *l*.

1943 *GL* StJ, Na'am, to scare or frighten anyone.

NAAMS see NYAAMS.

naan-nan vb dial; etym unknown. (Perh <*gnaw-gnaw*—BLB.) To hack, chop clumsily.

1956 Mc Man /náan-nan/ to cut (wood) with a blunt tool.

naan sita sb dial; prob <*non-suitor*. See *OED nonsuit, a.*

1956 Mc Man /náan sita/—(1) A nagging, cross, fussy person. (2) One who is always ready to quarrel over trifles.

naat see *nuoznaat*. *BL*

naavis see NERVOUS. *BL*

NACA-NACA see NAKA-NAKA.

NACCO, NACKO see NAGO.

NACRAM sb dial; etym unknown.

1943 *GL* Kgn, Nacram, a person who is not active.

nad sb dial. See quots.

1958 DeC StE /nad/ a spinner dumpling; Han, West /nad/ a boiled dumpling shaped like the letter C.

nada /náda/ pron dial; aphetic form of *another*; cf *aneda*, *neda*, *noda*. Another. *BL G*

1943 *GL* StAnn, Nadda, the other. 1957 JN StE, Gi nada somebody a chaance nuh.

NADA sb dial; <Sp *nada*, nothing. A negative expression inexactly representing the Spanish *nada*. *BL*

1943 *GL* Kgn, Nadas, nothing; StAnd, nadu, no; Tre, Nada, no.

NAGA, NAGER see NAYGA.

NAGGO see NAGO.

NAGIN see NOGGIN.

NAGO /nágo, náko/ sb now dial; <Ewe *anagó*, a Yoruba negro. [Note: Fante *anago*=night.]

1. A Yoruba-speaking people, many of whom were brought as slaves to Jamaica. Also attrib.

1775 *Ja Gazette* 25 Mar [A man] of the Nago country ..says his master died when he was a boy and has been run-away ever since. 1793 Edwards II 73, Many of the Whidah Negroes are found to be circumcised..It is practised universally by the Nagoes.

2. An individual of this origin.

1825 Bickell 43, Frank, a Nago, 5 ft 7½ in. no brand-mark, country marks on his face.

3. A term of contempt originally applied by Creole blacks to African-born slaves; now signifying a very black, ugly, or stupid negro.

1943 *GL* Kgn, Naggo, Coal black person; StAnd, Naggo, black man; Nacco, ugly; StJ, Naggo, a fool; StM, Nacko, ugly. 1954 LeP StE, Naggo—applied to the very black and stupid man.

NAHOO see NAPOOSHO, and next.

NAHU vb dial uncom; cf Twi *nna-hɔ́*, a deep sleep.

1943 *GL* StE, Nahu, to sleep.

NAHVAS see NERVOUS.

naint /naint/ vb dial; aphetic form of *anoint*, with the regular dial /ai/ for Std *oi*. Anoint.

1877 Murray *Feedin' 'Perrit* 4, Mek me tek little nut ile so nint it mek it soft. 1952 FGC StC, Spirit-weed for fever—mix with vinegar /naint yu badi/. *BL G N*

NAKA-NAKA /naka-naka/ vb and adj dial; prob merely var of NYAKA-NYAKA.

A. vb: 1. To pull to pieces, destroy.

1956 Mc Man /náka-náka/ to tear, destroy, disfigure something.

2. To patch up roughly or untidily.

1943 *GL* Clar, Naka-naka.

B. adj: Disordered; untidy; unsteady.

1943 *GL* Port, Naca-naca, rough. 1957 DeC StE /naka-naka/ unable to keep steady (as of a drunken man).

NAKED adj dial. =BARE, mere. *BA G*

1958 DeC StAnd /niekid/—the equivalent of *bare* in other parts of Jamaica, i.e. meaning mere, only; e.g. Rum in the old days cost only /a niekid kwati a glaas/.

NAKED-SKIN SNAIL sb dial; cf *EDD*: *Naked* adj. 1750, Naked snail.

1956 Mc Man /níekid skin sniel/ a slug.

NAMBO see next.

NAMBU /námbu/ sb dial; cf Twi *ɛ-nám*, meat, *e-búw*, nest, coop, cage, etc.

1. A field-bag, a NAMSACK.

1943 *GL* Clar, Nambo, side-bag used by cultivators; StC, Nambu, knapsack, a kit made of cloth; Namboo; also Port, StM. 1958 DeC Port /kotoku/ a sidebag made of canvas or sometimes of crocus bag, same as a /nambu/.

2. A temporary bag, made in the field, of grass or trash.

1958 DeC Kgn.

NAME vb dial; <*name* vb, or perh sb. In passive sense: to be named, to (deserve to) be called. *BL G N*

1957 JN [Girl speaking to little boy:] 'You come a me yard' (cutting her eyes); 'Come if you name man.' *Come if you are man enough.*

NAMI-NAMI see NYAMI-NYAMI.

NAMPREL sb dial rare; etym unknown.

1943 *GL* StM, Namprel, old horse.

NAMSACK /namsack/ sb dial; blend of *nam-* (cf NAMBU) and *knapsack*. *BA*

1. A side-bag.

1907 Jekyll 107, Everybody has his side-bag or namsack (knapsack). 1943 *GL* Man, Nansack. a sawyer's food-bag. 1955 FGC Man /namsak/. 1956 Mc Clar /námsák/ bag hung over shoulder, taken to ground. Also Man, Port, StE.

2. Generalized: any bag taken to the field.

1956 Mc StAnd, StT, Any bag taken to ground—perhaps crocus. 1958 DeC Port (Belmont), Here, a crocus bag with a drawstring, carried on the back, with the hands holding the mouth of the bag over the shoulder.

NAMSE see NYAAMS.

NANA /nána, náana/ sb dial; <Twi *nãná*, grandparent, grandfather, grandmother. *BL*

1. A grandmother or any old woman: often as a respectful term of address. *G N T*

1873 Rampini 127, Him curse him moder for a 'cra-cra' (careless)..'wenya-wenya' (meagre), 'nana' (old woman). 1922 Beckwith 84, N for Nana,* him cap trim with lace.. *Grandmother. 1927 Stafford 6, There's the stew for the Busha and Nana. 1954 LeP StAnn, Naana—grandmother, more used if she is very old.

2. A midwife.

1943 *GL* StE, Nana, midwife.

3. In the city: a nursemaid (of any age); a nanny (though this is an entirely different word, not Ja). *G*

c1915 FGC StAnd /náana/ nurse. [1960—still in use among Jamaicans.]

NANAY see NENE.

NANCE see ANANCY.

NANCHOR sb dial; by metanalysis of *an anchor*, producing *a nanchor*.

1907 Jekyll 258 [Song:] Him go long like a sailor nanchor.

NANCY see ANANCY.

NANCY BAG. Spider web; see ANANCY.

1873 Rampini 137 [The obeah man] gave them something in a nancy bag pounded up, which James Oliver put into the busha's drink. (From Slave Court Records, 1805–16, Portland.)

NANCY NEST sb dial; cf ANANCY; the second element prob means *nest*, but *net* is not impossible. A spider web.

1957 JN StAnn, see GWINE.

NANCY PRETTY sb dial; <*Nancy*, personifying name, +PRETTY. = **s** MISS PRETTY.

1952 FGC Port /nansi priti/ same as Banana Cudjo, Policeman.

NANCY STORY see ANANCY STORY.

NANGA sb dial; prob <NAGO—infl by BUNGO? A tribal name: see quot. *G*

1952 FGC Man, In St Catherine's parish there are Nangas—knowable by a decided depression in the centre of the forehead.

nangku sb dial; cf Twi *anyáŋ-kɔ́*, the action of going for wood or fuel.

1959 DeC StJ /nangku/ a temporary field bag made of trash or grass.

NANKA /nángka/ sb; <Twi *ɔ-nãŋkã́*, large horned snake. The Jamaican yellow snake: see quot 1940.

1940 Lynn Grant 116, Nanka, yellow snake—*Epicrates subflavus*. 1943 *GL* Clar, Port, Nanka, snake.

NANKEEN COTTON sb; *OED* 1797→. A variety of cotton with a naturally yellow staple.

1793 Edwards II 271, 3d Nankeen.—This differs but little in the seeds or otherwise from the species last mentioned [*sc* Brown Bearded], except in the colour of the wool, which is that of cloth called Nankeen. It is not so much in demand as the white. 1864 Grisebach 783, Nankeen Cotton: *Gossypium religiosum*.

NANNY-EYE CUFFEE sb dial. A nickname for certain fish with eyes like a goat's: see quot.

1943 *GL* Clar, Nan-yeye-cuffee, Shad or Alewives.

NANNY-EYE GRUNT sb dial. A variety of the grunt fish with eyes like a goat's.

1952 FGC StJ, StM /náni-yái grónt/.

NANNY (GOAT) sb chiefly dial. The ant-lion.

1952 FGC StAnd /nani/ same as /torkl/ ant-lion. 1960 J. Lewis StAnn, see PUGGO.

NANNY THATCH sb dial; <*Nanny*, prob in allusion to the namesake of Nanny Town, +*thatch*. A tree fern. (The leaves or fronds may be used as thatch; they resemble to some extent the leaves of long-thatch palms.)

1890 Thomas 88, Throughout..the Blue Mountains tree-ferns are to this day known to hog-hunters by no other name than that of 'Nanny thatch'. 1952 FGC StT, Nanny-thatch, tree fern.

NANSTAR adj dial rare; ? repr *oldster*.

1943 *GL* Clar, Nanstar, denoting age.

NANY see NENE.

NAPIER GRASS /níepya graas, níepa, neptyu(?)/ sb. The fodder grass *Pennisetum purpureum*.

1951 FGC Man, Napier grass used for cattle near Mandeville. 1952 FGC Man /níepa graas/ StAnn, StT, Napier grass has bone like cane, spike; drought-resistant. 1954 *FG* 238, Napier, Uganda, Elephant. The land should be well prepared for the planting of these grasses. 1956 Mc Man /neptyu gras/ a long-bladed grass with flag; grows in clumps.

napo see next.

NAPOOSHO, NAPOOSI sb, vb, and adj dial; etym mixed? cf Twi *nnɔpá-óó*, 'Sleep well!', *nna*, sleep; Engl slang *napoo*, finished, done for. Cf also *kananapo*, silence.

Definitions, as well as forms, differ considerably: the common core of meaning involves *sleep* (noun or verb uncert) in some way. The sense of stupidity may be connected here; the sense 'finish' is not clear. See quots. (Perh two words, not one.)

1943 *GL* Kgn, Narpoose, sleeping place; StE, nahoo, napoosi, to sleep; StE, napoosho, napooshoo, finish. 1956 Mc Man /napó/ stupid, dim-witted, 'half cracked'.

NARA /nára/ pron dial; aphetic form of *another*: /nada/ with flapped *r* for *d*. *BL*

1868 Russell 15, The Indefinite Pronouns..tara, (other) [;] nada nara (another). 1927 Anderson-Cundall 49 [Prov:] No tek narri somarri yeye so sleep. *Don't take another person's eyes to sleep with.*

NARM see NYAAMS.

NARO sb dial uncom; ?<*narrow*.

1943 *GL* Kgn, Naro navel. (1956 LeP StE, Known at Accompong but not at Elderslie.)

NARPOOSE see NAPOOSHO.

NARRI see NARA.

NASEBERRY (TREE) /niizberi/ sb; 1679 nasbury, 1696→ naseberry, 1756 nisberry, 1793 nesbury, 1801 neeseberry, 1851 neesberry; the Std pronunc *nase-* [neiz-] reflects the Sp name of the fruit, *néspera*, whereas the folk and earlier Std pronunc /niiz-/ represents the Sp name of the tree, *níspero*. *OED* 1698→.

The tree *Sapota achras* and its fruit. *N*

[1657 Continuation 46, Nispero, esteemed the best fruit in the Indies by the Spaniards.] 1679 Trapham 59, Tamarinds, Nasburies, sower Sops. 1696 Sloane 206, The Nispero Naseberry, or Sappatilla Tree. 1756 Browne 200, The Nisberry Tree. 1801 Dancer 364, Neeseberry (Achras sapota)—Seeds in Emulsion, a fine Bitter. 1814 Lunan II 2, Naseberry-Tree..The fruit is a round berry, covered with a rough brown coat..about the size of a small apple; ..the pulp..in colour, consistence, and taste, somewhat resembles that of the English pear, but sweeter. 1851 Gosse 268, The Naseberry, or neesberry, the *nispero* of the Spanish colonists..is one of the richest and most agreeable of West Indian fruits. 1952 FGC Port, StAnd, StAnn, StE, StJ, StM /níizbéri/ the general popular pronunc; 'naseberry' is the 'educated' form.

NASEBERRY BAT sb. In Gosse's use: Any of several bats of the genus *Artibeus* which feed on naseberries. See quot.

1851 Gosse 270, The Small Naseberry Bat. *Artibeus Jamaicensis*..; *ibid* 271, The Dusky Naseberry Bat. *Artibeus achradophilus*, Mihi. ('Αχρας, the wild-pear, the botanical name of the naseberry, and φιλέω, to love.) ..The Great Naseberry Bat. *Artibeus carpolegus*..The Brimstone Naseberry Bat. *Artibeus sulphureus*.

NASEBERRY BULLY-TREE or **BULLET (TREE)** sb; <NASEBERRY, general name for genus *Achras*+BULLY (TREE). The timber tree *Sapota sideroxylon*.

1756 Browne 201, Achras 3..The Bully, or Nisberry Bully-Tree. This is called the Bully-tree, because it generally grows the tallest of all the trees in the woods. [This explanation rests on the wrong sense of *bully*.] 1774 Long III 863, Naseberry bully-tree. 1820 Thomson 150, I have made several other trials with the bark of the lilac or hoop tree and the neeseberry bullet-tree, and have good reason to think they would prove serviceable. 1864 Grisebach 786, Naseberry-bully Tree. 1886 Hooper 30, Neesberry bullet tree. 1952 FGC StM, StT /niizberi buli-trii/—one type of bullet-wood, similar to /niizberi/ Tre /niezberi bulit/.

NASTINESS sb dial; cf *OED nasty* 1b. Bestiality, homosexuality, etc.

1958 FGC StAnd. 1962 BLB 63 /náasinis/.

NASTY (UP) vb dial; *OED* →1770. To render nasty or dirty. *G*

1873 Rampini 71, 'De putta-putta nasty every ting up', said Bob. (1960 Current, FGC.)

nata /náta, náata/ sb dial; aphetic form of ANATTA.

1943 *GL* StC, Natta, annato. 1956 Mc Clar /naata—yu kaal it anato/; Man /anáto/—some people say /naata/; StAnd /náta/ is what people say—/anato/ being 'the 'right' name.

NATAL TREE sb. A term said to be used for BIRTH TREE (though it is questionable whether 'natal' is a word generally known). See NAVEL-STRING TREE.

1953 Moore 30, The term 'natal tree' is used by Jamaican Negroes to denote the coconut tree under which the umbilical cord is buried. The fruit of this tree belongs to the child.

NATION sb dial. Applied to fowl: a species, a breed. Cf *OED nation* 6b. (Used broadly as StdE might use 'tribe' or 'race'.) *BL G*

1956 Mc StAnd (Dallas) /sense iz a nieshan tu itself/ *'Sense' fowl is a separate breed.*

NATTA-BIGE sb dial; *natter*, formed by metanalysis <*an atter(cop)*, a spider (see *OED Attercop* 1, 3), as in Scots NETTERCAP (see *SND*); +*bige*, bag. Cobweb.

1943 *GL* Port, Natta-bige, cobweb. 1957 DeC StE (Accom) /nata baag/ cobweb.

NAUNCE see NYAAMS.

NAVEL /níebl/ sb dial. The banana 'blossom', actually a sheath containing the blossoms and undeveloped fruits, at the end of the fruiting stem.

1956 Mc Man, StE /níebl/ Pink sheath of bananas at end of bunch, before opening.

NAVEL-STRING TREE sb. See quot. Cf BIRTH TREE.

1929 Beckwith 55, The mother must guard it [*sc* the navel cord] carefully and, before three days to a year from the time of birth, must bury it in the ground and plant a young tree over the spot, which henceforth becomes the property of the child and is called his 'navel-string tree'.

NAW see *naa*.

NAWGIN see NOGGIN.

NAWS sb dial; prob conn with *na*, *naa*, no (*EDD*).

1943 *GL* Tre, Naws, a small piece.

NAYGA /níega/ sb dial, also attrib; *OED Neger* comes closest to this by recording the pronunc [nī·gəɹ], which descended from this; in other words, present Ja folk pronunc preserves an Engl 17th-cent pronunc, when the first vowel was still the mid-front tense [e:], perhaps slightly diphthongized, corresp to the Continental European one. Infl of Sp *negro*, Fr *nègre*, Dut *neger* in the Caribbean area may have contributed to the retention of this older sound.

A negro. The term is avoided by whites, and resented by negroes if used of them by whites. As used among negroes it is a term more or less derogatory, commonly implying extra blackness, backwardness, laziness, stupidity, etc. Cf BLACK-NAYGA, *nigrish*, SALT-WATER NEGRO, etc. By some confused with NAGO. See also cpds in NEGRO-. *BL G*

1907 Jekyll 227. But a white man must not call them so. To say 'black nehgher' is an offense not to be forgiven. 1943 *GL* most parishes, Naga, Nayga, Naygar—black people; good for nothing. 1951 Murray 23 [Song:] Nayga kean bear fe see Nayga flourish. 1954 LeP Man, Nayga; StAnn, Neaga. 1954 Reckord *Della* typescript 18, Nayga pickney life cheap as yam. 1956 Mc Man /níega/ black person, negro.

NAYGA FISH sb dial. =NIGGER-FISH.

1952 FGC Port /níega fish/.

NAYGA HAIR sb dial. Negro hair. *T*

1957 JN Baillieston [Girl:] Fe her hair longer dan mine. Me have neaga hair.

NAYGA-MAN sb dial.

1. A negro.

1912 McK *Songs* 14, De cowitch under which we hab fe 'toop..Is killin' somet'ing for a naygur man.

2. A small black mudfish.

1952 FGC StE /níega-mán/ small sea fish that children play with with pin and thread.

NAYGAR see NAYGA.

NAYGA TRICK, NEGER-TRICK sb arch; cf NAYGA. A story told by a Creole negro to illustrate the 'tricks' played, or acts performed out of stupidity by the African-born or more backward negroes.

a 1818 Lewis (1834) 307, But the creole slaves are very fond of another species of tale, which they call 'Neger-tricks', and which bear the same relation to a Nancy-story which a farce does to a tragedy. The following is a specimen:—[Story of a man who tried to dupe his wives, but was instead beaten by them.] 1924 Beckwith 288, These old-fashioned slave stories..belong to the 'nager-trick' stories quoted by Lewis. 1929 Beckwith 215, Lewis found two classes of stories common in his day—'wonder tales', in which the supernatural element prevailed, and 'nager tricks', in which some stupid fellow served as the butt of his fellows..Today the last scarcely survives other than in an occasional noodle story told of a 'Congo nager', like that of the slave who, sent to bring home a clock from the repair shop, kicked it to pieces because it persisted in striking.

NAYGA YAM sb dial. =NEGRO YAM.

1956 Mc StAnd /níega yam/—nigro yam.

NAYGUR see NAYGA.

NAYM see NYAM.

NEACKA-NEACKA see NYAKA-NYAKA.

NEAGA see NAYGA.

NEAKA-NEAKA see NYAKA-NYAKA.

NEBAR, NEBBA, NEBBER, NEBER dial sp for *never*. *BL*

NEBY dial (part of speech uncert); perh for *never*—see prec.

1943 *GL* Tre, Neby, no.

NECK-BACK sb dial. The back of the neck, nape. *BL G*; *SC bakka-nékki*.

1907 Jekyll 275 [Song:] A whé the use you da hang da me neck-back, Married man me no want you. 1947 U.Newton III 39, When Mass Teeti (the barber) ran his shears down my 'neck-back'. 1956 Mc Man /nékbak/.

NECK STRING sb dial. The muscles in the neck. *BL G*

1950 Pioneer 61, An she start blow hard fe breat' an Her neck tring dem start fe swell.

neda indef pron or adj dial; aphetic form of *aneda*. Another. *G*

1957 JN Lowe River, Wi pick up waun neda wan.

NEDGE /nej/ vb; exactly parallel to *edge*, *OED* 3, 'To set (the teeth) on edge'. *Obs.* exc. *dial.* →1865; however, initial *n*- must be explained by metanalysis of the phr *on edge*: perhaps /mi tiit an-ej/ or similar phr was reanalysed as /mi tiit a-nej/ *my teeth hurt*. *BL*

1. intr. To be set on edge; to ache.

1948 Bennett 46, We teet is boun fi nedge [*Our teeth are sure to ache*]. 1952 FGC StC, Nedge-weed, good for when you teeth nedge or cramp.

2. trans. To set on edge; to cause to ache.

1960 P. Lyn StAnd, 'Stop doing that! /yu nej mi tiit/' *You're setting my teeth on edge!*

NEDGE-TEETH, NEDGE-WEED sb dial; see prec. A small plant with acidulous leaves: *Oxalis corniculata*.

1952 FGC StC, see NEDGE. 1955 *WIMJ* 159, Sour Grass; (N)edge Teeth; (Yellow or Wood) Sorrel.

NEEDLE-CASE sb; from the shape of the insect's body. The dragonfly. *BL N*

1943 *GL* StE, Needle case, dragon fly. 1952 FGC Han, Man, Port, StAnd, StT, West /niidl-kies, niigl kies/, dragonfly. 1956 Mc Man, Port /niigl kies/.

NEEDLE-POINT(ER) sb dial. A dragonfly.

1952 FGC Han, Needle-pointer, needle-case. 1956 Mc StAnd /níigl páint/ dragonfly.

NEEGRISH see *nigrish.*

ne-en, neen-a vb or vb phr dial; <*no,* not, +*en,* have, been, did—auxil of past tense; parallel to *naa.* Have not, did not, was not.

1943 *GL* Man, Nehena [=/ne+en+a/?]—was not. 1956 Mc Man /mi néen tel im nótn/ *I haven't told him anything.* /a hóu mi néen míit im/ *How is it that I did not meet her?* Also StE.

NEGA, NEGAR, NEGER sb dial; cf *OED neger* →1829. (Pronunc uncert; presumably it is /níiga/ but these spellings may be intended to represent /níega/.) =NAYGA. *G*

1877 Murray *Feedin' 'Perrit* 7, De kick him kick me, him plant me; I drop down ya, bif..She say 'Ef you ded tell me, I mek dem heng dat neger dis day'. 1943 *GL,* Nega, black people; West, Negar, negro.

NEGRESSA, NEGRESSEE sb dial; ?<*negress+-y.* The tree *Buchenavia capitata* (MOUNTAIN OLIVE).

1801 Dancer 363, Yellow Saunders..Negroes..call it Negressa. 1814 Lunan II 311, The negroes of Liguanea call this tree *Negressee,* and use the decoction of its bark to cure venereal taints. 1864 Grisebach 786, Negressee.

NEGRO BREAKFAST sb obs; cf BREAKFAST. A time of day: about 11 A.M., when there was a pause in work for the slaves to have breakfast.

1796 *Braco* 13 Feb, Finished Rio Bueno [cane] pieces at Negroe Breakfast then began to cut No. 1 and 2. *Ibid* 15 Feb, Finished No. 1 by Negro Breakfast. Continued cutting No. 2. *Ibid,* 1797 28 Mar, Finished No 5 at Negro Breakfast time & began to cut part of No 10.

NEGRO-COUNTRY YAM sb obs; i.e. GUINEA YAM.

1698 Sloane 219, Negro Country Yam. 1707 Sloane 140, *Negro* Country *Yams.* This has a great Root a Foot broad..They being cut into pieces and boiled or rosted. are eaten by *Negros,* Slaves, or *Europeans,* instead of Bread. 1864 Grisebach 789, Negro country yams: *Dioscorea alata.*

NEGRO-DAY sb obs. The day set aside for slaves to work their own provision-grounds: Saturday.

1828 Marly 65, Saturday being negro day, the two book-keepers..rode to the mountain, where the provision grounds were situated. *Ibid* 80, Till at last negro-day came.

NEGRO-DRIVER sb; cf *OED driver* 2 c 1796. A slave-driver. s.

1790 Beckford I 315–16, The negro-driver..was standing in front and leaning upon his stick; the other negroes were digging cane-holes.

NEGRO FRUIT sb obs. The kola nut; see quot.

1740 Importance 31, The *Besse* or Negroe Fruit, so call'd from their Fondness of it, grows like Cocoa in a Shell, a yellow Skin covers it when ripe; but is not very common.

NEGROFY vb obs; cf *OED,* 'Make into or as black as a negro', 1799 only. To infect with negro ideas—used as a contemptuous charge by whites who defended slavery against those who opposed it.

1839 Mc Mahon 212, If the black labourers spoke kindly of him, he would be exposed to the rancour of the overseer; and, under the character of a negrofied rascal, be dismissed from his employ.

NEGRO-GROUND sb obs. See quot.

1788–9 McNeill 3, Besides this, there is a portion of land belonging to every estate, denominated *Negro-Grounds,* of which each slave is allowed as much as he can cultivate, for his own use.

NEGRO GROUPER sb. A variety of the grouper fish with black skin.

1854–5 *TJSA* I 142, Serranus morio—Negro grooper.

NEGRO-HOUSE sb obs. Any of the houses in which the slaves were housed on an estate.

1834 Lewis (1845) 68–9, Breakfast was being got ready; as soon as it was over, I went down to the negro-houses to hear the whole body of Ebos lodge a complaint against one of the book-keepers. 1839 McMahon 85, Buckra constant punish we, only for..saying our prayers in negro-house. 1895 Banbury 32, see OLD SUCK.

NEGRO ITCH sb obs. =CRAW-CRAW.

1801 Dancer 361, *Cassia occidentalis*..the Root in Decoction, Diuretic. Expressed Juice, a cure for the Negro Itch, Craw-Craws, &c.

NEGRO PINE sb obs. A pineapple of poor quality. Cf BACKRA PINE.

1788 Marsden 86, And a third sort, called the Negro Pine, which is worst of all.

NEGRO-POT sb; *OED.* A heavy iron cooking-pot such as that generally used by negroes over open fires; nowadays it usually has a flared top, round bottom, and small legs. (In the first citation the sense seems to be transf to the contents of the pot.)

a 1818 Lewis (1834) 307, They boiled a negro-pot for him, but he was too ill to swallow a morsel. 1952 FGC StM, Negro pot—heavy iron, 3 legs.

NEGRO-TOWN sb dial. The villages of negroes formed in the hills by Maroons or runaway slaves before the settlement with the Maroons had been made; they were a base for raids upon the plantations.

1731 *Jrl. Assembly* 6, It is the opinion of the committees, that the soldiers be marched into the several negro-towns, and barracked there. 1733 *Jrl. Assembly* 132, That great quantities of eddoes, yams, and other provisions, remained in the ground in and about the said negro-town and barracks, which might and ought to have been dug up. 1774 Long II frontispiece map, Negro Town (on Anotta Bay River between George's R. and Flint R.).

NEGRO-WORM sb obs. The Guinea worm (*Filaria medinensis*): a subcutaneous worm with which many newcome slaves were infested.

1725 Sloane 362, A Cataplasme made of the green Leaves, Cassada-flower, and a little Oil..if apply'd with a green Leaf to the part, where Negro-worms lye, it softens and brings the Worm out.

NEGRO YAM sb; evid an abbr of NEGRO-COUNTRY YAM but note contrast with WHITE YAM; *OED* 1892 only. A species of white yam (*Dioscorea sativa*) of coarser texture than WHITE YAM.

1756 Browne 359, Dioscorea 1..The Negro Yam. 1814 Lunan II 308, This is commonly called the negro yam.. There are two kinds of negro yam, known by the names of cassada-yam and man-yam, the latter is considered the best, as being of a mealier better taste, and drier texture, but is not so productive; it is easily distinguished from the former by the stringy fibres which overspread its skin, which is smooth on the cassada-yam. The inside of both these yams is white, of a viscous or clammy nature; when roasted or boiled they are meally like a potatoe but of a closer texture, they are a very pleasant and nourishing food, in much esteem among the negroes. 1913 Harris 42, Negro yam and its varieties. 1952 FGC Port, StAnd, StJ /nígro yàm/; StE /niega yam/.

NEHENA see *ne-en, neen-a.*

NEHGHER see NAYGA.

NEITHER /niida/ adv dial; cf *OED* 2 'Now used only when the alternatives are expressed in clauses or sentences', →1513. Nor, or.

1956 Mc Man /mi duon iit di puok, niida di biif / *I don't eat pork, or beef.* *BL G T*

nej(-tiit) see NEDGE(-TEETH).

neks see NEXT.

NELL sb dial; by metanalysis of *an-ell* > *a-nell*. Cf NEDGE.

1943 *GL* Kgn, Nell, great amount: 'gi 'im a inch, 'im tek a nell'.

NELSON BALL PEAS sb dial; the allusion is prob to Lord Nelson (cf such other names as DUKE and COMMANDER coco) and implies superior quality. A bean with a somewhat spherical seed.

1952 FGC StC /nelsn-baal piiz/ grain is round.

nene sb dial; <Twi *nẽnẽ*, to discharge the bowels.

1943 *GL* Man, Nany or nanay, filt.

NEN-NEN sb dial; var of NANA, cf Twi *nãnã́*, grandmother, and Efik *n'né*, term of address to an old woman. (J. Berry.) *G T*

1954 LeP StT, Nennen, grandmother.

NENYAM, NENYANCE see NINYAM.

NEPHRITIC TREE sb arch; <*nephritic*, having to do with the kidneys. Cf *OED nephritic* 3. The tree *Pithecellobium unguis-cati*, which was once used as a medicine for kidney complaints. More often known as BLACK-BEAD SHRUB, BREAD-AND-CHEESE, etc.

a 1726 Barham (1794) 111, Nephritic tree. This tree is so called in Jamaica for its being a sovereign remedy for the stone. 1811 Titford Expl to Plate IX 6, see DOCTOR LONG. 1837 Macfadyen 306–7, Inga unguiscati..Browne calls it the *black-bead* shrub; and from others it receives the names of *Barbary-thorn* and *Nephritic-tree*. Barham tells us that it is a sovereign remedy for stone, gravel, and other urinary complaints, and also for obstruction of the liver and spleen. We are informed that it was first planted in the Island by a Spanish Bishop, who, in expatiating on the virtues of the plant, deduced that it must be useful in nephritic complaints, from the shape of the seeds resembling that of the kidney, and the white arillus corresponding to the fat in which the gland is imbedded. The bark is the part that is made use of, and Barham states, that in his time it was in such general use, that it was rare to meet with a tree that had not been barked. 1864 Grisebach 786.

NERVOUS /naavas, naavis/ adj dial. Foolish, without common sense; hence worried, tending to be neurotic. (Representing a settled state in an individual, not a temporary condition.)

1942 Bennett 22 [A woman who thinks she sees a ghost, etc.:] Me nahvas, yaw. 1956 Mc Port /naavis/ Used of a person who has 'not much sense', perhaps neurotic? 1960 Pat Wilmot StAnd, =neurotic.

NETTY adj dial uncom; perh <*nutty*, crazy (slang); cf CHICKEN NET.

1943 *GL* StC, Netty, to be funny.

NEUTRAL-UP vb phr dial; perh an individualism; <*neutral* adj, balanced, even, +*up*. To equalize, even up.

1955 Bennett *Vengeance*, Ef you kean do Good, no do no Bad, Try neutral up yuh deal.

NEVER adv dial. Hardly, barely. *BL*

1950 Pioneer 33, De wud nevah drop outa Puss mout' before Anancy run ovah Dog yard to tell him sey..[etc.].

NEVER-DEAD, NEVER-DIE sb dial; prob transl of Fr *immortelle*: cf *maatel*; but possibly an independent formation. A 'growing-stake'—one of the trees commonly planted to make live fences: *Glyricidia sepium*, or *Erythrina* species.

1952 FGC StT /neva-ded/; Tre, Never die—same as /pánya màshíet/.

NEW-NAYGA sb dial. A negro who has gone up in the world rapidly.

1943 *GL* Clar, New-nager, hurry-come-up.

NEW PLAGUE sb dial; an allusion to the Biblical plagues of Egypt?

1954 LeP Kgn, A louse, insect, etc.—New plague.

NEWS-BUG sb dial; because it is supposed to portend news to come. =NEWSMONGER.

1. See quot.

1952 FGC Han /nyuuz-bog/ whitish, size of a big peas, carries omen, bears news: knock him—if drops on back, bad news. Man /nyuuz-bog/ grayish-looking thing: when you catch it, spit on it and wish for good news; if it does not fly, bad news. Tre, News-bug, like tumble-bug but white colour, live in wood. StT, News bug, bring news: knock them down, turn on back, put on ashes: it's good news if they fly away after you knock them down.

2. Transf.

1954 LeP StE, A person who chats or gossips—a news bug.

NEWS-CARRIER sb dial. *G*

1954 LeP StAnn, Somebody who is always gossiping—News carrier.

NEWSMONGER /nyuuzmongga, nyuuz-bongga, nyuuzvongga/ sb now dial. Any of several wood-boring beetles which are popularly supposed to be harbingers of news, good or bad. See quots, and NEWS-BUG.

1756 Browne 428, Scarabeus 3..The Newsmonger. This insect is very like the foregoing [Tumble-Turd] both in size and appearance; but it is more rare, and seldom seen except it be in the inland parts of the island. It is of a light brown colour. 1951 FGC StAnd /nyuuz-bongga/ large beetle (2 in.) with flat back iridescent green-gold and red, flew with a loud buzzing sound. 1952 FGC Port /nyuuzvongga/; StAnd /nyuuzmongga/ lives in a hole in wood; Tre, Newsmonger = rain bug, news-bug.

NEW SUGAR sb. Newly made sugar from which the molasses has not been drained off. Also called WET SUGAR. *G*

1802 Nugent 70, Some pan sugar also, from Mrs Lewis. The new sugar is excellent, drank in cold water; and I like the pan sugar of all things. 1893 Sullivan 114, New Sugar. Is infinitely preferred by the natives to even 'shop sugar'. It is made in the island..and is sold in its unrefined state either as molasses, or, firmer, as pan-sugar. 1952 FGC StJ, StM, New sugar, wet sugar.

NEW YORK vb dial slang; in part imitative (see quot) but prob based on *Yawk* (*EDD*: to clear the throat, retch in vomiting).

1958 DeC gen /nu yaak/ i.e. New York, a crude and jocular verb meaning to vomit. The second syllable is commonly extended /yaaaak/ and strongly pharyngealized.

NEXT /neks/ adj; used in dial and pretty high up the social scale. Other; one more beyond that or those already mentioned: s. *BA BL G N T*

1948 A. Bustamante *Colonial Office Conference* II 24, You have given us £6,000,000 for building houses to supply two-thirds of the houses. We require a next one-third. 1956 Mc Man /yu sii a neks stiek de mam/ the second of four stakes marking property boundary. Port /wi liv de bot wi hav a neks hous doun ya/ *We live there but we have another house down here.* StAnd /get som néks frén kom óut/ *Invite some more friends.* 1957 JN Kgn, I ave a nex brother name Carl. . I use to go to a nex school.

NGA sb dial rare; etym unknown.

1943 *GL* StAnn, Nga, mouth.

NHANDIROBA sb bot; < Braz Pg *nhandi-roba* < Tupi. *Fevillea cordifolia* (Antidote cacoon).

1696 Sloane 85, Ghandiroba vel Nhandi-roba Brasiliensibus. 1774 Long II 418, Upon application to Dr Barham for advice, he gave him some *nhandiroba* kernels, to infuse in wine, and drink frequently; which cured him in time [of poisoning]. *Ibid* 419, The *nhandiroba* is a climbing plant. . [with] fruit like a green calabash with a circular black line round it. 1814 Lunan I 22, Nhandiroba. 1864 Grisebach 786. 1954 *WIMJ* 30.

NIAAMS see NYAAMS.

NICARAGO, NICARAGUA WOOD sb obs; *OED* 1703→. A species of *Cæsalpinia.*

1696 Sloane 213, Lignum Insulæ Bonaire Belgis. . Nicaragua Wood. 1756 Browne 17, Besides these. . exports of this Island. . there are large quantities of logwood, nicarago, braziletto. . [etc.]. *N* /nikarawa ud/.

NICE adj; an extension of *OED* sense 7. Proud, superior in manner.

1954 LeP Kgn, Proud, nice. 1960 LeP StAnd, Common usage, both lower and middle class (in addition to the sense of nice = pleasant, attractive): proud, haughty. /shi think shi nais/ *She thinks she's too good for us.*

NICE UP vb phr dial; < *nice* adj converted to vb + *up* adv. Be pleasant to, ingratiate oneself with. *G*

1952 FGC Han /mi trai tu nais ar op/.

NICHOL see NICKAR.

NICK vb and sb dial; cf *OED* 6, a particular throw at dice →1863.

A. vb: To throw (dice). *G*

1941 Kirkpatrick 20, Lak wen corpie ketch dem bwoy a nick dice a Race Course an dem run.

B. sb: See quot.

1943 *GL* StAnd, Nick, dice.

NICKAR, NICKER /níkal/ sb; 1696→ nickar, c1724→ nicker, 1920→ nickel, 1955 nichol; cf *OED knicker sb*[1], *nickar, nicker sb*[3], marble 1760→.

1. The related plants *Cæsalpinia bonduc* (YELLOW NICKER) and *C. bonducella* (GREY NICKER) and their seeds, respectively yellow and grey, which are used like marbles in boys' games, and medicinally. In the folk speech the pronunc is always /níkal/—cf recent spellings.

1696 Sloane 145, *The Ash-colour'd Nickar Tree.* Locis campestribus circa *Blewfields Bay* in Ins. Jam. a 1726 Barham (1794) 114, There are two sorts of these trees which are called nickers, the boys playing with the cone or fruit as they do with marbles: The one hath a yellow cone, the other an ash-coloured one. 1864 Grisebach 786, Nicker tree: *Guilandina.* 1920 Fawcett 92, Nickar tree; *ibid* 94. 1952 FGC Han, StAnn, StM, StT, Tre /níkal/. 1955 *WIMJ* 157, Yellow (Nicker) Nichol. . Grey (Nicker) Nichol; *ibid* 162, Nickel.

2. The tree *Ormosia jamaicensis* and its seeds, used similarly to those of sense 1. (The spellings 'nickel', 'nichol', are attempts to render the folk pronunc /níkal/. The implied restriction of this form to *Ormosia* is false: it is regularly used of *Cæsalpinia* also.)

1909 Harris 310 (see quot s.v. BEAD TREE). 1920 Fawcett 88, *O. jamaicensis*. . Nickel. . 'Nickel' is a corruption of 'necklace', as the beads are used to make necklaces. [This is an erroneous explanation; see etym above.] 1941 Swabey 13, Bead Tree. (Nickel.) *Ormosia jamaicensis.*

3. The game, like marbles, played by boys with nickers or 'nikals'.

1952 FGC Han.

NICKEL, NICKER see prec.

NICODEMUS sb dial; after the Biblical character (cf John iii. 1, etc.). One who comes by night. *BL*

1943 *GL* StAnd, Nikodemas, come by night.

nida indef pron dial; < *nada* or *neda.* Other. *BL*

1943 *GL* Tre, Nida, the next. [See NEXT.]

niega see NAYGA.

NIGGER-FISH sb dial. A type of 'skin fish' or OLD-WIFE, black in colour.

1952 FGC StAnn, StJ, StM, West /niga-fish/.

NIGGER-HEAD sb dial. The tree-nesting termite: see quot.

1942 *NHN* I 54, The first species met was the common 'nigger-head' or tree-nesting termite *Nasutitermes pilifrons.*

NIGGER NYACE sb dial; *nigger* + *nyaams.* = NEGRO YAM.

1943 *GL* StAnn, Niger nyace, negro yam.

NIGHT-BABY sb dial. Some unidentified nocturnal insect. See quot.

1952 FGC Port, Night-baby, like fly, black, has two big eyes.

NIGHT-BAT sb dial; < *night* + BAT. A night-flying moth, usually of the large kinds (the small being LAMP FLY, etc.).

1952 FGC Han, Man /nait-bat/ different sizes and colours.

NIGHT CHANGE sb dial. The time between midnight and about 1 A.M.

1958 DeC StAnd /nait-chienj/.

NIGHT DOCTOR-BIRD sb dial. A large nocturnal moth which, like the humming-bird, sucks from flower to flower. (Some moths are larger than some humming-birds.)

1952 FGC Tre, Night doctor-bird.

NIGHT-FLOWERING ACACIA sb bot. The tree *Calliandra portoricensis.*

1837 Macfadyen 318, Acacia vespertina. Night-flowering Acacia. . Common in Port Royal and St Andrew's mountains. . This plant has been confounded with *Mimosa comosa* of Swartz. It is very different, however, from that plant. I have given the specific designation of *Vespertina* to this species, from the circumstance that the flowers are at evening in their greatest perfection. 1920 Fawcett 142.

NIGHT GAULIN sb dial; < *night* + GAULIN. The Night Herons (*Nycticorax nycticorax, Nyctanassa violacea*).

1936 Bond 26–8, Black-Crowned Night Heron. . *Local names:*—Gaulin; Night Gaulin;. . Yellow-Crowned Night Heron. . *Local names:*—Gaulin; Night Gaulin. 1956 Jeffrey-Smith 124, Then there are the 'night gaulins'. . The black-crowned is not so often seen, for it is essentially a night bird; but the yellow-crowned is quite diurnal in its habits.

NIGHT GLASS sb dial, somewhat euphemistic. A chamber-pot.

1943 *GL* Clar, Powdie, night glass; StAnd, Poe, night glass.

NIGHTINGALE sb; *OED* of other birds. The bird *Mimus polyglottos*; also called JAMAICA NIGHTINGALE.

1725 Sloane 306, The Singing Bird, Mock Bird, or Nightingale. 1790 Beckford I 257–8, The nightingale, which is in Europe a timid bird, and loves to bury himself among the thickest shades, is yet in Jamaica pert, courageous, and intrusive; is oftentimes, particularly when watching its nest, not only impudently social, but does not seem to fear the hawk or man..it is in a continual flutter of gallantry and insult; but makes ample amends, in its quiet state, for its offences, and seems to implore forgiveness in the most enchanting and various modulations that the ear can possibly imbibe. 1836 Widow 13 [The 'mocking bird'] warbles forth its song both night and day, and from this circumstance it is commonly called the nightingale. 1952 FGC Man, StM /náitn-giel/ Han, StAnn, StAnd, StT /náitn-gèl/; StAnd —eat worm, put worm in their pickney head so people won't touch them.

NIGHT JANGA sb dial joc; <*night*+JANGA. The cockroach.

1943 *GL* StM, Night janga, roach.

NIGHTLY-WATCH sb obs.

1828 *Ordinances..Kingston* 10, For better ordering and regulating the town-guard, or nightly-watch, in the said city and parish.

NIGHT-PLAY sb dial. See quot, and cf SET-UP.

1958 DeC Port /nait-plie/ funeral celebrations held on the 2nd–8th nights.

NIGHT-SAGE sb dial; <*nightshade*, by consonantal metathesis, and prob by analogy to *sage*, very common in plant names. =NIGHTSHADE.

1952 FGC Han, StAnn, StE, StM, Tre /nait-siej/ deadly nightshade. 1960 *CLS* 149 /wi hád a búsh grúo, wi kál i naítshíej/.

NIGHTSHADE sb.

1. *Solanum* (as elsewhere; not a Jamaicanism).

2. Species of *Echites*, and *Urechites lutea*.

1927 Beckwith 23, Nightshade. *Urechites lutea*..A deadly poison; use 'Busy-nut' as an antidote. 1952 FGC Port, StAnd, StM /náit-shíed/—see NIGHT-SAGE. 1954 *FG* 244, Nightshade (*Echites* sp.) and Guinea Hen weed..are generally reckoned to be the two most noxious weeds of pastures. *Ibid* 576, Nightshade (*Urechites lutea*).

NIGHT WASP sb dial. See quots.

1952 FGC Han, Man /nait wasp/; Tre /nait was/ fly by night; small, red, make nest of clay in house; will sting. (Ordinary one in field, build nest like bees, make comb but no honey.)

nigretfl adj dial; prob <*neglectful*.

1958 DeC StC /nigrétfl/ pertaining to an irresponsible, no-account person.

nigrish, niigrish adj now dial; *OED negrish* 1735; cf *DA niggerish* 1825→. The quotations represent two pronunc: the first two based on NEGA, NEGAR (*OED Neger*), the third on *nigger*, both pronunc being current in Jamaica today.

[1723–35 John Atkins *Voyage to Guinea*..110, quoted in 1933 Williams 29, This country is governed by an absolute King, who lives in Negrish majesty at a town called Sabbee.] 1943 *GL* West, Neegrish, mean act. 1959 DeC West /nigrish/ applied to any person or custom considered backward or unenlightened.

NIGUM-BITEY see LIGNUM-VITÆ.

niidi sb dial; ?<*needle*. See quot.

1958 DeC Tre /niidi/—a hard and sharp growth, like a spur of bone, growing downward from the roof of the mouth, which appears in mules, donkeys, and occasionally cattle; as it interferes with the animal's eating, it must be cut out by the farrier.

nikal see NICKAR.

NINE-DAY sb dial; also attrib. The period of mourning after a funeral—nine days (and nights) of activities including a wake, burial, singing of hymns, and on the ninth night the laying of the ghost. Traditional practices kept up (though with many variations) in most parishes. *T*

1950 Pioneer 53, Ef dem set a nine-day baby Ghose fe teck yuh life, Yuh can go a Mada Banna balm. [*If they 'set' the ninth-day unlaid ghost of a dead baby on you (by Obeah)*..etc.] 1954 LeP Man, StE, StT, Nine day; StAnn, Nine days with black.

NINE-HAND BANANA, ~BUNCH sb. A bunch of bananas having nine HANDS, i.e. a full BUNCH. *BL*

1907 Jekyll 195 [Song:] The gal over yonder carry banana..A nine-hand banana. 1912 McK *Songs* 31, see PURE.

NINE-NIGHT /nain-nait, nai-nait/ sb dial; for *ninth night*. The celebration that concludes the NINE-DAY period of funeral activities: there are singing, dancing, games, storytelling, ring-play, etc. Details of the observance vary considerably throughout the Island. *BL G N T*

1929 Beckwith 77–8, The Jamaican Negroes believe that for nine nights after death the ghost rises out of the grave and returns to its familiar haunts..During this period every relative and friend gathers at the house of the dead to entertain the ghost, welcome his return, and speed him back to the grave. The idea seems to be that should the ghost mark one absentee he might later harm the recreant member..The ninth night is that demanding principal vigilance. 1946 Dunham 90, Nine-night—the ninth night after a Maroon burial, at which time the spirit of the dead person will wander back to its home to be 'entertained before being definitely consigned to the world of duppies'. 1954 LeP Man, StAnn, StE, StT, Feast held at the end of a period of mourning—Nine-night. 1956 Mc /nain nait/—gathering on the 9th night after death, when stories are told, riddles asked, etc. This is when the dead person's bed is brought in from outside.

NINE-NIGHT LIE sb dial.

1956 Mc Man /náinait lái/—A big lie (from the practice of telling tall stories at nine-night).

NINGAMBITY see LIGNUM-VITÆ.

NINGE-NINGE see *ningge-ningge*.

ninggam-baiti, ningkam-baiti see LIGNUM-VITÆ.

ningge-ningge sb dial; cf Efik *nìŋinìŋi*, a small quantity of something (J. Berry), and Amer Sp *nengue*, a very small child (Carambula). Very small thing, esp a lot of them together: see quots.

1943 *GL* Kgn, Ninge-ninge, small, meagre children; very small flies. 1958 DeC StE (Accom) /ningge-ningge/ Anything plentiful and small, e.g. flies, stones, etc.

NINT see *naint*.

NINYAM, NYAMNYAM /nyam-nyam, nyan-yam, ninyam, nenyam/ sb dial; 1826→ nyam-nyam, 1912 nenyam, 1942 ninyam, 1943 nynam, nenyance, ninyamphs, 1951 nyanyam; <NYAM, simply iterated or iterated and the first element reduced. In Ja, in general, the iterative has come to be the noun, as distinct from the uniterated verb NYAM.

1. Any foodstuff; food prepared for eating; a meal; the action of eating. (No attempt has

been made to separate the citations, since these senses usually overlap.)

1826 Williams 344, Warra debbil can poor negar hab in him cutacoo, but lilly bit nyamnyam? 1827 Hamel II 316, Your white man's country has room for you all, and land and nyam-nyam enough. 1873 Rampini 178 [Prov:] Nyam-nyam (eating) will fill belly, but breeze no fill gut. 1912 McK *Songs* 53, Buccra..Hab 'nuff nenyam fe waste. 1942 Bennett 9, Dem dah married de ninyam! Yuh kean get onion widout yuh buy Tomatis now me chile! 1943 *GL* Clar, Tre, Ninyam, Food; Man, StE, Nenyam, Food; StAnn, Nynam, Food; StM, Nyam-nyam, Food; Clar, Nenyance, Dinner; StAnd, Ninyamphs, Food. 1951 FGC Man, I don't have my nyanyam yet. 1956 Mc Man /nínyam/ food in general.

2. Specif: Yam.

1956 Mc StE (Accom) /ninyám/ yam.

NINYAMPHS see prec.

NINYAM-SURREY /ninyám-sóri/ sb dial; <NINYAM + *Surrey*, the eastern county of Ja. One who eats a great deal, or too much.

1943 *GL* Kgn, Port, StAnd, StAnn, StC, StT, Tre, Ninyam surrey, Ninyamsurry, Nenyam surrey—one that eats plentifully, a good eater, eat too much. 1955 FGC Man /nìnyám-sóri/ eat a lot, can't be satisfied. 1956 BLB Clar /nyam sori/ eat up the whole county of Surrey.

NIPPLE sb dial.

1958 DeC StC /nipl/ small finger-shaped dumpling, a SPINNER.

NIPPLE PEPPER sb. A variety of *Capsicum* pepper shaped like a nipple.

1814 Lunan I 357, Nipple Peppers..the fruit is shaped like a cone or nipple, broad at bottom, and narrowing to a point.

nit sb and vb dial.

A. sb: 1. A common folk pronunc of *nut* when it appears as the second element of compounds, e.g. CHIGGER-NUT, COCONUT, etc.

2. = BOOT sb[1].

1952 FGC StE, Nit—the young peanut when just formed on the plant.

B. vb: Of a plant: To form young fruit. (See prec sense.)

1952 FGC StE /nit/ to form young peanuts. 1956 BLB Man, Of mango trees, etc.: to nit—to put out young fruit.

NITTLE /nitl/ sb dial; a pronunc var of *nettle*. See METTLE. *G*

NIYABINGI /nàyabíngi/ sb cant, also attrib; <*Niya-Bhingi*, said to mean 'death to the white man'. A society of 'warriors' among the RASTAFARIAN cult, patterned on a supposed secret African order. See quot.

1960 *SAN Report* 11, On Dec. 7, 1935, the *Jamaica Times* published an account of the Niyabingi Order in Ethiopia and the Congo..This was just a few months after Italy had invaded Ethiopia. Both Ethiopia and Haile Selassie were in the news. According to the.. *Times* the Ethiopian Emperor was head of the Niyabingi Order, the purpose of which was the overthrow of white domination by racial war.

NIYAMAN sb dial; <*Niya*, abbr of NIYABINGI, +*man*. A member of the NIYABINGI.

1960 *SAN Report* 11, Some of those people who worshipped the Emperor and were locally known as 'Ras Tafaris' or 'Rastamen' came to describe themselves as 'Niyamen'—that is, members of Niyabingi.

NO[1] /na, no/ adv dial; <*no* (*EDD* 4), still widely in Engl dial, esp Nth and Sc (*SND* NA *adv*[1,2]). As a simple negative before a verb: Not.

1740 Importance 20, English Bacceroes no know one another. 1790 Moreton 153, No use me ill, Obisha! 1793 Edwards II 84, The Negro..exclaimed in the usual jargon, *You no hear Massa call you?* 1803 Dallas II 226, 'Dat no do for we poor Maroon'. 1877 Murray *Feedin' 'Perrit* 9, How him ugly dere, nobody no da go married to him when you gone. *Ibid*, Me no hab nobody fe cry fe me. *Ibid* 15, Da no none turckle me ben da eat. 1907 Jekyll 33, Annancy was so smart, no want fe Deat' catch him. 1954 Reckord *Della* typescript 7, Tonight pray him no harden him heart.

NO[2] /no/ adj dial; <*no*, = not any, the second of two related negatives, which has remained in dial use everywhere in the English-speaking world, while Std usage has substituted *any* as the second correlative. In correlative uses therefore, not a Jamaicanism. Any. *BL G*

1929 Beckwith 51 [Cry of man buying empty bottles:] No wine pin'! no ale pin'! no soda water bottle! [*Have you any wine pints for sale,* etc.]

NO[3] /no, na/ adv particle gen; writers of dialect spell *no*, *noh*, *nuh*; cf Sp *¿no?* is that not so? and similar tag-questions in other languages, esp Scots (*SND* NA *adv*[3]). *BA BL G T*

1. Following a statement or remark and inviting agreement or assent: Isn't that so? Don't you agree? (Not fully interrogative, as an answer is not necessarily expected: assent may be tacit.)

1823 Stewart 259, You want for make fool of me—no? 1941 Kirkpatrick 15, You tink is 'ere we stap nuh. [*You think we're going to stop here, eh?*] 1960 FGC StAnd /de waz faiv a dem, no?/ *There were five of them, weren't there?*

2. Following an order or request and (impatiently, pleadingly, etc.) inviting compliance: Won't you? (A response in terms not of words but of action is expected.)

1877 Murray *Feedin' 'Perrit* 4, Me say, Georgey comb you hed, no! 1877 Murray *Kittle* 25, Mudfish say, 'Bra unoo carry me go wid unoo, no?' 1950 Pioneer 71, But gimme few of dem nuh me frien? 1950 Pioneer 36, Hear Wasp, 'Anancy, me noh care how yuh sick, me haffe get me bite offa yuh head'. Anancy sey, 'Come noh, Bredda Wasp'. [*Come, why don't you? You might as well get it over with.*]

3. Introducing an exclamation, interrogative in form but requiring no answer: Isn't it (that), Don't you? (The effect is to call attention often disingenuously.)

1877 Murray *Feedin' 'Perrit* 13, No dis chupid pickney tek me one tuppy I hab, so go trow it way. [*Didn't this stupid child take my only twopence*..etc.] *Ibid* 15, No see it ya, sar. [*See, sir—here it is.*] 1907 Jekyll 92, No see how him mout' long. [*What a long mouth he has!*] 1950 Pioneer 34, Hear Dog, 'Who dat Bra Nancy?' Anancy sey, 'Noh Bredda Puss sar!' [*It's that Brother Puss!*]

NO-A /nuó-a/ adv dial; a dial spelling of an old-fashioned, now moribund pronunc of *no*. (*EDD* gives examples from Wilts and Lancs.) No.

1905 Smith 18, Chim-Chim say—'Hi! an' is him laugh at all since him dead?' An' dey say—'No-a'. c 1915 FGC StAnd [Schoolboy joke:] Master: 'Do you know who built the ark?' Country bumpkin: 'No-a sah'. Master: 'Correct!'

nobis sb dial; prob <*novice*, a term of reproach, used of a person who is awkward in manner or procedure.

1959 DeC Han /nobis/ A foolish, stupid, ignorant person.

NO BOY /no bwáai/ phr dial; <NO[1]+*boy*, ellipt for some such phr as *not for a boy* (*to try*)—i.e. difficult, requiring a man's strength. See quot. *BL*

1927 Anderson-Cundall 20 [Prov:] Go a heaben no bwoy. 'No bwoy' is a local expression meaning 'troublesome' or 'not easy'.

noda /nóda/ pron dial; in dial writing often sp *nudda*; aphet form of *another*: cf *nada*, *neda*. *G*

NO-EYE MEAL sb obs; <NO-EYE (PEA) +*meal*. Meal (flour) made from no-eye peas.

1855 *TJSA* II 41.

NO-EYE PEA sb; so called from the inconspicuousness of the hilum. A variety of the GUNGO PEA (*Cajanus cajan*): see quot 1920.

1837 Macfadyen 296, Cajanus flavus. No-Eye Pea..The general description of the preceding species [Pigeon or Congo Pea] applies, in nearly every respect, to this.. The exceptions are, that in this the corolla is of an uniform yellow colour..Of these two species the No-Eye Pea is the most delicate. 1920 Fawcett 71–2, C. cajan.. The 'No Eye Pea' has a corolla of a uniform yellow colour, whereas the 'Gungo' or 'Pigeon Pea' has the yellow corolla blotched with orange or red, and the calyx, pods and seeds are also marked with purple blotches or spots. 1954 *WIMJ* 28.

nof adj and adv dial; aphetic form of *enough*.

A. adj: 1. Many, numerous, plentiful; much; great. *BL G T*

1868 Russell 8 [Indication of plurality:] By the Adjectives *nuff*, *plenty-plenty*, *lat*; as Nuff cow pass ya; Plenty-plenty yam dig (etc.). 1950 Pioneer 64, You got nuff smaddy deh ah you yard? 1952 FGC StM, Bloodberry—tall tree, nuff branches. 1956 Mc Clar, To make calaban trap /tek nof lili tik/ *take a lot of little sticks*. StE /im bring im intu di ud—we iz nof big trii/ *He brought him into the wood—where there are many big trees.*

2. Comparative and superlative forms. *BL G*

1943 *GL* StC, Nuffer, more; no addr, Nuffist, most. 1954 LeP StAnn, Man you strong, you carry nuffer load dan him.

B. adv: Much, plentifully. *BL G*

1868 Russell 18, Adverbs of quantity—'Nuff (enough).

nof-nof adj adv and sb dial; iterative form of *nof*. *BL*

A. adj: Plentiful, a great many. *G*

1943 *GL* Tre, Nuff-nuff, Plenty or a sufficiency; also Kgn, Man, Port, StC, StJ. 1950 Pioneer 51, Race-Course..got ole heap a tan-op seat, An nuff-nuff parkin space!

B. adv: Much, a great deal. *G*

1956 Mc Man /mi pupa nof-nof taala an mi muma/ *my father is much taller than my mother.*

C. sb: What there is plenty of.

1956 BLB Man /gi mi som a di nof-nof no!/

NOGGIN sb dial; cf *OED noggin* 2, a small quantity of liquor. s; also s CURRENCY.

1. A farthing.

1943 *GL* Kgn Nawgin, farthing. 1955 FGC Man /nágin/ farthing.

2. A gill (three-farthings).

1943 *GL* Clar, Noggin, ¾*d*.; Kgn, Nawgin; Tre Nagin.

NOH see NO.

NOISY BUR sb dial; so called because the seeds make a light rattling sound.

1955 *WIMJ* 80, *Hyptis suaveolens*..Spikenard; Noisy Bur. This plant is still in use, to some extent, for the preparation of 'bush tea'..the seeds are used by some Mexican Indians both medicinally and as food.

nombari indef pron dial; pronunc of *nobody*, the intrusive *m* perh due to analogy with *somebody*.

1956 Mc Man /nómbari nó da a yáad disaya táim a díe ya/ *Nobody is at home at this time of day.* StE (Accom) /nombari/ and /sumadi/.

NO-MINE /no-main/ sb dial; <NO[1], not +*mind* vb. Carelessness; disobedience. (Cf StdE *don't-care.*) *BL*

1873 Rampini 178 [Prov:] No mind make ship run ashore. 1910 Anderson-Cundall 41, 'No-mine' mek ship run ashore.

NO MINE /no main/ vb phr dial; <NO[1], +*mind* vb. Never mind; regardless of. *BL G*

1910 Anderson-Cundall 8, No mine how cockroach drunk, him no walk pas' fowl-yard.

NO-MO adv dial; <*no more*, no sooner, hardly, barely. *BL*; *SC* nə̀mo.

1. No sooner, scarcely, only just.

1826 Williams 109 [In a Negro sermon on hell:] Dat time [when you die] no mo you begin for lib. [*When you die you are only then beginning to live.*] 1877 Murray *Kittle* 27, Well, I go sleep till bufo day, nummo come yerry dem Eboe fellow. [The comma after *day* should prob come two words later, after *come*.] *Well, I went to sleep till dawn had hardly come, hear those Eboe fellows..* [who sing a song].

2. Merely, only.

1826 Williams 109 [In a Negro sermon on hell:] You tink wha for Garamighty gib you black girl? No mo for rat trap for catch you sinful soul. [*Only as a trap..*]

NO-MO conj dial; prob <NO-MO adj, developing the idea of strict limitation into that of the single exception.

1. Except that; except for the fact that.

1826 Williams 109 [In a Negro sermon on hell:] Dem no gib you plantain—no so lead, no mo hot like hell, burn hole in you belly. [*—only lead, except that it's hot as hell..*] 1877 Murray *Feedin' 'Perrit* 12, 'Wha you mamma tell you? Don' him tell you so?' 'Yes, sar, no mo him say sar, das when me see you drink you rum, me mus'n't come close you'. 1907 Jekyll 31, So Annancy begin fe talk to himself: 'Bro'er Deat' say me fe go make up fire, but no mo so me no yerry'. [*Except that I didn't hear*, or in Jekyll's translation (p 34) *I must have failed to hear.*] 1958 DeC StT /no muo so/—conjunction meaning 'except for the fact that': /aldúo mi a pii-foul, mi hansom beriwel, no muor so mi fut so maaga/.

2. Except for, discounting.

1907 Jekyll 141, No, all the time me go down me an' Fowl a good friend, no mo' the little quarrel we have.

NO-MO adj dial; abbr of *no-more-than*, in the older form *no-mo* (*OED* →1813, *obs.*). Mere, only, alone. *SC nómo*.

1942 Bennett 10, One no mo' farden bump she buy! Wat a red kin 'oman mean! [*She has bought one mere farthing sweet! What a mean woman!*] 1943 *GL* Clar, Nummo, only; StAnn, Nomo, only; StM, Tre, Numo, only, no more. 1950 Pioneer 22, But it was ongle she an Dora no mo did know de song.

NO-MUS' /no-mos/ phr dial; for *mustn't* (*it be* (*so*)?). Mustn't it be (so)? What else can you expect? *G*

1952 FGC Man, 'No mus' hot, man?'—Said by one garage attendant to another who had touched the manifold of a car that had just been running.

NONE AT ALL /nuon-taal, non-taal/ adv phr dial; <*none at all*. A strong negative: not at all. *BA BL G*

1956 Mc Man /jíen no mémba wa mitél im se noun-táal/ *Jane has completely forgotten what I told her.* StE

/mi no sii di kóla a yu nuon táal/ *I can't see the colour of you at all.*

NONG /nong/ adv dial; dial sp (less common though phonemically better than NUNG). Now.

1912 McK *Ballads* 56, So-so trust nong every day Tell.. we get de little pay.

NOOCO see *nuku.*

NOOKOO sb[1] dial; cf Ewe *nɔkú,* 'Mother Death'.

1943 *GL* StM, Nookoo, ghost.

NOOKOO adj and sb[2] see *nuku.*

NOONOO BUSH /nunu bush/ sb dial; cf Twi *o-nunúm,* an aromatic plant, used like *ɛ-mɛ̃́* (=mint). 'The *Ocimum viride,* or *nunum* as it is known in Ashanti, is a common "medicine" to drive away ghosts' (1927 Rattray 57). A bush used in obeah practice: a kind of basil.

1942 Bennett 30, Me doan believe in obeah mam..an dis Is all an all ah do. Me wrap it up wid noonoo bush Same sweet bazley, yuh know..An' bury it a-me doa.

NORTH sb arch; *OED* B 4b 1699→; prob infl by Sp usage: *el norte,* the north wind. A wind from the north, liable to damage plantations, and bringing rough weather. The term is now being displaced by 'north wind' or 'norther'.

1679 Trapham 8–9, These norths are smart winds and cold, blowing from off the land with unusual force and continuance, being particular not general winds, either from the mountainous tracts of Jamaica itself, and then only to be felt on the south side, and not far to Sea, or else arising from Cuba, and then chiefly if not only remarked on the North side of Jamaica. 1788 Beckford 20 [The negro] cannot bear the cold; his hut should therefore be erected in a situation, impervious to the breeze at night, and under a local protection from the norths at noon, at the setting in of which (as they blow with uncommon keenness)..the chilly negroes..very sensibly feel. 1790 Beckford I 58, The north winds (or the Norths, as they are indiscriminately called in Jamaica) may sometimes be..prejudicial to the canes. 1847 Gosse 303, When the furious *norths* blow. 1952 FGC Port, West /naat/ (but StC, StM /naat win/). *BL*

NORTH SIDE

1. Specif. A part of an early legislative precinct, the second of the four estab in 1664.

1664 *Jrnls Assembly* 2–3, It is decreed that a quarter-sessions may be kept and held in every precinct, *viz.* in the parish of St Thomas, St David, comprehending Porto-Morant and Yallow, in one precinct; the parish of St John, comprehending Guanaboa and the North Side, for another precinct; the parish of St Andrew, comprehending Lygonee, for another precinct; the parish of Clarendon, comprehending the south west to Point-Negril, for another precinct.

2. Gen. The northern half of the island, generally moister than the South Side and subject to colder winds.

1679 Trapham 9, see NORTH. 1774 Long II 355, There is a remarkable difference between the woods of the North and South sides. 1873 Rampini 55, These mountain chains may be roughly said to divide the island into two halves, called respectively the North side and the South side. 1925 Beckwith 77 [Prov:] John-crow want fe go nort' side; why you t'ink breeze come tek him? (1960 Current, FGC.)

NORWEGIAN sb dial. A derogatory term for an albino negro, alluding to his light complexion.

1958 DeC StT /naawíijan/.

NOSEBURN TREE sb; a confusion? =BURN-NOSE (BARK).

1864 Grisebach 786, Noseburn tree: *Daphnopsis tenuifolia.*

NO SO adv phr dial arch; <NO[1] +*so,* particle of comparison. Nothing but, only.

1826 Williams 109 [In a negro sermon on hell:] No so boiling brimstone, nuttin else for drink..Dem no gib you plantain—no so lead. [*Only boiling brimstone.. nothing but lead.*]

NOT A MAN indef pron phr dial. Nobody. *G*

1957 JN StE, No-no, not a man a get this pretty one, *No, no; nobody shall have this pretty one!*

'NOUGH see *nof.*

NOWHERIAN adj dial; <*nowhere*+*-ian,* a person from nowhere (i.e. nowhere important).

1. Belonging to no fixed religious sect. *BA T*

1956 BLB Man.

2. From nowhere important; of no consequence. *BA G T*

1960 RJO StAnd /him jos a no-gud nowierian skachman/.

NO-WORTH /no wot/ adj dial; <NO[1] +*worth.* Worthless, good for nothing.

1826 Williams 19, Quamina..began to..curse the preacher's religion, since it was 'no worth'. 1912 McK *Ballads* 46, Me deh tell you say de Jackass no wut. (1956 Current, BLB.)

NOYAU sb; <Fr *noyau.* =KNOW-YOU.

NUBBA adv dial; <*never*; /b/ for Std /v/ is the normal reflex, but U (which may spell /u/ or /o/) is irreg.

1868 Russell 12, Nubba = never.

NUBBIN adj dial; cf DAE.

1943 *GL* StAnd, Nobin, small; StE, Nubbin, small.

NUDDA see *noda.*

1868 *TRSAA* I 66, see PASS I.

NUFF see *nof.*

NUFFER, NUFFIST see *nof* 2.

NUH see NO.

nuko, nuko-nuko, nuku adj and sb dial; cf Twi *nnukuu,* small pieces of cloth, Ewe *núkè,* smallish.

1943 *GL* StE, Nooco, short, nuko-nuko, small thing; StM, Nookoo, short.

NUMA /nuuma/ sb dial; cf *OED Noma,* 'A gangrenous ulceration of the throat, occurring mainly in young children'; also Colombian Sp *ñoma,* a large ulcer or sore. Pus.

1943 *GL* Clar, Han, Kgn, Numa, pus; StAnd, Nuema, pus.

NUMBER-ELEVEN MANGO sb. A variety of the mango (fruit of *Mangifera indica*): see quot 1837. *BL*

1837 Macfadyen 221, This valuable tree [Mango] was first introduced into this island in June 1782, being among a number of valuable plants taken in a French vessel, bound from the East Indies to St Domingo..There being a great number of plants, producing several varieties of the fruit, they were regularly numbered. Hence two of the most esteemed sorts have since come to be known by the names of No. 11 and No. 32. The No. 11 is a flat-sided green fruit, of a delicious aroma, and an agreeable subacid taste. 1862 Clutterbuck 143, The species of mangoes are distinguished by numbers, and number eleven is by far the best. 1952 FGC StE, StJ /nòmba lébm mànggo/; StAnd, StT /nòmba ilébm/. 1954 *FG* 475, Number Eleven. The most popular of the stringy varieties.

NUMBER THIRTY-TWO MANGO sb arch or obs. See quot.

1837 Macfadyen 221–2, The No. 32 resembles it [*sc* NUMBER ELEVEN] in form and fragrance, but is of a yellow colour, and possesses a more luscious sweetness.

NUMBER TWO sb dial.

1958 DeC Port /nomba tuu/ a cowtongue dumpling. StJ, a large round boiled dumpling, indented around the circumference so that it can be easily split in two.

NUMMO, NUMO see NO-MO.

NUNG adv dial; dial sp representing /nong/, i.e. *n* + nasalized *o*; cf DUNG, TUNG, etc. Now.

1941 Kirkpatrick 10, 'Im bowler a bruk dung nung. [*His bowlers are breaking down now.*] 1943 *GL* Kgn, Nung, now. 1954 LeP Kgn, Me hungry nung.

NUNG-NUNG adv dial; iterative of NUNG.

1943 *GL* Clar, Nungnung, right away.

nunus sb dial; abbr of, or element in, *bununus*.

1959 DeC StJ /nunús/ pet name for a child or sweetheart.

nuoz naat sb dial; <*nose* + *snot*. *BL*

1956 Mc StAnd, StE /nùoz-náat/ mucus from the nose.

NUSI sb dial; ?<*nursie*.

1943 *GL* Tre, Nusi, a small lizard.

NUT-OIL sb dial. Castor oil: oil from the OIL-NUT.

1877 Murray 4, Mek me tek little nut ile so nint [anoint] it mek it soft, no. 1960 LeP StAnd, Nut oil—Castor oil.

NYAAM, nyaamps see next.

NYAAMS, NYAMS /nyam, nyams, nyamps, nyans, nyaans, nyaas, nyaam, nyaams, naam/ sb[1] dial; for spelling-forms see quots; cf Mende *nyamisi*, yam (J. Berry). No single form can, however, be taken as the etymon; not only did many forms come to Ja from various Afr languages, but there is much overlapping among the languages themselves as between words for eating, for meat (animal flesh), for food in general, and for specific foods. (Ja folk use of the word FOOD, incidentally, reflects the basic position that yam held in the diet of West Africans and continues to hold among Jamaicans today.) See NYAM etym note. Yam. *N*

1877 Murray *Kittle* 27, Daddy, da de people da eat dem new nyams. 1943 *GL* Clar, Nyance, Nyaance—yam of any kind; Tre, Nyamce; Man, StJ, Nyaam; StAnd, Nyaams; StC, Nyamp; Man, Nyamps; StAnn, Nyace; no addr, Nyans; StC, Naams; no addr, Namse, Naunce; Man, StE, Narm. [These represent various attempts to spell a word which is normally oral, has no estab spelling, and contains sounds for which StdE does not provide.] 1954 LeP Kgn, Nyam; StE, Nyaam; StT, Niaams; StAnn, Nyasse. 1956 Mc StAnn /hóu yu núo se di nyáans raip yét/ also StAnd, StT /nyaams/.

NYAAMS /nyaams, nyaamps, nyamps/ sb[2] and vb dial; the similarity of forms with those of NYAAMS sb[1] is prob not accidental: the words are very likely related (certainly associated in people's thinking—cf NYAAMS-HEAD and the similar COCO-HEAD 2), but are treated separately here for convenience. Additional, perh related, Afr words are: Twi *nyằmoo*, lean, meagre, feeble, poor; *anyằmpá*, disgrace, disparagement; Ewe *nyama*, disorderly.

A. sb: 1. Foolishness, nonsense; something of no value. (Often exclamatory.)

1955 FGC Man /yu taakin nyaams/! 1957 LeP StE (Eld), I don't care a nyaams about him. (This may be a metaphorical use of sb[1].) 1957 JB StAnd, Nyamps—a derogatory exclamation, 'Not much good'. 1958 DeC Port /nyaamps/ idle, foolish talk.

2. Somebody who talks nonsense; an oaf; a weakling.

1900 Murray 8, see BUCK 1. 1943 *GL* StM, Nyawmce, idiot. 1951 D. Levy StE (Black R.) /nyaamps/ a stupid, unthinking, or silly person. 1954 LeP StE, Big, oafish man—nyaamse. 1958 DeC Port, A person who talks /nyaamps/.

B. vb: To make a frightening face.

1957 DeC StE (Accom) /nyaams/.

NYAAMS-HEAD sb dial; <NYAAMS sb[1] and sb[2] (a play on senses) + *head*. Cf YAM-HEAD.

1958 DeC StAnd /nyamsed/ a stupid fool.

NYAANCE, NYACE see NYAAMS.

NYACKA, NYAKKA-NYAKKA, NYAK-NYAKA see next.

NYAKA-NYAKA adj (adv), sb, and vb dial; cf Twi *nyằkã-nyằkã*, to cut into pieces. See also NAKA-NAKA.

A. adj: 1. Disorderly, untidy, dirty.

1868 Russell 10, Filthy-looking. . De yard look so nyaka-nyaka. African. 1943 *GL* Kgn, Neacka-neacka, neaka-neaka, untidy; StM, nyakka-nyakka, sloven; StT, nyak-nyaka.

2. Reduced to small mixed pieces.

1943 *GL* Kgn, Nyaka-nyaka, mangled; StAnn, Nyacka, scrambled.

3. Muddy, sloppy.

1959 DeC West /nyaka-nyaka/ adj. (of ground) wet, sloppy, muddy, especially if there is standing water.

B. sb: Ragged or rubbishy things; trash.

1959 DeC West /nyaka-nyaka/ miscellaneous rubbish or trash (also used to mean old ragged work clothes).

C. vb: 1. To hack or mangle (something) with a dull tool. Cf *saka-saka*.

1959 DeC West /nyaka-nyaka/ vb. To hack up anything with a dull knife.

2. Of an animal: to gnaw or rend.

1959 DeC West /nyaka-nyaka/ of a mouse, to gnaw.

NYAM /nyam/ vb and sb dial; 1788 1801 yam, 1790 knaum, 1835→ nyam, 1868 naym (?misprinted for *nyam*); the source is multiple: both verb (*eat*) and noun (*food*, or specific foods) existed in a number of W Afr languages, and many were brought to Ja: cf Wolof *ɲam*, *ɲamɲam*, to eat, Fula *ɲama*, *ɲamgo*, to eat; Hausa *na:ma*, flesh, meat, Efik *unam*, flesh, Twi *ɛnãm*, flesh, meat of any animal, Tshiluba *ɲama*, animal, Zulu *-nyama*, meat; Hausa *ɲamɲam*, *yamyam*, cannibal; Twi *ànyinam*, *ayam'kàw-dé*, species of yam; cf also NINYAM, NYAAMS, YAM. The resulting multiplicity has in the course of time become sorted out so that, in general, NYAM is the verb, NINYAM a noun (food), and NYAAMS a specific food (YAM). (Scots examples of *nyam*, *nyum-nyum* (*EDD*) are independent formations.) s YAM-YAMME.

A. vb: To eat, esp roughly or voraciously. (The word has never been an elegant one; its natural use today marks the most conservative speakers. Cf Cassidy-LePage, *CLS* II 29.) *N*

1788 Marsden 49, The negroes say, the black parroquets are good for *yam*, i.e. good to eat. 1790 Moreton 117 [Example of Creole talk:] Yellow Legs [a dog] come, and he knaum my—[excrement], and him puke. 1801 Dancer 174 [Dirt-eaters] display as much curiosity and nicety in their choice of the earth they *yam*, as snuff-takers or smokers in the kind of tobacco they make use of. 1835 Madden I 84, Nyaming of goat and wegitabs, instead of rashers of bacon and pratees. 1862 Clutterbuck 68, With sparkling eyes they purchased the congenial plant [*sc* sugar-cane], and nyaming greedily its fibre, were entranced with luscious joy. 1943 *GL* every parish. 1950 Pioneer 23, Anancy. . nyam off de whole a de cane dem. 1954 LeP Kgn, Me eatin' me dinner (*Nyam* is rude or coarse, or used with reference to animals); StAnn, Nyam —to eat (suggests eating ravenously). 1957 JN [School-girl:] When mi eat an mi belly full mi say mi can' nyam no more. *BL G T*

B. sb: Food; a meal.

1828 Marly 13, Eh! Mosquitoes hab grandy nyamn on dat new buckra! 1835 Madden I 188, Him want no nyam, no clothes, no sleep.

NYAMCE see NYAAMS.

NYAM-DOG /nyám-dáag/ sb dial; <NYAM +*dog*. A nickname for a Chinese, from the belief that the Chinese eat dog's meat.

1943 *GL* Port, Nyam dawg, a Chinese.

NYAMI-NYAMI sb, adj, and vb dial; cf NYAM, NINYAM, and Ewe *nyami-nyami*, smacking the lips. s YAM-YAMME.

A. sb: A greedy person.

1943 *GL* Kgn, Nami-nami, greedy person. 1955 FGC Man /nyami-nyami/.

B. adj: 1. Greedy.

1957 DeC StE (Accom) /nyami nyami/ greedy.

2. Eaten away, chewed. *G*

1956 Mc Man /nyami-nyami/ eaten (by insects, caterpillars, etc.—of cabbage leaves).

C. vb: To eat in random spots.

1957 DeC StE (Accom) /nyami-nyami/ to eat (of an insect—e.g. mosquitoes biting).

NYAMMING vbl sb dial; <NYAM.

1954 LeP Kgn, A dish of curried goat, nyamming.

NYAMN see NYAM.

NYAMNYAM see NINYAM.

NYAMP, NYAMPS see NYAAMS.

NYAMU sb dial uncom; <NYAM+-*u*?

1943 *GL* StJ, Nyamu, some flesh-eating animal.

NYANCE see NYAAMS.

NYANGA /nyangga/ sb and vb dial; cf Mende *nyàngá*, ostentation, giving oneself airs; Cameroons pidgin, same meaning (J. Berry); Ngombe *njangájálá*, pride. Cf YANGA.

A. sb: 1. Pride.

1896 Bates 38 [Prov:] Nyanga mek crab go sideways. 1943 *GL* StAnn, Nyanga, pride.

2. A person proud of himself; a dude.

1943 *GL* Man, A dude.

B. vb: To show oneself off, walking proudly or provocatively.

1943 *GL* Man, Nyanga, to play the dude. 1957 LeP in *Orbis* VI 384 /nyangga/ to walk proudly and provocatively, swinging the hips.

NYANYAM see NINYAM.

[**NYAPA** sb dial uncom; <Amer Sp *ñapa*, gift of little value which the seller gives to the buyer. Cf US Sth *lagniappe*. MAKE-UP, *braata*.

1943 *GL* Clar, Nyapa, buys then asks for make-up.]

NYASSE, NYAUS, NYAWMCE see NYAAMS.

nyata nuoz sb dial; etym unknown but presumably Afr.

1960 LeP StAnd /nyáta nuoz/—a very flat, broad nose; a person having such a nose.

nyeke-nyeke adj dial; cf the corresp verb NAKA-NAKA.

1956 Mc Man /nyéke-nyéke/ descriptive of something torn by a dog, a crow, etc.

NYLON ROAD sb. Any new very smooth asphalt-surfaced road—much smoother than the average Jamaican road. (From about 1958, FGC.)

NYNAM see NINYAM.

nyong /nyong/ adj dial; <*young*, under analogical infl from other words beginning /*ny*-/. Young. *SC njoen*, Gullah *noung*.

1862 Clutterbuck *passim*, *Nyoung* for *young* in representations of Negro speech. 1943 *GL* Han, StJ, Nyung, young. 1952 FGC StE (Quickstep) /nyong pikini/ young child.

NYOUNG, NYUNG see prec.

O /a/ particle dial; a var of A[8].

1877 Murray *Feedin' 'Perrit* 4, Dem would a hab fe smoke him de same like o when dem smoke horse.

OAGLY see UGLY adj.

OBEAH /uobia, obia, wobia, hobia/ sb and vb; 1760→ obeah, 1774 obeiah, 1788 1863 obea, 1789 obiah, 1794 1953 obia, c1800→ obi (plur 1823 obies), 1943 obah; the derivation is prob multiple—cf Efik *ubio*, 'a thing or mixture of things, put in the ground, as a charm to cause sickness or death '(*OED*); also the base of Twi *ɔ-bayifó*, witch, wizard, sorcerer (more literally sorcery-man, 'obeah-man', since -*fó* means *person*). *BA G N T*

A. sb: 1. The practice of malignant magic as widely known in Jamaica. Its origins are African; in practice it has never been clearly distinguished from MYAL: though the latter was supposedly curative of the ills caused by the former, both have shared the same methods to a great extent (MYAL with some admixture of elements derived from Christianity). Obeah is still practised throughout Jamaica—more than 35 terms for an OBEAH-MAN are locally current.

1760 *Jrl Assembly* 16 Dec (Vol v 245), The engrossed bill to remedy the evils arising from irregular assemblies of slaves. . and for preventing the practice of *obeah*. 1773 in 1835 Madden II 98, In the criminal record-book of the parish of St Andrews, I find the following obeah cases: 1773. Sarah, tried 'for having in her possession cats' teeth, cats' claws, cats' jaws, hair, beads, knotted cords, and other materials, relative to the practice of obeah. .'. 1862 Clutterbuck 98, *Obi* is the name of the religion, incantation, or devil-worship. . that prevails among the negroes. Obeah men, their high-priests or professors, are always native Africans, so are the women who practise its crafts. 1953 Moore gloss, Obeah [obia]—power over spirits. *BL*

2. The 'magic' so designed and supposedly achieved or 'worked' upon or in behalf of someone. See also PULL, PUT, SET, etc.

1842 in 1895 Banbury 21 [Song:] Dandy obeah da ya, oh! Me wi' pull he, oh! 1862 Clutterbuck 156, Which he knows to be a warning that *Obi is set for him*. [Here 'for' means *against*.] 1956 Mc Man /wok obia/ to perform obia. Also pronunc /hobia, wobia/.

3. The amulet containing the 'magic things' used by the obeah-man—a horn, box, pouch, or the like, full of rubbish; the contents of such an amulet. (The form 'obi' may have been preferred for this.)

c 1800 Mansong 11, Dr Mosely, in his treatise on Sugar, says—'I saw the obi of the famous negro robber, Three-Finger'd Jack, the terror of Jamaica, in 1780..It consisted of a goat's horn, filled with a compound of grave dirt, ashes, the blood of a black cat, and human fat, all mixed into a kind of paste: a cat's foot, a dried toad, a pig's tail, a slip of virginal parchment, of kid-skin, with characters marked with blood on it, were also in his obian bag. These, with a Keen sabre, and two guns, were all his obi. 1823 Koromantyn 177, The Obi is composed of a variety of materials; viz. blood, feathers..[etc.]. *BL*

4. The obeah materials, supposed to have magical powers, actually set out for the purpose of harming someone. In some cases the magical powers are supplemented with actual poisons derived from herbs. *BL*

1788 Marsden 40, They sometimes do much mischief by administering poisons, of which they have various kinds in the island, some of them very subtile and lingering in their effects. The general name with the negroes for these poisons is *obea*, which is frequently given to one another upon any slight cause; they do it in secret, and keep it so, nor is the person who administers it often found out. 1925 Beckwith 78 [Prov:] Keep sensa fowl fe pick obeah. [The belief is that the SENSE fowl will find and dig out buried obeah materials.]

B. vb: To work witchcraft against (someone).

a 1818 Lewis (1834) 146–7, If any negro from that time forward should be proved to have accused another of Obeahing him, or of telling another that he had been Obeahed, he should..never receive any favour from me in future. 1827 Hamel I 266, Or have you been wrestling with a duppie in your sleep—an incubus? Or have you been Obeah'd? 1950 Pioneer 53, Is betta smady obeah yuh Dan sell yuh a ole car! 1952 FGC StAnd, Is obeah dem obeah de man. 1956 Mc Clar /hobia im—put dopi an im/. *BL*

OBEAHISM, OBEISM sb; < the base syllable of OBEAH + *-ism*. The profession or practice of OBEAH. s.

1843 Philippo 248, see MYALISM. 1873 Rampini 141–2 (quoting from *Gleaner* 1869), Upon a gentleman remarking that the whole affair was a compound of Obeahism, Myalism, and Revivalism, some of the bystanders observed, that if the white people had not interfered the jar and money [being sought for by 'magic' means] would have been found.

OBEAH-MAN sb; *OED* 1764→. A male practitioner of OBEAH. Also attrib. *BA BL G T*

1760 Laws of Ja in 1774 Long II 489, *Obeiah-men*, pretended conjurors, or priests, upon conviction before two justices and three free holders of their practising as such, to suffer death, or transportation, at the discretion of the court. 1794 Edwards II 90–1, *Obia*-men or women..is now become in Jamaica the general term to denote those Africans who in that island practise witchcraft or sorcery, comprehending also the class of what are called Myalmen. 1954 LeP Man, Man who professes to kill or heal by magic—Obeah man. 1956 Mc Clar /obya man/.

OBEAHMAN BLUEBIRD, OBEAHMAN CUNNY sb dial. The ORANGE QUIT (*Euneornis campestris*); the name alludes to its cleverness in avoiding traps. Cf s OBEAHMAN DRUMMER.

1952 FGC StM /hobia-man bluubod/ orange, blue, red under throat; StT, Obeahman cunny—same as BLUE-SWEE; very smart.

OBEAH STICK sb dial; < OBEAH + *stick* sb. A stick supposedly given magical properties through OBEAH, therefore a dangerous weapon.

1863 Waddell 188 (year 1842), About the same time there was a riot at Running Gut Estate, caused by the new Africans having prepared what the Christians called an Obeah stick, which I took from them, as a dangerous club in a fight, and so quieted them.

OBEAH-WISDOM sb dial. Hypocrisy?

1954 LeP StAnn, A hypocrite—Obeah-wisdom.

OBEAH-WOMAN sb dial; *OED* 1840. A female practitioner of OBEAH. *BA BL G T*

1803 Dallas I 74 [Quao] was deterred from it [*sc* suing for peace] by an old obeah-woman, the only one of that sex known to have exercised the art. 1823 Koromantyn 177, The trade of an Obeah man or woman was not a little lucrative, as they manufactured and sold their obies, or spells, or preservatives, adapting them to different cases, and changing them accordingly. 1934 Williams 126, A notorious obeah-woman..known as 'Old Mother Austin'. She died on June 25, 1892.

OBEIAH see OBEAH.

OBEISM see OBEAHISM.

OBERDO see OVER-DO.

OBERSEER see BUSHA.

OBI, OBIA, OBIAH see OBEAH.

OBIAN adj dial rare; < *obi*, var of OBEAH + *-an*, adjective-forming suffix. Pertaining to OBEAH.

c 1800 Mansong 11, see OBEAH A 3. *Ibid* 8, Amalkir, the obian practitioner.

OBI HORN sb rare; < *obi*, var of OBEAH + *horn*. A goat's horn used as a container for OBEAH materials.

c 1800 Mansong 11, He again repaired to the cave of Amalkir, who hung an obi horn about his neck, rare for its supposed virtues.

OBI-RING sb; < *obi*, var of OBEAH + *ring*. A signet ring in which a hole has been drilled for the reception of an obeah charm or 'medicine'.

1934 Williams 143, One of the latest institutions of applied magic is known as the obi-ring, to which reference is made in the case of Ivanhoe Baker as cited in *The Daily Gleaner* of Feb 5, 1934. I can find no mention of it in any book to which I have had access, which leads me to the conclusion that it is of comparatively recent origin.

OBISHA see BUSHA.

OBI WEED sb dial; < *obi*, var of OBEAH + *weed*. An unidentified herb, used in obeah practice. (Prob not JOHN-CROW BUSH.)

1946 Dunham 156–7, Obi weed = Jonkra weed.

obrafo sb dial; cf Twi *ɔbrafo*, executioner, forerunner (J. Berry).

1956 Mc Port (Moore Town) /obrafo/ name for the 'town crier', man who shouts announcements from hill top.

OBROUNI sb dial; < Twi *obŭro-ni*, white man. White man.

1954 LeP Port (Moore Town), White man—obrouni. 1956 Mc Port, Obrouni.

OCEAN JACK sb. The Amber Jack fish. It is caught only in deep water or the ocean.

1952 FGC StC, StE /uoshan jak/.

OCEAN PIPER sb dial; < *ocean* + PIPER. The blue marlin. ('Piper' refers, in terms of a smaller fish, to the sharp beak of the marlin.)

1929 Beckwith 33, see POT-COVER. 1952 FGC StC, StE, StJ, West, 'Ocean piper' we call them—same as 'marlin'.

OCEAN SHARK sb dial. Among fishermen, the large sharks that are found out in deep water. (A general term.)

1952 FGC Port, StAnn /huoshan shaak/ the biggest, up to 13½ feet.

OCEAN TURBOT sb; <*ocean* + TURBOT.

1854–5 *TJSA* I 145, Balistes maculatus—Ocean Turbot.

OCTOBER-BIRD sb obs. The BUTTER-BIRD, which migrates from north to south America in the autumn, and returns in the spring, via the WI, being abundant in Jamaica from late September through October.

1793 Edwards I 99, The most delicious bird in the West Indies is the ortolan, or October-bird..I believe that they are not in the islands till the month of October—At least it is in that month that they visit Jamaica in prodigious flights, to feed on the seeds of the Guinea grass.

OCTOBER PINK sb; <*October* + PINK[1]. The BUTTER-BIRD, formerly called OCTOBER-BIRD.

1847 Gosse 229–30, Butter-Bird. Ortolan.—October Pink.—Ricebird..In ordinary seasons this well-known bird arrives in vast numbers from the United States, in the month of October, and..assembles in the guinea-grass fields, in flocks amounting to five hundred or more..Dr Chamberlayne..says:—..Their note..during their migration hither, is simply *ping, ping, ping*. 1956 Jeffrey-Smith 77.

oda see *uoda*.

ODUM sb dial; cf Twi *ɔ-dɔ́m*, a kind of tree, the bark of which is used in performing an ordeal. (See 1927 Rattray 31, 41.)

1934 Williams 36, The Ashanti name of *odum* for the silk-cotton tree perseveres in Jamaica both as regards its name and its characteristic association in popular superstition with duppies or ghosts who are supposed to make the odum tree their usual abode. [1955 FGC Man, Maroons called the cotton-tree the 'stormy okam' tree.]

OFF adv gen; cf *OED* A 5. *T*

1. Following a verb, indicating completion of the action. (Often where StdE would use *up*.) *G*

1950 Pioneer 75, When him baptize off all of dem, him siddown so nyam dem off clean. 1956 Mc StE /iz nat him hiiting aaf di jentilman shiip/ *He is not the one eating the gentleman's sheep*; /in iiti aaf/ *He ate it up*. 1958 DeC, Off—the old use of this with /nyam/ has carried over to /iit/ so that *eat off* is more common than *eat up* at all social levels. Ex. /hin nyam aaf aal in bikl/—peasant; /him iit it al aaf/—country schoolteacher; *He ate off his dinner*—upper-middle-class Kingston professional.

2. Following a verb, making it more emphatic.

1950 Pioneer 16, Nancy see one big picture a Puss pose off eena de book. [*Anancy saw a big picture of Puss striking a pose in the book.*] Hear Anancy..'But tap, a wen since Puss get so high dat him can prims off himself eena backra book?' [*—that he can show himself off in the white-man's book?*]

OFFICER'S TASSEL sb. = SOLDIER'S TASSEL.

1952 FGC StAnd.

OH int dial; prob Afr, though coinciding with Engl *oh*. Cf HAY, YE. A syllable frequently used at the end of the line or phrase in songs, meaningless, but prolonged by the singer or singers for its musical effect. *BL G*

1790 Moreton 157, O! laud, O! Tajo, tajo, tajo! 1895 Banbury 21 [Mial song from c1842:] Token show da night, oh! Da fe you day da behine oh! Sinna o, no mine, oh! 1907 Jekyll 162, Bad homan oh!—bad homan oh! 1951 Murray 2, Day oh! Day oh! *Ibid* 24, A Chi-Chi Bud oh!

OIL-NUT (TREE) /ail-not, hail-not/ sb now dial; *OED* 1707 only. The Castor-oil plant (*Ricinus communis*) and its nut-like seed. *BL*

1707 Sloane 126, The Oil-Nut-Tree..It seems not to be different from the common European *Ricinus*. a1726 Barham (1794) 120, Oil-nuts, see AGNUS CASTUS. 1774 Long III 712, Oil-nut tree..Ricinus Americanus..The oil-nut plant is now much cultivated in Jamaica. 1868 Russell 5, Eil-nut. Oil nut, castor oil. 1952 FGC Port /hail not/ seeds for /kyastorhail/. 1955 *WIMJ* 160, Castor Oil Plant; Oil Nut.

OIL OF — /áil a/ sb phr dial cant.

In the usage of the BALM-YARD, a phrase characterizing the names of BALM OILS. Many of these are genuine terms from the pharmacopoeia (e.g. *oil of peppermint, oil of cade, oil of origanum*, etc.), but others are 'magical', using religious terminology (as, *oil of Calvary, oil of salvation, oil of Virgin Mary*, etc.) or other terms suggesting their power or its effect (as, *oil of power, compellance, compliance, cat-o'-nine, dead-man, death, love*, etc.); some of the last are phrases to induce the retention of a lover or a lover's return, the disposal of a rival, luck in gambling, and so on (as *oil of stay-with-me, oil of come-back, oil of kill-him-dead, oil of bound-to-win*, etc.). These names are given to concoctions mixed with pharmaceutical odds and ends and herb medicines, and such effect as they may have is largely psychosomatic. (This kind of formation is not unknown elsewhere—cf Partridge s.v. oil: *oil of angels*—a bribe; *oil of barley*—beer; *birch, hazel*, or *strap oil*—a whipping; *oil of tongue*—flattery; etc.—but it is highly developed in this special sphere in Ja.) *BL*

1942 Bennett 29, An' den she..sprinkle it wid mus-powdah An' ile a-boun' fe win. *Ibid* 6, Jus' quatty ile-a kill-him-dead An' tro-pence buck-pon wall. 1943 *GL* Kgn, Ile a come back—healing oil and essence mixed; Ile a det—militated [?methylated] spirit; Ile af lub—Sweet oil and honey mixed. 1952 Kerr 102, The more exotic elements such as oil of come back. 1953 Moore 195, Aitai's color is light green or 'isle of trove'. 1955 Bennett *Long mout Doris*, For tropence ile-a-stay-wid-me Jus rub eena him head An him an her couldn' part at all So till one a dem dead.

OIL-PALM sb; *OED* 1866 only. Formerly called the PALM-OIL TREE.

1864 Grisebach 786, Oil-palm: *Elæis guineensis*.

OIL-PLANT sb arch; *OED* 1848. = WANGLA.

1756 Browne 270, Sesamum 1..The Vanglo, or Oil-plant. 1814 Lunan II 251, Vanglo, or Oil-Plant..The leaves are of a very mucilaginous nature, as well as the seeds, and the emulsion of both have been recommended as excellent remedies in dysentery. 1864 Grisebach 786, Oil-plant.

OKA sb dial; < Yoruba *ọkà*, corn, food made from prepared yam-flour, cassava, or other flour. (J. Berry.)

1959 DeC Han /oka/ a thick turned-cassava mush, served with a sauce boiled down from meat and okra.

OKRA, OKRO /okro/ occas /okra/ sb; 1679 ocra, 1696→ okra, 1756→ okro, 1801 ochrow, 1834→ ochra, 1913 ochro; Afr, exact form unknown—cf Twi *ŋkrũmã* (Christaller s.v. *kukuduúdùu*), Ibo *okuro*. *OED* 1707→. *BA T*

1. The plant *Hibiscus esculentus*, grown chiefly for its edible pods, but also having medicinal and other uses. Also MUSK OKRO. *G N*

1679 Trapham 59–60, As a food easy of digestion may well be admitted likewise the young Ocra an agreeable Food. 1696 Sloane 98, Alcea maxima, malvæ roseæ folio, fructu decagono. .[etc.]. Okra. 1756 Browne 285, Hibiscus 3. .The Okro Plant. a 1818 Lewis (1834) 152, The only native vegetable, which I like much, is the ochra, which tastes like asparagus, though not with quite so delicate a flavour. 1926 Fawcett 143, Ochra. Yields a good fibre. .The full but unripe fruit is an excellent vegetable. . either dressed plain or employed in soups. Inhalation of the vapour of the decoction is serviceable in allaying cough, hoarseness. .[etc.]. 1954 *FG* 469, Okroes.

2. In the names of other plants which, like okro, have a very mucilaginous nature: cf DINDI-OKRO, GOD-OKRO, *sipl-okro*. Also of especially slippery fish: cf OKRO PARROT, OKRA POLL, s OKRA FISH, s OKRA PATY.

OKRA POLL sb dial; <OKRA 2 + *poll* (as in poll-parrot? The wrasse is often classed by local fishermen as a PARROT). See quot.

1950 Smith 189, *Halichoeres garnoti*, the coral wrasse, is another attractive species. .it looks as if its colours have been painted on. The fisherfolk around St Mary, however, completely 'deglamourize' this fish by naming it 'okra poll' because it is slimy to touch as is boiled okra.

OKRO PARROT sb dial; <OKRO 2 + PARROT. A variety of the PARROT or similar fish—cf OKRA POLL.

1952 FGC Port, StM /ókro párat/—thin, flat fish—/swipl/ [i.e. slippery].

OLD-BADS /uol-bedz/ sb dial; <*old* + *bad* (*EDD* sb[2], Any article of clothing—Shet. Is.; *SND* Bad(d), Baud).

1958 DeC StT /uol-bedz/ ragged old clothes.

OLD BOY sb dial; perh suggesting the priority or stand-by quality of the wild yam, to which recourse is had when other food sources fail. (The sp is 'phonetic': /bwaai/.)

1954 LeP StE, Wild yam, Old Buoy.

OLD-BOY TREE sb dial; cf prec. See quot.

1952 FGC Tre /huol bwaai trii/—banana tree grown in poor soil with a bunch that shoots straight up.

OLD BROKE /uol brok/ sb dial; prob <*old* + BROKE for *broken*, but poss infl by *brock* (*EDD* sb[5] 2), or *broch* (*SND* n[2]).

1958 DeC Tre /uol brok/—old ragged work clothes.

OLD BUBA /uol búba/ sb dial; <*old* + BUBA.

1956 Mc Man /uol búba/ an old person who acts over-young.

OLD-CERASEE /ùol sórosi/ sb dial; <*old* + CERASEE. An old woman who is 'bitter as cerasee', nagging, uncontrolled. (Cf OUTLAW.)

1943 *GL* StM, Ole surrosy, nagging old woman. 1955 FGC Man /ùol sórosi/ old woman who is bitter, out of order, outlaw.

OLD DAMPA /uol dampa/ sb dial; <*old* + an unknown word; but cf DAMPA, vitality.

1958 DeC Man /uol dampa/ old ragged work clothes.

OLDER HEADS sb dial; cf *OED head sb* 7, but nothing very close to this is recorded since 17th cent. The old people of a community. (Common in Ja dial, but also used in Antigua, St Vincent, *BL*, *T*.)

1957 LeP StAnd /di huola hedz-dem wud sie dat/.

OLD HAG see next.

OLD-HIGE /ùol háig/ sb dial; <*old* + HIGE, hag. 1. A witch or OLD-WITCH; in popular stories and superstition she was said to take off her skin and fly at night (cf *kin-oul*) to suck people's (esp babies') blood (cf OLD SUCK). In this connection note the 'bat' in quot 1943. Cf *OED hag* 2. *BL G*

1895 Banbury 33–4, The locked jaw was always believed an invariable sign of the suck of an old hag. .The strangest thing in connection with this superstition is, that it was believed to be the living that acted the part of the 'old hige'. Women who were addicted to it had the power of divesting themselves of their skins, and with raw bodies issued out at nights in quest of blood. .Up to now any old shrivelled woman with skinny fingers and raw eyes is suspected of being a sucking hag in some parts of Jamaica and is feared accordingly. 1929 Beckwith 99, Old Hige is still a menace to infants in Jamaica, and it is from fear of her visit that they are guarded by a blue cross on the ninth night after birth. 1943 *GL* Kgn, Ol-hige, a sorceress. A bat whose appearance portends evil. 1956 Mc Man, The Old Hige could fly, change her skin, and take it off.

2. A nagging old woman. (Cf *OED hag* 3.)

1943 *GL* Clar, StT, Ole High, Ole Ige, a miserable person. 1954 LeP StAnn, StE, Nagging old woman—Ol' hige, Old higue. 1956 Mc Man, Port, StE, Ole Haig—a nagging old woman. *BL G*

3. A firefly. (Cf *OED hag* 4a.)

1958 DeC StT /uol haig/—small firefly. 1958 FGC StT, see HIGE sb 2.

OLD HIGUE see prec.

OLD JOE /úol júo/ sb dial. The pelican.

c 1915 FGC StAnd, Ol' Joe, pelican. 1943 *GL* StAnn, Olejoe, a pelican. 1952 FGC StAnn, StT, West /úol júo/—/pílikin/. 1956 Jeffrey-Smith 131 (St Catherine), Old Joe.

OLD JOHN /uol jan/ sb dial; cf similar appellations for the Devil, as, Old Nick, Old Boy, etc.

1943 *GL* StAnd, Ole Jan, devil.

OLD MAN sb[1], also attrib; cf *OED* 3 1694→.
1. The bird *Hyetornis pluvialis*, also called HUNTER, RAIN BIRD. (Found only in Jamaica.) *N*

1694 Ray in *Lett. Lit. Men* 200, The referring of the Old-men, or Rain-fowls, to the Cuckow. [From *OED*.] 1725 Sloane 313, Cuculus major, rostro longiore & magis recto. .Another Sort of Raine-Bird, or Old-Man. .They are call'd Old-Men from the light brown, or grey Colour their downy Feathers are of. 1873 Rampini 163, The old-man bird, with its long tail and slow solemn flight, every now and then appeared from out the branches of the cedar trees. 1952 FGC StAnd /húolman bórd/ darkish colour, says [high pitch:] ku-ku-ku-ku [low pitch:] ku-ku-ku-ku-ku-ku. Also Man /uol-man bod/ StAnn; StM /uol man bord/; StT, Old-man bird, big, brownish, long tail, almost size of ringtail, catch lizard in tree.

2. Either of two fish: see quot.

1950 Smith, Old man, *Abudefduf taurus*, *Microspathodon chrysurus*, Whitehouse [West].

OLD MAN sb[2] dial cant; prob <*old man* = the Devil. In the jargon of Revivalists, a spirit that 'possesses' a person at a Revival meeting.

1953 Moore 59.

(OLD-)MAN-BITTER-BUSH sb. See quots.

1927 Beckwith 23, Old-man-bitter-bush. *Vernonia arborescens*. .Take as tea for colic. 1953 *WIMJ* 243, Vernonia divaricata. .(Old) Man Bitter Bush; Fleabane.

OLD MAN'S BEARD sb; *OED* 1756 only. A parasitical plant, *Tillandsia usneoides*, having thin, curly greyish stems, and hanging from trees, electric wires, etc., like tufts of hair—whence the name. *G N*

1696 Sloane 77, Viscum Caryophylloides tenuissimum. . Ane Old Man's Beard. E ramis arborum in sylvis campestribus Insulæ Jamaicæ ubique dependet. a 1726

Barham (1794) 124, Old mens beard. 1756 Browne 193, Renealmia 1..Old-man's Beard. This slender parasitical plant is found upon the trees in many parts of Jamaica.. the sadlers and coach-makers..commonly stuff their pannels, cushions, &c. with this weed. 1864 Grisebach 786, Old-man's-beard (1960 Current, FGC.)

OLD MAN'S BEARD GRASS sb dial; <OLD MAN'S BEARD+*grass*: the grass presumably resembling the other plant in some respect. An unidentified plant; perh *Uniola virgata* when sterile.

1952 FGC Port, Old-man's-beard grass.

OLD MASSA sb dial.

1. One's master (an old man, or one who has been one's master for a long time)—as said by a slave.

1877 Murray *Kittle* 10, Put de tarn piece [stern-piece of a boat] wid ole massa han writin pon it, in a my coffin, too.

2. As a term of respectful or affectionate address to an old man.

c 1915 FGC StAnd, Morning, Ol' Massa.

3. God.

OLD MENS BEARD see OLD MAN'S BEARD.

OLD NAYGA BANANA sb dial; <*old*+NAYGA. A variety of banana—with a dark skin?

1952 FGC Port /uol niega/.

OLD NET sb dial; by metaphor, alluding to the holes in the net and the clothes.

1959 DeC StJ /uol net/ old and ragged work-clothes.

OLD NIGGER sb dial. A term of derogation applied to negroes by others: see quot. Cf. also NEW NAYGA. *G*

1954 LeP StAnn, Slovenly, untidy person, old nigger.

OLD SHOE SNAPPER sb dial; descriptive. A variety of the SNAPPER or similar fish.

1952 FGC Port, StM, Old-shoe snapper, same as dog-teeth snapper.

OLD SLUT /uol slot/ sb dial. The Savanna Blackbird (*Crotophaga ani*).

1952 FGC Man, some people call blackbird /uol slot/ old slut.

OLD SUCK sb dial; <*old*+*suck* sb, prob from the verb—cf *OED suck v* I c. =OLD HIGE.

1895 Banbury 32, It delights in human blood, especially that of new-born infants. In days gone by the 'Old Suck' (as she was also designated on account of her imagined propensity) was to be seen enveloped in a flame of fire, wending her way late at nights through the 'nigger house', or along the high road..Infants just born were guarded with the utmost care from the voracious creature of blood.

OLD TOM sb dial; cf OLD JOE. The pelican.

1900 Murray 3, The Old Tom and other sea birds floating..or perhaps rising suddenly with a denizen of the deep in its capacious bills.

OLD WENCH sb dial. =next.

OLD-WIFE sb chiefly dial. =ALEWIFE; also called NIGGER-FISH, OLD WENCH, TOBACCO FISH, TURBOT. Also in cpd names: SILVER, SPANISH, or TOBACCO ALEWIFE or OLD-WIFE. *BA BL N*

1892 Cockrell list, Old wench=old wife, *balistes vetula*.

OLD-WITCH sb dial. A witch, male or female, old or young. Transl Irish *sean-draoi*? (HPJ)

1873 Rampini 128, Now dere lib close to him an ole ole witch. 1907 Jekyll 65, One day there was a old-witch gal, an' Tacoma want the gal to marry. 1924 Beckwith 92, Part of the night, the Old Witch man comes in search of the girl. 1950 Pioneer 37, She had a ole-witch bredda name Downiwa. 1960 *CLS* 156 /nou ándro waz a uol wích bwái/ *Now Andrew was a old witch-boy. BL G*

OLD-WITCH GRUNT sb dial. A variety of the GRUNT, or similar fish.

1952 FGC StE /úol wích gront/.

OLD-WOMAN sb dial. A river shrimp or small crayfish.

1952 FGC Han /uol uman/—/shrints/ river crayfish without claws.

OLD-WOMAN BIRD sb; through correspondence with the OLD MAN bird. The Jamaican Lizard Cuckoo, of the same family as the OLD MAN and similar in appearance.

1936 Bond 176, *Saurothera vetula*..Old Woman Bird, Rain Bird.

OLD-WOMAN RAIN sb dial; prob by allusion to the proverb, 'Woman rain [i.e. tears] neber done' (1873 Rampini 182). A rain that continues for a long time. *BL*

1952 FGC Port /uol uman rien/ no waan' stop.

OLD-WOMAN'S BITTER sb; *OED* no quots.

1. Some species of *Citharexylon*: see quots.

1756 Browne 264, Citharexylon 1..The Old-woman's Bitter..This plant is very common in all the Savannas of Jamaica: it..seldom rises above eight or nine feet in height. 1774 Long III 821, It is uncertain as yet, whether or not we have the same tree [*sc* Quassi] in this island; but the *citharexylon*, or *old woman's bitter*, seems to have a very near affinity to it. 1811 Titford 79, see OVAL-LEAVED FIDDLEWOOD.

2. *Picramnia antidesma.*

1864 Grisebach 786, Old-woman's-bitter: *Picramnia Antidesma.* [1920 Fawcett 202, Majoe Bitter.] 1954 *WIMJ* 31, *Picramnia antidesma*..Majoe or Macary Bitters; Old Woman's Bitter. *Ibid* 29.

3. Species of *Eupatorium.* (The slight difference in the form of the name is prob not significant.)

1954 *WIMJ* 29, *E. triste, E. villosum*..Bitter Bush; Old Woman Bitter Bush; Hemp Agrimony.

OLD-WOMAN'S TOE sb dial. See quot.

1943 *NHN* II 68, *Bumelia retusa*?—Old Woman's Toe.. The wood is..coarse grained and yellow in colour. *Ibid* 89 [L. G. Perkins:] I have been told this name has reference to the roots of the tree, which are gnarled and knobby..very apt.

OLD-WOMAN'S TREE sb; *OED* 1866.

1864 Grisebach 786, Old-woman's-Tree: *Quiina jamaicensis.*

OLD WOOD YAM sb dial; prob descr of the texture of the yam, which is softer than that of NEGRO or WHITE YAM.

1958 DeC Port /uold wud yam/ one of the Portland Maroon names for the St Vincent yam.

OLD YAM sb dial.

1954 LeP StE, White yam—Old yam (term used when the white yam is found growing uncultivated in the bushes). [Cf OLD BOY.]

OLE HAIG, OLE HIGH, OLE IGH, OL-HIGE see OLD-HIGE.

OLIVE BARK-TREE sb bot; <*olive*, prob alluding to the fruit, +*bark-tree*, alluding to the use of the bark in tanning; *OED* 1866 only. The Black Olive tree, *Bucida buceras.*

1696 Sloane 156, Mangle Julifera..cortice ad coria densanda utili. Olive Bark-tree. 1814 Lunan II 20–1, Olive-Bark-Tree. Bucida..buceras. Barham mixed the bark of this tree with that of the mangrove, and says he made an excellent restringent styptic water of it. 1926 Fawcett 307, Olive Bark Tree. 1941 Swabey 27, see WILD OLIVE.

OLIVE MANGROVE (TREE) sb bot. The tree *Avicennia nitida*, which somewhat resembles the olive.

1756 Browne 263, The Olive Mangrove Tree..This tree is frequent near the sea, both on the north and south side of Jamaica; and remarkable on account of its cineritious colour, and the narrow form of its leaves. 1814 Lunan II 21–2, Olive Mangrove. Avicennia..there is only one species, a native of Jamaica. Tomentosa. 1864 Grisebach 785.

OLIVE PEPPER sb arch or obs; descr. A small *Capsicum* pepper shaped like an olive.

1774 Long III 857 [Among kinds of peppers:] Olive. 1814 Lunan I 357, Olive Peppers.—The fruit is of a beautiful yellow colour, and in shape like an olive, of which there is a pendulous and an upright variety.

OLIVE-SKIN sb. A colour term. *BA G*

1960 LeP StAnd, Olive-skin = Cool-skin; i.e. someone very dark but with a fine, smooth, and slightly purplish skin; very attractive.

OMAN, OOMAN sb dial; dial sp for *woman*. Cf *uman*. *BL G T*

1868 Russell 9, see MAN-COW. 1877 Murray *Feedin' 'Perrit* 4, Ef ooman hed sore it no look so bad. 1925 Beckwith 16 [Prov:] Ant follow fat, 'ooman follow man. 1950 Pioneer 16, Anancy wasa pass one ole oman yard.

OMAN PRIM sb dial; <OMAN + *Prim*, perh <*prince*: see quot, and cf MADA CANTINNY.

1951 Murray 18 [Song:] Dem sey dah me dah Cantinny, Dem sey dah me dah Oman Prim..[Note:] Oman Prim—A person of rank.

omi sb dial; <Yoruba *omi*, water, juice, sap. (J. Berry.) Water.

1959 DeC Han /omi/—word for 'water' common in Guinea Town.

ON /an/ prep dial. *G*

1. Against (a person)—freq in ref to quarrels. (Cf *OED* 21.)

1958 DeC gen, Create excitement on—to pick a fight with, arouse anger in: /duon kri-iet eni eksáitment an mi nou/. The use of *on* with this is regular.

2. In pregnant sense; referring to obeah practice: SET against or upon. *BL N*

1934 *Gleaner* 30 Jan, 'Duppy is on me and my shop' (cf DEALING STICK).

ona, onda see UNDER.

ONDLY /úondli/ adj dial; pronunc var of *only* with intrusive *d* produced by contextual articulation; cf *onggl*.

1912 McK *Ballads* 45, Dem wi' ondly try fe rob All de good you mighta hab.

ONE[1] /wan/ indef art dial; <*one* for *a*, *an*: cf *EDD one* 5, Sc. (OE *ān*, one, split in ME, and came into ModE as two words: *one*, numeral, and *a*, *an*, indef art. Ja folk use of *one* as indef art therefore in effect reverts to or reproduces the situation before the split.) *BA BL G*

1. A, an. (Unemphatic.)

1877 Murray *Kittle* 25, Mudfish say '..put me in a one packy o' water an I wi sing fe you'. 1950 Pioneer 16, Once upon a time Anancy wasa pass one ole oman yard. 1956 Mc Man /yu si wan hous tap die?/ *You see a housetop there?* 1957 JN Tre, Bredda Puntun dog a fight one nether woman dog name Rouby.

2. A, an. (Emphatic: an impressive, remarkable one; this is often heard from educated speakers as well as dial.)

1862 Clutterbuck 247, It is one crab, massa [i.e. a good big crab]. 1877 Murray *Kittle* 27, I wake Peter, My good sir, Peter mek up one face! nuff fe cruddle any milk! 1960 FGC StAnd, My dear, that was *one storm!*

ONE[2] /wan/ pron dial; cf *OED one* 22, 'An absolute form of *a*, to avoid repetition of a sb.: A person or thing of the kind already mentioned'. In Ja, used not only of persons or things, but, less concretely or definitely, of quantities, masses, kinds, etc. *BA BL G T*

1952 FGC StAnd, Throw away this water and put in some clean one.

ONE[3] /wan/ numeral adj or pron dial; cf *OED one* II: 'Emphatic numeral'; cf also sense 27 →1551. *BL G T*

1. Following and modifying a noun or pronoun: only, alone. *BA*

1803 Dallas II 165, You one buckra may pass this time, but the next we see we all fire. 1826 Williams 300, The girls [slaves]..told him he wanted them all for himself one. 1924 Beckwith 37, Anansi wanted the pig to eat an' he wanted to eat him one. [Note:] By himself, alone. 1955 Bennett *Me Dah Drive*, An ef dem tarra one no like it Den me one wi have de road. 1956 Mc Man /mii wan kyaang kyary-i/ *I can't carry it by myself;* /mék jéf wán táak/ *Let Geoff say it* [a poem] *by himself;* /jíen nyám aaf wan húol púdn him wán/ *Jane has eaten a whole pudding by herself.*

2. Single, same, identical, uniform.

1900 Murray 8, see GI'-ME-ME-BIT. 1942 Bennett 12, She is a sista to femme sista Lize, Me an' Lize nat wan mada, yuh know? [*Lize and I do not have the same mother, you know.*] 1956 Mc StAnd /di wan banaana hav plenti níem/ *The one variety of banana has several names;* StE /dem buot wier wan ting aal di taim—evriting wan ting/ *They both wear the same all the time—everything the same.*

ONE-A-MAN sb dial; see quot.

1959 DeC West /wan-a-man/ a large round boiled dumpling: one pound of flour makes one dumpling for one man.

ONE BLOW sb dial; <*one* + BLOW[1]. An unidentified plant, which has only one flower at a time.

1945 *NHN* II 143, 'One Blow'—a herb with purple berries, was very common.

ONE-EYE CUFFEE sb dial; for *one-eyed* + CUFFEE 3. A common, cheap fish: see quots.

1943 *GL* Clar, Wan-yeye-cuffee, shad or alewives; StT, One-eye Cuffe, shad. 1955 FGC Man /wan-yai-kofi/ herring.

ONE-FOOT MEAT sb dial joc; for *one-footed* + *meat*. Cf *jonjo*.

1958 DeC Port /wan-fut-miit/ name for edible fungus; 'meat with one foot' might be the joke involved.

ONE-ONE adv[1] and adj dial; iterative <*one*.

A. adv: 1. One at a time; one after another; singly in a sequence. *BA BL G T*

1924 Beckwith 1, Anancy..open his basket, take out the fishes one one, and say, 'Pretty little yallah-tail this!' an' put it aside. 1941 Kirkpatrick 7, Even dough is ongly a lickel bit we can sen' it we 'elp, becausen as de well beknownst sayin' go, one one full basket.

2. Now one and now another; one here and one there; occasionally, sporadic. *BA BL G T*

1820 Thomson 91, He told me the yaws came out *one, one*, and that they applied something that burnt his skin. 1956 Mc Man /dis iivnin nou yu sii dem wan wan, bot in di maanin yu sii aal siks wan taim/ *This afternoon you see them* [sc seacows] *occasionally, one at a time, but in the morning you may see as many as six at a time.* 1957 JN StJ, We got it but them don't bear, only one one pon one tree wha wi got.

B. adj: Occasional; isolated. *BL G T*

1952 FGC StJ, [Of garden-egg plants:] A few people have one-one trees—not so plenty. 1956 Mc StAnd /wán wan trii iz abóut di plíes/ *There's an odd tree here or there*; StE, 'Do you know Kromanti?' /úonggl wán wan niem/ *Just an odd word.*

ONE ONE adv[2] dial; iterative of ONE[3] 1. All alone, quite solitarily. *BA G*; *SC wawán.*

1927 Anderson-Cundall 93 [Prov:] Poor man pickney walk one one, rich man pickney walk gang-gang.

ONE TIME adv phr dial; abbr of *at one time.* At a time; together; simultaneously. *BA BL G T*

1873 Rampini 177 [Prov:] Man can't smoke an' whistle one time. 1956 Mc Man, see ONE-ONE A2; StE /somtaim aal siks did liv dier wan taim/ *Sometimes as many as six lived there together.*

onggl /óngl, hónggl, úonggl/ adv dial; often sp in dial *ongle*; <*only*, with *g* by articulative intrusion after a back nasal, and loss of *-y*. Cf ONDLY. Only.

1943 *GL* StJ, Ongle, only. 1956 Mc StE /iz óngl túu a dem buk kom yier/ *Only two of these books came here.* 1957 JN StAnn, Charles ongle sell coco.

ONGLE see prec.

ONION-PEEL OYSTER sb obs; descr of the shell. See quot.

1756 Browne 411, Glycymeris 1. Subrotunda, testa tenuissima subcitrina. The yellow Onion-peel Oyster.. This genus is distinguished by the hole in the centre of the under valve: the shells of all the species are very thin and delicate.

ONNOO, ONO, ONOO see UNU.

ON THE LOW adv phr dial; cf *EDD in the low*, below. Down on the floor: see quot.

1954 LeP Kgn, Bed—bed or mattress on the floor. (Sleeping on such a bed is sleeping on the low.)

OOMAN see OMAN.

OOMAN-BE-DYAM see WOMAN-BE-DAMNED.

OONA, OONOO see UNU.

OO-OO int dial; cf Twi 'óò, ô, *interj.* expressing admiration or surprise.' (Christaller.) *G*

1943 *GL* Tre, Oo-oo, African, approval.

OO-OU int dial; cf Twi 'ɔ́ɔ̀, ɔ̂, óò, ô, *interj.* expressing indignation or regret.' (Christaller.)

1943 *GL* Tre, Oo-ou, African, disapproval.

OPEN-GUARD (MACHETE) sb dial.

The type of MACHETE or CUTLASS having a blade gradually widening and (toward the end) somewhat bent back and the blade considerably flared. (Thus it is characterized today by the shape of the blade, though 'open guard' refers to the handle's being unprotected—which is the case with all present types of machete.)

[1803 Dallas II 58 [Of Cuban machetes:] The handle of the muschet is without a guard, but scalloped to admit the fingers and suit the grasp.] 1952 FGC Han, The flowers [of the SPANISH MACHETE tree] favour open-guard machete; StE [There are] two types of open-guard machete: 'Roslyn' and 'Mother Thomas' /úopm-gyáad/. 1954 LeP StE, Curved machete—open guard. 1956 BLB StJ /uopin gaad/.

OPEN PACKY vb phr dial; <*open* vb + PACKY. Fig. To express or reveal thoughts that one usually keeps hidden. *BL*

1943 *GL* Kgn, Open packy, Talk out your mind.

OPEN SHOAT sb dial; <*open* (but whether adj or vb is uncert) + *shoat*, evid a young pig (cf Engl dial and US usage); the whole compound should be compared with OPEN-GUARD MACHETE, and *shoat* with the other machete names BOAR and SOW; nevertheless the sense remains uncert.

1954 LeP StAnn, A straight machete—open shoat.

OPEN-WEB SPIDER sb dial. The kind of spider which spins a wheel-like web rather than a tube-like or other closed one.

1952 FGC Man /uopm-web spaida/—black.

OPERATE vb trans dial; cf *OED* 3 intr. To purge (someone). *BA BL G T*

1952 FGC StC, Cut off the point of the jocato plant before eating it, or it will operate you.

OPHE OPHE int dial rare; etym unknown.

1943 *GL* West, Ophe ophe, Yes.

ORANGE BIRD sb; see quots.

1. The Jamaican Spindalis.

1847 Gosse 231, Though not very numerous, this beautiful bird is well known, being conspicuous from his brillant colours..About Spanish Town, it is called the Orange-bird, not from its feeding on oranges, but from the resemblance of its plump and glowing brest to that beautiful fruit, as it sits among the dark green foliage. 1936 Bond 370, *Spindalis nigricephala*..Goldfinch; Orange Bird; Cashew Bird; Spanish Quail; Mark-head; Silver-head. 1956 Jeffrey-Smith 91–3.

2. The ORANGE QUIT.

1952 FGC StAnd, Orange bird: size of a grass-quit, favour /kinéri/; StAnn, Orange bird, same as orange quit.

ORANGE PINE sb obs. A variety of pineapple resembling the orange in some way: see CABBAGE PINE.

ORANGE QUIT sb; <*orange*, the fruit, a favourite food of the bird + QUIT. *OED* 1894 only. The Jamaican tanager *Euneornis campestris*. Also called BLUE-BADAS, ~-BAIZE, ~-GAY, ~-SWEE, FEATHER-TONGUE, LONG-MOUTH QUIT, OBEAHMAN BLUEBIRD, ~CUNNY, ORANGE BIRD, SOURSOP BIRD, SWEE.

1847 Gosse 236–7, Red-Throated Blue Tanager. Orange-quit..Towards the end of the year, when the dark and glossy foliage of the orange groves is relieved by the profuse golden fruit..this Tanager becomes numerous, hopping about the twigs, and pecking holes in the ripe fruit. 1936 Bond 312, Orange Quit..Long-mouthed Quit; Blue Baize; 'Swee'; Feather-tongue; Sour-sop Bird. 1956 Jeffrey-Smith 69–71.

ORANGE RIND MEAL sb obs. A kind of meal formerly made of orange rinds.

1855 *TJSA* II 41.

ORANGE WALK sb; <*orange*, the fruit + WALK. A grove of orange trees. *BL G*

1707 Sloane lxx, He..shew'd me the Woods wherein the Spaniards had usually planted their Cassada for the Town..They often in those Woods meet with Palisadoes, Orange-Walks, Limes, and other marks of formerly planted Ground. (1960 Current, FGC.)

ORELLIA, oriilya see ARALIA.

OSNABURG /áznbog/ sb dial; <*Osnaburg*; cf *OED*, and for pronunc cf *EDD*: *osenbrug*, Scot. See also and esp *SND*. *N*

1. Thick, coarse cloth, such as is used for prisoners' clothes. (Osnaburg was formerly given to slaves as work clothes.)

1956 Mc StAnd /áznbóg/; also StT.

2. Rough, shapeless clothes—e.g. made of sacking.

1956 Mc StT /áznbog/.

3. Very smart men's clothes.

1956 Mc Port.

OSTRICH FEATHER PALM sb bot; descr.

1951 FGC StAnd, Label on tree at Hope Gardens: Ostrich feather palm. *Chrysalidocarpus Intescens.*

OTAHEITE APPLE sb bot; *OED* 1858→.

1. The tree *Eugenia malaccensis* and its fruit, introduced into Jamaica in 1793. Variants of the name use both the forms *Otaheite* and *Tahiti*, and in the folk speech these have been further changed: cf ETAHOTI APPLE, ETHIOPIA APPLE, and quots 1952 ff.

1794 Broughton 17, Eugenia *nov. Sp.* Otaheite Apple [from] Otaheite [brought in] H.M.S. Providence, 1793. 1864 Grisebach 786, Otaheite-apple: *Jambosa malaccensis.* 1913 Harris 1, Apple, Otaheite..A very handsome tree with large, shining, leathery leaves, and particularly so when its branches are covered with a profusion of crimson flowers..The fruit is pear-shaped, bright red in colour, with a white pithy pulp. 1952 FGC Port /tiiti apl/ StAnd /hítioto apl/ StJ /ótoíiti apl/ StM /òtahíiti apl/. 1956 Mc Port /ítiúoti, húoti híiti hapl, huoti hapl/.

2. A secondary name for the JEW or JUNE PLUM, never much used. (This is the only sense in *OED*.)

1913 Harris 18, The Jew Plum or Otaheite apple is a native of Polynesia and was introduced to Jamaica in 1782 and again in 1792.

OTAHEITE CANE sb; *DAE* 1812→. A variety of sugar-cane introduced about 1791 to Jamaica from Otaheite by Capt Bligh. (Cf 1928 Earle 5.) It quickly became a favourite and long remained so.

1797 Braco 19 Sept, Planting Otaheite Canes on the Piece by Rio Bueno. 1957 *FFM* 336, The introduction of the Otaheite cane towards the close of the eighteenth century was to have equally far-reaching effects on sugar cultivation.

OTAHEITE CHESTNUT sb bot; see quot. The tree *Inocarpus edulis* and its seeds, introduced from Otaheite (Tahiti) to Jamaica in 1793, but never widely cultivated and now little known.

1913 Harris 5, Chestnut, Otaheite..This so-called chestnut is a native of the Pacific islands..The seeds are boiled or roasted and resemble the chestnut in flavour.

OTAHEITE GOOSEBERRY sb bot; from the place of origin and the appearance of the fruit. The tree *Phyllanthus distichus* (or *acidus*) and its fruit; current names are JIMBLING, CHEREMILA, and *baaj*.

1864 Grisebach 786, Otaheite-gooseberry: *Cicca disticha.* 1913 Harris 10, see JIMBLING. 1920 Fawcett 259, Otaheite Gooseberry..The fruits are not unlike gooseberries, but acid and astringent.

OTAHEITE PLUM sb. The tree *Spondias cytherea* and its fruit, introduced to Jamaica in the 1790's.

1802 Nugent 128, The Otaheite plum..it bears a bright pink blossom, like a tassel, and although some of the branches were covered with them, others were loaded with fruit quite green, others quite ripe. 1926 Fawcett 17–18, *S. cytherea*..Otaheite Plum..The flowers appear just before the young foliage begins to shoot in March or April. The fruit ripens in October and November; it has a subacid flavour and a fine aroma.

OTAHEITE WALNUT sb bot. The tree *Aleurites triloba* and its nut-like fruit; introduced from the East Indies, but never much cultivated and now little known.

1864 Grisebach 788, Otaheite Walnut: *Aleurites triloba. Ibid* 37, *A. triloba*..Naturalized in Jamaica..Antigua.. S. Vincent.

otahiiti apl see OTAHEITE APPLE.

OTHER-ELSE adj dial; cf *OED othersome.* Other.

1955 FGC Man, Irish potato or rice and other-else things.

OTHER-REST sb dial; cf OTHER-ELSE. The remainder. *BL G*

1956 Mc /di ada res av dem/.

otoiiti apl see OTAHEITE APPLE.

OTTEY sb dial rare; etym unknown.

1943 *GL* StC, Ottey, pot made from clay.

ou-di-du-dat sb dial; evid <*how-d'ye-do*+ an element of uncert origin, perh *that*, or perh some Hindustani word. A nickname for an East Indian.

1956 Mc Clar /ou di du dat/ a coolie; also salaam babu.

OUT vb dial; cf *OED out v* 1b →1653, '*Obs.* exc. dial.' *ODS* 1899. *BL*

1. To extinguish (a fire, flame, lamp, etc.).

1907 Jekyll 222, The brigade can't out the fire. 1924 Beckwith 166, He sees Water. 'Do, me good Water, I beg you out this fire.' 1952 FGC StAnd, Lamp-fly /hout/ de lamp at night. Also StM. *BA G T*

2. To put a player 'out' in cricket. (Note use in quot 1941 of a pleonastic adv *out* following the vb *out*.) *BA G T*

1941 Kirkpatrick 2, 'Im know 'im did stan' a good chance a gettin' out out fe sayin' it. 1957 JN Town-head, You noh out me you no.

3. To erase (e.g. the writing on a blackboard).

1960 BLB Man /a him out it out, tiicha/ *It's he who rubbed it out, teacher.*

OUT /out/ adv dial; cf *OED out adv*, esp senses 7 and 9—in Ja, however, *out* is appended more frequently to verbs, and to a wider range of verbs, than in StdE, to indicate extension or completion of the action of the verb. *BA BL G*

1952 FGC Han, Quok [a bird]..make a shrieking noise, warn out fish. 1956 Mc Man [Of an oil-nut tree:] /im ded out nou mam/ *It's died now.* 1957 JN, Teacher: Another pupil stole out her lunch. Boy: I see'm when im dia a eat it out, teacher.

OUT-AND-OUT adj dial; <*out-and-out*, 'complete, thoroughgoing'—*OED* B. Crude, indecent, OUTLAW. *BA*

1952 FGC Han, see *talawa* 2. 1956 Mc Man /óut-an-out piipl/ barbarous, intolerable people.

OUT-CHILD sb; cf OUTSIDE. A child born out of wedlock.

1873 Rampini 81–2, see BYE-CHILD.

OUTLAW, OUTLAWDED adj dial; the first form <*outlaw* sb; the second as 'double' past participle of *outlaw* vb, on analogy of such forms as *drownded*, *spayded*, etc. Indecent, outrageous, unrestrained.

1927 Stafford 41, Her song it was outlaw (fine folks say improper) But the music excuses the crude words. 1955 FGC Man, Outlaw—people don't control themself; wild; indecent. 1956 Mc Man /out-laadid piipl/ undesirable, barbarous.

OUT OF CROP see CROP.

OUTSIDE adj dial; cf *OED* B2, 3. Preceding and modifying a term referring to offspring: born out of wedlock. Cf OUT-CHILD, YARD-CHILD. *BL G N T*

1942 Bennett 1, Leah fadah outside darter son Wey dem call knock-knee Joe. 1952 Kerr 57, May has allowed her outside daughter, born before she married William, to build a house on the land.

OVAL-LEAVED FIDDLEWOOD sb bot obs. See quot.

1811 Titford 79, Oval Leaved Fiddlewood, Citharexylum Caudatum..French, Guittarin, and Bois Cotelet; called also Old Woman's Bitter.

OVER /úova, úoba/ prep and vb dial; also sp *ovah*. *BA G*

A. prep: Over to, over at. (Cf *EDD* 9.)

1912 McK *Songs* 118, We puppa ober May [*Our father is over at Mayfield*]. 1950 Pioneer 18, Ticks..go over Anancy yard; *ibid* 33, Anancy run ovah Dog yard go tell him. 1956 Mc StE (Accom), see BAWLING.

B. vb: To be over, to be finished. (Cf *EDD* 27.) *BL T*

1941 Kirkpatrick 15, Nutten wi' hender dis war ovahin' as quick as ever.

OVER-DO sb dial; <*over-do* vb. *BA*

1927 Anderson-Cundall 63 [Prov:] Oberdo nebber go a God. I.e. Ostentation does not appeal to God. 1943 *GL*, Oberdo, ostentation.

OVERHALE sb obs; <*overhale vb, OED* →a1641. A pad of woven plantain-trash thrown over other padding on a mule carrying burdens.

1823 Roughley 160, As soon as an under pad begins to fall to pieces, or gets wet, it should be replaced by the next pad to it, and a new one got as an overhale.

OVERHEAD RAIN sb dial.

1952 FGC StC, Overhead rain—a light rain; falls and stops.

OVERLOOK vb[1]; cf *OED* 3, 'now *rare* or *arch*.', but still the usual meaning in Ja, Barbados, and elsewhere in WI. To look (something) over or through; to peruse. *BA BL G*

1960 LeP StAnd, 'He overlooked my script' means, not he ignored it, but he read through it. I first noticed this from Frank Collymore in Barbados, and confirmed it with Shirley J. Reid and others in Jamaica.

OVERLOOK vb[2] dial; cf *OED* 7 →1895. To look at a living thing in such a way (e.g. through the 'evil eye') that one affects it adversely. (Babies that do not thrive are often thought, among the folk, to have been 'overlooked' in this way.) See next.

1952 FGC StM, Somebody overlook di baby, mek it sick. Also Man, West, etc.

OVERLOOK BEAN sb; see quot 1857. The large bean *Canavalia ensiformis*, believed to have a protective or 'overlooking' influence on provision grounds. Also *C. altissima*.

1837 Macfadyen I 291–2, Canavalia ensiformis. Overlook or Horse Bean..They are commonly planted, by the Negroes, along the margin of their provision grounds, from a superstitious notion, probably of African origin, very generally entertained, that the Overlook fulfils the part of a watchman, and, from some dreaded power ascribed to it, protects the provisions from plunder. Even the better informed adopt the practice, although they themselves may not place confidence in any particular influence which this humble plant can exercise. 1920 Fawcett 61, *C. ensiformis*..Horse Bean, Overlook Bean, Sword Bean, Jack Bean. *Ibid* 62, *C. altissima*..Overlook Bean. 1952 FGC Port, Overlook peas, guards others; StAnd /húobaluk/ always plant at fence side; StC /húovalúk biin/ plant in banana plantation as green mulch, like a watchman; StJ; StT.

OVERLOOKING vbl sb dial; <*overlook* vb[2]. The action of harming with the evil eye. *BL*

1952 Kerr 31, If overlooking takes place the baby's clothes must be burnt, and some of the ashes made into tea for him..After his bath crosses are marked with blue on his back and on the soles of his feet to prevent overlooking.

OVERNIGHT adj and sb dial. *BL*

A. adj: That has stood over night. *G*

1942 HPJ, Yu fyace faba obernite foofoo [*Your face looks like fufu that has stood overnight*].

B. sb: See quots.

1943 *GL*, see CHAKLATA. 1958 DeC StJ /uobanait/—food left over from the evening meal and saved for morning tea.

OVERNYAM vb dial; <*over* + NYAM—cf *over-eat*. To overeat. *G*

1954 LeP StE, Me a ova nyam meself.

OVERSEER sb. Special senses developed on sugar plantations: see quot. *BA G*

1790 Moreton 79, He who is chief in the superintendency of a plantation in Jamaica, is called an Overseer; and in the Windward Islands, a Manager; and the Overseer's Deputies are called Book-keepers; and in the Windward Islands Overseer's or Negro-Drivers.

OVERSIGHT vb trans; cf *OED v intr*. To pass over by an oversight. *G*

1958 LeP StAnd, 'Miss M—— had it but she oversighted it.'

OVER-WATER adj dial; for *over the water*. Foreign: introduced into Jamaica.

1900 Murray 10, I mus in not go near a ober water tree das growin 'pon de gate way side. *Ibid* 11, De talkin' tree is a ober water duppy tree. [The *Casuarina*.]

OWL-FACED BAT sb; *OED* identifies as *Chilonycteris Macleayii*, but without ref or quot. See quot.

1851 Gosse 326–7, The Owl-Faced Bat. May 24th, 1846. A pretty and interesting little Bat came into my hands, a species of the curious genus *Chilonycteris*.* *This closely resembles *Ch. Macleayii*..It differs, however, from that species in some of its admeasurements, and remarkably in colour. I therefore consider it distinct, and would thus describe it. *Chilonycteris grisea*, Mihi.

OWL-GAL sb dial or slang; the allusion is prob to the owl's nocturnal prowling.

1943 *GL* Clar, Han, Owl-gal, lewd type of girl.

OX-EYE BEAN sb; *OED* ref 1858. The climbing vine *Mucuna urens* and its large seeds, which resembles an ox's eye. (For details on the identification, cf 1920 Fawcett 52–3.)

1756 Browne 295, Zoophthalmum 1..The Ox-eye Bean. This plant is very common in the inland parts of Jamaica, and climbs to the top of the tallest trees in the wood. 1811 Titford 84, The ox-eye bean called by the French Yeux bourrique, is the seed of D. Urens, common in the West Indies. 1814 Lunan I 382–3, Horse or Ox-Eye Bean. 1920 Fawcett 52, *M. urens*..Ox Eye Bean. Rare; in fl. Sept. and Oct.

OYSTER-CRAB sb. A crab which lives in the shell of the mangrove oyster (*Pinnotheres geddesi* Miers). *G*

1756 Browne 420–1, Cancer 1..The Oyster-Crab. This little species is generally found with the Mangrove oysters, in their shells, where they always live in plenty, and spawn at the regular seasons..They are very small and tender, and nearly of the same length and breadth, seldom exceeding a quarter of an inch either way.

OYSTER PLANT sb; see quot. The plant *Rhoeo spathacea*, also called Moses in the Bulrushes.

1811 Titford Expl to Plate VII 3, Oyster Plant, (*tradescantia*), n.o. Ensat. This curious plant is commonly so called, from the upper part opening and shutting like the shell of an oyster, receiving in and protecting the small white flowers at night. (1963 current. FGC.)

paagi see PORGY.

PAAH see GOIN' PAAH.

paan see PAWN.

paani, pani sb dial; <PAN+*-y*. A PAN with a large handle.

1943 *GL* StJ, Pawnie, Big-handle pan—a Clarendon expression. 1955 FGC Man /pani/ in StM, a pan with a handle; in StJ, a pan-tub or tub-pan.

paanz-beli sb dial; <*paunch-bellied*; *OED* →1733.

1955 FGC Man /páanz-bèli/ a big-belly boy, bang-belly.

paanzo sb dial; <*paunch* (cf *paanz-beli*) +*-o*, which see.

1943 *GL* Port, Pawnzo, a big-belly boy. 1955 FGC Man /paanzo/ bang-belly.

paasl sb dial; a pronunc form of *parsley*—cf /pusl/ *pussley*, /baazli/ var of *basil*.

1952 FGC StE /paasl/ parsley.

PAA-TOOK see PATU.

pacasa, PACCASSAH see PAKASSA.

PACCY, PACKEY, PACKI(E) see next.

PACKY /páki/ sb dial; 1833→ packies, 1905 paccy, 1925 packey, 1943 packy (paki, pakie, packi, pakke); <Twi *apákyi*, a broad calabash with a cover; also the whole calabash. *BL*

1. The calabash tree (*Crescentia cujete*) and its spherical or oval gourd-like fruit. (Two varieties are widely known.)

.941 Swabey 16, Calabash—(Packy)..Tree seldom more than 20 ft high..Used for cattle yokes, tool handles, felloes of wheels, ribs in boat building. 1952 FGC Port /paki/—leaf good for cold; fruit, bake in oven or fire; juice, and drink.

2. The calabash fruit, usually dried, scooped out and used as a container or vessel for carrying liquids, food, etc.; it may be the entire shell, or only a part of it, often a cup or dish.

1833 Scott II 371, They [*sc* negro children] had all their little packies, or calabashes, on their heads, full of provisions. 1905 Dodd 34, Dey nebber would ah guess in dis wor'l dat rum could ah ina wet sugar ina paccy. 1925 Beckwith 21, Bowl go, packey come.. 'When the bowl goes, the packey comes'; implying an exchange of favors. Three varieties of gourd-bearing trees are distinguished in Jamaica: the 'calabash' bears a large fruit attached closely to the trunk; the 'packey' is a small fruit attached to the branches; and the 'took-took' bears fruit half way between in size. The peasants use these gourds for water carriers and drinking vessels. The largest, Long says, hold from 30 to 40 quarts. 1943 *GL* all parishes, Packie, Packy. 1952 FGC StAnd, StAnn, StJ, StM, StT /paki/ small calabash, used around every home for cups, plates, pot-spoons, etc. 1954 LeP Kgn, Man, StAnn, StE, A calabash—paki, pakie, packi, packie.

3. Fig. The head or skull. (The fruit is about the shape and often the size of the human head.)

1943 *GL* Port, Pakke, skull.

PACKY BUSH or **WEED** sb dial; <PACKY (prob from the resemblance of the leaves to those of the calabash) +BUSH or *weed*. IRON WEED (*Pseudelephantopus spicatus*).

1952 FGC StE, Packy-weed, iron weed; Tre, Packy-bush or -weed, iron weed. 1955 *WIMJ* 160, see IRON WEED.

PACKY-SPOON /páki-púun/ sb dial; <PACKY +*spoon*. A spoon made from a piece of calabash; see PACKY 2, quot 1952.

1956 BLB StAnd /wi kaal im pakipuun—nyam iina paki/ *We call him 'packy-spoon'—he eats from a packy.*

PACQUIE see PACKY.

PAD vb dial; cf *OED pad sb*[3] 2b, 3b, *sb*[4]; *EDD pad* sb[6]. *BA*

1868 Russell 5, see JACKASS. 1956 Mc Man, To harness a donkey: /pad/—but /sagl/ a horse.

pada, PADDA, PADDER see *pata* sb[1].

PAEN sb obs; unrecorded sp of *pagne* (*OED*). A garment worn by slave children.

1823 Koromantyn 123, A country cotton paen, or petticoat. *SC pângi*.

pagro, pugru /págró, púgrú/ sb dial; cf Sp *pagro*, the porgy fish.

1. A type of lobster.

1952 FGC StT /págró/ same as 'black hog', a stumpy black lobster.

2. A kind of fresh-water shrimp.

1956 Mc StT /púgrú/.

PAHA /páha/ sb dial; cf Sp *paja*, chaff, trash. See quots.

1943 *GL* Clar, Paha, an old mare. 1955 FGC Man /páha/ a horse too old and sick to work.

paia-paia sb dial; perh <*apparel* aphetized and iterated. One's only pieces of clothing.

1958 DeC StT /payapai/ the only item of clothing owned; i.e. a man's only hat, his only shoes, etc. 1961 BLB 24 /si hou da gal-ya lef mi paia-paia outa duo mek rien a wet dem/ *See! This girl has left my few pieces of clothes outdoors and let rain wet them.*

PAIN-A-EARS /píen-a-híez/ sb dial; like a number of other herbs, named after the complaint it is thought to cure (e.g. FRESH CUT, NEDGE-TEETH, etc.).

1952 FGC StC /píen-a-híez/ see GOD-COTTON.

PAIN-COCO sb dial; <*pain*+COCO. A plant of uncert identity (perh DUMB CANE?).

1929 Beckwith 129, Pain-cocoa and china cane: plants used in discovering the identity of a thief and causing him a pain.

paisa /páisa/ sb dial; <Hindi *paisā*, a copper coin. (Cf *OED pice*.) Money. *G T*

1943 *GL* Clar, Piesa, money; Kgn, Paisa, East Indian, money; Kgn, Port, Pisa, money; also Man, StC, StJ. 1956 Mc Man /páisa/ money.

PAKASSA /pakása/ sb chiefly dial; cf Hindi *pakká*, cooked, boiled.

1. A sauce of flour, coconut milk, and seasoning.

1943 *GL* Man, Paccassah, a sauce coloured with anatto, made of butter seasoning flour codfish; Tre, Pacasa, a sauce made of flour and Cocoanut milk. 1958 DeC Tre /pakása/ common local name for a coconut run-down; also /pokásii/.

2. A more elaborate dish: see quot.

1957 *FFM* 145, Banana Pakassa (Bananas, fish, meat, coconut, vegetables, annatto, seasoning).

PAKI, PAKIE, PAKKE see PACKY.

PALAM-PAM sb dial; echoic. Noise, confusion.

1955 Bennett *Back to Africa*, see BUMP-AND-BORE.

PALANCA, PALENKA /palángka/ sb dial; < Sp *palanca*, a stockade, but cf PALENQUE.

1. A fishing device consisting of many small lines, with hooks, hanging down from a single floating line: see quot 1873.

1873 Rampini 169 [Quot from a newspaper of 1870:] Another mode of fishing is with the 'palenka'. This is 'a line of almost interminable length, with any number of hooks affixed to it by other small lines. A common number is three. The largest has 550 hooks on it, at 2⅜ yards apart, which gives nearly a mile in length of fishing line.. As each hook is cast into the sea it is baited with pieces of fish..'

2. A kind of fishing-net.

1877 Murray *Feedin' 'Perrit* 3, Georgey Palanca..pursued the occupation of fisherman. His real name was Smith, but the sobriquet of 'Palanca' was bestowed upon him by the rest of the craft, from a peculiar kind of net so called, to which Georgey was especially partial. 1943 *GL* StAnn, Tre, Palanka, a net.

PALANKA see prec.

PALA-PALA adj and vb dial; iterative of *pala*, etym unknown. *G*

A. adj: Badly washed or polished; dirty.

1943 *GL* Kgn, StAnd, Pala-pala, Not properly washed or polished; StM, palla, bedaubed. 1955 FGC Man /pála-pála/ not properly washed or polished—said of plate, clothes, etc.

B. vb: To half-wash.

1957 DeC StE (Eld) /de onli pala-pala it iina di waata/ *They only daggled it in the water.*

PALE-FLOWERED TURKEY-BLOSSOM sb obs. In Macfadyen's use (186): *Kallstroemia maxima*, which, with Browne, he takes to be a *Tribulus* (sp *decolor*). See POLICE MACCA.

PALENKA see PALANCA.

PALENQUE sb arch or obs; 1662 penlico, 1663→ palenque, 1740 palink, 1757→ polink; < Amer Sp *palenque*, a stockade around a settlement, esp one in the mountains kept by runaway slaves (Alvarado, Pichardo, etc.). Cf PALANCA.

1. A stockaded settlement of runaway negroes in the mountains.

1662 *Jrls Assembly Ja* I Appendix 20, There are likewise a penlico of negroes, about one hundred and fifty, under one Boulo, which are lanciers and archers. 1663 *Cal State Papers Col* 1663 412, St Jago de-la-Vega, Feb 1: Proclamation of Sir Chas. Lyttleton, Deputy Governor..that Juan Luyola and the rest of the negroes of his *Palenque*.. shall have grants. 1740 Leslie map, 'Negro Palink' and 'Old Palink' [shown in southern part of St James parish].

2. A small farm or provision plantation.

1740 Leslie map, see prec quot. 1757 White 86, 360 Polinks and provision plantations..540 Pens and polinks. 1774 Long II 44, A great number of polinks, or places applied entirely to the cultivation of garden-stuff, fruits, and such sort of provision, for the town-market. 1790 Beckford II 187, The provision-grounds in the mountains, or polinks as they are called in the Island. 1889 Sanguinetti 51, In old land conveyances we come across the word 'Polink' which would be quite unintelligible to most of us now, as it has quite fallen into disuse.

3. A poultry run.

1707 Sloane xvii, A Palenque is here a place for bringing up of Poultry.

PALINK see prec.

PALLA-PALLA see PALA-PALA.

PALLETTE-TIP LIZARD sb obs; cf *OED palette* 4 *zool.*, and cf POLLY LIZARD. See quot.

1851 Gosse 254, This brief visit to the north side made me acquainted with a little Saurian of great beauty, the Ring-tail Pallette-tip (*Sphæriodactylus Richardsonii*). Its ground colour is pale red; the head is marked with irregular bands and stripes of brilliant yellow..The claw is sheathed, or protruded at will, on the *inner* side of the pallette, wherewith each toe is tipped. *Ibid* 284, The Eyed Pallette-tip. A very little species of Gecko (*Sphæriodactylus argus*), the smallest lizard that I am acquainted with, is not uncommonly seen in the dwelling-houses and out-buildings of Jamaica.

PALM sb and vb dial.

A. sb: The whole hand. (Cf FOOT = leg, HAND = arm.)

1956 Mc Man /paam/—the whole hand.

B. vb: To grasp, take hold of. (This may be a mishearing or 'interpretation' of *paan.*) *BL G*

1907 Jekyll 92, Parson Dog get fairly upstarted till him run in the ring an' palm Puss an begin to fight him.

PALMA CHRISTI OIL sb obs. NUT OIL (castor oil).

1774 Long III 909, Where glasses or boxes cannot be conveniently procured, the calibash..thoroughly dried, seasoned, and rubbed on the outside with *palma Christi* oil, may answer equally well.

PALM-BUCKLE vb dial; < PALM vb or *paan* (with assimilation of *n* > *m* before *b*) + BUCKLE vb. See quot.

1957 DeC /paambokl/ = /takl/: 1. trans. To tackle a job. 2. trans. To pick up something difficult to lift: a heavy load /masu/. 3. trans or intr. To fight: /him an mii páambokl wid súod/.

PALM-COCONUT sb dial. An unidentified palm; see quot.

1952 FGC StAnd /páam kùoknàt/—bear like coconut but smaller; bigger than macca-fat; same leaf, but boughs not as big.

PALMETTO THATCH sb bot; *OED* 1756→. The thatch-palm *Thrinax parviflora.*

1756 Browne 190–1, Corypha 1..Palmeto-Royal or Palmeto-Thatch..The tree is frequent in Jamaica, and covers whole fields in many parts of the island. 1864 Grisebach 788, Palmetto Thatch.

PALM GRASS sb. A low grass with broad blades somewhat resembling palm fronds.

1960 UCWI Herbarium, Palm grass, *Setaria palmifolia.*

palmiino sb dial; < Sp *palomino*, young pigeon. An unidentified bird, evid a dove, perh the PALOMA.

1952 FGC Man /palmíino/.

PALM-NUT TREE sb obs. The PALM-OIL TREE.

1823 Roughley 419, The palm-nut tree..whose luscious nut gives a fine flavoured, thick red oil.

PALM-OIL TREE sb obs; *OED* 1705→. The Guinea palm (*Elæis guineensis*).

1696 Sloane 176, Palma, foliorum pediculis spinosis, fructu pruniformi luteo oleoso..The Palm Oyl-tree. Hanc palmam Juniorem è Guinea Jamaicam allatam.. observavi.

PALM SWIFT sb ornith; see quot 1955. The swift *Tachornis phoenicobia*.

1847 Gosse 58, Palm Swift..This delicately-formed little Swift, conspicuous even in flight, from the broad belt of white across the black body, is a very common species in Jamaica, where it resides all the year. 1936 Bond 202, Antillean Palm Swift. 1955 Taylor 84, The Palm Swift.. is a very small bird only half the size of its two relations. The name comes from the fact that the birds roost and nest in large colonies in palm trees.

PALOMA sb; <Sp *paloma*, dove. The Mourning Dove.

1955 Taylor 91, The Mourning Dove is called the Long-tailed Pea Dove or Paloma.

PAM prep dial; var of *pan* prep. *G*

1943 *GL* Tre, Pam, upon.

PAM adv dial uncom; ?imitative.

1943 *GL* Kgn, Pam, quietly.

pam vb; etym uncert: perh <*spank*, or from **palm*, to apply the palm of the hand; or perh abbr of PAM-PAM. To spank (a child). *G*

1955 FGC Man /pam/ a child to quiet him.

pami sb dial; var of /pani/ cp *pam* for *pan*. (The same alternation is found in some Engl dial—cf *EDD pamber/pander, pame/pane, pamel/panel*, etc.) Cf next.

1957 DeC StAnd /pami/ a kerosene tin.

PAMMIE sb dial; cf *pannier* and alternation of *m/n*. This may be the same word as *pami*.

1943 *GL* West, Pammie, basket. Also Kgn.

PAM-PAM[1] sb dial.

1943 *GL* Tre, Pam-pam, a river snail.

PAM-PAM[2], **PLAM-PLAM** sb dial; cf Twi *pam'pàm*, to persecute; *pam'*, chase away, rout, dismiss, expel; ult echoic but cf also *pam*.

1. A flogging. *G*

1943 *GL* Kgn, Man, StJ, Pam-pam, plam-plam. 1955 FGC Man /plam-plam/.

2. A quarrel.

1943 *GL* Clar, Kgn, Pam-pam, plam-plam. 1955 FGC Man /pam-pam/.

pampas /pampas/ sb dial; a common var of *porpoise*, which is also widely used by fishermen in the reg dial form /paapas/. How this var can have arisen is uncert: perh through blending of *porpoise* with *grampus*, or infl of W Afr nasalization of vowels. The porpoise or similar cetacean. *BL*

1952 FGC [Port, StJ, StM /paapas/ blows like whale; head like pig, hole in head to spout; same as /pampas/ spoot water, generally go in bodies]; StC, StE, StJ, StT, West /pampas/ shape like shark but tail is cross-ways; black, harmless, have pointed mouth with small opening; go in large groups, jump; cast young ones [i.e. viviparous].

pampi sb dial; perh repr *Pompey*, a personalizing name. *BL*

1952 FGC StAnd /pampi/—man-crab; big, white, male.

PAMPIDOSIA adj dial; perh rel to *pompadour* or to *pomp* + *-ocious*.

1943 *GL* Kgn, Pampidosia, elaborate.

pampiduo jak sb dial; etym uncert: this may be a variant of Sp *pampano*, + JACK. An unidentified fish, perh of the genus *Caranx*, or a similar one.

1952 FGC StJ, StM /pámpidúo ják/.

pampi pig sb dial; cf *EDD pompey* sb 1. A small boy; a dwarf.

1952 FGC StAnn /pampi pig/ a winji or puny one.

PAMPUS sb obs; prob in some way related to *pompano* (Sp *pampano*), a fish of the *Carangidæ*; the quot assimilates the *pampus* to the *paru*, of the related family of *Stromateidæ*.

1725 Sloane 281, Paru pisci Brasiliensi Congener, sine pinnis ventralibus. A Pampus. This fish..was almost round in the fore Part, and from its broadest Place decreas'd by Degrees to the Tail.. it was all cover'd over with white small Scales..It was taken at Old Harbour.

PAN sb chiefly dial. In Jamaica (as in Yorkshire—cf *EDD*) used in many senses where there is no connotation of shallowness (see *OED*), and where StdE would favour *tin*, *can*, or *box* instead. *BL G T*

1957 JB StAnd, Pan—A box, as in money-pan, meaning money-box. 1958 DeC StT, Zinc pan—a Kerosene tin. 1960 LeP StAnd, Cash pan—a cash box; milk pan—a milk churn.

pan see PAWN.

pan /pan/ occas /pam/ prep and adv dial; in dial writing spelt *pon*, *pan*; aphetic form of *upon*: cf *OED upon*, form δ, *'pon*. Upon, in any of its senses, including some archaic ones now more idiomatically expressed in StdE by *on*, *in*, *at*, *against*, *for*, etc. *BL G N* Tobago

1868 Russell 1, One man was ya all a de time da look pon we (looking upon us all of the time). 1877 Murray *Kittle* 27, Tarra tell lie pon tarra. [*Each tells lies against the other.*] 1907 Jekyll 12, Annancy..gone run 'pon him rope. [*Annancy has gone running on his web.*] 1912 McK *Songs* 75, see *sampata* 2. 1924 Beckwith 3, Brer Ant say he kyan't depon haste. [*Brother Ant says he can't, he's in a hurry.*] *Ibid* 10, Anansi..drop in de trash, an' Tiger was upon hard sarchin' an' couldn't find Anansi until t'day!] 1942 Bennett 38, She come a yard pon a cryin' Sey she lose har jab. [*She comes to the yard crying, Says she has lost her job.*] *Ibid* 41, Me deh pon hase, me kean tap now. 1949 U.Newton v 16, He would yell: 'Come this way, cashew players! Two 'pon one! Two 'pon one!' [*Two for one!*] 1956 Mc Man /fi mi kunu pan sii ebri die/ *My boat is on the sea every day*; /di íeraplíen a flái pan tap a di kloud/ *The airplane is flying on top of the clouds*; /in no for pan di biich de/ *It's not far along the beach there.* 1958 DeC StAnd, StM /bra nansi stodi a brien pan im/ *Brother Nancy thought out a trick against him.*

PANAJAR see PANYA (JAR).

pana-pana sb dial; iterative of *pana*, perh <Sp *paño*, cloth, rag, (in pl) clothes. Cf PAEN.

1958 DeC Tre /pana-pana/—old ragged clothes.

PANCAKE sb dial. *BA*

1959 DeC West /pangkiek/ not the same as the American pancake, but rather a large fried dumpling, about a half-inch thick; synon. with *jack*.

panchalam, panchalan, panchalang, panchalong, panchelam see SPANISH ELM.

PAN COVER see PAN KIBBA.

PANEL (BED) sb. See quots. *G*

1958 DeC Man /pániil/ a metal bed with springs and a decorated headboard. 1960 LeP StAnd, A panel-bed has solid head-board and foot-board instead of bars.

PANG sb[1] dial; <Sp *pan*, bread, in the widespread pronunc [paŋ]. *BL*

1943 *GL* Clar, Kgn (2), Port, StM, Pang, bread.

PANG sb[2] dial; see quot, but this may well be Sp—cf prec. A variety of sweet-potato.

1952 FGC StE /pang/ sweet-potato—from a Chinaman so named.

pangge vb dial cant; etym unknown. In the language of St Thomas AFRICAN cult: to greet.

1953 Moore gloss.

panggra /pánggrá/ sb dial; etym unknown, but cf *pagro.*

1952 FGC /pánggrá/ a small fish, same as 'fowl-roost'; gray and black kinds; have mess in belly.

PANGSHALAM see SPANISH ELM.

PAN-HEAD sb dial; from the resemblance of his badge to a metal pan-cover. Cf PAN KIBBA. A district constable.

1941 Kirkpatrick 39, Dem a scatter scatter demself lak w'en pan 'ead run dung dem gambler bwoy..an' dem all run diffran way fe confusion de pan 'ead. 1943 *GL* Kgn, StAnn, StC, StJ, Tre, Pan-'ead—district constable. 1952 FGC Han, StM /páned/; StM /panhed/.

pani see *paani.*

PANIA see PANYA.

PANIA or **'PANIAR' MACHETE** see SPANISH MACHETE.

PANICKLE, PANICLE see PANNICLE.

paniil see PANEL (BED).

panish helem see SPANISH ELM.

'PANISH MACHETTE see SPANISH MACHETE.

PANJABA sb dial; ? < SPANISH ARBOUR (-VINE); cf *panchalam, panchuok.* One of the medicinal plants put into a fever-bath.

1954 Kirkland 170 (Port), Panjaba.

PAN KIBBA sb dial; < *pan cover,* the latter word being the gen dial form *kiver,* 'Sc. Irel. Eng. and Amer.' (*EDD.*) A district constable—cf PANHEAD.

1943 *GL* StAnd, Pan kibba, district constable.

PAN-MAN sb obs; *OED* 1879. The worker who tended the evaporation pans in a sugar mill or factory. *G*

1832 Davis letter, in 1955 Curtin, see FEEDER.

PANNICLE sb dial; prob < *pannikin,* infl by dimin suffix *-icle.* A small drinking vessel.

1907 Jekyll 172–3, 'Take fe you panicle', take your panicle, the tin mug out of which the morning sugar-water is drunk. 1943 *GL* Clar, Kgn, Port, StC, StT, Pannicle, Panicle, Panickle, a drinking mug or can. 1958 DeC Port /panikl/ a small tin mug.

PANNIER or **PANNYA MACHATE** see SPANISH MACHETE.

PANSEABLE adj dial; aphetic form of *responsible.*

1943 *GL* StE, Panseable, responsible.

PAN-SUGAR sb. Freshly made sugar taken from the pan at the end of the process of evaporation; as it is also carried in PANS for sale, the name is now understood in this sense.

1774 Long II 272, The ladies of this island eat large quantities of it [*sc* sugar] in sugar-cakes, or what is called *pan-sugar,** and confectionary. *The syrup in the tache, or last clarifier, adheres in a thick crust to the rim, somewhat resembling brown sugar-candy. This is taken off, and passes under the name of pan-sugar. 1802 Nugent 70, see NEW SUGAR. 1905 Dodd 31, Pan sugar is really better to trade in dan rum doh. (1960 still known in the country where sugar is made in small mills. FGC.) *BA G*

PANT sb[1] obs?; cf *OED sb*[2]. A disease of horses: see quot.

1802 Nugent 110, The horse, which drew the gig the whole way, died of the complaint they call the *pant,* which is very common with horses not bred in the West Indies.

PANT sb[2] chiefly dial; < *pants,* trousers, the plural inflection being absent, as it regularly is, from the dial. A pair of trousers.

1948 U.Newton iv 19, The boys would say: 'Newsy boy, you pant gone up'. 1952 FGC StAnd, That's a nice pant. [From educated middle-class lady.]

PANYA sb[1] dial; etym uncert: the word would correctly represent the dial form of *Spaniard,* i.e. Spanish, but there is no evidence to support this. *Pannier,* from the shape of the drum, and perh including an allusion to PAN, is another (but unconvincing) possibility.

1929 Beckwith 148, The Myal Man in the cockpits, however, claimed that two drums are required for the dance, a big drum called *bon* or *panya* played with sticks, and a gombay played with the fingers.

panya sb[2] dial; ? < *Spaniard*—see PANYA adj.

1958 DeC Port /panya/ A person, especially a girl, who always wants to dance and never misses an opportunity to do so; carries a faint connotation of disapproval, implying lack of seriousness.

PANYA adj dial; < *Spaniard. BL*

1. Spanish.

1943 *GL* Port, StAnn, StC, StJ, Panya, Pania, Spanish.

2. In compounds: cf PANYA JAR, PANYA MACHETE, etc.

PANYA (JAR) sb dial; < PANYA adj + *jar.* A large earthenware jar, often 4 ft high, used by the Spaniards when they held Jamaica, sometimes as a receptacle for valuables; also large clay or other jars of this general type. Cf SPANISH JAR.

1895 Banbury 36, These 'Panya jaws' are said to be of enormous sizes..[They are] believed to have been buried in the earth, or placed in caves by the Spaniards when they were leaving the country. 1929 Beckwith 47, In old days the calabash and the great clay jar called 'panya' (Spanish) were the common receptacles. 1943 *GL* Tre, Panajar, a big copper jar.

PANYA MASHATE, mashet, or **mashiet** see SPANISH MACHETE.

PAP /pap/ sb dial; < *pap.* The sp *pop* found in dial writing is due to the freq misapplication of the rule that Std Engl *o* is rendered in the dial by /a/: writers turn this about and render dial /a/ by *o,* as here, erroneously. *G T*

Porridge. (The association with infants or invalids (cf *OED sb*[2] 1) is not necessary in Ja.)

1924 Beckwith 50, Fish boiled some hot rice-pop. Anansi said, 'It no hot enough'. *Ibid* 57, So after de dinner de pop was hot. 1929 Beckwith 19, 'Pop', the approved dish for the sick or for delicate children, is made by boiling the grated corn and mixing it with milk and sugar. 1943 *GL* gen, Pap; Port, Pop, porridge.

pap vb dial; ? < *pop*—cf *OED v*[1] 5b; also POP. *BL*

1943 *GL* Clar, Pap, cheat by tricks; Han, To cheat or trick.

PAPA-LICK see PUPA-LICK.

PAPAW[1] sb obs exc hist; 1707 1825 Papa, 1725 Papau, 1739→ Papaw, 1775 Pappaw; 1793 Popo; 'Popo'—the name 'applied by the

Europeans to any slave coming from the Slave Coast west of the Yoruba country, the region in which the Ewe languages and their related dialects are spoken' (1960 LePage *CLS* 37, and map, 39). *BA G*

1. As a 'tribal'-geographic name: the area west of the Whydah, in Dahomey in which the people called Papaw dwelt, the port from which they were shipped, or the people themselves (references are often ambiguous). Freq attrib.

1707 Sloane liv, The Negros called Papas have most of these Scarifications. 1725 Sloane 376, Its use was first made known in Jamaica, by Papau-Negros. 1739 Leslie 323, They generally believe there are Two Gods..the First they call *Naskew* in the *Papaw* Language.

2. A slave of this origin.

1774 Long II 424, see EBOE. 1775 *Ja Gazette* 25 Mar, Choice Whydat, Pappaw and Gold Coast Slaves.. 1 Papaw, 1 Coromantee. 1825 Bickell [Advt for runaway slaves:] Betty, a Papa, 5 ft. 1 in.

[**PAPAW**[2]. The tree and its fruit *Carica papaya*. Not specif Jamaican.] *BL G T*

PAPAW MANGO sb obs; <PAPAW[2]+*mango*. A variety of mango having some resemblance to the papaw fruit (papaya).

1837 Macfadyen 222, 1. Carrot Mango..1. The Papaw Mango, of the same size with the last, but the pulp is juicy, and the taste a luscious sweet.

PAPAW WEED sb obs; <PAPAW[1]+*weed*. =BELLYACHE WEED.

1725 Sloane 376, [Addition to 1707 Sloane 228:] The fruit is like the wild Cucumber, but much less. Its use was first made known in Jamaica, by Papau-Negros, and thence call'd Papau-weed. a1726 Barham (1794) 19, Papaw weed.

PAPAW-WOOD sb obs; prob <PAPAW[2] (alluding to the manner of growth with a single bare trunk and a tuft of leaves on top) +*wood*. The MAIDEN PLUM tree.

1814 Lunan I 475, Maiden-plum tree. Comocladia.. This is sometimes called *burnwood* or *papaw-wood*, and grows very commonly in Jamaica, rising to the height of from twelve to sixteen feet, but never to any considerable thickness. About the top it is furnished with many.. leaves.

pap chau see POP-CHOW.

PAPER sb dial. An official paper—AGE-PAPER, BIRTH-PAPER, FREE-PAPER, etc. *BA BL G T*

a1818 Lewis (1845) 69, Venus..had purchased her freedom from my father..but by some neglect of the then attorney, Venus had never received any title, and she now came to beg 'massa so good as give paper'; otherwise she was still, to all intents and purposes, my slave.

PAPER-SKIN MANGO sb dial. The BLACK MANGO, which has a thin skin.

1952 FGC StAnn, StJ /píepa-skín/ green-skin or black mango.

PAPILIO (FLY) sb obs; <Lat *papilio*. A butterfly.

1774 Long II 125, The beautiful fork-tailed papilio flies are seen in swarms..they seem ever on the wing, and sometimes venture to soar over the highest pitch of these mountains. *Ibid* 128, A great variety of papilios and curculios.

papisho, PAPISHOE, PAPISHOW, papishuo see POPPY-SHOW.

paplas sb dial; ?<*poplar(s)*. An unidentified tree with soft wood; cf BEEFWOOD.

1952 FGC StAnn, Call it /paplas/ in Trelawny; in StAnn and St Catherine it's 'woman beefwood'.

PAPOOSE PLANTAIN sb dial; evid <*papoose*, American Indian child+*plantain*. A variety of plantain (*Musa paradisiaca*).

1952 FGC StT /papúus/ French plantain.

PAPPAJUCKATA sb obs; evid an early form or variant of JOCATO; cf Surinam Creole *Papa-Kalalóe*, where 'papa' seems to mean a large variety of calalu plant.

1774 Long III 918, Pappajuckata [Index reference to p 100, where only the form Juckata is given].

PAPPIE-SHOW, PAPPY-SHOW see POPPY-SHOW.

PARACUTA, PARACUTE see BARRACOUTA.

PARAGAN sb? or vb? dial; ?<*paragon*.

1943 *GL* Tre, Paragan, clinch.

PARAGATA sb; <Sp *alpargata*, a hemp-soled sandal.

1956 RWT StAnd, Paragáta, clogs worn by Chinese.

parai sb dial; <*Paroid*, brand name of a kind of roofing material.

1956 Mc Port /parái/ used on roofs of 'town houses', like /tapralin/; Kgn /parái/ also called /táiga ruufin/ used on house roof; StAnd /párai/.

PARAMBLE sb dial; <*peramble* (*EDD* Irel.), metathetic form of *preamble*.

1943 *GL* Tre, Paramble, statement.

PARANGLES sb dial; in this form either sing or plur; prob <PARAMBLE.

1. Complicated or involved matters.

1943 *GL* Kgn, Parangles, affairs. 1954 LeP Kgn, Dem jus' done wid a big parangles: Parangles means a thing with a lot of implications or elements.

2. Trinkets and over-adornments. (Cf BANGARANG, which seems similarly echoic. Or perh there is a blending of such words as *paraphernalia* and *bangles*.)

1955 FGC Man /parangglz/ trinklets; overdressed.

PARA-PARA sb dial; iterative of *para*, etym unknown. Cf PALA-PALA. A depreciatory term, the iteration furthering this sense: something poor, in bad condition, etc. Applied in a wide number of situations: see quots.

1943 *GL* Kgn, Parapara, rags. 1955 FGC Man /párapàra/ rags. 1957 DeC StE (Accom) /parapara/ anything in poor condition, e.g. clothes, house, etc. 1958 DeC StC /parapara/ soft and muddy; equiv to /poto-poto/. 1959 DeC West, Said of any plant which grows well but doesn't bear: /al di yam kom para-para/ the yams grew luxuriant tops but developed no food.

PARATEE sb; 1670 Pavathe, 1671 Perathe, 1774 Parrattee, 1826→ Paratee; prob <Sp *Pereda*, surname, the source of *Pedro*, in the same section of coastal StE (cf *Paratee Bay*, *Paratee Point*, *Pedro Point*, etc.). Early spellings show miscopyings from map to map: *v* for *r*, *th* for *tti*, etc.

Any of the inhabitants of a distinctive community at and near *Paratee Bay* in southeast StE. (Also attrib.)

[1670 Map in 1774 Long I, facing p 376, Parathe Bay. 1671 Ogilby, map facing p 336, Perathe bay. 1774 Long II 186, Parrattee bay..This part is swampy, and principally inhabited by Mulattoes, Quaterons, and other Casts; a poor, but peaceable and industrious race, who have long been settled here, and live by fishing and breeding poultry.] 1826 Williams 92, A marshalman..who had been shot at by a Paratee brown man who lived there. *Ibid* 95, I..related..the conversation I had held with the

Paratee. 1873 Rampini 160, In the great savanna of St Elizabeth's resides a curious colony of blacks whose origin has puzzled most travellers. They go by the name of Paratees, and build their huts in the little clumps of bush with which the plain is dotted. They have no religion, no tradition..it is supposed that they are of Indian origin. 1935 HPJ [From a servant:] Maroons are not Creoles, they are a different race; Paratees are a different race.

paravencha adv dial; <*peradventure. OED* '*arch.*' Perhaps. (Cf PERILVENTURE.)

1951 FGC Man /paravéncha/.

PARCHED-CORN sb dial; descr. A kind of beetle; it resembles a shiny kernel of parched corn.

1943 *NHN* II 70, Parched corn (*Cyclocephala tetrica*).

PARDALINE SNAKE sb obs; transl of species name. In Gosse's use: The Thunder snake, *Tropidophis pardalis*.

1851 Gosse 324–5, The Pardaline Snake..Four bands of reddish-brown run along each side of the back, and ten rows of round black spots.

PARDNER, PARTNER /paadna, paatna/ sb; the *d* form is the usual one, the *t* form adapted to StdE; evid abbr of *partnership*.

1. A savings club in which each member pays a set sum each week and each in turn gets the whole week's collection, lots being drawn to determine the sequence of the members' getting the total. (In Trinidad this is called a *susu*.)

1960 HPJ in *Gleaner* 9 Mar, If a man belongs to a *pardner*, he is under pressure to contribute regularly, while if he plans to put a certain amount in the Savings Bank every week, something will always prevent him. 1960 P. Lyn StAnd, I have to throw a pound for partner this week. I bag first draw in the partner. 1960 LeP StAnd [From a maid:] Can you let me have some money for a /paadna/? My /paadna/ money is due on Tuesday; there are twelve of us in this /paadna/.

2. The total sum of money collected in a pardner and paid each week.

1960 P. Lyn StAnd, I'm going to draw my partner this week.

3. Transf. A large sum of money derived from many small contributions—e.g. the prize won in a game of DROP-PAN. See also *tai shiin*.

1943 *GL* StAnd, Tieshin, partner. 1960 LeP StAnd, Drop pan is a kind of gambling Partner.

PARGIE see PORGY.

PARK NUT sb; etym obscure; perhaps a rationalized form of */pak not/, which would be a normal dial reflex of POP-NUT (see sense 2), an alternative name. (These may go back through folk versions to POPONAX.) The tree *Acacia lutea*.

1920 Fawcett 137–8, A. lutea..Wild Tamarind, Park Nut. 1941 Swabey 27, Parknut—(Popnut)..Wood useful for firewood and charcoal.

PAROQUET BUR sb. The wild bush *Triumfetta bartramia*.

1866 *Treas Bot* 1176, In Jamaica the name Paroquet Burr is..given to them [*sc* species of *Triumfetta*], on account of the green paroquets feeding on their ripe fruits or burrs. [From *OED*.] 1926 Fawcett 81–2, *T. Bartramia*.. Paroquet Bur.

PARROT-EYE sb dial.

1958 DeC Port /párat-yai/ a derogatory name for an albino Negro.

PARROT (FISH) sb; *OED* 1712→. Fish of the families *Sparisomidæ* and *Scaridæ*, but by Jamaican fishermen the term is used broadly to include other fish such as the wrasses (family *Coridæ*) which have the distinctive 'parrot mouth' and variegated colours. *BA N T*

1679 Trapham 66, Various Snappers..Sprat, Drummers, Parret fish, Dolphins..[etc.]. 1725 Sloane 281, The Parrot Fish. This Fish hath its Name from its Mouth, being like that of a Parrot. [Current in many compound names, which see.]

PARROT GUM-TREE sb obs. = GUM TREE (*Sapium jamaicense*).

1774 Long II 168, Among those..is the gum-tree, or sapium of Dr Brown, who, by some mistake, has described the parrot gum-tree for it, which is a species of manchineel. 1814 Lunan I 361, Gum Tree. Hippomane ..biglandulosa..It blossoms in the latter end of January and beginning of February, and is in some places called *parrot-gum tree*, which has been thought a different plant, owing to the difference in the leaves and appearance of the trees in its different stages.

PARROT MANGO sb. A variety of mango of variegated colours.

1837 Macfadyen 222, The Parrot Mango, an oval plump fruit, of a green colour with an erubescent tinge when ripe, juicy, with a somewhat turpentine flavour, subject to be infested with maggots. 1952 FGC StAnd, StT.

PARROTS' CORN sb rare; *OED* s.v. *parrot sb* 4 1857 only.

1854–5 *TJSA* I 64, Bastard Saffron, Parrots' Corn—*Carthamus tinctorius*.

PARROT WEED sb; *OED* lists, no quot.

1. *Bocconia frutescens*, now more commonly called JOHN-CROW BUSH, or *salandain*.

1756 Browne 244–5, Bocconia 1..Parrot-Weed. This shrubby plant is very common in all the shady gullies. 1801 Dancer 368, Juice of the Wild Celandine, or Parrot Weed. 1820 Thomson 54. 1914 Fawcett 223.

2. Said to be a name of Spirit-weed, but this is prob erron, due to mishearing of the folk pronunc of Spirit-weed: /pirit-, perit-wiid/.

1927 Beckwith 27, Spirit-weed. *Eryngium foetidum L.* 'Fat-bush', 'Fit-weed', 'Parrot-weed'.

PARROT WOOD sb.

1. A tree of uncert identity—perh *Cæsalpinia vesicaria*.

1811 Titford Expl to Plate VII, C. Bijuga (perhaps the parrot wood), nat. Jamaica.

2. = DRUMWOOD.

1952 FGC StAnn, Parrot-wood—parrots make holes, nests in it; it's soft and hollow.

PARRY-CART sb; etym unknown. A fly, trap, DINGHY, or similar light cart.

1942 HPJ, Fly—the parry cart. 1952 FGC West /párikyàat/ a dinghy: two-wheel cart for carrying people.

PARSLEY (PEAS) sb. See quot.

1811 Titford 123, Issong. The negro name for the Black Pea with a white spot; called by the people of Malabar, Ulinga; and in Jamaica, Parsley..a cure for all kinds of Head-Ache.

PARSON BROWN sb dial. A variety of orange.

1952 FGC StAnn /paasn broun/ big, reddish inside, sweet.

PARSON (CROW) sb dial. A white JOHN-CROW, either an albino one, or a young one before the head turns red. *G*

1943 *NHN* II 9, Parson—a John-Crow with white feathers. Like the Parson who was once invited to 'cut the cake' and was given the top layer, this crow is the first to begin eating the carrion. Also, the young John-Crow with head still black. [Paraphrased.] 1956 Jeffrey-Smith 2, Parson Crow. [Other names:] Jamaica Turkey, King Crow, Headman John-Crow.

PARSON'S PUSS sb. A children's game: The players sit in a circle and each in turn describes the Parson's Puss with an adjective, following the alphabet. Each player must repeat all the adjectives already said before adding his own.

1952 FGC Port (Pt Antonio).

PART-DAY sb dial.

1958 DeC Port /paat-die/ 9.00 a.m.–12 noon.

PARTNER see PARDNER.

PARTNER WORK sb dial. Work done by one cultivator for another in exchange for similar work done in return. *G*

1952 FGC Han, In cultivating yams—often do partner work.

PART-NIGHT sb dial.

1958 DeC StE /paat-nait/ midnight.

PARTRIDGE /páatrij, pártrij/ sb.

1. See quot.

1756 Browne 471, Tetrao 1..The Quail, commonly called a Partridge in Jamaica. These birds were introduced there from North America, and set loose in many parts of the island.

2. See quots.

1936 Bond 157, Ruddy Quail-Dove (*Oreopeleia montana*) Local names:—Partridge. 1952 FGC Han, Man, StAnd, StAnn, StM, StT. 1955 Taylor 91, The Ruddy Quail-dove is often erroneously referred to as the Partridge.

PARTRIDGE DOVE or **PIGEON** sb. The Ruddy Quail-dove (=PARTRIDGE 2).

1823 Stewart 78, The white-belly or white-breast, the mountain-witch, the partridge pigeon. 1847 Gosse 320 ff, Partridge Dove. Mountain Partridge. *Geotrygon montana*. [Gosse's name for the Mountain Witch is *Geotrygon sylvatica*.] 1956 Jeffrey-Smith 110, The Partridge Dove (*Oreopeleia montana*).

PARTY NEGRO sb obs. A negro slave member of any of the expeditionary parties sent against the Maroons and the runaways who had joined them, about 1730 to 1738/9.

1733 *Jrl Assembly* 120–1, Mr Arcedeckne presented to the house..a bill for raising and fitting out one or more parties, under command of Henry Williams and Ebenezer Lambe, to re-take the great negro-town, lately taken by the rebelious negroes..Resolved, That as soon as the party, to be enlisted or go out under captain Lambe and captain Williams, shall arrive at Robinson's plantation, the party negroes, now at windward, be ordered to return to their masters..Ayscough's Harry, Forrord's Jepong, Lawes's Fussow—very good party negroes, and have behaved with fidelity and bravery.

pasa-pasa sb dial; etym uncert: cf Sp *pasa*, it exceeds, it surpasses; the iteration is prob augmentative. (In various pidgin forms, Engl *pass* is used to show increased quantity, degree, etc.)

1943 *GL* Port, Passa-passa, plenty. 1955 FGC Man /pasa-pasa/ quantity.

pasa-pasa vb dial; etym unknown: perh iter of CB *-*pàc*-, to split.

1957 DeC StE (Accom) /pasa-pasa/ to mash up. =sipa-sipa.

PASAYRO, PASEARO, PASERO, pasiera see *pasiero*.

PASIAL /pasiál/ sb or vb dial; <Sp *pasear*, or Pg *passear*, to stroll. (Alternation between *l* and *r* is freq in the dial.) A stroll, to stroll.

1943 *GL* Kgn, Port StT, Pasial, Pasiale, Passial, a stroll, to go walking out on the streets. 1955 FGC Man, 'I goin' /pasiál/'.

PASIALE see prec.

pasiero /pasíero, pasíera/ sb chiefly dial; <Sp *pasajero* (Pg *passagéiro*) a traveller, a passenger: the sense is prob in origin that of SHIPMATE, or of Cuban Sp *carabela*, now weakened and less literal. A good friend or companion. *BL*

1943 *GL* Kgn, StAnn, Pasayro, Pasearo, a fellow, a friend. 1954 LeP StAnn, Passeiro—inseparable companion. 1955 FGC Man, A good friend: 'Me good /pasíero/'. 1956 Mc Port /pasíera/ a good friend. 1959 LeP StAnd, My pasero—my pal or best friend.

PASS /paas/ sb dial; prob an archaism: cf *OED pass sb*[1] 3c →1798. *SC pássi*.

1. A path, a road; perh a ford in a river—cf quot 1873. Also fig. Cf CROSS-PASS.

1823 Stewart 259, A master of an African trader.. inquired of a negro whom he met the way to Mr ——'s house. The negro recognizing him to be the captain of the ship in which he had been brought from his native country, eyed him with a look of ineffable contempt..he replied..'You want for make fool of me—no?—you can find pass go in a Guinea country bring me come here, but you can't find pass go in a massa house'. 1868 *TRSAA* 1 66, De two o' dem go out hunten. Annancey teck one pass, Green-lizard teck nudda. 1873 Rampini 177, If foot miss pass him no can find him. *Ibid* 179, Stranger no know where de deep water in de pass. 1952 FGC Tre /fala di paas/.

2. Transf. The aisle of a train or bus. (In this context indicates that the speaker is a country person.)

1942 Bennett 42, Move de bankra fram de pass Rose. 1943 Bennett 9, Yesiday ah put me leff foot In de pass an wasa aim Fe de conducta mash me pon i' An meck me sen' een claim.

PASS vb dial; cf *OED* 32 fig, 'to experience, undergo, endure..Now usually *pass through*' →1849. To pass through, survive. *BA T*

1956 Mc StAnd /dis hous páss about séven horikíen/

PASS /paas/ adv dial; prob abbr of *passing* adv. Common in creoles: cf *SC passà* <Pg *passar*. Beyond; more than; extremely.

1957 LeP (from BLB) in *Orbis* VI 386, Adverbs..The obsolete English word *passing* (for *surpassingly*) survives in such absolute forms in JC [*sc* Jamaican Creole] as /paas ogli/*extremely ugly*. *BL T*

PASSA-PASSA see *pasa-pasa* sb.

PASSEIRO see *pasiero*.

PASSIAL see *pasial*.

PASS MANGO sb dial; ?<PASS sb+*mango*. A kind of common mango; the reason for the name is uncertain.

1952 FGC StJ /paas manggo/ the Manchester name; in St Catherine, 'hairy-skin'.

pata, pada /páta, páda/ sb[1] dial; <Twi *patá*, a scaffold made of sticks on which plantains and other fruits are preserved; shed, hut; also *mpátá*, a scaffold, a litter, a bridge.

1. A framework hung in the kitchen or set up outside as a barbecue, on which food-crops, meat, and fish can be smoked or dried.

1890 Thomas 87, The men set to work at once to prepare for 'jerking' the pigs. Outside the hut they constructed a gridiron of green sticks about two feet from the ground. This is called about the Blue Mountain Valley a 'patta', while among the Maroons, and in the Cuna-Cuna district it is known as a 'caban'.. Underneath this a fire is kindled ..and the carcase laid skin downwards upon the sticks. 1943 *GL* Man, Pattah, a loft in the kitchen; StT, Potta, frail barbique of sticks or bamboo. 1956 Mc Clar /pata/ also /kreng-kreng, smuoka/ device for smoking corned meat over fire. 1958 DeC Tre /pata/ a temporary and makeshift barbecue for drying yam, etc.

2. A rough wooden kitchen table of boards or the like, for washing up, etc.; sometimes outdoors.

1943 *GL* Clar, Patta, a kitchen table; Clar, Pattah, a round wooden stand, table shape; Tre, Patta, table made of rails. 1958 DeC Port /pata/ a table (usually rough, with legs in front, nailed to wall in back) for drying dishes in kitchen.

3. A wooden frame to shade or protect young plants.

1958 DeC Port /pata/ a seed-flat or starting-frame for starting seedlings. Also StJ.

4. An outside kitchen or wash-place.

1943 *GL* StAnn, Pata, thatch kitchen. 1954 LeP Man, A washing place—pattah.

5. A rough hut used for shelter at a cultivation.

1943 *GL* Kgn, Padda, a peasant's ground-hut; Tre, Padder, hut; West, Patta, hut. 1954 LeP StAnn, StE, A thatched hut—Podder, Patta. 1955 FGC Man /pata/ temporary shelter. 1956 Mc West /pata/ a shelter built at ground, consisting of roof on poles, no walls.

6. See quot.

1954 LeP StT, Patta, an old dilapidated house.

7. A fowl-coop, a stand or other framework to hold a fowl nest.

1958 DeC StJ /pata/ a hen-coop built as a lean-to; StAnd, a bamboo fowl-nest (as described under BAMBOO POT); Tre, a hoop with a bottom woven of bamboo or withe, lined with trash, hung from a tree for hens to lay and set in.

8. A rough bed.

1956 Mc Man /pata/ a rough bed made of four upright pieces of wood with cross-pieces and laths.

9. A BUSH-BAG; see quot.

1958 DeC Man, StT /pata/ temporary bag made of grass or trash at the field.

pata /páta/ sb² and vb dial; prob <*paddle*, of which there is a Nth-country form *pattle* (*EDD*); cf esp *OED paddle sb*¹ 8a. There may be some influence also from *pata* sb¹, a very widespread word with many meanings. Cf CLAPPER sb. *G*

A. sb: See quots.

1956 Mc StJ /pata/ flat board for pounding on clothes being washed at the river. Also StE (Accom). 1959 DeC StJ /pata/ a wooden paddle used by women to beat clothes when washing at the stream; it is shaped like a ping-pong paddle, but with a handle two feet or longer.

B. vb: To beat clothes with a *pata* in washing them.

1956 Mc StE (Accom) /yu tek it pata kluoz/ *you use it to beat clothes.*

pata-kyat sb dial; <*pata* sb¹ 2+*cat*. A cat which raids the kitchen shelf, hence, transf, a thief. Cf *kamu kyat*.

1943 *GL* Kgn, Man, StT, Patta-cat, thief. 1955 FGC Man /pata-kyat/ a real thief, can't keep things away.

pat chau see POP CHOW.

PATCH-PATCH sb dial; iterative of *patch*.

1958 DeC StM /pach-pach/ old ragged clothes. *G*

PATIENCE adj dial; by conversion from the sb or by overcorrection of *patient* adj. Patient.

1873 Rampini 178 [Prov:] Patience man ride jackass.

pat kiba, pat kova see POT COVER. *G*

PATO see *patu*.

PATOAH dial sp for *patois*.

1942 Bennett 2, Me know sey she undahstan' Jamaica patoah.

PATOO, PATOOK see *patu*.

PATOOCK see POT-HOOK.

PATTA, PATTAH see *pata* sb¹.

PATTO, PATTOH see *patu*.

PATTOODOWDOW sb dial; <Twi *patú*, owl (cf PATU) + ?Twi *dódów*, to stammer, stutter.

1943 *GL* Man, Pattoodowdow, an ugly person.

PATTUX see POT-HOOK.

PATTY /pati/ sb; *OED* →1870. *T*

1. A semicircular pastry made by folding a circle of pastry upon itself over a filling of ground meat, fruit paste, or the like. (Also called a *tart* when made with fruit.) *BA G*

c 1915 FGC StAnd, Plantain patty. 1960, meat patties very popular.

2. See quot; dial.

1958 DeC Port /pati/—here meaning the same as /gato/ a dumpling which is rolled out flat, folded over, then folded again to produce four layers, then boiled or (usually) baked.

PATU /patu, patuk/ sb; in print usually sp *patoo*, *potoo*; <Twi *patú*, owl. (The vowel of the first syllable was originally *a*, and is still universally so in the folk speech. Forms with *o*—as those of Gosse, etc.—are due to a misapplication of the rule that Std Engl *o* as in *pot* is, in Ja dial, rendered by *a*; for the rule is not simply reversible.)

1. Properly applied to the bird *Nyctibius griseus*, related to the nightjars, but very widely applied also to owls.

1847 Gosse 41, The Potoo is not unfrequently seen in the evening, taking its station soon after sunset on some dead tree or fence-post, or floating by on noiseless wing, like an owl, which the common people suppose it to be. 1897 Heaven *The Negro Alphabet*, P for patook. 1943 *GL* gen, Patto, Paa-took, Pato, Pattoh, Patook, Potuck, Night owl; Potoo, night jar [this shows infl of book-learning]. 1950 Pioneer 31, Once upon a time Patto (night owl) was a very jokify an happy man an him get eena Bra 'Nancy company. 1952 FGC Man, StAnn, StM, StT /patu/ Han, StAnd /patuk/. (Stress about the same on both syllables.)

2. An ugly person. (Also a foolish person.)

[1873 Rampini 87, 'Him favour a patoo' (he is like a screech-owl)..[is said] of an ugly one [*sc* person].] 1956 Mc Man, Port /patu/ an ugly person (with comical implications); StAnd /patuk/ is a bird but they call people so /wen im fuufuul/. [1956 Jeffrey-Smith 14, The tiny curved beak seemed inadequate to the size of the bird, but the gape of the mouth more than compensated for this. Small wonder that in Jamaica a 'cuss-word' is, 'You mout favour potoo'. Another taunt is, 'You ugly like potoo'.]

3. Also attrib—see separate entries.

patu see PATU, POT-HOOK.

PATU-EYE sb dial; <PATU+*eye*. A derogatory term for an albino negro.

1958 DeC StT /patu-ai/.

patuk, patuks see PATU, POT-HOOK.

PATU LOBSTER sb dial; <PATU 2+LOBSTER. A type of sea crayfish with flattened body: the COCKROACH LOBSTER.

1952 FGC StM /pátu lábsta/ very ugly; shape of a roach, flat tail, no 'beard', no claws, sharp toes.

PATWA dial sp for *patois*. JC speech.

1943 *GL* Clar, Kgn, Man, Port.

PAW see GOIN' PAAH.

PA WILL, PUPA WILL sb dial; personifying name = 'Father William'. A variety of yam.

1952 FGC StC /pa wil, pupa wil/ yam, dig hole like coco hole, grows *up*.

PAWLI LIZARD see POLLY LIZARD.

PAWN /paan, pan/ vb dial; <*span*, vb (cf the similar /straan/ <*strand*). See *OED span* v^1 1, 'To grasp, lay hold of, seize. *Obs.*'→1513. Cp also Saramaccan *panjá*. Cf PALM. To take hold of, grasp, pick up. Also const *up*. **s.** *G*

1912 McK *Songs* 67, You..pawn you books an' went away. 1943 *GL* StE, StM, Pawn, take hold of, hold; StT, Paan, to clutch. 1950 Pioneer 24, So de po' gal open de door an Anancy pawn her up an carry her go gi de king. 1957 DeC /im gwain pan di wip/. 1958 DeC StT /pan op/ to pick up and carry something heavy.

PAWNIE see *paani*, *pani*.

PAYABLE (BUNCH) sb tech; <*payable*, that may or will be paid for (a sense not recorded in *OED*, *ODS*) +*bunch*. A 'count bunch' of bananas, also called simply 'bunch'—see quot.

1913 Fawcett 51, 'Payable bunches' or 'payables' mean nine hands and over; eight hands bring only three-fourths the price of nine hands, seven hands one half, six hands one-fourth. These are calculated into 'payable bunches'—for instance, 400 eight hands mean 300 'straights' or nine hands, 500 seven hands mean 250 'payables', 100 six hands mean 25 'payables'.

payapai see *paia-paia*.

PAYRIN see *periin*.

PEACE-CUP sb dial; <*peace* (implying death) +*cup*. A poisonous or infectious concoction used in obeah practice.

1934 Williams 126 [Quot from undated news clipping:] A notorious obeah-woman..known as 'Old Mother Austin'..died on June 25, 1892, after having lived and practiced her art at Llandewey in St David's..'Any way I send, death must come', is her boast. By means of a 'peace cup and spoon' she says she dropped off all the fingers and toes of a woman who had stolen from her.

PEACE-MAKER sb dial.

1. A male lover or sweetheart.

1954 LeP StE, Lover or sweetheart (man)—Peace-maker. 1956 Mc Man /píis-mieka/.

2. A policeman.

1956 Mc StT /piis-mieka/.

PEACE-MAN sb dial; cf PEACE-MAKER 2, PEACE-OFFICER.

1956 Mc StAnd /piis man/ a policeman.

PEACE-OFFICER sb dial; *OED* →1837. A constable. *BL*

1956 Mc Man, Port, StAnd /piis afisa, hafisa/ policeman.

PEACOCK sb dial. Applied to a male turkey.

1956 Mc Port, see *kwabla*.

PEACOCK FLOUNDER sb. The fish *Bothus lunatus*, which has spots suggesting the 'eyes' of a peacock's tail.

1950 Smith in *NHN* 13, The peacock flounder, belongs to that order of flattened fishes which swim on their sides and are adapted for life on the sea-bottom..Colour of specimen noted: Brownish with bright blue rings, crescents, spots, and dots.

PEADOVE sb; *OED* 1847. The dove *Zenaida aurita*, said to eat peas.

1840 Chamberlaine 19, Peadove—*Columba zenaida*. 1847 Gosse 308, The Pea-dove subsists on various fruits and seeds: pimento-berries, orange-pips, sop-seeds, castor-oil nuts, physic-nuts, maize, and the smaller seeds of pasture weeds are some of his resources. 1873 Rampini 164, Bald-pates, white-wings, and pea-doves were never wanting. 1955 Taylor 90, 92–3.

PEAHN-PEAHN, PEAH-PE-AH see *pyaa-pyaa*.

PEAKA-PEOW /piika-pyou, -pou/ sb; <Chinese, Hakka dial /piika-pyou/. A gambling game introduced and illegally run by Chinese: From a paper with 120 numbers on it, 30 are chosen by the throw of dice; each player marks 8 numbers on a paper, and if any of these corresponds to any of the 30, he wins.

1934 *Gleaner* 7 Mar 15, The police..were making a raid on a Peaka Peow bank premises and while they were holding those occupied in gambling there, in walked a Chinese holding a sheet of paper..with Chinese characters all over it. It turned out that the sheet of paper was..a vast number of peaka peow tickets. 1943 *GL* Kgn, Port, StAnd, StAnn, StC, Peaka-peow, Chinese lottery. ?1948 Calypso Tunes *Big Matty*, Me win Peaka Peow de odder day.

PEANIE see PEENY.

PEAN-PEAN see *pyaa-pyaa*.

PEAR /pie, pier/ sb. The usual term for the AVOCADO PEAR. *BL G*

PEAR-WALK sb. A grove of PEAR trees; cf WALK.

1958 DeC StT /pier-waak/.

PEAR-WITHE sb. A twining shrub in some way thought to resemble the PEAR: see quot.

1864 Grisebach 786, Pear-withe: *Tanæcium Jaroba*.

PEAS-WALK sb; <*peas*+WALK. A field of peas. (Appropriate for GUNGO PEAS, which grow on shrubs.)

1924 Beckwith 25, Anansi..tell them that he was about to die, an' he ask them this last request, that they bury him in the mids' of the peas-walk.

PEAW-PEAW see *pyaa-pyaa*.

PEBBAY sb dial rare; etym unknown.

1943 *GL* Kgn, Pebbay, Mix-up, quarrel.

PECATEM adj dial rare; etym unknown.

1943 *GL* Tre, Pecătem, not heavy.

PECHEERE, PECHEREE see PETCHARY.

PECK-PECK adv dial; perh suggesting chickens' manner of eating.

1. See quot.

1943 *GL* West, Peck-peck, God willing.

2. Vigorously.

1955 FGC Man /pek-pek/ 'I'm going to in it peck-peck; *must* have part'.

PECKY-PECKY see PICKY-PICKY.

PECTA sb dial; aphetic form.

1868 Russell 5, Pecta—Inspector.

PEDITA see *pitieta*.

PEE-GEE /píiji/ sb and vb; from pronunc of the letters 'P-G', abbr for 'Put-down-Go-'long' the name of a game, derived from the phrase used as a challenge during the game.

A. sb: A children's game: see quot, and cf *kontapiichi.*

1959 D. Macdonald Clar (Chapelton), Pee-Gee is the way we pronounced it at school. My own theory is that it is related to the challenge 'Put-down-Go-along', a sort of game called by us 'Puddung Gollang'. It is the result of one who has been unfortunate to be 'peegeed'. The other word which was pronounced 'kuntun' is sometimes confused with Pee-gee. Pee-gee was a game usually entered into for a period of a week or more. To 'join pee-gee' with another, both parties link their little fingers together and affirm their intention to abide by the conditions. Then a witness or arbitrator strikes a sharp blow with his hand on the joined fingers separating them, after which the pact comes into force. This means that one must continually be on guard not to be caught carrying any articles without having the little finger crossed over the fourth finger, for if the other party or parties should suddenly exhibit the sign and call out 'Pee-Gee' and you can't exhibit a counter-sign, all articles being carried become the property of the other (school appliances are exempt)..On the other hand 'Kuntun' refers to the crossing of the third finger over the second, but being so easily done, was not much played.

B. vb: To force a player of PEE-GEE to 'put-down-go-along'—i.e. to give up his possessions—by calling out 'Pee-gee' when he does not have his fingers crossed (see quot above).

PEEL-A'READY sb dial; for *peeled already.* Cf STRIP-ME-NAKED. Flour already prepared (alluding by contrast to flour prepared in the old way laboriously by hand).

1943 *GL* StM, Peel-a-ready, flour. 1954 LeP StAnn, Flour made from dried cassava—Peel already flour. 1955 FGC Man /piil arédi/—flour—no waste!

PEEL-HEAD /piil-ed/ adj dial; for *peeled-headed.* Bald. Also attrib. *BL*

1927 Anderson-Cundall 73, see *piipii.* 1950 Pioneer 21, Anancy sey, 'Mawning Sista Peel-head Fowl, weh you goin'?' Hear Peel-head: 'Me just going roun to de barba..'. Anancy [say]..'Lawd a Massi, me noh mean fe ceitful, but is how Peel-head a goh a barba an she noh got a "kench" a hair pon her head'. *Ibid* 81, One unconscionable peel-head johncrow Come tief it away. 1956 Mc Port /piil-ed/—same as /baal-ed/.

PEEL-NECK (FOWL) sb dial. A SENSAY FOWL. *BL G*

1934 Williams 34, see SENSAY FOWL. 1952 FGC StAnd, StAnn, StT, West /piilnek/ fowl. 1956 Mc Kgn, Port, StAnd, StT /piilnek/ fowl—a species of fowl that has no feathers on its neck.

PEEL-SKIN sb dial; <*peel* vb + *skin* sb; cf SKIN-FISH.

1958 DeC StT /piil-skin/ another name for turbot, so called because you peel off the skin instead of scaling.

PEENIE, PEENIE-WALLIE see PEENY, PEENY-WALLY. *BA*

PEENY sb[1]; prob abbr of PEENY-WALLY. *BL*

1. A large click-beetle (*Pyrophorus plagiophthalmus*) having two luminous spots on its head, often taken to be its eyes. The term is also freq applied to the smaller firefly (cf BLINKY, WINKY, etc.) with an intermittent light beneath its 'tail'.

1907 Jekyll 184, 'Peeny' is the Candlefly, which shines like my donkey's coat. 1912 McK *Songs* 33, Passin' by de peenies* sheddin' greenish light..*Fireflies. 1942 *GL* Clar, Kgn, Man, StAnn, StC, StM, West (i.e. chiefly in central parishes), Peanie, Peenie, Penie—a firefly. 1952 FGC Man /piini/ = /ka-pe/ and (old-time) 'candlefly'; Tre /piini/—two bright eyes, same as 'blinky'; West /piini/ but 'moony' more common. 1956 Mc Man /piini/—same as /wingki/ is bigger than /strienja/ and shows its light while flying.

2. See quot. (A rare, local meaning.)

1958 DeC Port /piini/—here meaning an insect which shines no light but gives out a distinctive 'bawl' something like /piiiu, piiiu/.

PEENY sb[2] dial; aphetic form of [sə'pinɪ], a common pronunc (in US etc.) of *subpœna.*

1943 *GL* StAnd, Peeny, subpœna.

PEENY /piini/ adj dial; prob var of BEENY, but cf *peeny*, small, puny (*EDD*, Yks), and PEENY-WEENY. Very small. *BA G*

1943 *GL* Clar, Pene, very small. 1957 DeC StE (Accom) /piini/ small.

PEENY BUSH sb dial; < PEENY sb[1] + BUSH 4. The shrub *Borreria lævis*; so called because, like the Peeny, it shines at night—the result of its having on its leaves the luminous fungus *Omphalia flavida.*

1961 DAP, known 20 years ago by this name in Trelawny.

PEENY-MOLLY sb dial; var of PEENY-WALLY showing *m/w* alternation and perh personifying folk-etym.

1956 DeC StT /piini-mali/ a firefly (small); this form with *m* attested by 3 informants, all in Yallahs; none of them would accept /-wali/ as the usage in Yallahs.

PEENY-WALLY /piini-wali, -waali/ sb; etym uncert, perh PEENY adj + Engl dial *wally* in one of its meanings (*EDD waul*, to roll the eyes, *waulie*, agile, nimble, *wallop*, a leap, *walliman*, a familiar spirit, etc.), and perh on the analogy of Scots *peelie-wally* (*SND* PEELIE). The click-beetle more often simply called PEENY. *BL* s TOM-TOM.

1943 *GL* Port, Kittibo, Peonie Waalie; StAnd, Peenie Wallie, blinkie. 1950 *NHN* IV 155, Peenie-wallies. 1952 FGC StAnd /piini-waali/—candlefly. 1956 Mc Port /piini-wali/ is smaller than /blingki/. 1957 DeC StE (Eld) /piini-wali/ a firefly.

PEENY-WEENY adj dial; PEENY adj + *weeny* (*EDD*). *G*

1954 LeP StAnn, Peeny-weeny, very small, tiny.

PEE-PEE see *piipii.*

PEEPER sb tech; <*peep* vb + *-er*. See quot.

1913 Fawcett 41, Even on the same property different fields require larger and smaller peepers* to be left according to the exposure or conformity of the land.. *'Peeper', a small pointed [banana] sucker, of about 4 to 12 in. high, starting below the level of the ground and sprouting through the earth, developing later into a 'sword sucker'.

PEEPY-EYED adj dial; <*peepy* (*OED*, *EDD*) + *eyed.* Having eyes that seem always partly closed. *G*

1877 Murray *Feedin' 'Perrit* 11, De ugly little peepee yeye ting.

PEFF adv dial arch and rare; prob for *pass*, which is used thus in African pidgin-English. A function-word of comparison: more.

1943 *GL* no addr, Peff young, younger.

PEG sb; <*peg* sb, descriptive of shape. (*F&W*, 'Brit. W. Indian'.)

1. One of the natural sections of an orange or similar fruit. *T*

c 1915 FGC StAnd, The pegs of any citrus fruit. 1956 LeP StAnd, Also applied to jackfruit.

2. By inference from PEG vb 2, a nut.

3. Attrib. Dividing into pegs.

1952 FGC StC /peg tumátis/ a kind of tomato that divides into pegs.

PEG vb; <PEG sb.

1. To divide (an orange) into its natural sections. *T*

1956 Mc StAnd, To peg an orange: to divide it into segments. Also used of peeling it by dividing the skin into 4 and tearing off.

2. To bear nuts.

1952 FGC StE, Peanuts start pegging: they send down *nits* or *boots*. 1957 EB Port, Of a tree: to bear nuts.

PEGGY sb dial; prob familiarizing name. See quot.

1958 DeC StAnd /pegi/ name of a soft white cane (but not the 'white cane').

PEGGYDONE sb dial obs; perh repr 'Peggy is done!'—cf *laad-mi-don*. An unidentified plant.

1868 Russell 5, Peggydone, A dangerous creeping prickle.

PEG-PEG sb dial; iterative of *peg*. Rough or lumpy processes dividing the surface of a vegetable product, or divisions of the product itself.

1929 Beckwith 18, see POLICE 2. 1952 FGC StAnd, Chocolate pod have some peg-peg outside the pod [i.e. the lengthwise ridges]; Tre, Akam..bear seeds, peg-peg and peg-peg.

PEG TOMATO see PEG sb 3.

PEG-TOP BOOT sb dial; cf *OED peg-top trousers*. See quots.

1956 Mc Man /peg-tap-buut/ Wellington boot, rubber knee-boot; Port, In Green Hill /peg-tap-buut/ is a short (mid-calf) rubber boot, a /fut puos-uol/ a long one.

PEG WOOD sb; prob from the appearance of the drupe. A tree: see quot.

1936 Fawcett 62, *Antirrhœa coriacea*..Peg Wood.

peke-peke[1], **PEKKEH-PEKKEH** see PICKY-PICKY[1].

PELICAN FLOWER sb; *OED* 1866→. A name for *Aristolochia grandiflora*, from the resemblance of the flower to a pelican.

1814 Lunan II 46–7, Pelican Flower, or Poison Hog-weed ..The flower is of a very singular structure..The tube is nearly nine inches in length, recurved or bent back..etc. 1854–5 *TJSA* I 67. 1864 Grisebach 786.

pempe see APIMPE, MAPEMPE.

pempem see MAPEMPE.

PEM-PEM, PEMPENY adj dial; cf Twi *apém* a thousand, *mpempem* thousands, *ɔ-pepém* a million. Plenty, plentiful. (1877 cit may illustrate a diff word.)

1877 Murray *Kittle* 25, Mudfish shake himself, den begin fe sing—'Yerry groomer corn pempeny'. 1943 *GL* Man, Pem-pem, plenty.

PEMPENG sb dial.

1943 *GL* StE, Pempeng, the male organ.

PEMPERRY sb rare; etym uncert. An unidentified tree, perh *pimploe*. See *plimpla*.

1943 *GL* no addr, Pemperry, a tree the suds of which leaves make an excellent shampoo.

PEN sb; 1695→ pen, 1774→1873 penn; cf *OED pen sb*[1], esp 2b, 1740→.

1. A cattle farm or enclosure. *BA BL*

c 1695 Acts & Laws 97, All Owners of Neat Cattle shall keep one white Man at each Pen, and two white Men at every Pen whereunto belongs above 200 Head of Cattle. 1774 Long I 495, Breeding penns 108,000 acres. *Ibid* II 206, Lowland-penns. 1801 Nugent 22, We drove to Lord B.'s Penn.* *[1934 ed. Cundall, note: For some reason the word 'pen', which, derived from the days when the wild cattle of the Spaniards were caught and penned, is used for a farm in Jamaica, is often spelled 'penn'.] 1835 Senior 103–4, The opinion greatly prevails..that what is called a 'large attorney'..is the most likely person to make a *sure return* and regular annual remittances, particularly in the case of a penn; because..he has, within his own controul, *that vent* for the surplus steers and mules annually bred in the place. 1860 Trollope 42, I saw various grazing farms—pens they are here called.

2. Any country estate not specifically a sugar, banana, or coconut property; a gentleman's estate or park.

1788 Marsden 10–11, At these pens or country-houses, and on the land adjoining, they breed plenty of hogs, sheep, goats, and poultry. 1826 Williams 66, His pen produces a superabundance of maize and guinea corn.. rice, if required, and every species of the bread kind in profusion. 1847 Gosse 137, Those beautiful parklike estates called *pens*. 1860 Trollope 14, The fact is, that hardly any Europeans, or even white creoles, live in the town. They have country seats, pens as they call them, at some little distance. 1960 StAnd [Present names:] Liguanea Pen, Bamboo Pen, etc.

3. Attrib.

1873 Rampini 164, To wash down all these delicacies we had penn punch, which seemed to consist mainly of brandy and cherry brandy.

PENCIL sb dial. A type of dumpling rolled out long and thin.

1958 DeC 32 /pentsl/ a thin spinner-dumpling.

PENGUIN, PENGUINED see PINGUIN, PINGUINED.

PENIE see PEENY.

PEN-KEEPER sb.

1. The man charged with the care of the cattle on a PEN (= PENNER 2).

1739 Leslie 248, If any Person whatsoever shall refuse, either by himself, Overseer, or Pen-keeper to discover, upon Oath, the true number of their Slaves, Horses, &c. it shall be lawful for the Justices & Vestry to tax such Person.. a 1818 Lewis (1845) 102, Prince should be instructed in farming business; and, in the meanwhile, should officiate as a pen-keeper to look after the cattle.

2. The owner of a cattle PEN. (= PENNER 1.)

1774 Long I 548, The pen-keepers and settlers should be encouraged..to breed them [*sc* cattle]. 1839 Mc Mahon 172, Let it be understood that pen-keepers in Jamaica, mean graziers, who are generally either attorneys, or old overseers..they generally reside on their pens, after purchasing them.

PENLICO see PALENQUE.

PENNER sb; <PEN + -*er*.

1. The owner of a PEN. Obs.

1873 Rampini 89, The inhabitants of the rural districts are coffee-planters among the hills, penners (cattle-farmers) in the interior parishes, and planters round the seaboard.

2. See quot.

1958 DeC StT, The *penner*, a man who drives the cattle on a large cattle pen; as this is a job with considerable responsibility and prestige, it is often used as an honorific title when addressing someone of lower 'rank' than a *busha* but still not a common laborer..[A man is a] /pena/ if he has only a few boys or menials under him.

PENNY-CATCHER /péni-kècha/ sb dial. A derisive or condemnatory term for one who will work for too little money.

1943 *GL* StAnd, Penny-ketcha, work for penny.

PENNYROYAL sb; cf *OED*. In Jamaica: The plant *Micromeria brownei*.

1927 Beckwith 23, Pennyroyal..'For any sort of complaint', boil into tea. 1955 *WIMJ* 81, Pennyroyal. The occasional use of this plant as an abortifacient..is confirmed.

PEN OVER vb phr; <*pen* vb+*over*. To fertilize (a field) by turning cattle into it temporarily to leave their droppings. Cf FLYING PEN.

1823 Stewart 104, A still more effectual mode of enriching the fields to be planted, is what is called penning them over—that is, penning or folding the cattle on successive divisions of the land, until the whole field is gone over. 1839 MacMahon 245, A cane-piece judiciously penned over seldom fails to give as good a return as a new planting. 1952 FGC StJ (Penning-over still practised on some estates).

PEONIE WAALIE see PEENY-WALLY.

PEPEERET see *pipieri*.

PEPPER AND SALT TO YOUR MAMMY! phr dial.

A phrase used to defy a *kin-oul* as it flies by: the witch is supposed to have taken off her skin and put on that of an owl so as to go abroad and suck people's blood; if pepper and salt are sprinkled in her skin while she is away it will cost her great pain to resume it—and this will presumably discourage her activities.

1929 Beckwith 85, A few nights after he had mentioned it to me, an owl had flown past the house crying 'Creech! creech! creech!' and that night someone had died in the hospital which directly fronted his house. One of Cundall's informants gives as formula to avert misfortune under such circumstances the words 'Pepper and salt to your mammy!' whatever that may mean.

PEPPER-ANT sb dial. A small ant having a 'burning' sting.

1952 FGC Han /pepa hants/ sting burn like pepper; very fine, red, like sugar ants.

PEPPER-ELDER sb; *OED* 1858→. Shrubs of the genus *Piper*, esp species *amalago*, and their fruit. Cf SPANISH ELDER.

1774 Long III 721, This plant [small-grained Black-Pepper] has generally been confounded with the pepper-elder, whose leaves have seven veins, or nerves, and which grows more luxuriantly. 1864 Grisebach 786, Pepper-elder. 1914 Fawcett 20, Pepper Elder, Joint Wood. 1952 FGC Tre, StM, StT /pepa-elda/ StAnd /-helda/ StT /-hilda/; use in tea, bath, soup.

PEPPER-FLY sb now chiefly dial.

1. A kind of small fly: see quot. *G*

1774 Long III 882, Pepper-Fly. Sand Fly. These are very troublesome insects, particularly in the neighbourhood of sandy bays, on the south-side coast..The first, if it happens to fall upon the tunicle of the eye, gives a very disagreeable smarting pain, resembling what is caused by pepper. 1952 FGC Han, Port, StAnd, West /pepa flai/ black, very small, burns in your eyes.

2. Transf. A lively quick-tempered person. *G*

1954 LeP StE.

3. A local name for a kind of firefly: see quot.

1958 DeC StT /pepa flai/ the large firefly, so called because it looks like PEPPER LIGHTS.

PEPPER-GRASS sb; *DAE* 1784→. Herbs of the genus *Lepidium*, used like cress in salads.

1696 Sloane 80, Pepper-grass. In Jamaica & omnibus Caribeis Insulis locis saxosis, & glareosis mediterraneis reperitur. 1754 Browne 272, The upright branchy Pepper-grass. This plant is a native of Jamaica, and grows wild in all the cooler hills of the island. 1914 Fawcett 242, Lepidium..Pepperwort. Peppergrass.

PEPPERLEAF SWEETWOOD sb. The tree *Nectandra coriacea* and its wood, used in making matchsticks, shoe heels, etc.

1946 *NHN* III 63, There are three kinds of 'Sweetwoods' in the forests bordering the trails to Corn Puss Gap. The 'Rock, Timber and Pepper-leaf Sweetwoods' are the best known. 1952 FGC StAnn, StE, StT, Tre /pepalíif swíit-wud/ soft wood, for shingle, matches.

PEPPER LIGHT sb dial. An electric-light bulb of the kind strung on Christmas trees—from their resemblance to small *Capsicum* peppers.

1958 DeC StT /pepa laits/ the lights strung on Christmas trees.

[**PEPPER OF JAMAICA** sb phr obs. =JAMAICA PEPPER, PIMENTO.]

PEPPER-POT sb; *OED* a1704→. *BA G T*

1. A rich soup traditional in WI cookery. Recipes vary, but essential ingredients are corned pork or beef, calalu, okra, and pepper; sometimes also CASSAREEP, but see quot 1873. *N*

1698 Ward 15, They make a rare Soop they call Pepper-pot; its an excellent Breakfast for a Salamander, or a good preparative for a Mountebanks Agent, who Eats Fire one day, that he may get better Victuals the next. 1835 Madden II 63, That he..will..renounce all the good things of negro life, the shads and herrings, and the relishing pickle that gave a flavour to all his messes—abjure the pepper-pot for mawkish vegetables.. 1873 Rampini 64–5, For here [in Chapelton], was I not introduced to 'pepper-pot' and mountain mullet? Not the Demerara pepper-pot..but a rich succulent potage, a very Meg Merrilees broth of pork and beef and fowl, ochroes and calaloo (the West Indian spinach), peppers, crayfish and negro yam; in colour a dark green, with the scarlet prawns appearing through the chaotic mass not unpicturesquely..With the negroes, pepperpot is a compound of the most heterogeneous description. Prawns or crayfish of some kind are *de rigueur*, but bamboo tops, cotton-tree tips, cabbage, pimpernel, pulse, and even the buds of the night-blowing cereus, occasionally find a place in its concoction. 1913 Harris 37, Pepper Pot. Get an earthen vessel. To every quart of water add three tablespoonsful of pure cassareep with salt to taste and a handful of bird peppers, or some cayenne pepper..It should be warmed every day and something should be added each day.

2. Fig. Anything having or supposed to have varied and tasty ingredients—e.g. written commentary, periodicals. (Cf *Pepperpot*, London, Spottiswoode, 1915→.)

PEPPER ROD sb; see quot 1952; *OED* 1866. Either of two common shrubs (see quot 1920) valued in folk medicine.

1864 Grisebach 786, Pepper-rod: *Croton humilis*. 1920 Fawcett 283, *C. humilis*; 284, *C. Wilsonii*—Pepper Rod. 1952 FGC StE, Pepper-rod burns violently if you touch it and put fingers to eyes; boil the root and sweeten /jringk di tii fi fiiva/. 1955 *WIMJ* 158, *Croton humilis*.. Pepper Rod; Small Seaside Balsam.

PEPPER SWEETWOOD sb. Perh confused: cf PEPPERLEAF SWEETWOOD and TIMBER SWEETWOOD.

1864 Grisebach 788, Pepper Sweet-wood: *Nectandra sanguinea*.

PEPPI see *piipii*.

pere-pere adj and sb dial; cf Tiv *pere pere*, light in weight. Small; small things, scraps; hence, (things) of little value.

1943 *GL* West, Perray-perray, small things. 1955 FGC Man /pere-pere—sumáal/ not worth while—e.g. oranges. 1956 Mc StJ, Scraps, remnants: /mi go a Bie, mi si song likl pere pere fish; mi kudn bai i/ *I went to the Bay,*

I saw some little rubbishy fish which I wouldn't buy. 1957 DeC StE (Accom) /pere-pere/ small things if flung in all directions, e.g. food thrown to chickens.

PERHAPSIN adv dial; <*perhaps* + *-n* suffix[1].

periin sb dial; perh repr *peering* (eyes).

1943 *GL* Kgn, Payrin, albino negro. 1958 DeC Port /perîin/ not-so-polite name for albino Negroes.

PERILVENTURE adv dial; <*peradventure.* Perhaps. (Cf *paravencha.*)

1959 C. Pickering Man.

PERINO sb obs; for etym see s. A fermented COOL-DRINK; see quot 1707.

[1663 Boyle *Useful Exp. in Nat. Philos.* II ii 100, In the Barbada's they have many drinks unknown to us; such as are Perino..] 1683 *Present State* 22. At the Sugar-works they make Drink of Malasses, in other places of Cassader, which they call Perinoe. 1707 Sloane xxix, To make Perino, a Drink much used here..Take a cake of bad Cassada Bread, about a foot over, and half an inch thick, burnt black on one side, break it to pieces..and put it to steep in two Gallons of water, let it stand in a Tub twelve hours, then add to it the froth of an Egg, and three gallons more water, and one pound of Sugar, let it work twelve hours, and Bottle it; it will keep good for a week.

PERIPLOCA-LEAVED BROOMWEED sb bot obs; cf BROOM-WEED. In Macfadyen's use: *Wissadula Fadyenii* (ident 1926 Fawcett 96).

1837 Macfadyen 85, Sida periplocifolia? *Periploca-leaved Broom-weed.*

PERRAY-PERRAY see *pere-pere.*

PERTINANT adj dial; aphetic form of *impertinent*, with reg change of *-ent* to /ant/.

1943 *GL* StAnd, Pertinant, impertinant.

PETCHARY /pichíeri/ sb; 1840 pecheere, 1843 pecheree, 1847→ petchary, 1955 petchery, petcherry; onomatopoeic—cf Puerto Rican and Cuban *pitirre*, Virgin Is *chicheri*, etc. *OED* 1860.

The common bird *Tyrannus dominicensis.* Its belligerence and its habit of pursuing the JOHN-CROW are noticed proverbially. Cf also COTTAHEAD, LOGGERHEAD, SEPTEMBER PECHARY, TOM FOOL 2; also *pipieri.*

1840 Chamberlaine 26, see *pipieri.* 1847 Gosse 171, That ceaseless shriek..very similar to the words *pecheery—pecheery—pecheer-ry*, from which they receive their name. 1936 Bond 243, Gray Kingbird..Local names:—Petchary (Jamaica)..*Ibid* 244 note, The various forms of this species have habitually been called 'Petcharies' by writers on West Indian birds as this was said to be the local Jamaican name for *Tolmarchus.* But the name 'Petchary' is applied only to the Gray Kingbird [*Tyrannus dominicensis*] in Jamaica, being, of course derived from the latter bird's distinctive three-syllabled note. 1952 FGC Han, Man, StAnd, StAnn, StT /pichíeri/ StT, Ordinary /pichíeri/ has black head, long beak, lays 70 feet in the air—two other kinds: loggerhead and September petchary.

PETCHERRY, PETCHERY see prec.

PETTA sb dial; familiarized form of *potato.*

1943 *GL* Man, StC, Petta, potato.

PETTIFOGGING /petifagin/ occas /petifiegin/ ppl adj chiefly dial. As a vaguely disdainful or derogatory term: small, insignificant; silly, funny. *BA G*

1942 Bennett 13, Tayma yuh like me no-toe boots Me buy it down de Lane. De 'oman was a show me wan Petty-fagg'n' wan, But me tell har me no want i. 1943 *GL* Kgn, Man, StC, StJ, Petty foggin, Petty faggin. 1955 FGC Man /pétifágin/ not worth while. 1956 Mc Port /cho, yu go we yu petifiegin gyal yu/ *Go away, you silly girl.*

PHACOMA see *fiekuma.*

PHEBA /fíba, fíiba/ sb arch. A female DAY-NAME now little remembered; it corresponded to the male name Cuffee, for a child born on Friday. (Both citations from oral sources are erroneous, indicating that the system is no longer well known.)

1774 Long II 427, Male..Cuffee, Female..Pheba, Friday. 1956 Mc Man, Fibba, name of girl born Tuesday? 1958 DeC StT /fiiba/ a female equivalent of QUASHIE.

PHINNEY MAN sb dial; Ko *mfini*, one who bewitches by 'eating the heart'. Cf *fini-fini* 2. A diabolical personage; specif an obeahman.

1924 Beckwith 83 [In the story the puppy barks to warn the old lady, its mistress, against a 'gentleman' who comes to court her, but she rejects the warning, sings to tell him to come, and he eventually kills her.] Nex' night, de gen'leman come back again, holla out, 'Hulloo!' Ol' lady sing, 'Heah, heah, Phinney man, Nobody heah, Phinney man'.

PHRYGIAN CAP sb obs. A kind of limpet; according to the quot, a name once current.

1756 Browne 397, Of pointed arching Limpets commonly called Phrygian-Caps. PATELLA 5..The rugged Phrygian-Cap Limpet.

piaang-piaang see *pyaa-pyaa.*

PIABA /píaba, píiaba/ sb dial; cf Ashanti (1927 Rattray 8) *piaa*, the plant *Hyptis brevipes* + *-ba*, young, small (of plants, etc.). A mint-like wild herb (*Hyptis pectinata*) much favoured in folk medicine. *BA BL G*

1905 Dodd 5, She go to bed, an' ah tek dis bush dem call 'Piobba' an a bwoil it down an mek some tea, gie 'er. 1927 Beckwith 24, For a cold, drink a tea made with three leaves of 'Piaba'..For headache take as tea. 'Number one for sores!' Squeeze the juice green upon a fresh wound. 1943 *GL* Clar, Piabbah; Man, Piabba. 1952 FGC StAnn, StC, StM, StT, Tre /píaba/. 1953 *WIMJ* 247, *Hyptis pectinata*..Piaba. Used to prepare tea..In Africa the plant is used for fever, chest complaints..etc. 1956 Mc Port /píiaba/ also called /strang-bak/.

PIABBA(H) see prec.

PIA MATER sb obs; prob from the colour of the wood—see quot. An unidentified tree (perh BREADNUT, which was used for timber, and the leaves for fodder).

1740 Importance 53, Pia Mater is a building Timber.. which is a hard Wood of a whitish Colour, and grows very large; the Leaf by some is esteem'd as the best Food for Horses, Sheep or Goats.

PIANGI see *pyanji(-pyanji).*

PIANO GRASS sb; see quot. The grass *Themeda arguens.*

1915 Harris in *Chronicle* 20 Sept 15, The species known here as 'Piano Grass', 'Christmas Grass' or 'Kangaroo Grass', which has spread over considerable areas in Trelawny and St James, also in St Thomas east of Morant Bay..so called because the seeds are supposed to have been introduced with packing material that came with a piano, has been known in Trelawny for at least twenty-five years. 1952 FGC StAnn, StT /piana graas/.

PIAZZA /píeza, piéza/ sb chiefly dial; cf *OED* 2, →1864, 'Now *rare*'.

1. The roofed and colonnaded veranda of early Jamaican dwelling-houses, sometimes open, sometimes with jalousies.

1774 Long II 21, Their [the Spaniards'] houses had no piazzas originally: the English made these additions, in order to render them more cool and pleasant. 1788 Marsden 8, The houses are in general of wood..They consist but of a room or two below stairs, with piazzas all round, and a story above: The inhabitants sit much in the piazzas in the evening to enjoy the breeze. 1826 Williams 314, The mansion [near Port Antonio] consists of an entrance-hall, with sleeping chambers on each side; and this hall leads to a piazza about fifty or sixty feet long, which forms the northern facade of the house. At one end of the piazza is likewise a chamber, and at the other a dining apartment or hall. . The piazza is about fifteen feet wide, furnished with a few chairs. . a spy-glass, a backgammon board, and chessmen. 1873 Rampini 21, Most of them [houses in Kingston] are fronted with covered verandahs called 'piazzas', provided with jalousies to fend off the vertical sun. 1952 FGC West /píeza/—veranda; StM /píeza/ is closed, veranda open.

2. See quot.

1907 Jekyll 266, The piazza, which is not pronounced in the Italian way but nearly rhymes with razor, is the long narrow entrance room of Jamaican houses.

3. The colonnaded entry-way to a shop, shaded by the extension of the story above (or of a roof); a series side by side form a covered walk for pedestrians.

1828 Ordinances 64, All railings and fencings obstructing the passage between piazzas, to be taken down. *Ibid* 76, No horse or mule to be suffered to stand. . in any Piazza in any Street, Lane, or Way, before or near the Shops of a Blacksmith or Farrier. 1952 FGC West, StAnn /píeza, piéza/ the part of a shop in front and below.

PICCANINI, PICCANNY see PICKNEY. *BA*

PICK vb trans now dial. s.

1. To gather (fodder: grass, cane-tops, etc.) wherever one can find it. *BA BL G*

1788–9 McNeill 6, As to the article of *picking grass*, on which so much has been said by late writers, no such thing now exists in this island. 1797 *Braco* 11 Feb, Small Gang Picking Tops on No 1.

2. To gather what one can find in (an area or place); to scavenge, clean up. Also const *up*.

1946 U.Newton I 6, Such work as 'picking up the yard'. 1956 Mc Man /ai pik op di maakit an born di robish/; /ai pik di biich an sel di shel/—*I pick up shells from the beach and sell them.*

PICK-AND-CHOOSE adj and sb; cf *OED pick v*[1] 7c. *BA BL G*

A. adj: Hard to please, finicky.

1950 Pioneer 37, Once upon a time dere was a very fine-fault an pick an choose gal.

B. sb: Fastidiousness, over-niceness.

1924 Beckwith 104, Pick an' choose isn't good. You wasn't pick an' choose, you wouldn't marry to Yellow Snake that was going to kill you now.

PICKANINNY, PICKANINY see PICKNEY.

PICKANINNY CHRISTMAS sb dial joc obs. Easter.

1707 Sloane lii, see LITTLE CHRISTMAS. 1835 Madden II 153, To. . spend piccanini Christmas (Easter) dancing.

PICKANINNY GANG sb obs; *OED* 1828. The THIRD GANG of slaves formerly used on estates for the lightest work; it was composed of children.

1828 Marly 93, A small gang called the pickeniny gang—these were the most numerous. The pickeniny gang consisted of the children. 1835 Senior 28, Pickaniny gang.

PICKANINNY MOTHER see PICKNEY-MUMMA.

PICKENINNY, PICKENINY see PICKNEY.

PICKER sb dial; <*picker*[1] (*OED*).

1. A pickaxe or mattock; also attrib. (*OED* 2 →1886.)

1907 Jekyll 158, Nothing more joyous can be imagined than a good 'digging-sing' from twenty throats, with the pickers—so they call their pickaxes—falling in regular beat. 1956 Mc StAnd [Song, Bury me me nana:] /pika man a dig uol fi beri mi/ *The grave-digger is digging a grave to bury me.*

2. A thief who 'picks up' small things in passing. (*OED* 1b →1822.)

1956 Mc Man /pika/ scuffler.

PICKERING'S HERB sb obs; see quot. The shrub *Ruellia paniculata.*

a1726 Barham (1794) 171–2, These herbs are called in Latin *prunella*, or alheal or self-heal. . The decoction of the herb, in wine or water, makes an excellent traumatic drink, to forward the healing of all wounds and stubborn ulcers. . Above twenty years past one captain Pickering, a gentleman I knew very well, had a stick with fire at the end of it darted at him, which happened to come just under the brow of his eye, and seemed to turn his eye out, and all despaired of his life. No surgeon being at hand, they sent for an old negro man, well skilled in plants; as soon as he came he ran and took of this herb that hath the bluish or purple flower, and washed it, reducing the eye as well as he could do to its place, and then laid on the bruised herb, bound it up, and the captain was carried home. The next day he sent for a surgeon; and when they came to open it, found it healed up. . This I heard from several worthy gentlemen who were there present. . and call it Pickering's herb to this day. 1725 Sloane 367, Pickerings Herb. 1814 Lunan II 64, Pickering's-Herb.

PICKER-MAN sb dial. A man who works with a PICKER.

1956 Mc StAnd, see PICKER 1.

PICKING GRASS, TOPS see PICK 1.

PICKINY, PICKINNIES see PICKNEY.

PICK-ME-ROUND /pik-mi-roun/ sb dial. Coconut cakes (eaten by picking the bits of coconut from the edges of the sugar fondant).

1943 *GL* StAnn, Pick-me-roun, coconut cake. 1946 U.Newton I 9, There we sat with. . some 'pick-me-roun' or 'coconut drops' (you know coconut and sugar cakes by that name; don't you?).

PICK-ME-TEETH /pik-mi-tiit/ sb dial joc. Salt fish: so nicknamed because the fibres get into one's teeth and force one to pick them after eating it.

1943 *GL* Tre, Pick-me-teeth, saltfish.

PICK-MOUTH sb dial; <*pick* (*OED v*[1] 8) +MOUTH 2. See quot.

1868 Russell 11, Pick-mout, Troublesome, teasing. Refers to one who teases another to quarrel. A pick-mout boy come again fe make quarrel.

PICKNE, PICKNIES see next.

PICKNEY /pikni/ also old-fashioned /pikini/. Sp of 'pickaninny': 1707 piganinnies, 1707 1838 pickaninny, 1826 pickeninny, 1828 pickeniny, 1834 1835 pickaniny, 1835 piccanini; sp of /pikini/: 1790 pickinnies, 1868 pickini; sp of /pikni/: 1845 piccanny, 1868 pickne, 1907 picny, 1910→ pickney, 1927 picknies, 1948 pickny. Prob <Pg pidgin (cf similar forms in Afr pidgin-English, e.g. Cameroons, Sierra Leone) <Pg *pequenino*. Cf *DA* 1653→. s. *BA BL G* Tobago.

1. A child, esp a very young child.

[1707 Sloane lii, Their Children call'd Piganinnies or rather Pequenos Ninnos, go naked till they are fit to be put to clean the Paths.] 1790 Moreton 152, Pickinnies (*i.e.* children). 1868 Russell 2, Pickne; *ibid* 6, Pickini—A child. African. 1907 Jekyll 40, Now Toad have twenty picny. 1927 Stafford 26, She drives away the picknies From the muscovado sugar.

2. Transf. The young of animals, birds, etc. See DUCK-PICKNEY.

3. Attrib. See also separate entries.

1956 McStE /pikni gal waak op an doung wan nait hie so/.

PICKNEY-MUMMA /píkni-múma/ sb dial; <PICKNEY + *muma*. *G*; *SC pikien-mamà*.

1. A nursing mother; the mother of a small child. Among slaves, these women were given extra provisions and certain privileges.

a1818 Lewis (1834) 191, There was also a dinner prepared at the house where the 'white people' reside, expressly for none but the *pickaniny-mothers*; that is, for the women who had children living. 1826 Barclay 318, When the child is about a couple of months old she takes it out to the field. All the '*pickeninny mummas*' go to the same work, and the children are put down together in some shade near the field. 1838 Kelly 33, The pickaninny mothers, as they are called, on coming into the field, gave the children to a nurse. 1910 Anderson-Cundall 37 [Prov:] Go a pickney mumma yard an' you sure fe get somet'ing. (1952 Current, FGC.)

2. Transf. Certain food plants that bear plentifully.

1952 FGC StE /píkini múma/ a kind of white coco; StJ /píkni múma/ a kind of sweet potato, 'bear plenty, always sure of some'.

3. Transf. Certain common bushes used medicinally: BLOODBERRY, SUCKY-BABY.

1952 FGC StAnn /píkni múma/ bloodberry, guma; draws boils; use for stomach-ache, cold.

PICKNEY-'PON-BACK sb dial. A name for the herb *Phyllanthus niruri* (also called CARRY-ME-SEED) from the way the small flower-heads hang along the underside of the leaf.

1961 FGC Man /pikni-pam-bak/—I know dat name since a boy. (From a man about age 40.)

PICK-NUT, PIG-NUT[2] sb dial; by folk-etym <*spikenard* (cf *OED*, *spignard* 1bc, *spiknard* 17–18c). The mint-like wild herbs *Leonotis nepetæfolia* and *Hyptis suaveolens*, much used in folk medicine.

1893 Sullivan 113, Pic-nut Tea. Boil the leaves for a tea; sweeten and serve hot or cold. 1927 Beckwith 24, Pig-nut. *Hyptis suaveolens*..For stomach-ache take a tea boiled with 'Piaba'. 1952 FGC StC, StM, Tre /piknat/ favour piaba. 1953 *WIMJ* 247, *Hyptis suaveolens*..Spikenard, Pig Nut. 1955 FGC Man /piknot/. 1955 *WIMJ* 159, *Leonotis nepetæfolia*..Labiatæ. Pick Nut; Christmas Candlesticks; Ball Head; Bald Head or Bush.

PICK-O'-BAIT sb dial; <*pick* (*OED sb*[2] 3) + *of* + *baits*. A small sea fish favoured for bait by fishermen.

1952 FGC StE /píkabiet/.

PICK-PICK vb dial; cf PICKER 2. To help oneself to things; to want everything one sees.

1956 Mc Port /yu pikpik tu moch/ *You want everything you see.*

PICK UP YOU' FOOT vb phr dial; cf Twi *mã wo nán so*, lift your feet, i.e., quicken your steps..make haste, (Christaller); perh also the military drill phr, 'Pick your feet up!' Cf PULL FOOT. To move fast. *BA*

1942 Bennett 9, Pick up yuh foot eena yuh han'..Run!!

PICKY-PICKY[1], **PECKY-PECKY** /piki-piki, peki-peki, peke-peke/ adj and adv dial; iteration of *picky*, choosy (cf US usage—*ADD*).

A. adj: 1. Finicky in eating.

1952 FGC StM /piki-piki/ eats very little. 1956 Mc StE (Eld) /peke-peke/ Fastidious in eating.

2. Greedy. Cf PICK-PICK.

1943 *GL* StM, Picky-picky, greedy.

3. Picked to bits; worm-eaten. (In the folk speech 'peck' vb falls in with 'pick'—cf 'wood-picker' for 'woodpecker', etc.) Also const *up*.

1943 *GL* StAnd, Peky-peky, pick [i.e. picked]; Pekkeh pekkeh. 1956 JN, See piece a de rotten pear..how it picky-picky up dey sah. 1959 DeC West /peke-peke/.. soft and rotten, especially common for wood eaten by termites.

B. adv: Fastidiously.

1950 Pioneer 56, Me kean nyam picky-picky! *I can't eat fastidiously!*

PICKY-PICKY[2] adj dial; etym unknown, but cf MEKE-MEKE. See quot.

1958 DeC Port /peke-peke/ sloppy, wet, and muddy.

PICKY-PICKY HEAD sb dial. The female equivalent of BLACK-PEPPER-BRAIN. *BL G*

1960 SJR /piki-piki hed/ when a girl's hair is very short, grows close to the scalp in little balls of fluff, very negroid.

PIC-NUT see PICK-NUT.

PICNY see PICKNEY.

PIECEN vb dial; cf *OED* →1887 '*local* or *techn.*' To add a piece of material on; to patch.

1907 Jekyll 121, Him buy..white flour, an'..he make it to paste an' piecen the quart pot bottom inside. *Ibid* 123, *Piecen*, a nice word. They use it also in speaking of the patching of old clothes. 1952 P. B. Caws StT, Piecen.

PIECES see TO PIECES.

PIESA see *paisa*.

PIGANINNIES see PICKNEY.

PIG CRAWL sb dial; <*pig* + CRAWL. A pigsty or pigpen.

1952 FGC StAnn /pig kral/ pig pen.

PIGEON PEAS sb; *OED* 1725→. The pea *Cajanus cajan* of which GUNGO PEAS is another variety; they are sometimes identified. *BA G*

1696 Sloane 140, Pigeon Pease. In Jamaica & Caribeis insulis..provenit. a1726 Barham (1794) 142, Pigeon-pease. They are so called from pigeons greedily feeding upon them. 1954 *WIMJ* 28, *Cajanus cajan*..Gungo (Congo) Pea; Pigeon Pea; No-eye Pea.

PIGEON-NECK POTATO sb dial. A variety of sweet-potato: see quot.

1952 FGC Port /píjin-nèk pitíeta/ when fruit bears, vine turns down like pigeon neck.

PIGEON-SHOOTER sb obs. One who lived by hunting game in the hills. Cf HOG-HUNTER.

1827 Hamel I 175, 'This', thought he, 'must be a hog-hunter, a Maroon, a pigeon-shooter'.

PIGEON WOOD sb; *OED* 1745→: 'so called for the marking or colouring' of the wood, is prob erron—see quots 1909, 1952. Various trees (*Diospyros tetrasperma*, *Dipholis salicifolia*, *Antirrhoea jamaicensis*) and their wood, used for cabinet work and in building.

1740 Importance 51, Pigeon Wood has a fine, smooth Skin; it has been sent home to dye with, but it did not answer for that End; it is used for inlaying Back-gammon Tables, and very serviceable in building. 1756 Browne 368, Pigeon Wood. This shrubby tree is greatly esteemed on account of its wood. 1864 Grisebach 786, Pigeon-wood: *Dipholis salicifolia* and *Diospyros tetrasperma*. 1909 Harris 310, Pigeon-wood (*Diospyros tetrasperma*,

Sw.). This is a small tree found chiefly on the limestone of the southern coast ranges. The timber is hard and is good for posts and scantlings. Wild pigeons feed on the berries. 1941 Swabey 21, Goldspoon—(Susan Wood, Pigeon wood, May Day Mahogany). *Antirrhoea jamaicensis*.. Wood is of a light red colour: fairly close grained. Good substitute for mahogany. *Ibid.* 27, Pigeon Wood—*Diospyros tetrasperma*..Small tree: wood hard: used for posts, rafters etc. 1952 FGC StAnn /pijin-wud/—in Portland this is the name of a species of sweetwood; flesh of pigeons is bitter when feeding on this; StE, next to gold-spoon; StT, for common house building; birds eat berries.

PIGFOOT, PIGTOE sb dial.

1952 FGC StT, Pigfoot, pigtoe—a small, useless kind of fish.

PIG-NOSE JACK sb dial. A variety of the Jack fish having a snout-like nose.

1952 FGC StM.

PIG-NUT[1] sb; *OED* in other senses.

The tree *Omphalea triandra* and its fruit: see quot 1814.

1814 Lunan I 203–4, Omphalea..1. Nucifera..This tree ..grows very commonly in Jamaica. The French call this *noisettier*, and in Jamaica it is known in some parishes by the name of *pig* or *hog* nut..The kernels of the nuts in the raw state are delicately sweet and wholesome;..when ripe, they burst from the pod and fall to the ground, where the hogs greedily devour them. 1864 Grisebach 786, Pig-nut: *Omphalea triandra*. 1913 Harris 5.

PIG-NUT[2] see PICK-NUT.

PIG'S-APPLE sb dial. =HOG-APPLE.

1952 FGC Port (Hector's River).

PIGSTY FENCE sb dial. A fence made with rows of sticks set diagonally side by side, sloping in opposite directions, and crossing at top and bottom so that they hold each other tight.

1952 FGC StE (Frenchman's Bay).

PIGTAIL BEAN sb dial. A very small bean similar to the banner-bean.

1952 FGC StT.

PIGTOE see PIGFOOT.

piiji see *kontapiichi*, PEE-GEE.

piini (wali) see PEENY, PEENY-WALLY.

piin-piin adj or sb dial; prob var of *pyaa-pyaa*.

1956 Mc /piin-piin/—simple, not important; inferior person or thing.

piipii sb dial; echoic. A small chick, esp a turkey chick. *BL G*

1927 Anderson-Cundall 73 [Prov:] Cuss John Crow 'peel-head', turkey pee-pee bex. 1943 *GL* Tre, Peppi, a young turkey. 1952 FGC StAnd, StAnn, StT, West /píipìi/.

piipiili see *pipili*.

pikin, pikini, pikni see PICKNEY. s *pikin*.

piknit sb dial; pronunc of *picnic*. *BL*

1956 Mc Man.

piknot see PICK-NUT.

pilikin sb dial; <*pelican*. (*OED* has a 16th-cent sp 'pillycane'.) The regular folk pronunc of 'pelican'. *BL*

1952 FGC Han, StJ /pílikan, pílikin/ StC, StT, West /pilikín/.

PILLUNG see next.

PILON, PYLON /pilóng, pílong/ sb; <Amer Sp (Cuba) *pilón (de tabaco)*, a pile or heap.

1. A pile of tobacco leaves set to cure.

1954 *FG* 373, When a good quantity of heads of tobacco is ready, they should be stapled together in a pile (pylon) of from 5 feet by 5 feet to 9 feet by 9 feet and 5 feet high.. Pylons should be built on plank floors.

2. A curing-house for tobacco.

1943 *GL* StM, Pillung, tobacco house. 1955 FGC Man, Tobacco factory, 'tobacco pilong'.

pilong see prec.

PILOT JACK sb dial. A fish of the Jack kind which swims in front of a school.

1952 FGC StC /pailat jak/ lead the troop.

PIMENTADE sb obs; <Fr *pimentade*. A peppery sauce.

1725 Sloane II 378, Pimentade is made of this [*sc* BIRD PEPPER], Juice of Lemons, and Manioc.

PIMENTO /piménta, priménta/ sb; p 1660 1672 piemente, 1662 1725 pimienta, 1679→ pimento, 1794 1797 piemento, dial sp 1905 premento; <Pg *pimenta (da Jamaica)*, allspice, the spelling in *-o* (now also so pronounced in Std Engl) is due to infl of Sp *pimiento*. *OED* 2 1690→. Cf *primenta*, a common pronc.

The tree *Pimenta officinalis*, and esp its fruit, an aromatic berry resembling black pepper, whence formerly called JAMAICA PEPPER, now (except in Jamaica) 'allspice'. *G N*

p 1660 State of Jamaica 611, Piemente growes plentifully in Mountaines and is a Spice of the forme of East India pepper of very curious gust haveing in it the mixt tast of diuers spices. 1662 Stubbe 47, That most delicate of Spices, call'd usually in England Pepper of Jamaica.. It is commonly called in Jamaica, Pimienta. 1671 Ogilby 338, A certain kind of Spice call'd Piemente..grows wild in the Mountains. 1672 Blome 13, Piemente. 1679 Trapham 38, The Bay Tree or Spicy Pimento perfume the woods with profitable sweets. 1725 Sloane vi, Fig. 2. the Jamaica Pepper, or Pimienta Tree. 1797 *Braco* 20 Sept, 8 Picking Piemento at Gordon Bank. 1905 Dodd 3 *et passim*, Premento. 1943 *GL* Clar, Primenta, pimento. 1952 FGC StAnd, StE, StM /primenta/.

PIMENTO DRAM sb. A kind of cordial made with PIMENTO berries steeped in rum, sugar, lime juice, etc.: see quot 1957.

1895 Sullivan 104, Pimento dram [2 recipes given]. 1907 *ODS*. 1952 FGC Port. 1957 *FFM* 280, Pimento Dram. 1 qt. ripe berries 1 qt. 18 [*sic*, prob for 80] proof rum.. Put on to boil sugar with water and cinnamon stick. When liquid is cold pour on to the berries..Add rum. Allow to stand for two weeks..Strain..and bottle.

PIMENTO GRASS sb; said to flourish in pimento walks. The pasture grass *Stenotaphrum secundatum*. *G*

1826 Williams 40, Two sorts of grass were pointed out to me, the pimento and the bahama. 1952 FGC StAnn /primento graas/ grows fat in pimento walk. 1954 *FG* 216, Crab grass of Manchester and the 'Pimento' grass of St Ann. This grass is also known as St Augustine grass.. the percentage of crab or pimento grass in these pastures varies considerably from paddock to paddock.

PIMENTO HORSE sb dial. The stick insect.

1945 *NHN* II 166, Through the English countryside they [frothy secretions made by insects] are known as 'Cuckoo Spit', but in Jamaica the popular name is 'Pimento-horse Spit', since they are believed to be the work of the 'Pimento-horse', which is the local name for the various species of Stick insects. 1952 FGC Tre /primenta haas/ stick insect.

PIMENTO HORSE SPIT sb dial. See prec, quot 1945.

PIMENTO THATCH sb dial. =SILVER THATCH.

1890 Thomas 71, see LONG THATCH.

PIMENTO-WALK sb; <PIMENTO+WALK. *OED* 1825. A grove of pimento trees.

1756 Browne 248, The leaves and bark are very warm.. which makes them extremely cautious of fire, in all Pimento-walks, where, if it should once catch, it runs with great fury. 1952 FGC StAnn, see PIMENTO GRASS.

pimpim sb dial; prob <*spin-spin*. A spinner dumpling.

1958 DeC Tre /pimpim/. 1959 DeC StJ /pimɒim/ small round fried dumplings about one inch diameter; West, Here a child's baby-talk word for dumpling /muma beg ya a piis a pimpim/.

PIMPLY-GUT sb dial. A disease in pigs caused by the PIMPLY-GUT WORM.

PIMPLY-GUT WORM sb dial. See quot.

1954 *FG* 710, The Pimply Gut Worm. This worm which lives in the large intestine is the cause of 'pimply gut' in pigs.

PIM-WOOD sb obs. An unidentified tree.

1756 Browne 142, Pavetta? 2. Subarborea major. Pim-wood.

PIN vb tech. In making a dugout *kunu*: To insert the square cedar pins that guide the boat-builder in reducing the sides to the proper thickness.

1952 FGC StM /pin di buot wid siida pin/.

PINCHERS sb dial; by folk-etym <*pilchard*, or the earlier form *pilcher*. A kind of sprat. (Cockrell's form 'pincers' is prob an attempt to 'standardize' the folk form.)

1892 Cockrell, Pincers—white bill. *Clupea humeralis*. 1952 FGC StJ /pinshaz/ a species of /prat/ use for bait; StM /pinchaz/ sprats, yellow stripes both sides; StT /pinchaz/ small sprat.

PINDAL(L) see next.

PINDAR /pínda/ sb now chiefly dial; 1696 pindall, 1707 1793 pindal, 1756→ pindar; <Kongo (Angola) *mpinda*, ground-nut, pea-nut. The *-l* and *-r* of spelling have no etym basis. *OED* 1707→. The ground-nut or peanut *Arachis hypogœa*. *BL*; *SC piendà*, Gullah *pinder*.

1696 Sloane 73, Earth Nuts or Pindalls. 1707 Sloane I lxxiii, I was assured that the Negroes feed on Pindals or Indian Earth-nuts, a sort of pea or bean producing its pods under ground. 1756 Browne 295, Arachis 1.. Pindar's, or Ground-Nuts..imported from Africa. 1873 Rampini 35, Then came by a woman with a basket of roasted pindar or ground nuts..on her head..We rather regretted when she turned the corner of a neighbouring street, and her 'Pindar buy, young gentlemen! Pindar buy, young ladies!..' was heard by us no more. 1952 FGC, all parishes /pinda/—StE 'common name'; Port 'less common than "peanut"'; StAnn, StJ 'old-time word, now throw-away—say "peanut"'.

PINDAR-CAKE sb. A confection having a base of brown muscovado sugar fondant with PINDAR nuts on top.

c1915 FGC StAnd. 1942 Bennett 10, 'Pinda-cake, wangla?'. *Ibid* 11, 'Buy peppermint—..Fresh pindacake!'

PINE sb; Amer Sp *piña*, pineapple; this was the first name for the fruit in English (cf *OED piña* →1622), until it was anglicized as *pine* about mid-17th cent (*OED pine sb*[2] 5 1661→, and see below 1657 etc.); in 1671 Ogilby 339 'pine-apple' still means a pine-tree cone, and 'ananas' is used for the pineapple; in Jamaica 'pine' has remained the usual name. *BL G*

1. The pineapple. *BA*

1657 *Continuation* 46, Fruits..Pyne, the best that ever was eat, in season almost all the year long. p1660 State of Jamaica 489, Soursops, Custard Apples.. besides plantings Pines &c. 1954 *FG* 392, The Sugar Loaf is only of importance as a fresh fruit. It is not a suitable pine for canning.

2. Also attrib: *pine balls, pine tarts*, etc.

c1915 FGC StAnd, Pine balls, made of pine cooked down and rolled with granulated sugar into balls. (1961 still current.) 1957 *FFM* 162, Pine tarts..Roll out and cut strips of pastry to make a criss-cross pattern and lay on top of pine filling.

PING-PONG vb colloq. To play at something, not doing it seriously or well.

1943 *GL* StAnd, Ping-pong, trying. 1960 NJL StC, A common Jamaican expression, if you say 'he ping-pongs at it' it means he doesn't do it very well—like me typing: I just ping-pong at it.

PINGUIN /ping-wing/ sb; 1679→pinguin, 1696 1835 penguin, 1756 pinquin; etym uncert, perh <*pin* (or PINE) +*whin*, prickly shrub (*OED* 2; note also Sc form *quhin*). The species name and the folk form PING-WING evid preserve an original first-syllable *i*, but through confusion of forms *penguin* developed early and is still occas found today. *OED* 1696→. *BL N*

1. The plant *Bromelia pinguin* and its fruit; because of its extremely prickly leaves it was used early to make hedges or 'fences'.

1679 Trapham 59, Tamarinds, Nasburies, sower Sops, Pinguins, with many other. 1696 Sloane 118, Penguins. In Jamaica & Caribeis Insulis ubique reperitur. 1835 Madden II 54, Pita..belongs to the same genus with the pine-apple and the common penguin. c1915 FGC StAnd /ping-wing/. 1933 McK 317, Ping-wing—A wild plant, cousin to the pineapple. 1955 *WIMJ* 71, Pinguin. The fruit provides a remedy for worms in children. 1956 Mc Man, Port, StAnd, StE /ping-wing/.

2. Also attrib: *pinguin hedge, pinguin fence*.

1756 Browne 147, This plant..found climbing upon all the pinquin-fences. 1778 Long II 208, With fringes of logwood, or penguin-fence. 1801 Nugent 22, Penguin hedges, which are like gigantic pineapples. 1950 Pioneer 81, Me wash it, me starch it, me iron it, Me hang it pan pingwing macka.

PINGUINED adj; <PINGUIN+*-ed*[2] (*OED*). Having pinguin bushes growing on it to form a hedge.

1823 Roughley 400, By a post and rail fence, or a double ditch, penguined over.

PING-WING see PINGUIN.

PING-WING YAM sb dial. A kind of yam similar to negro yam; apparently so called because the vine has prickles, like pinguin.

1952 FGC StAnd /ping-wing yam/.

PINIKIN sb dial; var form of *pilikin*, q.v.

1943 *GL* StAnd, Pinikin, pelican.

pinikl see PINNACLE.

PINK[1] sb; echoic, from the bird's cry. The BUTTER-BIRD. Also attrib. (Quot 1740 may belong with PINK[2].)

1740 Importance 38, Parrots, Parokets, Pink Birds, the little humming Bird. 1838 Kelly 27, They are called pinks, from their cry very closely resembling that word; but they are the real ortolan, of far-famed celebrity. 1952 FGC StAnd, StM, StM /pingk/—name from the sound it makes.

PINK[2] sb dial; from the colour. The Roseate Stilt, *Himantopus himantopus.*

1956 Jeffrey-Smith 118, Country folks near Jackson Town, where they used to be abundant, call them 'Pinks' and 'Stilts', and both names give the striking field characteristics.

PINK[3] sb dial slang; cf *ODS pink* B *adj* 3, 'slightly vulgar, indecent, or violent'. See quot.

1952 Kerr 89, There were few resident prostitutes [in 'Sugartown'] but during crop a number of ladies known locally as 'pinks' descended on the district [from Kingston].

PINK PARROT sb. A pink-coloured variety of the PARROT fish.

1952 FGC Port, StC, StE /pingk parat/.

PINK SAGE sb dial. A variety of 'sage' (*Lantana*) having pink flowers.

1952 FGC StM, Pink sage—wild sage.

PINK-WEED sb. Pink-root, *Spigelia anthelmia.*

1927 Beckwith 24, Pink-weed..To dose a baby for worms boil as tea and add a few drops of turpentine. 1954 *WIMJ* 31, Pink Root; Worm Grass, Pink Weed; Indian Pink.

PINNACLE /pínikl/ sb, also attrib; from the name of the estate.

The first well-organized camp of Rastafarians, established in May 1940 by Leonard Howell on behalf of the Ethiopian Salvation Society, on an abandoned estate near Sligoville, St Catherine parish. The name acquired symbolic associations for a time.

1941 *Gleaner* 25 Aug 16, Apart from himself, over five hundred members of the Society resided at Pinnacle. 1942 Bennett 46, Mass John come back fram pinnicle Yuh want see him beard Muma..Him tell we dat him get wey wen De police meck de raid. 1960 *SAN Report* 11–12, By the middle of 1941 the police were taking action against the Pinnacle community..Some brethen say that at Pinnacle, Howell represented himself as God and took the name of Gangungu Maraj or more familiarly, Gong.

PINQUIN see PINGUIN.

PINT sb dial.

1. Any ordinary glass bottle, whether it holds a pint or not. *BA*

1929 Beckwith 51 [Street cry of man buying empty bottles:] No wine pin'! no ale pin'! no soda water bottle! 1960 FGC Han [A boy asking for a Pepsi-Cola bottle so that he could collect the 1*d*. deposit:] /beg yu di paint/.

2. Slang: A sentence of six months in prison. Cf QUART.

1952 FGC Han.

PINTA see POINTER.

PINT-O'-WATER MANGO sb dial. A type of mango that is large and juicy.

1952 FGC StAnd /pàint-a-wáata/.

PIOBBA see PIABA.

PIPE vb rare obs; cf *OED v*[2] 3b. To convert (a cane or other plant) into a hollow tube by pulling out the inner part.

1790 Beckford I 52, The cattle, without extraordinary care, will frequently commit trespasses upon them [*sc* canes] in an early state: and as they pipe, or extract the heart-leaf, the future progress of the plant will be shortened, if not destroyed.

PIPER sb; cf *OED sb*[1] 2. Various fish of the family *Belonidæ*, genera *Strongylura* and *Tylosurus* (with both jaws much extended), and the family *Hemiramphidæ* (with only the lower jaw extended). *N*

1756 Browne 443, Esox 1..The Piper [see also Tab 45 fig 2]. 1851 Gosse 288–9, That species of Belone called indiscriminately Piper or Long-jaw. They are fond of congregating in little parties, containing from two or three to a dozen, skimming leisurely along near the surface. 1950 Smith in *NHN* 138, Piper, a local name for the needlefish, *Tylosurus notatus.* 1952 FGC StC, StT, West /paipa/ has long lower jaw; the one with long top jaw is 'jang-ho' or 'long-jaw'. StAnn /paipa/ same as trumpeter.

PIPE SNAPPER sb. A fish: see quot.

1854–5 *TJSA* I 142, *Centropristes tabacarius*—pipe snapper.

pipieri sb dial; echoic, from the bird's cry. The PETCHARY. Also fig: a pugnacious person.

1840 Chamberlaine 26, The Pecheere—Pepeeret—Tyrant Flycatcher. 1943 *GL* StT, Pippari, small fighting bird. Pugnacious person. 1956 Mc Port /pipíeri/ same as /pichíiri/.

pipili adj. dial; <*pipieri,* or an independent echoism of the same sort.

1. Greedy.

1956 Mc StE /piipiili/—/krievn, glotnos/.

2. Quarrelsome.

1956 Mc StJ /pipili/.

PIPPARI see *pipieri.*

PIRAMIDIG sb obs; echoic for the bird's cry. Gosse's name for the night-hawk *Chordeiles minor.*

1847 Gosse 33, Piramidig—Musquito-hawk..About an hour before the sun sets, we hear a loud, abrupt, and rapid repetition of four or five syllables in the air above our heads, resembling the sounds, *piramidig,* or *gi' me a bit.*

PISA see *paisa.*

PISSABED sb dial; a folk name transferred from the European dandelion to the very diff Ja dandelions. =DANDELION. *BL*

1801 Dancer 361, Stinking weed, or piss-a-bed (Cassia occidentalis). 1927 Beckwith 24, Pissibid..To regulate the bladder in case of stoppage. 1956 Mc Port /pisabed/ —tea bush.

PISSIBID see prec.

PISTAREEN sb obs; 1740 pistorine, 1808 pesterine, 1826 pistoreen, 1877 pistereen; *DA* 1774→. (Not specif Ja, but spellings and attrib use unrecorded in *OED, DAE, DA.*) A small Spanish silver coin once current in America and the WI.

1740 Importance 69, see DON PATINHO'S MONEY. 1808 Stewart 59, Pesterines and bitts, at 1*s*. 3*d*. and 7½*d*. (these are rare). 1826 Williams 103, A long stocking filled with dollars and pistoreens. 1877 Murray *Kittle* 12, Several doubloons, some 'half joes', Spanish dollars and 'pistereen bits'.

PITATA see *pitieta.*

PITCH vb chiefly dial; cf *OED v*[1] 8: 'Now *rare* or *arch.*' →1827; 18: →1857.

1. Of a flying thing: to alight or settle *on* or *upon* a spot. *BL*

1907 Jekyll 140, Fowl-Hawk..and..John Crow..go down till them pitch on a tree. 1910 Anderson-Cundall 28 [Prov:] You can't keep crow from flyin', but you can keep him from pitchin' 'pon you head. 1924 Beckwith 115, The bird came and perched on the housetop..then David Lawrence sang..Then the bird pitched off the house to the spot where he heard the singing. 1943 *GL* StE, see EMBO. 1960 *CLS* 159 /di rieza shàap tél if a flái pích pán i, i kót im/ *The razor is so sharp that if a fly settled on it, it would cut him.*

2. Fig: To stop somewhere for a short time.

1956 BLB StJ, see FOLLOW-LINE.

3. To fall headlong forward. *BA BL*

1943 *GL* StM, Pitch, fall voluntary or pushed. 1960 *CLS* 178, babíabúo..pích óut a di kátn tríi an dráp dóun a gróun so, búm!

PITCHY-PATCHY adj and sb dial; cf *EDD pitch* sb[3], v[2].

A. adj: Very much patched. *G*

1942 Bennett 24, Him put awn wan pitchy-patchy pants.

B. sb: 1. Old, ragged work clothes.

1959 DeC Tre /pichi-pachi/.

2. A person wearing ragged or patchy clothes.

1943 *GL* Port, Pitchy-patchy, one in tatters. 1956 Mc Port /pichi-pachi/ wearing worn but mended clothes; /raba/ is one in rags—*un*patched.

3. One of the stock characters in a John Canoe troupe.

1952 Kerr 144, The *Jockey*, and *Pitchy-Patchy*, who maintained order with a cattle-whip and kept the audience from crowding the dancers.

PITGAUL sb dial; <*spit*, an exact likeness (*EDD* sb[1] 19) +uncert element prob representing *gob*, a quantity of spittle (*EDD* sb[1] 3). An exact likeness.

1943 *GL* no addr, Pitgaul, bearing the same image.

PITH sb; cf *OED* 1. The young edible bud leaves of the cabbage palm.

1873 Rampini 155, The Mountain Cabbage..Its *pith*, as it is popularly called, *chou de palmiste*, as the French term it, is perhaps the most delicate vegetable in the tropics.

pitieta sb dial; cf *EDD*, *potato*. A common pronunc of *potato*. *BL*

1868 Russell 5, Marra, Marrow; Pedita, Potato. 1943 *GL* Clar, Pitata, sweet potato. 1961 FGC StAnd and gen /pitíeta/.

PITPIT sb dial; by iteration of the base of *pitieta*.

1943 *GL* Tre, Pitpit, potatoes.

PITY-ME-LITTLE sb dial; having the sense 'pity me who am so little'. A very small red ant with a very sharp sting.

1952 FGC Man, StT, Tre /pítimilítl/ 'red with black eyes', 'build nest in banana tree, very hot bite', 'sting you one place a thousand times'.

plaan sb dial; a reduced pronunc of *plantain*, which has such forms as [plá:n, plá:n̩, pláʔn, plá:ntn̩, plá:ntɪn]. *BL*

1943 *GL* Man, Plaan, plantain; StM, Plan'leaf, £1 note.

plaba, ploba sb dial; prob <*clabber* sb, naturally curdled milk. Cf CLABUB.

1. Sour milk.

1943 *GL* Kgn, plaba. 1957 DeC StAnd /plabop/—sour milk.

2. Boiled coconut sauce, custard, or rundown.

1943 *GL* Man, Plabo, remains from boiled coconut oil—custard. 1958 DeC Port /plobo/ whole banana boiled in a run-down.

3. An even more miscellaneous dish; a stew.

1955 FGC Man /plaba/—stew. 1956 Mc Port /plaba/ —A dish consisting of a variety of things all cooked together (no set constituents—may be ground provisions, with meat or fish, etc.).

4. A mix-up, a quarrel. (Cf *EDD claver* sb[2] 3, a dispute; and perh *palaver*.) s PALAVA.

1955 FGC Man /plaba/ quarrel. 1956 Mc Port /yu go get yosef in plaba/ *You will get yourself into a quarrel.*

plabop vb dial; <*plaba*+*up*. Of milk: to go sour.

1957 DeC StAnd.

PLABURNA sb (or vb?) dial rare; etym unknown, but see *plaba*.

1943 *GL* Clar, Plaburna, feast.

PLAIN CASE see PLAYING CASE.

PLAIT-HAT sb chiefly dial. A hat made by sewing together long strips of plaited palm-thatch.

1877 Murray *Feedin' 'Perrit* 4, 'Well, buy a liben [living] plait hat fe a tenpance, an kibber de poor head, no'.

PLAITING /platn/ sb dial; *OED* →1882. THATCH ready woven or plaited into strips for use in making hats, etc.

1956 Mc Man (Alligator Pond), People from country come buy up di plat'n fi cya' i' away.

plaka-plaka see *pyaka-pyaka*.

PLAM-PLAM see PAM-PAM.

plan-aas vb dial; perh <*plan*, echoic (cf PLAM-PLAM) +*arse*. *T*

1958 DeC West /plan-aas/ to hit someone with the flat of a cutlass.

PLANT see *plaan*.

PLANTAIN-BARK sb. The lower part of the plantain leaf which forms the sheaf or 'trunk' of the tree; it strips easily and is used to tie light bundles, and to make weak rope.

1925 Beckwith 23, When Tiger ole [old], dem tek plantain-bark lead him.

PLANTAIN BIRD sb obs. An unidentified bird, prob the BLUE-BAIZE.

1740 Importance 38, Bonana Birds, colour'd yellow, red and white, and have fine Notes; Plantane Birds, a little blew Bird.

PLANTAIN CHIPS sb. Slices of green plantain cooked in boiling fat. *BA BL G*

1952 FGC StM.

PLANTAIN DRINK sb obs; *OED* 1663 only. A COOL-DRINK made from the fruit of the plantain.

1707 Sloane xxix, Plantain Drink is stronger than any of the others, except Acajou Wine, though subject to grow sower in a short time.

PLANTAIN LEAF sb dial.

1. The large flat leaf of the plantain tree, put to many uses, as wrapping material, etc.

1925 Beckwith 63 [Prov:] If nager hate you, him gi' you basket fe carry water; but if you cleber, you put plantain-leaf a bottom. *BA BL G T*

2. Slang: A one-pound note (which is green).

1943 *GL* StM, see *plaan*.

PLANTAIN PORRIDGE sb. A kind of porridge made of green-plantain flour. *G*

1952 FGC StJ, Plantain porridge—beat it, sieve it like cassava, and make johnny-cake; Port, green plantain porridge, eat with coconut milk.

PLANTAIN TRASH sb. The dried leaves of the plantain tree, used as packing material and for many other uses. *BL G*

1952 FGC StAnd /plaantn trash kyang mek matras, mat/.

PLANTAIN-WALK sb. A grove or plantation of plantain trees. *BL G*

1661 Hickeringill 20, Cacoa-trees..especially in their Infancy must be protected from the scorching Sun by the favourable interposition of some shady Trees; and therefore the Plantane-Walks are usually made choice of, for such Nurseries. 1961 FGC still in use.

PLANTATION EEL sb joc obs. The yellow snake—once eaten under the guise of 'eel'.

1790 Moreton 22, *Old Hector and Sambo*—..plantation eels and cane rabbits will not hurt them.

PLANT-CANE sb; *OED* 1793. A sugar-cane top cut off and planted. *BA G*

1790 Beckford I 161, It is a common practice, where corn will grow, to plant it with the canes..Among plant-canes, I do not conceive it of consequence..but when it is planted among ratoons, I conceive it to be universally prejudicial. 1793 Edwards II 210–11, Plant-canes in this soil (which are those of the first growth) have been known in very fine seasons to yield two tons and a half of sugar per acre. 1957 JN /pláan kíen/—the first crop from a new planting. Subsequent crops are /ratuun/.

PLANT DOWN vb phr dial. Of the spirit of a dead person: to consign it finally to the grave; to lay (a ghost).

1929 Beckwith 76, In Mandeville it is the cut-eye bean that is used to plant down the ghost.

PLANTER'S MEDICINE sb joc obs. Flogging: see quot.

1839 McMahon 192–3, All persons in the hospital afflicted with ulcers..were flogged every Monday morning until the ulcers got better, and the patient was enabled to leave..discipline of this kind was customary on every estate..it was called planter's medicine.

PLANTING ESTATE sb. An estate especially suitable for planting.

1839 McMahon 244, see DRY-WEATHER ESTATE.

PLATTER sb dial joc; cf *EDD platter-foot*, flat-footed.

1943 *GL* StAnd, Platters, feet.

PLAW vb dial; prob <*claw* vb; cf *plaba* <*clabber*.

1943 *GL* Clar, Plaw, scratch.

PLAY sb dial; <*play* (*OED sb* 8).

1. An entertainment among plantation negroes, including singing, dancing, and feasting; one common occasion for this was, and continues to be, a wake, and especially NINE-NIGHT.

1774 Long II 475, A particular attention should also be had to their [the Coromantyns'] plays, for these have always been their rendezvous for hatching plots. 1788 Marsden 33, Every Saturday night many divert themselves with dancing and singing, which they stile plays; and, notwithstanding their week's labour, continue this violent exercise all night. 1825 De la Beche 40–1, Negroes in giving dances or plays sometimes go to great expense..The dance, or play, as it is sometimes called, commences about eight o'clock..and..continues to daybreak with scarcely any intermission, those of the old school preferring the goombay and African dances, and those of the new fiddles, reels, &c. 1833 Scott I 204, The following night there was to be a grand play or wake in the negro houses, over the head cooper, who had died in the morning.

2. Hence: *play-day*, a day's holiday; *play-night*, a night on which there is playing in connection with a funeral—see quot.

a1818 Lewis (1834) 89, Saturday's holiday (or *play-day*, in the negro dialect). *Ibid* 192, In addition to their holidays at Christmas, I gave them for play-days Good-Friday, the second Friday in October, and the second Friday in July ..The first is to be called 'the royal play-day', in honour of that excellent Princess, the Duchess of York..the July play-day is to be called 'the massa's'. 1958 DeC StT /plie-nait/ a funeral meeting on the 2nd to 8th nights, characterized by ring games and similar secular activity.

3. A dance or game (e.g. *baakini*, RING PLAY) of the kind played in connection with a funeral.

1956 Mc StE (Accom), The expression is 'to play baakini', and the baakini is called 'play': /kom plie di baakini, mek di liedi si—kom sho di plie/. 1957 DeC Clar, The word /plie/ seems to equal 'game': /dingki-mini/ described as 'ring play'.

PLAY vb dial; cf PLAY sb.

1. To indulge (oneself) in recreation. *BA G*

1796 *Braco* 26 Dec, All the Negroes having day to play themselves.

2. To hold a PLAY; to perform a play-dance.

1951 Murray 17 [Song:] Short an' stout gal a play we deh play. 1956 Mc StE (Accom) /kom plie di baakini/. *BL G*

3. In neg expr: not to be amusing oneself, to be serious about something. *BL G*

1927 Anderson-Cundall 64 [Prov:] When guinea-hen cry him say, 'ooman no fe play. 1952 Kerr 42, Henry said he was taught not to tell lies..He was flogged for doing it. His mother is not a 'playing woman'; she is very serious when she is vexed and 'will lash your head off' during this time.

4. To act by trickery or deception; const *off*, *out*—see quots. (Cf *OED play sb* 9.)

1912 McK *Ballads* gloss, play out: deceive. 1924 Beckwith 33, Tacoomah..was tried and sentenced to be hung. Anansi said, 'Brer Tacoomah, no fret! I'm a good liar; I play you off'.

PLAY-DAY see PLAY sb 2.

PLAYING-CASE sb dial. See quots.

1950 Moore 137, Playing case—another name for a 'playing drum' or treble drum. 1952 Kerr 145, Nobby showed us the drums and explained how they are made.. The name of the bass drum is Kynando, that of the other, Plain Case..Plain Case is made of trumpet wood.

PLAY-NIGHT sb dial. = PLAY-DAY; cf SET-UP.

1960 DeC StT, in 1961 *CLS* 72.

PLAY-SONG sb dial; <*play* (*OED sb* 6) +*song*. See quot.

1924 Beckwith 110, 'Massah, me kyan' stop him singing, because it mus' of been his little play-song* what he have singing'. *Jamaica children compose a 'secret song' which they amuse themselves with at play or sing when they are walking alone.

PLAY STICK vb phr; <*play* (*OED sb* 1c) +*stick*. To play a game of attack and defence with staves or strong sticks. (See STICK-LICKING.) *BA*

1924 Beckwith 46, When dey cut done, dey carry out in de open, dey begin to play stick, lick stick. Dem two go, dem two cut plantain, an' dem come out 'pon de open an' dem play.

PLAY-STONE sb dial; <*play* (*OED sb* 6) +*stone*. A stone thrown in play.

1873 Rampini 179 [Prov:] Play-stone kill bird.

PLEASE-ME sb dial.

1943 *GL* Han, Please-me, large round cakes.

PLEASURE /pléja/ vb refl dial; *OED* 1b a1619. To take (one's) pleasure; enjoy (oneself). *G*

1956 Mc StE (Accom) /dem pleja dem sel/ (take refreshments at nine-night).

PLEASURENESS sb dial.

1950 Moore 106, Pleasureness = pleasure.

PLENTY adj (often absol) and adv dial. *G*

1. In neg expr: not much, not many.

1952 FGC StJ, A few people have one-one trees—not so plenty (*not very many*). 1956 Mc Clar /it luk laik yu kyaan dringk plenti at aal/ *It seems you can't drink much* (to Mrs B, exhausted half way through a bottle of fizz).

2. Freq iterated: a very great deal; very many.

1868 Russell 8, It must be observed that plenty-plenty as an Adverb is more used by Coolies and other emigrants. 1952 FGC StAnd, Rain-bird [is] swallow; fly in great numbers, plenty plenty plenty, 'nuff 'nuff. 1954 LeP Port /ar ozban min drongk plenti plenti dat nait/. 1956 Mc Man /som a dem get plenti plenti moni/.

PLIERS sb dial. A kind of dumpling: see quots.

1958 DeC Port /plaiaz/ small finger-shaped dumplings, same as *spinners*; Tre, Any shape of boiled dumpling made with soda; this apparently makes the dumpling exceptionally tough.

PLIKS sb dial; echoic.

1959 DeC West /pliks/ a dumpling kneaded until very tough; so called from the sound made when bitten into.

plimpla sb dial; <*pin-pillow*, a pin-cushion, with reduction of unstressed vowels, assimilation of *n* to *m* before *p*, and assimilative intrusion of *l* in first syllable. Cf Barbados *pimploe*. The cactus *Opuntia tuna* and similar species. Also called TUNA. *BA G*

1943 *GL* no addr, Plimpla, a berry that yields a red dye. [Ref to cochineal insect, grown on tuna plants.] 1952 FGC StE /plímplà/ the tuna with large prickles. 1956 Mc Man /plímpla/ tuna.

plin sb dial; perh <*plim*, stout, fat, filled out; of bread, light (*EDD*). A boiled dumpling, specif a small, round one.

1958 DeC StT /plin/ a small, round, boiled dumpling; StE, a spinner dumpling.

plobo see *plaba*.

ploko-ploko see *pyaka-pyaka*.

plomi sb[1] dial; prob <*ploba*, with familiarizing -*y*.

1958 DeC Port /plomi/ coconut run-down.

plomi sb[2] see PLUMMY.

plongkas sb sing dial; cf *EDD plunk* sb[1] 3, a short, stout, and thick-set person, animal or thing; *plunky*, short, thick, heavy; -*as* may represent StdE -*ers*.

1. A heavy flour cake or dumpling.

1943 *GL* StE, Pluncas, flour cake. 1955 FGC Man /plongkas/ heavy cake, baked or fried. 1956 Mc Man /plongkas/ a big dumpling.

2. A heavy shoe.

1943 *GL* Kgn, Man, Pluncas, a heavy shoes. 1955 FGC Man /plongkas/ heavy, coarse shoes.

PLOUGH vb dial. To dig: the ordinary term in Ja. See next.

1956 Mc Man, To prepare the ground for planting /yu plóu it wit fáak/.

PLUG vb dial; prob <*plough*—cf *OED plugh(e)*, North-Engl pronunc. To dig; = PLOUGH.

1912 McK *Songs* 55, Aldough me heaby han' dem hab fe plug an' dig.

PLUM BANANA sb dial. A small variety of banana.

1952 FGC StJ /plom banana—likl shaat wan/.

PLUM-HEAD sb dial. A reddish fish similar to the snapper.

1952 FGC StE /plom hed/ like snapper; pale pink right through.

PLUMMY sb dial; <*plum* + -*y*.

1958 DeC StT /plomi/ a creased spinner dumpling; equivalent to COW-TONGUE.

PLUM(MY) MANGO sb; <*plum* (+ -*y*). See quots.

1837 Macfadyen 222, Plum Mango; a small variety of the fruit and scarcely eatable. 1952 FGC StAnd /plomi manggo/ very small.

PLUM TOMATO sb. A small variety of tomato resembling a plum. *G*

1952 FGC StC, StJ /plòm tumátis/.

PLUNCAS see *plongkas*.

PLUNDER vb dial.

1954 LeP Man, To hunt for food—to plunder.

PLY adv dial; echoic. A sound like that made by a strap striking someone. *G*

1868 Russell 19, A lick him *ply* wid de trap.

P.N.P. PARROT sb dial joc; <*P.N.P.*, initials of the People's National Party, which avowed interracial policies. A many-coloured variety of the PARROT fish.

1952 FGC StC /pii-en-pii parat/ same as rainbow parrot —all colours.

PO[1] /puo/ sb dial; <*po* (<Fr *pot de chambre*); neglected by *OED*, *EDD*, but see Partridge *Dict Slang*, low colloq, 19–20th cent. (Not specif Ja.) A chamber-pot, esp a common earthenware one; = PODIE. *BA BL G*

1943 *GL* Kgn, Po, the night-glass; StAnd, Poe. 1955 FGC Man /puo/ chimmy, clay pot, yabba. 1956 Mc Man, Eulin specified /puo/ as an earthenware chamber-pot; an enamel one is called /chiemba/ or /chimi/.

PO[2] sb; etym unknown: perh assoc with *po*, peacock (see *OED*).

1943 *GL* Port, Po, eunuch.

POADI-PAT see PODIE.

POCCO see POCO[1].

POCCOMEEA see POCOMANIA.

POCHO see POCO[1], PO' JOE.

POCKET-BOOK sb dial; from its flat, folded shape; cf the US pastry so called for the same reason. A kind of dumpling; also called COCO-BREAD, JACK.

1958 DeC StAnd /pakit-buk/ same as jack, a large fried dumpling. 1959 DeC Tre /pakit-buk; koko-bred/ two names for a cake made by rolling dough flat, folding once over, and baking; no sugar or leavening.

POCKET (SIDE) sb dial.

1958 DeC Port /paket, paket said/ a crocus bag hung from one shoulder.

POCKO-POCKO see *pyaka-pyaka*.

POCKWOOD sb now only bot; <*pock* sing of *pox*, syphilis, for which the gum was used as a medicine + *wood*. *OED* →1764. Also attrib. Lignum-vitæ.

1774 Long III 724, Gum lignum-vitæ, or Pock-wood Gum.—Gujacum. The gum is..in demand for its virtues in venereal taints. 1814 Lunan I 444, Pockwood tree. 1954 *WIMJ* 26, *Guiacum officinale*..Lignum Vitæ; Pockwood Tree..The wood and resin (gum guaiacum) were at one time officially included in the pharmacopœias.

POCO[1] /poko/ sb dial; prob abbr of POCOMANIA or of the forms from which it comes. The abbr may be due in part to euphemism, or perhaps to avoid the uncertainty of the last part of the word. = POCOMANIA.

1942 Bennett 32, Se po' Miss Hayes outside da gwa'n Like she dah jump poco. 1943 *GL* no addr, Poco, an African cult; Clar, Pocco, a mixture of African and Christian Religion; Port, Poco, a religeous set of dancers; Clar, Pocho, poco, pocomania meeting; StM, Pucco, pocomania.

POCO[2] /poko/ adv dial; appar an abbr of POCO-POCO.

1943 *GL* Kgn, Poco, boco, ordinary or not too bad.

POCO-MAN sb dial; < POCO[1] + *man*. One who goes in for POCOMANIA, or leads a pocomania group.

1943 HPJ, see JUMPER. 1956 Mc StE (Accom), see JUMP.

POCOMANIA [pouko'meinjə] /pòkomíia/ sb; origin obscure: the present established form is due to false hispanizing of a probably African form which may be **po-* (unidentified) + *kumona*, of which dances wildly performed under possession by 'ancestral spirits', and induced catalepsy, are the prominent features; another possibility is Twi *po*, to shake or tremble + *kɔ̀m*, to dance wildly in a state of frenzy + MYAL. Some combination of these is even possible; the forms of attempted spellings imply considerable variation. In folk use the short form POCO[1] is the normal one.

A cult mixing revivalism with ancestral-spirit-possession. See quots.

1929 Beckwith 176–7, Revivalist and Obeah Man unite in the particular religious cult known as the Pukkumerian. The name is used in derision, say the followers of this cult; for they are really Revivalists like all the rest. . The Pukkumerians hold their meetings near a grave-yard, and it is to the ghosts of their own membership that they appeal when spirits are summoned to a meeting. .'They jump and dance and sing and talk in a secret language because the spirits do not talk our language. .' In an open meeting, 'when the ghost comes they stretch out as if dead and the ghost talks to them'; nobody hears but the person in the trance. After the ghost leaves he comes out of the trance and tells everything the ghost says. 1943 *GL* Kgn, Pocomania, a religious cult; Man, Puccomina, revival; StT, Puck-co-myal, a kind of headan [heathen] Worshiping; Clar, Poccomeea, a legious mania. 1953 Moore 60, Pocomania, also called poco—The 'Black Israelites'. .'looked upon with disfavour by all the other cult groups' who consider it devil worship. In their ceremonies they use rum and ganja.

POCOMANIAN sb. A follower of the POCOMANIA cult.

1929 Beckwith 176–7, see POCOMANIA.

POCO-MUNGEE sb rare obs; < Amer Sp *pachamanca*, a meal, cooked in a hole in the ground with heated stones, and highly seasoned with capsicum or chili pepper; < Quichua. CAYAN-BUTTER.

1833–4 Hosack (1876) 98, A second course of forest game Was served. . With poco-mungee* and champagne. . *Poco-mungee—a name given by the maroons to a mixture of red bird-peppers and table salt ground together between two river stones.

POCO-POCO /poko-poko/ adv dial; iteration of Sp *poco*, small, not much—perh taken out of a longer phrase. In answer to the question 'How are you?' or the like: Fairly well. *BL G T*

1943 *GL* Kgn (several informants), Poco-poco: Reply to 'how-di-do' meaning 'not too good'; not too bad; StE, Not so bad but not too well. 1955 FGC Man /poko-poko/ not so bright, not so pleasant.

PODDER see *pata* sb[1].

PODIE /púodi/ sb dial; a hypocoristic form of *pot-de-chambre*; see PO[1], and cf US *potty*. A chamber-pot. Also attrib.

1943 *GL* Clar, Powdie, night glass; Kgn, Podie, chamber; Port, Poodie, urinary utensil; StM, Poudy, bedroom utensil; No addr, Poa-di-pat, chamber.

PODO sb; abbr of *Podocarpus*. Among foresters and planters: the introduced tree *Podocarpus usumbarensis*.

1952 FGC StAnn /púodò/ similar to yacca, found at Hardwar Gap. 1954 *FG* 254, Podo (Cape Yacca). This species is a native of South Africa and produces a light pine-type timber suitable for general constructional work.

POE see PO[1].

POINTER sb slang or cant. A knife.

1936 Martinez, see COCKS.

POINT-NOSE JACK sb dial. A fish of the Jack type with a pointed nose.

1952 FGC StC, StE, StT.

POISON-BERRY sb; *OED* 1756 only. Species of the genus *Cestrum*, several of which are native to Jamaica.

1696 Sloane 169, Syringa laurifolia Jamaicensis. . Poyson Berries. 1811 Titford 47, Rough-leaved Cestrum. . Is a native of Jamaica, and there are eight other species, one called Poison-berries. 1864 Grisebach 786, Poison-berry: *Cestrum*.

POISON CASSA'VA sb dial. = WILD CASSAVA.

1952 FGC StC /paizn kasava/. *BA*

POISON CHERRY sb. The shrub or small tree *Rhacoma crossopetalum*.

1926 Fawcett 29.

POISON DOGWOOD sb. = DOGWOOD 1, BITCHWOOD.

1952 FGC StT, Poison dogwood—beat and put in water to stun fish.

POISONED GROUPER see POISON GROUPER.

POISON(ED) HOGMEAT sb; <*poisoned* + HOGMEAT.

1. The vine *Aristolochia grandiflora*.

1756 Browne 329, see HOGMEAT. 1864 Grisebach 784, Poisoned Hog-meat. 1914 Fawcett 106, Poisoned Hog-Meat.

2. A kind of nightshade (convolvulaceous).

1952 FGC StM, Poison hogmeat—white nightsage.

POISONED HOGWEED sb. = POISONED HOGMEAT.

1864 Grisebach 784.

POISON GROUPER /pàizn grúpa/ sb; < *poison* + GROUPER. The fish *Scorpæna plumieri* and other similar species.

1756 Browne 454, Trigla 3. . The poisoned Grooper. The head of this fish is moderately large and full of prickly protuberances. 1851 Gosse 207, One of these was sufficiently hideous, and was no favourite with the old negro, who gave it the name of Poison-grouper. It was a species of *Apistes*. 1854–5 *TJSA* 1 142, *Scorpæna braziliensis*—poison grouper. 1892 Cockrell, Poison grouper, *Scorpæna stearnsii*. 1952 FGC Port, StC, StJ, StM, StT, West /paizn grupa/ brown colour; numb you; bone stick you, cramp you up.

POISONOUS CAPE GOOSEBERRY sb.

1954 *WIMJ* 22, *Physalis angulata* L. Poisonous Cape Gooseberry; Hog Weed; Winter Cherry.

POISON TOMATO sb dial. = COCKROACH BERRY.

1952 FGC StE /pàizn tumátis/.

P.O.J. CANE sb; acronym of *Præf-Station Oost-Java*, where this cane was developed. (Popularly thought to mean 'Pride of Java'.) A variety of sugar-cane. *G*

1952 FGC Port, StT, P.O.J. cane; StJ, StM, P.O.G. cane [erron].

PO' JOE /púojúo/ sb dial; prob <*poor Joe*. A small or young fish; also attrib of some variety of *wenshman*.

1943 *GL* Port, Pocho—a young or small kind of fish. 1952 FGC StJ /púojúo wénshmàn/.

pokasii see *pakasa*.

pok choi see POP-CHOW.

poko, poko-poko see POCO², POCO-POCO, *pyaka-pyaka*.

poko-tempo sb dial; <Sp *poco-tiempo*, a short time. Something temporary, slight, of little consequence. *BL*

1943 *GL* Port, Puccotempo, nothing of consequence. 1955 FGC Man, 'It's just a little /poko-tempo/' something temporary.

pok-pok sb dial; perh <*kapok*, the latter portion iterated. An unidentified tree—perhaps the Ceiba (Silk-cotton) or other like it.

1952 FGC StE /pok-pok/ (2 informants)—soft wood, similar to cotton; for boards, furniture; leaf something like pigeon-wood; tall tree; take it make ceiling, division.

pokro adj dial; etym unknown. Extremely poor.

1943 *GL* StJ, Puckro, poor. 1955 FGC Man /pokro/ very poor, just barely living.

POLEEN see *poliin*.

POLICE sb dial; *DAE* 1839, 1856 '*Colloq. obs.*'

1. A policeman. *BA BL G T*

1924 Beckwith 126, An' he sen' for a police an' tak up Anansi same time. 1957 JN, Him is a Police.

2. A variety of sweet-potato, perh in allusion to its roughness.

1929 Beckwith 18, [In Mandeville] 'police' is a round potato 'with peg-peg all over'.

3. In cpds: alluding to the police uniform (cf RED SEAM), and to the physical sternness of the police force. See separate entries below.

POLICE MACCA sb dial; <POLICE + MACCA: the name alludes to its sharp, punishing prickles. The plant *Kallstrœmia maxima*; sometimes also *Tribulus cistoides*; see quots.

1952 FGC Man, Police macca—because it catches you. 1954 *FG Kallstrœmia maxima*..The Police Macca is a creeping herb with a deceptively tender appearance. The fruits bear exceedingly sharp spines; the common name has been applied because ''im don' joke wi' dem 'im catch'. The closely related Jamaica Buttercup shares this quality. 1954 *WIMJ* 27, *Tribulus cistoides* L. Jamaica or Kingston Buttercup; Police Macca; Turkey Blossom; Kill Buckra.

POLICEMAN¹ sb dial. The red-striped variety of *Prepodes vittatus* (the FIDDLER BEETLE), the red stripes representing those on the Jamaican policeman's trousers.

1954 *NHN* VI 166.

POLICEMAN² /póliismán/ sb dial. The fish *Bodianus rufus* (and perh other similar species).

1952 FGC Port, Policeman, same as Nancy Pretty, Banana Cudjo; StE, Policeman—something like pangra, black above and yellow below.

POLICE TURBOT sb dial; <POLICE + TURBOT. A fish prob of the genus *Balistes*.

1952 FGC STC /poliis tórbit/ have a red stripe and two macca at the tail.

POLIEN see next.

poliin sb chiefly dial; <Amer Sp (Cuba) *polín*, a railway sleeper. (Santamaría.) A railway sleeper (on which the tracks are laid).

1943 *GL* Man, Port, Tre, Poleen, Poline, Polien, railway sleepers. 1952 FGC StE /pùolíin, políing/ take wild guinep and make /políin/ for railway. 1955 FGC Man /políin/.

poliing, POLINE see prec.

POLINK see PALENQUE.

POLL-HEAD (COW) sb dial. A polled cow.

1952 FGC StAnn, Poll-head—never had horns; West /puolhed/ clip cow horn-point.

POLLO sb dial; prob var of *poro*.

1943 *GL* West, Pollo, distress. 1960 LeP, known also at Elderslie, StE.

POLLY LIZARD /pali lizad/ sb chiefly dial; etym uncert—this may be a folk abbr of Gosse's PALLETTE-TIP LIZARD, but cf Bini *ozikpalo*, lizard (with falling pitch on *-palo*); folk-etym personification seems to have entered also. The smallest Jamaican lizards; see quots.

1940 Lynn-Grant 65 ff, 'Pawli'—Gonatodes fuscus.. *Sphærodactylus argus henriquesi*..[and four other species of *Sphærodactylus*]. 1952 FGC Man /pali lizad/ a little dark-looking thing 2½ inches, very clean, hide a lot, see them at night; StAnd /pali lizad/ smallest out o' all, dark brown, in house, harmless little creature, don't do you nothing; also StT, West /pali/.

polts vb dial; <*pulse* vb; see *OED*, *EDD* sb².

1958 DeC Clar /polts/ to pulp, as one does to coffee berries.

POMME D'OR sb; <Fr *pomme d'or*, golden apple. The vine *Passiflora laurifolia*, and its fruit.

1913 Harris 18, The Pomme d'Or, or Water-lemon..is quite the best of the smaller fruited edible Passifloras. 1926 Fawcett 235–6, *P. laurifolia*..Pomme d'Or, Golden Apple, Water Lemon. 1956 Mc StAnd /pam doa, pam duor/ a small yellow fruit with soft seeds inside, grows on /likl trii, ron laik wis/.

pom-pom yam, POMPON see PUMPUM YAM.

'PON see *pan*.

POND FISH sb dial. The giant water bug: see quot.

1944 *NHN* II 120, Of the Belastomids we have at least two species. The Giant Water bug, or 'Pond Fish' as it is locally called, sometimes reaches a length of four inches.

POND TILE sb dial; perh <*palm* or PAWN + unidentified element. The Elkhorn Coral (*Acropora palmata*).

1961 R. P. Bengry StAnd, 'Pond tile'—very common name for this coral among fishermen, though for what reason is unknown.

PONE /puon/ sb; <Amer Ind—see *DA*; *DA* 1612→ cakes made of maize or wheat; *potato pone DA* 1839→; *corn pone DA* 1859→ (diff sense in Ja); *sweet potato pone DA* '*obs.*' 1847, 1877 (= Ja senses 3, 2). *BA*; *BL* /pong/.

1. A cooking-utensil for baking cassava bread —corresponding to the present-day BAMMY IRON. (The citation is from Barbados, but cassava bread was made throughout the growing-area in much the same manner.)

1657 Ligon 29, They have a piece of Iron, which I guesse is cast round, the diameter of which, is about twenty inches, a little hollowed in the middle,..about halfe an inch thick at the brim or verge, but thicker towards the middle, with three feet like a pot, about six inches high, that fire may be underneath. To such a temper they heat this Pone, (as they call it) as to bake, but not burn. When 'tis made thus hot, the Indians, whom we trust to make it, because they are best acquainted with it, cast the meal upon the Pone, the whole breadth of it, and put it down with their hands, and it will presently stick together: And when they think that side almost enough, with a thing like a Battle-dore, they turn the other; and so turn and return it so often, till it be enough, which is presently done.

2. A baked sweet-potato? (This may be sense 3.) Obs. (Cf *DA sweet potato pone* quot 1877.)

1725 Sloane II 365, Patatas bak'd are excellent Food and call'd Pone[.] Mr Barham in his Observations.

3. A kind of pudding made of sweet-potato or maize, grated or as meal, with sugar and spices, and baked in an iron pot 'with fire above and below' called *pone*, or specif, *corn*, *potato*, or *sweet-potato pone*. See POTATO PUDDING. *G T*

1774 Long II 413, They make likewise a kind of pudding, with pounded maize; and sometimes of the sweet potato, which they call a potatoe-pone. *Ibid* III 774, The roots [of sweet potato] pounded are often made into a kind of pudding, called here a *pone*, which is baked. 1893 Sullivan 45, Sweet Potato Pone. [Recipe given.] 1952 FGC most parishes /púon/; StM, 'A St Elizabeth word—we don't have it here'; Port, StJ /puon/ is harder than pudding. 1956 Mc StAnd (Dallas) /kaan puon—grieta di kaan wi shuga/ boil in pot like dokunu. 1957 *FFM* 160, Potato Pone. 6 lb. grated pared raw sweet potatoes..(etc).

pong see POUND.

PONGO-RONG adv dial; echoic, but cf Twi *pòntóŋ-pòntóŋ*, expression imitative of the sound of drumming or of felling trees. The sound made by something heavy falling and rolling or thumping to a stop.

1868 Russell 19, De wood fall down *pongo-rong*.

PONY sb dial. A gelded horse. *G*

1956 Mc StAnd /puoni/—a /gyel haas/—called /stalyan/ before.

POO see GOIN PAAH.

POODIE see PODIE.

POOH see GOIN PAAH.

POOKA-POOKA adv dial; echoic. Imitation of the sound of water boiling in a kettle.

1929 Beckwith 202, Riddle: 'John Red-man tickle John Black-man till he laugh "pooka pooka"' alludes to the kettle singing over the fire.

POOM BAN see *pum-pan*.

POONOO sb dial; cf Akan dial of Twi *pũnu*, to become tumid or turgid, and the reduplicated form *pumpuŋ*; also PUMPUM YAM. (Cf also Sth US *poon-tang*, copulation.) *G*

1943 *GL* Tre, Poonoo, vulva.

POONYAAK see *punyaak*.

POOPALIK see PUPA-LICK.

POO PAN see *pum-pan*.

POOP-STINK PARROT sb dial; <*poop*, break wind +*stink*+PARROT. A variety of the parrot fish that is dark and soft (though it does not smell bad).

1952 FGC StC /pupstingk parat/.

POOR sb dial; by conversion <*poor* adj. Poverty.

1925 Beckwith 96 [Prov:] Poor ketch Cubba a low groun', him turn sarvent fe darg..If poverty finds Cubba ..destitute, he will be willing to serve even a poor man.

POOR JOE see PO' JOE.

POOR-MAN'S FRIEND sb dial.

1. The plant *Stylosanthes viscosa*.

1927 Beckwith 24, Poor-man's friend..For the kidneys boil and drink as tea. 1943 *GL* Kgn, Po man fren, a creeper used as medicine. 1954 *WIMJ* 18, S. viscosa.. Poor Man's Friend..used in decoction for the treatment of colds.

2. =POOR-MAN'S TEA, SEA(SIDE) THYME.

1943 *GL* Man, Po man fren, sea thyme.

POOR-MAN'S PUDDING sb dial.

1958 DeC 22 /pur-man-pudn/ pudding made with stale bread, breadfruit, etc.

POOR-MAN'S SAUCE sb; *OED* 1706 only.

1893 Sullivan 103, Poor man's sauce..Sliced ripe peppers, and..shalots..mustard seed..pork or herring pickle.. boiled twice over.

POOR-MAN'S TEA sb. A 'tea bush'; also called SEA(SIDE) THYME.

1927 Beckwith 25, Poor-man's tea. *Evolvulus arbuscula*.. Used in place of tea.

POOR ME BOY, POOR ME GAL int phr dial. An exclamation of self-pity in Jamaica characteristically adding 'boy', 'gal', or one's name, in apposition to the 'me' of the ordinary Engl phr 'poor me'. Note also the occas var 'me poor boy'. **s.**

1873 Rampini 105, Lard! I wish I never been barn. Poor me, Garg! [George]. I love Miss Lucy to distraction. 1877 Murray *Kittle* 25, Mudfish say, 'poor me boy, me done for to-day'. 1877 Murray *Feedin' 'Perrit* 7, Him hit it ya, bam; de door fly open. Liza say 'Por me gal, disha da massa in a de place'. 1907 Jekyll 187, Me want go home a yard oh! poor me boy me want go home. 1912 McK *Ballads* 28, 'O Mac, me feel so sick,' he said, 'I t'ink me poor boy soon wi dead'. 1942 Bennett 12, 'Po me charlie bwoy'; *ibid* 16, Po' me gal couldn' a did vote.

POOR-ROO see *poro*.

POOTU see *putu*.

POP sb see PAP.

POP /pap/ vb trans or intr.

1. To break, in any simple sense (no noise being necessarily involved); to crack, tear, come apart. *BA BL G*

1907 Jekyll 38, Then, as the Ratta dance, the high figure whé him make, him slide in the floor an' him trousies pop. 1924 Beckwith 37, While pulling, the tail broke in two. So Anansi had to give Foolman a piece of the tail that popped off. *Ibid* 80, An' Jack say, 'I gwine to pop de hen wing'. 1943 *GL* Kgn, Man, Port, StAnn, StE, Tre, Pop, break; StAnn, Pappi, break it. 1950 Pioneer 67, Den ah wi get ah chance fe pop him neck. 1956 Mc StE /yu gwen pap it/ *You'll break it* (a string of beads); /di glaas pap op/ *The glass was broken to pieces*.

2. To pop out: of a plant, to bud, to put out a shoot or a fruiting stalk. *BL*

1956 Mc Man /yam fut pap af di yam hed/ *A yam-foot grows from the yam-head;* /mi plaan tuu kuoknat intu it bot shi duon pap yet/ *I planted two coconuts in it, but they haven't begun to shoot yet.*

3. To break away from the place of attachment; const *out*. *BL G*

1956 Mc StJ /shi aalwiez pap-out grie hiez/ *She always pulls out grey hairs.*

4. To tell, reveal; also const *out*.

1942 Bennett 4, Pop-tory gimme Dela, all De labrish from yuh yard [*Tell me the story, Dela—give me all the gossip*]. 1943 *GL* StJ, Pop out, reveal. 1957 Bennett 59, Wa happen to dem sweet Jamaica Joke yuh use fe pop?

POP-BUR sb dial; <*pop* vb + *bur* sb. A common weed (*Salvia serotina*) with small 'burs' along the stem which pop when squeezed.

1952 FGC Man, Pop-bur, same as chicken-weed.

pop choi see next.

POP-CHOW, POP-CHOY sb; <Chinese (Cantonese) [baˀ tʃɔi], the second syllable prob infl by colloq *chow*, food. A green vegetable very similar to Swiss chard, introduced by the Chinese. *G*

1943 *GL* Kgn, Pop chow, Chineese, vegetable. 1952 FGC StAnd /pap chau/ at Cross Roads market; StC /pat chau/. 1960 NJL StC /pop choi/; EWM StAnd /pok choi/.

POPINAX see POPONAX.

POPISHO see POPPY-SHOW.

POP-NUT sb dial; POP + *nut*; but cf PARK NUT.

1. The tree *Omphalea triandra*. (This tree was much earlier called PIG NUT; it is possible that 'pop-' nut is altered from this.)

1920 Fawcett 320, Cob-nut, Pop-nut.

2. The trees *Acacia lutea* and *A. tortuosa*.

1941 Swabey 27, Parknut—(Popnut). 1943 *NHN* II 29, *Acacia tortuosa* Popnut Cashaw..It is said that the fruit, eaten by stock, swell to such an extent as to kill the animal [i.e. to make it burst or 'pop'].

3. The tree *Sloanea jamaicensis*, from the way in which the seed capsule (the 'nut') pops open.

1952 FGC StAnn, Pop-nut, same as break-axe, puss-head. (Said to be so called also in StE.)

4. The tree *Hernandia jamaicensis*.

1963 Proctor Institute of Ja, I have never heard the tree called anything but 'Popnut'.

POPO see PAPAW.

POP-OFF sb dial.

1. See quot 1955.

1943 *GL* StT, Pop-off, flour. 1955 FGC Man, Pop-off, flour and water mixed to make johnny-cake.

2. See quot 1960, and cf HOP-OFF.

1943 *GL* StM, Pop-off, 'stolen with pride'. 1960 NJL StC, Pop-off, an illegal rake-off, the proceeds of a 'racket' of some kind; a cut off the usual price, illegally received.

POPONAX sb; poponax 1725→, popinax 1727 1740; aphetic form of *opoponax*. The tree *Acacia tortuosa*; also called WILD POPONAX. *N*

1725 Sloane 384, This [*sc* 'Acacia Americana'] is call'd Poponax in Jamaica, where the root is us'd by Tanners to thicken their leather and to dye black. 1727 *Observations* 15, The fragrance of whose Flowers, intermixt with Jessamines or Popinaxes, is ready to overcome the Sense. 1740 Importance 54, Popinax, which has a very faint offensive smell, and stinks so much when it is cut, that nobody cares to go near it; it has a yellow everlasting Blossom. 1756 Browne 252, Mimosa 2..The Poponax. This shrub has been introduced to Jamaica, from the main continent. 1774 Long III 812–3, Poponax or Acacee..The person who first gave it introduction probably mistook it for the true *acacia*, which yields the medicinal gum. 1854–5 *TJSA* I 62, Poponax. Acacia tortuosa.

PO-POT sb dial; <PO[1] + *pot*. = PO[1], PODIE.

1943 *GL* Clar, Han, Po-pot, night glass.

POPPESHA see POPPY-SHOW.

POP-POP vb dial; iterative of POP. To break out in many places.

1952 FGC StAnd, Crab-yaws on foot-bottom, make your toes pop-pop.

POPPY-SHOW /papi-shuo, papisho/ sb, adj, and vb dial; <*poppy-show*, a peep-show, puppet-show (*EDD* poppy sb[2]), ult <*poppet*, puppet (*OED* 3). *BL*

A. sb: 1. A ridiculous exhibition; more generally, any kind of foolishness, as, ridiculous talk or actions. See quots. *G T*

1943 *GL* Clar, Papishoe, foolishness. 1950 Pioneer 45, All de ballerina head dem, tie wid ballerina bow, Ballerina glamour mix wid Ballerina pappy-show! 1956 Mc Man /papishuo/ a crowd of idlers.

2. A person who makes a foolish exhibition of himself. *G T*

1943 *GL* Kgn, Pappyshow, game stock; StJ, Popisho, a fool, Papishow, subject to ridicule. 1952 FGC Han /papi-shuo/ clown or idiot, stupid talking whether he knows it or not. 1954 LeP StE, A buffoon—a pappie show. 1956 Mc Man /a riil papisho/ a buffoon.

B. adj: (From sense 2 above.) Foolish, buffoonish, showing off. *N*

1896 Trowbridge in *Jrl Amer Folk-Lore* xxxv 282, Chuh, chil'! yo' too poppesha! *Ibid* 287, *Poppesha*. Foolish, stupid. 1943 *GL* StE, Poppy-show, ostentatious.

C. vb: To render ridiculous. *T*

1943 *GL* StAnd, Pappyshow, make a fool of.

POPS sb obs; see quot. *Passiflora fœtida*.

a 1726 Barham (1794) 136, Passion Flowers..Those called pops, because, if you squeeze the fruit, it pops off, being hollow. 1725 Sloane 376, The fruit..call'd vulgarly Pops in Jamaica..is eaten in that Island.

POP STORY see POP vb 4.

POP STYLE vb phr dial; <POP vb 4. To show off style; see quot.

1954 LeP Kgn, Of a woman: to walk in provocative fashion—pop style.

PORCUPINE YAM sb. A manner of serving yam so that it resembles a porcupine; see quot.

1913 Harris 44, Porcupine Yam. Two pounds yam, boil and mash with one egg and salt to taste. Shape the roll in beaten egg and vermicelli; fry.

PORGEE, PORGHEE, PORGO see next.

PORGY /paagi/ sb; <Pg, Sp *pargo*, sea bream.

1. Fish of the family *Sparidæ*, esp genus *Calamus*. *BA G N*

1679 Trapham 65, see GRUNT. 1725 Sloane 286, Pagrus lineis luteis varius..The Pargie. 1756 Browne 446, Sparus 2..The Porgee. This fish is very like the Bream both in form and appearance. 1952 FGC StC, StE, StT, West /paagi/.

2. The PORGY GRUNT.

1952 FGC Port /paagi/—a species of grunt.

PORGY GRUNT sb. A variety of the GRUNT fish that resembles the PORGY.

1854–5 *TJSA* I 142, Hæmulon heterodon, porghee grunt. 1952 FGC StJ, StM /paagi gront/.

poril sb dial rare; etym unknown. The STRAINER VINE.

1952 FGC StJ /póril/—strainer vine; long like /kwash/ can eat like chocho when young.

PORK GRUNT sb dial. Perh an error for PORGY GRUNT?

1952 FGC StM.

PORK WEED sb obs; erron for *poke-weed.* The poke-weed (*Phytolacca* sp.); also called JOCATO, MOUNTAIN CALALU.

1801 Dancer 368, Pork Weed—Jucato (*Phytolacca dodecand*). 1820 Thompson 152–3, I have often tried the pork weed, an ounce of the dried root, infused in a pint of wine.

poro, puru sb dial; for dial sp see quots; etym uncert, but cf Twi (Fante, Akuapem) *puróẃ*, vb, to stumble; to challenge to a fight; to excite aversion. *BL*

1942 *GL* Han, Port, StAnn, Purro, trouble; Clar, Poorroo; Kgn, Porrow; StC, Porrah, trouble. 1955 FGC Man /wat a puru/ trouble. 1956 Mc StE, Get into /poro/ get into trouble.

PORPOISE(-FISH) sb ?obs; evid from some resemblance to the porpoise. The puffer fish now named *Cheilichthys testudineus.*

1892 Cockrell list, Porpoise—*Tetrodon testudineus.* 1899 *JIJ* II 614, Porpoise-fish.

PORRAH, PORROW see *poro.*

PORTER-BUSH sb dial; <*porter* (*OED sb*[3]) +*bush.* The shrub *Flemingia strobilifera*; see quot 1952.

1927 Beckwith 25, Porter-bush. 1952 FGC StC /puota-bush/; StM, same as wild hops; makes draught porter.

PORTER CUP sb obs; etym uncert, but note that *port* wine was an ingredient of the *cup.* See quot.

1837 Patterson 397–8, [At Port Royal] a tavern..where we indulged in a copious draught, known by the name of porter cup, an excellent and refreshing beverage, made of Madeira wine, Port, and other ingredients.

PORTERWEED sb; the reason for the name is unknown.

1955 *WIMJ* 160, *Stachytarpheta jamaicensis*..Vervain; Porterweed.

PORTER-WITHOUT-FROTH sb dial; <*porter* (*OED sb*[3]). Fig. 'A ne'er-do-well, no-account person.'

1958 DeC StE.

PORTLANDIA sb; see quot 1756. The shrub *Portlandia grandiflora.*

1756 Browne 164–5, The large-leaf'd Portlandia..This plant is called by the name of Portlandia, after the present dutchess of Portland, who is a great lover of Botany. 1790 Beckford I 32, The silver-white and silky leaves of the portlandia. 1873 Rampini 144–5, It was pleasant..to..watch the humming-birds flitting about amongst the great trumpet-like flowers of the Portlandia.

PORTLAND RED PEAS sb. A variety of the bean *Vigna unguiculata* grown esp in the parish of Portland.

1952 FGC StC, Portland red peas, same as Nelson-ball: the grain is round; StT, Portland red, very fine. 1954 *FG* 420, Portland Red appears to be restricted to the parish whose name it bears. The grains are small and of a dark red colour.

PORTLAND YAM sb. The yampi, which grows especially well in the parish of Portland (cf 1954 *FG* 446).

1952 FGC StC, Portland yam, pink and white, same as /injin yam, yampi/.

PORTMANTEAU sb; the folk pronunc preserves an older one (cf *OED* 16–17th cent spellings, e.g. *portmantue*); cf also MANTRY-MAKER.

1958 DeC Tre /puotmantyúu/ a flat bangkra.

PORT-MORANT TOBACCO sb dial joc obs; <*Port Morant*, parish of St Thomas.

1814 Lunan II 245, see SUSUMBA.

PORTO sb chiefly dial; <*Portuguese.* See quot.

1960 *CLS* 91 (from HPJ), Portuguese immigration from Madeira and the Azores..hardly affected Jamaica; one or two hundred Portuguese peasants did arrive, and I understand that their descendants in the Montego Bay area are still known as *Portos.*

PORT ROYAL SENNA sb; <*Port Royal*, parish of St Andrew+*senna.* Sloane's specimen was from Port Royal (1920 Fawcett 110, *Sloane Herb.* vi 23, 24!); it was called 'C. Portu-regalis' by Bancroft (1837 Macfadyen 340). =JAMAICA SENNA.

1953 *WIMJ* 239, *Cassia obovata*..Port Royal..Senna.. At one time it was cultivated on the Palisadoes with a view to exporting the senna.

PORTUGEE, PORTUGUESE sb now dial; cf *ODS*: from *Portuguese*, regarded as a plur. Various kinds of butterfly fish (*Chætodontidæ*) or similar types. *BA*

1756 Browne 455, Rhomboida 3..The Portugise. 1952 FGC StAnn /pùotagíi/—green colour; StC, StM, West /pùotagíi/ most like angel-fish, white with dark stripe, red stripe, similar to BRIM; StE /pùotigíi/ 'hog-fish' we call them; StT.

PORTUGISE see prec.

POSE OFF vb phr; cf *OED pose v*[1] 4b. To put oneself into a striking or exaggerated attitude. *BA G*

1950 Pioneer 16, Nancy see one big picture a Puss pose off eena de book.

'POSE-UPON sb joc obs. An old nickname for salt-fish.

1873 Rampini 157, ''Pose-upon'* (as the negroes call salt fish)..*'Pose-upon' means 'impose-upon', and salt fish is a universal stand-by in Jamaica.

posl =*pussley* (purslane). See BABY PUZZLE.

POST-HOLDER sb dial. In the cant of cults (St Thomas parish): one of the lower officers, who holds the post of the centre of the booth.

1953 Moore 89, Post-holder (=co-worker, bearer)—initiates in Revival groups.

POST(S) sb dial. =BONE 3.

1958 DeC Man /puos/—the ribs of a bamboo basket, usually made from /huk, huuk, huok/ [i.e. HOOK].

pota-pota see *poto-poto.*

POTATO LOUSE sb. See quot.

1725 Sloane 193, Patata Louse. This is a small Insect very much troubling those who go amongst Patata-Pieces.. it has a very small, brown Head and Thorax, with six indifferently long Legs of a light brown Colour..the Abdomen, is..almost round, and of a black and yellow Colour mix'd.

POTATO-PIECE sb; <*potato*+*piece* (*OED sb* 2b). A potato field. *BA*

1725 Sloane 193, see POTATO LOUSE.

POTATO PỌNE see PONE 3. *BA*

POTATO PUDDING sb. See quot. *BA*

1958 DeC StJ /pitieta pudn/ name for what is more widely called *potato pone*, i.e. a baked pudding of sweet potato; in parts of StJ the word PONE is reserved for a pudding made with corn meal.

POTATO-SLIP sb; *DA* 1855 in sense 2.

1. The type of sweet-potato having a yellow root. (See also WILD POTATO-SLIP.) *G*

1756 Browne 154, Convolvulus 12..Bermudas Potatoes.. The Potatoe and Potatoe-slip. Both these plants are now cultivated all over America..they are hardly distinguished by the tops, but the roots of the latter are constantly of a yellow colour, and those of the former white: the plant rises equally from the bits and slips, though generally propagated by the latter, and is cultivated by laying a few short juncks of the stem..in shallow.. trenches, and covering them with..mould. 1774 Long III 774.

2. A piece of sweet-potato vine used for planting. *BA*

[1756 Browne 154, see quot above.] 1961 FGC gen.

POTATO SPARROW sb dial. See quots. (No record has been found of a bird so called.)

1958 FGC StT. 1958 DeC StT /potíeta-sparo/ a very thin person.

POT BAMMY sb dial. A kind of BAMMY made in an iron pot.

1929 Beckwith 21, The [cassava] 'trash' which remains in the towel may be used in various ways for food. Spread out in the breeze for two hours, then mixed with salt and baked, it is called 'pot bammie'.

POT-BELLY sb; cf *OED* (in medical sense) 1822–34. A protruding abdomen. *BA G T*

1820 Thomson 63, Pot-bellies, as they are called, without other signs of worms, are not infallible precursors. Many negro children who have naturally this appearance enjoy the best health; it disappears as they advance in life.

POT-COVER sb dial. A flat, dark, somewhat round fish: specif the *panggra* and some kinds of ANGEL-FISH.

1929 Beckwith 33, On the towing line are caught..ocean piper; grupper; 'pot-cover'; 'angel'. 1952 FGC StE /pát kóva/ gray and black kinds. 1956 Mc Man StC /pát kóva, pát kíba/ a flat fish, also called /hienjel fish/.

POT-HOOK /patuks, patuk, patu/ sb now dial; cf *OED* 1 c.

1. An instrument of punishment: see quots.

1707 Sloane lvii, For running away they put..Pottocks about their Necks, which are Iron Rings with two long Necks rivetted to them. 1739 Leslie 167, The Chain and Pot-hooks are painted by his own Order in the Picture I spoke of just now. These are Instruments which are used to punish slaves and Servants. 1943 *GL* Clar, Patoock, a ring to shackle slave.

2. A triangular yoke of wood put on an animal's neck to prevent its getting through fences, etc.

1943 *GL* no addr, Pattux, a wooden triangular bar to keep pigs from boring. 1957 DeC StE (Accom) /patu/ sort of collar of sticks put on animal.

POTOO see *patu*.

poto-poto /póto-póto/ also /póta-póta/ sb and adj dial; see dial sp in quots; a word of wide distribution in W Africa, hence poss of multiple source in Ja: cf Twi *pɔ̀tɔpɔtɔ, n.* slimy sediment, *a.* slimy, muddy, miry. Cf also PUT-PUT.

A. sb: 1. Mud. *G*

1873 Rampini 71, Black rich mud, full of decayed vegetation..was a couple of feet deep in more than one part of the road. 'De putta-putta nasty every ting up', said Bob. 1943 *GL* Clar, Tre, Puto-puto, mud. 1956 Mc StAnd /póto-póto/ muddy puddles; /pota-pota/ when dig and soften earth and mix with water—otherwise /mod/.

2. Construction of a house with wet clay applied to wattle.

1958 DeC Port /poto-poto/ wattle-and-daub house construction; informant..deriving the word from *putty*.

B. adj: 1. Muddy. *G*

1957 DeC StE /poto-poto/ sopping, muddy.

2. Of foods: Cooked too moist or soft.

1943 *GL* Clar, Puto-puto, to boil food so soft that it resembles soup. 1956 Mc Man /poto-poto/ used of pudding that is spoiled by being too moist.

3. Of people: Reduced to nothing.

1955 FGC Man /poto-poto/—down and out.

POT SNAPPER sb; the reason for the name is unknown, but cf CUTTER 1. The muttonfish *Lutianus analis*.

1892 Cockrell list, Pot snapper—[also called] rounder snapper, red snapper, mutton snapper. *Lutjanus analis*. 1952 FGC Port, StAnn, StE, StJ, StM /pat snapa/—red, with yellow streak.

POT SPOON sb dial; *OED* 1440 only. *BL*

1. A spoon used for cooking. *BA G*

1952 FGC StJ /paki/—slice in two, make /pat puun/ to scrape pot. 1956 Mc Man /pat spuun/ spoon kept on pot while cooking.

2. A soupspoon.

1956 Mc Man, Spoon used for drinking soup.

POT-STICK sb dial; *OED* →1869. A stirring stick. *BA G*

1952 FGC StE, Turned cornmeal: pour in cornmeal and turn with pot-stick till hard.

POTTA see *pata* sb[1].

POTTOCK see POT-HOOK.

POTTOO, POTUCK see *patu*.

POT-WATER sb dial. The liquid that remains in the pot after cooking.

1952 FGC West, Cook bananas and lean pork, drink the pot-water, 'you 'trong like cow!' Boil out stain from plantain—the pot water make you 'like iron!'

POUDY see PODIE.

POUND /poun, pong/ sb and vb. *BL G*

1. In all StdE senses of pound: freq pronunc /pong/.

2. As a past participle (for *pounded*).

1952 FGC StM [Of cleaning coffee berries:] It is /pound/ in a mortar.

POUND CRAB sb dial; prob so called from its weight. An unidentified crab.

1952 FGC StC /poun krab/ a sea-crab, can eat; round, pretty colours, red, white.

POUNDER sb. A fish of the herring kind; prob a Bony-fish or Ten-pounder (*Elops saurus*). *BA*

1725 Sloane 282, Harengus major, totus argenteus, squamis majoribus..A Pounder. This fish was eleven inches long..white lips, and within were rough small Teeth..This fish is very full of Bones..there are much larger of the same sort.

POUN PAN see *pum-pan*.

POUYAT BANANA [puˈjæt] /puyáak/ sb. A favourite banana, more often called GROS MICHEL.

1913 Fawcett 16, see quot s.v. MARTINIQUE BANANA. 1954 LeP Port, Puyaak—banana; StE, Poyawk—plantain. [The change of *t* > *k* made here is not unusual—see Introd.]

POVERTY-TRUCK sb dial. A small handcart?

1925 Beckwith 59 [Prov:] Horse-cart and poverty-truck a no one..A horse-cart is not the same as a 'poverty-truck'.

POWDIE see PODIE.

POWER sb dial; cf *OED sb* 4.

1. Psychic or spiritual power believed to be possessed by individuals; it fluctuates in degree; when it is high (cf phr 'in the power') it may manifest itself through unusual ability to speak (eloquence, 'cutting unknown tongue', etc.) and through increased influence upon others, e.g. to heal. *BA G T*

1929 Beckwith 173, When ányone goes to him who he says has a duppy, he gets into great power, jumps and speaks tongues. 1950 Pioneer 31, Wen de gal dem hear Anancy song de whole a dem run out an crowd roun' him. Anancy was eena powah. 1954 Reckord 2, Me tell you Lal, me did think one time that what mek me leave Shepherd was just a sudden mood; but it was a deep instinct surge up strong from the bottom a me. Me hate him power solid as de earth. *Ibid* 8, Me only breeze in an breeze out again fe warn her say yu power high.

2. Attrib and comb: see separate entries.

3. A type of sandal made from old automobile tyres. (The name alludes to their strength.) Also called JUMP-AND-JIVE.

1943 *GL* Clar, Powa, car-tire sandals; StAnd, StC, Power. 1952 FGC Man, StAnd /póua/ shoes of auto tyre. 1956 Mc Clar, Man, Port, StAnd /póua/ sandal made of tyre.

POWER KEY, POWER STONE sb dial. A stone used in cult practice (POCOMANIA), through which the power of the spirits of the dead is believed to flow.

1950 Moore 60, Power stone, a stone used in Pocomania service—placed on the 'altar' or table, and covered with a black cloth having a white cross on it. *Ibid* 96, Power key, the triangular stone around which a Pocomania ground-altar is built.

POWER RING sb dial. A ring used as a GUARD (2); see quot.

1950 Moore 49, Power rings are ordinary metal finger rings consecrated by an obeah man, or blessed by Roman Catholic priests, to serve as guards against harmful spirits.

POX sb obs. See quot.

1823 Roughley 178, A disorder, which breaks out in mules, called in that country [*sc* Jamaica] the pox, so termed by the negroes, and considered as such by the white people. Whether through ignorance, or by giving facility to such a term, to make the complaint or disorder better understood, is a thing I cannot determine. This disorder suddenly appears near the fetlocks..being neither more or less than a blood spavin.

POYAWK see POUYAT BANANA.

PRAG, praga see PROG, PROGGER.

praginz see PROGGINGS.

praia sb dial; an irreg but common pronunc of *prayer*.

1910 Anderson-Cundall 14, Darg wake a marnin' and say him pr'yer. 1952 FGC StAnn /pràia mîitn/. 1958 DeC StT /praia miitin/ funeral wake on first night after death.

praimali sb dial; <*primary*. Tree-pruning term: see quot.

1957 DeC StAnd /praimali/ a sucker which must be pruned; it shoots out sideways or even down from the branch or limb, then crooks and grows upward.

pram-pram see PRANG-PRANG.

PRAN see LICK AN' PRAN.

PRANG-PRANG /prang-prang, pran-pran, pram-pram/ sb and adj; iterative of *prong*, and infl by BRANG-BRANG and similar forms. Brambles or small sticks usable for kindling; the same as GRANG-GRANG, BRAM-BRAM.

1943 *GL* Clar, Prang-prang, brambles; Port, Prang prang, with many sprangs; Man, Pran-pran, small wood. 1955 FGC Man /prang-prang/ with many prickles. 1956 Mc Man /prang-prang/ pieces of wood, jag-jag. 1958 DeC Man /pram-pram/ small sticks used for firewood.

PRAN-PRAN see prec.

prap vb dial; <*pop*, burst, with intrusive *r*—cf *primenta* for pimento. Of corn: to pop.

1956 Mc StE (Accom), A: /dem kaal i prap kaan/. B: /aal a taim a did trai tu get it prap, it kudn prap/. A: *They call it pop-corn.* B: *Try as I would to get it to pop, it wouldn't.*

PRA-PRA vb and sb dial; <Twi *práp'ra* gather, sweep.

A. vb: 1. To pick up; to sweep things up into one's possession.

1943 *GL* Kgn, Pra-pra, to pick up. 1955 FGC Man, 'You pra-pra the whole of it and take it away'.—Say 'tek a likl' but they take up the whole.

2. To lift one's opponent in wrestling.

1943 *GL* Kgn, Proppa, to lift a person in wrestling.

B. sb. Taking possession of goods.

1910 Anderson-Cundall 39 [Prov:] Befo' pra-pra mek quarrel, mek ground s'ripple. Pra-pra = appropriation of goods *or* sometimes used to mean a fall.

PRAWNIE vb dial; prob in some way related to *prance*—cf *EDD pronsy, praunting*, etc.

1943 *GL* Clar, Prawnie, kick up.

PRAYER KEY sb dial; <*prayer*[1] (*OED*) + KEY. Some physical object associated with prayer in Revivalist practice—cf POWER KEY.

1929 Beckwith 163–4, Sometimes [at the meetings]..I feel to pray, and there isn't any chance to pray at the time, and I bow to squeeze the prayer-key. When you are in the spirit, you feel that the world is going around.

PREACHY-PREACHY sb dial; iterative <*preachy* adj. Continual preaching.

1826 Williams 19, Since there was so much preachy preachy, the lazy fellows did nothing but tief.

PRECKE, PRECKEH, PRECKY, PREKAE, PREKAY see next.

preke /preke/ occas /prekem/ sb, adj, and vb dial; for dial sp see quots; <Amer Sp *pereque*, quarrel, disturbance; intolerable person or thing. (Malaret.)

A. sb: 1. A surprising or upsetting occurrence; a predicament, a scrape; a painful situation.

1941 Kirkpatrick 29, Lawd, what a precke. You 'ear wey da Jarman broadcas' man say, 'im did t'ink im crackin' joke de odder night. *Ibid* gloss, Precke—an amazing occurrence. 1943 *GL* StAnd, Precke, predicament. 1950 Pioneer 48, Wat a precky wen dem fine out Is me sidung front dem yah.

2. A credulous person, a fool, one easily tricked; hence one considered inferior, a subject of derision; a clown; a good-for-nothing. The sense 'friend' is prob ironic, meaning a soft person who is taken advantage of. Specif. A low-class prostitute.

1943 *GL* Kgn, Preke, prekem, names of a very silly bird: 'You favour prekem'; StAnn, Prekeh, a scapegoat; Clar, Man, Port, Preckeh, an unworthy person, fool; Tre, Prekay, fool; Kgn, Precky, a name for one who is easily defeated; No addr, Prek-æ, a friend. 1955 FGC Man /preke/ tell him anything and he'll believe it. 1956 Mc Clar /him fieva preke/ he is going on foolishly; StE, The lowest class of prostitute (to call anyone /preke/ is a /bad kos/). 1958 DeC Port /preke/ a man of sloppy appearance, one who doesn't shave, wash, and dress carefully.

B. adj: 1. Foolish, easily taken advantage of.

1956 Mc StAnd /preke/ adj (of a willing worker:) at the beck and call of all and sundry.

2. Clownish; untidy or ill-organized.

1956 Mc StE (Eld), A preke game of cricket: anyone bowls.

C. vb: To get into trouble; to be forced to suffer.

1960 NJL StC /yu goin preke/ you're going to fart (be squeezed so hard that you fart), i.e. be in big trouble.

PREKEH, PREKEM see prec.

preke-preke adj dial; var of PICKY-PICKY.

1959 M. Jeffrey-Smith letter, I seem to remember hearing 'prekeh prekeh' used of a child who picks at his food, a fanciful eater.

prekprek see *pre-pre*[1].

PREMENTO see PIMENTO.

PREPRA sb dial; perh var of FRO-FRO[1].

1943 *GL* Port, Prepra, fire.

pre-pre[1] (also /preprek, prekprek/) sb, vb, and adj dial; perh < Twi *perɛ́pérɛ*, rash, hasty, precipitate. The forms with *k* may have been contaminated by *preke*.

A. sb: Loss of self-control; hysteria.

1950 Pioneer 38, De po gal was eena pre-pre now, she fine out say is Jackass she married to an she start fe bawl fe her bredda.

B. adj: Uncontrolled.

1957 DeC StE (Accom) /pre-pre/ adj. e.g. of a woman who giggles uncontrollably.

C. vb: To have diarrhœa; to void the bowels excessively.

1960 LeP StAnd /pre-pre/ when you take a laxative and then go to the lavatory, that's what you do; those darn dogs /preprek, prekprek/ all over the place.

pre-pre[2] see *pro-pro*.

PREPRE[3] adj dial; prob a reduced form of PRETTY-PRETTY. (If so, pronunc /pri-pri/.)

1943 *GL* Man, Prepre, pretty.

PRESS vb dial; cf *press* clothes with an iron. Cf PRESSER. To put in the foundation for a road by crushing chunks of limestone in place with a steam-roller; hence (since a surface of asphalt is finally put on) to pave. *BA*

1952 FGC Man (Christiana), They're going to press the road.

PRESSER sb dial; *press* vb + *-er*: see prec.

1956 Mc StT /presa/ a steam roller.

PRESS-OIL sb dial; < *pressed* + *oil*. Castor oil (which has to be squeezed out of the beans).

1952 FGC Han /pres-hail/.

PRETTY sb dial; < *pretty* adj. = NANCY PRETTY, a colourful fish.

1952 FGC StE /priti/ the name here for what is called porkfish in Portland.

PRETTY-PRETTY adj and sb chiefly dial; iterative of *pretty*. *G*

A. adj: Quite pretty, handsome, attractive.

1949 U.Newton v 23, And do you like pretty-pretty drinks? Drinks in bottles with crown corks shining above and carbonated beverages..yellow, orange, purple, pink and light green? 1950 Pioneer 38, Pretty-pretty man like yuh mus get any gal yuh want fe married to.

B. sb: Something very pretty—esp a dress.

1954 LeP Man, Yu a wear pretty-pretty. *You are wearing a very pretty dress.*

PRETTY-YELLOW, PRICKELALLA see PRICKLY-YELLOW.

PRICKLE-APPLE sb obs; *OED* 1681→. An old name for the SOURSOP, alluding to its fleshy spines.

[1657 Ligon 14, Anotto, Prickled apple, Prickled peare, Papa,..a good part of them bearing excellent fruit.] p 1660 State of Jamaica 489, Cashues, prickell peares, prickell apples Soursops, Custard Apples. 1672 Blome 25, Prickle-Aples, Prickle-Pears, Grapes.

PRICKLE-BUSH sb. Specif in Jamaica: *Randia aculeata*; see quot.

1936 Fawcett 53, Indigo Berry, Ink Berry, Box Briar, Prickle Bush..Branches..bearing here and there a pair of extra-axillary..sharp spines.

PRICKLED APPLE see PRICKLE-APPLE.

PRICKLE-GRASS sb. = BUR GRASS.

1952 FGC StM.

PRICKLE-ITCH sb dial. A dry rash on the skin.

1958 DeC StT /prikl-ich/.

PRICKLE-WALK sb dial; < *prickle* + WALK. A thick growth of prickly bushes.

1952 FGC StAnd, You mus' a drive in-a prickle-walk. (Said by garage man examining flat tyre.)

PRICKLY BREADFRUIT sb dial. A variety of breadfruit (*Artocarpus altilis*) with very rough, grater-like skin; not edible as breadfruit.

1952 FGC StT, Prickly breadfruit, same as monkey breadfruit.

PRICKLY CALALU sb; see CALALU. *Amarantus spinosus*; also called MACCA CALALU.

1756 Browne 340, Amaranthus 1..The prickly Calaloo. This plant is frequent in the mountains, as well as the lower hills of *Jamaica*; and much used as a green, when the more valuable sorts are scarce. 1914 Fawcett 130, Amarantus spinosus, Prickly Calalu, Spinach. 1954 *WIMJ* 28, Prickly Calalu; Spinach.

PRICKLY PEAR sb; *DAE* 1737→. The cactus *Opuntia tuna* and similar species. Also attrib.

1696 Sloane 194, Opuntia major..The Prickly Pear-tree. In Jamaica & Caribeis insulis ubique..reperitur. 1725 Sloane vi, The sort of Prickly Pear, thought in Jamaica to be that particular kind of Opuntia. 1926 Fawcett 27 6–7, *O. Tuna*..Prickly Pear (a name applied to this and allied species). *Ibid* 278. *BA G N*

PRICKLY-PEAR WITHE sb. = PRICKLY WITHE, GOD-OKRO.

a 1726 Barham (1794) 153, Prickly withe, which some call prickly pear withe.

PRICKLY-POLE sb; *OED* 1725. A small palm (*Bactris plumieriana*) covered, both trunk and leaves, with very sharp spines.

1696 Sloane 178, Palma spinosa minor..Prickly pole. 1740 Importance 51, The Prickly-Pole bears a pleasant Fruit or hard Berry, which they roast. 1828 Ordinances 107, No fence of penguins or prickly poles shall be made ..within the said city. 1864 Grisebach 787, Prickly-pole.

PRICKLY SENSITIVE-PLANT see CREEPING SENSITIVE-PLANT.

PRICKLY WHITE WOOD sb obs. A variety of PRICKLY-YELLOW.

a1726 Barham (1794) 153, Prickly white wood. 1774 Long III 828, Prickly white wood. *Zantoxylon, caudice spinosa, ligno albido*. This grows like the other [*sc* Prickly-Yellow], only the inner wood is very white.

PRICKLY-WITHE sb; *OED* 1725 only. The climbing cactus *Cereus triangularis*, which has a strong, wire-like withe at the centre.

1696 Sloane 196, Ficus Indica folio triangulari ensiformi ..Prickly With. 1814 Lunan I 413, Triangularis..Browne calls this the *strawberry pear*, and Sloane..the prickly-withe. 1926 Fawcett 280, Prickly Withe..Flowers opening at night, white..Fruit crimson.

PRICKLY-YELLOW (WOOD) sb; for forms see quots 1948 ff. The tree *Zanthoxylum martinicense* and its wood.

[1657 Ligon 14, Pickled [*sic*] yellow wood.] 1696 Sloane 138, Prickly yellow wood. In sylvis campestribus Insulæ Jamaicæ. 1756 Browne 189, Zanthoxylum 1..caudice spinosa, ligno subcroceo..Prickly Yellow-wood, or yellow Hercules. 1837 Macfadyen 194, Prickly Yellow.. This is a valuable timber tree: the wood is yellow, and used in house building. 1920 Fawcett 172, Prickly Yellow, Yellow Hercules. 1943 *NHN* II 67, Prickly yellow..Spines on the trunk give rise to the local name. 1948 U.Newton IV 29, At school we had so many trees with prickles or thorns e.g. the orange, tangerine, prickel-alla, Jerusalem Thorn. 1952 FGC StE /prikli yala/; StT, Tre /priti-yela, pritiala/.

PRIGE vb dial; a form of /prag/ (PROG), parallel to *baig*, bag, *raigin*, ragging, etc. = PROG.

1943 *GL* StAnn, Prige, to hunt.

primenta see PIMENTO.

PRIMROSE WILLOW sb bot. Various species of *Jussiæa*, or the closely related *Œnothera*.

1756 Browne 208, Oenothera 1. The smooth Primrose-willow..2. The hairy Primrose-willow..3. The small creeping Primrose-willow. 1864 Grisebach 787, Primrose-willow: *Jussiæa*.

PRIMS vb dial; prob <*primp* (*OED v dial* 1). To show (oneself) *off*. *BL*

1950 Pioneer 16, A wen since Puss get so high dat him can prims off himself eena backra book?

PRINCE-WOOD sb; see quot 1725; *OED* 'princes wood' 1686.

1. The large tree *Cordia gerascanthoides*, also called SPANISH ELM, following Sloane.

1696 Sloane 155, Spanish Elm or Prince Wood. 1725 Sloane 63, The Spanish Elm, or Prince Wood. This grows to be a very large and stately tree, affording very broad Boards to make Tables or Cabinets of its Wood, which is of the Softness and Grain of Elm, whence the Name of Spanish Elm, having many undulated light brown, or grey Lines in it, making a pleasant show, whence came the Name of Prince Wood amongst our Cabinet-Makers..The Flowers stand several together; they are.. of a sulphurous Colour. 1811 Lunan II 182, Spanish Elm, or Princewood. Cordia..gerascanthus. 1864 Grisebach 787, Prince-wood: *Hamelia ventricosa* and *Cordia gerascanthoides*. *Ibid* 783, Elm Spanish: (the same two trees named).

2. Following Grisebach (see prec quot), the small tree *Hamelia ventricosa*. (For Lunan, 1811 I 364, the genus 'Hamellia' had 'No English Name'.)

1936 Fawcett 45–6, *H. ventricosa*..Spanish Elm or Prince Wood (Sloane). [This identification would appear to be erroneous.]

PRINGA[1] sb dial; etym unknown.

1943 *GL* Tre, Pringa, a little country shop.

PRINGA[2]**, PRINJA** sb dial; <*spring* or *springe* + *-er*. A springe; a trap with a spring.

1943 *GL* Kgn, Prinja, a springe (for catching birds); Tre, Pringa, trap.

PRISON FARM SWEET-POTATO sb chiefly dial; from its origin at or assoc with the Prison Farm, StC. A variety of sweet-potato.

1929 Beckwith 18 [Mandeville:] 'Prison Farm' [is] white outside and pink inside. 1952 FGC StC /prizn faam/ plant it at St Catherine prison.

pritiala, priti-yela see PRICKLY-YELLOW.

PRIVILEGE sb obs. The best portion (about four-fifths) of a cargo of new slaves, for whom lots were drawn by prospective buyers.

1792 Stewart 3, Privilege—a term used to signify choice election: for it is now the practice, to estimate and proportion the privilege, to the extent of the demand.

PROAN see PRUAN.

PROCUMBENT BROOMWEED sb bot obs; cf BROOMWEED. In Macfadyen's use: *Sida ciliaris* (cf 1926 Fawcett 116).

1837 Macfadyen 79, Sida ciliaris. *Procumbent Broom-weed.*

PROFESSOR sb dial; cf *OED* 5. An obeah-man—euphemistic term.

1793 Edwards II 93, It is very difficult therefore for the white proprietor to distinguish the *Obeah professor* from any other Negro upon his plantation. 1827 Hamel II 8, 'I know the man,' said Mr Guthrie: 'he is reckoned a professor of Obeah'. 1862 Clutterbuck 98, see OBEAH 1. 1921 *Gleaner* 7 Mar 3, The female defendant told him that the male defendant, whom she called 'Professor', was able to cure him..The 'Professor' invited him in his room and told him that a woman 'ghost' was on him and that it was a former lover who had put the ghost on him.

PROG /prag/ vb dial; cf *OED prog*, intr →1876, trans →1656. To hunt, esp for food; to steal; also const *in*: to poke about in. See also PRIGE.

1943 *GL* Clar, Prag, hunt for food; Kgn, Prag, to steal. 1955 FGC Man, To /prag/ in a person's things. 1960 LeP StC /prag/ to steal; also other parishes.

PROGGER sb dial; PROG + *-er*.

1960 LeP StE /praga/—one who /pragz/. Common.

PROGGING DAY sb obs; cf PROG. Market day: the day for obtaining the goods one wants.

1873 Rampini 92, The weekly Saturday market of a country town..Family groups—for on 'progging day' no one ever dreams of staying at home—follow each other in quick succession.

PROGGINGS vbl sb dial; <PROG. The things that one has progged. *G* /pragz/

1960 LeP StE /praginz/—that which is got by a /praga/.

PROLIFIC BEAN sb bot. One of the varieties of *Phaseolus lunatus*.

1837 Macfadyen 281, Phaseolus fœcundus. Prolific or Hibbert Bean..This bean..is little inferior to the Lima bean, to which indeed it bears a considerable resemblance. 1913 Harris 25, There are several varieties of this plant known as Lima bean; broad bean, and prolific or Hibbert bean. 1920 Fawcett 64.

PROPERTY PONY sb dial; <*property*, an estate + *pony*. A beast of burden that belongs to 'the property' and which, therefore, many people use. Fig. A person.

1943 *GL* StT, Property ponie, one who does everything for everybody.

PROPPA see PRA-PRA[1].

pro-pro, pre-pre[2] sb dial; perh echoic—cf *kapkap*. See quots.

1952 FGC Port /pŕ-o-pŕ-o/ a black ant, big like red-ants, live in rotten wood. 1958 DeC Port /pre-pre/ large black stinging ants living in tree nests, especially in rotten wood.

PROVISION sb dial. A variety of sweet-potato that provides well.

1952 FGC StM, StT /provízhan/ big, red; brown, lasts long.

PROVISION GROUND see GROUND sb.

pruam see PRUAN.

PRUAN /prúan, prúam, próan/ sb chiefly dial; cf *OED prune sb*, 17–18th cent sp *pruen, pruan* (19th cent *dial*). The PRUNE TREE (*Prunus occidentalis*) and its fruit. Also attrib.

1893 Sullivan 105, Pruen liqueur. Half a bushel of pruen seeds..thrown into twelve gallons of proof rum. 1929 Beckwith 10, Upon this are laid sills cut and squared from..a tree called 'proan'. 1941 Swabey 28, Pruan—(Wild Prune, Prune Tree). 1946 *NHN* III 62, This Pruan tree was about 25 ft. in height..The bark of the Pruan is employed medicinally. 1952 FGC StE, StJ, Tre /prúan/; StT, Tre /próan/; StT /prúam/.

PRUEN (LIQUEUR) see prec.

PRUNE TREE sb bot; *OED* 1866. The tree *Prunus occidentalis*.

1850 Macfadyen 5, Cerasus occidentalis. Prune Tree.. The bark of the tree has an astringent taste, with a strong flavour of prussic acid, and is used in manufacturing an inferior description of Prune Dram. It is from the kernels of the drupe that the celebrated liqueur, the Noyau of Martinique, is prepared. 1864 Grisebach 787, Prune-tree. 1941 Swabey 28, see PRUAN.

PRUSSY, PRUSY adj dial; cf US *prissy*; and for *u* corresp to Std Engl *i*, cf RUBBA for *river*.

1943 *GL* Clar, Prusy, pert, womanish. 1957 JN Man [Said by a girl:] Come tan up now. Noh hear whey me say, Stand up, you prussy.

pspspsps int; <*puss*. The sound made to call a cat. *G*

c1915 FGC StAnd (remembered). 1957 DeC StAnd /pspspsps/ Call to cats.

PSYCHE sb; prob a rationalization of the sound of the bird's call. The honey creeper *Cœreba flaveola*.

1956 Jeffrey-Smith 71, see BANANA QUIT.

PUCCO see POCO[1].

PUCCOMINA see POCOMANIA.

PUCCOTEMPO see *poko-tempo*.

PUCK-CO-MYAL see POCOMANIA.

PUCKRO see *pokro*.

PUCKU see POCO[1].

PUCO-PUCO int dial; echoic. An imitation of the sound of boiling water.

1924 Beckwith 197 [Riddle:] John Redman tickle John Blackman till him laugh *puco-puco*.—[Answer:] Fire under boiling pot.

PUDDENWITH see next.

PUDDING-WITHE /pudn-wis/ sb; the stem seems to have been thought to resemble a 'pudding' (orig = sausage). The vines *Cissus sicyoides* and sometimes *C. trifoliata*. Also called BASTARD BRYONY, MARY BUSH, MARY-WITHE, SADDLE-WEED, SCRATCH WITHE, SNAKE BUSH or WITHE, SOLDIER WITHE, WALL SADDLE, WILD YAM, YAWS BUSH. *N*

1725 Sloane 371, It [*sc* Clematitis] is call'd in Jamaica Puddenwith, and is us'd to tye Rails. 1811 Titford 76–7, Traveller's Joy..It is also called Virgin's Bower and Pudding Withe. 1814 Lunan II 263, This plant grows in many parts of Jamaica, and commonly called Pudding Withe, or Traveller's Joy. 1952 FGC Port, StC, StT, Tre /pudn wis/ for poultice, boils, sore foot—colour is like pud'n when you boil it; StAnn, StM /puding wis/. 1954 *WIMJ* 29, *Cissus sicyoides*. 1955 *WIMJ* 158, *C. trifoliata*..Pudding Wys (Withe)?

PUDDUNG GOLLANG see PEE-GEE.

pudn wis see PUDDING-WITHE. *N*

pu-dong sb dial; <*put down*. A quarrel, a row. (Perhaps over claim and counter-claim to possession—cf PEE-GEE.)

1956 Mc Man /dem a ha wan pú-dong/ *They are having a row*.

PUFF sb; cf *OED sb* 5. A coconut-filled tart; = GIZADA. *BA*

1954 LeP StAnn, Puff, cake made with coconut. 1959 DeC Han /pof/ the pastry confection known in Kingston as /gizada/.

PUFFER, PUFF-FISH sb dial. See BALLOON-FISH. *G*

1952 FGC StJ, Puff-fish—a name sometimes used for bottle-fish.

PUFF-GUT sb dial. = PUFF-FISH.

1952 FGC Port.

PUFOON sb dial; etym unknown. = BAFFOON. (These are clearly in origin the same word; evidence is lacking to show which form is primary.)

1943 *GL* StE, Pufoon, a stench.

PUGGO sb dial. The ant-lion: see quot.

1960 Jack Lewis StAnn (Runaway Bay), Puggo is a little insect that the southern Americans call a doodlebug and is called nanny-goat in Jamaica (except as far as I know StAnn)—lives in round holes in dry ground.

pugru see *pagro*.

pu-kaak see PULL-CORK.

puka (yam) sb dial; < Twi *apúka*, a species of yam.

1956 Mc StAnd /puka/ a round, hard, white yam—another name for /renta, biejan/.

PUKE MANGO sb dial; <*puke*, vomit. An ill-tasting variety of mango.

1952 FGC StM /pyuk-manggo/ make you /tro op/.

puki sb dial; etym uncert, perh <*pooka*, hobgoblin (since the colour of the fish is blackish); -i is prob a familiarizing element; the word has the effect of a personal name or nickname such as is freq given to fish, birds, etc.

A fish. See quots.

1950 Smith, Pooky, *Holocentrus ascensionis*. 1952 FGC Port /púki/ kanggatuoni, wenshman; West, same as wenshman, except that puki is in shallow water, wenshman deep.

PUKKUMERIAN see POCOMANIA.

pukus see *putu*.

PULL vb chiefly dial. *BA*

1. To loosen, untie. *G*

c 1915 FGC StAnd, Pull the knot!

2. In witchcraft: to remove a spell; to take away the spirit which is supposed to be causing an illness in someone. (Cf *OED v* 11.)

c 1842 Song in 1895 Banbury 21, Dandy obeah da ya, oh! Me wi' pull he, oh! 1895 Banbury 7, [For the victim of Obeah] his only remedy is to have it 'pulled' out by another obeahman..An obeahman can always 'pull' as well as 'put', cure as well as kill. 1923 Beckwith 52 [Amber Song:] Pullee me ambah ye.

3. To extract a source of physical harm.

1922 Beckwith 44 [Song:] Yo' husban' jiggah nevah pull, Sabina, Yo' husban' shirt nevah patch [*Your husband's jiggers are never dug out*].

PULL-CORK sb dial. A corkscrew.

1956 Mc Man /pu-kaak/ a corkscrew.

PULLER sb dial; <PULL 2+*-er*.

1. An OBEAH-MAN.

1895 Banbury 13, The puller stoops over the spot, mutters some unintelligible words, looks into his *amber* and predicts exactly what is below.

2. A bottle-opener.

1956 Mc Man /púla/.

PULL FOOT vb phr; cf *OED pull* 19b →1876.

1. To run away. *G*

a 1818 Lewis (1834) 109, One of my ladies [*sc* a slave], after enjoying herself during the Saturday and Sunday.. chose to *pull foot*, and did not return from her hiding-place in the mountains till this morning. 1833 Scott I 351, The whole crew pulled foot as if Old Nick had held them in chase.

2. To move rapidly. *G*

1950 Pioneer 54, Me peep an se' one wite oman dah pull foot fe May shop.

PULL-(ME-)COAT sb dial. Species of *Portulaca*, used in folk medicine.

1943 *NHN* II 7, Portulaca (pull-me-coat). 1952 FGC Han, Pull-coat—mauve flowers; grows at river side; so called because it 'operates very strong'—for biliousness.

PULL ROOT /pú-rúut/ sb dial. BARBADOS or RENTA YAM.

1956 Mc StAnd /pu-ruut/.

PULP vb and adj dial; prob devel from *OED* sense 3, 'To remove the surrounding pulp from (coffee beans, or the like)'; cf PULPER.

A. vb intr: Of something soft or pulpy, esp the eyes: To bulge (as if being squeezed), protrude; to become extruded. Also const *out*, *up*. *BA G*

1952 FGC Han, StM /dem ai polp/—their eyes bulge; StAnd, 'Full' eyes /polp out/—stick out; Tre, Mango bug has two big eyes—pulp out; Han [To get rid of jiggers in the skin:] Pick it [with a pin] and they pulp up—pick out the whole bag. 1955 Bennett *Breeze Pass*, Dem y'eye dah pulp wid fright.

B. adj: Bulging, protruding—said esp of eyes.

1952 FGC StM, Pulp eyes, 'full' eyes. *BA G*

PULPER sb; *OED* 2 1874→. See quot.

1835 Senior 52–3, These ripe berries..go through a machine called a 'pulper', by which they are divested of the outside skin and glutinous substance between the skin and berry.

PUMBLE-FOOT sb chiefly dial; <*pummel-foot*, a club foot—cf *OED pommel* 8 →1895.

1. Attrib or for *pumble-footed*: clumsy in walking.

1942 Bennett 20, De pumble foot gal wey work wid me Teck careless so drop i' dung stairs.

2. A disease of poultry in which an abscess forms under the foot, deforming it and making the chicken walk with difficulty. Also pronounced 'bumble foot'.

1952 FGC StAnd, The chickens get pumble-foot. 1954 *FG* 723, Bumble Foot. When the bottom of the foot is badly bruised or cut..a fluid or a cheesy matter may accumulate in the spaces between the toes or on the ball of the foot, forming swellings.

pum-pan, pun-pan sb dial; <*pudden* dial Engl form of *pudding*; *OED pudding-pan* 1662 s.v. *pudding* 11b. A deep tin plate or basin (up to about 15 in. diameter) with sloping sides, having many uses (for mixing or cooking pudding or other foods, washing dishes, carrying light loads on the head, etc.).

1868 Russell 5, Poun pan, Pudding pan. 1943 *GL* Clar, Poo pan, dish pan; Kgn, Man, StE, Pumpan, pudding pan; StC, Pum pan, a deep tin plate; StM, Poom ban, pudding pan. 1952 FGC Tre /pun pan/. 1956 Mc Man, StC /pum pan/.

PUMPKIN CANE sb dial. A variety of sugar-cane.

1952 FGC Port /pongkin kien/—from the colour.

PUMPKIN SWEET-POTATO sb dial. A variety of sweet-potato with flesh the colour of a pumpkin's.

1952 FGC Port /pongkin/—sweet potato.

PUMPKIN-WOOD sb dial; the name refers to the sponginess of the wood. The tree *Hernandia jamaicensis*.

1952 FGC Tre /pongkin-wud/ chew for toothache; big tree, looks like anatto. 1961 Institute list.

PUMPUM sb dial; <Twi *pumpũŋ*, redup. <*pũŋ* vb, to become or to be tumid, turgid, distended. Something large and round, seeming swollen; esp in PUMPUM YAM. *BA*

1942 *GL* Kgn, Pumpum, lump.

PUMPUM YAM /pumpum yam/ see quots for sp; <PUMPUM+*yam*. A yam that grows as a round, lumpish tuber rather than the usual elongated one.

1929 Beckwith 16, Others are named for their shape, like the 'Pompon', which bears 'big and round'. 1934 Williams 36, In Jamaica, a yam that has developed spherically..is known as pumpum yam. 1941 *GL* Port, West, Pum-pum, round bumpy yellow yam; Tre, Poom-poom. 1958 DeC Clar, The afu (yellow) yam bears both a 'tall' food and also a drier, more powdery, round food called /pumpum/; Tre /pumpum/ a kind of white yam—it /bier roun/ and is highly prized.

PUNACK see *punyaak*.

PUNCHEON-WATER sb joc. Rum.

1896 Murray, P-stan fe puncheon-water, make you fight one anoder. 1922 Beckwith 83 (same).

PUNDRI sb dial rare; etym unknown.

1943 *GL* StE, Pundri, weakling.

PUNISH vb intr. With passive force: to undergo punishment; to suffer. *BA BL G*

1943 *GL* Kgn, Punish, to suffer. 1960 LeP StAnd, 'I going to punish' = I'm going to suffer.

PUNKO-MAN sb dial; <*punk*, poor, of inferior quality (see *EDD* 4) +*-o*, a suffix of obscure meaning added to many dial words +*man*.

1958 DeC StAnd /pongko-man/ an unreliable, ne'er-do-well, no-account man.

pun-pan see *pum-pan.*

PUNTEE sb obs; presumably Afr, but not found. See quot, and cf WATCHMAN.

1826 Williams 19, The old patriarch said, that 'formerly people minded the *puntees,* hung up in the trees and grounds as charms to keep off thieves'. 1827 Hamel I 152, Selling or giving away puntees, feathers, or glass bottles, to scare thieves from the orange or shaddock trees.

puntsi see *putu.*

punyaak sb dial obsolescent; <*poniard*; cf *OED* 17th cent sp *punyard.* A knife (of no special sort).

1943 *GL* Kgn, Poonyaak, kind of knife; StT, Punack, broken knife. 1955 FGC Man /punyaak/ old-time red wood-handle knife with one blade, a shirt-pocket knife. 1957 DeC StE /punyaak/ a knife.

PUNYARK see prec.

puo see PO.

puoa sb dial; etym unknown.

1959 DeC StJ /puoa/ a dumpling (large) 'baked in oil'.

puojuo see PO' JOE.

puoliin see *poliin.*

puoltris sb dial; <*poultice,* with intrusive *r*—cf SHORTRIGE.

1952 FGC StE, Corn-meal good for pain; /tek it mek puoltris/.

puotagii, puotigii see PORTUGEE.

PUPA /púpà/ sb dial; evid <*papa*—cf MUMA.

1. As a term of address or title: Father. *BL G*

1943 *GL* Kgn, Man, StAnd, StAnn, West, Puppa, father. 1956 Mc Clar, Man, StE, StT /púpá/ father.

2. Similarly: Grandfather. *BL*

1956 Mc StT, Affectionately: grandfather.

3. As a general title for an old man. (Cf PUPA WILL.) *BL G*

1956 Mc Man.

4. As an exclamation equiv to 'My Father!'—i.e. God. *BL G*

1942 Bennett 32, Pupa! Him 'ave awn boot a-foot An' helmit 'pon him head.

PUPA-CUTLASS sb dial. A 'father of a' cutlass; one having more authority or strength: see quot.

1943 *GL* StM, Puppa-cutlas, double-edged.

PUPA JESUS Term of address to God.

1962 BLB 66 /pupa jiizas/.

PUPA-LICK sb dial joc; <PUPA+LICK, father spank—the allusion being to the up-turned buttocks of one turning a somersault. A somersault. *BL*

1895 Banbury 16, He took to his heels and the beast after him. As it is expressed, the snake 'cutting papa-licks' (somersaults) after him all the way. 1900 Murray 3, A rum punchin mek a pupa lick an ef I didn't ben mek a move, all would a ben ober wid me. 1912 McK *Ballads* gloss, Pupperlicks: head over heels; turning somersaults. 1941 *GL* Clar, Kgn, Pupa-lick; StAnn, StJ, Pupa-lic, Poopa lik; StC, Bublic, somersault. 1943 Bennett 24, Po Italy kick pupa lick. 1956 Mc Man /pupa lik/ somersault.

PUPA WILL see PA WILL.

PUPPA see PUPA.

PUPPERLICK see PUPA-LICK.

PUPPY-FISH sb dial.

1. A fish similar to the angel fishes—perh *Peprilus paru* (1930 Jordan 266 'Poppyfish').

1892 Cockrell list, Puppy-fish, *stromateus alepidotus.* 1952 FGC StT, Puppy-fish—angel; has round mouth four stripes.

2. A sea fish perh of the genus *Bagre*—see quot.

1952 FGC StC, Puppy-fish—ten inches or so, has a beard; same as catfish, bobo.

PUPPY-MOUTH PARROT sb dial. A variety of PARROT fish with a mouth like that of a puppy.

1952 FGC StJ.

PUPPY SHARK sb dial. The fish *Carcharias limbatus* or similar species. *BA*

1854–5 *TJSA* I 145, Carcharias prionodon—Puppy Shark. 1952 FGC StAnn /popi shaak/ mouth comes over like puppy mouth; can eat [i.e. it is edible].

PUPPY TURBOT sb dial. A fish of the genus *Balistes* (species uncert).

1952 FGC StE /pópi tórbòt/ smaller than regular turbot; use to feed dogs.

PUPPY WORM sb. =ARROW-HEADED WORM.

pupu sb dial; <Engl *poop,* dung, perh infl by Afr words such as Twi *popoeéwó,* the first fæces of infants. *BL; SC poe póe.*

1956 Mc Man /púpu/ a sea slug.

PURE adj dial; an extension of *OED* sense 3a, b into contexts where it would be unlikely to be used in StdE. Nothing but, only. Cf BARE, SO-SO. *BL G N*

1912 McK *Songs* 31, Pure nine-han' bunch a car' de fame*. . *The nine-hand and only (pure) nine-hand bunches—none smaller, that is—grown by this old method have a fine reputation. 1942 Bennett 25, I was gwine to sen' pure orellia bush, As yuh wanted so-soh greens.

PURE-PURE adj dial; iterative of *pure.* Entire, complete, altogether. *BL*

1868 Russell 15, see BACKRA 4.

PURIFICATION sb dial. In *kumuna* practice, 'the rite of drumming sky and earthbound gods through the body of a goat preparatory to sacrificing it'.

1950 Moore 151.

PURPLE COCO sb. A variety of coco of a purplish colour.

1814 Lunan I 212, see COCO I.

PURPLE-FLOWERED BROOMWEED sb bot obs; cf BROOMWEED. In Macfadyen's use: *Abutilon pauciflorum* (cf 1926 Fawcett 102).

1837 Macfadyen 85, Sida peduncularis. *Purple-flowered Broom-weed.*

PURPLE GUAVA sb. A variety of guava.

1913 Harris 9, see STRAWBERRY GUAVA.

PURPLE-LIP sb bot. The GREENWITHE (Grisebach quotes Wright's description: 'perigonium rufescentivirens, labello rubro-marginato et punctato'—see 1910 Fawcett 17).

1864 Grisebach 787, Purple-lip: *Vanilla claviculata.*

PURPLE PEPPER sb obs. A variety of *Capsicum* pepper having a purplish cast.

1811 Titford xiii, Purple or Sore Throat Pepper. *Ibid* 47.

PURPLE SAGE sb dial. A variety of *Lantana* bush having a purplish flower.

1952 FGC StAnn, Purple sage, same as black sage, wild sage.

PURPLE YAM sb. A variety of the white yam having a reddish or purplish cast to the flesh. *G*

1814 Lunan II 309, see RED YAM.

PURPOSE adj dial; <*purpose* sb, or *purposeful*, prob with contamination of sense by *perverse*. Headstrong; contrary.

1946 U.Newton I 15, If you said: 'Kindly pick two breadfruits', he would pick twenty; while if you asked him to pick a few dozen he would most surely pick four or six. He was what you and I would call *a very purpose man.*

PURRO, puru[1] see *poro*.

puru[2] sb dial; perh <*puru*[1], trouble, or <*pull* vb. A kind of MACHETE.

1958 DeC StT /puru/ a cutlass with a round end and recurved tip (one kind of 'hook-point').

PUS-BLADDER sb dial; <*pus* + BLADDER. A type of jellyfish; see quot.

1944 *NHN* II 155, A large yellow species [of *Cyanea*] with great masses of tentacles is often seen in Kingston Harbour. It is known to fishermen as Pus Bladder.

PUSERY see PUSSERY.

PUSH-FOOT sb obs; cf such similar formations as *kick-foot, turn-hand.* A nickname for the Model-T Ford car, in which the low gear was engaged by pressing a foot pedal.

1943 *GL* StM, Push foot, old pedal-drive Ford car.

PUSS /pus/ sb.

1. The regular word for a cat throughout Jamaica; 'cat' is known but not much used. 'Puss' enters into many compound forms (separately listed). Also attrib. *BL G*

1774 Long II 449, One of the [negro] rebels exclaimed, that 'he had as many lives as a *puss*'. 1873 Rampini 178 [Prov:] Man no trabel, him no know puss hab cock-eye (squint); *ibid* 132, the obeah-man's 'puss-skin' wallet. 1957 JN, I gwen to buss da puss deh brain. *I'm going to smash that cat's brain.*

2. Abbr of PUSS BOOTS. (Sometimes pronounced /puus/.)

1943 *GL* Kgn, Port, StAnd, StE, StT, soft rubber-canvas shoes. 1950 U.Newton VI 19, And a pair of 'puss' or canvas shoes. 1956 Mc Man, Port /puus/—in distinction from /pus/ a cat.

3. A thief. *BL G*

1954 LeP StAnn, StE, Puss—a thief. 1956 Mc Port /pus/ a thief.

4. An albino negro; = PUSS-EYE.

1958 DeC StT /pus/ derogatory term for an albino Negro.

PUSS-BLOOD sb dial. = DOG BLOOD[1], the herb *Rivina humilis*.

1952 FGC Tre, Puss-blood; burst seeds—red like ink; similar to guma, bloodberry.

PUSS-BOOT sb chiefly dial; the allusion is to the silent tread—cf US 'sneakers'. Rubber-soled canvas shoes; more often called PUSS.

1942 Bennett 36, She. . Put awn wan tear-up frack Shove har foot eena wan ole puss boot An go.

PUSS-CLAW sb dial; from the sharp, curved prickles, cf CAT'S-CLAW.

1. The plant *Pisonia aculeata*, or FINGRIGO.

1952 FGC StAnd, Singgl-go, same as puss-claw; StAnn, Puss-claw has a gummy seed, called bramble, used to catch birds.

2. The plant *Prosopis juliflora*, or CASHAW.

1952 FGC StT /kasha/ very prickly, same as puss-claw.

PUSSERY sb dial; <PUSS 3 + -*ery*. Trickery; stealing.

1943 *GL* StE, Pusery, trickery. 1955 FGC Man, Pussery, stealing.

PUSS-EYE sb dial; cf PUSS 4. See quot. The allusion is to the squinting eyes: cf PUSS 1 quot 1873.

1958 DeC Port /pus-yai/. Derogatory name for an albino Negro.

PUSS-GUT sb dial.

1. The climbing cactus also called PRICKLY-WITHE, having a tough withe at the centre that is used to tie things together.

1952 FGC StAnn, Puss-gut, the wis from the sipl-okro.

2. See quot.

1955 *WIMJ* 158, *Desmodium* spp. . . Wild Pinder; Puss Gut.

PUSS-HEAD (TREE) sb dial; <PUSS + *head.* The tree *Sloanea jamaicensis*, from the resemblance of the mature seed capsule to the head of a cat.

1952 FGC StAnn, StT, Puss-head, same as combwood pop-nut.

PUSS-KITTEN sb dial; a redundant formation —cf HEAD-SKULL, MOUTH-LIP, etc. A kitten.

1956 Mc StAnd /pus-kitin/.

PUSS-PRAYERS sb dial joc; i.e. what the cat prays for. The avocado pear, which cats like.

1943 *GL* Kgn, Puss prayers, pear. 1955 FGC Man /pùs práiaz/ pear; puss love it.

PUSS-PUSS sb. A children's game.

1946 U.Newton I 3.

pus-yai see PUSS-EYE.

PUT vb dial; cf PUT HAND or MOUTH ON. *G*

1. To set the effect of obeah to work (on or upon someone), the antonym being to 'PULL'.

1793 Edwards II 95, Her step-mother (a woman of the Popo country. .) had put *obi* upon her, as she had also done upon those who had lately died. 1842 Song in 1895 Banbury 21, Lord, we come fe pull he oh, A no we put he, oh! [*We come to remove obeah; we did not put it on people*]. 1956 Mc Clar, see TURN 3.

2. To affect (someone) with the power of obeah, so that he is not responsible for his actions and will do anything wicked.

1895 Banbury 10, Dem put him so.

3. With *off*: to remove or pull obeah.

1950 Moore 92, Putting off things.

PUT ABOUT vb phr trans; see ABOUT.

PUT AND KENNY sb; etym unknown. See quot.

1943 *GL* no addr, Put and Kenny, A rich dish of beans meat and vegetables.

PUT AWAY conj phr dial; cf PUTTING OUT. Setting aside, apart from, disregarding.

1956 Mc Man /pút we sáiz, i nó tan gúd/ *Apart from its size it is not suitable.*

PUT-DOWN-GO-ALONG see PEE-GEE.

PUT HAND or **MOUTH ON** vb phr trans; cf *OED put* 23. *G*

1. *Put hand on*: to 'touch' or affect (someone) by spiritual or supernatural agency, bringing on illness or death.

1825 De la Beche 31–2, A negro woman..fancied her mother's ghost had appeared to her, and warned her of her death, and that whenever she attempted to take any nourishment, the spirit washed its hands in the broth.. —her expression was, that her mother had 'put her hand upon her'. 1895 Banbury 28, see KNOCK 1. 1954 LeP Kgn, StE, To have a spell or curse put on one's enemy—put han' pon 'im.

2. *Put mouth on*: to speak violently against, to say insulting things about; to curse.

1877 Murray *Kittle* 16, Ef dat gal put him mout pon you, my good sir, you tink say da tingree (sting ray) bite you.

PUT ON GOWN vb phr dial.

1942 HPJ, see DROP-DOWN.

PUTO-PUTO see *poto-poto.*

PUT-PUT /pot-pot/ sb dial; see *poto-poto.* Mud, or anything similar to it; also attrib.

1868 Russell 5, Put-put, mud. 1943 *GL* Han, StC, Put-put, Mud, anything muddy; StJ, Putt-putt, mud. 1957 DeC 5 /pot-pot/ adj. for muddy road or field.

putsi see PUTU.

PUTTA-PUTTA see *poto-poto.*

PUTTING OUT conj phr dial; cf PUT AWAY. Setting aside, excepting. *G*

1956 Mc /potn out sonde/ *Excepting Sunday.*

PUTT-PUTT see PUT-PUT.

putu, putus sb chiefly dial; prob of mixed origin, in part phonosymbolic—cf such words as Scots *pout, poot,* a term of affection for a child or young girl (*EDD poult* 3). (Note the many phonic variations.) A term of affection: darling, lovey.

1943 *GL* StJ, Pootu, love, darling. 1954 LeP StAnn, Putus—beautiful one, pretty one. 1958 DeC StAnd /putus/ darling, 'bona'; Tre /pukus/ pet name for a child or sweetheart; StJ /putsi/ same; StAnd /puntsi, putúm/ same.

putum, putsi see prec.

PUYAAK see POUYAT BANANA.

PWILE /pwail/ vb dial. A spelling for 'spoil' representing reduction of *sp-* to *p-* with labial off-glide *w* and archaic retention of 17–18th cent /ai/.

pyaam-pyaa, pyaang-pyaang see next.

pyaa-pyaa (the vowels, esp in the first syllable, are often nasalized) adj (and sb) dial; etym obscure. As in numerous Ja folk words, iteration is of Afr pattern; for the base *pyaa* cf Engl *pyah,* weak, paltry (Partridge), Scots *pyaavan,* peevish, sickly (*EDD*); but cf also and esp Amer Ind (Galibi, Tupi-Guarani) *piá, pián,* the disease *Polypapilloma tropicum* (Alvarado); and sometimes the term is used of *Frambœsia* (yaws). The weakening and degrading effects of disease are perhaps basic to the Jamaican word. (Friederici holds that *pian* is Amer Ind, and Alvarado states that it has entered the patois of negroes brought to Cayenne.)

Of a person or thing: weak; poor, inferior, insignificant, unimportant. (Shades of meaning are numerous.)

1941 Kirkpatrick Gloss, Pyaw-pyaw—picayune, small. 1943 *GL* [Attempts to spell the word:] West, peah-pe-ah; Port, peaw-peaw; Kgn, pyah-pyah; West, pyaw-pyaw; StT, peahn-peahn; StAnn, pean-pean; Kgn, pyawn-pyawn. 1955 FGC Man, This is /pyaang-pyaang/ to the one you have. 1956 Mc Man /pyaam-pyaa/ poor, badly off; shaky, wobbly in walking; Port, Funny, not proper, worthless. 1958 DeC Port, A /pyaa-pyaa man/ is defined as a /saaf-saaf man/: everybody can step on him and he will not stand up for his rights; he has no pride or self-respect, or at least is unwilling to fight to defend them.

PYACCA-PYACCA see *pyaka-pyaka.*

PYAH-PYAH see *pyaa-pyaa.*

pyaka-pyaka (also /pyata-pyata, plaka-plaka, ploko-ploko, pyoko-pyoko, poko-poko/) adj dial; these forms are clearly phonic variants, but evidence does not show which is primary; reading the series above in reverse, all could be speculatively derived from the commoner form (of same meaning) *poto-poto,* of Afr origin. Muddy; hence, untidy, messed up.

1943 *GL* Clar, Pyacka, muddy; Port, pyaka-pyaka, muddy; StT, pocko-pocko, untidy; Kgn, pyacca-pyacca, all muddled up. 1958 DeC Man /pyata-pyata; pyak/ adjectives for wet, muddy ground; the second seems to be a short version of /pyaka-pyaka/..The verb phrase /pyak op/ is also used with the same meaning. StT /plaka-plaka/; Han-West /ploko-ploko/; StJ /pyoko-pyoko/; Tre /poko-poko, pyoko-pyoko/ all meaning wet, sloppy, muddy (of a road).

pyak (op) see prec.

pyanji(-pyanji) adj dial; <*pyaan,* nasalized base of *pyaa-pyaa* + /ji/—cf *winji,* and similar words. Slight, small, weak.

1943 *GL* StAnn, Piangi, slight. 1955 FGC Man, A little /pyanji-pyanji/ pig.

pyata-pyata see *pyaka-pyaka.*

PYAWN-PYAWN, PYAW-PYAW see *pyaa-pyaa.*

PYLON see PILON.

pyoko-pyoko see *pyaka-pyaka.*

Q, QQ sb dial slang; initial letters of 'quarter-quart'.

1958 DeC gen /kyuu; kyuu-kyuu/ a quarter-quart of white rum.

QRUAW see QUAW 3.

QUABS see *kwabz.*

QUACKNO (BUSH) = GUACO.

QUACO[1] /kwaku, kwaaku/ sb chiefly dial; cf Twi *Kwàkú,* a male belonging to *Wukú,* personal Genius, because he was born on *Wukúda,* the fourth day. (See Christaller, Appendix B.)

1. The DAY-NAME for a boy born on Wednesday; this sense is now virtually out of use. *G*

1793 Edwards II 82, see MA.

2. Used of an unsophisticated negro by the more sophisticated: a rough, uncultivated person; an ignorant or stupid person.

1943 *GL* Port, Quaco, unimproved man; StAnd, Quakoo, country boy; StAnn, Quaco, Maroon. 1956 Mc Man /kwaaku/ ignorant, foolish person.

3. See quot.

1943 *GL* Tre, Quaco, a suspected person.

QUACO[2] see QUAQUA.

QUACO (BUSH) see GUACO (BUSH).

QUAHMIN see QUAMIN.

QUAIL /kwiel, kwail, kriel/ vb trans dial; cf *EDD* v^1 2, 'To grow flabby; of grass or any green vegetable matter.'

1. To cause to wilt. *G*

1952 FGC Port, StJ, To make dokunu, quail green banana-leaf; StM, Boil dokunu in a quailed green banana-leaf. 1959 DeC West /yu ha fi kriel di liif fos/—make a banana leaf soft (in preparing it for dokunu) by holding it over the fire.

2. To do away with, get rid of entirely; const *off*.

1950 Pioneer 64, It sweet him so tell him quail off de whole ah de bottle full.

QUAKOO see QUACO[1].

QUALITY adv and adj dial; evid abbr of phr *high-quality* or the like. Cf *OED quality, sb* 11.

A. adv: An intensifying word: Very, extremely.

1952 FGC Han [You have to] curse some quality bad words to get rid of a ghost.

B. adj: A vague word merely calling attention: Kind of, sort of—implying the unusual or unexpected.

1924 Beckwith 180 [Riddle:] Me mudder hab a whole shipload o' guinea-pig, all born at one quality head. [Answer:] Castor-oil bean. 1961 BLB 27 /bot hou Maasel bwai kom dat-de kwalati wie/ *But however did Marcel's son get that way?*

QUAMIN /kwaamin/ sb dial; cf Twi *Kwámè*, (Akan dial) *Kwámènά*, name for male born on the seventh day (*Ameŋ's* day).

1. The DAY-NAME for a boy born on Saturday; this sense is now virtually out of use. *G*

1954 LeP Man, Boy born on Saturday—Quahmin.

2. =QUACO[1] 2, though not as common: a bumpkin; a stupid person.

1943 *GL* Kgn, Quamin, a person of small mentality; StAnd, Quarmin, country lad; West, Quarmme, one slow of speech. 1958 DeC StE /kwaamin/ one slow of speech.

3. An eel. (Prob intended as a derogatory term.)

1943 *GL* Clar, Quamin, eel.

QUAO see QUAW.

QUARMIN, QUARMME see QUAMIN.

QUAQUA /kwakwa/ sb dial; ?<*Quaqua*. African tribal name (cf 1774 Long II 352). But cf Ko *kwa*, yam. Also attrib.

1. Cassava meal, flour, or starch. Cf COUSCOUS.

1855 *TJSA* II 41, Coco Meal and Second Meal—Quaqua starch. 1868 Russell 6, Qua-qua—Cassava in the form of a thick paste. African. [This may be sense 2.] 1893 Sullivan 38, Cassava Flour (Quaco). [Method of preparation described.] 1943 *GL* Kgn, Qua-qua, cassava flour; Tre, Qua-qua, cassava meal; Quaqua, the trash of the cassava remaining after the juice has been squeezed out. 1954 LeP Kgn, Flour from dried cassava—kwackwa; Dumpling made from cassava flour—kwackwa dumplin'. 1958 DeC StAnd /kwa-kwa/ flour—cassava head /kuskus/.

2. A cassava dish—see quot.

1958 DeC StE /kwakwa/—here meaning a special dish, a soft concoction..Cut up bitter cassava (don't grater, wash, or press), soak the /jongks/ overnight in salt water, dry in sun, pound in mortar, then bake with oil and seasonings.

QUARRY-QUARRY adj dial; iterative of *quarrel*, reduced by common loss of *l*. Quarrelsome.

1873 Rampini 124, You so quarry-quarry you no let I mek me old moder Fowl hear you flute?

QUART /kwaat/ sb dial slang. A year's sentence or term in prison; cf PINT.

1952 FGC Han /dem giim wan kwaat/ *They gave him one year in prison*; StM, Four full quart, a four-year sentence; Quart and flush, one and a half years.

QUARTER-DAY sb dial. See quot. Cf HALF-DAY, THREE-QUARTER DAY.

1958 DeC StAnd (Mavis Bank) /kwota-die/ a time of day (3.00 pm), so called because one-quarter of the working day still remains.

QUASHEBA see QUASHIBA.

QUASHEE, QUASHI see QUASHIE.

QUASHIBA sb; cf Twi *Akwàsiba*, name for a female corresp to QUASHIE.

1. A DAY-NAME for a girl born on Sunday; this sense is now virtually out of use. *G*

2. The coloured concubine of a white man.

1774 Long II 328, Europeans..are too easily led aside to give a loose to every kind of sensual delight: on this account some black or yellow *quasheba* is sought for, by whom a tawny breed is produced. 1790 Moreton 106, When pepper-pot and wine his blood alarms, He takes a quashiba unto his arms.

3. An uncultivated negro or coloured woman. (Cf QUASHIE 3.)

1808 Stewart 160, To use an expression in common use here, many of them [*sc* creole women] (who have not had the advantage of a judicious education, and introduction into polite company) exhibit much of the Quashiba.

4. A stupid or foolish woman. (Cf QUASHIE 4.)

1943 *GL* Tre, Quashiba, a fool woman.

QUASHIE /kwashi, kwaashi/ sb; cf Twi *Kwàsí*, name for a male born on *Kwasída* (*Ayisi's* day), the first day of the week. *OED* 1833→. Also attrib.

1. A DAY-NAME for a boy born on Sunday; this sense is now virtually out of use. *G*

c 1800 Mansong 16, Jack..beheld a negro beneath, armed, and bearing provisions..Jack..commanded him to deliver. Quashee, who was also bold and resolute, refused. *Ibid*, Quashee, before he set out, was christened, and his name changed to James Reeder.

2. A name typifying any male negro. *G*

1774 Long II 329, He [*sc* the educated mulatto son of a rich white planter] is soon..left to herd among his black kindred, and converse with Quashee and Mingo, instead of his school-fellows, Sir George, or My Lord. 1833 Scott I 353, Then [came] quashie himself, or a company of free blacks.

3. A peasant; a country bumpkin. (This sense merges imperceptibly with 2 and 4.)

1827 Hamel II 231, Quashie does not like to abandon house and furniture, his pigs, his turkies. 1952 FGC West, Bammy chips, thin as paper—not made by /kwashi/.

4. A stupid person, a fool; a backward person who refuses improvement. (Cf QUACO 2, QUAMIN 2.) *G*

1943 *GL* Man, Quashie, not intelligent; Tre, Quashi, a fool man. 1954 LeP StE, An insignificant person, of no account, Quashie.

5. In reference to peasant language—the speech of the common folk as opposed to educated speech.

1955 FGC StAnd, You're going to teach us to talk quashie? 1958 Kgn, *Quashie Lady*—title of Christmas pantomime modeled on *My Fair Lady*: a professor of language teaches a street girl to speak 'good English'.

6. Transf from sense 3 or 4; see quot.

1952 FGC StJ /kwashi/ half-full breadfruit.

7. Attrib: usu in sense 3; see quot.

1952 FGC StT, The sugar workers run it themselves—you might call it Quashie Government. 1956 BLB Port /ing woz roning jos a likl kwashi wedin/ *He was running just a little quashie wedding.*

QUATTIE /kwáti/ sb chiefly dial; <*quarter* (i.e. of a sixpence). The word is gradually falling into disuse and being replaced by /pinyíepini/ (penny-ha'-penny). See DeC 1961 *CLS* 67 and map 68. Money of the value of 1½*d*. Also called TUP, esp in western Ja.

1860 Trollope 20, 'And now de two quatties', he said. I knew nothing of quatties then, but I gave him the sixpence. 1873 Rampini 94, 'Quattie', a penny-half-penny—the 'quarter' of sixpence. 1905 Smith 15, Chim-chim come to town to get *quattie peas an' rice.. *Penny ha'penny. 1943 *GL* all parishes. s CURRENCY.

QUATTY see prec.

QUAW /kwá-o, kwá-u/ sb dial; cf Twi (Fante dial) *kwàw*, name for male born on the fifth day (*Yàw's* day); in senses 2 and 3 perh infl by *quaw*, *v*. 'to stare about foolishly or awkwardly' *EDD* (Northants).

1. A DAY-NAME for a boy born on Thursday. This sense is now virtually out of use.

1774 Long II 427, Quao.

2. A stupid, ugly person; one from the remote country parts.

1868 Russell 7, Quaw..Ugly, stupid. 1943 *GL* Tre, Quaw—mountain people.

3. An albino negro. Also called CEDAR, COME-BETWEEN, COPPER-COLOUR, *dundus*, *dunju*, *dunzdap*, *fliik*, FRECKLE-NATURE, GLIMPSE, GREY-BO, GREY BOZA, GREY JANE, GREY JOE, *ha-buo*, *hinigran*, *kriich-oul*, *kwaab*, *kwisel*, MANGO COLOUR, *mini-blista*, MONGOOSE, *mudu*, *muduk*, NORWEGIAN, PARROT-EYE, PATU-EYE, *periin*, PUSS, PUSS-EYE, QUAWY, RIPE BANANA, SIDE-PORK, SPECKLE, *ungguru*, WHITE COCKROACH, WHITE EBOE, WHITE LABOUR, WHITEY-WHITEY.

[1868 Russell 7, An ugly stupid looking man, with grey eyes, is called a 'Qruaw' by way of derision.] 1943 *GL* Kgn, Kwaw, Negro freak; No addr, Quaw, A very white person whose parents are black. 1952 FGC Man, Tre /kwaau/ albino negro. 1956 Mc Man, StE /kwa-o/.

QUAWE see next.

QUAWY /kwáa-i/ sb dial; <QUAW+-*y*. An albino negro. (Evid a familiarizing form =QUAW 3.)

1943 *GL* Clar, Quay, a red-colour person; Man, Quawe, albino.

QUAY see prec.

QUEEN sb; cf *OED* 5d.

1. The reigning leader of a SET; see also BLUES AND REDS. Obs. *BA*

1823 Stewart 274, Each party has its queen, who eclipses all the rest in the splendour of her dress. 1826 Barclay 11, A matron attends who possesses some degree of authority, and is called Queen of the Sett.

2. In a *kumona* 'entombment' ceremony, the leading female officer.

1950 Moore 130.

QUEEN COOT sb dial. The bird *Jacana spinosa*; see quot. s POND COOT.

1956 Jeffrey-Smith 114, The peasants do distinguish between the Red-Seal Coot and the White-Seal Coot, while the lovely Jacana is Queen Coot or Spanish Coot.

QUEEN CRAB sb dial; cf *Queen conch*. A common sea-crab (*Carpillius corallinus*) having a smooth, prettily spotted back shaped like a crown. Also called THUNDER CRAB.

1952 FGC Port, StE, StJ, StM, StT, West /kwiin kraab/ red shell, spotted, pretty; crown on back; if it hold you, won't let go till thunder rolls.

QUEEN-FISH sb dial; in contrast to king-fish. =CROSSBAR. *G*

QUEEN LOBSTER sb dial; <*queen*+LOBSTER. A kind of crayfish with short, flat body. Also called MOTHER LOBSTER.

1952 FGC Port, West /kwiin labsta/ flat, not so long; short toes, no tall horns.

QUEEN MULLET sb dial; cf *queen conch*. The fish *Upeneus maculatus*, or similar species, of splendid coloration. *BA*

1851 Gosse 208, There was a pair of King-mullets.. called also Queen-mullet..This is a beautiful fish; its general hue is pink, fading to white below, with three large livid spots on each side. 1950 Smith in *NHN* 188, Queen mullet—local name for one species of Goat-fish. 1952 FGC Port, StE, StJ, StM, StT, West /kwiin molit/.

QUEEN PINE sb; cf *OED pine*, 1661 only. A fine variety of pineapple.

1774 Long III 792, The queen pine, with leaves smooth, or sometimes spiked. 1959 Alma Norman StC, Queen pine grows only in some areas and is found for sale mainly in Kingston.

QUEE-QUEE, QUI-QUI adj and sb dial; echoic: that makes the sound /kwii-kwii/. Cf Ko *kwe-kwe*, squeak. Squeaky; a CRIER.

1905 Smith 16, Chim-Chim..put on him..*qui-qui shoe. *Squeaky. *Ibid* 34, Quee-quee shoe. 1935 HPJ, Criers—cf Quee-quee.

QUENG sb dial rare; etym unknown.

1943 *GL* StC, Queng, a wierd creature.

QUENTA, QUENTEH see CUENTA.

QUICHOLE sb dial; var pronunc of *krichuol*.

1943 *GL* Tre, Quichole, screech owl.

QUICK DANCE sb. See quot.

1860 Trollope 46–7 [Jamaica] 'I hope you dance quick dances' a lady said to me..In the West Indies, polkas and the like are quick dances; quadrilles and their counterparts are simply dead..And thus I soon became used to quick dances and long drinks—that is, in my vocabulary.

QUICK INCREASE PEAS sb; a rationalized form.

1913 Harris 33, see CUCKOLD'S INCREASE.

QUICK-QUICK adv dial; iterative of *quick*. At once. *G*

1956 Mc StAnd /mi wi sen fi yu kwik kwik/.

QUICK-STICK sb dial. A plant which grows when a stick of it is simply stuck into the ground—e.g. to make a live fence; applied most often to *Gliricidia sepium*, freq to *Erythrina* spp, and sometimes to other trees.

1952 FGC Han, StAnn, StM, Quick-stick, same as marangga; StM, Quick-stick, yes, but 'growin' stake' is the common word; StAnn, Quick-stick, same as sword-rose. 1955 *WIMJ* 158, *Gliricidia sepium*..Quick Stick; Grow Stick; Growing Stake; Maranga.

QUICK-TIME adv phr; *OED* 1816 only. Immediately; in a hurry. *BA G*

1952 FGC StAnd, You better come here quick time! ..Him run quick-time an' tell him mumma.

QUINGE vb dial; etym uncert, prob multiple: cf *OED quinch*, wince (→1627), *squinch*, screw or distort the face (1840); *DA squinch*, squeeze together; or <*cringe*, by substitution of /kw/ for /kr/—cf QUICHOLE. To crouch or huddle oneself together. *T*

1942 Bennett 28, Se har quinge up eena corner deh, Ah soh she shamey-shame. 1943 *GL* StE, Quinge, to shiver.

QUININE WEED sb. The herb *Phyllanthus niruri*; it has a bitter principle, whence the name; =CARRY-ME-SEED.

1927 Beckwith 13, Quinine Weed..For fever boil the sprigs as tea. 1954 *WIMJ* 31.

QUI-QUI see QUEE-QUEE.

QUISABA see CASSAVA.

QUIT sb; prob echoic—cf JOHN-CHEWIT. Any of several kinds of small birds. See quot 1847. See also BEENY QUIT and s SQUIT.

1847 Gosse 254, The name of *Quit* is applied without much discrimination by the negroes of Jamaica, to several small birds, such as the Banana Quit, which is a creeper, and the Blue Quit, and Grass Quits which are finches. (1961 Current, FGC.)

QUIT-QUIT sb dial; iterative of QUIT. A name for a small bird in stories.

1924 Beckwith 53–4, Quit-quit was the fiddler. Anansi was playing, 'tum, tum, tum' and all the girls were going round Brar Quit-quit.

QUITTER sb dial. *OED* →1689 of human beings. Suppurating matter, pus. s QUITTERING.

1943 *GL* Kgn, StJ, Quitta, pus, corruption; Man, Quitter, inflammation. 1952 FGC Han, Man /kwíta/ pus, corruption; comes out of a boil.

QUI YAH see KU.

QUOCK see next.

QUOK sb chiefly dial; echoic. Either of two species of night herons—see quot 1955.

1847 Gosse 344, Quok. Night-heron or Qua-bird..This fine bird is much oftener heard than seen. The superstitious negro..by night, is often startled by the loud and hoarse *quok* of this bird, suddenly emitted. 1952 FGC Han, Port, StAnd, StC, StM, StT /kwak/ or [kwɔk]. 1955 Taylor 64, The Yellow-crowned Night Heron (*Nyctanassa violacea*) and the Black-crowned Night Heron (*Nycticorax nycticorax*). In Jamaica they are both sometimes called Quock.

QUUALE see QUAIL.

raabaaba sb dial; perh <*raw*+BABA. See quot 1955.

1943 *GL* Kgn, Raw baba, hooligan; Port, Rababa, alias. 1955 FGC Man /raabáaba/ an alias-man, has many names; coarse person, rough in speaking.

raas sb vulg; prob by metathesis <*arse*, buttocks, but also possibly by metanalysis: *your-arse*>*you-rarse*. In favour of the first is the sense of raspberry, a disapproving, fart-like noise (Partridge), in which is a latent pun. The former would be earlier, before *r* ceased to be pronounced. If *rassa* in quot 1790 was a genuine folk form (which is possible: cf *ratta*, rat, etc.) and not merely a strained rhyme, it has since disappeared. *BL G*. But cf *SC lási*.

1. The buttocks; the word is more often used, however, in an exclamatory way to show strong opposition: scorn, anger, impatience, etc. It is considered very vulgar. *BA*

1943 *GL* Kgn, Rass, buttocks. (1961 Current, FGC.)

2. In phrases of obvious meaning.

1790 Moreton 154, Then missess fum me wid long switch And say him da for massa; My massa curse her, 'lying bitch!' And tell her 'buss my rassa!' c 1918 FGC StAnd /raas/ as in 'Raas to you!'—common among schoolboys.

raatid adj and int dial and slang; prob repr **wrothèd*, an overcorrection of *wroth* as if it were a ppl adj. (*Wroth* is a very common adjective in the Bible—Cruden lists 38 instances, e.g. 'Moses was wroth'.) Another possibility is **wroughted*, overcorrection of *wrought (up)*—cf *overwrought*.

1. Extremely angry or annoyed.

c 1915 FGC StAnd, Common among schoolboys, /a get raatid, yu si?/

2. An exclamation indicating anger or great annoyance, amazement, and the like.

1943 *GL* Port, Rawted, surprise; StAnd, Rawtid, exclamation of surprise. 1957 JN Tre [Child's account:] An him feed the hog mam and move the white goat. Him ben say ratid and hold the roap.

raba sb dial; ?<*raabaaba*. (If not, <*robber*.)

1956 Mc Port /rába/ a shabby, ill-kept person, one who wears torn, unmended clothes.

RABABA see *raabaaba*.

RACCA TONE see ROCK-STONE.

RACCOON sb obs; prob confused with CONY through similarity of the words; there is no evidence of there having been true raccoons in Jamaica. (Cf US *coon* for *raccoon*). An early name for the INDIAN CONY.

1683 *Present State* 19, Here's an Indian Coney, called Raccones, that is good Meat, but of a distastful shape, being something like an over-grown Rat. 1725 Sloane 329, The Racoons are commonly here in the Mountains, and live in hollow fiddlewood Trees. 1823 Stewart 75–6, They [*sc* rats] are of a much larger size than the European rat, especially that kind of them called by the negroes racoons.

RACE BALL sb obs; *OED* 1775 only. A ball held annually in connection with the horse-racing season.

1835 Senior 66, These balls are always genteelly patronized and handsomely managed. At a race ball, the stewards of the races officiate as stewards of the ball.

RACIAL adj dial slang. Generous, free-spending among friends.

1942 FGC Han /ríeshal/.

RACK TONE see ROCK-STONE. *BL*

RAFFLES ANT see TOM RAFFLES ANT.

rafi-dang sb dial; prob phonosymbolic: cf *rukudang*. A *tatu*.

1957 DeC StE (Accom) /rafi-dang/ a rough dwelling or temporary shelter in field.

RAFUL sb dial; etym unknown.

1943 *GL* StT, Raful, a kind of rice.

ragamofi, ragamorfi sb dial; <*ragamuffin*.

1958 DeC StM, old ragged clothes.

raga-raga, rag-rag sb, adj and vb dial; iterative of *rag* (+A[8]). Cf *rege-rege*.

A. sb: Old ragged clothes.

1958 DeC Tre /raga-raga, rag-rag/.

B. adj: In rags, ragged.

1943 *GL* Clar, StJ, Ragga-ragga, to be in rags. 1955 FGC Man /raga-raga/ raggity.

C. vb: To pull about, pull to pieces.

1943 *GL* StE, Ragga-ragga, ram-sack; StJ, raga-raga, hauling and pulling. 1955 FGC Man /raga-raga/ hauling & pulling; to tear in pieces. 1960 LeP StAnd, Raga-raga somebody—pull them about.

RAGGA-RAGGA see prec.

RAICHIE sb dial; prob familiarized form of *Rachel*. Either of two shrubs of the family *Sterculiaceæ*: see quot.

1954 *WIMJ* 24, *Melochia tomentosa* L. Tea Bush; Raichie. Used to make tea for colds. *Waltheria americana* L. Raichie.

raigin see RYGIN.

railo sb dial; cf *OED roil v*[1] 3 *dial*, to play or frolic. =SET-UP.

1958 DeC StT /railo/ a funeral wake on first night, with ring play, etc.

RAILWAY sb obs; for *railed way*. A passage protected with rails, communicating between the parts of a factory.

1823 Roughley 196, A strong high railway should be made, to reach across, between the grand copper and syphons, so that the negroes can pass, to draw the liquor from the syphon cocks with safety.

RAINBIRD sb. Any of several kinds of birds whose actions are thought to presage rain: 1. The OLD MAN BIRD; 2. The MANGROVE CUCKOO, the YELLOW-BILLED CUCKOO, and the OLD-WOMAN BIRD; 3. Swifts and swallows. (This group in other islands besides Jamaica—see Bond.)

1725 Sloane 312–13, An Old-Man, or, a Raine-Bird..It makes a Noise generally before Rain, whence it had its Name of Rain Bird. 1847 Gosse 273, Rainbird. *Saurothera vetula*. *Ibid* 277, Old Man.—Rainbird..The appellation of Rainbird is indiscriminately applied to both this and the preceding. 1952 FGC StJ, Rain bird coos—sign of rain; StT /rien bod/ same as /úol-màn briekú/ gives sign of rain. Man, StAnd, StAnn, StM /rien bord/ swallow, forked tail, long pointed wings, harmless, very stupid, thousands fly before rain. 1956 Jeffrey-Smith 19–20, 63.

RAINBOW sb dial joc.

1958 DeC Tre /rienbuo/ a tall, thin person.

RAINBOW OLD-WIFE sb dial. A many-coloured fish of the OLD-WIFE kind.

1952 FGC StM.

RAINBOW PARROT sb dial. A large, many-coloured fish of the PARROT kind.

1952 FGC StAnn, StC, StM, StT; in StC (Old Harbour) same as P.N.P. PARROT.

RAINBOW WOOD sb obs. A parti-coloured wood used in cabinet-making.

1774 Long III 864, Bread-nut Zebra Wood, or Rainbow Wood.

RAIN FLY sb. The termite (*Cryptotermes brevis*) in its winged phase, before it sheds its wings and begins another cycle of boring into wood; believed to come out in wet weather. *G T*

1944 *NHN* 137, Few ever connect 'chi-chi' with those hosts of winged creatures we call 'rain flies' which swarm around lights in late afternoons and early evenings, particularly during the months of March, April, and May.

RAIN-FOWL see OLD MAN, quot 1694.

RAIN-SEED sb dial; *ADD* 1892. See quot. s.

1873 Rampini 56, The advent of 'the seasons'..is..foretold..by the appearance in the sky..of light, cirrus clouds, which the negroes not inaptly nor unpoetically denominate 'rain-seeds'.

RAISE /riez/ sb dial; cf *OED* 5, 25, *DAE* 3, *DA* 2. *BA*

1. A contribution of money, either voluntary or extorted: a tip or required payment. *BL G T*

1912 McK *Ballads* 50, Last night me gie 'm de last-last tup, Yet now him come an bring me up..An' all because dese couple days Me couldn' gie 'm de usual raise. Note: Raise: contribution. 1952 FGC Han, StM /riez/—a tip; a small amount of money, earned or begged.

2. An opportunity to earn some money (or get it otherwise).

1952 FGC StAnd [Man asking to be taken on as guide:] /gi mi a riez no baas/. 1958 DeC StAnd /riez/—a chance to get some money, usually by employment, occasionally by begging or theft. The plea /a waan a riez/ usually is a request for a job, but is sometimes used by beggars.

3. Money earned or paid for something sold.

1952 FGC StJ /kyang get a riez gud fi kongk/ *You can get a good price for conch.*

RAISE /riez/ vb dial; <*raise* (special meanings).

1. Of provisions, money, etc.: to get by gift, loan, or other means. (Cf RAISE sb 1 and Std colloq 'raise a loan'. Cf *OED* 25.) *BL G*

1943 Bennett 12, Fe fine out if me could a raise Even a big-gill a de ile.

2. Of a yam hill: to make by heaping up dirt over a yam plant. (Cf *OED* 31.)

1823 Roughley 407, The gang must be set in with hoes to dig yam holes, or as it is termed, to raise yam hills. (1961 Current, FGC.)

3. Of the colour or complexion: to lighten from one generation to another. (Cf *OED* 34c.)

1952 Kerr 96, This attempt to get lighter children is called 'raising the colour'. *BL T*

RAISE A KITE vb phr dial or slang; prob a var of such phrases as *raise Cain*, *raise a row*. To grumble, complain.

1941 Kirkpatrick 8, De capen [captain] start raise a kite wid dem.

RAISE-MY-THOUGHTS sb dial slang. A drink of rum.

1907 Reynolds 18, see SEARCH-MY-HEART 2.

raj sb dial or cant; of uncert origin: perh conn with *rogue*, *roger*[1] (*OED*).

1943 *GL* StAnn, Radge, a rascal; smart man, one who is tricky. 1955 FGC Man /raj/ a sam-fai man, one who sets a plot, sams you.

RA-KA-NA-BUL see *kakanabu*.

raka-tuon see ROCK-STONE.

RAKE sb dial slang; cf US *rake-off*.

1. A 'hunch', an intuitive notion or impulse.

1952 FGC Han /kech di riek/ receive a sign or token that guides you in buying a drop-pan ticket. *BL*

2. A tricky device; a misleading answer that hides the truth of a situation.

1952 FGC Tre /dat waz jos Anansi riek/ *That was just Anancy's tricky reply.*

RAKISH adj dial; cf *OED rakish a*[1]. A forward, companionable person.

1943 *GL* StJ, Rakish, hedge-up [=edge-up?], companionish.

rakl-drom see RATTLE-DRUM.

rak-stuon, rak-tuon see ROCK-STONE.

RAM sb dial. The male of any animal: see RAM-GOAT, RAM-PUSS, etc. *BA*

RAMBLE vb dial. To go about rather aimlessly and blindly searching for something. *G*

1956 Mc StE (Accom) /yu gaan rámbl nou/.

RAMBLE AND TENGLE sb phr; prob for *wrangle and tangle*. Cf s *tenggl*.

1956 Mc StE (Accom) /rambl an tenggl/ quarrel, contention.

RAMBLING SHEPHERD sb dial; cf RAMBLE. An officer in Revivalist cult practices: see quot.

1950 Moore 84, The rambling shepherd has the job of whipping up the tempo of the ceremony, and leads the procession when it leaves the booth. He travels from one end of the procession to the other in order to keep in touch with the group all the time.

RAM-GOAT sb chiefly dial.

1. A ram. (*OED* →1634.) *BA BL G*

1954 LeP StAnn, Ran-goat. 1961 FGC gen /ramguot, rangguot/ ram.

2. As the name for various plants.

1864 Grisebach 787, Ram-goat: *Fagara microphylla*. [This may be an error for RAM-GOAT RATIONAL.]

RAM-GOAT BUSH or **SAGE** sb dial. =RAM-GOAT ROSE.

1943 *GL* Kgn, Rang goat bush, specie of sage plant. 1952 FGC StAnn, Ram-goat sage, garden periwinkle.

RAM-GOAT DASH-ALONG see RAM-GOAT RATIONAL.

RAMGOAT PRICKLY-YELLOW sb chiefly dial. A local name for the tree *Zanthoxylum insulare*; 'ramgoat' refers to its strong (though not unpleasant) smell; cf PRICKLY-YELLOW.

1961 W. E. Fulford Man.

RAM-GOAT RATIONAL, DASH-ALONG, NATIONAL, RUSH-ALONG, RASHICALI, REGULAR sb dial; < RAM-GOAT (prob for ram-goat's) +uncertain element altered phonically and by folk-etym into the many variant forms. The original form may well have been *ration* (the whole therefore meaning 'the goat's portion of food'), *-al* being added for unknown reasons; *regular* may be an abbreviated way of saying 'regular rations'. The word *ration* is well known and has been much used among the folk. Such folk explanations as that 'the plant dashes along the roadsides like a goat' are probably *ex post facto*.

The shrub *Turnera ulmifolia*, used in many folk remedies. Also called HOLLY ROSE.

1927 Beckwith 25, Ram-goat-dash (or rush)-along..For weakness, boil the leaf and stalk and bottle. It is of a bright red color and with sugar added has a fine flavor. 1952 FGC StT, Tre, Ramgoat dashalong; Han, StM /rangguot rashnal/ StAnn /rangguot rashikali/ Port /rámguot régyula/. 1954 Kirkland 170 [Among contents of a herb bath:] Ram-goat regular. 1954 *WIMJ* 32, Ram-goat Dash Along (R-g National or Rational).

RAM-GOAT ROSE sb dial; RAM-GOAT + ROSE. The common flower, often introduced into gardens, *Vinca rosea*.

1942 Bennett 25, But it nevah look nice, soh me put few Ramgoat roses in-betweens. 1952 FGC StAnd, etc., Ram-goat rose: there are white ones and purplish-pink. 1953 *WIMJ* 237, *Vinca rosea* L. Periwinkle; Ram Goat Rose; Brown Man's Fancy; Old Maid. This plant enjoys a widespread reputation in the treatment of diabetes.. Most investigations of this claim have shown negative results..In Jamaica it is also used as tea for colds.

RAM-GOAT RUSH-ALONG see RAM-GOAT RATIONAL.

RAM-GOAT SAGE see RAM-GOAT BUSH.

RAMOON (TREE) /raamuun, ramuun/ sb; < Sp *ramón*, browse-wood. 'When only "ramon" is said, the "ramón de caballos" (*Trophis racemosa*) is meant' (Roig y Mesa). *OED* 1756→. The tree *Trophis racemosa*, whose leaves are good fodder for cattle and horses.

1740 Importance 54, The Ramoon Tree Leaves are Food for their Horses, and fattens them. 1756 Browne 357, The Ramoon Tree. 1826 Williams 40, In cases of drought, the cattle are fed with the leaves of the bread-nut tree and the ramoon. 1952 FGC StM, StT /ráamúun/ also StAnn, Tre.

RAM-PUSS sb dial; < RAM + PUSS; cf *OED ram-cat*. A male cat. s.

1910 Anderson-Cundall 6 [Prov:] Neber buy rancid butter fe feed ram-puss. 1925 Beckwith 88, same. 1952 FGC StAnd, StT, West /ram-pus/ Tom-cat. 1954 LeP StAnn, The ram puss and the she cat meet up.

RAM'S-HORN PEPPER sb. A variety of *Capsicum* pepper having a twisted shape.

1774 Long III 857 [Peppers found in Jamaica:] Cherry, Ram's-horn, Coral. 1814 Lunan I 357, Rams-horn Peppers.—These are formed like the coral peppers, but are much longer and more spiral, and somewhat flatted.

RANCH sb dial; < Amer Sp *rancho*, =a poor man's hut. (Malaret.) A crude hut.

1954 LeP Kgn, Ranch—building made from bamboo poles. 1957 DeC StAnd (Irish Town) /ranch/—a hut or small and crudely built house; informant explained that his house blew down in the 1951 hurricane, and for the first year he was only able to build himself a little /ranch/.

RANGER sb obs? The shrub *Cæsalpinia pulcherrima*.

1854–5 *TJSA* I 15, The wood of the Poinciana pulcherima [*sic*], the common Barbadoes Pride, Flower Fence, or Ranger, is said to yield the best of Charcoals.

ranggatan sb dial; prob < *orang-utan*.

1. See quot. *G*

1959 DeC West /ranggatan/ a person of bad (i.e. disorderly) behavior.

2. See quot and cf *bangganarang*.

1958 DeC Han, West /ranggatan/ old ragged clothes.

RANG GOAT, rangguot see RAM-GOAT.

RANK BROOMWEED sb bot obs; cf BROOMWEED. In Macfadyen's use: *Sida rhombifolia* (see 1926 Fawcett 118).

1837 Macfadyen 80, Sida ruderata. *Rank Broom-weed.*

RAPPAW see WRAPPER.

RAPP-HOUSE sb obs; etym unknown. See quot.

1683 *Present State* 10, At the East by Port St Thomas, Port Morant, several Houses called Rapp-Houses, which serve for Store-Houses and Ale-Houses for the Neighbourhood, and such Vessels as use that Port.

RAQUETTE sb obs; <Fr *raquette*, a racket—see quot 1814. Prob never fully naturalized. The TUNA cactus. (Titford misapplies the name to the DILDO.)

1811 Titford 70, Raquette, Cactus Peruvianus. Is a dildo, but without prickles. 1814 Lunan I 409, The leaves, when fallen off, and cleared of their outward membrane, and pulp, shew a delicate reticulated texture, made by the nerves and filaments, variously branched, like the racquette used by tennis players, whence the plant received the name of *raquette* from the French.

RAS sb. A common abbreviation of RASTAFARI, RASTAFARIAN.

1961 *Gleaner* 8 June 1, see BUNGO MAN 2.

rash[1], rashi, rashin sb dial; <*ration(s)*. A meal; esp a quick or light meal.

1868 Russell 6, Rashe—A little hasty meal. 1912 McK *Ballads* 53, Man dem..Six long fortnight nyam me rash; Not a gill me caan' get. [*The men have been eating my snacks for six long fortnights, but I can't get three-farthings from them.*] 1943 *GL* Port, Rash-in, dinner. 1952 FGC StE, StM, West /rashin/ among poorer people, a quick meal; /mi tek op mi rashin/ have a big meal.

rash[2] sb dial; etym unknown—perh <*rash*[1].

1959 DeC Han /rash/ obeah.

rash-man sb dial; <*rash*[2]+*man*.

1959 DeC Han /rash-man/ obeah man.

RASS, RASSA see *raas*.

RASTAFARI, RASTAFARIAN [ˌræstəˈfarı] /ràstafarái/ attrib sb and sb; <*Ras Tafari*, Emperor of Ethiopa (Haile Selassie). s I[3].

A member of a cult which, taking Ras Tafari as their name-patron, hold that the Emperor of Ethiopia is God incarnate, and that they owe allegiance only to his government; they avow a desire to return to Africa; the men frequently let their beards and hair grow as a mark of their membership.

1960 *SAN Report* 11, see next.

RASTA (MAN) sb freq attrib; abbr of RASTAFARI (+*man*). An adherent of the RASTAFARI cult. s I[3], I-AND-I.

1955 Simpson 167, The 'Rasta' people consider Marcus Garvey..as the forerunner of their movement. 1960 *SAN Report* 11, Those people who worshipped the Emperor and were locally known as 'Ras Tafaris' or 'Rastamen' came to describe themselves as 'Niyamen'—that is, members of Niyabingi.

RAT-BAT sb; <*rat*+*bat*. A bat. (See also BAT.) *BL*

1851 Gosse 163, see BAT. c1935 HPJ, Rat-bat is the common term for a bat in Jamaica, where the word bat =moth, or cricket-bat.

RAT-BOOK sb obs.

1828 Marly 51, The rat-book, in which account was kept of rats killed.

RAT-CUT sb; abbr for *rat-cut berries* or *coffee*, those berries *cut* (i.e. chewed) by *rats*. The coffee berries which, since rats have bitten them, are not fit for marketing and are used at home. These are 'good berries' or the rats would not have 'cut' them.

1929 Beckwith 61, Coffee (especially the 'rot-cut' which is not fit for market). [This form shows misapplication of the rule for rendering dialect words into StdE form.] 1946 U.Newton I 17, Now when I did not want to do such things as clean the knives, or run to the shop near nightfall or pick up 'rat-cut' for the home in general, I would pretend that I was feeling bad. 1947 U.Newton III 18, Coffee was in bloom and rats were as usual cutting off the berries and tasting the sweet juices within. 1958 W. A. Roberts letter, 'Rat cut' coffee is valued rather than otherwise. The rats are said to know the good berries.

RAT-EARS sb dial. Any of certain plants having leaves shaped like a rat's ears, esp (1) *Peperomia pellucida*, but also (2) *Boerhavia scandens*, and (3) *Cissus trifoliata*.

1927 Beckwith 25, see RATTA-TEMPER. 1952 FGC StC, StM, StT /rát-íez/—kind of calalu with transparent stem, leaf shape of rat-ears—same as man-to-man; Han, Port, Rat-ears, juicy, transparent, like calalu—same as consumption weed. 1954 *WIMJ* 19, see RATTA-TEMPER. 1955 *WIMJ* 157, *Boerhavia scandens*..Rat Ears; Easy-to-Bruck. *Ibid* 155, *Cissus trifoliata*..Sorrel Vine; Rat Ears; ..to make tea for treating colds.

RATHER /réda/ vb dial; prob abbr of 'would rather have' or similar phrase. To prefer.

1924 Beckwith 156, De missis said to him..'Which one you rather?' He said, 'I rather de t'ree advice'. 1957 JN StE [Schoolgirl speaking:] Mi father come from Moore Town. Mi reddar mi mother. Mi going to England next year to mi mother. *BA BL G T*

RATID see *raatid*.

RATOON sb and vb; <Sp *retoño*, a fresh shoot or sprout. *OED* sb 1779→, vb 1756→.

A. sb: 1. A new shoot (of sugar-cane, 1756 Browne; indigo, 1774 Long; cotton, 1790 Beckford; banana, 1913 Fawcett; yam, ginger, 1956 Mc; or other cultivated plant) that springs from an old stock left in the ground. Also attrib. [Not specif Ja; cf *DAE* 1631→.] *BA G*

1756 Browne 132, The suckers that shoot from the roots left in the ground the foregoing season, which are generally called rattoons. 1774 Long III 680, This plant [indigo] gives ratoons, or re-produces, affording four or five crops in a year. 1954 *FG* 391 [Of pineapples:] Ratooning. A marked lessening in yields occurs after the first ratoon crop.

2. Transf. Something remaining after. Joc and slang.

1894 *Pop. Sci. Monthly* XLIV 493, The Jamaican reference to a meal made off the remnants of a previous feast as 'eating the rattoons'. [From *OED*.] 1958 DeC Clar /ratúun/ an unborn child fathered by a man who has left town and can't be traced.

B. vb: Of a plant: To put out a new shoot from the old stock.

1756 Browne 130, But you may be more free [in planting sugar-cane] where the ground is observed to produce a kind plant and to rattoon well. 1790 Beckford I 319, The Jamaica cotton will bear but one or two crops; whereas.. the French, will continue to ratoon for many years.

RAT-SPRING, RAT-SPRINGE sb. A trap activated by a spring, used against cane rats.

1823 Roughley 89, Bring the different cane-piece watchmen, with their weapons of defence on one side, and their rat-springs on the other, to the overseer's house, to see their success in destroying these hurtful creatures. *Ibid* 115, Every watchman..should always have a number of rat springes set in various directions.

RATTA sb dial; <*rat*+A[8]. (Cf Cameroons Pidgin *alœta, rata*; *SC aratta*.) *BL*

1. A rat; rats.

1873 Rampini 179 [Prov:] Ratta (rat) cunny (cunning), so when puss gone him make merry. 1943 *GL* most parishes, Ratta, rats.

2. Transf. Bulging muscle in the upper arm. *G*

1943 *GL* Kgn, Ratta, arm muscle. 1956 Mc Man /a lik yu pan yu rata/ ***I strike you on the muscle of your upper arm.***

RATTA-CASTLE sb dial joc; <RATTA+ *castle* (used ironically). This may be taken from an Anancy story in which Rat lives in a castle. An old house, esp one crowded with idlers. *BL*

1943 *GL* StAnd, Ratta-castle, an old house. 1955 FGC Man /ráta kyáasl/ old house with idlers.

RATTA-DRUM sb dial; evid <RATTA+*drum*, but cf RATTLE-DRUM. A tree-fern—from some reference to a noise it makes?

1921 Franck 429, The treefern, known locally as the 'rattadrum'.

RATTA-TEMPER sb dial; <RATTA+*temper*, bad-temper, anger. The herb *Peperomia pellucida*, used in folk medicine.

1927 Beckwith 25, Ratta-temper..'Rat-ears', 'Pepper-helda'. For a loose cough boil as tea. 1954 *WIMJ* 19, *Peperomia pellucida*..Pepper Elder; Rat Ears; Ratta Temper; Silver Bush [Grenadines]; Shiny Bush [Trinidad].

RATTLE-DRUM, RATTLER, RATTLING-DRUM /rakl-drom/ sb dial. The treble drum (smaller of a pair of drums often played together) with which the more complex rhythms are produced (while the bass drum keeps a steady beat); =TITTLE-DRUM.

1952 FGC Port /dis wan iz di rakl-drom/; Han /ratla/ the little drum; StM /ratlin drom/.

RATTLER see prec.

RATTLEWEED sb dial.

1. The plant *Priva lappulacea* (according to Beckwith's identification, which, however, is doubtful).

1927 Beckwith 25, see CLAMMY-BUR. 1954 *WIMJ* 31 (same).

2. Species of *Crotalaria*; =RATTLE-WORT.

1952 FGC StM, Rattle-weed—has pods like peas, rattle in wind when dry; blue and yellow flowers, different kinds.

RATTLE-WORT sb bot; *OED* 1866. Common wild species of *Crotalaria*.

1837 Macfadyen 238, Crotalaria. Rattle-wort. 1864 Grisebach 787. 1920 Fawcett 7.

RATTLING BUR sb dial. =RATTLEWEED 1.

1952 FGC StM.

RATTLING DRUM see RATTLE-DRUM.

RATTON sb obs; *OED* →1661. (This word may be the source of RATTA.) A rat.

1725 Sloane 294, It maintains it self principally on Snakes, Rattones, and Lizards, which it takes.

RATTOON see RATOON.

RAW adj chiefly dial. Smelling of fish. *BA BL*

1960 SJR StAnd, If meat smells 'raw', it means it smells fishy. Jamaican saying: When it rains, the Englishman smells raw behind the ears. [1960 LeP—this occurs in Andrew Salkey's novel, *A Taste of Violence*.]

RAW BABA see *raabaaba*.

RAW-CHAW /ráacháa/ sb; <*raw*+*chaw*, coarse food (or to chew coarsely). Of a person: coarse, rough, uncouth.

1941 Kirkpatrick 24, A real rawchaw mountain man wey like 'im onion an' garlic an' bwoy w'en 'im go fe nyam 'im nyam. 1956 Mc /mi no waant im roun mi at aal—im tuu raachaa/ *I do not wish to associate with her; she is too coarse.* 1960 NJL StC, Ordinary, common, loud—man or woman: He's /raachaa/.

RAWTED, RAWTID see *raatid*.

RAX (UP) vb (phr) dial; prob <*rack* (*OED* v^3).

1943 *GL* Kgn, Rax, to abuse someone. 1962 BLB 67 /raks-op/ berate, abuse.

RAZAM /rázam/ sb dial; <*rosin*, prob via a form with syllabic nasal: */razn/ or */razm/. *BL*

1943 *GL* StM, Razam, rosin.

razlin sb dial; phonologically this would represent *Rozlyn* or *Roslin* in StdE. Perh there is some conn with the Roslin estate (St Mary's) listed in 1792 *Proceedings of the Ja. House of Assembly*, App. XII (no page). A type of open-guard MACHETE.

1952 FGC StE /rázlin/ machete. 1958 DeC several parishes.

RAZOR GRASS sb; *OED* 1871→. Various sedges (*Scleria* spp) with sharp-edged leaves.

1864 Grisebach 787, Razor-grass: *Scleria scindens.* 1954 *FG* 587, Razor-grass..At least nine different kinds of Scleria occur in Jamaica, and all of them can be unpleasant weeds due to the cutting edges of the leaves. *G N*

RAZOR-MOUTH sb dial; cf *OED mouth* 17. The cutting edge of a razor.

1924 Beckwith 100 [Story:] As him sing out, razor-mout' tu'n over.

REACH vb dial. *BL G T*

1. Absol intr: To arrive. Also const *up*. (*EDD* 5.) *BA*

1907 Jekyll 110, 'Well,' he say, 'never min'; by the time me re'ch up me voice will come good'. 1950 Pioneer 63, When him reach him fine say cow no did-deh. [*When he arrived he found that cow was not there.*] 1956 Mc Man /yu riich op horli den/ you got here quite early.

2. Intr with *to*+obj: To arrive *at* (a place). (*OED* 16a →1802.)

1924 Beckwith 43, On reaching to the hole Anansi said, 'What a pretty hole'.

REACH THE SUNDIAL vb phr cant. See quot.

1950 Moore 101, If the spirits come and keep a cult member trumping under possession until high noon, they call this 'reaching the sun dial'. In other words, 'reaching the sun dial' is dancing Myal, or possession dance, throughout the morning hours of the sun until high noon.

READ /riid/ vb dial; *OED* 2 →1887. To interpret things without foreknowledge, to tell fortune or speak as a seer. Also const *up*. *BA G*

1956 Mc StE /di obya man bigin tu riid an tel yu liti ting/ *The obeah man begins to tell you little things about your affairs. Ibid* /if a diip streinja kud kom a yaad an riid mi op an tel mi ebriting/ *If a complete stranger could come along and tell me everything about my affairs. Ibid* /di swiitaat riid ar op/ (A woman has sung a song with a hidden meaning to warn her lover that her husband is at home) *The lover understood her warning.*

READY vb intr and refl dial. To make oneself ready, prepare oneself. *BA G*

1961 BLB 19 /dat taim im a redi fi go a daans nou/ *She was then getting ready to go to the dance.*

READY-MONEY LAND sb phr obs. Land on which a lucrative crop may be raised, but whose productivity will not last. *BA*

1774 Long I 463, What is vulgarly called ready-money land; which gives a present return in good sugar almost as soon as it is opened, but will soon fall off.

REBUSTA see ROBUSTA.

rech tai sb; ?<*retch*, reach, pull (*EDD*)+*tie* sb.

1956 Mc Man /rech tai/ way of tying head-scarf, with knot in front.

RED sb and adj dial; note that in Twi and other W Afr languages 'red' covers the range which, in European languages, includes red, orange, and yellow.

A. sb: The yolk of an egg.

1952 FGC StAnn, StJ, StM, West, Two parts of an egg: the /wait/ an' the /red/.

B. adj: 1. As a simple colour term, covering the range from yellow through orange to red and even purple: see RED-COAT PLUM, RED CRAB, RED-STICK CALALU, RED WASP, RED WATER-GRASS, RED YAM, etc. *G N*

2. As a complexion term, referring esp to the combination of a light or yellowish skin with crinkly hair or other negro features; often in derogatory use by negroes. See RED IBO, RED NAYGA, RED SKIN. *BA BL G T*

reda see RATHER. *BL*

RED-ARSED SPIDER sb obs. The BLACK SPIDER (and perhaps the BROWN WIDOW).

1756 Browne 419, Aranea 6..The red-arsed Spider. This insect is frequent in the woods, and its nip or bite said to be very venomous. The body is about an inch in length, and of an oblong form.

RED BANANA sb. The West Indies banana. (The word may not be Jamaican but has not been found in dictionaries or other books consulted.) *G*

1952 FGC Port, StJ, StM, StT /red banana/—small bunch with big fingers.

RED BATATAS sb obs; transl Fr *patates rouges*. The sweet-potato.

1606 Sloane 54, Convolvulus radice tuberosa esculenta minore purpurea..patates rouges comme les betes raves ..Red Batatas.

RED-BEAD TREE sb; *OED* 1756→ for diff tree. The tree *Adenanthera pavonina*.

1909 Harris 311, see CIRCASSIAN BEAD TREE. 1941 Swabey 13 (same). 1952 FGC StJ, StM, Tre, Red-bead tree.

RED-BEAD VINE sb; *OED* 1756→. The vine *Abrus precatorius*, also called JOHN-CROW BEAD, CRAB'S EYES.

1756 Browne 297–8, The Wild Liquorice, or Red-Bead Vine. This weakly climbing plant is very common among the bushes, in all the low lands of Jamaica. The infusion of the leaves and tops is much used in all our sugar-colonies. 1920 Fawcett 42–3, Wild Liquorice, Red Bead Vine, Crab's Eyes. 1955 *WIMJ* 157.

RED BEAN TREE sb; *OED* 1756→. The trees *Erythrina corallodendron* and *E. velutina*. Also called CORAL-BEAN TREE.

1756 Browne 288, The Coral or Red Bean Tree. This tree grows in many parts of Jamaica. 1864 Grisebach 781. 1920 Fawcett 50, 51.

RED BEEF-WOOD sb; *OED* 1891 only. The tree *Ardisia coriacea*.

1864 Grisebach 781, Red Beef-wood.

RED BELL-FLOWER sb. The vine *Ipomœa quamoclit*.

1814 Lunan I 399, see INDIAN CREEPER. 1864 Grisebach 781, Bell-flower, American red: *Ipomœa Quamoclit*.

RED-BELLY PARROT sb dial. A variety of the PARROT fish.

1952 FGC Port, StC, StJ, StM, Red-belly parrot—same as MACKENZIE PARROT.

RED-BELLY SNAPPER sb dial. A variety of the snapper fish.

1952 FGC West /red beli sinápa/—running snapper.

RED-BILLED DOCTOR BIRD or **STREAMER-TAIL** sb. The humming-bird *Trochilus polytmus*. (There is a black-billed variety.)

1956 Jeffrey-Smith 153. The red-billed streamer-tail is peculiar to Jamaica.

RED BIRCH sb. =BIRCH.

1920 Fawcett 206, Red Birch, West Indian Birch, Turpentine Tree, Mastic Tree. 1941 Swabey 13. 1955 *WIMJ* 157, *Bursera simaruba*..Red Birch.

RED BONAVIST sb; <*red*+BONAVIST. One of the varieties of the bean *Dolichos lablab*.

1696 Sloane 68, Phaseolus maximus perennis..semen ruffum hilo albido fere circumdante. Red bonavist.

RED BULLY or **BULLET (TREE)** sb. The tree *Dipholis nigra*, the wood sometimes having a deep red colour.

1826 Williams 290, Red bully tree (achras anona). 1864 Grisebach 782, Red Bully-tree. 1941 Swabey 15, see BULLY TREE. 1952 FGC StAnn, Tre /red bulit/ use for fence post.

RED CANDLEWOOD sb. *Amyris balsamifera*; cf RED KANTU.

1952 FGC Tre, Red candlewood, same as kantu, burn-eye.

RED CANELLA sb bot; <*red*+CANELLA. =MOUNTAIN CINNAMON.

RED CHAWSTICK sb. The plant *Gouania domingensis*, closely related to CHAWSTICK.

1864 Grisebach 782.

RED-COAT sb dial. An unidentified fish.

1952 FGC StM, Red-coat—deep pink; shape like bony fish.

RED-COAT PLUM sb dial. The plum tree *Spondias purpurea*, and its fruit, red when ripe.

[1837 Macfadyen 227, Leather-coat or Red Spanish-Plum.] 1952 FGC StAnd, Red-coat plum; StAnn, Red-coated plum; StM, Red plum. 1955 *WIMJ* 70, Red-coat Plum; Brazilian or Spanish Plum.

RED COCO sb dial. A variety of *Colocasia esculenta*. Also called RED MILADY.

1958 DeC Clar /red koko/ same as /red malíedi/—names for a reddish coco.

RED CRAB sb dial. The QUEEN CRAB.

1952 FGC StE /red krabz/—have red speckled back.

RED DANDELION sb dial; <*red*+DANDELION. The herb *Iresine paniculata*.

1955 *WIMJ* 70, Juba's Bush; Red Dandelion; Bitter Weed..This plant is said to provide an excellent tea described by one informant as diuretic—'flushes out all poison from the kidneys' (hence the name 'red dandelion'?).

REDDAR see *reda*.

RED-DEVIL PEPPER sb dial. The very hot red *Capsicum* pepper.

1952 FGC StM /red devl pepa/.

RED DISEASE OF GUIANA sb obs. COCO-BAY, evid from the colour of the pustules.

1801 Dancer 232, Leprosy and Coco-Bay, or Joint-Evil.* *Red Disease of Guiana.

RED DIVER sb dial. The Ruddy Duck, *Oxyura jamaicensis.*

1956 Jeffrey-Smith 139–40, One can understand this duck being called red diver, if seen with the sun shining on its plumage. It is of a lovely red chestnut, except for the crown of the head and the back of its neck, which are black.

RED DOVE sb obs. An unidentified dove; see BLUE-BELLY.

RED-EYE sb dial; perh an allusion to the mongoose?

1958 DeC StT /red-ai/—a greedy, miserly person. Also /haakshaa/.

RED-EYED FLYCATCHER sb obs; *OED* →1834. The Red-eyed Vireo.

1847 Gosse 194, Red-eyed Flycatcher—John-to-whit. *Vireosylva oliveacea.*

RED-EYE GINGER sb dial. A variety of ginger with red 'eyes' or sprouts.

1952 FGC Man /red-ai jinja/.

RED FIG sb. See quots.

1864 Grisebach 783, Red Fig: *Ficus pedunculata.* 1952 FGC StE, Red fig—has short leaf—/tek it saa buod/ *Use it for sawing into boards.*

RED-FOOTED BOOBY sb dial.

1956 Jeffrey-Smith 133, The White Booby (*Sula sula*) is mostly white and its bill is dark, while its feet are red; so it is known as the Red-footed Booby.

RED-FOOT JUMPER or **JUMPING DICK** sb dial. =HOPPING DICK.

1944 *NHN* II 130, Red-foot jumping Dick. 1952 FGC Man, Red-foot jumper.

RED GAL sb dial; the reason for the name is unknown—perh it refers to the yellow root. (See RED.) The herb *Morinda royoc,* used in folk medicine.

1954 *WIMJ* 30, see DUPPY POISON.

RED GAULIN sb; <*red*+GAULIN. The RED-NECKED GAULIN.

1956 Jeffrey-Smith 121, Locally they are distinguished only by colour, and are known severally as the Blue, the White and the Red Gaulin (the Red is very rare).

RED GRUNT sb dial. A fish of the GRUNT kind.

1946 *NHN* III 52, see RED GULLY. 1952 FGC StT /red gront/—there are red, yellow, and grass grunts.

RED GUAVA sb dial. According to Beckwith, a species of *Eupatorium.*

1927 Beckwith 18, Guava, red..For diarrhoea chew the leaves.

RED GULLY sb. An unidentified fish: see quot.

1946 *NHN* 51, Fish which are good to eat and afford good sport for fishermen are Blue Doctor, Red Grunt, Snapper, Red Gully, Rock Snapper. *Ibid* 52, The fish you can spear most easily around our cays are Parrots, Red Grunts, Snappers, and Gullies.

REDGUT BULLY-TREE sb. =RED BULLY.

1952 FGC StAnn, Redgut bullet (StE, Tre) = red or white bullet (StAnn) = cherry bullet (StC); StE /redgot bùlitrii/.

RED HAIRY-TAILED BAT sb. See quot.

1851 Gosse 279–80, The Red Hairy-Tailed Bat..He captured one, and on the next evening another, both of which were of one species, the Red Hairy-tail of the United States (Lasiurus rufus).

RED-HEAD sb chiefly dial; *OED* 1798 only, '?*Obs.*' The plant *Asclepias curassavica,* highly valued in herb medicine.

1801 Dancer 357, Red-head. 1814 Lunan I 64, see BASTARD IPECACUANHA. 1927 Beckwith 26, Red-head.. For a boil, 'rub it up', add laundry blue and rub on the sore to 'draw out the seed'. 1952 FGC Han, Port, StAnn, StT /reded/ good for warts, it 'operates' you; Han, StM, StT, Tre /red hed/.

RED HEDGE sb. The plant *Acalypha wilkesiana,* so called from the colour of its leaves and for its use in hedges.

1955 *WIMJ* 78, see COPPER LEAF.

RED IBO sb dial; <RED+IBO, Eboe. (The Ibo were originally of lighter colour than the other negroes; see 1960 *CLS* 79.) A light-coloured person with negroid characteristics. The term is always used insultingly.

1943 *GL* Kgn, Reddebo, mulatto; Port, Redibo, fair person. 1960 SJR StAnd, Red Ibo, pejorative term for a fair-skinned but otherwise negroid person.

RED JASMINE sb. The shrub *Plumieria rubra.*

1811 Titford ii, Red jasmine. Illust. Plate V 5.

RED KANTU sb dial; see *kantu.*

1952 FGC Tre /red kantu/ same as red candlewood, burn-eye, blind-eye.

[**REDLEGS** sb; *OED* 2, 1887 only. See quot.

1817 Williamson i 27, A ridge of hills, in the adjacent country, about the middle of the island [Barbados], is called Scotland, where a few of the descendants of a race of people transported in the time of Cromwell still live, called Redlegs. I saw some of them; tall, awkward made, and ill-looking fellows, much of a Quadroon colour; unmeaning, yet vain of ancestry; a degenerate and useless race as can be imagined.] *BA*

RED LIGHT sb dial. The tree *Erythroxylon areolatum,* so called near Portland Ridge.

1943 *NHN* II 26, Red Light..the wood is very hard, dark red in colour, and valued for posts.

RED MARY sb dial; cf RED+*Mary.* A variety of sugar-cane, yellowish within.

1958 DeC StAnd /red mieri/ a soft cane with black skin (nothing red about it).

RED MILADY sb dial; <RED+MILADY. A variety of coco similar to the SALLY. Also called RED COCO.

1952 FGC StJ /red mai liedi/ [careful pronunciation] = /sali/ but not so hard; red and white varieties. 1958 DeC Clar /red maliedi/ same as /red koko/, names for a reddish coco.

RED MISS KELLY PEAS sb dial; *red* + ?*Miskelly* (a surname in Jamaica at end of 18th cent: in 1798 John Miskelly was First Lieut of the town-guard of Kingston—cf 1798 Evidence 5) +*peas.* A variety of bean (prob *Vigna unguiculata*). Also called SKELLY PEAS.

1873 Rampini 90–1, Pease and pulse of all kinds—the 'red Miss Kelly' and the 'Black Betty'. 1929 Beckwith 19, ref to Rampini.

RED-MOUTH GRUNT sb dial. Some kind of fish of the GRUNT type—cf RED GRUNT.

1756 Browne 449, see DARK GRUNT. 1900 Murray 16, When de mout recober de blow it tun a sort of a red like, so dem boy usen fe call him 'red mout' grunt.

RED NAYGA sb dial. =RED (SKIN).

1954 LeP StE, Mulatto, red nayga. 1960 SJR StAnd /red niega/ having a very light skin—pass for white or Jamaica white, but crinkly hair.

RED-NECKED GAULIN sb; <*red-necked* + GAULIN. The Reddish Egret (*Dichromanassa rufescens*).

1847 Gosse 334, The red-necked gaulin—*Egretta ruficollis*. 1956 Jeffrey-Smith 123, The red-necked gaulin, the Reddish Egret (*Dichromanassa rufescens*)..is a very rare bird here.

RED PARROT(-FISH) sb. The fish *Sparisoma abilgardi*.

1950 Smith in *NHN* 199, Red Parrot-fish. 1952 FGC West, Red-Parrot—generally called here 'Mackenzie squab'.

RED PARTRIDGE sb.

1956 Jeffrey-Smith 112, Partridge Doves, once common, are rarely seen..Known as 'Red Partridge' they are still fairly common in the Cockpit Country.

RED PEA MEAL sb. A kind of meal (flour) once made from RED PEAS.

1856 *TJSA* II 41.

RED PEAS sb; *DAE* 1805→. A variety of *Vigna unguiculata*, or similar red beans. *BA G*

1727 *Observations* 13, Sugar-beans, Red-peas, Pigeon-peas, Garavonzas, and others. 1913 Harris 25.

RED PETCHARY sb obs?; < RED + PETCHARY. The LOGGERHEAD (*Tolmarchus caudifasciatus*), which has a yellow patch in its crown.

1847 Gosse 186, Red Petchary. Loggerhead. Great Crested Flycatcher.

RED-POP sb. An unidentified vine; = HOG POP.

RED RAIL sb; *OED* 1889–91. The rail *Amaurolimnas concolor*.

1847 Gosse 369, Red Rail. Water Partridge. 1936 Bond 90, Red Rail..*Local name:*—Water Partridge..Entire plumage reddish brown..*Range:*—Jamaica (*A.c. concolor*); possibly extinct.

RED RODWOOD sb; *OED* 1864. The tree *Eugenia axillaris*.

1864 Grisebach 787, Red Rod-wood. 1943 *NHN* II 53.

RED SAGE sb dial. The species of *Lantana* having a yellow-and-orange flower.

1952 FGC Han.

RED ST VINCENT YAM sb; cf RED. A variety of the St Vincent yam with purple or purplish flesh.

1952 FGC Port /réd sinvínsn/. 1963 BLB letter, The red St Vincent is not red at all, it is purple, just about the same colour as the purple cabbage.

REDS AND BLUES sb obs. = BLUES AND REDS.

1858 Chambre II 151–3, Christmas time is a great season for merrymaking amongst the negroes. We were fortunate in witnessing a ceremony or procession, called the 'Reds and the Blues..' On the north side of the island it is a splendid affair, but on the south side it is just the reverse..At Montego Bay, Lucea, and Falmouth, the rival factions of Reds and Blues represent all the great personages of the day, and their attendants. The ladies lend their jewels to be worn by the negro women who figure in the procession, and subscriptions are made by the residents to assist in purchasing the paraphernalia and dresses, which are really magnificent..Each set had a champion on their masters' horses, who made a great show, in armour..composed of guilt livery..Both being armed with lances and swords, they became so much excited, that the two pugnacious heroes defied each other to single combat in the street.

RED SEAM sb dial. A policeman. (The allusion is to the broad red stripe applied to the outer trousers seams.)

[1912 McK *Ballads* 62, Oh! where are..De frien's dat I used to hold dear?..have they all turned away from me now Becausen de red seam I wear?] 1943 *GL* StC, Red seam, policeman. 1956 Mc StAnd, StT /red siim/.

RED (SKIN) adj dial; < RED (+ *skin*, for *skinned*). Having a light-coloured (but not white) complexion; mulatto or lighter. (Not necessarily an insult, but sometimes used as such by darker people.) *BA G T*

1942 Bennett 10, Wat a red kin 'oman mean! [*What a mean, yellow-skinned woman!*]. 1943 Bennett 14, De 'oman..cut har y'eye an' pass Gawn sidung side a red-skin man. 1960 SJR, Red-skin: A negroid person with fair complexion—like people from St Elizabeth. Not pejorative, whereas RED IBO is.

RED SORREL sb; *OED* 1798. *Hibiscus sabdariffa*, whose pods are used to make SORREL DRINK. *BA*

1740 Importance 34, Two sorts of Sorrels, white and red, of both which they make Jellies and Marmalade, and a cool drink. 1756 Browne 285, Hibiscus 5..Red Sorrel.. The flower-cups and capsulæ..make very agreeable tarts; and the decoction of them, sweetened and fermented, is what people commonly call Sorrel Cool-drink. 1801 Dancer 360, Red sorrel..A cooling Diuretic Drink.. Preserved Sorrel..Sorrel Jam. 1954 *WIMJ* 30, see FRENCH SORREL.

RED SPANISH PLUM see LEATHER-COAT PLUM.

RED-STICK CALALU sb dial; <*red* + STICK I + CALALU. The wild PRICKLY CALALU.

1952 FGC StAnd, Red-stick calalu grow by themselves. 1954 Reckord 4, Me see dat lady Vie an she dress up like when red-stick calalu got seed.

RED-STICK CASSAVA sb dial; <*red* + STICK I + CASSAVA. The variety of cassava with a red stalk or stem. *G*

1952 FGC StT, Red-stick cassava, also black- and white-stick, in both bitter and sweet.

RED SWITCHY-TAIL sb dial. The young of the yellow snake—see quot.

1940 Lynn-Grant 116, *Epicrates subflavus*..The adult is a sturdy snake; the young so slender and thin necked that it is mistaken for a different snake by the natives and called the 'red switchy-tail'. The *Tropidophis* is considered, at least at Portland Point, to be the young *Epicrates*.

RED-TAILED SPIDER sb. = RED-ARSED SPIDER.

1774 Long III 877, Red-tailed Spider. It is of a glossy jet-black all over, except the tail, which glows with a vivid red.

RED-TAIL SNAPPER sb. The fish *Lutianus synagris*.

1854–5 *TJSA* I 142, *Messoprion uninotatus*—red tail snapper. 1952 FGC Port, StE /red-tiel snapa/. 1958 DeC StT.

RED TOM-FOOL see BIG TOM-FOOL.

REDUCE vb dial; cf *OED* 21d →1856. To weaken physically. (*OED*.)

1929 Beckwith 13, All whom I questioned agreed that fruit trees were good about a house with the exception of the pawpaw, which takes the richness from the soil or the strength from the householders themselves..The 'night jessamy', too, if planted near a house will 'reduce you'.

REDUCK vb trans; back-formation from *reduction* (perh used for *deduction*). To reduce, make a reduction in a calculation.

1952 FGC Man [A woman, given less change than she should have had:] I didn' see how you reduck it out.

RED WANDERING JEW see AUNTIE MAG.

RED WASP sb dial; < RED + *wasp*. The common yellow or tawny wasp (prob in contrast to the BLACK WASP).

1952 FGC StAnd, Red wasp /di was-dem sting hai/; Tre, Red wasp, big head and batty, waist small; /was-nes/ like comb, but no fat in it.

RED WATER-GRASS sb chiefly dial; see WATER-GRASS. The common wild plant *Zebrina pendula*, with red-purple leaves.

1952 FGC Man. 1954 *WIMJ* 32, see CREEPING JENNY.

RED-WEED see MOUNTAIN CALALU.

RED-WHITE SWEET-POTATO sb dial. A variety of sweet-potato with red skin and white flesh.

1952 FGC StC /red-wait/.

RED WITHE sb; *OED* 1866.

1. The climbing shrub *Combretum robinsonii*.

1864 Grisebach 787, Red-withe: *Combretum Jacquini*. 1926 Fawcett 312, Red withe.

2. The climbing shrub *Davilla rugosa*.

1926 Fawcett 172, *D. rugosa*..Red Withe..Stems useful for making baskets, &c.

RED WOOD sb.

[1. A kind of red wood, also called Guinea wood, formerly exported from Jamaica as a dye-wood.

1696 Sloane 213–14, Arbor quæ vel Brasiliensem rubedine superat..Redwood. E Guinea Jamaicam aliquando adfertur inde Europam Advehenda. 1725 Sloane 185, Red-wood.]

2. Species of *Erythroxylon*, now esp *E. areolatum*.

1756 Browne 278, Erythroxylum 1..Red-wood or Iron-wood, with oval leaves..Erythroxylum 2..The small round-leafed Erythroxylum, or Red-wood. 1837 Macfadyen 143, 144. 1920 Fawcett 160, *E. areolatum*.. Red Wood.

3. The large tree *Matayba apetala*.

1926 Fawcett 56, see CROMANTY 4. 1941 Swabey 18, Cobywood..Bastard Mahogany, Redwood.

RED YAM sb. A variety of the WHITE YAM: see quot 1814. *G*

1814 Lunan II 309, The red or purple yam appears to be only a variety of the white. 1924 Beckwith 173, So Anansi go to him ground, he have a yam name of 'red yam'.

REEF SNAPPER sb dial. A kind of SNAPPER that is found at the reefs. *BL*

1952 FGC StM, Reef snapper—yellowish; West /riif sinapa/ cuts pots—redder than mutton snapper.

rege sb dial; prob < *rag*—cf *rege-rege*. A nickname for foods: see quots.

1958 DeC StJ /rege/ coconut rundown; StT /rege/ a fritter.

rege-rege sb dial; iterative prob of a form of *rag*. Cf *raga-raga*. s REGGAE.

1. Rags, ragged clothing.

1954 LeP StT, Old, ragged clothes—Rege rege.

2. A quarrel, a row. (Cf *OED*, *EDD*, *rag vb* and *sb*.)

1959 DeC Han, Tre /rege-rege/ a quarrel, fuss, or *banggarang*.

REGJEGS sb[1] dial; prob reduced < *rags and jags*.

1943 *GL* StJ, Regjegs, rags.

REKAY-REKAY see next.

reke-reke adj and sb dial; iterative of some element suggesting weakness, e.g. *rack*, *wrack*, *wreck*; cf *racketty*, *rickety*. See quots.

1943 *GL* West, Rekay-rekay, weak. 1955 FGC Man /reke-reke/ a person weak from sickness.

RELISH sb dial; cf *OED sb*[1] 3b.

1. The part of a meal having distinctive flavour, in contrast to the bland starch foods that form the bulk of it.

1956 Mc StAnd, Relish, The savoury part of the meal as distinct from the /fuud/ (yam, coco, etc.)—i.e. fish, cabbage, etc.

2. Specif. The plant *alikasha* (ARRACACHA).

1956 Mc Port, Relish—a plant, also called /alikacha/; it is very like carrot, in colour and shape: /relish iz a plaant tu itself/. (Here the word is also used for bottled sauce.)

REMEDY sb dial joc; cf ASSISTANT. See quot.

1958 DeC StAnd, *Remedy* seems to mean any food which traditionally goes along with some other food and improves it, e.g. BREADFRUIT-REMEDY for run-down, SALTFISH-REMEDY for ackee. See SOUP-REMEDY.

RENEWAL sb dial.

1958 DeC StT /rinyúual/ a funeral celebration about a month after death.

rengk adj dial; < *rank*. s *rengk* vb.

1. Having an offensive smell (cf *OED* 12).

1943 *GL* StAnd, Renk, stink. *BL G*

2. Sour. (This perh refers to odour too.)

1943 *GL* Kgn, Wrenk, sour.

3. Impertinent (cf *OED* 14).

1955 FGC Man /rengk/ fierce, impertinent; 'You is renk!' 1956 Mc StAnd /rengk/ over-assured, pert.

RENK see prec.

RENKIN adj dial; evid < *ranking* < *rank* (*OED a.* 15. Of a..virulent type). Cf BANKING. Rank. (For *rank poison* cf 1513 Douglas *Æneis* II iv 37.)

1951 Murray 44 [Song:] Bitta Cassava kill Joe Brownie Bitta Cassava Renkin poison. *G*

renshman sb dial; occas var of *wenshman*: for alternation of *w* and *r* see also *ripri*, *sripl*. = *wenshman*.

1952 FGC StJ /renshman/.

RENT sb dial; *OED v*[2] →1898 (*EDD*). To rend, tear. *BA*

1952 FGC StM, see next.

renta yam sb chiefly dial; perh < *renter*, one who rends or tears (*OED sb*[2]). A widely grown variety of yam, white, soft, with hairy skin, which produces a very large foot. Also called BARBADOS YAM.

1942 Bennett, see COME-HERE-FE-HELP-WE. 1943 *GL* Clar, Kgn, Man, StM, Tre, Renta yam, Barbados yam. 1952 FGC StC /renta/ goes deep, St Lucia yam doesn't go deep; StM /renta/ same as Barbados—just tease up the surface and put it in—it rents the earth. 1958 DeC StC /rente/ St Vincent yam.

rento see prec.

REPATRILATE vb dial; < *repatriate* with intrusive *l*. To repatriate.

1942 Bennett 13, Him buy fus-class ticket goh dah Cuba An' had fe come back repatrilate.

REPEATER DRUM sb. A small, double-membraned drum, strung tight, used to 'play the melody' in drumming for *buru* dancing.

1960 *SAN Report* 18, see FUNDE DRUM.

RESIN HEIGHT sb phr tech obs. The point at which evaporating aloe juice is ready to be taken out of the evaporating vessel: see quot.

1814 Lunan I 13, The proper time to skip or ladle it out of the tache is when it is arrived at what is termed a resin height, or when it cuts freely, or in thin flakes, from the edges of a small wooden slice, that is dipped from time to time into the tache for that purpose.

REST DANCE sb dial. An inactive dance, with hugging, but little movement.

1952 FGC StM.

RESURRECTION LILY sb. A kind of lily which flowers about Easter time.

1927 Stafford 52, Then resurrection lilies bring, As white as snow that deck the Spring. 1952 FGC StC, Resurrection lily—comes up on Good Friday; bulb favour /huonyan/ (onion); white and green flower; smell sweet after four o'clock.

RHYGIN see RYGIN.

RHYME /raim/ sb dial; cf *rhyme*, to talk nonsense, tell lies (*EDD*). A joke, an amusing story. *BL*

1956 Mc Man /shi hab raim—shi hab plenti swiit taak/. 1960 BLB 9 /shi hav plenti raim/ *She is a joker.*

RHYMER /raima/ sb dial; *rhymer*: see prec. A person who can tell amusing stories or jokes.

1956 Mc Man /raima/ a person with a good repertoire of jokes /givz plenti juoks/.

RHYTHM UP vb phr dial. To play rhythmically.

1950 Pioneer 59, One guitar start fe rhythm up, An den me start fe sing.

RIAL /ráial/ sb dial; prob <*rial*, a coin of low value. Note: This is an old form of the word 'royal' and some people take this sense to be connected with the ordinary meaning of 'royal' (if so, used ironically); but this is hardly demonstrable. *EDD* has *royal* (Shropshire only) meaning 'independent, high and mighty —used in a bad sense', but again, connection with the Jamaican sense is by no means certain.

Hybrid. (Usu in cpds: CHINEY-RIAL, INDIAN-RIAL, MULE-RIAL, SPIDER-RIAL, TURKEY-RIAL.)

1943 *GL* Kgn, Rawyal, half-caste. 1958 DeC StC /ráial/ racial term: the offspring of East Indian woman and black man.

RIBAND CANE see next.

RIBBON CANE sb; *DAE* 1827→. A variety of sugar-cane with conspicuous vertical stripes, like a ribbon.

1811 Mathison 65, The *riband* or *striped cane* is no longer cultivated by judicious planters. The rind is hard. 1823 Roughley 287, In dry weather parishes..they are obliged to adopt a hardy callous species of cane to plant there, called the riband, and transparent cane, in order to withstand the force of the sun. 1952 FGC StJ, StT, Ribbon cane.

RIBBON COCO sb dial; <*ribbon*+COCO. A variety of *Colocasia* with a striped stalk.

1952 FGC StT, Ribbon coco.

RICE BITTERS sb dial.

1. The herb *Phyllanthus niruri*, which carries its flowers like small seeds ('rice') under the leaves; also called CARRY-ME-SEED.

1952 Kerr 26, Castor oil, rice bitters, and mojo bitters. 1952 FGC StT, Rice bitters—Chamba bitter.

2. See quot.

1953 *WIMJ* 234, *Andrographis paniculata*..Rice Bitters; Wild Rice. Used in Jamaica to prepare a general beverage..The tops are very bitter.

RICE-POP see PAP. *G*

RICE WEED sb dial. =SKELLION GRASS.

1952 FGC StJ, Rice weed—same as skellion grass: roots have knots, can't get rid of it; StM.

RICEY COCO sb; <*rice*+*-y*+*coco*, abbr of *coconut*. A dish made of rice flavoured with COCONUT MILK, sugar, and spices.

1893 Sullivan 65, Boil a pint of rice..add..coconut cream, nutmeg, cinnamon, rosewater, and sugar to taste. The people often eat this for their breakfast. 1952 FGC Port. 1957 *FFM* 254, Ricey Coco. (Recipe given.)

RICKY-RAK see next.

RICKY-ROCKY sb dial. The tree *Colubrina ferruginosa*.

1927 Beckwith 26, Ricky-rocky. The leaves of this tree are valued as an ingredient in a bath. 1929 Beckwith 12, About Mandeville..the lime-kiln [is built]..using preferably fiddlewood, and 'ricky-rocky' as wood. 1961 DAP Man, Ricky-rak, *Colubrina ferruginosa* Brongn.

RICKY-TEE sb dial; echoic. The bird *Myiarchus stolidus*; see quot.

1956 Jeffrey-Smith 49, The stolid flycatcher in St Elizabeth is called 'Ricky-tee' while in Trelawny it is known as Billy Green and as Stupid Jimmy, a name also given in Lower Trelawny to another 'little tom fool', which is the Great Antillean Pewee (*Blacicus caribaeus*) and which is also known as Willie Pee.

RIDDLE /ridl, rigl/ vb dial; cf *OED* v^1 2a, b →1773. To work out the meaning of; interpret. *G N*

1924 Beckwith 183 [Formula for introducing a riddle:] Riddle me riddle Guess me this riddle And perhaps not! 1927 Anderson-Cundall 121, Riddle me riddle, John me riddle, guess me dis riddle an' p'raps not. 1955 Bennett *Cricket Time*, Sinting a bruk a Jamma now, Riggle me guess is wat [*Some news is coming out in a jamma song—guess what it is!*]

RIDER sb dial.

1. An undesired shoot, esp on an orange tree.

1952 FGC StM /raida/ a false sucker on a tree.

2. A plant which climbs upon another: see CASSADA RIDER.

RIDGING GRASS sb.

1864 Grisebach 787, Ridging grass: *Anatherum bicorne.*

riel vb dial; prob <*rail*, *EDD* v^3, 'a dial. form of *reel*'. Of a woman: to move vigorously in sexual intercourse.

1958 DeC Clar /hou di gyal a riel pan di bed/.

RIFLE ANT sb obs; erron for RAFFLES ANT. =TOM RAFFLES ANT.

a 1818 Lewis (1834) 251 'St Thomas's in the East has been inoculated with another self-inflicted plague, under the name of 'the rifle-ant'.

RIGE sb or vb dial; a phonetically irreg form of *rag*: cf BULLYRIGE, RYGIN.

1943 *GL* StAnd, Rige, rag.

RIGHTED adj dial; <*right adj* (*OED* 13). In one's right mind; usu in neg. *G*

1942 Bennett 21, Lawd me no righted, me mad! me mad!

RIGIN, RI-GIN see RYGIN.

rigl see RIDDLE. *N*

RING sb dial. Ring play; a ring game. *G*

1957 JN Clar, We play ring and we play all kine of something. *Ibid*, Come outside and play; me and Stanley and Erol a play a ring [*are playing 'ring'*].

RING-BOAR sb dial. A wild boar whose tusks have grown around to form a 'ring' or spiral.

1952 FGC Tre /ring-buor—hav toch dat gruo roun—mek a ring/.

RING-DING sb dial; for etym see **s.**

1. Hilarity, lively entertainment. *G*

1907 Jekyll 234, Soldier da go way tomorrow, The last of the ring ding tomorrow. 1943 *GL* StAnn, Ring ding—hilarity. 1955 FGC Man /ring-ding/.

2. A quarrel. (Evid an ironic use of 1.) *G*

1943 *GL* Kgn, Ring-ding, a quarrel.

RING-DOWN adj and adv dial. **s.**

1. First-class, of the best quality.

1958 DeC StE (Accom) /di fela iz a ring doun uol wich/ *The fellow is a first-class witch.*

2. As an exclamation for emphasis.

1960 *CLS* 145 [Song:] 'Ring-down peas oi! hi! a ring down! Oh, ring down!' [Ring down is an emphatic epithet often used in mild oaths.]

RINGED GOWRIE sb. The Collared Swift.

1847 Gosse 51, Ringed Gowrie. 1955 Taylor 82, The Black Swift..and the Collared Swift (*Streptoprocne zonaris*), which is also known as the Cloud Swift or the Ringed Gowrie, are residents in Jamaica. 1956 Jeffrey-Smith 21, Ringed Gowrie (see CLOUD SWIFT).

RING JOHNNYCAKE sb dial.

1958 DeC StJ /ring-janikiek/ doughnut-shaped fried dumpling.

RING PLAY sb; <*ring* sb + PLAY. The playing of games by a ring of players, as at wakes, nine-night, and similar occasions. (For 'ring tunes' see 1907 Jekyll 190–215.) *G*

1953 Moore 156, Ring play: a nine-night entertainment—singing of bilah songs, but not country songs. 1958 DeC StT /ring plie/ a funeral wake characterized by ring play.

RINGTAIL PALLETTE-TIP see PALLETTE-TIP LIZARD.

RING-TAIL PIGEON (or **DOVE**) sb; *OED* 1865. The pigeon *Columba caribœa*.

1774 Long II 95, Shooting the ring-tail pigeons, which in this part of the country are very numerous. 1833–4 Hosack (1876) xiii 1 note, The ring-tail pigeons are so fat that in October the whole body is entirely covered with yellow fat. 1836 Lewis (1845) 53, Doves of all descriptions—of which the ring-tail has been allowed to rank with the most exquisite..by epicures. 1847 Gosse 291, Ring-tail pigeon..Of all our Doves, none is so exclusively arboreal as this. 1952 FGC Han, Man, StAnd, StE, StJ, StM, StT /ring-tiel (pijin)/.

RING-TING sb dial or slang; a rhyming form of *real thing*, perh infl by RING-DING. **s.**

1943 *GL* Port, Ring-ting, real thing.

RING-WORM sb obs. The Guinea worm; see NEGRO-WORM. *BA BL G*

1740 Importance 43, Ring-worms, which are very painful; they used to make a Fuss, winding them out a part at a time, but by a compressive Bandage and a drawing Plaister they do it much easier.

RINGWORM BUSH or **SHRUB** sb; *OED* 1756→. The shrub *Cassia alata*.

1756 Browne 224, Cassia 9. The Ring-worm Bush..The juice of the leaves or buds is said to cure the ring-worms. 1801 Dancer 368, Ring-worm bush (*Cassia herpetica*). 1820 Thomson 73, see FRENCH GUAVA TREE. 1864 Grisebach 787, Ringworm-shrub: *Cassia alata*. 1920 Fawcett 109, Ringworm Shrub.

RINGWORM WEED sb. See quot. (This may be an error.)

1927 Beckwith 26, Ringworm-weed. *Indigofera* ——.

RINGWORM YAWS sb obs; *OED* 1898. One of the effects of yaws which resemble ringworm infection.

1820 Thomson 83, see GUINEA-CORN YAWS.

RIO GRANDE SWEETWOOD sb; <*Rio Grande*, river in parish of Portland, Ja. A local name for the WHITE-WOOD or LOBLOLLY SWEET-WOOD tree (*Oreodaphne leucoxylon*).

1864 Grisebach 788, Rio Grande Sweet-wood.

RIPE adj dial; cf *OED* 6b. Of a person: old, of advanced age. *BA*

1943 *GL* StM, Ripe, aged. 1956 Mc Port /mi raip nou/ *I'm old now.* 1959 DeC West /raip/ aged, too old to work /hin duon wok de agén fram in get raip/.

RIPE sb dial; ellipt. See quot.

1958 DeC Tre /raip/ a junk of bitter cassava taken from the cassava-bag and dropped in soup to boil; this is recognized as risky, but apparently it imparts a fine flavour to the soup.

RIPE BANANA sb dial slang; allusion is to the colour of the skin.

1958 DeC StT /raip banana/ jocular and derogatory word for an albino.

RIPLEY PINE sb; <*Ripley* (see quot 1764) + PINE. A fine variety of pineapple.

[1764 Gordon in Mereness 381, At Mr John Ripleys near Kingston I saw eight acres of land under Pine Apple.] 1788 Marsden 86, A particular sort are ripe when quite black, and are reckoned to have the finest flavour, being most in esteem; this is the Ripley Pine. 1952 FGC StAnd, StAnn, StJ, StT /ripli pain/ smallest, but sweet; StM /ripl pain/.

ripl pain see prec.

ripre sb dial; occas var of *wipri* by substitution of /r/ for /w/: cf *renshman, sripl.* = *wipri.*

1952 FGC StC /ripre/.

RIST vb dial arch; prob overcorrection: formation of a weak-verb preterite from *rise* or *riz*? Rise.

1907 Jekyll 115, The mother say 'No', but him rist an' go. [*The mother says* (or *said*) *'No', but he rises* (or *rose*) *and goes* (or *went*).]

RIVER CANAAN CALALU sb dial; the reason for allusion to the Biblical name is uncert. A variety of CALALU that grows on river banks.

1952 FGC Port /riva kienyan kalalu/.

RIVER-COURSE TAMARIND sb dial. A kind of WILD TAMARIND.

1952 FGC StT, River-course tamarind, small, takes years to produce lumber.

RIVER DRUMMER sb. A fish of the DRUMMER type, found in rivers.

1952 FGC StM.

RIVER GAULIN sb dial. = LONG GAULIN.

RIVER MAID or **MUMMA** sb dial. A female deity associated with rivers, and sometimes brought into Revivalist worship; propitiatory offerings are left for her at springs and deep holes. (Practices differ considerably: see quots.) [Cf the Mammadillo (*maman de l'eau*) of St Lucia and Grenada. LeP.]

1893 Banbury 35–6, Rubba Mumma or Rubba Missis. This superstition most likely took its rise from the story of the *mermaid* or *water nymph* of England; she is believed to inhabit every fountainhead of an inexhaustible and considerable stream of water in Jamaica. For this reason the sources of such streams were worshipped, and sacrifices offered to the 'Rubba Missis'. It is a well-known fact that the slaves on water-works used to persuade their overseers or masters, to sacrifice an ox at the fountain-head of the water turning the mill in times of much drought. [She sat and combed her long black hair, appeared always at noon, disappeared when someone approached; if the comer saw her first and their eyes met, he was doomed; her comb was sometimes found; food was taken to the river head for her; mial songs and dances were done for her; fish from such rivers were considered her children, therefore not eaten (e.g. at Chester Castle, Hanover).] It was the opinion that wherever the river nymph resided, if the fountain was deep and blue, there was a table of pure gold. 1929 Beckwith 146. (Ref to Banbury.) 1952 FGC StAnd /riva muma, riva mied/ In Hope River, near Gordon Town, there's a blue hole where people drown; when water is low, have to pay River Muma as fishermen pay the sea—throw money in. West /riva muma/ at water head—has long flowing hair, disappears into water. 1953 Moore 86–7, the River Maid comes into Revival ceremonies during storm or rain, and may become the most important officer, superseding others. She is never harmed by water. *Ibid* 91, She has assistants: water shepherd, water shepherdess, water boy, and water girl.

RIVER MULLET sb. Any mullet which is found in rivers. *G*

1952 FGC Man, StJ, West /riva molit/ mouth round, body long, silvery; same that goes in rivers goes in sea.

RIVER MUMMA see RIVER MAID.

RIVER PINK sb; the reason for the name is unknown: it cannot refer to the colour or the song; perh the bird was thought of as similar in a general way to the PINK[1].

1847 Gosse 151, Water Thrush. *Bessy kick-up.—River-pink.* (Rob. MSS.) *Seiurus Noveboracensis.*

RIVERSIDE CALALU sb dial. Another name for the common COCO-CALALU.

1952 FGC StM.

RIVERSIDE TOBACCO sb; the name alludes to the shape of the leaf and to its growing by rivers. The herb *Pluchea odorata.*

1854–5 *TJSA* I 64, River Tobacco—Trixis? Conyza? 1864 Grisebach 788, Riverside Tobacco. 1936 Fawcett 201, *P. odorata*..Sweet scented Fleabane, Riverside Tobacco. 1955 *WIMJ* 76, Riverside Tobacco; Bitter Tobacco; Fox-leaf.

RIVER TOBACCO see prec.

R.M. SWEET-POTATO sb dial. A variety of sweet-potato with red skin, said to have been introduced by R. M. Little.

1952 FGC StT /hár hém/.

ROAD CATTLE sb. Oxen used for drawing loads of sugar to the wharf.

1823 Roughley 151, I would never put the road cattle, intended for carrying the crop to the wharf, to any other kind of work.

ROAST COCO vb phr dial; cf next. To make secret preparations, biding one's time; to scheme or plot.

1952 Kerr 157, Mr X..the Member of the House of Representatives, him gone sleep. Him a roast coco. We caan hear a thing 'bout him.

ROAST PLANTAIN (FOR SOMEONE) vb phr; cf prec, and BAKE BAMMY. To prepare to benefit by someone's downfall; by implication, to plot or scheme to bring this about.

1925 Beckwith 116 [Prov:] When John Crow see mauger cow, him roas' plantain fe him. (When the cow dies, the carrion crow will be ready to make a good meal.) 1960 P. Wilmot StAnd, Roasting plantain for someone.

ROAST PORK sb dial or slang. The cactus—prob the TUNA, whose fleshy flat leaves resemble bits of meat. (They are roasted for medicinal purposes.)

1943 *GL* Kgn, Roas pork, cactus.

ROBIN (MANGO) sb; prob an allusion to the colour when it ripens. A variety of mango—see quot 1954.

1952 FGC StE, StJ /rabin, raabin manggo/. 1954 *FG* 475, Robin. Found chiefly in the lowlands of St Elizabeth. Ripens with a pinkish tinge on one side. Very sweet, but hairy.

ROBIN (REDBREAST) sb; *OED* 1894. The bird *Todus todus*; see quots. *G*

1847 Gosse 73, Green Tody..Always conspicuous from its bright grass-green coat, and crimson velvet gorget, it.. has received a favourite name, that of Robin Redbreast. There is little resemblance, however, between the West Indian and the European namesakes. 1894 Newton *Dict. Birds* 791, *Robin*, a well-known nickname of the Redbreast..has been transplanted..to Jamaica in the case of the Green Tody. (From *OED*.) 1936 Bond 228, Jamaican Tody..Robin, Robin Redbreast. 1952 FGC Han, StAnd, StAnn, StM, StT /rábin réd brés, ráabin/.

ROBO YAM sb.

1954 LeP Kgn, Robo yam—coco yam.

ROBUSTA BANANA /robósta, rubósta/ sb; <Sp *robusta*, stout. A common variety of banana with stout fruit.

1943 *GL* no addr, Rebusta—a kind of banana. 1952 FGC Port, StAnd, StAnn, StJ, StM, StT /ròbósta/. 1956 Mc Port /rubósta/.

ROCCA-ROCCA adj dial; evid iterative of *rock* + A[8].

1943 *GL* StJ, Rocca-rocca, very rocky or stony.

ROCKA-TONE see ROCK-STONE.

ROCK BEAUTY sb; *OED* listed without quot. The many-coloured fish *Holacanthus tricolor.*

1892 Cockrell list, Rock beauty. 1953 Smith in *NHN* 9, see ANGEL-FISH.

ROCK BUSH sb.

1. The shrub *Phyllanthus epiphyllanthus.*

1920 Fawcett 261, see SOAP PLANT.

2. The shrub *Gesneria.*

1954 *WIMJ* 30, Gesneria sp..Rock Bush.

ROCK BUTTERFISH or **GROUPER** sb. The fish *Epinephelus striatus*; see HAMLET.

1892 Cockrell list, Rock grouper—*Epinephelus striatus.* 1952 FGC StC /rak grupa/ has stripes; StM, Rock grouper, same as rock butterfish, grass hamlet.

ROCK HIND sb; *OED* 1867; cf *hain.* One or more fish of the *Epinephelidæ* family: see quots.

1867 *TRSAA* I 25–6, Observing a prodigious large Rock-hind, Serranus catus, following close, a line was baited.. immediately the Rock-hind drove at it, gulped it, and was taken. 1892 Cockrell list, Rock hind, *Epinephelus apua.* 1952 FGC StAnn, StM /rak hainz/; StJ, West /rak hain/ larger than /hain/; also speckled.

ROCK MULLET sb.

1854–5 *TJSA* I 143, Mugil petrosus, Rock mullet.

ROCK ROSE sb dial; <*rock* + ROSE. The ROCK BUSH (2), *Gesneria neglecta.*

1944 *NHN* II 142, The 'Rock Rose'—a small plant with rosette-like leaves and a white flower with pink markings, almost hidden from view, pressed against the damp rocks. 1946 *NHN* III 59, The 'Rock Rose'—*Gesnera* [*sic*] *neglecta*—was noticed now and again in fruit.

ROCK-STONE /rak-tuon, raka-tuon, rak-stuon/ sb dial; *DAE* →1836. *BL G N*

1. A stone. (Cf for similar redundant const, HEAD-SKULL.) *BA*

1847 Gosse 274, The youth picked up a 'rock-stone', as pebbles are called in Jamaica, and delivered the missile with so skilful an aim, that the bird dropped to the ground. 1863 Waddell 182, The poor horses were plunging every step among rock stones, tree roots, and mud holes. 1868 Russell 5, Rocka-tone, Stone. 1943 *GL* Clar, Kgn, Man, StJ, Racca Tone, Rack tone; StC, rokka-tone.

2. Attrib. See quots.

1797 Braco 24 Aug, A Mule Died in the pastures from a fall & Broke it's foot in a rock stone Hole. 1956 Mc Man /raktuon lan/ bad, rocky land.

ROCK SWEETWOOD sb; <*rock* (implying hardness) + SWEETWOOD.

1. The tree *Nectandra sanguinea.*

1952 FGC StE, StT, Rock sweetwood—same as Timber sweetwood; very hard; the wood itself smells sweet; there are *white rock* and *black rock.*

2. The tree *Ocotea martinicensis* and its wood.

1946 *NHN* II 63, There are three kinds of 'Sweetwoods' in the forests bordering the trails to Corn Puss Gap. The 'Rock, Timber and Pepper-leaf Sweetwoods' are the best known..(c) 'Sweetwood Rock'. Ocotea martinicensis..a fairly large tree with obovate leaves tapering into a wedge-shaped base.

ROCK-WEED sb dial. A name for the wild *Begonia,* which grows along the faces of rocks.

1927 Beckwith 26, Rock-weed. *Begonia*——. For bowel complaint, boil three leaves, cool in a shut pan and drink cold with table-salt.

ROCK WIND sb. A wind which blows along the rocks, or from the rocks or hills out to sea.

1774 Long II 109, At certain times of the year..a wind blows, known here by the name of the rock-wind, and so called from its sweeping close along the shore from East to West..The rock-winds are always strong. 1952 FGC StAnn /rak win/ is a blow-an'-stop wind; blow high—good weather for a while; StC, Rock wind come from east-northeast; StJ /rak win iz lan briiz/ fisherman watch it, has a time to turn back; bring strong weather; StM, Rock win' come off de lan'.

ROCK WOOD sb. See quot.

1926 Fawcett 27, *Maytenus virens..*Rock Wood.

ROCKY-BUR sb. The wild plant *Priva lappulacea.*

1952 FGC StC, see FASTEN-MAN-COAT.

ROCKY-SWEET sb dial. = ROCK SWEETWOOD.

1952 FGC StAnn, Rocky Sweet = Timber Sweet.

RODNEY CASSADA sb dial; perh for Admiral Rodney—cf other honorific names: NELSON BALL PEAS, DUKE COCO. A variety of cassava.

1952 FGC StE /rádni kasáada/.

ROGGO adj dial; the base of *rogo-rogo.*

1943 *GL* StE, Roggo, rough.

rogo-rogo, roko-roko, rugo-rugo, ruku-ruku adj, vb, and sb dial; basically phonosymbolic, though perh infl by such similar words as *rough, rugged, rock* vb; cf also the related formations ROGGO, RUKUTO, *rukudang,* RUKUPANG.

The basic idea is that of unevenness: hence, inequality of surface (roughness), unsteadiness of movement (up and down, back and forth). Iterative structure makes the sense more emphatic. As usual in such words, one part of speech may be converted into another as sense requires without change of form.

A. adj: Rough; uneven; unsteady; shaky. *G*

1943 *GL* Kgn, Rooko-rooko, (a) rough, (b) rickety or shaky. 1955 FGC Man /rugo-rugo, ruku-ruku/ rough, shaky. 1956 Mc Man /roko-roko/ coarse-textured, rough (e.g. one's foot).

B. vb: To handle roughly; to shake; to mix. *G*

1943 *GL* StE, Rogo-rogo, to mix. 1957 DeC StE /rugo-rugo/ to shake or handle roughly, person or thing.

C. sb: A rough thing or action.

1943 *GL* StT, Ruggo-ruggo, rough things; Ruck-rucku, something done very roughly.

ROGUENESS sb dial; *rogue* + *-ness.* Roguery, trickery.

1942 Bennett 48, Me dah pray fe de war ovah An' watch dem Chiney man Se is who dem dah goh got dat time Fe put dem rogueness pon. [The Chinese shop-keepers have been profiting by wartime shortages.]

ROGUING ppl adj dial; *OED* →1672. That wanders about 'acquiring' whatever he finds; dishonest, scoundrelly; pilfering. Implied in ROGUING JOE.

ROGUING JOE (or **TOM**) sb dial.

1. A scuffler, scrounger, pilferer.

1955 FGC Man /ruogin juo/ man who goes round with a bag, picking up what he can.

2. A bag carried on the shoulders (or otherwise) by such a man.

1943 *GL* Clar, Roguin-Joe, a bag hang on the shoulder used as a stow away by pilferers. 1955 GHC Man, same. 1958 DeC StJ /ruogin tam/ a side-bag (any size) of canvas or crocus-bag.

3. A manner of carrying a miscellaneous load: see quot.

1958 DeC Kgn /ruogin-juo/ here meaning not a side-bag but a system of tying a very heavy load onto a man's back by means of grass, trash, string, or whatever else is handy; the load may be separate loose articles like field produce or may be one large object like a piece of furniture.

ROKKA-TONE see ROCK-STONE.

roko-roko see *rogo-rogo.*

ROLL COTTA vb phr; <*roll,* coil + COTTA. Lit, to form (plantain trash, cloth, etc.) into a head-pad; but this appears to have the transf sense of elation, being 'in one's salt' (q.v.).

1925 Beckwith 98 [Prov:] Puppy belly full, de tail roll catta. 1950 Pioneer 32 [Song:] Young Tung gal dem Dung Tung, Dem a roll dem catta sey youngo Tung, Anancy oh yuh timboley Dem a roll dem catta sey youngo Tung. [The girls are becoming excited by the singing.]

ROLL, ROLLING[1] vb and vbl sb; for *roar, roaring,* the second *r* altered by dissimilation and lambdacism. To roar; roaring. Cf ROLLING CALF.

1924 Beckwith 161, So de lion see de t'ree goat coming, he grunt like a great rolling. De mudder of de goat frighten. So when de lion..no see de two kid come back, commence to roll again.

ROLLING[2] vbl sb; evid *rolling,* as of a wheel, merged in sense with ROLLING[1]. *G*

1. The sound made by a heavy vehicle passing.

1956 Mc StE /wen a hier di ruolin/ *When I heard the sound of the truck.*

2. The sound made by an earthquake.

c1915 FGC StAnd.

ROLLING-CALF sb dial; <pres pple of ROLL, roar +*calf*.

1. An imaginary monster taking the form (usually) of a calf with fiery eyes, and haunting the roads and countryside at night. People who lead dishonest or wicked lives are said to 'turn rolling-calf' when they die.

1873 Rampini 83, The 'rolling calf', a spirit who haunts the city by night with a flaming eye, trailing a long chain behind him. 1877 Murray *Kittle* 10, Tom ded, mek him go; we no wan [him] fe come back ya; come da wander all bout worl like a ebel perit—da turn rollin calf, den da frighten ebery body. 1894 Spinner 48–9, Angelina shivered. She resolved to be always very good and never stay out late. It would be dreadful to be caught by a Rolling Calf, worse still to 'die wicked', and perhaps run the chance of becoming a Rolling Calf herself. 1895 Banbury 23, The belief in what are called Rollen (*roaring*) Calves. These are a set of animals, (or rather, as it is believed) evil spirits in the shape of animals, which travel about at nights, and are often seen by the people. 1907 Jekyll 176, 'Shop-keeper and butcher', so goes local tradition, 'tief too much and when they dead they turn Rolling Calf'. 1943 *GL* Kgn, Man; StAnd, Rollin Kyaffe, ghost. 1952 FGC Han, Rollin'-calf is a demon, not a ghost; travel around, has a chain trailing behind; looks like hog, size of a hog, eyes like fire itself; travels in darkness—can't counteract motor-car lights.

2. Transf. Some variety of angel-fish.

1950 Smith.

ROLLING-CALF BED sb dial; <ROLLING-CALF + *bed*.

1954 *WIMJ* 32, see CREEPING JENNY.

ROLLING CONCH sb dial. A small, round conch.

1952 FGC StJ /ruolin kongk/ lovely, pretty little shell.

ROLLING-PIN sb dial. An unidentified fish (perh some species of Elops), with a rounded body.

1952 FGC StM, Rollin'-pin—shape like bony-fish; eight inches; very scarce.

ROLL-OVER sb dial.

1959 DeC StJ /ruol uoba/ grated banana boiled in a run-down.

ROLL-'PON-GROUND sb.

1954 LeP StAnn, Roll pan grung—period of mourning after a funeral.

ROLL-'PON-KNEE sb dial.

1958 DeC StAnn, StC /ruol-pan-nii/ a cigar which is rolled (on the knee) from scraps of tobacco carried by the smoker..Not rolled until just before smoking.

ROLL ROCK-STONE sb dial.

A ring game played by boys at school, also at wakes: twelve players sit in a ring, the leader sings, others join in the chorus; a brick or large stone is passed meanwhile from player to player, each putting it on the ground in rhythm; the penalty of not keeping the rhythm is to have one's fingers mashed. (Cf 1922 Beckwith 90–1, Stone Pounding and Stone Passing.)

1952 FGC Han.

roloks sb dial; a metathetic variant of *loroks*.

1943 *GL* Kgn, Rollux, dirty, torn, old clothes. 1955 FGC Man /roloks/ old clothes.

ROMANCE BOY sb slang. A girl-chaser.

1952 FGC Han /im miit-op wit a romans-bwai/.

rompii, romplis, rontis sb dial; <*rump* + indeterminate elements: one may be *-less*. s.

1954 LeP Man, Fowl without tail-feathers—rumplis. 1956 Mc StAnd /rontis, rompii, romplis/ a fowl without a tail.

rondong, rondoun see RUNDOWN.

RONGARS sb dial; origin unknown.

1943 *GL* Clar, Rongars, bananas.

rontis see *rompii*.

ROOF sb tech.

1957 DeC StAnd /ruuf/. When a banana stump is split before replanting,..the *roof* (the round, outer, uncut surface) is always faced downwards [in planting].

ROOKAW sb dial obs; etym unknown. A musical instrument, similar to the SCRAPER.

1739 Leslie 326, They have other musical instruments, as ..the Rookaw, which is two Sticks jagged.

ROOKOOMBINE dial; etym uncert: see *rogo-rogo, bain*. A nonsense-word carrying sexual suggestion.

1951 Murray 33 [Song:] Rookoombine; [Refrain:] Oh Rookoombine eena Santa Fe.

ROOKO-ROOKO see *rogo-rogo*.

ROOSTER COCK sb dial; a redundant formation—cf *head-skull*, etc. A rooster or cock. *G*

1929 Beckwith 186, And a ram goat and one rooster cock!

ROOTER sb dial; <*root* vb + *-er*; cf RENTA.

1958 DeC Clar /ruta/ one of the Portland Maroon names for the St Vincent yam.

ROOTIE see *roti*.

ROPE LAY sb.

1952 FGC StE, Rope lay, the place where sisal ropes are twisted.

ropshan sb dial; an irreg form of *ruction*, disturbance (*OED* 1825→); perh infl by *eruption*.

1956 BLB Man /riez ropshan/ raise a ruction.

ROSE sb dial. The generic term for flowers: cf RAM-GOAT ROSE, ROCK ROSE, etc.

1907 Jekyll 266, 'Rose' means any kind of flowers. When they [*sc* speakers of dialect] want to indicate what we call roses they say 'sweet-rose'. 1952 FGC Han, Tre /ruoz, ruoziz/ flowers of any kind planted for their beauty in a garden.

ROSE-APPLE sb; <*rose*, for the rosy scent and flavour of the fruit + *apple*. *OED* 1812→. The tree *Eugenia jambos* and its fruit. *N*

1790 Beckford II 190, The orange, the rose-apple, the papa..and other productions. 1811 Titford 71, Fragrant Rose Apple, *Eugenia Fragrans*. 1913 Harris 19, The rose-apple..was introduced to Jamaica in 1762..The pale yellow fruits are about the size of a small apple, strongly impregnated with the odour of the rose. 1954 *FG* 254–5.

ROSE MANGO sb. A red-and-yellow variety of mango. *T*

1952 FGC Port.

ROSE-MARMALADE sb. A marmalade made from something with rose flavour—perh rose-apple?

1927 Stafford 6, Grenadilla and orange and guava For dolces and rose-marmalade.

ROSEMARY sb; <*rosemary* (which is similar). The common name for the shrub *Croton linearis*; in books called WILD or SPANISH ROSEMARY. *G*

1927 Beckwith 26, Rosemary..For a cold, fever or pain boil it for a bath or for tea..This fragrant herb is universally burned in the house to drive away evil influences or 'duppies'. 1952 FGC Han, StAnd, StJ, StM /rúoz méri/ make nice tea; cut into tobacco, smoke it; very small tree, leaf narrow and thick, like thyme. 1955 *WIMJ* 78 (Wild or Spanish) Rosemary. This plant, which has a pleasant aromatic odour, is much used by Jamaican peasants as a hair wash.

ROSES vb dial; <*roses* sb. To cover with flowers.

c 1930 Astley Clerk *A Soul Song*, Oh, when I die don't roses me at all, Put so-so one in me han' A sweet-smell one.

ROSEWOOD sb; cf *OED* 3 1756→.

1. The tree *Amyris balsamifera*. *G N*

1756 Browne 208, see WHITE CANDLEWOOD. 1920 Fawcett 192. 1941 Swabey 29, Rosewood—(Torchwood, Sandalwood, Amyriswood, White or Black Candlewood). *Amyris balsamifera*. . Wood hard, heavy and close-grained with aromatic smell.

2. *Linociera ligustrina*.

1864 Grisebach 787.

3. *Zanthoxylum rhodoxylon* (=CAESARWOOD).

4. *Drypetes ilicifolia*.

1920 Fawcett 270, Rose Wood.

roti /roti, ruti, ruuti/ sb dial; <Hindi *roṭī*, bread. s DUSTY ROTI.

1. A type of baked flour cake or bread made by East Indians (though more generally known).

1924 Beckwith *Hussay* 10, Unleavened bread, called *rotie*. 1943 *GL* Kgn, Ruttie, East Indian dish; Port, Rootie, East Indian journey cake; Tre, Ruti, roasted dumplin; also most other parishes. 1952 FGC StM /ruuti/. *G T*

2. Transf: see quot.

1958 DeC StAnd /roti/ here meaning curry-goat and rice served in a special way; it is put out on a large banana leaf and everyone gathers around to eat off this common 'dish'.

ROTIE see prec.

ROTTEN OFF vb phr dial; <*rotten* adj, or perh *rot* vb + -*n* suffix[1] or suffix[2]. To rot and fall off; to cause to rot and fall off. *BL G T*

1947 U.Newton II 8, Which made Ditha warn me that my fingers would 'rotten off'. 1952 FGC StAnd, Point finger at grave, it will rotten off. 1955 Bennett *Oonoo Lie!* All de lie gwine do de liard dem Is rotten off dem tongue!

ROUGH sb dial. See quot.

1958 DeC Kgn /rof/ a special kind of saltfish fritter; the saltfish is moistened, formed into a ball, covered with flour paste, then fried; also called /lapaz/.

ROUGH AND CRUSTY adv phr. In answer to the question 'How are you?': Pretty well.

1943 *GL* West, Poko-poko, rough and crusty. 1955 FGC Man, same.

ROUGH-HAIRED BUTTON-WEED see BUTTON-WEED.

ROUGH PUDDING sb dial.

1958 DeC Port /rof pudn/ a pudding made of old stale bread, sugar, etc.

ROUGH SEA sb dial joc. See quot.

1959 DeC West /rof sii/ a dumpling which is made with too much water, and so goes to pieces in the water, giving the appearance of white-capped waves.

ROUNCIVAL PEAS sb; *OED* →1856. The dial form may show infl of folk-etym in the last syllable ('full'). An unidentified pea or bean—today, the latter—of large size. *BA*

1696 Sloane 72, see SURINAM PEAS. 1952 FGC StC /rounsiful piiz/ old-time name.

ROUND-BILL sb dial; <*round* adj + BILL.

1959 DeC StJ /roun-bil/—an open-guard MACHETE (with widely rounded end and curving back).

ROUND CONCH sb dial. =ROLLING CONCH.

1952 FGC StJ /roun kongk/.

ROUND DOCK sb dial. A type of men's haircut.

1956 Mc Man, see DOCK B.

ROUNDER SNAPPER sb.

1892 Cockrell list, Rounder snapper—pot snapper.

ROUND-HEAD CONGO-TONY sb dial.

1952 FGC StM, Round-head /kanggatuoni/ same as deep-water wenshman.

ROUND-HEAD(ED) JACK sb. A variety of the jack or similar fish.

1851 Gosse 290, see BUNTUNG JACK. 1952 FGC StE, Round-head jack.

ROUND-LEAFED SENNA sb bot. An old name for *Cassia obovata* (1920 Fawcett 110).

1696 Sloane 148, Senna (2ᵃ.) Italica seu foliis obtusis. . Round-leav'd Sena.

ROUND PEPPER sb dial. A variety of *Capsicum* pepper which grows round (rather than long)—e.g. the SCOTCH-BONNET PEPPER.

1952 FGC StE, Roun' pepper is the hottest.

ROUND-POINT MANGO sb dial. A variety of COMMON MANGO.

1952 FGC StJ /roun-paint/ same as StC 'hairy-skin'. 1959 DeC Han /roun-paint/ name for a very stringy mango.

ROUND-RED PEA sb. See quot 1954.

1952 FGC StAnn, StE, StT /róun-rèd piiz/. 1954 *FG* 420, The True Red Pea is sometimes called the round-red, and, as the name implies, is characterized by a full roundness and a bright red colour.

ROUND ROBIN sb dial. A fish of uncertain identity (1930 Jordan 270 gives the name to *Decapterus punctatus*).

1952 FGC Port /roun rabin/ much like /brim-gront/ but prettier.

ROUND-THATCH PALM sb. A thatch palm with round (rather than long) leaves. (Species of *Thrinax*, etc.)

1952 FGC Port /roun-tach—laik krákasa, jípi-jàpa/.

ROUND-THE-ROAD sb dial; from the constant stirring necessary when it is cooking.

1. A coconut run-down.

1952 FGC StJ /roun-di-ruod/ stir to prevent it from going to oil. StM, Same as dip-an'-fall-back. 1958 DeC StM /roun-di-ruod/ coconut rundown.

2. See quot.

1943 *GL* Kgn, Roun de road, a dish of crab.

rounsiful piiz see ROUNCIVAL PEAS.

ROUTE /rout/ sb dial; <*route* (cf the midwest US pronunc). In the phr *this route*: in these parts, round here. *G*

1956 Mc StT /nát dis róut/ (said several times).

ROW /ruo/ sb dial; by conversion of *row*, vb, or perh by metathesis: /rúo/ < /úor/. An oar.

1956 Mc Kgn /yu rúo nák an it/; StC (Old Harbour) /rúo/ an oar of a sea-going /kúnu/.

ROWER sb. An agricultural implement for making trenches in rows to plant sugar-cane.

1952 FGC Tre /rúowa/.

ROWERSOME /róuasam/ adj or sb dial; <*row*, to quarrel + -*er*, suffix of agent + -*some*. Quarrelsome. *BL*

1943 *GL* Kgn, Rowasam, quarrelsome; StT, Rowersam, like to quarrel; also StJ, StM. 1955 FGC Man /róuasam/ raabaaba, make a row.

ROYAL see RIAL.

ROYAL MAROON sb dial. See quot.

1960 LeP in *CLS* 127, A few of the present Maroons have married non-Maroons, but even after many years of residence these immigrants are treated as outsiders and are never called 'royal Maroons'.

ROYAL TIMBIM see TIMBIM.

RUB, RUBBING vb and vbl sb dial. Of a violin or fiddle: to draw the bow across. See quot.

1907 Jekyll 39, The 'rubbing' of the fiddle, as they call it. *Ibid* 163, 'Rubbing' a fiddle conveys the exact idea of the way they play it. Holding it not up to the chin but resting on the biceps, they rub a short bow backwards and forwards across the strings.

RUB, RUB-UP sb dial. See quot, and cf MATTIE-BELLY.

1954 LeP StAnn, General term for dance or wild party—rub-up. Often said: 'Going to rub tonight'.

RUBADOO sb dial; prob <*rubadub*. To beat a drum.

1943 *GL* StE, Rubadoo, beat drum.

RUBBA sb dial; an irreg pronunc, the normal one being /riba/.

1943 *GL* StC, Rubba, river.

RUBBA MISSIS or **MUMMA** see RIVER MAID.

RUB (or **SCRUB**) **DRY YAWS** vb phr; allusion is to the itching which is relieved by rubbing. To curry favour. *G*

1943 *GL* StM, Rub-dry-yaws, connive, curry favour. 1955 FGC Man /krob drai yaaz/ get in well with someone to get favours in return.

rubosta see ROBUSTA BANANA.

RUCCUD sb dial; etym unknown.

1943 *GL* StC, Ruccud, an evil spirit.

RUCKODIMMO sb dial; cf *rogo-rogo*, shaky + *dima*.

1943 *GL*, Ruckodimmo, lame foot.

RUCK-RUCKU see *rogo-rogo*.

RUDE adj (and adv) dial; cf *OED* 4, 5. *BL T*

1. Forward, bold, impertinent; wild, violent, reckless. (The word is used in slightly more forceful senses, and far more commonly, than in StdE.) *BA G*

1956 Mc Man [Woman, to pig putting its head in the door:] /go bak, yu tuu ruud, go bak/. StE (Accom) [A little girl who had hurt herself by recklessness, described affectionately:] /dis wan ruud/.

2. Very aggressive sexually.

1952 FGC StM [Of a man who had many children by many mothers:] /him iz a ruud, ruud man/.

RUDENESS sb dial; cf RUDE 2. Sexual intercourse. *BA BL T*

1949 Forbes 59, 'Will you do me a rudeness?' is an invitation to pass an entertaining but not restful night. 1952 FGC Han /ruudnis/.

RUDE-TO-PARENTS sb dial joc. White proof rum, so called from its effect on the drinker.

1952 FGC Han /rúud tu píerents/ white proof rum—the customary term in Lucea.

RUFFO vb dial; evid <*rough* + *-o*, as in many other words, without very concrete meaning. To do something roughly and botch it.

1943 *GL* StE, Ruffo, to spoil.

RUGGAGE sb dial; <*rubbage*, rubbish: *OED* '*obs.* or *dial.*' (The alternation of *g* and *b* corresp to that of *k* and *p*: cf *plaa*, *plaba*, etc.)

1943 *GL* Kgn, Ruggage, no good. 1955 FGC Man /rogij/ rubbish.

rugo-rugo see *rogo-rogo*.

RUINATE /ruunit, ruunet/ adj and sb; <*ruinate*, adj.

A. adj: Of land: worn out by agriculture, and allowed to revert to wildness.

1835 Senior 54–5, Lands termed 'ruinate', which means such as have been used till worn out, and then allowed to grow up in bushes and weeds.. In three or four years after the ruinate is cleared up, the pimento begins to bear.

B. sb: A piece of formerly cultivated land that has 'gone back to bush'.

1895 Banbury 30, We would advise parents never to allow their little ones to wander about near woods, or ruinates by themselves. 1952 FGC StAnd, Tre, West /ruunit/ land once cultivated, now no good. Han, StAnn /ruunet/.

rukudang sb dial; cf *rogo-rogo*, and next. An old house, old bed—shaky, tumbledown. *G*

1943 *GL* StAnn, Roocoodang, a small ill-looking house. 1955 FGC Man /rukudang/ old house, old bed, etc.

RUKUPANG sb dial; cf *rogo-rogo*, and prec.

1943 *GL* Clar, Han, Rukupang, a bed.

ruku-ruku see *rogo-rogo*.

RUKUTO adj dial; cf *rogo-rogo*. *BL*

1943 *GL* StAnn, Rukuto, rough.

RUM-BUMP sb dial.

1. The Adam's apple.

1956 Mc Man /rom bomp/.

2. A swelling in the throat thought to be caused by excessive drinking of rum.

1950 Pioneer 37, Him head too lickle, him have rum-bump a him troat or him too ugly. 1956 Mc Man.

RUM-CANE sb. Sugar-canes which, having been damaged, are unfit for sugar and are therefore used to make rum. *G*

1790 Beckford I 50, And grinding the rum (or tainted canes). *Ibid*, Those who are very assiduous in collecting the rum-canes. (1952 Current, FGC.)

RUMMARIAN /romíerian/ sb dial; <*rum* + *-arian*, as in *unitarian*, *librarian*, etc. One who habitually drinks too much rum: a RUMMER. *G*

1943 *GL* StM, Rumarian, rum drunkard. 1955 FGC Man /romíerian/. s RUM-BUMPER.

RUMMER sb dial; cf RUMMARIAN. One who habitually gets drunk on rum.

1943 *GL* StM, Rumma, rum drunkard. 1955 FGC Man /roma/.

RUMPLIS, RUMPY see *rompii*.

RUN vb causative dial; cf *OED* 43. *G*

1. To drive away (someone—esp an evil spirit). *T*

1927 Beckwith 22, Marigold—Burn it in the house after a death 'to run away the spirits'. 1929 Beckwith 91–2, It is wise to carry a 'guard' of some kind to 'run duppy' if it is inclined to follow you. 1950 Pioneer 81 [Song:] Come we go down a Unity Fe see duppy run Miss Martin.

2. To purge (the bowels). *BL*

1925 Beckwith 114, What sweet billy-goat, a it da go run him belly.

RUN-AN'-'TAN'-UP sb dial joc.

1943 *GL* Kgn, Run and tan up, pumpkin [*Run and stand still*—alluding to the wandering vine].

RUNAWAY (LAND) sb. Land that breaks loose and slides down hill.

1827 Hamel II 250, In that quarter the ground is so broken, and precipitous, and loose withal, that it would be impossible to pass along it.. The weight of a man on the verge or the side of this (as it is there called) Runaway Land, would loosen a sufficiency of earth and rubbish to overwhelm a little army. 1952 FGC StAnn /rónawe/.

RUNDOWN sb dial.

1. A breakaway, a landslip. *G*

1952 FGC Tre /rondoun/.

2. A kind of sauce made by boiling coconut down till it becomes like custard (but stops short of becoming oil). In it may be cooked salt or pickled fish, banana, or other ingredients. It is served in a bowl in the middle of the table, into which one dips one's bread-kind. See DIP-AND-COME-BACK.

1943 *GL* Kgn, Rung-dung; StE, Rundung; StM, Rundown. 1952 FGC StAnn, StJ /rondoun/. 1956 Mc Man, StAnd /rondong/.

RUNDUNG, RUNGDUNG see prec.

runggus sb dial; etym obscure: *-gus* is prob to be conn with GUZU; cf *gunggus*. Tricks, cheats, usually with some implication of witchcraft.

1943 *GL* StAnn, Rungoos, tricks that baffle solution. 1950 Pioneer gloss, Roongoos, tricks. 1952 FGC StM /runggus/ trick, cheat, for example with false jewelry.

runkus sb dial; ? < *rumpus*. A wild party or dance. *G*

1954 LeP Man, Roonkus. 1956 Mc Man /runkus/.

RUNNING ANT sb. A SUGAR ANT. *G*

1952 FGC Han, Running ant, sugar ant; West, Doesn't bite; small and black; gets into sugar. *N* /ronin ans/.

RUNNING FISH sb dial. Fish that go in schools.

1952 FGC West, Grouper, a runnin' fish; in big baj [batch]; plentiful in Sept.–Oct.

RUNNING MARIGOLD see MARIGOLD.

RUNNING SNAPPER sb dial. Snapper fish that go in schools.

1952 FGC West /ronin sinápa/.

RUNNING WHEELS vb phr; cf RUN 1. The children's game of rolling hoops.

1946 U.Newton I; *ibid* II 12.

RUNNING YAWS sb dial. A variety of CRAB-YAWS characterized by peeling and fissuring of the sole of the foot and its periphery.

1959 O. D. Simons, UCWI Preventive Med.

RUN (ONE'S) MOUTH vb phr. To chatter or gossip. *BA G*

1954 LeP Kgn, Yu run yu mout fe not a ting, all de talk yu talk fe nutten. Man, to chat or gossip—run mouth.

RUSH sb dial. The central rib (or BONE) of a banana leaf.

1942 HPJ, see JAGGAY MAT.

RUSH vb chiefly dial. To berate or scold.

1956 BLB Man /we yu a rosh mi fa/ [*Why are you scolding me?*]

ruta see ROOTER.

ruti, RUTTIE, ruuti see *roti*.

RYAL see RIAL.

RYDIM /rídim/ sb dial; for *rhythm*. The hips or buttocks, from their swaying motion.

1943 Bennett 22, Ah put me han' pon me kimbo Ah meck a sudden movement Ah tun me rydim full gi' har. [*I put my hands at my waist, I make a sudden movement, I turn my hips hard around against her.*] *Ibid* 10, Not even a drapes trousiz or A pass de rydim coat. [*A coat which hangs below the hips.*] 1943 *GL* StC, Rydim—rump.

RYGIN /raigin/ adj (and adv) dial; prob < *ragging* < *rag* v^2 *OED* 'to scold, rate, speak severely to'—cf BULLYRIGE; also /baig, haig/ for *bag*, *hag*, etc. Angry, heated, severe; vigorous, lively, spirited; very able, top-notch—these senses passing insensibly into each other, and varying in range from very unfavourable to very favourable.

1943 *GL* StJ, Rigin, cross; Kgn, Rygin, heated; StAnd, Rygin, strong; Jones Pen, Rygin, hot or peppery, something very grand; Kgn, Rygin, of some prominence. 1950 Pioneer 32, Anancy temper get rygin. *Ibid* 96, Me can always do de wok, An' ri-gin wen me care. 1952 FGC StT [Song:] June and July Is a raigin hard time [a time of food shortage]. 1954 LeP Man, Lively, quick-tempered—raigin; StE, To walk (a woman) in a jaunty, provocative fashion—rhygin. 1955 FGC Man /raigin/ cross, lively; also, do a thing good /dat jaki a raigin raida/ *That jockey is a very spirited rider.*

sa, saa sb[2] dial; unstr and reduced < *sister*. *BL*

sa, sar /sa, sàr/ sb[1] dial; pronunc of *sir*, unstressed and stressed respectively. As a term of polite address: Sir; said to superiors or equals. Sometimes added to a statement merely for emphasis. *BL G*

1877 Murray *Kittle* 24, Ha Bra! buckra corn piece ripe, sa! 1877 Murray *Feedin' 'Perrit* 8, No egsvantage at all, sar, git up. 1960 BLB 9 /di skín-deng kyàn tín sa/ *The skins tend to be very thin.*

SAACA-SAACA, SAAKA-SAAKA see *saka* (*-saka*).

saal, SAAL see SALT.

saali adj dial; < SALT + *-y*. Attractive, nicely dressed.

1943 *GL* StM, Sauly, nice or attractive. 1956 Mc Port /saali/ dressed up (person); nicely dressed.

saalting sb dial; < *salt things*.

1. = SALT: any kind of salt meat or fish.

1943 *GL* Clar, Saalting, any kind of salt provision; StC, Salting, pickled fish. 1952 FGC StAnn, StE, StJ, StM, West /saalting, salting/: saltfish, corn-pork, herring, mackerel, shad. 1954 LeP Kgn, Salt-thing; Port, Saal ting—saltfish.

2. A general term for meat or fish, whether salt or fresh, in contrast with ground provisions, fruit, or other food.

1952 FGC Kgn, 'In the country', fish, flesh, or fowl, as distinct from 'breadkind'. 1954 LeP StAnn, Salt-ting, Salting—general term, meat or fish; StE; StT, Saalting. 1956 Mc StE /saalting/ fish or pork salted—/kyebij iz nat saalting, iz a vejitabl/ *Cabbage is not 'salting'; it is a vegetable.*

3. Anything eaten at a meal except the FOOD (i.e. the starch part: yam, coco, breadfruit, etc.).

1956 Mc Man /saalting/ anything eaten with /fuud/—may be meat or fish (whether fresh or salt) but also cabbage, calalu, susumba, etc: the non-starch part of the meal.

sab sb dial slang; from the motion-picture character, Sabu the Elephant-boy. A method of cutting a man's hair so that it is round, without tapering, at the back.

1952 FGC StM, Tre /sab/.

SABBATH FOOT sb dial; evid an allusion to there being no work on the Sabbath.

1943 *GL* StM, Sabbat fut, Lame or deformed foot. 1955 FGC Man /sábat fút/.

sabi-so sb dial; <*savvy*+*so*. Understanding; wisdom. *G*

1927 Anderson-Cundall 75, see *mek-so*.

SABO sb, in this sense obs; prob < Twi *asaabo*, kidney. [Prob the source of US *saba* bean.] The ANTIDOTE COCOON bean, *Fevillea cordifolia*, valued as a remedy against poison.

1725 Sloane 372 [Ref to vol 1, 200: Ghandiroba vel Nhandi-roba Brasiliensibus] The Negroes call them Sabo. (Barham.)

SAC see *sak*.

SACA-SACA see *saka(-saka)*.

SACKA /saka/ sb[1] dial; <*sack*, *OED sb*[4], a loose kind of gown worn by ladies; the final vowel may represent A[8], or perh *-er*. See quots.

1924 Beckwith 126–7, As Hanansi gone, de boy kill Hanansi mamma, tek off de [*sc* her] coat an' de sucker, put it on an' cook up de ol' lady. 1943 *GL* Clar, Sacka, Saka—a louse [*sic*] blouse; Kgn, Sacka, a loose bodice, an over-blouse.

SACKA sb[2] dial; <*sack*+?*-er*.

1954 LeP StE, Sacka, bed or mattress on the floor—often made of sacks (crocus bags).

SAD adj; <*sad OED* 2 '*Obs*: Settled, firmly established. . steadfast, firm, constant'; →1667. Yorks, Scots to late 19th cent (*EDD*, *SND*). *BL*

1943 *GL* No addr, Sad—good, excellent. 1952 C. Lindo, used at Jamaica College, 1920's, for example, of a dependable cricketer, 'He's a sad man'.

SADDLE sb dial. The ridge or coping of a roof.

1952 FGC West, The coping of a roof—black man call it /sadl/; the riddle 'When the back is sore, need a new saddle', refers to a house. *BA*

SADDLE-WEED sb dial. Cf JOCKEY-SADDLE. A climbing plant; prob *Cissus sicyoides*.

1951 FGC Man, Saddle-weed, snake-wis.

SAD FLYCATCHER sb ornith; the reason for the word 'sad' is uncertain: it may refer to the colour of the bird, or to its stolid manner.

1936 Bond 249, Sad Flycatcher (*Myiarchus barbirostris*). . Tom Fool; Little Tom Fool. 1956 Jeffrey-Smith 48.

SAGE /siej/ sb dial; cf *OED sb*[1] 1.

A term widely used in the folk names of plants (so much so that it is substituted for 'shade' in NIGHT-SAGE); applied primarily to genus *Lantana* (4 spp), but also to *Cordia* (2 spp), and *Salvia serotina*. Cf BLACK SAGE, WHITE SAGE, WILD SAGE. In the simple form (without modifying word) applied to *Miconia lævigata* and *Heliotropium parviflorum*. *BA G*

1954 *WIMJ* 29–31; 1955 *ibid* 158–9.

SAGE-ROSE sb bot. =HOLLY-ROSE.

sagi-sagi adj dial; ?<*shaggy*, with iteration.

1956 Mc Man /ságí-sàgi/ Shaggy. You comb donkey so that its hair won't be sagi-sagi.

sagwa sb dial; cf Twi *sã-guá*, place where drinkers are assembled; place where a king or chief holds a public reception. A medicine show, or the like; a carnival.

1943 *GL* Man, Sagwa, amusement; No addr, One who controls and performs with wild animals. 1955 FGC Man /sagwa/ medicine show, act on stage, paint face, snake-charming, sell ointment.

SAH see *sa*.

SAID ppl adj chiefly dial; cf *OED* 1, which however is virtually limited to legal use. Same, very, identical. *BA BL G*

1924 Beckwith 91, When she came, she didn't eat it for she knew it was the said fish. 1952 FGC Tre, The said one = the very same. 1956 Mc Man /a yú a i séd wan tél mi so/ *You are the very person who told me so*; StE /di séd iivn/ *The same evening*; StJ /ontíl tudé aa-m nát di séd pórsan/ *I am still not myself* (after illness).

SAINT sb obs; cf *OED* B 5 b, 1830→. A slavery abolitionist: see quots.

1826 Williams 37, Every thing is attributed, right or wrong, to the *Saints* (as they are called) in England, and their interference with the concerns of the proprietors in Jamaica has certainly excited a feeling of the greatest indignation. 1871 Rampini 69 [A planter's friend speaking:] It was the Saints that ruined us—St Wilberforce, St Macaulay, and their following.

[**ST HELENA ALMOND** sb bot obs. In MacFadyen's use: *Terminalia catappa*, the tree commonly called 'almond' today.

1850 Macfadyen 16, St Helena Almond. . Introduced into Jamaica in 1793 from St Helena.]

ST HILD'S COPPERS sb obs; the allusion to St Hild is not clear. The two first (and largest) in the set of seven coppers in which sugar-cane juice was formerly evaporated.

1788 Marsden 26, The boiling-house is near the mill, in which are seven coppers, decreasing in size after the two first, which are called *St Hild's coppers*.

ST JULIEN (MANGO) sb; app an honorific or ameliorative form of *Julie*, the name of the fruit in Martinique, Trinidad, etc. (Known in Trinidad from at least 1906.) A choice variety of mango popularized in Jamaica for the past 20–25 years. *BA*

1954 *FG* 475, St Julien or Julie. Similar to the Bombay but with fruit more flattened.

ST KITTS BREADFRUIT /singkít/ sb. A fine variety of breadfruit introduced from St Kitts.

1952 FGC Port, StT /singkít/.

ST KITTS COCO /singkít/ sb. A variety of COCO introduced from St Kitts.

1814 Lunan 1 212, The *St Kitt's coco*, which though of a much smaller size than the San Blas, is yet well worthy of cultivation. 1929 Beckwith 17, In Mandeville were enumerated. . the 'White Stalk', 'Too Good', 'Sinket', and 'Burban' [cocoes].

ST KITTS SUKIE see *suki* quot 1955.

ST LUCIA YAM /sinlúusha/ sb. A variety of yam introduced from St Lucia; some identify it with RENTA yam.

1952 FGC StC /sinlúusha/ doesn't go deep [into the ground], renta goes deep; StT, St Lucia—same as renta. 1956 Mc StAnd /sinlúusha/; StT /sintlúusha/ identified with renta.

ST MARY PINE sb. A pineapple associated with the parish of St Mary, Ja: see SUGAR PINE.

ST MARY TAMBRIK sb dial; <*St Mary* parish, Ja +*turmeric*, alluding to the bright yellow flesh? A variety of ginger.

1952 FGC Man, One kind of ginger is St Mary /tambrik/.

ST THOMAS /sìntámas/ sb. A variety of sweet-potato, evid conn with the parish of St Thomas, Jamaica. (Evidence is lacking; this may be St Thomas Is.)

1952 FGC StC /sint támas/ sweet potato, bears heavily.

ST VINCENT (PLUM) sb. A type of GROWING-STAKE, used for live fences: *Gliricidia sepium.*

1952 FGC Port, StAnd, StM /sinvínsn/; StAnn /sinvínsn plom/. 1954 *NHN* VI 166.

ST VINCENT YAM /sìnvínsn, simínsin/ sb. A variety of yam introduced from St Vincent; valued because it grows easily and makes an early crop.

1952 FGC gen /sìnvínsn/; Han, 'grow nearly wild in bush or forest land; plant in May, reap in December'. 1954 *FG* 445, The St Vincent is a heavy bearer, but it must be used when freshly cut.

sak sb dial; < *sa* sb[1] + *-k*, but cf also *seki*; cf *brak.*

1943 *GL* Clar, Sac—sister.

saka see SACKA, *saka(-saka)*, SAKE O'.

saka(-saka) /saka-saka, saaka-saaka/ sb dial; cf Kongo *saka*, to cut off; Ngombe *sáká*, sharp (of a knife); (Twi *sàkasàka*, disorder, confusion, turmoil). The second pronunciation perh shows infl of Engl *saw.*

To cut with a dull tool, hence, cut badly, saw poorly.

1868 Russell 17, To cut as with a saw; thus, Dis knife jis da saca-saca de meat. 1943 *GL* Clar, Sauka, sawker—cut with a dull knife; Kgn, Saaka-saaka; Port, Saaca-saaca—to cut with a dull weapon; StJ, Sucu-sucu—to cut. 1955 FGC Man /saka-saka/.

SAKE(-A) see next.

SAKE (O') /síeka/ prep dial; < (for the) *sake of.*

1. Because of. (*OED* 6b, → 1622.) *BL*

1912 McK *Songs* 14, De bank dem we de dig, . . dem caan' 'tan sake o' we naybor pig . . An' we caan' 'peak sake o' we naybor tongue. 1942 Bennett 13, Sake adah big mout' police-man Me nearly miss de train. 1943 *GL* gen, Saka, sayka, sake-a, săckah, because. 1956 Mc Man /síeka di drái, wi no ha nof yam dis íer/ *Owing to the drought, we have little yam this year.*

2. In such phrases as *For shame sake. BL G*

1941 Kirkpatrick 35, 'Im bone woulda rackle eena 'im grave fe shame sake. [*His bones would rattle in his grave from shame.*]

saku sb dial; cf Kongo *nsaku*, sack, bag, < Pg *saco* [saku]; also in US Gullah dial, a crocus bag; perh coincidentally reinforced in Ja by Engl *sack.* See quots.

1959 DeC StJ /saku/ a piece of canvas or burlap used for carrying a load; one merely holds the four corners together; Port, a large canvas bag fitted with a strap: carried either at side supported from shoulder, or on back supported by strap across forehead.

salaam-babu sb dial arch; cf *OED.* A 'coolie man' or East Indian, from their using the words as a greeting. (Still current c 1915; now virtually out of use.)

1943 *GL* Port, Salambaboo, Coolie man. 1956 Mc Clar, see *ou-di-du-dat.*

SALAD sb. In vegetable markets generally: a large sized tomato, the ox-heart or similar variety.

1952 FGC Port, StC, StJ /salad/. 1956 Mc Man /salad/: tomatoes, larger size.

salandain, salindain, salidain sb dial; < *celandine*—see quot 1837. The wild plant *Bocconia frutescens*, also called JOHN-CROW BUSH.

[1837 Macfadyen 23, All parts of the plant . . abound with a yellow juice; and Barham supposes that, from its resembling the common *Celandine* in this respect, it has received the same name.] 1943 *GL* No addr, Sallidine—Leaves for cleaning floor. 1952 FGC StAnn, StE, Tre /sálindàin/; StT /sàlandáin/—good to clean, stain floor; StT /sàlintáin/; StT /salidain/.

salimuon see *serimuon.*

SALINA /salíina/ sb; < Sp *salina*, salt-pit or -pan (*OED* 1697 → in other senses). A low, marshy piece of land along the sea; a salt marsh.

1756 Browne 356, This plant is common in all the Salinas on the south side of Jamaica. 1774 Long I 474, In making roads to traverse the salinas, or level grounds adjacent to the sea, and in swampy places, a *stratum* should first be laid. 1811 Titford xvi, Water Apple grows by the side of salinas and creeks. 1817 Williamson i 37, If there are selinas or marshes in the vicinity. (1960 still in use. FGC.)

SALLEE-MAN sb obs; cf *OED* 2, 1756 →. *OED*, 'A marine hydrozoan, *Velella vulgaris*'.

1756 Browne 387, The Sally-Man.

SALLIE see SALLY COCO.

SALLO see *salo.*

SALLY-COAT-BLUE sb dial; from the supposed words of the bird's song. The BLUE DOVE (2).

[1873 Rampini 76, Vain of her plumage the female of the blue pigeon (*Columba rufina*) cries 'Sally coat blue, Sally coat, true blue!'] 1952 FGC StT, Sally-coat-blue—blue dove.

SALLY COCO sb dial; prob < *Sally*, woman's name—perh one who grew the plant successfully. A soft variety of COCO; the feminine name may be contrastive with those of the hard COCOS: COMMANDER, DUKE, LEF' MAN.

1929 Beckwith 17 [Among cocos:] The 'Sally' and 'Minty' and the 'Green 'talk'. 1952 FGC Port, White /sali/ and red /sali/ StAnd, StC, StJ, StM, StT; 'stalk like black coco, but softer nature'. 1954 *FG* 447, The sallie (similar to the commander, but soft).

SALLY-MAN see SALLEE-MAN.

SALLY WATER sb; from the refrain of the song. Ring games: Little Sally Water and other games like it. *BA BL*

1907 Jekyll 76, They then begin to play *Sally Water . .* which goes on for an hour or two. *Ibid* 190, That informal kind of dancing . . known as 'playing in the ring' or 'Sally Water' has its origin in English children's games.

SALMON OF JAMAICA see JAMAICA SALMON.

salo sb dial arch; ? < Fr *salut*—cf quot 1907. A kind of dance (in which the dancers presumably saluted each other).

1907 Jekyll 263 [Song:] Jimmy Rampy a come oh! Sal oh! [Note:] 'Sal oh!' is perhaps a corruption of *salut.* Tradition associates a curtsey with the word. 1943 *GL* Kgn, Sallo, A kind of dance. 1955 FGC Man /sálo/ a way of dancing, sort of a MET. Old fashioned.

SAL OH see prec.

SALT /saal/ sb now dial; < *salt* sb or adj, but (as the pronunc shows) there may be infl also < *sowl(e), sawl, seawl*, a relish, dainty; anything eaten with bread; tasty, seasoned food—*EDD*, also attrib.

Salt fish (cod, mackerel, herring, etc.) or meat; in slavery days each slave was legally entitled to a weekly provision or allowance of 'salt'. Today it is still the basis of many dishes or sauces popularly eaten with starch foods. See also LONG SALT.

1825 Bickell 9–10, At Christmas..they [slaves] have an extra allowance of salt cod-fish, which they use in like manner; it generally goes with them under the name of salt, and they take a small portion of it at most of their meals, and put it in the pot to boil with the vegetables. 1837 James I, Massa give we no salt allowance, and no allowance at Christmas. 1943 *GL* Clar, Kgn, StM, Saal, salt provision, meat or fish; Clar, Saul. 1956 Mc Man /dem gí mi som háki an sáal/ *They gave me some ackee and salt* [*fish*].

SALT DOG /saal daag/ sb dial slang.

1943 *GL* Man, Sal dag, fritters.

SALT-FISH sb; cf *OED* a^1 2, c1460, 'any maner salt fish', only quot. *G*

1. Codfish preserved with salt, imported to the West Indies sugar colonies from North America and made a staple food of slaves and later the populace: now an ingredient of many favourite dishes. *BA N*

1774 Long II 425, She constantly bathed her body twice a day, and abstained wholly from salt-fish, and all sorts of rank food. 1927 Stafford 26, Soup of goongo-peas and salt-fish.

2. Attrib and comb: salt-fish and ackee, salt-fish and susumba; salt-fish fritters, etc. (Representative examples only; see also separate entries.)

1889 Sanguinetti 50, The well known compound dish of salt-fish and akee..was formerly known here as 'Bacal-lao', the Spanish equivalent of 'Codfish', its main ingredient. [Cf BACCALOW.] 1954 LeP StT, Saalfish flittas—codfish cakes. [Cf STAMP-AND-GO.] 1957 *FFM* 157, Saltfish and Ackees; *ibid* 222, Saltfish and Susumbers.

SALT-FISH CUCUMBER sb dial. The small wild cucumber, often eaten with salt-fish.

1952 FGC StM /saalfish kukumba/ have prickle, but not prickle to juk.

SALT-FISH MANGO sb dial. A variety of mango which is stringy, like salt-fish: the STRINGY MANGO.

1952 FGC Han.

SALT-FISH REMEDY sb dial joc; <SALT-FISH + REMEDY. See quot.

1958 DeC StAnd, salt-fish remedy—a nickname for ACKEE, 'because it is always cooked with and improves salt-fish'.

SALTING, SALT-THING, SALT-TING see *saalting*.

SALTPAN LAND sb; <*salt-pan* + *land*. Land lying low near the sea as natural meadow, though not used for saltpans. See quot.

1774 Long I 453, The richness of some of the savannah lands, which have been many years inclosed, in the neighbourhood of Spanish Town, and commonly distinguished by the name of the *Saltpan* lands, is really astonishing. Their natural grass, under moderate seasons of rain, is constantly luxuriant, with the aid of manure.

SALTPETRE sb dial.

1952 FGC StT, Saltpetre—disease of cocos: whitish, glitters at night.

SALT-WATER CREOLE sb obs. A person born on the voyage to Jamaica. (Had he been born in the island he would have been a full Creole.) Cf next.

1825 Bickell 44, Smart, a salt-water Creole, 5 ft. 5 in. marked IMC and NB. 1828 Marly 335, He was a salt-water Creole, having been born on his passage to Jamaica.

SALT-WATER NEGRO sb obs; *DAE, DA*, c1797. From the point of view of a West Indian negro, a negro born in Africa, across the ocean. *G*

1774 Long II 410, The Creole Blacks differ much from the Africans, not only in manners, but in beauty of shape, feature, and complexion. They hold the Africans in the utmost contempt, stiling them, 'salt-water Negroes', and 'Guiney birds'; but value themselves on their own pedigree.

SALT-WOOD sb; *DA* for diff plant. The tree *Neea nigricans*.

1961 DAP StE (Quickstep), see DICKY-BIRD BERRY.

SAM vb dial; abbr of *samfai*. To deceive; to cheat; as a *samfai* man does.

1943 *GL* StAnd, No sam, don't cheat. 1955 FGC Man, see *raj*.

samba sb dial uncom; cf Ko *nsampa*, hut.

1956 Mc Man /samba/ hut with wattle walls and banana-trash roof.

samba adj dial; ? <*sambo*.

1941 Kirkpatrick gloss, Samba—strong, firm; *ibid* 43, Fe we sojer dem 'tan' up samba.

SAMBO sb obs; prob <*sambo* in ref to the root or flower of the species (*decumbens*) which Sloane described: 'This has a great Root in respect of the Plant..of a white brown colour..The Flowers are..yellow.' (1707 193.) In Browne's use: Any of three species of *Cleome: spinosa, serrata*, and *decumbens*.

1756 Browne 273–4, Cleome..1. The prickly branched Sambo..2. The erect trifoliated Sambo..3. Sambo. 1864 Grisebach 787.

SAMBO BACKRA sb dial. A term of respect for a sambo (i.e. about three-quarters negro) man. Cf BLACK BACKRA.

1958 DeC StT /sambo bakra/.

SAME conj dial; by ellipsis <*the same* (*thing*) *as*, or similar phrase. Same as, identical with. (Used in equating two things.) *BL G T*

1935 HPJ, Burban coco same Black Juck. 1942 Bennett 30, Me wrap it up wid noonoo bush Same sweet barsley yuh know. 1956 Mc man /kraafish—siem labsta/, /pikni —siem pikini/; StE /keta-keta—siem bangga/.

SAME adj dial. Preceding certain nouns to form emphatic phrases: *same way*, just like that; *same time*, at once, just then; *same place*, right there (or here); *same one*, the very same (person or thing). *BA BL G T*

1905 Dodd 27, Ah might a risk it, an try mek ah fool dem same time. 1907 Jekyll 42, When him yerry, him 'tand up same place an' trimble. 1924 Beckwith 126, see POLICE. 1950 Pioneer 24, Same time a servant run out. *Ibid* 48, Eee-Hee Missis, is me same one Sidung yah all de time. 1955 Bennett '*Pendix*, Me eatin' jus as usual an' Me big an fat same way. 1956 Mc StE, Cawley: /we yu laan dat sang/?—Rowe: /siem plies hya/ *Right here*; Man /a yu síem wan tel mi so/ *You are the very person who told me so.*

SAME LIKE phr dial; cf *OED same* I. = Same as, just like. *BL G*

1952 FGC StAnd, Cane *flag*—same like corn. Abbay shape same like a coconut.

SAME ONE, PLACE, TIME, WAY see SAME adj. *BA BL G*

samfai /sámfái, sánfái, sángfái/ sb, vb, and adj; etym prob African, but no certain form has been found: the basic sense involves witchcraft in some way; related words may be Ewe *samedzi*, magic sign, Twi *asũmàŋfó*, owner of a charm; magician. (Sb freq attrib with *man.*) s.

A. sb: 1. An obeahman, or other person professing magic powers.

1943 *GL* Kgn, Samfi, a man who studies witchcraft. 1952 FGC StM /sámfái man/ a man that magic you, professing obeah. 1956 Mc Clar /sangfai man/ obeah man, guzu man, sayer, four-eye man.

2. One who tricks others by supposed magic powers; a confidence man.

1941 Kirkpatrick gloss, Sam fie—confidence man. *Ibid* 25, Lak w'en dem country bwoy come a town..an' befo' you know wey 'appen a sam fie man outa Wes' End sell dem Race Course or Tram cyar an' tek wey dem pocket full a money. 1943 *GL* Clar, Kgn, StAnd, Samfi, Samfiman, Samfieman, cheater, confidence trickster. 1952 W. C. Cassidy Kgn /san fai man/ a 'con' man: two work together to gull country men.

3. The trick of a samfai man.

1943 *GL* no addr, Sumfij, a ruse to show the alleged power of witchcraft.

4. (From sense 2). See quot.

1943 *GL* Man, Samfoi, Monkey or ugly person.

B. vb: To practise pretended witchcraft so as to trick people.

1943 *GL* Kgn, Samfy, to deceive; StAnn, Samfi, to fake, a false claim to magic.

C. adj: Dishonest, deceiving.

1943 *GL* StAnd, Samfie, crooked.

SAMFI(E), SAMFOI, SAMFY see prec.

SAMMY BLACKIE sb dial; < *Sammy*, a personifying name + *blackie*, alluding to their dark colour. Various species of small fish, including *Abudefduf saxatilis* and *Microspathodon chrysurus*.

1951 Smith in *NHN* 204, The princelings, to my mind, are represented by the pilot fish..and the yellow-tailed demoiselle..(they are known at Long Bay, St James, as 'Sammy Blackie').

sampata, shumpata sb chiefly dial; for variant forms see quots; <Pg *sapato*, Sp *zapato*, with prob infl of one or more African forms such as Twi *asepâteré*, shoe, itself derived from Pg *sapato*: but the relations among these sources are not clear. The Ja forms differ from the Sp-Pg esp in the intrusion of the nasal, and in the initial *sh-* being an alternative of *s-*, both of which features are uncharacteristic of Sp-Pg but characteristic of W Afr dialects; on the other hand the *e* vowels of the Twi word do not correspond with those of the Ja forms. If African forms were brought to Ja by the slaves, it would seem certain that they were influenced again by the Pg, or more likely the Sp form in the West Indies. Folk-etym has since produced further and numerous variants: for the first syllable, *sand-*, *sham-*, *slam-*, and even *shoe-*, for the rest of the word, *-patter* or *-platter*, combined in many ways. (The *s-* forms are chiefly eastern in Jamaica, the *sh-* forms western.) s SAMPLATTA FOOT.

1. A sandal with sole of wood or leather, more recently of automobile-tyre rubber, held on to the foot by leather or other straps. *BL*

1823 Roughley 110, His [a peasant's] foot clothed with a kind of sandal, (called in Jamaica a sand-patta). 1827 Hamel I 21, He espied a pair of shoepatters, a sort of coarse sandal. 1873 Rampini 93, Her [a country woman's] feet encased in sandals of untanned hide called 'sand patters'. 1933 McK 317, Sandplatters, sandals. 1943 *GL* Clar, StC, Samplata; Kgn, Samplatta; Tre, Shampatter; StAnn, Shamplata; Man, Shumpata, Shumpatta; Tre, Shumpatah; StAnd, Slampattor; Kgn, Slamplatta; West, Shoepata, Shupatta; StAnn, Shopata; StE, Shompoo (?erron form). 1952 FGC StAnd, StM /sámpáta/ Han, Tre /shámpáta/.

2. Attrib and fig.

1912 McK *Songs* 75, Ko 'pon you' jam samplatta* nose [*Look at your damn' samplatta nose!*] *A piece of leather cut somewhat larger than the size of the foot, and tied sandal-wise to it: said of anything that is flat and broad.

3. Old or shabby shoes. *BL*

1954 LeP StE, Shampatta is really shoes of wooden soles and one or two leather straps..It also denotes shabby shoes.

4. Anything old or broken down.

1943 *GL* Port.

SAMPATTA see *sampata.*

SAMPHIRE OF JAMAICA see JAMAICA(N) SAMPHIRE.

SAMPLATA, SAMPLATTA see *sampata.*

sananana sb dial; etym unknown.

1952 FGC Han /sànanána/ crab—pale yellow.

SAN BLAS COCO sb now dial; < *San Blas*, Mexico? + coco. See quots.

1814 Lunan I 212, The *San Blas coco*, which has come into general cultivation for some years past, grows to an enormous size in its stem or head, and the cocoes.. weigh three or four pounds or more each..The negroes are particularly partial to them. 1952 FGC StT /sam-blaast/ is soft coco.

SANCHY sb obs; perh < *sanctified*, evid a nickname. A negro who had embraced Methodism at the time when it was an active force for abolition of slavery. Cf SAINT.

1826 Williams 81, Mr Mathews cautioned me, at parting, against the sanchy, as he called my valet; adding that however well he might serve me, a saint was like a mule.

SANCOCHO see SANGKOCHIE.

SANDALWOOD sb; cf *OED* in diff senses. See quot. *G*

1941 Swabey 29, Rosewood..*Amyris balsamifera*.. Exported in small quantities as Sandalwood and Amyris-wood: produces the amyriswood oil of commerce (formerly West Indian Sandalwood Oil).

SAND-BAG TREE sb obs; an error for Sandbox tree.

1873 Rampini 158, The nut of a sand-bag tree, expanded with the heat, burst with a loud explosion.

SAND FISH sb; *OED* 1893. See quot 1854–5.

1854–5 *TJSA* I 144, Gobius soporator, Gobius ocellatus, Gobius multiocellatus, Gobius bacalaus: these are all called Sand Fish. 1952 FGC StC /san fish/—suck-stone; StJ /san fish/—sea galawas. *N*

SAND-GALL sb; cf *OED* 1787→.

1774 Long I 352, The savannah lands are for the most part clayey, or intermixed with sandy spaces, some of which are of great extent and depth. These are called sand-galls, and are wholly unproductive of trees, or any other vegetable than a small wire grass, unfit for pasturage.

SAN DOMINGO BULLET (TREE) sb. = BOB COOK.

SAND-PATTA, SAND-PATTER, SAND-PLATTER see *sampata. BL*

SAND SHARK sb. The goby fish.

1951 Smith in *NHN* 139, *Bathygobius soporator* (known in Jamaica as 'sand shark'), commonly found along the Palisadoes, particularly in tide pools.

SANDWICH vb dial or slang. To kiss: see quots.

1954 LeP StAnn, To Kiss—sandwich. 1958 DeC StAnd /sanwich/—to kiss with the tongue in the mouth.

sanfai, sangfai see *samfai.*

SANGKOCHIE /sàngkócho, sàngkúochi/ vb dial; evid <Amer Sp *sancocho*—soup of meat, cassava, plantain etc.—the 'olla podrida' of these countries (*sc* Ecuador and Puerto Rico): Malaret; cf also Revollo 240.

1. A rich soup; evidently also transf: a feast. Cf MACOOCHE, *kuochi wata.*

c 1915 FGC StAnd /sàngkócho/ remembered as current. 1943 *GL* StM, Sangkochie, feast at night after funeral surreptitiously.

2. Comb: *Sangkochie water*, a coconut rundown. (Connection with this form is not certain.)

1959 DeC West /som kuochi wata/ coconut run-down.

sangkocho see prec.

sangkuku /sàngkúku, sàngkútu/ vb dial; etym unknown. To stoop down, sit on one's heels; chiefly rural.

1943 *GL* Port, Sangkuku, to stoop; StT, Sancoocoo; Port, Sang-ko-ko, stoop down; Tre, Sankootoo; Port, Sanchocho. 1952 FGC Port /sángkuku/ manner of sitting on the heels with shoes flat and back resting against a wall. 1956 Mc Port /sángkuku/; StAnd /sangkuku doun/ to squat on the heels—butu.

sangkuma wis sb dial; evid <*Cinchona* (cf *OED* for confusion of this with *China, sb*[3]) +*wis*, vine. Cf *singkuma* banana. =CHINA WITHE.

1956 Mc StE (Accom) /sangkuma wis/ another name for /chieni-wis/.

SANKEY sb dial; <Ira David Sankey, singing evangelist and composer, pub *Sacred Songs and Solos* 1873, etc. *BA BL G*

1. A book of Sankey's religious songs.

1929 Beckwith 163, And I dreamt that I saw an angel, and he bids me get a Bible and a Sankey and a rod with a double fold.

2. A religious song or hymn.

1925 Beckwith 45 [Prov:] Ebery donkey hab him sankey. 'Every man to his own mind.' 1952 FGC Han /sangki/ a spiritual song. 1953 Moore 37, Sankey—hymn. 1956 Mc Man /sing sángki/ *sing hymns.*

SANPOORU sb dial rare; cf *sangkuku.*

1943 *GL* StM, Sanpooru, old man.

SANTA sb arch; etym unknown. A drink prepared with fruit juice, sugar, rum, and other ingredients; formerly much drunk.

1797 *Braco* 13 Oct, Observe two Coopers about the works Makeing Poles & a blowing of a Cask for Santa. 1828 Marly 46, They ceased [dancing] on being told that salt fish would be served out, along with a small allowance of sugar and santa, (a kind of shrub,) to the pickininy mothers. 1838 Kelly 21, The effects of the santa began to subdue and disperse them. 1952 FGC Han, [To make] /santa/: boil /tambrik/ [turmeric], strain, mix with wine.

SANTA (MARIA) /sàntamaráia/ sb; see quot 1837. The common form today is simply 'santa', esp in compounds.

1. The tree *Calophyllum jacquinii.* Cf WHITE SANTA MARIA. *BL N*

1696 Sloane 180, *Bastard Mammee Tree or Santa Maria.* In sylvis Jamaicæ Insulæ densis & opacis frequens est. a 1726 Barham (1794) 18. 1740 Importance 52, There is also a Tree call'd the Sancta Maria..The Spaniards pull off their Hats whenever they see the Tree. 1837 Macfadyen 136–7, Calophyllum Calaba..The name *Santa Maria*, was given, according to Barham, to this tree, from the juice..constituting a valuable balsam, useful in dressing wounds, known by the names of *Green balsam, Mary's balsam, Calaba balsam, &c.*.Calaba, was the name by which the tree was known among the Caribs. 1926 Fawcett 200, C. Jacquinii..Santa Maria, Wild Mammee. 1952 FGC StAnn, StM, StT, Tre /sànta maráia/ 'there is Red Santa and White Santa'.

2. The shrub *Piper umbellatum*, now generally called COW-FOOT, whose leaves are often used medicinally.

1696 Sloane 45, Piper longum racemosum malvaceum.. Santa Maria Leaves. a 1726 Barham (1794) 139, Piper longum racemosum malvaceum. This is commonly called *Santa Maria*, from its great virtues. 1801 Dancer 361, Santa Maria Leaf (*Piper umbellat*). Syrup made of the Decoction good in Colds, and an antidote to Poison.

santapii /sántapíi, sántapi/ sb dial; cf *OED centipede*, early spellings, and '*centipie, centapee*, in W. Indies and early navigators was prob. from Sp.' =*Centipede*; also called Forty-leg. s.

[1740 Importance 47, The Centipee is a long sort of an Insect with forty Feet.] 1952 FGC Port /sántapi/ StE /sántapíi/. *BA BL G T*

SAPODILLA sb; cf *OED* 1697→. *BA BL G N T*

1. The fruit usu called NASEBERRY in Jamaica; also its tree as a timber wood: *Sapota achras.*

p 1660 *State of Ja* 489, Manill [*sic*] supotas, supotillia, avocatas, cashues. 1672 Blome 25, Guavars, Mamees, Alumee[*sic*]-Supotas, Suppotillias, Avocatas. 1794 Barham 110, Naseberry-tree. It is also called by some sappadillos. 1952 FGC StE, Tre /sàpadíla/. 1954 *WIMJ* 31, Sapota achras..Naseberry; Sapodilla.

2. Transf: see quot.

1907 Jekyll 206, Sapadilla is really a fruit something like a medlar, but the name is given to all sorts of fruit, notably Granadilla.

3. =SAPODILLA BULLET: see next.

SAPODILLA BULLET sb; <SAPODILLA + BULLET. The tree *Mimusops excisa.*

1941 Swabey 30, Sapodilla—(Sapodilla bullet)..The wood is heavy, hard, close-grained, and dense, with a dark reddish colour.

sar see *sa* sb[2].

SARAH BIRD sb; evid a personifying name. The bird *Elænia fallax.*

1936 Bond 255, Greater Antillean Elænia..Sarah Bird. 1956 Jeffrey-Smith 50.

SAREY sb dial; ? <*Sarah*, personal name; cf MINTY, SALLY COCO. A variety of sweet-potato.

1929 Beckwith 18 [In Mandeville:] The 'Lewis Daley' is long and big; the 'Sarey', round and red.

SASAPHARILLA sb; an unrecorded spelling of *sarsaparilla*, illustrating *OED* γ form (which *OED* does not illustrate) with loss of *r* in pronunc. *G*

1672 Blome 13, China-Roots, Sasapharilla, Cashia Fistula, Tamerindes.

SATIN (FISH or SNAPPER) sb dial; descr. A fish very similar to the SILK, but fishermen make a consistent distinction: Satin is longer, rounder, and darker; however, they live with the Silk in deep water. Some species of *Lutianus*?

1952 FGC Port, StA, StE, StJ, StT, West /satn/; StM /satn fish/; StC /satn snapa/. 1961 FGC StC, Silk snapper is red, satin is black—otherwise the same.

SATISFY vb intr or refl dial. Be satisfied, satisfy yourself. *G T*

1896 Bates 122, Mudfish wouldn' satisfy. [*Mudfish would not be satisfied.*] 1900 Murray 8, see COW NECK. 1924 Beckwith 290, see BEFORE prep.

SAUCY adj dial; cf *OED* 1, quots →1630. Sharp to the taste.

1960 LeP StAnd, Saucy—sharp-flavoured, like jimbolin.

SAUKA see *saka(-saka)*.

SAUL see SALT.

SAULY see *saali*.

SAVANNA BIRD sb ornith; *OED* mistakenly identifies this with the SAVANNA BLACKBIRD; quots 1694 and 1725 only refer to the Savanna Bird. The Grasshopper Sparrow *Ammodramus savannarum*.

[1694 Ray in *Lett. Lit. Men* (Camden) 200, In referring the Savanna bird to the Lark-kind.] 1725 Sloane 306, The Savanna Bird..They sit on the ground in the Plains, and run thereon after the manner of Sky Larks, as low as they can, to avoid being discover'd. 1847 Gosse 242. 1936 Bond 394.

SAVANNA BLACKBIRD sb ornith; *OED* 1862 only. *Crotophaga ani*; cf BLACKBIRD 1, ANI.

1756 Browne 474, The Savanna Blackbird..they live chiefly upon ticks and other small vermin; and may be frequently seen jumping about all the cows and oxen in the fields. 1847 Gosse 282.

SAVANNA FLOWER sb bot; *OED* 1696→. Various species of *Echites* growing freely on the savannas, esp *E. jamaicensis*, with yellow flower.

1696 Sloane 89, Apocynum erectum..flore luteo.. Savanna Flour. In omnibus pratis campestribus Insulæ Jamaicæ floret elegantissima hæc planta. 1756 Browne 180, Nerium 2..The larger Savanna-flower..[climbs] among the neighbouring shrubs. All the parts of this plant are extremely poisonous. *Ibid* 182, Echites 1..The Savanna Flower, with a simple narrow flower-tube..This plant is common in the Savannas about Kingston. 1811 Titford Expl to Plate VI 2, Savanna Flower, (*echites suberecta*)..This is a small plant creeping among the grass in Savannahs, and only distinguishable by its small pale blue flowers. 1954 *WIMJ* 29, *Echites umbellata*..Maroon Weed; Savannah Flower.

SAVANNA GRASS sb; *DA* 1859→. See quots. *T*

1756 Browne 137, Gramen 8..The small Savanna Grass with echinated Valves..This little plant grows in the Savanna about Kingston, and seldom rises more than four or five inches above the ground. 1954 *FG* 232, Savannah Grass—Carpet Grass (*Anoxopus compressus*). This grass is widespread at low altitudes..In the West Indies it is an important pasture grass..It also makes a very satisfactory lawn grass.

SAVANNAH = SAVANNA.

SAVANNAH BROOMWEED sb bot obs; cf BROOMWEED. In Macfadyen's use: *Abutilon americanum* (ident 1926 Fawcett 101).

1837 Macfadyen 86, Sida abutiloides. *Savannah Broomweed.*

[**SAVANNAH-WATTLE** sb bot.

1864 Grisebach 787, Savannah-wattle, *Citharexylum quadrangulare* and *cinereum*.]

SAVANNA MUSTARD sb bot obs. Apparently *Brassica integrifolia*, 'Wild Mustard' (1914 Fawcett 240).

1756 Browne 273, Sinapis 2..The small Savanna Mustard ..commonly found wild among the grass, in all the Savannas. 1814 Lunan I 68. [Erroneous attribution of the name to Browne for *Cleome procumbens*.]

SAVANNA PURSLANE sb bot. *Portulaca halimoides.*

1850 Macfadyen 167–8. *Portulaca halimoides.* Savannah Purslane. This species is not very common..Towards Christmas the naked heath-like stems may be observed. 1914 Fawcett 170.

SAVANNA WEED sb obs. A weed used medicinally—prob what is now called PICK-NUT: *Hyptis suaveolens.*

1679 Trapham 100, Savanna Weed or Spiknard, as some call the same, being decocted make a fragrant and balsamick Bath to strengthen the cutaneous Fibres.

SAVE conj now dial; cf *OED* 2c *poetic*, →1897. Unless. *G*

1962 BLB 25 /yu kyaan kom iin-ya siev yu pie yu fier/ *You can't enter unless you pay your fare.*

SAVE-LIFE-QUICK sb dial joc.

1959 DeC StJ /sieb-laif-kwik/ turned cornmeal, apparently because it is easy and fast to prepare.

SAVEN TREE, SAVIN TREE sb; cf *OED savin.* Applied at first in Jamaica (as elsewhere) to Juniper and similar trees or shrubs (e.g. 1696 Sloane 128); later, and characteristically, to *Zanthoxylum fagara*, *Trichilium hirta* (= BASTARD IRONWOOD).

1756 Browne 146, Pterota..The Saven-tree, or bastard Ironwood. This shrub is very common in the lower lands of Jamaica. 1864 Grisebach 787, Savin tree. 1920 Fawcett 175. 1941 Swabey 23.

SAVVY adj dial; <*savvy* sb. 'practical sense, intelligence' (*OED*). Wise.

1927 Anderson-Cundall 118 [Prov:] De saby 'ooman hab yeye but no ear.

SAW-BILL sb dial; <*saw* sb + BILL.

1958 DeC StAnd /saa bil/ same as /baja bil/ i.e. a long machete, broad at tip, sharp both sides, used for billing grass or weeds.

SAW-HORN sb; cf *OED saw-horned beetle*, 1862. A beetle with serrated processes on its head.

1725 Sloane 210, Cantharis maxima..The large golden Saw-horn. Serra corn. max. Surin. e viridi aureo refulgens..I had it from Jamaica.

SAWKER see *saka(-saka)*.

SAWYER sb; cf *OED, DAE, DA*, 1789→. Any of various species of wood-boring beetles.

1756 Browne 428–9, Scarabeus 1..The little brown Sawyer. This is the least of the Beetle tribe I have met with in America..4..The great brown Sawyer..5..The small mottled Sawyer.

SAWYER-MAN DUMPLING sb dial; cf CART-MAN DUMPLING.

1958 DeC StT /saaya-man dompling/ a large round boiled dumpling. 1959 DeC Han, West, Not just any very large boiled dumpling (as in most of the island), but one which is cylindrical, 2–3 in. in diameter, 10–12 in. long; these are stood up in a ring around the side of the pot.

SAY see *se*.

SAYBALL see SEA-BAWL.

SAYKA see SAKE O'.

SAY-SAY see *sese*.

SCADE see SCARED.

SCALE sb dial; cf *OED* *sb*[1] II.

1958 DeC 32 /skiel/ a unit of weight (34 lbs) used in wholesaling foodkind; /wi dig tuu trii skiel a yam/ *We dig* (or *dug*) *two or three scale of yams.*

SCALE-YARD see SKILIAD.

SCALLION see SKELLION.

SCARCE-O'-FAT adj dial joc. Thin; also employed as a nickname. *BL*

1954 LeP StT, Scays-a-fat—meagre, thin. 1955 Bennett *Breeze Pass*, Koo 'Scarce-a-fat' an 'Buffooto' Eena de miggle street! 1958 DeC StT, see SNAKY-BONY.

SCARED vb infin dial; <*scared*, past form of *scare*. (Several other vb infinitives are formed in the same way—e.g. *broke, married, left, lost.*)

1943 *GL* Tre, Scade, to frighten.

SCARLET BEAN sb obs. Prob the CORAL-BEAN TREE.

1802 Nugent 97, Saw a most beautiful tree, called the Scarlet Bean. It is like a large coquelicot-geranium; for the leaves fall off as soon as the flowers make their appearance.

SCARLET CORDIA sb bot obs. The shrub *Cordia sebestena.*

[1756 Browne 202, The bushy Cordia, with large scarlet flowers.] 1790 Beckford I 32, The glowing red of the scarlet cordium. 1811 Lunan I 198, Adorned with large branches of fine scarlet flowers, (hence the name of *scarlet cordia*). [The part in parentheses is Lunan's; the rest quoted by him from Browne.]

SCARLET SEED sb bot. See quot 1864.

1756 Browne 368, The Scarlet-Seed..When the fruit is ripe, it..sheds its seeds..they are always inveloped in a greasy waxen substance of a scarlet colour. 1864 Grisebach 787, Scarlet-seed: *Ternstrœmia obovalis* and *Lœtia thamnia*. 1926 Fawcett 182.

SCATTER FOOT see *kyata fut.*

SCAVEECHED FISH /skobíich fish, skovíich ~/ sb; <Sp *escabeche*, pickled fish. A dish made with fish (snapper, king-fish, etc.) marinated in vinegar, with onion and spices. Also CAVEACH, ESCOVEITCHED FISH.

1889 Sanguinetti 50, We speak of 'Scaveched' fish but it is not generally known that in the original Spanish the word is 'Escaveached' or 'pickled'. 1893 Sullivan 115, Scaveeched King-fish. [Recipe given.] 1952 FGC StAnn /skovíicht fish/ fry; when cold, pepper and salt; StM /skobíich fish/; StT /skòvíich/.

SCENT vb intr dial; cf *OED* 3, 'now *rare* or *obs*.' To have or give off an odour. *BA G*

1956 Mc StE /di berrij sents gud/ *The lime drink smells good.* /jangko riid sent hai/ *Jangko reed has a strong (unpleasant) smell.*

SCHOOL-CALL sb dial; from the time when school begins or is 'called'. Locally: 9 A.M.

1958 DeC Port /skuul kal/ 9:00 a.m. Used by everybody in the district as a time of day. *BA G*

SCHOOLMASTER sb; cf *OED sb*[1] 1 e. A teacher of any sort; an adult in charge of the tutelage of a child, even quite informally. *BA*

1863 Waddell 161 (year 1839), 'Coolmassa'* one day passed his hut, and told him better he leave off rum. But he got angry and bawled after 'Coolmassa', and told him he would never leave off. *Teachers of all kinds were called schoolmasters. 1877 Murray *Feedin' 'Perrit* 14 [To a little girl who is keeping house for a man:] Wha you da mek monkey trick a'ter you coo'-massa for?

SCHOOL-TIME sb dial; cf SCHOOL-CALL. The time of day between 8 and 9 A.M. *G*

1958 DeC StT.

SCIENCE sb dial. = OBEAH. *BL G*

1943 *GL* Tre, Bunggusu, science.

SCIENCE MAN, SCIENTIFIC ~, SCIENTIST sb dial. = OBEAH-MAN. *G T*

1943 *GL* StM, Do good man, science man. 1952 Kerr 160, Busta seem to be a scientific man (magician). He told Sir Edward Denham that they both couldn't live under the same sky..Not long after this Sir Edward became ill and died. 1953 Moore 124, Scientist—obeah-man; so called by Cumina groups. 1959 DeC Tre.

SCISSORS-TAIL sb dial. *BL*

1. The Frigate Bird (*Fregata magnificens*), from the way it manipulates its spread tail-feathers as stabilizers when soaring. *G*

1936 Bond 18, Scissors-tail. 1952 FGC StJ /sízaz/—man o' war bird; have tail like scissors. 1956 Jeffrey-Smith 131, The Man o' War Bird..has..acquired a soubriquet of 'Scissors-Tail'.

2. The humming-bird *Trochilus polytmus.*

c1915 FGC StAnd, Scissors-tail humming-bird. 1956 Jeffrey-Smith 22, Streamer-Tail and Scissors-Tail are other local names which recall the appearance of the adult male in flight when the two long tail feathers stream out in all their beauty, or as it perches and crosses the feathers in question.

3. A variety of sweet-potato in which the leaves are divided and are thought to resemble scissors.

1929 Beckwith 18 [In Mandeville:] 'Costa Rica' is a white potato; 'Scissors Tail' (named from the shape of the leaf) bears a whole bunch of tubers. 1952 FGC StC.

SCOFULA see SCROFULOUS.

SCORN-THE-EARTH, SCORN-THE GROUND /kaan-di-ort, kaani-grong/ sb chiefly dial. Mistletoe, because it never touches the earth or ground. (See quot 1954 for names.) Cf also GOD-BUSH. *BL*

1943 *GL* Tre, Caandieart, Mistletoe. 1952 FGC Han /skàrn-di-órt/; Tre /káanigróng/. 1954 *WIMJ* 30–1, *Oryctanthus occidentalis*..God-bush; Scorn-the-Earth.. *Phthirusa pauciflora*..Mistletoe; Scorn-the-Earth. 1956 Mc Man /skáan-di-gráun, káanigróng/.

SCORPION WEED sb dial; see quots. = WILD CLARY (*Heliotropium indicum*) named from the shape of the flower and for its medicinal use.

[1814 Lunan II 248, The stalk is large, green, and hairy, rising about two feet high; the leaf like garden clary, having many five-leaved flowers, of a pale blue colour, set in a double row on the upper side of the branches, and turned like a scorpion's tail..It is boiled with cocoanut oil, to cure the sting of scorpions.] 1955 *WIMJ* 70, Wild Clary;..Scorpion Weed..it may be boiled with coconut oil to make a plaster for scorpion stings.

SCOTCH ATTORNEY sb; <*Scotch* + ATTORNEY. Cf *OED.* = SCOTCHMAN.

1864 Grisebach 787, Scotch attorney: *Clusia.* 1871 Kingsley v, The Matapalo (or Scotch Attorney, as it is rudely called here).

SCOTCH-BONNET PEPPER sb; cf *OED* 1858→. A variety of *Capsicum* pepper shaped like a Tam o' Shanter. Cf BONNET PEPPER.

1858 Simmonds *Dict. Trade*, quoted *OED.* 1873 Rampini 53, A dinner..highly seasoned with 'Scotch bonnets', or some other of the many varieties of the 'country peppers' (Capsicum). 1952 FGC Port /kach banit/; StAnd, StC, StM /skach banit/ bell-pepper, yellow, round.

SCOTCH GRASS sb; for origin see quots 1696, 1774; cf *OED* 1756, 1839 only. The pasture grass *Panicum molle.*

1696 Sloane 30 with addition from 218, *Scotch grass.* Circa locum dictum *Wague water & Agua alta* in Jamaica, & parte illa Insulæ Barbados Scotland dicta sponte in palustribus provenire audivi. 1774 Long III 761, Scotch-grass.—*Panicum majus.* This grass obtained its name from a part of Barbadoes, called Scotland; from whence it was originally brought. 1864 Grisebach 787.

SCOTCHMAN sb arch; cf SCOTCH ATTORNEY: the success of the Scotch in acquiring properties by managing them in their own interest is alluded to. Various species of *Clusia* and other vines which grow upon and around other trees until they kill them.

[1826 Williams 5, At first, a small delicate vine, it [the fig] attaches itself to the bark of the cotton tree..and..at last envelops it..Quashie compared it to the mortgagee strangling the proprietor, or the Scotchman hugging the Creole to death.] 1835 Scott xiv, Do you see that Scotchman hugging the Creole? 1860 Trollope 31. 1873 Rampini 172. 1952 FGC StT /kachman/ fig that eats up another tree.

SCOTRAN adj dial obs; ? < *Scotland*. Meaning uncert: strong? excellent? See quot.

1907 Jekyll 26 [Song:] My door is bar with a scotran bar oh, Fair an' gandelow steel.

SCOVEECH FISH see SCAVEECHED FISH.

SCRAPER sb dial. A crude 'musical' instrument, similar in principle to the JAWBONE: see quot. s REGGAE. *BL*

1953 Moore 172, The scraper, a corrugated stick across which is rubbed a plain stick [in pocomania and revivalist services].

SCRATCH vb; cf *OED* 3. To irritate (the mouth, skin, etc.) by pungency, acidity, etc. See CRATCH. (Freq in the names of plants—see separate entries.) *G*

1725 Sloane 367, Tayas or Eddos, are eaten in Jamaica, and cause a Heat in the Throat, call'd commonly there scratching the Throat, and this when well boil'd. They are therefore tho' eat only by Negroes. 1790 Beckford II 143, The Eboetoyer..is apt to scratch the mouth, if not properly boiled. 1960 FGC current; a folk word adopted generally.

SCRATCH-BUSH sb dial. One or more kinds of wild plants with fine hairs that cause itching or stinging of the skin upon contact. Specif *Urera baccifera, Indigofera suffruticosa. G*

1952 FGC Han, StAnn, Scratch-bush, 'a kind of stump cowitch', a stalky shrub, with tiny pink pea-like flowers and bunches of inch-long black pods; StT, Juicy stem, rough leaf: small stinging hairs under leaf and on stem. 1954 *FG* 585, The Scratch-bush or Cow-nettle..is an extremely annoying plant to the small farmer..because the entire plant is covered with stinging hairs.

SCRATCH COCO sb dial. Wild varieties of COCO (*Colocasia*) that SCRATCH the mouth or throat.

1756 Browne 332, Arum 6..The old roots are generally called *Scratch Coccos*, from a little pungency with which they are always impregnated. 1814 Lunan I 213. 1952 FGC Port, StM, StT /skrach kuoko/—wild, a whitish coco eaten by hogs; grow in swamp; scratch, frothy; StJ /krach kuoko/.

SCRATCH-MOUTH adj dial. That will SCRATCH the mouth; sharp, pungent, irritating.

1952 Topper 9, In certain areas small, degenerate, 'scratch-mouth' Red Spanish plants are called 'Cow Boy' [pineapples].

SCRATCH-SCRATCH sb dial. A skin disease that causes one to scratch continually; more often called *krach-krach.*

1952 FGC StM /skrach-skrach/—when children have /hiich/ finer than /ekzíima/. 1954 LeP StAnn, Dry, itching rash on the skin = scratch-scratch.

SCRATCH WITHE sb dial. PUDDING WITHE (*Cissus sicyoides*); used as a plaster against itching skin conditions.

1954 *WIMJ* 26, Pudding Wys (Withe);..Yaws Bush; Bastard Bryony; Scratch Wys. *Ibid* 34, Scratch Withe.

SCREBBEY see *skrebi.*

SCREECH-OWL /kríich òul/ sb dial. An albino negro. Also called QUAW.

1959 DeC Tre.

SCREW TREE sb; *OED* 1756 only. The tree *Helicteres jamaicensis*, with spirally twisted fruit.

1756 Browne 330, The Screw Tree..has much of the habit of the Mallows tribe; from which it is distinguished by the spiral form and connection of its capsular seed-vessels. 1854 *TJSA* I 8. 1926 Fawcett 156. 1954 *WIMJ* 23–4, Corkscrew; Screw Tree. With the wood and leaves, which are bitter, a tea is made for biliousness.

SCREWY sb dial. Any of the beetles (*Oncideres* spp) which 'saw' small limbs off trees by chewing round and round them.

1952 FGC StT, Screwy—bug; saws limbs off cotton tree and gungo.

SCRIPPLE see SRIPPLE.

SCROFULOUS /káfilos, kráfilos, skiáfilas/ sb dial; < *scrofulous* adj. A skin disease.

1943 *GL* Clar, Crafilous, a disease known as Scofula; Caffilus, disease on skin. 1957 EB Port /skiafilas/ a disease on the skin.

SCRUB DRY YAWS see RUB DRY YAWS.

SCRUSH see *skrosh.*

SCULL(ING) see *skol.*

SCUTTLE sb dial; descriptive. The TRUNK FISH.

1952 FGC StT, Scuttle—buck-buck, cony-buck, trunk-fish.

se conj dial; < Twi *sè*, 'after a previous verb.. introducing the words spoken.. = *saying*, is often not to be translated and serves as a mere quotation mark' (Christaller). This word is never pronounced like Engl *say*, but since the meaning is close (esp in such phrases as 'tell me say') it is often taken as the same word and written so. More accurate writers of the dialect, however, spell *sey*, *seh*, or as here *se. BL G N*

1. After verbs such as *think*, *know*, *believe*, *suppose*, *see*, or others involving communication, as, *tell*, *hear*, *promise*, introducing the object clause: virtually equiv to *that*. (Sometimes *that* is used redundantly after it.)

1837 James 10, And she think say, that I run away. 1907 Jekyll 8, Me tell you say them a call you name. 1950 Pioneer 16, Anancy..tek a oat [oath] seh him mus put himself eena Story Book. *Ibid*, Yuh no know sey Rat is nice Meat? *Ibid* 23, It look lika sey de people do fe purpose. 1952 FGC Tre, If a t'ief go a grung, it [wangla vine] wind off, drop off stick, and you know se t'ief go a you grung. 1956 Mc StE /mi si se a wuman tan up de/ *I can see that it's a woman standing there.*

2. Elliptically, without the object clause:

1956 Mc Man /im fieba se/ *It seems so*; /yu no hie mi tel yu se/ *Didn't you hear me tell you?*

3. Introducing direct speech.

1877 Murray *Kittle* 24, Him hax dem say, 'Bra, whi side unoo da go?'. 1907 Jekyll 7, I hear dem shing a shing a river side say: Yeshterday this time me a nyam Tiger fat. 1956 Mc StE /im tél im se, dúon kil/ *He says to him, 'Don't kill!'* /im tel im se, no bwai/ *He said, 'No, boy'.*

SEA-ANANCY sb dial. An unidentified creature—perh a sea-spider or spider crab.

1952 FGC StM, Sea-anancy—legs long and 'cranky' (thin).

SEA-BALL see SEA-BAWL.

SEA-BANANA sb chiefly dial.

1944 *NHN* II 168, I recognized it to be a sea-cucumber which I soon learnt was called by the people of the district [Montego Bay] a 'sea-banana'.

SEA-BAT sb; cf *OED* 2: *Malthe vespertilio.* The bat-fish. (Not the same as BAT-FISH.) *G*

1756 Browne 457, Lophius 2..The Sea-Batt..by the expansion of its side-fins and its small ventrals, represents a bat in some measure, whence its name. 1952 FGC StAnn.

SEA-BAWL sb dial; <*sea* + BAWL. A sheer hole in limestone rocks along the sea into which the waves wash with a roaring sound. (Also a similar hole inland.) Also attrib.

1890 Thomas 28, We made fair progress [climbing in the John-Crow Mountains]..until we came at chain No. 5, to the mouth of a bottomless pit, or, as the natives here call it a 'sea-bawl hole'. A cockpit I suppose, but with sides of laminated limestone, instead of the honey-comb rock which surrounds all those which I had hitherto seen. 1924 Beckwith 39, An' Brer Hawk fly along wid him till drop him into a sea-ball*..*A pit in the ground near the sea-coast, into which the waves wash is called a 'sea-ball'. 1943 *GL* Tre, Sayball, a deep hole in the mountain. 1961 *Gleaner* 9 June 5/7, 'I know a "sea-bawl" cave up there on my hut', Rose said. 'It sometimes makes a roaring noise like the sea.'

SEA-BEAN sb; *OED* 1696, 1867 only. The wild bean *Canavalia obtusifolia*, which grows commonly on the ground near the sea; cf SEA-SIDE BEAN.

1696 Sloane 70, The Sea bean. In arenosis maritimis Jamaicæ & Caribearum Insularum ubique provenit. 1707 Sloane 179. 1952 FGC Tre /síi-bíin/—flower reddish-purple like a coarse sweet-pea; vine prone along beach.

SEA-BEEF sb dial; a joc application of a nautical term (*OED* 1594–1850). A chiton: small edible jointed mollusc clinging to rocks by the sea. See quot 1960.

[1940 Perry 19, The Chiton..Natives of some of the West Indian Islands call it 'sea beef'.] 1946 *NHN* III 44, Those strange molluscs, the chitons, (sea beef). 1952 FGC StAnn, StE, StJ, StM, StT, West /sii-biif/ holds very hard to rock—get off with a machet or knife. 1956 Mc Kgn. 1960 R. P. Bengry, Institute of Ja, Members of at least four genera of chitons have been described for Jamaica. Among the common species are *Chiton tuberculatus, C. marmoratus, C. squamosus,* and *Ischnochiton purpurascens.*

SEA-BLADDER sb dial; *OED* 1860 only. The Portuguese man-o'-war. *BA BL G N*

[1756 Browne 386, The Portuguese Man of War. This is no more than a simple transparent bladder, furnished with a great number of *tentaculæ.*] 1952 FGC StE, StJ, StM /síi-bláda/ plenty afloat when there's to be hard wind; have legs below, sting, scratch.

SEA-BREEZE sb; *OED* 1697→. A breeze blowing inland off the sea. *BA BL G N*

1661 Hickeringill 10, The heat in the day time being alwaies alloy'd with the Sea Breezes; and the nights naturally cool, are..refreshed with Land Breezes. 1697 Nevill 20 May, But the land breeze dying we could not gett quite through the Kees so I anchored between them to take the next land-breeze to carry me out. 1774 Long III 600, The trade, or as it is called here, the sea-breeze. (1961 Current, FGC).

SEA BUTTERFLY sb; *OED* in diff meaning. A fish of the family Chætodontidæ; now commonly called Butterfly-fish.

1756 Browne 454, Chætodon 1..The Sea Butterfly.

SEA-CAT sb dial; <*sea* + prob *cat* = cat-o'-nine-tails; but cf Du *zeekat.* An octopus. Also called SEA-PUSS. *BA*

1946 *NHN* III 50, The familiar Jamaican 'sea-cat' or octopus. 1952 FGC gen /síi-kyat/.

SEA COCKROACH, SEA ROACH[1] sb; *OED* 1792 only. 'A crustacean of the genus *Remipes*' (*OED*). *BA BL*

1756 Browne 418, Pediculus 3..The Fish-Louse, or Sea Cock-Roach. 1952 FGC StE, StJ, West, Sea Cockroach, Sucks on fish; size of moony [large firefly—about 1½ in.]; rests inside gill of fish—holds on with stiff legs; hardish—not easily crushed. Port, StC, Sea roach.

SEA-COCONUT sb; cf *OED coco* 6, 'Sea Coco-nut of Jamaica'—no quot. Separate entry not this sense. The fruit of a palm (*Manicaria saccifera*) not native to Jamaica, but carried by the sea from the coast of Brazil and cast ashore all around the island. *BA*

1917 Guppy 127–8, The observant Jamaican native when he picks up on the beach the 'sea coco-nut', as he calls it, will tell you that it has been brought by the waves from a distance'. So also the Barbadians, who name it 'sea-apple', can have no acquaintance with the palm.. *Manicaria saccifera* is essentially a palm of the Amazon estuary. 1951 FGC StT, Tre, etc.

SEA-COTTON sb dial. The SEA-SIDE MAHOE.

1951 FGC StT.

SEA COWITCH sb dial; <*sea* + COWITCH. The sea-nettle; it floats in the sea and raises welts on the skin upon contact.

1952 FGC StAnn, StM, West /síi-kóuwich/—like a thread; floats in bundle; like spittle.

SEA-DOG sb dial. A kind of sea-worm with flat underside about 1 in. broad and 3 in. long—unidentified.

1952 FGC StM.

SEA-FIDDLER sb.

1892 Cockrell list, Sea-fiddler, *Rhinobatus undulatus.*

SEA-FLOWER sb dial; descr. The sea anemone.

1956 Mc Kgn /sìi-flóuaz/.

SEA-FOWL sb dial; <*sea* + FOWL. The spotted eagle ray (fish) *Aëtobatus narinari*, from its somewhat bird-like appearance.

1961 R. P. Bengry StAnd, This term (*sea-fowl*) is common among fishermen.

SEA-GALLIWASP sb; <*sea* + GALLIWASP; cf *OED*, 'A Jamaican name for *Elops saurus*'.

a 1705 Ray *Syn. Pisc.* 159 *Saurus maximus non maculatus;* The Sean fish or Sea Galley Wasp. [*OED*] 1725 Sloane 284, The Sein-Fish, or Sea-Gally-Wasp. 1952 FGC Port, StAnn, StE, StJ, StM, West /sii-gyálawas/—mouth resembles gallawas, gives it the name.

SEA-GAULIN sb dial; <*sea* + GAULIN. = GAULIN.

1907 Jekyll 74 [Anancy story:] An' by this time Sea-gaulin was passing an' hear what they are saying.

SEA GOD-A-ME sb dial; cf GOD-A-ME. A small fish; also called BLACK PIG.

1952 FGC West /sii gadami/.

SEA-GRUB sb dial. Worms used for fishing bait.

1956 Mc StC /sii grob/.

SEA-ICE sb dial. A white jelly-fish.

1956 Mc Kgn /síi-áis/ (heard from children).

SEAL sb dial; cf *OED sb*². In BALM-YARD ceremonies, a sort of altar on the ground; see quot.

1952 Kerr 138, The seal is a circle of stamped out red earth with a rope around it. Mother Evangeline says she often goes and works on the seal and draws visions there. It is consecrated.

SEAL vb dial. To shut off or make safe from evil influences (e.g. from spirits of the dead) by means of counter-agents and spells.

1952 FGC Han [Song:] Me seal me yard, Me seal i' wid white rum, Me seal i' wid lime and jeyes; No dead cyan' come in.

SEA LOBSTER sb. =LOBSTER, the spiny lobster, *Palinurus vulgaris* (actually a crayfish).

1725 Sloane 271, Locusta marina vulgaris dorso spinoso.. *Sea Lobster.* *G*

SEA-MAHMY sb dial; <*sea*+/maami/ one folk pronunc of *mama.* A mermaid, believed to inhabit the sea as the RIVER MUMMA does streams.

1907 Jekyll 124, Annancy..drop in the sea an' sink. An' when he go down a sea bottom he meet Sea-mahmy. *Ibid* 126, Sea-mahmy, Mermaid. *Ibid* xxxi, note 1 (Werner), One kind of duppy is a mermaid—but I can find no indication that she came from Africa.

SEA-MAHOE sb. =SEA-SIDE MAHOE. *BA*

1696 Sloane 95, Malva arborea maritima..flore luteo.. The *Sea Mahot.* 1707 Sloane 216.

SEA-MARBLE sb dial. A spherical seed (unidentified) ¾ in. diameter (thrown ashore in some quantity near Falmouth).

1952 FGC Tre /sii-maabl/.

SEA-NEEDLE sb dial; cf *OED* in diff sense. The black sea-egg with long, very sharp spines: Sloane's 'great long-prickled sea-egg'. (*Diadema antillarum.*)

1952 FGC StE, StM /sii-niigl, sii-niidl/.

SEAN FISH see SEINE FISH 1.

SEA-PLATE sb.

1756 Browne 394, Echinus 7..The Sea-Plate, or flat Sea-Egg.

SEA PLOVER sb.

1725 Sloane 319, Totanus dorso fusco albis maculis notato..The Sea Plover.

SEA POLICEMAN sb; cf POLICEMAN. The fish also called LEATHER-COAT.

1892 Cockrell list, Sea policeman, *Oligoplites saurus.*

SEA POTATO sb dial. =SEA-SIDE POTATO.

1952 FGC StM, Sea potato take out dead flesh from bad sore.

SEA-PRICK sb dial; cf *OED prick, sb* 17. A sea-cucumber. Also called SEA-BANANA.

1952 FGC StM, StT.

SEA-PUSS sb dial; <*sea*+PUSS; perh also infl by the last syllable of *octopus.* The SEA-CAT.

1943 *GL* West, Sea puss, octopus. 195 2FGC Port /sii pus/

SEA RAT-BAT sb dial; <*sea*+RAT-BAT. =BAT-FISH.

1952 FGC StC, StJ.

SEARCH-MY-HEART sb dial.

1. The herb *Rytidophyllum tomentosum,* used in 'tea' and believed to be good for the heart.

1893 Sullivan 114, Search-my-heart (in herb tea). 1927 Beckwith 26, Search-me-heart. For a fluttering heart, drink as tea. 1952 FGC Port, StAnn, StT /sorch-mi-haat/; StM, Tre /saach-mi-haat/ good heart medicine, nice tea, for pain in stomach.

2. A swallow of rum.

1907 Reynolds 18, Sammy resumed his position and produced the vial and after cock-eye Jimmy had swallowed a 'Sarch me heart' followed by a 'raise me toughts', he became greatly mollified.

SEA-ROACH[1] see SEA COCKROACH.

SEA-ROACH[2] sb dial. The COCKROACH LOBSTER. *BA*

1952 FGC StJ.

SEA ROSE sb obs; cf *OED* in diff sense. The fossil remains of a sea urchin or star-fish.

1696 Sloane 2, Lapidis astroiditis sive stellaris..*Sea Rose.*

SEA-SCORPION sb dial; cf *OED* in diff sense. = Sea centipede.

1952 FGC Port, StC, StE, StM, Tre /sii skáapyan/ bite and scratch.

SEA-SCRATCH sb dial; <*sea*+SCRATCH. A jelly-fish, Portuguese man-o'-war, sea-nettle, or other sea animal which 'stings' or sharply irritates the skin.

1952 FGC StE /síi skrách/ bladder or sea-cowitch.

SEA-SIDE BALSAM sb bot. See quots.

1756 Browne 347, CROTON 2. The small Sea-side Balsam. This plant is very common in the *Savannas* about Kingston: it is very hot and pungent upon the palate; and frequently used in baths and fomentations for nervous weaknesses..CROTON 4. The Sea-side Balsam. On breaking the more tender branches of any of these species, a large drop of thick balsamic liquor ouzes from the wound; from whence they have obtained this appellation. 1955 *WIMJ* 158, *Croton humilis*..Pepper Rod; Small Seaside Balsam.

SEA-SIDE BEAN sb. Any of several beans (see quots) growing beside the sea: the SEA-BEAN and others.

1837 Macfadyen 292, Purple-flowered Sea-side Bean; *ibid* 287, *Dolichos luteus.* Yellow Sea-side Bean. 1864 Grisebach 781, Seaside Bean: *Canavalia obtusifolia* and *Vigna luteola.*

SEA-SIDE BEECH sb arch or obs; *OED* 1777 (ref Ja) only. The tree *Exostema caribæum.*

1811 Titford Expl to Plate x 9, Caribbæan Bark, *C[inchona] Caribæa,* is called in Jamaica, Sea-side Beech. 1814 Lunan I 391, It grows near the sea-shore, and is called in Jamaica *sea-side beech.* 1864 Grisebach 781.

SEA-SIDE CANARY sb dial. *Dendroica petechia*; also called CHIPPIN' CHICK; see quot.

1956 Jeffrey-Smith 85, The Golden Warbler..is found by the seaside, and well merits its local name of Seaside Canary, Mangrove Warbler, and Mangrove Canary.

SEA-SIDE GERMANDER sb bot. *Stemodia maritima*; also called BASTARD GERMANDER.

1814 Lunan I 61. 1864 Grisebach 784.

SEA-SIDE JASMINE sb arch or obs. The flowering tree *Plumieria alba.*

1826 Williams 295–6, The rocks [somewhere in Portland parish] were lined with curious grotesque-looking trees.. they bore a large beautiful white flower, which is called here the sea-side jasmine. 1827 Hamel I 303, Oh he was sweet, like sea-side jessamine.

SEA-SIDE LAUREL sb. =SOAP PLANT.

1814 Lunan II 154, Sea-Side Laurel. Xylophylla [4 species listed]. 1920 Fawcett 261.

SEA-SIDE MAHOE sb. *BA*

1. *Hibiscus tiliaceus*; see quots.

1837 Macfadyen 69, Hibiscus tiliaceus. *Sea-side Mahoe*.. The bark affords a strong fibre equal to hemp or flax. 1926 Fawcett 141. 1941 Swabey 25, Mahoe, Seaside.. This is a small tree which yields a wood of purplish colour, variegated and having a satiny lustre.

2. *Thespesia populnea.*

1864 Grisebach 785. 1926 Fawcett 145.

SEA-SIDE OX-EYE sb bot; *OED* ref only 1866. The plant *Borrichia arborescens.*

1801 Dancer 368, Baths, or Fomentations..These may be made of the Leaves of Limes..Sea Side Ox-Eye (Bupth. marit.) a fine aromatic—etc. 1864 Grisebach 786. 1936 Fawcett 226.

SEA-SIDE PLUM TREE sb bot obs. See quot. This is the same as Macfadyen's MOUNTAIN PLUM; the division of species is no longer recognized; thus this is *Ximenia americana.*

1814 Lunan II 155–6, Sea-Side Plum Tree. *Ximenia*.. 1. Americana..2. Inermis.

SEA-SIDE POTATO sb. The plant *Ipomœa pes-capræ,* which grows along the sea-side and resembles the sweet-potato.

1801 Dancer 358, Sea-Side Potatoe Slip (Convolvulus brasiliens). Decoction of the Root in Dropsy. 1864 Grisebach 787. 1952 FGC StAnn, Seaside potato.

SEA-SIDE PURSLANE sb. The plant *Sesuvium portulacastrum.*

1801 Dancer 367, Gargles and Mouth Waters..Sea-Side Purslane (Sesuv. Portulac).—Decoction. 1864 Grisebach 787. 1952 FGC Han /síisaid pósl/ like land- /posl/ [i.e. pussley].

SEA-SIDE REED sb.

1756 Browne 138, Arundo 3. Erecta minor..the Sea-side Reed.

SEA(-SIDE) THYME sb. See quot 1955.

1943 *GL* Man, Po man fren, sea thyme. 1955 *WIMJ* 77, *Evolvulus arbuscula*..Sea(side) Thyme. This plant, a tea bush in its own right, is sometimes sold in the markets to the unwary as Poor Man's Friend (*Stylosanthes viscosa*). It is said to make a very pleasant beverage which is 'good for the heart, wind and belly-ache'.

SEA SOLDIER sb dial; <*sea*+SOLDIER. A soldier crab said to live in the sea.

1952 FGC StJ, Sea-soldier—same as land soldier, but would die on land. 1961 FGC StC, same.

SEASON sb[1]; cf *OED* 11b, 1707→. Cf also *DA. BA T*

1. A period of rainfall lasting one or more days that makes the ground fit to plant in; also the rain itself that falls seasonally.

1707 Sloane xxxii, These Seasons, as they are call'd, from their being fit to Plant in, are generally so over the whole Island..In the month of January is likewise expected a Season or Rain but this is not so constant nor violent as are the other two [*sc* May and October]. 1790 Moreton 38, At which time the rains, (or seasons as they are called) set in, and violently fall. 1817 Williamson ii 81, We had frequent and heavy rains during the month, as are usually expected under the name of October seasons. 1823 Roughley 241, The April and May seasons, (or showery weather). 1839 McMahon 248, On such low lands..the May seasons set in before the trash has been turned.

2. Weather favourable to planting. *G*

1952 FGC StT, A good season—a mingling of rain and sun; StM [Weather prov:] Rain and sun is good season.

3. Attrib.

1952 FGC StC, A season rain.

SEASON sb[2] chiefly dial; <*seasoning*. Any seasoning used in cooking or added to prepared food. *BL*

1877 Murray *Feedin' 'Perrit* 13, Liza, wha mek dis sesin [herring sauce] rancid so. It nuff to pisen a man. 1952 FGC Port /siizn/ said of thyme; StAnd, soup-season: skellion, thyme, etc.

SEASONING vbl sb and vb intr; cf *OED* 1d (quot 1c 1774 belongs here as first quot). *G*

A. vbl sb: The process of acclimatization to the West Indies.

1739 Leslie 328, Almost half of the new imported Negroes die in the Seasoning. 1790 Beckford II 283, The dread of seasoning, as it is called, has, I think, a visible effect upon the spirits of every stranger who visits the country.

B. vb intr: To become acclimatized.

1835 Senior 124, Unless..he [a newly arrived person] has no means of *seasoning* in the cooler part of the island.

SEA-SPONGE sb dial. A sponge found in the sea. *BA*

1952 FGC StAnn /síi-pónj/.

SEA-STING sb dial.

1. Some kind of irritating jelly-fish.

1961 FGC StC /sii-sting—bloba/.

2. Some kind of sea-worm that causes itching or stings the skin.

1952 FGC StJ /sii-sting/.

SEASTO sb obs; an anglicized form of *siesta* (the only form recorded in dictionaries) which prob indicates an actual early pronunc. Note use of *-o,* taken by English speakers as the mark of a Spanish word. (Cf *OED -ado* 2.)

1679 Trapham 59, I would change the times of eating in England, and that because of the too near heating Sun at high noon more inclining to a Seasto than anything else.

SEA-THIMBLE sb dial; descr. A small blue sea mollusc of the genus *Buccinum.*

1952 FGC StM /sii-timbl/.

SEA-TICK sb dial. =SEA COCKROACH.

1952 FGC StM /sii-tiks/—suck to fish; has joints and broad tail.

SEA-UNICORN sb obs; cf *OED* in diff sense. A saw-fish.

1774 Long II 72, A few years ago, a *Sierra Marina,* or sea-unicorn, was caught.

SEA-WASP sb dial.

1. The sea-nettle.

1952 FGC StT /síi-wás/ sea cowitch.

2. Some sort of jelly-fish?

1952 FGC StAnn /sii-was/ like jelly-fish, soft but in a case.

SEAWNY sb dial rare; etym unknown.

1943 *GL* Clar, Seawny, sugar.

SEA YAM sb dial. =GUINEA YAM (brought across the sea?).

1952 FGC StC /gini yam/ = /sii yam/—big, white inside.

SEBLEJACK see SUPPLE-JACK.

SECKEY see *seki.*

SECOND BREAKFAST sb now rural. See quots.

1802 Nugent 72, Had fruit for the children at 10; then second breakfast a little after 11.—Dined at 3. 1808 Stewart 190–1, The ladies here..sit down to breakfast about nine, or past it, have what they call second breakfast at twelve, dine at three or four, and drink tea at eight; but seldom eat much, if any supper..The meal called second breakfast is the most favourite..This meal has something peculiar in it. It must consist of certain favourite viands..This must be eaten with the assistance of the fingers alone; for knives and forks are on this occasion proscribed! In short, so fond are the ladies in general of this second breakfast, that they would.. relinquish all the other three, rather than part with this one. 1862 Clutterbuck 3, Snoring on the sofa after second breakfast (*Anglice,* lunch). 1958 DeC StT, Second breakfast = lunch (in contrast to MORNING-BREAKFAST).

SECOND COCK-CROW sb. About I A.M.

1826 Barclay 317, see COCK-CROW. 1873 Rampini 152, But immediately after second cock-crow is no uncommon hour for starting, especially when the day's journey is likely to be a long one.

SECOND GANG sb obs. The gang of slaves of medium strength—cf FIRST GANG, THIRD GANG.

1793 Edwards II 128–9, The second gang is composed of young boys and girls, women far gone with child, and convalescents, who are chiefly employed in weeding the canes, and other light work adapted to their strength. 1796 *Braco* 27 June, First Gang Digging Cane Holes on No 10. Second Gang Cutting plants on Rybona piece. 1823 Roughley 102. 1839 McMahon 117.

SECOND TABLE sb dial. In a pocomania service, the second phase, when the Bible is removed, fallen angels are invoked, and trumping and possessions follow.

1953 Moore 104.

SEE vb formally imperative, functionally demonstr. Introducing an adv of place, esp in certain phrases, of which the most frequent are: *See it here* (Here it is); *See him there* (There he is); etc. *BL G*

1877 Murray *Kittle* 15, Da de piece o' red herrin'..no see it ya, sar. [*That piece of red herring..here it is sir, don't you see?*]. 1907 Jekyll 192, Whe me lover dé? See-mya, see-mya. 1943 Bennett 14, Se' seat yah ole lady. [*Look, here's a seat, old lady.*] 1958 Mc StE /sii it dong dé so/ *There it is down there. Ibid* /sii it hou it blak-op/ *Look how black the sky's getting.*

SEED sb dial.

1. A single banana or plantain fruit; =FINGER.

1952 FGC Port, Jacob [banana] resemble fig [banana], but seed bigger; red banana—very big seed, bunch small; StT, Horse plantain has few seeds but very stout. 1956 Mc StE /dat wan tiela banaana—di siid av it big/.

2. The sucker which springs from the root of a banana or other crop plant, and is planted for the next crop; similarly a sugar-cane top.

1956 Mc Clar /siid/—banana sucker; StT, cabbage of the cane (sheath from which leaves come) is planted..It is also called the /siid/.

3. The testicles. *BA BL G*

1956 Mc Clar /ram pus—hav di siid/ /ram guot—dat we hav di siid heng doun/.

SEED-SEED sb dial; iterative. A great quantity of small seeds or things like seeds.

1952 FGC StE, Guinea corn, bear like seed-seed; StAnd, Chi-chi, live in wood, make seed-seed in you furniture. [The fecal pellets of termites.]

SEED-UNDER-LEAF sb dial. The medicinal weed *Phyllanthus niruri*. Also called CARRY-ME-SEED.

1952 FGC StAnd /siid-onda-liif/. 1954 *WIMJ* 31, Carry-me-seed; Seed-underleaf; Quinine weed.

SEED-YAM sb. A general term for any type of yam (all white yams) which bear seeds on the vine. *G*

1794 Barham 116, The plant..will have sometimes fifty knobs of different magnitude, just like the white seed-yam in Jamaica. *Ibid* 211–12, Two sorts of white, one of which is called the seed-yam, which is extraordinary white, and makes an admirable fine flour. 1952 FGC Han, Seed yam; StT, Seed yam includes renta, white, St Vincent, Mozella, and hard.

SEE JEE-JEE-COBER dial; cf *see-saw*, *jiji-* (as in *jiji-waina*) + *cober* < *come over*. To suggest a rocking motion. (In the song the rat gets across the flooding river on a piece of deal board.)

1951 Murray 48 [Song:] Me jump pon de deal bud Me see jee-jee-cober.

SEE-ME-CONTRACT see *simi-kantrak*.

sefwe vb dial; reduced from some such phr as *get safe away* or *take oneself away*, coinciding with Sp *se fue*. To make one's escape; to run away. *BL*

1956 BLB Man /az dem mek aata im, ing sefwe a bush/ [*As they made after him, he escaped into the bush*].

SEGRA-SEED sb; cf *OED*, 'Perh. a native W. Indian name'. =ANTIDOTE (COCOON), SABO.

1864 Grisebach 787, Segra-seed: *Feuillea cordifolia*. 1954 *WIMJ* 30, Segra Seed.

SEH see *se*.

SEINE FISH sb; *OED*: *obs. BA*

1. =SEA-GALLIWASP.

1725 Sloane 284.

2. A fish caught in a seine.

1952 FGC StT, Seine-fish, fish caught in net.

seki sb dial arch; cf Ewe *asíke*, concubine. A female tramp? (The meaning is becoming vague.)

1948 Bennett 1, Every seckey got him jeggeh [182:] *Every beggar has his bundle of rags.* 1958 DeC StAnd, StT /seki/—woman; word now..seldom heard..except in the common proverb /ebri seki tu dem boki/.

SELF[1] /self/ in cpds usu /sef/ pronom adj and adv dial; <*self*, *OED* 1a, →1579. *G*

A. adj: As an intensifier usu in negative const, following the noun: (not) even, itself, himself, etc. *BA T*

1877 Murray *Kittle* 21, 'Him no hab no cow?' 'No maam..Him no hab a cow horn ya self, misis.' 'Him hab sheep, dough?' 'Him no hab none, maam..Him no hab a piece o sheep wool self.' 1912 McK *Ballads* 49, How you sell wha' no wut gill self to black naygur for a bob. 1952 FGC StAnd /grábl sélf kyáang háada/ *Not even gravel is harder.* 1956 BLB Man /Mieri sef maita en waan go/ *Even Mary may have wanted to go.*

B. adv: Similarly, following a verb or participle: (not) even.

1907 Jekyll 259 [Song:] Not if the pork even purchase self Take it away for your labour. [*Not even if it was bought pork*, etc.]

SELF[2] pronom adj dial; <*self*, *OED* 1b, →1848: 'Now only *arch. rare.*' As an intensifier, preceding the noun: very same, self-same. *G T*

1960 FGC current: Is the self man do it, *It's that very man who did it.*

SELF-HEAL sb; cf *OED*, for diff plants. The medicinal herb *Ruellia paniculata*.

a 1726 Barham (1794) 171, Self-heal, or Alheal. See PICKERING'S HERB. 1801 Dancer 367, Self-Heal, or All-Heal..Decoction with Honey and Vinegar. 1854–5 *TJSA* 1 66, Christmas Pride, Self-heal. Ruellia paniculata.

SELF-HEATER sb. A kind of pressing iron in which charcoal is burned, with a chimney-like spout in front—still widely used by tailors, etc.

1956 Mc StE, StJ /self híita, selfíita/.

SELINA see SALINA.

SELL vb intr dial. To sell something to (someone). (The thing sold is not mentioned.) *G T*

1952 FGC StM [Boy asking gasoline-station attendant for service:] Sell me, no, man?

SEMEN CONTRA, SEMICONTRA, SEMOCONTRAC see *simi-kantrak.*

SEMPER VIVA see next.

SEMPERVIVE sb; <Lat *semper vivens*, ever living; cf *OED* '→1764, of the houseleek. The Ja forms begin with Trapham's but in folk speech very great alterations (phonetic and folk-etym) have come about; for forms see quots.

The plant *Aloes vulgaris*, valued for medicinal and household uses.

[1657 Ligon 99, The leaves of this Plant [Aloes], (which we call *semper vivens* in England, and growes neer the fire in Kitchins, hung up to a beam, with an oyl'd clout about the root)..is the best medicine in the world for a burn.] 1679 Trapham 106, A bitter sup of the juice of the Sempervive simple. 1696 Sloane 117, Aloe Dioscorid.. *Sempervive.* In Barbados, Jamaica, & Caribeis Insulis. a 1726 Barham (1794) 174, The leaf of Silk Grass is not so thick and juicy as semper vive, but much longer. 1740 Importance 36, Of Aloes there are different sorts. The *Semper vivum*, from whence the Gum comes that is used in Medicine. 1893 Sullivan 122, Slice, or rather split the leaves of semprevivy: roast them..etc. 1927 Beckwith 27, Sinkle-Bible (Semper viva). 1943 *GL* Port, StAnd, Sinklebible, Singlebible, Simplebible—Simpavievy, Sympaviver. 1952 FGC Port /sìngkaváivl, sìmpaváivis/; StAnn, StM, StT /singkl-baibl/; StT /singgl-baibl/; StAnd /síntl-báibl/. 1954 *WIMJ* 28.

SEMPREVIVY see prec.

SEND-OUT sb dial. Something newly sent out; specif, of a plant, a newly developed variety released to cultivators.

1952 FGC Tre /dat banaana de—iz a nyuu send-out/.

SENNA sb obs; cf *OED* s.v. *Senna*, Wild, 1866→. *Cæsalpinia pulcherrima*, now called BARBADOS PRIDE, etc. *G*

1792 Edwards 12, O'er the fragrant hedge..blows The crimson sena. *The botanic name is *poinciana.* It is commonly known by the name of Barbados pride. Sir Hans Sloane calls it *sena spuria*..or bastard sena.

SENSA see next.

SENSAY FOWL /sénsè/ sb chiefly dial; <Twi *asɛnsé*, a hen without a tail, a fowl with curled ruffled feathers. A variety of chicken having sparse, ruffled and uneven feathers. See quots for its relation to obeah. *BL G*

1929 Beckwith 120, 'If you promise sensay fowl anyt'ing, him wi' look fe it', is a saying which warns one to keep one's promises in an obeah transaction. 'Keep sensay fowl fe pick obeah', is the saying; and this means that if one 'plants' obeah, the ruffled fowl will 'dig it out'. 1934 Williams 34, Throughout the 'bush' there is a peculiar type of fowl with ruffled feathers and half-naked neck as if they had been partially plucked. The 'picknies' call them peel-neck, i.e. bald-neck, since peel-head means bald. These are technically known as senseh fowl. 1943 *GL* Kgn, Man, StJ, Sensay, Sensa, Sen-seh—ragged fowl. 1952 FGC gen /sense/.

sense (foul), SENSEH see prec.

SENSIBLE GRASS sb obs; cf *OED sensible* 10, 1725. The weed *Mimosa pudica*, now called SHAME-LADY, etc.

1725 Sloane 58, Sensible-Grass..It is so very sensible, that a Puff of Wind from your Mouth will make Impressions on it.

SENSIBLE TREE sb obs; cf *OED sensible* 10 The sensitive tree *Calliandra portoricensis.*

1696 Sloane 153, Mimosa arborea..Sensible Tree. Locis Red hills dictis copiose crescit.

SENSITIVE sb bot obs. *BL G*

1756 Browne 253–4, Mimosa 8..the larger smooth Sensitive..Mimosa 10..The..large-leafed Sensitive.. etc.

S'EP ME KING see KING.

SEPRE sb; cf Ewe *seblee*, thick, plump. A variety of the MAIDEN PLANTAIN.

1934 *Ja. Times* 19 May, see *fiekuma.*

SEPTEMBER PETCHARY sb. The grey petchary. (It migrates from Jamaica at the end of September and in early October.)

1952 FGC StT /septémba pichíeri/. 1960 E. S. Panton in *Gleaner* 7 May, The gray petchary or 'September'.

S'ER see SISTER quot 1912.

serimuon vb dial; evid a back-form from *ceremony*, blended with *moan* or *mourn.*

1943 *GL* Kgn, Serremone, to grieve over. 1956 BLB Man /salimuon/ to mourn.

SEROUCI see CERASEE.

SERREMONE see *serimuon.*

SERVICE MAN sb dial.

1958 DeC Port /sovis man/ a name for an obeah man.

sese /sésé/ sb dial; an iterative form of Twi *sè*, to say, tell; mention, speak of, redup *sise* (but whether the iteration came about in Jamaica or was from the African form is unknown). Quarrelling; a quarrel or argument. *BL*

1943 *GL* StJ, Sesseh, quarrel; No addr, Say-Say, quarrelling. 1956 Mc Clar /sese—kanfyuzhan/; Port /yu gwain faas in di piipl-dem sese/ *Are you going to interfere in these people's argument?*

SESSEH see prec.

SESUMBER see SUSUMBA.

SET vb¹ dial; cf *OED* 59.

1. To put or apply the supposed powers of OBEAH; also const *on, upon, for. BL G*

1793 Edwards II 93, When a Negro is robbed of a fowl or a hog, he applies directly to the Obeah man or woman; it is then made known among his fellow Blacks, that *Obi is set* for the thief; and as soon as the latter hears the dreadful news, his terrified imagination begins to work..he presently falls into a decline..etc. 1826 Barclay 191, see SHADOW CATCHER.

2. Specif. In the phr *set duppy.*

1942 Bennett 34, Yuh Dan set him grampa Duppy pon Sta Rose. [*Your Dan made his grandfather's ghost haunt Sister Rose.*] 1954 LeP StT /set dopi/ to have a spell or curse put upon one's enemy.

3. To prepare (drums) to recall dead spirits.

1953 Moore 126, Set the drums—to take the drums for a Cumina ceremony to the dancing floor, feed rum to the gods and other zombies..etc.

SET vb² dial. To take or perform (an intentional or prepared action).

1907 Jekyll 106, Annancy set a run with his bill chop at Cow neck.

SET sb obs; also attrib. **s.**

1. A group of girls (or others) dressed alike for the Christmas celebrations of the end of the 18th and early 19th centuries: see quots. The sets appear to have been introduced from the French islands, esp Haiti; they supplemented

and to some extent became mingled with the JOHN CANOE Christmas celebration; though the sets sought elegance in costume, dancing, singing, and general behaviour, whereas John Canoe was grotesque, wild, farcical and often disordered. (For fullest descriptions see 1816 Lewis (1845) 25–8; 1833 Scott I 346–52, and 1837 Belisario.)

1825 De la Beche 41, Many of the [negro] girls form themselves into what they call sets, in which the dresses are nearly alike; these sets travel preceded by flags, drums, and other music, from estate to estate, dancing at the houses of the white people, and in the negro villages, where they are given money, and very often entertained. 1826 Barclay 11, The young girls..form what they call 'a sett'..they..take the name of Blue Girls, Yellow Girls, &c. according to the dress and ribbon they have chosen. The airs they sing and dance to are simple and lively.

2. Attrib in *Set-girls*: the girls composing sets.

1837 Belisario Expl to Plate 2, Order of Procession of the Set Girls. Four Grand Masters to protect the Set. Adjutant bearing Flag. Hand-drum. Singer. Tambourine [etc., etc.] Commodore. Set Girls in equal numbers.

SET THE CHARGE vb phr; *OED set v* 86 →1770. To establish the cost; see quot. *G*

1961 Katzin 3, The passenger fare is fixed by a government agency, the Transport Board, but the driver sets the charge for the load..There is a customary charge for each market basket, hand basket, crocus bag, and bailing of a certain size.

SETTING-STICK sb dial. The stick which holds a CALABAN raised when the trap is set.

1952 FGC Man, The calaban is held up by a /setn stik/.

SETTLER sb. One who cultivates on a small scale, as distinct from a planter. Cf SMALL-SETTLER. *G*

1756 Browne 22, The inhabitants of this Island..whom I shall class into planters, settlers, merchants, and dependents; the most natural distinctions to communicate a satisfactory idea of the colony.

SET-UP sb dial; <*set*, sit +*up*; but cf *DAE setting up* 1. A wake or similar observance for the dead; the customs vary locally: see quots. For distribution of variant terms, see DeC map in 1961 *CLS* 72. *BL G T*

1952 Kerr 133 Death rituals:..The following contrasting attitudes to a 'set up' illustrate this point. 1952 FGC Han /sét-op/—wake, the first night a person is dead. 1956 Mc Man /set-op nait/—the parties held immediately after the death and again on the ninth night (the former now rarely observed). StAnd /di set-op iz wen sombady ded an duon beri yet/. 1958 DeC Port /set-op/—here meaning an all-night religious meeting the night before building the tomb (about a year after the death). Tre, The /set-op/ [is] on the first night [after the death], when there is usually no singing in this district. See also SILENCE WAKE, SINGING-MEETING.

SET UP vb phr intr; cf *OED set* 154 n; cf BLACK UP vb². Of rain-clouds: To get ready to come down as rain. *BA BL G*

1952 FGC StT, Clouds are setting up; West, Rain is setting up. c 1954 Reckord *Della* sc 5 typescript 17, It set up for rain. Storm going bus' tonight.

SEVEN-FINGER sb dial. An occasional variant form of the plant FIVE-FINGER (*Syngonium auritum*) in which two additional leaflets develop. The name is also applied loosely to other climbing plants with divided leaves.

[1814 Lunan I 298, Arum..auritum..The leaf has three lobes in the young plant, but, as it acquires age and strength, throws forth ears from the outward leaves, until it has frequently seven divisions, the hinder ones appearing like spurs to the others.] 1952 FGC StM, Seven-finger—Coco wis, China wis, wicker wis, etc.

SEVEN-MONTHS COCO sb dial. = MINTY COCO.

1952 FGC StT /sevm mons/—Minty coco.

SEVEN-STAR RAIN sb dial. A light, misty rain falling in June, of no use to the crops. (Referring to the Pleiades or some other constellation?)

1957 MacE. Leach.

SEVEN-YEAR PEAS sb now bot; *OED* only quot 1672. GUNGU PEAS.

a 1726 Barham (1794) 142, Pigeon peas..will keep bearing so for many years, which makes some call them seven-year pease. 1814 Lunan II 64. 1955 *WIMJ* 157, *Cajanus cajan*..Gungo Pea; Christmas Pea; Angola Pea; Seven-year Pea.

SEVEN-YEAR VINE sb; *OED* 1864; cf SEVEN-YEAR PEAS, and quot 1814. *Ipomœa tuberosa*.

1756 Browne 155–6, Ipomea 6. See SPANISH ARBOUR-VINE. 1774 Long III 804, Seven-year Vine..*Ipomea heptadactyla*..etc. 1814 Lunan I 400, This plant is called the *seven-year*..*vine* the leaves..have seven lobes, from whence it may probably have been called *seven-eared*, instead of *seven-yeared*, vine. 1864 Grisebach 787.

SEVILLE-SWEET ORANGE sb. = BITTER-SWEET ORANGE.

SEWI-SEWI, SEWY-SEWY see *swii-swii*.

SEY see *se*.

seya sb dial uncom; evid = *sayer*, one who says. An obeah-man.

1956 Mc Clar /obya man, guzu man, seya, fuo yai man/.

SEYMOUR GRASS sb; see quot 1915. The pasture grass *Andropogon pertusus*.

1915 H. H. Cousins in *Gleaner* I Sept, The introduction of this grass into Jamaica was apparently accidental..As the credit for recognizing and proving its practical agricultural utility in Jamaica is due to Mr G. Seymour Seymour of Retreat Pen..it is proposed to call the grass, which at present possesses no local name, 'Seymour Grass'. 1952 FGC StAnn, StT. 1954 *FG* 217.

SHABERS adj dial uncom; etym obscure, cf *OED shab*, a low fellow.

1943 *GL*, Shabers, not good company.

SHAD sb; *OED*: fish of genera *Alosa*, (US) *Dorosoma*. Applied in Jamaica to various small fish—see quots. *BA*

1892 Cockrell list, Shad = silverfish: *Gerres zebra*, *G. harengulus*. 1951 Smith in *NHN* 140, Shad—Jamaican name for a young Mojarra.

SHADBARK sb chiefly dial; <*shagbark*—cf *OED* 1691–6→, which also is in use in Ja. The tree *Pithecellobium alexandri*.

1920 Fawcett 148, Shag Bark, Shad Bark, Tamarind Shad Bark. 1941 Swabey 30, Shadbark..This is one of our most useful timber trees. ['Shagbark' not mentioned.] 1949 Forbes 54, The untidy shadbark tree. 1952 FGC StAnn, StE, StM, Tre—shadbark (5 instances), shagbark (once).

[**SHADDOCK (TREE)** sb; see quot 1707. The largest of the citrus fruits (and the tree it grows on): *Citrus decumana*. *BA G T*

1696 Sloane 212, Malus arantia, fructu rotundo maximo pallescente humanum caput excedente..The Shaddock Tree. In hortis & agris Insularum Jamaicæ & Barbados. 1707 Sloane 41, In Barbados the Shaddocks surpass those of Jamaica in goodness. The seed of this was first brought to Barbados by one Captain Shaddock, Commander of an East-India Ship, who touch'd at that Island in his Passage to England, and left the Seed there.]

SHADOW sb; cf *OED* 7. Formerly, a part of one's soul, in African belief thought to be manifested during life by one's shadow; now confused or combined with the concept of the DUPPY or spirit of a dead person: 'ghost'. *G N*

1826 Barclay 191, see SHADOW-CATCHER. 1877 Murray *Kittle* 10, Den if you no prinkle de fowl da me grabe, you want ebel perit fe go catch my shadder (shadow). Unno! 1895 Banbury 19, The mialman harms by depriving persons of their 'shadows' or setting the 'deaths' upon them. It is believed that after the shadow of anyone is taken he is never healthy; and if it be not caught, he must pine away until he dies. The shadow when taken is carried and nailed to the cotton tree. 1929 Beckwith 98, 'The soul goes to heaven, and it's not the body [that makes the duppy], for we know that goes away into the earth, but it's the shadow'. 1952 Kerr 131, He said that every man has two shadows, a good shadow and an evil one. The evil shadow will lure the good one away..bind [it]..etc. 1954 LeP StAnn, Shedda—ghost or spirit of a dead person.

SHADOW-CATCHER sb; cf *OED* in diff sense. A mialman or obeah-man, who professed to catch people's SHADOWS; see quots.

1826 Barclay 191 [At the trial of an obeahman in St David's parish:] One of the witnesses, a negro belonging to the same estate, was asked—'Do you know the prisoner to be an obeah-man?' '*Ees, massa, shadow-catcher, true.*' 'What do you mean by a shadow-catcher?' '*Him ha coffin*, (a little coffin produced,) *him set for catch dem shadow.*' 'What shadow do you mean?' '*When him set obeah for summary* (somebody), *him catch dem shadow and dem go dead*'; and too surely they were soon dead, when he pretended to have caught their shadows.

SHADOW-CATCHING vbl sb. Releasing a SHADOW that has been bound by obeah and restoring it to its owner.

1895 Banbury 23, The person suspected of having lost his shadow was taken to the cotton tree where it was spell bound, or to which it was 'nailed', as the people expressed it. The mialmen were accompanied thither by a large concourse of people. The victim was dressed all in white, with a white kerchief about his head. Eggs and fowls were taken along with cooked food to the cotton tree. The mialmen paraded up and down before the tree, with white cloths over their shoulders, singing and dancing; and all the people joining in the chorus. Alternately the cotton tree was pelted with eggs, and the necks of fowls rung off, and their bodies cast at it..the song and dancing proceeded more vigorously as the shadow began to make signs of leaving the tree. A white basin, with water to receive it, was held up..they all of a sudden caught up the person, and ran home, with him, affirming that the shadow was caught, covered up in a basin. Upon reaching home a cloth was wet in the water, and applied to the head of the patient and the shadow was said to be restored. This is the process of shadow-catching, for this piece of work they exacted six dollars, and were always readily paid.

SHADOW-TAKING sb. Capturing someone's SHADOW. (The distinction made here was not generally adhered to.)

1895 Banbury 19, In connection with shadow-taking is *shadow-catching*. That is, restoring the shadow to the person who had been deprived of it.

SHAGBARK see SHADBARK.

SHAGGY BUTTON-WEED see BUTTON-WEED.

SHAG-UP-MAN sb dial or slang; cf Engl slang *shag* = copulate, hence *shagged up*, exhausted: Partridge, etc.

1958 DeC Man /shag-op-man/ a lazy, no-account, worthless man.

SHAKA sb dial; 1837→ shaka; 1929 shakey; 1953 shaker; the normal reflex of Engl *shaker* in the folk speech would be /shieka/, or poss /sheka/; this word may have some infl, but *shaka* must be primarily from one or more African sources—cf Yoruba *shɛkɛre*, gourd, Hausa *chaki*, a rattle (Dalziel 13); Hause (20–1) derives such forms < *shagshag* (Arabic and Moorish).

A rattle made usually of a calabash on a stick, with JOHN-CROW BEADS or other seeds inside, used as a musical instrument—cf the Sp-Amer *maraca*. *BL*

1837 Belisario Expl to Plate 7, Shaka—a rattle used by the French Set Dancers. 1929 Beckwith 148, These two [drums]..are further supported by 'shakeys', held in a hand of each dancer and consisting in a gourd fastened to the end of a stick and filled with the shot-like seed of the wild canna or with small stones. 1952 FGC StAnd /shaka/—rattle made of gourd. 1953 Moore 172, The shaker, made from a gourd set on a stick; gloss /shakir/ a gourd rattle used in Cumina. 1956 Mc Port /shaka/ gourd shaken as accompaniment to calypso dancing.

SHAKA BIRD sb dial; < SHAKA + *bird*. A small bird (unidentified); see quot.

1952 FGC StT /shaka bord/ eats seeds of the shaka-bush; like goldfinch, but smaller.

SHAKA-BUSH sb dial; < SHAKA + *bush*. Another name for RATTLEWEED.

1952 FGC StT /shaka-bush/.

SHAKE FOOT vb phr dial; cf *EDD shake a foot*, 2 (2), esp Scot, Irel. To dance; cf next.

1954 LeP StE, Me lub fe shake foot cān' done. *BL*

SHAKEFOOT sb dial. A lively or wild dance.

1943 *GL* Kgn, Shakefoot, dance. 1954 LeP StE, StT, General term for dance or wild party—Shake-foot: mek we go a de shake-foot tonight. 1956 Mc Man, A dance, un bal: shake foot. *G*

SHAKER, SHAKEY see SHAKA.

SHAKE-UP sb dial; cf SHAKEFOOT.

1956 Mc Man /shiek-op/ a dance.

SHAKY-SHAKY[1] see s.

SHAKY-SHAKY[2] sb dial; iterated and familiarized form of *shake* (*OED sb*[1] 3b, 'The shock of an earthquake. Now only U.S.').

1914 FGC StAnd, Shaky-shaky, an earthquake. 1943 *GL* Kgn, Shaky-shaky, earthquake.

shali adj dial; evid for *shelly*.

1958 DeC Tre /shali/ loose, crumbly. (Cf GUM.)

SHALL-I /shálai/ sb dial joc; abbr of s.w. English *shalligonaked*, 'a thin, flimsy garment; cloth of an inferior kind' (*EDD*); the sense is evid the unanswerable alternative to buying the cloth or wearing the garment. Perh also infl by *challis*, *challie*.

1943 *GL* StM, Shall I, cheap material. 1955 FGC Man /shálai/ cheap material; 'shall I wear it?'—can't do otherwise.

SHALLOW-BELCHER sb dial. A plant (unidentified).

1952 FGC West /shàlo-bélsha/ small tree with bright orange-coloured berries.

SHAMA-DOG see SHAMER-DOG.

SHAMA(R) see SHAMER.

SHAMBRY sb dial; etym obscure—but cf *shambles*, a market (*DAE*).

1943 *GL* StJ, Shambry, a market.

SHAME vb or adj dial; aphetic and inflectionless form of *ashamed*, but cf *OED shame v* 1. [Note: Since there is no formal distinction, vb and adj are virtually one. The separation of quots below is therefore somewhat arbitrary.]

A. vb: To feel shame, be ashamed. *BA BL G T*

1955 Bennett *Cricket History*, Wat a way dem musa shame! [*How ashamed they must be!*]

B. adj: Ashamed. (Cf use in plant names: see next.) *BA BL G T*

1877 Murray *Feedin' 'Perrit* 17, You no shame O! [*Aren't you ashamed!*] 1952 Kerr 132, If she saw the duppy of a relative she would tell it that it should be 'shame' to come back like that.

SHAME-A-LADY, SHAME BROWN LADY, SHAME-BUSH, SHAME-LADY, SHAME-OL'-LADY sb dial; <SHAME + *lady* and other elements. = Next. *BL*

c1915 FGC StAnd, StAnn /shíem-líedi/. 1942 *NHN* I 8 10, The 'Sensitive Plant', 'Shama', or 'Shame Brown Lady' as it is variously called.. the slightest touch causes its leaflets to close. 1952 FGC StT /shíem-ùol-líedi/. 1954 *FG* 588, Shame-bush. 1954 *WIMJ* 30, see SHAMER.

SHAMER /shiema/ sb chiefly dial; evid <*shamer*, one who is ashamed, bashful.

The common weed *Mimosa pudica*, which shuts its leaves together at the slightest touch. Also called DEAD-AND-WAKE; FINE SHAMER; SENSITIVE; SHAME BROWN LADY, SHAME-LADY, ~OL'-LADY, ~WEED; SHAMER-MACCA, ~WEED; SHAMY, ~BUSH, ~DARLIN', ~DOG, ~MACCA, ~MARY; SHECKEL-WEED; SHUT-WEED.

1912 McK *Songs* 14, De cowitch under which we hab fe 'toop, De shamar lyin' t'ick like pumpkin soup, Is killin' somet'ing. 1942 *NHN* I 8 10, see SHAME BROWN LADY. 1952 FGC Han, StAnn, StM, StT /shíema/. 1954 *WIMJ* 30, Shame Weed; Sensitive Plant; Shama; Shame-a-Lady; Shut Weed; Dead and Awake.

SHAMER-DOG sb dial; <SHAME + *-er* + *dog*. A dog which should be ashamed; a shameful dog.

1877 Murray *Feedin' 'Perrit* 17 [Song:] You no shame O! Fe go tief de carn beef, Shama-dog O!—Tiefin' puss O!

SHAMER-MACCA, SHAMER-WEED, SHAME-WEED sb dial. = SHAMER.

1920 Fawcett 134. 1952 FGC StAnn, StC /shíema-máka/; Han /shíema-wiid/. 1954 *WIMJ* 30, see SHAMER. 1954 *FG* 588, see SHAME-BUSH.

SHAMPATTA, SHAMPATTER, SHAMPLATA see *sampata*.

SHAMROCK see JAMAICA SHAMROCK.

SHAM-SHAM sb dial; cf Twi *o-siãm*, parched and ground corn; meal. Cognate with ASHAM; but cf also Twi *sàmsam*, sandy, crumbly.

1. Parched and ground corn; if mixed with sugar, = ASHAM.

1943 *GL* Clar, Sham-sham, grind [= ground] parched corn; Port, parched corn mixed with sugar. 1952 FGC StE /sham-sham/ made from corn: parch, beat, sieve it out, add sugar, beat again. 1956 Mc Man.

2. The scrapings from cassava bread; this may be made into porridge.

1943 *GL* Man, Sham sham, scrapings of cassava bread. 1959 Mrs E. B. Hoyes, Kgn, Cassava flour.. is made into what we call 'Bammies', these are scraped after baking and it is this scraping that is called 'Sham-sham'. Can be eaten just like that or made into porridge.

3. Transf.

1959 Mc StE (Accom) /sham-sham/ The leavings of anything, as the scraps of straw, bark, etc. left from basket-making and rope-making, the dust and bits of leaf left over from cigar-making, etc.

SHAMY(-BUSH) sb dial; <SHAME + Y, familiarizing suffix + BUSH. = SHAMER.

1952 FGC StT /shíemi-búsh/; StAnn /shiemi/.

SHAMY-DARLIN', SHAMY-DOG, SHAMY MACCA, SHAMY-MARY sb dial; <SHAMY + various other elements. = SHAMER.

1943 *GL* Kgn, Shamy macca, briar. 1952 FGC Port /shíemi-dáalin/; StT /shíemi-dáag/. 1956 Mc Port /shíemi-dáalin/; StT /shíemi-míeri/.

SHANDELAY sb dial; etym unknown—perh no more than a nonsense refrain: cf JUMP SHAMADOR. Some kind of dance or caper.

1924 Beckwith 172 [Song:] Massa Puss an' Massa Rat a jump shandelay, Oh, jump shandelay, jump shandelay.

SHAPE UP TO vb phr dial. To take a position facing or opposing (someone). *BA G*

1958 DeC Port, To face up to, to turn at bay [said of a dog:] /it neba shiep op tu mi ar eniting/.

SHARK WAITING-BOY sb dial. The type of small fish that attends on (or is 'driven' by) a shark. See quot, and cf BARRACOUTA SLAVE.

1892 Cockrell list, Shark waiting-boy, *elacate canada*.

SHARLOT sb dial; perh <*Charlotte* (cf LIZA).

1943 *GL* StM, Sharlot, shad.

SHARP-LEAVED BROOMWEED sb bot obs; cf BROOMWEED. In Macfadyen's use: *Sida glabra* (ident 1926 Fawcett 113).

1837 Macfadyen 81, Sida arguta. *Sharp-leaved Broom-weed.*

SHA-SHA see SHAY-SHAY.

SHA-SHWA SNAPPER sb dial; etym unknown, but cf *shwuwa*, *shuwa*, the sound of meal frying in water, and Kongo *shiɔshia*, to splutter in cooking. = DOG-TEETH SNAPPER.

1952 FGC StC /sháshwa snápa/.

SHAVE sb dial; for *shaver*, or by assoc with such words as *spokeshave*. A small tool similar to a plane, used to shave ice for SNOWBALL drinks. *G*

1956 BLB Man /di shiev dol/ *The ice-shaver is dull.*

SHAW-KAW vb dial rare; etym unknown.

1943 *GL* StC, Shăw-kăw, to obligate.

SHAY-SHAY /shíe-she, shé-she/ sb dial; iterated prob <Fr *chassé*, as in dancing—cf the US *sashay*. Cf also Twi *sàw*, Fante *saa*, dance. A lively vigorous dance that takes various forms; see quot 1929.

c1915 FGC StAnd [Song:] Me wi' dance de shay-shay, Me wi' dance de katreel—Me wi' dance till de whole a me foot-battam peel. 1929 Beckwith 214, The shay-shay, that erotic dance to jazz music which is supposed to have originated in Africa but which DeLisser thinks derived from a Spanish dance called *mento*, *bamboula*, or *chica* and which 'consists of slow movements of the body.. the dancer never allows the upper part of the body to move as she writhes or shuffles over the ground'.. The shay-shay is danced with a single partner and always to song. 1933 McK 317, Shey-shey: barbecue song and dance. 1943 *GL* Man, Shay-shay, An African dance still practised in the wild areas of the island; also Clar, Port, StJ, StM. 1954 LeP StE, Sha-sha—general term for dance or wild party. 1963 T. Murray UWI, Shay-shay is a kind of shuffle dance, rhythmical but not violent.

SHEBBY sb dial; <*chevy*, chevy chase (BLB). Some kind of children's game played at school.

1957 JN StT, Yes mam they play with me a play shebby and Ketch.

SHECKEL-WEED sb dial; prob <*shackle*: see *OED sb*[1], or perh *sb*[2] *dial* 1, stubble. The sensitive plant *Mimosa pudica*, which has sharp thorns that annoy the field worker.

1927 Beckwith 26, Sheckel-weed.

SHED vb dial; cf *OED* 1 d →1659. Of ears of Indian corn: to separate themselves from the stalk against which they are formed. *BA G*

1912 McK *Songs* 109, Lilly, lilly, t'rough de corn, Till de pod dem shed..* *Until the pods are formed.

SHEDDA see SHADOW.

shedi-shedi adj dial; iterative of *shed*+-*y*.

1958 DeC Port /shedi-shedi/ crumbly, lacking cohesion; one must add shop-flour to a dumpling to prevent it from being this.

SHEE see *shi*(-*shi*).

SHEEP-HEAD sb dial; cf *OED* appl to diff fish. *Lactophrys trigonus* and similar species.

1952 FGC StC, StE, StJ /shiip-hed/ trunkfish without horns. *BL N*

SHEEP-WOOL sb dial joc; transf to clothes (the wool on Ja sheep hangs in lumps and flocks).

1959 DeC Tre /shiip-wul/ old ragged work clothes.

SHEG vb dial slang; prob < *shag v*[1], to toss about, to shake, *OED* →1572; cf present Engl slang *shag*, to have sexual intercourse with.

1. To annoy, to provoke, to trouble.

1943 *GL* no addr, Sheg, provoke; StT, Sheg, to bother. 1958 DeC StM, Sheg, to humbug (a man).

2. See quot—sense not clear.

1943 *GL* Tre, Sheg, put off.

3. See quot.

1958 DeC StM, Sheg, to seduce (a woman).

SHEG-UP sb dial slang; cf SHEG. A trickster who pretends innocence of the game.

1943 *GL* West /sheg up/ one who knows the thing but still plays as if he does not know.

SHEG-ROUND vb dial slang; cf SHEG. To commit petty dishonesties.

1943 *GL* West, Sheg-round, to fool around and knows the right.

SHEGBUG sb dial; <SHEG+*bug*.

1943 *GL* no addr, Shegbug, an old hut.

SHEKREY adj dial; var of *chekre*. Thin, run-down. *BL*

1943 *GL* StM, Shekrey, thin and light, meagre. 1955 FGC Man, Said of a person: /shekre/ in poor condition.

SHELL vb dial; cf *OED* 3: *shell off*. *G*

1958 DeC Port /shel/ to crumble and fall apart; wheat flour must be used in a dumpling to prevent this from happening.

SHELL-BLOW sb; <*shell*, a conch shell+*blow*; cf *OED* 1828→.

1. The blowing of the shell as a signal to begin or to cease work.

1825 Bickell 49, Many overseers have the first shell-blow, for dinner, at half past twelve o'clock, and the second at two, to go to the field again.

2. As a time of the day: the midday meal period when work ceases.

1796 Braco 13 Oct, Small Rain at Shell Blow. 1797 *Ibid* 2 Nov, Great Gang set in to clean Little Crompton Piece which they finished at Shell Blow. Afternoon Great Gang divided the one half planting Corn..etc. 1826 Barclay 329, At shell-blow numbers of the negroes are seen making traps or examining those they have got in the water.

SHELL COPPER, SHELL TACHE sb obs; cf *OED shell sb* 12. A copper or tache for the evaporation of cane-juice having a bottom made of a smooth hemisphere, rather than a cylinder with parts riveted together.

1797 Higgins 78, Shell teaches, being hemispherical, are preferable to those formerly used, because their bottoms are sufficiently concave for the purpose of ladling. 1823 Roughley 195, I should prefer shell coppers for manufacturing sugar, to those whose bottoms are rivetted to their tops.

SHELL-SHELL sb dial; iterative <*shell* sb. Many small bits of shell-like things (here, specif, the chitinous wing-covers of fireflies).

1929 Beckwith 110, 'Little blinkie head and wing and shell-shell, that's what the Obeah Men sell to the country people', ended Falconer with indignation.

SHELL TACHE see SHELL COPPER.

SHELL TURN-IN sb obs. Evid the cessation of work at the noon hour—cf SHELL-BLOW.

1797 Braco 16 Mar, Left off Cutting Plantain Walk piece at Shell turn inn & Began to Cutt No 4. *Ibid* 7 July, Finished Rio Bueno Grass Piece at shell turn inn & Began to Clean Rio Bueno Cane Piece.

SHELL TURN-OUT sb obs. The cessation of work at some time in the day, but it is not clear when this was. (App not used in contrast to SHELL TURN-IN.)

1837 James 14, I endeavoured to empty the pit of the water, but I could not do it from the heavy fall of rain which continued untill shell turn-out.

SHE-MI-A-PLAY-WID sb dial joc.

1954 LeP Kgn, She-mi-a-play-wid, sweetheart.

SHEPHERD, SHEPHERDESS sb; cf *OED* 2. In revivalist cults: The titles of leaders, male and female.

1953 Moore 38, etc.

SHEPPON see SHUT-PAN.

SHERIGO sb obs; etym unknown. *G*

1756 Browne 421, Cancer 6..The common Sea-Crab, or *Sherigo*. This species is very common in all the harbours of Jamaica, and furnisheth a good part of the food of the negro fishermen.

SHERRIF vb dial slang; ?<*sheriff*. To renege.

1941 Kirkpatrick 29, Den 'Itler gone go sherrif 'pon dem. 'Im not gwine get 'way so easy dough.

SHE-SHE see *shi*(-*shi*).

SHET-PAN see SHUT-PAN.

SHEVIL-NOSED SHARK sb obs; <*shevel*, distorted, twisted (of the mouth, etc.) +*nose* +-*ed*[2] (*OED*, *EDD*); this form has been superseded by *shovel-nosed* (*OED* 1707, *DAE* 1844).

1756 Browne 458, Squalus 4..The shevil-nosed Shark.

SHEY-SHEY see SHAY-SHAY.

shi pron dial; <*she*. Used without distinction of case: she, her. *BL G*

1833 Scott I 178, No flyin fis can beat shi. 1877 Murray *Feedin' 'Perrit* 10, I hate him, but I hate shi wus. 1952 *Big Sambo Gal* [recorded song], Sen' she back to she mumma.

shi see *shi*(-*shi*).

SHIELD sb dial. *G*

1958 DeC /shiil/ a scabbard or sheath for a cutlass.

shif-man sb dial; <*shift* (though whether the noun, meaning a woman's chemise—a word still in use by the oldest women—or the verb, implying instability, is uncertain) +*man*. See quots.

1958 DeC StT /shif-man/ an effeminate man, willingly does women's work; an unreliable, no-account person.

SHIM-SHAM sb dial; etym uncert, cf Twi *sinsiãm*, to strip off, pull, tear, etc.; but also SHAY-SHAY, and perh the *shimmy* dance of the 1920's.

1943 *GL* Kgn, Shim-sham, dance. 1955 FGC Man, Shim-sham, wild dance—old fashioned.

SHINE adj and sb dial; abbr or hypercorrection.

A. adj: Shiny, shining. *BL G*

1896 Bates 42, Daag hab shine teet' him b'long to butcher. 1952 FGC, It have a shine look; StE, Cutlass fish—flat, shine, good for frying. Port, Satin [fish] longer, rounder, shiner than silk [fish]. 1956 Mc StE /di muun waz veri shain/ *It was bright moonlight.*

B. sb: A very black negro with a smooth, clear skin. (In US for any negro.) *BL*

1954 LeP Man. 1956 Mc Man. 1958 DeC Port /shain/—racial term, neutral, not offensive, for clean, shiny, dark man.

SHINE-A-NIGHT sb dial; <*shine* vb (or perh SHINE adj) +A[1] 2+*night*. The weed also called MAN-HEART, used medicinally; cf PEENIE-BUSH.

1952 FGC StAnn.

SHINE AS DIAL see DIAL.

SHINE-EYE sb[1] (also attrib) and adj dial; <SHINE+*eye* or representing SHINE+*eye*+*-ed*[2] (*OED*). In the names of birds: shiny-eyed.

1. The white-eyed thrush, *Turdus jamaicensis.*

1847 Gosse 142–3, Shine-eye. [See GLASS-EYE.] 1952 FGC Man /shain-ai jompa/. 1956 Jeffrey-Smith 35–6, The Glass Eye..is known as the Long Day bird..other local names..Shine Eye..Fish Eye.

2. The Antillean Solitaire, *Myadestes genibarbis.*

1936 Bond 292, *Local names:*—Glass-eye (Jamaica).

3. The Greater Antillean Grackle, *Holoquiscalus niger.*

1952 FGC StAnd /sháin-ai babíedaz/; StM, Shine-eye blackbird; StT, Shine-eye—same as kling-kling.

SHINE-EYE sb[2] dial; <SHINE+*eye*. The PEENIE-WALLIE.

1959 DeC StJ /shain-ai/ large firefly with light coming from head.

SHINGLE-WOOD sb; cf *OED* 1864 only. The common tree *Nectandra antillana* formerly used to make shingles.

1864 Grisebach 787, Shingle-wood. 1914 Fawcett 215. 1941 Swabey 31, Sweetwood, Yellow—(Shinglewood, Whitewood, Longleaf Sweetwood)..It saws and splits easily but neither the boards nor the shingles are durable.

SHINY BUSH sb dial; descriptive of the leaves.

1954 *WIMJ* 19, *Peperomia pellucida* Kunth. Pepper Elder..; Rat Ears; Ratta Temper; Silver Bush [Grenadines]; Shiny Bush [Trinidad].

SHIPMATE sb dial obs; transf: cf *OED ship sb* 9. A fellow-slave who was brought from Africa in the same ship as another. Now forgotten, but cf *pasiero*. *G*

1823 Koromantyn 149, To their companions in misery, borne over the deep in the same ship, these sympathies are more peculiarly manifested; the term *shipmate* implying an union of the most endearing nature..an indissoluble bond. 1837 Sterne 16, Q. 'Are you and these four men friends?' A. 'The first is my son, one is my shipmate, Thompson is my Godson.' 1863 Waddell 107 (year 1836), His clean white Osnaburgh frock and trousers that a 'shipmate'*, good as a daughter to him, had always ready. *She was called his daughter. The attachment of the slaves, who had come in the same vessel, to each other was like that of blood relations.

shi(-shi) int dial. The sound made to drive away chickens and sometimes other fowl or sheep.

1943 *GL* Man, Shi, to get away; She-she, Go away; StT, Shee, cry used to drive sheep, fowls. 1955 FGC Man /shi-shi/ cry to chickens, etc.

SHITTEN CLOUD sb dial uncom; <*shitten* +*cloud* sb (*OED* 6). A brown-looking spot or patch on the skin.

1943 *GL* Man, Shitten cloud, liver spot.

SHOCKER sb dial. The lesser electric ray (*Narcine brasiliensis*), because of the electric shock which it gives when touched.

1961 R. P. Bengry StAnd, Shocker—term commonly used by fishermen.

SHOE-BLACK (FLOWER) sb; altered from SHOE-FLOWER; cf also *shoe* sb (*OED* 6c). The *Hibiscus rosa-sinensis*: see quot 1837.

1837 Macfadyen 66, The flowers, from the mucilaginous juice they contain, are employed to give a polish to the leather of shoes; and hence the plant has received the name of the *shoe-black.* 1873 Rampini 163. 1941 Kirkpatrick 4, Dat man tell lie dat woulda mek nodder man face tu'n redder dan a shoes black flowers.

SHOE-FLOWER sb; see quot; *OED shoe* 6c 1834. =SHOE-BLACK (FLOWER).

1814 Lunan I 176, They are also put to a use which seems little consistent with their elegance and beauty, that of blacking shoes, whence their names of *rosæ calceolariæ* and *shoe-flower.*

SHOEPATA, SHOEPATTER see *sampata.*

SHOES sb sg dial. *BL*

1. A pair of shoes. *BA G*

1950 Pioneer 49, Not a shoes no deh a worl Fe frighten me again. [*There's not a pair of shoes in the world that could astonish me any more.*] 1957 JN, Jean a get one pretty shoes man. (Later) She wear a new pretty red shoes; Man, Buy a tall-heel shoes for me.

2. A shoe.

1943 *GL* Tre, Shrip shap—an old shoes.

SHOESLACE sb dial; cf SHOES. A shoelace; a pair of shoelaces. *BL*

1942 Bennett 8–9, Shoeslace, powder puff!..Shoes lace! Toot' pace! buy quick no sah.

SHOLAY vb dial; etym unknown.

1943 *GL* StE, Sholay, to climb.

SHOMPOO see *sampata.*

SHOOKOTO sb dial; prob phonosymbolic of something shaky—perh infl by *shook*, past tense of *shake.*

1943 *GL* StE, Shookoto, rough bed.

SHOOKS see *shuks.*

SHOOLAH vb dial; cf *OED shool*, beg, sponge; skulk. To loaf about. *BL*

1943 *GL* Clar, Shoolah, to loaf. 1955 FGC Man, The person shoolah around.

SHOOTING sb dial; cf BEARING. The flowering stalk that shoots from certain plants, e.g. agave, banana, etc. *G*

1952 FGC StM, see *malela.*

SHOPATA see *sampata.*

SHOP FLOUR sb chiefly dial. *G*

1958 DeC /shap-floua, kounta-floua, hingglish-floua/ names for wheat flour. The last name is general for all grades; the first two mean the coarse grade sold in country shops. /kiek-floua/ the fine grade, as in US.

SHOP-MASTER sb dial.

1956 Mc Man /shap-maasa/ shopkeeper.

SHORANS see *shuorans.*

SHORT sb dial; prob < *short* adj, scarce. Shortage (of food). (Cf DRY, *drought.*) *BA BL G*

1956 Mc StT /wen it faal an shaat de, taaya iit laik eni hafu/ [*When it falls on short there,* etc.] *When things are short, taya can be eaten, just like afu.*

SHORT-BAG sb dial. Cf LONG-BAG. A small bag for carrying food, small tools, and other necessaries.

1958 DeC StT /shaat-bag/ = /fishim-bag/ a small (6–12 in. square) bag with handles, often used by hunters and fishermen. DeC Port, a /namsak/—satchel for carrying victuals to the field.

SHORTHAND sb dial. A substitute used when one is short-handed.

1952 FGC Tre, If we don't have manure /wi tek graas fa sháatán/—you call it now 'mulch'.

SHORT HEART sb phr; cf *OED short* 10b, c. A hasty temper.

1924 Beckwith 40, Now Anansi is a man with a very short heart.

SHORT-MOUTHED adj dial.

1907 Jekyll 4, Short-mout'ed. Quick at repartee.

SHORT-MOUTH(ED) (BLUE) QUIT sb. The bird *Pyrrhuphonia jamaica.*

1936 Bond 368, *Local names:*—Blue Quit; Cho-cho Quit; Short-mouthed Quit. 1955 Taylor 37, This very small bird is known locally as..the Short-mouthed Blue-quit. It is an entirely different bird from the Long-mouthed Blue-quit. 1956 Jeffrey-Smith 93, They are stocky little birds with short, much-thickened bills. This characteristic gives them the name of 'Short-mout' Quits'.

SHORTRIGE /sháatrij/ sb dial; < *shortage* with intrusive, assimilative *r.* *G*

1950 Pioneer 41, De country dah suffa from food shortrige.

SHOT vb dial occas; past tense of *shoot,* which is the usual dial form. *BL G*

1907 Jekyll 141, Me a beg you fe come a yard an' shot him fe me when him come.

SHOT sb obs; cf *OED sb*[1] 21 →1706. A man armed with a gun; cf BLACK SHOT. Also attrib.

1733 *Jrls Assembly* 153, Captain Cornish has left a few shot negroes, to help to reinforce me until the party comes. 1801 *Jrls Assembly* 1799 X 385, Return by the Superintendent of Charles-Town, of his Maroons: Officers 4, Men shot 69, Women 88, etc.

SHOVE-AND-LET-GO sb arch slang.

1943 *GL* StM, Shove-and-let-go, old pedal-drive Ford car.

SHOVEL-BEAK SHARK sb dial. = Shovel-nosed shark.

1952 FGC StJ.

SHOVEL-HEAD SHARK sb dial. = Shovel-nosed shark.

1952 FGC Port.

SHOVEL-MOUTH (SHARK) sb dial. = Shovel-nosed shark.

1952 FGC StC, StM, StT.

SHOW vb dial; cf *OED* 22d →1643. To show how. *BL G*

1957 JN StAnn, I give her the book and show her to write.

SHOW BELLY vb phr dial; < *show* + *belly* 1 (*OED*). To become visibly pregnant. *BA G*

1820 Thomson 113, Some [negro women] do not show belly, as they call it, till a few months before they are delivered. (1960 Current, BLB.)

SHOW-ME-CHUDLEIGH, SHOW-ME-SHOW-ME, SHOW-ME-TOWN sb dial; from the words spoken when the pupa is used in a game.

A pupa which, held in the palm of the hand, twists itself so as to 'point' at something: the person holding the pupa repeats a formula containing the words 'show me'; some of its variant forms are indicated by the names. Cf APEMPAY, *jiji-waina.*

1943 *GL* Man, Show-me Chudleigh, chrysalis. 1952 FGC Tre, Show-me-show-me—caterpillar; show-me-town, You say 'Suzie, Suzie, show me town', touch the show-me-town and it twist itself—reel and turn.

SHOWRANCE see *shuorans.*

SHREF-SHREF sb dial cant; etym unknown. In the so-called 'Maroon' talk of St Thomas AFRICAN cults: spirit.

1953 Moore gloss. See MAROON 2, quot 1953.

SHRIMP MAAMI sb dial; for *shrimp's* + MAAMI. The sea mantis—members of the *Stomatopoda,* which resemble huge shrimps.

1952 FGC StT /shrimp maami/ shape of a 40-leg, broader in back; if it sting you on Friday you're gone. 1960 Institute of Ja exhibit, Shrimp maami.

SHRINGSHA vb dial rare; perh < *scringe* vb[2], cringe, shrink (*EDD*) or similar dial form, + *-er.*

1943 *GL* StE, Shringsha, manlinger [= malinger].

SHRIP-SHAP see SLIP-SLOP.

SHRUBBY MOUNTAIN MAHOE sb bot obs. In Browne's use: *Malvaviscus sagræanus,* the Mahoe Rose.

1756 Browne 284, Hibiscus 2..The shrubby Mountain Mohoe. 1814 Lunan I 469.

SHRUBBY SWEETWOOD sb bot; *OED*; cf SWEETWOOD. *Amyris balsamifera.*

1756 Browne 209, Amyris 2..The smaller shrubby Sweetwood. 1774 Long III 750, Sweet-wood, or Shrubby Sweet-wood—Amyris. 1814 Lunan I 147, 149. 1864 Grisebach 788.

SHRUB COTTON sb; *OED* only quot 1858. The cotton shrub as distinct from cotton trees; *Gossypium* species (but not *Bombax,* etc.).

1793 Edwards II 270, Shrub Cotton, properly so called. The shrub..may be subdivided into several varieties, all of which however very nearly resemble each other. [Five varr named.] 1814 Lunan I 239.

shuks vb[1] dial; ? < *shook,* past tense of *shake*—cf US slang, to get rid of. To disappoint (someone), to leave in the lurch; hence, to hurt (one's) feelings. Cf also *EDD* SHUCK *v*[1].

1943 *GL* StJ, Shooks, deceive or disappoint. 1955 FGC Man, 'The person /shuks/ you—didn't come'. 1958 W. A. Roberts letter, To 'shooks' a person means, chiefly, to hurt his feelings.

shuks vb[2] dial; echoic—cf *chups,* to kiss.

1954 LeP StE, Shooks—to kiss.

SHUMPATA, SHUMPATAH, SHUMPATTA, SHUPATTA see *sampata.*

shuorans adj dial; aphetic form of *assurance.* Too self-assured; impudent. *G*

1907 Reynolds 18, You doan eben own a cow horn, let alone anyting else for de supportance of a wife. You surance fe true. [*What impudence!*] 1943 *GL* Han, Shorans, Impudent; Kgn, Showrance; StAnd, Surance, Forward; also StJ, StM.

SHUT-EYE LAND sb dial or slang; cf slang *shut-eye,* sleep. In phr, *to go to shut-eye land*: to die.

1943 Bennett 25, Wen smady pendictis bus, Dem gawn a shet-eye lan'.

SHUT-PAN /shét-pán, shé-pán/ sb; *OED* in diff sense.

A vessel of tin or other thin metal, cylindrical, with a cover having a flange that usually fits inside the upper edge and makes a tight closure; the cover frequently has a small fixed handle. The shut pan is chiefly used to carry food.

1929 Beckwith 147, The true Myal Man..'carries a sheppon [big covered pail] and the ghosts fall down from the tree and he catches them'. 1942 Bennett 11, Wan day, Cousin sue keiba up li bickle Eena wan lickle shet pan, De sort wey dem use fe ketch duppy yuh know. 1943 *GL* StC, Shet-pan, food container. 1950 U.Newton VI 32, So I opened the sugarpan, the shut-pan we call it in the country. 1960 The Native in *Gleaner* 4 July 10, Shut pan ..people (like myself) use it to secrete our loose change.

SHUT-WEED sb dial. The sensitive plant *Mimosa pudica,* which shuts its leaves together when touched.

1927 Beckwith 27, =DEAD-AND-WAKE. 1954 *WIMJ* 30, cf SHAMER.

shuwa, shwuwa sb dial; ult echoic—cf such words as Kongo *shiɔshia,* to splutter in cooking, Zulu *schwa,* sound of water spurting. The sound of frying; see quots.

1943 *GL* StAnn, Shwu-wa, the noise of frying meal. 1955 FGC Man /shúwa/ noise of meal frying with water.

sibi adj dial; cf *OED sievy* in diff sense. Having been sieved, hence in small floury particles—see quot.

1958 DeC Tre /sibi/ crumbly, lacking in cohesion; one must add shop-flour to qua-qua in making dumplings or it will be too /sibi/. (One informant corrected his pronunciation to /sivi/.)

sibl adj dial < *Seville (orange),* pronunc /síbl (árinj)/ =*sour (orange).* [This pronunc goes back at least to the 16th cent: Shakespeare *Much Ado* ii 1 304.] Sour, acid. (Applied usually but not necessarily to oranges.) *BL G*

1952 FGC /mi kyaang hiit it—it tuu sibl/.

sibl arinj =Seville orange. *BL*

sibljak see SUPPLEJACK.

sib-sib sb dial; iterative < *sieve* vb. Cassava, because it has to be sieved a great deal to produce the 'head' or flour.

1958 DeC StE /sib-sib/.

SICK vb trans dial; cf *OED* v^1 2 →a 1645. To sicken, to make sick. *G T*

1956 Mc Man /mi nyám píe tel i sík mi/ *I ate so many pears that I fell ill* [lit, —*that they made me ill*].

SIDE sb chiefly dial; this may in part be a loan-translation: cf Twi *ŋkyɛ́ŋ,* side, used to indicate position, location. *G*

In several more or less fixed phrases, with *side* preceded by a demonstr, interrog, possessive, or other pronoun: *this side,* here, in our neighbourhood; *that side,* yonder, over there; *what side, which side,* where; etc.

1862 Clutterbuck 42, What bring you dis side?*..*Here. 1868 Russell 2, De people dem dis side lib well fe true. 1873 Rampini 101, P.—What side you' ground is? W.—At Content. 1877 Murray *Kittle* 24, Bra, whi side unoo da go? 1924 Beckwith 41, 'What is all de strange news a fe you side?*..*In your district. 1952 FGC StAnn /ebribadi dis said/ *everybody in this locality.*

SIDE-BAG sb dial. A bag that hangs at one's side from a strap going over the shoulder. s SIDE-BASKET.

1907 Jekyll 107, Everybody has his side-bag or namsack (knapsack). 1924 Beckwith 22, Hanansi..tak de dog-head put into his side-bag. 1956 Mc Clar, Man /said-bag/ bag made of sacking (or fabric)—taken to /groun/.

SIDEMAN sb. A man on a motor lorry or truck who does what is required, apart from driving, to use the vehicle satisfactorily—e.g. keeping it shipshape, directing the driver when necessary, helping to load, etc.

1960 *Gleaner* 29 Aug. 1961 Katzin 10, The sidemen lifted the load to the truck while Miss A and Mamie climbed over the wheel..to find a seat.

SIDE-POCKET sb dial. =SIDE-BAG. *G*

1958 DeC Port /said-pakit/.

SIDE-PORK sb dial; from the sallow colour of a side of pork.

1958 DeC Port /said-puork/ derogatory name for an albino Negro.

SIDUN, SIDUNG vb phr dial. Common spelling among dialect writers to represent /sidong/ pronunc of *sit down.* *BA G*

1927 Anderson-Cundall 43, Sidun. 1950 Pioneer 101, Sidung.

SIEVE-SIEVE see *sib-sib.*

SIEVY see *sibi.*

siili sb dial; evid a person's name, but could be < *Celie, Seely, Sealy,* etc.

1952 FGC StAnd /siili/ a white sweet-potato.

sikin adj dial; < *sick* + *-i* + *-n.* Sick, in the colloq sense of weary, tired. *G*

1961 BLB 24 /mi sikin a hie dari bwai a braadkyaas nou/ *I am tired of hearing that boy broadcasting now.*

SILENCE WAKE, SILENT WAKE sb dial. See quots. The sense of 'silence' is not clear.

1958 DeC StAnd /sailant wiek, sailents wiek/ A set-up; StT /sailant wiek/ a funeral meeting which is hardly silent; usually this is the first night meeting, characterized here by singing long-metre all night; it is sometimes used also for the meetings on 2nd, 8th nights, characterized by ring games, Anancy stories, and riddles.

SILK (FISH or **SNAPPER)** sb; descr; cf *OED* 5a. The fish *Lutianus vivanus* and similar species.

a 1818 Lewis (1834) 104, Of the Sea Fish which I have hitherto met with, the Deep-water Silk appears to me the best. 1823 Stewart 81, The grooper, the silk, the snapper. 1892 Cockrell list, Silk, *Tropidinius dentatus.* 1952 FGC StE, StJ, West /silk/ Port, StAnn, StM /silk fish/ StC, StT /silk snapa/.

SILK GRASS sb obs; cf *OED* 1b 1753→. The fibres of various kinds of *Agave;* also the plant itself. *BA N*

1696 Sloane 110, Yuccæ folia folio in longissimum filamentum abeunte..*Silk Grass.* Ad margines viarum Insulæ Jamaicæ..observavi. a 1726 Barham (1794) 94,

Maguey, Of which they make a fine thread called *pita*, and we [in Jamaica] call it silk-grass. *Ibid* 174, Silk grass. This plant is of the aloetic kind..The chief use of this plant is to make silk; which..is quite coarse, but very white, hard, and strong; of this they make hammocks and ropes.

SILT SNAPPER sb; < SILK SNAPPER with substitution of *t* for *k*. = SILK SNAPPER.

1863 'Jamaica Notes' in *Intellectual Obs.* III 194, The deep-water Silt-Snappers include some five different species, all similar in colour (*OED*). 1867 *TRSAA* I 25, The deep-water-Silt Snappers.

SILVER-BACK FERN sb. The fern *Pityrogramma calomelanos*.

1946 *NHN* III 77, The 'Silver-Back Fern' is so called from its sori which form a silvery-grey powdery covering at the back of its frond.

SILVER BUSH sb dial; cf *OED* in diff senses. The shrub *Peperomia pellucida*; descr; cf SHINY BUSH.

SILVER DRUMMER sb. An unidentified fish of the DRUMMER kind: see quot.

1947 *NHN* III 93, Apart from the fact that the Silver Drummer is predacious, little is known of it. They do not appear to inhabit any river in sufficient numbers to have attracted special attention.

SILVER-FISH sb; *OED* 1703→. Silvery fish (family *Gerridæ*) of a number of species; see, specif, quot 1892.

1679 Trapham 65, The choice Mullet brings up the next division crowded with various Snappers...Mud fish, Cat fish, Silver fish, Pilchers, Sprat,..etc. 1892 Cockrell list, Silver fish—shad, *Gerres zebra*. 1952 FGC StC /silva fish/—shad; StJ, Silver-fish, broader and larger than shad.

SILVER GRUNT sb. Some fish of the family *Hæmulidæ*, perh the GREY GRUNT of today.

1756 Browne 447, Sciæna 2..The Silver Grunt.

SILVER HEAD sb. The Jamaican Spindalis.

1936 Bond 370, see MARK-HEAD. 1956 Jeffrey-Smith 92.

SILVER JACK sb. The fish *Vomer setapinnis cubensis*.

1950 Smith, 'Silver jack,' Lucea. 1952 FGC StC, StM /silva jak/ similar to old-wife.

SILVER OLD-WIFE sb. A fish, perh *Trachinotus goodei*. s SHEEPSHEAD ALE-WIFE.

1826 Williams 79, Baracootas, silver oldwives, trunk fish, and others. 1952 FGC StJ, West /silva uolwaif/ skinny—have to take off the skin; have a horn top of head.

SILVER SNAKE sb obs. The 'two-headed snake', *Typhlops jamaicensis*.

1756 Browne 460, Amphisbena 1. Subargentea..The Silver Snake. 1843 Phillippo 58, Of snakes, the silver, black and the yellow.

SILVER STRAW sb. = SILVER THATCH.

1929 Beckwith 45, Thatch, called 'silver straw'.

SILVER THATCH sb. The palm *Thrinax argentea*, the leaves of which are used for thatch.

1864 Grisebach 788, Silver Thatch. 1890 Thomas 71, see LONG THATCH. 1952 FGC Tre.

SILVER TREE sb obs; cf *OED* 2. A small tree, *Eugenia uniflora*—the Surinam cherry. (Ident 1926 Fawcett 334.)

1756 Browne 240, The shrubby *Philadelphus*, with Myrtle leaves; or the Silver Tree..This little tree is frequent in the red hills..it is now commonly called *Rod-wood* by the negroes.

siman-kwengkwe-man sb dial uncom; the last syllable is prob < Engl *man*, but may be partly reflected in Hausa *K'wank'wamai*, evil spirits supposed to cause lunacy; certain charms supposed to harm one who touches them (Bargery 682); for *siman*, cf Hausa *simi*, *sumi*, being silent because of fear, which has a combining-form *sumun-*.

1958 DeC StAnd /siman-kwengkwe-man/ obeah man.

SIMIDIMI sb dial uncom; ? < *semidemi-*, in allusion to the music. Cf SHIM-SHAM. *T*

1943 *GL* StE, Simidimi, dance.

simi-kantrak sb dial; < Sp *semencontra*, wormwood or other vermifuge (applied in Mexico and Cent Am to *Calea integrifolia*—Santamaría III 78) + -*k*, perh with folk-etym infl. The plant *Chenopodium ambrosioides*—see quots. s SINNER-CONTRACT.

1927 Beckwith 26, See-me-contract..'Worm-weed'. For worms or 'low stomach' drink as tea..Rub your body with it and scatter sprigs about the house 'to drive away all bad things'. The plant has a strong, pungent odor. 1929 Beckwith 94, Worm weed, called in Kromanti talk 'see-me-contract'. 1943 *GL* StE, Semocontrac. 1952 FGC StAnd, StM, Tre /simi-kantrak, simi-kantra, simo-kantrak/ also StC, StT. 1953 *WIMJ* 240, *Chenopodium ambrosioides L.* Semicontra (Semen Contra); Worm Weed; Worm Seed; Mexican Tea; Bitter Weed; Hedge Mustard. This species is the source of oil of chenopodium, the well-known anthelmintic. It is fairly commonly employed in Jamaica as a vermifuge.

SIMMINCE NYASSE sb dial; an attempt to indicate a dial pronunc of 'ST VINCENT YAM'; the sound intended was prob /simmínsi-nyáans/ showing assimilation of the first two syllables and of the last two; but see pronunc of YAM.

1954 LeP StAnn, Simmince nyasse—St Vincent Yam.

simo-kantrak see *simi-kantrak*.

simpavaivis, SIMPAVIEVY see SEMPERVIVE.

SIMPLE-BIBLE see SEMPERVIVE.

SIMPLE MAN sb dial; cf *OED simple sb* B 6. A man who deals in simples or medicinal herbs.

1956 Mc StE, see BETTER.

SINCE-WHEN adj and sb dial slang; from some such phrase as 'Since when did he—' indicating a changed way of living or acting. Newly rich, or a newly rich person. Cf HURRY-COME-UP.

1943 *GL* StM, Since-when, newly rich. 1955 FGC Man, Newly rich; people say 'Since when they get so fussy?'

SINDING see SOMETHING.

SING sb dial; < *sing* vb. What one sings, what is sung: a song. s.

1877 Murray *Kittle* 26, How de sing sweet Watchman him neber look 'pon Mudfish. [*The song pleased W. so much that he did not watch M.*] 1907 Jekyll 258, For these shortcomings the fiddler 'put her a sing', i.e. put her into a sing. 1956 Mc StAnd /jaabuon—dat a sing se 'mongki jaa buon so swiit', dat iz di babm av it/ *Jawbone—that's a song 'Monkey jawbone so sweet' that is the refrain of it.*
[Note: 'Jawbone' was understood for 'draw bone', i.e. to play the fiddle.]

SINGER sb. *BL G*

1912 McK *Songs* 79, Singer, a device on a kite—a *tongue* that buzzes.

singgl-baibl see SEMPERVIVE.

singgl-go, singgrigo see SINGLE-GO.

SINGING-MEETING sb dial. *BA*

1. A pseudo-Christian religious meeting not sanctioned by the church: see quot.

1837 Rampini 84, In some districts of the island, indeed, these [*sc* Christian religious services] are travestied at midnight meetings held under leafy booths erected for the purpose, which are carefully concealed from the knowledge of the parish minister. At these 'singing meetings' a woman sanctifies the bread and administers the elements. Hymns are sung, words are spoken, mysterious rites are observed.

2. A hymn-singing meeting on the night after the wake and funeral: see quots.

1958 DeC StJ /singin-miitn/ a funeral meeting on the second night; entirely religious; sing Sankey and long-meter all night. Tre, a funeral meeting held on the second night; sing Sankey all night (as opposed to the /set-op/ on the first night, when there is usually no singing in this district).

singkavaivl, singkl-baibl, SINGLE-BIBLE see SEMPERVIVE.

singkuma, zingkuma sb dial; cf Hausa *sunk'umi* (masc) *sunk'umā* (feminine), huge, swollen.

1. As the name or part of the name of a bull in an Anansi story.

1924 Beckwith 173, Den de bull was coming along, hear dem, say, [Song:] Oh who dey ca' me Timmo Limmo? Timmo Limmo, oh? Zinkuma Ya ya ya, oh, Zinkuma. [1959 Mr Harris Port (Moore Town), 'Sinkuma' means *strong, big.*]

2. A type of plantain similar to the MAIDEN PLANTAIN. Cf *fiekuma.*

1952 FGC Port /sangkuma, singkuma/—maiden plantain.

SINGLE-GO (MACCA) sb dial; <FINGRIGO, perh with concurrent infl of FINGLE, and with folk-etym. The plant FINGRIGO.

1952 FGC StAnd /sínggl-gò/ = puss-claw, cockspur; StAnn /sínggl-gò/ puss-claw—bears a gummy seed, called bramble, used to catch birds; StAnn, 'Single-go macca —natives distort it to /singgri-go/'.

SINGLINGS sb; from their having undergone only a single process of distillation; *OED* 1830→. The liquor produced by the first distillation of fermented sugar-cane juice.

1823 Roughley 161, Strong singlings, or low wine to wash them [mules] with where swelled, or bruised. *Ibid* 177, Warm singlings, or low wines, as it is termed in Jamaica.

SINKET sb dial. A sink or sink-hole in the ground surface above a limestone formation.

1943 *GL* Clar, Sinkets, Holes covered with grass, caverns, espec. in limestone areas. 1955 FGC Man /sínkit/ sink hole in limestone region.

SINKET (BREADFRUIT, COCO) see ST KITTS.

SINK-IN-THE-MIDDLE sb dial.

1958 DeC StT /singk-in-a-migl/ a name for the common long oval basket with a handle. Also called TOMATO BASKET, FISHERMAN BASKET.

SINKLE-BIBLE see SEMPERVIVE.

SINNICKY adj dial; for *sneaky*, with intrusive /i/—See Introd. An attempt to represent a dial pronunc, /siníki/ or /siníiki/.

1907 Jekyll 25, He sinnicky fe true, he is a horrid sneak.

sinti, sintin, sinting, SINTY see SOMETHING.

sintl-baibl see SEMPERVIVE.

sipa-sipa vb dial; perh <Sp *zipizape*, row, rumpus, scuffle.

1958 DeC StE (Accom) /sipa-sipa/ to mash up.

sipl adj and vb[1] dial; <*supple* adj; cf also *swipl.*

A. adj: Slippery, mucilaginous. Also in cpds.

1952 FGC StT /sipl/ said of a plant which exuded a mucilaginous juice from the stem when broken. 1956 Mc StE /okro iz a sipl vejitebl plaan/ *Okro is a slimy vegetable;* /di ruod is sipl an wet/; /a litl sipl hil/.

B. vb: To make supple or slippery.

1950 Pioneer 78, An' a pigeon meat im a sipple you jin'. [*Pigeon meat supples your joints.*] 1956 Mc StE (Accom) /im sibl i wi som okro/ *He made it slippery with some okro.*

sipl vb[2] dial; by metathesis <*slip*, or perh from *sipl* vb[1]. Const *away.* To slip away, escape.

1952 FGC StT, Them hold him, but Anansi /sipl awie/ *They caught him, but Anancy slipped away.*

sipljak see SUPPLEJACK.

sipl-kalalu sb dial; <*sipl* adj + *kalalu.* Slippery calalu. (All kinds have slippery juices; INDIAN KALE perhaps more than the others.)

1952 FGC StM /sipl-kalalu/ Indian Kale.

sipl-okro sb dial; <*sipl* + OKRO, a plant and esp fruit that is very mucilaginous. The climbing cactus *Cereus triangularis,* whose entire stem is very mucilaginous when cut. Also called GOD-OKRO.

1952 FGC StAnn /sipl-okro/. StM /swipl okro/ with fruit like a prickly-pear—climbing cactus, triangular cross-section.

SIPPLE see *sipl.*

sis, sista see next.

SISTER /sista, sis, sita, sta, sto, saa, sa, sor/ or /so/ sb dial. A polite term of address for a woman; usually preceding her name. *BL G*

1912 McK *Songs* 16, Me watch de vine dem grow, S'er t'row dung a de root. 1950 Pioneer 50, So me cotchin' wid Mass U, Miss Q, Sta P, an Cousin B. 1954 LeP Man, sah = sister; StAnn, Sitta = sister. (Some parents instruct the smaller ones of the family to use Bredda or Sitta before the names.) 1956 Mc Man, Sis—a general term of address, respectful /sita/ also /saa, sa/. 1958 DeC StT /sa-, sta-, so-, sto-/ sister, used with personal name only, e.g. /sa-jien/ [*Sister Jane*].

sita see prec.

SIT-DOWN sb dial.

1958 DeC /sit-down/ a funeral wake.

SIWI-SIWI see *swii-swii.*

SIX EYES sb phr. Symbolic of three people together being too many (cf the proverb 'Two's company, three's a crowd'). Cf MAKE FOUR EYES.

1910 Anderson-Cundall 17 [Prov:] When six yeye meet 'tory done.

SIX-MONTHS sb; tr of Fr *six-mois*, the Poinsettia. The shrub Poinsettia (*Euphorbia pulcherrima*), which remains in bloom for six months.

1933 McK 317, Six-months—'poinsettia'.

skaaf vb dial slang; <*scoff*—cf *OED v*[2]; the normal dial reflex of this, however, would be /skaf/ or /kaf/.

1958 DeC Port, To swallow down fast, to eat greedily; /let wi skaaf it op, bwaiz/.

skaan-di-graun, skarn-di-ort see SCORN-THE-EARTH.

skab vb chiefly dial; etym uncert: it could represent Std Engl *cob, scob, cab, scab,* and perh other words, of which none is known to have this sense. (Perh *scab* comes closest.) See *skrebi* vb.

1958 BLB Man /skab/ to cheat at lessons in school by copying another child's work.

skail droma see *kail droma.*

SKATE vb dial. To slide downhill on the sheath of a palm bough—common country game. *BA*

1959 LeP StAnd /kyabij paam bou. Wi yuuz dem tu skiet an—go op a litl hil, sit an, skiet dong an di graas/.

SKEAT see *kiet*.

SKELLION sb; <*scallion*. Scallion (*OED* c); so pronounced universally in Jamaica; cf the dial form *kelyan*.

1893 Sullivan 25, Let it stew gently for about an hour, then add a little pepper, skellions, tomatoes. 1924 Beckwith 72, It boil until it tell him to season in skelion. 1952 FGC Port, StAnd, StAnn, StC, StE, StM, StT /skelyan/.

SKELLION GRASS sb dial; <SKELLION+*grass*. The sedge Nut Grass (*Cyperus rotundus*); see RICE WEED.

1952 FGC StAnn (2) /skelyan graas/ same as rice-weed—all over Jamaica. 1961 FGC Man.

SKELLION LIZARD sb dial. A lizard—presumably a green one, or in some other way resembling or associated with SKELLION.

1952 FGC StT /skélyan lízad/.

SKELLY PEAS sb dial. =RED MISS KELLY.

1952 FGC StE /skeli piiz/.

SKEMP sb dial; prob <*skimp* (cf *EDD* 5). =KEMPS.

1943 *GL* Kgn, Skemp, small part.

SKENCH sb dial; prob <*skinch* vb, to be parsimonious or stingy (*EDD*), or an unrecorded *sk-* correspondent of *kinch* sb. =KENCH.

1943 *GL* StC, Skench, a small quantity. 1955 FGC Man.

SKEWER-STICK /skyuua stik/ sb dial.

1957 DeC /kyúa stik, skyúa stik/ a sharp pointed piece of bamboo for taking food from a pot.

skiafilas see SCROFULOUS.

SKID sb; cf *OED* 1c 1846→, *DA* 1800→. *BA*

1774 Long II 319 [Among seafaring terms introduced to Jamaica:] Skids. Poles, or levers used for putting casks into a boat from the shore.

skiit see *kiet*.

SKILIAD sb dial; ?for *scale-yard* (*OED* does not list this, but does list *scale-beam* and *steel-yard*), or perh <*still-yard* (*OED steel-yard*, α-form) with substitution of /k/ for /t/—cf Introd.

1943 *GL* Kgn, Skiliad, scale.

SKIN /kin/ sb and vb dial.

A. sb: 1. The body (as enclosed in the skin); esp in connection with washing or feeling pain.

1835 Madden I 156, She had *pain in her kin!* (pain in the skin means every sort of external ill that negro flesh is heir to). 1907 Jekyll 7, Bro'er Tiger go a river fe wash 'kin. 1924 Beckwith 61, O Brar Cock! from I lef' you heah, pain all over my skin so I go an' lie down, I couldn't look a t'ing. 1956 Mc Man, see BATHE. *G*

2. Abbr for KINCAT, KINOBA. *T*

1943 *GL* Kgn, Kin, turn. (Possibly the verb.)

B. vb: 1. Of the teeth: To become exposed by the drawing back of the skin (lips). Cf SKIN (ONE'S) TEETH. *BA G*

1958 DeC Clar /a tiit kin/ the teeth have 'skinned'—i.e. *he is dead*, the face has taken on the death grimace.

2. Abbr for SKIN (ONE'S) TEETH. *G T*

1943 *GL* Clar, Kin, grin.

SKIN-FISH sb dial. The kind of fish that has a skin (rather than scales) which must be taken off before it is eaten, such as TURBOT, OLD-WIFE, TOBACCO FISH, NIGGER-FISH, etc. *G*

1952 FGC StAnn, StT, etc.

SKIN (ONE'S) TEETH /kin tiit/ vb phr; <*skin* vb+*teeth*. To draw the lips back, revealing the teeth; to grin, to laugh, usu with pleasure, sometimes with chagrin. *BA BL G T*

1950 Pioneer 94, Go 'kin you teet' an show you smile. 1955 Bennett *Pleasuration*, Dem dah treat de gal like queen, all She dah do is kin her teet! 1956 Mc /yu kin yu tiit/ To laugh showing the teeth; to laugh enthusiastically.

SKIN-OVER see KINOBA.

SKIN-TEETH see KIN-TEET. *BA G*

SKIN UP (ONE'S) LIP vb phr chiefly dial. To wrinkle the upper lip with distaste or disdain. *BL G*

1955 Bennett *Breeze Pass*, Wid dem nose an mout-lip kin-up Like pet dog a view pig-sty.

SKIP vb and sb; cf *OED* v^2 a1818→, sb^4 1858→, 1885.

A. vb: In sugar-making, formerly: to carry forward the boiling cane liquor from one copper in the series to the next.

1797 Higgins 109 [Implied in the vbl sb:] As nothing of this kind is practicable in the skipping from the first teach; some new expedient is necessary. 1823 Roughley 348, It will take more boiling and perhaps more lime before it is fit to be skipped into the coolers.

B. sb: 1. The charge or quantity of sugar liquor that is held in one copper (and is skipped forward to the next after evaporation).

1823 Roughley 198, The stoke-hole..should be..capable of holding as much trash or fuel as will boil two skips of sugar.

2. The process of transferring or skipping the evaporated cane liquor from one copper forward to the next.

1797 Higgins 108, About twelve ladlings forward belong to a skip. *Ibid* 109, Some new expedient is necessary to prevent the burning-to which is manifested in every whole skip, by the hissing heat of the copper.

3. One of the vessels into which the evaporated, tempered sugar syrup was passed for granulation.

1835 Senior 51, The [evaporated] juice passes into the taitch, where it receives the temper-lime, &c., and being removed into flat vessels, called 'skips', proceeds gradually through the process of granulation. This completed, the skips are emptied into casks.

SKIPPING vbl sb; cf *OED vbl* sb^2 1826→.

1. In sugar-making: the carrying forward of the boiling cane liquor from one copper to the next: =SKIP sb 2.

1797 Higgins 29, The first..teach..in working ought always to be full, except at the time of skipping. 1823 Roughley 347, To ascertain the crisis for skipping sugar, from the tache into the coolers.

2. Attrib or comb: *skipping-gutter*, *skipping-time*, *skipping-trough*.

1797 Higgins 48, If the furnace be raised for a skipping trough to pass at right angles..the distance will be 33 inches. *Ibid* 108, At skipping time the instrument reserves some filtered syrup to recruit the emptied teach. 1823 Roughley 356, A strainer should be placed between the grand and second copper..and another still finer at the tache, on the skipping gutter.

skobiich fish see ESCOVEITCHED FISH, SCAVEECHED FISH.

skrab-yaaz see CRAB-YAWS.

skrebi adj, sb and vb; cf *OED scrubby*, insignificant, paltry; *EDD scrab, scrabbie*, stunted, knarled (Scots).

A. adj or sb: A person or thing of poor quality.

1943 *GL* Kgn, Screbbey, dunce. 1955 FGC Man /skrébi/ something not worth while—e.g. clothing.

B. vb: To copy from another pupil. (Here the word *crib* may be blended in.) See *skab*.

1956 Mc Clar /skrébi/ to copy, to look over a person's shoulder at his book, in school.

skribs sb dial; an occas pron of *squibs*.

1943 *GL* no addr, Scribs, clappers, fire-crackers.

skriil out vb phr dial; perh a metathetic form of *skirl* (cf *OED* v^1, *EDD*, Scotl, Irel, etc.), but the vowel perh shows analogical infl of *scream*. *G*

1958 DeC common, To cry out, scream out: /di gyol skriil out fi di beta/.

skrofi-routn sb dial; < *kofi-routn* with SCRUFFY blended into the first element. See *krofi-routn*.

skrosh vb and past ppl dial; hypercorrect form of *crush*; but cf Engl *scrunch*. *BL G*

A. vb: To crush.

1956 Mc StE /yu bail di banaana an skrosh it wi bota/.

B. past ppl: Crushed.

1956 Mc StE /skrosh banana/ a kind of pudding made from boiled bananas beaten with butter and set in a mould.

SKY GODS sb dial cant. The supposed deities of AFRICAN cults.

1953 Moore 189–204 (A list of some 39 names, many biblical, some perh African, most of them confused or corrupted in some way).

SLACK sb dial; < *slack* adj.

1. A slovenly person.

1956 Mc StT /slak/ slovenly untidy person.

2. A woman of loose morals.

1956 BLB Man /slak/ is used of girls of loose morals.

SLACKY-TIDY sb dial; < *slack* adj + *-y* + *tidy*, evid one who is slack about tidiness. A slovenly, untidy person.

1954 LeP StAnn, StE, Slacky-tidy. 1956 Mc Clar, Man /slaki-taidi/—dem don' carry demself tidy.

slaki-slaki adj dial; iterative of (*OED*) *slaky*, muddy (Berwick, Stirling), < *slake* sb^3 (chiefly Nth dial) mud, slime.

1958 DeC Man /slaki-slaki/ adjective for wet, muddy ground.

slaki-taidi see SLACKY-TIDY.

SLAM-BAM adv dial; < *slam-bang*, with the second element assim to the first by rhyme or partial iteration, and blending of *bam*. Suggesting the manner of sudden or direct action: certainly or without fail; immediately; emphatically. *BL*

1943 *GL* StM, Slam bam, straight on; StT, Slam bam, not until or not before. [See next quot.] 1956 Mc Clar /mi wi du it slam bam tumaro/ *I'll do it without fail* or *first thing tomorrow*.

SLAMPATTOR, SLAMPLATTA see *sampata*.

slandaz sb dial; var pronunc (by metath) of *sandals*.

SLANG sb; a particularization of the general term. A slang expression or usage. *BL G T*

1956 Mc Clar /aal duoz slangz/ *all those slang words*. 1958 A. K. Croston UCWI, Slangs = slang expressions. Frequently used in undergraduate essays.

SLAP(-BAM) adv dial; < *slap(-bang)*, the sense of intensiveness being transferred from time to place, and *bam* (as in SLAM-BAM) replacing *bang*. (*Slap*, all the way, is still current.) All the way, the entire distance. *BA BL*

1943 *GL* no addr, Slap-bam, a remote distance. 1962 BLB 42 /slap/ all the way, distance.

SLAVE-COURT sb obs. A court in which slaves were tried: see quots. *G*

1817 *An Act for the Subsistence* 124, He or she shall be tried at a slave-court. *Ibid* 136, And it is hereby declared, That at every court of quarter-sessions, held in each and every parish or precinct within this island the justices there assembled shall and may, after the usual business of the said court shall be done, form themselves into a court, for the purpose of inquiring into, hearing, and determining, all manner of offences for which any slave or slaves are liable to be punished with death, or transportation, or confinement to hard labour, as aforesaid, and shall open the said court by proclamation, declaring the same to be a slave-court for such purpose.

SLAVERY TANK sb. A water-tank of the kind that was used during slavery days.

1961 W. E. Fulford Man, Slavery tank—stonework tank for cattle, placed in a meadow where water would drain into it.

SLEEPY-HEAD PARROT sb dial. A variety of the PARROT fish which makes a sound like snoring when taken from the water.

1952 FGC StM.

SLIM sb dial. A cutlass or machete of slender shape and arched point.

1958 DeC Tre /slim/.

slimba adj dial; prob blend of *slim* and *limber*. Of a person: tall and thin.

1912 McK *Ballads* 54, see BALL-PAN MAN. 1958 DeC Tre /slimba/.

SLIMMY-LIKE adj dial; < *slim* + *-y* + *-like*. Slender.

1955 FGC Man.

SLING-BAG sb dial.

1959 DeC Han /sling-bag/ a crocus-bag rolled at the mouth so as to hook over the crown of the head or even over the forehead while the bag hangs down the man's back.

SLIP vb dial; cf *slip OED* vb^1 24 1652–1768 and *EDD* 9. In impers const: To escape (one's) memory. *BA BL G*

1956 Mc Man /im slíp mi unúo/ *It escapes me, you know*; /i slip Jien/ *Jane has forgotten*; /i slip im/ *He does not remember*.

SLIPPER-GRASS PARROT sb dial; for *slippery grass*. A variety of the PARROT fish associated in some way with slippery grass.

1952 FGC StAnn /slípa-gràas páarát/.

SLIPPERY-BUR sb dial. A type of broomweed having somewhat mucilaginous burs: *Corchorus siliquosus*. s BROWN WEED.

1927 Beckwith 27, Slippery-bur. . For cold or asthma. 1954 *WIMJ* 24, Brown Weed; Slippery Bur.

SLIPPERY-OKRO sb dial; <*slippery* + OKRO. Some kind of wild malvaceous plant with small hibiscus-like yellow flower. (Perh *Pavonia spinifex.*)

1951 FGC Man, StE.

SLIPPLE see SRIPPLE.

SLIP-SLOP sb dial; cf *OED* cit Bartlett 1859, '*Slip-slops*, old shoes turned down at the heel'.

1943 *GL* Tre, Shrip-shap, old shoes. 1955 FGC Man /slip-slap/. *G*

SLOBBER-SLOBBER /slaba-slaba/ sb dial; iterative of *slobbery*, untidy, slovenly (*EDD* 5). A slovenly, untidy person. (Cf also *laba-laba.*)

1954 LeP StAnn Slabber slabber. . used when the person is very untidy.

SLOGWOOD see SLUGWOOD.

SLOP-SLOP sb and adj dial; iterative of *slop*. (*OED sb*[2]).

1958 DeC StT /slap-slap/ n. and adj. Sloppy and muddy road or field; equiv to *potopoto*.

SLUG sb obs; prob dial var of *sloe*: *EDD* lists *slag* as one var.

1838 Kelly 26, About the ripe season of the slug (the fruit of the giant bully-tree).

SLUGWOOD /slogwud/ sb; prob <SLUG, in allusion to the black, succulent berries (like sloes), +*wood*. (*OED* has only Slog-wood, 1864.) Note folk-etym in quot 1952. The tree *Hufelandia pendula*, also called Slogwood.

1864 Grisebach 787, Slog-wood. 1914 Fawcett 204, Slog-wood or Slug-wood. 1941 Swabey 30, Slugwood—(Slogwood). 1952 FGC StAnn, StE; StT, Slugwood, has black berries like revolver bullets; pigeons feed on them.

SLUSH sb dial; cf *EDD slush* sb 3.

1954 LeP Kgn, Slush, a dish of curried goat.

SLUT sb dial; *OED* 3, '?Orig U.S.' but *DAE*, *DA* do not enter it; 1845→. *BL*

1943 *GL* Kgn, StE, Slut—bitch, she-dog.

smadi, S'MADI see SOMEBODY.

SMALL-EYE JACK = CAVALLY JACK.

1952 FGC StJ.

SMALL GREEN LIZARD see GREEN LIZARD.

SMALL HOUSE sb dial; cf Scots *wee hoosie*, US *little house*. *G*

1954 LeP StAnn, StE, Small house, latrine.

SMALL-LEAF sb dial.

1943 *NHN* II 59, *Exostema caribæum*—Small Leaf. . The rather small leaves give rise to the local name, but Fawcett and Rendle give the names 'Caribbee Bark Tree', 'Jamaica Jesuit's Bark', and 'Prince Wood Tree'.

SMALL-LEAVED CALALU sb bot; see CALALU. *Amarantus viridis*. *G*

1864 Grisebach 782, Calalu, small-leaved, *Euxolus caudatus*.

[SMALL-LEAVED IRONWOOD sb bot.

1864 Grisebach 784, Small-leaved Ironwood: *Mouriria myrtilloides*.]

[SMALL-LEAVED PIGEON-WOOD sb bot.

1864 Grisebach 786, Small-leaved Pigeon-wood: *Coccoloba punctata* and *leoganensis*.]

[SMALL-LEAVED ROD-WOOD sb bot.

1864 Grisebach 787, Small-leaved Rod-wood: *Eugenia monticola*.]

SMALL-LEAVED SWEETWOOD sb bot.

1914 Fawcett 217, *Nectandra coriacea*. . Sweetwood, Cap-berry sweetwood, small-leaved sweetwood.

SMALL-LEAVED WHITE BEEFWOOD see BEEFWOOD.

SMALL-LITTLE adj dial. *BL G*

1954 LeP StT, Very small, tiny (adj)—smaal-likl.

SMALL MATTERS /smáal-mátaz/ sd dial. Something of no consequence; a trifle. *BL G T*

1950 Pioneer 22, Bra 'Nancy, fas' as usual, fine himself a king yard goh tell king sey dat him Anancy can get de gal fe king. Hear him, 'Dat is shmall mattas king, shmall mattas. Just leave eveything to me'. 1954 LeP StT, Smaal mattas—something little, of no importance.

[SMALL PIGEON-WOOD sb bot.

1864 Grisebach 786, Small Pigeon-wood: *Coccoloba diversifolia*.]

SMALL-SEED (COTTON) sb obs. One of the varieties of *Gossypium*.

1793 Edwards II 271 [Varieties of SHRUB COTTON:] 4th, *French* or *Small-seed*, with a whitish beard. This is the cotton in general cultivation in Hispaniola. . On the whole, the most profitable sorts for general cultivation seem to be, the second of the Green-seed, the French or Small-seed, and the Brasilian. 1814 Lunan I 240.

SMALL-SETTLER sb; <*small*+*settler*. A CULTIVATOR who has only a small holding of land, enough for subsistence but not much more.

1936 Olivier 140, It was contrary to sound social policy to sell land to small settlers. 1951 FGC gen.

SMALL-SETTLING sb attrib; <**small-settle* vb, back-formed from SMALL-SETTLER, + -*ing*. Cultivation on a small settlement.

1952 FGC Tre, You can get a little small-settling work.

SMALL-STOCK sb; <*small*+*stock* (*OED* 54). Collectively: The poultry and smaller domestic animals kept on a property or estate. *BA*

1788 Marsden 22–3, The person who keeps the keys counts over the small stock every morning, and delivers in a list. 1790 Moreton 94, The first charge a book-keeper gets is that of the sheep, goats, swine, and poultry (called the small stock). 1797 *Braco* 13 July, Account of Small Stock. 2 Peacocks, 2 Do Henns, 5 Guinea Fowls. 1828 Ordinances. . Kingston 55. 1839 McMahon 184, When any one of them had killed a hog, a sheep, or other small stock. 1954 *FG* 538, Chapter XLV. Small stock and Poultry. (Covers pigs, goats, rabbits, poultry.)

smari see SOMEBODY.

SMARTLY TIME, ON A adv phr dial.

1958 DeC StT /an a smaatli taim/ promptly, early.

S'MODY see SOMEBODY.

SMOKE-MILL sb joc obs. A steam-engine.

1826 Barclay 239, I was much struck with their [the negroes'] admiration of the first 'steam-engine', or '*smoke-mill*', as they call it, that was set to work in the neighbourhood where I resided, and which they came from all quarters to see.

SMOKE PLANTAIN sb dial; prob for *smoky*. A variety of plantain, the fruit having a smoky colour.

1952 FGC Port, Smoke plantain = horse plantain.

SMOKER sb dial. A wire frame for hanging meat over the fire to smoke it; a *hangkra*.

1956 Mc Clar, StAnd /smúoka, sumúoka/—also /kreng-kreng, pata/.

SMOKY BANANA sb dial. A banana similar to the APPLE BANANA, but with a dark brown skin.

1952 FGC StAnd.

SMOOTH-LEAVED CERASEE sb bot.

1814 Lunan I 173, *Momordica balsamina*..This is called *smooth-leaved cerasee*, or *male balsam apple*. 1850 Macfadyen 139, Smooth-leaved Cerasee..Ainslie informs us that the Sanscrit name of the plant is *vahissee*, which sounds very like our *cerasee*.

SMOOTH-LEAVED COWITCH sb bot. The small tree *Acidoton urens*.

1756 Browne 336, The smooth-leafed Cowhage. 1920 Fawcett 303, *A. urens*..Mountain Cowitch, Smooth leaved Cowitch.

SMOOTH-LEAVED PINE sb obs? See KING PINE quot 1774.

SMUTTY adj dial; <*smutty* (cf *OED*). Ill-smelling. *BA*

1956 Mc StAnd /it smel smoti—it stingk/.

snaat-hed parat sb dial; from either *snot* or *snort* + *head* + PARROT. A variety of parrot fish.

1952 FGC StM /snaat-hed parat/—lets big lumps of slime out in pot; also StJ.

SNAKE BUSH sb dial. = PUDDING WITHE. (See quot 1954.)

SNAKE-CAP sb dial. An unidentified plant used medicinally—see quot.

1952 FGC StM /siníek-kyap/—have a /maav-kolor/ [mauve] flower; when children have /hiich/ [itch], bathe them with it—make skin smooth.

SNAKE-HEAD sb dial.

1958 DeC Kgn /sniek-hed/—a cutlass..20 in. long with an oblique lobed end.

SNAKE-ROOT sb dial. Prob the plant *Eryngium foetidum*, FIT WEED, used to 'revive' supposedly dead people in myalist practice.

1946 Dunham 159, Snake root..used in Obeah practices.

SNAKE WAITING-BOY sb dial. A lizard (species of *Celestus* or *Mabuya*—see quot 1940) said to attend on a snake. (Closely related to the GALLIWASP.) *BL*

1940 Lynn-Grant 101–3, 111, Snake waiting-boy: *Celestus Barbouri*..*Celestus Crusculus Crusculus*..*Celestus Crusculus Cundalli*..*Mabuya spilonotus*. 1943 *NHN* II 80, The snake-waiting-boy is another attractive, striped lizard. 1952 FGC StAnd /sníek wíetn-bwài/—plain thing, black; has legs but jus' wiggle-wiggle and run gone; head resembles snake; /eniwe im de, sniek duon lef far/ *Wherever it is, a snake is not far off*.

SNAKE-WEED sb dial; cf *OED* 1597 in diff senses.

1. An unidentified plant: see quot.

1927 Beckwith 27, Snake-weed (grass). For a snake-bite beat it up and bind over the bite.

2. ? = SPIRIT WEED.

1952 FGC StAnn, Snake-weed has prickles at tips and little prongs.

SNAKE WITHE sb.

1. *Cissus sicyoides*, so called because of the way it grows. Also called PUDDING-WITHE.

1926 Fawcett 77, Snake Withe, Wild Yam, Yaws Bush, Bastard Bryony..This species climbs to a great height on trees and rocks, sending down bundles of long cord-like fibres, which take root when they reach the ground. 1943 *NHN* I 128, Wall Saddle, also called Snake Withe or Soldier Withe. 1954 *WIMJ* 26.

2. A type of climbing cactus (*C. grandiflorus* or *C. flagelliformis*).

1952 FGC Han, Snake wis—a small, running, seven-side cactus.

SNAKE-WOOD sb; cf *OED* 2 1832→.

1. The TRUMPET TREE: *Cecropia peltata*.

1756 Browne 111, The Trumpet-tree, and Snake-wood. 1774 Long III 757, Snakewood. 1864 Grisebach 787, Snake-wood: *Cecropia peltata*. 1952 FGC Tre, Snake-wood, the Clarendon name for trumpet tree. 1954 *WIMJ* 28.

2. One kind of GREENHEART: *Colubrina ferruginosa*; perh also *C. reclinata*.

1926 Fawcett 68, *C. ferruginosa*..Greenheart, Snake Wood, Black Velvet, Wild or Mountain Ebony. 1941 Swabey 30, Snakewood. 1943 *NHN* II 89, Snake Wood. There are probably two species of trees called by this name. One species commonly occurs on the crest of the hill—it is scarcely more than a large shrub..On the lower slopes and coastal shelf, 'Snakewood' is unquestionably a tree. This tree may be *Colubrina reclinata*. 1952 FGC StAnn.

SNAKE YAM sb dial; descr. A variety of white yam in which the tubers are not thick but long.

1952 FGC StC /sniek yam/. 1954 LeP Man, Snake = white yam. So called because of the shape of the tuber. 1956 Mc Man, Snake yam—also called Braggin Tam.

SNAKY-BONY(-SCARCE-O'-FAT) adj and sb dial; <*snaky* + *bony* (+ SCARCE-O'-FAT). Very thin; a thin person.

1954 LeP StAnn, Snaky-boney—meagre, thin, adj. 1958 DeC StT /snieki-buoni-skies-a-fat/ a very thin person.

SNAP-DRAGON sb bot arch. *Ruellia tuberosa*, now usually called DUPPY GUN.

1756 Browne 268, Ruellia 2..Menow-weed, Spirit-weed, and Snap-Dragon. This plant is very common in most parts of Jamaica. 1814 Lunan II 191, Snap-Dragon..It hath..a four-square seed-vessel, about an inch long, containing a great many small brown flat seeds; which seed-vessel, touched with the least moisture, spring open with a little snap or noise. 1864 Grisebach 787, Snap-dragon.

SNAPPER sb; cf *OED* 1697→. Any of various fish of the genus *Lutianus* and similar ones. (The name is quite loosely applied by fishermen: see BLACK, MUTTON, POT, RED BELLY, RED TAIL, REEF, RUNNING, SATIN, SILK, YELLOW-TAIL and other kinds.) *BA BL G*

1679 Trapham 65, The next division crowded with various Snappers, Rock fish, Stone bass, Cavallies.

SNIPER-WIPER sb dial slang; origin uncert, but cf *EDD snipe*, to blow the nose with finger and thumb; if this is the source of the first element, *wiper* may be meant literally; but in view of the meaning, *wiper* may be a joc Vellerism for *viper*.

1956 Mc Man /snáipa-wáipa/ a snake in the grass, hypocrite.

SNIT /snit, sínít/ sb; <*sinnet*, early form of *OED sennet*[2]; *snit* is prob an overcorrection of *sinnet* by someone who took this to be a folk pronunciation (cf /simit/ for *smith*, /siniek/ for *snake*, etc.), and therefore considered the first vowel superfluous.

The Sennet fish: *Sphyræna borealis* or *S. picudilla*. *BA*

[1756 Browne 451, Perca? 1. Minor subargentea. The Sinnet.] 1854–5 *TJSA* I 144, Esox Americanus—the Snit? 1952 FGC Port, StM /snit/ favour barracouta; West /sinit/ round, long, but not as big as *snook*.

SNOWBALL sb.

1. A drink made of shaved ice with sweet fruit-flavoured syrup poured over. *BA T*

c 1915 FGC StAnd. 1948 Dunham 93. 1960 DeC in *Names* VIII 16, The snowball cart is primarily used for vending 'snowballs', i.e. fruit syrup poured over shaved ice, but one can usually also buy soft drinks, cakes, cookies, occasionally beer, and (rarely) an illegal tot of rum..The snowball cart..bears an elaborate and ornamental super-structure..[which] consists of racks for bottles, a glassed-in cabinet for cakes and cookies, and a roof.

2. Attrib or comb: *Snowball cart*, a brightly-painted push-cart from which snowballs are sold; *Snowball man*, seller of snowballs.

SNOW-BERRY sb bot; *OED* 1 1815→, *DAE* 1803→. The plant *Chiococca alba*, with white berries.

1756 Browne 164, Chiococca 1..Snow-berry, or David's-root..the berries are of a snowy colour. 1801 Dancer 363, Snowberry. 1936 Fawcett 70.

SNOWDROP TREE sb bot; *OED* 1864→. *Hænianthus incrassatus.*

1814 Lunan II 176, Snow-Drop-Tree. Chionanthus.. incrassata..petals white, concave, ending in a thread. 1864 Grisebach 787, Snowdrop Tree.

SO adv, conj, and pron; < Engl *so* adv and conj, but sometimes with concurrent infl of African words and syntax—e.g. of Twi *sò*, after the manner of, agreeing with the Engl sense *thus*. See separate senses.

A. adv: 1. Chiefly in exclamatory sentences: Postposed to the adjective it modifies, and emphasizing it. (Unstressed.) *BA BL G T*

1927 Anderson-Cundall 68, Pig ax him mumma say, wha mek him mout' long so. 1956 Mc StAnd /ou shi luk yong so/ *How young she looks!* /ou disa pikini ed baal so/ *How bald this child is!* /yu hafi tel mi wat unu a iit mek unu fat so/ *You must tell me what you eat to make you so fat!*

2. Postposed to sentences as a sort of concluding syllable, i.e. having a prosodic function, with little or no lexical meaning. *G T*

1956 Mc StAnd /jak fruut hav aal saiz—som smaala, som big so/ *Jackfruits can be any size, some smaller, some large.* StE /mi no kaal im síem we so/ *I didn't call him like that (as you say).* Man /iz hú did hav it so/ *Who had it?*

3. Postposed to and emphasizing adverbs or adverbial expressions of place: *de-so, ya-so*, etc. (See separate entries.) *G T*

B. conj: 1. In comparisons: like, as...as. (Unstressed.) *G T*

1941 Kirkpatrick 38, But if dem 'ead wuzen so cocoa mek dem follow da loud-mout man..(etc.) [*But if their head wasn't like a coco*,..etc.].

2. By reduction of *and so*: and, and thus. (But cf Twi *so*, *ɛso*, also, besides.) *BL*

1837 Belisario Expl to Plate 8, Him gone so lef me. 1910 Anderson-Cundall 5 [Prov:] You can't sit down 'pon cow back, so cuss cow 'kin. [*You can't curse cowskin while sitting on a cow's back*]. 1951 Murray 32, Ratta laugh, him laugh, him laugh, Him tumble dung so dead. 1950 Pioneer 63, Him meck up him mine fe carry some come offer de cow dem, so tell dem is fe him chewstick.

3. Expressing an immediate consequence: as, as soon as, the moment that. (Stressed.) *BL*

1877 Murray *Kittle* 25, Den so de pigeon dem da eat corn a top, Mudfish da da bottom da pick up wha drop, da eat. 1912 McK *Songs* 14, De bank dem we deh dig..dem caan' 'tan sake o' we naybor pig; For so we moul' it up he root it do'n. 1956 Mc Man /an so im klaim di trii, di fruut kom dong/; StE /só az him híer di náking, him ték a liti stík/.

C. pron: Such, that sort of thing. *G*

1912 McK *Songs* 43, De pan might leak Dem don't..eben try fe seek Some clay or so to mek it sound.

so see SISTER.

SOAKAPEE sb dial; < *soak* + uncert element, perh *pee*, urinate.

1941 Kirkpatrick gloss, Soakapee, sot, drunken dolt.

SOAKY-SWALLOW see SUCKY-SWALLOW.

SOAP-BERRY TREE sb; *OED* 3 1725→. The tree *Sapindus saponaria.*

1696 Sloane 185, Prunifera racemosa..fructu saponario.. The Sope-berry Tree. In omnibus sylvis camp. Jam. Ins. 1926 Fawcett 52, Soap Berry Tree..The fleshy exterior of the fruit can be used as soap. *N* /suop beri/.

SOAP-BUSH sb. *Clidemia hirta.*

1927 Beckwith 27, Soap-bush..Boil as tea. 1953 *WIMJ* 251, Indian Currant Bush; Soap Bush.

SOAP PLANT sb.

1920 Fawcett 261, *Phyllanthus..epiphyllanthus*..Seaside Laurel, Rock Bush, Soap Plant, Sword Bush..Soap is sometimes made from the ashes of the plant.

sobljak see SUPPLE-JACK.

sochilaik indef pron dial; < *such* + *-i* + *like*. Such-like; things like that.

1952 FGC Tre [Of a hunter attacked by a wild hog:] /dem huol yu doun an bait yu op an sochilaik—kil yu an di spat/; Tre, see VERVINE.

SODA-BLUFF sb.

c 1940 HPJ, Soda-bluff, a cake with soda in it.

sodad gront see SOUTH'ARD GRUNT.

SOFA sb dial. A rough, wooden single bed.

1954 LeP Kgn, A bed big enough for one person—sofa. 1958 DeC StT /suofa/ meaning not a sofa but a rough wooden bed.

SOFTLY adj dial; < *softly* adv. Quiet, soft.

1895 Bates 42 [Prov:] Sofely ribber run deep.

SOFT-SOFT adj dial. Easily taken advantage of. *BL*

1958 DeC Port, see *pyaa-pyaa*.

SOLDIER see CRACK-POT SOLDIER.

SOLDIER SOUP sb. Soup made of 'soldiers', or hermit crabs.

a 1818 Lewis (1845) 109, I have also tried the soldier soup, which is in great estimation in this island; but although it greatly resembled the very richest cray-fish soup, it seemed to me to be composed of crayfish which had been kept too long. The *soldiers* themselves were perfectly fresh, for they were brought to the kitchen quite alive and merry; but I was told that this taste of staleness is their peculiar flavour.

SOLDIER'S TASSEL sb. The plant *Russelia equisetiformis*, commonly planted in gardens; the flower is a long, slender bright-red tube, whence the name.

1952 FGC StAnd.

SOLDIER WITHE sb. = PUDDING WITHE.

1943 *NHN* I 28, see SNAKE WITHE. 1952 FGC StAnn, StE, Tre /soulja wis/.

SOLE sb tech; cf *OED* sb[1] 6. See quot.

1958 DeC StAnd, When a banana stump is split before replanting, the /suol/ is the flat, freshly-cut inside surface. In planting, this is always faced upwards. The *roof* (the round, outer, uncut surface) is always faced downwards.

solfit sb dial; < *surfeit*; cf *OED* 5b, 'an eruptive disease in horses'. Some kind of skin affliction (hives or the like): see quots.

1958 DeC StC /solfit/—an affliction of the skin, equiv to scratch-scratch. 1958 FGC StT /solfit/—when you hot and drink water, you get wheals [on your skin].

SOLID-NYAAMPS sb dial; < *solid* + NYAAMPS, but cf Twi *anyãmpa*, disgrace, dishonour, infamy.

1943 *GL* StM, Solid-nyaamps, worthless fellow.

SOLITAIRE sb ornith; *OED* 5b. The Antillean Solitaire bird, *Myadestes genibarbis solitarius*.

1847 Gosse 205, The temptation of these berries draws the Solitaires from their seclusion, and we not only hear their clear notes trilled from every part of the groves, but see them familiarly eating. 1890 Thomas 45, I was particularly struck by the mournful beauty of the cry of the solitaire. 1956 Jeffrey-Smith 36–9.

SOLOMON GUNDY the dish *salmagundi* (see *OED*).

SO LONG adv phr; < *so long as*. So long as. *G T*

1947 U.Newton III 28, He had a puppy which could tell the time by going outside (so long the day was sunny) looking at the sun..etc.

somadi, somari see next.

SOMEBODY /sómádi, sm-ádi/ occas /sómári, sm-ári/ sb dial; < *somebody*. Dial sp *s'mody* represents the pronunc with /d/, *summary* represents that with /r/. *BA*

1. A person; any person. *G*

1826 Barclay 191, see SHADOW-CATCHER: *summary* (somebody). 1826 Williams 195, 'You wicked somebody' [*You are a wicked person*]. 1873 Rampini 175 [Prov:] Braggin ribber nebber drown somebody (anybody). 1910 Anderson-Cundall 28, Fas' s'mody, *Impertinent people*, see FAST. 1927 Anderson-Cundall 49, see NARA. 1959 DeC Clar [When a man applied for a job and was refused:] /dem hàv nóf smádi arédi/.

2. A human being (as distinct from an animal).

1952 FGC Tre [Of a wild fruit:] /smádi híit it/ *Human beings (can) eat it.* *G*

3. In phrases following *every, some*.

1956 Mc Man, (Alligator Pond) /évri sómadi/ *everybody*, (Banana Ground) /sóm sómari/ *somebody*.

SOMETHING /somting, sonting, sonti, sompten, sinting, sintin, sinti/ sb dial; < *something*. (Cf *SC sánati, sanì*. Focke.) *BA G*

1. = Thing.

1826 Williams 194 [What dat sunting you hab day?] *What's that (thing) you have there?* 1912 McK *Songs* 92, De cowitch under which he hab fe 'toop..Is killin' some-t'ing for a naygur man. 1943 *GL* most parishes, Sunty, Sinting, Sinding, Sinty. 1956 Mc Man /yu a tek op yu sinting dem/ *You are gathering your belongings.* StE /yu gat tu moch somting fi go sel op de/ *You have too many things to go selling them all up.*

2. Of a person: A derogatory term that seems to deny him personality.

1954 LeP StAnn, Somebody of no account—Old black something.

som kuochi wata see SANGKOCHIE.

SO-MUCH see MUCH.

sompten, somting, sonti, sonting see SOMETHING.

SON-WIFE sb dial; for *son's wife*.

1954 LeP Kgn, Son-wife—daughter-in-law.

SOOKEY see *suki*.

SOOL vb dial; < *sowl*, to seize (a pig) by the ear. (*OED* v^3: Now *dial.*) →1892.

1943 *GL* No addr, Sool, The huntsman cry to incite a hound.

SOONGA sb obs; cf Ngombe *sóngbá*, sesame seeds. = WANGLA.

a 1726 Barham (1794) 121–2, Oily Pulse, Which is called *zesamum*, or *sesamum Africanum*. The first time I saw this plant, it was growing in a negro's plantation..[They have] seed vessels, full of small white seeds, which the negroes call *soonga*, or *wolongo*, which is much like the sago sold in shops, but very oily.

SOON-MAN see *suun-man*.

SOOTOOT sb dial uncom; < *surtout*.

1943 *GL* StE, Sootoot, an overall.

SOPHIE MANGO sb dial; prob personifying, but cf SALT-FISH MANGO. Some variety of mango.

1952 FGC StAnd /súofi manggo/.

sopljak see SUPPLE-JACK.

sor see SISTER.

SORASEE see CERASEE.

SORE-SORE sb dial; iterative of *sore*, sb. A collection of sores.

1952 FGC Man, Yaws, many people have it—/súor-sùor ùova dem fíes/.

SORE TOE sb dial.

1. Fig in phr *to mash one's sore toe*: to cause one pain or embarrassment, to touch a tender spot. *BL G*

1955 Bennett *Oonoo Lie!*, Beggin you pardon Jane, Me gwine mash oonoo sore-toe, But me haffe talk out plain.

2. Transf: A crude lamp; see quots.

1943 *GL* Man, Soretoe, a bottle lamp or torch made with a cork of porous paper, and supplied with kerosine oil. 1955 FGC Man.

sorosi see CERASEE.

SORREL /saril/ sb; *OED* 1760→ this sense.

1. The plant *Hibiscus sabdariffa*, from which a cool-drink, a jelly, etc. are made; also called FRENCH, INDIAN, JAMAICA(N), RED SORREL.

1707 Sloane xxix, Cool Drink made of Molossus and Water, Perino, Corn Drink, Cane Drink, that made of Sorrel or Pines, are all accounted unwholesom, they turning sower in twelve or twenty four hours..Although I have known some people drink nothing else, and yet have their health very well. 1913 Harris 20. 1952 FGC Han, StAnd, etc. /sáril/. *BA BL G T*

2. Attrib as in *sorrel cool-drink, sorrel jam*, etc. (see RED SORREL). *BA BL G T*

SORREL GRUNT sb; prob from the colour. Some variety of the GRUNT fish.

1854–5 *TJSA* I 143, Pristipoma..Are these the grunts usually denominated Sorrel grunts?

SORREL ROSE sb obs. The Jamaican wild rose.

1814 Lunan II 126, *Blakea..trinervia*..The petala of the flower have an agreeable acid taste, hence some have called this plant the *sorrel rose*.

SORREL VINE sb bot. The vine *Cissus trifoliata*; also called VINE-SORREL.

1837 Macfadyen 179, Cissus acida. *Sorrel-Vine*. 1864 Grisebach 787, Sorrel-vine: *Cissus acida*. 1926 Fawcett 78, Sorrel Vine. 1955 *WIMJ* 155, Cissus trifoliata L. Sorrel Vine; Rat Ears; Pudding Wys?; Wild Yam?

SORROW-FOR-POOR PEAS sb dial. A variety of 'peas' (i.e. beans) which are thought of as taking pity on the poor people who eat them. (Cf COME-HERE-FE-HELP-WE yam.)

1873 Rampini 90–1, Pease and pulse of all kinds—the 'red Miss Kelly' and the 'Black Betty',..and 'Sorrow for poor' crowd up all the available space. 1929 Beckwith 19, [ref to Rampini].

SO-SO /súo-so, só-so/ adj; prob < Pg Afr pidgin < Pg *so*, alone, sole, only; in sense 1 perh infl by Yoruba *sho-sho*, only; in sense 2 by English *so-so*, mediocre (*OED* so so B 1b).

1. Of a thing: alone, by itself, unaccompanied by something that one might have expected with it. *BL*

1907 Jekyll 165, So-so wahk him wahk suit me. [*Just the way she walks—apart from other things about her—suits me.*] 1924 Beckwith 94, So when she go long, she see so-so head in de road [i.e. a head without a body]. 1943 *GL* Clar, Kgn, Port, StJ, So-so—only, bare, plain, without; also Sosoh, Swoso. 1951 Murray 3–4 [Song:] Noh gimme so-soh bunch Me no horse wid bridle. [*Bunches alone*—a bunch being the heaviest load.] 1956 Mc Man /máin yu sóso hed ina di son/ *Be careful of your bare head in the sun* [without a hat].

2. Mere, ordinary. *BA BL G N*

1954 P. M. Sherlock, to LeP, 'I finally said, Well, bring me a dish of this "Cristofin" you're always talking about; and when they brought it, it was so-so cho-cho!'.

SO-SOH see SO-SO.

SOSUMA, SOSUMBA see SUSUMBA.

SOTAY, SO ȜAY, SOTEE, SOTEL, SO-TELL see next.

SO-TILL /so-tél, so-té, sotíl, sotíi/ conj and adv; < *so* adv 1 + *till* conj. (Cf Cameroons pidgin *sote:*, until. Schneider.) *BL G*

A. conj: Until. *SC sotê.*

1877 Murray *Feedin' 'Perrit* 3–4, Man hab him good, good head o' hair, take it go gie sun an sall water so tay it red de same like fox tail grass. 1943 *GL* StJ, StM, Tre, Sotay, Sotee, Sotel, until. 1950 Pioneer 35, Him proud a dem so till noh-mo-noh leff. [*Until he couldn't be prouder.*]

B. adv: Inexpressibly, excessively. (Derived by aposiopesis from such phrases as '— so till I can't express it', '—so till it couldn't be more'.)

1927 Stafford 42, I hate him so till! 1941 Kirkpatrick 2, 'Im cubbitch so tell, an' 'im no even know 'imself wey 'im want. 1950 Pioneer 76, When Brer Nancy hear dis, him frighten so tell, but him hab fe go. 1954 LeP StT, Dis ya man is di wos in a di distrik, im bad so till. 1956 Mc StT /ar ozban drongk da nait sotil/; Man /a glad fi si yu sotíia/ (emotional: exaggerated rise of pitch with lengthening).

sou, sb dial; prob < *sow*, female hog—cf BOAR, BOW (MACHETE); but perh infl by SWORD. A MACHETE, usually with a straight back, sometimes with flaring end.

1952 FGC Man, Machete—called /suord/ in St Thomas /sou/ in Vere. 1954 LeP Kgn, Port, StAnd, StE, StT /sou/. 1956 Mc StE /sou/ A straight machete—also open-guard.

SOUP-REMEDY sb dial joc; < *soup* + REMEDY. Vegetables to flavour soup.

1958 DeC StAnd /suup-remidi/ leginz.

SOUR-APPLE sb. An unidentified fruit: perhaps a variety of OTAHEITE APPLE.

1952 FGC StM, Sour-apple grows here: red, longer than Otaheite apple, sour.

SOURASEA see CERASEE.

SOUR BAAJ sb dial; < *sour* + *baaj*, which see.

1. The fruit of *Phyllanthus distichus* (or *acidus*).

1952 FGC Port, Know jimbilin, but /saua-baaj/ is the name here. 1956 Mc Port, Also called /soua-baaj/.

2. The fruit of *Averrhoa carambola*: see CHINESE JIMBLING quot 1959.

SOUR-FLY sb chiefly dial. A very small fly (*Drosophila* spp) that is attracted by souring foods, vinegar, etc. *BL G*

1952 FGC Han, StAnd /soua flai/ come when mango, pine juice, sour.

SOUR GRASS sb. The grass *Paspalum conjugatum*. *BA BL G*

1756 Browne 365, Andropogon 2..Sour-Grass..It is a strong detersive and agglutinant. 1864 Grisebach 787. 1954 *FG* 217.

SOUR ORANGE sb; *DAE* 1785→. The Seville orange: *Citrus vulgaris*. *BL N T*

[1725 Sloane 181, Orange trees are thought..to grow naturally in the Woods at Orange-Bay in Jamaica, both sweet and sour in great plenty.] 1837 Macfadyen 129–30, The sweet and the bitter Oranges are considered..as distinct species..In the parish of St John, in particular, the trees may be seen..laden with their golden-hued fruit, which for richness of flavour and for sweetness cannot be surpassed. In that district a bitter or a sour Orange is rarely to be met. 1952 FGC Port, StAnd, StE, StJ /sòuwa árinj/ = /sìbl árinj/.

SOUR PEPPER sb. A variety of *Capsicum*; see quot.

1954 *FG* 469, Sour Pepper, of similar growth and habits as the Bird, but bearing a much larger fruit..Largely used ..for making the various brands of hot pepper sauce.

SOURSOP BIRD sb; *OED* 1895→. The ORANGE QUIT, which frequently feeds on ripe soursops.

1847 Gosse 236, Orange-quit. Feather-tongue or Sour-sop bird. 1935 Bond 312, *Euneornis campestris*..Sour-sop Bird..*Range:*—Jamaica. 1956 Jeffrey-Smith 70, Its liking for certain fruit has originated besides the name of Orange Quit, that of Sour-Sop Bird.

SOURSOP FISH sb dial. A local name for the porcupine or HEDGEHOG fish, from its prickly exterior: *Diodon hystrix* and similar species.

1892 Cockrell list, Soursop fish—*diodon liturosus*. 1899 *Jrl Institute of Ja* 614, Sour-sop Fish. *Diodon maculatus.* 1952 FGC Port, StAnn, StC, StE, StM, StT, West /sauasap fish/.

SOURSOP TREE sb. The tree *Anona muricata*. (The fruit is the soursop.) *BA BL G N T*

[p1660 *State of Jamaica* see CUSTARD APPLE.] 1696 Sloane 204, *Anona maxima*..fructu maximo viridi conoide..The Sowre-sop Tree. 1756 Browne 255, The Sour-sop Tree. This..is one of the most common plants in every Savanna.

SOUR-WEED sb dial. Prob *Cissus trifoliata.*

1952 FGC StE /sauwa wiid/ vine sorrel.

SOUSHUMBER, SOUSOUMBER, SOUSUMBER see SUSUMBA.

SOUTH'ARD GRUNT sb; < *southward* + GRUNT. The WHITE GRUNT, so called in Old Harbour. See quot.

1952 FGC StC /sódad grónt/—'when you have weather [i.e. storms] they come from southward'.

SOUTH-SEA ROSE sb; *OED* 1753→. The garden plant *Nerium oleander.*

1740 Importance 35, With the South-sea Rose; The Flower is very beautiful,..the leaf and plant is something like the Osier. 1756 Browne 181, Nerium 3..The South-sea Rose. 1952 FGC StAnn, StE /sóut síi ruoz/ oleander.

SOUTH SIDE sb. That part of Jamaica which lies southward of the central mountainous ridge. See NORTH SIDE.

SOW-HOG /sou/ sb dial. *BA*

1943 *GL* StM, Sow-hog, sow.

SOWING-MATCH sb. A rural contest of seed-sowing.

1954 LeP Kgn, To sow the seeds—to have a sowing-match.

SOW-MOUTH sb dial. A fish with a mouth like a sow.

1952 FGC StE /sou-mout/ a hard-tailed squirrel.

spanchalam see SPANISH ELM.

SPANISH adj used in many cpds. As a colour word in early general and present dial use: bright yellow or gold: cf SPANISH CARNATION, COOT, ELM, etc. In reference to weapons it usually means very sharp, sharpened on both sides: cf SPANISH BILL, MACHETE. *T*

SPANISH ARBOUR-VINE sb; *OED* 1731→. The plant *Ipomœa tuberosa*, once much used on arbours.

1696 Sloane 55, Convolvulus major, heptaphyllos flore sulphureo odorato speciossimo. Spanish arbor vine, or Spanish woodbind. 1756 Browne 156, The Seven-year Vine, or Spanish Arbor-Vine..This plant has been probably introduced here from some part of the main continent..it is naturally a climber, and its thick foliage and large flowers, render it extremely fit for arbors. 1864 Grisebach 781.

SPANISH BEE sb. A variety of stingless bee (*Melipona*).

1764 Gordon 381, He has also a great quantity of Bees, some, which he calls Spanish Bees, have no stings. (1961 Current, FGC.)

SPANISH BILL sb dial. = SPANISH MACHETE.

1952 FGC StM.

SPANISH CALALU sb; see CALALU.

1. *Amarantus tristis.*

1811 Titford Expl to Plate XII 8, Spanish Colilu.. A[marantus] Viridis, of a green colour. 1914 Fawcett 130, Amarantus tristis..Spanish Calalu. 1954 *WIMJ* 28.

2. *Phytolacca octandra.*

1754 Browne 232, Phytolacca 1..Spanish Calaloe. This plant is a native of Jamaica, and now cultivated in most of the kitchen gardens in the island. 1814 Lunan II 80, *Phytolacca octandra*..This is the stature of the foregoing species [*P. decandra*], but the leaves are whiter; it is known by the name of *Spanish calalue.* 1864 Grisebach 782.

SPANISH CARNATION sb. One of the names of *Cæsalpinia pulcherrima.*

1696 Sloane 149, Sena spuria arborea spinosa..Flour fence of Barbados. Wild Sena or Spanish Carnations. a 1726 Barham (1794) 16, The flowers are elegantly mixed with red-yellow, and therefore called, by some, Spanish carnation. 1920 Fawcett 95.

SPANISH CEDAR sb.

1920 Fawcett 218, *Cedrela..odorata*..Jamaican, West Indian, Spanish, or Honduras Cedar. 1955 *WIMJ* 158.

SPANISH CHARDON sb obs; *OED Spanish cardon* →1707.

1756 Browne 314, The Cardoon, or Spanish-Chardon. This plant was lately introduced to Jamaica by Mr Wallen; and is now raised in many of the gardens.

SPANISH CONTRAYERVA sb arch or obs. Species of *Dorstenia,* in contrast to *Aristolochia,* the Jamaican plant so named. See CONTRAYERVA, quots 1794, 1887.

SPANISH COOT sb. The bird *Jacana spinosa*; see quot.

1956 Jeffrey-Smith 117, The Jacana..is known..as Spanish coot in St Catherine..It has a characteristic attitude on alighting..of lifting its wings to their fullest extent, thus displaying the lovely yellow of the underside of the wings.

SPANISH DAGGER sb; *DAE, DA* 1859→. *Yucca aloifolia*; see quot.

1811 Titford 56, Aloe-leaved Adam's Needle, *Yucca Aloifolia*..This beautiful plant grows in Jamaica..It is also called Dagger-plant and Spanish Dagger.

SPANISH DOG sb; cf *OED* 1787 only, in diff sense. A bloodhound, imported esp from Cuba, and used to track Maroons, runaway slaves, etc.

1803 Dallas II 161, They got immediately under arms, and proceeding in the direction of the sound, discovered a negro endeavouring to make his escape. One of the Spanish dogs was sent after him. 1862 Clutterbuck 99, Melhado said that he would send up to the Cinnamon tomorrow a brace of Spanish dogs, to be let loose on occasion of the next Obeah gathering..some of these dogs are extremely fierce. 'Do you mean that these are bloodhounds?' 'Yes, and beauties too..old Orritt, one of my skippers, brought them from Cuba.'

SPANISH DUPPY sb dial.

1956 Mc, Spanish Duppy—ghost of a person who died in slavery times.

SPANISH ELDER sb obs. *Piper aduncum,* one type of PEPPER-ELDER.

1696 Sloane 45, Piper longum folio nervoso pallide viridi, humilius..Spanish Elder. 1794 Barham 56–7, There is a shrub in Jamaica known by the name of Spanish elder, having a green jointed stem, full of pith, like English elder, but hath none of its fruit, but a sort of *julus,* like the long pepper. It cures the cholic.

SPANISH ELM for pronunc see quot 1952; sb; see PRINCE-WOOD 1 quot 1725; *OED* 1758→.

1. A large tree with sulphur-yellow flowers and wood with a grain like that of elm: *Cordia gerascanthoides.* Formerly also PRINCE-WOOD.

1696 Sloane 155, Spanish Elm or Prince Wood. 1725 Sloane 63. 1774 Long III 846, Spanish Elm, or Prince Wood. This is esteemed one of the best timber-trees in the island..The tree rises to a considerable height..The flowers are white. 1864 Grisebach 783, see PRINCE-WOOD. 1941 Swabey 20, Elm, Spanish—*Cordia gerascanthoides*.. Tree 60 ft to 80 ft high and 2 ft diameter: wood ornamental, resembling walnut..Wood tough and strong..Useful for cabinet work. 1952 FGC StAnn, StE, StM, StT /spànish hélem, spànish hálam, spánchalám, pánish hélem, pánchalám, pànchélam, pánchalán, pánchaláng/.

2. The shrub or small tree *Hamelia ventricosa* —so Grisebach (see PRINCE-WOOD 1), whom Fawcett follows (see PRINCE-WOOD 2).

1864 Grisebach 783. 1936 Fawcett 45–6.

SPANISH GILLY-FLOWER sb obs. = SAVANNA FLOWER.

1774 Long II 418–19, Dr Barham tells us that the savannah flower..has been made use of for this purpose [in a Myal ceremony]..It is one of the rankest poisons in the world ..Some call it the Spanish gilly-flower.

SPANISH GOOSEBERRY sb obs. An unidentified plant or fruit.

1807 Renny 86, Sapota, Spanish-gooseberry, and prickly-pear.

spanish halam, spanish helem see SPANISH ELM.

SPANISH HORSE sb obs. The praying mantis. Now called GOD-HORSE.

1756 Browne 433, Mantis 1..The Spanish-Horse.

SPANISH JAR sb; by 'correction' of PANYA (< *Spaniard*) to *Spanish*. A type of large earthenware jar commonly used by the Spanish in Jamaica, and in which valuables were often buried at the time of the English conquest; cf PANYA JAR.

1873 Rampini 140, During the past week the town of Lucea was kept in a state of considerable excitement, in consequence of a report..that a Spanish jar, containing a large quantity of gold coins, has been discovered. (1960 Current, FGC.)

SPANISH-LEAF (TOBACCO) sb. A broad-leaved variety of tobacco.

1952 FGC StM, Cow-tongue leaf, long but narrower than Spanish leaf; StAnn, Spanish leaf (tobacco) has a round leaf.

SPANISH MACHETE /pánya mashíet, ~mashét/ sb; forms beginning with *p-* are dial: cf PANYA.

1. A machete sharpened on both sides.

1954 LeP Man, Double edged machete—Spanish machete.

2. The CORAL-BEAN TREE, *Erythrina corallodendrum* or *E. velutina*, from the shape of the unopened flower.

1952 FGC Han /pánya mashíet, pánya mashét/ flowers favour open-guard machete. Also StT, Tre.

3. Fig. As a favourite symbol of something sharp, that can cut either way—hence, a hypocrite.

1895 Banbury 41, Pannya (Spanish) machate cut two side:—There are people who through deceit never give a fair and decided opinion on any subject, but will tell one thing to one and another thing to another when consulted. 1910 Anderson-Cundall 30, 'Paniar' machete cut two side. 1943 *GL* StJ, Panya mashate—Speaking against both sides. 1950 Pioneer 24, Soh Anancy bein' a 'panish machette goh to Ma Kayke an ax her..etc. 1954 LeP Man, Hypocrite—Spanish machete; StE, Pania machete; Pannier-machete.

SPANISH NETTLE sb bot. = Spanish needle, of which this was probably an erroneous form perpetuated by botanists, since the only current form is *needle*.

1814 Lunan II 184, *Bidens*..It is called in Jamaica, Spanish nettle, and is very common. 1864 Grisebach 786, Spanish Nettle. 1936 Fawcett 249. 1954 *WIMJ* 28, *Bidens pilosa*..Spanish Needle or Nettle.

SPANISH NIGHTINGALE sb. The Bahaman Mockingbird, *Mimus gundlachi hilli*.

a 1705 Ray *Syn. Avium & Piscium* (1713) 184, Icterus minor nidum suspendens..The Watchy Picket, or Spanish Nightingale. The American Hang-nest. 1935 Bond 277. 1956 Jeffrey-Smith 33.

SPANISH OAK sb. = FRENCH OAK: *Catalpa longissima*.

1909 Harris 316, see MAST-WOOD. 1952 FGC Port, StT /panchúok/ mastwood; StAnn, Spanish oak, called 'mast-wood' in St Thomas, 'Yokewood' in Portland; also StM.

SPANISH OLD-WIFE sb. The fish *Cantherines pullus*.

1951 Smith in *NHN* II, *Cantherines pullus* (known locally as 'Spanish oldwife') has a rather deep body covered with small bristles. 1952 FGC StM, Spanish oldwife—yellow tail; when boiled, colours water like /nata/ (anatta).

SPANISH PHEASANT sb obs. An unidentified bird.

1740 Importance 38, Among the curious are..Canary Birds, Spanish Pheasants..(etc.).

SPANISH PHYSIC-NUT sb bot. The FRENCH PHYSIC-NUT.

[1756 Browne 348–9, French Physic Nut..The seeds are purgative, but so very violent in their operations that they are now but rarely administered; tho' formerly, they were almost the only medicines of the purgative kind used among the Spaniards.] 1920 Fawcett 313, Spanish, or French Physic Nut.

SPANISH PLUM sb; *OED* 1823→.

1. The plum *Spondias purpurea*, including the RED COAT and YELLOW COAT plums. *N*

1727 *Observations* 13, Papahs, Spanish-plumbs, Coco-plumbs..(etc.). 1756 Browne 228–9, Spondias 1..The Spanish Plumb Tree. 1864 Grisebach 787. 1913 Harris 18, Plum, Spanish..The purple skinned fruit is especially pleasant with a sweet acid flavour, and it is much used. The yellow-skinned fruit is also possessed of an agreeable flavour, but, like the Hog Plum, it is often infested with the larvæ of a fruit fly. 1955 *WIMJ* 160.

2. The plum *Ximenia americana*. (1963 Proctor Institute of Ja.)

SPANISH QUAIL sb. The Jamaican Spindalis, prob so named from its yellow colour and the stripes on the face.

1936 Bond 370, *Spindalis nigricephala*..Gold finch.. Spanish Quail..(etc.). 1956 Jeffrey-Smith 92.

SPANISH ROSEMARY sb bot; *OED* 1753. The plant *Croton linearis*; = WILD ROSEMARY.

1696 Sloane 44, Ricino affinis odorifera..rorismarini folio..Wild Rosemary, or Spanish Rosemary. 1920 Fawcett 277. 1955 *WIMJ* 158.

SPANISH SHAD sb.

1892 Cockrell list, Spanish shad—*Gerres aprion*.

SPANISH THYME sb.

1955 *WIMJ* 80, *Coleus aromaticus*..French or Spanish Thyme..In Jamaica it is sometimes used in decoctions employed as cold remedies.

SPANISHTONIAN sb. A resident of Spanish Town.

1873 Rampini 20, The Spanishtonians, between whom and the Kingstonians there exists a feeling of jealousy.

SPANISH WALL sb. A kind of wall (of houses or other buildings) made by filling the interstices in a wooden frame with bits of broken stone and clayey earth, the whole being plastered up and usually whitewashed.

1927 Stafford 57, Wid a fist dat de 'Panish wall can break [i.e. *that can break a Spanish wall*]. 1929 Beckwith 10, The walls of the houses are..commonly of..'Spanish wall'. 1952 FGC Man, StE.

SPANISH WOODBIND sb obs; *OED* only 1731. *Ipomœa tuberosa*.

1696 Sloane 55, Spanish arbor vine, or Spanish wood-bind. 1864 Grisebach 789, Spanish Wood-bind.

SPANISH WOODPECKER sb dial. Probably the Yellow-bellied Sapsucker (*Sphyrapicus varius*), smaller than the Jamaican woodpecker.

1952 FGC Han, Spanish woodpecker—smaller sort, guinea-chick colour.

SPARE see IF LIFE SPARE.

SPATHODEA sb. The tree *Spathodea campanulata*; also called WATER-MAN.

1873 Rampini 64, Beside the court-house [in Chapelton] stood a splendid Spathodea in full blossom. (1960 Current, FGC.)

SPECIA /spiisha/ sb; <Sp *especia*, spice. A kind of sweetmeat made with cashew nuts or peanuts.

c1915 FGC StAnd.

SPECKLE sb dial.

1958 DeC StT /spekl/—name for an albino Negro.

SPECKLED GRASS sb. A kind of grass listed with 'Mountain' grasses by Long; unidentified.

1774 Long III 765, The Dutch, burr, cross, speckled, and manna grasses are among the best for fodder.

SPELL sb; <*spell* (*OED sb* 2). Oxen yoked up to do a spell of work, i.e. the amount of work done in one of the usual divisions of a working day.

1839 McMahon 43, If you allow me the benefit of a spell of steers and a cart, I can go to the pasture and bring home a load of the bones.

SPENGLE sb dial; etym unknown.

1943 *GL* No addr, Spengle, a kind of fighting cock.

SPICED GUN sb. A type of pastry in which a filling is rolled up into a cylinder resembling the barrel of a gun.

1926 Edmonds 30, Spiced Guns. Make a pastry, roll out and spread with butter, sprinkle with currants, cinnamon and mixed spice..Roll, cut in blocks, stand on end..in pie dish..Bake.

SPICEWOOD sb. The tree *Ocotea staminea*.

1914 Fawcett 213, Lignum dorum, Spice wood. 1941 Swabey 24, Lignum Durum—(spice wood)..*Lauraceæ*. It is common in the interior woodlands. 1952 FGC StAnn, Spicewood—wild cinnamon.

spichuudi sb dial; evid <US slang *patootie*, with *s*- by overcorrection, affrication of the first *t*, and voicing of the second. Cf *spituuti*.

1958 DeC StAnd /spichuudi/—a term of endearment.

SPIDER LILY sb; descr. Species of *Hymenocallis*: see EGG LILY, WHITE LILY.

1952 FGC StAnn, Spider lily—so called from the shape of the flower, with slender, spreading petals like the legs of a spider.

SPIDER-RIAL sb dial; <*spider*+RIAL. An imaginary monster, half-spider, half something else unspecified. (Possibly with allusion to Anancy the Spider, who was a sort of spiderman.)

1959 Mrs E. B. Hoyes Kgn, Every village has at least one person who bullies his or her way into public notice.. until one day his or her match comes into view; this opponent however has been long beset by his secret fear ..so in he jumps saying 'come sah you a bull-bucker, duppy-conqueror an me a macca-back spider riyal a wander'.

SPIGNARD see SPIKENARD.

spiish (also **spiich**) sb dial; back-formation <*species*. A species or kind.

1952 FGC StE /juuna iz a smaala spiish av wipri/ *Juna is a smaller type of whip-ray*. Also StAnd, StT, StE /tuu spiichiz av dem/.

SPIKENARD sb; *OED* 3c 1864. The medicinal herb *Hyptis suaveolens*. See PICK-NUT.

1679 Trapham 100, see SAVANNA WEED. 1696 Sloane 64 Mentastrum maximum, flore cœruleo, nardi odore..An Spignard, whereof a precious Oil may be made.. In pratis circa urbem St Jago de la Vega. 1756 Browne 257, Spikenard..It is one of the most grateful cephalics, and alexipharmics. 1864 Grisebach 787. 1954 *WIMJ* 247.

SPIN vb dial; a var pronunc of *spit* vb.

1957 JN Rural Hill, How me drink water..Gosh gosh a gwine to spin it back pan yuh Rickie..Nuh nuh spin pon the bway vaccinate. [*Don't spit on the boy's vaccination.*]

SPINACH sb. In Jamaica: Any edible species of *Amarantus*, but that of the markets is *A. viridis*. *BA N*

1914 Fawcett 130, *A. spinosus*..Prickly Calalu, Spinach.. In common use for greens, and by some preferred to the true spinach. *Ibid* 131, *A. viridis*..Green Calalu, Spinach. 1954 *WIMJ* 28, *A. spinosus, tristis*, and *viridis*—spinach.

spinij sb dial.

1958 DeC StT /spinij/—variant of /spinaz/ small, finger-shaped, boiled dumplings.

SPINNERS sb dial. A dumpling shaped by 'spinning' it between the hands.

1954 LeP, Spinners, small dumplings. 1955 FGC Man /spinaz/. 1958 DeC gen, Spinner—a small finger-shaped dumpling. See also PLIERS.

SPIRIT-LEAF sb; cf DUPPY-GUN. The common plant *Ruellia tuberosa*, whose pods burst when wet (whence perh the element 'spirit-').

1696 Sloane 52, An gentianella utriusque Indiæ impatiens foliis agerati..Spirit-leaf. a1726 Barham (1794) 179, Spirit-leaf. This plant is well known in Jamaica by this name. 1854–5 *TJSA* I 66, Spirit Leaf. 1864 Grisebach 787, Spirit-leaf, *Ruellia tuberosa*..

SPIRIT SICKNESS sb dial cant. In the langauge of St Thomas revivalist and kumuna cults: see quot.

1953 Moore 158, Spirit sickness: when a person is troubled with the wrong kind of spirit, and a 'working' by an obeah man is necessary to get rid of it, or 'take it off'; or else drugs, esp. 'incense from the doctor-shop'. Cumina dancing is used for spirit-sickness.

SPIRIT WEED sb; see quot 1927.

1. *Ruellia tuberosa*—i.e. identified (prob mistakenly) with SPIRIT LEAF.

1699 Sloane *Phil. Trans.* XXI 119, None is more surprising than one in Jamaica, called Spirit-weed (*OED*). 1756 Browne 268, Ruellia 2.., see SNAP-DRAGON. 1866 *Treas. Bot.* 1085/1, Spirit-leaf or Spirit-weed (*OED*).

2. *Eryngium fœtidum*. Also called FAT-BUSH, FIT-WEED, MYAL WEED, etc.

1850 Macfadyen 187. 1926 Fawcett 427, *E. fœtidum*.. Spirit Weed, Fit Weed. 1927 Beckwith 27, Spirit-weed. *Eryngium fœtidum L.* 'Fat-bush', 'Fit-weed', 'Parrot-weed'. Rub the plant over the body of a person in a fit and give him tea from the plant to drink..Because of its pungent odor the plant is universally employed like 'Rosemary' and 'See-me-contract' to 'drive away duppies'. 1954 *WIMJ* 29.

spituuti sb dial; overcorrection of US slang *patootie*. Cf *spichuudi*.

1958 DeC StT (2) /spituuti/ a girl friend.

SPLENDACIOUS adj dial; *OED* →1872. Splendid, highly decorative. *G*

1961 R. M. Murray in *Gleaner* 6 Aug 20, Remember, Belinda, you bangles bright, An sash splendacious begens dat night.

splif sb dial slang; cf US slang *spifflicate*, to make drunk; to bewilder, confuse (Berrey & Van den Bark 106.5, 174.4). A smoke of GANJA; concr, a ganja cigarette. **s.**

1936 Martinez in *Gleaner* 3 Oct 35, Here is the hot-bed of ganja smoking..and even the children may be seen at times taking what is better known as their 'spliff'. 1943 *GL* Clar, Splif, ganja cigarette. 1958 DeC Kgn /splif/ a ganja cigarette;..the splif is rolled in a long cone rather than a cylinder, the point of which is held in the mouth, the splif being held up vertically while smoking to prevent the ganja from falling out.

SPORTER sb dial; cf *DAE, DA*: sporting-house = brothel. A prostitute.

1952 Kerr 89, 'Well' she said 'when these big liners come in you know there are girls who go down to meet the boat. They are called "sporters"'.

SPORTIFY adj dial; < *sport + ify*—cf BOASIFY.

1956 Mc Man /im spuotifai laik—laik fi mek a porsn laaf/ *He is comical-like—likes to make a person laugh.*

SPOTTED-CHINNED SNAKE sb obs; cf *OED spotted* 5. In Gosse's use: The BROWN SNAKE.

1851 Gosse 384, The spotted-chinned snake. A pretty little Snake, hitherto unnoticed by zoologists, has occurred to my researches in the neighbourhood of Bluefields.. *Natrix callilæma*, mihi.

SPOTTED CREEPER sb ornith obs. In Gosse's use: The Cape May Warbler, *Dendroica tigrina.*

1847 Gosse 87, Spotted Creeper.

SPOTTING vbl sb; perh represents *sporting*, as heard by Beckwith. A kind of dance step; see quot.

1929 Beckwith 214, Of possibly African survivals danced among the folk one can see individual exhibitions. A servant girl in Westmoreland did a very pretty clog which she called 'spotting', and some young men in the Pedro Plains exhibited some remarkable muscular feats to the rhythm of music.

sprang sb dial; by overcorrection of *prong*. A prong; pointed twig; pointed wire. *BL G*

1943 *GL* Port, Prang-prang—with many sprangs. 1952 FGC StAnn, Snake-weed has prickles at tips and little /sprangz/; StJ /kriipa hav fuor sprang/ *A creeper has four prongs.*

SPRAT NET sb chiefly dial. A small net operated by one person for catching sprats and such small fish for bait.

1952 Smith in *NHN* 186, 'Goggle-eye sprat'..usually caught the evening before in a small 'sprat net'.

SPRAWL OUT vb phr dial. *BL G*

1. = BROAD-OUT.

2. To get fat.

1960 NJL StC.

SPRECKLE-SPRECKLE adj dial; iterative of *spreckle* for *spreckled*, speckled (*OED*: Scots and Nth dial).

1952 FGC StT /taiga plantin sprekl-sprekl/—spots all over the skin.

SPREE /sprii/ sb dial; perh abbr of **spree girl* —cf SPREE BOY. A girl friend. *BA*

1942 Bennett 12, Fe yuh muma granpa, bada Sam, Was fe me Granny oletime spree. 1943 *GL* Kgn, Spree, girl friend.

SPREE vb dial; cf *OED spree v. intr.*, to have or take part in a spree, 1855→. Refl: to enjoy (oneself). *BA G*

1942 Bennett 24, De sinting sweet me so tell, Fe se 'ow nayga man dah spree demself Eena wite peeple hotel. 1958 DeC StE (Accom) /sprii unuself/ *enjoy yourself.*

SPREE-BOY sb dial or slang. *BA*

1954 LeP Kgn, StE (Elderslie), A man 'dressed to kill'—spree-boy.

SPREE-CHILD sb dial slang. A very smartly dressed woman.

1954 LeP StT, Spree Chail—very smart-clothes woman.

SPRICKLE-SPRICKLE sb dial; iterative of sprickle, overcorrected or *sp-* variant form of *prickle.* A great many small prickles.

1952 FGC Port, Beef thyme—resemble tree-of-life, has sprickle-sprickle.

SPRING vb trans; cf *OED* 19. Of a receptacle or container: to let (the liquid in it) come out; to leak.

1960 LeP StAnd [Man inspecting a leak in an air-conditioner:] /hit springin waata/.

SPRUCY /prúusi/ adj dial; *OED* 1774 only.

1960 LeP StAnd, Sprucy—smart, or over-smartly dressed. Applied only to women, and to women who are over-particular about their dress, or who dress in an unsuitably glamorous way—especially older women who dress so as to look younger. (1961 BLB, 'I would not restrict this to women'.) *BA G*

SPUD sb dial slang; prob joc transf from *spud*, potato. *BA*

1943 *GL* Port, Spud, ripe banana.

SPUR sb dial; cf *OED* 'in dial glossaries' 1800→. A large buttressing root of such a tree as mountain guava, puss-head, cotton, etc. *N*

1952 FGC StT.

SPUR BUR sb. The wild plant *Pavonia spinifex*, with spined spurs on the burs: 'Spine-fruited Pavonia' (Macfadyen I 61).

1926 Fawcett 129, Spur Bur.

SPUR-TREE sb; cf *OED sb*[1] 14b.

1. A tree having a prominent spur or spurs—e.g. the large cotton-tree that has given its name to Spur-tree Hill, Manchester.

1886 Hooper 10, On the first December I visited Spur Tree Hill.

2. The tree *Petitia domingensis*—apparently = Lunan's *long-spiked fiddlewood* (I 292), whence the name.

1864 Grisebach 787.

SPUR YAWS sb dial. A variety of CRAB-YAWS in which a process resembling a spur grows out from the foot sole.

1959 O. D. Simons, UCWI Preventive Med.

SPYING SHEPHERD sb dial cant. In revivalist cults, the officer believed to have powers of divination and special knowledge of the spirit world.

1953 Moore 85.

SQUAB see *kwabz.*

SQUAB, SQUAB PARROT sb dial. In the names of fish:

1. See quot.

1952 FGC West /skwab/—name here for what is called /chob/ at Green Island (Han).

2. A variety of the PARROT fish; see quots.

1952 FGC StJ /kwáb páràt/ StM, Red squab parrot; West /skwáb páràt/ or Mackenzie squab—local name for red squab parrot: bigger and flatter than chub, but similar.

SQUALLY adj dial; cf WHITE SQUALL 2. Hungry.

1943 *GL* Han, StJ, Squallie, squally—hungry. 1955 FGC Man.

SQUAT DUCK sb; descr. The Masked Duck (*Oxyura dominica*).

1936 Bond 44.

SQUEEZE-EYE sb dial; for *squeezed-eyes*. A nickname for a Chinese. s 'QUEEZE-YEYE.

1942 Bennett 47, 'Queeze Yeye hooden sell me wan small tin.

SQUEEZER sb dial. Pince-nez eyeglasses.

1952 FGC StC.

SQUIB sb dial; <*squid*. The squid.

1952 FGC StM /skwibz/—bony, have a cup and spoon [Reference to the chitinous body]; StT /skwib/.

srints sb dial; pronunc var of *shrimps*.

1952 FGC Han /srints/ river crayfish without claws.

SRIPPLE adj dial; a phon alternant of *sipl*, *swipl*, showing interchange of *l* and *r* (freq in the dial), in this instance perh infl by *slipper(y)*. Slippery.

1910 Anderson-Cundall 39, S'ripple, see PRA-PRA. 1925 Beckwith 18 [Prov:] Before pra'pra' bring fight, mek ground slipple. [Alternate form:] s'ripple. 1943 *GL* StAnn, Scripple, slippery; StM, Sripple.

sta see SISTER.

STAFF sb dial. The central stem or rib of a fern leaf; cf BONE 1.

1952 FGC StT, Staff of maidenhair fern.

stagalang vb dial; <*stagger along*. To pick up and carry something heavy. Cf GRAPPLE.

STAG-FLY sb obs; *OED* →1693. See quot.

1725 Sloane 205, Scarabæus maximus platyceros, Taurus, nonnullis aliis, Lucanus, seu Cervus volans..The Stag-Fly. I had the Head of one of these given me which was.. said to be found in Jamaica.

STAGGER-BACK sb dial; by the agent being named for the action. Cf JOHN STAGGER-BACK. A kind of TIE-TEETH burnt-sugar confection.

1952 FGC StM /stágabàk/ black and tight; you stagger backway when you bite it.

stailit, tailits-plie sb dial; etym of first element unknown; +PLAY sb. See quots.

1958 DeC StAnd /stailit/ the name of one ring game, often used by extension for all ring play; StAnd /tailits-plie/ riddles.

STAIN sb; cf also STAINY.

1. The sap of trees, the juice of fruits (often but not necessarily unripe), or other vegetable exudation that might stain clothing, which is sticky, and which would taste tart or pucker the mouth. *BA*

1952 FGC West, Plantain—eat ripe or boil out stain. 1957 JB StAnd, Stain—the sap of a tree when it is cut.

2. Transf to the sense of taste: a gummy, tacky quality, more or less tart; sticky astringency.

1957 LeP StAnd (various informants), Stain—a taste that is not pleasant because it leaves the teeth and tongue furry. Stain—there is something sticky about the fruit, makes your lips stick together slightly.

STAINY adj; <STAIN+*-y*. Having a sticky or tacky quality, or astringency or tartness to the taste. *G*

1893 Sullivan 82, These ['jimblings'] are very stainy to the taste. 1952 FGC StT /stíeni/ tart; said of a plant or fruit. 1957 D. Manley StAnd, Some fruit have a sort of stainy taste—make you grit your teeth. 1960 Miss Mazely StAnd, Stainy—Guineps, even ripe, starapple when ripe, naseberry when not so ripe, unripe banana, are all stainy; they are sticky, tacky—your lips stick together even after you've cleaned your teeth. Does not mean 'sour'.

STAINY (BANANA) sb. A variety of banana that has more STAIN than others. *G*

1952 FGC StT /stíeni banána/ fingers have corners like plantain; *black stainy* is a darker green.

STAMP sb; abbr of STAMP-AND-GO, but note folk-etym explanation in quot 1958. A codfish fritter.

1952 FGC StJ /stamp/—salt fish. 1958 DeC StJ /stamp; aachi/ saltfish fritters. *Stamp* are molded in the hands and pressed flat (hence the name, says informant), whereas *aachi* are just dropped from the spoon into the pan. The informants who use *stamp* would not accept a suggested *stamp-and-go*.

STAMP-AND-GO sb chiefly dial; <*stamp-and-go*, 'An order given to sailors for the performance of certain duties' (*OED*); 'to step out at the capstan, or with hawsers, topsail-halyards, &c., generally to the fife or fiddle' (1867 Smyth *Sailor's Word-book*). [1833 Scott I 178, Stamp and go—the name of a boat.]

1. A simple codfish fritter, quickly made and a favourite provision for travellers.

1893 Sullivan 87, Stamp and go. These are rough cakes made with cornmeal and flour..salt-fish and a little butter and lard..fresh pepper is freely used..The country people as they travel stop at the way-side shops and buy these with a slice of bread for a trifle. Hence the name. 1952 FGC StAnn, StJ, StM, StT, West /stámpanggó, tàmpanggúo/ salt-fish fritter, fried very crisp.

2. Transf to other foods—sometimes quite different ones: see quots.

1958 DeC StT, Stamp-and-go, a name for fu-fu, i.e. food pounded in a mortar; Stamp-and-go—meaning here a confection of dropped coconut, sugar, etc.

stan see STAND.

STANCHA sb obs; < Sp *estancia*, farm, country house. A small plantation.

1672 Blome 44, The Spaniards that were in the Isle at the Landing of the English, keeping their slaves at their several small Plantations, or Stanchas.

STAND /stan, tan/ vb dial.

1. In phrases involving the basic sense (*OED* 1) of being on one's feet: *Stand* (one's) *heel*, to stand still in one place; *Stand steady*, be quiet, be silent; *Stand-up-stand-up*, to stand about for some time. Cf also *tan-de*. *BA BL G*

1907 Jekyll 109, Tiger creep out of the house with a great rolling of voice, can't 'tan' him heel. 1942 Bennett 45, Me tan-up tan-up 'bout de place Look-look pon everyting. 1943 *GL* Clar, Kgn, StAnn, StC, StJ, Tan tudy—keep still. 1956 Mc Clar /tan todi/ *Be silent!*

2. To be in a specified state, condition, position, etc. (*OED* 15e). *BA BL G*

1790 Moreton 105, I often laughed heartily at hearing a Creole master or miss say, 'Do, momma, get me some mauby, *mine* head no '*tand* good'. 1942 Bennett 47, Nuff bur-bur an' dutty all ovah him clothes. Yuh wahn se 'ow him tan! [*You should see the condition he's in!*] 1951 Murray 21, Ackee! Ackee! Red an pretty dem tan. 1956 Mc StAnd /hóu yu tán dis máanin/ *How are you this morning?*

3. To appear, to look, to seem to be. Also in impers phr *tan laik*, it seems, and *taka*. *BL G*

1877 Murray *Feedin' 'Perrit* 7, Well, de way how me top lip swell, I feel like it da pull me nose out o' place. When Liza see it, him bawl. Him put key pon it, but tan like key didn't gree wid it, so it swell wusser. 1956 Mc Man /beg yu sen mi wan fuotograaf mek mi sii hou mi tan/ *Would you please send me a photograph to let me see how I look?*

4. To be for a time, to stay, to remain. *BA G*

1956 Mc Man /shi tán wi mí íina díe/ *She stays with me during the day.*

5. As an exclamation (a self-directed imperative): Wait! Cf STOP.

1943 *GL* StM, Taun, expression of surprise. 1956 Mc StAnd /tan, mi no wen tel yu se notn du mi/ *Wait, I didn't tell you that anything was the matter with me.*

6. Phr, *tan-op!*—a call to stop mules or donkeys.

1958 DeC StAnd, etc. /tan-op/!

standariin, stanjariin sb dial; a hypercorrect *st-* variant of *tangerine.*

1952 FGC Port, StAnd /stándaríin/; Man, StAnd, StAnn /stánjaríin/.

STANDING LAND sb dial.

1954 LeP StE (Elderslie), Good fertile land—tanding lan'.

STAND MARSHAL vb phr obs; cf *OED* 15.

1774 Long I 394–5, Another bad effect..of this law..is the custom which many desperate debtors have fallen upon, of *standing marshal,* as it is called. After a series of persecution [*sic*] on the part of the creditor, iniquity in the officer, subterfuge and evasion in the debtor, the latter is driven at length to his intrenchments. He converts his *house* (literally speaking) into a castle, prepares to withstand a regular siege, and forms a garrison of armed slaves. Many have held out in this manner till their plantation has been entirely ruined for want of culture, and themselves reduced to a starving condition.

STAND-'PON-ROCK /támpánrát/ sb dial. A local name for WATERGRASS (*Commelina* species).

1952 FGC Tre /támpánrát/.

STANGERINE, stanjariin see *standariin.*

STANKO sb dial; etym unknown.

1954 LeP Kgn, Stanko, big, oafish man.

stap-an-guo see STOP-AND-GO.

stap a paas see STOP-(IT-)A-PASS.

STARAPPLE /sta-rápl, stàarápl/ sb; so called because the fruit in cross-section resembles a many-pointed figure; *OED* 1697→. *BA BL*

1. The tree *Chrysophyllum cainito* and its fruit.

1683 *Present State* 21, Supotilla, Aduecades, Star-Apples, Custard-Apples, and Prickle-Apples. 1696 Sloane 206, Anona..fructu rotundo majore..The Star Apple-tree. 1952 FGC StAnd, StAnn, StJ, Tre /sta-rápl/. *G N*

2. As a subject of popular comparisons: the tree never drops its fruit, hence it is considered CUBBITCH; the leaf has a different colour above and beneath, and often turns back in the wind, hence it is considered hypocritical: CEITFUL.

1954 LeP Man, Hypocrite—like starapple leaf.

STARCH BEAN sb. The YAM BEAN.

[1837 Macfadyen 286, The tubers may either be boiled plain, in which state they are a very good substitute for yams..or they may be submitted to a process similar to arrowroot, and a starch obtained.] 1952 FGC Port, StM /staach biin/ = yam bean; root like yam or potato, make starch.

STAR FERN sb; descr. The fern *Hemionitis palmata.*

1943 *NHN* I 12 10, There is the Star Fern, with an Ivy-shaped leaf. 1951 Proctor *Ferns* 8.

STAR FLOWER sb.

1955 *WIMJ* 159, *Isotoma longiflora*..Madam Fate; Horse Poison; Star Flower.

STARLIGHT sb. A firework 'sparkler'. *BA*

1947 U.Newton III 25. 1952 FGC Han.

STAR-OF-BETHLEHEM sb. A single-flowered lily-like plant: see quot.

1864 Grisebach 788, Star-of-Bethlehem: *Hypoxis decumbens.*

STAR-OF-NIGHT sb. A medium-sized tree clinging to other trees or rocks, with large, rose-coloured or whitish flowers, whence the name: see quot.

1864 Grisebach 788, Star-of-night: *Clusia rosea.*

STATION GUARD sb dial cant. An officer in revivalist and similar cults whose duty is to guard a 'station' in the ceremony. (Cf 'Stations of the Cross'.)

1929 Beckwith 168, Bedward was ordained Bishop of this church with the title of Shepherd, and there were 'station guards' and 'Mothers', after the Revivalist pattern.

STAVEWOOD sb; staves for rum casks were made of the wood. The tree *Simaruba glauca;* see quot 1920.

1778 Wright in *Trans. Royal Soc. Edinb.* (1790) II 76, *Quassia simaruba*..This tree is known in Jamaica by the name of Mountain Damson, Bitter Damson and Stave-wood. 1811 Titford 65, Stavewood tree. 1920 Fawcett 198, *S. glauca*..Bitter Damson, Bitter Dan, Mountain Damson, Stave Wood. *Ibid* 199 (notes on confusion with *S. amara* and *Quassia amara*). 1941 Swabey 14, Stave-wood.

STAY /ste, stie/ vb dial. *BA BL G*

1. = STAND 2: to be in a specified state, position, etc.

1924 Beckwith 16, Brar Nansi say to him, 'Brar Rabbit, *so* "daytime trouble" stay. So, as long as you live, never ask anybody to show it to you again!'. 1941 Kirkpatrick 3, You know dat man stay same way lak me an' you. 1952 FGC StAnd /kreng-kreng kalalu/ when dat boil, stay like okro. 1956 Mc StE /mi beg yu wan frak misiz—dis wan stie bad/ *Please give me a frock, misis—this one is in a bad way.*

2. = STAND 3: To appear, to seem to be.

1957 JN, Teacher, me father stay like de man that a write up de so. [*My father resembles the man..etc.*]

STAY-BACK sb dial. Left-overs of food.

1956 Mc StAnd /stie bak—wat yu iit an liiv/.

STEADY see *todi.*

STEAM BREAD sb. A kind of bread: see quot.

1952 FGC StJ (Montego Bay), Steam bread, bake in oven like milk bread.

STEAMER sb dial; cf *OED* 3 in diff sense. A crude kind of hookah for smoking ganja; see quot.

1958 DeC Kgn /stiima/—this is the other kind of pipe for smoking ganja [i.e. other than the CHILLUM]. It consists of a screw-topped jar, in the cover of which two holes are made. In the larger hole is soldered the stem of a /chilóng/, with the stem extending down below the water level in the jar; in the smaller hole is soldered a small tube, through which the smoker inhales.

STEAMER (BRAND) sb dial.

1958 DeC StM /tíima-brán/ a cutlass (so called because stamped 'Steamer Brand'). 1961 *CLS* 70 /stíima/.

STEAM FIRE sb dial. A low fire that makes a pot steam rather than boil.

1956 Mc StAnd /yu put it iina stiim faia—yu sii it duon get tu bon/ *You put it on a slow fire and see it doesn't burn.*

STEEL BOTTOM sb dial or slang; the allusion is obscure. A mixture of gin and wine.

1952 FGC Han. s. *BL*

STEM vb intr; cf *OED* v^2 1 →1570. To stop, to cease.

1958 DeC Tre /hin lif in han til i kount twelv, an in stem/ *He lifted his hand till he counted twelve and he stopped.*

STEPHEN-BASKET /stíibm-báaskit/ sb dial; see quot. A kind of market basket with a slightly raised centre and somewhat flaring sides.

1959 DeC StJ /stiibm-baskit/—This name is apparently a localism around Maroon Town, Flagstaff, and Flamstead. Informants explain that an old man (now long dead) used to make most of these baskets there; his name was /stiibm/.

STEPPY sb dial; <*step* (abbr) +-*y*. A step-mother.

1954 LeP StT, Stepmother—steppi.

STEP-SON sb dial. A son-in-law.

1954 LeP StAnn, Step-son = son-in-law [of Std Engl].

STEWART sb dial. A variety of sweet-potato with white flesh.

1929 Beckwith 18 [In Mandeville:] The 'Lewis Daley' is long and big;..the 'Stewart', white 'right through'.

STEW-BERRY sb dial; for *stewed berries.*

1958 DeC Port /stuu-beri/ a preserve made from sour barge.

STEW-DOWN sb dial. A local name for a coconut rundown.

1958 DeC Port /stuu-doun/.

STICK sb dial; cf *OED* sb^1 9 →1884.

1. The stem or stalk of various plants or their leaves—said of calalu, cassava, etc.; cf also BLACK-STICK CASSAVA and BLACK-STICK MAIDEN-HAIR. *G*

1952 FGC StAnn, etc.

2. = CORN-STICK; corncob.

1952 FGC StE, 'The stick has the grains on it'; 'To make grater-corn dumplings, keep the corn on the stick'.

STICK-IN-THE-MIDDLE sb dial. A dumpling. (The name does not seem to refer consistently to shape: perhaps it refers to the dumpling's lasting-powers inside the eater.)

1958–9 DeC StJ /stik-in-a-midl/ doughnut-shaped fried dumpling; StT /stik-in-a-migl/ a creased spinner dumpling; equivalent to COW-TONGUE.

stik-in-a-midl, stik-in-a-migl see prec.

STICK-LICKING sb dial; cf LICK, vb. *BA*

1. Fighting with long sticks (cf English *quarter-staff OED* 2); latterly, general rioting or fighting by hoodlums armed with sticks.

c 1920 FGC StAnd, Rioting and stick-licking. [1925 Beckwith 65 [Prov:] If you can't stan' lick, no play stick.]

2. Attrib.

1952 FGC StM, see HUSSAY.

STICK PRESS sb tech. In tobacco culture: a method of stacking cured tobacco stalks preparatory to stripping the leaves: see quot.

1954 *FG* 372, When the necessary quantity [of tobacco stalks] has been taken down, start making a 'stick press', that is, the bundles of plants with their dried leaves still hanging to them are placed in a staple with their heads or tops towards the centre, and the stalk end..outwards.

STIFF-OUT adv phr dial. Stiff, as in death. *G*

1961 BLB 15 /Bra Tombl tif-out ded/ *Brother Tumble has fallen stiff dead.*

STIFF-STONE /stíf-stúon, tíf-túon/ adv phr dial; <*stiff* (cf *OED* 2b) +*stone* attrib, as a stone. An intensive adverb (compounded of two others) prefixed to such words as *dead, drunk,* etc.: completely. *BL*

c 1915 FGC StAnd, Stiff-stone dead. 1954 LeP StAnn, Him husband was stiff ton drunk.

STIFFY adj dial; <*stiff*+-*y*. Stiff, of very thick consistency, difficult to stir or shape. Also in comb.

1952 FGC StM, John Baillie is sugar that becomes stiffy-like [from long boiling]. 1958 DeC StE /kwakwa/..a soft concoction the consistency of /stifi parij/.

STILLY sb dial; perh implying fidelity or steadiness?

1943 *GL* Kgn, Stilly, a lover; same as stucky.

STINGING BARBADOS CHERRY sb bot obs. The tree *Malpighia urens,* now called COWITCH CHERRY.

1814 Lunan I 50, This is called *stinging Barbadoes* or *cowhage* cherry..Leaves ending in acute points, sessile, covered with fine bristles..the bristles enter pretty deep, and stick close to whatever has forced them off.

STINGING BROOMWEED sb bot obs; cf BROOMWEED. In Macfadyen's use: *Sida urens* (ident 1926 Fawcett 110).

1837 Macfadyen 82, Sida urens. *Stinging Broom-weed.*

STINGING GROUPER sb. The fish *Scorpæna plumieri.*

1952 Smith in *NHN* 226, That it is capable of inflicting a most painful wound is definite but rumours that their venom has caused death have not, to my knowledge, been too reliable. It is known locally as the 'stinging grouper' though in proper ichthyological parlance a 'grouper' belongs to the family Serranidæ. 1952 FGC Port, StAnn, StJ /stíngin grúpa/ poison grupa.

STING-RAY see *tinggri.*

STINKING-BUSH sb.

1. = STINKING WEED: *Cassia occidentalis.*

1820 Thomson 73, We may wash the sores with the juice of the *stinking bush* (*cassia occidentalis*).

2. Some species of *Aristolochia* (prob *grandiflora*).

1952 FGC StAnn /stingkin bush/ wild, grows on vine, saxophone-shaped flower, mauvish colour with lightish-brown spots; has very strong unpleasant smell.

STINKING-OIL sb dial. Paraffin oil (kerosene).

1952 FGC Han, Stinking-oil, lamp-oil.

STINKING-PEAS sb.

1943 *NHN* II 45, *Cassia emarginata,* Stinking Peas.

STINKING TOE sb. The large *Hymenæa courbaril,* and its bean-like fruit resembling a large brown human toe, and having an unpleasant odour. *BA BL G N*

c 1915 FGC StAnd. 1920 Fawcett 121, Stinking Toe. 1941 Swabey 31, Stinking Toe—(West Indian Locust). 1952 FGC Port, StAnd, StM /tíngkin túo/.

STINKING WATER HORSE-TAIL sb bot obs.

1707 Sloane 69, Equisetum 13. sive fœtidum..Stinking Water Horse Tail..It is used for cleansing Household Goods.

STINKING WEED sb; *OED* 1756 only.

1. *Cassia occidentalis,* a common herb used as a substitute for coffee, and medicinally.

1756 Browne 224, Stinking-weed..The top is the only part used in Jamaica, where the plant is commonly employed in all resolutive baths. 1801 Dancer 361, Stinking weed or piss-a-bed (*Cassia occidentalis*).

Expressed Juice, a cure for the Negro Itch, Craw-Craws, &c. 1954 *WIMJ* 28, *C. occidentalis*..Wild Senna; Dandelion; Stinking Weed; Wild Coffee; John Crow Pea; Stinking Wood.

2. *Chenopodium ambrosioides*; also called WORM WEED, *simi-kantrak*, etc.

1952 FGC Tre /stingkin wiid/.

STINKING WOOD sb. = STINKING WEED 1. (This name is prob due to a typographical or other error; this plant is a shrub.)

1864 Grisebach 788, Stinking-wood: *Cassia occidentalis*. 1954 *WIMJ* 28, see STINKING WEED.

STINK-SORE sb dial. A sore on the foot which smells bad. *G*

1958 DeC StE (Accom) /stingk suo/.

STINK WEED sb dial; cf *OED* in diff sense. Species of *Pectis* (esp *P. febrifuga*?).

1927 Beckwith 28, Stink-weed. Pectis—for fever boil and drink as tea. 1954 *WIMJ* 31, Pectis spp Compositæ. Stink Weed.

STIRRING-STICK sb arch or obs. In early sugar-making: see quot. *G*

1823 Roughley 361, As soon as the sugar is skipped into a cooler, the head boiler is to take a stirring stick, a long stout rod, made flat for eighteen inches at one end, and three inches broad where it is flat, and with this stick work the sugar to and fro.

sto see SISTER.

STOCKADE see *takied*.

STOCKFISH WOOD sb obs; now superseded by TACK FISH. *OED* 1699 only. *Cæsalpinia vesicaria*; see TACK FISH (WOOD).

1718 *Courant* 30 July, 3/1. Logwood at 11*l*. and Stock-fishwood at 13*l*. per Tun. [a 1726 Barham (1794) 184, The Dutch gave this wood..the name of *stockvishhout*; but with us it is commonly called Nicaragua wood. It is but small to what logwood is, seems to be very tough, and is about the bigness of dried stockfish; which may be the reason the Dutch call it *stockvishhout*. It dyes a very fine red.]

STOLID FLYCATCHER sb ornith; trans of species name. The bird *Myiarchus stolidus*, or TOM FOOL.

[1847 Gosse 168, Foolish Petchary..*Myiobius stolidus*.—mihi.] 1936 Bond 248.

STOMACH EVIL sb obs; transl Fr *mal d'estomac*. DIRT-EATING, or the illness resulting therefrom.

1817 Williams I 110, What is known by the name of *mal d'estomac* among the French; among the British, the stomach evil, or dirt-eating.

STONE-BAR sb dial; back formation from STONE BASS understood as plural. The STONE BASS.

1892 Cockrell list, Stone bar, *Gerres plumierii*. 1952 FGC StJ /tuon bar shad/.

STONE BASS sb; *OED* 1698→. Fish of the family *Gerridæ*: shad. *N*

1679 Trapham 65, The choice Mullet brings up the next division crowded with various Snappers, Rock fish, Stone bass, Cavallies. 1725 Sloane 286, A Stone-Basse. 1854–5 *TJSA* I 143, *Gerres aprion*—Stone Bass of the market..The Gerres are our Shads and Silver Fish of the fishermen. 1952 FGC Port, StAnn, StM, West /tuon baas (shad)/; StC /stuon baalz/—like shad.

STONE-BEARD sb dial; cf *OED Tree-beard*. Some crassulaceous plant? Unidentified. Cf STONE-HAIR.

1952 FGC Port, Stone-beard—a kind of fat fine-leaved plant; grows on stone walls; good for baby tea.

STONE BREAM sb; <*stone*+*brim*. Some variety of the bream or similar fish.

1952 FGC StE /stuon brim/ yellow and with dark-colour stripes; square; same shape as porgy.

STONE-BRUISE sb dial; cf *OED*, less specif sense.

1. See quot. *BL G*

1956 Mc Clar /tuon bruuz/—A gathering under the foot, caused by 'squeezing' the foot in walking barefoot over rough ground.

2. A hairy caterpillar—from some fancied resemblance to sense 1?

1960 G. Underwood, UCWI Zool Dept.

STONE-BRUISE BUSH sb dial. An unidentified plant, used medicinally for stone-bruises, etc. *BA*

1952 FGC Port /tuon-bruuz bush/ good against /fisla/ [fistula] on finger.

STONE DRUMMER sb. Some variety of the drummer or similar fish.

1952 FGC StT /stuon droma/.

STONE-HAIR sb dial; cf STONE-BEARD.

1956 Mc StAnd /stuon ier/—lichen on rock.

STONE-HOLE sb dial. s.

1. A cave.

1907 Jekyll 78, As Monkey passing, Tiger was into a stone-hole an' jump out on the fellah an' catch him.

2. A deep place among rocks in a river.

1925 Beckwith 120 [Prov:] When river come down, 'tone-hole full.

STOOP vb dial. To sit on one's heels. *BA G*

1960 LeP StAnd, *Sankútu* means what we call 'to stoop' —that is to squat on the heels.

[Note: The ordinary sense of *stoop* is also fully current.]

STOP int; cf *OED* 15a, 20b. An exclamation of surprise, puzzlement, or the like: Hold on a minute! Esp in phr: *but stop!* Cf STAND 5.

1942 Bennett 12, Is Emeriah dah yuh muma bwoy? Den tap-tap, we dah fambily! [*Is Emeriah your mother, boy? Then hold on, we are relatives!*] 1955 LeP StE (Accom) /babiabuo se, bot stap! hu kaal mi niem—a hie mi niem kaal!/ *BA BL G*

STOP-AND-GO sb dial; by folk etym, or simple loss of the nasal. = STAMP-AND-GO.

1958 DeC Port /stap-an-guo/ a fritter.

STOP-(IT-)A-PASS /tap-a-pass, tap-i-a-paas/ sb dial; <*stop*+(*it*+) A[5]+*pass* vb.

1. A sauce made with coconut, salt fish, pepper and other ingredients, but not boiled all the way down: it is stopped from 'passing'—i.e. the coconut oil is prevented from separating. Cf RUNDOWN.

1943 *GL* Clar, Tappiapass, semi-clarified coconut oil and shad; StM, Tap-a-pass, half-boiled coconut oil; Tre, Tapi'anpass, A sauce made of flour and coconut milk. 1952 FGC Port, Stop-it-a-pass—coconut milk and salt cod, highly peppered, but don't boil or oil will separate. To make 'stuffed breadfruit' substitute this for the heart of a roasted breadfruit. StJ /tap i a pass/ 'name used in St Mary and St Catherine'. StM /stap a pass/ like dip-and-fall-back. 1956 Mc Clar /tapi a paas/ same as run-down, dip-an'-fall-back.

2. Transf. Left-over food, *bambai*.

1958 DeC Kgn /tap-it-a-pass/ here meaning left-over food, bumbai.

STORMY OKAM see ODUM.

STOSHE see STOSHY.

STOSHUS /stúoshos, túoshas/ adj dial; prob reduced <*ostentatious* (HPJ), with vowel *a* changed by analogy to such words as *precocious, ferocious*, etc. Cf SPLENDACIOUS. Well-dressed, smart, stylish; high-class.

1942 Bennett 27, Yuh want fe se de hotel dem Casha Blank an' Dacta Cleff. . dem stashius [*sic*] So-tell noh-mo-noh-leff. *You should see those hotels. . they're stylish till they couldn't be more so!*] 1943 *GL* Port, Stoshus, well-dressed, high class. 1950 Pioneer gloss, Stoshus—high class. 1956 Mc StAnd /túoshos gyal—shi waak stáilish/.

STOSHY /stúoshi/ sb dial; etym uncert: perh <*stosh-*, understood as the base of STOSHUS, +-*y*, familiarizing suffix; but cf *EDD stoushie*, a stout and healthy child.

1943 *GL* Port, Stoshe, boy friend. 1955 FGC Man /stúoshi/=/stóki/ boy friend.

STOVE sb dial. =COAL POT.

straani see STRAWNY.

STRAIGHT sb dial slang; prob <*straight*, a count bunch—see PAYABLE. In phr 'plate of straight': a banana.

1954 LeP Kgn, Plate a strait, dish of boiled bananas.

STRAIGHT MACHETE. See DeC in 1961 *CLS* 73.

STRAIGHT NOSE sb chiefly dial. A European type of nose, in contrast to the negroid type. *BA G*

1960 SJR StAnd.

STRAIGHT-POINT sb dial. A straight MACHETE with a slightly flaring end.

1959 DeC West /striet-paint/.

STRAINER (VINE) sb. The vine *Luffa cylindrica* and its fruit, whose netted, fibrous interior, when dry, was formerly used to strain liquids. *BA*

1850 Macfadyen 136, The Strainer Vine. . After the fruit has become ripe, and the pulp has decayed. . only the reticulated fibres are left. . In this state it. . has been applied to the purpose of straining lime-juice for. . *Punch*. 1864 Grisebach 288, Strainer-vine, *Luffa acutangula*. 1926 Fawcett 261. 1952 FGC StJ, StT, Tre.

STRANGER (FLY) sb dial; cf *EDD stranger* 6, 'A moth fluttering towards one, supposed to indicate the arrival of a stranger or a letter.' Caithness. A firefly (the small kind which flashes its light intermittently at its 'tail').

1952 FGC Man /strienja flai/ little flat one, give light at buttocks; Tre, Stranger fly=winker; West /strienja/ signal of a stranger coming: if flies high, a gentleman; if flies low, a lady. 1956 Mc Man /strienja/ firefly—the type which /shót aaf dem láit wen dem flái/.

STRAWBERRIES AND CREAM sb. A dish of starapple pulp mixed with oranges, etc. (Sometimes called *Matrimony*.)

1893 Sullivan 78, Oranges and Star Apples. [Recipe.] This is called 'strawberries and cream'. 1913 Harris 21, Star-apple. . The white, jelly-like pulp which surrounds the seeds is very sweet and agreeable and is either eaten alone or is mixed with orange-juice, a little sugar and grated nutmeg, with a spoonful of sherry all mixed together. This is called 'strawberries and cream'.

STRAWBERRY BANANA sb. =APPLE BANANA.

STRAWBERRY GUAVA sb.

1913 Harris 9, Guava, Purple. *Psidium Cattleianum*. . The *purple guava*, *China guava* or *strawberry guava* is indigenous to Brazil. . The pulp is. . sweet and acid, with a strawberry-like flavour.

STRAWBERRY PEAR sb; cf *OED* ref 1866. The fruit of the *Cereus triangularis*, which somewhat resembles the strawberry.

1756 Browne 238, Cactus 6. . triquetrus, scandens vel repens;. . The Strawberry Pear. 1814 Lunan I 413. 1913 Harris 33, *Cereus triangularis*. . The crimson fruit, known as 'Strawberry pear' contains a pleasant, sweet pulp enclosing numerous black seeds.

STRAWN UP vb phr dial; cf *EDD strawn* sb, strand. To pull into strawns or strands.

1952 FGC StC [Old man describing preparation of GOD-COTTON to stuff in ears:] /straan it op, straan it op/ *Pull the strands apart.*

STRAWNY adj dial; <*strawn*+-*y*. Full of strawns or strands. *G*

1952 FGC StE, Tie-teeth sugar—boil on fire, watch till it get /straani/.

STRAY-MINDED adj dial. Having a straying mind; wandering in one's thoughts; forgetful.

1958 FGC StAnd.

STREAMER-TAIL (HUMMING BIRD) sb. =LONG-TAILED HUMMING BIRD.

1929 Beckwith 122, The beautiful little streamer-tailed humming birds that flit about every flower garden in Jamaica. 1956 Bond 212–3, Red-Billed Streamer-Tail (*Aithurus polytmus*). . Black-Billed Streamer-Tail (*Aithurus scitulus*). 1956 Jeffrey-Smith 22.

STREAM MULLET sb. Some variety of mullet or similar fish.

1952 FGC StC.

STREELER /striila/ sb dial; <*streel*, to trail on the ground; stream, float at length (*OED* 'chiefly Anglo-Irish') +-*er*. A lady's sash.

1943 *GL* Port, Streela, sash worn round lady's waist. 1955 FGC Man /striila/ sash, tie a bow and hang down.

STRIKER sb dial; cf *OED* II, 1858 only, =harpoon. A fish spear.

1877 Murray *Feedin' 'Perrit* 4, As I da go so I see a baracouta, as I mek fe go tek me triker fe trike him. . de hat drop off o' my head.

STRIKING ppl adj dial; <*strike* vb as used in such phrases as *strike dead, blind, dumb* (*OED* 46). An intensifying epithet showing impatience, annoyance, or similar feeling. Cf GOD, LAW.

1956 BLB Man, etc., In one striking year. ., In ten striking years. .—used by speaker at a political meeting. 1957 JB, Can be used without a numeral, though more common with it: 'So many /straikin/ times I've told you to do so-and-so, and you haven't done it'.

STRINGY MANGO sb. =COMMON, HAIRY, SALT-FISH, or YELLOW MANGO.

1952 FGC Han, Port, StAnn, StJ, StT. 1959 DeC Han /stringi manggo/.

STRIPE(D) CANE sb. =RIBBON CANE.

1811 Mathison 65, see RIBBON CANE. 1952 FGC StE /straip-kien/ StJ /straipid kien/.

STRIPE(D)-HOLLAND sb; <*striped*+*Holland*, linen cloth (*OED*).

1. A striped variety of Holland cloth at one time widely used for clothing.

1877 Murray *Kittle* 6, With his clean striped holland shirt. 1952 FGC StAnd (see below).

2. *Dendroica pharetra* or *Mniotilta varia*, both birds prominently striped with black and white.

1952 FGC [StAnd, Ants-picker—striped dark and light, same as stripe-Holland cloth]; StT, Stripe-Holland—wood-searcher.

STRIP-ME-NAKED sb dial; cf *OED* in diff sense.

1. Flour (i.e. grain already cleaned and prepared for use—cf PEEL-A'READY).

1943 *GL* StM, Strip me naked, Flour.

2. See quot, and note diff interpretation.

1955 FGC Man /tríp-mi-níekid/—something made of flour —biscuits, cakes, food. Eat too much, you forget clothes. [I.e. you impoverish yourself and 'strip yourself naked' if you spend too much for food.]

STRIVE vb dial; common malapropism for *thrive*; *thrive* is normally reduced in the dial > *trive*, then by overcorrection or *st-* alternation made into *strive*. The proper sense of 'strive' prob blends in also. To thrive. *BL G*

1942 Bennett 34, De way people wash dem mout' pon yuh, Yuh naw go strive missis. 1952 FGC StAnd, StAnn, If you water the plant good it will strive.

STRONG-BACK sb dial; cf *OED strong a* 26, 1738 only: *Pittoniæ similis* (Bahamas).

1. Any of a number of plants used medicinally to strengthen the back. (Note diff interp quot 1956.) Those that have been identified are: a. *Cuphea parsonsia* (Beckwith *Parsonsia parsonsia*), b. *Sauvagesia brownei*, c. *Chrysanthellum americanum*, d. *Desmodium* spp (Beckwith *Meibomia supina*), e. *Morinda royoc*, f. *Hyptis pectinata*. *BL*

1927 Beckwith 28, Strong-back (a, b 'For a weak back drink a little as tea each day', c, d). 1952 FGC /trangbak/ 8 parishes. 1954 *WIMJ* 29–31 (a, b, c, d, e). 1956 Mc Port /strang bak/ another name for piaba (f)—so called because it is hard to pull.

2. A medicine—see quot.

1943 *GL* No addr, Trang-back, a medicine made of 3 or more kind of roots.

STRONG-BARK sb; cf *OED* this quot.

1864 Grisebach 788, Strong-bark: *Beureria*. [Perh erron for STRONG-BACK.]

STRONG-EYE adj and sb dial; perh loan-transl < Twi *n'ani yɛ deŋ*—strong-eye; insolent, self-willed, etc.

A. adj: Firm, determined; domineering.

1868 Russell 12, Trong-eye—Domineering, not easily brow-beaten. If Jim no bin trong-eye him wouldn't get de money. 1873 Rampini 87, A determined person is 'Mr Strong-eye'.

B. sb: Covetousness.

1907 Jekyll 122, Annancy. . through his strongy yeye an' his ungratefulness he want to shoot Tacoma cart a gully an' to kill his mule, that him one may be the master of the bank.

STRONG-MAN'S-WEED sb dial; evidently implying that it makes a man strong—cf STRONG-BACK. = GUINEA-HEN WEED.

1864 Grisebach 788, Strong-man's-weed: *Petiveria alliacea*. 1954 *WIMJ* 19, Strong man's weed. This plant has a strong smell of garlic. . The leaves are rubbed up and sniffed or tied on the head for headaches while the roots, steeped in white rum, are similarly used.

STRONG-MOUTH sb dial; perh loan-transl from some African word: cf STRONG-EYE. Insolence. *G*

1868 Russell 12, Trong-mout—Boisterous, brow-beating. De lawyer gain de case by trong-mout.

STRONG-PHYSIC adj and sb dial; fig < *strong physic*.

A. adj: Hot-tempered.

1868 Russell 12, *Trong-physic*—Hot tempered, bad. Creole pickni too trong-physic sista.

B. sb: A self-willed person.

1894 Banbury 43, Strong physic:—A hard headed and self-willed person.

[**STRUM-STRUM** sb obs; cf *OED* 1697, 1728. A crude stringed instrument of the Indians and negroes, the precursor of the banjo. See BANJA.

1725 Sloane Tab 232, Fidiculæ Indorum & Nigritarum, e cucurbitis inter se diversis, excavatis, pellibus tectis, confectæ, Strum Strumps. 1740 Importance 18, Some hundreds of them [*sc* negroes] will meet together, according to the Customs of their own Country (many of which they retain) with Strum-Strums and Calibashes, which they beat and make a horrid Noise with.]

STUCKEDEE sb dial; a 'stretched' form of STUCKY. s.

1943 *GL* StAnd, Stuckedee, sweetheart.

STUCKY /stoki/ sb dial; cf *EDD stucky*, robust (Dev.). Sweetheart, lover.

1933 McK 317, Stucky: sweetheart. 1943 *GL* Kgn, Stucky, lover (as com, me stucky). 1955 FGC Man /stoki/.

STUDERATION see TUDERATION.

STUDY vb dial. In phr: *study one's head*, think hard, rack one's brains; *study a brain*, *a plan*, etc., think out (a trick, a device). *BA BL G T*

1950 Pioneer 22, She tudy her head an sey she gwine fe lock up Dora. *Ibid* 18, Anancy. . study a brain fe work pon Ticks. 1956 Mc Clar /togi im ed/ consider; StE /im stódi a plan tu tiif im/ *He thought out a plan to rob him.*

stuon baalz see STONE BASS.

stuoshi see STOSHY.

STUPID JIMMY sb dial; < *stupid* + *Jimmy*, pers name, prob overlying Twi *gyimí*, vb to be stupid, foolish, senseless.

1. The bird LITTLE TOM FOOL, *Blacicus caribæus pallidus*.

1956 Jeffrey-Smith 148, The Jamaican Wood Pewee or Stupid Jimmy.

2. The Stolid Flycatcher.

1956 Jeffrey-Smith 49, see RICKY-TEE.

STYPTIC BUR sb bot. The weed *Priva lappulacea*, whose leaves naturally stick to the skin and can be used to cover small cuts.

1756 Browne 116, Verbena 5. . The stiptic or velvet Bur. This plant is a fine vulnerary and subastringent, and is commonly applied to bleeding wounds in either men or cattle by the inhabitants of the country parts of Jamaica. 1864 Grisebach 788, Styptic—or Velvet-bur: *Priva echinata*. 1954 *WIMJ* 25, see CLAMMY-BUR.

su int dial; < Twi *sú*, to set, place, or put. An exclamation made when one is suddenly handing something to another.

1943 *GL* StAnn, Su, hand. 1955 FGC Man, To hand abruptly, say 'Su!'

SUARRA WOOD sb; etym unknown.

1920 Fawcett 178, *Zanthoxylum spinosum*. . Lignum Rorum, Licca Tree, Suarra Wood.

SUBALTERNS' BUTTER sb obs. A nickname for avocado pears, once used as substitute for butter at sea (cf MIDSHIPMAN'S BUTTER) and ashore.

1862 Clutterbuck 110–1, Avocado (vulgarly, *alligator*) pears. . *Subalterns' butter!* yes, that was the familiar name we gave them in days when fresh butter was a thing unknown in Jamaica.

SUBLE-JACK, subljak see SUPPLE-JACK.

SUCHY-LIKE see *sochilaik*.

SUCK sb dial. The sucking disk of a sucking-fish.

1952 FGC Port, Sucking-fish have a suck—hold to boat or fish.

SUCK vb dial. To nag. See SUCKER.

SUCK-AX /sókaks/ sb dial; from the sponginess of the wood. The tree *Hernandia jamaicensis*; also called PUMPKIN WOOD.

1952 FGC StE /sókaks/—has soft back, red and green vertical stripes; good for colds.

SUCKER sb dial; cf OLD SUCK. See quot.

1954 LeP StAnn, Sucker—nagging old woman; [Kgn, Too suckin—nagging old woman].

SUCKER see SACKA.

SUCKEY-SWALLA see SUCKY-SWALLOW.

SUCKING DUPPY sb dial slang. Tuberculosis. (Cf OLD HIGE.)

1943 *GL* Kgn.

SUCKO-BOLO sb dial; etym uncert, but cf *suck*, suggesting babyishness + *-o* rhyming with *bolo*—for which cf BOLOW, COMBOLO. See also SUCK vb.

1943 *GL* no addr, Sucko-bolo, fretful, peevish person. 1955 FGC Man.

SUCK (ONE'S) TEETH vb phr; cf SUCK-TEETH. To make a sound of annoyance, displeasure, ill-nature, or disrespect by sucking air audibly through the teeth and over the tongue. *BA BL G N T*

c 1915 FGC StAnd, common. 1942 Bennett 13, No bada suck yuh teet'.

SUCK (ONE'S) TONGUE vb phr dial. To push the tongue forward in the mouth, with lips closed or only slightly parted, and suck it rhythmically, usu inaudibly. (A babyish activity.) *BL G*

1950 Pioneer 46, Tom stop suck him big finga, but May still dah suck her tongue.

SUCK-TEETH sb dial; <*suck* + TEETH. The action of 'sucking' one's teeth at someone as an insult or mark of scorn. *BL G T*

1947 U.Newton III 14; cf CUT-EYE.

SUCKY-BABY sb dial. A herb of uncertain identity: perh GUMA, also known as PICKNEY-MUMMA.

1927 Beckwith 28, Sucky-baby.

SUCKY-SWALLOW /sòki-swála/ sb dial; <*suck* + *-y* + *swallow*. (Note quot 1958: a diff origin is implied.) St Vincent yam, which is soft, and when boiled needs little chewing.

1943 *GL* Han, Sucky-swalla, St Vincent yams; Port, Suckey-swalla, Suck-an'-swalla. 1954 LeP Port, Soki swala; StE, Suckie-swalla. 1958 DeC Clar /suokiswalo/ one of the Portland Maroon names for St Vincent yam.

SUCTURE /sókcha/ sb dial; <*suck* vb + *-ture* (or perhaps altered from *suctorial disk*). A suction disk on an octopus's tentacle.

1952 FGC StE, Sea-cat is round, greyish, with several 'points'—send them out, have suctures where they suck.

SUCUMBER see SUSUMBA.

SUCU-SUCU see *saka(-saka)*.

SUEKETEE /swiikitii/ adj dial cant; prob 'stretched' form of *sweet* or *sweety*. In the language of St Thomas cults: sweet.

1953 Moore gloss, Sueketee..sweet.

SUFFICE /safíes/ sb dial; the pronunc is not the usual reflex. St Vincent yam.

1958 DeC Clar /safíes/ Portland Maroon name.

SUGAR-AND-WATER /shúgaan-wáata, shúgan-waata/ sb dial. s SUGAR TEA. *BA*

1. A beverage made of local brown (or new or wet) sugar and water, sometimes with added lime leaves or the like; drunk hot as morning TEA by the country people; also as a COOL-DRINK. *BL*

1942 Bennett 14, Pass de sugan-wata fe me chile.

2. Generalized: other sweetened beverages—lemonade, tamarind drink, etc.

1956 Mc Man /iz tamarin misiz—mek shuga an waata/ *It's tamarind; you make a drink with it.*

SUGAR-ANT sb. The ant *Tapinoma melanocephala*, which swarms over anything having sugar in it. *G N* /shuga ans/.

1740 Importance 48, There is also a very small sort, called the Sugar-Ant; they are very troublesome in Houses, by running over Victuals and whatever is uncover'd, but inoffensive else. 1952 FGC Han, Man, Port, StAnd, StE /shuga ants/; StT /shuga hants/: very fine, red, like pepper-ants.

SUGAR BARK sb.

1926 Fawcett 133, *Malvaviscus Sagræanus*..Sugar Bark, Morass Bark, Mahoe Rose.

SUGAR BEAN sb; *OED* only ref 1858. A variety of the common edible bean *Phaseolus lunatus*; also called JAMAICA BEAN or PEAS, LIMA BEAN.

1727 *Observations* 13, Sugar-beans, Red-peas,..and others I have forgot. 1740 Importance 34, Sugar-beans, which are broad and flat. 1756 Browne 292, Phaseolus 10 ..The Jamaica Bean, or Sugar-Bean. 1837 Macfadyen 282, Phaseolus saccharatus. Sugar-Bean..The Sugar-bean is very generally cultivated in the Lowlands. 1913 Harris 25, Bean, Sugar..There are several varieties of this plant known as Lima bean; broad bean, and prolific or Hibbert bean. 1920 Fawcett 64.

SUGAR CORN sb. Sweet corn (maize) in its young edible state.

1913 Harris 30, *Zea Mays*..Indian corn or maize..The young cobs or ears, while still tender and succulent, are brought to market..In this state they are known as 'sweet corn' or 'sugar corn' and are roasted and eaten.

SUGAR DRINK sb. A liquor made from sugar-cane juice—see quot.

1707 Sloane lxii, Sugar Drink is made with Sugar-Canes bruised in a Mortar, or Hand-Mill, and then boil'd with water, and wrought in a Cask: it is clear like water.

SUGAR-DRUGGING vbl sb obs; <*sugar* + vbl sb of *drog* (*OED*). The drogging (transporting in coasting vessels) of sugar.

1740 Importance 14, Others belong to the Shiping, or go coasting in Sloops, there called Sugar-drugging, carrying it to their Ports to embark for England.

SUGAR HEAD sb. A 'head' of sugar: a cylindrical lump formed by pouring new sugar into a tin and letting it solidify. Cf HEAD SUGAR.

1952 FGC StJ /shuga hed/.

SUGAR-LOAF PINE sb; *OED* 1796→. The commonest name in Jamaica of the China pineapple. Transl Sp *piña de pan de azúcar*.

1740 Importance 30, see CABBAGE PINE. 1774 Long III 792–3, Pine Apple. . There are several varieties of this delicious fruit. . Some of the sorts observable here, are,. . The pyramidical, or sugar loaf, with yellowish flesh, and deep green coat. The same, with a yellow coat. . Of these the sugar loaf is most esteemed. 1952 Topper 6, see next.

SUGAR PINE sb; < *sugar* + PINE. A variety of pineapple (technically, the *China*), the name emphasizing its flavour, whereas its synonym, SUGAR-LOAF PINE, emphasizes the shape.

1952 Topper 6, The China is only of importance as a fresh fruit. . This variety is also known as 'Sugar Loaf', 'Cheese', 'St Mary' and 'American Sugar Pine'. 1952 FGC StJ, StT.

SUGAR POT sb obs; *OED* 1681 only. A mould into which sugar was formerly poured to cure and form loaves.

1739 Leslie 339, In refining the Sugar, the first Degree of Pureness is effected by permitting the Molasses to drain away thro' the Hole at the Bottom of the Sugar-pots.

SUGAR-WATER sb. = SUGAR-AND-WATER.

1907 Jekyll 76, The guests are received by the godfather and given sugar-water and bread. *BA G*

SUGGY vb dial; < *sugg* (*EDD*) + *-y*, familiarizing or hypocoristic.

1943 *GL* StE, Suggy, to suck.

SUIT sb dial. Liking, satisfaction.

1954 Rowe StE (Accom) /im fiks'di laans tu im suut/ *He fixed the lance to his liking.* 1960 *CLS* 163.

suki sb dial; prob a personifying name. A variety of breadfruit: see quots.

1943 *GL* StJ, Sookey, kind of breadfruit. 1954 LeP StE, The Sukie breadfruit of a very large size which is rather spongy when cooked. 1955 FGC Man /súki/ also /síngkit súki/.

SUKIE see prec.

SULPHUR BANANA sb dial. A variety of banana with a sulphur taste: see quot.

1952 FGC Port, StAnn /solfa/ banana—stem bears straight up, then turns horizontal. Banana reddish, not the best to eat. Used to make ink, mark things.

SUMFIJ see *samfai*.

SUN sb dial. See quot. (No other evidence found—poss erron?)

1912 McK *Songs* 87, Cous' Sun*. . *Cousin James. Sun is the regular nickname for James.

SUNA adj dial; perh comparative degree of *soon*. (Cf Uncle Remus: 'Brer Rabbit was a mighty soon man'.) Cf also *suun-man*.

1943 *GL* Tre (2 informants), Suna, smart.

SUNDAY JINAL sb dial slang; < *Sunday* + *jinal*, literally, 'General'. A clergyman or preacher of any kind. (Since *jinal* means a trickster or one who deceives, this appears to be an antagonistic nickname.)

1957 JN /sonde jinal/.

SUN-HOT sb dial. Midday.

[1873 Rampini 179, Rockatone (stone) at ribber-bottom (bottom of the river) no know sun hot.] 1895 Banbury 36, Sometimes at 'sun hot' (noon) it would make its appearance. 1905 Dodd 5, Sun hot—noon. 1924 Beckwith 289, The man had some teeth a his mouth, they long like a Jackass a laugh a sun-hot.

SUNSHINE sb dial. One or more kinds of small fish, also called 'whiting', that have a silvery sheen.

1892 Cockrell list, Sunshine—*Malacanthus plumierii* [*sic*].

SUN SILK sb dial. A bright yellow variety of the silk-snapper.

1929 Beckwith 33, see BLACK SILK.

SUNSUM sb dial rare; < Twi *sũnsũm*, the soul or spirit of man. The spirit, the force of emotions within.

1934 Williams 165, The practice still in vogue in Jamaica of 'throwing words at the moon'. . You may tell the moon the most insulting things about a party within his hearing without being liable for libel. . It certainly 'cools the sunsum' of the speaker who goes away contented and satisfied.

SUNTING, SUNTY see SOMETHING.

sunu, sunu-man sb dial; aphet < *asunu*.

1958 DeC Tre /sunu, sunu-man/ a big, oafish, stupid man.

sunusunu see ASUNU.

suod see SWORD.

suosi apl sb dial; prob < *South Sea*, the Pacific ocean + *apple*; cf SOUTH SEA ROSE, etc. The Otaheite Apple.

1956 Mc StE (Accom) /súosi apl/ = /íiti-úoti/.

SUPE see *suup*.

supljak see next.

SUPPLE-JACK /supl-, subl-; sopl-, sobl-; sibl-, sipl-, swipl-/ sb; *OED* 1725→.

1. Climbing shrubs (*Paullinia barbadensis* and *P. jamaicensis*) with very flexible knobby stems. (Cf also MOUNTAIN and WILD SUPPLE-JACK.)

1696 Sloane 214, Planta fruticosa scandens ex cujus caule fiunt scipiones cinerei flexiles striati & tuberculati. . Supple Jacks. 1794 Barham 185, Supple-jack. . Is a withe so called, which is full of round knobs at every five or six inches distance. 1837 Macfadyen 158, Common Supple-jack. . The branches of this species, from their roughness and flexibility, are commonly employed as riding switches. 1926 Fawcett 44, 46. 1943 *GL* StAnd, Sebljack—supple-jack. 1952 FGC Han /sopljak/; StM /sobljak/; StAnn, Tre /subljak/.

2. A whip made from the shrub.

1834 Lewis (1845) 157, He struck her to the ground, beat her with a supplejack. [1837 James 7, And Mr Drake sometimes beat her himself with supplejack.] 1943 *GL* Man, Suble-jack: a suple whip made from the Toby Whitz. 1952 FGC StJ /im paan iz sobljak an wip di waif/.

SUPPLY vb tech; cf *OED* 3a; 4 →1859. To plant new canes in the places where ratoons have died out. *BA T*

1952 FGC Tre, If you don't want to replant the entire field, you have to supply.

SURANCE see *shuorans*.

SURINAM CALALU sb obs; see CALALU. MOUNTAIN CALALU.

1774 Long III 771–2, Surinam or Juckata Calalue. *Phytolacca assurgens ramosa.* 1814 Lunan II 79.

SURINAM COCO sb arch or obs; introduced from Surinam? A variety of *Colocasia esculenta*.

1814 Lunan I 212, The *Surinam coco*, which is by far the most delicate, but by no means so productive as the others; it bears at a greater distance from the main root than the other kinds, is much longer in proportion to its thickness, and creeps to a considerable distance in the earth.

SURINAM GRASS sb obs; *OED* only quot. An unidentified plant (not a 'grass' in the ordinary sense). See quot. *G*

1756 Browne 300, Lotus? 1. Erectus, foliis lanceolatis.. Surinam Grass. This plant was lately introduced to Jamaica, from some of the Dutch settlements, and cultivated in the mountains back of Bull-bay, where it thrives well.

SURINAM PEAS sb obs. Some kind of bean. (The name was not repeated by Sloane (1707 183), and the bean is not identified by Fawcett (1920).)

1696 Sloane 72, Phaseolus major erectus.. Surinam Pease, or Rouncivals.

SURINAM POISON sb; *OED* 1756 only. A leguminous plant (*Tephrosia toxicaria*) used to intoxicate fish.

1756 Browne 296, Surinam Poison, or the smaller shrubby Cytisus.. This plant has been introduced to Jamaica from the main.. The leaves and branches of this plant, being well pounded, and thrown into any river, pond, or creek, are observed to infect the waters very soon; by which all the fish are immediately intoxicated. 1864 Grisebach 788. 1920 Fawcett 18.

SURPRISED FOWL sb obs. See quots.

1774 Long II 567, The Negroe cooks, who are to dress what is called here a *surprized fowl*, or one which is required to be roasted or boiled with great expedition immediately after it is killed and plucked, pour lime-juice down the throat, and at the vent, to make the flesh tender and eatable. 1873 Rampini 54, In some houses.. his fare will be even rougher than that of the tavern. 'Beef' soup, .. a 'surprised' fowl knocked down as his buggy entered the gates.. and a coarse mass of sodden and over-baked 'cow meat'.. will probably form his repast.

SUSAN WOOD sb; etym unknown. The tree *Antirrhœa jamaicensis* and its wood.

1941 Swabey 21, Goldspoon—(Susan Wood, Pigeon wood, May Day Mahogany).

SUSU /súsu/ vb dial; cf Twi *susúw kã*, to utter a suspicion (also Gu *sú*, to relate, tell; Ewe *súsu*, to regard as, appear as, intend, think, believe; also the sb Twi *asú-tú*, whispering). To whisper (behind one's back); to gossip; to speak ill. *G*

1943 *GL* Han, StJ, Tre, Susu, to speak ill of someone, speak against another, talk behind back. StAnn, Sue-sue-sue-sue, to whisper. 1954 LeP Man, Susu—to chat or gossip. 1955 Bennett *Oonoo Lie!*, Dem su-su and dem sey-sey, an Dem labrish an disgrace.

SUSU sb dial rare; cf Ko *nsusu*, fowl.

1956 E. Seaga StAnd, Susu, a fowl.

SUSUMBA, SUSUMBER /susúmba/ sb; 1814 1864 1913 soushumber, 1839→ susumber, 1854–5 sousoumber, 1927 sosumba, 1929 sosuma, 1942 sesumber, 1943 sucumber, 1943 susumba, sushumber, 1954 sousumber; cf Ewe *sũsùmɛ*, *sũsumɛ*, an aromatic plant used in preparing soups; also Twi *nsúsŭaa*, a species of pot-herb, *mbá* (plur), the young of plants.

The very common wild and cultivated plants *Solanum torvum* and *S. mammosum*, used as a good bitter with salt-fish and in other dishes. Also called CAT-NAIL, GULLY BEANS, MACAW BUSH, PORT-MORANT TOBACCO, TURKEY-BERRY. *BL*

1814 Lunan II 245, There are two varieties, both very common in Jamaica, the berries about the size of small cherries.. they are.. known by the names *soushumber, cat-nail, Port-Morant tobacco*, and *macaw bush*. 1839 McMahon 27, He then ran after them, flogging, knocking them down, and tumbling them into the susumber bushes, full of thorns. 1913 Harris 42, The soushumber is used mainly by the natives who are very fond of it and consider it a wholesome vegetable. 1929 Beckwith 14, Salt cod cooked with.. the sosuma berry, is a favorite breakfast dish even upon the tables of the whites. 1954 *FG* 222, Salt Fish and Susumbers.

suun-man sb dial; perh <**soon* (cf *suna*, clever, smart) +*man*.

1958 DeC StT /suun-man/ an obeah man.

suup sb dial; <Hindi *sūp*, a fan for grain. See quot.

1943 *GL* No addr, Supe, a fanner for rice. 1955 FGC Man /suup/ Coolie word—fan for rice.

swaamp-swaamp adj dial; iterative of *swamp* for *swampy* (cf *shine* for *shiny*). *G*

1958 DeC StAnd /swaamp-swaamp/ muddy, swampy.

swaati adj dial; origin uncert—this would be a normal reflex of Std *swarthy*, Engl dial *swarty*, but the sense seems unrelated; less exactly it might represent *swatty* Engl dial form of *sweaty*, or perh *swaddy*, heavy. *BL*

1956 Mc StE /swaati/ Fat, bloated-looking; of a person, big, fat, muscle-less; of meat, slack-looking, saggy.

SWAG vb dial; cf *OED v* 3 →1802. To cause to swag or stagger.

1958 DeC Man, (Of a load) to be so heavy as to make a man stagger: /di luod a swagin im/.

SWALLOW ONE'S SPIT(TLE) vb phr dial. To keep silent, not to speak. *G*

[1793 Edwards II 61, An old and faithful Mandingo servant.. relates that.. in his own country Friday was constantly made a day of strict fasting. It was almost a sin, he observes, on that day, *to swallow his spittle*,—such is his expression.] 1942 Bennett 13, Well me hear him talk 'bout him cattles.. Me dis swallow me spit for all him 'ave Is wan big head maga cow.

swanzik sb dial; etym unknown.

1959 DeC StJ /swanzik/ a kind of cane.

SWEAT-TABLE sb dial; cf *DA sweat-cloth*, 'a cloth marked with figures, and used by gamblers'. 1843→1872.

1955 FGC Man /swet-tiebl/ a gambling table with oil-cloth cover; dice in a cup used on it.

SWEE =BLUE-SWEE.

SWEE, SWEE-SWEE see *swii, swii-swii*.

SWEET vb trans dial; *OED* v^1 2 c 1555→1602, then 1879 'West Indian Negro'. *G*

1. To please greatly.

1790 Moreton 157, You sweet me, mackey massa!.. I'll sweet my mackey massa! 1950 Pioneer 37 [Anancy speaks to Jackass, who is laughing at him:] Wat sweet yuh Bredda Jackass? 1956 Mc Man /wen mi waan sliip, no fuud no swiit mi/ *When I'm sleepy I don't enjoy food.*

2. Also const *up*: to try to please, be sweet to.

1950 Pioneer 94, Go sweet-up Joe, an' treat him nice.

SWEET adj dial; <*sweet*, but in senses now arch or obs in Std use. *G T*

1. Tipsy, slightly drunk. *BA BL*

1956 Mc Man.

2. Of a man: dressy, dandified. *BL*

1943 *GL* StAnd, Dandy-bwoy—sweet, fine, well-dressed. 1954 LeP StAnn, A man very elegantly got up—sweet man.

3. Entertaining, pleasing. *BA BL*

1957 DeC StAnd /im stuori muo swiit dan di wan ai tel yu/ *His story was better (more amusing) than mine.*

4. As a general term of commendation, rather emphatic; far more common in use than elsewhere: very nice, lovely. *N*

1862 Clutterbuck 249, Him will bery nice; make massa a sweet supper. 1905 Smith 14, An' Annancy say—'O me sweet frien' Tiger'. 1956 JN, cf BUNGO 3; Tre, We can get some sweet joke! Man, I love fi read because read sweet.

SWEET-AND-BITTER CASSAVA sb. See quot. *G*

a 1818 Lewis (1845) 107, The *sweet* cassava requires no preparation; the *bitter* cassava, unless the juice is carefully pressed out of it, is a deadly poison; there is a third kind, called the *sweet-and-bitter* cassava, which is perfectly wholesome till a certain age, when it acquires its deleterious qualities.

SWEET-APPLE sb obs; *OED* 1760 only. The ALLIGATOR APPLE.

1696 Sloane 205, Anona aquatica foliis laurinis atrovirentibus..*Water-Apple*, or *Sweet-Apple*. a 1786 Barham (1794) 205, Some call them Sweet-Apple.

SWEET-BASLEY sb dial; <*sweet* + BASLEY. Sweet-basil.

1942 Bennett 30, see SAME conj. 1955 Bennett *Sweepstake*, Me wrap it up wid noonoo bush, Same sweet-barsley yuh know.

SWEET-BROKE /swíit-brók/ sb dial. Sweetmeat(s).

1961 BLB 6 /so yu lob di swiit-brok, sa/ *How you do like sweetmeats!*

SWEET BROOM(WEED) sb bot; cf BROOMWEED. The plant *Scoparia dulcis*. *G*

1756 Browne 145, Scoparia 1..The Liquorish-weed, or sweet Broom-weed..it grows by a very branched stalk.. the tender shoots at the top are frequently used in diluting and pectoral infusions. 1814 Lunan I 455–6, Liquoriceweed or Sweet Broomweed. Scoparia..dulcis..The root is annual; the stalks woody and hexangular, rising two feet high, and sending out many branches..the leaves have a sweet taste like liquorice. 1864 Grisebach 782, Broomweed, sweet: *Scoparia dulcis*. 1927 Beckwith 28, Sweet broom, see Sweet-weed. 1954 Kirkland 170 [Contents of a bush-bath:] Sweet broom.

SWEET-CUP sb. The vine and its fruit *Passiflora maliformis*; also called *kangksnot*.

1850 Macfadyen 156. 1913 Harris 21, Sweet cup..A high climber with fruits the size of a small apple with the shell hard and of a yellow tinge when ripe, enclosing the seeds embedded in a sweet, sub-acid watery pulp. 1926 Fawcett 236. 1955 *WIMJ* 228.

SWEETEN (ONE'S) MOUTH vb phr; cf *OED sweeten* 7. To please (someone). *BA BL G*

1873 Rampini 172, We dismissed them [*sc* negroes] with a little extra largesse 'to sweeten their mouths', to use their own phrase.

SWEET GOURD sb. The vine *Lagenaria vulgaris*.

1913 Harris 31, Gourd, Sweet..This is also known as bottle gourd.

SWEETHEART LIFE sb dial.

1956 Mc StAnd /swíitaat làif/ living together unmarried.

SWEET IRONWOOD sb obs. See quot.

a 1726 Barham (1794) 86, Lignum Aloes. I met with a tree in Jamaica that had a very black heart, and a fine scent, much resembling lignum aloes, being very bitter. A carpenter who first shewed me this tree, called it sweet iron-wood.

SWEET JOHN TUWHIT sb. = JOHN CHEWIT.

1839 Hill in 1840 *Almanack* 32, This morning I heard the Musicapa Olivacea..with those two or three notes from which the children have given the bird the name of *Whip Tom Kelly* or *Sweet John Tuwhit*.

SWEET LIME sb; *OED* 1857 only. See quot 1913. *BL N*

1814 Lunan I 452, *Citrus lima*..Varieties:—French lime.. larger, sweet lime..between lime and lemon. 1913 Harris 11, *Citrus medica, var. acida*..*Sweet Lime*.—This is merely a variety of the sour lime.

SWEET-LIP GRUNT sb dial; cf perh *OED sweet-lips*, a delicate eater, epicure. Some variety of the Grunt fish.

1952 FGC StE /swiit-lip-gront/.

SWEET-MOUTH adj dial; for *sweet-mouthed*, *OED* →1611. Greedy, food-loving, gluttonous. *BA G*

1896 Heaven [Prov:] Sweet-mout fly follow coffin go a' hole. 1907 Jekyll 24, [Anancy denies having meat in his bag:] The fellow so sweet-mout' say in a cross way, 'No'. 1956 Mc StE /im a swiit-mout man—im lov tingz fi iit/ *He's a sweet-mouthed man*, etc.

SWEET-MOUTH sb dial. *BL G T*

1. The power of flattery or persuasion.

1835 Madden II 149, He is generally a shrewd, plausible fellow—has a good deal of Congo saw, or, in other negro parlance, sweet mouth. 1868 Russell 12, Some people tak sweet mout lib..[*Some people live by flattery or persuasiveness.*]

2. A flattering or persuasive person. (This may be for *sweet-mouthed*, adj.)

1868 Russell 12, Hendry wossa sweet-mout dan William.

SWEET-ORANGE sb chiefly dial. The ordinary orange, so called in contrast to the SOUR ORANGE. *BA*

1954 *WIMJ* 29, *C. aurantium L.*.Sweet Orange.

SWEET PEPPER sb. A variety of pepper (*Capsicum annuum*) that is not hot. *BL G T*

1913 Harris 36, Sweet Pepper—*Capsicum annuum*. 1952 FGC seven parishes.

SWEET PINE sb. = SUGAR-LOAF PINE.

1952 FGC StE /swiit pain/.

SWEET PLUM sb. The common plum *Spondias purpurea*.

1952 FGC 5 parishes.

SWEET-POTATO PONE see PONE 3. *BA G*

SWEET-ROSE sb dial. An ordinary garden or wild rose. *SC switi-rósoe*.

1907 Jekyll 266, see ROSE. 1912 McK *Songs* 72, Dogrose—A dark red sweet-rose.

SWEETSOP sb; *OED* 1696→. The tree *Annona squamosa* and its fruit: see quots. *BL*

1696 Sloane 205, Anona..fructu conoide squamoso parvo dulci. Sweet-sop. 1756 Browne 256, The Sweetsop, or Sugar Apple Tree..The fruit of this species is pretty much esteemed by many of the fair sex, tho' seldom served up at table. 1914 Fawcett 197, Sweet Sop ..The fruit is edible, sweet, and when grown in the hills, of excellent flavour, as good as the Cherimoya. 1953 *WIMJ* 236, For coughs sweetsop is said to be used with calabash to make a syrup.

SWEET-WEED sb; *OED* 1760, 1771. The wild plant *Scoparia dulcis*, used medicinally; also called LIQUORICE WEED, SWEET BROOM (WEED), WILD LIQUORICE.

1696 Sloane 81, Veronica fruticosa erecta dulcis..*Wild Liquorice or Sweet-weed*. a 1726 Barham (1794) 88–9. 1927 Beckwith 28, For a baby with pain, give a tea of 'Sweet-weed' with loaf sugar, salt and a little garlic. 1952 FGC Han.

SWEET WILLIAM sb; *OED* 1760 only. The climbing vine *Ipomœa quamoclit*; cf BARBADOS SWEET WILLIAM. *BA G*

1811 Titford 43, Indian Pink,..also called Sweet William ..of a most beautiful scarlet. 1951 FGC Man, Sweet William.

SWEETWOOD sb; *OED* 1607→ for other trees.

1. The tree *Misanteca triandra* and its wood.

1696 Sloane 136, Laurus folio longiore, flore hexapetalo racemoso..*Sweet wood.* [This is LONG-LEAVED SWEET-WOOD.] a1818 Lewis (1845) 33, The air, too, was delicious; the fragrance of the sweet-wood, and of several other scented trees..etc. 1914 Fawcett 205, *Misanteca triandra*..Sweet-wood. 1952 FGC StE, StM, Tre /swiitwud/—smell sweet, used for live fence, splitting shingle.

2. The tree *Nectandra coriacea* and its wood.

1914 Fawcett 217.

3. In combined forms: see CAP-BERRY, LONG-LEAVED, PEPPERLEAF, ROCK, SMALL-LEAVED, and TIMBER SWEETWOOD.

SWEET YAM sb dial. A variety of yam somewhat larger than yampi and without bitter flavour. *G*

1952 FGC Han, Sweet yam—white, flat, small, but very good; StJ, Bigger than yampi. 1958 DeC Clar /swiit yam/ very small, resembles the renta, has a very thin peel, 'have veil-like ears on it'; highly praised.

SWEET(Y) MANGO sb. A round, sweet variety of mango.

1952 FGC Port, StM.

SWELL-HAND sb dial. The manchineel tree, because the sap is highly irritant and vesicant.

1952 FGC StE /swel-han/ milk blister skin, swell you han'.

SWI adv dial; echoic. The sound made by the stroke of a whip. *G*

1868 Russell 19, I hit him wid de horse wip *swi, swi.*

SWIFT adj and sb dial; by ellipsis.

A. adj: =FAST: interfering, meddlesome. *BA*

1954 LeP Kgn, To meddle or interfere—swift. 1960 LeP StAnd, 'You're swift'—you're fast, inquisitive, meddling. (Common.) But not as a verb.

B. sb: Impatience, hastiness.

1925 Beckwith 15, A swift mek wass-wass no gader honey. 'It's because he was impatient that Wasp can't gather honey.' [He would not wait to learn from the bee.]

swii sb dial; echoic. The Orange Quit (*Euneornis campestris*); cf also BLUE-SWEE.

1936 Bond 312, *Local names:—*..Blue Baize; 'Swee'. 1956 Jeffrey-Smith 70.

swiidn sb dial; prob imitative of the bird's call: cf BLUE-SWEE. The blue quits, both LONG- and SHORT-MOUTH BLUE QUITS.

1952 FGC Han /swiidn/ short-mouth and long-mouth kinds; blue; small and bigger.

swii-swii sb; echoic.

1. The Jamaican Vireo (*Vireo modestus*).

1847 Gosse 192, Sewy-sewy. Vireo Noveboracensis..Its notes are very varied; sometimes a loud *chewurr*, or *sweet-will.* 1912 McK *Songs* 96, The swee-swees* on the wing. *Quits. The name imitates their chirping song. 1936 Bond 303, Local names:—Sewi-sewi; 'Furuh Bird'. 1952 FGC StAnd /swii swii/ a little bigger than beany, colour of grass-quit; StM, Sewy-sewy. 1956 Jeffrey-Smith 50, 52–3, Sewi-sewi.

2. For the *swii*, by iteration: the Orange Quit (*Euneornis campestris*).

1952 FGC StAnn /siwi-siwi/ very active in fruit trees; eat fruit. 1956 Mc Clar /swii swii bod/ a small bird, which eats the oranges.

swiit sb dial; dial pronunc of *suet*—cf *dwiit* for 'do it', etc.

swima-doun see next.

SWIMMER-DOWN sb dial; <*simmer*+*down.*

1958 DeC Man /swima-doun/ a coconut rundown.

swimps, swims, swimz sb dial; pronunc varr of *shrimps*. Also /shrints/ see OLD-WOMAN.

1952 FGC StAnn, West /swimps/ hardly ketch round this end. 1956 Mc StAnd /swimz/ StC /swims, swimz/.

SWINE-HEAD (JACK) sb dial. A variety of the jack fish whose head is thought to resemble a swine's.

1952 FGC StE /swáin-èd/.

SWINGE /swinj/ vb dial; phon var of *singe.*

1952 FGC StAnn, Supple-jack—swinge it in fire. *BA BL*

SWING-SANG see ZING-ZANG.

swipl adj dial; var of *sipl*, <*supple.* Slippery; more specif sometimes: muddy.

1941 Kirkpatrick gloss, Swipple—slippery. 1958 DeC /swipl/ muddy.

swipljak see SUPPLE-JACK.

SWIPPLE see *swipl* and s SWIPPLE-POLE.

SWIPS vb and adv dial; etym uncert, prob mixed: such Engl dial forms of *sweep* as *swip, swipe* (*EDD*) may be involved, but *whip*, with overcorrect *s*- form (common in Ja dial) is equally possible; blending with *slip* also. Cf *swipper, adj.* quick (*SND*). *BL G*

A. vb: 1. To pass swiftly and easily.

1943 *GL* Kgn, Swips, to pass swiftly. 1955 Bennett *Long mout Doris*, An she jus sidung deh wutless Meck him swips outa her han.

2. To drink at a quick draft.

1955 FGC Man, To swips off a drink—to drink it off 'swips'.

B. adv: Quickly and easily. (Perh in part echoic.)

1955 FGC Man, see prec.

swi-swi man sb dial; prob in some way conn with the name of the bird *swii-swii*, but the relationship is obscure. An obeah-man.

1954 LeP Port, Man professing to kill or heal by magic—Swii-swii man. 1958 DeC Port /swi-swi man/ obeah man.

[**SWITCHING NECK** sb dial; this may actually represent a spoken form **switchy-neck*; *OED* 1891. A local name for the Louisiana Heron, *Hydranassa tricolor*.

1936 Bond 23. 1955 Taylor 67, The Louisiana is perhaps the most snake-like of the Herons in the movements of its neck and bill and in consequence it is often known in Jamaica as Switching Neck.]

SWITCH-SORREL sb; *OED* 1864→. The plants *Dodonæa viscosa* and its variant *D. angustifolia.*

1756 Browne 191–2, Triopteris 1..The Switch-Sorrel.. This slender shrub is very common in the most barren parts of the red hills and seldom rises more than six or seven feet above the root: both the trunk and branches are very flexile and tapering. The taste of the whole plant is acerb and bitterish. 1864 Grisebach 787. 1926 Fawcett 59.

SWITCHY adj chiefly dial; *OED* 'rare', quots 1812→1879; common in Ja. Pliant.

1952 FGC StM [Of an okro plant:] Tall, switchy one.

SWITCHY-TAIL (WENSHMAN) sb dial. A variety of the Welshman fish, presumably having a pliant tail.

1952 FGC StJ, Switchy-tail wenchman; switchy-tail.

SWOGGY /swagi/ adj dial; phon var of *soggy*.

1952 FGC StAnn [Referring to jelly-moss:] It's very swoggy-like.

SWORD /suod/ sb dial. *BA*

1. A straight machete. See DeC in 1961 *CLS* 73, map.

1954 LeP Man. 1956 Mc Man, StE.

2. Attrib: *sword cutlass*—see quots.

1954 LeP StAnn, Double-edged machete—Sword Cutliss. 1956 Mc Man, A straight machete /súod kótlis/.

3. The blossom of the maize plant.

1959 DeC Han, StJ /di kaan bluo suod/ *The corn is beginning to blossom.*

4. The blossom of the bread-fruit, 6 in. long, and fleshy.

1957 *FFM* 251, Crystallised Breadfruit 'Sword' or Blossom..Pick breadfruit swords when just ripe (before they become brown and hard).

SWORD BEAN sb; *OED* 1883 only. The bean *Canavalia ensiformis*—the large pod somewhat resembling a sword.

1837 Macfadyen 291, Canavalia gladiata. Sword Bean.. Native of the East Indies. Cultivated in gardens to cover arbours. 1864 Grisebach 781. 1920 Fawcett 61, Horse Bean, Overlook Bean, Sword Bean, Jack Bean.

SWORD BUSH sb; descr.

1920 Fawcett 261, *Phyllanthus epiphyllanthus*..Seaside Laurel, Rock Bush, Soap Plant, Sword Bush.

SWORD FERN sb; descr.

1951 Proctor *Ferns* 8, *Nephrolepsis exaltata*..Sword fern.

SWORD LEAF sb. One of the first long, narrow leaves developed by a young banana tree or sucker.

1913 Fawcett 3, Its first leaves—'sword leaves'—are very long and narrow as compared with those developed later.

SWORD (MACHETE) see *sou*.

SWORD ROSE, SWORD TREE sb dial. The CORAL-BEAN TREE *Erythrina velutina*, or *E. corallodendron*, also called SPANISH MACHETE, from the resemblance of the keel of the flower to a machete or cutlass.

1952 FGC StAnn /suord ruoz/ = quick-stick; StT, Sword tree = Spanish machete: for live fence.

SWORD SUCKER sb. A type of banana sucker. Cf MAIDEN SUCKER.

1913 Fawcett 26, On moist soils 'sword suckers', cut down to within 8 in. of the bulb, may be used.

SWOSO see SO-SO.

SYMBOL vb dial; <*symbol* sb. See quot; cf also CUT UNKNOWN TONGUE.

1935 HPJ, Cimbal: to speak with tongues, in (i) Revivalist frenzy, (ii) Obeah. An example is given at the end of the Blue, 'Madam Satan'. Cimballed, 'Felix the Phantam', where more examples are given. (Astley Clerk: I think this word should be spelt symbol.)

SYMPAVIVER see SEMPERVIVE.

TA[1] sb dial; alternative of TATA, father. (But cf Ewe *ata*, father.) Father; also as a title of respectful or affectionate address. *N*

1793 Edwards II 82, see MA. 1807 Renny 167.

TA[2] sb dial; reduced form of *sta*, sister. (But cf Twi *ataá*, twin sister.) Sister. *BL*

1956 Mc StE (Elderslie).

TA[3] conj dial; prob <AFTER, B. Because, since.

1956 Mc StAnd /dem mos a go kech jangga gal, ta son so hat/ *They must be going to catch shrimps, girl, since the sun is so hot.*

taa (yam) sb dial; cf Twi *ɔ-dé*, Ewe *te*, *tayi*, a variety of yam. A variety of yam similar to AFU: see quots.

1943 *GL* Man, Tah, native yam nearly like affoo in taste. 1952 FGC Port /taa yam/—Lucea yam. 1955 FGC Man /taa/—a white yellow-yam, harder than yellow. 1956 Mc Clar /taa/—white afu. 1958 DeC Clar /taa/—a white yam also called /wait afu/.

taambrim sb dial; etym unknown.

1954 LeP StT, Lobster or crayfish—taambrim.

taat sb dial; <*thought*, *thaught*, thwart (see *OED*). A seat in a kunu or boat. *BL*

1952 FGC Port, StT, etc. /taat/ thwart (seat) in a fishing kunu—the regular word and pronunc. 1956 Mc Kgn, StC /taat/ seat of a kunu.

TAATA, TATA /táta, táata/ sb dial; <any of a number of African languages, e.g. Ewe *tatá*, Gĕ *tátà*, Ngombe *tatá*, Kimbundu *tata*, Bobangi *ta:ta*, Tshiluba *tatu*—all meaning father (sometimes grandfather) and used also as a term of address. Also attrib.

Father; also as a respectful and affectionate title, esp for an elderly person. *BL G*

1790 Moreton 153 [Song sung by slaves:] Since dem tief me from my tatta, Me can't go there. a1818 Lewis (1845) 122, In particular, the women called me by every endearing name they could think of. 'My son! my love! my husband! my father!' 'You no my massa, you my tata!' said one old woman. 1826 Barclay 212, Little negro children running to meet their master..and vociferating the endearing expression *Tata come*, *Tata come*. 1942 Bennett 41, Tahta John a-dead. 1943 *GL* reported from most parishes: Tata, Tawta, Tato. 1952 FGC StJ /tata/.

TAATA FAADA sb dial; <TAATA + *father*. God.

1943 *GL* Man, Tata Faada, Our Father. 1962 BLB 70 /taata faada/ term of address to God.

taat-bangk sb tech; <*taat*, kunu seat + *bank*, bench. A piece of wood placed inside a dugout kunu to support either end of a seat.

1952 FGC StJ /táat-bángk/.

taaya see TAYA.

TABAN sb dial; <*turbine*.

1951 Murray 8, London taban bwila bottom bus' kill ovah ninety man. [*London turbine boiler-bottom burst.*]

TABLE sb dial.

1. See quot.

1958 DeC Port /tiebl/—a funeral custom among the Portland Maroons. On the ninth night, all guests, friends and neighbors throw money on a table in order to cover all funeral expenses and final doctor bills. This is done with great ceremony and good humor and occupies the first part of the nine-night meeting.

2. See MOURNING TABLE.

TACHE sb obs; cf *OED*. Unrecorded spellings: 1788–90 teach; 1803 teache, taitch.

1788 Marsden 26, The smallest and last copper is called the teach. 1790 Beckford II 71, And last of all to the teach, where the liquor begins to granulate. 1803 Dallas I xcvi, The last, called the teache. *Ibid* II 347, The juice so purified is carried rapidly over an intense fire through the taitches.

tachi-mini sb dial; <*thatch*+-*y*+*mini*, cf *mini-mini*. See quot.

1956 BLB Man /tachimini/ old thatch house—a derisive term.

TACK sb dial; <*tack OED sb*[1], senses 7b and perh 10, though the latter may be blended with *tact*. A change in direction, a shift, a trick (corresp to *OED* 7b); holding quality, ability to shift so as not to be outwitted (perh corresp to *OED* 10). *BA G*

1924 Beckwith 28–9, So for every tack Anansi put up, Cunnie-mo'n-father break it down. Anansi said to Tiger, 'Look heah! ev'ry tack dat I put up, Cunnie-mo'n-father break it down..'. Anansi say, 'Well, the boy have tack! but we *mus'* ketch him'.

TACK FISH sb; <*stockfish*, evid misunderstood from folk pronunc /tak-fish/ and 'restored' so. (Fawcett has the further confused form 'Jack Fish Wood' 1920, 95.) =STOCKFISH WOOD. *Tack fish* is now the prevailing form.

1943 *NHN* II 45, *Cæsalpinia vesicaria*—Tack Fish.

TACKOMA, TACOMA see TACOOMA.

TACKRO(-TACKRO) see TAKRO(-TAKRO).

TACKY adj dial; <TACK, trick +*y*.

1. Tricky, hard to get the better of.

1956 Mc Man /taki/ tricky (person); lying; jinal.

2. Hard to beat; good.

1956 Mc Man /taki/ of high quality; a very good concert was described as 'sharp and tacky'.

TACOOMA /takuma, tukuma/ sb; 1868→ Tacooma, 1890 Tecuma, 1907 Tacoma, 1924 Tacoomah, 1943 Tackoma; <Twi *ntikũma*, son of Anansi (Christaller). In Anansi stories, the son of Anansi most often named. His character is not very distinctive, but he is sometimes seen in opposition to Anansi. *BL G*

1868 Russell 6, Tacooma—the Spider. 'African.' 1890 Milne-Home, quoted in 1896 Bates 127, Tecuma one spider, Anansi one Tecuma. Tecuma big and foolish, Anansi smaller and more cute. 1907 Jekyll v, Tacoma and the Old-Witch Girl. 1924 Beckwith vi, Tacoomah's Corn-piece. 1952 FGC Tre /bra tukuma/ *Brother Tacooma*.

TACOOMAH see prec.

TADPOLE sb obs. The larva of the mosquito.

1774 Long III 885, Muskeetos..deposite their eggs indifferently in all stagnant fluids..Their young, or tadpoles, in their smallest state, are so extremely minute as to be scarcely visible.

TAFFEE, TAFFIE see next.

TAFFY (GOAT or **RAM)** /táfi/ sb dial; perh an allusion to the mascot of the Royal Welch Fusiliers, a large white ram; the regiment has been stationed in Jamaica.

1. A ram goat.

1877 Murray *Kittle* 26, I did hear Misser Telford down dere hab a Taffy, an him say dat him wi gie de Taffy to any man dat wi eat him liber wid a grain o' salt. 1933 McK 317, Taffy goat: ram. 1943 *GL* Kgn, Port, StAnd, StJ, StT, Taffie, Taffee, Taffy, Toffee—a ram goat.

2. An old person. (Jocular but disrespectful.)

1956 Mc Clar, Man /táfi ram/.

TAFU CRAB sb dial; etym unknown. A brown crab with hair on its underside.

1952 FGC StE /táfu/ catch in pots, has big claw, can eat—rest used for bait; brown. 1960 LeP West /táfu kràb/ has brown hair on underside.

tagalang vb dial; evid <*stagger*+*along*. See quot; cf GRAPPLE, PAWN, *taga-taga*, *stagalang*.

1958 DeC StT /tagalang/ to pick up and carry something heavy.

taga-taga vb dial; prob of multiple etym: cf Hausa *tagataga* sb, swaying or staggering preparatory to a fall—e.g. after a blow; Engl *stagger*, normally pronunc /taga/, could be iterated.

1958 DeC StT /taga-taga/—to carry something so heavy that you stagger.

TAGGORAM sb dial; perh a personal name, or <*taffy-goat-ram*: cf TAFFY RAM 2. A very old person.

1948 Bennett 81, Tagooram. 1951 Murray 35 [Song:] Ef me even old like Taggoram An me wan' fe pose as twenty-one, Nobody's bus'ness but me own.

TAGOORAM see prec.

TAHITI APPLE /tíiti hápl/ sb; an early alternative, now largely displaced by OTAHEITE APPLE.

1873 Rampini 145, The ground was carpeted with the magenta blossoms of the Tahiti apple.

TAHTA see TAATA.

TAH (YAM) see *taa (yam)*.

taia see TAYA.

tailits-plie see *stailit*.

TAIL (OF A HURRICANE) sb; cf *OED* 4b 1872. The less violent winds that follow alongside the main force of a hurricane. *BA BL T*

1828 Marly 108, Marly casually enquired whether he had ever been informed, that the tail of a hurricane, about twenty years ago, had injured Happy Fortune estate.

TAILOR-SCISSORS (CRAB) sb dial. A sea crab with a very large claw resembling a tailor's scissors.

1952 FGC StM, Tailor-scissors—sea crab, very sharp claw, flat shell pointed at sides.

taimo sb dial. A variety of breadfruit (not identified).

1952 FGC StM /táimo/.

tai shiin /tái shíin/ sb; <Hakka dial of Chinese (or perh Cantonese): Great Spirit, divinely endowed human spirit. A book of numbered tickets, each representing something—e.g. a part of the body—and used in the gambling game DROP-PAN.

1943 *GL* Kgn, Tyshin, drop pan term; StAnd, Tieshin. 1952 FGC Han /tái shíin/.

tai-tai see *ti-tai*.

TAITCH see TACHE.

TAJO int dial obs; etym unknown. An exclamation of excitement and enjoyment.

1790 Moreton 157 [Song of slave girl dancing before her master:] Tajo, tajo, tajo! tajo, my mackey massa! O! laud, O! tajo, tajo, tajo! You work him, mackey massa!

TAK see TAKE.

taka /táka, tánka/ conj dial; <*stand* usu /tan/ +*ka*, perh abbr of LAKA, as if. It seems as if.

1943 *GL* StM, Tanka, it seems to be; Tre, Taka, it seems. 1956 BLB StAnd (Mt Charles) /insteda ing fi beta, ing taka im a wosa/ *Instead of his getting better, it seems as if he is worse;* /laad sa, ing taka ing suun chienj/ *Lord sir, it looks as if it will soon change.* Also /tanka/.

TAKADA sb and vb dial; <Sp *estacada*, stockade. (Beckwith's 'take-care-there' is erron.)

A. sb: A fence of wattle, bamboo, thatch, or the like around a house and yard or other building. See *takied*.

1927 Anderson-Cundall 84 [Prov:] When mango season plenty, neyger stoccado wear black pot. [The cooking-pot, unused, is upturned on the fence post.] 1929 Beckwith 10, About the house yard is set a wattled fence ..or a 'takada' (take-care-there) of close-set bamboo or of some other wood, carrying five rails.

B. vb: To make such a fence.

1943 *GL* Tre, Takāda, to thatch [presumably the fence or wall, as is done in booths].

taka-taka sb and vb dial; iterative of *tack* vb + A[8]. To fasten or sew roughly; rough sewing.

1943 *GL* Clar, Takka-takka—rough sewing. 1956 Mc Clar, To do something roughly, to patch up—e.g. in mending an old basket where the weaving has come undone /wi taka-taka it op/. *G*

TAKARI /takári, takáari, tàngkarí/ sb dial: Hindi *tarkāri*, vegetables. An East Indian dish of vegetables with curry.

1943 *GL* Tre, Takari, a sauce; curry. 1955 FGC Man /tàngkarí/ a dish: calalu, curry, etc. 1956 Mc Clar /takaari, dat hinjan fiid—kom fram yelo jinja, pongkin/.

TAKE /tek/ vb dial; <*take* in a number of its uses, with slight shades of difference. See MAKE, note. *BA*

1. To appropriate (things) to one's own use; a distinction from stealing is often claimed but not always clear. *BL G T*

1788 Marsden 43, Finding a pair of shoes..he took and converted them to his own use..he was ordered to be flogged,..the negro all the time of his punishment cried out, *Massa me no teevee, me takee.* 1828 Marly 41, Him no tief from Massa, him take from Massa. 1957 JN, Anything me find me gwine take it up.

2. Of adverse weather, illness, or the like: to overtake and have its effect on. Cf *OED* 8b. (Common.) *BL T*

1924 Beckwith 76, Him couldn't get away from de woman until rain tek him in de yard. *Ibid* 94, Come in here; late night goin' tek you. 1941 Kirkpatrick 38, see USUAL.

3. To set out on a certain course, move in a certain direction. Cf *OED* 25b. *BL G*

1956 Mc StE /di dopi ron aaf di step an tek roun di chaach/ *The duppy ran down the step and made off round the church.*

4. To make up one's mind or insist on doing something. *G*

1877 Murray *Kittle* 25, Bra me ben tell you say you mustn't come ya; da you hard ears you take so come ya. [*Brother, I told you you mustn't come here, but you obstinately insisted and came here.*]

5. Also const with adverbs: *take away, off, up*, etc. and with objects: see separate entries.

TAKE AWAY (ONE'S) SPEECH (FROM) vb phr; cf *OED take* 78. To cease to speak to, to 'cut' someone. *BA G*

1950 Pioneer 68, Ah did sorry fe true when Brer Tiger did tek way him speech from me.

TAKE BUSH, HOUSETOP vb phr; <*take*, abbr of *take to the* + BUSH 1, *housetop*, etc. To flee to a place of shelter. *BL G*

1907 Jekyll 9, So Bro'er Tiger have fe take bush an' Anancy run up a house top. 1924 Beckwith 13, When Anansi see him coming, he run away and tak house-top and since then he never come down.

TAKE CARE /tìkyá, tíkyà, tìkyíer/ vb phr; cf MIND. *BA*

1. Be careful that you do not; beware lest.

1877 Murray *Kittle* 26, Watchman say, 'I will do it, but take care you make me fool'. *Ibid* 27, Eat one leg o' de mutton..Ef de leg done before I come back, take care you touch any more! 1943 *GL* Most parishes, Tik-ya, take care. 1956 Mc /tikya yu no kom/ lit. *Mind lest you do not come*, i.e. *Be sure to come.* *BA G T*

2. In the rhyming phr *tikya-bikya*, lit 'take-care because'; this may somewhat reinforce the warning.

1943 *GL* Port, Tickia-bicia, take care.

TAKE GRUDGEFUL vb phr; <*take* + GRUDGEFUL sb. Cf *OED* 25b. To act enviously or spitefully.

1942 Bennett 34, see UP adv. 1950 Pioneer 18, Hei now Bredda Ticks, yuh se wey yuh do? De one deggeh goat me have you teck grudgeful kill him.

TAKE HOUSETOP see TAKE BUSH.

TAKE NOTICE vb phr; the phrase of official announcements used in simple sense. To notice, pay attention to. (Common.) *BA BL G*

1956 Mc StE /yu no mi neva tek nuotis a di suop/ *You know, I didn't look at the soap.* (She bought the wrong variety.)

TAKE OFF vb phr trans dial; cf *OED take* 83g. = PULL 2. *BL*

1953 Moore 52, 'Taking things off people' is the method used to release people from evil forces believed to have been placed on them for the purpose of making them sick, unlucky, unhappy, or in danger of being killed.

TAKE OFF CROP vb phr tech; cf *OED take* 83a. To cut the cane crop and make it into sugar and rum. Cf CROP.

1790 Moreton 52, Taking off crop is a very laborious piece of business. 1823 Roughley 248, They should adopt the mode of bringing in their crops [i.e. to the point of ripeness] to be taken off without intermission. (1961 Current, FGC.)

TAKE (ONE'S) GROUND vb phr. Cf *OED* 25. To stand steady, hold one's position.

1907 Jekyll 111, Blacksmit'..shub him [*sc* the iron] down Tiger t'roat. Tiger can't take him ground, iron too hot.

TAKE SET UPON vb phr dial; cf *OED set sb*[1] 7. To become actively opposed to, to begin to attack or continually victimize (someone); to haunt.

1956 BLB StAnd /no bada tek nong set pang mi/ *Don't try to make a victim of me now.*

TAKE SHAME vb phr. Cf *OED take* 25b. To be afraid of giving offence; to yield wisdom to politeness. *BL G*

1910 Anderson-Cundall 41 [Prov:] You tek shame, you shake cocobay-man han'. [*If you are too afraid of giving offence, you will shake the leper's hand.*] 1927 Beckwith 42 [Prov:] Don't tek shame and mak you' fr'en' pickney 'pwoil you beaver.

TAKE SPRING vb phr; cf *OED take* 52. Of a tuber: to begin to be fit to plant—to begin to have shoots.

1955 FGC Man /it get choui wen it gwain tek spring/.

TAKE TIME /tek-taim/ vb phr; prob reduction of *take your time* or the like. Cf *OED* 28.

1. Go slowly, be patient. Also as an exclamation. *BA BL G*

1873 Rampini 120, Stop, Breda! take time; my head hurt me so! 1894 Banbury 41, see HANCH. (1961 Current, FGC.)

2. Be cautious; be careful lest. (As an exclamation this may be anything from a simple warning to a threat.) Cf MIND.

1924 Beckwith 61, Cock tak time, tip on him toe. An' go long to one gourd, he hear Cockroach in a de gourd. 1956 Mc StAnd /tek taim nou/ *Go steady!* 1960 FGC Kgn /tek-taim ou yu huol mi/ *You'd better not try to take hold of me!*

TAKE UP vb phr. *BA*

1. To arrest, to seize by legal authority; *OED* 90b →1861. *G*

1952 FGC StAnn /dem goin tu tek op puo Anaansi/.

2. To take, catch (an ailment); cf *OED* 44b.

1956 BLB StE /main yu tek op a kuol doun de/ *Mind you don't catch a cold down there.*

TAKE UP WORK vb phr; cf *OED* 32b. Of a busha or head-man: to look over and judge the amount of work a man has done, so as to pay him.

1952 FGC Han, StAnd.

takied /takíed/ sb dial; <*stockade.*

1. A fence enclosing a yard or building; cf TAKADA.

1956 Mc StE (Accom) /takíed/ A high wall of painted bamboo..for a meeting hall.

2. A protective fence around a seed bed or young plant.

1956 Mc Man /takíed/ a low fence of pointed sticks round seed-bed.

TAKKA-TAKKA see *taka-taka.*

TAKOOMA see TACOOMA.

TAKRO(-TAKRO) /takro-takro/ also /takra-takra/ adj and vb dial; = *SC takroe* (1855 Focke).

A. adj: Ugly, unattractive, unkempt, rough, unrefined, forbidding in manner.

1868 Russell 10, Ugly, ill-proportioned. Dat is a takro-takro man. 'African.' 1873 Rampini 127, Him curse him moder for a 'cra-cra' (careless)..'takro-takro' (ugly).. 'nana' (old woman). 1943 *GL* StAnd, StJ, West, Tackro, shabby or ugly, ill-looking, rough and crusty; StC, Tre, Takro, unrefined, unkempt. 1959 D. Macdonald Clar (Chapelton), Tackro..is used to denote a person of austere disposition, uncooperative with others, and difficult to deal with..'Unprepossessing' is as close a definition as I can get.

B. vb: To do something roughly and badly.

1956 Mc Man /takra-takra it/.

takuma see TACOOMA.

talaban see *talawa.*

TALABERD see next.

talabred sb dial; <*thoroughbred,* with dissimilation of first *r.*

1943 *GL* StM, Talaberd, well-mannered. 1955 FGC Man /talabred/ horse or donkey.

talala see next.

talawa /tálawa, tálala, tálaban/ adj (sometimes indistinguishable from sb and vb) dial; cf Ewe (Gũ) *tálala,* direct, straightforward, thorough, to a high degree, entire, basic. **s.**

1. Sturdy, strong, not to be underestimated; tough, stubborn.

1943 *GL* Kgn, Talawah, great big, Tallaban, sturdy; StE, Tallawap, strong. 1952 FGC StM, Strong and stubborn; freq in the saying /im líkl bot im tálawa/. 1956 Mc Clar /talawa/ not to be taken lightly.

2. Cross-natured, dangerous, bad; of a girl: one who sets no limits in sexual matters.

1943 *GL* Man, Tallawah, trouble giver. 1952 FGC Han /talawa/ a girl who will disgrace herself; very bad—out-and-out. 1951 Murray 50 [Song:] Matty run a mile an' a half fe go tallala. (Note:) Meet her lover. 1956 Mc Clar /im talawa—miin 'kraas niecha'/.

TALAWAH see prec.

TALK vb dial.

1. In pregnant sense: to speak evil of, to slander. *BA*

1924 Beckwith 40, So they pass a law that anyone talk one another, that man will drop dead. *Ibid* 41, Anansi make law if anyone talk de odder one, he dead. 1962 BLB 33, Talk, to slander.

2. In phr: *to talk in one's head,* to think to oneself. *G*

1924 Beckwith 44, Hanansi come down an' talk in a head. He took up de han'kerchief an' say, 'Yah dere's a good red pocket-han'kerchief'.

TALKEE-TALKEE sb dial obs; *OED* 1808→. A ticket or pass giving the right to move about —formerly required of slaves away from their plantations.

1740 Importance 17, All Negroes must have written Tickets, which they call *Talkee, Talkee,* before they are suffer'd to pass.

TALKING vbl sb. A cause of much talk.

1929 Beckwith 20, One ['bearing' of cassava] exhibited at a fair, which weighed 56 pounds, 'was a talking among all the cultivators'. 1960 BLB /it woz di onggl taakin/ *It was a major topic of conversation.*

TALKING COW sb dial. A cow which, by persistent lowing, is believed to be predicting someone's death.

1929 Beckwith 85, Cundall's informant writes of the lowing of cattle: 'If cows surround a bull lowing sadly while the bull ploughs the earth with its horns, it is an omen of death', and in Mandeville I found that particular animals, called 'talking cows', were supposed to give the sign. *Ibid* 119.

TALKY-TALKY BOOTS sb dial obs. Cf TALKEE-TALKEE. Boots that squeak or CRY.

1873 Rampini 173, An incident occurred which amusingly illustrated his predilection for 'talky-talky' boots.

TALL adj dial; cf *OED* 7b.

1. Regularly used for 'long', of physical objects. *G*

1907 Jekyll 39, An' Donkey say..'I have long tail and long ear an' a very tall foot too'. (A very long leg.) 1952 FGC StE /taal kalalu/ with a long leaf. 1956 Mc StAnd /a taal mat, bout seven fiit—dem sliip an it/.

2. Transf to non-physical things—e.g. time.

1959 LeP StAnd, The mornings are getting tall (i.e. getting longer: it is getting light earlier).

3. Used for 'high'.

1956 Mc StE /taal-hiil shuu/ high-heeled shoe.

TALLABAN, TALLALA, TALLAWAH, TALLAWAP see *talawa.*

TALL BAAJ sb dial; <TALL 1. + *baaj.* The type of baaj with 'tall' (i.e. long) fruits: *Averrhoa carambola.* Also called CHINESE JIMBLING, COOLIE BAAJ.

1958 DeC.

TALL BROOMWEED sb bot obs; cf BROOMWEED. In Macfadyen's use: *Abutilon giganteum* (ident 1926 Fawcett 102).

1837 Macfadyen 87, Sida elata. *Tall Broom-weed.*

TALL-LEAF FERN sb dial; < TALL 1 + *leaf* + *fern*. Long-leaved fern.

1952 FGC StM /taal-liif-form/ fern used for flowers, dressing house.

TAMARIND see TAMBRAN, TAMBRIN. *BA G*

TAMARIND SHAD BARK sb. = SHADBARK.

TAMBAREEL sb dial; < *tambourine*, perh infl by Sp *tamboril*, tabour.

1943 *GL* StAnd, Tambareel, Tamborine.

TAMBO sb dial; cf Kongo *ntambu*, a trap. **s.**

1943 *GL* Port, Tambo, a bow-shaped Bird Trap.

TAMBRAN, TAMBRIN sb dial; the common folk pronunc of *tamarind* (through normal loss of *-d*, effect of vowel harmony changing *i* > *a*, and articulative intrusion of *b* after *m*). Tamarind. *BL G T*

1868 Russell 5, Tambran, Tamarind. 1943 *GL* StAnd, StAnn, StM, Tambran, tamarind. 1952 FGC Han, StAnn, StM /tambrin/; Port /tambran/.

TAMBRAN SEASON (or **TIME**) sb dial. The time of year (January to March) when tamarinds are in fruit, but other products are scarce: 'hard time'. Often fig. *BL*

1952 FGC Han /tambrin siizn or taim/ hard time; Port /tambran siizn/.

tambrik sb dial; < *turmeric*.

1952 FGC Han, see SANTA. 1958 DeC.

TAMBRIN JACK sb dial; < TAMBRIN + *jack*. A fish similar to the Jack; the name prob refers to thinness or small size.

1952 FGC StC /tambrin jak/ smaller than amber-jack.

tambu sb dial; etym uncert: cf Sp *tambor*, drum, but also and perh basically *tumba*, from African sources.

1. A drum. Cf *tumba, tumbe*.

1955 FGC Man /tambu/ among the Maroons, a rumba-box or Cuban drum.

2. A dance or musical entertainment. (Cf Santamaría *tambo* II.)

1943 *GL* StC, Tambus, holidays. 1955 FGC Man /tambu/ when many come together.

tampi sb dial; etym unknown.

1952 FGC Han /tampi/ ganja, a smoke of ganja.

TAMPONANNY see CHAMPONG-NANNY.

tam-tam sb dial; perh repr *Tom-Tom*. The PEENY-WALLY.

1959 DeC West /tamtam/ the large firefly with light coming from the head.

tan see STAND.

tana sb dial; aphetic form of *antana*. A rough bundle made with trash, bark, wis, etc. to carry provisions back from the field. Also called BUSH-BAG.

1943 *GL* Clar, StAnn, Tanna, a trash or grass bundle containing foodstuff, parcel. Tenna. 1955 FGC Man /tana/ ground provisions tied up in trash with wis—like string bag. 1956 Mc Man /tana/ bundle made on /groun/ when food is tied up in /jag-jag/ with /wis/. 1958 DeC Man /tana/. 1959 West /tanu/ variant of /tana/ a rough temporary field bag, made of trash.

tanchiin sb dial; < *stanchion*. A stand for putting things on; = *pata, dresa*.

1956 Mc Man /tànchíin/.

'TAND see STAND.

TANDA, TANDAY see next.

tan-de imperative phr dial; < *stand there*.

1. A magical formula to prevent someone or something from moving. Usually exclamatory —it has a variety of uses: to halt a ghost in its tracks, to stop a thief until he can be caught (cf TAN-YAH), but esp as part of funeral ceremonies to keep the departed spirit 'planted'. It enters into songs sung on such occasions.

1877 Murray *Kittle* 15 [Funeral song:] O! Tom, boy, tan da dutty, O!..Tom, boy, O! tan where you da, O! 1929 Beckwith 76, Falconer says the people in the bush take three grains of peas, tie them up in a piece of new calico, and, going to the grave a couple of minutes before the time of day at which the man died, they dig a hole, bury the bundle, and say, 'You 'tan 'deh wid dis'. *Ibid* 133, [The obeah man] sent everyone out of the room and then took a number of vials containing such drugs as drive away spirits and sprinkled them all about the room saying, 'Tan 'deh till I come!'. 1943 *GL* Clar, Tanda; StC, Tande; Tre, Tandeh, stand there; StJ, Tanday; Tre, Tandey, one of the rites of obeah. c1953 Wilson in *Gleaner* [Digging song:] *Bomma:* Go down, Go down— *Bobbin:* Tandey long. *Bomma:* Wheel and tandey— *Bobbin:* Tandey long [etc.].

2. The art of magic using this formula.

1929 Beckwith 125–6, Through Manchester there is a belief that a thief who enters a man's field can be made to stay and work until the owner comes and gives him a flogging. The art is called 'stand there' and depends upon impersonating the presence of a duppy..[etc.].

3. An illness believed to be due to obeah— it 'stands there' and is hard to cure.

1943 *GL* Man, Tandeh, any illness superstitiously believed to be inflicted by an obeah man. 1955 FGC Man /tande/ disease hard to cure.

TANDEH, TANDEY see prec.

TANGERINE ROSE sb. A way of serving a tangerine: see quot.

1957 *FFM* 148, Tangerine Rose. With paring knife, slice tangerines from stem near bottom in eights. Fold skin behind pegs. Remove strings from pegs. Garnish with sprig of mint.

tanka see *taka*.

TANNER see *tena*.

TANNIA, TANNIER see TANYA.

tan-pan-mi sb dial; < *stand* + *upon* + *me*.

1. A satchel or field bag for food and other supplies.

1958 DeC StAnn /tan-pan-mi/ same as /namsak/ or /heng-pan-mi/.

2. See quot.

1959 DeC West /tan-pan-mi/ old ragged work clothes, especially if very dirty.

tanu see *tana*.

TANYA /tanya/ sb; < Tupi *taña*. *OED tania*. A coarse type of COCO—more often called BADU.

1756 Browne 332, Arum 4..The purple Cocco, and Tannier. The tops of this plant are commonly used to feed the hogs; but the root is more valuable. 1929 Beckwith 17, The coco, variously known as the *eddo* or *tanya* in the West Indies. 1943 *GL* Man, Badu, root of wild coco (tannia); StC, Baddohead, headers tawna; Port, Tinya, Wild coco. 1955 *WIMJ* 158, Colocasia esculenta..Coco (Yam); Eddo; Tanya. *BA G T*

TAN-YAH sb dial; < *stand here*; see *tan-de*. The OVERLOOK BEAN.

1943 *GL* Man, Tan yah, A wild bean superstitiously believed to be able to hold thieves in ground in which it is planted till the owner goes there.

tap-a-paas, TAPI'ANPASS, tap-i-a-paas, tap-it-a-paas, TAPPIAPASS see STOP-(IT-)A-PASS.

tapnachik sb dial; < TWOPENNY CHICK. Either of the Jamaican thrushes. *BL N*

1952 FGC StAnn /tap-na-chik/ same as Hopping Dick; StM, Shine-eye /tap-n-a-chik/.

TAP-TAP see STOP.

TAR sb dial. *G*

1954 LeP StT, Taar—very black negro.

TARANTULA sb; cf *OED* 1 b, 1794→. Large, hairy spiders of the genus *Mygale*. *G*

1756 Browne 420, The black Tarantula. . The large brown Tarantula. . The large hairy Tarantula.

tarapom, tarapong see TARPON.

TAR-POD sb dial; < *tar* + *pod* (?for *pot*). A type of wild fig-tree.

1952 FGC Tre /taa-pad/ a large-leafed fig; 'plenty gum when you fall the tree'. 1961 DAP, Tar pod, *Clusia* spp.

TARPON /trapong, tarapong, tarapom/ sb; 1657 *terbum*, 1679 *tarpum*, 1756 *tropon*; etym unknown; *OED* 1685→. The fish *Tarpon atlanticus*. **s.** *BL*

[1657 Ligon 39, Snappers, red and gray, Cavallos, Terbums, Crabs, Lobsters.] 1679 Trapham 59, The choice Mullet brings up the next division crowded with various Snappers. . Porgoes, old Wives, Tarpums, Spanish Mackerel. 1756 Browne 442, Amia 1. . The Tropon. 1952 FGC Port, StAnn, StC, StM, StT /trápòng, tràpóng/ West /tarapom/ StJ /tarapong/.

TARPUM see TARPON.

TARRA adj dial; < *t'other*, with flapped *r* for *d* (dial reflex of voiced *th*). Cf *teda*. **s.** *BL G*

1. Other; the other.

1877 Murray 6, Bufo any of dem tarra fellow. 1943 *GL* most parishes, Tarra; StJ, Traw.

2. Second, next.

1950 Pioneer 23, Anancy 'tudy de song, an de tarra evenin' before Ma Kayke come, him goh a de door an sing de same song.

TARRA-TARRA sb dial; < TARRA, iterated. Miscellaneous things. *G*

1950 Pioneer 56, Bans a different-different knife an fork An spoon an tarra-tarra!

TARRY /tari/ vb dial; *OED v* 4b, '*arch.* exc. in U.S.' To remain for a period of time. *BA*

1956 Mc StE /shi muosli tari dong de/ *She passes most of the time down there;* /wi tari die/ *We stay there.*

TARRY(-TARRY) /taari/ adj dial; transf < *tarry*, of the nature of tar, etc.

1. Of a road: wet, sloppy, muddy.

1958 DeC StJ.

2. Sticky; like tar. *G*

1959 DeC West, adj for anything that 'comes tight'; e.g. wet sugar when boiling /kom taari-taari/.

TARSHAN sb dial; < *torchon*, *OED* →1908. See quots.

1943 *GL* StM, Tarshan, trimming. 1960 LeP StAnd /taashn lies/ a very coarse lace used in the country.

TAR (YAM) see *taa (yam)*.

TASSEL /tásl/ sb dial chiefly. The ARROW or FLAG of sugar-cane.

1961 *CLS* 69, see map showing distribution of variant terms.

TATA see TAATA.

tataz sb dial; etym uncert—phonologically derivable from *tatter*, *tata* or other words, but the sense is not clear.

1958 DeC Port /tataz/ salt fish fritters.

TATCH see THATCH.

tatlin sb dial; < *tackling* vbl sb; cf *EDD tattlin*, tackling.

1956 Mc StE (Accom) /tatlin/ mule pad.

TATO, TATTA see TAATA.

TATTRY sb dial; etym uncert: cf *tataz* and Ewe (Gẽ) *tátale*, banana pancakes.

1943 *GL*, Tattry, a small bammy.

tatu sb dial; attempts at phonetic sp: *tato*, *tattoo*, *tattu*; prob Afr, but no source found. A small house or hut, originally with a thatch roof. **s.**

1954 LeP Kgn, Thatched hut, Tattoo; StE, Tato; StT, Tattu. 1956 Mc Man /tatu/ a shelter consisting of thatch roof supported on (bamboo) posts, no walls; Man, StC, The thatch roof of a /buud/ (booth); StAnd, Any roughly built shelter with flat roof (not necessarily thatch) to be used by people as a stall (shop), shelter at ground, etc. 1958 DeC /tatu/ a small hut or shelter; in Kingston this is used for the shacks one finds in such places as Tinson Pen; in the country. . a shelter built at the field for the farmer or along the road for the road gangs; at Holland Bay. . for the fishermen's beach huts.

TAWNA see TANYA.

TAWTA see TAATA.

TAWYA see TAYA.

TAW (YAM) see *taa (yam)*.

TAY see TILL.

TAYA /taia, taya, taaya/ sb chiefly dial; < Tupi *taya*, Carib *taya*. *OED* enters *Tania* (see TANYA), a related form, but in Ja *taya* is the more frequent. A kind of COCO (*Xanthosoma* spp) with a yellow-fleshed root-stock which is eaten; see also EDDO, BADU, TANYA.

1696 Sloane 62, Aron maximum Ægyptiacum quod vulgo Colocasia. . *Tayas.* Ad rivulos Insulæ Jamaicæ frequenter & passim oritur. 1725 Sloane 367, Tayas or Eddos, are eaten in Jamaica, and cause a Heat in the Throat. 1756 Browne 332, The white Cocco, and Tyre. . The old heads are called White Coccos, and the young roots that shoot round the top, Tyres. 1803 Dallas 1 106, Yams, cocoas, toyaus. 1943 *GL* (Attempts to spell:) Port, Tiya, Tyeya; Tre, Tãyah; StAnn, StJ, Tawya; Kgn, Toya. 1952 FGC StT /táia/; Han, StT /taaya/; StAnn, StE, StJ, StM /taya/; Han, Hog-taya is Eddo. StAnn, Taya is river-coco, yellow—tek it feed pig.

TAYAH see prec.

TAYLOR BANANA sb. A variety of banana with a large fruit.

1956 Mc StE, see SEED 1.

TCHE see CHO.

te, tea see TILL.

TEA sb dial. *BA G T*

1. Any liquid taken as a beverage, usually hot—see COFFEE TEA, FISH TEA, SUGAR-AND-WATER. When brewed and taken for medicinal purposes, it is BUSH TEA.

[1740 Importance 44: They make several Infusions or Teas (as they call them) in Fevers.] 1912 McK *Songs* 87, See dem. . Comin' for de steamin' tea.*. . *Generic name for any non-alcoholic hot drink.

2. The peasant's or workman's first meal of the day, usually (but not necessarily) including some tea (sense I). See quots. Cf CHAKLATA, WASH-MOUTH. *BL N*

1907 Jekyll 62, At daylight, or soon after, it is the custom to drink tea. This is generally hot water and sugar with, or more often without, milk. Sometimes they make an infusion of the leaves of lime, orange, mint, fever-grass, cinnamon, pimento or search-me-heart. Coffee and chocolate are also occasionally used. These all grow in Jamaica, but, owing to its high price, actual tea is beyond the reach of the peasant. 1952 FGC StJ, StM, Tre, Tea—same as chaklata; StE, Tea at 6:30 A.M. chaklata at 7:30 to 8:00; StAnn, Tea—hot sugar-and-water with lime leaves. 1960 LeP StAnd, Tea, as a meal (the first *solid* food in the day) does not necessarily include any beverage at all. Our maids have bread-and-butter for their 'morning tea'.

TEA BUSH sb dial; <TEA I + BUSH. *BL G*

I. Any plant which may, in whole or in part, be used to make a TEA (sense I).

1952 FGC StAnd /piaba/ good tea-bush.

2. Specif: The plant *Melochia tomentosa*.

1954 *WIMJ* 24, Tea Bush; Raichie. Used to make tea for colds.

TEACH, TEACHE see TACHE.

TEACHERESS sb dial; *OED* →1657. A female teacher. (Cf BUTLERESS, DOCTRESS.)

1943 *GL* StT, Teatris, female teacher.

TEACHMENT sb dial; *OED* →a 1578. This is prob a new formation (on the analogy of preachment, etc.) rather than a survival.

1953 Moore 76, Teachment—teaching (through possession by spirits) received in the course of a Revival ceremony.

TEAH see TILL.

TEARING vbl sb dial.

1943 *GL* StJ, Tearin', a flogging.

TEAR-UP(-TEAR-UP) adj dial; for *torn-up*. Torn, very ragged. *BA G*

1868 Russell 11, You see one tear-up-tear-up dutty fella pass ya. 1956 Mc StE /uol tier-op kluoz/ *old ragged clothes*; /dem yuuz bad tier-op mat pan changga-bed/ *They use old torn mats on a changga bed.*

TEASE-TEASE vb dial; iterative of *tease*. To tease continually. *G*

1942 Bennett 5, Him gwan tease-tease de people dem, Him hooda nevah cease.

TEATRIS see TEACHERESS.

TEBBA sb dial; etym unknown. Sense uncertain (see quot: 'cocoa' might mean the chocolate drink, coco root, or something else).

1943 *GL* Port, Tebba, cocoa.

TEBE adj dial; cf perh Ewe *tébee*, full to the brim.

1943 *GL* StT, Tebe, big.

TECK see TAKE.

TECUMA see TACOOMA.

teda /teda, tida/ pron dial; <*t'other*, the other. The second, the other. *G*

1943 *GL* Port, Tedda, another; StJ, Tidda; Tre, Tida, the other. 1955 LeP StE, see A DA MEK. 1956 Mc Man /mi gi dem teda wan a chaans/ *I gave the other ones a chance*; /mi no nuo wish wan trangga an teda, jan ar jiemz/.

TEDDA see prec.

TEENAGER sb; <US *teenager*, one of any age from thirteen to nineteen. (The word has become very common, 1960–1. FGC.) A 'medium-sized cockroach' that is 'hard to control'—actually a separate species (*Blatella germanica*) which, when full-grown, remains smaller than the common cockroach. *BA BL*

1960 LeP StAnd, Teenager, teenage roach. 1961 FGC StAnd (called to notice by several informants).

TEE-TEE, TEE-TIE see *ti-tai*.

TEETH /tiit/ sb sing dial. s. *BL G N T*

I. A tooth, in any of the usual senses.

1943 Bennett 10, Bwoy, not even a gole teet or A gole chain roun yuh t'roat. 1956 Mc Man [Child, when a first tooth comes out:] /rata tek dis tiit an gi mi a nyuu wan/. 1957 JN Man, When my teeth comes out I just throw it away.

2. The tine of a fork.

1956 Mc Man /tiit/ the prong of a fork.

TEETH WIS sb dial; <TEETH + WIS. A vine used against toothache, prob the same as NEDGE-TEETH.

1952 FGC Tre /tiit-wis—wen di tiit a hat yu, yu tek it shub iin a yu tiit/.

TE-FEH see *tufe*.

TEG-A-REG, TEGGEREG see next.

TEG-REG, TEGGEREG sb dial; <*tag-rag*, *tag-and-rag*, 'of or belonging to the rabble' *OED* B a →1675. A rough, uncouth, trouble-making person.

[1826 Williams 326, Susanna, don't throw yourself away on any of the soldier buckras, nor tag-rag bookkeepers.] 1942 Bennett 27, Gwan gal you favah teggereg..Gloss: troublesome person. 1943 *GL* Man, Teg-reg, a coarse uncultured person; Port, Tegreg, parasite; No addr, a provocative person. Kgn, Teg-a-reg, a blushing woman [Error for 'unblushing'?]. 1950 Pioneer Gloss, Teggereg —bully.

TEGREY sb dial; etym unknown.

1943 *GL* Tre, Tegrey—donkey cart.

TEH see TILL.

TEK see TAKE.

TEKREHKI sb dial; <Twi *tekrekyi*, a bag or sack plaited like a mat.

1943 *GL* Tre, *Tekrehki*, a basket.

tel see TILL.

TELEPHONE WANTS YOU phr dial. You are wanted on the telephone. *G*

1959 FGC StAnd, 'The telephone wants you'—regularly said by maids, etc.

TELL[1] vb dial.

I. To say (a formula of greeting or parting).

1907 Jekyll 109, The gal..eat done an' tell goodbye. 1956 Mc /tel misis gu nait/ *Bid Missis good night.* *BA G T*

2. To reply, reveal one's decision. *G T*

1907 Jekyll 143, 'So you better put me fe guard you house from that tiefing Mr Ratta'. Dog was quite agree. Dog said:—'After dinner I will tell you better'. Quashy said 'Yes'.

TELL[2] see TILL.

TEMNE /timini/ sb now dial.

I. An African tribal and language name from Sierra Leone.

1943 *GL* No addr, Timini, A West African tribe.

2. A person of Temne origin; in Jamaica this implies short stature.

1952 FGC StAnd /timini man/ very short.

tempe sb dial; etym unknown: perh for *temper*? =DUPPY GUN.

1952 FGC StAnn /tempe/ duppy gun plant, trick-weed.

TEMPER-BUSH sb dial. The herb *Amyris balsamifera*, supposed to take away ill-temper.

1927 Beckwith 28, Temper-bush. *Amyris* ——. If any-one is angry with you, rub the body with the leaves and put some in your pocket and 'his anger will go back'. 1929 Beckwith 116, If a man is angry with you, rub up 'temper-bush'..and box him with it, and his mind will become friendly toward you.

TEMPTING POWDER sb dial. A medicine supposed to win a lover to one.

1895 Banbury 10, The obeahman gives what is called in English 'a love potion', but in Jamaica, 'tempting powder', which is a very nauseous draught and at times may prove dangerous.

tena sb dial; prob <*tanner*, sixpence. However, as *fip* <'fivepence' came to mean threepence, this may represent the old tenpence piece, i.e. *ten*+-*er*. Sixpence.

[1907 Jekyll 253, 'Tanner', for sixpence, is common in English slang but not here. It seems to have been derived in this case from the White soldiers at Newcastle.] 1943 *GL* Tre, Tenna, sixpence. 1952 FGC Han, StM /tena/ 6*d*.

tengge lans sb dial; perh <*teng* (*EDD*, Nth country form) <*tang*, the prong of a fork, barb of a hook or arrowhead +-*y*+*lance*. A fish-spear or similar device.

1956 Mc Man /tengge laans—saat av ting dat stik yu/ *An instrument for stabbing.*

TENGLE see RAMBLE AND TENGLE.

TENGRE see *tinggri*.

TENKE see next.

TENKY /tengki/ sb dial; <*thankee*, *thank-ye*, *OED* 'Vulgar colloq.' →1848. *G*

1. 'Thank you.' (Little used any more.) *N*

1943 *GL* Clar, Tenky—thanks; Tre, Tenke—thanks.

2. Ironically: Thanks and no more; no compensation made for good done.

1950 Pioneer 34 [Anancy, blaming Puss for ungratefulness:] Good me do a tenky me get. [*This is the thanks I get for the good I've done you!*]

3. A gift of various kinds. Cf TENKY-MASSA.

1943 *GL* Tre, Tenki, a bit of land given away free of rent to be cultivated.

TENKY-MASSA sb dial arch. A gift.

1920 FGC StAnd [Song—Quaco Sam:] Heng-kitcher tie me head, Tenky-Massa tie me t'roat. [*A handkerchief tied my head, a scarf (?) was about my throat.*] 1955 FGC Man /tengki-massa/ a gift.

TENKY-TITA sb dial; <TENKY+TITA. A small fish (lit, 'Thank you, Father'—evid the thanks given to God for small favours).

1943 *GL* Clar, Tenkitita, small fish.

TENNA see *tana*, *tena*.

TENNY sb dial; <*ten*+-*y* or -*ie*. A children's name for a yellow nicker, worth ten grey ones.

1952 FGC Han /teni/.

TEN O'CLOCK sb dial. A small plant of the Portulaca type with a star-shaped flower, said to bloom at 10 A.M.

1952 FGC StT (Ginger Hall).

TENPENCE sb now almost obs. A silver coin in existence in Jamaica at the end of the 18th cent and after; its value dropped so that it came to be worth only sixpence sterling, but a sixpence continued to be called 'tenpence' (so *fippence*=3*d*.). s CURRENCY.

[1808 Stewart 59, The silver coins are..tenpenny and five penny pieces; the latter is the smallest coin in use, there being no copper coin in circulation.] 1862 Clutterbuck 123, 'There's a tenpence to buy something'.. Domingo drew his bare foot along the floor in acknowledgement of the sixpence*..*Tenpence currency equal sixpence English. 1943 *GL* Tre, Tenpance—6*d*.

TENPENNY sb dial slang; perh in allusion to the tenpenny piece being of a large size.

1943 *GL* StAnd, Ten-penny, an enlarged abdomen.

tente sb dial; prob var of *intete*, but cf also ANTENNA, *tana*, *tete*.

1. See quots.

1958 DeC Port, StT /tente/ same as /intéte/ a temporary bag made in the field of grass or trash.

2. See quot.

1958 DeC Port /tente/ same as /intéte/ A special sort of basket that used to be used to carry jerked meat down to sell at Port Antonio market.

TENTED ppl adj obs? Of sugar-canes: blown or fallen together into heaps looking like tents.

1796 *Braco* 5 Apr, Continued cutting as Yesterday. Canes very much Tented. 1797 *Ibid*, same.

TEP sb dial; etym uncert: phonologically derivable from *step*, *tap*, and other words.

1943 *GL* Man, Tep, a small quantity. 1955 FGC Man /tep/ same.

TEP-TEP sb dial; etym unknown: perh alludes to ELEVEN STEPS.

1943 *GL* Kgn, Tep tep, trouble.

terenggl sb dial; by metath <*triangle*, musical instrument. See quot. Cf s *terenggl-fut*.

1955 FGC StAnd /plie terénggl/.

TERRAS(S) sb obs; evid a form of *terrace*. A series of boards laid alongside each other upon a sloping foundation (of masonry or the like) so as to 'line' it, or give it a smoother surface.

1774 Long III 676, They [*sc* indigo vats] are built with masonry, and lined with a strong terrass, like the steeper, or of close-grained plank (not cedar). 1807 Rennie 136, The curing-house is a large airy building, provided with a capacious melasses-cistern, the sides of which are sloped and lined with *terras* or boards. *Ibid* 142, To spread out the fresh coffee in the sun, in layers of about five inches in depth, on a sloping *terras*, or platform of boards.

TE TA TOE see *tii-taa-tuo*.

tete sb dial; var of *intete*. See quot.

1959 DeC Han /tete/ a temporary field bag made of trash or grass. (Heard only in Guinea Town; prob related to /intéte/ same meaning, heard only from Portland Maroons.)

tetes sb dial; origin uncert: perh phonosymbolic.

1. A friend, a lover.

1943 *GL* StT, Tetes, friend. 1943 Bennett 14, Is wat dem man a sey? Lawd sah Yuh musa har te-tes. [*What are those men saying? Lord, sir, you must be her sweetheart.*

2. A full-bosomed woman.

1961 BLB Kgn /mi gwaing aaks dem tuu fat tetes ya/.

3. See quot.

1955 FGC Man /tétés/ a bully.

TE TIE see *ti-tai.*

tetla sb dial; etym unknown. A deep-water LOBSTER or crayfish.

1952 FGC StM /tetla/ deepwater lobster—red and with spots; pretty.

TETY see *ti-tai.*

THANKGIVING TABLE sb dial; <*thanks-giving* + TABLE.

1954 LeP Kgn, Feast held at end of mourning period—thankgiving [*sic*] table.

THATCH sb. *BL*

1. Any of several round-leaved palms whose leaves are used to thatch houses and huts. See quot 1864. Cf BULL-HEAD, FAN, LONG, ROUND, SILVER THATCH.

1696 Sloane 179, Palma Brasiliensis prunifera folio.. *Thatch.* In sylvis saxosis & collibus sterilioribus Jamaicæ Insulæ ubique reperitur. 1864 Grisebach 788, Thatch: *Calyptronoma Swartzii* and *Copernicia tectorum.*

2. The leaf of such a palm, used for thatching roofs or weaving baskets, bags, hats, etc. *N*

1956 Mc Man /tach/—the leaf of a particular palm used for roofing. (Coconut palm leaves may be used.. but must be plaited).

3. Attrib in simple combinations (things made of thatch): thatch *hat, house, roof,* etc. See separate entries. *T*

THATCH BAG sb dial. A bag made of THATCH, a cutacoo.

1954 LeP StT, Palm-leaf bag, tatch bag.

THATCH-CUTTER sb. Men who cut down THATCH trees for the leaves and timber.

1890 Thomas 71, We saw the tracks of recent thatch-cutters.

THATCH HAT sb. A hat made of strips of plaited thatch sewn together.

1952 FGC Tre /tach hat/.

THATCH HOUSE sb. A house having wattled walls and thatch roof. Also called HUTCH, *kiba-bak. BL T*

1956 Mc Clar /tach ous/.

THATCH-POLE sb. The trunk of the PALMETTO THATCH. *N*

1756 Browne 191, The trunk seldom exceeds four or five inches in diameter; it is called the *Thatch-pole,* and is much used for piles in wharfs, and other buildings made in the sea; for it has been observed to stand the water very well and is never corroded or touched by the worms.

THATCH STICK sb obs. A piece of stick from the THATCH tree, formerly used as a drain for molasses in sugar-making.

1790 Beckford II 79–80, see CURER.

THATCH TREE sb. = THATCH 1.

1790 Beckford I 234, A beautiful and tufted clump of tall and verdant thatch trees, which spread their broad and shredded leaves (umbrella-like) in massy shadows. 1943 *GL* Kgn, Congo-jo, Bag made of leaves of.. the thatch-tree.

THATCH-WALK sb; < THATCH + WALK. A grove of thatch trees.

1890 Thomas 73, We were joined by another man on his way up to the thatch-walk.

THAW (YAM) see *taa (yam).*

THICK-LIP CONCH sb dial. A kind of conch with a thick opening.

1952 FGC StJ /tik-lip kongk/.

THICK-LIP GRUNT sb dial. A fish of the GRUNT type with prominent lips.

1952 FGC Port, StC, StM, StT, West.

THICK-S /tík-és/ sb dial; from the shape. A kind of broad, curved MACHETE.

1961 *CLS* 70.

THIEF, THIEVE see TIEF.

THIMBLE-BOTTOM BASKET sb dial. A large shallow round basket for produce with a thimble-shaped hump in the bottom (for carrying on the head), and straight flaring sides.

1958 DeC Tre /timbl-batam baskit/.

THINGS sb dial. Euphemistic or in pregnant sense: the 'magical' materials with which an obeah-man works: grave dirt, egg-shells, bones, herbs, etc.

1895 Banbury 9, Another obeahman with whom he had a quarrel, had burnt his 'things', which made him mad. It is the common opinion that when this is done, an obeah-man becomes good for nothing. He could never 'work' after that, and generally gets out of his head. (1961 still in use. FGC.)

THIRD GANG sb obs. The gang of slaves having the lightest work—composed of children, old people, etc. Cf FIRST GANG, PICKANINNY GANG. *BA*

1796 *Braco* July 21, Third Gang planting on No 9. 1839 Mc Mahon 119, Even the third gang, consisting of young children from nine to twelve years of age, were tasked to do an amount of work which kept them from dawn of day till dark.

THIRSTY adj dial; *OED* →1878. Of a plant: showing the effects of lack of moisture, not bearing as much sap or juice as is normal.

1952 FGC Tre /di plant tosti—it duon shuo fat/.

THIS SIDE see SIDE.

THOMAS sb dial; abbr of Doubting Thomas.

1958 DeC StT /tamas/ a stubborn and conceited man.

THOMAS MASU sb dial; < *Thomas* (perh a jocular dignifying of *tim* in *timbim*) + *masu,* lift, the whole suggesting difficulty or heaviness. Cf GEORGE.

1. A sore, swollen foot—a BIG-FOOT.

1943 *GL* StAnd, Thomas Massuh, a sore foot that is swollen. 1956 Mc StE /tamas masu/ enlarged foot /big-fut/.

2. Fig. A grave trouble, hard to be rid of.

1956 Mc StE, in phr /yu ha támas másu pan yu/ 'a trouble that can't cure'.

THOMPSON WEED sb dial; origin unknown. A local name for *Leonotis nepetæfolia,* more commonly called BALL-HEAD bush.

1952 FGC Man /tamsn wiid/ for coughs, colds, etc.

THORNBACK LOBSTER sb obs. = HORNED LOBSTER, LOBSTER.

1725 Sloane 270, Locusta marina vulgaris dorso spinoso. The Thornback Lobster.

THORNY BUTTON-WEED see BUTTON-WEED.

THREAD-BAG /tred-bag/ sb dial. A small cloth bag, tied or drawn closed with a thread or small string, and chiefly used by higglers for carrying their money. Often hung around the neck.

1923 Beckwith 52, Of the Amber he says, 'You must keep it quite nice in a little thread bag'. 1924 Beckwith 35, She drop and Goat cut her up an' put her in his tread-bag. 1942 Bennett 39, Me open me mout' wen ah se' har tread-Bag full up a money!

THREE-FINGERED JACK sb; *OED three a* and *sb* III 1a 1828.

1. Jack Mansong, a rebellious slave who hid in the mountains of Jamaica and raided the lowlands for several years until his capture in 1781. (See bibliography: c 1800 Mansong.)

2. The tree *Oreopanax capitatum.* (The name may be due to the fact that under each flower there are three scale-like bracteoles.)

1926 Fawcett 418, Woman Wood, Three fingered Jack, Growing Stick. 1941 *NHN* I 3 10, The typical species are Yacca..the Bloodwood or Beetwood..Three-fingered Jack.

THREE-FOOT HORSE sb dial; for *three-footed* horse. A supposed demon in the form of a horse with one foreleg and two hind legs, which haunts the countryside by night.

1905 in *Folklore* xv 91, The 'three-foot horse' is believed to be a kind of duppy with three legs, hence its name; and is able to gallop faster than any other horse. It goes about in moonlight nights, and if it meet any person it blows upon him and kills him. It will never attack you in the dark. It cannot hurt you on a tree. 1907 Jekyll 150, Devil ready to start, order his t'ree-foot horse saddle (i.e. to be saddled). 1952 FGC Han /trii-fut-haas/ one front leg and two back; shape like coffin and a little man sits on it; Have fire travels with it; will kill on sight; can't turn till they get to a crossroads; if you crawl under wire you're safe, but if you jump over, he can too and eat you. StAnd /chii-fut-aas/ if him buck you up a-night im blow bad breeze pon you.

THREE-GUTTER sb dial. A kind of MACHETE.

1958 DeC Port /trii gota/ a cutlass..so called because there are three 'gutters' (i.e. grooves) running the length of the blade.

THREE-GUTTER BED sb dial. See quot; the sense of the name is not clear, but cf THREE-GUTTER.

1954 LeP Kgn, Bed big enough for two persons—three-gutter bed.

THREE-PIECE sb dial. *BA BL G*

1952 FGC Han /chii-piis/ 'a suit with pants, weskit and coat of the same cloth'.

THREE-QUARTER adj tech. In banana-growing: fruit that are nearly but not quite FULL.

1952 FGC Han, Three-quarter bananas, not bursting full; StAnn, Three quarter, not really full.

THREE-QUARTER-DAY sb dial. See quot, and cf HALF-DAY, QUARTER-DAY.

1958 DeC StAnd /tri-kwota-die/ a time of day (9.00 a.m.) so called because three-quarters of the working day still remain.

THREE-THORNED CRAB sb obs.

1756 Browne 422, Cancer 14..The three-thorned Crab.

THROW vb dial.

1. To throw out, empty. *G*

1929 Beckwith 38, Come on, now, and we throw the water and the first one that is dry, that is the winner.

2. To contribute (money, one's payment, etc.). Formerly const *up.* *BA G*

1873 Rampini 139 (from Slave Court Records, Portland, 1805–16), He said in the mill-house that everyone must throw up money to kill the busha..[He heard] that money had been thrown up for the purpose of killing Mr Speed. 1960 LeP StAnd, 'I have to throw a partner this week' or 'I have to throw a pound for partner this week'.

3. Also in various phrases—see separate entries.

THROW-ABOUT adj dial. That throws things about; careless; untidy.

1943 *GL* StJ, Trow bout, careless and slack.

THROW (A) LICK vb phr (dial) slang; cf LICK, A sb.

1. To strike, to pummel. *G*

1941 Kirkpatrick 3, Is fe we intention fe trow lick ina 'Itler spine tell 'im cyan 'tan up.

2. To give (someone) a drink (cf US, a 'shot') of liquor.

1958 DeC StAnd, Throw a lick upon (someone)—buy (someone) a drink.

THROW OFF (UPON) vb phr dial slang. To give things (which one does not need) to someone poorer. *BA*

1941 Kirkpatrick 19, W'en dem did go ina Hollan' an' Belgium an France fus, dem did try fe trow off 'pon de people an' doan treat dem too bad fe mek dem ting say Jarmany is nat wutlis. 1960 FGC StAnd /mi no laik piipl truo aaf pan mi/.

THROW SARCASM vb phr dial. To relieve one's emotions by speaking out (to no one in particular) one's dislike for or sense of grievance against another. Cf THROW WORDS 2.

1835 Madden II 141 [From a letter to him as magistrate:] One Mrs Hope live in Brown Town. She began to through Casom and to abuse but which She Did not Call no Name ontill this last Monday. 1934 Rev. Powell, Manchester, MS, Throw sarcasm—vituperation by proxy.

THROW WORDS vb phr.

1. To use bad language; to swear. *G*

1955 Bennett *Bad Foot,* Takooma sey dat Nancy wasa T'row wud an dah cuss.

2. In phr *to throw words at the moon*: see quot.

1934 Rev. Powell, Manchester, MS, 'Throwing words at the moon'—the practice still in vogue in Jamaica, whereby you may tell the moon the most insulting things about a party within his hearing without being liable for libel.. Thus you in turn may be called 'a tief' or 'a liar fee true', every word reaching you and those who are standing about, and yet if you ask the vilifier what he is saying, the answer will be: 'Not you, sah, Him moon talk'.

THUNDER-BALL sb dial.

1. A thunderbolt; a clap of thunder. *BA T*

1942 Bennett 41, Wen..Him tun roun..Him se de sinting two yeye dem A roll like tunder-ball..It was a rollin' kealf! (Note: Appar confused: 'roll' means, of a rolling calf, 'roar', and thunder also makes a noise; but 'rolling' eyes do not.)

2. A stone celt remaining from Arawak Indian times. In Jamaica these are often kept in drinking-water receptacles in the belief that they keep the water cool. (=*OED thunder-bolt* 3.) *N*

1961 CBL Institute of Ja.

THUNDER CRAB sb dial. The QUEEN CRAB; see quot. Cf s THUNDER SNAKE.

1952 FGC StJ Thunder crab—if it hold you, won't let go till thunder rolls.

ti see TILL.

ti- prefix dial; <*to-*, unstressed. In *today, tonight*, the prefix is usually /ti-/ sometimes /tu-/. In dialect writing usu sp *te-*.

1868 Russell 18, Te-day, (to-day). 1950 Pioneer gloss, Tiday—today. 1957 Bennett 18, see TODAY DAY.

tichi sb dial; cf Ewe *títi*, small, tiny. Tiny creatures: ants. (Cf CHI-CHI.)

1924 Beckwith 204 [Riddle:] Little titchie above ground. [Answer:] Ants.

tichibu sb dial; cf *tichi*+*-bu*, bug, insect: cf Fanti *bũbũ*, insect. The large firefly, PEENY-WALLY; cf also *kitibu*.

1952 FGC Port /tichibu/.

TICHICRO sb; said to be echoic (cf CHI-CHI BUD) but note *tichi*. The small bird also known as a GRASS PINK. Cf CHICHI-CROW.

1847 Gosse 242, Tichicro..This modest little bird is not common, except in certain localities..It has a singular call, as it skulks in its grassy coverts, *cro-cro-tichicro*, whence its provincial name. 1956 Jeffrey-Smith 99–100, see GRASS PINK.

TICK-EATER sb; transl of the genus name. *OED* 1903. The bird *Crotophaga ani*, also called SAVANNA BLACKBIRD.

1774 Long III 893, Barbadoes and Savannah Blackbirds.. they are likewise extremely fond of the ticks, which infest cattle..These quadrupeds..very patiently suffer them to hop about their bodies, either when grazing, or lying down; the industrious birds (called for this reason *tick-eaters*) pick off all within their reach.

TICKET sb; *OED* →1675.

1. A written permission required of any slave away from his plantation to prove that he was on legitimate business; a pass or licence.

1683 Laws Pref d 3 b, Boats or Ferries, which dare carry no Negroes without a written Ticket or Licence from their Master or Overseer. 1739 Leslie 228, None shall give leave to any Negro-slave..to go out of their Plantations, without a Ticket or White-servant, in which Ticket is to be exprest their Name, from whence, and whither going, on Penalty of 40*s*. and paying for taking up as Runaways. 1793 Edwards II 165 [From Consolidated Slave Act, 1792:] Be it further Enacted..That no slave.. shall hereafter be suffered or permitted to go out of his or her master or owner's plantation or settlement, or to travel from one town or place to another, unless such slave shall have a ticket from his master..(etc.). *Ibid* 173, And be it further Enacted..That no ticket shall be granted to any slave or slaves for any time exceeding one calendar month.

2. A written permission formerly required before one was permitted to leave the Colony.

1663–4 *Jrnls Assembly* 2, 36. An act that no person have a ticket to go off without his name be up twenty-one days, and all underwritings cleared. 1889 Sanguinetti 52, In the old days a person had to put up his name at the Island Secretary's Office for a certain time before he could get his 'ticket' to leave the Colony.

TICKIA-BICIA see TAKE CARE.

TICKI-TICKI, TICKITICKY see TICKY-TICKY.

TICKLE-ME sb. A children's game.

1946 U.Newton I 3.

TICKS sb dial; plur form used as sg.

1. A tick.

1950 Pioneer 18 [Name of the tick in a story:] Anancy and Ticks. 1952 FGC Man, Kling-kling pick off every ticks off the cow; StM, Two kinds of oil-nut, 'one big as a ticks'.

2. In phr *to turn ticks on* (*someone*): To importune.

1956 BLB Man.

TICKY-TICKY[1] /tiki-tiki/ sb chiefly dial; cf Ewe *tikitiki*, Gẽ *tyíkityiki*, crowded, thronging; this coincides with an iterated dial derivative of Engl *thick*+*-y*, meaning very thick, numerous, closely packed. See TICKY-TICKY sb[2].

Any of several small fish found in large numbers in Jamaican waters, esp *Gambusia affinis* and *Limia caudifasciata*.

1774 Long III 866, Fresh-water Fish..Minnow, or Ticky-ticky. 1851 Gosse 84, *Poecilia melapleura*..The negroes call it Tickiticky, a term formed like our word Stickle-back..and alluding to the strong spine in the anal. 1942 *NHN* I 8 4, *Gambusia affinis*..A rather drab little fish, found in all the streams and swamps of Jamaica. 1943 *NHN* II 48, This fish, along with a close relative, our local 'ticki-ticki', has done and is still doing a great service by reducing our mosquito population. 1950 Smith in *NHN* 139, A poecilid or live-bearing toothcarp..*Limia caudifasciata*, known locally as 'tiki-tiki'. 1952 FGC Port /tikitiki/ come in thick schools; wash, parch, add salt, butter, eat with rice. StC, Silver fish and small shad. StJ, Any fine [i.e. very small] fish—same as fries. StT, same as /chuobiz/. West, smaller than fry.

TICKY-TICKY[2] sb dial; iterative <*thick* +*-y*, or *thicket*. Cf TICKY-TICKY. Land no longer cultivated and grown up in thickets.

1868 Russell 5, Ticky-ticky—ruinate land.

TIDA, TIDDA see *teda*.

TIE sb.

1. A quantity (of vegetables, etc.) as tied up for sale.

1952 FGC StAnd, A tie of watercress, Cross Roads market.

2. A vine or wis used for tying things; =*ti-tai*.

1960 LeP Man /hag-miit tai—a big wis gruo in di fiil/.

tie see TILL.

TIE BABY see BABY 4.

TIE-A-BUSH sb dial; <*tie* vb+A[1]+BUSH 3. An occas var of TIE-A-LEAF.

1958 DeC Port /taia bush/ dokunu.

TIE-A-LEAF, TIE-LEAF sb dial; <*tie* vb (+A[1])+*leaf*. =DOKUNU, alluding to its being tied up for cooking in a piece of banana or plantain leaf.

1943 *GL* StAnd, Tie a leaf, a kind of cornmeal pudding. 1947 U.Newton III 16, They like to eat parched corn, cut cake, tiealeaf, grated cake. 1952 FGC Port, StJ, West /tai-a-liif/; Port, StE, StM /tai-liif/.

TIE-A-TRASH sb dial; <*tie* vb+A[1]+TRASH. An occas var of TIE-A-LEAF.

1958 DeC Port /taia-trash/ the boiled dokunu.

TIEF /tiif/ sb and vb dial; <*thief*, *thieve*. *G T*

A. sb: A thief. (Usage corresp to that of Std Engl, only form differing.) *BA BL*

1873 Rampini 178 [Prov:] Man help tief [thief] to-day, 'noder time him help watchman. 1957 JN Man, Look here! a no mi pencil dis. You too tief—a no hit. (*You're a big thief* [Lit: *You're very thieving*]—*it isn't it!*)

B. vb: To steal; to steal from. (This is the reg dial usage and form, corresp to Std Engl *steal*.)

1788 Marsden 43, see TAKE 1. 1862 Clutterbuck 143, De busha (overseer) no tief nuttin hisself, and no allow nobody else for tief nuttin'. He too honest for true. 1873 Rampini 180 [Prov:] When black man tief, him tief half a bit (twopence farthing), when buckra tief, him tief whole estate. 1907 Jekyll 52, He will find out if it is the same watchman tiefing him [stealing from him]. 1956 Mc StE /im tiif haaf a di moni/ *He stole half the money;* /im stodi a plan tu tiif im/ *He thought of a plan to rob him.* *N*

TIEFINNESS, TIEFNESS sb dial; <*thieving* or *thief*+*-ness*. Thieving, thievery.

1950 Pioneer 57, Tiefenness gwine meck him bruck out Eena sore an shake an swell! 1957 Bennett 21, But as Anancy all ovah, him couldn' behave rightful, him had fe do lickle tiefniss.

TIEFIN TIEF sb dial; <*thieving*+*thief*. An utter, out-and-out thief. *G*

1950 Pioneer 57, see TIEF-TIEF.

TIEFNESS see TIEFINNESS.

TIEF-TIEF vb dial; iterative of TIEF. To steal repeatedly. *G*

1950 Pioneer 57, A tiefin-tief like dat deh tief Mus tief-tief till him dead.

TIE-HEAD sb chiefly dial; <*tie* vb+*head*. A head-scarf. (There are two ways of tying with the ends at the back: *butterfly* and *cocked-ear*. Mc.) *G*

1956 Mc Man /tai-hed/; StAnd /tai-hed, tai-ed, tai-yed/.

TIE ITS SIDES vb phr dial. Of Indian corn: to come into blossom. (The sense is obscure, but cf BABY 4.)

1958 DeC West /di kaan a tai in saidz/ *The corn is in blossom.*

TIE-TEETH sb dial; <*tie* vb+*teeth*. Any concoction in which the sugar is boiled until it becomes extremely gluey and difficult to chew. Also attrib.

c1915 FGC StAnd, Overcooked coconut cakes become tie-teeth. 1929 Beckwith 23, In a dry season the juice [of sugar-cane] will crystallize quickly, but in a wet season more lime must be used to prevent its turning into a spongy mass known as 'tie teeth'. 1952 FGC StE /tai-tiit shuga/ boil on fire, watch till it get /straani/; StJ /tai-tiit/ sugar boiled till /glami/ sort o' stretch; Tre, same as John Baillie: a tough sugar—/sorop/ dry out too much.

TIE-TIE see *ti-tai*.

TIE-TIE MANGO sb obs; <*ti-tai*, string + *mango*. See quot.

1837 Macfadyen 222, Tie-tie Mango; so named from the branches of the peduncle being long, and supporting the fruit like a bunch of onions; rather an inferior fruit.

TIE-TONGUE sb chiefly dial; for *tied tongue*, cf *tongue-tied* (*OED tie v* 2). A tied tongue, i.e. one not fully under control, producing defective speech. Also attrib. *BA BL G T*

c1915 FGC StAnd, A little tie-tongue boy. 1950 Pioneer 22, Anancy have bad tie-tongue yuh know.

TIE-UP adj and sb dial.

A. adj: 'Tied up'—pursed, tight-drawn.

1837 James 10, When Nanny come, her face 'tie up' (i.e. looked sour or displeased).

B. sb: See quot.

1959 DeC StJ /tai-op/—a bundle.

TIGER FERN sb dial. An unidentified fern.

1952 FGC StAnn /taiga form/ not very tall spray—more fluffy [i.e. bushy].

TIGER (PLANTAIN) sb dial; <*tiger*, usually equated with the leopard +*plantain*. A variety of plantain with speckled fruit.

1934 *Ja. Times* 19 May, see *fiekuma*. 1952 FGC Port, StT /taiga plantin/ spreckle-spreckle, spots all over the skin.

TIGER'S FOOT sb bot obs. In Browne's use: the convolvulus *Ipomœa quinquefolia*.

1756 Browne 155, Ipomea 4..The hairy Tiger's-foot.. Ipomea 5..The smooth-leaf'd Tiger's-foot. 1811 Lunan I 89, (Convolvulus) 4. Quinquefolius..This is Browne's ipomea five, who calls it the smooth leaved tiger's foot, and says it is frequent in the lowlands of Jamaica.

TIGHT adj dial; cf *OED* 1b →1677. Compact in texture or consistency.

1952 FGC StE, see TIGHT-FIT. 1956 Mc, Of close consistency, firm-textured, solid; /fu-fu—fúud bíitn in a máata tel it get táit/.

TIGHT-FIT sb dial. A food made from parched corn—see quot.

1952 FGC StE /tait-fit/ made from /shom-shom/—add hot water and beat it till it come tight in mortar.

TIGHT-HAND adj and sb dial; <*tight*, close-fisted (*OED a* 10b) +*hand* for *handed*. Mean; a person who is close with money. *G*

1958 DeC /tait-han/ a miserly man.

TIGHTY-TIGHTY adj dial; iterative from TIGHT+-*y*. =TIGHT. See quot.

1959 DeC StJ, Of dough, soil, etc: thick, gummy, cohesive; you put English flour with the cassava in a dumpling to make it /taiti-taiti/.

tiif see TIEF.

tiima-bran see STEAMER-BRAND.

tii-taa-tuo sb; cf Engl dial *tit-tat-toe*, US *tick-tack-toe*. The game of noughts-and-crosses. *BL*

1943 *GL* Kgn, StAnn, Te ta toe, a child's game. 1960 LeP StAnd /tíi tà túo, tii taa to/ the usual Jamaican term.

tiiti apl see OTAHEITE APPLE.

tiki-tiki see TICKY-TICKY.

tiki-tiki sb dial; iterative from *stick* sb+-*y*. Cf *tik-tik*. *G*

1959 DeC StJ /tiki-tiki/ small sticks used for firewood.

tiklbro sb dial; etym unknown. A small crab found in mangrove swamps.

1952 FGC StJ /tíklbro/ small crab, have red and white claw.

tik-siid sb dial; etym uncert; *tik* may represent *tick* or *thick*; *siid* appar means *seed*. An unidentified substance: see quot.

1952 FGC StT /Anaansi ful op im bag wid tik-siid/.

tik-tik sb dial; iterative from *stick* sb; cf *tiki-tiki*.

1958 DeC StAnd /tik-tik/ small sticks used for firewood.

tikya, tikyier see TAKE CARE.

til see TILL.

TILDEREE sb; echoic, from the bird's cry. The killdeer, *Charadrius vociferus*.

1847 Gosse 330, Killdeer plover. Tilderee.—Tell-tale.

TILL /til, tie, ti; tel, tea, te/ conj dial; for dial sp see quots. Cf SO-TILL. *BA*

1. Until. *G T*

1790 Moreton 154, An work him te-me weary. 1868 *TRSAA* I 65, Dem go a fiel' go work tay twelve o'clock. 1943 *GL* StC, Teh, until; Tre, Teah, until. 1950 Pioneer 71, So him siddung res himself tell him wife call him. 1956 Mc /tel/ common form for 'until', beside /til/.

2. By the time.

1957 JN /tie mi kech de, di man gaan/ By the time I arrived, the man was gone.

timbel sb dial; ?<*tumbrel*.

1958 DeC StT /timbel/ a small child's toy *buggy* with four wheels.

TIMBER sb tech. Either of the pieces of wood, bent or cut in a quarter-circle, which support the seat or *taat* of a *kunu* from above.

1956 Mc StC (Old Harbour) /timbaz/ the supports to the seat of a sea-going kunu.

TIMBER SWEETWOOD sb. Any of various sweetwoods, with some differences in naming among botanists. According to 1914 Fawcett, it has been applied to *Misanteca triandra* (Grisebach), *Nectandra antillana, N. membranacea* (Grisebach), and to *N. sanguinea* (Grisebach, Hooper). Fawcett recognizes only the last, and Swabey follows.

1864 Grisebach 788, Timber Sweet-wood. 1886 Hooper 29, Timber Sweetwood. 1914 Fawcett 217, *N. sanguinea* ..Timber Sweet Wood. 1941 Swabey 31, Sweetwood, Timber. 1946 *NHN* III 63, There are three kinds of 'Sweetwoods' in the forests bordering the trails to Corn Puss Gap. The 'Rock, Timber and Pepper-leaf Sweetwoods' are the best known..(b) 'Sweetwood Timber'.. has smaller leaves than the other two.

timbim sb dial; cf Twi *tim*, a sound suggesting heaviness, and *bima*, sore, ulcer. A sore or lame foot.

1943 *GL* Man, Royal tim-bim, soar-foot; StAnn timbim, an ulcer. Also Han, Port, StM. 1955 FGC Man /timbim/ lame foot, hard to be better.

TIME sb dial; *OED* 13c →1422. A season; a period of time considered in terms of the prevailing weather, or some effect thereof. Cf HUNGRY TIME. *BA BL G*

1956 Mc Man /di taim iz wet/ *It's a rainy period*; StE /di weda-taim/ *the stormy season.*

TIMELY adv dial; cf *OED* 2 →1842. At once (after something else); without loss of time. *BL*

1959 LeP StAnd [A man soldering, and cleaning the metal as he goes along:] You see what I'm doing—I'm trying to clean it up timely.

TIMINI see TEMNE.

timi-timi sb dial; cf Twi *tumẽtùmẽ*, a species of fern with fine flat fronds or leaves. The wild plant *Rivina humilis.*

1952 FGC StAnn, see DOG-BLOOD.

TIN-CASE sb now chiefly dial. A metal box or trunk, tinned and japanned.

1947 U.Newton II 5, I was..stuck into the 'Kingston Train' with my tin-case, a basket 'for Uncle Eddie and the little bag for Aunt Addie'.

ting vb dial; <*think*. A frequent reduction of *think*, but less common than /tingk/. *G*

1941 Kirkpatrick 42, Some a unnu people asways wan' ting say is defeat. [*Some of you people always are disposed to think that it's a defeat.*]

tinggri sb dial; <*sting-ray*; cf US and Austral *stingaree*. The sting-ray fish. *BL*

1877 Murray *Kittle* 16, Ef dat gal *put him mout* pon you.. you tink say da *tingree* (sting ray) *bite you.* 1952 FGC Port, StAnn, StE, StJ, StM, West /tinggri/ like /wipri/ and /kiit/ but smaller.

TING-LING see TING-TING.

TINGRY see *tinggri.*

TING-TING /ting-ting/ sb; 1847 tinkling, tin-tin, 1936 1951 ting-ting, 1956 ting-ling; imitative of the bird's cry. Local names for the TINKLING GRACKLE.

1847 Gosse 219, see KLING-KLING. 1936 Bond 351, Greater Antillean Grackle..'Ting-ting' (Jamaica). 1951 Murray 25, Some a Ting-ting. 1952 FGC StAnn /ting-ting/. 1956 Taylor 13, The Kling-kling..is also known.. in Jamaica as the Ting-ting or Ting-ling.

TINKLING (GRACKLE) sb; <*tinkling*, descriptive and echoic of the bird's cry. The bird *Holoquiscalus niger*, also called TING-TING, TIN-TIN, KLING-KLING, BARBADOS BLACKBIRD.

1847 Gosse 217–19, Tinkling Grakle..It is most amusing to stand where one is not observed, at a few yards' distance from a Tinkling at work..As he sits on a tree, he will now and then elevate the fan-like tail, ruffle up the plumage, throw back the head, and with the beak wide open, utter two or three most singular notes, which I can compare to nothing but the sounds produced by repeatedly striking with force a piece of sonorous metal, relieved occasionally by the creaking of a schoolboy's pencil upon a slate. 1936 Bond 351, Greater Antillean Grackle..Tinkling; 'Ting-ting' (Jamaica). 1956 Jeffrey-Smith 78–80.

TINNEN /tinin/ occas /tinan/ adj dial; *OED* →1653. *BA BL G T* (as sb.)

1. Made of tin or similar metal.

1952 FGC StM, A bucket is a /tinin/ thing.

2. Also in cpds, separately entered.

TINNEN FENCE sb dial; <TINNEN+*fence.* A fence made of corrugated galvanized iron. *G*

1956 Mc /tinin fens/.

TINNEN FUNK sb dial; <TINNEN+FUNK 3. A small, tin oil-lamp.

1958 DeC West /tinan fongk/—a small lamp made of tin with no chimney.

TINNEN LAMP sb dial; TINNEN+*lamp.* A small, tin oil-lamp; cf *jempe lamp. BA*

1956 Mc /tinin lamp/.

TIN-TIN see TING-TING.

TINTIRRIE sb dial rare; cf *titirre,* in 1936 Bond 243. Another name for the PETCHARY.

1943 *GL* no addr, Tintirrie, a fierce bird like an eagle in shape. [Not an accurate description.]

TINYA see TANYA.

TIP-AN'-PAWN sb dial; <*tip,* strike lightly +*and*+*span* (cf PAWN).

1. A cashew-nut game: see quot.

1954 LeP StE, 'Tip-and-Pawn' is a game played with cashew nuts. The seeds are thrown one at another and the distance between them spanned with outstretched fingers.

2. Transf. A man who limps. (The word suggests the unequal action of his feet.)

1954 LeP StE /tip-an-pawn/.

TIP-DOWN /tip-dong/ vb dial; cf *OED tip* v^2 8 (or a reduced form of *stoop* itself) + /dong/, *down.*

1943 *GL* StJ, tip-dung, stoop down.

TIPISS sb dial; <uncert element+*piss.*

1943 *GL* Tre, Tipiss, penis.

TIP-YOU-LAST sb dial; <*tip,* strike +*you* +*last.* A children's game; cf LAST-LICK.

1956 Mc Man, see BAP, BAPS B.

tishim, tisin int dial; echoic. The imitation of the sound of a sneeze, echoed to the sneezer by one who has just heard him. See quot. *G*

1960 BLB Man /tisin/ is to me the sound of sneezing. Also /tishim/. My mother always says it when a baby sneezes..I think it's supposed to ward off a serious cold or something.

TISSIN sb dial; echoic. Cf prec. 'Tee-hee'—the sound of giggling.

1924 Beckwith 3, Anancy laugh, 'Tissin, tissin, tissin!'

tista, tiista sb dial; <Scots form of *tester*[1]: *OED* gives *tyster, teester* as 15–16th cent. A canopy over a bed. *G*

1956 Mc StAnd /ton-puos bed hav tiista uova it/. 1958 DeC StT /tista/ a canopy used over a /ton-puos/ bed.

tita sb[1] dial; cf *titá*, Kpándò dial form of Ewe *tatá*, father. Father, and as a term of address; =TAATA, TATA.

1943 *GL* Han, StAnd, StC, Tre, Tita, father; Man, StJ, Titta, father. 1954 LeP StE, Titta, father.

tita sb[2] dial; prob reduction of *sister*, or pet-form based on it—cf STA, SITA. *BL G* (obs)

1956 Mc StT /tita/—Sister.

ti-tai /tì-tái/ sb dial; evid a reduced form of pidgin *tie-tie* (*OED tie-* 3: 'tie-tie,..a negro name for any string' 1883), iterative from *tie* vb. The form *tie-tie* in earlier printed sources may represent actual pronunc at the time, or 'correction' of the folk pronunc /ti-tai/ which alone survives today. *BL*; *SC tétéi.*

Anything used for tying, esp string and withes; also a piece of this tying something.

1774 Long II 427, see FUM-FUM. 1827 Hamel II 257, Stretching what they called a *tie-tie* of tent-ropes, hempen cordage, mahoe bark, and bush ropes, all spliced together, to form..a guide for those who could be induced to cross the bridge. 1868 Russell 5, Tety—A string. 1873 Rampini 180 [Prov:] When bull ole, you take hog-meat tee-tie (the trailing stem of a wild convolvulus) fe tie him. 1910 Anderson-Cundall 4, Same, sp 'ti-tie'. 1925 Beckwith 23 (cities Rampini, but respells 'tee-tee', which badly misrepresents the pronunc). 1943 *GL* 12 cits from 8 parishes, Te tie, titie. 1956 Mc Clar, Port StE /ti-tai/ string, vine, wis.

TITCHIE see *tichi.*

titibo sb dial; cf *tichibu*, firefly. The dry-wood termite, or CHI-CHI.

1956 Mc Clar /chichi—titibo, litl sonting iit op hud/ *Chi-chi—titibo, a little thing that eats up wood.*

titibu sb dial; cf *titibo, tichibu.* =*tichibu, kitibu* —the firefly PEENY-WALLY.

1952 FGC Port /titibu/ large firefly with light at its head. 1958 DeC Port /titibu/ firefly.

titi dompling sb dial; prob <*titty*, nipple, breast; but cf TITIMUS.

1959 DeC West /titi dompling/—a finger-shaped boiled dumpling.

TI-TIE see *ti-tai.*

TITIMUS sb dial. A var of CHICHI-MUS.

1943 *GL* StT, Titimus, The small finger.

TITTLE DRUM sb dial; in quot understood as echoic, and cf Bini *tititititititi*, the sound of a small drum, Mandingo *tyityi*, kind of drum, but analogy with *kittledrum*, kettledrum, may also have infl this. A treble drum; cf RATTLE DRUM.

1949 U.Newton v 30, In the distance we heard it: 'Bam.. bam'. 'Ti..ti..ti..tittle!' *Ibid* 32, Right in with the big drums, the tittle drums, the fifes.

TITTY-BITER sb dial. A small fresh-water creature which young girls put on their breasts in the belief that it will make them develop more quickly. Same as BUBBY-BITER.

1960 RJO StAnd.

TIYA see TAYA.

TLOOLOOLOOPS sb dial; var of *flululups*: phonosymbolic, but in an African pattern—cf Ewe *gblúlululu*, the tripping run of a stiff-legged animal, and similar words.

1943 *GL* Kgn, Tlooloooloops, fragments of meat.

TOAD-EYE CANE /tuod-ai/ sb dial. A variety of sugar-cane—see quots.

1952 FGC StJ /tuod-ai/ the Westmoreland name for what is called goat-shank in St Catherine. 1959 DeC West, Han /tuod-ai/ name of a cane with large eyes [i.e. buds].

TOADIE /tuodi/ sb dial; cf *OED*, Scots →c 1690.

1. A toad.

c 1915 FGC StAnd [Verse:] Toady, toady, mind you'self, Mind you'self mek a dig me grass..(etc.).

2. =TOADFISH.

TOATO see *tuoto.*

TOAYA see TAYA.

TOBACCO CONCH sb dial. A kind of shell-fish: see quot.

1952 FGC StJ /tubako kongk/ 3–5 inches long, twisted like tobacco.

TOBACCO-FISH, ~-OLD-WIFE, ~-TURBOT sb dial; from its having the shape of a tobacco leaf. See OLD-WIFE. Various fish of the family *Balistidæ*, esp genus *Balistes.*

1952 FGC Port, StAnn, StJ /tubáko fish/ skin greenish, favour tobacco leaf; a skin-fish, like ol'-wife, turbit. StC, StE /tubáko tórbit/ long and tapering, flat, like tobacco leaf; have sandpaper skin. StM /tubáko uól-wàif/ long, like tobacco leaf, skin very thin.

TOBEY-WITHE, TOBY-WITHE /tuobi-wis/ sb dial; <*Toby*? +*withe*. Certain plants of the *Malpighiaceæ* and *Sapindaceæ* families.

1927 Beckwith 28, Tobey-withe. *Stigmaphyllon emarginatum.* 1955 FGC Man /tuobi-wis/ supple-jack. When young, tie beast, bundle of wood.

TODAY-AND-TOMORROW MANGO sb dial. See quot.

1952 FGC StM /tidie-an-tumara manggo/ ripen on one side today, the other side tomorrow.

TODAY DAY /tíde-díe/ adv phr dial; the force of *today* is 'this present'. This very day. *BL G*

1907 Jekyll 38, He run into a hole, an' him make Ratta live into a hole up to to-day day. 1924 Beckwith 56, Dat is why you see Tumble-bug roll in filth to-day to-day [*sic*]. 1957 Bennett 18, Das why yuh se' crab have dat tick shell pon him back till teday day.

TODDY-RACK sb obs; <*toddy* + *rack sb*[7] (*OED*). A fermented liquor made from the sap of the coconut tree.

1794 Barham 132–3, If you expose the liquor [*sc* sap drawn from the coconut tree] in the sun, it will soon turn to vinegar; but, distilled in its ferment, it makes a spirit called *orraqua*, or *rack*, which far exceeds that made from rice; and these trees being called in some places *toddie*, it is therefore called toddie-rack.

todi adj dial; <*study* or *studdie*, Scots forms of *steady* (*OED*, *SND*). Steady, calm. *BL*

1943 *GL* StC, Tuddy, to be quiet. 1958 DeC Tre /todi/ steady; the first time I have heard this pronunciation except in the context *stand-steady*. Here it is /him iz a todi sensibl man/. This certainly confirms that /tan todi/ is *steady* rather than *sturdy*.

TOE sb. One of the nodes or lobes of a ginger root. Cf GINGER-TOE. *BL*

1952 FGC Man, Ginger has to be handled toe by toe. [Each one has to be peeled by hand.]

TOETO, TOETOE see *tuoto.*

toga-toga vb dial; prob <*tug* + A[8] iterated, but cf also *taga-taga.*

1958 DeC StT /toga-toga/ to partly carry, partly drag something heavy.

togi see STUDY.

toki haks see TUCKY AXE.

tokit sb dial; perh <*stock*, trunk or stem of a (living) tree (*OED sb*[1] 2).

1956 Mc StE /tokit/ trunk of a banana tree.

TOLAMOUT sb dial; etym unknown. [Perh 'hair' is miswritten for 'liar'.]

1943 *GL* StAnn, Tolamout, hair.

TOMALIE, TOMALY see *tumaali.*

TOMATICE, TOMATIS, TOMATTIS see *tumatis.*

TOMATO BASKET sb dial; see *tumatis* + *basket.* A basket having two bowl-like halves with a handle going over the middle between them.

1956 Mc Man /timótis báskit/. 1958 DeC StT /tamíeta baskit/—a name for the common long oval basket with handle. Also [called] /singk-in-a-migl/../fishaman baskit/.

TOMATO BERRY sb obs. The tomato.

1696 Sloane 109–10, Solanum secundum racemosum cerasorum forma..Tomato Berry. 1707 Sloane 237.

TOMATO FERN sb.

1951 Proctor 5, *Anisosorus hirsutus*..Tomato fern.

TOMAULIE see *tumaali.*

TOMB-BUILDING, ~-MAKING sb dial. = TOMBING; see quots.

1958 DeC Tre /tuum-bilding/—a meeting held about a year after a death to celebrate the building of the tomb..i.e. the concrete cover over the grave; singing and dancing all night long. StT /tuum-meking/. Six months to a year after death, to celebrate the building of the tomb; a big picnic feast and all-day outing, but nothing after dark.

TOMB DANCE sb dial. A dance held in connection with (and sometimes considered a part of) a TOMBING.

1929 Beckwith 84, In Long's day a feast with song and dance went with the 'covering', and today, if the bereaved person has money, he will hold a 'tomb dance' in the evening for his friends and kill a goat or hog for the feast.

TOMBEY see *tumba.*

TOMB-HEAD sb dial. A large head rounded at the top like a tomb; a person having such a head.

1960 LeP StAnd /tuum-hed/—a big head; someone with a big head.

TOMBING vbl sb dial; cf ENTOMBING. = TOMB-BUILDING; see quots.

1929 Beckwith 84, One last service remains for the proper burial of the dead, the 'tombing' ceremony, which took place in old days a month after burial, especially when a bereaved husband or wife wished to remarry, but which today allows a somewhat longer interval..The object is completely to cover the grave with an additional mound of earth. 1958 DeC StT /tuuming/ a funeral meeting held six months to a year after death..Some keep this just like the /jomp up/ others dance /kuumina/ all night long.

TOMB-MAKING see TOMB-BUILDING.

TOM BONTEIN'S BUSH sb bot; prob for Thomas Bontein, who was Clerk of the Naval Office in 1741 in Kingston; if he was or had been a planter, he may have been the person referred to in quot a 1726. *Picramnia antidesma,* also called MAJOE BITTERS.

a 1726 Barham (1794) 96, This plant was first shewn to me by a planter, who had done many excellent cures amongst his negro slaves, in old inveterate stubborn ulcers, and that by only boiling the bark and leaves..giving them plentifully to drink, and washing the sores with some of the decoction. 1801 Dancer 363, *Picramnia antidesma*.. Tom Bontein's Bush. 1814 Lunan I 477, This plant, sometimes called *Tom Bontein's bush,* and *old woman's bitter.* 1819 Dancer 377, Tom Bontin's bush [*ibid* 386, Bontein]. 1864 Grisebach 788, Tom-Bontrin's-bush [*sic*]. 1954 *WIMJ* 31, [repeats Grisebach's erroneous form].

TOM FOOL /tam fuul/ sb chiefly dial; <*Tom Fool,* a foolish person; but cf Fante *ɔ-tám,* a simple, silly fellow. *BL*

1. Formerly, the bird *Saurothera vetula*: see quot.

1847 Gosse 274, My little friend informed me that it was a Rain-bird, but that it had received also the title of Tom Fool, from its silly habit of gratifying its curiosity, instead of securing its safety.

2. The Flycatchers *Myiarchus stolidus* (so called in the other English-speaking islands also), and *Myiarchus barbirostris* (found only in Jamaica)—the latter also called LITTLE TOM FOOL, as is also *Blacicus caribæus.*

1952 FGC Han /taam fuul picheri/ doesn't fly when you throw stones at it; StAnd, Tom Fool, size of Grass Bird, jump-jump-jump-jump like him mad; StAnn, StM /litl tam fuul/ will let you put you han' on dem. 1956 Jeffrey-Smith 48, The name Tom Fool is given indiscriminately to different species of flycatchers from their habit of perching at the end of a low branch, taking a short flight to capture some passing insect, and returning to the identical spot to swallow the prey, within easy reach of the bystander's hand.

TOM FOOL DAY sb dial. 1 April. *BL T*

1943 *GL* StAnd, Tom fool day, All Fools Day, April 1st. StAnn, Tom fool day. Also Man.

TOMMY sb dial. A fish, prob the same as TOM SQUIRREL.

1952 FGC Han /taami/ same as kanggatuoni, wenshman.

tompa see TUMPA.

TOMPHARIAH vb dial arch or obs; etym unknown. See quot; this seems to be a var form of CONFARIA, but the sense relationship is obscure. Cf also CALIMBE, COMBOLO.

1943 *GL* Port, Tom-phariah, Ride on two poles.

TOM RAFFLES ANT /tàm ráfl, ~ ráflin/ sb; said to be named after a planter who brought them in to attack the young of the cane rat; Edwards (quot 1793) doubted stories of their rapacity and considered them indigenous. An ant (usually identified with MAD ANTS) said to be voracious; but cf quot 1942.

1790 Beckford I 56–7, An ant, which is known by the name of Tom Raffles:..in some places so excessive is their number, and so destructive their rapacity, that where they have not rats to encounter, they will attack the poultry; and have been even known to blind, by their numbers and perseverance..the eyes..of negro children. 1793 Edwards II 220, It is the *Formica omnivora* of Linnæus, and is called in Jamaica *Raffles'* ant, having been introduced there, as is commonly believed, by one Thomas Raffles, from the Havanna, about the year 1762.—But I conceive it was known in the island from the earliest times, and that it is precisely described by Sloane, as the *Formica fusca minima, antennis longissimis.* 1912 McK *Songs* 102, Tom Rafflins* hurry by. *Mad ants, which run very quickly. 1942 *NHN* I vii 8, In 1762, Thomas Raffle introduced from Cuba, the ant (*Formica omnivora*) which has since been known as 'Tom Raffle Ant' to prey upon young rats. These ants are said to have been very useful for many years, but gradually..they became a pest themselves. 1952 FGC Man, StT, Tre /tam rafl/ run up an' dong madly, = mad-ants, no bite; not as big as kap-kap but black; lives in nest in ground, dry places only; Man /tam raflin/; Port /rafl/—black, small; used to call mad-ants.

TOM SQUIRREL sb dial. Evidently some variety of squirrel fish (*Holocentrus*).

1929 Beckwith 33, 'Angel'; 'Tom squirrel'; bonito; dolphin.

TO MY GOD adv or int phr dial; abbr of *I swear to my God*, or the like. An intensifying phr. *BA BL G*

1961 BLB 16 /tu mi Gád mi kyaan bada wid dem/ *I really can't bother with them.*

tong see TUNG.

TONGUE sb. A lunette of thin paper strung under the bow at the top of a Jamaican hexagonal kite; it is made to buzz by pulling the kite, when aloft, sharply toward one. *BA BL*

c1915 FGC StAnd.

TONGUE CATTLE sb; <*tongue* (of a waggon) +*cattle.* The hindmost oxen in a team of three or more yoke of draught cattle. (Until the late 1950's used on sugar estates.)

1823 Roughley 151, The mill cattle out of crop, when in good order and when a large shipment is to be made with despatch, should be mixed with the road cattle for assistance, taking care to place them as middle cattle in the draft, but neither as tongue or leading cattle.

TONGUE STEER sb. One of a yoke or pair of TONGUE CATTLE.

1823 Roughley 130, Multitudes of fine serviceable cattle and mules taken off of Guinea grass pens, tongue steers especially. *Ibid* 133, Tongue steers, so much to be depended on for their strength, steadiness, and size.

TONGUE-TALLY sb dial; <*tongue*+*tally*, count. One whose tongue is going ceaselessly (like produce being tallied?).

1954 LeP StE, A word to describe someone who is always gossiping—tongue-tally.

ton han see TURN HAND.

ton-ton sb dial joc; iterative from /ton/ i.e. *turn*, the iteration indicating repeated action. TURNED CORNMEAL, which requires much stirring.

1952 FGC West /ton-ton/ turned cornmeal. 1958 DeC Port, same.

TOO /tu/ occas /tuu/ adv chiefly dial. *BL G*

1. Very, extremely, quite. *BA T*

1862 Clutterbuck 143, see TIEF B. 1873 Rampini 30, see TRICKIFIED. 1877 Murray *Kittle* 26, Watchman dance so, till de sweat drop off da him face. Him say, 'Mudfish, you sing too sweet'. 1907 Jekyll 4, The boy too trick [very tricky]. *Ibid* 21, Bro'er Annancy, me sorry fe you too much. 1929 Beckwith 17, see TOO GOOD.

2. Too much; excessively. (Before the vb.)

1877 Murray *Kittle* 13, 'Cho', said Sylvia, 'You too lub money. I can't bear you fe dat'. 1927 Stafford 41, You too lub chat. [*You like to gossip too much.*] 1943 Bennett 32, Me sorry but it serve her right She too have funny ways. *BA T*

3. In negative sentences: either.

1956 Mc Man /dem duon plie it op hya tu/ *They don't play it here either.*

TOO-FEY see *tufe.*

TOO GOOD sb dial; < TOO 1 +*good.* A variety of COCO, the name meaning 'very good'.

1929 Beckwith 17, In Mandeville were enumerated..the 'White Stalk', 'Too Good', 'Sinket'.

TOOKO-TOOKO, TOOKU-TOOKU see *tuku-tuku.*

TOOK-TOOK see *tuk-tuk.*

TOOMBAH see *tumba.*

TOOTHWORT sb bot; *OED* 1760→. The plant *Plumbago scandens*; for the name see quot a 1726.

a 1726 Barham (1794) 194, Toothwort..This plant is so called from the form and colour of the root, which is very white, and is composed, as it were, of a great many teeth.. It is counted a cooling, drying, and restringent plant. 1811 Lunan II 234, Tooth, or Lead Wort. Plumbago.. Scandens. 1864 Grisebach 788, Toothwort.

TOOTO sb dial; cf Hausa *tu:tu*, human excrement. *BL T*

1943 *GL* StE, Tooto, to urinate.

TOOTOOS see *tutu, tutus.*

TOP-AND-BOTTOM, FIRE-TOP-FIRE-BOTTOM sb dial. = PONE.

1958 DeC StT /tap-an-batam; faia-tap-faia-batam/ names for a /puon/ i.e. a pudding baked in a covered pot lined with banana leaf; fire is put both above and below the pot, hence the name.

TOP-A-TOP sb dial; reference is to the use of the leaves at the top of the plant, but the exact composition of the word is uncert—it could be iterative with A[8] inserted, or if A[1], it could be *top of the top.*

1740 Importance 34, see COCO-CALALU.

TO PIECES adv phr dial; from some such phr as *broken to pieces*, hence intensive in effect. Utterly, thoroughly, extremely. *BA*

1873 Rampini 87, 'Handsome to pieces', that is, handsome in every part of his body, is remarked of an Adonis. 1927 Anderson-Cundall 65. 1943 *GL* No addr, Handsome-to-pieces, extraordinarily handsome.

TOP-KNOT PLUM sb obs. A variety of the SPANISH PLUM with a knobby fruit.

a 1726 Barham (1794) 148, Some of them have a knob at the end, and are called the top-knot plum. 1774 Long III 827, Top-Knot Plum. Myrobalanus minor, fructu purpureo.

TOPSIDE adv and prep dial; cf BOTTOM-SIDE. Above; higher (up a hill, etc.) than something else. *G*

1943 *GL* StC, Tapside, above. 1952 FGC StT, Him live topside (up on a hill). 1956 Mc Man /mi stie tápsaid yo hóus/ *I live past your house (on higher ground).*

TOPSIDIN adv dial; < TOPSIDE + *-n* suffix[1].

1943 *GL* StC, Topsidin, above. 1962 BLB 35 /im lib tapsaidn di shap/ *He lives just above the shop.*

TORCH /tuoch, taach/ sb and vb dial.

A. sb: A crude kind of lamp (see quot). Cf SORE TOE. *BA*

1956 Mc StAnd /tuoch/ a bottle filled with kerosene, with paper stuffed in the neck, used for a light.

B. vb: To use a torch (sense 1) for fishing at night. *N*

1956 Mc Port /in guoan to tuoch/ *[He's] going to catch crayfish by torchlight.*

TORCHWOOD /túochwùd/ sb; see 1, quot 1725. s TORCH CACTUS. *N*

1. The smaller 'dildo' cactus, *Cereus gracilis. OED* 1866.

1696 Sloane 197, Cereus altissimus gracilior, fructu extus luteo..Dildo Tree the lesser or Torchwood. 1725 Sloane 158, Torch-wood..The inward Con-texture of the Fibres of this Plant remaining after the Weather has consum'd both the In and Outside of it, is used for a Torch by the Indians to catch Fish in the Night-Time, they hold it out of the Ends of their Canoes lighted, and the Fish leaping at it, they strike them with their Instruments. 1926 Fawcett 280, Torch-wood.

2. Two species of *Amyris* (*elemifera* and *balsamifera*). *OED* 1880.

1837 Macfadyen 231, Shrubby Torch-wood..Mountain fragrant Torch-wood. 1920 Fawcett 191–2. 1944 *NHN* II 94, see CANDLEWOOD. 1952 FGC Man, StAnn, StM,

Tre /tuoch-wud/ same as kantu, candlewood, burn-eye, blind-eye beyaca.

3. The tree *Casearia* (*Thiodia*) *serrata*.

1864 Grisebach 788, Torchwood: *Amyris balsamifera* and *Thiodia serrata*.

TORN-TORN adj dial; iterative from *torn*, pa ppl of *tear*. [Beckwith has prob 'corrected' this from *tear-tear*.] Cf TEAR-UP(-TEAR-UP). Torn to shreds.

1924 Beckwith 196 [Riddle:] Going up to town me coatie torn-torn and not a seamstress in a town could sew it. [Answer:] Banana leaf. (The banana leaf is easily shredded by the wind.)

TORTOISE FLY sb obs. A kind of beetle with back rounded like that of a tortoise: see quot.

1725 Sloane 208, *Scarabeolus Hemisphericus*..The Tortoise Fly..A hard Wing Case having several Holes or Cavities in them like those of a Thimble, were raised and something of the Shape of a Tortoise in the Middle.

TORTOISESHELL BIRD sb obs. In Gosse's use: the Least Bittern (*Ixobrychus exilis*); it refers to the colour of the plumage.

1847 Gosse 343, Little Yellow Bittern. Tortoiseshell-bird.

tosti see THIRSTY.

toti adj dial; cf *EDD* TUTTY *adj.*[2,3]. See quots.

1943 *GL* Man, Tutty, of stunted growth. 1955 FGC Man It /toti/ rather than stunted.

toto adj dial; ?<*total*. Single, sole.

c1935 BLB Man /mi no gat wan toto shilin fi gi im/ *I haven't got a single shilling to give her.*

TOTO, TOTOE see *tuoto*.

TOTOWATA see *tutu-wata*.

TOUCH vb; cf *OED* 11b →1850, of ships. To arrive at (a place). *BL G*

1957 JB StAnd, You haven't a hope to touch Spanish Town tonight..As soon as you touch Torrington Bridge you're in trouble with the traffic.

TOUCH /toch/ adj dial; for *touched* ppl adj; cf *OED v* 7 →1884. Tainted, rancid. *G*

1942 Bennett 17, Tell Fan me tenk her fe de pork, Doah it did lickle touch. [*Though it was a little tainted.*]

TOUCHING-STICK sb dial.

1956 Mc StC (Old Harbour) /tochin tik/ stick used to push a /kunu/ out from shore.

TOUGH adj and adv dial. In situations in which Std Engl would use *hard*. *G*

1943 *GL* StAnd, Dutty tough, earth [is] hard. 1957 DeC Western parishes mainly /wok tof/ work hard.

TOURIST BASKET see FANCY-BASKET.

TOWEL sb dial. A tablecloth.

1956 Mc Man /a blu towil we yu kyan pred ouba a tiebel/.

TOWN ORDER sb obs; *DAE, DA* 1833. See quot.

1835 Senior 126, There is no paper money, with the exception of island checks, and drafts on Kingston merchants, and other responsible individuals, which are common payments in the country parts, and denominated '*town orders*'.

TOWN TICKS sb dial; for *town tick*. Evid a countryman's term of derogation for something (or someone?) associated with the town: see quot. [Note that *ticks* is sg.]

1954 LeP StAnn, Town ticks, a louse, insects, despicable little things.

TOYA, TOYAUS see TAYA.

traika see STRIKER.

TRANSPARENT (CANE) sb chiefly dial. A variety of sugar-cane with a thin, clear-coloured skin.

1823 Roughley 287, see RIBBON CANE. 1959 DeC StJ /transpierants/ kind of cane.

trapong see TARPON.

TRAPONG FRY /trapong frai/ sb chiefly dial; <TARPON+*fry*, young fish. The fish *Cetengraulis edentulus*; they resemble tarpon, but are not their young.

1844-5 *TJSA* I 145, I suppose one or other of these Anchovies, will prove to be what our fishermen call Trapong fry. 1892 Cockrell list, Trapong fry—*cetengraulis edentulus*. 1952 FGC StJ /trapong frai/.

TRASH sb and vb; cf *OED sb*[1] 2, 1707→; *v*[3] 1793→. s THRASH.

A. sb: That part of any crop plant or vegetable product that is removed while it is growing, or left over from it when it is harvested, processed, or consumed. Specifically: *cane trash* (the dried leaves, the skin and pith after the juice is squeezed out); *plantain* or *banana trash* (the dried leaves); *coffee trash* (the skin of the berry); *chocolate trash* (the skin of cacao beans); *coconut trash* (the leaves, parts of the fruiting body, the gratings of the nut from which the milk has been squeezed); also the skins of fruits, peelings of vegetables, and the like. The word is universal and serves often instead of *skin, husk, pith*. *BA BL G*

c1695 Acts and Laws 131, Whoever shall wilfully fell any Trees, and cast the same, or any Cane, or Trash, or Rubbish into the same River..shall forfeit 5 l. 1774 Long III 911, The vacancies may be loosely filled with well-dried plantane trash, or dried corn-husks. 1873 Rampini 63, 'Cho! de nigger people call dem trash' (and he pointed to our treasures [*sc* epiphytes]), 'noting but logwood bush!'. 1946 Dunham 4, It was quite late when I crawled into the hard bed with its banana trash mattress. 1952 FGC StAnd, Bake chocolate berries and get off the thrash [overcorrection]; StAnn, The /trash/ of coffee comes off—berry is left; StAnd, /tro we trash of kuoknat —foul iit it/ StJ, Shell beans, t'row 'way de trash. 1958 DeC Port /kasada trash/—cassava head.

B. vb: 1. To remove unwanted parts of a vegetable product while it is growing or when it is being harvested, processed, or used. Also, to separate the product from the trash.

1790 Moreton 45, [The canes] have long blades..as they grow toward maturity, those blades wither and become burthensome to the stalk, so that they are obliged to be taken off, and this is called trashing. 1811 Mathison 75, To caution the planter against the common practice of *trashing high*, or stripping the trash and redundant leaves too indiscriminately from his canes at an early period of their growth. 1952 FGC StC, Of coffee: /trash it out di trash/; StT /trash-aaf/ the inner seed; StE, Of beans: /tek it op an trash it out/.

2. To bolster or support growing canes with bundles of trash. *BA*

1823 Roughley 217, The canes in those [sloping] places should be well trashed, or bolstered with trash, to keep them from lodging.

TRASH HAT sb dial. Prob an error for THATCH HAT: a hat made of palm thatch, of which the JIPPI-JAPPA is a fine variety. *G*

1949 Reid gloss, Trash hat—'jippi-jappa'.

TRASH-HOUSE sb obs; *OED* 1793. On a sugar plantation: a shed in which cane trash was put to dry until it could be used as fuel for the coppers. *BA G*

1790 Beckford II 34, Some trash-houses are upwards of one hundred feet long. 1827 Hamel I 312, I set fire to the trash-house at Mr Guthrie's. 1862 Clutterbuck 142, Trash-house. 1933 McK 317, Trash-house—a shed in which the refuse of the sugar cane is stored after the juice has been pressed out.

TRASHING vbl sb.

1790 Moreton 45, see TRASH vb I.

TRASH MAT sb dial. *G*

1954 LeP StT, Mat made from dry trash or grass—trash mat.

TRASH MATTRESS sb. A mattress stuffed with dried plantain leaves or similar material.

1827 Hamel II 83, The Obeah man..having seen his guest provided with a trash mattrass, left him. See TRASH A, quot 1946. *G*

TRASH-MYSELF (CANE) sb. =DROP-TRASH (CANE).

1952 FGC StJ /trash mi-self/ cane. 1959 DeC Tre /trash-miself/ name for a kind of cane whose trash falls cleanly.

TRASH-TRASH sb dial; iterative from TRASH. Trash. (The iteration implies a larger quantity or many small bits.)

1958 DeC Tre /trash-trash/ trash.

TRAW see TARRA.

TRAWN sb dial; <*straan*, strand.

1943 *GL* StJ, Trawn, strings or rags.

TREAD-BAG, tred-bag see THREAD-BAG.

TREE sb dial. The part of a plant above the ground: a bush, vine, tree.

1956 Mc Port /di trii [av hakam] gruo laik yam/; /pingwing hav trii laik karata/; /pi-aba—di trii av it gruo siem az paasli/.

TREE-OF-LIFE sb chiefly dial. =LEAF-OF-LIFE. *G*

1952 FGC Port; StC, Tree-of-life—there's two of them, one is for rose, one for medicine; StM; StT, Tree-of-life, same as leaf-of-life. 1958 DeC Clar /trii ov laif/ a small plant growing on rock; good for colds.

TREE-OYSTERS sb obs; *OED* 1767→. Oysters that 'grow on trees' by fastening themselves to the roots of the mangrove. *T*

1725 Sloane 261, Tree-Oysters, or, Mangrove-Oysters.

TREE PINE sb dial. =WILD PINE; a Bromeliad growing epiphytically on a tree.

1952 FGC Man, Tree-pine.

TREE ROSEMARY sb obs. In Barham's use: *Amyris balsamifera* (TORCHWOOD 2) or some similar tree.

a 1726 Barham (1794) 195, Tree-Rosemary. This I happened to meet with by chance..I carried some of the bark with me to England in the year 1717, which kept its scent very well. 1814 Lunan I 148, This species [*sc Amyris balsamifera*] is supposed to be the wood noticed by Barham, under the name *tree rosemary*.

TRELAWNY BLACKBIRD sb; <*Trelawny* parish, Ja +BLACKBIRD 3. The WILD PINE SERGEANT.

1956 Jeffrey-Smith 76, *Nesopsar nigerrimus.* Another member of the oriole family is the Black Banana Bird. James Bond lists it as Jamaican Blackbird. It is known as Trelawny Blackbird for it is found there, near and in the Cockpit area.

TREMBLE- see TRIMBLE-.

TREMBLER sb; *OED* 1832 for diff fish. The torpedo fish *Narcine brasiliensis*, an electric ray whose sting makes one tremble.

1854–5 *TJSA* I 145, Torpedo Bancroftii—The Trembler—la tremola. 1892 Cockrell list, Trembler—torpedo. *Narcine brasiliensis.*

TREMBLING GRASS sb obs; *OED* 1853. The grass *Briza media*.

1756 Browne 135, Briza I..The small trembling Grass. This little plant seldom rises above six or seven inches, and is sustained by a very slender weakly stalk.

TRESPASS adj dial; <*trespass* vb, or some form of it, e.g. *trespassing*. Prone to sin.

1929 Beckwith 167, And I said, 'Some of these sheep are very trespass'. And he said, 'You desire to bind these trespass sheep with cords, and the cords are the word of God'.

TRETCHAL sb dial; <*stretcher*, top of a door frame. (This word illustrates the dial reduction of *st*- > *t*-, and *r* > *l* by dissimilation.) The horizontal beam forming the top of a door frame.

1877 Murray *Feedin' 'Perrit* 7, I hit de back a me hed pon one piece o' block pon de door tretchal.

TREVELATION sb dial; <*tribulation*, with overcorrection of *b* > *v*, perh by analogy with *Revelation*. Tribulation.

1907 Jekyll 236–7 [Song:] Oh trial! Great trevelation children ho! Trial!..Note: There is no doubt about the word being *trevelation*, a mixture of Revelation, one of their favourite books in the Bible, and tribulation, for which it is intended.

TRICK adj dial; for *tricky*. Tricky, TRICKIFY.

1907 Jekyll 4, The boy too trick. 1943 *GL* StAnd, Trick, can't be trusted. 1962 BLB 71, Trick, adj—crafty.

TRICKIFIED, TRICKIFY /trikifai/ adj dial; <*trickified*; cf *trickify*, *OED* 1678, and -IFY. Tricky, crafty, shifty, not to be trusted.

1827 Hamel I 237, 'I'll have you put in the stocks forthwith, for an obstinate trickified ass'. 'Master, I'm no rickify hass.' *Ibid* II 48, The Brutchie walked by the side of the horseman with a hand on one of his reins, thinking that the trickified Missionary might give him the slip. 1873 Rampini 30, Jacob no pay no tax till after races oba'!! I know it!!! Jacob too trickify!!! 1907 Jekyll 39, An' Donkey wasn't agree, for he know that Toad is a very trickified thing. 1929 Beckwith 97, The belief that every man is accompanied by two duppies, a good and a bad, or 'a trickify one', as Wilfrid says. 1958 DeC StT /trikifai/.

TRICKING-CHICK sb; if this is the original form of the name, it may allude to the bird's propensity for digging up corn; cf CHICK-MAN-CHICK.

1740 Importance 38, see MOUNTAIN COCK.

TRICK-WEED sb dial; <*trick* sb, or perh TRICK+*weed*. The DUPPY GUN, from the way the seed pods suddenly burst open when wetted.

1952 FGC StAnn, Trick-weed—duppy gun /tempe/.

TRIMBLE vb dial; *OED* 'obs.' but *EDD*, *SND* both list as dial form. Tremble. *BL G T*

1907 Jekyll 42, When him yerry, him 'tand up same place 'an trimble. 1955 Bennett *Me Dah Drive*, Me no fraid an me no trimble.

TRIMBLE-LEAF, ~-WEED sb dial; <TRIMBLE +*leaf*, *weed*. The wild plant *Lycopodium cernuum*, which, when held in the hand however steadily, seems to tremble.

1952 FGC Port /trimbl-wiid/—fern-like; can't be held still. 1956 Mc Port /trimbl/ or /chimbl-liif/ a weed that trembles; used for decoration; also said to be boiled for a drink given to Maroon warriors to make them brave in battle.

TRIMONA, TRIMONIA sb dial; <*stramonium*, the species name. The thorn-apple, *Datura stramonium.*

1927 Beckwith 28, Trimona..For swelling, 'rub up' the leaf and bind upon the affected part. 1952 FGC Man /trimúonya/—grow on big bush; smoke for asthma. 1954 *WIMJ* 22, Thorn Apple; Trimona.

TRINIDAD YAM sb. =RENTA YAM; evid brought from the island of Trinidad.

1952 FGC Han, Trinidad yam and St Vincent grow practically wild in bush or forest land; StJ, Trinidad favor white yam. 1954 *FG* 445, The renta or Trinidad is a heavy bearer, and is grown and kept by the cultivators of Clarendon for family use. 1959 DeC Han /trinidad/ the renta yam.

TRIPE sb dial; cf *OED tripe*[1] 2, the intestines, bowels, guts.. →1806; *EDD* Sc, Irel, Wm →1883. Intestines (of a human being, in reference to constipation and other such conditions). Cf KNOT-GUT. *BL G*

1943 *GL* Man, Tripes, intestines. 1952 FGC Han /traip tai-op/; StM /di traip get twis/—constipation.

TROOPING pres pple and vbl sb dial; evid <*troop* vb, but cf TRUMP, an alternative term and perh var form. The action of inducing by hyperventilation semi-consciousness, and ultimately frenzy, at revivalist, pocomania, and similar cultist ceremonies: see quots.

1929 Beckwith 162, Once Margaret Williston began to breathe with a short sharp intake that sounded like the bark of a dog, an exercise which is called 'trooping' and which, if persisted in, will produce in the worker that semiconscious condition so favourable to the communications of spirits, and hence so coveted at a really successful Revivalist meeting. 1946 Dunham 74, I arrived in the midst of a 'possession'. As I approached I heard only the harsh, barking sound of the 'trooping' common to the Pilgrims when in ecstasy..A huge black man from Retirement was in the throes of spirit communication. His head was thrown back and his turban was awry. Rivulets of sweat ran from his face and off the ends of his mustache. He was slumped backward in the arms of the Shepherd and Shepherdess, eyes closed, mouth open just enough to let out the harsh choking, sound. The small circle of followers around them..were working into a frenzy, bodies jerking, eyes rolling, trooping for dear life.

TROPON see TARPON.

TROUBLE adj or sb attrib dial; for *troubled*, a *time* of *trouble*, or the like. Difficult.

1961 FGC StAnd, Poor fella, him havin' a very trouble time.

TRUMP (AND LABOUR) vb (phr) dial; prob repr *tromp* (cf US common var of *tramp*) +*and*+*labour*. Cf *chomp*. To perform the action of TRUMPING or TROOPING (and LABOURING).

1952 Moore 57, Trump—to dance, always counter-clockwise, around the altar at Revival meetings. *Ibid*, Trump and labor—to lose control at a revival service, and dance and show signs of possession.

TRUMPETER, (TRUMPET-FISH) sb; *OED* 1756→. Any of various fish of the order *Aulostomi*, with jaws and mouths that look like a trumpet, flute, or the like. Also called FIFER, FLUTE. *BA*

1756 Browne 441, Solenostomus 1..The Trumpeter, or Trumpet Fish..The head is long and narrow; the jaws closed up at the sides; the mouth very small; and the body long and slender. 1854–5 *TJSA* I 144, Fistularia tabaccaria—deep water Trumpeter. Aulostoma coloratum—shallow water Trumpeter. 1952 FGC StT, Trumpet; StM, Trumpet-fish; Port, StAnn, StE, West /trómpita/.

TRUMPET REED sb; *OED* 1866. The reed *Arundo occidentalis.*

1696 Sloane 33, Arundo alta gracilis, foliis è viridi cœruleis..The Trumpet Reed. 1811 Lunan 242, Trumpet-Reed. Zizania..aquatica. 1864 Grisebach 788, Trumpet-reed: *Arundo occidentalis.*

TRUMPET TREE sb; see quot a1726. *OED* 1756→. The tree *Cecropia peltata. N*

1696 Sloane 45–6, Yaruma de Oviedo..Trumpet-tree. In sylvis Jamaica..ubique copiosè oritur. a1726 Barham (1794) 195, Trumpet-tree..This is the common name this tree is called by in Jamaica, I suppose from its hollowness. 1756 Browne 111, The Trumpet-tree..The smaller branches, when cleared of the Septa, serve for wind instruments, and are frequently heard many miles among those echoing mountains; they yield an agreeable hollow sound: I have seen some cut and holed in the form of a German flute, and have not been displeased with their notes. 1886 Hooper 30, Trumpet tree. Cecropia peltata ..It does not yield a timber, but it is useful as shade, and in sundry other ways. 1953 *WIMJ* 252, Trumpet Tree; Snake Wood..A decoction of the leaves is used for colds and is said to be a sovereign remedy for a sore throat.

TRUMPING (AND LABOURING) vb (phr) dial; <TRUMP. As a part of revivalist and other cultist practices: inducing semi-consciousness and ultimately frenzy by hyperventilation: see quot, and cf TROOPING.

1953 Moore 57, Trumping—the process of sucking in the breath audibly as the body straightens from a bent position to an upright position while taking a hopping, walking step. Laboring is the term used to describe this same process as it becomes more emphatic and actually develops into an involuntary action.

TRUNK-CRAB sb obs. A crab with a shell shaped like a trunk. See quot.

1756 Browne 421, Cancer 8..The Trunk-Crab. The body of this curious shell-fish is large and roundish; and when it contracts its flatted claws, which lie close under the fore and lateral parts of the *scuta*, it seems but one continued shell, and has a very different appearance from any other sorts of the class.

TRUNK-FISH sb; *OED* 1804→. Any of various fish of the family *Ostraciidæ* with a hard box-like body. For other names see quot 1952. *N*

1756 Browne 457, Ostracion 5..The Trunck-fish. [Browne contrasts this with the Cuckold-fish, the latter having two additional horns over the eyes.] 1826 Williams 79, Baracootas, silver oldwives, trunk fish, and others with no less barbarous names. 1868 Hill 10, We have some eight different Ostraciones, all known by the name of *Trunk-fishes.* 1952 FGC, A general term among fishermen, local names being scuttle, buck-buck, cunny-buck, cow-fish, horny-money, /trongkfish/ and occas /chonk-fish/.

TRUNK FLEET sb joc obs. A series of servant women carrying trunks; see quots.

1835 Senior 30, Whenever the family makes an excursion from home..a number of women are seen moving along the road, smartly dressed, each carrying on her head a large band box, or light trunk..These are articles that would be injured by being strapped on the sumpter-saddle..As this party of carriers seldom separate on the journey, it is not inaptly termed 'the trunk fleet'. 1836 Widow 245, A string of about nine or ten negro girls, walking along the road, and sweating under the load of huge trunks and enormous band-boxes..I was told very gravely that it was the *trunk fleet*, the interpretation of which is neither more nor less than a company of waiting maids, to a visiting party of ladies, who thus transport the wardrobe of their mistresses from place to place.

TRUS, TRUSE see TRUST.

[**TRUSS-MADE** adj obs. Made like a truss; compactly built.

1823 Roughley 137, I would choose either for draft or back carriage, the young truss-made mule, not too tall.]

TRUST /tros/ sb and vb dial; cf *OED* 7 '*obs*' →1775. s. *BL N*

A. sb: Credit: when goods are given without immediate payment. *BA G T*

1873 Rampini 29 [From an advertisement:] A time to pay debts, and a time to trust again..We are happy to inform the public that 'poor old Trust' gave up the ghost on the 31st December. 1943 *GL* StC, Trus, credit. 1952 FGC StM /tros/ credit.

B. vb: 1. To give or to obtain (something) on credit; to give credit. *G T*

1873 Rampini 156, Excuse me, my friend, I cannot trust. 1910 Anderson-Cundall 37 [Prov:] Pay to-day, trus' to-morrow. 1942 Bennett 14, Ef she wen good she hooden want Fe trus' me li candy. [*If she were good she would not want to get a little candy from me on credit.*] 1943 *GL* Tre, Truse, to credit. 1952 FGC Han, Trus' me a bread until later. 1958 DeC StAnd /dem a tros lan uoba langkasta/.

2. To take a chance. *G*

1960 BLB Man /nuo, misis, mi kyaan tros/ *No, Missis, I won't take the chance* (*of doing it lest it doesn't turn out right*).

TRUVEL /trovl/ sb dial; <*trouble*, with over-correction of *b* to *v*. *BL G*

1942 Bennett 38, Yuh want get me eena truvel?

TUBBITTABRAWTA see TWO-BIT-O'-BRAATA.

TUBE sb dial. A tunnel on the railway.

1921 Frank 416, The train continues..through numerous 'tubes', as Jamaicans call a tunnel.

TUBITTY see TWO-BITTY.

TUCKO-TUCKO, TUCKY see *tuku-tuku*.

TUCKY AXE /toki haks/ sb dial; aphetic form of *Kentucky ax* (*DA*). A sturdy kind of axe; also the upper incisor teeth.

1956 Mc Clar /toki haks/ use to cut wood; Man /toki haks/ used [metaphorically] to describe strong, sharp teeth.

TUDDY see *todi*.

TUDERATION sb dial; <*study*+linking *r*+ *-ation*, on analogy of *education*, etc. Studying, thinking things out; scheming. (A word early used in dialect humour.) *G*

1925 Beckwith 106 [Prov:] Studeration better than education. 1943 *GL* Clar, Tuderation, education; StC, tudiration, thinking.

TUDIRATION see prec.

tufe /tú-fè/ sb dial; prob echoic or phonosymbolic—see Jekyll's note. Something worthless?

1907 Jekyll 59, An' the mumma say:—'You never better, tuffa'. [*You'll never be good for anything*]..Note: *tuffa*, with Italian *u* imitates spitting, a sign of contempt. 1943 *GL* Kgn, Too-fey; Man, Te-feh, nothing. 1955 FGC Man /tufe/.

TUFFA see prec.

TUKKU-TUKKU see *tuku-tuku*.

tuk-tuk, tuku-tuku[1] sb dial; said to be echoic, imitating the sound made when water is poured out, but cf Twi *o-dúku*, small cask, barrel, keg; and Ewe *takuu*, the noise of slapping like water in a pot. A calabash or gourd. (The distinctions made in quot 1925 are not made by all.) *BL*

1925 Beckwith 21, Three varieties of gourd-bearing trees are distinguished in Jamaica: the 'calabash' bears a large fruit attached closely to the trunk; the 'packey' is a small fruit attached to the branches; and the 'took-took' bears fruit half way between in size. 1943 *GL* StJ, Tucko-tucko, gourd; Tre, Took-took, a water gourd; West, Tukku-tukku, gourd or calabash. 1952 FGC StM, StJ /tuk-tuk/ small, name from sound it makes when water is poured out.

tuku(-tuku)[2], **tuki** adj dial; cf Ewe *túkui*, *túkutukui*, small, little; cf *dogi*. Short, small, stocky.

1943 *GL* Kgn, StAnn, StM, Tre, Tooku-tooku, Tucko-tucko, Tukku-tukku, small or very short person; Clar, Tucky, short. 1954 LeP StAnn, Short and tooko tooko, short, thickly built person. 1955 FGC Man /tuku/. *G*

TULIP TREE sb obs; *OED* mentions without quots. *Hibiscus elatus*.

1814 Lunan I 468, Hibiscus elatus..Browne calls this the *mountain mahoe*..In some places it is known by the name of tulip-tree. 1864 Grisebach 788, Tulip tree: *Paritium elatum*.

tumaali sb dial; cf *OED tomalley*; of Cariban origin. A dish made with crabs as the main ingredient.

1943 *GL* Kgn, Tumaldy, dish of stewed picked crabs and rice; Port, Tomalie, crab dish; StAnd, Tomaulie, a dish of crab; StM, Tomaly, soup prepared from crabs. 1955 FGC Man /tumáali/ dish of crabs—a StT word.

TUMALDY see prec.

tumatis sb dial; <*tomatoes*, taken as sg. The regular folk form of *tomato*. *BL N*

1877 Murray 9, Man you mout pretty! It dis faber a tun tomattis. 1943 *GL* Clar, Tomatice; StC, Tomatis, tomato. 1952 FGC StC /tumátis/.

tumba, tumbe sb dial; cf Twi *atũmpã̃ŋ*, big drum, Ewe *tímbò*, drum. Cf also Malaret *tumba* 4; Hause 8–14 lists four similar W Afr words.

1. A large drum (like certain African drums and tambourines, with snares and jingles). Cf *tambu* 1.

1914 Clerk 23–4, Today..the Maroons, at least those resident on the North side of the Island, use a drum; and a Toombah, a large piece of the Trumpet Tree, hollowed out, and three strings stretched across, and pieces of metal in place of shells, strung on each side. The Toombah is a variety of the banjo, guitar, and tambourine, and may probably be the Tabor of the Arawaks. 1943 *GL* StAnd, Tumboy, drums. 1958 DeC Port /tumbe/ the Portland Maroon equivalent of the Accompong /gumbe/ the drum.

2. A dance done to the accompaniment of the drum. Cf *tambu* 2.

1943 *GL* StJ, Tombey, African dance.

TUMBLE DOWN /tombl-dong/ vb phr dial. To fall down—a euphemism for having sexual intercourse; for an unwed girl, a first pregnancy. Cf BROKE FOOT. *BA G*

1951 Murray 50 [Song:] Matty run, Matty run, Matty tumble dung Matty run a mile an' a half fe go tallala.

TUMBLE-TURD /tombl-tod/ sb; *DAE* 1737→, *DA* →1758.

1. A large black horned beetle which rolls and buries dung.

1756 Browne 428, Scarabeus 2..The Tumble-Turd. This insect is of a thick round make, and furnished with strong limbs, as if nature had intended to fit all its parts for labour..The creature is a very expert mechanic..for, with its rising horn, it is observed to turn and roll over stones and lumps of dirt four or five times its own size.

2. Evid generalized to include other kinds of beetles. (The term *tumble-bug*, however, seems to keep the specific sense.)

1943 *GL* Tre, Tumble-tud, a boreing beetle. 1952 FGC Port /tombl-tod/—/hagvongga/ [i.e. newsmonger beetle]; StT /tombl-tod/ May bug.

3. Transf. A short, stocky person.

1943 *GL* StM, Tumble-tud, short man. 1954 LeP StE, Short, thickly-built person—tumble-tud. 1956 Mc Clar, A person may be likened to a /tombl-tod/ in jest: /yu jos go az likil tombl-tod/.

TUMBOY see *tumba*.

TUMBOZOO sb dial; cf Ewe *tímbo*, drum + *zɔ*, foot, leg; cf also *timbim* above.

1943 *GL* StAnn, Tumbozoo, a big foot, elephantiasis.

TUMFUTU sb dial; cf TUM-TUM.

1943 *GL* Tre, Tumfutu, a river fish.

TUMPA /tompa/ sb and adj dial; < *stump* + A[8] (or, sometimes, + *-y*, the English familiarizing suffix).

A. sb: 1. A stump, a piece left over after something has been cut off; hence, a part. Esp attrib: see separate entries. *G*

1907 Jekyll 139, Tumpa, stump. A man who has lost his arm is called a tumpa-hand man. 1943 *GL* StAnn, Tumpa, piece; StC, Tumpa, half; StC, Tumper, a piece.

2. A stocky person.

1954 LeP Kgn, A short, thickly-built person—Tumpa.

B. adj: Cut off short, stumpy, small. (In compounds often indistinguishable from the attrib sb.) Cf JUNKA. *G*

1907 Jekyll 143, One day Dog invite four Puss to dinner. The last one was Tumpy John because he has no tail. 1941 Kirkpatrick 40, Dem so tumpa, dem lickle better dan midget. 1942 Bennett 42, Pass me fe Leah tumpa knife. 1943 *GL* West, Tumpa, stout or round. 1956 Mc Clar /tompa man iz shaat/.

TUMPA-BILL, ~-CUTLASS sb dial; < TUMPA + BILL or CUTLASS. A bill or cutlass broken short but still kept in use.

1907 Jekyll 63, An he get into his house and take his tumpa bill coming to Cow force ace fe chop off Cow's neck. 1956 Mc Clar /tómpa kotlés/ A broken straight-machete, or the stump of a cutlass adapted as a tool for digging skellion.

TUMPA-FOOT sb and adj dial. *G*

A. sb: A stump leg (the lower part having been cut off); also, a wooden leg; hence, a person with a leg cut off or with a wooden leg.

1910 Anderson-Cundall 11 [Prov:] If you go a tump-a-foot dance, you must dance tump-a-foot. 1952 FGC Han /tompa-fut/ use two arm-stick; StAnd /tompa-fut/ with legs cut off; StM /tompa-fut/ one-foot man. 1956 Mc Clar /tompa fut/ a wooden peg-leg, or a person with a wooden leg.

B. adj: Having a leg cut off.

1943 *GL* Kgn, Tumpa-foot, one-legged.

TUMPA QUAW /tompa kwa-u/ sb dial; < TUMPA + QUAW.

1958 DeC Clar, see BLACK JANGA.

TUMPA TOE sb dial; < TUMPA + *toe*. (The sense of *tumpa* may be multiple: bad infestations of jiggers often reduced toes or the whole foot to stumps; on the other hand, this may refer to the big toes—cf TUMPY, the thumb.)

1912 McK *Songs* 75, An' chigger nyam you' tumpa toe.

TUMPA-TONGUE sb dial; < TUMPA + *tongue*. The stump of a tongue.

1896 Bates 124 [Prov:] Ef you wan' ooman fe' good, gib him 'tump o'tongue. [*If you want a woman to be good, give her a stump-tongue* (i.e. cut off her tongue).]

TUMPY[1] /tompi/ sb dial; etym prob multiple: cf TUMPA adj and *thumb*. The thumb—a nickname. Cf BIG FINGER, BIG TUMPY.

1943 *GL* StT, Thumpi, the thumb; No addr, Tumpy, a big finger. 1955 FGC Man /tompi/ big finger.

TUMPY[2] see TUMPA B.

TUM-TUM[1] /tum-tum/ sb now dial and arch; < Twi *túm tum*, imitative of the sound of pounding *fufuu* in a wooden mortar (Christaller). *OED sb*[3] 1833→. *G*; *SC tontón*.

1. = FUFU; plantain or any similar food pounded until it forms a sort of paste: see quots 1790.

1790 Beckford II 148–9, [Plantain] is..beaten up into a kind of paste, which the white people, as well as the negroes, are accustomed to eat with pepper pot, under the vulgar name of tum-tum. 1790 *Short Journey* 58–9, The constant accompanier of pepper-pot, is *fou-fou*, or *tum-tum*, two names for the same thing. This is only boiled plantain left to be stone cold, and then beat in a kind of wooden mortar—it both looks and eats like dough of a yellowish colour. 1895 Banbury 28, see FUM 2. 1943 *GL* West, Tum-tum, crushed or mashed food. 1959 DeC Han /tum-tum/ boiled food pounded in mortar until soft.

2. Attrib.

1895 Banbury 33, The old woman [old hige] got up, shook off her skin, placed it in a tum-tum mortar, and went out to suck.

TUM-TUM[2] /tom-tom/ sb dial; cf Ewe *tɔm-*, base of many words having to do with water. Minnows or other small fresh-water fish.

1943 *GL* Port, Tum-tum, a small fish. 1952 FGC Port, StAnn, StT /tom-tom/ minnows, small mullet. 1958 DeC Port /tom-tom/ a small herring-like fish eaten by the Maroons.

TUM-TUM[3] sb dial; echoic, but cf Fr *tam-tam*. A drum with a goatskin head.

1943 *GL* StJ, Tum-tum, a drum made of goatskin.

TUNG /tong/ sb dial. A common dial spelling for 'town', repr /tong/ (i.e. with a mid-back centred nasalized vowel, [ə̃]). Cf 'dung', down, etc. *G*

1868 Russell 5, Tung—Town. 1950 Pioneer 31, De two a dem goh dunga Oman Tung. [*The two of them went down to Woman Town.*]

TUNNEL sb dial. A cutting for a railway track.

1907 Jekyll 269 [Song:] Den number nine tunnel I would not work de..[Note:] The so-called tunnels are cuttings, Number nine had a very bad reputation.

tun-tun, tun-tus sb dial; varr of *dundun*, *dundus*[2]. See quots.

1958 DeC Port, Tre /tun-tun/ affectionate term used to a child or sweetheart; Port /tun-tus/ same.

TU'N-TU'N see *ton-ton*.

tuoshas, tuoshos see STOSHUS.

tuota see next.

tuoto sb dial; etym uncert: cf Fante *tõtõe*, roasted, but also Sp *torta*, round cake. A small cake (about 3 in. diameter and ½ in. thick) made of flour and brown sugar, sometimes with shredded coconut. *N*

1943 *GL* StM, Toato, sweet flour cakes with shredded coconuts; StT, Totoe, cake made from flour and coconut; West, Toeto. 1954 LeP StE, Sweet cake—Toto; StT, Toe-toe bulla [see BULLA]. 1956 Mc Clar, Man, Port, StE /tuoto/. 1958 DeC Port /tuota, tuoto, tuotuo/ a baked cake of gratered coconut, flour, sugar, baking powder.

tuotuo see prec.

TUP, TUPPY /top, topi/ sb dial; abbr of *twopence* (+-*y*, familiarizing suffix). (For map showing distribution see DeC in 1961 *CLS* 68). s CURRENCY. *G*

1. A penny half-penny; a QUATTIE. (Twopence in Ja currency was worth only 1½*d.* sterling—cf FIP.)

1877 Murray *Feedin' 'Perrit* 4, I buy a tup wut o' sal-fish. *Ibid* 13, No dis chupid pickney tek me one tuppy I hab, so go trow it way in a de shop so. 1912 McK 317, Tup—a penny ha'penny. 1943 *GL* Clar, StJ, Tre, Tup, 1½*d.*; Man, Tuppy; Tre, Tuppi, 1½*d.* 1952 FGC Han, StM /top/ quattie. 1956 Mc Man /topi/ same as quattie.

2. Fig. A very small amount.

1912 McK *Ballads* 46, You ca'an wuk a tup.

TUPPY-AN'-GILL sb dial. s CURRENCY.

1943 *GL* Han, Tuppy-an-gil, 2¼*d.*

TURBOT /torbat, torbit/ sb chiefly dial. See ALEWIFE. Various fish of the families *Balistidæ* and *Monacanthidæ*.

1892 Cockrell list, Turbot, *monacanthus hispidus*. 1952 FGC general /torbit, torbat/ a skin fish; StT /torbat/ is the Portland name for what is called alewife here; StE /torbit, torbat/ a specie [*sic*] of old-wife; West, more whitish than old-wife; StC /torbit/ same as /fani kaaka/.

TURKEY-BERRY sb bot; *OED* 1884. Either of two species of *Solanum* (see quot 1864); = SUSUMBA.

1756 Browne 174, Solanum 3..Turky Berries. Solanum 4..The larger Turky Berries. Both these species are very common in the low lands of Jamaica, and so like each other, that they have been commonly taken for the same plant..The berries, which generally are about the size of our European cherries, serve to feed the Turkies, from whence they have received the present appellation. 1864 Grisebach 788, Turkey-berry: *Solanum torvum* and *mammosum*. 1954 *WIMJ* 31.

TURKEY-BERRY TREE sb bot; *OED* 1858. The CLAMMY-CHERRY tree.

1756 Browne 167, Collococcus 1..The clammy Cherry, or Turkey-berry-tree..The berries are red, succulent, of the size of our smallest European cherries..The turkeys and other poultry feed much upon the fruit of this tree. 1864 Grisebach 788, Turkey-berry tree: *Cordia collococca*.

TURKEY-BLOSSOM sb bot; *OED* 1849. The flower (and plant) of *Tribulus cistoides*; see quot 1954. s TURKEY-WEED.

1756 Browne 220, Tribulus 1..The Turkey Blossom. This plant..is now very common about Kingston..The fowls are observed to feed much on the blossoms of this plant when it grows wild, and it is thought to heighten the flavour, as well as to contribute to the fattening of them. 1864 Grisebach 788, Turkey-Blossom: *Tribulus cistoides*. 1954 *WIMJ* 32, Jamaica or Kingston Buttercup; Police Macca; Kill Buckra; Turkey Blossom.

TURKEY-RIAL sb dial; <*turkey* + RIAL. A fowl thought to be a cross between a chicken and a turkey; it looks like a large chicken but with no feathers on its red neck.

1952 FGC StAnd, StAnn /tórki-ráial/ peel-neck [fowl].

TURK'S HEAD sb; *OED* 1725, 1760. The *Melocactus communis*, which resembles an elaborate turban.

1696 Sloane 198, Echinomelocactos..Turk's-head. 1756 Browne 238, Cactus 10..The Turk's-head, or Pope's-head Indian Fig. 1814 Lunan I 503, This is called *Turks* or *Pope's head*, and is common in Jamaica..Its roots are strong and many, which throw out a large round head of a greenish colour, deeply ribbed, and covered all over with prickles placed star-fashion. 1926 Fawcett 283, Turk's Head, Turk's Cap, Pope's Head, Melon Thistle.

TURKY BERRY see TURKEY-BERRY.

TURN /ton, torn/ vb.

1. Of a fruit: to begin to change colour, indicating that it is beginning to ripen. (Often used in the past pple form.) *BA BL G T*

1877 Murray *Feedin' 'Perrit* 9 [To a man who has been struck in the mouth:] Man you mout pretty! It dis faber a tun tomattis. 1893 Sullivan 30, Turned—half ripe. 'Turned' is when they [*sc* plantains] are between green and ripe. 1943 *GL* StE, Tun, start riping [ripening].

2. To turn into something else, enter a new phase, by natural or magical means. (Cf *OED* 35.) *BL G T*

1924 Beckwith 102 [Story:] One of the cow turn a beautiful young lady. I turn a piece of stick,..I turn a rock,—I turn all different things. 1956 Mc Port /mi a ton húol nou/ *I am getting old now.* Man /im ton big man nou/ (*The baby*) *is getting a big boy now.* 1957 JN StE, When mi turn big mi want to turn teacher. [*When I grow up I want to become a teacher.*]

3. Phr. *To turn* (someone) *down*: see quot.

1954 LeP StE, Tun-in-dung—to have a spell or curse put on one's enemy (*turn him down*). 1956 Mc Clar /ton im dong—huobia im—put dopi an im/.

TURN-BACK sb dial; prob by folk-etym <*thorn-back*. Cf THORN-BACK. A name for some kind of ray fish; said to mean that when it pricks you, you turn back (but this is prob an *ex post facto* explanation).

1943 *GL* Kgn, Turn back fish, specie of barracouta. 1952 FGC StC /ton bak/ kind of ray, black, carry lance in tail. 1961 FGC StC /ton-bak/—/wipri—wen im juk yu yu ton bak/.

TURN-BILL sb dial; for *turned bill*. A MACHETE having a turned or hooked end with which one pulls toward one the branches or stalks that are to be cut. Also called HOOK-POINT, HOOKY, HOOK BILL, etc.

1952 FGC StJ, Turn-bill, a bill with a turned-back end. 1956 Mc StE /ton bil/—/yu kot wi it an yu haal/.

TURN-CLAW sb dial. A HOOK BILL machete.

1959 DeC West /ton-klaa/ name for a cutlass with a large, rounded, hooked end.

TURN-COLOUR MAN sb; cf TURN 1.

1958 DeC StT /ton-kola man/ derogatory term for a nearly white person.

TURN(ED) CORNMEAL sb. Cornmeal boiled and stirred over the fire until quite thick. It may be seasoned in a number of ways. *BA*

1893 Sullivan 86, Turned cornmeal. One pint of cornmeal stirred over the fire with enough water to make it very stiff. 1952 FGC Port /ton/ or /torn kaanmiil/ Put on coconut milk, butter, seasoning, and boil; sprinkle in cornmeal and *keep turning*; grease bowl and turn into it; press down and turn over; can also fry. Gen.

TURN HAND vb phr; abbr of *turn one's hand to* (some task). Cf *OED* 56b. *G*

1943 *GL* Clar, Tun han, to buy and sell; StAnn, tun-han, to higgle. 1955 Bennett *Tun you han.* 1955 FGC Man /ton han/ buy and sell.

TURNING vbl sb. A musical variation.

1907 Jekyll 173, see CORNER.

TURN MACHETE. = HOOK BILL.

TURN (ONE'S) EYES vb phr dial. To influence (one's) mind in a certain direction.

1895 Banbury 9, To bring about an influence over the mind of any one, in order to gain some advantage from, or over him. This is called 'Turning his eyes'. ('Tun him yeye')..Females among the superstitious use this sort of incantation to prevent their sweethearts..leaving them for other women.

TURN-POINT (MACHETE) sb dial. =HOOK BILL.

1952 FGC West /ton paint/.

TURN-POST (BED) sb chiefly dial. A high hardwood bed having the corner posts turned by lathe, and having a canopy above. *BA G*

1956 Mc StAnd /ton puos bed hav tiista uova it an di fut hai af di groun/. 1958 DeC StAnd /torn-puos bed/ a high four-poster with canopy; StT /ton-puos/.

TURN STICK sb now dial.

1. In early sugar-making—a wooden stick for stirring the evaporating syrup; =STIRRING STICK. *G*

1823 Roughley 361, Before it [*sc* the sugar] is too cool, take the turn stick again and pass it over the surface gently to break the crust.

2. A wooden stick or spoon used to stir what is cooking in a pot.

1910 Anderson-Cundall 8 [Prov:] Cockroach neber lick turn 'tick. 1924 Beckwith 198 [Riddle:] Little Miss Nancy tie up her frock and wheel roun three times. [Answer:] Turn-stick in the pot. 1943 *GL* Kgn, Tun tik, wooden spoon; StC, Tuntick, wooden handle. 1956 Mc Clar /ton stik/ Man /ton tik/ used to stir pot on fire.

'TURN-T'ANKS sb dial. A thanksgiving service in church.

1907 Jekyll 77, The Sunday after the wedding is 'turn t'anks (return thanks). The married couple and their friends..ride to church dressed in their best. The bride and bridegroom, attended by the godfather and godmother, sit in 'couple bench', the rest of the party going to their own pews.

TURN-THROAT sb dial. A kind of MACHETE with hooked end. See HOOK BILL.

TURPENTINE MANGO sb. A variety of mango having a strong taste of turpentine.

1873 Rampini 157, Mango trees of all kinds..from the humble 'turpentine' to the proud 'No. 11'. 1952 FGC Port, StJ /torpintain/ StM /torpmtain/ StT /torpmtaim/ mango. *BL G T*

TURTLE sb. The ant-lion (genus *Myrmeleon*); also called NANNY(-GOAT), PUGGO.

1952 FGC StAnd /tórkl/ Nanny.

TURTLE APPLE sb dial. Prob =ALLIGATOR APPLE.

1952 FGC StE /torkl-apl/ wild soursop.

TURTLE-CRAB sb. 'A minute species of crab parasitic upon turtles and other marine animals' (*OED*).

1756 Browne 421, Cancer 2..I found this insect on the back of a turtle, near the western islands. The whole length of the trunk is not much above an inch, and the breadth of the body is nearly as much.

TURTLE CRAWL sb; <*turtle*+CRAWL; *OED* 1833→. An enclosure along the seashore in which turtles are kept. Also attrib.

1707 Sloane viii, Rivers on the North-side are..Porto Antonio River, Turtle Crawle Rivers, Priest Man's River..[etc.]. 1827 Hamel II 201–2, He shall have the boat that is hid in Turtle Crawl. 1833 Scott (1859) 420, The Turtle Crawls filled with beautiful clear water. 1873 Rampini 166, We subsequently visited a turtle 'crawl' in Sheffield Bay. It was a little fenced-in enclosure underneath some mangrove trees. Four green turtles were swimming about, preparatory to being sold. 1903 *Daily Mail* 9 Sept 5/3, A turtle crawl in Kingston, where over two hundred turtles were confined awaiting shipment.. was broken up by the force of the sea during the cyclone in Jamaica. 1935 HPJ, An enclosure for keeping live turtles [A. Clerk: *in the sea*] generally called 'a turtle crawl'.

TURTLE FAT sb.

1. The fat of sea-turtles, of a greenish colour, early sought after as a delicacy.

[1679 Trapham 61, The Bountiful Turtle,..gratifying the curious palate with extraordinary delicacy, exceeding that of marrow and fatness in any other Creature..the Flesh is truly solid but easy of digestion, like Fish in the last, but as flesh in the first, neither the lean nor the fat of a fishy taste.] [1707 Sloane xvii, Turtle, (Tortoises) are of several sorts, those of the Sea call'd green Turtle from their Fats being of that colour.]

2. The plant *Rhamnidium jamaicense*: see quot.

1943 *NHN* 59, Turtle Fat..The name is derived from the colour of the freshly cut heart wood which resembles that of green turtle fat.

3. Attrib in the names of other trees having greenish wood—see separate entries.

TURTLE-FAT MAHOE sb dial. The mahoe *Hibiscus elatus* (BLUE MAHOE), from a greenish cast in the wood, resembling turtle fat.

1952 FGC Tre, Turtle-fat mahoe..so called at Parleston West.

TURTLE-FAT SWEETWOOD sb dial. A species of *Amyris*; see quot.

1952 FGC StAnn, Turtle-fat sweetwood—gives off gum while burning, like pitch-pine.

TURTLE-FISHERY, ~-FISHING sb; *OED* 1707. The trade of catching and selling sea-turtles.

1707 Sloane lxxxvii, The Turtle-fishery there, and at the Caymanes were thought by Sir Henry Morgan to be ours by right..The same is to be said of the Turtle-fishing at the Island Vaches, off of Hispaniola.

TURTLE NET sb. A net used to catch sea-turtles; it is left floating with a COOTER or decoy; the turtle becomes tangled in the net when he comes to the decoy.

1952 FGC StM /tortl net/ float on water, with anchor.

TURTLER sb; *OED* 1697→.

1. 'A person, or a vessel, engaged in turtling; a turtle-catcher' (*OED*).

1697 Dampier (1729) I 395, The Jamaica Turtlers have such [nets]. 1707 Sloane lvi, The Turtlers who furnish the island with Turtle, may be reckoned among the trading ships. 1718 *Courant* 11 Feb 3, The Sloops (in their Persuit) met a Turtler, Augustine Golding Master, loaden with Cod from the ship Kingston.

2. A seller of turtle meat.

c 1695 *Acts & Laws* 106, No Butcher or Turtler shall sell any Meat, or Turtle, by retail, but in open Market.

TURTLE-SHELL MAHOE sb dial. Perh an error for TURTLE-FAT MAHOE.

1952 FGC StAnn, Turtle-shell mahoe—BLUE MAHOE.

tush /tush, tosh/ vb dial or slang. s.

1. To have a movement of the bowels.

c 1918 FGC StAnd (school-boy usage).

2. Of squibs: to take one that has not exploded, break it in two, and light the powder so that it squitters fire.

1952 FGC StAnd /tosh di klapaz/ light a fizzled fire-cracker.

tut int dial; cf Ewe *tútu*, closed. An intensifying, concluding exclamation: see quot.

1958 DeC Port /tut/ completely, utterly; this word is added at the end of a statement as a sort of intensive /anansi ton a haia wud agen, gaan, tut/ *Anancy went farther up into the forest, went clear away.*

TUTTUWATTA see *tutu-wata.*

TUTTY see *toti.*

tutu, tutus[1] sb dial; cf *dudus.* A darling, a pet.

1924 Beckwith 71 [Story:] Der once was a woman dat have a child. His name was Simon Tootoos. 1943 *GL* StAnn, Tutu, pet. 1945 Jacobs 281, Darling—me toto. 1955 FGC Man, tutu, a child, etc.

tutus[2] sb; etym unknown.

1. Male sexual organs.

1943 *GL* Clar, Tutus, testicle; Tre, Tootoos, male organ.

2. Transf. The head or fruit of the cat-tail reed. (This sense may belong elsewhere—perh as separate entry. Cf TOOTO.)

1952 FGC Han /tùtús/—cat-tail.

tutu-wata sb dial; echoic. A whistling call made with the fingers and palm.

1943 *GL* Man, Tuttuwatta, a sharp whistle produced by blowing air through the half-closed fingers and palm; No addr, Totowata, a schoolboy's call for his friend. 1953 FGC Man /tútu-wata/—two distinct sounds.

twe sb dial; prob phonosymbolic.

1943 *GL* Clar, Tweh, very small amount. 1955 FGC Man /twe/ a very small quantity.

TWEET-TO-WHIT sb; echoic. The bird *Vireo altiloquus.*

1949 Reid gloss, Tweet-to-whit—same as john-to-whit.

TWEH see *twe.*

TWENTY-EIGHT sb dial. See quot.

1959 DeC StJ /twenti-heit/ common name for the long (28 in.) variant of the cutlass. (Men in the western parishes measure the length of a cutlass overall (including handle). In the eastern parishes only the blade is measured; therefore this would be considered 22-inch.)

TWIGGY CASSIA sb obs. *Cassia viminea.* (An old name, never much used.)

1811 Titford Expl to Plate IX. 2, Weakly Senna Shrub, or Twiggy Cassia (*Cassia Viminea*), native of Jamaica.

TWILE sb dial; regularly derivable <*toil*, but the sense development is not clear.

1943 *GL* StE, Twile, rocking walk.

TWINING COWITCH

1920 Fawcett 306, see CREEPING COWITCH.

TWISTLETOE sb dial; by folk-etym <*mistletoe*, with infl of *twist.*

1952 FGC StAnn /twistltuo/ mistletoe.

TWO-BIT sb dial arch; <*two*+BIT. *G*

1943 *GL* StJ, Two-bit, 9*d*. s CURRENCY.

TWO-BIT-O'-BRAATA sb dial joc; <*two* +BIT+*of*+*braata.* A small addition (to what one has bought); hence, fig, one who goes along with another, a companion. *G*

1912 McK *Songs* 38, see *braata.* 1943 *GL* No addr, Tubbitta-brawta, companion.

TWO-BITTY adj dial or slang. Feeling like two-bits; not feeling up to much.

1943 *GL* Port, Tubitty, without energy.

TWO-MINDED adj dial. Confused. *G*

1953 Moore 100, Two minded—said of the Mother in a Pocomania ceremony, when, because of the presence of a white man, she sang the wrong song. She had a 'mixed spirit'—was drawn both ways, Poco and Revival. Afterwards she became 'one-minded'.

TWO-MOUTH /tuu mout/ sb dial.

A double-edged machete, hence, metaph, a deceitful person; cf SPANISH MACHETE. *BA G*

1954 LeP Kgn, Man.

TWOPENNY CHICK /tàpnachík, chàpnachík, chàpmachík, chìp-man-chíp, chìk-man-chík/ sb; <*twopenny*, perh in *OED* sense 2, as a disparaging epithet +*chick.* A thrush—the GLASS-EYE (*Turdus jamaicensis*); perhaps also the HOPPING DICK (*T. aurantius*). Cf CHICK-MAN-CHICK.

1774 Long III 895, Black-bird. This is commonly called here the two-penny chick..It is a very fearless, tame bird, and perks up its head and tail as it hops along the ground, like the English blackbird. 1840 Chamberlayne 22, The Two-Penny Chick..*Merula Jamaicensis*..This bird, resembling the European blackbird, is an inhabitant of the mountainous districts. 1847 Gosse 136, Twopenny chick—hopping dick. *Merula leucogenys.* 1873 Rampini 163, Black and golden banana birds, two-penny chicks, and mocking-birds. 1952 FGC, see present folk forms variously developed from this: *tapnachik, chapmachik, chapnachik,* CHICK-MAN-CHICK, CHIP-MAN-CHIP, etc.

TWO-SIDE BASKET sb dial. A flat BANKRA basket, which has two sideward bulges, the handle going over between.

1958 DeC Port /tuu-said baskit/.

TWO-TAIL sb dial. A swallow-tailed coat.

1961 R. M. Murray in *Gleaner* 6 Aug 20, Smood out mi two-tail, sarch fe me tie, We gwine katreel [quadrille], mi ole gal an I!

TYEYA see TAYA.

TYRE[1] sb dial; cf MICHELIN.

1958 DeC Tre /taia/ large, round, flat boiled dumpling.

TYRE[2] see TAYA.

-u /u/ particle dial arch; cf A[8], E[2], *-i.* A sound (now surviving only in the most conservative speech) early added to words ending in consonants to adapt them to W Afr patterns: cf, e.g., *musu*, mouse (which also exemplifies vowel harmony). *G*

UCROSOJA sb dial; <OKRO+SOLDIER? Meaning uncert: if etym analysis is right, this should be something slippery. Cf OKRO POLL.

1943 *GL* StAnn, Ucrosoja. [In a list of foods.]

UGLI (FRUIT) sb; <*ugly* (+*fruit*), alluding to the irreg shape and mottled colour. A hybrid citrus fruit, a blend of the grapefruit with others. **s.**

1934 *Gleaner* 26 Feb 19, Should the name of 'ugli' fruit be changed to a more beautiful name? 1955 Bennett *Food Alphabet*, U is fe ugly, dat ting nice you se. 1954 *FG* 317, *Ugli.* A type with loose peel developed at Trout Hall Orchards. Juicy and pleasantly acid.

UGLY /úogli, húogli/ adj dial; an irreg pronunc, emphatic (the unemphatic pronunc being the normal /ógli, hógli/).

1943 *GL* StJ, Oagly, ugly. 1952 FGC StJ /fragfish—beli red; stingk; huogli/.

UGLY sb dial; prob for *ugliness*, but perh <*ugly* adj. Sin, wickedness. *BL*

1803 Dallas II 226–7, 'Massa', said one of them, 'what you say we believe very good, but we no want to bring bad curse upon weselves, for Gar A'mighty no love ugly (that is wickedness)'. 1873 Rampini 177 [Prov:] Goramighty no lub ugly.

ULLO sb dial.

1943 *GL* Tre, Ullo, male organ.

ULU sb dial rare; cf Yoruba *olè*, thief.

1943 *GL* StC, Ulu, thief.

uman /úman, húman/ sb dial; a preservation of a former pronunc which was good upper-class usage from the 17th into the 19th century in England. Cf *OED, woman*. In Ja dial writing sp *'oman, ooman, homan*, etc. Woman. *BL G*

1877 Murray *Feedin' 'Perrit* 4, Ef ooman hed sore it no look so bad. 1907 Jekyll 162 [Song:] Bad homan oh! 1910 Anderson-Cundall 118, 'Ooman rain nebber done. 1957 Bennett 73, One oman pawn de finga, dip it right dung to de jint. *SC hóeman, óeman.*

UMBRELLA WEED sb. A small wild plant with round leaves standing horizontally above their stems like tiny umbrellas: *Dichondra repens*.

1952 FGC StAnn, Umbrella-weed; StC /ombráila wiid/.

UNACTIVE adj obs; *OED* 1 →1741. Sluggish, torpid.

1756 Browne 427, The Loggerhead Muskeeto. . They bite very sharp, but are so unactive that they are generally taken or killed.

UNARROWED adj obs. Of a sugar-cane: Not yet having produced an ARROW.

1823 Roughley 344–5, Well trashed, clean, unarrowed canes, take less lime than canes which. . are top-heavy from arrowing.

UNCLE sb. In the dial, given certain irreg pronunc; spellings in quots imply /angkul, ongkul/ or the like. (Regular pronunc would be /ongkl, hongkl/.) *G*

1868 Russell 5, Ancul, Uncle; *ibid* 9, Uncul. 1877 Murray *Feedin' 'Perrit* 11, Whenever she met him, she used to drop him two successive curtseys, 'Mannin' Ancool'.

UNCLE JOE =JOE LOUIS.

1952 FGC StE.

UNCONSCIONABLE adj; *OED* 1 b →1755. 'With depreciatory terms, as an intensive' (*OED*). *G*

1950 Pioneer 81 [Song:] One unconscionable peel-head john-crow Come tief it away. 1960 BLB, Unconscionable: grasping, avaricious, greedy, giving no thought to the needs of others.

UNCREOLIZED ppl adj; <*un-*+CREOLIZE+*-ed*. Not yet having adopted Creole manners of living.

1827 Hamel I 303, I must not give the story in its native simplicity, inasmuch as the lingo (I must not call it language) would be utterly unintelligible to all my uncreolized countrymen.

UNCUL see UNCLE.

UNDER /ona, onda, anda, aanda/ adv, prep. *G*

UNDER-OVERSEER sb obs. =BOOK-KEEPER.

1788 Marsden 22, The under-overseers or book-keepers are young men from home. . As two of them are usually kept on each plantation, they take it in turns to go to the field with the negroes, or to stay at home with the keys of the stores, which are constantly wanted.

UNDERTAKER, UNDERTAKER'S WIND sb. A name made recently as a counterpart to the old name DOCTOR for the sea-breeze: a wind blowing off the land toward the sea. (This is not a particularly unhealthful breeze, however; the new term is less apt than the old.)

1921 Frank 428, The fitful land breeze known as 'the undertaker'. 1949 Forbes 52, The 'Doctor's wind' blows in from the sea bringing a tang of salt and the savour of great spaces. In the evenings. . the 'Undertaker's wind' blows from the hills.

ungguru sb dial; cf Twi *guró̂w*, to break down, to languish.

1959 DeC West /unggúru/ an albino Negro.

UNI see UNU.

UNMANNERSABLE adj dial; <*un-*+MANNERSABLE. Unmannerly, ill-bred.

1942 Bennett 15 [Of a man who will not give his seat to a woman:] Dem man gwan unmannersable 'Pon de tramcar.

UNNO adv dial; cf I-NO. No, emphatically. *G*

1877 Murray *Kittle* 10, You want ebel perit fe go catch my shadder (shadow). Unno!

UNNO pron, see UNU.

UNO, UNOO see UNU.

UNTIDY adj dial. Indecent, vulgar.

1952 FGC Han /bóbi/ is the untidy word; /bos, bres/ are decent.

UNTRUTH /ontrúut/ adj dial; <*untruthful*. Untruthful. *G*

1957 JN [Girl:] Yuh too untrute! What de woman is a fasty woman! StT [Boy:] What Carlton Duncan? You untruth—nobody name so.

UNU /unu, uno, una, uni, hunu, wunu/ pron dial; dial spellings: *ono, onoo, oonoo, onnoo, oona, uno, unoo, unno, uni, unu, hunu, whunu, wunu*; <Ibo *unu*, you (plur). **s.** Tobago.

1. You (regularly in the plural). *BA BL N*

1868 Russell 13, Plur. 2nd.—Ono=you, ye. 1912 McK *Songs* 76, You t'ink Judge don't know unno well?* *Unno or Onnoo is an African word, meaning 'you' collectively. 1943 *GL* all parishes, Unoo, Onoo, Oonoo, Whunu—all of you. 1954 LeP StE, Uno help me move da rock tone ya.

2. You (occasionally in the singular).

1957 JN, Oona not sweeping out now. *Ibid*, Ono straighten de line. 1958 DeC StE, see SPREE, vb.

3. You, one (indefinite pronoun). *BL*

1957 DeC StE /uni kyaan kaal im niem/ *One can't call his name.*

uoda /óda, úoda, wúoda/ sb dial; etym unknown. (The folk pronunc would exactly represent StdE *odour*, but no connection has been demonstrated.) An unidentified tree: see quots.

1952 FGC StAnn /oda/ white lancewood [*Xylopia glabra*] is called /oda/ here—splits easily, pliable, used to wattle huts. StE /uoda, wuoda/ to make wattle; ? sweet-wood. Tre /uoda/ big tree, good for /wakl/ and post.

uol krebe sb dial; <*old*+*krebe*, a legacy.

1958 DeC Port /uol krebe/ old and ragged work clothes.

uonggl see *onggl*.

uonyan sb dial; var pronunc of *onion*. *BL*

1952 FGC Port, StC, StE /úonyan, húonyan/.

uovn /úovn/ sb dial; a common pronunc of *oven*. *BL*

1952 FGC StAnd /úovn/; also /húovn/.

UP /op/ adv and prep chiefly dial.

A. adv: Frequently added to verbs, participles, and adjectives with incremental or intensifying effect. *BA BL G*

1873 Rampini 121, But Annancy lash him up the more, till Tiger gallop. 1927 Beckwith 28, For swelling 'rub up' the leaf and bind on the affected part. 1942 Bennett 34, Counta yuh Jane teck grudgeful An' pwile up Fan new clothes. [*Because of you, Jane became spiteful and utterly spoiled Fan's new clothes*]. 1943 *GL* StAnd, Harris up [harass], tire up. 1956 Mc Man /di man biedid op/ *The man has a beard*; StAnd /get lili sinting rob op yosef/ *Get something to rub yourself with.* 1957 JN StJ, It name Guinea Pepper, a it first dark up when de rain goin start.

B. prep: Up at, up to. (Also in lower-class London usage. LeP.) *G*

1957 JN (What does your father do?) Him is a police. Up Crawle. 1957 JN, Up tailor mi should go but him send mi up Miss Sheila.

UPLIFTING TABLE sb cant. In the language of Revival cults: see quot.

1953 Moore 108–9 [The fifth type of Revival service:] Up-lifting table, 'To seek the promotion of understanding and prophecy'.

UPSTAIRS sb; evid abbr of *upstairs house*, *OED* B a 2. A two-storey house (i.e. one with an upstairs). *BA BL G*

1924 Beckwith 116, And she made a house with a hundred doors and a hundred windows and a large staircase; and the house is an upstairs, an' there both of them live. 1952 FGC StAnn, An upstairs—a two-storey house. 1958 DeC /yu sii wan uol opstierz de a kaana/ *You see an old two-storey house on the corner.*

URA interrog or rel pron dial arch or obs; prob analogical to *wara*. =WHOORA. *BL*

1943 *GL* West, Ura, who.

USEN vb dial; <*use* (for *used*, past tense) + -*n* suffix[2]. Cf *fishn, courtn*, etc. Used; was or were in the habit. *BA G*

1900 Murray 16, When de mout recober de blow it tun a sort of a red like, so dem boy usen fe call him 'red mout' grunt'. 1962 BLB 73 /yuuzn/ used.

USUAL /yuuzhal, yuujal/ adj or vb dial. (To be) habituated, in the habit.

1907 Jekyll 145, Tacoma usual to go an' knock it. 1912 McK *Songs* 38, De man who was usual to worry me life. 1941 Kirkpatrick 38, Man run twice as fas' as 'im ujual fe run w'en big 'fraid tek 'im.

VALANGHANNA sb obs; <Sp *berenjena*. Cf *OED verangene*. The egg-plant. Cf BOLANGENA.

1725 Sloane 377, This [*sc Solanum pomiferum*] is call'd Valanghanna in Jamaica by the Vulgar. 1774 Long 772, Brownjolly, Valinghanna, or Mad Apple. 1811 Titford 53, see EGG FRUIT.

VANGLA, VANGLO(E) see WANGLA.

VASSAL'S GRASS sb; see first quot. An unidentified grass.

a1818 Lewis (1834) 250, Many years ago, a new species of grass was imported into Jamaica, by Mr Vassal (to whom an estate near my own then belonged), as he said 'for the purpose of feeding his pigs and his book-keepers'. Its seeds being soon scattered about by the birds, it has taken possession of the cane-pieces, whence to eradicate it is an utter impossibility. . This nuisance, which is called 'Vassal's grass', from its original introducer, has now completely overrun the parish of Westmoreland. 1885 Brassey 262, The greater part of it was a coarse-looking but sweet herbage, called Vassal's grass.

VEGETABLE MARROW sb obs; cf *OED marrow* 3b [1763], 1866. The AVOCADO pear.

1788 Marsden 78, The Alicada. . is the fruit, the inside of which Sir Hans Sloane calls the vegetable marrow, and indeed it is equally good, as nutritive, and more pleasant to the taste than the finest marrow. [Not found in Sloane edd 1696, 1707, 1725.] a1818 Lewis (1845) 107, One of the best vegetable productions of the island is esteemed to be the Avogada pear, sometimes called 'the vegetable marrow'. . I could find no great merit in them.

VEGETABLE SULPHUR sb obs; *OED* 1855. A species of fungus or club moss; see quot.

1756 Browne 79, Clavaria Oblonga pulvere luteo referta. . This plant is frequent enough in the parish of Clarendon, and generally called the vegetable sulphur from the colour of its dust and seeds.

VELVET BUR sb bot; *OED* 1866. The wild plant *Priva lappulacea*, with burs having a velvet-like surface.

1756 Browne 116, see STYPTIC BUR. 1774 Long III 759. 1864 Grisebach 788. 1954 *WIMJ* 25, see CLAMMY BUR.

VELVET BUSH sb dial. =VELVET LEAF.

1953 *WIMJ* 251, *Cissampelos pareira*. . Velvet Leaf or Bush; False Pareira-brava.

VELVET LEAF sb; *OED* 1707→. The climbing shrub *Cissampelos pareira*, used in a number of folk remedies: see quots. Also attrib.

1696 Sloane 85, Clematis baccifera, glabra & villosa. . Velvet leaf. 1756 Browne 357, Cissampelos 1. . The Velvet-Leaf. . This plant is looked upon as an excellent diuretic, and in frequent use among the negroes in all obstructions of the urinary passages; but it has not been yet much known among the whites. 1893 Sullivan 113, Velvet Leaf Tea. Boil some leaves with some wild parsley . . [etc.]. 1914 Fawcett 193, *C. pareira*. . Velvet Leaf, Pareira Brava. 1952 FGC StAnd, StM, StT, Tre /velvit liif/ run like wis; round leaf, young leaf have back like velvet. 1958 DeC Clar /velvet liif/ a creeper with a very small leaf and velvety texture, used in obeah practice.

VELVET SEED(S) sb; *OED* 1866.

1. The tree *Guettarda elliptica*, and its fruit or seeds, of velvety texture.

1864 Grisebach 788, Velvet-seed: *Guettarda elliptica*. 1936 Fawcett 58, Velvet Seed.

2. The tree *Quiina jamaicensis*.

1926 Fawcett 205, *Q. jamaicensis*. . Velvet Seeds, Mountain Bay.

VENDUE sb obs; cf *OED vendue room* 1828. A building in which slaves were sold.

1823 *Koromantyn* 121, Above eight hundred [slaves]. . were seated on the floor of two spacious galleries of a large building called the vendue.

VENUS LIZARD sb obs; see quot: if Hill is right, the form 'Venus' is folk-etym. The GREEN GUANA lizard, *Anolis garmani*.

1851 Gosse 142, The Venus Lizard. The first time I met with that fine Iguaniform Lizard. . called Venus* by the negroes, and sometimes Green Guana, was on this ridge. . *This name has probably no allusion to the Goddess of beauty. Mr Hill writes to me as follows: 'The brilliant green Lizard you speak of is usually called the Green Venus. *Venus* in this case I take to be an Indian word; for I found it,—in a district of St Domingo (Yasica) in which all the rivers had Indian names,—as the name of one of the streams. We have an Indian name for another of our Lizards in *Iguana*'.

VERANDA(H)ED adj; *OED* a1818. Provided with a veranda; constructed like a veranda.

a1818 Lewis (1845) 42, The whole house is virandoed with shifting Venetian blinds to admit air.

VERBENE sb obs; anglicized <*verbena*; *OED* 1533. Cf VERVINE. Verbena.

1679 Trapham 99, Such a like discharge [of dropsical humour] the Herb Verbene, of which great store is to be found in Jamaica. . effecteth.

VERRYVINE see VERVINE.

VERVAIN HUMMING-BIRD sb; *OED* 1865. The smallest Jamaican humming-bird, *Mellisuga minima*.

1847 Gosse 127 *et seq*, Vervain Humming-Bird. . I have ventured to give to the present species a new appellation, derived from its habit of buzzing over the low herbaceous plants of pastures, which our other species do not. The West Indian vervain (*Stachytarpheta*) is one of the most common weeds in neglected pastures. 1936 Bond 217, Vervain Hummingbird. . Local names:—Doctor Bird; Little Doctor Bird. 1956 Jeffrey-Smith 25.

VERVINE sb; *OED*: 16–18th cent var of *vervain*, →1802. The vervain of Jamaica: *Stachytarpheta jamaicensis*, much valued as a TEA and in other folk remedies.

1756 Browne 116–7, Verbena 1. . The larger erect Vervine . . [etc.—used for 5 of the 6 kinds of Verbena listed]. 1893 Sullivan 112, Vervine tea. The leaves of the vervine plant the people use as a refreshing morning tea sweetened to taste. 1927 Beckwith 29, Verryvine (vervain). . For a purge, boil and give 9 mornings. 1952 FGC Han, Port, StAnn, StC, StT /vorvain/; Tre /voivain/—when you're hard to operate /fi porj blod an sochi-laik/.

VEX vb dial; for *vexed*; a 'corrected' form. =BEX. *BA G T*

1862 Clutterbuck 53, 'Don't vex', replied Leander [a negro groom], smiling. 1956 Mc StE /bot wái di man véks so/ *Why is the man so angry?*

VEXY adj dial; <VEX vb+-*y*, with the force of *-like* or *-ish*. Angryish, annoyed. *G*

1956 Mc Man /im get véksi/ *He became annoyed.*

VICTORY sb dial. A manner of cutting a man's hair so that it forms a V. (Current after Second World War.)

1952 FGC StM.

VIGE sb dial; prob an overcorrection (*v* for *b*) of BIGE, bag. See quots.

1943 *GL* StAnd, Vige, stealing; StAnn, Vige, something stolen.

VINC'N see *vinsen*.

VINEGAR MUMMA sb dial; for *vinegar mother*, mould that produces vinegar; *OED vinegar sb* 6 →1853.

1952 FGC Tre /víniga múma—dat iz di mada fi di viniga/.

VINE GUNGO PEA sb ?dial. See quot; if this is a folk term (as seems likely) it is joc—see COWITCH and GUNGO PEA.

1920 Fawcett 54, *Mucuna pruriens*. . Cowhage, Cowitch, Vine Gungo Pea.

VINE-SORREL sb bot. An alternative name for the SORREL VINE, *Cissus acida*.

a 1726 Barham (1794) 275, Cissus acida. . The vine sorrel. 1774 Long III 804, The Climbing, or Vine-sorrel. . This plant is very common in the woods, and raises itself to a considerable height with the help of the neighbouring shrubs. . The leaf. . has a very sharp sour taste like sorrel. 1814 Lunan II 262, Vine-Sorrel. 1864 Grisebach 788.

VING-VANG sb dial; prob echoic. See quot.

1943 *GL* Tre, Ving-vang, spinning toy made from a pear-stone [i.e. avocado pear seed].

vinsen sb dial; abbr. ST VINCENT YAM.

1954 LeP StAnn, StE, St Vincent yam—Vinc'n, Vinsen. 1956 Mc StE /vinsen/.

VIRANDOED see VERANDA(H)ED.

VIRGINIA BREADNUT sb bot obs. =JAMAICA WALNUT.

1811 Titford xvi, One sort [of *Juglans*] grows at Guanaboa . . with four nuts, which taste like a filbert, called by some, Virginia bread nut.

VISCID BROOMWEED sb bot obs; cf BROOMWEED. In Macfadyen's use: *Bastardia bivalvis* (ident 1926 Fawcett 121).

1837 Macfadyen 84, Sida viscosa. *Viscid Broom-weed.*

VISIT (ONE'S) INDIAN COUSIN vb phr dial joc. To get one's hair straightened: see quot.

1947 U.Newton II 2, Then comes the First Press. . That's the process whereby a heated iron comb is applied to the African kinks, producing nearly straight Indian Hair. That is why we girls say 'We are going to visit our Indian Cousins' instead of 'Going to the Hairdresser'.

vitl see BICKLE.

VOON-VAP vb dial; phonosymbolic. To play an organ badly.

1943 *GL* Kgn, Voon-vap. 1955 FGC Man /vum-vap/.

VOOPS /vups/ adv dial; cf BAPS, *flups*, and perh Engl *whoop(s)* (said when something unexpected suddenly happens), of which this may be a Vellerism.

1. A sound suggesting suddenness, or imitating sudden movement—e.g. of dashing away. *G T*

1943 *GL* Kgn, Voops, a quick sound; Voops, to disappear [i.e. suddenly]. 1950 Pioneer 32, Anancy start gwan bad an haul off de clothes dem offa Patto. As de clothes dem come off soh 'voops', a whole heap a feader fly ova Patto.

2. See quot.

1943 *GL*, Voops, an exclamatory expression showing satisfaction.

VOOTA /vuta/ sb dial; cf Ko *vuta*, sweet potato. Yam that has run wild.

1943 *GL* Port, Voota, St Vincent yam. 1954 LeP Port, Voota, Yellow yam dug in woods where someone has had a field some years previously; wild yam. 1956 Mc Port /vuta/ yellow yam gone wild.

vum-vap see VOON-VAP.

WA[1], WE[1] /wa, we/ pron dial; <*what* (cf northwest Engl dial form *wha*—*EDD*). Dial spellings: *wa, wah, wha*; *way, whé, weh, whey, wey*; cf also *wara*. *BL G T*

1. What. (Introductory interrog pron.)

1877 Murray *Kittle* 22, But maam, wha de good a all him 'complish an him no hab no sense? 1905 Dodd 12, A wah it good for? 1907 Jekyll 51, That's why I ask whé you name. 1956 Mc Man /a wá máta wíd im/ *What's the matter with him?* StAnd /wa yu se/ *What did you say?* /we mi fi du/ *What am I to do?*

2. What, which, who. (Relative pron.)

1877 Murray *Kittle* 5, Him is a regilar wa dem call *bosify Bony*. 1905 Dodd 11, But ah curious to know whey you travel dis way fur. *Ibid*, But weh me hav, you welcome to. 1941 Kirkpatrick 23, De steam motor cyar wey use fe explode widouten summuch as axin parden. 1956 Mc Man /him ha wán kóu we gí tén kwáat a mílk/ *He has a cow which gives ten quarts*. . ; /si-i human de we heng gi mi di maanggo/ *That's the woman who gave me the mango.*

WA[2], WE[2] interrog adv dial; <*where*. Dial spellings: *we, whe, wey, wha*. Where. . ?

1877 Murray *Kittle* 22, 'Den wha him jackass'. 'Him no hab none, missis.' 1924 Beckwith 26, Anansi. . said, 'whe' yo' get dat nasty t'ing from?' 1956 Mc StAnd /sis, wa plomi de/ *Sis, where is Plummy?* /a we dem a go/ *Where are they going?* /a we hunu ben de laas nait/ *Where were you (two) last night? BL G T* (WE)

waan vb auxil dial; <*want*. Should; do(es). *G*

1942 Bennett 47, Nuff bur-bur an' dutty all ovah him clothes. You wahn se 'ow him tan! [*You should see the condition he's in!*] 1952 FGC StAnd /injin kiel waan fieva koko/ *Indian kale looks like coco*; StC, Chinee yam grows a bunch of small ones /waan bier laik pinda/; StJ /wiliks; waan fieva suolja/ *Whelk looks like soldier-crab.*

WAANFU see next.

waang-fu vb, adj, and sb dial; <*want-food*. To hang about in the hope of being given food (sb, one who hangs about so; adj, of the kind that hangs about so); hence, undernourished (person). *G*

1943 *GL* Clar, Wanfoo, loaf for food; Waanfu, wait upon; Waunfo, hanker for food; Waunfou, to visit a person regularly at meal-times. Kgn, Wang-foo, sponging for food. 1955 FGC Man /waang-fu/ wanting food; /maaga/.

waantn sb dial; cf *OED wanty*, of which this is the Scot and Nth form: →1837. A rope passed all the way around a donkey and its load to hold the latter in place. Also attrib.

[1823 Roughley 160, There should be a strong wanty, of good length, likewise platted as the girths, to each mule.] 1943 *GL* Clar, Waunton, a long rope used in girthing load on an animal. Tre, Wanton, rope to steady load on animal's back. 1955 FGC Man /wáantn/. 1956 Mc StT /waantn ruop/.

waata krishiz, krisi, kushi see WATER CRISSY.

waat-melan sb dial; <*watermelon*. A common pronunc of *watermelon*. (In some forms the early and still widespread variant *-million* is also found. See *DA*.)

1952 FGC StAnd, StE, StJ /wáat-mélan/; Port, StC /wáat-mílan/.

waay, waay-uo int dial; perh <*waa, wae, woi*, Scot and Nth Engl forms of *woe*, int (cf *OED*) +*oh* or the prolonged *o* common in Ja folk-songs, esp at end of line, and in exclamatory portions: cf Twi *óò*. Dial sp: *wahi, whai, whoy, wi, woeyo, woio, woy*. *BL G*; *SC woi*.

1. Exclamation of pain, fright, surprise, sorrow.

1826 Williams 189, And make de buckra man cry *woio*. 1873 Rampini 127, 'Wi! O me moder me dead!'*..*An exclamation implying great fear and personal danger. 1877 Murray *Feedin' 'Perrit* 8, As I put de mug to my head—woy, I blige to pit [spit] it out. 1942 Bennett 43, Ah beg yuh pardon Carpi, lawd!..Wahi lady Come beg femme noh mah! 1943 *GL* Clar, Woeyo, oh my. 1951 Murray 40, Whai oh! Judy drownded.

2. Exclamation of great amusement, exultation, excitement.

1943 *GL* West, Whoy—joyful laughing. 1950 Pioneer 32, Whai, bwoy! As soon as de gal dem hear fe Patto sweet song dem run wey leff Anancy an crowd roun' Patto.

wa brok? interrog phr dial; <WA[1]+*brok* vb. What's going on? (Cf WA MEK?)

1959 FGC StE, Wha bruk? Used only in sense of festive activity. District where used—Potsdam. [Also elsewhere. FGC.]

WACKA-TAC sb dial; etym unknown.

1943 *GL* Kgn, Wacka-tac, disagreeable person.

WACKLE see WATTLE.

WACKY sb dial rare; etym unknown.

1907 Jekyll 101, Wacky, guava.

WA-FI-DO, wa-fi-du see *we-fi-du*. *G*

WAGATY adj dial; cf Yoruba *wágawàga*, clumsy, and *-ty, suffix*[1] (*OED*).

1943 *GL* Port, Wagaty, clumsy.

WAGA-WAGA adj and adv dial; etym unknown, prob Afr. Plentiful; plentifully.

1943 *GL* Kgn, Waga-waga, plenty; Wagga-whagga, Having things plentifully; StT, Wagga-wagga, plentiful. 1955 Bennett *Gawn a match*, Dem nagwine get a kemps more a Me wagga-wagga bickle.

WAGGA-WAGGA, ~-WHAGGA see prec.

WAGGON sb dial; cf *tea waggon*.

1956 Mc Man /wagan/ A dresser with several open shelves on which glasses, plates, etc are kept. Not mobile.

WAGGONETTE sb; cf WAGGON. *G*

1956 Mc Man /wagnat/ a dresser with open shelves above for plates, etc, with cupboard underneath.

wagnat see prec.

WAH see WA, WE.

WAHI see *waay*.

wail see WHILE, WILD, WILE.

waild baazli see WILD BASIL.

wail paip sb dial; <an uncert element, perh a var of QUAIL 2, referring to drinking +*pipe*. The Adam's-apple; but perh taken to be the swallowing-tube: cf RUM-BUMP.

1956 Mc Man, Adam's apple—/wail paip/ also /bomp-a-chuot/.

wais see WHILST. *G*

WAITING-BOY sb obs; *DAE* 1811→. A youth who waits on a gentleman; a personal attendant. Cf BARRACOUTA, SNAKE WAITING-BOY.

1798 Evidence, He attended me as a waiting-boy, and he is about 15 years of age.

WAIT (UP)ON vb phr; cf old-fashioned Engl and sth US usage. To wait for, delay for, attend the arrival of. *BL G*

1950 Pioneer 36, Anancy put de iron pot over him head an goh eena him bed fe wait pon Wasp. (Current, FGC.)

WAJA sb dial rare; etym unknown.

1943 *GL* Kgn, Waja, plant of the coco family, also called toya.

WAKE see SET-UP. *G*

WAKEE sb obs; etym unknown. An African 'tribal' or language name; a slave of this origin.

1825 Bickell 46, Sarah, a Wakee, 5 ft. 1 in. no brandmark.

WALA-WALA see WALLA-WALLA.

WALK sb; cf *OED sb*[1] 10c 1793→. A grove, usually planted, of trees, usually fruit trees but others also; cf separate entries: BANANA~, CHOCOLATE~, CITRUS~, COCOA~, COFFEE~, GUNGO~, PEAR~, PEAS~, PIMENTO~, PLANTAIN~, PRICKLE~, THATCH~. *BL G N*

p 1660 State of Jamaica 611, Cocoa of w[ch] this Island hath many large Walkes. 1756 Browne 248, [Pimento] is now cultivated, with great care, in many parts of the island, where it is planted in regular walks. 1774 Long I 495, Pimento walks..6000 acres. 1823 Koromantyn 84, These pimento groves are, in Jamaica, called *walks*. 1950 Pioneer 84 [Song:] Mattie run a mile and half in a Gungo Walk. 1952 FGC Man, In citrus walk, snails now used to clean trees.

WALK vb dial. *BA*

1. Of people: Used where Std Engl would ordinarily use 'come' or 'go'. *G*

1956 Mc Man /yu beta waak dis en/ *You'd better go this way*; StE /kom ier son—waak kom/ *Come here, son! Come!*

2. Of things that have no feet: to go.

1956 Mc StAnd /di bed hav tuu skruu—it kyan jos waak rait op/ *The bed has two screws—it can fold up*; StE /di ruod waak dong iina di goli/ *The road goes down into the gully*; StE [Of the funnel in a fish-pot:] /a we di fish waak go in/ *It's where the fish go in.*

WALK-AND-DROP sb dial. A limping person, whose gait is normal on one foot, light on the other. Cf JUCK-CUM-PENG.

1954 LeP StT, Waak-an-drap, man who limps.

WALK AND LANCE vb phr; cf *OED lance v* 2: To bound, spring, move quickly, rush.. *obs* exc *dial*, →1883.

1956 Mc Man /waak an laans/ To stride out, take long steps.

WALK-AND-NYAM sb dial. One who lives off others; a sponger.

1835 Madden I 92, On foot if he is only a poor walkand-nyam—a very significant negroism for a white man who has the sin of poverty and pedestrianism to answer for in Jamaica. [Cf WALKING BUCKRA.] 1894 Banbury 43, Walk an nyam:—One who goes about sponging on his neighbours, and will not work for his own support. 1925 Beckwith 112, Walk an' nyam..i.e. a sponger. 1962 BLB 72 /waak-an-nyam/.

WALK-'BOUT adj and sb dial. Wandering, straying; a person who does not stay at anything. *G*

1927 Anderson-Cundall 96, Walk-bout potato nebber bear. 1943 *GL* StJ, Walk-'bout, an unsteady person.

WALK DANDY-DUDE see DANDY DUDE.

WALK FOOT vb phr and ppl adj; <*walk* vb + aphetic form of *afoot*. **s.**

A. vb phr: To go afoot. *G*

1900 Murray 4, Yes squire, I walk foot from Lucea, chock to tung (Kingston).

B. ppl adj: Going afoot, pedestrian. (Cf WALKING BUCKRA.)

1873 Rampini 51, Women..washing clothes in the stream ..or a 'walk-foot buckra' resting under a tree. 1956 BLB Man /a trak fi walk-fut piipl/.

WALK GOOD! int or vb phr dial. A goodbye exclamation: Safe journey! (Used on ordinary occasions, not necessarily for long journeys.)

1929 Beckwith 199, 'Walk good, me love', says one to another setting out on a journey. 1958 FGC StAnd /waak gud/! *BL G N*; *SC wákka boen.*

WALKING BUCKRA sb arch or obs. See quot.

1828 Marly 45, Marly, not having yet procured a horse, he in consequence could not accompany them; no disgrace being considered so great in the island as that of a white man being seen walking on foot when away from his home. No person does it, but such as have forfeited their character and situation, and who, in consequence, are styled walking buckras, a name, synonimous to beggar, coupled with that of vagabond.

WALKING FERN sb. The fern *Thelypteris reptans*: see quot.

1943 *NHN* I 12 10, Then there is the Walking Fern which literally 'goes places'. The tip of a lead bends over and takes root in the ground and forms a new plant.

WALKING-SAAL sb dial joc; <*walking* ppl adj + *saal*, salt provisions, meat.

1943 *GL*, Walking-sawl, crab.

WALKING TRAIN sb dial. A local train.

1921 Frank 414, In the island dialect a local train is a 'walkin' train', and all Jamaican trains fall into this category.

WALLAH see next.

WALLA(-WALLA) /wala/ vb dial; <*wallow*, also iterated. See also *SND* WALLER.

1. To mix up something, or mix together things that are more or less liquid. *G*

1943 *GL* Port, Wallah, to mix with; StAnn, Walla, mixed. 1955 FGC Man, In mixing a cake, you 'walla it up'.

2. To smear something partly liquid upon; to smear with something partly liquid. *G*

1943 *GL* Kgn, Walla, to rub over; Kgn, Wall-walla, to handle all over; Tre, Walla walla, plaster.

3. To wash.

1943 *GL* Clar, StAnn, Walla, wash; Tre, Wala-wala, to wash. 1957 Bennett 92, Tercentenary Bush Bath an Walla walla committee.

4. To roll about. *BL G*

1956 BLB StJ /a-wé unu lóv wála wála unuséf an di fluor so?/ *Why do you all like to roll about on the floor so much?*

WALL-OKRO sb dial; <*wall* + OKRO 2. A climbing cactus which runs along stone walls and has a mucilaginous juice.

1952 FGC Tre /waal-okro/.

WALNUT sb.

1. The Jamaican walnut, *Picrodendron baccatum.*

1952 FGC StM /waal not/ on tree; pop them, grate, make oil.

2. The physic nut, *Jatropha* spp.

1952 FGC Port /waal not/ physic nut; bleeds at Easter time.

wa mek vb phr dial; elliptical for some such phr as *what makes it* (*that*), and in the pattern of such an expression as Ibo *gɛ nɛ mɛrɛ*, what makes, why? *G*

1. What is happening or going on?

1954 LeP StAnd, Wa mek? What are you doing?

2. Why? *BL*

1953 *GL* Port, Wamekso, why. 1954 Mc StE /wa mek dem de se so/ *Why do they say that?* 1955 Bennett *Over London*, Sometime me want ask a question, Wich part, wa meck, why or who.

WAMPARA /wámpara/ sb dial; <Cuban Sp *guampara*. A MACHETE; the word is applied to various sizes and shapes—see quot 1958. *BA*

1943 *GL* Kgn, StM, Wamparra, a kind of machete; cane knife; StJ, Wampara, A short cutlass for cutting cane tops. 1954 LeP Man, StAnn, Machete with hooked end —Wampera, Wampara, Wamparra. 1956 Mc Man, StAnd, StT /wámpara/ heavy machete with broad blunt end (cane bill); two-sided machete; machete with hooked end. 1958 DeC /wampara/ This cutlass name is known almost everywhere in Jamaica but with very uncertain meaning. Sometimes it is a general term. Informants have applied it to [most of the shapes]. The name usually carries a connotation of a heavy and broad cutlass, usually an old fashioned one..Many informants did not volunteer the term, but when suggested they remembered its use long ago.

WAMPARRA, WAMPERA see prec.

WAMPUS adj dial; cf US *catawampus*, imaginary fierce (and strong) animal.

1956 LeP StE /wat a wampas man/ big, stout.

WANDERER (**CANE**) sb dial. A variety of sugar-cane.

1952 FGC StJ /wándara/ cane—tough, straight.

WANFOO see *waang-fu*.

WANGA /wangga/ vb dial; cf YANGA. See quot.

1956 Mc Man /wangga/ to dance à la West Indies (shoulders raised, arms moving). A vulgar style of walking.

WANG-FOO see *waang-fu.*

wangga see WANGA.

WANGILA see next.

WANGLA /wánggla/ occas /wánggra/ sb now dial; 1756→ vanglo, 1801 1820 vangloe, 1817 vangla; [a 1726 (1794) wolongo], 1774 wongala, 1817→ wangla, 1823 wangola, 1835 whangra, 1895 wanglo; <Kongo *wangila.* Cf *OED vanglo* 1756→. *BL*

1. The small climbing *Sesamum orientale,* formerly valued for its oily seeds and other parts. Also called HOCKALENAH, OIL PLANT, VANGLOE.

[1696 Sloane 140, Laburnum humilius, siliquâ inter grana & grana junctâ, semine esculento. Another kind of Peason called Wandos of Battell.] a 1726 Barham (1794) 121–2, see SOONGA. 1756 Browne 270, The Vanglo.. These plants were introduced to Jamaica by the Jews, and are now cultivated in most parts of the island: the seeds are frequently used in broths, by many of our Europeans; but the Jews make 'em chiefly into cakes. 1774 Long III 809, Vanglo, Wongala, or Oil-plant. 1801 Dancer 362, Vangloe (*Sesamum*).—Emulsion of the seeds. 1823 Roughley 416–17, The wangola..whose leaf, when steeped for a short time in water,..makes it of a mucous, glutinous quality, and is deemed an excellent medicine in case of flux or dysentery. 1893 Sullivan 81, The natives make a sugar cake with..a bean called 'wangla'. 1952 FGC Tre /wánggla/—run like wis, grow like yam; if a tief go a grong, it wind off, drop off stick, and you know say tief go a you grong. StE /wánggla/ use to season up soup; also parch, beat, add sugar, sit and eat.

2. A sugar cake made with wangla seeds; also, latterly, one made with nuts—peanuts, cashew nuts. (The wangla seeds themselves are hardly used any more.)

1893, see quot above. 1942 Bennett 10, Candy Seller.. Nice young man come here, what you want? Pinda-cake, wangla? 1943 *GL* Clar, Kgn, Wangla, a peanut cake containing wangla seeds; StT, Wangra, a kind of candy. 1952 FGC Port, StM /wàngglá/ cakes of hard sugar with peanuts, formerly with wangla seeds.

3. The plant or its seeds as used in obeah practices: cf BURN WANGLA. (This is sometimes confused with *wanga,* in the French Antilles *ouanga,* witchcraft.) Also Gullah *waŋga*—1949 Turner 203.

1835 Madden II 88, A plant called whangra, used by obeah men, is of a deleterious quality. 193- Doris Evelyn *Empire Review* April. (Ref lost.)

WANGOLA, WANGRA see WANGLA.

WANIKA sb dial; etym obscure: evid a proper name (one implying fierce temper, toughness?). Cf Turner 177, Gullah personal name (woman) *wanika.* **s.**

1. A woman's name: see quots. *G*

a 1818 Lewis (1845) 71, A little fierce young devil of a Miss Whaunica flew at his [the driver's] throat, and endeavoured to strangle him. 1877 Murray *Kittle* 27, Yerry dem Eboe fellow—'Broke Whanica Penny comb Kill de debil moder Kill de debil moder'. [*Breaking Whanica's penny comb killed* (or *will kill*) *the devil's mother.*]

2. The tree *Matayba apetala,* or CROMANTY.

1926 Fawcett 55–6, Wanika. 1941 Swabey 18, Cobywood (Cromanty, Bastard Mahogany, Redwood, Wanika, Comanancy). *Matayba apetala.* 1952 FGC StAnn, StE, StM, StT /wánika/.

WANT see *waan.*

WANTON, WANTY see *waantn.*

wap[1], **wap-wap** sb and vb dial; *OED whop v,* to strike with heavy blows →1905. In senses somewhat diff from those of StdE: see quots. *BL G*

1943 *GL* Clar, Whap-whap, to flog or flogging. 1956 Mc StE /ing wop ing wi naif/ *He struck him with a knife.* /dem wap aaf guot hed/ *They chopped off Goat's head.*

wap[2] vb dial. A var form of GWAP.

1943 *GL* Kgn, Wop, eat greedily. 1956 Mc StAnd /wap i doun/ *to drink fast.*

wap[3] abbr of WAPPEN-BAPPEN. *G*

wapi sb dial; <*wap*[1] + *y,* familiarizing suffix.

1. A game of cards (quot 1958); also, in that game, a certain card (quot 1955). Also one of the tickets in DROP-PAN. *G*

1943 *GL,* Wappie, a game of cards. Kgn, Woppy, drop pan term. 1955 FGC Man /wapi/ in gambling with cards: the same number card (for example, 5) thrown by a second person. 1958 DeC StAnd, StT /wapi/ a game of cards in which each player is dealt six cards and one card is turned up; players alternately discard, the object being to go out first; players must either follow suit or follow number.

2. Sexual intercourse.

1958 DeC Clar /mi tuu taiad fi wapi tináit/. [Song:] /mada mek a luk mi wapi/.

WAPPEN-BAPPEN /wápm-bápm/ sb dial slang; prob phonosymbolic, suggesting the hammering-together of old tin, wood, etc. Cf *wap*[1], BAPS. A slum 'house' of one small room, made of miscellaneous pieces of wood and metal.

1936 Martinez in *Gleaner* 3 Oct 35, 'Ah deh go a mi wap' ..Banana Bertie was referring to his home, better known as a 'Wappen Bappen' to the wild gentry who reside in the more remote regions of Back O' Wall and Ackee Walk ..A 'Wappen-Bappen' is a tenement room, chiefly made of old packing cases, flattened out kerosene tins, old tar paper, orange box shooks, and even crocus bags. 1943 *GL* StAnd, Wappen bappen, a house of the slums; Whapm Bappm. 1955 FGC Man /wapm-bapm/ a shanty.

wara pron dial; <*what* + A[8]. A word early noticed by recorders of the dial: it represents the substitution of flapped *-r* for *t,* found widely in English speech; the African element is in addition of *-a. BL*

1. What, in all StdE senses. (Still in use in conservative areas.)

1826 Barclay 239, see *maasa-niega.* 1833 Foulks 45, Da wharrah make you bawl like a cow? 1868 Russell 14, Wara = wat or what, is now nearly obsolete. 1873 Rampini 118, 'Warra!' cried Tiger, 'who tell you dis one great big lie?' 1943 *GL* most parishes, Warra, what; Warra dah, what is that. 1956 Mc Man /a wara dwiim/ *What is the matter with him?* StAnd /wa yu se, wara/ *What did you say? What?*

2. Who. (Phonologically irreg; prob by analogy to 1.)

1943 *GL* Tre, Wara, who. 1956 Mc /a wara sii im wen im tiif di pitieta dem/?

wara-wara sb dial; iterative from *wara,* what, but coinciding with *were-were.* Miscellaneous small things, indefinite but fussy.

1950 Pioneer 56, Li kench a dis, li kemps a dat, Li chenks a warra-warra. [*Little bits of this, little pieces of that, Little bits of whatever-it-is.*]

wari sb dial arch; <Twi *wàre,* Fante *ɔware,* a game played with small balls moved in holes in a board. Nickers or nikals (see NICKAR)—used in playing the game. *BA*

1952 FGC StAnn /wari/ called them so in Portland as a boy—in StAnn & Tre called /nikal/.

WARIFY /wáarifai/ adj dial; <*war*+-IFY. Ready for 'war'; extremely angry.

1873 Rampini 126, Hi! but him well warify (in a great passion) when him yerry dis. 1962 BLB 72 /waarifai/ always ready for battle.

WARM FIRE vb phr dial; abbr. To warm oneself at the fire. Cf WARM SUN; also Fr Créole *sjofe dife*, ~*soley*, and Island Carib, 1650→1947 (Douglas Taylor).

1907 Jekyll 4, Negro..To warm fire. English..To warm oneself by the fire. [Note by A. Werner:] 'To warm fire' reminds one of the Bantu *Ku ot a moto*, of which it is almost a literal translation.

WARM-MOUTH sb dial; cf WASH-MOUTH. The first meal of the day.

1956 Mc StAnd /waam-mout/ 4 to 6 a.m., followed by breakfast at about 8 a.m.

WARM SUN vb phr dial; abbr. To warm oneself in the sun. Cf WARM FIRE.

1956 BLB Man /mek mi kyaa yu guop a baabikyu go waam son no/ *Let me take you up to the barbecue to warm (ourselves) in the sun.*

WARM-WARM sb dial; iterative from *warm*. Warmth; higher temperature than normal.

1956 BLB StJ /wen im tiidin im hav a likl waam-waam somtaim/ *When he's teething he sometimes becomes a little feverish.*

WARPO adj dial; perh based on *wap* (cf *whopping*, *whopper*), but cf Sp *guapo*, bold, ostentatious in manner.

1943 *GL* Kgn, Warpo, large.

WARRA, WARRA-WARRA see *wara*, *wara-wara*.

WARRIOR SHEPHERD sb dial cant. An officer of Revivalist cults, sometimes called 'captain': see quot.

1953 Moore 84–5, Warrior Shepherd..It is his duty to 'war the bounds', which means to protect the area being used for the service. He protects the service from human intervention and (evil) spiritual intrusion.

WART-BUSH sb dial; cf *OED wart-weed*. Any wild plant or 'milkweed' having milky juice, which is used to remove warts.

1952 FGC Han /waat-bush/ male milkweed; StT, milk-weed.

WART-HERB sb.

1864 Grisebach 788, Wart-herb: *Rhynchosia minima*.

WAS /woz/ vb dial. As auxiliary following the main verb and followed by an infinitive: indicating past time in the main verb. It is sometimes redundant (when past is already indicated). *BL G T*

1907 Jekyll 44, He didn' want was to receive his bite. *Ibid* 73, Annancy mean was to take away the gal from Rabbit. *Ibid* 87, Candlefly compel was to lef' without say a word. 1952 FGC Man, I had was to tell him; StC, Come back! You had was to repair the coil.

WAS see *was-was*. s WASSY.

WASH-BELLY sb dial; <*wash* vb+*belly*. The last child that a woman bears. *BL G*

1954 LeP Kgn, Man, Port, StAnn, StE, StT, Youngest child, wash-belly. 1956 Mc Man, Port, StE /wash-beli/ last child of child-bearing.

WASHERWOMAN sb. The bird BESSY KICK-UP. (Runaway Bay and vicinity.)

1956 Jeffrey-Smith 154, Northern Water Thrush, 'Washer-woman', *Seiurus noveboracensis*.

WASH-HEAD sb dial; abbr of *washed* CASSADA HEAD.

1959 DeC StJ /wash-hed/ moist, grated cassava which has been washed and wrung.

WASH-MOUTH /washmout/ sb dial joc; <*wash* vb+*mouth*. Cf WARM-MOUTH. Early morning TEA.

1943 *GL* StAnn, Wash mouth, anything eaten for tea. Tre, Washmout, food eaten in early morning. 1954 LeP StAnn, The first meal of the day, wash mout'. 1956 Mc StAnd /washmout/ first thing eaten in morning.

WASH (ONE'S) MOUTH (UPON) vb phr dial; cf *OED wash-mouth* sb, one who blabs out everything; a babbler. To say derogatory things about; to defame. *BA BL G*

1942 Bennett 19, Dah 'oman Miss Matty gwine look shame yuh se' Meck she gwan wash har mout' 'pon Nelly.

WASH-PAP sb dial; *wash* vb+*pap*. A kind of porridge made from green corn.

1952 FGC StE /wash pap/ grater green corn, use enough water to wash the grater and cook the corn, add milk and drink as porridge.

WASH SKIN vb phr dial. A phrase in which 'skin' is redundant in Std Engl. Cf BATHE (one's skin). *G*

1907 Jekyll 7, One day Annancy an' Bro'er Tiger go a river fe wash 'kin. 1910 Anderson-Cundall 1 [Prov:] De fus' time ant tas'e molasses him wash him 'kin ina it.

WASH SPAWN vb phr dial. Of BLACK CRABS (which annually 'run' from their inland haunts down to the sea for the purpose): To lay eggs.

1952 FGC StE, StJ /wash paan/.

WASH-WASH sb dial; iterative from *wash*. CASSAVA HEAD in one form or another: see quots.

1958 DeC Man /wash-wash/ the moist cassava from which the juice has been washed or pressed. 1959 DeC West /wash-wash/ here meaning any bits of cassava head which passed through the cloth during wringing; these are recovered from the starch by a second straining. *G*

WASHY adj dial; cf *OED* 6 →a 1721. Thin and sickly-looking, 'washed out'. *G*

1943 *GL* Clar, Washy, meager, sickly; Kgn, Washy, ill-looking (sickly).

WASHY sb dial; *wash* abbr +-*y*, familiarizing suffix. *G*

1. =WASH-BELLY. *BL*

1948 DeC StT /washi/ last child.

2. =WASH-WASH.

1956 Mc Man /washi/ cassava head.

WASP NEST sb dial; descr.

1958 DeC StT /waas nes/ confection of sugar and chopped coconut.

was-was sb dial; iterative from *was*, wasp. A wasp; wasps. *SC wassi-wássi*.

1877 Murray *Feedin' 'Perrit* 11, Him [a little girl] tan like him don't born good. Him wais dis faba a was-was. [*Her waist looks a wasp's.*] 1910 Anderson-Cundall 46, Was' was' buil' comb, but him can't put fat in it. 1952 FGC StT /was-was/ wasps.

wat see WHAT.

WAT-A-WAY see WHAT adv 2.

WATCH-DEAD sb dial; <*watch* vb+DEAD 1.

1958 DeC StT /wach-ded/ a funeral wake on first night.

WATCHICRACA sb obs. An unidentified bird. (Cf WATCHY-PICKET.)

1740 Importance 38, Among the curious are Flamingos, Corresoes, Cardinal Birds, Bill-Birds, Watchicracas, Canary Birds.

WATCHMAN sb.

1. A magical 'guard' put into a provision-ground to frighten thieves away. Cf PUNTEE.

1825 De la Beche 30–1, The negroes still continue to place watchmen (as they call them), in their provision grounds, though the practice is by no means so general as formerly, these are commonly composed of pieces of the wood-ant's nest, the roots of a particular grass, grave dirt, bunches of feathers, &c., either singly or together. Some people even make small boxes, resembling the coffins of infants, line them with black or white cloth, and then fill them up with earth, and very often grave dirt. These various 'watch-men' have ceased to be much attended to by the habitual plunderers of provision grounds. *BL G*

2. In the cant of kumona cults: see quot.

1953 Moore 159, The sky gods who guard the four corners of the earth [are the] Four Watchmen. They are similar to the function of the four Evangelists in Revival.

3. The piece of salt pork that is put on top of the beans in a pot or baking-dish.

1952 FGC StT.

WATCHY sb gen; familiarizing abbr of *watchman*. See *SND* WATCH II 3, WATCHIE, -Y. *BA*

1. A watchman. *G*

1943 *GL* StAnd, Watchie, watchman. 1956 LeP StAnd /wachi/ the familiar Jamaican form of watchman.

2. In the games of hide-and-whoop, hide-and-seek, etc.: The one who is 'it'.

1952 FGC Han /wachi/ The 'watchman' in the game of hide and whoop, played in water, also on land. Watchy turns his back; other boys whoop and dive. He is to catch one.

WATCHY PICKET sb ornith. The Jamaican oriole *Icterus leucopteryx.*

a 1705 Ray (1713) 184, Icterus minor nidum suspendens.. The Watchy Picket, or Spanish Nightingale [from *OED*]. 1725 Sloane 299–300, (Same). This bird was six inches long..[with] nests made of Old Mans Beard. 1847 Gosse 229, If an intruder attempt to rifle the nest when the young are there, both old birds fly round in excessive perturbation, and cry *Tom Paine's pick-a-ninny*, with vociferous shrillness..I presume this to be the *Watchy-picket* of Sloane. 1936 Bond 357, Banana Bird..; 'Watchy-picket'; Ma Katie; Auntie Katie.

WATER-APPLE sb; *OED* →1760. The ALLIGATOR APPLE, *Annona palustris.*

1696 Sloane 205, Anona aquatica..*Water-Apple*, or *Sweet-Apple*. Copiosissime crescit ad ripas fluvii *Black River* dicti prope pontem. 1725 Sloane 169, The Fruit is as big as one's Fist, turbinated like a Sour-sop..The Country people could say nothing of it but that it was edible, and called it Water, or, Sweet-Apple. 1854–5 *TJSA* I 59, Alligator or Water Apple or Cork Wood. 1952 FGC StAnn, Water-apple—like green-skin starapple.

WATER-BLABBER, ~-BLADDER sb dial; cf SEA-BLADDER. A jelly-fish.

1956 Mc Kgn.

WATER-BUCKET sb dial. A variety of sugar-cane: see quot.

1959 DeC West /wata-bokit/ name of a soft, red, especially juicy cane.

WATER-BURST /waata-bos/ sb dial; <*water* +*burst*. See quot.

1956 BLB Man, A river or stream in spate, or a road into which water has run during a shower of rain is called a /waata bos/.

WATER BUSH sb dial; <*water* sb+BUSH 3.

1952 FGC StAnd /waata-bush/ small branches with leaves, put on top of water in a container to keep it from splashing out when being carried.

WATER CABBAGE sb. An aroid water plant with leaves resembling those of the cabbage: *Pistia occidentalis.*

1943 *NHN* II 8, Water cabbage [growing on the river, with water hyacinth].

WATER COCONUT sb; cf COCONUT WATER. A coconut picked green for the sake of its water, rather than for the ripe nut meat. Cf JELLY COCONUT, in which there is still water, but the nut meat has begun to form. *BA BL G T*

c 1915 FGC StAnd. 1954 LeP StAnd.

WATER CRAB sb dial. A large, brown sea-crab.

1952 FGC StJ.

WATER CRISSY /wáata kríshiz, ~krísi, ~kúshi/ sb dial; <*water*+*cresses* (*OED*, 'Until 19 c. almost always in plural'); the folk forms result from reg loss of *-s*, change of internal *s*>*sh*, and prob further effects of folk-etym. Watercress.

1952 FGC Han /waata krisi/ watercress. 1955 *WIMJ* 159, Nasturtium fontanum..Water Cress; (Water Cushie or Crishes).

WATER-DIPPER sb dial; see quot. A large dragonfly. Cf NEEDLECASE.

1952 FGC Man, Tre /wáata dípa/ bigger than needlecase; dive at water and come up again.

WATER-DRY sb dial; <*water* sb+*dry* adj or vb; this could represent *water* sources running *dry*, or the land, people, etc. being *dry* or *drying* for lack of *water*: the syntactic relationship is not clear. Cf DRY sb. See quots.

1943 *GL* StJ, Wauta dry, thirst. 1955 FGC Man /waata-drai/ drought.

WATER-FETCHER sb dial. The smallest of a litter of pigs. (Allusion is to the first task of children in the country to fetch water to the home.) Cf *SND* WATER, *n.*, *v.* 6 (29) WATER-DROGER.

1952 FGC StAnd, StT /wáata-fécha/ undersized pig in a litter.

WATER-GRASS sb chiefly dial; <*water*+GRASS. Species of *Commelina* and *Zebrina* ('white' and 'red' water-grass)—creeping plants with juicy stems, valued in folk remedies.

1929 Beckwith 29, Water-grass. *Commelina longicaulis*.. For gonorrhoea, boil with red guava root..and drink as tea. 1952 FGC Han, Man, Port, StC, StE, StT /waata-graas/. 1954 *WIMJ* 29, *Commelina elegans*..Water Grass; *C. longicaulis*..Water Grass; French Weed. *Ibid* 32, *Zebrina pendula*..Red Water Grass. 1954 *FG* 583–4, Water Grass (*Commelina diffusa*). This plant is not a true grass. Several different kinds occur in Jamaica, most of them having small blue or white flowers. *N*

WATER HORSETAIL sb. The plant *Equisetum giganteum*, growing widely in lagoons and swamps in Jamaica.

1696 Sloane 215, Equisetum majus aquaticum..Great water Horsetail.

WATER LEMON sb bot; *OED* 1785→. The vines and fruit of two passion-flowers: *Passiflora laurifolia* and *P. maliformis.* The name refers to the shape and to the juicy pulp.

1756 Browne 328, Passiflora 4..The Water-Lemon. I have not known this plant to be yet cultivated in any of the gardens of Jamaica, tho a native: it grows frequent in the woods, and supplies the wild hogs with a great part of their food in the season. 1837 Macfadyen 157–8, *Passiflora laurifolia*. The Water-Lemon. 1913 Harris 18, The

Pomme d'Or, or Water-Lemon is frequently cultivated. It is a high climber so is best trained on an arbour, fence, or low tree. This is quite the best of the smaller fruited edible Passifloras. 1926 Fawcett 236.

WATER LIZARD sb. One of the POLLY LIZARDS: *Sphærodactylus argus henriquesi.*

1940 Lynn-Grant 71, Water Lizard.

WATER MAHOE sb; see quot 1946. The tree *Hernandia jamaicensis.* (Though not related to MAHOE, it has somewhat its appearance.)

1946 *NHN* III 63, Water mahoe. The wood is not of any value probably due to the fact that the trees are growing in such a damp habitat. The heartwood is soft and absorbs water to a very great extent. 1952 FGC StAnn, Water mahoe 'called "man Jack" in Portland'; StT, Water mahoe—/jetosi/.

WATER-MAN sb.

1. On a sugar estate: the man who does the irrigation.

1956 Mc StT (Serge Is.) /waata man/.

2. A habitual drinker. (*Water* here alludes to white rum.)

1956 Mc StT, In town, a 'water-man' is a drinker.

3. The tree *Spathodea campanulata.*

1952 FGC Man /wáata mán/—spathodea tree, because it draws up much water from the earth. (The blossoms are full of water.)

WATER-MAW sb dial. The bladder (of a cow).

1956 Mc StJ /waata maa/.

WATERMELON see *waatmelan.* *BA G*

WATER OATS sb obs; *DAE* 1817–18→. An old name for *wild rice* (*Zizania aquatica*); but the identification of this plant is in doubt.

1774 Long III 847, Water-oats, or Tare-grass. *Zizania pannicula effusa*..The plant is common in all the lagoons. It is also found in the swampy grounds of North-America; where the Indians eat the grain, instead of rice.

WATER PARTRIDGE sb.

1. The Red Rail, now 'possibly extinct' (Bond 90) in Jamaica: *Amaurolimnas concolor concolor.*

1847 Gosse 369, Red Rail. Water Partridge. *Rallus concolor.*—Mihi. The gallinaceous form common to the Rails, and the red hue of this species have given to it the provincial name of Water Partridge. 1936 Bond 90.

2. The QUOK.

1952 FGC StT (2 informants), Water-partridge, quok.

WATER-PLANTAIN sb obs.

1. The round-leafed Water-Hyacinth.

1756 Browne 195, Pontederia 1..The round-leafed Water-Plantain..I observed this plant in most of the Lagoons and rivers about the Ferry..it grows very luxuriantly, and throws up its flower-spike a good way beyond the surface of the water.

2. The water plant *Echinodorus cordifolius.*

1756 Browne 204–5, The Great Water-Plantain. This plant grows very common in all the stagnating waters about the Ferry. 1814 Lunan II 274–5, Water-Plantain, Great. Alisma..cordifolia.

WATER SCORPION sb. A genus of water insects: see quot. *G*

1944 *NHN* II 120, The *Ranatra* are among these, and as the two long air tubes stick together when wet, and resemble a sting, it is not surprising that this insect is generally known as the 'Water-scorpion'.

WATER SHEPHERD sb dial cant. An officer in Revivalist cults: see quot.

1929 Beckwith 146, see RIVER MAID. 1953 Moore 86, The Water Shepherd: [his duty is] to see that there is pure water available at all times.

WATER STARWORT sb obs. (Not as in *OED.*) An unidentified water plant.

1696 Sloane 75, Stellaria aquatica..Water-starwort. In Insula Jamaica, aquis fluentibus pigroribus ubique innatans reperitur.

WATER SUCKER sb techn. A young banana plant that grows out of the base or main root of a tree, but does not bear well. *G*

1913 Fawcett 42, Never leave a peeper on a stump [after-growth on the remains of a cut-down banana tree]..or a water sucker will result, producing for certain either a six or seven hand bunch.

WATER-VINE sb obs. = WATER WITHE.

1774 Long III vii, The plantane, the palma Christi, trumpet-tree, water-vines, withes and gourds.

WATER-WEED sb dial. The wild marigold *Wedelia trilobata,* used as a 'tea bush'.

1927 Beckwith 22, see GOLD-CUP. 1929 Beckwith 93–4, Another method, and probably the most successful, is to burn something in the house to keep away duppies.. [Various plants] and a water marigold called by my informant 'water weed'..are all used for this purpose. 1954 *WIMJ* 32, Wedelia trilobata..Wild or Running Marigold; Marygold; Creeping Ox-eye; Water Weed.

WATER-WITHE /waata wis/ sb; *OED* 1866. The wild grapevine—see quot 1756. (*Vitis tiliæfolia.*) *SC watra-tetéi.*

1696 Sloane 172, Vitis, fructu minore..Wild Vine or Water-with. 1756 Browne 178, VITIS. 1..The Jamaica Grape-vine, commonly called Water-withe. The withe of this grape-vine, when it grows luxuriant,..is so full of juice, that a junk of about 3 feet will yield near a pint of clear tasteless water; which has saved the lives of many who have wandered long in the woods, without any other refreshment of a liquid sort. 1835 Madden II 49, There is another singular plant called the water-withe..The stem is full of a tasteless water. 1864 Grisebach 788. 1926 Fawcett 74. 1952 FGC Tre /waata-wis/ wild grapevine.

WATER-WOOD sb; cf Fr name—quot 1850. The tree *Chimarrhis cymosa.*

1850 Macfadyen 215, Chimarris cymosa. The Water-wood..A tree of graceful port, with horizontally spreading branches..The French colonists style this, 'Bois de riviere'. It was first discovered by Jacquin in Martinique. 1864 Grisebach 788, Water-wood.

WATERY YAWS sb obs.

1820 Thomson 83, see GUINEA-CORN YAWS.

wat-lef /wat-lef, wat-liiv/ sb dial; for *what-is-left.* Things left over; usually, food left over from one meal and eaten at the next; also anything that remains partly used.

1947 U.Newton II 9, After we had eaten our 'what-left' and a bit of potato pudding. *Ibid* III 30, Watlef—food put aside for *bambie* (by and by) i.e. later on in the day. 1957 Bennett 50, Him got awn all Joe wat-lef Winta tings fram Merica [*left-over winter clothes*]. 1958 DeC Port /wat-liiv/ —leftovers (of food).

wat-liiv see prec.

WATTLE /watl, wakl/ vb dial; <*wattle,* flexible rod. Cf *EDD* 12, to beat, 1796→. To beat with a wattle or similar rod—or any similar implement, e.g. a whip. *G*

1924 Beckwith 33, An' de horse-whip lay out an' flog him, wattle him well till he holla. 1956 Mc StE /dem wátl im bák—dem watl im hot/ *They wattled his back—they wattled his hut.* [The latter is an ironical play on words.]

WATTLE-PANE sb dial. A panel of wattling: see quot.

1912 McK *Songs* 95, The torch-light glistens through the wattle-pane*..*The bedroom is separated from the kitchen by panes of undaubed wattle, through which is seen the glimmer of the burning torch-wood.

WATTLE-WOOD sb; *OED* 1864. The tree *Lætia thamnia*, used in wattling.

1837 Macfadyen 44, Lætia Thamnia..A very common shrub. It is sometimes called *Wattle-wood* by the Negroes, from their employing the long branches in constructing their houses. 1926 Fawcett 221, Wattle Wood. 1952 FGC Tre /wákl-ùd/, used in trapping animals.

WAUNFO(U) see *waang-fu*.

WAUNTON see *waantn*.

WAUTA DRY see WATER-DRY.

WAWEE sb obs. One of the 'tribal' and language names of negroes brought to Jamaica: prob Vai, from the coast of W. Africa south of Sierra Leone.

1835 Senior 34, Congo, Wawee, Nago, Eboe, Corromentee, Papa, etc.

WAX WOOD sb. The tree *Myrica microcarpa*; the name refers to the waxy appearance of the leaves and stems.

1914 Fawcett 32, Wax Wood.

WAXY adj dial. Of a person, a party, etc.—'nice', attractive, lively. See quots.

1943 *GL*, You waxy, you are nice. 1956 Mc StAnd /it jos a get waksi nong/ *Things are just warming up, it's getting good.*

WAY see WA[1], WE[1].

'WAY /we/ adv dial; aphetic form of *away*, very commonly used. Away. *G T*

1877 Murray *Feedin' 'Perrit* 4, I trow it way. 1907 Jekyll 78, Why you no' been get 'way when Bro'er Tiger catch you? 1950 Pioneer 61, Some scatta weh, some stagga back.

WAYSIDE BROOMWEED sb bot obs; cf BROOMWEED. In Macfadyen's use: *Sida acuta* (ident 1926 Fawcett 119).

1837 Macfadyen 78, Sida trivialis, Way-side Broom-weed.

WE[1, 2] see WA.

WE[3] /wi/ pron dial. As oblique case of the first pl pers pron: us, our. See *EDD* WE II 1, 2; *SND* WE 2.

1833 Scott II 355, Cousin Taam, what you bring we? 1912 McK *Songs* 14, We caan' 'peak sake o' we naybor tongue. [*We can't speak because of our neighbour's tongue.*] 1950 Pioneer 68, It surprise ebery one of we. *BL G*

WE[4] /wi/ vb dial. A common dial sp for /wi/ WILL.

WE[5] /we/ indef demons adj dial; etym uncert: /we/ in this use could represent, singly or merged, *what*, *which*, or *when* (before *n-*, as here). That, inexactly (whatever, whichever, or whenever). *G N T*

1956 Mc Man /him hózban ben blak-óp we náit/ *Her husband was very drunk that night.* (Informant insists on genuineness of this usage.)

WEATHER sb dial. Bad weather (a storm, heavy rain, etc.) extending over a period of days. Cf *OED sb*[1] 1h 'Now *dial.* and *Naut.*' Also attrib.

1952 FGC StJ, Lan' breeze, bring strong weather; fishermen watch it, have time to turn back; StT, When we have a weather, sea get rough! Han /wen weda taim/ ants shake their wings loose /ful op di huol plies wen weda gwain set in/. 1956 Mc StE /di weda taim, weda siizn, wen wi ha weda/ the rainy, stormy season (Aug–Sept). *BA BL*

WEATHER-BIRD sb dial; <WEATHER + *bird*. Sea birds that fly inland at the approach of stormy weather. *BA*

1952 FGC StT, Weather-bird—see them when there's going to be weather.

WEATHERY adj dial; < WEATHER + *-y*. Threatening a storm.

1952 FGC StC /it lúk wédari/ *It looks stormy.*

WEDDING-BESSY sb dial; <*wedding* + BESSY. A woman who comes to every wedding celebration. Cf BURYING-BESSY. *BL*

1943 *GL* Man, Wedden-bessie, one who attends weddings frequently. 1955 FGC Man /wedn-besi/.

WEEDING GANG sb techn obs. The THIRD GANG or PICKNEY GANG. *G*

1823 Roughley 103, The third or weeding gang. This corps, forming the rising generation.

WEED-MAN, WEEDY sb dial. An obeah-man, supposed to know poisonous and medicinal uses of weeds.

1958 DeC Clar, StT /wiid-man/ obeah man, so called because /him nuo plenty wiid/; Clar /wiidi/ short for the same, jocular but disrespectful.

WEENY sb dial; ?var of PEENY. A PEENY-WALLY (but this appears to be an erroneous form).

1937 R. Wright *Revels in Jamaica* 226, Lights twinkle out like 'weenies', as the natives call fireflies.

WEEPING WILLOW see WILLOW.

WEE-WEE adj dial; iterative from *wee*, small. Very small, tiny. *G*

1952 FGC StT, Pigtail bean, a wee-wee banner-bean type. *Ibid* /a likl wii-wii wan/.

we-fi-du (or **wa-fi-du**) vb phr and sb dial; <WA, WE + FI + *do*.

1. See quot 1907. *G*

1907 Jekyll 137, Whé fe do, what to do?..The implied answer is 'Nothing'. So the phrase means: 'It can't be helped'. 1943 *GL* StAnn, StM, Wey fe do, what to do. 1950 Pioneer 98, I is weary of dis worl'. But whey fe do, Cousin Mary.

2. A hat locally made of palm thatch (that one buys because it can't be helped—one cannot afford a better one). Often, one with a very wide brim.

1905 Dodd 18, A middle sized man with..small eyes and large 'weh-fe-do' hat. 1943 *GL* Clar (2), Weyfedo, Wa-fe-do, a big tatch hat made by natives. Man, Whe-fe-do, can't afford anything more expensive. StM, Wa-fi-do, broad-rimmed hat. 1952 FGC Tre /wa-fi-du/—/tach hat/.

WEH see 'WAY, WA[1], WE[1].

WEH-FE-DO see *we-fi-du*.

WEIGH-MEAT sb dial or slang; see quot. Bone that is weighed and paid for with meat (but is not meat in any other sense).

1893 Sullivan 22, But the butchers charge..for bone as well as meat, and sometimes one is disappointed to find that when the 'meat' is delivered, one half of it is 'weigh-meat' or large pieces of bone.

WEIGHT sb dial; cf *ODS* →1846. A quantity of goods constituting a unit in marketing. Specifically, 13 or 7½ lb of fish, 28 lb of potatoes, etc.: see quots.

1952 FGC StE, A weight of fish: 13 lbs furnished by a fisherman to a dealer and paid for as 12 lbs. (1958 DeC—this is true for most of the island, but in StT generally a weight is 7½ lbs.) 1958 DeC Kgn /wiet/—Potatoes and similar food are sold by weights, a weight being 28 lb. When selling by the pound it is common practice to give thirteen pounds for twelve, but there is no name for this.

WELL vb dial; <*well* adj, by ellipse of *to be*. To become well, to heal. Also const *up*. *BL*

1956 Mc Clar /dima—uol suo we neva wel/ *Old sore that never heals*; Man [Of a sprained foot:] /dis fut kaas mi trii poun fi wel/ *This foot cost me three pounds before it was right*; StAnd /it haad tu wel/ *It doesn't heal readily*. 1957 DeC StAnd /di trii wel-op—mi aam wel-op/ *The tree, my arm has got well, become whole.*

WELL adv dial; cf *OED* 16.

1. Modifying an adjective: very, extremely.

1868 Russell 10, Dis boy well cra-cra; *ibid* 18. 1950 Pioneer 71, Him well tired an hungry. 1954 LeP StAnn, Her husban well drunk dat nite. 1956 Mc Man /dat trak de ing wel bad/ *That track—it's very bad*. *BA G T*

2. Modifying a verb (and characteristically placed before it): very much. *BA T*

1924 Beckwith 2, Brer Nansi well want de mango. *Ibid* 42, Anansi tak up Hog put him in a bag and said, 'I well wan' fe eat you long time!' 1942 Bennett 42, Se fe yuh piece yah Berta! Yuh Well want i soh noh pose. [*You do really want it, so don't pretend.*]

3. In phr *well and*: quite; thoroughly; full well. (Cf colloq Engl 'good and'.) *BL G*

1896 Bates 122, Corn piece..hab plenty corn, an' de corn well an' ripe. 1956 BLB Man /yu wel an nuo se a fi-mi/ *You know very well that it is mine.*

WELL-HANDED adj obs. Well provided with hands, or labourers.

1707 Sloane lii, When a Plantation has many Men or Women, 'tis said to be well handed, or in case of few, it is said to be bad handed, or to want Hands. The expression comes, as some others, from the Planters of Jamaica, coming a long Voyage at Sea, whereby they get some of the Sea Phrases. 1778 Beckford 50, If the estate be not well handed, and abundant in cattle.

WELSHMAN sb obs.

1. The JABBERING CROW.

1774 Long III 896, Gabling Crow..When a flock of them assemble together, they are diverting enough to a traveler, with their strange, noisy gabble of guttural sounds, which imitate some human languages, and are thought to have much the confused vociferation of a parcel of Welsh folks exercising their lungs and tongues at a grand scolding match; hence these birds have been nick-named the Welshmen.

2. See *wenshman* (fish).

WEM see next.

WEN /wen/ occas /win, wem/ vbl particle dial; a parallel form to BEN, and evid a phon var of it.

1. Used without any other verb: was, were.

1942 Bennett 11, Me jump een an' 'pread me kitchief 'pon de seat, for it wen full up a dus [*For it was full of dust*]; *ibid* 14, see TRUST vb.

2. As auxiliary to another verb to express past time: did (+infinitive, with or without *fi*).

1942 Bennett 1, Me wen know 'ow much i-come to [*I knew how much it added up to*]; *ibid* 4, Me stop an ax har wats de time As me wen tink me late [*did think, thought*]. 1943 *GL* StC, Whem fe-dweit, was to do it; West, Win fe gu, was to go. 1956 Mc StAnd, see STAND 5; /we hunu wen de laas nait/ *Where were you (two) last night?* [*De* here = *be*.]

3. Combined with (and preceding) A[5], DA[3], or DE[4] to show durative or progressive action in the past. (Also subjunctive: see quot 1924.)

1924 Beckwith 26, Anansi said, 'Oh, no, Brar! you t'ink if you tell me wha' such good t'ings is, me wen' deh go mak trouble?' [*Did you think that if you tell me where such good things are, I was (or would be) going to make trouble?*] 1942 Bennett 3, Me write it out fe study it, Me jus' wena go start [*I was just going to start (reciting)*]; *ibid* 1, Ah wena dead fe bus out laugh [*I was dying to burst out laughing*].

wen, wena see WEN, BEN, BENA.

WENGA sb dial; var of WANGA.

1943 *GL* Port, Wenga, a vulgar style of walking.

wenshman sb dial; <*Welshman*. No effect of folk-etym appears to be present. Fish of the *Holocentridæ* family; Welshman. (Among the fishermen 'welshman' is known but 'wenshman' is almost universally used.)

1952 FGC Han, Port, StAnd, StAnn, StC, StJ, StM, StT, West /wenshman/. 1958 DeC StT /wenchman/.

wenshman dadi, ~pupa sb dial; for *wenshman's + daddy* or PUPA. Evid some variety of wenshman; see PO' JOE.

1952 FGC StJ /wenshman dadi, pupa/ Po' Joe.

wen-taim see WHEN-TIME.

WENYA-WENYA adj dial; cf Fon *winiwini*, fine, thin. Thin, 'maaga'.

1868 Russell 11, Wenya-wenya—Meagre not fat. Dat wenya-wenya boy 'trong. African. *Ibid* 19, Dat colt look so wenya-wenya. 1873 Rampini 127.

wepaat interrog or rel pron dial; <WE[1] or WE[2] +*part*, place. Where. *BL G*

1962 BLB 9 /a-wepaat di pikini-dem bena kom from/ *Where were the children coming from?*

wera-keta, wera-kete adj dial; etym unknown —perh Afr; cf *were-were*. Derogatory and of imprecise meaning: undersized, weak-looking, unkempt, etc. See quots. Cf. s *wera-keta fut*.

1943 *GL* Clar, Wherra-ketta, very small; Kgn, Wera-kete, funny, unstyled [in clothes?]; StM, Scrawny and weak; Wher-æ-ke-æ, a small woman. StAnn, Wereh-ceteh. 1955 FGC Kgn /wera-keta, wera-kete/ not looking good.

WEREH-CETEH see prec.

were-were (or **wiri-wiri**) sb and adj dial; cf Twi *w̃érὲ-w̃érὲ*, adv carelessly, negligently; Yoruba *wẹ̄rẹwẹ*, small, diminutive.

A. sb: see quots.

1943 *GL* StC, Werre werreh, torn garments, anything ragged. 1953 FGC Man /were-were/ a lot of little small things not worth while.

B. adj: see quot.

1943 *GL* StM, Wirry-wirry, meagre and small.

WERRE WERREH see prec.

WESLEY(AN) sb attrib. A Methodist-sponsored 'sing' and group labour activity, for which people were called together by the sound of a horn.

1912 McK *Songs* 95, Refreshing breezes fan me as I wake, and down the valley sounds the wesly* horn*..The wesly horn sounds when any work in common is to be undertaken. c 1955 Una Wilson 'Digging Songs' *Gleaner*, Wesley—a Wesleyan 'sing'—a gathering of friends to help dig yam hills, coco holes, etc.

WESLY HORN see prec.

WEST-INDIA EBONY sb.

1837 Macfadyen 301, see WEST-INDIAN EBONY.

WEST-INDIA MANGO sb obs. An old name for the tree *Grias cauliflora*, whose fruit was formerly pickled like the mango.

1774 Long III 810, Anchovy Pear, or West India Mango.

WEST INDIAN ALDER TREE see ALDER TREE.

WEST-INDIAN BARK sb. The tree *Exostema caribæum*, whose bark was once used as a substitute for Jesuits' bark. Also called CARIBBEE BARK-TREE.

1864 Grisebach 788, West-Indian-bark.

WEST-INDIAN BIRCH sb bot. =BIRCH.

1864 Grisebach 781, West Indian Birch. 1920 Fawcett 206. 1941 Swabey 13. 1955 *WIMJ* 157.

WEST-INDIAN CEDAR sb bot. =CEDAR, JAMAICA CEDAR.

1864 Grisebach 782, West Indian Cedar: *Cedrela odorata*. 1941 Swabey 17. 1955 *WIMJ* 158.

WEST-INDIA(N) CHERRY sb bot. A number of distinct trees, and their fruits: *Malpighia urens* (Cowitch Cherry) and *M. punicifolia* (Barbados Cherry); *Bunchosia jamaicensis*; *Eugenia uniflora* (Surinam Cherry).

1837 Macfadyen 146, Stinging West-India Cherry.. Pomegranate-leaved West-India Cherry. 1864 Grisebach 782, West Indian Cherry: *Malpighia* and *Bunchosia*. 1913 Harris 4, Cherry, West Indian. *Eugenia uniflora*.

WEST-INDIAN CHICKWEED sb. The herb *Drymaria cordata*.

1914 Fawcett 175, West Indian Chickweed.

WEST INDIAN CINNAMON TREE sb obs. =CANELLA.

1679 Trapham 38, The Bay Tree or spicy Piemento perfume the woods with profitable sweets, to which our Winter Bark or West Indian Cinnamon Tree adds its help to embalm the Air.

WEST-INDIA(N) EBONY sb. =EBONY.

1837 Macfadyen 301–2, Brya Ebenus. West-India Ebony ..When in blossom, with its long branches densely crowded with yellow flowers, it reminds the traveller of the broom of Europe. The wood is very hard and ponderous, and susceptible of a fine polish. 1920 Fawcett 26, West Indian Ebony. 1941 Swabey 20.

WEST-INDIAN ELM sb. The tree *Guazuma ulmifolia*, with elm-like leaves; usually called BASTARD CEDAR.

1955 *WIMJ* 158.

WEST-INDIAN GOOSEBERRY sb. The shrub *Pereskia aculeata*; also called BARBADOS GOOSEBERRY. *BA*

1926 Fawcett 273, West Indian Gooseberry..Often cultivated for its fruit.

WEST-INDIAN HONEYSUCKLE sb.

1864 Grisebach 784, West Indian Honeysuckle: *Tecoma capensis*.

WEST-INDIAN LAUREL sb. The tree *Prunus occidentalis*—more often called PRUAN.

1864 Grisebach 785, West Indian Laurel.

WEST-INDIA(N) LILAC sb bot. The tree *Melia azederach*.

1837 Macfadyen 167, Hoop-tree, or West-India Lilac.. A shrub, sometimes acquiring the port of a tree..The bark of this tree is bitter and astringent..The bark of the root is said to be a powerful anthelmintic. 1864 Grisebach 785, Lilac, West Indian. 1920 Fawcett 215–6.

WEST-INDIAN LOCUST (TREE) sb. The tree *Hymenæa courbaril*, commonly called STINKING TOE.

1920 Fawcett 121, West Indian Locust Tree. 1941 Swabey 31, West Indian Locust.

WEST INDIAN SANDALWOOD sb. Among cabinet-makers: The wood of the tree *Amyris balsamifera*.

1941 Swabey 29, see SANDALWOOD. 1944 *NHN* II 94, see AMYRIS WOOD.

WEST INDIA(N) SUMACH sb; *OED* 1866. The tree *Brunellia comocladifolia*.

1837 Macfadyen 195, West-India Sumach. 1864 Grisebach 788, West Indian Sumach. 1914 Fawcett 250.

WEST-INDIA(N) TEA sb. The bush *Capraria biflora*; see quot 1814.

1696 Sloane 90, Gratiolæ affinis frutescens..West-India Thea. 1814 Lunan II 277, West-India Tea..Under the name Goat-weed..it was omitted to be noticed that this plant had received the name of West India-Tea; as according to Long and Barham, the leaves not only resemble those of Tea, but make an equally agreeable decoction. 1864 Grisebach 788, West Indian Tea.

WEST INDIAN TREE DUCK sb. The duck *Dendrocygna arborea*, which builds its nest in trees.

1936 Bond 39, West Indian Tree Duck. 1956 Jeffrey-Smith 137, The..West Indian Tree Duck..was once very common; but today..it is rare.

WEST INDIES BANANA sb.

1952 FGC StT, West Indies Banana, red bananas.

WET-FOOT sb dial or slang; <*wet* vb+*foot*. One's being arrested for the first time.

1952 FGC StM /wet-fut/.

WET SUGAR Newly made unrefined cane sugar, with some of the molasses still in it: NEW SUGAR. It is used to make a beverage, confections, etc.

1952 FGC StE, StJ, StM, West /wet shuga/ make 'cut cakes' with wet sugar.

WEY see WA, WE.

WEY-FE-DO see *we-fi-du*.

WHA see WA, WE.

WHAI (OH) see *waay(-uo)*.

WHANGRA see WANGLA.

WHANICA see WANIKA.

WHARRA(H) see *wara*.

WHAT /wat, wa, we/ adv dial; *OED* B 4 →1556 and Mod Scots; cf WA, WE.

1. Introducing exclam expr: How.

1947 U.Newton II 38, Someone shouted: 'But what a boy can sleep! Wake up Newsy!' [*How that boy can sleep! What a boy for sleeping!*] 1954 LeP StAnn, What a boy can nyam mango! 1956 Mc Man /wat shi yong so/ *How young she is!*

2. In the exclam phr *What a way* (*how*): How (very much). Cf *OED* A 13b. *BL*

1952 FGC Han [Song:] What a way I would be gay if I win the sweepstake! 1954 LeP StE, Wat-a-way you dress pretty! 1956 Mc Man /wát a wé hou jamíeka get kúol nou/ *How cold Jamaica is getting*; StAnd /wat a we unu fat/ *How fat you are!* (*You are all getting too fat.*)

WHAT interrog pron dial. How much. *G T*

1954 LeP StAnd /wat a kwaat da milk/ *How much a quart is the milk?*

WHAT-LEFT see *wat-lef*.

WHAT SIDE adv phr dial; cf WHICH SIDE. Where. *BL G*

1896 Bates 122, Him hax wha' side Puss gone. [*He asked where Puss had gone.*]

WHAUNICA see WANIKA.

WHE see WA, WE.

WHEEL sb dial.

1. A coil.

1952 FGC StAnn, 'Jackass rope' tobacco is 'in a wheel'.

2. A ring; see quot.

1958 DeC Port /wiil/ an iron ring used with a bammy-iron in making bammy.

WHEELER sb dial; cf CART-WHEEL.

1952 FGC StE /wiila/ a round cake.

WHEELING SHEPHERD sb dial cant. An officer in Revivalist cults whose speciality is to wheel like a dervish around the ceremonial circle, sometimes with a glass of holy water on his head which he does not spill.

1953 Moore 78. *Ibid* 84, The principal shepherd in charge of most services and in over-all charge of the band [of revivalists] is the *wheeling shepherd*. His title denotes the pattern of his dance.

WHEEL-UP sb dial joc. Soup; the name alludes to the action of stirring it while cooking.

1943 *GL* StAnd, Wheel up, soup.

WHE-FE-DO see *we-fi-du*.

WHELK see *wilk(s)*.

WHENEVER TIME conj dial. Whenever.

1952 FGC StT [Story:] /weneva taim dem tiekin a baat, di haak kom/ *Whenever they were taking a bath, the hawk came.* 1961 BLB 14 /weneva-taim dat im kom im gwain plie a trik/ *When she comes she is going to play a prank.*

WHEN-TIME /wen-taim/ adv dial. When. *BL*

1962 BLB 10 /a-wentaim im ben hat imsef?/ *When did he hurt himself?*

WHERAEKEAE, WHERRA-KETTA see *wera-keta*.

WHEY see WA, WE.

WHEY FE DO see *we-fi-du*.

WHICH reg /wich/ also /wish, wishe, wishi/ interrog pron and adj dial. Irregular forms; see also WHICH PART. *G T*

1943 *GL* Tre, Wishey, which [This prob repr /wishi/]. 1956 Mc Man /a wísh wan a dém a fi yú/ *Which is yours?* /mi nó nuo wísh wan trángga an téda/ *I don't know which is the stronger.*

WHICH-PART /wish-paat, wishe-~, wich-~/ interrog and rel pron dial. Where, wherever. Cf next. *BL G T*

1952 FGC StM /mek i tan wish paat i de/ *Let it stay where it is.* 1954 LeP StT, Wish paat im live? 1955 Bennett *Goodbye Tramcar*, Wen me look pon dem road wich part Ole tram car line use fe lie! 1956 Mc Man /a wishe paat unu ben de laas nait/ *Where were you last night?* /a wíshe páat hin de nong/ *Where is he now?*

WHICH-SIDE /wich said, wi-said/ interrog and rel pron dial. Where. Cf prec. *BL G*

1877 Murray *Kittle* 21, Den wi side him horse day? [*Then where is his horse?*] Whi side him get horse, maam? 1943 *GL* Han, Whissay, where; Kgn, Whisa, where.

WHILE vb dial; cf *OED v* 1, To occupy or engage (a person) for a time..; to fill up the time of. To spend a lot of time with women.

1943 *GL* Clar, Whyle, to go out courting. 1955 FGC Man /wail/ run up and down with different women. *BA G*

WHILE /wail/ conj dial.

1. Provided that, so long as. (Cf *OED* B2 →1849.)

1956 Mc StE /mi mos riip aal i griin wanz tuu/ *Am I to pick the green ones too?* [Answer:] /wail it fit/ *So long as they're nearly ripe* [see FIT].

2. Since, seeing that.

1956 Mc StE /wail im a taak wat mi no se/ [*Since she has been reporting something I didn't say*].

WHILST /wais/ conj dial.

1. Provided that, so long as. (=WHILE 1.) *G*

1952 FGC StJ /it wil fluot aal di taim wais is katnwud/ *It will always float so long as it's cottonwood.* 1956 Mc Man /mi no-kyáa we i wan go wais hin no kómya/ *I don't care where he goes provided he doesn't come here.*

2. Since, because. (=WHILE 2.)

1956 Mc StAnd /mi wi sen fi yu kwik-kwik, wais mi laik yu/ *I shall send for you at once, because I like you.*

WHIP-RAY see *ripre, wipri*.

WHIP-TOM-KELLY sb obs; *OED* 1756→. The bird JOHN CHEWIT. (Gosse has cast doubt on the genuineness of the name but there appear to be independent reports in its favour.)

1756 Browne 476, Oriolus..The Whip-tom-kelly..It has not many notes, but these are loud and sweet. 1774 Long III 895, Fly-catcher, or Whip-tom-kelly. 1839 Hill in 1840 *Almanack* 32, see SWEET JOHN TUWHIT. 1843 Chamberlaine in *Almanack* 98. 1847 Gosse 195, I can scarcely understand how the call can be written 'Whip-Tom-Kelly', as the accent, if I may so say, is most energetically on the last syllable. Nor have I ever heard this appellation given to it in Jamaica. 1936 Bond 304, Black-whiskered Vireo (Vireo calidris). Local names:—John-to-whit;..Tom Kelly; Whip-Tom-Kelly..[etc.].

WHISA, WHISSAY see WHICH-SIDE.

WHIST see WIS.

WHISTLER sb dial. The SOLITAIRE.

1936 Bond 292, Local names:—Whistler; Mountain Whistler; Fiddler; Glass-eye (Jamaica). 195- *NHN* (ref lost), Quickstep, St Elizabeth.

WHISTLING COWBOY sb dial. A ghost or DUPPY associated with ROLLING CALF. See WHOOPING-BOY.

1952 FGC Han, Whistling cow-boy, another duppy.

WHISTLING TOAD sb. See quot.

1958 CBL, Members of the genus *Eleutherodactylus*, and especially the *E. martinicensis*, are called whistling toads.

WHITE adj dial. In the names of natural objects, plants, animals: used contrastively with BLACK, and often merely meaning comparatively light rather than dark. See such names as WHITE BEEFWOOD, WHITE CRAB, WHITE MASTIC, WHITE RAIN, WHITE SEA-EGG, WHITE-STICK (CASSADA, FERN, etc.). *BA G*

WHITE AFU (YAM) sb; <*white*+AFU.

1958 DeC Clar /taa/ a white yam also called /wait afu/.

WHITE ALBION (SUGAR) sb; <*white*+ALBION. A sugar of the kind first made at Albion estate, farther refined than BROWN ALBION.

1952 FGC StE, White Albion sugar, buy at shop.

WHITE-A-MIDDLE sb dial; <*white*+A[1]+*middle*. One who is only half Maroon or half negro. (Evid a Maroon term in the Moore Town orbit, Portland parish.)

1943 *GL* Port (2), White-a-middle, half Maroon; half Negro.

WHITEBACK (BUSH) sb dial; from the whitish colour of the underside of the leaf.

1. The wild herb *Chaptalia nutans*.

1952 FGC StT /wait-bak/ similar to the northern Dandelion. 1953 *WIMJ* 242, *Chaptalia nutans*..Kema Weed; Dandelion; White Back; Heal-I-and-Draw; Lion's Tail.

2. The wild herb *Senecio discolor*.

1955 *WIMJ* 76, White-back. Although we have been unable to trace analyses of this *Senecio* sp. several of them are said to be toxic.

WHITE-BACK FERN sb. =SILVER-BACK FERN.

1952 FGC Port.

WHITE-BARK sb. Another name for the LACE-BARK tree.

1941 Swabey 23, Lagetto, Whitebark. 1952 FGC StE (2) /wait-bark/ our name for lace-bark.

WHITE BEEFWOOD see BEEFWOOD.

WHITE-BELLIED see WHITE-BELLY.

WHITE-BELLY'D DUCK sb; cf *OED white-belly* 1889–91. A duck of uncert identity, perh the American Widgeon.

1725 Sloane 324, Anas fera ventre candido..the White-Belly'd Duck.

WHITE-BELLY (DOVE) sb. The wild dove *Leptotila jamaicensis*.

1725 Sloane 303, Columba minor ventre candido..The White-Belly'd Dove. 1823 Stewart 78, The white-belly, or white-breast, the mountain witch, the partridge pigeon. 1840 Chamberlaine in *Almanack* 18. 1847 Gosse 313–4, Whitebelly..This lovely Pigeon is chiefly confined to the upland districts; where its loud and plaintive cooing makes the woods resound. 1952 FGC Han, Man, StAnd, StAnn, StM; StT /wait-beli/ feeds on ground; wildest bird we have.

WHITE-BELLY MAID sb dial. The BESSY KICK-UP—said to accompany the White-belly Dove.

1952 FGC StM, White-belly maid, kick-up.

WHITE-BELLY RAT sb.

1. The CANE RAT.

1924 Beckwith 191 [Riddle:] My father plant a acre a kasava; only one white belly rat a eatey off. [Answer:] Grater for preparing kasava meal. 1952 FGC Man, StAnd, StT /wait-beli rat/.

2. Transf. A deceitful or hypocritical person.

1927 Anderson-Cundall 100, White-belly-ratta him bite and blow. 1954 LeP StAnd, A hypocrite—white belly rat; Kgn, StE, A deceitful person—white-belly rat; a white bellied rat is supposed to blow on the thing it bites so that the bite is not felt.

WHITE-BILL sb dial.

1892 Cockrell list [of fish], White bill—pincers, *Clupea humeralis*.

WHITE BITTER-WOOD sb.

1864 Grisebach 781, White Bitter-wood: *Trichilia spondioides*.

WHITE BONAVIST sb obs; <*white*+BONAVIST. The white colour-variant (others are 'whitish-red, dark purple, or black', 1920 Fawcett 71) of the bean *Dolichos lablab*.

1696 Sloane 67, Phaseolus maximus perennis..semen album..White bonavist. In hortis ad sepes plantatur.

WHITE BOOBY sb.

1. The booby bird *Sula sula* (also known as Red-footed Booby).

1936 Bond 13. 1956 Jeffrey-Smith 133, The White Booby is mostly white.

2. The booby bird *Sula dactylatra*, so called on Pedro Cays.

1936 Bond 12. 1956 Jeffrey-Smith 133, The 'white booby' found there [on Pedro Cays] is the Blue-faced Booby.

WHITE-BREAST (DOVE) sb. A euphemism that prob had little use: 1823 Stewart 78, see WHITE-BELLY DOVE.

WHITE BULLET-WOOD or **BULLY-TREE** sb. =BULLY (TREE). *N*

1774 Long III 748, White-bully tree, or Galimeta wood. 1864 Grisebach 782, Bully-tree, white: *Dipholis salicifolia*. 1941 Swabey 15, White Bully..White Bullet. 1952 FGC StE, StT /wáit bùlitríi/; StAnd, StAnn /wait bulit/.

WHITE CANDLEWOOD sb; cf CANDLEWOOD. *Amyris balsamifera*; also called BLACK CANDLEWOOD, ROSEWOOD, TORCHWOOD.

1756 Browne 208, Amyris. 1..White Candlewood, or Rosewood..This tree is found in the woods of *St Ann's*, and those back of *Bull-bay*..The wood is white..but grows of a dirty clouded ash-colour with age..The younger trees are frequently cut for fire-wood in the mountains; they are full of resin, burn very freely, and with a most agreeable smell. 1814 Lunan I 147, It is called *white candlewood*, because it burns so freely as frequently to be used for that purpose by the negroes. 1920 Fawcett IV 192. 1952 FGC Tre, White candlewood, same as torchwood.

WHITE CANE sb. A variety of sugar-cane with a whitish skin. *G*

1952 FGC Port, StAnd, StAnn, StE, StJ, StT /wait kien/ —very soft.

WHITE CASSADA sb. The non-poisonous kind of Cassava: Sweet cassava. *BA*

1707 Sloane lxxvi, There is a sort of White Cassada not poysonous, which boil'd as Yams are, may be eat like them.

WHITE CEDAR sb. The tree *Tecoma leucoxylon*; =WHITEWOOD CEDAR. *N*

1801 Dancer 367.

WHITE CINNAMON sb. The tree *Canella winterana*, whose bark was once valued in medicine.

1926 Fawcett 208, Wild Cinnamon, Whitewood Bark, White Cinnamon. 1955 *WIMJ* 157, see CANELLA.

WHITE-CLEARY sb.

1927 Beckwith 27, see MUSK-MELON.

WHITE COCKROACH sb dial. *G*

1958 DeC StT /wait kakruoch/ a name for an albino Negro.

WHITE COCO sb. A variety of *Colocasia esculenta* having white, relatively soft flesh.

1756 Browne 332, Arum 5..The white Cocco, and Tyre ..The old heads are called White Coccos. 1814 Lunan I 212, see COCO. 1823 Roughley 404, see BLACK COCO. 1952 FGC Han, StC, StE, StJ, StT /wait kuoko/ soft, for soup; bear large coco.

WHITE CRAB sb; in contrast to BLACK CRAB. See quots.

1952 FGC StAnd, StAnn, StJ, StM, StT /wait krab/ a land crab; see it only in April, May, June. 1960 Institute of Ja exhibit, White crab—*Cardisoma guanhumi*.

WHITE CROAKING-LIZARD sb; cf CROAKING-LIZARD. See quot.

1940 Lynn-Grant 81, *Xiphocerus valenciennesii*..it is locally known as the 'white croaking lizard' because of its similarity in locomotion to..the true croaking lizard. *Valenciennesii* is, of course, voiceless, while the 'croaking lizard' is a noisy fellow.

WHITE-DOVE see DOVE.

WHITE DRUMMER sb dial. A variety of the DRUMMER fish, of whitish colour.

1952 FGC StC, StT /wait droma/.

WHITE EBOE sb dial; <*white*+EBOE, IBO; cf RED IBO. See quot.

1942 HPJ, White Ebo, A Saint Elizabeth term for albinoes (Miss Reynolds); A term of abuse (Mr Parker).

WHITE EGG-BIRD sb obs. Gosse's name for the Royal Tern, *Thalasseus maximus.*

1847 Gosse 431, Crested Tern. White Egg-Bird, *Thalasseus Cayanus.*

WHITE-EYED THRUSH sb. The Hopping Dick (*Turdus jamaicensis*) which has conspicuously glassy eyes.

1936 Bond 284. 1956 Jeffrey-Smith 35, Gosse gave the other local names of Shine Eye and Fish Eye, and James Bond lists it as the White-eyed Thrush.

WHITE FIDDLEWOOD sb obs. A tree of uncert ident, perh *Citharexylum surrectum.*

a 1726 Barham (1794) 207–8, There is a particular tree in Jamaica whose wood is so very white it is distinguished from the other woods by the name of white wood, and is very often called white fiddle-wood. 1756 Browne 265, Citharexylon? 3..White Fiddle-wood..I have seen many of these trees in the mountains of St Elizabeth's. 1814 Lunan II 292 (ref to Browne).

WHITE FLUX sb dial obs; *OED white* II e, in diff sense. See quot.

1820 Thomson 34, A discharge of mucus (in dysentery) which they [negroes] call *white flux.*

WHITE FOWL sb dial joc. Mushroom or other edible fungus. (The folk look upon fungi as a poor substitute for meat—cf JUNJO.)

1954 LeP Man, StAnn, Mushroom—White fowl. 1956 Mc Man, StAnd /wait foul/ an edible fungus which grows on certain trees (e.g. trumpet tree).

WHITE-FRY sb dial; cf JACK-FRY. Tiny seafish, white-bait.

1956 Mc StAnd (Port Royal) /wait-frai/.

WHITE GAULIN sb; <*white* + GAULIN. Any of certain egrets or herons which are white when mature (*Ardea occidentalis repens, Egretta thula, Casmerodius albus*), or the white colour phase of other species when immature (*Florida cærulea*, the common BLUE GAULIN, or *Dichromanassa rufescens*, the rare RED-NECKED GAULIN). *BL*

1725 Sloane 314, *Ardea alba maxima*..The largest white Gaulding. 1950 Pioneer 78 [Song:] A tink you say you wouldn' drink white gawlin soup. 1956 Jeffrey-Smith 121–3.

WHITE GINGER sb; *OED ginger*, listed without ref or quot. One of the types of prepared ginger root: see quot. *BL*

1707 Sloane lxix, The white sort of Ginger is made by only scraping the fresh Root clean of its outward Membrane, and exposing it in the Sun till it be dry. This white Ginger is easily spoil'd by Worms.

WHITE GRUNT sb dial. One of the varieties of the GRUNT fish.

1952 FGC StE, StJ, StM, West /wait gront/. The 'white grunt' of StE is the SOUTH'ARD GRUNT of Old Harbour (Clar).

WHITE-GUM sb obs. A sea-snail which resembles the BLOODY-GUM except that its 'teeth' have no red coloration.

1756 Browne 399, Nerita 8..The coarser black *Nerite* commonly called the White Gum.

WHITE-HEAD sb.

1. The herb *Asclepias nivea*, very similar (except in the colour of the flower) to RED-HEAD (*A. curassavica*) and having similar uses in remedies.

1927 Beckwith 29, White-head..For a child with worms, squeeze the juice through a clean cloth and swallow clear. 1951 FGC Man /wait-hed/ a kind of 'milkweed'. 1953 *WIMJ* 238, White Head.

2. The herb *Parthenium hysterophorus*, with clumps of small flowers forming whitish 'heads'.

1864 Grisebach 788. 1953 *WIMJ* 243, see WILD WORMWOOD.

WHITE-HEADED PATU sb obs; <*white-headed* + PATU. A bird reported by Gosse on the information of others though with doubt. It is not reported by Bond or other modern writers. See quot.

1847 Gosse 49, White-headee Potoo. *Nyctibius pallidus.*—Mihi. The description below I have quoted..from Robinson's MSS., who has given an elaborately coloured figure of the species in his drawings. I have never met with it, but I think Mr Hill has..*Ibid* 51, Perhaps the present species may be 'the small wood Owle' of Sloane, ii. 296.

WHITE-HEAD GRASS sb dial. A small sedge having three horizontal blades at the top, all white at the middle where they join: *Dichromena colorata* or *D. ciliata.* s STAR-GRASS.

1952 FGC Port /wait-hed graas/.

WHITE-HEART BREADFRUIT sb. A variety of breadfruit with white flesh.

1952 FGC StAnd /wait-aat/; also gen.

WHITE-HORSE sb. The tree *Portlandia grandiflora.* (The reason of the name is unknown.)

1864 Grisebach 788, White-horse.

WHITEHOUSE BANANA sb; evid through some connection with Whitehouse, Westmoreland. Said to be the same as the GROS MICHEL.

1952 FGC Port, StAnn, StJ /wait-hous/.

WHITE IPECACUANHA sb bot.

1864 Grisebach 784, White Ipecacuanha: *Richardsonia scabra.*

WHITE JEG sb dial; <*white* + *jeg*, abbr of *jege-jege, reg-jeg*, or the like; cf US *white trash.* A 'poor white'.

1956 Mc StAnd /wait jeg/ a 'poor white'.

WHITE KUOBI. A variety of the *kuobi* sweet-potato.

1956 Mc Man.

WHITE LABOUR sb dial joc.

1956 DeC StE /wait lieba/ an albino Negro.

WHITE LANCEWOOD sb.

1. The tree *Xylopia glabra.*

1814 Lunan I 437–8, Uvaria lanceolata. [The Fruit is] white-lancewood berries. 1914 Fawcett 199, *X. glabra*—white lancewood. 1941 Swabey 23, Lancewood, white.. this is a medium sized tree with small branches.

2. The tree *Oxandra laurifolia.*

1941 Swabey 23, Lancewood, white..It is considered inferior to Black Lancewood.

WHITE LIGNUM-VITÆ sb. The tree *Polygala jamaicensis.*

1864 Grisebach 785, White Lignum-vitæ. 1920 Fawcett 244.

WHITE LILY sb. The common white lily *Pancratium caribæum.* *G*

1707 Sloane lx, In the Plains or Savannas, about Old Harbour, grows that fine Flower..called commonly in Jamaica White Lillies. *Ibid* 244, White Lilly..The Flowers of this Plant have a very fragrant smell. 1756 Browne 195, The White Lilly. This plant grows wild in most parts of Jamaica..The root is pretty acrid, and has been sometimes used in poultices by antiquated and pale-faced ladies, to raise a forced bloom in their fading cheeks.

WHITE LOGWOOD sb. The tree *Homalium racemosum*; the reason for the name is obscure, since it has hardly any resemblance to logwood.

1926 Fawcett 224.

WHITE MAHOE sb dial. A kind of mahoe wood of lighter colour than the wood of BLUE MAHOE.

1952 FGC Man, StAnn.

WHITE MAHOGANY sb. =GOLD SPOON.

1864 Grisebach 785.

WHITE MASTIC sb obs; see quot 1814. In Barham's use: *Bumelia rotundifolia.*

a 1726 Barham (1794) 103, see BLACK MASTIC. 1814 Lunan I 58, Bumelia..rotundifolia..Barham calls this tree white mastic, and says..'I observed they bore a fruit..and the gum that came out of it was in small little drops, white, and of the scent of mastick, for which reason the tree is called so'.

WHITE MILADY sb dial; <*white*+MILADY. A variety of coco, similar to the SALLY.

1952 FGC StJ, A white variety of MILADY. 1958 DeC Clar /wait malíedi/ same as /wait koko/.

WHITENING see WHITING.

WHITE PEOPLE'S PINE sb obs. =BUCKRA PINE.

WHITE RAIN sb dial. A rain which does not come from nimbus clouds: see quot, and cf WHITE SQUALL. *BA G*

1952 FGC Port /wait rien/ no big cloud over hill—take longer to fall.

WHITE ROCK SWEETWOOD see ROCK SWEETWOOD.

WHITE RODWOOD sb. The tree *Calyptranthes chytraculia*: see RODWOOD.

1864 Grisebach 787, White Rod-wood. 1943 *NHN* II 52, White Rodwood.

WHITES /waits/ sb dial slang; the *-s* in what is a sg form is a common overcorrection. A drink of white rum.

1961 C. Lindo Kgn, gen, Rum-shop lingo /gi mi a wáits/.

WHITE SAGE sb dial. The wild bush *Lantana camara*, used in folk medicine. (The species are not always clearly distinguished.)

1927 Beckwith 29, White-sage..For a cold, boil as tea. 1952 FGC Man, StAnn, StC, Tre /wait siej/—same as wild sage; light-coloured stem, white flowers. [*L. reticulata?*] 1954 *WIMJ* 25, *Lantana camara*..Wild Sage; White Sage.

WHITE SANTA (MARIA) sb. The tree *Calophyllum longifolium.*

1926 Fawcett 200. 1952 FGC, see SANTA MARIA.

WHITE SEA-EGG sb dial. The short-spined greenish sea-egg (called 'white' in contrast to the larger, long-spined black sea-egg or SEA-NEEDLE).

1952 FGC StAnn, White sea-egg close in to the shore.

WHITE SHARK sb. The shark *Carcharodon carcharias.*

1854–5 *TJSA* I 145, Squalus carcharias—White Shark. 1892 Cockrell list, White shark—ground shark, tiger shark. 1952 FGC StE, StM /wait shaak iz a manĺita/ *White shark is a man-eater.*

WHITE SHOT sb obs; a parallel formation to BLACK SHOT. A white man, or a band of whites, bearing firearms.

1736 House of Assembly (1915 Cundall 174) [Payments voted to a party raised to suppress rebellious negroes:] Each white shot, twenty shillings; each black shot, ten shillings; and each baggage-negro five shillings. 1793 Edwards (1801) III 310.

WHITE SORREL sb. The variety of *Hibiscus sabdariffa* having white 'heads'. *G*

1740 Importance 34, see RED SORREL. 1774 Long III 805, Red Sorrel..White Sorrel..The acid of the white (or rather yellow flowered) is somewhat fainter than the other ..The flowers are made, with the help of sugar, into very agreeable tarts and jellies; or fermented into a cooling beverage. 1958 FGC StAnd ('white sorrel' still said to distinguish from red).

WHITE SQUALL sb now chiefly dial; cf *OED squall sb*[2] I c, →1889.

[1. A squall in which there are no dark clouds; cf WHITE RAIN.

1858 Chambre II 83, They had not proceeded far before a white squall upset the boat, and many of the guests.. were drowned.]

2. Transf: Hunger. Cf SQUALLY.

1943 *GL* Man, Port, White squall, hunger. 1955 FGC Man, same.

WHITE SQUIRREL sb dial. A variety of the SQUIRREL fish with shiny scales.

1952 FGC StE /wait skweril/.

WHITE STALK (COCO) sb; cf WHITE. The type of coco with light-coloured (green) leaf-stalks.

1929 Beckwith 17, In Mandeville were enumerated the.. 'Jeremy' as the biggest, and the 'White Stalk'.

WHITE-STICK (CASSADA) sb; see quots. The variety of cassava which has green stalks.

1952 FGC StAnn, StE, StT /wait-stik kasaada/—there is also black-stick and red-stick. *G*

WHITE-STICK (FERN) sb dial; <WHITE+STICK. A fern having green leaf stems: see quots.

1927 Beckwith 14, For a cold or 'any sickness at all', wrap in a wad 3 leaves of Cashew-nut and a plant each of Maiden-hair fern, 'White-stick' and 'Rat-ears', boil them together strong and bottle for drinking. 1954 *WIMJ* 29, *Dryopteris* sp..? Whitestick.

WHITE SWEETWOOD sb. In Grisebach's use: *Nectandra coriacea* (Sweetwood, etc.) and *N. antillana* (Shingle-wood, etc.). (Fawcett.)

1756 Browne 214, see LOBLOLLY WHITEWOOD. 1864 Grisebach 788, White Sweet-wood: *Nectandra sanguinea* and *leucantha.*

WHITE-THORN sb bot. The tree *Macrocnemum jamaicense*, which, when in bloom, somewhat resembles the European whitethorn.

1814 Lunan II 277–8, White-thorn. Macrocnemum.. jamaicense..Mr Anthony Robinson says he found it plentifully on the road from Tony Abbott's to Clarendon Cross, where it was known by the name of White-Thorn. 1864 Grisebach 788. 1936 Fawcett 4.

WHITEWASHING vbl sb slang obs. Religious conversion accepted insincerely to save one's life.

1740 Importance 26, Sir Nicholas Laws sent his Letter.. to demand them [*sc* pirates] of the Spaniards, who answer'd, 'They were there as other Subjects of their Lord the King, being brought voluntarily over to the Holy Catholic Faith, and have received the Water of Baptism'; which those Rogues nick-name *white-washing*. So you may guess what sort of Converts they were, and what Credit they brought to their new Religion.

WHITE WATER-GRASS sb dial. The green-leaved WATER-GRASS (*Commelina* spp) in contrast to RED WATER-GRASS.

1951 FGC Man.

WHITE-WATER GRUNT sb dial. A fish of the GRUNT kind which is caught in rough water.

1952 FGC StM.

WHITE WATTLE sb.

1. The tree *Diospyros tetrasperma*, having white wood that is split to make wattles.

1943 *NHN* II 26, White Wattle.

2. The shrub *Miconia lævigata*, with white bark; it is used for wattles.

1952 FGC StM /wait wakl/. 1955 *WIMJ* 145, see FOWL BONE.

WHITE WENSHMAN sb dial. A light-coloured *wenshman* fish.

1952 FGC StJ /wait wenshman/ same as HORSE-EYE WENSHMAN.

WHITE WILLOW sb. The tree *Capparis indica*, which has light-coloured bark and some resemblance to the willow in its leaves.

1914 Fawcett 232, White willow.

WHITE-WING DOVE (or **PIGEON,** obs) sb. The wild dove *Zenaida asiatica*: see quots.

1840 Chamberlaine in *Almanack* 21, The white-wing pigeon (Columba leucoptera). 1847 Gosse 304, White-wing Dove..*Turtur leucopterus*..This is a turtle of much elegance. Its general aspect resembles that of the Pea-dove, but its colour is less warm, and its figure less plump. 1952 FGC Man, StAnd, StAnn, StC, StM, StT /wait wing/ feed in trees, fly in droves.

WHITE WITHE sb.

[1725 Sloane 26, This Shrub has a stalk no bigger than a Swan's Quill, cover'd with a whitish colour'd smooth, Bark.] 1920 Fawcett 233, see DRAGON WITHE.

WHITE-WOOD sb. *BA*

1. Two closely similar trees of the *Bignonia* family: *Tecoma leucoxylon* and *T. pentaphylla*.

1696 Sloane 154, Nerio affinis arbor..Leucoxylum.. White wood. 1725 Sloane 62, White Wood. This tree is as large as any of this Island, having a very great streight Trunc cover'd with a smooth whitish Bark, under which is its very hard Wood, which is white. 1756 Browne 263, Bignonia 1..White Cedar, or White-wood. 1814 Lunan II 278, White-Wood or Cedar. Bignonia. 1864 Grisebach 789.

2. The tree *Ocotea leucoxylon*.

[1756 Browne 214, see LOBLOLLY WHITEWOOD.] 1814 Lunan II 220, Laurus..leucoxylon. White-Wood. 1864 Grisebach 789. 1914 Fawcett 211, *O. leucoxylon*..White-wood, Loblolly Sweet-wood. 1941 Swabey 31.

3. The tree *Nectandra antillana*.

1864 Grisebach 789. 1914 Fawcett 215. 1941 Swabey 31, Sweetwood, Yellow—(Shinglewood, Whitewood, Long-leaf Sweetwood). *Nectandra antillana*..The wood is of a pale yellow colour and merges into the sapwood.

4. The tree *Drypetes lateriflora*.

1920 Fawcett 269, White Wood, Guiana Plum..The wood of this species is..of a rich, dark brown colour, with thick yellow sapwood. 1941 Swabey 22.

5. A tree of uncert identity.

a 1726 Barham (1794) 207–8, see WHITE FIDDLEWOOD.

WHITEWOOD BARK sb bot. The bark (and tree) *Canella winterana*.

1864 Grisebach 789, Whitewood-bark. 1926 Fawcett 208, Whitewood Bark. 1955 *WIMJ* 157, see CANELLA.

WHITEWOOD CEDAR sb. The tree *Tecoma leucoxylon*, once used medicinally against the poison of the Manchioneel.

1864 Grisebach 789, Whitewood-cedar: *Tecoma leucoxylon*.

WHITE YAM sb; <*white*+YAM. *Dioscorea alata*—a fine white-fleshed yam. *G*

1814 Lunan II 309, Dioscorea..alata..They are generally known by the name of white-yam, from the superior whiteness of their inside. 1864 Grisebach 789. 1913 Harris 42–3, *White yam* and its varieties belong to Dioscorea alata..The white yams are planted last and they take ten to twelve months to arrive at maturity. 1954 *FG* 444, The White Yam is considered the best of the yam family..There are three or four varieties of the white yam, but the finest is that known as the flour yam.

WHITEY-WHITEY sb; iterative from *white* +-*y*.

1959 DeC Han /waiti-waiti/ an albino Negro.

WHITING, WHITENING /waitn, waitning/ sb dial; the second form has internal intrusive *n*—cp *fishning*, *huntning*, etc. The fish *Chloroscombrus chrysurus*, which seems to be shiny white right through.

1892 Cockrell list, Whiting. 1950 Smith in *NHN* 225, Whiting—Jamaican name for the Bumper, one of the Jack fish. 1952 FGC StJ /waitn/ mos' like Jack. StE (2 informants) /waitning/ a flat, shine fish, same colour of a kingfish; catch on line; one kind has like a piece of tape on back fin, one inch long or more. Also Deep-water whitening.

WHITTAKER sb; surname. A variety of sweet-potato (prob named after someone who succeeded with it).

1952 FGC StC, StT /wítika/ white skin, generally round; slip is fine. *The plant has a thin stem.*

WHOOPING BOY /húupin bwáai/ sb dial. A ghost or 'duppy' which is supposed to haunt about at night: see quots. Also attrib.

1929 Beckwith 98–9, Whooping Boy rides three-foot Horse, whooping like a human being and dancing on the twigs in the woods. 1956 Mc StE (Accom) and from *Gleaner* 19 Aug 1956 /huupin bwai dopi/—a duppy who appears only at certain seasons and in certain places. He manifests himself with loud whoopings and cracking of whip, being the duppy of the man who used to pen the cattle on an estate in slavery times. He returns to where the cattle pen used to be.

WHOORA interrog or rel pron dial arch; prob <*who* by analogy to *wara*. The spp prob repr pronuncs /hura/ and /wura/. Who. =URA. *BL*

1896 Bates 122, You know whoora tek my fowl? 1943 *GL* StJ, Wurra, who.

WHOY see *waay*.

WHUNU see UNU.

WHYNE see WIND vb.

wi, WI see WE[3], WITH, WILL.

wich see WHICH.

WICH PART see WHICH PART.

WICKER-WITHE sb dial. A kind of 'wis'—a climbing plant of the philodendron kind—whose aerial roots are used as wicker.

1952 FGC StM /wika wis/ sucks to trees; roots hang down 30 to 40 feet; cut it, boil it, strip skin, make wicker chairs.

WIFE sb dial. A euphemism once applied to an overseer's mistress. *G*

1839 McMahon 186, The overseers in Jamaica generally kept one particular mistress, called by themselves 'housekeepers', but by the labourers their 'wives'.

WIG sb dial. A style of hair-cutting for men: see quot.

1952 FGC StJ (Falmouth), A wig—i.e. like a judge's wig, with a front peak, no razor line at the back. When the customer wants this, he says, therefore, to the barber, 'Try me!'

WIGGLE-WIGGLE vb dial; iterative from *wiggle*. To wriggle, to move with a sinuous motion.

1952 FGC StAnd, Snake waitin'-boy has legs but just wiggle-wiggle and run gone.

WILD ACKEE sb. The tree *Guarea glabra*; the name refers to the seed capsule which has cells containing the seeds and somewhat resembling the ackee pod.

1886 Hooper 32, see ALLIGATOR WOOD. 1920 Fawcett 215, see MUSK WOOD. 1952 FGC StAnd, StAnn, StM.

WILD BACHELOR-BUTTON sb dial. See CAESAR OBEAH. *G*

WILD BARSLEY see next.

WILD BASIL /wail-baazil, ~-baazl, ~-baazli/ occas /~-baazm/ sb. The herb *Ocimum micranthum*, valued in folk remedies.

1927 Beckwith 29, Wild-barsley..'Number one as a tea' in case of fever and also rub the leaves over the body. 1952 FGC Port, StE, StT /wail-baazl/; StT, Tre /wail-baazil/; StAnn, StM /wail baazli/; Tre /wail baazm/. 1953 *WIMJ* 247, Wild Barsley; Mosquito Bush, Wild Basil. Used as a general beverage.

WILD BRAZILETTO sb.

1914 Fawcett 251–2, see BASTARD BRAZILETTO.

WILD BROOM sb dial. One of the several kinds of BROOM-WEED: see quot 1955.

1952 FGC StM, Wild broom is a herb weed; black wild-broom has bunches of flowers; broomweed has pods. 1955 *WIMJ* 145, *Malachra alceæfolia*..Wild Broom; Wild Ochra.

WILD BUR /wail bor/ sb dial. One type of bur: see quots.

1952 FGC StM /wáil bór/; StT, see BUR-BUR 2.

WILD CABBAGE sb. = MOUNTAIN CABBAGE.

1952 FGC StJ /wail kyabij/ eat raw or cook.

WILD CANE sb. The canes *Arundo occidentalis* and *A. saccharoides*. *BA G*

1707 Sloane 109, The wild Cane. This rises to fifteen Foot high..It grows on all sides of the Rio Cobre, and in Marshy Grounds. 1756 Browne 138, Arundo 1..The larger wild or Bambu Cane. 1774 Long III 753, Wild-Cane. 1814 Lunan II 279, Wild-Cane or Reed. Arundo. 1952 FGC StM, StT /wail kien/ like bamboo.

WILD CARROT sb prob obs; see quot. The JOHN-CROW BUSH.

1837 Macfadyen 23, *Bocconia frutescens*. From the colour of the root, it commonly receives the name of the Wild Carrot.

WILD CASHEW sb. The tree *Byrsonima smallii*, with leaves somewhat resembling those of the cashew. *G*

1920 Fawcett 223, Wild Cashew.

WILD CASSADA sb dial. Because of the shape of the leaf: 1. The shrub *Jatropha gossypifolia* (also called BELLYACHE BUSH). Also, perh because of the fruit: 2. *Prunus myrtifolia* (also called ANTS-WOOD, CHINK WOOD, COCKROACH WOOD, MAROON LANCEWOOD). 3. The tree *Turpinia occidentalis* (also called IRON WOOD, CASSADA WOOD, MUTTON WOOD). *G*

1. See quots.

1696 Sloane 41, Ricinus minor..Wild Cassada. a 1726 Barham (1794) 35, There is another plant, called wild cassada, and is known by no other name by the people in Jamaica, but for what reason I cannot tell, it being in no respect like the other cassada. 1864 Grisebach 782, Wild Cassava. 1946 *NHN* III 13, Wild Cassada. 1954 *WIMJ* 30, see CASSADA MARBLE.

2. See quots.

1914 Fawcett 259, Wild Cassada; Ants' Wood. 1941 Swabey 17, Cassada, Wild..When green it may be cut very easily but becomes very tough and durable when dry.

3. See quot.

1926 Fawcett 38, Wild Cassada.

WILD CERASEE sb. The wild vine *Cayaponia racemosa*, that somewhat resembles Cerasee in its way of growing.

1926 Fawcett 269, see MOUNTAIN BRYONY.

WILD CHERIMOYA sb. The tree *Annona jamaicensis*.

1914 Fawcett 199, Wild Cherimoya.

WILD CINNAMON sb; *OED* 1858.

1. The tree *Canella winterana*.

1696 Sloane 165–6, Arbor baccifera, laurifolia, aromatica ..Wild Cinamon Tree. 1774 Long III 705, Wild Cinnamon—Canella alba, or Bastard Cortex winteranus. 1926 Fawcett 208, see WHITE CINNAMON. 1955 *WIMJ* 157, see CANELLA.

2. The tree *Amomis caryophyllata*.

1814 Lunan I 76, see WILD CLOVE TREE. 1864 Grisebach 782. 1926 Fawcett 326–7, *A. caryophyllata*..Wild Cinnamon, Wild Clove, Bay Rum Tree, Bay Berry Tree.. The leaves distilled yield..'oil of bay', the most important ingredient of bay rum.

(WILD) CLARY /klíeri, klíerit/ sb now dial; cf *OED clary sb*[2] 1 b. *Heliotropium indicum*, a wild plant valued for various medicinal uses; see quots.

1696 Sloane 94, Heliotropium Indicum hormini foliis latioribus..Wild Clary. Ubique circa urbem *St Jago de la Vega* reperitur. 1814 Lunan II 248 [citing Barham]: We have a very common plant, that grows every where in Jamaica, called wild clary..Like the *heliotropes*, it cleanseth and consolidates wounds and ulcers, and is good against the inflammations of the skin. It is boiled with cocoa-nut oil, to cure the sting of scorpions and the bite of a mad dog. 1952 FGC StT, Tre /klíeri/, StM, good to remove bumps on the face from shaving; Han, Blue /klíerit/ good for the eyes. [This preserves the folk belief from England, but adds a new form, evid by folk-etym.] 1955 *WIMJ* 158, *Heliotropium indicum* L. Boraginaceæ (Wild) Clary; Turnsoles; Scorpion Weed; Erysipelas Plant.

WILD CLEMATIS sb.

1914 Fawcett 190, *Clematis dioica*..Traveller's toy, Wild Clematis..The long, slender branches are used as withes.

WILD CLOVE (TREE) sb obs. = WILD CINNAMON.

1814 Lunan I 76, Myrtus..acris..It is commonly called *wild cinnamon*, or *wild clove tree*, and is said to be the *bayberry* of Hughes. 1926 Fawcett 327.

WILD COCO sb dial. = GROUND COCO 2. *G*

1910 Fawcett 113. 1952 FGC Port, StE, StT, Tree /wail koko/ same as scratch-coco; whitish, eaten by hogs; used to bait fish pots.

WILD COFFEE sb dial.

1. The bush *Cassia occidentalis*, whose seeds are used as a substitute for coffee. *G*

1920 Fawcett 104, C. occidentalis..Stinking Weed, Wild Coffee. 1953 *WIMJ* 239, see DANDELION.

2. The shrub *Faramea occidentalis*, somewhat resembling the coffee bush.

1864 Grisebach 783, Wild Coffee. 1936 Fawcett 81, Wild Jessamine (Browne); Wild Coffee.

3. The tree *Zuelania guidonia*, whose berries somewhat resemble coffee berries.

1864 Grisebach 783, Wild Coffee: *Zuelania lætioides.*

4. The shrub *Eugenia disticha*, whose reddish berry resembles that of coffee.

1864 Grisebach 783.

5. The shrub *Psychotria pubescens*, with coffee-like seeds.

1936 Fawcett 102, Wild Coffee.

6. The shrub *Palicourea domingensis*, with a berry somewhat like that of coffee.

1936 Fawcett 110, Wild Coffee.

WILD DAMSON sb. The tree *Eroteum theæoides*, having a fruit in shape and colour resembling the damson plum.

1926 Fawcett 185, Wild Damson.

WILD EBONY sb. The tree *Colubrina ferruginosa*, with wood somewhat like that of ebony, used in inlay work.

1926 Fawcett 68, see BLACK VELVET. 1941 Swabey 30, Snake-wood—(Greenheart, Wild or Mountain Ebony, Black Velvet).

WILD GINGER sb. *G*

1. The plant *Renealmia racemosa*, which grows from a root-stock resembling that of ginger.

1696 Sloane 61, Zinziber sylvestre minus..Wild Ginger. 1814 Lunan II 280, Wild-Ginger..Root fleshy, branches, having the smell and taste of ginger. 1864 Grisebach 784, Wild-Ginger: *Renealmia* and *Costus.*

2. The similar but larger plant *Costus spicatus*.

1814 Lunan II 281, Wild-Ginger. Costus. 1864 Grisebach 784 (see above). 1952 FGC Port, StE, Tre /wail jinja/.

WILD GRANADILLA sb dial. Vines and fruit of probably more than one kind; in StE a small *Passiflora*; in Tre, some kind of DUPPY PUMPKIN; in StT one having fruit like a cherry enclosed in a thin, papery membrane. *G*

1952 FGC.

WILD GRAPE sb. Any of various species of *Coccoloba*: *C. plumieri*, *C. swartzii*, *C. tenuifolia*, and *C. longifolia* (1954 Howard 85, 90, 94, 97); also *Vitis tiliæfolia*; see also quot 1941.

1864 Grisebach 784. 1914 Fawcett 115, Red Grape, Wild Grape; *ibid* 118. 1926 Fawcett 74, Water Withe, Wild Grape. 1941 Swabey 21, Grape, Wild—(Pigeon Plum). *Coccoloba laurifolia.*

WILD GUINEP sb. The tree *Exothea paniculata*, which resembles the guinep in its flowers and some other features.

1926 Fawcett 61–2, E. paniculata..Wild Ginep. 1941 Swabey 21, Wild Guinep. 1943 *NHN* II 68, Wild Guinep. 1952 FGC StAnn, Wild Guinep—same as mallet wood; fruit smaller, leaves finer than guinep. StE /wail genep—tek it mek poliin/ [i.e. sleepers] for railway.

WILD GUNGO sb dial. *Vernonia divaricata*; the bush has a superficial resemblance to that of GUNGO PEAS.

1955 *WIMJ* 76, (Old) Man Bitter Bush; Wild Gungo. The use of this plant to make tea for stomach upsets is confirmed.

WILD HOOK (CALALU) sb dial. A wild vine whose leaves are used as CALALU; identity uncert but prob *Syngonium auritum*.

1952 FGC Port, StC /wáil úk/ tangles on trees; when young, used for calalu. StJ /wáil húk/ use leaves for soup.

WILD HOPS sb.

1. The herb *Hyptis capitata*.

1696 Sloane 65, Sideritis spicata, scrophulariæ folio, flore albo..Wild Hoppes. 1801 Dancer 367, Gargles and Mouth Waters. Wild-hops (Clinopod. rugos.)—Infuse with honey and alum. 1814 Lunan II 282–3, Wild-Hops. Clinopodium..capitatum..Barham calls this plant Ironwort..Dr Wright notices it under the name of Wild Batchelor's Button. 1955 *WIMJ* 159, *Hyptis capitata*.. (Wild) Batchelor's Button; Cæsar Obeah; Wild Hops; Iron Wort.

2. The shrub *Flemingia strobilifera*, with flowers strikingly resembling hops.

1920 Fawcett 75, F. strobilifera..Wild Hops. 1954 *FG* 584, Wild Hops..This legume is a fast-spreading shrub that can be a serious pest in pastures.

3. The herb *Blechum brownei*, which, when young, has some resemblance to hops.

1946 *NHN* III 58, Plants of *Blechum Brownei*—The 'Wild Hops' with whitish flowers. 1954 *WIMJ* 28, Wild Hops; John Bush.

WILD INDIGO sb; *OED* 1866.

1. The shrub *Indigofera suffruticosa*.

1696 Sloane 142, Coluteæ affinis fruticosa argentea..Wild Indigo. 1756 Browne 302, The wild Indigo. This last species is very common in Jamaica, and grows wild in all the Savannas. 1920 Fawcett 16, Wild Indigo, Guatimala Indigo.

2. The shrub *Cassia tora*. Obs.

1696 Sloane 148, Sena minor herbacea..Wild Indigo.

WILD IPECACUANHA sb. = RED-HEAD (*Asclepias curassavica*).

1756 Browne 183, Asclepias 2..Wild or Bastard Ipecacuanha..The juice, and pounded plant, is applied to stop the blood in fresh wounds. 1954 *WIMJ* 28, Redhead; Bastard, Wild, Ipecacuanha; Blood Flower.

WILD JASMINE sb.

1. *Plumieria alba*.

1696 Sloane 154, Nerium arboreum altissimum..flore albo..The wild Jasmin Tree.

2. The shrub *Faramea occidentalis*, with very fragrant flowers resembling those of the jasmine.

1756 Browne 142, Pavetta?..The wild Jessamine..the flowers are pretty long and tubular, and retain both the smell and make of the garden Jessamine. 1864 Grisebach 784, Wild Jasmine. 1936 Fawcett 81, Wild Jessamine (Browne); Wild Coffee.

WILD LEMON sb obs. Evid some kind of *Amyris* or Sweetwood. [Lunan's index lists 'Wild Lemon' and refers to his treatment of Amyris, but the name is not used there.] *G*

1793 Edwards I 187, There are many beautiful varieties adapted for cabinet-work, among others the bread-nut, the wild-lemon, and the well-known mahogany.

WILD LIME sb.

1. The tree *Rheedia sessiliflora*, having a fruit somewhat of the shape of a lime.

1926 Fawcett 197, *R. sessiliflora*..Wild Lime.

2. The small tree *Palicourea pulchra*, having somewhat the appearance of a lime tree.

1936 Fawcett 107, *P. pulchra*..Wild Lime.

3. The small tree *Linociera ligustrina*: see quot.

1943 *NHN* II 82, *Linociera ligustrina*—Wild Lime..The common name is difficult to explain, but I am told the odour of the crushed leaves and fresh cut wood resembles that of a lime.

WILD LIQUORICE sb; *OED* 1760, 1866.

1. The vine *Abrus precatorius*, which has a strong smell of liquorice.

1696 Sloane 70–1, Phaseolus glycyrrhizites..Wild Liquorice. a 1726 Barham (1794) 88, We have two sorts of plants that have a liquorice-taste: The one is a vine, whose leaves have the true taste of liquorice, and is therefore called wild liquorice. [The other: LIQUORICE-WEED.] 1756 Browne 297, The Wild Liquorice, or Red-Bead Vine. 1920 Fawcett 43. 1954 *WIMJ* 28, see JOHN-CROW BEADS.

2. The bush now called LIQUORICE-WEED. Obs.

1696 Sloane 81, Veronica fruticosa..Wild Liquorice or Sweet-weed.

3. The vine *Rhynchosia phaseoloides*: see quot.

1920 Fawcett 74–5, *R. phaseoloides*..Seeds..somewhat like those of *Abrus precatorius*, and the plant is therefore sometimes (though wrongly) called 'Wild Liquorice'.

WILD MAHOE sb dial. = SEA-SIDE MAHOE.

1952 FGC Han, Wild mahoe—sea-cotton, down-cotton.

WILD MAHOGANY sb. The tree *Antirrhœa jamaicensis*, whose wood makes a good substitute for mahogany.

1864 Grisebach 785, White or Wild Mahogany. 1936 Fawcett 60, see GOLD SPOON.

WILD MAMMEE sb. *G*

1. The tree *Rheedia lateriflora*, with a fruit somewhat resembling the Mammee.

1926 Fawcett 196, Wild Mammee.

2. The tree *Calophyllum jacquinii*, with leaves somewhat like those of the Mammee.

1926 Fawcett 200, Santa Maria, Wild Mammee.

WILD MAMMEE-SAPOTA sb. A tree of the genus *Ternstrœmia*.

1926 Fawcett 182, Wild Mammee-Sapota, Scarlet Seed.

WILD MARIGOLD sb.

1954 *WIMJ* 32, see WATER-WEED.

WILD MELON sb. A wild vine producing a bitter, melon-like fruit: DUPPY MELON, CLIMBING MELON. *G*

1926 Fawcett 264, *Cionosicys pomiformis*..Wild Melon.

WILD MINT sb chiefly dial.

1. The shrub *Lantana involucrata*, with a smell more like sage than like mint.

1954 *WIMJ* 30, *L. involucrata*..Wild Sage; Wild Mint.

2. The herb *Micromeria viminea*: see quot.

1955 *WIMJ* 81, Peppermint; Wild Mint; All-Heal. Despite the fact that country people with whom we have talked say that *M. viminea* as found wild is not the same as the peppermint which they cultivate we have not, so far, been able to separate them botanically. It is certain, however, that the plants smell quite differently, only the cultivated plant having the characteristic peppermint odour.

3. The herb *Borreria lævis*.

1952 FGC Man /wail mint/.

WILD-NEGRO sb obs. A MAROON negro. ('Maroon': ult < Sp *cimarrón*, wild.)

1740 Importance 16–17, There are three sorts of Negroes, Free, Wild or Runaways, and Slaves..The Wild or Runaway Negroes are some of the descendants of those that took to the Woods, when the Spaniards deserted the Island. 1774 Long III 973, Marons (commonly called the Wild-Negroes).

WILD NUTMEG sb. An unidentified plant.

1940 Lynn-Grant 98, 'Wild nutmeg' seeds were found in the droppings [of the Guana lizard] on Goat Island.

WILD OATS sb bot. A wild grass *Pharus latifolius*.

1756 Browne 344, Wild Oats..This plant is pretty frequent in all the woody hills of Jamaica, and reckoned a hearty wholesome food for all sorts of cattle. 1864 Grisebach 786.

WILD OILNUT sb. The shrub *Jatropha divaricata*, named for its resemblance to the castor-oil bush.

1920 Fawcett 314, Wild Oil Nut.

WILD OKRA sb.

1. Species of *Malachra*, esp *M. alceæfolia*; these have mucilaginous sap: cf OKRA. *G*

1801 Dancer (1809) 385, The ochro, the wild ochro, &c. yield it [*sc* mucilage], I believe, in still greater abundance. [This may belong with 2.] 1864 Grisebach 786. 1926 Fawcett 122, *Malachra*..Wild Ochra. 1955 *WIMJ* 145, see WILD BROOM.

2. The MUSK OKRA, which is not eaten.

1926 Fawcett 142, *Hibiscus Abelmoschus*..Wild Ochra.

WILD OLIVE sb.

1. The tree *Bucida buceras*, with a fruit resembling the olive.

a 1726 Barham (1794) 102, There are several sorts [of mangrove]..The two most noted are, the red and black mangroves..There is another commonly called wild olive. 1891 Fawcett 18. 1941 Swabey 27, Olive, Wild—(Black Olive, Olive Bark Tree). *Bucida buceras*.

2. The small tree *Ximenia americana*, thought to resemble the olive.

1864 Grisebach 786, Wild Olive: *Ximenia americana*, *Bucida Buceras* and *capitata*.

3. The tree *Buchenavia capitata*, with wood like olivewood.

1864 Grisebach 786, see above. 1941 Swabey 33, Yellow Sanders—(Wild Olive)..Wood of light yellow colour; takes a good polish.

WILD ORANGE sb.

1. The tree *Esenbeckia pentaphylla*, with hard yellow wood.

1823 Stewart 210, They [*sc* floors] are formed of mahogany, wild orange, or other hard wood. [This may belong with another sense.] 1920 Fawcett 181, Wild Orange. 1941 Swabey 27, Orange, Wild.

2. The tree *Drypetes alba*.

1864 Grisebach 786, Wild Orange.

3. The tree *Sarcomphalus laurinus*; also called BASTARD LIGNUM-VITÆ.

1943 *NHN* II 59, Wild Orange.

WILD PAPAW sb. The tree *Carica jamaicensis*.

1696 Sloane 203, Papaya minor..The female wild Papaw Tree..The male wild Papaw Tree. 1926 Fawcett 246, *C. jamaicensis*..Wild Papaw.

WILD PASSION-FLOWER sb; *DAE* 1852→.

1801 Dancer 366, Wild passion-flower, or Contrayerva (*Passiflora normalis*).

WILD PEAR sb.

1. See quot.

1864 Grisebach 786, Wild Pear: *Clethra tinifolia*.

2. See quot.

1914 Fawcett 208, *Persea Harrisii*..Wild Pear.

WILD PEAS sb dial. Some kind of wild pea, unidentified.

1952 FGC Han /wail piiz/ similar to pinder but has a pod, round 2½ in.; dark reddish-purple seed.

WILD PHYSIC-NUT sb. The tree *Euphorbia punicea*, somewhat like the physic-nut.

1864 Grisebach 786, Wild Physic-nut: Euphorbia punicea. 1920 Fawcett 345, Wild Physic Nut.

WILD PIMENTO sb. Evid a name for a tree also called 'rod-wood'.

1847 Gosse 237, On a bush whose glossy black berries have obtained for it the name of *wild pimento*, but which is better known as rod-wood, we found a nest of the Orange Quit.

WILD PINDER sb. Any of certain species of *Desmodium* (see quot 1955); the plant somewhat resembles that of the peanut.

1927 Beckwith 12, Bee-bur..'Wild pinder', 'Strong-back', 'Bee-bush'..'Good fe weakness and pain fe true'. 1952 FGC Han, StT, Tre /wail pinda/. Also Man. 1955 *WIMJ* 158, *Desmodium axillare..D. procumbens..*; *D. supinum*..Wild Pinder; Fever Weed; French Honeysuckle.

WILD PINE sb; <*wild*+PINE; *OED* 1707→ Epiphytic plants of genus *Tillandsia*. *BA G N*

1696 Sloane 76–7, Wild Pine. Ubique in sylvis, truncis & ramis arborum..innascitur. 1794 Edwards (1801) III 347, All the water..was exhausted, and the enemy's only resource was in the leaves of the *wild-pine**..*It takes root on the body of a tree..By the conformation of its leaves, it catches and retains water from every shower. Each leaf resembles a spout, and forms at its base a natural bucket or reservoir. 1873 Rampini 42, Those noble [cotton] trees..covered up to the summit with wild pines and other parasitical plants. (1961 Current, FGC.)

WILD-PINE CRAB sb; <WILD PINE+*crab*. A small crab which lives in the epiphytic plants (which store water at the base of their leaves) on trees. (*Metopaulias depressus.*)

1961 Seen in Institute of Ja exhibit (FGC).

WILD-PINE SERGEANT sb. =BLACKBIRD 3.

1936 Bond 360, Jamaican Blackbird (*Nesopsar nigerrimus*) *Local names:*—Black Banana Bird; Corporal Bird; Wild Pine Sergeant. 1955 Taylor 88, The Wild-pine Sergeant ..which is related to the Orioles, is a glossy black bird with a pointed bill which it uses for rummaging in the wild-pines (*epiphytic bromeliads*) growing on the forest trees.

WILD PLANTAIN sb; *OED* 1756.

1. The tree *Heliconia bihai*, related to the plantain tree. *G N*

1696 Sloane 193, Musa humilior..Wild Plantans. 1725 Sloane 148, Wild-Plantains. 1756 Browne 364, Musa 3.. The wild Plantane Tree. This beautiful plant grows wild in most of the cooler mountains of Jamaica. (1961 Current, FGC.)

2. The herb more commonly called ENGLISH PLANTAIN.

1955 *WIMJ* 160, *Plantago major*..Wild Plantain.

WILD POMEGRANATE sb. See quot.

1936 Fawcett 51, *Casasia..longipes*..Wild Pomegranate ..A tree 25–30 ft. high..Berry on a pedicel..the pericarp thick and woody.

WILD POPONAX sb; <*wild*+POPONAX. The small tree *Acacia tortuosa*.

1920 Fawcett 138, A. tortuosa..Wild Poponax, Acacia Bush. 1941 Swabey 12, Acacia Bush—(Wild Poponax).. Wood used for fence posts, firewood and charcoal.

WILD POTATO(-SLIP) sb; <*wild*+POTATO-SLIP 1. Various wild convolvulaceous plants similar in appearance to the sweet-potato: see quots. *G*

1756 Browne 152, Convolvulus 1. Scandens, foliis trilobis..The wild Potato-slip. 1864 Grisebach 787, Wild Potato: *Ipomœa fastigiata*. 1952 FGC Han, StT /wàil pitieta/—sea-side potato [*Ipomœa pes-capræ*]. 1954 *FG* 581, Hogmeat or Wild Potato (*Ipomœa tiliacea*). The wild potato is a member of a large group of at least twenty-four species of related vines ('wiss'), which have large, funnel-shaped flowers, some of them very showy and beautiful. All of them can be serious pests.

WILD PRUNE sb.

1941 Swabey 28, see PRUAN.

WILD PUMPKIN sb dial. =WILD MELON.

1959 UCWI Herbarium, Wild pumpkin, *Cionosycis pomiformis*.

WILD RICE sb.

1953 *WIMJ* 234, see RICE BITTERS 2.

WILD ROSEMARY sb bot; *OED* (1611) 1753→. The shrub *Croton linearis*.

1696 Sloane 44, see SPANISH ROSEMARY. a1726 Barham (1794) 129, The leaf somewhat resembles..what they call wild rosemary in Jamaica. 1864 Grisebach 786, Wild Rosemary: Croton Cascarilla. 1955 *WIMJ* 78, *Croton linearis*..(Wild or Spanish) Rosemary. This plant, which has a pleasant aromatic odour, is much used by Jamaican peasants as a hair wash. As in Browne's day it is still used in baths for fever and colds.

WILD SAGE sb dial.

1. Any of the common wild *Lantana* species, used in folk medicine. See quot 1954.

1696 Sloane 163, Periclymenum rectum salviæ folio rugoso majore..The largest sort of wild sage..Periclymenum rectum salviæ folio rugoso minore..Wild Sage. 1756 Browne 268–9, Lantana 2..Wild Sage. Lantana 3.. Wild Sage with white flowers. 1952 FGC StAnn, Wild sage—black sage, purple sage, white sage. Also StM, StT, Tre. 1954 *WIMJ* 25, *Lantana camara*..Wild Sage ..*L. crocea..L. involucrata..L. trifolia*..It is highly probable that leaves of the above species of Lantana, together with others, are used indiscriminately to make a tea as a cold and fever remedy.

2. The herb *Salvia serotina* and perh other related species.

1864 Grisebach 787, Wild Sage: *Lantana* and *Salvia*. 1954 *WIMJ* 31, see CHICKEN-WEED.

WILD SAMPHIRE sb obs. In Sloane's use: The shrub *Heliotropium curassavicum*.

1696 Sloane 94, Heliotropium maritimum minus folio glauco..Wild Sampier. In palustribus maritimis. 1707 Sloane 213.

WILD SENNA sb bot; *OED* 1866.

1. The shrub *Cæsalpinia pulcherrima*, now generally called BARBADOS PRIDE.

1696 Sloane 149, Sena spuria arborea spinosa..Wild Sena or Spanish Carnations. a1726 Barham (1794) 16, see DOODLE-DOO. 1920 Fawcett 95.

2. Any of various small *Cassia* bushes used in folk remedies: see quots.

1927 Beckwith 15, Dandelion. *Cassia occidentalis*.. 'John Crow Pea', 'Wild Senna'..'Wild senna' tea cures constipation. *Ibid* 30, Wild-senna..*Cassia tora*. 1954 *WIMJ* 28, *C. obovata..C. occidentalis*..Wild Senna. (See DANDELION.)

WILD SHOT sb dial. =INDIAN SHOT.

1952 FGC StM, StT, Tre /wail shat/.

WILD SLIP sb dial. =WILD POTATO (SLIP).

1952 FGC StAnn (2), StE /wail slip/ wis. 1956 Mc Man /wail slip/ also /sip/ a creeper.

WILD SORREL sb. In Titford's use: A species of *Cissus*—perh *C. trifoliata*. *G*

1811 Titford Expl to Plate XIII, Wild Sorrel or Soursop, (Cissus) n.o. Hederaceæ. The leaves of this plant have an acid taste, and are used to make a cooling drink in fevers.

WILD SOURSOP sb.

1. =WILD SORREL; here the sourness is the reason for the name.

2. The tree *Annona montana*, and its fruit, closely related to the soursop; =DUPPY SOURSOP. *G*

1837 Macfadyen 7–8, see MOUNTAIN SOURSOP. 1914 Fawcett 195, Mountain or Wild Sour Sop..Fruit..dry, not edible.

3. Perh the small tree *Morinda citrifolia*, from the appearance of its fruit.

1952 FGC Han, Wild soursop. (Identity uncertain.)

WILD STARAPPLE sb. =DAMSON PLUM. *G*

1864 Grisebach 788, Wild Star-apple: *Chrysophyllum oliviforme*. 1952 FGC StE, Wild Starapple—in Clarkstown area called 'damsel'.

WILD STARCH sb dial. =STARCH BEAN, YAM BEAN. *G*

1873 Rampini 78, An almost level plateau, covered with grass, and ground orchids, and wild starch, and the lovely Bletia. 1952 FGC Han /wail staach/ take the root, like cassava, make starch.

WILD SUPPLE-JACK sb.

1. The shrub *Cardiospermum grandiflorum*.

1926 Fawcett 48, Wild Supple Jack..Stem to 25 ft. long, woody, pubescent.

2. Some species of *Cassia*.

1941 *NHN* I 3 9, Wild Supplejack (Cassia sp).

WILD SUSUMBER sb chiefly dial. GUMA (*Solanum nigrum*).

1944 *NHN* II 58, The genus *Solanum*..At the end of the scale it includes the wild Susumber, a small plant with black berries, and the Cockroach Poison, a thorny shrub with large bright orange coloured berries, both of which are very poisonous.

WILD TAMARIND /wail tambran, tambrin/ sb.

1. The tree *Pithecellobium arboreum*; *OED* 1833. *G*

1696 Sloane 151, Acacia arborea maxima..Wild Tamarinds. Circa urbem St Jago de la Vega. 1756 Browne 252, see MOUNTAIN TAMARIND. [*Ibid* 253, The shrubby wild Tamarind (1920 Fawcett 144, *Calliandra comosa*).] 1886 Hooper 28, Wild Tamarind, *Pithecolobium filicifolium*. 1920 Fawcett 148, Wild Tamarind..It saws freely,..is beautifully grained, takes a fine polish. 1952 FGC StAnd, StAnn, StM, StT.

2. =PARK NUT: *Acacia lutea*.

1920 Fawcett 138.

3. The herb *Phyllanthus niruri*, from the shape of the leaf.

1952 FGC StC /wail tambran/.

WILD TANSY sb bot. The herb *Ambrosia paniculata*, used in medicines.

1756 Browne 339–40, Ambrosia 1..Wild Tansey..This plant grows very common and luxuriant..It is a powerful vulnerary and resolutive. 1864 Grisebach 788, Wild Tansey. 1936 Fawcett 216, Wild Tansy..employed in baths and fomentations.

WILD THYME sb. The herb *Pilea microphylla*, with somewhat succulent stems and very small leaves, whence the name.

1927 Beckwith 11, 'Wild thyme'. For a woman in labour make it into a tea. 1954 *WIMJ* 25, see BABY PUZZLE.

WILD TOBACCO sb.

1. The shrub *Pluchea purpurascens*; so called from the shape of the leaf; =DOG BITTER.

1936 Fawcett 203, Wild Tobacco. 1952 FGC Han, StAnn, StC, StT, Tre /wàil tubáko/. 1955 *WIMJ* 76, Pluchea purpurascens..Bitter Tobacco; Wild Tobacco..used..to make a beverage which is thought useful in treating colds and fevers.

2. The closely related *Pluchea odorata*.

1953 *WIMJ* 243, *Pluchea odorata*..Riverside Tobacco; Wild Tobacco; Sweet-scented Fleabane.

WILD TOMATO sb. A wild solanaceous shrub with a fruit thought to resemble the tomato.

1955 *WIMJ* 153, *Physalis angulata*..Poisonous Cape Gooseberry; Wild Tomato..this species can be used to prepare tea to prevent an abortion after a fall during pregnancy.

WILD VINE sb obs.

1696 Sloane 172, see WATER-WITHE.

WILD WANGLA sb dial; <*wild*+WANGLA. =FUNK BUSH.

WILD WORMWOOD sb; *OED* 1696→. The herb *Parthenium hysterophorus*, used in folk medicine.

1696 Sloane 127, Artemisia humilior..Wild Wormwood. 1756 Browne 340, Parthenium 1..Wild Wormwood. This plant grows wild in most of the open fields round the island..It is observed to have much the same qualities with the Feverfew. 1864 Grisebach 789. 1953 *WIMJ* 243, *Parthenium hysterophorus*..Wild Wormwood; Dog-flea Weed; Whitehead; Mugwort; Bastard Feverfew.

WILD YAM sb; *OED* 1756→. *BL*

1. Plants of the genus *Dioscorea* or closely related genera, growing wild.

1725 Sloane 371, I have known this Root taken for wild Yams by Negroes, and eat by them, which purged them very much. Mr Barham MS. 1756 Browne 360, Dioscorea 3..The wild Yam. This plant grows wild in the inland woods of Jamaica, and bears very large capsules. It is not put to any use in that island. 1801 Dancer 363, see BASTARD SARSAPARILLA. 1864 Grisebach 789, Wild Yams: *Cissus sicyoides* and *Rajania pleioneura*. 1952 FGC Man, StAnd, etc. The term is used by country people (cultivators, etc) to include (1) native wild yams growing in the woods (cf AKAM, HIMBA), (2) escaped cultivated yams now in ruinate land, or (3) other plants having yam-like characteristics (as the twisting, winged or angular-stemmed vine, the leaves, the tuber)—e.g. *Smilax* spp.

2. The wild vine *Cissus sicyoides*; see also quot 1955. Also called PUDDING-WITHE.

1814 Lunan II 316, Cissus sicyoides..is known by the name of Wild Yam, it has a biting pungent taste, like that of arum, but dwells not so long upon the tongue. 1837 Macfadyen 178–9, *Cissus sicyoides*. Bastard Bryony..It has received the very ill-applied designation of 'the Wild Yam'. It is a favourite among the Negroes as an application to sores. 1864 Grisebach 789, see above. 1927 Beckwith 30, Wild-yam..'Mary bush'. For a bruise chop fine..Boil with 'pig-nut' for indigestion. 1954 *WIMJ* 26, 1955 *WIMJ* 158, C[issus] trifoliata..Sorrel Vine; Rat Ears; Pudding Wys (Withe)?; Wild Yam.

WILE vb[1] dial; ?<*wale*, to drive away (*EDD* *v.*[1] 9). [This would be phonetically irregular.] Evid, to drive, to chase. *BL*

1955 Bennett *Pedlar*, But me memba..All de vender dem ..Dah sell scissors an' fine teet' comb Till police wile dem weh.

WILE vb[2] dial; cf *OED Obs. rare*, to hoodwink, dupe. Also *SND* WILE *v.* 1. To trick, befool.

1956 BLB Man /mi dis a wail im/ *I am merely hoodwinking her* [mostly of tricking children].

wilk(**s**) sb dial; cf *OED whelk* β-form →1823. A whelk: but the form /wilk/ is universal among the fishermen and others; the word is often used in the plur with sg meaning.

1952 FGC Port (2), StC, StE, StJ, StM, StT, West /wilk, wilks/ StAnn /wiliks/. 1956 Mc StAnd (Port Royal) /wilks/ a sea shell-fish /jos laik a sniel/. 1958 DeC Clar /wilks/ grows in salt water, up to a quarter pound in weight and to three inches diameter.

WILL /wi/ vb dial; by ellipsis of (*to*) *be*. Will be.

1957 JB StAnd /efn mi kom dong a nait, it wi tuu haad fi kom op bak/ *If I come down at night, it will be too hard to come up again.*

WILLIAM BURKE CANE sb. A variety of sugar-cane connected in some way with William Burke.

1952 FGC Port.

WILLIE PEE sb dial; echoic. The bird *Blacicus caribæus.*

1956 Jeffrey-Smith 49, see RICKY-TEE.

WILLOW, (JAMAICA ~, WEEPING ~) sb.

1. The introduced tree *Casuarina equisetifolia*, now well known and widely cultivated.

1941 Swabey 17, Casuarina—(Willow). Introduced in 1788 and planted along sea coasts. 1944 *NHN* II 117–18, The Casuarina or 'Weeping Willow', as it is known in Jamaica is a native of Australia and the South Seas. We do not know just when it came to Jamaica..The specific name of our species..is *equisetifolia*. 1951 FGC StE (Malvern), Jamaica Willow. 1952 FGC StE, StM, Willow.

2. The introduced tree *Salix chilensis.*

1914 Fawcett 30–1, Willow. *S. chilensis*..Mr W. Harris states: 'The Salix trees at Troy were certainly planted, and I have never seen this species in a wild state'.

WIN vb dial. To defeat or beat (someone) in a contest of any kind. *BL G T; SC wíni.*

1924 Beckwith 121, So the two fellows who did bet him, he won them. *Ibid* 136. 1956 Mc StE /a wi win yu/ *I'll beat you.* 1958 DeC /hin win haavi, yu nyo/ *He defeated Harvey (in a lawsuit), you know.*

WIN see WEN.

WIND /win/ sb dial. Moving air taken as indicating the activity of spirits (usually evil ones). Cf BREEZE 2.

1953 Moore 33, Baptism is a protection of the child against 'bad wind'.

WIND /wain/ vb dial; cf *OED* v^1 4 →1887: '*Obs.* exc. *dial.*' To twist or turn the hips, esp provocatively, in dancing or walking.

1790 Moreton 156–7 [Girl dancing and singing:] Hip-saw! my deaa! You no shake like a-me! You no wind like a-me! 1943 *GL* Tre, Whyne, to roll. 1954 LeP StAnn, Wine, of a woman: to walk in a provocative fashion. 'Wine' to describe the swinging of hips. *BA BL G T*

WIND BUSH /win bush/ sb dial; <*wind* (flatulency) +BUSH 4. The shrub *Sida urens*, used as a carminative.

1955 *WIMJ* 145, Wind bush is used to make tea for a baby with 'gripe'.

WINDWARD /windad/ sb now chiefly dial. The eastern part of the Island. Also attrib. **s.**

1731–2 *Jrl. Assembly* 55, see LEEWARD. 1803 Dallas I 79, Windward Maroons—those settled in the eastern part of the island. 1956 Mc Man, Q. Where is X [a place]? A. /kwait tu windad/. *BA*

WINE see WIND vb.

WINGA, WINGEY, WINGI, WINGY, WINJE see next.

winji adj dial; <*winge*, to shrivel, as fruit kept too long (*EDD* v^2 *obs.*) +-*y*. Small, puny, weak, sickly-looking.

1943 *GL* Clar, StJ, Wingy, frail, weak and puny; Clar, Wingey, small; StE, Wingi, stunt[ed]; StE, Winga, slender; Kgn, Winje, sickly looking, undergrown, emaciated; StE, Winji, small (person). 1952 FGC StAnn, West /winji/ the smallest pig in a litter. 1956 Mc Man /dat lítl wínji píg/.

winji-winji vb dial; iterative from *winji*. To shrink together, make oneself small.

1950 Pioneer 34 [Anancy:] Se' yah Bra Puss, top wingy-wingy up yuhself pon me head yaw sah. [Puss is trying to hide in a basket on Anancy's head.]

WINKER, WINKY sb dial; <*wink* + -*er*, or -*y*. The firefly that 'winks' its light intermittently; =BLINKY.

1952 FGC Tre /wingka/ stranger fly. 1956 Mc Clar, Man /wingki/ a firefly.

WINTER'S CINNAMON sb obs; *OED* →1712. Winter's bark.

a 1726 Barham (1794) 42, Cinnamon. We have only one sort, called Winter's cinnamon, from one captain Winter, that first carried it to England.

WI-O see *waay-uo*.

wipri sb dial; <*whip-ray*. Whip-ray. (The StdE form is known to the fishermen but /wípri/ is virtually the only form they use.) *BL*

1952 FGC StE, StJ, StM /wípri/ has bone on tail, numbs you; bigger than /tinggri, kiit/, same as numb-fish.

WIRE-BACK JACK sb dial. A fish of the JACK kind that has a 'wire' or extension coming back from the dorsal fin.

1952 FGC StJ, StM /waia bak jak/.

WIRE-GRASS sb; *OED* 1864. In Jamaica, the grass *Paspalum filiforme.*

1864 Grisebach 789.

WIRE-RUSH sb obs; *OED wire sb* 16b, 1756. One or more varieties of *Scirpus.*

1756 Browne 126, Scirpus 1..The small Wire-rush.. Scirpus 2..The larger Wire-rush. Both these little plants are very frequent in the swamps of Jamaica.

WIRRY-WIRRY see *were-were.*

WIS, WIS-WIS /wis, wist/ sb and vb chiefly dial; <*withe* (or *withes*), a willow or other flexible tree wand: cf *OED* 3b.

A. sb: [1. In the West Indies, the sense of *withe* was early extended to include esp any flexible stem, vine or root that could be used to tie things. *Withe* is the current Std form in plant-names and botanical use.

1657 Ligon 87, And besides, the roots being far assunder, weeds grew up between, and worse then all weeds, Withs, which are of a stronger grouth then the Canes, and do much mischiefe where they are; for, they winde about them, and pull them down to the ground. 1679 Trapham 48, There grow large Withs, for so they are called,.. which being cut pour out a cleer well tasted and wholesome water to satiate the bewildered Traveller [see WATER-WITHE].]

2. In Jamaica, the universal folk forms are /wis/ and the iterated /wis-wis/: senses as in 1.

1896 Bates 42 [Prov:] Bull ole, you tek wis' wis' tie him [*When a bull is old, you can take a vine to tie him*]. 1907 Jekyll 63, Bro'er Cow, if you want to go with me you fe make me put one wiss-wiss over you harn. 1924 Beckwith 74 [Prov:] If you want fe lean, no lean 'pon wis. 1952 FGC StAnn /wist/—wis. 1957 JN Clar [Child speaking:] Me play cow, ma. Me tie whist on the children hand mam, and we run up and down. *N*

3. A temporary bag made at the field and tied up with wis. (Cf the verb.)

1958 DeC StAnd /wis-wis/ a temporary bag made of grass or trash.

4. In combination, in the names of a great many plants—see as separate entries.

B. vb: To tie up with wis or similar vegetable material.

1959 DeC Han, West/ wis/—to tie up with vines, trash, or grass; to make a /tana/ you /jos wis i op an truo pan fi-yu shuolda/. The reduplicative /wis-wis/ could be used in the same sentence.

WISDOM-WEED sb dial. One or more herbs thought to have the property of giving wisdom; specifically, GANJA. S WEED.

1954 Kirkland 170 [Among contents of a fever-bath:] Wisdom weed. [Unidentified.] 1958 CBL Kgn, Wisdom weed—a name esp among Rastafarians for ganja.

wish, wishi see WHICH.

wish-graaf sb dial; <*wish* vb + *graaf* vb.

1958 DeC Man /wish-graaf/ a mean and covetous person, because /hin waan graaf ebriting/.

WISHING COW sb dial. A cow that is believed to be wishing for someone's death. See quot.

1952 FGC StAnd /wishn kou/—one that bawl six, seven, eight time a night—mean someone gwine dead.

wishn pron interrog dial; <*which* (pronounced /wish/, a common variant) + *-n* suffix[1]. Which.

1952 FGC StT /a wishn a dem yu waan/ *Which of them do you want?*

wis-maami sb dial; <WIS + *maami*. The COCO-WIS, probably because it is so much larger than other vines. Cf SHRIMP-MAAMI.

1952 FGC Port /wis-maami—koko-wis/.

wist, WITH, WITHE see WIS, WIS-WIS.

WITHOUTEN /widoutn/ prep or conj dial; <*without* + *-n* suffix[1]. Without; unless. *BL G*

1962 BLB 36 /mi kyaan go widoutn moni/ *I can't go without money.* 1962 FGC gen /im wuon go widoutn yu go tu/ *He won't go unless you go too.*

WIZARD (MAN) sb dial.

1958 DeC StT /wizad, wizad man/ an obeahman.

WOEYO, WOIO see *waay-uo*.

WOLONGO see WANGLA.

WOMAN see *uman*.

WOMAN- sb attrib dial. Chiefly in the names of plants, but also of animals, etc.: Female, or having feminine characteristics (e.g. smoother skin, smaller size, softness); sometimes redundant. See as first element in separate entries. Cf also MAN-COW. *BL*

WOMAN-BE-DAMNED sb dial joc. A cooking arrangement whereby workmen may dispense with the help of a cook.

1943 *GL* StM, Ooman-be-dyam, Cooking can suspended from stick. 1955 FGC Man /úman-bi-dyám/.

WOMAN BEEFWOOD see BEEFWOOD quot 1952.

WOMAN-BREAST sb dial.

1958 DeC StAnd /wuman bres/ a small loaf of bread, about four inches long, weighing about a quarter pound, has a 'nipple' at each end.

WOMAN CAMFOR see *kyamfya yam* quot 1956.

WOMAN CANE sb dial. A variety of sugar-cane that is black and soft.

1952 FGC StJ /úman kíen/.

WOMAN-COW see MAN-COW quot 1868. *G*

WOMAN DANDELION sb dial. The shrub *Cassia tora*, lower, and with smaller, finer leaves than MAN DANDELION.

1952 FGC StM.

WOMAN DOCTOR FISH sb dial. A fish similar to the DOCTOR FISH, but rounder.

1952 FGC StC /uman dakta-fish/.

WOMAN KICK-'EM sb dial joc obs. A nickname for yellow yam. (The allusion may be to their being the least desirable kind of yam.)

1868 Russell 5, Oman-kick-am, Yellow yams.

WOMAN-MOUTH FERN sb dial. A kind of fern which crackles loudly when burning.

1952 FGC StAnn /wuman-mout forn/—when it burn it pop loud.

WOMAN OF COLOUR sb obs. The corresponding form to *man of colour*: a woman of mixed white and negro race. These terms were current in the latter part of the 18th century, but the preferred Jamaican term is BROWN. *G*

1839 McMahon 51, Steel was living in the fashion of the country, with a free woman of colour, named Miss Marshall.

WOMAN PIMENTO sb dial. The female pimento tree.

1868 Russell 9, see MAN COW.

WOMAN RAIN sb dial; for *woman's rain*. *BL*

1. Tears; weeping.

1873 Rampini 182 [Prov:] Woman rain neber done. 1910 Anderson-Cundall 47, same. 1925 Beckwith 124, (W)ooman rain neber done..i.e. a woman is always crying.

2. = OLD WOMAN RAIN. *G*

1956 BLB Man, Woman rain—a steady rain which continues for days.

WOMAN'S TONGUE (TREE) sb. *BA*

1. The tree *Albizzia lebbek* and its large flat bean.

1909 Harris 316, Woman's Tongue, or East Indian Walnut..An introduced tree, but now very common on the lowlands. 1941 Swabey 32, Woman's Tongue.. Introduced from India in 1782, and naturalised, being often regarded as a troublesome weed in pastures. 1944 *NHN* II 117, The scientific name of Woman's Tongue is *Albizzia lebbek*..It is..known as 'Woman's Tongue' because of the rustling of dry pods in the wind.

2. The tree *Cordia macrophylla*, whose large, stiff leaves make a clatter in the wind.

1961 W. E. Fulford Man, Woman's tongue.

WOMAN STRONG-BACK sb dial; <WOMAN- + STRONG-BACK. Cf MAN-BACK. See FLAT-BUR.

WOMAN-WOOD sb; from the softness of the wood.

1. The tree *Brunellia comocladifolia*.

1886 Hooper 30, Woman Wood or West Indian Sumac.. Worthless and indicative of a soil poor, or worn out by ground cultivation.

2. The tree *Oreopanax capitatum*.

1926 Fawcett 418, see THREE-FINGERED JACK.

3. The tree *Hernandia jamaicensis*.

1963 GHP Institute of Ja, C. B. Lewis has..recorded the name..'Womanwood'.

WONGALA see WANGLA.

WOOD /wud, hud/ sb vulg. The penis. *BL G T*

1943 *GL* Clar, Hood, genital. 1952 FGC Han /wud/ penis.

[**WOOD-ANT** sb; *OED* 1709? 1781. A termite: =DUCK ANT. *BL G*

1725 Sloane 197, This Spider..spreads some few Threads in Lieu of a Web, and catches in it Wood Ants, &c. 1774 Long II 427, Bug-a-bugs (wood-ants). 1835 Senior 77, Another terrible plague is the 'duck ant', or wood ant.. This ant resembles a nut-maggot, only that it is flat, has feet, and emits a very offensive smell. 1943 *GL* StAnd, Hoodance, wood ants.]

WOOD-CHINK sb. A wood-louse.

1756 Browne 434, Cimex 2..The small green Wood-Chink. This little insect is frequent in the woods of Jamaica..It is of a pale green colour mixed with very minute black specks in every part.

WOOD-CLOCK sb dial; <*wood*+*clock*, a beetle (*OED sb*³). A beetle that bores trees, esp the cotton-tree. See next.

1952 FGC Tre, Wood-clock, 'bore cotton-tree; start at 6 and keep on till 4 in the morning'.

WOOD-DIGGER sb ?obs. See quot, and see prec.

1756 Browne 433, Blatta 3..The Wood-Digger. This insect..digs frequently into soft pieces of timber, where it keeps a throbbing noise, not unlike our death-watches in Europe.

WOODEN-FOOT /wudn-fut, udn-~/ sb dial; <*wooden*+FOOT. A person with a wooden leg (in distinction to one with a stump, TUMPA-FOOT). Also attrib. *G*

1927 Anderson-Cundall 76, Wooden-foot man can' kick wid him good foot. 1952 FGC Han, StAnd, Tre /wudn-fut/. 1956 Mc Clar /udn fut man/ man having a wooden leg.

WOODEN-HEAD sb dial. A type of bait for fishing.

1956 Mc Kgn /wudn ed/.

WOODEN-HORN sb dial. A water creature similar to the crayfish but 'smaller than shrimps' with horns and sharp sting.

1956 Mc StAnd /wudn haan, wudn aan—it nieli fieva kriefish—smaala dan swimz/.

WOODEN PING-PING sb: ?fanciful. Some kind of worm that lives in the ground.

1924 Beckwith 77, Wooden ping-ping (there's a worm in the dirt name so) and Cock. So then Wooden Ping-ping hid in the earth and the Cock hunted for him, couldn't find him.

WOOD LIZARD sb. Perh some species of *Celestus*; cf WOOD-SLAVE 2.

1835 Senior 80, The 'wood lizard'..has a sleeky skin, like the common snake, and slips about in search of food.

WOOD OWL sb obs. The PATU (which is still being mistaken for an owl).

1725 Sloane 295, *Caprimulgi species*, a Wood Owle or Goat Sucker. *Raij. syn. p.* 180. A Wood Owle. *Ibid* 296, The Small Wood-Owle..along the upper Mandible were several bristly Hairs in a Line, like those of a Cats Mustachoes of a black Colour, the Aperture of the Chaps or Swallow, was extraordinarily large.

WOODPECKER sb. Cf PICKER.

1. A bird; in folk use more often pronounced /wud-pika/ than /wudpeka/. *G*

1952 FGC Han, Man, StAnn, StT.

2. A district constable or policeman—in allusion to the red colour on his uniform. (See RED SEAM.)

1952 FGC StM /wudpeka/.

WOOD-SKIN sb dial. The bark of a tree.

1924 Beckwith 115, By time dog return back, Hanansi gwine under wood 'kin an' hide, an' all de hunt Dog hunt, kyan't fin' him till dis day.

WOOD-SLAVE sb arch or obs; it dwells in rotten wood (*OED* identification erron).

1. The POLLY lizard (*Sphærodactylus* sp). *G T*

1725 Sloane 185, I saw one of these Spiders eat a small Lizard call'd a Woodslave, which was half out and half in his Mouth. *Ibid* 334, Salamandra minima, fusca, maculis albis notata..The Wood Slave. This is about an inch long from the end of the Snout, to that of the Tail..It lodges itself in old rotten Timber, and peeps out frequently frisking up and down in hot Weather.

2. The SNAKE WAITING-BOY (*Mabuya spilonotus*).

1851 Gosse 75, As he walks along the roads and lanes that divide the properties, he will perceive at every turn the smooth and trim little figures of the Wood-slaves.. basking on the loose stones of the dry-walls; their glossy fish-like scales glistening in the sun with metallic brilliance.

WOOD-SNAIL sb; *OED* 1831→.

1725 Sloane 230, Buccinum terrestre, minus..The long Wood Snail. This was about an Inch long, and of a greyish brown Colour..I found it in the Woods of Jamaica.

WOOD SORREL sb bot; *OED sb* 1 b 1770→.

1. The herbs *Oxalis corniculata* and *O. corymbosa*.

1756 Browne 231, Oxalis 1..The yellow Wood Sorrel. This plant is very common in the woods..It is a pleasant cooler and diuretic. 1814 Lunan II 304, Wood-sorrel. Oxalis..stricta. 1837 Macfadyen 183, Oxalis bipunctata. Bipunctated Wood-Sorrel..A weed in Gardens. 1955 *WIMJ* 159, *Oxalis corniculata*..Sour Grass; (N)edge Teeth; (Yellow or Wood) Sorrel.

2. The wild *Begonia*, esp *B. purpurea*. (Formerly CLIMBING SORREL.)

1864 Grisebach 787, Wood Sorrel: *Begonia acutifolia*. 1920 Fawcett 252, *B. purpurea*..Wood-sorrel.

WOOF /wuf/ adv dial; echoic. A word suggesting the sound of something dull or heavy falling to the ground. Cf BOOF.

1924 Beckwith 38, So while he was going on, hear some-t'ing drop '*woof!*'..At de same time den was Brar Dry-head drop off de tree.

WOOLLY VELVET-LEAF sb. A vine.

1854–5 *TJSA* I 59, Woolly Velvet Leaf. Cissampelos microcarpia [*sic*].

WOOZEN sb dial arch; <*weasand*, the wind-pipe (*OED* 2 →1798).

1943 *GL*, Woozen, the wind-pipe.

WOP, WOPPY see *wap*, *wapi*.

WORK vb dial. *BA G*

1. To earn.

1912 McK *Ballads* 35, De honest toil is pure as gold An' he who wuks a penny Can mek his life as much wort' while As he who earns a guinea.

2. To set about producing the effects of obeah.

1895 Banbury 7, The obeahman is retained as well as the lawyer, and at times he not only 'works' at home on the case, but goes into Court with his client.

WORKING vbl sb cant; cf *OED vbl sb* 5d. In the language of revivalist and similar groups: Any ceremony in which 'workings of the spirit' are sought; see quots.

1953 Moore 51–2, Private consultations between the minister of the Pentecostal Holiness Zion Tabernacle of Church Corners, Morant Bay, and his congregation members, during week days: faith meetings, protection from evil spirits, divination, or 'taking things off people'. *Ibid* 83, 'a working' = a Revivalist ceremony.

WORKING-TIME sb dial.

1958 DeC StT /wokin taim/ 7:00 A.M. Regularly used as time of day.

WORK-MAN sb dial; <WORK 2+*man*. An obeah-man. *G*

1958 DeC 5 /wok man/ a name for an obeah man.

WORK (ONE'S) BELLY vb phr dial. To produce diarrhœa. (Cf BELLY-WORK.)

1925 Beckwith 114 [Prov:] Wha' sweet [pleases] goat, always work him belly. *BA BL G T*

WORK (ONE'S) HEAD vb phr. To think hard, rack (one's) brain. Cf CONSIDER, STUDY (ONE'S) HEAD. *BL G*

1950 Pioneer 37, Same time Anancy start work him head pon Jackass, for him did bex bout how Jackass laugh after him.

WORM /wom, worom/ sb dial; *worm* has two chief dial forms /wom/ from reg loss of post-vocalic *r*, and /worom/ from intrusion of epenthetic vowel between *r* and *m*. Dial speakers also sometimes say /worm/. A worm.

1943 *GL* StAnd, StC, Worrum, worm; StE, Worum, worm. 1952 FGC StE, see WORMWOOD (TREE). *BL G*

WORM-BARK TREE sb obs; cf *OED worm* 17f: *worm-bark* c1791. The CABBAGE-BARK TREE, early used as an anthelmintic.

1777 Wright in *Phil. Trans.* LXVII 507, The Cabbage-bark tree, or Worm-bark tree, grows in..Jamaica.

WORM-EATER sb; *OED* 1760→. Evid the Warbler *Helmitheros vermivorus*.

1725 Sloane 310, Muscicapa pallide fusca..The Worm-Eater. 1847 Gosse 150, Worm-Eater. *Vermivora Pennsylvanica.* This is a scarce bird with us. [1936 Bond 329, Worm-Eating Warbler.]

WORM-GRASS sb; <*worm*+GRASS; *OED* 1756→.

1. The herb *Spigelia anthelmia.* (Distinctions between worm 'grass', 'bush', 'weed', etc. are not always made: see quot 1820.)

1756 Browne 156, Anthelmenthia 1..This plant..is now cultivated in many of the gardens of Jamaica..This vegetable has long been in use among the Negroes and Indians..and takes its present denomination from its peculiar efficacy in destroying of worms. 1820 Thomson 168, Worm-grass..There are many plants that go by this name; the real species, as described by Browne, is not common in this part of the island. 1864 Grisebach 789, Worm-grass: *Spigelia Anthelmia.* 1953 *WIMJ* 249, see INDIAN PINK 2.

2. The herb *Chenopodium ambrosioides,* also called WORM WEED.

1952 FGC StA, Tre, Worm-grass—/simo-kantrak, stinkin-wiid/.

WORM QUIT sb dial. The ANTS BIRD.

1952 FGC StAnn, Worm Quit.

WORM SEED sb.

1953 *WIMJ* 240, see *simi-kantrak.*

WORM TUBE sb; *OED* 1776→. 'The twisted shell or tube of a marine annelid or mollusc' (*OED*).

1756 Browne 396, Siphonium 1..The angular and variously writhed Worm-tube..2..The smooth, straight, shining Worm-tube [etc.].

WORM WEED sb. The herb *Chenopodium ambrosioides,* used in folk medicine, esp as a vermifuge. Also called *simi-kantrak.*

1927 Beckwith 26, See-me-contract..'Worm-Weed'. For worms or 'low stomach' drink as tea. 1953 *WIMJ* 240.

WORMWOOD (TREE) sb; from its use as a vermifuge. The CABBAGE-BARK (TREE). *BA*

1927 Beckwith 30, Worm-wood. *Andira inermis*..To carry off worms or phlegm, take one chip where the sun rises, two where it goes down, boil as tea and sweeten.. For a wound make a plaster of the grated nut. 1941 Swabey 16. 1952 FGC StE /wom wud, wen pikini hab wom/ cabbage bark; StT, Cabbage bark, wormwood tree: bark from the east side is best. 1954 *WIMJ* 28, *Andira inermis*..Cabbage (Bark) Tree; Bastard Cabbage; Worm Wood; Angeleen Tree.

worom, WORRUM see WORM. *BA BL*

WORTHLESS /wotlis/ adj and sb; has undergone the common phonetic alterations of a frequently-used word: reduction of *-less* > *-lis*; change of *t* > *k* (*wuck-*); metathesis of *r* and prec vowel (*writ-*), etc.: see dial sp in quots.

A. adj: A term of strong general condemnation: useless, of weak abilities, of low character (dishonest, trouble-making), etc. *G T*

1943 *GL* StJ, Wuckliss, worthless; Writless, worthless. 1956 Mc StAnd /wotlis—yu no wot notn/.

B. sb: Worthlessness.

1950 Pioneer 93, All because o' you, wid you' wuthless now.

WORUM see WORM.

WOSIS adj dial; cf *OED worsest, worst.* *BL G*

wotlis see WORTHLESS.

WOUNDED vb dial; for *wound,* by over-correction. To wound, to hurt. *BL G*

1955 Bennett *Me Dream* Ah swear dat ah mus fine a way Fe wounded cousin Rose.

wowatu /wowatú/ vb dial arch; <Twi *ye awâwâ-(a)túù,* to welcome by embracing. To make much of a person.

1956 Mc Port /im wowatú yu/ *He makes much of you.*

WOY, WOYO see *waay, waay-uo.*

WRAP sb dial.

1. A head-scarf knotted in front. Cf BANDEAU.

1956 Mc Man, StAnd /rap/. *BL G*

2. A BAG-A-BACK.

1958 DeC Port /rap/ a crocus bag whose mouth is rolled twice in such a manner that it may be hooked over the crown of the head.

WRAPPER sb dial.

1. A length of cloth formerly wrapped about the body by East Indians. Out of general use since about 1920.

c1930 A. Clerk *Songs* No 12, Me's a coolie, come from yanda Wid me wrapper roun' me shoulder. 1943 *GL* StC, Rappaw, East Indian Garment. 1956 Mc Clar /rápa/ Coolie loin cloth; StAnd /kúuli rápa/.

2. Attrib.

1952 FGC StM /rapa kuuli/ East Indian who wraps himself [in the old fashion, instead of wearing trousers].

WRAP-UP vb dial. To associate with intimately. *BL G*

1942 Bennett 35, Me noh wrap up wid dem, for I Pick an' choose me company. 1943 *GL* Kgn, Wrap up, associate. 1955 FGC Man /rap-op/ associate with equals.

WRATHED see *raatid.*

WRENK see *rengk.*

WRING sb dial; *OED sb*² 2 →1611. A wrench or sprain, generally of the ankle. *BA*

1952 FGC StT /ring/.

WRITE OFF vb phr. To copy (in writing). *G*

1956 Mc Man /mi mos ráit aaf dís an dís/ *I must copy this (writing) onto this (page).*

WRITLESS see WORTHLESS.

WRONG-SIDE adj dial; ellipt from some such phrase as *on the wrong side.* Inside out. *BL G*

1952 FGC StT /im shot rang-said/ *His shirt is inside out.*

WROTHED, WROUGHTED see *raatid.*

WUCKLISS see WORTHLESS.

WUNU see UNU.

wuoda see *uoda.*

WURRA see WHOORA.

WURRO-WURRO, WURRU-WURRU sb dial; <Yoruba *wúruwùru*, untidy, rough, in a confused mass.

See quots.

1943 *GL* StM, Wurry-wurro, bramble; StJ, Wurruwurru, hair.

wuse see HUSSAY.

WUSSARA adj dial; a triple comparative form: *worse*+*-er*+*-er*; cf *OED worser.* *BL G*

1943 *GL* Try Again, Wussara, worse.

WUSSEST adj dial; cf *OED worsest, worst.* *BLG*

wusu-wusu adj dial; prob W. Afr, but no source has been found.

1959 DeC StJ /wusu-wusu/ (of a man) big, lazy, stupid, clumsy.

WUTHLESS see WORTHLESS. *BA G*

WYNNE GRASS sb. The grass *Melinis minutiflora*, also called MOLASSES GRASS.

1952 FGC Man, Said to have been made popular by Mr Wynne, former owner of Brokenhurst Estate. 1954 *FG* 240, Wynne grass is a prolific seeder..The chief value of this grass lies in its ability to grow on areas of low fertility.

WYS see WIS, WITHE.

-Y¹ /i/ pron dial; a sp for *it* unstressed and in close juncture after a verb. =I¹: it. *BL G*

1924 Beckwith 22, He tak de packey, he dippy up full of de hot water. *Ibid* 53, You no have-y a han' you no sure of it.

-Y² /i/ additive sound dial arch; parallel to A⁸. In written dial also sp *-ie.* Cf CHANGIE FE CHANGIE. =*-i.* *BL*

YA¹ adv dial; <*here*, by reg loss of *r* and *h*; for details see Introduction: Phonology. Also sp *yah.* Here. *BL G N*

c 1842 in 1895 Banbury 21 [Song:] Dandy obeah da ya, oh! 1877 Murray *Feedin' 'Perrit* 11, So, calling her up, he said, 'Come ya, pickny'. 1907 Jekyll 8, Me tell you say them a call you name up ya. 1950 Pioneer 18, Him fas'en eena de bush yah.

YA² particle dial; perh <YA¹, perh phonosymbolic. A particle used to introduce echoic adverbial elements; if it has any semantic force this is something like 'like this'.

1877 Murray *Feedin' 'Perrit* 7, I yerry him kick open him room door ya bam. *Ibid*, Bam, him plant me agen, ya bif.

ya, yaa see YAH.

yaak see NEW YORK.

yaazi see YAWSY-. *BL*

YABA, YABBA /yaba/ sb chiefly dial; <Twi (Akan dial) *ayawá*, earthen vessel, dish. Dial sp *yabba, yabah, yaba.*

1. A native-made heavy earthenware vessel of any size (quite small bowls up to cooking pots holding several gallons); sometimes the clay material itself. *N*

1889 Sanguinetti 50, The familiar 'Yabba' or earthen vessel. 1929 Beckwith 27, Earthen bowls, hand turned and covered with a rude glaze, are always to be had in the Kingston market, but they are more rare in the hills where the old-time 'yabba' is being supplanted by tinware. 1942 Bennett 13, Now we can start fe nyam. Me gat de dip-dip yah Tayma Pass de yabah wid de yam. 1952 FGC StAnd, StM, Tre, West /yaba/ heavy earthenware, any shape.

2. Also attrib.

1954 LeP Kgn, Yabba-pot—cooking pot. 1956 Mc StAnd /yába pat—mek out a klie/.

YABBAH see ABBA.

YACCA (TREE) /yáka/ sb. A tree of the genus *Podocarpus*, of which there are two native species in Jamaica (see quot 1941), and one introduced (see PODO); also the wood.

1837 Macfadyen 176, Mahogany..No other wood, not even the Yacca, can rival it in its infinitely diversified shades. 1854–5 *TJSA* I 124, The Yacca tree forms a very conspicuous object on most of the high mountain ridges. 1941 Swabey 32, Yacca, Blue Mountain—*Podocarpus urbanii*..Yacca, St Ann's—*Podocarpus purdieanus.* 1952 FGC Port /yaka/.

yaga-yaga, yege-yege sb and vb dial; iterative from **yaga*, **yeg*, prob based on *rag*: cf *raga-raga, rege-rege*, and the 'Bungo talk' of Anansi the spider, who says /y-/ for /r-/ as in *red, ready* /yed, yedi/ etc. **s.**

A. sb: Rags, tatters; old unwanted things; rubbish.

1943 *GL* Port, Yaga-yaga, old rags; StM, Yagga-yagga, pieces of old rags; StAnn, Yeg-yeg, rags; Han, Yegeh-yegeh, rags. 1956 Mc StAnd /yaga-yaga—dat uol remnant—duon hav eni yuus agen/ *Yagga-yagga—that's old remnants—have no use any more.*

B. vb: See quot (the making into small ragged pieces seems to be the sense connection).

1954 LeP StT, To cut awkwardly or hack with a dull tool —yagga-yagga.

YAGGA-YAGGA see prec.

YAH /yaa, ya/ particle dial; <(*you*) *hear?.* Dial sp *yah, yaw.*

1. An emphatic concluding particle; it sometimes retains etymological meaning (though it does not require an answer), but very freq has lost virtually all lexical meaning.

1877 Murray *Feedin' 'Perrit*, Run go a market go buy tuppy pear yah. No go buy rotten pear, now..Run, yah! 1907 Jekyll 221 [Song:] Bring back me dumpling, yah? Note: 'Yah?'=Do you hear? 1942 Bennett 39, Gal tun back gu back home yaw, Doan falla me at all. 1956 Mc StAnd /mi da glad fi lili a di suup tu de ya/ *I'd be glad of a little of the soup today.* *Ibid* /laad man, maakit bad yáa/ *Market's bad!*

2. Occas followed by /sa/ *sir*.

1950 Pioneer 34, All of a sudden, hear Anancy, 'Se' yah Bra Puss, top wingy-wingy up yuhself pon me head yaw sah'. [*Stop twisting and squeezing yourself on my head, d'you hear sir?*]. 1957 JN Port [Child speaking:] Nuh meck wi play mumma yah sah. [*Suppose we play 'Mama', eh?*]

YAHSO see YA-SO.

yai, yaiz /yai, yaiz/ sb dial; by palatalization of initial vowel: cf Engl, Scots, US dial *yerb*, herb; *yerd*, earth; *yair*, air; etc. There may be some concurrent infl from Afr languages: cf Bambara *ɲe*, eye, *ye*, to see; Kpelle *ŋɛi*, eye; Nupe *eye*, eye. See compounds s.v. EYE.

Eye, eyes. (In the folk speech inflectional distinction between sg and plur is lost: each form is used in either number.) *BL G N*

1862 Clutterbuck 153, Nick like de bright yeyes. 1873 Rampini 182 [Prov:] Work is no evil. It is de yies (eyes) dat are cowards. 1943 *GL* Kgn, StAnd, StM, Yeye, eye. 1950 Pioneer 16, Anancy gi out 'bless we y'eye sight!' 1952 FGC Han /pepa-flai get in yai—born/ *Pepper-flies get in one's eyes—and burn!*

YALLER-TAIL see YELLOW-TAIL (BIRD).

YAM see NYAM.

YAM-BANK sb chiefly dial. The prevalent term in Han, StJ, West, for what is usually called a YAM-HILL. (For map showing distribution of these terms, see DeC in 1961 *CLS* 66.)

1952 FGC Han. *BA*

YAM-BANK PEAS sb dial. Beans grown on yam-banks: see quot.

1952 FGC StT (2 informants), Yam-bank peas, white with black or red spots.

YAM BEAN sb; *OED* 1864→. The bean *Pachyrhizus tuberosus*, which has edible beans and a tuber like yam. Also called STARCH BEAN.

1837 Macfadyen 285–6, Dolichos tuberosus. Yam-Bean.. The root is formed of a number of simple cord-like fibres, several feet in length..bearing..a succession of tubers. The beans are poisonous; but the root affords a very plentiful supply of very wholesome food. 1913 Harris 25–6, Bean, Yam..The very young pods are used like French beans..The ripe seeds are reputed to be poisonous, but the tubers afford..a substitute for yam, or they may be submitted to a process similar to arrowroot and a starch is obtained. 1920 Fawcett 70, *P. tuberosus*..Yam Bean.

YAM-CUTTER sb dial. The bird *Spindalis nigricephala.*

1952 FGC Man /yam-kota/ cuts yam sprout, also cho-cho vine; same as MARK-HEAD, GOLD-FRINGE.

YAM-FIELD sb dial.

1952 FGC Han, 'In StJ, West, they say "yam field"; in Han, "yam ground"'.

YAM-FINGER COCO sb dial. A kind of COCO which is like a 'finger' of yam (a subdivision or lobe of the tuber).

1952 FGC Han /yam-fingga koko/.

YAM FLY sb dial. An insect which appears when negro yam is in season; it is said to be black, stout like a bee, and to sting animals.

1952 FGC StT /yam flai/.

YAM-FOOT sb dial. A second tuber of yam which grows from the YAM-HEAD after the first tuber has been dug. *BA*

19 6 Mc Man /yam fut pap af di yam hed/.

YAM GROUND sb dial. *BA*

1952 FGC Han, see YAM FIELD.

YAM-HEAD sb dial. The piece of yam tuber from which the vine shoots, and from which the new tubers grow. *G*

1823 Roughley 407, A sufficiency of yam heads or plants ready to be put in the ground. 1956 Mc Man, see YAM-FOOT.

YAM HILL sb dial; *OED* 1864–5→. The heap of earth that is dug and into which the YAM-HEAD is planted. Cf YAM-BANK. *BL G*

1952 FGC Han; also gen.

YAM MANGO sb. A variety of mango with a firm, pale yellow flesh considered to resemble that of yellow yam.

1952 FGC StAnd, StJ, StM, StT /yam manggo/.

YAM-PATCH sb dial.

1958 DeC StT /yam pach/ equiv to /yam groun/.

YAMPEA see next.

YAMPEE /yámpi, yámpii/ sb; 1811 a1818 *yampoy*, 1811 *yampea*, 1823 *yampy*, 1862→ *yampee*, 1943 1954 *yampi*, 1954 *yampie*; cf Vai *dʒambi*, the wild yam; *OED* 1796→. A small variety of yam (*Dioscorea* sp) having fine white flesh. Also attrib. *BL*

1811 Titford Expl of Plate XII 6, A very delicious species [of yam] is small, purple outside, very white within, and called the Yampea or Yampoy. 1823 Stewart 63, There are a great variety of wholesome and nutritious roots produced in this island—as the yam (*diascorea*), the yampy, the coco, the sweet and bitter cassada. 1912 McK *Songs* 102, We sit beneat' de yampy shade. 1913 Harris 42, Indian yam or Yampee is *Dioscorea trifida*..With the exception of the yampee no variety of yam is equal to good Irish potatoes but..the latter are usually double the price of yams. 1952 FGC gen /yampi/; StJ, Three kinds /chaini, red, wait yampi/; Chiney is small, white inside, and has a /shain/ skin.

YAMPI, YAMPIE, YAMPOY, YAMPY see prec.

YAM WALK sb dial; <*yam*+WALK.

1958 DeC StT /yam walk/ (*sic*)—a yam-field.

YANGA /yángga/ vb dial; prob related to NYANGA; cf CB *-*yáng*-, dance about in joy, Ko -*yangalala*, be happy; perh infl by Amer Sp *yanga*, uncontrolled, carelessly done. To move (in dancing or in walking) in a shaking or swaying manner that is 'stylish' or provocative.

1925 Beckwith 81, Man da yawn, man da yonga!.. 'Yonga' is a dance in which 'the body is shaken in all directions'. 1943 *GL* Clar, Yanga, walk and stumble; Han, Yanga, swaying walk of women; Kgn, Yanga, a stylish way of stepping by women characterized by swinging of the arms, and swaying of the head. 1950 Pioneer 41, See yah de music sweet yuh se'! All de fowl dem start fe yanga an merenge roun' de room. 1955 FGC Man /yangga/ way of walking, step quite cute. *G*

YANGA sb dial; cf prec. A dance: see quots.

1925 Beckwith 81, 'Yonga' is a dance in which 'the body is shaken in all directions'. 1963 T. Murray UWI, Yanga is a fast dance rhythm. The dancer has hands on hips and pushes pelvis and knees forwards and back.

yangkuku apikibo sb dial; *yangkuku* has not been traced; *apikibo* is pidgin: *pikin*, child +*bo*, person, friend. A preserved Africanism: see quot.

1958 DeC Port (Moore Town) /yangkuku apíkibo/ Maroon children.

YAP sb dial slang; prob < surname. A Chinese.

1958 DeC StAnd /yap/.

YAP-YAP[1] vb and sb dial; iterative from *yap*, the mouth (slang).

A. vb: see quot.

1958 DeC StAnd /yap-yap/ to open the mouth wide out of hunger.

B. sb: see quot.

1959 DeC West /yap-yap/ bad language, obscenity, scurrilous talk.

YAP-YAP[2] sb dial; iterative from **yap* prob <*wrap* (cf *yeg*<*rag*).

1954 LeP StAnn, Yap-yap—old ragged clothes. (Change me good clothes and put on me yap-yap.)

YARD sb chiefly dial; cf *OED sb*[1] 3, *ODS*, 'Now *dial.* and *U.S.*'; Ja senses somewhat different. s. *BA*

1. The usual word for the land around and including a dwelling—a piece of private or particular property. *G T*

1877 Murray *Kittle* 21, My daughter, Molly tief pass, maam, den go da him yard. 1907 Jekyll 163, The immediate surroundings of the house are called the yard. They seldom speak of going to a friend's house. They say they are going to his yard. 1956 Mc StA /wi kyan go a mis mieri yaad/ *We can go to Miss Mary's place;* StE /im raid intu di man yaad/ *He rode into the man's place.*

2. Hence, more specif, the dwelling itself; often in phr /a yaad/ at home.

1950 Pioneer 71, Me gat tree pickney an dem mumma up a yard. 1954 LeP StAnn, Yard—a dwelling house. 1956 Mc Man /nómbari nó da a yáad nou/ *Nobody is at home now.* 1957 JN Arlington, Me have me broder a school and one de a yard.

YARD-CHILD sb dial. A child who lives in the household of its father; see quot.

1946 Dunham 19, Yard-children [are] those children who live with their father, rather than away from him in the household of their unmarried mother, the latter being called 'illegitimates'.

YARN sb dial. The CORATOE, because its leaves (like those of sisal) are the source of a useful fibre.

1956 Mc StAnd [Woman pointing to the plant:] /dis wan yaan—mek baaskit, shuuz, plenti ting/.

YA-SO /yá-so/ adv dial; YA[1]+SO adv 3. Here—but more emphatic than YA; cf DE-SO. *BL G*

1943 *GL* StC, Yaso—here; StAnd, StC, Yasso—right here; StAnd, Yahso—here; StAnd, Yasuh—this way.

YASSO, YASUH see prec.

YATWA sb dial rare; etym unknown.

1943 *GL* Port, Yatwa, dish made of breadfruit and coconut.

YAW, YAWS /yaa, yaaz/ sb, often in pl form with sg meaning; 'Cariban: Calinago *yáya*, Galibi *poétai ïaïa*' WD2. *OED* 1679→. Cf GUINEA-CORN ~, RINGWORM ~, WATERY YAWS.

1. The disease *Framboesia*, which greatly afflicted negroes on WI plantations. *BA G*

1679 Trapham 117, I must needs administer some relief to the Yaws. *Ibid* 120, The Yaws produced as before said from the unnatural mixture of humane with brutal seed. 1820 Thomson 82, The eruption of the yaws sometimes commences without any precursory symptoms of ill health. 1961, The disease is now rare; the word is still well known (FGC).

2. Various diseased conditions in cattle and esp in poultry: see quots. *BA G*

1790 Moreton 95, The yaws, a distemper very destructive amongst them [*sc* turkeys]. 1820 Thomson 90, Fowls, as well as pigeons, are liable to large swellings about the eyes and beak, which prevent the bird from feeding, thereby proving fatal; negroes call it the yaws. I have examined several..it was nothing else but *chigoes* which caused it. *Ibid* 91, Cattle are subject to an eruptive complaint, which is termed yaws; but it may be remarked that negroes give this appellation to every suspicious eruptive appearance either on themselves or the brute creation. 1893 Sullivan 81, Cashewnuts..Do not let your poultry get at them, they give them 'yaws', a disease of the neck and throat which kills them. 1954 *FG* 727, Fowl pox, sometimes called 'yaws', 'sore head', and 'canker', is a very infectious disease which exists in all countries where poultry are kept. It is caused by a filterable virus.

YAW vb obs; <YAW sb. Of a heated liquid: To take on the appearance of a skin affected with yaws, to blister and break out with bubbles and froth.

1797 Higgins 41, Each clarifier of 500 or 600 gallons yaws but slowly. *Ibid* 41, The reasons which limit us in the size of such a vessel, plainly forbid the use of two, were it only for the purpose of yawing.

YAW see YAH.

YAW BUMP sb dial. An eruption on coco: see quot.

1929 Beckwith 27, Other informants agreed that coco planted in May will show soft scaly bumps called 'yaw bumps'.

YAWS see YAW sb. *N*

YAWS BUSH sb chiefly dial. The vine *Cissus sicyoides*; the leaves are applied to sores—formerly to those of yaws. Also called PUDDING WITHE.

1926 Fawcett 77, *C. sicyoides*..Snake Withe, Wild Yam, Yaws Bush, Bastard Bryony. 1954 *WIMJ* 26.

YAWS-CHILDREN sb obs. Children suffering from yaws.

1811 Mathison 109, The yaws-children..kept as diseased subjects in a separate house.

YAWS-FILTH sb.

1959 O. D. Simons, UCWI Preventive Med, Yaws-filth—the pustules of papillary yaws.

YAW(S)-HOSPITAL, ~-HOUSE sb obs; *OED* 1822–7. A house on estates where slaves having the yaws were isolated till the disease had run its course.

1811 Mathison 109, The yaws-house is not to be removed on any pretence to a distant part of the estate. 1820 Thomson 86, From there being no yaw-house, the children mixed together at meals..*Ibid* 92, A yaw-hospital on every estate is absolutely necessary; it should be made warm and comfortable. 1907 Jekyll 250 [Song:] You tief Mister Dixon Brahma, You nyam ahm a Yaws-house level.

YAW SORE sb. The sore on the skin caused by infection with the disease of YAWS.

1679 Trapham 118, And so successively dress the Yawe sore with this Unguent.

YAWS-TRASH sb dial. The remains of yaws (when it has lost its first force); see quot.

1959 O. D. Simons, UCWI Preventive Med, Yaws-trash—the paling of the skin as in early secondary yaws.

YAWSY, YAWY adj and sb now chiefly dial; <YAW, YAWS+-*y*. *BL*

1. Affected with yaws. *G*

1679 Trapham 117–18, Opening both the Body of the Copper and that of the Yawy Patients. 1801 Dancer 220, White children, suckled for some time by Yawy Negroes. 1907 Jekyll 54, So there was a little yawzy fellah call

Soliday. 1924 Beckwith 105, There was two sister and they had a yawzy brudder whe the two sister didn't care about.

2. The yaws.

1924 Beckwith 100, But I have yawzy an' when de yawzy bite me, me mudder kill a cow an' tek de blood an' wash me.

YAWSY-KENGE sb dial; <YAWSY + KENGE (unknown element prob Afr). Cf next. One who has yaws.

1943 *GL* StM, Yawsikenge, one who has yaws. 1955 FGC Man /yaazi-kengge/ one who has yaws and walks on his heels.

YAWSY-SKIN sb dial; also attrib. One whose skin shows the scars and effects of yaws. *G*

1924 Beckwith 99, A woman have t'ree daughter an' one son, an' de son was a yawzy 'kin. *Ibid* 100, At de said time, de yawzy 'kin brudder Andrew was half Ol' Witch. 1960 Rowe in *CLS* 156, /ándro, di líkl yáazikin bréda/ *Andrew, the little yaws-skin [skin pitted from yaws] brother.*

YAW TAINT sb arch or obs. An effect of the yaws thought to carry over from one generation to the next, disposing the second toward contracting the disease.

1679 Trapham 122, The strange long Guinny Worms arising from the Yaw teint found especially in the Children and Youth of the Blacks.

YAW-WEED sb bot. The shrub *Morinda royoc*, once used as a medicine in treating yaws.

1774 Long III 750, Yaw-weed, or upright Woodbind, or Honey-suckle, with oval leaves—Morinda. 1811 Titford 98, Yaw weed, *Stilingia Silvatica*..is a cathartic and said to be a specific in syphilis and yaws. 1864 Grisebach 789. 1954 *WIMJ* 30, see DUPPY POISON.

YAYA /yaya, yaaya/ sb dial; cf Ko *yaya*, Ewe (Fɔ̃ dialect) *ya*, Yoruba *iya*, etc., mother. An affectionate term of address to one's grandmother, or to one's mother. *G*

1943 *GL* StJ, Yah yah—grandmother. 1958 DeC StJ /yaya; yaaya/—child's word for mother; StT /yaya/—same.

YE int dial. = HAY int.

1923 Beckwith 52, Pullee me ambah ye,..Pullee me ambah i ye..Pullee me ambah e. [In each case this element is given a full measure in the accompanying musical score.]

YEAR BEAN sb. A variety of *Phaseolus vulgaris*; the name prob refers to its bearing only once annually.

1837 Macfadyen 279, Year-Bean..This grows wild, and is very common in mountain thickets..It bears only once a year. The seeds have a great deal of the flavour of the Windsor-bean. 1864 Grisebach 781. 1920 Fawcett 64, Year Bean.

YEARLY-NIGHT sb dial.

1959 DeC West /yierli-nait/ a funeral wake held on the first anniversary of the death.

YEARRY see YERRY.

YEDDA adv dial; prob <*hither*.

1929 Beckwith 199, Such turns of speech as 'Come a little yedda' for 'further' or 'nearer'.

YEERIE see YERRY.

YEGEH-YEGEH, yeg-yeg see *yaga-yaga*.

YEHRI see YERRY.

YELLOW adj. A skin colour: mulatto or lighter; it may have favourable or unfavourable connotations. *BA N*

1831 *Courant* 5 July [Advt:] Absconded..a negro Girl named Jean..full eyes, and rather yellow skin'd. 1956 Mc Man /wan gud lukin yala fela/.

YELLOW BALSAM sb bot. The aromatic shrub *Croton flavens*.

1756 Browne 347, Croton 3. The Yellow Balsam..sometimes used in resolutive baths. 1864 Grisebach 781, Balsam, yellow. 1920 Fawcett 279.

YELLOW-BELLY /yelo-, yalo-beli/ adj dial; for *yellow-bellied*. Having yellow colour on its belly, or inside it—used as an epithet for animals, birds, fish, and by transf for vegetables, trees, etc.: *yellow-belly gutu*, *~sweet-potato*, *~sweetwood*, *~woodpecker*, etc. *G*

1952 FGC StE /yélo-bèli gútu/; StE /yalo-beli swiit-pitieta/; StAnn, StT /yelo-beli swiitwud/. 1956 Jeffrey-Smith 60, The Sapsucker. *Sphyrapicus varius*. There is another woodpecker, the Yellow-Bellied, which is not so handsome as the red-bellied.

YELLOW-BILLED PARROT sb ornith. See quots.

1936 Bond 166, *Amazona collaria*..*Local name:*—Yellow-billed Parrot..*Range:*—Jamaica. 1956 Jeffrey-Smith 55, Our parrots..The Yellow-billed..is larger and a more handsome bird than the Black-billed.

YELLOW-BILL(ED) SPRAT sb. A poisonous fish; see quots.

1801 Dancer 315, The Fish found Poisonous in this island are, the Yellow Billed Sprat, Barracuta, [etc.]. 1820 Thomson 41, The yellow-billed sprat in particular is to be dreaded, producing convulsions and sudden death. 1952 FGC Port /yala-bil sprat/ have pink stripes.

YELLOW BLAST sb obs; see quot. A disease of sugar-cane.

1790 Beckford I 52, The yellow and the black blast..It is called the yellow from its giving that colour to the leaves, and which is occasioned by large nests of insects that sap the root, relax the fibres, and bore into the substance of the canes; and from which particular property, they are called Borers, in the Leeward and French Islands.

YELLOW CANDLEWOOD sb. The tree *Cassia emarginata*; its wood is yellow and burns readily, whence the name.

1881 Harrison in *Handbook* 141, Yellow Candle Wood (Cassia emarginata)—This is more a dyewood. 1891 Fawcett 24, Yellow Candle Wood. Native of W. Indies. 1920 Fawcett 108. 1941 Swabey 16, Candlewood, Yellow—(Senna Tree)..Small tree to 20 ft in height: wood hard, but not large enough for general use, a first-class firewood.

YELLOW-COAT sb dial. A yellow-coloured fish similar to the mackerel.

1952 FGC StC, StT.

YELLOW-COAT PLUM sb. A yellow plum, either *Spondias Monbin* or *S. purpurea* form *lutea*.

1952 FGC StAnd, StAnn, Yellow-coat (plum).

YELLOW DOCTOR-FISH sb dial. A small fish similar to the DOCTOR FISH, but of yellow colour.

1952 FGC StM.

YELLOW-FACED GRASS-BIRD sb ornith. = Next.

1917 Panton in *Ja. Times* 3 Nov, The yellow faced grass-bird. 1936 Bond 381, Yellow-faced Grass Bird.

YELLOW-FACE(D) GRASS-QUIT sb. The bird *Tiaris olivacea*.

1847 Gosse 249, Yellow Face Grass-Quit. *Ibid* 251, In March, I have found the stomach of the Yellow-face full of seeds of the common pasture grasses. 1936 Bond 381, The song of the Yellow-faced Grassquit..is merely a weak trill.

YELLOW FIDDLEWOOD sb. Either of two similar, related trees: *Petitia domingensis* and *Citharexylum fruticosum*; cf FIDDLEWOOD.

1864 Grisebach 783, Yellow Fiddle-wood: *Petitia domingensis*. 1943 *NHN* II 69, *Citharexylum fruiticosum* [*sic*]—Yellow Fiddlewood. Attains a girth of 2½ feet, but the larger trees are always hollow. The wood is hard, tough, and yellow in colour.

YELLOW-FIN CAVALLY. Another name for the fish CAVALLY JACK.

1952 FGC StC, StE.

YELLOW FUSTIC sb obs. Some variety of FUSTIC or other similar tree.

1657 Continuation 45, Severall sorts of Wood.. 4. Cittano, of a yellow colour, a fathome about, excellent for dying, called in English, yellow Fustick.

YELLOW GINGER sb dial.

1954 *WIMJ* 30, see DUPPY POISON.

YELLOW GINGER-LILY see GINGER-LILY.

YELLOW GRUNT sb. Either of the similar species of GRUNT fish, *Hæmulon plumieri* and *H. flavolineatum*.

1892 Cockrell List, Yellow grunt, *Hæmulon arcuatum*. 1950–1 Smith 223, *Hæmulon flavolineatum*, the yellow grunt, is moderately elongated and compressed. (StM; common, Long Bay, StJ.) 1952 FGC StC, StE, StM, StT, West /yelo/ or /yala gront/.

YELLOW-HEART (BREADFRUIT) sb. A fine variety of breadfruit with yellow flesh.

1952 FGC StAnd /yela-aat/.

YELLOW-HERCULES sb bot; <*yellow*+*Hercules*, see quot 1774. A timber tree (*Zanthoxylum martinicense*) better known as PRICKLY-YELLOW.

1756 Browne 189–90, Zanthoxylum 1..Prickly Yellow-wood, or yellow Hercules..This tree is frequent in most parts of Jamaica..it is..esteemed a good timber-tree. 1774 Long III 828–9, Yellow hercules..This species Browne confounds with the first-mentioned; but it is much thicker set with pointed protuberances..The name given to it was founded on the resemblance it was supposed to bear to the club of Hercules. 1920 Fawcett 172, Prickly Yellow, Yellow Hercules. 1955 *WIMJ* 160.

YELLOW JACK sb dial. A fish of the JACK type.

1952 FGC StE, StM, West /yelo jak/ don't bite.

YELLOW-KUOBI /yela kuobi, ~kobi/ sb dial; the source of the second element is uncert; see COBY-WOOD, *kuobi*.

1952 FGC StE, StJ /yela kuobi/ a sweet-potato that is yellow inside, whitish outside. 1956 BLB StJ /yela kobi/ a variety of potato.

YELLOW MANGO sb. A common variety of the MANGO.

1837 Macfadyen 222, 3. Yellow kidney-shaped Mango, a very good fruit. 1915 FGC StAnd.

YELLOW MASTIC sb.

a 1726 Barham (1794) 103, see BLACK MASTIC.

YELLOW MASTWOOD sb.

1864 Grisebach 785, Yellow Mastwood: *Tobinia coriacea*.

YELLOW NICKER (or NIKAL) sb; <*yellow* + NICKER. The plant *Cæsalpinia bonduc* and its yellow fruit, a hard seed with which boys play games. It is also used medicinally. The folk pronunciation is always /níkal/.

1696 Sloane 144, *The Yellow Nickar Tree*. In Jamaica Insula circa urbem St Jago. 1920 Fawcett 92, *C. bonduc*, Nickar Tree, Yellow Nickar, Bonduc. 1952 FGC Han /níkal/ one yellow one is worth ten grey ones. 1953 *WIMJ* 239, see GREY NICKER.

YELLOW PLUM TREE sb; *DAE* 1707→. = YELLOW-COAT PLUM.

1696 Sloane 182, Myrobalanus..fructu luteo..The Yellow Plumb-tree. In Jamaicæ Insulæ sylvis copiose crescit.

YELLOW SANDERS sb; <*yellow*+*sanders*, sandalwood (cf *OED*, where see also *red sanders*).

1. An unidentified tree: see quot.

1756 Browne 372, Yellow Sanders. The wood of this tree is said to make good inside timbers: it is of a yellow colour, and a close smooth grain. It is very common in St James's and St Mary's, and grows to a considerable size.

2. The tree *Buchenavia capitata*, with light yellow wood and satiny grain.

1801 Dancer 363, Yellow saunders or mountain olive.. The bark, in decoction, cures venereal complaints. 1886 Hooper 29, Yellow sanders..*Bucida capitata*. 1926 Fawcett 308, Yellow Sanders, Mountain Wild Olive.

3. Two species of *Zanthoxylum*: *Z. elephantiasis* and *Z. flavum*, with yellow wood.

1920 Fawcett 172, Yellow Sanders; *ibid* 174, Jamaican Satin Wood, Yellow Sanders. 1941 Swabey 33, Yellow Sanders—(Jamaican Satinwood) *Zanthoxylum flavum*.

4. Some species of *Amyris*, perh *A. balsamifera*.

1814 Lunan I 148, Amyris...Maritima..This tree, which is called *yellow candlewood*, *rose wood*, and *yellow sanders*, appears not specifically different from the foregoing.. The wood is of a box colour, elegantly clouded and takes a fine polish.

5. One of the above (or perh still another tree) —not identified.

1927 Beckwith 30, Yellow senda. 'Works with "Doctor John"' either as tea or as an ingredient in a bath.

YELLOW SENDA see prec.

YELLOW SNAKE sb; *ODS* 1868→.

1. The yellow boa *Epicrates subflavus*, which reaches a length of 20 ft.

1725 Sloane 335, Serpens major subflavus..The yellow Snake. 1756 Browne 459, Cenchris 1..The Yellow Snake. 1851 Gosse 314, A serpent of the Boa kind..is commonly found around Bluefields, and I believe in most parts of the Island, and is distinguished by the appellation of Yellow Snake.

2. A mulatto. Obs.

1790 Moreton 59, see CACA A.

YELLOW SORREL sb.

1955 *WIMJ* 159, see WOOD SORREL.

YELLOW SWEETWOOD sb bot. The trees *Nectandra antillana* and *N. sanguinea*.

1864 Grisebach 788, Yellow Sweet-wood: *Nectandra sanguinea*. 1941 Swabey 31, Sweetwood, Yellow—(Shinglewood, Whitewood, Longleaf Sweetwood). *Nectandra antillana*..The wood is of a pale yellow colour and merges into the sapwood.

YELLOW-TAIL sb dial; *DA* 1775→. The common food fish *Ocyurus chrysurus*; also some other similar ones—see quot 1854–5. Among the folk the word has become symbolic of prettiness. *BA N*

1854–5 *TJSA* I 142, Leiostomos Xanthurus—Yellow-tail. 1892 Cockrell list, Yellowtail—*Ocyurus chrysurus*. 1910 Anderson-Cundall 18, see CACA-BELLY. 1950–1 Smith in *NHN* 221, *Ocyurus chrysurus*, the yellow tail..It is a graceful, stream-lined fish, elongate and compressed.. Head and body were brownish-red with reflections of gold on the back.

YELLOW-TAIL (BIRD) sb. See quot. *G*

1956 Jeffrey-Smith 125, Fishermen in Runaway Bay have a special name for white gaulins and for blue gaulins. They call the former 'Yaller-Tail', and the latter 'Hamlin' and 'Hamlet-Bud Dem' because they say that when the birds fly in flocks the fish that bear these local names are then 'running'.

YELLOW-TAIL JACK sb dial. A fish of the Jack type with a yellow tail.

1952 FGC StM.

YELLOW-TAIL SNAPPER sb. See quot 1854-5. *BA*

1854-5 *TJSA* I 142, *Messoprion chrysurus*—yellow tail snapper. 1952 FGC StAnn, StC /yala-, yela-tiel snapa/.

YELLOW TAMARIND sb. A tree: see quot.

1864 Grisebach 788, Yellow Tamarind: *Acacia villosa.*

YELLOW THISTLE sb. The herb *Argemone mexicana,* used in folk medicine.

1864 Grisebach 788, Yellow thistle. 1954 *WIMJ* 17, Mexican Poppy or Thistle; Prickly Poppy; Gamboge or Yellow Thistle. . This plant is used for colds, especially in children.

YELLOW-THROAT GUTU sb dial; <*yellow throat* (for *yellow-throated*) + GUTU. Cf YELLOW-BELLY. A variety of the small parrot fish called GUTU.

1952 FGC StE /yélo-trùot gútù/.

YELLOW TURTLE sb. s YELLOW-BILL TURTLE.

1873 Rampini 167, see MULATTO TURTLE.

YELLOW VELVET FISH sb ?obs. = GRASS GROUPER.

YELLOW WALL-FLOWER sb obs.

a 1726 Barham (1794) 204, Sir H. Sloane, in his Natural History of Jamaica, takes notice of a plant which he calls a yellow wall-flower, with a *polygala* leaf. . (Linn. *Cleome procumbens*).

YELLOW WASP see GALLIWASP.

YELLOW WATER-PLANTAIN sb obs.

1811 Titford 58, Yellow water-plantain, *Alisma flava*. . native to Jamaica.

YELLOW WOODPECKER sb obs. Cf YELLOW-BELLY (the woodpecker).

1725 Sloane 301, Pica luteonigra varia. . The Yellow Woodpecker.

YELLOW YAM sb. A species of *Dioscorea* having yellow flesh.

1913 Harris 42, *Yellow yam* and its varieties belong to *Dioscorea cayennensis.* 1952 FGC all parishes /yela-, yelo-, yala-yam/—afu or red afu yam. 1954 *FG* 444, The Yellow Yam is very popular with planters and does well almost anywhere.

yen demonstr adj dial arch; <*yen,* var form of *yon,* that (over there) (*EDD*). That.

1955 LeP StE (Accom) /yen tida wan/ *those other ones.*

YERA-YERA sb dial; cf *were-were,* sb.

1943 *GL* StM, Yera-yera, small food.

YERRAY-YERRAY see YERRY-YERRY.

yeri, YERRI, YERRIE see next.

YERRY /yeri/ vb dial arch (this word, once widespread, is now heard in traditional songs, proverbs, etc. and in quite old-fashioned speech); <*year* (Engl dial form of *hear,* N & W-country, *EDD*) + Y[2]. To hear, in its various senses (listen, obey). *BL*; *SC jéri,* Gullah *yeddy.*

1835 Madden II 153, Me always yeerie good advice. 1877 Murray *Kittle* 25 [Song:] Yerry groomer corn pempeny, Groomer yerry. 1907 Jekyll 111, 'Do, Bro'er Blacksmit', me yerry all whé you tell me this time'. 1943 *GL* most parishes, Yerri, yerrie, yearry, yehri.

YERRY-YERRY sb dial; etym unknown, but cf Yoruba *yẹ̀ri yẹ̀ri,* sparklingly, brightly.

1. Very small fish; minnows; TICKY-TICKY.

1912 McK *Ballads* 78, Bubbles like de turtle-berries Jostlin' wid de yerry-yerries*. . *yerry-yerries: minnows. 1943 *GL* Clar, Yerry-yerry, small fish useful for destroying mosquito larva. 1952 FGC StC /yieri-yieri/ 'Coolie call it'—same as *tiki-tiki.*

2. Transf.

1943 *GL* West, Yerray-yerray, small children.

YERZES see EARSES.

YEYE(S) see *yai, yaiz.*

YICKA vb dial; var of *nicker,* neigh; cf *ika.*

1943 *GL* Clar, Yicka, neigh.

YIES see *yai, yaiz.*

yiki adj dial. A BUNGO TALK pronunc of *little.*

yikl adj dial; reduced form of *little.*

1952 FGC Tre, a /yikl/ breadfruit tree.

YIMBA see HIMBA.

YIPPI YAPPA sb; <*Jipijapa,* Ecuador: a sp representing the Spanish pronunc of the initial sounds. = JIPPI-JAPPA.

c 1915 FGC StAnd /yípi-yàpa, ípi-àpa/ sp yippi-yappa. 1927 Stafford 8, Weaving hats of yippi yappi. 1952 FGC StM /ípiyápa/ straw /ípiápa/ broom.

yiti adj dial; = *yiki.*

YOKEWOOD sb; prob <*oak* (cf other Engl dial forms, as *years,* ears, *yerb,* herb, etc., and similar Jamaican dial forms, as *yai, yaiz*) + *wood.* (There is no evidence that this wood was especially used for making yokes.) The tree *Catalpa longissima*; for other names see quot 1941; also called FRENCH OAK, SPANISH OAK.

1886 Hooper 31, Yokewood. . *Catalpa longisiliqua*. . A fine well-grown tree. . It is easily sawn and used for general purposes in the form of boards and planks. 1941 Swabey 33, Yokewood—(French Oak, Mast Wood, Jamaica Oak). 1954 *FG* 254, Yokewood (Mastwood). Suitable for the lowlands under 1500 feet, particularly in dry and rocky areas.

YONGA see YANGA.

YOUNG-GAL-FANCY sb dial. An unidentified plant.

1952 FGC StAnn.

YOURICKY-YOURK sb dial. See quot.

1907 Jekyll 17, See de t'reepence he give me fe go buy youricky-yourk. *Ibid* 19, Youricky-yourk, a nonsense word for some kind of plaster.

YUBBA CANE /yúba/ sb dial; prob <*Uba* (1954 Stevenson 17, varieties, Indian and Hawaiian, brought to Barbados 1933-4), phonetically respelled, but cf CB *-*yùbá,* sugar-cane. A not very good variety of sugar-cane.

1949 Reid gloss, Yubba—poor species of sugar cane. 1952 FGC StAnn, StJ, StM /yúba/ switchy, tough cane; they are now getting rid of this.

YUCAM see next.

YUCCA[1] sb; cf *OED yucca, yuca.*

1. The name for CASSAVA in Central and much of South America—hardly used in Jamaica;

some early spellings not recorded in *OED*: *Jaccu*, *Yucam*.

1657 Continuation 42, And such abundance of Jaccu (a Root whereof the Savages once made their bread). 1657 True Des. 2, The Yucam (whereof Cassavi is made).

2. Prepared cassava: see quots.

1943 *GL* StT, Yucca—Cassava bread. 1955 FGC Man /yuuka/—sweet cassada boiled to eat.

YUCCA[2], YUCCO sb dial; prob conn with BEYACCA. Species of *Sapium*.

1909 Harris 300, Blind-eye or Yucco (*Sapium cuneatum*..). This tree appears to be found only in the western end of the island. It yields a valuable, lasting wood. 1941 Swabey 14, Blind-Eye—(Yucca, Beyacca, Gum tree, Milk-wood, Cantu, Cantoo) *Sapium jamaicense*.

YUH dial sp for /yu/ *you*. *BA G*

yuoko sb dial; <*yokewood*.

1956 Mc StAnd /yuoko/ a tree planted as shade-tree for coffee.

yuoyo see KNOW-YOU.

ZEBRA LIZARD sb zool; from its colour pattern. The common lizard *Anolis lineatopus lineatopus*.

[1851 Gosse 225, It appears to be replaced by the Zebra Anolis..a very handsome species..with fine contrasts of pale yellow and deep brown disposed in irregular transverse bands. *Ibid* 491, I also saw here *Anolis maculatus*, that zebra-marked Lizard.] 1940 Lynn-Grant 90, This anole has been named the 'zebra-lizard', probably only by visiting scientists. Males are basically brown. 1941 *NHN* I 2 8, The common 'bush lizard' or 'zebra lizard' varies from the typical subspecifically.

ZEBRA SNAKE sb zool obs.

1851 Gosse 324, Zebra snake.

ZEBRA WOOD sb; *OED* 1783→. Any of a number of trees, both large and small, whose wood is of variegated colour, or 'striped'. Not all can be identified from the citations; among those known to bear the name are *Eugenia fragrans*, *Coccoloba zebra*, and *Capparis cynophallophora*: see quots. *N*

1774 Long III 837–8, Pigeon Wood or Zebra Wood.. This is not what is commonly called zebra wood, although it well deserves the name for the uniformity of its stripes. The species of zebra wood at present in esteem among the cabinet-makers, is brought to Jamaica from the Mosquito shore; it is of a most lovely tint, and richly veined; but not in lists like the pigeon wood: the latter much better corresponds with the zebra skin in the disposition of its stripes, and the other seems to have the nearer resemblance in its general colouring and ground. 1802 Nugent 97, The floor..was of zebra wood, the ground like satin wood, the stripes mahogany colour. 1864 Grisebach 789, Zebra-wood: *Eugenia fragrans* var *cuneata*. 1914 Fawcett 113, *Coccoloba zebra*..'A very large timber tree; wood variegated'. (Griseb.) *Ibid* 231, *Capparis cynophallophora*..Black Willow, Zebra Wood. 1957 Howard 102, Zebra wood—*Coccoloba zebra*.

zeflin sb dial; <*zeppelin*. A kind of MACHETE (?from its shape).

1958 DeC StT /zeflin/ a cutlass.

zeflin baaskit sb dial; <*zeppelin* (the basket is quite round—balloon shaped).

1956 Mc StAnd /zeflin baaskit/ a very big market basket, narrow at top; has bands of thin metal going around it, from the mouth under the bottom.

ZELLA sb dial; cf Ewe (Fɔ̃ dialect) *zɛli*, a funeral drum. A NINE-NIGHT celebration, sometimes with an element of POCOMANIA added. Cf SET-UP.

1943 *GL* Port, Zella, playing games at a dead person's home. StM, Zella, the celebration of ninth night in the form of puckomania. 1955 FGC Man /zela/ pocomania regular service—wrap dem head, go in a sort of a myal.

ZEZEGARY sb bot; etym not found. A name under which WANGLA was imported at the end of the 18th cent, though it had already long been known and used; for a time it had a great reputation in the treatment of dysentery.

1801 Dancer 362, I cannot help thinking that a very undue importance has been given to the boasted one, of the specific virtues of *vangloe* (or the *zizigary* as it has been called), in dysentery. 1814 Lunan II 251, Sesamum ..orientale..This is a native of the East Indies, and lately brought to Jamaica, under the name of *Zezegary*, though Browne notices it as common in the island in his time. 1837 Macfadyen 69, The young shoots and leaves yield abundantly a fine mucilage, and they have been employed..as a substitute for the *vanglo* or *zezegary*, in Dysentery. 1864 Grisebach 789.

ZINC FENCE sb dial. A fence made of sheets of galvanized iron or similar metal. *G*

1960 LeP Kgn, A corrugated iron fence or fence of bashed-flat oil drums—zinc fence.

ZINC (PAN) sb dial; <*zinc*+PAN. A kerosene tin.

1956 Mc StAnd /zingk pan/ a kerosene tin, large metal tin, used esp for getting water. 1958 DeC StT /zingk pan/ a kerosene tin. 1960 FGC West, Zinc, a kerosene tin.

ZINC ROOF sb chiefly dial. A roof of corrugated galvanized iron. *BL*

1956 Mc StAnd /zingk ruuf/.

ZINC SUGAR sb dial; <ZINC+*sugar*. New sugar, because it is carried about for sale in a ZINC PAN.

1960 FGC West.

ZING vb dial; cf ZING-ZANG.

1943 *GL* Kgn, Zing, to swing.

zingkuma see *singkuma*.

ZING-ZANG sb; cf ZING, and the US Gullah *swiŋswaŋ*, a swing (Turner 237): phonosymbolic—cf *zig-zag*. A swing.

1943 *GL* Kgn, Zing zang, a swing. 1955 FGC Man /swing-sang/.

ZIZIGARY see ZEZEGARY.

ZOMBIE sb dial; cf Kongo *zumbi*, fetish. In the kumona cult: an ancestral spirit. *BA G*

1951 Moore 33–4, A zombie is a god, or an ancestor who was once possessed by a god or other ancestral zombie, or a living being who has been possessed by one of these.

ZUZU-MAN sb dial; cf *guzu*.

1958 DeC StT /zuzu-man/ a name for an obeahman.

ZUZU WAPP sb dial; prob <*zuzu*, obeahman+*whop*, to strike or beat. A children's ring game in which one player (named Zuzu Wapp) chases others, beating them. *BL*

1955 E. M. Burke Clar, letter.

SUPPLEMENT

ABNER sb dial; app < the proper name, perh a biblical allusion.

1959 HPJ, Abner: a word for child ghosts common in Hanover and some other parts of the island. c1970 DeB in Kingston *Gleaner* 'Take my Word', Abner:..the child ghost (NOT the same thing as a duppy)..a term common in Hanover..[also] Westmoreland and northern St Catherine.

afu buosan sb dial. = *buosan yam.*

1976 HPJ E. West, A third informant, in 1944, called the yam *affoo bosun*..He said the yam, being thwarted in its downward growth, spread sideways and became round *like the protuberance in hernia.* In fact, he regarded *boasun* as the word for hernia.

AMERICAN HANGNEST sb ornith obs. = SPANISH NIGHTINGALE: see quot a1705.

ANETTO, ANNETTO see ANATTA.

ANSWER IN THE PAN vb phr obs. In the production of sugar: To show good or bad qualities. Said of a soil (and perh of other factors such as the type of cane used). (The 'pan' is the container in which crystallization was completed, hence 'in the pan' symbolized the end of the process or the final result.)

1793 Edwards II 211, There is however a peculiar sort of land on the north side of Jamaica..that cannot be passed over unnoticed..few soils producing finer sugars, or such (I have been told by sugar refiners) *as answer so well in the pan*—an expression, signifying, as I understand it, a greater return of refined sugar than common.

ARTILLERY PLANT sb; see LACE PLANT 2.

AVOCADO PEAR sb. Add sp:

a1818 Lewis (1834) 241, One of the best vegetable productions of the island is esteemed to be the Avogada pear, sometimes called 'the vegetable marrow.'

AVOGADA see prec.

baakini sb dial. Add: Also Puerto Rico *baquiné, -í.* Also Dominica *baquini*, the wake at the death of an infant.

1974 Nazario 32 etc.

BABY-GRIPE BUSH sb. = *mirazmi bush.*

BABYLON sb. Add sense: 3. By extension: any part of the established 'white-man's' society in Jamaica or elsewhere.

1974 Jacobson *New York Mag* 4 Nov 78, And the movement is changing the face of Jamaica, which Rastas call, as they do everything outside of Ethiopia, Babylon.

BACCALOW sb dial. Delete the bracketed matter and substitute: (prob an early loan into West African pidgin; cf the *SC* cognate *bákjáu*—Focke).

BACKRA, BUCKRA sb. Add sense: 10. An albino negro. See quot s.v. S WHITE-NAYGA. See also S BUCCRA.

BACKRA BABY sb dial.

1976 Perkins StE, Letter: Buckra Baby..[name] applied in StAnn to the plant *Blakea trinervia.*

BAD adj. See *ef yu bad.*

BAD-BOTTOM SNAPPER sb dial. = DOG-TEETH SNAPPER, a variety caught over bad sea-bottoms.

1950 Smith, Treasure Beach: Bad bottom snapper, *Lutjanus jocu.*

BADDY BELLY n. Prob familiarized form of BAD BELLY. ?Indigestion.

1976 HPJ, In Feb. of 1973 I heard a secondary schoolgirl say, 'It can give you bady belly', presumably meaning just an upset stomach.

BAD-LUCKED /bad-lókid/ adj. Add quot:

1968 HPJ, My only reference is, 'That name is a bad-luckied name'..It was then explained to me that, for example, boys named Toby and Anthony 'grow up bad'.

bahu sb dial; attrib. Add quot to sense 2:

1976 HPJ, An article in the [Kgn] *Star* of 5 Dec 1969 has a lurid account of bahoo men (handcart men) at the Coronation Market in Kingston.

BAIT-BARKER sb. See CAESAR quot 1952.

BAIT-PICKER sb dial. A small fish which picks at bait but is not worth catching.

1950 Smith, Negril: bait-picker; Whitehouse: winsor—*Thalassoma nitida.*

baja bil see BADGER BILL.

BAKINNY see *baakini.*

balahu adj or sb dial; also attrib. Add earlier quot, sense 1:

1873 *The Morning Journal* 1 Oct [From HPJ], [An article] refers to 'balahoo' women on the Kingston streets at night.

BAMBOO sb dial vulg. The penis. Cf WOOD.

1971 Duffey StAnn, 'Bamboo for penis.'

BANANA PIECE sb. See INTERVAL quot 1956.

BANANA YOKEY sb dial. Add sense: 2. See quot.

1976 Perkins StE, Letter: Banana Yokie..Applied in St Eliz. not to the Banana Quit but to the Oriole.

BANANA YOKIE see prec.

BANJU SALE sb dial. Add earlier quot:

1903 Loscombe 39, A curious word is 'banjo'. In Jamaica parlance this..is..used to signify a sale by auction.

BARBADOS LEG sb. See JACKFRUIT FOOT quot 1943.

BARCKINY see *baakini.*

BAR-FLANKED GAMBET sb ornith obs. In Gosse's use: a type of sandpiper; see quot.

1847 Gosse 352, Bar-flanked Gambet. *Totanus melanoleucus?*

BARRAH see *bara.*

BAR-TAILED SANDPIPER sb ornith obs. In Gosse's use: see quot.

1847 Gosse 350, Bar-tailed Sandpiper. *Totanus chloropygius.*

BASSOO see *busu* sb[1].

BASTARD BLUE ROAN sb dial. A fish similar to the BLUE ROAN in colour but of a different species. See quot.

1950 Smith West (Whitehouse), Bastard blue roan, *Chromis cyaneus.*

BASTARD MARGARET sb dial; *bastard* + *margaret* (see MARGARET GRUNT). See quot.

1892 Cockrell list, Bastard margaret—*Hæmulon acutum.*

BASTARD PLEURISY sb obs. See quot.

1820 Thomson 24, The *bastard pleurisy*, as it is called.. peripneumonia notha..Unfortunately for the patient, it is generally confounded with pleurisy, to which, at the very commencement, it bears some resemblance. *Ibid* 32.

BAWKINNY see *baakini.*

BEANY SQUIT see next.

BEENY QUIT sb dial. Add sense: 2. See quot.

1974 Perkins StE, Beany Squit: (Not the same as Beany Bird) A dark coloured, medium sized bird that is swallow-like on the wing and arrives in numbers in Feb. in the Munro District.

BELLY-BAND sb dial. 1. The peritoneum. 2. A medicinal body-belt.

1976 HPJ [From S. O. Gayle, E. West] *Belly-ban'*.. peritoneum. He said *belly-bang* was a body belt worn in certain illnesses.

BELLY-BANG see prec.

BERMUDAS POTATO sb. See POTATO-SLIP quot 1756.

BERRY sb dial; etym unknown. A fish: see quot.

1950 Smith, Pedro Bay: Berry, *Chromis marginatus.*

beta no de phr dial; *better* + *not* + DE[3]. Better conditions are not yet present, or have not yet come; things are still bad.

1974 Jones in Kingston *Gleaner Mag* 19 May 5, BETTER NŌ DEH—In Jamaica it means the bad condition will continue.

BEZOAR NUT sb bot obs; <*bezoar*, an antidote + *nut*. The NICKAR.

1811 Titford Expl to plate VIII 6, illust III 12, Bezoar nuts.

BHUROO see *buru.*

BIG-BELLY adj dial. Add sense: 2. Pregnant.

1971 Duffey StAnn, A minatory saying I have heard here is: 'Open-bottom, big-belly, baby-come-soon.' It may be a girls' skipping song.

BISHOP sb; <*bishop*, the lady-bird (*OED* 6), here prob because the insect has the shape of a bishop's mitre. The common 'stink-bug': see quot.

c1948 *NHN*, Bishop—*Loxa flavicollis.*

BITTER JESSE sb dial. Add quot:

1976 Perkins StE, Letter: Bitter Jessie..Wild yam.

BLACK DOLLY sb dial; *black* + DOLLY. A fish: see quot.

1950 Smith, Whitehouse: Black dolly, *Cephalopholis punctatus.*

BLACK GRUNT sb dial. A dark variety of the GRUNT fish.

1952 FGC gen.

BLACK ISRAELITE sb dial. A member of one of the POCOMANIA cults.

1953 Moore 60, They are also called Black Israelites.

BLACK JACK COCO sb dial. A variety of coco: see quot.

1943 *GL* No addr, Black jack coco—Bourbon coco.

BLACK PORGY sb dial. A dark variety of the PORGY fish. *G*

1952 FGC StE /blak paagi/.

BLACK SHOT sb[2]. See quot.

1936 Olivier 33, The denuded limestone has left behind it small nodules of sulphate of iron known as 'black shot', which is poisonous to bananas.

BLACK-THATCH sb; *black* + THATCH. See quot.

1933 McK gloss, Black-thatch, common name for the tallest and stateliest of the tree ferns.

BLAKE'S EAR sb dial. [Folk-etym rendering of *Blakea* (the genus name), understood as *Blake-ear*].

1976 Perkins, Letter: Blake's ear..[name] applied in StAnn to the plant *Blakea trinervia.*

bloba see SEA-STING.

BLUE sb. A blues song. See SYMBOL quot 1935.

BLUE-BACK SPRAT sb dial. An unidentified fish.

1952 FGC StE.

BLUE-HEAD PATY sb dial; *paty* perh var pronunc of KATIE. A fish: see quot.

1950 Smith, Negril: *Thalassoma bifasciatus*, Blue-head paty.

BOASUN YAM see s BOSUN YAM.

BOGA sb dial; prob abbr of BUGABOO 1.

1974 Perkins StE, Bōga: Macaca grub. Larval stage of beetle.

BOOR-RU see *buru.*

BORAMBAY sb dial; etym unknown, but cf *bogobi*. A fish: see quot.

1950 Smith, Mouth of S. Negril river: Borambay, *Eleotris pisonia.*

BOSUN YAM sb dial; <BOSUN, boatswain, as an honorific title (cf COMMANDER COCO, DUKE COCO, etc.). See DENKE, *buosan.*

bout vb dial; aphetic form of ABOUT. To set a sugar mill going; hence, by extension, to cut and bring the crop to the mill to keep it in operation. (Cf. *EDD about* adj, 'While the harvest is about.' HPJ.)

1976 HPJ, I have two occurrences of *bouting*. Miss Cox has written to me mentioning *bout* as used [in West] to include the cutting of the cane..; there is no doubt about the usage.

bouting vbl sb, see prec.

BOX BRIAR sb bot. See INDIGO BERRY quot 1936.

BRACE-UP 'TOMACH sb dial; <*braced-up* + *stomach*. See quot.

1974 Jones in Kingston *Gleaner Mag* 19 May 5, BRACE-UP TOMACH—A girl with a full bust, often the envy of the flat-chested.

BRICKER sb dial <*breaker*[2] (*OED*).

1976 Perkins StE, Letter: Bricker (or Breaker)..A small

wooden cask, closed at both ends with a bung hole in the side. Made in pairs and used like hampers on a donkey for carrying water.

BROWN MAN sb. Add quot:

[a1818 Lewis (1834) 402, It seldom happens that mulattoes are in possession of plantations; but when a white man dies, who happens to possess twenty negroes, he will divide them among his brown family, leaving (we may say) five to each of his four children.]

BROWN WEED sb. Prob erron for BROOM-WEED. See SLIPPERY-BUR quot 1954.

BUCCRA sb chiefly dial; early sp of BACKRA, BUCKRA; see **s** KILL-BUCKRA, **s** WALK-FOOT, quot 1903.

BUCKLE-FOOT. Add adj dial, and var sense: see quot.

1974 Jones in Kingston *Gleaner Mag* 19 May 5, BUCKLE-FOOT—Bandi-legged or bow-legged.

BULLA sb dial. Cf Pg *bolo*, cake, dumpling. Senses 3, 4, add: Var etyms proposed as below, but prob < Ko *mbula*, act of striking.

3. 1976 HPJ, Lois Gayle in Kgn *Gleaner* 16 Sept. 1972 says the most common of its [*sc* bulla's] many meanings in her childhood [in E. West] was 'a parental rebuff'. 4. 1976 HPJ, In this sense, perh < Gaelic *bualad*,..a blow..Gaelic must have been spoken in Eastern Westmoreland [Parish] in some great houses during slavery.

BULLY (TREE) sb. Add: Perh folk-etym < Arawak *boerowè.*

buna, bunakin sb dial. Add quot:

1976 Perkins StE, Letter: Bunna Skin or Boona Skin.. Spathe of the Cabbage Palm. Used as an umbrella or for covering pimento etc., or barbecues in rainy weather.

BUNCH sb tech. Add earlier quot:

1913 Fawcett 44, Here a bookkeeper enters it in his book under its proper denomination as a bunch, or one of eight, seven, or six hands; or he may reject it as unmarketable for any one of several reasons—it is not 'full' enough or too 'full', the fingers are too small, there are not enough fingers on the lowest hand.

BUNGO sb. Add: See also *EDD bungow*, an idiot (1 example).

buosan sb dial. Add sense: 3. A bodily deformity in which a member swells out of shape.

1973 *Kingston Star* 2 June 10, 'I'd never buy said shoes for fear of getting boatswain.' [*Boatswain* here is a hypercorrection of *bosun*, taken to be the same as *bousan*.] 1976 HPJ, see **s** *afu buosan.*

BURAO see *buru.*

BURBAN see BOURBON COCO.

BURRA, BURROO, BURRU see *buru.*

buru-man sb dial. A man who does *buru* dancing.

1952 FGC StAnd.

BUSH-BATH sb. Add quot:

1972 *Gainesville* (Fla) *Sun* 22 Dec 4A, Jamaicans don't eat ganja. They smoke it, ..and they might even include some in their 'bush baths' for various aches and pains.

BUSQWINE sb. Add: HPJ reports (1976) that c1936 *Busquine* was a current personal name (StT), and appeared in the *Gleaner* death columns (Kgn 1973 and 1975) as a surname.

B'UTE /byuut/ sb dial; an arch pronunc of *brute*, repr BUNGO TALK, in this case the failure to pronounce *r*, a sound not native to Twi and other W. Afr. languages.

1907 Jekyll 33, Annancy say:—'Drop you b'ute!' [*Drop, you brute!*]

BUTTER ACKEE sb dial. A variety of ackee having a white pod.

1952 FGC Port.

BUTTERCUP see (JAMAICA) BUTTERCUP.

BUTTY vb dial; cf *butu.*

1943 *GL* No addr, Butty, to stoop.

BUZU see *busu* sb[1].

bwaai, bwai sb. See Introduction, Historical Phonology p. lxi.

BWILA sb. = boiler. See TABAN.

byuut see B'UTE.

CABANA CANE see **s** *kyabana.*

CALABA BALSAM see SANTA (MARIA) 1.

CALABAN sb dial. Add: Also *SC krafánga.* The source word is Pg *caravan*, a device or trick, prob adopted into Pg pidgin in Africa and spread by negroes in the Caribbean. See Cassidy, note in *American Speech* 1980.

CALALU sb. Add sp:

1903 Loscombe 41, K 'tan' for Kullaloo [*a kind of wild spinach*]; good when him bile [*good when it's boiled*].

CALALU WATER sb dial; by word-play: the water in which calalu is boiled is *thin.* See quot.

1974 Jones in Kingston *Gleaner Mag* 19 May 5, CALALOO WATER—having long thin legs. Applied chiefly to girls.

CAN' dial sp for *can't.*

CANE DRINK sb. A COOL-DRINK made from sugar-cane. See SORREL 1 quot 1707.

CANE OIL sb dial slang. Rum.

c1970 C. E. Palmer in Kingston *Gleaner*, His friend may order..a small flask of rum..I mean the 'good ole cane oil'.

CANNICLE sb dial; prob < *cannikin*, infl by dimin *-icle.* A small drinking vessel; = PANNICLE.

1954 FGC StAnd /kyánikl/.

CARRY-DOWN ARTIST sb dial slang.

c1970 C. E. Palmer in Kingston *Gleaner*, And if his [*sc* a country man's] defeat is due to someone who let him down, likely or not, he'll describe the latter as a 'carry down artist'.

CARVALLHY see CAVALLY.

CASHEW BUG sb. An insect that attacks the CASHEW: see quot.

c1948 *NHN*, Cashew bug, *Cosmopolites sordidus.*

CATALUE erron for CALALU.

a1818 Lewis (1834) 106.

CERFITICKET sb dial < *certificate* by metath and folk-etym, as if it were a kind of *ticket.*

1976 HPJ, Isn't *cerfiticket* for *certificate* worth recording? I think it can still be heard.

chaach sb dial; var pronunc of *church.* See quot s.v. TAKE 3.

CHAKUM-PECKLE sb dial rare; etym uncert; *-um* prob repr *and*, but other elements not clear. Cf CHOCK adv, CONFUSION.

1943 *GL* No addr, Chakum-peckle, confusion.

CHALICE /chalis/ sb cant. The RASTAFARIAN name for a GANJA pipe, having sacramental implications.

1977 Chris Lawrence.

CHARLEY LIZARD sb dial. The POLLY LIZARD.

c 1950 *NHN*.

CHICKEN-TEA sb dial; <*chicken*+TEA. A soup or broth the chief ingredient of which was chicken; the water in which chicken was boiled, drunk as a beverage.

1949 U.Newton v 20.

CHINESE OYSTER sb chiefly dial. The bivalve *Pinna muricata*, eaten locally by the Chinese.

c1946 *NHN*.

CHUN sb dial, perh for *churn* or *tun* or a blend of both.

1976 HPJ, In 1962 I was told of a word *chun* in north-east St Ann, applied to a *tun* in which meat was salted.

CLIMBING RIVINA see HOOP WITHE 1.

CLUCKING-HEN sb. Cf *N klukam hen*, Cayenne ibis; Miskito *klukum*, muscovy duck; Twi *krakúm*, turkey (cf Dut *kalkoen*, Danish *kalkun*).

COCOA-BAG error for COCOBAY.

a1818 Lewis (1834) 208.

COCOBAY sb dial. Add: Also *SC kokobé*.

COCOON see CACOON.

COI see CAY.

COLILU see CALALU.

COMBANCHA sb dial rare; ?Amer Sp. See quot.

1943 *GL* No addr, Combancha, a feast.

COMPARTNER sb dial. Prob infl by Sp *compadre*, in common use in Belize and other Central American creole English dialects with the sense of *close companion*.

CORE vb dial; <*score* (see Introduction, Phonology, 10). See quot.

1976 G. Buscher, UWI, Core: to make incisions in the skin of a fruit (I've heard it only of pawpaws) which has been picked green and is put down to ripen.

CORITO see CORATO

CORK-HEAD MULLET sb dial. A fish.

1950 Smith, Kingston: Cork-head mullet, *Mugil curema*.

CORN DRINK sb. A COOL-DRINK made from corn. See SORREL 1, quot 1707.

CORN PUSS sb dial; etym uncert: *corn* (perh repr *corned*) +PUSS; cf CANE-PIECE CAT.

1. In the Blue Mountains: prob the CONY.

1950, Corn Puss Gap, a gap in the mountains near Indian Cony River, StT.

2. A tricky, thieving cat.

1961 *Ja. Talk* 105.

CORROJUNGO Add quot:

1959 DeCamp StAnd /korojónggl/ (1) general trash, rubbish, and junk if piled around the yard so thick that the place is 'like a jungle' (2) thick bush growing up around a yard making the place 'like a jungle'.

COTTA[1] sb dial. Add quot to sense 1:

1976 Perkins StE, 'Cutting the Cotta' is not used *only* in connection with divorce [see quot 1774]. It also refers to when people living in the same house decide to part and reside separately. Since the cotta is used to bear a load, cutting the cotta means that burdens are no longer shared.

COTTA STICK see *kata-tik*.

COUNT BUNCH sb. See BUNCH quot 1952.

COUNTRY sb dial. One's home area or section. (*OED* Country sb. 4a →1855).

1976 HPJ, Early in 1968, a person before the [Petty Sessions] court spoke of 'a bus coming from my country' and a little later..a man referred in his evidence to 'a woman from my country', meaning in this case Port Antonio.

CREOLE sb. Add sense:

4. The broad vernacular spoken by Jamaicans; the name itself is a comparatively learned term, more common names being 'the dialect', PATWA, BUNGO TALK, *bad talk*, *broken talk* and other pejorative terms. (In Belize, by contrast, *creole* is the commonly accepted term.) [Note: the word was applied to language much earlier in reference to the vernacular patois of the francophone plantation colonies; e.g. in Mauritius, *Catéchisme en créole* 1828]. Now used generally by language scholars.

1868 Russell 1–2, The estates usually employ, besides Creoles, Africans, and these latter, even after they manage to speak 'creole', still retain the deep and harsh accentuation of their own language. 1957 LeP in *Orbis* 6, 375..most of the work to date has been done on Jamaican Creole. 1966 Bailey, B. L. *Jamaican Creole Syntax* (Cambridge University Press).

CRISS-MISS sb dial; <*kris*+*miss*, young woman. See quots.

1954 LeP Man, see *kris* 2. 1974 Jones in Kingston *Gleaner Mag* 19 May 5, CRISS-MISS—A pretentious girl who overrates herself.

CROMANTY BULLET sb. A tree, see CROMANTY 4.

CROSS-NATURE(D) adj; <*cross* (*OED a*, sense 5) quarrelsome, perverse+*natured*, by nature. See CROSS B. adj. Ill-tempered by disposition; quarrelsome.

1956 Mc Clar, see *talawa* 2.

CUBBY sb dial. Add sense: 2. Transf: A small drink (cf a *pony*, *OED* 4).

c1970 C. E. Palmer in Kingston *Gleaner*, A rummy doesn't ask his friend to buy him a drink anymore. 'Fire a shot, man!' He'll say. And so his friend may order a cubby, a small flask of rum.

CULLY /koli/ sb cant. The RASTAFARIAN name for the highest grade of GANJA.

1977 Chris Lawrence.

CUP AND SAUCER sb dial; from the appearance of the flower.

1976 Perkins, Letter: Cup and saucer..[name] applied in StAnn to the plant *Blakea trinervia*.

CURRENCY The entries under various coinage and currency headings in the first edition antedated the most recent currency reforms, and were assigned values in terms of £sd sterling, which had been the official currency since 1840. Many of them refer to the situation even prior to that date, when local Jamaican currency was valued below sterling (so that e.g. 5*d.* local currency = 3*d.* sterling). Since our first edition, the unit of the monetary system has been changed, initially to the Jamaican £, which in 1969 was replaced in value by two Jamaican dollars (J$) of 100 cents each. The Jamaica farthing (¼*d.*) was discontinued in 1957; the penny (1*d.*) and halfpenny (½*d.*) in 1969.

It has not been determined by us whether the old terms listed below have in fact survived monetary reform in popular usage; it may be that, even if remembered, it is without precise values in new currency terms. However, we list here their values in old local currency (where appropriate), in sterling and approximately in new Jamaican cents:

	Old local currency	Sterling	Approx. value in new Jamaican cents
BIT	Varied—see Dicty entry	4½*d.*	4
bit-an-fipans		7½*d.*	6
bit-an-fuopans		8½*d.*	7
bit-an-kwati		6*d.*	5
BOB-TENNER		1/6, 18*d.*	15
DOUBLOON	a guinea,	21 shillings, 252*d.*	210
fiiko		variable—see Dicty entry	
FIP, *fipans, fipens, fipini,* FIPNEY, *fipni,* FIPPENCE, FUP, *fupans*	5*d.*	3*d.*	2½
s FOUR-BIT, fuobit		1/6, 18*d.*	15
GILL	1*d.*	¾*d.*	½
JOE		6*d.*	5
kwati see QUATTIE			
MAC, MACARONI		1/-, 12*d.*	10
MAC-AND-FIP,-FIPNI etc.		1/3, 15*d.*	12½
s NOGGIN		1½*d.*	1¼
QUATTIE		1½*d.*	1¼
tena, TENNA, TEN-PENCE	10*d.*	6*d.*	5
TUP, TUPPY	2*d.*	1½*d.*	1¼
TUPPY-AN'-GILL	3*d.*	2¼*d.*	2
TWO-BIT		9*d.*	7½
s TWO-MAC		2/-, 24*d.*	20

CUT OIL vb phr dial; see CUT vb dial 2. See quot.

1976 G. Buscher, UWI, *Cut oil*: to separate, in speaking of coconut milk in a sauce made with it, e.g. a run-down, the liquid has to be boiled until it 'cuts oil', i.e. the oil separates from the other components.

CUTTING MOTHER see MOTHER 1.

CUT YANGA vb phr dial; < CUT 2 + YANGA sb and vb. See quot.

1974 Jones in Kingston *Gleaner Mag* 19 May 5, CUT YANGA—To show off by dressing up in a flashy style; also cutting capers or capoose when riding a horse. Much used in Nigeria.

CUWEDIE vb phr cant. Add: Cf Ko *kuwidi-ko,* you have not heard.

dajaka sb dial; etym unknown. Sandals made from old automobile tyres. Also called HITLER BOOT.

1952 FGC StAnd /dàjàka/.

DAY PEENY sb dial; *day* + PEENY. The lady-bird (*Prepodes* spp).

1952 FGC Port /die piini/.

DEAD-BREED sb dial; < *dead,* lifeless + *breed,* a genetic type, a family stock. See quot.

1976 HPJ, In Feb. of 1964, she told me of an expression 'dead-breed' applied to a short-lived stock: 'yo' no' come out a dead-breed' would be said to a person of long-lived stock.

DEADIE sb dial. Various small fish: see quot.

1950 Smith, Negril: Deadie, *Petrometopon cruentatus* and *Cephalopholis* spp.

DEAD MAN OIL sb dial. See OIL OF—. A supposed healing medicine.

1952 FGC StE, Dead-man oil.

DEEPWATER COD sb. See quot.

1892 Cockrell list, Deepwater cod, browned nose.

DENKY /dengki/ sb dial; cf DINKY. See quot.

1952 FGC, Denky, a mortar.

dibidibi see DIVI-DIVI.

DISGRACE vb dial; < *OED* disgrace *v,* 6, →1720. To speak disparagingly (of people).

1955 Bennett *Oonoo Lie!,* Dem su-su and dem sey-sey, an Dem labrish an disgrace.

DOLLY sb dial; < *dolly,* doll. (*Doll* is little used in Ja.) A small fish: see quot.

1950 Smith, Whitehouse: Dolly, *Cephalopholis fulvus.*

DO MI UNDERMUMBLE CONTUMBLE vb phr. Confused by oral use: *humble* and *contumely* may have been original components. A formula of surrender in boys' games. Perh now out of use.

1974 Jones in Kingston *Gleaner Mag* 19 May 5, DO MI UNDERMUNBLE [sic] CONTUMBLE—The plea of a boy to his conqueror in a fight to release him.

DONKEY EARS sb dial. A common plant with long, pointed, erect leaves; see quot.

c1950 Inst List, Sansevieria, Donkey ears.

DO OVER vb phr obs. To kill.

1790 Moreton 84.

DREADLOCKS sb cant. Add sense: 2. A Rastafarian.

1974 Jacobson in *New York Mag* 4 Nov 73, Reggae fa days. Rhythm wild!..A jus' man and man a do-it like-all de dread lock dem. Roots mon. [*I listened to reggae music for days. Wild rhythm!..It was just men playing like all the Dreadlocks. Deep stuff, man!*]

DROGO-BOWL sb dial. Add earlier quot:

1873 *Morning Journal* 2 Oct (?Kgn), Drogher bowl women. (1976 from HPJ).

DRUM-AND-FIFE CRACKERS sb pl. Some kind of biscuit. See HOT-AND-NICE quot. 1948.

DUCKANTEAL see *dokantiil.*

DUMB-THING sb dial. Add quot:

1976 HPJ, I came across a generalised use of the term [dumb thing] to mean the brute creation.

DUSTY ROTI sb dial. For etym substitute: < Hindi *dostī* (= *friendship*) *roṭī,* a term used esp by Muslims in India of two very thin *roṭī* placed together. See also *roti.*

DUTCHY MAID sb dial. = DUTCH POT.

1952 FGC Tre.

EDDO sb. Add quot:

1976 HPJ, I heard *eddoo* from someone from northern St Elizabeth in 1969.

EDDOE, EDDOO, EDDOW see EDDO.

EERIE adj dial. See s *T*³. Add quot:

1976 HPJ, This is *irie,* which sprang into prominence in 1974 as a word for 'grand' or 'lovely'. I have never heard it spontaneously pronounced by anybody, and Hibbert..did not seem certain of the pronunciation. I think it is Monk Lewis's word *eerie.*

EGG-BIRD sb obs. Birds which lay BOOBY EGGS.

c1945 NHN.

ejag see HEDGEHOG FISH.

EVELING sb dial. Add quot:

1976 R. Landale, Kgn, Letter: The new word 'eveling' for 'evening' seems to be firmly established now. I have been hearing it for over 40 years and now I seldom hear 'evening'.

EYE-BABY sb dial; <*eye*+BABY 1. See quot.

1974 Perkins StE, Eye-baby: There is a belief in St Elizabeth that there is a live baby in the pupil of every eye.

FAN SHELL sb dial. =CHINESE OYSTER.

1952 FGC StM.

FEECO see *fiiko.*

FEEDER sb. The worker who fed or inserted the canes into the rollers of a sugar mill.

1832 Davis letter, in 1955 Curtin 234, The minimum number needed to operate the sugar works..is given.. as follows: three men as cane carriers, two strong women as feeders, one woman to turn trash, six young women as trash carriers, one stocker-man, one pan-man, three boiler-men, one boatswain to superintend. These were all slaves.

FEKO see *fiiko.*

fiesti see FACETY.

FILTHER sb chiefly dial; <*filter,* by folk-etym and/or overcorrection. A filter.

1951 FGC Kgn, Oil-filther need cleaning.

FIRE ANT sb, An ant (*Solenopsis geminata*) which stings 'like fire'. *BL*

c1945 NHN.

flaig vb dial; cf *flaig* sb.

1976 HPJ, With regard to *flaig,* the late Mr Vermont, of St Mary, knew this as both verb and noun, but regarded it as local.

FLASH sb dial. *OED sb.*¹ 1 '*obs.* exc. *local*'. A pool.

1976 HPJ, Have you ever come across 'flash' as meaning a pool of water? I have heard it used of pools on the Palisadoes [Kgn Harbour].

FLUSH sb dial slang. Half a year in prison; =PINT 2.

FLY-BY-NIGHT PITCH-BY-DAY sb dial; *BY* is /bi, bai/; see PITCH vb 2. See quots.

1956 BLB StJ, see FOLLOW-LINE. 1974 Jones in Kingston *Gleaner Mag* 19 May 5, FLY-BE-NIGHT PITCH-BE-DAY—A worthless idle person of no fixed address.

FOUR-BIT see s CURRENCY.

FOUR-EYE DOG sb dial; see FOUR-EYE(D) MAN. See quot.

1974 Perkins StE, Four-eye dog: Some dogs have a dark spot over each eye and these spots are supposed to open into eyes at night and enable the dog to see duppies.

FOWL TICK sb dial. See quot.

c1945 NHN, Fowl tick, *Argas persicus.*

frainin pan sb dial: pronunc of *frying pan*—see **-n** /n/ suffix² dial.

1973 Majesty Pen recording of *Anansi, Rat-Bat, an' Tiger,* Im get im frainin pan an im get im ail.

FRENCH SET DANCERS sb. see SHAKA quot 1837.

FROSTING sb. See quot.

1974 Perkins StE, Frosting: Mist or very light rain.

FULL A. adj. Add quot: See s BUNCH 1913 Fawcett 44.

FUSS-FUSS adj and sb dial. See FESS, FESS-FESS quot 1958.

GIVE COCO FOR YAM vb phr. To reply or respond in the same terms; to give as good as one gets.

1862 Clutterbuck 182, He gib him coco for yam. 1889 *Amer. N & Q* III 47/1, Cocca for Yams:—What is the origin and original application of the expression—of West Indian derivation, I suspect..? [Further comment *Ibid* 78/1, 192/1, 216/1, mostly off the subject.]

GO COOK YOUR OWN BUSH vb phr. An exclamation used to discourage a sponger.

1974 Perkins StE, Go cook you' own bush: Go and eat in your own house.

GOD-MARK sb dial. A birthmark, thought to be given by God.

1972 Reported by John Figueroa, UWI.

GOLDEN CUP see GOLDEN APPLE 1.

GRANGI-GRANGI sb dial; familiarized <GRANG-GRANG. Sticks, brushwood.

1953 Murray 15 [Song:] Me look ina de water, Me see grangi-grangi.

GRASSHOPPER SPARROW sb; prob ref to the bird's habit of 'hopping' in the grass. See quot.

1955 Taylor 39, The Grasshopper Sparrow or Tichicro (*Ammodramus savannarum*), a nondescript little bird which..skulks among the grass tufts making short flights from one tuft to another.

GRASS-QUIT PLANT sb dial. A plant on which the GRASS-QUIT likes to feed: see quot.

c1950 Inst List, *Parthenium hysterophorus,* Grass-quit plant.

GRAY-EYE see LONG-DAY BIRD.

GREASE-PALM sb dial slang. A bribe.

c1970 C. E. Palmer in Kingston *Gleaner,* A country man will never speak of bribe. For him it is 'grease palm'.

GREAT CRAY-FISH see HORNED LOBSTER.

GREAT CRESTED FLYCATCHER see RED PETCHARY.

GREEN-BACK JACK sb dial. A fish: see quot.

1950 Smith, Negril: Green-back jack, *Caranx ruber.*

GREEN CONGRY see CONGRY.

GREEN EEL sb dial. =GREEN CONGRY.

1952 FGC StE.

GREENHEART FIDDLEWOOD sb obs. A species of *Chloroxylon.*

1756 Browne 264.

GREEN-PLANTAIN PORRIDGE sb dial. Porridge made from the flour of green plantains or by mashing boiled green plantains.

1952 FGC Port, StJ.

GREET vb dial. In the cant of *kumuna* groups: To invite gods and zombies to enter the heads of ceremonial drums by beating on them with specific rhythms.

1953 Moore 35.

GREY-BO sb dial. Add to etym: but prob also infl by the Liberian tribal name *Grebo.*

GREY-NAYGA sb dial. An albino negro.

1966 Cassidy-DeCamp in *Names* 14.131, The 'gray' list includes yet other terms: *Gray-nayga* (like *White-nayga*); and *Gray-owl, Gray-puss.*

GREY-OWL sb dial. An albino negro (in reference to skin pallor). See quot s.v. **s** GREY-NAYGA.

grong-bikl see **s** GROUND-BICKLE.

GROOPER see GROUPER.

GROUND-BICKLE sb dial; see BICKLE, BITTLE. Provisions grown at one's GROUND.

GROW-QUICK see GROWING STAKE.

GRUDGEFULNESS sb. see HEAR-SO quot.

grupa see GROUPER.

guaba dial pronunc of *guava.*

GUANA see GREEN GUAVA.

GUAVA CHEESE sb. A conserve of guavas, strained and boiled down with sugar to a solid consistency, which may be sliced like cheese.

c1915 FGC current generally.

GUINEA-HEN GRUNT sb dial. A variety of the GRUNT fish speckled like a guinea-hen.

1952 FGC West.

GULLY[1] sb. Add sense: 4. A concrete storm drain built in the bed of a gully (sense 1).

1955 LeP Kgn and StAnd, The Kingston Corporation was referred to as the 'Gully Government' because it built many storm drains.

hakam see *akam.*

HARD FERN sb chiefly dial. In the Blue Mountains: *Blechum occidentale*; in Trelawny *Polypodium polypodioides.*

c1950 *NHN.*

HARD-TAILED SQUIRREL see SOW-MOUTH.

HARD-TO-TAKE-UP sb dial. Fish of *Halichoeres* species, which are very slippery. See also OKRA POLL.

1950 Smith, Treasure Beach [StE]: Hard-to-take-up, 2 spp.

HAY GRASS sb. Grass grown for hay for animal feed. See HORSE-KIND quot 1936.

HEAVY MANNERS sb phr. Firm measures of control by the police.

1976 *Gleaner* 30 Aug p. 1 Kgn (Michael Manley speaking at PNP Youth Organisation annual conference), Comrades, if anybody asks you what is the Government's policy towards crime and violence, the answer is, 'heavy manners'. And if they ask you how long the heavy manners will remain, the answer is that it will remain as long as there is any threat of gunmanship and political violence.

heb vb dial. Var of HIB.

HEDGEHOG STONE sb obs. =ECHINI STONE.

heng auxil vbl particle. Var pronunc of *en.*

1956 Mc Man /si-i human de we heng gi mi di maanggo/ *That's the woman who gave me the mango.*

HOG-TAYA sb dial. A coarse kind of TAYA that is fed to hogs; =COCO CALALU 2.

1952 FGC Han.

HOMELY adj dial. (*OED homely,* adj 3, →1636.) Feeling 'at home', familiar.

1971 Duffey, StAnn, 'Dat dog soon homely'—a new puppy would soon feel at home.

HORSE DANCE sb. See HUSSAY quot 1952.

HO SENNY HO phr dial. [Chinese] Also in interrog form, **ho seni mau,** Is business good?

HOT adj dial. Add sense: 3. Of beer or other drinks: Unrefrigerated.

1971 Duffey, StAnn, Jamaicans distinguish between a cold drink and one that isn't iced by asking for a 'hot beer...' It is never a 'warm' drink or one 'off the shelf'.

HUG-UP sb. See FUN-FUN quot.

HUNTERMAN sb dial. Add sense: 2. Transf. An officer in revivalist cults: see also **s** HUNTING WOMAN.

1953 Moore 80–1.

HUNTING MOTHER see MOTHER 1.

HUNTING WOMAN sb dial. A female counterpart of a HUNTERMAN 2.

1953 Moore 80–1.

HUSBAND sb dial. A man who is kindly or protective towards a younger woman.

a1818 Lewis (1834) 240, The women called me by every endearing name they could think of. 'My son! my love! my husband! my father!' 1964 HPJ Kgn, Twice in March..a female news vendor described me as the 'husban'' of her little granddaughter, who was constantly with her and to whom I had always tried to be nice. 1976 HPJ, My assistant..mentioned a girl in Spanish Town (where she lives) who is now about 18. Some ten years ago this girl was sent frequently to a shop: the shopkeeper was very kind to her, and he was called her 'husband'.

I[3] /ai/ pron dial cant; <*I* strongly stressed; cf **s** I-AND-I.

Among Rastafarians, the singular personal pronoun, all genders and cases, adopted in preference to the general dial *me.* The sound is emphasized as in their pronunc of /ràstafarái/ (see RASTAFARI) and has become the dominant element in their alteration of many words, often by omitting consonants and replacing the first vowel with stressed *I*, e.g. *I-cient*, ancient; *I-tection*, protection; *Imes*, times; *I-bage*, cabbage; *I-rate*, create; *I-dure*, endure; and others they consider significant to their cult.

1977 Owens 65, The Rastas..would seem to perceive this creole pronoun 'me' as expressive of subservience, as representative of the self-degradation that was expected of the slaves by their masters. It makes persons into objects, not subjects. As a consequence the pronoun 'I' has a special importance to Rastas and is expressly opposed to the servile 'me'. Whether in the singular ('I') or the plural ('I and I' or briefly: 'I-n-I') or the reflexive ('I-self', 'I-n-I-self'), the use of this pronoun identifies the Rasta as an individual, as one beloved of Haile-I Selassie-I. Even the possessive 'my' and the objective 'me' are replaced by 'I' in the speech of the Rastas. *Ibid* 66–7, see list of Rasta words.

I-AND-I /àianái/ pron and sb dial cant; also sp I-n-I; from I^3 + *and* + I^3.

1. Rastafarian first personal pronoun (sg and pl) repeating 'I' for emphasis.

1974 Jacobson in *New York Mag* 4 Nov 73, I and I have fi check hard..It change I..now I and I [eat] jus' patty, hardo bread, from Yard. [*I was greatly affected..It changed me..Now I only eat patties, hard-dough bread, from Jamaica.*] 1977 Owens 65, Rastas use the plural form, I-n-I, quite naturally, and at first the unaccustomed ear is not certain that it is plural..In the end, however, it becomes clear that I-n-I is basically a substitute for 'we', and indeed a very significant one. It expresses at once the individualism that characterises the Rastas and the unity which they see among themselves by virtue of their unity with Jah.

2. A Rastafarian, Rastafarians. Also attrib.

1977 Owens 64, Once two Rastas told me that they had been forced out of a job because they were Rastas. As they had no locks and could not be visibly identified as Rastas, I inquired how the employer knew. They replied: 'By I-n-I argument. Man know I-n-I by I-n-I argument.' The word 'argument' as used by a Rasta does not connote querulousness, but indicates rather the activity of reasoning or the ability to state one's position on a subject.

INDIAN GIRL sb. A character in JOHN CANOE celebrations.

1952 Kerr 144.

I-n-I see S I-AND-I.

IRIE see S EERIE.

I-TAL sb dial cant; a Rastafarian word—see S I^3 and quot 1977.

1974 Jacobson in *New York Mag* 4 Nov 73, De I-tal reggie roots a Brooklyn. [*The genuine Rastafarian reggae is in Brooklyn.*] 1977 Owens 66, I-tal=(?) vital (meaning 'pure', 'natural', organic).

ITALIAN SENNA see JAMAICA SENNA.

JACATOO see JOCATO (CALALU).

JACCU see YUCCA sb^1 1.

JACKASS BISCUIT see JACKASS CORN.

JACKASS MARKET sb dial joc. See JACKASS quot 1956.

JACK BEAN see HORSE BEAN.

JACK-O'-THE-WOODS sb dial. = FATTEN BARROW; see quot 1957.

JAH sb dial. Add quot:

1977 Owens 64, Part of the fright which Rastas inspire in those members of the public who are not familiar with their ways is due to their aggressiveness in speaking out of the fullness of the truth that they have received from Jah.

jak panya see JACK-SPANIARD.

JAMAICA BLACK DOR see JAMAICA CLOCK.

JAMAICA(N) COAT-OF-ARMS sb joc. = S RICE-AND-PEAS, because it is such a favourite dish in Ja.

1949 U.Newton v 20, A big dish of rice-and-peas, otherwise known as Jamaican Coat of Arms.

JAMAICA CRAB sb. = BLACK CRAB, MOUNTAIN CRAB.

c 1830 *Waldie's Select Lib* II 88/3, The land crab, which is common to many of the West India islands, is more generally known as the Jamaica crab, because it has been described from observation in that island.

JAMAICA MOCK-BIRD see GOD'S-BIRD.

JAMAICAN CROW = GABBLING CROW.

JAMAICAN TODY see ROBIN (REDBREAST).

JAN CUNNOO, JANCUNOO, JANKOONO, JAN-KUNNAH see JOHN CANOE.

JESTER vb dial; evid a blend of *jester* sb and *gesture*, vb. To play the fool, to jest, to make motions without intending action.

1974 Jacobson *New York Mag* 4 Nov 79, Bob Marley, a Rasta, who may be the greatest political songwriter since Dylan, says of the government [of Jamaica], 'Dem a jestering.' He predicts a showdown and writes reggaes about it.

JESTERING vbl sb dial; < JESTER vb + *-ing*. Playing the fool, temporizing.

1976 *Gleaner* 31 Aug 2 Kgn (Eddie Seaga speaking at BITU annual conference), 'There are many within the ranks who want to deal with the questions of the "political prisoners" before it is too late..Many have resolved that it should not be allowed to continue until the elections. They should bear in mind that..after election day there will be no jestering.' Mr Seaga warned, to wild applause.

JEYESEY-AISE adj dial; < JEYES + -y + AISE. See quot, and compare YAWSY-SKIN.

1974 Jones in Kingston *Gleaner Mag* 19 May 5, Inferior, like a donkey with sore ears dressed with jeyes.

JIGGER sb. *OED* derives < *chigoe*, but in fact this word combines two sources: Cariban **chigo*, a flea (*Tunga penetrans*), which burrows under the skin and lays eggs, with West Afr **jiga*, a larval mite (family Trombiculidae) which irritates the skin, both parasites being widespread through tropical America. Among the Ja folk the Afr form clearly predominates, although the *-er* ending seems to reflect analogy with English agentive nouns. See *W3* and esp 1949 Turner 195.

JOCKATO, JOCOTO, JOKOTO, see JOCATO (CALALU), *jongkuto*.

JOCKEY sb. A character in JOHN CANOE celebrations.

1952 Kerr 144.

JOHN CONNU see JOHN CANOE.

JOHN-CROW SPELL sb obs? JOHN-CROW + *spell sb^3* (*OED*). The less desirable work period on sugar estates.

1826 Barclay 415, One spell was called *John Crow Spell*, and the other *Quality Spell*.

JOHN TAYLOR GRASS sb. (John Taylor is unidentified.)

c 1950 Inst List, John Taylor grass, *Trichachne insularis.*

JONCANOE, JONKANOO see JOHN CANOE.

JO PAN see DRUM PAN.

JUCATO, JUCKATA, JUCKOTO, JUKOTO see JOCATO (CALALU).

juk vb and sb dial. Add to etym: Perh reinforced by Pg *chocar*, push, thrust, represented in Saramaccan by *tjoko*. Also Gullah *chuk*.

JUNCOONU see JOHN CANOE.

JUST AS CHEAP adv phr. Equally well.

1977 HPJ Letter, Have you ever come across the expression: 'I had just as cheap go as stay'? [Remembered by FGC as current c 1915.]

kachapila sb dial; pronunc of *caterpillar*.

KATARRI /katári/ sb dial; cf Hindi *kuthārī*, an earthen vase. A mixed dish favoured by East Indians.

1943 *GL* No addr, Katarri, Indian delicacy. 1955 FGC StAnd.

KAY *see* CAY.

KAY DRUMMER sb dial; prob < CAY + DRUMMER. A fish: see quot.

1950 Smith, Palisadoes [Kgn]: Kay drummer, *Conodon nobilis.*

KEE *see* CAY.

KEIBA *see kiba.*

KEY see CAY.

KEY-HAULIN see KEEL-HAULING.

KIBBA, KIBBER see *kiba.*

kichibu, kikibu see *kitibu.*

KILL-BUCKRA sb dial. Add earlier quot:

1903 Loscombe 42, Kill-buccra..is..applied to a little yellow flower, like a buttercup, which comes into bloom at the beginning of the sickly season.

KINGSTONIAN sb. See SPANISHTONIAN quot.

kin uova see KINOBA.

kips, dial pronunc of *skip.*

1952 FGC StAnn /kip jak/ a fish [corrected to:] /kips jak/.

KNOCK WATER v phr dial. To drink rum.

1959 DeC Ginger Piece, /a duon nuo if ing gwaing gi mi a shiling tu guo an nak mi wata out a ruod dis iivning/.

KNOTTY int dial cant; from *knot*, referring to the way Rastafarians wear their hair—see DREADLOCKS. A Rastafarian greeting at meeting or parting.

1974 Jacobson in *New York Mag* 4 Nov 73, Ikes dread! Knotty! Hail dis!..I man a bus. More time soon. Knotty! [*Hi, brother Rasta!..I have to go. See you again brother!*]

KOO see KU.

krokro see *karakara.*

KULLALOO see CALALU.

kumuna sb dial. Add: Cf also CB *-*mįn*, dance.

KUNTANG-KUNTANG adv; onomatopoeic. See quot.

1974 Jones in Kingston *Gleaner Mag* 19 May 5, KUNTANG-KUNTANG—Going slowly but surely as a donkey does.

kyabana, kyavana sb dial; ?for *Habana* (Cuba) A variety of sugar-cane.

1952 FGC StT.

LADY PEAS sb sg; prob named for their pretty, variegated colour. Black-eye peas (*Vigna unguiculata*).

1952 FGC StAnd.

lamp vb, sb. To deceive; a deception.

1973 Majesty Pen recording of *Anansi, Rat-Bat, an' Tiger*, Breda Taiga gi im a argyument, so im disaid fi lamp im nou. Bot Taiga naa tek lamp suo iizi man.

LAND-PUSSLEY sb. Land-purslane, a plant, prob one of the purslanes or succulent herbs used in salads (Portulaca and similar species). See ITCH quot 1952; cf s TOONA, also s PUSLEY.

LANTERN-JAW SNOOK sb; descr. See quot.

1950 Smith, Lantern-jaw snook, *Centropomus undecimalis.*

LARN-MANNERS see DUPPY NEEDLE.

LASH LARUE sb dial slang. Nickname for a sexually overactive man. See quot s.v. LASHER.

LATED adj dial. Add earlier quot:

1903 Loscombe 294.37, It is apparent that he [= a Jamaican] is merely using a good old English expression. Yet another example is the invariable use of 'lated' where we should say 'late', which is of course a clipped form of 'belated'.

LIB-AN-NO-LIB vb phr dial; prob a calque from some African language. Now it's here and now it isn't.

1974 Jones in Kingston *Gleaner Mag* 19 May 5, LIB AN NO LIB—It is here or I have it; It is not here or I have not got it.

LIFT UP ONE'S MOUTH vb phr. To smile.

1971 Duffey, StAnn, 'Lif' up you mout' after you no see me so long'—our carpenter called this out to an old acquaintance, the meaning being 'Smile, don't you recognize me?'

lik-lik see LICKY-LICKY adj 2.

LILLY-LILLY adj dial; iter of *lili.* See FUM-FUM 1 quot 1774.

LILY GRASS sb; from the appearance of the head. = WHITE-HEAD GRASS, s STAR GRASS.

1952 FGC Port.

LIMBLESS sb dial. An unidentified plant.

1976 Perkins StE, Letter: Limbless..A weed that grows tall and straight and seldom branches

LINING OF THE WALLS vb phr dial. In the cant of *kumuna* cults: see quot.

1953 Moore 126, The principal zombies and ancestors come into the drum, then stand along the four walls of the house and watch the 'setting'..[This is called] the lining of the walls.

LINING PEG sb. A wooden peg to hold the string used as a guide to keep the rows straight when sugar-cane was being planted.

1823 Roughley 90, see DUNG BASKET.

lit, var pronunc of LICK.

LIVE WASH sb. In rum making: see quot.

1976 'Caribbean Tempo' (in *BWIA International Travel Mag.* 4.2) 29, Soon there are enough yeast cells to tackle the 24,000 gallons of 'live wash', as molasses-water mixture is called, which has been pumped into one of the fermenters.

LOCKS abbr of DREADLOCKS.

LONG-EARS see DRAB MULLET.

longga sb dial. Add: Cf Tonga *mulonga*, river.

LONG GUT see LONG BELLY.

LONG-SPIKED FIDDLEWOOD sb bot obs. A species or variety of *Citharexylon*.

1756 Browne 265.

LUCEA MANGO sb; <*Lucea*, town in parish of Hanover, Ja+*mango*. A variety of mango grown in and near Lucea.

1947 U.Newton II 13, Some famous mangoes called 'Lucea Mangoes'..the last word in mango-merriment. Large, fleshy, sugary, yielding and everything!

LUMVOTUVO phr dial. Add: Cf CB *-*tùmbò* belly.

MA sb dial. Add: Cf also CB *-*máá* (my) mother.

maami[2] sb dial. =MAMMEE APPLE. Note: /máami/ is the current folk form; see quot.

1976 G. Buscher, UWI, Marmee: I tried in vain to get mammy apples at Papine Market but was duly supplied with marmees once I'd learned that particular item.

maasa-niega sb dial. Add quot:

1833 Scott 144, Massa Niger, who put water in dis rum, eh?

MABIALE see FRENCH SET-GIRLS.

MACCA vb dial <MACCA sb. To prick; also metaph, to impress or affect deeply. See s *rengk* vb, quot 1974.

MACCA MAN sb dial; <MACCA+*man*. See quot.

c1970 C. E. Palmer in Kingston *Gleaner*, A very efficient or strong man is called a 'Macca man'. No one can successfully kick against the pricks so it is difficult for anyone to compete with a Macca man.

MACKA see MACCA.

MACKENZIE SQUAB see SQUAB 2.

MACONI WEED sb dial. A nickname for GANJA. See quot s.v. DRY GIN.

MALANTANG /malantáng/ sb dial; <*mulatto*. Any of several similar fish: see quot.

1950 Smith, lists five genera (and seven species) called 'Malantang' by Ja fishermen from Kgn to Morant Keys: *Blennius, Labrisomus, Malacoctenus, Cremnobates,* and *Rupiscartes*.

MAMMICK vb dial. Add sense: 2. To cause severe pain to (a human being).

1976 HPJ, The other day..a retired waitress, speaking of a spinal injury, said 'It mammock me..' The first time I heard the word was in 1956 or 1957, from someone born around 1935.

MAN DONE sb dial; abbr of such a phr as /im tingk im a man don/ he thinks he's a man already. See quot.

1974 Jones in Kingston *Gleaner Mag* 19 May 5, MAN-DONE—An undersized, but impertinent, precocious boy.

manggro see MANGROW.

MANGRO sb dial. =MANGROW.

MANGROVE CUCKOO sb. =RAINBIRD 2.

MANGROVE SNAPPER /mánggro snápa/ sb chiefly dial. See quots.

1950 Smith, Mangrove snapper, *Lutjanus griseus*.

MANILL SUPOTAS see MAMMEE SAPOTA quot p1660.

MANNA GRASS sb. See CROSS GRASS quot 1774.

MANNISH WATER sb dial. A type of meat and vegetable soup, served at weddings, and thought to fortify the male powers.

1976 G. Buscher, UWI, Mannish water [recipe from a Ja servant]: You will need one goat head, foot and tripe. Wash and scald the tripe. Cut up everything small and put to boil. Then you had [=add] some banana cut up with the skin, or potatoes or breadfruit, escallion and pepper and butter, and let it boil down like soup.

MARANGA COCO, MELANGA COCO sb (see MELANGA). Identified by Alvarado for Bolivia as <Am Sp *malanga* (=*Colocasia esculenta*), and for Cuba, Puerto Rico by Malaret as prob<AmSp<African (=*Arum sagittifolium*).

1952 FGC StM /marángga kóko/.

MARASMUS see *mirazmi*.

MARMEE see *maami*.

MAROONER sb obs; see *OED* 1: 'A buccanneer, pirate.'

1661 Hickeringill *Jamaica* 67, A few French Buckaneers, or hunting Marownaes [? *read* Marownars].

MAROWNAES see prec.

MARRYING vbl sb. The blending of rum of different kinds.

1976 'Caribbean Tempo' (in BWIA *International Travel Mag.* 4.2) 29, Rum is normally aged for a number of years in oak casks and when this process is completed the contents of each cask are tested by experienced blenders and then mixed in oak vats where the process of 'marrying' the blends takes place.

MARSHALMAN sb obs; cf *OED*. A bailiff.

1826 Williams 92.

MATTIE, MATTY sb dial; prob by merging of the familiar form of *Matilda* (see the popular Ja song by this name) with the chiefly nautical *matey*, companion (*OED* 1833→), and *matie* as in MATTIE-BELLY: a woman's name commonly symbolizing sexual easiness. SC *máti*.

1951 Murray 50 see quot s.v. *talawa* 2.

MAWGA-NANNY sb dial; <*maaga*, thin+NANNY, cf JIGGA NANNY.

1. A stock character in certain games; by the word's meaning, a very thin old woman.

1951 Murray 16, De play begin an' de ball gawn roun'; Mawga Nanny show me how de ball gawn roun'.

2. A very thin person; usu a girl.

1974 Jones in Kingston *Gleaner Mag* 19 May 5, MAWGA-NANNY—A very meagre girl.

MAYPOLE sb. (*OED* sense 2, 1750 Barbados →1848.) The coratoe plant, which shoots up a flowering spike about fifteen feet high, thought to resemble a maypole.

1825 De la Beche 41, The negroes have the amusements of the May-pole and Jack in the Green. A spike of yellow flowers of the American aloe is employed for the former purpose. 1977 FGC 'maypole' still current name for coratoe.

MECKAY-MECKAY see *mek-mek, meke-meke.*

MELANGA see s MARANGA COCO.

migl see MIDDLE.

MISS PRETTY sb dial; MISS+*pretty*. Any of various colourful fish, e.g. the Chaetodons.

1950 Smith.

MONEY LILY sb dial. =LUCKY LILY.

1952 FGC Tre.

MONGOOSE FERN sb dial. A fern which gives cover to the mongoose: see quot.

c1950 Inst List, *Lycopodium* (Portland).

MONKEY TAMARIND sb. Tree similar to tamarind tree. See DUPPY PUMPKIN quot 1946.

MOSQUITO-FOOT adj dial; <*mosquito*+FOOT, leg. Thin-legged.

1974 Jones in Kingston *Gleaner Mag* 19 May 5, MOSQUITO-FOOT—Having very meagre legs. Applied mostly to little girls.

MOTHER WATTIZOO sb dial; <*mother*+onomatopoeic element—cf *tutu-wata*. An unidentified bird.

1974 Perkins StAnn, Letter: Modda Wattizoo (Moneague District). I don't know which bird this refers to.

mou sb dial. Maw.

1952 FGC StE, see INSTRAL.

MOUNTAIN JUDY sb dial; <*mountain*+JUDY. =JUDY.

1955 Taylor 88.

MOUNTAIN PALM see MOUNTAIN CABBAGE.

MUGANGLE vb dial; prob representing *mug-handle*, pronc /mog ánggl/. See quot.

1974 Jones in Kingston *Gleaner Mag* 19 May 5, MUGANGLE—To hold or sling a girl by the arm, e.g. Man, mugangle the girl.

MULCH vb dial. To moult.

1974 Perkins StE, Mulch: To moult.

MULE sb[1] dial. =OBEAHMAN DRUMMER.

1950 Smith, Whitehouse: Mule, *Eques acuminatus.*

MULE sb[2] chiefly dial; often used as an insult. See quot.

1976 G. Buscher, UWI, Mule: a woman who has not borne a child..I think the Family Planning Unit could vouch for its importance as an autonomous semantic item.

MUSHET see MACHETE.

MUSSA sb dial. 1. Add earlier quot:

1797 *Columbian Mag* (HPJ), The Negroes call hasty pudding Mussa and like to eat it with their broths.

NAHHE see *maa-i.*

NASBURY see NASEBERRY (TREE).

NAUI see *maa-i.*

NEES(E)BERRY see NASEBERRY (TREE).

NEGRO-DRIVER sb. Add earlier quot:

1787 Robert Burns, Letter to Dr John Moore, London, 2 Aug, [when Burns was expecting to go to Jamaica as 'book-keeper' on an estate at Port Antonio]..even though it should never reach my ears a poor Negro-driver, or perhaps a victim of that inhospitable clime.

NEWTON sb dial; etym unknown.

1. The sapsucker—see YELLOW-BELLY.

1974 Perkins StE, Newton: The yellow-bellied Woodpecker.

2. The oriole.

1976 Perkins StE, Letter: Newton: Have heard this applied to both the Yellow-bellied Woodpecker and the Oriole.

NOGGIN sb dial. Add sense:

3. A penny-ha'penny. See s CURRENCY.

1903 Loscombe 38, In Jamaica..I found that 1½d., although usually called a 'quattie', is by old people in out-of-the-way places termed a 'noggin', and I accordingly suggest that these coins must have got their names from the amount of liquid measure they were severally able to purchase.

NONDESCRIPT sb. A character in former JOHN CANOE celebrations. See GOMBAY 2 quot 1833.

NONE-SO-PRETTY sb dial. =NANCY PRETTY.

1950 Smith.

NOSE sb tech. The looped end of a rope by which it is held steady while being made.

1952 FGC StE.

NOT HERE NOW, I'M vb phr dial. 'I'm not on duty'; see quot. Cf GONE vb.

1971 Duffey, StAnn, 'I'm not here now'—I have heard this from several people to indicate that the work for the day has been done and that they are leaving.

NUMB-FISH sb; *OED* →1867.

1. A small brown skate or sting-ray.

1952 FGC Port /nom-fish/ have bone on tail; StE /nom-fish/—after it juk you it cramp you.

2. In the Kingston area: *Urobatis sloani.*

1950 Smith.

NYAM-AN-GUWEH sb dial; <NYAM+*and* +*go away*. See quot.

1974 Jones in Kingston *Gleaner Mag* 19 May 5, NYAM-AN-GUWEH—One who likes to be present to partake of the meal, but being lazy, leaves soon after.

OBEAHISM Add earlier quot:

a1818 Lewis (1834) 291, This aunt..was haughty, ill-natured, and even suspected of Obeahism, for the occasional visits of an enormous black dog, whom she called Tiger, and whom she never failed to feed and caress with marked distinction.

OBEAHMAN DRUMMER sb dial. A type of drummer fish believed to have powers like those of an obeahman. See quot 1952. Also called MULE, SWALLOW FISH.

1950 Smith, St Mary: Obeah-man drummer, *Eques acuminatus.* 1952 FGC StJ /óbyaman jróma/—has two stones in his head; if he goes in a pot [fish trap] first, no other fish will.

OCHRA, OCHRO(W), OCRA see OKRA.

OKRA FISH sb dial. Cf OKRA POLL, s OKRA PATY. See quot.

1950 Smith, Hector's River: Okra fish, *Halichoeres radiatus.*

OKRA PATY sb dial; OKRA+?phon var of *katie* as in BANANA KATIE 2. See quot.

1950 Smith, Port Antonio to Negril: Okra parrot, poll, paty, *Halichoeres*, four species.

OLD-MAID DRUMMER sb dial. =s SWALLOWTAIL DRUMMER.

1950 Smith, Port Maria: Old-maid drummer, *Eques lanceolatus.*

OLD RUNNER sb dial. A fish: see quot.

1950 Smith, Port Antonio: Old runner, *Chromis marginatus.*

OLD WOMAN'S RAZOR sb dial. =DEVIL('S) HORSE-WHIP.

c1950 Inst List.

ombraila sb dial, a common pronunc of *umbrella.*

ONE-MINDED adj dial. See TWO-MINDED quot.

ORANGE DOG sb dial. A caterpillar which feeds on orange-tree leaves and has a face like that of a bulldog.

c1945 *NHN*, Orange dog, *Papilio* species.

PALAVA /palava, palaba/ sb dial; <Pg pidgin <Pg palavra, word, widespread in pidgin and creole languages. Prob the same as *plaba* 4. A noisy quarrel. But cf also *EDD* PALAVER 2. *Obs.* Noise, abuse. →1781.

1974 Jones in Kingston *Gleaner Mag* 19 May 5, PALAVA—A row.

pali (lizad) see POLLY LIZARD.

pampandam sb dial; etym unknown. =CROMANTY 4.

1952 FGC StT.

panchuok see SPANISH OAK.

PAN SHOWER sb dial. Just enough rain to fill a pan. See quot.

1970 EB (Mandeville) Man, Pan shower—a sudden heavy rainfall.

parakii sb dial, a pronunc of *parakeet.*

1952 FGC Han /pàrakíi/.

PARTLY adv chiefly dial. (Used for *practically*—by confusion of forms?) Practically, virtually, almost.

1973 Cawley *Anancy and the Pot* (story recorded at Accompong, 8 Dec), Cowskin beat 'im [=Anancy] such a way dat 'im partly kill 'im in de bush. 1976 HPJ, A curious variation appeared in a folk-tale I picked up in the 'thirties, 'Half a day partly..' It occurred in a *Gleaner* report of evidence in court in 1945, 'Sometimes people are partly naked', and in a Coronation Essay from 1952, 'In partly every possible street..' 'Clive conquered partly the whole of India' was written by a secondary school boy in 1935 or 1936. The usage is also found in Guyana.

PASSA-PASSA vb dial; prob <African pidgin-English <Pg *pasar* iterated. To pass repeatedly; see quot.

1974 Jones in Kingston *Gleaner Mag* 19 May 5, PASSA-PASSA—To use or distribute lavishly, e.g. 'Don't passa-passa the food'.

PAWN vb dial. Add: Concurrent infl of Pg *apanhar*, take, grasp, lay hold of (the prob source of Saramaccan *panjá* also) is likely.

PEE-PEE BED sb dial; <*pee-pee*, urine+*bed*, i.e. a bed that has been wet, or the action of bed-wetting. See quot.

1971 Duffey, St Ann, 'Pee-pee-beds'—the local name for millipedes that give off the smell suggested when disturbed.

peke-peke[2] adj dial; prob phonetic variant of *mek-mek, meke-meke.* Perh also infl by N. Engl & Scots *pick*, pitch, dirt, black mud (*SND, EDD*).

1958 DeC Port, /peke-peke/ sloppy, wet, and muddy.

PENCIL FLOWER see DONKEY WEED 2.

PERINO sb obs. Add: Prob hispanized form of an Arawak word, e.g. (Campa) *pearen*, cassava drink, or a Galibi word, e.g. *palinod*, beverage made by women.

perringkl see s *piniwingkl.*

PESTERINE see PISTAREEN.

PICCIN see PICKNEY, *pikin.*

PICK vb trans. Add sense: 3. To clean by taking out the unwanted part; specif to bone fish.

1940 HPJ, see BRAGADAP sb[1] 1.

PICKNEY. Add: Also *SC pikíen.* See also s *pikin.*

PICKNEY-MUMMA sb dial. Add: Also *SC pikíen-mamà.*

PIEMENTE, PIEMENTO see PIMENTO.

PIGEON PEPPER sb obs. A type of *Capsicum* pepper, evid favoured by pigeons; cf BIRD PEPPER.

1811 Titford XIII 47.

PIGEON 'TOMACH sb dial; <*pigeon+stomach.* See quot.

1974 Jones in Kingston *Gleaner Mag* 19 May 5, PIGEON TOMACH—A full breasted girl, same as 'brace-up 'tomach'.

pikin sb dial; <Pg *pequeno*, small, small child, prob via Pg pidgin, and parallel to Surinam creole *pikíen*, Cameroons creole *pikin*, Sierra Leone Krio *pikin*, etc. A child. See PICKNEY.

1903 Loscombe 41, Jamaica alphabet..O is an Orange; de piccins' (children's) delight.

PIMENTO TICK sb chiefly dial. A tick in some way associated with PIMENTO. See quot.

c1945 *NHN* Pimento tick, *Amblyomma maculatum*; Mandeville.

PINCERS see PINCHERS

piniwingkl sb dial; cf *EDD* PENNYWINKLE. The periwinkle (sea snail).

1952 FGC StE /piniwingkl/; [Port /pèrríngkl/].

PINK ROOT see INDIAN PINK 2.

PISTEREEN, PISTOREEN see PISTAREEN.

PLAYING-DRUM see PLAYING-CASE.

PLEASANT PLANTAIN sb obs. A medium-sized variety of plantain; see HORSE PLANTAIN quot 1725.

PLUCK-EYE adj dial; reduced <*plucked*, pulled outward + *eye*.

1974 Jones in Kingston *Gleaner Mag* 19 May 5, PLUCK-EYE—Having big, bulging, ugly eyes.

POD /pad/ sb dial. An ear of maize.

1912 McK *Songs* 109, see SHED.

POLLY GRUNT see *apali gront*.

POLOO-POLOO int dial arch or obs; cf *poro*.

1868 Russell 22, Interjections: Poloo-poloo, unfeelingness.

POND COOT sb. The bird *Jacana spinosa*; also called JACK SPENCE, LILY TROTTER, QUEEN COOT, S QUEEN OF BIRDS, S RIVER CHINK.

1955 Taylor 74.

POOKY sb dial; see *puki*.

POOKY SQUIRREL see *kanggatuoni* 1, *puki*.

POOM-POOM see PUMPUM YAM.

POOR MAN'S PEA see DUTCH RUNNER.

POOR ME BOY, POOR ME GAL Add earlier quot:

a1818 Lewis (1834) 292, The poor girl..endeavoured to beguile the time by singing—'Ho-day, poor me, O! / Poor me, Sarah Winyan, O!'

porot sb dial; a common pronunc of *parrot* (though the more regular /parat, paarat/ also occur).

POWER SHOES see POWER 3.

praima sb. A type of sugar-cane.

1952 FGC StM.

prap-kaan sb dial. <*prap* + *corn*. See *prap* quot 1956 Mc.

PRICKLY BOTTLE-FISH sb obs. In Browne's use: The porcupine fish. See BOTTLE-FISH.

PRICKLY FERN sb. Either of two ferns: see first quot; = MACCA FERN.

c1950 *NHN*, Macca fern, prickly fern, *Hypolepis nigrescens*, *Cyathea horrida*. 1952 FGC Port.

PROSPER adj dial; abbr from some such phr as 'It would prosper you'. Better, preferable.

1971 Duffey, StAnn, A tree-cutter indicating the best place for a tree to fall: 'Prosper to fall i' hya'.

puchin adj dial; etym unknown. Short; dwarfed.

1943 *GL* StAnn, Puchin, short, dwarfed. 1952 FGC StAnd.

PULP-EYE sb dial; <PULP vb (or perh adj) + *eye*: that makes the eyes pulp or bulge out. White rum.

c1970 C. E. Palmer in Kingston *Gleaner*, Another descriptive name for white rum is 'pulp eye'.

PURPLE PARROT sb. A fish: see quot.

1950 Smith, Long Bay: Purple parrot, *Pseudoscarus plumboeus*.

PUSLEY, PUSSLEY sb, var spp reflecting the Ja pron of *purslane*, a succulent herb (q.v. in *OED*). See S LAND-PUSSLEY, S TOONA quot 1893.

QUALITY SPELL see S JOHN-CROW SPELL.

QUARTER BUNCH sb tech. In the grading of bananas: see BUNCH quot 1952.

QUASH-QUASH sb dial; iterative from reduced form of *squash*. The fruit of the STRAINER (VINE).

c1950 Inst List

QUEEN DOVE sb dial cant; <QUEEN 2 + DOVE. A female leader in revivalist ceremonies.

1950 Moore 112–13.

QUEEN OF BIRDS sb. = S POND COOT.

'QUEEZE-YEYE see SQUEEZE-EYE and Introduction, Phonology §§10, 12.

QUI see KU.

QUITTERING sb dial; <*quitter* vb + *-ing* (*OED* → c1440). Filling with pus.

1974 Perkins StE, Quittering: Mattering (of a wound).

raabit sb dial, an occas pronunc of the more regular /rabit/ for *rabbit*.

RACE-BOOK sb. A paper-covered book cheaply printed for the racing season and including information about horses and races, advertising, jokes, etc.

1896 *Excelsior race book*. c1910–20 FGC StAnd.

RACECOURSE MACCA sb dial; from its growing plentifully on the Kingston racecourse, and its prickly stem (see MACCA). The JAMAICA BUTTERCUP.

1955 FGC StAnd.

RAGGITY adj. See *raga-raga* B.

RAIN BUG see NEWSMONGER.

RAIN SEED sb dial. Clouds that foretell rain. Add current quot:

1974 Perkins StE, Rain seed: mackerel sky.

RAMBLING MOTHER see MOTHER 1.

RAM-PUSS sb dial. Add earlier quot:

1903 Loscombe 39, In Jamaica a cat is invariably a 'puss' ..while the correct designation of grimalkin is a 'ram-puss'.

RAM-SACK vb dial; *ransack*, perh by folk-etym. *BA BL*

1943 *GL* StE, see *raga-raga* C.

RASHICALI adj dial; ?for *rascal(ly)*. See RAM-GOAT RATIONAL quot 1952.

RATCHET (KNIFE) sb. A folding knife whose blade springs out when released by a ratchet-like device in the handle.

1972 *Johnny Too Bad* (Reggae song), Walking down the road, with a ratchet in your waist..Johnny you're too bad, oh oh oh. 1976 D. Craig, UWI, Current.

RAT-TEETH PARROT sb dial. A variety of the PARROT fish with teeth sticking out of its mouth. Cf COCK-TEETH and HOG-TEETH PARROT.

1950 Smith, Kingston: Rat-teeth parrot, *Halichoeres garnoti*.

RED AFU (YAM) sb dial. A dark yellow variety of AFU YAM (contrasted with WHITE AFU).

1952 FGC StJ.

RED CALALU sb. =RED-STICK CALALU.

REDDEBO see RED IBO.

RED-EYE MULLET sb dial. (Contrast BLACK-EYE MULLET.)

1952 FGC StC.

RED-HEAD WATER FOWL sb dial. The Florida Gallinule (*Gallinula chloropus*).

1956 Jeffrey-Smith 114, The red shield has given it the name of Red-Head Water Fowl.

RED PEGGY sb dial. A nickname for the common 'red-ants' of Jamaica, known for their fierce biting.

1974 Perkins StE, Red Peggies: Red ants.

RED SANTA see SANTA (MARIA) I, quot 1952.

RED-SEAL COOT sb dial. The Florida Gallinule (*Gallinula chloropus*).

1956 Jeffrey-Smith 114, See QUEEN COOT.

RED SPANISH PLUM see LEATHER-COAT PLUM.

RED SPOTTED BEAN sb obs. An unidentified bean.

1696 Sloane 67, Phaseolus perennis..semine lato compresso, minore, rubro, maculis nigris notato..The small red-spotted bean.

[Note: The hyphen is erron. since the spots are black.]

REGGAE sb; a recently estab sp for *rege* (the basic sense of which is *ragged*—see *rege-rege* with possible ref to rag-time music (an early form of American jazz) but referring esp to the slum origins of this music in Kingston.

A type of music developed in Jamaica about 1964, based on s SKA, and usually having a heavy four-beat rhythm, using the bass, electric guitar, and drum, with the SCRAPER coming in at the end of the measure and acting as accompaniment to emotional songs often expressing rejection of established 'white-man' culture.

1973 *London Times Mag* 4 Feb, 'The Sound System: Reggae, and the Culture of the West Indians in London'. 1974 Jacobson *New York Mag* 4 Nov, 75, But the madness of 'new' Kingston couldn't be fully expressed in the simple grind of Rock Steady. A more complicated structure evolved to carry the weight of the lyrics, which were increasingly political (songs like 'Burning and Looting Tonight'). Sinuous music contrasted with cut-throat lyrics. But to most ears the resultant reggae.. still sounds 'unfinished'. Alton Ellis says,..—reggae music is unfinished because Jamaica is unfinished. 1976 *Time* 22 March 83, Created 15 years ago in the west Kingston ghettos by amateur musicians, reggae is characterized by a scratchy, staccato guitar, incessant drumming and full-volume bass. Its rhythm is distinctive because, unlike rock, it emphasizes the first beat instead of the second..'Reggae songs are the strongest way to reach the people', says [Jamaican] Songwriter Max Romeo. 1976 Jean Small, UWI, Reggae has now developed into different kinds,..[the] type that came from SKA, then there is a Rastafarian kind that is closely reminiscent of Rastafarian music.

rengk vb dial <*rengk* adj. See also s I-AND-I. To force (itself) upon, make a strong impression upon.

1974 Jacobson *New York Mag* 4 Nov 73, First year I and I site up De Harda Dey Come. It macka mi. Da one de renk mi a tell you.

RICE-AND-PEAS sb. *BA*

1. A dish made with rice, coconut oil, and usu RED PEAS (though CRAB-EYE PEAS or GUNGO PEAS are used). Also called s JAMAICA COAT-OF-ARMS.

c1915 FGC StAnd, common. 1947 U.Newton II 8, Some people call the midday meal 'lunch' but we always called it dinner on Sundays. As usual it consisted of a half moon of rice and peas; a few blocks of yams..etc.

2. The climbing vine *Quisqualis indica* whose clusters of red and white flowers are thought to resemble the dish.

c1915 FGC StAnd, Remembered. 1964 JAS *Flower Gardner* 85, Rice and Peas..A sturdy rampant creeper with flowers of three colours—white, rose and red.

RIDE AND GALLOP A JACKASS see JACKASS.

RIDING vbl sb. A step used in many ring games: see quot.

1922 Beckwith 61, *Riding*..a peculiar shuffling step.. one flat foot, one toe, without moving the feet from the ground, and turning slowly.

RIGHT LANGUAGE sb. Educated English in contrast to PATWA.

1956 McClar, /kabób/, in 'right language' Cobweb.

RIG-JUG sb dial; perh <*rig* sb[1] 6, a fuss (*EDD*)+*jig*. A noisy confusion. See BUMP-AND-BORE quot 1955.

RING-DING, RING-DOWN, RING-TING. The common first element in all these is Scots —see *SND*‡ RING v^3 (<reign) 3..freq used with intensive force=out and out, thorough-going etc. For DING, TING see *EDD* DING II I Dinger (b) anything of a superlative character.

RING-DOWN, RING-TING see prec.

RIVER CHINK sb dial; prob for *river chick*. The bird *Jacana spinosa*. Also called s POND COOT.

1955 Taylor 74.

RIVER COCO sb dial. =COCO CALALU 2

1952 FGC StAnn

ROCK STEADY sb. A type of music popular in Jamaica about 1960, intermediate between s SKA and s REGGAE. See quots.

1974 Jacobson *New York Mag* 4 Nov 75, Rock Steady is perhaps the slowest and most deliberate-tempoed popular music within memory. But the madness of 'new' Kingston couldn't be fully expressed in the simple grind of Rock Steady. 1976 Jean Small, UWI, Rock Steady is..a development of Ska that shows an increase in the influence of American popular music at that time [late 1950s, early 1960s]. Its rhythms are more complex than those of Ska.

ROCK SUCKER sb dial. A suckstone (fish with a suctorial disc).

1952 FGC StC, Rock sucker..suck on to a stone.

ROE MULLET sb dial. An unidentified variety of fish.

1952 FGC StC (from two informants).

rompii, romplis, rontis sb dial. Add: See also *SND*, *EDD* RUMP *v.*, to dock the tail of an animal; *rumpy*, tailless. *SND* RUNT *n.*[1], *v.*[1].. 4 (1) The tail of an animal; the rump.

ROOTS sb pl; see s ROOTS PEOPLE—the country people who best preserve African ways, of which Rastafarians approve; also those ways and values, hence use of the word for anything approved. [This antedates Alex Haley's use of the word.] Also attrib.

1974 Jacobson in *New York Mag* 4 Nov 73, The up-and-coming roots (nitty-gritty) reggae band. *Ibid*—see s DREADLOCKS 2.

ROOTS PEOPLE sb; cf *OEDS grass root.* Jamaicans who feel they belong in Africa rather than Ja. See quot.

1974 Jacobson *New York Mag* 4 Nov 78, Jamaican countrymen, called roots people have always felt 'misplaced' in their Jamaican 'paradise'.

ROYALIST see FRENCH SET-GIRLS.

RUMBA BOX /ròmba báks/ sb; <Amer Sp *rumba*, a dance+*box*. A musical instrument of the type of the African *zanza*. See quots. *BL*

1955 FGC Man, see *tambu*. 1961 *Ja. Talk* 266, The *rumba box*..simulates the tones of the bass viol by means of four pieces of metal of different gauges attached to a box (the resonance chamber), which vibrate when they are plucked with the fingers, and are tuned to correspond to the strings.

RUM-BUMPER sb dial; <RUM-BUMP+*-er*. =RUMMARIAN.

1952 FGC StAnd /ròm bómpa/.

RUN vb intr. See *OED* 8b, of fish 1887→, *DAE* 1743. Of the BLACK CRAB: To migrate to the sea from high land in order to spawn.

1826 Barclay 323, They are most plentiful in May, the season, at which they deposit their eggs, or '*run*', as the negroes express it.

RUNGLES sb dial; a var form of *runggus.*

c1915 FGC StAnd.

RUPTURE WORT see CRAB WITHE.

saach-mi-haat see SEARCH-MY-HEART.

saalchong sb dial; <*saal*+uncert element (perh *trunk*). A container for SALT provisions.

1952 FGC StAnd.

SADDLE A JACKASS see JACKASS.

SAID-SAME adj dial; *said* ppl. a. (*OED* 1) +*same.* A pleonastic emphatic equivalent of *same*: very same.

c1915 FGC StAnd, Remembered; current 1977.

samfai B vb. Add quot:

1972 Gainesville (Fla) *Sun* 22 Dec 4A, 'Samfied' means, loosely, led down the garden path. And anyone going to Jamaica, particularly with a foreign accent, would be samfied indeed, let alone, someone asking questions about ganja!

SAMPLATTA FOOT sb dial; <*sampata*+*foot*: Having a foot or feet resembling a rough sandal; see also *sampata* 2.

1974 Jones in Kingston *Gleaner Mag* 19 May 5, SAMPLATTA FOOT—A boy with deformed feet.

SAND BLACKIE sb dial. =SAMMY BLACKIE.

1950 Smith, Lucea: Sand blackie.

SAND-GUTU see GUTU.

santapii sb dial. Add: Prob <Pg *centope*, *centopie*: paralleled in Cameroon and Sierra Leone creoles.

SCHOOLMASTER SNAPPER sb dial. See DOG-TEETH SNAPPER, quot 1892.

SEA FORTY-LEG sb dial. The sea centipede.

1952 FGC gen.

SEA-GULF sb dial; by folk-etym <*seagull.*

1952 FGC StAnn.

SEE IT HERE, SEE IT THERE /siit ya; siit de/ vb phr dial.

c1915 FGC StAnd /siit ya; siit de/ common. 1971 Duffey, StAnn, 'See it here' 'See it there'—commonly used where Standard English would have 'Here it is' 'There it is'.

SENEGAL SENNA see JAMAICA SENNA.

SET sb obs. Sense 2, add earlier quot:

1833 Scott 245, But the beautiful part of the exhibition was the Set Girls. They danced along the streets, in bands of from fifteen to thirty. There were brown sets and black sets, and sets of all the intermediate gradations of colour. Each set was dressed pin for pin alike, and carried umbrellas or parasols of the same colour and size, held over their nice showy, well put on *toques*, or Madras handkerchiefs, all of the same pattern, tied round their heads, fresh out of the fold.—They sang, as they swam along the streets, in the most luxurious attitudes. I had never seen more beautiful creatures than there were amongst the brown sets—clear olive complexions, and fine faces, elegant carriages, splendid figures.

SET-GIRL see SET sb 2.

SEVEN SCENTS sb dial; from its mixture of odours. Sweet basil (*Ocimum basilicum*).

1974 Perkins StE, Seven scents: Sweet basil.

SEVEN-STAR WORM sb dial.

c1970 DeB in Kingston *Gleaner* 'Take my Word', An ex-Manchester penkeeper spoke of the 'seven-star worm', which, he says destroys large areas of good pasture about that time of year [*sc* June; see SEVEN-STAR RAIN].

SHAKY-SHAKY[1] sb dial. See EBOE DRUM quot a1818.

SHEEP-BUR see MUSK-MELON.

SHEEPSHEAD ALEWIFE sb dial. =SILVER OLD-WIFE.

1958 FGC Kgn.

SHEEP-TAIL sb dial. A piece of shirt protruding behind through torn pants; see quot. Also transf to the wearer.

1974 Jones in Kingston *Gleaner Mag* 19 May 5, SHEEP-TAIL—A boy with pants worn out or torn at the rump. To cover his rump, he draws down his shirt which sometimes protrudes and resembles a sheep's tail.

SHINE-EYE BARBADOS see SHINE-EYE sb[1] 3.

shing sb and vb dial. Var of *sing*. See *se* 3 quot 1907.

SHINY-MOON (SNAPPER) sb dial. =MOONSHINE SNAPPER.

1950 Smith, Negril: Shiny-moon, *Priacanthus arenatus* and *P. cruentatus.*

shrints see *swimps.*

SIDE-BASKET sb dial. =SIDE-BAG.

1952 FGC Man.

SIGHT UP v phr dial. To see.

1974 Jacobson in *New York Mag* 4 Nov 73, First year I and I site up De Harda Dey Come. It macka mi. [*Last year I saw the moving-picture 'The Harder They Come'. It affected me violently.*]

SILVER TICK sb dial; descr. A large cattle tick.

1952 FGC StT (2), Tre.

SING sb dial. Add earlier quot:

a 1818 Lewis (1834) 254, The woman's part is always chanted frequently in chorus, which the negroes call, 'taking up the sing'.

SINGING BIRD sb obs. See NIGHTINGALE quot 1725.

SINGLE-BIBLE see SEMPERVIVE.

SINNER-CONTRACT sb dial; by folk-etym < *simi-kantrak.*

c 1950 Inst List.

SKA sb; onomatopoeic. A type of popular music that originated in Jamaica in the mid-1950s, and later was developed into s ROCK STEADY and s REGGAE. See quots.

1974 Jacobson *New York Mag* 4 Nov 75, Drummond.. put together a band that is the cornerstone of reggae, the Skatalites. The music they played was called ska, after the sound the rhythm guitar made. 1976 Jean Small, UWI, SKA was taken up by the Jamaican government at that time [when it became popular] and identified as the *national sound*. This ensured its persistence and continued development in a way which had never before been possible for any other type of Jamaican music. 1976 Rex Nettleford, UWI, SKA: a type of music emerging from among the urban mass population in Jamaica during the mid-1950s, with evidence of influences from American recorded pop music, Rastafarian rhythms and elements of traditional (Revival and Pocomania) music.

skeng sb dial; prob abbr of *skengge.* A ratchet knife; a gun. See s SKENGAY quot 1976.

1976 D. Craig UWI, current.

SKENGAY /skengge/ n; echoic (see quot) but perh infl by *kengge.*

1974 Jacobson *New York Mag* 4 Nov 75, The Bunch are going through their oldies medley: 'Conquer Me' 'Nebuchadnezzar (King of Babylon)', and 'Johnny Too Bad', all superhits. Larry is shaking out the skeng-ay. The skeng-ay (updated ska) is the sound a Gibson guitar makes when a Jamaican strums it. It is very important. It keeps the reggae time..skeng-ay, skeng-ay..all reggae has it. 1976 Rex Nettleford, UWI [In Skengay] the sound of that guitar simulates gun-shots richocheting in the violence-prone backlanes of the depressed areas of Kingston, hence 'skeng' means a gun or 'iron'. The link between the music and the realities of contemporary ghetto life gives the words a particular cogency at this time.

SLAVE BEAD sb. See quot.

1972 Lechler in *JHSB* 5.188, The only item I found of any interest, was one tiny blue bead, which one of my more knowledgeable friends informed me was known in Jamaica as a 'slave bead'.

SMALL GANG see PICK I, PICKANINNY GANG.

SMALLPOX BUSH sb dial. *Parthenium hysterophorus*, formerly used to treat smallpox.

c 1950 Inst List.

SNOUK sb. Unrecorded sp for *snook*, the fish (genus *Centropomus*).

1790 Beckford I. 321, Snouk.

SORE THROAT PEPPER sb obs. A variety of *Capsicum* formerly used as a remedy for a sore throat. See PURPLE PEPPER.

SOUP-SEASON see SEASON sb[2].

SOW MACHETE see *sou.*

SPECKLE WOOD sb. See GRANADILLA (EBONY) (TREE) quot p1660.

splif sb dial. Add quot:

1972 Gainesville (Fla) *Sun* 22 Dec 4A, My grooms were very well paid, but they couldn't afford a 'spliff'. And anyway, very few Jamaicans use ganja.

SPYING MOTHER see MOTHER I.

SQUEECHY sb dial; prob phonosymbolic, suggesting tininess. The POLLY LIZARD. *BL*

c 1950 *NHN.*

SQUIT sb dial; overcorrection of QUIT sb. See s BEENY QUIT.

sred sb dial; a common pronunc of *shred.*

STANDING sb dial. A game played with cashew nuts; cf the marble game 'drops'.

1948 U.Newton IV 35, see KNOCK-AND-GO-ALONG.

STAR GRASS sb; from the appearance of the head. =WHITE-HEAD GRASS; also called s LILY GRASS.

1952 FGC Port, StAnd.

STAY-HOME see COMPELLING POWDER.

STEEL BOTTOM sb dial or slang. Add sense: 2. A drink of white rum followed by beer.

c 1970 C. E. Palmer in Kingston *Gleaner*, A white rum, chased with beer becomes a 'steel bottom'.

STINKING-ANTS sb dial; < *stinking* + ANTS. A black ant having a strong, acrid odour. See first quot.

c 1950 *NHN*, Stinking ant, *Crematogaster brevispinosa.* 1952 FGC gen.

STOCKER-MAN sb. The workman who saw to the stock of canes during grinding at a sugar mill.

1832 Davis letter, in 1955 Curtin 234, see s FEEDER.

STONE-HOLE 2. Add earlier quot:

1907 Jekyll 75, Gaulin..begun to fishening. An' as him put him head under a stone-hole the boy come down off the tree.

STREAMERS JACK sb dial. A fish of the Jack type with 'streamers' or ciliated fins.

1950 Smith, Lucea: Streamers jack, *Alectica ciliaris.*

STUCKEDEE sb dial; add quot:

1974 Jones in Kingston *Gleaner Mag* 19 May 5, STUCKIE or STUCKIDEE—A girl's young man or boy-friend.

STUCKIDEE, STUCKIE see STUCKEDEE, STUCKY.

SUGAR TEA sb dial; < *sugar* + TEA I. =SUGAR-AND-WATER.

1952 FGC StAnd.

SUPPORTER sb dial; folk-etym for *sapota* See MAMMEE SAPOTA.

SUSHUMBER see SUSUMBA.

SWALLOW FISH = s OBEAHMAN DRUMMER.

1950 Smith, Pedro Bay: Swallow fish, *Eques acuminatus.*

SWALLOWTAIL DRUMMER sb dial; descr. = s OLD-MAID DRUMMER.

1950 Smith, Pedro Bay: Swallowtail drummer, *Eques lanceolatus.*

SWEET-POTATO BUG sb dial. A stink-bug which attacks the sweet-potato plant.

c 1950 *NHN*, The sweet-potato bug, *Corecorus fuscus.* 1952 FGC StAnd, West.

SWIPPLE-POLE sb dial; <SWIPPLE+*pole.* The cochineal cactus, which has a slippery juice.

1952 FGC StE.

SWIVEL sb dial cant. = JACK sb[1] 2.

TAJA, an obs var sp of TAYA; see INDIAN KALE quot 1696.

takaari see TAKARI.

talawa Alternative etym: perh <*stalwart*, with reduction of consonant clusters (st, rt) and intrusion of A[8].

TALL CALALU sb dial. A variety of *Amarantus*: see quot.

1952 FGC StE /bakra kalalú luo, lim-lim, bot taal gruo striet op/ *Backra calalu is low and branching but tall calalu grows straight up.*

TAMBO sb dial. Add etym: cf also Guiana Arawak *tambo*, bowed fish trap (1928 De Goeje 253). These sources may be related or co-incidentally alike; if the latter, this is an instance of 'multiple etymology'.

tampanrat see STAND-'PON-ROCK.

tangkari see TAKARI.

tapralin dial pronunc of *tarpaulin*; see *parai* quot 1956.

TARPON sb. Add: Also *N tarpum*, prob <Miskito *tapam*: cf the related dial forms Sumu *tahpam*, Rama *tāpum*, Paya *ta'pam* (1932 Eduard Conzenius *Ethnographical Survey of the Miskito and Suma Indians of Honduras and Nicaragua* 66.) JH.

TARRA adj dial. Add: Also *SC tara*, Gullah *tarruh.*

tatu sb dial. Add quot:

1973 Majesty Pen recording of *Anansi, Rat-Bat, an' Tiger*, Im mek op a litl tatuu, an im get im frainin pan an im get im ail.

TEETH sb sing dial. Add: Also *SC tífi.* Also widely used as sg form in Scotland—see *SND* TUITH.

TEMPER LIME sb; <*temper* sb (*OED* 12b) +*lime*, calcium oxide. Quicklime formerly used to clarify cane juice in sugar-making.

1835 Senior 51.

tenggl vb dial; for *tangle.* Entangle.

1974 Jones in Kingston *Gleaner Mag* 19 May 5, NO TENGLE MI—Do not entangle me.

terenggl-fut sub dial; <*terenggl*, (musical) triangle+FOOT, leg. Thin-legged.

1974 Jones in Kingston *Gleaner Mag* 19 May 5, TERRENGLE-FOOT—A girl with meagre feet.

THICK-LIPPED MOUNTAIN MULLET sb dial. See quot.

1950 Smith, White River: Thick-lipped mountain mullet, *Agonostomus microps.*

THRASH sb usu dial; overcorrection for TRASH. See also BLACK ANANCY quot 1952.

THREE-KEEL sb dial; <*three*+*keel*, ref to the prominent dorsal ridges. The leatherback turtle.

c 1950 NHN, Three-keel, *Dermochelys coriacea*, Bull Bay.

THREE-QUARTER BUNCH sb techn. In the grading of bananas: see BUNCH quot 1952.

THUNDER SNAKE sb dial; cf THUNDER CRAB.

c 1950 NHN.

TICK-BIRD sb dial; *OED* 1871 only. See SAVANNA BLACKBIRD quot 1756, and BLACKBIRD 1 quot 1955.

TIE-LEAF see TIE-A-LEAF.

TIESHIN see *tai shiin.*

TOADFISH, TOADIE sb dial. The BOTTLE-FISH. *BL*

1952 FGC StC /tuodi, tuodfish, baklfish/.

TOAD-TRASH sb dial; <*toad* (for *frog*) +TRASH. The WILD-PINE, whose leaves retain rainwater in which tree frogs live.

1952 FGC StT.

TOASTER sb; cf *OED Toaster*[2]. The 'master of ceremonies' for an orchestra, singer, or singing group.

1976 Anon Informant (to FGC), The toaster has the microphone; he introduces the performers, comments, beats time and talks with the music—keeps things lively.

toch sb dial. = *tusk(s)*; see RING-BOAR quot.

TOM KELLY see WHIP-TOM-KELLEY.

TOM-TOM sb dial. (See PEENY-WALLY.)

1974 Perkins StE, Tom-tom: The firefly or Peenie Wallie.

TOONA /túuna/ sb. Tuna (cactus).

1893 Sullivan 118, 121, Pusley and Toona as Poultice.

TORCH CACTUS sb; see DILDO quot 1794 and TORCHWOOD 1. See quot.

c 1950 Inst List, Torch cactus, *C[ereus] grandicostatus.*

TRAMPOOZE vb dial; *OED* →1850. See quot.

1943 *GL* No addr. Trampooze, walk about from place to place. 1955 FGC StAnd.

TRINKLET sb dial; <*trinket* blended with *-let*, dimin suffix. A trinket.

1955 FGC StAnd /tríngklit/.

TRUST sb. See *SND* TRUST, *n.* 1. Also in *N*, Miskito, Cameroons, Fernando Po usage (JH).

tumoch adj or pron dial; cf TOO 1, PLENTY 2. Also *SC tóemoesi.* A great deal (of).

1907 Jekyll 21, Bro'er Annancy, me sorry fe you too much. 1978 LeP /im gat tumoch moni/ *He has a great deal of money.*

TURKEY WEED sb obs? = TURKEY-BLOSSOM.

1811 Titford Expl to plate XII, The turky weed..covers the road side from within about four miles from Kingston, where the negroes bring baskets to gather it when in flower, to feed the turkies and other poultry, who are extremely fond of it.

TURPENTINE TREE sb. = INCENSE TREE: see I quot 1920; also MULATTO TREE quot 1941.

TURTLE GRASS see MANATEE GRASS.

tush vb dial or slang. Add: cf Kimbundu *tuʒi*, Djerma *tosi*, human excrement.

1949 Turner 203.

TWIN-BREED n dial; <*twin* sb + *breed*, a genetic type, a family stock. A family that produces many twins.

1976 HPJ, Long before [1964], another informant told me that if a family had a pair or two of twins, people would say to the father or mother, 'Yo' come out a twin-breed'.

TWIN-COAT sb dial; <*twin* adj, dual + *coat*, covering. Hypocritical; cf STARAPPLE 2.

1974 Jones in Kingston *Gleaner Mag* 19 May 5, TWIN-COAT or TWIN-MOUT—Same as starapple leaf.

TWIN-MOUT' sb dial; <*twin* adj, dual + *mouth*, speaking. Hypocritical; see s TWIN-COAT quot.

TWIST TOBACCO sb dial; <*twist* (for *twisted*) or perh *twist* sb + *tobacco*. Tobacco leaves twisted to form a rope; = JACKASS ROPE.

1952 FGC StE, StM /twis-tubáka/.

TWO-MAC sb dial slang; <*two* + MAC. The sum of two shillings. s CURRENCY.

1952 FGC Han /a tuu-mak/ two shillin.

TYSHIN see *tai shiin*.

UGLI (FRUIT) sb. Add quot:

1951 *Am Speech* 35, Its rind..is rough and of an unattractive yellow-green color, whence the nickname, *ugly fruit*, which was applied in the 1930's, when the citrus first appeared in the Canadian market. The fruit is..a product of Jamaica, where it is extensively grown for export..under the trade name *Ugli*..The mother tree of this strange fruit was discovered near Brown's Town, Jamaica, about 1914, by a Mr. Levy. He judged it to be a natural hybrid of the Seville sweet orange and the variety of tangerine called the mandarin. However, general opinion regards it as a tangelo (*tangerine* + *pomelo*), i.e., a hybrid of a tangerine (*Citrus reticulata*) with the pomelo or grapefruit (*C. paradisi*).

UNKNOWN TONGUE see CUT UNKNOWN TONGUE

UNU pron dial. Add: Also *SC óenoe*, Gullah *hunna*. Cf CB **nu*, 2 pers pl infix.

uol man brieku sb dial, see RAINBIRD quot 1952.

VALINGHANNA see VALANGHANNA.

WALK-AND-COTCH vb phr dial. Of one whose legs are hurt: To lean on things for support while walking.

1955 Bennett *Bad Foot*, But Bra Nancy get a bad kick For him still a walk an cotch.

WALK-FOOT vb phr and ppl adj. Add quot:

1903 Loscombe 39, I have heard them [= West Indians] combine 'to go on foot' and 'to walk' into a single verb 'to walk-foot'. An English gentleman who, in a country where nearly every white man rides or drives, was addicted to pedestrian exercise, was invariably known to the peasants as 'Little buccra Walk-foot'.

WALK SAFE! int or vb phr dial. = WALK GOOD!

1971 Duffey, StAnn, The almost invariable Jamaican exhortation to 'Walk safe' or 'Have a safe journey', even if one is going only a short distance in clearly the safest of circumstances.

WALL-SADDLE sb dial; cf SADDLE-WEED. The wild vine *Cissus sicyoides*, which grows on the tops of walls and hangs down on either side.

1943 *NHN* I 128, see SNAKE WITHE. 1952 GHP.

WANIKA sb dial. Add: Also as a Surinam river name (Focke 37).

WARRIOR MOTHER see MOTHER I.

WASSY adj dial; <WAS, wasp + -*y*. Of people: potentially dangerous.

c 1970 C. E. Palmer in Kingston *Gleaner* Sometimes the same man [*sc* MACCA MAN] is said to be 'wassy'—much like the wasp.

WATER sb dial. In joc use: (white) rum. See PUNCHEON-WATER, WATER-MAN 2, etc.

WATER MOTHER see MOTHER I.

WATER SHEPHERDESS sb dial. See RIVER MAID quot 1953.

WATTLE-WALLING sb. The making of wattled walls.

1936 Olivier 47, All necessary materials for building a settler's house are to be found near at hand. Hardwood for framing, cedar for boarding and roofing-shingles and rods for wattle-walling are never far to seek.

WEED, THE sb chiefly dial; absol for WISDOM-WEED. GANJA.

wera-keta fut sb dial; <*wera-keta* + FOOT, leg. Thin-legged.

1974 Jones in Kingston *Gleaner Mag* 19 May 5, WERRAKETA-FOOT—Having spindly legs, like a goats [sic].

WERRAKETTA-FOOT see prec.

WHEELING MOTHER see MOTHER I.

WHITE-BIRD sb dial. A sea bird—gull or perh tern (see WHITE EGG-BIRD).

1952 FGC StT.

WHITE JOINTER sb dial; in contrast to BLACK JOINTER. A shrub of the genus *Piper*—prob *P. jamaicense*.

1952 FGC StC.

WHITE-MAN sb dial. An albino negro. Cf next.

1952 FGC Port.

WHITE-NAYGA /wàit-níega/ sb dial. An albino negro. Cf prec.

1966 Cassidy-DeCamp in *Names* 14.129, The approach to whiteness is also responsible for..*White-labor*, *White-nayga*, *Backra*, and *Backra-betters*.

WHITE-SEAL COOT sb dial. See quot.

1956 Jeffrey-Smith 115, There is a coot with a broad, entirely white shield, to which the name of Caribbean Coot (*Fulica caribaea*) has been given. (See *Ibid* 114, s.v. QUEEN COOT.)

WILD CERASEE sb. Add sense: 2. Also applied to *Melothria guadalupensis*—see MARY-SUCKY-BABY.

WINDWARD sb, attrib. Add later quot:

1968 HPJ, [In Petty Sessions court, Kgn] On April 11, ..a witness (I am pretty sure a policeman) said in his evidence: 'He carry him [escorted him] to the windward gate—beg pardon, the *eastern* gate.'

WINEY sb dial; for *wind* vb + *-y* familiarizing-suffix—see *jiji-waina*, APEMPAY, SHOW-ME TOWN.

1974 Perkins StE, Winey: Moth pupa, known as 'Apempey' in StAnn. Supposed to point the way by twisting its tail.

WINSOR sb dial; etym uncert: second element perh *-er*. = s BAIT-PICKER (see quot).

WINTER CHERRY see POISONOUS CAPE GOOSEBERRY.

WIRE WITHE sb obs? The inner cord of the PRICKLY-WITHE or PUSS GUT.

a 1726 Barham (1794) 153, In the centre of the green succulent part there is a strong wire withe, which planters use, and is very lasting.

WOOD SEARCHER see STRIPE(D) HOLLAND 2.

WORSERER see WUSSARA.

WUT dial sp of *worth*. See *n* pron, quot 1912.

yaak vb dial; see NEW YORK.

yaga-yaga. Add to A. sb: (Cf *SC jaga-jaga*, small branches chopped from felled trees.)

yala-yala adj dial; iterative of *yellow*. Yellowish.

1961 *Ja. Talk* 72.

YAM PIECE sb dial. A piece of land where yams are grown.

1952 FGC StAnd.

YAM-YAMME vb dial. < NYAM, iterated. In 18th cent accounts usually spelled without the N. See also NYAMI-NYAMI. To eat.

a 1818 Lewis (1834) 256, There's rice in the pot, take it, and yam-yamme.

YARD sb. Add sense: 3. Among Jamaicans abroad: home, Jamaica.

1974 Jacobson *New York Mag* 4 Nov 73, Alton has been on the hit parade down in Yard (what Jamaicans [in Brookyn] call home) ever since his first smash in 1959.

YAWY see YAWSY.

YEAR CLOTH sb dial obs. The annual issue of Osnaburgh cloth to slaves.

1797 *Columbian Mag* (HPJ), [Slaves] employed in husbandry receive annually some yards of Osnaburghs, which they call their year cloth; wherewith the men make a frock and trowsers, and the women a shift and coat.

yedi adj dial. The BUNGO TALK pronunc of *ready*.

YELLOW-BILLED CUCKOO sb ornith. *Coccyzus americanus*.

1847 Gosse 280, The stuttering voice of this yellow-billed cuckoo is heard among the prognostics of the coming rain. 1955 Taylor 33.

YELLOW-BILL TURTLE sb dial. Prob = YELLOW TURTLE.

1952 FGC StM.

YELLOW MINTER sb dial; etym unknown. An unidentified tree.

1974 Perkins StE, Yellow Minter: A tall straight tree allied to Dogwood.

YELLOW-SHANKS GAMBET sb ornith obs. In Gosse's use: A small wading bird: see quot.

1847 Gosse 351, Yellow-shanks Gambet. *Totanus flavipes*.

YELLOW-STRIPED GRUNT. A fish; see quot.

1950 Smith, Negril: Yellow-striped grunt, *Bathystoma striatum*.

YOUT /yuut/ sb [< *youth* spelled as it is pronounced in common speech].
The self-consciously and intentionally non-standard form of 'youth' adopted for themselves by the younger anti-conventional politically active people, chiefly of Kingston.

1976 Rex Nettleford, UWI, Needless to say that such words [as 'skeng'] have entered the everyday language of the youth population. Incidentally, the word '*YOUT*' is a real word now. The dropping of the aitch is a deliberate act of liberation, or should I say defiance?